P9-APZ-788

The Sports Encyclopedia: PRO FOOTBALL

David S. Neft · Roland T. Johnson · Richard M. Cohen

Text by: Jordan A. Deutsch

GROSSET & DUNLAP

Publishers · New York

PUBLISHED SIMULTANEOUSLY IN CANADA
LIBRARY OF CONGRESS CATALOG CARD NUMBER: 73-21141
ISBN: 0-448-11626-X

PRINTED IN THE UNITED STATES OF AMERICA

Contents

LEADERS AND FEATURES 475

Preface

The Sports Encyclopedia: Pro Football is the second reference book in a continuing series of major sports encyclopedias. The first book in this series, *The Sports Encyclopedia: Baseball,* was first published in May, 1974. Unlike the baseball encyclopedia, which represented a further evolution in the field of baseball research, this book marks the first complete statistical record on professional football. There is also an historical summary of professional football as it was played from its infancy in 1895 to the game as it is played today.

Although 1920 marked the establishment of the National Football League, the main body of statistical material does not begin until 1933. The reasons for starting that year are multiple. Aside from the fact that statistical material was not available until 1933, the year also signaled standardization of schedules, divisional play, and the first post-season championship match.

As with baseball, the authors have taken the liberty of arranging the material into various periods (1933-45, 1946-59, 1960-73). The 1933-45 period covers the time when football became organizationally cohesive and instilled public confidence. Then, in 1946, the All-American Football Conference came upon the scene and, although only surviving four years before a merger with the NFL took place, it served to bolster the "pro game" in cities which were previously considered unsuitable. The advent of the American Football League in 1960 accounts for the start of the most recent period — a time which planted the seeds for even further acceptance and growth.

It is because of this division of periods that the opportunity is available for fans to now gauge football history in a greater perspective. In each period, the authors have included a dearth of statistical matter and text in a year-by-year format. Additionally, there are register sections, championship games, Super Bowls, single-season and lifetime leaders, as well as a host of other featured material, all of which serves to make *The Sports Encyclopedia: Pro Football,* the most complete book of its kind.

For the authors, who could not have undertaken this project alone, there are many individuals and former professional players to thank whose assistance was necessary in helping to make this book a reality. Their contributions are extensive, and range from supplying demographic information to some of the color as it actually took place on the field. To these individuals, the authors express their deep appreciation that finally there is a book where you can "go and look it up."

Chief consultant in the preparation of the written manuscript—
John G. Hogrogian

Football Hall of Fame —
Jim Campbell, Research Librarian, who made available not only his facility, but also his endless knowledge, time, and co-operation in seeing this book to its fruition.
Don Smith, Public Relations Director

Stan Grosshandler — An independent contributor who coordinated and served as liaison with the following former professional players:

Chuck Bednarik
Jack Christiansen
Dutch Clark
Chuck Conerly
Ed Danowski
Art DeCarlo
Art Donovan
Buckets Goldenberg
Otto Graham
Pat Harder
Mel Hein
Clarke Hinkle
Crazy Legs Hirsch
Dick Hoerner
Henry Jordan
Don Kindt
Joe Kopcha
Dante Lavelli
Jim Mutscheller
Ernie Nevers
Johnny Sisk
Hank Soar
Ken Strong
Y. A. Tittle
Em Tunnell
Alex Wojciechowicz

Pro Football Weekly—
Art Arkush, Publisher
Bill Last, Associate Editor

Independent Contributors —
Bob Allen
Mark Swayne

Grosset & Dunlap —
Robert Markel, Editor-in-Chief
Irving Ross, Director of Production
Joe Sandler, Production
George Paturzo, Jacket design

Cover art by Bill Hoffman

The authors' wives, (a special thanks for once again displaying their faith and cooperation throughout the project): Naomi Neft, Judy Johnson, Nancy Cohen, and Thea Deutsch.

Since such a book of this magnitude will include errors the authors would appreciate, for the purpose of keeping future editions as accurate and complete as possible, if the readers will send any corrections and additions to:

SPORTS PRODUCTS, INC.
632 North Mountain Road
Newington, Conn. 06111

Codes and Explanations

In each section of the book, unfamiliar abbreviations, and bold facing may be shown. The following, by section, is an explanation of this matter:

Yearly Sections

Age — The age shown for each player is as Sept. 1 of that year.

Traded Players — Shown only on the team which the player played for most, along with a "from or to" reference.

Bold Facing — Indicates league leaders.

Team Name Line — Shown alongside the name of each team is the team Won-Lost-Tied record and the head coaches.

Home Team Indication — In a team's game-by-game scores, certain opponents appear in upper case. This means that the opponent played at that team's home park.

Opponent's Score — In a team's game-by-game scores the opponent's score always appears in the right hand column.

Rosters — Attempts to include, in a year, only those who actually played in a league game. The limitations of data, however, may have accidentally included men who did not get into a league game.

Position Abbreviations — (Applies to all sections. If a man played more than one position, the listing is in order of amount played at each position):

BB — Blocking back
C — Center
DB — Defensive back
DE — Defensive end
DG — Defensive guard
DT — Defensive tackle
FB — Fullback
FL — Flanker
G — Offensive and defensive guard
HB — Halfback
K — Punter or place kicker (and did not play any other position in a particular year)
LB — Linebacker
OG — Offensive guard
OE — Offensive end
OT — Offensive tackle
QB — Quarterback
T — Offensive and defensive tackle
TB — Tailback
TE — Tight end
WB — Wingback
WR — Wide receiver

Note: To see how these positions line up in the formation, see Formation Diagrams on pages 11–16.

Career Interruptions — Fully explained, but only covers a full year or career end interruption.

Team Abbreviations — (Applies to all sections)

Atl — Atlanta
Bal — Baltimore
Bkn — Brooklyn
Bos — Boston
Buf — Buffalo
Can — Canton
ChiB — Chicago Bears
ChiC — Chicago Cardinals
Cin — Cincinnati
Cle — Cleveland
C-P — Chicago Cardinals-Pittsburgh Steelers (merged)
C-S — Cincinnati Reds and St. Louis Gunners
Dal — Dallas
Day — Dayton
Dec — Decatur
Den — Denver
Det — Detroit
Dul — Duluth
Fra — Frankfurt
GB — Green Bay
Hou — Houston
KC — Kansas City
LA — Los Angeles
Mia — Miami
Min — Minnesota or Minneapolis
NE — New England
NO — New Orleans
Nwk — Newark
NYB — New York Bulldogs
NYG — New York Giants
NYJ — New York Jets
NYT — New York Titans
NYY — New York Yankees
Oak — Oakland
Phi — Philadelphia
Pit — Pittsburgh
P-P — Philadelphia Eagles-Pittsburgh Steelers (merged)
Port — Portsmouth
Pott — Pottsville
Prov — Providence
Roch — Rochester
SD — San Diego
SF — San Francisco
SI — Staten Island
StL — St. Louis
Was — Washington

Championship Section

Giveaways — Passes that were intercepted and fumbles lost.

Takeaways — Passes intercepted and opposing fumbles recovered.

Note: These two categories apply to team statistics only.

TAP — Indicates Tackled Attempting to Pass.

Register Sections

Players have been assigned to the various register sections according to what time period they played in most. The only exception to this is that anybody who played mostly before 1933 but overlapped his career beyond 1933, would appear in the 1933–45 Period Register Section.

Register sections, by period, are divided into an alphabetical register, and then into various statistical registers. In the alphabetical register, alongside each man's name are one or more reference numbers (1, 2, 3, 4, 5). These reference numbers are to serve as guides as where to find the player's

statistical record (if there is no reference number it means the player did not have enough minimum statistics to rate a ranking). The following are the reference numbers and their identification:

1 Passing
2 Rushing and receiving
3 Punt returns and kickoff returns
4 Punting
5 Kicking

The register sections are broken down into three periods, 1933–45, 1946–59, 1960–73.

Some of the unfamiliar information which appears in each alphabetical register is as follows:

Last name, Use name (name player was known as), nicknames which appear in parenthesis ( ):

Bailey, Howard (Screeno)

If a player used another name other than that he was "born as," his real name is indicated in parenthesis ( ) after the last name. Such as in the case of Rocky Thompson:

Thompson (Symonds), Rocky

Weight — Average weight for career.

HC — Indicates, for year or years, that the player was a head coach.

PC — Indicates, for year or years, that the player was a head coach while actively playing.

League Abbreviations — A (American Football League), AA (All-American Football Conference).

Other Major League Sports — Certain players also played professional basketball or major league baseball. The basketball information is indicated with the league in abbreviations: NBL—National Basketball League, NBA—National Basketball Association, BAA—Basketball Association of America.

Career Interruptions — If an abbreviation other than a league follows the year played, it means that only a full year was missed or a career end because of certain prevailing reasons. The codes and explanations follow:

AJ — Arm injury
BC — Broken collarbone
BH — Broken bone in hand
BL — Broken leg
BN — Broken ankle
BQ — Broken neck
CFL — Jumped to Canadian Football League
FJ — Foot or heel injury
HJ — Hand injury
HO — Holdout
IL — Illness
JJ — Injury or disabled list — type of injury unknown
KJ — Knee injury
MS — Military service
NJ — Ankle injury
SJ — Shoulder injury or shoulder separation
SL — Suspended by commissioner
VR — Voluntarily retired
XJ — Back injury

Pro Football's Offensive Formations

On the following pages are twelve different offensive formations presented in summary form. These formations have been included so that the reader may become acquainted with the various types of offensive formations and strategies which have evolved in pro football since 1933. Additionally, it is felt that these formations will provide an understanding of offensive positions in this book which are shown for the early years of pro football, as well as helping to avoid the confusion for those readers only familiar with the modern T-formation.

Single Wing

The single wing formation, which pre-dates pro football, derives its name from the fact that the right halfback acts as a wing back and is positioned just outside the end. This formation is basically executed by the ball being snapped under the center's legs directly to the tailback or the fullback.

The following are the strengths of the Single Wing:

. . . Two offensive men will be blocking each of the key defensive men on any particular play.

. . . More than normal amount of personnel on strong side where most of the running will take place.

. . . Effective ball-control type of offense.

. . . The biggest advantage is that the BB (Blocking Back), can be used as a blocker on running plays and does not hand off the football.

. . . It offers a deceptive offense in that many players are bunched and able to go in different directions.

. . . The defense is outnumbered at the point of the offensive attack.

. . . The defense cannot key directly to the strong side since the play can be run to the weak side.

The following are the weaknesses of the Single Wing:

. . . The plays are very slow in developing.

. . . Because of its slow development, there are seldom any long runs and long passes.

SINGLE WING — 1935 DETROIT

LE — Klewicki
LT — Johnson
C — Randolph
LG — Monahan
RG — Emerson
RT — G. Christensen
RE — Schneller
BB — F. Christensen
WB — Caddel
FB — Gutowski
TB — Clark

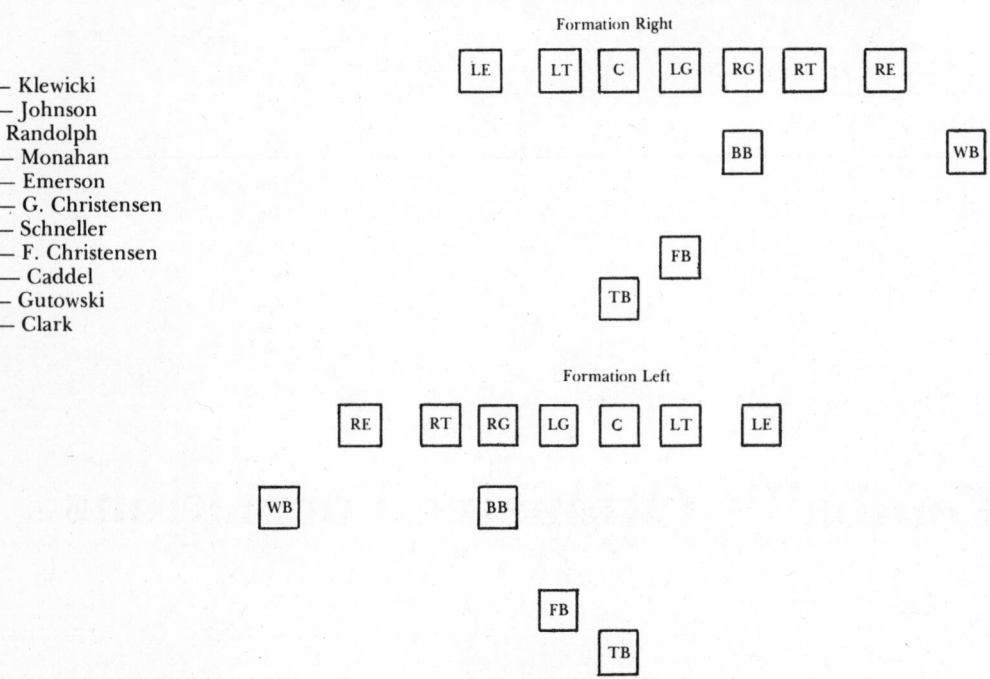

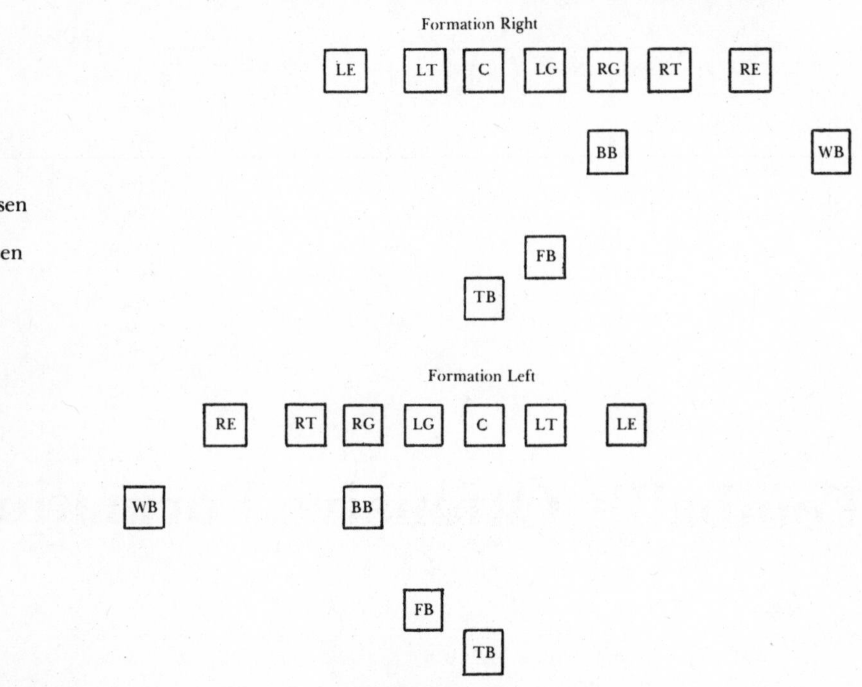

Standard Single Wing

In the Standard Single Wing the change from the formations lining up right to left, or vice versa, means that the backfield occupies the same exact position in relation to the line.

NOTRE DAME BOX — 1939 GREEN BAY

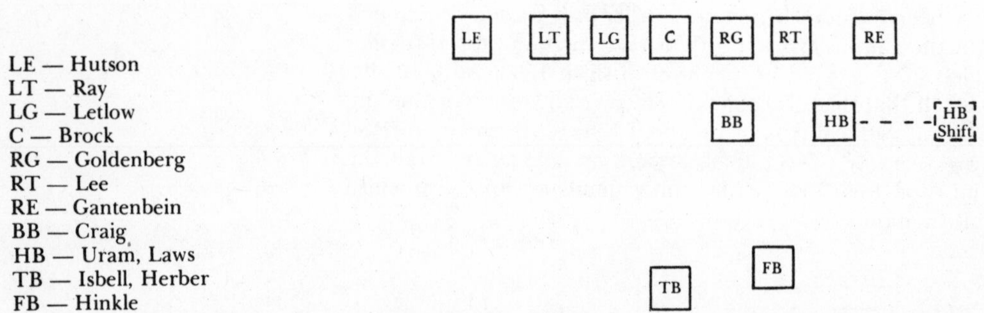

Notre Dame Box

This differs from the Standard Single Wing in that the line is balanced and the halfback frequently in tight between the tackle and the end.

The result of these two factors makes it easier to effect a running game to the weak side. Also, the halfback does more ball-carrying than the wing back in the Standard Single Wing.

SUTHERLAND SINGLE WING — 1941 BROOKLYN

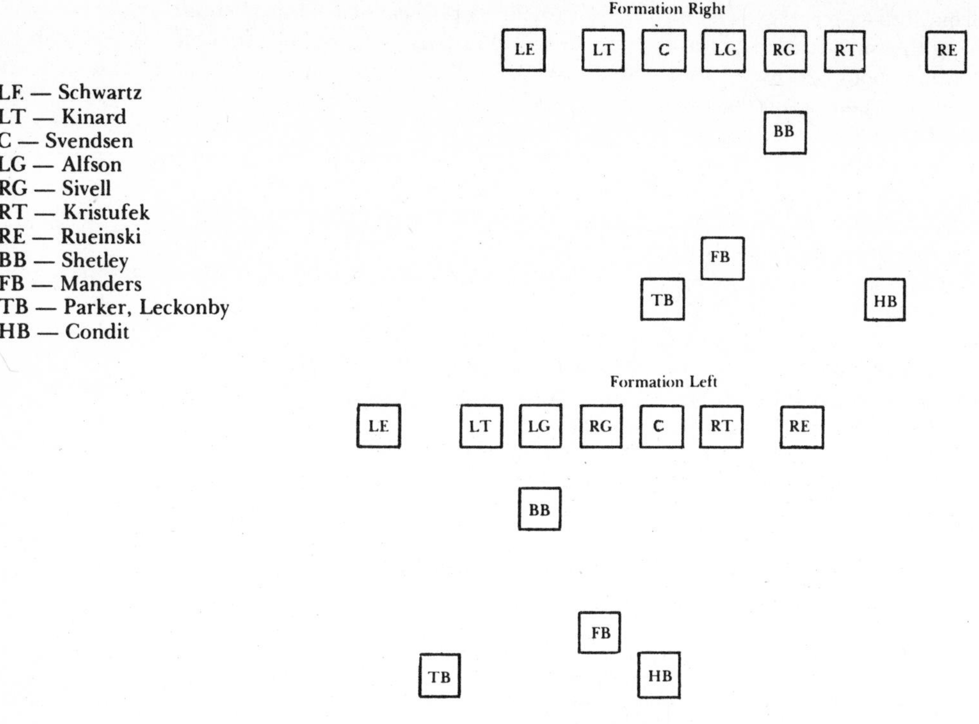

Sutherland Single Wing

The halfback is positioned very deep and also tighter than in the Standard Single Wing; the halfback and tailback actually switch positions when going to formation left.

This formation gives more flexibility in the backfield positions as both the tailback and the halfback are tripie threats (running, passing, receiving) when compared to the wing back in the Standard Single Wing who is normally only a receiver. The weakness of the Sutherland Single Wing is that on passing and the strong side end run, the wing back is not there for a quick reception and added blocking.

A — 1938 NEW YORK GIANTS

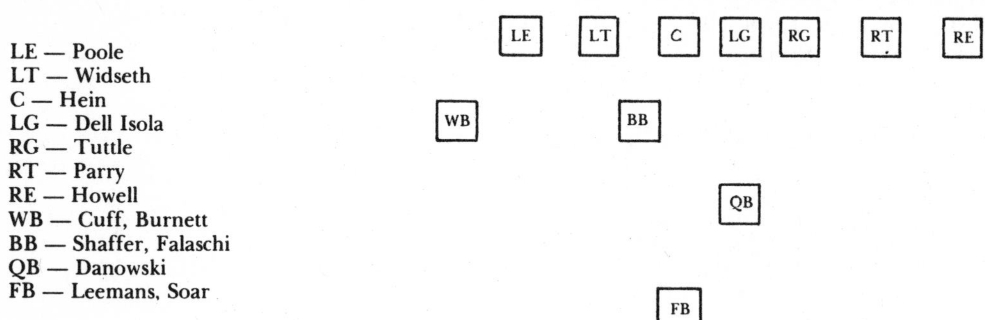

"A" Formation

This formation is quite unique in that a great center such as Mel Hein could snap to any of three men who had the option to go in either a left or right direction. This is also a great running formation designed to put pressure on the defensive tackle facing the strong side of the line.

The following are the differences from the Standard Single Wing:

. . . When the line forms right, the backs are strong left. When the line forms left, the backs form strong right.

. . . The quarterback, who is the primary passer, lines up closer to the line of scrimmage than the tailback in the Single Wing.

. . . The fullback is a potential passer.

The advantage of this formation is that because of its versatility in using any of three men, the defense is constantly off-balance. On the other hand, such a formation is a disadvantage in that it could not be effectively executed unless a team had a great center such as Hein. Perhaps for this reason the Giants were the only team to use this formation, giving them an advantage difficult to overcome.

T-Formations

The Chicago Bears, in 1931, under the direction of Ralph Jones, first introduced the T-formation—a strategy which revolutionized pro football. Following the introduction of this formation, its usage by most clubs came about because of the rule on substitutions, permitting teams to take advantage of players with specialized talents. Another rule influencing the T-formation was that in 1940 passing was allowed from anywhere behind the line of scrimmage, rather than the passer being positioned five yards back behind the line of the scrimmage. In this formation the line is always balanced and the quarterback is directly behind the center and takes the snap from between the center's legs and either handoffs or drops back to pass (or occasionally runs).

The strengths of the T-formation are as follows:

. . . Allows for speed, with great fakes and maneuvers by the backs—a factor which is the key to this formation's success.

. . . The backs can be running at full speed or close to full speed when taking the handoff from the quarterback.

. . . Quick openers and fast development of plays.

. . . Because of speed, double blocking is no longer necessary.

. . . Provides a pocket for pass protection.

. . . A running back can choose his "hole", whereas in the Single Wing he had to go to a specific "hole" and had very little choice if the "hole" closed.

. . . A more flexible, all-around offensive attack.

. . . The center becomes a more effective blocker as he can now directly face the blocker rather than having to keep his head positioned between his legs.

. . . More men in motion.

. . . Needs less versatile backs (more specialization).

The weaknesses of the T-formation are as follows:

. . . Requires specialized skills—the quarterback has to be a good ball handler and a good passer.

. . . Lacks the power of the Single Wing on short yardage situations.

. . . The quarterback is no longer a blocker after he has made his handoff.

T — 1940 CHICAGO BEARS

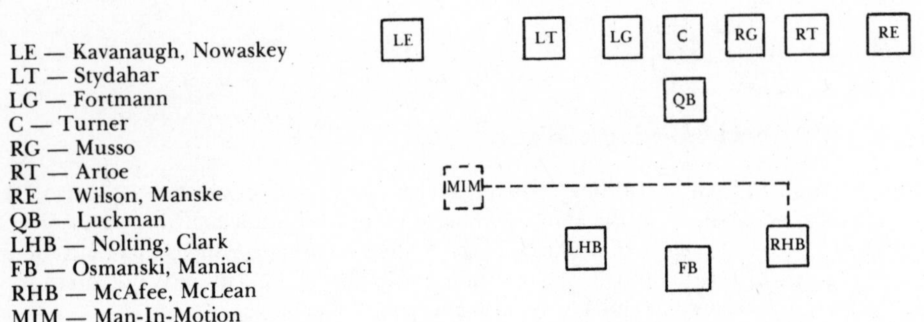

Chicago "T" (or Tight "T")

The Chicago "T", or Tight "T" as used by the Bears in the 1930's and 1940's employed fast running backs who had great faking and maneuvering ability. The great difference between the Chicago "T" and following T-formations was that the Bears tended to use only the long pass, not the quick short pass, as the alternative to a running play.

SLOT T — 1960 PHILADELPHIA EAGLES

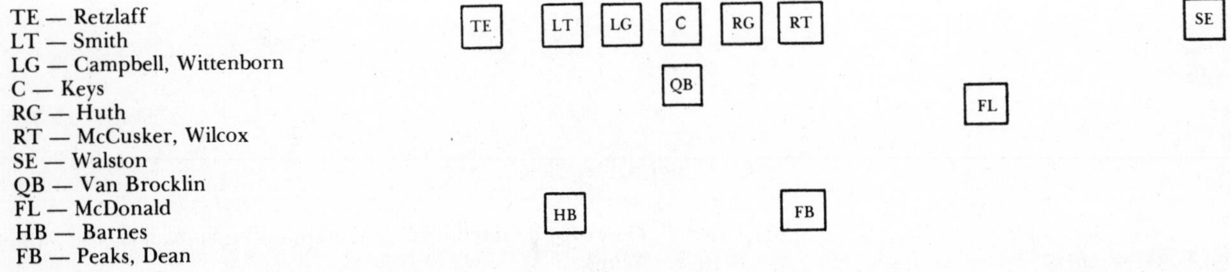

Slot T

The major difference from the Tight T is splitting the right end eight to ten yards outside the tackle and placing the right halfback as a flanker in the "slot" between the right tackle and the split right end.

Neither the split end or the flanker needs to be a good blocker that the right end or halfback are in the Tight T. Both are exclusively used for their pass-catching ability. The advantage of this formation is that it spreads the defense and isolates the split end or flanker into a one-on-one situation with the defense, a goal of all receivers. The major disadvantage of this formation is basically that it is pass oriented and has limited running potential.

PRO-SET T — 1971 DALLAS COWBOYS

WR LT LG C RG RT TE
QB
WR
HB FB

WR — Alworth
LT — Neely
LG — Niland
C — Manders
RG — Nye
RT — Wright
TE — Ditka, Truax
QB — Staubach
WR — Hayes
HB — Thomas
FB — Hill

Pro Set "T"

The basic reason for the Pro Set is the emphasis on the passing game. The Pro Set was developed due to the hash marks being moved more to the center of the field, thus providing room for a wide receiver on each side of the line (eight to ten yards outside the tackle or tight end).

The pressure on the defense to cover a fast wide receiver on each side of the line has caused an opening in zone defenses for the halfback and fullback to swing out of the backfield and receive short passes.

WISHBONE T OR Y

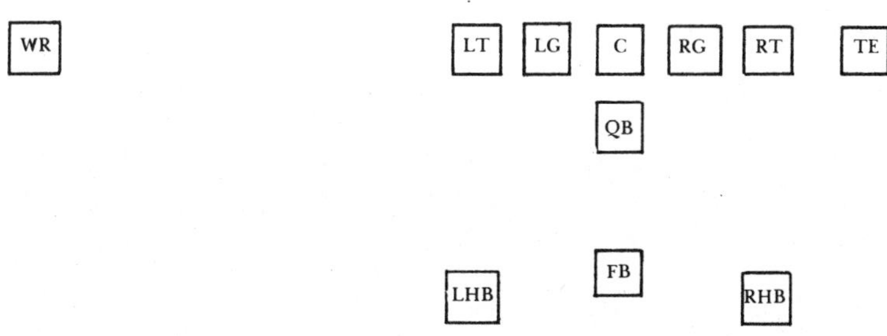

Wishbone T or Y

A new formation now developing is the Wishbone T or Y. This formation is now used with great regularity in the college game and has been used in the pros but not as the primary offensive formation. The basic advantage is that the quarterback has four options in this formation:

1. Handoff
2. Toss (laterally)
3. Keep & Run
4. Pass

This formation requires a more versatile quarterback with the ability to run as well as pass. It is likely to become a major formation as the colleges develop more quarterbacks using this formation.

The biggest advantage is the lateral options the quarterback can use, all of which generates a more versatile running attack.

The disadvantage of the Wishbone is that the play takes longer to develop, and long passing is limited because there is only one wide receiver as compared to two in the Pro Set.

SHOT GUN — 1959 SAN FRANCISCO 49ERS

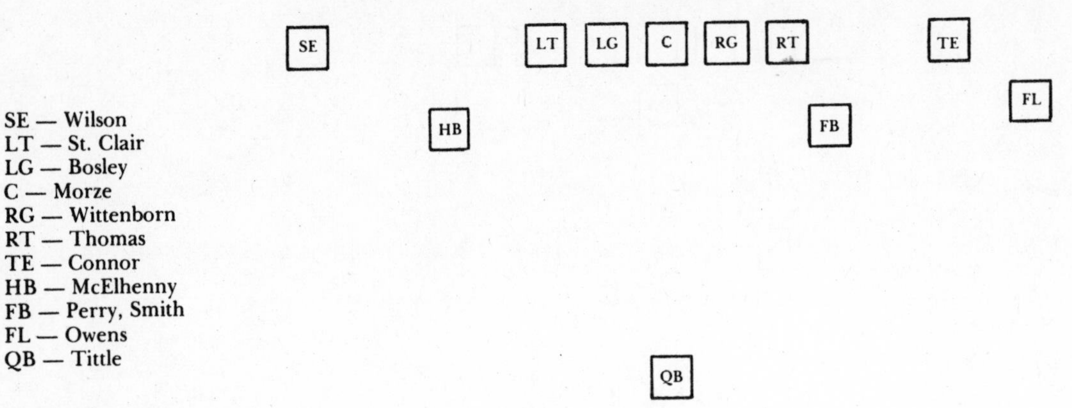

SE — Wilson
LT — St. Clair
LG — Bosley
C — Morze
RG — Wittenborn
RT — Thomas
TE — Connor
HB — McElhenny
FB — Perry, Smith
FL — Owens
QB — Tittle

The Shot Gun Formation

The Shot Gun is primarily a passing formation with very little running. In this formation, the center snaps the ball from under his legs directly to the quarterback who is seven to eight yards back; the quarterback is already in the pocket and is ready to throw as soon as he gets the ball. Also, there is the greatest opportunity to get five receivers downfield as soon as possible for a very quick pass to any of them.

The Shot Gun has never been used for an entire season as a main offensive formation by any team due to the inability to have a balanced attack. In this formation there is no potential for a screen, trap, or draw. Also, the quarterback is back all alone with no blockers in the backfield so he must quickly release the ball.

I — 1968 KANSAS CITY CHIEFS

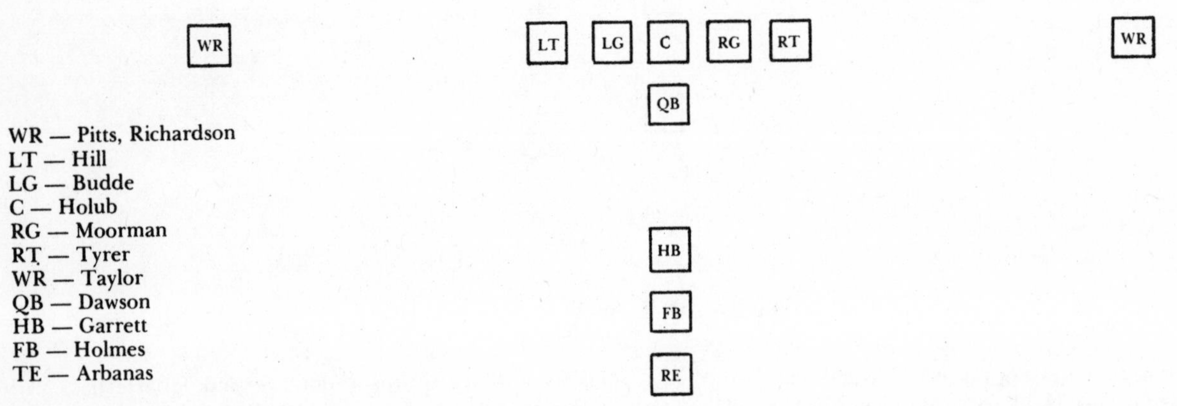

WR — Pitts, Richardson
LT — Hill
LG — Budde
C — Holub
RG — Moorman
RT — Tyrer
WR — Taylor
QB — Dawson
HB — Garrett
FB — Holmes
TE — Arbanas

The Tight-I and Normal-I

The Tight-I is shown in the diagram above. In the Normal-I the tight end moves to the line of scrimmage next to the right tackle.

This formation is a power running offense particularly directed up the middle with lots of blocking and deception (the ball is well hidden—it is hard to tell which back actually has the ball).

The weakness of this formation is that it takes too much time for the backs to go outside either for running or receiving.

In the above diagram the tight end (such as Fred Arbanas) is very similar to the single wing's blocking back and seldom, if ever, carries the ball.

1895–1919
From Latrobe to Thorpe, Two Legends in Any Time

All of our Super Sundays, multiyear contracts, and pro-football fever began in the Gay Nineties with a sixteen-year-old quarterback in Latrobe, Pennsylvania.

Amateur football clubs abounded in Pennsylvania in the 1890s. In 1895, the Latrobe YMCA sponsored a team which was to face a squad from neighboring Jeannette on August 31. Injury had cut down the Latrobe quarterback, and only a flash of American ingenuity rescued the team's chances. Overtures were made to sixteen-year-old John Brallier, a local high-school star about to enter college, to fill in for Latrobe. When he declined, an offer of ten dollars convinced Brallier to play. Latrobe defeated Jeannette 12-0, and despite claims that other players were paid as early as 1893, Brallier has traditionally been recognized as the first professional football player.

Of course, the game that day differed a bit from the current free-wheeling contests. Passing would not be legalized until 1906, and the offense relied exclusively on power running and kicking. The touchdown and field goal both counted for five points, and the very thick round ball, not designed for passing, lent itself very well to drop-kicking. All players went sixty minutes or were carried from the field, which was 110 yards long. The offense had three downs in which to gain five yards for a first down. The point after touchdown was attempted from the five-yard line directly opposite from where the touchdown was scored; if this angle was too acute, the team could punt the ball out and kick from where the punt was caught. Obviously, the extra point had not yet developed into the automatic play it is today. Referees received their pay from the host team and usually acceded quite willingly to the demands of a rabid home-town audience.

Following Latrobe's lead, many clubs began luring top players into their lineups with stipends. Latrobe and Greensburg each hired many college players in the next few years, as an assumed name enabled a dollarwise collegian to play for his school on Saturday and for a professional outfit on Sunday. Even college graduates often used phony names, since pro football had an unsavory reputation for dishonesty, vulgarity, and rowdiness. In order to attract non-college players, teams often helped the young athletes to find jobs.

The fans at these early contests approached hysteria. Either paying at the gate or throwing some change into a hat passed at halftime, the football fanatics in the stands charged games with life-and-death significance. The supporters of the victorious squad often piled out of the park and into the center of town in a boisterous and electric mob. The courthouse steeple in Latrobe had to be straightened on its base after one particularly spirited crowd had finished celebrating a home-town victory.

Baseball lent the fledgling sport a helping hand. Backed by Pirate owner Barney Dreyfuss, Pittsburgh fielded a team in 1898 with ex-Bucknell star Christy Mathewson at fullback, two years before Matty began his pitching career with the New York Giants. The Philadelphia Athletics fielded a football squad in 1902 which Connie Mack coached. Mack talked eccentric pitching star Rube Waddell into joining the team as a lineman. Rube made only a token appearance in each game, but Mack was happy just to be able to keep an eye on the boyish Waddell and shepherd him away from trouble. The Philadelphia Phillies that year also sponsored a team which met a squad from Syracuse in Madison Square Garden in New York City.

By 1904, though, financial and other problems put most of the Pennsylvania teams out of business. Although teams had sprung up in upper New York State, the main battlefield for the pro-football wars shifted to Ohio.

Starting in 1904, strong professional teams flourished in Canton, Massillon, Akron, Dayton, and Columbus. The Columbus Panhandles were organized by Joe Carr and numbered seven Nessers in its lineup—six Nesser brothers and a son of the oldest brother. To complete the family act, the father of the clan acted as waterboy, and the mother contributed her talents by washing the uniforms.

The Canton Bulldogs and Massillon Tigers squared off in a feverish rivalry starting in 1904. For three seasons both teams hired the top college players of the day to take part in the pitched battles that passed for football. For instance, Canton paid star Michigan back Willie Heston $600 to play one game against Massillon; the Tigers piled on Heston on the opening play, shaking him up, and held him to no yardage the rest of the afternoon.

Canton's coach offered one of his charges a bribe to throw a game against Massillon in 1906, and when this news hit the headlines, the wind went out of pro football's sails in Ohio and the great teams disbanded until a renewed public enthusiam called for large-scale pro football again in 1912.

When the teams regrouped that year, the game itself had changed. Passing had been legal for six years, though rarely used except in situations of despair. The touchdown now counted for six points, the field goal for three, the safety two, and the point after touchdown one. The field had shrunk slightly to 100 yards, and the offense now had four downs in which to gain ten yards. A rule prohibiting substituted players from re-entering the game in the same half simply reinforced the ethic that real men played sixty minutes.

The ball still resembled a short watermelon, making passing a risky tactic when attempted. The players lined up in a basic T formation, from which the primary play was a snap-back to the quarterback, who handed off to a back plowing up the middle. As far as end runs and reverses were concerned, they simply added a rare element of trickery to a team's repertoire.

The Ohio teams once again began drawing collegiate stars into their lineups with either straight salaries or with profit shares. An organized league was still eight years away in 1912, and each team arranged its own schedule with its chosen opponents. With no league, no restrictions existed on the hiring of players, and collegians played under aliases to preserve their amateur status as well as jumping from team to team to collect the best offers made week to week. An example of this involved the famed Knute Rockne, when a member of the Columbus club, reported facing Rockne six times in six weeks in six different uniforms, and Massillon once hired forty-five top players for one game simply to ensure that none of them would play for that week's opponent.

Despite the instabilities, the pro-football resurgence in Ohio flourished and reached a new peak in 1915. Canton pulled a coup by signing Jim Thorpe for $250 a game. A former star halfback at the Carlisle Indian School, the big Indian already was twenty-seven-years old and possessed a national reputation for his decathlon feats in the 1912 Olympic Games. In addition to playing pro baseball, Thorpe was coaching football at Indiana University when Canton beckoned.

Big Jim paralleled Babe Ruth in that he was a natural star who shone despite flaunting every training rule in the book. His 190 pounds distributed over a 6'1" frame packed a wallop few other players could muster. His zest for physical contact made him a dominant figure on both offense and defense. "When old Jim hits them, they rattle," Thorpe said. His open-field running involved a deceptive side step which he described by saying, "I gave them a leg for a second, then took it away." As a power runner, he was unmatched. He could pass, drop-kick, and punt in superior fashion, and his jarring tackles struck fear into his opponents. To go along with his talents, Thorpe armed himself with shoulder pads reinforced with sheet metal, a firm reminder to would-be tacklers to stand clear.

Although he did not always play at peak effort, Thorpe was a superstar, pro football's first glamorous drawing card. Before he joined the Bulldogs, Canton was averaging 1,200 paying fans per game; 8,000 customers showed up to see Thorpe make his local debut by leading the Bulldogs to victory over the hated Massillon Tigers.

With enthusiam (and profits) at a new high, the top Ohio teams hired All-Americans by the drove in 1916. The Canton line averaged a colossal 213 pounds and allowed only seven points in ten games. In the continuing Massillon-Canton rivalry, 10,000 fans turned out in Massillon on November 27 to view a scoreless tie—an exciting and frustrating battle that the Canton audience did not have to witness when their Bulldogs trounced the Tigers 24-0 in a December 4 rematch.

With the coming of the Great War, Uncle Sam began snapping up both players and fans for his own squad of battlers. Only Canton, Massillon, Akron, Youngstown, and Columbus fielded respectable teams in 1917, with the Bulldogs and Tigers splitting their annual two games. But by 1918 pro football had ground to a halt in the face of the national war effort.

Post-collegiate football, though, received a boost when the Great Lakes Naval Training Station team brought together many of the best collegiate players in the nation. George Halas held down an end position while Jimmy Conzelman and Paddy Driscoll starred in the backfield. The powerhouse squad rolled into the Rose Bowl and emerged victorious as an example of what post-graduate football could produce.

Nineteen-nineteen brought peace to Europe and a resumption of football war in Ohio. Most of the old teams returned and many new ones began play. Although a movement was afoot for organization of some sort, all the teams still existed as free-lance operations. Clubs signed new players who would grow to fame in the soon to be organized NFL. Canton hired Carlisle graduates Joe Guyon and Pete Calac to play in the backfield with Thorpe, while young Guy Chamberlin joined the Bulldogs as an end. George Halas was out of the Navy and playing for the Hammond Pros in Indiana. The Akron squad was sparked by halfback Fritz Pollard, a cat-quick runner from Brown University who was the first black pro-football star.

Up in Wisconsin, Curly Lambeau organized the Green Bay Packers with $500 provided by the Indian Packing Company. At the end of a 10-1 season, the players split the profits and received $16.75 apiece for their efforts. For the more established teams, the general pay scale provided $50 to $75 a game for star players and less for the always unsung linemen. Equipment remained primitive, with helmets and shoulder pads optional. Jim Thorpe, of course, retained his astronomical salary and lethal shoulder pads.

Thorpe led Canton to victory over Massillon twice during the postwar season. In the season's finale, the big Indian added fuel to his legend by scoring on a 50-yard drop-kick field goal to give Canton a 3-0 victory over Massillon. In the first contest between the two rivals, the Tigers appealed to Knute Rockne, then head coach at Notre Dame, to join the fray. Still young, in shape, and eager for the challenge, Rockne took the field in the Massillon striped jersey. Before a large crowd in Canton, Rockne knifed through the Bulldog blockers to nail Thorpe for a loss. The Indian genially warned Rockne, "Now all these people came to see old Jim run. You be a nice boy and let him run."

The next time Thorpe tried to turn the corner, Rockne again threw him for a loss. Smiling, Thorpe again lectured the Notre Dame man. Late in the game, Thorpe again headed around Rockne's end. As Rockne moved in for the tackle, Thorpe lowered his head and shoulders and charged. In Rockne's own words, "It was as if a locomotive had hit me and been followed by a ten-ton truck rambling over the remains." With Rockne sprawled on the turf, Thorpe raced 40 yards for a touchdown, trotted back to where Knute was lying, helped him to his feet, and said, "Thanks, young fella. You let old Jim run." Although Thorpe's words closed out a free-wheeling and courageous era, there was much more in store for pro football when the American Professional Football Association hoisted its colors in 1920.

1920 Gettin' Out the Starch

While Warren G. Harding pressed his presidential campaign with calls for a return to normalcy, George Halas was wooing players for a football team sponsored by the A. E. Staley Company of Decatur, Illinois. It was Staley himself who had hired Halas to play for the company baseball team and to run the football team—a move more designed to advertise the Staley Starchworks than to capitalize on the growing interest in football. In order to ease Halas' task, Staley provided his young hired star with fine package deals to offer prospective players and a year-round job with the starch company plus a share of the gate receipts were waved under the noses of all likely prospects. But it was Staley's promise to allow two hours of daily practice on company time that clinched the decision for many a serious player.

With such generous financial inducements, Halas brought many top-notch players onto his first team. The twenty-five-year-old coach himself played end. His old Navy buddy Jimmy Conzelman lined up at halfback, Guy Chamberlin left the Canton Bulldogs to hold down the end opposite Halas, George Trafton enlisted at center, Dutch Sternaman in the backfield, and a scrappy little quarterback named Charlie Dressen directed the Staley offense with as much verve as he would later direct several major-league baseball teams. The result of Halas' energetic vision was that the Decatur Staleys materialized into the best advertisement a starch factory or any company, for that matter, could desire. Then, with his team assembled and ready to set out in conquest of the world, or at least that part of the world he could reach, Halas began to contact existing teams to set up some games. It was one of these contacts, with Ralph Hay, manager of the Canton Bulldogs, which grew into a scheme even beyond Halas' wildest dreams. Hay told the younger man of plans to organize a league that autumn, and a preliminary meeting in Akron on August 20 led to a formal organizational conference in Canton on September 17.

Representatives of eleven clubs gathered in Hay's Hupmobile showroom on that muggy and historic evening. On the fenders of one of the cars hung buckets of beer. As those present stood on the running boards and leaned against the cars, the talk flowed and beer poured and the American Professional Football Association, predecessor of the National Football League, was born.

Two general principles formed the foundation of the new organization. To win the good will of college football (the rich kid on the gridiron block), all the teams present pledged to keep hands off undergraduates who still had eligibility remaining. The founders, seeing the necessity for consistent team images, also agreed not to tamper with players on other teams—a move that enabled fans to recognize the teams from week to week. The Canton Bulldogs, Massillon Tigers, Akron Pros, Dayton Triangles, Cleveland Indians, Rochester Jeffersons, Rock Island Independents, Muncie Tigers, Hammond Pros, Chicago Cardinals, and Decatur Staleys all cast their lots with the new league. To give the organization an air of substance, an admission fee of $100 per franchise was announced; however, according to George Halas, "I can testify that no money changed hands. I doubt if there was eleven hundred bucks in the whole room."

Jim Thorpe was named president, not so much for his administrative ability as for his glittering name. Big Jim continued to coach and play for Canton while his name adorned the league letterhead. The new league, which Thorpe presided over mostly as figurehead, was a loose and casual one. No schedule was issued, each club still arranged its own slate against both league and non-league opponents, standings or statistics were not kept, and players still jumped from team to team with some regularity.

Even membership in the league took on a casual air. Of the original eleven clubs, Massillon and Muncie disbanded even before the fall season began. Four additional clubs, not represented at the organizational meeting, played enough games against the league members to be considered part of the paper circuit as the Chicago Tigers, Detroit Heralds, Buffalo All-Americans, and Columbus Panhandles shared the dubious respectability of the loose Association. And most of the clubs, official members and not, had to struggle to stay one step ahead of the bill collector as the red ink flowed more readily than the black.

Canton, Buffalo, and Akron emerged as the cream of the circuit as the fall games progressed. Jim Thorpe continued to spark the Bulldogs, though age had begun to cut into his magnificent skills. Joe Guyon, who belted a 95-yard punt against the Chicago Tigers on November 14, provided a second Indian triple threat in the backfield. Fats Henry, a rotund 250-pounder who carried not an ounce of fat on his six-foot frame, joined Canton as a blue-chip tackle with a knack for piling up blockers on defense and for blocking kicks.

The Akron Pros went through the season undefeated, reaching a peak by defeating the Bulldogs before 6,000 fans in Canton on Thanksgiving Day. While Fritz Pollard, a black, did most of the ball carrying, there was another black on the squad, rookie end Paul Robeson from Rutgers, who would one day reach fame in show business and for his espousal of Marxism rather than for his pass receiving and tackling. The Pros also broke into the record book by selling tackle Bob Nash to Buffalo for $300 in the first pro-football trade.

Buffalo's stars were quarterback Tommy Hughitt from Michigan and halfback Elmer Oliphant of Army. The All-Americans arranged for a post-season playoff between Akron, Canton, and themselves for the league championship, and 15,000 spectators paid their way into New York's Polo Grounds to witness Buffalo's 7-3 defeat of Canton on December 4. After the game the Buffalo squad caught a train back to their upstate home town and there played Akron to a scoreless tie the next day to leave the championship title forever undecided.

While history was taking place in Buffalo, it was also occurring in Chicago, where not a championship but survival itself was at stake. When the owners of the Chicago Cardinals and the Chicago Tigers realized that continued box-office competition spelled only financial suicide, they decided to arrange a one-game playoff to decide which team would get Chicago's pro franchise. Star halfback Paddy Driscoll, to whom the Cardinals paid $300 a game, raced to a 40-yard touchdown in a 6-3 triumph to give the team sole but temporary pro-football rights in the Windy City.

An example depicting the tenor of play during pro football's first season could not have been more evident than as with Halas' Decatur Staleys. Despite finishing with ten wins, two ties, and one loss for the season, they posted a claim on the championship on the basis of holding undefeated Akron to a scoreless tie in their only meeting. Of course, Halas displayed his usual craftiness by coaxing Paddy Driscoll into playing for the Staleys for this one game. Although this violated the league rules, Thorpe's administration lacked the muscle to punish infractions of any sort.

Despite the fact of not finishing first in the standings, the Staleys fared the best when it came to renumeration. Each player received a $1,900 share of gate profits for the season, while few other teams in the circuit could claim $1,900 as their total profit for the season. But the Staleys earned every dollar they received, especially on the road, where life was as dangerous as it was exciting. At Rock Island, Illinois, a particularly rough game incited the crowd into a frenzy at the Staleys in general and at tough George Trafton in particular. It was such a rugged and bitterly fought contest that when the final gun sounded, Trafton raced for the bench and quickly slipped on a sweatshirt to cover his number as the spectators turned into an ugly mob bent on post-game revenge. So incensed was the crowd that, even after Trafton climbed into a cab waiting outside the park, a storm of rocks came crashing through the windows. Halas, meantime, took off on foot and finally flagged down a car. It was not until after he had crossed the state line into Iowa that he felt safe.

The one loss Decatur sustained came in a manner befitting a primitive league learning to crawl before it could walk. The Staleys squared off against the Cardinals in Chicago, and in mid-game the bleachers collapsed, spilling stunned but unhurt fans onto the ground. The unseated spectators then lined up along the sideline to watch the contest. Late in the game one of the Cardinals took a short pass near the sideline. About to be tackled, he ducked behind some spectators who had drifted onto the playing field. Deftly using his phalanx of impromptu blockers, the receiver glided to a touchdown behind the friendly wall of participating fans. The referee, fearful of the partisan crowd, allowed the score.

Thus was Halas first exposed to the Chicago football fan, and thus was the temperament and drama of pro football's first and glorious league season.

1921 Out of the Starchworks, into the Wind

Realizing that Jim Thorpe could run with the ball better than he could run a league, the league managers installed Joe Carr as the president of the American Professional Football Association at a reorganizational meeting in April. Long years as the manager of the Columbus Panhandles, plus extensive experience as a baseball executive, furnished the spectacled Carr with the administrative know-how Thorpe lacked. Although personally a gentle man, Carr governed pro football sternly through its formative stages until his death in 1939. Ironically, football installed its first great executive the same year that Judge Kenesaw Landis became the first Commissioner of Baseball.

In his first year, Carr presided over a league with eighteen members. Only thirteen of these teams completed the season, eleven of which were returning league members. Hammond, Evansville, Louisville, Minneapolis, and Muncie fielded teams early in the year but dropped out before the fall was up. Cincinnati and Green Bay entered the circuit for the first time, while the Decatur Staleys transferred to Chicago.

Carr's administration immediately showed some concrete results in upgrading the league operation. All member clubs paid an actual franchise fee of $50, thus providing the league office with a bit of leverage. Although standings were compiled, there were no set schedules, and teams still played both league and non-league opponents, making the standings not only difficult to keep but also the official records, which included the games of the non-league teams. To make matters even more confusing, the five teams which folded early were stricken from the books without a trace. But as ambiguous as the standings may have been, they provided a measure for the official awarding of a league championship—something not done in the previous season.

Yet, even with Carr's leadership, there were some situations the new president could not change. Newspapers rarely devoted more than a few lines to pro games, content to give the final score and little else. It was this lack of publicity which kept the paying crowds at a minimum while the financial woes of the teams piled higher and higher. The average football fan still preferred the college game for its pageantry, rah-rah spirit, and big-name stars and considered pro football rowdy, commercial, and drab.

George Halas worked hard against these and other obstacles to keep his team, the Decatur Staleys, in existence. A business recession had prompted the team's sponsor, Staley Starchworks of Decatur, to drop its pro-football team and A. E. Staley, the company's president, to suggest to Halas that he re-establish the club in Chicago. Halas accepted the offer and was aided by $5,000, which Staley gave him in return for retaining the team's name. Looking to save on a salary and to cut his risks in half, Halas made halfback Dutch Sternaman his partner in the new Chicago Staleys. After signing a lease to use Wrigley Field, the two young owners persuaded Guy Chamberlin and George Trafton to join them from the old Decatur squad as the core of the new team. Since neither owner expected the team to turn a profit the first year (it lost $71.63), Halas worked as a car salesman and Sternaman in a gas station to keep body and soul together.

The Acme Packing Company of Green Bay, which had acquired the Indian Packing Company, still saw fit to sponsor a pro team, so Curly Lambeau did not have to hustle for funds as frantically as did Halas. Lambeau, as coach and star player, led the Packers into the pro league after two years of free-lance play in Wisconsin.

Of the returning franchises, Akron continued strong with a 7-2-1 season's mark, while Canton dropped off to 4-3-3, owing partly to the defection of Jim Thorpe and Joe Guyon to the Cleveland Indians. But with Thorpe slowing down, Cleveland could still do no better than two wins in eight games with its two new stars. The Rock Island Independents underwent the only mid-game coaching change in football history. Frank Coughlin began the season as coach and starting tackle but lost so much respect when his line play fell below par that in the middle of a game the team owner sent future Hall of Famer Ed Healey into the lineup to replace Coughlin and to relay a message to quarterback Jimmy Conzelman, "You're the new coach. Mr. Flanagan wants you to take over." The twenty-three-year-old Conzelman expected a pay raise for his coaching, but his salary stayed exactly where it had been, at $150 a game.

The Buffalo All-Americans and the transplanted Staleys of Chicago raced out ahead of the field in pursuit of the league championship. Both clubs came into their November 15 confrontation with unbeaten records, though Buffalo had been tied twice in seven games. In the first half a Halas' pass reception set up a short touchdown run by Sternaman, but the important extra point was muffed by the Staleys. A second-half touchdown pass plus the conversion gave the Buffalo squad a 7-6 lead which it never lost.

The Staleys shut out the Green Bay Packers 20-0 the next week and headed into a rematch with Buffalo with renewed confidence. Guy Chamberlin returned an interception 70 yards for six points, and Sternaman added the extra point and a field goal to give the Staleys a 10-7 victory and first place. Chicago wound up with a 10-1-1 mark, Buffalo at 9-1-2, and the championship pennant flew over Wrigley Field. Buffalo objected, claiming that the Staley's final record included non-league games, but president Carr ruled that the championship was Chicago's.

As expected, the Staleys were not beloved champions in every city. Their annual game at Rock Island again saw the crowd up in arms and ready to charge the Staleys, with George Trafton singled out as a special target for a massaging. Sensing the crowd's reaction, Trafton readied himself to run from the stadium the second the game ended. Halas, also aware of the crowd's feeling, stuck the visitors' share of the gate receipts, amounting to $7,000, under Trafton's jersey just before the closing gun. As soon as time ran out, Trafton sprinted out of the park in full uniform, leaving the angry throng behind. Later, Halas explained the payroll handoff: "I knew that if trouble came, Trafton would be running for his live. I'd only be running for the seven thousand dollars."

1921

	W	L	T	Pct.
Chi Bears	10	1	1	.909
Buffalo	9	1	2	.900
Akron	7	2	1	.778
Green Bay	6	2	2	.750
Canton	4	3	3	.571
Dayton	4	3	1	.571
Rock Island	5	4	1	.556
Chi Cards	2	3	2	.400
Cleveland	2	6	0	.250
Rochester	2	6	0	.250
Detroit	1	7	1	.125
Columbus	0	6	0	.000
Cincinnati	0	8	0	.000

1922 The Birth of Young Papa Bear

In addition to playing a good game of football, George Halas showed a Midas touch when it came to giving names. With one stroke he changed the Chicago Staleys into the Chicago Bears, the most famous team in pro football. Then, at Halas' suggestion, the league itself was rechristened the National Football League. At the same time all the name changing was going on, pro football almost lost one of its legendary franchises when league boss Joe Carr booted the Green Bay Packers out in a move to preserve the circuit's integrity. Carr knew that the Packers had used college players under assumed names in the 1921 season and decided to make an example of the team by revoking the Green Bay franchise and returning the $50 franchise fee to the Acme Packing Company. Coach and quarterback Curly Lambeau would not quit so easily, though. He had $50 stored away with which he could buy back the Green Bay franchise, but he had to make a personal appearance at the league meeting in Canton, Ohio, to file his application. Unfortunately, Curly could not scrape up train fare to Ohio.

As a last resort, Lambeau turned to his friend Don Murphy for help. Not a player but a loyal fan, Murphy agreed to sell his car to raise the train fare, demanding in exchange that he start for the Packers in their opening game. Lambeau agreed, traveled to Canton, and purchased the Green Bay Packers franchise from the League for $50. Don Murphy started at tackle on opening day and retired happily after one minute of action.

While Green Bay found the means by which to survive, other franchises melted and shifted, and the league standings listed eighteen members, some of which played only a few games before disbanding for the season. With the scheduling still casual from week to week, a team doing poorly both afield and at the gate would simply fold up shop early in the season. Along with new league members Toledo, Racine, and Milwaukee, the most colorful was a team called the Oorang Indians, which Jim Thorpe had organized after his Cleveland franchise went out of business. Sponsored by a dog kennel and playing their home games in Marion, Ohio, the Indians fielded a 100 percent Redskin squad, headed by Thorpe, Joe Guyon, and Pete Calac. The years were adding up on this trio of Carlisle graduates, though, and the Indians compiled only a 2-6 record. But a good show was always provided, as the squad often ran onto the field in full war bonnets and buckskin over their football pants.

While Jim Thorpe directed the Indian squad, his old Canton Bulldogs rolled undefeated through the season to the first NFL championship. The Bulldogs fielded a new bunch of faces, led by coach and end Guy Chamberlin. The wiry end had played in Canton with Thorpe in 1919 and had starred for George Halas' champion 1921 Chicago Staleys before returning to direct the Bulldogs' return to the top of the pro-football hill.

Aside from Chamberlin, the stars of the Bulldogs were tackles Fats Henry and Link Lyman. Henry weighed 250 pounds, Lyman 246 pounds, and both moved like cats when quickness was in order. Just out of the University of Nebraska, Lyman confounded offenses with his last-second shifts in the defensive line. Henry approached being unstoppable on defense, and he was a great punter and drop-kicker to boot. His 50-yard drop-kick field goal against Toledo on November 13 set a record most probably never to be broken.

Running a close second to the Bulldogs were the Chicago Bears, newly named to create a relationship with the baseball Cubs in the public eye. The only two losses the Bears suffered came at the hands of the crosstown rival Cardinals; in both games Paddy Driscoll provided drop kicks enough for 6-0 and 9-0 Bear defeats.

The Bears also finished near the top in finances, turning a modest profit of $1,476.92 for owners Halas and Dutch Sternaman. On the other hand, the Green Bay Packers were plagued by constant bad weather and plunged to the bottom of the circuit at the box office, throwing Curly Lambeau into a deep financial hole very early in the year. But Lambeau and his Packers were saved by local businessmen. Realizing the value of the team for civic pride and advertisement, the merchants arranged for a $2,500 loan so that Lambeau could chase off the creditors hounding his steps. At the close of the season, a public non-profit corporation was set up to run the Packers. For five dollars, a Green Bay citizen could buy a share of the team and get a season's box seat thrown in as well. The townsfolk snapped up the shares, and the Packers had $5,000 in the bank by the time the next season rolled around.

In recounting the 1922 season, the annual brawl between the Chicago Bears and Rock Island Independents is worthy of mention—especially since it gave the impetus for the new NFL's first trade. Just before Thanksgiving the clubs squared off in muddy Wrigley Field with George Halas playing across the line from big Rock Island tackle Ed Healey. Halas devised a method of effectively blocking Healey from the play —namely, by holding onto the big man's jersey. Healey's appeals to the referee went unheeded, due perhaps to the fact that the home team at that time hired the officials. Healey warned Halas to cease and desist, but George persisted in this strategy on the next play. Halas, however, slipped in the mud after his block and rolled over just in time to see Healey's massive fist fly past his nose and imbed itself in the slop up to the wrist. Healey pulled his hand out of the ground with a sound like a bathroom plunger, and Halas took the hint, confining himself to legal blocks for the rest of the day.

The sight of Healey's wrist buried in the mud must have made a lasting impression on Halas, for on November 27 the Bears paid $100 to Rock Island for the big tackle's contract.

1922	W	L	T	Pct.
Canton	10	0	2	1.000
Chi Bears	9	3	0	.750
Chi Cards	8	3	0	.727
Toledo	5	2	2	.714
Rock Island	4	2	1	.667
Dayton	4	3	1	.571
Green Bay	4	3	3	.571
Racine	5	4	1	.556
Akron	3	4	2	.429
Buffalo	3	4	1	.429
Milwaukee	2	4	3	.333
Marion	2	6	0	.250
Minneapolis	1	3	0	.250
Evansville	0	2	0	.000
Louisville	0	3	0	.000
Rochester	0	3	1	.000
Hammond	0	4	1	.000
Columbus	0	7	0	.000

1923 Canton, the Single Wing, and Halas' Frantic Dash

In his second season as Canton coach, Guy Chamberlin brought home his second undefeated championship team, prompting some obseivers to wonder what he could do for an encore. None of the twenty league teams could defeat the Bulldogs, who rolled through their schedule with only one tie in eleven games to blemish a perfect record. Of course, coach Chamberlin's job was made considerably easier by player Guy Chamberlin, a stand-out two-way end. Tackles Fats Henry and Link Lyman continued to spark the leading defense in the circuit—and it was this brick-wall defense that insured a second championship as exemplified in the Bulldog's white-washing of the contending Chicago Bears, 6-0, for the Bears only loss of the season.

Beyond the race for the title, the spotlight fell on the game's strategy itself, as defense in general had been catching up with the basic T formation, leading to many low-scoring games and to many coaches' switching to other offensive setups. The short-punt formation stationed the quarterback five yards behind the center with the other backs closer to the line; this formation and the Notre Dame Box Formation grew in popularity among pro coaches. Just beginning to take hold in the pros was the single-wing formation, devised by Pop Warner at Stanford. In this deployment, a deep back called a tailback would take the snap and do most of the passing and running, while a wingback would be stationed near the line of scrimmage outside the end in a favorable pass-receiving position much like the modern flanker. The single wing provided powerful blocking for off-tackle plays and end runs and gradually became the dominant formation in the game up until World War II.

With the passing attack still badly needing some sprucing up, most teams still confined the aerial strictly to third-down situations. Only the Green Bay Packers used the air attack as often as the run. Curly Lambeau blended the pass into the regular Green Bay offense by frequently calling for as many as thirty passes a game, and his pioneering use of football aviation helped him develop a strong team from a squad of players recruited mostly from the immediate Wisconsin area.

Though the game was not as fancy and the press coverage minuscule in comparison with today, the NFL still produced star players whose names were often repeated in league cities. Eleven of 1923's gladiators eventually were enshrined in the Pro Football Hall of Fame in Canton. Linemen Fats Henry and Link Lyman of Canton and Ed Healey and George Trafton of the Chicago Bears won renown for their rugged work in the trenches, and Guy Chamberlin and George Halas have been enshrined among the ends. Future Hall of Famers among the backs included Jim Thorpe and Joe Guyon of the Oorang Indians, Curly Lambeau of the Green Bay Packers, Jimmy Conzelman of Milwaukee, and Paddy Driscoll of the Chicago Cardinals. In addition, Henry, Thorpe, Guyon, and Driscoll also starred as kickers, with Henry this year belting a 94-yard punt against Akron. Interestingly enough, all eleven have been recognized despite the absence of gaudy statistics to embellish their names.

Of all the legendary figures, it was Thorpe who managed to generate the most excitement on the field. Although no longer able to produce outstanding football for sixty minutes, opponents still feared the big Indian when aroused. Such a situation arose in a game against the Bears when Thorpe plunged for a short touchdown but fumbled on the two-yard line and George Halas scooped up the ball for the Bears. Halas started sprinting to the other end of the field with Thorpe in hot pursuit. Thorpe's calling card on defense was to throw the full force of his body high into the runner's back, and Halas realized what was coming if the Indian caught up with him. As Halas was later to remark, "I never ran faster in my life. I could feel Big Jim in the small of my back all the way." He must have, for his 98-yard touchdown return of a fumble, still standing as a record, owed much to the inspiration provided by Thorpe.

1923

	W	L	T	Pct.
Canton	11	0	1	1.000
Chi Bears	9	2	1	.818
Green Bay	7	2	1	.778
Milwaukee	7	2	3	.778
Cleveland	3	1	3	.750
Chi Cards	8	4	0	.667
Duluth	4	3	0	.571
Buffalo	5	4	3	.556
Columbus	5	4	1	.556
Racine	4	4	2	.500
Toledo	2	3	2	.400
Rock Island	2	3	3	.400
Minneapolis	2	5	2	.286
St. Louis	1	4	2	.200
Hammond	1	5	1	.167
Dayton	1	6	1	.143
Akron	1	6	0	.143
Marion	1	10	0	.091
Rochester	0	2	0	.000
Louisville	0	3	0	.000

1924 The Legislated Championship

The city of Canton, which had not lost a football game for two years, lost its pro-football team for 1924. In search of larger crowds and bigger profits in the big city, the invincible Bulldogs pulled up stakes and left their traditional home for the greener pastures of nearby Cleveland. Canton had hosted the best professional squads in the land, but rising salaries and expenses were forcing more of the smaller cities off the football stage.

Guy Chamberlin, Link Lyman, and most of the 1923 Bulldogs joined the team in Cleveland, but Fats Henry instead accepted an offer to play for the Pottsville Maroons, an independent pro team in the coal-mining district of Pennsylvania. But even without Henry, Chamberlin welded together a steel-tough Cleveland Bulldog club from his old team and from remnants of last year's Cleveland Indians.

The annual shuffle of teams saw five clubs drop out of the league and three join up, and one of the newcomers proved to be the Bulldogs' main competition for the championship. The Frankford Yellowjackets, based in a Philadelphia suburb, had played in the coal-mining circuit for years and were already a battle-hardened football machine upon entry into the NFL. Since Pennsylvania law then prohibited Sunday games, the Yellowjackets would usually play at home on Saturday and hit the road for an out-of-state Sunday game, thus building up a twenty-game season schedule and a lot of stamina.

As the season progressed, the Bulldogs lost their first game in three years, while the Yellowjackets endured two defeats out of the bushelful of games they played. Late in the year, both clubs scheduled games against weak clubs in order to inflate their records. But at the league's winter meeting, league head Joe Carr blew the whistle on this type of manipulation by declaring all games played after November 30 invalid for the league standings. This proclamation shrank Cleveland's record to 7-1-1 and Frankford's to 11-2-1, and Guy Chamberlin had his third championship in three years as Bulldog coach.

The Chicago Bears placed ahead of the Yellowjackets with a 6-1-4 mark, capturing the runner-up spot for the third year running. Halas and company lost their curtain raiser to Green Bay by a 5-0 count, but never again tasted defeat in ten league contests. The Bears refrained from scheduling late games to pump up the record, but their financial score needed no polishing at all as owners Halas and Dutch Sternaman split a $20,000 profit from the club at the end of the season.

The Oorang Indians disbanded before the season, and the Indians scattered to the wind. Pete Calac played for Buffalo, Joe Guyon joined the new Kansas City Cowboys, and Big Jim Thorpe signed on with the Rock Island Independents. Thorpe's spark had just about gone out, done in by his years of hard work and hard play, and the Independents used him mostly as a blocking back on offense. Still, rookie Steve Owen came into the league with a healthy respect for the Indian's blocking.

A 240-pound freshman tackle for the Kansas City Cowboys, Owen had played on a semi-pro team in the Midwest after the 1923 college season, and one opponent he faced was Thorpe, picking up a few extra dollars in the uniform of the Toledo Maroons.

Early in the game, Owen twice rushed right past Thorpe to nail the quarterback for a loss. After the second time, he remarked to a teammate, "Old Jim has slowed up. He won't block anymore." Owen shouldn't have said that; Thorpe heard him.

On the next play, young Owen again rushed in on the quarterback, paying no heed to Thorpe at all. In a flash, Owen was on his back with the wind knocked out of him, the victim of a Thorpe blindside body block. After the veteran had vindicated his reputation before the young upstart, he helped the rookie to his feet and offered him a bit of advice: "Son, always keep an eye on the old Indian."

1924

	W	L	T	Pct.
Cleveland	7	1	1	.875
Chi Bears	6	1	4	.857
Frankford	11	2	1	.846
Duluth	5	1	0	.833
Rock Island	6	2	2	.750
Green Bay	8	4	0	.667
Buffalo	6	4	0	.600
Racine	4	3	3	.571
Chi Cards	5	4	1	.556
Columbus	4	4	0	.500
Hammond	2	2	1	.500
Milwaukee	5	8	0	.385
Dayton	2	7	0	.222
Kansas City	2	7	0	.222
Akron	1	6	0	.143
Kenosha	0	5	1	.000
Minneapolis	0	6	0	.000
Rochester	0	7	0	.000

1925 Galloping Out of Oblivion

Even though the Four Horsemen of Notre Dame had graduated, college football still held the sporting spotlight in the autumn. The press treated pro football like a raggedy stepchild while trumpeting coast to coast the exploits of such teams as Dartmouth and the University of Washington. Although Washington's George (Wildcat) Wilson achieved a national reputation for his running, no football player could approach the fame of the Galloping Ghost—Red Grange of the University of Illinois.

Grange attained a standing next to Babe Ruth and Jack Dempsey on the sports pedestal by slipping and dodging to touchdowns by the bushelful. The shy redhead carried only 170 pounds, but he more than made up for his lack of bulk with quick changes of speeds and sharp cuts that left frustrated tacklers embracing his jet stream. His No. 77 disappearing downfield brought thousands to their feet cheering, not only in football stadiums but in movie houses which carried newsreels of his previous week's performance. With all the deserved publicity and fanfare, it was only inevitable that by the time autumn 1925 arrived, Grange was the hottest sports property around. Speculation grew over what No. 77 would do with his newfound fame. Most of his friends and the public advised him to go into acting or business and to avoid the dirty, profane world of pro football. When Grange finally revealed his choice, it wasn't a popular one, and suddenly America's redheaded golden boy was working at the dirtiest game in town.

But Grange figured that the most honest way to capitalize on his football fame was to play football. With C. C. Pyle, his fast-talking agent, conducting day-and-night secret negotiations with the Chicago Bears, Grange signed a professional contract with the team shortly after his final game with Illinois. In return for a hefty share of the gate receipts, Grange agreed to join the Bears for the remainder of their schedule and for a post-season barnstorming tour.

The public's loudly proclaimed disdain over the betrayal of their folk hero took no sides in the incident and blamed the pros as well as Grange. Colleges were incensed at the pros for signing Grange before he had graduated, and fans cursed him for contaminating himself with an unnatural professionalism. Grange himself shrugged off the criticism, openly admitting his desire to make big money before his glittering name evaporated from the public's eye. As far as the NFL was concerned, all the adjectives in the world couldn't harm them. They had finally gotten into the headlines, and the scorn was not nearly as large as the publicity.

Grange made his pro debut on Thanksgiving Day as the Bears hosted the Chicago Cardinals. An SRO crowd of 36,000 watched Grange pick up only 36 yards on the ground as the two Chicago rivals struggled to a scoreless tie. But three days later the Galloping Ghost galloped to 140 yards as the Bears beat Columbus 14–13 in a Chicago snowstorm.

To turn Grange's reputation into dollars, the Bears then set out on an Eastern tour that listed an exhausting eight games in twelve days. The first stop was St. Louis, where Red ran for four TDs against a hastily gathered squad of semi-pros. Three days later the Frankford Yellowjackets hosted the Bears in Philadelphia before a crowd of 35,000 eager to see some Grange magic. Heavy rain and deep mud ruled out any long runs, but Grange did score both touchdowns in a 14–7 Chicago victory. Immediately after the contest the Bears piled onto a train heading for New York.

The next day, Sunday, December 6, pro football won its spurs in New York City. The New York Giants had played their first year in virtual seclusion, but fans flooded the ticket windows to see the legendary halfback from the Midwest. The 73,000 paying customers set a record for professional football and saved Giant owner Tim Mara from a red-ink bath in his first year with the team.

The tired Bears took the field in the same wet uniforms they wore in Philadelphia. On the other hand, the Giants ran into action in spotless outfits, ready to put their best foot forward before the massive audience. Grange acted as a decoy for most of the game as Joe Sternaman, brother of the Bears' half-owner, broke away for a pair of touchdowns. The customers got their money's worth, though, when late in the contest Grange intercepted a Giant pass and trotted untouched for a touchdown to cap the 19–7 triumph for the Bears.

As the tour progressed all the Bears were dragging, nursing various wounds, and finding their stamina draining. Grange himself had been kicked in the neck in the New York game and was suffering from lack of rest due to the travel and to the demands of reporters. He kept on playing, though, spurred on by the healthy pile of dollars rolling his way with each game.

A listless Grange appeared before crowds in Washington, Boston, and Pittsburgh before finally sitting out a game in Detroit due to a badly swollen arm. The Bears ended the tour by hosting the Giants in a rematch at Chicago, and Red played before his home-town fans with only one arm at his disposal. Although the Giants won 9–0, the crowd applauded the local hero at the end of the day.

Grange pocketed $50,000 from the tour, and agent Pyle brought home the same amount. But after a short rest the Bears and Grange were off again—this time on a Southern and Western tour which would also gross $50,000 apiece for Grange and Pyle. When it was all over Grange found himself rich by playing eighteen games in less than three months. More important, though, and even beyond the profits the Bears and other teams realized, was that the NFL, at large, had finally broken into the national sports picture.

Despite Grange and his magnetism for publicity, there were other important events in the league which did not quite make the headlines. In the franchise shell game, three subtractions and five additions hiked the league membership to twenty-two.

The Canton Bulldogs were reorganized and readmitted, a Detroit franchise was granted to Jimmy Conzelman, a team was chartered in Providence, the Giants gave New York their first big-league football representation, and the Pottsville Maroons —veterans of the non-league coal-mining circuit in Pennsylvania—all cast their lot in what turned out to be a good year for joining the NFL. As the teams came, the players went. Some of the prominent ones who shifted their allegiance included Guy Chamberlin, who found Cleveland's lack of crowd support disheartening and moved over to the Frankford Yellowjackets as player and coach, Link Lyman and Fats Henry, who returned to Canton as the center of a mediocre squad, and Jim Thorpe, who started the year with the New York Giants but left the team after his aching legs kept him from showing any of his old spark at all.

The league championship went relatively unnoticed in the publicity over Red Grange. The Chicago Cardinals, led by Paddy Driscoll, and the Pottsville Maroons, the new boys on the block, entered their December 6 confrontation a half game apart in a contest which would decide the league championship. The Maroons easily downed the Cardinals 21–7 and seemingly won the championship in their first season in the circuit.

To celebrate the victory, the Maroons made the mistake of playing an all-star team of former Notre Dame players, including the Four Horsemen, in Philadelphia the next week—a game which Pottsville won, 9-7, and one which cost them the league title.

After the game, Frankford coach Guy Chamberlin filed an objection with the league office, claiming that Pottsville had violated his teams's territorial rights by playing Notre Dame in Philadelphia. League head Joe Carr agreed with Chamberlin and declared the title forfeited to the Cardinals as punishment.

Then, in a move to preserve some continuity in the record books, Carr instructed the Cardinals to play two more games to make their record better than Pottsville's. The Cardinals scheduled two games in four days, against Hammond and a Milwaukee club which had already dispanded for the season. They beat Hammond 13–0 and defeated Milwaukee in a farce of a game in which the quarters were only five minutes long to win perhaps the most unjust title in pro football's history.

To further the hypocrisy, Carr went on to fine the Milwaukee club $500 for using four high-school players in the post-season Cardinal match. While Carr was inventing champions he also took the time to reaffirm the league's policy of good will toward the colleges by ruling that no college player could be signed before his class had graduated. Why not? With Grange in the fold, the pros didn't need to bother the colleges for at least another ten years.

1925	W	L	T	Pct.
Chi Cards	11	2	1	.846
Pottsville	10	2	0	.833
Detroit	8	2	2	.800
N. Y. Giants	8	4	0	.667
Akron	4	2	2	.667
Frankford	13	7	0	.650
Chi Bears	9	5	3	.643
Rock Island	5	3	3	.625
Green Bay	8	5	0	.615
Providence	6	5	1	.545
Canton	4	4	0	.500
Cleveland	5	8	1	.385
Kansas City	2	5	1	.286
Hammond	1	3	0	.250
Buffalo	1	6	2	.143
Duluth	0	3	0	.000
Rochester	0	6	1	.000
Milwaukee	0	6	0	.000
Dayton	0	7	1	.000
Columbus	0	9	0	.000

1926 From Grange's Showcase to Nevers' Traveling Eskimos

C. C. Pyle quickly grew into a familiar face around the NFL. Affectionately known as "Cash and Carry," Pyle had driven a hard bargain as Red Grange's agent in negotiating a contract with the Chicago Bears, and now he was back asking for more.

Remembering the sell-out crowd at the Polo Grounds to see Grange with the Bears, Pyle requested a New York franchise of his own with which to showcase Grange. New York Giant owner Tim Mara hit the ceiling, claiming that Pyle was muscling in on his turf. The league lodge brothers backed up Mara's stand, and Pyle's proposed New York franchise was not admitted. Far from quitting, Pyle then began fighting for real. He announced the formation of the American Football League, a new circuit whose main attraction would be Red Grange of the New York Yankees.

Nine clubs made up the new loop. Aside from New York, new teams were placed in Philadelphia, Cleveland, Chicago, Boston, Brooklyn, and Newark; in addition, Rock Island jumped over from the NFL, and a road team nominally representing Los Angeles completed the membership. Each of the teams lured several established pros away from the NFL, and the young glamour backs of the league included Grange, Wildcat Wilson of the Los Angeles squad, and Brooklyn's Harry Stuhldreher, quarterback of the Four Horsemen of Notre Dame.

The old but hardly established NFL responded to Pyle's challenge by swelling its ranks to twenty-two teams, the largest roll call in league history. Brooklyn, Hartford, and Racine had been sufficiently impressed by the Grange tour in 1925 to take a fling at pro football, and homeless road clubs were established bearing the names of Los Angeles and Louisville. Oddly enough, Los Angeles, which unknowingly lent its name to two pro-football teams in the runaway franchise boom, never witnessed a game within its city boundaries.

Financially, everybody lost. It consistently rained Sunday after Sunday to keep the attendance to a minimum, and that fact of life, coupled with the high costs of a talent war, sent many an optimistic owner into hair-pulling fits and regret over entering such a booming field.

As the AFL season progressed through cloudbursts and empty seats, the New York Yankees and Philadelphia Quakers quickly rose to the top of the broth. The Quakers wound up as champs of the league, but only five clubs remained active until the end. Cleveland, Boston, Brooklyn, and Newark all walked off the stage before the final curtain to force the remaining troupe to fold its tent and reluctantly fade into history.

Although Red Grange did not have a spectacular season, he still drew enough people into Yankee Stadium to put a severe dent in Tim Mara's wallet. The Giants' owner dropped $60,000 during the year but tightened his belt and outlasted Pyle's threat.

NFL play went on as usual with Guy Chamberlin, as usual, piloting the champions. Chamberlin's Frankford Yellowjackets outsprinted the Chicago Bears and Pottsville Maroons in a three-way race for the crown. George Halas had strengthened the Bears by buying Paddy Driscoll from the Chicago Cardinals —an NFL preservation precipitated by the AFL's high offer to buy the versatile back's contract. The Maroons were paced by backs, Tony Latone and Barney Wentz.

Guy Chamberlin's best player at Frankford still remained himself, as was proven when the Bears invaded Frankford on a ten-game winning streak in a crucial late-season game. Chamberlin blocked a Driscoll extra-point attempt in the game's key play to allow a late touchdown and conversion to stand and give Frankford a 7-6 victory. The championship, which was Chamberlin's fourth in five years, turned out to be his last.

The biggest name on the NFL circuit this season was rookie Ernie Nevers of the Duluth Eskimos. A big, blond, handsome fullback, Nevers had built up a national reputation as an All-American at Stanford under Pop Warner. Nevers could crash a line like a truck, could pass from the single-wing formation, was a top-notch field-goal kicker, and played relentless defense. But to his fellow players, Ernie stood out first of all for his all-consuming desire for victory—a passion which kept him in the lineup when battered and hurt.

The NFL counted on Nevers' name to draw people to the park as much as Pyle depended on Grange, thus the Duluth squad was destined to play most of its games in larger cities away from Minnesota. The Eskimos played two home games, then hit the road on September 6 and did not return until February 5, after playing twenty-nine league and exhibition games in most of the circuit's cities.

Owner Ole Haugsrud agreed to pay Nevers $15,000 plus a percentage of the larger gates and was left with little money to hire other players. For most of the traveling road show, the Eskimos carried only thirteen players, making them truly "The Iron Men from the North," as Grantland Rice dubbed them. The owner and coach both suited up to cover the bare spots on the bench, but neither was of any help on the field itself. Ernie Nevers needed none of the nonexistent substitutes, as he played all but twenty-nine minutes of the tour, and his play topped whatever Red Grange had offered as a pro. Against Pottsville, Ernie completed seventeen consecutive passes, and in a game against Hartford he booted five field goals for a 15-0 victory. In Milwaukee, doctors advised him to sit out the game when abdominal pains signaled an oncoming appendicitis attack. But with the Eskimos losing 6-0, Nevers put himself into action, threw a 40-yard touchdown pass, and kicked the extra point to lodge a 7-6 Duluth triumph. The appendicitis attack couldn't cope with Ernie's natural defenses and fled before making itself felt.

However, in Canton, Nevers played against Jim Thorpe for the first and only time and had an experience he would never forget. The thirty-eight-year-old Thorpe had returned to the Bulldogs for his final campaign and left his calling card with the league's new superstar when he blindsided him after a pass reception. Thorpe helped the stunned Nevers to his feet and asked if he was all right. Nevers replied, "Sure, Jim, I'm O.K. But I'm glad I wasn't playing against you ten years ago." Later on, though, Nevers told of the full impact of the blow, and his description was a little more telling than that which he related to the big Indian: "I felt as though my ribs had been caved in, as if I'd been pile-driven three feet into the ground. Never before or since have I been hit as hard."

As far as the Eskimos' season itself went, the team played only slightly better than .500 ball against league teams, mostly because of the opportunity to concentrate exclusively on Nevers. Traveling by boat, car, and bus, the Eskimos finally returned to Minnesota with countless bruises and many lost pounds—a fact Nevers himself exemplified by dropping from 210 to 185 pounds during the five-month trip. But despite everything, Nevers won new accolades over and above his college honors and even gave owner Haugsrud a $4,000 profit from the tour.

1926	W	L	T	Pct.
Frankford	14	1	1	.933
Chi Bears	12	1	3	.923
Pottsville	10	2	1	.833
Kansas City	8	3	1	.727
Green Bay	7	3	3	.700
Los Angeles	6	3	1	.667
N. Y. Giants	8	4	0	.667
Duluth	6	5	2	.545
Buffalo	4	4	2	.500
Chi Cards	5	6	1	.455
Providence	5	7	0	.417
Detroit	4	6	2	.400
Hartford	3	7	0	.300
Brooklyn	3	8	0	.273
Milwaukee	2	7	0	.222
Akron	1	4	3	.200
Dayton	1	4	1	.200
Racine	1	4	0	.200
Columbus	1	6	0	.143
Canton	1	9	3	.100
Hammond	0	4	0	.000
Louisville	0	4	0	.000

1927 A Battered Knee, Broken Ribs, and the Mighty Giant Defense

All the teams that optimistically jumped into pro football in 1926 dropped out of the scene in 1927. The AFL went under entirely, and twelve NFL teams called it quits. C. C. Pyle's New York Yankees were taken into the NFL (which is what he wanted in the first place), and a new Cleveland team was admitted to bring the league membership to twelve clubs. Buffalo, however, dropped out in mid-season.

With the demise of the AFL, the NFL had cornered the market on post-graduate star backs. Red Grange came in with the Yankees, Ernie Nevers still played for Duluth, Wildcat Wilson signed with Providence, and ex-Michigan All-American Benny Friedman joined the new Cleveland team. While the other three primarily were runners, Friedman was known for his passing and play-calling, much like a modern quarterback, and he often startled many a fan and coach with his passes on firstdown, a "reckless" move definitely not in the 1927 "book."

None of these players or their teams, though, wound up with the championship. That trophy would go this year to the New York Giants, the possessors of the league's most bruising defense. Two-hundred-and-sixty-pound Cal Hubbard joined the team as a rookie but could not budge veteran stars Century Milstead and Steve Owen from tackle. Instead, Hubbard became the league's largest offensive end and welded the defense together as a large but quick linebacker. The hard-nosed Giants posted eleven shutouts, allowing only 20 points all year while grinding out 213 points for their side of the tally.

The Giants, in winning the title without a star back, managed to do so with a rugged triumph over the Chicago Bears, which was perhaps the key win of the season. Both clubs hit hard from the opening gun and hit harder as the game went on. On one play, George Halas tried to rush up and blindside Joe Guyon, winding up his career with the Giants. Indian Joe caught Halas in the corner of his eye, swung around at the last second, and drove his knee into George's side. Halas left the game with two broken ribs and a bit of advice from Guyon: "George, let that be a lesson to you. Never try to sneak up behind an Indian." What hurt George the most, though, was the clipping penalty he received for his efforts.

Steve Owen played tackle for the Giants that day and summed up the game: "It was the toughest, roughest football game I ever played. I played sixty minutes at tackle opposite Jim McMillen. When the final gun sounded, the two of us just sat on the ground. We shook hands but couldn't say anything. We were too exhausted. We just sat there."

The Giants also finished ahead of their rival at the gate, outdrawing the Yankees by a wide margin as Red Grange seriously injured his knee in a collision with George Trafton of the Bears in the third game of the year. With Red spending most of the season on crutches and making only token appearances in a few late games, the New York public showed little desire to see a Grangeless Yankee team when the Giants were driving on to a championship.

While Grange was on the sidelines, Ernie Nevers continued

in the lineup of the undermanned Duluth Eskimos. Playing a normal schedule this time, the Eskimos could win only one game in ten tries, as every opponent simply keyed on Nevers and safely ignored most of the other players. Ernie simply could not win all by himself, try as he would.

As pro football continued its search for stability, two of the game's legendary superstars moved down from their pinnacles. Jim Thorpe finally hung his shoulder pads up after fourteen years of dishing out and taking punishment, and Guy Chamberlin quit as Frankford coach and moved over to the Chicago Cardinals as a player, never again to be on a championship squad. Thorpe's performance over the years earned him recognition, even in eras to come, as the greatest athlete ever to appear on a football field.

1927	W	L	T	Pct.
N. Y. Giants	11	1	1	.917
Green Bay	7	2	1	.778
Chi Bears	9	3	2	.750
Cleveland	8	4	1	.667
Providence	8	5	1	.615
N. Y. Yankees	7	8	1	.467
Frankford	6	9	3	.400
Pottsville	5	8	0	.385
Chi Cards	3	7	1	.300
Dayton	1	6	1	.143
Duluth	1	8	0	.111
Buffalo	0	5	0	.000

1928 Nothing Much to Cheer About

The New York Giants swallowed a large dose of their own medicine in trying to defend their NFL championship. Billed as the league's top defensive club, the Giants themselves were shut out six times while springing enough leaks in that defense to allow 135 points. Sixth-place clubs, Tim Mara learned, draw fewer fans than do championship teams; a grand turnout of eighty diehards at one contest sent Mara scurrying for new players in the off season to prop up his ex-champs.

Fate smiled just as unkindly on the Green Bay Packers and Chicago Bears. The Packers dropped off into fourth place, convincing Curly Lambeau that he too needed to do some winter shopping in the football marketplace. The Bears' fifth-place standing could be chalked up to advancing age in key players like Paddy Driscoll, George Halas, and George Trafton, but also to a growing rift between owners Dutch Sternaman and Halas. Sternaman no longer played halfback but insisted on installing his own system into the Bear attack. As one Bear player later recalled, "We had two offenses—one devised by Halas, the other by Sternaman. Nobody knew what to expect on any play. Men ran into each other. The team lacked timing." The Bears were on a downhill slide, the worst of which was yet to come.

While these three famous teams were all retreating, the unheralded Providence Steamrollers grabbed off the league title with a 8-1-2 mark. Verteran Jimmy Conzelman doubled as coach and blocking back to become a member of a championship club for the first time since he joined the infant league in 1920. In powering the Steamrollers' attack to the top of the circuit, Conzelman's savvy was greatly aided by Wildcat Wilson's breakaway running.

The circuit, meantime, now counted only ten stops, with the dropping of Cleveland, Duluth, and Buffalo and the adding of a new Detroit outpost. Although Detroit was fortunate to have Benny Friedman, who threw passes like flies, the flies, unfortunately, outnumbered the paying customers. In fact, all the turnstiles slowed down throughout the league. The reason obviously enough was the absence of Red Grange and Ernie Nevers. Grange's knee had not responded well to treatment, so he decided to call it a day in pro football. Instead, he spent his autumn on the vaudeville circuit and in making a movie. Bad knee and all, the Grange name still was hot box-office material, in front of the camera as well as behind the line.

Nevers left pro football for something not so glamorous, returning to Stanford as an assistant coach under Pop Warner. On the side, though, Ernie picked up good money as a pitcher for the St. Louis Browns baseball team. Though his diamond career never reached the heights his football life did, Ernie did make it into baseball's record books. During Babe Ruth's record-setting sixty-home-run season of 1927, two of the Bambino's circuit clouts were served up by a St. Louis right-hander named Ernie Nevers.

1928	W	L	T	Pct.
Providence	8	1	2	.889
Frankford	11	3	2	.786
Detroit	7	2	1	.778
Green Bay	6	4	3	.600
Chi Bears	7	5	1	.583
N. Y. Giants	4	7	2	.364
N. Y. Yankees	4	8	1	.333
Pottsville	2	8	0	.200
Chi Cards	1	5	0	.167
Dayton	0	7	0	.000

1929 Harnessing the Bad Boys and a First Championship

Over the summer, Curly Lambeau turned the Green Bay Packers from a good team into the favorite for the championship by picking up three talented malcontents in Mike Michalske, Cal Hubbard, and Johnny Blood. Neither Michalske nor Hubbard had been happy in New York. The disbanding of the New York Yankees made guard Michalske a free agent, and he lost no time in putting his very quick 210 pounds to use in the Green Bay line. On defense, his favorite tactic was red-dogging the quarterback, long before this became a standard defensive weapon. Country boy Hubbard had tired of the bright New York lights and requested a trade to quiet Green Bay. The Giants granted his wish and lived to regret it, feeling the full pressure of his 265 pounds during a crucial game late in the season.

Blood combined the football skills of a Gale Sayers with the social talent of a Joe Namath. Nicknamed "The Vagabond Halfback," he had played for three NFL clubs before Lambeau picked up his contract from Pottsville. Blood could outsprint most other players, was a slashing inside runner, caught passes better than any back in the league, and was a first-rate defensive back and punter. In addition to all this, Blood led the league in times fined. He ignored training rules and never cared much about curfews; still, the handsome Irishman never let the Packers down on the field. But off the field, he saw as much action as Joe Namath without nearly as much green to lean on.

In negotiating his first contract with Lambeau, Johnny Blood showed where his values lay. The halfback wanted $100 a game, but Lambeau countered with an offer of $110 if Blood would lay off the booze after Tuesday of each week. Blood turned this down, asking Curly to accept Wednesday as the cutoff day for liquor. Lambeau threw his hands up and agreed, and his halfback stuck religiously to the agreement all year.

With these three in tow, Curly greatly improved a squad which already had some pretty fair players like tailback Red Dunn, halfback and premier punter Verne Lewellen, and end Lavie Dilweg. With supreme confidence, the Packers won their first five contests, all at home, with a bone-crushing defense and a wide-open offense featuring Dunn's passes and Blood's running and receiving. The true test remained, though, an eight-game road trip to complete the schedule. An enthusiastic crowd of 2,000 fans saw the team off at the station; true to form, Johnny Blood held the train up by showing up forty-five minutes late.

The Packers kept winning on the road, even after Red Dunn was knocked out of action with an injury, and they headed to New York for a November 24 showdown with the Giants. The New Yorkers also came into this confrontation undefeated and fully confident of knocking off the invaders from the Midwest. Owner Tim Mara had decided that passer Benny Friedman was the perfect prescription to heal his ailing Giants both on the field and at the ticket window. When the Detroit Wolverines refused to part with Benny, Mara simply whipped out his checkbook and bought the entire Detroit franchise, from the head coach down to the last sub.

An audience of 25,000 showed up at the Polo Grounds and witnessed a convincing upset by the Packers. Cal Hubbard and Mike Michalske led a pass rush which gave Benny Friedman no time at all to set up. Verne Lewellen consistently boomed sixty-yard punts to nail the Giants deep in their own territory, and Johnny Blood set up the first touchdown with a fumble recovery and scored the final one with a short run. All the Packers played the entire sixty minutes except guard Jim Bowdoin, who came out of the fray with an injury with only one minute left to play.

Green Bay ran through its final three games in eight days and headed back home as undefeated champions, the first since 1923. The send-off crowd of 2,000 had swelled into a welcoming party of 20,000 who danced and caroused in freezing temperatures all night when the Packers arrived.

A high note in the Packers' season was their three victories over the arch-rival Chicago Bears. The Bears were weak in the line and burdened with feuding co-owners, and they suffered their first losing season ever. After six games, the Bears stood at 4-1-1, but their final eight contests resulted in seven losses and a tie. Even the return of Red Grange to the Bears' backfield could not slow the backslide. Losses in the stock-market convinced Grange to accept Halas' offer to rejoin the Bears, but he no longer was the breakaway runner of old. Although his injured knee had robbed him of his speed and cutting ability, he more than earned his salary by developing into a good receiver, blocker, pass defender, and adequate inside runner.

Ernie Nevers also followed Grange back into the NFL fold, joining the Chicago Cardinals as a playing coach. In the annual Thanksgiving contest between the Cardinals and Bears, Ernie set a record yet untouched by scoring 40 points on six touchdowns and four extra points. In that same game, Jim Thorpe made a brief appearance for the Cardinals. As the Associated Press reported, "In his forties and musclebound, Thorpe was a mere shadow of his former self."

Passing Thorpe in the opposite direction was rookie back Ken Strong. The New York University star signed with the new Staten Island Stapletons when their offer of $5,000 plus a rent-free apartment topped an offer by the Giants. Strong threatened to score whenever he broke into an open field, and his toe added additional points to his tally with field goals and extra points on place kicks.

Staten Island came into the league along with Boston, Orange (N.J.), Buffalo, and Minneapolis. With Detroit, Pottsville, and the New York Yankees folding, the NFL lodge now numbered twelve brothers. Competing for the final time were the Dayton Triangles, charter members of the league in 1920. The Triangles lost all six of their contests this year and mercifully ceased operation after their final five seasons yielded a 2-24-3 record. Although Green Bay had won the championship, most of the smaller cities like Dayton were joining the Canton Bulldogs and Massillon Tigers in football's Valhalla.

1929

	W	L	T	Pct.
Green Bay	12	0	1	1.000
N. Y. Giants	12	1	1	.923
Frankford	9	4	5	.692
Chi Cards	6	6	1	.500
Boston	4	4	0	.500
Orange	3	4	4	.429
Stapleton (N. Y.)	3	4	3	.429
Providence	4	6	2	.400
Chi Bears	4	8	2	.333
Buffalo	1	7	1	.125
Minneapolis	1	9	0	.100
Dayton	0	6	0	.000

1930 Along Came Jones, There Goes Nagurski

George Halas decided that the Chicago Bears needed a housecleaning, so the first thing he did was to fire head coach George Halas. At the tender age of thirty-four, Halas called it quits as a player and coach to devote all his time to front-office duties. For a new coach, the Bears dipped into the college ranks for Ralph Jones, the head man at Lake Forest College and a leading proponent of the formation.

While most pro teams lined up in the Notre Dame box or the single wing, the Bears under Jones used the T with such refinements as split ends and a man in motion in the backfield—a role which was naturally enough given Red Grange for his ability to excel equally at grabbing passes as he was at clocking the defensive end.

Jones, whose refined T opened up the Bear offense with passes and end runs, climbed out on a shaky limb by promising a championship within three years. As the first step in rebuilding the Bears, Halas and Paddy Driscoll retired from the lineup and George Trafton simply was not invited back. Big George, though, could not be cut so easily. On his own, he showed up at the Bears' training camp and introduced himself to Jones. Told to return in uniform at 9:00 A.M. the next day, Trafton was ordered from the field when he arrived at 9:30. The next day he was ready to go at 8:45 and proceeded to win back his center job with some outstanding head-knocking in the pre-season.

To go with veterans like Trafton, Red Grange, and Link Lyman, Jones had a pair of rookie peaches in Bronko Nagurski and Carl Brumbaugh, the last of whom won the quarterback job and became the first great Bear passer in the T formation. Nagurski came out of the University of Minnesota as an All-American, both at fullback and at tackle. He stood 6' 2" and carried 230 solid pounds, and running with his head down like a battering ram, he quickly became the league's top power runner. Such was his play that teammate Red Grange, who had the good fortune to face Nagurski only in practice, was led to comment, "When you hit him, it was like getting an electric shock. If you hit him above the ankles, you were likely to get yourself killed." Another of Nagurski's feats—the kind which folklores are made of—took place on opening day when the Bears played the defending champion Packers. When the

Bears punted, Grange had the job of the blocking back and played up close to the line, while Nagurski was positioned farther back. Cal Hubbard, the Packers' mammoth tackle, asked Grange to let him past so he could test the rookie. Grange agreed, and Hubbard plowed into Nagurski with a full head of steam, only to bounce off the rookie like a rubber ball. Hubbard then came over to Grange and said, "Thanks, Red, but please don't do me any more favors."

Though the Bears went on to a successful season, the Packers won that opening game and each of their first eight contests. With an undefeated streak of twenty-two games, the Packers then lost to Ernie Nevers' Cardinals and the New York Giants on back-to-back weekends. Although the Giants took over first place with their victory over the Packers, a New York loss one week later returned first place to Green Bay for keeps. Boosted by a sensational rookie passer, Arnie Herber, the Packers squeaked past the Giants and Bears to become the first repeat champions since the Canton Bulldogs of 1922-23.

The Giants too had come up with a blue-chip rookie in runner Chris Cagle of Army to strengthen an already powerful squad. The most important game the Giants played this year, though, was not even a league contest but only an exhibition game. With the Great Depression throwing New Yorkers out of work in bunches, the Giants agreed to meet an All-Star team of Notre Dame graduates on December 14, with all the proceeds going to the New York Unemployment Fund.

Knute Rockne coached the Notre Dame squad, which included the Four Horsemen and other more recent graduates. Rockne never had thought much of the pros, so he told his charges, "These Giants are big but slow. Score two or three touchdowns in a hurry and then just hold them."

On the other hand, Benny Friedman and the Giants found the game a great opportunity to convince Rockne and the public of the quality of pro ball. Before a crowd of 55,000, Friedman led the Giants to a pair of quick touchdowns while allowing the Notre Dame players not even a first down. At halftime, Rockne asked that the Giants not make his boys look bad in a charity game, so most of the New York regulars sat out the remainder of the game. Nevertheless, the final score was a one-sided 22-0. Even Rockne had to admit the powerful showing of these paid professionals who made their living at football. The game ironically turned out to be Rockne's last, as he soon afterward died in a plane crash.

The Giants profited from the enormous publicity the press gave the contest, and no longer would the public shrug off the pros as clumsy goons. But more importantly, the New York Unemployment Fund collected $115,163.

The Chicago Bears and Cardinals also played an exhibition for unemployment relief. The Chicago game was most noteworthy because it was played indoors on an eighty yard field in Chicago Stadium as enough dirt was carted into the building and spread over the marble floor to form a six-inch-deep playing surface. But whereas the pros could lend some support to a stifled economy, they could do nothing to save some of their own lodge brothers, three of which—Boston, Buffalo, and Dayton—had to give up the ghost before the season started. To pick up the slack of the disbanded clubs, Brooklyn and Portsmouth (Ohio) came into the league. In addition, the New Jersey club in Orange moved its home over to larger Newark to give the NFL a final membership of eleven clubs.

After the conclusion of the college season, the league stole headlines when the Bears signed fullback Joe Savoldi of Notre Dame. The furor over recruiting Savoldi before his class graduated rivaled the 1925 uproar over Red Grange's turning professional, and president Joe Carr levied a $1,000 fine on the Bears for the premature signing. Yet as fate would have it, Savoldi lasted only four games. It was not that his play could really be faulted but simply that another rookie fullback, named Nagurski, proved to be too much competition to overcome.

1930

	W	L	T	Pct.
Green Bay	10	3	1	.769
N. Y. Giants	13	4	0	.765
Chi Bears	9	4	1	.692
Brooklyn	7	4	1	.636
Providence	6	4	1	.600
Stapleton (N.Y.)	5	5	2	.500
Chi Cards	5	6	2	.455
Portsmouth	5	6	3	.455
Frankford	4	14	1	.222
Minneapolis	1	7	1	.125
Newark	1	10	1	.091

1931 Nearly Unpacking the Pack

While the Green Bay Packers surprised few people by finishing on top of the NFL for the third straight year, few observers expected the Portsmouth Spartans to challenge Green Bay for the crown as closely as they did. The Spartans jumped up from eighth place to a strong runner-up spot with a fine trio of rookies in Dutch Clark, George Christensen, and Ox Emerson.

Christensen and Emerson beefed up the forward line, and tailback Clark made the Spartan ground attack as formidable as the ancient Greek infantry. Coming from Colorado College, Clark set the league on its ear with his dodging, jackrabbit-like frantic open-field running, his leadership on the field, his flawless play at safety, and his fine drop-kicking—the last of which was a dying art as the football gradually was slimmed down to help the passing game.

Clark signed for $140 a game but had more trouble getting his money than gaining yardage on the field. The Depression held the attendance down, and since the team bank account usually was no better than the last game's receipts, the last Spartan to get to the bank with his check usually could bounce it all the way home and nail it to the wall. At the end of the year, the team owed Clark $800 and paid him off in $1 bills, which were collected direct from the ticket window.

While the Spartans managed to survive off field on their wits, the Packers stuck to their on-field brick-wall defense to chalk up another fine season. To give further impetus to the Green Bay defense, the offense received a new shot in the arm in Arnie Herber's long passes to Johnny Blood and Verne Lewellen. The Packers ran off a winning streak of nine games to open the season before losing to Ernie Nevers and the Chicago Cardinals. When the Bears upset the Packers in the season's finale, only one game stood between Green Bay and Portsmouth, but Curly Lambeau conveniently ignored urgent calls by the Spartans for a playoff game.

The Bears played up to their potential in knocking off the Packers, but injuries during the year kept them from making a serious run at the top. The other pre-season favorite, the Giants, never got off the ground and finished at 6-6-1 despite a talented squad. Coach Leroy Andrews washed his hands of the team late in the season, and players Benny Friedman and

Steve Owen took the rudder as interim co-coaches for the last few games.

If the Giants had trouble, Minneapolis and Newark had more, as both clubs were forced to cease operations. Yet Cleveland once again gave the NFL a whirl to bring the membership up to ten clubs. The Depression, though, had all the teams on the financial ropes. But as long as there was a league, Joe Carr was going to use his authority as league president to keep everything within the guidelines. He levied $1,000 fines on the Bears, Green Bay, and Portsmouth for using players in the 1930 season whose college classes had not yet graduated. In addition to putting out fines, Carr's office also issued the first All-Pro team, selected by the league itself because no one else showed any interest in picking it. As would be expected, four Packers made the team—Johnny Blood, Lavie Dilweg, Cal Hubbard, and Mike Michalske—while the other selections were spread out among the Spartans, Bears, Cardinals, and Giants. Dutch Clark, Ernie Nevers, Red Grange, and Blood filled the backfield slots, Dilweg and New York's Red Badgro were honored at end, and Hubbard and George Christensen at tackle, Michalske and Butch Gibson of the Giants at guard, and center Frank McNally of the Cardinals won the interior line selections.

Of the three rookies who made this original All-Pro team, Clark and Christensen would have long distinguished careers in the NFL, while McNally would last only four seasons with the Cardinals. Another rookie center, Mel Hein of the Giants, who had to take a back seat to McNally this year, wasted no time in staking his claim on the All-Pro center spot as his personal property—a feat he managed throughout the remainder of the 1930s.

1931

	W	L	T	Pct.
Green Bay	12	2	0	.857
Portsmouth	11	3	0	.786
Chi Bears	8	4	0	.667
Chi Cards	5	4	0	.556
N. Y. Giants	6	6	1	.500
Providence	4	4	3	.500
Stapleton (N.Y.)	4	6	1	.400
Cleveland	2	8	0	.200
Brooklyn	2	12	0	.143
Frankford	1	6	1	.143

1932 The 80-Yard Circus

With the temperature plummeting to 30° below and several inches of snow on the ground, George Halas decided to move the NFL championship game indoors to Chicago Stadium for the sake of attendance. A decent turnout of 11,000 did fill the auditorium, but changes had to be made in the game itself to fit the building. As in a previous charity game played here in 1930, the field reached only eighty yards and was surrounded by a solid fence standing a few feet from the sidelines. The ground itself consisted of turf left behind by a circus, and a distinct aroma lingered on the playing field.

With these modifications, the Chicago Bears and Portsmouth Spartans clashed to resolve their deadlock for the championship. The Spartans played at a disadvantage because star runner Dutch Clark had gone home to coach the Colorado College basketball team for the winter and could not get back East for the game. Without Clark, the Spartans played a feverish defensive game and held the Bears scoreless until late in the contest. The Bears had the ball close to the Portsmouth goal, though, and the Spartans braced for a Bronko Nagurski plunge. Nagurski indeed took a handoff from Carl Brumbaugh, headed into the line, threw on his breaks, retreated a few steps, and tossed a soft pass to Red Grange all alone in the end zone.

The rules at this time said that a pass had to be thrown from at least five yards behind the line of scrimmage, and the Spartans complained that Bronko had not retreated far enough to make the pass legal. The officials allowed the score, and the Bears went on to a 9-0 triumph and their second NFL title, making good on Coach Ralph Jones's promise of a championship within three years. As an offshoot of this game, passing was legalized anywhere behind the line of scrimmage—one of several moves to open up the game.

This unusual title match had come about when Portsmouth won its final match and the Bears upset the Packers in their curtain-dropper. Green Bay evidently had been rolling to another title before stumbling at the finish line, dropping their last two games to the Spartans and Bears without scoring a point.

For the Packers, though, the season was far from a loss, since they added rookie fullback Clarke Hinkle to their backfield. At 200 pounds, the unheralded Hinkle hardly rivaled Bronko Nagurski in size, but he gave nothing away to the Bronk when it came to hitting and jolting. Bulldog Turner would later say of Hinkle, "When you hit him, it would just pop every joint all the way down to your toes." With Ernie Nevers retired this year, Hinkle joined Nagurski as the models for power backs in the 1930s.

The Bears also picked up a useful rookie in end Bill Hewitt, a colorful pass receiver whose tossing blond hair became his trademark, as he refused to wear a helmet until late in his career.

George Preston Marshall also came into the league with three partners as a rookie owner of the new Boston Braves. The Braves required a lot of courage from their owners by losing $46,000 in this first year, and Marshall's partners all washed their hands of pro football after the season. Marshall hung on, though, and would contribute many ideas for rules changes and pageantry to the league through the years.

More than balancing Boston's entry into the league were three casualties, Cleveland, Providence, and Frankford. Eight clubs turned out to be as low an enrollment as the NFL would fall to, and the tighter circuit gave rise to new and colorful rivalries, as well as the setup of two divisions, the Eastern and Western, whose winners would meet in the first official championship game in 1933.

Another new feature of the league was the keeping of individual statistics. Arnie Herber of Green Bay won the maiden passing crown, Luke Johnsos of the Bears caught the most passes, Staten Island rookie Bob Campiglio led all the rushers, and Dutch Clark took both the scoring and field-goal titles. A minuscule total of three field goals gave drop-kicker Clark the leadership in that category, due to the fact that the pros still were following the colleges by planting the goal posts on the back line of the end zone.

Only Dutch Clark and Cal Hubbard repeated on the second All-Pro team issued by the league. Newcomers included backs

Bronko Nagurski, Arnie Herber, and Portsmouth blocking back Father Lumpkin; ends Luke Johnsos of the Bears and Ray Flaherty of New York; and linemen Nate Barrager of Green Bay, Jules Carlson of the Bears, Walt Kiesling of the Cardinals, and Boston rookie Turk Edwards. The Bears and Packers each placed three players on the team, Portsmouth contributed two, and Boston, New York, and the Chicago Cardinals all had a single player honored.

But despite all the honors and all the statistics, the most important statistic remained the profit ledger. The Chicago Bears lost $18,000, prompting Dutch Sternaman to unload his half of the Bears for $38,000 to George Halas. Loans gave Halas the necessary down payment, and George scraped together the payments during 1934 to make the Chicago Bears an entirely George Halas production.

The crosstown Cardinals suffered through a dismal season with Ernie Nevers retired and no longer around to win games and fans. Tackle Duke Slater also called it a day before the season began. Aside from ending a fine ten-year career, Slater's retirement left the NFL with only one black player, tailback Joe Lillard of the Cardinals. When Lillard and rookie Ray Kemp of Pittsburgh were dropped after the 1933 season, it would not be until after World War II that the unofficial color line in pro football would be broken.

1932

	W	L	T	Pct.
Chi Bears	7	1	6	.875
Green Bay	10	3	1	.769
Portsmouth	6	2	4	.750
Boston	4	4	2	.500
N. Y. Giants	4	6	2	.400
Brooklyn	3	9	0	.250
Chicago Cards	2	6	2	.250
Stapleton	2	7	3	.222

1933—1945
Divide, Bring in the Goal Posts, and Conquer

While President Franklin D. Roosevelt was driving his New Deal legislation through Congress in early 1933, George Halas and George Preston Marshall were ushering in a New Deal of their own. NFL president Joe Carr presided over league meetings in February and July in which Halas, the strong-willed owner of the Chicago Bears, and Marshall, the equally stubborn owner of the Boston Redskins, led the club owners in adopting some needed innovations in their game and league.

Changes in the playing rules moved the goal posts from the back of the end zones up to the goal lines, permitted passing from any point behind the line of scrimmage (instead of from at least five yards behind the line), and moved the ball ten yards in from the sidelines on any play ending within five yards of the out-of-bounds line. Suddenly there were more field goals, more passes, more points scored, and more wide-open play in the NFL for 1933.

The division of the league into Eastern and Western divisions in that same year also spurred interest in the pro game, which was struggling against the financial hardships of the Depression plus the overwhelming emphasis put on college football by the media and fans. With two divisional races, more teams could now entertain title hopes into autumn, while the NFL championship game at the end of the season paralleled baseball's World Series and won big headlines in the newspapers.

The league had been shrinking since the start of the Depression, hitting a low of eight teams in 1932, but membership swelled to ten clubs in 1933 when Pittsburgh, Philadelphia, and Cincinnati joined after Staten Island folded. The league roll call stayed relatively stable through the rest of the 1930s. The only changes after 1933 were the folding of the Cincinnati team in 1934, the transfer of Portsmouth to Detroit in 1934, the shift of Boston to Washington in 1937, and the admittance of the Cleveland Rams in 1937.

With the small, steady number of clubs, league meetings were lively affairs where the tight circle of financially pressed owners heatedly thrashed out all proposals. Halas and Marshall, who loved to spar verbally with each other, were the main idea men of the organization. The other steady owners of the 1930s were Bert Bell of Philadelphia, who doubled as his team's head coach, general manager, and ticket salesman; Pittsburgh's Art Rooney, who founded his team with the winnings from a big day at the racetrack; Green Bay's Curley Lambeau, who had founded the Packers in 1919 before there was an NFL; New York's Tim Mara, who started his team in 1925 with the statement that "an exclusive franchise for anything in New York is worth $2,500," which was the admission fee; the Cardinals' Charles Bidwill, who bought his team in late 1933; Detroit's Dick Richards, an egocentric radio tycoon who barraged his coaches with suggestions and arguments; and Brooklyn's Dan Topping, who would later own the New York Yankees baseball team.

The game that these gentlemen presided over was gradually changing. Pro football in the 1920s was a running game, with passing only a desperation tactic. The passing attack grew more popular, however, when Green Bay's Arnie Herber and Washington's Sammy Baugh, both outstanding passers, broke into the league in the 1930s. The most spectacular newcomer, however, was Don Hutson of Green Bay, an end with a sprinter's speed plus slick moves. The slim Hutson was football's first modern wide receiver and for years was the NFL's top offensive threat.

Almost all of the league and divisional titles in the 1930s went to the Packers, Bears, Giants, and Redskins, with the other clubs perennial runners-up. Starting in 1940, however, the Chicago Bears rode roughshod over the rest of the competition with one of the greatest pro-football teams ever assembled. With limited substitution the rule of the day and most players required to play both offense and defense, the Bears had a roster deep in talent at all positions. But in addition to superior personnel, the Bears had a tactical advantage over their rivals. Aided by football genius Clark Shaughnessy, Halas had installed the first modern T-formation offense in the Bears. With an intelligent and talented quarterback in Sid Luckman to make it go, the Bears' T attack confused opponents with quick-opening running plays and a variety of passing plays. After the Bears crushed the Redskins 73-0 in the 1940 championship game, most of the NFL teams shifted from the single wing and similar formations to the T in the mid-1940s.

Other innovations changed the face of pro football in the 1930s. The football, which had been slimming down from the fat bladder it originally had been, reached its modern shape in 1933. This new ball was much easier to pass but practically impossible to drop-kick. Starting in 1934, the defending NFL championship team met a collection of college all stars in a pre-season contest for charity, and from 1936 through 1941 the New York Giants annually played a collection of NFL all stars. Colorful uniforms and halftime entertainment became common fare, with the Redskin marching band the best show in the field. A rule making helmets mandatory was passed late in the decade, and black players, never too common in the 1920s, disappeared completely behind an unspoken color bar.

One of the most important innovations was the draft of college players begun in 1936. With the weaker teams in the league picking first, this draft eliminated bidding over All-Americans and gave the weak teams a chance to build up. The Eagles made halfback Jay Berwanger of the University of Chicago their first pick in the initial draft, but Berwanger chose to go into business rather than engage in the shaky proposition of pro football. More and more big-name college players were turning pro, however, with Davey O'Brien and Whizzer White especially famous players signed to big NFL contracts.

As the 1930s turned into the 1940s, the personnel at the top of the league changed. Joe Carr died in 1939, and Elmer Layden, one of the Four Horsemen of Notre Dame, was named Commissioner in 1941. In 1940 Dan Reeves bought the Rams, Fred Mandel the Lions, and Alexis Thompson the Eagles, with Bert Bell and Art Rooney becoming partners in the Pittsburgh franchise. Hugh (Shorty) Ray took over as supervisor of officials and consultant on rule changes in 1938, and his long service to the league until his death in 1956 earned him election to the Pro Football Hall of Fame in 1966.

Through all the changes, the NFL survived. Attendance was modest, but the league outlasted two upstart competitors, the American Football League of 1936-37 and another league of the same name that operated in 1940-41.

But World War II almost put an end to the NFL. Starting in 1942, the military draft took away so many players that the league considered shutting down for the duration. The league persisted, however, with overage and draft-deferred men and with a truncated array of teams. The Rams went into mothballs for the 1943 season, the Steelers merged with the Eagles in 1943 and the Cardinals in 1944, and Brooklyn went out of action in 1945. The Boston Yanks, however, came into the league in 1944 and fleshed out the league roster a bit. Attendance fell off during the war years, as most star players were away in the service and other more pressing matters captured the attention of Americans on the home front. But the end of the war would bring a flood of top talent into the game, a spiraling boom in the nation's economy, and an incredible skyrocketing in the affairs of the game which had struggled through the first fifty years of its existence.

1933–1945 SINGLE SEASON LEADERS

RUSHING

Most Yards Rushing

		Team	Year	Yds.
1	Beattie Feathers	ChiB	1934	1004
2	Cliff Battles	Was	1937	874
3	Steve Van Buren	Phi	1945	832
4	Tuffy Leemans	NYG	1936	830
5	Ace Gutowsky	Det	1936	827
6	Jim Musick	Bos	1933	809
7	Swede Hanson	Phi	1934	805
8	Frank Akins	Was	1945	797
9	Dutch Clark	Det	1934	763
10	Bill Paschal	NYG	1944	737
	Cliff Battles	Bos	1933	736

Most Rushing Attempts

		Team	Year	Att.
1	Cliff Battles	Was	1937	216
2	Tuffy Leemans	NYG	1936	206
3	Bill Paschal	NYG	1944	196
4	Ace Gutowsky	Det	1936	191
5	John Grigas	C-P	1944	185
6	Cliff Battles	Bos	1936	176
7	Jim Musick	Bos	1933	173
8	George Grosvenor	ChiB-ChiC	1936	170
9	Bill Dudley	Pit	1942	162
10	Whizzer White	Pit	1938	152

Best Rushing Average
(Minimum 40 Attempts)

		Team	Year	Att.	Yds.	Avg.
1	Beattie Feathers	ChiB	1934	101	1004	9.9
2	George McAfee	ChiB	1941	65	474	7.3
3	Joe Maniaci	ChiB	1939	77	544	7.1
4	Ward Cuff	NYG	1943	80	523	6.5
5	Ernie Caddel	Det	1936	91	580	6.4
6	Frank Maznicki	ChiB	1942	54	343	6.4
7	Banks McFadden	Bkn	1940	65	411	6.3
8	Fred Gehrke	Cle	1945	74	467	6.3
9	Dutch Clark	Det	1934	122	763	6.3
10	Hugh Gallarneau	ChiB	1941	49	304	6.2

Most Touchdown Runs

		Team	Year	TD
1	Steve Van Buren	Phi	1945	15
2	Bill Paschal	NYG	1943	10
3	Johnny Drake	Cle	1939	9
	Johnny Drake	Cle	1940	9
	Bill Paschal	NYG	1944	9
6	Beattie Feathers	ChiB	1934	8
	Dutch Clark	Det	1934	8
	Hugh Gallarneau	ChiB	1941	8
	Gary Famiglietti	ChiB	1942	8
10	Bronko Nagurski	ChiB	1934	7
	Glenn Presnell	Det	1934	7
	Swede Hanson	Phi	1934	7
	Dutch Clark	Det	1936	7
	Fred Gehrke	Cle	1945	7

Most Yards Rushing per Game

		Team	Year	Yds/G
1	Steve Van Buren	Phi	1945	83
2	Frank Akins	Was	1945	80
3	Cliff Battles	Was	1937	79
4	Beattie Feathers	ChiB	1934	77
5	Bill Paschal	NYG	1944	74
6	Swede Hanson	Phi	1934	73
7	Tuffy Leemans	NYG	1936	69
8	Ace Gutowsky	Det	1936	69
9	Bill Osmanski	ChiB	1939	64
10	Bill Dudley	Pit	1942	63

PASSING

Most Yards Passing

		Team	Year	Yds.
1	Sid Luckman	ChiB	1943	2194
2	Cecil Isbell	GB	1942	2021
3	Sammy Baugh	Was	1943	1754
4	Sid Luckman	ChiB	1945	1725
5	Sammy Baugh	Was	1945	1669
6	Bob Waterfield	Cle	1945	1609
7	Sammy Baugh	Was	1942	1524
8	Cecil Isbell	GB	1941	1479
9	Tommy Thompson	Phi	1942	1410
10	Sammy Baugh	Was	1940	1367

Most Completed Passes

		Team	Year	Comp.
1	Cecil Isbell	GB	1942	146
2	Sammy Baugh	Was	1943	133
3	Sammy Baugh	Was	1942	132
4	Sammy Baugh	Was	1945	128
5	Bud Schwenk	ChiC	1942	126
6	Davey O'Brien	Phi	1940	124
7	Cecil Isbell	GB	1941	117
	Sid Luckman	ChiB	1945	117
9	Sammy Baugh	Was	1940	111
10	Sid Luckman	ChiB	1943	110

Best Completion Percentage
(Minimum 50 Attempts)

		Team	Year	Att.	Comp.	Pct.
1	Sammy Baugh	Was	1945	182	128	70.3
2	Sammy Baugh	Was	1940	177	111	62.7
3	Frankie Filchock	Was	1939	89	55	61.8
4	Sammy Baugh	Was	1942	225	132	58.7
5	Frankie Filchock	Was	1944	147	84	57.1
	Sid Luckman	ChiB	1941	119	68	57.1
7	Cecil Isbell	GB	1941	206	117	56.8
8	Sammy Baugh	Was	1944	146	82	56.2
9	Sammy Baugh	Was	1943	239	133	55.6
10	Sammy Baugh	Was	1939	96	53	55.2

Most Touchdown Passes

		Team	Year	TD
1	Sid Luckman	ChiB	1943	28
2	Cecil Isbell	GB	1942	24
3	Sammy Baugh	Was	1943	23
4	Sammy Baugh	Was	1942	16
5	Cecil Isbell	GB	1941	15
6	Sid Luckman	ChiB	1945	14
	Bob Waterfield	Cle	1945	14
8	Frankie Filchock	Was	1944	13
9	Sammy Baugh	Was	1940	12
	Frankie Sinkwich	Det	1944	12
	Irv Comp	GB	1944	12

Most Yards Passing per Game

		Team	Year	Yds/G
1	Sid Luckman	ChiB	1943	219
2	Cecil Isbell	GB	1942	184
3	Sammy Baugh	Was	1943	175
4	Sid Luckman	ChiB	1945	173
5	Sammy Baugh	Was	1945	167
6	Bob Waterfield	Cle	1945	161
7	Sammy Baugh	Was	1942	139
8	Cecil Isbell	GB	1941	134
9	Tommy Thompson	Phi	1942	128
10	Sammy Baugh	Was	1940	124

Most Yards per Passing Attempt
(Minimum 50 Attempts)

		Team	Year	Att.	Yds.	Yds/Att
1	Frankie Filchock	Was	1939	89	1094	12.3
2	Sid Luckman	ChiB	1943	202	2194	10.9
3	Charlie O'Rourke	ChiB	1942	88	951	10.8
4	Sid Luckman	ChiB	1941	119	1181	9.9
5	Sid Luckman	ChiB	1942	105	1023	9.7
6	Bob Waterfield	Cle	1945	171	1609	9.4
7	Sammy Baugh	Was	1945	182	1669	9.2
8	Sid Luckman	ChiB	1940	105	941	9.0
9	Bernie Masterson	ChiB	1937	72	615	8.5
10	Frankie Filchock	Was	1940	54	460	8.5

Fewest Percent Intercepted
(Minimum 50 Attempts)

		Team	Year	Att.	Int.	% Int
1	Sammy Baugh	Was	1945	182	4	2.20
2	Dwight Sloan	Det	1939	107	3	2.80
3	Foster Watkins	Phi	1940	85	3	3.53
4	Ed Danowski	NYG	1937	134	5	3.73
5	Bob Monnett	GB	1936	52	2	3.85
6	Ray Mallouf	ChiC	1941	96	4	4.17
7	Irv Comp	GB	1943	92	4	4.35
8	Sid Luckman	ChiB	1945	217	10	4.61
9	Ace Parker	Bkn	1938	148	7	4.73
10	Cecil Isbell	GB	1939	103	5	4.85

RECEIVING

Most Yards Receiving

		Team	Year	Yds.
1	Don Hutson	GB	1942	1211
2	Jim Benton	Cle	1945	1067
3	Don Hutson	GB	1944	866
4	Don Hutson	GB	1939	846
5	Don Hutson	GB	1945	834
6	Don Hutson	GB	1943	776
7	Don Hutson	GB	1941	738
8	Don Looney	Phi	1940	707
9	Gaynell Tinsley	ChiC	1937	675
10	Don Hutson	GB	1940	664

Most Receptions

		Team	Year	Rec.
1	Don Hutson	GB	1942	74
2	Don Looney	Phi	1940	58
	Don Hutson	GB	1941	58
	Don Hutson	GB	1944	58
5	Don Hutson	GB	1943	47
	Don Hutson	GB	1945	47
7	Don Hutson	GB	1940	45
	Jim Benton	Cle	1945	45
9	Don Hutson	GB	1937	41
	Gaynell Tinsley	ChiC	1938	41

Most Yards per Reception
(Minimum 400 Yards)

		Team	Year	Rec.	Yds.	Avg.
1	Ray McLean	ChiB	1942	19	571	30.1
2	Frank Liebel	NYG	1945	22	593	27.0
3	Don Hutson	GB	1939	34	846	24.9
4	Tony Bova	P-P	1943	17	419	24.6
5	Ray McLean	ChiB	1943	18	435	24.2
6	Jim Benton	Cle	1945	45	1067	23.7
7	Dave Diehl	Det	1944	18	426	23.7
8	Don Hutson	GB	1935	18	420	23.3
9	Harry Clark	ChiB	1943	23	535	23.3
10	Jeff Barrett	Bkn	1937	20	461	23.1

Most Touchdowns – Receiving

		Team	Year	TD
1	Don Hutson	GB	1942	17
2	Don Hutson	GB	1943	11
3	Don Hutson	GB	1941	10
	Frank Liebel	NYG	1945	10
5	Don Hutson	GB	1938	9
	Don Hutson	GB	1944	9
	Don Hutson	GB	1945	9
8	Don Hutson	GB	1936	8
	Jim Benton	Cle	1945	8

(Many with 7)

Most Yards Receiving per Game

		Team	Year	Yds/G
1	Don Hutson	GB	1942	110
2	Jim Benton	Cle	1945	107
3	Don Hutson	GB	1944	87
4	Don Hutson	GB	1945	83
5	Don Hutson	GB	1943	78
6	Don Hutson	GB	1939	77
7	Don Hutson	GB	1941	67
8	Don Looney	Phi	1940	64
9	Gaynell Tinsley	ChiC	1937	61
10	Don Hutson	GB	1940	60

INTERCEPTIONS

Most Passes Intercepted
(Starting 1940)

		Team	Year	Int.
1	Sammy Baugh	Was	1943	11
2	Irv Comp	GB	1943	10
3	Howie Livingston	NYG	1944	9
4	Bulldog Turner	ChiB	1942	8
	Don Hutson	GB	1943	8
6	Marshall Goldberg	ChiC	1941	7
	Art Jones	Pit	1941	7
	Don Hutson	GB	1942	7
	Joe Laws	GB	1943	7
	Alex Wojciechowicz	Det	1944	7
	Roy Zimmerman	Phi	1945	7

KICKING

Best Punting Average
(Minimum 30 punts – starting 1939)

		Team	Year	No.	Avg.
1	Sammy Baugh	Was	1940	35	51.3
2	Sammy Baugh	Was	1941	30	48.7
3	Sammy Baugh	Was	1942	37	46.6
4	Sammy Baugh	Was	1943	50	45.9
5	Len Barnum	Phi	1941	41	43.6
6	Sammy Baugh	Was	1945	33	43.3
7	Parker Hall	Cle	1940	57	43.2
8	Johnny Pingel	Det	1939	32	42.7
9	Jack Jacobs	Cle	1942	33	42.3
10	Ace Parker	Bkn	1939	40	42.0

Most Field Goals

		Team	Year	FG
1	Jack Manders	ChiB	1934	10
2	Clarke Hinkle	GB	1940	9
3	Jack Manders	ChiB	1937	8
4	Jack Manders	ChiB	1936	7
	Armand Niccolai	Pit	1936	7
	Ward Cuff	NYG	1939	7
	Joe Aguirre	Was	1945	7

(Many with 6)

Best Field Goal Percentage
(Minimum 5 attempts – starting 1936)

		Team	Year	FG	Att.	Pct.
1	Jack Manders	ChiB	1936	7	8	88
2	Regis Monahan	Det	1938	4	5	80
	Chuck Hanneman	Det	1939	4	5	80
	Andy Marefos	NYG	1941	4	5	80
	Ted Fritsch	GB	1942	4	5	80
	Frank Maznicki	ChiB	1942	4	5	80
7	Clarke Hinkle	GB	1940	9	14	64
8	Ward Cuff	NYG	1940	5	8	63
9	Don Hutson	GB	1943	3	5	60
10	Ward Cuff	NYG	1938	5	9	56

Most Points After Touchdown

		Team	Year	PAT
1	Bob Snyder	ChiB	1943	39
2	Don Hutson	GB	1943	36
	Pete Gudauskas	ChiB	1944	36
4	Don Hutson	GB	1942	33
5	Roy Zimmerman	Phi	1944	32
6	Jack Manders	ChiB	1934	31
	Don Hutson	GB	1944	31
	Bob Waterfield	Cle	1945	31
	Don Hutson	GB	1945	31
10	Roy Zimmerman	Phi	1945	29

Most PAT – No Misses

		Team	Year	PAT
1	Don Hutson	GB	1943	36
2	Pete Gudauskas	ChiB	1945	27
3	Ken Strong	NYG	1945	23
4	Ward Cuff	NYG	1942	18
5	Tilly Manton	NYG	1936	15
	Armand Niccolai	Pit	1939	15
7	Jack Manders	ChiB	1933	14
8	Tilly Manton	NYG	1937	12
9	Joe Maniaci	Bkn-ChiB	1938	11

SCORING

Most Points

		Team	Year	TD	FG	PAT	Pts.
1	Don Hutson	GB	1942	17	1	33	138
2	Don Hutson	GB	1943	12	3	36	117
3	Steve Van Buren	Phi	1945	18	0	2	110
4	Don Hutson	GB	1945	10	2	31	97
5	Don Hutson	GB	1941	12	1	20	95
6	Don Hutson	GB	1944	9	0	31	85
7	Jack Manders	ChiB	1934	3	10	31	79
8	Dutch Clark	Det	1934	8	4	13	73
	Dutch Clark	Det	1936	7	4	19	73
10	George McAfee	ChiB	1941	12	0	0	72
	Bill Paschal	NYG	1943	12	0	0	72

Most Points per Game

		Team	Year	PPG
1	Don Hutson	GB	1942	12.5
2	Don Hutson	GB	1943	11.7
3	Steve Van Buren	Phi	1945	11.0
4	Don Hutson	GB	1945	9.7
5	Don Hutson	GB	1941	8.6
6	Don Hutson	GB	1944	8.5
7	Bill Paschal	NYG	1943	7.2
8	Frankie Sinkwich	Det	1944	6.6
9	George McAfee	ChiB	1941	6.5
10	Jack Manders	ChiB	1937	6.3

1933–1945 PERIOD LEADERS

PASSING

(All Passers with at least 300 Attempts)

		Years	Att.	Comp.	Comp. Pct.	Yards	Yds/ Att.	TD	Int.	Pct. Int.
1	Sid Luckman	1939-45	942	494	52.4	8718	**9.3**	81	65	6.9
2	Sammy Baugh	1937-45	**1557**	**889**	**57.1**	**10897**	7.0	**96**	105	6.7
3	Cecil Isbell	*1938-42	818	411	50.2	5945	7.3	61	52	**6.4**
4	Ed Danowski	*1934-39,41	637	309	48.5	3818	6.0	39	43	6.8
5	Frankie Filchock	1938-41,44-45	505	254	50.3	3658	7.2	35	54	10.7
6	Arnie Herber	1933-40,44-45	1073	444	41.4	7394	6.9	70	89	8.3
7	Bernie Masterson	*1934-40	408	155	38.0	3372	8.3	35	38	9.3
8	Bob Monnett	*1933-38	340	158	46.5	2317	6.8	24	27	7.9
9	Irv Comp	1943-45	375	170	45.3	2686	7.2	26	36	9.6
10	Tommy Thompson	1940-42,45	421	205	48.7	2675	6.4	17	35	8.3
	Ace Parker	1937-41,45	603	279	45.3	3938	6.5	22	47	7.8
12	Parker Hall	1939-42	721	329	45.6	4033	5.6	29	67	9.3
13	Davey O'Brien	*1939-40	478	223	46.7	2614	5.5	11	34	7.1
14	Tuffy Leemans	*1936-43	383	167	43.6	2324	6.1	25	32	8.4
15	Roy Zimmerman	1940-45	384	155	40.4	2688	7.0	26	40	10.4
16	Dave Smukler	*1936-39,44	308	112	36.4	1357	4.4	16	32	10.4

RECEIVING

Most Receptions

		Years	Rec.
1	Don Hutson	*1935-45	488
2	Jim Benton	1938-40,42-45	190
3	Charley Malone	*1934-40,42	137
4	Joe Carter	1934-45	127
5	Bob Masterson	1938-45	126
6	Wayne Millner	*1936-41,45	124
7	Ward Cuff	1937-45	101
8	George Wilson	1937-45	100
9	Perry Schwartz	1938-42	99
10	Eddie Rucinski	1941-45	97

Most Yards

		Years	Yards
1	Don Hutson	*1935-45	7981
2	Jim Benton	1938-40,42-45	3309
3	Charley Malone	*1934-40,42	1922
4	Joe Carter	1934-45	1880
5	Ray McLean	1940-45	1749
6	Bob Masterson	1938-45	1702
7	Perry Schwartz	1938-42	1595
8	Wayne Millner	*1936-41,45	1578
9	Bill Hewitt	1933-39,43	1562
10	Bill Smith	1935-39	1509

Most Touchdowns

		Years	TD
1	Don Hutson	*1935-45	100
2	Jim Benton	1938-40,42-45	33
3	Bill Hewitt	1933-39,43	23
4	Joe Carter	*1933-45	21
5	Frank Liebel	1942-45	18
	Ray McLean	1940-45	18
	Bill Karr	*1933-38	18
8	Wilbur Moore	1939-45	16
9	George Wilson	1937-45	14
10	Joe Aguirre	1941,43-45	13
	Bob Masterson	1938-45	13
	Charley Malone	*1934-40,42	13
	Andy Farkas	*1938-45	13

Most Yards per Reception
(Minimum 40 Receptions)

		Years	Yds.	Rec.	Avg.
1	Frank Liebel	1942-45	1137	48	23.7
2	Ray McLean	1940-45	1749	75	23.3
3	Bill Karr	*1933-38	1042	48	21.7
4	Eggs Mansek	*1935-40	1467	70	21.0
5	Jeff Barrett	*1936-38	934	47	19.9

RUSHING

Most Yards

		Years	Yds.	Att.	Avg.
1	Clarke Hinkle	1933-41	3519	1043	3.4
2	Tuffy Leemans	*1936-43	3142	919	3.4
3	Cliff Battles	1933-37	3046	725	4.2
4	Ace Gutowsky	1933-39	3031	852	3.6
5	Pug Manders	1939-45	2529	690	3.7
6	Dutch Clark	1934-38	2296	468	4.9
7	Ray Nolting	*1936-43	2285	508	4.5
8	Bronko Nagurski	1933-37,43	2212	499	4.4
9	Ernie Caddel	*1933-38	2211	443	5.0
10	Andy Farkas	*1938-45	2103	587	3.6

Most Touchdowns

		Years	TD
1	Pug Manders	1939-45	33
2	Clarke Hinkle	1933-41	32
3	Dutch Clark	1934-38	24
	Ernie Caddel	*1933-38	24
	Johnny Drake	*1937-41	24
6	Bill Paschal	1943-45	21
	Andy Farkas	*1938-45	21
8	Gary Famiglietti	1938-45	20
	Cliff Battles	1933-37	20
10	Tuffy Leemans	*1936-43	17

KICKING

Most Field Goals

		Years	FG
1	Jack Manders	*1933-40	39
2	Armand Niccolai	*1934-42	34
3	Ward Cuff	1937-45	31
	Ralph Kercheval	*1934-40	31
5	Ken Strong	1933-35,39,44-45	29
6	Clarke Hinkle	1933-41	28

Most Points After Touchdown

		Years	PAT	Att.	Pct.
1	Don Hutson	*1935-45	172	184	93
2	Jack Manders	*1933-40	137	154	89
3	Ward Cuff	1937-45	98	102	96
4	Roy Zimmerman	1940-45	88	96	92
5	Ken Strong	1933-35,39,44-45	86	90	96
6	Bob Snyder	*1937-43	78	91	86
7	Armand Niccolai	*1934-42	71	77	92
	Bob Masterson	1938-45	71	79	90
9	Pete Gudauskas	*1940,43-45	64	67	96
10	Augie Lio	1941-45	63	68	93

SCORING

		Years	TD-Rush.	TD-Rec.	TD-other	FG	PAT	Points
1	Don Hutson	*1935-45	3	100	2	7	172	823
2	Jack Manders	*1933-40	11	6	2	39	137	368
3	Clarke Hinkle	1933-41	32	9	0	28	28	358
4	Ward Cuff	1937-45	6	12	2	31	98	311
5	Dutch Clark	1934-38	24	3	0	12	56	254
6	Ken Strong	1933-35,39,44-45	9	2	1	29	86	245
7	Andy Farkas	*1938-45	21	13	3	0	6	228
8	Jim Benton	1938-40,42-45	0	33	3	0	0	216
	Pug Manders	1939-45	33	2	1	0	0	216
10	Ralph Kercheval	*1934-40	4	4	2	31	32	185

*—Entire Career

NEW YORK GIANTS 11-3-0 Steve Owen

Scores of Each Game		
23	Pittsburgh	2
7	Portsmouth	17
10	Green Bay	7
20	Boston	21
56	PHILADELPHIA	0
21	BROOKLYN	7
10	Chic. Bears	14
13	PORTSMOUTH	10
7	BOSTON	0
3	CHIC. BEARS	0
17	GREEN BAY	6
10	Brooklyn	0
27	BROOKLYN	3
20	Philadelphia	14

Use Name	Pos.	Hgt	Wgt	Age	Int	Pts
Mel Hein	C-LB	6'2"	200	24		

Use Name – Tackles	Pos.	Hgt	Wgt	Age	Int	Pts
Len Grant	T	6'3"	222	27		
Tex Irvin (1 reception for 13 yd. touchdown)	T	6'	230	26		6
Bill Morgan	T	6'2"	226	23		
Bill Owen	T	6'	210	29		

Use Name – Guards	Pos.	Hgt	Wgt	Age	Int	Pts
John Cannella	G-C-LB	6'1"	198	25		
Butch Gibson	G	5'9"	205	29		
Potsy Jones	G	5'11"	210	23		
Steve Owen	G	5'10"	260	33		
Hank Reese	G-C-LB	5'11"	210	22		
Ollie Satenstein	G	6'	230	27		

Placed in the weaker Eastern Division, the Giants made themselves the pre-season favorites to win their circuit by picking up backs Harry Newman and Ken Strong. Rookie tailback Newman lived up to his All-American press clippings by leading the NFL in four passing categories, while Strong, signed after the Staten Island club left the NFL, balanced the passing game with his powerful running and accurate place kicking.

Coach Steve Owen already had at hand some first-rate football talent. Receivers Red Badgro, Ray Flaherty, and Dale Burnett furnished Newman with targets galore, and a line led by center Mel Hein gave Strong the daylight he needed. The defense, which prospered under coach Owen's philosophy of hitting harder than the opponents, was highlighted in a regular season's shutout victory over the Bears.

BROOKLYN DODGERS 5-4-1 Cap McEwen

Scores of Each Game		
0	CHIC. BEARS	10
27	CINCINNATI	0
7	New York	21
7	CHIC. CARDS	0
3	PITTSBURGH	3
32	Pittsburgh	0
3	Chic. Cards	0
14	BOSTON	0
0	NEW YORK	10
0	Cincinnati	10

Use Name	Pos.	Hgt	Wgt	Age	Int	Pts
George Chalmers	C-LB	6'	196			
Doc Morrison	C-LB	5'11"	210	24		

Use Name – Tackles	Pos.	Hgt	Wgt	Age	Int	Pts
Harold Ely	T	6'2"	270	23		
Don Greenshields	T	6'1"	190			
Lou Lubratovich	T	6'2"	230	26		
Saul Mielziner	T	6'1"	245			
Ralph Wright	T	6'	230			

Use Name – Guards	Pos.	Hgt	Wgt	Age	Int	Pts
Herman Hickman (2 PAT's in 3 attempts, 2 field goals)	G	5'10"	248	21		8
Bruce Jones	G	6'1"	222	28		
Hughie Rhea	G	6'3"	225	23		
Stu Worden	G	6'	210	23		

The Dodgers had two new owners and half a new backfield when Shipwreck Kelly and Chris Cagle, backs for the New York Giants, purchased the Brooklyn franchise for $25,000. The new playing owners hired Cap McEwen as head coach but freely dispensed their own instructions to the other players, thus clouding the chain of command.

No longer coach under the new regime, Benny Friedman still was a dangerous passer, and owner Kelly helped his team's cause by hauling in twenty-two tosses, tops in the league. Up front, big Herman Hickman made All-Pro in his second season. Though shallow in bench strength, the Dodgers posted a winning mark and finished second in the East, along with realizing a tidy profit.

BOSTON REDSKINS 5-5-2 Lone Star Dietz

Scores of Each Game		
7	Green Bay	7
0	Chic. Bears	7
21	Pittsburgh	6
21	NEW YORK	20
0	PORTSMOUTH	13
10	CHIC. CARDS	0
14	PITTSBURGH	16
10	CHIC. BEARS	0
0	New York	7
20	GREEN BAY	7
0	Brooklyn	14
0	Chic. Cards	0

Use Name	Pos.	Hgt	Wgt	Age	Int	Pts
Orien Crow	C-LB	6'	220			
Chief Johnson	C-LB	6'3"	205	24		

Use Name – Tackles	Pos.	Hgt	Wgt	Age	Int	Pts
Hal Cherne	T-C-LB	6'	230			
Turk Edwards	T	6'2"	235	25		
Marne Intrieri	T-C-OE-LB-DB	5'8"	250	25		
Jack Riley	T	6'2"	230			
John Scafide	T					

Use Name – Guards	Pos.	Hgt	Wgt	Age	Int	Pts
George Hurley	G	6'	200			
Jim Kamp	G	6'	210	24		
Jim MacMurdo	G	6'1"	210	22		
Mike Steponovich	G		205			
Dave Ward	G-OE-DE					
Dale Waters	G-OE-DE	6'	215			

Owner George Marshall kept his team in the news by renaming it the Redskins, hiring Lone Star Dietz, an Indian, as head coach, and signing several Indian players, none of whom played like Jim Thorpe. On opening day, the entire squad lined up for the team picture in war paint, feathers, and full headdress. The fun grew merrier when the Skins used one of Dietz's trick plays, such as the fake-fumble and broken-shoelace plays. As the enemy usually slapped down these razzle-dazzle moves, Dietz eventually had to bribe his signal callers into using them. Jim Musick and Cliff Battles hated the trick plays but showed enough speed behind conventional blocking to finish 1-2 in the NFL in rushing, while tackle Turk Edwards joined Battles on the All-Pro team.

Despite all the promotion, money was tight, and whenever a ball went into the stands, Marshall himself ran over and asked for its return.

PHILADELPHIA EAGLES 3-5-1 Lud Wray

Scores of Each Game		
0	New York	56
0	PORTSMOUTH	25
9	Green Bay	35
6	Cincinnati	0
3	CHIC. BEARS	3
25	PITTSBURGH	6
20	CINCINNATI	3
0	GREEN BAY	10
14	NEW YORK	20

Use Name	Pos.	Hgt	Wgt	Age	Int	Pts
Art Koeninger	C-LB	6'3"	205	25		
Bull Lipski	C-LB	5'11"	200			
Ray Smith	C-LB		220			

Use Name – Tackles	Pos.	Hgt	Wgt	Age	Int	Pts
Howie Auer (from CHIC)	T	6'1"	205	25		
Joe Carpe	T					
Paul Cuba	T	6'	215	26		
Bob Gonya	T	6'2"	210	23		
Larry Steinbach (from CHIC)	T	6'	212	29		
Guy Turnbow (1 field goal)	T-OE-DE	6'2"	217	25		3

Use Name – Guards	Pos.	Hgt	Wgt	Age	Int	Pts
Joe Kresky	G	6'	200	25		
Milt Leathers	G		198			
Roy Lechthaler	G	5'10"	198			
Henry Obst	G	5'11"	192			
Diddie Willson	G-OE-DE	5'10"	198	22		
Jim Zyntell (from NY)	G	6'1"	200	23		

The Philadelphia Eagles' first three NFL games left them nowhere to go but up. In New York, the Giants welcomed the Eagles into the league with a 56-0 shellacking, and 25-0 and 35-9 drubbings followed to rub salt in the open wound.

Bert Bell, a wealthy football fanatic who would later become the NFL commissioner, created this club by purchasing a Philadelphia franchise when the Pennsylvania laws forbidding Sunday sports were about to be dropped. Bell handled all the front-office duties, while partner Lud Wray held the coaching reigns on the shell-shocked team.

Surprisingly, the rookie-laden Eagles improved in mid-season, winning three games and shocking the Chicago Bears with a 3-3 tie that writers called the best football game in Philadelphia history.

PITTSBURGH PIRATES 3-6-2 Jap Douds

Scores of Each Game		
2	NEW YORK	23
14	CHIC. CARDS	13
6	BOSTON	21
17	CINCINNATI	3
0	Green Bay	47
0	Cincinnati	0
16	Boston	14
3	Brooklyn	3
0	BROOKLYN	32
6	Philadelphia	25
3	New York	27

Use Name	Pos.	Hgt	Wgt	Age	Int	Pts
Monty Lantz	C-LB	5'11"	185			
Cap Oehler	C-LB	6'	200	22		
Tom Whalen	BB-DB					

Use Name – Tackles	Pos.	Hgt	Wgt	Age	Int	Pts
Corwan Artman	T	6'2"	240			
Sam Cooper	T					
Jap Douds	T	5'10"	225	26		
Tiny Engebretsen (to CHIC, G) (1 field goal)	T	6'1"	225	23		3
Ray Kemp	T	6'1"	215			
Leo Raskowski (from BKN)	T	6'3"	220	26		
Don Rhodes	T		225			

Use Name – Guards	Pos.	Hgt	Wgt	Age	Int	Pts
Larry Critchfield	G	5'11"	195			
Nick DeCarbo	G	5'9"	185			
Clarence Janecek	G	6'	200	22		
Jim Letsinger	G		190			

After running a semi-pro team in Pittsburgh for a few years, thirty-two year-old Art Rooney organized the football Pirates with the announced legalization of Sunday sports in Pennsylvania. But a few days before the home opener, he learned that the new law did not go into effect until the Tuesday after the game. Rooney pleaded his case to the superintendent of police, who replied with "Give me a couple of tickets and I'll go to the game Sunday. That'll be the last place they'll look for me if they want to stop the game."

The game went on, and the fans got their first look at the new Pirates. Although the squad was a salad bowl of rookies, veterans of Rooney's semi-pro team, and marginal players from other NFL clubs, they managed three wins before the season ended.

TEAM TOTALS

	YARDS GAINED	OPPONENTS YARDS	PASS ATT.	PASS COMP.	COMP. PCT.	TOTAL POINTS	RUSH TD	PASS TD	OTHER TD	PAT	FG	SAF	OPPONENTS POINTS
NEW YORK	2970	2529	180	74	41.1	244	17	13	3	28	6	0	101
BROOKLYN	2207	1754	169	79	46.7	93	4	7	2	9	2	0	54
BOSTON	2823	2525	106	33	31.1	103	11	1	2	13	2	0	97
PHILADELPHIA	1786	2236	149	41	27.5	77	6	4	1	6	1	1	158
PITTSBURGH	1887	2761	195	61	31.3	67	5	3	0	5	4	1	208

							RUSHING				PASSING								RECEIVING				PUNTING		KICKING						PUNT RETURNS				KICKOFF RETURNS			
Use Name – Backs & Ends	Pos.	Age	Hgt	Wgt	Pts	Int	No.	Yds	Avg	TD	Att	Comp	%	Yds	Yd/Att	TD	Int–%	RK	No.	Yds	Avg	TD	No.	Avg	Pat	Att	%	FG	Att	%	No.	Yds	Avg	TD	No.	Yds	Avg	TD
NEW YORK GIANTS																																						
Harry Newman	TB-DB	23	5'8"	175	32		130	437	3.4	4	136	53	39	973	7.2	9	17–13	4							5	8	63	1										
Stu Clancy	TB-FB-DB	27	5'10"	190	18					3																												
Ken Strong	FB-DB	27	6'	198	59					2						1						2			14	15	93	5										
Kink Richards	FB-BB-TB-DB	22	5'11"	190	43		45	277	6.2	5						1						2			1	1	100											
Jack McBride	FB-TB-DB	31	5'11"	185	6											2									6	6	100											
Dale Burnett	WB-DB	24	6'1"	185	24																		3																
Hap Moran	WB-FB-DB	32	6'1"	190	7																		1			1	1	100 (Reception)											
Bo Molenda	BB-LB	27	5'10"	220	18					3																												
Max Krause	BB-LB	24	5'10"	197	7																		1			1	1	100 (Reception)											
Ray Flaherty	OE-DE	29	6'	187															11	187	17	0																
Red Badgro	OE-DE	30	6'	190	18																		2																
Glenn Campbell	OE-DE	28	5'11"	204	6																		1																
Tiny Feather	OE-WB-DE-DB	30	6'	200																																		
Joe Zapaustas	OE-DE		6'	198																																		
Tony Rovinski	OE-DE	24	5'9"	195																																		
BROOKLYN DODGERS																																						
Benny Friedman	TB-DB		5'10"	182	6						80	42	63	597	7.5	5	7–9	1							6	6	100											
Chris Cagle	TB-FB-DB	26	5'10"	170							74	31	42	385	5.2	2	9–12	7																				
Ollie Sansen	FB-DB	25	6'1"	187	6					1																												
Stumpy Thomason	FB-BB-DB-LB	27	5'7"	190																																		
Dick Richards	FB-BB-DB-LB		6'	194																																		
Shipwreck Kelly	WB-DB	23	6'2"	185	42					2									22	246	12	3												2				
Ben Douglas	WB-DB		6'	185	6																		1																
Bull Karcis	BB-LB	24	5'9"	230																																		
Dick Fishel	BB-TB-LB-DB		5'9"	190	6					1																												
Les Peterson	OE-DE	23	6'3"	205															13	170	13	0																
Paul Riblett	OE-DE	25	5'10"	184	6														12	172	14	1																
Tom Nash	OE-DE	25	6'3"	205	13																		2			1	2	50											
Van Rayburn	OE-DE		6'1"	180																																		
John Lyons	OE-DE		6'1"	210																																		
Harry Kloppenberg	OE-DE		6'1"	210																																		
BOSTON REDSKINS																																						
Cliff Battles	TB-DB	23	6'1"	198	27		146	737	5.0	3																		1						1				
Bob Campiglio	TB-DB	25	6'1"	185																																		
Louis Weller	TB-DB		5'6"	150	13					2															1	1	100											
Jim Musick	FB-DB	26	5'11"	195	44		173	809	4.7	5															11	12	92	1										
Roy Horstmann	FB-WB-DB		6'	185																																		
Ernie Pinckert	WB-DB	25	6'	195	6																																	
Marger Apsit	BB-LB		5'11"	205																																		
Benny LaPresta	BB-LB		5'9"	185	1																				1	1	100											
Ike Frankian	OE-DE	26	5'11"	210	6																		1																
Paul Collins	OE-DE	25	6'1"	195																																		
Steve Hokuf	OE-BB-DE-LB	22	6'	195																																		
PHILADELPHIA EAGLES																																						
Red Davis(from PORT,OE-DE)	TB-FB-DB		5'11"	195	10					1						1									4	7	57											
Lee Woodruff	TB-FB-DB-LB		6'	202	12					1																												
Nick Prisco	TB-DB		5'8"	193																																		
Swede Hanson	FB-TB-LB-DB	24	6'1"	192	24		133	494	3.7	3						1						1																
John White	FB-LB																																					
Porter Lainhart (from CHIC)	FB-LB	25	6'	180																																		
Jack Roberts	HB-DB		6'	210	6					1																												
Reb Russell (from NY,WB-DB)	HB-DB	26	6'1"	195																																		
Rick Lackman	HB-DB	21	5'11"	185																																		
Reds Kirkman	BB-DB	27	6'1"	195	7						73	22	30	354	4.8	2	13–18	9				1			1	2	50											
Dick Thornton	BB-DB		5'11"	195																																		
Harry O'Boyle	BB-DB		5'9"	180																																		
Joe Carter	OE-DE	23	6'1"	202	13																		2			1	1	100											
George Kenneally	OE-DE	31	6'	192																																		
Dick Fencl	OE-DE		5'10"	160																																		
Ev Rowan	OE-DE			190																																		
PITTSBURGH PIRATES																																						
Angie Brovelli	TB-BB-DB		6'	190	14					2															2	3	67											
Ed Westfall (from BOS)	TB-BB-DB		5'9"	175	13					1						1						1			1	1	100											
Walt Holmer (from BOS)	TB-BB-DB		6'	185	6					1																												
Bill Tanguay	TB-DB															1																						
Tony Holm	FB-LB		6'1"	215							52	16	31	406	7.8	2	13–25	8																				
Marty Kottler	FB-LB				6																																	
Jimmy Clark	HB-FB-DB		5'9"	170						1																												
Elmer Schwartz	HB-FB-DB-LB		6'	215																																		
Bucky Moore	HB-DB																																					
Frank Hood	HB-DB		6'	235																																		
Mose Kelsch	HB-DB	37	5'10"	225	11																				2	3	67	3										
Harp Vaughan	BB-HB-DB	26	5'7"	170	6																																	
George Shaffer	BB-DB			190																																		
Ray Tesser	OE-DE		6'2"	200															14	274	20	0																
Paul Moss	OE-DE		6'2"	180	12														13	383	29	2																
Bill Sortet	OE-DE	21	6'1"	185																																		
Ted Dailey	OE-DE		5'9"	170																																		
Gil Robinson	OE-DE																																					

CHICAGO BEARS 10-2-1 George Halas

Scores of Each Game		
14	Green Bay	7
7	BOSTON	0
10	Brooklyn	0
12	Chic. Cards	9
10	GREEN BAY	7
14	NEW YORK	10
0	Boston	10
3	Philadelphia	3
0	New York	3
17	PORTSMOUTH	14
22	CHIC. CARDS	6
17	Portsmouth	7
7	GREEN BAY	6

Use Name	Pos.	Hgt	Wgt	Age	Int	Pts
Ookie Miller	C-LB	6'	210	23		
Bert Pearson	C-LB	6'	208	28		
Dick Smith (from PHI)	C-LB	6'2"	225			

Use Name – Tackles	Pos.	Hgt	Wgt	Age	Int	Pts
Link Lyman	T	6'2"	252	34		
George Musso	T	6'2"	257	23		
Ray Richards	T-G	6'1"	225	27		
Dick Stahlman	T		216			

Use Name – Guards	Pos.	Hgt	Wgt	Age	Int	Pts
Bill Buckler	G-T-OE-DE	6'	230	32		
Zuck Carlson	G	6'	210	28		
Joe Kopcha	G	6'	220	27		

When owner George Halas decided to return to the sidelines as head coach, the Bears immediately made him look like a genius by winning their first six games. In the opener, end Bill Hewitt threw for one touchdown and scored another in the final two minutes for a 14-7 come-from-behind victory over the Green Bay Packers.

After the first six victories, the Bears hit the skids on an Eastern trip, losing to Boston and New York and tying Philadelphia. But four straight wins ended the season with the first Western title in the newly organized NFL structure, which split the ten teams into two divisions and set up the first official post-season championship.

Of the three Bears who made the All-Pro team—end Hewitt, guard Joe Kopcha, and fullback Bronko Nagurski—it was Nagurski who used his head as well as his legs when, after smashing into the wall behind the end zone on a touchdown run, he returned to the bench and said, "That last guy really hit me a good lick."

PORTSMOUTH SPARTANS 6-5-0 Potsy Clark

Scores of Each Game		
21	CINCINNATI	0
17	NEW YORK	7
7	CHIC. CARDS	6
0	Green Bay	17
13	Boston	0
25	Philadelphia	0
10	New York	13
7	GREEN BAY	0
7	Cincinnati	10
14	Chic. Bears	17
7	CHIC. BEARS	17

Use Name	Pos.	Hgt	Wgt	Age	Int	Pts
Clare Randolph	C-LB	6'2"	210	26		
John Wager	C-G-LB	5'11"	207			

Voluntarily retired – Dutch Clark

Use Name – Tackles	Pos.	Hgt	Wgt	Age	Int	Pts
Ben Boswell	T	6'	245			
George Christensen	T	6'2"	242	23		
Earl Elser	T	6'1"	230			
Harry Thayer	T-G	6'1"	215			

Use Name – Guards	Pos.	Hgt	Wgt	Age	Int	Pts
Maury Bodenger	G	5'10"	210	24		
Jim Bowdoin	G	6'1"	220	27		
Ray Davis	G		198			
Ox Emerson	G-C-LB	5'11"	205	25		

The Spartans began the season like a car without a spark plug when star tailback and field leader Dutch Clark stayed home as athletic director of the Colorado School of Mines.

Nevertheless, the Spartans challenged for the Western lead until a mid-season confrontation with the Bears. Portsmouth had gone ahead on a late touchdown pass, but Bronko Nagurski rumbled 55 yards to score on the first play after the kick off to break the back of the Spartans, as they never again threatened. Although finishing a distant second, there was some consolation in Glenn Presnell filling Clark's tailback slot admirably—leading the league in scoring—and winning a berth on the All-Pro squad.

GREEN BAY PACKERS 5-7-1 Curly Lambeau

Scores of Each Game		
7	BOSTON	7
7	CHIC. BEARS	14
7	NEW YORK	10
17	PORTSMOUTH	0
47	PITTSBURGH	0
7	Chic. Bears	10
35	PHILADELPHIA	9
14	Chic. Cards	6
0	Portsmouth	7
7	Boston	20
6	New York	17
10	Philadelphia	0
6	Chic. Bears	7

Use Name	Pos.	Hgt	Wgt	Age	Int	Pts
Larry Bettencourt	C-LB	5'11"	205	27		
Art Bultman	C-LB	6'2"	202	25		
Al Sarafiny	C-LB		235			
Paul Young	C-LB		195			

Voluntarily retired – Nate Barrager

Use Name – Tackles	Pos.	Hgt	Wgt	Age	Int	Pts
Cal Hubbard	T	6'2"	265	32		
Joe Kurth	T	6'1"	202	22		
Claude Percy	T-G	6'1"	210	31		
Jess Quatse (to and from PIT)	T	5'11"	230	26		

Use Name – Guards	Pos.	Hgt	Wgt	Age	Int	Pts
Rudy Comstock	G		208			
Lon Evans	G	6'2"	225	21		
Norm Greeney	G	5'11"	215	23		
Mike Michalske	G-T	6'	210	29		
Clyde Van Sickle	G		225			

The Packers fell hard and heavy, finishing with a losing record despite carrying the same players who won three straight NFL titles. One reason for the slump was the reduced effectiveness of Johnny Blood. Owner Curly Lambeau was losing patience with his *bon vivant*, and when Blood showed up at practice with a hangover, punted the ball, and fell flat on his back, Lambeau cut him from the squad.

Unfortunately for the Packers, Blood was not the only one to fall during the season. A spectator fell out of the bleachers during a game and sued for $25,000, forcing the club into bankruptcy. During the winter, reorganization and a new stock issue returned the team to solvency.

CINCINNATI REDS 3-6-1 Al Jolley, Mike Palm

Scores of Each Game		
0	Portsmouth	21
0	CHIC. CARDS	3
3	Pittsburgh	17
0	Brooklyn	27
0	PITTSBURGH	0
0	PHILADELPHIA	6
12	Chic. Cards	9
10	PORTSMOUTH	7
3	Philadelphia	20
10	BROOKLYN	0

Use Name	Pos.	Hgt	Wgt	Age	Int	Pts
Frank Abruzzino	C-BB-LB	6'	190	25		
Mil Berner	C-LB	6'2"	204	27		
John Rogers	C-LB	5'11"	205	23		

Use Name – Tackles	Pos.	Hgt	Wgt	Age	Int	Pts
Lloyd Burdick	T	6'4"	257	24		
John Burleson (from Port, G and PIT, T)	T	6'2"	237			
Walt Doell	T					
Leo Draveling	T	6'2"	210	23		
George Munday	T	6'2"	215	25		

Use Name – Guards	Pos.	Hgt	Wgt	Age	Int	Pts
Tom Blondin	G	6'	195	22		
Les Caywood	G	6'	230	28		
Rosie Grant	G	5'10"	198	24		
Biff Lee (1 field goal)	G	6'	225	25		3

Cincinnati came into the NFL for the second time, with the first venture hardly an encouraging example. In 1921, the Cincinnati Celts played eight games, lost eight games, and then dropped out of the league.

The new Reds fared slightly better with a 3-6-1 record, which was admirable considering that they resembled a modern expansion team, with a horde of rookies fresh from college and a handful of fringe players from other clubs. Of the veterans, Jim Mooney, a 197-pound end who ranked among the league's top punters, made the biggest splash, and one rookie, 5'6" speedster Gil LeFebvre, broke into the record books with a 98-yard punt return against Brooklyn in the season's finale.

CHICAGO CARDINALS 1-9-1 Paul Schissler

Scores of Each Game		
13	Pittsburgh	14
6	Portsmouth	7
3	Cincinnati	0
9	CHIC. BEARS	12
0	Boston	10
0	Brooklyn	7
6	GREEN BAY	14
9	CINCINNATI	12
0	BROOKLYN	3
6	Chic. Bears	22
0	BOSTON	

Use Name	Pos.	Hgt	Wgt	Age	Int	Pts
Frank McNally	C-T-LB	6'1"	205	26		6
Tim Moynihan	C-LB	6'1"	204	26		
Tom Yarr	C-LB	5'10"	205	25		

Use Name – Tackles	Pos.	Hgt	Wgt	Age	Int	Pts
Lou Gordon	T	6'5"	220	25		
Jess Tinsley	T	6'	204	25		
Jake Williams	T	6'	205	27		

Use Name – Guards	Pos.	Hgt	Wgt	Age	Int	Pts
Gil Bergerson (from CHI B)	G	6'6"	245	23		
Herb Blumer	G	6'1"	200	30		
Al Graham	G	6'	218	27		
Phil Handler	G	6'	218	24		
Walt Kiesling	G	6'3"	235	28		
Dave Ribble	G	6'1"	225	26		

On a slide since Ernie Nevers left after the 1931 season, the Cards hit bottom by compiling the worst record in a circuit with three expansion clubs.

With the Cards losing and the Bears headed for a championship, the Chicago pro-football rooter spent little of his time or money on the weaker of the city's franchises. It was this state of affairs which prompted owner Dr. David Jones to sell the club in mid-season to Charles Bidwill, a football fan who, until his death in 1947 remained at the head of the Cardinal organization despite never once being rewarded with a financially profitable season.

Although Walt Kiesling and Frank McNally gave new coach Paul Schissler some hope and the forward wall some toughness, the backfield, led by black tailback Joe Lillard, lacked the spark Nevers once had given it.

TEAM TOTALS

	YARDS GAINED	OPPONENTS YARDS	PASS ATT.	PASS COMP.	COMP. PCT.	TOTAL POINTS	RUSH TD	PASS TD	OTHER TD	PAT	FG	SAF	OPPONENTS POINTS
CHICAGO BEARS	**3029**	2326	**210**	**92**	43.8	133	3	11	2	15	**6**	**2**	82
PORTSMOUTH	2710	1983	170	65	38.2	128	11	5	0	14	**6**	0	87
GREEN BAY	2758	1929	209	88	42.1	170	15	6	3	20	2	0	107
CINCINNATI	1206	2319	101	24	23.8	38	2	0	1	3	5	1	110
CHICAGO CARDS	1508	2308	141	37	26.2	52	3	3	1	2	2	1	101

Use Name – Backs & Ends	Pos.	Age	Hgt	Wgt	Pts	Int	RUSHING				PASSING								RECEIVING				PUNTING		KICKING						PUNT RETURNS				KICKOFF RETURNS			
							No.	Yds	Avg	TD	Att	Comp	%	Yds	Yd/Att	TD	Int–%	RK	No.	Yds	Avg	TD	No.	Avg	Pat	Att	%	FG	Att	%	No.	Yds	Avg	TD	No.	Yds	Avg	TD
CHICAGO BEARS																																						
Keith Molesworth	QB-HB-DB	26	5'9"	160	6						50	19	38	421	8.4	5	4– 8	2				1																
Carl Brumbaugh	QB-DB	25	5'10"	165												1																						
Bronko Nagurski	FB-LB	24	6'2"	217	10		128	533	4.2	1															1	1	100	1										
Red Grange	HB-DB	29	6'	185	6											2																						
Johnny Sisk	HB-LB	26	6'2"	198	6																																	
Jack Manders	FB-HB-LB	24	6'	202	29		89	295	3.3	0															14	14	100	5										
Gene Ronzani	HB-FB-LB	24	5'9"	200	6		26	82	3.2	0												1																
John Doehring	HB-LB	23	6'	212												1																						
George Corbett	HB-DB	25	5'9"	180																																		
Paul Franklin	FB-OE-LB-DE	27	6'2"	205																																		
Bill Hewitt	OE-DE	23	5'9"	190	18											2			16	274	17	2																
Bill Karr	OE-DE	22	6'1"	194	24														8	184	23	3																
Luke Johnsos	OE-DE	26	6'2"	195	18														8	151	19	3																
Joe Zeller	G-OE-DE	25	6'1"	205	6																	1																
PORTSMOUTH SPARTANS																																						
Glenn Presnell	TB-DB	28	5'10"	190	63		118	522	4.4	6	125	47	38	774	6.2	4	12–10	6							12	13	92	5										
Elmer Schaake	FB-LB		5'11"	207	6		125	412	3.3	0												1																
Ace Gutowsky	FB-TB-LB-DB	23	5'11"	200	7		103	385	3.7	1						1									1	1	100											
Ernie Caddel	WB-DB	22	6'2"	198	30		74	286	3.9	4												1																
Mule Wilson	WB-DB		5'11"	203																																		
Father Lumpkin	BB-DB	25	6'2"	213	6																	1																
Gene Alford	BB-FB-DB-LB		5'9"	184	6																	1																
Harry Ebding	OE-DE	24	5'11"	207																																		
John Cavosie	OE-FB-BB-DE-LB-DB-T		6'	207	10																	1			1	2	50	1										
John Schneller	OE-DE	21	6'2"	200																																		
Buster Mitchell	T-OE-DE	27	6'	210																																		
Romney Hunter	OE-DE			178																																		
GREEN BAY PACKERS																																						
Arnie Herber	TB-HB-DB	23	5'11"	200	1						126	50	40	656	5.2	4	12–10	5							1	1	100											
Bob Monnett	TB-DB	23	5'9"	188	34		108	412	3.8	4	46	23	50	315	6.8	2	3– 7	3							10	11	91											
Clarke Hinkle	FB-LB	23	5'11"	200	30		139	393	2.8	4															0	1	0	2										
Buckets Goldenberg	FB-LB	22	5'10"	220	42					5																												
Hurdis McCrary	FB-LB			204																																		
Hank Bruder	HB-TB-DB	25	6'	194	12					2																												
Wuert Engelmann	HB-BB-TB-DB			195	12																	1			0	1	0											
Buster Mott	HB-DB			190																																		
Roger Grove	BB-DB	24	6'	188	8														15	217	14	0			8	9	89											
Johnny Blood	BB-HB-DB	28	6'1"	190	19																	3			1	1	100 (reception)											
Lavie Dilweg	OE-DE	29	6'3"	202															14	225	16	0																
Milt Gantenbein	OE-DE	23	6'	200	6																	1																
Al Rose	OE-DE	26	6'3"	204	6																	1																
Ben Smith	OE-DE	22	6'3"	205																																		
CINCINNATI REDS																																						
Lew Pope	TB-WB-FB-DB-LB	25	6'	195	6					1																												
Blake Workman	TB-DB	23	5'11"	185																																		
Seaman Squyers	TB-DB	23	6'3"	200																																		
Bill Senn	TB-DB	28	6'	185																																		
Red Corzine	FB-LB	24	6'	210	6					1																												
Ossie Wiberg	FB-LB																																					
Gil LeFebvre	WB-TB-DB	23	5'6"	157	6																													1				
Jim Bausch (from CHIC, FB-LB)	WB-DB	27	6'1"	200																																		
Lee Mulleneaux	WB-BB-FB-DB-LB	23	6'2"	215																																		
Mike Palm	WB-BB-DB	32	5'10"	172																																		
Chief Elkins	WB-DB																																					
Algy Clark	BB-DB	29	6'	190	15																				3	3	100	4										
Don Moses	BB-DB	26	5'11"	185																																		
Joe Crakes	OE-DE	24	6'1"	205																																		
Jim Mooney	OE-DE-T	25	5'11"	197																																		
Cookie Tackwell (from CHIB)	OE-DE	26	6'2"	212																																		
Chuck Braidwood	OE-DE	28	6'	210																																		
Kermit Schmidt	OE-DE	25	6'	200																																		
Hal Hilpert	OE-DE																																					
Dick Powell	OE-DE	26	6'2"	220																																		
CHICAGO CARDINALS																																						
Joe Lillard	TB-DB	25	6'	185	19					2						2									1	4	25	2										
Mike Koken	TB-BB-DB	23	5'11"	180	1											1									1	2	50											
Cliff Hansen	TB-DB		6'1"	190																																		
Bert Hinchman	FB-LB		5'10"	190																																		
Dick Nesbitt (from CHIB, HB-LB)	FB-LB		6'	206	6					1																												
Dock Ledbetter	FB-LB	25	5'10"	190																																		
Otto Vokaty	FB-LB	24	6'1"	195																																		
Hal Moe	WB-DB	23	5'10"	182	12																	2																
Howie Tipton	WB-TB-DB-G	22	5'11"	185	6																	1																
Les Malloy	BB-DB	24	6'	200																																		
Roy Lamb	BB-DB	30	5'6"	160																																		
Chuck Bennett	BB-DB	26	5'9"	198																																		
Bill Simas	BB-DB	24	6'	185																																		
Milan Creighton	OE-WB-DE-DB	25	6'	185																																		
Dave Nisbet	OE-DE	23	6'1"	180																																		
Charlie Kassel	OE-DE	29	6'1"	195																																		
George Rogge	OE-DE	26	6'	185																																		

NEW YORK GIANTS 8-5-0 Steve Owen

Scores of Each Game		
0	Detroit	9
6	Green Bay	20
14	Pittsburgh	12
16	Boston	13
14	BROOKLYN	0
17	PITTSBURGH	7
17	PHILADELPHIA	0
7	Chic. Bears	27
17	GREEN BAY	3
9	CHIC. BEARS	10
3	BOSTON	0
27	Brooklyn	0
0	Philadelphia	6

Use Name	Pos.	Hgt	Wgt	Age	Int	Pts
Mel Hein (1 reception for 13 yds.)	C-LB	6'2"	218	25		
Illness – Glenn Campbell						

Use Name – Tackles	Pos.	Hgt	Wgt	Age	Int	Pts
Knuckles Boyle	T	5'11"	232	25		
Len Grant	T-G	6'3"	225	28		
Tex Irvin	T	6'	230	27		
Bill Morgan	T	6'2"	230	24		
Bill Owen	T	6'	220	30		
Babe Scheuer	T	6'3"	240	22		

Use Name – Guards	Pos.	Hgt	Wgt	Age	Int	Pts
Bob Bellinger	G	5'11"	212	21		
John Cannella (to BKN)	G	6'1"	200	26		
Johnny Dell Isola	G-C-LB	5'11"	205	22		
Butch Gibson	G	5'9"	208	30		
Potsy Jones	G	5'11"	210	24		
Hank Reese	G-C-LB	5'11"	210	23		

When the Giants dropped their first two games of the season in Detroit and Green Bay, it took a large dose of Eastern Division opponents to get healthy. Steve Owen's charges then ran off a string of five victories to give them a final 7-1 record against their Eastern rivals and the title despite posting a 1-4 record against the Western clubs.

Unquestioningly, the Giants were the powers of the East. Center Mel Hein, guard Butch Gibson, and tackle Bill Morgan made All-Pro in the line; Red Badgro was honored for his two-way play at end, and Ken Strong's running and kicking won him a backfield spot on the dream team. Harry Newman did not make All-Pro and had to settle for the yards he racked up with his passing game.

BOSTON REDSKINS 6-6-0 Lone Star Dietz

Scores of Each Game		
7	Pittsburgh	0
6	Brooklyn	10
13	NEW YORK	16
39	PITTSBURGH	0
0	Detroit	24
6	PHILADELPHIA	0
9	CHIC. CARDS	0
0	GREEN BAY	10
0	CHIC. BEARS	21
14	Philadelphia	7
0	New York	3
13	BROOKLYN	3

Use Name	Pos.	Hgt	Wgt	Age	Int	Pts
Frank Bausch	C-LB	6'3"	215	26		
Orien Crow	C-LB	6'	220			

Use Name – Tackles	Pos.	Hgt	Wgt	Age	Int	Pts
Ben Boswell	T	6'	245			
Turk Edwards	T	6'2"	250	26		
Gail O'Brien	T	6'1"	220	22		
Steve Sinko	T	6'3"	230	23		

Use Name – Guards	Pos.	Hgt	Wgt	Age	Int	Pts
Rick Concannon	G	6'	220	25		
Marne Intrieri	G	5'8"	250	26		
Les Olsson	G	6'	220	25		
Frank Walton	G	5'11"	215	22		

Beginning the year with high hopes of overtaking the Giants in the East, Boston ended it by treading water in second place. While being able to consume the smaller fry around the circuit, they could not get by the Giants, Bears, and Lions—the powerhouses of the league.

A strong class of rookies fed the high expectations at the outset, but when play started for real, coach Lone Star Dietz found that his two best players still were speedy halfback Cliff Battles and 250-pound tackle Turk Edwards.

Even though the field operation found the going rough, the attendance figures showed enough progress to give owner George Marshall the encouragement that his bottom line would soon turn from red to black.

BROOKLYN DODGERS 4-7-0 Cap McEwen

Scores of Each Game		
10	BOSTON	6
7	CHIC. BEARS	21
0	New York	14
0	Detroit	28
21	PITTSBURGH	3
0	CHIC. CARDS	21
10	Philadelphia	7
10	Pittsburgh	0
0	PHILADELPHIA	13
0	NEW YORK	27
3	Boston	13

Use Name	Pos.	Hgt	Wgt	Age	Int	Pts
Doc Morrison	C-LB	5'11"	210	25		
Tony Siano	C-LB	5'8"	172	27		

Use Name – Tackles	Pos.	Hgt	Wgt	Age	Int	Pts
Chuck Brodnicki	T	6'2"	225			
Harold Ely	T	6'2"	260	24		
Lou Lubratovich	T	6'2"	228	27		
Saul Mielziner	T-C-LB	6'1"	245			

Use Name – Guards	Pos.	Hgt	Wgt	Age	Int	Pts
Jim Bowdoin	G-T	6'1"	215	28		
George DeMas	G	6'	190			
Tiny Engelbretsen (to GB, G)	G-T	6'1"	225	24		
Herman Hickman	G	5'10"	250	22		
Bruce Jones	G-T	6'1"	215	29		
Stu Worden	G	6'	210	24		

The season began with Chris Cagle selling his share of the Dodgers to Dan Topping, a future owner of the New York Yankees baseball team, and Benny Friedman retiring to coach college ball. Along with Friedman went the Dodgers' aerial attack, and the ground game—which still showed some muscle—became the victim of keying defenses.

During the campaign, guard Herman Hickman shone amidst the mediocrity with his size and speed, and his blocking kept the Dodger offense from becoming a complete corpse. In the backfield, 165-pound rookie Cliff Montgomery, heralded All-American from Columbia, failed to make the grade, but Ralph Kercheval from Kentucky won a starting halfback job with his running and punting. Shipwreck Kelly, still part owner, and Cagle, now only an employee, served well enough together on the field to eat up large chunks of yardage. Even Friedman, who returned late in the season, failed to improve the Dodgers' offense.

PHILADELPHIA EAGLES 4-7-0 Lud Wray

Scores of Each Game		
6	Green Bay	19
17	Pittsburgh	0
7	PITTSBURGH	9
0	DETROIT	10
0	Boston	6
0	New York	17
64	CINCINNATI	0
7	BROOKLYN	10
7	BOSTON	14
13	Brooklyn	0
6	NEW YORK	0

Use Name	Pos.	Hgt	Wgt	Age	Int	Pts
Chuck Hajek (1 PAT in 1 attempt)	C-LB	6'1"	210	23		1
Bull Lipski	C-LB	5'11"	200			

Use Name – Tackles	Pos.	Hgt	Wgt	Age	Int	Pts
Paul Cuba	T	6'	210	26		
Jim MacMurdo	T	6'1"	210	23		
Guy Turnbow	T	6'2"	217	26		
Vince Zizak	T	5'8"	208	25		

Use Name – Guards	Pos.	Hgt	Wgt	Age	Int	Pts
Joe Kresky	G	6'	220	26		
Barnes Milam	G					
Phil Poth	G					
Diddie Willson	G	5'10"	195	23		
Jim Zyntell	G	6'1"	200	24		

On November 4, a Philadelphia audience watched in shock as the Eagles destroyed the Cincinnati Reds 64-0, a bit of a surprise since the Eagles had not scored a point in their last three games.

The young club continued to improve as the season went along, and two second-year players attracted attention around the circuit. End Joe Carter grabbed sixteen forward passes to lead the league in receiving, while back Swede Hanson won a second-team All-Pro spot for his two-way play. Coach Lud Wray fielded a small team, but the young squad hit hard enough and often enough to annoy most of their opponents—one of which was the Giants, who dropped a 6-0 decision at Philadelphia in the season's finale en route to the championship game with the Bears.

PITTSBURGH PIRATES 2-10-0 Luby DiMelio

Scores of Each Game		
13	CINCINNATI	0
0	BOSTON	7
0	PHILADELPHIA	17
12	NEW YORK	14
9	Philadelphia	7
0	CHIC. BEARS	28
0	Boston	39
7	New York	17
3	Brooklyn	21
7	Detroit	40
0	St. Louis	6
0	BROOKLYN	10

Use Name	Pos.	Hgt	Wgt	Age	Int	Pts
Ben Ciccone	C-LB	5'10"	193	24		
Cap Oehler	C-LB	6'	206	23		

Use Name – Tackles	Pos.	Hgt	Wgt	Age	Int	Pts
John Dempsey (from PHI)	T	6'2"	225			
Armand Niccolai (1 PAT in 1 attempt, 3 field goals)	T	6'2"	220	22		10
Jess Quatse	T	5'11"	218	27		

Use Name – Guards	Pos.	Hgt	Wgt	Age	Int	Pts
Jap Douds	G-T	5'10"	216	27		
Norm Greeney	G-T	5'11"	210	24		
Zvonimir Kvaternick	G		210			
Basilio Marchi	G	6'2"	215	25		
Dave Ribble	G	6'1"	212	27		
Bull Snyder	G	6'2"	230	22		
Henry Weinberg	G-T		190			

Looking to build for his first championship, owner Art Rooney purchased brilliant but eccentric Johnny Blood from the Green Bay Packers. Rooney looked to Blood to shoot some fire into the Pirate offense and add a little color to the team's public image. Unfortunately, an early-season injury kept Blood on the sidelines most of the year, and the colorless Pirates finished in last place.

Two other Green Bay acquisitions—6'3" end Ben Smith, who came with Blood, and tackle Jess Quatse, who came in 1933—helped fill weak spots for new coach Luby DiMelio's lineup, as did rookie back Warren Heller, who came from the University of Pittsburgh to inject new offensive power into the team.

TEAM TOTALS

	YARDS GAINED	OPPONENTS YARDS	PASS ATT.	PASS COMP.	COMP. PCT.	TOTAL POINTS	RUSH TD	PASS TD	OTHER TD	PAT	FG	SAF	OPPONENTS POINTS
NEW YORK	2775	2342	154	63	40.9	147	12	5	1	16	7	1	107
BOSTON	3351	2606	138	39	28.3	107	10	4	2	8	1	0	94
BROOKLYN	1481	2687	161	43	26.7	61	5	1	1	7	4	0	153
PHILADELPHIA	2554	2237	163	47	28.8	127	11	7	1	10	1	0	85
PITTSBURGH	2527	3304	182	58	31.9	51	2	4	0	3	4	0	206

Use Name – Backs & Ends	Pos.	Age	Hgt	Wgt	Pts	Int	RUSHING No.	Yds	Avg	TD	PASSING Att	Comp	%	Yds	Yd/Att	TD	Int–%	RK	RECEIVING No.	Yds	Avg	TD	PUNTING No.	Avg	KICKING Pat	Att	%	FG	Att	%	PUNT RETURNS No.	Yds	Avg	TD	KICKOFF RETURNS No.	Yds	Avg	TD
NEW YORK GIANTS																																						
Harry Newman	TB-DB	24	5'8"	180	37		131	503	3.8	3	91	35	38	366	4.0	1	5–5	4							4	5	80	3										
Ed Danowski	TB-DB	22	6'1"	200							32	15	47	230	7.2	2	3–9																					1
Jack McBride	TB-DB	32	5'11"	185	1											1									1	1	100											
Ken Strong	FB-DB	28	6'	202	56		110	410	3.7	6															8	9	89	4	11	36								
Wee Willie Smith	FB-DB	24	5'6"	148	12		45	232	5.2	2						1																						
Kink Richards	FB-DB	23	5'11"	195	13					1												1			1	1	100											
Dale Burnett	WB-DB	25	6'1"	186	12														9	152	17	2																
Harry Stafford	WB-DB	24	5'11"	205																																		
Stu Clancy	WB-BB-DB-LB	28	5'10"	195																																		
John Norby (to PHI,HB-DB,to C-S)	WB-DB	23	6'	195																																		
Bo Molenda	BB-LB	28	5'10"	213	2																				2	2	100											
Max Krause	BB-LB	25	5'10"	206																																		
Red Badgro	OE-DE	31	6'	190	6														16	206	13	1																
Ray Flaherty	OE-DE	30	6'	190	6														8	79	10	1																
Ike Frankian	OE-DE	27	5'11"	207																																		
BOSTON REDSKINS																																						
Cliff Battles	TB-DB	24	6'1"	195	43		103	511	5.0	6												1			1	2	50											
Ted Wright	TB-DB	20	6'	185	8					1															2	4	50											
Hal McPhail	FB-DB	22	6'1"	230	21					1															3	5	60 (1 PAT on reception)											
Doug Wycoff	FB-BB-DB-LB	28	6'	225	6					1						1																						
Ernie Pinckert	WB-DB	26	6'	190	6					1																												
Pug Rentner	WB-DB	23	6'1"	195	6																	1																
Steve Hokuf	BB-LB	23	6'	200	5						51	13	25	203	4.0	3	10–20	7							2	3	67	1										
Arnie Arenz	BB-LB		6'2"	215																																		
Charley Malone	OE-DE	24	6'4"	200	12														11	121	11	2																
Paul Collins	OE-DE	26	6'1"	200																																		
Flavio Tosi	OE-DE	22	6'1"	190																																		
Chief Johnson	OE-DE-C-LB	25	6'3"	225																																		
BROOKLYN DODGERS																																						
Chris Cagle	TB-DB	27	5'10"	177												3																						
Shipwreck Kelly	TB-DB	24	6'2"	195	6					1																												
Cliff Montgomery	TB-DB	23	5'9"	165												1																						
Benny Friedman	TB-DB		5'10"	182																																		
Jack Grossman	FB-DB	24	6'1"	195	12											1			10	158	16	1												1				
Ollie Sansen	FB-DB	26	6'1"	195																																		
Ralph Kercheval	WB-DB	23	6'1"	195	36																	3			6	6	100	4										
Dick Nesbitt	WB-DB		6'	210																																		
Bull Karcis	BB-LB	25	5'9"	215																																		
Stumpy Thomason	BB-LB	28	5'7"	195																																		
Paul Riblett	OE-DE	26	5'10"	182	6																	1																
Wayland Becker (from CHIB)	OE-DE	23	6'	200																																		
Doc Cronkhite	OE-DE	23	6'5"	210																																		
Harry Kloppenberg	OE-DE		6'1"	210																																		
Phil Peterson	OE-DE	28	5'11"	195																																		
Tom Nash	OE-DE	26	6'3"	195																																		
Mike Stramiello	OE-DE	27	6'1"	207																																		
Joe Hugret	OE-DE	24	6'2"	195																																		
PHILADELPHIA EAGLES																																						
Ed Matesic	TB-DB	23	6'1"	195	7						60	20	33	272	4.5	3	5–8	3							1	1	100											
Dan Barnhart	TB-DB															1																						
Swede Hanson	FB-HB-LB-DB	25	6'1"	192	49		147	805	5.5	7												1			1	1	100											
Jim Leonard	FB-BB-LB	24	6'	204	6					1																												
Lorne Johnson	FB-LB																																					
Ed Storm	HB-FB-TB-DB	26	6'1"	195	12					2																												
Swede Ellstrom (from BOS,FB-DB)	HB-DB	26	6'1"	200	6					1						1									0	1	0											
Rick Lackman	HB-DB	22	5'11"	186																																		
Reds Weiner	HB-FB-DB-LB	23	5'9"	180	6											1									3	4	75	1	2	50								
Joe Knapper	HB-DB																																					
Reds Kirkman	BB-DB	28	6'1"	195	10											1						1			4	6	67											
Joe Carter	OE-DE	24	6'1"	203	24														16	238	15	4																
George Kenneally	OE-DE	32	6'	192																																		
Joe Pilconis	OE-DE	22	6'1"	192																																		
Bob Gonya	T-OE-DE	24	6'2"	205	6																	1																
PITTSBURGH PIRATES																																						
Warren Heller	TB-DB	24	5'11"	195	6		132	528	4.0	1	112	31	28	511	4.6	2	15–13	6																				
Harp Vaughan	TB-BB-HB-DB	27	5'7"	160							39	14	36	272	7.0	2	5–13																					
Jimmy Clark	FB-HB-DB		5'9"	177	6																	1																
Angie Brovelli	FB-HB-LB-DB		6'	195	6					1																												
Mose Kelsch	FB-LB	38	5'10"	220	5		3	12	4.0	0															2	5	40	1										
Pete Rajkovich	FB-LB																																					
Alex Rado	HB-DB	23	6'1"	200																																		
Johnny Blood	HB-DB	29	6'1"	188																																		
Jack Roberts (from PHI)	HB-FB-DB-LB		6'	220																																		
Jim Levey	HB-DB	27	5'10"	156																																		
George Kavel (to PHI)	HB-DB																																					
Bill Potts	HB-DB			200																																		
Silvio Zaninelli	BB-FB-LB-DB	20	5'10"	204																																		
Buster Mott (from C-S)	BB-DB			195																																		
Harry Marker	BB-DB																																					
Ben Smith	OE-DE	23	6'3"	210															12	190	16	0																
Joe Skladany	OE-DE			210	12														10	222	22	2																
Bill Sortet	OE-DE	22	6'1"	188	6																	1																
Ray Tesser	OE-DE		6'2"	207																																		

1934 N.F.L. — WEST

CHICAGO BEARS 13-0-0 George Halas

Scores of Each Game		
24	Green Bay	10
21	Cincinnati	3
21	Brooklyn	7
28	Pittsburgh	0
20	Chic. Cards	0
41	CINCINNATI	7
27	GREEN BAY	14
27	NEW YORK	7
21	Boston	0
10	New York	9
17	CHIC. CARDS	6
19	Detroit	16
10	DETROIT	7

Use Name	Pos.	Hgt	Wgt	Age	Int	Pts
Eddie Kawal	C-LB	6'2"	205	24		
Ookie Miller	C-G-LB	6'	204	24		
Bert Pearson	C-G-LB	6'	210	29		

Use Name – Tackles	Pos.	Hgt	Wgt	Age	Int	Pts
Art Buss	T	6'3"	218	23		
Link Lyman	T	6'2"	246	35		
George Musso	T	6'2"	268	24		
Ted Rosequist	T-G	6'4"	225	26		

Use Name – Guards	Pos.	Hgt	Wgt	Age	Int	Pts
Zuck Carlson	G	6'	210	29		
Walt Kiesling	G-T	6'3"	252	29		
Joe Kopcha	G	6'	226	28		
Joe Zeller	G	6'1"	198	26		

Rookie halfback Beattie Feathers of Tennessee, who helped battle the Bears to a scoreless tie in the first annual College All-Star Game, went on to rush for a record 1,004 yards, despite sitting out two games with a shoulder separation, to give the Bears the first perfect record in NFL history.

Joining Feathers on the All-Pro team were fullback Bronko Nagurski, whose locomotive blocking cleared the way for the rookie's runs, end Bill Hewitt, and guard Joe Kopcha. Tackle Link Lyman and center Eddie Kawal placed on the second team, and reserve fullback Jack Manders booted a record ten field goals to win a reputation as pro football's first great place kicker. Red Grange, reduced to a reserve, played his final season.

DETROIT LIONS 10-3-0 Potsy Clark

Scores of Each Game		
9	NEW YORK	0
6	CHIC. CARDS	0
3	Green Bay	0
10	Philadelphia	0
24	BOSTON	0
28	BROOKLYN	0
38	Cincinnati at Portsmouth	0
40	PITTSBURGH	7
17	Chic. Cards	13
40	ST. LOUIS	7
0	GREEN BAY	3
16	CHIC. BEARS	19
7	Chic. Bears	10

Use Name	Pos.	Hgt	Wgt	Age	Int	Pts
Chuck Bernard	C-LB	6'3"	225	22		
Clare Randolph	C-LB	6'2"	210	27		

Use Name – Tackles	Pos.	Hgt	Wgt	Age	Int	Pts
George Christensen	T	6'2"	240	24		
Bob Emerick	T-G	6'2"	220	21		
Jack Johnson	T	6'4"	220	24		
Sam Knox	T-G	6'	200	24		

Use Name – Guards	Pos.	Hgt	Wgt	Age	Int	Pts
Maury Bodenger	G	5'10"	195	25		
Ox Emerson	G	5'11"	220	26		
Tom Hupke	G	5'10"	194	23		
Ray Richards	G-T	6'1"	240	28		

Pro football returned to Detroit when George Richards purchased the financially shaky Portsmouth Spartans and transformed them into the Lions. Bright blue uniforms and halftime shows gave the fans a lot to look at, but the Lions themselves were the best show.

Led by Dutch Clark, open-field runner and safety *par excellence*, back after a year's retirement, and tackle George Christensen, the Lions shut out their first seven opponents and won their first ten games to stay even with the unbeaten Bears before the Packers broke the spell with a 3-0 upset. Detroit's Western title hopes then bit the dust via a pair of three-point losses to the Bears.

GREEN BAY PACKERS 7-6-0 Curly Lambeau

Scores of Each Game		
19	PHILADELPHIA	6
10	CHIC. BEARS	24
20	NEW YORK	6
0	DETROIT	3
41	CINCINNATI	0
15	CHIC. CARDS	0
14	Chic. Bears	27
10	Boston	0
3	New York	17
0	Chic. Cards	9
3	Detroit	0
0	Chic. Cards	6
21	St. Louis	14

Use Name	Pos.	Hgt	Wgt	Age	Int	Pts
Nate Barrager	C-G-LB	6'	210	27		
Art Bultman	C-LB	6'2"	200	26		
Frank Butler	C-LB	6'3"	226	25		

Use Name – Tackles	Pos.	Hgt	Wgt	Age	Int	Pts
Lon Evans	T-G	6'2"	220	22		
Carl Jorgensen	T-G	6'	200	23		
Joe Kurth	T	6'1"	202	23		
Claude Perry	T	6'1"	210	32		
Ade Schwammel (1 field goal)	T	6'2"	220	25		3

Use Name – Guards	Pos.	Hgt	Wgt	Age	Int	Pts
Bob Jones	G	6'2"	215	22		
Mike Michalske	G	6'	200	30		
Champ Seibold	G	6'4"	232	21		
Harry Wunsch	G					

After 1933's collapse, Curly Lambeau began remodeling the Packers. Johnny Blood was sold to Pittsburgh, Cal Hubbard retired, and Lambeau replaced both men with younger players. Veterans Arnie Herber, Clarke Hinkle, Buckets Goldenberg, Lon Evans, Mike Michalske, and Lavie Dilweg were still at their prime, though, and formed a solid gridwork around which Lambeau could quickly rebuild.

Still, the Packers fluctuated from game to game. After an embarrassing loss to the Chicago Cardinals in Milwaukee, Lambeau fined the entire squad half of one week's salary, saying they could have their money back by beating undefeated Detroit the next week, which they did, 3-0, via a 47-yard field goal by Clarke Hinkle. But another loss in the next Cardinal rematch sent Lambeau foaming.

CHICAGO CARDINALS 5-6-0 Paul Schissler

Scores of Each Game		
9	Cincinnati at Dayton	0
0	Detroit	6
16	Cincinnati	0
0	CHIC. BEARS	20
0	Green Bay	15
0	Boston	9
21	Brooklyn	0
13	DETROIT	17
9	GREEN BAY	0
6	Chic. Bears	17
6	GREEN BAY	0

Use Name	Pos.	Hgt	Wgt	Age	Int	Pts
Bernie Hughes	C-LB	6'1"	190	24		
Frank McNally	C-LB	6'1"	200	27		

Use Name – Tackles	Pos.	Hgt	Wgt	Age	Int	Pts
Harry Field	T	6'1"	230	22		
Lou Gordon	T	6'5"	230	26		
Ted Isaacson	T-C	6'4"	272	22		
Pete Mehringer	T	6'2"	200	24		
Paul Shenefelt	T	6'	195	23		

Use Name – Guards	Pos.	Hgt	Wgt	Age	Int	Pts
Bree Cuppoletti	G	5'10"	198	24		
Phil Handler	G	6'	215	25		
Howie Tipton	G-OE-DE	5'11"	180	23		
Bill Volok	G	6'2"	215	24		

After watching his newly purchased team stumble through a miserable 1933 campaign, owner Charles Bidwill decided that a new deal with the Cards was in order. Only six players returned from last year's team, while seventeen rookies filled the roster with inexperienced enthusiasm. Coach Paul Schissler molded this kiddie corps into a team good enough to win five games, all by shutouts, a vast improvement over the coach's first season with the Cardinals.

Of the returning veterans, end Milan Creighton, guard Phil Handler, and versatile Howie Tipton provided the best examples for the rookies to follow, and freshmen Doug Russell, Mike Mikulak, and Bill Smith were the gold nuggets in the recruit crop.

CINCINNATI REDS 0-8-0 Algy Clark – ST. LOUIS GUNNERS 1-2-0 Mike Palm

Scores of Each Game		
CINCINNATI		
0	Pittsburgh	13
0	CHIC. CARDS at Dayton	9
3	CHIC. BEARS	21
0	CHIC. CARDS	16
0	Green Bay	41
7	Chic. Bears	41
0	DETROIT At Portsmouth	38
0	Philadelphia	64
ST. LOUIS		
6	PITTSBURGH	0
7	Detroit	40
14	GREEN BAY	21

Use Name	Pos.	Hgt	Wgt	Age	Int	Pts
Tal Maples	C-LB	6'	195			
Russ McLeod	C-LB					
Lee Mulleneaux	C-LB	6'2"	216	24		
John Rogers	C-LB	5'11"	210	24		
Hal Weldin	C-LB					

Use Name – Tackles	Pos.	Hgt	Wgt	Age	Int	Pts
Charlie Diehl	T					
Earl Elser	T	6'1"	227			
Foster Howell	T	6'3"	205			
George Lyon	T		235			
Bill Montgomery	T-G					
George Munday	T-G	6'2"	206	26		
Sandy Sandberg	T	6'2"	225	24		
Cole Wilging	T-OE-DE	6'1"	185			
Charlie Zunker	T	6'4"	227			

Use Name – Guards	Pos.	Hgt	Wgt	Age	Int	Pts
Ed Aspatore (to & from CHI B)	G-T	6'1"	220			
Les Caywood	G	6'	230	29		
Rosie Grant	G	5'10"	198	25		
Homer Hanson	G	6'	210			
Russ Lay (from DET T-G)	G	5'11"	198	23		
Hilary Lee (1 PAT in 1 attempt)	G	6'	235	26		1
Len McGirl	G		206			
Homer Reynolds	G		185			
Harvey Sark	G					

When the Cincinnati Reds fell out of the NFL constellation, the St. Louis Gunners were created out of local rookies and castoffs from other clubs to finish out the remaining three games on the Reds' slate. Six Cincinnati players—Gene Alford, Red Corzine, Earl Elser, Russ Lay, Lee Mulleneaux, and George Munday—joined the new Gunners.

The team started out its short life with a burst of glory, knocking off the Pittsburgh Pirates 6-0 before a home-town crowd. The next two games with the Lions and Packers, though, were too much for the raggedy Gunners.

After finishing the three games, the Gunners returned to the oblivion from whence they came, and St. Louis would not have another team until the Chicago Cardinals were transplanted in 1960.

TEAM TOTALS

	YARDS GAINED	OPPONENTS YARDS	PASS ATT.	PASS COMP.	COMP. PCT.	TOTAL POINTS	RUSH TD	PASS TD	OTHER TD	PAT	FG	SAF	OPPONENTS POINTS
CHICAGO BEARS	3750	2119	192	57	29.7	286	22	15	0	34	10	0	86
DETROIT	3510	1960	144	43	29.9	238	27	3	2	22	8	0	59
GREEN BAY	3372	2523	188	73	38.8	156	8	10	1	16	8	1	112
CHICAGO CARDS	1598	1578	140	34	24.3	80	7	1	3	5	3	0	84
CIN–ST. LOUIS	1608	3488	173	49	28.3	37	3	1	0	4	3	2	304

Use Name – Backs & Ends	Pos.	Age	Hgt	Wgt	Pts	Int	RUSHING				PASSING								RECEIVING				PUNTING		KICKING						PUNT RETURNS				KICKOFF RETURNS			
							No.	Yds	Avg	TD	Att	Comp	%	Yds	Yd/Att	TD	Int–%	RK	No.	Yds	Avg	TD	No.	Avg	Pat	Att	%	FG	Att	%	No.	Yds	Avg	TD	No.	Yds	Avg	TD
CHICAGO BEARS																																						
Carl Brumbaugh	QB-DB	26	5'10"	180	13		7	9	1.3	0						4						2			1	1	100											
Bernie Masterson	QB-DB	23	6'3"	195	7		4	11	2.8	1	2	2	100	35	17.5	0	0– 0								1	1	100											
Beattie Feathers	HB-DB	25	5'10"	185	54		101	**1004**	**9.9**	**8**						1						1																
Bronko Nagurski	FB-LB	25	6'2"	230	43		123	586	4.8	7						2									1	2	50											
Gene Ronzani	HB-LB	25	5'9"	208	18		84	485	5.8	0	32	15	47	150	4.7	3	0– 0					3																
Jack Manders	FB-LB	25	6'	210	**79**		57	184	3.2	3															**31**	**32**	**97**	**10**										
Johnny Sisk	HB-LB	27	6'2"	200	6		41	156	3.8	1																												
Red Grange	HB-DB	30	6'	190	18		32	136	4.3	1												2																
Keith Molesworth	HB-QB-DB	27	5'9"	168	6		61	125	2.0	0						3																						
George Corbett	HB-DB	26	5'9"	184			30	119	4.0	1						1																						
John Doehring	HB-LB	24	6'	215			8	6	0.8	0						1																						
Bill Hewitt	OE-DE	24	5'9"	195	30		1	14	14.0	0									10	151	15	**5**																
Luke Johnsos	OE-DE	27	6'2"	198	6														6	94	16	1																
Bill Karr	OE-DE	23	6'1"	194	6														4	76	19	1																
DETROIT LIONS																																						
Dutch Clark	TB-DB	27	6'	190	73		122	763	6.3	**8**	49	23	**47**	383	**7.8**	0	3– 6	2							13	18	72	4										
Glenn Presnell	TB-DB	29	5'10"	200	63		117	413	3.5	7	57	13	23	236	4.1	2	9–16	7							9	12	75	4										
Ace Gutowsky	FB-LB	24	5'11"	205	30		141	517	3.7	5																												
Frank Christensen	FB-BB-LB-DB	24	6'1"	205	12					2																												
Bob Rowe	FB-WB-LB-DB	23	6'	200																																		
Ernie Caddel	WB-DB	23	6'2"	205	36		101	428	4.2	4						1			9	125	14	1																
Bill McWilliams	WB-DB	23	6'1"	205																																		
Father Lumpkin	BB-DB	26	6'2"	210	12					1												0																
Harry Ebding	OE-WB-DE-DB	25	5'11"	205	12														9	**257**	**29**	2																
John Schneller	OE-DE	22	6'2"	205																																		
Buster Mitchell	OE-DE	28	6'	210																																		
Bill McKalip	OE-DE	23	6'1"	195																																		
GREEN BAY PACKERS																																						
Arnie Herber	TB-DB	24	5'11"	203							**115**	**42**	37	**799**	6.9	**8**	12–10	**1**																				
Bob Monnett	TB-DB	24	5'9"	180	30					2	47	16	34	223	5.0	1	4– 9	5							6	7	86	4										
Clarke Hinkle	FB-LB	24	5'11"	200	26		112	384	3.4	1									10	110	11	1			5	5	100	3	7	43								
Roger Grove	HB-DB	25	6'	184	25					1												3			1	2	50											
Joe Laws	HB-DB	23	5'9"	185	12					1						1						1																
Hank Bruder	BB-FB-TB-DB-LB	26	6'	197	22					1												1			4	5	80											
Buckets Goldenberg	BB-FB-DB-LB	23	5'10"	215	12					2																												
Earl Witte	BB-DB	26	6'	188																																		
Milt Gantenbein	OE-DE	24	6'	193															10	165	17	0																
Lavie Dilweg	OE-DE	30	6'3"	195	12																	2																
Al Rose	OE-DE	27	6'3"	195	12																	2																
Les Peterson	OE-DE	24	6'3"	207																																		
Al Norgard	OE-DE	24	6'1"	194																																		
CHICAGO CARDINALS																																						
Doug Russell	TB-DB	22	6'	180	12					1																												
Homer Griffith	TB-WB-DB	22	5'11"	165	12																																	1
Bert Hinchman (to DET, BB-DB)	TB-DB		5'10"	190																														1				1
Mike Mikulak	FB-WB-LB-DB	21	6'1"	210	24					4																												
Roy Horstmann	FB-LB		6'	190																																		
Dave Cook	WB-DB	22	6'2"	200	4																				1	4	25	1										
Phil Sarboe (from BOS, TB-DB)	BB-DB	22	5'10"	165												1									0	1	0											
Frank Greene	BB-DB	23	5'11"	190																																		
Paul Pardonner	BB-DB	24	5'8"	170	3																							1										
Tom Murphy	BB-DB		5'11"	170																																		
Bill Smith	OE-DE	22	6'1"	198	25		5	74	14.8	2												1			4	6	67	1										
George Duggins	OE-DE	22	6'3"	200																																		
Milan Greighton	OE-DE	26	6'	190																																		
Bob Neuman	OE-DE	22	6'	200																																		
Joe Krejci	OE-DE		6'	190																																		
CINCINNATI REDS – ST. LOUIS GUNNERS																																						
Tom Bushby	TB-WB-DB	22	5'10"	200																																		
Tiny Feather	TB-DB	31	6'	205																																		
Syl Saumer(from & to PIT,FB-LB)	TB-DB	22	6'1"	195	6					1																												
Manny Rapp	TB-DB	21		215												1																						
Gil LeFebvre	TB-DB	24	5'6"	156																																		
Bill Senn	TB-DB	29	6'	175	3																							1	1	100								
Bill Lewis	TB-DB		5'11"	186																																		
Red Corzine	FB-LB	25	6'	210	6					1																												
Swede Johnston (from GB)	FB-LB	24	5'10"	200	6					1																												
Otto Vokaty	FB-LB	25	6'1"	190																																		
Ben Sohn	FB-LB																																					
Charlie McLaughlin	FB-LB																																					
Bill Parriott	FB-LB																																					
Lew Pope	WB-BB-DB	26	6'	196																																		
Gene Alford	WB-BB-DB		5'9"	170	6																				3	3	100	1	2	50								
Cy Casper (from GB,BB-DB)	WB-DB	22	6'	188																																		
Jabby Andrews	WB-DB			200																																		
Cliff Moore	WB-DB		6'1"	202																																		
Algy Clark (to PHI)	BB-DB	30	6'	190	3																				0	1	0	1										
Norris Steverson	BB-WB-DB		5'11"	190																																		
Blake Workman	BB-DB	24	5'11"	185																																		
Benny LaPresta	BB-DB		5'9"	185																																		
Jim Mooney	OE-DE	26	5'11"	197																																		
Cookie Tackwell	OE-DE	27	6'2"	218																																		
Paul Moss	OE-DE		6'2"	180	6																	1																
Mack Gladden	OE-DE	22		195																																		
George Rogge	OE-DE	27	6'	185																																		
Gump Ariail (from BKN)	OE-DE	22	5'11"	205																																		
Basil Wilkerson	OE-DE																																					

NEW YORK GIANTS 9-3-0 Steve Owen

Scores of Each Game		
42	Pittsburgh	7
7	Green Bay	16
20	Boston	12
10	BROOKLYN	7
17	BOSTON	6
13	CHIC. CARDS	14
3	CHIC. BEARS	20
3	Chic. Bears	0
10	PHILADELPHIA	0
21	Brooklyn	0
21	Philadelphia	14
13	PITTSBURGH	0

Use Name	Pos.	Hgt	Wgt	Age	Int	Pts
Johnny Dell Isola	C-G-LB	5'11"	198	23		
Mel Hein	C-LB	6'2"	225	26		

Use Name – Tackles	Pos.	Hgt	Wgt	Age	Int	Pts
Len Grant	T	6'3"	225	29		
Tex Irvin	T	6'	230	28		
Bill Morgan	T	6'2"	235	25		
Jess Quatse	T	5'11"	230	28		

Use Name – Guards	Pos.	Hgt	Wgt	Age	Int	Pts
Bob Bellinger	G	5'11"	220	22		
Potsy Jones	G	5'11"	224	25		
Bernie Kaplan	G	6'	210	22		
Bill Owen	G-T	6'	225	31		

The Giants stood so far above the competition in the East, they practically rebuilt the club in midstream and still won the division title. With a rock-hard defense leading the way, the New Yorkers never lost a game to an Eastern opponent, suffering their only defeats at the hands of the Packers, Bears, and Cardinals.

Coach Steve Owen mostly achieved the season's success by inserting new players in key spots. Second-year tailback Ed Danowski pushed Harry Newman to the bench on the strength of his passing and running, and Kink Richards took over Ken Strong's rushing job. Owen also eased ends Red Badgro and Ray Flaherty to the sidelines in favor of rookie Tod Goodwin, the league's leading receiver, and Ike Frankian. Others who had to be replaced were Butch Gibson, who retired, and Dale Burnett, who was injured. Nevertheless, whomever Owen plugged into the gap invariably worked, and the Giants, as always, triumphed in the East.

BROOKLYN DODGERS 5-6-1 Paul Schissler

Scores of Each Game		
3	Boston	7
12	Detroit	10
7	New York	10
14	Chic. Bears	24
17	PHILADELPHIA	6
13	Pittsburgh	7
3	Philadelphia	0
7	PITTSBURGH	16
14	CHIC. CARDS	12
0	NEW YORK	21
0	DETROIT	28
0	BOSTON	0

Use Name	Pos.	Hgt	Wgt	Age	Int	Pts
Walt McDonald	C-LB	5'10"	210	23		
Cap Oehler	C-LB	6'	205	24		

Use Name – Tackles	Pos.	Hgt	Wgt	Age	Int	Pts
Alex Eagle	T	6'2"	220	22		
Carl Heldt	T	6'2"	205	22		
Bill Lee	T	6'2"	240	23		
Lou Lubratovich	T	6'2"	220	28		
Jack Robinson	T	6'3"	220	23		

Use Name – Guards	Pos.	Hgt	Wgt	Age	Int	Pts
Gil Bergerson	G-T	6'6"	245	25		
Win Croft	G	5'11"	235	25		
Bo Kirkland	G	6'	215	22		
Frank Stojack	G	5'10"	190	23		

After seeing how the Chicago Cardinals had bettered themselves with an almost total rookie squad, the Dodgers hired Paul Schissler from the Cards tc run the same sort of rebuilding program in Brooklyn—and fifteen rookies were infused into the team. Old pros Chris Cagle, Shipwreck Kelly, and Herman Hickman retired before the season started to give the youngsters a chance. But the newcomers could not lift the team, and they finished with the same mediocre record as 1934. The tragic fault in the Dodgers still was the lack of a major-league passer, a fact which came home to roost when Kercheval's punts—one which covered 86 yards—proved more effective than the team's forward passing.

PITTSBURGH PIRATES 4-8-0 Joe Bach

Scores of Each Game		
17	Philadelphia	7
7	NEW YORK	42
7	CHIC. BEARS	23
0	Green Bay	27
6	PHILADELPHIA	17
17	CHIC. CARDS	13
6	BOSTON	0
7	BROOKLYN	13
16	Brooklyn	7
14	GREEN BAY	34
3	Boston	13
0	New York	13

Use Name	Pos.	Hgt	Wgt	Age	Int	Pts
Ben Ciccone	C-LB	5'10"	208	25		
Joe Malkovich	C-LB	6'3"	205	23		
Lee Mulleneaux	C-LB	6'2"	225	25		
Swede Pittman	C-LB	6'	215	27		
Ed Skoronski	C-LB	6'2"	208	23		

Use Name – Tackles	Pos.	Hgt	Wgt	Age	Int	Pts
Mule Bray	T	6'2"	220	26		
Stan Oleniczak	T	6'	220	23		6
Sandy Sandberg	T	6'2"	225	25		
Joe Wiehl	T	5'11"	254	25		

Use Name – Guards	Pos.	Hgt	Wgt	Age	Int	Pts
Al Arndt	G	5'11"	205	24		
Norm Greeney	G	5'11"	210	25		
Henry Hayduk	G	6'	200			
Bob Hoel	G	6'	212	22		
George Rado	G	5'9"	197	22		
Dave Ribble	G	6'1"	212	28		
Bull Snyder	G	6'2"	230	23		

With their third new head coach in as many years, the Pirates rushed into the season with a 17-7 triumph at Philadelphia. Coach Joe Bach got a look at the real Pirates, though, when his club opened its home schedule by letting the New York Giants roll to a 42-7 romp and then encountering three more straight losses to shrivel the attendance and spell another year of hardship for owner Art Rooney.

Yet before the season ended, the Pirates won four games, the highest total in their short history, with back-to-back victories over the then unbeaten Cardinals and Redskins. Although the Pirates' forward wall had good success against teams that relied heavily on running attacks, they were most vulnerable when it came to stopping the passing game. The Pittsburgh offense itself threatened no outbursts of points and relied instead on Armand Niccolai's field goals to win close games.

BOSTON REDSKINS 2-8-1 Eddie Casey

Scores of Each Game		
7	BROOKLYN	3
12	NEW YORK	20
7	DETROIT	17
6	New York	17
0	Pittsburgh	6
0	Detroit	14
6	PHILADELPHIA	7
14	CHIC. BEARS	30
0	CHIC. CARDS	6
13	PITTSBURGH	3
0	Brooklyn	0

Use Name	Pos.	Hgt	Wgt	Age	Int	Pts
Frank Bausch	C-LB	6'3"	210	27		
Chief Johnson	LB	6'3"	225	26		
Larry Siemering	C-LB	6'3"	202			

Use Name – Tackles	Pos.	Hgt	Wgt	Age	Int	Pts
Jim Barber	T	6'3"	205	23		
Turk Edwards	T	6'2"	260	27		
Gail O'Brien	T	6'1"	216	23		
Steve Sinko	T	6'3"	230	24		

Use Name – Guards	Pos.	Hgt	Wgt	Age	Int	Pts
Rick Concannon	G	6'	215	26		
Eddie Kahn	G	5'9"	190	23		
Jim Moran	G	6'1"	205	22		
Les Olsson	G	6'	225	27		

George Marshall had a perfect plan to draw more fans to the Redskin games. He hired Eddie Casey, an all-time great Harvard halfback, as his new head coach; with his previous college record and good looks, Casey would be a sure boost for the attendance. But the Marshall Plan did not work, and the Redskins bit the dust regularly from the start of the season.

Halfback Cliff Battles as usual made up almost the entire Boston offense with his end runs behind whatever blocking he could find. Without any passing game, a porous defense, and with owner Marshall sitting on the bench giving players instructions contradicting those of the coach, the Redskins were fortunate to win two games.

PHILADELPHIA EAGLES 2-9-0 Lud Wray

Scores of Each Game		
7	PITTSBURGH	17
0	Detroit	35
17	Pittsburgh	6
0	CHIC. BEARS	39
6	Brooklyn	17
7	Boston	6
0	BROOKLYN	3
3	Chic. Cards	12
0	New York	10
14	NEW YORK	21
6	GREEN BAY	13

Use Name	Pos.	Hgt	Wgt	Age	Int	Pts
Amy McPherson (from CHIB, G)	C-G-LB	5'11"	215	23		

Use Name – Tackles	Pos.	Hgt	Wgt	Age	Int	Pts
Howard Bailey	T	6'	205	22		
Bill Brian	T-C-LB	6'2"	200	22		
Paul Cuba	T	6'	212	27		
Carl Jorgensen (1 PAT in 1 attempt, 1 field goal)	T	6'	210	24		4
Joe Kresky (to and from PIT, G)	T-G	6'	220	27		
Jim MacMurdo	T	6'1"	210	24		
Leo Raskowski	T	6'3"	218	28		
Clyde Williams	T	6'2"	210	23		

Use Name – Guards	Pos.	Hgt	Wgt	Age	Int	Pts
Harry Benson	G	5'10"	218	25		
Tom Graham	G	6'3"	210			
Diddie Willson	G	5'10"	195	24		
Vince Zizak	G	5'8"	208	26		
Jim Zyntell	G	6'1"	200	25		

The Eagles slipped back from the gains they had made in 1934 by falling to a new low of two wins. A fine crowd of 20,000 turned out on opening day, but the Eagles promptly turned them off by losing 17-7 to the lowly Pittsburgh Pirates.

Although coach Lud Wray had essentially the same players back from last year, an injury to back Swede Hanson slowed the attack and could not be overcome by the collection of mediocre football talent. Of the newcomers, only Eggs Manske added much to the Eagles, teaming with Joe Carter to give the club a fine set of ends.

Wray at least showed an open mind about trying new talent. He gave Alabama Pitts, a graduate not of any college but of the Sing Sing big house, a crack at a backfield post. But the legendary prison athlete had left his best days behind the bars.

Use Name – Backs & Ends	Pos.	Age	Hgt	Wgt	Pts	Int	RUSHING No.	Yds	Avg	TD	PASSING Att	Comp	%	Yds	Yd/Att	TD	Int–%	RK	RECEIVING No.	Yds	Avg	TD	PUNTING No.	Avg	KICKING Pat	Att	%	FG	Att	%	PUNT RETURNS No.	Yds	Avg	TD	KICKOFF RETURNS No.	Yds	Avg	TD
NEW YORK GIANTS																																						
Ed Danowski	TB-DB	23	6'1"	198	12		130	335	2.6	2	113	57	50	795	7.0	11	9– 8	1																				
Harry Newman	TB-DB	25	5'8"	182	9						29	9	31	132	4.6	0									3	3	100	2										
Tony Sarausky	TB-FB-DB	23	5'11"	198	7					1	9	3	33	53	5.9	0									1	1	100											
John Mackorell	TB-DB		5'10"	178																																		
Kink Richards	FB-DB	24	5'11"	196	28		149	449	3.0	4									8	41	5	0			1	1	100	1										
Ken Strong	FB-DB	29	6'	205	29					1	3	0	0	0	0.0	0									11	12	92	4										
Stu Clancy	FB-WB-DB	29	5'10"	190	6					1																												
Max Krause	FB-DB	26	5'10"	200																																		
Dale Burnett	WB-DB	26	6'1"	188	36														12	199	17	6																
Leland Shaffer	WB-DB	23	6'2"	200															7	123	18	0																
Red Corzine	BB-LB	26	6'	210	6																																	
Bo Molenda	BB-LB	29	5'10"	215	11																				5	6	83											
Tod Goodwin	OE-DE	23	6'	184	24														26	432	17	4																
Ike Frankian	OE-DE	28	5'11"	207	6														7	39	6	0																
Walt Singer	OE-DE	22	6'	198	6																	1																
Red Badgro	OE-DE	32	6'	195																																		
Ray Flaherty	OE-DE	31	6'	195																																		
Les Borden	OE-DE		6'	185																																		
BROOKLYN DODGERS																																						
Red Franklin	TB-DB	23	5'10"	160	18					3	67	18	27	270	4.0	0		12																				
Jack Grossman	TB-DB	25	6'1"	190	13					2	35	9	26	149	4.3	1									1	1	100											
Wilbur White	TB-DB	23	6'	168							32	10	31	73	2.3	2																						
Bull Karcis	FB-LB	26	5'9"	220	6					1	5	2	40	23	4.6	0			5	58	12	0																
Stan Kostka	FB-LB	22	5'11"	215							6	0	0	0	0.0	0																						
Ralph Kercheval	HB-DB	24	6'1"	193	35						33	13	39	203	6.2	1			7	130	19	1			8	9	89	5	16	31								
Ollie Sansen	HB-DB	27	6'1"	198																																		
Father Lumpkin	BB-DB	27	6'2"	205																																		
John Norby	BB-DB	24	6'	195																																		
Jay Hornbeak	BB-DB		5'11"	185																																		
Wayland Becker	OE-DE	24	6'	185	6														10	131	13	1			0	1	0	0	3	0								
Ray Fuqua	OE-DE	23	6'	190	6														8	82	10	1																
Paul Riblett	OE-DE	27	5'10"	182															6	86	14	0																
Bud Hubbard	OE-DE		6'	190	6																	1																
PITTSBURGH PIRATES																																						
Johnny Gildea	TB-DB	25	6'2"	195							95	28	29	529	5.6	2		9																				
Warren Heller	TB-HB-DB	25	5'11"	195							41	9	22	88	2.1	0		14																				
Cy Casper	TB-BB-DB	23	6'	193	18					2	39	13	33	123	3.2	0			5	94	19	1																
John Doehring	TB-DB	25	6'	215							8	4	50	83	10.4	2																						
Silvio Zaninelli	FB-LB	21	5'10"	210																																		
Buzz Wetzel (from CHIB)	FB-LB	24	6'2"	205	6					1	8	2	25	21	2.6	0																						
Swede Ellstrom	FB-LB	27	6'1"	205							7	6	86	68	9.7	0																						
Art Strutt	HB-DB	22	6'	205	6		92	323	3.5	0	2	0	0	0	0.0	0			7	112	16	0																
Jim Levey	HB-DB	28	5'10"	170	24					2	5	1	20	12	2.4	0			11	112	10	2																
Heinie Weisenbaugh(to BOS,BB-LB)	HB-DB	21	5'11"	190	12						11	1	9	14	1.3	0			7	73	10	2																
Mike Nixon	HB-DB	23	5'11"	175																																		
John Turley	BB-DB	22	5'10"	180							27	6	22	92	3.4	1																						
Gene Augusterfer	BB-DB		5'9"	180																																		
Vic Vidoni	OE-DE	21	6'1"	210															11	111	10	0																
Ben Smith	OE-DE	24	6'3"	210															9	166	18	0																
Bill Sortet	OE-DE	23	6'1"	188															6	136	23	0																
Cliff Doloway	OE-DE		6'	215																																		
Glenn Campbell	OE-DE	30	5'11"	210																																		
Armand Niccolai	T-OE-DE	28	6'2"	220	28																				10	12	83	6										
BOSTON REDSKINS																																						
Bill Shepherd (to DET, FB-LB)	TB-BB-FB-DB-LB	23	5'9"	190	25		143	425	3.0	4	64	28	44	417	6.5	2		6							1	2	50											
Cliff Battles	TB-DB	25	6'1"	188	12		84	310	3.7	1	22	5	23	92	4.2	0									0	2	0											1
Pug Rentner	TB-BB-WB-DB	24	6'1"	182	13					1	50	9	18	148	3.0	1		12							1	1	100											
Doug Nott (from DET)	TB-DB	24	6'	195							34	9	26	169	5.0	1																						
Hal McPhail	FB-DB	23	6'1"	230							2	0	0	0	0.0	0																						
Jim Musick	FB-DB	28	5'11"	195	14					2	1	0	0	0	0.0	0									2	3	67											
Steve Hokuf	FB-BB-LB-OE-DE	24	6'	202																																		
Ernie Pinckert	WB-DB	27	6'	200															5	60	12	0																
Dick Baltzell	WB-DB	23	5'11"	205																																		
Ted Wright (to BKN, BB-DB)	BB-LB	21	6'	185	1						18	4	22	51	2.8	0									1	2	50											
Charley Malone	OE-DE	25	6'4"	210	12														22	433	20	2																
Flavio Tosi	OE-DE	23	6'1"	187	6														10	169	17	1																
Paul Collins	OE-DE	27	6'1"	200																																		
PHILADELPHIA EAGLES																																						
Ed Matesic	TB-DB	24	6'1"	195	6					1	64	15	23	284	4.4	2		10																				
Ed Storm	TB-DB	27	6'1"	195							44	15	34	372	8.5	3		5																				
Jim Leonard	FB-LB	25	6'	204	6					1	32	11	34	119	3.7	0																						
Izzy Weinstock	FB-BB-LB	22	6'	205							5	1	20	12	2.4	0			8	107	13	0																
Bob Rowe	FB-LB	24	6'	195																																		
Swede Hanson	HB-DB	26	6'1"	197							1	1	100	23	23.0	0	0– 0																					
Rick Lackman	HB-DB	23	5'11"	186	1						1	1	100	8	8.0	0	0– 0		5	49	10	0			1	1	100											
Mike Sebastian (to PIT)	HB-DB	25	5'11"	185							1	0	0	0	0.0	0																						
Alabama Pitts	HB-DB		5'10"	185																																		
Herald Frahm (to BOS, WB-DB)	HB-DB	29	5'10"	190																																		
Stumpy Thomason (from BKN)	BB-DB	29	5'7"	190																																		
Steve Banas (from DET)	BB-DB		6'	190																																		
Irv Kupcinet	BB-DB	23	6'1"	190																																		
Reds Kirkman	BB-DB	29	6'1"	195							10	3	30	30	3.0	1																						
Joe Carter	OE-DE	25	6'1"	203	12														11	260	24	2																
Eggs Manske	OE-DE	22	6'	185	24														9	205	23	4																
George Kenneally	OE-DE	33	6'	192																																		
Buke Robison	OE-DE-C-LB	25	6'4"	197																																		
Max Padlow	OE-DE	23	6'1"	198																																		
Hank Reese	C-LB	24	5'11"	210	7																				4	6	67	1										

TEAM TOTALS

	OFFENSE: FIRST DOWNS	RUSHING: Yards	TD	PASSING: Att.	Comp	Comp Pct.	Yards	Yds/ Att.	Yds/ Comp	TD	PENALTY: Yards	FUMBLES: Number	POINTS: Total	TD	PAT	FG	Saf	DEFENSE: Total Yards	Pass Att.	Pass Comp	Comp Pct.	No. Pass Int.	Oppos Fumb. Rec.	Points	TEAM TOTALS
NEW YORK	112	1451	9	154	69	44.8	980	6.4	14.2	11	175	20	180	23	21	7	0	2019	205	68	33.2	27	18	96	NEW YORK
BROOKLYN	90	1108	6	178	52	29.2	718	4.0	13.8	4	179	31	90	11	9	5	0	2960	163	55	33.7	26	38	141	BROOKLYN
PITTSBURGH	64	508	5	233	67	28.8	996	4.3	14.9	5	201	30	100	12	10	6	0	3204	189	66	34.9	21	27	209	PITTSBURGH
BOSTON	95	1263	5	175	47	26.9	752	4.3	16.0	3	166	30	65	10	5	0	0	1982	166	68	41.0	27	19	123	BOSTON
PHILADELPHIA	82	1054	2	158	47	29.7	848	5.4	18.0	6	330	28	60	8	6	2	0	2669	168	59	35.1	22	30	179	PHILADELPHIA

DETROIT LIONS 7-3-2 Potsy Clark

Scores of Each Game		
35	PHILADELPHIA	0
10	CHIC. CARDS	10
10	BROOKLYN	12
17	Boston	7
9	Green Bay	13
14	BOSTON	0
7	Chic. Cards	6
7	Green Bay	31
20	GREEN BAY	10
20	Chic. Bears	20
14	CHIC. BEARS	2
28	Brooklyn	0

Use Name	Pos.	Hgt	Wgt	Age	Int	Pts
Clare Randolph	C-LB	6'2"	205	28		
Elmer Ward	C-LB	6'2"	215	22		

Use Name – Tackles	Pos.	Hgt	Wgt	Age	Int	Pts
George Christensen	T	6'2"	238	25		
Jack Johnson	T	6'4"	210	25		
Red Stacy	T-G	6'2"	207	23		
Jim Steen	T	6'2"	205	22		

Use Name – Guards	Pos.	Hgt	Wgt	Age	Int	Pts
Ox Emerson	G	5'11"	190	27		
Roy Gagnon	G	5'11"	210	22		
Tom Hupke	G	5'10"	192	24		
Sam Knox	G	6'	220	25		
Regis Monahan	G	5'10"	215	26		

With a squad as deep as it was talented, the Lions were unbeaten in their last four games to edge the Packers and bring home the NFL crown in only their second year in the league.

The Lions stalked their opponents on the ground. Of the NFL's top ten rushers, Ernie Caddel, Dutch Clark, Bill Shepherd, and Ace Gutowsky all wore Detroit blue jerseys; Caddel and Shepherd relied on speed, Clark on shifty moves, and Gutowsky on straight-ahead power. Frank Christensen and Buddy Parker filled the blocking back position, and Glenn Presnell completed the platoon of backs with his running and place kicking. Clearing the way for the backs was a line featuring George Christensen, Ox Emerson, and Clare Randolph.

GREEN BAY PACKERS 8-4-0 Curly Lambeau

Scores of Each Game		
6	CHIC. CARDS	7
7	CHIC. BEARS	0
16	NEW YORK	7
27	PITTSBURGH	0
0	Chic. Cards	3
13	DETROIT	9
17	Chic. Bears	14
31	DETROIT	7
10	Detroit	20
34	Pittsburgh	14
7	Chic. Cards	9
13	Philadelphia	6

Use Name	Pos.	Hgt	Wgt	Age	Int	Pts
Nate Barrager	C-LB	6'	210	28		
Frank Butler	C-LB	6'3"	230	26		
George Svendsen	C-LB	6'4"	214	22		

Use Name – Tackles	Pos.	Hgt	Wgt	Age	Int	Pts
Cal Hubbard	T-DE	6'2"	265	34		6
Buster Maddox	T	6'3"	240	23		
Claude Perry	T	6'1"	215	33		
Ade Schwammel (3 PAT's in 4 attempts, 4 field goals)	T	6'2"	230	26		15
Champ Seibold	T	6'4"	240	22		

Use Name – Guards	Pos.	Hgt	Wgt	Age	Int	Pts
Tiny Engebretsen (1 PAT in 1 attempt)	G	6'1"	235	25		1
Lon Evans	G	6'2"	220	23		
Walt Kiesling	G	6'3"	260	30		
Mike Michalske	G	6'	200	31		
Bob O'Connor	G-T-BB-DE	6'1"	220	25		

Don Hutson's first play for the Green Bay Packers served notice that a new era had arrived. After the opening kickoff from the Bears, the frail end from Alabama split out to the left while Johnny Blood, back again in Green Bay, lined up as a flanker to the right. Since Blood had burned many a secondary, the Bears concentrated on him, while Hutson went down, faked the halfback to the outside, and outran the Bear safetyman down the middle. Arnie Herber cut loose with a perfect pass which Hutson carried for an 83-yard touchdown. Hutson brought a full bag of pass patterns and moves to go with his sprinter's speed to send defensive backs around the league back to the drawing board in the advent of pro football's first modern wide receiver.

Although the new pass combination shot the Packers back into contention in the Western Division, their three losses to the Chicago Cardinals torpedoed their title hopes in this discovery year of the bomb.

CHICAGO BEARS 6-4-2 George Halas

Scores of Each Game		
0	Green Bay	7
23	Pittsburgh	7
39	Philadelphia	0
24	BROOKLYN	14
14	GREEN BAY	17
20	New York	3
30	Boston	14
0	NEW YORK	3
20	DETROIT	20
2	Detroit	14
7	CHIC. CARDS	7
13	Chic. Cards	0

Use Name	Pos.	Hgt	Wgt	Age	Int	Pts
Eddie Kawal	C-LB-G-T	6'2"	198	25		6
Ookie Miller	C-LB	6'	204	25		
Frank Sullivan	C-LB	6'3"	203	23		

Use Name – Tackles	Pos.	Hgt	Wgt	Age	Int	Pts
Art Buss	T	6'3"	218	24		
Dub Miller	T-G	6'	210	23		
George Musso	T	6'2"	258	25		
Ted Rosequist	T-OE-DE	6'4"	213	27		
Milt Trost	T-OE-DE	6'1"	203	22		

Use Name – Guards	Pos.	Hgt	Wgt	Age	Int	Pts
Zuck Carlson	G-T	6'	198	30		
Joe Kopcha (1 field goal, missed 1 PAT attempt)	G	6'	226	29		3
Ray Richards	G	6'1"	235	29		
Joe Zeller	G	6'1"	203	27		

Although the Cardinals' 1934 bumper crop of rookies matured to give the team the toughest defense in the NFL, the offense still had the anemic look of recent years and relied heavily on Doug Russell's fine ball carrying, Phil Sarboe's passing, and Bill Smith's field-goal kicking. Mike Mikulak led the defense with his inspired linebacking, and rookie tackle Tony Blazine lent his weight to the brick-wall unit. The league honored fullback Mikulak and end Smith with All-Pro status and Sarboe and Blazine with second-team spots.

The young Cardinals rushed out to three straight victories before the Pirates handed them their first loss. After the fine start, their lack of offensive power brought them back into the pack. The Cardinals brought the Green Bay Packers down with them, though, dealing a fatal blow to the Pack's title hopes by beating them three times, capped by a late-season 9-7 decision.

CHICAGO CARDINALS 6-4-2 Milan Creighton

Scores of Each Game		
7	Green Bay	6
10	Detroit	10
3	GREEN BAY	0
13	Pittsburgh	17
14	New York	13
6	DETROIT	7
12	PHILADELPHIA	3
12	Brooklyn	14
6	Boston	0
9	GREEN BAY	7
7	Chic. Bears	7
0	CHIC. BEARS	13

Use Name	Pos.	Hgt	Wgt	Age	Int	Pts
Bernie Hughes	C-LB	6'1"	195	25		
Bert Pearson	C-LB	6'	205	30		

Use Name – Tackles	Pos.	Hgt	Wgt	Age	Int	Pts
Tony Blazine	T	6'	237	23		
Harry Field	T	6'1"	230	23		
Lou Gordon	T-G	6'5"	230	27		
Ted Isaacson	T-C	6'4"	272	23		

Use Name – Guards	Pos.	Hgt	Wgt	Age	Int	Pts
Bree Cupoletti	G	5'10"	198	25		
Phil Handler	G	6'	215	26		
Homer Hanson (to and from PHI, G)	G-C-LB	6'	220			
Pete Mehringer	G-T	6'2"	200	25		
Howie Tipton	G	5'11"	185	24		
Bill Volok (Missed 2 PAT attempts)	G-T	6'2"	215	25		6

The Bears struggled to a third-place tie with the Cardinals due to injuries and a costly retirement. A bad hip laid Bronko Nagurski up for most of the campaign, while halfback Beattie Feathers missed a few games with injuries and quarterback Carl Brumbaugh called it quits—all of which contributed to forcing the Bears to using practically a second-string backfield. Place-kicker Jack Manders and Gene Ronzani filled in well as runners but could not replace the great Nagurski. Bernie Masterson handled the quarterbacking but lacked the savvy of the departed Brumbaugh.

If the Bears had any continuity at all, it came from the forward line, as end Bill Karr, giant tackle George Musso, and guard Joe Kopcha all won All-Pro honors, and end Bill Hewitt barely missed the team.

Use Name – Backs & Ends	Pos.	Age	Hgt	Wgt	Pts	Int	Rushing No.	Rushing Yds	Rushing Avg	Rushing TD	Passing Att	Passing Comp	Passing %	Passing Yds	Passing Yd/Att	Passing TD	Passing Int–%	Passing RK
DETROIT LIONS																		
Dutch Clark	TB-DB	28	6'	180	55		120	412	3.4	4	26	11	42	133	5.1	2		
Glenn Presnell	TB-WB-DB	30	5'10"	190	28						45	15	33	193	4.3	0		11
Pug Vaughan	TB-DB	24	5'11"	180							15	7	47	104	6.9	2		
Ace Gutowsky	FB-LB	25	5'11'	195	12		102	295	2.9	2	9	5	56	95	10.6	2		
Buddy Parker	FB-BB-LB-DB	21	6'	190							1	0	0	0	0.0	0		
Tony Kaska	FB-LB	24	5'11"	185														
Ernie Caddel	WB-DB	24	6'2"	198	36		87	450	5.2	6	6	4	67	169	28.2	2		
Al Richins	WB-DB		5'9"	188														
Gil LeFebvre	WB-DB	25	5'6"	152														
Willie O'Neal	WB-DB		5'11"	187														
Frank Christensen	BB-DB	25	6'1"	195	8						21	6	29	92	4.4	0		
Harry Ebding	OE-DE	26	5'11"	195	6													
John Schneller	OE-DE	23	6'2"	205	12													
Butch Morse	OE-DE	23	6'2"	195														
Ed Klewicki	OE-DE	24	5'10"	210	12													
Buster Mitchell (to NY)	OE-DE	29	6'	205														
GREEN BAY PACKERS																		
Arnie Herber	TB-DB	25	5'11"	203	1						106	40	38	729	6.9	8	6– 6	4
Bob Monnett	TB-DB	25	5'9"	180	11		68	336	4.9	1	65	31	47	454	7.0	2	6– 9	3
Clarke Hinkle	FB-LB	25	5'11"	200	18		76	258	3.4	2								
Swede Johnston	FB-LB	25	5'10"	200	6					1								
George Sauer	HB-TB-DB	24	6'2"	204	24		89	334	3.8	3	21	9	43	177	8.4	1		
Johnny Blood	HB-DB	30	6'1"	190	24						33	11	33	164	5.0	0		
Joe Laws	HB-DB	24	5'9"	185	6					1	4	1	25	4	1.0	0		
Roger Grove	HB-DB	26	6'	185														
Buckets Goldenberg	BB-DB	24	5'10"	215														
Hank Bruder	BB-FB-DB-LB	27	6'	197	6						1	1	100	17	17.0	0		
Herm Schneidman	BB-DB	21	5'11"	205														
Don Hutson	OE-DE	22	6'1"	185	43													
Milt Gantenbein	OE-DE	25	6'	193	6													
Al Rose	OE-DE	28	6'3"	195														
Bob Tenner	OE-DE	22	6'	212														
Dom Vairo	OE-DE	21	6'2"	203														
Ernie Smith	T	25	6'2"	234	14													
CHICAGO BEARS																		
Bernie Masterson	QB-DB	24	6'3"	195	6						44	18	41	456	10.4	7	4– 9	2
Bob Dunlap	QB-DB	22	6'1"	187							37	11	30	111	3.0	1		
George Corbett	QB-DB	27	5'9"	177	3													
Gene Ronzani	FB-HB-LB	26	5'9"	190	15		79	356	4.5	1	41	16	39	230	5.6	3		6
Beattie Feathers	HB-DB	26	5'10"	177	18		56	280	5.0	3	14	5	36	53	3.8	0		
Keith Molesworth	HB-DB	28	5'9"	168	24		59	286	4.8	4	36	13	36	266	7.4	2		
Jack Manders	FB-LB	26	6'	198	19		69	245	3.6	0								
Red Pollock	HB-LB	23	6'2"	187	24					3	12	1	8	18	1.5	0		
George Grosvenor	HB-DB	24	6'	172							15	6	40	69	4.6	0		
Bronko Nagurski	FB-LB	26	6'2"	228	6		37	137	3.7	1	3	0	0	0	0.0	0		
Johnny Sisk	HB-LB	28	6'2"	195	6					1	1	1	100	1	1.0	0	0– 0	
Luke Johnsos	OE-DE	28	6'2"	187	24													
Bill Karr	OE-DE	24	6'1"	187	36													
Bill Hewitt	OE-DE	25	5'9"	182														
Fred Crawford	OE-DE-T	25	6'2"	200														
CHICAGO CARDINALS																		
Doug Russell	TB-DB	23	6'	180			140	499	3.6	0	28	7	25	108	3.9	0		
Ike Peterson	TB-DB	23	5'9"	185							25	6	24	121	4.8	1		
Gil Berry	TB-DB	23	5'10"	178							4	0	0	0	0.0	0		
Mike Mikulak	FB-LB	22	6'1"	210	6					1								
Mule Dowell	FB-LB	22	6'2"	210														
Al Nichelini	WB-DB	25	6'2"	203	24					4	1	1	100	16	16.0	0	0– 0	
Dave Cook	WB-DB	23	6'2"	200	6					1	1	1	100	7	7.0	0	0– 0	
Phil Sarboe	BB-DB	23	5'10"	165	12						67	31	46	368	5.5	1		8
Paul Pardonner	BB-DB	25	5'8"	170	4													
Hal Pangle	BB-FB-DB-LB	23	5'10"	205							4	1	25	15	3.8	0		
Bill Smith	OE-DE	23	6'1"	198	35													
Bill Wilson	OE-DE	23	5'10"	185														
Bob Neuman	OE-DE	23	6'	200	6													
Milan Creighton	OE-DE	27	6'	195														
Jim Mooney	OE-DE	27	5'11"	190														
Versil Deskin	OE-DE	22	6'	205														

Use Name – Backs & Ends	Receiving No.	Receiving Yds	Receiving Avg	Receiving TD	Punting No.	Punting Avg	Kicking Pat	Kicking Att	Kicking %	Kicking FG	Kicking Att	Kicking %	Punt Returns No.	Punt Returns Yds	Punt Returns Avg	Punt Returns TD	Kickoff Returns No.	Kickoff Returns Yds	Kickoff Returns Avg	Kickoff Returns TD
DETROIT LIONS																				
Dutch Clark	9	124	14	2			16	19	84	1										
Glenn Presnell				1			4	4	100	4						1				
Pug Vaughan																				
Ace Gutowsky																				
Buddy Parker																				
Tony Kaska																				
Ernie Caddel	10	171	17	0																
Al Richins																				
Gil LeFebvre																				
Willie O'Neal																				
Frank Christensen	5	57	11	1			2	2	100											
Harry Ebding	8	128	16	1																
John Schneller	7	149	21	2																
Butch Morse	6	63	11	0																
Ed Klewicki				2																
Buster Mitchell (to NY)																				
GREEN BAY PACKERS																				
Arnie Herber							1	1	100											
Bob Monnett							2	3	67	1										
Clarke Hinkle										2										
Swede Johnston	6	59	10	0																
George Sauer																				
Johnny Blood	25	404	16	3																
Joe Laws																				
Roger Grove																				
Buckets Goldenberg																				
Hank Bruder																				
Herm Schneidman																				
Don Hutson	18	420	23	7			1	1	100											
Milt Gantenbein	12	165	14	1																
Al Rose	8	91	11	0																
Bob Tenner																				
Dom Vairo																				
Ernie Smith							11	12	92	1										
CHICAGO BEARS																				
Bernie Masterson	7	99	14	1																
Bob Dunlap																				
George Corbett										1										
Gene Ronzani	8	122	15	1			3	4	75											
Beattie Feathers																				
Keith Molesworth	7	154	22	0																
Jack Manders							16	17	94	1	8	13								
Red Pollock	7	135	18	1																
George Grosvenor																				
Bronko Nagurski																				
Johnny Sisk																				
Luke Johnsos	19	298	16	4																
Bill Karr	9	220	24	6																
Bill Hewitt	5	80	16	0																
Fred Crawford																				
CHICAGO CARDINALS																				
Doug Russell																				
Ike Peterson																				
Gil Berry																				
Mike Mikulak	8	93	12	0																
Mule Dowell																				
Al Nichelini																				
Dave Cook																				
Phil Sarboe																2				
Paul Pardonner							1	2	50	1										
Hal Pangle																				
Bill Smith	24	318	13	2			5	8	63	6										
Bill Wilson																				
Bob Neuman																				
Milan Creighton																				
Jim Mooney																				
Versil Deskin																				

TEAM TOTALS — OFFENSE

TEAM TOTALS	FIRST DOWNS	RUSHING: Yards	RUSHING: TD	PASSING: Att.	PASSING: Comp	PASSING: Comp Pct.	PASSING: Yards	PASSING: Yds/Att.	PASSING: Yds/Comp	PASSING: TD	PENALTY: Yards	FUMBLES: Number	POINTS: Total	POINTS: TD	POINTS: PAT	POINTS: FG	POINTS: Saf
DETROIT	121	1773	15	141	57	40.4	920	6.5	16.1	9	195	21	191	25	22	5	2
GREEN BAY	125	1525	8	230	93	40.4	1545	6.7	16.6	11	295	29	181	23	19	8	0
CHICAGO BEARS	140	2096	13	211	73	34.6	1229	5.8	16.8	13	354	36	192	27	19	3	1
CHICAGO CARDS	107	1521	6	130	47	36.2	635	4.9	13.5	2	255	27	99	12	6	7	0

DEFENSE

TEAM TOTALS	Total Yards	Pass Att.	Pass Comp	Comp Pct.	No. Pass Int.	Oppos Fumb. Rec.	Points
DETROIT	2023	181	58	32.0	9	27	111
GREEN BAY	2161	191	61	31.9	27	21	96
CHICAGO BEARS	2337	194	59	30.4	37	30	106
CHICAGO CARDS	2068	153	58	37.9	24	23	97

BOSTON REDSKINS 7-5-0 Ray Flaherty

Scores of Each Game		
0	Pittsburgh	10
26	Philadelphia	3
14	Brooklyn	3
0	NEW YORK	7
2	Green Bay	31
17	PHILADELPHIA	7
13	CHIC. CARDS	10
3	GREEN BAY	7
0	CHIC. BEARS	26
30	BROOKLYN	6
30	PITTSBURGH	0
14	New York	0

Use Name	Pos.	Hgt	Wgt	Age	Int	Pts
Frank Bausch	C-LB	6'3"	215	28		
Larry Siemering	C-LB	6'3"	210			6

Use Name – Tackles	Pos.	Hgt	Wgt	Age	Int	Pts
Jim Barber	T	6'3"	215	24		
Vic Carroll	T-G	6'4"	212	23		6
Turk Edwards	T	6'2"	260	28		
Gail O'Brien	T	6'1"	220	24		
Steve Sinko	T	6'3"	235	25		

Use Name – Guards	Pos.	Hgt	Wgt	Age	Int	Pts
Rick Concannon	G	6'	217	27		
Eddie Kahn	G	5'9"	195	24		
Jim Karcher	G	6'	205	22		
Jim Morgan	G	6'1"	210	23		
Les Olsson	G	6'	220	27		

New coach Ray Flaherty made it known that he was in charge when he insisted that owner George Marshall stay off the field and in the stands. Flaherty's positive attitude, developed by years of winning in New York, soon spread to his players. Going without a real passer on the squad but still fortunate enough to have Cliff Battles and Turk Edwards as All-Pros, the Redskins won the Eastern title by defeating the Giants 14-0 in the final game of the season.

Although the Skins had won the crown, they had no place to hang their hat. With the team winning, owner Marshall had raised ticket prices on the day of a game without any advance notice, and both the public and the press blew a hurricane of protest over this shabby treatment of long-suffering fans. With angry winds beating about his head, Marshall simply folded up his tent and moved the championship game to New York.

PITTSBURGH PIRATES 6-6-0 Joe Bach

Scores of Each Game		
10	BOSTON	0
10	Brooklyn	6
10	NEW YORK	7
9	CHIC. BEARS	27
17	PHILADELPHIA	0
7	Chic. Bears	26
10	Green Bay	42
10	BROOKLYN	7
6	Philadelphia	0
3	Detroit	28
6	Chic. Cards	14
0	Boston	30

Use Name	Pos.	Hgt	Wgt	Age	Int	Pts
Lee Mulleneaux	C-LB	6'2"	225	26		
Buster Raborn	C-LB	6'	195	23		
John Turley	BB-DB	5'10"	185	23		

Use Name – Tackles	Pos.	Hgt	Wgt	Age	Int	Pts
Mule Bray	T	6'2"	220	27		
Ed Karpowich	T	6'4"	220	23		
(1 reception for –6 yds.)						
Sandy Sandberg	T	6'2"	225	26		

Use Name – Guards	Pos.	Hgt	Wgt	Age	Int	Pts
Win Croft	G	5'11"	235	26		
George Kakasic	G	5'10"	190	24		13
(1 PAT in 1 att., 2 FG, 1 rush for –8 yds.)						
Bill Lajousky	G	5'11"	200	23		
(1 rush for 1 yd.)						
Lindy Mayhew	G-T	6'1"	220	24		
George Rado	G	5'9"	198	23		

With a new unbalanced line offense, the Pirates roared out of the starting gate with victories over the Redskins, Dodgers, and Giants to grab the Eastern Division lead. If the Pirates had played only Eastern teams all year, they might have given owner Art Rooney his first championship. But such was not the case as they struck out in all five meetings against the Western clubs. The Pirates came into Boston on November 29 with a chance to ice away the crown by defeating the Redskins. Returning by train from an exhibition match in California the week before, the Bucs took the field tired and out of practice, and the sky-high Redskins blew them out of the stadium in a 30-0 rout. Rooney took the blame for scheduling the West Coast trip, for not even he had expected the Pirates to be in the title race as long as they were.

NEW YORK GIANTS 5-6-1 Steve Owen

Scores of Each Game		
7	Philadelphia	10
7	Pittsburgh	10
7	Boston	0
10	BROOKLYN	10
14	CHIC. CARDS	6
21	PHILADELPHIA	17
14	DETROIT	7
7	CHIC. BEARS	25
0	Detroit	38
14	GREEN BAY	26
14	Brooklyn	0
0	BOSTON	14

Use Name	Pos.	Hgt	Wgt	Age	Int	Pts
Len Dugan	C-LB	6'	210	24		
Mel Hein	C-LB	6'2"	225	27		
Chief Johnson	C-LB	6'3"	223	27		
Bob Tarrant	OE-DE	6'	180	22		
Bob Dunlap	DB	6'1"	195	23		

Use Name – Tackles	Pos.	Hgt	Wgt	Age	Int	Pts
Len Grant	T	6'3"	225	30		
Jack Haden	T	6'4"	230	21		
Cal Hubbard (from PIT, G-T)	T	6'2"	255	35		
Art Lewis	T-G	6'3"	225	23		6
Bill Morgan	T	6'2"	235	26		
Al Owen	T-G	6'	225	32		

Use Name – Guards	Pos.	Hgt	Wgt	Age	Int	Pts
Gaines Davis	G	5'11"	230	23		
Johnny Dell Isola	G-C-LB	5'11"	202	24		
Potsy Jones	G	5'11"	224	26		
Bernie Kaplan	G	6'	210	23		
Ewell Phillips	G	5'11"	210	26		
(1 reception for 5 yds.)						

When the Giants lost their first two contests to the Eagles and Pirates, the absence of some recently departed veterans stood out glaringly. Runner Ken Strong, second-string passer Harry Newman, end Red Badgro, and aging tackle Jess Quatse had all jumped to the outlaw American Football League, and end Ray Flaherty headed north to coach the Redskins. The young but talented Giants fought back into the Eastern title race behind the passing of Ed Danowski, the running of rookie Tuffy Leemans, and the line play of annual All-Pro Mel Hein. The division championship rode on the line in the season-ending confrontation between the Giants and Redskins in the Polo Grounds on December 6. Totally confident of victory, the Giants could not move the ball at all against the Skins and not only lost the game but also the first Eastern title since the divisions were formed in 1933.

BROOKLYN DODGERS 3-8-1 Paul Schissler

Scores of Each Game		
6	PITTSBURGH	10
3	BOSTON	14
18	PHILADELPHIA	0
10	New York	10
7	DETROIT	14
9	CHIC. CARDS	0
7	Pittsburgh	10
7	GREEN BAY	38
6	Boston	30
0	NEW YORK	14
13	Philadelphia	7
6	Detroit	14

Use Name	Pos.	Hgt	Wgt	Age	Int	Pts
Wagner Jorgensen	C-LB	6'2"	205	23		
Red Krause	C-LB	6'1"	205	22		
Cap Oehler	C-LB	6'	205	25		
Jim Hartman	OE-DE	6'2"	205			
Jack Grossman	DB	6'1"	195	26		

Use Name – Tackles	Pos.	Hgt	Wgt	Age	Int	Pts
Carl Heldt	T	6'2"	206	23		
(2 receptions for 39 yds.)						
Bill Lee	T	6'2"	225	24		
Jim Whatley	T-OE-DE	6'5"	220	23		
John Yezerski	T	6'4"	240			

Use Name – Guards	Pos.	Hgt	Wgt	Age	Int	Pts
Gil Bergerson	G-T	6'6"	245	26		
Verdi Boyer	G	5'10"	195	24		
Bo Kirkland	G	6'	215	23		
Justin Rukas	G	6'	205			
Frank Stojack	G	5'10"	198	24		

As usual, the Dodgers got along without any passing attack to mention. Obtained from the Cardinals in mid-season, passer Phil Sarboe failed to give the offense a needed second dimension. Although rookie Joe Maniaci helped the running game, punter Ralph Kercheval still was the chief offensive threat with his booming kicks. Tackle Bill Lee headed a fair line, but the Dodgers, in general, were on a downslide which only new blood gave any hope of stopping. Unfortunately for coach Paul Schissler, new blood was also brought in at the top as the team's three victories and fourth-place Eastern Division finish was just not enough to give him employment the following year.

PHILADELPHIA EAGLES 1-11-0 Bert Bell

Scores of Each Game		
10	NEW YORK	7
3	BOSTON	26
0	CHIC. BEARS	17
0	Brooklyn	18
0	DETROIT	23
0	Pittsburgh	17
7	Boston	17
17	New York	21
0	PITTSBURGH	6
0	Chic. Cards	13
7	CHIC. BEARS	28
7	BROOKLYN	13

Use Name	Pos.	Hgt	Wgt	Age	Int	Pts
Pete Stevens	C-LB	6'	215			
Max Padlow	OE-DE	6'1"	200	24		
Carl Kane	HB-DB	5'11"	195	23		

Use Name – Tackles	Pos.	Hgt	Wgt	Age	Int	Pts
Bill Brian	T	6'2"	220	23		
Art Buss	T	6'3"	220	25		
Jim MacMurdo	T	6'1"	210	25		6

Use Name – Guards	Pos.	Hgt	Wgt	Age	Int	Pts
Rudy Gollomb	G	5'11"	205	24		
Amy McPherson	G	5'11"	214	24		
Joe Pivaronik	G	5'9"	217	24		
Jim Russell	G-T	5'11"	210	25		
Vince Zizak	G	5'8"	208	27		

President of the Eagles since their birth, Bert Bell expanded his duties this year by taking over Lud Wray's job as head coach. On the side, Bell also made travel arrangements, sold tickets, promoted the club, and handled almost every job connected with the team.

In his first game on the sidelines, Bell watched his club upset the New York Giants 10-7 at home to get the season off to a flying start. But as where Bell could perform a solo show on the sidelines, he could do nothing in the game itself, and the Eagles skidded into an eleven-game losing streak. Before the season, in the first college draft, Bell had chosen Jay Berwanger, Heisman Trophy halfback from the University of Chicago, and promptly traded the negotiating rights to the Bears for veteran tackle Art Buss. When Berwanger decided against a pro-football career, Bell looked like a genius—at least until the Eagles took to the field.

Use Name – Backs & Ends	Pos.	Age	Hgt	Wgt	Pts	Int	Rushing No.	Rushing Yds	Rushing Avg	Rushing TD	Passing Att	Passing Comp	Passing %	Passing Yds	Passing Yd/Att	Passing TD	Passing Int–%	Passing RK	Receiving No.	Receiving Yds	Receiving Avg	Receiving TD	Punting No.	Punting Avg	Kicking Pat	Kicking Att	Kicking %	Kicking FG	Kicking Att	Kicking %	Punt Returns No.	Punt Returns Yds	Punt Returns Avg	Punt Returns TD	Kickoff Returns No.	Kickoff Returns Yds	Kickoff Returns Avg	Kickoff Returns TD
BOSTON REDSKINS																																						
Eddie Britt	TB-FB-DB	23	6'2"	205			72	180	2.5	0	44	18	41	294	6.7	3	5–11		6	106	18	0																
Ed Smith	TB-DB	23	6'2"	210	3		7	39	5.6	0	40	11	28	120	3.0	1	2–5											1										
Cliff Battles	FB-TB-DB	26	6'1"	195	42		176	614	3.5	5	52	18	35	242	4.7	1	6–12	9	6	103	17	1												1				
Pug Rentner	FB-DB	25	6'1"	186	18		95	404	4.3	1	39	15	38	198	5.1	0	6–15		4	33	8	0																
Don Irwin	FB-DB	23	6'1"	197	12		17	78	4.6	2	5	0	0	0	0.0	0	1–20		2	31	16	0																
Jim Musick	FB-DB	29	5'11"	205			6	14	2.3	0	1	1	100	9	9.0	0	0–0																					
Ernie Pinckert	WB-DB	28	6'	196			18	80	4.4	0									1	17	17	0																
Ed Justice	WB-DB	23	6'1"	205															8	132	17	0																
Riley Smith	BB-LB	25	6'2"	200	38		30	26	0.9	0	33	14	42	239	7.2	0	3–9		3	76	25	2			14	17	82	4										
Heinie Weisenbaugh	BB-LB	22	5'11"	190			3	9	3.0	0									3	37	12	0																
Wayne Millner	OE-DE	25	6'1"	190															18	211	12	0																
Charley Malone	OE-DE	26	6'4"	200	6														11	167	15	1																
Sam Busich	OE-DE	23	6'3"	190	10														6	57	10	1			1	2	50	1										
Bob McChesney	OE-DE	24	6'2"	195															5	62	12	0																
Flavio Tosi	OE-DE	24	6'1"	195	6														4	70	18	0																
PITTSBURGH PIRATES																																						
Ed Matesic	TB-DB	25	6'1"	205			46	58	1.3	0	138	64	46	850	6.2	5	16–12	3	1	13	13	0																
Max Fiske	TB-HB-DB	22	6'	195			58	92	1.6	0	15	6	40	64	4.3	0	3–20		7	96	14	0																
Jim Levey	TB-DB	29	5'10"	156			4	3	0.8	0																												
Bull Karcis	FB-LB	27	5'9"	220	13		89	272	3.1	2	4	0	0	0	0.0	0	2–50		8	71	9	0			1	1	100											
Wayne Sandefur	FB-LB	24	5'10"	195			7	13	1.9	0																												
Warren Heller	HB-DB	26	5'11"	195	18		106	332	3.1	0	5	0	0	0	0.0	0	1–20		12	160	13	3																
Art Strutt	HB-DB	23	6'	200	6		84	180	2.1	1	1	1	100	15	15.0	0	0–0		11	166	15	0																
Jim McDonald	HB-DB		6'	195			9	18	2.0	0									1	8	8	0																
Johnny Gildea	BB-HB-DB	26	6'2"	205			35	31	0.9	0	29	9	31	147	5.1	1	5–17		5	70	14	0																
Silvio Zaninelli	BB-FB-DB-LB	22	5'10"	200			31	61	2.0	0	6	1	17	2	0.3	0	1–17		2	12	6	0																
Bill Sortet	OE-DE	24	6'1"	188	6		1	47	47.0	0									14	197	14	1																
Ed Skoronski	OE-DE	24	6'2"	210	6														8	95	12	1																
Jeep Brett (from CHIC)	OE-DE	22	6'2"	205															7	139	20	0																
Vic Vidoni	OE-DE	22	6'1"	210															2	35	18	0																
Vinnie Sites	OE-DE	24	6'2"	215	6														2	22	11	1																
Armand Niccolai	T	24	6'2"	220	28																				7	8	88	7										
NEW YORK GIANTS																																						
Ed Danowski	TB-DB	24	6'1"	198			91	259	2.8	0	104	47	45	515	5.0	6	10–10	5																				
Tony Sarausky	TB-DB	24	5'11"	198	10		32	150	4.7	1	27	6	22	87	3.2	1	1–4								1	1	100	1										
Tuffy Leemans	FB-DB	23	6'	188	12		**206**	**830**	4.0	2	42	13	31	258	6.1	3	6–14		4	22	6	0																
Kink Richards	FB-DB	25	5'11"	196	12		114	421	3.7	1									7	146	21	1																
Dale Burnett	WB-DB	27	6'1"	188	18		10	0	0.0	0									16	246	15	3																
Max Krause	WB-DB	27	5'10"	210	6		11	37	3.4	0									5	47	9	1																
Tilly Manton	BB-LB	24	5'11"	187	21		30	86	2.9	0	5	3	60	27	5.4	0	0–0		5	81	16	1			15	15	**100**											
Red Corzine	BB-LB	27	6'	210	6		7	12	1.7	0									1	36	36	1																
Leland Shaffer	BB-LB	24	6'2"	200	6		3	10	3.3	0									2	30	15	1																
Tod Goodwin	OE-DE	24	6'	184	12		3	–1	–0.3	0									7	79	11	2																
Winnie Anderson	OE-DE		6'	185															7	74	11	0																
Gene Rose	OE-DE	25	6'1"	185			2	13	6.5	0									6	73	12	0																
Walt Singer	OE-DE	23	6'	198	6														6	38	6	0																
Buster Mitchell	OE-DE	30	6'	205															2	10	5	0																
BROOKLYN DODGERS																																						
Bobby Wilson	TB-DB		5'9"	147	24		104	505	4.9	3	40	11	28	148	3.7	0	9–22		1	12	12	1																
Red Franklin	TB-DB	24	5'10"	165	6		15	70	4.7	1	7	1	14	17	2.4	0	0–0																					
Joe Maniaci	TB-HB-DB	22	6'1"	204			35	70	2.0	0	4	1	25	1	0.3	0	0–0		1	30	30	0																
Mark Temple (to BOS)	TB-DB		5'10"	175	6		5	4	0.8	1	7	0	0	0	0.0	0	5–71		1	10	10	0																
John Biancone	TB-DB		5'6"	165			8	34	4.3	0	3	1	33	29	9.7	0	0–0																					
Dick Crayne	FB-DB	23	6'	210	7		64	203	3.2	1	2	1	50	52	26.0	0	0–0		1	32	32	0			1	2	50											
Tony Kaska	FB-DB	25	5'11"	200	6		9	29	3.2	1	1	0	0	0	0.0	0	1–100		1	5	5	0																
Dave Cook (from CHIC)	FB-DB	24	6'2"	208			10	24	2.4	0									1	2	2	0																
Ralph Kercheval	HB-DB	25	6'1"	193	37		66	261	4.0	2	25	6	24	92	3.7	0	3–12		7	63	9	0			4	8	50	5										
Father Lumpkin	BB-LB	28	6'2"	205			11	29	2.6	0									6	34	6	0																
Jeff Barrett	OE-DE	23	6'1"	185	6														14	268	19	1																
Paul Riblett	OE-DE	28	5'10"	186			2	4	2.0	0									4	49	12	0																
Red Badgro	OE-DE	33	6'	190															3	59	20	0																
Ray Fuqua	OE-DE	24	6'	190															1	2	2	0			0	1	0											
PHILADELPHIA EAGLES																																						
Swede Hanson	TB-DB	27	6'1"	197	6		119	359	3.0	1	15	0	0	0	0.0	0	3–20		3	33	11	0																
Don Jackson	TB-DB	22	5'11"	184			46	76	1.7	0	35	7	20	80	2.3	0	11–31																					
Walt Masters	TB-DB	29	5'10"	180			7	18	2.6	0	6	1	17	11	1.8	0	1–17																					
Reds Bassman	TB-HB-DB	23	5'11"	180			4	19	4.8	0	3	1	33	3	1.0	0	1–33		2	38	19	0																
Dave Smukler	FB-LB	22	6'1"	228	5		99	321	3.2	0	68	21	31	345	5.1	3	6–9	8							2	2	100	1										
John Kusko	FB-LB	22	5'11"	203	6		49	209	4.3	1	27	6	22	108	4.0	0	9–33																					
Stumpy Thomason	HB-FB-DB-LB	30	5'7"	190	1		109	333	3.1	0	10	1	10	11	1.1	0	2–20								1	1	100											
Jim Leonard	BB-TB-HB-DB	26	6'	200	6		33	72	2.2	0	6	2	33	45	7.5	0	2–33		5	46	9	1																
Glenn Frey	BB-DB	24	5'10"	195			7	8	1.1	0									3	65	22	0																
Eggs Manske	OE-DE	23	6'	185															17	325	19	0																
Joe Pilconis	OE-DE	24	6'1"	190	6														4	51	13	1																
Joe Carter	OE-DE	26	6'1"	202	6														4	42	11	1																
George Mulligan	OE-DE-LB	22	6'1"	198															1	3	3	0																
Hank Reese	C-LB	25	5'11"	215	9																				3	3	100	2										

TEAM TOTALS — **OFFENSE**

Team	First Downs	Rushing: No.	Rushing: Yards	Rushing: Avg. Yds.	Rushing: TD	Passing: Att.	Passing: Comp.	Passing: Comp. Pct.	Passing: Yards	Passing: Yds/Att.	Passing: Yds/Comp.	Passing: TD	Penalty: Yards	Fumbles: Number	Points: Total	Points: TD	Points: PAT	Points: FG	Points: Saf
BOSTON	113	425	1444	3.4	8	214	77	36.0	1102	5.1	14.3	5	275	31	149	19	15	6	1
PITTSBURGH	117	472	1100	2.3	3	198	81	40.9	1078	5.4	13.3	6	336	34	98	10	9	9	1
NEW YORK	146	509	1817	3.6	4	178	69	38.8	887	5.0	12.9	10	205	37	115	16	16	1	0
BROOKLYN	90	340	1300	3.8	9	141	43	30.5	621	4.4	14.4	2	210	25	92	12	5	5	0
PHILADELPHIA	99	463	1415	3.1	2	170	39	22.9	603	3.5	15.5	3	159	33	51	6	6	3	0

DEFENSE — **TEAM TOTALS**

Total Yards	Pass Att.	Pass Comp.	Comp. Pct.	No. Pass Int.	Oppos. Fumb. Rec.	Points	Team
2181	198	62	31.5	22	32	110	BOSTON
3032	163	**52**	31.9	25	26	187	PITTSBURGH
2841	149	60	40.3	19	24	163	NEW YORK
2798	174	65	37.4	24	27	161	BROOKLYN
2857	147	61	41.4	15	29	206	PHILADELPHIA

GREEN BAY PACKERS 10-1-1 Curly Lambeau

Scores of Each Game		
10	CHIC. CARDS	7
3	CHIC. BEARS	30
24	CHIC. CARDS	0
31	BOSTON	2
20	DETROIT	18
42	PITTSBURGH	10
21	Chic. Bears	10
7	Boston	3
38	Brooklyn	7
26	New York	14
26	Detroit	17
0	Chic. Cards	0

Use Name	Pos.	Hgt	Wgt	Age	Int	Pts
Frank Butler	C-LB	6'3"	246	27		
Tony Paulekas	C-LB	5'10"	210	24		
George Svendsen	C-LB	6'4"	224	23		
Al Rose	OE-DE	6'3"	205	29		

Use Name – Tackles	Pos.	Hgt	Wgt	Age	Int	Pts
Lou Gordon	T	6'5"	230	28		
Ade Schwammel	T	6'2"	230	27		8
(5 PAT's in 5 attempts, 1 field goal)						
Champ Seibold	T	6'4"	237	23		

Use Name – Guards	Pos.	Hgt	Wgt	Age	Int	Pts
Tiny Engelbretsen	G	6'1"	238	26		17
(2 PAT's in 2 attempts, 5 field goals)						
Lon Evans	G-T	6'2"	220	24		
Buckets Goldenberg	G-BB-DB-LB	5'11"	210	25		
(6 rushing attempts for 9 yds.)						
Walt Kiesling	G	6'3"	257	31		
Russ Letlow	G	6'	203	22		

The first great NFL passing combination put the Packers back on top in the West, as tailback Arnie Herber filled the air with footballs aimed at fleet end Don Hutson. Due to extremely stubby fingers, Herber gripped the ball with his thumb across the seams, but this unorthodox hold did not stop him from being the best long passer in the league. While introducing hard-cutting fakes to defensive backs, Hutson hauled in a record thirty-four passes for eight touchdowns. But, as a defensive end, the slight Hutson took a beating.

On the ground, rugged Clarke Hinkle handled the heavy-duty power running. Despite the retirement of Mike Michalske, the line was the class of the circuit, with tackle Ernie Smith and guard Lon Evans winning All-Pro honors.

CHICAGO BEARS 9-3-0 George Halas

Scores of Each Game		
30	Green Bay	3
17	Philadelphia	0
27	Pittsburgh	9
7	CHIC. CARDS	3
26	PITTSBURGH	7
12	DETROIT	10
10	GREEN BAY	21
25	New York	7
26	Boston	0
28	Philadelphia	7
7	Detroit	13
7	Chic. Cards	14

Use Name	Pos.	Hgt	Wgt	Age	Int	Pts
Eddie Kawal	C-LB	6'2"	198	26		
Ookie Miller	C-LB	6'	204	26		6
Frank Sullivan	C-LB	6'3"	203	24		
Bob Allman	OE-DE		198			

Use Name – Tackles	Pos.	Hgt	Wgt	Age	Int	Pts
George Musso	T	6'2"	258	26		
Joe Stydahar	T	6'4"	230	24		3
(3 PAT's in 4 attempts)						
Russ Thompson	T	6'5"	248	24		
Milt Trost	T	6'1"	203	23		

Use Name – Guards	Pos.	Hgt	Wgt	Age	Int	Pts
Zuck Carlson	G	6'	210	31		
Danny Fortmann	G	6'	210	20		
Eddie Michaels	G	5'11"	200	22		
Vern Oech	G	6'1"	207	23		
Joe Zeller	G	6'1"	206	28		

Three rookies led the Bears' charge back from the mediocrity of 1935. Halfback Ray Nolting exploded through small holes with his quick acceleration, while tough tackle Joe Stydahar provided running room for him and his fellow backs. When the Bears lost veteran guard Joe Kopcha when his medical studies forced a move to Detroit, rookie Danny Fortmann, also an aspiring doctor, more than made up for the loss with a hard-hitting internship in the line.

Veterans also contributed to the Chicago renaissance. Bronko Nagurski returned from his injury-filled 1935 season again to throw his weight around with considerable force and yards gained. Jack Manders booted seven field goals to lead the league for the third time, and bare-headed end Bill Hewitt won his third nod for All-Pro. With attendance up and both young and old players contributing, George Halas' heart was doubly warmed.

DETROIT LIONS 8-4-0 Potsy Clark

Scores of Each Game		
39	CHIC. CARDS	0
23	Philadelphia	0
14	Brooklyn	7
18	Green Bay	20
10	Chic. Bears	12
7	New York	14
28	PITTSBURGH	3
38	NEW YORK	0
14	Chic. Cards	7
13	CHIC. BEARS	7
17	GREEN BAY	26
14	BROOKLYN	6

Use Name	Pos.	Hgt	Wgt	Age	Int	Pts
Clare Randolph	C-LB	6'2"	207	29		
Del Ritchhart	C-LB	6'	195	25		6

Use Name – Tackles	Pos.	Hgt	Wgt	Age	Int	Pts
George Christensen	T	6'2"	238	26		
Jack Johnson	T	6'4"	210	26		
Red Stacy	T-G	6'2"	208	24		
Jim Steen	T	6'2"	205	23		

Use Name – Guards	Pos.	Hgt	Wgt	Age	Int	Pts
Ox Emerson	G	5'11"	192	28		
Tom Hupke	G	5'10"	192	25		
Sam Knox	G	6'	220	26		
Joe Kopcha	G	6'	226	30		
Regis Monahan	G-T	5'10"	215	27		6
Sid Wagner	G	5'11"	190	23		

Detroit went into key late-season contests without the services of fullback Ace Gutowsky, halfback Ernie Caddel, and center Clare Randolph, to lose all chances of repeating as Western Division winners.

The Detroit offense remained highly potent due largely to Dutch Clark's off-tackle slants and drop-kicking; from all his talents, Clark collected a league-leading 73 points. The loss of Randolph hurt the forward wall, but beefy George Christensen and small guard Ox Emerson opened more than a few holes for Clark to race through. No one could cover for Randolph at linebacker, though, and his absence hurt the defense the same way that Gutowsky's robbed the offense of its only solid power runner.

CHICAGO CARDINALS 3-8-1 Milan Creighton

Scores of Each Game		
7	Green Bay	10
0	Detroit	39
0	Green Bay	24
3	Chic. Bears	7
6	New York	14
0	Brooklyn	9
10	Boston	13
13	PHILADELPHIA	0
14	PITTSBURGH	6
7	DETROIT	14
14	CHIC. BEARS	7
0	GREEN BAY	0

Use Name	Pos.	Hgt	Wgt	Age	Int	Pts
Bernie Hughes	C-LB	6'1"	190	26		
Al Lind	C-LB					
Bert Pearson	C-LB	6'	210	31		
Milan Creighton	DE	6'	190	28		

Use Name – Tackles	Pos.	Hgt	Wgt	Age	Int	Pts
Conway Baker	T	5'11"	225	25		
Tony Blazine	T	6'	225	24		
Harry Field	T	6'1"	225	24		
Pete Mehringer	T	6'2"	218	26		
Jack Robinson (from BKN)	T	6'3"	220	24		

Use Name – Guards	Pos.	Hgt	Wgt	Age	Int	Pts
Ross Carter	G	6'	200	22		
Bree Cuppoletti	G	5'10"	200	26		
Phil Handler	G	5'	210	27		
Homer Hanson	G	6'	220			
Dub Miller	G	6'	225	24		
Howie Tipton	G-OE-DE	5'11"	185	25		
(1 reception for 15 yds.)						
Bill Volok	G	6'2"	215	26		

Despite slipping back into their losing ways, the Cardinals did experience one very satisfying moment. For the first time since Thanksgiving of 1929, when Ernie Nevers scored 40 points, the Cardinals defeated the Bears.

Aside from the Bear game, though, sparkling moments were few and far between for the Redbirds. With Doug Russell, the leading runner, knocked out for most of the year with an injury, the Cardinal offense went nowhere in a hurry. To pick up some of the backfield slack, the Cardinals obtained George Grosvenor from the Bears—who, predictably enough, turned in a key performance in the victory over his former teammates. Also helping Grosvenor in the backfield, especially on defense, was Mike Mikulak.

Use Name – Backs and Ends	Pos.	Age	Hgt	Wgt	Pts	Int	RUSHING				PASSING								RECEIVING				PUNTING		KICKING						PUNT RETURNS				KICKOFF RETURNS			
							No.	Yds	Avg	TD	Att	Comp	%	Yds	Yd/Att	TD	Int–%	RK	No.	Yds	Avg	TD	No.	Avg	Pat	Att	%	FG	Att	%	No.	Yds	Avg	TD	No.	Yds	Avg	TD
GREEN BAY PACKERS																																						
Arnie Herber	TB-DB	26	5'11"	195			20	−32	−1.6	0	173	77	45	1239	7.2	11	13– 8	1																				
Bob Monnett	TB-HB-DB	26	5'9"	185	3		104	224	2.2	0	52	20	38	280	5.4	4	2– 4	4	13	169	13	0			3	3	100											
Harry Mattos	TB-DB		6'	200			1	2	2.0	0	12	4	33	32	2.7	0	2– 17																					
Clarke Hinkle	FB-LB	26	5'11"	205	31		100	476	4.8	5	2	1	50	10	5.0	0	0– 0								1	1	100											
George Sauer	FB-HB-LB-DB	25	6'2"	208	18		94	305	3.2	3	4	2	50	26	6.5	0	1– 25		6	110	18	0																
Swede Johnston	FB-LB	26	5'10"	192	6		42	110	2.6	1									2	11	6	0																
Joe Laws	HB-DB	25	5'9"	185	18		50	296	5.9	1	4	1	25	22	5.5	1	0– 0		10	132	13	2																
Paul Miller	HB-DB	23	5'11"	175	18		52	227	4.4	1	1	0	0	0	0.0	0	1–100		8	113	14	2																
Johnny Blood	HB-DB	31	6'1"	185	19		13	65	5.0	0	6	3	50	20	3.3	1	0– 0		7	147	21	2			1	1	100 (Run)											
Hank Bruder	BB-DB	28	6'	197			4	−7	−1.7	0									2	25	13	0																
Cal Clemens	BB-DB	24	6'1"	195	1		3	−8	−2.7	0	1	0	0	0	0.0	0	0– 0		1	18	18	0			1	1	100											
Herm Schneidman	BB-DB	22	5'11"	200	6														3	68	23	1																
Don Hutson	OE-DE	23	6'1"	185	54		1	−3	−3.0	0									34	526	15	8																
Milt Gantenbein	OE-DE	26	6'	208	6														15	231	15	1																
Wayland Becker	OE-DE	25	6'	190	6														5	66	13	1																
Bernie Scherer	OE-DE	23	6'1"	183	6														2	13	7	0																
Ernie Smith	T	26	6'2"	220	29																				17	18	94	4										
CHICAGO BEARS																																						
Bernie Masterson	QB-DB	25	6'3"	195	12		9	−7	−0.8	2	42	10	24	292	7.0	3	6– 14		1	28	28	0																
Carl Brumbaugh	QB-DB	28	5'10"	178	12		9	−1	−0.1	0	28	8	29	140	5.0	5	3– 11		5	39	8	2			0	1	0											
George Corbett	QB-HB-DB	28	5'9"	180	6		13	45	3.5	0	13	5	38	64	4.9	0	1– 8		3	69	23	1																
Bronko Nagurski	FB-LB	27	6'2"	228	19		122	529	4.3	3	5	1	20	8	1.6	1	2– 40		1	12	12	0			1	1	100											
Ray Nolting	HB-DB	22	5'11"	185	6		76	352	4.6	0	13	3	23	30	2.3	2	1– 8		2	50	25	1																
Beattie Feathers	HB-DB	27	5'10"	185	12		97	350	3.6	2	11	1	9	10	0.9	0	2– 18		2	5	3	0																
Keith Molesworth	HB-QB-DB	29	5'9"	170			60	276	4.6	0	31	15	48	188	6.1	4	4– 13		9	146	16	0																
Jack Manders	FB-LB	27	6'	210	62		63	207	3.3	3	3	2	67	52	17.3	0	0– 0		1	4	4	1			17	21	81	7	8	88								
Gene Ronzani	HB-QB-LB-DB	27	5'9"	200	12		37	186	5.0	0	12	8	67	170	14.2	1	2– 17		4	58	15	2																
Johnny Sisk	HB-LB	29	6'2"	195			41	163	4.0	0									1	39	39	0																
John Doehring	HB-QB-LB	26	6'	215			18	101	5.6	0	12	5	42	145	12.1	1	0– 0		1	19	19	0																
Red Pollock	HB-LB	24	6'2"	200															1	15	15	0																
Bill Hewitt	OE-DE	26	5'9"	190	42		2	−9	−4.5	0									15	358	24	6																
Bill Karr	OE-DE	25	6'1"	190	18		4	11	2.8	1									6	121	20	2																
Luke Johnsos	OE-DE	29	6'2"	198	12														5	121	24	2																
Ted Rosequist	OE-DE-T	28	6'4"	225															1	15	15	0																
DETROIT LIONS																																						
Dutch Clark	TB-DB	29	6'	180	73		123	628	5.1	7	71	38	54	467	6.6	4	6– 8	2	1	5	5	0			19	23	83	4										
Glenn Presnell	TB-DB	31	5'10"	190	15		48	201	4.2	1	36	15	42	221	6.1	2	7– 19								6	8	75	1										
Ace Gutowsky	FB-LB	26	5'11"	194	36		191	827	4.3	6	13	2	15	21	1.6	0	4– 31		1	30	30	0																
Bill Shepherd	FB-LB	24	5'9"	200	13		74	292	3.9	1	9	3	33	57	6.3	0	1– 11								1	1	100											
Ernie Caddel	WB-DB	25	6'2"	198	30		91	580	6.4	4	4	1	25	30	7.5	0	2– 50		19	150	8	1																
Ike Peterson	WB-TB-DB	24	5'9"	185			60	276	4.6	3	6	0	0	0	0.0	0	1– 17		8	38	5	0																
Wilbur White	WB-DB	24	6'	165			8	21	2.6	0	1	0	0	0	0.0	0	0– 0		2	21	11	0																
Frank Christensen	BB-DB	26	6'1"	197	6		2	−2	−1.0	0	6	2	33	22	3.7	0	1– 17		2	58	29	1																
Buddy Parker	BB-DB	22	6'	190			6	21	3.5	0									1	15	15	0																
Harry Ebding	OE-DE	27	5'11"	195	24														10	194	19	3																
John Schneller	OE-DE	24	6'2"	205	6														7	124	18	1																
Butch Morse	OE-DE	24	6'2"	195															5	83	17	0																
Ed Klewicki	OE-DE	25	5'10"	210															4	90	23	0																
Bill McKalip	OE-WB-DE-DB	25	6'1"	185			7	39	5.6	0									1	10	10	0																
CHICAGO CARDINALS																																						
Phil Sarboe (to BKN)	TB-DB	24	5'10"	170			83	103	1.2	0	114	47	41	680	6.0	3	13– 11	6	1	18	18	0																
Pug Vaughan	TB-DB	25	5'11"	182			67	79	1.2	0	79	30	38	546	6.9	3	10– 13	7																				
George Grosvenor (from CHIB, HB-DB)	TB-DB	25	6'	175	30		170	612	3.6	4	34	12	35	173	5.1	0	6– 18		1	6	6	0												1				
Clarence Kellogg	FB-DB		5'10"	205	9		66	164	2.5	0									4	11	3	0			6	7	86	1										
Mule Dowell	FB-DB	23	6'2"	202			54	151	2.8	0	2	1	50	6	3.0	0	0– 0																					
Hal Pangle	FB-BB-DB-LB	24	5'10"	196	6		38	101	2.7	1	2	0	0	0	0.0	0	0– 0		9	195	22	0																
Swede Ellstrom	FB-DB	28	6'1"	205			4	12	3.0	0																												
Al Nichelini	WB-DB	26	6'2"	210	6		55	189	3.4	0									9	133	15	1																
Jimmy Lawrence	WB-DB	22	5'11"	195			26	84	3.2	0	2	0	0	0	0.0	0	1– 50		8	98	12	0																
Doug Russell	WB-DB	24	6'	190			3	11	3.7	0	1	0	0	0	0.0	0	0– 0																					
Mike Mikulak	BB-LB	23	6'1"	210			24	56	2.3	0									6	62	10	0																
Charlie McBride	BB-LB				6		2	1	0.5	0									1	38	38	1																
Bill Smith	OE-DE	24	6'1"	198	11		2	13	6.5	0	1	0	0	0	0.0	0	1–100		20	414	21	1			2	3	67	1										
Versil Deskin	OE-DE	23	6'	190	6														3	60	20	1																
Bob Neuman	OE-DE	24	6'	195			1	3	3.0	0									3	41	14	0																
Ray Davis	OE-DE			198															1	36	36	0																
Bill Wilson	OE-DE	24	5'10"	182															1	12	12	0																

TEAM TOTALS	OFFENSE	RUSHING:				PASSING:							PENALTY:	FUMBLES:	POINTS:					DEFENSE							TEAM TOTALS
	FIRST DOWNS	No.	Yards	Avg. Yds.	TD	Att.	Comp.	Comp Pct.	Yards	Yds/ Att.	Yds/ Comp.	TD	Yards	Number	Total	TD	PAT	FG	Saf	Total Yards	Pass Att.	Pass Comp.	Comp. Pct.	No. Pass Int.	Oppos Fumb. Rec.	Points	
GREEN BAY	148	490	1664	3.4	11	255	108	42.4	1629	6.4	15.1	17	478	23	248	31	30	10	1	2664	227	81	35.7	31	19	118	GREEN BAY
CHICAGO BEARS	145	552	2206	4.0	11	170	58	34.1	1099	6.5	18.9	17	435	24	222	30	21	7	0	3000	227	86	37.9	35	24	94	CHICAGO BEARS
DETROIT	170	610	2883	4.7	22	146	61	41.8	818	5.6	13.4	6	290	20	235	32	26	5	1	2489	194	70	36.1	21	13	102	DETROIT
CHICAGO CARDS	138	552	1509	2.7	5	183	68	37.2	1123	6.1	16.5	4	415	34	74	10	8	2	0	2725	176	67	38.1	24	35	143	CHICAGO CARDS

WASHINGTON REDSKINS 8-3-0 Ray Flaherty

Scores of Each Game			Use Name	Pos.	Hgt	Wgt	Age	Int	Pts	Use Name – Tackles	Pos.	Hgt	Wgt	Age	Int	Pts	Use Name – Guards	Pos.	Hgt	Wgt	Age	Int	Pts
13	NEW YORK	3	Eddie Kawal	C-LB	6'2"	198	27			Jim Barber	T	6'3"	215	25			Dick Bassi	G	5'11"	210	22		
14	CHIC. CARDS	21	George Smith	C-LB	6'2"	205	23			Chuck Bond	T	6'2"	240	23			Vic Carroll	G-T-C-LB	6'4"	225	24		
11	BROOKLYN	7								Turk Edwards	T	6'2"	255	29			Eddie Kahn	G	5'9"	198	25		6
0	PHILADELPHIA	14	Nelson Peterson	WB-DB	5'8"	182	22			Bill Young	T	6'1"	240	23			Jim Karcher	G	6'	207	23		
34	PITTSBURGH	20															Eddie Michaels	G	5'11"	195	23		
10	Philadelphia	7															Les Olsson	G	6'	250	28		
21	Brooklyn	0																					
13	Pittsburgh	21																					
16	Cleveland	7																					
14	GREEN BAY	6																					
49	New York	14																					

Long, lean rookie Sammy Baugh gave the transplanted Redskins the passing arm needed to round out their attack. In a pre-season practice, coach Ray Flaherty told Baugh to hit a downfield receiver in the eye with the ball, and Sammy calmly replied, "Which eye, Coach?"

In the Redskins' Washington debut, Baugh completed eleven of his sixteen passes and played the full sixty minutes in a 13-3 triumph over the Giants. By mid-season, his bullet aerials had meshed with Cliff Battle's running to give Washington the NFL's most explosive attack.

The New York Giants kept pace with the Redskins, though, and it took the season's finale—where 8,000 Washington fans traveled to New York—before the Skins could put a claim to the title in an upset victory.

NEW YORK GIANTS 6-3-2 Steve Owen

Scores of Each Game			Use Name	Pos.	Hgt	Wgt	Age	Int	Pts	Use Name – Tackles	Pos.	Hgt	Wgt	Age	Int	Pts	Use Name – Guards	Pos.	Hgt	Wgt	Age	Int	Pts
3	Washington	13	Stan Galazin	C-LB	6'3"	215	22			Jerry Dennerlein	T	6'2"	235	24			Pete Cole	G	5'11"	200	21		
10	Pittsburgh	7	Mel Hein	C-LB	6'2"	225	28			Len Grant	T	6'3"	225	31			Johnny Dell Isola	G-LB	5'11"	206	25		
16	Philadelphia	7	(1 reception for 7 yds.)							Jack Haden	T	6'4"	233	22			Kayo Lunday	G-C-LB	6'3"	215	24		
21	PHILADELPHIA	0	Chief Johnson	C-LB	6'3"	225	28			Ox Parry	T	6'4"	230	22			Orville Tuttle	G	5'9"	210	24		
21	BROOKLYN	0								Ed Widseth	T	6'1"	225	25			Tarzan White	G	5'9"	210	21		
3	CHIC. BEARS	3																					
17	PITTSBURGH	0																					
0	DETROIT	17																					
10	GREEN BAY	0																					
13	Brooklyn	13																					
14	WASHINGTON	49																					

With seventeen rookies on the twenty-five-man roster, the Giants surprised most observers by going into their final game as favorites for the Eastern title before falling to Washington in a 49-14 offensive blitz.

Starring on the revamped club was rookie Ward Cuff, who made the starting lineup as a wingback, while young veteran Ed Danowski did the passing and second-year-man Tuffy Leemans added his ball-carrying to the pot. Center Mel Hein, guard John Dell Isola, and rookie tackle Ed Widseth starred in a line which helped shut out four opponents during the season. The rebirth on the field sent the turnstiles clicking, with 50,000 fans turning out at the Polo Grounds to witness a 3-3 tie with the Chicago Bears.

PITTSBURGH PIRATES 4-7-0 Johnny Blood

Scores of Each Game			Use Name	Pos.	Hgt	Wgt	Age	Int	Pts	Use Name – Tackles	Pos.	Hgt	Wgt	Age	Int	Pts	Use Name – Guards	Pos.	Hgt	Wgt	Age	Int	Pts
27	PHILADELPHIA	14	Mike Basrak	C-LB	6'2"	220	24			Frank Billock	T	6'	230				Byron Gentry	G	5'11"	230	23		
21	Brooklyn	0	Buster Raborn	C-LB	6'	200	24			Joe Cardwell	T-DE	6'3"	240	23			George Kakasic	G	5'10"	203	25		2
7	NEW YORK	10								Tex Holcomb (to PHI)	T	6'2"	235	24			(2 PAT's in 2 attempts)						
0	CHIC. BEARS	7	Bill Harris	OE-DE			23			Ed Karpowich	T	6'4"	223	24			Walt Kiesling	G	6'3"	250	32		
3	Detroit	7								(1 rush for 15 yds.)							Lindy Mayhew	G	6'1"	225	25		
20	Washington	34	Wayne Sandefur	DB	5'10"	195	25			Sandy Sandberg (to BKN)	T	6'2"	235	27			John Perko	G	6'1"	210	21		
7	CHIC. CARDS	13															(1 rush for 5 yds.)						
16	PHILADELPHIA	7																					
0	New York	17																					
21	WASHINGTON	13																					
0	BROOKLYN	23																					

Looking to push the Pirates to the top in the East, owner Art Rooney brought in the unpredictable Johnny Blood as head coach and big Walt Kiesling as his assistant. Both men—who played with Ernie Nevers on the 1926 Duluth Eskimos—played part time while directing their younger mates through a mediocre season.

The Pirates as usual lost all their games with Western teams but this time managed to split eight contests within their own division and upset the title-bound Redskins with a 21-13 triumph, but the defection of passer Ed Matesic to the rival American Football League left the burden of the attack on short-yardage runners like Bull Karcis and did not help the Pirates' cause.

BROOKLYN DODGERS 3-7-1 Potsy Clark

Scores of Each Game			Use Name	Pos.	Hgt	Wgt	Age	Int	Pts	Use Name – Tackles	Pos.	Hgt	Wgt	Age	Int	Pts	Use Name – Guards	Pos.	Hgt	Wgt	Age	Int	Pts
13	Philadelphia	7	Norm Cooper	C-LB	6'4"	210	24			John Golemgeske	T-G	6'2"	225	22			Sig Andrusking	G	5'8"	187			
0	PITTSBURGH	21	(1 reception for 14 yds.)							Pat Harrison	T	6'2"	215				Red Krause (to WAS, C-LB)	G	6'1"	215	23		
9	CLEVELAND	7	Wagner Jorgensen	C-LB	6'2"	225	24			Roy Ilowit	T	6'2"	220	20			Rube Leisk	G	6'	195			
7	Washington	11								Bill Lee (to GB)	T	6'2"	225	25			Don Nelson	G	5'9"	205			
0	Detroit	30	Fred King	BB-LB	6'2"	205	24			Jim Whatley	T-DE	6'5"	223	24			Ed Skoronski (to CLE, T-C-LB)	G-T	6'2"	220	25		
0	New York	21	Father Lumpkin	BB-LB	6'2"	220	29																
0	WASHINGTON	21																					
10	PHILADELPHIA	14																					
7	Chic. Bears	29																					
23	Pittsburgh	0																					
13	NEW YORK	13																					

The Dodgers finally found an offensive leader when former Duke tailback Ace Parker joined the club in November. Parker had been playing professional baseball and only late in the fall received permission from the Philadelphia Athletics to play football. Excelling both as a passer and runner, Parker immediately added a new punch to the Brooklyn offense, and he gave the Dodgers what Dutch Clark had long given the Detroit Lions, a general on the field.

With Ace, and a new coach in Potsy Clark, the Dodgers improved vastly, capping their season with a 23-0 victory at Pittsburgh and a 13-13 tie with the heavily favored Giants. Joe Maniaci and Ralph Kercheval scored all the Brooklyn points in the Giant game, finding their jobs easier with a real passer in the lineup.

PHILADELPHIA EAGLES 2-8-1 Bert Bell

Scores of Each Game			Use Name	Pos.	Hgt	Wgt	Age	Int	Pts	Use Name – Tackles	Pos.	Hgt	Wgt	Age	Int	Pts	Use Name – Guards	Pos.	Hgt	Wgt	Age	Int	Pts
14	Pittsburgh	27	Moose Harper	C-LB	6'4"	218	23		6	Art Buss	T	6'3"	220	26			Bill Hughes	G	6'1"	220	22		
7	BROOKLYN	13	Hank Reese	C-LB	5'11"	215	26		3	John Dempsey	T	6'2"	225				Amy McPherson	G	5'11"	240	25		
3	CLEVELAND	21	(3 PAT's in 3 attempts)							Fritz Ferko	T	6'1"	238	24			George Rado (from PIT)	G	5'9"	197	24		
6	CHIC. CARDS	6								Charlie Knox	T	5'11"	185				Jim Russell	G-T	5'11"	210	26		
7	NEW YORK	16	Herb Roton	OE-DE	6'2"	210	24			Jim MacMurdo	T	6'1"	206	26			Mule Stockton	G-T	6'1"	218	23		
14	Washington	0								Ray Spillers	T	6'3"	218	22			Vince Zizak	G	5'8"	208	28		
0	New York	21	Jim Leonard	BB-DB	6'	200	27																
7	WASHINGTON	10																					
7	Pittsburgh	16																					
14	Brooklyn	10																					
7	Green Bay	37																					

Coach Bert Bell had the satisfaction of seeing his Eagles improve 100 percent over their 1936 season; they won two games this year instead of one. Bell had no worries about losing his job, though, since he owned the team.

For the second straight year, Bell traded off the first-draft choice, sending back Sam Francis of Nebraska to the Bears for veteran end Bill Hewitt. The bare-headed Hewitt turned in another All-Pro performance, while rookie back Emmett Mortell came through as a ball-carrier, and second-year man Dave Smukler grew into an effective runner and passer to complement Mortell. The only seasoned body in a youth-laden line was center Hank Reese.

Use Name – Backs & Ends	Pos.	Age	Hgt	Wgt	Pts	Int	RUSHING No.	Yds	Avg	TD	PASSING Att	Comp	%	Yds	Yd/Att	TD	Int–%	RK	RECEIVING No.	Yds	Avg	TD	PUNTING No.	Avg	KICKING Pat	Att	%	FG	Att	%	PUNT RETURNS No.	Yds	Avg	TD	KICKOFF RETURNS No.	Yds	Avg	TD
WASHINGTON REDSKINS																																						
Sammy Baugh	TB-DB	23	6'2"	185	6		86	240	2.8	1	171	81	47	1127	6.6	8	14– 8	2																				
Dixie Howell	TB-DB	23	5'11"	175			5	9	1.8	0	6	1	17	14	2.3	0	3–50																					
Cliff Battles	FB-TB-DB	27	6'1"	195	42		216	874	4.0	5	33	13	39	142	4.3	0	3– 9		9	81	9	1																
Don Irwin	FB-DB	24	6'1"	196	12		89	315	3.5	2	3	0	0	0	0.0	0	0– 0		8	112	14	0																
Max Krause	FB-BB-DB-LB	28	5'10"	198	6		21	47	2.2	1									2	13	7	0																
Eddie Britt	FB-DB	24	6'2"	205			7	21	3.0	0																												
Ed Justice	WB-DB	24	6'1"	205	18		8	35	4.4	0									9	150	17	3																
Ernie Pinckert	WB-DB	29	6'	195	6		2	10	5.0	0									10	145	15	1																
Riley Smith	BB-LB	26	6'2"	200	55		12	39	3.3	2	9	4	44	33	3.7	3	0– 0		11	93	8	0			22	26	85	5										
Charley Malone	OE-DE	27	6'4"	200	24														28	419	15	4																
Wayne Millner	OE-DE	26	6'1"	190	18		2	6	3.0	0									14	216	15	2																
Bob McChesney	OE-DE	25	6'2"	195															6	50	8	0																
Ben Smith	OE-DE	26	6'3"	208															2	37	19	0																
NEW YORK GIANTS																																						
Ed Danowski	QB-DB	25	6'1"	195	6		66	95	1.4	1	134	66	49	814	6.1	8	5– 4	3																				
Mickey Kobrosky	QB-DB	22	6'	187			13	41	3.2	0	13	2	15	18	1.4	0	2–15																					
Tony Sarausky	QB-DB	25	5'11'	205			4	18	4.5	0	10	3	30	31	3.1	0	0– 0																					
Hank Soar	FB-DB	23	6'2"	207	17		120	442	3.7	0	21	5	24	83	4.0	1	2–10		6	77	13	1			2	3	67	1										
Tuffy Leemans	FB-DB	24	6'	192	6		144	429	3.0	0	20	5	25	64	3.2	1	1– 5		11	157	14	1																
Kink Richards	FB-DB	26	5'11"	196	18		89	327	3.7	1									10	149	15	2																
Jim Neill	FB-DB	22	6'1"	190			7	55	7.9	0	3	1	33	0	0.0	0	1–33																					
Ward Cuff	WB-DB	24	6'1"	198	30		4	32	8.0	2									5	117	23	2						2										
Dale Burnett	WB-DB	28	6'1"	188	6		7	4	0.6	0									10	121	12	1																
Red Corzine	BB-LB	28	6'	218	6		8	23	2.9	0	1	0	0	0	0.0	0	0– 0		9	75	8	1																
Leland Shaffer	BB-DB	25	6'2"	200			8	35	4.4	0									7	72	10	0																
Tilly Manton	BB-LB	25	5'11"	187	27		8	16	2.0	0	1	1	100	14	14.0	0	0– 0		3	15	5	0			12	12	100	5										
Will Walls	OE-DE	22	6'4"	205															7	55	8	0																
Jim Poole	OE-DE	21	6'3"	215	12														5	79	16	2																
Ray Hanken	OE-DE	22	5'11"	190															4	51	13	0																
Jim Lee Howell	OE-DE	22	6'6"	200															4	32	8	0																
Chuck Gelatka	OE-DE	24	6'1"	195															1	17	17	0																
PITTSBURGH PIRATES																																						
Johnny Gildea	TB-BB-DB	27	6'2"	215	6		49	65	1.3	1	47	14	30	288	6.1	2	9–19		3	47	16	0																
Max Fiske	TB-DB	23	6'	205			28	44	1.6	0	43	17	40	318	7.4	4	4– 9		1	0	0	0																
Tuffy Thompson	TB-HB-DB	22	5'11"	175	6		43	80	1.9	0	14	6	43	100	7.1	1	4–29		6	126	21	1																
Bull Karcis	FB-LB	28	5'9"	225	18		128	511	4.0	3	3	1	33	2	0.7	1	1–33		2	18	9	0																
Stu Smith	FB-TB-LB-DB	21	6'	195			65	211	3.2	0	2	0	0	0	0.0	0	1–50																					
Izzy Weinstock	FB-BB-LB	24	6'	212	4		33	88	2.7	0															4	6	67											
Bill Davidson	HB-TB-DB	22	6'	182	24		101	293	2.9	1	24	8	33	81	3.4	0	5–21		4	169	42	2																
Johnny Blood	HB-BB-TB-DB	32	6'1"	185	30		9	37	4.1	0	25	10	40	115	4.6	1	2– 8		10	168	17	4																1
By Haines	HB-DB	23	5'11"	185			24	29	1.2	0	6	1	17	14	2.3	0	1–17		2	17	9	0																
Bill Breeden	HB-OE-DB	23	6'1"	210	1		10	25	2.5	0									6	59	10	0			1	1	100											
Silvio Zaninelli	BB-DB	23	5'10"	215			4	14	3.5	0									2	12	6	0																
Bill Sortet	OE-DE	25	6'1"	188	6														9	121	13	1																
Jeep Brett	OE-DE	23	6'2"	200	6														8	135	17	1																
Mac Cara	OE-DE	23	5'10"	185															2	36	18	0																
Vinnie Sites	OE-DE	25	6'2"	215															2	10	5	0																
Armand Niccolai	T	25	6'2"	225	17																				5	7	71	4										
BROOKLYN DODGERS																																						
Ace Parker	TB-DB	25	6'	184	13		34	26	0.8	1	61	28	46	514	8.4	1	7–11	7							1	2	50							1				
Reino Nori	TB-DB	24	5'8"	168			26	81	3.1	0	23	11	48	168	7.3	1	3–13																					
Carl Brumbaugh	TB-DB	29	5'10"	180			13	–3	–0.2	0	18	5	28	87	4.8	0	3–17																					
(from CLE, BB-DB, to CHI B, QB-DB)																																						
Shipwreck Kelly	TB-DB	27	6'2"	195			16	29	1.8	0	12	2	17	21	1.8	0	3–25		1	7	7	0																
Red Franklin	TB-DB	25	5'10"	165			4	12	3.0	0	4	0	0	0	0.0	0	0– 0																					
Joe Maniaci	FB-HB-DB	23	6'1"	220	23		92	433	4.7	2	4	1	25	0	0.0	0	2–50		3	11	4	0			5	5	100	2										
Dick Crayne	FB-DB	24	6'	200	3		47	135	2.9	0	4	2	50	20	5.0	0	0– 0		1	4	4	0						1										
Bert Johnson	FB-TB-DB	25	6'	205			41	59	1.4	0	11	0	0	0	0.0	0	1– 9		1	3	3	0																
Vannie Albanese	FB-BB-DB-LB	24	6'	184			21	53	2.5	0	2	1	50	5	2.5	0	0– 0																					
Ralph Kercheval	HB-TB-DB	26	6'1"	193	13		48	84	1.8	1	19	11	58	154	8.1	1	1– 5		5	57	11	0			1	3	33	2										
Tony Kaska	BB-LB	26	5'11"	196			1	4	4.0	0									4	84	21	0																
Jeff Barrett	OE-DE	24	6'1"	180	18		1	8	8.0	0									20	461	23	3																
Jim Austin	OE-DE	24	6'2"	200															13	185	14	0																
Buster Mitchell	OE-DE	31	6'	205	6														8	115	14	1																
Frank Cumiskey	OE-DE		6'2"	205															5	50	10	0																
PHILADELPHIA EAGLES																																						
Emmett Mortell	TB-DB	23	6'1"	182			100	312	3.1	0	71	18	25	320	4.5	1	8–11	11	1	0	0	0																
Dave Smukler	FB-LB	23	6'1"	229	17		92	247	2.6	1	118	42	36	432	3.7	6	14–12	10	1	–4	–4	0			8	9	89	1										
Swede Hanson	FB-LB	28	6'1"	193	6		18	59	3.3	1	2	0	0	0	0.0	0	0– 0																					
Rabbit Keen	WB-TB-DB	22	5'9"	174			34	154	4.5	0	6	1	17	86	14.3	1	0– 0		5	45	9	0																
Bob Masters	WB-DB	26	5'11"	200			9	32	3.6	0									4	60	15	0																
Winnie Baze	WB-TB-DB	23	5'11"	190			3	14	4.7	0	3	0	0	0	0.0	0	0– 0		1	2	2	0																
Jay Arnold	WB-BB-DB	23	6'1"	206			5	7	1.4	0									8	142	18	0																
John Kusko	BB-TB-DB	23	5'11"	190			17	27	1.6	0	7	2	29	11	1.6	0	2–29		2	47	24	0																
Glenn Frey	BB-DB	25	5'10"	190			5	11	2.2	0									4	19	5	0																
Bill Hewitt	OE-DE	27	5'9"	190	30														16	197	12	5																
Joe Carter	OE-DE	27	6'1"	208	18														15	282	19	3																
Joe Pilconis	OE-DE	25	6'1"	184	6		2	21	10.5	0									6	59	10	0																

TEAM TOTALS	OFFENSE FIRST DOWNS	RUSHING: No.	Yards	Avg. Yds.	TD	PASSING: Att.	Comp.	Comp. Pct.	Yards	Yds/ Att.	Yds/ Comp.	TD	Int.	Pct. Int.	FUMBLES: Number	PENALTY: Yards	POINTS: Total	TD	PAT	FG	Saf	DEFENSE Total Yards	Pass Att.	Pass Comp.	Comp. Pct.	No. Pass Int.	Oppos. Fumb. Rec.	Points	TEAM TOTALS
WASHINGTON	149	448	1596	3.6	11	222	99	44.6	1316	5.9	13.3	11	20	9.0	38	338	195	26	22	5	1	2123	171	66	38.6	17	24	120	WASHINGTON
NEW YORK	127	478	1517	3.2	4	203	83	40.9	1024	5.0	12.3	10	11	5.4	25	275	128	15	14	8	0	2158	182	71	39.0	30	14	109	NEW YORK
PITTSBURGH	105	496	1417	2.9	5	164	57	34.8	918	5.6	16.1	9	27	16.5	31	358	122	16	12	4	1	2232	185	60	32.4	17	23	145	PITTSBURGH
BROOKLYN	88	375	978	2.6	5	179	64	35.8	995	5.6	15.5	4	23	12.8	28	190	82	10	7	5	0	2821	165	74	44.8	21	16	174	BROOKLYN
PHILADELPHIA	68	285	884	3.1	2	207	63	30.4	849	4.1	13.5	8	24	11.6	17	146	86	12	11	1	0	3150	196	79	40.3	19	17	177	PHILADELPHIA

CHICAGO BEARS 9-1-1 George Halas

Scores of Each Game		
14	Green Bay	2
7	Pittsburgh	0
20	Cleveland	2
16	CHIC. CARDS	7
28	DETROIT	20
3	New York	3
14	GREEN BAY	24
29	BROOKLYN	7
13	Detroit	0
15	CLEVELAND	7
42	Chic. Cards	28

Use Name	Pos.	Hgt	Wgt	Age	Int	Pts
Frank Bausch	C-LB	6'2"	224	29		
Bill Conkright	C-LB	6'1"	200	23		
Frank Sullivan	C-LB	6'3"	203	25		
Henry Hammond	OE-DE	5'11"	190			
George Corbett	DB	5'9"	178	29		
Kay Bell	T	6'2"	210	22		
Del Bjork	T	6'1"	218	23		
Joe Stydahar	T	6'4"	230	25		
Russ Thompson	T	6'5"	248	25		
Milt Trost	T	6'1"	203	24		
Zuck Carlson	G	6'	198	22		
Danny Fortmann	G	6'	210	21		
George Musso	G	6'2"	258	27		
Joe Zeller	G	6'1"	203	29		

As the only NFL club still using the T formation, the Bears passed the word that they were back by winning their first five contests before the New York Giants held them to a 3-3 tie. A loss to the Green Bay Packers caused some people to doubt the Bears, but the Halas men ran off four straight victories to ice away the Western championship.

On the road to the top, quarterback Bernie Masterson had his pick of three hard-charging runners on ground plays. Halfback Ray Nolting relied on quickness to break clear, while both Bronko Nagurski and Jack Manders were straight-ahead power runners and blockers.

Up in the line, Joe Stydahar, George Musso, Danny Fortmann, and Frank Bausch all made either first-or second-team All-Pro with their trench play, and rookie George Wilson capably filled the traded Bill Hewitt's end slot.

GREEN BAY PACKERS 7-4-0 Curly Lambeau

Scores of Each Game		
7	CHIC. CARDS	14
2	CHIC. BEARS	14
26	DETROIT	6
34	CHIC. CARDS	13
35	Cleveland	10
35	CLEVELAND	7
14	Detroit	13
24	Chic. Bears	14
37	PHILADELPHIA	7
0	New York	10
6	Washington	14

Use Name	Pos.	Hgt	Wgt	Age	Int	Pts
Darrell Lester	C-LB	6'3"	220	27		
Bud Svendsen	C-LB	6'1"	195	22		
George Svendsen	C-LB	6'4"	230	24		
(1 reception for 11 yds.)						
Swede Johnston	FB-LB	5'10"	195	27		
Averell Daniell (to BKN)	T	6'3"	215			
Lou Gordon	T	6'5"	230	29		
Champ Seibold	T	6'4"	235	24		
Ernie Smith	T	6'2"	222	27		15
(12 PAT's in 14 attempts, 1 FG)						
Lyle Sturgeon	T	6'3"	250			
Tiny Engebretsen	G	6'1"	240	27		8
(5 PAT's in 6 attempts, 1 FG)						
Lon Evans	G	6'2"	230	25		
Russ Letlow	G	6'	210	23		
Mike Michalske	G	6'	230	33		
Bud Schammel	G-DE	6'2"	235			6

A bad hip and some added pounds around the middle cut down on Arnie Herber's never great mobility—enough to make him vulnerable to a strong pass rush—and the Cardinals and Bears applied enough pressure to hand the Packers two quick losses at the start of the season that even a seven-game winning streak could not make up for.

Herber's arm still sent many a long pass onto Don Hutson's outstretched fingertips for huge chunks of yardage. To balance this airmail service, fullback Clarke Hinkle carried the mail on the ground with enough power to merit All-Pro honors. Guards Russ Letlow and Lon Evans and center George Svendsen opened up holes for Hinkle and shielded Herber from too much hostile interference. But even with so much running talent, the Packers again stumbled at the end of the year by dropping games to the Giants and Redskins.

DETROIT LIONS 7-4-0 Dutch Clark

Scores of Each Game		
28	Cleveland	0
16	CHIC. CARDS	7
6	Green Bay	26
7	PITTSBURGH	3
30	BROOKLYN	0
20	Chic. Bears	28
13	GREEN BAY	14
27	CLEVELAND	7
17	New York	0
16	Chic. Cards	7
0	CHIC. BEARS	13

Use Name	Pos.	Hgt	Wgt	Age	Int	Pts
Del Ritchhart	C-LB	6'	195	26		
Dixie Stokes	C-LB	6'	205	24		
Frank Christensen	BB-DB	6'1"	198	27		
Ray Reckmack (from BKN)	BB-DB	6'	200			
Charley Payne	WB-DB					
George Christensen	T-G	6'2"	238	27		
Jack Johnson	T	6'4"	212	27		6
Bob Reynolds	T	6'4"	218	23		
Red Stacy	T	6'2"	215	25		
Hal Cooper	G	5'10"	207			
Ox Emerson	G	5'11"	196	29		
Bill Feldhaus	G-T	6'	230	25		
Tom Fena	G		200			
Tom Hupke	G	5'10"	188	26		6
Sid Wagner	G	5'11"	190	24		

Dutch Clark had been running the Lions on the field since the team began, so it was only natural that he be chosen head coach when Potsy Clark decided to pack it in during the spring. Under Dutch's direction, the Lions lost only to the Packers and Bears. Clark's best player was an aging but still dangerous tailback named Dutch Clark.

Others who stood out in the Detroit lineup were Ace Gutowsky, who still crashed into the center of the line, Ernie Caddel, who still carried the ball to the outside, and George Christensen and Ox Emerson, both of whom helped stiffen the line. Although the Lions essentially had the same club that won the championship in 1935, they lacked the spark of that previous season and were beginning to get the label of a good team mired in a mediocre rut.

CHICAGO CARDINALS 5-5-1 Milan Creighton

Scores of Each Game		
14	Green Bay	7
7	Detroit	16
21	Washington	14
6	Philadelphia	6
6	Cleveland	0
13	Green Bay	34
7	Chic. Bears	16
13	Pittsburgh	7
13	CLEVELAND	7
7	DETROIT	16
28	CHIC. BEARS	42

Use Name	Pos.	Hgt	Wgt	Age	Int	Pts
Len Dugan	C-LB	6'	220	25		
Ham Harmon	C-LB		220			
John Reynolds	C-LB					
Milan Creighton	DE	6'	190	29		
Bill Muellner	OE-DE					
Conway Baker	T	5'11"	225	26		6
(6 PAT's in 6 attempts)						
Tony Blazine	T	6'	230	25		
(1 reception for 2 yds.)						
Earl Nolan	T	6'1"	205			
(Missed 1 PAT attempt)						
Jack Robinson	T	6'3"	220	25		
Hal Carlson	G					
Ross Carter	G	6'	200	23		
Bree Cuppoletti	G	5'10"	200	27		
Bob Hoel	G	6'	212	24		
Dub Miller	G	6'	220	25		
John Morrow	G	5'11"	230			
Bill Volok	G	6'2"	215	27		
(1 reception for 9 yds.)						

The Cardinals flew back up to the .500 mark on the wings of a new passing combination to rival Herber & Hutson in Green Bay. Coming from LSU as a unit, passer Pat Coffee and receiver Gaynell Tinsley found NFL defenses not much more difficult than what they had faced in college. Tinsley gained 675 yards to set a receiving record, part of which came on a 97-yard pass play from Coffee in a game against the Bears.

While the two rookies ate up yardage, Doug Russell and Bill Smith again were hampered with injuries and played below their par. Both men had been promising young players two years before but found themselves aging prematurely because of the injury hex. Although George Grosvenor helped the running game, the Cardinals relied mostly on their new air express.

CLEVELAND RAMS 1-10-0 Hugo Bezdek

Scores of Each Game		
0	DETROIT	28
21	Philadelphia	3
7	Brooklyn	9
0	CHIC. CARDS	6
2	CHIC. BEARS	20
10	GREEN BAY	35
7	Green Bay	35
7	Chic. Cards	13
7	Detroit	27
7	WASHINGTON	16
7	Chic. Bears	15

Use Name	Pos.	Hgt	Wgt	Age	Int	Pts
Chuck Cherundolo	C-LB	6'1"	210	21		
Ookie Miller	C-LB	6'	215	27		
Jim Turner	C-LB	6'2"	210			
Ollie Savatsky	OE-DE	6'2"	215	25		
Joe Williams	DB	5'9"	178	23		
Bob Emerick	T	6'2"	230	24		
Ted Livingston	T-G	6'3"	215	23		
Primo Miller	T	6'2"	220	21		6
Dale Prather	T-DE	6'2"	190	25		
Ted Rosequist	T	6'4"	225	29		
Wayne Underwood	T	6'1"	190			
Forrest Burmeister	G-T	6'3"	215			
Ralph Isselhardt (from DET)	G			27		
Dick Zoll	G	5'11"	220	23		

The first new club in the league since 1933, the Rams played like an expansion team by winning one out of eleven games. The offense scored the least points in the NFL, while the defense sprang for the most.

Coach Hugo Bezdek, the only man who managed a major-league baseball team and coached in the NFL, built his squad from a slew of rookies, a few defectors from the outlaw American Football League, and a handful of NFL veterans. Most of the rookies came from Midwest schools like Purdue and Ohio State, and the gems of the bunch were back Johnny Drake, the club's leading rusher, and center Chuck Cherundolo, a lineman who would have a long NFL career. The team's top passer, Bob Snyder, left the AFL along with five others to join the new NFL franchise. Two veterans of the Chicago Bears, center Ookie Miller and tackle Ted Rosequist, helped bring the club some respectability.

Use Name – Backs & Ends	Pos.	Age	Hgt	Wgt	Pts	Int	RUSHING				PASSING								RECEIVING				PUNTING		KICKING						PUNT RETURNS				KICKOFF RETURNS			
							No.	Yds	Avg	TD	Att	Comp	%	Yds	Yd/Att	TD	Int–%	RK	No.	Yds	Avg	TD	No.	Avg	Pat	Att	%	FG	Att	%	No.	Yds	Avg	TD	No.	Yds	Avg	TD
CHICAGO BEARS																																						
Bernie Masterson	QB-DB	26	6'3"	195	6		30	21	0.7	1	72	26	36	615	8.5	8	7–10	4																				
Ray Buivid	QB-HB-DB	22	6'1"	195	6		19	24	1.3	0	35	17	49	215	6.1	6	2– 6		1	4	4	1																
Gene Ronzani	QB-HB-DB	28	5'9"	190	6		12	17	1.4	0	13	4	31	84	6.5	0	1– 8		2	40	20	1																
Ray Nolting	HB-DB	23	5'11"	185	12		106	424	4.0	2	4	0	0	0	0.0	0	1–25		4	64	16	0																
Bronko Nagurski	FB-LB	28	6'2"	238	6		73	343	4.7	1	2	1	50	35	17.5	1	0– 0																					
Jack Manders	HB-DB	28	6'	200	69		73	319	4.4	0									7	155	22	3			15	20	75	8										
Beattie Feathers	HB-DB	28	5'10"	185	6		66	211	3.2	1	6	2	33	12	2.0	0	0– 0																					
Sam Francis	FB-LB	22	6'	205	7		48	129	2.7	0	6	3	50	34	5.7	1	2–33		1	9	9	0			1	1	100											
Pug Rentner	HB-DB	26	6'1"	185	6		21	70	3.3	0									6	101	17	1																
Keith Molesworth	HB-QB-DB	30	5'9"	168	1		20	53	2.7	0	6	1	17	4	0.7	0	0– 0		4	21	5	0			1	1	100											
John Doehring	HB-DB	27	6'	225			9	33	3.7	0	3	2	67	25	8.3	0	0– 0																					
Les McDonald	OE-DE	22	6'4"	200	24														11	179	16	4																
Eggs Manske	OE-DE	24	6'	185	24														9	225	25	3																
Bill Karr	OE-DE	26	6'1"	187	12		1	10	10.0	0									7	188	27	2																
Dick Plasman	OE-DE	23	6'3"	210	8														3	18	6	1			2	4	50											
George Wilson	OE-DE	23	6'1"	190	6														1	20	20	0																
GREEN BAY PACKERS																																						
Arnie Herber	TB-DB	27	5'11"	195			5	9	1.8	0	104	47	45	676	6.5	7	10–10	6																				
Bob Monnett	TB-HB-DB	27	5'9"	180	6		87	161	1.9	1	73	37	51	580	7.9	9	8–11	1	4	32	8	0																
Herb Banet	TB-HB-DB		6'2"	200			9	29	3.2	0	7	1	14	2	0.3	0	2–29		1	6	6	0																
Ray Peterson	TB-DB			190							6	3	50	47	7.8	0	0– 0																					
Ed Smith	TB-DB	24	6'2"	204							2	0	0	0	0.0	0	1–50																					
Clark Hinkle	FB-LB	27	5'11"	205	56		129	552	4.3	5	3	2	67	43	14.3	0	0– 0		8	116	15	2			8	9	89	2										
Ed Jankowski	FB-LB	24	5'9"	205	25		61	325	5.3	2									1	60	60	1			1	1	100											
George Sauer	FB-LB	26	6'2"	212			7	17	2.4	0																												
Joe Laws	HB-DB	26	5'9"	185	12		74	310	4.2	2	11	5	45	49	4.5	0	2–18		10	121	12	0																
Paul Miller	HB-DB	24	5'11"	180	6		71	265	3.7	0									6	66	11	1																
Hank Bruder	BB-TB-DB	29	6'	200	6		15	56	3.7	1	6	0	0	0	0.0	0	2–33																					
Herm Schneidman	BB-DB	23	5'11"	200	6		5	17	3.4	0									2	35	18	1																
Buckets Goldenberg	BB-G-DB-LB	26	5'10"	220	6		4	18	4.5	0																												
Don Hutson	OE-DE	24	6'1"	180	42		14	26	1.9	0	4	0	0	0	0.0	0	1–25		41	552	13	7																
Milt Gantenbein	OE-DE	27	6'	200	12														12	237	20	2																
Bernie Scherer	OE-DE	24	6'1"	190	12														7	148	21	2																
Wayland Becker	OE-DE	26	6'	205			2	4	2.0	0									2	13	7	0																
DETROIT LIONS																																						
Dutch Clark	TB-DB	30	6'	180	45		96	468	4.9	5	39	19	49	202	5.2	1	3– 8		2	33	17	1			6	10	60	1										
Bill Shepherd	TB-FB-DB-LB	25	5'9"	190	31		93	325	3.5	2	46	19	41	297	6.5	1	7–15								7	8	88	2										
Ace Gutowsky	FB-LB	27	5'11"	202	6		126	361	2.9	1	8	1	13	30	3.8	0	2–25																					
Lee Kizzire	FB-LB		6'	200			7	20	2.9	0																												
Ernie Caddel	WB-DB	26	6'2"	195	18		76	429	5.6	3	4	0	0	0	0.0	0	0– 0		9	80	9	0																
Lloyd Cardwell	WB-DB	24	6'2"	195	6		36	181	5.0	0									3	51	17	1																
Vern Huffman	BB-TB-WB-DB	23	6'2"	210	6		35	187	5.3	0	23	5	22	102	4.4	2	6–26		8	104	13	0																
Ed Klewicki	OE-WB-DE	26	5'10"	210	6		10	53	5.3	0									8	134	17	0																
Butch Morse	OE-DE	25	6'2"	202	6		1	−3	−3.0	0									8	131	16	1																
Harry Ebding	OE-DE	28	5'11"	195	18														5	89	18	1																
Chuck Hanneman	OE-DE	22	6'	195	6		2	53	26.5	1									1	9	9	0																
Regis Monahan	G	28	5'10"	215	20																				5	5	100	5										
CHICAGO CARDINALS																																						
Pat Coffee	TB-DB		5'11"	185	6		55	157	2.9	1	119	52	44	804	6.8	5	11– 9	5																				
George Grosvenor	TB-DB	26	6'	175	12		137	461	3.4	2	50	21	42	325	6.5	3	7–14	9																				
Hal Pangle	FB-DB	25	5'10"	200	12		61	203	3.3	2	2	0	0	0	0.0	0	1–50		5	58	12	0			0	1	0											
Buddy Parker	FB-DB	23	6'	195	7		50	115	2.3	1	1	0	0	0	0.0	0	0– 0		2	14	7	0			1	2	50											
Bill Crass	FB-DB		6'	205			5	8	1.6	0	1	0	0	0	0.0	0	0– 0																					
Doug Russell	WB-DB	25	6'	190	12		23	76	3.3	0	11	4	36	94	8.5	1	2–18		12	263	22	1												1				
Jimmy Lawrence	WB-DB	23	5'11"	185	6		19	60	3.2	1	3	0	0	0	0.0	0	0– 0		3	32	11	0																
Rock Reed	WB-DB	22	5'8"	170	6		10	33	3.3	0	1	0	0	0	0.0	0	0– 0		2	26	13	1																
Howie Tipton	BB-LB	26	5'11"	185			9	23	2.6	0									1	2	2	0																
Pete Tyler	BB-LB		5'11"	190	6		5	−5	−1.0	0	1	0	0	0	0.0	0	0– 0		7	60	9	1																
Bill May	BB-LB		5'11"	185	10		4	16	4.0	0															4	5	80	2										
Gaynell Tinsley	OE-DE	21	6'1"	195	36		1	2	2.0	0									36	675	19	5																
Bill Smith	OE-DE	25	6'1"	198	9														3	52	17	0			3	3	100											
Versil Deskin	OE-DE	24	6'	200	6														3	48	16	1																
Bill Wilson	OE-DE	25	5'10"	185															1	2	2	0																
CLEVELAND RAMS																																						
Bob Snyder	TB-DB	24	6'	190	16		82	232	2.8	1	66	25	38	378	5.7	2	6– 9	8	3	20	7	0			7	7	100	1										
Ed Goddard (from BKN)	TB-WB-DB	22	5'10"	180	13		57	162	2.8	1	41	13	32	180	4.4	2	8–20		6	61	10	0			1	1	100											
Harry Mattos	TB-DB		6'	195	8		26	16	0.6	1	22	5	23	94	4.3	1	4–18								2	2	100											
Joe Keeble	TB-WB-DB		6'	190	6		12	40	3.3	0	9	2	22	25	2.8	0	3–33		1	42	42	1																
Bud Cooper	TB-FB-DB		6'1"	204			19	45	2.4	0	5	2	40	21	4.2	0	1–20																					
Bill O'Neill	TB-DB						4	12	3.0	0	2	1	50	20	10.0	0	1–50																					
Ray Johnson	TB-FB-DB		6'1"	200			7	28	4.0	0																												
Johnny Drake	FB-WB-LB-DB	21	6'1"	205	30		98	333	3.4	3	1	0	0	0	0.0	0	0– 0		10	172	17	2																
Mark Barber	FB-LB		5'11"	192			14	35	2.5	0	3	1	33	7	2.3	0	0– 0																					
John Bettridge (from CHIB)	FB-LB		5'10"	188			22	35	1.6	0									1	17	17	0																
Julie Alfonse	WB-TB-DB	23	5'8"	180			33	60	1.8	0	10	4	40	48	4.8	0	0– 0		5	113	23	0																
Mike Sebastian	WB-DB	27	5'11"	185			6	4	0.7	0																												
Stan Pincura	BB-DB	23	5'11"	175			5	−22	−4.4	0	27	9	33	92	3.4	0	3–11		12	139	12	0																
Wayne Gift	BB-DB		5'8"	175			3	7	2.3	0	3	0	0	0	0.0	0	0– 0		3	20	7	0																
Sam Busich	OE-DE	24	6'3"	190															13	136	10	0																
Paul Halleck	OE-DE		6'	195															3	57	19	0																
Phil Bucklew	OE-DE		6'1"	205															3	51	17	0																
Walt Uzdavinis	OE-DE		6'2"	210															1	15	15	0																

TEAM TOTALS — OFFENSE

TEAM TOTALS	FIRST DOWNS	RUSHING: No.	Yards	Avg. Yds.	TD	PASSING: Att.	Comp.	Comp Pct.	Yards	Yds/ Att.	Yds/ Comp.	TD	Int.	Pct. Int.	FUMBLES: Number	PENALTY: Yards	POINTS: Total	TD	PAT	FG	Saf
CHICAGO BEARS	114	479	1654	3.5	5	147	56	38.1	1024	7.0	18.3	16	13	8.8	26	505	201	26	19	8	1
GREEN BAY	140	483	1789	3.7	11	216	95	44.0	1397	6.5	14.7	16	26	12.0	18	291	220	30	26	4	1
DETROIT	120	482	2074	4.3	12	120	44	36.7	631	5.3	14.3	4	18	15.0	17	139	180	23	18	8	0
CHICAGO CARDS	99	379	1149	3.0	7	189	77	40.7	1243	6.6	16.1	9	21	11.1	30	305	135	19	15	2	0
CLEVLEAND	88	368	930	2.5	6	168	59	35.1	836	5.0	14.2	4	23	13.7	28	228	175	10	10	1	1

DEFENSE

Total Yards	Pass Att.	Pass Comp.	Comp. Pct.	No. Pass Int.	Oppos. Fumb. Rec.	Points	TEAM TOTALS
2255	195	78	40.0	17	21	100	CHICAGO BEARS
2297	197	70	35.5	22	11	122	GREEN BAY
2102	165	59	35.8	25	17	105	DETROIT
2526	204	73	35.8	24	21	165	CHICAGO CARDS
2702	155	67	43.2	15	15	207	CLEVELAND

NEW YORK GIANTS 8-2-1 Steve Owen

Scores of Each Game		
27	Pittsburgh	14
10	Philadelphia	14
10	PITTSBURGH	13
10	Washington	7
17	PHIALDELPHIA	7
28	BROOKLYN	14
6	CHIC. CARDS	0
28	CLEVELAND	0
15	GREEN BAY	3
7	Brooklyn	7
36	WASHINGTON	0

Use Name	Pos.	Hgt	Wgt	Age	Int	Pts
Stan Galazin	C-LB	6'3"	215	23		
Mel Hein	C-LB	6'2"	225	29		6
Cliff Johnson	C-LB	6'3"	225	29		

Use Name – Tackles	Pos.	Hgt	Wgt	Age	Int	Pts
Frank Cope	T	6'2"	213	22		
Jack Haden	T	6'4"	233	23		
John Mellus	T	6'	210	21		
Ox Parry	T	6'4"	230	23		
Ed Widseth	T	6'1"	225	26		

Use Name – Guards	Pos.	Hgt	Wgt	Age	Int	Pts
Pete Cole	G	5'11"	220	22		
Johnny Dell Isola	G-LB	5'11"	198	26		
Kayo Lunday	G-C-LB	6'3"	215	25		
Orville Tuttle	G	5'9"	210	25		
(1 reception for –2 yds.)						
Tarzan White	G	5'9"	205	22		

When the league awarded its first Most Valuable Player Award to Mel Hein, it was not a surprising choice, as the New York center had just made the All-Pro team for the sixth straight year. Hein's season performance was highlighted in a game against Green Bay when he picked off a pass at mid-field and rambled 50 yards for the only touchdown of his NFL career. Ed Danowski and Ed Widseth joined teammate Hein on the All-Pro team, and Tuffy Leemans barely missed a spot. Coach Owen had stockpiled so much talent, he formed two separate squads which alternated in the game by quarters, and after two early losses to the Eagles and Pirates, the deep Giants marched undefeated through the bulk of their schedule. With the Eastern crown again on the line, the Giants crushed the Redskins 36-0 in the final game of the year in New York.

WASHINGTON REDSKINS 6-3-2 Ray Flaherty

Scores of Each Game		
26	Philadelphia	23
16	BROOKLYN	16
37	CLEVELAND	13
7	NEW YORK	10
7	Detroit	5
20	PHILADELPHIA	14
6	Brooklyn	6
7	Pittsburgh	0
7	Chic. Bears	31
15	PITTSBURGH	0
0	New York	36

Use Name	Pos.	Hgt	Wgt	Age	Int	Pts
Vic Carroll	C-LB	6'4"	230	25		
Bud Erickson	C-LB	6'1"	195	22		
Red Krause	C-LB	6'1"	216	24		
Mickey Parks	C-LB	6'	220	21		
Rink Bond	BB-LB	5'10"	200	24		

Use Name – Tackles	Pos.	Hgt	Wgt	Age	Int	Pts
Jim Barber	T	6'3"	228	26		
Chuck Bond	T	6'2"	232	24		
Turk Edwards	T	6'2"	256	30		6
Willie Wilkin	T	6'4"	247	22		
Bill Young	T	6'1"	242	24		6
(1 reception for 62 yd. touchdown)						
Roy Young	T	6'2"	215	21		

Use Name – Guards	Pos.	Hgt	Wgt	Age	Int	Pts
Hank Bartos	G	6'1"	216	24		
Jim Karcher	G	6'	207	24		
Les Olsson	G	6'	243	29		
Clem Stralka	G	5'10"	202	24		

When Cliff Battles retired and the Eagles separated Sammy Baugh's shoulder early in the season's first game, visions of a long year passed before the Redskins' eyes. Two rookies, passer Bill Hartman and runner Andy Farkas, rushed to the rescue, though, pulled out a victory over the Eagles, and kept the Skins in contention in the East.

Although Baugh returned to action in mid-season below peak efficiency, and Washington kept pace with New York—thanks to an outstanding line led by tackles Turk Edwards and Jim Barber—the Skins could not duplicate last year's efforts and lost in the finale to the Giants with the Eastern crown at stake.

BROOKLYN DODGERS 4-4-3 Potsy Clark

Scores of Each Game		
16	Washington	16
3	PITTSBURGH	17
13	CHIC. CARDS	0
17	Pittsburgh	7
7	Green Bay	35
14	New York	28
6	WASHINGTON	6
10	Philadelphia	7
32	PHILADELPHIA	14
6	CHIC. BEARS	24
7	NEW YORK	7

Use Name	Pos.	Hgt	Wgt	Age	Int	Pts
Norm Cooper	C-LB	6'4"	205	25		
Lou Mark	C-LB	6'	195	23		
Gene Moore	C-LB	6'3"	205	25		
Eddie Britt	DB	6'2"	195	25		

Use Name – Tackles	Pos.	Hgt	Wgt	Age	Int	Pts
Leo Disend	T	6'2"	224	22		
John Golemgeske	T	6'2"	225	23		
Bruiser Kinard	T	6'1"	210	23		
Jim Whatley	T	6'5"	227	25		

Use Name – Guards	Pos.	Hgt	Wgt	Age	Int	Pts
Ox Emerson	G	5'11"	200	30		
Ed Merlin	G	5'10"	200	22		
Len Noyes	G	6'	214	24		
Jim Sivell	G	5'9"	200	24		

Though the Dodgers never threatened to take the lead in the Eastern Division, coach Potsy Clark had to consider the year a success. The team broke even in wins and losses for the first time in five years, and more young talent was gathering in Brooklyn.

Ace Parker developed into an All-Pro tailback in his first full pro season, excelling in all aspects of play and shining brightest as a passer. Each game, though, Parker had to wonder who his backfield mates would be. Veteran Beattie Feathers and rookie Boyd Brumbaugh were racked up with injuries, and Joe Maniaci was traded to the Bears in mid-year. Only fullback Scrapper Farrell kept Parker from being a one-man show, along with rookie tackle Bruiser Kinard, who, living up to his nickname, hit enough people to win second-team All-Pro honors.

PHILADELPHIA EAGLES 5-6-0 Bert Bell

Scores of Each Game		
23	WASHINGTON	26
27	Pittsburgh at Buffalo	7
14	NEW YORK	10
6	CHIC. BEARS	28
7	New York	17
14	Washington	20
7	CHIC. CARDS	0 at Erie
7	BROOKLYN	10
14	Brooklyn	32
14	PITTSBURGH	7 at Charleston W.Va.
21	Detroit	7

Use Name	Pos.	Hgt	Wgt	Age	Int	Pts
Moose Harper	C-LB	6'4"	223	24		
John Kusko	HB-DB	5'11"	190	24		
Bob Masters	BB-DB	5'11"	200	27		

Use Name – Tackles	Pos.	Hgt	Wgt	Age	Int	Pts
Drew Ellis	T	6'1"	215	23		
Fritz Ferko	T	6'1"	245	25		
Wimpy Giddens	T	6'2"	220	23		
Ray Keeling	T	6'3"	263	22		
Bob Pylman	T	6'4"	215	24		6
(1 reception for 1 yd.)						
Clem Woltman	T	6'1"	218	22		

Use Name – Guards	Pos.	Hgt	Wgt	Age	Int	Pts
Bill Fiedler	G	5'9"	200	22		
Bill Hughes	G	6'1"	227	23		
George Rado	G-DE	5'9"	185	25		
Ted Schmitt	G	5'11"	214	21		
Mule Stockton	G	6'1"	210	24		

The Eagles rewarded Bert Bell's hard work by winning five games, their best showing ever. The young players he had brought together jelled enough to finish the year with two strong victories and hope for the future.

Central to this rebirth was the development of Dave Smukler and Emmett Mortell into good ball carriers. The Eagle line progressed as the youngsters holding down trench slots were force-fed a diet of experience by more established opponents. Both starting tackles were rookies, and the two guards were just two-year pros. To steady the kids, Bell fielded veterans Bill Hewitt and Joe Carter at the ends and Hank Reese at center.

PITTSBURGH PIRATES 2-9-0 Johnny Blood

Scores of Each Game		
7	Detroit	16
14	NEW YORK	27
7	PHILADELPHIA at Buffalo	27
17	Brooklyn	3
13	New York	10
7	BROOKLYN	17
0	Green Bay	20
0	WASHINGTON	7
7	Philadelphia at Charleston,W.Va.	14
0	Washington	15
7	CLEVELAND at New Orleans	13

Use Name	Pos.	Hgt	Wgt	Age	Int	Pts
Mike Basrak	C-LB	6'2"	220	25		
Joe Maras	C-T-LB	6'1"	205	22		
Karl McDade	C-LB	6'3"	195	24		
Lou Tsoutsouvas	C-LB	5'11"	210	22		
Bill Wilson (to PHI)	OE-DE	5'10"	185	26		
Bernie Lee (from PHI)	BB-LB	5'11"	190	24		
Clarence Tommerson	DB	6'2"	197	23		

Use Name – Tackles	Pos.	Hgt	Wgt	Age	Int	Pts
Joe Cardwell	T	6'3"	230	24		
Ted Doyle	T	6'2"	220	24		
Ed Karpowich	T	6'4"	225	25		
Lou Lassahn	T-DE	6'	205	25		
John Nosich	T	6'3"	230	22		
Red Rorison	T	6'3"	250	24		

Use Name – Guards	Pos.	Hgt	Wgt	Age	Int	Pts
Shipley Farroh	G					
Byron Gentry	G	5'11"	220	24		
George Kakasic	G	5'10"	202	26		
Walt Kiesling	G	6'3"	248	33		
Lindy Mayhew	G	6'1"	223	26		
John Perko	G	6'1"	210	22		

When Colorado halfback Whizzer White learned that he could delay his acceptance of a Rhodes scholarship, he signed a $15,800 contract with the Pirates. With the largest salary in the league, White received a lot of publicity before his debut against the Detroit Lions—so much so that as he lined up to take the opening kickoff, the jitters descended and the ball hit him squarely in the eye. White recovered from his embarrassment and black eye, though, to lead the NFL in yards gained rushing. While White got better as the season progressed, the Pirates, in general, got worse. But following three quick losses, Johnny Blood's merry men rose up and ambushed the Dodgers and Giants. Then, unknown to Blood, owner Art Rooney sold rookie Frankie Filchock, the team's main passer, to Washington. After that, the team never again won, as injuries and more sales chopped the Pirates down to mere bathtub sailors.

Use Name – Backs & Ends	Pos.	Age	Hgt	Wgt	Pts	Int	Rushing No.	Rushing Yds	Rushing Avg	Rushing TD	Passing Att	Passing Comp	Passing %	Passing Yds	Passing Yd/Att	Passing TD	Passing Int–%	Passing RK	Receiving No.	Receiving Yds	Receiving Avg	Receiving TD	Punting No.	Punting Avg	Kicking Pat	Kicking Att	Kicking %	Kicking FG	Kicking Att	Kicking %	Punt Returns No.	Punt Returns Yds	Punt Returns Avg	Punt Returns TD	Kickoff Returns No.	Kickoff Returns Yds	Kickoff Returns Avg	Kickoff Returns TD
NEW YORK GIANTS																																						
Ed Danowski	QB-DB	26	6'1"	198	6		48	215	4.5	1	129	70	54	848	6.6	7	8– 6	2																				
Len Barnum	QB-WB-DB	25	6'	200	6		35	97	2.8	1	6	1	17	45	7.5	0	1–17		3	37	12	0																
Tuffy Leemans	FB-QB-DB	25	6'	192	24		121	463	3.8	4	42	19	45	249	5.9	3	6–14		4	68	17	0																
Hank Soar	FB-DB	24	6'2"	207	13		122	401	3.3	2	7	1	14	0	0.0	0	3–43		13	164	13	0			1	1	100											
Bull Karcis (from PIT)	FB-LB	38	5'9"	225	30		89	212	2.4	4																												
Kink Richards	FB-DB	27	5'11"	195	2		25	111	4.4	0	1	0	0	0	0.0	0	1–100		1	8	8	0			2	2	100											
Red Wolfe	FB-DB	25	6'	205			15	19	1.3	0	1	0	0	0	0.0	0	0– 0		2	23	12	0			0	1	0											
Ward Cuff	WB-DB	25	6'1"	198	45		18	38	2.1	0									8	114	14	1			18	20	90	5	9	56								
Dale Burnett	WB-DB	29	6'1"	188	6		6	13	2.2	0									13	145	11	1																
Leland Shaffer	BB-DB	26	6'2"	200	12		1	4	4.0	0									12	86	7	2																
Nello Falaschi	BB-LB	24	6'	195			1	6	6.0	0																												
Johnny Gildea	BB-LB	28	6'2"	205			1	2	2.0	0									1	3	3	0																
Jim Lee Howell	OE-DE	23	6'6"	200	12														12	163	14	2																
Chuck Gelatka	OE-DB	25	6'1"	185	12														7	106	15	1			0	1	0											
Jim Poole	OE-DE	22	6'3"	215	6														7	98	14	1																
Ray Hanken	OE-DE	25	5'11"	190	12														5	73	15	2																
Hap Barnard	OE-DE	23	6'2"	190															1	33	33	0																
Will Walls	OE-DE	23	6'4"	205															1	23	23	0																
WASHINGTON REDSKINS																																						
Sammy Baugh	TB-DB	24	6'2"	185			15	35	2.3	0	128	63	49	853	6.7	6	11– 9	4																				
Bill Hartman	TB-DB	23	6'	190			71	195	2.7	0	77	38	49	558	7.4	3	10–13	9	1	6	6	0																
Andy Farkas	FB-DB	22	5'10"	190	37		75	315	4.2	6									9	66	7	0			1	1	100											
Max Krause	FB-DB	29	5'10"	195	18		25	214	8.6	2									2	62	31	1																
George Karamatic	FB-DB	21	5'8"	187	11		50	185	3.7	0									4	99	25	1			2	3	67	1	2	50								
Don Irwin	FB-WB-TB-DB	25	6'1"	196	6		66	130	2.0	1	6	0	0	0	0.0	0	2–33		16	138	9	0			0	1	0											
Ed Justice	WB-DB	25	6'1"	200	6		10	11	1.1	0									14	173	12	1																
Ernie Pinckert	WB-DB	30	6'	198			3	7	2.3	0									3	20	7	0																
Riley Smith	BB-LB	27	6'2"	200	15		3	–7	–2.3	0	4	1	25	18	4.5	0	0– 0		4	131	33	1			3	6	50	2	5	40								
Jay Turner	BB-LB	24	5'10"	198			5	25	5.0	0									2	10	5	0																
Tilly Manton (from NY)	BB-LB	26	5'11"	187	5		2	3	1.5	0															2	3	67	1	4	25								
Charley Malone	OE-DE	28	6'4"	210	6														24	257	11	1																
Wayne Millner	OE-DE	27	6'1"	190	6		3	5	1.7	0									18	232	13	1																
Bob Masterson	OE-DE	23	6'1"	186	14		3	89	29.7	0									10	213	21	1			5	6	83	1	1	100								
Bob McChesney	OE-DE	26	6'2"	193	6														3	49	16	1																
Hal Bradley (from CHIC)	OE-DE	24	6'4"	205															1	14	14	0																
BROOKLYN DODGERS																																						
Ace Parker	TB-DB	26	6'	180	29		93	253	2.7	2	148	63	43	865	5.8	5	7– 5	5	1	19	19	1			5	7	71											
Tony Sarausky	TB-DB	26	5'11"	203			8	42	5.3	0	8	2	25	10	1.3	0	0– 0																					
Scrapper Farrell (from PIT)	FB-DB	23	5'9"	202	18		108	425	3.9	3																												
Boyd Brumbaugh	FB-DB	23	5'11"	193	6		45	191	4.2	0									1	5	5	1																
Vannie Albanese	FB-DB	25	6'	183			27	97	3.6	0	1	0	0	0	0.0	0	0– 0																					
Stan Kosel	FB-DB	21	5'11"	190			13	43	3.3	0	1	0	0	0	0.0	0	0– 0																					
Beattie Feathers	HB-DB	29	5'10"	185	12		28	94	3.4	2									3	34	11	0																
Ralph Kercheval	HB-TB-DB	27	6'1"	193	28		51	86	1.7	1	9	3	33	98	10.9	0	1–11		11	136	12	0			7	9	78	5	13	38								
Wendell Butcher	BB-FB-LB-DB	24	6'1"	200	6		30	99	3.3	1									3	44	15	0																
Tony Kaska	BB-LB	27	5'11"	192			2	1	0.5	0									2	77	39	0																
Bill Reissig	BB-LB-DE	23	6'	195	6																							2	2	100								
Jim Austin	OE-DE	25	6'2"	196	6														14	180	13	1																
Jeff Barrett	OE-DE	25	6'1"	182	12		2	3	1.5	0									13	205	16	2																
Perry Schwartz	OE-DE	23	6'2"	204	6		2	–3	–1.5	0									8	132	17	1																
John Druze	OE-DE	24	6'	195															4	29	7	0																
Harold Hill	OE-DE	22	6'1"	200															3	61	20	0																
Bill Waller	OE-DE	23	6'	190															3	15	5	0																
PHILADELPHIA EAGLES																																						
Emmett Mortell	TB-DB	24	6'1"	183			110	296	2.7	0	57	12	21	201	3.5	7	7–12	14																				
Dick Riffle	TB-FB-DB	23	6'1"	194	6		65	227	3.5	1	31	9	29	178	5.7	1	4–13																					
Dave Smukler	FB-LB	24	6'1"	226	18		96	313	3.3	1	102	42	41	524	5.1	7	8– 8	6							6	6	100	0	1	0								
Joe Bukant	FB-LB	22	6'	214			48	119	2.5	0	1	1	100	14	14.0	0	0– 0																					
Jay Arnold	HB-DB	24	6'1"	209	27		19	22	1.2	0									6	74	12	2			3	3	100											
Rabbit Keen	HB-DB	23	5'9"	165			3	10	3.3	0																												
Woody Dow	BB-DB	21	6'	195	6		4	20	5.0	0									5	88	18	1																
John Cole	BB-FB-LB	23	5'9"	197			1	4	4.0	0									2	9	5	0																
Joe Carter	OE-DE	28	6'1"	195	48														27	386	14	7																
Bill Hewitt	OE-DE	28	5'9"	190	24														18	237	13	4																
Red Ramsey	OE-DE	23	6'	190	6														5	122	24	1																
Hank Reese	C-LB	27	5'11"	220	13																				10	13	77	1	6	17								
PITTSBURGH PIRATES																																						
Whizzer White	TB-HB-DB	21	6'1"	185	24		152	567	3.7	4	73	29	40	393	5.4	2	18–25	16	7	88	13	0																
Frankie Filchock (to WAS)	TB-DB	21	5'11"	188	6		69	198	2.9	1	101	41	41	469	4.6	3	11–11	13	2	4	2	0																
Max Fiske	TB-DB	24	6'	190			29	83	2.9	0	37	11	30	121	3.3	0	4–11																					
Stu Smith	FB-BB-LB	22	6'	195			80	241	3.0	0									3	30	10	0																
Swede Hanson	FB-DB	29	6'1"	190			15	50	3.3	0									1	2	2	0																
Bob Douglas	FB-DB	23	6'	195			4	10	2.5	0																												
Tuffy Thompson	HB-DB	23	5'11"	172	6		39	139	3.6	1	7	0	0	0	0.0	0	3–43		9	55	6	0																
Bill Davidson	HB-OE-DB	23	6'	183			33	52	1.6	0	2	2	100	10	5.0	0	0– 0		12	229	19	0																
John Oelerich (to CHIB)	HB-DB	21	6'	192			14	23	1.6	0	1	1	100	10	10.0	0	0– 0		3	23	8	0																
Johnny Blood	BB-DB	33	6'1"	184			21	–5	–0.2	0									2	5	3	0																
Tom Burnette (to PHI)	BB-LB	22	6'1"	194			1	0	0.0	0	1	0	0	0	0.0	0	0– 0		1	3	3	0						0	1	0								
Izzy Weinstock	BB-LB	25	6'	215			1	0	0.0	0																												
Eggs Manske (to CHIB)	OE-HB-DE-DB	25	6'	185	18		5	29	5.8	0									19	310	16	2																
Bill Sortet	OE-DE	26	6'1"	188	24		1	–5	–5.0	0									11	166	15	4																
Paul McDonough	OE-DE	21	6'4"	215															6	86	14	0																
George Platukas	OE-DE	23	6'	188			3	6	2.0	0									4	82	21	0																
Mac Cara	OE-DE	24	5'10"	200			1	–1	–1.0	0									4	18	5	0																
Jess Tatum	OE-DE	23	6'1"	215															1	16	16	0																
Armand Niccolai	T	26	6'2"	230	13																				10	10	100	1	5	20								

TEAM TOTALS — OFFENSE

Team	First Downs	Rushing: No.	Rushing: Yards	Rushing: Avg. Yds.	Rushing: TD	Passing Att.	Passing Comp	Comp Pct.	Yards	Yds/ Att.	Yds/ Comp	TD	Int.	Pct. Int.	Fumbles: Number	Penalty: Yards	Points: Total	Points: TD	Points: PAT	Points: FG Att.	Points: FG	Points: Saf
NEW YORK	132	467	1550	3.3	12	186	91	48.9	1142	6.1	12.5	10	19	10.2	23	233	194	26	21	11	5	1
WASHINGTON	147	399	1424	3.6	10	248	114	46.0	1536	6.2	13.5	9	27	10.9	45	410	148	20	13	12	5	0
BROOKLYN	96	379	1212	3.2	9	169	69	40.8	992	5.9	14.4	6	8	4.7	24	332	131	16	12	15	7	1
PHILADELPHIA	86	346	1011	2.9	2	191	64	33.5	917	4.8	14.3	15	19	9.1	13	220	154	22	19	9	1	0
PITTSBURGH	103	474	1414	3.0	5	194	72	37.1	916	4.7	12.7	5	33	17.0	14	225	79	11	10	6	1	0

DEFENSE — TEAM TOTALS

Total Yards	Pass Att.	Pass Comp.	Comp. Pct.	No. Pass Int.	Oppos. Fumb. Rec.	Points	Team
2029	226	77	34.1	34	14	79	NEW YORK
2174	195	69	35.4	19	9	154	WASHINGTON
2958	246	105	42.7	28	9	161	BROOKLYN
3270	197	97	49.2	16	17	164	PHILADELPHIA
2626	185	74	40.0	14	8	169	PITTSBURGH

GREEN BAY PACKERS 8-3-0 Curly Lambeau

Scores of Each Game		
26	CLEVELAND	17
0	CHIC. BEARS	2
28	CHIC. CARDS	7
24	Chic. Cards at Buffalo	22
7	DETROIT	17
35	BROOKLYN	7
20	PITTSBURGH	0
28	Cleveland	7
24	Chic. Bears	17
28	Detroit	7
3	New York	15

Use Name	Pos.	Hgt	Wgt	Age	Int	Pts
Darrell Lester	C-LB	6'3"	220	28		
Ookie Miller	C-LB	6'	215	28		
Lee Mulleneaux (from CHIC)	C-LB	6'2"	225	28		
Roy Schoemann	C-LB	6'1"	192			
Tony Borak	OE-DE	6'1"	190	25		
Voluntarily retired – Bud Svendsen						
Voluntarily retired – Ernie Smith						

Use Name – Tackles	Pos.	Hgt	Wgt	Age	Int	Pts
Frank Butler	T	6'3"	246	29		
Leo Katalinas	T	6'2"	240	22		
Bill Lee	T	6'2"	225	26		
Baby Ray	T	6'6"	250	23		
Champ Seibold	T	6'4"	240	25		

Use Name – Guards	Pos.	Hgt	Wgt	Age	Int	Pts
Tiny Engelbretsen	G	6'1"	240	28		15
(9 PAT's in 9 attempts, 2 FG in 4 attempts)						
Buckets Goldenberg	G-LB	5'10"	225	27		
Swede Johnston	G-LB	5'10"	195	28		
Potsy Jones	G	5'11"	230	28		
Russ Letlow	G	6'	212	24		
Pete Tinsley	G	5'8"	205	25		

With Arnie Herber slowing up, coach Curly Lambeau brought in a new rookie tailback with a strong passing arm. Cecil Isbell not only could throw the ball but could also carry it around the end for good yardage. Lambeau broke the rookie in gradually, alternating him with Herber at tailback and sometimes playing them both in the same backfield. Isbell hauled in a few Herber aerials, and the rookie sometimes caught defenses napping by throwing to the lead-footed Herber. Of course, both men often found their main targets in Don Hutson, who was heading for his usual receiving championship when he hurt his knee in Detroit on November 13. After the injury, the Packers grimly hung onto the lead in the West and won the title despite a 15-3 loss to the Giants in the finale.

DETROIT LIONS 7-4-0 Dutch Clark

Scores of Each Game		
16	PITTSBURGH	7
17	Cleveland	21
17	Green Bay	7
5	WASHINGTON	7
10	CHIC. CARDS	0
13	Chic. Bears	7
6	CLEVELAND	0
7	GREEN BAY	28
7	Chic. Cards	3
14	CHIC. BEARS	7
7	PHILADELPHIA	21

Use Name	Pos.	Hgt	Wgt	Age	Int	Pts
Jack Mackenroth	C-LB	6'2"	215	22		
Dixie Stokes	C-LB	6'	208	25		
Alex Wojciechowicz	C-LB	5'11"	204	23		
Lou Barle	BB-DB	6'1"	210	22		

Use Name – Tackles	Pos.	Hgt	Wgt	Age	Int	Pts
George Christensen	T	6'2"	250	28		
Jack Johnson	T	6'4"	220	28		
Tony Matisi	T	6'2"	230	24		
Bob Reynolds	T	6'4"	223	24		
Bill Rogers	T	5'11"	240	25		

Use Name – Guards	Pos.	Hgt	Wgt	Age	Int	Pts
Bill Feldhaus	G	6'	225	26		
Les Graham	G	6'	215	22		
Bill Radovich	G	5'10"	235	23		
Sid Wagner	G	5'11"	197	25		

The Lions' first game in spacious Briggs Stadium drew 55,000 spectators to see a close loss to the Washington Redskins. The irony of the season was that popular support should now be growing when the team was beginning to slip.

With Dutch Clark shelved by a bad ankle, Bill Shepherd handled most of the outside running until injuries sidelined him near the end of the season. Ace Gutowsky kept spinning into the line with elbows and knees flashing, and Lloyd Cardwell caught passes and defended well enough to make All-Pro. The forward wall also blended veterans with newcomers. George Christensen still excelled at tackle, while rookie Alex Wojciechowicz made a bigger name for himself with his hitting on both lines. With all the lineup changes, the Lions still had a chance to tie for the top with a final win, but the Eagles upset them 21-7.

CHICAGO BEARS 6-5-0 George Halas

Scores of Each Game		
16	CHIC. CARDS	13
2	Green Bay	0
28	Philadelphia	6
7	Cleveland	14
34	Chic. Cards	28
21	CLEVELAND	23
7	DETROIT	13
17	GREEN BAY	24
31	WASHINGTON	7
24	Brooklyn	6
7	Detroit	14

Use Name	Pos.	Hgt	Wgt	Age	Int	Pts
Frank Bausch	C-LB	6'2"	224	30		
Bill Conkright	C-OE-LB-DE	6'1"	200	24		6
(1 reception for 2 yd. touchdown)						
Frank Sullivan	C-LB	6'3"	203	26		
Red Corzine	LB	6'	218	29		

Use Name – Tackles	Pos.	Hgt	Wgt	Age	Int	Pts
Del Bjork	T	6'1"	218	24		
Lou Gordon	T	6'5"	230	30		
Joe Stydahar	T	6'4"	230	26		
Russ Thompson	T	6'5"	248	26		
Milt Trost	T	6'1"	208	25		

Use Name – Guards	Pos.	Hgt	Wgt	Age	Int	Pts
Dick Bassi	G	5'11"	210	23		6
Danny Fortmann	G	6'	210	22		
George Musso	G	6'2"	270	28		
Gust Zarnas	G	5'10"	212	23		
Joe Zeller	G	6'1"	203	30		6

With the veterans of the 1930s aging and the stars of the 1940s not yet arrived, the Bears—who sometimes displayed a powerful football machine—sputtered enough times to end with five losses, a calamity which had not occurred since the season of 1929.

Although Joe Maniaci ran well after his mid-season purchase from Brooklyn, he could not fill the gaping hole Bronko Nagurski's retirement left at the fullback spot. Quarterback Bernie Masterson passed infrequently but for good mileage, and Ray Nolting, Sam Francis, and Jack Manders picked up moderate yardage on the ground, but fumbles continually plagued the offense in an off-again, on-again year. The inconsistency of the Bear squad became evident by their victories over Green Bay and Washington and their double losses to Cleveland and Detroit.

CLEVELAND RAMS 4-7-0 Hugo Bezdek, Art Lewis

Scores of Each Game		
17	Green Bay	26
6	CHIC. CARDS	7
13	Washington	37
21	DETROIT	17
14	CHIC. BEARS	7
23	Chic. Bears	21
7	GREEN BAY	28
0	Detroit	6
0	New York	28
17	Chic. Cards	31
13	Pittsburgh at New Orleans	7

Use Name	Pos.	Hgt	Wgt	Age	Int	Pts
Chuck Cherundolo	C-LB	6'1"	220	22		
Gerry Conlee	C-LB	5'11"	190	22		
Jack May	C-LB	5'10"	210	23		
Jack Giannoni	OE-DE	6'1"	210	22		
Dale Prather	OE-DE	6'2"	190	26		

Use Name – Tackles	Pos.	Hgt	Wgt	Age	Int	Pts
Bill Krause	T	6'	210	23		
Art Lewis	T	6'3"	223	25		
Ted Livingston	T	6'3"	218	24		
Primo Miller	T	6'2"	220	22		
Chuck Ream	T	6'2"	225	23		
Jack Robinson (from PITT, T)	T-G	6'3"	218	26		

Use Name – Guards	Pos.	Hgt	Wgt	Age	Int	Pts
Red Chesbro	G	5'11"	190	23		
Tom Hupke	G	5'10"	195	27		
Vic Markov	G-T	6'	215	22		
Phil Ragazzo	G	6'	190	23		
Dick Zoll	G-T	5'11"	215	24		
(1 PAT in 1 attempt)						

Coach Hugo Bezdek handed in his resignation when the first four games resulted in only one victory, and assistant Art Lewis was given the thankless job of interim head coach for the rest of the year. Little did Lewis know what lay directly ahead. Two matches with the Chicago Bears approached, and the Rams surprised everyone by winning both. Although four losses followed, a final victory over Pittsburgh ended the season on a high note. On a team filled with rookies, only two Rams were older than twenty-five. Of these, first-draft choice Corby Davis bulled his way to enough hard yardage to lead the team in rushing, while tall end Jim Benton provided a big target for veteran Bob Snyder. The top breakaway runner was once again Johnny Drake.

CHICAGO CARDINALS 2-9-0 Milan Creighton

Scores of Each Game		
13	Chic. Bears	16
7	Cleveland	6
7	Green Bay	28
22	GREEN BAY at Buffalo	24
0	Brooklyn	13
28	CHIC. BEARS	34
0	Detroit	10
0	Philadelphia at Erie	7
0	New York	6
3	DETROIT	7
31	CLEVELAND	17

Use Name	Pos.	Hgt	Wgt	Age	Int	Pts
Phil Dougherty	C-LB	5'11"	185			6
Len Dugan	C-LB	6'	220	26		

Use Name – Tackles	Pos.	Hgt	Wgt	Age	Int	Pts
Al Babartsky	T	6'	220	23		
Conway Baker	T	5'11"	225	27		
(missed 1 field goal attempt)						
Jon Bilbo	T-G	6'	195			
Tony Blazine	T	6'	230	26		6
Elwyn Dunstan	T	6'3"	235	23		
Bob McGee	T	6'	210			
Earl Nolan	T	6'1"	205			

Use Name – Guards	Pos.	Hgt	Wgt	Age	Int	Pts
Ross Carter	G	6'	200	24		
Bree Cuppoletti	G	5'10"	200	28		
Bob Hoel	G	6'	200	25		
John Morrow	G	5'11"	230			
Bill Volok	G	6'2"	215	28		

After breaking even last year, the Cardinals backslid, and coach Milan Creighton's efforts could only result in two wins over the Cleveland Rams. Of all his charges, end Gaynell Tinsley stood out for his All-Pro performance amidst the shambles. Making the honor roll a second time in two years, Tinsley grabbed forty-one passes to lead the NFL despite constant double coverage and the absence of a consistent passer for the Cardinals. In the only time he reached the end zone, Tinsley excited the crowd on a 98-yard pass play from Doug Russell in the second victory over Cleveland.

Use Name – Backs & Ends	Pos.	Age	Hgt	Wgt	Pts	Int	Rushing No.	Rushing Yds	Rushing Avg	Rushing TD	Passing Att	Passing Comp	Passing %	Passing Yds	Passing Yd/Att	Passing TD	Passing Int–%	Passing RK	Receiving No.	Receiving Yds	Receiving Avg	Receiving TD	Punting No.	Punting Avg	Kicking Pat	Kicking Att	Kicking %	Kicking FG	Kicking Att	Kicking %	Punt Returns No.	Punt Returns Yds	Punt Returns Avg	Punt Returns TD	Kickoff Returns No.	Kickoff Returns Yds	Kickoff Returns Avg	Kickoff Returns TD
GREEN BAY PACKERS																																						
Cecil Isbell	TB-HB-DB	23	6'1"	190	12		85	445	5.2	2	91	37	41	659	7.2	7	10–11	8	5	104	21	0																
Bob Monnett	TB-HB-DB	28	5'9"	180	7		75	225	3.0	0	57	31	**54**	465	**8.2**	**9**	4– 7	1	1	23	23	0			7	7	100											
Arnie Herber	TB-DB	28	5'11"	200	12		6	−1	−0.2	0	55	22	40	336	6.1	4	4– 7	11	5	84	17	2						0	1	0								
Clarke Hinkle	FB-LB	28	5'11"	203	**58**		114	299	2.6	3	2	1	50	6	3.0	0	0– 0		7	98	14	4			7	8	88	3	9	33								
Ed Jankowski	FB-LB	25	5'9"	195	14		24	124	5.1	2															2	3	67											
John Howell	FB-BB-LB	23	5'10"	185			7	7	1.0	0																												
Joe Laws	HB-DB	27	5'9"	185	12		60	253	4.2	0	5	0	0	0	0.0	0	2–40		6	55	9	1																
Andy Uram	HB-DB	23	5'10"	187	12		28	145	5.2	2									4	46	12	0																
Paul Miller	HB-DB	25	5'11"	185			20	48	2.4	0									4	36	9	0																
Dick Weisgerber	BB-DB	23	5'10"	205			6	13	2.2	0																												
Herm Schneidman	BB-DB	24	5'11"	200			4	8	2.0	0																												
Hank Bruder	BB-DB	30	6'	200			2	6	3.0	0									2	14	7	0																
Don Hutson	OE-DE	25	6'1"	185	57		3	−1	−0.3	0									32	**548**	17	**9**			3	3	100											
Milt Gantenbein	OE-DE	28	6'	205	6														12	164	14	1																
Wayland Becker	OE-DE	27	6'	205															7	166	24	0																
Moose Mulleneaux	OE-DE	21	6'3"	210	12														4	97	24	2																
Bernie Scherer	OE-DE	25	6'1"	193	6														2	31	16	1																
DETROIT LIONS																																						
Vern Huffman	TB-DB	24	6'2"	220	6		69	181	2.6	1	85	27	32	382	4.5	2	8– 9	15	1	17	17	0																
Dutch Clark	TB-DB	31	6'	190	8		7	25	3.6	0	12	6	50	50	4.2	1	2–17								2	2	100	2	2	100								
Bill Shepherd	FB-TB-LB-DB	26	5'9"	205	23		100	455	4.6	3	32	8	25	167	5.2	0	6–19								2	2	100	1	2	50								
Ace Gutowsky	FB-LB	28	5'11"	205	12		131	444	3.4	2	7	3	43	41	5.9	0	0– 0		1	25	25	0																
Paul Szakash	FB-LB	25	6'	215			20	55	2.8	0									1	0	0	0																
Lloyd Cardwell	WB-DB	25	6'2"	195	30		73	294	4.0	4	1	1	100	35	35.0	0	0– 0		9	138	15	1																
Rip Ryan	WB-DB	23	6'2"	190			24	180	7.5	0	9	2	22	27	3.0	0	0– 0		7	78	11	0																
Dick Nardi	WB-FB-DB	22	5'10"	200			20	109	5.5	0																												
Ernie Caddel	WB-DB	27	6'2"	195	6		14	38	2.7	1	2	2	100	45	22.5	0	0– 0		1	6	6	0																
Fred Vanzo	BB-LB	22	6'2"	230															4	52	13	0																
Jim McDonald	BB-DB	22	6'1"	190															2	41	21	0																
Maury Patt	OE-DE	24	6'2"	207			3	30	10.0	0									7	80	11	0																
Monk Moscrip	OE-DE	24	6'	195	12														6	118	20	1			6	6	100	0	1	0								
Chuck Hanneman	OE-DE	23	6'	212	6		1	6	6.0	0									4	80	20	1																
Ed Klewicki	OE-WB-DE	27	5'10"	198			10	76	7.6	0									3	57	19	0																
Butch Morse	OE-DE	26	6'2"	206															3	55	18	0																
Regis Monahan	G	29	5'10"	220	14																				2	4	50	4	5	**80**								
CHICAGO BEARS																																						
Bernie Masterson	QB-DB	27	6'3"	195			13	−16	−1.2	0	112	46	41	848	7.6	7	9– 8	3	1	4	4	0																
Ray Buivid	QB-HB-DB	23	6'1"	195			32	65	2.0	0	48	17	35	295	6.1	5	2– 4		1	8	8	0																
George Corbett	QB-DB	30	5'9"	177	6		7	29	4.1	0	9	3	33	32	3.6	0	3–33		1	10	10	0																
Carl Brumbaugh	QB-DB	30	5'10"	175			3	−15	−5.0	0	4	2	50	25	6.3	0	0– 0		1	23	23	0																
Gene Ronzani	QB-DB	29	5'9"	190			7	12	1.7	0	1	0	0	0	0.0	0	0– 0																					
Reino Nori	QB-DB	25	5'8"	165			1	1	1.0	0																												
Joe Maniaci (from BKN)	FB-HB-LB	24	6'1"	210	32		88	345	3.6	3	2	1	50	19	9.5	1	0– 0		9	127	14	0			11	11	**100**	1	3	33								
Ray Nolting	HB-DB	24	5'11"	185	12		63	297	4.7	1	11	0	0	0	0.0	0	3–27		4	90	23	1																
Sam Francis	FB-HB-DB	23	6'	205	18		85	297	3.5	3	3	1	33	0	0.0	0	0– 0		1	8	8	0			0	2	0											
Jack Manders	HB-DB	29	6'	200	37		67	263	3.9	2	1	0	0	0	0.0	0	0– 0		2	27	14	1			10	12	83	3	9	33								
Bert Johnson	FB-LB	26	6'	215	12		37	138	3.7	2	2	1	50	4	2.0	0	0– 0																					
Bob Swisher	HB-DB	24	5'11"	165			22	133	6.0	0	4	1	25	8	2.0	0	1–25		4	65	16	0																
Gary Famiglietti	FB-LB	23	6'	214			33	129	3.9	0																												
Dick Schweidler	HB-DB	23	6'	185			16	57	3.6	0	1	0	0	0	0.0	0	0– 0		1	21	21	0																
Bill Karr	OE-DE	27	6'1"	187	24		1	6	6.0	0									14	253	18	4																
Les McDonald	OE-DE	23	6'4"	200	7		1	0	0.0	0									9	175	19	1			1	1	100											
Dick Plasman	OE-DE	24	6'3"	210	6														8	117	15	1																
George Wilson	OE-DE	24	6'1"	190	6														4	81	20	1																
Ferd Dreher	OE-DE	25	6'3"	205	6														3	69	23	1																
CLEVELAND RAMS																																						
Bob Snyder	TB-DB	25	6'	205	10		44	78	1.8	0	87	36	41	631	7.3	6	9–10	7	1	16	16	0			7	10	70	1	2	50								
Ed Goddard	TB-WB-DB	23	5'10"	185	7		40	−16	−0.4	0	43	19	44	238	5.5	0	6–14		6	128	21	1			1	1	100											
Dick Tuckey (from WAS)	TB-DB	24	6'2"	205	2		43	76	1.8	0	32	8	25	140	4.4	1	3– 9		1	10	10	0			2	3	67											
Bob Davis	TB-DB	24	6'	175			22	100	4.5	0	26	6	23	49	1.9	0	2– 8		3	31	10	0			0	1	0											
Carl Littlefield	TB-DB	22	6'	200	6		19	69	3.6	0	15	1	7	23	1.5	0	5–33		1	9	9	0																
Ray Johnson	TB-DB		6'1"	190							5	3	60	45	9.0	0	1–20																					
Corby Davis	FB-LB	23	5'11"	215	19		71	202	2.8	3	1	0	0	0	0.0	0	0– 0		1	2	2	0			1	1	100											
Johnny Drake	FB-WB-LB-DB	22	6'1"	210	6		74	188	2.5	1	3	1	33	8	2.7	0	0– 0		2	13	7	0																
Nelson Peterson	WB-TB-DB	23	5'8"	168	20		21	70	3.3	1	6	0	0	0	0.0	0	2–33		4	43	11	1			2	2	100	2	2	100								
Julie Alfonse	WB-DB	24	5'8"	180	12		16	16	1.0	1	2	2	100	19	9.5	0	0– 0		2	47	24	0																
Stan Pincura	BB-DB	24	5'11"	175	6		2	−6	−3.0	0	33	13	39	240	7.3	2	7–21		6	72	12	1																
Vic Spadaccini	BB-WB-DB	22	6'	215			9	46	5.1	0									8	101	13	0																
Carl Brazell	BB-DB	21	5'10"	195			4	14	3.5	0									7	100	14	0																
Jim Benton	OE-DE	21	6'3"	205	36														21	418	**20**	5																
Ray Hamilton	OE-DE	22	6'4"	210															10	187	19	0																
Johnny Kovatch	OE-DE	23	5'11"	172	6														8	97	12	1																
Johnny Stephens	OE-DE	22	6'1"	190															6	75	13	0																
Phil Bucklew	OE-DE		6'1"	205															1	14	14	0																
CHICAGO CARDINALS																																						
John Robbins	TB-DB	22	6'2"	185			63	213	3.4	0	97	52	54	577	5.9	2	9– 9	10																				
Dwight Sloan	TB-DB	23	5'10"	180			56	126	2.3	0	79	37	48	333	4.2	1	7– 9	12	1	10	10	0																
Pat Coffee	TB-DB		5'11"	180	12		40	169	4.2	2	39	16	41	200	5.1	0	4–10																					
Ray Burnett	TB-DB						1	−10	−10.0	0	2	1	50	19	9.5	0	0– 0																					
Sam Agee	FB-DB	24	6'1"	208	6		48	178	3.7	1	2	2	100	27	13.5	0	0– 0		2	5	3	0																
Buddy Parker	FB-DB	24	6'	195	12		45	144	3.2	2	2	2	100	21	10.5	0	0– 0		16	142	9	0																
Ed Cherry	FB-DB	23	6'	205			6	18	3.0	0																												
Milt Popovich	FB-WB-DB	21	5'11"	190			6	13	2.2	0									1	8	8	0																
Jimmy Lawrence	WB-DB	24	5'11"	190	18		78	207	2.7	3	11	3	27	65	5.9	0	4–36		14	105	8	0																
Doug Russell	WB-DB	26	6'	190	6		31	60	1.9	1	7	1	14	98	14.0	1	2–29		6	36	6	0																
Frank Patrick	BB-LB	22	5'11"	190	17		1	1	1.0	0	1	0	0	0	0.0	0	0– 0		1	21	21	1			8	8	100	1	4	25								
Pete Tyler	BB-LB		5'11"	190	6		1	1	1.0	0									2	24	12	1																
Hal Pangle	BB-LB	26	5'10"	200			2	3	1.5	0									2	14	7	0																
Bill May	BB-LB		5'11"	190															1	16	16	0			0	2	0	0	1	0								
Gaynell Tinsley	OE-DE	22	6'1"	195	6		4	26	6.5	0									**41**	516	13	1																
Bill Smith	OE-DE	26	6'1"	198	16														18	338	19	1			4	5	80	2	2	100								
Versil Deskin	OE-DE	25	6'	200															6	57	10	0																
Ev Fisher	OE-BB-DE-LB	23	5'11'	205															3	48	16	0																

TEAM TOTALS	OFFENSE: First Downs	Rushing: No.	Rushing: Yards	Rushing: Avg. Yds.	Rushing: TD	Passing: Att.	Passing: Comp.	Passing: Comp. Pct.	Passing: Yards	Passing: Yds/Att.	Passing: Yds/Comp.	Passing: TD	Passing: Pct. Int.	Passing: Pct. Int.	Fumbles: Number	Penalty: Yards	Points: Total	Points: TD	Points: PAT	Points: FG Att.	Points: FG	Points: Saf	DEFENSE: Total Yards	Pass Att.	Pass Comp.	Comp. Pct.	No. Pass Int.	Oppos. Fumb. Rec.	Points	TEAM TOTALS
GREEN BAY	134	434	1571	3.6	9	210	91	43.3	1466	**7.0**	16.1	**20**	20	9.5	18	250	**223**	**30**	**28**	14	5	0	2594	232	92	39.7	21	12	118	GREEN BAY
DETROIT	129	472	**1893**	**4.0**	11	148	49	33.1	747	5.0	15.2	3	16	10.8	18	345	119	14	12	10	7	1	2199	205	77	37.6	23	13	108	DETROIT
CHICAGO BEARS	141	462	1686	3.6	11	197	72	36.5	1222	6.2	**17.0**	12	18	9.1	56	350	194	26	22	12	4	**2**	2187	190	76	40.0	24	14	148	CHICAGO BEARS
CLEVELAND	101	351	798	2.3	6	247	88	35.6	1363	5.5	15.5	9	34	13.8	23	195	131	18	14	4	3	0	3020	**172**	77	44.8	23	16	215	CLEVELAND
CHICAGO CARDS	121	382	1149	3.0	9	240	**114**	47.5	1340	5.6	11.8	4	26	10.8	34	286	111	15	12	8	3	0	2558	182	80	44.0	18	10	168	CHICAGO CARDS

NEW YORK GIANTS 9-1-1 Steve Owen

Scores of Each Game		
13	Philadelphia	3
0	Washington	0
14	Pittsburgh	7
27	PHILADELPHIA	10
16	CHIC. BEARS	13
7	Brooklyn	6
14	Detroit	18
17	CHIC. CARDS	7
23	PITTSBURGH	7
28	BROOKLYN	7
9	WASHINGTON	7

Use Name	Pos.	Hgt	Wgt	Age	Int	Pts
Stan Galazin	C-LB	6'3"	204	24		
Mel Hein	C-LB	6'2"	225	30		
Chief Johnson	C-LB	6'3"	225	30		

Use Name – Tackles	Pos.	Hgt	Wgt	Age	Int	Pts
Pete Cole	T	5'11"	225	23		
Frank Cope	T	6'2"	215	23		
John Mellus	T	6'	220	22		
Ox Parry	T	6'4"	230	24		
Ed Widseth	T	6'1"	220	27		

Use Name – Guards	Pos.	Hgt	Wgt	Age	Int	Pts
Johnny Dell Isola	G-LB	5'11"	200	27		
Kayo Lunday	G-C-LB	6'3"	215	26		
Doug Oldershaw	G-LB	6'	195	24		
Orville Tuttle	G	5'9"	202	26		
Tarzan White	G	5'9"	216	23		

With Hitler's blitzkrieg rolling through Europe this fall, the New York Giant defense was a lot sturdier than the Maginot Line. The blue-jerseyed Giants rudely turned back attempts to trespass on their turf, allowing enemies only 85 points in eleven confrontations. Aerial attacks did not bother the New Yorkers, as they intercepted thirty-five passes, a league high. The steadfast front line was manned by Mel Hein, Johnny Dell Isola, Orville Tuttle, Frank Cope, Ed Widseth, Jim Poole, and Will Walls, and if the enemy did get through these troops, mobile units in the secondary usually rushed to the scene and grounded the invader.

The Giants also could launch a powerful counterattack, Ed Danowski pinpointed his passes better than any artillery could, and Tuffy Leemans ground out tough yardage in the infantry. When the smoke cleared, the Giants stood triumphant on the Eastern front.

WASHINGTON REDSKINS 8-2-1 Ray Flaherty

Scores of Each Game		
7	Philadelphia	0
0	NEW YORK	0
41	BROOKLYN	13
44	PITTSBURGH	14
21	Pittsburgh	14
14	Green Bay	24
7	PHILADELPHIA	6
42	Brooklyn	0
28	CHIC. CARDS	7
31	DETROIT	7
7	New York	9

Use Name	Pos.	Hgt	Wgt	Age	Int	Pts
Bud Erickson	C-LB	6'1"	200	23		
Mickey Parks	C-LB	6'	228	22		
(Missed 1 PAT attempt)						

Use Name – Tackles	Pos.	Hgt	Wgt	Age	Int	Pts
Jim Barber	T	6'3"	230	27		
Vic Carroll	T-C-LB	6'4"	230	28		
Turk Edwards	T	6'2"	270	31		
(Missed 1 PAT attempt)						
Willie Wilkin	T	6'4"	260	23		
(Missed 1 PAT attempt)						
Bill Young	T	6'1"	240	25		

Use Name – Guards	Pos.	Hgt	Wgt	Age	Int	Pts
Dick Farman	G	6'	215	23		
Jim Karcher	G	6'	200	25		
(8 punts for 39 yd. average)						
Clyde Shugart	G	6'1"	212	22		
Steve Slivinski	G	5'10"	210	22		
Clem Stralka	G	5'10"	210	25		
Steve Uhrinyak	G	6'2"	218	24		

For the fourth straight year, a large group of Washington fans traveled up to New York to see the Eastern Division championship decided between the Giants and Redskins on the final Sunday of the season. This year, a punishing defensive battle came down to a field-goal attempt by Washington's Bo Russell with forty-five seconds left. Alas, Russell missed, and New York picked up all the chips with a 9-7 win. Along the way to this showdown, coach Ray Flaherty kept Sammy Baugh in one piece by playing him only thirty minutes a game. Frankie Filchock handled the tailback job for two quarters a game and kept the offense moving with his own accurate passing. Alternating by quarters, both passers stayed healthy, and the Redskins' offense glowed.

Top honors went to halfback Andy Farkas and tackle Jim Barber, who capped the season with All-Pro performances.

BROOKLYN DODGERS 4-6-1 Potsy Clark

Scores of Each Game		
12	PITTSBURGH	7
23	CLEVELAND	12
7	Detroit	27
0	Philadelphia	0
13	Washington	41
23	PHILADELPHIA	14
6	NEW YORK	7
17	PITTSBURGH	13
0	WASHINGTON	42
0	GREEN BAY	28
7	New York	28

Use Name	Pos.	Hgt	Wgt	Age	Int	Pts
Paul Humphrey	C-LB	6'	195	22		
Lou Mark	C-LB	6'	195	24		
Joe Ratica	C-LB	6'	205	22		
George Lenc	OE-DE	6'3"	204	21		
Scrapper Farrell	FB-DB	5'9"	205	24		
Dick Falk	FB-DB	6'	200	23		

Use Name – Tackles	Pos.	Hgt	Wgt	Age	Int	Pts
Leo Disend	T	6'2"	224	23		
Bob Haak	T-G	6'1"	245	23		
Carl Kaplanoff	T-G	6'	235	22		
Bruiser Kinard	T	6'1"	210	24		7
(7 PAT's in 7 attempts)						
Alec Shellogg (from CHI B)	T	6'	215	24		

Use Name – Guards	Pos.	Hgt	Wgt	Age	Int	Pts
John Golemgeske	G-T	6'2"	225	24		
Ralph Heikkenen	G	5'10"	180	22		
Les Lane	G	6'3"	193	23		
Ed Merlin	G	5'10"	200	23		
Jim Sivell	G	5'9"	200	25		

The Dodgers were running harder and harder on a treadmill and going no place. Coach Potsy Clark brought in some veterans and signed some rookies, but the Dodgers still wallowed in mediocrity. After a decade in the league, they showed no signs of challenging the Giants and Redskins as powers in the NFL East. In the last few years, the Dodgers had added one top-notch rookie to their ranks, and this year's sparkler was runner Pug Manders, Jack's brother of the Chicago Bears, a straight-ahead plunger. Tailback Ace Parker and tackle Bruiser Kinard, prize finds the last two years, led their teammates and won reputations as first-rate players on a second-rate team. Fullback Ace Gutowsky came over to Brooklyn from the Detroit Lions, but he, Beattie Feathers, and Ralph Kercheval all had left their best running behind them. None of the other linemen came close to matching Kinard's ferocity.

PHILADELPHIA EAGLES 1-9-1 Bert Bell

Scores of Each Game		
0	WASHINGTON	7
3	NEW YORK	13
0	BROOKLYN	0
10	New York	27
14	Brooklyn	23
6	Washington	7
16	GREEN BAY	23
14	Chic. Bears	27
17	PITTSBURGH	14
12	Pittsburgh	24
13	Cleveland at Colorado Springs	35

Use Name	Pos.	Hgt	Wgt	Age	Int	Pts
Zed Coston	C-LB	6'2"	222	23		
Moose Harper	C-LB	6'4"	230	25		
Jake Schueble	LB	6'	196	22		
Rankin Britt	DE	6'2"	206	24		

Use Name – Tackles	Pos.	Hgt	Wgt	Age	Int	Pts
Drew Ellis	T-FB	6'1"	216	24		
(6 rushing attempts for 1 yd.)						
Ray Keeling	T	6'3"	255	23		
Bob Pylman	T	6'4"	215	25		
George Somers	T	6'2"	242	23		
Clem Woltman	T	6'1"	212	23		

Use Name – Guards	Pos.	Hgt	Wgt	Age	Int	Pts
Bree Cuppoletti	G	5'10"	205	29		
Bill Hughes	G	6'1"	232	24		
Emmett Kriel	G	6'2"	200	23		
Hank Reese	G-C-LB	5'11"	216	28		7
(1 PAT in 1 attempt, 2 FG in 4 attempts)						
Ted Schmitt	G	5'11"	214	22		6
Allie White	G-T	5'11"	212	24		

Weighing in at 150 pounds, little Davey O'Brien learned to throw the ball often while an All-American at Texas Christian University, and Eagle owner Bert Bell gambled that the 5'7" passer would find pro defenses no more difficult to crack than college units. After luring O'Brien into uniform with a $12,000 contract, Bell insured his slight rookie against injury with Lloyds of London. The insurance policy called for a payment of $1,500 to the Eagles for each game O'Brien missed with an injury. Davey never missed a single game, and he lived up to expectations as a passer. He set a league record for yards gained in a season, surpassing Arnie Herber's 1936 mark. His twenty-one completions in one game also set a new standard. But O'Brien's passes could not help the Eagles win more than one game. After a strong 1938 campaign, the Eagles lapsed back into their losing ways again.

PITTSBURGH STEELERS 1-9-1 Johnny Blood, Walt Kiesling

Scores of Each Game		
7	Brooklyn	12
0	CHIC. CARDS	10
0	CHIC. BEARS	32
7	NEW YORK	14
14	Washington	44
14	WASHINGTON	21
14	Cleveland	14
13	Brooklyn	17
7	New York	23
14	Philadelphia	17
24	PHILADELPHIA	12

Use Name	Pos.	Hgt	Wgt	Age	Int	Pts
Ted Grabinski	C-LB	6'2"	200	24		
Joe Maras	C-T-LB	6'1"	202	23		
John Tosi (to BKN)	C-T-G-LB	5'10"	225	24		
Wayland Becker	OE-DE	6'	205	28		
Max Fiske	OE-DB	6'	205	25		
Johnny Blood	BB-DB	6'1"	185	34		
Earl Bartlett	HB-DB	6'	200			
Clarence Tommerson	HB-DB	6'2"	195	24		
Joe Williams	HB-DB	5'9"	178	25		

Use Name – Tackles	Pos.	Hgt	Wgt	Age	Int	Pts
Don Campbell	T	6'	215	22		
Ted Doyle	T-G	6'2"	220	25		
Ed Karpowich	T	6'4"	222	26		

Use Name – Guards	Pos.	Hgt	Wgt	Age	Int	Pts
Vinnie Farrar	G-BB-LB	6'	200	26		
Byron Gentry	G	5'11"	230	25		
George Kakasic	G	5'10"	205	27		
Lou Midler	G-T	6'1"	225	24		
Stan Pavkov	G	6'1"	215	24		
John Perko	G	6'1"	205	23		

Voluntarily retired – Whizzer White

An opening-day loss to Brooklyn was bad enough, but when the lowly Cardinals shut the Pirates out 10-0 and the Bears then shellacked them 32-0, Pittsburgh coach Johnny Blood packed his bags and quit. Two and a half years of losing was all the old star could take.

The coaching reigns fell to big Walt Kiesling, Blood's assistant for two years. Kiesling worked the players hard, a complete turnaround from Blood's country-club atmosphere, but the discipline did not stop the club from losing. With two games remaining, the Pirates started a home-and-away series with the Eagles in search of their first win, as was Philadelphia. The first game went to the Eagles 17-14, but Kiesling's men came back to win the curtain-dropper in Pittsburgh to end the season on the only positive note of the year.

Use Name – Backs & Ends	Pos.	Age	Hgt	Wgt	Pts	Int	RUSHING No.	Yds	Avg	TD	PASSING Att	Comp	%	Yds	Yd/Att	TD	Int–%	RK	RECEIVING No.	Yds	Avg	TD	PUNTING No.	Avg	KICKING Pat	Att	%	FG	Att	%	PUNT RETURNS No.	Yds	Avg	TD	KICKOFF RETURNS No.	Yds	Avg	TD
NEW YORK GIANTS																																						
Ed Danowski	QB-DB	27	6'1"	198			25	21	0.8	0	101	42	42	437	4.3	3	6–6	10					29	38														
Len Barnum	QB-WB-DB	26	6'	200	24		91	237	2.6	2	27	8	30	141	5.2	3	1–4		3	50	17	0	29	41	3	3	100	3	7	43								
Eddie Miller	QB-DB	22	5'10"	165	6		30	99	3.3	1	23	13	57	195	8.5	2	2–9						5	37														
Tuffy Leemans	FB-DB	26	6'	195	30		128	429	3.4	3	26	12	46	198	7.6	0	2–8		8	185	23	2																
Hank Soar	FB-DB	25	6'2"	210	20		66	158	2.4	2									12	134	11	0			2	2	100	0	1	0								
Kink Richards	FB-DB	28	5'11"	195	6		40	117	2.9	1									2	8	4	0	1	39														
Bull Karcis	FB-LB	30	5'9"	225			31	93	3.0	0																												
Al Owen	FB-BB-DB-LB	26	6'	188	6		8	11	1.4	0									2	45	23	1																
Ken Strong	FB	33	6'	200	19		1	1	1.0	0													5	55	7	7	100	4	8	50								
Ward Cuff	WB-DB	26	6'1"	185	39		23	102	4.4	0									10	83	8	2			6	6	100	7	16	44								
Dale Burnett	WB-DB	30	6'1"	186			1	3	3.0	0									8	86	11	0																
Leland Shaffer	BB-DB	27	6'2"	205			3	6	2.0	0									2	8	4	0																
Nello Falaschi	BB-LB	25	6'	195			1	4	4.0	0									4	27	7	0																
Jim Poole	OE-DE	23	6'3"	215															7	99	14	0																
Chuck Gelatka	OE-DB	26	6'1"	180															6	71	12	0																
Jim Lee Howell	OE-DE	24	6'6"	200	12														5	112	22	2																
Jiggs Kline	OE-DE	25	6'1"	195	6														4	44	11	1																
Will Walls	OE-DE	24	6'4"	212															2	19	10	0																
WASHINGTON REDSKINS																																						
Frankie Filchock	TB-DB	22	5'11"	190	6		103	413	4.0	1	89	55	62	1094	12.3	11	7–8	1																				
Sammy Baugh	TB-DB	25	6'2"	182			14	46	3.3	0	96	53	55	518	5.4	6	9–9	9					26	38.4														
Jimmy German	TB-DB	22	6'	180	12		20	58	2.9	2	12	6	50	97	8.1	1	2–17																					
Andy Farkas	FB-DB	23	5'10"	190	68		139	547	3.9	5									16	437	27	5			2	3	67	0	1	0								1
Wilbur Moore	FB-DB	23	5'11"	190			27	100	3.7	0									1	2	2	0																
Don Irwin	FB-WB-DB	26	6'1"	196	6		10	63	6.3	1									1	8	8	0																
Jim Meade	FB-DB	25	6'1"	195			13	34	2.6	0									1	1	1	0	8	37														
Dick Todd	WB-FB-DB	24	5'11"	170	38		57	266	4.7	2	4	3	75	86	21.5	0	0–0		19	230	12	3	5	32	2	3	67							1				
Jimmy Johnston	WB-DB	22	6'1"	190	7		7	47	6.7	0									11	111	10	1	8	39	1	1	100											
Ed Justice	WB-DB	26	6'1"	200	18		5	56	11.2	1									7	124	18	1																
Boyd Morgan	WB-DB	24	6'	196			1	0	0.0	0									1	4	4	0																
Ernie Pinckert	BB-LB	31	6'	198			5	17	3.4	0																												
Max Krause	BB-LB	30	5'10"	202			3	23	7.7	0																												
John Spirida	BB-OE-DE	23	6'	195			2	5	2.5	0									2	95	48	0	10	39														
Jay Turner	BB-LB	25	5'10"	205			2	1	0.5	0									2	15	8	0	1	33														
Wayne Millner	OE-DE	28	6'1"	190	24		4	12	3.0	0									19	294	15	4																
Charley Malone	OE-DE	29	6'4"	210	18														18	274	15	3			0	1	0											
Bob Masterson	OE-DE	24	6'1"	200	15														10	114	11	1			6	8	75	1	6	17								
Bob McChesney	OE-DE	27	6'2"	190	6		1	5	5.0	1									9	86	10	0																
Bo Russell	T	23	6'1"	218	24																				15	16	94	1	6	17								
BROOKLYN DODGERS																																						
Ace Parker	TB-DB	27	6'	168	33		104	271	2.6	5	157	72	46	977	6.2	4	13–8	8	1	5	5	0	40	42	0	1	0	1	5	20								
Ray Carnelly	TB-HB-DB	22	6'2"	187			15	64	4.3	0	14	3	21	35	2.5	0	3–21		1	5	5	0						0	1	0								
Bill Leckorby	TB-DB	21	6'1"	185			4	–1	–0.2	0	1	0	0	0	0.0	0	0–0																					
Pug Manders	FB-BB-DB-LB	26	6'	210	12		114	482	4.2	2									3	22	7	0																
Sam Francis (from PIT)	FB-HB-DB	24	6'	210	6		76	230	3.0	1									2	5	3	0	13	38														
Ace Gutowsky	FB-DB	29	5'11"	205			58	202	3.5	0	1	1	100	5	5.0	0	0–0																					
Len Janiak	FB-BB-DB	23	6'1"	195			18	56	3.1	0									2	6	3	0																
Ralph Kercheval	HB-DB	28	6'1"	193	21		34	99	2.9	0	1	1	100	7	7.0	0	0–0		3	8	3	0	28	39	3	3	100	6	13	46								
Beattie Feathers	HB-DB	30	5'10"	185			8	21	2.6	0									1	12	12	0																
Wendell Butcher	BB-LB	25	6'1"	200			2	2	1.0	0									9	73	8	0																
Stan Kosel	BB-LB	22	5'11"	190	6		2	6	3.0	0									2	40	20	1																
Bill Reissig	BB-LB-DE	24	6'	195	3																				0	1	0	1	1	100								
Perry Schwartz	OE-DE	24	6'2"	200	18														33	550	17	3																
Waddy Young	OE-DE	23	6'3"	205															8	100	13	0																
Harold Hill	OE-DE	23	6'1"	200															7	150	21	0																
Herman Hodges	OE-DE	24	6'1"	195	6														4	45	11	0																
PHILADELPHIA EAGLES																																						
Davey O'Brien	QB-DB	22	5'7"	150	6		108	–14	–0.1	1	201	99	49	1324	6.6	6	17–8	6					3	40	0	1	0 (Pass)											
Emmett Mortell	QB-DB	25	6'1"	178			37	88	2.4	0	41	12	29	134	3.3	1	0–0						23	43														
Dave Smukler	FB-LB	25	6'1"	224			45	218	4.8	0	20	7	35	56	2.8	0	4–20						10	48														
Franny Murray	HB-DB	23	6'	200	26		47	137	2.9	1									13	144	11	1	33	37	8	12	67	2	4	50								
Joe Bukant	FB-HB-LB	23	6'	223	18		59	136	2.3	3	1	0	0	0	0.0	0	0–0						1	54														
Dick Riffle	HB-QB-DB	24	6'1"	197			18	61	3.4	0	4	1	25	2	0.5	0	1–25		6	57	10	0	17	40														
Jay Arnold	HB-DB	25	6'1"	207	12		8	1	0.1	1									13	207	16	1	1	42														
Chuck Newton	HB-FB-DB	22	6'	205	6		1	0	0.0	0									9	123	14	1																
Woody Dow	FB-LB	22	6'	195			1	–7	–7.0	0									5	58	12	0																
Red Ramsey	OE-DE	24	6'	192	6														31	359	12	1																
Joe Carter	OE-DE	29	6'1"	200	12		1	4	4.0	0									24	292	12	2																
Bill Hewitt	OE-DE	29	5'9"	190	6		1	1	1.0	0									15	243	16	1																
Elmer Kolberg	OE-DB	23	6'4"	200															3	33	11	0																
PITTSBURGH STEELERS																																						
Hugh McCullough	TB-DB	23	6'	185	6		60	96	1.6	1	100	32	32	443	4.4	2	12–12	12	4	57	14	0	31	33														
Coley McDonough (from CHIC)	TB-DB	24	6'1"	195	6		27	75	2.8	0	47	17	36	365	7.8	2	8–17		1	3	3	1	10	37														
Lou Tomasetti	TB-HB-DB	23	6'	188	6		49	86	1.8	1	47	13	28	140	3.0	1	7–15		4	22	6	0	3	37														
Ernie Wheeler (to CHIC)	TB-DB	24	6'1"	180			17	0	0.0	0	17	5	29	94	5.5	1	7–41						10	46														
Boyd Brumbaugh (from BKN)	FB-TB-DB	24	5'11"	195	18		111	343	3.1	2	10	3	30	121	12.1	2	1–10		5	95	19	1	1	34														
Swede Johnston	FB-DB	29	5'10"	195	12		59	220	3.7	2													10	47														
Carl Littlefield	FB-DB	23	6'	200			39	141	3.6	0									1	18	18	0																
Bob Masters	HB-TB-DB	28	5'11"	195			9	39	4.3	0	3	1	33	9	3.0	0	1–33		2	12	6	0																
Bill Davidson	HB-TB-DB	24	6'	180			21	27	1.3	0	7	1	14	8	1.1	0	0–0		6	27	5	0																
Dick Nardi (to BKN)	HB-TB-DB	23	5'10"	200			10	15	1.5	0	5	2	40	12	2.4	0	1–20		1	3	3	0	1	19														
Karl Schuelke	FB-DB		5'10"	200			2	2	1.0	0																												
Rink Bond	BB-LB	25	5'10"	200			1	4	4.0	0																												
Jack Lee	BB-LB	22	5'10"	205			1	–11	–11.0	0	1	0	0	0	0.0	0	0–0						1	44														
Sam Boyd	OE-DE	25	6'1"	190	12														21	423	20	2																
Bill Sortet	OE-DE	27	6'1"	185	6														16	196	12	1																
George Platukas	OE-DE	24	6'	186	18														7	170	24	3																
Bernie Scherer	OE-DE	26	6'1"	195															2	49	25	0																
Frank Souchak	OE-DE	24	6'	205															1	12	12	0																
Armand Niccolai	T-G	27	6'2"	230	24																				15	15	100	3	8	38								

TEAM TOTALS — OFFENSE

TEAM TOTALS	FIRST DOWNS	RUSHING: No.	Yards	Avg.	TD	PASSING: Att.	Comp.	Comp. Pct.	Yards	Yds. Att.	Yds. Comp.	TD	Int.	Pct. Int.	FUMBLES: Number	PENALTY: Yards	POINTS: Total	TD	PAT	FG Att.	FG	Saf
NEW YORK	109	448	1281	2.9	9	177	75	42.4	971	5.5	13.0	8	11	6.2	21	267	168	18	18	32	14	0
WASHINGTON	125	413	1693	4.1	13	201	117	58.2	1795	8.9	15.3	18	18	9.0	33	332	242	35	26	13	2	0
BROOKLYN	113	400	1332	3.3	7	176	77	43.8	1024	5.8	13.3	4	16	9.1	21	210	108	12	10	20	8	1
PHILADELPHIA	97	332	626	1.9	6	267	119	44.6	1516	5.7	12.7	7	22	8.2	28	237	105	14	9	8	4	0
PITTSBURGH	113	432	1137	2.6	7	221	70	31.7	1084	4.9	15.5	8	34	15.4	25	279	114	15	15	8	3	0

DEFENSE

Total Yards	Pass Att.	Pass Comp.	Comp. Pct.	Int.	Points	TEAM TOTALS
2482	222	89	40.1	35	85	NEW YORK
2116	243	90	37.0	24	94	WASHINGTON
3113	195	92	47.2	22	219	BROOKLYN
2954	210	97	46.2	17	200	PHILADELPHIA
3100	193	88	45.6	11	216	PITTSBURGH

GREEN BAY PACKERS 9-2-0 Curly Lambeau

Scores of Each Game		
14	CHIC. CARDS	10
21	CHIC. BEARS	16
24	CLEVELAND	27
27	CHIC. CARDS	20
26	DETROIT	7
24	WASHINGTON	14
27	Chic. Bears	30
23	Philadelphia	16
28	Brooklyn	0
7	Cleveland	6
12	Detroit	7

Use Name	Pos.	Hgt	Wgt	Age	Int	Pts
Charley Brock	C-LB	6'2"	193	23		6
Tom Greenfield	C-LB	6'4"	200	21		6
Bud Svendsen	C-LB	6'1"	183	24		6
Al Moore	DE	6'2"	218	25		
Frank Steen	OE-DE	6'1"	190	23		
Dick Weisgerber	BB-DB	5'10"	202	24		
Voluntarily retired – Champ Seibold						

Use Name – Tackles	Pos.	Hgt	Wgt	Age	Int	Pts
Paul Kell	T	6'2"	217	22		
Wally Kilbourne	T	6'3"	240	23		
Bill Lee	T	6'2"	224	27		
Baby Ray	T	6'6"	238	24		
Charlie Schultz	T	6'3"	228	22		
Ernie Smith	T	6'2"	220	29		3
(3 PAT's in 4 attempts)						

Use Name – Guards	Pos.	Hgt	Wgt	Age	Int	Pts
Jack Brennan	G	6'1"	204	22		
Buckets Goldenberg	G-LB	5'10"	222	28		
Russ Letlow	G	6'	213	25		
Pete Tinsley	G	5'8"	196	26		
Frank Twedell	G	5'11"	220	22		
Gust Zarnas (from BKN)	G	5'10"	222	24		

In the middle of a game against the Lions, Curly Lambeau made a switch which added a few years to Don Hutson's career. Lambeau assigned rookie Larry Craig, a 205-pound bruiser, to play blocking back on offense and end on defense, freeing Hutson to use his speed at safety. His new secondary post spared Hutson the pounding of defensive line play and left him more energy for his pass-catching on offense. Passes from Cecil Isbell and Arnie Herber kept Hutson busy, while the running corps gained enough yards to make the Packers the top offensive club in the league. The foundation for this attack was a solid line featuring guards Russ Letlow and Buckets Goldenberg, all of which combined to give Green Bay a return trip to the championship game.

CHICAGO BEARS 8-3-0 George Halas

Scores of Each Game		
30	CLEVELAND	21
16	Green Bay	21
32	Pittsburgh	0
35	Cleveland	21
44	CHIC. CARDS	7
13	New York	16
0	DETROIT	10
30	GREEN BAY	27
23	Detroit	13
27	PHILADELPHIA	14
48	Chic. Cards	7

Use Name	Pos.	Hgt	Wgt	Age	Int	Pts
Frank Bausch	C-LB	6'2"	225	31		
Chet Chesney	C-LB	6'2"	227	22		
Frank Sullivan	C-LB	6'3"	205	27		
Chuck Apolskis	OE-DE	6'2"	207	22		
Charlie Heileman	OE-DE	6'2"	197	23		
Anton Stofa	QB-DB	6'	195	21		

Use Name – Tackles	Pos.	Hgt	Wgt	Age	Int	Pts
Joe Stydahar	T	6'4"	230	27		4
(1 reception for 9 yds., 4 PAT's in 6 attempts)						
Russ Thompson	T	6'5"	250	27		
John Torrance	T	6'3"	285	25		
Milt Trost	T	6'1"	208	26		

Use Name – Guards	Pos.	Hgt	Wgt	Age	Int	Pts
Dick Bassi	G	5'11"	210	24		
Ray Bray	G	6'	224	22		
Aldo Forte	G-T	6'	212	21		
Danny Fortmann	G-LB	6'	210	23		
George Musso	G	6'2"	270	29		

A single-wing tailback at Columbia University, rookie Sid Luckman had to start from scratch in learning to be a T-quarterback, and at first he was tripping over his own feet before getting the hang of handing off and faking. George Halas believed in the intelligent young man, though, and broke him in gradually at halfback while turning him over to veterans Carl Brumbaugh and Bernie Masterson for quarterback training. By the season's end, Luckman was settled in his new job, and the Bears had a new leader at quarterback. The club also came up with a new fullback in Bill Osmanski, a quick-starting rookie who played with his spikes filed sharp. The leading rusher in the league, Osmanski, joined veteran linemen Joe Stydahar and Danny Fortmann on the All-Pro team.

DETROIT LIONS 6-5-0 Gus Henderson

Scores of Each Game		
21	CHIC. CARDS	13
27	BROOKLYN	7
17	Chic. Cards	3
15	CLEVELAND	7
7	Green Bay	26
10	Chic. Bears	0
18	NEW YORK	14
13	CHIC. BEARS	23
3	Cleveland	14
7	Washington	31
7	GREEN BAY	12

Use Name	Pos.	Hgt	Wgt	Age	Int	Pts
Tony Calvelli	C-G-LB	5'10"	190	23		
Dixie Stokes	C-LB	6'	205	26		
Tony Tonelli	C-G-LB	6'	210	22		
John Wiatrak	C-LB	6'	220	26		
Alex Wojciechowicz	C-LB	5'11"	200	24		
Connie Mack Berry	OE-DE	6'3"	200	23		
Hal Brill	TB-DB	5'10"	175	25		
Elvin Hutchinson	WB-DB	5'11"	195	26		

Use Name – Tackles	Pos.	Hgt	Wgt	Age	Int	Pts
Ray George	T	6'	230	23		
Jack Johnson	T	6'4"	220	29		
Steve Maronic	T	6'	225	23		
Bill Rogers	T	5'11"	240	26		

Use Name – Guards	Pos.	Hgt	Wgt	Age	Int	Pts
Bill Feldhaus	G-LB	6'	225	27		
Phil Martinovich	G	5'10"	220	24		9
(3 field goals in 6 attempts)						
Bill Radovich	G	5'10"	225	24		
Cal Thomas	G	6'2"	210	24		
John Wiethe	G-LB	6'	195	22		
(2 receptions for 5 yds.)						

With a new broom sweeping away many of the stars of the past decade, the Lions took the field a vastly different outfit from last year. Tailback Dutch Clark left Detroit to be head coach at Cleveland, tackle George Christensen became assistant coach at Brooklyn, Ace Gutowsky was sold to the Dodgers, and Ernie Caddel retired. For better or worse, new coach Gus Henderson had to go with a patchwork squad in the midst of rebuilding. At first, Henderson looked like a genius, as the Lions won their first four games and six of their first seven. But then the bottom fell out and the league-leading Lions lost their final four games to sink back into the mire in the Western Division.

CLEVELAND RAMS 5-5-1 Dutch Clark

Scores of Each Game		
21	Chic. Bears	30
12	Brooklyn	23
27	Green Bay	24
21	CHIC. BEARS	35
7	Detroit	15
24	Chic. Cards	0
14	PITTSBURGH	14
14	CHIC. CARDS	0
14	DETROIT	3
6	GREEN BAY	7
35	PHILADELPHIA at Colorado Springs	13

Use Name	Pos.	Hgt	Wgt	Age	Int	Pts
Chuck Cherundolo	C-LB	6'1"	217	23		
Bill Conkright	C-LB	6'1"	204	25		
Gerry Dowd	C-LB	6'	210	23		6
Mike Perry	BB-LB	5'11"	197	22		

Use Name – Tackles	Pos.	Hgt	Wgt	Age	Int	Pts
Chet Adams	T	6'3"	227	23		5
(5 PAT's in 5 attempts)						
Ben Friend	T	6'5"	248	22		
Art Lewis	T-G	6'3"	230	26		
Ted Livingston	T-G	6'3"	222	25		
Ralph Neihaus	T	6'4"	220			
Nate Schenker	T	6'2"	220	21		

Use Name – Guards	Pos.	Hgt	Wgt	Age	Int	Pts
Alex Atty	G	5'8"	216	22		
Lew Bostick	G	6'	197	22		2
(1 punt for 55 yds., 2 PAT's in 2 attempts)						
Tom Hupke	G	5'10"	190	28		
Riley Matheson	G-LB	6'2"	203	24		
Barney McGarry	G-LB	6'1"	205	21		
Phil Ragazzo	G-T	6'	210	24		

With Dutch Clark taking over as non-playing head coach, the Rams started the year with a rookie coach and a very inexperienced squad. Despite an upset of Green Bay, the early games chiefly gave the young Rams a chance to get used to each other while losing. But then, suddenly, in mid-season, the team jelled. The Rams twice shut out the Cardinals and upset the fading Lions before a record 25,000 home-town fans. After a close loss to the Packers, the Rams evened their final record by beating the Eagles. Rookie Parker Hall, known as "Bullet", was at center stage during the resurgence, topping all passers in the league statistics and winning the league MVP Award, and Jim Benton, Vic Spadaccini, Johnny Drake, and Chet Adams all blossomed during the second half of the season as the team rolled up 107 points to their opponents' 37.

CHICAGO CARDINALS 1-10-0 Ernie Nevers

Scores of Each Game		
13	Detroit	21
10	Green Bay	14
10	Pittsburgh	0
3	DETROIT	17
20	Green Bay	27
7	Chic. Bears	44
0	CLEVELAND	24
0	Cleveland	14
7	New York	17
7	Washington	28
7	CHIC. BEARS	48

Use Name	Pos.	Hgt	Wgt	Age	Int	Pts
Henry Adams	C-LB	6'1"	190	23		
Ki Aldrich	C-LB	6'	195	23		
Len Dugan (to PIT)	C-LB	6'	220	27		
Charlie Gainor	DE		190			
Don Cosner	WB-DB	6'2"	200	22		
Jim Neill	WB-DB	6'1"	180	24		
Holdout – Gaynell Tinsley						

Use Name – Tackles	Pos.	Hgt	Wgt	Age	Int	Pts
Al Babartsky	T	6'	220	24		6
Conway Baker	T	5'11"	225	28		
Jim Bilbo	T	6'	195			
Tony Blazine	T	6'	230	27		
Elwyn Dunstan (to CLE)	T	6'3"	235	24		
(3 rushing attempts for 2 yds)						
Frank Zelencik	T	6'1"	220	24		

Use Name – Guards	Pos.	Hgt	Wgt	Age	Int	Pts
Ross Carter	G-C-LB	6'	195	25		
Frank Huffman	G-LB	6'2"	205	24		
Mike Kochel	G-LB	5'11"	195	23		
Regis Monahan	G	5'10"	215	30		4
(1 PAT in 1 attempt, 1 FG in 1 attempt)						
Glynn Rogers	G		220			
Andy Sabados	G	5'11"	208	22		
Jim Thomas	G	5'11"	200	22		
Bill Volok	G	6'2"	215	29		

To try and get the Cardinals back into a winning habit, owner Charles Bidwill hired all-time great Ernie Nevers to coach the club. Nevers had played with a never-say-die fervor, but that attitude didn't rub off on his charges. Right from training camp, the Cards did not expect to do much better than the two wins they picked up in 1938. As it turned out, they won only a single contest. The disorganized Cardinals suffered a mortal loss when end Gaynell Tinsley, the best player on the team, held out for more money and then retired to coach a high-school team. His absence killed any passing attack the team had.

Never's one consolation for the year came in the appearance of two blue-chip rookies, 195-pound center Ki Aldrich and All-American back Marshall Goldberg. A fine defensive back as well as a dangerous runner, Goldberg would last with the Cardinals into their winning days in the late 1940s.

Use Name – Backs & Ends	Pos.	Age	Hgt	Wgt	Pts	Int	Rushing No.	Rushing Yds	Rushing Avg	Rushing TD	Passing Att	Passing Comp	Passing %	Passing Yds	Passing Yd/Att	Passing TD	Passing Int–%	Passing RK	Receiving No.	Receiving Yds	Receiving Avg	Receiving TD	Punting No.	Punting Avg	Kicking Pat	Kicking Att	Kicking %	Kicking FG	Kicking Att	Kicking %	Punt Returns No.	Punt Returns Yds	Punt Returns Avg	Punt Returns TD	Kickoff Returns No.	Kickoff Returns Yds	Kickoff Returns Avg	Kickoff Returns TD
GREEN BAY PACKERS																																						
Arnie Herber	TB-DB	29	5'11"	200	6		18	−11	−0.6	1	139	57	41	1107	8.0	8	9– 6	4	1	18	18	0	24	40														
Cecil Isbell	TB-HB-DB	24	6'1"	190	15		132	407	3.1	2	103	43	42	749	7.3	6	5– 5	3	9	71	18	0	4	31	3	3	100											
Jim Lawrence (from CHIC,WB-DB)	TB-DB	25	5'11"	190			7	6	0.9	0	4	1	25	15	3.8	0	1–25		3	41	14	0	3	38														
Clarke Hinkle	FB-LB	29	5'11"	195	35		135	381	2.8	5									4	70	18	0	43	41	2	3	67	1	10	10								
Ed Jankowski	FB-LB	26	5'9"	202	12		75	278	3.7	2									1	5	5	0																
Frank Balasz	FB-LB	21	6'2"	215			11	41	3.7	0									1	11	11	0	1	35														
Andy Uram	HB-DB	24	5'10"	187	18		52	272	5.2	1	1	0	0	0	0.0	0	0– 0		7	93	13	2																
Joe Laws	HB-DB	28	5'9"	184	24		55	162	2.9	2	1	0	0	0	0.0	0	0– 0		11	177	16	1																
Tuffy Thompson	HB-DB	24	5'11"	170			6	9	1.5	0									1	1	1	0												1				
Larry Buhler	HB-BB-DB	22	6'2"	204			5	3	0.6	0																												
Larry Craig	BB-DB-DE	23	6'1"	205			2	6	3.0	0									3	44	15	0																
Hank Bruder	BB-DB	31	6'	202	6														5	65	16	1																
Don Hutson	OE-DE-DB	26	6'1"	185	38		5	26	5.2	0									34	846	25	6			2	2	100											
Moose Mulleneaux	OE-DE	22	6'3"	206	6														12	218	18	1																
Milt Gantenbein	OE-DE	29	6'	195	6														7	127	18	1																
Harry Jacunski	OE-DE	23	6'2"	195	12														5	104	21	2																
Tiny Engebretsen	G	29	6'1"	245	30																				18	19	95	4	8	50								
CHICAGO BEARS																																						
Bernie Masterson	QB-DB	28	6'3"	195	12		21	−31	−1.5	2	113	44	39	914	8.1	8	9– 8	5	2	37	19	0			0	1	0(Pass)											
Sid Luckman	QB-HB-DB	22	6'	193	6		24	42	1.8	0	51	23	45	636	12.5	5	4– 8						27	44														
Billy Patterson	QB-HB-DB	20	5'10"	167	1		14	34	2.4	0	38	14	37	227	6.0	3	4–11						8	38	1	1	100											
Bob Snyder	QB-DB	26	6'	205	4		15	56	3.7	0	12	5	42	135	11.3	0	1– 8						7	42	1	2	50	1	1	100								
Solly Sherman	QB-DB	21	6'1"	190	6		3	−5	−1.7	0	4	2	50	43	10.8	0	0– 0		1	42	42	0																
Bill Osmanski	FB-LB	22	5'11"	195	48		121	699	5.8	7									3	65	22	1																
Joe Maniaci	FB-LB	25	6'1"	210	37		77	544	7.1	4	2	1	50	10	5.0	0	0– 0								4	8	50	1	2	50								
Ray Nolting	HB-DB	25	5'11"	185	24		50	216	4.3	2									6	87	15	1	12	39														
Bob Swisher	HB-DB	25	5'11"	165	18		30	192	6.4	2									7	228	33	1	3	31														
Gary Famiglietti	FB-LB	24	6'	214	1		33	128	3.9	0									3	72	24	0			1	1	100											
Bob MacLeod	HB-DB	22	6'	190	30		17	88	5.2	1									10	231	23	3																
Jack Manders	HB-DB	30	6'	200	50		25	63	2.5	3									1	29	29	1			17	20	85	3	7	43								
Dick Schweidler	HB-DB	24	6'	185			5	15	3.0	0									2	43	22	0																
Dick Plasman	OE-DE	25	6'3"	210	21						1	0	0	0	0.0	0	0– 0		19	403	21	3			3	3	100	0	1	0								
Les McDonald	OE-DE	24	6'4"	200	18		1	−2	−2.0	0									16	261	16	3																
Eggs Manske	OE-DE	26	6'	185	12														10	321	32	2																
George Wilson	OE-DE	25	6'1"	190															5	66	13	0																
John Siegal	OE-DE	21	6'1"	196	6														3	71	24	1																
DETROIT LIONS																																						
Dwight Sloan	TB-DB	24	5'10"	180	24		79	225	2.8	4	107	45	42	658	6.1	2	3– 3	7					1	43														
Darrell Tully	TB-DB	22	6'1"	200	6		31	50	1.6	1	69	20	29	356	5.2	2	13–19	13																				
Johnny Pingel	TB-DB	23	6'	180	6		72	301	4.2	1	48	27	56	343	7.1	3	4– 8						32	43														
Bill Shepherd	FB-LB	27	5'9"	205	18		85	420	4.9	2	1	0	0	0	0.0	0	0– 0		14	143	10	1	23	37														
Howie Weiss	FB-LB	22	6'	210			37	150	4.1	0									4	25	6	0																
Lloyd Cardwell	WB-DB	26	6'2"	200	18		29	141	4.9	1									13	250	19	2																
Jim McDonald	WB-FB-DB	23	6'1"	195			25	80	3.2	0									5	71	14	0																
Rip Ryan	WB-DB	24	6'2"	195	12		8	41	5.1	1									7	46	7	1	3	37														
Gordon Gore	WB-DB	26	6'	215			8	7	0.9	0	1	0	0	0	0.0	0	0– 0		1	20	20	0																
Fred Vanzo	BB-LB	23	6'1"	230			5	46	9.2	0									4	110	28	0																
Paul Szakash	BB-DB	26	6'	215			3	11	3.7	0															0	1	0											
Monk Moscrip	OE-DE	25	6'	195	15		1	8	8.0	0									14	176	13	0			9	12	75	0	1	0								
Chuck Hanneman	OE-DE	24	6'	212	29														12	257	21	2	1	31	5	5	100	4	5	80								
Bill Moore	OE-DE	27	6'1"	195	6		1	7	7.0	0									6	82	14	1																
Jim Austin	OE-DE	26	6'2"	200															5	102	20	0																
Ray Hamilton	OE-DE	23	6'4"	215															3	53	18	0																
Dave Diehl	OE-DE	20	6'	190															1	12	12	0																
Ray Clemons	G	26	6'	215															1	5	5	0	15	43														
CLEVELAND RAMS																																						
Parker Hall	TB-DB	22	6'	205	12		120	458	3.8	2	208	106	51	1227	5.9	9	13– 6	2	1	−16	−16	0	58	41														
Marty Slovak	TB-DB	22	5'9"	176			42	135	3.2	0	27	13	48	97	3.6	2	5–19						1	15														
Kelly Moan	TB-DB	26	6'	193	1		2	−15	−7.5	0	9	3	33	77	8.6	1	2–22						1	30	1	1	100											
Bronko Smilanich	TB-DB	23	5'11"	180			1	−3	−3.0	0	2	1	50	11	5.5	0	0– 0																					
Johnny Drake	FB-DB-LB	23	6'1"	214	54		118	453	3.8	9									5	53	11	0																
Gaylon Smith	FB-WB-DB	23	5'11"	205	12		58	98	1.7	2	5	4	80	3	0.6	0	0– 0		3	57	19	0																
Corby Davis	FB-LB	24	5'11"	214	13		13	15	1.2	1									3	49	16	0	10	39	4	4	100	1	2	50								
Bill Lazetich	WB-DB	22	6'	200	6		6	23	3.8	0									8	44	6	1																
Doug Russell (from CHIC)	WB-DB	27	6'	190	6		9	21	2.3	0	1	0	0	0	0.0	0	0– 0		5	67	13	1	8	41														
Bill McRaven	WB-DB	21	5'11"	170			7	29	4.1	0									2	14	7	0																
Vic Spadaccini	BB-DB	23	6'	225	18														32	292	9	1			12	16	75											
Mike Rodak	BB-LB-DE	22	5'10"	195			1	−1	−1.0	0	1	0	0	0	0.0	0	1–100		4	54	14	0																
Lou Barle	BB-LB	23	6'1"	200															2	16	8	0																
Jim Benton	OE-DE	22	6'3"	197	48		7	19	2.7	0									27	388	14	7																
Maury Patt	OE-DE	25	6'2"	202			6	20	3.3	0									15	165	11	0																
Johnny Wilson	OE-DE	23	6'3"	200	6														8	108	14	1																
Paul McDonough	OE-DE	22	6'4"	218	6														8	73	9	1																
Joel Hitt	OE-DE	21	6'1"	180			1	3	3.0	0									4	51	13	0																
CHICAGO CARDINALS																																						
John Robbins	TB-DB	23	6'2"	180			38	97	2.6	0	85	36	42	499	5.9	4	10–12	11	2	12	6	0	2	41														
Frank Patrick	TB-DB	23	5'11"	190	7		30	84	2.8	1	79	22	28	291	3.7	1	13–16	14					16	40	1	1	100											
Bert Johnson (from CHIB,FB-LB)	TB-DB	27	6'	215			38	95	2.5	0	40	14	35	208	5.2	0	5–12						14	37														
Marshall Goldberg	FB-TB-DB	21	5'11"	184	18		56	152	2.7	2	7	1	14	4	0.6	0	1–14		5	90	18	1																
Sam Agee	FB-DB	25	6'1"	218	6		45	137	3.1	1	3	0	0	0	0.0	0	0– 0		1	6	6	0																
Ed Cherry (to PIT)	FB-DB	24	6'	210			10	30	3.0	0																												
Milt Popovich	WB-FB-DB	22	5'11"	190	6		26	78	3.0	0	6	5	83	52	8.7	0	0– 0		2	10	5	0	27	33														
Rock Reed	WB-DB	24	5'8"	175			5	−6	−1.2	0	1	1	100	2	2.0	0	0– 0		3	67	22	0																
George Faust	BB-LB	22	6'1"	205	1		22	71	3.2	0	5	0	0	0	0.0	0	1–20		4	85	21	0	25	44	1	1	100	1	1	0								
Ev Fisher	BB-OE-LB-DE	24	5'11"	205			18	63	3.5	0									6	62	10	0																
Buddy Parker	BB-LB	25	6'	196			12	37	3.1	0									5	33	7	0																
Earl Crowder	BB-LB	23	6'	198			6	−5	−0.8	0	7	2	29	6	0.9	0	0– 0		2	59	30	0																
Bill Smith	OE-DB	27	6'1"	198	36		1	3	3.0	0									21	387	18	4	1	36	6	8	75	2	8	25								
Joel Mason	OE-DB	26	6'	190															18	188	10	0																
Versil Deskin	OE-DE	26	6'	200															4	84	21	0																
John Klump	OE-DE	22	6'3"	195															4	21	5	0																
Hal Bradley (from WAS)	OE-DE	25	6'4"	205															3	29	10	0																
Keith Birlem (to WAS,WB-DB)	OE-DB	25	5'11"	198															2	17	9	0																

TEAM TOTALS	OFFENSE: First Downs	Rushing: No.	Yards	Avg.	TD	Passing: Att.	Comp.	Comp. Pct.	Yards	Yds. Att.	Yds. Comp.	TD	Int.	Pct. Int.	Fumbles: Number	Penalty: Yards	Points: Total	TD	PAT	FG Att.	FG	Saf	DEFENSE: Total Yards	Pass Att.	Pass Comp.	Comp. Pct.	Int.	Points	TEAM TOTALS
GREEN BAY	149	515	1574	3.1	13	248	101	40.7	1871	7.5	18.5	14	15	6.0	16	259	233	31	28	18	5	2	2770	239	106	44.4	26	153	GREEN BAY
CHICAGO BEARS	148	438	2043	4.7	21	221	89	40.3	1965	8.9	22.1	16	18	8.1	33	416	298	42	31	11	5	0	2604	319	133	41.7	25	157	CHICAGO BEARS
DETROIT	133	384	1487	3.9	10	226	92	40.7	1357	6.0	14.8	7	20	8.8	27	304	145	18	14	12	7	1	2603	217	92	42.4	14	150	DETROIT
CLEVELAND	131	390	1260	3.2	14	253	127	50.2	1415	5.6	11.1	12	21	8.3	28	220	195	28	24	2	1	0	2785	199	78	39.2	23	164	CLEVELAND
CHICAGO CARDS	101	325	835	2.6	4	248	84	33.9	1170	4.7	13.9	5	33	13.9	36	238	84	11	9	10	3	0	2998	201	86	42.8	12	254	CHICAGO BEARS

WASHINGTON REDSKINS 9-2-0 Ray Flaherty

Scores of Each Game		
24	BROOKLYN	17
21	NEW YORK	7
40	Pittsburgh	10
28	CHIC. CARDS	21
34	Philadelphia	17
20	Detroit	14
37	PITTSBURGH	10
14	Brooklyn	16
7	CHIC. BEARS	3
7	New York	21
13	PHILADELPHIA	6

Use Name	Pos.	Hgt	Wgt	Age	Int	Pts
Steve Andrako	C-LB	6'	210	24		
Mickey Parks	C-LB	6'	230	23		
Bob Titchenal	C-LB	6'2"	197	22		
Boyd Morgan	BB-LB	6'	200	25		
Keith Birlem – military service						

Use Name – Tackles	Pos.	Hgt	Wgt	Age	Int	Pts
Jim Barber	T	6'3"	230	28		
Vic Carroll	T-C-LB	6'4"	228	27		
Turk Edwards	T	6'2"	275	32		
Bob Fisher	T	6'2"	220	23		
Bo Russell	T	6'1"	228	24		14
(11 PAT's in 13 attempts, 1 FG in 1 attempt)						
Willie Wilkin	T	6'4"	265	24		
Bill Young	T	6'1"	250	26		

Use Name – Guards	Pos.	Hgt	Wgt	Age	Int	Pts
Dick Farman	G	6'	220	24		
Clyde Shugart	G	6'	226	23		
Steve Slivinski	G	5'10"	215	23		
Clem Stralka	G	5'10"	210	26		

In a late-season meeting between Chicago and Washington, the Bears had the ball on the Redskins' 6-yard line and were trailing 7-3 with time left for one play. Sid Luckman drilled a pass that hit Bill Osmanski in the chest and bounced away, and the entire Bear team screamed that Redskin Frankie Filchock had interfered with Osmanski. The officials didn't see it that way, so the Redskins were winners. But when Washington owner George Marshall commented to the press, "The Bears are front runners, quitters. They're not a second-half team, just a bunch of cry-babies," it gave the Bears something to ponder when they returned in three weeks for the championship game.

Although the Redskins took the Eastern title on a high-octane offense centered around Sammy Baugh's rifle passes and the playing of Dick Todd, Wayne Millner, Jim Barber, Wee Willie Wilkin, and Steve Slivinski, they could not overcome Marshall's words nor the Bears' playing when it came time for the NFL title.

BROOKLYN DODGERS 8-3-0 Jock Sutherland

Scores of Each Game		
17	Washington	24
10	Pittsburgh	3
30	PHILADELPHIA	17
21	PITTSBURGH	0
7	Chic. Bears	16
21	Philadelphia	7
7	NEW YORK	10
16	WASHINGTON	14
29	CLEVELAND	14
14	CHIC. CARDS	9
14	New York	6

Use Name	Pos.	Hgt	Wgt	Age	Int	Pts
Lou Mark	C-LB	6'	195	25		
Bud Svendsen	C-G-LB	6'1"	190	25		
Si Titus	C-LB	6'	195	21		
Sherrill Busby	DE	6'2"	200	22		
Bob Winslow (from DET)	DE	6'2"	205			

Use Name – Tackles	Pos.	Hgt	Wgt	Age	Int	Pts
John Golemgeske	T	6'2"	225	25		
Red Heater	T	6'2"	220	21		
Bruiser Kinard	T	6'1"	210	25		
Frank Kristufek	T	6'	210	24		
Walt Merrill	T	6'2"	220	23		

Use Name – Guards	Pos.	Hgt	Wgt	Age	Int	Pts
Ty Coon	G	6'	215	25		
Mike Gussie	G-LB	6'	204	22		6
(1 reception for 9 yd. touchdown)						
Art Jacher	G	6'1"	202	24		6
(1 reception for 2 yd. touchdown)						
Matt Kober	G					
Steve Petro	G-LB	5'10"	200	25		
Jim Sivell	G	5'9"	215	26		

The hiring of Dr. Jock Sutherland, famous coach at the University of Pittsburgh, started the most successful Dodger season off on the right foot. Sutherland emphasized hard work and team spirit, and the Dodgers responded by chasing the Washington Redskins to the wire in the Eastern Division. With losses only to the Redskins, Bears, and Giants, Brooklyn's final record equaled the Bears' season mark. Centered around league MVP Ace Parker, a lively offense highlighted the Brooklyn revival. Passing, running, and punting with flair, Parker sparked a squad of some highly gifted football talent. Rookie Banks McFadden helped Pug Manders with the ball-carrying, end Perry Schwartz caught passes, blocked, and tackled well enough to win All-Pro honors, and Bruiser Kinard starred in a line which Sutherland had welded together into an effective unit. In all, it was enough of a pleasant change of pace from the recent menu to give Brooklyn fans something to shout about.

NEW YORK GIANTS 6-4-1 Steve Owen

Scores of Each Game		
10	Pittsburgh	10
7	Washington	21
20	Philadelphia	14
17	PHILADELPHIA	7
12	PITTSBURGH	0
21	CHIC. BEARS	37
10	Brooklyn	7
0	CLEVELAND	13
7	GREEN BAY	3
21	WASHINGTON	7
6	BROOKLYN	14

Use Name	Pos.	Hgt	Wgt	Age	Int	Pts
Wen Goldsmith	C-LB	6'	202	22		
Mel Hein	C-LB	6'2"	223	31		
Kayo Lunday	C-G-LB	6'3"	215	27		
Jiggs Kline	DE	6'1"	195	26		
Carl Tomasello	DE	6'	210	23		

Use Name – Tackles	Pos.	Hgt	Wgt	Age	Int	Pts
Frank Cope	T	6'2"	218	24		
Jerry Dennerlein	T	6'2"	245	27		
Gil Duggan	T	6'3"	235	22		
Monk Edwards	T	6'3"	218	20		
Ed McGee	T	6'1"	210	24		
John Mellus	T	6'	223	23		
Ed Widseth	T	6'1"	220	28		

Use Name – Guards	Pos.	Hgt	Wgt	Age	Int	Pts
Pete Cole	G	5'11"	223	24		
Johnny Dell Isola	G-LB	5'11"	200	28		
Ken Moore	G	6'	212	23		
Doug Oldershaw	G-LB-OE-DE	6'	195	25		
Orville Tuttle	G	5'9"	205	27		

Complacency caught up with the Giants, and so did the Washington Redskins. After two years on top of the Eastern Division, the New Yorkers fell off into third place despite a wealth of championship players. Even without the retired Ed Danowski, the offense moved the ball, and the defense was no pushover, but the spark that turns good players into a great team simply wasn't there. The club looked sluggish in an opening-day tie with Pittsburgh, and a loss to Washington the next week threw the Giants into a hole they never climbed out of.

There was nothing wrong with the line; Mel Hein made All-Pro, while guard Doug Oldershaw and tackle John Mellus won second-team honors. Tuffy Leemans, Eddie Miller, Leland Shaffer, and Ward Cuff kept the backfield in good shape. Yet the Giants lost four games and closed the season by bowing to Brooklyn, 14-6, to cast some shadow on the day the team chose to honor Mel Hein.

PITTSBURGH STEELERS 2-7-2 Walt Kiesling

Scores of Each Game		
7	CHIC. CARDS	7
10	NEW YORK	10
10	Detroit	7
3	BROOKLYN	10
10	WASHINGTON	40
0	Brooklyn	21
0	New York	12
3	Green Bay	24
10	Washington	37
7	PHILADELPHIA	3
0	Philadelphia	7

Use Name	Pos.	Hgt	Wgt	Age	Int	Pts
Ted Grabinski	C-G-LB	6'2"	204	25		
Joe Maras	C-T-LB	6'1"	203	24		
John Schmidt	C-LB	6'3"	210			
Frank Sullivan	C-LB	6'3"	220	28		
Sam Boyd	OE-DE	6'1"	185	26		
Rocco Pirro	HB-DB	6'	205	23		
John Yurchey	HB-DB	5'11"	188	22		

Use Name – Tackles	Pos.	Hgt	Wgt	Age	Int	Pts
Don Campbell	T	6'	235	23		
Ted Doyle	T	6'2"	220	26		
Clark Goff	T	6'3"	235	22		
John Woudenberg	T	6'3"	225	22		

Use Name – Guards	Pos.	Hgt	Wgt	Age	Int	Pts
Frank Bykowski	G	6'	205	22		
Carl Nery	G	6'	212	23		
Stan Pavkov	G	6'	208	25		
John Perko	G	6'1"	195	24		
Jack Sanders	G	6'	225	23		

By tying the Cardinals and Giants and beating the Lions, the Pirates stood undefeated after three games. This impossible dream proved to be just that, as the Bucs dropped their next six games to return to the depths of the East. Even with a large recruitment of new players, coach Walt Kiesling simply couldn't keep his battered craft afloat.

Tailback Bill Patterson came over from the Bears but brought no winning magic with him. Rookies Merl Condit and George Kiick carried the ball conscientiously but not spectacularly. Kiesling strung together a respectable defense, but the Pittsburgh offense could not put more than 10 points on the scoreboard in any one game, nor score a touchdown in five of their contests. After the season, owner Art Rooney finally despaired and sold the team. But Rooney's exodus was only temporary, as he would be back on the Pittsburgh pro-football scene before the next season rolled around.

PHILADELPHIA EAGLES 1-10-0 Bert Bell

Scores of Each Game		
20	Green Bay	27
13	Cleveland	21
14	NEW YORK	20
17	Brooklyn	30
7	New York	17
17	WASHINGTON	34
7	BROOKLYN	21
3	Pittsburgh	7
0	DETROIT	21
7	PITTSBURGH	0
6	Washington	13

Use Name	Pos.	Hgt	Wgt	Age	Int	Pts
Chuck Cherundolo	C-LB	6'1"	212	24		
Moose Harper	C-LB	6'4"	230	26		
Ted Schmitt	C-LB	5'11"	220	23		
(1 rush for 6 yds., 1 reception for 8 yds.)						
Woody Dow	DB	6'	195	23		

Use Name – Tackles	Pos.	Hgt	Wgt	Age	Int	Pts
Ray George	T	6'	228	24		
Phil Ragazzo	T	6'	223	25		
Russ Thompson	T	6'5"	250	28		
Milt Trost	T	6'1"	210	27		
Clem Woltman	T	6'1"	212	24		

Use Name – Guards	Pos.	Hgt	Wgt	Age	Int	Pts
Dick Bassi	G	5'11"	215	25		
Jerry Ginney	G	5'11"	217	24		
Bill Hughes	G	6'1"	228	25		
Elbie Schultz	G	6'4"	242	22		

Whatever flying the Eagles did was on the right wing of little Davey O'Brien. Blessed with a fine rookie receiver in Don Looney and cursed with a weak running corps and a porous line, O'Brien kept passing as a means of self-preservation to keep his 150-pound frame from being unduly manhandled by onrushing linemen. While O'Brien set new records for pass attempts and completions for a season, Looney reeled in enough aerials to set a receiving record. With little else besides the passing combination, the Eagles dropped their first nine games before beating the Pirates in a sort of Futility Bowl. The final game of the year, against the Redskins, turned into an aerial circus, with O'Brien pitted against fellow TCU graduate Slingin' Sammy Baugh. In a battle of the arms, little Davey sent a record sixty passes sailing off into the autumn air for thirty-three completions. But as usual, the Eagles lost, and Davey quit football to join the FBI.

Use Name – Backs & Ends	Pos.	Age	Hgt	Wgt	Pts	Int	RUSHING No.	RUSHING Yds	RUSHING Avg	RUSHING TD	PASSING Att	PASSING Comp	PASSING %	PASSING Yds	PASSING Yd/Att	PASSING TD	PASSING Int–%	PASSING RK	RECEIVING No.	RECEIVING Yds	RECEIVING Avg	RECEIVING TD	PUNTING No.	PUNTING Avg	KICKING Pat	KICKING Att	KICKING %	KICKING FG	KICKING Att	KICKING %	PUNT RETURNS No.	PUNT RETURNS Yds	PUNT RETURNS Avg	PUNT RETURNS TD	KICKOFF RETURNS No.	KICKOFF RETURNS Yds	KICKOFF RETURNS Avg	KICKOFF RETURNS TD
WASHINGTON REDSKINS																																						
Sammy Baugh	TB-DB	26	6'2"	183			20	16	0.8	0	177	111	63	1367	7.7	12	10–6	1					35	51.3														
Frankie Filchock	TB-DB	23	5'11"	195	12		50	126	2.5	2	54	28	52	460	8.5	6	9–17																					
Roy Zimmerman	TB-FB-DB	22	6'2"	197			31	127	4.1	0	12	4	33	53	4.4	0	3–25						7	37														
Jimmy Johnston	FB-DB	23	6'1"	195	42		84	256	3.0	3									29	350	12	3	3	40														
Bob Seymour	FB-DB	24	6'2"	195	24		57	170	3.0	4									2	3	2	0																
Wilbur Moore	FB-WB-DB	24	5'11"	190	18		15	89	5.9	2									2	26	13	1																
Andy Farkas	FB-DB	24	5'10"	190			1	0	0.0	0																												
Dick Todd	WB-FB-DB	25	5'11"	165	54		76	408	5.4	4	1	1	100	7	7.0	0	0–0		20	402	20	4	12	36										1				
Jim Meade	WB-DB	26	6'1"	198			48	115	2.4	0									4	39	10	0	9	40														
Ed Justice	WB-DB	27	6'1"	200	12		3	34	11.3	0									15	170	11	2																
Max Krause	BB-LB	31	5'10"	206			4	21	5.3	0																												
Ernie Pinckert	BB-LB	32	6'	205															2	27	14	0																
Bob Hoffman	BB-LB	22	6'1"	200			3	7	2.3	0																												
Ray Hare	BB-WB-LB-DB	22	6'1"	205			1	2	2.0	0																												
Wayne Millner	OE-DE	29	6'1"	190	18		3	31	10.3	0									22	233	11	3																
Charley Malone	OE-DE	30	6'4"	215															20	222	11	0																
Bob Masterson	OE-DE	25	6'1"	210	42		1	0	0.0	0									18	283	16	4			15	17	88	1	2	50								
Bob McChesney	OE-DE	28	6'2"	198	6														9	119	13	1																
Sandy Sanford	OE-DE	24	6'1"	210	3														1	13	13	0			3	4	75	0	2	0								
BROOKLYN DODGERS																																						
Ace Parker	TB-DB	28	6'	168	49	6	89	306	3.4	3	111	49	44	817	7.4	10	7–6	2	3	139	46	2	49	38	19	22	86											
Dick Cassiano	TB-HB-DB	22	5'11"	175	12		35	84	2.4	0	30	9	30	128	4.3	1	2–7		2	67	34	2																
George Cafego	TB-HB-DB	25	5'10"	180			41	109	2.7	0	17	7	41	105	6.2	1	2–12		9	105	12	0	1	18														
Bill Leckonby	TB-DB	22	6'1"	185	12		19	53	2.8	0	13	7	54	74	5.7	0	0–0		1	8	8	1	2	27														
Ralph Kercheval	TB-DB	29	6'1"	185	15		11	19	1.7	0	7	4	57	38	5.4	1	0–0		1	17	17	0	8	46	3	3	100	4	11	36								
Banks McFadden	HB-DB		6'2"	180	18		65	411	6.3	1	8	3	38	103	12.9	1	1–12		9	97	11	2																
Pug Manders	FB-DB	27	6'	212	36		80	311	3.9	5	1	0	0	0	0.0	0	0–0		1	38	38	1																
Sam Francis	FB-DB	25	6'	207	6		44	217	4.9	1													16	45				0	1	0								
Frank Zadworney	HB-DB	23	6'	202			2	5	2.5	0																												
Rhoten Shetley	BB-LB	22	5'11"	200	6		7	30	4.3	0	4	1	25	2	0.5	0	1–25		8	126	16	1																
Ben Kish	BB-LB	23	6'	200															9	124	14	0	3	44														
Wendell Butcher	BB-LB	26	6'1"	200															2	21	11	0																
Perry Schwartz	OE-DE	25	6'2"	200	18														21	370	16	3																
Waddy Young	OE-DE	24	6'3"	205			1	1	1.0	0									7	85	12	0																
Herman Hodges	OE-DE	25	6'1"	195															3	38	13	0																
Bill Bailey	OE-DE	24	6'3"	205															1	12	12	0																
Harold Hill	OE-DE	24	6'1"	200															1	9	9	0																
NEW YORK GIANTS																																						
Eddie Miller	QB-DB	22	5'10"	165	6		65	206	3.2	1	73	35	48	505	6.9	3	7–10	6					19	39														
Kay Eakin	QB-DB	23	6'	183			14	20	1.4	0	43	17	40	199	4.6	0	3–7						11	41														
Len Barnum	QB-FB-DB	27	6'	198	9		48	128	2.7	0	23	9	39	150	6.5	3	2–9		1	15	15	0	39	40	6	7	86	1	4	25								
Grenny Landsdell	QB-DB	22	6'	190			7	9	1.3	0	3	2	67	23	7.7	1	0–0																					
Tuffy Leemans	FB-DB	27	6'	195	6		132	474	3.6	1	31	15	48	159	5.1	2	3–10																					
Walt Nielsen	FB-DB	23	6'3"	220	6		73	269	3.7	1	1	0	0	0	0.0	0	0–0		2	17	9	0	1	42														
Hank Soar	FB-DB	26	6'2"	207	12		80	246	3.1	1									4	36	9	1						0	1	0								
Dom Principe	FB-DB	23	6'	195			11	8	0.7	0																												
Ward Cuff	WB-DB	27	6'1"	185	42		15	86	5.7	1									13	220	17	1			9	9	100	5	8	63								
Leland Shaffer	WB-BB-DB	28	6'2"	202	18		7	20	2.9	1									15	121	8	2																
Nello Falaschi	BB-LB	26	6'	195															2	9	5	0																
Al Owen	BB-LB	27	6'	188			2	10	5.0	0									1	5	5	0																
Jack Hinkle	BB-LB	22	6'	190															3	23	8	0																
John McLaughry	BB-LB	23	6'1"	205															1	–1	–1	0																
Jim Lee Howell	OE-DE	25	6'6"	205	12														14	255	18	2																
Jim Poole	OE-DE	24	6'3"	217	18														10	156	16	3																
Chuck Gelatka	OE-DB	27	6'1"	182															6	56	9	0																
Max Harrison	OE-DE	24	6'1"	208															4	96	24	0																
Bolo Perdue	OE-DE	23	5'10"	207															2	28	14	0																
PITTSBURGH STEELERS																																						
Billy Patterson	TB-DB	21	5'10"	167			87	171	2.0	0	117	34	29	529	4.5	3	15–13	13					43	39														
Tommy Thompson	TB-HB-DB	24	6'1"	190			40	39	1.0	0	28	9	32	145	5.2	1	3–11		4	55	14	0																
Coley McDonough	TB-DB	25	6'1"	190	6		15	33	2.2	1	14	8	57	92	6.6	0	3–21						4	40														
Lou Tomasetti	HB-DB	24	6'	202	12		68	246	3.6	1	6	3	50	30	5.0	0	2–33		6	129	22	1																
George Kiick	FB-DB	23	6'	200			66	212	3.2	0	2	0	0	0	0.0	0	1–50		3	22	7	0																
Merl Condit	HB-DB	23	5'11"	195	6		52	205	3.9	0	15	2	13	33	2.2	0	2–13		4	30	8	1	12	38														
Swede Johnston	FB-DB	30	5'10"	205			41	113	2.8	0													8	40														
Boyd Brumbaugh	FB-DB	25	5'11"	195			32	79	2.5	0	7	2	29	46	6.6	0	1–14		1	0	0	0	6	32														
John Noppenberg	FB-OE-DB	22	6'	202			2	4	2.0	0									4	74	19	0	4	34														
Hank Bruder	BB-LB	32	6'	205															5	49	10	0																
Ev Fisher	BB-LB	25	5'11"	205															2	12	6	0																
George Platukas	OE-DE	25	6'	200	12														15	290	19	2																
Bill Sortet	OE-DE	28	6'1"	184															7	112	16	0																
Walt Kichefski	OE-DE	24	6'1"	210															4	26	7	0																
John Klumb (from CHIC)	OE-DE	23	6'3"	205															3	76	25	0																
Armand Niccolai	T	28	6'2"	230	24																				6	6	100	6	14	43								
PHILADELPHIA EAGLES																																						
Davey O'Brien	QB-DB	23	5'7"	151	6		100	–180	–1.8	1	277	124	45	1290	4.7	5	17–6	5					6	41														
Foster Watkins	QB-DB	22	5'9"	160	2		14	–76	–5.4	0	85	28	33	565	6.6	1	3–4	10							2	2	100											
Dick Riffle	HB-FB-DB	25	6'1"	197	30		81	238	2.9	4									8	58	7	1	14	34														
Elmer Hackney	FB-LB	24	6'2"	210	6		32	101	3.2	1									2	4	2	0																
Frank Emmons	FB-HB-LB	22	6'1"	213	12		29	77	2.7	1									3	19	6	1																
John Cole	FB-LB	25	5'9"	197	6		26	75	2.9	0									2	11	6	0	10	34	3	5	60	1	1	100								
Joe Bukant	FB-HB-LB	24	6'	220	6		18	50	2.8	1									1	13	13	0																
Jay Arnold	HB-DB	26	6'1"	213			3	9	3.0	0									7	145	21	0																
Franny Murray	HB-DB	24	6'	200	6		8	7	0.9	0									12	125	10	0	30	37	6	7	86	0	1	0								
Chuck Newton	HB-DB	23	6'	204															1	22	22	0																
Don Looney	OE-DB	22	6'2"	190	30		2	–4	–2.0	1									58	707	12	4																
Red Ramsey	OE-DE	25	6'	192															17	143	8	0																
Les McDonald (to DET)	OE-DE	25	6'4"	206			2	–2	–1.0	0									15	309	21	0																
Joe Carter	OE-DE	30	6'1"	200			1	–3	–3.0	0									12	201	18	0																
Joe Wendlick	OE-DE	24	6'	208															8	67	8	0																
Elmer Kolberg	OE-HB-DB	24	6'4"	198															6	43	7	0																
George Somers	T	24	6'2"	260	7																				1	1	100	2	9	22								

TEAM TOTALS	OFFENSE FIRST DOWNS	RUSHING No.	RUSHING Yds.	RUSHING Avg. Yds.	RUSHING TD	PASSING: Att.	Comp.	Comp. Pct.	Yds.	Yds/ Att.	Yds/ Comp.	TD	Int.	Pct. Int.	PUNT RETURNS Yds.	PUNT RETURNS TD	KICKOFF RETURNS Yds.	KICKOFF RETURNS TD	INT. RETURNS: No.	Yds.	Avg. Yds.	TD	PEN. Yds.	FUM. No.	POINTS: Total	PAT	FG Att.	FG Mde.	Saf	DEFENSE Total Yards	Pass Att.	Pass Comp.	Comp Pct.	Oppos. Fumb. Rec.	Points	TEAM TOTALS
WASHINGTON	147	397	1402	3.5	15	244	144	59.0	1887	7.7	13.1	18	22	9.0	591	1	741	0	18	212	11.8	1	427	40	245	29	5	2	0	2847	287	125	43.6	9	142	WASHINGTON
BROOKLYN	115	394	1546	3.9	10	191	80	41.9	1267	6.6	15.8	14	13	6.8	408	0	793	1	18	287	15.9	0	285	23	186	22	12	4	1	2836	259	113	43.6	14	120	BROOKLYN
NEW YORK	127	454	1476	3.3	6	174	78	44.8	1036	6.0	13.3	9	15	8.6	448	0	282	0	23	224	9.7	0	349	28	131	15	13	6	1	2219	234	91	38.9	11	133	NEW YORK
PITTSBURGH	97	362	1102	3.0	2	189	58	30.7	875	5.2	15.1	4	27	14.3	441	0	843	0	8	62	7.8	0	336	26	60	6	14	6	0	2742	192	83	43.2	15	178	PITTSBURGH
PHILA.	122	317	298	0.9	9	362	152	42.0	1855	5.1	12.2	6	20	5.5	393	0	667	0	12	148	12.3	0	215	14	111	12	11	3	0	2780	151	80	53.0	13	211	PHILA.

CHICAGO BEARS 8-3-0 George Halas

Scores of Each Game		
41	Green Bay	10
7	Chic. Cards	21
21	Cleveland	14
7	DETROIT	0
16	BROOKLYN	7
37	New York	21
14	GREEN BAY	7
14	Detroit	17
3	Washington	7
47	CLEVELAND	25
31	CHIC. CARDS	23

Use Name	Pos.	Hgt	Wgt	Age	Int	Pts
Frank Bausch	C-LB	6'2"	225	32		
Chet Chesney	C-LB	6'2"	227	23		
Bulldog Turner	C-LB	6'1"	235	21		
Young Bussey	DB	5'9"	183	22		

Use Name – Tackles	Pos.	Hgt	Wgt	Age	Int	Pts
Lee Artoe	T	6'3"	218	24		4
(1 PAT in 2 attempts, 1 FG in 1 attempt)						
Ed Kolman	T	6'2"	225	22		
Joe Mihal	T	6'3"	230	24		
Joe Stydahar	T	6'4"	230	28		
John Torrance	T	6'3"	285	26		

Use Name – Guards	Pos.	Hgt	Wgt	Age	Int	Pts
Al Baisi	G	6'	215	22		
Ray Bray	G	6'	224	23		
Aldo Forte	G	6'	210	22		
Danny Fortmann	G-LB	6'	210	24		
Phil Martinovich	G	5'10"	220	25		6
(2 field goals in 2 attempts)						
George Musso	G	6'2"	270	30		

When Commissioner Bert Bell looked at the pre-season roster, he said, "Nobody's going to beat the Bears. They're the greatest team ever assembled." Bell's remarks were prompted by an exceptional class of rookies which had transformed the Bears into the class of the league. One freshman was George McAfee, an explosive open-field runner who broke a 93-yard kickoff return in his first pro game. The others included end Ken Kavanaugh, tackles Lee Artoe and Ed Kolman, and center Bulldog Turner—a ferocious blocker and tackler who was as quick as he was big. Add these newcomers to veterans Luckman, Stydahar, Fortmann, Osmanski, Nolting, Maniaci, Musso, and Wilson, and the West had a new champion.

The Bears did lose three games, though, the last one a 7-3 defeat at Washington. After the game, Redskin owner George Marshall called the Bears "quitters" and "crybabies"—remarks he would later regret.

GREEN BAY PACKERS 6-4-1 Curly Lambeau

Scores of Each Game		
27	PHILADELPHIA	20
10	CHIC. BEARS	41
31	CHIC. CARDS	6
31	CLEVELAND	14
14	DETROIT	23
24	PITTSBURGH	3
7	Chic. Bears	14
28	Chic. Cards	7
3	New York	7
50	Detroit	7
13	Cleveland	13

Use Name	Pos.	Hgt	Wgt	Age	Int	Pts
Charley Brock	C-LB	6'2"	205	24		
Tom Greenfield	C-LB	6'4"	218	22		
George Svendsen	C-LB	6'4"	240	25		
George Seeman	OE-DE	6'1"	195	22		
Dick Weisgerber	BB-DE	5'10"	194	25		
(1 reception for 37 yds.)						

Use Name – Tackles	Pos.	Hgt	Wgt	Age	Int	Pts
Leo Disend	T	6'2"	224	24		
Paul Kell	T	6'2"	217	23		
Bill Lee	T	6'2"	235	28		
Baby Ray	T	6'6"	248	25		
Charlie Schultz	T	6'3"	230	23		
Champ Seibold	T	6'4"	246	27		

Use Name – Guards	Pos.	Hgt	Wgt	Age	Int	Pts
Tiny Engebretsen	G	6'1"	245	30		11
(8 PAT's in 8 attempts, 1 FG in 5 attempts)						
Buckets Goldenberg	G-LB	5'10"	225	29		
Smiley Johnson	G-LB	5'9"	200	23		
Russ Letlow	G	6'	215	26		
Lou Midler	G	6'1"	220	25		
Pete Tinsley	G-LB	5'8"	214	27		
Gust Zarnas	G	5'10"	225	25		

When the Chicago Bears trounced the Packers 41-10 to open their season, Green Bay fans knew that when 1941 rolled around they would no longer be the West's defending champions. The Packers still were a rugged team but unfortunately not as rugged as George Halas' powerhouse. After losses to the Lions, Bears again, and Giants, owner-coach Curly Lambeau became convinced that his team needed a body-building course before they could overtake the Bears.

But nothing was wrong with Don Hutson's body, as he bounced back from last year's knee injury to lead the NFL in scoring. The quick end found most of his passes coming from Cecil Isbell, with Arnie Herber getting less playing time at tailback. The same solid supporting cast filled the Green Bay line and backfield, with Clarke Hinkle and Russ Letlow shining especially bright to give the Packers a respectable but frustrating role as runners-up.

DETROIT LIONS 5-5-1 Potsy Clark

Scores of Each Game		
0	Chic. Cards at Buffalo	0
7	PITTSBURGH	10
6	CLEVELAND	0
43	CHIC. CARDS	14
0	Chic. Bears	7
23	Green Bay	14
14	WASHINGTON	20
0	Cleveland	24
17	CHIC. BEARS	14
21	Philadelphia	0
7	GREEN BAY	50

Use Name	Pos.	Hgt	Wgt	Age	Int	Pts
Tony Calvelli	C-LB	5'10"	190	24		6
Sam Tsoutsouvas	C-LB	6'	205			
Alex Wojciechowicz	C-LB	5'11"	200	25		6
Glenn Morris	OE-DE	6'	200	28		
Voluntarily retired – Paul Szakash						

Use Name – Tackles	Pos.	Hgt	Wgt	Age	Int	Pts
Clem Crabtree	T-G	6'3"	220	21		
Tony Furst	T	6'1"	220	22		
Johnny Hackenbruck	T	6'2"	215	25		
Jack Johnson	T	6'4"	220	30		6
(1 reception for 48 yds. touchdown)						
Steve Maronic	T	6'	225	24		
(Missed 1 field goal attempt)						
Bill Rogers	T	5'11"	240	27		
Harry Smith	T	5'11"	215			

Use Name – Guards	Pos.	Hgt	Wgt	Age	Int	Pts
Bill Feldhaus	G-LB	6'	225	28		
Bill Radovich	G	5'10"	225	25		
Harry Speelman	G	5'11"	220			
Cal Thomas	G	6'2"	210	25		
John Wiethe	G-LB	6'	195	23		

After being tipped off about an unheralded college center, owner George Richards ordered coach Gus Henderson to pick Bulldog Turner of Hardin-Simmons as Detroit's first draft choice. Richards then slipped Turner some money and free dental treatment to tell all other teams that he wasn't interested in pro football. But on the day of the draft, Henderson inexplicably named Doyle Nave of USC as his first pick, and George Halas promptly claimed Turner. Richards fired Henderson, who then revealed Richards' secret wooing of Turner. The league fined Richards $5,000, and he promptly sold the team to Fred Mandel and got out of pro football.

Although Nave didn't make the team, Mandel got Whizzer White, back from a year at Oxford, to play for the Lions. Preparing to enter Yale Law School, White led the NFL in rushing on a Detroit club that had few other good players.

CLEVELAND RAMS 4-6-1 Dutch Clark

Scores of Each Game		
21	PHILADELPHIA	13
0	Detroit	6
14	CHIC. BEARS	21
14	Green Bay	31
26	CHIC. CARDS	14
7	Chic. Cards	17
24	DETROIT	0
13	New York	0
14	Brooklyn	29
25	Chic. Bears	47
13	GREEN BAY	13

Use Name	Pos.	Hgt	Wgt	Age	Int	Pts
Bill Conkright	C-LB	6'1"	204	26		
Shag Goolsby	C-LB	6'2"	195	23		
Jack Haman	C-LB	6'1"	210	22		6
(1 reception for 5 yds.)						
Hank Rockwell	C-G-LB	6'4"	225	23		6
(1 rush for 5 yds., 1 reception for 5 yd. TD)						
Connie Mack Berry	OE-DE	6'3"	210	24		
Mike Kinek	OE-DE	6'1"	200	23		
Harvey Murphy	OE-DE	5'10"	194			
Jack Nix	WB-DB	6'	175			
Glenn Olson	BB-DB	6'	195			

Use Name – Tackles	Pos.	Hgt	Wgt	Age	Int	Pts
Stan Anderson	T	6'2"	220	22		
Boyd Clay	T	6'1"	215	27		
(Missed 1 field goal attempt)						
Elwyn Dunstan	T	6'3"	235	25		
(1 rush for 4 yds.)						
Ted Livingston	T	6'3"	222	26		
Fred Shirey (from GB)	T	6'2"	225	24		

Use Name – Guards	Pos.	Hgt	Wgt	Age	Int	Pts
Pete Gudauskas	G-LB	6'2"	210	23		1
(1 PAT in 3 attempts)						
Riley Matheson	G-LB	6'2"	208	25		
Barney McGarry	G-LB	6'1"	205	22		
Ralph Stevenson	G-LB	5'10"	196			

When the Rams opened the season with a 21-13 victory over the Eagles, Cleveland fans expected the good showing of late 1939 to continue. But the Lions ended the spell, 16-0. The Bears and Packers then took on the Rams and dispelled whatever title hopes existed. With the Rams exposed as bogus contenders, the river of paying customers dried up, and the red ink began flowing in the front office—as even with back-to-back shutouts of the Lions and Giants later in the season, it was too late to rekindle the high hopes and enthusiasm of the fans.

For the most part, Johnny Drake and Parker Hall entertained the small audiences that remained loyal. Drake made All-Pro with his determined running, and Hall, a tailback, gave the rooters a treat with his passing, running, and punting.

CHICAGO CARDINALS 2-7-2 Jimmy Conzelman

Scores of Each Game		
7	Pittsburgh	7
0	DETROIT at Buffalo	0
21	CHIC. BEARS	7
6	Green Bay	31
14	Detroit	43
21	Washington	28
14	Cleveland	26
17	CLEVELAND	7
7	GREEN BAY	28
9	Brooklyn	14
23	Chic. Bears	31

Use Name	Pos.	Hgt	Wgt	Age	Int	Pts
Ki Aldrich	C-LB	6'	195	24		
Andy Chisick	C-LB	6'1"	205	23		
Rex Williams	C-LB	6'2"	195	24		
Keith Ranspot	OE-DE	6'3"	205	25		
Ev Elkins	WB-DB	5'11"	190	22		
Jimmy German	TB-DB	6'	180	23		
Herm Schneidman	BB-LB	5'11"	200	26		

Use Name – Tackles	Pos.	Hgt	Wgt	Age	Int	Pts
Conway Baker	T	5'11"	225	29		
Ed Beinor	T-DE	6'2"	230	22		
Tony Blazine	T	6'	230	28		
Ray Busler	T	6'1"	220	25		
Bill Davis	T	6'1"	235	23		
Bob Wood	T	6'2"	230			

Use Name – Guards	Pos.	Hgt	Wgt	Age	Int	Pts
Frank Huffman	G-LB	6'2"	205	25		
Joe Kuharich	G-LB	5'11"	195	23		
(Missed 1 field goal attempt)						
Bill Murphy	G	6'	205	26		
Rupert Pate	G	6'1"	205	23		
Andy Sabados	G	5'11"	210	23		
Tarzan White	G	5'9"	220	24		

With witty Jimmy Conzelman taking over as head coach, the Cardinals went into the season a loose if not a powerful team. With end Gaynell Tinsley back in action and Hugh McCullough the new tailback, the relaxed Cardinals tied the Pirates and Lions in their first two games before moving on to Comiskey Park and the Bears.

Conzelman wanted nothing better than to beat his friendly rival George Halas, and the Cardinals took the lead by driving to a quick touchdown. A little later, rookie Lloyd Madden took a handoff on a reverse and broke into the clear. Forgetting that pro goal posts are planted on the goal line and not behind the end zone, Madden quit running around the 10-yard line and was quickly tackled. But despite the mental error, the Cardinals went on to a 21-7 victory over their powerful neighbors—a great and lasting triumph in the face of the fact that Conzelman and company would win only one more game all year.

Use Name – Backs & Ends	Pos.	Age	Hgt	Wgt	Pts	Int	RUSHING				PASSING								RECEIVING				PUNTING		KICKING						PUNT RETURNS				KICKOFF RETURNS			
							No.	Yds	Avg	TD	Att	Comp	%	Yds	Yd/Att	TD	Int–%	RK	No.	Yds	Avg	TD	No.	Avg	Pat	Att	%	FG	Att	%	No.	Yds	Avg	TD	No.	Yds	Avg	TD
CHICAGO BEARS																																						
Sid Luckman	QB-DB	23	6'	197			23	−65	−2.8	0	105	48	46	941	9.0	4	9– 9	4					27	42														
Bernie Masterson	QB-DB	29	6'3"	195	7		10	−7	−0.7	1	23	9	39	212	9.2	2	3– 13								1	1	100											
Bob Snyder	QB-DB	27	6'	205	7		7	12	1.7	0	22	5	23	145	6.6	1	1– 5						5	35	4	6	67	1	4	25								
Solly Sherman	QB-DB	22	6'1"	190			8	10	1.3	0	4	1	25	15	3.8	1	0– 0																					
Ray Nolting	HB-DB	26	5'11"	185	12		78	373	4.8	1	2	1	50	38	19.0	0	0– 0		3	36	12	0	2	34														1
Joe Maniaci	FB-LB	26	6'1"	210	19		84	368	4.4	2									1	−5	−5	0			1	1	100											
Gary Famiglietti	FB-HB-LB	25	6'	214	24		93	320	3.4	4									1	11	11	0																
Harry Clark	HB-DB	22	6'	180	18		56	258	4.6	2	3	0	0	0	0.0	0	2– 67		3	80	27	0	1	30														
George McAfee	HB-DB	22	6'	182	18		47	253	5.4	2	11	4	36	50	4.5	2	0– 0		7	117	17	0	22	39														1
Bill Osmanski	FB-LB	23	5'11"	197	18		50	192	3.8	3									1	13	13	0																
Bob Swisher	HB-DB	26	5'11"	165			15	70	4.7	0	1	0	0	0	0.0	0	0– 0		2	106	53	0																
Jack Manders	HB-DB	31	6'	200	23		8	20	2.5	0															17	18	95	2	3	67								
Ray McLean	HB-DB	24	5'10"	168	25		14	10	0.7	1									6	138	23	2			1	1	100 (reception)							1				
Ken Kavanaugh	OE-DE	23	6'3"	205	18														12	276	23	3																
Dick Plasman	OE-DE	26	6'3"	210	15														11	245	22	2			3	3	100											
Eggs Manske	OE-DE	27	6'	185															6	81	14	0																
Bob Nowaskey	OE-DE	22	6'	205	12		1	4	4.0	0									5	105	21	2																
George Wilson	OE-DE	26	6'1"	190	6														4	90	23	1																
John Siegal	OE-DE	22	6'1"	205	6														4	53	13	0																
Hamp Pool	OE-DE	25	6'3"	215															2	55	28	0																
GREEN BAY PACKERS																																						
Cecil Isbell	TB-DB	25	6'1"	190	24		97	270	2.8	4	150	68	45	1037	6.9	9	12– 8	3					2	32														
Arnie Herber	TB-DB	30	5'11"	208			6	−23	−3.8	0	89	38	43	560	6.3	5	7– 8	7					13	39														
Hal Van Every	TB-HB-DB	22	6'	195			38	154	4.1	0	41	12	29	199	4.9	4	6– 15		4	41	10	0	17	36														
Clarke Hinkle	FB-LB	30	5'11"	200	48		109	383	3.5	2									4	28	7	1	22	37	3	3	100	9	14	64								
Andy Uram	HB-DB	25	5'10"	188	19		71	270	3.8	1									10	188	19	2			1	2	50											
Ed Jankowski	FB-LB	27	5'9"	205	12		48	211	4.4	2																												
Harry Buhler	FB-HB-LB-DB	23	6'2"	210			36	118	3.3	0									1	17	17	0																
Frank Balasz	FB-LB	22	6'2"	213	6		25	107	4.3	1	1	0	0	0	0.0	0	1–100		1	7	7	0																
Lou Brock	HB-DB	22	6'	205			18	60	3.3	0	2	0	0	0	0.0	0	0– 0		5	97	19	0	3	42														
Joe Laws	HB-DB	29	5'9"	186	6		7	21	3.0	0									5	60	12	1																
Beattie Feathers	HB-DB	31	5'10"	190			4	19	4.8	0																												
Larry Craig	BB-DE	24	6'1"	206			3	9	3.0	0									6	67	11	0																
Bob Adkins	BB-LB-DE	23	6'1"	210	13		1	5	5.0	0									4	73	18	1			1	1	100	0	1	0								
Don Hutson	OE-DB	27	6'1"	185	57	6													45	664	15	7			15	16	94											
Moose Mulleneaux	OE-DE	23	6'3"	205	42														16	288	18	6																
Ray Riddick	OE-DE	22	6'1"	210															11	148	13	0																
Dick Evans	OE-DB	23	6'3"	195															2	40	20	0																
Harry Jacunski	OE-DE	24	6'2"	198															2	29	15	0																
Milt Gantenbein	OE-DE	30	6'	195															1	12	12	0																
DETROIT LIONS																																						
Whizzer White	TB-FB-DB	23	6'1"	190	32		**146**	**514**	3.5	5	80	35	44	461	5.8	0	11– 14	11	4	55	14	0	52	41	2	3	67	0	1	0								
Cotton Price	TB-DB	21	6'1"	185	16		42	122	2.9	2	66	33	50	456	6.9	3	7– 11	8					9	41	4	6	67											
Dwight Sloan	TB-DB	25	5'10"	180			58	225	3.9	0	46	18	39	260	5.7	0	8– 17						2	27														
Howie Weiss	FB-LB	23	6'	210	24		79	298	3.8	3									4	56	14	0																
Bill Shepherd	FB-DB	28	5'9"	205			24	67	2.8	0									2	12	6	0	1	40														
Lloyd Cardwell	WB-DB	27	6'2"	200	18		48	186	3.9	2	1	0	0	0	0.0	0	0– 0		20	349	17	1																
Rip Ryan	WB-FB-DB	25	6'2"	195		6	22	42	1.9	0	2	0	0	0	0.0	0	0– 0		9	96	11	0	9	39														
Jack Morlock	WB-DB		5'10"	165			1	0	0.0	0																												
Fred Vanzo	BB-LB	24	6'2"	230			1	−1	−1.0	0									7	75	11	0																
Bill Callihan	BB-DB	24	6'3"	210															4	38	10	0																
Paul Moore	BB-LB	22	5'9"	210	6		2	4	2.0	0									4	29	7	1																
Chuck Hanneman	OE-DE	25	6'	212	16														14	228	16	0			10	10	100	2	4	50								
Dave Diehl	OE-DE	21	6'	190	6														12	131	11	0																
Stillman Rouse	OE-DE	23	6'2"	205			2	0	0.0	0									2	17	9	0																
Butch Morse	OE-DE	27	6'2"	195															1	13	13	0																
Bill Fisk	OE-DE	23	6'	190			2	0	0.0	0									1	10	10	0																
CLEVELAND RAMS																																						
Parker Hall	TB-DB	23	6'	205	6		94	365	3.9	1	183	77	42	1108	6.1	6	16– 9	9					**57**	43														
Marty Slovak	TB-DB	23	5'9"	182	6		53	129	2.4	1	28	17	61	234	8.4	1	4– 14																					
Ken Heineman	TB-DB	22	5'9"	170	1		6	−5	−0.8	0	8	3	38	74	9.3	1	1– 12						2	32	1	1	100											
Jim Gillette	TB-DB	22	6'1"	185			1	1	1.0	0	4	0	0	0	0.0	0	2– 50																					
Fred Gehrke	TB-DB	22	5'11"	180							1	0	0	0	0.0	0	0– 0		1	−2	−2	0																
Johnny Drake	FB-DB-LB	24	6'1"	214	56		134	480	3.6	**9**	4	2	50	16	4.0	2	0– 0		8	81	10	0			2	6	25	0	1	0								
Len Janiak	FB-DB	24	6'1"	210			19	44	2.3	0									1	3	3	0	1	30														
Ollie Cordill	WB-DB	24	6'2"	190	12		24	73	3.0	0									14	158	11	2	5	45														
Dante Magnani	WB-DB	23	5'10"	183	6		7	19	2.7	0									11	119	11	1																
Vic Spadaccini	BB-DB	24	6'	225	23						1	0	0	0	0.0	0	0– 0		22	276	13	2			5	5	100											
Gaylon Smith	BB-TB-LB	24	5'11"	205			19	18	0.9	0	18	10	56	150	8.3	2	2– 11		3	65	22	0	11	36														
Earl Crowder	BB-LB	24	6'	198															2	33	17	0																
Mike Rodak	BB-LB	23	5'10"	196			1	4	4.0	0																												
Jim Benton	OE-DE	23	6'3"	197	18		1	0	0.0	0									22	351	16	3																
Paul McDonough	WB-OE-DE	23	6'4"	223	6		2	5	2.5	0									12	315	**26**	1																
Johnny Wilson	OE-DE	24	6'3"	200	6														7	93	13	1																
Maury Patt	OE-DE	26	6'2"	202	6		1	0	0.0	0									2	52	26	1																
Chet Adams	T-OE-DE	24	6'3"	228	10														2	28	14	0			7	10	70	1	5	20								
CHICAGO CARDINALS																																						
Hugh McCullough	TB-DB	24	6'	185	19		52	278	5.3	3	116	43	37	529	4.6	4	21– 18	12					30	40	1	3	33	0	1	0								
Beryl Clark	TB-DB	22	6'	200	3		39	9	0.2	0	58	25	43	316	5.4	2	6– 10		1	20	20	0	28	33	3	3	100											
Bob Kellogg	TB-DB			165			9	31	3.4	0	18	6	33	42	2.3	0	4– 22						2	27														
Marshall Goldberg	FB-TB-DB	22	5'11"	188	18		87	325	3.7	2	2	0	0	0	0.0	0	0– 0		2	29	15	1	1	47														
Mario Tonelli	FB-DB	23	5'11"	200	6		51	148	2.9	1									5	53	11	0	1	15														
Milt Popovich	FB-DB	23	5'11"	190			41	138	3.4	0									5	32	6	0	5	42														
Marty Christiansen	FB-DB	23	6'	200	6		32	71	2.2	1																												
John Hall	WB-DB	23	6'	195	30		39	88	2.3	1	3	0	0	0	0.0	0	2– 67		4	111	28	2																1
Lloyd Madden	WB-DB	21	6'1"	195	18		29	186	6.4	2									4	90	23	1																
Buddy Parker	BB-LB	26	6'	195	9		6	8	1.3	1									6	45	8	0			3	3	100	0	1	0								
Bert Johnson	BB-LB	28	6'	210			6	15	2.5	0	1	1	100	25	25.0	0	0– 0		2	52	26	0	1	19														
Lou Zontini	BB-LB	23	5'9"	180	16		1	1	1.0	0													2	46	10	10	**100**	2	5	40								
Gaynell Tinsley	OE-DE	24	6'2"	205	6		1	17	17.0	0									16	165	10	1																
Al Coppage	OE-DE	24	6'1"	195	6														15	163	11	1																
John Shirk	OE-DE	22	6'4"	200															11	91	8	0																
Pop Ivy (from PIT)	OE-DE	24	6'3"	200															2	32	16	0																
Bill Dewell	OE-DE	23	6'4"	205															2	29	15	0																

TEAM TOTALS	OFFENSE																													DEFENSE						TEAM TOTALS
		RUSHING:				PASSING:									PUNT RETURNS		KICKOFF RETURNS		INT. RETURNS:				PEN.	FUM.	POINTS:											
	FIRST DOWNS	No.	Yds.	Avg. Yds.	TD	Att.	Comp.	Comp. Pct.	Yds.	Yds/ Att.	Yds/ Comp.	TD	Int.	Pct. Int.	Yds.	TD	Yds.	TD	No.	Yds.	Avg. Yds.	TD	Yds	No.	Total	PAT	FG Att.	FG Mde.	Saf	Total Yards	Pass Att.	Pass Comp.	Comp. Pct.	Oppos. Fumb. Rec.	Points	
CHI. BEARS	141	**494**	**1818**	3.7	**16**	171	68	39.8	1401	**8.2**	**20.6**	10	15	8.8	500	1	798	2	27	271	10.0	2	**605**	35	238	28	10	6	0	2750	269	133	49.4	11	152	CHI. BEARS
GREEN BAY	**154**	463	1604	3.5	10	283	118	41.7	1796	6.3	15.2	**18**	26	9.2	494	0	381	0	**40**	414	10.4	1	295	21	238	28	**20**	**10**	0	2532	252	98	38.9	7	155	GREEN BAY
DETROIT	133	427	1457	3.4	12	195	86	44.1	1177	6.0	13.7	3	26	13.3	300	0	714	0	29	298	10.3	2	259	27	138	16	6	2	1	2357	177	77	43.5	**20**	153	DETROIT
CLEVELAND	113	364	1142	3.1	11	247	109	44.1	1582	6.4	14.5	12	25	10.1	349	0	655	0	25	306	12.2	2	260	26	171	16	7	1	1	3102	247	99	40.1	14	191	CLEVELAND
CHI. CARDS	112	393	1315	3.3	11	198	75	37.9	912	4.6	12.2	6	33	16.7	346	0	632	1	23	389	**16.9**	1	331	23	139	17	8	2	1	2783	186	**69**	37.1	19	222	CHI.CARDS

NEW YORK GIANTS 8-3-0 Steve Owen

Scores of Each Game		
24	Philadelphia	0
17	Washington	10
37	Pittsburgh	10
16	PHILADELPHIA	0
28	PITTSBURGH	7
13	Brooklyn	16
7	CHIC. CARDS	10
20	DETROIT	13
49	CLEVELAND	14
20	WASHINGTON	13
7	BROOKLYN	21

Use Name	Pos.	Hgt	Wgt	Age	Int	Pts
Lou DeFilippo	C-LB	6'1"	225	25		
Chet Gladchuk	C-T-LB	6'4"	245	24	1	
Mel Hein	C-LB	6'2"	230	32	1	
Kayo Lunday	C-G-LB	6'3"	215	28	1	
Dick Horne	DE	6'2"	212	23		
Don Vosberg	OE-DE	6'2"	188	21		

injured – Ed Widseth (broken leg)

Use Name – Tackles	Pos.	Hgt	Wgt	Age	Int	Pts
Tony Blazine	T	6'	240	29		
Frank Cope	T	6'2"	226	25		6
John Mellus	T	6'	220	24		
Win Pedersen (1 field goal in 1 attempt)	T	6'3"	220	26	1	3

Use Name – Guards	Pos.	Hgt	Wgt	Age	Int	Pts
Monk Edwards	G-T-LB	6'3"	210	21		
Doug Oldershaw	G-DE-LB	6'	195	26	1	6
Ben Sohn	G	6'2"	220	22		
Orville Tuttle	G	5'9"	215	28		
Len Younce	G-LB	6'1"	205	24	2	

With the Eastern Division championship already won, the Giants closed out their regular season by facing the Brooklyn Dodgers in the Polo Grounds on December 7. During the first half the public-address announcer urgently called out, "All armed forces personnel are requested to report to their commands immediately. Repeat . . ." Finally, at half time, the Giants heard the news of Pearl Harbor over the radio. They finished the game by losing in what turned out to be an insignificant contest in the face of all that was to come.

Soon to be broken up by the military draft, this Giant team rebounded from an off year to reassert its claim on the Eastern crown. Rookie backs Len Eshmont and Andy Manefos took some of the rushing burden off veteran Tuffy Leemans' shoulders, and freshman Len Younce helped John Mellus, Monk Edwards, Mel Hein, and the other linemen.

BROOKLYN DODGERS 7-4-0 Jock Sutherland

Scores of Each Game		
14	DETROIT	7
24	Philadelphia	13
0	Washington	3
7	Green Bay	30
6	CHIC. CARDS	20
16	NEW YORK	13
15	PHILADELPHIA	6
13	WASHINGTON	7
7	Pittsburgh	14
35	PITTSBURGH	7
21	New York	7

Use Name	Pos.	Hgt	Wgt	Age	Int	Pts
Ray Frick	C-LB	6'1"	205			
Joe Koons	C-LB	6'2"	195	24		
Tom Robertson	C-LB	6'	215	24		
Bud Svendsen (1 punt return for 2 yds.)	C-LB	6'1"	195	26	1	
Si Titus	C-LB-DE	6'	195	22	2	
Russ Cotton	BB-LB	6'2"	197	26		

Use Name – Tackles	Pos.	Hgt	Wgt	Age	Int	Pts
Pete Dobrus	T	6'	215	24		
Andy Fronczek	T	6'	200	24		
Mike Jurich	T	6'1"	225	22		
Bruiser Kinard (3 PAT's in 5 attempts)	T	6'1"	218	26		9
Frank Kristufek	T	6'	208	25		
Walt Merrill	T	6'2"	215	24		

Use Name – Guards	Pos.	Hgt	Wgt	Age	Int	Pts
Warren Alfson	G-LB	6'	198	26	2	
George Kinard	G-LB	6'1"	195	24		
Steve Petro	G-LB	5'10"	190	26		
Jim Sivell	G	5'9"	210	27		

The Dodgers enjoyed beating the local rival Giants twice during the year, but the Giants laughed last by finishing in first place ahead of Brooklyn. While the Giants lost only one other game besides the Brooklyn matches, the Dodgers dropped decisions to the Packers, Cardinals, Pirates, and Redskins to leave coach Jock Sutherland's boys one game away from the Eastern crown. Four young veterans pumped the life blood into the team. Tackle Bruiser Kinard held the line together and made up for his unimposing 218-pound frame by hitting often and hitting hard. End Perry Schwartz caught passes on offense and rushed passers on defense. Fullback Pug Manders cracked into enough holes narrowly to edge out George McAfee for the NFL rushing title, and the glue uniting all the parts was supplied by Ace Parker, the premier passer, runner, punter, defensive back, and team leader.

WASHINGTON REDSKINS 6-5-0 Ray Flaherty

Scores of Each Game		
10	NEW YORK	17
3	BROOKLYN	0
24	Pittsburgh	20
21	Philadelphia	17
17	CLEVELAND	13
23	PITTSBURGH	3
7	Brooklyn	13
21	Chic. Bears	35
13	New York	20
17	GREEN BAY	22
20	PHILADELPHIA	14

Use Name	Pos.	Hgt	Wgt	Age	Int	Pts
Ki Aldrich (4 PAT's in 5 attempts, 1 FG in 3 attempts)	C-LB	6'	215	25	2	7
Vic Carroll (1 reception for 31 yds.)	C-G-LB	6'4"	230	28	2	6
George Smith	C-LB	6'2"	222	27		
Bob Titchenal	C-DE-LB	6'2"	195	23	2	
Ken Dow	FB-DB	5'10"	198	22		

Use Name – Tackles	Pos.	Hgt	Wgt	Age	Int	Pts
Jim Barber	T	6'3"	235	29		
Fred Davis	T	6'3"	240	23		
Jim Stuart	T	6'	212	22		
Willie Wilkin	T	6'4"	260	25		
Bill Young	T	6'1"	255	27		

Use Name – Guards	Pos.	Hgt	Wgt	Age	Int	Pts
Dick Farman	G	6'	225	27		
Clyde Shugart	G	6'1"	220	24		
Steve Slivinski	G	5'10"	215	24	1	
Clem Stralka	G	5'10"	215	27		

With fullback Andy Farkas back from a knee injury and center Ki Aldrich obtained in a trade with the Cardinals, the Redskins looked stronger than last year. But a 17-10 opening-game loss to New York raised some doubts and rekindled the rumor that the team had not overcome the beating suffered at the hands of the Bears in the 1940 championship game. Although the Skins laughed at such suggestions and came back to win five in a row, Brooklyn upset them 13-7, the Bears soundly beat them 35-21, and the Giants and Packers edged out close victories to leave only thoughts of next year.

Prime in the Skins' attack was Sammy Baugh, who had some hard luck passing but managed to lead the league in punting as a result of his unexpected quick kicks, a line-drive punt on third down which often caught the defense flat-footed.

PHILADELPHIA EAGLES 2-8-1 Greasy Neale

Scores of Each Game		
0	NEW YORK	24
10	Pittsburgh	7
13	BROOKLYN	24
0	New York	16
17	WASHINGTON	21
21	CHIC. CARDS	14
6	Brooklyn	15
7	PITTSBURGH	7
17	Detroit	21
14	CHIC. BEARS	49
14	Washington	20

Use Name	Pos.	Hgt	Wgt	Age	Int	Pts
Frank Bausch	C-LB	6'2"	225	33		
Bob Bjorklund	C-LB	6'2"	225	23		
Bernie Feibish	C-LB	6'2"	223		1	
Lyle Graham	C-LB	6'3"	210	25	2	
Gran Harrison	DE	6'3"	212	24		

Use Name – Tackles	Pos.	Hgt	Wgt	Age	Int	Pts
John Eibner	T	6'2"	220	25		
Joe Frank	T	6'1"	220	26		
Phil Ragazzo	T	6'	223	26		
Vic Sears	T	6'3"	208	23		
Cecil Sturgeon	T	6'2"	254	22		
Hodges West	T	6'1"	220	22		

Use Name – Guards	Pos.	Hgt	Wgt	Age	Int	Pts
Tony Cemore	G	6'	210	24	1	
Enio Conti (1 rush for –1 yd.)	G	5'11"	200	28		
Dave diFilippo	G	5'10"	210	23		
Ralph Fritz	G	5'9"	202	23		
Woody Gerber	G	6'	225	21		
Bob Suffridge	G	6'	190	26		

The Philadelphia and Pittsburgh franchises were passed around during the off season like hot potatoes. Art Rooney started the ball rolling by selling the Pirates to Alexis Thompson in December and then buying a half interest in the Eagles from his friend Bert Bell. In April, Thompson mentioned a preference for a Philadelphia franchise, and Rooney, eager to return to Pittsburgh, talked Bell into swapping franchises.

Thompson started his Philadelphia tenure by hiring Greasy Neale, a long-time college coach, and Neale installed Tommy Thompson as his T-formation quarterback. Blind in one eye, Thompson was an uncanny long passer and a strong leader on a team almost totally comprised of rookies.

PITTSBURGH STEELERS 1-9-1 Bert Bell, Buff Donelli, Walt Kiesling

Scores of Each Game		
14	Cleveland	17
7	PHILADELPHIA	10
10	NEW YORK	37
20	WASHINGTON	24
7	New York	28
7	Chic. Bears	34
3	Washington	23
7	Philadelphia	7
14	BROOKLYN	7
7	GREEN BAY	54
7	Brooklyn	35

Use Name	Pos.	Hgt	Wgt	Age	Int	Pts
Chuck Cherundolo	C-LB	6'1"	210	25	1	
Moose Harper	C-LB	6'4"	235	27		
John Schiechl	C-LB	6'2"	232	24	1	
Dick Dolly (1 rush for 2 yds.)	OE-DE	6'3"	210	23		

Use Name – Tackles	Pos.	Hgt	Wgt	Age	Int	Pts
Joe Coomer	T	6'6"	265	22		
Ted Doyle	T	6'2"	222	27		
Royal Kahler	T	6'2"	225	23		
George Somers (Missed 2 field goal attempts)	T	6'2"	250	25		
John Woudenberg	T	6'3"	235	23		

Use Name – Guards	Pos.	Hgt	Wgt	Age	Int	Pts
Dick Bassi (1 reception for 6 yds.)	G	5'11"	225	26		
Carl Nery	G	6'	215	24		
Jack Sanders (5 PAT's in 5 attempts)	G	6'	227	24		5
Elbie Schultz	G	6'4"	245	23		
Don Williams	G	5'8"	210	22		

When Art Rooney sold the Pirates to Alexis Thompson after the 1940 season, he soon felt an itch to get back to the Steel City, and a complicated franchise swap saw Thompson get the Eagles and Rooney and Bert Bell wind up as co-owners of the newly renamed Steelers. Never again would Rooney wash his hands of Pittsburgh pro football. With Bell handling the coaching reigns, Rooney watched a pre-season workout for a few minutes, turned to a bystander, and sneered, "Well, we've got a new team, a new coach, a new nickname, and new uniforms, but they look like the same old Pirates to me." The bystander turned out to be a reporter, and Rooney's remarks made big news in the papers. With team morale undercut, Bell handed the coaching duties over to Buff Donelli after two games, but Walt Kiesling was back in charge by mid-season. Winning one game for the three coaches, the Steelers were off to a flying start.

TEAM TOTALS

OFFENSE	First Downs: Tot	by Rsh	by Pas	by Pen	Rushing: No.	Yds.	Avg. Yds.	TD	Passing: Att.	Com	Comp. Pct.	Yds.	Avg. Yds. Att.	Avg. Yds. Comp	TD	Int.	Pct. Int.
N.Y.	110	68	33	9	433	1318	3.0	16	156	68	43.6	1088	7.0	16.0	11	12	7.7
BKN.	132	82	44	6	444	1665	3.7	14	202	90	44.6	1134	5.6	12.6	5	18	8.9
WASH.	135	62	64	9	406	1097	2.7	7	262	134	51.1	1563	6.0	11.7	11	30	11.5
PHIL.	128	60	59	9	360	849	2.4	6	249	115	46.2	1367	5.5	11.9	10	27	10.8
PITT.	75	49	18	8	381	1223	3.2	9	168	42	25.0	654	3.9	15.6	5	34	20.2

OFFENSE	Punting: No.	Avg. Yds.	Punt Returns: No.	Yds.	Avg. Yds.	TD	Kickoff Returns: No.	Yds.	Avg. Yds.	TD	Interception Returns: No.	Yds.	Avg. Yds.	TD	Penalties: No.	Yds.	Fumbles: No.	Lost	Points: Tot	PAT	FG Att	FG	Saf.
N.Y.	64	41.5	47	717	15.3	0	20	467	23.4	0	29	569	19.6	1	40	323	25	14	238	28	20	10	0
BKN.	60	41.5	41	343	8.4	0	28	616	22.0	0	20	228	11.4	1	38	371	27	10	158	18	14	4	1
WASH.	55	45.9	45	675	15.0	3	28	580	20.7	0	23	291	12.7	1	50	402	23	11	176	20	14	6	0
PHIL.	69	41.0	27	210	7.8	0	31	734	23.7	0	21	213	10.1	0	54	407	24	15	119	14	8	3	0
PITT.	87	37.4	28	372	13.3	0	44	930	21.1	0	19	186	9.8	0	44	363	32	15	103	13	6	2	0

							RUSHING				PASSING								RECEIVING				PUNTING		KICKING						PUNT RETURNS				KICKOFF RETURNS			
Use Name – Backs & Ends	Pos.	Age	Hgt	Wgt	Pts	Int	No.	Yds	Avg	TD	Att	Comp	%	Yds	Yd/Att	TD	Int–%	RK	No.	Yds	Avg	TD	No.	Avg	Pat	Att	%	FG	Att	%	No.	Yds	Avg	TD	No.	Yds	Avg	TD
NEW YORK GIANTS																																						
Ed Danowski	QB	29	6'1"	198							24	12	50	179	7.5	2	2–8		1	12	12	0	2	36.5														
Marion Pugh	QB-DB	21	6'1"	187			24	50	2.1	0	24	12	50	161	6.7	1	0–0								0	1	0				1	5	5	0				
Kay Eakin	QB-WB-DB	24	6'	178	6	2	27	17	0.6	0	19	5	26	71	3.7	1	4–21		5	81	16	1	20	47.4				0	1	0								
Tuffy Leemans	FB-DB	28	6'	200	24	3	100	332	3.3	4	66	31	47	475	7.2	4	5–8	5													14	170	12	0				
Len Eshmont	FB-DB	24	5'11"	180			50	164	3.3	0	3	2	67	32	10.7	1	0–0		1	4	4	0	11	38.9							6	131	22	0				
Andy Marefos	FB-DB	24	6'	225	30	2	60	153	2.5	2	8	2	25	79	9.9	1	1–12		1	5	5	0			6	6	100	4	5	80								
Frank Reagan	FB-DB	22	5'11"	185	24	1	35	146	4.2	4	6	1	17	16	2.7	0	0–0						13	37.5							6	113	19	0				
Hank Soar	FB-DB	27	6'2"	207	3	2	29	90	3.1	0	5	3	60	75	15.0	1	0–0								3	3	100				4	54	14	0				
Red McClain	FB-DB	23	5'9"	182	12	1	9	36	4.0	2																												
Ward Cuff	WB-DB	28	6'1"	190	46	4	28	157	5.6	0									19	317	17	2			19	20	95	5	13	38	1	10	10	0				
George Franck	WB-FB-DB	22	6'	175	24	4	48	101	2.1	3	1	0	0	0	0.0	0	0–0		8	95	12	1	18	39.8							13	194	15	0				
Howie Yeager	WB-DB	26	5'11"	173	24		22	67	3.0	1									11	237	22	3									2	40	20	0				
Dom Principe	BB-LB	24	6'	205			1	5	5.0	0									4	54	14	0																
Leland Shaffer	BB-DB	29	6'2"	205		1													1	5	5	0																
Nello Falaschi	BB-LB	27	6'	195		1													1	3	3	0																
Jim Poole	OE-DE	25	6'3"	220	18	1													6	74	12	2																
Will Walls	OE-DE	26	6'4"	220															4	69	17	0																
Jim Lee Howell	OE-DE	26	6'6"	218	6														4	62	16	1																
Vince Dennery	OE-DE	24	5'11"	190	6														1	65	65	1																
Jack Lummus	OE-DE	23	6'3"	194															1	5	5	0																
BROOKLYN DODGERS																																						
Ace Parker	TB-DB	29	6'	180		1	85	301	3.5	0	102	51	50	642	6.3	2	8–8	8	3	66	22	0	27	39.5							16	153	10	0				
Bill Leckonby	TB-DB	23	6'1"	185	6	3	54	202	3.7	0	64	25	39	299	4.7	1	5–8	11	1	9	9	1	15	39.2							15	119	8	0				
Dean McAdams	TB-HB-DB	23	6'1"	195	9	1	38	99	2.6	0	27	12	44	176	6.5	2	3–11		7	94	13	0	16	47.6	3	3	100	2	3	67	2	11	6	0				
Leo Stasica	TB-DB	25	5'11"	185			3	17	5.7	0	2	1	50	14	7.0	0	0–0														2	14	7	0				
Pug Manders	FB-DB	28	6'	200	42	4	111	486	4.4	6									6	67	11	0																
Merl Condit	HB-DB	23	5'11"	185	41	3	91	357	3.9	4	6	1	17	3	0.5	0	1–17		5	32	6	0	1	38.0	11	12	92	2	11	18	5	44	9	0				
George Kracum	FB-DB	23	6'1"	212	18	1	52	169	3.3	3									2	17	9	0																
Thurman Jones	FB-DB	23	5'10"	195			1	3	3.0	0																												
Larry Peace	HB-DB	24	5'11"	185	1		4	2	0.5	0															1	1	100											
Rhoten Shetley	BB-LB	23	5'11"	210	6	1	1	7	7.0	1	1	0	0	0	0.0	0	0–0		5	63	13	0																
Ben Kish	BB-LB	24	6'	200		1													4	50	13	0	1	35.0														
Wendell Butcher	BB-LB	27	6'1"	190			1	2	2.0	0																												
Perry Schwartz	OE-DE	26	6'2"	195	12		1	7	7.0	0									24	343	14	2																
Eddie Rucinski	OE-DE	25	6'2"	196	6		2	13	6.5	0									17	204	12	1																
Herman Hodges	OE-DE	26	6'1"	200															12	128	11	0																
Don Wemple	OE-DE	23	6'2"	195	6														2	37	19	1																
Bill Bailey	OE-DE	25	6'3"	220															1	14	14	0																
Dave Parker	OE-DE	23	6'3"	200															1	10	10	0																
WASHINGTON REDSKINS																																						
Sammy Baugh	TB-DB	27	6'2"	185		4	27	12	0.4	0	193	106	55	1236	6.4	10	19–10	4					30	48.7														
Frankie Filchock	TB-DB	24	5'11"	198	12		115	383	3.3	0	68	28	41	327	4.8	1	11–16	12					1	35.0							7	157	22	1				
Andy Farkas	FB-DB	25	5'10"	195	18	4	85	224	2.6	2									12	77	6	0									14	152	11	1				
Dick Todd	FB-DB	26	5'11"	170	18		55	138	2.5	1									8	125	16	1	10	43.5														
Bob Seymour	FB-WB-DB	25	6'2"	205	24	2	62	137	2.2	2									6	85	14	2									10	128	13	0				
Lee Gentry	FB-DB	22	6'	198		1	5	13	2.6	0																					14	238	17	1				
Roy Zimmerman	WB-FB-DB	23	6'2"	198			20	54	2.7	0	1	0	0	0	0.0	0	0–0		5	36	7	0	14	42.4														
Wilbur Moore	WB-BB-DB	25	5'11"	188	6		10	48	4.8	1									2	6	3	0																
Ed Justice	WB-DB	28	6'1"	198	6	2	4	−8	−2.0	0									8	149	19	1																
Ray Hare	BB-LB	23	6'1"	200	6		11	48	4.4	1									12	87	7	0																
Cecil Hare	BB-LB	22	5'11"	190	1		6	22	3.7	0									1	25	25	0																
Bob Hoffman	BB-LB	23	6'1"	194			1	2	2.0	0																												
Wayne Millner	OE-DE	30	6'1"	190			2	8	4.0	0									20	262	13	0																
Bob Mc Chesney	OE-DE	29	6'2"	195	12														19	213	11	2																
Bob Masterson	OE-DE	26	6'1"	220	23	1	1	3	3.0	0									11	135	12	1			8	8	100	3	6	50								
Joe Aguirre	OE-DE	22	6'4"	220	26														10	103	10	2			8	9	89	2	5	40								
Ed Cifers	OE-DE	25	6'2"	218	6														10	94	9	1																
Al Krueger	OE-DB	22	6'1"	190	6	1													7	123	18	1																
Frank Clair	OE-DE	24	6'1"	204															2	12	6	0																
PHILADELPHIA EAGLES																																						
Tommy Thompson	QB-DB	25	6'1"	187	6	3	54	28	0.5	0	162	86	53	974	6.0	8	14–9	7	2	10	5	1	1	43.0							5	27	5	0				
Len Barnum	QB-HB-FB-DB	28	6'	200	8	2	35	64	1.8	0	55	19	35	260	4.7	0	10–18		1	11	11	0	41	43.6	2	2	100	2	6	33								
Foster Watkins	QB-HB-DB	23	5'9"	165			15	11	0.7	0	10	6	60	51	5.1	1	0–0		3	27	9	0									3	17	6	0				
Jim Castiglia	FB-LB	22	5'11"	205	24	1	60	183	3.1	4	7	0	0	0	0.0	0	1–14		4	24	6	0																
Dan DeSantis	HB-DB	22	6'	180	1	2	45	125	2.8	0	7	3	43	78	11.1	1	1–14		4	53	13	0	7	29.4	1	1	100				9	80	9	0				
Terry Fox	FB-LB	22	6'1"	208			21	97	4.6	0									6	71	12	0																
Jack Banta	HB-DB	23	5'11"	192	6		29	93	3.2	1									2	42	21	0	9	45.6														
Sam Bartholomew	FB-LB	23	5'11"	188		1	21	71	3.4	0									3	15	5	0									1	1	1	0				
Mort Landsberg	HB-DB	22	5'11"	180		2	23	69	3.0	0									5	51	10	0									2	15	8	0				
Fred Gloden	HB-DB	22	5'10"	187			22	55	2.5	0									2	13	7	0																
Mike Basca	HB-DB	24	5'8"	170	18	3	14	43	3.1	1	4	0	0	0	0.0	0	1–25		2	45	23	0	10	34.8	9	9	100	1	2	50	1	8	8	0				
Lou Tomasetti (to DET,WB-DB)	HB-DB	25	6'	195	6	1	16	41	2.6	0									2	40	20	1									3	48	16	0				
Wes McAfee	HB-DB	22	5'11"	175	8		9	6	0.7	0	4	1	25	4	1.0	0	0–0		3	30	10	1	1	32.0	2	2	100				3	21	7	0				
Lou Ghecas	HB-DB	23	5'9"	175			2	3	1.5	0																					1	11	11	0				
Dick Humbert	OE-DB	22	6'1"	175	18	1													29	332	11	3																
Bob Krieger	OE-DE	21	6'1"	190	12														19	232	12	2																
Hank Piro	OE-DB	23	6'	186	6	1													10	141	14	1																
Kirk Hershey (from CLE)	OE-DE	22	6'2"	215															9	81	9	0																
Larry Cabrelli	OE-DE	24	5'11"	195	6														4	90	23	1																
John Shonk	OE-DB	23	6'1"	190		1													4	43	11	0																
Jack Ferrante	OE-DE	25	6'1"	195															2	22	11	0																
PITTSBURGH STEELERS																																						
Boyd Brumbaugh	TB-FB-DB	26	5'11"	197	12		68	114	1.7	2	41	13	32	260	6.3	2	8–20		1	1	1	0									7	60	9	0				
Coley McDonough	TB-DB	26	6'1"	182			20	64	3.2	0	41	12	29	200	4.9	1	5–12						7	37.1							2	28	14	0				
Art Jones	TB-HB-DB	22	6'2"	190	30	7	52	239	4.6	4	23	6	26	86	3.7	0	3–13		4	121	30	1	47	37.7							14	232	17	0				
Al Donelli	TB-HB-DB	22	5'7"	165		1	15	32	2.1	0	8	2	25	13	1.6	1	3–37		2	25	13	0	1	41.0							1	11	11	0				
Les Dodson	TB-DB	25	6'1"	180			2	−4	−2.0	0	8	1	13	7	0.9	0	3–37						1	34.0														
Ben Starret	TB-BB-LB	23	5'10"	200			7	9	1.3	0	2	0	0	0	0.0	0	1–50																					
Frank Zopetti	TB-DB		5'11"	185							1	0	0	0	0.0	0	0–0																					
Dick Riffle	FB-TB-DB	26	6'1"	210	12	6	109	388	3.6	1	39	8	21	88	2.3	1	9–23		2	24	12	1	7	35.3							3	38	13	0				
Elmer Hackney	FB-DB	25	6'2"	204	6		63	253	4.0	1	1	0	0	0	0.0	0	0–0		1	10	10	0									1	3	3	0				
Joe Hoague	FB-DB	23	6'2"	200	12		33	112	3.4	1	1	0	0	0	0.0	0	0–0		2	21	11	1	17	37.1														
John Noppenberg (to DET)	HB-TB-DB	23	6'	190			11	16	1.5	0	3	0	0	0	0.0	0	0–0						7	38.6														
Jay Arnold	BB-HB-LB	27	6'1"	215		1	2	4	2.0	0									1	5	5	0																
Rocco Pirro	BB-LB	24	6'	215		1	1	1	1.0	0									2	31	16	0																
John Patrick	BB-LB	23	6'	200		1													1	12	12	0																
Don Looney	OE-DB	23	6'2"	177	6														10	186	19	1																
Joe Wendlick	OE-DE	25	6'	206															7	84	12	0																
Walt Kichefski	OE-DE	25	6'1"	214	6														5	111	22	1																
George Platukas	OE-DE	26	6'	194															2	15	8	0																
Elmer Kolberg	OE-DE	25	6'4"	200															1	2	2	0																
Armand Niccolai	T	29	6'2"	230	14																				8	9	89	2	4	50								

TEAM TOTALS

	FIRST DOWNS:				RUSHING:				PASSING:									PUNTING:		PUNT RETURNS:				KICKOFF RETURNS:				INTERCEPTION RETURNS:				PENAL-TIES:		FUM-BLES:		POINTS:					
DEFENSE	Tot	by Rsh	by Pas	by Pen	No.	Yds.	Avg. Yds.	TD	Att.	Com	Comp. Pct.	Yds.	Avg. Yds. Att.	Avg. Yds. Comp	TD	Int.	Pct. Int.	No.	Avg. Yds.	No.	Yds.	Avg. Yds.	TD	No.	Yds.	Avg. Yds.	TD	No.	Yds.	Avg. Yds.	TD	No.	Yds.	No.	Lost	Tot	PAT	FG Att	FG	Saf.	DEFENSE
N.Y.	116	64	47	5	408	1166	2.9	9	218	103	47.2	1212	5.6	11.8	6	29	13.3	75	40.3	33	469	14.2	1	45	1007	22.4	0	12	105	8.8	1	47	371	34	13	114	12	11	4	0	N.Y.
BKN.	110	58	45	7	376	1210	3.2	6	189	86	45.5	1169	6.2	13.6	6	20	10.6	72	40.1	34	463	13.6	1	29	625	21.6	0	18	261	14.5	1	47	370	17	8	127	13	10	4	0	BKN.
WASH.	129	66	56	7	410	1110	2.7	16	229	103	45.0	1338	5.8	13.0	14	23	10.0	65	41.6	28	351	12.5	0	36	698	19.4	0	30	309	10.3	0	37	269	33	12	174	19	13	5	1	WASH.
PHIL.	126	72	47	7	432	1498	3.5	14	238	100	42.0	1369	5.8	13.7	13	21	8.8	66	38.4	37	519	14.0	0	22	443	20.1	0	27	492	18.2	2	50	455	21	10	218	26	14	8	0	PHIL.
PITT.	116	72	34	10	426	1550	3.6	17	189	84	44.4	1168	6.2	13.9	10	19	10.1	65	40.6	41	416	10.1	0	21	536	25.5	1	34	596	17.5	2	54	495	17	8	276	34	12	4	1	PITT.

CHICAGO BEARS 10-1-0 George Halas

Scores of Each Game		
25	Green Bay	17
48	Cleveland	21
53	CHIC. CARDS	7
49	DETROIT	0
34	PITTSBURGH	7
14	GREEN BAY	16
31	CLEVELAND	13
35	WASHINGTON	21
24	Detroit	7
49	Philadelphia	14
34	Chic. Cards	24
	WEST playoff	
33	GREEN BAY	14

Use Name	Pos.	Hgt	Wgt	Age	Int	Pts
Bill Hughes	C-LB	6'1"	222	26	1	
(1 punt return for 6 yds.)						
Al Matuza	C-LB	6'2"	200	22	2	
Bulldog Turner	C-LB	6'1"	230	22	1	

Use Name – Tackles	Pos.	Hgt	Wgt	Age	Int	Pts
Lee Artoe	T	6'3"	230	25		6
(3 PAT's in 4 attempts, 1 FG in 7 attempts)						
John Federovich	T	6'5"	260	24	1	
Ed Kolman	T	6'2"	230	23		
Joe Mihal	T	6'3"	225	25		
Joe Stydahar	T	6'4"	230	29	1	4
(4 PAT's in 4 attempts)						

Use Name – Guards	Pos.	Hgt	Wgt	Age	Int	Pts
Al Baisi	G	6'	215	23		
Ray Bray	G	6'	245	24		
Aldo Forte	G	6'	212	23		
Danny Fortmann	G-LB	6'	207	25	3	
Hal Lahar	G	6'	225	22		4
(1 PAT in 3 attempts, 1 FG in 1 attempt)						
George Musso	G	6'2"	255	31		

As strong as the Bears looked last year, they were in even better shape this year. Two new horses, Norm Standlee and Hugh Gallarneau, were yoked into the backfield, and George McAfee grew into the most feared runner in the NFL. Combining a deer's speed with a rabbit's moves, McAfee led the league in average yards per carry, threatened to break punt and kickoff returns into touchdowns, and intercepted six passes as a cornerback on defense. But even with McAfee's overall play, Standlee's power running, Sid Luckman's passing, and the Bears averaging 36 points a game—capped by routs of 53-7 over the Cardinals and 49-0 over the Lions—it took a playoff game with the Green Bay Packers before the Western Division championship could be decided, as both clubs took turns to mar each other's perfect records and force the post-season game.

GREEN BAY PACKERS 10-1-0 Curly Lambeau

Scores of Each Game		
23	DETROIT	0
24	CLEVELAND	7
17	CHIC. BEARS	25
14	CHIC. CARDS	13
30	BROOKLYN	7
17	Cleveland	14
24	Detroit	7
16	Chic. Bears	14
17	CHIC. CARDS	9
54	Pittsburgh	7
22	Washington	17
	WEST Playoff	
14	Chic. Bears	33

Use Name	Pos.	Hgt	Wgt	Age	Int	Pts
Charley Brock	C-LB	6'2"	205	25		
Tom Greenfield	C-LB	6'4"	220	23		
George Svendesn	C-LB	6'4"	240	26	1	
Bob Adkins	BB-DE	6'1"	210	24	2	3
(3 PAT's in 3 attempts)						
Larry Buhler	BB-DE	6'2"	215	24		
Bill Johnson	DE	6'1"	196	24		

Use Name – Tackles	Pos.	Hgt	Wgt	Age	Int	Pts
Bill Lee	T	6'2"	240	29		
Ernie Pannell	T	6'2"	220	24	1	6
Baby Ray	T	6'6"	250	26		
Charlie Schultz	T	6'3"	235	24		

Use Name – Guards	Pos.	Hgt	Wgt	Age	Int	Pts
Amadeo Bucchianeri	G	5'10"	210	24		
Tiny Engebretsen	G	6'1"	245	31		3
(1 field goal in 3 attempts)						
Buckets Goldenberg	G-LB	5'10"	230	30	1	
Smiley Johnson	G-LB	5'9"	195	24	1	
Bill Kuusisto	G	6'	230	23		
Russ Letlow	G	6'	215	27		
Lee McLaughlin	G	6'1"	226	24		
Pete Tinsley	G-LB	5'8"	205	28	1	

With the Chicago Bears destroying all their opponents in the early going, everyone but Curly Lambeau was calling the Bears a superteam. Lambeau reminded his Packers that the Bears were only human and due for a fall, and when the two clubs met in mid-season, the hard-nosed Green Bay defense shut off the Bears and led the Packers to a 16-14 upset victory. That triumph made up for an opening-day loss to the Bears and led to both clubs having identical records when the regular season closed.

The Packers went into the playoff game with the NFL's premier receiver and league MVP in Don Hutson, a superb passer and strategist in Cecil Isbell, a stable of hard-charging runners headed by Clarke Hinkle, and a tough forward wall featuring Baby Ray and Buckets Goldenberg. But with all their talent, the Packers came up empty and fell before the George Halas machine 33-14.

DETROIT LIONS 4-6-1 Bill Edwards

Scores of Each Game		
0	Green Bay	23
7	Brooklyn	14
14	Chic. Cards	14
17	CLEVELAND	7
0	Chic. Bears	49
7	GREEN BAY	24
14	Cleveland	0
13	New York	20
21	PHILADELPHIA	17
7	CHIC. BEARS	24
21	CHIC. CARDS	3

Use Name	Pos.	Hgt	Wgt	Age	Int	Pts
Bob Nelson	C-T-LB	6'1"	215	21	1	
Dunc Obee	C-LB	5'11"	200	23		
Alex Wojciechowicz	C-LB	5'11"	205	26		
Paul Moore	BB-LB	5'9"	205	23		
Injured – Mike Rodak (broken leg)						

Use Name – Tackles	Pos.	Hgt	Wgt	Age	Int	Pts
Clem Crabtree	T	6'3"	230	22		
Tony Furst	T	6'1"	215	23	1	
Andy Logan	T	6'	222	23		
Ted Pavelic	T	6'	213	22		
Alex Schibanoff	T	6'1"	220	21		
John Tripson	T	6'3"	210	21		
Emil Uremovich	T	6'2"	220	24		

Use Name – Guards	Pos.	Hgt	Wgt	Age	Int	Pts
Stan Batinski	G	5'10"	215	24		
John Mattiford	G	5'10"	216	25		
(1 reception for 21 yds.)						
Bill Radovich	G	5'10"	230	26		
John Wiethe	G-LB	6'	200	24	2	

The Lions were offensive pussy cats, with no passing attack and a line that pushed no one around. Although they picked up four wins by beating the Rams twice, the Cardinals, and the Eagles, the stronger clubs lost no sleep over them. Against the Packers, Detroit dropped games by scores of 23-0 and 24-7, and the Bears took a pair via counts of 49-0 and 24-7—as the only score the Lions managed in the two games was a 101-yard kickoff return by Billy Jefferson.

New coach Bill Edwards, who had inherited a deteriorating club which would sink lower before starting to climb, also lost his ace Whizzer White after the season. White, who stood out amidst the rubble for his 100 percent effort at all times, went into military service and then on to pursue a legal career, which would lead to an appointment as Associate Justice of the United States Supreme Court.

CHICAGO CARDINALS 3-7-1 Jimmy Conzelman

Scores of Each Game		
6	CLEVELAND	10
14	DETROIT	14
13	Green Bay	14
7	Chic. Bears	53
20	Brooklyn	6
14	Philadelphia	21
10	New York	7
9	Green Bay	17
7	Cleveland	0
3	Detroit	21
24	CHIC. BEARS	34

Use Name	Pos.	Hgt	Wgt	Age	Int	Pts
Ray Apolskis	C-LB	5'11"	200	22	1	
Andy Chisick	C-LB	6'1"	208	24	1	
Fred Shook	C-LB	6'	218	22		
Walt Rankin	FB-DB	5'11"	190	23		
holdout – Gil Duggan						

Use Name – Tackles	Pos.	Hgt	Wgt	Age	Int	Pts
Al Bahartsky	T	6'	220	25		
Conway Baker	T	5'11"	230	30		
Ed Beinor (to WAS)	T	6'2"	215	23		
Ray Busler	T	6'1"	220	26		
Bill Davis	T	6'1"	235	24		6
John Kuzman	T	6'1"	235	25		

Use Name – Guards	Pos.	Hgt	Wgt	Age	Int	Pts
John Higgins	G-LB	6'1"	210	21		
Frank Huffman	G-LB	6'2"	210	26		
Joe Kuharich	G-LB	5'11"	195	24	1	
(1 punt for 45 yds.)						
Joe Lokanc	G-LB	5'11"	205	22		
(1 reception for 2 yds.)						
Bill Murphy	G	6'	200	27		
Tarzan White	G	5'9"	225	25		

When the Bears trounced the Cardinals 53-7 in their first meeting of the season, Jimmy Conzelman knew he wouldn't be beating George Halas this year. But the coach could take satisfaction from other achievements. The Cardinals climbed up into fourth place in the West, finishing out of the last-place dungeon for the first time in four years, and their three wins included impressive upsets over Brooklyn and New York. With a better final record than Cleveland, Philadelphia, and Pittsburgh, the Cardinals felt they were making progress. Personal achievements also brightened the season. Guard Joe Kuharich won All-Pro status in his second pro year, and fullback Marshall Goldberg took a second-team place on the honor roll with his all-around play. Goldberg, whose reputation on defense was undisputed around the circuit, also led the NFL at mid-season in rushing, punt and kickoff returning, and interceptions.

CLEVELAND RAMS 2-9-0 Dutch Clark

Scores of Each Game		
17	PITTSBURGH	14
10	Chic. Cards	6
7	Green Bay	24
21	CHIC. BEARS	48
7	Detroit	17
14	GREEN BAY	17
13	Washington	17
0	DETROIT	14
13	Chic. Bears	31
14	New York	49
0	CHIC. CARDS	7

Use Name	Pos.	Hgt	Wgt	Age	Int	Pts
Bill Conkright	C-LB	6'1"	200	27	1	
Jack Haman	C-LB	6'1"	214	23	1	
Bill Rieth	C-LB	5'11"	203	25		
Frank Maher (from PIT)	DB	6'1"	195	23		

Use Name – Tackles	Pos.	Hgt	Wgt	Age	Int	Pts
Graham Armstrong	T	6'4"	225	23		
Boyd Clay	T	6'1"	213	28		4
(1 PAT in 1 attempt, 1 FG in 2 attempts)						
Elwyn Dunstan	T	6'3"	245	26		6
(1 punt return for 35 yd. TD)						
Mike Kostiuk	T	6'	215	22		
Del Lyman (from GB)	T	6'3"	225	23		
Fred Shirey	T	6'2"	220	25		

Use Name – Guards	Pos.	Hgt	Wgt	Age	Int	Pts
John Gregory	G	6'2"	210	25		
Riley Matheson	G-LB	6'2"	203	26	1	
Barney McGarry	G-LB	6'1"	200	23		
Hank Rockwell	G-C-LB	6'4"	225	24	1	
Milt Simington	G	6'2"	213	23		
Wilfred Thorpe	G-LB-DE	6'3"	200	24	1	
Gordon Wilson	G-T	6'	225	25		

Looking to buy an NFL franchise he could eventually move to Los Angeles, Dan Reeves bought a controlling interest in the Cleveland Rams. In the opening game against Pittsburgh, Reeves and part owner Fred Levy were brought to their feet by Dante Magnani's opening kickoff which he returned 95 yards for a touchdown. When the Rams beat the Steelers and the Cardinals in their first two games, Reeves and Levy thought they had gotten into an easy business. But the bubble burst as the Rams lost their last nine contests.

Although coach Dutch Clark kept his job under the new ownership, he could not shake the Rams out of their mediocre habits. Parker Hall and Johnny Drake, as usual, handled the bulk of the passing and running but could not make up for the new blood which was needed in the backfield. And despite Riley Matheson's fine defensive work, the line also needed a transfusion.

TEAM TOTALS

OFFENSE	FIRST DOWNS: Tot	by Rsh	by Pas	by Pen	RUSHING: No.	Yds.	Avg Yds.	TD	PASSING: Att	Com	Comp Pct.	Yds.	Avg. Yds. Att.	Avg. Yds. Comp	TD	Int	Pct. Int.	PUNTING: No.	Avg. Yds.
CHI. B.	181	112	56	13	495	2290	4.6	30	196	98	50.0	2002	10.2	20.4	19	11	5.6	32	38.7
G.B	166	82	69	15	467	1550	3.3	13	253	133	52.6	1731	6.8	13.0	17	13	5.1	53	42.1
DET.	86	51	29	6	361	1009	2.8	7	187	58	31.0	848	4.5	14.6	5	20	10.6	79	39.7
CHI. C.	138	66	64	8	386	1098	2.8	8	252	117	46.4	1658	6.6	14.2	6	20	7.9	79	39.3
CLEVE.	121	68	44	9	343	984	2.9	4	285	123	43.2	1352	4.7	11.0	10	35	12.3	79	40.4

OFFENSE	PUNT RETURNS: No.	Yds.	Avg. Yds.	TD	KICKOFF RETURNS: No.	Yds.	Avg. Yds.	TD	INTERCEPTION RETURNS: No.	Yds.	Avg. Yds.	TD	PENALTIES: No.	Yds.	FUMBLES: No.	Lost	POINTS: Tot	PAT	FG Att	FG	Saf.	OFFENSE
CHI. B.	27	546	20.2	2	29	685	23.6	1	34	566	16.6	3	77	677	37	19	396	45	11	5	0	CHI. B.
G.B	41	487	11.9	1	28	567	20.3	0	25	455	18.2	1	47	509	20	11	258	28	20	10	1	G.B.
DET.	35	502	14.3	1	37	980	26.5	1	18	327	18.2	2	52	455	24	11	121	16	9	1	0	DET.
CHI. C.	32	311	9.7	0	31	705	22.7	0	16	145	9.1	1	41	446	19	12	127	13	12	4	0	CHI. C.
CLEVE.	32	343	10.7	1	41	820	20.0	1	15	141	9.4	0	29	265	25	8	116	14	4	2	0	CLEVE.

Use Name – Backs & Ends	Pos.	Age	Hgt	Wgt	Pts	Int	Rushing No.	Yds	Avg	TD	Passing Att	Comp	%	Yds	Yd/Att	TD	Int–%	RK	Receiving No.	Yds	Avg	TD	Punting No.	Avg	Kicking Pat	Att	%	FG	Att	%	Punt Returns No.	Yds	Avg	TD	Kickoff Returns No.	Yds	Avg	TD
CHICAGO BEARS																																						
Sid Luckman	QB-DB	24	6'	198	6	3	18	18	1.0	1	119	68	57	1181	9.9	9	6– 5	1					13	41.0														
Young Bussey	QB-DB	23	5'9"	185		2	13	9	0.7	0	40	13	33	353	8.8	5	3– 7						2	37.0							1	40	40	0				
Bob Snyder	QB-DB	28	6'	190	26	1	7	–10	–1.4	0	28	13	46	353	12.6	3	2– 7						2	38.0	20	24	83	2	2	100								
George McAfee	HB-DB	23	6'	180	72	6	65	474	7.3	6	3	1	33	44	14.7	1	0– 0		7	144	21	3	12	35.8							5	158	32	1				1
Norm Standlee	FB-LB	22	6'2"	230	30	2	81	414	5.1	5									2	–3	–1	0	2	63.0														
Bill Osmanski	FB-LB	24	5'11"	198	24	3	76	361	4.8	4	1	0	0	0	0.0	0	0– 0		4	52	13	0																
Hugh Gallarneau	HB-DB	24	6'	190	66	1	49	304	6.2	8									11	204	19	2	1	0.0							2	36	18	0				
Ray Nolting	HB-DB	27	5'11"	185	6		40	169	4.2	1	5	3	60	71	14.2	1	0– 0		4	68	17	0									4	50	13	0				
Bob Swisher	HB-DB	27	5'11"	160	18	1	37	149	4.0	0									6	179	30	2									7	101	14	0				
Harry Clark	HB-DB	23	6'	185	1	2	28	122	4.4	0									2	61	30	0			1	1	100				4	56	14	0				
Gary Famiglietti	FB-HB-LB	26	6'	220	6		36	101	2.8	1																												
Joe Maniaci	FB-LB	27	6'1"	215	29		28	95	3.4	3									2	21	11	0			8	8	100	1	1	100								
Ray McLean	HB-DB	25	5'10"	168	18	3	13	78	6.0	1									5	84	17	1									3	99	33	1				
Dick Plasman	OE-DE	27	6'3"	215	6		1	1	1.0	0									14	283	20	0			6	9	67											
Bob Nowaskey	OE-DE	23	6'	205	13		3	5	1.7	0									12	199	17	1			1	2	50											
Ken Kavanaugh	OE-DE	24	6'3"	206	37	1													11	314	29	6			1	1	100											
John Siegal	OE-DE	23	6'1"	205	18														9	220	24	3																
Hamp Pool	OE-DE	26	6'3"	225	6														5	101	20	1																
George Wilson	OE-DE	27	6'1"	200															4	75	19	0																
GREEN BAY PACKERS																																						
Cecil Isbell	TB-DB	26	6'1"	190	6	1	72	317	4.4	1	206	117	57	1479	7.2	15	11– 5	2	1	–1	–1	0									3	19	6	0				
Hal Van Every	TB-DB	23	6'	195	18	3	25	127	5.1	2	30	11	37	195	6.5	0	2– 7		1	3	3	0	13	38.8							4	58	15	0				
Tony Canadeo	TB-DB	22	5'11"	190	18	2	43	137	3.2	3	16	4	25	54	3.4	2	0– 0						10	40.5							4	26	7	0				
Clarke Hinkle	FB-LB	31	5'11"	198	56	1	129	393	3.0	5									8	78	10	1	22	44.5	2	2	100	6	14	43	2	61	31	0				
Andy Uram	HB-DB	26	5'10"	188	6	2	49	258	5.3	0									6	124	21	0									7	121	17	1				
George Paskvan	FB-DB	23	6'	190		2	38	116	3.1	0																												
Ed Jankowski	FB-LB	28	5'9"	200	4	1	47	65	1.4	0															1	2	50	1	1	100								
Joe Laws	HB-DB	30	5'9"	190	6	2	21	58	2.8	0									4	48	12	1									2	3	2	0				
Lou Brock	HB-DB	23	6'	197	12	2	14	44	3.1	0									22	307	14	2	3	42.7							15	153	10	0				
Herm Rohrig	HB-DB	23	5'8"	190	4	1	21	2	0.1	0	1	1	100	3	3.0	0	0– 0		11	58	5	0	5	42.8	1	1	100	1	1	100	4	46	12	0				
Larry Craig	BB-DE	25	6'1"	208			1	1	1.0	0									2	13	7	0																
Don Hutson	OE-DB	28	6'1"	185	95	1	4	22	5.5	2									58	738	13	10			20	24	83	1	1	100								
Moose Mulleneaux	OE-DE	24	6'3"	210	12														9	216	24	2																
Harry Jacunski	OE-DE	25	6'2"	200															4	48	12	0																
Ray Riddick	OE-DE	23	6'1"	215															3	33	11	0																
Ed Frutig	OE-DB	21	6'1"	185			1	11	11.0	0									2	40	20	0																
Alex Urban	OE-DE	24	6'3"	200	6														2	26	13	1																
DETROIT LIONS																																						
Whizzer White	TB-WB-DB	24	6'1"	185	24	1	89	238	2.7	2	62	22	35	338	5.5	2	5– 8	9	5	158	32	1	48	41.6							19	262	14	0				
Billy Jefferson	TB-DB	23	6'2"	205	12	1	56	164	2.9	1	72	18	25	181	2.5	0	9–12	13	2	14	7	0	20	37.5							7	69	10	0				1
Cotton Price	TB-DB	22	6'1"	182			16	36	2.3	0	33	9	27	112	3.4	0	4–12		1	6	6	0	5	38.2							3	48	16	0				
Harry Hopp	FB-DB	22	6'	205	6	1	69	202	2.9	1	3	0	0	0	0.0	0	1–33		2	7	4	0	2	42.0														
Steve Belichick	FB-LB		5'8"	190	18	1	28	118	4.2	2									1	13	13	0									1	77	77	1				
Milt Piepul	FB-LB	22	6'1"	215			20	56	2.8	0	1	1	100	23	23.0	0	0– 0						1	35.0														
Lloyd Parsons	FB-LB	23	5'11"	197			5	9	1.8	0									1	3	3	0																
Dick Booth	WB-DB	23	6'1"	190	6	1	29	79	2.7	1	8	5	63	135	16.9	2	1–12		7	103	15	0	1	25.0														
Ned Mathews	WB-DB	23	5'10"	185	6	5	31	56	1.8	0	8	3	38	59	7.4	1	0– 0		6	56	9	0	1	26.0							1	3	3	0				
Lloyd Cardwell	WB-DB	28	6'2"	195			10	19	1.9	0																					3	25	8	0				
Bill Callihan	BB-DB	25	6'3"	217															4	34	9	0																
Fred Vanzo (to CHIC)	BB-LB	25	6'2"	228															2	20	10	0																
Bill Fisk	OE-DE	24	6'	198	12														9	140	16	2																
Stan Anderson (from CLE)	OE-DE-T	23	6'2"	215															7	79	11	0																
John Jett	OE-DE	23	6'7"	225															4	50	13	0																
Chuck Hanneman (to CLE)	OE-DE	26	6'	215	13														4	48	12	1			4	4	100	1	4	25								
Paul Szakash	OE-DE-DB	28	6'	210															3	77	26	0																
Maury Britt	OE-DE	22	6'4"	210	6														1	45	45	1																
Augie Lio	G-LB	23	6'	225	18	3																	1	28.0	12	13	92	0	5	0								
CHICAGO CARDINALS																																						
Johnny Clement	TB-DB	21	6'	190	6		61	94	1.5	1	100	48	48	690	6.9	3	7– 7	6					4	31.3							13	113	9	0				
Ray Mallouf	TB-DB	23	5'11"	180			43	104	2.4	0	96	48	50	725	7.6	2	4– 4	3					28	41.0							4	11	3	0				
Hugh McCullough	TB-DB	25	6'	185			15	34	2.3	0	32	12	38	133	4.2	0	5–16						3	40.7							3	35	12	0				
Marshall Goldberg	FB-TB-DB	23	5'11"	190	24	7	117	427	3.6	3	19	9	47	110	5.8	1	1– 5		16	313	20	1									12	152	13	0	12	290	24	0
Bob Morrow	FB-DB	23	6'	220	6	1	37	128	3.5	1																												
Frank Balasz (from GB)	FB-DB	23	6'2"	210	1		23	81	3.5	0	4	0	0	0	0.0	0	2–50		2	17	9	0	7	37.0	1	1	100											
Milt Popovich	FB-G-LB	24	5'11"	200			5	4	0.8	0																												
John Hall	WB-DB	24	6'	200	24		53	165	3.1	2	1	0	0	0	0.0	0	0– 0		16	302	19	2																
John Martin	WB-DB	23	6'1"	192	12	1	25	56	2.2	1									4	53	13	1	24	39.9														
Avery Monfort	WB-DB	22	5'10"	178			3	8	2.7	0																												
Buddy Parker	BB-LB	27	6'	192		2	1	–1	–1.0	0									8	122	15	0			0	1	0											
Bert Johnson	BB-WB-LB-DB	29	6'	210	6	1	3	7	2.3	0									4	90	23	1																
Lou Zontini	BB-LB	24	5'9"	190	5		1	–9	–9.0	0									1	22	22	0	12	37.1	5	5	100	0	4	0								
Bill Dewell	OE-DE	24	6'4"	200	6		1	–1	–1.0	0									28	352	13	1																
Pop Ivy	OE-DE	25	6'3"	205	12	1													20	183	9	0																
Al Coppage	OE-DE	25	6'1"	195															8	117	15	0																
Bill Daddio	OE-DE	25	5'11"	202	20														5	39	8	0			8	9	89	4	8	50								
Dick Evans	OE-DE	24	6'3"	203															3	34	11	0																
CLEVELAND RAMS																																						
Parker Hall	TB-DB	24	6'	195	12	2	57	232	4.1	2	190	84	44	883	4.6	7	19–10	9					49	40.1							13	125	10	0				
Marty Slovak	TB-DB	24	5'9"	180			46	132	2.9	0	54	27	50	287	5.3	2	9–17														4	30	8	0				
Owen Goodnight	TB-DB	23	6'	195		2	21	–8	–0.4	0	36	12	33	182	5.1	1	5–14						16	39.8							2	27	14	0				
Johnny Drake	FB-DB	25	6'1"	220	18	2	101	246	2.4	2	2	0	0	0	0.0	0	0– 0		16	211	13	1																
Corby Davis	FB-BB-LB	26	5'11"	212			31	110	3.5	0									13	64	5	0	2	37.5							1	6	6	0				
Gaylon Smith	FB-DB	25	5'11"	195		1	11	22	2.0	0	2	0	0	0	0.0	0	1–50						1	23.0							1	33	33	0				
Len Janiak	FB-BB-DB	25	6'1"	200		1	14	20	1.4	0									2	5	3	0																
Dante Magnani	WB-DB	24	5'10"	175	12	2	24	137	5.7	0									14	189	14	1									5	54	11	0				
George Morris	WB-DB	22	5'11"	188			24	69	2.9	0									9	17	2	0									5	33	7	0				
Tony Gallovich	WB-DB	22	5'9"	170			1	1	1.0	0																												
Charlie Seabright	BB-LB	23	6'2"	195							1	0	0	0	0.0	0	1–100		5	44	9	0																
Rudy Mucha	BB-G-LB	23	6'1"	228			1	0	0.0	0									1	3	3	0	11	44.4														
Red Hickey	OE-DE	24	6'2"	195	24		7	7	1.0	0									21	294	14	4																
Paul McDonough	OE-DE	24	6'4"	230	12														14	198	14	2																
Maury Patt	OE-DE	27	6'2"	206	6		5	16	3.2	0									17	163	10	1																
Johnny Wilson	OE-DE	25	6'3"	205	6														5	115	23	1																
Ray Prochaska	OE-DE	22	6'3"	205															4	29	7	0																
Chet Adams	T	25	6'3"	230	16																				13	14	93	1	2	50								

TEAM TOTALS

DEFENSE	First Downs: Tot	by Rsh	by Pas	by Pen	Rushing: No.	Yds.	Avg. Yds.	TD	Passing: Att.	Com	Comp. Pct.	Yds.	Avg. Yds. Att.	Avg. Yds. Comp	TD	Int.	Pct. Int.	Punting: No.	Avg. Yds.	Punt Returns: No.	Yds.	Avg. Yds.	TD	Kickoff Returns: No.	Yds.	Avg. Yds.	TD	Interception Returns: No.	Yds.	Avg. Yds.	TD	Penalties: No.	Yds.	Fumbles: No.	Lost	Points: Tot	PAT	FG Att	FG	Saf.	DEFENSE
CHI. B.	143	60	63	20	373	1076	2.9	6	265	106	40.0	1463	5.5	13.8	9	34	12.8	56	39.5	20	340	17.0	2	48	1187	24.7	1	11	214	19.5	0	42	448	26	14	147	18	7	3	0	CHI. B.
G.B.	124	76	41	7	356	1221	3.4	10	233	104	44.6	1343	5.8	12.9	8	25	10.7	58	40.5	31	432	13.9	1	39	880	22.6	0	13	170	13.1	0	63	539	41	23	120	12	12	4	0	G.B.
DET.	160	89	61	10	475	1404	3.0	8	247	112	45.3	1605	6.5	14.3	8	18	7.3	67	42.8	40	546	13.7	1	29	628	21.7	0	20	215	10.8	0	36	415	20	12	195	24	18	9	0	DET.
CHI. C.	110	61	42	7	384	1301	3.4	13	196	90	45.9	1305	6.7	14.5	12	16	8.2	62	43.3	40	552	13.8	1	30	596	19.9	0	20	340	17.0	1	47	437	27	15	197	23	6	2	0	CHI. C.
CLEVE.	138	82	44	12	436	1547	3.5	23	206	90	43.7	1425	6.9	15.8	14	15	7.3	68	40.1	51	418	8.2	1	18	484	26.9	1	35	409	11.7	3	49	419	20	11	244	28	15	4	0	CLEVE.

1942 N.F.L. — EAST

WASHINGTON REDSKINS 10-1-0 Ray Flaherty

Scores of Each Game		
28	PITTSBURG	14
7	NEW YORK	14
14	Philadelphia	10
33	CLEVELAND	14
21	Brooklyn	10
14	Pittsburgh	0
30	PHILADELPHIA	27
28	CHIC. CARDS	0
14	New York	7
23	BROOKLYN	3
15	Detroit	3

Use Name	Pos.	Hgt	Wgt	Age	Int	Pts
Ki Aldrich	C-LB	6'	210	26		6
(1 kickoff return for 8 yds.)						
George Smith	C-LB	6'2"	215	28		
(Missed 1 field goal attempt)						
Bob Titchenal	OE-LB	6'2"	200	24	1	
(1 reception for 7 yds.)						

Use Name – Tackles	Pos.	Hgt	Wgt	Age	Int	Pts
Ed Beinor	T	6'2"	220	24		
Vic Carroll	T-G-C	6'4"	235	29		
Fred Davis	T	6'3"	240	24		
George Watts	T	6'1"	225	24		
Willie Wilkin	T	6'4"	265	26		8
(1 kickoff return for 15 yds.)						
Bill Young	T	6'1"	250	28		

Use Name – Guards	Pos.	Hgt	Wgt	Age	Int	Pts
Dick Farman	G	6'	220	26		
Clyde Shugart	G	6'1"	220	25		
Steve Slivinski	G	5'10"	216	25		
Clem Stralka	G	5'10"	220	28		
Joe Zeno	G	5'10"	220	23		

In the only game the Redskins lost, they held the Giants to no first downs and still dropped a rain-soaked 14-7 heartbreaker. After this early setback, the Washington offense caught up with the defense and led the Skins to nine straight wins, including a rematch with the Giants. In the last four games, the defense brilliantly held up its end of the bargain by allowing only one touchdown.

Although the defense, led by tackle Willie Wilkin, was the heart of the team, the explosive attack won most of the newsprint. Sammy Baugh drilled his passes from the tailback slot, Andy Farkas bulled his way to hard rushing yardage, and Dick Todd and Bob Masterson corraled most of Baugh's slings. Despite the loss of Wayne Millner, Frankie Filchock, and Jim Barber in the military buildup, the Redskins were armed to the teeth and hungry for revenge over the Bears in the upcoming championship game.

PITTSBURGH STEELERS 7-4-0 Walt Kiesling

Scores of Each Game		
14	PHILADELPHIA	24
14	Washington	28
13	NEW YORK	10
7	Brooklyn	0
14	Philadelphia	0
0	WASHINGTON	14
17	New York	9
35	Detroit	7
19	CHIC. CARDS	3
13	BROOKLYN	0
21	Green Bay	24

Use Name	Pos.	Hgt	Wgt	Age	Int	Pts
Art Albrecht	C-T-LB	6'1"	200	20		
Chuck Cherundolo	C-LB	6'1"	212	26	1	
Clure Mosher	C-G-LB	6'1"	215	22		
Hal Hinte (from GB)	DE	6'1"	195	22		
Ralph Wenzel	DE	6'	205	24		
John Naioti	DB	5'10"	175	20		

Use Name – Tackles	Pos.	Hgt	Wgt	Age	Int	Pts
Ted Doyle	T	6'2"	220	28		
Eberle Schultz	T	6'4"	250	24		
George Somers	T	6'2"	260	26		1
(1 PAT in 1 attempt, missed 1 FG attempt)						
John Woudenberg	T	6'3"	220	24		
(1 reception for – 1 yd.)						

Use Name – Guards	Pos.	Hgt	Wgt	Age	Int	Pts
Joe Lamas	G	5'10"	216	26		6
Hubbard Law	G-LB	6'1"	210	21	1	
(1 rush for 6 yds.)						
Frank Pastin	G-LB	5'10"	197	21		
Mike Rodak	G-DE	5'10"	195	25		
Jack Sanders	G-LB	6'	215	25	1	7
(7 PAT in 8 attempts)						
Milt Simington	G	6'2"	220	24		4
(1 FG in 1 attempt, 1 PAT in 2 attempts)						
George Sirochman	G	6'2"	220	24		

After two early losses, the Steelers shockingly came alive and won seven of their last nine contests. In this totally unexpected transformation of the chaotic Steelers into contenders, rookie tailback Bill Dudley made the big difference.

Although Dudley stood only 5'10", had problems outrunning some linemen, and passed the ball with an awkward side-arm motion, he was a born winner. He ran slowly but knew how to use his blockers, which hole to hit, and when to cut back across an open field. He looked funny passing, but he completed passes, and his running, passing, kick-returning, defensive work, punting, and place-kicking all testified to a competitor's heart burning in his small body. He introduced himself to the league by running 55 yards for a touchdown in the first minute of play on opening day. Like Eddie Stanky in baseball, Bill Dudley had limited talent but always found a way to win.

NEW YORK GIANTS 5-5-1 Steve Owen

Scores of Each Game		
14	Washington	7
10	Pittsburgh	13
35	PHILADELPHIA	17
7	Chic. Bears	26
7	Brooklyn	17
9	PITTSBURGH	17
14	Philadelphia	0
7	WASHINGTON	14
21	GREEN BAY	21
21	CHIC. CARDS	7
10	BROOKLYN	0

Use Name	Pos.	Hgt	Wgt	Age	Int	Pts
Emmett Barrett	C-LB	6'2"	192	23		
Harold Hall	C-LB	6'2"	210			
Mel Hein	C-LB	6'2"	232	33	1	
Ed Hiemstra	C-G-LB	6'	200	22	1	
Jiggs Kline	DE	6'1"	198	28		
Harry Buffington	BB-LB	6'	195	23	1	

Use Name – Tackles	Pos.	Hgt	Wgt	Age	Int	Pts
Kay Bell	T	6'2"	230	27		
Al Blozis	T	6'6"	250	23		
Frank Cope	T	6'2"	220	26		
Paul Stenn	T	6'2"	236	24		

Use Name – Guards	Pos.	Hgt	Wgt	Age	Int	Pts
Chuck Avedisian	G-LB	5'9"	200	24		
Monk Edwards	G-T-LB	6'3"	210	22		
Ed Lechner	G-T	6'1"	200	22		
Red Seick	G-LB	6'	195	31		

Cold in mid-season, hot at the end, the Giants finished a lukewarm third in the Eastern Division. Starting out with a victory over the Redskins, the Giants hoped to repeat as Eastern champs, but a three-game losing skid in October laid that ambition to rest, and the club had to win its last two games just to break even for the year.

The New Yorkers lost a lot of blood to the military, with runner Len Eshmont, blocking back Nello Falaschi, end Jim Poole, and tackle John Mellus lining up in different formations to the music of different signals. To compensate, Tuffy Leemans concentrated more on passing than on running, leaving the bulk of the ball-carrying to rookie Merle Hapes. The line was bolstered by rookie tackle Al Blozis, a 6'6" broth of a man who was a world champion shot-putter at Georgetown University. But the incoming talent hardly balanced the men trading in their blue jerseys for olive drab.

BROOKLYN DODGERS 3-8-0 Mike Getto

Scores of Each Game		
35	Philadelphia	14
28	Detroit	7
0	PITTSBURGH	7
10	WASHINGTON	21
17	NEW YORK	7
0	CLEVELAND	17
0	CHIC. BEARS	35
7	PHILADELPHIA	14
3	Washington	23
0	Pittsburgh	13
0	New York	10

Use Name	Pos.	Hgt	Wgt	Age	Int	Pts
Art Deremer	C-LB	6'3"	208	24		
Don Pierce	C-LB	6'1"	186	23		
Tom Robertson	C-LB	6'	218	25	1	
(1 kickoff return for 9 yds.)						
Si Titus	C-LB-DE	6'	195	23		
Mike Nixon	WB-DB	5'11"	187	30		
Bob Gifford	BB-LB	6'	200	23		

Use Name – Tackles	Pos.	Hgt	Wgt	Age	Int	Pts
Mike Jurich	T	6'1"	235	23		
Duce Keahey (from NY)	T-G	6'2"	215	25		
Bruiser Kinard	T	6'1"	220	27		
Walt Merrill	T	6'2"	215	25		
Bernie Weiner	T-G	5'11"	222	24		

Use Name – Guards	Pos.	Hgt	Wgt	Age	Int	Pts
Bob Jeffries	G	6'2"	206	23		
Art Jocher	G	6'1"	207	26		
Bernie Kapitansky	G	6'1"	212	21		
George Kinard	G	6'1"	205	25		
Jim Sivell	G	5'9"	205	28		
Bud Svendsen	G-C-LB	6'1"	195	27	1	

With owner Dan Topping, coach Jock Sutherland, and star tailback Ace Parker all in the military, the Dodgers made an about-face. Sutherland had been the organizational genius and Parker the inspirational leader. Without their presence the team wandered through the season with very little direction. Mike Getto coached the club but could not replace Sutherland. Losers before the Scot arrived in Brooklyn, the Dodgers turned back into losers as soon as he left.

Dean McAdams played indifferently at tailback and could not fill Parker's shoes as a leader. Bruiser Kinard and Perry Schwartz kept up their good work on the line, and runners Pug Manders and Merl Condit gained yardage consistently although their jobs were tougher now that Parker's passes were no longer a threat. The Dodgers won only three games all year, but a victory over the rival Giants salvaged some of their local pride.

PHILADELPHIA EAGLES 2-9-0 Greasy Neale

Scores of Each Game		
24	Pittsburgh	14
14	Cleveland	24
14	BROOKLYN	35
10	WASHINGTON	14
17	New York	35
0	PITTSBURGH	14
14	Chic. Bears	45
27	Washington	30
0	NEW YORK	14
14	Brooklyn	7
0	GREEN BAY	7

Use Name	Pos.	Hgt	Wgt	Age	Int	Pts
Ray Graves	C-LB	6'1"	205	23	1	1
(1 PAT in 1 attempt)						
Ken Hayden	C-LB	6'	205	22	1	
Basilio Marchi	C-LB	6'2"	225	33		
Bob Wear	C-LB	5'11"	205	23		
Tex Williams	C-LB	5'11"	190	23		
Jack Smith	OE-DE	6'1"	200	25		
(1 kickoff return for 13 yds.)						
Al Thacker	DB	5'10"	200	23		
Jim Lankas	FB-LB	6'2"	215	24		

Use Name – Tackles	Pos.	Hgt	Wgt	Age	Int	Pts
Leo Brennan	T	6'	210	22		
Leon Cook	T					
John Eibner	T	6'2"	235	26		
Joe Frank	T	6'1"	215	27		
Bill Halverson	T	6'3"	242	24		
Frank Hrabetin	T	6'4"	235	26		
(1 kickoff return for 7 yds.)						
Ed Kasky	T	6'1"	220	23		
(Missed 1 field goal attempt)						
Steve Levanitis	T	6'1"	220	23		
Vic Sears	T	6'3"	210	24		6

Use Name – Guards	Pos.	Hgt	Wgt	Age	Int	Pts
Enio Conti	G	5'11"	205	29		
Woody Gerber	G	6'	220	22	1	
Bernie Kaplan	G	6'	205	29		
Al Milling	G	5'9"	170	22		
Rupert Pate	G	6'1"	205	25		6

Good ball players were scattered as rarely as four-leaf clovers on the Eagles, but Uncle Sam picked a handful of these gems for his own team. Linemen Bob Suffridge and Phil Ragazzo, starting end Bob Kreiger, and backs Jim Castiglia, Dan DeSantis, and Terry Fox (last year's top three rushers) all marched off into the military. Coach Greasy Neale made up for the losses by inviting hordes of rookies to training camp and keeping the best.

Tommy Thompson beat the draft because he could see in only one eye, and he spent the year directing the Eagles' T-formation offense. He led the team to an opening-day 24-14 victory over the Steelers, but eight straight losses followed for the young Eagles, and that fact, coupled with the prospect of more players being drafted, prompted the Eagles to merge with the Steelers when the 1943 season rolled around.

TEAM TOTALS

OFFENSE	First Downs: Tot	by Rsh	by Pas	by Pen	Rushing: No.	Yds.	Avg. Yds.	TD	Passing: Att	Com	Comp Pct.	Yds.	Avg. Yds. Att.	Avg. Yds. Comp	TD	Int	Pct. Int.	Punting: No.	Avg. Yds.
WASH.	149	71	66	12	413	1521	3.7	9	257	137	**53.3**	1600	6.2	11.7	16	17	6.6	63	**44.3**
PITT.	130	86	29	**15**	**490**	1851	3.8	15	161	51	31.7	686	4.3	13.5	2	11	6.8	75	36.6
N.Y.	105	65	36	4	401	1221	3.0	10	148	67	45.3	957	6.5	14.3	10	14	9.5	65	38.5
BKN.	109	76	23	10	431	1495	3.5	9	159	56	35.2	714	4.5	12.8	3	24	15.1	73	40.6
PHI.	124	66	50	8	407	1105	2.7	8	213	96	45.1	1416	6.6	14.8	8	17	8.0	72	37.2

OFFENSE	Punt Returns: No.	Yds.	Avg. Yds.	TD	Kickoff Returns: No.	Yds.	Avg. Yds.	TD	Interception Returns: No.	Yds	Avg. Yds.	TD	Penalties: No.	Yds.	Fumbles: No.	Lost	Points: Tot	PAT	FG Att	FG	Saf.
WASH.	**45**	544	12.1	0	23	640	**27.8**	**2**	19	225	11.8	0	67	610	26	13	227	28	9	3	2
PITT.	43	**662**	**15.4**	**2**	30	699	23.3	1	21	**420**	**20.0**	0	58	383	22	10	167	20	**16**	3	0
N.Y.	31	393	12.7	0	24	564	23.5	0	15	269	17.9	1	48	437	15	**7**	155	20	**16**	3	0
BKN.	29	309	10.7	0	31	656	21.2	0	14	229	16.4	1	32	288	23	10	100	13	6	3	0
PHI.	42	596	14.2	1	**42**	**882**	21.0	1	18	179	9.9	0	47	392	26	11	134	17	8	3	0

Use Name – Backs & Ends	Pos.	Age	Hgt	Wgt	Pts	Int	RUSHING				PASSING								RECEIVING				PUNTING		KICKING						PUNT RETURNS				KICKOFF RETURNS			
							No.	Yds	Avg	TD	Att	Comp	%	Yds	Yd/Att	TD	Int–%	RK	No.	Yds	Avg	TD	No.	Avg	Pat	Att	%	FG	Att	%	No.	Yds	Avg	TD	No.	Yds	Avg	TD
WASHINGTON REDSKINS																																						
Sammy Baugh	TB-DB	28	6'2"	185	6	5	20	61	3.1	1	225	132	59	1524	6.8	16	11–5	1					37	46.6							5	63	13	0				
Dick Poillon	TB-DB	22	6'	185	5		55	148	2.7	0	15	2	13	52	3.5	0	3–20						11	38.5	2	2	100	1	2	50	1	0	0	0	3	65	22	0
Roy Zimmerman	TB-DB	24	6'2"	200	4		12	56	4.7	0	10	2	20	13	1.3	0	2–20						4	50.5	1	1	100	1	1	100					1	25	25	0
Andy Farkas	FB-DB	26	5'10"	192	39	3	125	468	3.7	3									11	143	13	2			3	3	100				16	219	14	0	4	206	52	1
Bob Seymour	FB-DB	26	6'2"	208	6	3	54	190	3.5	1									3	20	7	0									4	79	20	0				
Steve Juzwik	FB-DB	24	5'8"	190	15		15	75	5.0	2															3	3	100				3	33	11	0	1	22	22	0
Rufus Deal	FB-DB	24	6'	205			5	12	2.4	0																												
Dick Todd	WB-FB-DB	27	5'11"	170	26	2	65	195	3.0	0	6	1	17	11	1.8	0	1–17		23	328	14	4	11	40.2	2	3	67				13	143	11	0	2	92	46	0
Wilbur Moore	WB-BB-DB	26	5'11"	190	12	3	10	25	2.5	0									10	114	11	2									1	3	3	0	1	24	24	0
Ed Justice	WB-DB	29	6'1"	195	6	1	3	–1	–0.3	0									9	108	12	1																
John Goodyear	WB-DB	22	6'1"	190			2	1	0.5	0																												
Ray Hare	BB-LB	24	6'1"	205	12	1	27	197	7.3	1									5	57	11	0									1	0	0	0	1	95	95	1
Cecil Hare	BB-LB	23	5'11"	195	12		14	57	4.1	1									3	35	12	1									1	4	4	0	1	11	11	0
Marv Whited	BB-LB	24	5'10"	210			1	3	3.0	0																												
Bob Masterson	OE-DE	27	6'1"	220	32		3	12	4.0	0	1	0	0	0	0.0	0	0–0		22	308	14	2			17	19	89	1	5	20					3	45	15	0
Ed Cifers	OE-DE	26	6'2"	225	18														18	196	11	1													2	0	0	0
John Kovatch	OE-DE	22	6'3"	190	6														12	90	8	1													1	13	13	0
Al Krueger	OE-DE	23	6'1"	185															9	65	7	0													1	19	19	0
Bob McChesney	OE-DE	30	6'2"	200	12		2	22	11.0	0									8	100	13	2																
Charley Malone	OE-DE	32	6'4"	200															3	29	10	0																
PITTSBURGH STEELERS																																						
Bill Dudley	TB-DB	21	5'10"	175	36	3	162	696	4.3	5	94	35	37	438	4.7	2	5–5	9	1	24	24	0	18	32.0							20	271	14	0	11	298	27	1
Andy Tomasic	TB-DB	22	6'	175	6	2	60	214	3.6	0	54	11	20	174	3.2	0	5–9		1	27	27	0	17	35.5	0	1	0				12	199	17	1	4	94	24	0
Dick Riffle	FB-DB	27	6'1"	204	25	4	118	467	4.0	4	8	3	38	64	8.0	0	1–12		3	50	17	0	1	40.0	1	1	100				1	8	8	0	7	137	20	0
Joe Hoague	FB-DB	24	6'2"	200	6	1	65	168	2.6	1	1	0	0	0	0.0	0	0–0						2	44.0														
Curt Sandig	HB-DB	24	5'10"	170	24	5	50	116	2.3	3	4	2	50	10	2.5	0	0–0		6	103	17	0	37	38.8							6	142	24	1	7	168	24	0
George Gonda	HB-DB		5'10"	175	12	1	17	147	8.6	2									1	7	7	0									2	17	9	0				
John Binotto (to PHI)	HB-DB	22	5'10"	185	1		17	47	2.8	0															1	1	100				2	25	13	0				
Al Donelli (to PHI)	HB-DB	23	5'7"	165			2	–4	–2.0	0																												
Vern Martin	BB-LB	22	5'10"	195	12														7	64	9	1																
Russ Cotton	BB-LB	27	6'2"	195		1													2	58	29	0																
Walt Kichefski	OE-DE	26	6'1"	210															15	189	13	0																
Don Looney	OE-DB	24	6'2"	180	6														7	59	8	1																
Tom Brown	OE-DE	21	6'2"	216	6														4	69	17	0																
Tony Bova	OE-DB	25	6'1"	190		1													3	37	12	0													1	2	2	0
Armand Niccolai	T	30	6'2"	230	15																				9	9	100	2	14	14								
NEW YORK GIANTS																																						
Tuffy Leemans	QB-DB	29	6'	200	18		51	116	2.3	3	69	35	51	555	8.0	7	4–6	4	1	–10	–10	0									2	26	13	0				
Andy Marefos	QB-FB-DB	25	6'	220	6	1	48	138	2.9	1	29	11	38	176	6.1	1	5–17											0	2	0								
Bob Trocolor	QB-DB	23	6'2"	205			26	18	0.7	0	5	3	60	52	10.4	1	1–20						16	41.3							2	24	12	0	1	35	35	0
Bill Hutchinson	QB-DB	26	5'9"	180			7	27	3.9	0	4	1	25	–3	–0.7	0	2–50						2	32.5							1	1	1	0				
Merle Hapes	FB-DB	23	5'10"	185	30	3	95	363	3.8	3	2	2	100	–12	–6.0	0	0–0		10	79	8	2	15	37.1							11	170	15	0	9	215	24	0
Hank Soar	FB-DB	28	6'2"	210	8	3	49	187	3.8	1	10	3	30	34	3.4	0	1–10						3	42.0	2	3	67	0	2	0	3	29	10	0	5	134	27	0
Leo Cantor	FB-DB	23	6'1"	195	12	2	67	124	1.9	2	29	12	41	155	5.3	1	1–3						20	38.1							5	69	14	0	1	24	24	0
Ward Cuff	WB-DB	29	6'	195	39	1	38	189	5.0	0									16	267	17	2			18	18	100	3	11	27	4	54	14	0	3	78	26	0
Don Lieberum	WB-DB	24	6'	175			11	29	2.6	0									6	65	11	0									1	0	0	0	1	12	12	0
Al Owen	BB-LB	29	6'	205			8	27	3.4	0									1	20	20	0									2	20	10	0				
Leland Shaffer	BB-LB	30	6'2"	205			1	3	3.0	0									3	20	7	0													2	40	20	0
Dom Principe	BB-LB	25	6'	210															2	33	17	0	1	32.0														
John Chickerneo	BB-LB	25	6'1"	205		1																	8	37.8														
Jim Lee Howell	OE-DE	27	6'6"	218															10	115	12	0																
Will Walls	OE-DE	27	6'4"	220	12														7	190	27	2													2	26	13	0
Neal Adams	OE-DE	23	6'3"	195	24	1													6	87	15	3																
John Lascari	OE-DE	24	6'2"	210	6														3	38	13	1						0	1	0								
Frank Liebel	OE-DE	22	6'1"	203															2	53	27	0																
BROOKLYN DODGERS																																						
Dean McAdams	TB-DB	24	6'1"	190	2		110	314	2.9	0	89	35	39	441	5.0	2	15–17	11	3	11	4	0	52	41.3	2	2	100				6	95	16	0	7	165	24	0
Harold McCullough	TB-DB	24	5'11"	170			21	11	0.5	0	38	12	32	211	5.6	1	3–8						12	35.2							1	0	0	0				
Gerry Courtney	TB-DB	24	6'	195	6	1	8	12	1.5	1	4	1	25	14	3.5	0	2–50		1	1	1	0																
Curt Mecham	TB-DB	22	6'	180			3	0	0.0	0	4	1	25	9	2.3	0	0–0																					
Meril Condit	HB-DB	25	5'11"	185	37	6	129	647	5.0	2	17	5	29	27	1.6	0	3–18		9	111	12	0	7	45.0	10	10	100	3	6	50	21	210	10	0	8	172	22	0
Pug Manders	FB-DB	29	6'	200	36	2	93	316	3.4	6	1	0	0	0	0.0	0	0–0		4	53	13	0													9	210	23	0
Bob Robertson	HB-DB	25	5'11"	185		2	46	132	2.9	0	3	1	33	1	0.3	0	1–33		5	61	12	0	1	32.0							1	4	4	0				
Walt Fedora	FB-DB	23	5'11"	190			16	34	2.1	0																									4	75	19	0
Jack Vetter	HB-DB	21	6'2"	198			1	4	4.0	0																												
Thurman Jones	FB-DB	24	5'10"	200	1		1	2	2.0	0															1	1	100											
Rhoten Shetley	BB-LB	24	5'11"	210	6	1													3	19	6	1																
Wendell Butcher	BB-LB	28	6'1"	195															1	16	16	0																
Perry Schwartz	OE-DE	27	6'2"	195	6		2	20	10.0	0									13	200	15	1													2	25	13	0
Eddie Rucinski	OE-DE	26	6'2"	198	6														9	99	11	1																
Herman Hodges	OE-DE	27	6'1"	200															4	74	19	0																
Joe Tofil	OE-DB	24	6'1"	205															3	33	11	0																
Don Eliason	OE-DE	24	6'2"	205															1	36	36	0																
PHILADELPHIA EAGLES																																						
Tommy Thompson	QB-DB	26	6'1"	190	6	4	92	9	0.1	1	203	95	47	1410	6.9	8	16–8	5													7	60	9	0	5	76	15	0
Len Barnum	QB-DB	29	6'	200	16	1	30	64	2.1	0	9	1	11	6	0.7	0	1–11		3	54	18	0	50	38.1	7	8	88	3	7	43	1	44	44	0	1	16	16	0
Bob Davis	HB-DB	28	6'	180	18	2	43	207	4.8	2									6	93	16	1									10	84	8	0	8	140	18	0
Ted Williams	FB-LB	25	5'11"	185	12		50	183	3.7	2									9	58	6	0													3	58	19	0
Bosh Pritchard (from CLE)	HB-DB	23	5'11"	165	6	3	38	166	4.4	0									2	4	2	0	19	34.7							11	107	10	0	4	158	40	1
Ernie Steele	HB-DB	24	6'	190	13	2	24	124	5.2	0									7	114	16	1	2	30.5	1	1	100				10	264	26	1	7	160	23	0
Lou Tomasetti	HB-DB	26	6'	195		1	45	102	2.3	0									4	22	6	0									3	37	12	0	4	90	23	0
Dick Erdlitz	HB-DB	22	5'10"	182	14	1	21	69	3.3	1									5	78	16	0			8	8	100								1	25	25	0
Billy Jefferson (to BKN)	HB-DB	24	6'2"	210			12	58	4.8	0	4	1	25	11	2.8	0	0–0						2	49.5											3	74	25	0
Bert Johnson	HB-DB	30	6'	215	12		27	54	2.0	0									9	123	14	2													2	40	20	0
Jack Stackpool	FB-LB	24	6'1"	207			15	47	3.1	0									2	59	30	0													1	13	13	0
Irv Hall	FB-LB	28	6'	210			8	14	1.8	0									2	18	9	0	1	36.0											1	22	22	0
Bob Masters	HB-DB	31	5'11"	200			1	3	3.0	0																												
Fred Meyer	OE-DE	23	6'2"	190	6		2	13	6.5	0									16	304	19	1													1	14	14	0
Larry Cabrelli	OE-DE	25	5'11"	195	6														15	249	17	1																
Len Supulski	OE-DB	21	6'	175	6	1	1	1	1.0	0									8	149	19	1																
Bob Priestley	OE-DE	30	5'11"	192															4	47	12	0																
Bill Combs	OE-DB	22	5'11"	183	6														4	44	11	1																

TEAM TOTALS

DEFENSE	FIRST DOWNS: Tot	by Rsh	by Pas	by Pen	RUSHING: No.	Yds.	Avg Yds.	TD	PASSING: Att.	Com	Comp Pct.	Yds.	Avg. Yds. Att.	Avg. Yds. Comp	TD	Int.	Pct. Int.	PUNTING: No.	Avg. Yds.	PUNT RETURNS: No.	Yds.	Avg. Yds.	TD	KICKOFF RETURNS: No.	Yds.	Avg. Yds.	TD	INTERCEPTION RETURNS: No.	Yds.	Avg. Yds.	TD	PENALTIES: No.	Yds.	FUMBLES: No.	Lost	POINTS: Tot	PAT	FG Att	FG	Saf.	DEFENSE
WASH.	111	52	46	13	367	848	2.3	5	216	81	37.5	1093	5.1	13.5	5	19	8.8	83	38.1	30	375	12.5	0	37	829	22.4	2	17	319	18.8	1	43	340	16	7	102	12	8	4	0	WASH.
PITT.	114	59	50	5	366	1205	3.3	6	211	100	47.4	1183	5.6	11.8	9	21	10.0	71	41.3	40	412	10.3	0	27	500	18.5	0	11	131	11.9	0	60	512	19	7	119	14	17	5	0	PITT.
N.Y.	159	86	62	11	466	1485	3.2	13	228	114	50.0	1401	6.1	12.3	4	15	6.6	64	37.6	40	500	12.5	1	35	826	23.6	1	14	215	15.4	0	41	290	36	19	139	16	8	3	0	N.Y.
BKN.	131	77	49	5	426	1630	3.8	13	199	89	44.7	1175	5.9	13.2	9	14	7.0	62	40.0	37	551	14.9	1	22	526	23.9	0	24	173	7.2	0	61	495	26	12	168	21	13	3	0	BKN.
PHI.	131	78	40	13	464	1727	3.7	20	178	79	44.4	1241	7.0	15.7	12	18	10.1	65	40.5	31	446	14.4	0	26	632	24.3	1	17	224	13.2	0	51	452	20	10	239	32	9	3	0	PHI.

CHICAGO BEARS 11-0-0 George Halas

Scores of Each Game		
44	Green Bay	28
21	Cleveland	7
41	CHIC. CARDS	14
26	NEW YORK	7
45	PHILADELPHIA	14
16	DETROIT	0
35	Brooklyn	0
38	GREEN BAY	7
42	Detroit	0
47	CLEVELAND	0
21	Chic. Cards	7

Use Name	Pos.	Hgt	Wgt	Age	Int	Pts
Stu Clarkson	C-LB	6'2"	198	23		
Al Matuzo	C-LB	6'2"	205	23	2	
Bulldog Turner	C-LB	6'1"	240	23	8	12
(1 kickoff return for 6 yds.)						
Clint Wager	OE-DE	6'6"	215	21		
Voluntarily retired – Bob Snyder						

Use Name – Tackles	Pos.	Hgt	Wgt	Age	Int	Pts
Lee Artoe	T	6'3"	230	26		20
(20 PAT's in 22 attempts, missed 1 FG attempt)						
Bill Hempel	T	6'	235	22		
Al Hoptowit	T	6'1"	216	26		
Ed Kolman	T	6'2"	230	24		
Joe Stydahar	T	6'4"	240	30		5
(5 PAT's in 8 attempts)						

Use Name – Guards	Pos.	Hgt	Wgt	Age	Int	Pts
Len Akin	G-LB	5'11"	207	36	1	
Ray Bray	G	6'	245	25		
Chuck Drulis	G-LB	5'10"	215	24	1	
Danny Fortmann	G-LB	6'	210	26	4	6
Nick Kerasiotis	G-LB	5'11"	197	24		
George Musso	G	6'2"	255	32		

With the Bears' first three fullbacks in the service, George Halas stuck fourth-stringer Gary Famiglietti into the lineup, and he simply responded by leading the club in rushing and winning a berth on the All-Pro team. Another Bear hero was rookie Frank Maznicki, who filled in for Navy-departed George McAfee with his own brand of speedy running. End Dick Plasman was also gone, as was tackle Joe Stydahar, who was called late in the year. Even George Halas was summonded back into the Navy in mid-season. But nothing could stop the talent-heavy Bears. They won eleven straight, easy games, by 14 points or more.

Halas left the club in the hands of assistants Hunk Anderson, Luke Johnsos, and Paddy Driscoll, and this triumvirate had close to a pushbutton job. They got passing from Sid Luckman, long-yardage receiving from halfback Scooter McLean, and superb line play from Bulldog Turner, Danny Fortmann, Lee Artoe, and George Wilson.

GREEN BAY PACKERS 8-2-1 Curly Lambeau

Scores of Each Game		
28	CHIC. BEARS	44
17	Chic. Cards	13
38	DETROIT	7
45	CLEVELAND	28
28	Detroit	7
55	CHIC. CARDS	24
30	Cleveland	12
7	Chic. Bears	38
21	New York	21
7	Philadelphia	0
24	PITTSBURGH	21

Use Name	Pos.	Hgt	Wgt	Age	Int	Pts
Charley Brock	C-LB	6'2"	210	26	6	6
Bob Flowers	C-LB	6'1"	205	25		
Bob Ingalls	C-LB	6'3"	200	23	1	6
Earl Ohlgren	DE	6'2"	210	24		
John Stonebraker	OE-DE	6'3"	200	24		
Ben Starret	BB-LE	5'11"	210	24		
(1 punt for 43 yds.)						

Use Name – Tackles	Pos.	Hgt	Wgt	Age	Int	Pts
Paul Berezney	T	6'2"	220	25		
(1 kickoff return for 7 yds.)						
Tiny Croft	T	6'3"	300	21		
Royal Kahler	T	6'2"	226	24		
Bill Lee	T	6'2"	240	30		
Ernie Pannell	T	6'2"	220	25		
Baby Ray	T	6'6"	245	27		

Use Name – Guards	Pos.	Hgt	Wgt	Age	Int	Pts
Buckets Goldenberg	G-LB	5'10"	220	31	4	
Bill Kuusisto	G	6'	225	24		
Russ Letlow	G	6'	222	28		
Pete Tinsley	G-LB	5'8"	205	29	1	
Fred Vant Hull	G-LB	6'	214	22		

Don Hutson caught lightning in a bottle this year, in addition to a lot of passes. With the Packer offense stressing the air game, Hutson set new NFL season records for receptions, yards gained on receptions, touchdown passes caught, and points scored. Passer Cecil Isbell set a few records himself, in yards gained passing and in touchdown passes. No one in the league had yet learned how to cover the crafty Hutson, and Isbell rarely missed the receiver in the open. Hutson also kicked extra points for Green Bay, building up a record 138 points that went unmatched until Paul Hornung came along in 1960.

Even with this premier combination, however, the Packers were only the second-best team in the league. They lost twice all year, but unfortunately did so at the hands of the unbeaten Bears. No excuses could be offered, as even with Clarke Hinkle in the Coast Guard, youngsters Ted Fritsch, Charlie Sample, and Tony Canadeo picked up the slack.

CLEVELAND RAMS 5-6-0 Dutch Clark

Scores of Each Game		
0	Chic. Cards	7
24	PHILADELPHIA	14
14	Detroit	0
7	CHIC. BEARS	21
14	Washington	33
28	Green Bay	45
7	CHIC. CARDS	3
17	Brooklyn	0
12	GREEN BAY	30
27	DETROIT	7
0	Chic. Bears	47

Use Name	Pos.	Hgt	Wgt	Age	Int	Pts
Bill Conkright	C-LB	6'1"	205	28	2	
Don Johnson	C-LB	6'	205	21		
Bill Rieth	C-LB	5'11"	203	26		
Hank Rockwell	C-LB-DE	6'4"	230	25	1	
Herb Godfrey	OE-DE	6'1"	187	23		
Maury Patt	DE	6'2"	205	28		

Use Name – Tackles	Pos.	Hgt	Wgt	Age	Int	Pts
Boyd Clay	T	6'1"	225	29		4
(4 PAT's in 4 attempts)						
Jake Fawcett	T	5'11"	225	23		
Tex Mooney	T	6'5"	270	25		
Joe Pasqua	T	6'1"	228	24		1
(1 PAT in 1 attempt)						

Use Name – Guards	Pos.	Hgt	Wgt	Age	Int	Pts
Larry Brahm	G-LB	5'10"	204	26	1	
Riley Matheson	G-LB	6'2"	205	27	1	
Barney McGarry	G-LB	6'1"	200	24		
Roy Stuart	G-LB	5'8"	185	22	1	
Wilfred Thorpe	G-LB	6'3"	210	25	1	

The Cleveland rise to a 5-6-0 record looked more impressive than it really was, since the five wins came against the Cardinals, Dodgers, Eagles, and Lions, all weaker sisters on the circuit. On the other hand, the Bears beat the Rams 21-7 and 47-0, the Packers stopped them 45-28 and 30-12, and the Redskins took a 33-14 decision. The Cardinals even downed the Rams 7-0 in their first meeting. The improved record showed only that the Rams were the best of the bad.

Although fullback Johnny Drake hung up his spikes, Dante Magnani developed into a good overall runner and receiver. Two of the linemen, Chet Adams and Riley Matheson, won compliments for their play, but neither Dan Reeves nor Fred Levy were around to add their praise. Both co-owners had been called back into the military and received permission to suspend operation for 1943 with their players being spread around the league.

CHICAGO CARDINALS 3-8-0 Jimmy Conzelman

Scores of Each Game		
7	CLEVELAND	0
13	DETROIT	0
13	GREEN BAY	17
14	Chic. Bears	41
7	Detroit	0
3	Cleveland	7
24	Green Bay	55
0	Washington	28
3	Pittsburgh	19
7	New York	21
7	CHIC. BEARS	21

Use Name	Pos.	Hgt	Wgt	Age	Int	Pts
Ray Apolskis	C-LB	5'11"	200	23	2	
Vince Banonis	C-LB	6'1"	220	21	2	
Ben Ciccone	C-LB	5'10"	220	33		
Ernie Wheeler	DB	6'1"	200	27		
(1 punt for 40 yds.)						
Dick Evans	OE-DE	6'3"	210	25		

Use Name – Tackles	Pos.	Hgt	Wgt	Age	Int	Pts
Joe Allton	T	6'2"	235	21	1	
Al Babartsky	T	6'	225	26		
Chet Bulger	T	6'3"	235	24		
Gil Duggan	T	6'3"	225	24	1	
Ross Nagel	T	6'4"	225	19		
Carl Olson	T	6'2"	206	25		
Champ Siebold	T	6'4"	237	29	1	6

Use Name – Guards	Pos.	Hgt	Wgt	Age	Int	Pts
Conway Baker	G	5'11"	225	31		
Libero Bertagnolli	G-LB	5'9"	190	26		
Frank Bohlmann	G	5'11"	212	25		
Ralph Fife	G-LB	6'	202	22		
Bob Maddock	G-LB	6'	200	22		
Gordon Wilson	G	6'	230	26		

With last year's top passer, receiver, and lineman in military service, the Cardinals expected a rough time this year. But even without Johnny Clement, Bill Dewell, and Joe Kuharich, the Cardinals opened the season by shutting out the Rams and Lions. Whatever faint hopes this beginning raised, eight losses in the next nine matches dashed them like crockery on the rocks. Bud Schwenk, the new passer, was no Sammy Baugh, but at least he kept busy by throwing the most passes in the league, and veteran end Pop Ivy grabbed twenty-seven aerials, a very distant second to Don Hutson's seventy-four receptions. Marshall Goldberg continued to be the backfield ace on offense and defense, but no one made up for Kuharich's loss in the line. After his third mediocre team in a row, coach Jimmy Conzelman quit to work in the front office of the St. Louis Browns baseball team. He would be back, though, bringing better times with him.

DETROIT LIONS 0-11-0 Bill Edwards, Bull Karcis

Scores of Each Game		
0	Chic. Cards	13
0	CLEVELAND	14
7	BROOKLYN	28
7	Green Bay	38
0	CHIC. CARDS	7
7	GREEN BAY	28
0	Chic. Bears	16
7	PITTSBURGH	35
7	Cleveland	27
0	CHIC. BEARS	42
3	WASHINGTON	15

Use Name	Pos.	Hgt	Wgt	Age	Int	Pts
Tony Arena	C-LB	6'	200	24		
Sloko Gill	C-G-LB	5'10"	185	24	1	
John Schiechl (from PIT)	C-LB	6'2"	245	25		
Alex Wojciechowicz	C-LB	5'11"	210	27	2	
(4 receptions for 44 yds., 3 kickoff rets. for 30 yds.)						
Bill Kennedy	DE	5'11"	194	23		

Use Name – Tackles	Pos.	Hgt	Wgt	Age	Int	Pts
Henry Goodman	T	6'3"	220	23		
Ted Pavelic	T	6'	210	23		3
(1 field goal in 2 attempts)						
Alex Schibanoff	T	6'1"	215	22		
George Speth	T	6'2"	220	24		
Emil Uremovich	T	6'2"	230	25		

Use Name – Guards	Pos.	Hgt	Wgt	Age	Int	Pts
Larry Sartori	G	6'	208	25		
(1 punt for 42 yds.)						
John Wiethe	G-LB	6'	200	25		
Tony Zuzzio	G	5'11"	210	26		

These Lions had no bite, no scratch, no offense, and no defense. The attack scored only five touchdowns all year, never posting more than 7 points in any one game, while the defense sprang so many leaks that 263 enemy points rushed through in a torrent. The closest the feeble Lions came to victory was a 7-0 loss to the Cardinals.

After three games, coach Bill Edwards quit, and Bull Karcis picked up the coaching reigns. The nightmare kept on going, though, and Karcis may have been tempted to play fullback himself, as none of his young backs showed any magnetism for the end zone. The only thing worse than the feeble passing attack was the attendance, a sparse 100,508 for seven home games. But owner Fred Mandel showed no discouragement. He never made any move to sell the club nor to fold for the duration of the war, as some other clubs had. In fact, Mandel insisted that the NFL and his team go on.

TEAM TOTALS

	FIRST DOWNS:				RUSHING:				PASSING:									PUNTING:		PUNT RETURNS:				KICKOFF RETURNS:				INTERCEPTION RETURNS:				PENALTIES:		FUMBLES:		POINTS:					
OFFENSE	Tot	by Rsh	by Pas	by Pen	No.	Yds.	Avg. Yds.	TD	Att	Com	Comp Pct.	Yds.	Avg. Yds. Att.	Avg. Yds. Comp	TD	Int	Pct. Int.	No.	Avg. Yds.	No.	Yds.	Avg. Yds.	TD	No.	Yds.	Avg. Yds.	TD	No.	Yds.	Avg. Yds.	TD	No.	Yds.	No.	Lost	Tot	PAT	FG Att	FG	Saf	OFFENSE
CHI.B.	155	98	48	9	470	1911	4.1	23	194	94	48.5	1974	10.2	21.0	21	29	14.9	49	38.9	39	459	11.8	1	21	537	25.6	0	33	402	12.2	3	99	905	27	15	376	46	6	4	0	CHI.B
G.B.	176	65	97	14	422	1274	3.0	10	330	172	52.1	2407	7.3	14.0	28	18	5.5	58	37.4	32	327	10.2	0	36	769	21.4	1	33	349	10.6	1	38	312	13	8	300	39	10	5	0	G.B.
CLEVE.	103	26	60	7	310	1035	3.3	5	249	109	43.8	1537	6.2	14.1	13	27	10.8	77	40.3	30	307	10.2	0	39	739	18.9	0	23	255	11.1	0	45	315	20	8	150	19	6	3	1	CLEVE.
CHI. C.	132	58	59	15	366	1021	2.8	4	316	131	41.5	1432	4.5	10.9	6	29	9.2	74	39.5	32	364	11.4	0	36	855	23.8	1	25	263	10.5	1	46	400	25	11	98	11	10	5	0	CHI.C.
DET.	115	67	40	8	342	1261	3.7	4	222	73	32.9	885	4.0	12.1	1	33	14.9	71	40.6	34	378	11.1	0	38	687	18.1	0	18	188	10.4	0	43	364	35	23	38	5	6	1	0	DET.

Use Name – Backs & Ends	Pos.	Age	Hgt	Wgt	Pts	Int	RUSHING No.	Yds	Avg	TD	PASSING Att	Comp	%	Yds	Yd/Att	TD	Int–%	RK	RECEIVING No.	Yds	Avg	TD	PUNTING No.	Avg	KICKING Pat	Att	%	FG	Att	%	PUNT RETURNS No.	Yds	Avg	TD	KICKOFF RETURNS No.	Yds	Avg	TD
CHICAGO BEARS																																						
Sid Luckman	QB-DB	25	6'	200	6	4	13	24	1.8	0	105	57	54	1023	9.7	10	13–12	3					24	40.6							6	55	9	0				
Charlie O'Rourke	QB-DB	25	5'11"	175	6	3	18	–17	–0.9	1	88	37	42	951	10.8	11	16–18	6					23	35.5							2	8	4	0				
Gary Famiglietti	FB-LB	27	6'	225	48	1	118	503	4.3	8									1	12	12	0			0	1	0								1	9	9	0
Frank Maznicki	HB-DB	22	5'9"	178	45	4	54	343	6.4	1	1	0	0	0	0.0	0	0– 0		2	17	9	1			21	22	95	4	5	80	6	50	8	0	1	33	33	0
Hugh Gallarneau	HB-DB	25	6'	190	42		68	292	4.3	4									14	291	21	3									9	101	11	0	6	151	25	0
Harry Clark	HB-DB	24	6'	190	36		58	273	4.7	4									6	131	22	2									5	76	15	0	5	159	32	0
Ray Nolting	HB-DB	28	5'11"	185	18		57	245	4.3	3									2	23	12	0									3	23	8	0	1	10	10	0
John Petty	FB-LB	23	6'1"	225	12	1	41	149	3.6	2									4	53	13	0	2	57.0														
Ray McLean	HB-DB	26	5'10"	165	54	3	26	63	2.4	0									19	571	30	8									6	118	20	1	4	106	27	0
Bill Geyer	HB-DB	22	5'10"	170			9	18	2.0	0									1	22	22	0									2	28	14	0				
Bill Osmanski	FB-LB	25	5'11"	198			2	9	4.5	0																												
Frank Morris	FB-LB	24	6'2"	214			3	7	2.3	0									3	24	8	0																
Adolph Kissell	HB-DB	21	5'11"	190			2	–1	–0.5	0																									2	63	32	0
John Siegal	OE-DE	24	6'1"	202	12														13	263	20	2																
Hamp Pool	OE-DE	27	6'3"	225	30														10	321	32	5																
George Wilson	OE-DE	28	6'1"	205	12	1													9	89	10	0																
Bob Nowaskey	OE-DE	24	6'	200			1	3	3.0	0									6	128	21	0																
Connie Mack Berry	OE-DE	26	6'3"	212	12														4	29	7	0																
GREEN BAY PACKERS																																						
Cecil Isbell	TB-DB	27	6'1"	190	6	6	36	83	2.3	1	268	146	54	2021	7.5	24	14– 5	2					4	35.3							1	14	14	0	3	44	15	0
Tony Canadeo	TB-HB-DB	23	5'11"	190	18	1	89	272	3.1	3	59	24	41	310	5.3	3	4– 7		10	66	7	0	18	35.8							7	76	11	0	6	137	23	0
Charlie Sample	FB-LB	22	5'9"	200	30		57	255	4.5	4									6	35	6	1													3	91	30	0
Lou Brock	FB-HB-DB	24	6'	192	20	2	95	237	2.5	2									20	139	7	1	32	38.1	2	2	100	0	1	0	8	86	11	0	9	179	20	0
Ted Fritsch	FB-LB	21	5'10"	210	13		74	223	3.0	0									9	60	7	0	3	40.7	1	1	100	4	5	80	1	31	31	0	2	43	22	0
Joe Laws	HB-DB	31	5'9"	180	6	3	29	100	3.4	0	3	2	67	76	25.3	1	0– 0		6	96	16	1									7	56	8	0	2	36	18	0
Andy Uram	HB-DB	27	5'10"	188	31	2	24	75	3.1	0									21	420	20	4			1	1	100				7	50	7	0	8	208	26	1
Bob Kahler	HB-DB	25	6'3"	200			8	4	0.5	0									2	21	11	0									1	14	14	0				
Dick Weisgerber	BB-DE	27	5'10"	198	2		5	21	4.2	0															2	2	100											
Larry Craig	BB-DE	26	6'1"	205			2	0	0.0	0																									2	24	12	0
Don Hutson	OE-DB	29	6'1"	185	138	7	3	4	1.3	0									74	1211	15	17			33	34	97	1	4	25								
Harry Jacunski	OE-DE	26	6'2"	204	6														8	125	16	1																
Joel Mason	OE-DE	29	6'	195															7	86	12	0																
Ray Riddick	OE-DE	24	6'1"	202	6														6	104	17	1																
Joe Carter	OE-DE	32	6'1"	200	6														2	19	10	1																
Keith Ranspot (from DET)	OE-DB	27	6'3"	190	6														1	25	25	1																
CLEVELAND RAMS																																						
Parker Hall	TB-DB	25	6'	195	6	3	41	–3	–0.1	1	140	62	44	815	5.8	7	19–14	8					36	38.8							12	148	12	0	10	155	16	0
Jack Jacobs	TB-DB	23	6'1"	180		4	32	91	2.8	0	93	43	46	640	6.9	6	6– 6	7					33	42.3							8	63	8	0	4	83	21	0
Gaylon Smith	FB-DB	26	5'11"	205	12	4	83	332	4.0	2	12	2	17	49	4.1	0	1– 8		3	66	22	0									6	62	10	0	6	109	18	0
George Morris	FB-DB	23	5'11"	188		2	22	65	3.0	0																					1	2	2	0	1	15	15	0
Corby Davis	FB-DB	27	5'11"	205		1	28	55	2.0	0	2	1	50	22	11.0	0	1–50		2	18	9	0	7	39.3														
Dante Magnani	WB-DB	25	5'10"	178	30		59	344	5.8	1	1	0	0	0	0.0	0	0– 0		24	276	12	4									2	27	14	0	11	250	23	0
Len Janiak	WB-FB-DB	26	6'1"	205	6		34	108	3.2	0	1	1	100	11	11.0	0	0– 0		6	51	9	1																
Bill Lazetich	WB-DB	25	6'	195	12		3	19	6.3	1									6	65	11	1													1	27	27	0
Jack Boone	WB-DB	24	5'11"	175	6	1	3	–1	–0.3	0									2	58	29	1									1	5	5	0				
Art Elston	BB-LB	23	5'11"	195			1	15	15.0	0									4	58	15	0													2	46	23	0
Warren Plunkett	BB-LB	22	6'	200															2	16	16	0													1	4	4	0
John Petchel	BB-LB	23	5'11"	185			1	–2	–2.0	0									1	16	16	0													2	26	13	0
Jim Benton	OE-DE	25	6'3"	195	6														23	345	15	1																
Ben Hightower	OE-DB	23	6'2"	183	18														19	312	16	3																
Johnny Wilson	OE-DE	26	6'3"	205	12														6	113	19	1																
Joe Gibson	OE-DE	23	6'3"	204															6	79	13	0																
George Platukas	OE-DE	27	6'	205	12	1													5	64	13	1																
Chet Adams	T	26	6'3"	235	23																				14	15	93	3	6	50								
CHICAGO CARDINALS																																						
Bud Schwenk	TB-DB	24	6'2"	205	12	1	111	313	2.8	2	295	126	43	1360	4.6	6	27– 9	9					3	38.0											2	24	12	0
Joe Bukant	TB-DB	26	6'	210			17	34	2.0	0	15	4	27	56	3.7	0	2–13																					
John Knolla	TB-WB-DB	23	5'10"	180		1	15	43	2.9	0	6	1	17	16	2.7	0	0– 0		8	48	6	0									6	64	11	0	1	24	24	0
Marshall Goldberg	FB-DB	24	5'11"	195	12	3	116	369	3.2	1									9	108	12	0									6	60	10	0	15	393	26	1
Bob Morrow	FB-DB	24	6'	225	6		45	145	3.2	1																												
John Martin	WB-DB	24	6'1"	195		6	30	10	0.3	0									22	312	14	0	36	39.3							4	50	13	0	8	202	25	0
Steve Lach	WB-DB	22	6'2"	205	25	4	30	97	3.2	0									18	261	15	4	31	40.1	1	1	100				13	158	12	0	7	164	23	0
Lloyd Cheatham	WB-DB	23	6'2"	198	6	1	1	1	1.0	0									6	29	5	1									3	32	11	0	2	37	19	0
Buddy Parker	BB-LB	28	6'	190			1	9	9.0	0									2	7	4	0																
Milt Popovich	BB-G-LB	25	5'11"	208		1													2	21	11	0	3	36.3														
Pop Ivy	OE-DE	26	6'3"	220	2														27	259	10	0			2	2	100											
Al Coppage	OE-DE	26	6'1"	197															20	196	10	0													1	11	11	0
Bill Daddio	OE-DE	26	5'11"	204	29	1													11	108	10	1			8	8	100	5	10	50								
Ray Ebli	OE-DE	22	6'2"	210															6	83	14	0																
DETROIT LIONS																																						
Harry Hopp	TB-DB	23	6'	210		1	66	230	3.5	0	68	20	29	258	3.8	0	13–19	12					27	40.7							9	98	11	0	5	108	22	0
Chet Wetterlund	TB-DB	24	6'2"	185		1	23	6	0.3	0	44	13	30	230	5.2	0	10–23						11	40.8							3	26	9	0	5	89	18	0
Tom Colella	TB-DB	24	6'	185		1	23	51	2.2	0	41	18	44	178	4.3	0	4–10						16	38.1							2	14	7	0	4	74	19	0
Ned Mathews	TB-WB-DB	24	5'10"	185			21	79	3.8	0	22	6	27	43	2.0	1	2– 9		3	38	13	0									7	82	12	0	5	97	19	0
Joe Stringfellow	TB-OE-DB	22	6'	185			16	41	2.6	0	13	5	38	67	5.2	0	2–15		8	89	11	0	9	40.3											2	54	27	0
Elmer Hackney	FB-LB	26	6'2"	200	12		34	208	6.1	2									3	22	7	0													1	4	4	0
Frank Grigonis	FB-LB	23	5'10"	182	6	1	37	131	3.5	1									1	17	17	0													2	49	25	0
John Polanski	FB-LB	23	6'2"	212		1	17	67	3.9	0																												
Harry Seltzer	FB-LB	23	5'9"	195			14	44	3.1	0									2	23	12	0																
Mickey Sanzotta	WB-TB-DB	21	5'9"	185		2	71	268	3.8	0	15	4	27	45	3.0	0	0– 0		5	16	3	0	1	42.0							5	46	9	0				
Lloyd Cardwell	WB-DB	29	6'2"	190	6	2	6	78	13.0	1									5	125	25	0									2	45	23	0	1	13	13	0
Emil Banjavic	WB-DB	23	6'1"	194	6	1	11	67	6.1	0									5	50	10	1	5	47.0							2	29	15	0	4	69	17	0
John Hall	WB-DB	25	6'	190		1	2	–8	–4.0	0	1	0	0	0	0.0	0	0– 0		1	42	42	0									4	38	10	0	4	86	22	0
Paul Szakash	BB-DB	29	6'	210															5	53	11	0																
Bill Callihan	BB-DB	26	6'3"	215		3					1	0	0	0	0.0	0	1–100		4	48	12	0	1	44.0														
Murray Evans	BB-DB	23	6'1"	205			1	–1	–1.0	0	17	7	41	64	3.8	0	1– 6		2	32	16	0																
Bill Fisk	OE-DE	25	6'	200															15	177	12	0													1	10	10	0
Charlie Behan	OE-DE	22	6'3"	195															4	63	16	0																
Gran Harrison	OE-DE	25	6'3"	210															3	21	7	0																
Larry Knorr	OE-DE	25	6'2"	192															2	18	9	0																
Perry Scott	OE-DE	25	6'2"	210															1	7	7	0																
Augie Lio	G-LB	24	6'	235	5	1																			5	5	100	0	4	0					1	4	4	0

TEAM TOTALS

DEFENSE	FIRST DOWNS: Tot	by Rsh	by Pas	by Pen	RUSHING: No.	Yds.	Avg. Yds.	TD	PASSING: Att.	Com	Comp Pct.	Yds.	Avg. Yds. Att.	Avg. Yds. Comp	TD	Int.	Pct. Int.	PUNTING: No.	Avg. Yds.	PUNT RETURNS: No.	Yds.	Avg. Yds.	TD	KICKOFF RETURNS: No.	Yds.	Avg. Yds.	TD	INTERCEPTION RETURNS: No.	Yds.	Avg. Yds.	TD	PENALTIES: No.	Yds.	FUMBLES: No.	Lost	POINTS: Tot	PAT	FG Att	FG	Saf.	DEFENSE
CHI. B.	98	35	47	16	294	519	1.8	3	280	111	39.6	1179	4.2	10.6	7	33	11.8	76	38.2	25	298	11.9	1	60	1194	19.9	0	29	282	9.7	1	34	324	33	18	84	12	2	0	0	CHI. B.
G.B.	147	79	59	9	376	1559	4.1	17	242	100	41.3	1471	6.1	14.7	8	33	13.6	56	37.0	38	395	10.4	0	45	1058	23.5	1	18	282	15.7	2	63	539	22	15	215	27	9	6	1	G.B.
CLEVE.	165	92	60	13	463	1764	3.8	11	262	125	47.7	1740	6.6	13.9	17	23	8.8	56	40.6	40	504	12.6	0	27	545	20.2	0	27	310	11.5	0	46	387	21	10	207	25	9	4	1	CLEVE.
CHI. C.	114	61	44	9	390	1495	3.8	11	214	84	39.3	1502	7.0	17.9	15	25	11.7	75	40.2	44	532	12.1	1	26	530	20.4	0	29	390	13.4	2	71	636	19	8	209	26	9	3	0	CHI. C.
DET.	128	69	51	8	440	1463	3.3	13	219	103	47.0	1623	7.4	15.8	22	18	8.2	69	41.0	32	326	10.2	0	15	388	25.9	1	33	453	13.7	1	53	441	20	10	263	33	9	2	1	DET.

WASHINGTON REDSKINS 6-3-1 Dutch Bergman

Scores of Each Game		
27	BROOKLYN	0
33	Green Bay	7
13	CHIC. CARDS	7
48	Brooklyn	10
14	Phil-Pitt	14
42	DETROIT	20
21	CHIC. BEARS	7
14	PHIL-PITT	27
10	New York	14
7	NEW YORK	31
	EAST Playoff	
28	New York	0

Use Name	Pos.	Hgt	Wgt	Age	Int	Pts
Ken Hayden	C-LB	6'	205	23		
George Smith	C-LB	6'2"	214	29	2	
(1 punt return for 3 yds.)						
Jack Smith	OE-DE	6'1"	200	26		
Joe Gibson*	BB-LB-DE	6'3"	210	24		
Coye Dunn	WB-DB	6'	198			

Use Name – Tackles	Pos.	Hgt	Wgt	Age	Int	Pts
Joe Pasqua*	T	6'1"	225	25		1
(1 PAT in 1 attempt)						
Lou Rymkus	T	6'4"	223	24	1	12
Willie Wilkin	T	6'4"	270	27		
Joe Zeno	T	5'10"	235	24		

Use Name – Guards	Pos.	Hgt	Wgt	Age	Int	Pts
Dick Farman	G-LB	6'	216	27		
Al Fiorentino	G-LB	5'7"	200	26		
Tony Leon	G-LB	5'9"	195	26		
Angelo Paternoster	G-LB					
Frank Ribar	G-LB	6'1"	190			
Clyde Shugart	G-T-LB	6'1"	220	26	1	
Steve Slivinski	G-LB	5'10"	215	26	1	

After seven games, the Redskins were undefeated and sitting pretty atop the Eastern Division. Dutch Bergman was directing the club as coach, with Ray Flaherty in the Navy, and he worried only a little when the Skins lost to the war-mergered Eagles-Steelers club. A home-and-away series with the New York Giants capped the season for the Skins, who needed only a win or a tie to clinch the Eastern crown. But they got neither, as the Giants won both games to deadlock the title race. Expected to fold completely in the playoff game, the fading Redskins shot back into focus as Sammy Baugh threw for three touchdowns in a 28-0 put-down of the New Yorkers.

Baugh starred all year in the passing game. He ranked with Sid Luckman as the top passer in pro ball—and he also intercepted the most aerials by picking off eleven wayward tosses. On offense or defense, passes were Baugh's trademark.

NEW YORK GIANTS 6-3-1 Steve Owen

Scores of Each Game		
14	Phil-Pitt	28
20	Brooklyn	0
42	PHIL-PITT	14
21	GREEN BAY	35
0	Detroit	0
7	CHIC. BEARS	56
24	CHIC. CARDS	13
24	BROOKLYN	7
14	WASHINGTON	10
31	Washington	7
	EAST Playoff	
0	WASHINGTON	28

Use Name	Pos.	Hgt	Wgt	Age	Int	Pts
Mel Hein	C-LB	6'2"	234	34	1	
(Attempted 1 pass – incomplete)						
Bill Piccolo	C-LB	5'11"	185	23		
Hub Barker	BB-LB	5'10"	195	24		

Use Name – Tackles	Pos.	Hgt	Wgt	Age	Int	Pts
Verlin Adams	T-DE	6'	205	25		
Al Blozis	T	6'6"	250	24		6
(1 reception for 15 yds.)						
Vic Carroll	T	6'4"	230	30		
Frank Cope	T	6'2"	232	27		
Frank Umont	T	5'11"	220	25		

Use Name – Guards	Pos.	Hgt	Wgt	Age	Int	Pts
Chuck Avedisian	G-LB	5'9"	200	25		6
Walt Dubzinski	G-C-LB	5'10"	205	23	1	
Sal Marone	G	5'10"	195	25		
Tom Roberts	G-T	6'1"	215	28		
Larry Visnic	G-LB	5'11"	195	24		

Against the Bears, the New York defense looked like a kitchen strainer trying to hold water. Chicago quarterback Sid Luckman riddled the Giants with pinpoint passes, throwing for 433 yards and a record seven touchdowns in a 56-7 romp. After this performance, few expected the Giants to contain Sammy Baugh's slings, but the New Yorkers stiffened their defense and upset the Redskins 14-10 and 31-7 in a home-and-away series which ended the season with a tie for the Eastern lead. But the pass defense turned back into a pumpkin in the playoff game by allowing 28 points, while the offense never got to the scoreboard.

During the year, the young and the old helped the club. Rookie Bill Paschal bulled his way to a league-leading 572 yards behind the tough blocking of second-year tackle Al Blozis. Balancing this youth was thirty-four-year-old center Mel Hein, an instructor at Union College during the week and the pivot of the New York line on Sunday.

PHILADELPHIA EAGLES – PITTSBURGH STEELERS 5-4-1 Greasy Neale, Walt Kiesling

Scores of Each Game		
17	BROOKLYN	H 0
28	NEW YORK	H 14
21	Chic. Bears	48
14	New York	42
34	CHIC. CARDS	P 13
14	WASHINGTON	H 14
7	Brooklyn	13
35	DETROIT	P 34
27	Washington	14
28	GREEN BAY	H 38

H = at Philadelphia
P = at Pittsburgh

Use Name	Pos.	Hgt	Wgt	Age	Int	Pts
Ray Graves	C-LB	6'1"	205	24	1	
Al Wukits	C-LB	6'3"	190	23	1	6
Ray Reutt	DE	6'	195			
Hugh McCullough	DB	6'	185	27		

Use Name – Tackles	Pos.	Hgt	Wgt	Age	Int	Pts
Ted Doyle	T	6'2"	220	29		
Joe Frank	T	6'1"	215	28		
Bucko Kilroy	T	6'2"	240	22		
Elbie Schultz	T	6'4"	250	25		
Vic Sears	T	6'3"	220	25		
(1 kickoff return for 15 yds.)						
Al Wistert	T	6'1"	205	22		

Use Name – Guards	Pos.	Hgt	Wgt	Age	Int	Pts
Rocco Canale	G	5'11"	225	26		
Enio Conti	G	5'11"	205	30	1	
Eddie Michaels	G	5'11"	210	29		
Gordon Paschka	G	6'	205	23		2
(2 PAT's in 2 attempts)						

Faced with draining financial and manpower resources, the Eagles and Steelers merged into one team for a season. Philadelphia and Pittsburgh split the home schedule, coaches Greasy Neale and Walt Kiesling shared the reigns, and both teams pooled their players.

But with stars Bill Dudley and Tommy Thompson off to military service, the team was a true potpourri on the field. The Redskins sold Roy Zimmerman, Sammy Baugh's understudy, to the Phi-Pitt squad to play quarterback. Free-agent halfback Jack Hinkle shone as a ball carrier, while second-year tackle Vic Sears won a spot on the UPI All-Pro team. Rookies Al Wistert and Bucko Kilroy helped in the line, and veteran end Bill Hewitt came out of retirement, even wearing a helmet for the first time in his career. There was even a left-handed passer, Allie Sherman, who played little but whom coach Neale called "the smartest football player I ever coached." With a varied cast, the merged team managed to win five games.

BROOKLYN DODGERS 2-8-0 Pete Cawthorn

Scores of Each Game		
0	Detroit	27
0	Phil-Pitt	17
0	Washington	27
0	NEW YORK	20
21	Chic. Bears	33
10	WASHINGTON	48
7	CHIC. CARDS	0
13	PHIL-PITT	7
7	GREEN BAY	31
7	New York	24

Use Name	Pos.	Hgt	Wgt	Age	Int	Pts
Bill Conkright (from WAS)*	C-LB	6'1"	205	29	1	
Vaughn Stewart (from CHIC)	C-LB	6'1"	200	23		
Bud Svendsen	C-LB	6'1"	180	28	1	
John Bandura	OE-DE	6'	206	24		
Herm Schmaar	DE	6'2"	210	28		

Use Name – Tackles	Pos.	Hgt	Wgt	Age	Int	Pts
Bill Davis	T	6'1"	235	25		
Jake Fawcett*	T	5'11"	225	24		
John Matisi	T	6'2"	215	22	1	
Tex Mooney*	T	6'5"	290	26		
George Sergienko	T	6'1"	240	25		

Use Name – Guards	Pos.	Hgt	Wgt	Age	Int	Pts
Bill Armstrong	G	6'1"	210	23		
George Grandinette	G	5'9"	215	26		
Al Gutknecht	G-LB	6'	210	26		
Lew Jones	G-LB	6'	215	31	1	
(1 kickoff return for 5 yds.)						
Pete Owens	G-C-LB	5'11"	205	26		
Phil Swiadon	G	6'	220	28		

* = Property of CLEVELAND RAMS who suspended operations for the 1943 season.

Brooklyn sports fans suffered through a long year, as both baseball and football Dodgers plodded through dismal seasons. Although the baseball team finished seventh, it had a colorful manager in Leo Durocher and a flashy star in Dixie Walker. The football Dodgers also lost regularly, finishing dead last in the East, but had none of the color of their baseball brethren. Pete Cawthorn handled the coaching reigns on the war-ravaged football team, fielding a lineup which had problems scoring points. Dean McAdams again played tailback, and the fans again talked wistfully of the absent Ace Parker. McAdams' task was not made any easier when end Perry Schwartz went into the service, but runners Pug Manders and Merlin Condit kept the running game respectable and Bruiser Kinard starred in a patchwork line. Only wins over Philadelphia-Pittsburgh and the Cardinals broke the sports gloom hanging over Brooklyn.

TEAM TOTALS

OFFENSE	FIRST DOWNS: Tot	by Rsh	by Pas	by Pen	RUSHING: No.	Yds.	Avg. Yds.	TD	PASSING: Att.	Com	Comp. Pct.	Yds.	Avg. Yds. Att.	Avg. Yds. Comp	TD	Int.	Pct. Int.
WASH.	112	55	49	8	320	1069	3.3	7	254	139	54.7	1837	7.2	13.2	24	20	7.9
N.Y.	102	72	24	6	386	1436	3.7	14	149	63	42.3	760	5.1	12.1	8	9	6.0
PHI-PIT	138	96	32	10	459	1730	3.8	18	175	65	37.1	1138	6.5	17.6	11	20	11.4
BKN.	80	39	35	6	333	610	1.8	4	205	90	43.9	969	4.7	10.8	5	21	10.2
DEFENSE																	
WASH.	110	68	34	8	406	1330	3.3	10	193	77	39.9	1026	5.3	13.3	9	26	13.5
N.Y.	118	63	51	4	366	1006	2.7	8	229	119	52.0	1724	7.5	14.5	16	18	7.9
PHI-PIT	96	42	41	13	312	793	2.5	18	221	102	46.2	1393	6.3	13.7	15	22	10.0
BKN.	128	75	44	9	404	1562	3.9	16	219	86	39.3	1552	7.1	18.0	15	15	6.9

OFFENSE	PUNTING: No.	Avg. Yds.	PUNT RETURNS: No.	Yds.	Avg. Yds.	TD	KICKOFF RETURNS: No.	Yds.	Avg. Yds.	TD	INTERCEPTION RETURNS: No.	Yds.	Avg. Yds.	TD	PENALTIES: No.	Yds.	FUMBLES: No.	Lost	POINTS: Tot	PAT	FG Att	FG	Saf.	TEAM TOTALS OFFENSE
WASH.	65	43.1	41	442	10.8	0	26	616	23.7	0	26	247	9.5	1	35	499	30	11	229	28	7	1	0	WASH.
N.Y.	69	39.5	35	466	13.3	0	20	436	21.8	0	18	205	11.4	1	42	293	21	5	197	26	10	3	0	N.Y.
PHI-PIT	62	34.4	32	335	10.5	0	40	802	20.1	0	22	304	13.8	2	54	484	37	15	225	30	6	1	0	PHI-PIT
BKN.	89	36.2	30	268	8.9	0	40	968	24.2	0	15	163	10.9	0	36	292	22	9	65	8	6	1	0	BKN.
DEFENSE																								DEFENSE
WASH.	76	37.0	28	267	9.5	0	31	726	23.4	0	20	231	11.6	2	44	349	16	8	137	17	6	2	0	WASH.
N.Y.	76	37.2	39	391	10.0	0	41	791	19.3	0	9	135	15.0	0	49	329	33	10	170	23	7	1	0	N.Y.
PHI-PIT	60	39.9	28	348	12.4	0	34	772	22.7	2	20	258	12.9	1	59	466	20	8	230	29	11	1	0	PHI-PIT
BKN.	60	37.3	34	430	12.6	1	10	225	22.5	0	21	193	9.2	1	56	435	26	9	234	27	14	7	0	BKN.

Use Name – Backs & Ends	Pos.	Age	Hgt	Wgt	Pts	Int	RUSHING				PASSING								RECEIVING				PUNTING		KICKING						PUNT RETURNS				KICKOFF RETURNS			
							No.	Yds	Avg	TD	Att	Comp	%	Yds	Yd/Att	TD	Int–%	RK	No.	Yds	Avg	TD	No.	Avg	Pat	Att	%	FG	Att	%	No.	Yds	Avg	TD	No.	Yds	Avg	TD
WASHINGTON REDSKINS																																						
Sammy Baugh	TB-DB	29	6'2"	180		**11**	19	−42	−2.2	0	**239**	**133**	**56**	1754	7.3	23	19– 8	2					**50**	**45.9**							2	13	7	0				
Leo Stasica	TB-DB	27	5'11"	195		1	9	−10	−1.1	0	6	1	17	34	5.7	0	1– 17						1	38.0							1	11	11	0				
Andy Farkas	FB-DB	27	5'10"	195	54		110	331	3.0	5									19	202	11	4									**15**	168	11	0	9	279	31	0
Bob Seymour	FB-DB	27	6'2"	205	12	2	65	232	3.6	0									17	167	10	2									13	173	13	0	2	34	17	0
Frank Akins	FB-LB	24	5'10"	200			10	25	2.5	0									1	51	51	0	3	18.0														
Jack Jenkins	FB-LB	23	6'1"	210	1		4	20	5.0	0															1	1	100											
Wilbur Moore	WB-DB	27	5'11"	180	54	2	40	231	5.8	2									30	537	18	7									2	2	1	0	1	18	18	0
Frank Seno	WB-DB	22	6'	185		1	26	152	5.8	0									12	195	16	0									2	27	14	0	3	61	20	0
Ray Hare	BB-LB	25	6'1"	205		3	21	96	4.6	0									2	9	5	0									1	5	5	0	2	36	18	0
Joe Aguirre	OE-DE	24	6'4"	220	48														37	420	11	7			6	9	67	0	2	0					3	21	7	0
Bob Masterson	OE-DE	28	6'1"	220	41														16	200	13	3			20	21	95	1	5	20					2	66	33	0
Alex Piasecky	OE-DE	26	6'2"	197	6	1													3	17	6	1													1	17	17	0
Ted Lapka	OE-DE	23	6'1"	190															2	39	20	0																
NEW YORK GIANTS																																						
Tuffy Leemans	QB-DB	30	6'	202			37	69	1.9	0	87	37	43	366	4.2	5	5– 6	7													3	66	22	0	2	29	15	0
Emery Nix	QB-DB	23	5'11"	180		2	19	26	1.4	0	53	24	45	390	7.4	3	3– 6	4													4	50	13	0	1	12	12	0
Bob Trocolor	QB-DB	24	6'2"	205			6	−4	−0.7	0	7	2	29	4	0.6	0	1– 14						5	31.0							1	17	17	0	2	64	32	0
Bill Paschal	FB-DB	22	6'	195	72		**147**	**572**	3.9	**10**									9	74	8	2	12	35.0							9	92	10	0	7	183	26	0
Carl Kinscherf	FB-DB	23	6'1"	185	6		49	77	1.6	1									2	4	2	0	32	40.7											2	57	29	0
Bull Karcis	FB-LB	34	5'9"	225			12	25	2.1	0									1	1	1	0													1	21	21	0
Ward Cuff	WB-FB-DB	30	6'1"	192	53	3	80	523	**6.5**	3	1	0	0	0	0.0	0	0– 0		7	52	7	0			26	27	96	**3**	9	33	9	120	13	0	3	59	20	0
Dave Brown	WB-DB	24	5'11"	190		6	32	131	4.1	0									5	29	6	0									7	106	15	0				
Hank Soar	WB-DB	29	6'2"	210		3	2	8	4.0	0																					2	15	8	0				
Leland Shaffer	BB-LB	31	6'2"	200		1	1	3	3.0	0									3	66	22	0																
Joe Sulatis	BB-DE	22	6'2"	210			1	6	6.0	0									1	12	12	0																
Will Walls	OE-DE	28	6'4"	220	12														14	231	17	2													1	3	3	0
Frank Liebel	OE-DE	23	6'1"	203	18														11	199	18	3																
Neal Adams	OE-DE	24	6'3"	195	12														8	65	8	1													1	8	8	0
Steve Pritko*	OE-DE	21	6'2"	205	6														1	12	12	0																
Len Younce	G-LB	26	6'1"	205	6	1																	20	42.5				0	1	0								
PHILADELPHIA EAGLES – PITTSBURGH STEELERS																																						
Roy Zimmerman	QB-DB	25	6'2"	200	35	5	33	−41	−1.2	1	124	43	35	846	6.8	9	17– 14	6					44	34.6	26	28	93	1	6	17					3	55	18	0
Allie Sherman	QB-DB	20	5'11"	160	6		17	−20	−1.2	1	37	16	43	208	5.6	2	1– 3																					
Jack Hinkle	HB-DB	25	6'	215	24	4	116	571	4.9	4									1	3	3	0	4	19.5							4	45	11	0	11	217	20	0
Ernie Steel	HB-DB	25	6'	190	36		85	409	4.8	4	1	0	0	0	0.0	0	1–100		9	168	19	2									12	152	13	0	11	236	21	0
Johnny Butler	HB-DB	24	5'10"	185	18		87	362	4.2	3	13	6	46	84	6.5	0	1– 8		3	63	21	0	11	37.0							13	108	8	0	6	92	15	0
Bob Thurbon	HB-DB	25	5'10"	172	36	1	71	291	4.1	5									6	100	17	1									2	19	10	0	6	150	25	0
Charlie Gauer	FB-LB-DE	22	6'2"	215		1	12	69	5.8	0									2	18	9	0																
Ben Kish	FB-DB	26	6'	200	12	5	22	50	2.3	0									8	67	8	1	1	42.0														
Ted Laux	HB-DB	25	5'10"	185	2	1	9	23	2.6	0									2	19	10	0			2	2	100				1	11	11	0				
Bob Masters (to CHI B)	FB-LB	32	5'11"	200			4	16	4.0	0																									2	37	19	0
Steve Sader	FB-LB		5'11"	180			3	5	1.7	0																												
Dean Steward	HB		6'	210			1	−6	−6.0	0													2	42.0														
Tony Bova	OE-DB	26	6'1"	190	30		1	11	11.0	0									17	419	**25**	5																
Larry Cabrelli	OE-DB	26	5'11"	195	12	1													12	199	17	1																
Tom Miller	OE-DE	25	6'2"	198	6	1													3	60	20	1																
Bill Hewitt	OE-DE	33	5'9"	190															2	22	11	0																
BROOKLYN DODGERS																																						
Dean McAdams	TB-DB	25	6'1"	195		3	41	−38	−0.9	0	75	37	49	315	4.2	0	7– 9	10	2	6	3	0	36	37.6							4	54	14	0	5	102	20	0
Ken Heineman	TB-DB	25	5'9"	165		2	49	126	2.6	0	57	19	33	285	5.0	3	8– 14	12					14	34.6							10	78	8	0	**16**	**442**	28	0
George Cafego (to WAS)	TB-DB	28	5'10"	180			34	−12	−0.4	0	45	22	49	258	5.7	1	3– 7						21	34.3							6	52	9	0	9	218	24	0
Cecil Johnson	TB-HB-DB	21	5'11"	204	12	1	26	38	1.5	0	8	4	50	16	2.0	0	1– 12		9	136	15	2	10	34.9											3	68	23	0
Frank Sachse	TB-HB-DB	26	6'	195			8	14	1.8	0	9	5	56	72	8.0	1	1– 11		3	26	9	0									2	37	19	0				
Pug Manders	FB-LB	30	6'	200	24		89	266	3.0	3	5	4	80	31	6.2	1	0– 0		5	68	14	1													1	19	19	0
Jody Marek	FB-LB	27	5'11"	182			6	9	1.5	0									1	0	0	0						0	1	0								
Marshall Edwards	FB-LB						1	5	5.0	0									1	−4	−4	0																
Merl Condit	HB-DB	26	5'11"	185	12	1	67	190	2.8	1	6	0	0	0	0.0	0	1– 17		7	101	14	1	19	38.1				0	3	0	6	47	8	0	6	178	30	0
Frank Martin	HB-DB	24	5'10"	165		2	25	50	2.0	0	4	2	50	15	3.8	0	0– 0		13	152	12	0									5	38	8	0				
Tilly Manton	BB-DB	31	5'11"	190			2	−7	−3.5	0	4	2	50	26	6.5	0	0– 0		6	26	4	0						0	1	0								
Joe Setcavage	BB-DB	25	5'11"	190		1	1	3	3.0	0	1	0	0	0	0.0	0	0– 0		5	26	5	0									1	2	2	0	1	5	5	0
Bill Brown	BB-DB	26	6'	190															4	42	11	0																
Andy Kowalski	OE-DE	23	6'	197		1													11	145	13	0																
Keith Ranspot	OE-DE	28	6'3"	190															7	80	11	0																
George Webb	OE-DE	27	6'1"	180															7	60	9	0																
Ray Wehba	OE-DE	27	6'	215															4	43	11	0													1	15	15	0
Bruiser Kinard	T	28	6'1"	218	17														5	62	12	1			8	9	89	1	1	100								

CHICAGO BEARS 8-1-1 Luke Johnsos, Hunk Anderson

Scores of Each Game			Use Name	Pos.	Hgt	Wgt	Age	Int	Pts	Use Name – Tackles	Pos.	Hgt	Wgt	Age	Int	Pts	Use Name – Guards	Pos.	Hgt	Wgt	Age	Int	Pts
21	Green Bay	21	Al Matuza	C-LB	6'2"	195	24			Al Babartsky	T	6'	225	27			Danny Fortmann	G-LB	6'	210	27		
27	Detroit	21	Fred Mundee	C-LB	6'1"	220	30	1		Bernie Digris	T-G		212				Pete Gudauskas	G-LB	6'2"	222	26		
20	CHIC. CARDS	0	Bulldog Turner	C-LB	6'1"	235	24			Al Hoptowit	T	6'1"	218	27			Tony Ippolito	G-LB		220		1	
48	PHIL–PITT	21								Dom Sigillo	T	6'	230	30			Jim Logan	G		190			
33	BROOKLYN	21	Joe Vodicka	HB-DB	5'10"	190	22			Bill Steinkemper	T		220				(1 kickoff return for 2 yds.)						
35	DETROIT	14															Monte Merkel	G	5'10"	215			
21	GREEN BAY	7															George Musso	G	6'2"	270	33		
56	New York	7																					
7	Washington	21																					
35	Chic. Cards	24																					

Still strong from working his farm, thirty-four-year-old Bronko Nagurski ended his five-year retirement to rejoin the draft-depleted Bears as a tackle. Nagurski played in the line until the final game of the schedule against the Cardinals. Needing a victory to clinch the Western title, the Bears trailed the Cardinals 24-14 at the end of three quarters. Coach Hunk Anderson then told the old pro to take over at his old fullback spot, and seven plays later Bronko smashed over for a touchdown after a 62-yard drive. The Bears later had the ball on fourth down with 4 yards to go; Nagurski plowed off-tackle for 6 yards and a first down, and a Sid Luckman touchdown pass to Harry Clark soon put the Bears ahead for keeps. Picking up 84 yards in sixteen carries, Nagurski said, "That game gave me my greatest kick out of football."

GREEN BAY PACKERS 7-2-1 Curly Lambeau

Scores of Each Game			Use Name	Pos.	Hgt	Wgt	Age	Int	Pts	Use Name – Tackles	Pos.	Hgt	Wgt	Age	Int	Pts	Use Name – Guards	Pos.	Hgt	Wgt	Age	Int	Pts
21	CHIC. BEARS	21	Charley Brock	C-LB	6'2"	210	27	4		Chet Adams*	T	6'3"	240	27		3	Sherwood Fries	G-LB	6'1"	238	22	2	
28	Chic. Cards	7	Bob Flowers	C-LB	6'1"	215	26	1		(1 field goal in 6 attempts)							Buckets Goldenberg	G-LB	5'10"	220	32	2	
35	DETROIT	14	Amy McPherson	C-DT	5'11"	248	31			Paul Berezney	T	6'2"	220	26			Bill Kuusisto	G	6'	230	25		
7	WASHINGTON	33								Tiny Croft	T	6'3"	298	22			Glen Sorenson	G	6'	225	22		
27	Detroit	6	Don Perkins	LB	6'	195	25			Baby Ray	T	6'6"	250	28			(Missed 2 field goal attempts)						
35	New York	21								Ade Schwammel	T	6'2"	230	34			Pete Tinsley	G-LB	5'8"	205	30	1	
7	Chic. Bears	21																					
35	CHIC. CARDS	14																					
31	Brooklyn	7																					
38	Phil–Pitt	28																					

Don Hutson had hauled many a pass into the end zone, but he got a chance to get on the other end of the pipe on one play. Hutson took a handoff and headed off on what looked like an end run. With all the defense converging on him, the fast end pulled up short and tossed a 38-yard pass to Harry Jacunski all alone in the end zone. After the play, the poker-faced Hutson broke into a grin. Passing, it seemed, was not that difficult. Most of the Green Bay passes were thrown by Tony Canadeo and Irv Comp, since star tailback Cecil Isbell had quit to coach at Purdue University. Isbell explained why he quit when still young: "I hadn't been up in Green Bay long when I saw Lambeau go around the locker room and tell players like Herber and Gatenbein and Hank Bruder that they were all done with the Packers. I sat there and watched and then I vowed it would never happen to me. I'd quit before they came around to tell me."

DETROIT LIONS 3-6-1 Gus Dorais

Scores of Each Game			Use Name	Pos.	Hgt	Wgt	Age	Int	Pts	Use Name – Tackles	Pos.	Hgt	Wgt	Age	Int	Pts	Use Name – Guards	Pos.	Hgt	Wgt	Age	Int	Pts
35	CHIC. CARDS	17	Gerry Conlee	C-LB	5'11"	200	27	1		Al Kaporch	T	5'10"	215	29	1		Stan Batinski	G	5'10"	212	26		
27	BROOKLYN	0	(1 kickoff return for 15 yds.)							Alex Ketzko	T		215				Sonny Liles	G-LB	5'9"	185	24		
21	CHIC. BEARS	27	Ernie Rosteck	C-LB	6'1"	210	21			Ed Opalewski	T	6'3"	220	23			Riley Matheson*	G-LB	6'2"	205	28		
14	Green Bay	35	Alex Wojciechowicz	C-LB	5'11"	210	28	2		Lloyd Wickett	T	6'1"	205	23			Ted Pavelic	G	6'	225	24		
7	Chic. Cards at Buffalo	0	(1 kickoff return for 17 yds.)														Lyle Rockenbach	G	5'9"	192			
																	Tony Rubino	G	5'10"	205	22		
6	GREEN BAY	27	Sam Busich	DE	6'3"	188	30		1								Roy Stuart*	G-LB	5'8"	185	23		
14	Chic. Bears	35	(1 PAT in 1 attempt)																				
0	NEW YORK	0	Bob Layden	DE	6'	195																	
20	Washington	42																					
34	Phil–Pitt	35																					

New coach Gus Dorais took over a team that had no offense, a porous defense, and lost every game in 1942. To soup up the attack, Dorais selected Georgia tailback Frankie Sinkwich as the Lions' first draft pick, and the rookie made the passing game respectable and led the club in rushing. With the Cleveland Rams in mothballs for the year, guard Riley Matheson spent the season in Detroit, joining Alex Wojciechowicz and Augie Lio in a line far from the worst in the league. Most importantly, Dorais never let the club slip back into the chaos of last year. The new coach got the Lions off to a roaring start with a 35-17 victory over the Cardinals and a 27-0 shellacking of Brooklyn, outscoring last year's entire point total in two games. The offense did cool off, though, and in the game with the Giants both teams moved up and down the field without scoring, the last 0-0 tie to date.

CHICAGO CARDINALS 0-10-0 Phil Handler

Scores of Each Game			Use Name	Pos.	Hgt	Wgt	Age	Int	Pts	Use Name – Tackles	Pos.	Hgt	Wgt	Age	Int	Pts	Use Name – Guards	Pos.	Hgt	Wgt	Age	Int	Pts
17	Detroit	35	Don Pierce	C-LB	6'1"	186	24			Art Albrecht	T-C	6'1"	200	21			Vern Ghersanich	G-LB	5'11"	210		1	
7	GREEN BAY	28								Clarence Booth	T	6'	220	23			Lou Marotti	G	5'10"	195	25		
0	Chic. Bears	20	Buddy Parker	BB-LB	6'	190	29			Chet Bulger	T	6'3"	235	25		1	Floyd Rhea	G-LB	6'	215	22		
0	DETROIT at Buffalo	7	Andy Puplis	WB-DB	5'9"	180		1		(1 PAT in 1 attempt)							(1 kickoff return for 10 yds.)						
			(1 kickoff return for 9 yds.)							Gil Duggan	T	6'3"	225	25			Marshall Robnett	G-LB	6'	200	24		
7	Washington	13															(1 kickoff return for 12 yds.)						
13	Phil–Pitt	34															Gordon Wilson	G	6'	230	27		
0	Brooklyn	7															(1 kickoff return for 6 yds.)						
14	Green Bay	35																					
13	New York	24																					
24	CHIC. BEARS	35																					

With Jimmy Conzelman working in baseball, long-time assistant coach Phil Handler took over as head man. Handler may have been looking for another sport to pursue after the Cardinals dropped all ten games on their schedule. The high note of the season was the final game against the Bears, in which Bronko Nagurski's heroics foiled a fine effort by the Cardinals to upset their big neighbors. Outside of that game, the Cardinals pressed their opponents very little.

For the second straight year, the team's top passer and receiver marched off into the service. To replace absent passer Bud Schwenk and end Pop Ivy, coach Handler put rookie Ronnie Cahill in the lineup at tailback and veteran Eddie Rucinski at end. Shining through the darkness of the winless season, Rucinski snagged enough passes to win a spot on the wire-service All-Pro teams. Few of the other Cardinals heard praise, though.

TEAM TOTALS	FIRST DOWNS:				RUSHING:				PASSING:									PUNTING:		PUNT RETURNS:				KICKOFF RETURNS:				INTERCEPTION RETURNS:				PENALTIES:		FUMBLES:		POINTS:					TEAM TOTALS
OFFENSE	Tot	by Rsh	by Pas	by Pen	No.	Yds.	Avg. Yds.	TD	Att.	Com	Comp. Pct.	Yds.	Avg. Yds. Att.	Avg. Yds. Comp	TD	Int.	Pct. Int.	No.	Avg. Yds.	No.	Yds.	Avg. Yds.	TD	No.	Yds.	Avg. Yds.	TD	No.	Yds.	Avg. Yds.	TD	No.	Yds.	No.	Lost	Tot	PAT	FG Att	FG	Saf.	OFFENSE
CHIC. B.	161	84	66	11	424	1651	3.9	14	229	117	51.1	2310	10.1	19.7	28	17	7.4	48	37.2	28	359	12.8	0	29	722	24.9	1	24	219	9.1	0	86	748	27	18	303	39	7	2	0	CHIC. B.
G.B.	134	60	66	8	397	1442	3.6	13	253	114	45.1	1909	7.5	16.7	21	19	7.5	52	36.0	32	371	11.6	0	28	661	23.6	0	42	606	14.4	2	52	403	15	6	264	36	15	4	0	G.B.
DET.	106	49	46	11	294	817	2.8	10	248	93	37.5	1290	5.2	13.9	11	37	14.9	65	41.4	32	436	13.6	1	36	815	22.6	1	19	304	16.0	2	59	472	12	5	178	22	12	2	0	DET.
CHIC. C.	102	48	43	11	334	709	2.1	5	219	88	40.2	1095	5.0	12.4	6	39	17.8	56	38.7	16	163	10.2	0	31	569	18.4	0	16	243	15.2	0	45	389	17	5	95	11	5	2	0	CHIC. C.
DEFENSE																																									DEFENSE
CHIC. B.	100	49	33	18	332	1282	3.9	14	203	64	31.5	980	4.8	15.3	8	24	11.8	62	38.9	31	426	13.7	0	50	1145	22.9	0	17	314	18.5	1	57	475	22	6	157	22	10	1	0	CHIC. B.
G.B.	122	62	56	4	350	1112	3.2	9	242	111	45.9	1420	5.9	12.8	16	42	17.4	55	36.6	28	332	11.9	0	31	660	21.3	0	19	188	9.9	0	51	391	22	9	172	22	3	0	0	G.B.
DET.	130	69	54	7	381	1213	3.2	14	227	109	48.0	1606	7.1	14.7	16	19	8.4	66	41.9	29	291	10.0	0	29	615	21.2	0	37	436	11.8	1	58	501	23	12	218	29	10	3	0	DET.
CHIC. C.	131	75	48	8	396	1166	2.9	13	198	101	51.0	1607	8.1	15.9	21	16	8.1	51	37.2	29	355	12.2	0	24	655	27.3	0	39	536	13.7	2	65	634	19	12	238	31	7	1	0	CHIC. C.

							RUSHING				PASSING								RECEIVING				PUNTING		KICKING						PUNT RETURNS				KICKOFF RETURNS			
Use Name – Backs & Ends	Pos.	Age	Hgt	Wgt	Pts	Int	No.	Yds	Avg	TD	Att	Comp	%	Yds	Yd/Att	TD	Int–%	RK	No.	Yds	Avg	TD	No.	Avg	Pat	Att	%	FG	Att	%	No.	Yds	Avg	TD	No.	Yds	Avg	TD
CHICAGO BEARS																																						
Sid Luckman	QB-DB	26	6'	195	6	4	22	–40	–1.8	1	202	110	54	**2194**	**10.9**	**28**	12– 6	1					34	35.9							4	46	12	0	1	7	7	0
Bob Snyder	QB-DB	30	6'	205	45	1	6	–20	–3.3	0	26	7	27	116	4.5	0	4– 15						10	37.8	**39**	**42**	93	2	7	29								
Harry Clark	HB-DB	25	6'	180	60	5	120	556	4.6	3	1	0	0	0	0.0	0	1–100		23	535	23	7									10	158	16	0	13	326	25	0
Dante Magnani*	HB-DB	26	5'10"	178	24	2	51	310	6.1	2									6	88	15	1									4	40	10	0	6	171	29	1
Gary Famiglietti	FB-LB	28	6'	225	12		64	229	3.6	2									1	10	10	0																
Ray Nolting	HB-DB	29	5'11"	190	6	1	38	209	5.5	1									5	90	18	0									2	13	7	0	2	40	20	0
Ray McLean	HB-DB	27	5'10"	168	18	4	35	127	3.6	1									18	435	24	2									7	94	13	0	4	105	26	0
Bill Osmanski	FB-LB	26	5'11"	198	6		37	102	2.8	1																												
Bronko Nagurski	T-FB-LB	34	6'2"	235	6		16	84	5.3	1																												
Doug McEnulty	HB-DB	21	6'3"	215	6	1	16	45	2.8	0									1	10	10	1	4	46.8														
Bill Geyer	HB-DB	23	5'10"	170	24	2	16	36	2.3	2									5	123	25	2									1	8	8	0	2	71	36	0
Bob Steuber	HB-DB	21	6'2"	200			1	3	3.0	0																												
George Wilson	OE-DE	29	6'1"	205	30	2													21	293	14	5																
Hamp Pool	OE-DE	28	6'3"	215	30														18	363	20	5																
Jim Benton*	OE-DE	26	6'3"	195	18														13	235	18	3																
Connie Mack Berry	OE-DE	27	6'3"	218	12														4	99	25	2																
John Siegal	OE-DE	25	6'1"	205															2	29	15	0																
GREEN BAY PACKERS																																						
Tony Canadeo	TB-DB	24	5'11"	195	30	2	94	489	5.2	3	129	56	43	875	6.8	9	12– 9	5	3	31	10	2	3	34.0							8	93	12	0	10	242	24	0
Irv Comp	TB-DB	24	6'2"	192	24	10	77	182	2.4	3	92	46	50	662	7.2	7	4– **4**	3					12	37.8							1	20	20	0	4	81	20	0
Lou Brock	TB-HB-DB	25	6'	195	18	1	45	67	1.5	2	22	9	41	274	12.5	3	1– 5		4	57	14	1	32	36.4							8	126	16	0	5	112	22	0
Joe Laws	HB-DB	32	5'9"	188		7	43	232	5.4	0									5	33	7	0									10	84	8	0	2	47	24	0
Tony Falkenstein	FB-LB	28	5'10	210	6		58	198	3.4	1									3	39	13	0													2	47	24	0
Ted Fritsch	FB-LB	22	5'10"	205	24		54	169	3.1	4									2	55	28	0	5	30.2				0	2	0					4	99	25	0
Andy Uram	HB-TB-DB	28	5'10"	190	12	2	15	53	3.5	0	6	2	33	60	10.0	1	1– 7		10	212	21	2									5	48	10	0				
Bob Kabler	HB-DB	26	6'3"	200			1	5	5.0	0																												
Jim Lankas	FB-LB	25	6'2"	225			2	2	1.0	0																												
Larry Craig	BB-DE	27	6'1"	208			1	3	3.0	0																												
Ben Starret	BB-DE	25	5'11"	215		1	1	1	1.0	0																												
Don Hutson	OE-DB	30	6'1"	178	**117**	8	6	41	6.8	0	4	1	25	38	9.5	1	1– 25		**47**	**776**	17	**11**			36	36	**100**	**3**	5	**60**								
Harry Jacunski	OE-DE	27	6'2"	198	18	1													24	528	22	3													1	33	33	0
Joel Mason	OE-DE	30	6'	200	12														8	107	13	2																
Dick Evans	OE-DB	26	6'3"	210															8	71	9	0																
DETROIT LIONS																																						
Frankie Sinkwich	TB-DB	22	5'11"	185	12	1	93	266	2.9	1	126	50	40	699	5.5	7	20– 16	8	1	8	8	0	12	45.9				0	1	0	11	**228**	**21**	0	5	128	26	0
Chuck Fenenbock	TB-WB-DB	25	5'9"	172	6	1	46	180	3.9	0	58	20	34	338	5.8	3	9– 16	11	5	45	9	1	4	46.0							6	54	9	0	11	224	20	0
Tom Colella	TB-DB	25	6'	185			15	25	1.7	0	31	11	35	103	3.3	0	4– 13		1	–1	–1	0	6	46.7							2	11	6	0				
Harry Hopp	FB-LB-DB	24	6'	200	54	2	56	99	1.8	5	8	5	63	60	7.5	0	0– 0		17	229	13	3	42	39.1							1	–7	–7	0	3	57	19	0
Elmer Hackney	FB-LB	27	6'2"	200	18	2	27	87	3.2	2	3	1	33	–1	–0.3	0	0– 0		5	51	10	0									1	40	40	**1**	2	36	18	0
Mike Corgan	FB-LB		5'10"	188			5	14	2.8	0									1	9	9	0																
Ned Mathews	WB-TB-DB	25	5'10"	184	18	4	38	124	3.3	1	12	4	33	76	6.3	1	0– 0		9	193	21	1	1	35.0							4	37	9	0	7	246	**35**	1
Art Van Tone	WB-DB	24	5'10"	185	6	2	2	1	0.5	0	3	1	33	7	2.3	0	1– 33		6	112	19	1									3	47	16	0				
Lloyd Cardwell	WB-DB	30	6'2"	190			3	6	2.0	0									1	9	9	0									2	21	11	0	3	56	19	0
Bob Keene	WB-DB	24	5'11"	190			1	1	1.0	0									1	27	27	0													1	12	12	0
Bill Callihan	BB-DB	27	6'3"	230	24	1	5	17	3.4	1	2	0	0	0	0.0	0	1– 50		8	108	14	3									2	5	3	0				
Murray Evans	BB-DB	24	6'1"	206			2	3	1.5	0	5	1	20	8	1.6	0	2– 40		3	31	10	0																
Jack Matheson	OE-DE	23	6'2"	204	6														13	156	12	1													1	19	19	0
Bill Fisk	OE-DE	26	6'	198															11	137	12	0													1	5	5	0
Ben Hightower*	OE-DB	24	6'2"	185	6	1	1	–6	–6.0	0									10	172	17	1																
Bert Kuczynski	OE-DE	23	6'	197															1	4	4	0																
Augie Lio	G-LB	25	6'	235	27	1																			21	23	91	2	**11**	18								
CHICAGO CARDINALS																																						
Ronnie Cahill	TB-DB	26	5'8"	170			62	–11	–0.2	0	109	50	46	608	5.6	3	21– 19	8					3	29.3							1	19	19	0	3	56	19	0
Joe Bukant	TB-DB	27	6'	208			42	87	2.1	0	40	14	35	109	2.7	1	5– 12		1	0	0	0	5	36.2														
Walt Masters	TB-DB	36	5'10"	200			14	–17	–1.2	0	45	17	38	249	5.5	2	7– 16						10	36.8							1	13	13	0	2	39	20	0
John Grigas	FB-DB	23	6'	205	18	5	105	333	3.2	3	19	4	21	98	5.2	0	4– 21		19	225	12	0									2	–2	–1	0	3	72	24	0
Bob Morrow	FB-DB	25	6'	225	12	2	38	129	3.4	2									3	20	7	0													3	66	22	0
George Smith	FB-DB		6'1"	200			4	12	3.0	0									1	18	18	0																
Walt Rankin	FB-DB	25	5'11"	200		3	2	1	0.5	0									10	44	4	0													4	57	14	0
John Martin	WB-DB	25	6'1"	195		1	30	98	3.3	0									7	138	20	0	30	39.6							9	95	11	0	7	130	19	0
John Hall	WB-DB	26	6'	200	6	2	22	51	2.3	0	4	2	50	24	6.0	0	2– 50		7	82	12	0									1	17	17	0	2	35	18	0
Marshall Goldberg	WB-DB	25	5'11"	190	6	1	6	6	1.0	0									4	31	8	1									1	15	15	0	2	53	27	0
Cal Purdin	WB-DB	21	6'2"	190			9	20	2.2	0	2	1	50	7	3.5	0	0– 0		3	35	12	0	8	42.6							1	6	6	0	1	24	24	0
Eddie Rucinski	OE-DE	27	6'2"	198	18														26	398	15	3																
Don Currivan	OE-DE	22	6'	195	12														5	79	16	1																
Freeman Rexer	OE-DE	25	6'1"	210															1	14	14	0																
Clint Wager	OE-DE	22	6'6"	220															1	11	11	0																
Conway Baker	G	32	5'11'	235	14																				5	6	83	1	2	50								
Dixie Stokes	C-LB	30	6'	200	8																				5	6	83	1	3	33								

1944 N.F.L. — EAST

NEW YORK GIANTS 8-1-1 Steve Owen

Scores of Each Game		
22	Boston	10
14	Brooklyn	7
23	CARD–PITT	0
17	PHILADELPHIA	24
31	BOSTON	0
21	Philadelphia	21
24	GREEN BAY	0
7	BROOKLYN	0
16	WASHINGTON	13
31	Washington	0

Use Name	Pos.	Hgt	Wgt	Age	Int	Pts
Mel Hein	C-LB	6'2"	230	35	3	
Bill Piccolo	C-LB	5'11"	185	24	2	
Larry Visnic	BB-LB	5'11"	195	25	2	
Roy Clay	WB-DB	6'	185	21		

Use Name – Tackles	Pos.	Hgt	Wgt	Age	Int	Pts
Al Blozis	T	6'6"	250	25		
(Killed in military service – Jan. 31, 1945)						
Roland Caranci	T	6'1"	227	23		
Vic Carroll	T	6'4"	235	31	1	8
(1 punt return for 28 yd. touchdown)						
Frank Cope	T	6'2"	220	28		
Frank Damiani	T	6'1"	225	22		
Herb Kane	T	6'1"	215	23		

Use Name – Guards	Pos.	Hgt	Wgt	Age	Int	Pts
Chuck Avedisian	G-LB	5'9"	210	26	1	6
Jim Sivell (from BKN)	G	5'9"	205	30		
Frank Umont	G-T	5'11"	220	26		

When passer Arnie Herber showed up at training camp, he was so overweight that one reporter called him "a tub of lard." The ex-Packer worked hard, though, shook off the cobwebs of his three-year retirement, and soon recaptured his fine touch at throwing the bomb. With Herber throwing and the tough defense hanging up five shutouts, the Giants edged out the Eagles for the Eastern Division title. Among the whitewashings were a satisfying 24-0 triumph over Herber's old mates in Green Bay and a 31-0 victory over Washington to clinch the divisional crown.

Coach Steve Owen built this year's squad with parts salvaged from many sources. Herber and kicker Ken Strong came out of retirement, Mel Hein commuted from his full-time job at Union College, Bill Paschal was a second-year pro, and Howie Levingston came out of the service. Fortunately, Ward Cuff, Frank Cope, Al Blozis, and Len Younce were no farther than the locker room.

PHILADELPHIA EAGLES 7-1-2 Greasy Neale

Scores of Each Game		
28	Boston	7
31	WASHINGTON	31
38	BOSTON	0
24	New York	17
21	Brooklyn	7
21	NEW YORK	21
37	Washington	7
7	CHIC. BEARS	28
34	BROOKLYN	0
26	CLEVELAND	13

Use Name	Pos.	Hgt	Wgt	Age	Int	Pts
Vic Lindskog	C-LB	6'1"	205	28	1	6
Bap Manzini	C-LB	5'11"	200	24	1	
Walt Nowak	OE-DB	5'11"	185	17		
John Yovicsin	DE	6'3"	195			
Vic Sears (broken ankle)						

Use Name – Tackles	Pos.	Hgt	Wgt	Age	Int	Pts
Rocco Canale	T	5'11"	235	27		
Bob Friedman	T	6'2"	215	22	1	
Bucko Kilroy	T	6'2"	240	23		
Al Wistert	T	6'1"	215	23		

Use Name – Guards	Pos.	Hgt	Wgt	Age	Int	Pts
Bruno Banducci	G	5'11"	205	22		
Enio Conti	G	5'11"	205	31		
Carl Fagiolo	G	6'	200			
Mike Mandarino	G-T-C	5'11"	240	23		
Duke Maronic	G	5'9"	205	23	1	
Eddie Michaels	G	5'11"	210	30		

Shucking off the Steelers to go it alone, the Eagles abruptly shot into the upper reaches of the NFL. Coach Greasy Neale was building a powerhouse which had not reached its peak, yet just missed winning the Eastern Division championship. The chief addition to the flock was Steve Van Buren, a hard-charging runner with a halfback's moves and a fullback's power. Running with head down and knees pumping furiously, Van Buren usually bowled over tacklers in his way, and he could cut and dance his way through an open field when he wanted to, so much so that in the late 1940s he was the league's dominant runner.

Coach Neale fielded other good players around Van Buren. Passer Roy Zimmerman, runner Jack Hinkle, and defensive ace Ernie Steele stocked the backfield with quality, and Al Wistert, Bucko Kilroy, and Bruno Banducci filled the line with able-bodied bruisers.

WASHINGTON REDSKINS 6-3-1 Dud DeGroot

Scores of Each Game		
31	Philadelphia	31
21	Boston	14
17	BROOKLYN	14
42	CARD–PITT	20
14	CLEVELAND	10
10	Brooklyn	0
7	PHILADELPHIA	37
14	BOSTON	7
13	New York	16
0	NEW YORK	31

Use Name	Pos.	Hgt	Wgt	Age	Int	Pts
Nick Campofreda	C-DT	6'1"	240	30		
Vern Foltz	C-LB	6'1"	205	26		
Chief Johnson	C-LB	6'3"	233	35		
Pete Marcus	DE	6'2"	200	25		

Use Name – Tackles	Pos.	Hgt	Wgt	Age	Int	Pts
Jack Keenan	T	5'10"	220	25		
Jim North	T	6'3"	235	25		
Ev Sharp	T	6'1"	220	25		
Mitch Ucovich	T	5'11"	208	28		
Joe Ungerer	T	6'	225	27		
Joe Zeno	T	5'10"	240	25		

Use Name – Guards	Pos.	Hgt	Wgt	Age	Int	Pts
Tom Bedore	G-LB	5'11"	193	18		
Al Fiorentino	G-LB	5'7"	204	27	1	
(1 kickoff return for 5 yds.)						
Ed Merkle	G-LB	5'10"	215	27		
Ray Monaco	G-LB	5'10"	208	26		
Clyde Shugart	G	6'1"	230	27		
Frank Walton	G	5'11"	240	32		

With long-time coach Ray Flaherty in the Navy, owner George Marshall again started going through field managers like water. This year's head man, Dud DeGroot, brought the T-formation with him to Washington, forcing Sammy Baugh to learn a completely new system of offense. Sammy missed the old single-wing and double-wing attack at first, but he slowly got the hang of taking a direct snap from the center. Fresh out of the Navy, Frankie Filchock split the quarterback duties with Baugh and celebrated his civilian status by leading the league in passing. With these two arms throwing to Joe Aguirre, Wilbur Moore, and Les Dye, the Redskins won five straight games after an opening-day tie to climb to the top in the East. Although three losses in their last four matches placed the Skins in a third-place finish, they were hopeful that Baugh and the new offensive system would soon produce a winner.

BOSTON YANKS 2-8-0 Herb Kopf

Scores of Each Game		
7	PHILADELPHIA	28
10	NEW YORK	22
14	WASHINGTON	21
0	Philadelphia	38
17	Brooklyn	14
0	New York	31
7	Chic. Bears	21
13	BROOKLYN	6
7	Washington	14
7	Detroit	38

Use Name	Pos.	Hgt	Wgt	Age	Int	Pts
Walt Dubzinski	C-LB	5'10"	205	24		
Ed Korisky	C-LB	6'1"	210	26	1	
Jim Magee	C-LB	6'1"	200	23		
Morgan Tiller	OE-DE	6'1"	195	24		
(1 kickoff return for 12 yds.)						
Bob McRoberts	HB-DB	5'11"	190	20		
Frank Santora	QB-DB	5'10"	166	18		
(1 kickoff return for 27 yds.)						

Use Name – Tackles	Pos.	Hgt	Wgt	Age	Int	Pts
Art Albrecht	T	6'1'	210	22		
Ed Franco	T	5'8"	205	28		
Wimpy Giddens	T	6'2"	220	29		
Ed McGee	T	6'1"	230	28	1	
Thron Riggs	T	6'1"	225	23		

Use Name – Guards	Pos.	Hgt	Wgt	Age	Int	Pts
Vince Commisa	G	5'9"	190			
Frank Gaziano	G	5'8"	218	28		
John Morelli	G-LB	5'10"	190	21		12
Bill Walker	G	6'	220	23		

While singer Kate Smith was selling lots of war bonds, her manager, Ted Collins, was buying a pro-football team. He purchased an NFL franchise for Boston and set up the Yanks, hiring Herb Kopf to run the club on the field. The first Yank roster listed both rookies and veteran pros cut loose by other teams. The top passer, George Cafego, had been the first player picked in the 1940 collegiate draft, but he had shown little since then for the Brooklyn Dodgers and Washington Redskins. Of the leading runners, Bob Davis had bounced around with three clubs since 1938, while Milt Crain was playing his first pro season. The Yanks were end Keith Ranspot's seventh team in four years, but he settled in Boston long enough to lead the club in receiving. Of the interior linemen, only ex-Lion Augie Lio would have started elsewhere. With the league's weakest attack, the Yanks could beat only the inept Brooklyn Tigers.

BROOKLYN TIGERS 0-10-0 Pete Cawthorn, Ed Kuhale, Frank Bridges

Scores of Each Game		
7	Green Bay	14
14	Detroit	19
7	NEW YORK	14
14	Washington	17
14	BOSTON	17
7	PHILADELPHIA	21
0	WASHINGTON	10
6	Boston	13
0	New York	7
0	Philadelphia	34

Use Name	Pos.	Hgt	Wgt	Age	Int	Pts
George Smith	C-LB	6'2"	215	30	1	
(6 punts for 37.2 yd. average)						
Vaughn Stewart	C-LB	6'1"	180	24		
(1 punt for 58 yds.)						
George Weeks	DE	6'2"	200			

Use Name – Tackles	Pos.	Hgt	Wgt	Age	Int	Pts
George Doherty	T	6'1"	215	23		
George Sergienko	T	6'1"	250	26		
Frank Strom	T	6'2"	252	28		
Charlie Ware	T	6'3"	245	26		

Use Name – Guards	Pos.	Hgt	Wgt	Age	Int	Pts
John Ellis	G	5'10"	212	24		
Tony Leon	G-LB	5'9"	197	27	1	
Floyd Rhea	G-LB	6'	215	23	1	
Gordon Wilson (from BOS)	G	6'	230	28		

The old Dodgers were rechristened the Tigers, but the only bite was on owner Dan Topping's wallet. Brooklyn fans never warmed up to the new name, and they didn't bother coming out to see the winless squad. After all, a ticket to a Tiger game gave the buyer the privilege of watching a parade of scatter-arm passers throw lots of incompleted passes. Or the paying customer could watch fullback Pug Manders, a good runner, fling himself at nonexistent holes that were never cleared out by the line. If he appreciated line play, the fan could watch Bruiser Kinard get double- and triple-teamed while some of his trench mates were ignored by the enemy. The Tigers unfortunately never played the Card-Pitt squad; one of them would have had to win, if only one could score some points. Although the Card-Pitt team hardly was an encouraging example, owner Topping arranged a merger for next year with the Boston Yanks—and Brooklyn would never return to the NFL.

TEAM TOTALS

	FIRST DOWNS:				RUSHING:				PASSING:								
OFFENSE	Tot	by Rsh	by Pas	by Pen	No.	Yds.	Avg. Yds.	TD	Att.	Com	Comp. Pct.	Yds.	Avg. Yds. Att.	Avg. Yds. Comp	TD	Int.	Pct. Int.
N.Y.	99	72	23	4	416	1532	3.7	11	125	47	37.6	857	6.9	18.2	9	17	13.6
PHIL.	110	73	27	10	424	1661	3.9	23	136	55	40.4	941	6.9	17.1	9	12	8.8
WASH.	133	59	70	4	342	904	2.6	6	299	170	56.9	2021	6.8	11.9	17	17	5.7
BOSTON	87	36	41	10	324	471	1.5	3	197	85	43.1	1030	5.2	12.1	6	22	11.2
BKN.	110	53	47	10	365	964	2.6	6	213	76	35.7	996	4.7	13.1	3	29	13.6
DEFENSE																	
N.Y.	137	66	64	7	374	1000	2.7	6	258	114	44.2	1290	5.0	11.3	3	34	13.1
PHIL.	86	43	35	8	321	558	1.7	7	231	105	45.5	1379	6.0	13.1	12	33	14.3
WASH.	123	71	47	5	409	1492	3.7	15	188	84	44.7	1166	6.2	13.9	9	19	10.1
BOSTON	126	81	44	1	446	1575	3.5	20	166	76	45.8	1131	6.8	14.9	11	16	9.6
BKN.	95	41	41	13	362	1181	3.3	14	181	78	43.1	1227	6.8	15.7	9	10	5.5

	PUNTING:		PUNT RETURNS:				KICKOFF RETURNS:			
OFFENSE	No.	Avg. Yds.	No.	Yds.	Avg. Yds.	TD	No.	Yds.	Avg. Yds.	TD
N.Y.	60	38.6	33	399	12.1	1	17	466	27.4	0
PHIL.	55	39.9	41	563	13.7	1	26	630	24.2	1
WASH.	59	39.0	26	269	10.3	0	37	682	18.4	0
BOSTON	72	35.0	27	457	12.3	0	39	797	20.4	0
BKN.	74	38.0	31	359	11.6	1	26	578	22.2	0
DEFENSE										
N.Y.	60	37.2	32	323	10.1	1	40	957	23.9	0
PHIL.	71	39.8	26	265	10.2	0	46	830	18.0	1
WASH.	55	36.6	32	426	13.3	0	26	566	21.8	0
BOSTON	62	35.8	42	483	11.5	2	18	425	23.6	0
BKN.	71	38.6	35	465	13.3	0	15	293	19.5	0

	INTERCEPTION RETURNS:				PENALTIES:		FUMBLES:		POINTS:					TEAM TOTALS
	No.	Yds.	Avg. Yds.	TD	No.	Yds.	No.	Lost	Tot	PAT	FG Att	FG	Saf.	OFFENSE
	34	549	16.1	4	68	502	14	7	206	25	16	7	2	N.Y.
	33	544	16.4	3	66	523	36	20	267	33	8	4	0	PHIL.
	19	177	9.3	0	68	545	28	12	169	19	8	4	0	WASH.
	16	236	14.8	0	34	228	29	8	82	10	9	2	0	BOSTON
	10	76	7.6	0	81	639	27	8	69	9	6	0	0	BKN.
														DEFENSE
	17	197	11.5	0	54	412	30	11	75	9	10	4	0	N.Y.
	12	160	13.3	0	79	570	29	4	131	14	5	1	0	PHIL.
	17	302	17.7	3	60	421	22	9	180	21	13	5	0	WASH.
	22	302	13.7	1	77	561	24	11	233	30	7	5	1	BOSTON
	29	268	9.2	1	63	539	21	9	166	19	13	3	0	BKN.

Use Name – Backs & Ends	Pos.	Age	Hgt	Wgt	Pts	Int	RUSHING				PASSING								RECEIVING				PUNTING		KICKING						PUNT RETURNS				KICKOFF RETURNS			
							No.	Yds	Avg	TD	Att	Comp	%	Yds	Yd/Att	TD	Int–%	RK	No.	Yds	Avg	TD	No.	Avg	Pat	Att	%	FG	Att	%	No.	Yds	Avg	TD	No.	Yds	Avg	TD
NEW YORK GIANTS																																						
Arnie Herber	QB	34	5'11"	210			7	-58	-8.3	0	86	36	42	651	7.6	6	8- 9	7					1	39.0														
Joe Sulatis	QB-DE	23	6'2"	210			9	38	4.2	0	17	4	24	53	3.1	1	4- 24																					
Hank Soar	QB-DB	30	6'2"	210		1	9	10	1.1	0	10	4	40	113	11.3	2	1- 10														6	52	9	0				
Bill Paschal	FB-DB	23	6'	200	54		196	737	3.8	9	8	2	25	31	3.9	0	2- 25						1	6.0							7	102	15	0	9	260	29	0
Howie Livingston	FB-DB	22	6'1"	190	18	9	84	313	3.7	1	1	0	0	0	0.0	0	1-100		1	12	12	1	2	39.5							4	44	11	0	4	114	29	0
Carl Kinscherf	FB-DB	24	6'1"	190		1	9	21	2.3	0									1	9	9	0																
Ken Strong	FB	38	6'	210	41		2	-2	-1.0	0													1	44.0	23	24	96	6	12	50								
Ward Cuff	WB-DB	31	6'1"	195	17	2	76	425	5.6	0									11	135	12	2			2	2	100	1	4	25	11	115	10	0	2	63	32	0
Bill Petrilas	WB-DB	26	6'1"	195	12	5	12	29	2.4	0																					4	58	15	0				
Keith Beebe	BB-DB	23	5'9"	180		3	8	12	1.5	0	3	1	33	9	3.0	0	1- 11						7	30.0														
Len Calligaro	BB-LB	23	5'11"	190	6		3	4	1.3	1									2	11	6	0																
Hub Barker	BB-LB	25	5'10"	190			1	3	3.0	0									3	34	11	0																
Neal Adams	OE-DE	25	6'3"	195	6														14	342	24	1													2	29	15	0
Frank Liebel	OE-DB	24	6'1"	205	36	1													13	292	22	5																
Verlin Adams	OE-DE	26	6'	205															1	12	12	0																
John Weiss	OE-DB	22	6'3"	195															1	10	10	0																
Len Younce	G-LB	27	6'1"	210		3																	48	40.4														
PHILADELPHIA EAGLES																																						
Roy Zimmerman	QB-DB	26	6'2"	200	62	4	26	-84	-3.2	3	105	39	37	785	7.5	8	10- 10	9					39	39.3	32	34	94	4	8	50								
Allie Sherman	QB-DB	21	5'11"	175	6	2	22	-42	-1.9	1	31	16	52	156	5.0	1	2- 6						1	27.0														
Steve Van Buren	HB-DB	23	6'	200	42	5	80	444	5.6	5													1	35.0							15	230	15	1	8	266	33	1
Jack Hinkle	HB-DB	26	6'	195	18	2	92	421	4.6	2									2	34	17	0									4	32	8	0	6	134	22	0
Mel Bleeker	HB-DB	24	5'11"	185	48	1	60	315	5.3	4									8	299	37	4									1	3	3	0				
Ernie Steele	HB-DB	26	6'	180	30	6	59	247	4.2	5									1	22	22	0									11	181	16	0	5	128	26	0
Jack Banta	HB-DB	26	5'11"	190	18	1	38	198	5.2	3									1	8	8	0	9	44.2							7	81	12	0	3	54	18	0
Ben Kish	FB-LB	27	6'	200	7	4	22	96	4.4	0									5	73	15	1	4	45.5	1	1	100								2	36	18	0
Art Macioszczyk	FB-LB	23	5'9"	210			16	55	3.4	0									3	28	9	0									1	14	14	0	1	4	4	0
Toimi Jarvi	HB-DB	24	6'	200		1	5	16	3.2	0									1	9	9	0									2	22	11	0				
Ted Laux	HB-DB	26	5'10"	185			2	-1	-0.5	0									1	6	6	0	1	18.0														
Larry Cabrelli	OE-DB	27	5'11"	190	6		1	-2	-2.0	0									14	169	12	1																
Tom Miller	OE-DE	26	6'2"	205	6	1	1	-2	-2.0	0									8	135	17	0													1	8	8	0
Flip McDonald (from BKN)	OE-DB	23	6'2"	195	6	1													4	26	7	1																
Jack Ferrante	OE-DE	28	6'1"	205	6														3	66	22	1																
Charlie Gauer	OE-DE	23	6'2"	215		1													2	35	18	0																
John Durko	OE-DE	25	6'4"	235	6														2	31	16	1																
WASHINGTON REDSKINS																																						
Frankie Filchock	QB-HB-DB	27	5'11"	198			33	-34	-1.0	0	147	**84**	**57**	1139	7.7	**13**	9- 6	**1**	3	51	17	0									3	5	2	0	3	42	14	0
Sammy Baugh	QB-DB	30	6'2"	180		4	19	-38	-2.0	0	146	82	56	849	5.8	4	8- **5**	4	1	0	0	0	44	40.5							4	23	6	0				
Larry Weldon	QB-DB	27	6'	198	4		8	8	1.0	0	6	4	67	33	5.5	0	0- 0								4	4	100								3	28	9	0
Bob Seymour	FB-DB	28	6'2"	208	36	2	92	315	3.4	3									19	263	14	3	10	35.5							1	6	6	0				
Frank Akins	FB-LB	25	5'10"	205	6		46	154	3.3	1									5	27	5	0	1	39.0											1	14	14	0
Frank Seno	HB-DB	23	6'	195		2	43	140	3.3	0									17	146	9	0									10	129	13	0	8	193	24	0
Wilbur Moore	HB-DB	28	5'11"	185	42	5	37	140	3.8	2									33	424	13	5									1	12	12	0	8	143	18	0
Mike Micka	FB-DB	23	6'	190		1	25	94	3.8	0									2	16	8	0	2	21.0														
Andy Farkas	FB-HB-DB	28	5'10"	192		3	21	85	4.0	0									4	29	7	0									7	94	13	0	11	229	21	0
Bob Sneddon	HB-DB	23	5'10"	180		1	14	30	2.1	0									3	42	14	0																
Larry Fuller	HB-DB	21	5'10"	187	6		4	10	2.5	0									5	82	16	1																
Andy Natowich	HB-DB		5'10"	175																															1	16	16	0
Joe Aquirre	OE-DE	25	6'4"	234	51														34	410	12	4	2	43.5	15	18	83	4	8	50								
Les Dye	OE	26	6'1"	182	12														24	281	12	2																
Doug Turley	OE-DE	25	6'2"	212	6														8	112	14	1													1	12	12	0
Alex Piasecky	OE-DE	27	6'2"	197															8	77	10	0																
Ted Lapka	OE-DE	24	6'1"	196	6														4	61	15	1																
BOSTON YANKS																																						
George Cafego	QB-DB	29	5'10"	180	6	1	61	31	0.5	1	73	35	48	454	6.2	3	7- 10	10	2	8	4	0	16	36.4							4	49	12	0	3	48	16	0
Leo Stasica	QB-DB	28	5'11"	185		1	22	-16	-0.7	0	47	21	45	225	4.8	1	7- 15						1	38.0							3	30	10	0	3	75	25	0
Scott Gudmundson	QB-DB	23	5'10"	175			14	-21	-1.5	0	38	16	42	226	5.9	1	4- 11						12	33.5							1	27	27	0	3	55	18	0
Frank Turbert	QB-DB		5'11"	200			14	-16	-1.1	0	14	5	36	37	2.6	0	0- 0		1	16	16	0									1	7	7	0				
Bob Davis	HB-DB	32	6'	190	6	4	95	363	3.8	1	18	8	44	88	4.9	1	2- 11		19	97	5	0	3	20.0							**22**	**271**	12	0	7	152	22	0
Milt Crain	FB-LB	23	6'2"	225		1	26	78	3.0	0									1	16	16	0	1	40.0							2	10	5	0	2	33	17	0
Ken Steinmetz	FB-LB	20	6'	186			11	24	2.2	0	1	0	0	0	0.0	0	0- 0						1	17.0														
Ted Williams	HB-DB	27	5'11"	180	6	1	52	13	0.3	1	6	0	0	0	0.0	0	2- 33		6	28	5	0									1	13	13	0	6	82	14	0
John Martin (from C-P)	HB-DB	26	6'1"	195		3	19	7	0.4	0									6	56	9	0	41	36.4							3	50	17	0	8	265	33	0
Dave Smukler	FB-LB	27	6'1"	225			2	7	3.5	0													2	24.5														
Paul Sanders	HB-DB	25	5'11"	192			6	4	0.7	0									4	5	1	0																
Tony Falkenstein (from BKN,BB)	FB-LB	29	5'10"	200			4	2	0.5	0									1	21	21	0																
Keith Ranspot	OE-DE	29	6'3"	205	18														19	269	14	3						0	1	0					3	37	12	0
Joe Crowley	OE-DB	25	6'	190	18	1													13	279	21	3																
Harry Wynne	OE-DE	24	6'4"	205															10	205	21	0													1	11	11	0
Sam Goldman	OE-DE	27	6'3"	220															2	21	11	0													1	0	0	0
Dick Harrison	OE-DB	28	6'	195															1	9	9	0																
Augie Lio	G-LB	26	6'	235	16	2																			10	11	91	2	8	25								
BROOKLYN TIGERS																																						
Charlie McGibbony	TB-DB	26	5'10"	160		1	26	81	3.1	0	48	18	38	262	5.5	1	10- 21						8	36.8							5	66	13	0	2	40	20	0
Frankie Sachse	TB-DB	27	6'	197			9	13	1.4	0	45	18	40	226	5.0	0	5- 11														1	23	23	0	1	25	25	0
Cecil Johnson	TB-DB	22	5'11"	190			30	41	1.4	0	25	10	40	193	7.7	2	4- 16						23	**42.6**							7	102	15	0				
Kenny Fryer	TB-DB	25	6'	200			15	15	1.0	0	24	9	38	91	3.8	0	2- 8						7	39.0														
Johnny Butler (from C-P,HB-DB)	TB-DB	25	5'10"	185	12	3	60	94	1.6	0	23	8	35	107	4.7	0	1- 4		3	109	36	2	13	37.3							9	99	11	0	4	92	23	0
Steve Marko	TB-DB	20	6'	200			6	10	1.7	0	7	1	14	2	0.3	0	2- 29																		3	80	27	0
John McMichaels	TB-DB	26	5'11"	190			3	1	0.3	0	1	0	0	0	0.0	0	1-100						2	42.5							1	5	5	0				
Pug Manders	FB-LB	31	6'	200	30	1	127	430	3.4	5	34	9	26	96	2.8	0	4- 12		6	78	13	0						0	1	0					11	227	21	0
Ray Hare	HB-FB-DB	26	6'1"	202	6	1	72	196	2.7	0	1	0	0	0	0.0	0	0- 0		9	206	23	1									2	5	3	0	4	120	30	0
Bill Reynolds	HB-DB	25	5'8"	175	6		11	71	6.5	1																					1	12	12	0	1	18	18	0
Frank Martin	HB-DB	25	5'10"	180		1	11	18	1.6	0	1	1	100	7	7.0	0	0- 0		3	15	5	0	1	2.0							3	16	5	0				
Bob Trocolor	HB-DB	25	6'2"	210			3	8	2.7	0													1	10.0														
Charlie Taylor	BB-LB	24	5'10"	210			7	19	2.7	0									2	22	11	0									2	25	13	0	1	12	12	0
Bill Brown	BB-LB	27	6'	205		1	4	10	2.5	0	3	1	33	11	3.7	0	0- 0		2	10	5	0									2	16	8	0	1	12	12	0
Bob Masterson	OE-DE	29	6'1"	218	6						1	1	100	1	1.0	0	0- 0		24	258	11	1	4	34.0				0	5	0								
Joe Carter	OE-DE	34	6'1"	197															13	143	11	0	9	36.1														
Andy Kowalski	OE-DE	24	6'1"	200	6														9	155	17	1																
Rocky Uguccioni	OE-DE	26	6'	195	6														7	94	13	0									1	12	12	1				
Bill LaFitte	OE	18	6'1"	170															1	15	15	0																
Bruiser Kinard	T	29	6'1"	218	9	1																			9	9	**100**								1	22	22	0

GREEN BAY PACKERS 8-2-0 Curly Lambeau

Scores of Each Game		
14	BROOKLYN	7
42	CHIC. BEARS	28
27	DETROIT	6
34	CARD–PITT	7
30	CLEVELAND	21
14	Detroit	0
0	Chic. Bears	21
42	Cleveland	7
0	New York	24
35	Card–Pitt	20

Use Name	Pos.	Hgt	Wgt	Age	Int	Pts
Charley Brock	C-LB	6'2"	210	28	1	
Bob Flowers	C-LB	6'1"	210	27		
Amy McPherson	C-DT	5'11"	240	32		
Bob Kercher	DE	6'2"	196	26		
Bob Kahler	DB	6'3"	204	27		

Use Name – Tackles	Pos.	Hgt	Wgt	Age	Int	Pts
Paul Berezney	T	6'2"	220	27		
Tiny Croft	T	6'3"	285	23		
Baby Ray	T	6'6"	250	29		
Ade Schwammel	T	6'2"	215	35		

Use Name – Guards	Pos.	Hgt	Wgt	Age	Int	Pts
Amadeo Bucchianeri	G	5'10"	215	27		
Buckets Goldenberg	G-LB	5'10"	220	33		
Bill Kuusisto	G	6'	230	26		
Glen Sorenson	G-LB	6'	215	23		1
(Missed 2 FG attempts, 1 PAT in 1 attempt)						
Pete Tinsley	G-LB	5'8"	210	31		
Charlie Tollefson	G	6'	215	27		

Far from the greatest Green Bay team ever, this year's edition of the Packers was good enough to win the Western Division crown. The Packers ran off six straight victories at the start of the season and coasted home the rest of the way, leaving the Bears and Lions to snarl over the second-place spoils. Although Don Hutson, as usual, burned defensive backs for long gains, most of the faces in the Green Bay backfield were new. Rangy Irv Comp was Hutson's new passing partner, and popular Ted Fritsch picked up the tough yardage on the ground as Clarke Hinkle once did. Baby Ray, Buckets Goldenberg, and Charlie Brock gave the strong forward line a veteran flavor. Like most wartime clubs, the Packers mixed veterans and youngsters together with a salad-bowl effect that was sometimes interesting and sometimes boringly inept. But with Don Hutson on hand, Green Bay remained the best around.

CHICAGO BEARS 6-3-1 Luke Johnsos, Hunk Anderson, Paddy Driscoll

Scores of Each Game		
28	Green Bay	42
7	Cleveland	19
34	CARD–PITT	7
21	DETROIT	21
28	CLEVELAND	21
21	GREEN BAY	0
21	BOSTON	7
21	Detroit	41
28	Philadelphia	7
49	Card–Pitt	7

Use Name	Pos.	Hgt	Wgt	Age	Int	Pts
Fred Mundee	C-LB	6'1"	220	31	1	
Bulldog Turner	C-LB-HB	6'1"	255	25	2	6
(1 rush for 48 yd. TD, 1 punt return for 9 yds.)						
Elmo Kelly	DE	6'1"	210	27		
Max Burnell	HB-DB					
Harley Greenich	HB-DB	5'11"	185			

Use Name – Tackles	Pos.	Hgt	Wgt	Age	Int	Pts
Al Babartsky	T	6'	225	28		
Al Hoptowit	T	6'1"	222	28		
Tom Roberts	T	6'1"	215	28		
Dom Sigillo	T	6'	220	31		
Jake Sweeney	T	6'3"	240	22		

Use Name – Guards	Pos.	Hgt	Wgt	Age	Int	Pts
George Musso	G	6'2"	260	34		
Paul Podmajersky	G	5'11"	220			
Ed Sprinkle	G-LB	6'1"	200	20	1	
George Zorich	G-LB	6'2"	210	25	1	

The Bears dropped their first two games of the year to Green Bay and Cleveland, then spent the rest of the season trying to catch up with the Packers. Although they had to settle for a second-place tie, the Bears received several noteworthy performances. Quarterback Sid Luckman spent most of his week in the Merchant Marine but usually got away on Sunday to direct the attack. Sid's understudy was thirty-five-year-old Gene Ronzani, back in the NFL for the first time since 1938.

Bulldog Turner kept up his superior work at center, but also showed hidden talent as a ball carrier. When several Bears were ejected for fighting in a game against the Card-Pitt team, Bulldog volunteered for emergency duty at halfback. The only time he got the ball he plowed straight ahead for a 48-yard touchdown. Card-Pitt coach Walt Kiesling was so angry he kicked Turner in the rump the next time there was a pile-up in front of his bench.

DETROIT LIONS 6-3-1 Gus Dorais

Scores of Each Game		
6	Green Bay	27
19	BROOKLYN	14
17	CLEVELAND	20
21	Chic. Bears	21
0	GREEN BAY	14
27	Card–Pitt	6
21	CARD–PITT	7
41	CHIC. BEARS	21
26	Cleveland	14
38	BOSTON	7

Use Name	Pos.	Hgt	Wgt	Age	Int	Pts
Ed Eiden (from PHI)	C-LB	6'	205	22		
Ernie Rosteck	C-LB	6'1"	226	22		
Alex Wojciechowicz	C-LB	5'11"	220	29	7	
Paul Blessing	OE-DE	6'4"	215	25		
Dale Nansen	DE-T	6'3"	225	23		
Freeman Rexer (from BOS)	DE	6'1"	212	26		
John Greene	BB-DB	6'	215	24	2	

Use Name – Tackles	Pos.	Hgt	Wgt	Age	Int	Pts
Joe D'Orazio	T	5'11"	220			
Tony Furst	T	6'1"	215	26		
Tom Kennedy	T	6'	218	24		
Luther Lindon	T	5'10"	240	27		
Ed Opalewski	T	6'3"	240	24		
Bill Rogers	T	5'11"	250	31		

Use Name – Guards	Pos.	Hgt	Wgt	Age	Int	Pts
Stan Batinski	G	5'10"	218	27		
Al Kaporch	G-LB	5'10"	215	30	1	
(1 punt return for 14 yds.)						
Sonny Liles	G-LB	5'9"	185	25	1	
(1 punt return for 5 yds.)						
George Sirochman	G	6'2"	210	26		

The Lions began the season by posting a 1-3-1 record. But then, with the emergence of a powerful offense, Detroit won its last five games to climb up into a second-place perch along with the Bears. One of the victories in the closing streak was a 41-21 upset over the Chicagoans that fatally slashed their slim title hopes. Although the Lions never threatened to catch the Packers, Detroit fans relished the turn-around in form by a team which only two years ago had not won a single game all season.

Leading the resurgence was tailback Frankie Sinkwich, a strong passer, shifty runner, and a top-notch punter. Coach Gus Dorais constructed his offense around Sinkwich's passes to end Jack Matheson, and the tailback spurred the Lions on well enough to win the league MVP Award and put some teeth back in his team's attack.

CLEVELAND RAMS 4-6-0 Buff Donelli

Scores of Each Game		
30	Card–Pitt	28
19	CHIC. BEARS	7
20	Detroit	17
21	Green Bay	30
21	Chic. Bears	28
10	Washington	14
7	GREEN BAY	42
33	Card–Pitt	6
14	DETROIT	26
13	Philadelphia	26

Use Name	Pos.	Hgt	Wgt	Age	Int	Pts
Bill Conkright	C-LB	6'1"	205	30		
Joe Gibson	C-LB-DE	6'3"	220	25		
Bill Rieth	C-LB	5'11"	203	28	1	
Mike Scarry	C-T-LB	6'	220	24	1	
Floyd Konetsky	DE	6'	195	24		
Howie Carson	HB-DB	6'1"	190			

Use Name – Tackles	Pos.	Hgt	Wgt	Age	Int	Pts
Boyd Clay	T	6'1"	225	31		
Jake Fawcett	T	5'11"	220	25		
(1 reception for 9 yds., 2 kickoff rets. for 2 yds.)						
Del Lyman	T	6'3"	220	27		
Norm Olsen	T	6'2"	220	22		
(1 kickoff return for 19 yds.)						
Chet Pudloski	T	6'1"	210	29		

Use Name – Guards	Pos.	Hgt	Wgt	Age	Int	Pts
Tom Corbo	G-LB	5'11"	210	26	1	
Al Gutknecht	G-LB	6'	200	27		
Les Lear	G-LB	5'11"	223	26		
Riley Matheson	G-LB	6'2"	205	29	3	
Charley Riffle	G-LB	6'	210	26		

After a year in deep freeze, the Rams rushed back into the football wars, hiring Buff Donelli as head coach and recalling their players who had been spread around the league in 1943. Returning to Cleveland were Jim Benton, Bill Conkright, Jake Fawcett, Joe Gibson, Riley Matheson, John Petchel, and Bill Rieth, the only seven Rams still active. Donelli bolstered this nucleus with rookies and free agents. At the heart of the attack was passer Albie Reisz and runner Walt West, both rookies. With the team pasted together again, the Rams celebrated their rebirth with a 30-28 victory over Card-Pitt. The next week they upset the Bears 19-7 and then beat Detroit 20-17. Green Bay, as expected, burst the bubble by downing the Rams 30-21, throwing them into a tailspin which lasted the rest of the year.

CHICAGO CARDINALS – PITTSBURGH STEELERS 0-10-0 Phil Handler, Walt Kiesling

Scores of Each Game		
28	CLEVELAND	P 30
7	Green Bay	34
7	Chic. Bears	34
0	New York	23
20	Washington	42
6	DETROIT	P 27
7	Detroit	21
6	CLEVELAND	C 33
20	GREEN BAY	C 35
7	CHIC. BEARS	P 49

P=at Pittsburgh
C=at Chicago

Use Name	Pos.	Hgt	Wgt	Age	Int	Pts
Vince Banonis	C-LB	6'1"	220	23		
Al Wukits	C-LB	6'3"	215	24		

Use Name – Tackles	Pos.	Hgt	Wgt	Age	Int	Pts
Clarence Booth	T	6'	225	24		
Chet Bulger	T	6'3"	245	26		
(1 kickoff return for 5 yds.)						
Ted Doyle	T	6'2"	230	30		
Gil Duggan	T	6'3"	225	26		
Al Merkovsky	T	6'1"	238	27		
Elbie Schultz	T	6'4"	250	26		6
(touchdown on kickoff return lateral)						

Use Name – Guards	Pos.	Hgt	Wgt	Age	Int	Pts
Lou Marotti	G	5'10"	212	26		
(1 kickoff return for 2 yds.)						
John Perko	G	6'1"	210	28	1	
(1 kickoff return for 3 yds.)						

Known affectionately around the league as the Carpets, this joint effort of the Cardinals and Steelers lost every time it took the field. Pittsburgh, in 1943, had merged with the Eagles, and this year pooled resources with the hard-pressed Cards. The losing season was a true team effort, with both organizations liable for the blame. Co-coaches Phil Handler and Walt Kiesling fielded a line in which only Conway Baker and Vince Banonis were big-league players. John Grigas threw and ran more than any other back, grinding out enough yardage to rank second in the league rushing statistics, and veteran end Eddie Rucinski played well as a receiver.

The closest the Carpets came to getting off the floor was a close 30-28 opening-game loss to Cleveland. After that, they were rarely long in the game after the opening gun. After their disastrous combined showing, both clubs decided to go it alone in 1945.

TEAM TOTALS

	FIRST DOWNS:				RUSHING:				PASSING:									PUNTING:		PUNT RETURNS:				KICKOFF RETURNS:				INTERCEPTION RETURNS:				PENAL-TIES:		FUM-BLES:		POINTS:					
OFFENSE	Tot	by Rsh	by Pas	by Pen	No.	Yds.	Avg. Yds.	TD	Att.	Com	Comp. Pct.	Yds.	Avg. Yds. Att.	Avg. Yds. Comp	TD	Int.	Pct. Int.	No.	Avg. Yds.	No.	Yds.	Avg. Yds.	TD	No.	Yds.	Avg. Yds.	TD	No.	Yds.	Avg. Yds.	TD	No.	Yds.	No.	Lost	Tot	PAT	FG Att	FG	Saf.	OFFENSE
G.B.	147	70	63	14	395	1517	3.8	16	253	105	41.5	1471	5.8	14.0	15	24	9.5	48	36.9	27	241	8.9	0	30	612	20.4	0	29	454	15.6	3	62	558	11	7	238	32	6	0	1	G.B.
CHIC. B.	140	73	57	10	412	1562	3.8	16	217	107	49.3	1616	7.4	15.1	21	18	8.3	57	36.6	29	263	9.1	0	31	670	21.6	0	24	387	16.1	0	121	1025	24	14	258	36	0	0	0	CHIC. B.
DET.	106	52	47	7	326	1141	3.5	14	207	89	43.0	1475	7.1	16.6	16	28	13.5	54	40.5	31	440	14.2	0	25	589	23.6	1	26	307	11.8	0	56	417	22	8	216	24	8	2	0	DET.
CLEVE.	104	51	43	10	358	1141	3.2	11	209	85	40.7	1261	6.0	14.8	13	26	12.4	57	38.4	28	326	11.6	0	41	923	22.5	0	27	310	11.5	0	64	441	28	15	188	20	7	4	0	CLEVE.
CARD-PITT	109	56	44	9	360	1019	2.8	7	258	87	33.7	1257	4.9	14.4	8	41	15.9	60	32.7	17	159	9.4	0	53	1119	21.1	1	16	146	9.1	0	65	479	30	12	108	12	2	0	0	CARD-PITT
DEFENSE																																									DEFENSE
G.B.	114	56	49	9	357	1130	3.2	10	227	89	39.4	1224	5.4	13.8	10	29	12.8	57	36.8	18	193	10.7	0	34	804	23.6	0	24	344	14.3	1	88	700	25	12	141	18	2	1	0	G.B.
CHIC. B.	110	49	38	23	298	954	3.2	14	208	69	33.2	1052	5.1	15.2	10	24	11.5	58	38.4	32	393	12.3	0	46	949	20.6	1	18	283	15.7	2	59	489	23	10	172	22	6	2	0	CHIC. B.
DET.	129	63	57	9	403	1216	3.0	7	246	106	43.1	1442	5.9	13.6	15	26	10.5	57	35.8	20	252	12.6	0	39	898	23.0	0	28	351	12.5	0	51	405	25	16	151	19	3	0	0	DET.
CLEVE.	116	69	41	6	387	1412	3.7	16	206	87	42.3	1434	7.0	16.5	16	27	13.1	55	38.5	24	290	12.1	0	36	872	24.2	1	26	289	11.1	0	77	627	27	17	224	27	3	1	1	CLEVE.
CARD-PITT	109	56	46	7	365	1394	3.8	25	204	98	48.0	1575	7.7	16.1	22	16	7.8	50	37.2	39	386	9.9	0	25	472	18.8	0	41	690	16.8	2	77	633	23	12	328	41	7	1	1	CARD-PITT

Use Name – Backs & Ends	Pos.	Age	Hgt	Wgt	Pts	Int	Rushing No.	Rushing Yds	Rushing Avg	Rushing TD	Passing Att	Passing Comp	Passing %	Passing Yds	Passing Yd/Att	Passing TD	Passing Int–%	Passing RK	Receiving No.	Receiving Yds	Receiving Avg	Receiving TD	Punting No.	Punting Avg	Kicking Pat	Kicking Att	Kicking %	Kicking FG	Kicking Att	Kicking %	Punt Returns No.	Punt Returns Yds	Punt Returns Avg	Punt Returns TD	Kickoff Returns No.	Kickoff Returns Yds	Kickoff Returns Avg	Kickoff Returns TD
GREEN BAY PACKERS																																						
Irv Comp	TB-DB	25	6'2"	214	18	6	52	134	2.6	2	177	80	45	1159	6.5	12	21–12	7	2	16	8	1									2	32	16	0	2	37	19	0
Tony Canadeo	TB-DB	25	5'11"	190			31	149	4.8	0	20	9	45	89	4.5	0	0–0		1	12	12	0	13	36.9							1	4	4	0	1	12	12	0
Tex McKay	TB-DB	24	6'	190			5	12	2.4	0	14	6	43	72	5.1	1	2–14						8	37.1							2	19	10	0				
Dick Bilda	TB-DB		6'	200		1					1	0	0	0	0.0	0	0–0																					
Ted Fritsch	FB-LB	23	5'10"	210	30	6	94	322	3.4	4									3	5	2	0	10	40.8											11	288	26	0
Don Perkins	FB-LB	26	6'	197	12	2	58	207	3.6	0									1	1	1	0	1	31.0											2	34	17	0
Joe Laws	HB-DB	33	5'9"	190	24	3	45	200	4.4	3	4	1	25	15	3.8	0	1–25		7	61	9	1									15	118	8	0	8	132	17	0
Lou Brock	HB-DB	26	6'	190	30		36	200	5.6	3	21	5	24	94	4.5	2	0–0		4	74	19	2	14	35.0							4	36	9	0	2	41	21	0
Paul Duhart	HB-DB	23	6'	180	24	4	51	183	3.6	2	13	3	31	42	3.2	0	0–0		9	176	20	2									3	32	11	0	1	18	18	0
Larry Craig	BB-DE	28	6'1"	205		1													2	17	9	0													1	17	17	0
Ben Starret	BB-DE	26	5'11"	220	12		10	21	2.1	2									1	6	6	0	2	33.0											11	13	13	0
Don Hutson	OE-DB	31	6'1"	180	85	4	12	87	7.3	0	3	0	0	0	0.0	0	0–0		58	866	15	9			31	33	94	0	3	0								
Harry Jacunski	OE-DE	28	6'2"	205															9	151	17	0																
Ray Wehba	OE-DE	28	6'	215		1													6	67	11	0																
Alex Urban	OE-DE	27	6'3"	210			1	2	2.0	0									1	10	10	0													1	20	20	0
Joel Mason	OE-DE	31	6'	210															1	9	9	0																
CHICAGO BEARS																																						
Sid Luckman	QB-DB	27	6'	200	6	2	20	–96	–4.8	1	143	71	50	1018	7.1	11	11–8	2					20	34.2							1	6	6	0				
Gene Ronzani	QB-DB	35	5'9"	210		3	12	26	2.2	0	56	26	46	448	8.0	9	5–9	2																				
John Long	QB-DB	29	6'	185			24	2	0.1	0	14	9	64	128	9.1	1	1–7						7	35.4							2	14	7	0	1	14	14	0
Bill Glenn	QB-DB	26	6'	157			1	1	1.0	0	4	1	25	22	5.5	0	1–25																					
Hank Margarita	HB-DB	23	5'11"	175	24	3	88	463	5.3	4									15	130	9	0	1	34.0							5	9	2	0	12	279	23	0
Jim Fordham	FB-LB	27	5'11"	215	24		73	381	5.2	4									1	13	13	0													2	42	21	0
Al Grygo	HB-DB	26	5'10"	172	12	4	53	322	6.1	2									5	42	8	0	4	30.8							11	100	9	0	7	162	23	0
Gary Famiglietti	FB-LB	29	6'	238	18		63	282	4.5	2									1	23	23	1																
Tipp Mooney	HB-DB	25	6'	187	6	1	29	88	3.0	0									2	74	37	1									1	46	46	0	3	65	22	0
Ray McLean	HB-DB	28	5'10"	165	42	3	29	35	0.9	2									19	414	22	5									8	79	10	0	4	102	26	0
Doug McEnulty	HB-DB	22	6'3"	227	6	1	8	11	1.4	0									2	10	5	1	25	39.8														
Bob Masters	FB-LB	33	5'11"	204			11	9	0.8	0																												
George Wilson	OE-DE	30	6'1"	205	24														24	265	11	4																
Connie Mack Berry	OE-DE	28	6'3"	212	36														21	378	18	6																
Abe Craft	OE-DB	22	6'	180	12	1													9	140	16	2																
Rudy Smeja	OE-DE	23	6'2"	195	6														7	110	16	1													1	7	7	0
Dick Plasman	OE-DE	30	6'3"	220															1	17	17	0													1	–1	–1	0
Pete Gudauskas	G-LB	27	6'2"	220	36	1																			36	37	97											
DETROIT LIONS																																						
Frankie Sinkwich	TB-DB	23	5'11"	195	66	3	150	563	3.8	6	148	58	39	1060	7.2	12	20–14	6					45	41.0	24	30	80	2	8	25	11	148	13	0	6	144	24	0
Russ Lowther	TB-DB	21	5'8"	165		1	9	18	2.0	0	10	7	70	54	5.4	0	2–20						5	41.0							2	28	14	0				
Bob Westfall	FB-TB-LB	25	5'8"	195	30	1	65	277	4.3	3	47	23	49	342	7.3	4	6–13		16	218	14	2	1	11.0							3	38	13	0	3	79	26	0
Elmer Hackney	FB-LB	28	6'2"	198	30	3	58	184	3.2	4	1	1	100	19	19.0	0	0–0		8	48	6	1																
Fred Dawley	FB-LB		5'9"	190			2	16	8.0	0																												
Art Van Tone	WB-DB	25	5'10"	185	36	4	25	30	1.2	1	1	0	0	0	0.0	0	0–0		9	237	26	4	2	47.0							5	78	16	0	9	227	25	1
Bob Keene	WB-DB	25	5'11"	190	12	2	9	26	2.9	0									5	91	18	2	1	30.0							7	120	17	0	4	93	23	0
Tony Aiello (to BKN,HB-DB)	WB-DB	23	5'6"	165			6	22	3.7	0																					1	9	9	0				
Bill Callihan	BB-DB	28	6'3"	220			1	3	3.0	0									8	67	8	0													3	46	15	0
Buzz Trebotich	BB-DB	23	5'10"	210			1	2	2.0	0																												
Jack Matheson	OE-DE	24	6'2"	220	18	1													23	361	16	3																
Dave Diehl	OE-DE	25	6'	200	24														18	426	24	4																
Wayne Clark	OE-DE	26	6'3"	210															2	27	14	0																
CLEVELAND RAMS																																						
Albie Reisz	TB-DB	26	5'10"	170	12	3	69	134	1.9	2	113	49	43	777	6.9	8	10–9	5					24	40.0							5	68	14	0	12	285	24	0
Tom Colella	TB-DB	26	6'	190	21	4	53	208	3.9	2	76	27	36	336	4.4	4	10–13	12	2	64	32	1	33	37.8				1	1	100	4	65	16	0	10	241	24	0
Walt West	FB-DB	25	6'	197	12	2	66	220	3.3	0									9	64	7	0			6	8	75				1	0	0	0	1	15	15	0
Mike Kabealo	HB-DB	28	5'8"	185	6	2	47	152	3.2	1	1	1	100	54	54.0	1	0–0		2	20	10	0									7	64	9	0	4	126	32	0
Harvey Jones	FB-DB	23	6'	175	6	3	38	133	3.5	1									6	59	10	0									6	66	11	0	1	33	33	0
Jim Gillette	HB-DB	26	6'1"	185	12	3	26	131	5.0	2																					1	16	16	0	4	115	29	0
Lou Zontini	HB-DB	27	5'9"	190	47	2	33	105	3.2	3	2	2	100	18	9.0	0	0–0		3	88	29	1			14	16	88	3	6	50	4	47	12	0	3	66	22	0
Roy Huggins	FB-LB	25	5'11"	195			12	41	3.4	0									1	0	0	0																
Stan Skoczen	HB-DB		5'11"	187			1	0	0.0	0																												
John Karrs	BB-LB	28	6'1"	210			7	0	0.0	0	10	4	40	49	4.9	0	4–40																					
John Petchel	BB-DB	25	5'11"	185	6	1	5	11	2.2	0	3	2	67	27	9.0	0	0–0		1	43	43	1													1	17	17	0
Dave Bernard	BB-LB	31	5'10"	190			1	6	6.0	0	4	0	0	0	0.0	0	2–50																					
Jim Benton	OE-DE	27	6'3"	195	42														39	505	13	6													2	4	2	0
Steve Pritko	OE-DE	22	6'2"	210	18	1													18	296	16	3																
Ray Hamilton	OE-DE	28	6'4"	210	6														3	113	38	1																
CHICAGO CARDINALS – PITTSBURGH STEELERS																																						
John McCarthy	QB-DB	28	5'8"	160			6	–49	–8.2	0	67	20	30	250	3.6	0	13–19						24	33.4							1	9	9	0				
Tony Bova	QB-OE-DB	27	6'1"	192	12		14	–22	–1.6	0	30	6	20	96	3.2	0	1–3		19	287	15	2																
Coley McDonough	QB-DB	29	6'1"	190			3	7	2.3	0	23	10	43	208	9.0	2	4–17																					
Walt Masters	QB	37	5'10"	197			1	–14	–14.0	0	7	1	14	13	1.9	0	2–29						2	45.5														
John Grigas	FB-LB	24	6'	203	18	1	185	610	3.3	3	131	50	38	690	5.3	6	21–16	11	2	33	17	0	12	35.1							5	40	8	0	23	471	20	0
Bob Thurbon	HB-DB	26	5'10"	176	30	2	69	185	2.7	4									7	134	19	1	15	30.0							1	2	2	0	12	291	24	0
George Magulick	HB-DB	25	5'9"	150		2	17	102	6.0	0									6	48	8	0									7	86	12	0	5	101	20	0
John Popovich	HB-DB	26	5'8"	160			8	29	3.6	0									3	1	0	0													3	75	25	0
Walt Rankin	FB-LB	26	5'11"	200		2	3	13	4.3	0									4	18	5	0																
Bernie Semes	HB-DB	25	5'7"	188		1	17	38	2.2	0									3	22	7	0																
Eddie Rucinski	OE-DB	28	6'2"	198	6	4	16	72	4.5	0									22	284	13	1													3	67	22	0
Don Currivan	OE-DB	23	6'	195	12														7	163	23	2													1	14	14	0
Walt Kichefski	OE-DE	28	6'1"	215															6	85	14	0																
Clint Wager	OE-DE	23	6'6"	222															5	73	15	0																
Marshall Robnett	C-G-LB	25	6'	208	1	1																	1	14.0	1	1	100	0	2	0								
Conway Baker	G	33	5'11"	230	11																				11	15	73											

WASHINGTON REDSKINS 8-2-0 Dud DeGroot

Scores of Each Game		
20	Boston	28
14	Pittsburgh	0
24	PHILADELPHIA	14
24	New York	14
24	CHIC. CARDS	21
34	BOSTON	7
28	CHIC. BEARS	21
0	Philadelphia	16
24	PITTSBURGH	0
17	NEW YORK	0

Use Name	Pos.	Hgt	Wgt	Age	Int	Pts
Ki Aldrich	C-LB	6'	215	29		
Ernie Barber	C-LB	6'1"	225	30		
Al DeMao	C-LB	6'2"	200	25	1	
Lee Pressley (1 rush for 1 yd.)	C-FB-LB	6'2"	230	22		
John Watson	C-LB	6'	205	24		
Larry Weldon (1 PAT in 1 attempt)	DE	6'	198	28		1

Use Name – Tackles	Pos.	Hgt	Wgt	Age	Int	Pts
John Adams	T	6'7"	245	25		
Earl Audet	T	6'2"	250	24		
Fred Davis	T	6'3"	240	27		
John Koniszewski	T	6'3"	228	26		
Ev Sharp	T	6'1"	225	26		
Joe Ungerer	T	6'	260	28		

Use Name – Guards	Pos.	Hgt	Wgt	Age	Int	Pts
Elzaphan Hanna	G	5'10"	218	28		
Jack Keenan	G	5'10"	208	26		
Al Lolotai (1 kickoff return for 15 yds.)	G-T	6'	215	24	1	
Reid Lennan	G	6'	228	23		
Clem Stralka	G	5'10"	228	31		
Frank Walton	G	5'11"	235	33		
Marv Whited	G	5'10"	205	27	1	

An arm, a toe, and a pair of legs gave the Redskins sharp weapons in their drive to the top of the East. The arm, quarterback Sammy Baugh, completed a record 70.3 percent of his passes and kept the Washington attack moving in the air. The toe, Joe Aguirre, belted seven field goals, with one of them beating the Cardinals 24-21 in the last minute of play. To complete this tale of limbs, Steve Bagarus' quick legs often sprang the little halfback into the open on pass plays and end runs, one time leaving the Bears in the jet stream of a 55-yard weaving dash which made the difference in a 28-21 Redskin victory. An anatomy of the Washington offense would place these three players at the heart of the attack.

The framework for this talent was the T formation which had given Sammy Baugh trouble last year. But now that he was used to it, Sammy said he could play in top hat and tails—a remark fostered by his having no running duties in the T formation.

PHILADELPHIA EAGLES 7-3-0 Greasy Neale

Scores of Each Game		
21	CHIC. CARDS	6
24	Detroit	28
14	Washington	24
28	CLEVELAND	14
45	Pittsburgh	3
38	NEW YORK	17
30	PITTSBURGH	6
16	WASHINGTON	0
21	New York	28
35	BOSTON	7

Use Name	Pos.	Hgt	Wgt	Age	Int	Pts
Terry Fox	LB	6'1"	208	26		
Vic Lindskog	C-LB	6'1"	200	29	1	
Mike Mandarino	C	5'11"	240	24		
Bap Manzini	C-LB	5'11"	190	25		
Charlie Gauer	DE	6'2"	210	24		
Red Ramsey	DE	6'	210	30		
Milt Smith	DB-OE	6'3"	185	25		

Use Name – Tackles	Pos.	Hgt	Wgt	Age	Int	Pts
Rocco Canale	T	5'11"	235	28		
George Fritts	T	5'11"	205	25		
Bucko Kilroy (1 kickoff return for 7 yds.)	T	6'2"	240	24		
Vic Sears	T	6'3"	215	27		
Art Shires	T	6'2"	220	26		
John Smith	T	6'2"	200	26		
Al Wistert	T	6'1"	215	24		

Use Name – Guards	Pos.	Hgt	Wgt	Age	Int	Pts
Bruno Banducci	G	5'11"	205	23		
Enio Conti	G	5'11"	207	32		
Duke Maronic	G	5'9"	205	24		
Eddie Michaels	G	5'11"	215	31		
Jack Sanders	G	6'	210	28		
Bob Suffridge	G	6'	220	30		

With his weak left arm useless for straight-arm tactics, Steve Van Buren had to get past tacklers by trampling them under his pistonlike legs. He did enough trampling, with some dodging thrown in, to win his first rushing title as well as the scoring championship. The Lions tasted Van Buren's wares when he stormed to a 69-yard touchdown run, and the Giants had to endure a 98-yard Van Buren kickoff return. With Van Buren snorting up yardage in storms, the Eagles stayed close to the Redskins until the Giants shot them down, 28-21, in their second meeting of the year.

Rock-hard tackles Al Wistert and Vic Sears also starred in this campaign. Passer Tommy Thompson was discharged from the Army and balanced the run-oriented attack as coach Greasy Neale was slowly but surely assembling a championship team.

NEW YORK GIANTS 3-6-1 Steve Owen

Scores of Each Game		
34	Pittsburgh	6
13	Boston	13
7	PITTSBURGH	21
14	WASHINGTON	24
17	CLEVELAND	21
17	Philadelphia	38
35	DETROIT	14
14	GREEN BAY	23
28	PHILADELPHIA	21
0	Washington	17

Use Name	Pos.	Hgt	Wgt	Age	Int	Pts
Lou DeFilippo	C-LB	6'1"	225	29		
Mel Hein	C-LB	6'2"	230	36	2	
Bill Piccolo	C-LB	5'11"	185	25		6
Elmer Barbour	BB-LB	6'1"	200	23		
Hub Barker	BB-LB	5'10"	195	26		
Bob Morrow	BB-LB	6'	220	27		
Leland Shaffer (2 kickoff returns for 42 yds.)	BB-LB	6'2"	210	33		
Bill Petrilas	DB	6'1"	195	27	2	

Use Name – Tackles	Pos.	Hgt	Wgt	Age	Int	Pts
Vic Carroll	T-C	6'4"	235	32		
Frank Cope	T	6'2"	235	29		
Lou Eaton	T	6'2"	215	30		
Herb Kane	T	6'1"	220	24		
Tom Kearns	T	6'4"	245	25		
Jim Little	T	6'1"	200	24		
Win Pedersen	T	6'3"	225	30		
Phil Ragazzo	T	6'	223	30	1	
Army Tomaini	T	6'	235	27		

Use Name – Guards	Pos.	Hgt	Wgt	Age	Int	Pts
Verlin Adams	G-LB-DE	6'	205	27	1	
Bob Garner	G	6'	238	22		
Carl Grate	G-LB	6'	215	25		
Virgil Lindahl (1 reception for 32 yds.)	G-OE-LB	6'1"	197	24		
Jim Sivell	G	5'9"	205	31		
Frank Umont	G	5'11"	215	27		
Larry Visnic (1 kickoff return for 0 yds.)	G-LB	5'11"	180	26	1	
Tarzan White	G	5'9"	225	29		

The death of Al Blozis in France began the year on a tragic note which made the football games seem less important. Lieutenant Blozis met a hero's death when he went back for a missing member of his platoon and stopped a German bullet, cutting short a brilliant NFL career that lasted only three seasons.

Guard Len Younce also joined the military, and fullback Bill Paschal spent half the season in service, leaving the Giants a much weaker team. From its perch atop the Eastern Division, New York tumbled into third place with a squad made up of untried rookies and overaged veterans. One of the old-timers, passer Arnie Herber, had a last fling at glory in a late-season game against the Eagles. After Philadelphia had built up a big first-half lead, Herber came into the game in the second half and threw three touchdown passes to Frank Liebel in a five-minute span, bringing the Giants back to victory.

BOSTON YANKS 3-6-1 Herb Kopf

Scores of Each Game		
28	PITTSBURGH	7
28	WASHINGTON	20
13	NEW YORK	13
14	Green Bay	38
10	Pittsburgh	6
9	DETROIT	10
7	Washington	34
0	GREEN BAY	28
7	Cleveland	20
7	Philadelphia	35

Use Name	Pos.	Hgt	Wgt	Age	Int	Pts
Jim Magee	C-LB	6'1"	200	24	1	
Jack Sachse	C-LB	6'	210	24		
Bill Anderson	DE	6'2"	190	24		
Andy Kowalski	DE	6'1"	200	25		
Lou Mark	DE-LB	6'	200	30		

Use Name – Tackles	Pos.	Hgt	Wgt	Age	Int	Pts
Don Deeks	T	6'4"	240	22		
George Doherty	T	6'1"	220	24		
Ed McGee	T	6'1"	225	29		
George Sergienko	T	6'1"	250	27		

Use Name – Guards	Pos.	Hgt	Wgt	Age	Int	Pts
Al Fiorentino	G	5'7"	200	28		
Ellis Jones	G-LB	6'	190	24		
Tony Leon	G	5'9"	210	28		
John Morelli	G-LB	5'10"	192	22	1	
Floyd Rhea	G	6'	220	24		
Bill Walker (1 kickoff return for 3 yds.)	G	6'	220	24		

The Brooklyn Tigers joined forces with the Yanks for this year, but the marriage of two weak clubs only gave birth to an anemic offspring. Playing four home games in Boston and one in New York, the Yanks inherited the pop-gun offense characteristic of both parent squads. Even worse, the Yanks were duds at the box office in both cities, forcing owner Ted Collins to use the team as a tax write-off. The other NFL clubs also wrote off the Yanks as serious threats on the field. But the team did win three games, two from Pittsburgh plus an upset of Washington, and stayed very close in several losses. The lack of scoring punch was a ball and chain on the Yanks' movement. Passer Scott Gudmundson never showed a major-league arm, and leading runner Pug Manders ranked only fifteenth in the league statistics. The biggest asset on the Brooklyn roster, tackle Bruiser Kinard, was snatched away by Uncle Sam before he could make it to New England.

PITTSBURGH STEELERS 2-8-0 Jim Leonard

Scores of Each Game		
7	Boston	28
6	NEW YORK	34
0	WASHINGTON	14
21	New York	7
6	BOSTON	10
3	PHILADELPHIA	45
23	CHIC. CARDS	0
6	Philadelphia	30
7	Chic. Bears	28
0	Washington	24

Use Name	Pos.	Hgt	Wgt	Age	Int	Pts
Art Brandau	C-LB	6'2"	215	23		
Chuck Cherundolo	C-LB	6'1"	215	29	1	
Vern Foltz	C-LB	6'1"	205	27		
Si Titus	C-LB-DE	6'	195	26		
Al Wukits	C-LB	6'3"	230	25		
Carmine DePascal	OE-DB	6'	188	27		
John Pierre (1 kickoff return for 10 yds.)	OE-DE	6'	185	24		
Julie Koshlap	HB-DB			27		

Use Name – Tackles	Pos.	Hgt	Wgt	Age	Int	Pts
Joe Cibulas	T	6'	220	22		
Joe Coomer (missed 1 FG attempt)	T	6'6"	290	26		
Ted Doyle	T	6'2"	240	31	1	6
Len Frketich	T	6'1"	290	27		
John Kondria	T	6'	185	25		
Ed McNamara	T	6'2"	225	25		
Ross Sorce	T	6'4"	255	25		
Glenn Stough (1 kickoff return for 6 yds.)	T	6'5"	240	24		

Use Name – Guards	Pos.	Hgt	Wgt	Age	Int	Pts
Carl Buda	G	5'11"	220	26		
Garth Chamberlain	G	6'	215	20		
Henry DePaul	G	5'11"	225	28		
Hubbard Law	G	6'1"	210	24		
Al Merkovsky	G-T	6'1"	210	28		
John Perko	G	6'1"	210	29		
Bill Brown	BB-DB	6'	205	28		
John Partick	BB-FB-LB	6'	200	27		
Mel O'Dell	HB-DB	5'8"	176			

After two years in merger situations, the Steelers decided that they could field a last-place team without help from any other club. Under coach Jim Leonard, the Steelers beat the Cardinals and Giants for their only wins, a pretty good showing for a team that didn't throw a single touchdown pass all year. The bright note of the season was the return of tailback Bill Dudley. In his first game back in uniform, Dudley ran for two touchdowns in leading his team to victory over the Cardinals. In the four games he played, Dudley scored more points than any other Pittsburgh back could score in the entire year.

TEAM TOTALS

OFFENSE	First Downs: Tot	by Rsh	by Pas	by Pen	Rushing: No.	Yds.	Avg Yds.	TD	Passing: Att	Com	Comp Pct.	Yds.	Avg. Yds. Att.	Avg. Yds. Comp	TD	Int	Pct. Int.	Punting: No.	Avg. Yds.
WASH.	154	77	**71**	6	394	1708	4.3	15	228	**146**	**64.0**	1838	8.1	12.6	12	**11**	**4.8**	33	**43.3**
PHIL.	131	74	47	10	391	1647	4.2	**26**	192	98	51.0	1321	6.9	13.5	11	14	7.3	47	37.8
N.Y.	98	50	38	10	317	791	2.5	6	201	92	45.8	1534	7.6	16.7	**16**	16	8.0	50	38.4
BOSTON	83	44	30	9	345	846	2.5	9	160	66	41.3	1000	6.3	15.2	6	21	13.1	**66**	36.4
PITT.	96	56	30	10	367	951	2.6	8	164	61	37.2	652	4.0	10.7	0	21	12.8	65	39.3
DEFENSE																			
WASH.	111	60	39	12	337	1003	3.0	8	209	95	45.5	**1121**	**5.4**	**11.8**	9	16	7.7	46	40.1
PHIL.	**104**	54	**37**	13	**318**	**817**	2.6	8	205	89	43.4	1243	6.1	14.0	10	19	9.3	63	37.5
N.Y.	140	77	55	8	395	1643	4.2	17	**186**	99	53.2	1410	7.6	14.2	**6**	13	7.0	44	40.0
BOSTON	133	62	61	10	387	1364	3.5	15	227	104	45.8	1427	6.3	13.7	10	**30**	**13.2**	43	38.9
PITT.	116	64	49	**3**	363	1371	3.8	16	191	102	53.4	1617	8.5	15.9	14	13	6.8	48	38.2

OFFENSE	Punt Returns: No.	Yds.	Avg. Yds.	TD	Kickoff Returns: No.	Yds.	Avg. Yds.	TD	Interception Returns: No.	Yds.	Avg. Yds.	TD	Penalties: No.	Yds.	Fumbles: No.	Lost	Points: Tot	PAT	FG Att	FG	Saf.
WASH.	31	390	12.6	0	29	628	21.7	0	16	233	14.6	0	**80**	**672**	23	9	209	26	**13**	**7**	0
PHIL.	37	452	12.2	0	30	734	**24.5**	**1**	19	257	13.5	0	61	529	27	10	**272**	**32**	8	4	0
N.Y.	26	277	10.7	0	30	649	21.6	0	13	116	8.9	0	56	492	27	9	179	23	**13**	6	0
BOSTON	27	233	8.6	0	41	845	20.6	0	**30**	264	8.8	0	61	533	31	15	123	15	6	4	0
PITT.	32	361	11.3	0	30	652	21.7	0	13	212	16.3	1	53	436	26	8	79	7	5	4	0
DEFENSE																					
WASH.	**23**	**254**	11.1	**0**	37	692	18.7	**0**	11	140	12.7	**0**	49	411	23	6	**121**	**16**	5	1	**0**
PHIL.	28	288	10.3	**0**	39	866	22.2	**0**	14	**127**	**9.1**	**0**	56	422	22	7	133	**16**	6	3	**0**
N.Y.	28	305	10.9	**0**	30	825	27.5	1	16	336	21.0	2	55	472	31	14	198	24	14	6	**0**
BOSTON	38	461	12.1	1	25	678	27.1	**0**	21	252	12.0	1	**94**	**811**	22	8	211	25	16	8	**0**
PITT.	42	436	10.4	**0**	25	520	20.8	**0**	21	229	10.9	**0**	61	600	**40**	14	220	25	8	5	**0**

Use Name – Backs & Ends	Pos.	Age	Hgt	Wgt	Pts	Int	RUSHING				PASSING								RECEIVING				PUNTING		KICKING						PUNT RETURNS				KICKOFF RETURNS			
							No.	Yds	Avg	TD	Att	Comp	%	Yds	Yd/Att	TD	Int–%	RK	No.	Yds	Avg	TD	No.	Avg	Pat	Att	%	FG	Att	%	No.	Yds	Avg	TD	No.	Yds	Avg	TD
WASHINGTON REDSKINS																																						
Sammy Baugh	QB-DB	31	6′2″	185	1	4	19	−71	−3.7	0	182	128	70	1669	9.2	11	4–2	1					33	43.3	1	1	100											
Frankie Filchock	QB-HB-DB	28	5′11″	190		1	9	21	2.3	0	46	18	39	169	3.7	1	7–15		3	33	11	0									1	17	17	0				
Frank Akins	FB-LB	26	5′10″	210	36		147	797	5.4	6									8	57	7	0													1	21	21	0
Wilbur Moore	HB-DB	29	5′11″	180	12		29	206	7.1	1									13	115	9	1									1	10	10	0				
Merl Condit	HB-DB	28	5′11″	185	19		36	173	4.8	3									3	16	5	0			1	1	100											
Steve Bagarus	HB-DB	26	6′	170	36		39	154	3.9	1									35	517	15	5									21	251	12	0	12	325	27	0
Bob Seymour	FB-DB	29	6′2″	208	18	4	30	102	3.4	2									8	91	11	1																
Bill deCorrevont	HB-DB	26	6′	185			22	91	4.1	0									4	36	9	0									3	45	15	0	11	210	19	0
Sal Rosato	FB-LB	27	6′1″	220	12		23	85	3.7	2									1	7	7	0													1	17	17	0
Mike Micka (to BOS)	FB-LB	24	6′	190		1	19	62	3.3	0									2	74	37	0													2	31	16	0
Dick Todd	HB-DB	30	5′11″	182		4	7	54	7.7	0																					5	67	13	0				
Bob DeFruiter	HB-DB	28	6′	190			7	36	5.1	0									1	19	19	0																
Vito Ananis	HB-DB	29	5′10″	195			3	8	2.7	0																												
Ceril Hare	HB-DB	26	5′11″	200			3	0	0.0	0									3	83	28	0													2	30	15	0
Jim Gaffney	HB-DB	24	6′1″	208			1	−6	−6.0	0																												
Doug Turley	OE-DE	26	6′2″	210	6														17	185	11	1																
Joe Aguirre	OE-DE	26	6′4″	230	44														16	289	18	0			23	24	96	7	13	54								
Wayne Millner	OE-DE	34	6′1″	190	12														13	130	10	2																
Tom Miller	OE-DE	27	6′2″	198															11	84	8	0																
Les Dye	OE	27	6′1″	180	12														7	84	12	2																
Alex Piasecky	OE-DE	28	6′2″	198															1	18	18	0																
PHILADELPHIA EAGLES																																						
Roy Zimmerman	QB-DB	27	6′2″	205	47	7	29	−11	−0.4	1	132	67	51	991	7.5	9	8–6	4					47	37.8	29	33	88	4	8	50	1	7	7	0				
Allie Sherman	QB-DB	22	5′11″	173	6		16	−7	−0.4	1	29	15	52	172	5.9	2	3–10																					
Tommy Thompson	QB-DB	29	6′1″	190		2	8	−13	−1.6	0	28	15	54	146	5.2	0	2–7																					
Steve Van Buren	HB-DB	24	6′	205	110	1	143	832	5.8	15	1	0	0	0	0.0	0	0–0		10	123	12	2			2	2	100				14	154	11	0	13	373	29	1
Ernie Steele	HB-DB	27	6′	190	12	1	20	212	10.6	2	2	1	50	12	6.0	0	1–50		3	42	14	0									2	22	11	0	3	72	24	0
Mel Bleeker	HB-DB	25	5′11″	195	12		50	167	3.3	2									3	32	11	0									4	37	9	0				
Sonny Karnofsky	HB-DB	22	5′10″	175	12	1	41	134	3.3	2									5	113	23	0									7	103	15	0	6	164	27	0
Ben Kish	FB-LB	28	6′	215		1	9	82	9.1	0									8	78	10	0																
Johnny Butler	HB-DB	26	5′10″	185	6	1	21	61	2.9	1									2	14	7	0													1	21	21	0
Jack Banta	HB-DB	27	5′11″	192	6		15	49	3.3	1									1	10	10	0									4	74	19	0	2	37	19	0
Gil Steinke	HB-DB	25	6′	180	6		7	46	6.6	1									2	12	6	0									2	27	14	0	1	18	18	0
Jack Hinkle	HB-DB	27	6′	193		1	11	40	3.6	0									1	8	8	0									3	28	9	0	1	17	17	0
Jim Castiglia	FB-LB	26	5′11″	210			13	29	2.2	0																												
Dick Erdlitz	HB-DB	25	5′10″	180		1	6	24	4.0	0																												
John Rogalla	FB-LB	27	6′	215	1		2	2	1.0	0									2	22	11	0			1	1	100											
Jack Ferrante	OE-DE	29	6′1″	195	42	1													21	474	23	7																
Larry Cabrelli	OE-DB	28	5′11″	190		1													15	140	9	0													2	25	13	0
Fred Meyer	OE-DE	26	6′2″	195	6														11	125	11	1																
Flip McDonald	OE-DB	24	6′2″	195	6														8	75	9	1																
Dick Humbert	OE-DB	26	6′1″	185															6	53	9	0																
NEW YORK GIANTS																																						
Arnie Herber	QB	35	5′11″	220			6	−27	−4.5	0	80	35	44	641	8.0	9	8–10	5					1	51.0														
Marion Pugh	QB	25	6′1″	187			24	−52	−2.2	0	58	27	47	390	6.7	3	3–5																					
John Hovious	QB	26	5′8″	180			22	−7	−0.3	0	46	22	48	373	8.1	4	5–11																		1	20	20	0
Joe Sulatis	QB-WB	24	6′2″	205			10	37	3.7	0	13	7	54	126	9.7	0	0–0		2	12	6	0													3	50	17	0
Bill Paschal	FB-DB	24	6′	196	12		59	247	4.2	2	1	0	0	0	0.0	0	0–0		2	11	6	0													2	43	22	0
Steve Filipowicz	FB-LB	24	5′8″	200	12		53	142	2.7	1	2	0	0	0	0.0	0	0–0		4	49	12	1									1	18	18	0	1	32	32	0
Howie Livingston	FB-DB	23	6′1″	190	30	3	40	109	2.7	3									14	250	18	2	13	37.0							13	106	8	0	4	104	26	0
Ward Cuff	WB-DB	32	6′1″	187		1	48	214	4.5	0									12	172	14	0									10	124	12	0	4	105	26	0
George Franck	WB-DB	26	6′	180			29	61	2.1	0	1	1	100	4	4.0	0	0–0		3	39	13	0	22	37.8											3	58	19	0
Jack Doolan (from WAS)	WB-DB	26	6′1″	190			10	26	2.6	0									6	50	8	0													3	87	29	0
Mike Klotovich	WB-DB	28	5′10″	180			5	26	5.2	0									1	7	7	0	11	38.4														
Ed Shedlosky	WB-DB	25	6′	185			9	11	1.2	0									2	15	8	0									1	19	19	0	2	40	20	0
Frank Martin (from BOS)	WB-DB	26	5′10″	185	6	1	3	11	3.7	0									4	67	17	1									1	10	10	0	1	18	18	0
Frank Liebel	OE-DB	25	6′1″	205	60	1													22	593	27	10																
Sam Fox	OE-DE	25	6′2″	215	12														10	120	12	2													1	14	14	0
John Weiss	OE-DB	23	6′3″	195	6														4	82	21	1													2	36	18	0
Hal Springer	OE-DE	23	6′4″	212															4	63	16	0																
Harry Wynne	OE-DE	25	6′4″	200															2	25	13	0																
Ken Strong	K	39	6′	210	41																		3	44.7	23	23	100	6	13	46								
BOSTON YANKS																																						
Scott Gudmundson	QB-DB	24	5′10″	180		2	23	4	0.2	0	43	17	40	299	7.0	1	5–12		1	−8	−8	0	17	36.0							4	36	9	0				
George Cafego	QB-DB	30	5′10″	178		1	19	−51	−2.7	0	26	13	50	149	5.8	0	3–12		2	20	10	0	6	35.5							1	0	0	0	2	47	24	0
Ace Parker	QB-DB	33	6′	187			18	−49	−2.7	0	24	10	42	123	5.1	0	5–21						7	32.0														
Frank Sachse	QB-DB	28	6′	198		2	5	9	1.8	0	21	9	43	203	9.7	2	1–5																					
Hugh McCullough	QB-DB	29	6′	185			2	1	0.5	0	5	0	0	0	0.0	0	3–60		1	17	17	0	2	32.0														
Pug Manders	FB-LB	32	6′	200	36	3	76	238	3.1	6	9	5	56	42	4.7	0	1–11																		2	10	5	0
John Martin	HB-DB	27	6′1″	198	12	1	39	191	4.9	1									2	20	10	0	14	41.1							4	7	2	0	13	302	23	0
John Grigas	FB-LB	25	6′	203	12	1	64	160	2.5	2	14	5	36	85	6.1	0	1–7		5	54	11	0													4	65	16	0
Ned Mathews	HB-DB	27	5′10″	185	6	3	27	146	5.4	0	1	0	0	0	0.0	0	0–0		4	56	14	1													4	108	27	0
Bob Davis	HB-DB	31	6′	190		6	29	91	3.1	0	10	5	50	73	7.3	3	0–0		9	56	6	0	3	41.0							10	91	9	0	6	131	22	0
Babe Dimancheff	HB-DB	23	5′11″	178		1	30	69	2.3	0									1	15	15	0									8	99	12	0	4	123	31	0
Paul Duhart (from PIT)	HB-QB-DB	24	6′	180	6		17	17	1.0	1	9	3	33	27	3.0	0	2–22																		4	81	20	0
Ken Steinmetz	FB-LB	21	6′	190		1	4	12	3.0	0													8	30.0														
Don Currivan	OE-DB	24	6′	190	24														16	397	25	4													1	3	3	0
Bob Masterson	OE-DE	30	6′1″	220															15	191	13	0						0	1	0								
Keith Ranspot	OE-DE	30	6′3″	205															8	117	15	0																
Joe Crowley	OE-DB	26	6′	198		1													1	12	12	0																
Augie Lio	G-LB	27	6′	230	27	3																			15	16	94	4	5	80								
George Smith	C-LB	31	6′2″	225		2																	9	39.4											1	0	0	0
PITTSBURGH STEELERS																																						
Busit Warren (from PHI, HB-DB)	TB-DB	28	5′11″	175	12	1	96	285	3.0	2	92	36	39	368	4.0	0	10–11	10	1	−1	−1	0									13	168	13	0	5	137	27	0
Bill Dudley	TB-DB	24	5′10″	176	20	2	57	204	3.6	3	32	10	31	58	1.8	0	2–6						2	18.0	2	3	67				5	20	4	0	3	65	22	0
Ed Stofko	TB-DB	25	6′1″	192			13	−16	−1.2	0	17	7	41	94	5.5	0	4–24						3	36.3														
Toimi Jarvi	TB-DB	25	6′	200			9	24	2.7	0	10	4	40	50	5.0	0	3–30						2	34.5														
Russ Lowther	TB-DB	22	5′8″	165			15	54	3.6	0	4	0	0	0	0.0	0	1–25						1	35.0	0	1	0				2	35	18	0	1	20	20	0
Al Postus	TB-DB	23	5′10″	180			2	4	2.0	0	5	2	40	73	14.6	0	1–20																		1	14	14	0
John Lucente	FB-LB	23	5′9″	200	12		82	242	3.0	1									11	45	4	0													5	102	20	0
Art Jones	HB-DB	26	6′2″	193		1	15	64	4.3	0									5	8	2	0									6	62	12	0	1	26	26	0
George Kiick	HB-DB	28	6′	195	6		15	45	3.0	1									1	−2	−2	0													1	19	19	0
John Petrella	HB-DB	25	5′7″	160		1	15	33	2.2	0																					6	52	9	0	3	85	28	0
John Itzel	FB-LB	20	6′	190		1	4	11	2.8	0									1	4	4	0																
Al Nichols	FB-LB	28	5′10″	205			10	5	0.5	0																												
Sid Tinsley	HB-DB	24	5′9″	168		1	5	3	0.6	0													57	40.4														
John Popovich	HB-DB	27	5′8″	160			4	−8	−2.0	0																									1	39	39	0
John Naioti	HB-DB	23	5′10″	185	4		1	−17	−17.0	0									2	14	7	0			4	4	100											
Leon Pense	BB-DB	23	6′	170		3	6	1	0.2	0									1	32	32	0													1	21	21	0
John Petchel	BB-DB	26	5′11″	185		1	2	2	1.0	0	1	1	100	8	8.0	0	0–0		2	25	13	0																
Tony Bova	OE-HB-DB	28	6′1″	185			6	11	1.8	0	1	0	0	0	0.0	0	0–0		15	220	15	0									1	24	24	0				
Morgan Tiller	OE-DE	25	6′1″	195															10	141	14	0													3	47	16	0
Dick Dolly	OE-DE	27	6′3″	212															8	122	15	0																
Al Olszewski	OE-DB	24	6′2″	185															2	28	14	0																
Frank Kimble	OE-DE	27	6′5″	205															2	16	8	0																
Ben Agajanian (from PHI)	K	26	6′	195	13																				1	2	50	4	4	100								

CLEVELAND RAMS 9-1-0 Adam Walsh

Scores of Each Game		
21	CHIC. CARDS	0
17	CHIC. BEARS	0
27	Green Bay	14
41	Chic. Bears	21
14	Philadelphia	28
21	New York	17
20	GREEN BAY	7
35	Chic. Cards	21
28	Detroit	21
20	BOSTON	7

Use Name	Pos.	Hgt	Wgt	Age	Int	Pts
Dave Bernard	LB	5'10"	197	32		
Bob deLauer	C-LB	6'1"	218	25		
Roger Harding	C-LB	6'2"	195	22	1	
George Phillips	LB	6'3"	215	24		
Bill Rieth	C-G-LB	5'11"	203	29		
Mike Scarry	C-LB	6'	220	25	4	
Joe Winkler	C-LB	6'1"	200	23	1	
Floyd Konetsky	DE	6'	195	25		
Bob Shaw (1 kickoff return for 1 yd.)	OE-DE	6'4"	229	24		

Use Name – Tackles	Pos.	Hgt	Wgt	Age	Int	Pts
Graham Armstrong	T	6'4"	215	27		
Gil Bouley	T	6'2"	233	24		
Roger Eason	T	6'2"	220	27		
Len Levy	T	6'	260	24		
Elbie Schultz	T	6'4"	245	27		
Rudy Sikich	T	6'1"	220	24		

Use Name – Guards	Pos.	Hgt	Wgt	Age	Int	Pts
Mike Lazetich	G-LB	6'1"	195	24		
Les Lear	G-LB	5'11"	223	27		
Sonny Liles (from DET)	G-LB	5'9"	195	26	1	
Riley Matheson (1 punt return for 5 yds.)	G-LB	6'2"	210	30	2	
Art Mergenthal	G-LB	5'11"	215	25		
Ray Monaco	G-LB	5'10"	215	27		

The husband of movie star Jane Russell and a Rose Bowl star at UCLA, rookie quarterback Bob Waterfield added to his credits by leading the Rams to the NFL championship. At the controls of Cleveland's new T offense, Waterfield loved to throw the long ball, ran the bootleg play with great poise, and had a knack for rallying his teammates when faced with defeat. He also found time to kick field goals, punt, and intercept six passes while on defense. Injuries could not stop him; taped like a mummy because of torn rib muscles, he hit end Jim Benton with ten passes for 303 yards in defeating Detroit and clinching the Western crown. Waterfield got lots of help from running backs, Fred Gehrke, Jim Gillette, and Don Greenwood, while ends Benton and Steve Pritko both were mentioned on All-Pro teams. But even with such a fine squad, owner Dan Reeves still lost $50,000 in this championship season.

DETROIT LIONS 7-3-0 Gus Dorais

Scores of Each Game		
10	Chic. Cards	0
21	Green Bay	57
28	PHILADELPHIA	24
26	CHIC. CARDS	0
16	CHIC. BEARS	10
10	Boston	9
35	Chic. Bears	28
14	New York	35
21	CLEVELAND	28
14	GREEN BAY	3

Use Name	Pos.	Hgt	Wgt	Age	Int	Pts
Frank Kring	LB	6'	190	26		
Bob Nelson (1 field goal in 4 attempts)	C-LB	6'1"	215	25	1	3
Frank Szymanski	C-LB	6'	225	22	1	
Rex Williams	C-LB	6'2"	210	29		
Alex Wojciechowicz	C-LB	5'11"	220	31		
Ted Grefe	OE-DE	6'	205	27		
Larry Knorr	OE-DB	6'2"	195	28		
Vince Mazza	DE	6'1"	210	24		
Arch Milano	OE-DE	6'	197	26		
Lake Robertson	DE	6'1"	210	26		

Use Name – Tackles	Pos.	Hgt	Wgt	Age	Int	Pts
Al Kaporch	T	5'10"	215	31	1	
Mike Kostiuk	T	6'	210	26		
Luther Lindon	T	5'10"	245	28		
Joe Manzo	T	6'1"	220	28		
Dick Mesak	T	6'2"	225	25		
Garvin Mugg	T	6'1"	215	24		
Dom Sigillo	T	6'	230	32		
Emil Uremovich	T	6'2"	240	28		
Joe Krol (2 punts for 37.0 average)	DB	6'1"	210	26		
Bob Sneddon	WB-DB	5'10"	180	24		

Use Name – Guards	Pos.	Hgt	Wgt	Age	Int	Pts
Stan Batinski	G	5'10"	215	28		
Bill Radovich	G	5'10"	240	30		
Larry Sartori	G	6'	208	28		
Damon Tassos	G-LB	6'1"	220	21	3	

Star tailback Frankie Sinkwich spent the year in the service, but Uncle Sam made up for it by discharging two linemen who immediately beefed up the Detroit line. Emil Uremovich and Bill Radovich put their military training to use in the football trenches and opened up enough holes for Detroit runners to carry the club to a second-place finish. Bob Westfall, ex-GI Chuck Fenenbock, and newly acquired Andy Farkas blasted away for enough yards to compensate for the loss of Sinkwich's passing. On defense, the Lions saw lots of passes. On October 7, Green Bay's Don Hutson burned the secondary for four touchdown catches in just the second period of a 57-21 Packer romp. And in a late-season showdown with the Rams, the Lions watched sure-handed Jim Benton haul in ten passes for 303 yards in a 28-21 Cleveland win, to more than point up the Lions' inability to deal with the aerial attack.

GREEN BAY PACKERS 6-4-0 Curly Lambeau

Scores of Each Game		
31	CHIC. BEARS	21
57	DETROIT	21
14	CLEVELAND	27
38	BOSTON	14
33	CHIC. CARDS	14
24	Chic. Bears	28
7	Cleveland	20
28	Boston	0
23	New York	14
3	Detroit	14

Use Name	Pos.	Hgt	Wgt	Age	Int	Pts
Charley Brock	C-LB	6'2"	210	29	4	12
Bob Flowers	C-LB	6'1"	210	28	1	
Bob Adkins	BB-G-DE	6'1"	220	28		
Larry Craig (1 kickoff return for 11 yds.)	BB-DE	6'1"	215	29		6
Ken Keuper (1 punt for 12 yds.)	BB-DE	6'	215	27		

Use Name – Tackles	Pos.	Hgt	Wgt	Age	Int	Pts
Solon Barnett	T	6'1"	235	24		
Tiny Croft	T	6'3"	285	24		
Paul Lipscomb	T	6'4"	230	22		
Amy McPherson	T-C	5'11"	240	33		
Ed Neal	T	6'4"	287	27		
Ernie Pannell (1 kickoff return for 10 yds.)	T	6'2"	220	28		
Baby Ray	T	6'6"	256	30		

Use Name – Guards	Pos.	Hgt	Wgt	Age	Int	Pts
Amadeo Bucchianeri	G	5'10"	210	28		
Bernie Crimmins	G-LB	5'11"	195	26	1	6
Ray Frankowski	G	5'11"	220	26		
Buckets Goldenberg	G	5'10"	220	34		
Bill Kuusisto	G	6'	230	27		
Glen Sorenson (missed 1 field goal attempt)	G	6'	210	24		
Pete Tinsley	G-LB	5'8"	205	32	1	
Charlie Tollefson	G	6'	215	28		

After the 1944 season, Don Hutson announced his retirement by saying, "If I every play on this field again, I'll jump off the Empire State Building." Evidently, he changed his mind, since he was back in uniform at the start of the season with no sign of carrying out his threat. Even though the Packers fell off to third place, Hutson still soared above all the receivers in the NFL. In the second quarter of the October 7 game against Detroit, Hutson caught four touchdown passes and kicked five extra points, chalking up a record 29 points in one period. The Packers also had a colorful twenty-seven-year-old rookie tackle named Ed Neal. Bulldog Turner best described him: "Ed Neal weighed two hundred and eighty-seven pounds stripped. His arms were as big as my leg and as hard as a table." Turner's remarks were not ill-founded, as Neal would break Turner's nose five times during the course of their many encounters.

CHICAGO BEARS 3-7-0 Luke Johnsos, Hunk Anderson, George Halas

Scores of Each Game		
21	Green Bay	31
0	Cleveland	17
7	CHIC. CARDS	16
21	CLEVELAND	41
10	Detroit	16
28	GREEN BAY	24
28	DETROIT	35
21	Washington	28
28	PITTSBURGH	7
28	Chic. Cards	20

Use Name	Pos.	Hgt	Wgt	Age	Int	Pts
Forest Masterson	C-G	6'3"	246	26		
Fred Mundee	C-LB	6'1"	220	32		
John Schiechl	C-LB	6'2"	245	28		
Bulldog Turner	C-LB	6'1"	230	26		
Milt Vucinich	C-LB	6'	215	25		
Charlie Mitchell	DB	6'	185	24		

Use Name – Tackles	Pos.	Hgt	Wgt	Age	Int	Pts
Lee Artoe (Missed 1 field goal attempt)	T	6'3"	237	29		
Al Barbartsky	T	6'	225	29		
Glen Burgeis	T	6'1"	220	23		
Jim Daniell (1 kickoff return for 14 yds.)	T	6'2"	230	27		
Al Hoptowit	T	6'1"	212	29		
Frank Ramsey	T	6'1"	240	29		
Tom Roberts	T	6'1"	215	29		
Joe Stydahar	T	6'4"	230	33		

Use Name – Guards	Pos.	Hgt	Wgt	Age	Int	Pts
Chuck Drulis	G-LB	5'10"	215	27		
Nick Kerasiotis	G-LB	5'11"	193	27		
Rudy Mucha (from CLE)	G	6'1"	246	27		
Pete Perez	G	5'9"	220	21		
Ed Sprinkle	G-DE	6'1"	200	21		
George Zorich	G	6'2"	210	26		

After eight games, the Bears had won only once. Too many players had gone off into the military for coaches Hunk Anderson, Luke Johnsos, and Paddy Driscoll to keep the Bears on top of the NFL heap. The club was practicing on Thanksgiving morning when Sid Luckman noticed a middle-aged man in a Navy uniform walking across the field, and when he waved he knew that George Halas was back. With two games left on the slate, Papa Bear again took over the coaching reigns of the once Monsters of the Midway.

Other prewar Bears also started trickling back as Ken Kavanaugh, Joe Stydahar, George McAfee, and Hugh Gallarneau all put the Chicago jersey back on after years of military uniforms. When McAfee reported in time for a game against Pittsburgh, Halas promised to use him sparingly. True to his word, Halas used him for only twelve minutes; in that time, McAfee ripped off three quick touchdowns.

CHICAGO CARDINALS 1-9-0 Phil Handler

Scores of Each Game		
0	DETROIT	10
0	Cleveland	21
6	Philadelphia	21
16	Chic. Bears	7
0	Detroit	26
14	Green Bay	33
21	Washington	24
0	Pittsburgh	23
21	CLEVELAND	35
20	CHIC. BEARS	28

Use Name	Pos.	Hgt	Wgt	Age	Int	Pts
Ray Apolskis	C-LB	5'11"	200	26		
Bill Campbell	C-LB-DB	6'	195	25		
Larry Fuller (from WAS)	LB	5'10"	196	22		
Bob Norman	C-LB	6'1"	185	25		
Hal Robl	LB	6'	227	27		
Marshall Robnett	C-LB	6'	208	26		
Cliff Speegle	C-LB	6'1"	195	27	2	
John Durko	DE	6'4"	235	26		
Pop Ivy	DE	6'3"	205	29	1	
Freeman Rexer	OE-DE	6'1"	210	27		
Les Bruckner (1 kickoff return for 13 yds.)	FB-LB	6'1"	195	26		
Hal Blackwell (17 punts for 38.9 yd. average)	HB-DB	6'1"	205	26		

Use Name – Tackles	Pos.	Hgt	Wgt	Age	Int	Pts
Chet Bulger	T	6'3"	235	27		6
Ray Busler	T	6'1"	225	30		
Gil Duggan	T	6'3"	225	27		
Bob Eckl	T	6'1"	233	27		
Ralph Foster	T	6'1"	230	28		
Mitch Ucovich	T	5'11"	208	29		
Bob Zimny (1 kickoff return for 12 yds.)	T	6'1"	220	24		
Chet Maeda (1 pass attempt – incomplete)	HB-DB	5'10"	187	26		

Use Name – Guards	Pos.	Hgt	Wgt	Age	Int	Pts
Conway Baker (Missed 1 FG and 1 PAT attempt)	G	5'11"	230	34		
Libero Bertagnolli	G		188	29		
Dave Braden	G-LB	6'	210	26		
Steve Enich	G	5'10"	212	22		
Ralph Fife	G-LB	6'	210	25		
Lou Marotti	G	5'10"	223	27		
Vic Obeck	G	6'	225	27		
Gordon Wilson	G	6'	225	29		

Although the Cardinals still finished in last place, owner Charles Bidwill and coach Phil Handler were laying the groundwork for future success. Imitating the Bears, Handler remodeled the offense with the T-formation. To run this new offense, Bidwill signed quarterback Paul Christman of Missouri, a fine passer who suffered a rough rookie season but grew into a crafty field general with time. Further reinforcements came from military returnees Bill Dewell and Joe Kuharich and from ex-Redskin Frank Seno. Dewell especially helped Christman, giving him a target to aim at while enemy linemen poured through the thin Cardinal line at him. The new attack got off the ground slowly, scoring 98 points and only beating the Bears, the one team they most wanted to beat.

TEAM TOTALS

OFFENSE	First Downs: Tot	by Rsh	by Pas	by Pen	Rushing: No.	Yds.	Avg Yds.	TD	Passing: Att	Com	Comp Pct.	Yds.	Avg. Yds. Att.	Avg. Yds. Comp	TD	Int	Pct. Int.	Punting: No.	Avg.	Punt Returns: No.	Yds.	Avg. Yds.	TD	Kickoff Returns: No.	Yds.	Avg. Yds.	TD	Interception Returns: No.	Yds.	Avg. Yds.	TD	Penalties: No.	Yds.	Fumbles: No.	Lost	Points: Tot	PAT	FG Att	FG	Saf.	OFFENSE
CLEVE.	137	68	60	9	372	**1714**	**4.6**	19	199	100	50.3	1767	**8.9**	17.7	**16**	20	10.1	47	40.1	31	353	11.4	0	26	458	17.6	0	28	398	14.2	0	67	593	34	18	244	31	3	1	0	CLEVE.
DET.	102	40	47	15	313	857	2.7	8	238	87	36.6	1544	6.5	17.7	15	36	15.1	53	38.0	**39**	**563**	**14.4**	1	30	662	22.1	0	23	424	18.4	1	66	673	32	10	195	25	7	2	1	DET.
G.B.	131	73	44	14	377	1325	3.5	15	218	81	37.2	1536	7.0	**19.0**	14	24	11.0	46	39.9	34	310	9.1	0	33	670	20.3	0	24	**464**	**19.3**	5	69	**723**	**21**	7	258	31	**13**	5	1	G.B.
CHIC. B.	**164**	**86**	60	**18**	**422**	1497	3.5	13	244	128	52.5	**1857**	7.6	14.5	14	12	4.9	44	35.7	17	165	9.7	0	39	677	17.4	0	15	101	6.7	0	67	666	**21**	10	192	27	3	1	0	CHIC. B.
CHIC. C.	115	47	51	17	334	933	2.8	8	**267**	99	37.1	1328	5.0	13.4	5	18	6.7	62	36.7	27	276	10.2	0	**46**	**924**	20.1	0	12	133	11.1	0	50	389	35	13	98	12	4	0	1	CHIC. C.

Use Name – Backs & Ends	Pos.	Age	Hgt	Wgt	Pts	Int	Rushing No.	Rushing Yds	Rushing Avg	Rushing TD	Passing Att	Passing Comp	Passing %	Passing Yds	Passing Yd/Att	Passing TD	Passing Int–%	RK
CLEVELAND RAMS																		
Bob Waterfield	QB-DB	25	6'1"	190	64	6	18	18	1.0	5	171	88	52	1609	9.4	14	16–9	2
Albie Reisz	QB-DB	27	5'10"	170		2	12	-2	-0.2	0	21	9	43	146	7.0	2	4–19	
Jack Jacobs	QB-DB	26	6'1"	180			2	0	0.0	0	5	3	60	12	2.4	0	0–0	
Steve Nemeth	QB-DB	23	5'10"	172							1	0	0	0	0.0	0	0–0	
Fred Gehrke	HB-DB	27	5'11"	190	48	4	74	467	6.3	7								
Jim Gillette	HB-DB	27	6'1"	185	6	4	63	390	6.1	1								
Don Greenwood	FB-LB	24	6'	190	24		101	376	3.7	4								
Tom Colella	HB-DB	27	6'	185	24		46	224	4.9	2	1	0	0	0	0.0	0	0–0	
George Koch	HB-DB	26	6'	200			12	101	8.4	0								
Ralph Ruthstrom	FB-LB	24	6'5"	208		1	10	74	7.4	0								
Pat West	FB-LB	22	6'	204			19	45	2.4	0								
Harvey Jones	HB-DB	24	6'	175	6	2	8	15	1.9	0								
Jim Worden	HB-DB	29	5'10"	180			4	3	0.8	0								
Walt Zirinsky	HB-DB	24	5'11"	187			3	3	1.0	0								
Jim Benton	OE-DE	28	6'3"	195	48													
Steve Pritko	OE-DE	23	6'2"	210	24													
Red Hickey	OE-DE	28	6'2"	195														
Ray Hamilton	OE-DE	29	6'4"	210														
DETROIT LIONS																		
Chuck Fenenbock	TB-DB	27	5'9"	175	12	1	72	143	2.0	1	110	45	41	752	6.8	7	11–10	7
Charley Price	TB-DB	26	6'1"	185		1	24	71	3.0	0	52	16	31	256	4.9	3	8–15	
Dave Ryan	TB-DB	22	5'10"	190	15	3	36	93	2.6	1	44	13	30	331	7.5	3	10–23	
Dick Weber	TB-DB	26	5'11"	195			7	10	1.4	0	22	6	27	72	3.3	0	5–23	
Bob Westfall	FB-LB	26	5'8"	190	54		82	234	2.9	6	4	3	75	91	22.8	1	0–0	
Andy Farkas	FB-WB-LB	29	5'10"	195	12		31	137	4.4	0								
Elmer Hackney	FB-LB	29	6'2"	203			6	13	2.2	0								
Dick Booth	WB-DB	27	6'1"	190	6		4	20	5.0	0								
Art Van Tone	WB-DB	26	5'10"	185			3	14	4.7	0								
Bob Brumley	WB-DB	23	6'	200			5	18	3.6	0								
Jim Thomason	WB-DB	25	6'	200			9	9	1.0	0								
Tippy Madarik	WB-DB	23	5'11"	197		1	2	5	2.5	0								
Bob Keene	WB-DB	26	5'11"	193			2	2	1.0	0								
Bill Callihan	BB-FB-LB	29	6'3"	230	31	2	27	85	3.1	0	5	3	60	34	6.8	1	2–40	
Chuck DeShane	BB-DB	26	6'1"	192	12	3												
Buzz Trebotich	BB-DB	24	5'10"	210		3	3	3	1.0	0	1	1	100	8	8.0	0	0–0	
John Greene	OE-DB	25	6'	215	30	3												
Jack Matheson	OE-DE	25	6'2"	210	14													
Ed Frutig (from GB)	OE-DB	25	6'1"	185	6													
Dave Diehl	OE-DE	26	6'	200														
GREEN BAY PACKERS																		
Irv Comp	TB-DB	26	6'2"	205	18	2	57	75	1.3	1	106	44	43	865	8.2	7	11–10	6
Tex McKay	TB-DB	25	6'	195	12	3	71	231	3.3	2	89	32	36	520	5.8	5	9–10	9
Lou Brock	TB-HB-DB	27	6'	195	18	3	46	196	4.3	3	22	5	23	151	6.9	2	4–18	
Ted Fritsch	FB-LB	24	5'10"	210	57	1	88	282	3.2	7								
Don Perkins (to CHIB)	FB-LB	27	6'	198	12		46	273	5.9	2								
Bruce Smith	HB-DB	25	6'	197			21	94	4.5	0								
Joe Laws	HB-DB	34	5'9"	185		3	16	82	5.1	0								
Russ Mosley	HB-DB	27	5'10"	170			16	49	3.1	0	1	0	0	0	0.0	0	0–0	
Ken Snelling	FB-LB	26	6'	210			3	10	3.3	0								
Charlie Sample	FB-LB	25	5'9"	210			2	2	1.0	0								
Ben Starret	BB-DE	27	5'11"	220		1	5	26	5.2	0								
Don Hutson	OE-DB	32	6'1"	180	97	4	8	60	7.5	1								
Nolan Luhn	OE-DE	24	6'3"	200	6													
Clyde Goodnight	OE-DB	21	6'1"	195	18		8	26	3.3	0								
Moose Mulleneaux	OE-DE	28	6'3"	210														
Alex Urban	OE-DE	28	6'3"	210														
Joel Mason	DE	32	6'	200														
CHICAGO BEARS																		
Sid Luckman	QB-DB	28	6'	205			36	-118	-3.3	0	217	117	54	1725	7.9	14	10–5	2
Gene Ronzani	QB-DB	36	5'9"	210			3	-20	-6.7	0	24	10	42	119	5.0	0	2–8	
John Long	QB-DB	30	6'	185			2	3	1.5	0								
Hank Margarita	HB-DB	24	5'11"	175	30	6	112	497	4.4	3								
Hugh Gallarneau	HB-DB	28	6'	190	18	2	75	260	3.5	2								
Gary Famiglietti	FB-LB	30	6'	235	18		65	235	3.6	3								
Jim Fordham	FB-LB	28	5'11"	215	6		45	153	3.4	1								
George McAfee	HB-DB	27	6'	185	24	1	16	139	8.7	3	1	0	0	0	0.0	0	0–0	
Tipp Mooney	HB-DB	26	6'	187			17	105	6.2	0								
Al Grygo	HB-DB	27	5'10"	173	6	3	23	98	4.3	0	1	1	100	13	13.0	0	0–0	
Special Delivery Jones	HB-DB	26	5'10"	175			8	41	5.1	0	1	0	0	0	0.0	0	0–0	
Ray McLean	HB-DB	29	5'10"	168		1	9	22	2.4	0								
John Hunt	HB-DB	26	6'	192			1	1	1.0	0								
Bob Swisher	HB-DB	31	5'11"	160		1												
George Wilson	OE-DE	31	6'1"	200	18													
Ken Kavanaugh	OE-DE	28	6'3"	205	36													
Connie Mack Berry	OE-DE	29	6'3"	218														
Abe Croft	OE-DB	23	6'	185														
John Morton	OE-DB	23	6'	190														
Rudy Smeja	OE-DE	24	6'2"	195														
Pete Gudauskas	G-LB	28	6'2"	222	30	1												
CHICAGO CARDINALS																		
Paul Christman	QB	27	6'	218	6		30	-34	-1.1	1	219	89	41	1147	5.3	5	12–5	8
Paul Collins	QB	22	5'11"	178			10	13	1.3	0	17	3	18	43	2.5	0	2–12	
Vince Oliver	QB	26	5'11"	180			11	-3	-0.3	0	10	4	40	22	2.2	0	0–0	
Frank Seno	HB-DB	24	6'	185	12	1	93	355	3.8	2	1	0	0	0	0.0	0	0–0	
Leo Cantor	HB-DB	26	6'	195	30	5	83	291	3.5	5	18	3	17	116	6.4	0	4–22	
Buzz Mertes	HB-DB	24	6'	195			24	107	4.5	0								
Ernie Bonelli	FB-LB	25	5'11"	197		1	32	93	2.9	0								
Al Drulis	FB-LB	24	5'10"	195			12	49	4.1	0								
John Knolla	HB-DB	26	5'10"	180			15	36	2.4	0	1	0	0	0	0.0	0	0–0	
Walt Rankin	FB-LB	27	5'11"	190		1	7	11	1.6	0								
Bill Reynolds	HB-DB	26	5'8"	190			7	10	1.4	0								
Walt Watt	HB-DB	23	6'	187			6	7	1.2	0								
Al Lindow	HB-DB																	
Joe Vodicka (from CHIB)	HB-DB	24	5'10"	187			3	-1	-0.3	0								
Frank Balasz	FB-LB	27	6'2"	210			1	-1	-1.0	0								
Bill Dewell	OE-DE	28	6'4"	200	6													
Eddie Rucinski	OE-DE	29	6'2"	195	12													
Jim Poole (to NY)	OE-DE	29	6'3"	220	12	1												
Joe Carter	OE-DE	35	6'1"	200														
Clint Wager	OE-DE	24	6'6"	215														
Joe Kuharich	G-LB	28	5'11"	195	12													

Use Name – Backs & Ends	Receiving No.	Receiving Yds	Receiving Avg	Receiving TD	Punting No.	Punting Avg	Kicking Pat	Kicking Att	Kicking %	Kicking FG	Kicking Att	Kicking %	Punt Returns No.	Punt Returns Yds	Punt Returns Avg	Punt Returns TD	Kickoff Returns No.	Kickoff Returns Yds	Kickoff Returns Avg	Kickoff Returns TD
CLEVELAND RAMS																				
Bob Waterfield					39	40.7	31	34	91	1	3	33	2	34	17	0				
Albie Reisz	1	11	11	0	7	34.4							8	78	10	0				
Jack Jacobs					1	43.0							1	6	6	0				
Steve Nemeth																				
Fred Gehrke	8	90	11	1									8	120	15	0	9	173	19	0
Jim Gillette	6	48	8	0									7	53	8	0	4	66	17	0
Don Greenwood	3	72	24	0													5	106	21	0
Tom Colella	7	64	9	2									1	10	10	0	3	89	30	0
George Koch																	1	7	7	0
Ralph Ruthstrom													3	47	16	0				
Pat West	1	-2	-2	0																
Harvey Jones	2	36	18	1																
Jim Worden																				
Walt Zirinsky																				
Jim Benton	45	1067	24	8													3	16	5	0
Steve Pritko	19	255	13	4																
Red Hickey	4	76	19	0																
Ray Hamilton	4	50	13	0																
DETROIT LIONS																				
Chuck Fenenbock	1	24	24	0	29	37.2							5	69	14	0	7	192	27	0
Charley Price					4	37.0							3	32	11	0	4	79	20	0
Dave Ryan	2	67	34	1	17	39.3				1	3	33	15	220	15	0	6	138	23	0
Dick Weber					1	42.0											1	24	24	0
Bob Westfall	12	209	17	3									1	16	16	0	2	26	13	0
Andy Farkas	9	132	15	2									7	101	14	0	8	165	21	0
Elmer Hackney																				
Dick Booth	3	90	30	1									2	8	4	0	1	26	26	0
Art Van Tone	3	67	22	0																
Bob Brumley	2	27	14	0																
Jim Thomason	1	6	6	0																
Tippy Madarik																				
Bob Keene																				
Bill Callihan	4	88	22	1			25	27	93											
Chuck DeShane	2	29	15	0									5	107	21	1				
Buzz Trebotich																				
John Greene	26	450	17	5																
Jack Matheson	19	341	18	1									1	10	10	0				
Ed Frutig (from GB)	2	5	3	1													1	12	12	0
Dave Diehl	1	9	9	0																
GREEN BAY PACKERS																				
Irv Comp	1	50	50	1									4	36	9	0	5	110	22	0
Tex McKay					44	41.2							7	66	9	0	4	67	17	0
Lou Brock	4	87	22	0									4	37	9	0	1	12	12	0
Ted Fritsch	3	13	4	0						3	8	38					8	279	35	0
Don Perkins (to CHIB)	2	11	6	0	1	13.0														
Bruce Smith													6	67	11	0	2	46	23	0
Joe Laws	2	11	6	0									11	71	6	0	4	72	18	0
Russ Mosley	1	10	10	0									1	13	13	0				
Ken Snelling																				
Charlie Sample																				
Ben Starret																	1	3	3	0
Don Hutson	47	834	18	9			31	35	89	2	4	50					4	37	9	0
Nolan Luhn	10	151	15	1																
Clyde Goodnight	7	283	40	3													1	8	8	0
Moose Mulleneaux	3	31	10	0																
Alex Urban	1	55	55	0																
Joel Mason													1	20	20	0	1	15	15	0
CHICAGO BEARS																				
Sid Luckman					36	36.0											2	31	16	0
Gene Ronzani													1	6	6	0	1	0	0	0
John Long					1	42.0							1	12	12	0				
Hank Margarita	23	394	17	2	1	29.0							7	66	9	0	10	155	16	0
Hugh Gallarneau	7	58	8	1									3	30	10	0	6	90	15	0
Gary Famiglietti	4	42	11	0						0	1	0					1	19	19	0
Jim Fordham	4	34	9	0																
George McAfee	3	85	28	1	2	31.0							1	8	8	0	5	98	20	0
Tipp Mooney	2	10	5	0													3	51	17	0
Al Grygo	5	82	16	1	2	43.0											4	80	20	0
Special Delivery Jones	1	0	0	0													2	72	36	0
Ray McLean	8	107	13	0									3	41	14	0	3	60	20	0
John Hunt					2	27.0														
Bob Swisher	2	4	2	0																
George Wilson	28	259	9	3									1	2	2	0				
Ken Kavanaugh	35	539	22	6													1	7	7	0
Connie Mack Berry	12	202	17	0																
Abe Croft	2	12	6	0																
John Morton	1	18	18	0																
Rudy Smeja	1	11	11	0																
Pete Gudauskas							27	27	100	1	2	50								
CHICAGO CARDINALS																				
Paul Christman																	1	44	44	0
Paul Collins																				
Vince Oliver																				
Frank Seno	7	129	18	0									10	103	10	0	19	408	21	0
Leo Cantor	15	159	11	0	5	33.2							5	59	12	0	6	123	21	0
Buzz Mertes	2	1	1	0									1	7	7	0	1	12	12	0
Ernie Bonelli	3	9	3	0									3	37	12	0	2	45	23	0
Al Drulis	6	49	8	0													4	44	11	0
John Knolla	1	15	15	0	2	33.0							3	43	14	0	6	114	19	0
Walt Rankin	3	25	8	0													1	14	14	0
Bill Reynolds					38	36.4														
Walt Watt	1	22	22	0													1	18	18	0
Al Lindow													1	18	18	0	1	13	13	0
Joe Vodicka (from CHIB)	1	3	3	0									4	9	2	0	1	20	20	0
Frank Balasz	1	15	15	0																
Bill Dewell	26	370	14	1																
Eddie Rucinski	23	400	17	2																
Jim Poole (to NY)	6	82	14	2																
Joe Carter	3	17	6	0													1	44	44	0
Clint Wager	1	32	32	0																
Joe Kuharich							12	13	92	0	3	0								

TEAM TOTALS

DEFENSE	First Downs: Tot	by Rsh	by Pas	by Pen	Rushing: No.	Yds.	Avg. Yds.	TD	Passing: Att.	Com	Comp. Pct.	Yds.	Avg. Yds. Att.	Avg. Yds. Comp	TD	Int.	Pct. Int.
CLEVE.	129	67	51	11	349	1026	2.9	10	253	99	39.1	1463	5.8	14.8	9	28	11.1
DET.	105	46	42	17	356	912	2.6	7	227	89	39.2	1615	7.1	18.1	17	23	10.1
G.B.	137	65	57	15	388	1349	3.5	16	231	111	48.1	1708	7.4	15.4	9	24	10.4
CHIC. B.	126	63	44	19	357	1464	4.1	20	195	83	42.6	1283	6.6	15.5	10	15	7.7
CHIC. C.	110	57	43	10	382	1320	3.5	17	187	87	46.5	1490	8.0	17.1	15	12	6.4

DEFENSE	Punting: No.	Avg. Yds.	Punt Returns: No.	Yds.	Avg. Yds.	TD	Kickoff Returns: No.	Yds.	Avg. Yds.	TD	Interception Returns: No.	Yds.	Avg. Yds.	TD	Penalties: No.	Yds.	Fumbles: No.	Lost	Points: Tot	PAT	FG Att	FG	Saf.
CLEVE.	52	36.4	28	333	11.9	0	45	923	20.5	0	20	353	17.7	0	43	391	31	16	136	19	4	1	0
DET.	64	35.5	32	314	9.8	0	37	614	16.6	0	36	334	9.3	2	64	568	27	10	194	24	5	4	2
G.B.	59	37.2	25	283	11.3	0	39	725	18.6	0	24	376	15.6	0	68	701	31	17	173	23	2	0	0
CHIC. B.	42	39.7	24	353	14.7	0	37	688	18.6	0	12	236	19.6	2	63	581	24	6	235	30	7	3	1
CHIC. C.	52	41.6	33	353	10.7	0	20	368	18.4	0	18	220	12.2	0	77	749	26	11	228	27	8	3	0

WORLD WAR II - MILITARY SERVICE

Full seasons missed by active players
(Only men who played in an official N.F.L. game before entering military service are listed.)

BROOKLYN DODGERS and TIGERS, BOSTON YANKS (1941=11 1942=25 1943=46 1944=51 1945=57)

41	42	43	44	45	Player
				45	Art Albrecht
	42	43	44	45	Warren Alfson
	42	43	44	45	Bill Bailey
41	42	43	44	45	Sherrill Busby
41	42				George Cafego
41	42	43	44	45	Dick Cassiano
			44		Merl Condit
41	42	43	44	45	Ty Coon
		43	44	45	Gerry Courtney
		43	44	45	Art Deremer
				45	Walt Dubzinski
		43	44	45	Don Eliason
				45	Tony Falkenstein
		43	44	45	Walt Fedora
41	42	43	44	45	Sam Francis
	42	43	44	45	Ray Frick
	42	43	44	45	Andy Fronczek
		43	44	45	Bob Gifford
				45	Sam Goldman
41	42	43	44	45	Mike Gussie
				45	Dick Harrison
			44	45	Ken Heineman
		43	44	45	Herman Hodges
		43	44	45	Bob Jeffries
		43	44	45	Art Jocher
				45	Cecil Johnson
			44	45	Lew Jones
		43	44	45	Thurman Jones
		43	44	45	Mike Jurich
		43	44	45	Bernie Kapitansky
		43	44	45	Duce Keahey
41	42	43	44	45	Ralph Kercheval
				45	Bruiser Kinard
		43	44	45	George Kinard
	42				Ben Kish
	42	43	44	45	Joe Koons
	42	43	44	45	George Kracum
	42	43	44	45	Frank Kristufek
				45	Bill LaFitte
	42	43	44	45	Bill Leckonby
41	42	43	44		Lou Mark
			44	45	John Matisi
41	42	43	44	45	Banks McFadden
		43	44	45	Curt Mecham
		43	44	45	Walt Merrill
			44	45	Tex Mooney
	42	43	44		Ace Parker
	42	43	44	45	Dave Parker
	42	43	44	45	Larry Peace
	42	43	44	45	Steve Petro
				45	Thron Riggs
		43	44	45	Bob Robertson
		43	44	45	Tom Robertson
				45	Frank Santora
		43	44	45	Perry Schwartz
		43	44	45	Rhoten Shetley
		43			Jim Sivell
			44	45	Bud Svendsen
		43	44		Si Titus
		43	44	45	Joe Tofil
				45	Rocky Uguccioni
		43	44	45	Jack Vetter
		43	44	45	Bernie Weiner
	42				Don Wemple (killed in action June 23, 1943)
41	42	43	44		Waddy Young (shot down and killed during first B-29 raid over Tokyo)
41	42	43	44	45	Frank Zadworney

NEW YORK GIANTS (1941=5 1942=27 1943=44 1944=47 1945=41)

41	42	43	44	45	Player
				45	Neal Adams
		43	44		Emmett Barrett
			44	45	Dave Brown
		43	44	45	Harry Buffington
		43	44		Leo Cantor
		43	44	45	John Chickerneo
41	42	43	44	45	Pete Cole
				45	Frank Damiani
	42	43	44	45	Ed Danowski
	42	43	44		Lou DeFilippo
	42	43	44	45	Vince Dennery
	42	43	44	45	Kay Eakin
		43	44	45	Mank Edwards
	42	43	44	45	Len Eshmont
	42	43	44	45	Nello Falaschi
	42	43	44		George Franck
41	42	43	44	45	Chuck Gelatka
	42	43	44	45	Chet Gladchuk
		43	44	45	Merle Hapes
		43	44	45	Ed Hiemstra
	42	43	44	45	Dick Horne
		43	44	45	Jim Lee Howell
		43	44		Jiggs Kline
41	42	43	44		Grenny Landsdell
		43	44	45	John Lascari
		43	44	45	Ed Lechner
		43	44	45	Don Lieberum
	42	43	44		Jack Lummus (killed in action)
	42	43	44	45	Kayo Lunday
		43	44	45	Andy Marefos
	42	43	44	45	Red McClain
	42	43	44	45	John Mellus
41	42	43	44	45	Eddie Miller
41	42	43	44	45	Walt Nielsen
			44	45	Emery Nix
	42	43	44	45	Doug Oldershaw
		43	44	45	Al Owen
	42	43	44		Win Pedersen
	42	43	44		Jim Poole
		43	44	45	Dom Principe
	42	43	44		Marion Pugh
	42	43	44	45	Frank Reagan
		43	44	45	Red Seick
				45	Hank Soar
	42	43	44	45	Ben Sohn
		43	44	45	Paul Stenn
	42	43	44	45	Orville Tuttle
	42	43	44	45	Don Vosberg
			44	45	Will Walls
	42	43	44	45	Howie Yeager
				45	Len Younce

Al Blozis–played in 1944–killed in action Jan. 31, 1945

PHILADELPHIA EAGLES (1941=1 1942=28 1943=47 1944=48 1945=40)

41	42	43	44	45	Player
	42	43			Jack Banta
		43	44	45	Len Barnum
	42	43	44	45	Sam Bartholomew
	42	43	44		Mike Basca (killed in action in France in 1944)
		43	44	45	John Binotti
	42	43	44	45	Bob Biorklund
		43	44	45	Leo Brenner
	42	43	44	45	Tony Cemore
	42	43	44		Jim Castiglia
		43	44	45	Bill Combs
	42	43	44	45	Dan DeSantis
	42	43	44	45	Dave diFilippo
		43	44	45	Al Donelli
		43	44	45	John Eibner
41	42	43	44	45	Frank Emmons
		43	44		Dick Erdlitz
	42	43	44	45	Bernie Feibish
	42	43	44		Terry Fox
			44	45	Joe Frank
	42	43	44	45	Ralph Fritz
		43	44	45	Woody Gerber
	42	43	44	45	Lou Ghecas
	42	43	44	45	Fred Gloden
	42	43	44	45	Lyle Graham
			44	45	Ray Graves
		43	44	45	Irv Hall
		43	44	45	Bill Halverson
	42				Jack Hinkle
		43	44	45	Frank Hrabetin
	42	43	44		Dick Humbert
		43	44	45	Ed Kasky
	42	43	44	45	Bob Krieger
	42	43	44	45	Mort Landsberg
		43	44	45	Steve Levanitis
				45	Art Macioszczyk (also 1946)
		43	44	45	Basilio Marchi
	42	43	44	45	Wes McAfee
	42				Hugh McCullough
		43	44		Fred Meyer
		43	44	45	Rupert Pate
	42	43	44	45	Hank Piro
		43	44	45	Bosh Pritchard
	42	43	44		Phil Ragazzo
	42	43	44	45	John Shonk
		43	44	45	Jack Stackpool
	42				Leo Stasica
			44	45	Dean Steward
	42	43	44		Bob Suffridge
		43			Len Supulski (killed in airplane crash in France in 1944)
		43	44		Tommy Thompson
		43	44	45	Lou Tomasetti
	42	43	44	45	Foster Watkins
	42	43	44	45	Hodges West
		43	44	45	Tex Williams

PITTSBURGH STEELERS (1941=3 1942=14 1943=33 1944=30 1945=21)

41	42	43	44	45	Player
	42	43	44	45	Dick Bassi
		43	44	45	Tom Brown
		43	44		Chuck Cherundolo
	42	43	44		Joe Coomer
		43	44	45	Russ Cotton
		43			Milt Crain
	42	43	44		Dick Dolly
		43	44		Bill Dudley
41	42	43	44	45	Clark Goff
		43	44	45	Goerge Gonda
	42	43	44	45	Moose Harper
		43	44	45	Joe Hoague
	42	43	44		Art Jones
		43			Walt Kichefski
41	42	43	44		George Kiick
		43	44	45	Joe Lamas
		43	44		Hubbard Law
		43	44	45	Don Looney
		43	44	45	Vern Martin
	42	43			Coley McDonough
		43	44	45	Clure Mosher
	42	43	44	45	Carl Nery
	42	43	44		John Patrick
41	42	43	44	45	Stan Pavkov
	42	43	44	45	Rocco Pirro
		43	44	45	Mike Rodak
		43	44		Jack Sanders
		43	44	45	Curt Sandig
		43	44	45	Andy Tomasic
		43	44	45	Ralph Wenzel
	42	43	44	45	Don Williams
		43	44	45	John Woudenberg
	42	43	44	45	Frank Zopetti

WASHINGTON REDSKINS (1941=7 1942=14 1943=33 1944=37 1945=34)

41	42	43	44	45	Player
		43	44		Ki Aldrich
41	42	43	44	45	Steve Andrako
	42	43	44	45	Jim Barber
		43	44	45	Ed Beinor
41	42				Keith Birlem (killed in action, May 7, 1943)
		43	44	45	Ed Cifers
	42	43	44	45	Frank Clair
		43	44		Fred Davis
		43	44	45	Rufus Deal
	42	43	44	45	Ken Dow
	42	43			Frankie Filchock
	42	43	44	45	Lee Gentry
		43	44	45	John Goodyear
		43	44		Cecil Hare
			44	45	Ken Hayden
	42	43	44	45	Bob Hoffman
			44	45	Jack Jenkins
		43	44	45	Ed Justice
		43	44	45	Steve Juzwik
		43	44	45	John Kovatch
		43	44	45	Al Krueger
				45	Ted Lapka
		43			Charley Malone
		43	44	45	Bob McChesney
41	42	43	44	45	Jim Meade
				45	Ed Merkle
	42	43	44		Wayne Millner
41	42	43	44	45	Boyd Morgan
				45	Andy Natowich
41	42	43	44	45	Mickey Parks
		43	44	45	Dick Poillon
			44	45	Frank Ribar
41	42	43	44	45	Bo Russell
			44	45	Lou Rymkus
41	42	43	44	45	Sandy Sanford
			44	45	Jack Smith
		43	44		Clem Stralka
		43	44	45	Bob Titchenal
		43	44		Dick Todd
		43	44	45	George Watts
		43	44		Marv Whited
			44	45	Willie Wilkin
		43	44	45	Bill Young
				45	Joe Zeno

WORLD WAR II - MILITARY SERVICE

Full seasons missed by active players
(Only men who played in an official N.F.L. game before entering military service are listed.)

CHICAGO BEARS (1941=1 1942=15 1943=31 1944=43 1945=32)

41	42	43	44	45	Player
		43	44	45	Len Akin
		43	44		Lee Artoe
	42	43	44	45	Al Baisi
		43	44	45	Ray Bray
	42	43	44		Young Bussey (missing in action Jan. 7, 1945)
41	42	43	44	45	Chet Chesney
			44	45	Harry Clark
		43	44	45	Stu Clarkson
		43	44		Chuck Drulis
	42	43	44	45	John Federovich
	42	43	44	45	Aldo Forte
			44	45	Danny Fortmann
		43	44		Hugh Gallarneau
			44	45	Bill Geyer
		43	44	45	Bill Hempel
	42	43	44	45	Bill Hughes
			44	45	Tony Ippolito
	42	43	44		Ken Kavanaugh
		43	44		Nick Keriasotis
		43	44	45	Adolph Kissell
		43	44	45	Ed Kolman
	42	43	44	45	Hal Lahar
			44	45	Jim Logan
	42	43	44	45	Joe Maniaci
	42	43	44	45	Phil Martinovich
			44	45	Al Matuza
		43	44	45	Frank Maznicki
	42	43	44		George McAfee
			44	45	Monte Merkel
	42	43	44	45	Joe Mihal
		43	44	45	Frank Morris
		43	44	45	Bob Nowaskey
		43	44	45	Charlie O'Rourke
			44	45	Bill Osmanski
		43	44	45	John Petty
	42	43			Dick Plasman
			44	45	Hamp Pool
			44	45	John Siegal
	42	43	44	45	Norm Standlee
			44		Bill Steinkemper
			44	45	Bob Steuber
		43	44		Joe Stydahar
	42	43	44		Bob Swisher
			44		Joe Vodicka

CHICAGO CARDINALS (1941=5 1942=22 1943=36 1944=42 1945=30)

41	42	43	44	45	Player
		43	44	45	Joe Allton
		43	44		Ray Apolskis
	42	43	44		Frank Balasz
		43			Vince Banonis
		43	44		Libero Bertagnolli
			44	45	Joe Bukant
	42	43	44		Ray Rusler
			44	45	Ronnie Cahill
		43	44	45	Lloyd Cheatham
	42	43	44	45	Andy Chisick
	42	43	44	45	Johnny Clement
		43	44	45	Al Coppage
		43	44	45	Bill Daddio
	42				Bill Davis
	42	43	44		Bill Dewell
		43	44	45	Ray Elli
41	42	43	44	45	Ev Elkins
		43	44		Ralph Fife
			44	45	Marshall Goldberg
	42	43	44	45	John Higgins
	42	43	44	45	Frank Huffman
		43	44		Pop Ivy
41	42	43	44	45	Jimmy Johnston
		43	44		John Knolla
	42	43	44		Joe Kuharich
	42	43	44	45	John Kuzman
		43	44	45	Steve Lach
	42	43	44	45	Joe Lokenc
		43	44	45	Bob Maddock
	42	43	44	45	Ray Mallouf
	42	43	44	45	Avery Monfort
			44		Bob Morrow
	42	43	44	45	Bill Murphy
			44	45	Andy Puplis
			44	45	Cal Purdin
		43	44	45	Bud Schwenk
41	42	43	44	45	John Shirk
	42	43	44	45	Fred Shook
			44	45	George Smith
41	42	43	44		Marin Tonelli
	42	43	44	45	Fred Vanzo
		43	44	45	Ernie Wheeler
	42	43	44		Tarzan White
41	42	43	44	45	Bob Wood

CLEVELAND RAMS (1941=4 1942=18 1943=36 1944=39 1945=38)

41	42	43	44	45	Player
			44	45	Chet Adams
	42	43	44		Graham Armstrong
		43	44	45	Jack Boone
				45	Boyd Clay
41	42	43	44	45	Ollie Cordill
		43	44	45	Corby Davis
		43	44	45	Art Elston
				45	Jake Fawcett
41	42	43	44		Fred Gehrke
				45	Joe Gibson
41	42	43			Jim Gillette
	42	43	44	45	Owen Goodnight
		43	44	45	Parker Hall
	42	43	44	45	Jack Haman
	42	43	44	45	Kirk Hershey
	42	43	44		Red Hickey
			44	45	Ben Hightower
		43	44		Jack Jacobs
		43	44	45	Ben Janiak
		43	44	45	Don Johnson
	42	43	44		Mike Kostiuk
		43	44	45	Bill Lazetich
	42	43	44	45	Ted Livingston
			44	45	Dante Magnani
	42	43	44	45	Frank Maher
	42	43	44	45	Paul McDonough
		43	44	45	Barney McGarry
		43	44	45	George Morris
	42	43	44		Rudy Mucha
			44	45	Joe Pasqua
		43	44		Maury Patt
		43	44	45	George Platukis
		43	44	45	Warren Plunkett
	42	43	44	45	Ray Prochaska
				45	Chet Pudloski
		43			Bill Rieth
				45	Charley Riffle
		43	44	45	Hank Rockwell
	42	43	44	45	Charlie Seabright
	42	43	44	45	Marty Slovak
		43	44	45	Gaylon Smith
	42	43	44	45	Vic Spadaccini
41	42	43	44	45	Ralph Stevenson
			44	45	Roy Stuart
		43	44	45	Wilfred Thorpe
		43	44	45	Johnny Wilson
				45	Lou Zontini

DETROIT LIONS (1941=6 1942=23 1943=45 1944=54 1945=42)

41	42	43	44	45	Player
	42	43	44	45	Stan Anderson
		43	44	45	Tony Arena
		43	44	45	Emil Baniavcic
	42				Stan Batinski
		43	44		Charlie Behan (killed in action May 18, 1945—Okinawa)
	42	43	44	45	Steve Belichick
	42	43	44		Dick Booth
	42	43	44	45	Maury Britt (right arm amputated after being wounded in combat)
41	42	43	44	45	Tony Calvelli
			44	45	Gerry Conlee
			44	45	Mike Corgan
	42	43	44	45	Clem Crabtree
			44	45	Murray Evans
			44		Chuck Fenenbock
			44	45	Bill Fisk
	42	43			Tony Furst
		43	44		Sloko Gill
		43	44	45	Henry Goodman
		43	44	45	Frank Grigonis
41	42	43	44	45	John Hackenbruck
		43	44	45	Gran Harrison
			44	45	Harry Hopp
		43	44	45	Bill Kennedy (also 1946)
			44		Alex Ketzko (killed in action Dec. 23, 1944)
		43	44		Larry Knorr
			44	45	Bert Kuczynski
	42	43	44	45	Andy Logan
	42	43	44	45	John Mattiford
	42	43	44		Paul Moore
41	42	43	44	45	Butch Morse
	42	43	44		Bob Nelson
	42	43	44	45	Dunc Obee
	42	43	44	45	Lloyd Parsons
			44	45	Ted Pavelic
		43	44	45	John Polanski
	42	43	44		Cotton Price
	42	43	44		Bill Radovich
			44	45	Lyle Rockenbach
41	42	43	44	45	Stillman Rouse
			44	45	Tony Rubino
41	42	43	44	45	Rip Ryan
		43	44	45	Mickey Sanzotta
		43	44		Larry Sartori
		43	44	45	Alex Schibanoff
		43	44		John Schiechl
		43	44	45	Perry Scott
		43	44	45	Harry Seltzer
				45	Frankie Sinkwich
41	42	43	44	45	Dwight Sloan
		43			Dave Smukler
		43	44	45	George Speth
		43	44	45	Joe Stringfellow
		43	44	45	Paul Szakash
	42	43	44	45	John Tripson
		43	44		Emil Uremovich
		43			Chet Wetterlund (killed in action Sept. 5, 1944)
			44	45	Lloyd Wickett
	42	43	44	45	Whizzer White
		43	44	45	Tony Zuzzio

GREEN BAY PACKERS (1941=1 1942=16 1943=25 1944=27 1945=23)

41	42	43	44	45	Player
	42	43	44		Bob Adkins
				45	Tony Canadeo
		43			Joe Carter
			44	45	Dick Evans
			44	45	Sherwood Fries
	42	43	44		Ed Frutig
	42	43	44		Tom Greenfield
	42	43	44	45	Clarke Hinkle
		43	44	45	Bob Ingalls
	42	43	44	45	Ed Jankowski
	42	43	44	45	Bill Johnson
	42	43	44		Smiley Johnson (killed in action at Iwo Jima)
				45	Bob Kahler
			44	45	Jim Lankas
		43	44	45	Bill Lee
		43	44	45	Russ Letlow
	42	43	44	45	Lee McLaughlin
	42	43	44		Moose Mulleneaux
		43	44		Ernie Pannell
	42	43	44	45	George Paskvan
		43	44	45	Ray Riddick
	42	43	44	45	Herm Rohrig
		43	44		Charlie Sample
	42	43	44	45	Charlie Schultz
	42	43	44	45	George Svendsen
			44	45	Andy Uram
	42	43			Alex Urban
	42	43	44	45	Hal Van Every
		43	44	45	Fred Vant Hull
				45	Ray Wehba
		43	44	45	Dick Weisgerber
41	42	43	44	45	Gust Zarnas

Total N.F.L. 1941=44 1942=202 1943=376 1944=418 1945=358

Championship Games 1933–1936

1933
December 17 at Chicago
(Attendance: Approximately 26,000)

Beginning History on a Seesaw

Two strong divisional champions and clear, crisp weather set a perfect table for the NFL's first championship game between the Bears and Giants. Both clubs moved the ball in the first half, the Bears mostly by running and the Giants by passing, but the defenses had limited the scoring to a pair of Jack Manders field goals for Chicago and a 29-yard touchdown pass from Harry Newman to Red Badgro plus the conversion for New York. In the third quarter, Manders' third field goal put the Bears on top 9-7, and the Giants came right back with a 61-yard drive, capped by Max Krause's 1-yard plunge into the end zone. Six plays later, the Bears recaptured the lead on an 8-yard pass from Bronko Nagurski to Bill Karr after a fake run. With Chicago leading 16-14, the Giants scored on the first play of the final quarter. With the ball on the Chicago 8-yard line, Newman pitched out to Ken Strong, who lateraled back to Newman when trapped behind the line; after scrambling around for a few seconds, Newman then threw a pass to Strong in the end zone. But with their backs to the wall, and under three minutes left, Nagurski passed to Bill Hewitt, who took a few steps and lateraled to Bill Karr, who went all the way to give the Bears a 23-21 win.

SCORING

NEW YORK	0	7	7	7–21
CHICAGO	3	3	10	7–23

1st Qtr: CHI.	Manders, FG 16 yards
2nd Qtr: CHI.	Manders, FG 40 yards
N.Y.	Badgro, 29 yard pass from Newman PAT–Strong (kick)
3rd Qtr: CHI.	Manders, FG 28 yards
N.Y.	Krause, 1 yard rush PAT–Strong (kick)
CHI.	Karr, 8 yard pass from Nagurski PAT–Manders (kick)
4th Qtr: N.Y.	Strong, 8 yard pass from Newman PAT–Strong (kick)
CHI.	Karr, 36 yards on lateral from Hewitt on pass from Nagurski PAT–Manders (kick)

TEAM STATS

CHI.		N.Y.
12	First Downs	13
161	Rushing Yardage	99
16	Pass Attempts	20
7	Pass Completions	14
.438	Completion Percentage	.700
147	Passing Yardage	200
1	Interceptions	1
10	Punts	13
39.8	Punting Average	28.6
58	Punt Return Yards	59
0	Fumbles Lost	0
7	Penalties	3
40	Penalty Yards	15

1934
December 9 at New York
(Attendance: 35,059)

Sneaking to the Throne

Although the Bears had gone undefeated through the season and the Giants had lost three of their last six games to barely hold onto first place in the East, injuries and the weather leveled the differences between the clubs. Bears guard Joe Kopcha and rookie sensation Beattie Feathers were left at home with injuries, while the Giants had to play without passer Harry Newman and end Red Badgro. Overnight rain and freezing temperatures turned the field into a sheet of ice that favored neither team. Both clubs slipped and skidded on the ice through the first half, with the Bears leading 10-3 at halftime. When the Giants came out for the second half, the Bears and spectators were surprised to see most of them wearing sneakers instead of football cleats. The only score of the third quarter was a Jack Manders field goal which put the Bears ahead 13-3, but the Giants exploded for 27 points in the fourth quarter. With the sneakers providing better footing on the icy turf, the Giants closed the gap to 13-10 on a 28-yard pass from Ed Danowski to Ike Frankian. Then, in short order, Ken Strong ran 42 yards past the sliding Bears for a touchdown, and the Giants added two more touchdowns by Strong and Danowski to ice away the victory 30-13.

SCORING

CHICAGO	0	10	3	0–13
NEW YORK	3	0	0	27–30

1st Qtr: N.Y.	Strong, FG 38 yards	
2nd Qtr: CHI.	Nagurski, 1 yard rush	PAT–Manders (kick)
CHI.	Manders, FG 17 yards	
3rd Qtr: CHI.	Manders, FG 24 yards	
4th Qtr: N.Y.	Frankian, 28 yard pass from Danowski	PAT–Strong (kick)
N.Y.	Strong, 42 yard rush	PAT–Strong (kick)
N.Y.	Strong, 11 yard rush	PAT–Strong–(No Good)
N.Y.	Danowski, 6 yard rush	PAT–Strong (kick)

TEAM STATS

N.Y.		CHI.
7	First Downs	7
170	Rushing Yardage	93
13	Pass Attempts	13
7	Pass Completions	6
.538	Completion Percentage	.462
115	Passing Yardage	74
2	Interceptions	3
6	Punts	9
38	Punting Average	35
2	Fumbles Lost	0
0	Penalty Yards	30

1935
December 15 at Detroit
(Attendance: 15,000)

Finding Glory in the Mud

A muddy field, freezing rain, and biting wind gave an advantage to the Lions, who were a running club, and hurt the Giants, who relied on the pass. On the first series after the opening kickoff, however, the Lions completed two long passes in a 61-yard drive climaxed by Ace Gutowsky's 5-yard smash into the end zone. The Giants drove back to the Detroit 13-yard line, but Ken Strong's field-goal attempt was unsuccessful; even more costly for New York on this drive were two broken ribs receiver Tod Goodwin suffered in making a catch. Detroit added a second touchdown late in first quarter when Dutch Clark broke loose for a 40-yard run to make the score 13-0. In the second the Giants closed the gap to 13-7 with a 42-yard pass from Ed Danowski to Ken Strong. New York struggled to get the tying touchdown in the fourth quarter, but fell short with a streak of bad luck. With three minutes left to play, the Lions blocked Danowski's punt and recovered it on the New York 26-yard line. Six plays later, Ernie Caddell skirted around end from the one-foot line for the clinching points. With Danowski then heaving desperation passes, Buddy Parker picked one off and returned it to the Giant 10. Three plays later, Parker carried the ball in but missed the extra point in a final 26-7 outcome.

SCORING

NEW YORK	0	7	0	0– 7
DETROIT	13	0	0	13–26

1st Qtr: Det.	Gutowsky, 2 yard rush	PAT–Presnell (kick)
Det.	Clark, 40 yard rush	PAT–Clark (No Good)
2nd Qtr: N.Y.	Strong, 42 yard pass from Danowski	PAT–Strong (kick)
3rd Qtr:	None	
4th Qtr: Det.	Caddel, 4 yard rush	PAT–Clark (kick)
Det.	Parker, 9 yard rush	PAT–Parker (No Good)

TEAM STATS

N.Y.		DET.
8	First Downs	13
106	Rushing Yardage	235
13	Pass Attempts	5
4	Pass Completions	2
.308	Completion Percentage	.400
88	Passing Yardage	68
2	Interceptions	0
5	Punts	4
43	Punting Average	39
3	Fumbles Lost	4
15	Penalty Yards	25

1936
December 13 at New York
(Attendance: 29,543)

Getting Neutralized on Neutral Ground

With the game scheduled for the home park of the Eastern champion, Redskin owner George Marshall showed his contempt for what he considered Boston's poor support of his team by moving the title match to the neutral Polo Grounds in New York. The orphaned Redskins were given little chance of upending the favored Green Bay Packers, and when star runner Cliff Battles was injured on the first Boston series of downs, they faced a bleak afternoon. Moments after Battles left the field, Green Bay's Arnie Herber launched a 43-yard pass play to Don Hutson that swung momentum completely over to the Packers. The Redskins fought gamely back and drove seventy-eight yards, capped by Pug Rentner's plunge from the one-yard line. Riley Smith's conversion attempt sailed wide, however, and the Skins still trailed 7-6. The Packers upped the count to 14-6 by driving 74 yards in six plays after the second-half kickoff. The key play in the drive was a 52-yard pass play from Herber to veteran Johnny Blood, and the touchdown itself came on an 8-yard pass from Herber to Milt Gantenbein. The Redskins meanwhile suffered a further blow when Frank Bausch, their only healthy center, was ejected from the game for fighting. In the final period, the Packers again scored after blocking a Boston punt to run the score to 21-6.

SCORING

GREEN BAY	7	0	7	7–21
BOSTON	0	6	0	0– 6

1st Qtr: G.B.	Hutson, 43 yard pass from Herber PAT–E. Smith (kick)
2nd Qtr: Bos.	Rentner, 1 yard rush PAT–R. Smith (No Good)
3rd Qtr: G.B.	Gantenbein, 8 yard pass from Herber PAT–E. Smith (kick)
4th Qtr: G.B.	Monnett, 2 yard rush PAT–E. Smith (kick)

TEAM STATS

G.B.		BOS.
7	First Downs	8
67	Rushing Yardage	39
23	Pass Attempts	26
9	Pass Completions	7
.391	Completion Percentage	.269
153	Passing Yardage	77
2	Interceptions	1
10	Punts	7
34	Punting Average	35
4	Punt Returns	5
27	Punt Return Yards	58
2	Fumbles	5
1	Fumbles Lost	2
3	Penalties	4
15	Penalty Yards	25

1937

December 12, at Chicago
(Attendance 15,878)

Washington and the Golden Arm

Sammy Baugh, Washington's marvelous rookie passer, showed the Bears his skill and daring by passing from his own end zone to Cliff Battles for a 43-yard gain on the Redskins' first play from scrimmage. The Redskins were forced to punt, but they did drive 53 yards the next time they got the ball, with Battles going over from the seven-yard line for the score. The Bears fought back and, with Jack Manders, Bronko Nagurski, and Eggs Manske leading the way, scored two touchdowns to make the halftime score 14-7 in favor of Chicago. Baugh hit Wayne Millner with a 55-yard bomb to tie the score in the third quarter, but the Bears used the power of Nagurski and Manders to smash away at the Redskins for another touchdown, making the count 21-14, Chicago. But Baugh then unleashed the full power of his arm. On the first play after the kickoff, he hit Millner for a 78-yard touchdown, and minutes later he threw 35 yards to Ed Justice to take the lead, 28-21. Although the fourth quarter was enlivened by a free-for-all, the 28-21 Washington lead stayed untouched, as the Bears simply could not mount a passing attack any thing like what Slingin' Sam had done.

SCORING

WASHINGTON	7	0	21	0–28
CHIC. BEARS	14	0	7	0–21

First Quarter

Was.	Battles, 7 yard rush PAT–R. Smith (kick)	8:04
Chi.	Manders, 10 yard rush PAT–Manders (kick)	11:12
Chi.	Manders, 39 yard pass from Masterson PAT–Manders (kick)	14:25

Third Quarter

Was.	Milner, 55 yard pass from Baugh PAT–R. Smith (kick)	1:13
Chi.	Manske, 4 yard pass from Masterson PAT–Manders (kick)	5:56
Was.	Milner, 78 yard pass from Baugh PAT–R. Smith (kick)	6:26
Was.	Justice, 35 yard pass from Baugh PAT–R. Smith (kick)	14:06

TEAM STATISTICS

CHI.			WASH.
14	First Downs	– Total*	22
8		– by Rushing	9
6		– by Passing	13
0		– by Penalty	0
2	Punt Returns	– Number	1
3	Fumbles	– Number	4
1		– Times Lost Ball	3
1	Penalties	– Number	1
15		– Yards Penalized	5

*includes Touchdowns

INDIVIDUAL STATISTICS

CHICAGO	No.	Yds.	Avg.	WASHINGTON	No.	Yds.	Avg.
			RUSHING				
Manders	10	64	6.4	Battles	17	51	3.0
Nagurski	7	47	6.7	Irwin	10	33	3.3
Nolting	10	38	3.8	Baugh	3	32	10.7
Buivid	1	6	6.0	Justice	1	4	4.0
Rentner	1	0	0.0	Krause	1	4	4.0
Masterson	1	–2	–2.0	Milner	1	–2	–2.0
Ronzani	1	–3	–3.0		33	122	3.7
	31	150	4.8				
			RECEIVING				
Manske	2	55	27.5	Milner	8	181	22.6
Plasman	2	44	22.0	Battles	3	82	27.3
McDonald	2	39	19.5	Justice	3	63	21.0
Manders	1	37	37.0	Malone	3	27	9.0
Rentner	1	32	32.0	R. Smith	2	20	10.0
	8	207	25.9	Pinckert	1	18	18.0
				Irwin	1	7	7.0
					21	398	19.0
			PUNTING				
Nolting	4		45.0	Baugh	5		23.2
Francis	1		62.0	R. Smith	1		12.0
Feathers	1		44.0	Battles	1		27.0
	6		49.5		7		24.8

PASSING

CHICAGO	Att.	Comp.	Comp. Pct.	Att	Int.	Yds/ Att.	Yds/ Comp.	Yards Lost Tackled
Masterson	17	4	23.5	131	2	7.7	32.8	1– 7
Buivid	11	3	27.3	41	1	3.7	13.7	2–18
Molesworth	1	1	100.0	35	0	35.0	35.0	
Nagurski	1	0	0.0	0	0	0.0	0.0	
	30	8	26.7	207	3	6.9	25.9	3–25
WASHINGTON								
Baugh	34	17	50.0	358	1	10.5	21.1	1–26
Battles	5	3	60.0	23	1	4.6	7.7	2– 6
R. Smith	2	1	50.0	17	1	8.5	17.0	1–13
	41	21	51.2	398	3	9.7	19.0	4–45

1938

December 12, at New York
(Attendance 48,120)

Start with Defense, End with Victory

Two blocked punts gave the Giants an early first-quarter lead before the largest crowd yet to see an NFL championship game. The first blocked kick led to Ward Cuff's 13-yard field goal; the second led to Tuffy Leemans' six-yard run for a touchdown. Trailing 9-0 although holding the New York offense, the Packers came back in the second quarter on a 40-yard pass from Arnie Herber to Moose Mulleneaux, who was the Packers' primary receiver because Don Hutson was injured. The teams traded touchdowns before the half ended to bring the score up to 16-14 in favor of the Giants at halftime. Within the first three minutes of the second half, the Packers had taken the lead on a Tiny Engebretsen field goal, but the Giants promptly drove 61 yards behind Hank Soar's running and Ed Danowski's passing for the winning touchdown in the 23-17 contest.

SCORING

GREEN BAY	0	14	3	0–17
NEW YORK	9	7	7	0–23

First Quarter

N.Y.	Cuff, 13 yard Field Goal
N.Y.	Leemans, 6 yard rush PAT–Gildea (No Good)

Second Quarter

G.B.	C. Mulleneaux, 40 yard pass from Herber PAT – Engebretsen (kick)
N.Y.	Barnard, 20 yard pass from Danowski PAT – Cuff (kick)
G.B.	Hinkle, 1 yard rush PAT – Engebretsen (kick)

Third Quarter

G.B.	Engebretsen, 15 yard Field Goal
N.Y.	Soar, 23 yard pass from Danowski PAT – Cuff (kick)

TEAM STATISTICS

N.Y.			G.B.
13	First Downs	– Total*	16
7		– by Rushing	10
4		– by Passing	6
2		– by Penalty	0
2	Fumbles	– Number	4
0		– Times Lost Ball	2
2	Penalties	– Number	3
10		– Yards Penalized	20

*includes Touchdowns

INDIVIDUAL STATISTICS

NEW YORK	No.	Yds.	Avg.	GREEN BAY	No.	Yds.	Avg.
			PUNT RETURNS				
Leemans	2	34	17.0	Monnett	1	10	10.0
				Herber	1	0	0.0
				Uram	1	0	0.0
					3	10	3.3
			KICKOFF RETURNS				
Cuff	1	20	20.0	Laws	1	29	29.0
Soar	1	16	16.0	Hinkle	1	22	22.0
Howell	1	12	12.0	Herber	1	15	15.0
Shaffer	1	8	8.0		3	66	22.0
	4	56	14.0				
			INTERCEPTION RETURNS				
Danowski	1	0	0.0	Engebretsen	1	0	0.0

INDIVIDUAL STATISTICS

NEW YORK	No.	Yds.	Avg.	GREEN BAY	No.	Yds.	Avg.
			RUSHING				
Soar	21	65	3.1	Hinkle	18	63	3.5
Leemans	13	42	3.2	Monnett	4	29	7.3
Barnum	3	8	2.7	Herber	3	22	7.3
Danowski	1	4	4.0	Isbell	11	20	1.8
Karcis	3	3	1.0	Laws	4	20	5.0
Cuff	2	–7	–3.5	Janowski	3	14	4.7
	43	115	2.7	Uran	2	–1	–0.5
				Miller	1	–3	–3.0
					46	164	4.6
			RECEIVING				
Soar	3	41	13.7	Becker	2	79	39.5
Howell	2	3	1.5	C. Mulleneaux	2	54	27.0
Barnard	1	20	20.0	Uram	1	24	24.0
Barnum	1	20	20.0	Isbell	1	22	22.0
Leemans	1	5	5.0	Scherer	1	19	19.0
Perry	0	8	–	Gantenbein	1	6	6.0
	8	97	12.1	Hutson	0	10	–
					8	214	26.8
			PUNTING				
Danowski	6		39.5	Herber	3		41.3
Gildea	1		55.0	Hinkle	2		18.5
Barnum	1		33.0	Isbell	1		0.0
	8		40.6		6		26.8

PASSING

NEW YORK	Att.	Comp.	Comp. Pct.	Yds.	Int.	Yds/ Att.	Yds/ Comp.
Danowski	11	7	63.6	77	0	7.0	11.0
Leemans	2	1	50.0	20	1	10.0	20.0
Barnum	1	0	0.0	0	0	0.0	0.0
Soar	1	0	0.0	0	0	0.0	0.0
	15	8	53.3	97	1	6.5	12.1
GREEN BAY							
Herber	14	5	35.7	123	0	8.8	24.6
Isbell	5	3	60.0	91	1	18.2	30.3
	19	8	42.1	214	1	11.3	26.8

1939

December 10, at Milwaukee
(Attendance 32,279)

Shackles and Humiliation

The Packers avenged last year's championship-game loss by completely shackling the Giants and running off to a 27-0 victory. The Green Bay defense kept the Giants bottled up in their own territory most of the game, with the Packer line constantly smashing through into the New York backfield. The only score of the first half was a seven-yard pass from Arnie Herber to Milt Gantenbein, plus the conversion, but the Packers put the game away in the second half on touchdowns by Joe Laws and Ed Jankowski and field goals by Tiny Engebretsen and Ernie Smith. Unable to launch an attack all day, the Giants suffered the worst championship beating yet.

SCORING

NEW YORK	0	0	0	0– 0
GREEN BAY	7	0	10	10–27

First Quarter

G.B.	Gantenbein, 7 yard pass from Herber PAT – Engebretsen (kick)

Third Quarter

G.B.	Engebretsen, 29 yard Field Goal
G.B.	Laws, 27 yard pass from Isbell PAT – Engebretsen (kick)

Fourth Quarter

G.B.	Smith, 42 yard Field Goal
G.B.	Jankowski, 1 yard rush PAT – Smith (kick)

TEAM STATISTICS

G.B.			N.Y.
13	First Downs	– Total*	9
7		– by Rushing	5
4		– by Passing	3
2		– by Penalty	1
2	Fumbles	– Number	1
0		– Times Lost Ball	0
4	Penalties	– Number	5
50		– Yards Penalized	21

*includes Touchdowns

INDIVIDUAL STATISTICS

GREEN BAY	No.	Yds.	Avg.	NEW YORK	No.	Yds.	Avg.
			PUNT RETURNS				
Laws	1	15	15.0	Leemans	2	25	12.5
Uram	1	10	10.0				
	2	25	12.5				
			KICKOFF RETURNS				
				Leemans	3	41	13.7
	None			Cuff	1	13	13.0
					4	54	13.5
			INTERCEPTION RETURNS				
Brock	2	14	7.0	Miller	1	5	5.0
Svendson	1	15	15.0	Barnum	1	0	0.0
Uram	1	10	10.0	Cuff	1	0	0.0
Gantenbein	1	5	5.0		3	5	1.7
Lawrence	1	0	0.0				
	6	44	7.3				

INDIVIDUAL STATISTICS

GREEN BAY	No.	Yds.	Avg.	NEW YORK	No.	Yds.	Avg.
			RUSHING				
Uram	10	38	3.8	Leemans	12	24	2.0
Isbell	14	28	2.0	Miller	2	19	9.5
Hinkle	13	23	1.8	Soar	4	14	3.5
Laws	3	20	6.7	Richards	7	12	1.7
Janowski	7	14	2.0	Cuff	3	7	2.3
Jacunski	1	11	11.0	Barnum	4	4	1.0
Herber	2	3	1.5	Kline	1	1	1.0
Hutson	1	3	3.0	Owen	1	–2	–2.0
	51	140	2.7		34	79	2.3
			RECEIVING				
Hutson	2	21	10.5	Shaffer	2	16	8.0
Craig	2	6	3.0	Falaschi	2	6	3.0
Jacunski	1	31	31.0	Leemans	1	37	37.0
Laws	1	31	31.0	Gelatka	1	24	24.0
Gantenbein	1	7	7.0	Barnum	1	6	6.0
	7	96	13.7	Cuff	1	5	5.0
					8	94	11.8
			PUNTING				
Hinkle	5		22.6	Danowski	4		42.5
Herber	2		34.5	Barnum	2		36.0
	7		26.0		6		40.3

PASSING

GREEN BAY	Att.	Comp.	Comp. Pct.	Yds.	Int.	Yds/ Att.	Yds/ Comp.	Yards Lost Tackled
Herber	8	5	62.5	59	3	7.4	11.8	1–6
Isbell	2	2	100.0	37	0	18.5	18.5	
	10	7	70.0	96	3	9.6	13.7	1–6
NEW YORK								
Danowski	12	4	33.3	48	3	4.0	12.0	
Miller	6	3	50.0	40	1	6.7	13.3	1–9
Leemans	4	1	25.0	6	1	1.5	6.0	
Barnum	3	0	0.0	0	1	0.0	0.0	
	25	8	32.0	94	6	3.8	11.8	1–9

1940

December 8, at Washington
(Attendance 36,034)

SCORING

CHIC. BEARS	21	7	26	19–73
WASHINGTON	0	0	0	0– 0

First Quarter

Chi.	Osmanski, 68 yard rush PAT – Manders (kick)	00:55
Chi.	Luckman, 1 yard rush PAT – Snyder (kick)	10:50
Chi.	Maniaci, 42 yard rush PAT – Martinovick (kick)	12:25

Second Quarter

Chi.	Kavanaugh, 30 yard pass from Luckman PAT – Snyder (kick)	11:45

Third Quarter

Chi.	Pool, 15 yard interception return PAT – Plasman (kick)	00:45
Chi.	Nolting, 23 yard rush PAT – Plasman (No Good)	4:25
Chi.	McAfee, 35 yard interception return PAT – Stydahar (kick)	5:12
Chi.	Turner, 20 yard interception return PAT – Maniaci (No Good)	12:56

Fourth Quarter

Chi.	Clark, 44 yard rush PAT – Famiglietti (no Good)	4:47
Chi.	Famiglietti, 2 yard rush PAT – Maniaci, pass from Sherman	6:15
Chi.	Clark, 1 yard rush PAT – Snyder, pass (No Good)	12:36

TEAM STATISTICS

WASH.		CHI.
15	First Downs – Total*	26
3	– by Rushing	20
10	– by Passing	5
2	– by Penalty	1
0	Fumbles – Number	1
0	– Times Lost Ball	0
6	Penalties – Number	7
71	– Yards Penalized	36

* – includes touchdowns

The Worst Vengence Ever

Still bristling from a 7-3 loss to the Redskins three weeks earlier, the Bears administered the worst beating ever in an NFL game by crushing Washington 73-0 in a perfect display of football. Using their T-formation instead of the single wing generally used around the league, the Bears served notice right at the start that this afternoon was theirs. On the second play from scrimmage, Bill Osmanski went around end for 68 yards for a touchdown, sprung loose by George Wilson's flying block which erased the two last Redskin defenders in one shot. Washington's Max Krause then returned the kickoff back to the Chicago 39-yard line, and five plays later Sammy Baugh threw a perfect pass to Charlie Malone all alone on the five. Malone dropped it, and the Redskins never came close again. By the end of the first quarter the score was 21-0 and the game was turning into a rout. With the Chicago defense shutting off the Redskin runners and intercepting passes freely, the score mounted to 28-0 at halftime. Rather than slack off in the second half, the Bears poured it on, running the final score to 73-0 with three fourth-quarter touchdowns.

INDIVIDUAL STATISTICS

WASHINGTON	No	Yds	Avg.	CHICAGO	No	Yds	Avg.
			PUNT RETURNS				
Moore	1	6	6.0	McAfee	1	17	17.0
				Clark	1	9	9.0
				Luckman	1	3	3.0
					3	29	9.7
			INTERCEPTION RETURNS				
				Maniaci	2	26	13.0
				McAfee	1	35	35.0
				Turner	1	20	20.0
				Pool	1	15	15.0
				Nolting	1	10	10.0
				McLean	1	0	0.0
				Osmanski	1	0	0.0
					8	106	13.3

INDIVIDUAL STATISTICS

WASHINGTON	No	Yds	Avg.	CHICAGO	No	Yds	Avg.
			RUSHING				
Filchock	2	20	10.0	Osmanski	10	107	10.7
Seymour	4	17	4.3	Clark	7	75	10.7
Johnson	4	14	3.5	Nolting	11	67	6.1
Justice	1	2	2.0	Maniaci	5	62	12.4
Zimmerman	1	2	2.0	McAfee	7	32	4.6
	12	55	4.6	Famiglietti	4	19	4.8
				McLean	3	18	6.0
				Nowaskey	1	7	7.0
				Snyder	1	2	2.0
				Manders	2	1	0.5
				Luckman	1	1	1.0
					52	391	7.5
			RECEIVING				
Millner	6	94	15.7	Maniaci	2	44	22.0
Masterson	3	34	11.3	Kavanaugh	2	32	16.0
Johnson	3	9	3.0	Swisher	1	36	36.0
Malone	2	51	25.5	Mihal	1	14	14.0
Hoffman	2	8	4.0	Nolting	1	12	12.0
Farkas	1	19	19.0		7	138	19.7
Seymour	1	7	7.0				
Justice	1	4	4.0				
McChesney	1	0	0.0				
	20	226	11.3				
			PUNTING				
Zimmerman	1		61.0	Luckman	1		58.0
Todd	1		35.0	McAfee	1		38.0
Baugh	1		31.0		2		48.0
	3		42.3				
			KICKOFF RETURNS				
Filchock	3	65	21.7	Nolting	1	22	22.0
Krause	1	51	51.0				
Farkas	1	35	35.0				
Zimmerman	1	33	33.0				
Pinckert	1	10	10.0				
Malone	1	9	9.0				
	8	203	25.4				

PASSING

WASHINGTON	Att	Comp	Comp Pct.	Yds	Int	Yds/ Att.	Yds/ Comp	Yards Lost Tackled
Filchock	23	8	34.8	101	4	4.4	12.6	1–17
Baugh	16	9	56.3	91	2	5.7	10.1	1–16
Zimmerman	12	3	25.0	34	2	2.8	11.3	1–17
	51	20	39.2	226	8	4.4	11.3	3–50
CHICAGO								
Luckman	6	4	66.7	102	0	17.0	25.5	
Snyder	3	3	100.0	36	0	12.0	12.0	1–10
McAfee	1	0	0.0	0	0	–	–	
	10	7	70.0	138	0	13.8	19.7	1–10

1941

December 21, at Chicago
(Attendance 13,341)

SCORING

NEW YORK	6	0	3	0– 9
CHIC. BEARS	3	6	14	14–37

First Quarter

Chi.	Snyder, 14 yard Field Goal	10:34
N.Y.	Franck, 31 yard pass from Leemans PAT – Cuff (No Good)	12:40

Second Quarter

Chi.	Snyder, 39 yard Field Goal	0:44
Chi.	Snyder, 37 yard Field Goal	9:58

Third Quarter

N.Y.	Cuff, 17 yard Field Goal	4:25
Chi.	Standlee, 2 yard rush PAT – Snyder (kick)	7:48
Chi.	Standlee, 7 yard rush PAT – Maniaci (kick)	13:05

Fourth Quarter

Chi.	McAfee, 5 yard rush PAT – Artoe (kick)	10:55
Chi.	Kavanaugh, 42 yard fumble return PAT – McLean (kick)	14:51

The Anticlimactic Affair

With attendance held down by concern over the recent attack on Pearl Harbor, the Bears wore the Giants down in the first half and broke the game open in the final half for a 37-9 victory. After the first thirty minutes the score read 9-6, with the Bears tallying three Bob Snyder field goals and the Giants a 31-yard touchdown pass from Tuffy Leemans to George Franck. A Ward Cuff field goal tied the score at 9-9 early in the third quarter, but the Bears took charge from that point on. With Sid Luckman's passes on target and Norm Standlee almost unstoppable on short yardage plays, the Bears drove 71 yards for six points, with Standlee taking it over from the two. Minutes later, Standlee climaxed another Bear drive with a seven-yard dash into the end zone, with the extra point making the score 23-9 at the end of three quarters. The deep Bears completely routed the Giants in the final period, notching two touchdowns and adding the final extra point on a drop kick, already a forgotten play in football.

TEAM STATISTICS

CHI.		N.Y.
20	First Downs	8
192	Rushing Yardage	84
19	Passing – Attempts	15
11	– Completions	3
57.9	– Completion Pct.	20.0
182	– Yards	73
9.6	– Yards per Attempt	4.9
16.5	– Yards per Completion	24.3
0	– Intercepted	3
2	Punting – Number	5
53.5	– Average Yards	38.6
3	Fumbles – Number	2
1	– Times Lost Ball	2
9	Penalties – Number	3
80	– Yards Penalized	31

1942

December 13, at Washington
(Attendance 36,006)

SCORING

CHIC. BEARS	0	6	0	0– 6
WASHINGTON	0	7	7	0–14

Second Quarter

CHI.	Artoe, 52 yard fumble return PAT – Artoe (No Good)	1:22
WAS.	Moore, 39 yard pass from Baugh PAT – Masterson (kick)	8:56

Third Quarter

Was.	Farkas, 1 yard rush PAT – Masterson (kick)	7:25

TEAM STATISTICS

WASH.		CHI.
10	First Downs – Total	10
6	– by Rushing	6
2	– by Passing	3
2	– by Penalty	1
1	Fumbles – Number	1
1	– Times Lost Ball	1
4	Penalties – Number	7
26	– Yards Penalized	47

Somewhat Healing the Wounds

The Redskins won a measure of revenge for their 1940 humiliation by beating the undefeated Chicago Bears 14-6 for the NFL championship. The Washington line played inspired football, completely shredding the Chicago running game and rushing the Bear passers. With Sammy Baugh averaging over 50 yards per punt, the Bears spent most of the game mired in their own territory. Chicago did score first, with no thanks to their offense, as tackle Lee Artoe returned a fumble 52 yards for a touchdown. Baugh hit Wilbur Moore for a 39-yard touchdown pass, and the extra point made it 7-6 Washington at the halftime break. With the Bear attack unable to get untracked, the Redskins added an Andy Farkas touchdown in the second half for the 14-6 win.

INDIVIDUAL STATISTICS

WASHINGTON	No	Yds	Avg.	CHICAGO	No	Yds	Avg.
			KICKOFF RETURNS				
Hare	1	29	29.0	McLean	1	25	25.0
Moore	1	23	23.0	Nolting	1	23	23.0
	2	52	26.0	Clark	1	21	21.0
					3	69	23.0
			INTERCEPTION RETURNS				
Moore	1	14	14.0	Nolting	1	0	0.0
Baugh	1	0	0.0	O'Rourke	1	0	0.0
Hare	1	0	0.0		2	0	0.0
	3	14	4.7				

INDIVIDUAL STATISTICS

WASHINGTON	No	Yds	Avg.	CHICAGO	No	Yds	Avg.
			RUSHING				
Farkas	13	46	3.5	Osmanski	13	38	2.9
Seymour	14	34	2.4	Nolting	8	26	3.3
Todd	2	12	6.0	Famiglietti	7	22	3.1
Hare	4	7	1.8	Maznicki	5	14	2.8
Baugh	2	6	3.0	McLean	1	3	3.0
Masterson	1	–1	–1.0	Gallarneau	1	0	0.0
	36	104	2.9	Petty	3	–1	–0.3
					38	102	2.7
			RECEIVING				
Moore	2	41	20.5	McLean	3	26	8.7
Todd	1	9	9.0	Siegel	2	11	5.5
Cifers	1	8	8.0	Maznicki	1	39	39.0
Masterson	1	8	8.0	Nowaskey	1	32	32.0
	5	66	13.2	Nolting	1	11	11.0
					8	119	14.9
			PUNTING				
Baugh	1		52.5	Luckman	6		42.0
			PUNT RETURNS				
Todd	2	5	2.5	Gallarneau	1	13	13.0
Farkas	2	0	0.0				
Seymour	2	0	0.0				
	6	5	0.8				

PASSING

WASHINGTON	Att	Comp	Comp Pct.	Yds	Int	Yds/ Att.	Yds/ Comp	Yards Lost Tackled
Baugh	13	5	38.5	66	2	5.1	13.2	
CHICAGO								
Luckman	11	4	36.4	9	2	0.8	2.3	3–33
O'Rourke	6	4	66.7	110	0	18.3	27.5	
Maznicki	1	0	0.0	0	1	–	–	
	18	8	44.4	119	3	6.6	14.9	3–33

1943

December 26, at Chicago
(Attendance 34,320)

Five Strikes for Luckman, One Kick for Baugh

Sid Luckman turned in a marvelous all-around performance in leading the Bears to a 41-21 triumph over the Washington Redskins. Luckman threw five touchdown passes, ran for 64 yards, deftly picked the Redskin defense apart with his play-calling, and intercepted two passes on defense. Sammy Baugh, Luckman's opposite number on the Redskins, missed most of the first half when kicked in the head while making a tackle. With George Cafego filling in at tailback, the Redskins drew first blood when Andy Farkas bucked over from the one-yard line. Luckman went to work after that and soon put the game out of reach. A 31-yard pass play to Harry Clark tied the score, and a 3-yard plunge by Bronko Nagurski, back from five years of retirement, gave the Bears a 14-7 halftime edge. In the first few minutes of the second half, halfback Dante Magnani twice went all the way with short passes, running 36 and 66 yards to break the game wide open. Sammy Baugh, still dizzy from a mild concussion, returned to action in the third quarter and rallied his mates to a touchdown before the end of the period. The Bears, leading 27-14 after three quarters, completely dominated the final quarter. They held onto the ball for the first eleven minutes and fifty seconds of the period by launching an extended drive that resulted in a Jim Benton touchdown, then recovered an onside kick and again marched steadily downfield for another score.

SCORING

WASHINGTON	0	7	7	7–21
CHIC. BEARS	0	14	13	14–41

Second Quarter		
Was.	Farkas, 1 yard rush PAT – Masterson (kick)	0:02
Chi.	Clark, 31 yard pass from Luckman PAT – Snyder (kick)	2:23
Chi.	Nagurski, 3 yard rush PAT – Snyder (kick)	12:57
Third Quarter		
Chi.	Magnani, 36 yard pass from Luckman PAT – Snyder (kick)	2:59
Chi.	Magnani, 66 yard pass from Luckman PAT – Snyder (No Good)	11:33
Was.	Farkas, 17 yard pass from Baugh PAT – Masterson kick	13:44
Fourth Quarter		
Chi.	Benton, 29 yard pass from Luckman PAT – Snyder (kick)	3:30
Chi.	Clark, 16 yard pass from Luckman PAT – Snyder (kick)	11:50
Was.	Aguirre, 26 yard pass from Baugh PAT – Aguirre (kick)	12:02

TEAM STATISTICS

CHI.		WASH.
14	First Downs	11
169	Rushing Yardage	50
27	Passing – Attempts	24
15	– Completions	11
55.6	– Completion Pct.	45.8
276	– Yards	199
10.2	– Yards per Attempt	8.3
18.4	– Yards per Completion	18.1
0	– Had Intercepted	4
5	Punting – Number	5
32.0	– Average Yards	40.8
3	Punt Returns – Number	2
60	– Yards	37
20.0	– Average Yards	18.5
2	Kickoff Returns – Number	7
21	– Yards	107
10.5	– Average Yards	15.3
0	Fumbles – Number	1
0	– Times Lost Ball	0
9	Penalties – Number	3
81	– Yards Penalized	35

1944

December 17, at New York
(Attendance 46,016)

One Decoy and a Lot of Defense

Although the Giants had beaten them 24-0 only four weeks earlier, the Packers won the NFL championship by downing New York 14-7 in a strong defensive battle. The Giants got next to nothing out of runner Bill Paschal, who hurt his ankle in the final game of the regular season, so they relied on their defense to keep them in the game. The Packers knew that the Giants would have to double-team end Don Hutson, so they wisely used him as a decoy most of the afternoon and hit at the weakened sectors of the New York defense. After a scoreless first quarter, the Packers returned a New York punt to the Giant 48-yard line to start a drive at the beginning of the second period. On the first play, Joe Laws broke through the line for 20 yards, and Ted Fritsch ran 27 yards down to the one on the next play. The Giants held firm for three plays, but Fritsch plunged over on fourth down for the touchdown. Later in the quarter they started another drive from their own 38-yard line. On third and three, Irv Comp hit Hutson with a pass good for 24 yards down to the New York 30, and three plays later, with the Giants concentrating on Hutson, Comp hit Fritsch with a pass which he ran untouched all the way to the end zone. Hutson added the extra point after both touchdowns to give Green Bay a 14-0 bulge at the half. The teams traded punts and interceptions through the third quarter until a long pass from ex-Packer Arnie Herber to Frank Liebel gave the Giants a first down on the Green Bay one-yard line when the period ended. On the first play of the final quarter, Ward Cuff drove in for New York's only touchdown of the day, with the extra point making the count 14-7. The Giants launched a final drive to tie the game late in the period, only to have a long pass by Herber intercepted by Paul Duhart on the 20-yard line.

SCORING

GREEN BAY	0	14	0	0–14
NEW YORK	0	0	0	7– 7

Second Quarter		
G.B.	Fritsch, 1 yard rush PAT – Hutson (kick)	2:26
G.B.	Fritsch, 28 yard pass from Comp PAT – Hutson (kick)	13:43
Fourth Quarter		
N.Y.	Cuff, 1 yard rush PAT – Strong (kick)	0:03

TEAM STATISTICS

N.Y.		G.B.
9	First Downs – Total	13
6	– by Rushing	10
2	– by Passing	3
1	– by Penalty	0
2	Fumbles – Number	2
0	– Times Lost Ball	0
11	Penalties – Number	4
90	– Yards Penalized	48

INDIVIDUAL STATISTICS

NEW YORK	No	Yds	Avg.	GREEN BAY	No	Yds	Avg.
RUSHING							
Cuff	12	76	6.3	Fritsch	18	59	3.3
Livingston	12	22	1.8	Laws	13	72	5.5
Paschal	2	4	2.0	Comp	7	42	6.0
Sulaitis	1	–1	–1.0	Duhart	7	15	2.1
	27	101	3.7	Perkins	2	–4	–2.0
					47	184	3.9
RECEIVING							
Liebel	3	70	23.3	Hutson	2	46	23.0
Cuff	2	23	11.5	Fritsch	1	28	28.0
Livingston	2	21	10.5		3	74	24.7
Barker	1	0	0.0				
	8	114	14.3				
PUNTING							
Younce	10		41.0	L. Brock	6		36.8
				Fritsch	4		41.0
					10		38.5
PUNT RETURNS							
Cuff	3	29	9.7	Comp	4	46	11.5
Livingston	1	2	2.0	Laws	3	37	12.3
	4	31	7.8	Duhart	1	5	5.0
					8	88	11.0
KICKOFF RETURNS							
Cuff	1	24	24.0	Laws	1	9	9.0
Livingston	1	22	22.0				
Herber	1	17	17.0				
Sulaitis	1	16	16.0				
	4	79	19.8				
INTERCEPTION RETURNS							
Younce	1	5	5.0	Laws	3	28	9.3
Livingston	1	0	0.0	Duhart	1	0	0.0
Hein	1	–3	–3.0		4	28	7.0
	3	2	0.7				

PASSING

NEW YORK	Att	Comp	Comp Pct.	Yds	Int	Yds/ Att.	Yds/ Comp	Yards Lost Tackled
Herber	22	8	36.4	114	4	5.2	14.3	3–16
GREEN BAY								
Comp	10	3	30.0	74	3	7.4	24.7	2–21
L. Brock	1	0	0.0	0	0	–	–	
	11	3	27.3	74	3	6.7	24.7	2–21

1945

December 16, at Cleveland
(Attendance 32,178)

Goal Posts and Crossbars

As young Bob Waterfield led his Cleveland Rams against the Washington Redskins and veteran passing star Sammy Baugh, a strong wind whipping across the field directly figured in the first score of the game and eventual outcome. Early in the first quarter the Skins stopped a Cleveland drive on the five-yard line. Baugh then faded back into his end zone to throw a long pass, but when he let it fly a gust of wind blew it into the goal post. The ball bounced back into the end zone, which was a safety under the rules then in effect. The 2-0 lead held up through the first quarter, but Baugh didn't; bruised ribs knocked him out of action in the opening period, and he played only a few minutes in the second half. Frankie Filchock took over at tailback and hit Steve Bagarus with a 38-yard touchdown pass, but Cleveland took a 9-7 lead before the half on a Waterfield to Jim Benton pass covering 37 yards. Waterfield's extra-point try hit the crossbar, bounced up in the air and dropped over, giving the Rams a point which proved to be the winning margin, as both teams scored a touchdown in the third period although Cleveland missed the conversion to give them a final 15-14 victory.

SCORING

WASHINGTON	0	7	7	0–14
CLEVELAND	2	7	6	0–15

First Quarter	
Cle.	Safety – Automatic; Baugh's pass from inside of end zone hit goal post.
Second Quarter	
Was.	Bagarus, 38 yard pass from Filchock PAT – Aguirre (kick)
Cle.	Benton, 37 yard pass from Waterfield PAT – Waterfield (kick)
Third Quarter	
Cle.	Gillette, 53 yard pass from Waterfield PAT – Waterfield (No Good)
Was.	Seymour, 8 yard pass from Filchock PAT – Aguirre (kick)

TEAM STATISTICS

CLE.		WASH.
14	First Downs	8
180	Rushing Yardage	35
27	Passing – Attempts	20
14	– Completions	9
51.9	– Completion Pct.	45.0
192	– Yards	179
7.1	– Yards per Attempt	9.0
13.7	– Yards per Completion	19.9
2	– Had Intercepted	2
8	Punting – Number	7
38	– Average Yards	36
1	Fumbles Lost	1
60	Yards Penalized	34

INDIVIDUAL STATISTICS

CLEVELAND	No	Yds	Avg.	WASHINGTON	No	Yds	Avg.
KICKOFF RETURNS							
Greenwood	2	33	16.5	Condit	1	34	34.0
Nemeth	1	5	5.0	Bagarus	1	24	24.0
	3	38	12.7		2	58	29.0
INTERCEPTION RETURNS							
West	1	23	23.0	Aldrich	2	11	5.5
Reisz	1	15	15.0				
	2	38	19.0				

Use Name (Nicknames) – Positions	Team by Year	See Section	Hgt	Wgt	College	Int	Pts
Abbruzzino, Frank C-BB-LB	31Bkn 33Cin		6'	190	Colgate		
Adams, Chet DT-OT-OE-DE	39-42Cle 43GB 44-45MS	5	6'3"	233	Ohio U.	1	173
	46-48CleAA 49BufAA 50NYY						
Adams, Henry C-LB	39ChiC		6'1"	190	Pittsburgh		
Adams, Neal OE-DE	42-44NYG 45MS 46-47BknAA	2	6'3"	195	Arkansas	1	54
42-43 played in N.B.L.							
Adams, Verlin DE-T-G-OE-LB	43-45NYG		6'	205	Morris Harvey	1	
Adkins, Bob BB-DE-G-LB	40-41GB 42-44MS 45GB		6'1"	213	Marshall	2	16
Agee, Sam FB-DB	38-39ChiC	2	6'1"	218	Vanderbilt		12
Aquirre, Joe OE-DE	41,43-45Was 46-49LA-AA	2 5	6'4"	225	St. Mary's		310
Aiello, Tony WB-DB	44Det 44Bkn		5'6"	165	Youngstown		
Akin, Len G-LB	42ChiB 43-45MS		5'11"	207	Baylor	1	
Akins, Frank FB-LB	43-46Was	2	5'10"	208	Washington State		42
Albanese, Vannie FB-DB-BB-LB	37-38Bkn	2	6'	184	Syracuse		
Albrecht, Art T-C-LB	42Pit 43ChiC 44Bos 45MS		6'1"	203	Wisconsin		
Aldrich, Ki C-LB-G	39-40ChiC 41-42Was 43-44MS		6'	207	Texas Christian	7	19
	45-47Was						
Alfonse, Julie WB-DB-TB	37-38Cle	2	5'8"	180	Minnesota		12
Alford, Gene BB-DB-WB-FB-LB	31-33Port 34C-S		5'9"	177	Texas Tech		12
Alfson, Warren G-LB	42-45MS		6'	198	Nebraska	2	
Allman, Bob OE-DE	36ChiB			198	Michigan State		
Allton, Joe T	42ChiC 43-45MS		6'2"	235	Oklahoma	1	
Ananis, Vito HB-DB	45Was		5'10"	195	Boston College		
Anderson, Bill DE	45Bos		6'2"	190	West Virginia		
Anderson, Hunk G	22-25ChiB HC42-45ChiB		5'11"	195	Notre Dame		
Anderson, Stan T-OE-DE	40-41Cle 41Det 42-45MS		6'2"	218	Stanford		
Anderson, Winnie OE-DE	36NYG		6'	185	Colgate		
Andrako, Steve C-LB	40Was 41-45MS		6'	210	Ohio State		
Andrews, Jabby WB-DB	34C-S			200	Texas		
Andruskina, Sig G	37Bkn		5'8"	187	Detroit		
Apolskis, Chuck OE-DE	39ChiB		6'2"	207	DePaul		
Apsit, Marger BB-LB	31Fra 31Bkn 32GB 33Bos		5'11"	205	Southern Calif.		
Arena, Tony C-LB	42Det 43-45MS		6'	200	Michigan State		
Arenz, Arnie BB-LB	34Bos		6'2"	215	St. Louis		
Ariail, Gump OE-DE	34Bkn 34C-S		5'11"	205	Auburn		
Armstrong, Bill G	43Bkn		6'1"	210	U. C. L. A.		
Arndt, Al G	35Pit		5'11"	205	S. Dakota State		
Arnold, Jay HB-DB-BB-WB-LB	37-40Phi 41Pit	2	6'1"	210	Texas	2	39
Artman, Corwan T	31NYG 32Bos 33Pit		6'2"	240	Stanford		
Artoe, Lee T	40-42ChiB 43-44MS 45ChiB 46-47LA-AA	5	6'3"	234	Santa Clara,		31
	48BalAA				California		
Aspatore, Ed T-G	34C-S 34ChiB 34C-S		6'1"	220	Marquette		
Atty, Alex G	39Cle		5'8"	216	West Virginia		
Auer, Howie T	33ChiC 33Phi		6'1"	205	Michigan		
Augusterfer, Gene BB-DB	35Pit		5'9"	180	Catholic		
Austin, Jim OE-DE	37-38Bkn 39Det	2	6'2"	199	St. Mary's		6
Avedisian, Chuck G-LB	42-44NYG		5'9"	203	Providence	1	12
Babartsky, Al T	38-39,41-42ChiC 43-45ChiB		6'	223	Fordham		6
Bach, Joe	HC35-36,52-53Pit				Notre Dame		
Badgro, Red OE-DE	27NYY 30-35NYG 36Bkn	2	6'	191	Southern Calif.		24
29-30 played major league baseball							
Bailey, Bill OE-DE	40-41Bkn 42-45MS		6'3"	213	Duke		
Bailey, Howard (Screeno) T	35Phi		6'	205	Tennessee		
Baisi, Al G	40-41ChiB 42-45MS 46ChiB 47Phi		6'	217	West Virginia		
Baker, Conway T-G	36-43ChiC 44C-P 45ChiC	5	5'11"	228	Centenary		31
Balasz, Frank FB-LB-DB	39-41GB 41ChiC 42-44MS 45ChiC	2	6'2"	212	Iowa		7
Baltzell, Dick WB-DB	35Bos		5'11"	205	Southwestern –		
					(Kansas)		
Banas, Steve BB-DB	35Det 35Phi		6'	190	Notre Dame		
Bandura, John OE-DE	43Bkn		6'	206	Southwestern La.		
Banet, Herb TB-HB-DB	37GB		6'2"	200	Manchester		
Banjavic, Emil WB-DB	42Det 43-45MS		6'1"	194	Arizona	1	6
Barber, Ernie C-LB	45Was		6'1"	225	San Francisco		
Barber, Jim T	35-36Bos 37-41Was 42-45MS		6'3"	223	San Francisco		
Barber, Mark FB-LB	37Cle		5'11"	192	S. Dakota State		
Barbour, Elmer BB-LB	45NYG		6'1"	200	Wake Forest		
Barker, Hubert BB-LB	43-45NYG		5'10"	193	Arkansas		
Barle, Lou (Fats) BB-DB-LB	38Det 39Cle		6'1"	205	none		
39-43 played in N. B. L.							
Barnard, Hap OE-DE	38NYG		6'2"	190	Central St. – Okla.		
Barnett, Solon T-G	45-46GB		6'1"	235	Baylor		
Barnhart, Dan (Chief) TB-DB	34Phi		6'2"	200	Centenary		
Barnum, Len (Feets, Bear Tracks) QB-DB-FB-WB-HB		12 45	6'	200	West Va. Wesleyan	3	63
	38-40NYG 41-42Phi 43-45MS						
Barrager, Nate C-LB-G	30Min 30-31Fra 31-32,34-35GB		6'	210	Southern Calif.		
Barrett, Emmett C-LB	42NYG 43-44MS		6'2"	192	Portland		
Barrett, Jeff OE-DE	36-38Bkn	2	6'1"	182	Louisiana State		36
Bartholomew, Sam FB-LB	41Phi 42-45MS		5'11"	188	Tennessee	1	
Bartlett, Earl HB-DB	39Pit		6'	200	Centre		
Bartos, Hank G	38Was		6'1"	216	North Carolina		
Basca, Mike HB-DB	41Phi 42-44MS – killed in action		5'8"	170	Villanova	3	18
Basrak, Mike C-LB	37-38Pit		6'2"	220	Duquesne		
Bassi, Dick G-LB	37Was 38-39ChiB 40Phi 41Pit		5'11"	214	Santa Clara	1	6
	42-45MS 46-47SF-AA						
Bassman, Reds TB-HB-DB	36Phi		5'11"	180	Ursinus		
Batinski, Stan G	41Det 42MS 43-47Det 48Bos 49NYB		5'10"	215	Temple		
Battles, Cliff TB-DB-FB	32-36Bos 37Was HC46-47Bkn AA	12	6'1"	194	West Va. Wesleyan		166
Baugh, Sammy QB-TB-DB	37-52Was HC60-61NYA HC64HouA	12 4	6'2"	182	Texas Christian	28	55
Bausch, Frank (Pete) C-LB	34-36Bos 37-40ChiB 41 Phi		6'3"	220	Kansas		
Bausch, Jim FB-WB-LB-DB	33ChiC 33Cin		6'1"	200	Kansas		
Baze, Winnie WB-TB-DB	37Phi		5'11"	190	Texas Tech		
Becker, Wayland OE-DE	34ChiB 34-35Bkn 36-38GB 39Pit	2	6'	198	Marquette		12
Bedore, Tom G-LB	44Was		5'11"	193	none		
Beebe, Keith BB-DB	44NYG		5'9"	180	Occidental	3	
Behan, Charlie OE-DE	42Det 43-44MS – killed in action		6'3"	195	Northern Illinois		
Beinor, Ed T-DE	40-41ChiC 41-42Was 43-45MS		6'2"	222	Notre Dame		
Belichick, Steve FB-LB	41Det 42-45MS	2	5'8"	190	Case Reserve	1	18
Bell, Bert	HC38-40Phi HC41Pit				Pennsylvania		
Bell, Kay T	37ChiB 42NYG		6'2"	220	Washington State		
Bellinger, Bob G	34-35NYG		5'11"	216	Gonzaga		
Bennett, Chuck BB-DB	30Port 33ChiC		5'9"	198	Indiana		
Benson, Harry G	35Phi		5'10"	218	Western Maryland		
Benton, Jim (Big Jim) OE-DE	38-40,42Cle 43ChiB	2	6'3"	200	Arkansas		288
	44-45Cle 46-47LA						
Berezney, Paul T	42-44GB 46MiaAA		6'2"	221	Fordham		
Bergerson, Gil G-T	32-33ChiB 33ChiC 35-36Bkn		6'6"	245	Oregon State		
Bergman, Dutch	HC43Was				Notre Dame		
Bernard, Chuck C-LB	34Det		6'3"	225	Michigan		
Bernard, Dave LB-BB	44-45Cle		5'10"	194	Mississippi		
Berner, Mil C-LB	33Cin		6'2"	204	Syracuse		
Berry, Connie Mack DE-OE	39Det 40Cle 42-46ChiB	2	6'3"	215	N. Carolina State		60
39-46 played in N.B.L.	47ChiAA						
Berry, Gil TB-DB	35ChiC		5'10"	178	Illinois		
Bertagnolli, Libero G-LB	42ChiC 43-44MS 45ChiC		5'9"	189	Washington-St. L		
Bettencourt, Larry C-LB	33GB		5'11"	205	St. Mary's		
28, 31-32 played major league baseball							
Bettridge, John FB-LB	37ChiB 37Cle		5'10"	188	Ohio State		
Bezdek, Hugo	HC37-38Cle				none		
17-19 manager – major league baseball							
Biancone, John TB-DB	36Bkn		5'6"	165	Oregon State		
Bilbo, Jon T-G	38-39ChiC		6'	195	Mississippi		
Bilda, Dick TB-DB	44GB		6'	200	Marquette	1	
Billock, Frank T	37Pit		6'	230	St. Mary's (Minn.)		
Binotto, John HB-DB	42Pit 42Phi 43-45MS		5'10"	185	Duquesne		1
Birlem, Keith DB-OE-WB	39ChiC 39Was		5'11"	198	San Jose State		
	40-42MS – killed in action						
Bjork, Del T	37-38ChiB		6'1"	218	Oregon		
Bjorklund, Bob C-LB	41Phi 42-45MS		6'2"	225	Minnesota		
Blackwell, Hal HB-DB	45ChiC		6'1"	205	South Carolina		
Blazine, Tony T	35-40ChiC 41NYG		6'	232	Ill. Wesleyan		6
Bleeker, Mel HB-DB	44-46Phi 47LA	2	5'11"	189	Southern Calif.	2	66
Blessing, Paul OE-DE	44Det		6'4"	215	Kearney State		
Blondin, Tom G	33Cin		6'	195	West Va. Wesleyan		
Blood (born McNally), Johnny HB-BB-DB-TB	25-26Mil	12	6'1"	187	St. John's – Minn.		92
	26-27Dul 28Pott 29-33GB 34Pit 35-36GB PC37-39Pit						
Blozis, Al (The Human Howitzer) T	42-44NYG		6'6"	250	Georgetown		6
	MS – killed in action						
Blumer, Herb T-G	25-30, 33ChiC		6'1"	200	Missouri		
Bodenger, Maury G	31-33Port 34Det		5'10"	203	Tulane		
Bohlmann, Frank G	42ChiC		5'11"	212	Marquette		
Bond, Chuck T	37-38Was		6'2"	236	Washington		
Bond, Rink BB-LB	38Was 39Pit		5'10"	200	Washington		
Bonelli, Ernie FB-LB-HB-DB	45ChiC 46Pit	2	5'11"	194	Pittsburgh	1	
Boone, Jack WB-DB	42Cle 43-45MS		5'11"	175	Elon	1	6
Booth, Clarence T	43ChiC 44C-P		6'	223	S. M. U.		
Booth, Dick WB-DB	41Det 42-44MS 45Det	2	6'1"	190	Case Reserve	1	12
Borak, Tony DE	38GB		6'1"	190	Creighton		
Borden, Les OE-DE	35NYG		6'	185	Fordham		
Bostick, Lew G	39Cle		6'	197	Alabama		2
Boswell, Ben T	33Port 34Bos		6'	245	Texas Christian		
Bova, Tony OE-DB-DE-QB-HB	42Pit 43P-P 44C-P 45-57Pit	12	6'1"	190	St. Francis – Pa.	1	44
Bowdoin, Jim G-T	28-31GB 32NYG 32Bkn 33Port 34Bkn		6'1"	218	Alabama		
Boyd, Sam OE-DE	39-40Pit	2	6'1"	188	Baylor		12
Boyer, Verdi G	36Bkn		5'10"	195	U. C. L. A.		
Boyle, Knuckles T	34NYG		5'11"	232	none		
Braden, Dave G-LB	45ChiC		6'	210	Marquette		
Bradley, Hal OE-DE	38ChiC 38-39Was 39ChiC		6'4"	205	Elon		
Brahm, Larry G-LB	42Cle		5'10"	204	Temple		
Braidwood, Chuck OE-DE	30Port 31Cle 32ChiC 33Cin		6'	210	Tenn. – Chattanooga		
Bray, Mule T	35-36Pit		6'2"	220	S. M. U.		
Brazell, Carl BB-DB	38Cle		5'10"	195	Baylor		
Breeden, Bill HB-OE-DB	37Pit		6'1"	210	Oklahoma		
Brennan, Jack G	39GB		6'1"	204	Michigan		
Brennan, Leo T	42Phi 43-45MS		6'	210	Holy Cross		
Brett, Jeep OE-DE	36ChiC 36-37Pit	2	6'2"	203	Washington State		6
Brian, Bill T-C-LB	35-36Phi		6'2"	210	Gonzaga		
Bridges, Frank	HC44Bkn				Baylor		
Brill, Hal TB-DB	39Det		5'10"	175	Wichita State		
Britt, Eddie DB-TB-FB	36Bos 37Was 38Bkn	12	6'2"	202	Holy Cross		
Britt, Maury OE-DE	41Det 42-45MS – arm amputated		6'4"	210	Arkansas		6
Britt, Rankin DE	39Phi		6'2"	206	Texas A & M		
Brock, Charley C-LB	39-47GB		6'2"	207	Nebraska	17	24
Brock, Lou HB-DB-FB-TB	40-45GB	12 34	6'	195	Purdue	8	98
Brodnicki, Chuck T	34Bkn		6'2"	225	Villanova		
Brovelli, Angie DB-TB-FB-HB-BB-LB	33-34Pit		6'	193	St. Mary's		20
Brown, Bill BB-DB-LB	43-44Bkn 45Pit		6'	202	Texas Tech	1	
Brown, Tom OE-DE	42Pit 43-45MS		6'2"	216	William & Mary		6
Bruckner, Les FB-LB	45ChiC		6'1"	195	Michigan State		
Bruder, Hank BB-DB-LB-TB-FB-HB	31-39GB 40Pit		6'	199	Northwestern		52
Brumbaugh, Boyd FB-TB-DB-HB	38-39Bkn 39-41Pit	12	5'11"	195	Duquesne		36
Brumbaugh, Carl QB-DB-TB-BB	30-34,36ChiB 37Cle 37Bkn	12	5'10"	176	Florida		25
	37-38ChiB						
Brumley, Bob WB-DB	45Det		6'	200	Rice		
Bucchianeri, Amadeo G	41,44-45GB		5'10"	212	Indiana		
Buckler, Bill G-T-OE-DE	26-28,31-33ChiB		6'	230	Alabama		
Bucklew, Phil OE-DE	37-38Cle		6'1"	205	Xavier – Ohio		
Buda, Carl G	45Pit		5'11"	220	Creighton, Tulsa		
Buhler, Larry FB-HB-BB-DB-LB-DE	39-41GB	2	6'2"	210	Minnesota		
Buivid, Ray QB-HB-DB	37-38ChiB	12	6'1"	195	Marquette		6
Bukant, Joe (Buckin' Joe) FB-TB-HB-LB-DB	38-40Phi	12	6'	215	Washington – St. L.		24
	42-43ChiC 44-45MS						
Bultman, Art C-LB	31Bkn 32-34GB		6'2"	201	Marquette		
Burdick, Lloyd (Tiny, Shorty) T	31-32ChiB 33Cin		6'4"	257	Illinois		
Burgeis, Glen T	45ChiB		6'1"	220	Tulsa		
Burleson, John T-G	33Port 33Pit 33Cin		6'2"	237	S. M. U.		
Burmeister, Forrest G-T	37Cle		6'3"	215	Purdue		
Burnell, Max HB-DB	44ChiB				Notre Dame		
Burnett, Dale WB-DB	30-39NYG	2	6'1"	187	Kansas St. Teach.		102
Burnett, Ray TB-DB	38ChiC				none		
Burnette, Tom BB-LB	38Pit 38Phi		6'1"	194	North Carolina		
Busby, Sherrill DE	40Bkn 41-45MS		6'2"	200	Troy State		
Bushby, Tom TB-WB-DB	34C-S		5'10"	200	Kansas State		
Busich, Sam OE-DE	36Bos 37Cle 43Det	2	6'3"	189	Ohio State		10
Busler, Ray T	40-41ChiC 42-44MS 45ChiC		6'1"	222	Marquette		
Buss, Art T	34-35ChiB 36-37Phi		6'3"	219	Michigan State		
Bussey, Young DB-QB	40-41ChiB	1	5'9"	184	Louisiana State	2	
	42-44MS – missing in action						
Butcher, Wendell BB-LB-FB-DB	38-42Bkn	2	6'1"	197	Gustavus-Adolphus		6
Butler, Frank C-LB-T	34-36,38GB		6'3"	237	Michigan State		
Butler, Johnny HB-DB-TB	43P-P 44C-P 44Bkn 45Phi	12	5'10"	185	Tennessee	4	36
Bykowski, Frank G	40Pit		6'	205	Purdue		
Cabrelli, Larry OE-DE-DB	41-42Phi 43P-P 44-47Phi	2	5'11"	194	Colgate	2	36

Use Name (Nicknames) – Positions	Team by Year	See Section	Hgt	Wgt	College	Int	Pts
Caddel, Ernie WB-DB	33Port 34-38Det	2	6'2"	198	Stanford		156
Cafego, George (Bad News) QB-TB-DB-HB	40Bkn 41-42MS 43Bkn 43Was 44-45Bos	12 4	5'10"	180	Tennessee	2	6
Cagle, Chris (Red) TB-DB-FB	30-32NYG 33-34Bkn	1	5'10"	174	Army, Southwestern La.		
Cahill, Ronnie TB-DB	43ChiC 44-45MS	12	5'8"	170	Holy Cross		
Calligaro, Len BB-LB	44NYG		5'11"	190	Wisconsin		6
Callihan, Bill BB-DB-LB-FB	40-45Det	2 5	6'3"	217	Nebraska	6	55
Calvelli, Tony C-LB-G	39-40Det 41-45MS 47SF-AA		5'10"	189	Stanford	1	6
Campbell, Don (Pop) T	39-40Pit		6'	225	Carnegie-Mellon		
Campbell, Glen (Turtle) OE-DE	29-33NYG 34IL 35Pit		5'11"	207	Kansas St. Teach.		6
Campiglio, Bob TB-DB	32SI 33Bos		6'1"	185	W. Liberty State		
Campofreda, Nick C-DT	44Was		6'1"	240	West. Maryland		
Canale, Rocco T-G	43P-P 44-45Phi 46-47Bos		5'11"	240	Boston College		
Cannella, John G-C-LB	33-34NYG 34Bkn		6'1"	199	Fordham		
Cantor, Leo DB-HB-FB	42NYG 43-44MS 45ChiC	12 4	6'	195	U.C.L.A.	7	42
Cara, Mac OE-DE	37-38Pit		5'10"	193	N. Carolina State		
Caranci, Roland T	44NYG		6'1"	227	Colorado		
Cardwell, Joe T-DE	37-38Pit		6'3"	235	Duke		
Cardwell, Lloyd WB-DB-FB	37-43Det	2	6'2"	195	Nebraska	2	78
Carlson, Hal G	37ChiC				DePaul		
Carlson, Zuck G-T	29-37ChiB		6'	205	Oregon State		
Carnelly, Ray TB-HB-DB	39Bkn		6'2"	187	Carnegie-Mellon		
Carpe, Joe T	26-27Fra 28Pott 29Bos 33Phi				Millikin		
Carroll, Vic T-C-G-LB-OE	36Bos 37-42Was 43-47NYG		6'4"	231	Nevada	4	32
Carson, Howie HB-DB	44Cle		6'1"	190	Illinois		
Carter, Joe OE-DE	33-40Phi 42GB 43MS 44Bkn 45ChiC	2	6'1"	201	S.M.U.		139
Carter, Ross (Timber Beast) G-C-LB	36-39ChiC		6'	199	Oregon		
Casey, Eddie B	20Buf HC35Bos				Harvard		
Casper, Cy DB-BB-TB-WB	34GB 34C-S 35Pit	1	6'	190	Texas Christian		18
Cassiano, Dick TB-HB-DB	40Bkn 41-45MS	12	5'11"	175	Pittsburgh		12
Cavosie, John OE-DE-FB-LB-BB-DB-T	31-33Port		6'	207	Butler		10
Cawthorn, Pete	HC43-44Bkn				Texas Tech		
Caywood, Les G	26KC 26Buf 27Cle 27Pott 27NYG 28Det 29-30NYG 31ChiC 31-32NYG 32Bkn 33Cin 34C-S		6'	230	St. John's–Minn.		
Cemore, Tony G	41Phi 42-45MS		6'	210	Creighton	1	
Chalmers, George C-LB	33Bkn		6'	196	N.Y.U.		
Chamberlain, Garth G	45Pit		6'	215	Brigham Young		
Cherne, Hal T-C-LB	33Bos		6'	230	DePaul		
Cherry, Ed FB-DB	38-39ChiC 39Pit		6'	208	Hardin-Simmons		
Cherundolo, Chuck C-LB	37-39Cle 40Phi 41-42Pit 43-44MS 45-48Pit		6'1"	215	Penn State	4	
Chesbro, Red G	38Cle		5'11"	190	Colgate		
Chesney, Chet C-LB	39-40ChiB 41-45MS		6'2"	227	DePaul		
Chickerneo, John (Chick) BB-LB	42NYG 43-45MS		6'1"	205	Pittsburgh	1	
Chisick, Andy C-LB	40-41ChiC 42-45MS		6'1"	207	Villanova	1	
Christiansen, Marty FB-DB	40ChiC	2	6'	200	Minnesota		6
Christensen, Frank BB-DB-FB-LB	34-37Det	1	6'1"	199	Utah		26
Christensen, George T-G	31-33Port 34-38Det		6'2"	241	Oregon		
Cibulas, Joe T	45Pit		6'	220	Duquesne		
Ciccone, Ben (Scaggie)	34-35Pit 42ChiC		5'10"	207	Duquesne		
Clair, Frank OE-DE	41Was 42-45MS		6'1"	204	Ohio State		
Clancy, Stu DB-FB-WB-TB-BB-LB	30Nwk 31-32SI 32-35NYG		5'10"	192	Holy Cross		24
Clark, Algy BB-DB	30Bkn 31Cle 32Bos 33Cin PC34C-S 34Phi		6'	190	Ohio State		18
Clark, Beryl TB-DB	40ChiC	12 4	6'	200	Oklahoma		3
Clark, Dutch TB-DB	31-32Port 33VR 34-36,PC37-38Det HC39-42Cle	12 5	6'	182	Colorado College		254
Clark, Harry HB-DB	40-43ChiB 44-45MS 46-48LA-AA 48ChiAA	23	6'	189	West Virginia	9	139
Clark, Jimmy FB-HB-DB	33-34Pit		5'9"	174	Pittsburgh		6
Clark, Potsy	HC30-33Port HC34-36Det HC37-39Bkn HC40Det				Illinois		
Clark, Wayne OE-DE	44Det		6'3"	210	Utah		
Clay, Boyd T	40-42,44Cle 45MS		6'1"	220	Tennessee		8
Clay, Roy WB-DB	44NYG		6'	185	Colorado State		
Clemens, Cal BB-DB	36GB		6'1"	195	Southern Calif.		1
Clemons, Ray G	39Det		6'	215	Central St.–Okla.		
Coffee, Pat TB-DB	37-38ChiC	12	5'11"	183	Louisiana State		18
Cole, John (King) FB-LB-BB	38,40Phi	2	5'9"	197	St. Joseph's–Pa.		6
Cole, Pete G-T	37-40NYG 41-45MS		5'11"	222	Trinity (Texas)		
Colella, Tom DB-HB-TB	42-43Det 44-45Cle 46-48CleAA 49BufAA	1234	6'	187	Canisius	26	93
Collins, Paul (Rip) OE-DE	32-35Bos		6'1"	198	Pittsburgh		
Collins, Paul QB	45ChiC		5'11"	178	Missouri		
Combs, Bill OE-DB	42Phi 43-45MS		5'11"	183	Purdue		6
Commisa, Vince G	44Bos		5'9"	190	Notre Dame		
Comstock, Rudy G	23Can 24Cle 25Can 26-29Fra 30NYG 31-33GB			208	Georgetown		
Concannon, Rick G	32SI 34-36Bos		6'	217	N.Y.U.		
Condit, Merl (Merlyn the Magician) HB-DB	40Pit 41-43Bkn 44MS 45Was 46Pit	12345	5'11"	187	Carnegie-Mellon	10	125
Conkright, Bill (Red) C-LB-OE-DE	37-38ChiB 39-42Cle 43Was 43Bkn 44Cle HC62OakA		6'1"	203	Oklahoma	4	6
Conlee, Gerry C-LB	38Cle 43Det 44-45MS 46-47SF-AA		5'11"	203	St. Mary's	1	
Conti, Enio G	41-42Phi 43P-P 44-45Phi		5'11"	204	Bucknell	1	
Conzelman, Jimmy BB-DB	20Dec 21-22RI 23-24Mil 25-26Det 27-29Prov HC40-42ChiC 43-45MS HC46-48ChiC		6'	180	Washington–St. L		
Cook, Dave DB-WB-FB	34-36ChiC 36Bkn		6'2"	203	Illinois		10
Cook, Leon T	42Phi				Northwestern		
Coon, Ty G	40Bkn 41-45MS		6'	215	N. Carolina State		
Cooper, Bud TB-FB-DB	37Cle		6'1"	204	Penn State		
Cooper, Hal G	37Det		5'10"	207	Detroit		
Cooper, Norm C-LB	37-38Bkn		6'4"	210	Howard (Ala.)		
Cooper, Sam T	33Pit				Geneva		
Cope, Frank T	38-47NYG		6'2"	225	Santa Clara		6
Coppage, Al OE-DE-DB	40-42ChiC 43-45MS 46CleAA 47BufAA	2	6'1"	195	Oklahoma		18
Corbett, George QB-HB-DB	32-38ChiB	2	5'9"	179	Millikin		15
Corbo, Tom G-LB	44Cle		5'11"	210	Duquesne	1	
Cordill, Ollie WB-DB	40Cle 41-45MS	2	6'2"	190	Rice		12
Corgan, Mike FB-LB	43Det 44-45MS		5'10"	188	Notre Dame		
Corzine, Red (Lefty) LB-BB-FB	33Cin 34C-S 35-37NYG 38ChiB	2	6'	213	Davis & Elkins		30
Cosner, Don WB-DB	39ChiC		6'2"	200	Montana State		
Coston, Zed C-LB	39Phi		6'2"	222	Texas A&M		
Cotton, Russ BB-LB	41Bkn 42Pit 43-45MS		6'2"	196	Texas–El Paso	1	
Courtney, Gerry TB-DB	42Bkn 43-45MS		6'	195	Syracuse	1	6
Crabtree, Clem T-G	40-41Det 42-45MS		6'3"	225	Wake Forest		

Use Name (Nicknames) – Positions	Team by Year	See Section	Hgt	Wgt	College	Int	Pts
Craig, Larry (Superman) BB-DE-LB-OE-DB	39-49GB	2	6'1"	211	South Carolina	1	6
Crain, Milt FB-LB	44Bos	2	6'2"	225	Baylor	1	
Crakes, Joe OE-DE	33Cin		6'1"	205	South Dakota		
Crass, Bill FB-DB	37ChiC		6'	205	Louisiana State		
Crawford, Fred OE-DE-T	35ChiB		6'2"	200	Duke		
Crayne, Dick (Baldy) FB-DB	36-37Bkn	2	6'	205	Iowa		10
Creighton, Milan DE-OE-WB-DB	31-34,PC35-37,HC38ChiC		6'	190	Arkansas		
Crimmins, Bernie G-LB	45GB		5'11"	195	Notre Dame	1	6
Critchfield, Larry G	33Pit		5'11"	195	Grove City		
Croft, Abe OE-DB	44-45ChiB	2	6'	183	S.M.U.	1	12
Croft, Tiny T	42-47GB		6'3"	287	Ripon		
Croft, Win G	35Bkn 36Pit		5'11"	235	Utah		
Cronkhite, Doc OE-DE	34Bkn		6'5"	210	Kansas State		
Crow, Orien C-LB	33-34Bos		6'	220	Haskell Indian		
Crowder, Earl BB-LB	39ChiC 40Cle		6'	198	Oklahoma		
Crowley, Joe OE-DB	44-45Bos	2	6'	194	Dartmouth	2	18
Cuba, Paul T	33-35Phi		6'	212	Pittsburgh		
Cuff, Ward WB-DB-HB-FB	37-45NYG 46ChiC 47GB	23 5	6'1"	192	Marquette	11	417
Cumiskey, Frank OE-DE	37Bkn		6'2"	205	Ohio State		
Cuppoletti, Bree G	34-38ChiC 39Phi		5'10"	200	Oregon		
Daddio, Bill DE-OE	41-42ChiC 43-45MS 46BufAA	2 5	5'11"	207	Pittsburgh	1	52
Dailey, Ted OE-DE	33Pit		5'9"	170	Pittsburgh		
Damiani, Frank T	44NYG 45MS		6'1"	225	Manhattan		
Daniell, Averell T	37GB 37Bkn		6'3"	215	Pittsburgh		
Daniell, Jim T	45ChiB 46CleAA		6'2"	230	Ohio State		
Danowski, Ed QB-TB-DB	34-39,41NYG 42-45MS	12 4	6'1"	198	Fordham		24
Davidson, Bill HB-DB-TB-OE	37-39Pit	12	6'	182	Temple		24
Davis, Bill T	40-41ChiC 42MS 43Bkn 46MiaAA		6'1"	234	Texas Tech		6
Davis, Bob (Twenty Grand) HB-DB-TB	38Cle 42Phi 44-46Bos	123	6'	185	Kentucky	19	30
Davis, Corby FB-LB-DB-BB	38-39, 41-42Cle 43-45MS	2	5'11"	212	Indiana	1	32
Davis, Gaines G	36NYG		5'11"	230	Texas Tech		
Davis, Ray G-OE-DE	32-33Port 36ChiC			198	Howard (Ala.)		
Davis, Red TB-FB-DB-OE-DE	33Port 33Phi		5'11"	195	Geneva		10
Dawley, Fred FB-LB	44Det		5'9"	190	Michigan		
Deal, Rufus FB-DB	43-45MS		6'	205	Auburn		
DeCarbo, Nick G	33Pit		5'9"	185	Duquesne		
DeFilippo, Lou C-LB-DT	41NYG 42-44MS 45-47NYG		6'1"	230	Fordham		
Dell Isola, Johnny G-LB-C	34-40NYG		5'11"	201	Fordham		
DeMas, George G	32ST 34Bkn		6'	190	Wash. & Jefferson		
Dempsey, John T	34Phi 34Pit 37Phi		6'2"	225	Bucknell		
Dennerlein, Jerry T	37,40NYG		6'2"	240	St. Mary's		
Dennery, Vince OE-DE	41NYG 42-45MS		5'11"	190	Fordham		
DePascal, Carmine DB-OE	45Pit		6'	188	Wichita State		
DePaul, Henry G	45Pit		5'11"	225	Duquesne		
Deremer, Art C-LB	42Bkn 43-45MS		6'3"	208	Niagara		
DeSantis, Dan HB-DB	41Phi 42-45MS	2	6'	180	Niagara	2	1
Deskin, Versil OE-DE	35-39ChiC	2	6'	199	Drake		12
Diehl, Charlie T-G	30-31ChiC 34C-S				Idaho		
Diehl, Dave OE-DE	39-40,44-45Det	2	6'	195	Michigan State		30
Dietz, Lone Star	HC33-34Bos				Carlisle		
diFilippo, Dave G	41Phi 42-45MS		5'10"	210	Villanova		
Digris, Bernie T-G	43ChiB			212	Holy Cross		
Dilweg, Lavie OE-DE	26Mil 27-34GB	2	6'3"	199	Marquette		12
DiMelio, Luby	HC34Pit				Pittsburgh		
Disend, Leo (Moose) T	38-39Bkn 40GB		6'2"	224	Albright		
Dohrus, Pete T	41Bkn		6'	215	Carnegie-Mellon		
Dodson, Les TB-DB	41Pit		6'1"	180	Mississippi		
Doehring, John (Bull) HB-LB-TB-DB-QB	32-34ChiB 35Pit 36-37ChiB	2	6'	216	none		
Doell, Walt T	33Cin				Texas		
Doloway, Cliff OE-DE	35Pit		6'	215	Carnegie-Mellon		
Dolly, Dick OE-DE	41Pit 42-44MS 45Pit		6'3"	211	West Virginia		
Donelli, Al TB-HB-DB	41-42Pit 42Phi 43-45MS		5'7"	165	Duquesne	1	
Donelli, Buff	HC41Pit HC44Cle				Duquesne		
Dorais, Gus	HC43-47Det				Notre Dame		
D'Orazio, Joe T	44Det		5'11"	220	Ithaca		
Douds, Jap T-G	30Prov 30-31Port 32ChiC PC33-34Pit		5'10"	220	Wash. & Jefferson		
Dougherty, Phil C-LB	38ChiC		5'11"	185	Santa Clara		6
Douglas, Ben WB-DB	33Bkn		6'	185	Grinnell		6
Douglas, Bob FB-DB	38Pit		6'	195	Kansas State		
Dow, Ken FB-DB	41Was 42-45MS		5'10"	198	Oregon State		
Dow, Woody (Rowdy, Cub) BB-FB-DB-LB	38-40Phi	2	6'	195	W. Texas State		6
Dowd, Gerry C-LB	39Cle		6'	210	St. Mary's		6
Dowell, Mule FB-DB-LB	35-36ChiC	2	6'2"	206	Texas Tech		
Doyle, Ted T-G	38-42Pit 43P-P 44C-P 45Pit		6'2"	224	Nebraska	1	6
Drake, Johnny FB-DB-LB-WB	37-41Cle	2	6'1"	213	Purdue	2	164
Draveling, Leo (Firpo) T	33Cin		6'2"	210	Michigan		
Dreher, Fred OE-DE	38ChiB		6'3"	205	Denver		6
Druze, John OE-DE	38Bkn		6'	195	Fordham		
Dubzinski, Walt LB-C-G	43NYG 44Bos 45MS		5'10"	205	Boston College	1	
Dugan, Len C-LB	36NYG 37-39ChiC 39Pit		6'	218	Wichita State		
Duggan, Gil (Cactus Face) T	40NYG 41HO 42-43ChiC 44C-P 45ChiC 46LA-AA 47BufAA		6'3"	229	Oklahoma	1	
Duggins, George OE-DE	34ChiC		6'3"	200	Purdue		
Duhart, Paul HB-DB-QB	44GB 45Pit 45Bos	2	6'	180	Florida	4	30
Dunlap, Bob DB-QB	35ChiB 36NYG	1	6'1"	191	Oklahoma		
Dunn, Coye WB-DB	43Was		6'	198	Southern Calif.		
Dunstan, Elwyn T	38-39ChiC 39-41Cle		6'3"	238	Portland		6
Durko, John DE-OE	44Phi 45ChiC		6'4"	235	Albright		6
Dye, Les OE	44-45Was	2	6'1"	181	Syracuse		24
Eagle, Alex T	35Bkn		6'2"	220	Oregon		
Eakin, Kay QB-DB-WB-HB	40-41NYG 42-45MS 46MiaAA	12 4	6'	180	Arkansas	4	6
Eaton, Lou T	45NYG		6'2"	215	California		
Ebding, Harry (Irish) OE-DE-WB-DB	31-33Port 34-37Det	2	5'11"	199	St. Mary's		60
Eckl, Bob T	45ChiC		6'1"	233	Wisconsin		
Edwards, Bill (Big Bill)	HC41-42Det				Wittenberg		
Edwards, Marshall FB-LB	43Bkn				Wake Forest		
Edwards, Monk G-T-LB	40-42NYG 43-45MS 46NYG		6'3"	213	Baylor		
Edwards, Turk T	32-36Bos 37-40,HC46-48Was		6'2"	258	Washington State		6
Eibner, John T	41-42Phi 43-45MS 46Phi		6'2"	228	Kentucky		
Eiden, Ed C-LB	44Phi 44Det		6'	205	Scranton		

Use Name (Nicknames) – Positions	Team by Year	See Section	Hgt	Wgt	College	Int	Pts
Eliason, Don OE-DE	42Bkn 43-45MS 46Bos		6'2"	215	Hamline		
Elkins, Chief WB-DB	28-29Fra 29ChiC 33Cin				Haskell Indian		
Elkins, Ev WB-DB	40ChiC 41-45MS		5'11"	190	Marshall		
Ellis Drew T-FB	38-39Phi		6'1"	215	Texas Christian		
Ellis, John G	44Bkn		5'10"	212	Vanderbilt		
Ellstrom, Swede FB-DB-HB-LB	34Bos 34Phi 35Pit 36ChiC		6'1"	203	Oklahoma		6
Elser, Earl T	33Port 34C-S		6'1"	229	Butler		
Ely, Harold T	32ChiB 32-34Bkn		6'2"	265	Iowa		
Emerick, Bob T-G	34Det 37Cle		6'2"	225	Miami–Ohio		
Emerson, Ox G-LB-C	31-33Port 34-37Det 38Bkn		5'11"	200	Texas		
Emmons, Frank FB-HB-LB	40Phi 41-45MS	2	6'1"	213	Oregon		12
Engebretsen, Tiny G-T	32ChiB 33Pit 33ChiC 34Bkn	5	6'1"	238	Northwestern		88
	34-41GB						
Engelmann, Wuert DB-HB-BB-TB	30-33GB			195	S. Dakota State		12
Enich, Steve G	45ChiC		5'10"	212	Marquette		
Erdlitz, Dick HB-DB	42Phi 43-44MS 45Phi 46MiaAA	2 5	5'10"	181	Northwestern	3	48
Erickson, Bud C-LB	38-39Was		6'1"	198	Washington		
Evans, Dick OE-DB-DE	40GB 41-42ChiC 43GB 44-45MS	2	6'3"	205	Iowa		
Evans, Lon G-T	33-37GB		6'2"	223	Texas Christian		
Evans, Murray BB-DB	42-43Det 44-45MS		6'1"	205	Hardin-Simmons		
Fagiolo, Carl G	44Phi		6'	200	none		
Falaschi, Nello (Flash) BB-LB	38-41NYG 42-45MS		6'	195	Santa Clara	1	
Falkenstein, Tony FB-LB-BB	43GB 44Bkn 44Bos 45MS	2	5'10"	205	St. Mary's		6
Famiglietti, Gary FB-LB-HB	38-45ChiB 46Bos	2	6'	225	Boston U.	1	151
Farkas, Andy FB-DB-HB-WB-LB	38-44Was 45Det	23	5'10"	192	Detroit	10	228
Farman, Dick G-LB	39-43Was		6'	219	Washington State		
Farrar, Vinnie G-BB-LB	39Pit		6'	200	N. Carolina State		
Farrell, Scrapper FB-DB	38Pit 38-39Bkn	2	5'9"	204	Muhlenberg		18
Farroh, Shipley G	38Pit				Iowa		
Faust, George BB-LB	39ChiC		6'1"	205	Minnesota		1
Fawcett, Jake T	42Cle 43Bkn 44Cle 45MS 46LA		5'11"	223	S.M.U.	1	
Feather, Tiny OE-TB-DB-DE-WB	27Cle 28Det 29-30NYG		6'	203	Kansas State		
	31SI 31-33NYG 34C-S						
Feathers, Beattie HB-DB	34-37ChiB 38-39Bkn 40GB	12	5'10"	185	Tennessee		102
Federovich, John T	41ChiB 42-45MS 46ChiB		6'5"	261	Davis & Elkins	1	
Fedora, Walt FB-DB	42Bkn 43-45MS		5'11"	190	George Washington		
Feibish, Bernie C-LB	41Phi 42-45MS		6'2"	223	N. Y. U.	1	
Feldhaus, Bill G-LB-T	37-40Det		6'	226	Cincinnati		
Fena, Tom G	37Det			200	Denver		
Fencl, Dick OE-DE	33Phi		5'10"	160	Northwestern		
Ferko, Fritz T	37-38Phi		6'1"	242	West Chester St.		
Fiedler, Bill G	38Phi		5'9"	200	Pennsylvania		
Field, Harry T	34-36ChiC		6'1"	228	Oregon State		
Fife, Ralph G-LB	42ChiC 43-44MS 45ChiC 46Pit		6'	207	Pittsburgh		
Filchock, Frankie TB-QB-DB-HB	38Pit 38-41Was	12	5'11"	193	Indiana	1	48
	42-43MS 44-45Was 46NYG 47-49DE 50Bal HC60-61DenA						
Filipowicz, Steve LB-FB-BB	45-46NYG	2	5'8"	200	Fordham	4	30
44-45, 48 played major league baseball							
Fiorentino, Al G-LB	43-44Was 45Bos		5'7"	201	Boston College	1	
Fishel, Dick BB-TB-LB-DB	33Bkn		5'9"	190	Syracuse		6
Fisher, Bob T	40Was		6'2"	220	Southern Calif.		
Fisher, Ev (King) BB-LB-OE-DE	38-39ChiC 40Pit	2	5'11"	205	Santa Clara		
Fisk, Bill OE-DE	40-43Det 44-45MS 46-47SF-AA 48LA-AA	2	6'	199	Southern Calif.		18
Fiske, Max (Baxie) TB-DB-OE-HB	36-39Pit	12	6'	199	DePaul		
Flaherty, Ray OE-DE	27-28NYY 28-29, 31-35NYG HC36Bos	2	6'	190	Gonzaga		6
	HC37-42Was 43-45MS HC46-48NY-AA HC49ChiAA						
Folk, Dick FB-DB	39Bkn		6'	200	Arkansas State,		
					Ill. Wesleyan		
Foltz, Vern C-LB	44Was 45Pit 46MS		6'1"	205	St. Vincent		
Fordham, Jim FB-LB	44-45ChiB	2	5'11"	215	Georgia		30
Forte, Aldo G-T	39-41ChiB 42-45MS 46Det 46ChiB 47GB		6'	213	Montana		
Fortmann, Danny G-LB	36-43ChiB 44-45MS		6'	210	Colgate	7	6
Foster, Ralph T	45-46ChiC		6'1"	230	Oklahoma State		
Fox, Sam OE-DE	45NYG	2	6'2"	215	Ohio State		12
Fox, Terry FB-LB	41Phi 42-44MS 45Phi 46MiaAA	2	6'1"	208	Miami (Fla.)		
Frahm, Herald DB-WB-HB	32SI 35Phi 35Bos		5'10"	190	Nebraska		
Francis, Sam FB-DB-HB-LB	37-38ChiB 39Pit 39-40Bkn	2 4	6'	207	Nebraska		37
	41-45MS						
Franck, George WB-DB-FB	41NYG 42-44MS 45-47NYG	2 4	6'	176	Minnesota	5	48
Franco, Ed T	44Bos		5'8"	205	Fordham		
Frank, Joe T	41-42Phi 43P-P 44-45MS		6'1"	217	Georgetown		
Frankian, Ike OE-DE	33Bos 34-35NYG		5'11"	208	St. Mary's		12
Franklin, Paul FB-LB-OE-DE	30-33ChiB		6'2"	205	Franklin (Ind.)		
Franklin, Red TB-DB	35-37Bkn	1	5'10"	163	Oregon State		24
Frey, Glenn (Wackie) BB-DB	36-37Phi		5'10"	193	Temple		
Frick, Ray C-LB	41Bkn 42-45MS		6'1"	205	Pennsylvania		
Friedman, Benny TB-DB	27Cle 28Det 29-31NYG	1			Michigan		6
	PC32, 33-34Bkn						
Friedman, Bob T	44Phi		6'2"	215	Washington	1	
Friend, Ben T	39Cle		6'5"	248	Louisiana State		
Fries, Sherwood G-LB	43GB 44-45MS		6'1"	235	Colorado State	2	
Fritts, George T	45Phi		5'11"	205	Clemson		
Fritz, Ralph G	41Phi 42-45MS		5'9"	202	Michigan		
Frketich, Len T	45Pit		6'1"	290	Penn State		
Fronczek, Andy T	41Bkn 42-45MS		6'	200	Richmond		
Frutig, Ed OE-DB-DE	41 GB 42-44MS 45GB 45-46Det	2	6'1"	190	Michigan		18
Fryer, Kenny TB-DB	42-43MS 44Bkn		6'	200	West Virginia		
Fuller, Larry HB-DB-LB	44-45Was 45ChiC		5'10"	192	none		6
Fuqua, Ray OE-DE	35-36Bkn		6'	190	S.M.U.		6
Furst, Tony T	40-41Det 42-43MS 44Det		6'1"	217	Dayton	1	
Gagnon, Roy (Rosy) G	35Det		5'11"	210	Oregon		
Gainor, Charlie DE	39ChiC			190	North Dakota		
Galazin, Stan C-LB	37-39NYG		6'3"	211	Villanova		
Gallarneau, Hugh HB-DB	41-42ChiB 43-44MS 45-47ChiB	2	6'	190	Stanford	4	210
Gallovich, Tony WB-DB	41Cle		5'9"	170	Wake Forest		
Gantenbein, Milt OE-DE	31-40GB	2	6'	199	Wisconsin		42
Garner, Bob G	45NYG		6'	238	none		
Gauer, Charlie DE-FB-OE-LB	43P-P 44-45Phi		6'2"	213	Colgate	2	
Gaziano, Frank G	44Bos		5'8"	218	Holy Cross		
Gelatka, Chuck OE-DB-DE	37-40NYG 41-45MS	2	6'1.'	185	Mississippi State		12
Gentry, Byron (Pills) G	37-39Pit		5'11"	227	Southern Calif.		
Gentry, Lee FB-DB	41Was 42-45MS		6'	198	Tulsa	1	
George, Ray T	39Det 40Phi		6'	229	Southern Calif.		
Gerber, Woody G	41-42Phi 43-45MS		6'	223	Alabama	1	

Use Name (Nicknames) – Positions	Team by Year	See Section	Hgt	Wgt	College	Int	Pts
German, Jimmy TB-DB	39Was 40ChiC		6'	180	Centre		12
Getto, Mike	HC42Bkn				Pittsburgh		
Geyer, Bill HB-DB	42-43ChiB 44-45MS 46ChiB	2	5'10"	173	Colgate	2	24
Ghecas, Lou HB-DB	41Phi 42-45MS		5'9"	175	Georgetown		
Ghersanich, Vern G-LB	43ChiC		5'11"	210	Auburn	1	
Giannoni, Jack OE-DE	38Cle		6'1"	210	St. Mary's		
Gibson, Butch G	30NYG 30Nwk 31-34NYG		5'9"	206	Grove City	1	
Gibson, Joe LB-DE-C-OE-BB	42Cle 43Was 44Cle 45MS		6'3"	213	Tulsa		
	46-47BknAA						
Giddens, Wimpy T	38Phi 44Bos		6'2"	220	Louisiana Tech		
Gifford, Bob BB-LB	42Bkn 43-45MS		6'	200	Denver		
Gift, Wayne BB-DB	37Cle		5'8"	175	Purdue		
Gildea, Johnny TB-BB-DB-LB-HB	35-37Pit 38NYG	12	6'2"	205	St. Bonaventure		6
Gill, Sloko C-LB-G	42Det 43-44MS		5'10"	185	Youngstown	1	
Ginney, Jerry G	40Phi		5'11"	217	Santa Clara		
Gladden, Mack OE-DE	34C-S			195	Missouri		
Glenn, Bill QB-DB	44ChiB		6'	157	Eastern Illinois		
Gloden, Fred HB-DB	41Phi 42-45MS 46MiaAA	2	5'10"	187	Tulane		6
Goddard, Ed (Rip) TB-DB-WB	37Bkn 37-38Cle	12	5'10"	183	Washington State		20
Godfrey, Herb OE-DE	42Cle		6'1"	187	Washington State		
Goff Clark T	40Pit 41-45MS		6'3"	235	Florida		
Goldberg, Marshall (Biggie) DB-FB-HB-TB-WB	39-43ChiC	123	5'11"	190	Pittsburgh	17	102
	44-45MS 46-48ChiC						
Goldenberg, Buckets G-LB-BB-DB-FB	33-45GB		5'10"	220	Wisconsin	7	60
Goldsmith, Wen C-LB	40NYG		6'	202	Kansas St. Teach.		
Golemgeske, John T-G	37-40Bkn		6'2"	225	Wisconsin		
Gollomb, Rudy G	36Phi		5'11"	205	Carroll (Wis.)		
Gonda, George HB-DB	42Pit 43-45MS		5'10"	175	Duquesne	1	12
Gonya, Bob T-OE-DE	33-34Phi		6'2"	208	Northwestern		6
Goodman, Henry T	42Det 43-45MS		6'3"	220	West Virginia		
Goodnight, Owen TB-DB	41Cle 42-45MS	1	6'	195	Hardin-Simmons	2	
Goodwin, Tod OE-DE	35-36NYG	2	6'	184	West Virginia		36
Goodyear, John WB-DB	42Was 43-45MS		6'	190	Marquette		
Goolsby, Shag C-LB	40Cle		6'2"	195	Mississippi State		
Gordon, Lou T-G	30ChiC 31Bkn 31-35ChiC 36-37GB		6'5"	228	Illinois		
	38ChiB						
Gore, Gordon WB-DB	39Det		6'	215	SW State–Okla.		
Grabinski, Ted LB-C-G	39-40Pit		6'2"	207	Duquesne		
Graham, Al G	25-29Day 30Port 30-31Prov 32-33ChiC		6'	218	none		
Graham Les G	38Det		6'	215	Tulsa		
Graham Lyle C-LB	41Phi 42-45MS		6'3"	210	Richmond	2	
Graham, Tom G	35Phi		6'3"	210	Temple		
Grandinette, George G	43Bkn		5'9"	215	Fordham		
Grange, Red (The Wheaton Iceman) HB-DB	25ChiB 27NYY 28KJ	2	6'	188	Illinois		24
	29-34ChiB						
Grant, Len T-G	30-37NYG		6'3"	204	N. Y. U.		
Grant, Rosie G	32SI 33Cin 34C-S		5'10"	198	N. Y. U.		
Grate, Carl G-LB	45NYG		6'	215	Georgia		
Graves, Ray C-LB	42Phi 43P-P 44-45MS 46Phi		6'1"	205	Tennessee	2	1
Greene, Frank (Toadie) BB-DB	34ChiC		5'11"	190	Tulsa		
Greeney, Norm G-T	34-35Pit		5'11"	212	Notre Dame		
Greenfield, Tom C-LB	39-41GB 42-44MS		6'4"	213	Arizona		6
Greenich, Harley HB-DB	44ChiB		5'11"	185	Mississippi		
Greenshields, Don T	32-33Bkn		6'1"	190	Penn State		
Grefe, Ted OE-DE	45Det		6'	205	Northwestern		
Gregory, John G	41Cle		6'2"	210	Tenn.–Chattanooga		
Griffith, Homer TB-DB-WB	34ChiC		5'11"	165	Southern Calif.		12
Grigas, John FB-LB-DB	43ChiC 44C-P 45-47Bos	123	6'	204	Holy Cross	8	66
Grigonis, Frank FB-LB	42Det 43-45MS	2	5'10"	182	Tenn.–Chattanooga	1	6
Grossman, Jack DB-FB-TB	32,34-36Bkn	12	6'1"	193	Rutgers		25
Grosvenor, George TB-DB-HB	35-36ChiB 36-37ChiC	12	6'	174	Colorado		42
Grove, Roger (Roy) HB-DB-BB	31-35GB	2 5	6'	186	Michigan State		33
Grygo, Al HB-DB	44-45ChiB	2	5'10"	173	South Carolina	7	18
Gudauskas, Pete G-LB	40Cle 43-45ChiB	5	6'2"	219	Murray State	2	67
Gudmundson, Scott QB-DB	44-45Bos	12 4	5'10"	178	George Washington	2	
Gussie, Mike G-LB	40Bkn 41-45MS		6'	204	West Virginia		6
Gutknecht, Al G-LB	43Bkn 44Cle		6'	205	Niagara		
Gutowsky, Ace FB-LB-DB-TB	32-33Port 34-38Det 39Bkn	12	5'11"	201	Oklahoma City		103
Haak, Bob (Spanky) T-G	39Bkn		6'1"	245	Indiana		
Hackenbruck, Johnny T	40Det 41-45MS		6'2"	215	Oregon State		
Hackney, Elmer FB-LB-DB	40Phi 41Pit 42-46Det	2	6'2"	202	Kansas State	5	72
Haden, Jack T	36-38NYG		6'4"	232	Arkansas		
Haines, By HB-DB	37Pit		5'11"	185	Washington		
Hajek, Chuck C-LB	34Phi		6'1"	210	Northwestern		1
Halas, George OE-DE	PC20Dec PC21-29,HC33-42ChiB		6'	164	Illinois		
	43-45MS HC46-55,58-68ChiB						
19 played major league baseball							
Hall, Harold C-LB	42NYG		6'2"	210	Springfield		
Hall, Irv FB-LB	42Phi 43-45MS		6'	210	Brown		
Hall, John WB-DB	40-41ChiC 42Det 43ChiC	2	6'	196	Texas Christian	3	60
Hall, Parker (Bullet) TB-DB-QB	39-42Cle 43-45S 46SF-AA	1234	6'	198	Mississippi	5	36
Halleck, Paul OE-DE	37Cle		6'	195	Ohio U.		
Halverson, Bill T	42Phi 43-45MS		6'3"	242	Oregon State		
Haman, Jack C-LB	40-41Cle 42-45MS		6'1"	212	Northwestern	1	6
Hamilton, Ray OE-DE	38Cle 39Det 44-45Cle 46-47LA	2	6'4"	212	Arkansas		12
Hammond, Henry OE-DE	37ChiB		5'11"	190	SW at Memphis		
Handler, Phil (Motsy) G	30-36, HC43,45,49ChiC HC44C-P		6'	215	Texas Christian		
Hanken, Ray OE-DE	37-38NYG		5'11"	190	George Washington		12
Hanna, Elzaphan G	45Was		5'10"	218	South Carolina		
Hanneman, Chuck OE-DE	37-41Det 41Cle	2 5	6'	209	Eastern Michigan		70
Hansen, Cliff TB-DB	33ChiC		6'1"	190	Luther		
Hanson, Homer G-C-LB	34C-S 35ChiC 35Phi 35-36ChiC		6'	217	Kansas State		
Hanson, Swede FB-DB-LB-TB-HB	31Bkn 32SI 33-37Phi	2	6'	194	Temple		85
	38Pit						
Hapes, Merle FB-DB	42NYG 43-45MS 46NYG 47-49DE	2 4	5'10"	190	Mississippi	4	60
Hare, Cecil BB-LB-DB-HB	41-42Was 43-44MS 45Was 46NYG		5'11"	195	Gonzaga	1	12
Hare, Ray BB-LB-DB-WB-HB-FB	40-43Was 44Bkn 46NY-AA	2	6'1"	204	Gonzaga	5	24
Harmon, Ham C-LB	37ChiC			220	Tulsa		
Harper, Moose C-LB	37-40Phi 41Pit 42-45MS		6'4"	227	Austin		6
Harris, Bill OE-DE	37Pit				Hardin-Simmons		
Harrison, Dick OE-DB	44Bos 45MS		6'	195	Boston College		
Harrison, Gran DE-OE	41Phi 42Det 43-45MS		6'3"	211	Mississippi State		
Harrison, Max OE-DE	40NYG		6'1"	208	Auburn		
Harrison, Pat T	37Bkn		6'2"	215	Howard (Ala.)		

Use Name (Nicknames) – Positions	Team by Year	See Section	Hgt	Wgt	College	Int	Pts
Hartman, Bill TB-DB	38Was	12	6'	190	Georgia		
Hartman, Jim OE-DE	36Bkn		6'2"	205	Colorado State		
Hayden, Ken C-LB	42Phi 43Was 44-45MS		6'	205	Arkansas	1	
Hayduk, Henry G	35Pit		6'	200	Washington State		
Heater, Red T	40Bkn		6'2"	220	Syracuse		
Heikkenen, Ralph G	39Bkn		5'10"	180	Michigan		
Heileman, Charlie OE-DE	39ChiB		6'2"	197	Iowa State		
Hein, Mel C-LB	31-45NYG HC47LA-AA		6'2"	225	Washington State	8	6
Heineman, Ken TB-DB	40Cle 43Bkn 44-45MS	12	5'9"	168	Texas-El Paso	2	1
Heldt, Carl T	35-36Bkn		6'2"	206	Purdue		
Heller, Warren TB-DB-HB	34-36Pit	12	5'11"	195	Pittsburgh		24
Hempel, Bill T	42ChiB 43-45MS		6'	235	Carroll (Wis.)		
Henderson, Gus	HC39Det				Oberlin		
Herber, Arnie (Flash) TB-DB-QB-HB	30-40GB 44-45NYG	12 4	5'11"	203	Regis		20
Hershey, Kirk OE-DE	41Cle 41Phi 42-45MS		6'2"	215	Carroll (Wis.)		
Hewitt, Bill OE-DE	32-36ChiB 37-39Phi 43P-P	2	5'9"	188	Michigan		150
Hickman, Herman G	32-34Bkn		5'10"	249	Tennessee		8
Hiemstra, Ed LB-C-G	42NYG 43-45MS		6'	200	Sterling	1	
Higgins, John G-LB	41ChiC 42-45MS		6'1"	200	Trinity (Texas)		
Hightower, Ben OE-DB	42Cle 43Det 44-45MS	2	6'2"	184	Sam Houston St.	1	24
Hill, Harold OE-DE	38-40Bkn	2	6"	200	Howard (Ala.)		
Hilpert, Hal OE-DE	30NYG 33Cin				Oklahoma City		
Hinchman, Bert FB-TB-DB-LB-BB	33-34ChiC 34Det		5'10"	190	Butler		
Hinkle, Clarke FB-LB	32-41GB 42-45MS	2 45	5'11"	201	Bucknell	1	358
Hinkle, Jack HB-DB-BB-LB	40NYG 42MS 43P-P 44-47Phi	2	6'	195	Syracuse	9	42
Hinte, Hal DE	42GB 42Pit		6'1"	195	Pittsburgh		
Hitt, Joel OE-DE	39Cle		6'1"	180	Mississippi Coll.		
Hoague, Joe FB-DB-LB	41-42Pit 43-45MS 46Bos	2	6'2"	203	Colgate	2	18
Hodges, Herman (Country) OE-DE	39-42Bkn 43-45MS	2	6'1"	198	Howard (Ala.)		6
Hoel, Bob G	35Pit 37-38ChiC		6'	208	Pittsburgh		
Hokuf, Steve BB-LB-OE-DE-FB	33-35Bos	1	6'	199	Nebraska		5
Holcomb, Tex T	37Pit 37Phi		6'2"	235	Texas Tech		
Holm, Tony FB-LB	30Prov 31Port 32ChiC 33Pit	1	6'1"	215	Alabama		
Holmer, Walt TB-DB-BB	29-30ChiB 31-32ChiC 33Bos		6'	185	Northwestern		6
	33Pit						
Hood, Frank HB-DB	33Pit		6'	235	Pittsburgh		
Hopp, Harry FB-DB-TB-LB-QB-BB	41-43Det 44-45MS	12 4	6'	209	Nebraska	5	78
	46BufAA 46MiaAA 47LA-AA						
Hoptowit, Al T	42-45ChiB		6'1"	217	Washington State		
Hornbeak, Jay BB-DB	35Bkn		5'11"	185	Washington		
Horstmann, Roy FB-LB-DB-WB	33Bos 34ChiC		6'	188	Purdue		
Hovious, John QB	45NYG	1	5'8"	180	Mississippi		
Howell, Dixie TB-DB	37Was		5'11"	175	Alabama		
Howell, Foster T	34C-S		6'3"	205	Texas Christian		
Howell, Jim Lee OE-DE	37-42NYG 43-45MS 46-48NYG	2	6'6"	210	Arkansas		42
	HC54-60NYG						
Howell, John FB-LB-BB	38GB		5'10"	185	Nebraska		
Hrabetin, Frank T	42Phi 43-45MS 46BknAA 46MiaAA		6'4"	233	Loyola (L.A.)		
Hubbard, Bud OE-DE	35Bkn		6'	190	San Jose State		6
Hubbard, Cal T-G-DE	27-28NYG 29-33,35GB 36Pit 36NYG		6'2"	262	Centenary,		6
					Geneva		
Huffman, Frank G-LB 38-39 played in N.B.L.	39-41ChiC 42-45MS		6'2"	207	Marshall		
Huffman, Vern TB-DB-BB-WB	37-38Det	12	6'2"	215	Indiana		12
Huggins, Roy FB-LB	44Cle		5'11"	195	Vanderbilt		
Hughes, Bernie C-LB	34-36ChiC		6'1"	192	Oregon		
Hughes, Bill (Hoss) G-C-LB	37-40Phi 41ChiB 42-45MS		6'1"	226	Texas	1	
Hugret, Joe OE-DE	34Bkn		6'2"	195	N. Y. U.		
Humphrey, Paul C-LB	39Bkn		6'	195	Purdue		
Hunt, John HB-DB	45ChiB		6'	192	Marshall		
Hunter, Romney OE-DE	33Port			178	Marshall		
Hupke, Tom G	34-37Det 38-39Cle		5'10"	192	Alabama		6
Hurley, George G	32-33Bos		6'	200	Washington State		
Hutchinson, Bill QB-DB	42NYG		5'9"	180	Dartmouth		
Hutchinson, Elvin (The Red Oak Express) WB-DB	39Det		5'11"	195	Whittier		
Hutson, Don OE-DB-DE	35-45GB	2 5	6'1"	183	Alabama	30	823
Ilowit, Roy T	37Bkn		6'2"	220	C.U.N.Y.-City		
Ingalls, Bob C-LB	42GB 43-45MS		6'3"	200	Michigan	1	6
Intrieri, Marne G-T-C-LB-DE-OE	32SI 33-34Bos		5'8"	250	Loyola (Balt.)		
Ippolito, Tony G-LB	43ChiB 44-45MS			220	Purdue	1	
Irvin, Tex T	31Prov 32-35NYG		6'	230	Davis & Elkins		6
Irwin, Don FB-DB-WB-TB	36Bos 37-39Was	2	6'1"	196	Colgate		36
Isaacson, Ted T-C	34-35ChiC		6'4"	272	Washington		
Isbell, Cecil TB-DB-HB	38-42GB HC47-49BalAA	12	6'1"	190	Purdue	7	63
Isselhardt, Ralph G	37Det 37Cle				Franklin (Ohio)		
Itzel, John FB-LB	45Pit		6'	190	Pittsburgh,	1	
					Georgetown		
Ivy, Pop DE-OE	40Pit 40-42ChiC 43-44MS 45-47ChiC	2	6'3"	208	Oklahoma	3	20
	HC58-59ChiC HC60-61StL HC62-63HouA						
Jackson, Don TB-DB	36Phi	12	5'11"	184	North Carolina		
Jacunski, Harry OE-DE	39-44GB	2	6'2"	200	Fordham	1	36
Janecek, Clarence (Janny) G	33Pit		6'	200	Purdue		
Janiak, Len DB-FB-BB-WB	39Bkn 40-42Cle 43-45MS	2	6'1"	203	Ohio U.	1	6
Jankowski, Ed FB-LB	37-41GB 42-45MS	2	5'9"	201	Wisconsin	1	67
Jarvi, Toimi DB-TB-HB	44Phi 45Pit		6'	200	Northern Illinois	1	
Jefferson, Billy TB-DB-HB	41Det 42Phi 42Bkn	12	6'2"	208	Mississippi State	1	12
Jeffries, Bob G	42Bkn 43-45MS		6'2"	206	Missouri		
Jett, John OE-DE	41Det		6'7"	225	Wake Forest		
Jocher, Art G	40,42Bkn 43-45MS		6'1"	205	Manhattan		6
Johnson, Bert (Warhorse) DB-LB-FB-BB-TB-HB-WB	37Bkn	12	6'	212	Kentucky	1	30
	38-39ChiB 39-41ChiC 42Phi						
Johnson, Bill DE	41GB 42-45MS		6'1"	196	Minnesota		
Johnson, Cecil TB-DB-HB	43-44Bkn 45MS	12 4	5'11"	197	East Texas State	1	12
Johnson, Chief LB-C-OE-DE	33-35Bos 36-39NYG 44Was		6'3"	223	Haskell Indian		
Johnson, Don C-LB	42Cle 43-45MS		6'	205	Northwestern		
Johnson, Jack T	34-40Det		6'4"	216	Utah		12
Johnson, Lorne FB-LB	34Phi				Temple		
Johnson, Ray DB-TB-FB	37-38Cle		6'1"	195	Denver		
Johnson, Smiley G-LB	40-41GB		5'9"	198	Georgia	1	
	42-44MS-Killed in action						
Johnsos, Luke OE-DE	29-36,38,HC42-45ChiB	2	6'2"	195	Northwestern		72
Johnston, Jimmy DB-FB-WB-HB	39-40Was 41-45MS 46ChiC	2	6'1"	193	Washington	1	49
Johnston, Swede FB-LB-DB-G	34GB 34C-S 35-38GB	2	5'10"	197	Elmhurst,		30
	39-40Pit				Marquette		
Jolley, Al (Rocky) T	22Akr 23Day 29Buf 30Bkn 31Cle				Marietta,		
	HC33Cin				Kansas State		

Use Name (Nicknames) – Positions	Team by Year	See Section	Hgt	Wgt	College	Int	Pts
Jones, Art DB-HB-TB	41Pit 42-44MS 45Pit	2 4	6'2"	192	Richmond	8	30
Jones, Bob G	34GB		6'2"	215	Indiana		
Jones, Bruce G-T	27-28GB 30Nwk 31-34Bkn		6'1"	219	Alabama		
Jones, Ellis G-LB	45Bos		6'	190	Tulsa		
Jones, Harvey DB-FB-HB	44-45Cle 47Was	2	6'	175	Baylor	5	12
Jones, Lew G-LB	43Bkn 44-45MS		6'	215	Weatherford J.C.	1	
Jones, Potsy G	30Min 30-31Fra 32-36NYG 38GB		5'11"	220	Bucknell		
Jones, Thurman FB-DB	41-42Bkn 43-45MS		5'10"	198	Abilene Christian		1
Jorgensen, Carl T-G	34GB 35Phi		6'	205	St. Mary's		4
Jorgensen, Wagner C-LB	36-37Bkn		6'2"	215	St. Mary's		
Jurich, Mike T	41-42Bkn 43-45MS		6'1"	230	Denver		
Justice, Ed WB-DB-OE	36Bos 37-42Was 43-45MS	2	6'1"	200	Gonzaga	3	66
Kabealo, Mike HB-DB	44Cle	2	5'8"	185	Ohio State	2	6
Kahler, Bob DB-HB	42-44GB 45MS		6'3"	201	Nebraska		
Kahler, Royal T	41Pit 42GB		6'2"	226	Nebraska		
Kahn, Eddie (King Kong) G	35-36Bos 37Was		5'9"	194	North Carolina		6
Kakasic, George (Bunko) G	36-39Pit		5'10"	200	Duquesne		15
39 played as George Kase							
Kamp. Jim G	32SI 33Bos		6'	210	Oklahoma City		
Kane, Carl HB-DB	36Phi		5'11"	195	St. Louis		
Kane, Herb T	44-45NYG		6'1"	218	EC State-Okla.		
Kapitansky, Bernie G	42Bkn 43-45MS		6'1"	212	Long Island U.		
Kaplan, Bernie G	35-36NYG 42Phi		6'	208	Western Maryland		
Kaplanoff, Carl T-G	39Bkn		6'	235	Ohio State		
Kaporch, Al T-G-LB	43-45Det		5'10"	215	St. Bonaventure	3	
Karamatic, George (Automatic) FB-DB	38Was	2	5'8"	187	Gonzaga		11
Karcher, Jim G	36Bos 37-39Was		6'	205	Ohio State		
Karcis, Bull (Five Yards)FB-LB-BB	32-35Bkn 36-38Pit	2	5'9"	223	Carnegie-Mellon		67
	38-39NYG HC42Det 43NYG						
Karpowich, Ed T 38-39 played as Ed Karp	36-39Pit		6'4"	223	Catholic		
Karr, Bill OE-DE	33-38ChiB	2	6'1"	190	West Virginia		120
Karrs, John BB-LB	44Cle		6'1"	210	Duquesne		
Kaska, Tony FB-LB-BB-DB	35Det 36-38Bkn		5'11"	193	Ill. Wesleyan		6
Kasky, Ed T	42Phi 43-45MS		6'1"	220	Villanova		
Kassel, Charlie OE-DE	27ChiB 27-28Fra 29-33ChiC		6'1"	195	Illinois		
Katalinas, Leo T	38GB		6'2"	240	Catholic		
Kavel, George HB-DB	34Pit 34Phi				Carnegie-Mellon		
Kawal, Eddie C-LB-G-T	31,34-36ChiB 37Was		6'2"	200	Illinois		6
Keahey, Duce T-G	42NYG 42Bkn 43-45MS		6'2"	215	George Wash.		
Keeble, Joe TB-WB-DB	37Cle		6'	190	U.C.L.A.		6
Keeling, Ray (King Kong) T	38-39Phi		6'3"	259	Texas		
Keen, Rabbit WB-DB-HB-TB	37-38Phi	2	5'9"	170	Arkansas		
Keenan, Jack T-G	44-45Was		5'10"	214	South Carolina		
Keene, Bob WB-DB	43-45Det		5'11"	191	Detroit	2	12
Kell, Paul T	39-40GB		6'2"	217	Notre Dame		
Kellogg, Bob TB-DB	40ChiC			165	Tulane		
Kellogg, Clarence FB-DB	36ChiC	2	5'10"	205	St. Mary's		9
Kelly, Elmo DE	44ChiB		6'1"	210	Wichita State		
Kelly, Shipwreck DB-WB-TB	32NYG 33-34,37Bkn	2	6'2"	192	Kentucky		48
Kelsch, Mose HB-FB-DB-LB	33-34Pit		5'10"	223	none		16
Kemp, Ray T	33Pit		6'1"	215	Duquesne		
Kenneally, George OE-DE	26-28Pott 29Bos 30ChiC		6'	192	St. Bonaventure		
	32Bos 33-35Phi						
Kennedy, Tom T	44Det		6'	218	Wayne State		
Kerasiotis, Nick G-LB	42ChiB 43-44MS 45ChiB		5'11"	195	St. Ambrose		
Kercher, Bob DE	44GB		6'2"	196	Georgetown		
Kercheval, Ralph DB-HB-TB-WB	34-40Bkn 41-45MS	12 45	6'1"	192	Kentucky		185
Ketzko, Alex T	43Det 44MS-killed in action			215	Michigan State		
Kichefski, Walt OE-DE	40-42Pit 43MS 44C-P	2	6'1"	212	Miami (Fla.)		6
Kiesling, Walt G-T	26-27Dul 28Pott 29-33ChiC 34ChiB		6'3"	250	St. Thomas		
	35-36GB 37-38,HC39-42Pit HC43P-P HC44C-P HC54-56Pit						
Kiick, George DB-FB-HB	40Pit 41-44MS 45Pit	2	6'	198	Bucknell		6
Kilbourne, Wally (Cleats) T	39GB		6'3"	240	Minnesota		
Kimble, Frank OE-DE	45Pit		6'5"	205	West Virginia		
Kinard, Bruiser T	38-44Bkn 45MS 46-47NY-AA	5	6'1"	216	Mississippi	1	42
Kinard, George G-LB	41-42Bkn 43-45MS 46NY-AA		6'1"	202	Mississippi		
Kinek, Mike OE-DE	40Cle		6'1"	200	Michigan State		
King, Fred BB-LB	37Bkn		6'2"	205	Hobart		
Kinscherf, Carl FB-DB	43-44NYG	2 4	6'1"	188	Colgate	1	6
Kirkland, Bo G	35-36Bkn		6'	215	Alabama		
Kirkman, Reds BB-DB	33-35Phi	1	6'1"	195	Wash. & Jefferson		17
Kish, Ben LB-FB-BB-DB	40-41Bkn 42MS 43P-P 44-49Phi	2	6'	207	Pittsburgh	16	25
Kissell, Adolph HB-DB	42ChiB 43-45MS		5'11"	190	Boston College		
Kizzire, Lee FB-LB	37Det		6'	200	Wyoming		
Klewicki, Ed OE-DE-WB	35-38Det	2	5'10"	209	Michigan State		18
Kline, Jiggs DE-OE	39-40,42NYG 43-44MS		6'1"	196	Kansas St. Teach.		6
Kloppenberg, Harry OE-DE	30SI 31,33-34Bkn		6'1"	210	Fordham		
Klotovich, Mike WB-DB	45NYG		5'10"	180	St. Mary's		
Klumb, John OE-DE	39-40ChiC 40Pit		6'3"	200	Washington State		
Knapper, Joe HB-DB	34Phi				Ottawa (Kansas)		
Knolla, John DB-HB-TB-WB	42ChiC 43-44MS 45ChiC	2	5'10"	180	Creighton	1	
Knorr, Larry OE-DE-DB	42Det 43-44MS 45 Det		6'2"	194	Dayton		
Knox, Charlie T	37Phi		5'11"	185	St. Edmonds		
Knox, Sam (Dutch) G-T	34-36Det		6'	213	New Hampshire		
Kober, Matt G	40Bkn				Villanova		
Kobrosky, Mickey QB-DB	37NYG		6'	187	Trinity (Conn.)		
Kochel, Mike G-LB	39ChiC		5'11"	195	Fordham		
Koeninger, Art C-LB	31Fra 32SI 33Phi		6'3"	205	Tenn.-Chattanooga		
Koken, Mike TB-DB-BB	33ChiC		5'11"	180	Notre Dame		1
Kolberg, Elmer OE-DB-DE-HB	39-40Phi 41Pit	2	6'4"	199	Oregon State		
Kolman, Ed T	40-42ChiB 43-45MS 46-47ChiB 49NYG		6'2"	232	Temple		
Kondria, John T	45Pit		6'	185	St. Vincent		
Konetsky, Floyd DE	44-45Cle 47BalAA		6'	197	Florida	1	
Koons, Joe C-LB	41Bkn 42-45MS		6'2"	195	Scranton		
Kopcha, Joe (Doc) G	29,32-35ChiB 36Det		6'	225	Tenn.-Chattanooga		3
Kopf, Herb	HC44-46Bos				Wash. & Jefferson		
Korisky, Ed C-LB	44Bos		6'1"	210	Villanova	1	
Kosell, Stan FB-DB-BB-LB	38-39Bkn		5'11"	190	Albright		6
Koshlap, Julie HB-DB	45Pit				Georgetown		
Kostiuk, Mike T	41Cle 42-44MS 45Det		6'	212	Detroit Tech		
Kostka, Stan FB-LB	35Bkn		5'11"	215	Minnesota		
Kottler, Marty FB-LB	33Pit				Centre		6

Use Name (Nickname) – Positions	Team by Year	See Section	Hgt	Wgt	College	Int	Pts
Kovatch, Johnny OE-DE	38Cle		5'11"	172	Northwestern		6
Kowalski, Andy OE-DE	43-44Bkn 45Bos	2	6'1"	199	Mississippi State	1	6
Kracum, George FB-DB	41Bkn 42-45MS	2	6'1"	212	Pittsburgh	1	18
Krause, Bill T	38Cle		6'	210	Baldwin-Wallace		
Krause, Max (Bananas) BB-DB-LB-FB-WB	33-36NYG 37-40Was	2	5'10"	202	Gonzaga		37
Krause, Red C-LB-G	36-37Bkn 37-38Was		6'1"	212	St. Louis		
Krejci, Joe OE-DE	34ChiC		6'	190	Penn State		
Kresky, Joe G-T	32Bos 33-35Phi 35Pit 35Phi		6'	220	Wisconsin		
Krieger, Bob OE-DE	41Phi 42-45MS 46Phi	2	6'1"	190	Dartmouth		12
Kriel, Emmett (Sally) G	39Phi		6'2"	200	Baylor		
Kring, Frank LB	45Det		6'	190	Texas Christian		
Kristufek, Frank T	40-41Bkn 42-45MS		6'	209	Pittsburgh		
Krol, Joe DB	45Det		6'1"	210	Western Ontario		
Krueger, Al OE-DE-DB	41-42Was 43-45MS 46LA-AA	2	6'1"	188	Southern Calif.	1	12
Kubale, Ed	HC44Bkn				Centre		
Kuczynski, Bert OE-DE	43Det 44-45MS 46Phi		6'	196	Pennsylvania		6
43 played major league baseball							
Kuharich, Joe G-LB	40-41ChiC 42-44MS 45,HC52ChiC HC54-58Was HC64-68Phi	5	5'11"	195	Notre Dame	1	12
Kupcinet, Irv BB-DB	35Phi		6'1"	190	North Dakota		
Kurth, Joe T	33-34GB		6'1"	202	Notre Dame		
Kusko, John FB-LB-DB-BB-TB-HB	36-38Phi	12	5'11"	194	Temple		6
Kuusisto, Bill G	41-46GB		6'	228	Minnesota		
Kvaternick, Zvonimir G	34Pit			210	Kansas		
Lackman, Rick HB-DB	33-35Phi		5'11"	186	none		1
LaFitte, Bill OE	44Bkn 45MS		6'1"	170	Ouachita Baptist		
Lainhart, Porter FB-LB	33ChiC 33Phi		6'	180	Washington State		
Lajousky, Bill G	36Pit		5'11"	200	Catholic		
Lamas, Joe G	42Pit 43-45MS		5'10"	216	Mt. St. Mary's		6
Lamb, Roy BB-DB	25RI 26-27,33ChiC		5'6"	160	Lombard		
Lambeau, Curly TB-DB	PC21-29,HC30-49GB HC50-51ChiC HC52-54Was		6'	195	Notre Dame		
Landsberg, Mort HB-DB	41Phi 42-45MS 47LA-AA	2	5'11"	180	Cornell	2	
Landsdell, Grenny QB-DB	40NYG 41-44MS		6'	190	Southern Calif.		
Lane, Les G	39Bkn		6'3"	193	South Dakota		
Lankas, Jim FB-LB	42Phi 43GB 44-45MS		6'2"	220	St. Mary's		
Lantz, Monty C-LB	33Pit		5'11"	185	Grove City		
Lapka, Ted OE-DE	43-44Was 45MS 46Was		6'1"	193	St. Ambrose		12
LaPresta, Benny BB-LB-DB	33Bos 34C-S		5'9"	185	St. Louis		1
Lascari, John OE-DE	42NYG 43-45MS		6'2"	210	Georgetown		6
Lasahn, Lou T-DE	38Pit		6'	205	West. Maryland		
Laux, Ted HB-DB	43P-P 44Phi		5'10"	185	St. Joseph's–Pa.	1	2
Law, Hubbard G-LB	42Pit 43-44MS 45Pit		6'1"	210	Sam Houston St.	1	
Lawrence, Jimmy WB-DB-TB	36-39ChiC 39GB	2	5'11"	190	Texas Christian		24
Laws, Joe HB-DB	34-45GB	123	5'9"	186	Iowa	18	126
Lay, Russ G-T	34Det 34C-S		5'11"	198	Michigan State		
Layden, Bob DE	43Det		6'	195	Southwestern–(Kansas)		
Lazetich, Bill WB-DB	39,42Cle 43-45MS	2	6'	198	Montana		18
Leathers, Milt G	33Phi			198	Georgia		
Lechner, Ed G-T	42NYG 43-45MS		6'1"	200	Minnesota		
Lechthaler, Roy G	33Phi		5'10"	198	Lebanon Valley		
Leckonby, Bill (Wild Bill) TB-DB	39-41Bkn 42-45MS	12	6'1"	185	St. Lawrence	3	18
Ledbetter, Doc FB-LB	32SI 32-33ChiC		5'10"	190	Arkansas		
Lee, Bernie BB-LB	38Phi 38Pit		5'11"	190	Villanova		
Lee, Biff G	31Cle 31Port 33Cin 34C-S		6'	230	Oklahoma		4
Lee, Bill T	35-37Bkn 37-42GB 43-45MS 46GB		6'2"	231	Alabama		
Lee, Jack (Whitey) BB-LB	39Pit		5'10"	205	Carnegie-Mellon		
Leemans, Tuffy FB-DB-QB	36-43NYG	12	6'	195	George Wash.	3	120
LeFebvre, Gil (Frenchy) WB-TB-DB	33Cin 34C-S 35Det		5'6"	155	none		6
Leisk, Rube G	37Bkn		6'	195	Louisiana State		
Lenc, George (Chilly) OE-DE	39Bkn		6'3"	204	Augustana		
Leon, Tony G-LB	43Was 44Bkn 45-46Bos		5'9"	203	Alabama	1	
Leonard, Jim BB-FB-DB-LB-TB-HB	34-37Phi HC45Pit	12	6'	202	Notre Dame		18
Lester, Darrell C-LB	37-38GB		6'3"	220	Texas Christian		
Letlow, Russ G	36-42GB 43-45MS 46GB		6'	214	San Francisco		
Letsinger, Jim G	33Pit			190	Purdue		
Levanitis, Steve T	42Phi 43-45MS		6'1"	220	Boston College		
Levey, Jim HB-DB-TB	34-36Pit	2	5'10"	163	none		24
30-33 played major league baseball							
Lewis, Art T-G	36NYG PC38, 39Cle		6'3"	226	Ohio U.		6
Lewis, Bill TB-DB	34C-S		5'11"	186	Texas Christian		
Liebel, Frank OE-DE-DB	42-47NYG 48ChiC	2	6'1"	211	Norwich	7	144
Lieberum, Don WB-DB	42NYG 43-45MS		6'	175	Manchester		
Liles, Sonny G-LB	43-45Det 45Cle		5'9"	188	Oklahoma State	2	
Lillard, Joe TB-DB	32-33ChiC		6'	185	Oregon State		19
Lindahl, Virgil G-LB-OE	45NYG		6'1"	197	Wayne St. (Neb.), Kentucky		
Lind, Al C-LB	36ChiC				Northwestern		
Lindon, Luther T	44-45Det		5'10"	243	Kentucky		
Lindow, Al HB-DB	45ChiC				Washington–St. L		
Lio, Augie G-LB	41-43Det 44-45Bos 46Phi 47BalAA	5	6'	234	Georgetown	10	172
Lipski, Bull C-LB	33-34Phi		5'11"	200	Temple		
Little, Jim T	45NYG		6'1"	200	Kentucky		
Littlefield, Carl (Moon Eyes) DB-FB-TB	38Cle 39Pit	2	6'	200	Washington State		6
Livingston, Ted T-G	37-40Cle		6'3"	219	Indiana		
Logan (born Wyhowanec), Andy T	41Det 42-45MS		6'	222	Case Reserve		
Logan, Jim G	43ChiB 44-45MS			190	Indiana		
Lokanc, Joe G-LB	41ChiC 42-45MS		5'11"	205	Northwestern		
Long, John QB-DB	44-45ChiB	2	6'	185	Colgate		
Looney, Don OE-DB	40Phi 41-42Pit 43-45MS	2	6'2"	182	Texas Christian		42
Lowther, Russ TB-DB	44Det 45Pit		5'8"	165	Detroit	1	
Lubratovich, Lou T	31-35Bkn		6'2"	226	Wisconsin		
Lurente, John FB-LB	45Pit	2	5'9"	200	West Virginia		12
Luckman, Sid QB-DB-HB	39-50ChiB	12 4	6'	197	Columbia	14	37
Lummus, Jack OE-DE	41NYG 42-44MS—killed in action		6'3"	194	Baylor		
Lumpkin, Father BB-DB-LB	30-33Port 34Det 35-37Bkn		6'2"	211	Georgia Tech		18
Lunday, Kayo LB-G-C	37-41NYG 42-45MS 46-47NYG		6'3"	217	Arkansas	1	
Lyman, Del T	41GB 41,44Cle		6'3"	223	U.C.L.A.		
Lyman, Link T	22-23Can 24Cle 25Can 25Fra 27-28,30-31,33-34ChiB		6'2"	249	Nebraska		
Lyon, George T	29NYG 30Port 31ChiB 31Cle 32Bkn 34C-S			235	Kansas State		

Use Name (Nickname) – Positions	Team by Year	See Section	Hgt	Wgt	College	Int	Pts
Lyons, John OE-DE	33Bkn		6'1"	210	Tulsa		
Mackenroth, Jack C-LB	38Det		6'2"	215	North Dakota		
Mackorell, John TB-DB	35NYG		5'10"	178	Davidson		
MacLeod, Bob HB-DB	39ChiB	2	6'	190	Dartmouth		30
MacMurdo, Jim (Big Jim) T-G	32-33Bos 34-37Phi		6'1"	209	Pittsburgh		6
Madden, Lloyd WB-DB	40ChiC	2	6'1"	195	Colorado Mines		18
Maddock, Bob G-LB	42ChiC 43-45MS 46ChiC		6'	200	Notre Dame		
Maddox, Buster T	35GB		6'3"	240	Kansas State		
Maeda, Chet HB-DB	45ChiC		5'10"	187	Colorado State		
Magee, Jim C-LB	44-46Bos		6'1"	202	Villanova	1	
Magulick, George HB-DB	44C-P		5'9"	150	St. Francis–Pa.	2	
Maher, Frank DB	41Pit 41Cle 42-45MS		6'1"	195	Toledo		
Malkovich, Joe (Hunk) C-LB	35Pit		6'3"	205	Duquesne		
Malloy, Les BB-DB	31-33ChiC		6'	200	Loyola (Chic.)		
Malone, Charley OE-DE	34-36Bos 37-40, 42Was 43MS	2	6'4"	206	Texas A&M		78
Mandarino, Mike C-G-T	44-45Phi		5'11"	240	LaSalle		
Manders, Jack FB-LB-HB-DB	33-40ChiB	2 5	6'	203	Minnesota		368
Manders, Pug FB-LB-DB-BB	39-44Bkn 45Bos 46NY-AA 47BufAA	12	6'	202	Drake	10	234
Maniaci, Joe FB-LB-HB-DB-TB	36-38Bkn 38-41ChiB 42-45MS	2 5	6'1"	212	Fordham		140
Manske, Eggs OE-DE-HB-DB	35-36Phi 37ChiB 38Pit 38-40ChiB	2	6'	185	Northwestern		84
Manton, Tilly BB-LB-DB	36-38NYG 38Was 43Bkn	2 5	5'11"	188	Texas Christian		53
Manzini, Bap C-LB	44-45,48Phi		5'11"	195	St. Vincent	1	
Manzo, Joe T	45Det		6'1"	220	Boston College		
Maples, Tal C-LB	34C-S		6'	195	Tennessee		
Maras, Joe C-LB-T	38-40Pit		6'1"	203	Duquesne		
Marchi, Basilio G-C-LB	34Pit 42Phi 43-45MS		6'2"	220	N.Y.U.		
Marcus, Pete DE	44Was		6'2"	200	Kentucky		
Marefos, Andy (Anvil Andy) FB-DB-QB-LB	41-42NYG 43-45MS 46LA-AA	12	6'	223	St. Mary's	3	62
Marek, Jodey FB-LB	43Bkn		5'11"	182	Texas Tech		
Margarita, Hank HB-DB	44-46ChiB	2	5'11"	178	Brown	9	54
Mark, Lou LB-C-DE	38-40Bkn 41-44MS 45Bos		6'	196	N. Carolina State		
Marker, Harry BB-DB	34Pit				West Virginia		
Marko, Steve TB-DB	44Bkn		6'	200	none		
Markov, Vic G-T	38Cle		6'	215	Washington		
Marone, Sal G	43NYG		5'10"	195	Manhattan		
Maronic, Steve T	39-40Det		6'	225	North Carolina		
Marotti, Lou G	43ChiC 44C-P 45ChiC		5'10"	210	Toledo		
Martin, Frank DB-HB-WB	43-44Bkn 45Bos 45NYG	2	5'10"	177	Alabama	4	6
Martin, John DB-WB-HB	41-43ChiC 44C-P 44-45Bos	234	6'1"	195	Oklahoma	12	24
Martin, Vern BB-LB	42Pit 43-45MS		5'10"	195	Texas		12
Mason, Joel OE-DE-DB	39ChiC 42-45GB	2	6'	199	Western Michigan		12
42-43 played, 46-47 coached in N.B.L.							
Masters, Bob (Chief) DB-HB-LB-FB-WB-BB-TB	37-38Phi 39Pit 42Phi 43P-P 43-44ChiB	2	5'11"	200	Baylor		
Masters, Walt TB-DB-QB	36Phi 43ChiC 44C-P	1	5'10"	192	Pennsylvania		
31,37,39 played major league baseball							
Masterson, Bernie QB-DB	34-40ChiB	12	6'3"	195	Nebraska		50
Masterson, Bob OE-DE	38-43Was 44Bkn 45Bos 46NY-AA	2 5	6'1"	213	Miami (Fla.)	2	173
Masterson, Forest C-G	45ChiB		6'3"	246	Iowa		
Matesic, Ed TB-DB	34-35Phi 36Pit	12	6'1"	198	Pittsburgh		13
Matheson, Jack OE-DE	43-46Det 47ChiB	2	6'2"	221	Western Michigan	2	38
Matheson, Riley G-LB	39-42Cle 43-45MS 46-47LA 48SF-AA		6'2"	207	Texas–El Paso	14	
Mathews, Ned DB-HB-WB-TB	41-43Det 45Bos PC46ChiAA 46-47SF-AA	12	5'10"	187	U.C.L.A.	18	78
Matisi, John T	43Bkn 44-45MS 46BufAA		6'2"	218	Duquesne	1	
Matisi, Tony T	38Det		6'2"	230	Pittsburgh		
Mattiford, John G	41Det 42-45MS		5'10"	216	Marshall		
Mattos, Harry TB-DB	36GB 37Cle	12	6'	198	St. Mary's		8
Matuza, Al C-LB	41-43ChiB 44-45MS 46JJ		6'2"	200	Georgetown	4	
May, Bill BB-LB	37-38ChiC		5'11"	188	Louisiana State		10
May, Jack C-LB	38Cle		5'10"	210	Centenary		
Mayhew, Lindy G-T	36-38Pit		6'1"	223	Texas–El Paso		
McAdams, Dean TB-DB-HB	41-43Bkn	12 4	6'1"	193	Washington	4	11
McAfee, Wes HB-DB	41Phi 42-45MS		5'11"	175	Duke		8
McBride, Charlie BB-LB	36ChiC				Washington State		6
McBride, Jack DB-TB-FB	25-29NYG 30-32Bkn 32-34NYG		5'11"	185	Syracuse		7
McCarthy, John QB-DB	44C-P	1	5'8"	160	St. Francis–Pa.		
McChesney, Bob OE-DE	36Bos 37-42Was 43-45MS	2	6'2"	195	U.C.L.A.		42
McClain, Red FB-DB	41NYG 42-45MS		5'9"	182	S.M.U.	1	12
McCrary, Hurdis FB-LB	29-33GB			204	Georgia		
McCullough, Harold TB-DB	42Bkn	1	5'11"	170	Cornell		
McCullough, Hugh DB-TB-QB	39Pit 40-41ChiC 42MS 43P-P 45Bos	12 4	6'	185	Oklahoma		25
McDade, Karl C-LB	38Pit		6'3"	195	Portland		
McDonald, Jim HB-DB	36Pit		6'	195	Duquesne		
McDonald, Flip OE-DB-DE	44Bkn 44-46Phi 48NY-AA	2	6'2"	200	Oklahoma	1	6
McDonald, Jim DB-WB-BB-FB	38-39Det	2	6'1"	193	Ohio State		
McDonald, Les OE-DE	37-39ChiB 40Phi 40Det	2	6'4"	202	Nebraska		49
McDonald, Walt C-LB	35Bkn		5'10"	210	Utah		
McDonough, Coley TB-DB-QB	39ChiC 39-41Pit 42-43MS 44C-P	12	6'1"	189	Dayton		12
McDonough, Paul OE-DE-WB	38Pit 39-41Cle 42-45MS	2	6'4"	222	Utah		24
McEnulty, Doug HB-DB	43-44ChiB	4	6'3"	221	Wichita State	2	12
McEwen, Cap	HC33-34Bkn				Army		
McFadden, Banks HB-DB	40Bkn 41-45MS	2	6'2"	180	Clemson		18
McGarry, Barney G-LB	39-42Cle 43-45MS		6'1"	203	Utah		
McGee, Bob T	38ChiC		6'	210	Santa Clara		
McGee, Ed T	40NYG 44-46Bos		6'1"	224	Temple	1	
McGibbony, Charlie TB-DB	44Bkn	12	5'10"	160	Arkansas State	1	
McGirl, Len G	34C-S			206	Missouri		
McKalip, Bill OE-DE-WB-DB	31-32Port 34,36Det		6'1"	190	Oregon State		
McKay, Tex DB-TB-FB-HB	44-47GB	12 4	6'	193	Texas	4	21
McLaughlin, Charlie FB-LB	34C-S				Wichita State		
McLaughlin, Lee G	41GB 42-45MS		6'1"	226	Virginia		
McLaughry, John BB-LB	40NYG		6'1"	205	Brown		
McLean, Ray (Scooter) HB-DB	40-47ChiB HC53,58GB	23 5	5'10"	167	St. Anselm's	17	225
McLeod, Russ C-LB	34C-S				St. Louis		
McMichaels, John TB-DB	44Bkn		5'11"	190	Birmingham–South.		
McNally, Frank C-LB-T	31-34ChiC		6'1"	203	St. Mary's		6
McNamara, Ed T	45Pit		6'2"	225	Holy Cross		
McPhail, Hal FB-DB	34-35Bos		6'1"	230	Army, Xavier–Ohio		21

Use Name (Nicknames) – Positions	Team by Year	See Section	Hgt	Wgt	College	Int	Pts
McPherson, Amy C-G-T-LB	35ChiB 35-37Phi 43-45GB		5'11"	233	Nebraska		
McRaven, Bill (Bullet Bill) WB-DB	39Cle		5'11"	170	Murray State		
McRoberts, Bob HB-DB	44Bos		5'11"	190	Wisconsin-Stout		
McWilliams, Bill WB-DB	34Det		6'1"	205	Iowa		
Meade, Jim DB-WB-FB	39-40Was 41-45MS	2	6'1"	197	Maryland		
Mecham, Curt TB-DB	42Bkn 43-45MS		6'	180	Oregon		
Mehringer, Pete (Champ) T-G	34-36ChiC		6'2"	206	Kansas		
Mellus, John T	38-41NYG 42-45MS 46SF-AA 47-49Bal AA		6'	214	Villanova		7
Mergenthal, Art G-LB	45Cle 46LA		5'11"	215	Notre Dame		
Merkel, Monte G	43ChiB 44-45MS		5'10"	215	Kansas		
Merkle, Ed G-LB	44Was 45MS		5'10"	215	Oklahoma State		
Merkovsky, Al T-G	44C-P 45-46Pit		6'1"	223	Pittsburgh		
Merlin, Ed G	38-39Bkn		5'10"	210	Vanderbilt		
Merrill, Walt T	40-42Bkn 43-45MS		6'2"	217	Alabama		
Mesak, Dick T	45Det		6'2"	225	St. Mary's		
Meyer, Fred OE-DE	42Phi 43-44MS 45Phi	2	6'2"	193	Stanford		12
Michaels, Eddie G	36ChiB 37Was 43P-P 44-46Phi 47CFL		5'11"	205	Villanova		
Michalske, Mike G	27-28NYY 29-35,37GB		6'	210	Penn State		
Midler, Lou G-T	39Pit 40GB		6'1"	223	Minnesota		
Mielziner, Saul T-C-LB	29-30NYG 31-34Bkn		6'1"	245	Carnegie-Mellon		
Mihal, Joe T	40-41ChiB 42-45MS 46LA-AA 47ChiAA		6'3"	234	Purdue		
Mikulak, Mike FB-LB-BB-WB-DB	34-36ChiC	2	6'1"	210	Oregon		30
Milam, Barnes G	34Phi				Austin		
Milano, Arch OE-DE	45Det		6'	197	St. Francis-Pa.		
Miller, Dub G-T	35ChiB 36-37ChiC		6'	218	Chadron State		
Miller, Eddie QB-DB	39-40NYG 41-45MS	12	5'10"	165	New Mexico State		12
Miller, Ookie C-LB-G	32-36ChiB 37Cle 38GB		6'	209	Purdue		6
Miller, Paul HB-DB	36-38GB	2	5'11"	180	S. Dakota State		24
Miller, Primo T	37-38Cle		6'2"	220	Rice		6
Miller, Tom DE-OE	43P-P 44Phi 45Was 46GB	2	6'2"	202	Hampden-Sydney	2	12
Milling, Al G	42Phi		5'9"	170	Richmond		
Millner, Wayne OE-DE	36Bos 37-41Was 42-44MS 45Was	2	6'1"	190	Notre Dame		78
	HC51Phi						
Mitchell, Buster OE-DE-T	31-33Port 34-35Det	2	6'	207	Davis & Elkins		6
	35-36NYG 37Bkn						
Moan, Kelly TB-DB	39Cle		6'	193	West Virginia		1
Moe, Hal WB-DB	33ChiC		5'10"	182	Oregon State		12
Molenda, Bo BB-FB-LB	27-28NYY 29-32GB 32-35NYG		5'10"	216	Michigan		31
Molesworth, Keith (Rabbit) DB-HB-QB	31-37ChiB HC53Bal	12	5'9"	167	Monmouth (Ill.)		37
Monaco, Ray G-LB	44Was 45Cle		5'10"	212	Holy Cross		
Monahan, Regis (Monty) G-T	35-38Det 39ChiC	5	5'10"	216	Ohio State		44
Monfort, Avery WB-DB	41ChiC 42-45MS		5'10"	178	New Mexico		
Monnett, Bob TB-DB-HB	33-38GB	12 5	5'9"	182	Michigan State		91
Montgomery, Bill T-G	34C-S				St. Louis		
Montgomery, Cliff TB-DB	34Bkn		5'9"	165	Columbia		
Mooney, Jim OE-DE-T	30Nwk 30-31Bkn 33Cin 34C-S		5'11"	195	Georgetown		
	35ChiC						
Mooney (born Schupbach), Tex T	42Cle 43Bkn 44-45MS		6'5"	280	West Texas State		
Mooney, Tipp HB-DB	44-45ChiB	2	6'	187	Abilene Christian	1	6
Moore, Al DE	39GB		6'2"	218	Texas A&M		
Moore, Bill OE-DE	39Det		6'1"	195	North Carolina		6
Moore, Bucky HB-DB	32ChiC 33Pit				Loyola (N. Orl.)		
Moore, Cliff WB-DB	34C-S		6'1"	202	Penn State		
Moore, Gene C-LB	38Bkn		6'3"	205	Colorado		
Moore, Ken G	40NYG		6'	212	West Va. Wesleyan		
Moore, Paul (June) BB-LB	40-41Det 42-44MS		5'9"	208	Presbyterian		6
Moore, Wilbur DB-WB-HB-FB-BB	39-46Was	2	5'11"	187	Minnesota	12	144
Moran, Hap DB-WB-FB	25-27Fra 27ChiC 28Pott 28-33NYG		6'1"	190	Grinnell, Carnegie-Mellon		7
Moran, Jim G	35-36Bos		6'1"	208	Holy Cross		
Morelli, John G-LB	44-45Bos		5'10"	191	Georgetown		
Morgan, Bill T	33-36NYG		6'2"	232	Oregon		
Morgan, Boyd (Red) BB-LB-WB-DB	39-40Was 41-45MS		6'	198	Southern Calif.		
Morlock, John WB-DB	40Det		5'10"	165	Marshall		
Morris, Frank FB-LB	42ChiB 43-45MS		6'2"	214	Boston U.		
Morris, George DB-WB-FB	41-42Cle 43-45MS	2	5'11"	188	Baldwin-Wallace	2	
Morris, Glenn OE-DE	40Det		6'	200	Colorado State		
Morrison, Doc C-LB	33-34Bkn		5'11"	210	Michigan		
Morrow, Bob FB-DB-BB-LB	41-43ChiC 44MS 45NYG 46NY-AA	2	6'	222	Ill. Wesleyan	3	24
Morrow, John G	37-38ChiC		5'11"	230	Kearney State		
Morse, Butch OE-DE	35-38,40Det 41-45MS	2	6'2"	199	Oregon		6
Mortell, Emmett TB-DB-QB	37-39Phi	12	6'1"	181	Wisconsin		
Moscrip, Monk OE-DE	38-39Det	2 5	6'	195	Stanford		27
Moses, Don BB-DB	33Cin		5'11"	185	Southern Calif.		
Mosher, Clure C-G-LB	42Pit 43-45MS		6'1"	215	Louisville		
Mosley, Russ DB-HB	45-46GB		5'10"	170	Alabama	2	
Moss, Paul OE-DE	33Pit 34C-S	2	6'2"	180	Purdue		18
Mott, Buster DB-BB-HB	33GB 34C-S 34Pit			193	Georgia		
Moynihan, Tim C-LB	32-33ChiC		6'1"	204	Notre Dame		
Mucha, Rudy G-LB-BB	41Cle 42-44MS 45Cle 45-46ChiB	4	6'1"	236	Washington		
Muellner, Bill OE-DE	37ChiC				DePaul		
Mugg, Garvin T	45Det		6'1"	215	North Texas State		
Mulleneaux, Lee (Brute) LB-C-DB-WB-BB-FB	32NYG 33Cin		6'2"	221	Utah State		
	34C-S 35-36Pit 38ChiC 38GB						
Mulleneaux, Moose DE-OE	38-41GB 42-44MS 45-46GB	2	6'3"	209	Utah State		72
Mulligan, George OE-DE-LB	36Phi		6'1"	198	Catholic		
Munday, George (Sunny) T-G	31Cle 31-32NYG 33Cin 34C-S		6'2"	210	Kansas St. Teach.		
Mundee, Fred C-LB	43-45ChiB		6'1"	220	Notre Dame	2	
Murphy, Bill G	40-41ChiC 42-45MS		6'	203	Washington-St.L.		
Murphy, Harvey OE-DE	40Cle		5'10"	194	Mississippi		
Murphy, Tom BB-DB	34ChiC		5'11"	170	Arkansas		
Murray, Franny HB-DB	39-40Phi	2 45	6'	200	Pennsylvania		32
Musick, Jim FB-DB	32-33, 35-36Bos	2 5	5'11"	198	Southern Calif.		58
Musso, George G-T	33-44ChiB		6'2"	262	Millikin		
Nagurski, Bronko FB-LB-T	30-37, 43ChiB	2	6'2"	229	Minnesota		90
Naioti, John DB-HB	42, 45Pit		5'10"	180	St. Francis-Pa.		4
Nardi, Dick DB-WB-HB-TB-FB	38Det 39Pit 39Bkn	2	5'10"	200	Ohio State		
Nash, Tom OE-DE	28-32GB 33-34Bkn		6'3"	200	Georgia		13
Natowich, Andy HB-DB	44Was 45MS		5'10"	175	Holy Cross		
Neihaus, Ralph T	39Cle		6'4"	220	Dayton		
Neill, Jim DB-FB-WB	37NYG 39ChiC		6'1"	185	Texas Tech		
Nelson, Don G	37Bkn		5'9"	205	Iowa		

Use Name (Nicknames) – Positions	Team by Year	See Section	Hgt	Wgt	College	Int	Pts
Nery, Carl G	40-41Pit 42-45MS		6'	214	Duquesne		
Nesbitt, Dick FB-LB-WB-HB-DB	30-33ChiB 33ChiC 34Bkn		6'	208	Drake		6
Neuman, Bob OE-DE	34-36ChiC		6'	198	Ill. Wesleyan		6
Nevers, Ernie FB-DB-TB	26-27Dul 28VR PC29-31ChiC		6'	205	Stanford		
26-28 played major league baseball							
Newman, Harry TB-DB	33-35NYG	12 5	5'8"	179	Michigan		78
Newton, Chuck HB-DB-FB	39-40Phi	2	6'	205	Washington		6
Niccolai, Armand (Nick) T-G-DE-OE	34-42Pit	5	6'2"	226	Duquesne		173
Nichelini, Al WB-DB	35-36ChiC	2	6'2"	207	St. Mary's		30
Nichols, Al FB-LB	45Pit		5'10"	205	Temple		
Nielsen, Walt FB-DB	40NYG 41-45MS	2	6'3"	220	Arizona		6
Nisbet, Dave OE-DE	33ChiC		6'1"	180	Washington		
Nix, Emery QB-DB	43NYG 44-45MS 46NYG	12	5'11"	180	Texas Christian	2	
Nix, Jack WB-DB	40Cle		6'	175	Mississippi State		
Nixon (born Nicksick), Mike DB-HB-WB	35Pit 42Bkn		5'11"	181	Pittsburgh		
	HC59-61Was HC65Pit						
Nolan, Earl T	37-38ChiC		6'1"	205	Arizona		
Nolting, Ray HB-DB	36-43ChiB	12	5'11"	186	Cincinnati	1	96
Noppenberg, John DB-HB-FB-TB-OE	40-41Pit 41Det		6'	196	Miami (Fla.)		
Norby, John DB-WB-BB-HB	34NYG 34Phi 34C-S 35Bkn		6'	195	Idaho		
Norgard, Al OE-DE	34GB		6'1"	194	Stanford		
Nori, Reino TB-DB-QB	37Bkn 38ChiB	2	5'8"	167	Northern Illinois		
Norman, Bob C-LB	45ChiC		6'1"	185	none		
North, Jim T	44Was		6'3"	235	Central Wash. St.		
Nosich, John T	38Pit		6'3"	230	Duquesne		
Nott, Doug TB-DB	38Det 35Bos	1	6'	195	Detroit		
Nowak, Walt OE-DB	44Phi		5'11"	185	Villanova		
Noyes, Len G	38Bkn		6'	214	Montana		
Obee, Dunc C-LB	41Det 42-45MS		5'11"	200	Dayton		
O'Boyle, Harry BB-DB	28-29,32GB 33Phi		5'9"	180	Notre Dame		
O'Brien, Davey (Slingshot) QB-DB	39-40Phi	12	5'7"	151	Texas Christian		12
O'Brien, Gail T	34-36Bos		6'1"	219	Nebraska		
Obst, Henry G	31SI 33Phi		5'11"	192	Syracuse		
O'Connor, Bob G-T-DE-BB	35GB		6'1"	220	Stanford		
O'Delli, Mel HB-DB	45Pit		5'8"	176	Duquesne		
Oech, Vern G	36ChiB		6'1"	207	Minnesota		
Oehler, Cap C-LB	33-34Pit 35-36Bkn		6'	204	Purdue		
Oelerich, John HB-DB	38Pit 38ChiB		6'	192	St. Ambrose		
Ohlgren, Earl DE	42GB		6'2"	210	Minnesota		
Oldershaw, Doug G-LB-DE-OE	39-41NYG 42-45MS		6'	195	Cal.–Santa Barbara	1	6
Oleniczak, Stan (Oleo) T	35Pit		6'	220	Pittsburgh		6
Oliver, Vince QB	45ChiC		5'11"	180	Indiana		
Olsen, Norm T	44Cle		6'2"	220	Alabama		
Olson, Carl T	42ChiC		6'2"	206	U.C.L.A.		
Olson, Glenn BB-DB	40Cle		6'	195	Iowa		
Olsson, Les (Swede) G	34-36Bos 37-38Was		6'	232	Mercer		
Olszewski, Al OE-DB	45Pit		6'2"	185	Penn State, Pittsburgh		
O'Neal, Willie WB-DB	35Det		5'11"	187	St. Benedict's		
O'Neill, Bill TB-DB	37Cle				George Washington		
Opalewski, Ed T	43-44Det		6'3"	230	Eastern Michigan		
Osmanski, Bill FB-LB	39-43ChiB 44-45MS 46-47ChiB	2	5'11"	197	Holy Cross	4	126
Owen, Al BB-LB-FB-DB	39-40,42NYG 43-45MS		6'	194	Mercer		6
Owen, Bill (Red) T-G	25-26KC 27Cle 28Det 29-36NYG		6'	220	Oklahoma State		
Owen, Steve T-G	24-25KC 26-30,PC31,33,HC32,34-53NYG		5'10"	260	Phillips		
Owens, Pete G-C-LB	43Bkn		5'11"	205	Texas Tech		
Padlow, Max OE-DE	35-36Phi		6'1"	199	Ohio State		
Palm, Mike DB-WB-BB	25-26NYG,PC33Cin HC34C-S		5'10"	170	Penn State		
Pangle, Hal FB-DB-LB-BB	35-38ChiC	2	5'10"	200	Oregon State		18
Pannell, Ernie T	41-42GB 43-44MS 45GB		6'2"	220	Texas A&M	1	6
Pardonner, Paul (Pudge) BB-DB	34-35ChiC		5'8"	170	Purdue		7
Parker, Ace TB-DB-QB	37-41Bkn 42-44MS 45Bos 46NY-AA	12 45	6'	178	Duke	7	148
37-38 played major league baseball							
Parker, Buddy BB-LB-FB-DB	35-36Det 37-43,HC49ChiC	2	6'	193	Centenary	2	28
	HC51-56Det HC57-64Pit						
Parker, Dave OE-DE	41Bkn 42-45MS		6'3"	200	Hardin-Simmons		
Parks, Mickey C-LB	38-40Was 41-45MS 46ChiAA		6'	225	Oklahoma		
Parriott, Bill FB-LB	34C-S				West Virginia		
Parry, Ox T	37-39NYG		6'4"	230	Baylor		
Parsons, Lloyd FB-LB	41Det 42-45MS		5'11"	197	Gustavus-Adolphus		
Paschal, Bill FB-DB-LB	43-47NYG 47-48Bos	23	6'	201	Georgia Tech		210
Paskvan, George FB-DB	41GB 42-45MS	2	6'	190	Wisconsin	2	
Pasqua, Joe T	42Cle 43Was 44-45MS 46LA		6'1"	226	S.M.U.		2
Pastin, Frank G-LB	42Pit		5'10"	197	Waynesburg		
Pate, Rupert G	40ChiC 42Phi 43-45MS		6'1"	205	Wake Forest		6
Paternoster, Angelo G-LB	43Was				Georgetown		
Patt, Maury (Babe) OE-DE	38Det 39-42Cle 43-44MS	2	6'2"	205	Carnegie-Mellon		12
Patterson, Billy TB-DB-QB-HB	39ChiB 40Pit	12 4	5'10"	167	Baylor		1
Patrick, Frank TB-DB-BB-LB	38-39ChiC	12	5'11"	190	Pittsburgh		24
Patrick, John BB-LB-FB	41Pit 42-44MS 45-46Pit		6'	202	Penn State	1	
Paulekas, Tony C-LB	36GB		5'10"	210	Wash. & Jefferson		
Pavelic, Ted T-G	41-43Det 44-45MS		6'	218	Detroit		3
Pavkov, Stan G	39-40Pit 41-45MS		6'	212	Idaho		
Payne, Charley WB-DB	37Det				Detroit		
Peace, Larry HB-DB	41Bkn 42-45MS		5'11"	185	Pittsburgh		1
Pearson, Bert C-LB-G	29-34ChiB 35-36ChiC		6'	208	Kansas State		
Pederson, Win T	41NYG 42-44MS 45NYG 46Bos		6'3"	223	Minnesota	1	3
Pense, Leon BB-DB	45Pit		6'	170	Arkansas	3	
Perdue, Bolo DE-OE	40NYG 46BknAA		5'10"	206	Duke		
Perez, Pete G	45ChiB		5'9"	220	Illinois		
Perkins, Don FB-LB	43-45GB 45-46ChiB	2	6'	198	Wis-Platteville	2	24
Perko, John G-LB	37-40Pit 44C-P 45-47Pit		6'1"	207	Duquesne	1	
Perry, Claude T-G	27-31GB 31Bkn 32-35GB		6'1"	212	Alabama		
Perry, Mike (Iron Mike) BB-LB	39Cle		5'11"	197	St. Mary's		
Petchel, John BB-DB-LB	43-44Cle 45Pit		5'11"	185	Duquesne	2	6
Peterson, Ike TB-DB-WB	35ChiC 36Det	12	5'9"	185	Gonzaga		18
Peterson, Les OE-DE	31Port 32SI 32GB 33Bkn 34GB	2	6'3"	206	Texas		
Peterson, Nelson WB-DB-TB	37Was 38Cle		5'8"	175	West Va. Wesleyan		20
Peterson, Phil OE-DE	34Bkn		5'11"	195	Wisconsin		
Peterson, Ray TB-DB	37GB			190	San Francisco		
Petrella, John HB-DB	45Pit		5'7"	160	Penn State	1	
Petrilas, Bill DB-WB	44-45NYG		6'1"	195	none	7	12
Petro, Steve G-LB	40-41Bkn 42-45MS		5'10"	195	Pittsburgh		

Use Name (Nicknames) – Positions	Team by Year	See Section	Hgt	Wgt	College	Int	Pts
Petty, John FB-LB	42ChiB 43-45MS	2	6'1"	225	Purdue	1	12
Phillips, Ewell G	36NYG		5'11"	210	Okla. Baptist		
Phillips, George LB	45Cle		6'3"	215	U. C. L. A.		
Piasecky, Alex OE-DE	43-45Was	2	6'2"	197	Duke	1	6
Piccolo, Bill C-LB	43-45NYG		5'11"	185	Canisius	2	6
Piepul, Milt FB-LB	41Det		6'1"	215	Notre Dame		
Pierce, Don C-LB	42Bkn 43ChiC		6'1"	186	Kansas		
Pierre, John OE-DE	45Pit		6'	185	Pittsburgh		
Pilconis, Joe OE-DE	34,36-37Phi	2	6'1"	189	Temple		12
Pinckert, Ernie WB-DB-BB-LB	32-36Bos 37-40Was	2	6'	197	Southern Calif.		18
Pincura, Stan BB-DB	37-38Cle	12	5'11"	175	Ohio State		6
Pingel, Johnny TB-DB	39Det	12 4	6'	180	Michigan State		6
Piro, Hank OE-DB	41Phi 42-45MS	2	6'	186	Syracuse	1	6
Pittman, Swede C-LB	35Pit		6'	215	Hardin-Simmons		
Pitts, Alabama HB-DB	35Phi		5'10"	185	none		
Pivaronik, Joe G	36Phi		5'9"	217	Notre Dame		
Plasman, Dick DE-OE-T	37-41ChiB 42-43MS 44ChiB	2 5	6'3"	218	Vanderbilt		56
	46-47ChiC						
Platukas, George OE-DE	38-41Pit 42Cle 43-45MS	2	6'	196	Duquesne	1	42
Plunkett, Warren BB-LB	42Cle 43-45MS		6'	200	Minnesota		
Podmajersky, Paul G	44ChiB		5'11"	220	Illinois		
Pollock, Red HB-LB	35-36ChiB		6'2"	194	PMC Colleges		24
Pool, Hamp OE-DE	40-43ChiB 44-45MS PC46MiaAA	2	6'3"	221	Stanford		66
	HC47ChiAA HC52-54LA						
Poole, Jim OE-DE	37-41NYG 42-44MS 45ChiC 45-46NYG	2	6'3"	218	Mississippi	2	84
Pope, Lew (Chicken) DB-WB-TB-BB-FB-LB	31Prov 33Cin		6'	196	Purdue		6
	34C-S						
Popovich, John HB-DB	44C-P 45Pit		5'8"	160	St. Vincent		
Popovich, Milt FB-DB-WB-LB-G-BB	38-42ChiC	2 4	5'11"	196	Montana	1	6
Postus, Al TB-DB	45Pit		5'10"	180	Villanova		
Poth, Phil G	34Phi				Gonzaga		
Potts, Bill HB-DB	34Pit			200	Villanova		
Powell, Dick (Tiny) OE-DE	32NYG 33Cin		6'2"	220	Davis & Elkins		
Prather, Dale OE-DE-T	37-38Cle		6'2"	190	George Washington		
Presnell, Glenn TB-DB-WB	31-33Port 34-36Det	12 5	5'10"	193	Nebraska		169
Pressley, Lee C-LB-FB	45Was		6'2"	230	Oklahoma		
Price, Cotton TB-DB-QB	40-41Det 42-44MS 45Det	12	6'1"	183	Texas A&M	1	16
	46MiaAA						
Priestley, Bob OE-DE	42Phi		5'11"	192	Brown		
Principe, Dom LB-BB-FB-DB	40-42NYG 43-45MS 46BknAA	2	6'	205	Fordham		12
Prisco, Nick TB-DB	33Phi		5'8"	193	Rutgers		
Prochaska, Ray OE-DE	41Cle 42-45Ms HC61StL		6'3"	205	Nebraska		
Pudloski, Chet T	44Cle 45MS		6'1"	210	Villanova		
Pugh, Marion QB-DB	4INYG 42-44MS 45NYG 46MiaAA	12	6'1"	187	Texas A&M		12
Puplis, Andy WB-DB	43ChiC 44-45MS		5'9"	180	Notre Dame	1	
Pylman Bob T	38-39Phi		6'4"	214	S. Dakota State		6
Quatse, Jess T	33GB 33Pit 33GB 34Pit 35NYG		5'11"	226	Pittsburgh		
Raborn, Buster C-LB	36-37Pit		6'	198	S. M. U.		
Rado, Alex (Pug, Moose) HB-DB	34Pit		6'1"	200	West Va. Tech.		
Rado, George (Mousie) G-DE	35-37Pit, 37-38Phi		5'9"	194	Duquesne		
Radovich, Bill G	38-41Det 42-44MS 45Det 46-47LA-AA		5'10"	238	Southern Calif.		
Ragazzo, Phil T-G	38-40Cle 40-41Phi 42-44MS 45-47NYG		6'	216	Case Reserve		
Rajkovich, Pete FB-LB	34Pit				Detroit		
Ramsey, Frank T	45ChiB		6'1"	240	Oregon State		
Ramsey, Red OE-DE	38-40Phi	2	6'	196	Texas Tech		12
Randolph, Clare C-LB	30ChiC 31-33Port 34-36Det		6'2"	208	Indiana		
Rankin, Walt LB-FB-DB	41,43ChiC 44C-P 45-47ChiC	2	5'11"	197	Texas Tech	8	
Ranspot, Keith OE-DE-DB	40ChiC 42Det 42GB 43Bkn	2	6'3"	199	S. M. U.		24
	44-45Bos						
Rapp, Manny TB-DB	34C-S			215	St. Louis		
Raskowski, Leo T	32SI 33Bkn 33Pit 35Phi		6'3"	219	Ohio State		
Ratica, Joe C-LB	39Bkn		6'	205	St. Vincent		
Ray, Baby T	38-48GB		6'6"	249	Vanderbilt	1	
Rayburn, Van OE-DE	33Bkn		6'1"	180	Tennessee		
Ream, Chuck T	38Cle		6'2"	225	Ohio State		
Reckmack, Ray BB-DB	37Bkn 37Det		6'	200	Syracuse		
Reed, Rock WB-DB	37,39ChiC		5'8"	173	Louisiana State		6
Reese, Hank C-LB-G	33-34NYG 35-39Phi	5	5'11"	214	Temple		39
Reissig, Bill BB-LB-DE	38-39Bkn		6'	195	Ft. Hays Kan. St.		9
Reisz, Albie TB-DB-QB	44-45Cle 46LA 47BufAA	12 4	5'10"	174	Southeastern La.	5	12
Rentner, Pug DB-WB-FB-HB-TB-BB	34-36Bos 37ChiB	12	6'1"	187	Northwestern		43
Reutt, Ray DE	43P-P		6'	195	V. M. I.		
Rexer, Freeman DE-OE	43ChiC 44Bos 44Det 45ChiC		6'1"	211	Tulane		
Reynolds, Bill HB-DB	44Bkn 45ChiC	4	5'8"	183	Mississippi		6
Reynolds, Bob T	37-38Det		6'4"	221	Stanford		
Reynolds, Homer G	34C-S			185	Tulsa		
Reynolds, John C-LB	37ChiC				Baylor		
Rhea, Floyd G-LB	43ChiC 44Bkn 45Bos 47Det		6'	218	Oregon	1	
Rhea, Hughie G	33Bkn		6'3"	225	Nebraska		
Rhodes, Don T	33Pit			225	Wash. & Jefferson		
Ribar, Frank G-LB	43Was 44-45MS		6'1"	190	Duke		
Ribble Dave (Tex, Babe) G	32Port 33ChiC 34-35Pit		6'1"	216	Hardin-Simmons		
Riblett, Paul OE-DE	32-36Bkn	2	5'10"	184	Pennsylvania		12
Richards, Dick FB-DB-BB-LB	33Bkn		6'	194	Kentucky		
Richards, Kink FB-DB-BB-TB	33-39NYG	2	5'11"	195	Simpson		
Richards, Ray G-T	30Fra 33ChiB 34Det 35ChiB		6'1"	233	Nebraska		
	HC55-57ChiC						
Richins, Al WB-DB	35Det		5'9"	188	Utah		
Riddick, Ray DE-OE	40-42GB 43-45MS 46GB	2	6'1"	211	Fordham		6
Rieth, Bill C-LB-G	41-42Cle 43MS 44-45Cle		5'11"	203	Carnegie-Mellon	1	
Riffle, Dick DB-FB-TB-HB-QB	38-40Phi 41-42Pit	12 4	6'1"	200	Albright	10	73
Riggs, Thron T	44Bos 45MS		6'1"	225	Washington		
Riley, Jack T	33Bos		6'2"	230	Northwestern		
Ritchhart, Del C-LB	36-37Det		6'	195	Colorado		
Robbins, John TB-DB	38-39ChiC	12	6'2"	183	Arkansas		
Roberts,Jack HB-DB-FB-LB	32Bos 32SI 33-34Phi 34Pit		6'	215	Georgia		6
Roberts, Tom T-G	43NYG 44-45ChiB		6'1"	215	DePaul		
Robertson, Bob HB-DB	42Bkn 43-45MS	2	5'11"	185	Southern Calif.	2	
Robertson, Lake DE	45Det		6'1"	210	Mississippi		
Robertson, Tom C-LB	41-42Bkn 43-45Ms 46NYAA		6'	219	Tulsa	1	
Robinson, Gil OE-DE	33Pit				Catawba		
Robinson, Jack T-G	35-36Bkn 36-37ChiC 38Pit 38Cle		6'3"	220	NE Missouri St.		
Robison, Buke OE-DE-C-LB	35Phi		6'4"	197	Brigham Young		
Robl, Hal LB	45ChiC		6'	227	Wis. St. – Oshkosh		

Use Name (Nicknames) – Positions	Team by Year	See Section	Hgt	Wgt	College	Int	Pts
Robnett, Marshall LB-C-G	43ChiC 44C-P 45ChiC		6'	205	Texas A&M	1	1
Rockenbach, Lyle G	43Det 44-45MS		5'9"	192	Michigan State		
Rockwell, Hank C-G-LB-DE	40-42Cle 43-45MS 46,48LA-AA		6'4"	231	Arizona State	2	6
Rodak, Mike BB-LB-DE-G	39-40Cle 41BL 42Pit 43-45MS		5'10"	196	Case Reserve		
Rogalla, John FB-LB	45Phi		6'	215	Scranton		1
Rogers, Bill T	38-40, 44,Det		5'11"	243	Villanova		
Rogers, Glynn G	39ChiC			220	Texas Christian		
Rogers, John (Bee) C-LB	33Cin 34C-S		5'11"	208	Notre Dame		
Rogge, George OE-DE	31-33ChiC 34C-S		6'	185	Iowa		
Ronzani, Gene QB-HB-DB-LB-FB	33-38,44-45ChiB	12	5'9"	200	Marquette	3	57
	HC50-53GB						
Rorison, Red T	38Pit		6'3"	250	Southern Calif.		
Rose, Al OE-DE	30-31Prov 32-36GB		6'3"	200	Texas		18
Rose, Gene OE-DE	36NYG		6'1"	185	Tennessee		
Rosequist, Ted T-G-DE-OE	34-36ChiB 37Cle		6'4"	222	Ohio State		
Rosteck, Ernie C-LB	43-44Det		6'1"	218	none		
Roton, Herb (Bummy) OE-DE	37Phi		6'2"	210	Auburn		
Rouse, Stillman OE-DE	40Det 41-45MS		6'2"	205	Missouri		
Rovinski, Tony OE-DE	33NYG		5'9"	195	Holy Cross		
Rowan, Ev OE-DE	30,32Bkn 33Phi			190	Ohio State		
Rowe, Bob FB-LB-WB-DB	34Det 35Phi		6'	198	Colgate		
Rubino, Tony G	43Det 44-45MS 46Det		5'10"	208	Wake Forest		
Rucinski, Eddie OE-DE-DB	41-42Bkn 43ChiC 44C-P	2	6'2"	197	Indiana	4	48
	45-46ChiC						
Rukas, Justin G	36Bkn		6'	205	Louisiana State		
Russell, Bo T	39-40Was 41-45MS	5	6'1"	223	Auburn		38
Russell, Doug WB-DB-TB	34-39ChiC 39Cle	12	6'	187	Kansas State		36
Russell, Jim G-T	36-37Phi		5'11"	210	Temple		
Russell, Reb DB-HB-WB	33NYG 33Phi		6'1"	195	Northwestern		
Ryan, Rip WB-DB-FB	38-40Det 41-45MS	2	6'2"	193	Utah State	6	12
Sabados, Andy G	39-40ChiC		5'11"	209	The Citadel		
Sachse, Frank DB-TB-QB-HB	43-44Bkn 45Bos	1	6'	197	Texas Tech	2	
43-45 played in N.B.L.							
Sachse, Jack C-LB	45Bos		6'	210	Texas		
Sader, Steve FB-LB	43P-P		5'11"	180	Temple		
Sample, Charlie FB-LB	42BG 43-44MS 45GB	2	5'9"	205	Toledo		30
Sandberg, Sandy T	34C-S 35-37Pit 37Bkn		6'2"	228	Iowa Wesleyan		
Sandefur, Wayne FB-LB-DB	36-37Pit		5'10"	195	Purdue		
Sanders, Jack G-LB	40-42Pit 43-44MS 45Phi	5	6'	219	S. M. U.	1	12
Sanders, Paul HB-DB	44Bos		5'11"	192	Utah State		
Sandig, Curt HB-DB	42Pit 43-45MS 46BufAA	2 4	5'10"	173	St. Mary's (Tex.)	5	30
Sanford, Sandy OE-DE	40Was 41-45MS		6'1"	210	Alabama		3
Sansen, Ollie DB-FB-HB	32-35Bkn		6'1"	193	Iowa		6
Santora, Frank DB-QB	44Bos 45MS		5'10"	166	none		
Sanzotta, Mickey WB-DB-TB	42Det 45-45MS 46Det	2	5'9"	188	Case Reserve	2	
Sarafiny, Al C-LB	33GB			235	St. Edward's		
Sarausky, Tony TB-DB-QB-FB	35-37NYG 38Bkn	12	5'11"	201	Fordham		17
Sarboe, Phil DB-TB-BB	34Bos 34-36ChiC 36Bkn	12	5'10"	167	Washington State		12
Sark, Harvey G	31 NYG 34C-S				Phillips		
Sartori, Larry G	42Det 43-44MS 45Det		6'	208	Fordham		
Satenstein, Ollie G	29-32SI 33NYG		6'	230	N. Y. U.		
Sauer, George HB-FB-DB-LB-TB	35-37GB	2	6'2"	208	Nebraska		42
Saumer, Syl TB-DB-FB-LB	34Pit 34C-S 34Pit		6'1"	195	St. Olaf		6
Savatsky, Ollie OE-DE	37Cle		6'2"	215	Miami-Ohio		
Scafide, John T	33Bos				Tulane		
Scarry Mike C-LB-T	44-45Cle 46-47CleAA		6'	214	Waynesburg	7	
Schaake, Elmer (Dutch) FB-LB	33Port	2	5'11"	207	Kansas		6
Schammel, Bud G-DE	37GB		6'2"	235	Iowa		6
Schenker, Nate T	39Cle		6'2"	220	Howard (Ala.)		
Scherer Bernie OE-DE	36-38GB 39Pit	2	6'1"	190	Nebraska		24
Scheuer, Babe T	34NYG		6'3"	240	N. Y. U.		
Schibanoff, Alex T	41-42Det 43-45MS		6'1"	218	Franklin & Marsh.		
Schiechl, John C-LB	41-42Pit 42Det 43-44MS 45-46ChiB		6'2"	244	Santa Clara	6	
	47-SF-AA						
Schissler, Paul	HC33-34ChiC HC35-36Bkn				Nebraska		
Schmaar, Herm DE	43Bkn		6'2"	210	Catholic		
Schmidt, John C-LB	40Pit		6'3"	210	Carnegie-Mellon		
Schmidt Kermit (Dutch) OE-DE	32Bos 33Cin		6'	200	Cal. St. Polytech		
Schmitt, Ted G-C-LB	38-40Phi		5'11"	216	Pittsburgh		6
Schneidman, Herm (Biff) BB-DB-LB	35-38GB 40ChiC		5'11"	201	Iowa		12
Schneller, John OE-DE	33Port 34-36Det	2	6'2"	204	Wisconsin		18
Schoemann, Ray C-LB	38GB		6'1"	192	Marquette		
Schuehle, Jake LB	39Phi		6'	196	Rice		
Schuelke, Karl FB-DB	39Pit		5'10"	200	Wisconsin		
Schultz, Charlie T	39-41GB 42-45MS		6'3"	231	Minnesota		
Schultz, Elbie T-G	40Phi 41-42Pit 43P-P 44C-P 45Cle		6'4"	252	Oregon State		6
	46-47LA						
Schwammel Ade (Tar) T	34-36, 43-44GB		6'2"	225	Oregon State		26
Schwartz, Elmer HB-DB-FB-LB	31Port 32ChiC 33Pit		6'	215	Washington State		
Schwartz, Perry OE-DE	38-42Bkn 43-45MS 46NY-AA	2	6'2"	199	California		60
Schweidler, Dick HB-DB	38-39, 46ChiB	2	6'	182	St. Louis	1	18
Scott, Perry OE-DE	42Det 43-45MS		6'2"	210	Muhlenberg		
Sebastian, Mike DB-HB-WB	35Phi 35Pit 37Cle		5'11"	185	Pittsburgh		
Seeman, George OE-DE	40GB		6'1"	195	Nebraska		
Seibold, Champ T-G	34-38GB 39VR 40GB 42ChiC		6'4"	238	Wisconsin	1	6
Seick, Red G-LB	42NYG 43-45MS		6'	195	Manhattan		
Seltzer, Harry FB-LB	42Det 43-45MS		5'9"	195	Morris Harvey		
Semes, Bernie HB-DB	44C-P		5'7"	188	Duquesne	1	
Senn, Bill TB-DB	26-31ChiB 31Bkn 33Cin 34C-S		6'	180	Knox		3
Sergienko, George T	43-44Bkn 45Bos 46BknAA		6'1"	248	American Inter.		
Setcavage, Joe BB-DB	43Bkn		5'11"	190	Duquesne	1	
Seymour, Bob DB-FB-HB-WB	40-45Was 46LA-AA	23	6'2"	205	Oklahoma	17	138
Shaffer, George BB-DB	33Pit			190	Wash. & Jefferson		
Shaffer, Leland BB-DB-LB-WB	35-43,45NYG	2	6'2"	203	Kansas State	2	36
Sharp, Ev T	44-45Was		6'1"	223	Cal. St. Polytech		
Shedlosky, Ed WB-DB	45NY,G		6'	185	Tulsa, Fordham		
Shellogg, Alec T	39ChiB 39Bkn		6'	215	Notre Dame		
Shenefelt, Paul T	34ChiC		6'	195	Manchester		
Shepherd, Bill FB-LB-TB-DB-BB	35Bos 35-40Det	12 5	5'9"	199	Western Maryland		110
Sherman, Allie QB-DB	43P-P 44-47Phi HC61-68NYG	12	5'11"	170	C. U. N. Y. – Bklyn.	2	24
Sherman, Solly QB-DB	39-40ChiB		6'1"	190	Chicago		6
Shetley, Rhoten BB-LB-FB	40-42Bkn 43-45MS 46BknAA	2	5'11"	208	Furman	2	18
Shires, Art T	45Phi		6'2"	220	Tennessee		

Use Name (Nicknames) – Positions	Team by Year	See Section	Hgt	Wgt	College	Int	Pts
Shirey, Fred T	40-41Cle		6'2"	223	Nebraska		
Shirk, John OE-DE	40ChiC41-45MS	2	6'4"	200	Oklahoma		
Shonk, John OE-DB	41Phi 42-45MS		6'1"	190	West Virginia	1	
Shook, Fred C-LB	41ChiC 42-45MS		6'	218	Texas Christian		
Shugart, Clyde G-LB-T	39-44Was		6'1"	221	Iowa State	1	
Siano, Tony C-LB	32Bos 34Bkn		5'8"	172	Fordham		
Siegal, John OE-DE	39-43ChiB 44-45MS	2	6'1"	203	Columbia		42
Siemering, Larry C-LB	35-36Bos		6'3"	206	San Francisco		6
Sigillo, Dom T	45Det		6'	230	Xavier-Ohio		
Sikich, Rudy T	45Cle		6'1"	220	Minnesota		
Simas, Bill BB-DB	32-33ChiC		6'	185	St. Mary's		
Simington, Milt G	41Cle 42Pit		6'2"	217	Arkansas		4
died Jan 18, 1943—heart attack							
Singer, Walt OE-DE	35-36NYG		6'	198	Syracuse		12
Sinko, Steve T	34-36Bos		6'3"	232	Duquesne		
Sinkwich, Frankie TB-DB-HB	43-44Det 45MS 46-47NY-AA	12 45	5'11"	190	Georgia	4	78
	47BalAA						
Sirochman, George G	42Pit 44Det		6'2"	215	Duquesne		
Sisk, Johnny (Big Train) HB-LB	32-36ChiB	2	6'2"	197	Marquette		18
Sites, Vinnie OE-DE	36-37Pit		6'2"	215	Pittsburgh		6
Sivell, Jim (Happy) G	38-42Bkn 43MS 44Bkn 44-45NYG		5'9"	205	Auburn		
	46MiaAA						
Skladany, Joe (Muggsy) OE-DE	34Pit	2		210	Pittsburgh		12
Skoczen, Stan HB-DB	44Cle				Case Reserve		
Skoronski, Ed OE-DE-C-LB-G-T	35-36Pit 37Bkn 37Cle		6'2"	213	Purdue		6
Slivinski, Steve G-LB	39-43Was		5'10"	214	Washington	2	
Sloan, Swight (Paddlefoot) TB-DB	38ChiC 39-40Det 41-45MS	12	5'10"	180	Arkansas		24
Slovak, Marty (The Elliston Eel) TB-DB	39-41Cle	12	5'9"	179	Toledo		6
	42-45MS						
Smeja, Rudy OE-DE	44-45ChiB 46Phi	2	6'2"	195	Michigan		6
Smilanich, Bronko TB-DB	39Cle		5'11"	180	Arizona		
Smith, Ben (Big Ben) OE-DE	33GB 34-35Pit 37Was	2	6'3"	208	Alabama		
Smith, Bill OE–DE	34-39ChiC	2 5	6'1"	198	Washington		132
Smith, Dick C-LB	33Phi 33ChiB		6'2"	225	Ohio State		
Smith, Ed TB-DB	36Bos 37GB	1	6'2"	207	N. Y. U.		3
Smith, Ernie T	35-37GB 38VR 39GB	5	6'2"	224	Southern Calif.		61
Smith, Gaylon FB-DB-LB-WB-BB-TB	39-42Cle 43-45MS	12	5'11"	202	SW at Memphis	6	54
	46Cle AA						
Smith, George C-LB	37,41-43Was 44Bkn 45Bos 47SF-AA		6'2"	220	California	6	
Smith, George FB-DB	43ChiC 44-45MS		6'1"	200	Villanova		
Smith, Harry T	40Det		5'11"	215	Southern Calif.		
Smith, Jack DE-OE	42Phi 43Was 44-45MS		6'1"	200	Stanford		
Smith, John T	45Phi		6'2"	200	Florida		
Smith, Milt DB-OE	45Phi		6'3"	185	U. C. L. A.		
Smith, Ray C-LB	30Port 30-31Prov 33Phi			220	Missouri		
Smith, Riley (General) BB-LB	36Bos 37-38Was	12 5	6'2"	200	Alabama		108
Smith, Stu FB-LB-TB-DB-BB	37-38Pit	2	6'	195	Bucknell		
Smith, Wee Willie FB-DB	34NYG	2	5'6"	148	Idaho		12
Smukler, Dave (Dynamite) FB-LB	36-39Phi 43MS 44Bos	12 5	6'1"	226	Temple		40
Sneddon, Bob DB-HB-WB	44Was 45Det 46LA-AA		5'10"	180	St. Mary's	2	
Snelling, Ken FB-LB	45GB		6'	210	U. C. L. A.		
Snyder, Bob QB-DB-TB	37-38Cle 39-41ChiB 42VR 43ChiB	12 5	6'	200	Ohio U.	2	108
	HC47LA						
Snyder, Bull G	34-35Pit		6'2"	230	Ohio U.		
Soar, Hank DB-FB-WB-QB	37-44NYG 45MS 46NYG	12 5	6'2"	209	Providence	12	73
47-48 coached in B. A. A.							
Sohn, Ben G	41NYG 42-45MS		6'2"	220	Southern Calif.		
Sohn, Ben FB-LB	34C-S				Washington		
Somers, George T	39-40Phi 41-42Pit	5	6'2"	253	LaSalle		8
Sorce, Ross T	45Pit		6'4"	255	Georgetown		
Sorenson, Glen G-LB	43-45GB		6'	217	Utah State		1
Sortet, Bill OE-DE	33-40Pit	2	6'1"	187	West Virginia		48
Souchak, Frank OE-DE	39Pit		6'	205	Pittsburgh		
Spadaccini, Vic BB-DB-WB	38-40Cle 42-45MS	2 5	6'	222	Minnesota		41
Speegle, Cliff C-LB	45ChiC		6'1"	195	Oklahoma	2	
Speelman, Harry G	40Det		5'11"	220	Michigan State		
Speth, George T	42Det 43-45MS		6'2"	220	Murray State		
Spillers, Ray (Brush) T	37Phi		6'3"	218	Arkansas		
Spirida, John BB-DE-OE	39Was		6'	195	St. Anselm's		
Springer, Hal OE-DE	45NYG		6'4"	212	Central St.–Okla.		
Squyres, Seaman (Cob) TB-DB	33Cin		6'3"	200	Rice		
Stackpool, Jack FB-LB	42Phi 43-45MS		6'1"	207	Washington		
Stacy, Red T-G	35-37Det		6'2"	210	Oklahoma		
Stafford, Harry WB-DB	34NYG		5'11"	205	Texas		
Stahlman, Dick T	24Ham 24Ken 24-25Akr 26RI			216	DePaul,		
	27-28,30NYG 31-32GB 33ChiB				Northwestern		
Starrett, Ben BB-DE-LB-TB	41Pit 42-45GB		5'11"	213	St. Mary's	2	12
Stasica, Leo DB-QB-TB	41Bkn 42MS 43Was 44Bos	12	5'11"	185	Colorado	2	
Steele, Ernie HB-DB	42Phi 43P-P 44-48Phi	23	6'	187	Washington	24	115
Steen, Frank OE-DE	39GB		6'1"	190	Rice		
Steen, Jim T	35-36Det		6'2"	205	Syracuse		
Steinbach, Larry T	30-31ChiB 31-33ChiC 33Phi		6'	212	St. Thomas		
Steinkemper, Bill T	43ChiB 44MS			220	Notre Dame		
Steinmetz, Ken FB-LB	44-45Bos		6'	188	none	1	
Stephens, Johnny OE-DE	38Cle		6'1"	190	Marshall		
Steponovich, Mike G	33Bos			205	St. Mary's		
Stevens, Pete C-LB	36Phi		6'	215	Temple		
Stevenson, Ralph G-LB	40Cle 41-45MS		5'10"	196	Oklahoma		
Steverson, Norris BB-DB-WB	34C-S		5'11"	190	Arizona State		
Steward, Dean HB	43P-P 44-45MS		6'	210	Ursinus		
Stewart, Vaughn C-LB	43ChiC 43-44Bkn		6'1"	190	Alabama		
Stockton, Mule G-T	37-38Phi		6'1"	214	McMurry		
Stofko, Ed TB-DB	45Pit		6'1"	192	St. Francis-Pa.		
Stojack, Frank (Toughie) G	35-36Bkn		5'10"	194	Washington State		
Stokes, Dixie C-LB	37-39Det 43ChiC		6'	205	Centenary		8
Stolfa, Anton QB-DB	39ChiB		6'	195	Luther		
Stonebraker, John OE-DE	42GB		6'3"	200	Southern Calif.		
Storm, Ed TB-DB-HB-FB	34-35Ph	1	6'1"	195	Santa Clara		12
Stough, Glenn T	45Pit		6'5"	240	Duke		
Stralka, Clem (Little Bull) G	38-42Was 43-44MS		5'10"	215	Georgetown		
	45-46Was						
Stramiello, Mike OE-DE	30-32Bkn 32SI 34Bkn		6'1"	207	Colgate		
Stringfellow, Joe TB-DB-OE	42Det 43-45MS		6'	185	Southern Miss.		
Strom, Frank T	44Bkn		6'2"	252	Claremore J. C.		
Strong, Ken FB-DB-K	29-32SI 33-35,39,44-47NYG	2 5	6'	206	N. Y. U.		319
Strutt, Art HB-DB	35-36Pit	2	6'	202	Duquesne		12
Stuart, Jim T	41Was		6'	212	Oregon		

Use Name (Nicknames) – Positions	Team by Year	See Section	Hgt	Wgt	College	Int	Pts
Stuart, Roy G-LB	42Cle 43Det 44-45MS 46BufAA		5'8"	188	Tulsa		
Sturgeon, Cecil T	41Phi		6'2"	254	N. Dakota State		
Sturgeon, Lyle T	37GB		6'3"	250	N. Dakota State		
Stydahar, Joe T	36-42ChiB 43-44MS 45-46ChiB	5	6'4"	233	West Virginia	1	28
	HC50-51LA HC53-54ChiC						
Suffridge, Bob G	41Phi 42-44MS 45Phi		6'	205	Tennessee		
Sullivan, Frank C-LB	35-39ChiB 40Pit		6'3"	206	Loyola (N. Orl.)		
Supulski, Len OE-DB	42Phi 43-44MS-killed in action		6'	175	Dickinson	1	6
Sutherland, Jock	HC40-41Bkn 42-45MS HC46-47Pit				Pittsubrgh		
Svendsen, Bud C-LB-G	37,39GB 38VR 40-43Bkn 44-45MS		6'1"	190	Minnesota	3	6
Svendsen, George C-LB	35-37, 40-41GB 42-45MS		6'4"	230	Minnesota	1	
37-39 played in N.B.L.							
Sweeney, Jake T	44ChiB		6'3"	240	Cincinnati		
Swiadon, Phil G	43Bkn		6'	220	N. Y. U.		
Swisher, Bob HB-DB	38-41ChiB 42-44MS 45ChiB	2	5'11"	163	Northwestern	2	36
Szakash, Paul (Socko) BB-DB-FB-LB-OE-DE	38-39Det 40VR		6'	213	Montana		
	41-42Det 43-45MS						
Tackwell, Cookie OE-DE	30Min 30-31Fra 31-33ChiB		6'2"	215	Kansas State		
	33Cin 34C-S						
Tanguay, Bill TB-DB	33Pit				N. Y. U.		
Tarrant, Bob OE-DE	36NYG		6'	180	Kansas State C.		
Tatum, Jess OE-DE	38Pit		6'1"	215	N. Carolina State		
Taylor, Charlie BB-LB	44Bkn		5'10"	210	Ouachita Baptist		
Temple, Mark TB-DB	36Bkn 36Bos		5'10"	175	Oregon		6
Tenner, Bob OE-DE	35GB		6'	212	Minnesota		
Tesser, Ray OE-DE	33-34Pit	2	6'2"	204	Carnegie-Mellon		
Thacker, Al DB	42Phi		5'10"	200	Morris Harvey		
Thayer, Harry T-G	33Port		6'1"	215	Tennessee		
Thomas, Cal G	39-40Det		6'2"	210	Tulsa		
Thomas, Jim G	39ChiC		5'11"	200	Oklahoma		
Thomason, Jim WB-DB	45Det		6'	200	Texas A&M		
Thomason, Stumpy BB-DB-FB-LB-HB	30-35Bkn 35-36Phi	2	5'7"	191	Georgia Tech		1
Thompson, Russ T	36-39ChiB 40Phi		6'5"	249	Nebraska		
Thompson, Tuffy HB-DB-TB	37-38Pit 39GB	2	5'11"	172	Minnesota		12
Thornton, Dick BB-DB	33Phi		5'11"	195	Missouri–Rolla		
Thorpe, Wilfred G-LB-DE	41-42Cle 43-45MS		6'3"	205	Arkansas	2	
Thurbon, Bob HB-DB	43P-P 44C-P 46BufAA	2	5'10"	176	Pittsburgh	3	66
Tiller, Morgan OE-DE	44Bos 45Pit	2	6'1"	195	Denver		
Tinsley, Gaynell OE-DE	37-38ChiC 39HO 40ChiC	2	6'1"	198	Louisiana State		48
Tinsley, Jess T	29-33ChiC		6'	204	Louisiana State		
Tinsley, Pete G-LB	38-45GB		5'8"	205	Georgia	4	
Tinsley, Sid HB-DB	45Pit	4	5'9"	168	Clemson	1	
Tipton, Howie G-OE-DE-LB-DB-BB-WB-TB	33-37ChiC		5'11"	186	Southern Calif.		6
Titchenal, Bob LB-OE-C-DE	40-42Was 43-45MS 46SF-AA	2	6'2"	194	San Jose State	3	12
	47LA-AA						
Titus, Si C-LB-DE	40-42Bkn 43-44MS 45Pit		6'	195	Holy Cross	2	
Todd, Dick DB-HB-WB-FB	39-42Was 43-44MS 45-48Was	234	5'11"	172	Texas A&M	14	208
	HC51Was						
Tofil, Joe OE-DB	42Bkn 43-45MS		6'1"	205	Indiana		
Tollefson, Charlie G	44-46GB		6'	215	Iowa		
Tomaini, Army T	45NYG		6'	235	Catawba		
Tomasello, Carl DE	40NYG		6'	210	Scranton		
Tomasic, Andy TB-DB	42Pit 43-45MS 46Pit	12	6'	175	Temple	2	6
49 played major league baseball							
Tommerson, Clarence DB-HB	38-39Pit		6'2"	196	Wisconsin		
Tonelli, Mario FB-DB	40ChiC 41-44MS	2	5'11"	200	Notre Dame		6
Tonelli, Tony C-LB-G	39Det		6'	210	Southern Calif.		
Torrance, John T	39-40ChiB		6'3"	285	Louisiana State		
Tosi, Flavio (Bull) OE-DE	34-36Bos	2	6'1"	191	Boston College		12
Tosi, John C-LB-T-G	39Pit 39Bkn		5'10"	225	Niagara		
Trebotich, Buzz BB-DB-LB-FB	44-45Det 47Bal AA		5'10"	208	St. Mary's	3	
Tripson, John T	41Det 42-45MS		6'3"	210	Mississippi State		
Trocolor, Bob QB-DB-HB	42-43NYG 44Bkn	2	6'2"	207	Alabama		
Trost, Milt (Bud) T-DE-OE	35-39ChiB 40Phi		6'1"	206	Marquette		
Tsoutsouvas, Lou C-LB	38Pit		5'11"	210	Stanford		
Tsoutsouvas, Sam C-LB	40Det		6'	205	Oregon State		
Tuckey, Dick TB-DB	38Was 38Cle	12	6'2"	205	Manhattan		2
Tully, Darrell TB-DB	39Det	12	6'1"	200	East Texas State		6
Turbert, Frank QB-DB	44Bos		5'11"	200	Morris Harvey		
Turley, John BB-DB	35-36Pit	1	5'10"	183	Ohio Wesleyan		
Turnbow, Guy T-OE-DB	33-34Phi		6'2"	217	Mississippi		3
Turner, Jay BB-LB	38-39Was		5'10"	202	George Washington		
Turner, Jim C-LB	37Cle		6'2"	210	Oklahoma State		
Tuttle, Orville G	37-41NYG 42-45MS 46NYG		5'9"	210	Oklahoma City		
Twedell, Frank G	39GB		5'11"	220	Minnesota		
Tyler, Pete BB-LB	37-38ChiC		5'11"	190	Hardin-Simmons		12
Ucovich, Mitch T	44Was 45ChiC		5'11"	208	San Jose State		
Uguccioni, Rocky OE-DE	44Bkn 45MS		6'	195	Murray State		6
Uhrinyak, Steve G	39Was		6'2"	218	Franklin & Marsh.		
Umont, Frank G-T	43-45NYG		5'11"	218	none		
Underwood, Wayne T	37Cle		6'1"	190	Davis & Elkins		
Ungerer, Joe T	44-45Was		6'	243	Fordham		
Uram, Andy HB-DB-TB	38-43GB 44-45MS	2	5'10"	188	Minnesota	6	98
Urban, Alex DE-OE	41GB 42-43MS 44-45GB		6'3"	207	South Carolina		6
Uremovich, Emil T	41-42Det 43-44MS 45-46Det 48ChiAA		6'2"	233	Indiana	1	
Uzdavinis, Walt DE-OE-T	37Cle		6'2"	210	Fordham		
Vairo, Dom OE-DE	35GB		6'2"	203	Notre Dame		
Van Every, Hal TB-DB-HB	40-41GB 42-45MS	12 4	6'	195	Minnesota	3	18
Van Sickle, Clyde G	32-33GB			225	Arkansas		
Vant Hull, Fred G-LB	42GB 43-45MS		6'	214	Minnesota		
Van Tone, Art WB-DB	43-45Det 46BknAA	2	5'10"	185	Southern Miss.	7	60
Vanzo, Fred (Chopper) BB-LB	38-41Det 41ChiC 42-45MS	2	6'2"	230	Northwestern		
Vaughan, Harp DB-BB-TB-HB	33-34Pit	1	5'7"	165	Indiana (Pa.)		6
Vaughan, Pug TB-DB	35Det 36ChiC	12	5'11"	181	Tennessee		
Vetter, Jack HB-DB	42Bkn 43-45MS		6'2"	198	McPherson		
Vidoni, Vic (Putt) OE-DE	35-36Pit	2	6'1"	210	Duquesne		
Visnic, Larry LB-G-BB	43-45NYG		5'11"	190	St. Benedict's	3	
Vodicka, Joe HB-DB	43ChiB 44MS 45ChiB 45ChiC		5'10"	189	none		
Vokaty, Otto FB-LB	31Cle 32NYG 33ChiC 34C-S		6'1"	193	Heidelberg		
Volok, Bill G-T	34-39ChiC		6'2"	215	Tulsa		6
Vosberg, Don OE-DE	41NYG 42-45MS		6'2"	188	Marquette		
Vucinich, Milt C-LB	45ChiB		6'	215	Stanford		
Wager, Clint OE-DE	42ChiB 43ChiC 44C-P 45ChiC		6'6"	218	St. Mary's (Minn.)		
43-46,47-49 played in N. B. L., 49-50 played in N. B. A.							
Wager, John C-LB-G	31-33Port		5'11"	207	Carthage		
Wagner, Sid G	36-38Det		5'11"	192	Michigan State		

Use Name (Nicknames) – Positions	Team by Year	See Section	Hgt	Wgt	College	Int	Pts
Walker, Bill G	44-45Bos		6'	220	V.M.I.		
Waller, Bill OE-DE	38Bkn		6'	190	Illinois		
Walls, Will OE-DE	37-39,41-43NYG 44-45MS	2	6'4"	214	Texas Christian		24
Walsh, Adam	HC45Cle HC46LA				Notre Dame		
Walton, Frank (Tiger) G	44-45Was		5'11"	230	Pittsburgh		
Ward, Dave G-OE-DE	33Bos				New Mexico		
Ward, Elmer (Bear) C-LB	35Det		6'2"	215	Utah State		
Ware, Charlie T	44Bkn		6'3"	245	Birmingham–South.		
Warren, Busit TB-DB-HB	45Phi 45Pit	12	5'11"	175	Tennessee	1	12
Waters, Dale G-OE-DE	31Cle 31Port 32-33Bos		6'	215	Florida		
Watkins, Foster (Flippin') QB-DB-HB	40-41Phi 42-45MS	12	5'9"	163	West Texas State		2
Watson, Jim C-LB	45Was		6'	205	U. of Pacific		
Watt, Walt HB-DB	45ChiC		6'	187	Miami (Fla.)		
Watts, George T	42Was 43-45MS		6'1"	225	Appalachian State		
Wear, Bob C-LB	42Phi		5'11"	205	Penn State		
Webb, George OE-DE	43Bkn		6'1"	180	Texas Tech		
Weber, Dick TB-DB	45Det		5'11"	195	St. Louis		
Weeks, George DE	44Bkn		6'2"	200	Alabama		
Wehba, Ray OE-DE	43Bkn 44GB 45MS	2	6'	215	Southern Calif.	1	
Weinberg, Henry G-T	34Pit			190	Duquesne		
Weiner, Bernie T-G	43-45MS		5'11"	222	Kansas State		
Weiner, Reds HB-DB-FB-LB	34Phi		5'9"	180	Muhlenberg		6
Weinstock, Izzy LB-FB-BB	35Phi 37-38Pit	2	6'	211	Pittsburgh		4
Weisenbaugh, Heinie BB-LB-HB-DB	35Pit 35-36Bos	2	5'11"	190	Pittsburgh		12
Weisgerber, Dick BB-DE-DB	38-40,42GB 43-45MS		5'10"	200	Willamette		2
Weiss, Howie FB-LB	39-40Det	2	6'	210	Wisconsin		24
Weiss, John OE-DB	44-46NYG		6'3"	198	none		12
Weldin, Hal C-LB	34C-S				Northwestern		
Weldon, Larry QB-DB-DE	44-45Was		6'	198	Presbyterian		5
Weller, Louis (Rabbit) TB-DB	33Bos		5'6"	150	Haskell Indiana		13
Wemple, Don OE-DE	41Bkn 42-44MS–killed in action		6'2"	195	Colgate		6
Wendlick, Joe OE-DE	40Phi 41Pit	2	6'	207	Oregon State		
Wenzel, Ralph DE	42Pit 43-45MS		6'	205	Tulane		
West, Hodges T	41Phi 42-45MS		6'1"	220	Tennessee		
West, Walt FB-DB	44Cle	2	6'	197	Pittsburgh	2	12
Westfall, Bob FB-LB-TB	45-47Det	12	5'8"	190	Michigan	1	96
Westfall, Ed TB-DB-BB	32-33Bos 33Pit		5'9"	175	Ohio Wesleyan		13
Wetterlund, Chet TB-DB	42Det 43-44MS–killed in action	1	6'2"	185	Ill. Wesleyan	1	
Wetzel, Buzz FB-LB	35ChiB 35Pit		6'2"	205	Ohio State		6
Whalen, Tom BB-DB	33Pit				Catholic		
Whatley, Jim T-DE-OE	36-38Bkn		6'5"	223	Alabama		
Wheeler, Ernie DB-TB	39Pit 39,42ChiC 43-45MS		6'1"	190	N. Dakota State		
Whire, John FB-LB	33Phi				Georgia		
White, Allie G-T	39Phi		5'11"	212	Texas Christian		
White, Tarzan G	37-39NYG 40-41ChiC 42-44MS 45NYG		5'9"	217	Alabama		
White, Whizzer TB-DB-HB-FB-WB	38Pit 39VR 40-41Det 42-45MS	12 4	6'1"	187	Colorado	1	80
White, Wilbur (Red) TB-DB-WB	35Bkn 36Det	1	6'	167	Colorado State		
Whited, Marv LB-BB-G	42Was 43-44MS 45Was		5'10"	208	Oklahoma	1	
Wiatrak, John C-LB	39Det		6'	220	Washington		
Wiberg, Ossie FB-LB	27Cle 28Det 30NYG 32Bkn 33Cin				Neb. Wesleyan		
Wickett, Lloyd T	43Det 44-45MS 46Det		6'1"	208	Oregon State		
Widseth, Ed T	37-40NYG 41BL		6'1"	223	Minnesota		
Wiehl, Joe (Tiny) T	35Pit		5'11"	254	Duquesne		
Wiethe, John G-LB	39-42Det		6'	198	Xavier–Ohio	2	
Wilging, Cole T-OE-DE	34C-S		6'1"	185	Xavier–Ohio		
Wilkerson, Basil OE-DE	32SI 32Bos 34C-S				Oklahoma City		
Wilkin, Willie (Wee Willie) T	38-43Was 44-45MS PC46ChiAA		6'4"	261	St. Mary's		8
Williams, Clyde T	35Phi		6'2"	210	Georgia Tech		
Williams, Don G	41Pit 42-45MS		5'8"	210	Texas		
Williams, Jake T	29-33ChiC		6'	205	Texas Christian		
Williams, Joe DB-HB	37Cle 39Pit		5'9"	178	Ohio State		
Williams, Rex (Pinky) C-LB	40ChiC 45Det		6'2"	203	Texas Tech		
Williams, Ted FB-LB-HB-DB	42Phi 44Bos	2	5'11"	183	Boston College	1	18
Williams, Tex C-LB	42Phi 43-45MS 46MiaAA		5'11"	193	Auburn	1	
Willson, Diddie G-OE-DE	33-35Phi		5'10"	196	Pennsylvania		
Wilson, Bill OE-DE	35-37ChiC 38Pit 38Phi		5'10"	184	Gonzaga		
Wilson, Bobby TB-DB	36Bkn	12	5'9"	147	S.M.U.		24
Wilson, George OE-DE	37-46ChiB HC57-64Det HC66-69MiaA	2	6'1"	199	Northwestern	3	108
Wilson, Gordon G-T	41Cle 42-43ChiC 44Bos 44Bkn 45ChiC		6'	228	Texas–El Paso		
Wilson, Johnny (Long John) OE-DE	39-42Cle 43-45MS	2	6'3"	203	Case Reserve		30
Wilson, Mule WB-DB	26Buf 26KC 27-30NYG 30SI 30-31GB 32-33Port		5'11"	203	Texas A&M		
Winkler, Joe C-LB	45Cle		6'1"	200	Purdue	1	
Winslow, Bob DE	40Det 40Bkn		6'2"	205	Southern Calif.		
Witte, Earl BB-DB	34GB		6'	188	Gustavus-Adolphus		
Wojciechowicz, Alex C-LB	38-46Det 46-50Phi		5'11"	217	Fordham	14	6
Wolfe, Red FB-DB	38NYG		6'	205	Texas		
Woltman, Clem T	38-40Phi		6'1"	214	Purdue		
Wood, Bob T	40ChiC 41-45MS		6'2"	230	Alabama		
Woodruff, Lee TB-DB-FB-LB	31Prov 32Bos 33Phi		6'	202	Mississippi		12
Worden, Jim HB-DB	45Cle		5'10"	180	Waynesburg		
Worden, Stu G	30,32-34Bkn		6'	210	Hampden-Sydney		
Workman, Blake (Sheriff) DB-TB-BB	33Cin 34C-S		5'11"	185	Tulsa		
Wray, Lud C-LB	20-21Buf 22Roch HC32Bos HC33-37Phi				Pennsylvania		
Wright, Ralph T	33Bkn		6'	230	Kentucky		
Wright, Ted TB-DB-BB-LB	34-35Bos 35Bkn		6'	185	North Texas State		9
Wukits, Al LB-C-G	43P-P 44C-P 45Pit 46BufAA 46MiaAA		6'3"	213	Duquesne	3	6
Wunsch, Harry G	34GB				Notre Dame		
Wycoff, Doug FB-DB-BB-LB	27NYG 29-30SI 31NYG 32SI 34Bos		6'	225	Georgia Tech		
Wynne, Harry OE-DE	44Bos 45NYG	2	6'4"	203	Arkansas		
Yarr, Tom C-LB	33ChiC		5'10"	205	Notre Dame		
Yeager, Howie WB-DB	41NYG 42-45MS	2	5'11"	173	Cal.–Santa Barbara		24
Yezerski, John T	36Bkn		6'4"	240	St. Mary's		
Younce, Len G-LB	41,43-44NYG 45MS 46-48NYG	45	6'1"	208	Oregon State	10	49
Young, Bill (Bubbles) T	37-42Was 43-45MS 46Was		6'1"	247	Alabama		6
Young, Paul	33GB			195	Oklahoma		
Young, Roy T	38Was		6'2"	215	Texas A&M		
Young, Waddy OE-DE	39-40Bkn 41-44MS–killed in action	2	6'3"	205	Oklahoma		
Yovicsin, John DE	44Phi		6'3"	195	Gettysburg		
Yurchey, John HB-DB	40Pit		5'11"	188	Duquesne		
Zadworney, Frank HB-DB	40Bkn 41-45MS		6'	202	Ohio State		
Zaninelli, Silvio BB-DB-LB-FB	34-37Pit	2	5'10"	207	Duquesne		6
Zapustas, Joe OE-DE	33NYG		6'	198	Fordham		
Zarnas, Gust G	38ChiB 39Bkn 39-40GB 41-45MS		5'10"	220	Ohio State		
Zelencik, Frank T	39ChiC		6'1"	220	Oglethorpe		
Zeller, Joe G-OE-DE	32GB 33-38ChiB		6'1"	203	Indiana		12
Zeno, Joe G-T	42-44Was 45MS 46-47Bos		5'10"	234	Holy Cross	1	
Zimmerman, Roy QB-DB-TB-FB-WB	40-42Was 43P-P 44-46Phi 47Det 48Bos	12 45	6'2"	201	San Jose State	19	229
Zirinsky, Walt HB-DB	45Cle		5'11"	187	Lafayette		
Zizak, Vince G-T	34-37Phi		5'8"	208	Villanova		
Zoll, Dick G-T	37-38Cle		5'11"	218	Indiana		1
Zontini, Lou HB-LB-DB-BB-FB	40-41ChiC 44Cle 45MS 46BufAA	2 45	5'9"	189	Notre Dame	3	110
Zopetti, Frank TB-DB	41Pit 42-45MS		5'11"	185	Duquesne		
Zorich, George G-LB	44-45ChiB 46MiaAA 47BalAA		6'2"	213	Northwestern	1	
Zunker, Charlie T	34C-S		6'4"	227	SW Texas State		
Zuzzio, Tony G	42Det 43-45MS		5'11"	210	Muhlenberg		
Zyntell, Jim G	33NYG 33-35Phi		6'1"	200	Holy Cross		

Lifetime Statistics - 1933-1945 Players Section 1 - **PASSING**
(All men with 25 or more passing attempts)

Name	Years*	Att.	Comp.	Comp. Pct.	Yards	Yds./ Att.	TD	Int.	Pct. Int.
Len Barnum	38-42	120	38	31.7	602	5.0	6	15	12.5
Cliff Battles	*35-37	107	36	33.6	476	4.4	1		
Sammy Baugh	37-52	2995	1693	56.5	21886	7.3	188	203	6.8
Johnny Blood	*35-39	64	24	37.5	299	4.7	2		
Tony Bova	42-47	31	6	19.4	96	3.1	0	1	3.2
Eddie Britt	36-38	44	18	40.9	294	6.7	3	5	11.4
Lou Brock	40-45	67	19	28.4	519	7.7	7	5	7.5
Boyd Brumbaugh	38-41	58	18	31.0	427	7.4	4	10	17.2
Carl Brumbaugh	*36-38	50	15	30.0	252	5.0	10	6	12.0
Ray Buivid	37-38	83	34	41.0	510	6.1	11	4	4.8
Joe Bukant	38-40,42-43	57	19	33.3	179	3.1	1	7	12.3
Young Russey	40-41	40	13	32.5	353	8.8	5	3	7.5
Johnny Butler	43-45	36	14	38.9	191	5.3	0	2	5.6
George Cafego	40,43-45	161	77	47.8	966	6.0	5	15	9.3
Chris Cagle	*33	74	31	41.9	385	5.2	5	9	12.2
Ronnie Cahill	43	109	50	45.9	608	5.6	3	21	19.3
Leo Cantor	42,45	47	15	31.9	271	5.8	1	5	10.6
Cy Casper	*35	39	13	33.3	123	3.2	0		
Dick Cassiano	40	30	9	30.0	128	4.3	1	2	6.7
Frank Christensen	*35-36	27	8	29.6	114	4.2	0		
Beryl Clark	40	58	25	43.1	316	5.4	2	6	10.3
Dutch Clark	34-38	197	97	49.2	1235	6.3	8		
Pat Coffee	37-38	158	68	43.0	1004	6.4	4	15	9.5
Tom Colella	42-49	149	56	37.6	617	4.1	4	18	12.1
Merl Condit	40-43,45-46	48	10	20.8	152	3.2	1	7	14.6
Ed Danowski	34-39,41	637	309	48.5	3819	6.0	39	43	6.8
Bill Davidson	37-39	33	11	33.3	99	3.0	0	5	15.2
Bob Davis	38,42,44-46	55	20	36.4	177	3.2	4	4	7.3
Bob Dunlap	35-36	37	11	29.7	111	3.0	1		
Kay Eakin	40-41,46	107	41	38.3	601	5.6	3	12	11.2
Beattie Feathers	*35-40	31	8	25.8	75	2.4	1		
Frankie Filchock	38-41,44-46,50	677	342	50.5	4921	7.3	47	79	11.7
Max Fiske	36-38	95	34	35.8	503	5.3	4	11	11.6
Red Franklin	35-37	78	19	24.4	287	3.7	1		
Benny Friedman	*33	80	42	52.5	597	7.5	5	7	8.7
Johnny Gilden	35-38	171	51	29.8	964	5.6	5		
Ed Goddard	37-38	84	32	38.1	418	5.0	2	14	16.7
Marshall Goldberg	39-43,46-48	28	10	35.7	114	4.1	1	2	7.1
Owen Goodnight	41	36	12	33.3	182	5.1	1	5	13.9
John Grigas	43-47	166	60	36.1	889	5.4	6	27	16.3
Jack Grossman	*35-36	35	9	25.7	149	4.3	2		
George Grosvenor	35-37	99	39	39.4	567	5.7	3		
Scott Gudmundson	44-45	81	33	40.7	525	6.5	2	9	11.1
Ace Gutowsky	*35-39	38	12	31.6	192	5.1	3		
Parker Hall	39-42,46	729	331	45.4	4048	5.6	29	67	9.2
Bill Hartman	38	77	38	49.4	558	7.4	3	10	13.0
Ken Heineman	40,43	65	22	33.8	359	5.5	4	9	13.8
Warren Heller	34-36	158	40	25.3	599	3.8	2		
Arnie Herber	33-40,44-45	1073	444	41.4	7394	6.9	70	89	8.3
Steve Hokuf	*34	51	13	25.5	203	4.0	3	10	19.6
Tony Holm	33	52	16	30.8	406	7.8	2	13	25.0
Harry Hopp	41-43,46-47	101	36	35.6	508	5.0	0	14	13.9
John Hovious	45	46	22	47.8	373	8.1	4	5	10.9
Vern Huffman	37-38	108	32	29.6	484	4.5	4	14	13.0
Cecil Isbell	38-42	818	411	50.2	5945	7.3	61	52	6.4
Don Jackson	36	35	7	20.0	80	2.3	0	11	31.4
Billy Jefferson	41-42	76	19	25.0	192	2.5	0	9	11.8
Bert Johnson	37-42	54	16	29.6	237	4.4	0	6	11.1
Cecil Johnson	43-44	33	14	42.4	209	6.3	2	5	15.2
Ralph Kercheval	*35-40	94	38	40.4	592	6.3	3		
Reds Kirkman	*33.35	83	25	30.1	384	4.6	4		
John Kusko	36-38	34	8	23.5	119	3.5	0	11	32.3
Joe Laws	*35-45	32	10	31.3	166	5.2	3		
Bill Leckonby	39-41	78	32	41.0	373	4.8	1	5	6.4
Tuffy Leemans	36-43	383	167	43.6	2324	6.1	25	32	8.4
Jim Leonard	*35-36	38	13	34.2	164	4.3	0		
Sid Luckman	39-50	1657	904	54.6	14683	8.9	137	131	7.9
Pug Manders	39-47	53	20	37.7	183	3.5	1	5	9.4
Andy Marefos	41-42,46	37	13	35.1	255	6.9	2	6	16.2
Walt Masters	36,43-44	58	19	32.8	273	4.7	2	10	17.2
Bernie Masterson	34-40	408	155	38.0	3372	8.3	35	38	9.3
Ed Matesic	34-36	262	99	37.8	1406	5.4	10		
Ned Mathews	41-43,45-47	46	14	30.4	204	4.4	3	2	4.3
Harry Mattos	36-37	34	9	26.5	126	3.7	1	6	17.6
Dean McAdams	41-43	191	84	44.0	932	4.9	4	25	13.1
John McCarthy	44	67	20	29.9	250	3.6	0	13	19.4
Harold McCullough	42	38	12	31.6	211	5.6	1	3	7.9
Hugh McCullough	39-43,45	253	87	34.4	1105	4.4	6	41	16.2
Coley McDonough	39-41,44	125	47	37.6	865	6.9	5	20	16.0
Charlie McGibbony	44	48	18	37.5	262	5.5	1	10	20.8
Tex McKay	44-47	103	38	36.9	592	5.7	6	11	10.7
Eddie Miller	39-40	96	48	50.0	700	7.3	5	9	9.4
Keith Molesworth	*33,35-37	123	48	39.0	879	7.1	14		
Bob Monnett	33-38	340	158	46.5	2317	6.8	24	27	7.9
Emmett Mortell	37-39	169	42	24.9	655	3.9	9	15	8.9
Harry Newman	33-35	256	97	37.9	1471	5.7	10		
Emery Nix	43,46	72	34	47.2	546	7.6	5	3	4.2
Ray Nolting	36-43	35	7	20.0	139	4.0	3	5	14.3
Doug Nott	35	34	9	26.5	169	5.0	1		
Davey O'Brien	39-40	478	223	46.7	2614	5.5	11	34	7.1
Ace Parker	37-41,45-46	718	335	46.7	4701	6.5	30	50	7.0
Billy Patterson	39-40	155	48	31.0	756	4.9	6	19	12.3
Frank Patrick	38-39	80	22	27.5	291	3.6	1	13	16.2
Ike Peterson	35-36	31	6	19.4	121	3.9	1		
Stan Pincura	37-38	60	22	36.7	332	5.5	2	10	16.7
Johnny Pingel	39	48	27	56.3	343	7.1	3	4	8.3
Glenn Presnell	33-36	263	90	34.2	1424	5.4	8		
Cotton Price	40-41,45-46	225	94	41.8	1308	5.8	8	24	10.7
Marion Pugh	41,45-46	200	94	47.0	1159	5.8	9	15	7.5
Albie Reisz	44-47	134	58	43.3	923	6.9	10	14	10.4
Pug Rentner	*35-37	89	24	27.0	346	3.9	1	6	15.4
Dick Riffle	38-42	82	21	25.6	332	4.0	2	15	18.3
John Robbins	38-39	182	88	48.4	1076	5.9	6	19	10.4
Gene Ronzanir	*34-38,44-45	179	79	44.1	1201	6.7	16		
Doug Russell	*35-39	48	12	25.0	300	6.3	2		
Frank Sachse	43-45	75	32	42.7	501	6.7	3	7	9.3
Tony Sarausky	35-38	54	14	25.9	181	3.4	1		
Phil Sarboe	*35-36	181	78	43.1	1048	5.8	5		
Bill Shepherd	*36-40	88	30	34.1	521	5.9	3	14	15.9
Allie Sherman	43-47	135	66	48.9	823	6.1	9	9	6.7
Frankie Sinkwich	43-44,46-47	301	121	40.2	1913	6.4	19	42	14.0
Dwight Sloan	38-40	232	100	43.1	1251	5.4	3	18	7.8
Marty Slovak	39-41	109	57	52.3	618	5.7	5	18	16.5
Ed Smith	36-37	42	11	26.2	120	2.9	1	3	7.1
Gaylon Smith	39-42,46	37	16	43.2	202	5.5	2	4	10.8
Riley Smith	36-38	46	19	41.3	290	6.3	3	3	6.5
Dave Smukler	36-39,44	308	112	36.4	1357	4.4	16	32	10.4
Bob Snyder	37-41,43	241	91	37.8	1758	7.3	12	23	9.5
Hank Soar	37-46	53	16	30.2	305	5.8	4	7	13.2
Leo Stasica	41,43-44	55	23	41.8	273	5.0	1	8	14.5
Ed Storm	*35	44	15	34.1	372	8.5	3		
Andy Tomasic	42,46	66	15	22.7	227	3.4	0	6	9.1
Dick Tuckey	38	32	8	25.0	140	4.4	1	3	9.4
Darrel Tully	39	69	20	29.0	356	5.2	2	13	18.8
John Turley	35	27	6	22.2	92	3.4	1		
Hal Van Every	40-41	71	23	32.4	394	5.5	4	8	11.3
Harp Vaughan	*34	39	14	35.9	272	7.0	2	5	12.8
Pug Vaughan	35-36	94	37	39.4	650	6.9	5		
Bursit Warren	45	92	36	39.1	368	4.0	0	10	10.9
Foster Watkins	40-41	95	34	35.8	616	6.5	2	3	3.2
Bob Westfall	44-47	53	27	50.9	428	8.1	5	7	13.2
Chet Wetterlund	42	44	13	29.5	230	5.2	0	10	22.7
Whizzer White	38,40-41	215	86	40.0	1192	5.5	4	34	15.8
Wilbur White	35-36	33	10	30.3	73	2.2	2		
Bobby Wilson	36	40	11	27.5	148	3.7	0	9	22.5
Roy Zimmerman	40-48	708	291	41.1	4801	6.8	44	70	9.9

* - Years shown are years for which the man's passing statistics are available. Touchdown passes include all years beginning with 1933. An asterisk (*) before the information in the "Years" column indicates that the man played, and may have thrown touchdown passes, in 1933, 1934, or 1935 when his other passing statistics were not available.

Lifetime Statistics - 1933-1945 Players Section 2 - **RUSHING and RECEIVING**
(All ment with 25 or more rushing attempts or 10 or more receptions)

Name	Years*	RUSHING Att.	Yards	Avg.	TD	RECEIVING Rec.	Yards	Avg.	TD
Neal Adams	42-47					43	719	16.7	7
Sam Agee	38-39	93	315	3.4	2	3	11	3.7	0
Joe Aquirre	41-49	3	16	5.3	0	160	2262	14.1	29
Frank Akins	43-46	244	1142	4.7	7	16	150	9.4	0
Vannie Albanese	37-38	48	150	3.1	0				
Julie Alfonse	37-38	49	76	1.6	1	7	160	22.9	0
Jay Arnold	37-41	37	43	1.2	1	35	573	16.4	3
Jim Austin	37-39					32	467	14.6	1
Red Badgro	*34,36					19	265	13.9	3
Frank Balasz	39-41,45	60	228	3.8	1	5	50	10.0	0
Len Barnum	38-42	239	590	2.5	3	11	167	15.2	0
Jeff Barrett	36-38	3	11	3.7	0	47	934	19.9	6
Cliff Battles	33-37 + *36-37	725	3046	4.2	20	15	184	12.3	3
Sammy Baugh	37-52	318	324	1.0	9	1	0	0.0	0
Wayland Becker	35-39	2	4	2.0	0	24	376	15.7	2
Steve Belichick	41	28	118	4.2	2	1	13	13.0	0
Jim Benton	38-40,42-47	8	19	2.4	0	288	4801	16.7	45
Connie Mack Berry	39-40,42-47					45	766	17.0	8
Mel Bleeker	44-47	139	586	4.2	6	14	360	25.7	4
Johnny Blood	*36-39+*35-39	43	97	2.3	0	44	724	16.5	12
Ernie Bonelli	45-46	38	100	2.6	0	4	35	8.8	0
Dick Booth	41-45	33	99	3.0	1	10	193	19.3	1
Tony Bova	42-47	21	0	0.0	0	60	1134	18.9	7
Sam Boyd	39-40					21	423	20.1	2
Jeep Brett	36-37					15	274	18.3	1
Eddie Britt	36-38	79	201	2.5	0	6	106	17.7	0
Lou Brock	40-45	254	804	3.2	10	59	761	12.9	6
Boyd Brumbaugh	38-41	256	727	2.8	4	8	101	12.6	2
Carl Brumbaugh	*34,36-38+*36-38	32	−10	−0.3	1	6	62	10.3	4
Larry Buhler	39-41	41	121	3.0	0	1	17	17.0	0
Ray Buivid	37-38	51	89	1.7	1	2	12	6.0	1
Joe Bukant	38-40,42-43	184	426	2.3	4	2	13	6.5	0
Dale Burnett	*36-39+*34-39	24	20	0.8	0	68	949	14.0	16
Sam Busich	36-37,43					19	193	10.2	1
Wendell Butcher	38-42	33	103	3.1	1	15	154	10.3	0
Johnny Butler	43-45	168	517	3.1	4	8	186	23.3	2
Larry Cabrelli	41-47	1	−2	−2.0	0	68	945	13.9	5
Ernie Caddel	33-38+*34-38	443	2211	5.0	22	48	532	11.1	3
George Cafego	40,43-45	155	77	0.5	1	13	133	10.2	0
Ronnie Cahill	43	62	−11	−0.2	0				
Bill Callihan	40-45	33	105	3.2	1	32	383	12.0	4
Leo Cantor	42,45	150	415	2.8	7	15	159	10.6	0
Lloyd Cardwell	37-43	205	905	4.4	8	51	922	18.1	5
Joe Carter	*34-45	2	1	0.5	0	127	1880	14.8	21
Dick Cassiano	40	35	84	2.4	0	2	67	33.5	2
Marty Christiansen	40	32	71	2.2	1				
Beryl Clark	40	39	9	0.2	0	1	20	20.0	0
Dutch Clark	34-38+*35-38	468	2296	4.9	24	12	162	13.5	3
Harry Clark	40-43,46-48	390	1711	4.4	11	51	1022	20.0	11
Pat Coffee	37-38	95	326	3.4	3				
John Cole	38,40	27	79	2.9	0	4	20	5.0	0
Tom Colella	42-49	199	754	3.8	8	18	215	11.9	5
Merl Condit	40-43,45-46	421	1713	4.1	11	32	323	10.1	2
Al Coppage	40-42,46-47					65	736	11.3	3
George Corbett	*34,36-38+*36-38	50	193	3.9	0	4	79	19.8	1
Ollie Cordill	40	24	73	3.0	0	14	158	11.3	2
Red Corzine	*36-38	15	35	2.3	2	10	111	11.1	2
Larry Craig	39-49	10	16	1.6	0	14	155	11.1	0
Milt Crain	44	26	78	3.0	0	1	16	16.0	0
Dick Crayne	36-37	111	338	3.0	1	2	36	18.0	0
Abe Croft	44-45					11	152	13.8	2
Joe Crowley	44-45					14	291	20.8	3
Ward Cuff	37-47	344	1851	5.4	7	106	1559	14.7	13
Bill Daddio	41-42,46					16	147	9.2	1
Ed Danowski	*35-39,41	360	925	2.6	4	1	12	12.0	0
Bill Davidson	37-39	155	370	2.4	1	22	425	19.3	2
Bob Davis	38,42,44-46	230	904	3.9	3	47	427	9.1	2
Corby Davis	38-39,41-42	143	382	2.7	4	19	133	7.0	0
Dan DeSantis	41	45	125	2.8	0	4	53	13.3	0
Versil Deskin	*36-39					16	249	15.6	2
Dave Diehl	39-40,44-45					32	578	18.1	4
Lavie Dilweg	*33					14	225	16.1	2
John Doehring	*34,36-37+*36-37	35	140	4.0	0	1	19	19.0	0
Woody Dow	38-40	5	13	2.6	0	10	146	14.6	1
Mule Dowell	*36	54	151	2.8	0				
Johnny Drake	37-41	525	1700	3.2	24	41	530	12.9	3
Paul Duhart	44-45	68	200	2.9	3	9	176	19.6	2
Les Dye	44-45					31	365	11.8	4
Kay Eakin	40-41,46	56	−4	−0.1	0	11	148	13.5	1
Harry Ebding	*34-37					32	668	20.9	7
Frank Emmons	40	29	77	2.7	1	3	19	6.3	1
Dick Erdlitz	42,45-46	53	131	2.5	2	12	109	9.1	0
Dick Evans	40-43					13	145	11.2	0
Tony Falkenstein	43-44	62	200	3.2	1	4	60	15.0	0
Gary Famiglietti	38-46	528	1981	3.8	24	12	187	15.6	1
Andy Farkas	38-45	587	2103	3.6	21	80	1086	13.6	13
Scrapper Farrell	38-39	109	425	3.9	3				
Beattie Feathers	34-40+*36-40	360	1979	5.5	16	6	51	8.5	1
Frankie Filchock	38-41,44-46,50	477	1478	3.1	6	8	88	11.0	0
Steve Filipowicz	45-46	55	145	2.6	2	11	133	12.1	2
Ev Fisher	38-40	18	63	3.5	0	11	122	11.1	0
Bill Fisk	40-43,46-48	2	0	0.0	0	69	791	11.5	3
Max Fiske	36-38	115	219	1.9	0	8	96	12.0	0
Ray Flaherty	*33-34					19	267	14.1	1
Jim Fordham	44-45	118	534	4.5	5	5	47	9.4	0

Name	Years*	RUSHING Att.	Yards	Avg.	TD	RECEIVING Rec.	Yards	Avg.	TD
Sam Fox	45					10	120	12.0	2
Terry Fox	41,45-46	33	123	3.7	0	9	98	10.9	0
Sam Francis	37-40	253	873	3.5	5	4	22	5.5	0
George Franck	41,45-47	144	525	3.6	3	27	536	19.9	5
Ed Frutig	41,45-46	1	11	11.0	0	12	117	9.8	3
Hugh Gallarneau	41-42,45-47	343	1421	4.1	26	51	794	15.6	7
Milt Gantenbein	*34-40					69	1101	16.0	7
Chuck Gelatka	37-40					20	250	12.5	1
Bill Geyer	42-43,46	25	54	2.2	2	6	145	24.2	2
Johnny Gildea	*36-38	85	98	1.2	1	9	120	13.3	0
Fred Gloden	41,46	35	79	2.3	1	2	13	6.5	0
Ed Goddard	37-38	97	146	1.5	2	12	189	15.8	1
Marshall Goldberg	39-43,46-48	476	1644	3.5	11	60	775	12.9	5
Tod Goodwin	35-36	3	−1	−0.3	0	33	511	15.5	6
Red Grange	*34 + *	32	136	4.3	2				2
John Grigas	43-47	465	1581	3.4	10	30	374	12.5	1
Frank Grigonis	42	37	131	3.5	1	1	17	17.0	0
Jack Grossman	*+*34				2	10	158	15.8	1
George Grosvenor	*36-37	307	1073	3.5	6	1	6	6.0	0
Roger Grove	*+*33				1	15	217	14.5	3
Al Grygo	44-45	76	420	5.5	2	10	124	12.4	1
Scott Gudmundson	44-45	37	−17	−0.5	0	1	-8	-8.0	0
Ace Gutowsky	33-39+*36-39	852	3031	3.6	16	2	55	27.5	1
Elmer Hackney	40-46	220	846	3.8	10	19	135	7.1	1
John Hall	40-43	116	296	2.6	3	28	537	19.2	5
Parker Hall	39-42,46	329	1083	3.3	6	3	9	3.0	0
Ray Hamilton	38-39,44-47					40	682	17.2	2
Chuck Hanneman	37-41	3	59	19.7	1	35	622	17.8	4
Swede Hanson	*33-34,36-38+*36-38	432	1767	4.1	12	4	35	8.8	2
Merel Hapes	42-46	146	524	3.6	8	13	119	9.2	2
Ray Hare	40-44,46	132	539	4.1	2	28	359	12.8	1
Bill Hartman	38	71	195	2.7	0	1	6	6.0	0
Ken Heineman	40-43	55	121	2.2	0				
Warren Heller	*34,36+*36	238	860	3.6	1	12	160	13.3	3
Arnie Herber	36-40,44-45	68	−143	−2.1	1	6	102	17.0	2
Bill Hewitt	33-39,43	4	6	1.5	0	97	1562	16.1	23
Ben Hightower	42-43	1	−6	−6.0	0	29	484	16.7	4
Harold Hill	38-40					11	220	20.0	0
Clarke Hinkle	33-41+*34,36-41	1043	3519	3.4	32	41	500	12.2	9
Jack Hinkle	40,43-47	238	1067	4.5	6	7	68	9.7	0
Joe Hoague	41-42,46	99	282	2.8	2	3	25	8.3	1
Herman Hodges	39-42					23	285	12.4	0
Harry Hopp	41-43,46-47	262	801	3.1	9	24	294	12.3	3
Jim Lee Howell	37-42,46-47					61	921	15.1	7
Vern Huffman	7-38	104	368	3.5	1	9	121	13.4	0
Don Hutson	35-45	56	262	4.7	3	488	7981	16.4	100
Don Irwin	36-39	182	586	3.2	6	27	289	10.4	0
Cecil Isbell	38-42	422	1522	3.6	10	15	174	11.6	0
Pop Ivy	40-42,45-47					53	513	9.7	1
Don Jackson	36	46	76	1.7	0				
Harry Jacunski	39-44					52	985	18.9	6
Len Janiak	39-42	85	228	2.7	0	11	65	5.9	1
Ed Jankowski	37-41	255	1003	3.9	8	2	65	32.5	1
Billy Jefferson	41-42	68	222	3.3	1	2	14	7.0	0
Bert Johnson	37-42	152	368	2.4	2	16	268	16.8	3
Cecil Johnson	43-44	56	79	1.4	0	9	136	15.1	2
Luke Johnsos	33-36					38	664	17.5	10
Jimmy Johnston	39-40,46	97	321	3.3	3	40	461	11.5	4
Swede Johnston	*36-40+*35-40	142	443	3.1	5	8	70	8.8	0
Art Jones	41,45	67	303	4.5	4	9	129	14.3	1
Harvey Jones	44-45,47	46	148	3.2	1	8	95	11.9	1
Ed Justice	36-42	33	127	3.8	1	70	1006	14.4	9
Mike Kabealo	44	47	152	3.2	1	2	20	10.0	0
George Karamatic	38	50	185	3.7	0	4	99	24.8	1
Bull Karcis	*36-39,43+*35-39,43	349	1113	3.2	10	16	148	9.3	0
Bill Karr	*36-38+33-38	6	27	4.5	1	48	1042	21.7	18
Rabbit Keen	37-38	37	164	4.4	0	5	45	9.0	0
Clarence Kellogg	36	66	164	2.5	0	4	11	2.8	0
Shipwreck Kelly	*37+*33,37	16	29	1.8	3	23	253	11.0	3
Ralph Kercheval	*36-40+*35-40	210	549	2.6	4	34	411	12.1	4
Walt Kichefski	40-42,44					30	411	13.7	1
George Kiick	40,45	81	257	3.2	1	4	20	5.0	0
Carl Kinscherf	43-44	58	98	1.7	1	3	13	4.3	0
Ben Kish	40-41,43-49	74	344	4.6	1	38	420	11.1	2
Ed Klewicki	*36-38	20	129	6.5	0	15	281	18.7	2
John Knolla	42,45	30	79	2.6	0	9	63	7.0	0
Elmer Kolberg	39-41					10	78	7.8	0
Andy Kowalski	43-45					20	300	15.0	1
George Kracum	41	52	169	3.3	3	2	17	8.5	0
Max Krause	*36-40	64	342	5.3	3	9	122	13.6	3
Bob Krieger	41,46					21	279	13.3	2
Al Krueger	41-42,46					35	401	11.5	2
John Kusko	36-38	66	236	3.6	1	2	47	23.5	0
Mort Landsberg	41,47	25	58	2.3	0	6	51	8.5	0
Jimmy Lawrence	36-39	130	357	2.7	4	28	276	9.9	0
Joe Laws	*36-45	400	1714	4.3	10	66	794	12.0	9
Bill Lazetich	39,42	9	42	4.7	1	14	109	7.8	2
Bill Leckonby	39-41	77	254	3.3	0	2	17	8.5	2
Tuffy Leemans	36-43	919	3142	3.4	17	28	422	15.1	3
Jim Leonard	*36-37	33	72	2.2	2	5	46	9.2	1
Jim Levey	*36+*35	4	3	0.8	2	11	112	10.2	2
Frank Liebel	42-48					82	1755	21.4	23
Carl Littlefield	38-39	58	210	3.6	0	2	27	13.5	0
John Long	44-45	26	5	0.2	0				
Don Looney	40-42	2	−4	-2	1	75	952	12.7	6

* — Years shown are years for which the man's rushing and receiving statistics are available. Touchdowns include all years beginning with 1933. An asterisk (*) before the information in the "Years" column indicates that the man played, and may have had touchdowns, in 1933, 1934, or 1935 when his other statistics were not available.

Lifetime Statistics - 1933-1945 Players Section 2 - **RUSHING and RECEIVING** (continued)
(All men with 25 or more rushing attempts or 10 or more receptions)

Name	Years*	RUSHING Att.	Yards	Avg.	TD	RECEIVING Rec.	Yards	Avg.	TD
John Lucente	45	82	242	3.0	1	11	45	4.1	0
Sid Luckman	39-50	204	-209	-1.0	4	1	15	15.0	0
Bob MacLeod	39	17	88	5.2	1	10	231	23.1	3
Lloyd Madden	40	29	186	6.4	2	4	90	22.5	1
Charley Malone	34-40,42					137	1922	14.0	13
Jack Manders	33-40+*36-40	451	1596	3.5	11	11	215	19.5	6
Pug Manders	39-47	742	2712	3.7	36	28	375	13.4	2
Joe Maniaci	36-41	404	1855	4.6	14	16	184	11.5	0
Eggs Manske	35-40	5	29	5.8	0	70	1467	21.0	11
Tilly Manton	36-38,43	42	98	2.3	0	14	122	8.7	1
Andy Marefos	41-42,46	138	384	2.8	7	2	18	9.0	0
Hank Margarita	44-46	204	960	4.7	7	38	524	13.8	2
Frank Martin	43-45	39	79	2.0	0	20	234	11.7	0
John Martin	41-45	143	362	2.5	2	41	579	14.1	1
Joel Mason	39,42-45					34	390	11.5	2
Bob Masters	37-39,42-44	34	99	2.9	0	6	72	12.0	0
Bernie Masterson	*34,36-40+*35-40	87	-29	-0.3	7	11	168	15.3	1
Bob Masterson	38-46	8	104	13.0	0	136	1821	13.4	13
Ed Matesic	*36	46	58	1.3	1	1	13	13.0	0
Jack Matheson	43-47					73	1044	14.3	5
Ned Mathews	41-43,45-47	186	752	4.0	4	34	494	14.5	6
Harry Mattos	36-37	27	18	0.7	1				
Dean McAdams	41-43	189	375	2.0	0	12	111	9.3	0
Bob McChesney	36-42	3	27	9.0	1	59	679	11.5	6
Hugh McCullough	39-43,45	129	409	3.2	4	5	74	14.8	0
Flip McDonald	44-46,48					15	131	8.7	2
Jim McDonald	38-39	25	80	3.2	0	7	112	16.0	0
Les McDonald	37-40	4	-4	-1.0	0	51	924	18.1	8
Coley McDonough	39-41,44	65	179	2.8	1	1	3	3.0	1
Paul McDonough	38-41	2	5	2.5	0	40	672	16.8	4
Banks McFadden	40	65	411	6.3	1	9	97	10.8	2
Charlie McGibbony	44	26	81	3.1	0				
Tex McKay	44-47	100	288	2.9	3				
Ray McLean	40-47	152	412	2.7	6	103	2222	21.6	21
Jim Meade	39-40	61	149	2.4	0	5	40	8.0	0
Fred Meyer	42,45	2	13	6.5	0	27	429	15.9	2
Mike Mikulak	*36 + *35-36	24	56	2.3	5	14	155	11.1	0
Eddie Miller	39-40	95	305	3.2	2				
Paul Miller	36-38	143	540	3.8	1	18	215	11.9	3
Tom Miller	43-46	1	-2	-2.0	0	22	279	12.7	1
Wayne Millner	36-41,45	14	62	4.4	0	124	1578	12.7	12
Buster Mitchell	*36-37	2	4	2.0	0	10	125	12.5	1
Keith Molesworth	*34-37+*35-37	200	739	3.7	5	20	321	16.1	1
Bob Monnett	*33,35-38+*36-38	442	1358	3.1	8	18	224	12.4	0
Tipp Mooney	44-45	46	193	4.2	0	4	84	21.0	1
Wilbur Moore	39-46	183	901	4.9	8	91	1224	13.5	16
George Morris	41-42	46	134	2.9	0	9	17	1.9	0
Bob Morrow	41-43,45-46	128	456	3.6	4	4	26	6.5	0
Butch Morse	35-38,40	1	-3	-3.0	0	23	345	15.0	1
Emmett Mortell	37-39	247	696	2.8	0	1	0	0.0	0
Monk Moscrip	38-39	1	8	8.0	0	20	294	14.7	1
Paul Moss	*33					13	383	29.5	3
Moose Mulleneaux	38-41,45-46					44	850	19.3	11
Franny Murray	39-40	55	144	2.6	1	25	269	10.8	1
Jim Musick	*33,36	179	643	3.6	7				
Bronko Nagurski	33-37,43+*36-37,43	499	2212	4.4	14	1	12	12.0	0
Dick Nardi	38-39	30	124	4.1	0	1	3	3.0	0
Harry Newman	*33-34+*	261	940	3.6	7				0
Chuck Newton	39-40	1	0	0.0	0	10	145	14.5	1
Al Nichelini	*36	55	189	3.4	4	9	133	14.8	1
Walt Nielsen	40	73	269	3.7	1	2	17	8.5	0
Emery Nix	43,46	27	1	0.0	0				
Ray Nolting	36-43	508	2285	4.5	11	30	508	16.9	3
Reino Nori	37-38	27	82	3.0	0				
Davey O'Brien	39-40	209	-194	-0.9	2				
Bill Osmanski	39-43, 46-47	374	1743	4.7	20	12	170	14.2	1
Hal Pangle	*36-38	101	307	3.0	3	16	267	16.7	0
Ace Parker	37-41,45-46	498	1292	2.6	14	8	229	28.6	3
Buddy Parker	*36-43	121	333	2.8	4	40	378	9.5	0
Bill Paschal	43-48	677	2430	3.6	27	32	326	10.2	8
George Paskvan	41	38	116	3.1	0				
Maury Patt	38-42	15	66	4.4	0	41	460	11.2	2
Billy Patterson	39-40	101	205	2.0	0				
Frank Patrick	38-39	31	85	2.7	1	1	21	21.0	1
Don Perkins	43-46	138	585	4.2	2	5	53	10.6	0
Ike Peterson	*36	60	276	4.6	3	8	38	4.8	0
Les Peterson	*34					13	170	13.1	0
John Petty	42	41	149	3.6	2	4	53	13.3	0
Alex Piasecky	43-45					12	112	9.3	1
Joe Pilconis	*36-37	2	21	10.5	0	10	110	11.0	1
Ernie Pinckert	*36-40+*35-40	28	114	4.1	1	21	269	12.8	1
Stan Pincura	37-38	7	-28	-4.0	0	18	211	11.7	1
Johnny Pingel	39	72	301	4.2	1				
Hank Piro	41					10	141	14.1	1
Dick Plasman	37-41,44,46-47	1	1	1.0	0	56	1083	19.3	7
George Platukas	38-42	3	6	2.0	0	33	621	18.8	6
Hamp Pool	40-43,46					38	903	23.8	11
Jim Poole	37-41,45-46					65	895	13.8	13
Milt Popovich	38-42	78	233	3.0	0	10	71	7.1	0
Glenn Presnell	*33-34,36+*36	283	1136	4.0	14				1
Cotton Price	40-41,45-46	97	174	1.8	2	3	23	7.7	0
Dom Principe	40-42,46	51	152	3.0	2	9	112	12.4	0
Marion Pugh	41,45-46	77	-127	-1.6	2	4	43	10.8	0
Red Ramsey	38-40,45					53	624	11.8	2
Walt Rankin	41,43-37	20	30	1.5	0	17	87	5.1	0

Name	Years*	RUSHING Att.	Yards	Avg.	TD	RECEIVING Rec.	Yards	Avg.	TD
Keith Ranspot	40,42-45					35	491	14.0	4
Albie Reisz	44-47	83	164	2.0	2	1	11	11.0	0
Pug Rentner	*36-37	116	474	4.1	2	10	134	13.4	2
Paul Riblett	*36+*33,35-36	2	4	2.0	0	22	307	14.0	2
Kink Richards	*33,35-39+*35-39	462	1702	3.7	13	28	252	9.0	6
Ray Riddick	40-42,46					20	285	14.3	1
Rick Riffle	38-42	391	1381	3.5	10	19	189	9.9	2
John Robbins	38-39	101	310	3.1	0	2	12	6.0	0
Bob Robertson	42	46	132	2.9	0	5	61	12.2	0
Gene Ronzani	33-38,44-45+*35-38,44-45	260	1144	4.4	1	14	220	15.7	8
Eddie Rucinski	41-46	18	85	4.7	0	99	1408	14.2	8
Doug Russell	*35-39+*36-39	206	667	3.2	2	23	366	15.9	2
Rip Ryan	38-40	54	263	4.9	1	23	220	9.6	1
Charlie Sample	42,45	59	257	4.4	4	6	35	5.8	1
Curt Sandig	42,46	72	168	2.3	4	8	118	14.8	0
Mickey Sanzotta	42,46	77	340	4.4	0	7	35	5.0	0
Tony Sarausky	*36-38	44	210	4.8	2				
Phil Sarboe	*36	83	103	1.2	0	1	18	18.0	0
George Sauer	35-37+*36-37	190	656	3.5	6	6	110	18.3	0
Elmer Schaake	33+*	125	412	3.3	0				1
Bernie Scherer	36-39					13	241	18.5	3
John Schneller	*35-36					14	273	19.5	3
Perry Schwartz	38-42,46	5	24	4.8	0	104	1677	16.1	10
Dick Schweidler	38-39,46	41	166	4.0	3	4	75	18.8	0
Bob Seymour	40-46	397	1311	3.3	12	72	817	11.3	11
Leland Shaffer	*36-43,45+35-43,45	24	81	3.4	1	52	531	10.2	5
Bill Shepherd	35-40+*36-40	519	1984	3.8	12	16	155	9.7	1
Allie Sherman	43-47	92	-44	-0.5	4				
Rhoten Shetley	40-42,46	17	58	3.4	1	17	218	12.8	2
John Shirk	40					11	91	8.3	0
John Siegal	39-43					31	636	20.5	6
Frankie Sinkwich	43-44,46-47	321	1090	3.4	7	2	11	5.5	0
Johnny Sisk	*34,36	82	319	3.9	3	1	39	39.0	0
Joe Skladany	34					10	222	22.2	2
Dwight Sloan	38-40	193	576	3.0	4	1	10	10.0	0
Marty Slovak	39-41	141	396	2.8	1				
Rudy Smeja	44-46					11	166	15.1	1
Ben Smith	*34-35,37					23	393	17.1	0
Bill Smith	*34,36-39+*35-39	8	90	11.3	2	86	1509	17.5	9
Gaylon Smith	39-42,46	233	710	3.0	9	16	261	16.3	0
Riley Smith	36-38	45	58	1.3	2	18	300	16.7	3
Stu Smith	37-38	145	452	3.1	0	3	30	10.0	0
Wee Willie Smith	34	45	232	5.2	2				
Dave Smukler	36-39,44	334	1106	3.3	2	1	-4	-4.0	0
Bob Snyder	37-41,43	161	348	2.2	1	4	36	9.0	0
Hank Soar	37-46	478	1545	3.2	6	35	411	11.7	2
Bill Sortet	*35-40	2	42	21.0	0	63	928	14.7	8
Vic Spadaccini	38-40	9	46	5.1	0	62	669	10.8	3
Leo Stasica	41,43-44	34	-9	-0.3	0				
Ernie Steele	42-48	258	1337	5.2	14	31	520	16.8	4
Ken Strong	*34-35,39,44-47	113	409	3.6	9				2
Art Strutt	35-36	176	503	2.9	1	18	278	15.4	0
Bob Swisher	38-41,45	104	544	5.2	2	21	582	27.7	3
Ray Tesser	*33					14	274	19.6	0
Stumpy Thomason	*36+*	109	333	3.1	0				0
Tuffy Thompson	37-39	88	228	2.6	1	16	182	11.4	1
Bob Thurbon	43-44,46	143	478	3.3	9	14	231	16.5	2
Morgan Tiller	44-45					10	141	14.1	0
Gaynell Tinsley	37-38,40	6	45	7.5	0	93	1356	14.6	7
Bob Titchenal	40-42,46-47	2	2	1.0	0	15	264	17.6	0
Dick Todd	39-42,45-48	368	1573	4.3	11	119	1826	15.3	20
Andy Tomasic	42,46	60	214	3.6	0	1	27	27.0	0
Mario Tonelli	40	51	148	2.9	1	5	53	10.6	0
Flavio Tosi	*35-36					14	239	17.1	1
Bob Trocolor	42-44	35	22	0.6	0				
Dick Tuckey	38	43	76	1.8	0	1	10	10.0	0
Darrell Tully	39	31	50	1.6	1				
Andy Uram	38-43	239	1073	4.5	4	58	1083	18.7	10
Hal Van Every	40-41	63	281	4.5	2	5	44	8.8	0
Art Van Tone	43-46	34	55	1.6	1	25	568	22.7	8
Fred Vanzo	38-41	6	45	7.5	0	17	257	15.1	0
Pug Vaughan	*36	67	79	1.2	0				
Vic Vidoni	35-36					13	146	11.2	0
Will Walls	37-39,41-43					35	587	16.8	4
Busit Warren	45	96	285	3.0	2	1	-1	-1.0	0
Foster Watkins	40-41	29	-65	-2.2	0	3	27	9.0	0
Ray Wehba	43-44					10	110	11.0	0
Izzy Weinstock	*37-38+35,37-38	34	88	2.6	0	8	107	13.4	0
Heinie Weisenbaugh	*36+35-36	3	9	3.0	0	10	110	11.0	2
Howie Weiss	39-40	116	448	3.9	3	8	81	10.1	0
Joe Wendlick	40-41					15	151	10.1	0
Walt West	44	66	220	3.3	0	9	64	7.1	0
Bob Westfall	44-47	209	697	3.3	11	47	588	12.5	5
Whizzer White	38,40-41	387	1319	3.4	11	16	301	18.8	1
Ted Williams	42,44	102	196	1.9	3	15	86	5.7	0
Bobby Wilson	36	104	505	4.9	3	1	12	12.0	1
George Wilson	37-46					111	1342	12.1	15
Johnny Wilson	39-42					26	429	16.5	4
Harry Wynne	44-45					12	230	19.2	0
Howie Yeager	41	22	67	3.0	1	11	239	21.7	3
Waddy Young	39-40	1	1	1.0	0	15	185	12.3	0
Silvio Zaninelli	*36-37	35	75	2.1	0	4	24	6.0	0
Roy Zimmerman	40-48	200	244	1.2	7	5	36	7.2	0
Lou Zontini	40-41,44,46	48	133	2.8	3	4	110	27.5	1

+ - Indicates that Rushing statistics and Receiving statistics are available for different years, Rushing years are before the +, and Receiving years are after the +.

Section 3 – PUNT RETURNS and KICKOFF RETURNS

(All men with 25 or more Punt Returns or 25 or more Kickoff Returns)

Name	Years	PUNT RETURNS No.	Yards	Avg.	TD	KICKOFF RETURNS No.	Yards	Avg.	TD
Lou Brock	P 42-45	39	438	11.2	0	17	344	20.2	0
Harry Clark	P 42-43,46-48	26	379	14.6	0	32	854	26.7	0
Tom Colella	42-49	32	487	15.2	1	26	553	21.3	0
Merl Condit	P 42-43,45-46	35	332	9.5	0	17	369	21.7	0
Ward Cuff	P 42-47	37	447	12.1	0	12	305	25.4	0
Bob Davis	42,44-46	55	576	10.5	0	26	515	19.8	0
Andy Farkas	P 42-45	59	734	12.4	1	32	879	27.5	2
(includes 1 kickoff return touchdown in 1939)									
Marshall Goldberg	41-43,46-48	21	259	12.3	0	34	844	24.8	1
John Grigas	43-47	7	38	5.4	0	32	635	19.8	0
Parker Hall	P 42,46	25	273	10.9	0	11	177	16.1	0
Joe Laws	P 42-45	45	332	7.4	1	16	287	17.9	0
(includes 1 punt return touchdown in 1939)									
John Martin	P 42-45	20	202	10.1	0	36	899	25.0	0
Ray McLean	P 42-47	39	575	14.7	3	20	461	23.1	0
(includes 1 punt return touchdown in 1940)									
Bill Paschal	43-48	29	395	13.6	0	53	1245	23.5	0
Bob Seymour	P 42-46	46	597	13.0	0	6	121	20.2	0
Ernie Steele	42-48	56	889	15.9	1	38	763	20.1	0
Dick Todd	P 42,45-48	44	581	13.2	3	17	378	22.2	0
(includes 1 punt return touchdown in 1939 and 1 punt return touchdown in 1940)									

Kickoff Return statistics start in 1942.
Punt Return statistics start in 1941.

P – includes Punt Return statistics for 1941.

Section 4 – PUNTING

(All men with 25 or more punts)

Name	Years	No.	Avg.
Len Barnum	39-42	159	40.5
Sammy Baugh	39-52	338	44.9
Lou Brock	40-45	84	37.2
George Cafego	40,43-45	44	34.9
Leo Cantor	42,45	25	37.1
Beryl Clark	40	28	33.0
Tom Colella	42-49	196	37.4
Merl Condit	40-43,45-46	39	39.4
Ed Danowski	39,41	31	37.9
Kay Eakin	40-41,46	68	43.1
Sam Francis	39-40	29	41.7
George Franck	41,45-47	63	39.2
Scott Gudmundson	44-45	29	35.0
Parker Hall	39-42	200	41.0
Merle Hapes	42,46	27	38.3
Arnie Herber	39-40,44-45	39	40.0
Clarke Hinkle	39-41	87	40.9
Harry Hopp	41-43,46-47	86	38.2
Cecil Johnson	43-44	33	40.2
Art Jones	41,45	47	37.7
Ralph Kercheval	39-40	36	40.6
Carl Kinscherf	43-44	32	40.7
Sid Luckman	39-50	230	38.4
John Martin	41-45	145	38.8
Dean McAdams	41-43	104	41.0
Hugh McCullough	39-43,45	66	36.5
Doug McEnulty	43-44	29	40.8
Tex McKay	44-47	124	41.9
Rudy Mucha	41,45-46	34	40.7
Franny Murray	39-40	63	37.0
Ace Parker	39-41,45-46	150	38.3
Billy Patterson	39-40	51	39.1
Johnny Pingel	39	32	42.7
Milt Popovich	39-42	35	34.6
Albie Reisz	44-47	88	37.6
Bill Reynolds	44-45	38	36.4
Dick Riffle	39-42	39	37.0
Curt Sandig	42,46	41	38.8
Frankie Sinkwich	43-44,46-47	64	41.5
Sid Tinsley	45	57	40.4
Dick Todd	39-42,45-48	38	38.7
Hal Van Every	40-41	30	37.3
Whizzer White	40-41	100	41.4
Len Younce	41,43-44,46-48	70	40.6
Roy Zimmerman	40-48	278	39.8
Lou Zontini	40-41,44,46	58	36.8

Punting statistics start in 1939.

Section 5 – KICKING

(All men with 10 or more PAT or Field Goal Attempts)

Name	Years	PAT	PAT Att.	PAT Pct.	FG	FG Att.	FG Pct.
Chet Adams	39-43,46-50	122	131	93	13	40	33
Joe Aguirre	41-49	85	95	89	17	39	44
Lee Artoe	40-42,45-48	25	30	83	2	10	20
Conway Baker	36-45	22	28	79	1	3	33
Len Barnum	38-42	18	20	90	9	24	38
Bill Callihan	40-45	25	27	93			
Dutch Clark	34-38	56	72	78	12		
Merl Condit	40-43,45-46	26	27	96	5	22	23
Ward Cuff	37-47	156	162	96	43		
Bill Daddio	41-42,46	19	20	95	9	18	50
Tiny Engebretsen	33-41	43	45	96	15		
Dick Erdlitz	42,45-46	30	30	100	2	7	29
Roger Grove	33-35	9	11	82			
Pete Gudauskas	40,43-45	64	67	96	1	2	50
Chuck Hanneman	37-41	19	19	100	7	13	54
Clarke Hinkle	33-41	28	32	88	28		
Don Hutson	35-45	172	184	93	7	17	41
Ralph Kercheval	34-40	32	41	78	31		
Bruiser Kinard	38-47	27	30	90	1	1	100
Joe Kuharich	40-41,45	12	13	92	0	4	0
Augie Lio	41-47	109	115	95	17	52	33
Jack Manders	33-40	137	154	89	39		
Joe Maniaci	36-41	29	33	88	5		
Tilly Manton	36-38,43	29	30	97	6		
Bob Masterson	38-46	71	79	90	8	32	25
Ray McLean	40-47	44	52	85	0	1	0
Regis Monahan	35-39	8	10	80	10		
Bob Monnett	33-38	28	31	90	5		
Monk Moscrip	38-39	15	18	83	0	2	0
Franny Murray	39-40	14	19	74	2	5	40
Jim Musick	33,35-36	13	15	87	1		
Harry Newman	33-35	12	16	75	6		
Armand Niccolai	34-42	71	77	92	34		
Ace Parker	37-41,45-46	25	32	78	1	5	20
Dick Plasman	37-41,44,46-47	14	19	74	0	1	0
Glenn Presnell	33-36	31	37	84	14		
Hank Reese	33-39	21	26	81	6		
Bo Russell	39-40	26	29	90	2	7	29
Jack Sanders	40-42,45	12	13	92			
Bill Shepherd	35-40	11	13	85	3		
Frankie Sinkwich	43-44,46-47	24	30	80	2	9	22
Bill Smith	34-39	24	33	73	12		
Ernie Smith	35-37,39	43	48	90	6		
Riley Smith	36-38	39	49	80	11		
Dave Smukler	36-39,43-44	16	17	94	2		
Bob Snyder	37-43,47	78	91	86	8		
Hank Soar	37-46	10	12	83	1		
George Somers	39-42	2	2	100	2	12	17
Vic Spadaccini	38-40	17	21	81			
Ken Strong	33-35,39,44-47	142	147	97	35		
Joe Stydahar	36-42,45-46	28	35	80	0	2	0
Len Younce	41,43-44,46-48	37	38	97	2	9	22
Roy Zimmerman	40-48	133	144	92	18	42	43
Lou Zontini	40-41,44-46	59	62	95	9	23	39

Field Goal Attempts statistics start in 1938.
Other kicking statistics start in 1933.

1946—1959
Beginning and Ending with Confrontation

The postwar boom in the American economy put money in the pockets of football fans, and a new professional league took the field in 1946 to win a share of that money. The All-American Football Conference, organized by Arch Ward, sports editor of the Chicago Tribune, had wealthy owners backing almost every franchise, and the new league lured over 100 players away from the NFL and drove player salaries up to new heights. With ex-Notre Dame star Jim Crowley as commissioner, the AAFC brought good-quality football to New York, Brooklyn, Buffalo, Miami, Cleveland, Chicago, San Francisco, and Los Angeles in 1946.

To face this challenge, the NFL named Bert Bell, part owner of the Pittsburgh Steelers, as its commissioner. A tough, likable man with an immense love of football, Bert would guide the NFL through fourteen crucial years in which pro football reached a dazzling level of prosperity.

The 1946 season was prosperous for few pro-football clubs, as the high price of financial warfare put most of the clubs in the red for the season. The most notable exception was the Cleveland Browns of the AAFC. Captivating a city which the NFL champion Rams had abandoned, the Browns drew an average of 57,000 fans to each of their home games as they swept to the league championship.

But although the financial picture suffered in 1946, pro football advanced on several fronts. Both leagues placed clubs in California, with the NFL Rams moving from Cleveland to Los Angeles and the AAFC fielding teams in San Francisco and Los Angeles. Pro football became the first major-league sport to invade the West Coast.

Both leagues also employed black players, who had been unofficially barred from pro football since the early 1930s. The AAFC Browns signed fullback Marion Motley and guard Bill Willis, while the NFL Rams hired halfback Kenny Washington and end Woody Strode. These players had to walk the same unpleasant path of abuse that baseball player Jackie Robinson walked in 1947, but the football pioneers have never received anything close to the publicity that Robinson attracted.

The 1946 season also gave NFL Commissioner Bell his first test of leadership. On the morning of the championship game between the Giants and Bears, Bell learned that New York players Frank Filchock and Merle Hapes had been offered bribes to throw the game. Although neither had accepted the bribes, neither had reported the offer to the authorities. Bell released the news to the press, keeping everything out in the open so as to preserve confidence in the game, and he suspended Hapes while allowing Filchock to play. Although Filchock played an outstanding game in a 24-14 Bear win, Bell later suspended him indefinitely from NFL competition. The cumulative effect of the incident was to underline Bell's determination to lead the NFL firmly and openly.

Most pro teams continued to lose money in the late 1940's as the war between the leagues raged. Attendance was high in both leagues in 1946 and 1947, but the bidding war over players washed away most of the ticket revenues. When the postwar economic boom died out in 1948 and attendance dropped, the clubs felt a tight financial pinch—a major factor in the new league beginning to prod the NFL for peace terms. AAFC Commissioner Jonas Ingram, who succeeded Crowley in 1947, tried in vain to arrange a merger after the 1948 season. With Scrappy Kessing as its new commissioner, the league hobbled through 1949 before finally reaching a merger agreement with the NFL. The merger was dictated along NFL terms. The Cleveland Browns, San Francisco '49ers, and Baltimore Colts were admitted from the AAFC into the NFL, but the other four clubs in the young league were disbanded. The players on these four clubs went into a special pool and were distributed among the NFL teams, with the Giants profiting most by obtaining several stars from the AAFC Yankees.

The NFL entered the 1950s with the field to itself and with wise leadership in Commissioner Bell. One of the most important innovations of Bell's administration was the free-substitution rule. This rule, temporarily adopted during World War II and given a one-year trial in 1949, allowed coaches to develop separate platoons for offense and defense. Permanently adopted in 1950, the rule gave full bloom to the era of specialists who would charge the game with their highly polished skills. Another innovation after the merger was face masks, which became standard equipment on helmets and spared modern players the battle scars old-time players carried around on their faces.

But Bell's master stroke was a wise and firm policy toward the young medium of television. Bell insisted on permitting only road games to be televised into a team's home city. Television thus brought in added revenues without hurting paid attendance, and a national contract signed with the Columbia Broadcasting System in 1956 spread the game's following throughout the country.

Pro football soared in popularity in the 1950s and rivaled baseball as the national pastime. The total NFL attendance of 1,977,556 in 1950 set a new record for the sport, and the record continued to mount year by year in a steady climb through the end of the decade. Attendance broke two million in 1952 and went over three million in 1958. The team owners who had stuck out the frugal days of the Depression and the war with the AAFC suddenly found themselves raking in money hand over fist.

The NFL entered the 1950s with a lineup of thirteen clubs, but not all the teams shared in the prosperity. The Baltimore Colts franchise folded after the 1950 season, and the New York Yanks became the Dallas Texans in 1952. When pro football flopped in Texas, the team was transferred to Baltimore for the 1953 campaign, and the Colts took root in this second chance to give the NFL twelve solid franchises.

As the decade drew to a close, a new group of businessmen were looking to get into the game. But when Lamar Hunt and Bud Adams were turned down in applications for NFL clubs, they held organizational meetings and formed a new American Football League in the summer of 1959, with plans to start play in 1960. Once again, the NFL prepared itself to go to war. A new general would have to be found for the struggle, however, for as Commissioner Bell was watching the Eagles and Steelers play in Philadelphia on October 11, 1959, a massive heart attack ended his life in the very setting where he had spent most of his energies.

1946–1959 SINGLE SEASON LEADERS

RUSHING

Most Yards Rushing

		Team	Year	Yds.
1	Jimmy Brown	Cle	1958	1527
2	Spec Sanders	NY-AA	1947	1432
3	Jimmy Brown	Cle	1959	1329
4	Steve Van Buren	Phi	1949	1146
5	Rich Casares	ChiB	1956	1126
6	Tony Canadeo	GB	1949	1052
7	Joe Perry	SF	1954	1049
8	J. D. Smith	SF	1959	1036
9	Joe Perry	SF	1953	1018
10	Steve Van Buren	Phi	1947	1008

Most Rushing Attempts

		Team	Year	Att.
1	Jimmy Brown	Cle	1959	290
2	Eddie Price	NYG	1951	271
3	Steve Van Buren	Phi	1949	263
4	Jimmy Brown	Cle	1958	257
5	Rick Casares	ChiB	1956	234
6	Spec Sanders	NY-AA	1947	231
7	Steve Van Buren	Phi	1947	217
8	Alan Ameche	Bal	1955	213
9	Tony Canadeo	GB	1949	208
	Rob Goode	Was	1951	208

Best Rushing Average (Minimum 50 Attempts)

		Team	Year	Att.	Yds.	Avg.
1	Chuck Fenenbock	LA-AA	1946	50	420	8.4
2	Marion Motley	CleAA	1946	73	601	8.2
3	Hugh McElhenny	SF	1954	64	515	8.0
4	Lenny Moore	Bal	1956	86	649	7.5
5	Kenny Washington	LA	1947	60	444	7.4
6	Tom Wilson	LA	1956	64	470	7.3
7	Joe Perry	SF-AA	1948	77	562	7.3
8	Lenny Moore	Bal	1958	82	598	7.3
9	Skeets Quinlan	LA	1953	97	705	7.3
10	Spec. Del. Jones	CleAA	1947	77	539	7.0

Most Touchdown Runs

		Team	Year	TD
1	Spec Sanders	NY-AA	1947	18
2	Jimmy Brown	Cle	1958	17
3	Jimmy Brown	Cle	1959	14
4	Steve Van Buren	Phi	1947	13
5	Rick Casares	ChiB	1956	12
6	Steve Van Buren	Phi	1949	11
	Johnny Lujack	ChiB	1950	11
	Dan Towler	LA	1954	11
	Tobin Rote	GB	1956	11

(8 tied with 10)

Most Yards Rushing per Game

		Team	Year	Yds/G
1	Jimmy Brown	Cle	1958	127
2	Jimmy Brown	Cle	1959	111
3	Spec Sanders	NY-AA	1947	102
4	Steve Van Buren	Phi	1949	96
5	Rick Casares	ChiB	1956	94
6	Tony Canadeo	GB	1949	88
7	Joe Perry	SF	1954	87
8	J. D. Smith	SF	1959	86
9	Joe Perry	SF	1953	85
10	Steve Van Buren	Phi	1947	84

Best KICKOFF RETURN Average (Minimum 10 Attempts)

		Team	Year	No.	Yds.	Avg.
1	Lenny Lyles	Bal	1958	11	398	36.1
2	Ollie Matson	ChiC	1958	14	497	35.5
3	Lynn Chadnois	Pit	1952	17	599	35.2
4	Joe Arenas	SF	1953	16	551	34.4
5	Buddy Young	Bal	1953	11	378	34.4
6	Vitamin Smith	LA	1950	22	742	33.7
7	Chet Mutryn	BufAA	1947	21	691	32.9
8	Russ Craft	Phi	1946	10	327	32.7
9	Lynn Chandnois	Pit	1951	12	390	32.5
10	Tom Wilson	LA	1956	15	477	31.8

Best PUNT RETURN Average (Minimum 10 Attempts)

		Team	Year	No.	Yds.	Avg.
1	Herb Rich	Bal	1950	12	276	23.0
2	Jack Christiansen	Det	1952	15	322	21.5
3	Rex Bumgardner	BufAA	1948	16	336	21.0
4	Red Cochran	ChiC	1949	15	314	20.9
5	Jerry Davis	ChiC	1948	16	334	20.9
6	Buddy Young	NYY	1951	12	231	19.3
7	Billy Grimes	GB	1950	29	555	19.1
8	Jack Christiansen	Det	1951	18	343	19.1
9	Ollie Matson	ChiC	1955	13	245	18.8
10	Chuck Fenenbock	LA-AA	1946	16	299	18.7

PASSING

Most Yards Passing

		Team	Year	Yds.
1	Sammy Baugh	Was	1947	2938
2	Johnny Unitas	Bal	1959	2899
3	Billy Wade	LA	1958	2875
4	Otto Graham	Cle	1952	2816
5	Otto Graham	CleAA	1949	2785
6	Otto Graham	CleAA	1947	2753
7	Otto Graham	Cle	1953	2722
8	Otto Graham	CleAA	1948	2713
9	Sid Luckman	ChiB	1947	2712
10	Johnny Lujack	ChiB	1949	2658

Most Completed Passes

		Team	Year	Comp.
1	Sammy Baugh	Was	1947	210
2	Norm Van Brocklin	Phi	1958	198
3	Johnny Unitas	Bal	1959	193
4	Norm Van Brocklin	Phi	1959	191
5	Sammy Baugh	Was	1948	185
	Glen Dobbs	LA-AA	1948	185
7	Otto Graham	Cle	1952	181
	Billy Wade	LA	1958	181
9	Tobin Rote	GB	1954	180
10	Sid Luckman	ChiB	1947	176
	Y. A. Tittle	SF	1957	176

Best Completion Percentage (Minimum 100 Attempts)

		Team	Year	Att.	Comp.	Pct.
1	Otto Graham	Cle	1953	258	167	64.7
2	Y. A. Tittle	SF	1957	279	176	63.1
3	Otto Graham	CleAA	1947	269	163	60.6
4	John Brodie	SF	1958	172	103	59.9
5	Sammy Baugh	Was	1947	354	210	59.3
6	Eddie LeBaron	Was	1957	167	99	59.3
7	Otto Graham	Cle	1954	240	142	59.2
8	Sammy Baugh	Was	1948	315	185	58.7
9	Milt Plum	Cle	1959	266	156	58.6
10	Billy Wade	LA	1959	261	153	58.6

Most Touchdown Passes

		Team	Year	TD
1	Johnny Unitas	Bal	1959	32
2	Frankie Albert	SF-AA	1948	29
3	Frankie Albert	SF-AA	1949	27
4	Bobby Layne	Det	1951	26
5	Sammy Baugh	Was	1947	25
	Otto Graham	CleAA	1947	25
	Tommy Thompson	Phi	1948	25
	Otto Graham	CleAA	1948	25
9	Sid Luckman	ChiB	1947	24
	Johnny Unitas	Bal	1957	24

Most Yards Passing per Game

		Team	Year	Yds/G
1	Sammy Baugh	Was	1947	245
2	Johnny Unitas	Bal	1959	242
3	Billy Wade	LA	1958	240
4	Otto Graham	Cle	1952	235
5	Otto Graham	Cle	1953	227
6	Sid Luckman	ChiB	1947	226
7	Johnny Lujack	ChiB	1949	222
8	Norm Van Brocklin	LA	1954	220
9	Norm Van Brocklin	Phi	1959	218
10	Sammy Baugh	Was	1948	217

Most Yards per Passing Attempt (Minimum 100 Attempts)

		Team	Year	Att.	Yds.	Yd/Att.
1	Tom O'Connell	Cle	1957	110	1229	11.2
2	Otto Graham	Cle	1953	258	2722	10.6
3	Otto Graham	CleAA	1946	174	1834	10.5
4	Otto Graham	CleAA	1947	269	2753	10.2
5	Norm Van Brocklin	LA	1954	260	2637	10.1
6	Ed Brown	ChiB	1956	168	1667	9.9
7	Otto Graham	CleAA	1949	285	2785	9.8
8	Eddie LeBaron	Was	1958	145	1365	9.4
9	Otto Graham	Cle	1955	185	1721	9.3
10	Eddie LeBaron	Was	1957	167	1508	9.0

Fewest Percent Intercepted (Minimum 100 Attempts)

		Team	Year	Att.	Int.	% Int
1	Chuck Conerly	NYG	1959	194	4	2.06
2	Ace Parker	NY-AA	1946	115	3	2.61
3	Johnny Unitas	Bal	1958	263	7	2.66
4	Milt Plum	Cle	1959	266	8	3.01
5	Y. A. Tittle	SF	1954	295	9	3.10
6	Y. A. Tittle	BalAA	1948	289	9	3.11
7	Harry Gilmer	Det	1955	122	4	3.28
8	Jim Hardy	LA	1948	211	7	3.32
9	Otto Graham	Cle	1953	258	9	3.50
10	Paul Christman	ChiC	1948	114	4	3.51
	Otto Graham	CleAA	1949	285	10	3.51

RECEIVING

Most Yards Receiving

		Team	Year	Yds.
1	Crazy Legs Hirsch	LA	1951	1495
2	Billy Howton	GB	1952	1231
3	Bob Boyd	LA	1954	1212
4	Billy Howton	GB	1956	1888
5	Mac Speedie	CleAA	1947	1146
6	Harlon Hill	ChiB	1956	1128
7	Harlon Hill	ChiB	1954	1124
8	Tom Fears	LA	1950	1116
9	Del Shofner	LA	1958	1097
10	Pete Pihos	Phi	1953	1049

Most Receptions

		Team	Year	Rec.
1	Tom Fears	LA	1950	84
2	Tom Fears	LA	1949	77
3	Mac Speedie	CleAA	1947	67
4	Bob Mann	Det	1949	66
	Crazy Legs Hirsch	LA	1951	66
6	Jim Keane	ChiB	1947	64
7	Jim Benton	LA	1946	63
	Pete Pihos	Phi	1953	63
9	Mac Speedie	CleAA	1949	62
	Mac Speedie	Cle	1952	62
	Pete Pihos	Phi	1955	62

Most Yards per Reception (Minimum 400 Yards)

		Team	Year	Rec.	Yds.	Avg.
1	Don Currivan	Bos	1947	24	782	32.6
2	Ray Renfro	Cle	1957	21	589	28.0
3	Jimmy Orr	Pit	1958	33	910	27.6
4	Ken Kavanaugh	ChiB	1947	32	818	25.6
5	Cloyce Box	Det	1953	16	403	25.2
6	Harlon Hill	ChiB	1954	45	1124	25.0
7	Elbie Nickel	Pit	1949	26	633	24.3
8	Harlon Hill	ChiB	1956	47	1128	24.0
9	Elbie Nickel	Pit	1950	22	527	24.0
10	Ray Renfro	Cle	1958	24	573	23.9

Most Touchdowns – Receiving

		Team	Year	TD
1	Crazy Legs Hirsch	LA	1951	17
2	Cloyce Box	Det	1952	15
3	Mal Kutner	ChiC	1948	14
	Alyn Beals	SF-AA	1948	14
	Ray Berry	Bal	1959	14
6	Ken Kavanaugh	ChiB	1947	13
	Billy Howton	GB	1952	13
8	Alyn Beals	SF-AA	1949	12
	Bob Shaw	ChiC	1950	12
	Leon Hart	Det	1951	12
	Hugh Taylor	Was	1952	12
	Harlon Hill	ChiB	1954	12
	Billy Howton	GB	1956	12

Most Yards Receiving per Game

		Team	Year	Yds/G
1	Crazy Legs Hirsch	LA	1951	125
2	Billy Howton	GB	1952	103
3	Bob Boyd	LA	1954	101
4	Billy Howton	GB	1956	99
5	Harlon Hill	ChiB	1956	94
6	Tom Fears	LA	1950	93
7	Del Shofner	LA	1958	91
8	Jim Benton	LA	1946	89
9	Pete Pihos	Phi	1953	87
10	Bob Mann	Det	1949	85

SCORING

Most Points

		Team	Year	TD	FG	PAT	Pts.
1	Doak Walker	Det	1950	11	8	38	128
2	Spec Sanders	NY-AA	1947	19	0	0	114
	Gordie Soltau	SF	1953	6	10	48	114
	Bobby Walston	Phi	1954	11	4	36	114
5	Pat Harder	ChiC	1948	6	7	53	110
6	Johnny Lujack	ChiB	1950	11	3	34	109
7	Jimmy Brown	Cle	1958	18	0	0	108
8	Doak Walker	Det	1954	5	11	43	106
9	Pat Harder	ChiC	1947	7	7	39	102
	Pat Harder	ChiC	1949	8	3	45	102
	Choo-Choo Roberts	NYG	1949	17	0	0	102
	Crazy Legs Hirsch	LA	1951	17	0	0	102

Most Points per Game

		Team	Year	PPG
1	Doak Walker	Det	1950	10.7
2	Gordie Soltau	SF	1953	9.5
	Bobby Walston	Phi	1954	9.5
4	Pat Harder	ChiC	1948	9.2
5	Ted Fritsch	GB	1946	9.1
6	Johnny Lujack	ChiB	1950	9.1
7	Jimmy Brown	Cle	1958	9.0
8	Doak Walker	Det	1954	8.8
9	Pat Harder	ChiC	1947	8.5
	Pat Harder	ChiC	1947	8.5
	Choo-Choo Roberts	NYG	1949	8.5
	Crazy Legs Hirsch	LA	1951	8.5

KICKING

Best Punting Average (Minimum 30 punts)

		Team	Year	No.	Avg.
1	Glenn Dobbs	LA-AA	1948	68	49.1
2	Frankie Albert	SF-AA	1949	31	48.2
3	Glenn Dobbs	BknAA	1946	80	47.8
4	Joe Muha	Phi	1948	57	47.2
5	Yale Lary	Det	1959	45	47.1
6	Pat Brady	Pit	1953	80	46.9
7	Horace Gillom	Cle	1952	61	45.7
8	Tommy Davis	SF	1959	59	45.7
9	Bob Cifers	Det	1946	30	45.6
10	Horace Gillom	Cle	1951	73	45.4

Most Field Goals

		Team	Year	FG
1	Lou Groza	Cle	1953	23
2	Pat Summerall	NYG	1959	20
3	Lou Groza	Cle	1952	19
4	Sam Baker	Was	1956	17
5	Lou Groza	Cle	1954	16
	Fred Cone	GB	1955	16
7	Ben Agajanian	LA-AA	1947	15
	Lou Groza	Cle	1957	15
9	Sam Baker	Was	1957	14
	Paige Cothren	LA	1958	14
	Tom Milner	Pit	1958	14

Best Field Goal Percentage (Minimum 10 attempts)

		Team	Year	FG	Att.	Pct.
1	Lou Groza	Cle	1953	23	26	88
2	Bobby Layne	Det	1956	12	15	80
3	Bill Dudley	Was	1951	10	13	77
4	Ray Poole	NYG	1951	12	16	75
5	Steve Nemeth	ChiAA	1946	9	12	75
	Bobby Walston	Phi	1957	9	12	75
7	Fred Cone	GB	1957	12	17	71
8	Pat Harder	ChiC	1947	7	10	70
9	Pat Summerall	NYG	1959	20	29	69
10	Lou Groza	Cle	1950	13	19	68

Most Points After Touchdown

		Team	Year	PAT
1	Joe Vetrano	SF-AA	1948	62
2	Joe Vetrano	SF-AA	1949	56
3	Bob Waterfield	LA	1950	54
4	Pat Harder	ChiC	1948	53
5	Lou Groza	CleAA	1948	51
6	Cliff Patton	Phi	1948	50
	Steve Myhra	Bal	1959	50
8	Harvey Johnson	NY-AA	1947	49
9	Gordie Soltau	SF	1953	48
	Steve Myhra	Bal	1958	48

Most PAT – No Misses

		Team	Year	PAT
1	Joe Vetrano	SF-AA	1949	56
2	Pat Harder	ChiC	1948	53
3	Cliff Patton	Phi	1948	50
4	Rex Grossman	BalAA	1948	43
	Lou Groza	Cle	1951	43
	Doak Walker	Det	1954	43
7	Paige Cothren	LA	1958	42
8	Les Richter	LA	1954	38
	Paige Cothren	LA	1957	38
10	Bob Waterfield	LA	1946	37
	Harvey Johnson	NY-AA	1948	37
	George Blanda	ChiB	1955	37

INTERCEPTIONS

Most Passes Intercepted

		Team	Year	Int.
1	Night Train Lane	LA	1952	14
2	Don Sandifer	Was	1948	13
	Spec Sanders	NYY	1950	13
4	Bob Nussbaumer	ChiC	1949	12
	Don Doll	Det	1950	12
	Woodley Lewis	LA	1950	12
	Jack Christiansen	Det	1953	12
8	Otto Schnellbacher	NY-AA	1948	11
	Don Doll	Det	1949	11
	Otto Schnellbacher	NYG	1951	11
	Tom Keane	Bal	1953	11
	Will Sherman	LA	1954	11
	Lindon Crow	ChiC	1955	11
	Jimmy Patton	NYG	1958	11

1946–1959 PERIOD LEADERS

PASSING

(All passers with at least 1000 attempts)

		Years	Att.	Comp.	Comp. Pct.	Yards	Yds/ Att.	TD	Int.	Pct. Int.
1	Otto Graham	*1946-55	2626	1464	55.8	**23584**	**9.0**	**174**	135	5.1
2	Norm Van Brocklin	1949-59	2611	1400	53.6	21140	8.1	149	161	6.2
3	Johnny Unitas	1956-59	1129	611	54.1	8954	7.9	84	**48**	**4.3**
4	Y. A. Tittle	1948-59	2960	**1627**	55.0	21937	7.4	142	177	6.0
5	Sammy Baugh	1946-52	1436	804	**56.0**	10989	7.7	92	98	6.8
6	Chuck Conerly	1948-59	2593	1308	50.4	17900	6.9	158	152	5.9
7	Bobby Layne	1948-59	**3109**	1520	48.9	22063	7.1	163	193	6.2
8	Frankie Albert	*1946-52	1564	831	53.1	10795	6.9	115	98	6.3
9	George Ratterman	*1947-56	1396	737	52.8	10473	7.5	91	96	6.9
	Tommy Thompson	1946-50	1003	527	52.5	7725	7.7	74	68	6.8
11	Bobby Tomason	*1949,51-57	1346	687	51.0	9480	7.0	68	90	6.7
12	Bob Waterfield	1946-52	1446	725	50.1	10240	7.1	84	111	7.7
13	Tobin Rote	1950-59	2450	1082	44.2	15144	6.2	119	158	6.4
14	Eddie LeBaron	1952-53,55-59	1104	538	48.7	8068	7.3	59	88	8.0
15	Jim Finks	*1949-55	1382	661	47.8	8622	6.2	55	88	6.4
16	Adrian Burk	*1950-56	1079	500	46.3	7001	6.5	61	89	8.2
17	Lamar McHan	1954-59	1120	481	42.9	7383	6.6	57	86	7.7

SCORING

		Years	TD-Rush	TD-Rec.	TD-Other	FG	PAT	Points
1	Lou Groza	1946-59	0	1	0	161	512	1001
2	Gordie Soltau	*1950-58	0	25	0	70	284	644
3	Bobby Walston	1951-59	0	40	0	48	247	631
4	George Blanda	1949-58	5	0	0	88	247	541
5	Doak Walker	*1950-55	12	21	1	49	183	534
6	Pat Harder	*1946-53	33	5	0	35	198	531
7	Bob Waterfield	1946-52	8	0	0	59	284	509
8	Ben Agajanian	1947-49,53-57	0	0	0	76	263	491
9	Joe Perry	1948-59	67	11	1	1	6	483
10	Fred Cone	1951-57	12	4	0	53	200	455

RECEIVING

Most Receptions

		Years	Rec
1	Billy Wilson	1951-59	404
2	Tom Fears	*1948-56	400
3	Crazy Legs Hirsch	*1946-57	387
4	Dante Lavelli	*1946-56	386
5	Pete Pihos	*1947-55	373
6	Mac Speedie	*1946-52	349
7	Billy Howton	1952-59	342
8	Elbie Nickel	*1947-57	329
9	Hugh Taylor	*1947-54	272
10	Gordie Soltau	*1950-58	249

Most Yards

		Years	Yards
1	Crazy Legs Hirsch	*1946-57	7029
2	Dante Lavelli	*1946-56	6488
3	Billy Howton	1952-59	6091
4	Billy Wilson	1951-59	5851
5	Pete Pihos	*1947-55	5619
6	Mac Speedie	*1946-52	5602
7	Tom Fears	*1948-56	5397
8	Hugh Taylor	*1947-54	5233
9	Elbie Nickel	*1947-57	5131
10	Harlon Hill	1954-59	4467

Most Touchdowns

		Years	TD
1	Dante Lavelli	*1946-56	62
2	Pete Pihos	*1947-55	61
3	Crazy Legs Hirsch	*1946-57	60
4	Hugh Taylor	*1947-54	58
5	Alyn Beals	*1946-51	49
6	Billy Wilson	1951-59	48
7	Billy Howton	1952-59	44
8	Harlon Hill	1954-59	40
	Bobby Walston	1951-59	40
10	Tom Fears	*1948-56	38

Most Yards Per Reception
(Minimum 100 receptions)

		Years	Yds.	Rec.	Avg.
1	Ken Kavanaugh	1946-50	2493	114	21.9
2	Mal Kutner	*1946-50	3060	145	21.1
3	Cloyce Box	*1949-50,52-54	2665	129	20.7
4	Ray Renfro	1952-59	3576	174	20.6
5	Bob Boyd	*1950-57	3611	176	20.5
6	Harlon Hill	1954-59	4467	218	20.5
7	Hugh Taylor	*1947-54	5233	272	19.2
8	Crazy Legs Hirsch	*1946-57	7029	387	18.2
9	Billy Hillenbrand	*1946-48	1987	110	18.1
10	Gene Schroeder	*1951-52,54-57	1870	104	18.0

RUSHING

Most Attempts

		Years	Att.
1	Joe Perry	1948-59	1607
2	Steve Van Buren	1946-51	1097
3	Bob Hoernschemeyer	*1946-55	1059
4	Ollie Matson	1952,54-59	922
5	Rick Casares	1955-59	916
6	Alan Ameche	1955-59	884
7	Marion Motley	*1946-53,55	828
8	Hugh McElhenny	1952-59	782
9	Tank Younger	*1949-58	770
10	Jimmy Brown	1957-59	749

Most Yards

		Years	Yards
1	Joe Perry	1948-59	8496
2	Marion Motley	*1946-53,55	4720
3	Steve Van Buren	1946-51	4584
4	Bob Hoernschemeyer	*1946-55	4548
5	Ollie Matson	1952,54-59	4194
6	Hugh McElhenny	1952-59	3941
7	Rick Casares	1955-59	3838
8	Jimmy Brown	1957-59	3798
9	Alan Ameche	1955-59	3782
10	Tank Younger	*1949-58	3640

Most Touchdowns

		Years	TD
1	Joe Perry	1948-59	67
2	Steve Van Buren	1946-51	48
3	Otto Graham	*1946-55	44
4	Dan Towler	*1950-55	43
5	Jimmy Brown	1957-59	40
6	Alan Ameche	1955-59	37
7	Hugh McElhenny	1952-59	35
	Tobin Rote	1950-59	35
9	Tank Younger	*1949-58	34
	Rick Casares	1955-59	34

Most Yards per Attempt
(Minimum 500 Attempts)

		Years	Yds.	Att.	Avg.
1	Marion Motley	*1946-53,55	4720	828	5.7
2	Spec Sanders	*1946-48,50	2900	540	5.4
3	Joe Perry	1948-59	8496	1607	5.3
4	Chet Mutryn	*1946-50	3031	583	5.2
5	Dan Towler	*1950-55	3493	672	5.2
6	Johnny Strzykalski	*1946-52	3415	662	5.2
7	Tobin Rote	1950-59	3078	601	5.1
8	Charlie Trippi	*1947-55	3506	687	5.1
9	Jimmy Brown	1957-59	3798	749	5.1
10	Hugh McElhenny	1952-59	3941	782	5.0

PUNT RETURNS

(Minimum 50 Returns)

		Years	Ret.	Yards	Avg.	TD
1	Jim Cason	*1948-52,54-56	67	948	14.1	0
2	Charlie Trippi	*1947-55	63	864	13.7	2
3	Chuck Fenenbock	1946-48	50	678	13.6	0
4	Billy Grimes	*1949-52	68	901	13.3	2
5	Ray Mathews	1951-59	61	779	12.8	3
6	Jack Christiansen	*1951-58	85	1084	12.8	8
7	Bill Dudley	1946-51,53	99	1224	12.4	3
8	George McAfee	1946-50	106	1265	11.9	1
9	Bosh Pritchard	1946-51	84	965	11.5	2
10	Ollie Matson	1952,54-59	62	585	9.4	3

KICKOFF RETURNS

(Minimum 50 Returns)

		Years	Ret.	Yards	Avg.	TD
1	Lynn Chadnois	*1950-56	92	2720	29.6	3
2	Buddy Young	*1947-55	125	3465	27.7	4
3	Ollie Matson	1952,54-59	103	2821	27.4	6
4	Joe Arenas	*1951-57	139	3798	27.3	1
5	Joe Scott	*1948-53	54	1467	27.2	1
6	Monk Gafford	*1946-48	55	1469	26.7	0
7	Chet Mutryn	*1946-50	73	1902	26.1	1
8	Vitamin Smith	*1949-53	57	1453	25.5	3
9	Al Carmichael	1953-58	153	3907	25.5	2
10	Steve Van Buren	1946-51	55	1391	25.3	1

INTERCEPTION RETURNS

(in order by Returns)

		Years	Ret.	Yards	Avg.	TD
1	Em Tunnell	1948-59	76	1260	16.6	4
2	Jack Butler	*1951-59	52	827	15.9	4
	Bobby Dillon	*1952-59	52	976	18.8	5
4	Night Train Lane	1952-59	57	935	19.9	4
5	Jack Christiansen	*1951-58	46	717	15.6	3
6	Warren Lahr	*1948-59	44	562	12.8	5
7	Don Doll	*1949-54	41	617	15.0	2
8	Tom Keane	*1948-55	40	349	8.7	1
9	Jim David	*1952-59	36	259	7.2	0
10	Ray Ramsey	*1947-53	35	663	18.9	1

PUNTING

(Minimum 150 Punts)

		Years	No.	Avg.
1	Glenn Dobbs	*1946-49	231	46.40
2	Pat Brady	*1952-54	223	44.52
3	Don Chandler	1956-59	239	44.23
4	Sam Baker	1953,56-59	221	43.76
5	Horace Gillom	*1947-56	492	43.11
6	Frankie Albert	*1946-52	299	43.02
7	Joe Muha	*1946-50	179	42.94
8	Norm Van Brocklin	1949-59	463	42.83
9	Bob Waterfield	1946-52	276	42.66
10	Jim Smith	*1948-53	196	42.37

KICKING

Most Field Goals

		Years	FG	Att.	Pct.
1	Lou Groza	1946-57	161	300	54
2	George Blanda	1949-58	88	201	44
3	Ben Agajanian	1947-49,53-57	76	147	52
4	Pat Summerall	1952-59	73	152	48
5	Gordie Soltau	*1950-58	70	138	51
6	Bob Waterfield	1946-52	59	107	55
7	Sam Baker	1953,56-59	54	96	56
8	Fred Cone	1951-57	53	89	60
9	Doak Walker	*1950-55	49	87	56
10	Bobby Walston	1951-59	48	97	49

Most Points After Touchdowns

		Years	PAT	Att.	Pct.
1	Lou Groza	1946-59	512	528	97.0
2	Bob Waterfield	1946-52	284	302	94.0
	Gordie Soltau	*1950-58	284	302	94.0
4	Ben Agajanian	1947-49,53-57	263	268	98.1
5	George Blanda	1949-58	247	250	98.8
	Bobby Walston	1951-59	247	260	95.0
7	Fred Cone	1951-57	200	214	93.5
8	Pat Harder	*1946-53	198	204	97.1
9	Joe Vetrano	*1946-49	187	203	92.1
10	Doak Walker	*1950-55	183	191	95.8

* – Entire Career

NEW YORK GIANTS 7-3-1 Steve Owen

Scores of Each Game		
17	Boston	0
17	Pittsburgh	14
14	Washington	24
28	CHIC. CARDS	24
14	CHIC. BEARS	0
14	Philadelphia	24
45	PHILADELPHIA	17
28	BOSTON	28
7	PITTSBURGH	0
21	LOS ANGELES	31
31	WASHINGTON	0

Use Name	Pos.	Hgt	Wgt	Age	Int	Pts
Lou DeFilippo	C-DT	6'1"	240	30		
Chet Gladchuk	C-DT	6'4"	245	29		
Lou Palazzi	C-LB	6'	195	25		
Pete Gorgone	BB-LB	6'	220	25		

Use Name – Tackles	Pos.	Hgt	Wgt	Age	Int	Pts
Joe Byler	T	6'5"	240	23		
Vic Carroll	T	6'4"	240	33		
(1 kickoff return for 11 yds.)						
Frank Cope	T	6'2"	230	30		
Tex Coulter	T	6'4"	225	21		
Phil Ragazzo	T	6'	220	31		
Jim White	T	6'2"	225	25		6

Use Name – Guards	Pos.	Hgt	Wgt	Age	Int	Pts
Bob Dobelstein	G-LB	5'11"	210	24		
Monk Edwards	G-LB	6'3"	215	26		
Kayo Lunday	G	6'3"	220	33		
Orville Tuttle	G	5'9"	215	33		
Len Younce	G-LB	6'1"	210	29	1	
(1 punt for 10 yds.)						

The Giants bounced back from an off year to grab the Eastern Division championship with a tough defense and recharged offense. The new battery in the attack was tailback Frankie Filchock, a flashy performer obtained from the Washington Redskins. Unchained from Sammy Baugh's shadow after six seasons Filchock came into his own with elusive running and a strong passing arm, winning an All-Pro berth for his efforts. The defense was built on the shoulders of a strong line stocked with healthy young men like Jim White, Frank Cope, Tex Coulter, Len Younce, Monk Edwards, and Chet Gladchuk. Even with the departure of veterans Mel Hein, Arnie Herber, and Ward Cuff, the Giants flexed too much muscle for their Eastern opponents. And at the box office, the Giant fans showed their own power, turning out for an average crowd of 50,000 at each home game, making the season profitable both in the standings and in the financial accounts.

PHILADELPHIA EAGLES 6-5-0 Greasy Neale

Scores of Each Game		
25	Los Angeles	14
49	BOSTON	25
7	GREEN BAY	19
14	Chic. Bears	21
28	Washington	24
24	NEW YORK	14
17	New York	45
7	Pittsburgh	10
10	WASHINGTON	27
10	PITTSBURGH	7
40	Boston	14

Use Name	Pos.	Hgt	Wgt	Age	Int	Pts
Ray Graves	C-LB	6'1"	205	27		
Henry Gude	C-G	6'1"	225	24		
(1 kickoff return for 0 yds.)						
Vic Lindskog	C-LB	6'1"	200	30	1	
Alex Wojciechowicz	C-LB	5'11"	225	31		
(from DET)						
Bob Friedlund	OE-DE	6'3"	210	26		
Bert Kuczynski	OE-DE	6'	195	26		6
(1 reception for 9 yd. touchdown)						
Flip McDonald	OE-DE	6'2"	200	25		
Art Macioszczyk – military service						

Use Name – Tackles	Pos.	Hgt	Wgt	Age	Int	Pts
Otis Douglas	T	6'1"	220	34		
John Eibner	T	6'2"	230	30		
Bucko Kilroy	T	6'2"	240	25	1	
Jay MacDowell	T-OE	6'2"	210	27		2
(1 reception for 28 yds.)						
Vic Sears	T	6'3"	225	28		
Al Wistert	T	6'1"	215	25	1	

Use Name – Guards	Pos.	Hgt	Wgt	Age	Int	Pts
Duke Maronic	G	5'9"	205	25	1	
Bob McDonough	G	5'11"	205	29		
Eddie Michaels	G	5'11"	210	32		
Cliff Patton	G	6'2"	240	22		
John Wyhonic	G	6'	210	26		

The lackluster Eagle record hid the fact that coach Greasy Neale was still adding talent to his developing club. This year's new arrivals were Alex Wojciechowicz, a tough veteran center and linebacker picked up from Detroit, ex-Boston guard Augie Lio, rookie fullback and linebacker Joe Muha, and wiry half-back Bosh Pritchard. Already settled in at quarterback was Tommy Thompson. Steve Van Buren had made a habit of storming through the enemy like a one-man stampede, while linemen Vic Sears, Al Wistert, and Bucko Kilroy made opponents pay a price for facing the Eagles.

But this season the array of talent did not quite jell into a first-class team. Although the defense still needed some patchwork and the offense sputtered when injuries shelved Steve Van Buren, the Eagles still looked like a team on the verge of breaking through.

WASHINGTON REDSKINS 5-5-1 Turk Edwards

Scores of Each Game		
14	PITTSBURGH	14
17	DETROIT	16
24	NEW YORK	14
14	Boston	6
24	PHILADELPHIA	28
7	Pittsburgh	14
7	BOSTON	14
20	Chic. Bears	24
27	Philadelphia	10
7	GREEN BAY	20
0	New York	31

Use Name	Pos.	Hgt	Wgt	Age	Int	Pts
Ki Aldrich	C-LB	6'	206	30	3	6
Al DeMao	C-LB	6'2"	205	26	2	
Clyde Ehrhardt	C-LB	6'1"	240	26	1	
Ralph Schilling	DE-OE	6'3"	218	25		
(to BUF AA) (1 reception for 14 yds.)						

Use Name – Tackles	Pos.	Hgt	Wgt	Age	Int	Pts
John Adams	T	6'7"	245	26		
Don Avery	T	6'4"	245	25		
John Koniszewski	T	6'3"	250	27		
Paul Stenn	T	6'2"	245	28		
Bill Young	T	6'1"	254	32		

Use Name – Guards	Pos.	Hgt	Wgt	Age	Int	Pts
Oscar Britt	G	5'11"	193	28		
Al Couppee	G-FB	6'	225	27		
(3 rushing attempts for 22 yds.)						
John Jaffurs	G	5'10"	200	24		
John Steber	G	6'	200	23		
Clem Stralka	G	5'10"	228	32		
Bill Ward	G	6'	230	25		
(1 kickoff return for 2 yds.)						

George Marshall did New York owner Tim Mara a favor and ended up suffering because of it. Sending passer Frankie Filchock to the punchless Giants, Marshall figured that Sammy Baugh was all the quarterback any team needed. As things turned out, injuries to Baugh left the Skins without a passer for several games, while Filchock sparked the Giants to the Eastern title. But more than Baugh's hurts caused the drop to third place. Owner Marshall refused to compete with the AAFC in offering high salaries to his players, and with offers too good to resist, the new league lured away ace tackle Willie Wilkin, star end and kicker Joe Aguirre, and even head coach Dud DeGroot.

Despite these losses, coach Turk Edwards kept the team in the race through the autumn, with wins needed in the last two games to clinch the crown. The Packers killed the title hopes with a 20-7 win, and then the Giants added insult to injury with a 31-0 triumph.

PITTSBURGH STEELERS 5-5-1 Jock Sutherland

Scores of Each Game		
14	CHIC. CARDS	7
14	Washington	14
14	NEW YORK	17
16	BOSTON	7
7	Green Bay	17
33	Boston	7
14	WASHINGTON	7
7	Detroit	17
10	PHILADELPHIA	7
0	New York	7
7	Philadelphia	10

Use Name	Pos.	Hgt	Wgt	Age	Int	Pts
Art Brandau	C-LB	6'2"	204	24		
Chuck Cherundolo	C-LB	6'1"	222	30	1	
George Titus	C-LB	5'10"	185	24		
Jim Reynolds	DB	6'	193	25		
John Patrick	BB-LB	6'	205	28		
Vern Foltz – military service						

Use Name – Tackles	Pos.	Hgt	Wgt	Age	Int	Pts
Joe Coomer	T	6'6"	280	27		
Earl Klapstein	T	6'	220	24		
Art McCaffray	T	5'11"	190	25		
Al Merkovsky	T	6'1"	220	29		
Joe Repko	T	6'	235	25		
Jack Wiley	T	5'11"	203	25		

Use Name – Guards	Pos.	Hgt	Wgt	Age	Int	Pts
Ray Bucek	G-LB	6'	186	26		
Ralph Fife	G-LB	6'	208	26		
(2 kickoff returns for 31 yds.)						
Frank Mattioli	G-LB	6'	210	23		
John Perko	G-LB	6'1"	210	30		
Nick Skorich	G-LB	5'9"	200	25		

With stern coach Jock Sutherland running a tight ship, and with Bill Dudley in uniform for the whole year, owner Art Rooney felt that the Steelers were on the road to the top in the East. Rooney could not have expected, however, that the coach and star player would immediately grow to dislike each other. Dudley always chewed out teammates who put out less than a full effort, and Sutherland saw this as overstepping his bounds. Deciding that Dudley had become a prima donna in the Army, Sutherland chose to reassert his authority over the Steelers by constantly needling the back about his running style and side-arm passing. Dudley accepted his coach's distain and sarcasm in silence, answering him with his performance on the field. He led the NFL in rushing and in interceptions, and he spurred the mediocre team into a third-place finish. At the end of the season, Dudley finally answered his hostile coach: He quit professional football.

BOSTON YANKS 2-8-1 Herb Kopf

Scores of Each Game		
0	NEW YORK	17
25	Philadelphia	49
7	Pittsburgh	16
6	WASHINGTON	14
7	PITTSBURGH	33
14	CHIC. CARDS	28
14	Washington	17
28	New York	28
40	LOS ANGELES	21
34	Detroit	10
14	PHILADELPHIA	40

Use Name	Pos.	Hgt	Wgt	Age	Int	Pts
Joe Domnanovich	C-LB	6'1"	205	27		
Gene Lee	C-LB	6'3"	226	24	1	
(1 kickoff return for 0 yds.)						
Jim Magee	C-LB	6'1"	205	25		
Joe Sulatis	LB	6'2"	210	25		
Sam Bailey	OE-DE	6'2"	195	22		

Use Name – Tackles	Pos.	Hgt	Wgt	Age	Int	Pts
Ralph Calacagni	T	6'3"	225	24		
Tom Dean	T	6'2"	248	22		
Don Deeks	T	6'4"	235	23		
Rube Juster	T	6'2"	230	22		
Ed McGee	T	6'1"	230	30		
Win Pedersen	T	6'3"	225	31		
Steve Sierocinski	T	6'3"	245	24		

Use Name – Guards	Pos.	Hgt	Wgt	Age	Int	Pts
John Badaczewski	G	6'1"	235	24		
Rocco Canale	G	5'11"	253	29		
Tony Leon	G	5'9"	210	29		
(1 kickoff return for 6 yds.)						
Joe Zeno	G	5'10"	238	27	1	

With New York regularly drawing 50,000 fans to home games, with the Los Angeles Rams averaging 38,700 despite AAFC competition, the Boston Yanks still drew very few paying customers to their games. Owner Ted Collins still used the team mainly as a tax write-off, with the operation showing no signs of turning a profit after three years in existence. On the field, the team set no records either, although rookie Paul Governali did give the Yanks a solid passing threat, beating out first draft choice Boley Dancewicz for the signal-calling job. Veteran runners Gary Famiglietti and Jim Gillette joined the club through trades, but both had too much mileage to help the attack. The line folded under pressure like an accordion, and the Yanks could only shake their heads when guard Augie Lio was traded to the Eagles and immediately made All-Pro.

TEAM TOTALS

OFFENSE	FIRST DOWNS: Tot	by Rsh	by Pas	by Pen	RUSHING: No.	Yds.	Avg. Yds.	TD	PASSING: Att.	Com	Comp. Pct.	Yds.	Avg. Yds. Att.	Avg. Yds. Comp	TD	Int.	Pct. Int.
N.Y.	163	81	63	19	413	1467	3.6	15	194	100	51.5	1450	7.5	14.5	14	25	12.9
PHIL.	156	75	69	12	422	1263	3.0	12	217	116	53.5	1641	7.6	14.1	14	19	8.8
WASH.	161	84	67	10	435	1492	3.4	10	221	112	50.7	1613	7.3	14.4	10	22	10.0
PITT.	120	75	35	10	414	1307	3.2	13	161	58	36.0	970	6.0	16.6	4	13	8.1
BOSTON	147	67	59	21	365	1109	3.0	10	239	103	43.1	1566	6.6	15.1	15	18	7.5

OFFENSE	PUNTING: No.	Avg. Yds.	PUNT RETURNS: No.	Yds.	Avg. Yds.	TD	KICKOFF RETURNS: No.	Yds.	Avg. Yds.	TD	INTERCEPTION RETURNS: No.	Yds.	Avg. Yds.	TD	PENALTIES: No.	Yds.	FUMBLES: No.	Lost	POINTS: Tot	PAT	FG Att	FG	Saf.
N.Y.	50	43.4	33	378	11.5	0	24	625	26.0	0	19	295	15.5	1	76	785	36	16	236	32	9	4	0
PHIL.	57	38.2	39	504	12.9	1	41	881	21.5	0	26	413	15.9	1	86	769	54	27	231	29	15	8	2
WASH.	45	44.1	43	470	10.9	0	36	784	21.8	0	24	337	14.0	1	85	843	36	22	171	21	18	6	0
PITT.	70	39.7	37	498	13.5	0	26	474	18.2	0	14	295	21.1	1	69	534	38	15	136	16	9	2	0
BOSTON	72	40.2	29	363	12.5	0	52	1063	20.4	1	17	236	13.9	1	83	691	33	18	189	21	2	0	0

							RUSHING				PASSING								RECEIVING				PUNTING		KICKING						PUNT RETURNS				KICKOFF RETURNS			
Use Name – Backs & Ends	Pos.	Age	Hgt	Wgt	Pts	Int	No.	Yds	Avg	TD	Att	Comp	%	Yds	Yd/Att	TD	Int–%	RK	No.	Yds	Avg	TD	No.	Avg	Pat	Att	%	FG	Att	%	No.	Yds	Avg	TD	No.	Yds	Avg	TD
NEW YORK GIANTS																																						
Frankie Filchock	QB	29	5'11"	190	12		98	371	3.8	2	169	87	51	1262	7.5	12	25–15	8													6	50	8	0	4	109	27	0
Emery Nix	QB	26	5'11"	180			8	−25	−3.1	0	19	10	53	156	8.2	2	0– 0																					
Bill Paschal	FB-DB	25	6'	200	36		117	362	3.1	4									9	78	9	2	1	47.0							9	111	12	0	6	158	26	0
Frank Reagan	FB-DB	27	5'11"	185	12		62	246	4.0	2	6	3	50	32	5.3	0	0– 0		4	71	18	0	20	42.8							5	48	10	0	2	77	39	0
Merle Hapes	FB-DB	27	5'10"	195	30	1	51	161	3.2	5									3	40	13	0	12	39.9							2	5	3	0	2	43	22	0
Hank Soar	FB-DB	32	6'2"	215		3	1	3	3.0	0																					3	57	19	0				
George Franck	WB-DB	27	6'	180	6		43	270	6.3	0									6	137	23	1	16	39.0											6	162	27	0
Howie Livingston	WB-DB	24	6'1"	195	18	4	10	38	3.8	1									2	36	18	1													1	30	30	0
Jack Doolan	WB-DB	27	6'1"	195			12	33	2.8	0									3	28	9	0									3	49	16	0				
Dave Brown	WB-DB	27	5'11"	190			9	5	0.6	0																					1	0	0	0				
Steve Filipowicz	BB-LB	25	5'8"	200	18	4	2	3	1.5	1									7	84	12	1									4	58	15	0	1	16	16	0
Cecil Hare	BB-LB	27	5'11"	195															2	30	15	0													1	19	19	0
Jim Poole	OE-DE	30	6'3"	225	18														24	307	13	3																
Frank Liebel	OE-DB	26	6'1"	220	24	5													18	360	20	4																
Jim Lee Howell	OE-DE	31	6'6"	215															9	141	16	0																
John Weiss	OE-DB	24	6'3"	205	6														4	70	18	1																
Don McCafferty	OE-DE	25	6'4"	220	6														3	38	13	1																
Jack Mead	OE-DB	24	6'3"	215		1													3	26	12	0																
Ken Strong	K	40	6'	210	44																				32	32	100	4	9	44								
PHILADELPHIA EAGLES																																						
Tommy Thompson	QB	30	6'1"	190			34	−116	−3.4	0	103	57	55	745	7.4	6	9– 9	3																				
Roy Zimmerman	QB-DB	28	6'2"	200	14	3	23	43	1.9	1	79	41	50	597	7.6	4	8–10	6					23	38.7	2	2	100	2	4	50								
Allie Sherman	QB	23	5'11"	170			20	8	0.4	0	33	17	52	264	8.0	4	2– 6																					
Steve Van Buren	HB-DB	25	6'	205	36		116	529	4.6	5	1	1	100	35	35.0	0	0– 0		6	55	9	0	1	41.0							5	89	18	1	11	319	29	0
Bosh Pritchard	HB-DB	27	5'11"	170	36	3	42	218	5.2	3	1	0	0	0	0.0	0	0– 0		14	309	22	3	7	34.6							12	166	14	0	8	164	21	0
Gil Steinke	HB-DB	26	6'	175	24	6	38	154	4.1	1									5	107	21	2									8	116	15	0	3	92	31	0
Ernie Steele	HB-DB	28	6'	190	6	3	31	108	3.5	1									5	69	14	0									9	82	9	0	8	120	15	0
Russ Craft	HB-DB	26	5'9"	175		3	27	108	4.0	0									4	48	12	0									4	47	12	0	4	86	22	0
Jim Castiglia	FB-LB	27	5'11"	210	6		39	87	2.2	1									11	51	5	0													1	17	17	0
Joe Muha	FB-LB	25	6'1"	205		1	12	41	3.4	0													22	38.3											1	23	23	0
Jack Hinkle	HB-DB	28	6'	195		2	18	33	1.8	0																					1	4	4	0	1	25	25	0
Pete Kmetovic	HB-DB	26	5'9"	173			5	30	6.0	0									4	68	17	0																
Ben Kish	FB-LB	29	6'	215		1	6	13	2.2	0									3	16	5	0	4	40.8														
Elliott Ormsbee	HB-DB	24	5'11"	185			4	12	3.0	0																									1	5	5	0
Mel Bleeker	HB-DB	26	5'11"	190			6	−7	−1.2	0									3	29	10	0																
Jack Ferrante	OE-DE	30	6'1"	195	24														28	451	16	4																
Dick Humbert	OE-DB	27	6'1"	175	18		1	2	2.0	0									18	191	11	3													1	18	18	0
Larry Cabrelli	OE-DE	29	5'11"	195	6														8	98	12	1																
Rudy Smeja	OE-DE	25	6'2"	196															3	45	15	0													1	12	12	0
Bob Krieger	OE-DE	26	6'1"	190															2	47	24	0																
Augie Lio	G	28	6'	235	51																				27	27	100	6	11	55								
WASHINGTON REDSKINS																																						
Sammy Baugh	QB	32	6'2"	180	6		18	−76	−4.2	1	161	87	54	1163	7.2	8	17–11	7					33	45.1														
Jim Youel	QB-DB	24	6'	175	6	2	13	60	4.6	1	48	20	42	352	7.3	2	3– 6						2	34.0							13	150	12	0	2	29	15	0
Jack Jacobs	QB-HB-DB	27	6'1"	185		2	18	34	1.9	0	12	5	42	98	8.2	0	2–17		4	53	13	0	10	42.8							2	23	12	0				
Dick Todd	HB-DB	31	5'11"	173	30	4	41	266	6.5	3									8	107	13	2									5	64	13	0	3	47	16	0
Sal Rosato	FB-LB	28	6'1"	228	12		62	238	3.8	2									1	17	17	0									1	12	12	0				
Eddie Saenz	HB-DB	23	5'11"	170	24	1	55	213	3.9	1									12	242	20	3													11	264	24	0
Jack Jenkins	FB-LB	26	6'1"	205	6	3	64	200	3.1	1									2	27	14	0									2	14	7	0				
Steve Bagarus	HB-DB	27	6'	170	18	4	53	168	3.0	0									31	438	14	3									18	192	11	0	13	332	26	0
Frank Akins	FB-LB	27	5'10"	215			41	166	4.0	0									2	15	8	0																
Jim Gaffney	HB-DB	25	6'1"	200	6		25	96	3.8	0									7	85	12	1													1	24	24	0
Wilbur Moore	HB-DB	30	5'11"	190		2	15	62	4.1	0																					1	2	2	0				
Dick Poillon	HB-DB	26	6'	186	45		25	45	1.8	1									7	114	16	0			21	21	100	6	16	38	1	13	13	0	5	86	17	0
Bob DeFruiter	HB-DB	29	6'	190			2	−2	−1.0	0									1	9	9	0																
Jim Peebles	OE-DE	26	6'4"	218	6														9	164	18	1						0	2	0								
Doug Turley	OE-DE	27	6'2"	210															6	105	18	0																
John Kovatch	OE-DE	26	6'3"	200															6	67	11	0																
Don Lookabaugh	OE-DE	26	6'4"	212															6	67	11	0																
Ed Cifers	OE-DE	30	6'2"	234															6	61	10	0																
Ted Lapka	OE-DE	26	6'1"	192	6														3	28	9	0																
PITTSBURGH STEELERS																																						
Bill Dudley	TB-DB	25	5'10"	172	48	10	146	604	4.1	3	90	32	36	452	5.0	2	9–10	10	4	109	27	1	60	40.0	12	14	86	2	7	29	27	385	14	0	14	280	20	0
Johnny Clement	TB-DB	26	6'	190	6		43	60	1.4	1	47	16	34	345	7.2	1	3– 6		1	22	22	0	9	35.0							3	26	9	0	3	66	22	0
Andy Tomasic	TB-DB	26	6'	175							12	4	33	53	4.4	0	1– 8						1	56.0							1	20	20	0				
Tony Campagno	FB-DB	25	5'11"	200	6	1	67	217	3.2	1									7	77	11	0													1	27	27	0
Bill Dutton	HB-DB	25	5'10"	180	12		53	169	3.2	2	6	4	67	31	5.2	0	0– 0		2	68	34	0									3	36	12	0	1	22	22	0
Merl Condit	HB-DB	29	5'11"	186	10		46	141	3.1	1	4	2	50	89	22.3	1	0– 0		4	33	8	0			4	4	100	0	2	0	3	31	10	0	3	19	6	0
Steve Lach	FB-DB	26	6'2"	200	30	1	42	111	2.6	5	1	0	0	0	0.0	0	0– 0		2	11	6	0																
Ernie Bonelli	HB-DB	26	5'11"	190			6	7	1.2	0									1	26	26	0																
Walt Gorinski	FB-DB	26	6'1"	207			1	3	3.0	0																												
Max Kielbasa	HB-DB	25	6'1"	185			2	−2	−1.0	0																												
Cullen Rogers	HB-DB	25	5'10"	178			6	−8	−1.3	0	1	0	0	0	0.0	0	0– 0																					
Charlie Seabright	BB-LB	28	6'2"	210	6	1													4	77	19	1																
Bill Garnaas	BB-LB	25	5'11"	195	6														3	56	19	1													2	29	15	0
Val Jansante	OE-DE	25	6'1"	188	6		2	5	2.5	0									10	136	14	1																
Charlie Mehelich	OE-DE	24	6'1"	205															10	116	12	0																
Tony Bova	OE-DE	29	6'1"	190															6	171	29	0																
Sam Gray	OE-DE	26	6'	195															1	20	20	0																
Bob Davis	OE-DE	25	5'11"	195	6														1	13	13	0																
BOSTON YANKS																																						
Paul Governali	QB	25	5'11"	195	12		33	−187	−5.7	2	192	83	43	1293	6.7	13	10– 5	5					11	43.7														
Boley Dancewicz	QB-DB	21	5'10"	185		1	14	81	5.8	0	34	13	38	162	4.8	1	5–15																					
Howie Maley	QB-HB-DB	24	5'11"	188			13	67	5.2	0	8	3	38	71	8.9	1	2–25		2	35	18	0	60	39.4							3	12	4	0	1	3	3	0
John Grigas	FB-LB	26	6'	205	18	1	84	426	5.1	2	2	1	50	16	8.0	0	1–50		3	61	20	1	1	45.0											1	8	8	0
Babe Dimancheff	HB-DB	24	5'11"	178	6	1	57	238	4.2	0									5	121	24	1									7	98	14	0	5	96	19	0
Bob Davis	HB-DB	31	6'	190	6	7	41	143	3.5	0	1	1	100	7	7.0	0	0– 0		10	150	15	1									13	130	10	0	5	92	18	0
Jim Gillette	HB-DB	28	6'1"	185	12	1	30	99	3.3	1									5	96	19	1									2	62	31	0	3	43	14	0
Sonny Karnofsky	HB-DB	23	5'10"	175	18		36	84	2.3	1									8	139	17	1									2	38	19	0	21	599	29	1
Mike Micka	HB-DB	25	6'	184	6	2	20	76	3.8	0																												
Gary Famiglietti	FB	31	6'	238	24		23	54	2.3	4	1	1	100	6	6.0	0	0– 0		1	17	17	0						0	1	0								
Lou Abbruzzi	HB-DB	27	5'10"	175			6	26	4.3	0	1	1	100	11	11.0	0	0– 0		2	55	28	0									1	1	1	0	8	127	16	0
Joe Hoague	FB-LB	28	6'2"	210		1	1	2	2.0	0									1	4	4	0																
Rudy Romboli	FB-LB	23	5'10"	215		1	1	−3	−3.0	0																												
Hal Crisler	OE-DE	22	6'4"	215	30		4	6	1.5	0									32	385	12	5													2	22	11	0
Sam Goldman	OE-DE	29	6'3"	228			2	−3	−1.5	0									15	154	10	0													2	41	21	0
Don Currivan	OE-DB	25	6'	195	24														11	262	24	4									1	22	22	0	1	14	14	0
Nick Scollard	OE-DE	26	6'4"	218	33														7	78	11	1			21	24	88	0	1	0					1	12	12	0
Don Eliason	OE-DE	28	6'2"	225															1	9	9	0			0	1												

TEAM TOTALS

	FIRST DOWNS:				RUSHING:				PASSING:									PUNTING:		PUNT RETURNS:				KICKOFF RETURNS:				INTERCEPTION RETURNS:				PENALTIES:		FUMBLES:		POINTS:					TEAM TOTALS
OFFENSE	Tot	by Rsh	by Pas	by Pen	No.	Yds.	Avg Yds.	TD	Att	Com	Comp Pct.	Yds.	Avg. Yds. Att.	Avg. Yds. Comp	TD	Int	Pct. Int.	No.	Avg. Yds.	No.	Yds.	Avg. Yds.	TD	No.	Yds.	Avg. Yds.	TD	No.	Yds.	Avg. Yds.	TD	No.	Yds.	No.	Lost	Tot	PAT	FG Att	FG	Saf.	OFFENSE
N.Y.	161	77	72	12	394	1289	3.3	12	258	128	49.6	1823	7.7	14.3	9	19	7.4	58	38.9	28	250	8.9	0	52	1279	24.6	2	25	246	9.8	1	94	837	42	26	162	21	9	5	0	N.Y
PHIL.	146	72	56	18	418	1123	2.7	19	220	95	43.2	1360	6.2	14.3	11	26	11.8	64	40.2	30	356	11.9	0	40	822	20.5	0	19	380	20.0	1	91	817	36	18	220	26	10	4	1	PHIL.
WASH.	147	71	56	20	407	1103	2.7	16	216	101	46.8	1342	6.2	13.3	10	24	11.1	58	41.0	28	404	14.4	0	32	652	20.4	0	22	459	20.9	4	66	552	29	10	191	24	13	3	1	WASH.
PITT.	147	94	44	9	466	1754	3.8	9	162	64	39.5	939	5.8	14.7	6	14	8.6	68	42.2	32	247	7.7	0	28	684	24.4	0	13	131	10.1	0	75	707	28	17	117	15	10	4	0	PITT.
BOSTON	182	104	69	9	452	1852	4.1	22	227	106	46.7	1642	7.3	15.5	15	17	7.5	52	38.7	49	705	14.4	1	36	670	18.6	0	18	346	19.2	0	84	871	34	14	273	34	14	5	1	BOSTON

CHICAGO BEARS 8-2-1 George Halas

Scores of Each Game		
30	Green Bay	7
34	Chic. Cards	17
28	LOS ANGELES	28
21	PHILADELPHIA	14
0	New York	14
10	GREEN BAY	7
27	Los Angeles	21
24	WASHINGTON	20
42	DETROIT	6
28	CHIC. CARDS	35
45	Detroit	24

Use Name	Pos.	Hgt	Wgt	Age	Int	Pts
Stu Clarkson	C-LB	6'2"	215	27	3	6
John Schiechl	C-LB	6'2"	250	29	3	
Bulldog Turner	C-LB	6'1"	240	27	1	
(1 kickoff return for 2 yds.)						
Walt Lamb	DE-OE	6'1"	195	25		
(1 reception for 10 yds.)						
Bill Geyer	HB-DB	5'10"	180	26		
(1 kickoff return for 14 yds.)						
Hank Margarita	HB-DB	5'11"	185	25		
(4 rushing attempts for 0 yds.)						
injured — Al Matuza						

Use Name – Tackles	Pos.	Hgt	Wgt	Age	Int	Pts
Fred Davis	T	6'3"	245	28		
John Federovich	T	6'5"	262	29		
Mike Jarmoluk	T	6'5"	260	23		
Ed Kolman	T	6'2"	235	28		
Walt Stickel	T	6'3"	245	24		
Joe Stydahar	T	6'4"	250	34		12
(12 PAT 's in 13 attempts, 2 missed FG attempts)						

Use Name – Guards	Pos.	Hgt	Wgt	Age	Int	Pts
Al Baisi	G	6'	215	28		
Ray Bray	G	6'	240	29		
Chuck Drulis	G-LB	5'10"	215	28	1	
Aldo Forte (from DET)	G	6'	215	28		
Pat Preston	G-LB	6'2"	215	23		

With World War II over, Americans wanted to return to a normal life without war bonds, ration stamps, and blackouts. The Chicago Bears did their part to recreate the prewar scene by recapturing the NFL flag with a platoon of old Bears back from the war. George McAfee, Bill Osmanski, and Hugh Gallarneau ran with the ball just as in the good old days, while Ken Kavanaugh and Ray Bray again filled the line. Sid Luckman, Bulldog Turner, and George Wilson had been around right through the war and kept up their good work now that the big boys were back. To round out the squad, newcomers like tough Ed Sprinkle, Fred Davis, and Dante Magnani gave George Halas new troops to deploy. Many key players were aging, but the Bears looked more experienced than old in easily taking the Western Division crown.

LOS ANGELES RAMS 6-4-1 Adam Walsh

Scores of Each Game		
14	PHILADELPHIA	25
21	Green Bay	17
28	Chic. Bears	28
35	DETROIT	14
10	Chic. Cards	34
41	Detroit	20
21	CHIC. BEARS	27
17	CHIC. CARDS	14
21	Boston	40
31	New York	21
38	GREEN BAY	17

Use Name	Pos.	Hgt	Wgt	Age	Int	Pts
Bod deLauer	C-LB	6'1"	218	26		
(Missed 2 FG attempts)						
Roger Harding	C-LB	6'2"	215	23	1	
Fred Naumetz	C-LB	6'1"	220	24	1	
Albie Reisz	DB	5'10"	175	28		

Use Name – Tackles	Pos.	Hgt	Wgt	Age	Int	Pts
Gil Bouley	T	6'2"	235	25		
Jake Fawcett	T	5'11"	220	27	1	
Clyde Johnson	T	6'6"	265	29		
Joe Pasqua	T	6'1"	225	28		
Elbie Schultz	T	6'4"	260	28		

Use Name – Guards	Pos.	Hgt	Wgt	Age	Int	Pts
Roger Eason	G	6'2"	225	28		
Mike Lazetich	G-LB	6'1"	215	25		
Les Lear	G-LB	5'11"	227	28	1	
Len Levy	G	6'	260	25		6
Riley Matheson	G-LB	6'2"	210	31	4	
Art Mergenthal	G-LB	5'11"	215	26		

Less than a month after the Cleveland Rams had won the 1945 championship, owner Dan Reeves picked them up and replanted them in the promised land of Southern California. The other NFL owners had been reluctant to approve the switch, but an average attendance of 38,700 in the face of AAFC competition convinced the doubters that Los Angeles indeed was ready for big-league sports. The team, though, by never winning more than two games in a row, could not capture another title for its new home. Bob Waterfield kept shooting passes to Jim Benton, but the rest of the squad never reached the edge of last year. Three newcomers kept the team interesting if not victorious. Tommy Harmon, the 1940 Heisman Trophy winner, came out of the Army to make a solid debut in the NFL, and two UCLA graduates, Kenny Washington and Woody Strode, won attention as the first blacks in the league since 1933.

GREEN BAY PACKERS 6-5-0 Curly Lambeau

Scores of Each Game		
7	CHIC. BEARS	30
17	LOS ANGELES	21
19	Philadelphia	7
17	PITTSBURGH	7
10	DETROIT	7
7	Chic. Bears	10
19	Chic. Cards	7
9	Detroit	0
6	CHIC. CARDS	24
20	Washington	7
17	Los Angeles	38

Use Name	Pos.	Hgt	Wgt	Age	Int	Pts
Charley Brock	C-LB	6'2"	210	30		
Bob Flowers	C-LB	6'1"	210	29		
Les Gatewood	C-LB	6'2"	195	25		
Tom Miller	DE-OE	6'2"	208	28		
Moose Mulleneaux	DE	6'3"	210	29		
Ray Riddick	DE	6'1"	220	28		
Ken Keuper	BB-DB	6'	205	28	3	
(1 kickoff return for 6 yds.)						
Al Zupek	BB-DE	6'1"	205	23		
Charlie Mitchell	DB	6'	190	25	1	
Russ Mosley	DB	5'10"	170	28	1	

Use Name – Tackles	Pos.	Hgt	Wgt	Age	Int	Pts
Tiny Croft	T	6'3"	275	25		
Bill Lee	T	6'2"	225	34		
Paul Lipscomb	T	6'4"	240	23		
Urban Odson	T	6'3"	255	27		2
Baby Ray	T	6'6'	250	31	1	

Use Name – Guards	Pos.	Hgt	Wgt	Age	Int	Pts
Solon Barnett	G	6'1"	235	25		
Earl Bennett	G-LB	5'8"	188	26		
Bill Kuusisto	G	6'	225	28		
Russ Letlow	G	6'	218	32		
Ed Neal	G-T	6'4"	290	28		
Merv Pregulman	G-LB	6'3"	215	24		
Al Sparlis	G-LB	5'11"	185	26		
Charlie Tollefson	G	6'	215	29		
Dick Wildung	G	6'	220	24		

Green Bay lost a hero and Curly Lambeau an ace when Don Hutson finally made his retirement stick. The Packers long had counted on the wiry end to put points on the scoreboard, and not until the coming of Vince Lombardi would the team adjust to his loss. To make matters worse, the new AAFC was driving player salaries up to the sky, making it hard for the non-profit Packers to sign new talent.

Coach Lambeau relied on a strong running game to make up for the diminished air attack. Ex-GI Tony Canadeo, veteran Ted Fritsch, and rookie Walt Schlinkman handled the bulk of the ball-carrying with little help from passer Irv Comp and his undistinguished receivers. Quick losses to the Bears and Rams uncovered chinks in the Packer defense, and a strong mid-season spurt petered out into two losses in the last three games.

CHICAGO CARDINALS 6-5-0 Jimmy Conzelman

Scores of Each Game		
7	Pittsburgh	14
34	DETROIT	14
17	CHIC. BEARS	34
36	Detroit	14
24	New York	28
34	LOS ANGELES	10
28	Boston	14
7	GREEN BAY	19
14	Los Angeles	17
24	Green Bay	6
35	Chic. Bears	28

Use Name	Pos.	Hgt	Wgt	Age	Int	Pts
Vince Banonis	C-LB	6'1"	230	24	2	
Bill Campbell	C-LB	6'	195	26		
(1 kickoff return for 17 yds.)						
Dick Plasman	DE	6'3"	230	32		
Al Drulis	FB-LB	5'10"	195	25		
(1 rush for 0 yds.)						

Use Name – Tackles	Pos.	Hgt	Wgt	Age	Int	Pts
Chet Bulger	T	6'3"	238	28		
Ralph Foster	T	6'1"	230	29		
Tom Kearns	T	6'4"	248	26		
Stan Mauldin	T	6'2"	224	26		
(1 kickoff return for 16 yds.)						
Walt Szot	T	6'1"	215	27		
Bob Zimny	T	6'1"	230	25		

Use Name – Guards	Pos.	Hgt	Wgt	Age	Int	Pts
Ray Apolskis	G-LB	5'11"	215	27	1	
Lloyd Arms	G	6'1"	215	27		
Jake Colhouer	G	6'1"	210	24		
Bill Conoly	G	6'	227	26		
Bob Maddock	G-LB	6'	200	26		
Buster Ramsey	G-LB	6'1"	210	26	1	
(1 rush for 5 yds.)						

Owner Charles Bidwill opened his wallet wide, shelling out enough money to buy a championship nucleus for the Cardinals. He started the renovation by luring Jimmy Conzelman back as coach and giving him a marvelous rookie crop to work with. Bruising fullback Pat Harder lived up to expectations as a first draft choice, while Elmer Angsman starred at halfback despite a lack of press clippings. Speedster Mal Kutner gave the team a deep pass threat, and linemen Buster Ramsey and Stan Mauldin plugged holes in the line with hard-hitting bulk. Veterans Paul Christman, Marshall Goldberg, and Bill Dewell blended in with the newcomers to turn the Cardinals into a winning team with a bright future. The final game of the year with the Bears ended the season on an up note. With the score tied 28-28 and time for one more play, Paul Christman ignored Conzelman's signals for a field goal and threw a 5-yard touchdown pass to Mal Kutner for the victory.

DETROIT LIONS 1-10-0 Gus Dorais

Scores of Each Game		
14	Chic. Cards	34
16	Washington	17
14	CHIC. CARDS	36
14	Los Angeles	35
7	Green Bay	10
20	LOS ANGELES	41
17	PITTSBURGH	7
0	GREEN BAY	9
6	Chic. Bears	42
10	BOSTON	34
24	CHIC. BEARS	45

Use Name	Pos.	Hgt	Wgt	Age	Int	Pts
Elmer Hackney	LB	6'2"	200	30		
Walt Jurkiewicz	C-LB	6'1"	220	27		
Frank Szymanski	C-LB	6'	215	23		
Vince Mazza	OE-DE	6'1"	210	25		
Bill Kennedy — military service						

Use Name – Tackles	Pos.	Hgt	Wgt	Age	Int	Pts
Leon Fichman	T	6'1"	215	25		
Jim Montgomery	T	6'4"	235	24		
Russ Thomas	T	6'3"	230	22	1	
Emil Uremovich	T	6'2"	240	29		
Lloyd Wickett	T	6'1"	210	26		

Use Name – Guards	Pos.	Hgt	Wgt	Age	Int	Pts
Stan Batinski	G	5'10"	215	29		
Tony Rubino	G	5'10"	210	25		
Damon Tassos	G	6'1"	225	22	1	3
(3 PAT's in 3 attempts, missed 1 FG attempt)						
Walt Vezmar	G	5'11"	235	21		

The Lions lost tailback Frankie Sinkwich to the military after the 1944 season, and when he got his discharge from the service he signed with the New York Yankees of the new AAFC instead of with Detroit. That defection killed the Lions' passing game, and a rash of pre-season injuries to backs and linemen wiped out the running game. With the offense thus crippled, coach Gus Dorais watched his team drop six games before it beat the Steelers 17-7. Any hopes the victory may have raised were dashed to bits when the Lions ran out the season with four more losses.

This year's collapse underlined the deterioration of last year's team. Tailback Chuck Fenenbock jumped to the AAFC, runner Andy Farkas retired, and center Alex Wojciechowicz was traded to Philadelphia early in the campaign, and those players who stayed behind in Detroit never reached the heights of last year's second-place finish.

TEAM TOTALS

	FIRST DOWNS:				RUSHING:				PASSING:									PUNTING:		PUNT RETURNS:				KICKOFF RETURNS:				INTERCEPTION RETURNS:				PENALTIES:		FUMBLES:		POINTS:					TEAM TOTALS
OFFENSE	Tot	by Rsh	by Pas	by Pen	No.	Yds.	Avg Yds.	TD	Att	Com	Comp Pct.	Yds.	Avg. Yds. Att.	Avg. Yds. Comp	TD	Int	Pct. Int.	No.	Avg. Yds.	No.	Yds.	Avg. Yds.	TD	No.	Yds.	Avg. Yds.	TD	No.	Yds.	Avg. Yds.	TD	No.	Yds.	No.	Lost	Tot	PAT	FG Att	FG	Saf.	OFFENSE
CHIC. B.	211	112	82	17	506	1762	3.5	19	253	120	47.4	1950	7.7	16.2	18	19	7.5	58	38.1	29	336	11.6	0	37	800	21.6	0	27	465	17.2	1	104	940	35	16	289	37	11	4	0	CHIC. B.
L.A.	214	102	91	21	404	1683	4.2	15	326	153	46.9	2080	6.4	13.6	19	24	7.4	45	44.4	26	295	11.3	0	43	934	21.7	1	23	376	16.3	1	80	764	31	20	277	37	11	6	0	L.A.
G.B.	160	112	34	14	561	1765	3.1	12	178	54	30.3	841	4.7	15.5	4	18	10.1	65	42.8	28	284	10.2	0	34	739	21.7	0	24	399	16.6	0	82	693	24	11	148	15	17	9	2	G.B.
CHIC. C.	175	77	84	14	371	1529	4.1	16	266	115	43.2	1951	7.3	16.9	17	20	7.5	50	39.6	23	255	11.1	0	40	825	20.6	1	24	262	10.9	0	84	761	44	29	260	33	12	5	1	CHIC. C.
DET.	120	49	59	12	274	470	1.7	7	287	119	41.5	1674	5.8	14.6	11	33	11.5	67	43.4	28	332	11.9	0	59	1127	19.1	0	13	230	17.7	0	82	635	26	12	142	17	6	3	2	DET.

Use Name – Backs & Ends	Pos.	Age	Hgt	Wgt	Pts	Int	RUSHING No.	Yds	Avg	TD	PASSING Att	Comp	%	Yds	Yd/Att	TD	Int–%	RK	RECEIVING No.	Yds	Avg	TD	PUNTING No.	Avg	KICKING Pat	Att	%	FG	Att	%	PUNT RETURNS No.	Yds	Avg	TD	KICKOFF RETURNS No.	Yds	Avg	TD
CHICAGO BEARS																																						
Sid Luckman	QB-DB	29	6'	195		1	25	-76	-3.0	0	229	110	48	**1826**	**8.0**	17	16–7	1					33	37.4														
Tom Farris	QB-DB	25	6'1"	185		4	22	17	0.8	0	21	8	38	108	5.1	1	3–14		1	16	16	0									2	4	2	0	1	27	27	0
Hugh Gallarneau	HB-DB	29	6'	190	48		112	476	4.3	6									12	185	15	1									10	99	10	0	5	115	23	0
Bill Osmanski	FB-LB	29	5'11"	200	30	1	78	343	4.4	5									4	40	10	0									1	10	10	0	8	203	25	0
Dante Magnani	HB-DB	29	5'10"	180	6	1	68	277	4.1	0									14	156	11	1													3	50	17	0
Joe Osmanski	FB-LB	27	6'2"	220	12		55	201	3.7	2									2	14	7	0													3	54	18	0
Noah Mullins	HB-DB	27	5'11"	185		3	20	117	5.9	0	1	1	100	16	16.0	0	0–0														4	50	13	0	1	22	22	0
Don Perkins	FB-LB	28	6'	200			34	105	3.1	0									2	41	21	0									1	14	14	0	1	25	25	0
Dick Schweidler	HB-DB	31	6'	175	18	1	20	94	4.7	3									1	11	11	0									1	13	13	0	3	63	21	0
Lloyd Reese	FB-LB	24	6'2"	240	12		18	84	4.7	2																												
George McAfee	HB-DB	28	6'	180	18	3	14	53	3.8	0	2	1	50	0	0.0	0	0–0		10	137	14	3									1	24	24	0	3	96	32	0
Frank Maznicki	HB-DB	26	5'9"	185	37	2	19	43	2.3	0									2	38	19	0			25	26	96	4	9	44	1	12	12	0	2	65	33	0
Ray McLean	HB-DB	30	5'10"	170	18	2	16	29	1.8	1									17	348	20	2									7	86	12	0	3	53	18	0
Ken Kavanaugh	OE-DE	29	6'3"	210	30														18	337	19	5																
Jim Keane	OE-DE	22	6'4"	220	18														14	331	24	3	2	39.5							1	23	23	0				
George Wilson	OE-DE	32	6'1"	210	6														11	104	9	1																
Ed Sprinkle	OE-DE	22	6'1"	205	18	1													7	124	18	2													2	11	6	0
Connie Mack Berry	OE-DE	30	6'3"	220															4	58	15	0																
Rudy Mucha	G	28	6'1"	235			1	-1	-1.0	0													23	39.0														
LOS ANGELES RAMS																																						
Bob Waterfield	QB-DB	26	6'1"	190	61	5	16	-60	-3.7	1	**251**	**127**	51	1747	7.0	**18**	17–7	2					39	44.6	**37**	**37**	**100**	6	9	**67**	1	12	12	0				
Jim Hardy	QB-DB	24	6'	185		1	10	-10	-1.0	0	64	24	38	285	4.5	1	7–11	13					5	41.8														
Fred Gehrke	HB-DB	28	5'11"	190	30	3	71	371	5.2	3	1	1	100	29	29.0	0	0–0		11	83	8	2									8	59	7	0	8	186	23	0
Tommy Harmon	HB-DB	26	6'1"	197	30	3	47	236	5.0	2									10	199	20	2									5	57	11	0	6	134	22	0
Pat West	FB-LB	23	6'	200	6		40	226	5.7	1																									4	49	12	0
Mike Holovak	FB-LB	26	6'1"	220	18		55	211	3.8	3									2	6	3	0													1	18	18	0
Jack Banta	HB-DB	28	5'11"	192	6	2	44	209	4.7	0									8	81	10	1	1	44.0							2	26	13	0	8	142	18	0
Bob Hoffman	FB-LB	28	6'1"	210	18		42	162	3.9	3																												
Jack Wilson	HB-DB	28	6'	200	6	1	19	120	6.3	0									3	30	10	1									5	99	20	0	6	145	24	0
Kenny Washington	HB-DB	28	6'1"	200	6		23	114	5.0	1	8	1	13	19	2.4	0	0–0		6	83	14	0													2	39	20	0
Tom Farmer	HB-DB	25	5'11"	195	6		28	90	3.2	1	2	0	0	0	0.0	0	0–0		6	17	3	0									4	40	10	0	4	129	32	0
Steve Sucic	FB-LB	25	6'	200			7	18	2.6	0									1	1	1	0													1	20	20	0
Ralph Ruthstrom	FB-LB	25	6'5"	208			2	-4	-2.0	0									1	9	9	0									1	2	2	0				
Jim Benton	OE-DE	29	6'3"	206	36														**63**	**981**	16	6																
Steve Pritko	OE-DE	24	6'2"	210	12														18	185	10	2																
Red Hickey	OE-DE	29	6'2"	203	18														8	213	27	3													1	14	14	0
Ray Hamilton	OE-DE	30	6'4"	210															8	92	11	0																
Bob Shaw	OE-DE	25	6'4"	225	18														4	63	16	2													1	52	52	1
Woody Strode	OE-DE	31	6'3"	205															4	37	9	0													1	6	6	0
GREEN BAY PACKERS																																						
Irv Comp	TB-DB	27	6'2"	205	6	2	61	62	1.0	1	94	27	29	333	3.5	1	8–9	12																	1	29	29	0
Cliff Aberson	TB-DB	24	6'	195		3	48	161	3.4	0	41	14	34	184	4.5	0	5–12																		3	69	23	0
Tony Canadeo	TB-HB-DB	27	5'11"	190		1	122	476	3.9	0	27	7	26	189	7.0	1	3–11		2	25	13	0									6	76	13	0	6	163	27	0
Bruce Smith	TB-DB	26	6'	197			22	119	5.4	0																					2	12	6	0	1	20	20	0
Ted Fritsch	FB-LB	25	5'10"	210	**100**	1	128	444	3.4	**9**									2	13	7	1	1	52.0	13	15	87	**9**	17	53					3	68	23	0
Walt Schlinkman	FB	24	5'8"	190	12		97	379	3.9	2									1	5	5	0													2	43	22	0
Tex McKay	FB-DB	26	6'	193	8	1	21	34	1.6	1													**64**	42.7	2	2	100								2	41	21	0
Bob Nussbaumer	HB-DB	22	5'11"	175		3	29	43	1.5	0	1	1	100	10	10.0	0	0–0		10	143	14	0									12	98	8	0	6	148	25	0
Bob Forte	HB-DB	24	6'	195		2	17	73	4.3	0	7	3	43	28	4.0	1	1–14		2	5	3	0																
Herm Rohrig	HB-TB-DB	28	5'8"	190		5	15	-23	-1.6	0	8	2	25	97	12.1	1	1–12		2	30	15	0									8	98	12	0	5	106	21	0
Larry Craig	BB-DE	30	6'1"	218			1	-3	-3.0	0																									2	18	9	0
Clyde Goodnight	OE-DB	22	6'1"	195	6														16	308	19	1																
Nolan Luhn	OE-DE	25	6'3"	200	14														16	224	14	2													2	28	14	0
Don Wells	OE-DE	24	6'2"	200															2	74	37	0																
Hal Prescott	OE-DB	25	6'2"	210															1	8	8	0																
CHICAGO CARDINALS																																						
Paul Christman	QB	28	6'	210	18		28	-61	-2.2	3	229	100	44	1656	7.2	13	18–8	4																				
Ray Mallouf	QB-DB	28	5'11"	180		1	4	6	1.5	0	34	14	41	260	7.6	4	2–6						15	34.5														
Pat Harder	FB-LB	24	5'11"	205	35		106	545	5.1	4									11	128	12	1			5	5	100				1	10	10	0	5	92	18	0
Elmer Angsman	HB	20	5'11"	190	12		48	328	**6.8**	2	1	0	0	0	0.0	0	0–0		2	44	22	0													1	13	13	0
Marshall Goldberg	HB-DB	28	5'11"	192	24	4	43	210	4.9	3									17	152	9	1									1	11	11	0	5	108	22	0
Frank Seno	HB-DB	25	6'	185	12	4	62	191	3.1	0	1	0	0	0	0.0	0	0–0		12	124	10	1									17	176	10	0	13	408	**31**	**1**
Jim Strausbaugh	HB-DB	28	5'9"	180	18		37	183	4.9	3	1	1	100	35	35.0	0	0–0		5	56	11	0									2	34	17	0	6	104	17	0
Ward Cuff	HB-DB	33	6'1"	192	55		13	78	6.0	1									5	82	16	1			28	30	93	5	12	42	2	24	12	0				
Jimmy Johnston	HB-DB	29	6'1"	195		1	6	18	3.0	0																									2	22	11	0
Bill Montgomery	FB-LB	23	6'	205			8	11	1.4	0																												
George Sutch	HB-DB						5	4	0.8	0																									1	4	4	0
Walt Rankin	FB-LB	28	5'11"	197		2	5	1	0.2	0																									1	11	11	0
Paul Sarringhaus	HB-DB	25	6'	185			2	1	0.5	0																												
Bill Dewell	OE-DE	29	6'4"	210	42														27	643	**24**	7																
Mal Kutner	OE-DB	25	6'2"	197	30	4	1	-1	-1.0	0									27	634	23	5													3	30	10	0
Pop Ivy	OE-DE	30	6'3"	210	6	1													4	39	10	1																
Eddie Rucinski	OE-DB	30	6'2"	195															2	23	12	0																
Joe Parker	OE-DE	23	6'1"	220															2	17	9	0													1	0	0	0
Al Hust	OE-DE	25	6'1"	220															1	9	9	0																
Bill Blackburn	C-LB	24	6'6"	225	8	3	1	10	10.0	0													35	41.9														
DETROIT LIONS																																						
Dave Ryan	TB-DB	23	5'10"	190	12	4	71	65	0.9	1	**154**	73	47	965	6.3	6	17–11	9	1	-5	-5	0									7	57	8	0	15	308	21	0
Jim Callahan	TB-DB	25	5'11"	185	12	2	52	86	1.7	2	68	22	32	359	5.3	2	7–10	11					4	45.5							6	71	12	0	6	133	22	0
Bill deCorrevont	TB-WB-DB	27	6'	185	12		8	-32	-4.0	0	19	8	42	155	8.2	2	2–11		10	278	28	2	5	58.6							6	81	14	0	10	183	18	0
Joel McCoy	TB-DB	26	5'10"	170			19	-29	-1.5	0	18	6	33	72	4.0	0	4–22														1	8	8	0	1	7	7	0
Tippy Madarik	TB-WB-DB	24	5'11"	200		3	8	7	0.9	0	14	7	50	104	7.4	1	0–0		6	38	6	0									5	71	14	0	5	131	26	0
Jim Jones	TB		6'	180			3	3	1.0	0	4	0	0	0	0.0	0	1–25						1	-9.0														
Camp Wilson	FB-LB	24	6'2"	200	18		64	207	3.2	3									7	62	9	0	22	34.9											7	127	18	0
Bob Westfall	FB-LB	27	5'8"	190	6		28	54	1.9	1	2	1	50	-5	-5.0	0	1–50		17	142	8	0													4	58	15	0
Mickey Sanzotta	WB-DB	25	5'9"	190			6	72	12.0	0	1	0	0	0	0.0	0	0–0		2	19	10	0									2	41	21	0	2	40	20	0
Gene Spangler	WB-DB	23	5'10"	195			1	1	1.0	0									2	1	1	0													2	30	15	0
Bob Cifers	BB-DB	25	5'11"	200	24		8	18	2.3	0	6	2	33	24	4.0	0	1–17		4	178	45	5	30	**45.6**							1	3	3	0				
Ivan Schottel	BB-DB	25	6'2"	200	6		4	12	3.0	0									4	146	36	1	5	41.6											1	20	20	0
Chuck DeShane	BB-LB	27	6'1"	218	10	1	2	3	1.5	0	1	0	0	0	0.0	0	0–0		2	13	7	0			10	10	100	0	1	0								
John Greene	OE-DE	26	6'	210	14														20	289	14	2													2	29	15	0
Jack Matheson	OE-DE	26	6'2"	235		1													17	178	10	0													1	17	17	0
Ted Cremer	OE-DE	27	6'2"	205															15	179	12	0																
Ed Frutig	OE-DE	26	6'1"	200	12														8	72	9	2																
Ralph Jones	OE-DE	25	6'3"	200															4	84	21	0													3	44	15	0
Jack Helms	DE	25	6'4"	215	13																				4	6	67	3	4	75								

TEAM TOTALS

DEFENSE	FIRST DOWNS: Tot	by Rsh	by Pas	by Pen	RUSHING: No.	Yds.	Avg. Yds.	TD	PASSING: Att.	Com	Comp. Pct.	Yds.	Avg. Yds. Att.	Avg. Yds. Comp	TD	Int.	Pct. Int.	PUNTING: No.	Avg. Yds.	PUNT RETURNS: No.	Yds.	Avg. Yds.	TD	KICKOFF RETURNS: No.	Yds.	Avg. Yds.	TD	INTERCEPTION RETURNS: No.	Yds.	Avg. Yds.	TD	PENALTIES: No.	Yds.	FUMBLES: No.	Lost	POINTS: Tot	PAT	FG Att	FG	Saf.	DEFENSE
CHIC. B.	138	57	68	12	**334**	**1044**	3.1	12	257	108	42.0	1610	6.3	14.9	14	27	10.5	59	44.6	**24**	256	10.6	**0**	50	799	**16.0**	**0**	19	300	15.8	0	76	716	38	22	193	25	11	4	**0**	CHIC. B.
L.A.	170	76	75	19	402	1325	3.3	14	265	112	42.3	2154	8.1	19.2	21	23	8.7	51	40.2	27	350	13.0	**0**	52	1301	25.0	1	24	386	16.1	0	89	702	35	15	257	30	11	5	1	L.A.
G.B.	158	84	59	15	367	1372	3.7	15	214	94	43.9	1288	6.0	13.7	**6**	24	11.2	60	41.8	35	414	11.8	**0**	**28**	683	24.4	**0**	18	275	15.3	1	76	628	**45**	**28**	158	20	7	4	**0**	G.B.
CHIC. C.	176	95	66	15	438	1249	2.9	12	273	118	43.2	1603	5.9	14.9	14	25	9.2	57	41.3	29	399	13.8	**0**	46	748	16.3	**0**	20	355	17.8	0	80	673	39	20	198	25	10	5	1	CHIC. C.
DET.	203	104	78	21	481	1698	3.5	21	249	123	49.4	1975	7.9	16.0	20	13	5.2	52	40.3	33	334	10.1	**0**	**28**	**601**	21.5	**0**	33	430	13.0	0	**100**	**912**	31	16	310	38	15	8	1	DET.

NEW YORK YANKEES 10-3-1 Ray Flaherty

Scores of Each Game		
21	San Francisco	7
21	BUFFALO	10
17	Chicago	17
7	Cleveland	24
21	Buffalo	13
0	CLEVELAND	7
21	BROOKLYN	10
31	Los Angeles	17
24	MIAMI	21
17	LOS ANGELES	12
10	SAN FRANCISCO	9
28	CHICAGO	38
21	Brooklyn	7
31	Miami	0

Use Name	Pos.	Hgt	Wgt	Age	Int	Pts
Jack Baldwin	C-LB	6'3"	225	25		
Tom Robertson	C-LB	6'	225	29		
Lou Sossamon	C-LB	6'1"	207	25		
Ray Hare	BB-LB	6'1"	205	28		

Use Name – Tackles	Pos.	Hgt	Wgt	Age	Int	Pts
George Bentz	T	6'2"	230	27		
Nate Johnson	T	6'3"	240	26		
Bruiser Kinard	T	6'1"	218	31		
Harley McCollum	T	6'4"	245	28		
Darrell Palmer	T	6'2"	245	24		
Roman Piskor	T	6'	245	28		

Use Name – Guards	Pos.	Hgt	Wgt	Age	Int	Pts
Mike Karmazin	G	5'11"	210	27		
George Kinard	G	6'1"	205	29		
Charley Riffle	G	6'	212	28		
Joe Yackanich	G	5'10"	205	24		

His Brooklyn team had not done well in the NFL, so owner Dan Topping jumped the club into the AAFC as the Yankees. After a year in mothballs, the team took back its players from the Boston franchise and set up shop in Yankee Stadium. With ex-Redskin coach Ray Flaherty at the helm, the Yankees won the Eastern title with a mixed squad of NFL veterans and freshmen pros. Tailback Ace Parker, a step slower than in his prewar days, directed the single-wing attack, and old Dodgers Bruiser Kinard, Pug Manders, Perry Schwartz, and Bob Masterson rejoined Parker in the lineup. The brightest star, however, was rookie Spec Sanders, a standout runner, passer, receiver, and defensive back. Of the three games the Yankees lost, two came at the hands of the powerful Cleveland Browns.

BROOKLYN DODGERS 3-10-1 Mal Stevens, Cliff Battles

Scores of Each Game		
27	Buffalo	14
14	Los Angeles	20
13	San Francisco	32
7	Cleveland	26
21	CHICAGO	21
10	New York	21
30	MIAMI	7
21	Chicago	14
14	BUFFALO	17
14	LOS ANGELES	19
14	SAN FRANCISCO	30
7	NEW YORK	21
14	CLEVELAND	66
20	Miami	31

Use Name	Pos.	Hgt	Wgt	Age	Int	Pts
Joe Gibson	C-LB-DE	6'3"	215	27		
Russ Morrow	C-LB-OE	6'7"	200	22		12
(1 reception for 8 yds. and TD, 22 yds. on rushing lateral)						
Caleb Warrington	C-LB	6'2"	210	25		
Bolo Perdue	DE	5'10"	205	29		

Use Name – Tackles	Pos.	Hgt	Wgt	Age	Int	Pts
Nick Daukas	T	6'4"	225	23	1	
(2 receptions for 19 yds.)						
Frank Hrabetin (to MIA)	T	6'4"	230	30		
(1 reception for 17 yds.)						
Herb Maack	T	6'2"	210	29		
Ed Mieszkowski	T	6'2"	220	21		
George Perpich	T	6'2"	230	26		
(1 punt return for 16 yds.)						
Martin Ruby	T	6'3"	250	26		
(1 reception for 3 yds.)						
George Sergienko	T	6'1"	250	28		

Use Name – Guards	Pos.	Hgt	Wgt	Age	Int	Pts
George Bernhardt	G	5'10"	210	27		
(1 kickoff return for 13 yds.)						
John Billman	G	6'1"	202	26		
Harry Buffington	G	6'	210	27		
Jack Freeman	G	6'	198	24		
Vic Obeck	G	6'	225	28		
(1 punt return for 3 yds.)						

Brooklyn fans supported the baseball Dodgers in royal style but treated the football team like an unwanted stepchild as the attendance averaged under 20,000 per game. This edition of the Dodgers gave fans little reason to turn out, winning only three games all year and ending the season with a six-game losing streak. The entire offense rested on the shoulders of rookie tailback Glen Dobbs, a great passer who won the league MVP Award. Receivers Saxon Judd and Joe Davis kept the offense alive with their catches, but the runners made no headway at all. Even with All-Pro tackle Martin Ruby, the line sprang many leaks. The losing, both of games and money, cost coach Mal Stevens his job after seven games, but replacements Cliff Battles and Tom Scott offered no magic potions for victory.

BUFFALO BISONS 3-10-1 Red Dawson

Scores of Each Game		
14	BROOKLYN	27
10	New York	21
0	CLEVELAND	28
35	Chicago	38
21	LOS ANGELES	21
13	NEW YORK	21
14	MIAMI	17
17	SAN FRANCISCO	14
49	CHICAGO	17
14	San Francisco	27
17	Brooklyn	14
14	Miami	21
17	Cleveland	42
14	Los Angeles	62

Use Name	Pos.	Hgt	Wgt	Age	Int	Pts
Sam Brazinsky	C-LB	6'1"	215	24	2	
Jim Martinelli	C-LB	6'	227	26	1	
Felto Prewitt	C-LB	5'11"	210	22	4	
Bill Daddio	DE	5'11"	215	30		3
(3 PAT's in 3 attempts)						
Ralph Schilling	DE-OE	6'3"	218	25		
(from WAS-NFL)						
John Fekete	HB-DB	5'11"	200	25		
(1 rush for –1 yd.)						

Use Name – Tackles	Pos.	Hgt	Wgt	Age	Int	Pts
Jack Dugger	T-DE-OE	6'3"	225	23		6
(1 reception for 15 yds.)						
Chubby Grigg	T	6'2"	330	20		
Jack Kramer	T	6'	220	23		
John Matisi	T	6'2"	220	25		
Ben Pucci	T	6'4"	260	21		
C.B. Stanley	T	6'4"	225	27		

Use Name – Guards	Pos.	Hgt	Wgt	Age	Int	Pts
George Doherty (from NY)	G	6'1"	218	25		
(1 kickoff return for 0 yds.)						
Elmer Jones	G-LB	6'	233	26	2	
Al Klug	G	6'1"	220	25		
Hal Lahar	G	6'	225	27		
Jim Lecture	G	5'10"	220	22		
John Perko	G	6'1"	225	27		
Rocco Pirro	G	6'	235	29		
Roy Stuart	G-LB	5'8"	195	26		
Gene White	G	6'	205	27		

Buffalo had tried pro football several times before and now took another shot at it in the AAFC. In the early 1920s the Buffalo All-Americans had been a powerful contender for the championship of professional football. As late as 1929 Buffalo had held a franchise in the NFL, and in 1940-41 she had been part of the outlaw American Football League. Undaunted by the litter of these past failures, Sam Cordovano purchased a franchise.

Under the direction of coach Red Dawson, the Bisons had a lot of problems keeping other teams out of the end zone. They lost games 38-35 to Chicago, 42-17 to Cleveland, and 62-14 to Los Angeles. Yet, with a pair of tough runners in Vic Kulbitski and Steve Juzwik, the Bisons also broke out with a flurry of points, as the Chicago Rockets learned in a 49-17 Buffalo blitzkrieg.

MIAMI SEAHAWKS 3-11-0 Jack Meagher, Hamp Pool (retired as player when named head coach)

Scores of Each Game		
0	Cleveland	44
14	San Francisco	21
14	Los Angeles	30
7	SAN FRANCISCO	34
17	Buffalo	14
7	Chicago	28
7	Brooklyn	30
21	New York	24
7	CHICAGO	20
21	BUFFALO	14
21	LOS ANGELES	34
0	CLEVELAND	34
0	NEW YORK	31
31	BROOKLYN	20

Use Name	Pos.	Hgt	Wgt	Age	Int	Pts
Daryl Cato	C-LB	6'2"	195	26	1	
(3 yds. rushing on lateral)						
John Tavener	C-LB	6'	225	25		
Ken Whitlow	C-LB	6'1"	190	28	2	
Tex Williams	C-LB	6'	195	27	1	
Al Wukits (from BUF)	C-LB-G	6'3"	218	26	2	
Stan Stasica	HB-DB	5'10"	175	25		

Use Name – Tackles	Pos.	Hgt	Wgt	Age	Int	Pts
Paul Berezney	T	6'2"	225	29		
Bill Davis	T	6'1"	230	29		
Gene Ellenson	T	6'1"	210	25		
George Hekkers	T	6'4"	225	23		
Mitch Olenski	T	6'3"	218	26		
(1 kickoff return for 2 yds.)						

Use Name – Guards	Pos.	Hgt	Wgt	Age	Int	Pts
Ed Bell	G	6'1"	210	24		
Hal Jungmichel	G	5'9"	200	26	1	
Joe Krivonak	G	6'2"	230	28		
Jim Sivell	G	5'9"	200	32		
Charlie Taylor	G	5'11"	205	26		
George Zorich	G	6'2"	215	27		
(1 punt return for 18 yds.)						

Miami may have been a booming city, but it hardly was ready to support a pro-football team. Playing before tiny home crowds, the Seahawks gave their fans little reason to come back a second time, as they lost eleven games, most of them by lopsided scores. A collection of marginal NFL veterans and undistinguished rookies filled the Miami roster but left the victory column of the standings close to empty. The year began with a 44-0 trouncing in Cleveland, and only wins over Brooklyn and Buffalo (twice) broke the monotony.

As unimpressive as they were on the field, the Seahawks were the financial albatross around the AAFC's neck. The Miami owners quickly sank into a sea of red ink, and only contributions from other clubs kept the Seahawks from drowning in mid-season. But the scant attendance finally sent the Seahawks to Davey Jones's locker after one season.

TEAM TOTALS

	FIRST DOWNS:				RUSHING:				PASSING:									PUNTING:		PUNT RETURNS:				KICKOFF RETURNS:				INTERCEPTION RETURNS:				PENALTIES:		FUMBLES:		POINTS:					
OFFENSE	Tot	by Rsh	by Pas	by Pen	No.	Yds.	Avg Yds.	TD	Att	Com	Comp Pct.	Yds.	Avg. Yds. Att.	Avg. Yds. Comp	TD	Int	Pct. Int.	No.	Avg. Yds.	No.	Yds.	Avg. Yds.	TD	No.	Yds.	Avg. Yds.	TD	No.	Yds.	Avg. Yds.	TD	No.	Yds.	No.	Lost	Tot	PAT	FG Att	FG	Saf.	OFFENSE
N.Y.	158	98	54	6	512	1880	3.7	17	274	129	47.1	1645	6.0	12.8	13	21	7.7	79	36.0	51	778	15.3	3	44	1050	23.9	1	16	266	16.6	1	65	558	63	24	270	36	9	6	0	N.Y.
BKN.	135	54	70	11	374	1017	2.7	9	327	162	49.5	2258	6.9	13.9	17	23	7.0	90	46.5	30	389	13.0	1	55	1005	18.3	0	12	209	17.4	0	56	453	43	17	226	27	11	5	2	BKN.
BUFF.	147	85	45	17	501	2046	4.1	13	238	96	40.3	1367	5.7	14.2	16	23	9.7	88	35.6	37	534	14.4	0	59	1265	21.4	0	22	297	13.5	1	46	296	55	35	249	33	8	4	0	BUFF.
MIAMI	121	50	59	12	408	848	2.1	13	295	131	44.4	1725	5.9	13.2	10	33	11.2	80	40.6	27	301	11.1	0	61	1344	22.0	0	24	279	11.6	0	56	402	47	23	167	23	7	2	0	MIAMI
DEFENSE																																									DEFENSE
N.Y.	119	61	47	11	449	1055	2.3	9	252	123	48.4	1564	6.2	12.7	13	16	6.3	88	42.3	40	432	10.8	0	47	968	20.6	0	21	392	18.7	1	51	449	39	18	192	22	16	8	1	N.Y.
BKN.	192	114	69	9	575	2458	4.3	24	255	132	51.9	2077	8.2	15.7	19	12	4.7	73	40.6	44	619	14.1	1	46	1182	25.7	1	23	354	15.4	1	53	395	56	26	339	42	16	5	3	BKN.
BUFF.	170	94	68	8	497	2075	4.2	21	295	146	49.5	2370	8.0	16.2	23	22	7.5	67	41.5	47	810	17.2	2	42	1046	24.9	1	23	208	9.0	1	73	588	42	29	370	49	9	3	0	BUFF.
MIAMI	155	93	53	9	528	2248	4.3	24	252	123	48.4	1876	7.4	15.3	19	24	9.5	51	42.0	44	595	13.5	1	37	685	18.5	0	33	559	16.9	3	68	625	47	20	378	45	16	13	0	MIAMI

							RUSHING				PASSING								RECEIVING				PUNTING		KICKING						PUNT RETURNS				KICKOFF RETURNS			
Use Name – Backs & Ends	Pos.	Age	Hgt	Wgt	Pts	Int	No.	Yds	Avg	TD	Att	Comp	%	Yds	Yd/Att	TD	Int–%	RK	No.	Yds	Avg	TD	No.	Avg	Pat	Att	%	FG	Att	%	No.	Yds	Avg	TD	No.	Yds	Avg	TD
NEW YORK YANKEES																																						
Ace Parker	TB-DB	34	6'	180	24		75	184	2.5	3	115	62	54	763	6.6	8	3– 3	3					27	33.7							8	85	11	0	2	27	14	0
Spec Sanders	TB-WB-DB	27	6'1"	196	72	2	140	709	5.1	6	79	33	42	411	5.2	4	9–11		17	259	15	3	33	36.6							17	257	15	1	13	395	30	1
Bob Perina	TB-DB	25	6'1"	205	6	2	45	135	3.0	1	48	21	44	279	5.8	1	4– 8						11	37.5							15	205	14	0	4	81	20	0
Frankie Sinkwich	TB-DB	25	5'11"	190			7	20	2.9	0	12	5	42	61	5.1	0	2–17																					
Eddie Prokop	FB-DB	24	5'11"	200	18	1	65	236	3.6	1	11	4	36	72	6.5	0	0– 0		5	52	10	1									4	116	29	1	2	47	24	0
Bob Kennedy	FB-DB	25	5'11"	195	12	3	58	179	3.1	2	6	2	33	45	7.5	0	3–50		11	59	5	0	7	37.0							3	20	7	0	4	105	26	0
Pug Manders	FB-LB	33	6'	200	18		49	168	3.4	3	3	2	67	14	4.7	0	0– 0		3	49	16	0													1	26	26	0
Dewey Proctor	FB-LB	25	5'11"	215	12		23	76	3.3	1									3	32	11	1																
Harvey Johnson	FB-LB	27	5'11"	210	54		16	63	3.9	0									2	19	10	0			36	36	100	6	8	75								
Lowell Wagner	WB-DB	22	6'	193	12		15	29	1.9	0									9	126	14	1									2	55	28	1	4	119	30	0
Bob Sweiger	WB-DB	27	6'	209	6	4	7	22	3.1	0									8	55	7	1	1	52.0							1	14	14	0	5	103	21	0
Lloyd Cheatham	BB-LB	27	6'2"	215	6	1	3	2	0.7	0									4	54	14	1									1	26	26	0	1	7	7	0
Bob Morrow	BB-LB	28	6'	220			8	54	6.8	0									1	6	6	0																
Jack Russell	OE-DE	26	6'1"	215	24														23	223	10	4																
Bruce Alford	OE-DB	25	6'	190															13	173	13	0													1	62	62	0
Harry Burrus	OE-WB-DB	25	6'1"	195	6	2	1	3	3.0	0									10	251	25	1																
Bob Masterson	OE-DE	31	6'1"	225		1													10	119	12	0						0	1	0					5	55	11	0
Perry Schwartz	OE-DE	31	6'2"	200															5	82	16	0													2	23	12	0
Mel Conger	OE-DE	27	6'2"	225															3	61	20	0																
Henry Stanton	OE-DE	26	6'2"	200															2	25	13	0																
BROOKLYN DODGERS																																						
Glenn Dobbs	TB-DB	26	6'4"	210	36	2	95	208	2.2	4	269	135	50	1886	7.0	13	15– 6		1	–5	–5	0	80	47.8							7	146	21	1	12	214	18	0
Lew Mayne	TB-DB	26	6'1"	190	12		70	191	2.7	1	25	14	56	219	8.8	3	4–16		5	9	2	0	3	26.3							6	47	8	0	4	90	23	0
Charlie Armstrong	TB-DB	27	5'10"	180		2	22	78	3.6	0	21	9	43	126	6.0	1	2–10						6	38.5							6	97	16	0	3	93	31	0
Harry Connolly	TB-DB	26	5'11"	190			8	18	2.3	0	8	2	25	29	3.6	0	1–12														1	6	6	0	2	41	21	0
Dom Principe	FB-LB	29	6'	210	12		39	139	3.6	2									3	25	8	0													6	117	20	0
Charlie Timmons	FB-LB	28	5'10"	210			23	65	2.8	0									1	4	4	0																
Bill Daley (to MIA)	FB-LB	26	6'2"	210			14	63	4.5	0									2	–5	–2	0													1	10	10	0
Rhoten Shetley	FB-LB	28	5'11"	210			9	21	2.3	0									1	10	10	0																
Cal Purdin (to MIA,HB-DB)	WB-DB	24	6'2"	185			10	12	1.2	0	1	1	100	–2	–2.0	0	0– 0		12	108	9	0									4	52	13	0	4	77	19	0
Doyle Tackett	WB-BB-DB	22	6'	201	12	1	11	–6	–0.5	0									10	191	19	2									1	3	3	0	5	76	15	0
Art Van Tone	WB-DB	27	5'10"	185	18	1	4	10	2.5	0									7	152	22	3									1	5	5	0	2	25	13	0
Dub Jones (from MIA,HB-DB)	WB-DB	21	6'4"	200			43	163	3.8	0	2	1	50	0	0.0	0	1–50														1	6	6	0	6	91	15	0
Mickey Colmer	BB-LB	27	6'2"	218	6	1	46	155	3.4	0									22	327	15	1									1	9	9	0	1	9	9	0
Walt McDonald (from MIA,QB)	BB-DB	25	6'1"	210		2	4	–11	–2.7	0	3	1	33	24	8.0	0	1–33		12	126	11	0													3	32	11	0
Saxon Judd	OE	25	6'1"	190	30														34	443	13	4													3	54	18	0
Joe Davis	OE-DE	25	6'2"	195	7														22	337	15	1			1	1	100								2	32	16	0
Neal Adams	OE-DE	27	6'3"	195	12														12	225	15	2																
Jim McCarthy	OE-DE	24	6'1"	205	23	1													11	296	27	3			5	7	71	0	1	0					1	8	8	0
Bob McCain	OE-DE	24	5'11"	195															3	27	9	0																
Phil Martinovich	G	31	5'10"	220	36																				21	22	95	5	10	50								
BUFFALO BISONS																																						
George Terlep	QB-DB	24	5'10"	180	6		36	29	0.8	1	123	48	39	574	4.7	7	14–11	9					1	31.0											1	23	23	0
Al Dekdebrun	QB-DB	25	5'11"	180		3	25	–55	–2.2	0	66	28	42	517	7.8	8	8–12																		6	116	19	0
Ken Stofer	QB-DB	27	5'9"	188			16	36	2.3	0	26	9	35	86	3.3	1	1– 4		1	14	14	0	3	36.0							5	53	11	0	2	81	41	0
Harry Hopp	QB-FB-LB	27	6'1"	215	18		61	218	3.6	3	22	11	50	190	8.6	0	0– 0		2	–1	0	0	15	30.7											6	113	19	0
Vic Kulbitski	FB-LB	25	5'11"	205	12	1	97	605	6.2	2									1	0	0	0													5	81	16	0
Steve Juzwik	HB-DB	28	5'8"	184	42	5	71	455	6.4	3									23	357	16	3									11	135	12	0	21	452	22	0
Chet Mutryn	HB-DB	25	5'9"	180	30		57	289	5.1	1									7	168	24	3									5	57	11	0	4	79	20	0
Pres Johnston (from MIA)	FB-LB	25	6'	205	19	1	45	218	4.8	2	1	1	100	9	9.0	0	0– 0		6	54	9	1	28	39.7	1	1	100								2	21	11	0
Lou Tomasetti	HB-DB	30	6'	198	12	1	43	139	3.2	1									6	81	14	1									7	138	20	0	2	85	43	0
Andy Dudish	HB-DB	25	5'11"	180			30	106	3.5	0									2	33	17	0									5	73	15	0	7	196	28	0
Curt Sandig	HB-DB	28	5'10"	175	6		22	52	2.4	1									2	15	8	0	4	38.8							2	20	10	0	2	43	22	0
Jim Thibaut	FB-LB	27	5'11"	205	6		10	48	4.8	1																												
Lou Zontini	FB-LB	29	5'9"	195	42	1	13	36	2.8	0	1	0	0	0	0.0	0	0– 0						44	36.3	30	31	97	4	8	50					1	19	19	0
Blondy Black	FB-DB	26	5'11"	195		1	1	10	10.0	0									1	21	21	0									2	58	29	0				
Bob Thurbon	HB-DB	28	5'10"	180			3	2	0.7	0									1	–3	–3	0													1	15	15	0
Fay King	OE	24	6'3"	195	36														30	466	16	6																
Al Vandeweghe	OE-DE	25	5'11"	200	12														6	67	11	1													1	15	15	0
Herb Nelson	OE-DE	25	6'4"	218			1	1	1.0	0									4	47	12	0																
John Batorski	OE-DE	25	6'2"	238															2	27	14	0																
Marty Comer	OE-DE	28	6'	202	6														2	17	9	0																
Ray Ebli	OE-DE	26	6'2"	210	6														2	15	8	1																
Nick Klutka	OE-DE	25	5'11"	200															1	9	9	0																
MIAMI SEAHAWKS																																						
Marion Pugh	QB	26	6'1"	187	12		29	–125	–4.3	2	118	55	47	608	5.2	5	12–10	8	4	43	11	0													1	24	24	0
Cotton Price	QB	27	6'1"	180			15	–55	–3.7	0	74	36	49	484	6.5	2	5– 7		2	17	9	0	4	26.3											2	32	16	0
Kay Eakin	QB-HB-DB	29	6'	180		2	15	–41	–2.7	0	45	19	42	331	7.4	2	5–11		6	67	11	0	37	41.4							3	30	10	0	4	51	13	0
Jimmy Nelson	HB-QB-DB	27	5'11"	180	12	2	39	163	4.2	2	24	8	33	135	5.6	0	4–17		4	20	5	0	16	39.7							7	71	10	0	10	192	19	0
Jim Tarrant	QB	25	5'9"	160			5	–46	–9.2	0	12	5	42	95	7.9	1	0– 0																					
Ken Holley	QB	26	5'10"	185			2	–22	–11.0	0	11	3	27	36	3.3	0	4–36																					
Frank Trigilio (from LA)	FB-LB	27	5'11"	200	6		41	126	3.1	1																												
Don Reece	FB-LB-T	26	6'1"	230	12	1	30	109	3.6	2									1	5	5	0																
Bob Paffrath (from BKN,BB-DB)	HB-DB	28	5'8"	190	12		31	100	3.2	2	1	0	0	0	0.0	0	0– 0		4	–6	–1	0	1	50.0							1	1	1	0	4	76	19	0
Jim Reynolds	FB-LB	26	6'1"	190		2	32	96	3.0	0									1	32	32	0	1	39.0											1	13	13	0
Monk Gafford (from BKN, WB-DB)	HB-DB	25	5'11"	195	30	4	24	66	2.8	1	5	1	20	–3	–0.6	0	2–40		14	270	19	4	13	40.3							9	117	13	0	11	345	31	0
Stan Koslowski	FB-LB	21	6'1"	200			18	61	3.4	0									2	27	14	0									1	4	4	0	3	72	24	0
Dick Erdlitz	HB-DB	26	5'10"	180	34	1	26	38	1.5	1	1	1	100	10	10.0	0	0– 0		7	31	4	0			22	22	100	2	7	29					6	104	17	0
Terry Fox	FB-LB	27	6'1"	208			12	26	2.2	0									3	27	9	0	2	44.0											1	24	24	0
Fred Gloden	HB-DB	27	5'10"	187	6		13	24	1.9	1																									1	20	20	0
Fondren Mitchell	HB-DB	25	6'	185		1	5	17	3.4	0									8	131	16	0													4	52	13	0
John Vardian	HB-DB	21	5'8"	165			5	–8	–1.6	0	1	1	100	–4	–4.0	0	0– 0		7	108	15	0													1	23	23	0
Lamar Davis	OE-DB	25	6'1"	185	12	4	14	64	4.6	0									22	275	13	2									4	54	14	0	5	235	47	0
Lamar Blount	OE-DB	26	6'1"	190	6														13	218	17	1																
Prince Scott	OE-DB	27	6'1"	190	12	1													13	180	14	2									1	6	6	0	2	28	14	0
Dick Horne	OE-DE	28	6'2"	215															5	48	10	0																
Hub Ulrich	OE-DE	25	6'	205	6														4	75	19	1																
Hamp Pool	OE-DE	31	6'3"	225															3	63	21	0																

CLEVELAND BROWNS 12-2-0 Paul Brown

Scores of Each Game		
44	MIAMI	0
20	Chicago	6
28	Buffalo	0
24	NEW YORK	7
26	BROOKLYN	7
7	New York	0
31	LOS ANGELES	14
20	SAN FRANCISCO	34
16	Los Angeles	17
14	San Francisco	7
51	CHICAGO	14
42	BUFFALO	17
34	Miami	0
66	Brooklyn	14

Use Name	Pos.	Hgt	Wgt	Age	Int	Pts
Frank Gatski	C-LB	6'3"	210	24	1	6
Mel Maceau	C-LB	6'	203	24		
Mike Scarry	C-LB	6'	208	26	2	

Use Name – Tackles	Pos.	Hgt	Wgt	Age	Int	Pts
Chet Adams (5 PAT's in 5 attempts)	T	6'3"	228	30	1	17
Ernie Blandin	T	6'4"	245	27		
Jim Daniell	T	6'2"	230	28		
Lou Rymkus	T	6'4"	230	27		

Use Name – Guards	Pos.	Hgt	Wgt	Age	Int	Pts
George Cheroke	G	5'9"	195	25		
Lin Houston	G	6'	205	25		
Alex Kapter	G	6'	205	24		
Bob Kolesar	G	5'10"	200	25		
Ed Ulinski (1 rush for 2 yds.)	G	5'11"	200	25		
Bill Willis	G	6'2"	206	25		

Cleveland lost a champion when the Rams left but gained a dynasty with the birth of the Browns. Coached by Paul Brown and manned by a platoon of war-hardened ex-GIs, the Browns overwhelmed their opponents and went on to take the newly created All American Football Conference championship. Cleveland fans were captivated as they never were by the Rams, turning out for a record average attendance of 57,000 per game, with an opening-day crowd of 60,000 watching the Browns destroy the Miami Seahawks 44-0.

With Paul Brown welding the parts together with a rigorous discipline, the Browns boasted of a full squad of first-rate players. Leading the pack was quarterback Otto Graham, a fine passer, safetyman, and field leader. Ends Mac Speedie and Dante Lavelli gave Graham a superb pair of targets, tackle Lou Groza led the league in scoring on the strength of his toe, Tom Colella picked off the most enemy passes, and Marion Motley and Bill Willis, two black players signed by Brown, gave Cleveland the league's best fullback and guard.

SAN FRANCISCO 49ers 9-5-0 Buck Shaw

Scores of Each Game		
7	NEW YORK	21
21	MIAMI	14
32	BROOKLYN	13
7	Chicago	21
34	Miami	7
23	Los Angeles	14
14	Buffalo	17
34	Cleveland	20
27	BUFFALO	14
7	CLEVELAND	14
9	New York	10
30	Brooklyn	14
14	CHICAGO	0
48	LOS ANGELES	7

Use Name	Pos.	Hgt	Wgt	Age	Int	Pts
Gerry Conlee	C-LB	5'11"	210	30		
Art Elston	C-LB	5'11"	190	27	1	
Ed Forrest	C-LB	5'11"	210	25		
Bill Remington	C-LB	6'1"	185	25		

Use Name – Tackles	Pos.	Hgt	Wgt	Age	Int	Pts
Bob Bryant	T	6'3"	225	27		
John Kuzman	T	6'1"	230	30		6
John Mellus (1 PAT in 2 attempts and missed 1 FG attempt)	T	6'	210	29		1
John Woudenberg	T	6'3"	225	28		

Use Name – Guards	Pos.	Hgt	Wgt	Age	Int	Pts
Bruno Banducci	G	5'11"	215	24		
Dick Bassi	G-LB	5'11"	215	31	1	
Garland Gregory (1 kickoff return for 0 yds.)	G-LB	5'11"	185	27		
Visco Grgich	G	5'11"	210	23		
Charlie Pavlich	G	6'2"	210	25		
Bob Thornton	G	5'10"	205	27		

When the NFL brushed off his application for a franchise, Tony Morabito organized the '49ers for the AAFC. In this debut season, the '49ers established that they were the second-best franchise in the league, trailing the Browns not only this year but for the whole span of the AAFC. Both in attendance and in the standings, San Francisco would grow accustomed to being listed right below Cleveland.

Coach Buck Shaw built the team around quarterback Frankie Albert, a little left-handed passer who scrambled before it was fashionable. Albert's favorite receiver was Alyn Beals, a quick end from Santa Clara who loved to run deep patterns. Ex-Bear Norm Standlee was the top runner and ex-Eagle Bruno Banducci the leading lineman.

LOS ANGELES DONS 7-5-2 Dud DeGroot

Scores of Each Game		
20	BROOKLYN	14
30	MIAMI	14
21	Buffalo	21
21	Chicago	9
14	SAN FRANCISCO	23
14	Cleveland	31
17	NEW YORK	31
17	CLEVELAND	16
12	New York	17
19	Brooklyn	14
34	Miami	21
62	BUFFALO	14
7	San Francisco	48
17	CHICAGO	17

Use Name	Pos.	Hgt	Wgt	Age	Int	Pts
Don Nolander	C-LB	6'1"	210	25	1	
Hank Rockwell	C-G	6'4"	230	29		
John McQuary	HB-DB	6'1"	208	26		

Use Name – Tackles	Pos.	Hgt	Wgt	Age	Int	Pts
Lee Artoe ((1 kickoff return for 13 yds., 1 PAT in 2 attempts)	T	6'3"	240	30		1
Earl Audet	T	6'2"	252	25		
Gil Duggan	T	6'3"	235	28		
Joe Mihal	T	6'3"	240	30		
Paul Mitchell	T	6'3"	225	26		

Use Name – Guards	Pos.	Hgt	Wgt	Age	Int	Pts
Ray Frankowski	G	5'11"	220	27		6
Al Lolotai	G	6'	220	25		
Bill Radovich	G	5'10"	255	31		
Frank Yokas	G	5'11"	210	22		

After having no pro teams last year, Los Angeles suddenly had two, the Rams and Dons, and both of them lost money in the battle for paying customers—a financial bleeding which would go on until the Dons gave up the ghost in 1949.

The Dons raked in points like leaves on an October Saturday, but their opponents in return marched all over the Los Angeles defense. Even with 1943 Heisman Trophy winner Angelo Bertelli injured, veteran pro backs Charlie O'Rourke, John Kimbrough, Chuck Fenenbock, and Harry Clark kept the ball moving steadily. Dale Gentry was the team's top receiver, and Bob Nelson, Lee Artoe, Bill Radovich, and Bob Reinhard gave the Dons four of the AAFC's best linemen. The defense did turn in a standout game in a 17-16 upset of the Browns, but a 48-7 trouncing by San Francisco pointed out the leaks in the dam.

CHICAGO ROCKETS 5-6-3 Dick Hanley, Bob Dove, Ned Mathews, Willie Wilkin, Pat Boland

Scores of Each Game		
6	CLEVELAND	20
17	NEW YORK	17
38	BUFFALO	35
21	SAN FRANCISCO	7
9	LOS ANGELES	21
21	Brooklyn	21
28	MIAMI	7
17	Buffalo	49
14	BROOKLYN	21
20	Miami	7
14	Cleveland	51
38	New York	28
0	San Francisco	14
17	Los Angeles	17

Use Name	Pos.	Hgt	Wgt	Age	Int	Pts
Herb Coleman (1 kickoff return for 20 yds.)	C-LB	6'	200	23	1	
Mickey Parks	C-LB	6'	220	29		

Use Name – Tackles	Pos.	Hgt	Wgt	Age	Int	Pts
Jim Brutz	T	6'	230	27		
Charlie Huneke	T	6'3"	225	25		
Quentin Kenk (from BUF)	T	6'2"	225	27		
Norm Verr	T	6'1"	240	23		
Lloyd Wasserbach (1 kickoff return for 13 yds.)	T	5'11"	205	25	1	
Willie Wilkin (3 yds. receiving on lateral)	T	6'4"	260	30		

Use Name – Guards	Pos.	Hgt	Wgt	Age	Int	Pts
Jim O'Neal	G	6'1"	230	22		
Jim Pearcy	G	5'11"	210	27		
Joe Ruetz	G-LB	6'	200	29	2	
Tony Sumpter	G	6'1"	215	24		
Evan Vogds	G	5'10"	204	23		

The Rockets faced the hardest road in the AAFC, sharing the Chicago football dollar with the NFL Bears and Cardinals. With the Bears perennial champions and the Cardinals on the rise, the Rockets had problems enough without the chaos in their higher command. Dick Hanley began the year as coach but quit after three games. Then three players, Bob Dove, Ned Mathews, and Willie Wilkin, took over as a committee of coaches for five games, with Pat Boland finally coming in as full-time coach for the last six contests.

Through all these changes, the Rockets managed to stay around the break-even point in wins and losses. Bob "Hunchy" Hoernschemeyer sparked the offense with his passing and running, and Elroy "Crazy Legs" Hirsch added his speed to the team.

TEAM TOTALS

OFFENSE	First Downs: Tot	by Rsh	by Pas	by Pen	Rushing: No.	Yds.	Avg Yds.	TD	Passing: Att	Com	Comp Pct.	Yds.	Avg. Yds. Att.	Avg. Yds. Comp	TD	Int	Pct. Int.
CLEVE.	146	79	60	7	494	2007	4.1	27	237	123	51.9	2266	9.6	18.4	22	7	3.0
S.F.	170	113	52	5	592	2175	3.7	22	252	130	51.6	1721	6.8	13.2	18	21	8.3
L.A.	183	92	84	7	549	1949	3.6	17	322	176	54.7	2193	6.8	12.5	19	30	9.3
CHI.	149	76	63	10	511	1559	3.1	10	310	144	46.5	1898	6.1	13.1	18	29	9.4
DEFENSE																	
CLEVE.	160	89	56	15	546	1616	3.0	8	299	125	41.8	1317	4.4	10.5	8	41	13.7
S.F.	140	56	79	5	425	873	2.1	7	359	185	51.5	2150	5.9	11.6	15	21	5.8
L.A.	144	71	65	8	451	1356	3.0	19	284	138	48.6	2101	7.4	15.2	17	20	7.0
CHI.	129	69	50	10	475	1718	3.6	16	259	119	46.0	1618	6.3	13.6	19	31	12.0

OFFENSE	Punting: No.	Avg. Yds.	Punt Returns: No.	Yds.	Avg. Yds.	TD	Kickoff Returns: No.	Yds.	Avg. Yds.	TD	Interception Returns: No.	Yds.	Avg. Yds.	TD	Penalties: No.	Yds.	Fumbles: No.	Lost	Points: Tot	PAT	FG Att	FG	Saf.	OFFENSE
CLEVE.	58	39.2	39	537	13.8	0	36	841	23.4	1	41	589	14.4	4	71	600	54	30	423	52	29	13	1	CLEVE.
S.F.	67	40.6	51	640	12.5	0	37	777	21.0	0	21	391	18.6	1	56	440	35	21	307	35	8	4	1	S.F
L.A.	57	44.2	49	724	14.8	0	57	1307	22.9	1	20	293	14.7	1	50	379	31	13	305	37	17	6	2	L.A.
CHI.	91	41.9	48	652	13.6	3	54	1323	24.5	2	31	516	16.6	1	63	514	40	18	263	32	12	9	0	CHI.
DEFENSE																								**DEFENSE**
CLEVE.	71	41.6	39	510	13.1	1	61	1397	22.9	0	7	116	16.6	0	48	326	58	23	137	17	9	4	0	CLEVE.
S.F.	87	38.8	34	483	14.2	1	61	1360	22.3	1	21	292	13.9	1	47	377	46	26	189	24	9	3	0	S.F.
L.A.	84	38.7	36	530	14.7	1	54	1161	21.5	2	30	387	12.9	0	50	329	32	17	290	35	12	7	0	L.A.
CHI.	89	40.0	48	626	13.0	0	55	1117	20.3	0	29	532	18.3	3	73	553	48	22	315	41	14	6	2	CHI.

Use Name – Backs & Ends	Pos.	Age	Hgt	Wgt	Pts	Int	Rushing No.	Rushing Yds	Rushing Avg	Rushing TD	Passing Att	Passing Comp	Passing %	Passing Yds	Passing Yd/Att	Passing TD	Passing Int–%	Passing RK	Receiving No.	Receiving Yds	Receiving Avg	Receiving TD	Punting No.	Punting Avg	Kicking Pat	Kicking Att	Kicking %	Kicking FG	Kicking Att	Kicking %	Punt Returns No.	Punt Returns Yds	Punt Returns Avg	Punt Returns TD	Kickoff Returns No.	Kickoff Returns Yds	Kickoff Returns Avg	Kickoff Returns TD
CLEVELAND BROWNS																																						
Otto Graham	QB-DB	24	6'1"	190	12	5	30	–125	–4.2	1	174	95	55	1834	10.5	17	5– 3	1													12	129	11	0				
Cliff Lewis	QB-DB	23	5'11"	165		5	24	–34	–1.4	0	30	11	37	125	4.2	1	1– 3														8	133	17	0	3	70	23	0
Bud Schwenk	QB	28	6'2"	200	6		6	–1	–0.2	1	23	15	65	276	12.0	4	0– 0																					
Marion Motley	FB-LB	26	6'1"	218	36	1	73	601	8.2	5									10	188	19	1									1	0	0	0	3	53	18	0
Special Delivery Jones	HB-DB	27	5'10"	195	36	2	77	539	7.0	4	4	1	25	4	1.0	0	0– 0		4	120	30	1									7	73	10	0	12	307	26	1
Don Greenwood	HB-DB	25	6'	198	36	2	77	274	3.6	6	1	1	100	27	27.0	0	0– 0		4	0	0	0													5	105	21	0
Gaylon Smith	FB-LB	30	5'11"	200	30	1	62	240	3.9	5									7	73	10	0																
Tom Colella	HB-DB	28	6'	187	18	10	30	118	3.9	2									1	12	12	1	47	40.3							8	172	22	0	1	29	29	0
Ray Terrell	HB-DB	27	6'	185	6	3	39	117	3.0	0	2	0	0	0	0.0	0	0– 0		4	21	5	0													3	80	27	0
Gene Fekete	FB-LB	24	6'	195	6		26	106	4.1	1									1	2	2	0													1	21	21	0
Bill Lund	HB-DB	22	5'10"	180	18	1	23	72	3.1	1									4	64	16	2									2	30	15	0	1	32	32	0
Al Akins	HB-DB	25	6'1"	195	6	1	5	42	8.4	1																									2	74	37	0
Fred Evans	HB-DB	25	5'11"	185		1	8	27	3.4	0									1	7	7	0	8	37.0							1	0	0	0				
Bob Steuber	HB-DB	24	6'2"	200		1	8	19	2.4	0									1	9	9	0													2	53	27	0
Lou Saban	FB-LB	24	6'	198		4	4	–4	–1.0	0	3	0	0	0	0.0	0	1–33		1	45	45	0																
Dante Lavelli	OE	23	6'	190	48		1	14	14.0	0									40	843	21	8																
Mac Speedie	OE-DE	26	6'3"	200	43														24	564	24	7	3	28.0	1	1	100								1	1	1	0
John Harrington	OE-DE	24	6'3"	198															8	136	17	0													2	16	8	0
John Yonaker	OE-DE	25	6'5"	218	12														7	98	14	2																
George Young	OE-DE	22	6'3"	210															3	37	12	0																
Al Coppage	OE-DE	30	6'1"	195															2	34	17	0																
John Rokisky	OE-DE	26	6'2"	200	1														1	13	13	0			1	1	100											
Lou Groza	T	22	6'3"	215	84																				45	47	96	13	29	45								
SAN FRANCISCO 49ers																																						
Frankie Albert	QB-DB	26	5'10"	160	24		69	–10	–0.1	4	197	104	53	1404	7.1	14	14– 7	2					54	41.0							1	6	6	0	4	74	19	0
Jess Freitas	QB-DB	25	5'10"	170		2	6	–21	–3.5	0	44	22	50	234	5.3	3	7–16														1	10	10	0				
Parker Hall	QB-DB	29	6'	192			17	31	1.8	0	8	2	25	15	1.9	0	0– 0		2	25	13	0													1	22	22	0
Norm Standlee	FB-LB	27	6'2"	245	12		134	651	4.9	2									2	–5	–2	0	1	34.0											1	33	33	0
Earle Parsons	HB-DB	26	6'	180	12		74	362	4.9	2									8	52	7	0									15	198	13	0	4	94	24	0
Johnny Strzykalski	HB-DB	23	5'9"	190	12	3	79	346	4.4	2									9	80	9	0									3	26	9	0	7	142	20	0
Len Eshmont	HB-DB	29	5'11"	178	54		73	340	4.7	6	2	1	50	42	21.0	1	0– 0		17	287	17	2									2	25	13	0	10	264	26	0
Don Durdan	HB-DB	26	5'9"	175	6	2	32	132	4.1	0									2	27	14	1	6	39.8							3	37	12	0				
Ken Casanega	HB-DB	25	5'11"	175	12	8	29	90	3.1	1									5	102	20	1									18	248	14	0	3	61	20	0
Dick Renfro	FB-LB	27	5'10"	200	18		18	85	4.7	3																									1	20	20	0
Joe Vetrano	HB-DB	24	5'9"	170	49	3	23	69	3.0	1									4	37	9	0	6	39.3	31	38	82	4	7	57	7	84	12	0	3	49	16	0
Ken Roskie	FB-LB	26	6'1"	230			9	16	1.8	0									0	7	–	0																
Pete Franceschi	HB-DB	26	5'9"	170	12		8	–5	–0.6	1									3	35	12	1									1	6	6	0				
Alyn Beals	OE-DB	25	6'	185	61		2	–7	–3.5	0									40	586	15	10			1	1	100											
Bill Fisk	OE-DE	29	6'	200	6														19	186	10	1																
Bob Titchenal	OE-DE	28	6'2"	190	12		1	2	2.0	0									7	160	23	2																
Nick Susoeff	OE-DE	25	6'1"	210															5	98	20	0													1	10	10	0
Ed Balatti	OE-DB	22	6'1"	190	8														4	15	4	0			2	2	100											
Hank Norberg	OE-DE	27	6'2"	225		1													3	29	10	0																
LOS ANGELES DONS																																						
Charlie O'Rourke	QB-DB	29	5'11"	175	6		47	50	1.1	1	182	105	58	1250	6.9	12	14– 8	4					8	39.0											1	28	28	0
Angelo Bertelli	QB	25	6'1"	190	6		11	–16	–1.5	1	127	67	53	917	7.2	7	14–11	7					2	38.0														
Bob Mitchell	QB-DB	25	5'11"	195		1	8	–12	–1.5	0	10	3	30	19	1.9	0	2–20		1	1	1	0	1	44.0														
John Kimbrough	FB-LB	28	6'2"	210	42		122	473	3.9	6									9	162	18	1													5	111	22	0
Chuck Fenenbock	HB-DB	28	5'9"	175	24		50	420	8.4	3	1	0	0	0	0.0	0	0– 0		11	67	6	0									16	299	19	0	17	479	28	1
Harry Clark	HB-DB	28	6'	195	12	2	62	250	4.0	0									10	123	12	2									2	24	12	0	2	48	24	0
Earl Elsey	HB-DB	27	5'8"	175		2	47	165	3.5	0									14	179	13	0									9	147	16	0	15	335	22	0
Bob Seymour	HB-DB	30	6'2"	208	18	4	37	165	4.5	0									17	188	11	3									18	211	12	0	4	87	22	0
Buzz Mertes	HB-DB	25	6'	195	6	1	40	111	2.8	0									5	61	12	1													2	35	18	0
Bernie Nygren	HB-DB	26	5'9"	193	6	2	26	111	4.3	0									13	170	13	1													4	88	22	0
Andy Marefos	FB-LB	29	6'	225	26		30	93	3.1	4									1	13	13	0			2	2	100											
John Polanski	FB-LB	27	6'2"	210	12	1	28	77	2.7	1									2	15	8	1																
Paul Vinnola	HB-DB	24	5'10"	180		1	23	36	1.6	0									4	39	10	0									2	24	12	0	5	83	17	0
Bob Sneddon	HB-DB	25	5'10"	180		1	3	6	2.0	0									2	11	6	0																
Dale Gentry	OE-DE	29	6'3"	223	30		5	29	5.8	1									24	341	14	3									1	14	14	0				
Al Krueger	OE-DE	27	6'1"	190	6														19	213	11	1																
Bob Nowaskey	OE-DE	28	6'	200	24	1	3	14	4.7	0									19	198	10	3									1	5	5	0				
Joe Aguirre	OE-DE	27	6'4"	225	55		2	–5	–2.5	0	1	0	0	0	0.0	0	0– 0		14	246	18	2	2	45.5	31	32	97	4	11	36								
Bill Kerr	OE-DE	30	6'	220		1	1	10	10.0	0									7	122	17	0																
John Morton	OE-DE	24	6'	200	6	1													4	44	11	1																
Bob Reinhard	T	25	6'4"	225	6		1	–30	–30.0	0	1	1	100	7	7.0	0	0– 0						44	45.4														
Bob Nelson	C-LB	26	6'1"	215	9	1																			3	5	60	2	6	33					1	0	0	0
CHICAGO ROCKETS																																						
Bob Hoernschemeyer	TB-DB	20	5'11"	192		1	111	375	3.4	0	193	95	49	1266	6.6	14	14– 7	6	1	11	11	0	11	44.0							6	91	15	0	9	275	31	0
Walt Williams	TB-DB	27	6'1"	195	12	2	21	19	0.9	1	30	13	48	226	7.5	1	5–17		1	3	3	0	24	41.6							1	6	6	0	1	18	18	0
Steve Nemeth	TB-DB	24	5'10"	175	59		4	10	2.5	0	23	5	22	68	3.0	0	0– 0						2	46.0	32	33	97	9	12	75	1	14	14	0				
Bill Schroeder	TB-DB	23	6'	190		1	12	42	3.5	0	2	1	50	10	5.0	0	0– 0		1	9	9	0									0	7	–	0	1	19	19	0
Norm Cox	TB	20	6'2"	210			1	12	12.0	0																												
Walt Clay	HB-TB-DB	22	5'11"	195	6	6	65	283	4.4	1	27	12	44	140	5.2	2	3–11		4	48	12	0	1	45.0							8	70	9	0	2	43	22	0
Crazy Legs Hirsch	HB-DB	22	6'2"	190	36	6	87	226	2.6	1	20	12	60	156	7.8	1	2–10		27	347	13	3			0	1	0				17	235	14	1	14	384	27	1
Bill Kellagher	FB-LB	26	5'11"	205	18		49	178	3.6	3	3	2	67	15	5.0	0	1–33		2	36	18	0	1	56.0											3	48	16	0
Billy Hillenbrand	HB-DB	24	6'	188	48	3	50	175	3.5	2	3	0	0	0	0.0	0	2–67		21	315	15	4									13	180	14	1	8	220	28	1
Ernie Lewis	FB-LB	22	6'1"	215	6	1	57	164	2.9	1	8	4	50	17	2.1	0	1–12		2	26	13	0	50	41.7											2	22	11	0
Ned Mathews (to SF)	HB-DB	28	5'10"	192	18	2	30	109	3.6	1	1	1	100	26	26.0	0	0– 0		6	100	17	2													6	118	20	0
Pete Lamana	FB-LB	25	5'11"	210	6	1	6	21	3.5	0																					0	20	–	1	1	18	18	0
Don Griffin	HB-DB	23	5'11"	195		1	28	13	0.5	0	1	0	0	0	0.0	0	1–100		5	28	6	0													2	31	16	0
Bill Boedecker	HB-DB	22	5'11"	190	6	1	6	8	1.3	0									5	82	16	1									2	29	15	0	2	84	42	0
Ralph Heywood	OE-DE	25	6'2"	195	24														20	287	14	4	2	28.5														
Tom Lahey	OE-DE	28	6'2"	218		1	1	–2	–2.0	0									17	203	12	0													1	5	5	0
Frank Quillen	OE-DE	24	6'5"	225	12	1													13	143	11	2													1	13	13	0
Bob Motl	OE-DE	26	6'3"	195	6														9	124	14	1																
Bob Dove	OE-DE	25	6'2"	220	6														7	67	10	1																
Max Morris	OE-DE	21	6'2'	200			1	20	20.0	0									3	66	22	0																

N.F.L. — December 15, at New York (Attendance 58, 436)

Hapes and Filchock, and Luckman's Run

On the morning of the game, news broke that Merle Hapes and Frankie Filchock, two New York backs, were under investigation in a bribe attempt. Hapes, who had declined a bribe to throw the game but had not reported the attempt, was suspended by Commissioner Bert Bell, but Filchock, who knew of the bribe offer only through Hapes, was allowed to play. With suspicion hanging over his head, Filchock played a hard fifty minutes, despite a broken nose, in the Giants' losing effort against the Bears. Chicago, with a host of stars back from military service, scored two touchdowns in the first quarter, the first after recovering a fumble and the second on an interception return. Filchock cut the Bear lead down with a 38-yard touchdown pass to Frank Liebel late in the quarter. At the start of the second half, the Giants recovered a Chicago fumble deep in Bear territory, and a short pass from Filchock to Steve Filipowicz plus the extra point knotted the score at 14 all. The tie held until early in the fourth quarter, when, aided by a 16-yard punt by Howie Livingston of New York, the Bears drove to a first down on the Giant 19. Sid Luckman, who never ran with the ball, then shocked the Giants by running for the touchdown to put the game out of reach. For Filchock, it was all bad news, as he was also suspended soon after the game for his failure to report what Hapes had told him.

SCORING

NEW YORK	7	0	7	0–14
CHIC. BEARS	14	0	0	10–24

First Quarter

Chi.	Kavanaugh, 21 yard pass from Luckman PAT – Maznicki (kick)	4:36
Chi.	Magnani, 19 yard interception return PAT – Maznicki (kick)	8:52
N.Y.	Liebel, 38 yard pass from Filchock PAT – Strong (kick)	13:26

Third Quarter

N.Y.	Filipowicz, 5 yard pass from Filchock PAT – Strong (kick)	3:44

Fourth Quarter

Chi.	Luckman, 19 yard rush PAT – Maznicki (kick)	2:45
Chi.	Maznicki, 26 yard Field Goal	9:44

TEAM STATISTICS

N.Y.		CHI.
13	First Downs	10
120	Rushing Yardage	101
26	Pass Attempts	23
9	Pass Completions	9
34.6	Completion Percentage	39.1
128	Passing Yardage	144
4.9	Average Yards per Attempt	6.3
14.2	Average Yards per Comp.	16.0
6	Passes had Intercepted	2
4	Punts	7
31.7	Average Punt Distance	42.3
9	Punt Return Yards	13
3	Fumbles	2
2	Lost Ball	1
6	Penalties	9
70	Yards Penalized	112

A.A.F.C. — December 22, at Cleveland (Attendance 41,181)

Nearly Avoiding a Futile Finish

The Cleveland Browns had beaten the New York Yankees twice during the season, by scores of 24-7 and 7-0, and were clear favorites to sweep the first AAFC championship game. New York did not roll over dead for the Browns, however, and fought them closely all afternoon. The Yankees got up on the scoreboard in the first period after Eddie Prokop picked off an Otto Graham pass and returned it to the Cleveland 34-yard line. After an Ace Parker—Jack Russell pass and a Spec Sanders run netted two first downs, the New York drive stalled on the Cleveland four, and Harvey Johnson booted a 12-yard field goal to make the score 3-0. The Browns knew they were in for a rough afternoon when they had a first down on the Yankee six-yard line, and the New York defense held for four downs. The Browns again reached New York territory early in the second quarter, only to have Lou Groza's field-goal attempt fail. Late in the period, the Browns took possession after a punt on their own 30, and Graham passes to Dub Jones, Mac Speedie, and Dante Lavelli moved the ball quickly to the New York 12. Marion Motley carried the ball in from there on two running plays; Groza's conversion made the score 7-3. The Yankees took a 9-7 lead in the third period on Spec Sanders' two-yard run after an 80-yard drive, but the extra-point attempt was blocked. With defeat staring them in the face, the Browns drove 22 yards on eleven plays, most of them passes, with the score coming on a 16-yard Graham-to-Lavelli pass with under five minutes left in the game. New York's final drive ended when Graham picked off Parker's pass on the Cleveland 30-yard line, and the game ended 14-9 in favor of Cleveland.

SCORING

CLEVELAND	0	7	0	7–14
NEW YORK	3	0	6	0– 9

First Quarter

N.Y.	H. Johnson, 12 yard F.G.	5:31

Second Quarter

Cle.	Motley, 1 yard rush PAT – Groza (kick)	13:58

Third Quarter

N.Y.	Sanders, 2 yard rush PAT – H. Johnson (No Good)	9:28

Fourth Quarter

Cle.	Lavelli, 16 yard pass from Graham PAT – Groza (kick)	10:47

TEAM STATISTICS

CLE.		N.Y.
18	First Downs – Total	10
8	by Rushing	6
10	by Passing	4
0	by Penalty	0
3	Fumbles – Number	2
0	Lost Ball	1
5	Penalties – Number	4
25	Yards Penalized	20

INDIVIDUAL STATISTICS

RUSHING

CLEVELAND	No	Yds	Avg.	NEW YORK	No	Yds	Avg.
Motley	13	98	7.5	Sanders	14	55	3.9
Jones	10	16	1.6	Parker	9	5	0.6
Greenwood	5	14	2.8	Prokop	5	5	1.0
Colella	4	14	3.5	Wagner	1	0	0.0
Terrell	1	–4	–4.0		29	65	2.2
Lavelli	1	–7	–7.0				
Graham	3	–19	–6.3				
	37	112	3.0				

RECEIVING

CLEVELAND	No	Yds	Avg.	NEW YORK	No	Yds	Avg.
Lavelli	6	87	14.5	Russell	5	58	11.6
Speedie	6	71	11.8	Schwartz	1	12	12.0
Jones	3	45	15.0	Masterson	1	7	7.0
Yonakor	1	8	8.0	Prokop	1	4	4.0
Greenwood	(Lat)	2	–		8	81	10.1
	16	213	13.3				

PUNTING

CLEVELAND	No	Yds	Avg.	NEW YORK	No	Yds	Avg.
Colella	2		38.5	Parker	4		29.0
				Sanders	1		45.0
					5		32.2

PUNT RETURNS

CLEVELAND	No	Yds	Avg.	NEW YORK	No	Yds	Avg.
Graham	5	20	4.0	Perina	1	5	5.0

KICKOFF RETURNS

CLEVELAND	No	Yds	Avg.	NEW YORK	No	Yds	Avg.
Greenwood	2	25	12.5	Sanders	2	52	26.0
Jones	1	12	12.0	Morrow	1	25	25.0
	3	37	12.3		3	77	25.7

INTERCEPTION RETURNS

CLEVELAND	No	Yds	Avg.	NEW YORK	No	Yds	Avg.
Graham	1	4	4.0	Prokop	1	16	16.0

PASSING

Cleveland	Att	Comp	Comp Pct.	Yds	Int	Yds/ Att.	Yds/ Comp
Graham	27	16	59.3	213	1	7.9	13.3
New York							
Parker	18	8	44.4	81	1	4.5	10.1
Sanders	2	0	0.0	0	0	–	–
	20	8	40.0	81	1	4.1	10.1

N.F.L. —December 28, at Chicago (Attendance 30,759)

Icing the Eagles

The Cardinals had beaten the Eagles 45-21 during the season and had a strategy designed to exploit Philadelphia's 5-2-4 defensive. Midway through the first quarter, on an icy field, the Cards double-teamed the Eagle defensive guard and sent Charlie Trippi roaring up the middle. Since there was no middle linebacker in the Philadelphia defense, Trippi went 44 yards for a touchdown. The Cards scored again in the second quarter on another quick opener through the Eagle defense, but just before the half Tommy Thompson's long pass to Pat McHugh made the score 14-7. With the Cardinal offense stalled, the Eagles hoped to climb back into the game, only to have Trippi return a punt 75 yards to make the score 21-7. Another Eagle touchdown brought them within seven points, but Elmer Angsman's 70-yard dash through the center of the line nailed down the championship.

SCORING

CHIC. Cards	**7**	**7**	**7**	**7—28**
PHILADELPHIA	**0**	**7**	**7**	**7—21**

First Quarter
- Chi. Trippi, 44 yard rush — 6:22
  - PAT — Harder (kick)

Second Quarter
- Chi. Angsman, 10 yard rush — 6:54
  - PAT — Harder (kick)
- Phi. McHugh, 70 yard pass from Thompson — 14:00
  - PAT — Patton (kick)

Third Quarter
- Chi. Trippi, 75 yard punt return — 8:44
  - PAT — Harder (kick)
- Phi. Van Buren, 1 yard rush — 13:10
  - PAT — Patton (kick)

Fourth Quarter
- Chi. Angsman, 70 yard rush — 7:30
  - PAT — Harder (kick)
- Phi. Craft, 1 yard rush — 10:30
  - PAT — Patton (kick)

TEAM STATISTICS

CHI.		PHIL.
11	First Downs—Total	22
7	First Downs—Rushing	10
2	First Downs—Passing	11
1	First Downs—Penalty	1
282	Rushing Yardage	60
14	Pass Attempts	44
3	Pass Completions	27
21.4	Completion Percentage	61.4
54	Passing Yardage	297
3.9	Average Yards per Attempt	6.8
18.0	Average Yards per Comp.	11.0
8	Punts	8
32	Average Distance	34.5
3	Interception Returns	3
45	Yards	11
15.0	Average Yards	3.7
4	Punt Returns	4
150	Yards	10
37.5	Average Yards	2.5
3	Kickoff Returns	5
70	Yards	63
23.3	Average Yards	12.6
2	Fumbles	2
1	Fumbles Lost	0
10	Penalties	7
97	Yards Penalized	55

A.A.F.C.— December 14, at New York (Attendance 60,103)

A Fumble, Roughness, and Cleveland Makes it Two

The rematch between the Browns and Yankees again was a defensive battle, although they had played two high-scoring games during the season. The Browns launched the first extended drive of the game late in the first quarter. Starting from their own 32-yard line, the Browns drove down to the New York one-yard line, with the key play in the drive a 51-yard end run by Marion Motley. Otto Graham snuck over for the touchdown, and Lou Groza added the extra point. The Yankees came right back with a drive of their own, as little Buddy Young and Spec Sanders led the New Yorkers down to the Cleveland five-yard line, where the attack petered out. Harvey Johnson salvaged three points with a 12-yard field goal, bringing the score to 7-3. Groza missed two three-point tries before halftime broke the action. Neither club could mount a consistent attack in the third quarter, but the Browns got a break when Tom Colella picked off a Sanders pass and returned it to the New York 41. Martion Motley then ran for 16 yards, Graham threw to Dub Jones for eleven more, and Lew Mayne hauled in another Graham pass for eight more yards. Two power plays with Jones carrying the ball gave Cleveland a first down on the 4-yard line. On the next play, Graham faked handoffs to Motley and Mayne and gave the ball to Jones, who made it to the end zone unmolested. The Yanks had two scoring threats left, marching to Cleveland's 19-yard line before losing the ball on a fumble and reaching the 29 late in the game, only to have an unnecessary-roughness penalty push them back out of scoring range.

SCORING

NEW YORK	**0**	**3**	**0**	**0— 3**
CLEVELAND	**7**	**0**	**7**	**0—14**

First Quarter
- Cle. Graham, 1 yard rush — 13:00
  - PAT — Groza (kick)

Second Quarter
- N.Y. H.Johnson, 12 field goal — 4:14

Third Quarter
- Cle. Jones, 4 yard rush — 10:04
  - PAT — Saban (kick)

TEAM STATISTICS

N.Y.		CLE.
13	First Downs—Total*	17
8	by Rushing	12
5	by Passing	4
0	by Penalty	1
3	Fumbles—Number	2
2	Lost Ball	1
3	Penalties—Number	7
21	Yards Penalized	45
0	Field Goals Missed	2

*—Includes Touchdowns

INDIVIDUAL STATISTICS

NEW YORK	No	Yds	Avg.	CLEVELAND	No	Yds	Avg.
RUSHING							
Young	16	69	4.3	Motley	33	109	8.4
Sanders	12	40	3.3	Jones	10	27	2.7
Prokop	5	14	2.8	Graham	4	21	5.3
	33	123	3.7	Lewis	1	9	9.0
				Colella	1	6	6.0
				Mayne	4	0	0.0
					33	172	5.2
RECEIVING							
Young	2	25	12.5	Speedie	4	25	6.3
Sweiger	2	12	6.0	Lavelli	3	37	12.3
Kurrasch	1	20	20.0	Jones	3	31	10.3
Davis	1	18	18.0	Colella	2	7	3.5
Russell	1	14	14.0	Mayne	1	8	8.0
	7	89	12.7	Lewis	1	4	4.0
					14	112	8.0
PUNTING							
Kennedy	6		36.0	Gillom	5		45.0
PUNT RETURNS							
Young	2	4	2.0	Lewis	3	25	8.3
Prokop	1	10	10.0	Motley	1	2	2.0
	3	14	4.7		4	27	6.8
KICKOFF RETURNS							
Young	2	51	25.5	Colella	1	16	16.0
Sanders	1	32	32.0	Allen	1	10	10.0
	3	83	27.7		2	26	13.0
INTERCEPTION RETURNS							
None				Colella	1	13	13.0

PASSING

	Att	Comp	Comp Pct.	Yds	Int	Yds/ Att.	Yds/ Comp.
NEW YORK							
Sanders	17	7	41.2	89	1	5.2	12.7
Prokop	1	0	0.0	0	0	–	–
	18	7	38.9	89	1	4.9	12.7
CLEVELAND							
Graham	21	14	66.7	112	0	5.3	8.0

PHILADELPHIA EAGLES 8-4-0 Greasy Neale

Scores of Each Game		
45	WASHINGTON	42
23	NEW YORK	0
7	Chic. Bears	40
24	Pittsburgh	35
14	LOS ANGELES	7
38	Washington	14
41	New York	24
32	BOSTON	0
14	Boston	21
21	PITTSBURGH	0
21	CHIC. CARDS	45
28	GREEN BAY	14
	EAST playoff	
21	Pittsburgh	0

Use Name	Pos.	Hgt	Wgt	Age	Int	Pts
Roger Harding	C-LB	6'2"	215	24		
Vic Lindskog	C-LB	6'1"	205	31	1	
Boyd Williams	C-LB	6'3"	218	25		
Alex Wojciechowicz	C-LB	5'11"	225	32	1	
Larry Cabrelli	DE	5'11"	195	30		
John Green	DE	6'1"	190	25		
Eddie Michaels – Canadian Football League						

Use Name – Tackles	Pos.	Hgt	Wgt	Age	Int	Pts
Alf Bauman (from CHI-AAFC)	T	6'2"	218	27		
T.G. Campion	T	6'2"	235	26		
Otis Douglas	T	6'1"	224	35		
Jim Kekeris	T	6'1"	275	23		2
(Missed 1 Field Goal Attempt, 2 PAT in 3 attempts)						
Jay MacDowell	T	6'2"	220	28		
Vic Sears	T	6'3"	230	29		
(1 punt return for 6 yds.)						
Don Talcott	T	6'2"	235	25		
Al Wistert	T	6'1"	215	26		

Use Name – Guards	Pos.	Hgt	Wgt	Age	Int	Pts
Al Baisi	G	6'	225	29		
Bucko Kilroy	G	6'2"	245	26		
Duke Maronic	G	5'9"	205	26		
Don Weedon	G	5'11"	220	26		
John Wyhonic	G	6'	210	27		

With Steve Van Buren running over defenders for a record 1,008 yards rushing and Tommy Thompson making his infrequent passes count for good yardage, the Philadelphia offense kept the Eagles flying high in the Eastern Division. Greasy Neale's T-formation attack jelled in fine fashion, with the addition of end Pete Pihos adding the finishing touch. A fullback in college, Pihos blocked like an avalanche, hugged every pass like a falling baby, and joined Jack Ferrante in the toughest end combination in the league. Enemy runners found it hard to move against a line of Pihos, Ferrante, Vic Sears, annual All-Pro Al Wistert, Vic Lindskog, and Bucko Kilroy, with linebackers Alex Wojciechowicz and Joe Muha around to erase any mistakes.

PITTSBURGH STEELERS 8-4-0 Jock Sutherland

Scores of Each Game		
17	DETROIT	10
7	LOS ANGELES	48
26	Washington	27
30	Boston	14
35	PHILADELPHIA	24
38	New York	21
18	Green Bay	17
21	WASHINGTON	14
24	NEW YORK	7
7	Chic. Bears	49
0	Philadelphia	21
17	BOSTON	7
	EAST playoff	
0	PHILADELPHIA	21

Use Name	Pos.	Hgt	Wgt	Age	Int	Pts
Chuck Cherundolo	C-LB	6'1"	215	31		
Bryant Meeks	C-LB	6'2"	190	21		
Frank Sinkovitz	C-LB	6'1"	217	24	3	6
Tony Bova	OE-DE	6'1"	190	30		2
(1 kickoff return for 16 yds.)						
Sam Gray	DE	6'	194	27		
Al Drulis	BB-LB	5'10"	188	26		

Use Name – Tackles	Pos.	Hgt	Wgt	Age	Int	Pts
Ralph Calacagri	T	6'3"	235	25		2
Bill Hornick	T	6'1"	207	28		
Joe Repko	T	6'	230	26		6
Paul Stenn	T	6'2"	240	29		
Jack Wiley	T	5'11"	206	26		
Frank Wydo	T	6'4"	208	23		

Use Name – Guards	Pos.	Hgt	Wgt	Age	Int	Pts
Bill Creyar	G-LB	5'11"	190	22		
John Mastrangelo	G	6'1"	215	21		6
Bill Moore	G	5'11"	215	24		
John Perko	G-LB	6'1"	207	31		
Nick Skorich	G-LB	5'9"	192	26		

When Bill Dudley made it definite that he was not returning, owner Art Rooney reluctantly traded him to Detroit. Although he considered Dudley "the best all-around ballplayer I've ever seen," Rooney still was confident that coach Jock Sutherland could mold the remaining players into a winning team. Stressing teamwork on a club with no superstars, Sutherland spurred the anonymous Steelers into a first-place tie with the Eagles. The two clubs had split their meetings during the season, but the Steelers headed into the Eastern playoff with tailback Johnny Clement shelved with injuries, and the Eagles held the nameless Steelers pointless via a 21-0 score.

BOSTON YANKS 4-7-1 Clipper Smith

Scores of Each Game		
7	NEW YORK	7
7	DETROIT	21
14	PITTSBURGH	30
14	New York	0
7	Chic. Cards	27
24	CHIC. BEARS	28
27	Los Angeles	16
0	Philadelphia	32
21	PHILADELPHIA	14
27	WASHINGTON	24
7	Pittsburgh	17
13	Washington	40

Use Name	Pos.	Hgt	Wgt	Age	Int	Pts
Joe Domnanovich	C-LB	6'1"	210	28	1	
Bill Godwin	C-LB	6'3"	236	28	2	
Joe Sabasteanski	C-LB	6'	205	26	1	
Sam Goldman	DE-OE	6'3"	224	30		
(1 reception for 9 yds.)						
Ed Fiorentino	DE	6'1"	210	25		
Bob Long	HB-DB	5'10"	190	25		

Use Name – Tackles	Pos.	Hgt	Wgt	Age	Int	Pts
Rocco Canale	T	5'11"	253	30		
Tom Dean	T	6'2"	247	23		
Tom Rodgers	T	6'	248	24		
Alex Sidorik	T	6'	255	25		
Carroll Vogelaar	T	6'3"	238	27		

Use Name – Guards	Pos.	Hgt	Wgt	Age	Int	Pts
John Badaczewski	G	6'1"	235	25		
Fritz Barzilauskas	G	6'1..	228	26		
Bill Collins	G	5'8"	195	25		
Bill Kennedy	G	5'11"	205	28		
Bob McClure	G	6'1"	224	23		
(1 kickoff return for 12 yds.)						
Jim Wright	G	6'1"	222	26		
Joe Zeno	G	5'10"	238	28		

The Yanks welcomed new coach Clipper Smith to Boston by winning a new high of four games, but few fans paid their way in to see the resurgence. Of the victories, a 14-0 shutout over New York and a 21-14 upset of the Philadelphia Eagles especially would have caused the fans to buzz if there had been any fans. The Yanks even boasted of a statistical leader, as Frank Seno tied for top honors in interceptions. The new coach revamped his offense, trading quarterback Paul Governali to the Giants for fullback Bill Paschal and installing second-year man Boley Dancewicz as signal-caller—all to no avail, either on the field or at the box office.

WASHINGTON REDSKINS 4-8-0 Turk Edwards

Scores of Each Game		
42	Philadelphia	45
27	PITTSBURGH	26
28	NEW YORK	20
10	Green Bay	27
20	CHIC. BEARS	56
14	PHILADELPHIA	38
14	Pittsburgh	21
21	Detroit	38
45	CHIC. CARDS	21
24	Boston	27
10	New York	35
40	BOSTON	13

Use Name	Pos.	Hgt	Wgt	Age	Int	Pts
Ki Aldrich	C-G-LB	6'	215	31	2	
Al DeMao	C-LB	6'2"	211	27	2	
Jack Sommers	C-LB	6'3"	232	28		
(Missed 1 field goal attempt)						
Harvey Jones	HB-DB	6'	175	26		
(1 kickoff return for 30 yds.)						

Use Name – Tackles	Pos.	Hgt	Wgt	Age	Int	Pts
John Adams	T	6'7"	254	27		
Don Avery	T	6'4"	258	26		
(2 kickoff returns for 24 yds.)						
Don Deeks (from BOS)	T	6'4"	232	24		
John Sanchez (from CHI-AAFC and DET)	T	6'3"	234	26	1	
Ernie Williamson	T	6'4"	235	24		
(1 kickoff return for 28 yds.)						

Use Name – Guards	Pos.	Hgt	Wgt	Age	Int	Pts
Fred Boensch	G-LB	6'4"	225	27	1	
Mike Garzoni	G	5'11"	213	23		
Bill Gray	G	5'11"	210	24		
Hank Harris	G	6'	260	24		
Leo Nobile	G-LB	5'10"	210	25		
John Steber	G	6'	220	24		

The tone of the season was set on opening day when the Skins lost a 45-42 shootout with the Eagles. Scoring points came easy for the Skins; it was stopping the other team that presented problems. At the helm of the attack was passer Sammy Baugh, improving with age in his eleventh pro season. Slingin' Sam was honored with a special day before a game against the strong Chicago Cardinals, and the Washington linemen pledged as their gift to keep the passer off the ground and safe from Cardinal pass-rushers. With the blockers coming through as promised, Baugh riddled the Cardinals for twenty-five completions in thirty-three attempts, good for 355 yards, six touchdown passes, and a 45-21 victory.

But even with top performances from Baugh, runner Jim Castiglia, and halfback Bob Nussbaumer, the Redskins could win only four games. They exploded for 40 or more points against the Eagles, Cardinals, and Boston Yanks, but tasted their own medicine against the Eagles and Bears. Sammy Baugh had hit his peak, but the Redskins in general were on a steady downhill slide.

NEW YORK GIANTS 2-8-2 Steve Owen

Scores of Each Game		
7	Boston	7
0	Philadelphia	33
20	Washington	28
0	BOSTON	14
21	PITTSBURGH	38
7	Detroit	35
21	PHILADELPHIA	41
7	Pittsburgh	24
24	GREEN BAY	24
35	CHIC. CARDS	31
35	WASHINGTON	10
10	Los Angeles	35

Use Name	Pos.	Hgt	Wgt	Age	Int	Pts
Lou DeFilippo	C-LB	6'1"	235	31		
Chet Gladchuk	C-DT	6'4"	255	30		
Lou Palazzi	C-LB	6'	200	26		
Bill Miklich	BB-LB	6'	208	26		
(1 reception for –5 yds.)						
Declared ineligible – Frankie Filchock, Merle Hapes						

Use Name – Tackles	Pos.	Hgt	Wgt	Age	Int	Pts
Frank Cope	T	6'2"	240	31		
Phil Ragazzo	T	6'	225	32		
Bill Schuler	T	6'	215	25		
Jim White	T	6'2"	228	26	1	6

Use Name – Guards	Pos.	Hgt	Wgt	Age	Int	Pts
Bob Dobelstein	G-LB	5'11"	212	25	1	6
Bill Hachten	G-LB	6'	210	22		
Kayo Lunday	G	6'3"	225	34		
George Tobin	G-LB	5'10"	205	26		
Leo Younce	G-LB	6'1"	210	30	3	4
(1 PAT in 1 att., 1 FG in 1 att., 1 punt for 43 yds.)						

With Frankie Filchock and Merle Hapes suspended by the league for not reporting a bribe offer to throw the 1946 championship game, the Giants headed into the season without a quarterback to run the attack. Not until Paul Governali was obtained from Boston in mid-season did the Giants come up with a major-league passer, but by then it was too late to salvage the season. New York lost seven games before it won a contest, dropping to the bottom of the East for keeps. Coach Steve Owen had expected the season to be a rebuilding year, with a slew of rookies on the roster, but he could not anticipate what fate had in store. The only bright notes were a 35-31 upset of the Cardinals and top-notch seasons by Len Younce and Frank Reagen.

TEAM TOTALS

OFFENSE	FIRST DOWNS: Tot	by Rsh	by Pas	by Pen	RUSHING: No.	Yds.	Avg Yds.	TD	PASSING: Att	Com	Comp Pct.	Yds.	Avg. Yds. Att.	Avg. Yds. Comp	TD	Int	Pct. Int.
PHILA.	203	109	68	26	474	1971	4.2	21	223	116	52.0	1761	7.9	15.2	18	19	8.5
PITT.	176	108	57	11	496	1948	3.9	15	209	86	41.1	1410	6.8	16.4	10	19	9.1
BOSTON	117	49	52	16	343	973	2.8	5	238	95	39.9	1661	6.9	17.5	15	27	11.3
WASH.	242	76	140	26	384	1343	3.5	11	416	231	55.5	3336	8.0	14.4	28	18	4.3
N.Y.	149	56	71	22	366	1195	3.3	7	293	123	42.0	1999	6.8	16.4	17	26	8.9

OFFENSE	PUNTING: No.	Avg. Yds.	PUNT RETURNS: No.	Yds.	Avg. Yds.	TD	KICKOFF RETURNS: No.	Yds.	Avg. Yds.	TD	INTERCEPTION RETURNS: No.	Yds.	Avg. Yds.	TD	PENALTIES: No.	Yds.	FUMBLES: No.	Lost	POINTS: Tot	PAT	FG Att	FG	Saf.
PHILA.	63	42.4	54	716	13.3	2	44	854	19.4	1	23	287	12.5	0	92	848	37	14	308	38	20	4	0
PITT.	68	41.1	40	583	14.6	0	50	975	19.5	0	18	397	22.1	4	60	527	28	16	240	30	14	6	3
BOSTON	93	40.6	25	378	15.1	1	52	1130	21.7	0	28	336	12.0	0	93	855	21	8	168	21	4	3	0
WASH.	52	40.3	36	445	12.4	0	66	1456	22.1	2	21	172	8.2	0	102	860	34	21	295	37	7	4	0
N.Y.	77	42.3	44	371	8.4	0	48	905	18.9	0	27	435	16.1	0	98	945	30	16	190	25	6	3	0

Use Name – Backs & Ends	Pos.	Age	Hgt	Wgt	Pts	Int	RUSHING No.	Yds	Avg	TD	PASSING Att	Comp	%	Yds	Yd/Att	TD	Int–%	RK	RECEIVING No.	Yds	Avg	TD	PUNTING No.	Avg	KICKING Pat	Att	%	FG	Att	%	PUNT RETURNS No.	Yds	Avg	TD	KICKOFF RETURNS No.	Yds	Avg	TD
PHILADELPHIA EAGLES																																						
Tommy Thompson	QB	31	6'1"	195	12		23	52	2.4	2	201	106	53	1680	8.4	16	15– 7	3																				
Bill Mackrides	QB	22	5'11"	187	6		7	−15	−2.1	0	17	8	47	58	3.4	2	3– 8																					
Allie Sherman	QB	24	5'11"	173	6		17	17	1.0	1	5	2	40	23	4.6	0	1– 20																					
Steve Van Buren	HB-DB	26	6'	205	84	1	217	1008	4.5	13									9	79	9	0													13	282	29	1
Bosh Pritchard	HB-DB	28	5'11"	160	24	1	69	294	4.3	1									16	315	20	3	2	32.0							24	271	11	0	8	148	19	0
Pat McHugh	HB-DB	27	5'11"	165	12	3	22	171	7.8	1									2	16	8	0									10	156	16	1	3	50	17	0
Ernie Steele	HB-DB	29	6'	182	6	6	26	138	5.3	1									4	62	16	0									11	183	17	0	2	17	9	0
Joe Muha	FB-LB	26	6'1"	205	15		27	107	4.0	2									1	10	10	0	53	43.5				1	5	20					3	55	18	0
Art Macioszczyk	FB-LB	26	5'9"	215			30	104	3.5	0									3	20	7	0													2	36	18	0
Gil Steinke	HB-DB	27	6'	172	6	1	16	50	3.1	0									4	90	23	1									6	69	12	0				
Noble Doss	HB-DB	27	6'	180		2	11	45	4.1	0									2	17	9	0																
Jack Hinkle	HB-DB	29	6'	185			1	2	2.0	0																												
Russ Craft	HB-DB	27	5'9"	175	6	1	5	−1	−0.2	0									2	66	33	1									1	5	5	0				
Ben Kish	FB-LB	30	6'	212		1	3	−1	−0.3	0									1	12	12	0	8	37.6											1	10	10	0
Pete Pihos	OE-DE	23	6'1"	210	48														23	382	17	7									1	26	26	1	1	17	17	0
Jack Ferrante	OE-DE	31	6'1"	200	24														18	341	19	4													7	99	14	0
Neill Armstrong	OE-DB	21	6'2"	188	12														17	197	12	2													3	38	13	0
Dick Humbert	OE-DB	28	6'1"	175		2													13	139	11	0																
Hal Prescott	OE-DB	26	6'2"	200		3													1	15	15	0																
Cliff Patton	G	23	6'2"	255	45																				36	40	90	3	14	21								
PITTSBURGH STEELERS																																						
Johnny Clement	TB	27	6'	188	24		129	670	5.2	4	123	52	42	1004	8.2	7	9– 7	8	1	6	6	0													1	24	24	0
Walt Slater	TB-DB	27	5'11"	187		4	46	167	3.6	0	39	18	46	215	5.5	1	5– 13														28	435	16	0	22	480	22	0
Gonzales Morales	TB-DB	24	6'	190		1	29	96	3.3	0	27	8	30	78	2.9	1	4– 15														6	88	15	0	5	113	23	0
Gene Hubka	TB-DB	23	5'10"	175			2	4	2.0	0																									3	59	20	0
Steve Lach	FB	27	6'2"	215	54		120	372	3.1	8	5	2	40	12	2.4	1	0– 0		11	77	7	1																
Bob Cifers	HB-DB	26	5'11"	198		1	87	356	4.1	0	3	2	67	28	9.3	0	0– 0		3	58	19	0	68	41.1											2	30	15	0
Tony Compagno	FB-DB	26	5'11"	197	30	4	34	126	3.7	2									9	190	21	1													2	32	16	0
Paul White	HB-DB	25	6'1"	183		2	22	85	3.9	0	3	1	33	21	7.0	0	0– 0		2	55	28	0									5	50	10	0	3	50	17	0
Bob Sullivan	HB-TB-DB	22	5'9"	187	12		21	61	2.9	1	9	3	33	52	5.8	0	1– 11		4	72	18	1									1	10	10	0	4	86	22	0
Paul Davis	FB-DB	22	6'1"	185			4	5	1.3	0																												
Joe Glamp	HB-DB	24	5'11"	185	48		1	2	2.0	0															30	31	97	6	14	43								
Bill Garnaas	WB	26	5'11"	183	12														5	144	29	2													1	17	17	0
Charlie Seabright	BB-LB	29	6'2"	201	6	3	1	4	4.0	0									7	16	2	0													3	23	8	0
Val Jansante	OE-DE	26	6'1"	190	32														35	599	17	5													2	42	21	0
Bob Davis	OE-DE	26	5'11"	190															5	145	29	0													1	3	3	0
Charlie Mehelich	OE-DE	25	6'1"	195															3	38	13	0																
Elbie Nickel	OE-DE	24	6'1"	188															1	10	10	0																
BOSTON YANKS																																						
Boley Dancewicz	QB	22	5'10"	190	6		47	145	3.1	1	169	66	39	1203	7.1	11	18– 11	11					1	40.0														
Howie Maley	QB-HB	25	5'11"	185			32	132	4.1	0	12	6	50	144	12.0	1	1– 8						92	40.6											1	23	23	0
Bill Paschal (from NY)	FB-LB	26	6'	205	6		78	263	3.4	1	1	0	0	0	0.0	0	0– 0		4	70	18	0									1	11	11	0	5	103	21	0
Frank Seno	HB-DB	26	6'	195	12	10	69	212	3.1	0									12	118	10	1									12	213	18	1	27	636	24	0
Frank Maznicki	HB-DB	27	5'9"	180	37	4	34	77	2.3	0	1	0	0	0	0.0	0	1–100		6	76	13	0			19	21	90	2	2	100	2	48	24	0				
Joe Golding	HB-DB	26	6'	180	18	5	26	71	2.7	1									6	52	9	2									7	63	9	0	9	173	19	0
Jim Mello	FB-LB	26	5'10"	190		1	33	62	1.9	0									2	26	13	0																
John Griggs	FB-LB	27	6'	205			27	52	1.9	0									1	1	1	0													1	19	19	0
Rudy Romboli	FB-LB	24	5'10"	215		1	23	50	2.2	0									4	30	8	0													3	64	21	0
John Poto	HB-DB	21	5'10"	197	6		6	27	4.5	1																					1	12	12	0	4	99	25	0
Mike Micka	HB-DB	26	6'	193		2	1	−4	−4.0	0									2	11	6	0																
Walt Williams	HB-DB	28	6'1"	192							1	0	0	0	0.0	0	1–100		1	2	2	0									1	14	14	0				
Hal Crisler	OE-DE	23	6'4"	215	12														25	363	15	2																
Don Currivan	OE-DB	26	6'	192	60	1													24	782	33	9																
Bill Chipley	OE-DB	27	6'3"	200	6		1	3	3.0	0									5	105	21	1																
Nick Scollard	OE-DE	27	6'4"	218	5														2	18	9	0			2	2	100	1	4	25								
WASHINGTON REDSKINS																																						
Sammy Baugh	QB	33	6'2"	182	12		25	47	1.9	2	354	210	59	2938	8.3	25	15– 4	1					35	43.7														
Jim Youel	QB	25	6'	174	6		10	44	4.4	1	62	21	34	398	6.4	3	3– 5						2	17.5														
Jim Castiglia (from BAL-AAFC)	FB	28	5'11"	210	30		104	426	4.2	5									11	88	8	0													1	10	10	0
Sal Rosato	FB-LB	29	6'1"	236	6		74	297	4.0	0									7	107	15	1													2	36	18	0
Eddie Saenz	HB-DB	24	5'11"	168	36		51	143	2.8	0									34	598	18	4									24	308	13	0	29	797	27	2
Bob Nussbaumer	HB-DB	23	5'11"	170	24	1	43	136	3.2	0									47	597	13	4									2	15	8	0	8	154	19	0
Dick Poillon	HB-DB	27	6'	197	85	2	28	104	3.7	2									20	250	13	4	15	35.5	37	41	90	4	6	67	3	37	12	0	4	23	6	0
Jack Jenkins	FB-LB	27	6'1"	202		1	16	54	3.4	0									5	96	19	0																
Dick Todd	HB-DB	32	5'11"	173		4	10	45	4.5	0									4	84	21	0									4	48	12	0	19	189	21	0
Tom Farmer	HB-DB	26	5'11"	183	6	6	15	29	1.9	1									8	137	17	0													4	118	30	0
Tommy Mont	HB-DB	25	6'	192		1	1	7	7.0	0									2	14	7	0									3	37	12	0				
Ralph Ruthstrom	FB-LB	26	6'5"	215			2	5	2.5	0																									1	5	5	0
George Wilde	HB-DB	24	6'1"	193	6		4	−1	−0.2	0									6	45	8	1													1	19	19	0
Vince Pacewic	HB-DB	25	6'1"	205															5	42	8	0																
Hugh Taylor	OE	24	6'4"	197	36		1	7	7.0	0									26	511	20	6																
Paul McKee	OE-DE	24	6'3"	214	12														16	242	15	2																
Joe Duckworth	OE-DE	26	6'2"	220	18														14	250	18	3																
Joe Tereshinski	OE-DE	23	6'2"	205	6														10	76	8	1																
Doug Turley	OE-DE	28	6'2"	215	6														6	95	16	1													1	10	10	0
John Lookabaugh	OE-DE	27	6'4"	220	6														6	78	13	1																
Jim Peebles	OE-DE	27	6'4"	232															4	26	7	0						0	1	0					1	13	13	0
NEW YORK GIANTS																																						
Paul Governali (from BOS)	QB	26	5'11"	194	12		40	151	3.8	2	252	108	43	1775	7.0	17	22– 9	7					4	35.5														
Jerry Niles	QB	27	6'1"	195			8	24	3.0	0	57	19	33	269	4.7	1	7– 12																		1	12	12	0
Frank Reagan	QB-DB	28	5'11"	180		10	14	22	1.6	0	25	12	48	191	7.6	1	2– 8						61	42.8							27	182	17	0	2	35	18	0
Art Faircloth	QB-DB	27	6'	190			10	9	0.9	0	5	3	60	30	6.0	1	0– 0						4	39.7											2	62	31	0
Choo-Choo Roberts	FB	23	5'11"	188	6		86	296	3.5	1									4	58	15	0													8	141	18	0
Jim Blumenstock	FB-DB	28	5'11"	190	12		54	168	3.1	2	8	4	50	48	6.0	0	1– 13		4	15	4	0									1	8	8	0	2	77	39	0
Gordon Paschka	FB-LB	27	6'	220	12		48	143	3.0	2									1	−6	−6	0													1	20	20	0
George Cheverko	WB-DB	26	6'1"	195	18	3	19	63	3.3	0									17	300	18	3									5	88	18	0	7	135	19	0
Howie Livingston	WB-DB	25	6'1"	190	18	4	19	87	4.6	0									12	273	23	3													9	203	23	0
George Franck	WB-DB	28	6'	180	18	1	24	93	3.9	0									10	265	27	3	7	42.4							6	60	10	0	7	121	17	0
Dave Brown	WB-DB	28	5'11"	190			6	5	0.8	0									1	5	5	0									4	22	6	0	1	30	30	0
Joe Sulatis	BB-LB-DE	26	6'2"	210		1													7	53	8	0													2	23	12	0
John Cannady	BB-LB	23	6'2"	220		1	1	14	14.0	0									1	3	3	0																
Duke Iverson	BB-LB	27	6'2"	200															1	11	11	0													1	16	16	0
Ray Poole	OE-DE	25	6'2"	215	24	1													24	395	17	4																
Frank Liebel	OE-DE	27	6'1"	220	6														16	258	16	1													1	12	12	0
Tex Coulter	OE-T	22	6'4"	262	6														8	107	13	1													2	16	8	0
Vic Carroll	OE-T	34	6'4"	240	12	1													7	123	18	2																
Jack Mead	OE-DE	25	6'3"	210															6	91	15	0																
Jim Lee Howell	OE-DE	32	6'6"	220															3	41	14	0																
Greg Browning	OE	25	6'	190															1	12	12	0																
Ken Strong	K	41	6'	210	30																				24	25	96	2	5	40								

TEAM TOTALS

DEFENSE	FIRST DOWNS: Tot	by Rsh	by Pas	by Pen	RUSHING: No.	Yds.	Avg. Yds.	TD	PASSING: Att.	Com	Comp. Pct.	Yds.	Avg. Yds. Att.	Avg. Yds. Comp	TD	Int.	Pct. Int.	PUNTING: No.	Avg. Yds.	PUNT RETURNS: No.	Yds.	Avg. Yds.	TD	KICKOFF RETURNS: No.	Yds.	Avg. Yds.	TD	INTERCEPTION RETURNS: No.	Yds.	Avg. Yds.	TD	PENALTIES: No.	Yds.	FUMBLES: No.	Lost	POINTS: Tot	PAT	FG Att	FG	Saf.	DEFENSE
PHILA.	188	75	86	27	380	1329	3.5	13	334	152	45.5	2410	7.2	16.0	19	23	6.9	70	38.4	32	350	10.9	0	49	989	20.2	1	19	236	12.4	2	110	1017	28	13	242	32	10	2	0	PHILA.
PITT.	170	88	68	14	403	1622	4.0	11	244	98	40.2	1847	7.6	18.8	20	18	7.4	70	42.5	30	330	11.0	0	43	892	20.7	0	19	287	15.1	0	78	622	34	14	259	34	7	5	0	PITT.
BOSTON	219	112	94	13	493	2020	4.1	18	303	158	52.1	2042	6.7	12.9	17	28	9.2	61	41.8	63	913	14.5	1	32	562	17.6	0	27	236	8.7	1	99	1030	34	17	256	29	11	3	1	BOSTON
WASH.	196	80	88	28	409	1564	3.8	18	282	146	51.8	2422	8.6	16.6	26	21	7.5	60	40.8	38	512	13.5	0	51	1130	22.2	1	18	428	23.8	3	87	745	24	8	367	47	17	8	1	WASH.
N.Y.	190	101	75	14	457	1836	4.0	18	276	121	43.8	2015	7.3	16.6	19	27	9.8	70	41.8	50	719	14.4	1	47	859	18.3	1	26	350	13.5	2	95	861	33	12	309	39	17	8	0	N.Y.

CHICAGO CARDINALS 9-3-0 Jimmy Conzelman

Scores of Each Game		
45	DETROIT	21
31	CHIC. BEARS	7
14	Green Bay	10
7	Los Angeles	27
27	BOSTON	7
17	LOS ANGELES	10
17	Detroit	7
21	GREEN BAY	20
21	Washington	45
31	New York	35
45	Philadelphia	21
30	Chic. Bears	21

Use Name	Pos.	Hgt	Wgt	Age	Int	Pts
Vince Banonis	C-LB	6'1"	230	25	3	6
Bill Blackburn	C-LB	6'6"	225	25	3	
(1 punt for 19 yds.)						
Bill Campbell	LB	6'	195	27		
Clarence Esser	DE-T	6'	190	23		
Pop Ivy	DE	6'3"	210	31		
(Missed 1 field goal attempt)						
Joe Parker	DE	6'	220	24		

Use Name – Tackles	Pos.	Hgt	Wgt	Age	Int	Pts
Chet Bulger	T	6'3"	238	29		
Joe Coomer	T	6'6"	287	28		
Caleb Martin	T	6'4"	245	24		
Stan Mauldin	T	6'2"	225	27	1	
Dick Plasman	T-DE	6'3"	238	33		
Walt Szot	T	6'1"	225	28		
Bob Zimny	T	6'1"	235	26		

Use Name – Guards	Pos.	Hgt	Wgt	Age	Int	Pts
Plato Andros	G	6'	235	26		
Ray Apolskis	G-LB	5'11"	210	28		
Lloyd Arms	G	6'1"	215	28		
Jake Colhover	G	6'1"	210	25		
(2 kickoff returns for 16 yds.)						
Ham Nichols	G-LB	5'11"	200	23	1	
Buster Ramsey	G-LB	6'1"	220	27	4	

Owner Charles Bidwill had slowly built up a championship team, but he never lived to see it. He died on April 19, just as the Cardinals were on the verge of climbing to the top of the NFL mountain. Another tragedy was the death of rookie Jeff Burkett in a plane crash on October 24. Just before his death, Bidwill signed rookie halfback Charley Trippi, the final member of the Dream Backfield with Paul Christman, Pat Harder, and Elmer Angsman. But even with a solid line, the Cardinals could not shake the Bears until beating them 30-21 in the season's finale.

CHICAGO BEARS 8-4-0 George Halas

Scores of Each Game		
20	Green Bay	29
7	Chic. Cards	31
40	PHILADELPHIA	7
33	DETROIT	24
56	Washington	20
28	Boston	24
20	GREEN BAY	17
41	Los Angeles	31
49	PITTSBURGH	7
34	Detroit	14
14	LOS ANGELES	17
21	CHIC. CARDS	30

Use Name	Pos.	Hgt	Wgt	Age	Int	Pts
Stu Clarkson	C-LB	6'2"	215	28	2	
Thurman Garrett	C-G	6'3"	275	23	1	
(Missed 1 field goal attempt)						
Bulldog Turner	C-LB	6'1"	235	28	2	6
Allen Smith	DE	6'2"	215	24		
(2 kickoff returns for 18 yds.)						
Russ Reader	DB	6'	185	28		

Use Name – Tackles	Pos.	Hgt	Wgt	Age	Int	Pts
Fred Davis	T	6'3"	245	29		
Ed Ecker	T	6'7"	290	24		
Fred Hartman	T	6'1"	235	27	1	6
Ed Kolman	T	6'2"	235	29		
Walt Stickel	T	6'3"	250	25		

Use Name – Guards	Pos.	Hgt	Wgt	Age	Int	Pts
Ray Bray	G	6'	240	30		
Chuck Drulis	G-LB	5'10"	215	29	1	
Bill Johnson	G-LB	6'	210	26		
Bill Milner	G-LB	6'1"	212	23	1	
Pat Preston	G-LB	6'2"	215	24		

The Bears got off to a sluggish start with a 29-20 loss to Green Bay, then hit rock bottom with a 31-7 humiliation at the hands of the rising Cardinals. Staring prospects for a dismal season straight in the face, George Halas rallied his defending champs and drove them back into the Western Division race. Going into the final game with the Cardinals, both Chicago clubs were tied for the division lead. On the first play after the opening kickoff, Cardinal quarterback Paul Christman launched an 80-yard touchdown pass to speedy halfback Babe Dimancheff, and the Bears spent the rest of the afternoon trying to catch up. They never did.

Even with the final disappointment, the Bears boasted of several outstanding individual performances. Sid Luckman, Ken Kavanaugh, and Fred Davis all won All-Pro honors, while second-year end Jim Keane led the league in receiving. Center Bulldog Turner won applause for his 96-yard return of an interception in which he dodged and weaved more like a 180-pound halfback than a 235-pound center.

GREEN BAY PACKERS 6-5-1 Curly Lambeau

Scores of Each Game		
29	CHIC. BEARS	20
17	LOS ANGELES	14
10	CHIC. CARDS	14
27	WASHINGTON	10
34	DETROIT	17
17	PITTSBURGH	18
17	Chic. Bears	20
20	Chic. Cards	21
24	New York	24
30	Los Angeles	10
35	Detroit	14
14	Philadelphia	28

Use Name	Pos.	Hgt	Wgt	Age	Int	Pts
Charley Brock	C-LB	6'2"	210	31	2	
Bob Flowers	C-LB	6'1"	210	30	1	
Les Gatewood	C-LB	6'2"	200	26		
John Kovatch	DE	6'3"	200	27		
Bob Skoglund	DE	6'1"	198	22		
Don Wells	DE	6'2"	200	25		
Bob McDougal	FB-LB	6'2"	205	26		

Use Name – Tackles	Pos.	Hgt	Wgt	Age	Int	Pts
Tiny Croft	T	6'3"	280	26		
Paul Lipscomb	T	6'5"	245	24		
Urban Odson	T	6'3"	250	28		
Baby Ray	T	6'6"	250	32		

Use Name – Guards	Pos.	Hgt	Wgt	Age	Int	Pts
Ed Bell	G	6'1"	233	25		
Ray Clemons	G	5'10"	220	26		
Ralph Davis	G	5'11"	205	25		
Aldo Forte	G	6'	215	29		
Ed Neal	G-T	6'4"	290	29		6
Damon Tassos	G	6'1"	225	23		
Dick Wildung	G	6'	220	25		2

Curly Lambeau installed the T formation at Green Bay and developed a respectable passing attack; but quarterback Jack Jacobs was no Cecil Isbell, and ends Nolan Luhn and Clyde Goodnight were no Don Hutsons. What Lambeau did have was a short-passing offense which moved the ball sporadically but couldn't break games open like the old Packer air combinations. Tony Canadeo and Walt Schlinkman kept the running game healthy, moving behind a line which stayed strong despite the retirement of Bill Lee and Russ Letlow. The Packers were a solid if unspectacular team, with only a cruel streak of bad luck killing their title hopes, as they lost 18-17 to Pittsburgh, 20-17 to the Bears, and 21-20 to the Cardinals.

LOS ANGELES RAMS Bob Snyder 6-6-0

Scores of Each Game		
48	Pittsburgh	7
14	Green Bay	17
27	Detroit	13
27	CHIC. CARDS	7
7	Philadelphia	14
10	Chic. Cards	17
16	BOSTON	27
21	CHIC. BEARS	41
28	DETROIT	17
10	GREEN BAY	30
17	Chic. Bears	14
34	NEW YORK	10

Use Name	Pos.	Hgt	Wgt	Age	Int	Pts
Jack Martin	C-LB	6'3"	235	25	1	
Fred Naumetz	C-LB	6'1"	223	25	1	
Woody Strode – Canadian Football League						

Use Name – Tackles	Pos.	Hgt	Wgt	Age	Int	Pts
Gil Bouley	T	6'2"	238	26		6
(1 reception for 15 yds., 1 punt return for 24 yds.)						
Ed Champagne	T	6'3"	225	25		
Dick Huffman	T	6'2"	250	24		6
Clyde Johnson	T	6'6"	273	30		
Elbie Schultz	T	6'4"	274	29		
Bill Smyth	T-OE	6'3"	245	25		
(3 receptions for 26 yds.)						

Use Name – Guards	Pos.	Hgt	Wgt	Age	Int	Pts
Bob David	G-LB	6'	222	25		
Hal Dean	G-LB	6'	205	24		
Roger Eason	G	6'2"	230	29		
Jack Finlay	G-LB	6'1"	216	26		
Mike Lazetich	G-LB	6'1"	212	26		
Riley Matheson	G-LB	6'2"	210	32	1	

After the season ended, Rams fans could talk about Kenny Washington's 92-yard run against the Cardinals on November 2. Or else they could remember Bob Waterfield's 86-yard punt in the October 5 game with Green Bay. Unfortunately, the Rams lost both games, and the fans preferred not to discuss the team's mediocre season record.

The Rams fluctuated from one extreme to another like an excited Geiger counter. They impressed all observers with a 48-7 victory over Pittsburgh, a 27-7 upset of the title-bound Cardinals, and a 17-14 late-season triumph over the Bears. But mixed in with these gems were a 27-16 loss to the anemic Boston Yanks, a 41-21 trouncing at the hands of the Bears, and a 30-10 defeat by the Packers.

New head coach Bob Snyder directed an explosive squad which just as often laid a dud as detonated. Bob Waterfield kept winging the ball to steady Jim Benton, Kenny Washington developed into a dangerous runner, Tommy Harmon starred as a defensive back, 250-pound tackle Dick Huffman ate enemy ball carriers alive, and the rest of the squad listed lots of top-drawer players. Still, the Rams stumbled, bumbled, and butted no one in the end.

DETROIT LIONS Gus Dorais 3-9-0

Scores of Each Game		
10	Pittsburgh	17
21	Chic. Cards	45
21	Boston	7
13	LOS ANGELES	27
24	Chic. Bears	33
17	Green Bay	34
35	NEW YORK	7
7	CHIC. CARDS	17
38	WASHINGTON	21
17	Los Angeles	28
14	CHIC. BEARS	34
14	GREEN BAY	35

Use Name	Pos.	Hgt	Wgt	Age	Int	Pts
Reed Nelson	C-LB	6'	230	26		
Merv Pregulman	C-LB	6'3"	215	25	2	
(1 punt return for 9 yds.)						
Dick Stovall	C-LB	6'	208	23	1	
Frank Szymanski	C-LB	6'	225	24		

Use Name – Tackles	Pos.	Hgt	Wgt	Age	Int	Pts
Jack Dugger	T	6'3"	240	24	1	
Leon Fichman	T	6'1"	215	26		
George Hekkers (from BAL-AAFC)	T	6'4"	225	24		
Mitch Olenski	T	6'3"	225	27		
Ed Stacco	T	6'2"	250	22		
Russ Thomas	T	6'3"	235	23		

Use Name – Guards	Pos.	Hgt	Wgt	Age	Int	Pts
Stan Batinski	G	5'10"	215	30		
Ben Chase	G	6'3"	235	24		
Chuck DeShane	G	6'1"	218	28		
Bob Ivory	G	6'2"	212	23		
Elmer Jones	G	6'	225	27		
Les Lear	G	5'11"	227	29		
Floyd Rhea	G					
Walt Vezmer	G	5'11"	235	22		
Bill Ward (from WAS)	G	6'	230	26		

When Steeler tailback Bill Dudley announced his retirement, the Lions traded two players and a first draft choice to Pittsburgh for rights to talk to the star player. During the spring, Lion coach Gus Dorais visited Dudley at the University of Virginia, where he was coaching, and offered him a three-year contract at $20,000 per year. Dudley could not turn down a pact which made him the highest paid pro player. The other Lion players at first were apprehensive, hearing rumors that the back was arrogant and pushy. But from the first day of training, Dudley kept his mouth shut and put out 100 percent effort, and the Lion players elected him team captain as a sign of their respect. Unfortunately, this did not help the defense. In six games against the Cardinals, Bears, and Packers, the Lions allowed an average of 33 points per game.

TEAM TOTALS

OFFENSE	First Downs: Tot	by Rsh	by Pas	by Pen	Rushing: No.	Yds.	Avg Yds.	TD	Passing: Att	Com	Comp Pct.	Yds.	Avg. Yds. Att.	Avg. Yds. Comp	TD	Int	Pct. Int.	Punting: No.	Avg. Yds.
CHIC. C.	241	101	110	30	468	1735	3.7	20	340	160	47.1	2580	7.6	16.1	18	25	7.4	56	40.8
CHIC. B.	263	122	123	18	448	1959	4.4	21	378	194	51.3	3093	8.2	15.9	29	35	9.3	38	41.5
G.B.	206	105	82	19	510	2149	4.2	14	253	112	44.3	1724	6.8	15.4	17	19	7.5	65	43.6
L.A.	206	112	82	19	459	2171	4.7	15	293	123	42.0	1660	5.7	13.5	13	28	9.6	72	40.1
DET.	189	77	93	19	333	1234	3.7	6	348	167	48.0	2446	7.1	14.7	23	34	9.8	65	43.0

OFFENSE	Punt Returns: No.	Yds.	Avg. Yds.	TD	Kickoff Returns: No.	Yds.	Avg. Yds.	TD	Interception Returns: No.	Yds.	Avg. Yds.	TD	Penalties: No.	Yds.	Fumbles: No.	Lost	Points: Tot	PAT	FG Att	FG	Saf.	OFFENSE
CHIC. C.	27	370	13.7	0	43	716	16.7	0	27	438	16.2	2	89	688	32	16	306	39	10	7	0	CHIC. C.
CHIC. B.	39	495	12.7	0	41	872	21.3	0	27	491	18.2	3	107	1020	34	23	363	45	1	0	0	CHIC. B
G.B.	45	563	12.5	0	42	874	20.8	0	30	428	14.3	1	104	1019	24	13	274	33	29	13	2	G.B.
L.A.	44	640	14.5	2	36	727	20.2	0	24	288	12.0	1	87	800	33	20	259	31	17	8	0	L.A.
DET.	34	452	13.3	1	50	926	18.5	0	25	226	9.0	1	78	704	30	18	231	30	11	5	0	DET.

Use Name – Backs & Ends	Pos.	Age	Hgt	Wgt	Pts	Int	RUSHING				PASSING								RECEIVING				PUNTING		KICKING						PUNT RETURNS				KICKOFF RETURNS			
							No.	Yds	Avg	TD	Att	Comp	%	Yds	Yd/Att	TD	Int–%	RK	No.	Yds	Avg	TD	No.	Avg	Pat	Att	%	FG	Att	%	No.	Yds	Avg	TD	No.	Yds	Avg	TD
CHICAGO CARDINALS																																					
Paul Christman	QB	29	6'	208	12		8	11	1.4	2	301	138	46	2191	7.3	17	22-7	4																			
Ray Mallouf	QB	29	5'11"	180			5	13	2.6	0	36	21	58	340	9.4	1	2-6					43	39.9														
Elmer Angsman	HB	21	5'11"	205	48		110	412	3.7	7										5	138	28	1													2	17	9	0
Charlie Trippi	HB-DB	24	6'	190	18	1	83	401	4.8	2	2	1	50	49	24.5	0	1-50		23	240	10	0									8	141	18	0	15	321	21	0
Pat Harder	FB-LB	25	5'11"	205	102		113	371	3.3	7									9	78	9	0			39	40	98	7	10	70								
Marshall Goldberg	HB-FB-DB	29	5'11"	190			51	155	3.0	0									7	52	7	0	proper								1	21	21	0				
Bill deCorrevont	HB-DB	28	6'	190	6	1	29	149	5.1	1									4	52	13	0									8	61	8	0	7	102	15	0
Babe Dimancheff	HB	25	5'11"	175	24		30	116	3.9	0									22	438	20	4													10	180	18	0
Red Cochran	FB-DB	25	6'	200	12	8	14	36	2.6	1	1	0	0	0	0.0	0	0-0		1	7	7	1	1	25.0							10	147	15	0	4	46	12	0
Vic Schwall	HB	23	5'8"	190			12	33	2.8	0																									1	20	20	0
Charlie Smith	HB-DB	24	5'11"	170		1	9	23	2.6	0									1	-6	-6	0													1	14	14	0
Walt Rankin	FB-LB	29	5'11"	202			3	4	1.3	0																												
Mal Kutner	OE-DB	26	6'2"	195	48	3													43	944	22	7																
Bill Dewell	OE-DE	30	6'4"	210	24														42	576	14	4																
Jeff Burkett – died Oct. 24	OE-DB	26	6'1"	190	6	1	1	11	11.0	0									2	44	22	1	11	47.4														
Jack Doolan	OE-DB	28	6'1"	190																1	17	17	0																
CHICAGO BEARS																																					
Sid Luckman	QB	30	6'	197	7		10	86	8.6	1	323	176	54	2712	8.4	24	31-10	2	1	15	15	0	5	35.4	1	1	100											
Nick Sacrinty	QB-DB	23	5'11"	185		1	4	4	1.0	0	48	15	31	299	6.2	5	3-6																					
Tom Farris	QB-DB	26	6'1"	185		1	1	-3	-3.0	0	2	0	0	0	0.0	0	0-0																					
Joe Osmanski	FB-LB	28	6'2"	220	6		64	328	5.4	1									7	134	19	0																
Mike Holovak	FB-LB	27	6'1"	215	6		51	281	5.5	1									7	119	17	0													2	47	24	0
Don Kindt	HB-DB	21	6'1"	200	12	3	61	266	4.4	2									2	24	12	0													10	220	22	0
George Gulyanics	HB-DB	26	6'	195	24	2	35	212	6.1	4	2	1	50	55	27.5	0	1-50		3	22	7	0	23	44.8							1	7	7	0	5	124	25	0
George McAfee	HB-DB	29	6'	175	24	1	63	209	3.3	3									32	490	15	1	2	35.5							18	261	15	0	1	23	23	0
Bob Fenimore	HB-DB	21	6'1"	195	18	2	53	189	3.8	1	3	2	67	27	9.0	0	0-0		15	219	15	2									2	16	8	0				
Frank Minini	HB-DB	23	6'1"	215	12	1	26	132	5.1	2									2	23	12	0													11	261	24	0
Hugh Gallarneau	HB-DB	30	6'	190	36	1	39	89	2.3	6									7	56	8	0													2	43	22	0
Ray McLean	HB-DB	31	5'10"	165	50	1	10	58	5.8	0									11	125	11	1			44	52	85	0	1	0	5	58	12	0	2	35	18	0
Noah Mullins	HB-DB	28	5'11"	185		6	9	55	6.1	0									1	4	4	0									13	153	12	0				
Bill Osmanski	FB	30	5'11"	195			10	37	3.7	0																									3	67	22	0
Eddie Allen	FB-LB	29	6'1"	200			12	16	1.3	0													8	37.4														
Jim Keane	OE-DE	23	6'4"	220	60														64	910	14	10																
Ken Kavanaugh	OE-DE	30	6'3"	210	78														32	818	26	13																
Ed Sprinkle	OE-DE	23	6'1"	207																4	43	11	0																
Ed Cifers	OE-DE	31	6'2"	228	12	1													3	48	16	1													2	33	17	0
Mike Jarmoluk	OE-T	24	6'5"	250	6														2	33	17	1																
Jack Matheson	OE-DE	27	6'2"	235																1	8	8	0																
GREEN BAY PACKERS																																					
Jack Jacobs	QB-DB	28	6'1"	190	6	4	18	64	3.6	1	242	108	45	1615	6.7	16	17-7	5					57	43.5							1	4	4	0				
Irv Comp	QB-DB	28	6'2"	205		5	5	46	9.2	0	1	0	0	0	0.0	0	1-100														1	0	0	0				
Tony Canadeo	HB-DB	28	5'11"	190	12		103	464	4.5	2	8	3	38	101	12.6	1	1-13														10	111	11	0	15	312	21	0
Walt Schlinkman	FB	25	5'8"	190	12		115	439	3.8	2									2	-6	-3	0																
Bruce Smith	HB-DB	27	6'	197	14	2	47	288	6.1	1									4	50	13	1									1	22	22	0	3	61	20	0
Ted Fritsch	FB-LB	26	5'10"	210	56	1	68	247	3.6	6															2	2	100	6	13	46					5	100	20	0
Jim Gillette	HB-DB	29	6'1"	185	6		50	207	4.1	0									12	224	19	1									11	168	15	0	3	66	22	0
Ed Cody	FB-DB	24	5'10"	190	12		56	263	4.7	2									1	2	2	0									2	30	15	0	10	269	27	0
Bob Forte	HB-DB	25	6'	195	18	8	29	80	2.4	0	2	1	50	8	4.0	0	0-0		7	80	11	2									1	15	15	0	2	28	14	0
Herm Rohrig	HB-DB	29	5'8"	190		5	7	22	3.1	0																					18	213	12	0	1	15	15	0
Ken Keuper	HB-DB	29	6'	209		2	6	14	2.3	0									2	37	19	0																
Tex McKay	HB	27	6'	195	1		3	11	3.7	0													8	43.8	1	1	100										
Ward Cuff	HB-DB	34	6'1"	192	51		1	7	7.0	0															30	30	100	7	16	44								
Nolan Luhn	OE-DE	26	6'3"	200	42														42	696	17	7													2	30	15	0
Clyde Goodnight	OE-DB	23	6'1"	195	36		1	-1	-1.0	0									38	593	16	6													1	7	7	0
Gene Wilson	OE-DB	21	5'10"	175			1	-2	-2.0	0									3	34	11	0																
Larry Craig	OE-DE	31	6'1"	218																1	14	14	0																
LOS ANGELES RAMS																																					
Bob Waterfield	QB-DB	27	6'1"	193	54	5	3	6	2.0	1	221	96	43	1210	5.5	8	18-8	10	2	14	7	0	59	42.4	27	30	90	7	16	44	1	2	2	0				
Jim Hardy	QB	25	6'	175			3	-6	-2.0	0	57	23	40	388	6.8	5	7-12						10	26.3														
John Ksionzyk	QB	26	5'10"	190							7	1	14	17	2.4	0	2-29																					
Kenny Washington	HB-DB	29	6'1"	215	30		60	444	7.4	5	5	2	40	14	2.8	0	1-20		3	40	13	0									3	44	15	0	2	52	26	0
Tommy Harmon	HB-DB	27	6'1"	200	24	8	60	306	5.1	1	3	1	33	31	10.3	0	0-0		5	89	18	1									27	392	15	1	9	208	23	0
Fred Gehrke	HB-DB	29	5'11"	190	13	1	59	304	5.2	0									6	19	3	0			4	4	100	1	1	100	4	112	28	1	2	29	15	0
Jack Banta	HB-DB	29	5'11"	190	6	2	40	193	4.8	1									14	198	14	0	3	41.7							2	19	10	0	2	50	25	0
Dante Magnani	HB	30	5'10"	184	6		48	178	3.7	0									4	57	14	1													6	186	31	0
Pat West	FB-LB	24	6'	200	12	1	42	162	3.9	2																									1	21	21	0
Bob Hoffman	FB-LB	29	6'1"	210	18	1	42	159	3.8	3									2	22	11	0													1	12	12	0
Dick Hoerner	FB-LB	25	6'4"	217	12		30	124	4.1	2									1	20	20	0																
Mel Bleeker	HB-DB	27	5'11"	187	6	1	23	111	4.8	0																									3	50	17	0
Gerry Cowhig	FB-LB	26	6'2"	217		1	25	104	4.2	0																									2	29	15	0
Les Horvath	HB-DB	26	5'10"	168			18	68	3.8	0									3	29	10	0									4	29	7	0	3	58	19	0
Steve Bagarus	HB-DB	28	6'	178		1	3	15	5.0	0																					2	18	9	0	1	11	11	0
Jack Wilson	HB-DB	29	6'	200			3	3	1.0	0									1	-5	-5	0																
Jim Benton	OE-DE	30	6'3"	216	36														35	511	15	6																
Red Hickey	OE-DE	30	6'2"	212	12														12	196	16	2																
Ray Hamilton	OE-DE	31	6'4"	214	6														12	193	16	1													1	10	10	0
Steve Pritko	OE-DE	25	6'2"	200																10	101	10	0																
Jack Zilly	OE-DE	25	6'2"	206																7	75	11	0													1	10	10	0
Frank Hubbell	OE-DE	25	6'2"	222	12														2	60	30	2																
DETROIT LIONS																																					
Clyde LeForce	QB-DB	24	5'11"	178		3	18	143	7.9	0	175	94	54	1384	7.9	13	20-11	6													6	78	13	0	4	98	25	0
Roy Zimmerman	QB	29	6'2"	205	51		13	28	2.2	1	138	57	41	867	6.3	7	9-7	9					49	42.4	30	31	97	5	11	45								
Joe Margucci	QB-HB-DB	24	5'10"	180	12		26	97	3.7	1	31	13	42	171	5.5	1	5-16		10	125	13	1									2	23	12	0	5	94	19	0
Camp Wilson	FB-LB	25	6'2"	205			89	412	4.6	0									5	96	19	0													3	46	15	0
Bill Dudley	HB-DB	26	5'10"	178	66	5	80	302	3.8	2	4	3	75	24	6.0	2	0-0		27	375	14	7	15	43.8							11	182	17	1	15	359	24	0
Bob Westfall	FB-LB	28	5'8"	185	6		34	132	3.9	1									2	19	10	0													2	27	14	0
Bob Wiese	HB-DB	24	6'3"	200		5	20	61	3.1	0									5	53	11	0	1	61.0														
Tippy Madarik	HB-DB	25	5'11"	200	6		19	29	1.5	1									4	75	19	0									1	7	7	0	3	49	16	0
Pete Kmetovic	HB-DB	27	5'9"	177	12		14	23	1.6	0									6	143	24	0									3	26	9	0	4	62	16	0
Joe Watt (from BOS)	HB-DB	26	5'11"	183	12	2	11	7	0.6	0									4	104	26	2									10	143	14	0	4	68	17	0
Steve Sucic (from BOS)	FB-LB	26	6'	210			3	3	1.0	0									1	20	20	0													1	18	18	0
Bill O'Brien	HB-DB	23	6'	180			1	2	2.0	0																												
Ken Reese	HB-DB	25	5'11"	175			3	1	0.3	0																									2	40	20	0
Bill Hillman	FB-LB		5'11"	200			2	0	0.0	0									1	25	25	0													1	15	15	0
Tommy James	HB-DB	23	5'10"	180			2	-1	-0.5	0																					1	2	2	0				
Bob DeFruiter (from WAS)	HB-DB	30	6'	190		3	1	-2	-2.0	0																												
John Greene	OE-DE	27	6'	200	30														38	621	16	5													2	19	10	0
Kelley Mote	OE-DB	24	6'2"	193	6	1													16	180	11	1													1	17	17	0
Cecil Souders	OE-DE	25	6'1"	210	6														15	184	12	1																
Ralph Heywood	OE-DE	26	6'2"	205	12														13	198	15	2																
Ted Cremer	OE-DE	28	6'2"	212	6														13	117	9	1																
Ted Cook	OE-DB	26	6'2"	195	6	2													7	111	16	1									1	10	10	0	2	14	7	0

TEAM TOTALS

OFFENSE	FIRST DOWNS: Tot	by Rsh	by Pas	by Pen	RUSHING: No.	Yds.	Avg Yds.	TD	PASSING: Att	Com	Comp Pct.	Yds.	Avg. Yds. Att.	Avg. Yds. Comp	TD	Int	Pct. Int.	PUNTING: No.	Avg. Yds.	PUNT RETURNS: No.	Yds.	Avg. Yds.	TD	KICKOFF RETURNS: No.	Yds.	Avg. Yds.	TD	INTERCEPTION RETURNS: No.	Yds.	Avg. Yds.	TD	PENALTIES: No.	Yds.	FUMBLES: No.	Lost	POINTS: Tot	PAT	FG Att	FG	Saf.	DEFENSE
CHIC. C.	201	90	101	10	400	1759	4.4	10	314	148	47.1	2206	7.3	14.9	18	27	8.6	58	41.2	36	337	9.4	0	53	1037	19.6	0	25	331	13.2	0	90	852	25	18	231	30	14	5	0	CHIC. C.
CHIC. B.	206	78	96	32	392	1423	3.6	6	345	161	46.7	2449	7.1	15.2	20	27	7.8	64	42.4	27	433	16.0	2	57	1000	17.5	0	35	408	11.7	0	75	580	27	20	241	29	15	8	1	CHIC. B.
G.B.	193	96	71	26	433	1606	3.7	13	277	122	44.0	1790	6.5	14.7	14	30	10.8	65	43.5	44	483	11.0	0	48	1034	21.5	0	19	293	15.4	1	88	759	41	21	210	25	11	5	1	G.B
L.A.	209	99	93	17	453	1544	3.4	12	306	145	47.4	2059	6.7	14.2	14	24	7.8	76	41.1	29	352	12.1	0	47	1002	21.3	0	28	487	17.4	1	76	761	34	24	214	26	6	4	1	L.A.
DET.	220	96	106	18	461	1975	4.3	18	310	156	50.3	2430	7.8	15.6	21	25	8.1	55	42.2	39	584	15.0	1	45	929	20.6	0	34	442	13.0	2	112	1039	23	18	305	38	15	5	0	DET.

1947 A.A.F.C. — EAST

NEW YORK YANKEES 11-2-1 Ray Flaherty

Scores of Each Game		
24	Buffalo	28
48	CHICAGO	26
30	Los Angeles	14
21	San Francisco	16
21	Baltimore	7
17	Cleveland	26
31	BROOKLYN	7
28	Chicago	7
35	BALTIMORE	21
24	SAN FRANCISCO	16
16	LOS ANGELES	13
28	CLEVELAND	28
35	BUFFALO	13
20	Brooklyn	17

Use Name	Pos.	Hgt	Wgt	Age	Int	Pts
Fred Cardinal	LB	5'11"	220	22		
Paul Duke	C-LB	6'1"	210	21		
Lou Sossamon	C-LB	6'1"	207	26		6
Ralph Stewart	C-LB	6'	205	21		
Ray Ruskusky	DE	6'3"	200	26	1	
Henry Stanton	DE	6'2"	200	27		

Use Name – Tackles	Pos.	Hgt	Wgt	Age	Int	Pts
Jack Durishan	T-G	6'2"	230	25		
(1 kickoff return for 3 yds.)						
Charlie Elliott	T	6'2"	240	25		
Nate Johnson	T	6'3"	240	27		
Bruiser Kinard	T	6'1"	218	32		
Ted Ossowski	T	6'	218	25		
Darrell Palmer	T	6'2"	245	25		
Vic Schleich	T	6'3"	240	26		

Use Name – Guards	Pos.	Hgt	Wgt	Age	Int	Pts
Dick Barwegan	G	6'1"	215	24		
Roman Bentz	G	6'2"	230	28		
Charley Riffle	G	6'	212	29		
Ed Sharkey	G	6'3"	215	21		
Joe Yackanich	G	5'10"	205	25		

Yankee coach Ray Flaherty had no stars like Joe DiMaggio on his squad, but he did have a versatile tailback in Spec Sanders, a quick scatback in 5'5" rookie Buddy Young, a tough two-way end in John Russell, and solid linemen in Nate Johnson, Bruiser Kinard, Dick Barwegan, and Lou Sossamon. Sanders slithered and sprinted to a pro record of 1,432 yards rushing, passed well, and played defensive back, replacing the retired Ace Parker as backfield leader on the team. Building around Sanders, Flaherty programmed a hard-hitting attack that averaged 27 points a game. But the New Yorkers could not escape the Browns' shadow. In their first meeting, the Browns won a 26-17 decision. In the rematch, the Yankees had the Browns down 28-0, but let them get off the hook for a 28-28 tie—a tipoff how the championship game would go.

BUFFALO BILLS 8-4-2 Red Dawson

Scores of Each Game		
28	NEW YORK	24
14	Cleveland	30
28	CHICAGO	20
31	Chicago	14
24	SAN FRANCISCO	41
27	Los Angeles	25
20	BALTIMORE	15
14	Brooklyn	14
35	BROOKLYN	7
7	CLEVELAND	28
25	LOS ANGELES	0
33	Baltimore	14
13	New York	35
21	San Francisco	21

Use Name	Pos.	Hgt	Wgt	Age	Int	Pts
Bert Corley	C-LB	6'2"	210	27	1	
Joe Haynes	C-G	6'3"	225	26		
Felto Prewitt	C-LB	5'11"	210	23	2	
John Morton	OE-DE	6'	200	25		

Use Name – Tackles	Pos.	Hgt	Wgt	Age	Int	Pts
Jack Carpenter	T	6'	235	24		
Gil Duggan	T	6'3"	235	29		
John Kerns	T	6'3"	245	24		
Chet Kozel	T	6'2"	207	27		
(1 kickoff return for 11 yds.)						

Use Name – Guards	Pos.	Hgt	Wgt	Age	Int	Pts
George Doherty	G	6'1"	218	26		
George Groves	G	5'11"	195	26		
Hal Lahar	G	6'	225	28		
John Maskas	G	5'11"	212	27		
Rosco Pirro	G	6'	235	30		
Vin Scott	G	5'8"	215	25		

The Bills came up with a new name, a new quarterback, and a new lease on life. While the change of name from the Bisons to the Bills didn't help the team on the field, the arrival of passer George Ratterman certainly did. The rookie quarterback from Notre Dame stepped right in as a starter, zipping passes to ends Fay King and Al Baldwin from the first game on. With the new passer spreading out the defenses, halfback Chet Mutryn blossomed into a fine runner, and the Bills suddenly were scoring points in a steady flow. Up until the final two weeks of the season, the Bills were in the running for the Eastern Division crown, but a 35-13 defeat by the Yankees ended any hopes of a mini-miracle. The fans reacted to the new winning image by almost doubling the 1946 attendance, a favor much appreciated by the owners.

BROOKLYN DODGERS 3-10-1 Cliff Battles

Scores of Each Game		
7	San Francisco	23
7	Baltimore	16
7	CLEVELAND	55
21	Los Angeles	48
35	Chicago	31
7	New York	31
14	BUFFALO	14
7	Buffalo	35
7	CHICAGO	3
12	Cleveland	13
21	BALTIMORE	13
12	LOS ANGELES	16
7	SAN FRANCISCO	21
17	NEW YORK	20

Use Name	Pos.	Hgt	Wgt	Age	Int	Pts
Lou Daukas	C-LB	6'	203	26	1	
(1 kickoff return for 1 yd.)						
Joe Gibson	LB-DE	6'3"	215	28	1	
Ed Gustatson	C-LB	6'3"	205	25		
Frank Laurinaitis	LB	5'10"	200	25		
Russ Morrow	LB-DE	6'7"	210	23		
Caleb Warrington	C-G	6'2"	210	26		
(2 yds. on pass reception lateral)						
Neal Adams	OE-DE	6'3"	195	28		
Mel Conger	DE	6'2"	225	28		
Mike Patanelli	DE	6'2"	215	22		
Bernie Nygren	HB-DB	5'9"	193	27		
Adolph Kowalski	BB-DB	6'3"	205	26		
Doyle Tackett	BB-DB	6'	205	23	1	
(25 yds. on pass reception lateral)						

Use Name – Tackles	Pos.	Hgt	Wgt	Age	Int	Pts
Nick Daukas	T	6'4"	225	24		
Charlie Huneke (from CHI)	T	6'3"	225	26		
Ed Mieszkowski	T	6'2"	220	22		
Martin Ruby	T	6'3"	250	27		
Leroy Schneider	T	5'11"	237	24		
Harlan Wetz	T	6'5"	265	22		
Garland Williams	T	6'3"	220	26		

Use Name – Guards	Pos.	Hgt	Wgt	Age	Int	Pts
George Bernhardt	G	5'10"	215	28		
Harry Buffington	G	6'	210	28		
Amos Harris	G	6'	210	26		
Ed Jeffers	G	6'3"	215	24		
Billy Jones	G	6'	220	27		

Tailback Glen Dobbs learned how quickly football fame can evaporate. Last year, he led the AAFC in passing, made the All-League team, won the first league MVP Award, and established himself as a rising star in the pro-football sky. This year, he got off to a slow start and found out how short coach Cliff Battles' memory was when the Dodgers traded with Chicago for tailback Bob Hoernschemeyer. Before the season was over, Hoernschemeyer had won the starter's position, and Dobbs was playing for the Los Angeles Dons.

Since Hoernschemeyer ran with the ball better than he passed, the Brooklyn offense shifted focus by concentrating on a ground attack. Fullback Mickey Colmer helped Hoernschemeyer with the running and also led the league in punting. Up front, only Martin Ruby was above average. With good players scattered thinly across the roster, the Dodgers lost all but three games, and with fans scattered thinly throughout the stands, the front office lost quite a few dollars.

BALTIMORE COLTS 2-11-1 Cecil Isbell

Scores of Each Game		
16	BROOKLYN	7
7	San Francisco	14
0	Cleveland	28
7	NEW YORK	21
28	SAN FRANCISCO	28
15	Buffalo	20
10	LOS ANGELES	38
0	Los Angeles	56
21	New York	35
21	Chicago	27
14	Brooklyn	21
14	BUFFALO	33
14	CHICAGO	7
0	CLEVELAND	42

Use Name	Pos.	Hgt	Wgt	Age	Int	Pts
Dick Handley	C-LB	6'1"	215	25		
Joe Kodba	C-LB	5'11"	190	26		
Mike Phillips	C-LB	6'	208	25		
Bill Baumgartner	OE-DE	6'3"	202	26		
Floyd Konetsky	DE	6'	200	27	1	
Armand Cure	HB-DB	6'4"	198	28		
(2 rushing attempts for –1 yd.)						

Use Name – Tackles	Pos.	Hgt	Wgt	Age	Int	Pts
George Hekkers (to DET-NFL)	T	6'4"	225	24		
Mike Kasap	T	6'2"	255	26		
Al Klug	T	6'1"	212	26		
Jim Landrigan	T	6'4"	235	24		
John Mellus	T	6'	210	30		
(5 yds. on pass reception lateral)						
George Perpich	T	6'2"	235	27		

Use Name – Guards	Pos.	Hgt	Wgt	Age	Int	Pts
Barry French	G	6'	225	26		
(1 kickoff return for 11 yds.)						
Ed Grain (from NY)	G	6'	230	25		
Luke Higgins	G	6'	210	26		
Vic Marino	G	5'8"	205	28		
Frank Yokas	G	5'11"	210	23		
George Zorich	G	6'2"	215	28		

When the Miami Seahawks ran aground on financial reefs, the franchise was set afloat in the virgin football waters of Baltimore. The new owners started building their team by hiring Cecil Isbell as head coach. The ex-Packer star emphasized the passing game, and he came up with a representative quarterback in Bud Schwenk, Otto Graham's backup in 1946 and an NFL veteran. Schwenk kept the fans alert by throwing spades of passes to end Lamar Davis and halfback Billy Hillenbrand; he had to keep throwing, since the running attack had all the force of a feather. The Colts picked up former Detroit Lion star Frankie Sinkwich in mid-season, but he was past his prime and less effective in the T formation. Isbell did acquire two good linemen in tackle John Mellus and guard Augie Lio, but the rest of the line badly needed shoring up. Even though the Colts won only two games, they won enough of a following to come back for a second year.

TEAM TOTALS

OFFENSE	First Downs: Tot	by Rsh	by Pas	by Pen	Rushing: No.	Yds.	Avg. Yds.	TD	Passing: Att.	Com	Comp. Pct.	Yds.	Avg. Yds. Att.	Avg. Yds. Comp.	TD	Int	Pct. Int.
N.Y.	187	120	54	13	534	2930	5.5	27	216	111	51.4	1795	8.3	16.2	16	18	8.3
BUFFALO	175	109	59	7	496	2217	4.5	18	267	129	48.3	1891	7.1	14.7	24	23	8.6
BKN.	138	92	39	7	495	1936	3.9	21	232	92	39.7	1060	4.6	11.5	4	17	7.3
BALT.	161	65	85	11	417	1161	2.8	7	352	177	50.3	2337	6.6	13.2	13	24	6.8
DEFENSE																	
N.Y.	140	67	60	13	371	1237	3.3	13	304	144	47.4	1910	6.3	13.3	17	17	5.6
BUFFALO	182	109	64	9	507	2218	4.4	22	260	133	51.2	1929	7.4	14.5	14	18	6.9
BKN.	178	112	57	9	514	2516	4.9	16	265	124	46.8	2130	8.0	17.2	21	16	6.0
BALT.	183	118	59	6	571	2665	4.7	29	239	124	51.9	1791	7.5	14.4	17	14	5.9

OFFENSE	Punting: No.	Avg. Yds.	Punt Returns: No.	Yds.	Avg. Yds.	TD	Kickoff Returns: No.	Yds.	Avg. Yds.	TD	Interception Returns: No.	Yds.	Avg. Yds.	TD	Penalties: No.	Yds.	Fumbles: No.	Lost	Points: Tot	PAT	FG Att	FG	Saf.
N.Y.	55	40.0	32	489	15.3	2	53	1351	25.5	3	17	342	20.1	1	67	522	45	17	378	49	8	7	1
BUFFALO	57	37.0	42	545	13.0	0	50	1282	25.6	2	18	404	22.4	2	48	390	36	17	320	38	4	2	0
BKN.	84	42.8	32	425	13.3	0	56	1296	23.1	0	16	157	9.8	0	46	374	37	13	181	22	20	3	0
BALT.	78	36.2	33	546	16.5	0	59	1356	23.0	1	14	213	15.2	0	47	360	36	23	167	21	10	4	1
DEFENSE																							
N.Y.	78	41.4	39	473	12.1	0	68	1401	20.6	0	18	237	13.2	1	54	382	33	12	239	26	15	7	0
BUFFALO	64	42.8	29	312	10.8	0	58	1357	23.4	0	23	327	14.2	2	52	456	34	14	288	36	10	4	3
BKN.	55	40.0	50	744	14.9	1	37	1032	27.9	2	17	219	12.9	3	43	261	40	20	340	40	18	12	0
BALT.	56	40.0	46	627	13.6	1	38	646	17.0	1	24	417	17.4	4	59	488	50	25	377	50	12	3	0

Use Name – Backs & Ends	Pos.	Age	Hgt	Wgt	Pts	Int	RUSHING				PASSING								RECEIVING				PUNTING		KICKING						PUNT RETURNS				KICKOFF RETURNS			
							No.	Yds	Avg	TD	Att	Comp	%	Yds	Yd/Att	TD	Int–%	RK	No.	Yds	Avg	TD	No.	Avg	Pat	Att	%	FG	Att	%	No.	Yds	Avg	TD	No.	Yds	Avg	TD
NEW YORK YANKEES																																						
Spec Sanders	TB-DB	28	6'1"	196	**114**	3	**231**	**1432**	6.2	**18**	171	93	54	1442	8.4	14	17– 10	3	1	13	13	0	46	42.1							6	164	**27**	0	**22**	593	27	1
Ben Raimondi	TB	22	5'10"	175			6	11	1.8	0	15	3	20	54	3.6	0	0– 0																					
Buddy Young	FB-HB-DB	21	5'5"	170	42		116	712	6.1	3	2	1	50	13	6.5	0	0– 0		27	303	11	2									8	127	16	**1**	12	332	28	**1**
Eddie Prokop	FB-DB	25	5'11"	200	30	3	76	324	4.3	4	8	4	50	137	17.1	2	1– 13		3	79	26	1									7	78	11	0	7	188	27	0
Bob Kennedy	FB-DB	26	5'11"	195	6	2	44	258	5.9	1	3	2	67	56	18.7	0	0– 0						5	25.2							6	44	7	0				
Dewey Proctor	FB-LB	26	5'11"	215	6	1	15	15	1.0	1	1	0	0	0	0.0	0	0– 0		1	4	4	0													1	15	15	0
John Sylvester	HB-DB	25	6'	183			17	101	5.9	0	1	0	0	0	0.0	0	0– 0		1	5	5	0	1	42.0							3	37	12	0	1	25	25	0
Harry Burrus	WB-DB	26	6'1"	195	12	1	1	5	5.0	0									8	192	24	2																
Harmon Rowe	HB-DB	25	6'	182		2	2	−3	−1.5	0																									1	18	18	0
Lowell Wagner	WB-DB	23	6'	193	6														4	50	13	1																
Bob Sweiger	BB-LB	28	6'	209	12	2	9	44	4.9	0									11	108	10	1													1	12	12	0
Lloyd Cheatham	BB	28	6'2"	215	12		1	−2	−2.0	0									4	124	31	2																
Harvey Johnson	BB-LB	28	5'11"	210	70																				**49**	**51**	98	7	8	**88**								
Jack Russell	OE-DE	27	6'1"	215	18	1													20	368	18	2													4	66	17	0
Bruce Alford	OE-DB	26	6'	190	42	1													20	298	15	5									1	34	34	1	2	90	45	1
Van Davis	OE-DE	25	6'2"	215															8	179	22	0													1	9	9	0
Roy Kurrasch	OE-DE	25	6'2"	195															2	53	27	0																
Ollie Poole	OE-DE	25	6'3"	220															1	19	19	0									1	5	5	0				
BUFFALO BILLS																																						
George Ratterman	QB	20	6'1"	175	6		17	−49	−2.9	1	244	124	51	1840	7.5	22	20– 8	3							0	1	0											
George Terlep	QB-DB	25	5'10"	180		1	4	11	2.8	0	23	5	22	51	2.2	2	3– 13														1	17	17	0				
Albie Reisz	QB	29	5'10"	180			2	32	16.0	0													57	37.0														
Chet Mutryn	HB-DB	26	5'9"	180	73	1	140	868	6.2	9									10	176	18	2			1	2	50				13	187	14	0	21	**691**	**33**	1
Julie Rykovich	HB-DB	23	6'2"	200	24	2	92	414	4.5	4									4	44	11	0									7	93	13	0	12	257	21	0
Lou Tomasetti	HB-DB	31	6'	198	18	1	92	326	3.5	2									13	125	10	0													4	74	19	0
Vic Kulbitski	FB-LB	26	5'11"	205	31	1	56	249	4.4	1									9	117	13	4			1	1	100				1	13	13	0	1	19	19	0
George Koch	HB-DB	28	6'	200	6	3	37	149	4.0	1									1	10	10	0									4	84	21	0	1	12	12	0
Steve Juzwik	HB-DB	29	5'8"	184	40		26	130	5.0	0									5	35	7	1			28	32	88	2	3	67	4	36	9	0	1	20	20	0
Alex Wizbicki	HB-DB	25	5'11"	188	6		9	44	4.9	0																					9	105	12	0	5	164	33	1
Pug Manders	FB-LB	34	6'	200			3	15	5.0	0																												
Buckets Hirsch	FB-LB	26	5'10"	205	6	3	4	7	1.8	0																												
Fay King	OE	25	6'3"	195	36														26	382	15	6																
Al Baldwin	OE-DB	24	6'2"	187	42	2													25	468	19	7													1	6	6	0
Al Coppage	OE-DB	31	6'1"	195	12														20	226	11	2													2	28	14	0
Paul Gibson	OE-DB	22	6'2"	190															8	154	19	0																
Ray Kuffel	OE-DE	25	6'3"	210															3	37	12	0																
Marty Comer	OE-DE	29	6'	202	6														2	75	38	1																
Vince Mazza	OE-DE	26	6'1"	210		1													2	11	6	0																
Graham Armstrong	T	28	6'4"	240	8																				8	10	80	0	1	0								
BROOKLYN DODGERS																																						
Bob Hoernschemeyer (from CHI)	TB-DB	21	5'11"	192	36	1	152	704	4.6	5	173	73	42	926	5.4	4	11– 6	9	1	4	4	1	2	28.0							1	19	19	0	1	11	11	0
Bob Perina	TB-HB-DB	26	6'1"	205	24	4	67	116	1.7	3	24	11	46	91	3.8	0	2– 8		9	67	7	1	7	29.9							4	27	7	0	3	67	22	0
Dub Jones	TB-DB	22	6'4"	200	6	2	43	136	3.2	1	15	3	20	37	2.5	0	2– 13														14	157	11	0	7	121	17	0
Mickey Colmer	FB-LB	28	6'2"	224	60		152	578	3.8	9	3	1	33	20	6.7	0	0– 0		18	190	11	1	56	44.7											3	77	26	0
Monk Gafford	HB-DB	26	5'11"	195	6	3	46	232	5.0	1									8	113	14	0									11	186	17	0	21	565	27	0
Al Akins	HB-DB	26	6'1"	195	12	1	15	79	5.3	1									6	101	17	1									1	17	17	0	5	131	26	0
Lee Tevis	FB-LB	25	5'11"	190		2	4	44	11.0	0	3	0	0	0	0.0	0	0– 0						5	49.2														
George Benson	HB-DB	28	6'1"	205			2	5	2.5	0																												
Elmore Harris	HB	24	5'11"	175			3	−2	−0.7	0																									14	329	24	0
Walt McDonald	BB	26	6'1"	210			1	1	1.0	0									3	30	10	0									1	19	19	0				
Saxon Judd	OE	26	6'1"	190	6														18	204	11	1													2	5	3	0
Hal Thompson	OE-DE	25	6'1"	205			1	4	4.0	0									15	148	10	0																
Jim McCarthy	OE-DE	25	6'1"	205							2	1	50	17	8.5	0	1– 50		10	147	15	0																
Herb Nelson	OE-DE	26	6'4"	218															2	17	9	0																
Ed Scruggs	OE-DE	24	6'1"	195															2	9	5	0																
Bob Hein	OE-DE	26	6'3"	220															1	7	7	0																
Phil Martinovich	G	32	5'10"	220	31																				22	25	88	3	20	15								
BALTIMORE COLTS																																						
Bud Schwenk	QB	29	6'2"	200	6		25	58	2.3	1	**327**	**168**	51	2236	6.8	13	20– 6	5																				
Ernie Case	QB-DB	27	5'10"	170	4	2	1	0	0.0	0	11	4	36	49	4.5	0	1– 9						5	30.4	1	1	100	1	1	100	2	18	9	0	4	104	26	0
John Galvin	QB	27	5'10"	170			1	−4	−4.0	0	6	3	50	34	5.7	0	0– 0						**66**	36.0											2	38	19	0
Steve Nemeth	QB	25	5'10"	175	1		1	1	1.0	0	6	2	33	18	3.0	0	2– 33						3	42.0	1	1	100	0	1	0								
Buzz Mertes	FB	26	6'	205	12		95	321	3.4	2									2	28	14	0																
Frankie Sinkwich (from NY, TB)	HB-DB	26	5'11"	190			71	241	3.4	0	15	8	53	93	6.2	0	0– 0		1	3	3	0	7	37.1							1	15	15	0	5	118	24	0
Billy Hillenbrand	HB-DB	25	6'	188	60	1	66	204	3.1	2	1	0	0	0	0.0	0	1–100		39	702	18	7									13	201	15	0	18	466	26	1
John Wright	FB-LB	26	5'11"	225		1	38	113	3.0	0																												
Rudy Mobley	HB-DB	25	5'7"	155	12	2	26	90	3.5	1									11	121	11	1									5	74	15	0	1	18	18	0
John Vardian	HB-DB	22	5'8"	168	6	3	35	57	1.6	0									16	280	18	1									5	66	13	0	6	128	21	0
Ray Terrell (to CLE)	HB-DB	28	6'	185		1	26	48	1.8	0									6	21	4	0									1	18	18	0	9	204	23	0
Blondy Black	HB-DB	27	5'11"	195			5	39	7.8	0									1	7	7	0																
Andy Dudish	HB-DB	26	5'11"	180	12		28	30	1.1	1									7	130	19	1									5	121	24	0	8	184	23	0
Jim Castiglia (to WAS–NFL)	FB	28	5'11"	210	6		9	18	2.0	0									1	10	10	0																
Buzz Trebotich	FB-LB	26	5'10"	205			3	−4	−1.3	0																									1	17	17	0
Lamar Davis	OE-DB	26	6'1"	185	12	1	3	14	4.7	0	1	0	0	0	0.0	0	0– 0		46	515	11	2									1	33	33	0	2	44	22	0
Hub Bechtol	OE-DE	21	6'3"	200	6	1	2	−1	−0.5	0									17	167	10	1													1	13	13	0
Lamar Blount (from BUF)	OE-HB-DB	27	6'1"	190			4	5	1.3	0									8	148	19	0																
Sig Sigurdson	OE-DE	28	6'2"	206															8	104	13	0																
Elmer Madar	OE-DB	26	5'11"	185															8	53	7	0													1	14	14	0
Ralph Jones	OE-DE	26	6'3"	200															3	23	8	0																
Gorham Getchell	OE-DE	27	6'4"	225															2	17	9	0																
Gil Meyer	OE-DE	26	6'2"	200															1	3	3	0																
Augie Lio	G	29	6'	230	28																				19	20	95	3	8	38								

CLEVELAND BROWNS 12-1-1 Paul Brown

Scores of Each Game		
30	BUFFALO	14
55	Brooklyn	7
28	BALTIMORE	0
41	Chicago	21
26	NEW YORK	17
10	LOS ANGELES	13
31	CHICAGO	28
14	San Francisco	7
28	Buffalo	7
13	BROOKLYN	12
37	SAN FRANCISCO	14
28	New York	28
27	Los Angeles	17
42	Baltimore	0

Use Name	Pos.	Hgt	Wgt	Age	Int	Pts
Frank Gatski	C-LB	6'3"	210	25	2	
(1 kickoff return for 17 yds.)						
Mel Maceau	C-LB	6'	203	25		
Lou Saban	LB	6'	198	25	2	10
(10 PAT in 11 attempts)						
Mike Scarry	C-LB	6'	208	27		
George Young	DE	6'3"	210	23		

Use Name – Tackles	Pos.	Hgt	Wgt	Age	Int	Pts
Ernie Blandin	T	6'4"	245	28		
(1 rush for –6 yds.)						
Roman Piskor	T	6'	245	29		
Lou Rymkus	T	6'4"	230	28		
Len Simonetti	T	5'11"	225	28	1	

Use Name – Guards	Pos.	Hgt	Wgt	Age	Int	Pts
Bob Gaudio	G-LB	5'10"	215	22		
Lin Houston	G	6'	205	26		
Weldon Humble	G-LB	6'1"	215	26	2	
(1 rush for 0 yds.)						
Ed Ulinski	G	5'11"	200	26		
Bill Willis	G	6'2"	206	26		

Since the Browns obviously outclassed the rest of the AAFC, people already were discussing how they would fare in the established NFL. The Browns lost only one game this year, and the Cleveland fans kept turning out in the highest numbers in pro football. The team's riches began with coach Paul Brown, a demanding leader who combined Spartan discipline with endless blackboard analyses. The attack dazzled opponents with passes as quarterback Otto Graham calmly shot unstoppable sideline passes to Dante Lavelli and Mac Speedie, then crossed up the defense with an occasional long bomb. The linemen made sure Graham had plenty of time to sight his receivers, and fullback Marion Motley kept defenses honest with his pile-driving running. The Browns also had a lot of heart, showing their mettle when they fell behind 28-0 to the New York Yankees and came back to salvage a 28-28 tie.

SAN FRANCISCO 49ers 8-4-2 Buck Shaw

Scores of Each Game		
23	BROOKLYN	7
17	LOS ANGELES	14
14	BALTIMORE	7
16	NEW YORK	21
41	Buffalo	24
28	Baltimore	28
42	CHICAGO	28
7	CLEVELAND	14
26	Los Angeles	16
16	New York	24
14	Cleveland	37
41	Chicago	16
21	Brooklyn	7
21	BUFFALO	21

Use Name	Pos.	Hgt	Wgt	Age	Int	Pts
Jack Baldwin (from NY)	C-LB	6'3"	225	26		
Tony Calvelli	C-LB	5'10"	187	31	1	
Gerry Conlee	C-LB	5'11"	210	31		
(1 punt return for 1 yd.)						
John Schiechl	C-LB	6'2"	250	30	2	
George Smith	C-LB	6'2"	245	33	1	

Use Name – Tackles	Pos.	Hgt	Wgt	Age	Int	Pts
Bob Bryant	T	6'3"	225	28		
Odis Crowell	T	6'2"	220	23		
Visco Grgich	T	5'11"	210	24		
(1 kickoff return for 21 yds.)						
Al Satterfield	T	6'3"	225	25		
Bob Thornton	T	5'10"	205	28		
(1 punt return for 32 yds.)						
John Woudenberg	T	6'3"	225	29		
(1 kickoff return for 2 yds.)						

Use Name – Guards	Pos.	Hgt	Wgt	Age	Int	Pts
Bruno Banducci	G	5'11"	215	25		
(1 punt ret. for 19 yds., 1 kickoff ret. for 27 yds.)						
Dick Bassi	G-LB	5'11"	215	32		
Art Elston	G-C-LB	5'11"	190	28	2	
Ed Forrest	G-LB	5'11"	210	26		
Garland Gregory	G-LB	5'11"	185	28		
(1 punt return for 31 yds.)						

Althought the '49ers could not challenge the Browns for first place, quarterback Frankie Albert kept fans and players buzzing with his magical ball-handling and unpredictable play-calling. Little Frankie dealt out fakes in the backfield like the girl next door by sending defenders in hot pursuit of runners who didn't even have the ball. Close to the end zone, he often would fake to all three backs, hide the ball behind his hip, and roll unmolested around end for a touchdown. Although his long passes wobbled like a crippled pigeon, Albert never hesitated to throw the ball to ends Alyn Beals and Nick Susoeff on quick short patterns or on deep bombs. With Albert deftly shuffling pass plays, handoffs to his running backs, and bootleg keepers, enemy defenders never knew what was coming next.

LOS ANGELES DONS 7-7-0 Dud DeGroot, Mel Hein, Ted Shipkey

Scores of Each Game		
24	Chicago	21
14	San Francisco	17
14	NEW YORK	30
48	BROOKLYN	21
25	BUFFALO	27
13	Cleveland	10
38	Baltimore	10
56	BALTIMORE	0
16	SAN FRANCISCO	26
0	Buffalo	25
13	New York	16
16	Brooklyn	12
17	CLEVELAND	27
34	CHICAGO	14

Use Name	Pos.	Hgt	Wgt	Age	Int	Pts
John Brown	C-LB	6'4"	230	25	1	
Dick Danahe	C-T	6'2"	235	22		
(8 yds. on pass reception lateral)						
Bob Steuber	FB-LB	6'2"	200	25		
(1 rush for 2 yds.)						

Use Name – Tackles	Pos.	Hgt	Wgt	Age	Int	Pts
Lee Artoe	T	6'3"	240	31		
(1 kickoff return for 16 yds.)						
Earl Audet	T	6'2"	252	26		
Pete Berezney	T	6'2"	240	23		
Paul Mitchell	T	6'3"	225	27		
Jim Smith	T	6'4"	270	23		

Use Name – Guards	Pos.	Hgt	Wgt	Age	Int	Pts
Ray Frankowski	G	5'11"	220	28		
Bernie Gallagher	G	6'	235	24		
Reid Lennan	G	6'	235	25		
Len Levy	G	6'	252	26		
Al Lolotai	G	6'	220	26		
Bill Radovich	G	5'10"	255	32		

Los Angeles football fans warmed up to the Dons by more than doubling the total attendance to a figure of 304,177. The Browns alone outdrew the Dons in the AAFC, and only a handful of NFL clubs could match their total. Even with the healthy ticket sales, the club still lost money because of high costs in this time of football war.

But the Dons did field an interesting team which could rise to dazzling heights. They hung the only loss of the season on the Cleveland Browns in a 13-10 upset. They trounced the Baltimore Colts 56-0 and 38-10 and downed Brooklyn 48-21. Yet the Dons also lost three close games by a total of 8 points to bring their final record down to the break-even point. The fans could single out any number of players for fine play, with John Kimbrough, Dale Gentry, Len Levy, and Bob Nelson especially worthy of attention from the newly found customers. Coach Dud DeGroot also drew attention; he was fired in mid-season.

CHICAGO ROCKETS 1-13-0 Jim Crowley, Hamp Pool

Scores of Each Game		
21	LOS ANGELES	24
26	New York	48
20	Buffalo	28
14	BUFFALO	31
21	CLEVELAND	41
31	BROOKLYN	35
28	San Francisco	42
28	Cleveland	31
7	NEW YORK	28
3	Brooklyn	7
27	BALTIMORE	21
16	SAN FRANCISCO	41
7	Baltimore	14
14	Los Angeles	34

Use Name	Pos.	Hgt	Wgt	Age	Int	Pts
Herb Coleman	C-LB	6'	200	24		
Pete Lamana	C-LB	5'11"	210	26		
Fred Negus	C-LB	6'1"	205	25		
Cliff Rothrock	C-LB	5'10"	198	25		
Connie Mack Berry	DE	6'3"	230	31		

Use Name – Tackles	Pos.	Hgt	Wgt	Age	Int	Pts
Alf Bauman (to PHI-NFL)	T	6'2"	218	27		
Chubby Grigg	T	6'2"	330	21		
John Kuzman	T	6'1"	230	31		
(1 kickoff return for 7 yds.)						
Harley McCollum	T	6'4"	245	29		
(1 kickoff return for 9 yds.)						
Joe Mihal	T	6'3"	240	31		
Bruno Niedziela	T	6'2"	225	24		
Ben Pucci	T	6'4"	260	22		
John Sanchez (to DET-NFL & WAS-NFL)	T	6'3"	234	26		
Norm Verry	T	6'1"	240	24		
Lloyd Wasserbach	T	5'11"	205	26		

Use Name – Guards	Pos.	Hgt	Wgt	Age	Int	Pts
Alex Agase (from LA)	G-LB	5'10"	210	25	1	
John Billman	G-LB	6'1"	202	27		
Al Hecht	G	6'	235	25		
Fran Mattingly	G-LB	5'11"	215	27	1	
Jim O'Neal	G	6'1"	230	23		
Jim Pearcy	G	5'11"	210	28		
Tony Sumpter	G	6'1"	215	25		
Evan Vogds	G	5'10"	204	24		

Jim Crowley resigned as AAFC commissioner to take over as general manager and head coach of the Rockets, leading some people to doubt his sanity. As general manager, Crowley had to worry about a 33 percent drop in attendance and the renewed gate pull of the NFL Bears and Cardinals. As coach, he watched his team lose its first ten games and end the season with only one victory. In an effort to get the Rockets moving, general manager Crowley fired head coach Crowley, replacing him with Hamp Pool, and when new ownership took over the club after the season, general manager Crowley joined his alter ego on the unemployment line.

On the field, the Rockets hardly fielded a team equal to the Cardinals and Bears. Injuries robbed the club of backs Angelo Bertelli, Crazy Legs Hirsch, and Ray Ramsey for stretches of action, and none of the remaining players could stop the skid to the bottom.

TEAM TOTALS

OFFENSE	First Downs: Tot	by Rsh	by Pas	by Pen	Rushing: No.	Yds.	Avg. Yds.	TD	Passing: Att.	Com	Comp. Pct.	Yds.	Avg. Yds. Att.	Avg. Yds. Comp	TD	Int.	Pct. Int.
CLEVE.	214	108	91	15	479	2557	5.3	24	296	174	58.8	2990	10.1	17.2	26	12	4.1
S.F.	218	138	72	8	587	2767	4.7	22	297	147	49.5	1993	6.7	13.6	22	19	6.4
L.A.	161	86	62	13	487	1780	3.7	17	300	141	47.0	2127	7.1	15.1	19	25	8.3
CHICAGO	155	69	75	11	401	1520	3.8	9	341	157	46.0	2353	6.9	15.0	23	26	7.6
DEFENSE																	
CLEVE.	188	102	75	11	503	2181	4.3	12	303	129	42.6	1707	5.6	13.2	11	32	10.6
S.F.	178	87	78	13	405	1631	4.0	10	332	177	53.3	2502	7.5	14.1	23	24	7.2
L.A.	160	76	68	16	461	1668	3.6	9	310	157	50.6	2376	7.7	15.1	24	24	7.7
CHICAGO	200	116	76	8	564	2752	4.9	34	288	140	48.6	2206	7.7	15.8	20	19	6.6

OFFENSE	Punting: No.	Avg. Yds.	Punt Returns: No.	Yds.	Avg. Yds.	TD	Kickoff Returns: No.	Yds.	Avg. Yds.	TD	Interception Returns: No.	Yds.	Avg. Yds.	TD	Penalties: No.	Yds.	Fumbles: No.	Lost	Points: Tot	PAT	FG Att	FG	Saf.
CLEVE.	52	43.6	32	503	15.7	1	42	889	21.2	0	32	474	14.8	3	80	650	29	16	410	50	20	8	0
S.F.	50	43.5	44	500	11.4	1	43	845	19.7	0	24	406	16.9	1	58	472	47	18	327	39	12	4	0
L.A.	58	45.0	47	583	12.4	0	55	1287	23.4	0	24	345	14.4	2	58	478	29	14	328	39	24	15	2
CHICAGO	67	39.1	28	289	10.3	0	69	1483	21.5	0	19	400	21.1	3	38	264	50	26	263	33	9	4	1
DEFENSE																							
CLEVE.	58	43.0	31	506	16.3	0	63	1449	23.0	0	12	208	17.3	1	47	385	40	19	185	23	11	4	0
S.F.	62	37.1	24	324	13.5	1	58	1346	23.2	1	19	356	18.7	1	56	416	37	21	264	34	10	4	1
L.A.	75	40.9	30	324	10.8	0	60	1494	24.9	1	25	465	18.6	0	59	507	43	13	256	26	13	6	1
CHICAGO	53	39.7	41	570	13.9	1	45	1067	23.7	1	26	512	19.7	0	72	610	32	20	425	56	18	7	0

Use Name – Backs & Ends	Pos.	Age	Hgt	Wgt	Pts	Int	RUSHING				PASSING								RECEIVING				PUNTING		KICKING						PUNT RETURNS				KICKOFF RETURNS			
							No.	Yds	Avg	TD	Att	Comp	%	Yds	Yd/Att	TD	Int–%	RK	No.	Yds	Avg	TD	No.	Avg	Pat	Att	%	FG	Att	%	No.	Yds	Avg	TD	No.	Yds	Avg	TD
CLEVELAND BROWNS																																						
Otto Graham	QB-DB	25	6'1"	190	6	1	19	72	3.8	1	269	163	**61**	**2753**	**10.2**	**25**	11– 4	1													10	121	12	0				
Ermal Allen	QB-DB	28	5'11"	165		4	7	11	1.6	0	13	4	31	88	6.8	0	0– 0						4	33.8							4	28	7	0				
Cliff Lewis	QB-DB	24	5'11"	165		4	11	66	6.0	0	11	5	45	70	6.4	1	1– 9														7	84	12	0	4	71	18	0
Marion Motley	FB-LB	27	6'1"	218	60	1	146	889	6.1	8									7	73	10	1													13	322	25	0
Special Delivery Jones	HB-DB	28	5'10"	195	36		69	443	**6.4**	5	3	2	67	79	26.3	0	0– 0		5	92	18	1									2	37	19	0	2	48	24	0
Bill Boedecker	HB-DB	23	5'11"	190	30		31	194	6.3	4									8	175	22	1									3	82	27	0	6	133	22	0
Bob Cowan	HB-DB	24	5'11"	185	18		38	181	4.8	2									5	60	12	1													3	55	18	0
Spiro Dellerba	FB-LB	24	5'11"	200	6		29	176	6.1	0									1	14	14	0													1	34	34	0
Bill Lund	HB-DB	23	5'10"	180	18	2	14	105	7.5	1									6	110	18	1													2	37	19	0
Tony Adamle	FB-LB	23	6'	210	6	1	23	95	4.1	1									1	22	22	0									0	36	–	0	1	22	22	0
Don Greenwood	HB-DB	26	6'	198		4	18	94	5.2	0									5	49	10	0																
Tom Colella	HB-DB	29	6'	187	24	**6**	11	77	7.0	1									4	63	16	1	1	36.0							5	113	23	1	1	13	13	0
Lew Mayne	HB-DB	27	6'1"	190	18		41	75	1.8	0									6	238	40	3													5	102	20	0
Jim Dewar	HB-DB	25	6'1"	190	6	1	14	64	4.6	1																					1	2	2	0	1	25	25	0
Mac Speedie	OE	27	6'3"	200	42		1	–7	–7.0	0									**67**	**1146**	17	6																
Dante Lavelli	OE	24	6'	190	54														49	799	16	9													1	10	10	0
John Yonaker	OE-DE	26	6'5"	218	12														6	95	16	2													1	0	0	0
Marshall Shurnas	OE-DE	25	6'1"	205															2	30	15	0																
Horace Gillom	OE-DE	26	6'1"	208		1													2	24	12	0	47	44.6														
Lou Groza	T	23	6'3"	214	60																				39	42	93	7	19	37								
Chet Adams	T	31	6'3"	228	4																				1	2	50	1	1	100								
SAN FRANCISCO 49ers																																						
Frankie Albert	QB	27	5'10"	160	30		46	179	3.9	5	242	128	53	1692	7.0	18	15– 6	2					40	44.0	0	2	0								1	23	23	0
Jess Freitas	QB	26	5'10"	170		1	6	–9	–1.5	0	33	13	39	215	6.5	4	2– 6						8	42.0														
Bev Wallace	QB	24	6'2"	180							16	5	31	48	3.0	0	2–13						2	39.0														
Johnny Strzykalski	HB-DB	24	5'9"	190	48	2	143	906	6.3	5	4	1	25	38	9.5	0	0– 0		15	258	17	3									8	70	9	0	6	124	21	0
Norm Standlee	FB-LB	28	6'2"	245	48		145	585	4.0	8									2	22	11	0													3	24	8	0
Len Eshmont	HB-DB	30	5'11"	178	12	**6**	84	381	4.5	0									19	303	16	2									1	3	3	0	9	177	20	0
Ned Mathews	HB-DB	29	5'10"	192	30	4	39	238	6.1	2	2	0	0	0	0.0	0	0– 0		6	51	9	2									4	44	11	0	2	46	23	0
Len Masini	FB-LB	26	6'	225	12	1	38	167	4.4	2																												
Earle Parsons	HB-DB	27	6'	180	12		33	125	3.8	0									9	163	18	2									10	106	11	0	4	99	25	0
Wally Yonamine	HB-DB	23	5'9"	180		1	19	74	3.9	0									3	40	13	0									2	29	15	0	7	127	18	0
Ed Carr	HB-DB	20	6'	185		2	11	42	3.8	0									4	41	10	0									1	20	20	0	2	42	21	0
Ed Robnett	FB-LB	27	5'8"	205			7	18	2.6	0																												
Joe Vetrano	HB-DB	25	5'9"	170	50		10	11	1.1	0															38	43	88	4	12	33	12	137	11	0	5	117	23	0
Don Durdan	HB-DB	27	5'9"	175			1	2	2.0	0																												
Alyn Beals	OE-DB	26	6'	185	60	1	5	48	9.6	0									47	655	14	**10**																
Nick Susoeff	OE-DE	26	6'1"	210	12														24	223	9	2																
Ed Balatti	OE-DB	23	6'1"	190	13														8	98	12	1			1	1	100				2	8	4	1	1	16	16	0
Bill Fisk	OE-DE	30	6'	200															5	39	8	0																
Dick Horne	OE-DE	29	6'2"	215															3	69	23	0																
Hank Norberg	OE-DE	28	6'2"	225															2	31	16	0																
LOS ANGELES DONS																																						
Charlie O'Rourke	QB-TB	30	5'11"	175	6		24	55	2.3	1	178	89	50	1449	8.2	13	16– 9	7																	1	24	24	0
Glenn Dobbs (from BKN)	TB-DB	27	6'4"	210	12	5	42	131	3.1	1	143	61	43	762	5.3	7	8– 6	8	2	21	11	0	44	43.4							**19**	**215**	11	0	5	119	24	0
Bill Reinhard	TB-DB	25	5'10"	165	6	1	1	2	2.0	1	2	0	0	0	0.0	0	0– 0														2	22	11	0				
John Kimbrough	FB	29	6'2"	210	66		131	562	4.3	8									16	281	18	3													4	96	24	0
Bob Kelly	HB-DB	22	5'10"	190	18	2	51	205	4.0	2									9	68	8	1									4	69	17	0	3	61	20	0
Chuck Fenenbock	HB-DB	29	5'9"	175	36		58	185	3.2	3	7	1	14	7	1.0	0	2–29		20	276	14	2									17	210	12	0	18	452	25	0
Harry Clark	HB-DB	29	6'	195	12		44	173	3.9	2									3	54	18	0									3	38	13	0	8	225	28	0
Bert Pigott	HB-DB	26	6'2"	195	6	1	46	161	3.5	0									7	63	9	1									1	7	7	0	5	120	24	0
Bob Reinhard	FB-DT	26	6'4"	230	6	1	41	150	3.7	0	4	2	50	21	5.3	0	0– 0		3	34	11	1	28	**45.7**											3	42	14	0
Bob Mitchell	HB-DB	26	5'11"	195	6	2	32	85	2.7	0									3	36	12	1													6	119	20	0
Walt Clay (from CHI)	HB-DB	23	5'11"	195		1	9	42	4.7	0									1	52	52	0																
Mort Landsberg	HB-DB	28	5'11"	180			2	–11	–5.5	0									1	0	0	0																
Harry Hopp	BB-DB	28	6'	215		1	10	52	5.2	0									3	59	20	0													1	13	13	0
Walt Heap	BB-DB	25	6'1"	210	12	5	5	3	0.6	0									2	0	0	1																
Dale Gentry	OE-DE	30	6'3"	223	12														22	352	16	2																
Burr Baldwin	OE-DE	25	6'1"	200	6														12	275	23	1																
Ezz Anderson	OE-DE	27	6'4"	215	6		3	24	8.0	0									11	126	11	1																
Joe Aguirre	OE-DE	28	6'4"	225	24														8	158	20	4																
Bob Nowaskey	OE-DE	29	6'	200		2													8	106	13	0									1	22	22	0				
Bob Titchenal	OE-LB	29	6'2"	190			1	0	0.0	0									7	97	14	0																
Bob Nelson	C-LB-OE	27	6'1"	215	12	2													3	61	20	1																
Ben Agajanian	K	28	6'1"	210	84																				39	40	**98**	**15**	**24**	63								
CHICAGO ROCKETS																																						
Sam Vacanti	QB	25	5'11"	200	6		11	–9	–0.8	1	**225**	96	43	1571	7.0	16	16– 7	6																				
Al Dekdebrun	QB-TB-DB	26	5'11"	180			20	71	3.6	0	75	45	60	556	7.4	5	7– 9																					
Angelo Bertelli	QB	26	6'1"	190			1	2	2.0	0	7	2	29	–5	–0.7	0	2–29											0	1	0								
Norm Cox	QB	21	6'2"	210			1	–3	–3.0	0	2	1	50	9	4.5	0	0– 0																					
Bill Daley	FB-DB	27	6'2"	210	24		121	447	3.7	4	6	3	50	70	11.7	1	1–17		12	116	10	0									1	3	3	0	7	145	21	0
Ray Ramsey	HB-DB	26	6'2"	170	60	5	70	433	6.2	2									35	768	22	8									11	131	12	0	16	406	25	0
Bill Kellagher	FB-DB	27	5'11"	205		**6**	42	243	5.8	0									3	22	7	0																
Fred Evans (from BUF)	HB-DB	26	5'11"	185	12		31	124	4.0	1	2	0	0	0	0.0	0	0– 0		5	84	17	1	2	36.5							5	30	6	0	9	159	18	0
Crazy Legs Hirsch	HB-DB	23	6'2"	190	24		23	51	2.2	1	1	0	0	0	0.0	0	0– 0		10	282	**28**	3									2	24	12	0	6	172	29	0
Ernie Lewis	FB-LB	23	6'1"	215			13	47	3.6	0													65	39.2														
Bill Schroeder	HB-DB	24	6'	190	18	4	11	45	4.1	0									2	19	10	1													5	92	18	0
Bill Bass	HB-DB	25	5'10"	180	12	2	28	44	1.6	0	1	1	100	14	14.0	0	0– 0		8	79	10	1									10	85	9	0	12	264	22	0
Ted Scalissi	HB-DB	25	5'8"	173	12		35	37	1.1	0									5	67	13	2									2	26	13	0	8	171	21	0
Max Morris	OE	22	6'2"	200	12														22	239	11	1													1	13	13	0
John Harrington	OE	25	6'3"	198	18														17	233	14	3																
Tom Lahey	OE-DE	29	6'2"	218															13	148	11	0													2	18	9	0
Frank Quillen	OE-DE	25	6'5"	225	6														7	113	16	1																
Jerry Mulready	OE-DE	25	6'1"	205															7	108	15	0																
Bob Dove	OE-DE	26	6'2"	220	6														6	61	10	1													1	16	16	0
Ray Elbi	OE-DE	27	6'2"	210	6														4	38	10	1																
John Rokisky	OE-DE	27	6'2"	200	45														1	8	8	0			33	35	94	4	8	50								

PHILADELPHIA EAGLES 9-2-1 Greasy Neale

Scores of Each Game		
14	Chic. Cards.	21
28	Los Angeles	28
45	NEW YORK	0
45	Washington	0
12	CHIC. BEARS	7
34	Pittsburgh	7
35	New York	14
45	BOSTON	0
42	WASHINGTON	21
17	PITTSBURGH	0
14	Boston	37
45	DETROIT	21

Use Name	Pos.	Hgt	Wgt	Age	Int	Pts
Vic Lindskog	C-LB	6'1"	205	32		
Bap Manzini	C-LB	5'11"	195	28		
Frank Szymanski	C	6'	230	25		
Alex Wojciechowicz	C-LB	5'11"	232	33	1	
John Green (2 kickoff returns for 24 yds.)	OE-DE	6'1"	192	26		
Hal Prescott	OE-DB	6'2"	193	27		
Al Johnson (1 punt for 5 yards)	DB	6'	175	23		

Use Name – Tackles	Pos.	Hgt	Wgt	Age	Int	Pts
Otis Douglas	T	6'1"	225	36		
Fred Hartman	T	6'1"	222	28		
Jay MacDowell	T	6'2"	215	29		
George Savitsky	T	6'2"	245	24		
Vic Sears	T	6'3"	225	30		
Al Wistert	T	6'1"	214	27		

Use Name – Guards	Pos.	Hgt	Wgt	Age	Int	Pts
Walt Barnes	G	6'1"	233	30		2
Mario Giannelli	G	6'	270	27		
Bucko Kilroy	G	6'2"	244	27		
John Magee	G	5'10"	220	25		
Duke Maronic	G	5'9"	210	27		

An opening-day loss to the defending champion Cardinals didn't discourage the Eagles from riding roughshod over the Eastern Division for another trip to the championship game. Coach Greasy Neale had the best of everything at his command—the league's best runner in Steve Van Buren, a passer in Tommy Thompson, second only to Sammy Baugh in the NFL, an outstanding two-way end in Pete Pihos, fine tackles in Al Wistert and Vic Sears, a league-leading kicker in Cliff Patton, and a league-leading punter in Joe Muha. Aided by a supporting cast of strong players, the Eagles confidently entered into the title rematch with the Cardinals.

WASHINGTON REDSKINS 7-5-0 Turk Edwards

Scores of Each Game		
17	PITTSBURGH	14
41	NEW YORK	10
7	Pittsburgh	10
0	PHILADELPHIA	45
23	Green Bay	7
59	BOSTON	21
23	Boston	7
46	DETROIT	21
21	Philadelphia	42
13	Chic. Bears	48
13	LOS ANGELES	41
28	New York	21

Use Name	Pos.	Hgt	Wgt	Age	Int	Pts
Don Corbitt	C-LB	6'4"	224	24		
Al DeMao	C-LB	6'2"	223	28	1	
Clyde Ehrhardt	C-LB	6'1"	232	28	2	
Jim Peebles (1 PAT in 2 attempts)	DE	6'4"	234	28		1
Hal Shoener	DE	6'3"	207	25		
Art Macioszczyk	FB-LB	5'9"	200	27		
Howie Livingston	DB	6'1"	197	26		

Use Name – Tackles	Pos.	Hgt	Wgt	Age	Int	Pts
John Adams	T	6'7"	237	28		
Carl Butkus (to NY-AAFC)	T	6'1"	245	26		
Weldon Edwards	T	6'	225	24		
John Koniszewski	T	6'3"	252	29		2
Mike Roussos	T	6'3"	235	22		
John Sanchez	T	6'3"	240	27		
Ed Stacco	T	6'2"	272	23		

Use Name – Guards	Pos.	Hgt	Wgt	Age	Int	Pts
Fred Boensch	G	6'4"	230	28		
Bill Gray	G	5'11"	210	25		
Hank Harris	G-T	6'	270	25		
Mike Katrishen	G	6'1"	215	25		
John Steber	G	6'	233	25		

The time had come to groom a successor for Sammy Baugh, so the Redskins drafted Alabama quarterback Harry Gilmer. Owner George Marshall had been so impressed by Gilmer's college career that he sold the draft rights to rookie passer Charlie Conerly to the New York Giants. It was a decision that Marshall would regret, as Gilmer's career became plagued with injuries while Conerly played fourteen years as the Giant quarterback.

Baugh, meantime, wasn't so old that he couldn't hold down the fort. Against the Boston Yanks, he threw for 446 yards in driving the Skins to a 59-21 laugher, and the Skins' offense pumped out points at a steady clip. But the defense had a talent for making mediocre passers look like Baugh himself. Opponents passed so often against the Skins that rookie safetyman Dan Sandifer wound up with a record thirteen interceptions.

NEW YORK GIANTS 4-8-0 Steve Owen

Scores of Each Game		
27	Boston	7
10	Washington	41
0	Philadelphia	45
35	CHIC. CARDS	63
34	PITTSBURGH	27
14	Chic. Bears	35
14	PHILADELPHIA	35
37	LOS ANGELES	52
49	Green Bay	3
28	BOSTON	14
28	Pittsburgh	38
21	WASHINGTON	28

Use Name	Pos.	Hgt	Wgt	Age	Int	Pts
John Cannady	C-LB	6'2"	225	24	2	
Carl Fennema	C-LB	6'2"	210	22		6
Art Faircloth (1 rush for –1 yd.)	DB-HB	6'	190	28	3	
Ken Keuper	DB	6'	200	30	1	

Declared ineligible – Frankie Filchock, Merle Hapes

Use Name – Tackles	Pos.	Hgt	Wgt	Age	Int	Pts
Larry Beil	T	6'2"	235	24		
Tex Coulter	T	6'4"	245	23		
Bill Schuler	T	6'	215	26		
John Treadaway	T	6'5"	250	28		
Jim White (1 kickoff return for 6 yds.)	T	6'2"	228	27		6
Ernie Williamson	T	6'4"	250	25		

Use Name – Guards	Pos.	Hgt	Wgt	Age	Int	Pts
Bob Dobelstein	G-LB	5'11"	212	26	1	6
Bill Erickson	G-LB	6'2"	210	26		
Don Ettinger	G-LB	6'2"	210	25	2	
Mike Garzoni (to NY-AAFC)	G	5'11"	220	24		
Ed Royston (1 kickoff return for 5 yds.)	G	6'1"	220	25		

The Redskins did the Giants more favors than anyone in the last few years. The Skins had sent Frankie Filchock to New York in 1946, and Filchock promptly led the Giants to an Eastern title. This year, the Redskins sold the draft rights to passer Chuck Conerly to the Giants. Although he demonstrated his passing ability by completing a record thirty-six passes in fifty-three attempts against the Steelers, Pittsburgh won the game 38-28—a game that seemed to summarize the Giants' season. The New Yorkers could score but could not stop their opponents from doing the same. Seven times they gave up 35 or more points in a game, grounding the offense with a handicap too heavy to overcome. Since Conerly was not a gifted runner, and the Giants did not have an outstanding center like Mel Hein (a necessity for a successful A-formation team), Steve Owen installed the T formation as the Giants basic offense in mid-season. So 1948 was truly a "rebuilding" season for New York.

PITTSBURGH STEELERS 4-8-0 John Michelosen

Scores of Each Game		
14	Washington	17
24	BOSTON	14
10	WASHINGTON	7
7	Boston	13
27	New York	34
7	PHILADELPHIA	34
38	GREEN BAY	7
7	CHIC. CARDS	24
14	Detroit	17
0	Philadelphia	17
38	NEW YORK	28
14	Los Angeles	31

Use Name	Pos.	Hgt	Wgt	Age	Int	Pts
Chuck Cherundolo	C-LB	6'1"	220	32		
Bryant Meeks	C-LB	6'2"	195	22		
Frank Sinkovitz	C-LB	6'1"	215	25	1	
Roy Kurrasch	DE	6'2"	195	26		
Ed Ryan	DE	6'2"	200	22		
Bill Garnaas (1 kickoff return for 18 yds.)	WB	5'11"	183	27		

Use Name – Tackles	Pos.	Hgt	Wgt	Age	Int	Pts
John Mastrangelo	T	6'1"	225	22		
Carl Samuelson	T	6'4"	245	25	1	
Hubert Shurtz	T	6'3"	235	25		
Jack Wiley	T	5'11"	210	27		
Frank Wydo	T	6'4"	215	24		

Use Name – Guards	Pos.	Hgt	Wgt	Age	Int	Pts
Bill Cregar	G-LB	5'11"	200	23		
Bill Moore	G	5'11"	220	25		
Leo Nobile	G-LB	5'10"	215	26		
Nick Skorich	G	5'9"	200	27		
Steve Suhey (1 kickoff return for 11 yds.)	G	5'11"	215	26		

Coach Jock Sutherland was scouring the South for talent in April when his recurrent headaches forced him into the hospital. Within six days he was dead of a brain tumor. Assistant John Michelosen took over as head coach but could not inspire the team to perform as Sutherland had done. The single-wing offense rolled like a steamroller some days and rolled over dead on others. The defense also fluctuated between generous and miserly, and the team's fortunes, consistently tough under Sutherland, went from Jekyll to Hyde from week to week.

BOSTON YANKS 3-9-0 Clipper Smitn

Scores of Each Game		
0	GREEN BAY	31
7	NEW YORK	28
14	Pittsburgh	24
17	Detroit	14
13	PITTSBURGH	7
27	Chic. Cards	49
21	Washington	59
7	WASHINGTON	23
0	Philadelphia	45
17	CHIC. BEARS	51
14	New York	28
37	PHILADELPHIA	14

Use Name	Pos.	Hgt	Wgt	Age	Int	Pts
Joe Domnanovich (1 punt return for 29 yds.)	C-LB	6'1"	215	29	1	
Bill Godwin	C-LB	6'3"	245	29		
Vaughn Mancha	C-LB	6'1"	230	27		
George Sullivan	OE-DE	6'2"	205	22		
Mike Micka (4 rushing attempts for 3 yds.)	DB-HB	6'	185	27	3	
Dave Ryan (3 rushing attempts for 1 yd.)	DB-HB	5'10"	190	25		

Use Name – Tackles	Pos.	Hgt	Wgt	Age	Int	Pts
Bob Davis	T	6'4"	235	21		
Mike Jarmoluk	T	6'5"	252	25	2	
John Nolan	T	6'2"	230	22		
George Roman	T	6'4"	232	23		
Carroll Vogelaar	T	6'3"	260	28		

Use Name – Guards	Pos.	Hgt	Wgt	Age	Int	Pts
John Badaczewski (to CHIC)	G	6'1"	235	26		
Fritz Barzilauskas	G	6'1"	230	27		
Stan Batinski	G	5'10"	215	31		
Bob McClure (2 kickoff returns for 14 yds.)	G	6'1"	224	24		
Joe Sabasteanski	G-LB	6'	208	27	2	

The fact that a low number of fans showed up to see the Yanks did not stop them from having some shining moments in yet another losing season. In one mid-season stretch, the defense got tough enough to post back-to-back victories over the Lions and Steelers. Aided by Philadelphia's overconfidence, the Yanks reached their highest peak when they upset the title-bound Eagles 37-14 in a late-season encounter. They lost their other nine games, though—most of them not even close—and wound up with a financial statement far short of the break-even point. The fact was enough to prompt owner Ted Collins to move the club to New York for the 1949 season.

TEAM TOTALS

OFFENSE	First Downs: Tot	by Rsh	by Pas	by Pen	Rushing: No.	Yds.	Avg. Yds.	TD	Passing: Att.	Com	Comp. Pct.	Yds.	Avg. Yds. Att.	Avg. Yds. Comp	TD	Int.	Pct. Int.	Punting: No.	Avg. Yds.
PHIL.	241	119	99	23	528	2378	4.5	21	301	159	52.8	2241	7.5	14.1	27	16	5.3	62	45.9
WASH.	236	93	120	23	434	1603	3.7	11	360	202	56.1	2861	7.9	14.2	24	26	7.2	51	42.2
N.Y.	212	81	114	17	362	1219	3.4	12	363	191	52.6	2504	6.9	13.1	24	16	4.4	78	38.6
PITT.	210	122	68	20	510	1934	3.8	17	266	108	40.6	1529	5.8	14.2	8	29	10.9	63	39.0
BOSTON	121	55	55	11	365	1170	3.2	4	261	101	38.7	1308	5.0	13.0	13	34	13.0	93	42.0

OFFENSE	Punt Returns: No.	Yds.	Avg. Yds.	TD	Kickoff Returns: No.	Yds.	Avg. Yds.	TD	Interception Returns: No.	Yds.	Avg. Yds.	TD	Penalties: No.	Yds.	Fumbles: No.	Lost	Points: Tot	PAT	FG Att	FG	Saf.
PHIL.	51	554	10.9	1	32	681	21.3	0	23	228	9.9	0	86	773	35	18	376	50	17	8	1
WASH.	34	370	10.9	0	54	1164	21.6	1	24	482	20.1	2	122	1100	30	17	291	34	7	5	1
N.Y.	24	212	8.8	0	57	1238	21.7	1	39	561	14.4	2	95	815	36	20	297	40	8	1	1
PITT.	36	353	9.8	0	42	846	20.1	0	13	320	24.6	1	63	616	43	17	200	26	10	4	0
BOSTON	40	507	12.7	0	54	1090	20.2	0	18	374	20.8	3	81	813	40	20	174	21	7	3	0

Use Name – Backs & Ends	Pos.	Age	Hgt	Wgt	Pts	Int	Rushing No.	Yds	Avg	TD	Passing Att	Comp	%	Yds	Yd/Att	TD	Int–%	RK	Receiving No.	Yds	Avg	TD	Punting No.	Avg	Kicking Pat	Att	%	FG	Att	%	Punt Returns No.	Yds	Avg	TD	Kickoff Returns No.	Yds	Avg	TD
PHILADELPHIA EAGLES																																						
Tommy Thompson	QB	32	6'1"	195	6		12	46	3.8	1	246	141	57	1965	8.0	25	11– 4	2																				
Bill Mackrides	QB	23	5'11"	180			7	4	0.6	0	53	18	34	276	5.2	2	4– 8																					
Steve Van Buren	HB-DB	27	6'	205	60	2	201	945	4.7	10	1	0	0	0	0.0	0	0– 0		10	96	10	0													14	292	21	0
Bosh Pritchard	HB-DB	29	5'11"	163	48		117	517	4.4	4									27	252	9	2									24	282	12	1	9	249	28	0
Noble Doss	HB-DB	28	6'	189			62	193	3.1	0									8	96	12	0									1	0	0	0	1	26	26	0
Jim Parmer	HB-DB	21	6'	190	18	1	30	167	5.6	3																									1	14	14	0
Jack Myers	FB-LB	23	6'2"	200	6	2	21	118	5.6	1									7	57	8	0																
Ben Kish	FB-LB	31	6'	210	6	3	10	106	10.6	1																					1	0	0	0				
Ernie Steele	HB-DB	30	6'	186	12	6	13	99	7.6	1	1	0	0	0	0.0	0	1–100		2	43	22	1									1	5	5	0	2	30	15	0
Joe Muha	FB-LB	27	6'1"	205	6		25	90	3.6	0									2	22	11	1	57	47.2				0	5	0								
Russ Craft	HB-DB	28	5'9"	170	12		13	67	5.2	0									4	138	35	2									3	32	11	0				
Gil Steinke	HB-DB	28	6'	172			5	17	3.4	0																									1	17	17	0
Pat McHugh	HB-DB	28	5'11"	165		2	4	12	3.0	0																					18	220	12	0				
Les Palmer	HB-DB	24	6'	180																			4	37.0							1	8	8	0	1	20	20	0
Pete Phios	OE-DE	24	6'1"	215	66		8	–3	–0.4	0									46	766	17	11													1	9	9	0
Jack Ferrante	OE-DE	32	6'1"	205	42														28	444	16	7																
Neill Armstrong	OE-DB	22	6'2"	188	18	2													24	325	14	3																
Dick Humbert	OE-DB	29	6'1"	180		4													1	2	2	0									2	7	4	0				
Cliff Patton	G	24	6'2"	240	74																				50	50	100	8	12	67								
WASHINGTON REDSKINS																																						
Sammy Baugh	QB	34	6'2"	180	6		4	4	1.0	1	315	185	59	2599	8.3	22	23– 7	1																				
Tommy Mont	QB-DB	26	6'	197	6	2	11	103	9.4	1	28	12	43	157	5.6	2	2– 7																					
Harry Gilmer	QB	22	6'	160							5	2	40	69	13.8	0	0– 0																					
Jim Castiglia	FB	29	5'11"	205	12		97	330	3.4	0									7	73	10	2													1	18	18	0
Ed Quirk	FB-LB	23	6'1"	230	24		77	328	4.3	4									9	40	4	0																
Dick Poillon	HB	28	6'	198	66		71	233	3.3	1									9	105	12	1	51	42.2	33	38	87	5	7	71								
Dick Todd	HB-DB	33	5'11"	174	42		57	201	3.5	1									37	550	15	6									3	21	7	0	3	50	17	0
Tom Farmer	HB-DB	27	5'11"	193	18		52	188	3.6	1									12	148	12	2									4	34	9	0	8	192	24	0
Dan Sandifer	HB-DB	21	6'1"	190	24	13	18	67	3.7	0									9	181	20	1									20	236	12	0	26	594	23	1
Bob Nussbaumer	HB-DB	24	5'11"	176	6		23	59	2.6	0									19	252	13	1									1	–8	–8	0	2	38	19	0
Howard Hartley	HB-DB	24	6'	185	6	3	5	40	8.0	1									1	10	10	0									2	41	21	0	4	64	16	0
Eddie Saenz	HB-DB	25	5'11"	168			8	21	2.6	0									4	62	16	0									2	26	13	0	8	173	22	0
John Hollar	FB-LB	26	6'	220			4	7	1.8	0																												
Tippy Madarik	HB-DB	26	5'11"	205			2	7	3.5	0																									1	20	20	0
Steve Bagarus	HB-DB	29	6'	173	6		3	6	2.0	0									15	100	7	1													1	15	15	0
Hal Crisler	OE-DB	24	6'4"	215	36	2													33	599	18	6									2	20	10	0				
Hugh Taylor	OE	25	6'4"	192	18						1	0	0	0	0.0	0	0– 0		20	341	17	3																
Paul McKee	OE-DE	25	6'3"	220															14	171	12	0																
Doug Turley	OE-DE	29	6'2"	230	6														8	111	14	0																
Joe Tereshinski	OE-DE	24	6'2"	214	6														4	98	25	1																
NEW YORK GIANTS																																						
Charlie Conerly	QB	24	6'1"	183	30		40	160	4.0	5	299	162	54	2175	7.3	22	13– 4	6					17	39.9											4	72	18	0
Paul Governali	QB	27	5'11"	190			6	–48	–8.0	0	56	27	48	280	5.0	1	1– 2																					
Choo-Choo Roberts	FB	24	5'11"	188	18		145	491	3.4	0									14	222	16	3									1	10	10	0	7	160	23	0
Joe Scott	HB-DB	22	6'1"	200	30	5	48	198	4.1	2									17	235	14	2									3	25	8	0	20	569	28	1
Ray Coates	HB-DB	24	6'1"	190	18		50	176	3.5	3	2	1	50	26	13.0	1	0– 0																		6	107	18	0
Skippy Minisi	HB-DB	21	5'11"	190	12	2	36	160	4.4	1	3	0	0	0	0.0	0	2– 67		13	123	9	1									3	25	8	0	4	82	21	0
Em Tunnell	HB-DB	26	6'1"	187	6	7	17	43	2.5	0	2	1	50	23	11.5	0	0– 0		4	32	8	0									12	115	10	0	1	21	21	0
George Cheverko (from WAS)	HB-WB-DB	27	6'1"	195		6	3	10	3.3	0									1	41	41	0									1	5	5	0	3	80	27	0
John Atwood	HB-WB-DB	23	5'11"	185	6	1	9	6	0.7	0									10	141	14	1									4	32	8	0	3	58	19	0
Frank Williams	FB-LB	26	6'	212	4														1	5	5	0			4	5	80	0	1	0								
Jules Siegle	FB-LB	25	6'	210			2	6	3.0	0																									1	12	12	0
Joe Sulatis	BB-DE	27	6'2"	210	12		5	18	3.6	1	1	0	0	0	0.0	0	0– 0		26	298	11	1													4	66	17	0
Joe Johnson	WB-DB	23	6'2"	195	12														19	217	11	2																
Frank Reagan	DB	29	5'11"	180		9																	61	38.2														
Bill Swiacki	OE	23	6'2"	195	60														39	550	14	1													1	0	0	0
Ray Poole	OE-DE	26	6'2"	215	26														35	492	14	3																
Bruce Gehrke	OE-DB	23	6'2"	190	6														9	109	12	1																
Joyce Pipkin	OE-DE	24	6'1"	203															2	28	14	0																
Paul Walker	OE-DB	23	6'3"	210		1													1	11	11	0																
Len Younce	G-LB	31	6'1"	210	39																				39	37	97	1	7	14								
PITTSBURGH STEELERS																																						
Ray Evans	TB-DB	26	6'1"	195	12		99	343	3.5	2	137	64	47	924	6.7	5	17– 12	11	7	93	13	0	1	0.0							10	133	13	0	7	122	17	0
Johnny Clement	TB	28	6'	190	12		67	261	3.9	2	58	18	32	281	4.8	3	7– 12																					
Gonzales Morales	TB-DB	25	6'	185	6	1	13	29	2.2	0	4	3	75	30	7.5	0	0– 0														8	83	10	0	3	62	21	0
Norm Mosley	TB-DB	26	5'9"	185	6		13	39	3.0	1	2	0	0	0	0.0	0	0– 0														7	52	7	0	1	31	31	0
Bob Cifers	HB-DB	27	5'11"	195	6		112	361	3.2	1	4	0	0	0	0.0	0	1– 25		4	55	14	0	62	39.6							1	8	8	0	9	245	27	0
George Papach	FB-DB	23	6'2"	205	18		60	324	5.4	2									4	72	18	1													1	16	16	0
Jerry Shipkey	FB-DB	23	6'1"	210	48		64	199	3.1	8									10	106	11	0													2	34	17	0
Joe Glamp	HB-DB	25	5'11"	185	56		28	167	5.9	1	1	0	0	0	0.0	0	0– 0		9	138	15	2			26	27	96	4	10	40	1	15	15	0	7	158	23	0
Jerry Nuzum	HB-DB	25	6'1"	195		1	26	109	4.2	0									2	37	19	0									1	7	7	0	6	122	20	0
Tony Compagno	FB-DB	27	5'11"	200	6	7	24	101	4.2	0									1	4	4	0									4	21	5	0				
Paul Davis	FB-DB	23	6'1"	190		1	2	–1	–0.5	0																					4	34	9	0	1	13	13	0
Joe Gasparella	BB-LB	21	6'4"	225			1	5	5.0	0	57	23	40	294	5.2	0	4– 7																					
Charlie Seabright	BB-LB	30	6'2"	205	6	1					1	0	0	0	0.0	0	0– 0		8	63	8	1													1	4	4	0
Val Jansante	OE	27	6'1"	190	18		1	–3	–3.0	0									39	623	16	3																
Elbie Nickel	OE-DE	25	6'1"	190	6														22	324	15	1																
Bob Davis	OE-DE	27	5'11"	190															2	14	7	0													1	8	8	0
Charlie Mehelich	OE-DE	26	6'1"	195							2	0	0	0	0.0	0	0– 0																		1	2	2	0
BOSTON YANKS																																						
Roy Zimmerman	QB	30	6'2"	205	16		13	72	5.5	0	107	46	43	649	6.1	7	13– 12	12					51	43.4	13	15	87	1	4	25								
Jim Youel (to WAS)	QB	26	6'	175	6		19	79	4.1	1	36	9	25	99	2.8	2	4– 11		1	20	20	0	2	32.5														
Boley Dancewicz	QB	23	5'10"	188	6		4	3	0.8	1	35	17	49	186	5.3	0	5– 14																					
Gene Malinowski	TB-DB	23	6'1"	210		1	11	21	1.9	0	54	15	28	218	4.0	3	7– 13		3	–10	–3	0																
Phil Slosburg	TB-HB-DB	21	5'10"	170			32	89	2.8	0	20	8	40	119	6.0	1	3– 15		2	29	15	0									10	141	14	0	1	37	37	0
Frank Nelson	TB-HB-DB	25	5'9"	167		1	18	60	3.3	0	17	8	47	71	4.2	0	2– 12		1	10	10	0									2	27	14	0	3	34	11	0
Al Dekdebrun (from NY-AAFC)	TB-DB	27	5'11"	185			2	14	7.0	0	3	1	33	2	0.7	1	1– 33																					
Bill Paschal	FB-LB	27	6'	212	30		80	249	3.1	1									8	93	12	4	2	40.0							3	79	26	0	24	498	21	0
Frank Seno	HB-DB	27	6'	204	18	1	71	242	3.4	0									13	322	25	3									13	99	8	0	8	171	21	0
Frank Muehlheuser	FB-LB	22	6'2"	215	6		38	169	4.4	1									3	19	6	0	1	46.0											1	27	27	0
Rudy Romboli	FB-LB	25	5'10"	210	6		25	90	3.6	1									8	77	10	0													1	22	22	0
Joe Golding	HB-DB	27	6'	184	36	4	24	36	1.5	0									9	159	18	4									10	129	13	0	7	192	27	0
John Poto	HB-DB	22	5'10"	190			13	32	2.5	0									10	101	10	0									1	3	3	0	1	16	16	0
Bob Hazelhurst	HB-DB	23	6'	188			11	15	1.4	0													2	50.0											2	31	16	0
Ralph Heywood (from DET)	OE-DE	27	6'2"	205	18		1	11	11.0	0									14	208	15	1	46	38.4											1	8	8	0
Bill Chipley	OE-DB	28	6'3"	192	12	3													13	131	10	1																
Jim Tyree	OE-DE	26	6'3"	204	6														13	106	8	0													1	17	17	0
Steve Pritko	OE-DE	26	6'2"	210	6														3	42	14	0													2	23	12	0
Nick Scollard	OE-DE	28	6'4"	215	14														2	23	12	0			8	8	100	2	3	67								

TEAM TOTALS

DEFENSE	First Downs: Tot	by Rsh	by Pas	by Pen	Rushing: No.	Yds.	Avg Yds.	TD	Passing: Att	Com	Comp Pct.	Yds.	Avg. Yds. Att.	Avg. Yds. Comp	TD	Int	Pct. Int.	Punting: No.	Avg. Yds.	Punt Returns: No.	Yds.	Avg. Yds.	TD	Kickoff Returns: No.	Yds.	Avg. Yds.	TD	Interception Returns: No.	Yds.	Avg. Yds.	TD	Penalties: No.	Yds.	Fumbles: No.	Lost	Points: Tot	PAT	FG Att	FG	Saf.	DEFENSE
PHIL.	158	62	83	13	376	1209	3.2	5	338	139	41.1	1951	5.8	14.0	14	23	6.8	88	38.8	38	411	10.8	0	48	990	20.6	0	16	257	16.1	2	87	860	33	16	156	21	5	1	0	PHIL.
WASH.	233	114	93	26	482	1958	4.1	17	289	135	46.7	1953	6.8	14.5	20	24	8.3	52	43.8	30	383	12.8	0	44	1079	24.5	1	26	389	15.0	0	81	771	40	18	287	38	10	3	0	WASH.
N.Y.	227	109	106	12	481	2168	4.5	26	311	157	50.5	2406	7.7	15.3	25	39	12.5	57	39.5	55	812	14.8	2	56	1242	22.2	0	16	216	13.5	1	104	880	34	11	388	52	8	4	0	N.Y.
PITT.	188	90	83	15	434	1648	3.8	7	279	149	53.4	1987	7.1	13.3	18	13	4.7	67	42.8	33	374	11.3	1	35	622	17.8	0	29	378	13.0	0	106	927	22	18	243	30	16	7	0	PITT.
BOSTON	244	124	100	20	511	2320	4.5	19	356	161	45.2	2463	6.9	15.3	27	18	5.1	69	40.2	51	469	9.2	0	36	702	19.5	0	34	507	14.9	0	104	929	46	24	372	48	11	6	0	BOSTON

CHICAGO CARDINALS 11-1-0 Jimmy Conzelman

Scores of Each Game		
24	PHILADELPHIA	21
17	CHIC. BEARS	28
17	Green Bay	7
63	New York	35
49	BOSTON	27
27	Los Angeles	22
56	DETROIT	20
24	Pittsburgh	7
27	LOS ANGELES	24
28	Detroit	14
42	GREEN BAY	7
24	Chic. Bears	21

Use Name	Pos.	Hgt	Wgt	Age	Int	Pts
Vince Banonis	C-LB	6'1"	232	26	2	
Bill Blackburn	C-LB	6'6"	230	26	2	12
Bill Campbell	LB	6'	195	28		
Bob Dove (1 rush for −2 yds.)	DE	6'2"	220	27		
Sam Goldman	DE	6'3"	235	31		
Frank Liebel	OE-DE	6'1"	220	28		
Jack Doolan	DB	6'1"	190	29		
Marshall Goldberg	DB	5'11"	195	30	2	
Bob Ravensburg	DB	6'	190	23	1	

Use Name – Tackles	Pos.	Hgt	Wgt	Age	Int	Pts
Chet Bulger	T	6'3"	238	30		
Joe Coomer	T	6'6"	283	29		
Marv Jacobs	T	6'2"	235	23		
Dick Loepfe	T	6'2"	230	27		
Stan Mauldin (died of heart attack – September 24.)	T	6'2"	226	28		
Walt Szot	T	6'1"	218	29		
Bob Zimny	T	6'1"	235	27		

Use Name – Guards	Pos.	Hgt	Wgt	Age	Int	Pts
Plato Andros	G	6'	242	27		
Ray Apolskis	G-LB	5'11"	210	29		
Lloyd Arms	G	6'1"	215	29		
Jake Colhauer	G	6'1"	215	26		
Ham Nichols	G-LB	5'11"	210	24		
Buster Ramsey	G-LB	6'1"	215	28	1	
Dick Wedel	G	5'11"	205	25		

After the opening-day victory over the Eagles, the Cardinal clubhouse should have been a scene of jubilation. Instead, tragedy and grief filled the room. Star tackle Stan Mauldin had keeled over after the game and died of a heart attack. The Cardinals rekindled their spirits, though, and came down to the final game of the season tied with the Bears for the Western Division lead. Earlier in the year, the Bears had beaten the Cardinals 28-17, but this time the Cardinals came through with a 24-21 victory and the Western crown.

CHICAGO BEARS 10-2-0 George Halas

Scores of Each Game		
45	Green Bay	7
28	Chic. Cards	17
42	LOS ANGELES	21
28	DETROIT	0
7	Philadelphia	12
35	NEW YORK	14
21	Los Angeles	6
7	GREEN BAY	6
51	Boston	17
48	WASHINGTON	13
42	Detroit	14
21	CHIC. CARDS	24

Use Name	Pos.	Hgt	Wgt	Age	Int	Pts
Stu Clarkson	C-LB	6'2"	220	29	2	
Thurman Garrett	C	6'3"	260	24		
Bulldog Turner	C-LB	6'1"	235	29	2	
Ed Cifers (1 rush for 5 yds.)	OE-DE	6'2"	230	32		
Hank Norberg (1 reception for 4 yds.)	OE-DE	6'2"	225	29		

Use Name – Tackles	Pos.	Hgt	Wgt	Age	Int	Pts
Alf Bauman	T	6'2"	235	28		
George Connor (1 kickoff return for 5 yds.)	T	6'3"	240	23		
Fred Davis	T	6'3"	248	30		
Paul Stenn	T	6'2"	240	30		
Walt Stickel	T	6'3"	245	26		

Use Name – Guards	Pos.	Hgt	Wgt	Age	Int	Pts
Ray Bray (1 kickoff return for 8 yds.)	G	6'	240	31		
Chuck Drulis	G-LB	5'10"	215	30	1	
Bill Milner	G-LB	6'1"	215	24		
Pat Preston	G-LB	6'2"	220	25		
Wash Serini	G	6'2"	235	24		

George Halas opened his wallet wide to outbid the AAFC for three blue-chip rookies, quarterbacks Johnny Lujack and Bobby Layne and tackle George Connor. Lujack signed an $18,000 contract, Layne got a $10,000 bonus to ink a $22,500 pact, and Connor signed a no-cut contract, all exceptional deals for freshman pro-football players. With veteran Sid Luckman still running the offense, Lujack played mostly on defense, while Layne mostly sat and watched and Connor saw action both on offense and defense.

Yet even with these fine rookies, it was the veteran ball players who kept the Bears in the running for the Western Division crown right to the end. Going into the season's finale with the Cardinals, the two Chicago teams were tied for the lead, but the Cardinals won a return trip to the championship game with a 24-21 victory. Once again, the Bears had been beaten at the wire.

LOS ANGELES RAMS 6-5-1 Clark Shaughnessy

Scores of Each Game		
44	DETROIT	7
28	PHILADELPHIA	28
21	Chic. Bears	42
0	Green Bay	16
34	Detroit	27
22	CHIC. CARDS	27
6	CHIC. BEARS	21
52	New York	37
24	Chic. Cards	27
24	GREEN BAY	10
41	Washington	13
31	PITTSBURGH	14

Use Name	Pos.	Hgt	Wgt	Age	Int	Pts
Jack Martin	C-LB	6'3"	240	26		
Fred Naumetz	C-LB	6'1"	222	26	4	
Don Paul	C-LB	6'1"	230	23		
Bob DeFruiter (3 rushing attempts for 4 yds.)	DB-HB	6'	190	31		

Use Name – Tackles	Pos.	Hgt	Wgt	Age	Int	Pts
Gil Bouley (1 reception for 15 yds., 1 kickoff return for 8 yds.)	T	6'2"	235	27		
Ed Champagne	T	6'3"	240	26		
Dick Huffman	T	6'2"	256	25		
Joe Repko	T	6'	240	27		
Al Sparkman	T	6'6"	253	23		

Use Name – Guards	Pos.	Hgt	Wgt	Age	Int	Pts
Bob David (to CHI-AAFC)	G-LB	6'	215	26		
Hal Dean	G-LB	6'	205	25	1	
Roger Eason	G	6'2"	230	30		
Jack Finlay	G-LB	6'1"	215	27		
Mike Lazetich	G-LB	6'1"	214	27		
Ray Yagiello	G-LB	6'	220	25		

When the Rams made Clark Shaughnessy their new head coach, they brought in one of football's greatest strategic minds. George Halas had hired the ex-Stanford coach as a consultant in the early 1940s, and Shaughnessy added subtle changes to the T formation which made the Bears the scourge of the league. Rams owner Dan Reeves had hoped that the little tactician could give the Los Angeles attack some of the same medicine he had provided the Bears. But even with some of the players resenting Shaughnessy's strict method of dealing with them, all were amazed by the scope of his football theories.

And score the Rams did, despite the loss of last year's top passing combination. Big Jim Benton called it a career, leaving quarterback Bob Waterfield without his favorite receiver, and Waterfield himself soon was on the sidelines with an injury. Shaughnessy gave the quarterback job to second-stringer Jim Hardy and turned the vacant end position over to rookie Tom Fears. Freezing defensive backs with a variety of moves, Fears caught the most passes of any end in the league. Hardy also came through in fine fashion, shining most brightly by passing for 406 yards in a game against the Cardinals. But a soft defense held the Rams down in third place as enemy quarterbacks simply ran their plays away from big tackle Dick Huffman.

GREEN BAY PACKERS 3-9-0 Curly Lambeau

Scores of Each Game		
31	Boston	0
7	CHIC. BEARS	45
33	DETROIT	21
7	CHIC. CARDS	17
16	LOS ANGELES	0
7	WASHINGTON	23
20	Detroit	24
7	Pittsburgh	38
6	Chic. Bears	7
3	NEW YORK	49
10	Los Angeles	24
7	Chic. Cards	42

Use Name	Pos.	Hgt	Wgt	Age	Int	Pts
Lloyd Baxter	C	6'2"	210	25		
Bob Flowers	C-LB	6'1"	210	31	4	
Jay Rhodemyre	C-LB	6'1"	210	26	1	
Larry Craig	DE-LB	6'1"	218	32		
Ted Cremer	DE	6'2"	210	29		
Don Wells	DE	6'2"	200	26		

Use Name – Tackles	Pos.	Hgt	Wgt	Age	Int	Pts
Ed Bell	T	6'1"	233	26		
Jim Kekeris	T	6'1"	257	24		
Paul Lipscomb	T	6'5"	245	25		
Urban Odson	T	6'3"	250	29		
Baby Ray	T	6'6"	250	33		
Dick Wildung	T	6'	220	26		

Use Name – Guards	Pos.	Hgt	Wgt	Age	Int	Pts
Ralph Davis	G	5'11"	205	26		
Don Deeks	G	6'4"	245	25		
Ed Neal	G	6'4"	290	30		
Larry Olsonoski	G	6'2"	214	23		
Damon Tassos	G	6'1"	225	24		
Evan Vogds	G	5'10"	215	25		

After an early-season 17-7 loss to the Cardinals, coach Curly Lambeau fined the entire squad half of one week's salary for "indifferent play." The players did not feel they had been indifferent, but they believed that a good game against the Rams would get their money back. The Packers easily downed the Rams 16-0, bringing their season's record up to 3-2-0. Expecting an extra-large paycheck, the players blew their stacks when they did not get back the fine money. Morale dropped to zero, and the Packers lost every other game this year. Finally, in January, when it was too late, Lambeau returned the players' money.

DETROIT LIONS 2-10-0 Bo McMillin

Scores of Each Game		
7	Los Angeles	44
21	Green Bay	33
14	BOSTON	17
0	Chic. Bears	28
27	LOS ANGELES	24
24	GREEN BAY	20
20	Chic. Cards	56
21	Washington	46
17	PITTSBURGH	14
14	CHIC. CARDS	28
14	CHIC. BEARS	42
21	Philadelphia	45

Use Name	Pos.	Hgt	Wgt	Age	Int	Pts
Larry Ellis	LB	6'1"	204	26		
Roger Harding	C-LB	6'2"	215	25		
Bob Wiese	LB	6'3"	195	25		
Max Bumgardner	DE	6'2"	190	24		
Ivan Schottel	DE	6'2"	208	27		
Earl Maves	DB-WB	5'9"	180	25		

Use Name – Tackles	Pos.	Hgt	Wgt	Age	Int	Pts
Paul Briggs	T	6'4"	248	28		
Jack Dugger	T	6'3"	227	25		
Dale Hansen	T	6'3"	220	27		
George Hekkers	T	6'4"	230	25		
Russ Thomas	T	6'3"	240	24		

Les Lear – Canadian Football League

Use Name – Guards	Pos.	Hgt	Wgt	Age	Int	Pts
Les Bingaman	G	6'3"	240	23		
Howie Brown	G	5'11"	215	25		
Chuck DeShane	G-LB	6'1"	217	29		
Elmer Jones	G-LB	6'	215	28		
Bill Miklich (from NY)	G-LB	6'	208	27		
Dick Stovall	G-LB	6'	200	24		
Bill Ward	G	6'	230	27		

New owner D. Lyle Fyfe dipped into the college ranks for a new head coach and came up with ex-Indiana mentor Bo McMillin, whom he wooed with a lucrative five-year contract. Many of the players thought that the aging McMillin was behind the times in his thinking, and Bo's opinion of his players wasn't too high when they won only two games all year. Rookie quarterback Fred Enke kept the offense moving fairly steadily, but the defense gave up twice as many points as the attack could score—which prompted McMillin to have lots of new faces in next year's lineup.

TEAM TOTALS

OFFENSE	First Downs: Tot	by Rsh	by Pas	by Pen	Rushing: No.	Yds.	Avg. Yds.	TD	Passing: Att.	Com	Comp. Pct.	Yds.	Avg. Yds. Att.	Avg. Yds. Comp	TD	Int.	Pct. Int.	Punting: No.	Avg. Yds.	Punt Returns: No.	Yds.	Avg. Yds.	TD	Kickoff Returns: No.	Yds.	Avg. Yds.	TD	Interception Returns: No.	Yds.	Avg. Yds.	TD	Penalties: No.	Yds.	Fumbles: No.	Lost	Points: Tot	PAT	FG Att	FG	Saf.	OFFENSE
CHIC. C.	233	135	81	17	531	2560	4.8	25	285	134	47.0	2134	7.5	15.9	22	12	4.2	66	39.7	35	669	19.1	4	38	915	24.1	0	23	350	15.2	2	83	749	21	16	395	53	21	8	0	CHIC. C.
CHIC. B.	242	134	93	15	557	2452	4.4	24	287	142	49.5	1894	6.6	13.3	22	19	6.6	69	42.8	55	781	14.2	1	29	751	25.9	1	30	388	12.9	1	122	1066	33	21	375	51	7	2	0	CHIC. B.
L.A.	239	100	123	16	427	1743	4.1	13	395	201	50.9	2748	7.0	13.7	28	25	6.3	63	41.8	41	514	12.5	0	42	894	21.3	1	19	223	11.7	1	98	859	32	17	327	39	11	6	0	L.A.
G.B.	172	89	58	25	446	1759	3.9	11	274	109	39.8	1364	5.0	12.5	8	29	10.6	78	40.3	47	527	11.2	0	47	926	19.7	0	29	405	14.0	0	104	941	30	19	154	16	16	6	0	G.B.
DET.	187	84	92	11	389	1360	3.5	6	324	151	46.6	2288	7.1	15.2	20	26	8.0	67	35.4	33	289	8.8	0	61	1114	18.3	0	14	91	6.5	0	49	395	35	20	200	26	6	2	0	DET.

TEAM TOTALS

							RUSHING				PASSING								RECEIVING				PUNTING		KICKING						PUNT RETURNS				KICKOFF RETURNS			
Use Name – Backs & Ends	Pos.	Age	Hgt	Wgt	Pts	Int	No.	Yds	Avg	TD	Att	Comp	%	Yds	Yd/Att	TD	Int–%	RK	No.	Yds	Avg	TD	No.	Avg	Pat	Att	%	FG	Att	%	No.	Yds	Avg	TD	No.	Yds	Avg	TD
CHICAGO CARDINALS																																						
Ray Mallouf	QB	30	5'11"	180	6		13	17	1.3	1	143	73	51	1160	8.1	13	6–4	4					45	39.0														
Paul Christman	QB	30	6'	212	6		8	6	0.8	1	114	51	45	740	6.5	5	4–4	9																				
Charley Eikenberg	QB	25	6'2"	205			2	9	4.5	0	19	6	32	116	6.1	3	2–11						2	36.0														
Charlie Trippi	HB	25	6'	185	60		128	690	5.4	6	8	4	50	118	14.8	1	0–0		22	228	10	2	13	43.4							11	213	19	2	16	354	22	0
Elmer Angsman	HB	22	5'11"	205	54		131	638	4.9	8									9	142	16	1																
Pat Harder	FB-LB	26	5'11"	205	110		126	554	4.4	6									13	93	7	0			53	53	100	7	17	41								
Vinnie Yablonski	FB-LB	26	5'8"	195	3		48	233	4.9	0									1	13	13	0						1	4	25								
Babe Dimancheff	HB	26	5'11"	180	24		27	117	4.3	1									13	260	20	3													6	118	20	0
Vic Schwall	HB	24	5'8"	185	6		15	107	7.1	1	1	0	0	0	0.0	0	0–0		2	13	7	0																
Jerry Davis	HB-DB	26	5'10"	175	12	4	12	77	6.4	0																					16	334	21	2	15	437	29	0
Corwin Clatt	FB-DB	25	6'	210		1	6	38	6.3	0																												
Red Cochran	HB-DB	26	6'	190		7	3	15	5.0	0													6	38.2							8	122	15	0	1	6	6	0
Bob Hanlon	HB-DB	23	6'1"	195		1	6	11	1.8	0																												
Mal Kutner	OE-DB	27	6'2"	197	90	2	5	50	10.0	1									41	943	23	14																
Bill Dewell	OE-DE	31	6'4"	215	12														33	442	13	2																
CHICAGO BEARS																																						
Sid Luckman	QB	31	6'	195			8	11	1.4	0	163	89	55	1047	6.4	13	14–9	8					10	38.4														
Johnny Lujack	QB-DB	23	6'	185	50	8	15	110	7.3	1	66	36	55	611	9.3	6	3–5								44	46	96	0	3	0								
Bobby Layne	QB	21	6'1"	198	6		13	80	6.1	1	52	16	31	232	6.4	3	2–4						1	24.0				0	1	0								
George Gulyanics	HB	27	6'	198	30		119	439	3.7	4									8	130	16	1	55	44.2														
George McAfee	HB-DB	30	6'	175	48	2	92	392	4.3	5	4	0	0	0	0.0	0	0–0		17	227	13	2	1	18.0							30	417	14	1	1	25	25	0
Joe Osmanski	FB	29	6'2"	215	6		74	341	4.6	1									9	43	5	0													2	26	13	0
J. R. Boone	HB-DB	22	5'8"	158	42	1	48	266	5.5	5	1	1	100	4	4.0	0	0–0		10	143	14	2									11	137	12	0	2	31	16	0
Mike Holovak	FB-LB	28	6'1"	205	12	1	30	228	7.6	2									4	30	8	0																
Noah Mullins	HB-DB	29	5'11"	180	36	7	36	208	5.8	1	1	0	0	0	0.0	0	0–0		9	127	14	4									3	33	11	0	1	41	41	0
Don Kindt	FB-LB	22	6'1"	210	12	1	54	189	3.5	2									11	137	12	0																
Frank Minini	HB	24	6'1"	212	30		24	79	3.3	2									1	14	14	1													12	370	31	1
Al Lawler	HB-DB	24	5'10"	175	6		9	44	4.9	0									3	40	13	0			3	3	100	1	1	100	5	81	16	0	3	85	28	0
Bill deCorrevont	HB-DB	29	6'	185		5	16	25	1.5	0									2	7	4	0									4	61	15	0	6	160	27	0
Fred Evans (frim CHI-AAFC)	HB-DB	27	5'11"	186	12		10	15	1.5	0									1	−2	−2	0									1	15	15	0				
Dick Flanagan	HB-DB	21	6'	205			5	14	2.8	0																												
Jim Canady	HB-DB	22	5'10"	178			2	8	4.0	0																					1	37	37	0				
Jim Keane	OE-DE	24	6'4"	218	18														30	414	14	3																
Ken Kavanaugh	OE-DE	31	6'3"	207	42														18	352	20	6																
Ed Sprinkle	OE-DE	24	6'1"	207	18		1	−2	−2.0	0									10	132	13	3																
Joe Abbey	OE-DE	22	6'1"	198															5	67	13	0																
Allen Smith	OE-DE	25	6'2"	220															3	29	10	0																
Fred Venturelli	K	30	5'11"	235	7																				4	4	100	1	2	50								
LOS ANGELES RAMS																																						
Jim Hardy	QB	26	6'	180			5	14	2.8	0	211	112	53	1390	6.6	14	7–3	4					3	50.3														
Bob Waterfield	QB-DB	28	6'1"	193	56	4	7	12	1.7	0	180	87	48	1354	7.5	14	18–10	7					43	42.6	38	44	86	6	11	55								
Paul Rickards	QB	22	6'1"	190			2	21	10.5	0	2	2	100	4	2.0	0	0–0																					
Dick Hoerner	FB-DB	26	6'4"	214	36	1	76	354	4.7	4									18	227	13	2									1	6	6	0	2	35	18	0
Kenny Washington	HB-DB	30	6'1"	220	18	2	57	301	5.3	2	1	0	0	0	0.0	0	0–0		6	104	17	1									1	12	12	0	2	54	27	0
Fred Gehrke	HB-DB	30	5'11"	190	19	2	56	246	4.4	1	1	0	0	0	0.0	0	0–0		16	173	11	1			1	1	100				19	217	11	0	17	464	27	1
Gerry Cowhig	FB-DB	27	6'2"	214	12	1	46	206	4.5	2									3	18	6	0									1	3	3	0	1	3	3	0
Dante Magnani	HB	31	5'10"	193	6		38	144	3.8	0									3	28	9	1													3	49	16	0
Les Horvath	HB-DB	27	5'10"	176	6	2	30	118	3.9	0									4	42	11	0									13	203	16	0	2	31	16	0
Jack Banta	HB-DB	30	5'11"	188			32	105	3.3	0									4	34	9	0	17	37.6							1	14	14	0	6	119	20	0
Bob Hoffman	FB-LB	30	6'1"	212	30		22	68	3.1	4									3	28	9	1													2	19	10	0
Bruce Smith (from GB)	HB-DB	28	6'	197			18	59	3.3	0	1	0	0	0	0.0	0	0–0		4	29	7	0									1	10	10	0				
Bob Alger	HB-DB	25	6'1"	205			8	41	5.1	0																												
Joe Corn	HB-DB	26	5'6"	168			11	27	2.5	0																					4	49	12	0	5	112	22	0
Tom Keane	HB-DB	21	6'1"	196	12		7	16	2.3	0									11	195	18	2																
Jim Mello (to CHI-AAFC)	FB-DB	27	5'10"	190			7	3	0.4	0									1	17	17	0																
Tom Fears	OE-DB	24	6'2"	216	30	2	2	8	4.0	0									51	698	14	4																
Red Hickey	OE-DE	31	6'2"	215	42														30	509	17	7																
Jack Zilly	OE-DE	26	6'2"	210	24														13	169	13	4																
Don Currivan (from BOS)	OE-DB	27	6'	192	24		1	−4	−4.0	0									12	218	18	3																
Frank Hubbell	OE-DE	26	6'2"	222	6														10	134	13	1																
Bill Smyth	OE-DE	26	6'3"	235	6														6	66	11	1																
Larry Brink	OE-DE	25	6'5"	217			1	−3	−3.0	0									4	36	9	0																
GREEN BAY PACKERS																																						
Jack Jacobs	QB-DB	29	6'1"	190	6		24	73	3.0	1	184	82	45	848	4.6	5	21–11	13					69	40.3							1	3	3	0				
Irv Comp	QB-DB	29	6'2"	205		5	3	3	1.0	0	49	16	33	335	6.8	1	7–14														3	35	12	0				
Perry Moss	QB	24	5'10"	170			5	2	0.4	0	17	4	24	20	1.2	0	0–0																					
Tony Canadeo	HB-DB	29	5'11"	190	24	3	123	598	4.8	4	8	2	25	24	3.0	0	0–0		9	81	9	0	1	38.0							4	55	14	0	9	166	18	0
Walt Schlinkman	FB	26	5'8"	193	24		106	441	4.2	4																									4	89	22	0
Ted Fritsch	FB-LB	27	5'10"	210	29	1	37	173	4.7	0															5	6	83	6	16	38					1	17	17	0
Ralph Earhart	HB-DB	25	5'10"	165	18		30	140	4.7	1									17	194	11	2									11	137	12	0	2	51	26	0
Fred Provo	HB-DB	26	5'9"	185			29	90	3.1	0	1	1	100	20	20.0	1	0–0		4	−9	−2	0									18	208	12	0	10	205	21	0
Oscar Smith	HB-DB	25	6'	185			27	85	3.1	0									12	121	10	0									8	71	9	0	12	287	24	0
Ed Cody	FB-DB	25	5'10"	190	11		26	58	2.2	0															11	13	85								2	31	16	0
Bob Forte	HB-DB	26	6'	195	6	5	12	30	2.5	0									6	63	11	1													2	30	15	0
Jug Girard	HB-DB	21	5'11"	175		1	13	26	2.0	0	14	4	29	117	8.4	1	1–7		1	2	2	0	8	40.0											1	20	20	0
Pat West (from LA)	FB	25	6'	200			4	24	6.0	0									3	37	12	0																
Clyde Goodnight	OE-DB	24	6'1"	195	18														28	448	16	3													1	12	12	0
Nolan Luhn	OE-DE	27	6'3"	200	12														17	285	17	2													3	18	6	0
Ted Cook	OE-DB	27	6'2"	195		6													13	156	12	0									2	18	9	0				
Gene Wilson	OE-DB	22	5'10"	180		2													2	23	12	0																
DETROIT LIONS																																						
Fred Enke	QB	23	6'1"	200			74	365	4.9	0	221	100	45	1328	6.0	11	17–8	10	1	6	6	0													5	76	15	0
Clyde LeForce	QB-WB-DB	25	5'11"	175	30	1	28	86	3.1	1	101	50	50	912	9.0	9	8–8	6	8	122	15	3									1	9	9	0	1	10	10	0
Charley Sarratt	QB-DB	24	6'1"	185			3	3	1.0	0	1	1	100	48	48.0	0	0–0		1	3	3	0	5	33.2							1	2	2	0				
Camp Wilson	FB	26	6'2"	200	12		157	612	3.9	2									2	9	5	0													10	228	23	0
Bill Dudley	HB-WB-DB	27	5'10"	176	42	1	33	97	2.9	0	1	0	0	0	0.0	0	1–100		20	210	11	6	23	35.9							8	67	8	0	10	204	20	0
Joe Watt	HB-DB	27	5'11"	183		4	20	54	2.7	0									2	29	15	0									8	87	11	0	12	180	15	0
Paul Sarringhaus	HB	27	6'	185			19	38	2.0	0									1	−1	−1	0													5	95	19	0
Ken Roskie (from GB)	FB-LB	28	6'1"	220	6	1	6	29	4.8	1																									1	30	30	0
Steve Sucic	FB-LB	27	6'	210			6	20	3.3	0																												
Andy Dudish	HB-DB	27	5'11"	185			1	5	5.0	0																					2	10	5	0	2	38	19	0
Jim Gillette	HB-DB	30	6'1"	185		6	2	3	1.5	0									1	8	8	0									2	10	5	0				
Joe Margucci	WB-DB	25	5'10"	184	30		34	14	0.4	3									36	450	13	2									10	100	10	0	10	199	20	0
George Grimes	WB-DB	26	5'11"	190	6	1	1	8	8.0	0									1	17	17	1	28	35.9							1	4	4	0				
Mel Groomes	WB-DB	21	6'	175			2	1	0.5	0									2	18	9	0																
Bob Mann	OE	24	5'11"	170	18		6	46	7.6	0									33	560	17	3													1	16	16	0
John Greene	OE-DE	28	6'	210	30														25	595	24	5													1	11	11	0
Kelley Mote	OE	25	6'2"	182															13	212	16	0													3	27	9	0
Cecil Souders	OE-DE	26	6'1"	210															2	19	10	0																
Merv Pregulman	C-LB	26	6'3"	214	32	1																			26	27	96	2	6	33								

TEAM TOTALS

DEFENSE	First Downs: Tot	by Rsh	by Pas	by Pen	Rushing: No.	Yds.	Avg. Yds.	TD	Passing: Att.	Com	Comp. Pct.	Yds.	Avg. Yds. Att.	Avg. Yds. Comp	TD	Int.	Pct. Int.	Punting: No.	Avg. Yds.	Punt Returns: No.	Yds.	Avg. Yds.	TD	Kickoff Returns: No.	Yds.	Avg. Yds.	TD	Interception Returns: No.	Yds.	Avg. Yds.	TD	Penalties: No.	Yds.	Fumbles: No.	Lost	Points: Tot	PAT	FG Att	FG	Saf.	DEFENSE
CHIC. C.	190	85	94	11	408	1516	3.7	8	336	159	47.3	2520	7.5	15.8	22	23	6.8	72	39.2	42	504	12.0	0	64	1207	18.9	1	12	143	11.9	0	87	743	30	24	226	28	11	2	0	CHIC. C.
CHIC. B.	174	71	70	33	384	1254	3.3	8	336	139	41.4	1646	4.9	11.8	12	30	8.9	82	39.5	45	413	9.2	0	59	1101	18.7	0	19	225	11.8	0	72	633	29	16	151	17	8	4	1	CHIC. B.
L.A.	204	90	97	17	441	1570	3.6	13	309	164	53.1	2143	6.9	13.1	20	19	6.1	77	41.0	32	445	13.9	1	53	1157	21.8	1	25	311	12.4	3	77	719	42	24	269	33	11	6	1	L.A.
G.B.	222	132	74	16	537	2153	4.0	21	260	134	51.5	1626	6.3	12.1	13	29	11.2	70	43.3	38	473	12.4	1	22	611	27.8	1	29	457	15.8	2	91	771	23	15	290	38	14	6	0	G.B.
DET.	253	135	103	15	495	2382	4.8	27	302	161	53.3	2176	7.2	13.5	25	14	4.6	56	40.5	32	492	15.4	1	39	908	23.3	0	26	539	20.7	4	94	894	28	19	407	51	16	6	1	DET.

BUFFALO BILLS 7-7-0 Red Dawson

Scores of Each Game		
14	San Francisco	35
42	CHICAGO	7
13	CLEVELAND	42
28	SAN FRANCISCO	38
31	BROOKLYN	21
13	NEW YORK	14
14	Cleveland	31
35	Los Angeles	21
35	BALTIMORE	17
26	Brooklyn	21
20	LOS ANGELES	27
39	Chicago	35
35	New York	14
15	Baltimore	35
	EAST Playoff	
28	Baltimore	17

Use Name	Pos.	Hgt	Wgt	Age	Int	Pts
Jack Baldwin	C-LB	6'3"	220	27		
Bob Callahan	C-LB	6'	205	24		
Buckets Hirsch	LB	5'10"	205	27		
Felto Prewitt	C-LB	5'11"	204	24		
Art Statuto	C	6'2"	220	23		
(2 yds. on pass reception lateral)						
Jerry Whalen	C-G	6'1"	235	20		
Bob Stefik	DE	5'11"	180	24		
(missed 1 PAT attempt)						
Ed Balatti (from SF and NY)	DE	6'1	205	24		
Vince Mazza	DE	6'1"	224	27		6
Carl Schuette	DB	6'1"	200	26	4	6
Alex Wizbicki	DB	5'11"	188	26	3	
(3 punt returns for 33 yds.)						

Use Name – Tackles	Pos.	Hgt	Wgt	Age	Int	Pts
Jack Carpenter	T	6'	242	25		
John Kerns	T	6'3"	240	25		
(1 kickoff return for 3 yds.)						
(2 yds. on punt return lateral)						
John Kissell	T	6'3"	234	25		

Use Name – Guards	Pos.	Hgt	Wgt	Age	Int	Pts
Ed King	G-DE	6'	218	23		
Hal Lahar	G	6'	207	29		
Rocco Pirro	G	6'	230	31		
Vin Scott	G	5'8"	215	26		
John Wyhonic	G	6'	214	28		

In the Eastern Division, a mere 7-7 record earned the Bills a share of the division lead and forced a playoff game with the Colts in Baltimore for the Eastern title. After three quarters, the Colts were sitting on a 17-7 lead before a dancing crowd of 27,327. But early in the final period George Ratterman hit Bill Gompers for a 66-yard touchdown pass to bring the count up to 17-14. A few minutes later, the Bills started on another drive deep in their own territory. Buffalo picked up two first downs before star halfback Chet Mutryn took a short pass, ran a few steps, and dropped the ball. The Colts recovered the ball, but the officials ruled it an incomplete pass. Six plays later, Al Baldwin scored on a 35-yard pass, and Buffalo wound up with a final 28-17 victory and a trip to Cleveland.

BALTIMORE COLTS 7-7-0 Cecil Isbell

Scores of Each Game		
45	NEW YORK	28
14	Chicago	21
27	New York	14
35	BROOKLYN	20
10	CLEVELAND	14
14	SAN FRANCISCO	56
29	Los Angeles	14
10	San Francisco	21
17	Buffalo	35
7	Cleveland	28
38	CHICAGO	24
14	LOS ANGELES	17
38	Brooklyn	20
35	BUFFALO	15
	EAST Playoff	
17	BUFFALO	28

Use Name	Pos.	Hgt	Wgt	Age	Int	Pts
Herb Coleman (from CHI)	C-LB	6'	200	25		
Bert Corley	C-LB	6'2"	210	28		
Len McCormick	C-LB	6'3"	232	25	1	
Ralph Stewart (from NY)	C-LB	6'	205	22		
John Sylvester	DB	6'	183	26	1	
(2 punt returns for 16 yds.)						
injured – Barry French						

Use Name – Tackles	Pos.	Hgt	Wgt	Age	Int	Pts
Lee Artoe	T	6'3"	240	32		
Pete Berezney	T	6'2"	240	24		
Ernie Blandin	T	6'4"	245	29		
John Mellus	T	6'	210	31		
Alex Sidorik	T	6'	245	26		
Jim Spruill	T	6'3"	225	25		

Use Name – Guards	Pos.	Hgt	Wgt	Age	Int	Pts
Dick Barwegan	G-LB	6'1"	215	25	1	
Bill Garrett	G	6'1"	235	24		
(1 kickoff return for 6 yds.)						
Ed Grain	G	6'	230	26		
George Groves	G-LB	5'11"	195	27		
Al Klug	G	6'1"	212	27		
Jack Simmons	G	6'4"	235	22		

The Cleveland Browns were set at quarterback with Otto Graham, so they dealt Baltimore the draft rights to a rookie passer from LSU. Y.A. Tittle, his hair already thinning, proved just the medicine to make the Colts well. In his pro debut, Tittle threw four touchdown passes to lead the Colts to a 45-28 upset of the New York Yankees. With Y.A. throwing the ball to halfback Billy Hillenbrand and end Lamar Davis, and with Buzz Mertes carrying the ball on the ground, the offense heated up enough to carry the club to a tie for first place in the Eastern Division. Two newcomers, tackle Lee Artoe and guard Dick Barwegan, beefed up the line, and rookie back Rex Grossman led the league in field goals.

NEW YORK YANKEES 6-8-0 Ray Flaherty, Red Strader

Scores of Each Game		
21	Brooklyn	3
28	Baltimore	45
0	San Francisco	41
14	BALTIMORE	27
10	Los Angeles	20
14	Buffalo	13
7	SAN FRANCISCO	21
7	Cleveland	35
42	CHICAGO	7
38	LOS ANGELES	6
21	BROOKLYN	7
21	CLEVELAND	34
14	BUFFALO	35
28	Chicago	7

Use Name	Pos.	Hgt	Wgt	Age	Int	Pts
Joe Magliolo	LB	6'	210	26	1	
Roland Nabors	C-LB	6'2"	200	24	1	
Frank Perantoni	C	6'	220	24		
Lou Sossamon	C-LB	6'1"	207	27		
John Rokisky	DE	6'2"	205	28		
Harmon Rowe	DB	6'	182	25		
(1 punt return for 12 yds.)						
Steve Sieradzki	DB	6'	194	23		

Use Name – Tackles	Pos.	Hgt	Wgt	Age	Int	Pts
Carl Butkus (from WAS-NFL)	T	6'1"	245	26		
Bill Chambers	T	6'2"	230	25		
Denver Crawford	T	6'	210	27		
Nelson Greene	T	6'2"	235	25		
Glenn Johnson	T	6'4"	260	26		
Clayton Lane	T	6'	215	26		
Paul Mitchell (from LA)	T	6'3"	240	28		
Darrell Palmer	T	6'2"	245	26		
Marion Shirley	T	6'4"	260	26		
Arnie Weinmeister	T	6'4"	235	25		

Use Name – Guards	Pos.	Hgt	Wgt	Age	Int	Pts
Mike Garzoni (from NYG-NFL)	G	5'11"	220	24		
Charley Riffle	G-LB	6'	212	30	1	
Ed Sharkey	G-LB	6'3"	215	22		
Joe Signiago	G	6'1"	215	25		
Dick Werder	G	5'9"	210	26		
Joe Yackanich	G	5'10"	205	26		

Even with a trio of blue-chip rookies, the Yankees could not repeat as Eastern champions. Tackle Arnie Weinmeister took over for the retired Bruiser Kinard with little drop in efficiency. Pete Layden, after finishing the baseball season as an outfielder with the St. Louis Browns, joined the football Yankees and backed up Spec Sanders at tailback. Defensive back Otto "The Claw" Schnellbacher earned his nickname by leading the league with eleven interceptions and then spent the winter playing professional basketball. But when the Yankees offense sputtered and faltered, they dropped six of their first eight contests. Coach Ray Flaherty paid with his job despite his two divisional crowns, and a late-season spurt under new coach Red Strader left the Yankees one game out of first place at the end of the disappointing campaign.

One mark of the team's decline is found in their two games with the Cleveland Browns. In 1947, the New Yorkers lost a close decision and then held the Browns to a tie. This year, however, the Browns took easy 35-7 and 34-21 victories.

BROOKLYN DODGERS 2-12-0 Carl Voyles

Scores of Each Game		
3	NEW YORK	21
20	San Francisco	36
7	Los Angeles	17
20	Baltimore	35
21	Buffalo	31
17	Cleveland	30
21	CHICAGO	7
35	Chicago	14
0	LOS ANGELES	17
21	BUFFALO	26
7	New York	21
40	SAN FRANCISCO	63
20	BALTIMORE	38
21	CLEVELAND	31

Use Name	Pos.	Hgt	Wgt	Age	Int	Pts
Jim Cooper	C-LB	6'	205	24		
Ed Gustafson	C-LB	6'3"	205	26		
(1 rush for 7 yds.)						
George Strohmeyer	C-LB	5'10"	200	24	4	
(1 punt return for 5 yds.)						
Caleb Warrington	C-G	6'2"	210	27		
Tom Mikula	FB-LB	5'10"	200	21		
Jim Dewar	WB-DB	6'1"	190	26		
John Klasnic	WB-DB	6'	185	21		
Doyle Tackett	BB-DB	6'	205	24		
(1 punt return for 10 yds.)						
Pepper Martin	K	5'8"	183	44		

Use Name – Tackles	Pos.	Hgt	Wgt	Age	Int	Pts
John Clowes	T	6'1"	235	26		
Charlie Huneke	T	6'3"	225	27		
Herb Nelson	T-DE	6'4"	220	27		
Martin Ruby	T	6'3"	250	28		6
Ralph Sazio	T	6'1"	220	26		
(5 yds. on rushing lateral)						
Joe Spencer	T	6'3"	235	25		
Garland Williams	T	6'3"	220	27		

Use Name – Guards	Pos.	Hgt	Wgt	Age	Int	Pts
Harry Buffington	G	6'	210	29		
Amos Harris	G	6'	210	27		
(1 kickoff return for 10 yds.)						
Bob Leonetti (from BUF)	G	6'	230	25		
Herb St. John	G	5'10"	215	22		
John Wozniak	G-LB	6'	210	27	1	
(13 yds. on rushing lateral)						

Branch Rickey had built the baseball Dodgers into a successful franchise, and now he wanted to take a crack at football. At Rickey's suggestion, the baseball club purchased the football Brooklyn Dodgers. The success of the baseball team didn't wear off on their football counterparts, as they won only two of their fourteen games. Had the Chicago Rockets not been around for the Dodgers to beat twice, Brooklyn may never have won on the gridiron. The team's only bright spots included fullback Mickey Colmer, tailbacks Bob Hoernschemeyer and Bob Chappuis, and tackle Martin Ruby—a quartet that earned the highest marks on the club.

The fans who filled Ebbets Field in the summer stayed away from the ballpark on fall Sundays. By the end of the year, Rickey and the owners of the baseball team had had enough of pro football, and they turned the club back to the league—a move which necessitated the Dodgers' merger with the New York Yankees for the 1949 season.

TEAM TOTALS

	FIRST DOWNS:				RUSHING:				PASSING:									PUNTING:		PUNT RETURNS:				KICKOFF RETURNS:				INTERCEPTION RETURNS:				PENALTIES:		FUMBLES:		POINTS:					
OFFENSE	Tot	by Rsh	by Pas	by Pen	No.	Yds.	Avg Yds.	TD	Att	Com	Comp Pct.	Yds.	Avg. Yds. Att.	Avg. Yds. Comp	TD	Int	Pct. Int.	No.	Avg. Yds.	No.	Yds.	Avg. Yds.	TD	No.	Yds.	Avg. Yds.	TD	No.	Yds.	Avg. Yds.	TD	No.	Yds.	No.	Lost	Tot	PAT	FG Att	FG	Saf.	OFFENSE
BUFFALO	223	120	89	14	539	2738	5.1	29	360	177	49.2	2683	7.5	15.2	17	26	7.2	63	38.7	33	557	**16.9**	**3**	53	1033	19.5	0	14	294	**21.0**	**2**	88	644	34	13	360	43	3	1	1	BUFFALO
BALT.	218	120	84	14	532	2166	4.1	22	340	185	54.4	**2899**	**8.5**	15.7	19	**13**	**3.8**	66	38.6	40	597	14.9	1	52	1062	20.4	0	22	262	11.9	0	84	743	33	21	333	43	18	**10**	1	BALT.
N.Y.	178	93	70	15	464	1977	4.3	20	316	139	44.0	1966	6.2	14.1	15	24	7.6	77	40.4	39	515	13.2	1	49	1128	23.0	0	27	**461**	17.1	1	84	690	35	15	265	37	7	2	0	N.Y.
BKN.	194	101	79	14	409	1787	4.4	12	**410**	188	45.9	2524	6.2	13.4	20	32	7.8	63	42.8	30	314	10.5	1	**60**	**1336**	22.3	0	25	438	17.5	1	56	410	41	15	253	31	8	2	0	BKN.
DEFENSE																																									DEFENSE
BUFFALO	207	98	95	14	463	1983	4.3	25	414	211	51.0	2829	6.8	13.4	23	14	3.4	67	43.5	40	620	15.5	1	57	1333	23.4	**0**	26	447	17.2	**0**	76	616	**44**	**26**	358	49	11	5	**0**	BUFFALO
BALT.	224	125	84	15	504	2522	5.0	21	364	177	48.6	2438	6.7	13.8	18	22	6.0	58	43.4	31	318	**10.3**	**0**	61	1176	19.3	**0**	**13**	208	16.0	2	73	556	30	14	327	43	11	2	1	BALT.
N.Y.	192	94	85	13	467	2015	4.3	18	341	160	46.9	2767	8.1	17.3	19	27	7.9	64	41.3	48	566	11.8	1	47	944	20.1	**0**	24	341	14.2	1	**89**	733	35	16	301	37	12	6	**0**	N.Y.
BKN.	226	146	72	8	585	3146	5.4	30	**296**	160	54.1	**1985**	6.7	**12.4**	23	25	8.4	51	39.8	38	699	18.4	2	48	1007	21.0	1	32	321	10.3	1	82	775	37	17	387	48	12	7	**0**	BKN.

Use Name – Backs & Ends	Pos.	Age	Hgt	Wgt	Pts	Int	RUSHING				PASSING								RECEIVING				PUNTING		KICKING						PUNT RETURNS				KICKOFF RETURNS			
							No.	Yds	Avg	TD	Att	Comp	%	Yds	Yd/Att	TD	Int-%	RK	No.	Yds	Avg	TD	No.	Avg	Pat	Att	%	FG	Att	%	No.	Yds	Avg	TD	No.	Yds	Avg	TD
BUFFALO BILLS																																						
George Ratterman	QB	21	6'1"	182	18		12	-18	-1.5	3	335	168	50	2577	7.7	16	22-7	4																				
Jim Still	QB-DB	24	6'3"	190		1	5	-26	-5.2	0	14	5	36	89	6.4	1	3-21						47	38.8														
Chet Mutryn	HB-DB	27	5'9"	173	96		147	823	5.6	10	6	2	33	21	3.5	0	0-0		39	794	20	5									10	171	17	1	19	500	26	0
Lou Tomasetti	HB	32	6'	205	48		134	716	5.3	7									22	213	10	1													2	14	7	0
Bob Steuber	FB-LB	26	6'2"	200	41		69	437	6.3	3	2	1	50	-4	-2.0	0	0-0		2	14	7	0	1	40.0	20	23	87	1	2	50					6	123	21	0
Bill Gompers	HB-DB	20	6'1'	185	6	2	48	219	4.6	1																					1	10	10	0	4	62	16	0
Vic Kulbitski	FB-LB	27	5'10"	206	14		40	152	3.8	0									3	37	12	0			8	10	80								1	18	18	0
Rex Bumgardner	HB-DB	24	5'11"	193	12	2	14	82	5.9	0									1	63	63	0									16	336	21	2	9	141	16	0
Don Schneider	HB	24	5'9"	170			15	70	4.7	0									1	14	14	0									1	4	4	0	4	77	19	0
Chick Maggioli	HB-DB	26	5'11"	180		1	11	27	2.5	0	1	1	100	0	0.0	0	0-0		3	23	8	0	2	47.5							1	0	0	0	2	38	19	0
Al Akins (from BKN)	HB-DB	27	6'1"	208			4	-9	-2.2	0									3	12	4	0																
Al Baldwin	OE	25	6'2"	198	48														54	916	17	8			0	1	0											
Bill O'Connor	OE-DE	22	6'4"	220	12														31	301	10	2													1	0	0	0
Paul Gibson	OE-DB	23	6'2"	190															11	216	20	0																
Marty Comer	OE-DE	30	6'	205	6														5	66	13	1																
George Kisiday	OE-DE	25	6'1"	220															1	20	20	0																
Graham Armstrong	T	29	6'4"	240	15														1	0	0	0			15	17	88	0	1	0					1	9	9	0
BALTIMORE COLTS																																						
Y. A. Tittle	QB	21	6'	190	24		52	157	3.0	4	289	161	56	2522	8.7	16	9-3	1																				
Charlie O'Rourke	QB	31	5'11"	175	6		7	15	2.1	1	51	24	47	377	7.4	3	4-8						66	38.6														
Buzz Mertes	FB	27	6'	205	24		155	680	4.4	4									6	56	9	0													1	15	15	0
Billy Hillenbrand	HB-DB	26	6'	188	78		100	510	5.1	7									50	970	19	6									18	231	13	0	16	356	22	0
Bob Pfohl	HB-DB	22	6'	200	36		107	455	4.3	4									13	134	10	1									2	102	51	1	17	366	22	0
Lu Gambino	FB-LB	24	6'1"	205	6		54	194	3.6	1									6	28	5	0													3	57	19	0
Jake Leicht	HB-DB	27	5'9"	170	12	5	20	88	4.4	1									12	134	11	1									8	139	17	0	4	83	21	0
Aubrey Fowler	HB-DB	28	5'10"	160		3	6	30	5.0	0																					4	41	10	0	2	16	8	0
Lew Mayne	HB-DB	28	6'1"	190			14	26	1.9	0									2	33	17	0									2	24	12	0	3	61	20	0
John Vardian	HB-DB	23	5'8"	168			6	13	2.2	0									3	26	9	0									3	34	11	0	3	66	22	0
Spiro Dellerba	FB-LB	25	5'11"	200		2	2	0	0.0	0																									1	12	12	0
Rex Grossman	FB-LB	24	6'1"	215	73	2	8	-3	-0.4	0															43	43	100	10	18	56								
Lamar Davis	OE-DB	27	6'1"	185	42	5													41	765	19	7									1	10	10	0				
Win Williams	OE	25	6'2"	185	12														32	360	11	2													1	20	20	0
John North	OE-DB	27	6'2"	198	12	1													8	204	26	1																
Joe Smith	OE-DB	26	6'1"	183	6	1	1	1	1.0	0									8	131	16	1																
Hub Bechtol	OE-DE	22	6'3"	200															2	25	13	0													0	4	–	0
Bob Nowaskey (from LA)	OE-DE	30	6'	200															1	31	31	0																
Ollie Poole	OE-DE	26	6'3"	220															1	2	2	0																
NEW YORK YANKEES																																						
Spec Sanders	TB-DB	29	6'1"	196	54	1	169	759	4.5	9	168	78	46	918	5.5	5	11-7	9					42	40.6							13	128	10	0	9	217	24	0
Pete Layden	TB-DB	28	5'11"	195	18	3	95	576	6.1	3	105	43	41	816	7.8	9	8-8	7					21	42.1							7	64	9	0	8	211	26	0
Al Dekdebrun (to BOS-NFL)	TB-DB	27	5'11"	185		1	7	24	3.4	0	20	10	50	149	7.5	0	2-10														1	12	12	0	1	15	15	0
Bud Schwenk	TB	30	6'2"	200			3	6	2.0	0	17	6	35	52	3.1	0	3-18																					
Tom Casey	TB-DB	24	5'11"	175	6		18	75	4.2	0	5	2	40	31	6.2	1	0-0						6	40.3							9	229	25	1	7	170	24	0
Buddy Young	FB-DB	22	5'5"	170	30		70	245	3.5	1									21	259	12	4									2	11	6	0	12	303	25	0
Bill Daley	FB-DB	28	6'2"	210	6		40	102	2.6	1									4	31	8	0	1	41.0											4	88	22	0
Lowell Tew	FB	21	5'11"	195	30		24	95	4.0	5									7	97	14	0													3	75	25	0
Bob Kennedy	FB-DB	27	5'11"	195	6	4	33	90	2.7	1	1	0	0	0	0.0	0	0-0		5	23	5	0	7	33.9							1	14	14	0	2	20	10	0
Lowell Wagner	WB-DB	24	6'	193	6	1													6	99	17	1																
Duke Iverson	WB-DB	28	6'2"	188		1													4	30	8	0																
Lloyd Cheatham	BB	29	6'2"	215			2	1	0.5	0									7	76	11	0													1	18	18	0
Bob Sweiger	BB-LB	29	6'	209			3	4	1.3	0									12	129	11	0													1	3	3	0
Howie Parker	BB-LB	22	6'2"	220															1	17	17	0																
Harvey Johnson	BB-LB	29	5'11"	210	43														1	6	6	0			37	37	100	2	7	29								
Bruce Alford	OE	27	6'	190	18														32	578	18	3																
Jack Russell	OE-DE	28	6'1"	215	36	1													23	433	19	6																
Otto Schnellbacher	OE-DB	25	6'2"	185	6	11													5	72	14	0									5	45	9	0				
Van Davis	OE-DE	26	6'2"	215	6	1													4	49	12	1																
Paul Cleary	OE-DE	26	6'1"	196															4	37	9	0													1	8	8	0
Flip McDonald	OE-DE	27	6'2"	210															3	30	10	0																
BROOKLYN DODGERS																																						
Bob Chappuis	TB-DB	25	6'	190	6		52	310	6.0	1	213	100	47	1402	6.6	8	15-7	8													1	8	8	0	3	55	18	0
Bob Hoernschemeyer	TB-WB-DB	22	5'11"	192	42		110	574	5.2	3	155	71	46	854	5.5	8	15-10	10	11	173	16	3	1	40.0							1	3	3	0	6	138	23	0
Monk Gafford	TB-WB-DB	27	5'11"	195	30		30	51	1.7	1	39	17	44	268	6.9	4	2-5		15	274	18	4									14	130	9	0	23	559	24	0
Mickey Colmer	FB-LB	29	6'2"	218	60		164	704	4.3	6	1	0	0	0	0.0	0	0-0		21	372	18	4	56	42.5											8	163	20	0
Morrie Warren	FB-LB	24	5'11"	208			1	1	1.0	0																									1	36	36	0
Bob Sullivan	FB-LB	23	5'9"	195			2	-1	-0.5	0																									1	22	22	0
Lee Tevis	FB-LB	26	5'11"	190	10						1	0	0	0	0.0	0	0-0		1	-8	-8	0	5	42.8	4	4	100	2	7	29	6	59	10	0	2	40	20	0
Nick Forkovitch	FB-LB	28	5'11"	195			1	4	4.0	0																												
Ray Ramsey	WB-DB	27	6'2"	170	18	7	22	48	2.2	0	1	0	0	0	0.0	0	0-0		13	315	24	2									5	82	16	1	10	233	23	0
Jim Camp	WB-DB	24	6'	170		1	8	43	5.4	0									1	43	43	0													1	12	12	0
Hardy Brown	WB-DB	24	6'	185	37	1	6	23	3.8	1									3	36	12	1			25	29	86	0	1	0								
Hugo Marcolini	WB-DB	25	6'	203			5	11	2.2	0									2	38	19	0													2	33	17	0
Carl Allen	WB-DB	27	6'	175	6	2	1	9	9.0	0																					1	17	17	0				
Jim Smith (from BUF)	WB-DB	23	6'1"	188		4	1	7	7.0	0													14	38.4							1	1	1	0				
Walt McDonald	BB-DB	27	6'1"	210	6	3	6	15	2.5	0									7	41	6	1																
Saxon Judd	OE	27	6'1"	190	12														32	350	11	2																
Max Morris	OE	23	6'2"	200	6														28	372	13	1													1	14	14	0
Dan Edwards	OE-DE	22	6'1"	200															23	176	8	0													1	21	21	0
Hank Foldberg	OE-DE	25	6'1"	200	6														16	129	8	0																
Harry Burrus (from CHI)	OE-DB	27	6'1"	195	8	3	1	-3	-3.0	0									10	227	23	1			2	3	67											
Hal Thompson	OE-DE	26	6'1"	205	6														4	37	9	1																
Ed Scruggs	OE-DE	25	6'1"	195															1	8	8	0																

CLEVELAND BROWNS 14-0-0 Paul Brown

Scores of Each Game		
19	LOS ANGELES	14
42	Buffalo	13
28	Chicago	7
21	CHICAGO	10
14	Baltimore	10
30	BROOKLYN	17
31	BUFFALO	14
35	NEW YORK	7
28	BALTIMORE	7
14	SAN FRANCISCO	7
34	New York	21
31	Los Angeles	14
31	San Francisco	28
31	Brooklyn	21

Use Name	Pos.	Hgt	Wgt	Age	Int	Pts
Frank Gatski	C	6'3"	220	26		
Mel Maceau	C-LB	6'	203	26		
Lou Saban	LB	6'	198	26	5	
Frank Kosikowski	DE	6'1"	200	22		
injured – Warren Lahr						

Use Name – Tackles	Pos.	Hgt	Wgt	Age	Int	Pts
Chet Adams	T	6'3"	230	32		
Chubby Grigg	T	6'2"	280	22		
Ben Pucci	T	6'4"	245	23		
Lou Rymkus	T	6'4"	230	29		
Len Simonetti	T	5'11"	225	29		

Use Name – Guards	Pos.	Hgt	Wgt	Age	Int	Pts
Alex Agase	G-LB	5'10"	212	26		
Bob Gaudio (1 rush for 2 yds.)	G-LB	5'10"	215	23		
Lin Houston	G	6'	205	27		
Weldon Humble	G-LB	6'1"	215	27	1	
Ed Ulinski	G	5'11"	200	27		
Bill Willis	G	6'2"	210	27		

They hardly needed any strengthening, but the Browns went into the season with new help in halfback Dub Jones, guard Weldon Humble, linebacker Tony Adamle, and end and punter Horace Gillom. With last year's powerhouse intact, the Browns ripped through the league undefeated, untied, and unthreatened by any other team. Only San Francisco had hopes of knocking off the Browns, and their two meetings became the high points of the AAFC season. A pulsating crowd of 82,769 in Cleveland watched the Browns tumble the '49ers from the undefeated ranks with a hard-fought 14-7 decision. Their rematch in San Francisco drew an audience of 59,785 and wound up in a 31-28 Brown victory.

A look at the Cleveland roster explained their dominance of the league. Eight Browns won spots on the first or second All-League teams, with Otto Graham, Marion Motley, Mac Speedie, Dante Lavelli, Lou Rymkus, Bill Willis, Ed Ulinski, and Lou Saban thus honored. With San Francisco disposed of, the title game against the Eastern champion Buffalo Bills had to be anticlimactic.

SAN FRANCISCO 49ers 12-2-0 Buck Shaw

Scores of Each Game		
35	BUFFALO	14
36	BROOKLYN	20
41	NEW YORK	0
36	LOS ANGELES	14
38	Buffalo	28
31	Chicago	14
56	Baltimore	14
21	New York	7
21	BALTIMORE	10
44	CHICAGO	21
7	Cleveland	14
63	Brooklyn	40
28	CLEVELAND	31
38	Los Angeles	21

Use Name	Pos.	Hgt	Wgt	Age	Int	Pts
Art Elston	C-G-LB	5'11"	190	29	1	
Bill Johnson	C-LB	6'3"	210	22	1	
Walt McCormick	C-LB	6'1"	215	21		
Joel Williams	C-LB	6'1"	215	20		
Ken Casanega	HB-DB	5'11"	175	27		

Use Name – Tackles	Pos.	Hgt	Wgt	Age	Int	Pts
Bob Bryant (1 punt return for 14 yds.)	T	6'3"	225	29		
Floyd Collier	T	6'1"	215	24		
Charlie Elliott (from CHI)	T	6'2"	240	26		
Visco Grgich	T	5'11"	210	25		
Fred Land	T-G	6'1"	220	23		
Bob Mike	T	6'1"	220	24		
Hal Puddy	T	6'3"	220	23		
John Woudenberg	T	6'3"	225	30		

Use Name – Guards	Pos.	Hgt	Wgt	Age	Int	Pts
Bruno Banducci	G	5'11"	215	26		
Roman Bentz (from NY)	G	6'2"	230	29		
Don Clark	G-LB	5'11"	197	24	1	
Jim Cox	G-LB	6'1"	208	27		
Paul Evansen	G	6'3"	240	26		
Riley Matheson	G-LB	6'2"	210	33	2	

Joe "the Jet" Perry got his pro career off the ground with a flash of light when, on his first play, he jetted 58 yards to the end zone. Perry would face insults and violence because of his black skin, but his talents and determination kept him in the league long after the black man had made his mark in pro football. But Perry was just one back on the team with the greatest running in the history of pro football. The '49ers gained 3,663 yards rushing, averaged 6.1 yards per carry, 262 yards per game, scored thirty-five rushing TDs, and a total of 495 points, all records which still stand. The starting backfield of Albert, Strzykalski, Eshmont and Standlee rushed for 2,122 yards on 337 carries, and the second-string unit of Wallace, Lillywhite, Hall, and Standlee racked up 1,016 yards on only 174 attempts! The stand-out linemen leading the way for these ball carriers were tackles Visco Grgich and John Woudenberg and guards Bruno Banducci and Riley Matheson. Despite this, the '49ers still were bridesmaids for the Browns and their superior defense.

LOS ANGELES DONS 7-7-0 Jim Phelan

Scores of Each Game		
7	Chicago	0
14	Cleveland	19
17	BROOKLYN	7
14	San Francisco	36
20	NEW YORK	10
49	CHICAGO	28
14	BALTIMORE	29
21	BUFFALO	35
17	Brooklyn	0
6	New York	38
27	Buffalo	20
17	Baltimore	14
14	CLEVELAND	31
21	SAN FRANCISCO	38

Use Name	Pos.	Hgt	Wgt	Age	Int	Pts
John Brown	C-LB	6'4"	230	26	1	
Jack Flagerman (6 yds. on pass reception lateral)	C-LB	6'	218	26		
Bob Nelson (1 rush for –7 yds.)	C-LB	6'1"	215	28	1	
Ezz Anderson – Canadian Football League						

Use Name – Tackles	Pos.	Hgt	Wgt	Age	Int	Pts
Earl Audet	T	6'2"	252	27		
Don Avery	T	6'4"	260	27		
Dick Danabe	T	6'2"	235	23		
Clyde Johnson	T	6'6"	270	31		
Mike Perrotti (7 yds. on pass reception lateral)	T	6'3"	240	25		
Bill Smith (from CHI)	T	6'2"	250	21		
Bernie Winkler	T	6'1"	232	22		

Use Name – Guards	Pos.	Hgt	Wgt	Age	Int	Pts
Ray Frankowski	G	5'11"	230	29		
Len Levy	G	6'	252	27		
Al Lolotai	G	6'	233	27		
Knox Ramsey	G	6'1"	210	22		
Hank Rockwell (6 yds. on pass reception lateral)	G-C	6'4"	245	31		

Attendance at Dons' games dropped off this year, but wealthy owner Ben Lindheimer kept shelling out money to sign new talent. He brought halfback Herm Wedemeyer into the fold with a $12,000 contract, which was big money for a rookie. He signed Len Ford, a 230-pound end who would later become a great defensive end for the Browns. But all of Lindheimer's money couldn't get the Dons past Cleveland or San Francisco.

But the Dons did showcase some excellent football players. Glen Dobbs regained his 1946 form and gave the team a top passer and good runner. Veteran Joe Aguirre and rookie Wedemeyer both gave Dobbs easy targets to throw to, linemen Bob Nelson and Bob Reinhard gave the passer plenty of time to set up, and place-kicker Ben Agajanian put his toeless right foot to good use in belting field goals—enough of an array of talent to claim show money in a difficult field.

CHICAGO ROCKETS 1-13-0 Ed McKeever

Scores of Each Game		
0	LOS ANGELES	7
7	Buffalo	42
21	BALTIMORE	14
7	CLEVELAND	28
10	Cleveland	21
14	SAN FRANCISCO	31
28	Los Angeles	49
7	Brooklyn	21
14	BROOKLYN	35
7	New York	42
21	San Francisco	44
24	Baltimore	38
35	BUFFALO	39
7	NEW YORK	28

Use Name	Pos.	Hgt	Wgt	Age	Int	Pts
Pete Lamana	C-LB	5'11"	210	27	1	
Fred Negus	C-LB	6'1"	205	26	5	6
John Rapacz	C	6'4"	230	23		
Farnham Johnson (2 PAT in 2 attemnts)	DE	6'	210	24		2
Ike Owens	DE	6'1"	190	27		
Fred Evans (to CHIB-NFL)	HB-DB	5'11"	186	27		
Joe Prokop	HB-DB	6'2"	170	27		

Use Name – Tackles	Pos.	Hgt	Wgt	Age	Int	Pts
Jim Brutz	T	6'	230	29		
Ziggy Czarobski	T	6'	225	25		
Ed Ecker	T	6'7"	285	25		
Nate Johnson	T	6'3"	240	28		
Roman Piskor	T	6'	245	30		
Emil Uremovich	T	6'2"	235	31	1	
Bill Bass – Canadian Football League						

Use Name – Guards	Pos.	Hgt	Wgt	Age	Int	Pts
George Bernhardt (from BKN)	G	5'10"	215	29		
Bob David (from LA-NFL)	G	6'	215	26		
Chet Kozel (from BUF)	G	6'2"	215	28		
Jim Pearcy	G	5'11"	220	29		
Joe Ruetz	G	6'	200	31		
Gasper Urban	G-LB	6'1"	215	25	1	

For the third straight year, the Rockets had new owners and a new coach. This year's head coach was Ed McKeever, privileged with a sideline seat for the Rockets' miserable season. The Rockets had the worst situation of any pro-football franchise; in addition to battling both the Bears and Cardinals for the Chicago sports dollar, the Rockets had to contend with constant turnover in their own leadership. Their pitiful performance on the field drove whatever fans they had away and forced this year's owners to look for a new buyer.

The Rockets fielded a collection of rookies, NFL rejects, and marginal veterans in their march to nowhere. The only player on the roster destined to go far in pro football spent most of the season in a hospital bed. Elroy "Crazy Legs" Hirsch got hit in an early game and didn't get up; when he awoke, he was in the hospital with a fractured skull and a loss of body coordination. Doctors told him to forget football; he instead forgot the doctors' advice and worked his way back to become a star pass receiver in the 1950s.

TEAM TOTALS

	FIRST DOWNS:				RUSHING:				PASSING:									PUNTING:	
OFFENSE	Tot	by Rsh	by Pas	by Pen	No.	Yds.	Avg. Yds.	TD	Att.	Com	Comp. Pct.	Yds.	Avg. Yds. Att.	Avg. Yds. Comp	TD	Int.	Pct. Int.	No.	Avg. Yds.
CLEVE.	243	123	104	16	544	2557	4.7	25	344	178	51.7	2809	8.2	15.8	26	16	4.7	56	35.0
S.F.	227	152	67	8	603	3663	6.1	35	288	162	56.3	2104	7.3	13.0	30	14	4.9	44	42.6
L.A.	186	78	93	15	400	1554	3.9	11	406	195	48.0	2497	6.2	12.8	21	24	5.9	76	47.2
CHICAGO	180	102	65	13	484	1719	3.6	8	341	146	42.8	2290	6.7	15.7	19	38	11.1	60	44.7
DEFENSE																			
CLEVE.	171	84	74	13	436	1519	3.5	10	354	159	44.9	2097	5.9	13.2	14	24	6.8	73	39.7
S.F.	203	100	90	13	468	1906	4.1	11	374	184	49.2	2615	7.0	13.2	23	32	8.6	68	40.5
L.A.	209	125	70	14	514	2456	4.8	14	344	164	47.7	2473	7.5	15.7	24	24	7.0	67	40.7
CHICAGO	217	117	81	19	538	2614	4.9	33	318	155	48.7	2568	7.8	16.0	23	19	6.0	57	42.3

PUNT RETURNS:				KICKOFF RETURNS:				INTERCEPTION RETURNS:				PENALTIES:		FUMBLES:		POINTS:					TEAM TOTALS
No.	Yds.	Avg. Yds.	TD	No.	Yds.	Avg. Yds.	TD	No.	Yds.	Avg. Yds.	TD	No.	Yds.	No.	Lost	Tot	PAT	FG Att	FG	Saf.	OFFENSE
39	385	9.9	0	40	752	18.8	0	24	283	11.8	0	77	761	25	11	389	51	19	8	1	CLEVE.
44	676	15.4	0	45	1098	24.4	1	32	357	11.2	2	89	794	38	21	495	64	8	5	1	S.F.
44	730	16.6	1	56	1093	19.5	0	24	295	12.3	2	77	715	36	16	258	33	15	5	0	L.A.
32	348	10.9	0	60	1265	21.1	0	19	247	13.0	0	78	659	51	27	202	28	4	2	0	CHICAGO
																					DEFENSE
32	356	11.1	0	48	1151	24.0	0	16	359	22.4	1	76	657	44	16	190	25	8	3	0	CLEVE.
24	314	13.1	0	70	1511	21.6	0	14	119	8.5	0	72	567	35	20	248	32	5	2	0	S.F.
52	644	12.4	1	45	962	21.4	0	24	206	8.6	0	76	805	38	16	305	38	12	7	3	L.A.
36	605	16.8	2	39	683	17.5	0	38	636	16.7	3	89	707	30	14	439	58	11	3	0	CHICAGO

Use Name – Backs & Ends	Pos.	Age	Hgt	Wgt	Pts	Int	RUSHING				PASSING								RECEIVING				PUNTING		KICKING						PUNT RETURNS				KICKOFF RETURNS			
							No.	Yds	Avg	TD	Att	Comp	%	Yds	Yd/Att	TD	Int–%	RK	No.	Yds	Avg	TD	No.	Avg	Pat	Att	%	FG	Att	%	No.	Yds	Avg	TD	No.	Yds	Avg	TD
CLEVELAND BROWNS																																						
Otto Graham	QB-DB	26	6'1"	190	36	1	23	146	6.3	6	333	173	52	2713	8.1	25	15–5	3													1	12	12	0				
Cliff Lewis	QB-DB	25	5'11"	165		9	5	44	8.8	0	8	4	50	69	8.6	1	0–0						1	18.0							26	258	10	0	7	147	21	0
George Terlep (from BUF)	QB	26	5'10"	180			1	4	4.0	0	4	1	25	27	6.8	0	2–50																					
Marion Motley	FB-LB	28	6'1"	220	42		157	964	6.1	5	1	0	0	0	0.0	0	0–0		13	192	15	2													14	337	24	0
Special Delivery Jones	HB	29	5'10"	195	60		100	400	4.0	5									14	293	21	5																
Bill Boedecker	HB-DB	24	5'11"	190	30		78	254	3.3	3									13	237	18	2									2	8	4	0	4	61	15	0
Dub Jones	HB-DB	23	6'4"	200	18		33	149	4.5	1									9	119	13	2													2	35	18	0
Ara Parseghian	HB-DB	25	5'10"	192	12	1	32	135	4.2	1									2	31	16	1													2	41	21	0
Ollie Cline	FB-LB	22	6'	200			29	129	4.4	0																									3	55	18	0
Bob Cowan	HB-DB	25	5'11"	185	30		33	99	3.0	1									15	265	18	4													3	53	18	0
Tony Adamle	FB-LB	24	6'	210	6		17	88	5.2	1																												
Tom Colella	HB-DB	30	6'	187	6	2	14	60	4.3	1									1	7	7	0	49	35.0							5	60	12	0				
Dean Sensenbaugher	HB-DB	23	5'9"	190	6		18	59	3.3	1																												
Tommy James	HB-DB	24	5'10"	180		4	1	8	8.0	0									1	44	44	0									5	47	9	0				
Mac Speedie	OE	28	6'3"	200	24		1	7	7.0	0									58	816	14	4													1	13	13	0
Dante Lavelli	OE	25	6'	190	30		1	9	9.0	0									25	463	19	5													1	0	0	0
Horace Gillom	OE-DE	27	6'1"	208	6														20	295	15	1	6	37.8											3	10	3	0
John Yonaker	OE-DE	27	6'5"	218		1													5	27	5	0																
George Young	OE-DE	24	6'3"	210	6														2	20	10	0																
Lou Groza	T	24	6'3"	215	75																				51	52	98	8	19	42								
SAN FRANCISCO 49ers																																						
Frankie Albert	QB	28	5'10"	160	49		69	349	5.1	8	264	154	58	1990	7.6	29	10–4	2	1	1	1	0	35	44.8	1	2	50											
Bev Wallace	QB	25	6'2"	180			3	2	0.7	0	22	8	36	114	5.2	1	3–14						4	38.4														
Johnny Strzykalski	HB-DB	25	5'9"	190	66	3	141	915	6.5	4	1	0	0	0	0.0	0	0–0		26	485	19	7									13	201	15	0	9	185	21	0
Joe Perry	FB-DB	21	6'	195	72	1	77	562	7.3	10									8	79	10	1													4	145	36	1
Forrest Hall	HB	25	5'8"	155	12		66	413	6.3	2									4	87	22	0									3	97	32	0	13	369	28	0
Verl Lillywhite	HB-DB	21	5'10"	185	18	3	53	340	6.4	3	1	0	0	0	0.0	0	1–100		1	–1	–1	0	3	25.3							3	41	14	0				
Len Eshmont	HB-DB	31	5'11"	178	12	1	50	296	5.9	1									14	214	15	0													1	32	32	0
Norm Standlee	FB-LB	29	6'2"	245	18		52	261	5.0	3									1	1	1	0													1	31	31	0
Jim Cason	HB-DB	21	6'	168	18	5	20	146	7.3	2									4	99	25	1									22	309	14	0	10	212	21	0
Bob Sullivan	HB-DB	25	5'10"	190	6	1	33	121	3.7	0									4	58	15	1													2	40	20	0
Ed Carr	HB-DB	21	6'	185	12	7	14	121	8.6	1									3	40	13	0													1	16	16	0
Joe Vetrano	HB	26	5'9"	170	83		12	71	5.9	1									1	34	34	0	1	38.0	62	66	94	5	8	63					1	38	38	0
Paul Crowe	HB-DB	24	6'1"	195	12	5	12	65	5.4	0									0	16	–	1									2	14	7	0	2	18	9	0
Alyn Beals	OE	27	6'	185	84														46	591	13	14																
Nick Susoeff	OE-DE	27	6'1"	210	6														27	237	9	1													1	12	12	0
Hal Shoener	OE-DE	25	6'3"	200	18														15	76	5	3																
Gail Bruce	OE-DE	24	6'1"	205			1	1	1.0	0									5	49	10	0																
Norm Maloney	OE-DE	25	6'1"	190	7														1	29	29	1			1	1	100											
Clarence Howell	OE-DE	21	6'1"	188		1													1	9	9	0																
LOS ANGELES DONS																																						
Glenn Dobbs	TB-DB	28	6'4"	210	24	1	91	539	5.9	4	369	185	50	2403	6.5	21	20–5	5	2	11	6	0	68	49.1											2	38	19	0
Herm Wedemeyer	TB-HB	24	5'10"	178	12		79	249	3.2	0	30	9	30	79	2.6	0	3–10		36	330	9	2	1	10.0							23	368	16	0	11	240	22	0
Bill Reinhard	TB-HB-DB	26	5'10"	170	12	4	6	31	5.2	0	5	0	0	0	0.0	0	0–0		5	48	10	0									16	276	17	1	2	41	21	0
Walt Clay	HB-DB	24	5'11"	195	24	2	86	293	3.4	3									10	118	12	1													4	48	12	0
John Kimbrough	FB	30	6'2"	210	30		76	189	2.5	3									10	131	13	0													4	54	14	0
Mike Graham	FB-LB	23	6'	200	6	1	19	69	3.6	1									0	2	–	0													6	145	24	0
Jeff Durkota	FB-LB	24	6'	205		1	14	66	4.7	0									2	12	6	0													9	198	22	0
Lin Sexton	HB-DB	22	6'	180		1	7	39	5.6	0																					3	47	16	0	3	49	16	0
Bob Reinhard	FB-DT	27	6'4"	238			1	21	21.0	0									4	54	14	0	6	34.0							1	23	23	0	3	51	17	0
Len Masini (from SF)	FB-LB	27	6'	225			3	12	4.0	0									1	–1	–1	0																
Bob Kelly	HB-DB	23	5'10"	193		3	3	10	3.3	0																												
John Naumu	HB	27	5'8"	175			1	0	0.0	0													1	34.0											6	131	22	0
Walt Heap	BB-DB	26	6'1"	210	6	5	3	12	4.0	0									2	9	5	0																
Dick Ottele	BB-DB	21	6'3"	210			2	11	5.5	0																									3	47	16	0
Bob Mitchell	BB-DB	27	5'11"	195		3	2	–2	–1.0	0	2	1	50	15	7.5	0	1–50																					
Joe Aguirre	OE-DE	29	6'4"	225	56														38	599	16	9			2	3	67								1	10	10	0
Len Ford	OE-DE	22	6'4"	230	42	1													31	598	19	7													1	24	24	0
Dale Gentry	OE-DE	31	6'3"	223															28	308	11	0																
Burr Baldwin	OE-DE	26	6'1"	195															10	96	10	0																
Bill Fisk	OE-DE	31	6'	205															9	102	11	0																
Lou Mihajlovich	OE	23	5'11"	175															4	42	11	0																
Ben Agajanian	K	29	6'	215	46																				31	32	97	5	15	33								
CHICAGO ROCKETS																																						
Jess Freitas	QB	27	5'10"	170			24	25	1.0	0	167	84	50	1425	8.5	14	16–10	5																				
Sam Vacanti (to BAL)	QB	26	5'11"	200	12		7	7	1.0	2	116	47	41	633	5.5	2	15–13	11																				
Angelo Bertelli	QB	27	6'1"	190			2	–1	–0.5	0	32	7	22	60	1.9	1	3–9																					
Tom Farris	QB	27	6'1"	185			4	5	1.3	0	9	3	33	24	2.7	0	3–33																					
Julie Rykovich (from BUF)	HB-DB	24	6'2"	200	36	3	96	425	4.4	6	1	1	100	12	12.0	0	0–0		5	71	14	0									1	23	23	0	7	129	18	0
Eddie Prokop	HB-DB	26	5'11"	200	24		54	266	4.9	1	1	0	0	0	0.0	0	0–0		7	223	32	3									6	80	13	0	15	323	22	0
Jim Mello (from LA-NFL)	FB-DB	27	5'10"	190	6		50	243	4.9	1									3	38	13	0													2	30	15	0
Dewey Proctor	FB-LB	27	5'11"	215	6		47	190	4.0	1									2	18	9	0																
Bob Livingstone	HB-DB	26	6'	175	12		55	174	3.2	0									15	240	16	2									3	24	8	0	9	211	23	0
Chuck Fenenbock (from LA)	HB-DB	30	5'9"	175	6		43	174	4.0	0	15	4	27	136	9.1	2	1–7		8	111	14	1									17	169	10	0	14	311	22	0
Floyd Simmons	HB-DB	23	6'1"	200	12		36	121	3.4	1									2	60	31	1													3	77	26	0
Bill Kellagher	FB-LB	28	5'11"	205	6		33	97	2.9	1																									3	54	18	0
Crazy Legs Hirsch	HB-DB	24	6'2"	190	6	2	23	93	4.0	0									7	101	14	1									2	27	14	0	1	10	10	0
Harry Clark (from LA)	HB-DB	30	6'	195			22	79	3.6	0									4	38	10	0									2	27	14	0	4	96	24	0
Ernie Lewis	FB-LB	24	6'1"	215			13	54	4.2	0									1	6	6	0	60	44.7														
Steve Juzwik	HB	30	5'8"	184	5		13	19	1.5	0									1	5	5	0			5	5	100											
Bob Perina	HB-DB	27	6'1"	205		6	6	1	0.2	0									2	13	7	0									2	14	7	0	3	52	17	0
Fay King	OE	26	6'3"	195	42														50	647	13	7													1	11	11	0
Bob Jensen	OE-DE	22	6'4"	207	6														20	276	14	1													1	10	10	0
Ray Kuffell	OE-DE	26	6'3"	215	18														19	365	19	3													1	16	16	0
Jim McCarthy	OE-DE	26	6'1"	205	27														3	30	10	0			21	21	100	2	3	67								

N. F. L. – December 19, at Philadelphia (Attendance 36,309)

Fit for Neither Man Nor Beast

A heavy snowstorm that fell throughout the game made football a makeshift operation in this championship game. Although the tarpaulin was taken off the field only thirty minutes before the opening kickoff, snow had completely obliterated all yard markers by the time the contest began; all first down and out-of-bounds decisions were pure judgment decisions by the officials. Before the game was very old, several inches of snow coated the field and made secure footing a pipe dream. A consistent passing attack was out of the question, but both clubs had a full stable of strong runners. On their first play from scrimmage, the Eagles went for broke, with Tommy Thompson heaving a long bomb which Jack Ferrante hauled 65 yards to the end zone; an offside penalty nullified the score, however, and the game settled into a contest of power running. The Cardinals used smashes by Elmer Angsman, Pat Harder, and Charlie Trippi to move the ball down to the Philadelphia 29-yard line, where the attack stalled. Several Cardinal players cleared a spot with their hands for the ball to be spotted for a field-goal attempt, but Harder's boot sailed wide. The Eagles had a scoring opportunity in the second quarter when they recovered Angsman's fumble on the Chicago 21. The Cards then intercepted one of Thompson's passes but put the ball into play on the 7-yard line, within the shadow of their own goal post. After three plays, Ray Mallouf punted out to the 45, but Philadelphia's Pat McHugh returned the ball to the 21. Sticking strictly to running plays and one screen pass, Thompson drove his team down to the 8-yard line before the Cards stiffened, but Cliff Patton's field-goal attempt from the 12 missed the mark. The half ended with the score 0-0, with visibility cut to a minimum and with snowbanks piling up on the field and along the sidelines. The hardy fans stayed with the game, waiting to see which club would get a break to enable them to score. On the first series of downs in the second half, the Cards recovered Steve Van Buren's fumble at mid-field and drove down to the 30-yard line before losing the ball when a fourth-and-one power play failed. The big break finally came near the end of the third quarter, when the Eagles recovered Angsman's fumble on the Chicago 17. Bosh Pritchard then ran through the left side for six yards as the quarter ended. After the teams went to the other end of the field and the officials lined the ball up as closely as they could, Joe Muha plowed through the middle down to the eight. Thompson then snuck down to the 5, and Van Buren blasted through a big hole on the right side for the remaining yardage. Cliff Patton added the extra point to make the score 7-0, a truly imposing lead in these weather conditions. The Eagles later in the period were pinned deep in their own territory, with a third down and 16 to go on their own 8-yard line. Thompson got the Eagles out of the hole by faking a pitch-out to Van Buren and running up the middle for 17 yards and the first down. The Eagles ate up most of the remaining time and were camped on the Chicago five-yard line when the clock ran out and mercifully sent the players and fans to the warmth of their homes.

INDIVIDUAL STATISTICS

PHILADELPHIA	No	Yds	Avg.	CHICAGO	No	Yds	Avg.
RUSHING							
Van Buren	26	98	3.8	Angsman	10	33	3.3
Pritchard	16	67	4.2	Harder	11	30	2.7
Thompson	11	50	4.5	Trippi	9	26	2.9
Myers	2	7	3.5	Mallouf	2	5	2.5
Muha	2	3	1.5	Clatt	1	2	1.2
	57	225	3.9	Schwall	1	0	0.0
					34	96	2.8
RECEIVING							
Ferrante	1	7	7.0	Kutner	2	19	9.5
Pihos	1	0	0.0	Dewell	1	16	16.0
	2	7	3.5		3	35	11.7
PUNTING							
Muha	5		38.6	Mallouf	8		37.4
PUNT RETURNS							
McHugh	2	22	11.0	Trippi	2	11	5.5
KICKOFF RETURNS							
McHugh	1	18	18.0	Schwall	1	20	20.0
				Trippi	1	15	15.0
					2	35	17.5
INTERCEPTION RETURNS							
Steele	1	0	0.0	Cochran	2	20	10.0

PASSING

PHILADELPHIA	Att	Comp	Comp Pct.	Yds	Int	Yds/ Att.	Yds/ Comp
Thompson	12	2	16.7	7	2	0.6	3.5
CHICAGO							
Mallouf	7	3	42.9	35	0	5.0	11.7
Trippi	2	0	0.0	0	0	–	–
Eikenburg	2	0	0.0	0	1	–	–
	11	3	27.3	35	1	3.2	11.7

SCORING

PHILADELPHIA	0	0	0	7–7
CHICAGO CARDS	0	0	0	0–0

Fourth Quarter
Phi. Van Buren, 5 yard rush
PAT – Patton (kick) 1:04

TEAM STATISTICS

PHIL.		CHIC.
16	First Downs – Total	6
15	by Rushing	3
0	by Passing	3
1	by Penalty	0
1	Fumbles – Number	3
1	Lost Ball	2
3	Penalties – Number	4
17	Yards	33
3	Field Goals Missed	1

A. A. F. C – December 19, at Cleveland (Attendance 22,981)

Handily Capping a Perfect Season

The game was considered no contest before it even started, and that was exactly how it turned out. The Cleveland Browns, champions of the Western Division, had swept undefeated through their fourteen-game schedule with a blistering offense and stubborn defense. The Eastern champion Buffalo Bills had a potent offense but allowed almost as many points as they scored. They evenly split their fourteen games and had to beat Baltimore in a divisional playoff to take the title in the weak Eastern sector. The Browns began by converting an interception into a first-quarter touchdown. After Tommy James returned the ball 30 yards to the Buffalo 20-yard line, the Browns took seven plays to cover the distance, with Special Delivery Jones's three-yard run scoring the points. Completely stymying George Ratterman's passes, the Browns got their second first-half score when George Young returned Rex Bumgardner's fumble 18 yards for a touchdown. The score was 14-0 at halftime, but the Browns really poured it on in the second half. Within three minutes they had intercepted a Ratterman pass and driven 21 yards for the score, with an Otto Graham to Special Delivery Jones pass covering the final nine yards. Later in the quarter, Marion Motley ran 29 yards to score, with Lou Groza's conversion running the score to 28-0. With the game now out of hand, the Bills replaced Ratterman at quarterback with Jim Still and promptly went on to score their only touchdown of the afternoon. After making one first down on the drive, Still punted the ball to Cleveland, but the Bills retained possession on a roughing-the-kicker penalty. On the next play, Still passed to Bumgardner for 25 yards, bringing the ball down to the Cleveland 28. After one running play, Still passed to Bill O'Connor for another first down on the 10-yard line. A pass to Al Baldwin then put the Bills on the scoreboard, and Graham Armstrong's kick made it 28-7. The Browns added on three fourth-period touchdowns to make the final count an embarrassing 49-7. Dub Jones returned the kickoff after the Buffalo score 46 yards down to the Bills' 34-yard line, and after Jones ran the ball for three yards Marion Motley blasted through the Bills for the final 31 yards. The final two touchdowns came after interceptions, the first on a drive of 60 yards and the second on Lou Saban's 39-yard return of the pilfered pass, and by the time the clock ended the match, both clubs had their second-stringers on the field.

SCORING

CLEVELAND	7	7	14	21–49
BUFFALO	0	0	7	0– 7

First Quarter
Cle. E. Jones, 3 yard rush 14:50
PAT – Groza (kick)

Second Quarter
Cle. Young, 18 yard fumble return PAT – Groza (kick) 3:25

Third Quarter
Cle. E. Jones, 9 yard pass from Graham 2:02
PAT – Groza (kick)
Cle. Motley, 29 yard rush 10:35
PAT – Groza (kick)
Buf. A. Baldwin, 10 yard pass from Still 14:56
PAT – Armstrong (kick)

Fourth Quarter
Cle. Motley, 31 yard rush 0:44
PAT – Groza (kick)
Cle. Motley, 5 yard rush 9:44
PAT – Groza (kick)
Cle. Saban, 39 yard pass interception (by Still) 11:49
PAT – Groza (kick)

TEAM STATISTICS

CLE.		BUF.
20	First Downs – Total*	13
10	by Rushing	4
8	by Passing	7
2	by Penalty	2
6	Fumbles – Number	3
3	Lost Ball	3
9	Penalties – Number	7
90	Yards	27
1	Field Goals Missed	0

* – Includes Touchdowns

INDIVIDUAL STATISTICS

CLEVELAND	No	Yds	Avg.	BUFFALO	No	Yds	Avg.
RUSHING							
Motley	14	133	9.5	Bumgardner	11	34	3.1
E. Jones	8	29	3.6	Tomasetti	11	20	1.8
D. Jones	5	22	4.4	Mutryn	8	8	1.0
Cline	1	20	20.0	Kulbitski	2	1	0.5
Parseghian	4	14	3.5	Still	1	0	0.0
Sensenb'her	2	2	1.0		33	63	1.9
Colella	1	1	1.0				
Graham	1	0	0.0				
Adamle	2	−1	−0.5				
Terlep	2	−5	−2.5				
	40	215	5.4				
RECEIVING							
E. Jones	3	39	13.0	O'Connor	3	41	13.7
Speedie	2	22	11.0	Mutryn	2	5	2.5
Lavelli	2	16	8.0	Bumgardner	1	25	25.0
D. Jones	2	13	6.5	Kulbitski	1	14	14.0
Gillom	1	15	15.0	A. Baldwin	1	10	10.0
Motley	1	13	13.0	Gibson	1	7	7.0
	11	118	10.7	Snyder	1	4	4.0
				Tomasetti	1	−2	−2.0
					11	104	9.5
PUNTING							
Colella	2		31.0	Still	6		42.5
Gillom	1		36.0				
	3		32.7				
PUNT RETURNS							
Lewis	2	10	5.0	None			
Colella	1	18	18.0				
Terlep	1	13	13.0				
	4	41	10.3				
KICKOFF RETURNS							
D. Jones	1	46	46.0	Schneider	2	33	16.5
Motley	1	20	20.0	Mutyrn	1	18	18.0
	2	66	33.0		3	51	17.0
INTERCEPTION RETURNS							
James	2	36	18.0	Maggioli	1	2	2.0
Saban	1	39	39.0				
Adamle	1	4	4.0				
Colella	1	1	1.0				
	5	80	16.0				

PASSING

CLEVELAND	Att	Comp	Comp Pct.	Yds	Int	Yds/ Att.	Yds/ Comp
Graham	24	11	45.8	118	1	4.9	10.7
E. Jones	2	0	0.0	0	0	–	–
	26	11	42.3	118	1	4.5	10.7
BUFFALO							
Still	18	6	33.3	80	2	4.4	13.3
Ratterman	18	5	27.8	24	3	1.3	4.8
	36	11	30.6	104	5	2.9	9.5

N.F.L. – December 18, at Los Angeles (Attendance 27,980)

Flying High in the Mud

A steady downpour of rain turned the playing field into a quagmire. It was a terrain which helped the Eagles, who relied on their big backs to move the ball on the ground, and hurt the Rams, who were primarily a passing team. Both teams slid around in the mud all afternoon, with only Steve Van Buren of the Eagles showing any ability to run in the mud; he picked up 196 yards rushing to set a new championship-game record. The Eagles' first-half touchdown came on a 63-yard drive during which Tommy Thompson completed three key passes, a weapon that the Rams could not ignite today. Thompson hit Jack Ferrante for 11 yards on one toss, hit him again for 15 yards, and fired a deep pass over the middle to Pete Pihos that covered 31 yards and scored six points. The Rams meanwhile could get no attack rolling in the mud, and a blocked punt in the third quarter made the final margin 14-0, Philadelphia.

SCORING

LOS ANGELES	0	0	0	0– 0
PHILADELPHIA	0	7	7	0–14

Second Quarter
Phi. Pihos, 31 yard pass from Thompson
PAT – Patton (kick)

Third Quarter
Phi. Skladany, 2 yard blocked punt return
PAT – Patton (kick)

TEAM STATISTICS

L.A.		PHIL.
7	First Downs – Total	17
0	First Downs – Rushing	12
6	First Downs – Passing	4
1	First Downs – Penalty	1
9	Punts	6
38.1	Average Punt Distance	36.3
17	Punt Return Yards	14
1	Fumbles	4
0	Fumbles Lost	1
4	Penalties	6
25	Yards Penalized	40

INDIVIDUAL STATISTICS

RUSHING

LOS ANGELES	No	Yds	Avg.	PHILADELPHIA	No	Yds	Avg.
Gehrke	3	13	4.3	Van Buren	31	196	6.3
V. T. Smith	6	11	1.8	Parmer	15	41	2.7
Hoerner	7	10	1.4	Scott	6	23	3.8
Waterfield	2	3	1.5	Thompson	4	7	1.8
Hirsch	2	0	0.0	Ziegler	3	4	1.3
Kalmanir	2	0	0.0	Pritchard	1	2	2.0
Van Brocklin	2	–16	–8.0	Myers	1	1	1.0
	24	21	0.9		61	274	4.5

PASSING

LOS ANGELES	Att	Comp	Comp Pct.	Yds	Int	Yds/ Att.	Yds/ Comp
Waterfield	13	5	38.5	43	1	3.3	8.6
Van Brocklin	14	5	35.7	55	0	3.9	11.0
	27	10	37.0	98	1	3.6	9.8
PHILADELPHIA							
Thompson	9	5	55.6	68	2	7.6	13.6

A.A.F.C. – December 11, at Cleveland (Attendance 22,550)

The Final Championship

With the league not arranged into divisions this year, a playoff system was installed in which the first- and fourth-place and the second- and third-place teams played each other. In these first-round matches the Browns beat Buffalo 31-21 and the '49ers beat New York 17-7, putting Cleveland and San Francisco into the championship game. Several days before the contest news broke that the NFL and the AAFC would merge, so that it was fitting for the two most successful AAFC clubs to play in the final league game. Attendance at the game was unusually low, but the Browns and '49ers fought a spirited battle in the snow and slush for the final AAFC crown. The Browns had won each previous championship but had never before faced the '49ers in the title game. This year's playoff system gave the '49ers, always finishing second behind Cleveland in the Western Division, their first shot at all the marbles. The Browns' defense turned out to be the key of the game, foiling the running of Norm Standlee and Joe Perry and rushing Frankie Albert whenever he attempted to pass. The only score of the first half came when Cleveland's Special Delivery Jones blasted into the end zone from two yards out, with Lou Groza adding the extra point. When Marion Motley broke loose on a trap play for a 63-yard touchdown in the third quarter, San Francisco's prospects appeared bleak. A Frankie Albert to Paul Salata touchdown pass brought the '49ers back to within seven points of the Browns in the final period, but a final Cleveland touchdown ended the game 21-7 and gave the Browns a complete set of AAFC championship trophies.

SCORING

CLEVELAND	7	0	7	7–21
SAN FRANCISCO	0	0	0	7– 7

First Quarter
Cle. E. Jones, 2 yard rush
PAT – Groza (kick) 7:20

Third Quarter
Cle. Motley, 63 yard rush
PAT – Groza (kick) 9:30

Fourth Quarter
S.F. Salata, 23 yard pass from Albert 0:14
PAT – Yetrano (kick)
Cle. D. Jones, 4 yard rush
PAT – Groza (kick) 6:13

TEAM STATISTICS

CLE.		S. F.
16	First Downs – Total	14
11	by Rushing	7
5	by Passing	7
0	by Penalty	0
0	Fumbles – Number	2
0	Lost Ball	0
1	Penalties – Number	0
5	Yards Penalized	0
0	Field Goals Missed	1

INDIVIDUAL STATISTICS

CLEVELAND	No	Yds	Avg.	SAN FRANCISCO	No	Yds	Avg.
RUSHING							
Motley	8	75	9.4	Albert	5	41	8.2
E. Jones	16	63	3.9	Perry	6	36	6.0
Graham	9	62	6.9	Standlee	10	21	2.1
Lahr	1	7	7.0	Garlin	3	13	4.3
James	2	7	3.5	Cathcart	9	11	1.2
D. Jones	4	2	0.5		33	122	3.7
Lewis	1	1	1.0				
	41	217	5.3				
RECEIVING							
Lavelli	4	56	14.0	Salata	3	47	15.7
Speedie	1	37	37.0	Beals	3	26	8.7
D. Jones	1	25	25.0	Shoener	2	25	12.5
E. Jones	1	10	10.0	Garlin	1	10	10.0
	7	128	18.3		9	108	12.0
PUNTING							
Gillom	4		43.0	Albert	6		44.0
PUNT RETURNS							
Lewis	3	38	12.7	Cathcart	1	13	13.0
Lahr	2	23	11.5	Cason	1	10	10.0
	5	61	12.2		2	23	11.5
KICKOFF RETURNS							
Lahr	2	41	20.5	Cathcart	1	22	22.0

PASSING

CLEVELAND	Att	Comp	Comp Pct.	Yds	Int	Yds/ Att.	Yds/ Comp
Graham	17	7	41.2	128	0	7.5	18.3
SAN FRANCISCO							
Albert	24	9	37.5	108	0	4.5	12.0
Lillywhite	1	0	0.0	0	0	–	–
	25	9	36.0	108	0	4.3	12.0

Scores of Each Game		
PHILADELPHIA EAGLES 11-1-0 Greasy Neale		
7	N.Y. Bulldogs	0
22	Detroit	14
28	CHIC. CARDS	3
21	Chic. Bears	38
49	WASHINGTON	14
38	Pittsburgh	7
38	LOS ANGELES	14
44	Washington	21
42	N.Y. BULLDOGS	0
34	PITTSBURGH	17
24	N.Y. Giants	3
17	N.Y. GIANTS	3

Use Name	Pos.	Hgt	Wgt	Age	Int	Pts
Chuck Bednarik	C-LB	6'3"	230	24		
Vic Lindskog	C	6'1"	200	33		
Alex Wojciechowicz	C-LB	5'11"	235	34	2	
Leo Skladany	DE	6'1"	205	22		
Jay MacDowell	DE-T	6'2"	222	30		
Dick Humbert	DB-OE	6'1"	186	30	7	
(1 reception for 14 yds.)						

Use Name – Tackles	Pos.	Hgt	Wgt	Age	Int	Pts
Otis Douglas	T	6'1"	226	37		
Mike Jarmoluk (from NYB)	T	6'5"	265	26	1	
George Savitsky	T	6'2"	242	25		
Vic Sears	T	6'3"	225	31		
Al Wistert	T	6'1"	217	28		

Use Name – Guards	Pos.	Hgt	Wgt	Age	Int	Pts
Walt Barnes	G	6'1"	240	31		
Mario Giannelli	G	6'	265	28		2
Bucko Kilroy	G	6'2"	248	28		
John Magee	G	5'10"	222	26		
Duke Maronic	G	5'9"	215	28		

The Eagles may have been champions, but the high expenses of running the team were making a pauper of owner Alexis Thompson. Thus, before the season opened, a group of 100 Philadelphians, each paying $3,000, bought themselves the NFL champions.

The Eagles welcomed their new benefactors by rolling through their schedule to an easy Eastern Division title. The Philadelphia attack moved mostly on the ground, with Steve Van Buren and Bosh Pritchard punching out yardage play after play. Especially devastating was the Eagles' end run, with both guards and fullback Joe Muha leading Van Buren around the flank. To complement his powerful offense, coach Greasy Neale devised a 5-2-4 defense which stopped enemy passers cold in the new era of aerial warfare.

Scores of Each Game		
PITTSBURGH STEELERS 6-5-1 John Michelosen		
28	N.Y. GIANTS	7
14	WASHINGTON	27
14	DETROIT	7
21	N.Y. Giants	17
24	N.Y. BULLDOGS	13
7	PHILADELPHIA	38
14	Washington	27
7	LOS ANGELES	7
30	Green Bay	7
17	Philadelphia	34
21	Chic. Bears	30
27	N.Y. Bulldogs	0

Use Name	Pos.	Hgt	Wgt	Age	Int	Pts
Bob Balog	C-LB	6'2"	225	25		
Vince Ragunas	LB	5'11"	200	25		
Frank Sinkovitz	C-LB	6'1"	215	26	1	
Bill Walsh	C	6'2"	230	22		
Bob Davis	DE	5'11"	190	28		
Bill McPeak	DE	6'1"	200	24		
Charlie Mehelich	DE	6'1"	200	27		

Use Name – Tackles	Pos.	Hgt	Wgt	Age	Int	Pts
Pete Barbolak	T	6'3"	235	23		
Carl Samuelson	T	6'4"	245	26		8
Walt Szot	T	6'1"	225	30		
Jack Wiley	T	5'11"	210	28		
(1 reception for 10 yds.)						
Frank Wydo	T	6'4"	215	25		
(2 receptions for 21 yds.)						

Use Name – Guards	Pos.	Hgt	Wgt	Age	Int	Pts
Darrell Hogan	G-LB	5'10"	210	23	1	
Bill Moore	G	5'11"	220	26		
Leo Nobile	G-LB	5'10"	215	27	1	
Steve Suhey	G	5'11"	215	27		

With every other team in the league lining up in the explosive T formation, the Steelers stuck with the hard-hitting, conservative single-wing attack. While other clubs were throwing the ball in what old-timers considered reckless fashion, Pittsburgh still ground out its yardage with off-tackle power plays and wingback reverses. Rookie Joe Geri was the last of the triple-threat tailbacks, but his passing was much less threatening than his running and kicking. With the attack relying almost completely on the running of Jerry Nuzum and Geri, the Steelers needed a rock-rib defense to win six games. The free-substitution rule, in on a trial basis this year, enabled coach John Michelosen to devote certain players like rookie end Bill McPeak exclusively to defense and to save his entire starting offensive backfield of Seabright, Geri, Nuzum and Papich from the rigors of playing defense.

Scores of Each Game		
NEW YORK GIANTS 6-6-0 Steve Owen		
7	Pittsburgh	28
38	N.Y. Bulldogs	14
45	Washington	35
17	PITTSBURGH	21
35	CHIC. BEARS	28
41	Chic. Cards	38
24	N.Y. BULLDOGS	31
30	Green Bay	10
21	DETROIT	45
23	WASHINGTON	7
3	PHILADELPHIA	24
3	Philadelphia	17

Use Name	Pos.	Hgt	Wgt	Age	Int	Pts
John Cannady	LB	6'2"	225	25	1	
Tex Coulter	C	6'4"	245	24		
Carl Fennema	C-LB	6'2"	210	23		
George Kershaw	DE	6'4"	210	22		
Declared ineligible – Frankie Filchock, Merle Hapes						

Use Name – Tackles	Pos.	Hgt	Wgt	Age	Int	Pts
Bill Austin	OT	6'1"	218	20	1	
Carl Butkus	T	6'1"	245	27		
Al DeRogatis	DT	6'4"	235	22		6
Ralph Hutchinson	T	6'2"	230	24		
Ed Kolman	DT	6'2"	235	30		
(2 kickoff returns for 24 yds.)						
John Sanchez (from WAS)	T	6'3"	240	28		
Jim White	OT	6'2"	225	28		

Use Name – Guards	Pos.	Hgt	Wgt	Age	Int	Pts
Jon Baker	G-LB	6'2"	210	26		
Jake Colhouer	G	6'1"	210	27		
Don Ettinger	G-LB	6'2"	215	26	2	
Ed Royston	G	6'1"	220	26		

Gaping holes were still evident in the Giants' lineup as coach Steve Owen slowly filled his squad with young quality players. Second-year pro Chuck Conerly had staked out the quarterback job for his own with his pinpoint passing. Halfback Choo-Choo Roberts had a real taste for the end zone, scoring seventeen touchdowns to lead the league in TDs and scoring, and, with free substitution now in effect, coach Owen began developing specialists in the modern tradition. Sophomore safetyman Em Tunnell was a ball hawk for interceptions and a one-man offense when returning a punt or interception. Two rookie linemen were assigned to the different platoons, Bill Austin to the offense and Al DeRogatis to the defense, while Ben Agajanian—a fourth-year man—provided Owen with a kicking specialist.

Scores of Each Game		
WASHINGTON REDSKINS 4-7-1 John Whelchel, Herman Ball		
7	Chic. Cards.	38
27	Pittsburgh	14
35	N.Y. GIANTS	45
38	N.Y. BULLDOGS	14
14	Philadelphia	49
14	N.Y. Bulldogs	14
27	PITTSBURGH	14
21	PHILADELPHIA	44
21	CHIC. BEARS	31
7	N.Y. Giants	23
30	GREEN BAY	0
27	Los Angeles	53

Use Name	Pos.	Hgt	Wgt	Age	Int	Pts
Al DeMao	C-LB	6'2"	210	29	1	
Clyde Ehrhardt	C	6'1"	223	29		
Jim Peebles	DE	6'4"	232	29		
(1 rushing attempt for –3 yds.)						
Herb Shoener	DE	6'3"	202	26		6
Frank Seno	DB	6'	190	28		
(2 kickoff returns for 39 yds.)						

Use Name – Tackles	Pos.	Hgt	Wgt	Age	Int	Pts
John Adams	T	6'7"	230	29		
Bob Hendren	T	6'8"	240	26		
Laurie Niemi	T	6'1"	236	24		
Len Szafaryn	T	6'2"	212	21		

Use Name – Guards	Pos.	Hgt	Wgt	Age	Int	Pts
John Badaczewski	G	6'1"	237	27		
Mike Katrishen	G	6'1"	212	26		
Herb Siegert	G-LB	6'3"	210	25	2	
Joe Soboleski (from CHI-AAFC)	G	6'	215	23		
John Steber	G	6'	230	26		
Dick Stovall	G-LB	6'	198	25		

Owner George Marshall decided that his team needed discipline, so he hired John Whelchel, a retired admiral and ex-coach at Navy, as his new head coach. As things turned out, Whelchel got along fine with the players but couldn't stomach interference from the owner. Marshall figured that Whelchel was using his players all wrong, so he came to a practice and told the coach where to play his men. Whelchel looked Marshall in the eye, pulled an about-face, and marched off the field. Marshall turned a dark shade of purple, gathered a few of the players together, and yelled, "How could you let that man ruin the ball club?" When the players answered that Whelchel, after all, was the coach, the owner replied, "Hell, I hired him for a disciplinarian, not for a goddamn coach." This behavior, plus Marshall's unwillingness to sign any black players on the Redskins, assured Washington fans of another losing season.

Scores of Each Game		
NEW YORK BULLDOGS 1-10-1 Charley Ewart		
0	PHILADELPHIA	7
14	N.Y. GIANTS	38
0	GREEN BAY	19
14	Washington	38
13	Pittsburgh	24
14	WASHINGTON	14
31	N.Y. Giants	24
20	CHIC. CARDS	65
0	Philadelphia	42
20	Los Angeles	42
27	Detroit	28
0	PITTSBURGH	27

Use Name	Pos.	Hgt	Wgt	Age	Int	Pts
Bill Campbell (from CHIC)	LB	6'	195	29		
Joe Domnanovich	C-LB	6'1"	215	30	1	
Herb Ellis	C-LB	6'2"	205	23		
Merv Pregulman	C	6'3"	214	27		
Sam Tamburo	DE	6'2"	200	23		
Joe Watt	DB	5'11"	185	28	1	
Al Dekdebrun – Canadian Football League						

Use Name – Tackles	Pos.	Hgt	Wgt	Age	Int	Pts
Tom Blake	T	6'2"	220	23		
(1 punt return for 6 yds.)						
Frank Gaul	T	6'	200	23		
John Nolan	T	6'2"	240	23		
George Roman	T	6'4"	245	24		
Carroll Vogelaar	T	6'3"	260	29		

Use Name – Guards	Pos.	Hgt	Wgt	Age	Int	Pts
Fritz Barzilauskas	G	6'1"	230	28		
Stan Batinski	G	5'10"	215	32		
Larry Olsonoski (from GB)	G	6'2"	214	24		
Joe Sabasteanski	G	6'	208	28		
John Weaver	G	6'2"	215	23		

Owner Ted Collins moved his Boston Yanks to New York in hopes for a colorful season as the Bulldogs. Using the Polo Grounds when the Giants were away, the Bulldogs played before echoing, empty stands; not even half-time circus acts brought customers in. The show on the field resembled a circus, too. Collins bought quarterback Bobby Layne from the Bears, and Layne learned how to eat the ball without flinching behind his pitiful offensive line. Coach Charley Ewart wanted to run a ball-control offense like the Eagles, but, according to Layne, "We didn't have any Steve Van Burens." Layne was even forced to make up plays in the huddle by drawing pass patterns in the dirt with his finger. With no one paying money to see this show, Collins cut expenses by releasing many of the squad, and by season's end only nineteen players were suiting up.

TEAM TOTALS

OFFENSE	FIRST DOWNS: Tot	by Rsh	by Pas	by Pen	RUSHING: No.	Yds.	Avg Yds.	TD	PASSING: Att	Com	Comp Pct.	Yds.	Avg. Yds. Att.	Avg. Yds. Comp	TD	Int	Pct. Int.	PUNTING: No.	Avg. Yds.
PHIL.	243	143	87	13	632	2607	4.1	25	251	130	51.8	1909	7.6	14.7	18	14	5.6	53	40.8
PITT.	189	126	50	13	535	2209	4.1	19	209	81	38.8	1310	6.3	16.2	10	18	8.6	77	40.9
N.Y.G.	177	75	87	15	419	1404	3.4	15	322	155	48.1	2157	6.7	13.9	17	23	7.1	73	36.9
WASH.	217	78	121	18	407	1579	3.9	14	394	197	50.0	2816	7.1	14.3	22	29	7.4	68	40.4
N.Y.B	183	76	88	19	353	1184	3.4	9	343	172	50.1	2025	5.9	11.8	10	23	6.7	77	41.2

PUNT RETURNS: No.	Yds.	Avg. Yds.	TD	KICKOFF RETURNS: No.	Yds.	Avg. Yds.	TD	INTERCEPTION RETURNS: No.	Yds.	Avg. Yds.	TD	PENALTIES: No.	Yds.	FUMBLES: No.	Lost	POINTS: Tot	PAT	FG Att	FG	Saf.	OFFENSE
48	577	12.0	2	25	542	21.7	0	29	409	14.1	2	81	729	29	12	364	47	19	9	1	PHIL.
34	449	13.2	0	37	792	21.4	0	22	310	14.1	1	52	460	31	9	224	30	7	2	1	PITT.
39	457	11.7	1	37	961	26.0	1	22	336	15.3	2	88	800	23	10	287	35	13	8	0	N.Y.G.
35	377	10.8	0	55	1113	20.2	0	18	223	12.4	0	85	675	24	13	268	34	7	4	0	WASH.
37	211	5.7	0	58	1191	20.5	0	14	211	15.1	1	51	420	41	22	153	18	10	3	0	N.Y.B.

Use Name – Backs & Ends	Pos.	Age	Hgt	Wgt	Pts	Int	Rushing No.	Rushing Yds	Rushing Avg	Rushing TD	Passing Att	Passing Comp	Passing %	Passing Yds	Passing Yd/Att	Passing TD	Passing Int–%	Passing RK	Receiving No.	Receiving Yds	Receiving Avg	Receiving TD	Punting No.	Punting Avg	Kicking Pat	Kicking Att	Kicking %	Kicking FG	Kicking Att	Kicking %	Punt Returns No.	Punt Returns Yds	Punt Returns Avg	Punt Returns TD	Kickoff Returns No.	Kickoff Returns Yds	Kickoff Returns Avg	Kickoff Returns TD
PHILADELPHIA EAGLES																																						
Tommy Thompson	QB	33	6'1"	195	12		15	17	1.1	2	214	116	54	1727	8.1	16	11– 5	2																				
Bill Mackrides	QB	24	5'11"	182	6		14	17	1.2	1	36	14	39	182	5.1	2	2– 6																					
Steve VanBuren	HB	28	6'	200	72		263	1146	4.4	11									4	88	22	1													12	288	24	0
Bosh Pritchard	HB	30	5'11"	163	30		84	506	6.0	3	1	0	0	0	0.0	0	1–100		8	185	23	2									13	99	8	0	5	99	20	0
Frank Ziegler	HB-DB	25	5'11"	175	6	1	84	283	3.4	1									3	33	11	0									2	20	10	0	1	21	21	0
Jim Parmer	HB-DB	22	6'	190	30	2	66	234	3.5	5									5	33	7	0																
Clyde Scott	HB	25	6'	175	18		40	195	4.9	1									8	148	19	1									5	114	23	1	1	54	54	0
Jack Myers	FB	24	6'2"	200	6		48	182	3.8	1									7	98	14	0													2	27	14	0
Joe Muha	FB-LB	28	6'1"	205	11	2	3	19	6.3	0									1	10	10	0	45	40.0	5	5	100	0	1	0	1	2	2	0	1	20	20	0
Russ Craft	HB-DB	29	5'9"	172	6	1	11	5	0.5	0									1	37	37	0									3	50	17	0				
Pat McHugh	HB-DB	29	5'11"	165	6	6	2	5	2.5	0																					3	26	9	0				
Ben Kish	FB-LB	32	6'	207			2	–2	–1.0	0																												
Frank Reagan	DB	30	5'11"	180	6	7																	8	45.3							21	266	13	1				
John Green	DE	27	6'1"	194																															2	33	17	0
Jack Ferrante	OE	33	6'1"	205	30														34	508	15	5																
Pete Pihos	OE-DE	25	6'1"	210	24														34	484	14	4													1	0	0	0
Neill Armstrong	OE-DB	23	6'2"	188	30														24	271	11	5																
Cliff Patton	G	25	6'2"	240	69																				42	43	98	9	18	50								
PITTSBURGH STEELERS																																						
Joe Geri	TB	25	5'10"	180	45		133	543	4.1	5	77	31	40	554	7.2	5	5– 6						43	43.2	12	13	92	1	1	100	2	28	14	0				
Jim Finks	TB-DB	22	6'	175	12	1	35	135	3.9	1	71	24	34	322	4.5	2	8– 11		1	17	17	1																
Bob Gage	TB-DB	22	5'11"	175	18	5	46	228	5.0	3	36	17	47	329	9.1	2	4– 11		1	8	8	0	4	40.8							16	254	16	0	1	25	25	0
Jerry Nuzum	HB	26	6'1"	200	42		139	611	4.4	5	1	1	100	21	21.0	0	0– 0		4	81	20	2													1	17	17	0
George Papach	FB	24	6'2"	210			99	407	4.1	0	1	0	0	0	0.0	0	0– 0		6	18	3	0													3	57	19	0
Don Samuel	HB-TB-DB	25	5'11"	190	6	1	39	163	4.2	1	21	7	33	67	3.2	0	1– 5		1	2	2	0									7	80	11	0				
Jerry Shipkey	FB-DB	24	6'1"	210	30	3	26	93	3.6	5									2	32	16	0																
Bob Hanlon	HB-DB	24	6'1"	195		3	6	13	2.2	0									1	4	4	0													11	213	19	0
Joe Hollingsworth	FB	24	6'	200			6	13	2.2	0	1	0	0	0	0.0	0	0– 0																					
Joe Glamp	HB	26	5'11"	185	21		3	–8	–2.7	0									1	14	14	0			18	18	100	1	7	14								
Charlie Seabright	BB	31	6'2"	208							1	1	100	17	17.0	1	0– 0		4	4	1	0													1	24	24	0
Frank Minini	BB	25	6'1"	200			1	5	5.0	0																									16	390	24	0
Howard Hartley	DB	25	6'	185		6																									9	87	10	0				
Elbie Nickel	OE	26	6'1"	190	18														26	633	24	3													1	20	20	0
Val Jansante	OE	28	6'1"	190	24														29	445	15	4													3	46	15	0
Bill Long	OE	23	6'1"	200			2	6	3.0	0									2	21	11	0	30	37.6														
NEW YORK GIANTS																																						
Chuck Conerly	QB	25	6'1"	185			23	42	1.8	0	305	152	50	2138	7.0	17	20– 7	4					2	35.0														
Ray Mallouf	QB-DB	31	5'11"	180		1	1	–1	–1.0	0	16	3	19	19	1.2	0	2– 13						57	37.4														
Choo-Choo Roberts	HB	25	5'11"	188	102		152	634	4.2	9	1	0	0	0	0.0	0	1–100		35	711	20	8													1	16	16	0
Joe Scott	HB-DB	23	6'1"	200	42	1	70	224	3.2	6									15	111	7	1													7	203	29	0
Bob Greenhalgh	FB	25	6'1"	200			62	188	3.0	0									3	23	8	0																
Jack Salscheider	HB	24	5'10"	185	6		26	105	4.0	0									4	9	2	0	14	35.4											15	474	32	1
Clete Fischer	HB-DB	24	5'9"	170	6	2	26	72	2.8	0									3	45	15	1									7	64	9	0	8	188	24	0
Ray Coates	HB-DB	25	6'1"	200	6	1	27	55	2.0	0									8	152	19	1									6	78	13	0				
Buzz Mertes (from BAL-AAFC)	FB	28	6'	205			16	46	2.9	0									2	14	7	0																
Joe Sulatis	FB-DE	28	6'2"	215			14	42	3.0	0									3	35	12	0													1	27	27	0
Noah Mullins	HB-DB	30	5'11"	177	6	3	2	–3	–1.5	0									2	45	23	1																
Em Tunnell	HB-DB	27	6'1"	187	18	10													1	7	7	0									26	315	12	1	2	26	13	0
Bill Swiacki	OE	24	6'2"	195	24														47	652	14	4																
Ray Poole	OE-DE	27	6'2"	215	6														25	277	11	1													1	3	3	0
Dick Hensley	OE-DE	23	6'4"	210															3	24	8	0																
Frank LoVuolo	OE-DE	25	6'2"	210	6														2	37	19	0																
Dick Duden	OE-DE	22	6'3"	212															2	15	8	0																
Ben Agajanian	K	30	6'	210	59																				35	36	97	8	13	62								
WASHINGTON REDSKINS																																						
Sammy Baugh	QB	35	6'2"	182	12		13	67	5.2	2	255	145	57	1903	7.5	18	14– 5	1					1	53.0														
Harry Gilmer	QB-HB	23	6'	164			31	167	5.4	0	132	49	37	869	6.6	4	15– 11	12	5	77	15	0																
Tommy Mont	QB-HB	27	6'	192	12		14	75	5.4	0	7	3	43	44	6.3	0	0– 0		8	105	13	2													1	22	22	0
Rob Goode	HB-DB	22	6'4"	210	12	2	61	261	4.3	2									16	279	17	0													3	50	17	0
Pete Stout	FB-LB	26	6'	200	36	1	62	245	4.0	4									8	102	13	2																
Harry Dowda	HB-DB	25	6'2"	194	18	3	65	239	3.7	2									11	187	17	1																
Eddie Saenz	HB	26	5'11"	168			53	170	3.2	0									23	251	11	0									17	178	10	0	24	465	19	0
Ed Quirk	FB	24	6'1"	226	6		40	139	3.5	1									5	33	7	0																
Tom Cochran	FB	25	6'	209	6		34	135	4.0	1									7	82	12	0													1	19	19	0
Dan Sandifer	HB-DB	22	6'1"	190	18	5	20	64	3.2	0									19	293	15	3									18	199	11	0	24	518	22	0
John Hollar (from DET)	FB	27	6'	225	12		13	35	2.7	1									4	38	10	1																
Dick Poillon	HB	29	6'	198	46		7	5	0.7	0									1	8	8	0	66	40.9	34	37	97	4	7	57								
Howie Livingston	HB-DB	27	6'1"	190	6	4	1	1	1.0	1									3	41	14	0																
Hugh Taylor	OE	26	6'4"	192	54														45	781	17	9																
Hal Crisler	OE	25	6'4"	207	24														26	388	15	4																
Clyde Goodnight	OE-DE	25	6'1"	200															11	150	14	0																
Joe Tereshinski	OE-DE	25	6'2"	214															4	36	9	0																
Ed Berrang	OE-DE	24	6'2"	203															1	5	5	0																
NEW YORK BULLDOGS																																						
Bobby Layne	QB	22	6'1"	198	18		54	196	3.6	3	299	155	52	1796	6.0	9	18– 6	6																				
Johnny Rauch	QB-DB	22	6'	200	6	2	3	46	15.3	1	25	11	44	169	6.8	1	3– 12																					
Bob DeMoss	QB	22	6'2"	185			5	1	0.2	0	18	6	33	60	3.3	0	2– 11																					
Joe Osmanski (from CHIB)	FB	30	6'2"	215	12		81	312	3.8	2									18	138	8	0													4	46	12	0
Joe Golding	HB-DB	28	6'	184	18	1	63	240	3.8	0									12	78	7	2									5	27	5	0	13	289	22	0
Paul Shoults	HB	24	5'11"	178			46	124	2.7	0									10	124	12	0									8	27	3	0	14	271	19	0
Phil Slosburg	HB-DB	22	5'10"	170	6	1	37	121	3.3	1									4	11	3	0									4	32	8	0	4	98	25	0
Jim Cànady (from CHIB)	HB-DB	23	5'10"	178		5	23	91	4.0	0									5	80	16	0									4	36	9	0	10	233	23	0
Dean Sensenbaugher	HB	24	5'9"	190	6		20	36	1.8	1																					1	9	9	0	3	81	27	0
Frank Nelson	HB-DB	26	5'9"	167		1	8	26	3.3	0																					3	14	5	0	3	52	17	0
Oscar Smith (from GB)	HB-DB	26	6'	185		2	16	24	1.5	0																					5	31	6	0	2	36	18	0
Jim Wade	HB-DB	23	5'11"	175		1	9	23	2.6	0									4	58	15	0									7	32	5	0	3	58	19	0
Frank Muehlheuser	FB-LB	23	6'2"	220	6		9	10	1.1	1									2	26	13	0	1	0.0											1	40	40	0
Mike Boyda	FB-LB	26	6'1"	205		1					1	0	0	0	0.0	0	0– 0						56	44.2														
Bill Chipley	OE	29	6'3"	205	12														57	631	11	2													1	7	7	0
Ralph Heywood	OE	28	6'2"	205	24		3	–6	–2.0	1									37	499	13	3	20	34.9														
Hal Prescott (from PHI)	OE	28	6'2"	193	6														10	162	16	1																
Joe Abbey (from CHIB)	OE-DE	23	6'1"	205															8	110	14	0																
Nick Scollard	OE-DE	29	6'4"	225	39	1													3	81	27	2			18	21	86	3	10	30	1	6	6	0	2	16	8	0
Bob Sponaugle	OE-DE	20	6'1"	203															2	26	13	0																

TEAM TOTALS

DEFENSE	First Downs: Tot	by Rsh	by Pas	by Pen	Rushing: No.	Yds.	Avg Yds.	TD	Passing: Att	Com	Comp Pct.	Yds.	Avg. Yds. Att.	Avg. Yds. Comp	TD	Int	Pct. Int.	Punting: No.	Avg. Yds.	Punt Returns: No.	Yds.	Avg. Yds.	TD	Kickoff Returns: No.	Yds.	Avg. Yds.	TD	Interception Returns: No.	Yds.	Avg. Yds.	TD	Penalties: No.	Yds.	Fumbles: No.	Lost	Points: Tot	PAT	FG Att	FG	Saf.	DEFENSE
PHIL.	148	60	68	20	353	1217	3.4	5	303	121	39.9	1607	5.3	13.3	11	29	9.6	81	38.6	36	384	10.7	0	53	1087	20.5	0	14	241	17.2	1	62	533	30	14	134	17	8	5	0	PHIL.
PITT.	210	100	98	12	463	1862	4.0	17	337	161	47.8	2043	6.1	12.7	9	22	6.5	66	40.7	27	373	13.8	1	35	687	19.6	0	18	334	18.6	1	97	862	26	9	214	25	14	7	0	PITT.
N.Y.G.	232	104	110	18	465	1664	3.6	20	374	193	51.6	2460	6.7	12.7	16	22	5.9	65	38.6	52	598	11.5	2	48	1092	22.8	0	23	226	9.8	1	64	559	32	18	298	40	12	6	0	N.Y.G.
WASH.	233	120	95	18	487	2316	4.8	23	316	148	46.8	2409	7.6	16.3	24	18	5.7	59	40.7	38	442	11.6	0	42	917	21.8	0	29	377	13.0	0	74	676	30	13	339	42	15	5	0	WASH.
N.Y.B.	238	131	92	15	535	2360	4.4	20	303	147	48.5	2132	7.0	14.5	25	14	4.6	63	39.7	52	660	12.7	2	31	618	19.9	0	23	356	15.5	1	90	766	33	14	368	47	12	7	0	N.Y.B.

LOS ANGELES RAMS 8-2-2 Clark Shaughnessy

Scores of Each Game		
27	DETROIT	24
48	Green Bay	7
31	Chic. Bears	16
21	Detroit	10
35	GREEN BAY	7
27	CHIC. BEARS	24
14	Philadelphia	38
7	Pittsburgh	7
28	Chic. Cards	28
42	N. Y. BULLDOGS	20
27	CHIC. CARDS	31
53	WASHINGTON	27

Use Name	Pos.	Hgt	Wgt	Age	Int	Pts
Jack Martin	C-LB	6'3"	240	27		
Fred Naumetz	C-LB	6'1"	223	27		
Don Paul	LB	6'1"	230	24	2	
(2 kickoff returns for 32 yds.)						
Larry Brink	DE	6'5"	230	26		
George Sims	DB	5'11"	170	21	9	6

Use Name – Tackles	Pos.	Hgt	Wgt	Age	Int	Pts
Gil Bouley	T	6'2"	235	28		
Ed Champagne	T	6'3"	240	27		
Dick Huffman	T	6'2"	256	26		
(2 receptions for 36 yds.)						
Joe Repko	T	6'	240	28		
Al Sparkman	T	6'6"	253	24		

Use Name – Guards	Pos.	Hgt	Wgt	Age	Int	Pts
Hal Dean	G	6'	205	26		
(1 kickoff return for 0 yds.)						
Jack Finlay	G-LB	6'1"	216	28		
Mike Lazetich	G-LB	6'1"	214	28		2
Ray Yagiello	G	6'	220	26		

Clark Shaughnessy, one of the creators of the modern T offense, came up with another far-reaching innovation this year. Already blessed with two fine ends in Tom Fears and Bob Shaw, Shaughnessy wanted to use newly acquired halfback Crazy Legs Hirsch as a wide receiver, and he did so by cleverly splitting Hirsch wide as a flanker. With three fine targets to aim at, quarterbacks Bob Waterfield and rookie Norm Van Brocklin directed pro football's most dynamic air show.

But after winning their first six games on the strength of their offense, the Rams took on the defensive-minded Philadelphia Eagles and lost. The match proved to be the Rams' Waterloo, and they struggled through the rest of their games with great difficulty. Yet the Rams did beat the Bears twice during that season to finish ahead of Halas' squad by percentage points and to win the first divisional crown for the West Coast.

CHICAGO BEARS 9-3-0 George Halas

Scores of Each Game		
17	Green Bay	0
17	Chic. Cards	7
16	LOS ANGELES	21
38	PHILADELPHIA	21
28	N. Y. Giants	35
24	Los Angeles	27
24	GREEN BAY	3
27	DETROIT	24
31	Washington	21
28	Detroit	7
30	PITTSBURGH	21
52	CHIC. CARDS	21

Use Name	Pos.	Hgt	Wgt	Age	Int	Pts
Stu Clarkson	LB	6'2"	220	30	2	
Frank Szymanski	C	6'	215	26		
Bulldog Turner	C-LB	6'1"	235	30		
Bill Milner	DE	6'1"	215	25		
Bill deCorrevont	DB-HB	6'	185	30	4	
(1 reception for 44 yds.)						

Use Name – Tackles	Pos.	Hgt	Wgt	Age	Int	Pts
Alf Bauman	T	6'2"	235	29		
George Connor	T	6'3"	240	24		
(3 receptions for 51 yds.)						
Fred Davis	T	6'3"	245	31		
Paul Stenn	T	6'2"	245	31		
(2 receptions for 11 yds.)						
Walt Stickel	T	6'3"	245	27		

Use Name – Guards	Pos.	Hgt	Wgt	Age	Int	Pts
Ray Bray	G	6'	235	32		
Chuck Drulis	G-LB	5'10"	215	31	1	
Dick Flanagan	G-FB	6'	210	22		
(5 kickoff returns for 88 yds.)						
Pat Preston	G-LB	6'2"	215	26		
Wash Serini	G	6'2"	235	25		

George Halas started the season by selling quarterback Bobby Layne to the New York Bulldogs. Although the move would later haunt him, it was not a foolish decision at the time. When veteran Sid Luckman was sidetracked for most of the season with a thyroid condition, Halas considered himself fortunate to have Johnny Lujack, the former Heisman Trophy winner from Notre Dame. Showing a strong arm and unexpected poise, Lujack came through in flying colors, leading the Bears to a season-ending six-game winning streak which fell just short of the title. With Lujack capping his successful season by passing for a record 468 yards, and six touchdowns against the Cardinals in the season finale, and the presence of a third quarterback in promising rookie George Blanda, there was no evidence of the passing misfortunes which would haunt the Bears within a few short years.

CHICAGO CARDINALS 6-5-1 Buddy Parker, Phil Handler

Scores of Each Game		
38	WASHINGTON	7
7	CHIC. BEARS	17
3	Philadelphia	28
39	Green Bay	17
7	DETROIT	24
38	N. Y. GIANTS	41
42	Detroit	19
65	N. Y. Bulldogs	20
28	LOS ANGELES	28
41	GREEN BAY	21
31	Los Angeles	27
21	Chic. Bears	52

Use Name	Pos.	Hgt	Wgt	Age	Int	Pts
Vince Banonis	C-LB	6'1"	232	27	4	6
Bill Blackburn	C-LB	6'6"	230	27	3	6
(1 kickoff return for 4 yds.)						
Jim Cain	DE	6'1"	210	22		
Bob Dove	DE	6'2"	220	28		
Corwin Clatt	DB	6'	210	26	2	
(1 punt return for 22 yds.)						
Jerry Davis	DB	5'10"	175	27	6	6
(1 punt return for 14 yds.)						
Bob Nussbaumer	DB	5'11"	170	25	12	
(1 punt return for 16 yds.)						

Use Name – Tackles	Pos.	Hgt	Wgt	Age	Int	Pts
Chet Bulger	T	6'3"	238	31		
Joe Coomer	T	6'6"	283	30		
Bill Fischer	T	6'2"	250	22	1	
John Goldsberry	T	6'2"	245	23	1	
Dick Loepfe	T	6'2"	230	28		
George Petrovich	T	6'2"	225	24		
Bob Zimny	T	6'1"	235	28		

Use Name – Guards	Pos.	Hgt	Wgt	Age	Int	Pts
Plato Andros	G	6'	242	28		
Ray Apolskis	G-LB	5'11"	210	30	1	
Ham Nichols	G-LB	5'11"	210	25		
Buster Ramsey	G-LB	6'1"	220	29	1	2
(1 kickoff return for 0 yds.)						

The championship squads of 1947-48 slowly were breaking up on the reefs of time. The death of Stan Mauldin robbed the Cardinals of a great lineman, defensive back Marshall Goldberg retired, and injuries were turning Paul Christman into an ordinary passer. To further worsen the team's plight, head coach Jimmy Conzelman decided to quit after the 1948 season—a move which left the widow of late owner Charles Bidwill in a dither. She couldn't decide between assistants Phil Handler and Buddy Parker for the vacated spot—and unwisely made them co-coaches, a chaotic arrangement which lasted half a year and four losses in six games before Handler moved into the front office. But it was too late for Parker to do more than bring the club up above the break-even point, or prevent the 52-21 trouncing by the Bears in the season's finale, which returned the Cardinals to the roll of bridesmaid in Chicago.

DETROIT LIONS 4-8-0 Bo McMillin

Scores of Each Game		
24	Los Angeles	27
14	PHILADELPHIA	22
7	Pittsburgh	14
10	LOS ANGELES	21
24	Chic. Cards	7
14	Green Bay	16
19	CHIC. CARDS	42
24	Chic. Bears	27
45	N. Y. Giants	21
7	CHIC. BEARS	28
28	N. Y. BULLDOGS	27
21	GREEN BAY	7

Use Name	Pos.	Hgt	Wgt	Age	Int	Pts
George Karstens	C	6'4"	205	25		
Bob Pifferini	C-LB	6'	210	24	3	
Jack Simmons	C-T	6'4"	240	23		
Abe Addams	DE	6'2"	220	23		
Sam Goldman	DE	6'3"	235	32		
Ollie Poole	DE	6'3"	220	27		
Chick Maggioli	DB-HB	5'11"	174	27	3	6
(1 reception for 9 yds.)						
Jim Mello	DB	5'10"	190	28	3	
(3 kickoff returns for 37 yds.)						

Use Name – Tackles	Pos.	Hgt	Wgt	Age	Int	Pts
George Hekkers	T	6'4"	240	26		
John Prchlik	T	6'4"	230	24		
Mike Roussos (from WAS)	T	6'3"	240	23		
Al Russas	T-DE	6'2"	210	25		
Cecil Souders	T-DE	6'1"	210	27		
(1 kickoff return for 7 yds.)						
Russ Thomas	T	6'3"	242	25		
John Treadway	T	6'5"	266	29		

Use Name – Guards	Pos.	Hgt	Wgt	Age	Int	Pts
Les Bingaman	DG	6'3"	250	24		
Howie Brown	G-T	5'11"	215	26		
Mario DeMarco	G-LB	5'11"	200	22		
Chuck DeShane	G-LB	6'1"	217	30	1	
Bill Ward	G	6'	230	28		

Even while mired in mediocrity, the Lions were sowing the seeds for a defensive unit which would win as much press space as many offensive units. Coach Bo McMillin uncovered some of these specialists this year who would man the great Detroit defense of the early 1950s.

A pair of backs, Don Doll and Jim Smith, each showed a flair for picking off interceptions and running them back a long way. Smith ran one of his nine thefts back 102 yards for a score against the Bears, and Doll averaged over 25 yards a return for his eleven interceptions. At middle guard, Les Bingaman plugged up holes with his considerable bulk; one writer said that Bingaman stops runners the same way Pepper Martin stopped ground balls, with his stomach. Once Bingaman was taking a rest in practice, and a teammate yelled, "Move around Bing, you're killing the grass." Thus, it seemed, the Lions were on their way.

GREEN BAY PACKERS 2-10-0 Curly Lambeau

Scores of Each Game		
0	CHIC. BEARS	17
7	LOS ANGELES	48
19	N. Y. Bulldogs	0
17	CHIC. CARDS	39
7	Los Angeles	35
16	DETROIT	14
3	Chic. Bears	24
10	N. Y. GIANTS	30
7	PITTSBURGH	30
21	Chic. Cards	41
0	Washington	30
7	Detroit	21

Use Name	Pos.	Hgt	Wgt	Age	Int	Pts
Ben Flowers	C-LB	6'1"	210	32		
Roger Harding (from NYB)	C-LB	6'2"	215	26	1	
Ed Neal	C-T	6'4"	290	31		
Jay Rhodemyre	C-LB	6'1"	210	27	4	
Larry Craig	DE-LB	6'1"	218	33		
Ralph Olsen	DE	6'4"	220	25		
Don Wells	DE	6'2"	200	27		
Irv Comp	DB	6'2"	205	30	3	
Ken Kranz	DB	5'10"	190	25		

Use Name – Tackles	Pos.	Hgt	Wgt	Age	Int	Pts
Ed Bell	T	6'1"	233	27		
Lou Ferry	T	6'2"	233	22		
Glenn Johnson	T	6'4"	265	27		6
Paul Lipscomb	T	6'5"	245	26		
Urban Odson	T	6'3"	250	30		
Dick Wildung	T	6'	220	27		

Use Name – Guards	Pos.	Hgt	Wgt	Age	Int	Pts
Buddy Burris	G-LB	5'11"	215	26	1	
Roger Eason	G	6'2"	230	31		
Damon Tassos	G-LB	6'1"	225	25	1	
Evan Vogds	G	5'10"	215	26		
(1 kickoff return for 0 yds.)						

With the wolves howling for Curly Lambeau's head, the Packers ran the gauntlet of their worst season in history. Outside of gutsy runner Tony Canadeo, the Packers fielded a pitiful team which won only twice all year. In addition, the Packer organization tottered on the brink of bankruptcy, relying on a new sale of shares to restock the team treasury. The governing board wanted a larger voice in running the club, while Lambeau still insisted on concentrating power in his own hands. When the coach and governing board reached an impasse over the issue, Lambeau read the handwriting on the wall and resigned on February 1, 1950. Some of the executives heaved a sigh of relief, but former player Buckets Goldenberg summed up popular opinion: "I don't see how the Packers can last without him. He was the Packers."

TEAM TOTALS

OFFENSE	First Downs: Tot	by Rsh	by Pas	by Pen	Rushing: No.	Yds.	Avg Yds.	TD	Passing: Att	Com	Comp Pct.	Yds.	Avg. Yds. Att.	Avg. Yds. Comp	TD	Int	Pct. Int.
L.A.	245	103	**125**	17	445	1732	3.9	17	366	192	**52.5**	2819	7.7	14.7	23	27	7.4
CHIC. B.	**248**	111	119	18	483	1785	3.7	18	385	193	50.1	**3055**	**7.9**	15.8	**24**	30	7.8
CHIC. C.	207	106	82	19	467	2130	**4.6**	21	307	138	45.0	1763	5.8	12.8	21	26	8.5
DET.	206	81	104	**21**	397	1381	3.5	10	**399**	178	44.6	2291	5.8	12.9	18	28	7.0
G.B	182	99	68	15	50[illegible]	2061	4.1	7	299	91	30.4	1291	4.3	14.2	5	29	9.7

OFFENSE	Punting: No.	Avg. Yds.	Punt Returns: No.	Yds.	Avg. Yds.	TD	Kickoff Returns: No.	Yds.	Avg. Yds.	TD	Interception Returns: No.	Yds.	Avg. Yds.	TD	Penalties: No.	Yds.	Fumbles: No.	Lost	Points: Tot	PAT	FG Att	FG	Saf.
L.A.	52	**44.4**	43	**624**	14.5	2	37	690	18.6	0	30	359	12.0	4	83	795	29	18	360	45	17	**9**	0
CHIC. B.	52	43.3	**52**	583	11.2	0	38	874	23.0	0	27	257	9.5	2	**92**	**901**	25	18	332	42	16	8	1
CHIC. C.	65	40.9	30	546	**18.2**	2	51	1013	19.9	0	**33**	486	14.7	3	67	590	**20**	16	360	46	11	8	1
DET.	62	37.9	39	557	14.3	2	49	1064	21.7	0	32	**656**	**20.5**	2	71	662	34	21	237	30	14	5	0
G.B.	**87**	40.2	37	310	8.4	1	42	815	19.4	0	20	187	9.4	0	76	722	32	16	114	12	**22**	6	0

Use Name – Backs & Ends	Pos.	Age	Hgt	Wgt	Pts	Int	RUSHING No.	Yds	Avg	TD	PASSING Att	Comp	%	Yds	Yd/Att	TD	Int–%	RK	RECEIVING No.	Yds	Avg	TD	PUNTING No.	Avg	KICKING Pat	Att	%	FG	Att	%	PUNT RETURNS No.	Yds	Avg	TD	KICKOFF RETURNS No.	Yds	Avg	TD
LOS ANGELES RAMS																																						
Bob Waterfield	QB	29	6'1"	200	76		5	-4	-0.8	1	296	154	52	2168	7.3	17	24– 8	4					49	44.4	43	45	98	9	16	56								
Norm Van Brocklin	QB	23	6'1"	190			4	-1	-0.3	0	58	32	55	601	10.3	6	2– 3						2	45.5														
Bobby Thomason	QB	21	6'1"	198							12	6	50	50	4.2	0	1– 8																					
Dick Hoerner	FB	27	6'4"	220	36		155	582	3.8	6									17	213	13	0	1	43.0														
Crazy Legs Hirsch	HB-DB	25	6'2"	192	36	2	68	287	4.2	2									22	326	15	4																
Tommy Kalmanir	HB	23	5'8"	170	12		29	218	7.5	1									2	36	18	0									14	164	12	1	18	403	22	0
Fred Gehrke	HB-DB	31	5'11"	190	32		58	203	3.5	3									9	140	16	2			2	3	67	0	1	0								
Tank Younger	HB-FB	21	6'3"	217			52	191	3.7	0									7	119	17	0																
Vitamin Smith	HB	25	5'8"	180	24		40	117	2.9	2									5	63	13	1									27	427	16	1	13	235	18	0
Jerry Williams	HB-DB	25	5'10"	165	24	5	19	103	5.4	3									7	102	15	0									2	33	17	0				
Gerry Cowhig	FB-DB	28	6'2"	214	12	4	10	32	3.2	1																									2	20	10	0
Bob Agler	FB-LB	26	6'1"	210			4	7	1.8	0																												
Tom Fears	OE	25	6'2"	216	54		1	-3	-3.0	0									77	1013	13	9																
Bob Shaw	OE-DE	28	6'4"	225	36														29	535	18	6																
Tom Keane	OE-DB	22	6'1"	196															4	70	18	0																
Don Currivan	OE-DB	28	6'	190	6	5													3	78	26	1																
Jack Zilly	OE-DE	27	6'2"	210															3	35	12	0													1	0	0	0
Frank Hubbell	OE-DE	27	6'2"	222	6	1													3	32	11	0																
Bill Smyth	OE-DE	27	6'3"	245															2	21	11	0																
CHICAGO BEARS																																						
Johnny Lujack	QB	24	6'	185	57		8	64	8.0	2	**312**	**162**	52	**2658**	**8.2**	**23**	22– 7	3					3	41.0	42	44	98	1	1	100								
Sid Luckman	QB	32	6'	195			3	4	1.3	0	50	22	44	200	4.0	1	3– 6						1	16.0														
George Blanda	QB-LB	21	6'1"	195	27		2	9	4.5	1	21	9	43	197	9.4	0	5–24						19	39.3				7	15	47								
George Gulyanics	HB	28	6'	195	36		102	452	4.4	5	1	0	0	0	0.0	0	0– 0		16	165	10	1	29	**47.2**														
Julie Rykovich	HB	25	6'2"	208	48		88	340	3.9	6									16	210	13	2																
John Hoffman	FB	23	6'2"	215	18		53	216	4.1	1									25	373	15	2													10	249	25	0
Wally Dreyer	HB	24	5'10"	170			45	172	3.8	0									7	94	13	0									13	130	10	0	13	338	26	0
George McAfee	HB-DB	31	6'	175	30	6	42	161	3.8	3									9	157	17	1									24	279	12	0				
Don Kindt	FB-DB	23	6'1"	207		2	41	118	2.9	0									12	118	10	0																
J.R. Boone	HB-DB	23	5'8"	160	18	1	35	111	3.2	0									14	336	24	3									14	170	12	0				
Dante Magnani	HB	32	5'10"	178			33	59	1.8	0									3	29	10	0																
Ed Cody	FB-DB	26	5'10"	195	6	2	11	25	2.3	0																					1	4	4	0	8	181	23	0
Bob Perina	HB-DB	28	6'1"	205		6	4	4	1.0	0									3	33	11	0													1	10	10	0
Jim Keane	OE	25	6'4"	215	36														47	696	15	6																
Ken Kavanaugh	OE-DE	32	6'3"	207	54														29	655	23	**9**																
Ed Sprinkle	OE-DE	25	6'1"	207	2		1	5	5.0	0	1	0	0	0	0.0	0	0– 0		4	69	17	0																
Jack Dugger	OE-DE	26	6'3"	230															1	11	11	0													1	8	8	0
CHICAGO CARDINALS																																						
Paul Christman	QB	31	6'	212			4	34	8.5	0	151	75	50	1015	6.7	11	13– 9	7																				
Jim Hardy	QB	27	6'	180	6		7	6	0.9	1	150	63	42	748	5.0	10	13– 9	11					5	36.0														
Elmer Angsman	HB	23	5'11"	205	36		125	674	5.4	6	1	0	0	0	0.0	0	0– 0		5	57	11	0													5	66	13	0
Charlie Trippi	HB-DB	26	6'	185	54		112	553	4.9	3	2	0	0	0	0.0	0	0– 0		34	412	12	6	8	36.5							10	160	16	0	18	427	24	0
Pat Harder	FB-LB	27	5'11"	205	**102**		106	447	4.2	7									12	100	8	1			45	**47**	98	3	5	60								
Babe Dimancheff	HB	27	5'11"	180	24		38	151	4.0	3									10	130	13	1													2	43	22	0
Vinnie Yablonski	FB-LB	27	5'8"	195	16		32	97	3.0	0									6	35	6	0			1	1	100	5	6	**83**								
Red Cochran	HB	27	6'	190	24		20	87	4.4	1	1	0	0	0	0.0	0	0– 0		7	107	15	1	52	42.0							15	314	**21**	**2**	20	410	21	0
Vic Schwall	HB	25	5'8"	185	12		12	47	3.9	0	2	0	0	0	0.0	0	0– 0		3	8	3	2													4	63	16	0
Clarence Self	HB-DB	24	5'8"	170		1	4	16	4.0	0																					2	20	10	0				
Mal Kutner	OE-DB	28	6'2"	197	30		5	10	2.0	0									30	465	16	5																
Bill Dewell	OE-DE	32	6'4"	215	12														20	235	12	2																
Bob Ravensburg	OE	24	6'1"	190	18		2	8	4.0	0									10	203	20	3																
Tom Wham	OE-DE	25	6'2"	215	6	1													1	11	11	0																
DETROIT LIONS																																						
Frank Tripucka	QB	21	6'2"	180	6		12	36	3.0	1	145	62	43	833	5.7	9	14–10	10					28	38.4														
Fred Enke	QB	24	6'1"	200	6		36	134	3.7	1	142	63	44	793	5.6	6	5– 4	8	1	14	14	0																
Clyde LeForce	QB	26	5'11"	175	6		13	58	4.5	1	112	53	47	665	5.9	3	9– 8	9																				
Bill Dudley	HB	28	5'10"	176	81		125	402	3.2	3									27	190	7	2	32	39.9	30	32	97	5	14	36	11	199	18	1	13	246	19	0
Camp Wilson	FB	27	6'2"	200	6		68	222	3.3	1									6	31	5	0																
Wally Triplett	HB	22	5'10"	175	12		53	221	4.2	1									8	90	11	0									21	281	13	1				
Jim Smith (from CHI-AAFC)	HB-DB	24	6'1"	190	6	9	33	162	4.9	0									2	16	8	0									2	25	13	0	7	172	25	0
Cloyce Box	HB	25	6'4"	220	24		30	62	2.1	0									15	276	18	4													3	50	17	0
John Panelli	FB-LB	23	5'11"	200		1	10	37	3.7	0									1	13	13	0													1	16	16	0
Don Doll	HB-DB	22	5'10"	185	12	11	8	25	3.1	1									1	-5	-5	0									5	52	10	0	21	**536**	26	0
Mel Groomes	HB-DB	22	6'	180	6	1	1	1	1.0	0									3	33	11	1																
Bob Mann	OE	25	5'11"	167	24														66	**1014**	15	4																
John Greene	OE	29	6'	210	42														42	542	13	7																
Kelley Mote	OE	26	6'2"	190															4	58	15	0																
Bernie Hafen	OE	26	6'2"	195															1	10	10	0																
GREEN BAY PACKERS																																						
Jug Girard	QB-HB-DB	22	5'11"	175	6	1	45	198	4.4	1	175	62	35	881	5.0	4	12– 7	12	1	13	13	0	**69**	39.0							11	70	6	0	2	45	23	0
Stan Heath	QB	22	6'1"	190	6		10	25	2.5	1	106	26	25	355	3.3	1	14–13	14																				
Jack Jacobs	QB-DB	30	6'1"	190		2					16	3	19	55	3.4	0	3–19						17	44.5							1	9	9	0				
Tony Canadeo	HB	30	5'11"	190	24		208	1052	5.1	4									3	-2	-1	0													2	20	10	0
Ted Fritsch	FB	28	5'10"	210	32		69	227	3.3	1	1	0	0	0	0.0	0	0– 0		6	81	14	0			11	13	85	5	**20**	25					1	23	23	0
Walt Schlinkman	FB	27	5'8"	190			47	196	4.2	0																									1	23	23	0
Bob Forte	HB-DB	27	6'	195		2	40	135	3.4	0	1	0	0	0	0.0	0	0– 0		7	85	12	0									1	13	13	0	7	159	23	0
Bob Summerhays	FB	22	6'1"	207			29	101	3.5	0									1	34	34	0																
Ralph Earhart	HB	26	5'10"	165	6		20	54	2.7	0									5	109	22	0									14	161	12	1	11	187	17	0
Bob Cifers	HB	28	5'11"	210			23	52	2.3	0									1	5	5	0	1	49.0														
Jack Kirby	HB-DB	26	5'11"	185			3	6	2.0	0																					8	48	6	0	14	315	23	0
Ted Cook	OE-DB	28	6'2"	195	6	5													25	442	18	1													1	7	7	0
Bill Kelley	OE	23	6'2"	195	6														17	222	13	1																
Nolan Luhn	OE-DE	28	6'3"	200	6														15	169	11	1																
Steve Pritko (from NYB)	OE-DE	27	6'2"	215	12														7	98	14	2																
Dan Orlich	OE-DE	24	6'5"	215															4	39	10	0																
Joe Ethridge	T	21	6'	230	4																				1	1	100	1	2	50								

TEAM TOTALS

DEFENSE	FIRST DOWNS: Tot	by Rsh	by Pas	by Pen	RUSHING: No.	Yds.	Avg Yds.	TD	PASSING: Att	Com	Comp Pct.	Yds.	Avg. Yds. Att.	Avg. Yds. Comp	TD	Int	Pct. Int.	PUNTING: No.	Avg. Yds.	PUNT RETURNS: No.	Yds.	Avg. Yds.	TD	KICKOFF RETURNS: No.	Yds.	Avg. Yds.	TD	INTERCEPTION RETURNS: No.	Yds.	Avg. Yds.	TD	PENALTIES: No.	Yds.	FUMBLES: No.	Lost	POINTS: Tot	PAT	FG Att	FG	Saf.	DEFENSE
L.A.	213	101	92	20	472	1679	3.6	14	335	144	43.0	2084	6.2	14.5	16	30	9.0	68	44.2	**26**	**215**	8.3	0	55	**1144**	20.8	0	27	229	**8.5**	1	72	676	30	18	239	30	13	5	1	L.A.
CHIC. B.	170	**56**	95	19	428	**1196**	**2.8**	6	320	152	47.5	2147	6.7	14.1	20	27	8.4	78	41.4	32	359	11.2	0	44	963	21.9	0	30	499	16.6	2	56	521	27	16	218	29	7	5	0	CHIC. B.
CHIC. C.	231	113	107	11	446	1874	4.2	19	383	174	45.4	2617	6.8	15.0	18	**33**	8.6	59	**38.4**	43	361	8.4	1	54	1252	23.2	1	26	401	15.4	1	67	625	26	**21**	301	37	14	6	0	CHIC. C.
DET.	204	103	85	16	491	1827	3.7	15	312	149	47.8	1814	5.8	**12.2**	14	32	**10.3**	59	43.5	38	367	9.7	1	38	712	**18.7**	0	28	365	13.0	4	73	700	31	17	259	32	15	5	1	DET.
G.B.	218	110	89	19	501	2077	4.1	20	**292**	138	47.3	2123	7.3	15.4	15	20	6.8	68	39.8	50	932	18.6	3	**29**	583	20.1	0	29	406	14.0	4	91	836	23	15	329	40	26	11	2	G.B.

CLEVELAND BROWNS 9-1-2 Paul Brown

Scores of Each Game		
28	Buffalo	28
21	BALTIMORE	0
14	NEW YORK	3
28	Baltimore	20
42	LOS ANGELES	7
28	San Francisco	56
61	Los Angeles	14
30	SAN FRANCISCO	28
35	CHICAGO	2
7	BUFFALO	7
31	New York	0
14	Chicago	6

Use Name	Pos.	Hgt	Wgt	Age	Int	Pts
Frank Gatski	C	6'3"	240	27		
Lou Saban	LB	6'	215	27	2	17
(11 for 11 PAT – 0 for 2 Field Goal Attempts)						
Tommy Thompson	C-LB	6'1"	220	22	1	
Bill O'Connor	DE	6'4"	220	23		
John Yonaker	DE	6'5"	227	28		
(1 punt return for 1 yd.)						
George Young	DE	6'3"	215	25		

Use Name – Tackles	Pos.	Hgt	Wgt	Age	Int	Pts
Chubby Grigg	T	6'2"	280	23		
(2 yds. on reception lateral)						
Darrell Palmer	T	6'2"	235	27		
Lou Rymkus	T	6'4"	235	30		
(1 kickoff return for 16 yds.)						
Joe Spencer	T	6'3"	240	26		

Use Name – Guards	Pos.	Hgt	Wgt	Age	Int	Pts
Alex Agase	G-LB	5'10"	210	27	3	
Bob Gaudio (1 rush for –2 yds.)	G	5'10"	225	24		
Lin Houston	G	6'	215	28		
(19 yds. on reception lateral)						
Weldon Humble	G-LB	6'1"	225	28	2	
Ed Ulinski	G	5'11"	210	28		
Bill Willis	G	6'2"	215	28	1	

The Browns looked so good on paper that many experts predicted a second straight perfect season. Otto Graham and Co. began the campaign with a tie and then four straight victories before running their unbeaten streak to twenty-seven games over three seasons. But then, out on the Coast, the '49ers knocked the complacent Browns from their pedestal with a whopping 56-28 upset. On the flight back to Cleveland, coach Paul Brown entertained his players with a blistering tirade and the team went on to five wins and one tie.

Although the Browns proved the class of their breed, the AAFC was not considered the class of pro football, and when the two leagues merged to begin the 1950 season, Cleveland heroes like Otto Graham, Marion Motley, Mac Speedie, Dante Lavelli, Bill Willis, Lou Groza, and Lou Rymkus welcomed the chance to show they could win in any league.

SAN FRANCISCO 49ers 9-3-0 Buck Shaw

Scores of Each Game		
31	BALTIMORE	17
42	CHICAGO	7
42	LOS ANGELES	14
17	Buffalo	28
42	Chicago	24
56	CLEVELAND	28
51	BUFFALO	7
3	New York	24
28	Cleveland	30
28	Baltimore	10
41	Los Angeles	24
35	NEW YORK	14

Use Name	Pos.	Hgt	Wgt	Age	Int	Pts
Bill Johnson	C-LB	6'3"	210	23	1	6
Tino Sabuco	C	6'1"	206	22		
Pete Wissman	C-LB	6'	215	25	1	

Use Name – Tackles	Pos.	Hgt	Wgt	Age	Int	Pts
Bob Bryant	T	6'3"	230	30		
Jack Carpenter	T	6'	242	26		
(from BUF, 2 receptions for 20 yds.)						
Ray Evans	T	6'1"	225	25		
Bob Mike	T	6'1"	220	25		
Joe Morgan	T	6'1"	245	20		
(–1 yd. on rushing lateral)						
Charley Quilter	T	6'1"	240	23		
John Woudenberg	T	6'3"	225	31		

Use Name – Guards	Pos.	Hgt	Wgt	Age	Int	Pts
Bruno Banducci	G	5'11"	220	27		
Don Clark	G-LB	5'11"	197	25	1	
Visco Grgich	G	5'11"	220	26		
Homer Hobbs	G	5'11"	210	26		

The '49ers enjoyed their finest moment in the AAFC when the Cleveland Browns came into Kezar Stadium for a mid-season clash. The Browns had last been beaten early in the 1947 season, but behind Frankie Albert's passing and the running of Joe Perry and Johnny Strzykalski, the '49ers destroyed the Browns' cloak of invincibility with a convincing romp. As the Browns left town, the '49ers moved into first place—a position which their fans had almost forgotten existed.

But injuries to halfbacks Strzykalski and Ed Carr the next week crippled the San Francisco running game, and the '49ers lost two in a row, 24-3 to the Yankees and 30-28 to the Browns, once again to lock the team into the familiar surroundings of second place.

NEW YORK YANKEES 8-4-0 Red Strader

Scores of Each Game		
17	Buffalo	14
3	Cleveland	14
10	LOS ANGELES	7
38	Chicago	24
24	Baltimore	21
24	SAN FRANCISCO	3
21	BALTIMORE	14
14	BUFFALO	17
14	CHICAGO	10
0	CLEVELAND	31
17	Los Angeles	16
14	San Francisco	35

Use Name	Pos.	Hgt	Wgt	Age	Int	Pts
Brad Ecklund	C-LB	6'3"	215	27		
Frank Perantoni	C	6'	220	25		

Use Name – Tackles	Pos.	Hgt	Wgt	Age	Int	Pts
Paul Mitchell	T	6'3"	240	29		
(1 punt return for 15 yds.)						
Martin Ruby	T	6'3"	250	29	1	6
Marion Shirley	T	6'4"	260	27		
Arnie Weinmeister	T	6'4"	235	26		
Ralph Sazio – Canadian Football League						
Spec Sanders (knee injury)						

Use Name – Guards	Pos.	Hgt	Wgt	Age	Int	Pts
George Brown	G	6'2"	223	26		
Bill Chambers	G	6'2"	230	26		
Bill Erickson	G-LB	6'2"	210	27		
John Mastrangelo	G	6'1"	235	23		
Ed Sharkey	G-LB	6'3"	215	23	1	
Joe Signiago	G	6'1"	225	26		
John Wozniak	G-LB	6'	218			

Although the New York Yankees and Brooklyn Dodgers were the most hated of rivals in baseball, their football namesakes could not afford such luxury and ended their feuding and pooled their players under the banner of the New York Yankees when economics forced the Brooklyn management out of business. Yet while the cluster of talent produced a solid team, it did not contain a passer.

The Yankees got help from Tiny Buddy Young, a halfback, who bounced up sprightly after each tackle and threatened to break away for big yardage every time he got the ball, and Arnie Weinmeister, Martin Ruby, and Joe Signaigo, who ranked among the best linemen in the league. The Yankees even had two outstanding young defensive backs in Otto Schnellbacher and rookie Tom Landry. But the lack of a passer put a ceiling on the team's progress.

BUFFALO BILLS 5-5-2 Red Dawson, Clem Crowe

Scores of Each Game		
14	Chicago	17
28	CLEVELAND	28
14	NEW YORK	17
28	SAN FRANCISCO	17
28	BALTIMORE	35
28	Los Angeles	42
7	San Francisco	51
17	LOS ANGELES	14
17	New York	14
7	Cleveland	7
10	CHICAGO	0
38	Baltimore	14

Use Name	Pos.	Hgt	Wgt	Age	Int	Pts
Hal Herring	C-LB	6'1"	215	25	1	
Buckets Hirsch	LB	5'10"	210	28		
Bill Schroll	LB	6'	210	23	1	
Carl Schuette	C-LB	6'1"	205	27		
Art Statuto	C	6'2"	223	24		
Bob Logel	DE	6'3"	210	21		
Vince Mazza	DE	6'1"	224	28		
Bill Stanton	DE	6'2"	210	24		

Use Name – Tackles	Pos.	Hgt	Wgt	Age	Int	Pts
John Kerns	T	6'3"	245	26		
John Kissell	T	6'2"	247	26		
John Maskas	T	5'11"	212	29		
Vin Scott – Canadian Football League						

Use Name – Guards	Pos.	Hgt	Wgt	Age	Int	Pts
Abe Gibron	G	5'10"	231	23		
(3 yds. on reception lateral)						
Ed King	G	6'	218	24		
Rocco Pirro	G	6'	235	32		
Odell Stautzenberger	G	6'	218	24		
Vic Vasicek	G	5'11"	220	23		
(5 yds. on reception lateral)						
John Wyhonic	G	6'	218	29		

The Bills became the only team in AAFC history to go through a season without losing to the Cleveland Browns. In both their meetings, the Bills and Browns battled to a draw, by scores of 28-28 and 7-7. The rest of the schedule saw the Bills on a treadmill, as they lost four of their first six games, then won four of their final six. Their final resting place was in the middle of the pack.

But off-the-field developments angered Buffalo fans more than did the stumbling Bills. The merger of the NFL and the AAFC was announced at the end of the season, with the Cleveland Browns, San Francisco '49ers, and Baltimore Colts all admitted into the established league. Buffalo, whose fans had supported the team, was consigned to pro football's junk pile along with the other AAFC teams.

Use Name – Backs & Ends	Pos.	Age	Hgt	Wgt	Pts	Int	RUSHING				PASSING								RECEIVING				PUNTING		KICKING						PUNT RETURNS				KICKOFF RETURNS			
							No.	Yds	Avg	TD	Att	Comp	%	Yds	Yd/Att	TD	Int–%	RK	No.	Yds	Avg	TD	No.	Avg	Pat	Att	%	FG	Att	%	No.	Yds	Avg	TD	No.	Yds	Avg	TD
CLEVELAND BROWNS																																						
Otto Graham	QB	27	6'1"	195	18		27	107	4.0	3	285	161	56	2785	9.8	19	10– 4	1																				
Cliff Lewis	QB-DB	26	5'11"	168	6	6	9	–17	–1.9	1	10	5	50	144	14.4	2	2–20														20	174	9	0				
Marion Motley	FB-LB	29	6'1"	238	48		113	570	5.0	8									15	191	13	0													12	262	22	0
Dub Jones	HB	24	6'4"	204	30		77	312	4.1	4									12	241	20	1													8	204	26	0
Bill Boedecker	HB	25	5'11"	195	18		50	269	5.4	1									11	371	34	2													9	189	21	0
Special Delivery Jones	HB	30	5'10"	205	42		43	127	3.0	4	1	0	0	0	0.0	0	0– 0		9	130	14	3													1	15	15	0
Ed Susteric	FB-LB	25	6'	205	6		23	114	5.0	1									1	7	7	0													2	39	20	0
Tony Adamle	FB-LB	25	6'	215		4	17	64	3.8	0									1	13	13	0																
Warren Lahr	HB-DB	25	5'11"	185	6	4	9	36	4.0	1									1	20	20	0	4	31.3							6	83	14	0				
Les Horvath	HB-DB	28	5'10"	175	18	2	10	35	3.5	1									2	71	36	1									3	19	6	0				
Ara Parsegian	HB	26	5'10"	195			12	31	2.6	0									1	2	2	0																
Tommy James	HB-DB	25	5'10"	185	6	4	10	28	2.8	0																												
Mac Speedie	OE	29	6'3"	205	42														62	1028	17	7																
Dante Lavelli	OE	26	6'	192	42														28	475	17	7																
Horace Gillom	OE-DE	28	6'1"	220			2	8	4.0	0									23	359	16	0	54	37.2														
Lou Groza	T	25	6'3"	235	40																				34	35	97	2	9	22					1	2	2	0
SAN FRANCISCO 49ers																																						
Frankie Albert	QB	29	5'10"	170	18		35	249	7.1	3	260	129	50	1862	7.2	27	16– 6	3					31	48.2	0	1	0											
Bev Wallace	QB	26	6'2"	180	6		2	2	1.0	1	23	9	39	95	4.1	0	4–17						1	30.0														
Joe Perry	FB	22	6'	195	66		115	783	6.8	8	2	0	0	0	0.0	0	0– 0		11	146	13	3													14	337	24	0
Sam Cathcart	HB-DB	24	6'	175	6	1	69	412	6.0	1									12	182	15	0									18	306	17	0	7	138	20	0
Johnny Strzykalski	HB	26	5'9"	190	24		66	287	4.3	3									6	99	17	1									2	19	10	0	2	57	29	0
Verl Lillywhite	HB-DB	22	5'10"	185	24	1	69	263	3.8	2									8	82	10	2	4	50.5											1	16	16	0
Norm Standlee	FB	30	6'2"	230	24		44	237	5.4	4													8	34.5														
Len Eshmont	HB-DB	32	5'11"	180	12	3	25	164	6.6	0									3	107	36	2													1	13	13	0
Ed Carr	HB-DB	22	6'	185	42	7	19	120	6.3	2									7	165	24	3									1	6	6	0				
Don Garlin	HB-DB	22	5'11"	188	6	1	21	113	5.4	1									6	64	11	0													1	21	21	0
Jim Cason	HB-DB	22	6'	168	6	9	21	70	3.3	1	2	1	50	38	19.0	1	0– 0		5	38	38	0									21	351	17	0	11	247	22	0
Joe Vetrano	HB	27	5'9"	170	65		11	50	4.5	0															56	56	100	3	7	43	1	16	16	0				
Lowell Wagner	HB-DB	25	6'	193	6	6	3	17	5.7	0																					1	2	2	0				
Alyn Beals	OE	28	6'	190	73		4	32	8.0	0									44	678	15	12			1	1	100											
Paul Salata	OE	22	6'2"	190	24														24	289	12	4																
Hal Shoener	OE	26	6'3"	200															7	84	12	0									1	8	8	0	1	17	17	0
Nick Susoeff	OE-DE	28	6'1"	215	6														5	52	10	1																
Gail Bruce	OE-DE	25	6'1"	205		1													1	9	9	0													1	8	8	0
Norm Maloney	OE-DE	26	6'1"	190																											1	5	5	0				
NEW YORK YANKEES																																						
Don Panciera	QB	26	6'1"	195			10	–4	–0.4	0	150	51	34	801	5.3	5	16–11	9																				
Gil Johnson	QB	28	5'11"	195			3	21	7.0	0	36	12	33	179	5.0	0	5–14																					
Buddy Young	HB	23	5'5"	170	48		76	495	6.5	5									12	171	14	2									9	171	19	0	11	316	29	1
Bob Kennedy	FB-HB-LB	28	5'11"	195	36	2	118	490	4.2	5	1	1	100	27	27.0	0	0– 0		7	55	8	1													1	15	15	0
Sherman Howard	HB-DB	25	5'11"	192	18	1	117	459	3.9	3									1	24	24	0													4	95	24	0
Lou Kusserow	FB	25	6'1"	200			39	136	3.5	0	1	0	0	0	0.0	0	0– 0																		6	136	23	0
Eddie Prokop	FB-LB	27	5'11"	200	12		31	109	3.5	2									1	7	7	0													3	62	21	0
Mickey Colmer	FB	30	6'2"	215			36	100	2.8	0	1	0	0	0	0.0	0	0– 0		2	10	5	0	5	46.4											1	16	16	0
Pete Layden	HB-DB	29	5'11"	195	6	7	19	96	5.1	0	10	2	20	25	2.5	0	1–10		1	0	0	0	15	41.7							29	287	10	0	1	28	28	0
Tom Landry	HB-DB	24	6'1"	195		1	29	91	3.1	0									6	109	18	0	51	44.1							3	52	17	0	2	39	20	0
Lowell Tew	HB	22	5'11"	195	6		14	65	4.6	1																									1	17	17	0
Duke Iverson	HB-DB	29	6'2"	198		1	6	50	8.3	0																									2	18	9	0
Harmon Rowe	DB-HB	26	6'	182	3		6	21	3.5	0																												
Noble Doss	HB	29	6'	189			5	15	3.0	0																									1	22	22	0
Dewey Proctor	FB-LB	28	5'11"	215			1	–1	–1.0	0																												
Bruce Alford	OE	28	6'	190	6														11	213	19	1													2	31	16	0
Dan Garza	OE	25	6'3"	200															9	193	21	0													1	21	21	0
Jack Russell	OE-DE	29	6'1"	215	12	1													7	130	19	1																
Barney Poole	OE-DE	26	6'2"	220		1													6	83	14	0									1	6	6	0				
Van Davis	OE-DE	27	6'2"	215															2	26	13	0																
Otto Schnellbacher	DB-OE	26	6'2"	185		4													1	11	11	0									4	31	8	0				
Harvey Johnson	G-LB	30	5'11"	210	46	1																			25	25	100	7	15	47								
BUFFALO BILLS																																						
George Ratterman	QB	22	6'1"	190	24		36	85	2.4	4	252	146	58	777	7.1	14	13–15	2																				
Jim Still	QB	25	6'3"	195			2	6	3.0	0	12	6	50	86	7.2	1	1– 8						16	38.4														
Jess Freitas	QB	28	5'10"	170			3	13	4.3	0	9	4	44	10	1.1	0	2–22																					
Chet Mutryn	HB	28	5'9"	183	30		131	696	5.3	5									29	333	11	0									7	77	11	0	10	224	22	0
Ollie Cline	FB	23	6'	200	18		125	518	4.1	3									15	110	7	0													1	21	21	0
Rex Bumgardner	HB	25	5'11"	193	30		101	391	3.9	1									7	168	24	4									4	35	9	0	9	163	18	0
Lou Tomasetti	HB	33	6'	205	18		54	249	4.6	2									9	56	6	1									2	13	7	0	1	19	19	0
Joe Sutton	HB-DB	25	5'11"	180	6		9	63	7.0	0									5	63	13	1									6	62	10	0	4	82	21	0
Vito Kissell	FB-LB	22	5'10"	205		1	10	19	1.9	0									3	37	12	0													1	1	1	0
Larry Joe	HB	26	5'9"	190			2	18	9.0	0									2	52	26	0													1	12	12	0
Wilbur Volz	HB-DB	25	6'	192	6		4	7	1.8	1									1	6	6	0													3	43	14	0
Tom Colella	HB-DB	31	6'	187		3	7	–9	–1.3	0									2	6	3	0	44	35.3							5	42	8	0	7	107	15	0
Alex Wizbicki	HB-DB	27	5'11"	188		1	5	–10	–2.0	0																									1	22	22	0
Bob Livingstone (from CHI)	HB-DB	27	6'	175	6	1	1	0	0.0	0									3	80	27	0									17	292	17	1	6	85	14	0
Al Baldwin	OE	26	6'2"	210	42		2	1	0.5	0									53	719	14	7																
Jim Lukens	OE	25	6'4"	205	12														24	249	10	2																
Paul Gibson	OE-DE	24	6'2"	205		1													3	32	11	0																
Bob Oristaglio	OE-DE	25	6'2"	210															1	14	14	0																
Chet Adams	T	33	6'3"	240	44																				32	32	100	4	11	36								

CHICAGO HORNETS 4-8-0 Ray Flaherty

Scores of Each Game		
17	BUFFALO	14
7	San Francisco	42
23	Los Angeles	21
35	BALTIMORE	7
24	SAN FRANCISCO	42
24	NEW YORK	38
17	Baltimore	7
14	LOS ANGELES	24
2	Cleveland	35
10	New York	14
0	Buffalo	10
6	CLEVELAND	14

Use Name	Pos.	Hgt	Wgt	Age	Int	Pts
Fred Negus	C-LB	6'1"	210	27	2	6
John Rapacz	C	6'4"	235	24		
George Strohmeyer	C-LB	5'10"	210	25	3	
Paul Cleary	DE	6'1"	196	27		
Bob Heck	DE	6'3"	207	24		
Ray Kuffel	DE	6'3"	215	27		

Use Name – Tackles	Pos.	Hgt	Wgt	Age	Int	Pts
John Clowes	T	6'1"	239	27		
Ziggy Czarobski	T	6'	235	26		
Ted Hazelwood	T	6'1"	235	25		
Nate Johnson	T	6'3"	245	29		
Homer Paine	T	6'	235	26		
Joe Soboleski (to WAS-NFL)	T	6'	215	23		

Use Name – Guards	Pos.	Hgt	Wgt	Age	Int	Pts
Jim Bailey	G	6'2"	215	22		
Jim Pearcy	G	5'11"	210	30		
Ray Richeson (1 kickoff return for 0 yds.)	G	6'	235	26		
Herb St. John	G	5'10"	215	23		
Marty Wendell	G	5'10"	215	22		

The AAFC Chicago franchise began the season with its fourth set of new owners, a new nickname in the Hornets, a new coach in Ray Flaherty, and paper-thin chances for survival. Chicago simply would not support three pro-football franchises, and the Hornets offered no competition for the Bears and Cardinals, who already were set with established followings and colorful teams. The Rockets had starved for customers for three years, and as the Hornets, the dollar famine got worse. An unappetizing production on the field killed any hopes the franchise had of beating the squeeze play in the oncoming merger. Those fans who did show up this year saw a club greatly improved over last year's punching bag, as the Hornets used a much tighter defense to chalk up four victories, their highest total since 1946.

LOS ANGELES DONS 4-8-0 Jim Phelan

Scores of Each Game		
49	BALTIMORE	17
21	CHICAGO	23
14	San Francisco	42
7	New York	10
7	Cleveland	42
42	BUFFALO	28
14	CLEVELAND	61
14	Buffalo	17
24	Chicago	14
24	SAN FRANCISCO	41
21	Baltimore	10
16	NEW YORK	17

Use Name	Pos.	Hgt	Wgt	Age	Int	Pts
John Brown	C-LB	6'4"	230	27	3	12
Dick Woodward	C-LB	6'2"	220	23	2	6
Dan Dworsky (1 kickoff return for 14 yds.)	BB-LB	6'	211	21	1	
Joyce Pipkin	BB	6'1"	205	25		

Use Name – Tackles	Pos.	Hgt	Wgt	Age	Int	Pts
Ed Henke (1 reception for 15 yds.)	T-G	6'3"	217	21		
Ed Kelley (1 rush for –2 yds.)	T	6'4"	230	25		
Mike Perrotti	T	6'3"	245	26		
Bob Reinhard (1 reception for 2 yds.)	T	6'4"	236	28		
Bob Tinsley	T	6'4"	245	25		
Ernie Williamson	T	6'4"	250	26		

Use Name – Guards	Pos.	Hgt	Wgt	Age	Int	Pts
Bob Dobelstein	G	5'11"	220	27		
Ollie Fletcher	G	6'3"	210	26		
Al Lolotai	G	6'	230	28		
Knox Ramsey	G	6'1"	216	23		
Ben Whaley	G	5'11"	210	22		

The Dons gave one the impression of a man going the wrong way on an escalator. The attendance never improved, the team's record kept slipping, and more of the press coverage was captured by the Rams. Owner Ben Lindheimer couldn't be faulted though, as he unstintingly shelled out good money after bad to keep the Dons going. Several other AAFC franchises also owed their lives to Lindheimer. The Los Angeles owner contributed some of his own funds to help the tottering Chicago Hornets, and the Baltimore Colts tasted Lindheimer's hospitality in a unique player deal. When the Colts traded for Los Angeles halfback Herm Wedemeyer, they found out that they couldn't afford his $12,000 contract. Lindheimer told the Colts that if they could pay $8,000, he would take care of the rest.

BALTIMORE COLTS 1-11-0 Cecil Isbell, Walt Driskill

Scores of Each Game		
17	San Francisco	31
17	Los Angeles	49
0	Cleveland	21
7	Chicago	35
20	CLEVELAND	28
35	Buffalo	28
21	NEW YORK	24
7	CHICAGO	17
14	New York	21
10	SAN FRANCISCO	28
10	LOS ANGELES	21
14	BUFFALO	38

Use Name	Pos.	Hgt	Wgt	Age	Int	Pts
Warren Beson	C	6'	205	22		
Spiro Dellerba	LB	5'11"	200	26		
Felto Prewitt	C-LB	5'11"	204	25		
Ralph Ruthstrom	LB	6'5"	215	28	1	
Al Tillman	C-LB	6'	210	26		
Hub Bechtol	DE	6'3"	205	23	1	
Bill Leonard (1 kickoff return for 25 yds.)	DE	6'2"	200	22	1	
Bob Nowaskey	DE	6'	220	31	1	

Use Name – Tackles	Pos.	Hgt	Wgt	Age	Int	Pts
Ernie Blandin	T	6'4"	245	30		
Jon Jenkins	T	6'2"	225	23		
John Mellus	T	6'	210	32		
Alex Sidorik	T	6'	245	27		
Jim Spruill	T	6'3"	225	26		

Use Name – Guards	Pos.	Hgt	Wgt	Age	Int	Pts
Dick Barwegan	G	6'1"	230	26		
Ken Cooper	G	6'1"	205	26		
Barry French	G	6'	225	28		
Bill Garrett	G	6'1"	235	25		

It was the theory of some onlookers that Y.A. Tittle developed his strong passing arm while throwing the ball with tacklers constantly on his back. While the pass protection leaked like a strainer, the running attack was so anemic that Y.A. had little choice but to retreat a few steps and try to hit a receiver while defensive linemen clawed and pummeled him. Tittle came out of the year healthy, but the Colts wound up with a sickly 1-11-0 record. Outside of the quarterback, few of the Colts showed any long-range potential. Only guard Dick Barwegan would make his weight felt in the NFL in coming years. Although coach Cecil Isbell paid in mid-season for the lack of talent with his job, his replacement, Walt Driskill, had no Midas touch when it came to turning losers into winners. Consequently, the Colts, doormats of the AAFC, would also play the same role when joining the NFL in 1950.

Use Name – Backs & Ends	Pos.	Age	Hgt	Wgt	Pts	Int	RUSHING				PASSING								RECEIVING				PUNTING		KICKING						PUNT RETURNS				KICKOFF RETURNS			
							No.	Yds	Avg	TD	Att	Comp	%	Yds	Yd/Att	TD	Int–%	RK	No.	Yds	Avg	TD	No.	Avg	Pat	Att	%	FG	Att	%	No.	Yds	Avg	TD	No.	Yds	Avg	TD
CHICAGO HORNETS																																						
Bob Hoernschemeyer	TB	23	5'11"	195	12		**133**	456	3.4	2	167	69	41	1063	6.4	6	11– 7	6					4	48.8							1	4	2	0	14	373	27	0
Johnny Clement	TB	29	6'	185	30		106	388	3.7	5	114	58	51	906	7.9	6	13–11	5																				
Bob Chappuis	TB	26	6'	190			4	13	3.3	0	14	2	14	40	2.9	0	4–29																					
John Donaldson (from LA)	TB-DB	24	5'10"	180			1	−2	−2.0	0	1	0	0	0	0.0	0	0– 0														1	18	18	0	1	27	27	0
Rip Collins	FB-DB	22	6'	190		1	28	88	3.1	0	1	0	0	0	0.0	0	0– 0		6	161	27	0	41	42.1											2	23	12	0
Ernie Lewis	FB	25	6'1"	210	6		11	43	3.9	1													16	42.5														
George Buksar	FB-LB	23	6'	200	6		13	16	1.2	1	1	0	0	0	0.0	0	0– 0																					
Frank Aschenbrenner	FB	24	5'10"	188			8	14	1.8	0									2	−4	−2	0													2	35	18	0
Hardy Brown	FB-DB	25	6'	185		3	1	2	2.0	0									1	10	10	0	10	39.7														
Ray Ramsey	WB-DB	28	6'2"	165	24	2	32	43	1.3	0									17	366	22	4									8	64	8	0	14	407	**29**	0
Paul Patterson	WB-DB	23	5'9"	185	24	3	2	0	0.0	0									16	304	19	4									4	33	8	0				
Jim Smith (to DET-NFL)	WB	24	6'1"	190															1	31	31	0																
Bob Sweiger	BB-LB	30	6'	209		1	3	17	5.7	0									11	126	11	0													3	59	20	0
Walt McDonald	BB	28	6'1"	210			1	0	0.0	0																												
Dan Edwards	OE	23	6'1"	203	24														42	573	14	3													2	29	15	**1**
Hank Foldberg	OE-DE	26	6'1"	205															15	202	13	0																
Fay King	OE	27	6'3"	195	6														9	88	10	1													1	13	13	0
Jim McCarthy	OE-DE	27	6'1"	205	39														4	58	15	0			21	23	91	6	13	46								
Bob Jensen	OE-DE	23	6'4"	222															2	14	7	0																
LOS ANGELES DONS																																						
Glenn Dobbs	TB	29	6'4"	214	18		34	161	4.7	3	153	65	42	825	5.4	4	9– 6	6					39	42.3														
George Taliaferro	TB	22	5'11"	195	42		95	472	5.0	5	124	45	36	790	6.4	4	14–11	8	0	42	–	1	27	36.4							2	53	27	**1**	13	313	24	0
Walt Clay	TB	25	5'11"	198			9	34	3.8	0	1	1	100	8	8.0	0	0– 0																					
Hosea Rodgers	FB	27	6'1"	192	30		131	494	3.8	5	1	0	0	0	0.0	0	0– 0		7	97	14	0																
Billy Grimes	HB	22	6'1"	192	36		83	429	5.2	4	3	3	100	105	35.0	1	0– 0		13	189	15	2									5	67	13	0	16	411	26	0
Earl Howell	HB	24	5'10"	189	12		31	116	3.7	1									5	11	2	1									1	7	7	0	4	74	19	0
Jimmie Spavital	FB-LB	23	6'1"	215		4	15	44	2.9	0									1	−1	−1	0									6	58	10	0	1	32	32	0
Harper Davis	DB-HB	23	5'11"	175	6	2	13	33	2.5	1									2	13	7	0									2	37	19	0	4	87	22	0
Tom McWilliams	DB-HB	23	5'11"	185		2	3	15	5.0	0	2	0	0	0	0.0	0	0– 0														8	112	14	0				
Bob Kennedy	DB-HB	21	6'	178		1	2	14	7.0	0																												
Paul Crowe (from SF)	DB-FB	25	6'1"	195	6	1	3	2	0.7	0																					6	96	16	0				
Bob Hoffman	BB-LB	31	6'1"	220		1													2	21	11	0													1	14	14	0
George Murphy	BB	22	6'	200			1	0	0.0	0									1	17	17	0																
Len Ford	OE-DE	23	6'4"	235	6	1													36	577	16	1																
Dick Wilkins	OE	23	6'2"	192	18		8	28	3.5	0	1	0	0	0	0.0	0	0– 0		32	589	18	3																
Lew Holder	OE	25	6'1"	191			1	−1	−1.0	0									5	71	14	0																
Joe Aguirre	OE-DE	30	6'4"	225	6														3	37	12	1																
Ab Wimberly	OE-DE	23	6'2"	212	12	1													3	22	7	0																
Burr Baldwin	OE-DB	27	6'1"	195		2	1	1	1.0	0									2	26	13	0																
Bob Nelson	C-LB	29	6'1"	210	43																				34	35	97	3	6	50								
BALTIMORE COLTS																																						
Y. A. Tittle	QB	22	6'	190	12		29	89	3.1	2	**289**	148	51	2209	7.6	14	18– 6	4																				
Sam Vacanti	QB	27	5'11"	210	3		7	10	1.4	0	27	11	41	134	5.0	0	1– 4								3	3	100	0	2	0					1	10	10	0
Charlie O'Rourke	QB	32	5'11"	175							7	1	14	12	1.7	0	1–14						28	39.2														
Herm Wedemeyer	HB	25	5'10"	178			64	291	4.5	0	1	0	0	0	0	0	1–100		10	112	11	0	3	18.0							16	221	14	0	**30**	**602**	20	0
Lu Gambino	FB	25	6'1"	205	6		56	208	3.7	0									10	67	7	1																
Billy Stone	HB	23	6'	190	48		51	205	4.0	2									31	621	20	6													1	25	25	0
Bob Pfohl	HB	23	6'	200	12		67	205	3.1	2									7	62	9	0													4	98	25	0
Chick Jagade	FB	22	6'	200	12		33	174	5.3	2									8	44	6	0													6	75	13	0
Paul Page	HB-DB	22	6'	180			25	81	3.2	0									4	62	16	0									1	16	16	0	4	108	27	0
Bob Kelly	HB-DB	24	5'10"	193		3	9	17	1.9	0									2	25	13	0													2	31	16	0
Buzz Mertes (to NYG-NFL)	FB	28	6'	205	6		11	8	0.7	0									2	22	11	1																
Wayne Kingery	HB-DB	22	5'11"	175		1	3	3	1.0	0									1	−2	−2	0	3	36.3							2	19	10	0				
Bob Cowan	HB-DB	26	5'11"	185		3	1	0	0.0	0									1	26	26	0																
Jake Leicht	HB-DB	28	5'9"	170		1	6	−7	−1.2	0									1	12	12	0									9	109	12	0	8	171	21	0
Lamar Davis	OE-DB	28	6'1"	185	6	1													38	548	14	1													1	13	13	0
John North	OE	28	6'2"	200	24														25	490	20	4																
Win Williams	OE	26	6'2"	185	6														20	266	13	1																
Rex Grassman	K	25	6'1"	215	37						1	0	0	0	0.0	0	1–100						28	38.8	19	19	100	6	11	**55**								

TEAM TOTALS

	FIRST DOWNS:				RUSHING:				PASSING:									PUNTING:		PUNT RETURNS:				KICKOFF RETURNS:				INTERCEPTION RETURNS:				PENAL-TIES:		FUM-BLES:		POINTS:					TEAM TOTALS
OFFENSE	Tot	by Rsh	by Pas	by Pen	No.	Yds.	Avg. Yds.	TD	Att	Com	Comp. Pct.	Yds.	Avg. Yds. Att.	Avg. Yds. Comp	TD	Int.	Pct. Int.	No.	Avg. Yds.	No.	Yds.	Avg. Yds.	TD	No.	Yds.	Avg. Yds.	TD	No.	Yds.	Avg. Yds.	TD	No.	Yds.	No.	Lost	Tot	PAT	FG Att	FG	Saf.	OFFENSE
CLEVE.	176	62	**100**	**14**	403	1682	4.2	24	296	**166**	56.1	**2929**	**9.9**	**17.6**	21	**12**	**4.1**	58	36.8	30	277	9.2	0	34	727	21.4	0	29	331	11.4	2	**72**	**617**	33	21	339	45	11	2	0	CLEVE.
S.F.	175	**117**	53	5	506	**2798**	**5.5**	**26**	287	139	48.4	1995	7.0	14.4	**28**	20	7.0	44	**45.5**	46	**713**	**15.5**	0	39	854	21.9	0	**32**	**474**	14.8	**3**	65	595	47	22	**416**	**57**	7	3	**1**	S.F.
N.Y.	135	91	37	7	**510**	2143	4.2	16	199	66	33.2	1032	5.2	15.6	5	22	11.1	**71**	43.8	**47**	562	12.0	0	36	816	22.7	**1**	24	321	13.4	2	52	358	35	20	196	25	**15**	**7**	0	N.Y.
BUFFALO	**184**	111	61	12	492	2047	4.2	16	273	156	**57.1**	1873	6.9	12.0	15	16	5.9	60	36.1	34	400	11.8	**1**	40	729	18.2	0	9	84	9.3	0	59	454	34	18	236	32	11	4	0	BUFFALO
CHICAGO	122	46	63	13	342	1080	3.2	9	297	129	43.4	2009	6.8	15.6	12	28	9.4	**71**	42.2	21	240	11.4	0	43	989	23.0	**1**	15	323	**21.5**	0	63	426	**29**	19	179	21	13	6	**1**	CHICAGO
L.A.	157	82	63	12	430	1838	4.3	19	286	114	39.9	1728	6.0	15.2	9	23	8.0	66	39.9	30	430	14.3	**1**	41	972	**23.7**	0	21	316	15.0	2	59	536	31	**17**	253	34	6	3	0	L.A.
BALT.	151	66	78	7	362	1284	3.5	8	**325**	160	49.2	2355	7.3	14.7	14	22	6.8	62	37.9	28	365	13.0	0	**58**	**1158**	20.0	0	13	113	8.7	0	49	369	32	21	172	22	13	6	0	BALT.
DEFENSE																																									DEFENSE
CLEVE.	156	75	67	14	437	1905	4.4	13	304	120	**39.5**	**1677**	**5.5**	14.0	**9**	29	9.5	63	39.6	**27**	**314**	11.6	**0**	**32**	694	21.7	**0**	12	**153**	12.8	**0**	45	359	32	13	**171**	**22**	10	**3**	1	CLEVE.
S.F.	150	74	68	8	401	1364	3.4	12	318	137	43.1	1949	6.1	14.2	15	**32**	**10.1**	75	39.3	**27**	317	11.7	**0**	61	1216	19.9	**0**	20	229	11.5	1	51	374	27	15	227	29	10	6	**0**	S.F.
N.Y.	**129**	**55**	68	**6**	**360**	**1134**	**3.2**	**8**	316	159	50.3	2189	6.9	**13.8**	13	24	7.6	**78**	41.8	44	485	**11.0**	1	44	994	22.6	1	22	349	15.9	3	56	414	33	17	206	26	**9**	6	**0**	N.Y.
BUFFALO	139	69	62	8	385	1616	4.2	13	282	132	46.8	2109	7.5	16.0	18	9	3.2	58	42.4	29	343	11.8	**0**	41	959	23.4	**0**	16	250	15.6	1	54	419	34	22	256	35	16	**3**	1	BUFFALO
CHICAGO	163	92	61	10	467	2309	4.9	24	**197**	**107**	54.3	1732	8.8	16.2	**9**	15	7.6	54	**37.6**	44	583	13.3	1	36	868	24.1	1	28	335	12.0	2	**73**	521	**52**	**37**	268	37	10	**3**	**0**	CHICAGO
L.A.	174	89	69	16	484	2148	4.4	20	290	148	51.0	2414	8.3	16.3	22	21	7.2	52	40.0	30	398	13.3	**0**	43	824	**19.2**	**0**	23	268	**11.7**	1	68	**678**	35	17	322	40	12	6	**0**	L.A.
BALT.	189	121	**60**	8	511	2396	4.7	28	256	127	49.6	1851	7.2	14.6	18	13	5.1	52	40.7	35	547	15.6	**0**	34	**690**	20.3	**0**	22	378	17.2	1	72	590	28	17	341	47	**9**	4	**0**	BALT.

1950 Gathering in the Best of the Flock

The death of the AAFC gathered all the strong clubs into the NFL under a strong commissioner in Bert Bell and exiled the weaker franchises into the history books. The Cleveland Browns, San Francisco '49ers, and Baltimore Colts moved into the established league, swelling its membership up to 13 clubs, while the players from the defunct teams went into a pool and were spread around the league.

The new era also brought with it the permanent adoption of the "free substitution" rule which relieved coaches of the necessity of playing most men both ways and that gave the opportunity to develop offensive and defensive specialists who would excel in one aspect of the game. This division of labor made pro football a faster, more exciting game to watch, and while sold-out stadiums were still the exception rather than the rule, attendance soared to a record total of 1,977,556.

Only the new medium of television did not fit smoothly into the picture. The Los Angeles Rams televised all their games, both home and away, and watched their attendance shrink to almost half of the 1949 total despite a very attractive football team. It was an example that Bell would later use to support the TV blackout of all home games throughout the league.

AMERICAN CONFERENCE

Cleveland Browns—The NFL schedule-maker indulged his sense of drama by pitting the 1949 NFL champion Philadelphia Eagles against the 1949 AAFC champion Cleveland Browns on the Saturday night before the other teams opened their seasons. The oddsmakers favored the Eagles, but coach Paul Brown had his team ready to break into the established league with a bang. A crowd of 71,000 jammed Philadelphia's Municipal Stadium but found little cause for cheering. With Otto Graham slinging sideline passes to Mac Speedie, Dub Jones, and Dante Lavelli, the Browns ran away from the Eagles in the second half for a stunningly easy 35-10 upset. The Browns then marched briskly through their NFL opponents, winning ten games and losing twice to the New York Giants. But in the conference playoff, the Browns rebounded to down New York 8-3.

New York Giants—The death of the AAFC Yankees brought back to the Giants defensive tackle Arnie Weinmeister and defensive backs Otto Schnellbacher, Tom Landry, and Harmon Rowe, while the college draft brought scrappy fullback Eddie Price into the fold. Coach Steve Owen built his offense around runners Price and Choo-Choo Roberts, and he constructed the famous "umbrella defense" to defuse free-passing clubs like the Browns. In this defense, the two defensive ends dropped off the line to cover receivers, while backs Em Tunnell, Landry, Schnellbacher, and Rowe formed the "umbrella" in the zone pass defense.

Philadelphia Eagles—A tight budget and an injured foot killed the Eagles' chances of repeating as NFL champs. The tight budget of the front office did not allow for any pay raises, and several holdouts riddled the club with dissension. Coach Greasy Neale had no use for owner Jim Clark when he rewarded the holdouts with raises after most of the players agreed to play for the same salary as last year, and their deteriorating relations came to a head when the players had to pull Neale off Clark in the Polo Grounds dressing room. The injured foot belonged to Steve Van Buren. An off-season operation failed to heal properly and left the punishing halfback a shadow of his former self. But with Tommy Thompson throwing the ball, Frank Ziegler running it, and young Chuck Bednarik bolstering the defense at linebacker, the Eagles stayed close behind the Browns and Giants until dropping their last four games.

Pittsburgh Steelers—The Steeler offense still looked like something out of the 1930s. While every other pro team now used the T formation, coach John Michelosen still stuck with the conservative single wing. Although tailback Joe Geri picked up yardage in bits and pieces with off-tackle smashes, his pass completions came few and far between. The earthbound Steelers scored only 180 points, less than half of what the pass-oriented Rams tallied, but a hard-nosed defense, led by lineman Bill McPeak and Ernie Stautner, kept them in most of their games. Of their six victories, the most impressive was a 17-6 triumph over the New York Giants. The most characteristic win, though, was a bruising 9-7 fray with the Eagles in which all the Steeler points came on three Geri field goals. Coach Michelosen liked this kind of hard-hitting football so much that he let Jim Finks, a promising passer, waste away unused.

Chicago Cardinals—After thirty-one years in Green Bay, Curly Lambeau began anew as coach of the Cards, but he brought with him none of the magic of his six NFL championships with the Packers. Still emphasizing the pass, he elevated strong-armed Jim Hardy from second string to starting quarterback. Hardy enjoyed some good days, such as the game in which he threw five touchdown passes to end Bob Shaw, but he also had his bad days—one of which made the record books when the Eagles intercepted him eight times. Despite Hardy's inconsistency, Lambeau had to stick with him, since he had unloaded incumbent quarterback Paul Christman before the season.

Washington Redskins—Quarterback Harry Gilmer still showed no signs of growing into the starting lineup, and heralded rookie Choo-Choo Justice impressed no one with his running. Only fullback Rob Goode and end Hugh Taylor helped aging Sammy Baugh and Bill Dudley shoot some life into the attack, and despite rookie Chuck Drazenovich's fine play at linebacker, the defense had as much trouble stopping the enemy as the offense had moving the ball. The result was predictable, as the Skins went on an eight-game losing streak in mid-season to turn the year into a shambles. But coach Herman Ball somehow survived and would be back for more next year.

NATIONAL CONFERENCE

Los Angeles Rams—The modern passing attack hit a new peak as the Rams threw their way to the top of the National Conference by chalking up 466 points, sixty-four touchdowns, and 70 points in one game—all records. New head coach Joe Stydahar, replacing the fired Clark Shaughnessy, managed a superb pair of quarterbacks in young Norm Van Brocklin and veteran Bob Waterfield. Ends Tom Fears and Crazy Legs Hirsch and halfback ex-Army star Glenn Davis were all among the league's top receivers. The defense fell far short of immovable, but the offense carried the team into a tie with the Bears for the conference crown. In the playoff game, Fears, who had set a new season's receiving record, hauled in three touchdown passes as the Rams won 24-14.

Chicago Bears—Johnny Lujack was completing his passes, but he wasn't getting his usual zing into the ball. After the season, the word leaked out that Lujack had hurt his shoulder and, with veteran Sid Luckman unable to play for any extended stretch, had to keep playing with the injury. The young passer boosted the Bears into a tie for the conference title, but his arm was never again the same. In engineering a strong offense, Lujack ran well, hit end Jim Keane with short passes, and often handed off to George Gulyanics. George Connor and Dick Barwegan excelled in the offensive line with Connor doubling as a big linebacker on defense.

New York Yanks—Ted Collins still owned the team, but the Yanks were a far different outfit from last year's Bulldogs. The club had a new name, moved to Yankee Stadium, had a respected coach in Red Strader, and a practically whole new cast of players. Only three men returned from the Bulldog roster, with most of the squad recruited from AAFC veterans. Quarterback George Ratterman, runners Sherman Howard, George Taliaferro, and Buddy Young, receiver Dan Edwards, linemen Joe Signiago and Martin Ruby, and defensive back Spec Sanders all came from the AAFC to bring the franchise alive. Add solid rookie seasons from runner Zollie Toth and end Art Weiner, and the Yanks had a pretty fair team. Only two things remained the same: New Yorkers still kept away from the ballpark, and Collins kept losing money.

Detroit Lions—The Lions hadn't won a championship since 1935, but they gathered together a nucleus of players who would soon bring the NFL title to Detroit. Quarterback Bobby Layne was puchased from the New York Bulldogs, giving the squad a leader both on the field and off it. Layne sparkled on long, time-consuming downfield marches, as well as on late-night extra curricular activities. Like Babe Ruth, however, Layne could ignore all training rules and still turn in an outstanding performance on the gridiron. The rookie crop yielded a fine runner, receiver, and kicker in Doak Walker, a bruising two-way end in Leon Hart, and a tough tackle in Thurman McGraw. Further additions included halfback Bob Hoernschemeyer and offensive lineman Lou Creekmur, both from AAFC rosters.

Green Bay Packers—New coach Gene Ronzani inherited a deteriorating squad, and constant front-office interference didn't make his task any easier. Some new talent, however, kept the season from being a total loss. Rookie quarterback Tobin Rote showed flair both in passing and running, end Al Baldwin and halfback Billy Grimes both fit into the attack after coming over from the AAFC, and rookie Clayton Tonnemaker graded out as the best Packer lineman. But the defense leaked horrendously, five times allowing 40 or more points, while the offense was inconsistent.

San Francisco '49Ers—Fullback Joe Perry and halfback Johnny Strzykalski both carried the ball above and beyond the call of duty, but they could not make up for a weakened passing attack. Saddled with his first losing season in San Francisco, coach Buck Shaw did uncover two fine rookies, pass receiver and place kicker Gordy Soltau and tackle Leo Nomellini, a brute of a tackle equally effective in the offensive or defensive line.

Baltimore Colts—The Colts started out their NFL career by dropping all seven of their pre-season games and six of their regular season's games. Only at quarterback were the Colts well fortified, with Y. A. Tittle and rookie Adrian Burk both worthy of better supporting casts. But even these two were not enough to keep attendance from dwindling, the club from continually losing, and owner Abraham Watner from selling the franchise back to the league.

FINAL TEAM STATISTICS

OFFENSE

	BALT.	CHI.B.	CHI.C.	CLEVE.	DET.	G.BAY	L.A.	N.Y.G.	N.Y.Y.	PHIL.	PITT.	S.F.	WASH.
FIRST DOWNS:													
Total	188	234	194	199	209	174	**278**	173	210	231	177	201	187
by Rushing	56	141	84	104	92	82	112	114	94	**142**	97	107	92
by Passing	109	85	87	86	98	70	**142**	53	102	79	68	83	84
by Penalty	23	10	23	9	19	22	**24**	6	14	10	12	11	11
RUSHING:													
Number	345	574	386	457	389	398	404	515	397	**581**	477	460	410
Yards	1148	2308	1604	2089	1626	1706	1711	**2336**	1832	2328	1659	1955	1773
Average Yards	3.3	4.0	4.2	4.6	4.2	4.3	4.2	4.5	**4.6**	4.0	3.5	4.3	4.3
Touchdowns	12	25	8	20	14	15	**28**	21	16	13	12	14	10
PASSING:													
Attempts	438	296	368	260	403	367	**453**	187	355	285	255	326	314
Completions	206	135	165	139	176	140	**253**	81	174	121	100	164	154
Completion Percent	47.0	45.6	44.8	53.5	43.7	38.1	**55.8**	43.3	49.0	42.5	39.2	50.3	49.0
Yards	2687	1927	2375	1984	2772	1831	**3709**	1338	2894	1836	1729	1875	2093
Avg. Yards per Att.	6.1	6.5	6.5	7.6	6.9	5.0	**8.2**	7.2	8.2	6.4	6.8	5.8	6.7
Avg. Yards per Comp.	13.0	14.3	14.4	14.3	15.8	13.1	14.7	16.5	16.6	15.2	**17.3**	11.4	13.6
Touchdowns	14	5	21	15	22	14	**31**	12	29	15	10	14	18
Interceptions	31	24	31	21	29	37	27	**10**	26	28	29	25	25
Percent Intercepted	7.1	8.1	8.4	8.1	7.2	10.1	6.0	**5.3**	7.3	9.8	11.4	7.7	8.0
PUNTING:													
Number	**83**	66	76	66	68	74	63	78	72	56	61	63	64
Average Distance	40.2	41.7	40.6	**43.2**	40.2	38.1	40.5	37.1	42.2	41.4	41.3	38.7	40.6
PUNT RETURNS:													
Number	26	**60**	33	30	36	44	45	42	27	52	33	33	43
Yards	378	601	338	469	389	**729**	393	410	305	401	387	406	407
Average Yards	15.5	10.0	10.2	15.6	10.8	**16.6**	8.7	9.8	11.3	7.7	11.7	12.3	9.5
Touchdowns	1	0	1	1	0	**2**	0	0	0	0	0	0	1
KICKOFF RETURNS:													
Number	**66**	35	51	32	40	56	56	25	58	38	32	40	51
Yards	1286	818	1064	670	1067	1233	**1424**	592	1280	867	748	800	1242
Average Yards	19.5	23.4	20.9	20.9	**26.7**	22.0	25.4	23.7	22.1	22.8	23.4	20.0	24.4
Touchdowns	0	0	0	0	1	0	**3**	0	1	1	0	0	0
INTERCEPTION RETURNS:													
Number	**34**	16	22	31	31	27	31	27	30	31	22	22	19
Yards	**571**	283	190	262	480	337	512	408	438	401	295	304	221
Average Yards	16.8	**17.7**	8.6	8.5	15.5	12.5	16.5	15.1	14.6	12.9	13.4	13.8	11.6
Touchdowns	**4**	**4**	0	2	3	2	1	0	2	3	0	1	2
PENALTIES:													
Number	63	85	76	104	86	85	**110**	68	85	63	57	93	80
Yards	579	738	609	968	804	757	**1038**	562	762	612	477	851	829
FUMBLES:													
Number	32	**23**	25	26	35	35	30	36	32	32	41	35	42
Number Lost	21	17	14	**12**	18	20	17	20	13	15	29	21	22
POINTS:													
Total	213	279	233	310	321	244	**466**	268	366	254	180	213	232
PAT Attempts	31	35	31	38	43	34	**63**	35	51	33	22	29	31
PAT Made	27	34	29	38	39	31	**59**	30	48	32	22	27	31
FG Attempts	4	20	12	21	18	17	14	12	9	**22**	14	8	10
FG Made	0	9	6	**14**	8	3	7	6	2	8	8	4	5
Percent FG Made	0.0	45.0	50.0	**66.7**	44.5	17.6	50.0	50.0	22.2	36.4	57.1	50.0	50.0
Safeties	0	1	0	1	0	0	1	2	**3**	0	1	0	0

DEFENSE

	BALT.	CHI.B.	CHI.C.	CLEVE.	DET.	G.BAY	L.A.	N.Y.G.	N.Y.Y.	PHIL.	PITT,	S.F.	WASH.
FIRST DOWNS:													
Total	257	178	216	184	200	220	217	176	249	**141**	198	204	217
by Rushing	150	67	126	96	70	91	113	87	119	**66**	111	111	110
by Passing	96	88	79	71	113	110	88	76	112	**65**	77	81	90
by Penalty	11	23	11	17	17	19	16	13	18	**10**	**10**	12	17
RUSHING:													
Number	514	**388**	525	451	399	422	431	473	434	391	460	443	462
Yards	2857	1449	2132	1573	**1367**	1885	1882	1387	2445	1603	1889	1662	1944
Average Yards	5.6	3.7	4.1	3.5	3.4	4.5	4.4	**2.9**	5.6	4.1	4.1	3.8	4.2
Touchdowns	28	14	21	10	13	23	12	8	28	**5**	12	17	17
PASSING:													
Attempts	304	354	**269**	292	381	379	385	295	396	277	300	347	328
Completions	156	169	130	121	191	185	165	145	189	**102**	146	164	145
Completion Percent	51.3	47.7	48.3	41.4	50.1	48.8	42.9	49.2	47.7	**36.8**	48.7	47.3	44.2
Yards	2545	2265	2075	**1581**	2580	2818	2576	1848	2775	1621	1801	2289	2276
Avg. Yards per Att.	8.4	6.4	7.7	**5.4**	6.8	7.4	6.7	6.3	7.0	5.9	6.0	6.6	6.9
Avg. Yards per Comp.	16.3	13.4	16.0	13.1	13.5	15.2	15.6	12.7	14.7	15.9	**12.3**	14.0	15.7
Touchdowns	31	11	14	**8**	23	24	26	11	17	10	10	16	19
Interceptions	**34**	16	22	31	31	27	31	27	30	31	22	22	19
Percent Intercepted	11.2	4.5	8.2	10.6	8.1	7.1	8.1	9.1	7.6	**11.2**	7.3	6.3	5.8
PUNTING:													
Number	56	**87**	57	69	73	72	72	77	58	77	70	62	60
Average Distance	39.1	39.7	43.3	41.5	42.7	42.7	40.2	41.2	**38.8**	38.9	40.8	39.4	40.3
PUNT RETURNS:													
Number	44	**24**	46	32	45	49	28	43	53	32	35	37	36
Yards	531	303	400	**210**	529	372	394	420	699	392	504	413	446
Average Yards	12.1	12.6	8.7	**6.6**	11.8	7.6	14.1	9.8	13.2	12.3	14.4	11.2	12.4
Touchdowns	**0**	1	1	**0**	**0**	**0**	**0**	**0**	**0**	1	1	**0**	2
KICKOFF RETURNS:													
Number	**36**	44	46	43	54	41	48	55	53	38	37	41	44
Yards	900	848	1063	988	1218	845	1411	1166	1148	834	**710**	1014	946
Average Yards	25.0	19.3	23.1	23.0	22.6	20.6	29.4	21.2	21.7	21.9	**19.2**	24.7	21.5
Touchdowns	1	**0**	**0**	**0**	2	**0**	2	**0**	**0**	**0**	**0**	1	**0**
INTERCEPTION RETURNS:													
Number	31	24	31	21	25	37	27	**10**	26	28	29	25	25
Yards	622	396	410	262	372	575	294	**120**	343	289	244	429	346
Average Yards	20.1	16.5	13.2	12.5	12.8	15.5	10.9	12.0	13.2	10.3	**8.4**	17.2	13.8
Touchdowns	2	2	1	1	**0**	5	3	**0**	2	1	1	3	3
PENALTIES:													
Number	**96**	77	93	62	86	95	93	70	88	73	77	71	74
Yards	**967**	671	876	554	803	919	859	553	824	590	733	599	638
FUMBLES:													
Number	29	24	37	37	35	34	31	**43**	28	32	30	39	25
Number Lost	14	16	24	24	24	15	15	**27**	14	17	16	21	12
POINTS:													
Total	462	207	287	144	285	406	309	150	367	**141**	195	300	326
PAT Attempts	63	27	38	19	39	55	43	19	49	**17**	25	39	43
PAT Made	61	24	35	18	37	50	42	18	46	**15**	24	35	42
FG Attempts	13	12	18	**11**	**11**	13	13	**11**	17	18	12	14	18
FG Made	7	5	8	4	4	6	**3**	6	9	8	5	7	8
Percent FG Made	53.8	41.7	44.4	36.4	36.4	46.1	**23.1**	54.5	53.0	44.4	41.7	50.0	44.4
Safeties	1	**0**	**0**	**0**	1	1	**0**	**0**	**0**	**0**	3	2	1

SCORING

CLEVELAND	**7**	**6**	**7**	**10—30**
LOS ANGELES	**14**	**0**	**14**	**0—28**

First Quarter

L.A. Davis, 82 yard pass from Waterfield
PAT—Waterfield (Kick)

Cle. Jones, 27 yard pass from Graham
PAT—Groza (Kick)

L.A. Hoerner, 3 yard rush
PAT—Waterfield (Kick)

Second Quarter

Cle. Lavelli, 37 yard pass from Graham
PAT—Bad Center Snap

Third Quarter

Cle. Lavelli, 39 yard pass from Graham
PAT—Groza (Kick)

L.A. Hoerner, 1 yard rush
PAT—Waterfield (Kick)

L.A. Brink, 6 yard Fumble return
PAT—Waterfield (Kick)

Fourth Quarter

Cle. Bumgardner, 14 yard pass from Graham
PAT—Groza, (Kick)

Cle. Groza, 16 yard field goal

TEAM STATISTICS

CLEVE.		L.A.
22	First Downs	22
116	Rushing Yardage	106
33	Pass Attempts	32
22	Pass Completions	18
66.7	Completion Percentage	56.3
298	Passing Yardage	312
9.0	Avg. Yards per Attempt	9.8
13.5	Avg. Yards per Completion	17.3
1	Had Intercepted	5
5	Number of Punts	4
38.4	Average Punt Distance	50.8
22	Punt Return Yardage	14
3	Fumbles	0
3	Fumbles Lost	0
3	Penalties	4
25	Yards Penalized	48

1950
CHAMPIONSHIP GAME
December 24, at Cleveland
(Attendance 29,751)

Different League, Same Title

In their first season in the NFL the Browns beat the Giants in a playoff for the Eastern title, and now only the Rams stood in the way of the league championship. Both clubs depended on strong passing attacks, and footballs filled the air right from the start of the game. On the first play from scrimmage, Bob Waterfield hit Glenn Davis on a fly pattern good for 82 yards and a touchdown. Within three minutes Cleveland tied the score on an Otto Graham to Dub Jones pass, but Los Angeles again went ahead by driving 81 yards in eight plays after the kickoff. Both teams slowed up for the rest of the quarter, but the Browns struck again midway through the second period. With the ball on the Los Angeles 37-yard line, Dante Lavelli grabbed a Graham pass between two Ram defenders on the 8-yard line and ran it in for six points. On the extra point, holder Tommy James fumbled the snap, so the Browns trailed 14-13 at the half. Graham hit Lavelli with another touchdown pass four minutes into the third quarter to put Cleveland into the lead 20-14, but the Rams came right back with a score of their own. Waterfield hit on three straight passes to bring the ball down to the Cleveland 17, and then he turned to fullback Dick Hoerner. The powerful Hoerner carried the ball seven straight times, scoring from the 1-yard line on fourth down. On the first play after the kickoff, Marion Motley fumbled deep in his own territory, and Ram end Larry Brink scooped the ball up and carried it in for the second Los Angeles touchdown in twenty-one seconds. Waterfield's conversion made it 28-20, with the Browns' missed extra point looking very large. The Cleveland defense, however, tightened up and gave the offense a chance to get back in the game. Late in the third period, Warren Lahr intercepted a Waterfield pass on his own 35-yard line, and Graham then drove his team 65 yards with nine completed passes, including five in a row to Lavelli, with the touchdown coming on a diving catch by Rex Bumgardner. Now Cleveland trailed by only one point, but the Ram defense followed Cleveland's in stiffening up. Neither team could launch an extended drive, trading punts for most of the fourth quarter. With two minutes left in the game, Cliff Lewis returned Waterfield's punt to the Brown 32-yard line, giving Cleveland one last shot at winning it. Graham kept the ball and ran 19 yards on the first play, then passed to Bumgardner for 10 more yards. His next pass was incomplete, but completions to Jones and Bumgardner then brought the ball down to the Ram 11. After a quarterback sneak to get the ball in the center of the field, Graham turned the ball over to kicker Lou Groza. The kick from the 16 split the goal posts with only twenty-eight seconds left, and the Browns took the NFL crown with a 30-28 win.

1950 N.F.L. — American Conference

CLEVELAND BROWNS 10-2-0 Paul Brown

Scores of Each Game		
35	Philadelphia	10
31	Baltimore	0
0	N.Y. GIANTS	6
30	Pittsburgh	17
34	CHIC. CARDS	24
13	N.Y. Giants	17
45	PITTSBURGH	7
10	Chic. Cards	7
34	SAN FRANCISCO	14
20	WASHINGTON	14
13	PHILADELPHIA	7
45	Washington	21
	Playoff	
8	N.Y. GIANTS	3

Use Name	Pos.	Hgt	Wgt	Age	Int	Pts
Lou Groza	OT	6'3"	235	26		74
Lou Rymkus	OT	6'4"	235	31		
Abe Gibron	OG	5'11"	236	24		
Lin Houston	OG	6'	215	29		
Weldon Humble	OG	6'1"	225	29		
Frank Gatski	C	6'3"	240	28		
Bill Willis	DG	6'3"	215	29		
Len Ford	DE	6'4"	238	24		
George Young	DE	6'3"	215	26		
Jim Martin	OT-DE	6'2"	215	26	2	
Chubby Grigg	DT	6'2"	280	24		12
John Kissell	DT	6'3"	247	27		2
Darrell Palmer	DT	6'2"	235	28		
John Sandusky	DT	6'1"	250	24		
Alex Agase	LB	5'10"	212	28	1	
Tommy Thompson	LB	6'1"	220	23		
Hal Herring	C-LB	6'1"	210	26	2	
Tony Adamle	FB-LB	6'1"	220	26	1	
Ken Gorga	DB	6'2"	200	21	6	
Warren Lahr	DB	5'11"	185	26	8	12
Cliff Lewis	QB-DB	5'11"	168	27	1	
Tommy James	HB-DB	5'10"	185	26	9	
Otto Graham	QB	6'1"	195	28		36
Rex Baumgardner	HB	5'11"	193	26		18
Ken Carpenter	HB	6'1"	192	24		6
Dub Jones	HB	6'4"	205	25		66
Dom Moselle	HB	6'	192	24		
Don Phelps	DB-HB	5'11"	185	25	1	18
Emerson Cole	FB	6'2"	215	22		
Marion Motley	LB-FB	6'1"	238	30		24
Dante Lavelli	OE	6'	192	27		30
Mac Speedie	OE	6'3"	205	30		6
Horace Gillom	DE-OE	6'1"	225	29		6

Chick Jagade – Broken Foot
Special Delivery Jones – Canadian Football League

NEW YORK GIANTS 10-2-0 Steve Owen

Scores of Each Game		
18	Pittsburgh	7
6	Cleveland	0
21	Washington	17
6	PITTSBURGH	17
17	CLEVELAND	13
3	Chic. Cards	17
24	WASHINGTON	21
51	CHIC. CARDS	21
55	Baltimore	20
7	PHILADELPHIA	3
51	N.Y. YANKS	7
9	Philadelphia	7
	Playoff	
3	Cleveland	8

Use Name	Pos.	Hgt	Wgt	Age	Int	Pts
John Sanchez	OT	6'3"	240	29		
Jim White	OT	6'2"	230	29		
George Roman	DT-OT	6'4"	250	25		
Bill Austin	OG	6'1"	220	21		
Don Ettinger	OG	6'2"	215	27		
John Mastrangelo	LB-OG	6'1"	235	24		
Joe Sulaitis	BB-OG	6'2"	215	29		
John Rapacz	LB-C	6'4"	260	25		
Jim Duncan	DE	6'2"	205	24		
Ray Poole	DE	6'2"	215	28	1	45
Leo Skladany	DE	6'1"	210	23		
Al DeRogatis	DT	6'4"	240	23		6
Arnie Weinmeister	DT	6'4"	235	27		
Jon Baker	LB	6'2"	215	27		
John Cannady	LB	6'2"	225	26	2	
Bill Milner	LB	6'1"	225	26		
Dick Woodward	C-LB	6'2"	225	24	1	6
Tom Landry	DB	6'1"	195	25	2	6
Harmon Rowe	DB	6'	182	27	3	
Otto Schnellbacher	DB	6'2"	190	27	8	
Em Tunnell	DB	6'1"	187	28	7	
Chuck Conerly	QB	6'1"	185	26		6
Travis Tidwell	QB	5'10"	185	25		12
Forrest Griffith	HB	5'11"	190	21		12
Jim Ostendarp	HB	5'8"	178	25		12
Joe Scott	HB	6'1"	200	24		18
Randy Clay	DB-HB	6'	185	22	2	15
Choo-Choo Roberts	DB-HB	5'11"	188	26		32
Bob Jackson	FB	5'11"	210	25		12
Eddie Price	FB	5'11"	190	24		24
Bob McChesney	OE	6'2"	190	23		36
Bill Swiacki	OE	6'2"	195	25		18
Ellery Williams	OE	6'	185	24		
Kelley Mote	DE-OE	6'2"	190	27	1	6

Dick Hensley – Military Service

PHILADELPHIA EAGLES 6-6-0 Greasy Neale

Scores of Each Game		
10	CLEVELAND	35
45	Chic. Cards	7
56	LOS ANGELES	20
24	Baltimore	14
17	Pittsburgh	10
35	WASHINGTON	3
7	PITTSBURGH	9
33	Washington	0
10	CHIC. CARDS	14
3	N.Y. Giants	7
7	Cleveland	13
7	N.Y. GIANTS	9

Use Name	Pos.	Hgt	Wgt	Age	Int	Pts
Al Wistert	OT	6'1"	217	29		
Vic Sears	DT-OT	6'3"	237	32		
John Magee	OG	5'10"	220	27		
Duke Maronic	OG	5'9"	209	29		
Cliff Patton	OG	6'2"	240	26		56
Bucko Kilroy	OT-DT-OG	6'2"	240	29		
Vic Lindskog	C	6'1"	205	34		
Walt Barnes	OG-DG	6'1"	248	32		
Mario Gianelli	OG-DG	6'	265	29		
John Green	DE	6'1"	192	28		6
Norm Willey	DE	6'2"	210	23	1	6
Walt Stickel	DT	6'3"	245	28		
Mike Jarmoluk	DE-DT	6'5"	250	27		
Jay MacDowell	DE-DT	6'2"	215	31		
Joe Muha	LB	6'1"	206	29	2	6
Chuck Bednarik	C-LB	6'3"	233	25	1	
Alex Wojciechowicz	C-LB	5'11"	232	35	1	
Russ Craft	HB-DB	5'9"	172	30	7	6
Pat McHugh	HB-DB	5'11"	166	30	4	
Frank Reagan	HB-DB	5'11"	180	31	4	6
Dan Sandifer (from SF)	HB-DB	6'2"	190	23	2	
Joe Sutton	HB-DB	5'11"	180	26	8	
Tommy Thompson	QB	6'1"	196	33		
Bill MacKrides	QB	5'11"	179	25		
Clyde Scott	HB	6'	175	26		
Steve Van Buren	HB	6'	205	29		24
Frank Ziegler	HB	5'11"	172	26		18
Toy Ledbetter	DB-HB	5'10"	190	23		18
Jack Myers	LB-FB	6'2"	200	25		
Jim Parmer	DB-FB	6'	189	23		48
Jack Ferrante	OE	6'1"	188	34		18
Billy Hix	OE	6'2"	215	22		
Pete Pihos	DE-OE	6'1"	215	26		36
Neill Armstrong	DB-OE	6'2"	188	24	3	6

Bosh Pritchard – Injury

PITTSBURGH STEELERS 6-6-0 John Michelosen

Scores of Each Game		
7	N.Y. GIANTS	18
7	Detroit	10
26	Washington	7
17	CLEVELAND	30
17	N.Y. Giants	6
10	PHILADELPHIA	17
7	Cleveland	45
9	Philadelphia	7
17	BALTIMORE	7
28	Chic. Cards	17
7	WASHINGTON	24
28	CHIC. CARDS	7

Use Name	Pos.	Hgt	Wgt	Age	Int	Pts
Lou Allen	OT	6'3"	215	27		
Frank Wydo	OT	6'4"	220	26		
Jack Wiley	DT-OT	5'11"	210	29		
George Hughes	OG	6'1"	225	25		
Dick Tomlinson	OG	6'1"	205	22		
Bob Balog	C	6'2"	225	26		
Bill Walsh	C	6'2"	230	23		
Bob Davis	DE	5'11"	195	29		
George Hays	DE	6'2"	210	25		
Bill McPeak	DE	6'1"	200	25		
Carl Samuelson	DT	6'4"	250	27		
Ernie Stautner	DT	6'1"	218	25		2
Walt Szot	DT	6'1"	225	31		
Darrell Hogan	LB	5'10"	210	24	1	
George Nicksich	OG-LB	6'	225	22	3	
Frank Sinkovitz	C-LB	6'1"	220	27	2	
Joe Hollingsworth	FB-LB	6'	200	25		
Jerry Shipkey	FB-LB	6'1"	210	25	2	18
Don Samuel	DB	5'11"	190	26		
Jim Finks	TB-DB	6'	175	23		
Tom McWilliams	TB-DB	5'11"	180	24	2	
Howard Hartley	WB-DB	6'	185	26	5	
Joe Geri	TB	5'10"	190	26		64
Bob Gage	DB-TB	5'11"	175	23	4	30
Lynn Chandnois	WB	6'2"	195	26		
Jerry Nuzum	HB	6'1"	200	27		12
Fran Rogel	FB	5'11"	200	23		24
Joe Gasparella	BB	6'4"	220	23		
Charlie Seabright	BB	6'2"	210	32		6
Truett Smith	BB	6'2"	210	26		
Val Jansante	OE	6'1"	190	29		
Elbie Nickel	OE	6'1"	195	27		24
Bill Long	DE-OE	6'1"	200	24		
Charlie Mehelich	DE-OE	6'1"	200	28		

CHICAGO CARDINALS 5-7-0 Curly Lambeau

Scores of Each Game		
7	PHILADELPHIA	45
55	BALTIMORE	13
6	Chic. Bears	27
24	Cleveland	34
38	Washington	28
17	N.Y. GIANTS	3
7	CLEVELAND	10
21	N.Y. Giants	51
14	Philadelphia	10
17	PITTSBURGH	28
20	CHIC. BEARS	10
7	Pittsburgh	28

Use Name	Pos.	Hgt	Wgt	Age	Int	Pts
Plato Andros	OT	6'	240	29		
Bill Fischer	OT	6'2"	250	23		
John Hock	OT	6'2"	217	22		
George Petrovich	OG	6'2"	225	25		
Buster Ramsey	OG	6'1"	225	30		
Knox Ramsey	OG	6'1"	210	24		
Ed Bagdon	LB-OG	5'10"	200	24		
Bill Blackburn	C	6'6"	230	28		
Bob Dove	DE	6'2"	220	29	1	
Jerry Hennessey	DE	6'2"	211	24		
Tom Wham	DE	6'2"	215	26		6
John Goldsberry	DT	6'2"	245	24		
Lloyd McDermott (from DET)	DT	6'2"	240	24		
Jack Jennings	OT-DT	6'4"	245	23		
Jim Lipinski	OT-DT	6'4"	238	23		
Gerry Cowhig	LB	6'2"	214	29		
Bill Svoboda	LB	6'	210	23		
Ray Apolskis	OG-LB	5'11"	210	31	1	
Vince Banonis	C-LB	6'1"	235	28		
Red Cochran	DB	6'	190	28		
Jerry Davis	DB	5'10"	180	28	9	
Bob Nussbaumer	DB	5'11"	170	26		
Mike Swistowicz	DB	5'10"	185	25		
Don Paul	HB-DB	6'	185	24	4	12
Ray Ramsey	OE-DB	6'2"	165	29	1	
Jim Hardy	QB	6'	180	28		6
Frank Tripucka	QB	6'2"	175	22		6
Elmer Angsmann	HB	5'11"	197	24		12
Babe Dimancheff	HB	5'11"	180	28		
Vic Schwall	HB	5'8"	190	26		
Charlie Trippi	HB	6'	185	27		24
Fred Gehrke (from SF)	DB-HB	5'11"	190	32	3	12
Pat Harder	FB	5'11"	200	28		40
Vinnie Yablonski	FB	5'8"	195	28		19
Fran Polsfoot	OE	6'3"	200	23		36
Bob Shaw	OE	6'4"	225	29		72
Mal Kutner	DB-OE	6'2"	197	29	3	

WASHINGTON REDSKINS 3-9-0 Herman Ball

Scores of Each Game		
38	Baltimore	14
21	Green Bay	35
7	PITTSBURGH	26
17	N.Y. GIANTS	21
28	CHIC. CARDS	38
3	Philadelphia	35
21	N.Y. Giants	24
0	PHILADELPHIA	33
14	Cleveland	20
38	BALTIMORE	28
24	Pittsburgh	7
21	CLEVELAND	45

Use Name	Pos.	Hgt	Wgt	Age	Int	Pts
Laurie Niemi	OT	6'1"	247	25		
Bob Hendren	DT-OT	6'8"	246	27		
Jerry Houghton	DT-OT	6'2"	226	24		
John Badaczewski	OG	6'1"	238	28		
Herb Siegert	OG	6'3"	213	26		
John Steber	OG	6'	240	27		
Slug Witucki	OG	5'11"	240	22		
Gene Pepper	OT-DT-LB-OG	6'2"	230	23		
Harry Ulinski	C	6'4"	226	25		
Dan Brown	DE	6'1"	200	25		
Roland Dale	DE	6'3"	210	23		
Ed Berrang	OE-DE	6'2"	203	25		
Lou Karras	DT	6'4"	240	23		
Paul Lipscomb	DT	6'5"	248	27		
Al DeMao	C-LB	6'2"	215	30		
Ed Quirk	C-LB	6'1"	228	25	2	
Chuck Drazenovich	FB-LB	6'1"	225	23	2	6
Pete Stout	FB-LB	6'	202	27	1	
Hardy Brown (from BAL)	DB-LB	6'	195	26	1	
Joe Bartos	HB-DB	6'2"	194	24		
Harry Dowda	HB-DB	6'2"	197	26	4	6
Hall Haynes	HB-DB	6'	190	21	4	6
Eddie Saenz	HB-DB	5'11"	166	27	1	12
Sammy Baugh	QB	6'2"	184	36		6
Nick Sebek	QB	6'	194	23		
Harry Gilmer	HB-QB	6'	170	24		6
Choo-Choo Justice	HB	5'10"	172	26		12
Frank Spaniel (from BAL)	HB	5'10"	185	22	1	12
George Thomas	HB	6'1"	184	22		
Bill Dudley	DB-HB	5'10"	175	29	2	64
Rob Goode	LB-FB	6'4"	220	23	2	36
Clyde Goodnight	OE	6'1"	195	26		12
Hugh Taylor	OE	6'4"	191	27		54
Joe Tereshinski	DE-OE	6'2"	209	26		

CLEVELAND BROWNS

RUSHING

Last Name	No.	Yds	Avg	TD
Motley	140	810	5.8	3
Jones	83	384	4.6	6
Bumgardner	67	231	3.4	2
Phelps	39	198	5.1	2
Carpenter	35	181	5.2	1
Graham	55	145	2.6	6
Cole	26	105	4.0	0
Moselle	5	39	7.8	0
Adamle	3	8	2.7	0
James	1	−1	−1.0	0
Lewis	2	−1	−0.5	0
Humble	1	−10	−10.0	0

RECEIVING

Last Name	No.	Yds	Avg	TD
Speedie	42	548	13	1
Lavelli	37	565	15	5
Jones	31	458	15	5
Motley	11	151	14	1
Bumgardner	9	112	12	1
Carpenter	5	45	16	0
Gillom	2	54	27	1
Phelps	1	28	28	0
Groza	1	23	23	1

PUNT RETURNS

Last Name	No.	Yds	Avg	TD
Phelps	13	174	13	1
Moselle	7	126	18	0
Gorgal	4	83	21	0
Carpenter	4	58	15	0
Lewis	2	13	7	0
James	0	15	0	0

KICKOFF RETURNS

Last Name	No.	Yds	Avg	TD
Phelps	12	325	27	0
Moselle	5	107	21	0
Carpenter	5	98	20	0
Adamle	4	53	13	0
Gillom	3	51	17	0
Cole	1	22	22	0
Martin	1	14	14	0
Rymkus	1	0	0	0

PASSING – PUNTING – KICKING Statistics

PASSING	Att	Comp	%	Yds	Yd/Att	TD	Int–%	RK
Graham	253	137	54	1943	7.7	14	20– 8	2
Lewis	4	1	25	38	9.5	1	0– 0	
Gillom	1	1	100	3	3.0	0	0– 0	
Carpenter	1	0	0	0	0	0	1–100	
Groza	1	0	0	0	0	0	0– 0	

PUNTING	No	Avg
Gillom	66	43.2

KICKING	XP	Att	%	FG	Att	%
Groza	29	29	100	13	19	68
Grigg	9	9	100	1	2	50

NEW YORK GIANTS

RUSHING

Last Name	No.	Yds	Avg	TD
Price	126	703	5.6	4
Roberts	116	483	4.2	4
Scott	72	322	4.5	2
Clay	74	254	3.4	2
Griffith	45	162	3.6	2
Ostendarp	18	144	8.0	2
Tidwell	29	133	4.6	2
Jackson	12	113	9.4	2
Conerly	23	22	0.9	1

RECEIVING

Last Name	No.	Yds	Avg	TD
Swiacki	20	280	14	3
McChesney	19	380	20	6
Roberts	11	144	13	1
Scott	9	240	27	1
Clay	7	69	10	0
Williams	4	78	20	0
Mote	4	72	18	1
Price	4	30	8	0
Griffith	1	26	26	0
Weinmeister	1	16	16	0
Sulaitis	1	3	3	0

PUNT RETURNS

Last Name	No.	Yds	Avg	TD
Tunnell	31	305	10	0
Ostendarp	7	60	9	0
Schnellbacher	3	22	7	0
Scott	1	23	23	0

KICKOFF RETURNS

Last Name	No.	Yds	Avg	TD
Scott	14	351	25	0
Sulaitis	4	112	28	0
Ostendarp	3	68	23	0
Clay	1	25	25	0
Roberts	1	13	13	0
Poole	1	12	12	0
Swiacki	1	11	11	0

PASSING	Att	Comp	%	Yds	Yd/Att	TD	Int–%	RK
Conerly	132	56	42	1000	7.6	8	7– 5	6
Tidwell	55	25	45	338	6.2	4	3– 5	

PUNTING	No	Avg
Landry	58	36.8
Conerly	20	38.0

KICKING	XP	Att	%	FG	Att	%
Poole	30	34	88	5	11	45
Clay	0	1	0	1	1	100

PHILADELPHIA EAGLES

RUSHING

Last Name	No.	Yds	Avg	TD
Ziegler	172	733	4.3	1
Van Buren	188	629	3.3	4
Ledbetter	67	320	4.8	1
Parmer	60	203	3.4	7
Myers	29	159	5.5	0
MacKrides	21	82	3.9	0
Reagan	3	55	18.3	0
Craft	8	52	6.5	0
Scott	13	46	3.5	0
Thompson	15	34	2.3	0
McHugh	4	14	3.5	0
Sandifer	1	3	3.0	0
Sutton	1	1	1.0	0

RECEIVING

Last Name	No.	Yds	Avg	TD
Pihos	38	447	12	6
Ferrante	35	588	17	3
Ziegler	13	216	17	2
Myers	12	204	17	0
Armstrong	8	124	16	1
Parmer	6	103	17	1
Ledbetter	4	81	20	2
Van Buren	2	34	17	0
Hix	2	25	13	0
Craft	1	14	14	0

PUNT RETURNS

Last Name	No.	Yds	Avg	TD
Sandifer	15	155	10	0
Craft	19	113	6	0
Sutton	9	75	8	0
Reagan	6	38	6	0
Ziegler	3	20	7	0

KICKOFF RETURNS

Last Name	No.	Yds	Avg	TD
Craft	10	327	33	1
Ziegler	10	204	20	0
Van Buren	5	110	22	0
Sandifer	5	108	22	0
McHugh	2	45	23	0
Muha	2	28	14	0
Myers	2	25	13	0
Sutton	1	21	21	0
Green	1	14	14	0
Maronic	1	4	4	0

PASSING	Att	Comp	%	Yds	Yd/Att	TD	Int–%	RK
Thompson	239	107	45	1608	6.7	11	22– 9	11
MacKrides	46	14	30	228	5.0	4	6–13	

PUNTING	No	Avg
Reagan	54	42.0
Muha	2	24.0

KICKING	XP	Att	%	FG	Att	%
Patton	32	33	97	8	17	47
Muha	0	0	0	0	5	0

PITTSBURGH STEELERS

RUSHING

Last Name	No.	Yds	Avg	TD
Geri	188	705	3.8	2
Rogel	92	418	4.5	3
Chandnois	71	216	3.0	0
Nuzum	57	154	2.7	1
Gage	39	106	2.7	3
McWilliams	10	39	3.9	0
Shipkey	18	17	0.9	3
Finks	1	2	2.0	0
Hollingsworth	1	2	2.0	0

RECEIVING

Last Name	No.	Yds	Avg	TD
Jansante	26	353	14	0
Rogel	24	304	13	1
Nickel	22	527	24	4
Chandnois	7	158	23	0
Nuzum	6	142	24	1
Gage	6	127	21	2
Seabright	3	37	12	1
Hartley	2	27	14	0
Mehelich	2	18	9	0
Geri	1	33	33	1
Gasparella	1	3	3	0

PUNT RETURNS

Last Name	No.	Yds	Avg	TD
Gage	14	192	14	0
McWilliams	11	139	13	0
Hartley	5	23	5	0
Chandnois	3	33	11	0

KICKOFF RETURNS

Last Name	No.	Yds	Avg	TD
Chandnois	12	351	29	0
Gage	9	196	22	0
Nuzum	2	47	24	0
McWilliams	3	45	15	0
Hartley	1	44	44	0
Hollingsworth	1	22	22	0
Rogel	1	20	20	0
Mehelich	2	16	8	0
Wydo	1	7	7	0

PASSING	Att	Comp	%	Yds	Yd/Att	TD	Int–%	RK
Geri	113	41	36	866	7.7	6	15–13	16
Gage	58	21	36	294	5.1	1	5– 9	
Gasparella	54	23	43	383	7.1	3	5– 9	
Finks	9	5	56	35	3.9	0	1–11	
McWilliams	8	5	63	113	14.1	0	1–13	
Chandnois	6	1	17	5	0.8	0	2–33	
Rogel	4	3	75	30	7.5	0	0– 0	
Seabright	3	1	33	3	1.0	0	0– 0	

PUNTING	No	Avg
Geri	55	40.7
Gage	3	48.7
McWilliams	3	45.0

KICKING	XP	Att	%	FG	Att	%
Geri	22	22	100	8	14	57

CHICAGO CARDINALS

RUSHING

Last Name	No.	Yds	Avg	TD
Harder	99	454	4.6	1
Trippi	99	426	4.3	3
Angsman	102	362	3.5	1
Schwall	17	114	6.7	0
Yablonski	30	110	3.7	1
Gehrke	25	73	2.9	1
Paul	14	80	5.7	0
Tripucka	4	35	8.8	1
Hardy	10	14	1.4	1
Dimancheff	8	5	0.6	0

RECEIVING

Last Name	No.	Yds	Avg	TD
Shaw	48	971	20	12
Polsfoot	38	653	17	6
Trippi	32	270	8	1
Harder	15	111	7	0
Yablonski	7	71	10	0
Angsman	7	56	8	1
Paul	5	93	19	1
Dimancheff	5	53	11	0
Gehrke	5	26	5	1
Kutner	4	74	19	0
Bagdon	1	19	19	0
Schwall	1	7	7	0

PUNT RETURNS

Last Name	No.	Yds	Avg	TD
Paul	18	194	11	1
Swistowicz	4	59	15	0
Trippi	7	54	8	0
Gehrke	5	44	9	0
Davis	3	29	10	0
Blackburn	1	2	2	0

KICKOFF RETURNS

Last Name	No.	Yds	Avg	TD
Paul	28	693	25	0
Trippi	8	139	17	0
Harder	6	112	19	0
Gehrke	2	57	29	0
Wham	2	53	27	0
Davis	3	25	8	0
Schwall	1	21	21	0
Bagdon	1	11	11	0
Hennessey	1	5	5	0
Hock	1	5	5	0

PASSING	Att	Comp	%	Yds	Yd/Att	TD	Int–%	RK
Hardy	257	117	46	1636	6.4	17	24– 9	10
Tripucka	108	47	44	720	6.8	4	7– 6	13
Trippi	3	1	33	19	6.3	0	0– 0	

PUNTING	No	Avg
Hardy	56	39.4
Tripucka	18	43.7
Trippi	2	47.0

KICKING	XP	Att	%	FG	Att	%
Harder	22	24	92	4	9	44
Yablonski	7	7	100	2	3	67

WASHINGTON REDSKINS

RUSHING

Last Name	No.	Yds	Avg	TD
Goode	136	560	3.4	5
Dudley	66	339	5.1	1
Justice	59	285	4.8	0
Drazenovich	35	155	4.1	1
Gilmer	22	145	6.6	1
Saenz	20	64	3.2	1
Stout	9	53	5.9	0
Dowda	23	47	2.0	0
Thomas	20	41	2.1	0
Bartos	9	36	4.0	0
Baugh	7	27	3.9	1
Spaniel	15	22	1.5	1
Haynes	2	20	10.0	0

RECEIVING

Last Name	No.	Yds	Avg	TD
Taylor	39	833	21	9
Dudley	22	172	8	1
Justice	19	180	9	2
Goode	19	160	8	1
Tereshinski	17	148	9	0
Goodnight	12	185	15	2
Saenz	10	165	17	1
Spaniel	5	84	17	0
Drazenovich	3	38	13	0
Dowda	2	16	8	0
Stout	2	15	8	0
Thomas	2	7	4	0
Berrang	1	14	14	0
DeMao	1	4	4	0

PUNT RETURNS

Last Name	No.	Yds	Avg	TD
Dudley	12	185	15	1
Saenz	14	125	9	0
Justice	7	46	7	0
Haynes	3	22	7	0
Thomas	3	15	5	0
Spaniel	2	11	6	0

KICKOFF RETURNS

Last Name	No.	Yds	Avg	TD
Saenz	12	347	29	0
Spaniel	14	316	23	0
Justice	9	223	25	0
Haynes	5	214	43	0
Thomas	8	169	21	0
Dudley	1	43	43	0
Drazenovich	3	38	13	0
Goodnight	1	12	12	0
H. Brown	3	21	7	0
Siegert	1	0	0	0

PASSING	Att	Comp	%	Yds	Yd/Att	TD	Int–%	RK
Baugh	166	90	54	1130	6.8	10	11– 7	6
Gilmer	141	63	45	948	6.7	8	12– 9	13
Justice	4	1	25	15	3.8	0	0– 0	
Sebek	3	0	0	0	0.0	0	2–67	

PUNTING	No	Avg
Justice	22	41.3
Haynes	19	39.8
Dudley	14	41.8
Baugh	9	39.1

KICKING	XP	Att	%	FG	Att	%
Dudley	31	31	100	5	10	50
H. Brown	0	1	0	0	0	0

1950 N.F.L. — National Conference

LOS ANGELES RAMS 9-3-0 Joe Stydahar

Scores of Each Game	
20 CHIC. BEARS	24
45 N.Y. YANKS	28
35 San Francisco	14
20 Philadelphia	56
30 Detroit	28
70 BALTIMORE	27
65 DETROIT	24
28 SAN FRANCISCO	21
45 Green Bay	14
43 N.Y. Yanks	35
14 Chic. Bears	24
51 GREEN BAY	14
Playoff	
24 CHIC. BEARS	14

Use Name	Pos.	Hgt	Wgt	Age	Int	Pts
Gil Bouley	DT-OT	6'2"	235	29		
Ed Champagne	DT-OT	6'3"	240	28		6
Harry Thompson	OG	6'2"	225	23		
Jack Finlay	LB-OG	6'1"	215	29		
Dave Stephenson	DG-OG	6'2"	235	24		
Art Statuto	C	6'2"	220	25		
Fred Naumetz	LB-C	6'1"	223	28	1	
Stan West	DG	6'2"	245	23		
Larry Brink	DE	6'5"	235	27		2
Jack Zilly	DE	6'2"	215	28		
Bill Smyth	OE-DE	6'3"	245	28		
Dick Huffman	OT-DT	6'2"	256	27		
Bob Reinhard	OT-DT	6'4"	240	29		6
Mike Lazetich	OG-LB	6'1"	195	24		
Vic Vasicek	OG-LB	5'11"	225	24	1	
Don Paul	C-LB	6'1"	230	25	3	
Tank Younger	HB-FB-LB	6'3"	220	22		12
Woodley Lewis	DB	6'1"	185	25	12	6
George Sims	DB	5'11"	170	22	1	
Jerry Williams	HB-DB	5'10"	175	26	3	12
Tom Keane	OE-DB	6'1"	195	23	6	6
Norm Van Brocklin	QB	6'1"	190	24		6
Bob Waterfield	QB	6'1"	200	30		81
Paul Barry	HB	6'	210	24		12
Glenn Davis	HB	5'11"	170	25		42
Tommy Kalmanir	HB	5'8"	175	24		6
Vitamin Smith	HB	5'8"	175	26		48
Ralph Pasquariello	FB	6'2"	240	23		6
Dan Towler	FB	6'2"	225	22		36
Dick Hoerner	LB-FB	6'4"	220	28		66
Bob Boyd	OE	6'2"	205	22		24
Tom Fears	OE	6'2"	215	26		42
Crazy Legs Hirsch	DB-OE	6'2"	190	26	4	47

CHICAGO BEARS 9-3-0 George Halas

Scores of Each Game	
24 Los Angeles	20
32 San Francisco	20
21 Green Bay	31
27 CHIC. CARDS	6
28 GREEN BAY	14
27 N.Y. Yanks	38
35 Detroit	21
28 N.Y. YANKS	20
17 SAN FRANCISCO	0
24 LOS ANGELES	14
10 Chic. Cards	20
6 DETROIT	3
Playoff	
14 Los Angeles	24

Use Name	Pos.	Hgt	Wgt	Age	Int	Pts
Paul Stenn	OT	6'2"	245	32		
George Connor	LB-OT	6'3"	240	25	1	
Dick Barwegan	OG	6'1"	230	27		
Frank Dempsey	OT-OG	6'3"	235	25		
Wash Serini	DG-OG	6'2"	235	26		2
Wayne Hansen	LB-OG	6'2"	228	22		
Bulldog Turner	LB-C	6'1"	235	31		
Ed Bradley	DE	6'	208	24		
Ed Sprinkle	OE-DE	6'1"	207	26		
Bill Wightkin	OE-DE	6'3"	235	23		
Alf Bauman	DT	6'2"	235	30		
Bill Garrett	DT	6'1"	240	26		6
Fred Davis	OT-DT	6'3"	245	32		
Ray Bray	OG-DG	6'	240	33		
Fred Negus	LB	6'1"	212	28		
Jerry Weatherley	LB	6'5"	215	21	2	12
Stu Clarkson	C-LB	6'2"	225	31		
Ed Cody	DB	5'10"	190	27		
Red O'Quinn	DB	6'2"	195	25	3	6
J.R. Boone	HB-DB	5'8"	163	24		
Al Campana	HB-DB	5'11"	185	24	1	6
Harper Davis	HB-DB	5'11"	172	24	5	6
George McAfee	HB-DB	6'	175	32	2	
Don Kindt	FB-DB	6'1"	205	24		6
George Blanda	DB-LB-QB	6'1"	198	22		18
Sid Luckman	QB	6'	195	33		
Steve Romanik	QB	6'1"	190	26		
Johnny Lujack	DB-QB	6'	185	25	1	109
George Gulyanics	HB	6'	195	29		12
Chuck Hunsinger	HB	6'	188	25		12
Julie Rykovich	HB	6'2"	205	26		42
Curley Morrison	FB	6'2"	215	24		6
John Hoffman	LB-FB	6'2"	218	24	1	18
Jim Keane	OE	6'4"	215	26		
Ken Kavanaugh	OE	6'3"	207	33		18

NEW YORK YANKS 7-5-0 Red Strader

Scores of Each Game	
21 San Francisco	17
28 Los Angeles	45
44 DETROIT	21
44 Green Bay	31
29 SAN FRANCISCO	24
35 GREEN BAY	17
38 CHIC. BEARS	27
20 Chic. Bears	28
35 LOS ANGELES	43
14 Detroit	49
7 N.Y. Giants	51
51 BALTIMORE	14

Use Name	Pos.	Hgt	Wgt	Age	Int	Pts
John Nolan	OT	6'2"	226	24		
Jon Jenkins (from BAL)	DT-OT	6'2"	225	24		
Carroll Vogelaar	DT-OT	6'1"	255	30		
John Clowes	OG-DT-OT	6'1"	240	28		
George Brown	OG	6'2"	220	27		
Joe Signiago	OG	6'1"	220	27		
John Wozniak	OG	6'	220	29		
Brad Ecklund	LB-C	6'3"	215	28		
John Yonaker	DE	6'5"	227	29	1	
Barney Poole	OE-DE	6'2"	220	27		6
Chet Adams	DT	6'3"	240	34		51
Nate Johnson	DT	6'3"	255	30		
Paul Mitchell	DT	6'3"	240	30		
Martin Ruby	DT	6'4"	245	30		2
Bob Kennedy	LB	5'11"	195	29	1	
Jim Champion	OT-LB	6'	230	23		2
Ed Sharkey	OG-LB	6'3"	240	24	1	
Joe Domnanovich	C-LB	6'1"	215	31		
Lou Kusserow	FB-LB	6'1"	200	26		
Duke Iverson	DB	6'2"	208	30	3	8
Pete Layden	DB	5'11"	185	30	3	3
Joe Golding	HB-DB	6'	187	29	7	12
Spec Sanders	HB-DB	6'1"	197	31	13	
George Ratterman	QB	6'1"	180	23		18
Johnny Rauch	QB	6'	195	23		
Sherman Howard	HB	5'11"	192	26		54
George Taliaferro	HB	5'11"	195	23		54
Buddy Young	HB	5'5"	170	24		12
Ben Aldridge	DB-HB	6'	195	23	1	
Zollie Toth	FB	6'2"	215	26		48
Bruce Alford	OE	6'	190	29		6
Dan Edwards	OE	6'1"	195	24		36
Art Weiner	DE-OE	6'3"	212	26		36
Jack Russell	DE-OE	6'1"	215	30		18

DETROIT LIONS 6-6-0 Buddy Parker

Scores of Each Game	
45 Green Bay	7
10 PITTSBURGH	7
21 N.Y. Yanks	44
24 SAN FRANCISCO	7
28 LOS ANGELES	30
27 San Francisco	28
24 Los Angeles	65
21 CHIC. BEARS	35
24 GREEN BAY	21
49 N.Y. YANKS	14
45 Baltimore	21
3 Chic. Bears	6

Use Name	Pos.	Hgt	Wgt	Age	Int	Pts
Gus Cifelli	OT	6'4"	240	24		
Floyd Jaszewski	OT	6'4"	230	23		
Howie Brown	OG	5'11"	215	27		
Joe Sobeleski	OG	6'	210	24		
Lou Creekmur	DT-OG	6'4"	240	23		
Dick Flanagan	LB-OG	6'	220	23		
Jack Simmons	C	6'4"	240	24		
Les Bingaman	DG	6'3"	250	25		
Jim Cain	OE-DE	6'1"	200	23		6
Bernie Hafen	OE-DE	6'2"	195	27		
Thurman McGraw	DT	6'5"	235	23	1	
John Prchlik	DT	6'4"	235	25		
Chet Bulger	OT-DT	6'3"	250	32		
Ray Lininger	C-LB	5'11"	217	23	3	
Joe Watson	C-LB	6'3"	235	24	1	
Rex Grossman (From BAL)	FB-LB	6'1"	215	26		16
John Panelli	FB-LB	5'11"	200	24		
Bill Schectt	FB-LB	6'1"	215	24	2	
Don Doll	DB	5'10"	185	12	12	6
Jim Smith	DB	6'1"	185	25	5	6
Don Panciera	QB-DB	6'1"	195	27	1	
Gerry Krall	HB-DB	5'10"	185	23		
Clarence Self	HB-DB	5'8"	185	25	3	6
Bobby Layne	QB	6'1"	195	23		25
Fred Enke	HB-QB	6'1"	200	25		
Bob Hoernschemeyer	HB	5'11"	195	24		12
Dante Magnani	HB	5'10"	185	33		
Lindy Pearson	HB	6'	195	21		12
Wally Triplett	HB	5'10"	173	23		12
Doak Walker	DB-HB	5'11"	173	23	1	128
Ollie Cline	FB	6'	200	24		12
Cloyce Box	OE	6'4"	220	26		66
John Greene	OE	6'	210	30		18
Leon Hart	OE	6'5"	262	21		6
Dick Rifenburg	OE	6'3"	195	23		6

GREEN BAY PACKERS 3-9-0 Gene Ronzani

Scores of Each Game	
7 DETROIT	45
35 WASHINGTON	21
31 CHIC. BEARS	21
31 N.Y. YANKS	44
14 Chic. Bears	28
17 N.Y. Yanks	35
21 Baltimore	41
14 LOS ANGELES	45
21 Detroit	24
25 SAN FRANCISCO	21
14 Los Angeles	51
14 San Francisco	30

Use Name	Pos.	Hgt	Wgt	Age	Int	Pts
Ed Ecker	JT	6'7"	270	27		
Dick Wildung	DT-OT	6'	220	28		
Ray DiPierro	OG	5'11"	210	23		
Willie Manley	OT-OG	6'2"	210	24		
Len Szafaryn	LB-OG	6'2"	230	22		
Ed Neal	DG-C	6'4"	275	32		
Dan Orlich	DE	6'5"	215	26	1	6
Steve Pritko	OE-DE	6'2"	210	28		12
Ab Wimberly	OE-DE	6'1"	210	24	1	
Clarence McGeary	DT	6'5"	250	24		
Don Stansauk	DT	6'1"	255	25		
Joe Spencer	OT-DT	6'3"	240	27	1	
Buddy Burris	LB	5'11"	215	27		
Chuck Drulis	LB	5'10"	220	32		
Carl Schuette	LB	6'1"	210	28	1	
Bob Summerhays	LB	6'1"	207	23	1	
Clayton Tonnemaker	C-LB	6'2"	235	22	1	1
Rebel Steiner	DB	6'1"	185	24	7	6
Alex Wizbicki	DB	5'11"	188	28	2	
Tony Cannava	HB-DB	5'10"	180	26		
Wally Dreyer	HB-DB	5'10"	170	25	5	6
Bob Forte	HB-DB	6'	205	28	1	
Jug Girard	HB-DB	5'11"	175	23	1	
Paul Christman	QB	6'	200	32		6
Tom O'Malley	QB	5'11"	185	26		
Tobin Rote	QB	6'3"	200	22		
Bill Boedecker (to PHI)	HB	5'11"	195	26		
Larry Coutre	HB	5'10"	175	21		18
Billy Grimes	HB	6'1"	197	23		48
Breezy Reid (From ChiB)	HB	5'10"	187	23		18
Tony Canadeo	FB	5'11"	190	31		24
Jack Cloud	FB	5'10"	220	25		18
Ted Fritsch	FB	5'10"	215	29		39
Ted Cook	OE	6'2"	195	29		18
Bob Mann	OE	5'11"	175	26		6
Al Baldwin	DB-OE	6'2"	210	27	5	18

Stan Heath – Canadian Football League
Jack Jacobs – Canadian Football League

SAN FRANCISCO FORTY NINERS 3-9-0 Buck Shaw

Scores of Each Game	
17 N.Y. YANKS	21
20 CHIC. BEARS	32
14 LOS ANGELES	35
7 Detroit	24
24 N.Y. Yanks	29
28 DETROIT	27
17 BALTIMORE	14
21 Los Angeles	28
14 Cleveland	34
0 Chic. Bears	17
21 Green Bay	25
30 GREEN BAY	14

Use Name	Pos.	Hgt	Wgt	Age	Int	Pts
Charley Quilter	OT	6'1"	240	24		
Harley Dow	OG-OT	6'2"	220	25		
Leo Nomellini	DT-OT	6'3"	270	25		
Bruno Banducci	OG	5'11"	220	28		6
Ray Evans	OG	6'1"	225	26		
Homer Hobbs	OG	5'11"	210	26		
Charlie Shaw	OG	6'2"	220	23		
Bill Johnson	LB-C	6'3"	210	24		
Hal Shoener	DE	6'3"	200	27	1	
Gail Bruce	OE-DE	6'1"	205	26	1	
Don Campora	DT	6'3"	270	23		
Ray Collins	DT	5'11"	230	22		
Clay Matthews	DT	6'3"	215	22		
Don Burke	LB	6'	230	24		
Visco Grgich	LB	5'11"	220	27	1	
Pete Wissman	C-LB	6'	215	26	1	
Norm Standlee	FB-LB	6'2"	230	31		6
Jim Powers	QB-LB	6'	185	22	5	
Nerl Lillywhite	HB-DB	5'10"	185	23	1	
Howie Livingston (From WAS)	HB-DB	6'1"	190	28	5	18
Lowell Wagner	HB-DB	6'	195	26	4	
Frankie Albert	QB	5'10"	170	30		18
Royal Cathcart	HB	6'	185	24		
Don Garlin	HB	5'11"	188	23		
Emil Sitko	HB	5'8"	180	26		12
Johnny Strzykalski	HB	5'9"	190	27		18
Jim Cason	DB-HB	6'	168	23	1	24
Sam Cathcart	DB-HB	6'	175	25	3	
Joe Perry	FB	6'	195	23		36
Alyn Beals	OE	6'	190	29		18
Alex Loyd	OE	6'4"	198	23		
Jack Nix	OE	6'2"	200	22		1
Gordie Soltau	OE	6'2"	195	25		44

BALTIMORE COLTS 1-11-0 Clem Crowe

Scores of Each Game	
14 WASHINGTON	38
0 CLEVELAND	31
13 Chic. Cards	55
14 PHILADELPHIA	24
27 Los Angeles	70
14 San Francisco	17
41 GREEN BAY	21
7 Pittsburgh	17
20 N.Y. GIANTS	55
28 Washington	38
21 DETROIT	45
14 N.Y. Yanks	51

Use Name	Pos.	Hgt	Wgt	Age	Int	Pts
Barry French	OT	6'	225	29		
Ernie Blandin	DT-OT	6'4"	245	31		
Ken Cooper	OG	6'1"	205	27		
Ed King	OG	6'	215	25		
Earl Murray	OG	6'2"	240	24		
John Schweder	OG	6'1"	220	23		
Bob Nelson	LB-C	6'1"	210	30		
Bob Jensen	DE	6'4"	224	24		
Bob Nowaskey	DE	6'	210	32		
Art Spinney	OE-DE	6'	215	23		
Don Colo	DT	6'3"	245	25		
Art Donovan	OT-DT	6'2"	245	25		
Sisto Averno	LB	5'11"	230	24		
Ollie Fletcher	OG-LB	6'3"	210	26		
Joel Williams	C-LB	6'1"	225	22		6
George Buksar	FB-LB	6'	202	24	6	
Vito Kissell	FB-LB	5'10"	205	23	2	11
Chick Maggioli	DB	5'11"	180	28	8	
Bob Livingstone	HB-DB	6'	170	28	3	
Bob Perina	HB-DB	6'1"	205	29		
Herb Rich	HB-DB	5'11"	180	21	3	12
Billy Stone	HB-DB	6'	190	24	6	30
Adrian Burk	QB	6'2"	185	22		6
Frankie Filchock	QB	5'11"	200	33		
Y.A. Tittle	QB	6'	190	23		12
Gino Mazzanti	HB	5'11"	190	21		6
Chet Mutryn	HB	5'9"	180	29		24
Rip Collins	DB-HB	6'	190	23	1	
Ernie Zaleiski	DB-HB	6'	185	23	2	12
Leon Campbell	FB	6'	207	23		
Jimmie Spavital	FB	6'1"	205	24		18
Hal Crisler	OE	6'4"	215	26		30
John North	OE	6'2"	200	29		
Paul Salata (From SF)	OE	6'2"	192	23		24
Bob Oristaglio	DE-OE	6'2"	215	26		
Jim Owens	DE-OE	6'3"	205	23	1	6

LOS ANGELES RAMS

RUSHING

Last Name	No.	Yds	Avg	TD
Davis	88	416	4.7	3
Hoerner	95	381	4.0	10
Smith	51	250	4.9	1
Barry	50	231	3.4	2
Towler	46	130	2.8	6
Williams	13	108	8.3	1
Kalmanir	20	83	4.2	0
Pasquariello	7	31	4.4	1
Younger	8	28	3.5	2
Van Brocklin	15	22	1.5	1
Hirsch	2	19	9.5	0
Waterfield	8	14	1.8	1
Boyd	1	−2	−2.0	0

RECEIVING

Last Name	No.	Yds	Avg	TD
Fears	**84**	**1116**	13	7
Hirsch	42	687	16	7
Davis	42	592	14	4
Hoerner	26	446	17	1
Smith	16	279	17	4
Boyd	9	220	24	4
Towler	8	63	8	0
Barry	7	122	17	0
Kalmanir	5	58	12	1
Champagne	4	52	13	1
Williams	4	21	5	1
Smyth	2	10	5	0
Keane	1	19	19	0
Bouley	1	11	11	0
Reinhard	1	11	11	1
Pasquariello	1	2	2	0

PUNT RETURNS

Last Name	No.	Yds	Avg	TD
Smith	22	218	10	0
Kalminir	13	116	9	0
Williams	6	35	6	0
Davis	3	24	8	0
Lewis	1	0	0	0

KICKOFF RETURNS

Last Name	No.	Yds	Avg	TD
Smith	22	**742**	**34**	**3**
Kalmanir	13	358	28	0
Davis	8	167	21	0
Towler	5	47	9	0
Lewis	2	47	24	0
Vasicek	2	30	15	0
Finlay	2	14	7	0
Pasquariello	1	14	14	0
Stephenson	1	5	5	0

PASSING – PUNTING – KICKING

PASSING	Att	Comp	%	Yds	Yd/Att	TD	Int–%	RK
Van Brocklin	233	127	55	2061	**8.8**	**18**	14– 6	**1**
Waterfield	213	122	**57**	1540	7.2	11	13– 6	2
Davis	5	3	60	97	19.4	2	0– 0	
Smith	1	1	100	11	11.0	0	0– 0	
Hirsch	1	0	0	0	0.0	0	0– 0	

PUNTING	No.	Avg
Waterfield	52	40.1
Van Brocklin	11	42.4

KICKING	XP	Att	%	FG	Att	%
Waterfield	**54**	**58**	93	7	14	50
Hirsch	5	5	100	0	0	0

CHICAGO BEARS

RUSHING

Last Name	No.	Yds	Avg	TD
Gulyanics	146	571	3.9	2
Lujack	63	397	**6.3**	**11**
Rykovich	122	394	3.2	7
Hunsinger	61	326	5.3	2
Morrison	66	252	3.8	1
Hoffman	42	154	3.7	0
Campana	45	134	3.0	1
H. Davis	10	57	5.7	1
Boone	13	15	1.2	0
Kindt	1	4	4.0	0
McAfee	2	4	2.0	0
Luckman	2	1	.5	0
Sprinkle	1	−1	−1.0	0

RECEIVING

Last Name	No.	Yds	Avg	TD
Keane	36	433	12	0
Rykovich	21	344	16	0
Kavanaugh	17	331	19	2
Morrison	13	86	7	0
Gulyanics	12	137	11	0
Hoffman	8	161	20	2
Boone	8	139	17	0
Campana	5	58	12	0
Sprinkle	4	70	18	0
Kindt	3	72	24	1
Wightkin	3	24	8	0
H. Davis	2	15	8	0
Connor	1	21	21	0
Hunsinger	1	20	20	0
Lujack	1	16	16	0

PUNT RETURNS

Last Name	No.	Yds	Avg	TD
McAfee	**33**	284	9	0
Boone	17	215	13	0
Hoffman	7	75	11	0
H. Davis	1	19	19	0
Kindt	1	4	4	0
Hunsinger	1	4	4	0

KICKOFF RETURNS

Last Name	No.	Yds	Avg	TD
Hunsinger	12	343	29	0
Morrison	10	261	26	0
Campana	4	54	14	0
Hoffman	2	52	26	0
Kindt	2	33	17	0
McAfee	1	23	23	0
Stenn	1	16	16	0
H. Davis	1	13	13	0
Bauman	1	9	9	0
Sprinkle	1	5	5	0
Connor	0	9	0	0

PASSING – PUNTING – KICKING

PASSING	Att	Comp	%	Yds	Yd/Att	TD	Int–%	RK
Lujack	254	121	48	1731	6.8	4	21– 8	12
Luckman	37	13	35	180	4.9	1	2– 5	
Romanik	2	0	0	0	0.0	0	0– 0	
Gulyanics	1	1	100	16	16.0	0	0– 0	
Blanda	1	0	0	0	0.0	0	0– 0	
McAfee	1	0	0	0	0.0	0	1–100	

PUNTING	No.	Avg
Morrison	57	**43.3**
Gulyanics	6	33.5
Blanda	2	15.0
Rykovich	1	48.0

KICKING	XP	Att	%	FG	Att	%
Blanda	0	0	0	6	15	40
Lujack	34	35	97	3	5	60

NEW YORK YANKS

RUSHING

Last Name	No.	Yds	Avg	TD
Toth	131	636	4.9	5
Taliaferro	88	411	4.7	4
Howard	71	362	5.0	3
Young	76	334	4.6	1
Aldridge	16	69	4.3	0
Rauch	2	12	6.0	0
Kusserow	1	6	6.0	0
Golding	1	2	2.0	0
Ratterman	11	0	0.0	3

RECEIVING

Last Name	No.	Yds	Avg	TD
Edwards	52	775	15	6
Weiner	35	722	21	6
Taliaferro	21	299	14	5
Young	20	302	15	1
Toth	15	189	13	3
Howard	12	278	23	5
Russell	10	177	18	2
Poole	4	82	21	1
Aldridge	4	56	14	0
Alford	1	14	14	0

PUNT RETURNS

Last Name	No.	Yds	Avg	TD
Taliaferro	9	129	14	0
Sanders	6	93	16	0
Young	9	54	6	0
Aldridge	2	17	9	0
Howard	1	12	12	0

KICKOFF RETURNS

Last Name	No.	Yds	Avg	TD
Young	20	536	27	0
Taliaferro	25	473	19	0
Howard	8	240	30	1
Poole	2	8	4	0
Russell	2	8	4	0
Kennedy	1	15	15	0

PASSING – PUNTING – KICKING

PASSING	Att	Comp	%	Yds	Yd/Att	TD	Int–%	RK
Ratterman	294	140	48	2251	7.7	**22**	24– 8	4
Rauch	51	29	57	502	9.8	6	2– 4	
Taliaferro	7	3	43	83	11.9	1	0– 0	
Sanders	3	2	67	58	19.3	0	0– 0	

PUNTING	No.	Avg
Sanders	71	42.3
Taliaferro	1	39.0

KICKING	XP	Att	%	FG	Att	%
Adams	45	48	94	2	9	22
Layden	3	3	100	0	0	0

DETROIT LIONS

RUSHING

Last Name	No.	Yds	Avg	TD
Hoernschemeyer	84	471	5.6	1
Walker	83	386	4.7	5
Layne	56	250	4.5	4
Cline	69	227	3.3	2
Triplett	14	92	6.6	0
Pearson	31	82	2.6	2
Panelli	32	82	2.6	0
Enke	9	16	1.8	0
Self	3	9	3.0	0
Magnani	3	7	2.3	0
Schroll	1	1	1.0	0
Krall	3	0	0.0	0

RECEIVING

Last Name	No.	Yds	Avg	TD
Box	50	1009	20	11
Walker	35	534	15	6
Hart	31	505	16	1
Greene	22	368	17	2
Rifenburg	10	96	10	1
Hoernschemeyer	8	78	10	1
Cline	7	18	3	0
Triplett	6	70	12	0
Krall	2	61	31	0
Panelli	2	9	5	0
Self	1	12	12	0
Cain	1	8	8	0
Grossman	1	4	4	0
Pearson	1	4	4	0

PUNT RETURNS

Last Name	No.	Yds	Avg	TD
Self	12	129	11	0
Triplett	11	94	9	0
Walker	5	77	15	0
Doll	5	71	14	0
Krall	1	9	9	0
Pearson	1	6	6	0
Enke	1	3	3	0

KICKOFF RETURNS

Last Name	No.	Yds	Avg	TD
Triplett	8	411	51	1
Walker	10	225	23	0
Self	6	155	25	0
Pearson	7	120	17	0
Doll	2	52	26	0
Panelli	2	48	24	0
Cline	1	20	20	0
Grossman	1	15	15	0
Enke	1	11	11	0
Cain	1	10	10	0
Brown	1	0	0	0

PASSING – PUNTING – KICKING

PASSING	Att	Comp	%	Yds	Yd/Att	TD	Int–%	RK
Layne	**336**	152	45	**2323**	6.9	16	18– 5	4
Enke	53	22	42	424	8.0	5	7– 13	
Walker	7	1	14	6	.9	0	0– 0	
Hoernschemeyer	4	1	25	19	4.8	1	1– 25	
Pearson	3	0	0	0	0.0	0	3–100	

PUNTING	No	Avg
Smith	32	40.9
Walker	32	39.9
Hoernschemeyer	4	36.8

KICKING	XP	Att	%	FG	Att	%
Walker	38	41	93	8	18	44
Layne	1	2	50	0	0	0
Grossman	16	19	84	0	3	0

GREEN BAY PACKERS

RUSHING

Last Name	No.	Yds	Avg	TD
Grimes	84	480	5.7	5
Reid	87	394	4.5	1
Coutre	41	283	6.9	1
Canadeo	93	247	2.6	4
Rote	27	158	5.9	0
Cloud	18	52	2.9	3
Girard	14	39	2.8	0
Christman	7	18	2.6	1
Boedecker	8	16	2.0	0
Fritsch	7	13	1.9	0
Forte	9	13	1.4	0
Cannava	1	2	2.0	0
Dreyer	1	0	0.0	0
O'Malley	1	−9	−9.0	0

RECEIVING

Last Name	No.	Yds	Avg	TD
Baldwin	28	555	20	3
Grimes	17	261	15	1
Coutre	17	206	12	2
Pritko	17	125	7	2
Cook	16	182	11	3
Reid	11	120	11	2
Canadeo	10	54	5	0
Mann	6	89	15	1
Manley	5	66	13	0
Girard	4	89	22	0
Cloud	3	19	6	0
Wimberly	2	18	9	0
Forte	2	9	5	0
Cannava	1	28	28	0
Boedecker	1	10	10	0

PUNT RETURNS

Last Name	No.	Yds	Avg	TD
Grimes	29	**555**	19	**2**
Canadeo	5	68	14	0
Boedecker	5	49	10	0
Dreyer	3	48	16	0
Cannava	2	9	5	0

KICKOFF RETURNS

Last Name	No.	Yds	Avg	TD
Grimes	26	600	23	0
Canadeo	16	411	26	0
Forte	3	73	24	0
DiPierro	3	42	14	0
Fritsch	2	34	17	0
Girard	1	25	25	0
Boedecker	1	20	20	0
Burris	3	18	6	0
Canava	1	10	10	0

PASSING – PUNTING – KICKING

PASSING	Att	Comp	%	Yds	Yd/Att	TD	Int–%	RK
Rote	224	83	37	1231	5.5	7	24– 11	17
Christman	126	51	40	545	4.3	7	7– 6	15
O'Malley	15	4	27	31	2.1	0	6– 40	
Forte	2	2	100	24	12.0	0	0– 0	

PUNTING	No	Avg
Girard	71	38.2
Forte	3	35.7

KICKING	XP	Att	%	FG	Att	%
Fritsch	30	33	91	3	17	18
Tonnemaker	1	1	100	0	0	0

SAN FRANCISCO FORTY NINERS

RUSHING

Last Name	No.	Yds	Avg	TD
Perry	124	647	5.2	5
Strzykalski	136	612	4.5	2
Albert	53	272	5.1	3
Cason	38	129	3.4	1
Sitko	23	105	4.6	1
S. Cathcart	33	76	2.3	0
Standlee	12	23	1.9	1
Wagner	2	5	2.5	0
R. Cathcart	3	5	1.7	0
Powers	3	4	1.3	0
Lillywhite	7	4	.6	0
Garlin	3	3	1.0	0
Shoener	1	1	1.0	0
Livingston	1	0	0.0	0

RECEIVING

Last Name	No.	Yds	Avg	TD
Loyd	32	402	13	0
Cason	30	374	12	3
Strzykalski	24	187	8	1
Beals	22	315	14	3
Soltau	14	170	12	1
Perry	13	69	5	1
Nix	9	114	13	0
S. Cathcart	7	99	14	0
Livingston	5	156	31	2
Sitko	3	43	14	1
Bruce	1	10	10	0
Lillywhite	1	6	6	0
Banducci	0	11	0	1

PUNT RETURNS

Last Name	No.	Yds	Avg	TD
S. Cathcart	16	185	12	0
Cason	11	173	16	0
Wagner	1	4	4	0
Livingston	2	3	2	0

KICKOFF RETURNS

Last Name	No.	Yds	Avg	TD
S. Cathcart	13	311	24	0
Perry	12	223	19	0
Shoener	4	53	13	0
Cason	2	48	24	0
Lillywhite	2	36	18	0
Garlin	1	24	24	0
Standlee	1	17	17	0
Matthews	1	10	10	0
Evans	1	2	2	0

PASSING – PUNTING – KICKING

PASSING	Att	Comp	%	Yds	Yd/Att	TD	Int–%	RK
Albert	306	155	51	1767	5.8	14	23– 8	8
Powers	20	9	45	108	5.4	0	2– 10	

PUNTING	No.	Avg
Albert	37	38.5
Lillywhite	26	39.1

KICKING	XP	Att	%	FG	Att	%
Soltau	26	28	93	4	7	57
Nix	1	1	100	0	0	0

BALTIMORE COLTS

RUSHING

Last Name	No.	Yds	Avg	TD
Mutryn	108	355	3.3	2
Spavital	58	246	4.2	2
Stone	14	113	8.1	1
Collins	69	101	1.5	0
Campbell	20	93	4.7	0
Tittle	20	77	3.9	2
Williams	0	50	0.0	1
Buksar	12	44	3.7	0
Mazzanti	7	22	3.1	1
Burk	11	19	1.7	1
Kissell	2	6	3.0	0
Rich	2	6	3.0	0
Zalejski	7	−2	−0.3	1
Livingston	1	−3	−3.0	0

RECEIVING

Last Name	No.	Yds	Avg	TD
Salata	50	618	12	4
Mutryn	36	379	13	2
Spavital	21	238	11	1
Crisler	19	307	16	5
Collins	19	295	16	0
Owens	19	188	10	0
Oristaglio	14	134	10	0
Stone	12	324	27	4
North	5	90	18	0
Spinney	2	19	10	0
Fletcher	2	18	9	0
Buksar	2	2	1	0
Blandin	1	16	16	0
Mazzanti	1	11	11	0
Campbell	1	5	5	0
Zalejski	1	1	1	0

PUNT RETURNS

Last Name	No.	Yds	Avg	TD
Rich	12	276	**23**	1
Mutryn	6	45	8	0
Livingstone	3	33	11	0
Zalejski	3	17	6	0
Stone	2	7	4	0

KICKOFF RETURNS

Last Name	No.	Yds	Avg	TD
Rich	17	434	26	0
Mutryn	19	408	21	0
Zalejski	7	101	14	0
Stone	2	35	18	0
Collins	2	33	17	0
Oristaglio	2	32	16	0
Blandin	3	31	10	0
Owens	2	29	15	0
Kissell	2	19	10	0
Salata	3	12	4	0
Livingston	1	11	11	0

PASSING – PUNTING – KICKING

PASSING	Att	Comp	%	Yds	Yd/Att	TD	Int–%	RK
Tittle	315	**161**	51	1884	6.0	8	19– 6	8
Burk	119	43	36	798	6.7	6	12– 10	17
Filchock	3	1	33	1	.3	0	0– 0	
Mutryn	1	1	100	4	4.0	0	0– 0	

PUNTING	No.	Avg
Burk	**81**	40.0
Collins	2	45.5

KICKING	XP	Att	%	FG	Att	%
Kissell	11	11	100	0	1	0

1951 Blackout: Rams, Fadeout: Colts

One franchise saw the error of its ways, while another never saw the light of the season. The Los Angeles Rams this year telecast only their road games, reversing last year's policy of showing all their games on TV. With the home giveaway stopped, fans poured back into the Coliseum to see the explosive Rams, shooting attendance up to the highest in pro football. Commissioner Bert Bell, the leading proponent of the television blackout of home games, grew even firmer in his position because of this Los Angeles episode.

Bell had a less pleasant experience dealing with the Baltimore Colts franchise. After losing money on the team for several seasons, team owner Abraham Watner turned the franchise back to the league at the NFL meeting in February. Although Baltimore fans protested loudly, their team was dismantled and the players spread around the league as part of the collegiate draft. By-products of the death of the Colts were the strengthening of the remaining teams and the reduction of league membership to a more manageable twelve clubs.

The wire services recognized the modern shape of the game by naming for the first time separate All-Pro teams for the offense and defense. Although the two-platoon system now was common, many players still played both ways, due partly to the low roster limit of thirty-three men.

AMERICAN CONFERENCE

Cleveland Browns—When the '49ers beat the Browns 24-10 on opening day, the other clubs in the conference took hope that Cleveland was ready to fall from the top. By the end of the season, however, the Browns, as usual, had captured the conference flag. After that opening loss, Paul Brown's men had won all their games, with only two of the victories by less than 10 points. Sportswriters began comparing the Browns to the great Chicago Bears of 1940-41. Both had inspirational coaches in George Halas and Paul Brown, and both had marvelous quarterbacks in Sid Luckman and Otto Graham. With Marion Motley slowing up, the Cleveland running game could not match the old Bears' ground attack, but ends Dante Lavelli and Mac Speedie caught more passes than any of the early Chicago receivers. The comparisons could never be resolved, but one thing was definite: With nine men named to All-Pro teams, the Browns had to be called the best of the present—until someone could prove otherwise.

New York Giants—The Giants were a strong team, but their tragic flaw was an inability to beat Cleveland. In their first meeting, the Browns squeezed by with a 14-13 victory, and their November rematch wound up with the Browns ahead 10-0. The Giants won all their other games, but the two losses were enough to shut them into a second-place finish. The losses to Cleveland, however, could not dull several stellar individual performances. Fullback Eddie Price, a small man for his position, hustled his way to the rushing championship and set a record for rushing attempts in one season. Defensive lineman Arnie Weinmeister, Al Derogatis, and linebacker Jon Baker all won All-Pro honors, as did offensive tackle Tex Coulter.

Washington Redskins—When the Redskins dropped their first three games, owner George Marshall predictably fired head coach Herman Ball. Marshall then offered the pilot's position to Hunk Anderson, an assistant coach for the Bears. Anderson was willing, but George Halas refused to let him out of his contract with the Bears unless Washington sent star tackle Paul Lipscomb to Chicago. Marshall called Halas a few uncomplimentary names, and named former Redskin star Dick Todd as his new coach. The Skins came alive under Todd, winning their first two games and climbing up to third place by the season's end.

Philadelphia Eagles—With the firing of Greasy Neale and the retirement of Tommy Thompson, the Eagles needed a new head coach and quarterback for 1951. They came up with an adequate quarterback in Adrian Burk, a survivor of the Baltimore Colts, but the appointment of Bo McMillin as coach ended in tragedy. A highly successful college coach at Indiana, McMillin came to Philadelphia after three unspectacular seasons with the Detroit Lions. The Eagles won their first two games for the new coach, but then McMillin resigned, revealing that stomach cancer made it impossible for him to continue. With assistant Wayne Millner at the helm, the Eagles lost their next three games and finished a weak fifth. Steve Van Buren's continued foot ailments figured greatly in the collapse, with both the Eagles and Van Buren looking as if they would never be the same.

Pittsburgh Steelers—Jock Sutherland had been in his grave for over three years, but the Steelers still looked like a Sutherland team. Coach John Michelosen, an assistant under the stern Scot, still deployed the Steelers in the single-wing formation on offense. The defense still was a hard-nosed unit which only grudgingly allowed points. And the Steelers still were a faceless outfit, one without a dynamic star who would make good copy for the reporters. One thing had changed, though: The rest of the NFL teams had developed high-power passing attacks which could leave the Steelers hopelessly behind with one good outburst. Only when the defense held the enemy to 14 points or less did the Steelers win, and although Bill McPeak, Ernie Stautner, Dale Dodrill, Howard Hartley, Jack Butler, Jerry Shipkey, and the other defenders six times limited the opponent to two touchdowns or less, the Steelers still could win only four games.

Chicago Cardinals—In dire need of a quarterback, the Cards moved Charlie Trippi to the signal caller's position after four years at halfback. Although he had starred as a single-wing tailback in college, Trippi was not the sort of quarterback who could lift this talent-thin club above mediocrity. As if below-average personnel were not problem enough, club president Walter Wolfner and coach Curly Lambeau quarreled all year, Wolfner claiming that the coach was lax on discipline, Lambeau saying that the front office was meddling in coaching matters. With two games left on the schedule, Lambeau bitterly resigned, leaving the club in the hands of his assistants, but a moment of glory still remained for the Cards. Losing 14-0 at halftime, the Cards came back to defeat the Bears on the final Sunday and end the Bears' hopes for a conference crown.

NATIONAL CONFERENCE

Los Angeles Rams—Large crowds consistently turned out to see the Rams, the most dynamic club in pro football. The explosive offense had two superb quarterbacks in Norm Van Brocklin and Bob Waterfield, one of whom was bound to be hot on the day of a game, and two superb receivers in Tom Fears and Crazy Legs Hirsch. Tying Don Hutson's season record of seventeen touchdown catches, Hirsch also set a new standard of 1,495 yards gained receiving in one year. Coach Joe Stydahar came up with an innovation in his "bull elephant" backfield, with three big fullbacks in Dan Towler, Dick Hoerner, and Tank Younger giving the Rams unmatched pass blocking and power running. The offense kept the club at the head of the conference most of the season, but the Lions knocked the Rams out of first place with a 24-22 upset one week from the end. Los Angeles snuck back into first, however, by beating the Packers while San Francisco beat Detroit on the final Sunday.

Detroit Lions—New coach Buddy Parker had much less of the schoolmaster in him than deposed coach Bo McMillin, and the Lions reacted to the relaxed atmosphere by going all out for victory. Attendance at Briggs Stadium doubled as the Lions ran neck and neck with the Rams all season. Quarterback Bobby Layne, runner Bob Hoernschemeyer, two-way end Leon Hart, offensive guard Lou Creekmur, and defensive guard Les Bingaman all starred as the Lions just missed the title by losing to the '49ers 21-17 on the last Sunday of the season. However, the Lions were finally on their way.

San Francisco '49ers—It took them a year to get used to NFL competition, but the '49ers finished with three straight wins to recapture their usual second-place spot. The quarterback for these final three games was Y. A. Tittle, the refugee from Baltimore who had been taken aboard when the Colts sank. For most of the campaign Tittle sat on the bench, watched Frankie Albert run the team, and learned the San Francisco system. Coach Buck Shaw started "the Bald Eagle" down the stretch, and the results established Tittle as Albert's successor. Fullback Joe Perry, receivers Gordy Soltau and Billy Wilson, and tackle Leo Nomellini also contributed to the strong finish and gave the club a youthful look. The '49ers played the spoiler role to the hilt, handing the Browns their only loss, knocking off the Rams in mid-season, and twice beating the Lions late in the year.

Chicago Bears—An era ended for the Bears when Sid Luckman, George McAfee, and Ken Kavanaugh, all stars of the 1940s, retired. Coach George Halas especially could have used a young Luckman, as quarterback Johnny Lujack was plagued with a sore shoulder that turned his bullet passes into easy floaters. With the air game crippled, the Bears relied on runners Kayo Dottley, George Gulyanics, and Julie Rykovich to bang out the yardage on the ground. The offensive line did its part to make the running game work, as George Connor, Dick Barwegan, and veteran Bulldog Turner all cleared the way for the backs. Connor also starred on the adequate defensive unit which three times broke down and gave up 40 or more points. With all their problems, the Bears still could have tied the Rams for the conference lead by winning their final game, but the Cards upset them.

Green Bay Packers—The Packers lost their last seven games to finish a limp fifth in the National Conference. Even the hapless New York Yanks downed the Packers 31-28 for their only win of the season. Coach Gene Ronzani looked high and low for running backs, and the best he could find were Fred Cone, whose kicking far surpassed his ball-carrying, and Tony Canadeo, a veteran of the Lambeau era who had long ago left his best days behind. That left the burden of the running as well as the throwing to quarterback Tobin Rote. Ends Bob Mann and Ray Pelfrey caught many of Rote's passes, but so, unfortunately, did enemy defensive backs.

New York Yanks—The year got off to a flying start when quarterback George Ratterman, fullback Lou Kusserow, tackle Martin Ruby, and end Jack Russell decided to do their football playing in the Canadian League. But Ratterman did not find Canada to his liking and rejoined the Yanks, still winless, in mid-season. With Ratterman and Bob Celeri sharing the passer's job, the Yanks showed some life down the stretch, tying the '49ers and beating the Packers on successive weekends. They ended their season by bowing to the Giants.

FINAL TEAM STATISTICS

OFFENSE

	CHI.B.	CHI.C.	CLEVE.	DET.	G.BAY	L.A.	N.Y.G.	N.Y.Y.	PHIL.	PITT.	S.F.	WASH.
FIRST DOWNS:												
Total	256	224	203	231	218	272	151	211	200	172	237	199
by Rushing	141	108	92	109	75	114	81	89	111	76	134	128
by Passing	90	101	99	105	115	130	54	99	73	79	92	62
by Penalty	25	15	12	17	28	28	16	23	16	17	11	9
RUSHING:												
Number	539	440	415	410	313	426	491	364	509	425	523	547
Yards	2408	1963	1708	1841	1196	2210	1713	1337	1562	1428	2366	2151
Average Yards	4.5	4.5	4.1	4.5	3.8	5.2	3.5	3.7	3.1	3.4	4.5	3.9
Touchdowns	24	14	20	11	8	22	10	12	13	9	18	14
PASSING:												
Attempts	315	334	271	351	478	373	210	428	284	330	281	226
Completions	143	161	151	158	231	189	101	172	120	130	154	99
Completion Percentage	45.4	48.2	55.7	45.0	48.3	50.2	48.1	40.2	42.3	39.4	54.8	43.8
Yards	2239	2244	2273	2500	2846	3296	1432	2634	1713	1842	1955	1508
Avg. Yards per Attempt	7.1	6.7	8.4	7.1	6.0	8.8	6.8	6.2	6.0	5.6	7.0	6.8
Avg. Yards per Completion	15.7	13.9	15.1	15.8	12.3	17.4	14.2	15.3	14.3	14.2	12.7	15.2
Touchdowns	12	13	18	29	26	26	11	16	17	10	14	8
Interceptions	20	24	17	24	29	22	26	27	29	26	19	25
Percent Intercepted	6.3	7.2	6.3	6.8	6.1	5.9	12.4	6.3	10.2	7.9	6.8	11.1
PUNTING:												
Number	62	70	73	58	61	52	87	81	77	80	54	59
Average Distance	38.5	39.8	45.5	41.3	41.0	41.5	40.2	38.3	39.1	38.6	43.6	38.7
PUNT RETURNS:												
Number	44	30	30	32	29	37	48	29	43	47	35	40
Yards	374	192	230	483	213	344	675	379	382	464	407	333
Average Yards	8.5	6.4	7.7	15.1	7.3	9.3	14.1	13.1	8.9	9.9	11.6	8.3
Touchdowns	1	0	0	4	0	1	4	1	0	1	1	0
KICKOFF RETURNS:												
Number	46	43	27	45	60	44	28	55	48	34	38	47
Yards	974	1051	496	1053	1449	826	724	1256	920	858	820	896
Average Yards	21.2	24.4	18.4	23.4	24.2	18.8	25.9	22.8	19.2	25.2	21.6	19.1
Touchdowns	0	0	0	0	0	0	1	1	0	0	0	0
INTERCEPTION RETURNS:												
Number	21	27	22	15	22	19	41	22	18	30	33	18
Yards	216	390	235	235	292	193	542	235	256	461	498	166
Average Yards	10.3	14.4	10.7	15.7	13.3	10.2	13.2	10.7	14.2	15.4	15.1	9.2
Touchdowns	0	0	2	0	1	1	4	0	0	3	1	0
PENALTIES:												
Number	118	82	117	80	90	94	64	63	51	75	67	67
Yards	1107	729	1017	746	790	813	569	605	428	694	560	560
FUMBLES:												
Number	23	26	26	19	23	22	27	22	36	31	26	34
Number Lost	15	20	19	9	15	15	13	9	18	17	20	18
POINTS:												
Total	286	210	331	336	254	392	254	241	234	183	255	183
PAT Attempts	38	27	43	44	35	51	31	31	31	23	33	22
PAT Made	37	27	43	43	29	47	30	31	28	22	31	21
FG Attempts	19	13	23	17	8	24	16	14	11	14	18	13
FG Made	7	7	10	9	5	13	12	6	6	7	6	10
Percent FG Made	36.8	53.8	43.5	52.9	62.5	54.2	75.0	42.9	54.5	50.0	33.3	76.9
Safeties	0	0	0	1	0	0	1	0	1	1	1	0

DEFENSE

	CHI.B.	CHI.C.	CLEVE.	DET.	G.BAY	L.A.	N.Y.G.	N.Y.Y.	PHIL.	PITT.	S.F.	WASH.
FIRST DOWNS:												
Total	228	212	201	235	236	231	174	257	183	188	188	241
by Rushing	100	116	88	102	127	125	60	125	92	97	91	135
by Passing	101	83	81	107	95	84	103	118	77	74	84	92
by Penalty	27	13	32	26	14	22	11	14	14	17	13	14
RUSHING:												
Number	372	476	428	454	496	478	392	464	462	499	417	464
Yards	1958	1977	1454	1509	2152	2206	913	2397	1816	1859	1549	2093
Average Yards	5.3	4.2	3.4	3.3	4.3	4.6	2.3	5.1	3.9	3.7	3.7	4.5
Touchdowns	15	15	8	13	22	17	8	23	12	13	9	20
PASSING:												
Attempts	337	265	330	374	313	329	377	355	287	266	353	295
Completions	160	123	151	181	157	140	162	182	119	136	158	140
Completion Percentage	47.5	46.4	45.8	48.4	50.2	42.6	43.0	51.3	41.5	51.1	44.7	47.4
Yards	2431	1973	1978	2608	2535	1992	2337	2776	1748	1687	2313	2104
Avg. Yards per Attempt	7.2	7.4	6.0	7.0	8.1	6.1	6.2	7.8	6.1	6.3	6.5	7.1
Avg. Yards per Completion	15.2	16.0	13.1	14.4	16.1	14.2	14.4	15.2	14.7	12.4	14.6	15.0
Touchdowns	21	18	10	18	25	13	11	24	17	12	15	16
Interceptions	21	27	22	15	22	19	41	22	18	30	33	18
Percent Intercepted	6.2	10.2	6.7	4.0	7.0	5.8	10.9	6.2	6.3	10.3	9.4	6.1
PUNTING:												
Number	66	62	69	56	62	75	86	66	70	77	70	55
Average Distance	37.7	40.9	39.8	41.6	37.6	40.9	40.2	39.9	44.4	40.7	40.4	40.8
PUNT RETURNS:												
Number	25	47	49	33	38	33	54	33	34	40	21	37
Yards	251	677	340	386	564	375	399	333	261	411	140	349
Average Yards	10.0	14.4	6.9	11.7	14.8	11.4	7.4	10.1	7.7	10.3	6.7	9.5
Touchdowns	0	4	0	1	2	3	0	1	1	0	0	1
KICKOFF RETURNS:												
Number	38	42	34	58	40	54	49	48	41	32	44	35
Yards	977	801	763	1328	741	1478	1002	1077	923	597	957	679
Average Yards	25.7	19.1	22.4	22.9	18.5	27.4	20.4	22.4	22.5	18.7	21.8	19.4
Touchdowns	0	0	0	0	0	0	1	1	0	0	0	0
INTERCEPTION RETURNS:												
Number	20	24	17	24	29	22	26	27	29	26	19	25
Yards	321	342	95	277	387	313	280	299	475	446	223	261
Average Yards	16.1	14.3	5.6	11.5	13.3	14.2	10.8	11.1	16.4	17.2	11.7	10.4
Touchdowns	0	1	1	0	1	1	0	1	2	3	0	2
PENALTIES:												
Number	102	80	59	81	99	107	60	87	53	84	68	71
Yards	1022	711	505	656	924	1028	506	797	458	725	526	630
FUMBLES:												
Number	25	21	35	22	23	26	37	18	28	30	22	28
Number Lost	21	16	29	16	13	10	12	12	19	16	9	15
POINTS:												
Total	282	287	152	259	375	261	161	382	264	235	205	296
PAT Attempts	39	38	20	32	50	35	20	49	32	30	24	40
PAT Made	37	38	18	31	49	33	20	44	31	28	22	38
FG Attempts	5	17	14	22	17	12	15	18	21	12	24	13
FG Made	3	7	4	12	8	6	7	12	13	7	13	6
Percent FG Made	60.0	41.2	28.6	54.5	47.0	50.0	46.7	66.7	61.9	58.3	54.2	46.2
Safeties	1	0	1	0	1	0	0	1	1	0	0	0

1951 CHAMPIONSHIP GAME

December 23, at Los Angeles
(Attendance 59,475)

SCORING

LOS ANGELES	0	7	7	10	–24
CLEVELAND	0	10	0	7	–17

Second Quarter

L.A.	Hoerner, 1 yard rush PAT–Waterfield (Kick)	5:44
Cle.	Groza, 52 yard field goal	11:08
Cle.	Jones, 17 yard pass from Graham PAT–Groza (Kick)	12:54

Third Quarter

L.A.	Towler, 1 yard rush PAT–Waterfield (Kick)	6:16

Fourth Quarter

L.A.	Waterfield, 17 yard field goal	3:10
Cle.	Carpenter, 5 yard rush PAT–Groza (Kick)	7:10
L.A.	Fears, 73 yard pass from Van Brocklin PAT–Waterfield (Kick)	7:35

TEAM STATISTICS

L.A.		CLEVE.
20	First Downs–Total	22
9	First Downs–Rushing	6
9	First Downs–Passing	16
2	First Downs–Penalty	0
2	Fumbles	4
1	Fumbles Lost	1
5	Penalties	6
25	Yards Penalized	41
1	Field Goals Missed	1

Van Brocklin to Fears to the Championship

In the rematch with the Rams, the Browns were not as precise as in last year's game, as Lou Groza missed a 23-yard field goal on the first drive. The first quarter ended with the match still scoreless, but Bob Waterfield led the Rams 55 yards in twelve plays, mixing passes and runs, with Dick Hoerner plowing into the end zone from the 1-yard line. Leading 7-0, the Rams bothered Otto Graham with blitzing linebackers, but the Browns put three points on the scoreboard with a 52-yard field goal by Groza. After three plays, the Rams kicked the ball back to the Browns, and then Otto Graham began picking the Los Angeles defense apart. First he hit Mac Speedie for 14 yards, then passed to Marion Motley over the middle for 23 yards, and finally threw to Dub Jones for 17 yards and a touchdown. The Browns took a 10-7 lead into the locker room at halftime, but the Rams went ahead six minutes into the third period. Otto Graham was back to pass on his own 24-yard line when Los Angeles end Larry Brink blindsided him and knocked the ball loose. Andy Robustelli picked it up and ran it all the way down to the 2. From there, Dan Towler needed three attempts to make it into the end zone, and Waterfield's conversion made it 14-10. The Rams upped the lead to 17-10 with a fourth-quarter Waterfield field goal, but the Browns drove 70 yards in ten plays to tie the score at 17-17. Less than a minute later, however, Norm Van Brocklin, who had relieved Waterfield at quarterback for the Rams, hit Tom Fears with a perfect pass that resulted in a 73-yard touchdown and the championship.

INDIVIDUAL STATISTICS

LOS ANGELES	No.	Yds	Avg.	CLEVELAND	No.	Yds	Avg.
RUSHING							
Towler	16	36	2.3	Graham	5	43	8.6
Younger	4	20	5.0	Motley	5	23	4.6
Smith	9	15	1.7	Carpenter	4	14	3.5
Waterfield	2	8	4.0	Jones	9	12	1.3
Hoerner	5	5	1.0		23	92	4.0
Van Brocklin	1	3	3.0				
Davis	6	–6	–1.0				
	43	81	1.9				
RECEIVING							
Fears	4	146	36.5	Speedie	7	81	11.6
Hirsch	4	66	16.5	Lavelli	4	66	16.5
Davis	3	10	3.3	Jones	4	62	15.5
Smith	1	18	18.0	Carpenter	3	48	16.0
Hoerner	1	13	13.0	Motley	1	23	23.0
	13	253	19.5		19	280	14.7
PUNTING							
Waterfield	5		43.4	Gillom	4		37.0
PUNT RETURNS							
None				Lewis	1	13	13.0
				Carpenter	1	1	1.0
					2	14	7.0
KICKOFF RETURNS							
Williams	1	21	21.0	Carpenter	5	132	26.4
INTERCEPTION RETURNS							
Johnson	1	35	35.0	James	1	0	0.0
Paul	1	26	26.0	Lahr	1	0	0.0
Williams	1	15	15.0		2	0	0.0
	3	76	25.3				

PASSING

LOS ANGELES	Att	Comp	Comp Pct.	Yds	Int	Yds/ Att.	Yds/ Comp	Yards Lost Tackled
Waterfield	24	9	37.5	125	2	5.2	13.9	0
Van Brocklin	6	4	66.7	128	0	21.3	32.0	0
	30	13	43.3	253	2	8.4	19.5	0
CLEVELAND								
Graham	40	19	47.5	280	3	7.0	14.7	5–47
Carpenter	1	0	0	0	0	–	–	0
	41	19	46.3	280	3	6.8	14.7	5–47

CLEVELAND BROWNS 11-1-0 Paul Brown

Scores of Each Game		
10	San Francisco	24
38	Los Angeles	23
45	WASHINGTON	0
17	PITTSBURGH	0
14	N.Y. GIANTS	13
34	Chic. Cards	17
20	PHILADELPHIA	17
10	N.Y. Giants	0
42	CHIC. BEARS	21
49	CHIC. CARDS	28
28	Pittsburgh	0
24	Philadelphia	9

Use Name	Pos.	Hgt	Wgt	Age	Int	Pts
Lou Groza	OT	6'3"	235	27		73
Lou Rymkus	OT	6'4"	235	32		
John Sandusky	OT	6'1"	250	25		
Bob Gaudio	OG	5'10"	220	26		
Abe Gibron	OG	5'11"	230	25		
Lin Houston	OG	6'	215	30		
Frank Gatski	C	6'3"	240	29		
Bill Willis	DG	6'2"	215	30		
Len Ford	DE	6'4"	230	25		
George Young	DE	6'3"	215	27		6
Bob Oristaglio	OE-DE	6'2"	215	27		6
Chubby Grigg	DT	6'2"	280	25		
John Kissell	DT	6'3"	247	28		
Darrell Palmer	DT	6'2"	235	29		
Tony Adamle	LB	6'	215	27	1	
Alex Agase	LB	5'10"	210	29	2	
Tommy Thompson	LB	6'1"	220	24	2	
Hal Herring	C-LB	6'1"	210	27	1	
Chick Jagade	FB-LB	6'	210	24		
Tommy James	DB	5'10"	185	27	2	
Warren Lahr	DB	5'11"	185	27	5	12
Don Shula	DB	5'11"	190	21	4	
Cliff Lewis	QB-DB	5'11"	168	28	5	
Carl Taseff	HB-DB	5'11"	192	22		12
Otto Graham	QB	6'1"	195	29		24
Rex Baumgardner	HB	5'11"	193	27		12
Ken Carpenter	HB	6'	187	25		36
Dub Jones	HB	6'4"	205	26		72
Don Phelps	HB	5'11"	185	26		6
Emerson Cole	FB	6'2"	215	23		6
Marion Motley	LB-FB	6'	238	31		6
Dante Lavelli	OE	6'	192	28		36
Mac Speedie	OE	6'3"	205	31		18
Horace Gillom	DE-OE	6'1"	220	30		6

Ken Gorgal – Military Service

Art Spinney – Military Service

NEW YORK GIANTS 9-2-1 Steve Owen

Scores of Each Game		
13	Pittsburgh	13
35	Washington	14
28	CHIC. CARDS	17
26	PHILADELPHIA	24
13	Cleveland	14
37	N.Y. YANKS	31
28	WASHINGTON	14
0	CLEVELAND	10
10	Chic. Cards	0
14	PITTSBURGH	0
23	Philadelphia	7
27	N.Y. Yanks	17

Use Name	Pos.	Hgt	Wgt	Age	Int	Pts
Tex Coulter	OT	6'4"	260	26		
Herb Hannah	OT	6'3"	220	29		
Ray Krouse	DT-OT	6'3"	250	24		
Earl Murray	OG	6'2"	240	25		
Bill Albright	OT-DT-OG	6'1"	232	22		
Fritz Barzilaukas	LB-OG	6'1"	230	30		
Duke Maronic	LB-OG	5'9"	218	30		
Joe Sulaitis	BB-OG	6'2"	215	30		
John Rapacz	C	6'4"	260	26		
Jim Duncan	DE	6'2"	205	25	2	
Ray Poole	DE	6'2"	215	29		66
Al DeRogatis	DT	6'4"	240	24		
Arnie Weinmeister	DT	6'4"	235	28		
Joh Baker	LB	6'2"	215	28		
John Cannady	LB	6'2"	225	27	3	
Dick Woodward	C-LB	6'2"	225	25	2	
Tom Landry	DB	6'1"	195	26	8	18
Harmon Rowe	DB	6'	182	28	2	2
Otto Schnellbacher	DB	6'2"	190	28	11	12
Em Tunnell	DB	6'1"	183	29	9	24
John Amberg	HB-DB	5'11"	195	23	3	
Bob Wilkinson	OE-DB	6'3"	215	24	1	6
Chuck Conerly	QB	6'1"	185	27		6
Travis Tidwell	QB	5'10"	185	26		
Forrest Griffith	HB	5'11"	190	22		
Jim Ostendarp	HB	5'8"	178	26		
Kyle Rote	HB	6'	195	22		6
Joe Scott	HB	6'1"	195	25		18
Bob Jackson	FB	5'11"	210	26		
Eddie Price	FB	5'11"	190	25		42
Bob Hudson	OE	6'4"	215	21		
Bob McChesney	OE	6'2"	190	24		12
Bill Stribling	OE	6'1"	205	24		12
Kelley Mote	DE-OE	6'2"	190	28		24

Bill Austin – Military Service
Randy Clay – Military Service
Dick Hensley – Military Service
Choo-Choo Roberts – Canadian Football League

WASHINGTON REDSKINS 5-7-0 Herman Ball Dick Todd

Scores of Each Game		
17	Detroit	35
14	N.Y. GIANTS	35
0	Cleveland	45
7	CHIC. CARDS	3
27	Philadelphia	23
0	CHIC. BEARS	27
14	N.Y. Giants	28
22	Pittsburgh	7
31	LOS ANGELES	21
21	PHILADELPHIA	35
20	Chic. Cards	17
10	PITTSBURGH	20

Use Name	Pos.	Hgt	Wgt	Age	Int	Pts
Laurie Niemi	OT	6'1"	256	26		
Gene Pepper	OG-OT	6'2"	244	24		
Jim Peebles	DE-OT	6'4"	237	31		
Buddy Brown	OG	6'1"	211	24		
Herb Siegert	OG	6'3"	225	27		
Slug Witucki	OG	5'11"	239	23		
Harry Ulinski	C	6'4"	230	26		
John Badaczewski	DG	6'1"	255	29		
Jim Ricca	DG	6'4"	268	24		
Walt Yowarsky	DE	6'2"	230	23		
Bob Hendren	OT-DE	6'8"	245	28		
Lou Karras	DT	6'4"	248	24		
Paul Lipscomb	DT	6'5"	252	28	1	
Jim Staton	DT	6'4"	246	24		
George Buksar	LB	6'	202	25	1	
Ed Quirk	LB	6'1"	240	26		
Al DeMao	C-LB	6'2"	220	31	1	
Chuck Drazenovich	FB-LB	6'1"	222	24	2	18
Jack Dwyer	DB	5'11"	175	24	1	
Neil Ferris	DB	5'11"	178	23		
Ed Salem	QB-DB	5'11"	193	23	5	
Billy Cox	HB-DB	6'3"	194	22	2	
Harry Dowda	HB-DB	6'2"	200	27		
Sammy Baugh	QB	6'2"	175	37		
Harry Gilmer	DB-QB	6'	162	25	5	
Johnny Papit	HB	6'	190	23		
Eddie Saenz	HB	5'10"	170	28		
Bill Dudley	DB-HB	5'10"	175	30		69
George Thomas	DB-HB	6'1"	180	23		12
Rob Goode	FB	6'4"	224	24		54
Leon Heath	FB	6'1"	202	23		
Gene Brito	OE	6'1"	216	26		
Hugh Taylor	OE	6'4"	190	28		18
Joe Tereshinski	DE-LB-OE	6'2"	217	27		12

Hall Haynes – Military Service
Choo-Choo Justice – Military Service

PITTSBURGH STEELERS 4-7-1 John Michelosen

Scores of Each Game		
13	N.Y. GIANTS	13
33	Green Bay	35
24	SAN FRANCISCO	28
0	Cleveland	17
28	Chic. Cards	14
13	PHILADELPHIA	34
28	GREEN BAY	7
7	WASHINGTON	22
17	Philadelphia	13
0	N.Y. Giants	14
0	CLEVELAND	28
20	Washington	10

Use Name	Pos.	Hgt	Wgt	Age	Int	Pts
Lou Allen	OT	6'3"	215	28		
Frank Wydo	OT	6'4"	220	27		
Paul Lea	DT-OT	6'2"	240	21		
George Hughes	OG	6'1"	225	26		
Dick Tomlinson	OG	6'1"	205	23		
Lou Levanti	C-OG	6'1"	215	25		
Tony Momsen	C	6'1"	215	24		
Bill Walsh	C	6'2"	230	24		
Bill McPeak	DE	6'1"	200	26		
Charlie Mehelich	DE	6'1"	200	29		2
George Hays	DT-DE	6'2"	210	26		
Carl Samuelson	DT	6'4"	260	28		
Ernie Stautner	DT	6'1"	230	26		
Dale Dodrill	LB	6'1"	205	26		
Darrell Hogan	LB	5'10"	210	25	1	
Frank Sinkovitz	LB	6'1"	220	28	2	
John Schweder	OG-LB	6'1"	225	24	1	
Jack Butler	DB	6'	195	23	5	6
Howard Hartley	DB	6'	185	27	10	
Jerry Shipkey	DB	6'1"	215	26	6	6
Jim Finks	TB-DB	6'	175	24	3	6
Joe Geri	TB	5'10"	185	27		61
Chuck Ortmann	DB-TB	6'1"	190	22	1	
Jerry Nuzum	HB	6'1"	200	28		6
Ray Mathews	DB-HB	6'	185	22	1	6
Lynn Chandnois	TB-HB	6'2"	195	27		42
Joe Hollingsworth	FB	6'	200	26		
Fran Rogel	FB	5'11"	200	24		18
Joe Gasparella (to Chic C)	BB	6'4"	220	24		
Dick Hendley	BB	6'	198	25		
Truett Smith	BB	6'2"	205	27		
Val Jansante (to GB)	OE	6'1"	190	30		6
Tom Jelley	OE	6'5"	225	24		
Henry Minarik	OE	6'2"	200	24		6
Elbie Nickel	OE	6'1"	195	28		18

PHILADELPHIA EAGLES 4-8-0 Bo McMillin Wayne Millner

Scores of Each Game		
17	Chic. Cards	14
21	SAN FRANCISCO	14
24	Green Bay	37
24	N.Y. Giants	26
23	WASHINGTON	27
34	Pittsburgh	13
17	Cleveland	20
10	DETROIT	28
13	PITTSBURGH	17
35	Washington	21
7	N.Y. GIANTS	23
9	CLEVELAND	24

Use Name	Pos.	Hgt	Wgt	Age	Int	Pts
Bucko Kilroy	OT	6'2"	235	30		
Vic Sears	DT-OT	6'3"	225	33		
Walt Barnes	OG	6'1"	230	33		
Ray Romero	OG	5'11"	213	24		
Dick Steere	OG	6'4"	240	24		
Al Wistert	OG	6'1"	214	30		
John Magee	LB-OG	5'10"	220	28		
Vic Lindskog	C	6'1"	203	35		
Mario Gianelli	DG	6'	260	30		
John Green	DE	6'1"	190	29		
Jay MacDowell	DE	6'2"	220	32		
Norm Willey	DE	6'2"	215	24		
Bud Grant	OE-DE	6'3"	200	24		
Walt Stickel	DT	6'3"	250	29		2
Roscoe Hansen	OT-DT	6'3"	215	22		
Mike Jarmoluk	DE-DT	6'5"	250	28	1	
Gerry Cowhig	LB	6'2"	218	30		6
Chuck Bednarik	C-LB	6'3"	230	26		
Ken Farragut	C-LB	6'4"	230	23		
Ebert Van Buren	FB-LB	6'2"	210	26	1	
Russ Craft	DB	5'9"	175	31	2	
Pat McHugh	DB	5'11"	166	31	1	
Frank Reagan	DB	5'11"	185	32	4	
Joe Sutton	DB	5'11"	180	27	2	
Neill Armstrong	OE-DB	6'2"	195	25	4	
Adrian Burk	QB	6'2"	190	23		6
Bill MacKrides	QB	5'11"	179	26		
Al Pollard (from NYY)	HB	6'	196	23		
Bosh Pritchard (to NYG)	HB	5'11"	163	32		6
Clyde Scott	HB	6'	170	27		24
Steve Van Buren	HB	6'	202	30		36
Frank Ziegler	HB	5'11"	175	27		12
Dan Sandifer	DB-HB	6'2"	190	24	1	12
Jim Parmer	DB-FB	6'	195	24		12
Bobby Walston	OE	6'	190	22		94
Red O'Quinn (from ChiB)	OE	6'2"	195	26		
Pete Pihos	DE-OE	6'1"	205	27	2	30

Toy Ledbetter – Military Service

CHICAGO CARDINALS 3-9-0 Curley Lambeau

Scores of Each Game		
14	PHILADELPHIA	17
28	CHIC. BEARS	14
17	N.Y. Giants	28
3	Washington	7
14	PITTSBURGH	28
17	CLEVELAND	34
21	Los Angeles	45
27	San Francisco	21
0	N.Y. GIANTS	10
28	Cleveland	49
17	WASHINGTON	20
24	Chic. Bears	14

Use Name	Pos.	Hgt	Wgt	Age	Int	Pts
Bill Fischer	OT	6'2"	250	24		
Jack Jennings	OT	6'4"	245	24		
Ed Bagdon	OG	5'10"	200	25		
Lynn Lynch	OG	6'2"	225	23		
Buster Ramsey	LB-OG	6'1"	225	31		
Knox Ramsey	LB-OG	6'1"	210	25		
Jack Simmons	C	6'4"	240	25		
Bob Dove	DE	6'2"	225	30		
Jerry Hennessey	DE	6'2"	215	25		
Tony Klimak	DE	5'11"	200	25	3	
Tom Wham	DE	6'2"	220	27		
Lou Ferry	DT	6'2"	243	24		
Don Joyce	DT	6'3"	250	21		
Lloyd McDermott	DT	6'2"	240	25	1	
Jerry Groom	LB	6'3"	235	22		
Jerry Houghton	LB	6'2"	226	25		
Fred Wallner	LB	6'2"	230	22	1	
Cliff Patton	OT-LB	6'2"	240	27	3	34
Leo Sanford	C-LB	6'1"	220	22	1	
John Panelli	FB-LB	5'11"	200	25		
Bill Svoboda	FB-LB	6'	210	24		
Billy Gay	DB	5'11"	180	23		
Lindy Lauro	DB	5'10"	195	27		
S.J. Whitman	DB	5'11"	185	25	7	
Jerry Davis	HB-DB	5'10"	180	29	2	
Tom Bienemann	OE-DB	6'3"	220	23	1	
Ray Ramsey	OE-DB	6'2"	165	30	5	
Jim Hardy	QB	6'	180	29		
Charlie Trippi	QB	6'	185	28		24
Frank Tripucka	QB	6'2"	175	23		
Elmer Angsman	HB	5'11"	197	25		24
Billy Cross	HB	5'6"	155	22		36
Emil Sitko	HB	5'8"	185	27		
Don Paul	DB-HB	6'	180	25	3	36
Ralph Pasquariello	FB	6'2"	235	24		6
Vinnie Yablonski	FB	5'8"	195	29		14
Fran Polsfoot	OE	6'3"	200	24		24
Don Stonesifer	OE	6'	200	24		12

Bob Shaw – Canadian Football League

John Hock – Military Service

CLEVELAND BROWNS

RUSHING

Last Name	No.	Yds	Avg	TD
Jones	104	492	4.7	7
Carpenter	85	402	4.7	4
Motley	61	273	4.5	1
Cole	46	252	5.5	1
Bumgardner	45	126	2.8	1
Phelps	16	65	4.1	1
Taseff	13	49	3.8	2
Jagade	7	30	4.3	0
Graham	35	29	.8	3
Lewis	3	−10	−3.3	0

RECEIVING

Last Name	No.	Yds	Avg	TD
Lavelli	43	586	14	6
Speedie	34	589	17	3
Jones	30	570	19	5
Carpenter	12	183	15	2
Gillom	11	164	15	0
Motley	10	52	5	0
Bumgardner	5	61	12	1
Cole	4	30	8	0
Oristaglio	1	20	20	1
Taseff	1	18	18	0

PUNT RETURNS

Last Name	No.	Yds	Avg	TD
Carpenter	14	173	12	0
Lewis	14	48	3	0
Taseff	1	6	6	0
Phelps	1	3	3	0

KICKOFF RETURNS

Last Name	No.	Yds	Avg	TD
Carpenter	9	196	22	0
Bumgardner	3	75	25	0
Phelps	3	66	22	0
Taseff	3	56	19	0
Jagade	2	36	18	0
Cole	2	28	14	0
Gillom	2	25	13	0
Gaudio	1	8	8	0
Shula	1	6	6	0
Gibron	1	0	0	0

PASSING – PUNTING – KICKING

PASSING	Att	Comp	%	Yds	Yd/Att	TD	Int–%	RK
Graham	265	147	55	2205	8.3	17	16– 6	1
Lewis	6	4	67	68	11.3	1	1–17	

PUNTING	No	Avg
Gillom	73	45.5

KICKING	XP	Att	%	FG	Att	%
Groza	43	43	100	10	23	43

NEW YORK GIANTS

RUSHING

Last Name	No.	Yds	Avg	TD
Price	271	971	3.6	7
Scott	94	367	3.9	1
Griffith	54	115	2.1	0
Rote	21	114	5.4	1
Conerly	17	65	3.8	1
Amberg	7	35	5.0	0
Tidwell	11	14	1.3	0
Jackson	5	9	1.8	0

RECEIVING

Last Name	No.	Yds	Avg	TD
Scott	23	356	15	2
Stribling	18	226	13	2
McChesney	14	230	16	2
Mote	11	187	17	4
Wilkinson	11	182	17	1
Rote	8	62	8	0
Price	5	19	4	0
Hudson	4	122	31	0
Sulaitis	4	25	6	0
Griffith	2	19	10	0
Murray	1	−4	−4	0
Hannah	0	8	0	0

PUNT RETURNS

Last Name	No.	Yds	Avg	TD
Tunnell	34	489	14	3
Ostendarp	2	57	29	0
Schnellbacher	7	32	5	0
Landry	1	0	0	0

KICKOFF RETURNS

Last Name	No.	Yds	Avg	TD
Tunnell	6	227	38	1
Rote	6	185	31	0
Scott	6	154	26	0
Sulaitis	1	37	37	0
Griffith	2	28	14	0
Jackson	1	27	27	0
Ostendarp	1	15	15	0
Coulter	1	12	12	0
Landry	1	0	0	0
Murray	1	0	0	0

PASSING – PUNTING – KICKING

	Att	Comp	%	Yds	Yds/Att	TD	Int–%	RK
Conerly	189	93	49	1277	6.8	10	22–12	11
Tidwell	21	8	38	155	7.4	1	4–19	

PUNTING	No	Avg
Conerly	72	39.7
Landry	15	42.5

KICKING	XP	Att	%	FG	Att	%
Poole	30	31	97	12	16	75

WASHINGTON REDSKINS

RUSHING

Last Name	No.	Yds	Avg	TD
Goode	208	951	4.6	9
Dudley	91	398	4.4	2
Papit	44	175	4.0	0
Heath	64	159	2.5	0
Gilmer	19	141	7.4	0
Thomas	42	130	3.1	0
Dowda	29	111	3.8	0
Drazenovich	34	76	2.2	3
Saenz	3	8	2.7	0
Cox	2	7	3.5	0
Baugh	11	−5	−0.5	0

RECEIVING

Last Name	No.	Yds	Avg	TD
Taylor	29	444	15	3
Brito	24	313	13	0
Dudley	22	303	14	1
Thomas	7	193	28	2
Tereshinksi	6	74	12	2
Goode	3	45	15	0
Papit	3	43	14	0
Dowda	2	54	27	0
Drazenovich	1	27	27	0
Saenz	1	9	9	0
Heath	1	3	3	0

PUNT RETURNS

Last Name	No.	Yds	Avg	TD
Dudley	22	172	8	0
Gilmer	6	132	22	0
Dwyer	7	22	3	0
Saenz	2	6	3	0
Ferris	2	1	1	0
Buksar	1	0	0	0

KICKOFF RETURNS

Last Name	No.	Yds	Avg	TD
Dowda	13	341	26	0
Dudley	11	248	23	0
Saenz	9	145	16	0
Buksar	4	56	14	0
Brito	4	39	10	0
Lipscomb	2	27	14	0
Hendren	2	21	11	0
Dwyer	1	19	19	0
Siegert	1	0	0	0

PASSING – PUNTING – KICKING

PASSING	Att	Comp	%	Yds	Yd/Att	TD	Int–%	RK
Baugh	154	67	44	1104	7.2	7	17–11	16
Gilmer	68	31	46	391	5.8	1	6– 9	
Salem	3	0	0	0	0.0	0	2–67	
Dudley	1	1	100	13	13.0	0	0– 0	

PUNTING	No	Avg
Cox	28	40.0
Dudley	27	34.9
Baugh	4	55.3

KICKING	XP	Att	%	FG	Att	%
Dudley	21	22	95	10	13	77

PITTSBURGH STEELERS

RUSHING

Last Name	No.	Yds	Avg	TD
Rogel	109	385	3.5	3
Chandnois	108	332	3.1	2
Ortmann	59	327	5.5	0
Geri	90	252	2.8	3
Nuzum	27	56	2.1	1
Mathews	21	37	1.8	0
Finks	3	27	9.0	0
Hollingsworth	7	11	1.6	0
Smith	1	1	1.0	0

RECEIVING

Last Name	No.	Yds	Avg	TD
Minarik	35	459	13	1
Chandnois	29	490	17	5
Nickel	28	447	16	3
Jansante	16	200	13	1
Rogel	10	59	6	0
Smith	4	71	18	0
Ortmann	4	62	16	0
Nuzum	2	43	22	0
Geri	2	9	5	0
Jelley	1	8	8	0

PUNT RETURNS

Last Name	No.	Yds	Avg	TD
Mathews	15	231	15	1
Hartley	18	156	9	0
Chandnois	12	55	5	0
Finks	1	20	20	0
Butler	1	2	2	0

KICKOFF RETURNS

Last Name	No.	Yds	Avg	TD
Chandnois	12	390	33	0
Mathews	13	327	25	0
Geri	2	108	54	0
Hartley	1	14	14	0
McPeak	3	10	3	0
Rogel	2	9	5	0
Wydo	1	0	0	0

PASSING – PUNTING – KICKING

PASSING	Att	Comp	%	Yds	Yd/Att	TD	Int–%	RK
Ortmann	139	56	40	671	4.8	3	13– 9	17
Geri	90	29	32	506	5.6	2	7– 8	
Chandnois	43	16	37	256	6.0	2	4– 9	
Mathews	31	15	48	208	6.7	2	0– 0	
Finks	24	14	58	201	8.4	1	1– 4	
Gasparella	2	0	0	0	0.0	0	1–50	
Rogel	1	0	0	0	0	0	0– 0	

PUNTING	No	Avg
Geri	73	38.2
Ortmann	7	43.1

KICKING	XP	Att	%	FG	Att	%
Geri	22	23	96	7	14	50

PHILADELPHIA EAGLES

RUSHING

Last Name	No.	Yds	Avg	TD
Ziegler	113	418	3.7	2
S. Van Buren	112	327	2.9	6
Parmer	92	316	3.4	2
Scott	45	161	3.6	1
Pollard	26	121	4.7	0
Sandifer	35	113	3.2	1
E. Van Buren	16	60	3.8	0
Pritchard	42	29	.7	0
Burk	28	12	.4	1
MacKrides	7	9	1.3	0

RECEIVING

Last Name	No.	Yds	Avg	TD
Pihos	35	536	15	5
Walston	31	512	17	8
Parmer	13	80	6	0
Scott	10	212	21	3
Pritchard	8	103	13	0
Ziegler	8	59	7	0
S. Van Buren	4	28	7	0
O'Quinn	3	58	19	0
Armstrong	3	44	15	0
Pollard	3	35	12	0
Sandifer	2	36	18	1
Lindskog	0	21	0	0
Magee	0	7	0	0

PUNT RETURNS

Last Name	No.	Yds	Avg	TD
Pollard	18	148	8	0
Pritchard	11	147	13	1
Sandifer	14	137	10	0
Scott	4	72	18	0
Grant	1	9	9	0
Craft	2	0	0	0

KICKOFF RETURNS

Last Name	No.	Yds	Avg	TD
Pollard	19	464	22	0
Scott	8	171	21	0
Sandifer	8	147	18	0
Pritchard	7	120	17	0
Walston	5	57	11	0
Craft	2	53	27	0
Pihos	3	40	13	0
Kilroy	1	18	18	0
Barnes	1	15	15	0
Cowhig	1	12	12	0

PASSING – PUNTING – KICKING

PASSING	Att	Comp	%	Yds	Yd/Att	TD	Int–%	RK
Burk	218	92	42	1329	6.1	14	23–11	15
MacKrides	54	23	43	333	6.2	3	5– 9	

PUNTING	No	Avg
Burk	67	39.5
Reagan	10	36.7

KICKING	XP	Att	%	FG	Att	%
Walston	28	31	90	6	11	55

CHICAGO CARDINALS

RUSHING

Last Name	No.	Yds	Avg	TD
Trippi	78	501	6.4	4
Angsman	121	380	3.1	3
Cross	53	283	5.3	3
Pasquareillo	53	251	4.7	1
Paut	37	247	6.7	3
Sitko	52	183	3.5	0
Hardy	12	38	3.2	0
Panelli	13	38	2.9	0
Yablonski	14	20	1.4	0
Svoboda	5	15	3.0	0
Tripucka	1	14	14.0	0
Davis	1	−7	−7.0	0

RECEIVING

Last Name	No.	Yds	Avg	TD
Polsfoot	57	796	14	4
Stonesifer	27	343	13	2
Paul	23	398	17	3
Cross	18	322	18	3
Angsman	9	195	22	1
R. Ramsey	8	135	17	0
Svoboda	6	−9	−1	0
Sitko	4	28	7	0
Davis	4	24	6	0
Pasquariello	2	−9	−5	0
Bieneman	1	8	8	0
Yablonski	1	8	8	0
Panelli	1	5	5	0

PUNT RETURNS

Last Name	No.	Yds	Avg	TD
Paul	19	143	8	0
Cross	7	39	6	0
Davis	4	10	3	0

KICKOFF RETURNS

Last Name	No.	Yds	Avg	TD
Sitko	17	429	25	0
Paul	15	424	28	0
Panelli	2	57	29	0
Angsman	2	51	26	0
Bieneman	2	34	17	0
Svoboda	1	29	29	0
Jennings	1	16	16	0
Hennessy	1	11	11	0
Fischer	1	0	0	0
R. Ramsey	1	0	0	0

PASSING – PUNTING – KICKING

PASSING	Att	Comp	%	Yds	Yd/Att	TD	Int–%	RK
Trippi	191	88	46	1191	6.2	8	13– 7	10
Hardy	114	56	49	809	7.1	3	10– 9	14
Tripucka	29	17	59	244	8.4	2	1– 3	

PUNTING	No	Avg
Polsfoot	47	40.7
Trippi	12	37.2
Tripucka	11	39.0

KICKING	XP	Att	%	FG	Att	%
Patton	19	19	100	5	8	63
Yablonski	8	8	100	2	5	40

LOS ANGELES RAMS 8-4-0 Joe Stydahar

Scores of Each Game		
54	N.Y. YANKS	14
23	CLEVELAND	38
27	Detroit	21
28	Green Bay	0
17	San Francisco	44
23	SAN FRANCISCO	16
45	CHIC. CARDS	21
48	N.Y. YANKS	21
21	Washington	31
42	Chic. Bears	17
22	DETROIT	24
42	GREEN BAY	14

Use Name	Pos.	Hgt	Wgt	Age	Int	Pts
Tom Dahms	OT	6'5"	240	23		
Don Simensen	OT	6'2"	220	24		
Dick Daugherty	OG	6'1"	214	22		
Bill Lange	OG	6'1"	245	24		
Harry Thompson	DE-DG-OG	6'2"	225	24		
Leon McLaughlin	C	6'2"	228	25		
Stan West	DG	6'2"	258	24		
Larry Brink	DE	6'5"	240	28		
Andy Robustelli	DE	6'1"	220	25		
Jack Zilly	DE	6'2"	215	29		
Charlie Toogood	DT	6'	233	23	1	
Jim Winkler	DT	6'2"	248	24		
Bobby Collier	OT-DT	6'3"	230	21		
Jack Halliday	OT-DT	6'3"	238	23		
Don Paul	LB	6'1"	230	26	1	
Jack Finlay	OG-LB	6'1"	222	30		
Joe Reid	C-LB	6'3"	225	21		
Tank Younger	HB-FB-LB	6'3"	226	23	1	6
Woodley Lewis	DB	6'	195	26	3	
Herb Rich	DB	5'11"	180	22	3	
Marvin Johnson	HB-DB	5'11"	180	23		
Jerry Williams	HB-DB	5'10"	176	27	3	24
Bob Boyd	OE-DB	6'2"	198	23	2	6
Norb Hecker	OE-DB	6'2"	190	24	3	6
Norm Van Brocklin	QB	6'1"	200	25		12
Bob Waterfield	QB	6'1"	200	31		98
Glen Davis	HB	5'11"	170	26		12
Tommy Kalmanir	HB	5'8"	170	25		12
Vitamin Smith	HB	5'8"	180	27		12
Dick Hoerner	FB	6'4"	220	29		42
Dan Towler	FB	6'2"	220	23		36
Tom Fears	OE	6'2"	215	27		24
Tom Keane	DB-OE	6'1"	190	24	2	
Crazy Legs Hirsch	HB-OE	6'2"	190	27		102

Paul Barry – Military Service
Dick Huffman – Canadian Football League

DETROIT LIONS 7-4-1 Buddy Parker

Scores of Each Game		
35	WASHINGTON	17
37	N. Y. Yanks	10
21	LOS ANGELES	27
24	N.Y. YANKS	24
23	CHIC. BEARS	28
24	Green Bay	17
41	Chic. Bears	28
28	Philadelphia	10
52	GREEN BAY	35
10	SAN FRANCISCO	20
24	Los Angeles	22
17	San Francisco	21

Use Name	Pos.	Hgt	Wgt	Age	Int	Pts
Gus Cifelli	OT	6'4"	240	25		
Floyd Jaszewski	OT	6'4"	230	24		
Dan Rogas	DT-OT	6'1"	225	24		
Barry French	OG	6'	225	30		
Bob Momsen	OG	6'3"	225	21		
Bruce Womack	OG	6'3"	210	22		
Lou Creekmur	DT-OG	6'4"	230	24		
Vince Banonis	LB-C	6'1"	235	29	1	
Les Bingaman	DG	6'3"	260	26		
Ed Berrang (From WAS)	DE	6'2"	203	26	1	
Jim Martin	OT-DE	6'2"	220	27		
Jim Doran	OE-DE	6'2"	195	23	1	12
Thurman McGraw	DT	6'5"	235	24		
John Prchlik	DT	6'4"	235	26		2
Dick Flanagan	OG-LB	6'	215	24	2	
Roy Lininger	C-LB	5'11"	217	24		
Lavern Torgeson	C-LB	6'	210	22	1	
Art Murakowski	FB-LB	6'	195	25		
Jack Christiansen	DB	6'1"	180	22	2	24
Don Doll	DB	5'10"	185	24	1	
Jim Hill	DB	6'	185	22		
Clarence Self	DB	5'8"	185	26		
Jim Smith	DB	6'1"	195	26	3	
Fred Enke	QB	6'1"	200	26		
Bobby Layne	QB	6'1"	190	24		6
Bob Hoernschemeyer	HB	5'11"	195	25		30
Lindy Pearson	HB	6'	200	22		
Doak Walker	HB	5'11"	173	24		97
Ollie Cline	FB	6'	200	25		
Pete D'Alonzo	FB	5'10"	210	21		
Pat Harder	FB	5'11"	202	29		57
Leon Hart	OE	6'5"	262	22	2	72
Bill Swiacki	OE	6'2"	195	26		
Dorne Dibble	DB-OE	6'2"	195	22	1	36

Cloyce Box – Military Service
Jim Cain – Military Service
Wally Triplett – Military Service

SAN FRANCISCO FORTY NINERS 7-4-1 Buck Shaw

Scores of Each Game		
24	CLEVELAND	10
14	Philadelphia	21
28	Pittsburgh	24
7	Chic. Bears	13
44	LOS ANGELES	17
16	Los Angeles	23
19	N. Y. GIANTS	14
21	CHIC. CARDS	27
10	N. Y. Yanks	10
20	Detroit	10
31	GREEN BAY	19
21	DETROIT	17

Use Name	Pos.	Hgt	Wgt	Age	Int	Pts
Ray Collins	OT	5'11"	230	23		
Leo Nomellini	DT-OT	6'3"	270	26		6
Bruno Banducci	OG	5'11"	220	29		
Bob Downs	OG	5'10"	210			
Nick Feher	OG	6'	220	24		
Dave Sparks	OG	6'1"	222	22		
Bill Johnson	C	6'3"	225	25		
Gail Bruce	DE	6'1"	210	27		1
Ed Henke	DT-DE	6'3"	225	23		
Al Carapella	DT	6'	235	24	1	
Hamp Tanner	OT-DT	6'2"	280	24		2
Hardy Brown	LB	6'	196	27	1	
Don Burke	OG-LB	6'	235	25		
Visco Grgich	OG-LB	5'11"	225	28		
Pete Wissman	C-LB	6'	220	27	2	
Norm Standlee	FB-LB	6'2"	240	32		
Lowell Wagner	DB	6'	195	27	9	
Jim Powers	QB-DB	6'	185	23	4	
Rex Berry	HB-DB	5'11"	180	25	4	
Jim Cason	HB-DB	6'	168	24	3	6
Bob White	HB-DB	5'11"	174	22	1	
Frankie Albert	QB	5'10"	170	31		18
Y. A. Tittle	QB	6'	190	24		6
Joe Arenas	HB	5'11"	180	25		24
Jim Monachino	HB	5'10"	190	22		12
Pete Schabarum	HB	5'11"	185	22		12
Johnny Strzykalski	HB	5'9"	190	28		18
Verl Lillywhite	DB-HB	5'10"	185	24	3	12
Joe Perry	FB	6'	210	24		24
Bishop Strickland	FB	5'10"	195	22		
Alyn Beals	OE	6'	190	30		
Bill Jessup	OE	6'1"	190	22		6
Gordie Soltau	OE	6'2"	195	26		90
Billy Wilson	OE	6'3"	195	24		18

Clay Mathews – Military Service

CHICAGO BEARS 7-5-0 George Halas

Scores of Each Game		
31	Green Bay	20
14	Chic. Cards	28
24	N. Y. YANKS	21
13	SAN FRANCISCO	7
28	Detroit	23
27	Washington	0
28	DETROIT	41
24	GREEN BAY	13
21	Cleveland	42
17	LOS ANGELES	42
45	N. Y. Yanks	21
14	CHIC. CARDS	24

Use Name	Pos.	Hgt	Wgt	Age	Int	Pts
Paul Stenn	DT-OT	6'2"	245	33		
George Conner	LB-OT	6'3"	240	26	2	
Dick Barwegan	OG	6'1"	228	28		
Frank Dempsey	OG	6'3"	235	26		
Wayne Hansen	OG	6'2"	230	23		
Wash Serini	OG	6'2"	235	27		
Bob Moser	C	6'3"	240	22		
Bulldog Turner	OG-C	6'1"	235	32		
Ed Neal (From GB)	DG-C	6'4"	275	33		
Les Cowan	DT-DE	6'5"	235	24		
Ed Sprinkle	OE-DE	6'1"	207	27	1	12
Fred Davis	OT-DT	6'3"	248	33		
Ray Bray	DG	6'	235	34		
Jerry Stoutberg	OG-LB	6'2"	228	23		
Stu Clarkson	LB	6'2"	225	32	1	
J. R. Boone	HB	5'8"	163	25		
Al Campana	HB-DB	5'11"	180	25		
Billy Stone	HB-DB	6'	188	25	4	12
Don Kindt	FB-DB	6'1"	208	25	4	6
Gene Schroeder	OE-DB	6'3"	190	22	5	18
Steve Romanik	QB	6'1"	190	27		6
Bob Williams	QB	6'1"	198	22		
George Blanda	LB-DB-QB	6'1"	204	23	1	44
Johnny Lujack	DB-QB	6'	188	26	3	52
George Gulyanics	HB	6'	204	30		24
Chuck Hunsinger	HB	6'	188	26		24
Brad Rowland	HB	6'1"	190	23		
Julie Rykovich	HB	6'2"	205	27		24
Wilford White	HB	5'9"	172	23		16
Kayo Dottley	FB	6'1"	200	23		24
Curley Morrison	FB	6'2"	215	25		
Jim Keane	OE	6'4"	215	27		6
Bill Wightkin	OE	6'3"	238	24		6
John Hoffman	LB-OE	6'2"	218	25		12

Jerry Weatherley – Military Service

GREEN BAY PACKERS 3-9-0 Gene Ronzani

Scores of Each Game		
20	CHIC. BEARS	31
35	PITTSBURGH	33
37	PHILADELPHIA	24
0	LOS ANGELES	28
29	N. Y. Yanks	27
17	DETROIT	24
7	Pittsburgh	28
13	Chic. Bears	24
35	Detroit	52
28	N. Y. YANKS	31
19	San Francisco	31
14	Los Angeles	42

Use Name	Pos.	Hgt	Wgt	Age	Int	Pts
Willie Manley	OG-OT	6'2"	225	25		
Joe Spencer	DT-OT	6'3"	240	28		
Dick Wildung	DT-OT	6'	220	29		
Ray DiPierro	OG	5'11"	210	24		
Dave Stephenson	OG	6'2"	235	25		
Buddy Burris	LB-OG	5'11"	215	28		
Jay Rhodemyre	C	6'1"	210	29		
Dick Afflis	DG	6'	252	22		
Art Felker	DE	6'3"	205	23		
John Martinkovic	DE	6'3"	235	24		
Dan Orlich	OE-DE	6'5"	215	26		
Ab Wimberly	OE-DE	6'1"	215	25		
Howie Ruetz	DT	6'3"	265	23	1	
Don Stansauk	DT	6'1"	255	26		
Ed Ecker	OT-DT	6'7"	270	28		
Walt Michaels	LB	6'	225	22		
Bill Schroll	LB	6'	218	25		
Bob Summerhays	LB	6'1"	215	24	2	6
Ham Nichols	OG-LB	5'11"	215	27		
Carl Schuette	C-LB	6'1"	210	29		
Bob Nussbaumer	DB	5'11"	170	27		
Rebel Steiner	DB	6'	185	25	3	
Rip Collins	HB-DB	6'	190	24	2	
Harper Davis	HB-DB	5'11"	172	25	4	
Jug Girard	HB-DB	5'11"	175	24	5	12
Ace Loomis	HB-DB	6'1"	190	23	4	
Tobin Rote	QB	6'3"	200	23		18
Bobby Thomason	QB	6'1"	197	22		
Tony Canadeo	HB	5'11"	190	32		18
Billy Grimes	HB	6'1"	197	24		12
Breezy Reid	HB	5'10"	180	24		
Dom Moselle	DB-HB	6'	192	25	1	18
Jack Cloud	FB	5'10"	220	26		12
Fred Cone	FB	5'11"	197	25		50
Carl Elliott	OE	6'4"	215	24		30
Bob Mann	OE	5'11"	172	27		48
Dick Moje	OE	6'2"	210	24		
Ray Pelfrey	HB-OE	6'	190	23		30

Larry Coutre – Military Service
Bob Forte – Military Service

Len Szafaryn – Military Service
Clayton Tonnemaker – Military Service

NEW YORK YANKS 1-9-2 Red Strader

Scores of Each Game		
14	Los Angeles	54
10	DETROIT	37
21	Chic. Bears	24
24	Detroit	24
27	GREEN BAY	29
31	N. Y. Giants	37
14	San Francisco	19
21	Los Angeles	48
10	SAN FRANCISCO	10
31	Green Bay	28
21	CHIC. BEARS	45
17	N. Y. GIANTS	27

Use Name	Pos.	Hgt	Wgt	Age	Int	Pts
Jim Champion	DT-OT	6'	245	24		
John Clowes (To DET)	DT-OT	6'1"	245	29		
Ross Nagel	DT-OT	6'4"	243	28	1	
Jim Cullom	OG	5'11"	235	25		
Sisto Averno	LB-OG	5'11"	228	25		
Wayne Siegert	OT-LB-OG	6'3"	225	21		
Joe Domnanovich	C	6'1"	215	32		
Brad Ecklund	C	6'3"	215	29		
Barney Poole	DE	6'2"	220	28		
Breck Stroschein	DE	6'1"	205	22		
Art Tait	DE	5'11"	205	22		12
Don Colo	DT	6'3"	252	26		
Art Donovan	DT	6'2"	240	26		
Mike McCormack	DT	6'4"	230	24		
Paul Mitchell	DT	6'3"	240	31		
Harvey Johnson	LB	5'11"	220	32		49
Vito Kissell	LB	5'10"	205	24		
John Wozniak	OG-LB	6'	220	30		
Ben Aldridge	DB	6'	195	24	5	
Joe Golding	DB	6'	187	30	2	
Bobby Griffin	DB	6'	180	23	4	
Duke Iverson	DB	6'2"	208	31		
Darrell Meisenheimer	DB	5'10"	195	25	3	
Paul Crowe	HB-DB	6'1"	195	27	3	
Bob Celeri	QB	5'10"	180	24		6
George Ratterman	QB	6'1"	180	24		
Johnny Rauch (To PHI)	QB	6'	195	24		
Bev Wallace	QB	6'2"	180	28		
Sherman Howard	HB	5'11"	192	27		42
Buddy Young	HB	5'5"	170	25		36
George Taliaferro	DB-QB-HB	5'11"	195	24	4	30
Zollie Toth	FB	6'2"	215	27		24
Bruce Alford	OE	6'	190	30		
Dan Edwards	OE	6'1"	195	25		18
Dan Graza	OE	6'3"	205	27		24
Bill O'Connor	DE-OE	6'4"	220	25		

Lou Kusserow – Canadian Football League
Martin Ruby – Canadian Football League
Jack Russell – Canadian Football League

LOS ANGELES RAMS

RUSHING

Last Name	No.	Yds	Avg	TD
Towler	126	854	6.8	6
Hoerner	94	569	6.1	6
Younger	36	223	6.2	1
Davis	64	200	3.1	1
Smith	52	143	2.8	1
Williams	21	106	5.0	2
Kalmanir	16	61	3.8	0
Waterfield	9	49	5.4	3
Hirsch	1	3	3.0	0
Van Brocklin	7	2	.3	2

RECEIVING

Last Name	No.	Yds	Avg	TD
Hirsch	66	1495	23	17
Fears	32	528	17	3
Smith	16	278	17	1
Towler	16	257	16	0
Keane	12	133	11	0
Boyd	9	128	14	1
Hoerner	8	102	13	1
Davis	8	90	11	1
Kalmanir	6	91	15	1
Younger	5	72	14	0
Williams	5	49	10	0
Hecker	4	35	9	1
Johnson	2	38	19	0

PUNT RETURNS

Last Name	No.	Yds	Avg	TD
Smith	12	139	12	0
Kalmanir	5	86	17	1
Davis	15	85	6	0
Williams	4	22	6	0
Lewis	1	12	12	0

KICKOFF RETURNS

Last Name	No.	Yds	Avg	TD
Smith	15	274	18	0
Davis	9	179	20	0
Williams	6	133	22	0
Kalmanir	6	120	20	0
Lewis	4	67	17	0
Hoerner	1	22	22	0
Simensen	1	13	13	0
Towler	1	10	10	0
Collier	1	8	8	0

PASSING – PUNTING – KICKING

PASSING	Att	Comp	%	Yds	Yd/Att	TD	Int–%	RK
Van Brocklin	194	100	52	1725	8.9	13	11– 6	2
Waterfield	176	88	50	1566	8.9	13	10– 6	2
Davis	2	1	50	5	2.5	0	0– 0	
Keane	1	0	0	0	0	0	1–100	

PUNTING	No	Avg
Van Brocklin	48	41.5
Waterfield	4	41.5

KICKING	XP	Att	%	FG	Att	%
Waterfield	41	43	95	13	23	57
Fears	6	7	86	0	0	0
Hirsch	0	1	0	0	0	0
Hecker	0	0	0	0	1	0

DETROIT LIONS

RUSHING

Last Name	No.	Yds	Avg	TD
Hoernschemeyer	132	678	5.1	2
Harder	101	380	3.8	6
Walker	79	356	4.5	2
Layne	61	290	4.8	1
Pearson	22	88	4.0	0
Doran	2	23	11.5	0
Cline	3	15	5.0	0
D'Alonzo	2	11	5.5	0
Enke	4	6	1.5	0
Hart	4	–6	–1.5	0

RECEIVING

Last Name	No.	Yds	Avg	TD
Hart	35	544	16	12
Dibble	30	613	20	6
Hoernschemeyer	23	263	11	3
Walker	22	421	19	4
Harder	17	193	11	2
Swiacki	16	188	12	0
Doran	10	225	23	2
Pearson	5	43	9	0
Martin	0	10	0	0

PUNT RETURNS

Last Name	No.	Yds	Avg	TD
Christiansen	18	343	19	4
Walker	7	85	12	0
Doll	5	39	8	0
Hoernschemeyer	2	16	8	0

KICKOFF RETURNS

Last Name	No.	Yds	Avg	TD
Walker	15	408	27	0
Christiansen	11	270	25	0
Doll	9	220	24	0
Hoernschemeyer	3	78	26	0
Cline	3	48	16	0
Harder	1	14	14	0
Prchlik	1	12	12	0
French	1	3	3	0
Murakowski	1	0	0	0

PASSING – PUNTING – KICKING

PASSING	Att	Comp	%	Yds	Yd/Att	TD	Int–%	RK
Layne	332	152	46	2403	7.2	26	23– 7	6
Enke	9	2	22	22	2.4	0	1–11	
Walker	5	2	40	29	5.8	1	0– 0	
Hoernschemeyer	4	2	50	46	12.0	2	0– 0	
Harder	1	0	0	0	0.0	0	0– 0	

PUNTING	No	Avg
Smith	49	42.5
Walker	9	35.1

KICKING	XP	Att	%	FG	Att	%
Walker	43	44	98	6	12	50
Harder	0	0	0	3	5	60

SAN FRANCISCO FORTY NINERS

RUSHING

Last Name	No.	Yds	Avg	TD
Perry	136	677	5.0	3
Lillywhite	67	397	5.9	1
Schabarum	76	311	4.1	2
Strzykalski	81	296	3.7	3
Arenas	34	183	5.4	3
Strickland	34	165	4.9	0
Albert	35	146	4.2	3
Monachino	21	74	3.5	2
Standlee	16	65	4.1	0
White	8	33	4.1	0
Tittle	13	18	1.4	1
Cason	1	5	5.0	0
Soltau	1	–4	–4.0	0

RECEIVING

Last Name	No.	Yds	Avg	TD
Soltau	59	826	14	7
Wilson	18	268	15	3
Perry	18	167	9	1
Beals	12	126	11	0
Strzykalski	12	105	9	0
Lillywhite	11	125	11	1
Schabarum	10	162	16	0
Jessup	7	99	14	1
White	3	36	12	0
Arenas	1	12	12	1
Berry	1	12	12	0
Cason	1	8	8	0
Monachino	1	6	6	0
Johnson	0	3	0	0

PUNT RETURNS

Last Name	No.	Yds	Avg	TD
Arenas	21	272	13	0
Cason	13	115	9	0
Nomellini	1	20	20	1

KICKOFF RETURNS

Last Name	No.	Yds	Avg	TD
Arenas	21	542	26	0
Cason	10	196	20	0
Perry	1	32	32	0
Nomellini	2	27	14	0
Strickland	1	14	14	0
Collins	1	6	6	0
Banducci	1	3	3	0
Wilson	1	0	0	0

PASSING – PUNTING – KICKING

PASSING	Att	Comp	%	Yds	Yd/Att	TD	Int–%	RK
Albert	166	90	54	1116	6.7	5	10– 6	9
Tittle	114	63	55	808	7.1	8	9– 8	8
Perry	1	1	100	31	31.0	1	0– 0	

PUNTING	No	Avg
Albert	34	44.3
Lillywhite	20	42.4

KICKING	XP	Att	%	FG	Att	%
Soltau	30	32	94	6	18	33
Bruce	1	1	100	0	0	0

CHICAGO BEARS

RUSHING

Last Name	No.	Yds	Avg	TD
Dottley	127	670	5.3	3
Gulyanics	105	403	3.8	4
Rykovich	83	399	4.8	4
Hunsinger	73	369	5.1	3
Lujack	47	171	3.6	7
Stone	30	123	4.1	1
Morrison	29	96	3.3	0
White	9	86	9.6	1
Rowland	10	50	5.0	0
Romanik	12	23	1.9	1
Boone	3	9	3.0	0
Kindt	2	5	2.5	0
Schroeder	1	4	4.0	0
Campana	2	3	1.5	0
Williams	5	0	0.0	0
Hoffman	1	–3	–3.0	0

RECEIVING

Last Name	No.	Yds	Avg	TD
Hoffman	28	394	14	2
Schroeder	24	461	19	3
Stone	18	320	18	1
Keane	15	247	16	1
Dottley	14	225	16	1
Gulyanics	13	146	11	0
Rykovich	6	133	22	0
Boone	6	117	20	0
Hunsinger	6	59	10	1
White	4	45	11	1
Kindt	4	39	10	1
Sprinkle	2	11	6	1
Wightkin	1	47	47	0
Rowland	1	–2	–2	0
Morrison	1	–3	–3	0

PUNT RETURNS

Last Name	No.	Yds	Avg	TD
White	14	131	9	0
Stone	14	120	9	0
Boone	14	113	8	0
Hunsinger	1	7	7	0
Wightkin	1	3	3	1

KICKOFF RETURNS

Last Name	No.	Yds	Avg	TD
Morrison	13	353	27	0
Rowland	15	350	23	0
Stone	5	108	22	0
Hunsinger	4	66	17	0
Davis	3	26	9	0
Hansen	1	23	23	0
Blanda	2	19	10	0
Schroeder	1	18	18	0
Connor	1	9	9	0
Sereni	1	2	2	0

PASSING – PUNTING – KICKING

PASSING	Att	Comp	%	Yds	Yd/Att	TD	Int–%	RK
Lujack	176	85	48	1295	7.4	8	8– 5	5
Romanik	101	43	43	791	7.8	3	9– 8	11
Williams	33	14	42	146	4.4	1	2– 6	
Rykovich	3	0	0	0	0.0	0	1–33	
Morrison	1	1	100	7	7.0	0	0– 0	
White	1	0	0	0	0.0	0	0– 0	

PUNTING	No	Avg
Morrison	57	39.1
Williams	4	36.3
Rowland	1	18.0

KICKING	XP	Att	%	FG	Att	%
Blanda	26	26	100	6	17	35
Lujack	10	11	91	0	0	0
White	1	1	100	1	2	50

GREEN BAY PACKERS

RUSHING

Last Name	No.	Yds	Avg	TD
Rote	76	523	6.9	3
Cone	56	190	3.4	1
Canadeo	54	131	2.4	1
Grimes	44	123	2.8	1
Reid	23	73	3.2	0
Cloud	29	61	2.1	1
Pelfrey	3	44	14.7	0
Moselle	12	23	2.0	1
Girard	4	20	5.0	0
Mann	2	9	4.5	0
Collins	5	4	.8	0
Thomason	5	–5	–1.0	0

RECEIVING

Last Name	No.	Yds	Avg	TD
Mann	50	696	14	8
Pelfrey	38	462	12	5
Elliott	35	317	9	5
Cone	28	315	11	0
Canadeo	22	226	10	2
Grimes	15	170	11	1
Moselle	14	233	17	2
Girard	10	220	22	2
Reid	9	115	13	0
Cloud	3	16	5	1
Davis	1	15	15	0
Moje	1	11	11	0
Wimberly	1	10	10	0
Loomis	1	9	9	0
Orlich	1	9	9	0
Collins	1	5	5	0
Rote	0	11	0	0

PUNT RETURNS

Last Name	No.	Yds	Avg	TD
Grimes	16	100	6	0
Moselle	9	80	9	0
Davis	2	21	11	0
Girard	1	9	9	0
Wussbaumer	1	3	3	0

KICKOFF RETURNS

Last Name	No.	Yds	Avg	TD
Grimes	23	582	25	0
Moselle	20	547	27	0
Canadeo	4	101	25	0
Michaels	5	86	17	0
Collins	1	40	40	0
Martinkovic	2	34	17	0
Summerhays	1	21	21	0
Cone	1	20	20	0
Elliott	1	14	14	0
Wimberly	2	4	2	0

PASSING – PUNTING – KICKING

PASSING	Att	Comp	%	Yds	Yd/Att	TD	Int–%	RK
Rote	256	106	41	1540	6.0	15	20– 8	11
Thomason	221	125	57	1306	5.9	11	9– 4	4
Reid	1	0	0	0	0.0	0	0– 0	

PUNTING	No	Avg
Girard	52	40.4
Pelfrey	5	44.0
Collins	2	40.5
Rote	1	55.0
Cone	1	47.0

KICKING	XP	Att	%	FG	Att	%
Cone	29	35	83	5	7	71
Michaels	0	0	0	0	1	0

NEW YORK YANKS

RUSHING

Last Name	No.	Yds	Avg	TD
Toth	119	384	3.2	4
Howard	94	343	3.6	4
Taliaferro	62	330	5.3	3
Young	46	165	3.6	1
Celeri	36	107	3.0	0
Rauch	7	26	3.7	0
Ratterman	3	9	3.0	0
Wallace	1	–8	–8.0	0

RECEIVING

Last Name	No.	Yds	Avg	TD
Edwards	39	509	13	3
Young	31	508	16	3
Garza	31	470	15	4
Howard	21	447	21	3
Taliaferro	16	230	14	2
O'Connor	14	192	14	0
Toth	10	100	10	0
Alford	4	65	16	0
Crowe	3	20	7	0
Celeri	2	71	36	1
Wozniak	1	4	4	0

PUNT RETURNS

Last Name	No.	Yds	Avg	TD
Young	12	231	19	1
Taliaferro	9	68	8	0
Griffin	4	46	12	0
Aldridge	1	0	0	0

KICKOFF RETURNS

Last Name	No.	Yds	Avg	TD
Taliaferro	27	622	23	0
Young	14	427	31	1
Averno	3	28	9	0
Iverson	1	14	14	0
Mitchell	1	11	11	0
O'Connor	1	10	10	0
Johnson	1	4	4	0
Siegert	1	2	2	0
McCormack	1	0	0	0

PASSING – PUNTING – KICKING

PASSING	Att	Comp	%	Yds	Yd/Att	TD	Int–%	RK
Celeri	238	102	43	1797	7.6	12	15– 6	7
Rauch	94	30	32	288	3.1	1	4– 4	
Ratterman	67	31	46	340	5.1	2	6– 9	
Taliaferro	33	13	39	251	7.6	1	3– 9	
Wallace	8	1	13	9	1.1	0	0– 0	

PUNTING	No	Avg
Taliaferro	76	37.9
Celeri	5	44.8

KICKING	XP	Att	%	FG	Att	%
Johnson	31	31	100	6	14	43

1952 Texas: Everything but the Pros

Two rookies joined the league who perfectly illustrated the modern pro game. Both Hugh McElhenny of San Francisco and Ollie Matson of the Cardinals had blazing speed and the ability to bring a crowd to its feet with a breakaway run or pass reception. Pro football in general was fast, offense-oriented, and spiced with exciting stars on most of the teams and the fans showed their approval by turning out in a record number of 2,052,126 for seventy-two league games.

Eleven of the clubs prospered in these booming times, but the twelfth franchise was a pain in the neck for the league. Tired of losing money, New York Yank owner Ted Collins sold his franchise back to the league. Bert Bell and the league then sold the team to a group from Dallas, Texas. Long a hotbed for college and high-school football, Texas looked like an untapped source of riches just waiting for an NFL team. Instead, the Dallas Texans went through their first few games waiting for customers, while the fans ignored the team. After four home games, the Texans were averaging under 15,000 attendance per game, convincing the owners to get out immediately. They turned the club over to the league in mid-season, and the commissioner's office operated the Texans as a road team for the remainder of the year.

AMERICAN CONFERENCE

Cleveland Browns—Even in an off year, the Browns marched off with a conference title. They lost four games, the most in the history of the team, yet still came home a game ahead of the Giants and Eagles. The Giants beat the Browns twice but had problems with the rest of the league. The Eagles downed the Browns in their second meeting but lost two of their last three contests to fall out of contention. The other Cleveland loss was administered by the Detroit Lions, the Browns' opponent in the upcoming championship game. The Browns nevertheless headed into the title match with a lot of guns at their side. Lou Groza and Horace Gillom fueled the potent kicking game, Otto Graham and Mac Speedie hooked up in a dangerous passing combination, Marion Motley came back from knee injuries to have a good year, and Len Ford and Bill Willis kept the defensive backbone stiff.

New York Giants—Safetyman Em Tunnell gave the New York defense a lot of offensive power. Very fast and shifty, Tunnell returned interceptions, punts, and kickoffs with such electric flair that he actually outgained the league rushing leader in yards gained. Dan Towler of Los Angeles won the running title with 894 yards, while Tunnell, never lining up on offense, ran for 924 yards on his various returns. But even with Tunnell, Tom Landry, and Arnie Weinmeister starring on defense, and with Eddie Price sparking the offense, the Giants still finished short of the title in second place.

Philadelphia Eagles—The Eagles broke in a new coach and lost their greatest star during the pre-season. Jim Trimble took over the coaching reigns but never had the pleasure of using Steve Van Buren in action. In a training-camp scrimmage, a hard tackle ripped up Van Buren's knee, ending the powerful halfback's glowing career. Trimble rallied his forces, however, and drove the Eagles through the season fast on the heels of the Cleveland Browns. The new coach installed Bobby Thomason, a pick-up from Green Bay, as quarterback, and youngsters Bud Grant and Bobby Walston as the offensive ends, shifted tough Pete Pihos to the defensive unit, and was smart enough to leave Chuck Bednarik alone at linebacker.

Pittsburgh Steelers—The Steelers came out of the dark ages this year, led by a coach from the 1930s. Joe Bach had coached the team back in 1935-36 and had been canned by owner Art Rooney, at whose wedding he had been best man. Now Rooney rehired him, saying, "I never should have let him get away in the first place. That bull-headed Dutchman was the best organizer I ever had." An all-out passing attack from the T-formation is what Bach organized for this year. The single wing went out, and passer Jim Finks came off the bench to take over as quarterback. The Steelers still lost more than they won, but their new system generated more offense and more excitement.

Chicago Cardinals—The Cards won three of their first four games but hardly had the personnel to keep that pace up. Under freshman coach Joe Kuharich, the Cards dropped seven of their last eight contests, as the offense had problems scoring more than two touchdowns. Quarterback Charlie Trippi ran the ball well but could not give the team a real passing threat; essentially, he was a halfback playing quarterback out of necessity. Filling one halfback spot was rookie Ollie Matson, a marvelous overall athlete who combined power and speed in his 6' 2", 205-pound frame. The bronze medal winner in the 400-meter sprint at the 1952 Olympics, Matson returned kicks explosively, gave the Cards a breakaway threat in the backfield, and played defense often enough and well enough to win All-Pro honors as a cornerback.

Washington Redskins—Owner George Marshall canned another coach, replacing Dick Todd with Curly Lambeau before the regular season even began, but the fans were concerned more with the imminent departure of Sammy Baugh. Breaking his hand in a pre-season contest, Slingin' Sam spent most of the year holding the ball on place kicks and coaching little Eddie LeBaron in the tricks of quarterbacking. Like most recent seasons, this campaign was a dismal one, with the Redskins riding a six-game losing streak heading into their final two games. At this point Baugh returned to the starting lineup for his pro finale and rallied the team to beat the Giants 27-17 and knock them out of the conference race, and then Sammy wrapped up his career as the Redskins topped the Eagles 27-21.

NATIONAL CONFERENCE

Detroit Lions—The Lions dropped two of their first three contests, but then Bobby Layne and his merry men roared back to deadlock the Rams for the National Conference title. Even with Doak Walker hurt most of the year, the Lion attack moved on Bob Hoernschemeyer's legs, Layne's arm, receiver Cloyce Box's hands, and blocker Lou Creekmur's shoulders. The Lions also developed a defensive unit which fans would recognize and applaud as much as the offense. Big Les Bingaman, quick and clever as a fox, held down the middle of the line, mean Thurman McGraw piled up runners and passers from his tackle spot, and Jack Christiansen, Yale Lary, Jim David, and Jim Smith gave the Lion secondary strength matched only by the Giants—all of which was enough to give the Lions their first conference crown when, on a foggy Sunday in Los Angeles, they ended the Rams' reign with a 31-21 playoff triumph.

Los Angeles Rams—All of a sudden the high-riding Rams were rolling in the dirt. The defense wasn't holding anybody, head coach Joe Stydahar was feuding with chief assistant Hamp Pool, and the club lost its last three pre-season games. When the Browns murdered the Rams 37-7 on opening day, the internal feud came to a head. Stydahar quit, leaving the club in Pool's control, and the Rams quickly dropped to a 1-3 mark. Then, in mid-October, the defending champs regrouped. The defense shaped up, thanks largely to defensive backs Herb Rich and Night Train Lane, a free-agent rookie who picked off a record fourteen passes, while the offense regained its top stride.

San Francisco '49ers—With five straight wins to begin the year, the '49ers were on the way to a conference crown until one play turned it all around. With the '49ers ahead of the Bears 17-10 in the second half, Frankie Albert dropped back deep to punt. When he got the ball, he instead decided to run for the first down, only to be dropped short of the needed yardage. The Bears quickly drove to a tying touchdown and won the game on a last-minute 48-yard field goal by George Blanda. After that, relations between Albert and coach Buck Shaw were strained, contributing to a second-half collapse by the team. Thus, a season highlighted by the arrival of Hugh McElhenny, a long-legged halfback who was the best open-field runner since Red Grange and George McAfee, ended in bitterness.

Green Bay Packers—The Packers got away from their limp-rag image of recent years, showing enough life to break even in wins and losses for the first time since 1947. The team for once signed a strong crop of rookies. Tackle Dave Hanner, a jolly bald-headed man who used his tremendous strength on the field, and smart back Bobby Dillon, who was blind in one eye, shored up a defense which sorely needed reinforcements, while Babe Parilli and Billy Howton broke into the offensive lineup. Parilli shared the quarterback job with Tobin Rote, and both men found the sure-handed Howton open for many key passes. The veterans on the squad may have had a funny feeling when the Packers, for the first time ever in a regular season game, lined up against a Curly Lambeau team. Sentiment went out the window, though, as the Packers defeated Lambeau's Redskins 35-20.

Chicago Bears—Four years ago George Halas had a marvelous stable of quarterbacks in Sid Luckman, Johnny Lujack, and Bobby Layne; now Luckman was gracefully retired, Lujack had quit with a bad shoulder, and Layne was leading the Detroit Lions to a league championship. Stuck with a pair of unproven quarterbacks in George Blanda and Steve Romanik, the Bears dropped below the .500 mark for the first time since 1945 and only the second time since 1929.

Dallas Texans—It was a promising venture that ended as a joke. The league transferred the New York Yanks franchise to Dallas, but after four echo-filled games in the Cotton Bowl, the club owners threw in the sponge and turned the operation over to the league. For the second half of the season the Texans traveled the country as a road team, using Hershey, Pennsylvania, as their home base for loosely organized practices. With morale lower than the floor, the Texans shocked the world by beating the Bears 27-23 on Thanksgiving Day in Akron, Ohio, before a rousing throng of 3,000 paid customers for the only win of their existence.

FINAL TEAM STATISTICS

OFFENSE

	CHI.B.	CHI.C.	CLEVE.	DALLAS	DET.	G.BAY	L.A.	N.Y.	PHIL.	PITT.	S.F.	WASH.
FIRST DOWNS:												
Total	194	176	228	172	219	197	205	155	181	187	213	206
by Rushing	90	91	105	79	92	84	92	78	72	67	97	95
by Passing	87	74	119	78	115	95	102	66	98	110	104	90
by Penalty	17	11	4	15	12	18	11	11	11	10	12	21
RUSHING:												
Number	411	477	394	381	442	405	411	442	434	384	421	467
Yards	1543	1748	1786	1397	1780	1485	1811	1636	1370	1204	1905	1655
Average Yards	3.8	3.7	4.5	3.7	4.0	3.7	4.4	3.7	3.2	3.1	4.5	3.5
Touchdowns	11	10	12	13	14	11	17	11	10	12	16	10
PASSING:												
Attempts	347	289	374	352	362	337	329	280	361	365	342	286
Completions	141	124	184	149	171	161	167	121	154	167	177	147
Completion Percentage	40.6	42.9	49.2	42.3	47.2	47.8	50.8	43.2	42.7	45.8	51.8	51.4
Gross Yards	2015	1512	2839	1807	2495	2688	2438	1713	2272	2504	2371	2127
Yards Lost Tackled	280	301	273	423	287	314	146	321	307	313	396	387
Net Yards	1735	1211	2566	1384	2208	2374	2292	1392	1965	2191	1975	1740
Avg. Yards per Attempt (Gross)	5.8	5.2	7.6	5.1	6.9	8.0	7.4	6.1	6.3	6.9	6.9	7.4
Avg. Yards per Comp. (Gross)	14.3	12.2	15.4	12.1	14.6	16.7	14.6	14.2	14.8	15.0	13.4	14.5
Touchdowns	18	10	22	12	24	26	17	16	13	21	19	20
Interceptions	27	22	26	20	28	25	31	22	19	23	23	21
Percent Intercepted	7.8	7.6	7.0	8.5	7.7	7.4	9.4	7.9	5.3	6.3	6.7	7.3
PUNTS:												
Number	66	76	61	84	66	65	59	82	83	81	68	68
Average Yards	42.4	37.3	45.7	36.7	44.1	40.7	42.8	41.0	40.2	43.0	42.6	41.3
PUNT RETURNS:												
Number	41	49	55	21	35	38	38	41	53	47	40	41
Yards	223	450	410	160	520	370	527	502	446	557	436	452
Average Yards	5.4	9.2	7.5	7.6	14.9	9.7	13.9	12.2	8.4	11.9	10.9	11.0
Touchdowns	0	0	1	0	3	0	2	0	2	3	2	2
KICKOFF RETURNS:												
Number	50	45	47	67	39	52	40	45	47	39	36	51
Yards	1168	1008	823	1586	882	1085	967	999	1173	1128	798	1052
Average Yards	23.4	22.4	17.5	23.7	22.6	20.9	24.2	22.2	25.0	28.9	22.2	20.6
Touchdowns	2	2	0	0	0	0	0	0	0	2	0	0
INTERCEPTION RETURNS:												
Number	20	25	22	28	32	22	38	28	20	27	17	18
Yards	281	232	250	307	477	254	712	371	290	409	252	301
Average Yards	14.1	9.3	11.4	14.2	14.9	11.5	18.7	13.3	14.5	15.1	14.8	16.7
Touchdowns	0	0	0	1	2	1	4	1	3	1	1	1
PENALTIES												
Number	73	87	85	67	77	83	100	64	80	57	79	69
Yards	583	743	744	621	799	739	891	626	747	520	628	669
FUMBLES:												
Number	39	33	21	35	17	40	32	27	43	27	26	32
Number Lost	24	23	11	25	10	31	17	14	22	14	13	17
POINTS:												
Total	245	172	310	182	344	295	349	234	252	300	285	240
PAT Attempts	31	24	35	27	43	39	45	29	31	42	37	32
PAT Made	31	22	35	20	42	37	44	28	31	36	35	26
FG Attempts	28	18	33	4	28	21	19	17	20	11	12	10
FG Made	8	2	19	0	14	6	11	10	11	4	6	4
Percent FG Made	28.6	11.1	57.6	0.0	50.0	28.6	57.9	58.8	55.0	36.4	50.0	40.0
Safeties	2	0	1	0	1	0	1	1	1	0	2	2

DEFENSE

	CHI.B.	CHI.C.	CLEVE.	DALLAS	DET.	G.BAY	L.A.	N.Y.	PHIL.	PITT.	S.F.	WASH.
FIRST DOWNS:												
Total	209	176	186	197	195	202	212	189	187	224	167	189
by Rushing	98	85	78	97	74	87	93	72	81	100	81	96
by Passing	98	82	95	90	105	97	97	110	93	115	76	80
by Penalty	13	9	13	10	16	18	22	7	13	9	10	13
RUSHING:												
Number	463	455	411	421	353	415	441	404	408	460	412	426
Yards	1921	1588	1386	2334	1145	1507	1613	1303	1396	1744	1566	1817
Average Yards	4.1	3.5	3.4	5.5	3.2	3.6	3.7	3.2	3.4	3.8	3.8	4.3
Touchdowns	20	8	11	17	8	16	10	8	12	8	10	19
PASSING:												
Attempts	311	307	348	310	382	340	360	337	343	369	342	275
Completions	160	149	141	150	182	162	161	162	157	167	151	121
Completion Percentage	51.4	48.5	40.5	48.4	47.6	47.6	44.7	48.1	45.8	45.3	44.2	44.0
Gross Yards	2350	1942	2028	2394	2421	2205	2252	2514	2164	2765	1929	1817
Yards Lost Tackled	259	177	339	346	321	443	369	336	470	220	291	237
Net Yards	2091	1765	1689	2048	2100	1762	1883	2178	1754	2545	1638	1580
Avg. Yards per Attempt (Gross)	7.6	6.3	5.8	7.7	6.3	6.5	6.3	7.5	6.3	7.5	5.6	6.6
Avg. Yards per Comp. (Gross)	14.7	13.0	14.4	16.0	13.3	13.6	14.0	15.5	13.8	16.6	12.8	15.0
Touchdowns	16	16	17	31	15	17	18	18	19	24	15	12
Interceptions	20	25	22	28	32	22	38	28	20	27	17	18
Percent Intercepted	6.4	8.1	6.3	9.0	8.4	6.5	10.6	8.3	5.8	7.3	5.0	6.5
PUNTS:												
Number	67	69	84	50	73	72	66	84	88	73	78	55
Average Yards	41.5	42.1	40.6	43.3	40.6	39.0	42.8	40.5	41.3	42.4	41.3	41.2
PUNT RETURNS:												
Number	38	54	39	36	41	36	22	52	55	50	29	47
Yards	612	600	307	399	305	281	178	348	571	483	359	610
Average Yards	16.1	11.1	7.9	11.1	7.4	7.8	8.1	6.7	10.4	9.7	12.4	13.0
Touchdowns	2	1	0	3	0	1	0	2	1	1	1	3
KICKOFF RETURNS:												
Number	36	35	47	35	63	51	48	49	44	56	52	42
Yards	906	774	1107	732	1338	1312	1149	357	1111	1024	1242	1017
Average Yards	25.2	22.1	23.6	20.9	21.2	25.7	23.9	19.5	25.3	18.3	23.9	24.2
Touchdowns	2	2	0	0	0	0	0	0	0	2	0	0
INTERCEPTION RETURNS:												
Number	27	22	26	30	28	25	31	22	19	23	23	21
Yards	323	240	389	632	364	339	518	306	187	426	299	203
Average Yards	12.0	10.9	15.0	21.1	13.0	13.6	16.7	13.9	9.8	18.5	13.0	9.7
Touchdowns	0	0	1	4	1	3	3	0	1	0	0	2
PENALTIES												
Number	91	91	46	91	62	96	77	66	74	71	65	91
Yards	795	883	425	926	596	752	746	518	699	623	530	817
FUMBLES:												
Number	44	30	23	27	34	28	26	35	36	26	31	32
Number Lost	26	18	14	18	25	19	18	17	19	13	18	16
POINTS:												
Total	326	221	213	427	192	312	234	231	271	273	221	287
PAT Attempts	43	28	27	56	25	40	30	30	37	35	27	37
PAT Made	40	25	25	54	21	39	28	27	31	35	27	35
FG Attempts	20	20	11	24	15	20	16	19	14	18	21	23
FG Made	8	8	4	11	7	11	6	8	4	8	10	10
Percent FG Made	40.0	40.0	36.3	45.8	46.7	55.0	37.5	42.1	28.6	44.4	47.6	43.5
Safeties	2	2	1	2	0	1	0	0	0	2	1	0

1952
CHAMPIONSHIP GAME
December 28 at Cleveland
(Attendance 50,934)

Roaring Back After Seventeen Years

The Browns came into the game with a long injury list but hurt themselves more with mistakes during the contest. Dub Jones, Mac Speedie, and John Kissell all missed the game, and Lou Groza played with cracked ribs, which made him miss all three of his field-goal attempts. The Browns made their first mistake in the opening quarter when Horace Gillom got off a poor 22-yard punt which gave Detroit the ball at mid-field. Bobby Layne then took the Lions into the end zone after eight plays, with the touchdown scored by Layne himself on a quarterback sneak. The Detroit defense meanwhile kept the Browns scoreless, and the halftime score was 7-0 in favor of the Lions. Doak Walker, the versatile halfback out most of the season with injuries, lengthened the lead to 14-0 in the third quarter with a 67-yard dash through a massive hole opened on the right side. After the kickoff, the Browns went on their only extended drive of the game, driving 67 yards to make the score 14-7. Then the mistakes started flowing. The Browns had a first down on the Detroit 5-yard line, only to lose the ball on downs. In the fourth quarter, Ken Carpenter fumbled a punt, which the Lions converted into a Pat Harder field goal and their first NFL title in seventeen years.

SCORING

DETROIT	0	7	7	3	–17
CLEVELAND	0	0	7	0	– 7

First Quarter
None

Second Quarter
Det. Layne, 2 yard rush; PAT – Harder (kick)

Third Quarter
Det. Walker, 67 yard rush; PAT – Harder (kick)
Cle. Jagade, 7 yard rush; PAT – Groza (kick)

Fourth Quarter
Det. Harder, 36 yard Field Goal

TEAM STATISTICS

DET.		CLE.
10	First Downs – Total	22
8	– by Rushing	15
2	– by Passing	7
0	– by Penalty	0
34	Rushing – Attempts	34
199	– Yards	227
5.9	– Average Yards	6.7
10	Passing – Attempts	36
7	– Completions	20
68	– Yards	191
0	– Had Intercepted	1
6	Punts – Number	3
40.8	– Average Distance	43.3
18	Punt Return Yards	18
0	Fumbles – Number	1
0	– Times Lost Ball	1
3	Penalties – Number	7
25	– Yards Penalized	65
0	Giveaways	2
2	Takeaways	0
+2	Difference	–2

INDIVIDUAL STATISTICS

RUSHING	No.	Yds.	Avg.	RECEIVING	No.	Yds.	Avg.
Cleveland							
Jagade	15	104	6.9	Bumg'ner	4	43	10.8
Motley	6	74	12.3	Lavelli	4	23	5.8
Graham	7	23	3.3	Renfro	4	26	6.5
Carpenter	3	13	4.3	Motley	3	21	7.0
Renfro	3	13	4.3	Brewster	2	53	26.5
				Carpenter	2	7	3.5
				Gillom	1	8	8.0
Detroit							
Walker	10	97	9.7	Harder	2	18	9.0
Layne	9	47	5.2	Walker	2	11	5.5
Harder	8	28	3.5	Hart	1	15	15.0
Horn'meyer	7	27	3.9	Swiacki	1	14	14.0
				Box	1	10	10.0

PASSING

	Att.	Comp	Comp Pct.	Yds	Yds/ Att	Yds/ Comp
Cleveland						
Graham	35	20	57.1	191	5.5	9.6
Motley	1	0	00.0	0	–	–
Detroit						
Layne	9	7	77.8	68	7.6	9.7
Walker	1	0	00.0	0	–	–

CLEVELAND BROWNS 8-4-0 Paul Brown

Scores of Each Game		
37	LOS ANGELES	7
21	Pittsburgh	20
9	NEW YORK	17
49	Philadelphia	7
19	WASHINGTON	15
6	Detroit	17
28	CHIC. CARDS	13
29	PITTSBURGH	28
20	PHILADELPHIA	28
48	Washington	24
10	Chic. Cards	0
34	New York	37

Use Name	Pos.	Hgt	Wgt	Age	Int	Pts
Lou Groza	OT	6'3"	235	28		89
John Sandusky	OT	6'1"	250	26		
Bob Gain	DT-OT	6'3"	245	24		3
Abe Gibron	OG	5'11"	240	26		
Lin Houston	OG	6'	215	31		
Joe Skibinski	OG	5'11"	220	24		
Frank Gatski	C	6'3"	240	30		
Bill Willis	DG	6'2"	215	31		
Len Ford	DE	6'4"	240	26		6
George Young	DE	6'3"	215	28		2
Jerry Helluin	DT	6'2"	280	22		
John Kissell	DT	6'3"	247	29		
Darrell Palmer	DT	6'2"	235	30		
Walt Michaels	LB	6'	215	23	4	
Tommy Thompson	LB	6'1"	220	25	1	
Ed Sharkey	OG-LB	6'3"	240	25		
Hal Herring	C-LB	6'1"	210	28		
Emerson Cole (to Chi B)	DB-LB	6'2"	215	24		
Tommy James	DB	5'10"	185	28	4	
Warren Lahr	DB	5'11"	185	28	5	
Don Phelps	DB	5'11"	185	27		
Bert Rechichar	DB	6'1"	200	22	6	
Don Shula	DB	5'11"	190	22		
Otto Graham	QB	6'1"	195	30		24
George Ratterman	QB	6'1"	185	25		
Ken Carpenter	HB	6'	190	26		30
Sherman Howard	HB	5'11"	195	28		18
Dub Jones	HB	6'4"	205	27		36
Ray Renfro	HB	6'1"	185	21		
Rex Bumgardner	DB-HB	5'11"	193	28	2	
Chick Jagade	FB	6'	210	25		18
Marion Motley	LB-FB	6'1"	238	32		18
Darrell Brewster	OE	6'3"	210	22		6
Dante Lavelli	OE	6'	192	29		24
Mac Speedie	OE	6'3"	205	32		30
Horace Gillom	DE-OE	6'1"	225	31		6

Tony Adamle – Voluntarily retired
Ken Gorgal – Military Service
Carl Taseff – Military Service
Art Spinney – Military Service

NEW YORK GIANTS 7-5-0 Steve Owen

Scores of Each Game		
24	Dallas	6
31	Philadelphia	7
17	Cleveland	9
23	CHIC. CARDS	24
10	PHILADELPHIA	14
28	Chic. Cards	6
23	SAN FRANCISCO	14
3	GREEN BAY	17
14	Washington	10
7	Pittsburgh	63
17	WASHINGTON	27
37	CLEVELAND	34

Use Name	Pos.	Hgt	Wgt	Age	Int	Pts
Dick Yelvington	OT	6'2"	230	25		
Hal Mitchell	OG-OT	6'1"	225	20		
Ray Krouse	DT-OT	6'3"	250	25		
Bill Albright	OG	6'1"	232	23		
Ray Beck	OG	6'2"	220	20		
George Kennard	OG	6'	205	23		
Bob Patton	OG	6'	226	24		
John Rapacz	C	6'4"	260	27		
Tex Coulter	OT-C	6'4"	260	27		
Jim Duncan	DE	6'2"	205	26	2	
Ray Poole	DE	6'2"	215	30	1	56
Horrace Sherrod	OE-DE	6'	190	25		6
Al DeRogatis	DT	6'4"	240	25		
Arnie Weinmeister	DT	6'4"	235	29		2
Jon Baker	LB	6'2"	215	29		
John Cannady	LB	6'2"	225	28	2	
Joe Sulaitis	OG-BB-LB	6'2"	215	31		
Pat Knight	DE-BB-LB	6'2"	200	23		
Don Menasco	DB	6'	185	22	4	
Harmon Rowe	DB	6'	182	29	1	
Em Tunnell	DB	6'1"	183	30	7	
Tom Landry	QB-DB	6'1"	195	27	8	12
John Amberg	HB-DB	5'11"	195	24	2	
Fred Benners	QB	6'3"	195	22		
Chuck Conerly	QB	6'1"	185	28		2
Kyle Rote	HB	6'	195	23		24
Joe Scott	HB	6'1"	195	26		24
George Thomas	HB	6'1"	185	24		
Frank Gifford	DB-HB	6'1"	190	22	1	
Eddie Price	FB	5'11"	190	26		30
Bob Hudson	OE	6'4"	215	22		
Bob McChesney	OE	6'2"	190	25		36
Bill Stribling	OE	6'1"	205	25		30
Kelley Mote	DE-OE	6'2"	190	29		
Bob Wilkinson	HB-DB-OE	6'3"	215	25		12

Bill Austin – Military Service
Randy Clay – Military Service

PHILADELPHIA EAGLES 7-5-0 Jim Trimble

Scores of Each Game		
31	Pittsburgh	25
7	NEW YORK	31
26	PITTSBURGH	21
7	CLEVELAND	49
14	New York	10
10	Green Bay	12
38	WASHINGTON	20
10	CHIC. CARDS	7
28	Cleveland	20
22	Chic. Cards	28
38	DALLAS	21
21	Washington	27

Use Name	Pos.	Hgt	Wgt	Age	Int	Pts
Lum Snyder	OT	6'5"	225	22		
Frank Wydo	OT	6'4"	235	28		
Bill Horrell	OG	5'11"	222	22		
Maury Nipp	OG	6'	218	22		
John Magee	OG	5'10"	220	29		
Dan Rogas	OG	6'1"	230	25		
Joe Tyrrell	OG	5'11"	216	23		
Ken Farragut	LB-C	6'4"	240	24		
Bucko Kilroy	OT-DG	6'2"	240	31		
Bob Oristaglio	DE	6'2"	215	28		
Jack Zilly	DE	6'2"	215	30		
Norm Willey	OG-DE	6'2"	225	25	1	
Mike Jarmoluk	DT	6'5"	240	29	2	12
Vic Sears	DT	6'3"	230	34	1	6
Chuck Bednarik	C-LB	6'3"	230	27	2	
Wayne Robinson	C-LB	6'2"	220	22		
Ebert Van Buren	HB-LB	6'2"	210	27		8
Bob Stringer	FB-LB	6'1"	200	22	1	
Russ Craft	DB	5'9"	175	32	1	6
Joe Restic	DB	6'2"	180	22		
Joe Sutton	DB	5'11"	180	28	3	
Neil Ferris (from WAS)	HB-DB	5'11"	185	24		6
Bibbles Bawel	OE-DB	6'1"	186	22	8	6
Adrian Burk	QB	6'2"	190	24		
Fred Enke	QB	6'1"	200	27		
Bobby Thomason	QB	6'1"	195	23		
Ralph Goldston	HB	5'11"	195	24		18
Al Pollard	HB	6'	197	24		6
Don Stevens	HB	5'9"	176	25		6
Frank Ziegler	HB	5'11"	175	28		24
John Brewer	FB	6'4"	230	24		12
John Huzvar	FB	6'4"	240	23		12
Jim Parmer	FB	6'	190	25		
Bud Grant	OE	6'3"	198	25		42
Bobby Walston	OE	6'	185	23		82
Pete Pihos	DE-OE	6'1"	215	28		12

Neill Armstrong – Canadian Football League
Roscoe Hansen – Military Service
Toy Ledbetter – Military Service
Red O'Quinn – Canadian Football League
Ray Romero – Military Service
Steve Van Buren – Knee Injury

PITTSBURGH STEELERS 5-7-0 Joe Bach

Scores of Each Game		
25	PHILADELPHIA	31
20	CLEVELAND	21
21	Philadelphia	26
24	WASHINGTON	28
34	Chic. Cards	28
24	Washington	23
6	DETROIT	31
28	Cleveland	29
17	CHIC. CARDS	14
63	NEW YORK	7
24	San Francisco	7
14	Los Angeles	28

Use Name	Pos.	Hgt	Wgt	Age	Int	Pts
Dick Fugler	OT	6'2"	235	22		
George Hughes	OG-OT	6'1"	225	27		
Rudy Andabaker	OG	6'	205	23		
Earl Murray	OG	6'2"	240	26		
Pete Ladygo	LB-OG	6'2"	215	24		
Bill Walsh	C	6'2"	230	25		
George Hays	DE	6'2"	210	27	1	12
Bill McPeak	DE	6'1"	200	27		
George Tarasovic	DE	6'4"	235	23		
Lou Ferry	DT	6'2"	245	25		6
Ernie Stautner	DT	6'1"	230	27		
Dale Dodrill	LB	6'1"	210	27		6
Darrell Hogan	LB	5'10"	210	26	4	6
John Schweder	OG-LB	6'1"	225	25		
Lou Levanti	C-LB	6'1"	215	26		
Frank Sinkovitz	C-LB	6'1"	220	29	1	
Jerry Shipkey	FB-LB	6'1"	215	27	2	
Jim Brandt	DB	6'1"	200	24		
Howard Hartley	DB	6'	185	28	4	
Claude Hipps	DB	6'1"	188	26	3	
Ed Kissell	DB	6'1"	190	24	5	
Jack Butler	OE-DB	6'	195	24	7	12
Pat Brady	QB	6'1"	195	24		
Jim Finks	QB	6'	175	25		30
Gary Kerkorian	QB	5'11"	185	23		47
Tom Calvin	HB	6'	200	26		
Lynn Chandnois	HB	6'2"	195	28		30
Ray Mathews	HB	6'	185	23		43
Ed Modzelewski	FB	6'	210	23		18
Fran Rogel	FB	5'11"	200	25		18
Jack Spinks	FB	6'	238	22		
Dick Hensley	OE	6'4"	210	26		12
Elbie Nickel	OE	6'1"	195	29		54
George Sulima	OE	6'2"	200	25		6

CHICAGO CARDINALS 4-8-0 Joe Kuharich

Scores of Each Game		
7	WASHINGTON	23
21	CHIC. BEARS	10
17	Washington	6
24	New York	23
28	PITTSBURGH	34
6	NEW YORK	28
13	Cleveland	28
7	Philadelphia	10
14	Pittsburgh	17
28	PHILADELPHIA	22
0	CLEVELAND	10
7	Chic. Bears	10

Use Name	Pos.	Hgt	Wgt	Age	Int	Pts
Volney Peters	DT-OT	6'4"	225	24		6
Jack Jennings	OT	6'4"	245	25		
Bill Fischer	OG	6'2"	245	25		
Ed Listopad	OG	6'2"	230	22		
Mike Sikora	OG	6'2"	230	24		
Jack Simmons	C	6'4"	230	26		
Tom Bienemann	DE	6'3"	220	24		
Bob Dove	DE	6'2"	225	31		
Tony Klimek	DE	5'11"	200	26	2	
Don Joyce	DT	6'3"	250	22		
Mike Mergen	DT	6'5"	245	23		
Jerry Groom	C-DT	6'3"	235	23		
Eli Popa	LB	5'10"	202	21		
Bill Svoboda	LB	6'	210	25	2	
Fred Wallner	LB	6'2"	230	23		
Gordon Polofsky	OG-LB	6'1"	218	21		
Leo Sanford	OG-LB	6'1"	220	23	2	
John Panelli	FB-LB	5'11"	200	26	3	
Roy Barni	DB	5'11"	185	25	6	
Billy Gay	DB	5'11"	180	24		
S. J. Whitman	DB	5'11"	185	26	3	
Don Paul	HB-DB	6'	180	26		6
Ray Ramsey	OE-DB	6'2"	165	31	5	
Don Panciera	QB	6'1"	185	29		
Charlie Trippi	HB-QB	6'	185	29		24
Elmer Angsman	HB	5'11"	200	26		6
Billy Cross	HB	5'6"	150	23		24
Joe Geri	HB	5'10"	185	28		28
Johnny Karras	HB	5'11"	187	24		6
Emil Sitko	HB	5'8"	185	28		6
Wally Triplett	HB	5'10"	175	25		
Ralph Pasquariello	FB	6'2"	235	25		
Ollie Matson	DB-FB	6'2"	205	22	2	54
Cliff Anderson	OE	6'2"	215	22		12
Fran Polsfoot	OE	6'3"	200	25		
Don Stonesifer	OE	6'	200	25		
Ralph Thomas	DE-OE	5'11"	195	22		

John Hock – Military Service

WASHINGTON REDSKINS 4-8-0 Curly Lambeau

Scores of Each Game		
23	Chic. Cards	7
20	Green Bay	35
6	CHIC. CARDS	17
28	Pittsburgh	24
15	Cleveland	19
23	PITTSBURGH	24
20	Philadelphia	38
17	SAN FRANCISCO	23
10	NEW YORK	14
24	CLEVELAND	48
27	New York	17
27	PHILADELPHIA	21

Use Name	Pos.	Hgt	Wgt	Age	Int	Pts
Joe Moss	OT	6'1"	221	22		
Laurie Niemi	DT-OT	6'1"	257	27		
Ed Bagdon	OG	5'10"	213	26		7
Buddy Brown	OG	6'1"	212	25		
Jim Clark	OG	6'1"	230	23		
Knox Ramsey (from PHI)	LB-OG	6'1"	225	26		
Gene Pepper	OT-DT-DG-OG	6'2"	237	25		
Tony Momsen	C	6'1"	215	25		
Dick Woodward	C	6'2"	225	26		
Jim Ricca	OT-DG	6'4"	267	25		
Ed Berrang	DE	6'2"	211	27	2	
Jerry Hennessey	DE	6'2"	224	26		2
John Yonaker	DT-DE	6'5"	225	31		
Lou Karras	DT	6'4"	234	25		
Paul Lipscomb	DT	6'5"	255	29	1	
Ed Ecker	OT-DT	6'7"	265	29		
Al DeMao	C-LB	6'2"	220	32		
George Buksar	FB-LB	6'	220	26		24
Chuck Drazenovich	FB-LB	6'1"	226	25	3	18
Joe Tereshinski	OE-LB	6'2"	217	28	1	
Dick Alban	DB	6'	185	23	1	
Andy Davis	DB	6'	188	25		
Billy Cox	HB-DB	6'3"	184	23	3	
Harry Dowda	HB-DB	6'2"	200	28	2	6
Johnny Williams	HB-DB	5'11"	170	25	5	18
Sammy Baugh	QB	6'2"	175	38		
Eddie LeBaron	QB	5'9"	173	22		18
Harry Gilmer	HB-QB	6'	172	26		6
Choo-Choo Justice	HB	5'10"	178	28		6
Johnny Papit	HB	6'	188	24		6
Julie Rykovich	HB	6'2"	200	28		13
Sam Venuto	HB	6'1"	195	24		6
Jack Cloud	FB	5'10"	220	27		
Leon Heath	FB	6'1"	198	24		18
Bob Sykes	FB	6'1"	218	24		
Gene Brito	OE	6'1"	215	27		12
Hugh Taylor	OE	6'4"	188	29		72

Bill Dudley – Voluntarily Retired
Rob Goode – Military Service
Hall Haynes – Military Service
Harry Ulinski – Military Service
Slug Witucki – Military Service
Walt Yowarsky – Military Service

CLEVELAND BROWNS

RUSHING

Last Name	No.	Yds	Avg	TD
Motley	104	444	4.3	1
Carpenter	72	408	5.7	3
Jagade	57	373	6.5	2
Jones	65	270	4.2	2
Graham	42	130	3.1	4
Howard	34	95	2.8	0
Bumgardner	9	38	4.2	0
Renfro	10	26	2.6	0
Ratterman	1	2	2.0	0

RECEIVING

Last Name	No.	Yds	Avg	TD
Speedie	62	911	15	5
Jones	43	651	15	4
Lavelli	21	336	16	4
Carpenter	16	136	9	1
Motley	13	213	16	2
Howard	11	219	20	3
Jagade	9	203	23	1
Brewster	4	117	29	1
Gillom	4	45	11	1
Renfro	1	8	8	0

PUNT RETURNS

Last Name	No.	Yds	Avg	TD
Renfro	22	169	7	0
Carpenter	10	139	14	1
Rechichar	14	58	4	0
Bumgardner	4	24	6	0
Phelps	5	15	3	0
Skibinski	0	5	0	0

KICKOFF RETURNS

Last Name	No.	Yds	Avg	TD
Carpenter	11	234	21	0
Renfro	8	130	16	0
Cole	5	99	20	0
Bumgardner	5	89	18	0
Motley	3	88	29	0
Rechichar	4	70	18	0
Jagade	3	58	19	0
Sharkey	2	24	12	0
Howard	1	22	22	0
Michaels	1	16	16	0
Brewster	1	11	11	0
Skibinski	1	8	8	0
Gillom	1	2	2	0
Gain	1	0	0	0
Gibron	1	0	0	0

PASSING – PUNTING – KICKING

PASSING	Att	Comp	%	Yds	Yd/Att	TD	Int–%	RK
Graham	364	181	50	2816	7.7	20	24– 7	2
Ratterman	6	2	33	20	3.3	1	2–33	
Jones	2	1	50	3	1.5	1	0– 0	
Motley	2	0	0	0	0.0	0	0– 0	

PUNTING	No	Avg
Gillom	61	45.7

KICKING	XP	Att	%	FG	Att	%
Groza	32	32	100	19	33	58
Gain	3	3	100	0	0	0

NEW YORK GIANTS

RUSHING

Last Name	No.	Yds	Avg	TD
Price	183	748	4.1	5
Rote	103	421	4.1	2
Gifford	38	116	3.1	0
Conerly	27	115	4.3	0
Scott	38	107	2.8	3
Landry	7	40	5.7	1
Amberg	7	27	3.9	0
Wilkinson	26	26	1.0	0
Thomas	6	18	3.0	0
Benners	5	16	3.2	0
McChesney	2	2	1.0	0

RECEIVING

Last Name	No.	Yds	Avg	TD
Stribling	26	399	15	5
McChesney	21	430	20	6
Rote	21	240	11	2
Scott	14	251	18	1
Price	11	36	3	0
Wilkinson	6	148	24	2
Gifford	5	36	7	0
Mote	4	45	11	0
Hudson	4	40	10	0
Sulaitis	4	31	8	0
Amberg	3	40	13	0
Coulter	1	9	9	0
Thomas	1	8	8	0

PUNT RETURNS

Last Name	No.	Yds	Avg	TD
Tunnell	30	411	14	0
Landry	10	88	9	0
Gifford	1	3	3	0

KICKOFF RETURNS

Last Name	No.	Yds	Avg	TD
Tunnell	15	364	24	0
Scott	7	190	27	0
Gifford	4	124	31	0
Rote	6	110	18	0
Sulaitis	4	91	23	0
Sherrod	2	33	17	0
McChesney	3	28	9	0
Price	1	21	21	0
Landry	1	20	20	0
Stribling	1	11	11	0
Kennard	1	0	0	0
Beck	0	7	0	0

PASSING – PUNTING – KICKING

PASSING	Att	Comp	%	Yds	Yd/Att	TD	Int–%	RK
Conerly	169	82	49	1090	6.5	13	10– 6	9
Benners	58	25	43	320	5.5	0	5– 9	
Landry	47	11	23	172	3.7	1	7–15	
Rote	4	2	50	113	28.3	1	0– 0	
Gifford	2	1	50	18	9.0	1	0– 0	

PUNTING	No	Avg
Landry	82	41.0

KICKING	XP	Att	%	FG	Att	%
Poole	26	27	96	10	17	59
Conerly	2	2	100	0	0	0

PHILADELPHIA EAGLES

RUSHING

Last Name	No.	Yds	Avg	TD
Huzvar	105	349	3.3	2
Goldston	65	210	3.2	3
Brewer	50	188	3.8	2
Pollard	55	186	3.4	1
Ziegler	67	172	2.6	2
Stevens	33	95	2.9	0
Thomason	17	88	5.2	0
Burk	7	28	4.0	0
Enke	14	25	1.8	0
Parmer	12	23	1.9	0
Ferris	11	22	2.0	1
Stringer	2	5	2.5	0
E. Van Buren	7	1	0.1	0

RECEIVING

Last Name	No.	Yds	Avg	TD
Grant	56	997	18	7
Walston	26	469	18	3
Stevens	13	174	13	0
Huzvar	13	37	2	0
Pihos	12	219	18	1
Ziegler	8	120	15	2
Pollard	8	59	7	0
Brewer	5	19	4	0
E. Van Buren	4	73	18	0
Bawel	2	60	30	0
Enke	2	19	10	0
Goldston	2	12	6	0
Parmer	2	10	5	0
Ferris	1	8	8	0
Stringer	1	4	4	0

PUNT RETURNS

Last Name	No.	Yds	Avg	TD
Bawel	34	261	8	1
Stevens	16	172	11	1
Walston	2	13	7	0
Ferris	2	11	6	0
E. Van Buren	1	0	0	0

KICKOFF RETURNS

Last Name	No.	Yds	Avg	TD
Pollard	21	528	25	0
Stevens	16	433	27	0
Ziegler	4	82	21	0
Ferris	3	76	25	0
Sears	1	45	45	0
Parmer	2	33	17	0
Stringer	1	22	22	0
Craft	1	18	18	0
E. Van Buren	1	12	12	0

PASSING – PUNTING – KICKING

PASSING	Att	Comp	%	Yds	Yd/Att	TD	Int–%	RK
Thomason	212	95	45	1334	6.3	8	9– 4	10
Burk	82	37	45	561	6.8	4	5– 6	
Enke	67	22	33	377	5.6	1	5– 7	

PUNTING	No	Avg
Burk	83	40.2

KICKING	XP	Att	%	FG	Att	%
Walston	31	31	100	11	20	55

PITTSBURGH STEELERS

RUSHING

Last Name	No.	Yds	Avg	TD
Mathews	66	315	4.8	0
Chandnois	97	298	3.1	1
Rogel	84	230	2.7	3
Modzelewski	82	195	2.4	3
Spinks	22	94	4.3	0
Finks	23	37	1.6	5
Kerkorian	2	20	10.0	0
Calvin	7	14	2.0	0
Shipley	1	1	1.0	0

RECEIVING

Last Name	No.	Yds	Avg	TD
Nickel	55	884	16	9
Mathews	33	543	16	5
Chandnois	28	370	13	2
Hensley	12	217	18	2
Rogel	12	140	12	0
Modzelewski	11	109	10	0
Sulima	9	176	20	1
Butler	3	37	12	2
Spinks	2	22	11	0
Calvin	2	4	2	0
Hughes	0	2	0	0

PUNT RETURNS

Last Name	No.	Yds	Avg	TD
Mathews	26	397	15	2
Chandnois	17	111	7	0
Hartley	1	34	34	0
Calvin	2	12	6	0
Hays	1	3	3	1

KICKOFF RETURNS

Last Name	No.	Yds	Avg	TD
Chandnois	17	599	35	2
Mathews	14	367	26	0
Calvin	5	120	24	0
Brandt	1	24	24	0
Murray	1	14	14	0
Ladygo	1	4	4	0

PASSING – PUNTING – KICKING

PASSING	Att	Comp	%	Yds	Yd/Att	TD	Int–%	RK
Finks	336	158	47	2307	6.9	20	19– 6	4
Mathews	13	3	23	104	8.0	0	1– 8	
Kerkorian	11	5	45	79	7.2	1	3–27	
Brady	3	1	33	14	4.7	0	0– 0	
Chandnois	2	0	0	0	0.0	0	0– 0	

PUNTING	No	Avg
Brady	17	43.2
Finks	4	39.0

KICKING	XP	Att	%	FG	Att	%
Kerkorian	35	41	85	4	9	44
Kissell	0	0	0	0	2	0
Mathews	1	1	100	0	0	0

CHICAGO CARDINALS

RUSHING

Last Name	No.	Yds	Avg	TD
Trippi	72	350	4.9	4
Sitko	88	348	4.0	1
Cross	71	347	4.9	2
Matson	96	344	3.6	3
Pasquariello	48	129	2.7	0
Angsman	46	114	2.5	0
Geri	20	50	2.5	0
Karras	24	42	1.8	0
Paul	6	28	4.7	0
Panciera	4	6	1.5	0
Peters	1	–7	–7.0	0

RECEIVING

Last Name	No.	Yds	Avg	TD
Stonesifer	54	617	11	0
Cross	17	234	14	2
Anderson	11	191	17	2
Matson	11	187	17	3
Pasquariello	7	46	7	0
Trippi	5	66	13	0
Karras	5	63	13	1
Paul	4	32	8	1
Angsman	4	22	6	1
Ramsey	3	27	9	0
Sitko	2	16	8	0

PUNT RETURNS

Last Name	No.	Yds	Avg	TD
Cross	21	177	8	0
Paul	10	97	10	0
Matson	9	86	10	0
Karras	4	47	12	0
Triplett	2	26	13	0
Barni	2	17	9	0
Peters	1	0	0	0

KICKOFF RETURNS

Last Name	No.	Yds	Avg	TD
Matson	20	624	31	2
Cross	9	169	19	0
Karras	4	69	17	0
Paul	3	54	18	0
Stonesifer	2	27	14	0
Sitko	1	19	19	0
Mergen	1	13	13	0
Pasquariello	1	13	13	0
Anderson	1	8	8	0
Peters	1	4	4	0
Fischer	1	0	0	0

PASSING – PUNTING – KICKING

PASSING	Att	Comp	%	Yds	Yd/Att	TD	Int–%	RK
Trippi	181	84	46	890	4.9	5	13– 7	12
Panciera	96	35	36	582	6.1	5	9– 9	

PUNTING	No	Att
Geri	29	37.7
Trippi	16	36.8

KICKING	XP	Att	%	FG	Att	%
Geri	22	24	92	2	18	11

WASHINGTON REDSKINS

RUSHING

Last Name	No.	Yds	Avg	TD
Heath	90	388	4.3	2
Gilmer	100	365	3.7	0
Rykovich	94	361	3.8	1
LeBaron	43	164	4.0	2
Justice	36	129	3.6	0
Papit	34	102	3.0	0
Drazenovich	29	66	2.3	3
Cloud	7	21	3.0	0
Venuto	4	16	4.0	1
Sykes	4	10	2.5	0
Dowda	6	5	.8	0
Williams	2	3	1.5	0
Buksar	3	3	1.0	0
Baugh	1	1	1.0	0
Cox	3	–1	–0.3	0

RECEIVING

Last Name	No.	Yds	Avg	TD
Taylor	41	961	23	12
Heath	12	146	6	1
Brito	21	270	13	2
Rykovich	16	283	18	1
Gilmer	15	143	10	1
Justice	11	106	10	1
Drazenovich	4	62	16	0
Papit	3	71	24	1
Dowda	3	20	7	1
Cox	2	19	10	0
Tereshinski	2	19	10	0
Buksar	2	3	2	0
Williams	1	13	13	0
Sykes	1	5	5	0
Karras	1	–2	–2	0

PUNT RETURNS

Last Name	No.	Yds	Avg	TD
Williams	24	366	15	2
Justice	12	47	4	0
Gilmer	3	28	9	0

KICKOFF RETURNS

Last Name	No.	Yds	Avg	TD
Williams	20	486	24	0
Justice	10	209	21	0
Gilmer	7	157	22	0
Buksar	4	43	11	0
Venuto	2	28	14	0
Papit	1	25	25	0
Cloud	1	18	18	0
Brito	2	5	3	0
Lipscomb	1	5	5	0

PASSING – PUNTING – KICKING

PASSING	Att	Comp	%	Yds	Yd/Att	TD	Int–%	RK
LeBaron	194	95	49	1420	7.3	14	15– 8	5
Gilmer	58	31	53	555	9.6	4	4– 7	
Baugh	33	20	61	152	4.6	2	1– 3	
Justice	1	0	0	0	0.0	0	1–100	

PUNTING	No	Att
LeBaron	51	42.2
Justice	11	39.2
Cox	5	35.4
Baugh	1	48.0

KICKING	XP	Att	%	FG	Att	%
Buksar	15	18	83	3	7	43
Bagdon	4	6	67	1	3	33
LeBaron	6	7	86	0	0	0
Rykovich	1	1	100	0	0	0

DETROIT LIONS 9-3-0 Buddy Parker

Scores of Each Game		
3	San Francisco	17
17	Los Angeles	14
0	SAN FRANCISCO	28
24	LOS ANGELES	16
52	Green Bay	17
17	CLEVELAND	6
31	Pittsburgh	6
43	DALLAS	13
23	Chic. Bears	24
48	GREEN BAY	24
45	CHIC. BEARS	21
41	Dallas	6
	Playoff	
31	Los Angeles	21

Use Name	Pos.	Hgt	Wgt	Age	Int	Pts
Gus Cifelli	OT	6'4"	240	26		
Bob Miller	DT-OT	6'3"	235	22		
Stan Campbell	OG	6'	215	22		
Dick Stanfel	OG	6'3"	240	25		
Lou Creekmur	OT-OG	6'4"	230	25		
Vince Banonis	C	6'1"	235	30		
Les Bingaman	DG	6'3"	285	27	1	
Blaine Earon	DE	6'1"	195	23		
Sonny Gandee (from DAL)	DE	6'1"	210	23		2
Jim Doran	OE-DE	6'2"	195	24		6
Pat Summerall	OE-DE	6'4"	220	22		
Thurman McGraw	DT	6'5"	235	25		
John Prchlik	DT	6'4"	235	27		
Dick Flanagan	OG-LB	6'	215	25	1	
Jim Martin	OG-LB	6'2"	220	28		
Lavern Torgeson	C-LB	6'	210	23	5	6
Jim David	DB	5'11"	172	25	7	
Don Doll	DB	5'10"	185	25	2	
Jim Hill	DB	6'	185	23	1	
Yale Lary	DB	6'	180	21	4	6
Jack Christiansen	HB-DB	6'1"	180	23	2	24
Clyde Scott (from PHI)	HB-DB	6'	175	28	1	
Jim Smith	HB-DB	6'1"	195	27	9	6
Tom Dublinski	QB	6'2"	190	22		
Jim Hardy	QB	6'	180	30		1
Bobby Layne	QB	6'1"	190	25		8
Byron Bailey	HB	5'10"	185	22		12
Jug Girard	HB	5'11"	175	25		24
Bob Hoernschemeyer	HB	5'11"	195	26		24
Doak Walker	HB	5'11"	173	25		14
Ollie Cline	FB	6'	200	26		6
Pete D'Alonzo	FB	5'10"	210	22		
Pat Harder	FB	5'11"	202	30		85
Cloyce Box	OE	6'4"	220	28		90
Leon Hart	OE	6'5"	262	23		24
Bill Swiacki	OE	6'2"	195	27		6

Jim Cain – Military Service
Dorne Dibble – Military Service

LOS ANGELES RAMS 9-3-0 Hamp Pool

Scores of Each Game		
7	Cleveland	37
14	DETROIT	17
30	Green Bay	28
16	Detroit	24
31	CHIC. BEARS	7
42	DALLAS	20
27	Dallas	6
40	Chic. Bears	24
35	SAN FRANCISCO	9
34	San Francisco	21
45	GREEN BAY	27
28	PITTSBURGH	14
	Playoff	
21	DETROIT	31

Use Name	Pos.	Hgt	Wgt	Age	Int	Pts
Tom Dahms	OT	6'5"	240	24		
Don Simensen	OT	6'2"	220	25		
Len Teeuws	OT	6'4"	235	25		
Dick Daugherty	OG	6'1"	214	23		
Bill Lange	OG	6'1"	245	25		
Bud McFadin	OG	6'3"	245	24		
Harry Thompson	DE-OG	6'2"	225	25		
Leon McLaughlin	C	6'2"	228	26		
Stan West	DG	6'2"	240	25	1	
Larry Brink	DE	6'5"	240	29		
Andy Robustelli	DE	6'1"	220	26	1	12
Ken Casner	DT	6'2"	245	22		6
Charlie Toogood	DT	6'	233	24		
Jim Winkler	DT	6'2"	248	25		
Duane Putnam	OG-LB	6'	215	24		
Don Paul	C-LB	6'1"	230	27	2	
Tank Younger	HB-FB-LB	6'3"	226	24	2	6
Jack Dwyer	DB	5'11"	176	25	4	12
Night Train Lane	DB	6'1"	190	24	14	14
Herb Rich	DB	5'11"	180	23	8	6
Woodley Lewis	HB-DB	6'	195	27	1	12
Jerry Williams	HB-DB	5'10"	176	28	4	
Norb Hecker	OE-DB	6'2"	190	25	1	
Don Klosterman	QB	5'10"	180	22		
Norm Van Brocklin	QB	6'1"	200	26		
Bob Waterfield	QB	6'1"	200	32		83
Paul Barry	HB	6'	200	26		6
Carl Mayes	HB	6'	190	22		
Skeets Quinlan	HB	5'11"	175	24		18
Vitamin Smith	HB	5'8"	180	28		36
Jack Myers	FB	6'2"	202	27		6
Dan Towler	FB	6'2"	226	24		60
Bob Carey	OE	6'5"	215	24		12
Tom Fears	OE	6'2"	215	28		36
Crazy Legs Hirsch	OE	6'2"	190	28		24

Bob Boyd – Military Service

SAN FRANCISCO FORTY NINERS 7-5-0 Buck Shaw

Scores of Each Game		
17	DETROIT	3
37	Dallas	14
28	Detroit	0
40	Chic. Bears	16
48	DALLAS	21
17	CHIC. BEARS	20
14	New York	23
23	Washington	17
9	Los Angeles	35
21	LOS ANGELES	34
7	PITTSBURGH	24
24	GREEN BAY	14

Use Name	Pos.	Hgt	Wgt	Age	Int	Pts
Ray Collins	DT-OT	5'11"	230	24		
Leo Nomellini	DT-OT	6'3"	265	27		
Bruno Banducci	OG	5'11"	220	30		
Nick Feher	OG	6'	225	25		
Jerry Smith	LB-OG	6'1"	230	22		
Bill Johnson	C	6'3"	240	26		
Ed Henke	DE	6'3"	225	24		
Pat O'Donahue	DE	6'1"	200	22		7
Charley Powell	DE	6'2"	215	20		2
Al Endriss	OE-DE	6'2"	200	23		
Don Campora	DT	6'3"	265	25		
Al Carapella	OT-DT	6'	235	25		
Bob Toneff	OT-DT	6'2"	252	22		
Hardy Brown	LB	6'	196	28	1	
Don Burke	OG-LB	6'	235	26	1	6
Visco Grgich	OG-LB	5'11"	225	29		
Bob Momsen	OG-LB	6'3"	225	22		2
Pete Wissman	C-LB	6'	220	28		
Jim Cason	DB	6'	168	25	2	
Rex Berry	HB-DB	5'11"	180	26	2	
Sam Cathcart	HB-DB	6'	175	27	3	
Lowell Wagner	HB-DB	6'	195	28	6	
Jim Powers	LB-QB-DB	6'	185	24	2	
Frankie Albert	QB	5'10"	170	32		6
Y. A. Tittle	QB	6'	190	25		
Ben Aldridge	HB	6'	195	25		6
Joe Arenas	HB	5'11"	180	26		6
Hugh McElhenny	HB	6'1"	198	23		60
Johnny Strzykalski	HB	5'9"	190	29		
Bob White	HB	5'11"	174	23		18
J. R. Boone	DB-HB	5'8"	163	26		6
Bob Meyers	FB	6'2"	284	22		
Joe Perry	FB	6'	210	25		48
Norm Standlee	FB	6'2"	240	33		
Bill Jessup	OE	6'1"	200	23		6
Gordie Soltau	OE	6'2"	195	27		94
Billy Wilson	OE	6'3"	195	25		18

Werl Lillywhite – Military Service
Clay Mathews – Military Service
Pete Schabarum – Military Service
Dave Sparks – Military Service

GREEN BAY PACKERS 6-6-0 Gene Ronzani

Scores of Each Game		
14	CHIC. BEARS	24
35	WASHINGTON	20
28	LOS ANGELES	30
24	Dallas	14
17	DETROIT	52
12	PHILADELPHIA	10
41	Chic. Bears	28
17	New York	3
42	DALLAS	14
24	Detroit	48
27	Los Angeles	45
14	San Francisco	24

Use Name	Pos.	Hgt	Wgt	Age	Int	Pts
Dick Afflis	OT	6'	250	23		
Steve Dowden	OT	6'2"	235	23		
Bob Dees	DT-OT	6'4"	245	22		
Ray Bray	OG	6'	240	35		
Steve Ruzich	OG	6'2"	225	24		
Dave Stephenson	OG	6'2"	235	26		
Dick Logan	DT-OG	6'2"	225	22		
Jay Rhodemyre	C	6'1"	210	30		
John Martinkovic	DE	6'3"	235	25		12
Ab Wimberly	DE	6'1"	215	26	1	
Dave Hanner	DT	6'2"	245	23		
Tom Johnson	DT	6'2"	230	22		
Howie Ruetz	DT	6'3"	255	24		
Wash Serini	OG-DT-DG	6'2"	240	28		
Deral Teteak	OG-LB	5'10"	210	23	1	
George Schmidt	C-LB	6'2"	230	25		
Bob Forte	HB-LB	6'	205	30	4	
Hal Faverty	C-DE-LB	6'2"	220	25		
Bobby Dillon	DB	6'1"	185	22	4	
Marvin Johnson (from LA)	DB	5'11"	185	24	2	
Ace Loomis	DB	6'1"	190	24	4	6
Dom Moselle	DB	6'	192	26	3	
Dan Sandifer	DB	6'2"	190	25	2	
Clarence Self	DB	5'8"	180	27	1	
Babe Parilli	QB	6'1"	190	22		6
Tobin Rote	QB	6'3"	200	24		18
Tony Canadeo	HB	5'11"	190	33		18
Billy Grimes	HB	6'1"	195	25		
Lindy Pearson (from DET)	HB	6'	200	23		
Breezy Reid	HB	5'10"	185	25		24
Bill Robinson	HB	6'	195	23		
Fred Cone	FB	5'11"	198	26		53
Bobby Jack Floyd	FB	6'	210	23		6
Bill Reichardt	FB	5'11"	210	22		26
Billy Howton	OE	6'2"	185	22		78
Jim Keane	OE	6'4"	215	28		6
Bob Mann	OE	5'11"	170	28		36
Carl Elliott	DE-OE	6'4"	215	25		6

Larry Coutre – Military Service
Len Szafaryn – Military Service
Clayton Tonnemaker – Military Service

CHICAGO BEARS 5-7-0 George Halas

Scores of Each Game		
24	Green Bay	14
10	Chic. Cards	21
38	DALLAS	20
16	SAN FRANCISCO	40
7	Los Angeles	31
20	San Francisco	17
28	GREEN BAY	41
24	LOS ANGELES	40
24	DETROIT	23
23	Dallas	27
21	Detroit	45
10	CHIC. CARDS	7

Use Name	Pos.	Hgt	Wgt	Age	Int	Pts
Bulldog Turner	OG-OT	6'1"	235	33		
George Connor	LB-OT	6'3"	240	27	2	
Dick Barwegan	OG	6'1"	230	29		
Ed Bradley	OG	6'	215	26		
Bob Moser	C	6'3"	240	23		
Wayne Hansen	OG-C	6'2"	233	24		
Jack Hoffman	DE	6'5"	230	23	1	
Ed Sprinkle	OE-DE	6'1"	207	28		6
Bill Bishop	DT	6'4"	248	21		
Fred Williams	DT	6'4"	250	22	1	
Bob Cross	OT-DT	6'4"	240	21		
Jerry Weatherley	LB	6'5"	220	23	3	
Herman Clark	OG-LB	6'3"	260	21	1	
Frank Dempsey	OG-LB	6'3"	234	27	1	
John Hoffman	OE-LB	6'2"	212	26	2	
Bill George	OG-DT-LB	6'2"	235	21		
Al Campana	HB-DB	5'11"	180	26		
Jim Dooley	HB-DB	6'4"	200	22	5	
Jimmy Lesane	HB-DB	5'10"	172	21		
Billy Stone	HB-DB	6'	194	26	1	24
Don Kindt	FB-DB	6'1"	208	26	3	2
Steve Romanik	QB	6'1"	190	28		
Bob Williams	QB	6'1"	195	23		
George Blanda	DB-QB	6'1"	200	24		54
Babe Dimancheff	HB	5'11"	175	30		12
George Gulyanics	HB	6'	200	31		
Chuck Hunsinger	HB	6'	188	27		12
Eddie Macon	HB	6'	175	24		12
Wilford White	HB	5'9"	172	24		7
Leon Campbell	FB	6'	197	25		6
Kayo Dottley	FB	6'1"	200	24		24
Curley Morrison	FB	6'2"	215	26		24
Bill McColl	OE	6'4"	230	22		12
Bill Wightkin	DE-OE	6'3"	238	25		12
Gene Schroeder	DB-OE	6'3"	190	23		36

Stu Clarkson – Canadian Football League
Johnny Lujack – Shoulder Injury

DALLAS TEXANS 1-11-0 Jimmy Phelan

Scores of Each Game		
6	NEW YORK	24
14	SAN FRANCISCO	37
20	Chic. Bears	38
14	GREEN BAY	24
21	San Francisco	48
20	Los Angeles	42
6	LOS ANGELES	27
13	Detroit	43
14	Green Bay	42
27	CHIC. BEARS	23
21	Philadelphia	38
6	DETROIT	41

Use Name	Pos.	Hgt	Wgt	Age	Int	Pts
Ken Jackson	OT	6'2"	225	23		
Jim Lansford	OT	6'3"	235	22		
Hamp Tanner	OT	6'2"	280	25		
Sisto Averno	OG	5'11"	235	26		
Weldon Humble	OG	6'1"	225	31		
George Robison	OG	6'2"	215	21		
John Wozniak	OG	6'	220	31		
Brad Ecklund	C	6'3"	215	30		
Art Tait	DE	5'11"	205	23		
Gino Marchetti	OT-DE	6'4"	235	26		6
Barney Poole	OE-DE	6'2"	225	29		
Joe Campanella	DT	6'2"	235	21		
Don Colo	DT	6'3"	252	27	1	
Art Donovan	DT	6'2"	260	27		
Chubby Grigg	DT	6'2"	280	26		9
Joe Soboleski	DT	6'	210	26		
Pat Cannamela	LB	6'	195	23		8
Keever Jankovich	LB	6'	215	23		
Joe Reid	DG-LB	6'3"	225	22	1	
Keith Flowers	C-LB	6'	211	21	1	3
Jerry Davis	DB	5'10"	180	30	3	6
Dick McKissack	DB	6'2"	208	26		
Will Sherman	DB	6'2"	197	23	1	
Billy Baggett	HB-DB	5'11"	175	23	1	6
Johnny Petitbon	HB-DB	5'11"	185	21	5	
Tom Keane	OE-DB	6'1"	190	25	10	
Stan Williams	OE-DB	6'2"	195	23	5	6
Bob Celeri	QB	5'10"	180	25		6
Chuck Ortmann	QB	6'1"	190	23		
Frank Tripucka (from CHI C)	QB	6'2"	180	24		18
Hank Lauricella	HB	5'11"	175	22		
Buddy Young	HB	5'5"	180	26		30
George Taliaferro	QB-HB	5'11"	200	25		12
Dick Hoerner	FB	6'4"	220	30		12
Zollie Toth	FB	6'2"	215	28		24
Dan Edwards	OE	6'1"	195	26		
Gene Felker	OE	6'1"	198	23		6
Ray Pelfrey (to CHI C)	OE	6'	190	24		12
Dick Wilkins	OE	6'2"	195	26		18

Mike McCormack – Military Service

DETROIT LIONS

RUSHING

Last Name	No.	Yds	Avg	TD
Hoernschemeyer	106	457	4.3	4
Layne	94	411	4.4	1
Harder	81	244	3.0	2
Girard	61	222	3.6	2
Christiansen	19	148	7.8	2
Walker	26	106	4.1	0
Bailey	19	74	3.9	2
Doran	1	36	36.0	0
Cline	13	36	2.8	1
Hardy	5	16	3.2	0
Smith	3	12	4.0	0
Hart	3	10	3.3	0
D'Alonzo	5	7	1.4	0
Dublinski	1	3	3.0	0
Scott	2	–2	–1.0	0

RECEIVING

Last Name	No.	Yds	Avg	TD
Box	42	924	22	15
Hart	32	376	12	4
Girard	17	316	19	2
Swiacki	17	213	13	1
Hoernschemeyer	17	139	8	0
Harder	14	142	10	1
Walker	11	90	8	0
Doran	10	147	15	1
Christiansen	3	32	11	0
Cline	2	45	23	0
Bailey	2	28	14	0
D'Alonzo	2	4	2	0
Scott	1	21	21	0
Smith	1	18	18	0

PUNT RETURNS

Last Name	No.	Yds	Avg	TD
Christiansen	15	322	21	2
Lary	16	182	11	1
Scott	3	14	5	0
Hill	1	2	2	0

KICKOFF RETURNS

Last Name	No.	Yds	Avg	TD
Christiansen	16	409	26	0
Lary	12	303	25	0
Scott	3	68	23	0
Girard	2	31	16	0
Earon	3	25	8	0
Bailey	1	23	23	0
Hoernschemeyer	1	23	23	0
Miller	1	0	0	0

PASSING – PUNTING – KICKING

PASSING	Att	Comp	%	Yds	Yd/Att	TD	Int–%	RK
Layne	287	139	48	1999	7.0	19	20– 7	6
Hardy	59	28	48	434	7.4	3	5– 8	
Dublinski	6	1	17	39	6.5	0	1–17	
Hoernschemeyer	4	2	50	14	3.5	2	1–25	
Girard	4	0	0	0	0.0	0	0– 0	
Walker	2	1	50	9	4.5	0	1–50	

PUNTING	No	Avg
Smith	61	44.7
Lary	5	36.2

KICKING	XP	Att	%	FG	Att	%
Harder	34	35	97	11	23	48
Walker	5	5	100	3	5	60
Layne	2	2	100	0	0	0
Hardy	1	1	100	0	0	0

LOS ANGELES RAMS

RUSHING

Last Name	No.	Yds	Avg	TD
Towler	156	**894**	5.7	**10**
Younger	63	331	5.3	1
Quinlan	52	224	4.3	1
Smith	57	133	2.3	3
Lewis	19	114	6.0	0
Myers	27	82	3.0	1
Williams	11	65	5.9	0
Mayes	5	2	0.4	0
Fears	1	0	0.0	0
Barry	2	–1	–0.5	0
Klosterman	1	–9	–9.0	0
Van Brocklin	7	–10	–1.4	0
Waterfield	9	–14	–1.6	1

RECEIVING

Last Name	No.	Yds	Avg	TD
Fears	48	600	13	6
Carey	36	539	15	1
Hirsch	25	590	24	4
Smith	16	254	16	3
Quinlan	14	265	19	2
Younger	12	73	6	0
Towler	11	68	6	0
Barry	2	43	22	1
Myers	2	1	1	0
Waterfield	1	5	5	0

PUNT RETURNS

Last Name	No.	Yds	Avg	TD
Lewis	19	351	18	2
Quinlan	14	167	12	0
Williams	1	9	9	0
Smith	2	0	0	0
Rich	1	0	0	0
Towler	1	0	0	0

KICKOFF RETURNS

Last Name	No.	Yds	Avg	TD
Quinlan	17	440	26	0
Lewis	16	345	22	0
Smith	5	158	32	0
Towler	1	9	9	0
West	1	0	0	0

PASSING – PUNTING – KICKING

PASSING	Att	Comp	%	Yds	Yd/Att	TD	Int–%	RK
Van Brocklin	205	113	**55**	1736	**8.5**	14	17– 8	3
Waterfield	109	51	47	655	6.0	3	11–10	15
Klosterman	10	3	30	47	4.7	0	3– 3	
Quinlan	4	0	0	0	0.0	0	0– 0	
Smith	1	0	0	0	0.0	0	0– 0	

PUNTING	No	Avg
Waterfield	30	42.5
Van Brocklin	29	43.1

KICKING	XP	Att	%	FG	Att	%
Waterfield	**44**	45	98	11	18	**61**
Carey	0	0	0	0	1	0

SAN FRANCISCO FORTY-NINERS

RUSHING

Last Name	No.	Yds	Avg	TD
Perry	158	725	4.6	8
McElhenny	98	684	7.0	6
Arenas	44	183	4.2	0
Albert	22	87	4.0	1
Boone	24	72	3.0	0
Strzykalski	16	53	3.3	0
Aldridge	13	36	2.8	0
White	24	33	1.4	1
Cathcart	6	21	3.5	0
Standlee	2	8	4.0	0
Berry	1	7	7.0	0
Nomellini	1	5	5.0	0
Meyers	1	2	2.0	0
Tittle	11	–11	–1.0	0

RECEIVING

Last Name	No.	Yds	Avg	TD
Soltau	55	774	14	7
McElhenny	26	367	14	3
Boone	25	461	18	1
Wilson	23	304	13	3
Perry	15	81	5	0
White	12	173	14	2
Jessup	6	108	18	1
Arenas	5	47	9	1
Aldridge	4	22	6	1
Cathcart	2	15	8	0
Henke	1	13	13	0
Wagner	1	6	6	0
Strzykalski	1	4	4	0
Banducci	1	–4	–4	0

PUNT RETURNS

Last Name	No.	Yds	Avg	TD
McElhenny	20	284	14	1
Boone	11	66	6	0
Arenas	7	40	6	0
Cathcart	1	23	23	0
O'Donahue	1	23	23	1

KICKOFF RETURNS

Last Name	No.	Yds	Avg	TD
McElhenny	18	396	22	0
Arenas	11	291	26	0
Brown	2	31	16	0
Burke	1	25	25	0
Cathcart	1	20	20	0
Nomellini	1	18	18	0
O'Donahue	2	17	9	0

PASSING – PUNTING – KICKING

PASSING	Att	Comp	%	Yds	Yd/Att	TD	Int–%	RK
Tittle	208	106	51	1407	6.8	11	12– 6	6
Albert	129	71	55	964	7.5	8	10– 8	8
Perry	2	0	0	0	0.0	0	0– 0	
Arenas	1	0	0	0	0.0	0	0– 0	
Cathcart	1	0	0	0	0.0	0	1–100	
Powers	1	0	0	0	0.0	0	0– 0	

PUNTING	No	Avg
Albert	68	42.6

KICKING	XP	Att	%	FG	Att	%
Soltau	34	36	94	6	12	50
O'Donahue	1	1	100	0	0	0

GREEN BAY PACKERS

RUSHING

Last Name	No.	Yds	Avg	TD
Rote	58	313	5.4	2
Cone	70	276	3.9	2
Floyd	61	236	3.9	1
Canadeo	65	191	2.9	2
Reid	58	156	2.7	2
Reichardt	39	121	3.1	1
Parilli	32	106	3.3	1
Grimes	17	59	3.5	0
Robinson	3	4	1.3	0
Pearson	5	2	0.4	0
Self	0	21	21.0	0

RECEIVING

Last Name	No.	Yds	Avg	TD
Howton	53	**1231**	23	13
Mann	30	517	17	6
Keane	18	191	11	1
Reid	12	250	21	2
Elliott	12	114	10	1
Floyd	11	129	12	0
Canadeo	9	86	10	1
Cone	8	98	12	1
Reichardt	5	18	4	0
Rote	1	28	28	1
Pearson	1	16	16	0

PUNT RETURNS

Last Name	No.	Yds	Avg	TD
Grimes	18	179	10	0
Loomis	8	83	10	0
Moselle	7	77	11	0
Dillon	2	22	11	0
Sandifer	2	5	3	0
Canadeo	1	4	4	0

KICKOFF RETURNS

Last Name	No.	Yds	Avg	TD
Grimes	18	422	23	0
Loomis	10	207	21	0
Self	3	85	28	0
Moselle	5	83	17	0
Floyd	5	75	15	0
Canadeo	2	62	31	0
Robinson	2	49	25	0
Cone	2	23	12	0
Dees	1	20	20	0
Reichardt	1	19	19	0
Schmidt	1	14	14	0
Martinkovic	1	0	0	0

PASSING – PUNTING – KICKING

PASSING	Att	Comp	%	Yds	Yd/Att	TD	Int–%	RK
Parilli	177	77	44	1416	8.0	13	17–10	11
Rote	157	82	52	1268	8.1	13	8– 5	**1**
Forte	2	2	100	4	2.0	0	0– 0	
Canadeo	1	0	0	0	0.0	0	0– 0	

PUNTING	No	Avg
Parilli	65	40.7

KICKING	XP	Att	%	FG	Att	%
Cone	32	34	94	1	1	100
Reichardt	5	5	100	5	20	25

CHICAGO BEARS

RUSHING

Last Name	No.	Yds	Avg	TD
Morrison	95	367	3.9	3
Dottley	65	302	4.6	3
Stone	50	196	3.9	2
Macon	30	194	6.5	1
Hunsinger	58	139	2.4	0
Dimancheff	17	106	6.2	1
Blanda	20	104	5.2	1
Campbell	24	76	3.2	0
B. Williams	11	33	3.0	0
Campana	9	14	1.6	0
Kindt	3	13	4.3	0
Romanik	6	9	1.5	0
Lesane	1	5	5.0	0
Gulyanics	2	4	2.0	0
Dooley	1	0	0.0	0
White	19	–19	–1.0	0

RECEIVING

Last Name	No.	Yds	Avg	TD
Schroeder	39	660	17	6
McColl	20	277	14	2
Hunsinger	16	170	11	2
Stone	13	283	22	2
Morrison	10	129	13	1
Dottley	9	113	13	1
White	8	152	19	0
Macon	8	25	3	0
Wightkin	7	120	17	2
Dimancheff	5	69	1	1
Campbell	2	1	1	0
Jo. Hoffman	1	9	9	0
Campana	1	3	3	0
Sprinkle	1	2	2	1
Turner	1	2	2	0

PUNT RETURNS

Last Name	No.	Yds	Avg	TD
White	23	117	5	0
Macon	7	74	11	0
Lesane	9	25	3	0
Kindt	1	7	7	0
Dimancheff	1	0	0	0

KICKOFF RETURNS

Last Name	No.	Yds	Avg	TD
Hunsinger	15	308	21	0
Macon	9	299	33	1
White	5	134	27	0
Dimancheff	4	110	28	0
Campbell	2	106	53	1
Morrison	4	41	10	0
Stone	2	40	20	0
Sprinkle	4	39	10	0
Jo. Hoffman	2	34	17	0
Turner	1	29	29	0
McColl	1	0	0	0

PASSING – PUNTING – KICKING

PASSING	Att	Comp	%	Yds	Yd/Att	TD	Int–%	RK
Blanda	131	47	36	664	5.1	8	11– 8	14
Romanik	126	49	39	772	6.1	4	11– 9	15
B. Williams	87	45	52	579	6.7	6	5– 6	
White	2	0	0	0	0.0	0	0– 0	
Lesane	1	0	0	0	0.0	0	0– 0	

PUNTING	No	Avg
Morrison	64	42.3
Williams	2	45.0

KICKING	XP	Att	%	FG	Att	%
Blanda	30	30	100	6	25	24
White	1	1	100	2	3	67

DALLAS TEXANS

RUSHING

Last Name	No.	Yds	Avg	TD
Taliaferro	100	419	4.2	1
Toth	82	266	3.2	4
Young	71	243	3.4	3
Hoerner	56	162	2.9	2
Celeri	17	135	7.9	0
Baggett	19	65	3.4	0
Lauricella	19	55	2.9	0
Tripucka	10	25	2.5	3
Ortmann	8	24	3.0	0

RECEIVING

Last Name	No.	Yds	Avg	TD
Wilkins	32	416	13	3
Young	22	269	12	2
Taliaferro	21	244	12	1
Pelfrey	20	264	13	2
Toth	13	54	4	0
Hoerner	10	172	17	0
Williams	9	123	14	0
Felker	6	63	11	1
Celeri	4	37	9	1
Keane	3	73	24	0
Baggett	3	41	14	1
Edwards	3	22	7	0
Poole	2	23	12	0
Marchetti	1	17	17	1
Petitbon	1	11	11	0
Wozniak	1	–1	–1	0

PUNT RETURNS

Last Name	No.	Yds	Avg	TD
Baggett	13	102	9	0
Young	6	35	6	0
Davis	1	11	11	0
Keane	1	8	8	0
Taliaferro	1	4	4	0

KICKOFF RETURNS

Last Name	No.	Yds	Avg	TD
Young	**23**	**643**	28	0
Baggett	**23**	567	25	0
Taliaferro	6	146	24	0
Jankovich	3	45	15	0
Campanella	3	40	13	0
Pelfrey	2	34	17	0
Hoerner	1	33	33	0
Lauricella	1	26	26	0
Tanner	1	19	19	0
Toth	1	18	18	0
Humble	1	17	17	0
Reid	1	17	17	0
Petitbon	1	11	11	0
Wozniak	1	4	4	0
Tait	1	0	0	0

PASSING – PUNTING – KICKING

PASSING	Att	Comp	%	Yds	Yd/Att	TD	Int–%	RK
Tripucka	186	91	49	809	4.3	3	17– 9	13
Celeri	75	31	40	490	6.5	3	3– 4	
Taliaferro	63	16	25	298	4.7	2	6–10	
Lauricella	22	11	50	177	8.1	4	2– 9	
Ortmann	15	5	33	73	4.9	0	1– 7	
Young	3	0	0	0	0.0	0	1–33	

PUNTING	No	Avg
Lauricella	58	35.1
Tripucka	36	36.7
Celeri	21	41.7

PASSING	XP	Att	%	FG	Att	%
Grigg	9	12	75	0	3	0
Cannamela	8	10	80	0	1	0
Flowers	3	5	60	0	0	0

1953 Bring on the Defense

This season's rookie class sprouted no spectacular runners or passers, but blockers and defenders who would star in the league for years made a mass debut. Offensive linemen like Rosey Brown, Jack Stroud, Ray Wietecha, Bob St. Clair, Jim Ringo, Harley Sewell, and Charlie Ane and defensive behemoths like Joe Schmidt, Doug Atkins, Big Daddy Lipscomb, Dick Modzelewski, and Bill Pellington excited crowds with the violence of their crunching blocks and punishing tackles. The offense had dominated the game in recent years, but now the defense was getting some brawny reinforcements to help it catch up.

The league itself got some help from the courts and from the citizens of Baltimore. Federal Judge Allan K. Grim ruled that the TV blackout of home games did not violate the anti-trust laws, thus giving legal approval to Commissioner Bert Bell's television policy. The citizens of Baltimore did their share to help the NFL by buying 15,000 season's tickets for the new Baltimore Colts, who took the place of the wandering Dallas Texans. With Carroll Rosenbloom at the head of the organization, the Colts drew an average attendance of 28,000 and gave the league twelve solid franchises. The Baltimore renaissance helped boost the total NFL attendance 5 percent more to another new record of 2,164,585. The one tragic footnote to the year came in March when Jim Thorpe, pro football's first superstar and its first league president, passed away.

EASTERN CONFERENCE

Cleveland Browns—Owner and founder Mickey McBride sold the team to Dave R. Jones, but the Browns kept right on winning under the new regime. Now at the peak of his powers, quarterback Otto Graham picked defenses apart like a safecracker and shot his arrow passes like another William Tell picking off apples. Mac Speedie jumped to the Canadian League, but Dante Lavelli still hauled in Graham's passes regularly. In addition, young halfback Ray Renfro showed talent both as a receiver and a runner. With Marion Motley's bad knees bothering him, Chick Jagade answered the call to duty at fullback, and the Cleveland defense as always was tough. The Browns rolled through their first eleven games in blitzkrieg fashion, but let up and dropped their finale 42-27 to the Eagles.

Philadelphia Eagles—When offensive end Bud Grant skipped up to Canada to play and eventually to begin a coaching career, Eagle pilot Jim Trimble replaced him by using Pete Pihos mostly on offense. A tough character who had played a lot at defensive end, Pihos nonetheless had sure hands which sucked in any passes thrown his way. With Pihos and Bobby Walston at the ends, quarterback Bobby Thomason kept the Eagles moving with a flood of passes. The defense, featuring pass-rushing Norm Willey and hard-tackling Chuck Bednarik, improved on last year's performance, and only an outstanding year by the Browns kept the surprising Eagles off the Eastern throne.

Washington Redskins—The world saw one last glimpse of Curly Lambeau's genius as he molded the Redskins into a very tough outfit down the stretch. Of the final six games, Washington won four and lost the other two by a grand total of four points. Lambeau used Eddie LeBaron at quarterback but kept the little man alive by spelling him often with rookie Jack Scarbath. Halfback Choo-Choo Justice pleasantly surprised the team by looking like the runner he was in college instead of like the lackluster pro he had been. Sparked by end Gene Brito, rookie tackle Dick Modzelewski, linebacker Chuck Drazenovich, and cornerback Don Doll, the defense shone in the second half of the season, with a 10-0 shutout of the Eagles. That triumph was Lambeau's 231st NFL victory and his last.

Pittsburgh Steelers—Owner Art Rooney still was waiting for his first NFL title after twenty-one years in the league. After World War II, Jock Sutherland had almost made it to the top with a hard-running single-wing attack, and now coach Joe Bach had the Steelers throwing the ball around the clock from the T-formation. Bach, unfortunately, did not even get as close as did Sutherland, with this club reaching the break-even point only by winning its last two games. After a good start, the offense had bogged down, so the defense had to carry the team to those final two victories.

New York Giants—Despite a fine catch of raw material for the offensive line in rookies Rosey Brown, Jack Stroud, and Ray Wietecha, the Giants were far from a finished masterpiece. With workhorse fullback Eddie Price hurt, the New York offense ground to a halt, with Sonny Grandelius, Kyle Rote, and Frank Gifford hardly able to take up the slack. The Giants put only 30 points on the scoreboard in their opening three losses, which shot all their hopes to pieces. Injuries and Ray Poole's jumping to Canada plagued the defense, and young Gifford often found himself going both ways as a running back and cornerback, wearing himself ragged in the process. One week from the end came the crowning humiliation, a 62-14 shellacking by the Cleveland Browns. The Mara family, owners and operators of the club, took action after the season by firing Steve Owen as coach after over thirty-one years at the helm, closing the book on a large chapter in Giant history.

Chicago Cardinals—Joe Stydahar's only previous port of call as a head coach had been at Los Angeles, where his Rams always finished on top. He was thus hardly prepared for the situation of the Chicago Cardinals, who won only a single game all year. Stydahar tried to install the same free-wheeling passing attack he had used in Los Angeles, but his passer here was neither Norm Van Brocklin nor Bob Waterfield but instead a very average quarterback named Jim Root. The only speed on the team marched off into the Army in the person of Ollie Matson, leaving Stydahar with no game-breaker to spark the attack. Through eleven games the Cards were winless, although they did manage a very satisfying tie against the coach's old charges, the Rams. But the Cards did save the best for last, whipping the Bears 24-17 in the finale to avoid a shutout for the year.

WESTERN CONFERENCE

Detroit Lions—Even though they were the defending champions, the Lions signed an immensely talented bunch of rookies. Offensive linemen Harley Sewell, Charlie Ane, and Ollie Spencer, tough linebacker Joe Schmidt, and halfback Gene Gedman all fit right in with this winning club. In addition, all the key veterans returned to drive for another title. Bobby Layne still ran the offense and inspired his teammates with his infectious enthusiasm, Bob Hoernschemeyer and Doak Walker again gave the club a pair of versatile halfbacks, and Lou Creekmur and Dick Stanfel kept up their good work in the offensive line. On defense, Les Bingaman guided his 300-pound body with an uncanny knack for smelling out plays, while Jack Christiansen had a nose for picking off enemy passes.

San Francisco '49ers—The '49ers jumped off to early wins over the Eagles and Rams but ran into disaster in their next game against the Lions. On a quarterback keeper play near the goal line, passer Y.A. Tittle was knocked out of action with a triple fracture of his cheekbone. Defensive back Jim Powers doubled as the back-up quarterback, and while he could not avoid a 24-21 loss to the Lions, he did drive his team to a 35-28 victory the next week against the Bears. In the rematch with the Lions, however, Detroit triumphed 14-10, practically ending San Francisco's title hopes.

Los Angeles Rams—Even with Bob Waterfield retired, the Rams felt strong enough to grab the Western Conference title back from the Lions, and they proved their point by beating Detroit in both their meetings. The only problem was that the Rams couldn't reach the same peak effort in all their games. They lost twice to San Francisco, once to the Bears, and settled for a tie with the lowly Cardinals. At their best, though, the Rams were a spectacularly exciting football team, with Norm Van Brocklin, Dan Towler, Skeets Quinlan, and Crazy Legs Hirsch the stars on offense and Andy Robustelli, Big Daddy Lipscomb, Don Paul, and Night Train Lane the defensive standouts.

Chicago Bears—No doubt about it, this was the worst Bear team ever. Bulldog Turner had retired, leaving none of the 1940-41 champions in action for this dismal 3-8-1 season, while the George Halas well of talent had dried up. Although there were a few good players, such as George Connor, Jim Dooley, Bill George, and Ed Sprinkle, they were scattered like diamonds in a pigsty. The once powerful backfield had no runners of note and an erratic quarterback in George Blanda, whose kicks hit the mark more often than his passes. On defense, the secondary especially needed patching up. But even with all these holes, the Bears still could recapture their old glory on occasion, as when they dealt a fatal blow to Los Angeles' title hopes by knocking the Rams off 24-21 late in the year.

Baltimore Colts—Only thirteen Dallas players caught on with the Colts, but among them were All-Pro cornerback Tom Keane and defensive linemen Gino Marchetti and Art Donovan, both of whom would be around when the team started winning championships. The Colts began the season in fine fashion, beating the Bears 13-9 as cornerback Bert Rechichar ran a George Blanda interception back 39 yards for a touchdown and also kicked a record 56-yard field goal in his first NFL attempt. The Colts slipped back into the pack by losing their last seven games, but this time the Colts were here to stay.

Green Bay Packers—The Packers fell back into last place, and the executive committee openly second-guessed coach Gene Ronzani at every opportunity. Certain members of the committee even asked players what they thought the coach was doing wrong. The players backed up their coach, but the turmoil did not help a team that was weak to start with. Finally, with two games left on the schedule, the committee fired Ronzani, issuing a statement that he had resigned. Assistants Chuck Drulis, Hugh Devore, and Ray McLean were appointed to take over, but after three days the committee dropped Drulis from the triumvirate.

FINAL TEAM STATISTICS

OFFENSE

	BALT.	CHI.B.	CHI.C.	CLEVE.	DET.	G.BAY	L.A.	N.Y.	PHIL.	PITT.	S.F.	WASH.
FIRST DOWNS:												
Total	157	214	184	213	206	189	214	166	**256**	206	243	181
by Rushing	75	79	75	79	105	93	105	66	97	98	**128**	90
by Passing	66	119	95	122	96	79	104	87	**144**	97	99	82
by Penalty	16	16	14	12	5	**17**	5	13	15	11	16	9
RUSHING:												
Number	376	367	322	379	427	424	426	398	410	432	**443**	413
Yards	1459	1129	1179	1577	1812	1665	2148	1049	1722	1549	**2230**	1726
Average Yards	3.9	3.1	3.7	4.2	4.2	3.9	**5.0**	2.6	4.2	3.6	5.0	4.2
Touchdowns	7	9	7	20	12	14	23	6	22	13	**26**	10
PASSING:												
Attempts	319	**446**	408	303	316	352	324	345	438	416	322	278
Completions	126	206	181	191	144	147	173	158	**224**	189	174	107
Completion Percentage	39.5	46.2	44.4	**63.0**	45.6	41.8	53.4	45.8	51.1	45.4	54.0	38.5
Gross Yards	1625	2637	2191	3059	2309	1833	2772	1985	**3357**	2014	2407	1736
Yards Lost Tackled	368	138	328	245	163	278	**107**	274	268	164	239	228
Net Yards	1257	2499	1863	2814	2146	1555	2565	1711	**3089**	1850	2168	1508
Avg. Yards per Attempt (Gross)	5.1	5.9	5.4	**10.1**	7.3	5.2	8.6	5.8	7.7	4.8	7.5	6.2
Avg. Yards per Comp. (Gross)	12.9	12.8	12.1	16.0	**16.0**	12.5	16.0	12.6	15.0	10.7	13.8	16.2
Touchdowns	13	15	14	16	18	9	19	16	**25**	10	22	12
Interceptions	27	30	27	**9**	27	34	18	34	31	21	19	29
Percent Intercepted	8.5	6.7	6.6	**3.0**	8.5	9.7	5.6	9.9	7.1	5.0	5.9	10.4
PUNTS:												
Number	83	66	76	63	68	80	60	**86**	53	80	42	68
Average Yards	38.4	42.6	41.6	43.8	40.6	37.6	42.2	39.2	42.4	**46.9**	40.6	38.5
PUNT RETURNS:												
Number	29	38	50	43	35	39	**55**	**55**	46	50	33	36
Yards	184	143	**349**	175	233	348	326	334	166	269	250	306
Average Yards	6.3	4.0	7.0	4.1	6.7	**8.9**	5.9	6.1	3.6	5.4	7.6	8.5
Touchdowns	**1**	0	0	0	**1**	**1**	**1**	0	0	0	0	0
KICKOFF RETURNS:												
Number	53	48	50	30	43	**56**	48	41	37	44	43	41
Yards	**1258**	1089	1120	579	926	1197	1136	1077	787	1101	1105	797
Average Yards	23.7	22.7	22.4	19.3	21.5	21.4	23.7	**26.3**	21.3	25.0	25.7	19.4
Touchdowns	**1**	0	0	0	0	0	0	0	0	**1**	0	0
INTERCEPTION RETURNS:												
Number	29	14	24	25	**38**	28	30	23	24	21	23	27
Yards	308	292	439	246	**663**	351	417	412	299	273	388	247
Average Yards	10.6	**20.9**	18.3	9.8	17.4	12.5	13.9	17.9	12.5	13.0	16.9	9.1
Touchdowns	1	1	2	1	2	2	**3**	1	1	1	1	2
PENALTIES:												
Number	69	61	73	86	52	67	73	44	84	54	**90**	49
Yards	623	530	611	680	427	624	597	411	**779**	546	772	408
FUMBLES:												
Number	34	32	39	27	24	29	32	**19**	37	28	28	31
Number Lost	21	21	21	15	15	14	22	**9**	15	14	19	18
POINTS:												
Total	182	218	190	348	271	200	366	179	352	211	**372**	208
PAT Attempts	23	27	23	40	33	25	48	24	**49**	28	**49**	25
PAT Made	21	27	23	39	31	23	45	22	46	27	**48**	25
FG Attempts	18	21	24	**26**	23	16	25	12	15	12	18	22
FG Made	7	7	9	**23**	14	5	11	3	4	4	10	11
Percent FG Made	38.9	33.3	37.5	**88.5**	60.9	31.3	44.0	25.0	26.7	33.3	55.6	50.0
Safeties	1	1	1	0	0	0	0	**2**	0	**2**	0	0

DEFENSE

	BALT.	CHI.B.	CHI.C.	CLEVE.	DET.	G.BAY	L.A.	N.Y.	PHIL.	PITT.	S.F.	WASH.
FIRST DOWNS:												
Total	232	213	216	206	194	199	194	189	186	**184**	206	210
by Rushing	121	94	95	89	91	95	91	81	69	**63**	99	102
by Passing	95	109	111	101	96	**91**	92	99	98	110	95	93
by Penalty	16	10	10	16	**7**	13	11	9	19	11	12	15
RUSHING:												
Number	445	437	440	374	404	407	375	385	**331**	366	398	455
Yards	2315	1776	1662	1560	1580	1746	1570	1360	**1117**	1125	1548	1886
Average Yards	5.2	4.1	3.8	4.2	3.9	4.3	4.2	3.5	3.4	**3.1**	3.9	4.1
Touchdowns	21	15	24	11	10	24	10	12	**6**	9	12	15
PASSING:												
Attempts	321	364	341	389	354	**312**	366	368	374	372	356	350
Completions	165	174	176	164	159	**144**	161	173	167	193	173	171
Completion Percentage	51.4	47.8	51.6	**42.2**	44.9	46.2	44.0	47.0	44.7	51.9	48.6	48.9
Gross Yards	2411	2530	2619	2271	2162	2341	2181	2558	2289	2413	2100	**1950**
Yards Lost Tackled	240	154	255	256	197	236	299	177	**408**	157	223	198
Net Yards	2171	2376	2364	2015	1965	2105	1882	2381	1881	2256	1877	**1752**
Avg. Yards per Attempt (Gross)	7.5	7.0	7.7	5.8	6.1	7.5	6.0	6.5	6.1	6.5	5.9	**5.6**
Avg. Yards per Comp. (Gross)	14.6	14.5	14.9	13.8	13.6	16.3	13.5	14.8	13.7	18.5	12.1	**11.4**
Touchdowns	21	14	17	10	13	15	15	20	17	22	17	**8**
Interceptions	23	14	24	25	**38**	28	30	23	24	21	23	27
Percent Intercepted	9.0	3.8	7.0	6.4	**10.7**	9.0	8.2	6.3	6.4	5.6	6.5	7.7
PUNTS:												
Number	55	73	74	72	62	66	75	72	79	**83**	60	54
Average Yards	40.3	**36.5**	42.0	40.8	40.4	41.7	40.5	43.0	42.5	42.5	41.0	41.7
PUNT RETURNS:												
Number	40	34	44	35	41	41	45	69	45	50	**27**	38
Yards	307	234	**68**	156	275	232	356	521	257	403	109	165
Average Yards	7.7	6.9	**1.5**	4.5	6.7	5.7	7.9	7.6	5.7	8.1	4.0	4.3
Touchdowns	1	1	**0**	**0**	1	1	**0**	**0**	**0**	**0**	**0**	**0**
KICKOFF RETURNS:												
Number	40	36	**35**	46	54	40	59	36	49	37	59	43
Yards	724	844	852	1114	1193	851	1600	705	1208	**604**	1264	1213
Average Yards	18.1	23.4	24.3	24.2	22.1	21.3	27.1	19.6	24.7	**16.3**	21.4	28.2
Touchdowns	**0**	**0**	**0**	**0**	**0**	**0**	**0**	1	1	**0**	**0**	**0**
INTERCEPTION RETURNS:												
Number	27	30	27	**9**	27	34	18	34	31	21	19	29
Yards	469	449	202	**94**	426	407	373	526	351	373	204	461
Average Yards	17.4	15.0	**7.5**	10.4	15.8	12.0	20.7	15.5	11.3	17.8	10.7	15.9
Touchdowns	3	3	**0**	1	2	2	2	1	1	1	**0**	2
PENALTIES:												
Number	**87**	79	72	40	53	84	51	68	63	66	71	68
Yards	**757**	711	615	335	463	617	465	625	606	603	615	596
FUMBLES:												
Number	**42**	34	23	25	31	28	22	32	27	29	33	34
Number Lost	**27**	23	12	16	15	19	13	14	17	14	17	17
POINTS:												
Total	350	262	337	**162**	205	338	236	277	215	263	237	215
PAT Attempts	46	33	45	**22**	26	43	29	35	27	33	30	25
PAT Made	45	31	43	**20**	23	41	27	34	26	32	30	25
FG Attempts	16	30	**13**	**13**	19	22	23	20	18	19	16	23
FG Made	9	11	8	**2**	6	11	11	9	9	11	9	12
Percent FG Made	56.3	36.7	61.5	**15.4**	31.6	50.0	47.8	45.0	50.0	57.9	56.3	52.2
Safeties	1	**0**	**0**	2	1	**0**	1	**0**	**0**	**0**	**0**	2

1953 CHAMPIONSHIP GAME

December 27 at Detroit
(Attendance 54,577)

SCORING

DETROIT	7	3	0	7	–17
CLEVELAND	0	3	7	6	–16

First Quarter		
Det.	Walker, 1 yard rush; PAT – Walker (kick)	4:05
Second Quarter		
Cle.	Groza, 13 yard FG	0:09
Det.	Walker, 23 yard FG	13:45
Third Quarter		
Cle.	Jagade, 9 yard rush; PAT – Groza (kick)	6:48
Fourth Quarter		
Cle.	Groza, 15 yard FG	0:44
Cle.	Groza, 43 yard FG	10:50
Det.	Doran, 33 yard pass from Layne; PAT – Walker (kick)	12:52

TEAM STATISTICS

DET.		CLE.
18	First Downs – Total	11
10	by Rushing	9
7	by Passing	1
1	by Penalty	1
3	Fumbles – Number	2
2	Times Lost Ball	2
4	Penalties – Number	4
50	Yards Penalized	30
4	Giveaways	4
4	Takeaways	4
0	Difference	0

Throwing It Up and Away

Even with Otto Graham suffering through his worst day as a professional, the Browns battled the Lions evenly through most of the game. Graham's long afternoon of frustration began when Lavern Torgeson made him fumble deep in his own territory on the first series of downs in the game. Les Bingaman recovered the ball on the 13-yard line, and the Lions took six plays to cover that distance, with Doak Walker crashing over from the 1-yard line. The Browns returned the favor by recovering a Detroit fumble on the Lion 6-yard line, but they had to settle for three points on a Lou Groza field goal. Late in the second quarter, Jim David picked off a Graham pass, and Doak Walker converted this turnover into three points with a 23-yard field goal. Trailing 10-3 at halftime, the Browns quickly tied the game up in the third period. Ken Gorgal intercepted a Bobby Layne pass and returned it to the Cleveland 49; the Browns then covered 51 yards in eight plays, with only one pass in the drive. Neither team could break the 10-10 deadlock in the third quarter, but Lou Groza booted a 15-yard field goal forty-four seconds into the final period to put the Browns ahead 13-10. Detroit's bid to tie the game failed when Walker's 33-yard field-goal attempt sailed wide, and Groza added another three-pointer with less than five minutes left in the game to make the score 16-10. After Groza kicked the ball into the end zone for a touchback, Bobby Layne marched his club downfield on a winning drive. He hit Jim Doran with a pass good for 17 yards, and after two incompleted passes he again threw to Doran, this time for 18 yards. Cloyce Box then hauled in a pass for 9 yards, and after Bob Hoernschemeyer failed to get the first down, Layne picked up 3 yards on a keeper play. With a first down on the Cleveland 33, Layne then hit Doran with a deep pass that carried all the way to the end zone. Doak Walker's extra point gave the Lions a 17-16 lead with two minutes left, and Otto Graham's first pass was intercepted to insure defeat for the Browns in the championship game for the third consecutive year.

INDIVIDUAL STATISTICS

RUSHING

DETROIT	No.	Yds	Avg.	CLEVELAND	No.	Yds	Avg.
Horn'meyer	17	47	2.8	Jagade	15	104	6.9
Layne	11	46	4.2	Jones	3	28	9.3
Gedman	8	29	3.6	Reynolds	6	16	2.7
Walker	3	7	2.3	Carpenter	3	14	4.7
	39	129	3.3	Renfro	4	11	2.8
				Graham	5	9	1.8
					36	182	5.1

RECEIVING

DETROIT	No.	Yds	Avg.	CLEVELAND	No.	Yds	Avg.
Doran	4	95	23.8	Jagade	1	18	18.0
Box	4	54	13.5	Lavelli	1	13	13.0
Horn'meyer	2	–2	–1.0	Reynolds	1	7	7.0
Dibble	1	22	22.0		3	38	12.7
Walker	1	10	10.0				
	12	179	14.9				

PUNTING

DETROIT	No	Avg	CLEVELAND	No.	Avg.
Lary	4	49.3	Gillom	5	42.6

PUNT RETURNS

DETROIT	No.	Yds	Avg.	CLEVELAND	No.	Yds	Avg.
None				Reynolds	2	32	16.0
				Carpenter	1	3	3.0
					3	35	11.7

KICKOFF RETURNS

DETROIT	No.	Yds	Avg.	CLEVELAND	No.	Yds	Avg.
Girard	2	39	19.5	Jagade	1	29	29.0
Walker	1	7	7.0	Reynolds	1	21	21.0
	3	46	15.3	Carpenter	1	18	18.0
				Young	1	2	2.0
					4	70	17.5

INTERCEPTION RETURNS

DETROIT	No.	Yds	Avg.	CLEVELAND	No.	Yds	Avg.
David	1	36	36.0	Gorgal	2	9	4.5
Karilivacz	1	12	12.0				
	2	48	24.0				

PASSING

	Att	Comp	Comp Pct.	Yds	Yds/ Att.	Yds/ Comp	Yds Lost Tackled
Detroit							
Layne	25	12	48.0	179	7.2	14.9	
Walker	1	0	0.0	0	–	–	
	26	12	46.2	179	6.9	14.9	2–15
Cleveland							
Graham	15	2	13.3	20	1.3	10.0	
Ratterman	1	1	100.0	18	18.0	18.0	
	16	3	18.8	38	2.4	12.7	3–28

1953 N.F.L. — Eastern Conference

CLEVELAND BROWNS 11-1-0 Paul Brown

Scores of Each Game		
27	Green Bay	0
27	Chic. Cards	7
37	PHILADELPHIA	13
30	Washington	14
7	New York	0
27	WASHINGTON	3
34	PITTSBURGH	16
23	SAN FRANCISCO	21
20	Pittsburgh	16
27	Chic. Cards	16
62	NEW YORK	14
27	Philadelphia	42

Use Name	Pos.	Hgt	Wgt	Age	Int	Pts
Lou Groza	OT	6'3"	240	29		108
John Sandusky	OT	6'1"	258	27		
Don Steinbrunner	OT	6'3"	220	21		
Gene Donaldson	OG	5'9"	215	23		
Abe Gibron	OG	5'11"	245	27		
Lin Houston	OG	6'	225	32		
Chuck Noll	OG	6'1"	218	21		
Frank Gatski	C	6'3"	240	31		
Bill Willis	DG	6'2"	218	32		
Doug Atkins	DE	6'8"	250	23		
Len Ford	DE	6'4"	254	27	1	
George Young	DE	6'3"	220	29		
Don Colo	DT	6'3"	258	28		
Jerry Helluin	DT	6'2"	292	23		6
Darrell Palmer	DT	6'2"	242	31		

Use Name	Pos.	Hgt	Wgt	Age	Int	Pts
Walt Michaels	LB	6'	232	24	1	6
Tommy Thompson	LB	6'1"	227	26	2	
Tom Catlin	C-LB	6'1"	210	22	1	
Ken Gorgal	DB	6'2"	200	24	4	
Tommy James	DB	5'10"	185	29	5	6
Kenny Konz	DB	5'10"	182	25	5	
Warren Lahr	DB	5'11"	192	29	5	
Sherman Howard	HB-DB	5'11"	196	29	1	

Tony Adamle – Voluntarily Retired
Bob Gain – Military Service
John Kissell – Canadian Football League
Joe Skibinski – Military Service
Mac Speedie – Canadian Football League

Use Name	Pos.	Hgt	Wgt	Age	Int	Pts
Otto Graham	QB	6'1"	200	31		36
George Ratterman	QB	6'1"	182	26		
Ken Carpenter	HB	6'	195	27		30
Dub Jones	HB	6'4"	200	28		
Ray Renfro	HB	6'1"	185	22		54
Billy Reynolds	HB	5'10"	188	21		18
Chick Jagade	FB	6'	220	26		24
Marion Motley	LB-FB	6'1"	238	33		
Darrell Brewster	OE	6'3"	205	23		24
Dante Lavelli	OE	6'	192	30		36
Horace Gillom	DE-OE	6'1"	225	32		

PHILADELPHIA EAGLES 7-4-1 Jim Trimble

Scores of Each Game		
21	San Francisco	31
21	WASHINGTON	21
13	Cleveland	37
23	PITTSBURGH	7
56	Chic. Cards	17
35	Pittsburgh	7
30	NEW YORK	7
45	BALTIMORE	14
38	CHIC. CARDS	0
28	New York	37
0	Washington	10
42	CLEVELAND	27

Use Name	Pos.	Hgt	Wgt	Age	Int	Pts
Lum Snyder	OT	6'5"	230	23		
Frank Wydo	OT	6'4"	235	29		
George Mrkonic	DT-OT	6'2"	225	24		
John Magee	OG	5'10"	220	30		
John Michels	OG	5'11"	200	22		
Maury Nipp	OG	6'	218	23		
Ken Farragut	LB-C	6'4"	245	25		
Bucko Kilroy	DG	6'2"	245	32		
Tom Scott	DE	6'2"	210	23		6
Norm Willey	DE	6'2"	225	26		
Willie Irvin	OE-DE	6'3"	203	23		
Mike Jarmoluk	DT	6'5"	250	30	1	
Jess Richardson	DT	6'2"	235	23		
Vic Sears	DT	6'3"	220	35		

Use Name	Pos.	Hgt	Wgt	Age	Int	Pts
Wayne Robinson	LB	6'2"	220	23		
Ebert Van Buren	LB	6'2"	210	28	1	
Chuck Bednarik	C-LB	6'3"	230	28	6	6
Bob Stringer	FB-LB	6'1"	193	23	1	
Tom Brookshier	DB	6'	185	21	8	
Russ Craft	DB	5'9"	175	33	4	
Bob Hudson	DB	6'4"	220	23	3	
Al Pollard	FB-DB	6'	195	25		1

Bibbles Bawel – Military Service
Ralph Goldston – Broken Leg
Bud Grant – Canadian Football League
Roscoe Hansen – Military Service
Bill Horrell – Military Service
Ray Romero – Military Service

Use Name	Pos.	Hgt	Wgt	Age	Int	Pts
Adrian Burk	QB	6'2"	190	25		18
Bob Gambold	QB	6'4"	215	23		
Bobby Thomason	QB	6'1"	193	24		6
Skippy Giancanelli	HB	5'10"	173	24		36
Don Johnson	HB	6'	187	22		42
Toy Ledbetter	HB	5'10"	200	26		18
Jerry Williams	HB	5'10"	176	29		24
Frank Ziegler	HB	5'11"	176	29		30
John Brewer	FB	6'4"	230	25		6
Jim Parmer	DB-FB	6'	195	26		12
Bob Schnelker	OE	6'3"	208	23		
Bobby Walston	OE	6'	188	24		87
Pete Pihos	DE-OE	6'1"	212	29		60

WASHINGTON REDSKINS 6-5-1 Curly Lambeau

Scores of Each Game		
24	Chic. Cards	13
21	Philadelphia	21
13	NEW YORK	9
14	CLEVELAND	30
17	Baltimore	27
3	Cleveland	27
28	CHIC. CARDS	17
24	CHIC. BEARS	27
24	New York	21
17	Pittsburgh	9
10	PHILADELPHIA	0
13	PITTSBURGH	14

Use Name	Pos.	Hgt	Wgt	Age	Int	Pts
Don Boll	OT	6'2"	265	26		
Ted Hazelwood	OT	6'1"	235	29		
Laurie Niemi	DT-OT	6'1"	257	28		6
Slug Witucki	OG	5'11"	245	25		
Gene Pepper	OT-OG	6'2"	242	26		
Jim Clark	OT-DT-LB-OG	6'1"	230	24		
Harry Ulinski	C	6'4"	225	28		
Jim Ricca	OT-DT-DG	6'4"	268	26		
Jerry Hennessey	DE	6'2"	224	27		
Bill Hegarty (from PIT)	DT-DE	6'4"	240	23		
Joe Tereshinski	LB-DE	6'2"	220	29		
Gene Brito	OE-DE	6'1"	223	28		
Don Campora	DT	6'3"	270	26		
Paul Lipscomb	DT	6'5"	250	30		
Dick Modzelewski	DT	6'	248	22		

Use Name	Pos.	Hgt	Wgt	Age	Int	Pts
Knox Ramsey	OG-LB	6'1"	222	27		
Al DeMao	C-LB	6'2"	220	33		
Jack Cloud	FB-LB	5'10"	222	28	2	6
Chuck Drazenovich	FB-LB	6'1"	222	26		6
Dick Alban	DB	6'	190	24	4	
Don Doll	DB	5'10"	185	26	10	
Johnny Williams	DB	5'11"	180	26	6	
Harry Dowda	HB-DB	6'2"	200	29	5	6
Hall Haynes	HB-DB	6'	190	24		

Billy Cox – Military Service
Rob Goode – Military Service
Walt Yowarsky – Military Service
Harry Gilmer – Injury

Use Name	Pos.	Hgt	Wgt	Age	Int	Pts
Eddie LeBaron	QB	5'9"	168	23		12
Jack Scarbath	QB	6'2"	205	23		
Paul Barry	HB	6'	210	27		
Bill Dudley	HB	5'10"	175	32		58
Choo-Choo Justice	HB	5'10"	175	29		24
Johnny Papit (to GB)	HB	6'	190	25		6
Julie Rykovich	HB	6'2"	210	29		6
Sam Baker	FB	6'2"	210	21		6
Leon Heath	FB	6'1"	208	25		24
Paul Dekker	OE	6'5"	220	22		6
Fran Polsfoot	OE	6'3"	210	26		
Hugh Taylor	OE	6'4"	190	30		48

PITTSBURGH STEELERS 6-6-0 Joe Bach

Scores of Each Game		
21	Detroit	38
24	NEW YORK	14
31	CHIC. CARDS	28
7	Philadelphia	23
31	GREEN BAY	14
7	PHILADELPHIA	35
16	Cleveland	34
14	New York	10
16	CLEVELAND	20
9	WASHINGTON	17
21	Chic. Cards	17
14	Washington	13

Use Name	Pos.	Hgt	Wgt	Age	Int	Pts
George Hughes	OT	6'1"	225	28		
Bob Gaona	DT-OT	6'3"	235	23		
Marv McFadden	OG	6'	215	23		
John Schweder	LB-OG	6'1"	225	26		
Lou Tepe	C	6'2"	205	23		
Bill Walsh	C	6'2"	225	26		
John Alderton	DE	6'1"	200	22		
Bill McPeak	DE	6'1"	200	28		
George Tarasovic	DE	6'4"	240	24		
Lou Ferry	DT	6'2"	245	26		2
Tom Palmer	DT	6'2"	240	25		
Ernie Stautner	DT	6'1"	235	28		
Nick Bolkovac	OT-DT	6'1"	230	26		45

Use Name	Pos.	Hgt	Wgt	Age	Int	Pts
Dale Dodrill	LB	6'1"	210	28	1	6
Dick Flanagan	LB	6'	220	26	2	
Darrell Hogan	LB	5'10"	210	27		
Marv Matuszak	OG-LB	6'3"	230	22	1	
Art DeCarlo	DB	6'2"	195	23	5	
Ed Fullerton	DB	5'10"	190	23		
Claude Hipps	DB	6'1"	190	27	2	
Jack Butler	OE-DB	6'	195	25	9	12

Pete Ladygo – Injury
Rudy Andabaker – Military Service
Ed Kissell – Military Service
Ed Modzelewski – Military Service

Use Name	Pos.	Hgt	Wgt	Age	Int	Pts
Pat Brady	QB	6'1"	195	25		
Jim Finks	QB	6'	175	26		12
Bill Mackrides (to NY)	QB	5'11"	185	27		6
Ted Marchibroda	QB	5'10"	170	22		
Tom Calvin	HB	6'	200	27		
Lynn Chandnois	HB	6'2"	195	29		24
Jim Brandt	DB-HB	6'1"	200	25		18
Ray Mathews	DB-HB	6'	185	24	1	44
Leo Elter	FB-HB	5'10"	200	24		
Fran Rogel	FB	5'11"	205	26		12
Ed Barker	OE	6'3"	198	22		6
Elbie Nickel	OE	6'1"	195	30		24
George Sulima	OE	6'2"	200	26		

NEW YORK GIANTS 3-9-0 Steve Owen

Scores of Each Game		
7	Los Angeles	21
14	Pittsburgh	24
9	Washington	13
21	CHIC. CARDS	7
0	CLEVELAND	7
23	Chic. Cards	20
7	Philadelphia	30
10	PITTSBURGH	14
21	WASHINGTON	24
37	PHILADELPHIA	28
14	Cleveland	62
16	DETROIT	27

Use Name	Pos.	Hgt	Wgt	Age	Int	Pts
Rosey Brown	OT	6'3"	245	20		
Everett Douglas	OT	6'3"	240	21		
Dick Yelvington	OT	6'2"	230	26		
Bill Austin	OG	6'1"	225	24		
George Kennard	OG	6'	205	24		
Chester Lagod	OG	6'2"	220	25		
Jack Stroud	OG	6'1"	215	24		
Bill Albright	DT-OG	6'1"	232	24		6
John Rapacz	C	6'4"	260	28		
Jim Duncan	DE	6'2"	205	27	3	
Joe Sulaitis	LB-DE	6'2"	215	32	1	
Ray Krouse	DT	6'3"	250	26		
Arnie Weinmeister	DT	6'4"	235	30		

Use Name	Pos.	Hgt	Wgt	Age	Int	Pts
John Cannady	LB	6'2"	225	29	1	
Bob Peviani	LB	6'1"	210	21		
Joe Ramona	OG-LB	6'1"	210	22		
Ray Wietecha	C-LB	6'1"	215	24	1	
Dick Woodward	C-LB	6'2"	225	27	1	
Tom Landry	DB	6'1"	195	28	3	
Don Menasco	DB	6'	185	23	1	
Leo Miles	DB	6'	200	21		
Em Tunnell	DB	6'1"	183	31	6	
Randy Clay	HB-DB	6'	190	25	2	32

Ray Beck – Military Service
Tex Coulter – Canadian Football League
Pat Knight – Military Service
Ray Poole – Canadian Football League

Use Name	Pos.	Hgt	Wgt	Age	Int	Pts
Chuck Conerly	QB	6'1"	185	29		
Arnie Galiffa	QB	6'2"	195	26		
Sonny Grandelius	HB	6'	195	23		6
Kyle Rote	HB	6'	195	24		36
Frank Gifford	DB-HB	6'1"	190	23	1	47
Cutter Long	DB-HB	6'1"	190	21	3	14
Clarence Avinger	FB	6'1"	215	24		
Merwin Hodel	FB	6'2"	205	22		
Eddie Price	FB	5'11"	190	27		18
Cliff Anderson (from CHI C)	OE	6'2"	215	23		
Ray Pelfrey	OE	6'	190	25		18
Joe Scott	OE	6'1"	195	27		
Bill Stribling	OE	6'1"	205	26		

CHICAGO CARDINALS 1-10-1 Joe Stydahar

Scores of Each Game		
13	WASHINGTON	24
7	CLEVELAND	27
28	Pittsburgh	31
7	New York	21
17	PHILADELPHIA	56
20	NEW YORK	23
17	Washington	28
24	LOS ANGELES	24
0	Philadelphia	38
16	Cleveland	27
17	PITTSBURGH	21
24	Chic. Bears	17

Use Name	Pos.	Hgt	Wgt	Age	Int	Pts
Jack Jennings	OT	6'4"	245	26		
Tom Higgins	DT-OT	6'2"	230	24		
Volney Peters	DT-OT	6'4"	225	25		
Bill Fischer	OG	6'2"	245	26		
Dave Suminski (from WAS)	OG	5'11"	230	22		
Jerry Watford	DE-OG	6'3"	205	23		
Ed Husmann	LB-OG	6'	218	22		
Jack Simmons	C	6'4"	230	27		
Tom Bienemann	DE	6'3"	220	25		
Keever Jankovich	DE	6'	215	24		
George Schmidt	DE	6'2"	230	26		2
Pat Summerall	DE	6'4"	220	23		50
Jerry Groom	DT	6'3"	235	24		
Don Joyce	DT	6'3"	250	23		
George Gilchrist	DG-DT	6'	260	25		

Use Name	Pos.	Hgt	Wgt	Age	Int	Pts
John Panelli	LB	5'11"	200	27	1	
Bill Svoboda	LB	6'	210	26	1	
Nick Chickillo	OG-LB	5'11"	220	22		
Gordon Polofsky	OG-LB	6'1"	218	22		
Leo Sanford	C-LB	6'1"	220	24	2	6
Roy Barni	DB	5'11"	185	26		
Jim Psaltis	DB	6'1"	190	26	2	
Dan Sandifer (from GB)	DB	6'2"	190	26		
Tony Curcillo	HB-DB	6'1"	200	22	2	
Don Paul	HB-DB	6'	180	27	5	12
Ray Ramsey	OE-DB	6'2"	165	32	10	6

Ralph Pasquariello – Injury
Dick Fugler – Military Service
Ollie Matson – Military Service

Use Name	Pos.	Hgt	Wgt	Age	Int	Pts
Ray Nagel	QB	5'11"	177	26		
Steve Romanik (from Chi B)	QB	6'1"	190	29		6
Jim Root	QB	6'1"	185	22		6
Billy Cross	HB	5'6"	147	24		12
Wally Triplett	HB	5'10"	175	26		
Charlie Trippi	HB	6'	185	30		12
Al Campana	DB-HB	5'11"	180	27		
Willie Carter	DB-HB	5'11"	198	22		
Johnny Olszewski	FB	5'11"	195	22		30
Jack Spinks	FB	6'	235	23		
Gern Nagler	OE	6'2"	190	20		36
Don Stonesifer	OE	6'	200	26		12

Ralph Thomas – Military Service
Fred Wallner – Military Service

CLEVELAND BROWNS

RUSHING

Last Name	No.	Yds	Avg	TD
Renfro	60	352	5.9	4
Jagade	86	344	4.0	4
Reynolds	72	313	4.3	3
Carpenter	46	195	4.2	3
Motley	32	161	5.0	0
Graham	43	143	3.3	6
Howard	7	42	6.0	0
Jones	31	28	0.9	0
Ratterman	2	6	3.0	0
Gibron	0	−7	–	0

RECEIVING

Last Name	No.	Yds	Avg	TD
Lavelli	45	783	17	6
Renfro	39	722	19	4
Brewster	32	632	20	4
Jones	24	373	16	0
Jagade	20	193	10	0
Reynolds	9	120	13	0
Carpenter	9	109	12	2
Gillom	7	80	11	0
Motley	6	47	8	0

PUNT RETURNS

Last Name	No.	Yds	Avg	TD
Reynolds	18	111	6	0
Renfro	17	53	3	0
Jones	1	7	7	0
Konz	1	4	4	0
Carpenter	6	0	0	0

KICKOFF RETURNS

Last Name	No.	Yds	Avg	TD
Carpenter	16	367	23	0
Reynolds	4	74	19	0
Motley	3	60	20	0
Micheals	2	40	20	0
Steinbrunner	1	23	23	0
Donaldson	1	7	7	0
Howard	1	6	6	0
Noll	1	2	2	0
Young	1	0	0	0

PASSING – PUNTING – KICKING

PASSING	Att	Comp	%	Yds	Yd/Att	TD	Int–%	RK
Graham	258	167	65	2722	10.6	11	9– 3	1
Ratterman	41	23	56	301	7.3	4	0– 0	
Renfro	3	1	33	36	12.0	1	0– 0	
Jones	1	0	0	0	0.0	0	0– 0	

PUNTING	No	Avg
Gillom	63	43.8

KICKING	XP	Att	%	FG	Att	%
Groza	39	40	98	23	26	88

PHILADELPHIA EAGLES

RUSHING

Last Name	No.	Yds	Avg	TD
Johnson	83	439	5.3	5
Williams	61	345	5.7	3
Ziegler	83	320	3.9	5
Parmer	38	158	4.2	2
Giancanelli	44	131	3.0	1
Ledbetter	41	120	2.9	1
Brewer	17	85	5.0	1
Burk	8	54	6.8	3
Pollard	23	44	1.9	0
Thomason	9	23	2.6	1
Stringer	1	5	5.0	0
Gambold	2	−2	−1.0	0

RECEIVING

Last Name	No.	Yds	Avg	TD
Pihos	**63**	**1049**	17	**10**
Walston	41	750	18	5
Williams	31	438	14	1
Giancanelli	20	346	17	5
Ziegler	15	211	14	0
Parmer	14	89	6	0
Ledbetter	13	137	11	2
Johnson	12	227	19	2
Pollard	7	33	5	0
Brewer	4	43	11	0
Schnelker	4	34	9	0

PUNT RETURNS

Last Name	No.	Yds	Avg	TD
Pollard	20	106	5	0
Williams	15	25	2	0
Johnson	5	14	3	0
Giancanelli	4	11	3	0
Hudson	2	10	5	0

KICKOFF RETURNS

Last Name	No.	Yds	Avg	TD
Williams	14	343	25	0
Pollard	13	301	23	0
Johnson	4	69	17	0
Giancanelli	2	45	23	0
Parmer	1	18	18	0
Stringer	1	11	11	0
Hudson	1	0	0	0
Scott	1	0	0	0

PASSING – PUNTING – KICKING

PASSING	Att	Comp	%	Yds	Yd/Att	TD	Int–%	RK
Thomason	304	162	53	2462	8.1	**21**	20– 7	4
Burk	119	56	47	788	6.6	4	9– 8	8
Gambold	14	6	43	107	7.6	0	2–14	
Ziegler	1	0	0	0	0.0	0	0– 0	

PUNTING	No	Avg
Burk	41	43.0
Bednarik	12	40.3

KICKING	XP	Att	%	FG	Att	%
Walston	45	48	94	4	13	31
Pollard	1	1	100	0	2	0

WASHINGTON REDSKINS

RUSHING

Last Name	No.	Yds	Avg	TD
Justice	115	616	5.4	2
Heath	76	266	3.5	4
Rykovich	73	251	3.4	0
Barry	56	218	3.9	0
Papit	17	102	6.0	1
Scarbath	22	98	4.5	0
LeBaron	21	95	4.5	2
Baker	17	72	4.2	1
Drazenovich	11	27	2.5	1
Dudley	5	15	3.0	0
Cloud	3	7	2.3	0
Dowda	1	3	3.0	0
Haynes	2	0	0.0	0

RECEIVING

Last Name	No.	Yds	Avg	TD
Taylor	35	703	20	8
Justice	22	434	20	2
Dekker	14	182	13	1
Polsfoot	11	164	15	0
Barry	8	70	9	0
Rykovich	7	73	10	1
Heath	5	45	9	0
Brito	2	35	18	0
Baker	2	21	11	0
Papit	1	9	9	0

PUNT RETURNS

Last Name	No.	Yds	Avg	TD
Williams	18	172	10	0
Haynes	5	92	18	0
Dudley	8	34	4	0
Justice	4	6	2	0
Doll	1	2	2	0

KICKOFF RETURNS

Last Name	No.	Yds	Avg	TD
Williams	9	224	25	0
Baker	9	186	21	0
Haynes	7	123	18	0
Barry	6	112	19	0
Cloud	4	68	17	0
Rykovich	2	39	20	0
Papit	2	38	19	0
Justice	1	20	20	0
Boll	1	11	11	0
Lipscomb	1	8	8	0
Brito	1	6	6	0

PASSING – PUNTING – KICKING

PASSING	Att	Comp	%	Yds	Yd/Att	TD	Int–%	RK
LeBaron	149	62	42	874	5.9	3	17–11	17
Scarbath	129	45	35	862	6.7	9	12– 9	13

PUNTING	No	Avg
LeBaron	51	39.3
Baker	17	36.1

KICKING	XP	Att	%	FG	Att	%
Dudley	25	25	100	11	22	50

PITTSBURGH STEELERS

RUSHING

Last Name	No.	Yds	Avg	TD
Rogel	137	527	3.8	2
Chandnois	123	470	3.8	3
Mathews	65	260	4.0	2
Brandt	42	106	2.5	3
Elter	26	81	3.1	0
Calvin	13	65	5.0	0
Mackrides	14	27	1.9	1
Marchibroda	1	15	15.0	0
Finks	12	0	0.0	2

RECEIVING

Last Name	No.	Yds	Avg	TD
Nickel	62	743	12	4
Chandnois	43	412	10	0
Mathews	27	346	13	4
Rogel	19	95	5	0
Barker	17	172	10	1
Sulima	10	131	13	0
Calvin	4	28	7	0
Elter	3	29	10	0
Butler	2	43	22	1
Brandt	2	15	8	0

PUNT RETURNS

Last Name	No.	Yds	Avg	TD
Mathews	16	128	8	0
Chandnois	26	101	4	0
Brandt	6	34	6	0
Butler	1	5	5	0
DeCarlo	1	1	1	0

KICKOFF RETURNS

Last Name	No.	Yds	Avg	TD
Chandnois	21	610	29	1
Mathews	10	261	26	0
Brandt	6	135	23	0
Tepe	3	47	16	0
Marchibroda	1	25	25	0
Elter	1	23	23	0
Gaona	1	0	0	0
Hughes	1	0	0	0

PASSING – PUNTING – KICKING

PASSING	Att	Comp	%	Yds	Yd/Att	TD	Int–%	RK
Finks	292	131	45	1484	5.1	8	14– 5	8
Mackrides	109	54	50	506	4.6	2	8– 7	12
Marchibroda	22	9	41	66	3.0	1	2– 9	
Chandnois	3	1	33	11	3.7	0	0– 0	
Mathews	2	0	0	0	0.0	0	0– 0	
Brady	1	0	0	0	0.0	0	0– 0	
Brandt	1	0	0	0	0.0	0	0– 0	
Rogel	1	0	0	0	0.0	0	0– 0	

PUNTING	No	Avg
Brady	**80**	**46.9**

KICKING	XP	Att	%	FG	Att	%
Bolkovac	27	28	96	4	12	33

NEW YORK GIANTS

RUSHING

Last Name	No.	Yds	Avg	TD
Grandelius	108	278	2.6	1
Rote	63	213	3.4	1
Price	101	206	2.0	2
Gifford	50	157	3.1	2
Conerly	24	91	3.8	0
Long	20	58	2.9	0
Clay	16	26	1.6	0
Hodel	5	11	2.2	0
Avinger	5	6	1.2	0
Galiffa	5	1	0.2	0

RECEIVING

Last Name	No.	Yds	Avg	TD
Rote	26	440	17	5
Price	26	233	9	1
Gifford	18	292	16	4
Anderson	17	266	16	0
Pelfrey	17	233	14	3
Stribling	16	175	11	0
Grandelius	15	80	5	0
Long	14	220	16	2
Clay	5	51	10	1
Avinger	2	8	4	0
Hodel	2	−15	−7	0
Scott	1	10	10	0

PUNT RETURNS

Last Name	No.	Yds	Avg	TD
Tunnell	**38**	223	6	0
Gifford	16	106	7	0
Landry	1	5	5	0

KICKOFF RETURNS

Last Name	No.	Yds	Avg	TD
Tunnell	17	479	28	0
Gifford	13	327	25	0
Long	7	198	28	0
Landry	2	38	19	0
Clay	1	20	20	0
Sulaitis	1	15	15	0

PASSING – PUNTING – KICKING

PASSING	Att	Comp	%	Yds	Yd/Att	TD	Int–%	RK
Conerly	303	143	47	1711	5.7	13	25– 8	8
Galiffa	13	4	31	129	9.9	1	5–38	
Rote	8	2	25	45	5.6	0	1–13	
Gifford	6	3	50	47	7.8	1	0– 0	

PUNTING	No	Avg
Landry	44	40.3
Avinger	42	38.1

KICKING	XP	Att	%	FG	Att	%
Clay	20	22	91	2	7	29
Gifford	2	2	100	1	5	20

CHICAGO CARDINALS

RUSHING

Last Name	No.	Yds	Avg	TD
Trippi	97	433	4.5	0
Olszewski	106	386	3.6	4
Cross	51	196	3.8	1
Paul	16	114	7.1	0
Curcillo	8	29	3.6	0
Root	26	12	0.5	1
Nagel	4	8	2.0	0
Triplett	3	1	2.7	1
Romanik	2	1	0.5	1
Spinks	6	0	0.0	0
Carter	2	−3	−1.5	0
Campana	2	−5	−2.5	0

RECEIVING

Last Name	No.	Yds	Avg	TD
Stonesifer	56	684	12	2
Nagler	43	610	14	6
Olszewski	21	210	10	1
Cross	17	285	17	1
Paul	16	167	10	2
Ramsey	12	118	10	0
Trippi	11	87	8	2
Triplett	3	15	5	0
Spinks	1	6	6	0

PUNT RETURNS

Last Name	No.	Yds	Avg	TD
Trippi	21	239	**11**	0
Paul	18	85	5	0
Sandifer	3	35	12	0
Carter	4	20	5	0
Cross	6	5	1	0
Olszewski	1	0	0	0

KICKOFF RETURNS

Last Name	No.	Yds	Avg	TD
Cross	12	257	21	0
Triplett	10	253	25	0
Trippi	8	199	25	0
Carter	8	178	22	0
Paul	4	106	27	0
Campana	3	56	19	0
Curcillo	1	17	17	0
Olszewski	1	17	17	0
Jennings	1	15	15	0
Svoboda	1	15	15	0
Joyce	1	7	7	0

PASSING – PUNTING – KICKING

PASSING	Att	Comp	%	Yds	Yd/Att	TD	Int–%	RK
Root	192	80	42	1149	6.0	8	11– 6	7
Romanik	125	51	41	650	5.2	4	11– 9	15
Nagel	62	30	48	192	3.1	0	5– 8	
Trippi	34	20	59	195	5.7	2	1– 3	
Paul	2	1	50	13	6.5	0	0– 0	
Olszewski	1	0	0	0	0.0	0	1–100	

PUNTING	No	Avg
Trippi	54	42.9
Simmons	22	38.4

KICKING	XP	Att	%	FG	Att	%
Summerall	23	23	100	9	24	38

DETROIT LIONS 10-2-0 Buddy Parker

Scores of Each Game		
38	PITTSBURGH	21
27	Baltimore	17
24	SAN FRANCISCO	21
19	LOS ANGELES	31
14	San Francisco	10
24	Los Angeles	37
17	BALTIMORE	7
14	Green Bay	7
20	Chic. Bears	16
34	GREEN BAY	15
13	CHIC. BEARS	7
27	New York	16

Use Name	Pos.	Hgt	Wgt	Age	Int	Pts
Charlie Ane	OT	6'2"	265	22		
Ollie Spencer	OT	6'2"	230	22		
Lou Creekmur	OG-OT	6'4"	250	26		
Dick Stanfel	OG	6'3"	235	26		
Harley Sewell	LB-OG	6'1"	220	22	1	
Vince Banonis	C	6'1"	235	31		
Les Bingaman	OG	6'3"	300	28	1	
Jim Cain	DE	6'1"	200	26		
Bob Dove (from Chi C)	DE	6'2"	225	32		
Blaine Earon	DE	6'1"	195	24		
Sonny Gandee	DE	6'1"	210	24	1	
Jim Doran	OE-DE	6'2"	195	25		
Thurman McGraw	DT	6'5"	235	26	1	
John Prchlik	DT	6'4"	235	28		
Bob Miller	OT-DT	6'3"	235	23	1	

Use Name	Pos.	Hgt	Wgt	Age	Int	Pts
Joe Schmidt	LB	6'1"	218	21	2	
Jim Martin	OG-LB	6'2"	225	29	1	10
Lavern Torgeson	C-LB	6'	215	24	5	
Jack Christiansen	DB	6'1"	185	24	12	6
Jim David	DB	5'11"	175	26	4	
Carl Karilivacz	DB	6'	185	22		
Yale Lary	DB	6'	185	22	5	6
Jim Smith	HB-DB	6'1"	195	28	3	

Stan Campbell – Military Service
Jim Hill – Military Service

Use Name	Pos.	Hgt	Wgt	Age	Int	Pts
Tom Dublinski	QB	6'2"	190	23		
Bobby Layne	QB	6'1"	195	26		
Gene Gedman	HB	5'11"	195	21		18
Jug Girard	HB	5'11"	175	26		
Bob Hoernschemeyer	HB	5'11"	195	27		54
Doak Walker	HB	5'11"	172	26		93
Lew Carpenter	DB-HB	6'1"	200	21	1	6
Ollie Cline	FB	6'	200	27		6
Pat Harder	FB	5'11"	202	31		
Bob Smith	FB	6'	204	24		
Cloyce Box	OE	6'4"	220	29		12
Dorne Dibble	OE	6'2"	195	24		18
Leon Hart	OE	6'5"	265	24		42

SAN FRANCISCO FORTY NINERS 9-3-0 Buck Shaw

Scores of Each Game		
31	PHILADELPHIA	21
31	LOS ANGELES	30
21	Detroit	24
35	Chic. Bears	28
10	DETROIT	14
24	CHIC. BEARS	14
31	Los Angeles	27
21	Cleveland	23
37	Green Bay	7
38	Baltimore	21
48	GREEN BAY	14
45	BALTIMORE	14

Use Name	Pos.	Hgt	Wgt	Age	Int	Pts
Hal Miller	OT	6'4"	230	23		
Bob St. Clair	OT	6'9"	245	22		
Doug Hogland	OG-OT	6'3"	225	22		
Bruno Banducci	OG	5'11"	220	31		
Nick Feher	OG	6'	225	26		
Jerry Smith	LB-OG	6'1"	230	23		
Bill Johnson	C	6'3"	240	27		
Clay Mathews	DE	6'3"	220	25		
Charley Powell	DE	6'2"	220	21		
Bob Van Doren	DE	6'3"	215	24		
Al Carapella	DT	6'	235	26		
Leo Nomellini	OT-DT	6'3"	252	28		

Jim Cason – Canadian Football League
Ed Henke – Military Service

Use Name	Pos.	Hgt	Wgt	Age	Int	Pts
Hardy Brown	LB	6'	196	29	1	
John Morton	LB	6'2"	220	24	2	
Don Burke	OG-LB	6'	235	27		
Art Michalik	OG-LB	6'2"	225	23		
Pete Brown	C-LB	6'2"	210	22		
Jack Manley	C-LB	6'3"	215	24		
Rex Berry	DB	5'11"	180	27	7	6
Fred Bruney	DB	5'10"	177	22	5	
Lowell Wagner	HB-DB	6'	195	29	6	
Jim Monachino	FB-DB	5'10"	187	24		

Bill Jessup – Military Service
Pat O'Donahue – Military Service
Dave Sparks – Military Service
Bob Toneff – Military Service

Use Name	Pos.	Hgt	Wgt	Age	Int	Pts
Hal Ledyard	QB	6'	185	22		
Y. A. Tittle	QB	6'	190	26		36
Jim Powers	DB-QB	6'	185	25		
Hugh McElhenny	HB	6'1"	198	24		30
Joe Arenas	DB-HB	5'11"	180	27	2	42
Billy Mixon	DB-HB	5'11"	185	23		6
Pete Schabarum	DB-HB	5'11"	185	24		
Ken Bahnsen	FB	5'10"	200	23		
Joe Perry	FB	6'	210	26		78
Harry Babcock	OE	6'2"	195	22		
Gordie Soltau	OE	6'2"	195	28		114
Billy Wilson	OE	6'3"	190	26		60

Bob White – Military Service
Verl Lillywhite – Military Service

LOS ANGELES RAMS 8-3-1 Hamp Pool

Scores of Each Game		
21	NEW YORK	7
30	San Francisco	31
38	Green Bay	20
31	Detroit	19
38	CHIC. BEARS	24
37	DETROIT	24
27	SAN FRANCISCO	31
24	Chic. Cards	24
21	Baltimore	13
21	Chic. Bears	24
45	BALTIMORE	2
33	GREEN BAY	17

Use Name	Pos.	Hgt	Wgt	Age	Int	Pts
Tom Dahms	OT	6'5"	240	25		
Bob Fry	OT	6'4"	220	22		
Len Teeuws	DT-OT	6'4"	235	26		
Dick Daugherty	OG	6'1"	214	24		
John Hock	OG	6'2"	235	25		
Duane Putnam	OG	6'	215	25		
Harry Thompson	DE-OG	6'2"	225	26		
Leon McLaughlin	C	6'2"	228	27		
Stan West	DG	6'2"	230	26	1	
Larry Brink	DE	6'5"	240	30		
Big Daddy Lipscomb	DE	6'5"	272	22		
Andy Robustelli	DE	6'1"	220	27		
Charlie Toogood	DT	6'	233	25	1	
Frank Fuller	C-DT	6'4"	235	24		

Use Name	Pos.	Hgt	Wgt	Age	Int	Pts
Bud McFadin	LB	6'3"	245	25	1	
Don Paul	LB	6'1"	225	28	3	
Harland Svare	LB	6'	210	22	1	
Bob Griffin	C-LB	6'3"	215	24		
Jack Dwyer	DB	5'11"	175	26	2	6
Neil Ferris	DB	5'11"	180	25		
Night Train Lane	DB	6'1"	190	25	3	12
Herb Rich	DB	5'11"	180	24	3	6
Woodley Lewis	HB-DB	6'	195	28	7	12
Norb Hecker	OE-DB	6'2"	190	26	7	

Bob Carey – Military Service
Don Klosterman – Military Service

Use Name	Pos.	Hgt	Wgt	Age	Int	Pts
Rudy Bukich	QB	6'1"	193	22		6
Norm Van Brocklin	QB	6'1"	200	27		
Tom McCormick	HB	5'11"	190	23		
Brad Myers	HB	6'1"	200	23		18
Skeets Quinlan	HB	5'11"	175	25		36
Vitamin Smith	HB	5'8"	180	29		18
Dan Towler	FB	6'2"	226	25		48
Tank Younger	LB-HB-FB	6'3"	226	25		54
Tom Fears	OE	6'2"	215	29		32
Crazy Legs Hirsch	OE	6'2"	190	29		28
Bob Boyd	DB-OE	6'2"	200	25	1	24
Ben Agajanian	K	6'	215	34		66

CHICAGO BEARS 3-8-1 George Halas

Scores of Each Game		
9	Baltimore	13
17	Green Bay	13
14	BALTIMORE	16
28	SAN FRANCISCO	35
24	Los Angeles	38
14	San Francisco	24
21	GREEN BAY	21
27	Washington	24
16	DETROIT	20
24	LOS ANGELES	21
7	Detroit	13
17	CHIC. CARDS	24

Use Name	Pos.	Hgt	Wgt	Age	Int	Pts
Kline Gilbert	OT	6'2"	224	22		
Art Davis	DT-OT	6'2"	235	23		
George Connor	OG-LB-OT	6'3"	240	28		
John Badaczewski	OG	6'1"	235	31		
John Hatley	OG	6'3"	245	22		
Billy Autrey	C	6'3"	220	20		
Bob Moser	C	6'3"	235	24		
Wayne Hansen	OT-OG-LB-C	6'2"	235	25		
Ed Sprinkle	DE	6'1"	210	29		6
Bill Wightkin	OE-DE	6'3"	233	26		6
Bill Bishop	DT	6'4"	250	22	1	
John Kreamcheck	DT	6'5"	255	25		
Fred Williams	DT	6'4"	250	23		

Ed Bradley – Canadian Football League
Herman Clark – Military Service

Use Name	Pos.	Hgt	Wgt	Age	Int	Pts
John Helwig	LB	6'2"	208	25		
Jerry Shipkey	LB	6'1"	215	28		
Jerry Weatherley	LB	6'5"	218	24	1	
Frank Dempsey	OG-LB	6'3"	235	28		
Bill George	OG-LB	6'2"	240	22		
George Figner	DB	6'	185	24	1	
Don Kindt	DB	6'1"	208	27	6	6
Howie Livingston	DB	6'1"	198	31		
Rex Proctor	DB	5'10"	180	24	1	
S. J. Whitman (from Chi C)	DB	5'11"	185	27	3	
Billy Anderson	HB-DB	6'	198	24		
Lloyd Lowe	HB-DB	5'10"	155	24	1	

Bob Cross – Military Service
Jack Hoffman – Military Service
Chuck Hunsinger – Canadian Football League
Jimmy Lesane – Military Service

Use Name	Pos.	Hgt	Wgt	Age	Int	Pts
George Blanda	QB	6'1"	197	25		48
Tom O'Connell	QB	5'11"	182	21		
Willie Thrower	QB	5'11"	182	23		
Eddie Macon	HB	6'	175	25		18
Billy Stone	HB	6'	195	27		36
John Hoffman	DE-LB-OE-FB-HB	6'2"	215	27	1	24
Leon Campbell	FB	6'	197	26		
Kayo Dottley	FB	6'1"	200	25		6
Bobby Jack Floyd	FB	6'	210	24		
Curley Morrison	HB-FB	6'2"	215	27		12
Jim Dooley	OE	6'4"	198	23		24
Dick Hensley	OE	6'4"	218	27		2
Bill McColl	OE	6'4"	230	23		30

Gene Schroeder – Military Service
Bob Williams – Military Service

BALTIMORE COLTS 3-9-0 Keith Molesworth

Scores of Each Game		
13	CHIC. BEARS	9
17	DETROIT	27
16	Chic. Bears	14
14	Green Bay	37
27	WASHINGTON	17
24	GREEN BAY	35
7	Detroit	17
14	Philadelphia	45
13	LOS ANGELES	21
21	SAN FRANCISCO	38
2	Los Angeles	45
14	San Francisco	45

Use Name	Pos.	Hgt	Wgt	Age	Int	Pts
Ernie Blandin	OT	6'4"	260	34		
Ken Jackson	OT	6'2"	235	24		
Jack Little	OT	6'4"	235	22		
Dick Barwegan	OG	6'1"	230	30		
Bill Lange	OG	6'1"	230	26		
Sisto Averno	LB-OG	5'11"	245	27		
Brad Ecklund	C	6'3"	215	31		
Barney Poole	DE	6'2"	250	30		
Art Spinney	DE	6'	235	26		
Elmer Wingate	DE	6'3"	230	25		
Joe Campanella	DT	6'2"	245	22		
Art Donovan	DT	6'2"	270	28		2
Tom Finnin	DT	6'2"	255	25		
Gino Marchetti	DT	6'4"	245	27		
Jim Winkler	OG-DT	6'2"	255	26		

Use Name	Pos.	Hgt	Wgt	Age	Int	Pts
Alex Agase	LB	5'10"	220	31	1	
Bill Pellington	LB	6'2"	235	24	2	
Ed Sharkey	OG-LB	6'3"	240	26		
Ed Mioduszewski	QB-DB	5'10"	185	23	1	
Bert Rechichar	HB-DB	6'1"	210	23	7	33
Don Shula	HB-DB	5'11"	190	23	3	
Carl Taseff	HB-DB	5'11"	195	24	2	12
Tom Keane	OE-DB	6'1"	185	26	11	

Johnny Petitbon – Military Service
Mike McCormack – Military Service
Stan Williams – Canadian Football League
John Wozniak – Canadian Football League
Zollie Toth – Knee Injury

Use Name	Pos.	Hgt	Wgt	Age	Int	Pts
Jack Del Bello	QB	6'1"	190	25		
Fred Enke	QB	6'1"	205	28		
Dick Flowers	QB	6'	190	25		
Larry Coutre (from GB)	HB	5'10"	175	24		
Tommy Kalmanir	HB	5'8"	170	27		6
Buddy Young	HB	5'5"	180	27		24
George Taliaferro	QB-HB	5'11"	200	26		24
John Huzvar	FB	6'4"	250	24		30
Buck McPhail	FB	6'1"	195	23		27
Dan Edwards	OE	6'1"	190	27		18
Mel Embree	OE	6'3"	190	26		6
Monte Brethauer	DB-OE	6'1"	175	22	1	

GREEN BAY PACKERS 2-9-1 Gene Ronzani Hugh Devore Ray McLean

Scores of Each Game		
0	CLEVELAND	27
13	CHIC. BEARS	17
20	LOS ANGELES	38
37	BALTIMORE	14
14	Pittsburgh	31
35	Baltimore	24
21	Chic. Bears	21
7	DETROIT	14
7	SAN FRANCISCO	37
15	Detroit	34
14	San Francisco	48
17	Los Angeles	33

Use Name	Pos.	Hgt	Wgt	Age	Int	Pts
Gus Cifelli	OT	6'4"	250	27		
Len Szafaryn	OG-OT	6'2"	230	25		
Dick Afflis	DG-OT	6'	250	24		
Buddy Brown	OG	6'1"	220	26		
Steve Ruzich	OG	6'2"	230	25		
Dick Logan	DT-OG	6'2"	230	23		
Jim Ringo	C	6'1"	225	22		
Dave Stephenson	OG-C	6'2"	225	27		
John Martinkovic	DE	6'3"	240	26		
George Hays	DE	6'2"	215	28		
Carl Elliott	OE-DE	6'4"	220	26		6
Dave Hanner	DT	6'2"	250	24	1	
Howie Ruetz	DT	6'3"	250	25		
Dick Wildung	DT	6'	230	31		

Use Name	Pos.	Hgt	Wgt	Age	Int	Pts
Bob Forte	LB	6'	205	31		
Clayton Tonnemaker	LB	6'2"	235	25		
Deral Teteak	OG-LB	5'10"	210	24		
Roger Zatkoff	DE-LB	6'2"	215	22		
Bill Forester	DT-LB	6'3"	230	22	1	
Ben Aldridge	DB	6'	195	26	5	
Bobby Dillon	DB	6'1"	180	23	9	6
Marvin Johnson	DB	5'11"	185	25	4	
Ace Loomis	DB	6'1"	190	25	4	
Val Joe Walker	DB	6'1"	180	22	4	6

Clarence Self – Military Service

Use Name	Pos.	Hgt	Wgt	Age	Int	Pts
Babe Parilli	QB	6'1"	190	23		24
Tobin Rote	QB	6'3"	200	25		
Byron Bailey (from DET)	HB	5'10"	198	23		
Al Carmichael	HB	6'1"	190	23		6
Gib Dawson	HB	5'11"	180	23		6
Breezy Reid	HB	5'10"	188	26		18
Don Barton	DB-HB	5'11"	175	23		6
J. R. Boone	DB-HB	5'8"	167	27		6
Fred Cone	FB	5'11"	197	27		74
Howie Ferguson	FB	6'2"	210	23		
Billy Howton	OE	6'2"	188	23		24
Bob Mann	OE	5'11"	175	29		12
Clive Rush	OE	6'2"	197	22		

DETROIT LIONS

RUSHING

Last Name	No.	Yds	Avg	TD
Hoernschemeyer	101	482	4.8	7
Layne	87	343	3.9	0
Walker	66	337	5.1	2
Gedman	83	255	3.1	3
Cline	42	169	4.0	0
Girard	19	73	3.8	0
B. Smith	6	51	8.5	0
Dublinski	6	39	6.5	0
Carpenter	7	24	3.4	0
Harder	8	21	2.6	0
Lary	1	21	21.0	0
Hart	1	2	2.0	0
Christiansen	0	–5	–	0

RECEIVING

Last Name	No.	Yds	Avg	TD
Walker	30	502	17	3
Hart	25	472	19	7
Hoernschemeyer	23	282	12	2
Box	16	403	25	2
Dibble	16	274	17	3
Gedman	14	121	9	0
Cline	10	126	13	1
Doran	6	75	13	0
Girard	2	24	12	0
Harder	1	19	19	0
J. Smith	1	11	11	0

PUNT RETURNS

Last Name	No.	Yds	Avg	TD
Lary	13	115	9	1
Girard	9	86	10	0
Christiansen	8	22	3	0
Gedman	4	10	3	0
Schmidt	1	0	0	0

KICKOFF RETURNS

Last Name	No.	Yds	Avg	TD
Girard	9	252	28	0
Christiansen	10	183	18	0
Carpenter	8	172	22	0
Walker	4	139	35	0
Lary	6	116	19	0
Gedman	2	47	24	0
Hoernschemeyer	1	10	10	0
Stanfel	1	4	4	0
Bingaman	1	3	3	0
Cline	1	0	0	0

PASSING – PUNTING – KICKING

PASSING	Att	Comp	%	Yds	Yd/Att	TD	Int–%	RK
Layne	273	125	46	2088	7.7	16	21– 8	5
Dublinski	30	14	47	174	5.8	0	5–17	
Walker	7	3	43	31	4.4	1	0– 0	
Hoernschemeyer	5	2	40	16	3.2	1	1–20	
Girard	1	0	0	0	0.0	0	0– 0	

PUNTING	No	Avg
J. Smith	40	41.2
Lary	28	39.7

KICKING	XP	Att	%	FG	Att	%
Walker	27	29	93	12	19	63
Martin	4	4	100	2	4	50

SAN FRANCISCO FORTY NINERS

RUSHING

Last Name	No.	Yds	Avg	TD
Perry	192	1018	5.3	10
McElhenny	112	503	4.5	3
Arenas	72	380	5.3	6
Mixon	25	176	7.0	1
Schabarum	18	104	5.8	0
Tittle	14	41	2.9	6
Monachino	4	10	2.5	0
Wagner	1	4	4.0	0
Ledyard	1	3	3.0	0
Bahnsen	1	1	1.0	0
Powers	3	–10	–3.3	0

RECEIVING

Last Name	No.	Yds	Avg	TD
Wilson	51	840	16	10
Soltau	43	620	14	6
McElhenny	30	474	16	2
Perry	19	191	10	3
Arenas	10	113	11	1
Schabarum	10	96	10	0
Babcock	7	59	8	0
Monachino	2	9	5	0
Mixon	1	7	7	0
Hogland	1	–2	–2	0

PUNT RETURNS

Last Name	No.	Yds	Avg	TD
McElhenny	15	104	7	0
Arenas	8	93	12	0
Berry	7	42	6	0
Bruney	1	11	11	0
Schabarum	2	0	0	0

KICKOFF RETURNS

Last Name	No.	Yds	Avg	TD
Arenas	16	551	34	0
McElhenny	15	368	25	0
Schabarum	2	50	25	0
Bruney	2	46	23	0
Berry	1	37	37	0
Perry	2	21	11	0
Bahnsen	1	21	21	0
Nomellini	1	5	5	0
Babcock	2	3	2	0
H. Brown	1	3	3	0

PASSING – PUNTING – KICKING

PASSING	Att	Comp	%	Yds	Yd/Att	TD	Int–%	RK
Tittle	259	149	58	2121	8.2	20	16– 6	3
Powers	49	22	45	259	5.3	1	2– 4	
Ledyard	9	0	0	0	0.0	0	1–11	
McElhenny	3	2	67	13	4.3	1	0– 0	
Perry	1	1	100	14	14.0	0	0– 0	
Arenas	1	0	0	0	0.0	0	0– 0	

PUNTING	No	Avg
Powers	42	40.6

KICKING	XP	Att	%	FG	Att	%
Soltau	48	49	98	10	15	67
Perry	0	0	0	0	3	0

LOS ANGELES RAMS

RUSHING

Last Name	No.	Yds	Avg	TD
Towler	152	879	5.8	7
Quinlan	97	705	7.3	4
Younger	84	350	4.2	8
Myers	40	124	3.1	3
McCormick	20	29	1.5	0
Bukich	14	28	2.0	1
Smith	8	26	3.3	0
Van Brocklin	8	11	1.4	0
Lewis	2	2	1.0	0
Hirsch	1	–6	–6.0	0

RECEIVING

Last Name	No.	Yds	Avg	TD
Hirsch	61	941	15	4
Boyd	24	548	23	4
Fears	23	278	12	4
Younger	20	259	13	1
Quinlan	17	260	15	2
Towler	11	125	11	1
Smith	6	151	25	3
McCormick	5	72	14	0
Myers	4	13	3	0
Hecker	2	25	13	0

PUNT RETURNS

Last Name	No.	Yds	Avg	TD
Lewis	35	267	8	1
Smith	12	30	3	0
Boyd	5	26	5	0
McCormick	2	2	1	0
Myers	1	1	1	0

KICKOFF RETURNS

Last Name	No.	Yds	Avg	TD
Lewis	32	830	26	0
McCormick	5	134	27	0
Smith	2	44	22	0
Myers	3	42	14	0
Quinlan	2	38	19	0
Younger	1	24	24	0
Toogood	1	19	19	0
McFadin	1	5	5	0
Thompson	1	0	0	0

PASSING – PUNTING – KICKING

PASSING	Att	Comp	%	Yds	Yd/Att	TD	Int–%	RK
Van Brocklin	286	156	55	2393	8.4	19	14– 5	2
Bukich	32	14	44	169	5.3	0	3– 9	
Quinlan	4	2	50	60	15.0	0	1–25	
Smith	2	1	50	50	25.0	0	0– 0	

PUNTING	No	Avg
Van Brocklin	60	42.2

KICKING	XP	Att	%	FG	Att	%
Agajanian	36	37	97	10	24	42
Fears	5	6	83	1	1	100
Hirsch	4	5	80	0	0	0

CHICAGO BEARS

RUSHING

Last Name	No.	Yds	Avg	TD
Morrison	95	307	3.2	2
Stone	72	169	2.3	2
Dottley	58	150	2.6	1
Macon	40	130	3.3	1
Campbell	22	130	5.9	0
Hoffman	32	95	3.0	3
Floyd	16	70	4.4	0
Blanda	24	62	2.6	0
O'Connell	7	16	2.3	0

RECEIVING

Last Name	No.	Yds	Avg	TD
Dooley	53	841	16	4
McColl	36	453	13	4
Stone	34	376	11	4
Hoffman	28	341	12	1
Morrison	16	214	13	0
Floyd	9	63	7	0
Macon	6	24	4	2
Campbell	5	74	15	0
Dottley	5	21	4	0
Hensley	4	117	29	0
Lowe	4	34	9	0
Anderson	3	33	11	0
Wightkin	2	22	11	0
Connor	1	17	17	0
Blanda	0	7	0	0

PUNT RETURNS

Last Name	No.	Yds	Avg	TD
Macon	17	68	4	0
Lowe	15	51	3	0
Stone	4	12	3	0
Anderson	1	7	7	0
Dempsey	1	5	5	0

KICKOFF RETURNS

Last Name	No.	Yds	Avg	TD
Campbell	19	455	24	0
Macon	13	373	29	0
Anderson	5	127	25	0
Morrison	4	43	11	0
Hoffman	2	32	16	0
Lowe	1	26	26	0
Connor	1	21	21	0
Helwig	1	12	12	0
Sprinkle	1	0	0	0
Wightkin	1	0	0	0

PASSING – PUNTING – KICKING

PASSING	Att	Comp	%	Yds	Yd/Att	TD	Int–%	RK
Blanda	362	169	47	2164	6.0	14	23– 7	6
O'Connell	67	33	49	437	6.5	1	4– 6	
Thrower	8	3	38	27	3.4	0	1–13	
Macon	1	0	0	0	0.0	0	0– 0	

PUNTING	No	Avg
Morrison	65	42.6
Anderson	1	46.0

KICKING	XP	Att	%	FG	Att	%
Blanda	27	27	100	7	20	35
George	0	0	0	0	1	0

BALTIMORE COLTS

RUSHING

Last Name	No.	Yds	Avg	TD
Huzvar	119	515	4.3	4
Taliaferro	102	479	4.7	2
McPhail	53	138	2.6	0
Young	40	135	3.4	0
Enke	28	91	3.3	0
Kalmanir	16	53	3.3	0
Coutre	22	39	1.8	0
Mioduszewski	3	33	11.0	0
Del Bello	14	14	1.0	0
Taseff	1	1	1.0	1

RECEIVING

Last Name	No.	Yds	Avg	TD
Edwards	35	312	9	3
Embree	23	272	12	1
Taliaferro	20	346	17	2
Young	12	201	17	3
Brethauer	10	133	13	0
McPhail	10	38	4	0
Huzvar	6	55	9	1
Rechichar	3	151	50	2
Keane	3	61	20	0
Kalmanir	3	31	10	1
Shula	1	6	6	0
Coutre	1	–4	–4	0
Marchetti	0	19	0	0

PUNT RETURNS

Last Name	No.	Yds	Avg	TD
Taseff	1	71	71	1
Coutre	5	43	9	0
Taliaferro	10	31	3	0
Kalmanir	2	19	10	0
Mioduszewski	4	13	3	0
Young	6	9	2	0
Keane	1	3	3	0
Rechichar	1	0	0	0

KICKOFF RETURNS

Last Name	No.	Yds	Avg	TD
Young	11	378	34	1
Taliaferro	16	331	21	0
Coutre	12	318	27	0
Taseff	4	87	22	0
Kalmanir	3	51	17	0
Jackson	3	37	12	0
Rechichar	1	28	28	0
Mioduszewski	1	25	25	0
Poole	2	24	12	0
Finnin	1	18	18	0
Campanella	2	13	7	0

PASSING – PUNTING – KICKING

PASSING	Att	Comp	%	Yds	Yd/Att	TD	Int–%	RK
Enke	169	71	42	1054	6.2	8	15– 9	11
Del Bello	61	27	44	229	3.8	1	5– 8	
Taliaferro	55	15	27	211	3.8	2	5– 9	
Mioduszewski	30	11	37	113	3.8	2	2– 7	
Flowers	4	2	50	18	4.5	0	0– 0	

PUNTING	No	Avg
Taliaferro	65	37.5
Keane	18	41.8

KICKING	XP	Att	%	FG	Att	%
McPhail	21	23	91	2	5	40
Rechichar	0	0	0	5	13	38

GREEN BAY PACKERS

RUSHING

Last Name	No.	Yds	Avg	TD
Reid	95	492	5.2	3
Cone	92	301	3.3	5
Carmichael	49	199	4.1	1
Rote	33	180	5.5	0
Parilli	42	171	4.1	4
Ferguson	52	134	2.6	0
Barton	7	40	5.7	0
Bailey	13	29	2.2	0
Boone	7	24	3.4	0
Dawson	5	18	3.6	0
Rush	1	–6	–6.0	0

RECEIVING

Last Name	No.	Yds	Avg	TD
Howton	25	463	19	4
Mann	23	327	14	2
Cone	18	165	9	1
Ferguson	15	86	6	0
Rush	14	190	14	0
Elliott	13	150	12	0
Carmichael	12	131	11	0
Reid	10	100	10	0
Bailey	8	119	15	0
Boone	6	55	9	1
Barton	2	51	26	1

PUNT RETURNS

Last Name	No.	Yds	Avg	TD
Carmichael	20	199	10	0
Dawson	7	72	10	1
Boone	5	24	5	0
Barton	2	13	7	0
Aldridge	1	0	0	0

KICKOFF RETURNS

Last Name	No.	Yds	Avg	TD
Carmichael	26	641	25	0
Ferguson	7	123	18	0
Dawson	4	102	26	0
Reid	4	82	21	0
Teteak	2	62	31	0
Bailey	2	34	17	0
Loomis	1	19	19	0
Barton	1	14	14	0
Martinkovic	2	12	6	0
Forester	1	12	12	0
Wildung	1	6	6	0

PASSING – PUNTING – KICKING

PASSING	Att	Comp	%	Yds	Yd/Att	TD	Int–%	RK
Rote	185	72	39	1005	5.4	5	15– 8	14
Parilli	166	74	45	830	5.0	4	19–11	16
Boone	1	1	100	–1	–1.0	0	0– 0	

PUNTING	No	Avg
Rush	60	37.7
Parilli	19	36.1
Rote	1	57.0

KICKING	XP	Att	%	FG	Att	%
Cone	23	25	92	5	16	31

1954 Putting Some Tarnish on the Golden Glow

The sun was shining brightly on the NFL, giving the team owners a radiant financial glow. Attendance climbed to another new record total of 2,190,571, and most of the clubs had lucrative local TV contracts to line the owners' pockets doubly with green. The veteran owners like Tim Mara, George Marshall, Art Rooney, and George Halas now raked in the dollars faster than they had lost them in the rugged 1930s and 1940s. Another old-time owner, Bert Bell, was also making out well. With his contract as commissioner renewed for twelve years, the frog-voiced Bell combined universal popularity with complete authority and an unblemished record of making the right move at the right time.

But one mosquito from the north buzzed annoyingly around the NFL's head. The Canadian Football League had also been growing fat off the postwar boom and now felt strong enough to make some inroads south of the border. American fans could watch a Canadian game every Saturday on television, often recognizing famous American players who had been lured north with healthy contracts. Nineteen fifty-two Heisman Trophy winner Billy Vessels had scorned the Baltimore Colts to cross the border, and NFL veterans Arnie Weinmeister, Eddie LeBaron, and Gene Brito this year signed with Canadian teams. But the American teams responded with their own raids, and NFL clubs soon were drawing Canadian stars south.

EASTERN CONFERENCE

Cleveland Browns—When the Browns dropped two of their first three games, the second a 55-27 loss to the Steelers, the other Eastern clubs smelled the blood of a dying champion. The obituaries were premature, however, as the Browns then won every game until the final Sunday of the season again to take their conference crown. The slow settling in of Mo Bassett, Mike McCormack, and Walt Michaels as replacements for the retired Marion Motley, Bill Willis, and Tommy Thompson partly accounted for the slow start, but renewed concentration by the long-time champs got the club back on the winning path. Led by charging end Len Ford, the defense allowed only nine touchdowns in the last nine games, while quarterback Otto Graham kept the attack moving through the air.

Philadelphia Eagles—The Eagles opened the season perfectly by beating Cleveland 28-10 and then won their next three contests to take the Eastern lead. The Philadelphia passing game drove the club, as when quarterback Adrian Burk threw seven touchdown passes in a 49-21 romp over the Redskins. But, suddenly, the attack dried up, as the Steelers, Packers, Giants, and Browns beat the Eagles in a mid-season stretch of five games. A rematch with the Redskins helped retune the offense, but with the Browns by then in high gear, the Eagles could not make up the lost ground.

New York Giants—With long-time coach Steve Owen gone, the Giants began a new era with a fantastic influx of coaching talent. Jim Lee Howell, a popular Giant end in the 1930s and 1940s, took over as head coach with the philosophy of keeping his troops loose as well as disciplined. Coming in from West Point to take control of the offense was Vince Lombardi, a forty-one-year-old inspirational leader and master tactician. Lombardi installed the power sweep, in which both guards escorted the runner around end, and the halfback option, in which the back may either pass or run as the play develops. Promoted to playing coach in charge of the defense was Tom Landry, another football genius who kept his All-Pro status as a cornerback as well as technically refining the modern 4-3-4 defense as a coach.

Pittsburgh Steelers—Promoted to head coach for the third time, Walt Kiesling got the Steelers off to a rousing 4-1 start highlighted by a 55-27 trouncing of the mighty Cleveland Browns. Most pre-season predictions had expected little of the Steelers, and the club finally lived up to those small expectations by losing six of their last seven starts. The defense, led by Ernie Stautner, Dale Dodrill, and Jack Butler, stayed tough all season, but the offense faded away after a great start.

Washington Redskins—New head coach Joe Kuharich never had much of a chance to build a winning team this year. Even before the season started, quarterback Eddie LeBaron and defensive end Gene Brito, both key performers, jumped the team to play in the Canadian League. To make matters worse, the trade of Don Doll to the Rams and the retirement of Bill Dudley left the defensive secondary quite threadbare. A 41-7 thrashing by the '49ers started the Skins on their way to five quick losses and a trip to the basement in the East, as passing teams found the Washington defense easy to throw against. Seven times the Redskins gave up over 35 points, with a 62-3 loss to Cleveland the height of the club's ineptitude. Finally, to crown an ineffective year with tragedy, guard Dave Sparks died of a heart attack after the 34-14 loss to Cleveland on December 5.

Chicago Cardinals—Even with Ollie Matson back from military service, the Cards plunged to the depths of the standings right from the first Sunday of the season. Five quick losses established the Cardinals as doormats, and the team was fortunate to beat Pittsburgh and Washington for its only victories. The offense never found the proper groove, as rookie quarterback Lamar McHan floundered about in his inexperience. Matson starred as an explosive runner and receiver, using his powerful legs to break tackles when he couldn't outrun a defender. He also found time to fill in on defense, often joining ex-runner Charlie Trippi and ex-Ram Night Train Lane in the secondary. A bargain pick-up, Lane led the league with ten interceptions.

WESTERN CONFERENCE

Detroit Lions—For the third time running, the Lions convincingly won the Western Conference title with the same cast of starring characters. Bobby Layne engineered long drives with his wobbly passes, imaginative play-calling, and driving enthusiasm, while reporters wrote stories of equal length about his late-night carousing. Doak Walker, so slight that he looked fragile, ran well behind his blockers and kicked long field goals regularly. Big Les Bingaman, a bulky 320-pounder whose tiny feet seemed out of place with his giant frame, moved like a cat both in diagnosing enemy plays and in pursuing enemy runners. The defensive secondary, dubbed Chris's Crew after safetyman Jack Christiansen, won cheers from even offense-minded fans, while Layne did his best to publicize the unsung offensive linemen.

Chicago Bears—George Halas hadn't lost the Midas touch after all, as his refurbished Bears won their last four games to capture second place in the West and re-establish themselves as NFL powers. Halas regenerated the offense with talented newcomers in key spots. Rookie Harlon Hill, a tall, lanky end from tiny Florence State College in Alabama, set the league on its ear with his spectacular grabs of long bombs and short sideline passes. At quarterback, Halas alternated rookie Zeke Bratkowski with veteran George Blanda, while ex-Brown Chick Jagade juiced up the running game at the fullback spot. Two more rookies, Stan Jones and Larry Strickland, won jobs in the offensive line, partially offsetting the loss of George Connor to injuries. The Bears grew stronger as the year progressed, and while they began the season with a 48-23 loss to Detroit, they ended it by beating those same Lions 28-24.

San Francisco '49ers—Undefeated after five games, the '49ers then fell apart, dropping three straight games to fall back into the Western Conference pack. The slide began when halfback Hugh McElhenny, heading for the league rushing title, was sidelined with a shoulder separation. Joe Perry and rookie John Henry Johnson, recruited from the Canadian Football League, both ate up yardage with their power running but could not make up for the breakaway threat lost in McElhenny. The defense also collapsed during the three-game skid, giving up 121 points to the Bears, Rams, and Lions in that span. But even with the fatal slump, the '49ers still showcased many top stars, as Perry and Johnson finished 1-2 in the NFL rushing statistics. After this season, Coach Buck Shaw was fired, taking with him a nine-year winning record but no championship trophies to grace his den.

Los Angeles Rams—Despite a 48-0 opening-day victory over Baltimore, the Rams could win only two of their first six games. The offense was still explosive, with Norm Van Brocklin passing, Tank Younger and Dan Towler running, and speedy Bob Boyd joining Tom Fears and Crazy Legs Hirsch as dangerous receivers, but the explosions now came in spurts instead of with machine-gun rapidity. Even as the attack scored 35 or more points four times, it chalked up fewer than 20 points four times. Les Richter, for whom the Rams had traded eleven players to the Dallas Texans in 1952, came out of the Army to make his pro debut as a linebacker, but the defense still coughed up 49 points more than in 1953.

Green Bay Packers—New coach Lisle Blackbourn hardly endeared himself to the populace as the Packers lost their first three games, but the club suddenly came alive, beating the Rams, Eagles, and Colts twice for four wins in their next five tilts. Blackbourn hardly had time to enjoy the renaissance, though, as the Lions twice, the '49ers, and the Rams handed the Packers four straight losses to end the year.

Baltimore Colts—In looking for a new head coach to direct the team's rebuilding, owner Carroll Rosenbloom narrowed the field down to two of Paul Brown's assistants at Cleveland. He first offered the job to Blanton Collier, only to be turned down when Collier instead chose the head job at the University of Kentucky. Then Weeb Ewbank was offered the post, and the stubby Cleveland lieutenant accepted the challenge of building the Colts into champions. Ewbank set a timetable of five years to reach the top and immediately began bringing together the players who would win the title.

FINAL TEAM STATISTICS

OFFENSE

	BALT.	CHI.B.	CHI.C.	CLEVE.	DET.	G.BAY	L.A.	N.Y.	PHIL.	PITT.	S.F.	WASH.
FIRST DOWNS:												
Total	169	219	184	238	236	207	255	197	221	205	252	188
by Rushing	66	63	83	113	91	79	115	85	66	71	125	94
by Passing	90	144	86	112	134	112	125	99	139	115	109	76
by Penalty	13	12	15	13	11	16	15	13	16	19	18	18
RUSHING:												
Number	364	353	418	476	393	321	432	380	401	368	442	427
Yards	1275	1142	1612	1793	1608	1328	2140	1482	1196	1282	2498	1626
Average Yards	3.5	3.2	3.9	3.8	4.1	4.1	5.0	3.9	3.0	3.5	5.7	3.8
Touchdowns	4	8	10	23	11	13	24	8	4	10	28	9
PASSING:												
Attempts	313	429	349	295	395	412	321	334	401	386	340	257
Completions	163	208	148	174	215	195	171	163	206	189	187	116
Completion Percentage	52.1	48.5	42.4	59.0	54.4	47.3	53.3	48.8	51.4	49.0	55.0	45.1
Gross Yards	2005	3299	1903	2557	2972	2454	3180	2467	2982	2321	2444	1813
Yards Lost Tackled	336	195	241	226	147	295	133	141	375	148	238	319
Net Yards	1669	3104	1662	2331	2825	2159	3047	2326	2607	2173	2206	1494
Avg. Yards per Attempt (Gross)	6.4	7.7	5.5	8.7	7.5	6.0	9.9	7.4	7.4	6.0	7.2	7.1
Avg. Yards per Comp. (Gross)	12.3	15.9	12.9	14.7	13.8	12.6	18.6	15.1	14.5	12.3	13.1	15.6
Touchdowns	9	26	8	14	25	14	15	27	33	15	10	15
Interceptions	22	35	30	22	21	19	23	22	30	26	12	32
Percent Intercepted	7.0	8.2	8.6	7.5	5.3	4.6	7.2	6.6	7.5	6.7	3.5	12.5
PUNTS:												
Number	72	57	63	52	63	72	44	64	73	66	60	62
Average Yards	37.2	40.1	39.2	42.9	41.0	41.7	42.6	42.5	40.0	43.2	37.0	40.2
PUNT RETURNS:												
Number	33	42	39	61	37	40	44	52	49	32	36	26
Yards	168	186	208	324	364	394	201	305	273	110	205	121
Average Yards	5.1	4.4	5.3	5.3	9.8	9.9	4.6	5.9	5.6	3.4	5.7	4.7
Touchdowns	0	0	1	0	2	1	0	1	0	0	0	0
KICKOFF RETURNS:												
Number	48	50	58	31	39	49	56	29	45	45	39	69
Yards	899	942	1420	783	822	1193	1202	662	946	987	930	1380
Average Yards	18.7	18.8	24.5	25.3	21.1	24.3	21.5	22.8	21.0	21.9	23.8	20.0
Touchdowns	0	0	3	0	1	0	1	0	0	0	0	1
INTERCEPTION RETURNS:												
Number	20	27	24	23	30	19	23	33	28	30	19	18
Yards	166	458	294	369	372	285	274	370	326	569	282	133
Average Yards	8.3	17.0	12.3	16.0	12.4	15.0	11.9	11.2	11.6	19.0	14.8	7.4
Touchdowns	0	1	0	4	2	1	1	0	1	3	2	0
PENALTIES:												
Number	71	71	91	83	75	57	77	61	85	54	73	54
Yards	662	592	819	796	689	522	757	502	874	471	614	455
FUMBLES:												
Number	20	30	32	25	22	21	27	25	38	28	30	41
Number Lost	12	15	23	17	11	12	18	15	22	17	13	23
POINTS:												
Total	131	301	183	336	337	234	314	293	284	219	313	207
PAT Attempts	13	38	23	41	43	29	41	36	39	28	40	27
PAT Made	12	37	21	40	43	27	41	36	36	25	37	26
FG Attempts	23	22	19	24	23	16	16	25	10	13	21	10
FG Made	11	12	8	16	12	9	9	13	4	8	12	5
Percent FG Made	47.8	54.5	42.1	66.7	52.2	56.3	56.3	52.0	40.0	61.5	57.1	50.0
Safeties	1	0	0	1	0	0	0	1	1	1	0	2

DEFENSE

	BALT.	CHI.B.	CHI.C.	CLEVE.	DET.	G.BAY	L.A.	N.Y.	PHIL.	PITT.	S.F.	WASH.
FIRST DOWNS:												
Total	234	221	226	147	199	228	240	195	171	221	207	282
by Rushing	95	94	85	56	85	101	92	77	64	120	74	108
by Passing	120	106	123	73	99	119	129	110	84	93	122	163
by Penalty	19	21	18	18	15	8	19	8	23	8	11	11
RUSHING:												
Number	425	427	400	372	397	403	368	415	354	466	348	400
Yards	1630	1917	1532	1050	1520	1871	1615	1332	1063	2193	1371	1888
Average Yards	3.8	4.5	3.8	2.8	3.8	4.6	4.4	3.2	3.0	4.7	3.9	4.7
Touchdowns	21	15	13	4	13	13	14	9	8	14	8	20
PASSING:												
Attempts	330	369	356	300	357	374	393	352	345	295	374	387
Completions	178	177	193	126	150	208	219	164	143	167	193	217
Completion Percentage	53.9	48.0	54.2	42.0	42.0	55.6	55.7	46.6	41.4	56.6	51.6	56.1
Gross Yards	2513	2432	3006	1784	2390	2690	2697	2322	2030	2458	3015	3060
Yards Lost Tackled	203	244	212	176	164	211	130	306	346	281	366	155
Net Yards	2310	2188	2794	1608	2226	2479	2567	2016	1684	2177	2649	2905
Avg. Yards per Attempt (Gross)	7.6	6.6	8.4	5.9	6.7	7.2	6.9	6.6	5.9	8.3	8.1	7.9
Avg. Yards per Comp. (Gross)	14.1	13.7	15.6	14.2	15.9	12.9	12.3	14.2	14.2	14.7	15.6	14.1
Touchdowns	12	13	29	15	10	17	16	11	13	18	24	33
Interceptions	20	27	24	23	30	19	23	33	28	30	19	18
Percent Intercepted	6.1	7.3	6.7	6.4	10.0	5.1	5.9	9.4	8.1	10.2	5.1	4.7
PUNTS:												
Number	57	65	55	84	65	64	58	71	71	54	59	45
Average Yards	39.8	39.4	41.7	40.1	39.3	40.1	43.0	40.2	42.3	39.9	41.0	39.6
PUNT RETURNS:												
Number	45	40	46	38	29	43	32	45	49	44	40	40
Yards	150	430	55	128	67	290	373	152	304	302	269	411
Average Yards	3.3	10.8	1.2	3.4	2.3	6.7	11.7	3.4	6.2	6.9	6.7	10.3
Touchdowns	0	2	0	1	0	1	0	0	1	0	0	0
KICKOFF RETURNS:												
Number	29	47	36	51	61	45	46	53	52	42	57	39
Yards	587	1018	832	1060	1257	832	1058	1274	1235	1003	1145	865
Average Yards	20.2	21.7	23.1	20.8	20.6	18.5	23.0	24.0	23.8	23.9	20.1	22.2
Touchdowns	0	1	1	0	0	0	0	1	2	1	0	0
INTERCEPTION RETURNS:												
Number	22	35	30	22	21	19	23	22	30	26	12	32
Yards	232	397	397	368	187	380	293	352	476	332	167	317
Average Yards	10.5	11.3	13.2	16.7	8.9	20.0	12.7	16.0	15.9	12.8	13.9	9.9
Touchdowns	1	2	1	2	0	1	1	1	2	1	0	3
PENALTIES:												
Number	92	87	74	58	53	72	63	65	58	97	51	82
Yards	834	696	716	608	489	666	605	562	589	823	426	739
FUMBLES:												
Number	28	31	30	26	22	22	18	38	32	31	29	32
Number Lost	10	18	19	19	12	14	6	22	22	20	18	18
POINTS:												
Total	279	279	347	162	189	251	285	184	230	263	251	432
PAT Attempts	36	34	44	22	23	33	34	23	27	34	32	56
PAT Made	36	32	42	21	21	32	33	20	25	33	32	54
FG Attempts	19	25	16	9	18	14	26	15	28	17	19	16
FG Made	9	13	11	3	10	7	16	8	13	8	9	12
Percent FG Made	47.4	52.0	68.8	33.3	55.6	50.0	61.5	53.3	46.4	47.1	47.4	75.0
Safeties	0	2	1	0	0	0	0	1	2	1	0	0

1954 CHAMPIONSHIP GAME

December 26 at Cleveland
(Attendance 43,827)

1954 Nearly Leaving on a Laugher

This was to be Otto Graham's last game, and he wanted to go out a winner. His first pass of the day was intercepted, leading to a Detroit field goal, but every move after that helped the Browns to a crushing 56-10 victory over the Lions. Before the first quarter had ended, the Browns led 14-3 on touchdown passes from Graham to Ray Renfro and Darrell Brewster. A 52-yard run by Lew Carpenter set up Detroit's only touchdown of the game in the second quarter, but the Browns scored three times before the half to run the score to 35-10; Graham made two touchdowns himself and passed to Renfro for another. The Cleveland defense shut the Lions out in the second half, while Graham and Co. poured it on. Graham and Fred Morrison scored in the third period, and Chet Hanulak added a final touchdown in the fourth quarter. It was a perfect farewell for Graham, but he would be back for a curtain call.

SCORING

CLEVELAND	14	21	14	7	—56
DETROIT	3	7	0	0	—10

First Quarter
- Det. Walker, 36 yard Field Goal
- Cle. Renfro, 35 yard pass from Graham — PAT – Groza (kick)
- Cle. Brewster, 8 yard pass from Graham — PAT – Groza (kick)

Second Quarter
- Cle. Graham, 1 yard rush — PAT – Groza (kick)
- Det. Bowman, 5 yard rush — PAT – Walker (kick)
- Cle. Graham, 5 yard rush — PAT – Groza (kick)
- Cle. Renfro, 31 yard pass from Graham — PAT – Groza (kick)

Third Quarter
- Cle. Graham, 1 yard rush — PAT – Groza (kick)
- Cle. Morrison, 12 yard rush — PAT – Groza (kick)

Fourth Quarter
- Cle. Hanulak, 10 yard rush — PAT – Groza (kick)

TEAM STATISTICS

DET.		CLE.
16	First Down – Total	17
5	by Rushing	8
9	by Passing	6
2	by Penalty	3
3	Fumbles – Number	2
3	Times Lost Ball	2
4	Penalties – Number	5
49	Yards Penalized	50
9	Giveaways	4
4	Takeaways	9
–5	Difference	+5

INDIVIDUAL STATISTICS

DETROIT	No	Yds	Avg.	CLEVELAND	No	Yds	Avg.
RUSHING							
Carpenter	8	34	8.0	Hanulak	5	44	8.8
Bowman	7	61	8.7	Graham	9	27	3.0
Walker	3	13	4.3	Bassett	8	27	3.4
Layne	7	7	1.0	Morrison	10	19	1.9
Horn'meyer	2	2	1.0	Reynolds	6	16	2.7
Dublinski	2	–11	–5.5	Jones	3	3	1.0
	29	136	4.7	Renfro	3	2	1.5
				Ratterman	1	2	2.0
					45	140	3.1
RECEIVING							
Carpenter	6	17	2.8	Renfro	5	94	18.8
Girard	5	57	11.4	Brewster	2	53	26.5
Dibble	4	63	15.8	Bassett	1	10	10.0
Walker	2	39	19.5	Lavelli	1	6	6.0
Hart	1	19	19.0		9	163	18.1
Bowman	1	0	0.0				
	19	195	10.3				
PUNT RETURNS							
Girard	1	0	0.0	Reynolds	1	42	42.0
				Konz	1	0	0.0
					2	42	21.0
KICKOFF RETURNS							
Girard	3	52	17.3	Reynolds	3	85	28.3
Christianson	2	36	18.0				
Walker	1	20	20.0				
	6	108	18.0				
INTERCEPTION RETURNS							
Schmidt	1	14	14.0	Ford	2	46	23.0
Christianson	1	0	0.0	Konz	2	28	14.0
	2	14	7.0	Paul	1	31	31.0
				Michaels	1	17	17.0
					6	122	20.3
PUNTING							
Girard	6		41.3	Gillom	4		43.0

PASSING

	Att	Comp	Comp Pct.	Yds	Yds/ Att.	Yds/ Comp	Yds Lost Tackled	Int
DETROIT								
Layne	42	18	42.9	177	4.2	9.8	0–0	6
Dublinski	2	1	50.0	18	9.0	18.0	0–0	0
	44	19	43.2	195	4.4	10.3	0–0	6
CLEVELAND								
Graham	12	9	75.0	163	13.6	18.1	0–0	2

CLEVELAND BROWNS 9-3-0 Paul Brown

Scores of Each Game		
10	Philadelphia	28
31	CHIC. CARDS	7
27	Pittsburgh	55
35	Chic. Cards	3
24	NEW YORK	14
62	WASHINGTON	3
39	Chic. Bears	10
6	PHILADELPHIA	0
16	New York	7
34	Washington	14
42	PITTSBURGH	7
10	DETROIT	14

Use Name	Pos.	Hgt	Wgt	Age	Int	Pts
Lou Groza	OT	6'3"	235	30		85
John Sandusky	OT	6'1"	250	28		
Don King	DT-OT	6'3"	260	24		
Harold Bradley	OG	6'2"	230	25		
Herschel Forester	OG	6'	230	24		
Abe Gibron	OG	5'11"	240	28		
Frank Gatski	C	6'3"	240	32		
Mike McCormack	DG	6'4"	248	27	1	
Doug Atkins	DE	6'8"	250	24		
Len Ford	DE	6'4"	250	28		2
Carlton Massey	DE	6'2"	215	25		
Don Colo	DT	6'3"	260	29		
John Kissell	DT	6'3"	238	31		
Bob Gain	OT-DG-DT	6'3"	250	26		
Tony Adamle	LB	6'	218	30		
Walt Michaels	LB	6'	225	25	1	
Chuck Noll	OG-LB	6'1"	210	22		
Tom Catlin	C-LB	6'1"	210	23	1	
Ken Gorgal	DB	6'2"	200	25	1	6
Kenny Konz	DB	5'10"	180	26	7	15
Don Paul	DB	6'	190	28	3	
Tommy James	HB-DB	5'10"	185	30	4	
Warren Lahr	HB-DB	5'11"	190	30	5	6
Otto Graham	QB	6'1"	205	32		48
George Ratterman	QB	6'1"	185	27		6
Chet Hanulak	HB	5'10"	180	21		24
Dub Jones	HB	6'4"	200	29		12
Ray Renfro	HB	6'1"	190	23		6
Billy Reynolds	HB	5'10"	190	22		12
Mo Bassett	FB	6'1"	230	24		36
Curley Morrison	FB	6'2"	215	28		12
Darrell Brewster	OE	6'3"	210	24		24
Dante Lavelli	OE	6'	190	31		42
Horace Gillom	DE-OE	6'1"	225	33		

Joe Skibinski – Military Service

PHILADELPHIA EAGLES 7-4-1 Jim Trimble

Scores of Each Game		
28	CLEVELAND	10
35	Chic. Cards	16
24	PITTSBURGH	22
49	Washington	21
7	Pittsburgh	17
14	GREEN BAY	37
30	CHIC. CARDS	14
14	New York	27
0	Cleveland	6
41	WASHINGTON	33
13	Detroit	13
29	NEW YORK	14

Use Name	Pos.	Hgt	Wgt	Age	Int	Pts
Gus Cifelli (to PIT)	OT	6'4"	250	28		
Lum Snyder	OT	6'5"	225	24		
Frank Wydo	OT	6'4"	235	30		
Ken Huxhold	OG	6'1"	215	25		
John Magee	OG	5'10"	220	31		
Menil Mavraides	OG	6'1"	235	20		
Tom Higgins	OT-OG	6'2"	230	25		
Ken Farragut	LB-C	6'4"	245	26		
Bucko Kilroy	DG	6'2"	250	33	4	
Tom Scott	DE	6'2"	218	24		
Don Luft	OE-DE	6'5"	220	25		
Norm Willey	OE-DE	6'2"	225	27		6
Mike Jarmoluk	DT	6'5"	250	31		
Jess Richardson	DT	6'2"	240	24	1	
Wayne Robinson	LB	6'2"	230	24	4	
Chuck Bednarik	C-LB	6'3"	230	29	1	
Ed Sharkey	OT-OG-LB	6'3"	230	27	1	
Roy Barni	DB	5'11"	185	27	2	
Harry Dowda	DB	6'2"	200	30	2	
Ralph Goldston	DB	5'11"	195	26		
Bob Hudson	DB	6'4"	220	24	8	
Don Miller (from GB)	DB	6'2"	195	23		
Bud Roffler	DB	6'1"	200	25		
Don Stevens	DB	5'9"	176	27		
Jerry Norton	HB-DB	5'11"	183	24	5	6
Adrian Burk	QB	6'2"	190	26		
Bobby Thomason	QB	6'1"	200	25		
Skippy Giancanelli	HB	5'10"	173	25		24
Don Johnson	HB	6'	187	23		
Toy Ledbetter	HB	5'10"	200	27		24
Jerry Williams	HB	5'10"	185	30		24
Dom Moselle	DB-HB	6'	193	28		18
Jim Parmer	FB	6'	195	27		
Neil Worden	FB	5'10"	190	24		6
Bobby Walston	OE	6'	190	25		114
Pete Pihos	DE-OE	6'1"	210	30		60

Bibbles Bawel – Military Service
Tom Brookshier – Military Service

Bill Horrell – Military Service
Maury Nipp – Military Service

NEW YORK GIANTS 7-5-0 Jim Lee Howell

Scores of Each Game		
41	Chic. Cards	10
14	Baltimore	20
51	Washington	21
31	CHIC. CARDS	17
24	WASHINGTON	7
14	Cleveland	24
30	Pittsburgh	6
27	PHILADELPHIA	14
16	LOS ANGELES	17
7	CLEVELAND	16
24	PITTSBURGH	3
14	Philadelphia	29

Use Name	Pos.	Hgt	Wgt	Age	Int	Pts
Rosey Brown	OT	6'3"	245	21		
Dick Yelvington	OT	6'2"	230	27		
Bill Austin	OG	6'1"	225	25		
John Bauer	OG	6'3"	235	22		
Russ Carroccio	OG	6'1"	235	23		
George Kennard	OG	6'	215	25		
Jack Stroud	OG	6'1"	215	25		
Bill Albright	OT-DT-OG	6'1"	235	25		
John Rapacz	C	6'4"	260	29		
Barney Poole	DE	6'2"	250	31		
Pat Knight	LB-DE	6'2"	210	25	3	
Ray Collins	DT	5'11"	235	26		
Ray Krouse	DT	6'3"	260	27		
Billy Shipp	DT	6'5"	275	23		
John Cannady	LB	6'2"	245	30	2	
Pete Mangum	LB	6'	218	22		
Bill Svoboda	LB	6'	210	27	1	
Ray Wietecha	C-LB	6'1"	225	25		
Cliff Livingston	DE-LB	6'3"	205	24		
Tom Landry	DB	6'1"	195	29	8	
Dick Nolan	DB	6'1"	185	22	6	2
Herb Rich	DB	5'11"	180	25	5	
Em Tunnell	DB	6'1"	185	32	8	
Wayne Berry	HB-DB	6'	175	21		
Bobby Clatterbuck	QB	6'3"	195	22		6
Chuck Conerly	QB	6'1"	185	30		7
Don Heinrich	QB	6'	185	22		
Frank Gifford	HB	6'1"	195	24		18
Herb Johnson	HB	5'10"	172	25		12
Cutter Long	HB	6'1"	195	22		12
Kyle Rote	HB	6'	195	25		12
Bobby Epps	FB	5'9"	195	22		
Eddie Price	FB	5'11"	190	28		30
Ken MacAfee	OE	6'2"	205	24		48
Bob Schnelker	OE	6'3"	215	24		48
Bob Topp	OE	6'2"	190	22		18
Dick Wilkins	OE	6'2"	195	28		6
Ben Agajanian	K	6'	215	35		74

Ray Beck – Military Service
Arnie Weinmeister – Canadian Football League

PITTSBURGH STEELERS 5-7-0 Joe Bach Walt Kiesling

Scores of Each Game		
21	Green Bay	20
37	WASHINGTON	7
22	Philadelphia	24
55	CLEVELAND	27
17	PHILADELPHIA	7
14	Chic. Cards	17
6	NEW YORK	30
14	Washington	17
3	SAN FRANCISCO	31
20	CHIC. CARDS	17
3	New York	24
7	Cleveland	42

Use Name	Pos.	Hgt	Wgt	Age	Int	Pts
Bob Gaona	OT	6'3"	245	24		
George Hughes	OT	6'1"	225	29		
Nick Bolkovac	DT-OT	6'1"	230	27		12
Joe Matesic	DT-OT	6'4"	250	26		
Rudy Andabaker	OG	6'	210	25		
Pete Ladygo	OG	6'2"	220	26		
John Schweder	LB-OG	6'1"	225	27		
Bill Walsh	C	6'2"	238	27		
Dewey Brundage	DE	6'3"	210	23		
Bill McPeak	DE	6'1"	200	29		2
Joe Zombek	DE	6'1"	195	22		
Ernie Cheatham (to BAL)	DT	6'4"	245	26		
Lou Ferry	DT	6'2"	245	27		
Tom Palmer	DT	6'2"	240	26		
Ernie Stautner	DT	6'1"	235	29	1	
Dale Dodrill	LB	6'1"	210	29	3	
Dick Flanagan	LB	6'	220	27	3	
Stan Sheriff	C-LB	6'1"	230	23	1	
Lou Tepe	C-LB	6'2"	205	24	3	
Paul Cameron	DB	6'	185	23	7	
Russ Craft	DB	5'9"	180	34	3	6
Ed Kissell	DB	6'1"	195	26	1	14
Jack Butler	OE-DB	6'	195	26	4	12
Dewey McConnell	OE-DB	6'	190	25	3	
Jim Finks	QB	6'	175	27		
Paul Held	QB	6'2"	195	26		23
Tom Calvin	HB	6'	200	28		
Lynn Chandnois	HB	6'2"	195	30		6
Johnny Lattner	HB	6'1"	195	22		42
Ray Mathews	HB	6'	185	25		48
Jim Brandt	DB-HB	6'1"	200	26		6
Burrell Shields	DB-HB	6'2"	205	22	1	
Leo Elter	FB	5'10"	200	25		
Fran Rogel	FB	5'11"	205	27		12
Elbie Nickel	OE	6'1"	195	31		30
George Sulima	OE	6'2"	200	27		6
Jack O'Brien	DE-OE	6'2"	215	23		
Pat Brady	K	6'1"	195	26		

Marv Matuszak – Military Service
Marv McFadden – Military Service
Ed Modzelewski – Military Service
George Tarasovic – Military Service

WASHINGTON REDSKINS 3-9-0 Joe Kuharich

Scores of Each Game		
7	San Francisco	41
7	Pittsburgh	37
21	NEW YORK	51
21	PHILADELPHIA	49
7	New York	24
24	BALTIMORE	21
3	Cleveland	62
17	PITTSBURGH	14
16	Chic. Cards	38
33	Philadelphia	41
14	CLEVELAND	34
37	CHIC. CARDS	20

Use Name	Pos.	Hgt	Wgt	Age	Int	Pts
Don Boll	OT	6'2"	274	27		
Dave Sparks – died Dec. 5	OT	6'1"	238	25		
Ken Barfield	DT-OT	6'2"	238	25		
Slug Witucki	OG	5'11"	253	26		
Marv Berschet	DE-OG	6'2"	220	25		
Ron Hansen	LB-OG	6'	220	22		
Harry Ulinski	C	6'4"	228	29		
Jim Schrader	OT-C	6'2"	233	22		
Jim Ricca	OT-DT-DG	6'4"	274	27		8
Chet Ostrowski	DE	6'1"	225	24	1	
Walt Yowarsky	DE	6'2"	235	26		
Dick Modzelewski	DT	6'	260	23		2
Volney Peters	DT	6'4"	230	26		
Bob Morgan (from Chi C)	OT-DT	6'	235	21		
Nick Adducci	LB	5'10"	210	25		
Walt Cudzik	C-LB	6'2"	215	21		
Joe Tereshinski	DE-LB	6'2"	220	30		
Chuck Drazenovich	FB-LB	6'1"	224	27	1	
Ralph Felton	FB-LB	5'11"	210	22	2	19
Dick Alban	DB	6'	192	25	9	
Jim Kincaid	DB	5'11"	180	23		1
Don Menasco	DB	6'	185	24		
George Rosso	DB	5'11"	177	24	4	
Scooter Scudero	HB-DB	5'10"	175	24	1	6
Al Dorow	QB	6'	194	24		18
Jack Scarbath	QB	6'2"	208	24		
Vic Janowicz	HB	5'9"	184	24		21
Choo-Choo Justice	HB	5'10"	178	30		18
Billy Wells	HB	5'9"	178	22		24
Harry Gilmer	DB-HB	6'	173	28		
Dale Atkeson	FB	6'2"	210	24		18
Rob Goode	FB	6'4"	226	27		6
Ed Barker	OE	6'3"	193	31		18
Johnny Carson	OE	6'3"	200	24		
Hugh Taylor	OE	6'4"	208	31		48
Sam Morley	OE	6'2"	182	22		

Sam Baker – Military Service
Gene Brito – Canadian Football League
Billy Cox – Military Service
Art DeCarlo – Military Service
Paul Dekker – Canadian Football League

Norb Hecker – Canadian Football League
Eddie LeBaron – Canadian Football League

CHICAGO CARDINALS 2-10-0 Joe Stydahar

Scores of Each Game		
10	NEW YORK	41
16	PHILADELPHIA	35
7	Cleveland	31
17	New York	31
3	CLEVELAND	35
17	PITTSBURGH	14
14	Philadelphia	30
17	Los Angeles	28
38	WASHINGTON	16
17	Pittsburgh	20
7	CHIC. BEARS	29
20	Washington	37

Use Name	Pos.	Hgt	Wgt	Age	Int	Pts
Jack Jennings	OT	6'4"	248	27		
Len Teeuws	OT	6'4"	245	27		
Ledio Fanucchi	DT-OT	6'2"	225	23		
Dick Fugler	DT-OT	6'2"	240	24		
John Hatley	OG	6'3"	245	23		
Jerry Watford	DE-OG	6'3"	205	24		
Bill Lange	LB-OG	6'1"	230	27		
Jack Simmons	C	6'4"	230	28		
Tom Bienemann	DE	6'3"	215	26		
Leo Sugar	DE	6'1"	200	25		6
Pat Summerall	DE	6'4"	220	24		45
Jerry Groom	DT	6'3"	235	25		
Chuck Ulrich	DT	6'4"	225	23		
Gordon Polofsky	OG-LB	6'1"	220	23		
Fred Wallner	OG-LB	6'2"	230	25		
Leo Sanford	C-LB	6'1"	220	25	2	
Elmer Arterburn	DB	5'10"	175	25		
Al Brosky	DB	5'11"	175	24	2	
Ellsworth Kingery	DB	5'11"	180	25	1	
Charley Oakley	DB	5'10"	170	23		
Bill Bredde	HB-DB	6'1"	195	21	2	6
George Kinek	OE-DB	6'2"	190	25	2	
Night Train Lane	OE-DB	6'1"	190	26	10	
Lamar McHan	QB	6'1"	190	22		6
Steve Romanik	QB	6'1"	190	30		6
Paul Barry	HB	6'	210	28		
Emmett King	HB	5'9"	195	21		6
George Brancato	DB-HB	5'9"	177	23		
Les Goble	DB-HB	5'11"	160	22	1	18
Ollie Matson	DB-HB	6'2"	210	24	1	54
Jimmy Sears	DB-HB	5'11"	178	23		
Charlie Trippi	DB-HB	6'	185	31	3	6
Johnny Olszewski	FB	5'11"	195	23		12
Jack Crittendon	OE	6'1"	190	23		
Mel Embree	OE	6'3"	190	27		
Jim Ladd	OE	6'4"	205	21		
Don Stonesifer	OE	6'	200	27		18

Ed Husmann – Military Service
Gern Nagler – Military Service
Jim Root – Military Service
Dave Suminski – Canadian Football League
Ralph Thomas – Military Service

CLEVELAND BROWNS

RUSHING

Last Name	No.	Yds	Avg	TD
Bassett	144	588	4.1	6
Hanulak	59	296	5.0	4
Morrison	54	234	4.3	2
Jones	51	231	4.5	0
Reynolds	64	180	2.8	2
Renfro	29	151	5.2	0
Graham	63	114	1.8	8
Lahr	3	18	6.0	0
James	1	–6	–6.0	0
Ratterman	8	–13	–1.6	1

RECEIVING

Last Name	No.	Yds	Avg	TD
Lavelli	47	802	17	7
Brewster	42	676	16	4
Bassett	20	205	10	0
Jones	19	347	18	2
Renfro	13	228	18	1
Morrison	12	81	7	0
Reynolds	10	76	8	0
Hanulak	6	80	13	0
Gillom	5	62	12	0

PUNT RETURNS

Last Name	No.	Yds	Avg	TD
Reynolds	25	138	6	0
Hanulak	27	92	3	0
Paul	1	57	57	0
Konz	7	37	5	0
Gorgal	1	0	0	0

KICKOFF RETURNS

Last Name	No.	Yds	Avg	TD
Reynolds	14	413	30	0
Hanulak	9	213	24	0
Konz	2	53	27	0
Paul	1	31	31	0
Renfro	1	24	24	0
Bassett	1	20	20	0
Gorgal	1	11	11	0
Massey	1	10	10	0
Morrison	1	8	8	0

PASSING – PUNTING – KICKING Statistics

PASSING	Att	Comp	%	Yds	Yd/Att	TD	Int–%	RK
Graham	240	142	59	2092	8.7	11	17– 7	3
Ratterman	53	32	60	465	8.8	3	3– 5	
Lahr	1	0	0	0	0.0	0	1–100	
Renfro	1	0	0	0	0.0	0	1–100	

PUNTING	No	Avg
Gillom	52	42.9

KICKING	XP	Att	%	FG	Att	%
Groza	37	38	97	16	24	67
Konz	3	3	100	0	0	0

PHILADELPHIA EAGLES

RUSHING

Last Name	No.	Yds	Avg	TD
Parmer	119	408	3.4	0
Ledbetter	81	241	3.0	1
Williams	47	183	3.9	1
Worden	58	128	2.2	1
Moselle	29	114	3.9	1
Giancanelli	33	47	1.4	0
Thomason	10	45	4.5	0
Burk	15	18	1.2	0
Johnson	7	16	2.3	0
Pihos	1	–1	–1.0	0
Norton	1	–3	–3.0	0

RECEIVING

Last Name	No.	Yds	Avg	TD
Pihos	60	872	15	10
Williams	44	668	15	3
Walston	31	581	19	11
Moselle	17	242	14	2
Ledbetter	15	192	13	3
Giancanelli	14	195	14	4
Parmer	12	40	3	0
Worden	7	63	9	0
Luft	3	59	20	0
Willey	2	50	25	0
Johnson	1	20	20	0

PUNT RETURNS

Last Name	No.	Yds	Avg	TD
Williams	23	153	7	0
Norton	21	89	4	0
Bednarik	2	26	13	0
Sharkey	1	5	5	0
Barni	1	0	0	0
Cifelli	1	0	0	0

KICKOFF RETURNS

Last Name	No.	Yds	Avg	TD
Giancanelli	17	387	23	0
Ledbetter	8	175	22	0
Johnson	6	152	25	0
Moselle	7	149	21	0
Bednarik	3	40	13	0
Roffler	1	19	19	0
Snyder	2	17	9	0
Stevens	1	6	6	0

PASSING – PUNTING – KICKING Statistics

PASSING	Att	Comp	%	Yds	Yd/Att	TD	Int–%	RK
Burk	231	123	53	1740	7.5	23	17– 7	5
Thomason	170	83	49	1242	7.3	10	13– 8	14

PUNTING	No	Avg
Burk	73	40.0

KICKING	XP	Att	%	FG	Att	%
Walston	36	39	92	4	10	40

NEW YORK GIANTS

RUSHING

Last Name	No.	Yds	Avg	TD
Price	135	555	4.1	2
Gifford	66	368	5.6	2
Johnson	42	168	4.0	1
Epps	30	110	3.7	0
Conerly	24	107	4.5	1
Long	32	106	3.3	1
Rote	30	59	2.0	0
Berry	1	30	30.0	0
Heinrich	1	0	0.0	0
Clatterbuck	19	–21	–1.1	1

RECEIVING

Last Name	No.	Yds	Avg	TD
Schnelker	30	550	18	8
Rote	29	551	19	2
Price	28	352	13	3
MacAfee	24	438	18	8
Gifford	14	154	11	1
Long	13	178	14	1
Johnson	10	89	9	0
Topp	6	90	15	3
Epps	5	20	4	0
Wilkins	4	45	11	1

PUNT RETURNS

Last Name	No.	Yds	Avg	TD
Johnson	16	164	10	1
Tunnell	21	70	3	0
Long	6	54	9	0
Gifford	8	12	2	0
Rich	1	5	5	0

KICKOFF RETURNS

Last Name	No.	Yds	Avg	TD
Johnson	10	251	25	0
Long	10	237	24	0
Tunnell	5	98	20	0
Gifford	1	29	29	0
Svoboda	1	21	21	0
Kennard	1	16	16	0
Topp	1	10	10	0

PASSING – PUNTING – KICKING Statistics

PASSING	Att	Comp	%	Yds	Yd/Att	TD	Int–%	RK
Conerly	210	103	49	1439	6.9	17	11– 5	7
Clatterbuck	101	50	50	781	7.7	6	7– 7	12
Heinrich	9	4	44	56	6.2	0	2– 22	
Gifford	8	4	50	155	19.4	3	1– 13	
Rote	6	2	33	36	6.0	1	1– 17	

PUNTING	No	Avg
Landry	64	42.5

KICKING	XP	Att	%	FG	Att	%
Agajanian	35	35	100	13	25	52
Conerly	1	1	100	0	0	0

PITTSBURGH STEELERS

RUSHING

Last Name	No.	Yds	Avg	TD
Rogel	111	415	3.7	1
Mathews	80	242	3.0	2
Lattner	69	237	3.4	5
Chandnois	45	147	3.3	1
Brandt	19	82	4.3	1
Calvin	12	57	4.8	0
Elter	13	54	4.2	0
Shields	7	28	4.0	0
Finks	9	17	1.9	0
Held	3	3	1.0	0

RECEIVING

Last Name	No.	Yds	Avg	TD
Mathews	44	652	15	6
Nickel	40	584	15	5
Sulima	30	439	15	1
Lattner	25	305	12	2
Chandnois	22	176	8	0
Rogel	18	51	3	1
Elter	4	16	4	0
Shields	1	22	22	0
Calvin	1	19	19	0
Butler	1	12	12	0
Brandt	1	9	9	0
O'Brien	1	9	9	0
McConnell	1	2	2	0
Gaona	0	25	0	0

PUNT RETURNS

Last Name	No.	Yds	Avg	TD
Lattner	17	73	4	0
Cameron	2	19	10	0
Chandnois	8	12	2	0
Mathews	2	6	3	0
Shields	3	0	0	0

KICKOFF RETURNS

Last Name	No.	Yds	Avg	TD
Lattner	16	413	26	0
Chandnois	13	256	20	0
Shields	9	183	20	0
Mathews	4	88	22	0
Elter	2	32	16	0
Calvin	1	15	15	0

PASSING – PUNTING – KICKING Statistics

PASSING	Att	Comp	%	Yds	Yd/Att	TD	Int–%	RK
Finks	306	164	54	2003	6.6	14	19– 6	7
Held	73	24	33	305	4.2	1	6– 8	
Mathews	4	0	0	0	0.0	0	1– 25	
Chandnois	3	1	33	13	4.3	0	0– 0	

PUNTING	No	Avg
Brady	66	43.2

KICKING	XP	Att	%	FG	Att	%
Held	14	16	88	3	5	60
Kissell	8	9	89	2	4	50
Bolkovac	3	3	100	3	4	75

WASHINGTON REDSKINS

RUSHING

Last Name	No.	Yds	Avg	TD
Wells	100	516	5.2	3
Goode	108	462	4.3	0
Justice	56	254	4.5	1
Atkeson	68	176	2.6	2
Dorow	34	117	3.4	3
Scarbath	17	36	2.1	0
Gilmer	6	19	3.2	0
Scudero	21	19	0.9	0
Janowicz	6	13	2.2	0
Felton	3	8	2.7	0
Drazenovich	8	6	0.8	0

RECEIVING

Last Name	No.	Yds	Avg	TD
Taylor	37	659	18	8
Barker	23	353	15	3
Wells	19	295	16	1
Carson	12	139	12	0
Justice	11	242	22	2
Atkeson	4	75	19	0
Scudero	4	32	8	1
Goode	4	4	1	0
Drazenovich	1	15	15	0
Janowicz	1	–1	–1	0

PUNT RETURNS

Last Name	No.	Yds	Avg	TD
Scudero	14	53	4	0
Atkeson	4	29	7	0
Wells	3	24	8	0
Rosso	4	15	4	0
Felton	1	0	0	0

KICKOFF RETURNS

Last Name	No.	Yds	Avg	TD
Atkeson	24	623	26	1
Wells	17	319	19	0
Goode	16	284	18	0
Scudero	3	70	23	0
Felton	2	18	9	0
Janowicz	1	18	18	0
Drazenovich	1	17	17	0
Yowarsky	1	13	13	0
Ostrowski	3	9	3	0
Ricca	1	9	9	0

PASSING – PUNTING – KICKING Statistics

PASSING	Att	Comp	%	Yds	Yd/Att	TD	Int–%	RK
Dorow	138	70	51	997	7.2	8	17– 12	15
Scarbath	109	44	40	798	7.3	7	13– 12	16
Gilmer	7	2	29	18	2.6	0	1– 14	
Justice	2	0	0	0	0.0	0	1– 50	
Janowicz	1	0	0	0	0.0	0	0– 0	

PUNTING	No	Avg
Justice	61	40.3
Janowicz	1	32.0

KICKING	XP	Att	%	FG	Att	%
Felton	16	17	94	1	2	50
Janowicz	9	9	100	4	8	50
Kincaid	1	1	100	0	0	0

CHICAGO CARDINALS

RUSHING

Last Name	No.	Yds	Avg	TD
Matson	101	506	5.0	4
Olszewski	106	352	3.3	1
King	57	167	2.9	0
Barry	50	156	3.1	0
Trippi	18	152	8.4	1
McHan	34	152	4.5	1
Bredde	13	57	4.4	1
Goble	30	42	1.4	1
Brancato	2	26	13.0	0
Romanik	7	2	0.3	1

RECEIVING

Last Name	No.	Yds	Avg	TD
Stonesifer	44	607	14	3
Matson	34	611	18	3
Ladd	22	254	12	0
Olszewski	12	133	11	1
Barry	7	29	4	0
King	6	43	7	1
Crittendon	5	48	10	0
Lane	4	58	15	0
Bredde	3	44	15	0
Brancato	3	28	9	0
Trippi	3	18	6	0
Embree	2	20	10	0
Goble	1	–1	–1	0

PUNT RETURNS

Last Name	No.	Yds	Avg	TD
Matson	11	100	9	1
Trippi	6	57	10	0
Goble	22	51	2	0

KICKOFF RETURNS

Last Name	No.	Yds	Avg	TD
Goble	27	749	28	2
Matson	17	449	26	1
Barry	5	80	16	0
Sears	2	38	19	0
Olszewski	1	21	21	0
Bredde	1	19	19	0
King	1	19	19	0
Trippi	1	17	17	0
Hatley	1	11	11	0
Jennings	1	10	10	0
Sugar	1	7	7	0

PASSING – PUNTING – KICKING Statistics

PASSING	Att	Comp	%	Yds	Yd/Att	TD	Int–%	RK
McHan	255	105	41	1475	5.8	6	22– 9	17
Romanik	79	36	46	343	4.3	2	5– 6	
Trippi	13	7	54	85	6.5	0	3– 23	
Matson	2	0	0	0	0.0	0	0– 0	

PUNTING	No	Avg
Trippi	59	39.1
McHan	4	39.8

KICKING	XP	Att	%	FG	Att	%
Summerall	21	23	91	8	18	44
Crittendon	0	0	0	0	1	0

1954 N.F.L. — Western Conference

DETROIT LIONS 9-2-1 Buddy Parker

Scores of Each Game		
48	CHIC. BEARS	23
21	LOS ANGELES	3
35	BALTIMORE	0
31	San Francisco	37
27	Los Angeles	24
27	Baltimore	3
48	SAN FRANCISCO	7
21	Green Bay	17
28	GREEN BAY	24
13	PHILADELPHIA	13
24	Chic. Bears	28
14	Cleveland	10

Use Name	Pos.	Hgt	Wgt	Age	Int	Pts
Charlie Ane	OT	6'2"	250	23		
Lou Creekmur	DT-OT	6'4"	255	27		
Dick Stanfel	OG	6'3"	240	27		
Harley Sewell	LB-OG	6'1"	225	23		6
Andy Miketa	C	6'2"	210	23		
Les Bingaman	DG	6'3"	320	29		
Jim Cain	DE	6'1"	200	27		
Bob Dove	DE	6'2"	220	33		
Sonny Gandee	DE	6'1"	220	25	3	
Hal Turner	DE	6'2"	235	24		
Jim Doran	OE-DE	6'2"	200	26		24
Gil Mains	DT	6'2"	235	24		
Jerry Perry	DT	6'4"	235	23		
Thurman McGraw	OT-DT	6'5"	235	27		
Bob Miller	OT-DT	6'3"	235	24		

Use Name	Pos.	Hgt	Wgt	Age	Int	Pts
Joe Schmidt	LB	6'1"	220	22	2	
Jim Martin	OG-LB	6'2"	230	30		3
Lavern Torgeson	C-LB	6'	215	25	2	
Jack Christiansen	DB	6'1"	190	25	8	12
Jim David	DB	5'11"	175	27	7	
Carl Karilivacz	DB	6'	185	23	2	6
Bill Stits	DB	6'	190	23	6	

Stan Campbell – Military Service
Gene Gedman – Military Service
Jim Hill – Military Service
Yale Lary – Military Service
Ollie Spencer – Military Service

Use Name	Pos.	Hgt	Wgt	Age	Int	Pts
Tom Dublinski	QB	6'2"	190	24		6
Bobby Layne	QB	6'1"	200	27		12
Bob Hoernschemeyer	HB	5'11"	195	28		18
Doak Walker	HB	5'11"	172	27		106
Dick Kercher	DB-HB	6'2"	205	22		
Lew Carpenter	FB-HB	6'1"	200	22		30
Jug Girard	OE-HB	5'11"	175	27		42
Bill Bowman	FB	6'2"	210	23		30
Bob Smith	FB	6'	205	25		
Cloyce Box	OE	6'4"	220	30		
Dorne Dibble	OE	6'2"	195	25		36
Leon Hart	OE	6'5"	250	25		6

CHICAGO BEARS 8-4-0 George Halas

Scores of Each Game		
23	Detroit	48
10	Green Bay	3
28	BALTIMORE	9
24	SAN FRANCISCO	31
38	Los Angeles	42
31	San Francisco	27
28	GREEN BAY	23
10	CLEVELAND	39
28	Baltimore	13
24	LOS ANGELES	13
29	Chic. Cards	7
28	DETROIT	24

Use Name	Pos.	Hgt	Wgt	Age	Int	Pts
Stan Jones	OT	6'1"	255	23		
Bill Wightkin	OT	6'3"	233	27		
George Connor	LB-OT	6'3"	240	29	1	
Kline Gilbert	OG	6'2"	235	23		
Fred Williams	OG	6'4"	250	24		
Larry Strickland	C	6'4"	255	23		
Larry Brink	DE	6'5"	240	31		6
Ted Daffer	DE	6'	198	24		
Ed Meadows	DE	6'2"	220	22		
Ed Sprinkle	DE	6'1"	210	30	1	
Bill Bishop	DT	6'4"	245	23		
John Kreamcheck	DT	6'5"	255	26		
Paul Lipscomb (from WAS)	DT	6'5"	250	31		

Frank Dempsey – Canadian Football League

Use Name	Pos.	Hgt	Wgt	Age	Int	Pts
Herman Clark	LB	6'3"	255	23		
John Helwig	LB	6'2"	208	26	3	
Jerry Weatherley	C-LB	6'5"	218	25	2	6
Bill George	OG-LB	6'2"	240	23	2	25
Pete Perini	FB-LB	6'	225	26		1
Wayne Hansen	OT-OG-C-LB	6'2"	235	26	1	6
Lloyd Lowe	DB	5'10"	155	25		
McNeil Moore	DB	6'	185	21	3	
Stan Wallace	DB	6'3"	208	22	4	
S. J. Whitman	DB	5'11"	185	28	5	6
Don Kindt	HB-DB	6'1"	208	28	2	
Ray Gene Smith	HB-DB	5'10"	188	24	2	

Jack Hoffman – Military Service
Eddie Macon – Canadian Football League
Tom O'Connell – Military Service

Use Name	Pos.	Hgt	Wgt	Age	Int	Pts
George Blanda	QB	6'1"	207	26		47
Zeke Bratkowski	QB	6'2"	202	22		6
Ed Brown	DB-QB	6'2"	205	25	1	
Bucky McElroy	HB	5'11"	195	25		
Billy Stone	HB	6'	190	28		36
Billy Anderson	DB-HB	6'	198	25		
John Hoffman	OE-HB	6'2"	215	28		12
Leon Campbell	FB	6'	197	27		
Chick Jagade	FB	6'	220	27		18
Jim Dooley	OE	6'4"	198	24		42
Harlon Hill	OE	6'3"	198	22		72
Bill McColl	OE	6'4"	230	24		12
Gene Schroeder	OE	6'3"	190	25		6

Bob Williams – Military Service

SAN FRANCISCO FORTY NINERS 7-4-1 Buck Shaw

Scores of Each Game		
41	WASHINGTON	7
24	Los Angeles	24
23	Green Bay	17
31	Chic. Bears	24
37	DETROIT	31
27	CHIC. BEARS	31
34	LOS ANGELES	42
7	Detroit	48
31	Pittsburgh	3
13	Baltimore	17
35	GREEN BAY	0
10	BALTIMORE	7

Use Name	Pos.	Hgt	Wgt	Age	Int	Pts
Bob St. Clair	OT	6'9"	262	23		
Doug Hogland	OG-OT	6'3"	235	23		
Bruno Banducci	OG	5'11"	220	32		
Ted Connolly	OG	6'3"	225	22		
Nick Feher	OG	6'	225	27		
Bob Hantla	LB-OG	6'1"	220	22		
Bill Johnson	C	6'3"	240	28		
Jack Brumfield	DE	6'2"	215	22		
Clay Matthews	DE	6'3"	220	26		
Al Carapella	DT	6'	235	27	2	
Leo Nomellini	OT-DT	6'3"	252	29		
Bob Toneff	DT-DG	6'2"	252	24	1	
Marion Campbell	OT-DE-DT	6'3"	245	25		

Fred Bruney – Military Service

Use Name	Pos.	Hgt	Wgt	Age	Int	Pts
Hardy Brown	LB	6'	196	30	3	6
Don Burke	OG-LB	6'	240	28		
Art Michalik	OG-LB	6'2"	230	24		
Pete Brown	C-LB	6'2"	210	23	1	
Pete Wissman	C-LB	6'	220	30		
Frank Cassara	FB-LB	6'	215	27		
Rex Berry	DB	5'11"	180	28	3	6
Johnny Williams	DB	5'11"	180	27	3	
Jim Cason	HB-DB	6'	175	27		
Billy Mixon	HB-DB	5'11"	197	24	2	
Billy Tidwell	HB-DB	5'9"	178	23		
Floyd Sagely	OE-DB	6'1"	187	22		

Ed Henke – Military Service
Pat O'Donahue – Military Service
Charley Powell – Military Service

Use Name	Pos.	Hgt	Wgt	Age	Int	Pts
Maury Duncan	QB	6'1"	185	23		
Arnie Galiffa	QB	6'2"	190	27		
Y. A. Tittle	QB	6'	190	27		24
John Henry Johnson	HB	6'2"	205	24		54
Hugh McElhenny	HB	6'1"	198	25		36
Joe Arenas	DB-HB	5'11"	180	28	3	
Pete Schabarum	DB-HB	5'11"	185	25	1	6
Joe Perry	FB	6'	210	27		57
Bill Jessup	OE	6'1"	195	25		18
Gordie Soltau	OE	6'2"	195	29		76
Billy Wilson	OE	6'3"	190	27		30
Harry Babcock	DE-OE	6'2"	195	23		

Verl Lillywhite – Military Service
Jerry Smith – Military Service
Bob White – Military Service

LOS ANGELES RAMS 6-5-1 Hamp Pool

Scores of Each Game		
48	Baltimore	0
24	SAN FRANCISCO	24
3	Detroit	21
17	Green Bay	35
42	CHIC. BEARS	38
24	DETROIT	27
42	San Francisco	34
28	CHIC. CARDS	17
17	New York	16
13	Chic. Bears	24
21	BALTIMORE	22
35	GREEN BAY	27

Use Name	Pos.	Hgt	Wgt	Age	Int	Pts
Bob Cross	OT	6'4"	250	23		
Tom Dahms	OT	6'5"	240	26		
Duane Putnam	OG	6'	230	26		
Harry Thompson	OG	6'2"	225	27		
Art Hauser	DT-OG	6'	230	23		
Leon McLaughlin	C	6'2"	228	28		
Stan West	DG	6'2"	235	27	1	
Duane Wardlow	DE	6'4"	215	22		
Paul Miller	C-DE	6'2"	215	22	1	
Andy Robustelli	DE	6'1"	220	28		6
Big Daddy Lipscomb	DT	6'6"	280	23		
Charlie Toogood	OT-DT	6'	235	26	1	

Rudy Bukich – Military Service

Use Name	Pos.	Hgt	Wgt	Age	Int	Pts
Bob Griffin	LB	6'3"	220	25		
Les Richter	LB	6'3"	240	23	1	62
Harland Svare	LB	6'	210	23		
Don Paul	C-LB	6'1"	230	29		
Bud McFadin	OG-DT-LB	6'3"	245	26		
Bill Bowers	DB	6'	198	23		
Don Doll	DB	5'10"	185	27	5	
Jack Dwyer	DB	5'11"	175	27	4	6
Hall Haynes	DB	6'	185	25	1	
Ed Haynes	DB	6'1"	185	26	2	
Will Sherman	DB	6'2"	200	25	6	

Dick Daugherty – Military Service
Bob Fry – Military Service

Use Name	Pos.	Hgt	Wgt	Age	Int	Pts
Norm Van Brocklin	QB	6'1"	200	28		
Billy Wade	QB	6'2"	215	23		6
Tom McCormick	HB	5'11"	190	24		
Skeets Quinlan	HB	5'11"	175	26		36
Woodley Lewis	DB-OE-HB	6'	195	29		6
Tank Younger	LB-FB-HB	6'3"	226	26		48
Dan Towler	FB	6'2"	226	26		66
Bob Boyd	OE	6'2"	200	26		36
Bob Carey	OE	6'5"	215	26		5
Tom Fears	OE	6'2"	215	30		19
Crazy Legs Hirsch	DB-OE	6'2"	190	30	1	18

Don Klosterman – Military Service
Brad Myers – Military Service

GREEN BAY PACKERS 4-8-0 Lisle Blackbourn

Scores of Each Game		
20	PITTSBURGH	21
3	CHIC. BEARS	10
17	SAN FRANCISCO	23
35	LOS ANGELES	17
7	Baltimore	6
37	Philadelphia	14
23	Chic. Bears	28
24	BALTIMORE	13
17	DETROIT	21
24	Detroit	28
0	San Francisco	35
27	Los Angeles	35

Use Name	Pos.	Hgt	Wgt	Age	Int	Pts
Art Hunter	OT	6'4"	240	21		
Len Szafaryn	OT	6'2"	225	26		
Al Barry	OG	6'2"	225	23		
Buddy Brown	OG	6'1"	225	27		
Dave Stephenson	C-OG	6'2"	230	28		
Jim Ringo	C	6'1"	230	23		
Dick Afflis	OT-OG-DG	6'1"	250	25	1	
Carl Elliott	DE	6'4"	230	27		
Gene Knutson	DE	6'2"	205	22		
John Martinkovic	DE	6'3"	245	27		
Gene White	DE	6'2"	205	22	1	
Dave Hanner	DT	6'2"	260	25		
Jerry Helluin	DT	6'2"	280	24		

Use Name	Pos.	Hgt	Wgt	Age	Int	Pts
Bill Forester	LB	6'3"	235	23	1	
Deral Teteak	LB	5'10"	210	25	1	
Clayton Tonnemaker	LB	6'2"	240	26	1	
Roger Zatkoff	LB	6'2"	215	23	1	
Steve Ruzich	OT-OG-DT-LB	6'2"	230	26		
Bobby Dillon	DB	6'1"	180	24	7	6
Jim Psaltis	DB	6'1"	190	27		
Clarence Self	DB	5'8"	185	29	2	
Val Joe Walker	DB	6'1"	178	23	4	

Babe Parilli – Military Service

Use Name	Pos.	Hgt	Wgt	Age	Int	Pts
Bob Garrett	QB	6'1"	198	22		
Tobin Rote	QB	6'3"	205	26		48
Al Carmichael	HB	6'1"	190	24		
Joe Johnson	HB	6'	185	24		6
Breezy Reid	HB	5'10"	190	27		30
Verl Switzer	DB-HB	5'11"	190	22		24
Fred Cone	FB	5'11"	200	28		54
Howie Ferguson	FB	6'2"	210	24		
Billy Howton	OE	6'2"	190	24		12
Gary Knafelc (from Chi C)	OE	6'4"	205	22		
Max McGee	OE	6'2"	203	22		54

BALTIMORE COLTS 3-9-0 Weeb Ewbank

Scores of Each Game		
0	LOS ANGELES	48
20	NEW YORK	14
9	Chic. Bears	28
0	Detroit	35
6	GREEN BAY	7
21	Washington	24
3	DETROIT	27
13	Green Bay	24
13	CHIC. BEARS	28
17	SAN FRANCISCO	13
22	Los Angeles	21
7	San Francisco	10

Use Name	Pos.	Hgt	Wgt	Age	Int	Pts
Jack Little	OT	6'4"	235	23		
Ken Jackson	OG-OT	6'2"	240	25		
Dick Barwegan	OG	6'1"	235	31		
Gene Pepper	OG	6'2"	242	27		
Alex Sandusky	OG	6'1"	220	22		
Art Spinney	OG	6'	235	27		
Sisto Averno	LB-OG	5'11"	245	28		
George Radosevich	C	6'2"	230	27		
Buzz Nutter	LB-C	6'4"	225	23		
Don Joyce	DE	6'3"	255	24		
Bob Langas	DE	6'4"	230	24		
Gino Marchetti	DE	6'4"	245	28		
Jim Mutscheller	OE-DE	6'1"	220	24		
Art Donovan	DT	6'2"	270	29		
Tom Finnin	DT	6'2"	275	26		2

Use Name	Pos.	Hgt	Wgt	Age	Int	Pts
Doug Eggers	LB	6'	210	24	3	
Bill Pellington	LB	6'2"	230	25		
Charley Robinson	OG-LB	6'	240	26		6
Joe Campanella	OT-DT-LB	6'2"	245	23	1	
Bob Leberman	DB	6'1"	180	22	2	
Jimmy Lesane (fron Chi B)	DB	5'10"	180	23		
Chuck McMillan	DB	6'3"	175	23		
Bert Rechichar	DB	6'1"	210	24	2	19
Tom Keane	HB-DB	6'1"	190	27	5	
Don Shula	HB-DB	5'11"	190	24	5	

Monte Brethauer – Military Service
Johnny Petitbon – Military Service

Use Name	Pos.	Hgt	Wgt	Age	Int	Pts
Cotton Davidson	QB	6'1"	180	23		
Fred Enke	QB	6'1"	205	29		
Gary Kerkorian	QB	5'11"	185	25		32
George Taliaferro	HB	5'11"	195	27		6
Royce Womble	HB	6'	185	22		18
Buddy Young	HB	5'5"	170	28		30
Carl Taseff	DB-HB	5'11"	195	25	2	6
John Huzvar	FB	6'4"	250	25		
Zollie Toth	FB	6'2"	230	30		6
Lloyd Colteryahn	OE	6'2"	220	24		
Dan Edwards	OE	6'1"	200	28		6
Jack Bighead	DE-OE	6'3"	215	24		

DETROIT LIONS

RUSHING

Last Name	No.	Yds	Avg	TD
Carpenter	104	476	4.6	3
Bowman	96	397	4.1	2
Hoernschemeyer	94	242	2.6	2
Walker	32	240	7.5	1
Layne	30	119	4.0	2
Dublinski	21	76	3.6	1
Girard	9	36	4.0	0
Box	1	20	20.0	0
Kercher	3	1	0.3	0
Smith	3	1	0.3	0

RECEIVING

Last Name	No.	Yds	Avg	TD
Dibble	46	768	17	6
Bowman	34	288	8	2
Walker	32	564	18	3
Girard	27	421	16	7
Hart	24	377	16	0
Hoernschemeyer	20	153	8	1
Carpenter	16	145	9	2
Doran	10	203	20	4
Box	6	53	9	0

PUNT RETURNS

Last Name	No.	Yds	Avg	TD
Christiansen	23	225	10	1
Walker	3	117	29	1
Girard	9	22	2	0
Schmidt	1	0	0	0

KICKOFF RETURNS

Last Name	No.	Yds	Avg	TD
Girard	12	248	21	0
Bowman	6	178	30	1
Walker	8	172	22	0
Christiansen	5	102	20	0
Hoernschemeyer	4	73	18	0
Carpenter	2	46	23	0
Mains	1	3	3	0
Sewell	1	0	0	0

PASSING – PUNTING – KICKING

PASSING	Att	Comp	%	Yds	Yd/Att	TD	Int–%	RK
Layne	246	135	55	1818	7.4	14	12– 5	1
Dublinski	138	77	56	1073	7.8	8	7– 5	4
Hoernschemeyer	7	3	43	81	11.6	3	1–14	
Walker	4	0	0	0	0.0	0	1–25	

PUNTING	No	Avg
Girard	63	41.0

KICKING	XP	Att	%	FG	Att	%
Walker	43	43	100	11	17	65
Martin	0	0	0	1	6	17

CHICAGO BEARS

RUSHING

Last Name	No.	Yds	Avg	TD
Jagade	157	498	3.2	3
Stone	79	306	3.9	3
Hoffman	39	178	4.6	1
Blanda	19	41	2.2	0
Campbell	18	38	2.1	0
Brown	9	36	4.0	0
Bratkowski	15	35	2.3	1
Perini	4	11	2.8	0
Anderson	3	8	2.7	0
Kindt	10	–9	–0.9	0

RECEIVING

Last Name	No.	Yds	Avg	TD
Hill	45	1124	25	12
Stone	35	395	11	3
Dooley	34	658	19	7
Hoffman	28	354	13	1
McColl	24	368	15	2
Jagade	24	172	7	0
Kindt	9	101	11	0
Perini	5	56	11	0
Campbell	3	0	0	0
Schroeder	1	71	71	1

PUNT RETURNS

Last Name	No.	Yds	Avg	TD
Moore	11	80	7	0
Smith	7	43	6	0
Stone	14	40	3	0
Hoffman	1	5	5	0
Lowe	2	4	2	0
Kindt	1	1	1	0

KICKOFF RETURNS

Last Name	No.	Yds	Avg	TD
Stone	8	215	27	0
Jagade	11	195	18	0
Moore	8	156	20	0
Campbell	3	77	26	0
Perini	3	44	15	0
Smith	2	38	19	0
Connor	2	32	16	0
Hoffman	1	23	23	0
McElroy	1	21	21	0
Meadows	1	17	17	0
Anderson	1	15	15	0
Kindt	1	10	10	0
Sprinkle	3	8	3	0
Lowe	1	0	0	0

PASSING – PUNTING – KICKING

PASSING	Att	Comp	%	Yds	Yd/Att	TD	Int–%	RK
Blanda	281	131	47	1929	6.9	15	17– 6	11
Bratkowski	130	67	52	1087	8.4	8	17–13	12
Brown	17	10	59	283	16.7	3	1– 6	

PUNTING	No	Avg
Bratkowski	39	41.0
Brown	18	38.0

KICKING	XP	Att	%	FG	Att	%
Blanda	23	23	100	8	16	50
George	13	14	93	4	6	67
Perini	1	1	100	0	0	0

SAN FRANCISCO FORTY NINERS

RUSHING

Last Name	No.	Yds	Avg	TD
Perry	**173**	**1049**	6.1	8
J.H. Johnson	129	681	5.3	9
McElhenny	64	515	**8.0**	6
Schabarum	21	79	3.8	1
Arenas	11	77	7.0	0
Tittle	28	68	2.4	4
Mixon	7	19	2.7	0
Cassara	3	17	5.7	0
Galiffa	1	2	2.0	0
Tidwell	1	1	1.0	0
Cason	2	1	0.5	0
Jessup	1	–5	–5.0	0
P. Brown	1	–6	–6.0	0

RECEIVING

Last Name	No.	Yds	Avg	TD
Wilson	**60**	830	14	5
Jessup	30	565	19	3
J.H. Johnson	28	183	7	0
Perry	26	203	8	0
Soltau	22	316	14	2
McElhenny	8	162	20	0
Babcock	6	91	15	0
Schabarum	4	70	18	0
Arenas	2	12	6	0
Cassara	1	12	12	0

PUNT RETURNS

Last Name	No.	Yds	Avg	TD
Arenas	23	117	5	0
McElhenny	8	78	10	0
Schabarum	2	10	5	0
Tidwell	3	0	0	0

KICKOFF RETURNS

Last Name	No.	Yds	Avg	TD
Arenas	16	362	23	0
Tidwell	10	287	29	0
McElhenny	8	210	26	0
Schabarum	1	34	34	0
J.H. Johnson	2	25	13	0
Toneff	1	10	10	0
Hogland	1	2	2	0

PASSING – PUNTING – KICKING

PASSING	Att	Comp	%	Yds	Yd/Att	TD	Int–%	RK
Tittle	295	170	58	2205	7.5	9	9– **3**	2
Duncan	14	4	29	82	5.9	0	2–14	
Cason	13	7	54	40	3.1	0	1– 8	
Galiffa	12	3	25	54	4.5	0	0– 0	
J.H. Johnson	2	1	50	10	5.0	1	0– 0	
P. Brown	1	1	100	19	19.0	0	0– 0	
Perry	1	1	100	34	34.0	0	0– 0	
Schabarum	1	0	0	0	0.0	0	0– 0	
Tidwell	1	0	0	0	0.0	0	0– 0	

PUNTING	No	Avg
P. Brown	49	37.5
H. Brown	10	38.4
Berry	1	0.0

KICKING	XP	Att	%	FG	Att	%
Soltau	31	33	94	11	18	61
Perry	6	7	86	1	3	33

LOS ANGELES RAMS

RUSHING

Last Name	No.	Yds	Avg	TD
Younger	91	610	6.7	8
Towler	149	599	4.0	**11**
Quinlan	82	490	6.0	4
Wade	28	190	6.8	1
McCormick	48	173	3.6	0
Lewis	26	72	2.8	0
Fears	1	10	10.0	0
Hirsch	1	6	6.0	0
Van Brocklin	6	–10	–1.7	0

RECEIVING

Last Name	No.	Yds	Avg	TD
Boyd	53	**1212**	23	6
Fears	36	546	15	3
Hirsch	35	720	21	3
Quinlan	18	324	18	2
Towler	10	127	13	0
Younger	8	76	10	0
Carey	5	49	10	0
McCormick	3	58	19	0
Lewis	2	19	10	0
Robustelli	1	49	49	1

PUNT RETURNS

Last Name	No.	Yds	Avg	TD
Sherman	6	89	15	0
Lewis	22	82	4	0
Dwyer	6	18	3	0
McCormick	7	8	1	0
Quinlan	1	4	4	0
Doll	1	0	0	0
Hughes	1	0	0	0

KICKOFF RETURNS

Last Name	No.	Yds	Avg	TD
Lewis	**34**	**836**	25	1
Sherman	6	130	22	0
Quinlan	4	69	17	0
Dwyer	3	65	22	0
McCormick	3	49	16	0
Dahms	2	23	12	0
Putnam	1	13	13	0
Toogood	1	11	11	0
Lipscomb	1	6	6	0
Robustelli	1	0	0	0

PASSING – PUNTING – KICKING

PASSING	Att	Comp	%	Yds	Yd/Att	TD	Int–%	RK
Van Brocklin	260	139	53	**2637**	**10.1**	13	21– 8	6
Wade	59	31	53	509	8.6	2	1– 2	
Quinlan	2	1	50	34	17.0	0	1–50	

PUNTING	No	Avg
Van Brocklin	44	42.6

KICKING	XP	Att	%	FG	Att	%
Richter	38	38	100	8	15	53
Carey	2	2	100	1	1	100
Fears	1	1	100	0	0	0

GREEN BAY PACKERS

RUSHING

Last Name	No.	Yds	Avg	TD
Reid	99	507	5.1	5
Rote	67	301	4.5	8
Ferguson	83	276	3.3	0
Carmichael	33	130	3.9	0
Switzer	15	59	3.9	0
Johnson	7	31	4.4	0
Cone	15	18	1.2	0
McGee	1	9	9.0	0
Garrett	1	–3	–3.0	0

RECEIVING

Last Name	No.	Yds	Avg	TD
Howton	52	768	15	2
Ferguson	41	398	10	0
McGee	36	614	17	9
Carmichael	18	251	14	0
Switzer	17	166	10	2
Reid	14	129	9	0
Johnson	10	72	7	1
Knafelc	5	48	10	0
Cone	4	19	5	0

PUNT RETURNS

Last Name	No.	Yds	Avg	TD
Switzer	24	**306**	**13**	1
Carmichael	9	43	5	0
Johnson	5	38	8	0
Dillon	1	7	7	0
Psaltis	1	0	0	0

KICKOFF RETURNS

Last Name	No.	Yds	Avg	TD
Carmichael	20	531	27	0
Switzer	20	500	25	0
Johnson	4	91	23	0
Ferguson	2	31	16	0
Cone	1	22	22	0
Forester	1	18	18	0
Brown	1	0	0	0

PASSING – PUNTING – KICKING

PASSING	Att	Comp	%	Yds	Yd/Att	TD	Int–%	RK
Rote	**382**	**180**	47	2311	6.1	14	18– 5	10
Garrett	30	15	50	143	4.8	0	1– 3	

PUNTING	No	Avg
McGee	72	41.7

KICKING	XP	Att	%	FG	Att	%
Cone	27	29	93	9	16	56

BALTIMORE COLTS

RUSHING

Last Name	No.	Yds	Avg	TD
Young	70	311	4.4	2
Toth	86	303	3.5	1
Taseff	41	228	5.6	0
Womble	60	174	2.9	0
Taliaferro	48	157	3.3	0
Kerkorian	22	36	1.6	1
Davidson	11	31	2.8	0
Huzvar	19	29	1.5	0
Shula	2	3	1.5	0
Enke	5	3	0.6	0

RECEIVING

Last Name	No.	Yds	Avg	TD
Edwards	40	531	13	1
Colteryahn	30	384	13	0
Womble	30	338	11	3
Taseff	16	159	10	1
Young	15	272	18	3
Taliaferro	14	122	9	1
Toth	11	51	5	0
Bighead	6	89	15	0
Mutscheller	1	49	49	0

PUNT RETURNS

Last Name	No.	Yds	Avg	TD
Young	14	60	4	0
Taseff	8	52	7	0
Taliaferro	5	34	7	0
Rechichar	6	22	4	0
Lesane	6	13	2	0

KICKOFF RETURNS

Last Name	No.	Yds	Avg	TD
Young	13	308	24	0
Womble	9	170	19	0
Taseff	7	167	24	0
Taliaferro	7	134	19	0
Lesane	4	91	23	0
Rechichar	3	26	9	0
Pellington	2	26	13	0
Robinson	1	19	19	0
Langas	1	18	18	0
Joyce	1	13	13	0
Toth	1	13	13	0
McMillan	1	5	5	0
Huzvar	1	0	0	0
Radosevich	1	0	0	0

PASSING – PUNTING – KICKING

PASSING	Att	Comp	%	Yds	Yd/Att	TD	Int–%	RK
Kerkorian	217	117	54	1515	7.0	9	12– 6	7
Davidson	64	28	44	309	4.8	0	5– 8	
Enke	28	17	61	171	6.1	0	3– 7	
Taliaferro	2	0	0	0	0.0	0	1– 50	
Keane	1	1	100	0	0.0	0	0– 0	
Lesane	1	0	0	0	0.0	0	0– 0	
Toth	1	0	0	0	0.0	0	1–100	

PUNTING	No	Avg
Davidson	72	37.2

KICKING	XP	Att	%	FG	Att	%
Kerkorian	11	12	91	5	10	50
Rechichar	1	1	100	6	13	46

1955 Continuing the Bloodless War

Disarmament talks between the United States and Canada fell through in February, but no ambassadors spoke at these meetings, and nuclear weapons never were mentioned. Representatives of the Canadian Football League and NFL commissioner Bert Bell were trying to thrash out a "no raiding" treaty for each other's players. No agreement was signed, leaving some clubs free to pirate players across national borders. The NFL captured Eddie LeBaron, Gene Brito, and Norb Hecker, all of whom had fled north a year ago, and also Alex Webster, a talented Canadian League runner. The Toronto Argonauts of the CFL signed quarterback Tom Dublinski of the Detroit Lions, but the Lions went to court and forced Dublinski to sit out this year before joining the Canadian club. But this was more a war of threats than of deeds, as most players simply stayed right where they were.

On the field itself, the players in the NFL were witnessing a gradual change in defensive tactics. The six-man line, standard at the start of the decade, had gradually turned into a 5-2-4 defense geared to deal with strong passing attacks. Now the five-man line was slowly evolving into a four-man line, as more and more teams replaced the middle guard with a mobile middle linebacker who could cover both the pass and the run. By the end of the decade, the 4-3-4 defense was used throughout the league, and middle linebackers like Joe Schmidt, Bill George, and Sam Huff were winning as many cheers as any of the offensive stars.

EASTERN CONFERENCE

Cleveland Browns—Coach Paul Brown was ready to defend the NFL championship without retired quarterback Otto Graham, but when the Browns looked pitiful in their pre-season games, Brown sent out an S.O.S. for his veteran passer. Answering the call in time for the final exhibition game, Graham still could not prevent an opening-day loss to the improved Washington Redskins. But after this warm-up, Graham and his mates hit their stride, winning their next six contests and driving to a conference crown for the tenth straight year.

Washington Redskins—The Redskins shed their recent mediocrity to make a surprisingly strong run at the Browns for the Eastern crown. Returning to the NFL after a year in Canada were quarterback Eddie LeBaron, defensive end Gene Brito, and defensive back Norb Hecker. Along with Brito's strong defensive work and little LeBaron's slick ball-handling, Vic Janowicz's all-around talent highlighted the club's dramatic rise. Abandoning his baseball career with the Pittsburgh Pirates, Janowicz combined his dogged running with accurate place-kicking to finish eight points behind scoring leader Doak Walker.

New York Giants—The Giants had too much talent to keep losing, as they did in their first three games, and all the parts finally did fit together over the second half of the schedule. In the last seven games, the Giants won five, lost one, and tied one to finish in a rush behind Cleveland and Washington in the East. Head coach Jim Lee Howell needed time to blend rookies Mel Triplett, Rosie Grier, Jimmy Patton, and ex-Canadian star Alex Webster into the lineup, but the late-season results upheld the coach's faith in the newcomers. Of the holdovers, halfback Frank Gifford, guard Bill Austin, and safetyman Em Tunnell made All-Pro teams. Gifford blossomed into stardom with his ability to run the pass-option play, run behind his blockers, and catch passes. Relieved of any duties on defense, the handsome Gifford concentrated on honing his offensive skills to a fine point.

Chicago Cardinals—New head coach Ray Richards tasted sweet victory when his Cards met the Bears late in the year for their annual intercity battle. The Bears were riding a six-game winning streak to the Western Division crown, but the Cards derailed them with a stunning 53-14 upset. Aside from the Bear game, however, highlights for the Cardinals fell widely over the landscape. Ollie Matson continued to quicken pulses with his dramatic kick returns and runs from scrimmage, while Night Train Lane kept up his good work in the defensive backfield. Lane did take a few turns as an offensive end, though, and on one shift he grabbed a 97-yard TD pass from Ogden Compton.

Philadelphia Eagles—Coming from 10 points behind to beat the New York Giants on opening day, the Eagles nevertheless began the year on a bad note as middle guard Bucko Kilroy, playing in his 101st consecutive game, tore ligaments in his knee. Outstanding seasons by Norm Willey, Tom Scott, Chuck Bednarik, and Bibbles Bawel kept the defense on an even keel, but the offense dragged its feet with a sluggish performance for the year. Quarterbacks Adrian Burk and Bobby Thomason found ends Pete Pihos and Bill Stribling open for frequent passes, but no Eagle runner consistently moved the ball on the ground.

Pittsburgh Steelers—Coach Walt Kiesling needed a back-up quarterback to spell Jim Finks, so he brought three young passers to training camp—Ted Marchibroda, Vic Eaton, and John Unitas. A ninth-round draft pick from the University of Louisville, Unitas never caught Kiesling's eye and was cut without ever getting into even a pre-season game. So, while Unitas spent the season quarterbacking the semi-pro Bloomington Rams, the Steeler offense struggled along under Finks, Marchibroda, and Eaton, scoring 20 points only three times all season.

WESTERN CONFERENCE

Los Angeles Rams—The Rams looked high and low for a new head coach, and they came up with unheralded Sid Gillman of the University of Cincinnati. A master organizer and offensive genius, Gillman took the Rams right to the top of the Western Conference for the first time since 1951. Rookies Ron Waller and Don Burroughs were the only key newcomers, as veterans Norm Van Brocklin, Tank Younger, Tom Fears, and Crazy Legs Hirsch spearheaded the attack, while Andy Robustelli and Will Sherman led the defense. Two mid-season losses to the Bears pushed the Rams back into second place, but three straight wins at the end of the year enabled them to sneak into first when the Cardinals upset the Bears two weeks from the end of the season. With a tougher defense and a breakaway runner in Waller to complement Van Brocklin's passing, the Rams were looking forward again to fighting the Browns for the NFL crown.

Chicago Bears—Told that George Halas was retiring as coach after the season, the Bears went all out to win the championship for their departing leader. Three losses to open the year doubled the players' determination to win, and the Bears then took off on a six-game winning streak, twice beating the Rams to take the lead in the West. Second-year man Ed Brown, a superb short passer, took charge at quarterback, rookies Rick Casares and Bobby Watkins beefed up the running attack, and Harlon Hill again starred as a pass receiver. Of the linemen, Bill Wightkin and Stan Jones stood out on offense, Bill George and George Connor on defense. The tough Bears were riding high until the Cards shot the horse out from under them with a 53-14 upset.

Green Bay Packers—Armed with a rejuvenated offense, the Packers moved up into third place by evenly splitting their season with wins and losses. Howie Ferguson, a hustling fullback, developed into a top-flight runner and gave the club a strong ground game to balance the attack. Tobin Rote's passes to Billy Howton and Gary Knafelc ate up yardage in large bites, keeping enemy defenses spread for Ferguson's runs. Spearheaded by linebacker Roger Zatkoff and safety Bobby Dillon, the defense kept the Packers in most of their games, while field-goal kicker Fred Cone helped win some close contests with his toe.

Baltimore Colts—Rookie fullback Alan Ameche broke into the professional ranks with a thunderbolt of a run. On his first play from scrimmage, he took a handoff, banged through the middle of the line, and rumbled 79 yards for a touchdown. The Colts went on to win that game, and Ameche went on to take the NFL rushing crown. Besides Ameche, the strong rookie crop turned up quarterback George Shaw, halfback L.G. Dupre, sure-handed end Ray Berry, and linemen George Preas and Dick Szymanski. After a fine beginning of three straight wins, the Colts fell off into mediocrity, but winning was less important right now to coach Weeb Ewbank than the building process.

San Francisco '49ers—For a second straight year, injuries bothered Hugh McElhenny, and for a second straight year the '49ers offense had problems scoring points. The bad foot which hobbled McElhenny robbed the attack of football's premier breakaway runner and left it without punch. The Redskins beat the '49ers 7-0, the first shutout hung on them since 1950, and the Browns and Packers just missed blanking them in other games. A five-game mid-season losing streak did nothing to improve new head coach Red Strader's disposition, and owner Tony Morabito sent Strader packing after just one season on the job.

Detroit Lions—Two off-season events sent the Lions reeling down into the Western Conference basement after three years in the penthouse. Middle guard Les Bingaman, literally the center of the defense, decided to quit, and a horse on which Bobby Layne's young son was riding bolted and separated Papa Layne's shoulder. Layne didn't miss any time from the lineup, but he left the zip in his arm back on a horse trail in Texas. With the offense thus crippled, the defense had problems of its own, trying to replace Bingaman's bulk and brains in the defensive line. Coach Buddy Parker eventually shifted offensive lineman Lou Creekmur to the middle guard spot, but by that time the Lions had lost their first six games.

FINAL TEAM STATISTICS

OFFENSE

	BALT.	CHI.B.	CHI.C.	CLEVE.	DET.	G.BAY	L.A.	N.Y.	PHIL.	PITT.	S.F.	WASH.
FIRST DOWNS:												
Total	206	235	150	224	224	213	233	189	219	211	204	193
by Rushing	93	118	84	111	88	106	118	92	71	74	102	101
by Passing	92	101	53	98	119	95	103	86	128	119	89	71
by Penalty	21	16	13	15	17	12	12	11	20	18	13	21
RUSHING:												
Number	456	487	438	536	392	433	451	414	392	420	408	478
Yards	1833	2388	1626	2020	1477	1883	1943	1693	1317	1284	1713	2000
Average Yards	4.0	4.9	3.7	3.8	3.8	4.3	4.3	4.1	3.4	3.1	4.2	4.2
Touchdowns	15	19	10	20	11	11	17	13	9	13	12	17
PASSING:												
Attempts	266	306	280	234	400	348	344	292	400	390	303	257
Completions	134	145	106	130	204	159	175	137	198	189	151	101
Completion Percentage	50.4	47.4	37.9	55.6	51.0	45.7	50.9	46.9	49.5	48.5	49.8	39.3
Gross Yards	1795	2108	1520	2225	2542	2004	2206	1865	2696	2550	2225	1549
Yards Lost Tackled	164	180	175	275	132	225	145	105	224	163	287	201
Net Yards	1631	1928	1345	1950	2410	1779	2061	1760	2472	2387	1938	1348
Avg. Yards per Attempt (Gross)	6.7	6.9	5.4	9.5	6.4	5.8	6.4	6.4	6.7	6.5	7.3	6.0
Avg. Yards per Comp. (Gross)	13.4	14.5	14.3	17.1	12.5	12.6	12.6	13.6	13.6	13.5	14.7	15.3
Touchdowns	11	17	14	21	15	17	9	17	19	12	17	11
Interceptions	22	23	25	11	22	19	18	15	24	30	28	21
Percent Intercepted	8.3	7.5	8.9	4.7	5.5	5.5	5.2	5.1	6.0	7.7	9.2	8.2
PUNTS:												
Number	55	57	75	58	67	56	60	75	61	71	63	62
Average Yards	39.3	39.9	40.3	41.2	41.0	43.2	44.6	40.3	42.9	38.4	40.6	41.6
PUNT RETURNS:												
Number	48	35	34	44	41	36	44	36	41	46	39	43
Yards	178	147	408	337	224	280	229	230	95	88	118	407
Average Yards	3.7	4.2	12.0	7.7	5.5	7.8	5.2	6.4	2.3	1.9	3.0	9.5
Touchdowns	0	0	2	1	0	1	1	2	0	0	0	2
KICKOFF RETURNS:												
Number	40	44	44	41	45	39	44	39	39	44	51	43
Yards	941	1085	835	949	839	1002	1013	848	922	1157	1147	1097
Average Yards	23.5	24.7	19.0	23.1	18.6	25.7	23.0	21.7	23.6	26.3	22.5	25.5
Touchdowns	0	0	0	0	0	1	0	1	1	0	0	1
INTERCEPTION RETURNS:												
Number	19	19	29	25	15	31	31	23	16	10	21	19
Yards	260	299	368	287	224	400	353	250	302	85	242	215
Average Yards	13.7	15.7	12.7	11.5	14.9	12.9	11.4	10.9	18.9	8.5	11.5	11.3
Touchdowns	0	0	3	3	1	0	3	0	2	0	1	0
PENALTIES:												
Number	59	57	82	64	51	41	64	50	61	67	64	60
Yards	565	498	695	603	526	401	612	458	542	604	541	648
FUMBLES:												
Number	18	23	35	27	28	37	23	25	35	26	25	25
Number Lost	8	18	20	18	19	25	10	16	21	17	18	21
POINTS:												
Total	214	294	224	349	230	258	260	267	248	195	216	246
PAT Attempts	26	37	29	45	29	30	31	34	31	27	30	33
PAT Made	25	37	23	44	27	30	30	33	29	21	27	30
FG Attempts	26	16	21	22	17	24	32	15	26	18	12	21
FG Made	11	11	9	11	9	16	14	10	11	4	3	6
Percent FG Made	42.3	68.8	42.9	50.0	52.9	66.7	43.8	66.7	42.3	22.2	25.0	28.6
Safeties	0	1	0	1	1	0	1	0	0	0	0	0

DEFENSE

	BALT.	CHI.B.	CHI.C.	CLEVE.	DET.	G.BAY	L.A.	N.Y.	PHIL.	PITT.	S.F.	WASH.
FIRST DOWNS:												
Total	234	216	224	171	217	196	245	209	174	176	250	189
by Rushing	120	96	100	65	95	118	95	77	89	98	132	73
by Passing	98	106	102	83	110	71	122	119	69	67	103	104
by Penalty	16	14	22	23	12	7	28	13	16	11	15	12
RUSHING:												
Number	448	398	465	351	449	475	423	418	455	494	538	391
Yards	2035	2100	1902	1189	1851	2174	1624	1441	1637	1814	2135	1275
Average Yards	4.5	5.3	4.1	3.4	4.1	4.6	3.8	3.4	3.6	3.7	4.0	3.3
Touchdowns	18	17	11	12	16	18	10	10	12	11	24	8
PASSING:												
Attempts	320	354	371	323	304	259	351	373	272	242	311	340
Completions	158	177	154	126	163	118	198	181	124	123	147	165
Completion Percentage	49.4	50.0	41.5	39.0	53.6	45.6	55.0	48.5	45.6	50.8	47.3	48.5
Gross Yards	2288	2369	2146	1775	2304	1768	2518	2543	1810	1530	2045	2189
Yards Lost Tackled	201	312	138	123	140	80	209	176	216	235	172	274
Net Yards	2087	2057	2008	1652	2164	1688	2309	2367	1594	1295	1873	1915
Avg. Yards per Attempt (Gross)	7.2	6.7	5.8	5.5	7.6	6.8	7.2	6.8	6.7	6.3	6.6	6.4
Avg. Yards per Comp. (Gross)	14.5	13.4	13.9	14.1	14.1	15.0	13.0	14.0	14.6	12.4	13.9	13.3
Touchdowns	12	14	16	15	18	13	18	16	12	19	10	17
Interceptions	19	19	29	25	15	31	31	23	16	10	21	19
Percent Intercepted	5.9	5.4	7.8	7.7	4.9	12.0	8.8	6.2	5.9	4.1	6.8	5.6
PUNTS:												
Number	56	65	61	70	60	52	56	64	74	80	57	65
Average Yards	39.9	42.0	40.6	39.1	40.6	41.8	42.4	41.6	39.1	42.1	42.6	41.2
PUNT RETURNS:												
Number	37	40	42	37	42	36	41	52	36	42	40	42
Yards	71	201	288	186	152	223	264	181	206	304	369	296
Average Yards	1.9	5.0	6.9	5.0	3.6	6.2	6.4	3.5	5.7	7.2	9.2	7.0
Touchdowns	0	1	2	1	0	1	0	0	1	1	1	1
KICKOFF RETURNS:												
Number	36	43	46	50	44	48	35	54	40	38	37	42
Yards	724	943	1133	1220	942	1157	690	1370	987	779	867	1023
Average Yards	20.1	21.9	24.6	24.4	21.4	24.1	19.7	25.4	24.7	20.5	23.4	24.4
Touchdowns	0	0	0	1	0	0	0	2	0	0	0	1
INTERCEPTION RETURNS:												
Number	22	23	25	11	22	19	18	15	24	30	28	21
Yards	269	247	261	181	306	268	338	194	228	494	299	200
Average Yards	12.2	10.7	10.4	16.5	13.9	14.1	18.8	12.9	9.5	16.5	10.7	9.5
Touchdowns	0	0	0	1	1	1	0	2	0	5	2	1
PENALTIES:												
Number	69	54	65	58	62	56	50	46	57	66	58	79
Yards	681	530	677	560	544	490	430	439	463	657	528	694
FUMBLES:												
Number	24	28	23	21	33	27	20	34	27	35	19	36
Number Lost	14	15	18	15	24	18	15	16	20	19	13	24
POINTS:												
Total	239	251	252	218	275	276	231	223	231	285	298	222
PAT Attempts	30	32	31	29	36	36	29	30	28	36	37	28
PAT Made	29	26	31	23	35	36	27	26	27	33	36	27
FG Attempts	14	24	29	15	23	17	17	20	23	25	24	19
FG Made	10	11	11	7	8	8	10	5	12	12	12	9
Percent FG Made	71.4	45.8	37.9	46.7	34.8	47.1	58.8	25.0	52.2	48.0	50.0	47.4
Safeties	0	0	1	0	0	0	0	1	0	0	2	0

Winning on a Final Bow

Paul Brown had talked Otto Graham out of retirement last fall, so Graham was back for his second farewell performance in the championship game. This year's opponent was the Los Angeles Rams, whom rookie coach Sid Gillman had led to the Western title for the first time since 1951. The Rams intercepted a Graham pass early in the game, but the Browns promptly picked off a Norm Van Brocklin pass and turned it into a 26-yard Lou Groza field goal. Cleveland's Don Paul intercepted another Van Brocklin pass early in the second quarter and returned it 65 yards for a touchdown, making the score 10-0. The Rams quickly scored on a Van Brocklin to Skeets Quinlan pass, but a 50-yard pass from Graham to Dante Lavelli ran the halftime count to 17-7. The second half was all Cleveland, as the Browns' pass rush kept Van Brocklin off balance, and Graham ran for a pair of touchdowns and threw to Ray Renfro for a third. The Rams added a touchdown late in the game, and the final score was 38-14 in favor of Cleveland, a championship for Paul Brown and a final bow for Otto Graham.

1955 CHAMPIONSHIP GAME

December 26 at Los Angeles
(Attendance 87,695)

SCORING

LOS ANGELES	0	7	0	7–14
CLEVELAND	3	14	14	7–38

First Quarter
- Cle. Groza, 26 yard Field Goal – 12:21

Second Quarter
- Cle. Paul, 65 yard Interception Return – 4:12
  PAT – Groza (kick)
- L.A. Quinlan, 67 yard pass from Van Brocklin – 6:04
  PAT – Richter (kick)
- Cle. Lavelli, 50 yard pass from Graham – 14:21
  PAT – Groza (kick)

Third Quarter
- Cle. Graham, 15 yard rush – 8:06
  PAT – Groza (kick)
- Cle. Graham, 1 yard rush – 12:44
  PAT – Groza (kick)

Fourth Quarter
- Cle. Renfro, 35 yard pass from Graham – 0:11
  PAT – Groza (kick)
- L.A. Waller, 4 yard rush – 12:42
  PAT – Richter (kick)

TEAM STATISTICS

CLE.		L.A.
17	First Downs – Total	17
7	by Rushing	8
10	by Passing	8
0	by Penalty	1
0	Fumbles – Number	1
0	Times Lost Ball	1
5	Penalties – Number	2
74	Yards Penalized	10
3	Giveaways	8
8	Takeaways	3
+5	Difference	–5

INDIVIDUAL STATISTICS

CLEVELAND	No.	Yds.	Avg.	LOS ANGELES	No.	Yds.	Avg.
RUSHING							
Modzelewski	13	61	4.7	Towler	14	64	4.6
Bassett	11	49	4.5	Walker	11	48	4.4
Morrison	11	33	3.0	Wade	1	4	4.0
Graham	9	21	2.3		26	116	4.5
Jones	1	3	3.0				
Smith	3	2	0.7				
	48	169	3.5				
RECEIVING							
Modzelewski	5	34	6.8	Quinlan	5	116	23.2
Lavelli	3	95	31.7	Waller	3	18	6.0
Renfro	2	49	24.5	Fears	1	16	16.0
Jones	1	11	11.0	Hirsch	1	9	9.0
Brewster	1	9	9.0	Towler	1	7	7.0
Morrison	1	7	7.0		11	166	15.1
Bassett	1	4	4.0				
	14	209	14.9				
PUNT RETURNS							
Konz	2	27	13.5	Lewis	1	9	9.0
Paul	1	0	0.0				
	3	27	9.0				
KICKOFF RETURNS							
Smith	2	41	20.5	Lewis	4	127	31.8
Paul	1	0	0	Waller	3	88	29.3
	3	41	13.7		7	215	30.7
INTERCEPTION RETURNS							
Konz	2	12	6.0	Burroughs	1	24	24.0
Paul	1	65	65.0	Morris	1	22	22.0
James	1	11	11.0	Hughes	1	0	0.0
Palumbo	1	10	10.0		3	46	15.3
Michaels	1	5	5.0				
Ford	1	0	0.0				
	7	103	14.7				
PUNTING							
Gillom	3		42.7	Van Brocklin	4		45.0

PASSING

	Att	Comp	Comp Pct.	Yds	Yds/ Att.	Yds/ Comp	Yds Lost Tackled	Int
Cleveland								
Graham	25	14	56.0	209	8.4	14.9	1– 7	3
Los Angeles								
Van Brocklin	25	11	44.0	166	6.6	15.1	0– 0	6
Wade	3	0	0.0	0	–	–	2–23	1
	28	11	39.3	166	5.9	15.1	2–23	7

CLEVELAND BROWNS 9-2-1 Paul Brown

Scores of Each Game		
17	WASHINGTON	27
38	San Francisco	3
21	PHILADELPHIA	17
24	Washington	14
41	GREEN BAY	10
26	Chic. Cards	20
24	NEW YORK	14
17	Philadelphia	33
41	PITTSBURGH	14
35	New York	35
30	Pittsburgh	7
35	CHIC. CARDS	24

Use Name	Pos.	Hgt	Wgt	Age	Int	Pts
Lou Groza	OT	6'3"	242	31		77
Mike McCormack	OT	6'4"	248	28		
John Sandusky	DT-OT	6'1"	252	29		
Harold Bradley	OG	6'2"	230	26		
Herschel Forester	OG	6'	230	25		
Abe Gibron	OG	5'11"	250	29		
Frank Gatski	C	6'3"	240	33		
Bob Gain	DG	6'3"	250	27		
Len Ford	DE	6'4"	258	29		
Carlton Massey	DE	6'2"	218	26	1	
Don Colo	DT	6'3"	250	30		
John Kissell	DT	6'3"	248	32		
Tom Jones	OT-DT	6'2"	255	24		

Use Name	Pos.	Hgt	Wgt	Age	Int	Pts
Walt Michaels	LB	6'	230	26	1	6
Chuck Noll	LB	6'1"	220	23	5	8
Sam Palumbo	C-LB	6'2"	225	24		
Pete Perini (from Chi B)	FB-LB	6'	225	27		
Chuck Weber	OG-DE-LB	6'1"	225	26		
Kenny Konz	DB	5'10"	182	27	5	6
Warren Lahr	DB	5'11"	194	31	5	
Don Paul	DB	6'	195	29	4	6
Bob White (to BAL)	DB	5'11"	180	26		
Tommy James	HB-DB	5'10"	185	31	2	
Johnny Petitbon	HB-DB	5'11"	195	24	2	

Tom Catlin – Military Service
Chet Hanulak – Military Service

Use Name	Pos.	Hgt	Wgt	Age	Int	Pts
Otto Graham	QB	6'1"	205	33		36
George Ratterman	QB	6'1"	180	28		6
Henry Ford	HB	6'	175	24		
Dub Jones	HB	6'4"	200	30		6
Curley Morrison	HB	6'2"	218	29		18
Ray Renfro	HB	6'1"	190	24		48
Bob Smith	HB	5'10"	195	23		6
Mo Bassett	FB	6'1"	232	25		18
Ed Modzelewski	FB	6'	215	26		48
Darrell Brewster	OE	6'3"	210	25		36
Dante Lavelli	OE	6'	192	32		24
Horace Gillom	DE-OE	6'1"	225	34		

Billy Reynolds – Military Service

WASHINGTON REDSKINS 8-4-0 Joe Kuharich

Scores of Each Game		
27	Cleveland	17
31	Philadelphia	30
10	CHIC. CARDS	24
14	CLEVELAND	24
14	Baltimore	13
7	New York	35
34	PHILADELPHIA	21
7	SAN FRANCISCO	0
31	Chic. Cards	0
23	Pittsburgh	14
20	NEW YORK	27
28	PITTSBURGH	17

Use Name	Pos.	Hgt	Wgt	Age	Int	Pts
Don Boll	OT	6'2"	263	28		
Mike Davlin	OT	6'1"	230	27		
Fred Miller	OT	6'3"	225	24		
Walt Houston	OG	6'	217	22		
Ron Marciniak	OG	6'1"	218	23		
Red Stephens	OG	6'	230	25		
Slug Witucki	OG	5'11"	257	27		
Johnny Allen	C	6'2"	217	23		
Harry Ulinski	C	6'4"	235	30		
Gene Brito	DE	6'1"	230	30		
Chet Ostrowski	DE	6'1"	228	25		
Marv Berschet	OG-DE	6'2"	220	26		
J. D. Kimmel	DT	6'4"	245	26		
Volney Peters	DT	6'4"	242	27		
Jim Norman	OT-DT	6'2"	248	21		

Use Name	Pos.	Hgt	Wgt	Age	Int	Pts
Nick Adducci	LB	5'10"	204	26		
Ralph Felton	LB	5'11"	210	23		
Lavern Torgeson	C-LB	6'	222	26	3	
Chuck Drazenovich	FB-LB	6'1"	227	28	2	
Dick Alban	DB	6'	197	26	2	
Roy Barni (from PHI)	DB	5'11"	187	28	1	6
Hal Norris	LB-DB	5'11"	194	23		
Scooter Scudero	HB-DB	5'10"	176	25	5	12
Norb Hecker	OE-DB	6'2"	190	28	6	8

Sam Baker – Military Service
Art DeCarlo – Military Service
Jim Schrader – Military Service
Billy Wells – Military Service

Use Name	Pos.	Hgt	Wgt	Age	Int	Pts
Al Dorow	QB	6'	190	25		
Ralph Guglielmi	QB	6'1"	200	22		6
Eddie LeBaron	QB	5'9"	168	25		24
Vic Janowicz	HB	5'9"	190	25		88
Jim Monachino	HB	5'10"	185	26		12
Bert Zagers	HB	5'10"	186	22		18
Dale Atkeson	FB	6'2"	210	25		12
Leo Elter	HB-FB	5'10"	197	26		24
Johnny Carson	OE	6'3"	203	25		18
Billy Cox	OE	6'3"	190	26		
Charlie Jones	OE	6'1"	202	26		
Ralph Thomas	OE	5'11"	190	25		18

NEW YORK GIANTS 6-5-1 Jim Lee Howell

Scores of Each Game		
17	Philadelphia	27
17	Chic. Cards	28
23	Pittsburgh	30
10	CHIC. CARDS	0
17	PITTSBURGH	19
35	WASHINGTON	7
14	Cleveland	24
17	BALTIMORE	7
31	PHILADELPHIA	7
35	CLEVELAND	35
27	Washington	20
24	Detroit	19

Use Name	Pos.	Hgt	Wgt	Age	Int	Pts
Rosey Brown	OT	6'3"	245	22		
Dick Yelvington	OT	6'2"	230	28		
Bill Austin	OG	6'1"	225	26		
George Kennard	OG	6'	215	26		
Jack Stroud	OG	6'1"	215	26		
Ray Beck	DG-OG	6'2"	225	23		
Ray Wietecha	C	6'1"	225	26		
Stan West	OG-DG	6'2"	235	28		
John Hall	DE	6'1"	220	22		
Cliff Livingston	DE	6'3"	205	25		6
Walt Yowarsky (from DET)	DE	6'2"	235	27		
Rex Boggan	DT	6'3"	245	25		
Rosey Grier	DT	6'5"	260	22		
Ray Krouse	DT	6'3"	260	28		

Use Name	Pos.	Hgt	Wgt	Age	Int	Pts
Pat Knight	LB	6'2"	210	26	2	
Harland Svare	LB	6'	215	24	2	
Bill Svoboda	LB	6'	210	28	1	
Tom Landry	DB	6'1"	195	30	2	
Dick Nolan	DB	6'1"	185	23	1	
Jimmy Patton	DB	6'	180	23	1	12
Herb Rich	DB	5'11"	180	26	6	
Em Tunnell	DB	6'1"	185	33	7	6
Larry Weaver	HB-DB	5'11"	190	22		

Bill Albright – Canadian Football League
Ray Collins – Canadian Football League
Billy Shipp – Canadian Football League

Use Name	Pos.	Hgt	Wgt	Age	Int	Pts
Bobby Clatterbuck	QB	6'3"	195	23		
Chuck Conerly	QB	6'1"	185	31		1
Don Heinrich	QB	6'	185	23		12
Frank Gifford	HB	6'1"	195	25		42
Joe Heap	HB	5'11"	185	23		
Kyle Rote	HB	6'	195	26		48
Alex Webster	HB	6'3"	210	24		36
Bobby Epps	FB	5'9"	195	23		12
Eddie Price	FB	5'11"	190	29		
Mel Triplett	FB	6'1"	215	23		
Ken MacAfee	OE	6'2"	205	25		6
Bob Schnelker	OE	6'3"	215	25		18
Cutter Long	HB-OE	6'1"	195	23		6
Ben Agajanian	K	6'	215	36		62

CHICAGO CARDINALS 4-7-1 Ray Richards

Scores of Each Game		
7	Pittsburgh	14
28	NEW YORK	17
24	Washington	10
0	New York	10
24	PHILADELPHIA	24
20	CLEVELAND	26
27	PITTSBURGH	13
14	Green Bay	31
0	WASHINGTON	31
53	CHIC. BEARS	14
3	Philadelphia	27
24	Cleveland	35

Use Name	Pos.	Hgt	Wgt	Age	Int	Pts
Burt Delevan	OT	6'2"	235	25		
Jack Jennings	OT	6'4"	245	28		
Len Teeuws	DT-OT	6'4"	245	28		
Larry Hartshorn	OG	6'	225	22		
John Hatley	OG	6'3"	245	24		
Bill Lange	LB-OG	6'1"	245	28		
Jack Simmons	C	6'4"	240	29		
Tom Bienemann	DE	6'3"	225	27	2	
Leo Sugar	DE	6'1"	210	26	1	
Pat Summerall	DE	6'4"	225	25	1	53
Jerry Groom	DT	6'3"	240	26		
Tony Pasquesi	DT	6'4"	235	21		
Chuck Ulrich	DT	6'4"	240	24		

Use Name	Pos.	Hgt	Wgt	Age	Int	Pts
Fred Wallner	LB	6'2"	230	26	2	
Harry Thompson	OG-LB	6'2"	230	28		
Leo Sanford	C-LB	6'1"	225	26	3	6
Lindon Crow	DB	6'1"	187	22	3	
Jimmy Hill	DB	6'2"	190	26		
Tom Keane	DB	6'1"	190	28	6	
Jim Psaltis	DB	6'1"	190	28	4	6
Charlie Trippi	DB	6'	185	32		
Night Train Lane	OE-DB	6'1"	190	27	6	6

Ed Husmann – Military Service
Jim Root – Military Service
Jimmy Sears – Military Service

Use Name	Pos.	Hgt	Wgt	Age	Int	Pts
Ogden Compton	QB	6'1"	180	22		
Lamar McHan	QB	6'1"	197	23		12
Dave Leggett	DB-QB	6'2"	198	21		
Dave Mann	HB	6'1"	190	22		33
Ollie Matson	HB	6'2"	210	25		30
Frank Bernardi	DB-HB	5'9"	180	22	1	5
Jimmy Carr	DB-HB	6'1"	195	22		
Les Goble	DB-HB	5'11"	155	23		
Mal Hammack	FB	6'2"	200	22		12
Johnny Olszewski	FB	5'11"	200	24		6
Max Boydston	OE	6'2"	207	22		6
Gern Nagler	OE	6'2"	190	22		18
Don Stonesifer	OE	6'	200	28		30
Dick Brubaker	DE-OE	6'	205	23		
Frank McPhee	DB-OE	6'3"	195	24		

PHILADELPHIA EAGLES 4-7-1 Jim Trimble

Scores of Each Game		
27	NEW YORK	17
30	WASHINGTON	31
17	Cleveland	21
7	Pittsburgh	13
24	Chic. Cards	24
24	PITTSBURGH	0
21	Washington	34
33	CLEVELAND	17
7	New York	31
21	LOS ANGELES	23
27	CHIC. CARDS	3
10	Chic. Bears	17

Use Name	Pos.	Hgt	Wgt	Age	Int	Pts
Lum Snyder	OT	6'5"	230	25		
Jim Weatherall	OT	6'4"	235	25		
Frank Wydo	OT	6'4"	235	31		
Tom Higgins	OG-OT	6'2"	230	26		
Ken Huxhold	OG	6'1"	215	26		
Buck Lansford	OG	6'2"	230	22		
John Magee	OG	5'10"	220	32		
Ed Sharkey (to SF)	OG	6'3"	235	28		
*Russ Carroccio	OT-DG-DT-OG	6'1"	235	24	1	
Bob Kelley	C	6'2"	225	26		
Bucko Kilroy	DG	6'2"	250	34		
Jim Ricca (from DET)	OT-DT-DG	6'4"	270	28	1	
Tom Scott	DE	6'2"	220	25		
Norm Willey	OE-DE	6'2"	225	28		
Jess Richardson	DT	6'2"	235	25		
Mike Jarmoluk	DG-DT	6'5"	250	32		

Use Name	Pos.	Hgt	Wgt	Age	Int	Pts
Wayne Robinson	LB	6'2"	220	25	1	
Chuck Bednarik	C-LB	6'3"	230	30	1	
Eddie Bell	DB	6'1"	205	24	1	
Harry Dowda	DB	6'2"	200	31		
Bob Hudson	LB-DB	6'4"	220	25	3	
Ralph Goldston	HB-DB	5'11"	195	27		
Bibbles Bawel	OE-DB	6'1"	185	25	9	12

Tom Brookshier – Military Service
Menil Mavraides – Military Service
Maury Nipp – Military Service
Neil Worden – Military Service

*(from NY)

Use Name	Pos.	Hgt	Wgt	Age	Int	Pts
Adrian Burk	QB	6'2"	190	27		12
Bobby Thomason	QB	6'1"	200	26		
Skippy Giancanelli	HB	5'10"	180	26		18
Don Johnson	HB	6'	187	24		
Toy Ledbetter	HB	5'10"	200	28		6
Jim Parmer	HB	6'	195	28		6
George Taliaferro	HB	5'11"	195	28		
Ted Wegert	HB	5'11"	195	23		12
Jerry Norton	DB-HB	5'11"	200	25	1	18
Dick Bielski	FB	6'1"	215	23		56
Rob Goode (from WAS)	FB	6'4"	230	28		
Pete Pihos	OE	6'1"	210	31		42
Bill Stribling	OE	6'1"	205	28		36
Bobby Walston	HB-OE	6'	190	26		30

PITTSBURGH STEELERS 4-8-0 Walt Kiesling

Scores of Each Game		
14	CHIC. CARDS	7
26	Los Angeles	27
30	NEW YORK	23
13	PHILADELPHIA	7
19	New York	17
0	Philadelphia	24
13	Chic. Cards	27
28	DETROIT	31
14	Cleveland	41
14	WASHINGTON	23
7	CLEVELAND	30
17	Washington	28

Use Name	Pos.	Hgt	Wgt	Age	Int	Pts
Bob Gaona	OT	6'3"	250	25		
Frank Varrichione	OT	6'1"	235	23		
Nick Feher	OG	6'	225	28		
Dick Oniskey	OG	6'2"	225			
John Schweder	LB-OG	6'1"	225	28		
Fred Broussard (to NY)	C	6'3"	235	22		
Dick Flanagan	C	6'	220	28		
Bill McPeak	DE	6'1"	215	30		
Ed Meadows	DE	6'2"	218	23		
Joe O'Malley	DE	6'2"	220	22		6
Lou Ferry	DT	6'2"	250	28		
Willie McClung	DT	6'2"	215	26		
Dick Modzelewski	DT	6'	250	24		
Ernie Stautner	OG-DT	6'1"	235	30		

Use Name	Pos.	Hgt	Wgt	Age	Int	Pts
Dale Dodrill	LB	6'1"	210	30	2	
Marv Matuszak	LB	6'3"	235	24	1	
Art Michalik	LB	6'2"	230	25		12
John Reger	OG-LB	6'	220	24	2	
Lou Tepe	C-LB	6'2"	215	25		
Marion Motley	FB-LB	6'1"	240	35		
Jack Butler	DB	6'	195	27		
Dick Doyle	DB	6'	195	24	1	
Jim Hill	DB	6'	195	26	1	
Richie McCabe	DB	6'1"	185	21	3	6
Vic Eaton	QB-DB	6'2"	200	22		

Paul Cameron – Military Service
Johnny Lattner – Military Service
Marv McFadden – Military Service

Use Name	Pos.	Hgt	Wgt	Age	Int	Pts
Jim Finks	QB	6'	175	28		24
Ted Marchibroda	QB	5'10"	180	24		6
Lynn Chandnois	HB	6'2"	205	31		30
Ray Mathews	HB	6'	185	26		42
Sid Watson	HB	5'11"	185	22		6
Leon Campbell	FB	6'	197	28		
Fran Rogel	FB	5'11"	205	28		12
Ed Bernet	OE	6'3"	200	22		6
Jack McClairen	OE	6'4"	215	24		
Elbie Nickel	OE	6'1"	195	32		12
Jack O'Brien	DE-OE	6'2"	215	24		12
Tad Weed	K	5'5"	140	22		21

Stan Sheriff – Military Service
George Tarasovic – Military Service

CLEVELAND BROWNS

RUSHING Last Name	No.	Yds	Avg	TD
Morrison	156	824	5.3	3
Modzelewski	185	619	3.3	6
Bassett	38	174	4.6	3
Smith	37	142	3.8	1
Graham	68	121	1.8	6
Renfro	29	90	3.1	0
Jones	10	44	4.4	0
Petitbon	3	10	3.3	0
Ratterman	6	8	1.3	1
James	1	2	2.0	0
H. Ford	2	1	0.5	0
Perini	2	0	0.0	0
Gillom	1	−15	−15.0	0

RECEIVING Last Name	No.	Yds	Avg	TD
Brewster	34	622	18	6
Lavelli	31	492	16	4
Renfro	29	603	21	8
Modzelewski	13	113	9	2
Morrison	9	185	21	0
Bassett	9	83	9	0
Jones	3	115	38	1
Smith	2	12	6	0
Perini	1	3	3	0

PUNT RETURNS Last Name	No.	Yds	Avg	TD
Paul	19	148	8	1
Konz	17	138	8	0
White	2	28	14	0
H. Ford	4	15	4	0
Smith	1	5	5	0
Renfro	1	3	3	0

KICKOFF RETURNS Last Name	No.	Yds	Avg	TD
White	14	400	29	0
Smith	13	320	25	0
Bassett	7	151	22	0
Paul	5	109	23	0
Konz	3	66	22	0
Michaels	3	45	15	0

PASSING	Att	Comp	%	Yds	Yd/Att	TD	Int–%	RK
Graham	185	98	53	1721	9.3	15	8– 4	1
Ratterman	47	32	68	504	10.7	6	3– 6	
Renfro	2	0	0	0	0.0	0	0– 0	

PUNTING	No	Avg
Gillom	58	41.2

KICKING	XP	Att	%	FG	Att	%
Groza	44	45	98	11	22	50

WASHINGTON REDSKINS

RUSHING Last Name	No.	Yds	Avg	TD
Janowicz	93	397	4.3	4
Zagers	89	395	4.4	2
Elter	97	361	3.7	3
Atkeson	77	300	3.9	1
Monachino	46	207	4.5	2
LeBaron	37	190	5.1	4
Guglielmi	18	51	2.8	1
Dorow	8	49	6.1	0
Scudero	6	27	4.5	0

RECEIVING Last Name	No.	Yds	Avg	TD
Carson	23	443	19	3
Zagers	14	306	22	0
Elter	13	219	17	1
Janowicz	11	149	14	3
Thomas	9	105	12	2
Atkeson	9	81	9	1
Monachino	8	74	9	0
Cox	5	71	14	0
Jones	4	58	15	0
Hecker	3	31	10	1
Drazenovich	1	−3	−3	0

PUNT RETURNS Last Name	No.	Yds	Avg	TD
Scudero	25	241	10	1
Zagers	7	125	18	1
Monachino	6	26	4	0
Adduci	1	10	10	0
Felton	1	5	5	0
Alban	3	0	0	0

KICKOFF RETURNS Last Name	No.	Yds	Avg	TD
Scudero	25	699	28	1
Zagers	11	280	25	0
Atkeson	4	106	27	0
Felton	1	12	12	0
Barni	1	0	0	0
Marciniak	1	0	0	0

PASSING	Att	Comp	%	Yds	Yd/Att	TD	Int–%	RK
LeBaron	178	79	44	1270	7.1	9	15– 8	12
Guglielmi	62	20	32	242	3.9	2	4– 7	
Dorow	12	2	17	37	3.1	0	1– 8	
Janowicz	5	0	0	0	0.0	0	1–20	

PUNTING	No	Avg
LeBaron	62	41.6

KICKING	XP	Att	%	FG	Att	%
Janowicz	28	31	90	6	20	30
Hecker	2	2	100	0	1	0

NEW YORK GIANTS

RUSHING Last Name	No.	Yds	Avg	TD
Webster	128	634	5.0	5
Epps	95	375	3.9	2
Gifford	86	351	4.1	3
Triplett	34	138	4.1	0
Price	30	109	3.6	0
Rote	10	46	4.6	0
Heap	8	29	3.6	0
Conerly	12	10	0.8	0
Heinrich	7	4	0.6	2
Weaver	3	0	0.0	0
Clatterbuck	1	−3	−3.0	0

RECEIVING Last Name	No.	Yds	Avg	TD
Gifford	33	437	13	4
Rote	31	580	19	8
Schnelker	25	326	13	2
Webster	22	269	12	1
MacAfee	11	170	15	1
Long	6	64	11	1
Epps	5	8	2	0
Triplett	3	9	3	0
Price	1	2	2	0

PUNT RETURNS Last Name	No.	Yds	Avg	TD
Tunnell	25	98	4	1
Patton	3	69	23	1
Heap	8	63	8	0

KICKOFF RETURNS Last Name	No.	Yds	Avg	TD
Heap	12	230	19	0
Patton	5	229	46	1
Long	6	172	29	0
Gifford	5	114	23	0
Triplett	3	47	16	0
Kennard	3	36	12	0
Brown	1	14	14	0
West	1	6	6	0
Yowarsky	3	0	0	0

PASSING	Att	Comp	%	Yds	Yd/Att	TD	Int–%	RK
Conerly	202	98	49	1310	6.5	13	13– 6	7
Heinrich	67	31	46	413	6.2	2	2– 3	
Clatterbuck	16	6	38	46	2.9	0	0– 0	
Gifford	6	2	33	96	16.0	2	0– 0	
Rote	1	0	0	0	0.0	0	0– 0	

PUNTING	No	Avg
Landry	75	40.3

KICKING	XP	Att	%	FG	Att	%
Agajanian	32	33	97	10	15	67
Conerly	1	1	100	0	0	0

CHICAGO CARDINALS

RUSHING Last Name	No.	Yds	Avg	TD
Matson	109	475	4.4	1
Mann	87	336	3.9	4
Olszewski	84	326	3.9	1
McHan	56	194	3.5	2
Hammack	51	160	3.1	2
Carr	30	115	3.8	0
Bernardi	8	17	2.1	0
Goble	7	11	1.6	0
Compton	6	−8	−1.3	0

RECEIVING Last Name	No.	Yds	Avg	TD
Stonesifer	28	330	12	5
Matson	17	237	14	2
Mann	16	137	9	1
Carr	9	157	17	0
Olszewski	9	37	4	0
Nagler	7	218	31	3
Brubaker	6	125	21	0
Hammack	5	13	3	0
Bernardi	4	77	19	1
Boydston	3	79	26	1
Lane	2	110	55	1

PUNT RETURNS Last Name	No.	Yds	Avg	TD
Matson	13	245	19	2
Bernardi	19	163	9	0
Carr	1	0	0	0
Hill	1	0	0	0

KICKOFF RETURNS Last Name	No.	Yds	Avg	TD
Matson	15	368	25	0
Goble	8	160	20	0
Mann	6	136	23	0
Carr	4	93	23	0
Hammack	2	32	16	0
Olszewski	2	26	13	0
Hatley	2	13	7	0
Simmons	1	7	7	0
Delevan	2	0	0	0
Lange	2	0	0	0

PASSING	Att	Comp	%	Yds	Yd/Att	TD	Int–%	RK
McHan	207	78	38	1085	5.2	11	19– 9	14
Compton	61	22	36	339	5.6	1	6–10	
Mann	10	5	50	53	5.3	2	0– 0	
Leggett	1	0	0	0	0.0	0	0– 0	
Matson	1	1	100	43	43.0	0	0– 0	

PUNTING	No	Avg
Mann	43	40.1
Trippi	32	40.7

KICKING	XP	Att	%	FG	Att	%
Summerall	23	25	92	8	19	42
Mann	0	2	0	1	1	100
Keane	0	0	0	0	1	0
McHan	0	2	0	0	0	0

PHILADELPHIA EAGLES

RUSHING Last Name	No.	Yds	Avg	TD
Giancanelli	97	385	4.0	2
Goode	83	297	3.6	0
Norton	36	144	4.0	1
Burk	36	132	3.7	2
Parmer	34	129	3.8	1
Wegert	26	120	4.6	2
Bielski	28	67	2.4	1
Ledbetter	21	48	2.3	0
Thomason	17	29	1.7	0
Johnson	3	1	0.3	0
Taliaferro	3	−2	−0.7	0
Walston	1	−3	−3.0	0
Goldston	14	−7	−0.5	0

RECEIVING Last Name	No.	Yds	Avg	TD
Pihos	62	864	14	7
Stribling	38	568	15	6
Walston	27	443	16	3
Giancanelli	25	379	15	1
Goode	11	152	14	0
Norton	11	125	11	1
Bielski	8	48	6	0
Ledbetter	7	88	13	1
Taliaferro	3	17	6	0
Wegert	3	17	6	0
Goldston	2	8	4	0
Bawel	1	6	6	0
Parmer	1	−4	−4	0

PUNT RETURNS Last Name	No.	Yds	Avg	TD
Norton	20	33	2	0
Bawel	15	32	2	0
Giancanelli	5	30	6	0
Hudson	1	0	0	0

KICKOFF RETURNS Last Name	No.	Yds	Avg	TD
Norton	8	281	35	1
Giancanelli	11	267	24	0
Bawel	8	169	21	0
Wegert	4	87	22	0
Goode	2	36	18	0
Snyder	3	34	11	0
Ledbetter	1	21	21	0
Taliaferro	1	16	16	0
Sharkey	1	11	11	0

PASSING	Att	Comp	%	Yds	Yd/Att	TD	Int–%	RK
Burk	228	110	48	1359	6.0	9	17– 8	11
Thomason	171	88	51	1337	7.8	10	7– 4	2
Norton	1	0	0	0	0.0	0	0– 0	

PUNTING	No	Avg
Burk	61	42.9

KICKING	XP	Att	%	FG	Att	%
Bielski	23	24	96	9	23	39
Walston	6	7	86	2	3	67

PITTSBURGH STEELERS

RUSHING Last Name	No.	Yds	Avg	TD
Rogel	168	588	3.5	2
Chandnois	105	353	3.4	5
Mathews	57	187	3.3	1
Finks	35	76	2.2	4
Campbell	18	42	2.3	0
Watson	29	31	1.1	0
Motley	2	8	4.0	0
Marchibroda	6	−1	−0.2	1

RECEIVING Last Name	No.	Yds	Avg	TD
Mathews	42	762	18	6
Nickel	36	488	14	2
Chandnois	27	385	14	0
Rogel	24	222	9	0
Bernet	22	276	13	1
Watson	19	223	12	1
O'Brien	9	105	12	2
Campbell	9	76	8	0
McClairen	1	13	13	0

PUNT RETURNS Last Name	No.	Yds	Avg	TD
Eaton	23	73	3	0
Watson	23	15	1	0

KICKOFF RETURNS Last Name	No.	Yds	Avg	TD
Watson	27	716	27	0
Chandnois	9	223	25	0
Campbell	4	133	33	0
Rogel	1	81	81	0
Gaona	2	4	2	0
Matuszak	1	0	0	0

PASSING	Att	Comp	%	Yds	Yd/Att	TD	Int–%	RK
Finks	344	165	48	2270	6.6	10	26– 8	10
Marchibroda	43	24	56	280	6.5	2	3– 7	
Eaton	2	0	0	0	0.0	0	0– 0	
Chandnois	1	0	0	0	0.0	0	1–100	

PUNTING	No	Avg
Eaton	66	38.2
Zombek	5	40.2

KICKING	XP	Att	%	FG	Att	%
Weed	12	12	100	3	6	50
Michalik	9	15	60	1	12	8

LOS ANGELES RAMS 8-3-1 Sid Gillman

Scores of Each Game		
23	San Francisco	14
27	PITTSBURGH	26
17	Detroit	10
28	Green Bay	30
24	DETROIT	13
20	CHIC. BEARS	31
27	SAN FRANCISCO	14
3	Chic. Bears	24
17	Baltimore	17
23	Philadelphia	21
20	BALTIMORE	14
31	GREEN BAY	17

Use Name	Pos.	Hgt	Wgt	Age	Int	Pts
Bob Cross	OT	6'4"	250	24		
Glenn Holtzman	OT	6'3"	240	25		
Charlie Toogood	OT	6'	228	27		
Jack Ellena	OG	6'1"	226	23		
Sid Fournet	OG	6'	238	22		
John Hock	OG	6'2"	230	27		
Duane Putnam	OG	6'	230	27		
Leon McLaughlin	C	6'2"	228	29		
Paul Miller	DE	6'2"	220	23		
Andy Robustelli	DE	6'1"	230	29	1	12
Art Hauser	DT	6'	236	24		
Big Daddy Lipscomb	DT	6'6"	286	24		
Bud McFadin	OT	6'3"	250	27		3
Frank Fuller	OG-DE-DT	6'4"	245	26		
Don Paul	LB	6'1"	222	30		
Les Richter	LB	6'3"	230	24	2	69
Bob Griffin	C-LB	6'3"	230	26	1	2
Larry Morris	HB-LB	6'2"	210	21		6
Don Burroughs	DB	6'4"	176	24	9	
Jim Cason	DB	6'	175	28	5	6
Hall Haynes	DB	6'	182	26		
Ed Hughes	DB	6'1"	180	27		
Will Sherman	DB	6'2"	194	26	11	
Norm Van Brocklin	QB	6'1"	200	29		
Billy Wade	QB	6'2"	195	24		
Tom McCormick	HB	5'11"	180	25		6
Skeets Quinlan	HB	5'11"	170	27		6
Ron Waller	HB	5'11"	174	22		48
Corky Taylor	DB-HB	5'10"	192	21	2	12
Dan Towler	FB	6'2"	226	27		18
Tank Younger	FB	6'3"	228	27		30
Jack Bighead	OE	6'3"	215	25		
Bob Boyd	OE	6'2"	200	27		18
Tom Fears	OE	6'2"	203	31		12
Crazy Legs Hirsch	OE	6'2"	190	31		12
Woodley Lewis	OE	6'	188	30		

Rudy Bukich – Military Service
Dick Daugherty – Military Service
Bob Fry – Military Service
Brad Myers – Military Service
Duane Wardlow – Military Service

CHICAGO BEARS 8-4-0 George Halas

Scores of Each Game		
17	Baltimore	23
3	Green Bay	24
19	SAN FRANCISCO	20
38	BALTIMORE	10
34	San Francisco	23
31	Los Angeles	20
52	GREEN BAY	31
24	LOS ANGELES	3
24	Detroit	14
14	Chic. Cards	53
21	DETROIT	20
17	PHILADELPHIA	10

Use Name	Pos.	Hgt	Wgt	Age	Int	Pts
Kline Gilbert	OT	6'2"	235	24		
Bill Wightkin	OT	6'3"	235	28		
Stan Jones	OG	6'1"	255	24		
Herman Clark	LB-OG	6'3"	255	24		
Larry Strickland	C	6'4"	250	24		
Doug Atkins	DE	6'8"	255	25		
John Helwig	DE	6'2"	208	27		
Ed Sprinkle	DE	6'1"	207	31		
Jack Hoffman	OE-DE	6'5"	235	26		
Bill Bishop	DT	6'4"	250	24	1	
John Kreamcheck	DT	6'5"	255	27		
Fred Williams	DT	6'4"	250	25		
Joe Fortuanto	LB	6'	225	25		
Bill George	LB	6'2"	240	24	2	
George Connor	OT-LB	6'3"	240	30	1	6
Ralph Jecha	OG-LB	6'2"	235	24		
Wayne Hansen	C-DT-LB	6'2"	235	27		
Ken Gorgal	DB	6'2"	200	26	6	
Charlie Sumner	DB	6'1"	190	25	7	
Don Kindt	HB-DB	6'1"	208	29		
Ray Gene Smith	HB-DB	5'10"	188	25	2	
George Blanda	QB	6'1"	207	27		82
Ed Brown	QB	6'2"	205	26		12
Bob Williams	QB	6'1"	197	26		
Henry Mosley	HB	6'2"	210	25		
Bobby Watkins	HB	5'10"	195	23		48
Ron Drzewiecki	DB-HB	5'11"	185	23		6
Harry Hugasian (from BAL)	DB-HB	6'1"	192	24		
John Hoffman	FB-OE-HB	6'2"	215	29		8
Rick Casares	FB	6'2"	225	24		30
Chick Jagade	FB	6'	220	28		12
Harlon Hill	OE	6'3"	200	23		54
Bill McColl	OE	6'4"	230	25		24
Gene Schroeder	OE	6'3"	190	26		12

Zeke Bratkowski – Military Service
Jim Dooley – Military Service
McNeil Moore – Military Service
Tom O'Connell – Military Service
Stan Wallace – Military Service

GREEN BAY PACKERS 6-6-0 Lisle Blackbourn

Scores of Each Game		
20	DETROIT	17
24	CHIC. BEARS	3
20	BALTIMORE	24
30	LOS ANGELES	28
10	Cleveland	41
10	Baltimore	14
31	Chic. Bears	52
31	CHIC. CARDS	14
27	SAN FRANCISCO	21
10	Detroit	24
28	San Francisco	7
17	Los Angeles	31

Use Name	Pos.	Hgt	Wgt	Age	Int	Pts
Tom Dahms	OT	6'5"	240	27		
Len Szafaryn	OT	6'2"	230	27		6
Buddy Brown	OG	6'1"	225	28		
Joe Skibinski	OG	5'11"	228	27		
Jack Spinks	OG	6'	240	25		
Jim Ringo	C	6'1"	230	24		
Dave Stephenson	C	6'2"	230	29		
Nate Borden	DE	6'	205	23		
John Martinkovic	DE	6'3"	245	28		
Pat O'Donahue	DE	6'1"	215	25		
Dave Hanner	DT	6'2"	250	26		
Jerry Helluin	DT	6'2"	260	25		
Bill Lucky	DT	6'3"	250	24		
Tom Bettis	LB	6'2"	225	22		
Bill Forester	LB	6'3"	235	24	4	
Deral Teteak	LB	5'10"	210	26	2	
Roger Zatkoff	LB	6'2"	215	24	3	
Hank Bullough	OG-LB	6'	220	21		
George Timberlake	OG-LB	6'1"	220	23		
Billy Bookout	DB	5'11"	180	23	2	
Bobby Dillon	DB	6'1"	180	25	9	
Doyle Nix	DB	6'1"	188	22	5	
Clarence Self	DB	5'8"	180	30		
Val Joe Walker	DB	6'1"	178	24	6	
Jim Capuzzi	QB-DB	6'	190	23		
Charlie Brackins	QB	6'2"	202	23		
Paul Held	QB	6'2"	194	27		
Tobin Rote	QB	6'3"	215	27		30
Al Carmichael	HB	6'1"	190	25		12
Joe Johnson	HB	6'	180	25		6
Breezy Reid	HB	5'10"	190	28		18
Al Romine	DB-HB	6'2"	190	22		
Veryl Switzer	DB-HB	5'11"	190	23		6
Bob Clemens	FB	6'2"	200	23		
Fred Cone	FB	5'11"	200	29		78
Howie Ferguson	FB	6'2"	212	25		24
Billy Howton	OE	6'2"	190	25		30
Jim Jennings	OE	6'3"	195	22		
Gary Knafelc	OE	6'4"	215	23		48
Dick Deschaine	K	6'	190	25		

Al Barry – Military Service
Max McGee – Military Service
Art Hunter – Military Service
Gene Knutson – Military Service
Babe Parilli – Military Service

BALTIMORE COLTS 5-6-1 Weeb Ewbank

Scores of Each Game		
23	CHIC. BEARS	17
28	DETROIT	13
24	Green Bay	20
10	Chic. Bears	38
13	WASHINGTON	14
14	GREEN BAY	10
14	Detroit	24
7	New York	17
17	LOS ANGELES	17
26	SAN FRANCISCO	14
14	Los Angeles	20
24	San Francisco	35

Use Name	Pos.	Hgt	Wgt	Age	Int	Pts
Dick Chorovich	OT	6'4"	260	22		
Ken Jackson	OT	6'2"	235	26		
George Radosevich	OT	6'2"	225	28		
George Preas	OG-OT	6'2"	228	23		
Alex Sandusky	OG	6'1"	215	23		
Art Spinney	OG	6'	230	28		
Buzz Nutter	LB-C	6'4"	220	24		
Don Joyce	DE	6'3"	255	25		
Gino Marchetti	DE	6'4"	245	29		
Art Donovan	DT	6'2"	265	30		
Tom Finnin	DT	6'2"	255	27		
Bob Myers	DT	6'	260	24		
Doug Eggers	LB	6'	210	25		
Bill Pellington	LB	6'2"	230	26	2	
Jack Patera	OG-LB	6'1"	230	23	1	
Dick Szymanski	C-LB	6'3"	230	23		
Joe Campanella	OT-DT-LB	6'2"	245	24	2	
Bert Rechichar	DB	6'1"	210	25	6	55
Don Shula	DB	5'11"	190	25	5	
Jesse Thomas	DB	5'10"	180	26	1	
Walter Bryant	HB-DB	6'1"	185	22	1	
Carl Taseff	HB-DB	5'11"	190	26	1	
Monte Brethauer	OE-DB	6'1"	180	24		
Gary Kerkorian	QB	5'11"	185	26		9
George Shaw	QB	6'1"	180	22		18
L. G. Dupre	HB	5'11"	190	23		6
Dean Renfro	HB	5'11"	180	22		
Burrell Shields	HB	6'2"	200	23		
Royce Womble	HB	6'	185	23		
Buddy Young	HB	5'5"	176	29		12
Alan Ameche	FB	6'	217	22		54
Dick Young	HB-FB	5'11"	210	24		
Ray Berry	OE	6'2"	190	22		
Lloyd Colteryahn	OE	6'2"	220	25		18
Jim Mutscheller	OE	6'1"	218	25		42

Cotton Davidson – Military Service

SAN FRANCISCO FORTY NINERS 4-8-0 Red Strader

Scores of Each Game		
14	LOS ANGELES	23
3	CLEVELAND	38
20	Chic. Bears	19
27	Detroit	24
23	CHIC. BEARS	34
38	DETROIT	21
14	Los Angeles	27
0	Washington	7
21	Green Bay	27
14	Baltimore	26
7	GREEN BAY	28
35	BALTIMORE	24

Use Name	Pos.	Hgt	Wgt	Age	Int	Pts
Bob St. Clair	OT	6'9"	263	24		
Leo Nomellini	DT-OT	6'3"	252	30		
Doug Hogland	OG	6'3"	240	24		
Eldred Kraemer	OG	6'2"	225	25		
Lou Palatella	LB-OG	6'2"	230	22		
Bob Hantla	DE-LB-OG	6'1"	220	23		
Ed Beatty	C	6'3"	230	23		
Bill Johnson	C	6'3"	240	29		
Clay Matthews	DE	6'3"	220	27	1	
Charley Powell	DE	6'2"	230	23		
Marion Campbell	DT	6'3"	245	26	1	
Al Carapella	DT	6'	235	28		
Sid Youngelman	DT	6'3"	240	23		
Hardy Brown	LB	6'	196	31	2	
Paul Carr	LB	6'	205	23	1	
Matt Hazeltine	LB	6'1"	205	22		
Tom Stolhandske	DE-LB	6'2"	210	23	1	
Bob Toneff	DT-LB	6'2"	252	25		
Rex Berry	DB	5'11"	180	29	3	6
Bobby Luna	DB	5'11"	183	22	2	
George Maderos	DB	6'1"	187	22	2	
Lowell Wagner	DB	6'	195	31		
Dick Moegle	HB-DB	6'	180	21	6	30
Ernie Smith	HB-DB	6'3"	190	22		
Maury Duncan	QB	6'1"	185	24		
Y. A. Tittle	QB	6'	190	28		
Carroll Hardy	HB	6'	185	22		24
Hugh McElhenny	HB	6'1"	198	26		36
Joe Arenas	DB-HB	5'11"	180	29	1	12
John Henry Johnson	DB-HB	6'2"	205	25	1	6
Lem Harkey (from PIT)	FB	6'1"	205	21		
Bud Laughlin	FB	6'1"	200	24		
Joe Perry	FB	6'	210	28		18
Harry Babcock	OE	6'2"	190	24		
Gordie Soltau	OE	6'2"	194	30		42
Billy Wilson	OE	6'3"	190	28		42
Ted Vaught	DE-OE	6'	208	23		

Bill Jessup – Injury
Fred Bruney – Military Service
Ted Connolly – Military Service
Ed Henke – Canadian Football League
Verl Lillywhite – Military Service
Jerry Smith – Military Service

DETROIT LIONS 3-9-0 Buddy Parker

Scores of Each Game		
17	Green Bay	20
13	Baltimore	28
10	LOS ANGELES	17
24	SAN FRANCISCO	27
13	Los Angeles	24
21	San Francisco	38
24	BALTIMORE	14
31	Pittsburgh	28
14	CHIC. BEARS	24
24	GREEN BAY	10
20	Chic. Bears	21
19	NEW YORK	24

Use Name	Pos.	Hgt	Wgt	Age	Int	Pts
Charlie Ane	OT	6'2"	260	24		
Jim Salsbury	OG-OT	6'1"	220	23		
George Atkins	OG	6'1"	210	23		
Stan Campbell	OG	6'	220	25		
Harley Sewell	OG	6'1"	235	24		
Dick Stanfel	OG	6'3"	245	28		
Andy Miketa	C	6'2"	210	24		
Lou Creekmur	OT-DG	6'4"	250	28		
Jim Cain	DE	6'1"	200	28		
Sonny Gandee	LB-DE	6'1"	220	26		6
Walt Jenkins	DT-DE	6'1"	223	24		
Gil Mains	DT	6'2"	235	25		6
Darris McCord	DT	6'4"	248	22		
Bob Miller	DT	6'3"	235	25		
Jim Martin	LB	6'2"	230	31		
Joe Schmidt	LB	6'1"	220	23		
Ted Topor	LB	6'1"	210	25		
Leon Cunningham	C-LB	6'2"	215	24		
Bob Long	DE-LB	6'3"	223	21		2
Jack Christiansen	DB	6'1"	195	26	3	
Jim David	DB	5'11"	175	28	3	
Dom Fucci	DB	5'11"	190	27		
Carl Karilivacz	DB	6'	185	24	2	
Lee Riley	DB	6'1"	190	23	2	
Dick Woit	DB	5'8"	175	24		
Harry Gilmer	QB	6'	180	29		
Bobby Layne	QB	6'1"	200	28		
Bob Hoernschemeyer	HB	5'11"	195	29		6
Bill Stits	DB-HB	6'	190	24	3	6
Doak Walker	DB-HB	5'11"	172	28	1	96
Lew Carpenter	FB-HB	6'1"	200	23		48
Jug Girard	OE-HB	5'11"	175	28		
Dave Middleton	OE-HB	6'1"	190	22		30
Leon Hart	OE-FB	6'5"	255	26		6
Dorne Dibble	OE	6'2"	195	26		12
Jim Doran	OE	6'2"	200	27		12

Bill Bowman – Military Service
Tom Dublinski – Canadian Football League
Gene Gedman – Military Service
Yale Lary – Military Service
Jerry Perry – Military Service
Ollie Spencer – Military Service

LOS ANGELES RAMS

RUSHING

Last Name	No.	Yds	Avg	TD
Waller	151	716	4.7	7
Younger	138	644	4.7	5
Morris	40	148	3.7	1
Towler	43	137	3.2	3
Taylor	26	95	3.7	0
Quinlan	15	70	4.7	0
McCormick	16	66	4.1	1
Wade	11	43	3.9	0
Van Brocklin	11	24	2.2	0

RECEIVING

Last Name	No.	Yds	Avg	TD
Fears	44	569	13	2
Hirsch	25	460	18	2
Waller	24	228	10	1
Boyd	22	383	17	3
Quinlan	19	245	13	0
Lewis	19	199	10	0
Taylor	7	47	7	1
Younger	6	51	9	0
Towler	6	25	4	0
McCormick	3	−1	−0	0

PUNT RETURNS

Last Name	No.	Yds	Avg	TD
Lewis	29	105	4	0
Waller	14	60	4	0
Quinlan	1	55	55	1
Ellena	0	9	0	0

KICKOFF RETURNS

Last Name	No.	Yds	Avg	TD
Waller	17	461	27	0
Lewis	20	450	23	0
McCormick	2	42	21	0
Lipscomb	2	32	16	0
Hauser	2	17	9	0
Toogood	1	11	11	0

PASSING – PUNTING – KICKING

PASSING	Att	Comp	%	Yds	Yd/Att	TD	Int–%	RK
Van Brocklin	272	144	53	1890	7.0	8	15– 6	6
Wade	71	31	44	316	4.5	1	3– 4	
Waller	1	0	0	0	0.0	0	0– 0	

PUNTING	No	Avg
Van Brocklin	60	44.6

KICKING	XP	Att	%	FG	Att	%
Richter	30	31	97	13	24	54
McFadin	0	0	0	1	5	20
Fears	0	0	0	0	3	0

CHICAGO BEARS

RUSHING

Last Name	No.	Yds	Avg	TD
Casares	125	672	5.4	4
Watkins	110	553	5.0	8
Jo. Hoffman	94	454	4.8	0
Jagade	72	309	4.3	2
Brown	43	203	4.7	2
Williams	13	79	6.1	0
Drzewiecki	10	54	5.4	1
Blanda	15	54	3.6	2
Hugasian	12	34	2.8	0
Mosley	3	10	3.3	0

RECEIVING

Last Name	No.	Yds	Avg	TD
Hill	42	789	19	9
McColl	35	502	14	4
Schroeder	17	315	19	2
Casares	16	136	9	1
Jo. Hoffman	11	153	14	1
Jagade	7	16	2	0
Ja. Hoffman	6	86	14	0
Watkins	6	79	13	0
Hugasian	3	32	11	0
Kindt	2	15	8	0
Smith	1	13	13	0
Drzewiecki	1	1	1	0

PUNT RETURNS

Last Name	No.	Yds	Avg	TD
Drzewiecki	20	100	5	0
Smith	12	47	4	0
Kindt	1	0	0	0
Sumner	1	0	0	0

KICKOFF RETURNS

Last Name	No.	Yds	Avg	TD
Drzewiecki	25	591	24	0
Sumner	10	288	29	0
Watkins	5	145	29	0
Smith	1	24	24	0
Jagade	1	23	23	0
Mosley	1	14	14	0
Hugasian	1	0	0	0

PASSING – PUNTING – KICKING

PASSING	Att	Comp	%	Yds	Yd/Att	TD	Int–%	RK
Brown	164	85	52	1307	8.0	9	10– 6	4
Blanda	97	42	43	459	4.7	4	7– 7	
Williams	40	15	38	256	6.4	3	5–13	
Casares	3	2	67	27	9.0	1	1–33	
McColl	2	1	50	59	30.0	0	0– 0	

PUNTING	No	Avg
Brown	44	40.1
Williams	13	39.1

KICKING	XP	Att	%	FG	Att	%
Blanda	37	37	100	11	16	69

GREEN BAY PACKERS

RUSHING

Last Name	No.	Yds	Avg	TD
Ferguson	192	859	4.5	4
Rote	74	332	4.5	5
Reid	83	303	3.7	2
Johnson	49	210	4.3	0
Switzer	16	101	6.3	0
Carmichael	6	45	7.5	0
Cone	12	25	2.1	0
Held	1	8	8.0	0

RECEIVING

Last Name	No.	Yds	Avg	TD
Howton	44	697	16	5
Knafelc	40	613	15	8
Ferguson	22	153	7	0
Carmichael	16	222	14	1
Switzer	14	104	7	1
Reid	13	138	11	1
Johnson	9	71	8	1
Cone	1	7	7	0

PUNT RETURNS

Last Name	No.	Yds	Avg	TD
Switzer	24	158	7	0
Carmichael	10	89	9	0
Szafaryn	1	28	28	1
Johnson	1	5	5	0
Romine	1	0	0	0

KICKOFF RETURNS

Last Name	No.	Yds	Avg	TD
Switzer	17	445	26	0
Carmichael	14	418	30	1
Forester	3	52	17	0
Johnson	2	46	23	0
Reid	2	21	11	0
Ferguson	1	20	20	0

PASSING – PUNTING – KICKING

PASSING	Att	Comp	%	Yds	Yd/Att	TD	Int–%	RK
Rote	342	157	46	1977	5.8	17	19– 6	7
Held	4	2	50	27	6.8	0	0– 0	
Brackins	2	0	0	0	0.0	0	0– 0	

PUNTING	No	Avg
Deschaine	56	43.2

KICKING	XP	Att	%	FG	Att	%
Cone	30	30	100	16	24	67

BALTIMORE COLTS

RUSHING

Last Name	No.	Yds	Avg	TD
Ameche	213	961	4.5	9
Dupre	88	338	3.8	1
Shaw	68	301	4.4	3
B. Young	32	87	2.7	1
D. Young	17	39	2.3	0
Shields	10	34	3.4	0
Kerkorian	6	20	3.3	1
Renfro	4	13	3.3	0
Bryant	2	4	2.0	0
Womble	4	2	0.5	0

RECEIVING

Last Name	No.	Yds	Avg	TD
Mutscheller	33	518	16	7
Ameche	27	141	5	0
Colteryahn	21	251	12	3
B. Young	19	426	22	1
Berry	13	205	16	0
Dupre	10	153	15	0
Shields	3	27	9	0
D. Young	2	15	8	0
Womble	1	14	14	0
Pellington	1	10	10	0
Taseff	1	3	3	0

PUNT RETURNS

Last Name	No.	Yds	Avg	TD
Rechichar	30	121	4	0
Taseff	14	46	3	0
Pellington	1	6	6	0
D. Young	1	3	3	0
Patera	1	2	2	0
B. Young	1	0	0	0

KICKOFF RETURNS

Last Name	No.	Yds	Avg	TD
Rechichar	9	235	26	0
B. Young	9	222	25	0
Taseff	7	162	23	0
Ameche	4	60	15	0
D. Young	2	37	19	0
Pellington	2	36	18	0
Berry	2	27	14	0
Renfro	1	20	20	0

PASSING – PUNTING – KICKING

PASSING	Att	Comp	%	Yds	Yd/Att	TD	Int–%	RK
Shaw	237	119	50	1586	6.7	10	19– 8	9
Kerkorian	29	15	52	209	7.2	1	3–10	

PUNTING	No	Avg
Brethauer	55	39.3

KICKING	XP	Att	%	FG	Att	%
Rechichar	25	26	96	10	24	42
Kerkorian	0	0	0	1	2	50

SAN FRANCISCO FORTY NINERS

RUSHING

Last Name	No.	Yds	Avg	TD
Perry	156	701	4.5	2
McElhenny	90	327	3.6	4
Moegle	41	235	5.7	5
Arenas	37	150	4.1	0
Tittle	23	114	5.0	0
J. Johnson	19	69	3.6	1
Laughlin	20	58	2.9	0
Hardy	15	37	2.5	0
Harkey	6	27	4.5	0
Duncan	1	−5	−5.0	0

RECEIVING

Last Name	No.	Yds	Avg	TD
Wilson	53	831	16	7
Soltau	26	358	14	1
Perry	19	55	3	1
Arenas	13	255	20	2
Hardy	12	338	28	4
McElhenny	11	203	18	2
Laughlin	8	54	7	0
Moegle	4	94	24	0
Babcock	3	31	10	0
J. Johnson	2	6	3	0

PUNT RETURNS

Last Name	No.	Yds	Avg	TD
Arenas	21	55	3	0
Moegle	8	36	5	0
Berry	1	11	11	0
McElhenny	7	10	1	0
J. Johnson	1	6	6	0
Carapella	1	0	0	0

KICKOFF RETURNS

Last Name	No.	Yds	Avg	TD
Arenas	24	594	25	0
Moegle	10	249	25	0
McElhenny	9	189	21	0
Hardy	3	65	22	0
Laughlin	1	25	25	0
Toneff	1	13	13	0
Hazeltine	1	9	9	0
Powell	1	2	2	0
Palatella	1	1	1	0

PASSING – PUNTING – KICKING

PASSING	Att	Comp	%	Yds	Int–%	TD	Int–%	RK
Tittle	287	147	51	2185	7.6	17	28–10	5
Duncan	12	4	33	40	3.3	0	0– 0	
Perry	2	0	0	0	0.0	0	0– 0	
Arenas	1	0	0	0	0.0	0	0– 0	
Moegle	1	0	0	0	0.0	0	0– 0	

PUNTING	No	Avg
Luna	63	40.6

KICKING	XP	Att	%	FG	Att	%
Soltau	27	30	90	3	12	25

DETROIT LIONS

RUSHING

Last Name	No.	Yds	Avg	TD
Carpenter	137	543	4.0	6
Middleton	59	201	3.4	2
Stits	46	165	3.6	0
Hart	35	159	4.5	0
Layne	31	111	3.6	0
Hoernschemeyer	36	109	3.0	1
Walker	23	95	4.1	2
Gilmer	15	67	4.5	0
Girard	10	27	2.7	0

RECEIVING

Last Name	No.	Yds	Avg	TD
Middleton	44	663	15	3
Carpenter	44	312	7	2
Doran	38	552	15	2
Girard	23	301	13	0
Walker	22	428	19	5
Dibble	17	179	13	2
Hart	9	54	6	1
Hoernschemeyer	5	36	7	0
Stits	5	17	3	0

PUNT RETURNS

Last Name	No.	Yds	Avg	TD
Riley	14	107	8	0
Christiansen	12	87	7	0
Girard	9	25	3	0
Walker	2	5	3	0
David	1	0	0	0
Karilivacz	1	0	0	0
Schmidt	1	0	0	0
Stits	1	0	0	0

KICKOFF RETURNS

Last Name	No.	Yds	Avg	TD
Middleton	11	188	17	0
Christiansen	7	169	24	0
Girard	7	117	17	0
Riley	5	111	22	0
Hart	4	86	22	0
Carpenter	4	78	20	0
Walker	1	24	24	0
Martin	1	14	14	0
Cunningham	1	13	13	0
Toper	1	13	13	0
Woit	1	13	13	0
Gandee	1	7	7	0
Schmidt	1	6	6	0

PASSING – PUNTING – KICKING

PASSING	Att	Comp	%	Yds	Yd/Att	TD	Int–%	RK
Layne	270	143	53	1830	6.8	11	17– 6	3
Gilmer	122	58	48	633	5.2	2	4– 3	
Walker	3	0	0	0	0.0	0	0– 0	
Hornschemeyer	2	1	50	17	8.5	1	1–50	
Stits	2	2	100	62	31.0	1	0– 0	
Girard	1	0	0	0	0.0	0	0– 0	

PUNTING	No	Avg
Girard	56	41.3
Walker	9	40.2
Fucci	2	36.0

KICKING	XP	Att	%	FG	Att	%
Walker	27	29	93	9	16	56
Martin	0	0	0	0	1	0

1956 Wiring the Quarterback

The television tube now was creating pro-football fans in every corner of the country, as the NFL signed a lucrative contract with the Columbia Broadcasting System for TV coverage of all league games. With home contests blacked out for a fifty-mile radius, CBS captured huge audiences every Sunday afternoon with regional telecasts of most games and coast-to-coast coverage of all post-season action. Besides handsomely rewarding the teams financially, the TV contract further fueled the league's already skyrocketing attendance and started some people to thinking of pro football as the new national pastime.

The world of electronics did create some problems for Commissioner Bert Bell, as walkie-talkie radios came into vogue on the field. Instead of sending plays into the quarterback via alternating guards, as had been his custom, Cleveland coach Paul Brown installed radio receivers in his quarterbacks' helmets and called the plays by radio. Very quickly, several teams were broadcasting their signals from the bench, leading other clubs to tune in on the enemy's wave length to try to decode their messages. The Pittsburgh Steelers even installed special wiring in the turf at Forbes Field to aid radio reception, but Bell quickly ended this sideshow by banning, on October 19, all such electronic gadgetry.

Bell this year faced no threats from Canada, as the Canadian teams had tired of waging a raiding war, but he did face a new adversary in the new NFL players' association. This union was seeking benefits such as the establishment of a pension and a minimum salary of $5,000, but the owners felt strong enough to ignore this group for now.

EASTERN CONFERENCE

New York Giants—The Giants moved into Yankee Stadium this year, and once the New Yorkers beat the quick-starting Chicago Cards in a mid-season showdown, they easily charged down the home stretch. While the offense jelled after several seasons of playing together, the defense was bolstered by four fine newcomers. Defensive coach Tom Landry, no longer a player, replaced himself in the secondary with ex-Ram Ed Hughes, installed rookie Sam Huff, whose crunching tackles won him a hero's status with Giant fans, as a full-time middle linebacker, and traded for two excellent linemen in ex-Ram Andy Robustelli and ex-Steeler Dick Modzelewski. Em Tunnell and Rosie Grier shone among the returning defenders, and although the Chuck Conerly-led offense consistently ground out points, it was the defensive unit that gave this team its image and won the fans' imagination.

Chicago Cardinals—For a team with an unsure quarterback, the Cards got off to an amazing start by beating the Browns, Giants, Redskins, and Eagles in their first four games. Directing the attack through these victories was young Lamar McHan, a talented passer whose lack of confidence required constant pep talks from his teammates, even in the huddle. After the opening spurt, however, the entire Card team faded into inconsistency. Although Night Train Lane and Lindon Crow starred in the secondary, the improved defense fell into a mid-season skid when injuries shelved tackles Chuck Ulrich and Tony Pasquesi.

Washington Redskins—One evening during training camp, halfback Vic Janowicz was riding in a friend's car when the vehicle left the road in an accident. Janowicz was thrown from the car against a tree, suffering brain damage, which ended his football career. The Redskins as a team were shocked by the loss of their star back, but the players as individuals were repelled by owner George Marshall's policy toward the crippled Janowicz. Stating that the accident happened on off-duty hours, Marshall put the injured player off the Redskin payroll. Fully aware of the staggering medical costs facing him, each Redskin player contributed $10 each week to help Janowicz through the crisis. Morale on the squad sank to an ugly level, and although injuries to quarterbacks Eddie LeBaron and Al Dorow hurt the team, the Redskin season was unalterably ruined before it began.

Cleveland Browns—All monarchies eventually fall, and the Browns this year ran into a revolt by their former abject subjects in the Eastern Conference. The retirement of Otto Graham left the dynasty on shaky ground, with four losses in the first five games signaling the death of the king. George Ratterman began the year at quarterback but ripped up his knee in the season's fourth game. Babe Parilli was next on the firing line, lasting three games before a shoulder separation shelved him and left the Browns without a quarterback. In desperation, the team signed free-agent Tom O'Connell, who did surprisingly well in the remaining games. A loss to the Cards in the final game of the year saddled the Browns with their first losing season ever, but this cloudy season had a silver lining. With an early pick in the collegiate draft, the Browns would wind up with Jimmy Brown.

Pittsburgh Steelers—The Steelers' rebuilding program fielded several promising first- and second-year men. Youngsters Joe Krupa, John Reger, and Gary Glick worked their way onto the defensive platoon, while Frank Varrichione, Willie McClung, and Lowell Perry got their feet wet on offense. Of all these young gems, Perry shone the brightest, with his darting speed put to good use as a pass receiver and a punt returner until a mid-season tackle fractured his pelvis and ended his career before it really began. But even with Perry's loss, the Steelers played respectable football while breaking in the new men.

Philadelphia Eagles—Pete Pihos was gone, Bucko Kilroy was gone, and any resemblance to the championship teams of the Greasy Neale era was gone. The Eagles still had not signed any reliable, heavy-duty runner, relying instead on Bobby Thomason and Adrian Burk to pass the club to victory in the face of expectant enemy defenses. With the sticky-finger Pihos retired, even the air attack bogged down, with the offense dropping 105 points off from its 1955 production.

WESTERN CONFERENCE

Chicago Bears—This season both started a new era in Bear history and recaptured the glory of the pre-World War II Bear teams. Although George Halas still called the shots from the front office, he kept his promise to install a younger coach by turning over the reigns to long-time assistant Paddy Driscoll, who was a full two years younger. But even without Halas prowling the sidelines, this Bear club looked a lot like the team which won four straight divisional crowns from 1940 to 1943. The defense, led by Bill George, stood like a granite wall for enemy offenses to beat their heads against, while the Bear attack combined hard running with accurate passing.

Detroit Lions—With Bobby Layne's shoulder healed and Joe Schmidt's coming into his own as a middle linebacker, the Lions had an inspirational leader at the head of both the offensive and defensive platoons. With last year's collapse to motivate them further, the Lions roared out of the pack with six straight wins and ran head and head with the Bears for the Western crown. Two weeks from the end of the year, Detroit took a half-game lead by destroying the Bears 42-10, and that same slim margin was on the line when the clubs again met on the last day of the season. With Detroit favored to win, disaster struck when Chicago's Ed Meadows blindsided Layne, knocking him out of action with a concussion. Bitterness and anger filled the field, and when the final gun sounded, Chicago had won 38-21.

San Francisco '49ers—Popular ex-quarterback Frankie Albert returned to the '49ers as head coach but couldn't make up his mind on which quarterback to use. At the start of the year, he benched veteran Y. A. Tittle and gave the starting job to rookie Earl Morrall. Pro football, however, had reached the stage where no rookie could step right into the lineup and turn a club into a winner, so Albert put Tittle back into the signal caller's spot and the '49ers rallied to four wins and a tie in their last five games.

Baltimore Colts—When a hard tackle by the Bears' Fred Williams broke quarterback George Shaw's kneecap in the Colts' fourth game, into the lineup trotted rookie Johnny Unitas, signed as an unheralded free agent during training camp. With Unitas' timing rusty from inactivity, the Colts kept fumbling the ball, and the Bears coasted to a 58-27 triumph. With little expected from him, Unitas then led the Colts to successive upsets over the Packers and Browns and later engineered a 56-21 thrashing of the Rams. Two other key newcomers figured in the mid-season surge—rookie speedster Lenny Moore and ex-Ram defensive tackle Big Daddy Lipscomb.

Green Bay Packers—On successive weekends the Packers knocked the Lions temporarily out of first place with a 24-20 triumph, then killed the Cardinals' Eastern Division hopes with a 24-21 upset. But outside of these two spoiler victories, the season bogged down in a swamp of internal turmoil. The team executive committee began growling at head coach Lisle Blackbourn when the Packers won only two of their first eight games. One executive member blasted Blackbourn for not playing first draft choice Jack Losch more often, another wanted Blackbourn's head for trading off defensive end John Martinkovic.

Los Angeles Rams—The Rams' decisive loss in last year's championship game led coach Sid Gillman to replace some of the parts in his football machine, only to have the entire unit break down in the process. Gillman unloaded Andy Robustelli, Big Daddy Lipscomb, and Ed Hughes from the defensive unit and started young Billy Wade at quarterback over Norm Van Brocklin. With ten rookies on the thirty-five-man roster, the Rams opened the season by beating the Eagles 27-7 and then dropped three straight to reveal the flaws in the new lineup.

FINAL TEAM STATISTICS

OFFENSE

	BALT.	CHI.B.	CHI.C.	CLEVE.	DET.	G.BAY	L.A.	N.Y.	PHIL.	PITT.	S.F.	WASH.
FIRST DOWNS:												
Total	216	244	191	173	247	212	227	223	160	184	221	176
by Rushing	106	140	116	94	122	86	103	124	73	83	101	91
by Passing	99	92	63	63	111	112	111	82	74	83	107	71
by Penalty	11	12	12	16	14	14	13	17	13	18	13	14
RUSHING:												
Number	432	536	527	480	507	337	384	499	418	413	419	501
Yards	2202	2468	2053	1845	2011	1421	1978	2129	1377	1350	1836	1743
Average Yards	5.1	4.6	3.9	3.8	4.0	4.2	5.2	4.3	3.3	3.3	4.4	3.5
Touchdowns	21	22	14	8	21	13	15	18	11	14	17	5
PASSING:												
Attempts	279	250	214	202	301	353	329	275	249	318	297	215
Completions	158	135	100	105	160	171	170	133	122	136	162	104
Completion Percentage	56.6	54.0	46.7	52.0	53.2	48.4	51.7	48.4	49.0	42.8	54.5	48.4
Gross Yards	2210	2193	1492	1358	2250	2591	2601	1601	1556	1793	2262	1335
Yards Lost Tackled	289	124	123	183	55	193	182	34	279	127	285	117
Net Yards	1921	2069	1369	1175	2195	2398	2419	1567	1277	1666	1977	1218
Avg. Yards per Attempt (Gross)	7.9	8.8	7.0	6.7	7.5	7.3	7.9	5.8	6.2	5.6	7.6	6.2
Avg. Yards per Comp. (Gross)	14.0	16.2	14.9	12.9	14.1	15.2	15.3	12.0	12.8	13.2	14.0	12.8
Touchdowns	14	19	13	8	13	21	18	17	6	14	8	11
Interceptions	18	19	14	18	23	18	28	14	27	24	19	18
Percent Intercepted	6.5	7.6	6.5	8.9	7.6	5.1	8.5	5.1	10.8	7.5	6.4	8.4
PUNTS:												
Number	58	44	55	50	52	62	48	60	68	77	59	63
Average Yards	38.4	39.3	37.8	41.9	41.3	42.7	43.1	41.8	41.8	38.2	38.4	42.4
PUNT RETURNS:												
Number	42	30	32	41	43	30	43	36	36	45	35	29
Yards	297	195	305	317	233	239	253	162	241	299	160	273
Average Yards	7.1	6.5	9.5	7.7	5.4	8.0	5.9	4.5	6.7	6.6	4.6	9.4
Touchdowns	1	1	1	1	1	0	1	0	0	0	1	0
KICKOFF RETURNS:												
Number	54	37	33	34	33	59	44	35	45	40	51	44
Yards	1043	830	700	830	687	1442	1011	719	1073	1042	1257	864
Average Yards	19.3	22.4	21.2	24.4	20.8	24.4	23.0	20.5	23.8	26.1	24.6	19.6
Touchdowns	0	1	1	0	0	1	1	0	0	0	1	0
INTERCEPTION RETURNS:												
Number	13	23	33	18	28	19	20	17	16	18	17	18
Yards	134	420	451	274	360	406	328	198	246	312	126	148
Average Yards	10.3	18.3	13.7	15.2	12.9	21.4	16.4	11.6	15.4	17.3	7.4	8.2
Touchdowns	0	3	1	1	1	1	2	0	1	0	1	0
PENALTIES:												
Number	53	67	78	52	66	42	57	52	59	74	57	44
Yards	507	553	626	457	668	393	583	474	542	614	562	383
FUMBLES:												
Number	18	18	29	18	14	24	32	27	25	16	17	29
Number Lost	14	10	21	12	11	11	18	13	11	10	12	17
POINTS:												
Total	270	363	240	167	300	264	291	264	143	217	233	183
PAT Attempts	38	47	30	19	36	35	38	35	18	29	28	19
PAT Made	33	45	30	18	36	33	36	34	17	26	26	16
FG Attempts	16	28	22	20	25	8	19	15	14	9	20	25
FG Made	3	12	10	11	16	5	9	6	6	5	13	17
Percent FG Made	18.8	42.9	45.5	55.0	64.0	62.5	47.4	40.0	42.9	55.6	65.0	68.0
Safeties	0	0	0	1	0	0	0	1	0	1	0	1

DEFENSE

	BALT.	CHI.B	CHI.C.	CLEVE.	DET.	G.BAY	L.A.	N.Y.	PHIL.	PITT.	S.F.	WASH.
FIRST DOWNS:												
Total	238	207	211	188	181	246	224	188	200	167	236	188
by Rushing	109	80	117	108	81	129	109	82	110	93	124	97
by Passing	115	113	79	62	84	104	100	90	69	66	103	83
by Penalty	14	14	15	18	16	13	15	16	21	8	9	8
RUSHING:												
Number	447	384	478	463	373	512	473	415	513	468	481	446
Yards	1916	1483	2075	2032	1503	2619	1944	1443	1893	1743	2192	1570
Average Yards	4.3	3.9	4.3	4.4	4.0	5.1	4.1	3.5	3.7	3.7	4.6	3.5
Touchdowns	16	14	14	13	9	20	21	10	10	14	23	15
PASSING:												
Attempts	297	332	287	226	297	260	290	297	243	234	279	240
Completions	165	159	129	107	138	144	156	149	114	128	147	120
Completion Percentage	55.6	47.9	44.9	47.3	46.5	55.4	53.8	50.2	46.9	54.7	52.7	50.0
Gross Yards	2463	2413	1670	1215	2045	2166	2374	1890	1506	1646	2115	1739
Yards Lost Tackled	203	220	146	112	140	75	212	252	173	203	145	110
Net Yards	2260	2193	1524	1103	1905	2091	2162	1638	1333	1443	1970	1629
Avg. Yards per Attempt (Gross)	8.3	7.3	5.8	5.4	6.9	8.3	8.2	6.4	6.2	6.8	7.6	7.2
Avg. Yards per Comp. (Gross)	14.9	15.2	12.9	11.4	14.8	15.0	15.2	12.7	13.2	12.9	14.4	14.5
Touchdowns	22	16	8	7	11	17	17	12	15	14	12	11
Interceptions	13	23	33	18	28	19	20	17	16	18	17	18
Percent Intercepted	4.4	6.9	11.5	8.0	9.4	7.3	6.9	5.7	6.6	7.7	6.1	7.5
PUNTS:												
Number	56	64	52	59	59	50	58	62	68	65	42	61
Average Yards	44.4	40.0	39.2	40.7	39.4	40.8	42.0	36.5	41.0	41.6	40.7	40.7
PUNT RETURNS:												
Number	39	29	28	26	32	49	31	34	50	45	35	44
Yards	153	243	132	137	197	280	342	337	283	451	123	296
Average Yards	3.9	8.4	4.7	5.3	6.2	5.7	11.0	9.9	5.7	10.0	3.5	6.7
Touchdowns	2	1	0	0	0	1	0	0	0	1	0	2
KICKOFF RETURNS:												
Number	43	47	40	33	48	48	52	46	27	43	42	40
Yards	1015	1249	889	819	1041	924	1068	1033	666	817	988	989
Average Yards	23.6	26.6	22.2	24.8	21.7	19.3	20.5	22.5	24.7	19.0	23.5	24.7
Touchdowns	1	1	0	0	1	0	1	0	0	0	0	1
INTERCEPTION RETURNS:												
Number	18	19	14	18	23	18	28	14	27	24	19	18
Yards	275	343	173	279	243	312	331	235	365	364	330	153
Average Yards	15.3	18.1	12.4	15.5	10.6	17.3	11.8	16.8	13.5	15.2	17.4	8.5
Touchdowns	2	1	0	0	1	3	0	1	0	3	0	0
PENALTIES:												
Number	62	60	60	61	48	52	62	56	76	69	37	58
Yards	486	624	543	529	519	493	512	495	686	606	321	548
FUMBLES:												
Number	23	24	23	11	16	17	13	32	17	39	27	25
Number Lost	15	15	12	8	12	8	8	16	11	22	17	16
POINTS:												
Total	322	246	182	177	188	342	307	197	215	250	284	225
PAT Attempts	43	34	23	21	21	44	39	25	25	33	34	29
PAT Made	40	33	21	21	21	42	37	24	23	31	32	25
FG Attempts	19	18	16	17	20	18	20	16	21	16	25	15
FG Made	8	3	7	10	11	12	12	7	14	7	14	8
Percent FG Made	42.1	16.7	43.8	58.8	55.0	66.7	60.0	43.8	66.7	43.8	56.0	53.3
Safeties	0	0	1	0	1	0	0	1	0	0	0	1

1956 CHAMPIONSHIP GAME

December 30, at New York
(Attendance 56,836)

Icing the Bears on Giant Footing

Just as in 1934, the Giants and Bears met for the NFL title on an icy field in New York, with the Giants again getting superior footing from sneakers. New York established itself right at the outset as Gene Filipski ran the opening kickoff 53 yards back to the Chicago 38-yard line. Four plays later, Mel Triplett barged 17 yards over left tackle for the first touchdown of the game. Two plays after the kickoff, the Giants recovered Rick Casares' fumble deep in his own territory and converted it into three points on Ben Agajanian's toe. After Jimmy Patton picked off an Ed Brown pass, Agajanian kicked another field goal to make the score 13-0 at the end of the first quarter. Three minutes into the second period, Alex Webster's three-yard run plus the extra point ran the lead to 20-0. With a rout staring them in the face, the Bears got a break when Em Tunnell fumbled a punt on the New York 25-yard line and John Mellekas recovered for Chicago. Five plays later, Rick Casares ran nine yards for the Bears' only touchdown of the day. The Giants put the game in their hip pocket with a pair of touchdowns late in the second period. The Giants drove 72 yards in five plays, with a 50-yard pass from Chuck Conerly to Alex Webster the key play. Within two minutes, New York's Ray Beck blocked Ed Brown's punt, and Henry Moore fell on it in the end zone for another Giant touchdown. The halftime score of 34-7 convinced quite a few fans to leave the frigid stadium for the warmth at home. The Bears, however, had to endure a second half in which the Giant linemen constantly pressured Ed Brown and George Blanda, the linebackers hounded fullback Rick Casares, and the secondary blanketed ace receiver Harlon Hill. The Chicago attack was throttled so completely that the Bears abandoned the T formation and switched to the double wing in the third quarter. The Giants, however, scored the only points of the period by driving 80 yards in four plays, with the final nine yards coming on a Conerly-to-Kyle Rote pass as Conerly continued to pick on rookie defensive back J.C. Caroline. Conerly's 14-yard touchdown pass to Frank Gifford midway through the final period ran the score to 47-7, and that total stood up through the final eight minutes of the game. By the end of the game, third-string quarterback Bobby Clatterbuck was directing the New York offense, but the Bears were able to keep him from lengthening the lead.

SCORING

NEW YORK	13	21	6	7—47
CHIC. BEARS	0	7	0	0— 7

First Quarter

N. Y.	Triplett, 17 yard rush PAT – Agajanian (kick)	2:40
N. Y.	Agajanian, 17 yard Field Goal	4:59
N. Y.	Agajanian, 43 yard Field Goal	12:21

Second Quarter

N. Y.	Webster, 3 yard rush PAT – Agajanian (kick)	2:34
Chi.	Casares, 9 yard rush PAT – Blanda (kick)	6:52
N. Y.	Webster, 1 yard rush PAT – Agajanian (kick)	9:54
N.Y.	Moore, recovered blocked punt in end zone PAT – Agajanian (kick)	11:32

Third Quarter

N.Y.	Rote, 9 yard pass from Conerly PAT – Agajanian (No Good)	10:10

Fourth Quarter

N.Y.	Gifford, 14 yard pass from Conerly PAT – Agajanian (kick)	6:23

TEAM STATISTICS

N.Y.		CHI.
16	First Downs – Total	19
8	First Downs – Rushing	8
8	First Downs – Passing	10
0	First Downs – Penalty	1
126	Rushing Yardage	67
20	Pass Attempts	47
11	Pass Completions	20
55.0	Completion Percentage	42.5
228	Yards Gained Passing	247
6	Yards Lost Attempting to Pass	34
222	Net Passing Yards	213
11.4	Average Yards per Attempt	5.3
20.7	Average Yards per Completion	12.4
3	Punts	8
37	Average Punting Distance	34
46	Punt Return Yardage	1
2	Interceptions	0
48	Interception Return Yardage	0
6	Penalties	4
40	Yards Penalized	50
3	Fumbles	2
2	Fumbles Lost	1

NEW YORK GIANTS 8-3-1 Jim Lee Howell

Scores of Each Game			Use Name	Pos.	Hgt	Wgt	Age	Int	Pts
38	San Francisco	21	Rosey Brown	OT	6'3"	245	23		
27	Chic. Cards	35	Dick Yelvington	OT	6'2"	235	29		
21	Cleveland	9	Bill Austin	OG	6'1"	225	27		
38	PITTSBURGH	10	Jerry Huth	OG	6'	215	23		
20	PHILADELPHIA	3	Jack Spinks (from GB)	OG	6'	235	26		
17	Pittsburgh	14	Jack Stroud	OG	6'1"	235	27		
23	CHIC. CARDS	10	Ray Wietecha	C	6'1"	225	27		
7	Washington	33	Ray Beck	OG-DG	6'2"	225	24	1	
17	CHIC. BEARS	17	Jim Katcavage	DE	6'3"	235	21		
28	WASHINGTON	14	Andy Robustelli	DE	6'1"	235	30		2
7	CLEVELAND	24	Walt Yowarsky	DE	6'2"	235	28		
21	Philadelphia	7	Rosey Grier	DT	6'5"	275	23		
			Dick Modzelewski	DT	6'	260	25		

Use Name	Pos.	Hgt	Wgt	Age	Int	Pts
Sam Huff	LB	6'1"	230	21	3	
Cliff Livingston	LB	6'3"	210	26		
Harland Svare	LB	6'	215	25		
Bill Svoboda	LB	6'	210	29	2	
Ed Hughes	DB	6'1"	185	28	1	
Dick Nolan	DB	6'1"	185	24	2	
Jimmy Patton	DB	6'	180	24	1	
Herb Rich	DB	5'11"	185	27	1	
Em Tunnell	DB	6'1"	200	34	6	
Henry Moore	HB-DB	6'1"	195	22		

Use Name	Pos.	Hgt	Wgt	Age	Int	Pts
Bobby Clatterbuck	QB	6'3"	195	24		
Chuck Conerly	QB	6'1"	185	32		
Don Heinrich	QB	6'	180	24		
Don Chandler	HB	6'2"	205	21		3
Gene Filipski	HB	5'11"	185	25		6
Frank Gifford	HB	6'1"	205	26		65
Alex Webster	HB	6'3"	210	25		60
Mel Triplett	FB	6'1"	215	24		36
Ken MacAfee	OE	6'2"	215	26		24
Kyle Rote	OE	6'	205	27		24
Bob Schnelker	OE	6'3"	215	26		6
Ben Agajanian	K	6'	215	37		38

CHICAGO CARDINALS 7-5-0 Ray Richards

Scores of Each Game			Use Name	Pos.	Hgt	Wgt	Age	Int	Pts
9	CLEVELAND	7	Tom Dahms	OT	6'5"	247	28		
35	NEW YORK	27	Burt Delevan	OT	6'2"	236	26		
31	Washington	3	Jack Jennings	OT	6'4"	245	29		
20	Philadelphia	6	John Dittrich	OG	6'1"	230	23		
14	WASHINGTON	17	Doug Hogland	OG	6'3"	240	25		
28	PHILADELPHIA	17	Bob Konovsky	OT-OG	6'2"	245	22		
10	New York	23	Jack Simmons	C	6'4"	240	30		
7	Pittsburgh	14	Stan West	OG	6'2"	235	29		
38	PITTSBURGH	27	Tom Bienemann	DE	6'3"	225	28	1	
21	GREEN BAY	24	Leo Sugar	DE	6'1"	210	27		
3	Chic. Bears	10	Pat Summerall	DE	6'4"	225	26		60
24	Cleveland	7	Chuck Ulrich	DT	6'4"	250	25		
			Len Teeuws	DT	6'4"	245	29		
			Tony Pasquesi	LB-DT	6'4"	250	22		

Use Name	Pos.	Hgt	Wgt	Age	Int	Pts
Carl Brettschneider	LB	6'1"	220	24		
Hardy Brown (from SF)	LB	6'	196	32		
Ed Husmann	OG-LB	6'	225	25		
Leo Sanford	C-LB	6'1"	230	27	5	
Chuck Weber (from CLE)	DE-LB	6'1"	225	27	1	
Lindon Crow	DB	6'1"	187	23	11	
Jimmy Hill	DB	6'2"	190	27	5	
Woodley Lewis	DB	6'	195	31	1	
Julian Spence	DB	5'11"	175	27	1	
John Roach	QB-DB	6'4"	190	23		
Night Train Lane	OE-DB	6'1"	190	28	7	6

Mal Hammack – Military Service
Jimmy Sears – Military Service

Use Name	Pos.	Hgt	Wgt	Age	Int	Pts
Lamar McHan	QB	6'1"	197	24		30
Jim Root	QB	6'1"	185	25		12
Alex Burl	HB	5'10"	165	24		6
Ollie Matson	HB	6'2"	210	26		48
Frank Bernardi	DB-HB	5'9"	180	23	1	6
Dave Mann	OE-HB	6'1"	190	23		6
Joe Childress	FB	6'	195	22		6
Johnny Olszewski	FB	5'11"	200	25		12
Max Boydston	OE	6'2"	207	23		12
Gern Nagler	OE	6'2"	190	23		24
Don Stonesifer	OE	6'	200	29		12
Charlie Anderson	DE-OE	6'	230	22		

WASHINGTON REDSKINS 6-6-0 Joe Kuharich

Scores of Each Game			Use Name	Pos.	Hgt	Wgt	Age	Int	Pts
13	Pittsburgh	30	Don Boll	OT	6'2"	270	29		
9	Philadelphia	13	Johnny Miller	DT-OT	6'5"	242	22		2
3	CHIC. CARDS	31	H. Jagielski (from Chi C)	DT-OT	6'	250	24		
20	CLEVELAND	9	Dick Stanfel	OG	6'3"	230	29		
17	Chic. Cards	14	Red Stephens	OG	6'	227	26		
18	DETROIT	17	Slug Witucki	OG	5'11"	234	28		
33	NEW YORK	7	Bill Fulcher	LB-OG	6'	190	22	1	
20	Cleveland	17	Johnny Allen	C	6'2"	224	24		
14	New York	28	Jim Schrader	C	6'2"	235	24		
19	PHILADELPHIA	17	Harry Ulinski	C	6'4"	232	31		
0	PITTSBURGH	23	Gene Brito	DE	6'1"	230	31	1	
17	Baltimore	19	Erik Christensen	DE	6'3"	235	25		
			Chet Ostrowski	DE	6'1"	232	26	1	
			Ralph Thomas	OE-DE	5'11"	184	26		
			J. D. Kimmel	DT	6'4"	250	27		
			Volney Peters	DT	6'4"	237	28		
			John Paluck	DE-DT	6'2"	235	23		6

Use Name	Pos.	Hgt	Wgt	Age	Int	Pts
Chuck Drazenovich	LB	6'1"	224	29		
Ralph Felton	LB	5'11"	210	24		
Tony Sardisco (to SF)	LB	6'2"	215	23		
Lavern Torgeson	LB	6'	220	27	1	
Roy Barni	DB	5'11"	184	29	2	
Art DeCarlo	DB	6'2"	193	26	1	
Norb Hecker	DB	6'2"	196	29	8	6
Gary Lowe	DB	5'11"	198	22	1	
Hal Norris	LB-DB	5'11"	194	24		
Scooter Scudero	HB-DB	5'10"	170	26	2	

Vic Janowicz – Brain injury in automobile accident
Ralph Guglielmi – Military Service
Bert Zagers – Military Service

Use Name	Pos.	Hgt	Wgt	Age	Int	Pts
Al Dorow	QB	6'	190	26		
Eddie LeBaron	QB	5'9"	165	26		
Fred Wyant	QB	6'	200	22		
Jerry Planutis	HB	5'9"	175	26		
Tom Runnels	HB	5'10"	184	22		6
Billy Wells	HB	5'9"	178	24		12
Dick James	DB-HB	5'9"	174	22		18
Dale Atkeson	FB	6'2"	212	26		6
Sam Baker	FB	6'2"	210	24		67
Leo Elter	FB	5'10"	202	27		12
Johnny Carson	OE	6'3"	198	26		18
Steve Meilinger	OE	6'2"	220	26		30

CLEVELAND BROWNS 5-7-0 Paul Brown

Scores of Each Game			Use Name	Pos.	Hgt	Wgt	Age	Int	Pts
7	Chic. Cards	9	Lou Groza	OT	6'3"	240	32		51
14	Pittsburgh	10	Mike McCormack	OT	6'4"	248	29		
9	NEW YORK	21	John Macerelli	OG-OT	6'2"	230	26		
9	Washington	20	Harold Bradley	OG	6'2"	230	27		
16	PITTSBURGH	24	Herschel Forester	OG	6'	230	26		
24	Green Bay	7	Abe Gibron (to PHI)	OG	5'11"	240	30		
7	BALTIMORE	21	Frank Gatski	C	6'3"	240	34		
16	Philadelphia	0	Art Hunter	DE-DT-C	6'4"	225	23		
17	WASHINGTON	20	Len Ford	DE	6'4"	250	30		
17	PHILADELPHIA	14	Carlton Massey	DE	6'2"	220	27		
24	New York	7	Jim Ray Smith	DE	6'3"	220	25		
7	CHIC. CARDS	24	Horace Gillom	OE-DE	6'1"	225	35		
			Don Colo	DT	6'3"	245	31	1	
			John Kissell	DT	6'3"	248	33		
			Don Goss	OT-DT	6'5"	260	24		
			Bob Gain	DE-LB-DT	6'3"	250	28		

Use Name	Pos.	Hgt	Wgt	Age	Int	Pts
Galen Fiss	LB	6'	215	~~26~~	1	
Walt Michaels	LB	6'	230	27		
Chuck Noll	LB	6'1"	220	24	1	6
Sam Palumbo	C-LB	6'2"	220	25		
Kenny Konz	DB	5'10"	180	28	4	6
Warren Lahr	DB	5'11"	190	32	3	
Don Paul	DB	6'	190	30	7	6
Johnny Petitbon	DB	5'11"	185	25		
Junior Wren	DB	6'	185	26	1	2
Billy Kinard	HB-DB	6'	185	22		6

Tom Catlin – Military Service
Chet Hanulak – Military Service
Billy Reynolds – Military Service

Use Name	Pos.	Hgt	Wgt	Age	Int	Pts
Tom O'Connell	QB	5'11"	190	24		12
Babe Parilli	QB	6'1"	190	26		
George Ratterman	QB	6'1"	185	29		6
Preston Carpenter	HB	6'2"	190	22		
Curley Morrison	HB	6'2"	215	30		12
Skeets Quinlan (from LA)	HB	5'11"	170	28		
Mo Bassett	FB	6'1"	230	26		12
Ed Modzelewski	FB	6'	215	27		12
Darrell Brewster	OE	6'3"	210	26		6
Dante Lavelli	OE	6'	192	33		6
Ray Renfro	HB-FL	6'1"	192	25		24

PITTSBURGH STEELERS 5-7-0 Walt Kiesling

Scores of Each Game			Use Name	Pos.	Hgt	Wgt	Age	Int	Pts
30	WASHINGTON	13	Bob Gaona	OT	6'3"	245	26		
10	CLEVELAND	14	Frank Varrichione	OT	6'1"	240	24		
21	PHILADELPHIA	35	Ralph Jecha	OG	6'2"	235	25		
10	New York	38	Marv McFadden	OG	6'	230	26		
24	Cleveland	16	Bob O'Neil	DE-OG	6'1"	220	23		
14	NEW YORK	17	John Cenci	C	6'	215	22		
7	Philadelphia	14	Jim Taylor	C	6'2"	230	22		
14	CHIC. CARDS	7	Bill McPeak	DE	6'1"	220	31		2
27	Chic. Cards	38	Joe O'Malley	DE	6'2"	215	23		
30	LOS ANGELES	13	George Tarasovic	C-LB-DE	6'4"	245	27	3	
7	Detroit	45	Joe Krupa	DT	6'2"	240	23		
23	Washington	0	Ernie Stautner	DT	6'1"	230	31		
			Willie McClung	OT-DT	6'2"	245	27		

Use Name	Pos.	Hgt	Wgt	Age	Int	Pts
Dale Dodrill	LB	6'1"	210	31	1	
Marv Matuszak	LB	6'3"	230	25	2	
Art Michalik	LB	6'2"	230	26		
John Reger	LB	6'	220	25	2	
Dick Alban	DB	6'	195	27	2	
Fred Bruney (from SF)	DB	5'10"	180	25	1	
Gary Glick	DB	6'2"	195	25		28
Art Davis	HB-DB	6'1"	195	22		
Jack Butler	OE-DB	6'	195	28	6	12

Paul Cameron – Military Service
Johnny Lattner – Military Service
Richie McCabe – Military Service

Use Name	Pos.	Hgt	Wgt	Age	Int	Pts
Ted Marchibroda	QB	5'10"	180	25		12
Jack Scarbath	QB	6'2"	205	26		
Lou Baldacci	HB	6'2"	200	22		
Lynn Chandnois	HB	6'2"	205	32		30
Sid Watson	HB	5'11"	185	23		37
Henry Ford	DB-HB	6'	184	25	1	12
Fran Rogel	FB	5'11"	205	29		12
Charlie Shepard	HB-FB	6'2"	215	23		
Fred Glatz	OE	6'1"	200	22		
Ray Mathews	OE	6'	190	27		30
Jack McClairen	OE	6'4"	210	25		
Elbie Nickel	OE	6'1"	210	33		30
Jack O'Brien	OE	6'2"	210	25		
John Stock	OE	6'2"	210	22		
Lowell Perry	HB-OE	6'	195	24		12

PHILADELPHIA EAGLES 3-8-1 Hugh Devore

Scores of Each Game			Use Name	Pos.	Hgt	Wgt	Age	Int	Pts
7	Los Angeles	27	Dick Murley (from PIT)	OT	6'	247	22		
13	WASHINGTON	9	Frank Wydo	OT	6'4"	228	32		
35	Pittsburgh	21	Tom Dimmick	C-LB-OT	6'6"	250	25		
6	CHIC. CARDS	20	Ken Huxhold	OG	6'1"	230	27		
3	New York	20	Maury Nipp	OG	6'	220	26		
17	Chic. Cards	28	Frank D'Agostino	OT-OG	6'1"	244	22		
14	PITTSBURGH	7	Buck Lansford	OT-OG	6'2"	235	23		
0	CLEVELAND	16	Bob Kelley	C	6'2"	238	27		
10	SAN FRANCISCO	10	Tom Scott	DE	6'2"	225	26	1	
14	Cleveland	17	Norm Willey	DE	6'2"	230	29		
17	Washington	19	Marion Campbell	DT	6'3"	250	27	1	
7	NEW YORK	21	Jess Richardson	DT	6'2"	275	26		
			Jim Weatherall	DT	6'4"	245	26		
			Sid Youngelman	DT	6'3"	255	24		

Use Name	Pos.	Hgt	Wgt	Age	Int	Pts
Chuck Bednarik	LB	6'3"	235	31	2	
Wayne Robinson	LB	6'2"	236	26		
Bob Pellegrini	OG-LB	6'2"	237	21		
Jim Ricca	OT-DT-LB	6'4"	270	29		
Bibbles Bawel	DB	6'1"	185	26	1	
Eddie Bell	DB	6'1"	212	25	4	6
Tom Brookshier	DB	6'	195	24	1	
Jerry Norton	DB	5'11"	200	26	2	
Lee Riley	DB	6'1"	200	24	3	
Rocky Ryan	HB-DB	6'1"	202	24	1	

Bob Hudson – Voluntarily Retired
Menil Mavraides – Military Service
Lum Snyder – Military Service
Neil Worden – Military Service

Use Name	Pos.	Hgt	Wgt	Age	Int	Pts
Adrian Burk	QB	6'2"	194	28		
Bobby Thomason	QB	6'1"	190	27		12
Will Berzinski	HB	6'2"	195	22		
Skippy Giancanelli	HB	5'10"	180	27		6
Ken Keller	HB	5'11"	185	22		24
Bob Smith (from CLE)	HB	5'10"	195	24		
Ted Wegert	HB	5'11"	210	24		6
Jim Parmer	FB-HB	6'	195	29		
Dick Bielski	FB	6'1"	225	24		6
Don Schaefer	FB	6'	210	22		12
John Bredice	OE	6'1"	213	22		6
Hank Burnine (from NY)	OE	6'2"	185	24		12
Pete Retzlaff	OE	6'1"	208	26		
Bill Stribling	OE	6'1"	205	29		
Bobby Walston	OE	6'	190	27		53

NEW YORK GIANTS

RUSHING

Last Name	No.	Yds	Avg	TD
Gifford	159	819	5.2	5
Webster	178	694	3.9	7
Triplett	125	515	4.1	5
Filipski	13	85	6.5	1
Conerly	11	11	1.0	0
Chandler	1	7	7.0	0
Rote	3	5	1.7	0
Patton	2	–1	–0.5	0
Moore	2	–2	–1.0	0
Heinrich	5	–4	–0.8	0

RECEIVING

Last Name	No.	Yds	Avg	TD
Gifford	51	603	12	4
Rote	28	405	14	4
Webster	21	197	9	3
MacAfee	14	184	13	4
Schnelker	9	122	14	1
Triplett	6	48	8	1
Filipski	3	37	12	0
Chandler	1	5	5	0

PUNT RETURNS

Last Name	No.	Yds	Avg	TD
Tunnell	22	120	5	0
Filipski	1	25	25	0
Patton	12	17	1	0

KICKOFF RETURNS

Last Name	No.	Yds	Avg	TD
Filipski	19	390	21	0
Patton	13	283	22	0
Hughes	1	27	27	0
Triplett	1	2	2	0

PASSING – PUNTING – KICKING

PASSING	Att	Comp	%	Yds	Yd/Att	TD	Int–%	RK
Conerly	174	90	52	1143	6.6	10	7– 4	3
Heinrich	88	37	42	369	4.2	5	5– 6	
Clatterbuck	7	4	57	54	7.7	0	1– 14	
Gifford	5	2	40	35	7.0	2	1– 20	
Rote	1	0	0	0	0.0	0	0– 0	

PUNTING	No	Avg
Chandler	59	41.9
Conerly	1	33.0

KICKING	XP	Att	%	FG	Att	%
Agajanian	23	23	100	5	13	38
Gifford	8	9	89	1	2	50
Chandler	3	3	100	0	0	0

CHICAGO CARDINALS

RUSHING

Last Name	No.	Yds	Avg	TD
Matson	192	924	4.8	5
Olszewski	157	598	3.8	2
Childress	43	203	4.7	0
McHan	58	161	2.8	5
Mann	45	116	2.6	0
Root	17	45	2.6	2
Bernardi	14	4	0.3	0
Burl	1	2	2.0	0

RECEIVING

Last Name	No.	Yds	Avg	TD
Stonesifer	22	320	15	2
Olszewski	17	182	11	0
Matson	15	199	13	2
Nagler	14	268	19	4
Mann	13	170	13	1
Boydston	6	116	19	2
Childress	6	82	14	1
Bernardi	4	56	14	0
Burl	2	24	12	1
Lane	1	75	75	0

PUNT RETURNS

Last Name	No.	Yds	Avg	TD
Bernardi	18	217	12	1
Matson	5	39	8	0
Lewis	5	22	4	0
Crow	1	21	21	0
Sanford	1	6	6	0
Lane	2	0	0	0

KICKOFF RETURNS

Last Name	No.	Yds	Avg	TD
Matson	13	362	28	1
Mann	7	131	19	0
Bernardi	4	101	25	0
Burl	3	59	20	0
Olszewski	3	25	8	0
Lewis	1	22	22	0
Weber	2	3	2	0
Childress	1	0	0	0

PASSING – PUNTING – KICKING

PASSING	Att	Comp	%	Yds	Yd/Att	TD	Int–%	RK
McHan	152	72	47	1159	7.6	10	8– 5	6
Root	57	28	49	333	5.8	3	5– 9	
Matson	3	0	0	0	0.0	0	0– 0	
Mann	2	0	0	0	0.0	0	1– 50	

PUNTING	No	Avg
Mann	36	37.4
Roach	11	40.8
McHan	8	35.6

KICKING	XP	Att	%	FG	Att	%
Summerall	30	30	100	10	22	46

WASHINGTON REDSKINS

RUSHING

Last Name	No.	Yds	Avg	TD
Elter	145	544	3.8	2
Runnels	96	334	3.5	0
James	58	280	4.8	1
Wells	69	185	2.7	1
Atkeson	63	163	2.6	1
Baker	25	117	4.7	0
Dorow	30	105	3.5	0
LeBaron	11	6	0.5	0
Planutis	2	6	3.0	0
Scudero	2	3	1.5	0

RECEIVING

Last Name	No.	Yds	Avg	TD
Carson	39	504	13	3
Meilinger	24	395	16	5
Elter	11	99	9	0
James	7	127	18	2
Wells	6	86	14	0
Runnels	6	56	9	1
Atkeson	6	28	5	0
Baker	4	35	9	0
Planutis	1	5	5	0

PUNT RETURNS

Last Name	No.	Yds	Avg	TD
Runnels	8	91	11	0
James	6	84	14	0
Scudero	10	50	5	0
Wells	2	36	18	0
Atkeson	1	12	12	0
Baker	1	0	0	0
Lowe	1	0	0	0

KICKOFF RETURNS

Last Name	No.	Yds	Avg	TD
Runnels	17	375	22	0
James	9	181	20	0
Scudero	9	157	17	0
Elter	4	87	22	0
Atkeson	1	25	25	0
Sardisco	1	15	15	0
Kimmel	1	12	12	0
Wells	1	12	12	0
Thomas	1	0	0	0

PASSING – PUNTING – KICKING

PASSING	Att	Comp	%	Yds	Yd/Att	TD	Int–%	RK
Dorow	112	55	49	730	6.5	8	8– 7	11
LeBaron	98	47	48	554	5.7	3	10– 10	
Runnels	3	1	33	34	11.3	0	0– 0	
Wyant	2	1	50	17	8.5	0	0– 0	

PUNTING	No	Avg
Baker	59	42.5
LeBaron	4	40.3

KICKING	XP	Att	%	FG	Att	%
Baker	16	19	84	17	25	68

CLEVELAND BROWNS

RUSHING

Last Name	No.	Yds	Avg	TD
Carpenter	188	756	4.0	0
Modzelewski	107	431	4.0	2
Morrison	83	340	4.1	1
Bassett	41	129	3.1	1
Parilli	18	65	3.6	0
O'Connell	24	40	1.7	2
Kinard	1	27	27.0	1
Quinlan	12	25	2.1	0
Renfro	4	24	6.0	0
Ratterman	10	19	1.9	1

RECEIVING

Last Name	No.	Yds	Avg	TD
Brewster	28	417	15	1
Lavelli	20	344	17	1
Renfro	17	325	19	4
Carpenter	16	124	8	0
Modzelewski	10	27	3	0
Quinlan	7	87	12	0
Morrison	6	29	5	1
Bassett	4	29	7	1

PUNT RETURNS

Last Name	No.	Yds	Avg	TD
Konz	13	187	14	1
Paul	17	103	6	0
Quinlan	14	50	4	0
Carpenter	1	18	18	0

KICKOFF RETURNS

Last Name	No.	Yds	Avg	TD
Carpenter	15	381	25	0
Quinlan	12	256	21	0
Kinard	7	196	28	0
Morrison	1	17	17	0

PASSING – PUNTING – KICKING

PASSING	Att	Comp	%	Yds	Yd/Att	TD	Int–%	RK
O'Connell	96	42	44	551	5.7	4	8– 8	
Ratterman	57	39	68	398	7.0	1	3– 5	
Parilli	49	24	49	409	8.4	3	7– 14	

PUNTING	No	Avg
Morrison	38	41.1
Gillom	12	44.7

KICKING	XP	Att	%	FG	Att	%
Groza	18	18	100	11	20	55

PITTSBURGH STEELERS

RUSHING

Last Name	No.	Yds	Avg	TD
Rogel	131	476	3.6	2
Watson	112	298	2.7	4
Marchibroda	39	152	3.9	2
Baldacci	31	140	4.5	0
Chandnois	44	118	2.7	4
Shepard	30	91	3.0	0
Perry	2	37	18.5	0
Ford	12	26	2.2	2
Scarbath	4	19	4.8	0
Davis	5	6	1.2	0
Varrichione	0	–2	–	0
Mathews	3	–11	–3.7	0

RECEIVING

Last Name	No.	Yds	Avg	TD
Mathews	31	540	17	5
Nickel	27	376	14	5
Rogel	23	88	4	0
Perry	14	334	24	2
Watson	12	138	12	0
Chandnois	7	71	10	1
O'Brien	6	71	12	0
Baldacci	5	62	12	0
McClairen	5	56	11	0
Ford	3	7	2	0
Shepard	1	31	31	0
Butler	1	10	10	1
Davis	1	9	9	0

PUNT RETURNS

Last Name	No.	Yds	Avg	TD
Ford	25	145	6	0
Perry	11	127	12	0
Bruney	5	20	4	0
Davis	3	5	2	0
Watson	1	2	2	0

KICKOFF RETURNS

Last Name	No.	Yds	Avg	TD
Chandnois	8	291	36	0
Bruney	9	235	26	0
Perry	9	219	24	0
Ford	6	135	23	0
Watson	4	110	28	0
Mathews	1	26	26	0
Reger	1	13	13	0
Varrichione	1	8	8	0
Matuszak	1	5	5	0

PASSING – PUNTING – KICKING

PASSING	Att	Comp	%	Yds	Yd/Att	TD	Int–%	RK
Marchibroda	275	124	45	1585	5.8	12	19– 7	10
Scarbath	41	12	29	208	5.1	2	5– 12	
Baldacci	1	0	0	0	0.0	0	0– 0	
Chandnois	1	0	0	0	0.0	0	0– 0	

PUNTING	No	Avg
Baldacci	26	38.8
Shepard	26	36.6
Glatz	25	39.4

KICKING	XP	Att	%	FG	Att	%
Glick	16	17	94	4	7	57
Watson	10	12	83	1	1	100
Michalik	0	0	0	0	1	0

PHILADELPHIA EAGLES

RUSHING

Last Name	No.	Yds	Avg	TD
Keller	112	433	3.9	4
Schaefer	102	320	3.1	2
Bielski	52	162	3.1	1
Giancanelli	42	148	3.5	1
Wegert	47	127	2.7	1
Berzinski	15	72	4.8	0
Burk	17	61	3.6	0
Thomason	21	48	2.3	2
Smith	11	18	1.6	0
Parmer	1	–2	–2.0	0

RECEIVING

Last Name	No.	Yds	Avg	TD
Waltson	39	590	15	3
Schaefer	13	117	9	0
Retzlaff	12	159	13	0
Burnine	10	208	21	2
Bredice	10	146	15	1
Giancanelli	10	104	10	0
Bielski	8	63	8	0
Keller	7	36	5	0
Wegert	6	46	8	0
Berzinski	3	35	12	0
Stribling	2	11	6	0
Ryan	1	31	31	0
Riley	1	10	10	0

PUNT RETURNS

Last Name	No.	Yds	Avg	TD
Keller	15	146	10	0
Riley	17	73	4	0
Giancanelli	4	22	6	0

KICKOFF RETURNS

Last Name	No.	Yds	Avg	TD
Riley	15	381	25	0
Keller	15	353	24	0
Giancanelli	8	187	23	0
Pellegrini	2	47	24	0
Willey	2	32	16	0
Norton	1	31	31	0
Bawel	1	25	25	0
Bednarik	1	17	17	0
Smith	1	14	14	0

PASSING – PUNTING – KICKING

PASSING	Att	Comp	%	Yds	Yd/Att	TD	Int–%	RK
Thomason	164	82	50	1119	6.8	4	21– 12	12
Burk	82	39	48	426	5.2	1	6– 7	
Schaefer	3	1	33	11	3.7	1	0– 0	

PUNTING	No	Avg
Burk	68	41.8

KICKING	XP	Att	%	FG	Att	%
Walston	17	18	94	6	13	46
Bielski	0	0	0	0	1	0

CHICAGO BEARS 9-2-1 Paddy Driscoll

Scores of Each Game		
21	Baltimore	28
37	Green Bay	21
31	SAN FRANCISCO	7
58	BALTIMORE	27
38	San Francisco	21
35	Los Angeles	24
38	GREEN BAY	14
30	LOS ANGELES	21
17	New York	17
10	Detroit	42
10	CHIC. CARDS	3
38	DETROIT	21

Use Name	Pos.	Hgt	Wgt	Age	Int	Pts
Kline Gilbert	OT	6'2"	235	25		
John Mellekas	OT	6'3"	255	23		
Bill Wightkin	OT	6'3"	235	29		
Herman Clark	OG	6'3"	255	25		
Stan Jones	OG	6'1"	255	25		
Tom Roggeman	OG	6'	235	25		
Dick Klawitter	C	6'7"	270	26		
Larry Strickland	C	6'4"	245	25		
Doug Atkins	DE	6'8"	255	26		
John Helwig	DE	6'2"	208	28		
Jack Hoffman	DE	6'5"	235	27		
Ed Meadows	DE	6'2"	220	24		
Bill Bishop	DT	6'4"	250	25		
Fred Williams	DT	6'4"	245	26	1	
M. L. Brackett	DE-LB-DT	6'5"	248	23	1	
Joe Fortunato	LB	6'	225	26	2	6
Bill George	LB	6'2"	240	25	2	
Wayne Hansen	LB	6'2"	230	28	1	
Ken Gorgal (to GB)	DB	6'2"	200	27	2	
McNeil Moore	DB	6'	185	23	3	
Ray Gene Smith	DB	5'10"	185	26	4	
Stan Wallace	DB	6'3"	207	24	1	
J. C. Caroline	HB-DB	6'1"	190	23	6	24
George Blanda	QB	6'1"	207	28		81
Ed Brown	QB	6'2"	205	27		12
Jim Haluska	QB	6'	190	23		
Don Bingham	HB	6'	185	26		6
Harland Carl	HB	6'	195	25		6
Perry Jeter	HB	5'7"	178	22		18
Bobby Watkins	HB	5'10"	195	24		18
John Hoffman	FB-HB	6'2"	215	30		12
Rick Casares	FB	6'2"	225	25		84
Jim Dooley	OE	6'4"	198	26		
Harlon Hill	OE	6'3"	198	24		66
Bill McColl	OE	6'4"	230	26		24
Gene Schroeder	OE	6'3"	195	27		6

Zeke Bratkowski — Military Service
Ron Drzewiecki — Military Service
Charlie Sumner — Military Service

DETROIT LIONS 9-3-0 Buddy Parker

Scores of Each Game		
20	Green Bay	16
31	Baltimore	14
24	LOS ANGELES	21
20	SAN FRANCISCO	17
16	Los Angeles	7
17	San Francisco	13
17	Washington	18
27	BALTIMORE	3
20	GREEN BAY	24
42	CHIC. BEARS	10
45	PITTSBURGH	7
21	Chic. Bears	38

Use Name	Pos.	Hgt	Wgt	Age	Int	Pts
Lou Creekmur	OT	6'4"	250	29		
Ollie Spencer	OT	6'2"	245	25		
Jim Salsbury	OG-OT	6'1"	235	24		
Stan Campbell	OG	6'	225	26		
Harley Sewell	OG	6'1"	235	25		
Charlie Ane	C	6'2"	260	25		
Bob Lusk	C	6'1"	222	23		
Gene Cronin	OG-DE	6'2"	230	23		
Gil Mains	DT-DE	6'2"	235	26		
Ray Krouse	DT	6'3"	265	29		
Darris McCord	DT	6'4"	240	23		
Bob Miller	DT	6'3"	245	26		
Jerry Perry	DT	6'4"	235	25		
Sonny Gandee	LB	6'1"	220	27		
Jim Martin	LB	6'2"	225	32		15
Joe Schmidt	LB	6'1"	220	24	1	
Bob Long	DE-LB	6'3"	230	22	2	
Jack Christiansen	DB	6'1"	195	27	8	6
Jim David	DB	5'11"	175	29	7	
Carl Karilivacz	DB	6'	185	25	1	
Yale Lary	DB	6'	185	25	8	6
Bill Stits	HB-DB	6'	200	25	1	
Harry Gilmer	QB	6'	180	30		
Bobby Layne	QB	6'1"	200	29		99
Jerry Reichow	OE-QB	6'2"	210	21		6
Hopalong Cassady	HB	5'10"	178	22		
Gene Gedman	HB	5'11"	195	24		48
Don McIlhenny	HB	6'	195	21		30
Jug Girard	OE-HB	5'11"	175	29		
Bill Bowman	FB	6'2"	215	25		12
Leon Hart	FB	6'5"	248	27		36
Tom Tracy	FB	5'9"	200	24		
Dorne Dibble	OE	6'2"	195	27		12
Jim Doran	OE	6'2"	200	28		
Dave Middleton	OE	6'1"	195	23		30

Lew Carpenter — Military Service

SAN FRANCISCO FORTY NINERS 5-6-1 Frankie Albert

Scores of Each Game		
21	NEW YORK	38
33	LOS ANGELES	30
7	Chic. Bears	31
17	Detroit	20
21	CHIC. BEARS	38
13	DETROIT	17
6	Los Angeles	30
17	Green Bay	16
10	Philadelphia	10
20	Baltimore	17
38	GREEN BAY	20
30	BALTIMORE	17

Use Name	Pos.	Hgt	Wgt	Age	Int	Pts
Bob Cross	OT	6'4"	250	25		
Bob St. Clair	OT	6'9"	265	25		
John Gonzaga	DE-OT	6'3"	240	23		
Ted Connolly	OG	6'3"	240	24		
Lou Palatella	OG	6'2"	230	23		
Ed Beatty	C	6'3"	230	24		
Bill Johnson	C	6'3"	240	30		
Bruce Bosley	DE	6'2"	240	22		
Ed Henke	DE	6'3"	227	28		
Charley Powell	DE	6'2"	220	24		
Charlie Smith	DE	6'2"	205	23	1	
Bill Herchman	DT	6'2"	240	23		
Leo Nomellini	DT	6'3"	255	31		
Bob Toneff	OG-DG-DT	6'3"	263	26		
Matt Hazeltine	LB	6'1"	205	23	1	
Leo Rucka	LB	6'3"	212	24		
Stan Sheriff	LB	6'1"	218	25		
Ed Sharkey	OG-LB	6'3"	235	30	1	
George Morris	C-LB	6'2"	220	25		
Paul Carr	DB-LB	6'	205	24	2	
Rex Berry	DB	5'11"	185	30	3	
Bob Holladay (from LA)	DB	5'11"	175	23	1	
George Maderos	DB	6'1"	187	23	2	
Ernie Smith	DB	6'3"	190	23		
J. D. Smith (from Chi B)	DB	6'1"	200	23		
Earl Morrall	QB	6'1"	190	22		
Y. A. Tittle	QB	6'	190	29		24
Joe Arenas	HB	5'11"	180	30		18
Tom McCormick	HB	5'11"	180	26		
Hugh McElhenny	HB	6'1"	198	27		48
Dick Moegle	HB-DB	6'	185	22	6	6
John Henry Johnson	FB-HB	6'2"	205	26		12
Paul Goad	FB	6'	195	21		
Joe Perry	FB	6'	210	29		18
Clyde Conner	OE	6'2"	195	23		6
Floyd Sagely	OE	6'1"	195	24		
Gordie Soltau	OE	6'2"	195	31		71
Billy Wilson	OE	6'3"	190	29		30
Bill Jessup	FL-OE	6'1"	195	27		

BALTIMORE COLTS 5-7-0 Weeb Ewbank

Scores of Each Game		
28	CHIC. BEARS	21
14	DETROIT	31
33	Green Bay	38
27	Chic. Bears	58
28	GREEN BAY	21
21	Cleveland	7
3	Detroit	27
56	LOS ANGELES	21
17	SAN FRANCISCO	20
7	Los Angeles	31
17	San Francisco	30
19	WASHINGTON	17

Use Name	Pos.	Hgt	Wgt	Age	Int	Pts
Dick Chorovich	OT	6'4"	260	23		
Tom Feamster	DE-OT	6'7"	260	25		24
Ken Jackson	OG-OT	6'2"	235	27		
Alex Sandusky	OG	6'1"	230	24		
Art Spinney	OG	6'	230	29		
George Preas	OT-LB-OG	6'2"	230	24		
Buzz Nutter	C	6'4"	225	25		
George Radosevich	OT-C	6'2"	230	29		
Don Joyce	DE	6'3"	255	26		
Gino Marchetti	DE	6'4"	245	30		
Art Donovan	DT	6'2"	265	31		
Tom Finnin	DT	6'2"	255	28		
Big Daddy Lipscomb	DT	6'6"	282	25		
Jerry Peterson	DT	6'3"	290	22		
Joe Campanella	LB	6'2"	245	25		
Doug Eggers	LB	6'	215	26	1	
Bill Koman	LB	6'2"	220	22		
Jack Patera	LB	6'1"	240	24	2	
Bill Pellington	LB	6'2"	230	27	1	
Jim Harness	DB	5'11"	180	22		
John Hermann (from NY)	DB	6'1"	180	22		
Tommy James	DB	5'10"	185	32		
Don Shula	DB	5'11"	190	26	1	
Jesse Thomas	DB	5'10"	180	27	2	6
Bert Rechichar	HB-DB	6'1"	210	26	4	17
Carl Taseff	HB-DB	5'11"	190	27	2	12
Gary Kerkorian	QB	5'11"	185	27		1
George Shaw	QB	6'1"	180	23		
Johnny Unitas	QB	6'1"	190	23		6
L. G. Dupre	HB	5'11"	190	24		24
Lenny Moore	HB	6'1"	190	23		54
Billy Vessels	HB	6'	190	25		18
Royce Womble	HB	6'	185	24		12
Dick Nyers	DB-HB	5'11"	178	22		
Alan Ameche	FB	6'	217	23		48
Dick Young	FB	5'11"	210	25		
Ray Berry	OE	6'2"	190	23		12
Lloyd Colteryahn	OE	6'2"	220	26		
Bernie Flowers	OE	6'2"	190	26		
Jim Mutscheller	OE	6'1"	210	26		36

Cotton Davidson — Military Service
Dick Szymanski — Military Service

GREEN BAY PACKERS 4-8-0 Lisle Blackbourn

Scores of Each Game		
16	DETROIT	20
21	CHIC. BEARS	37
38	BALTIMORE	33
42	LOS ANGELES	17
21	Baltimore	28
7	CLEVELAND	24
14	Chic. Bears	38
16	SAN FRANCISCO	17
24	Detroit	20
24	Chic. Cards	21
20	San Francisco	38
21	Los Angeles	49

Use Name	Pos.	Hgt	Wgt	Age	Int	Pts
Bob Skoronski	OT	6'3"	250	23		
Don King (from PHI)	DT-OT	6'3"	265	26		
John Sandusky	DT-OT	6'1"	250	30		
Buddy Brown	OG	6'1"	225	29		
Joe Skibinski	OG	5'11"	230	28		
Jerry Smith (from SF)	OG	6'1"	230	26		
Len Szafaryn	OG	6'2"	225	28		
Forrest Gregg	OT-DT-OG	6'4"	240	23		
Larry Lauer	C	6'3"	235	27		
Jim Ringo	C	6'1"	235	25		
Emery Barnes	DE	6'6"	235	27		
Nate Borden	DE	6'	225	24		
Gene Knutson	DE	6'2"	230	24		
John Martinkovic	DE	6'3"	245	29		
Dave Hanner	DT	6'2"	255	27		
Jerry Helluin	DT	6'2"	265	26		
Tom Bettis	LB	6'2"	230	23		
Bill Forester	LB	6'3"	235	25	4	
Deral Teteak	LB	5'10"	210	27	2	
Roger Zatkoff	LB	6'2"	215	25		
Billy Bookout	DB	5'11"	180	24	1	
Jim Capuzzi	DB	6'	190	24	2	
Bobby Dillon	DB	6'1"	180	26	7	6
Hank Gremminger	DB	6'1"	195	23	2	
Val Joe Walker	DB	6'1"	180	25	1	
Glenn Young	DB	6'2"	205	26		
Tobin Rote	QB	6'3"	215	28		66
Bart Starr	QB	6'1"	200	23		
Al Carmichael	HB	6'1"	190	26		12
Joe Johnson	HB	6'	180	26		
Jack Losch	HB	6'1"	205	23		
Breezy Reid	HB	5'10"	190	29		
Bill Roberts	HB	6'	200	27		
Fred Cone	FB	5'11"	200	30		72
Howie Ferguson	FB	6'2"	215	26		
Billy Howton	OE	6'2"	190	26		72
Gary Knafelc	OE	6'4"	215	24		36
Dick Deschaine	K	6'	210	26		

Al Barry — Military Service
Hank Bullough — Military Service
Max McGee — Military Service
Doyle Nix — Military Service

LOS ANGELES RAMS 4-8-0 Sid Gillman

Scores of Each Game		
27	PHILADELPHIA	7
30	San Francisco	33
21	Detroit	24
17	Green Bay	42
7	DETROIT	16
24	CHIC. BEARS	35
30	SAN FRANCISCO	6
21	Chic. Bears	30
21	Baltimore	56
13	Pittsburgh	30
31	BALTIMORE	7
49	GREEN BAY	21

Use Name	Pos.	Hgt	Wgt	Age	Int	Pts
Bob Fry	OT	6'4"	225	25		
Glenn Holtzman	OT	6'3"	250	26		
Charlie Toogood	OT	6'	230	28		
John Hock	OG	6'2"	234	28		
Duane Putnam	OG	6'	230	28		
John Morrow	OG-DE-C	6'3"	237	23		
Dick Daugherty	OG-LB-C	6'1"	223	27		
Paul Miller	DE	6'2"	215	24		
Duane Wardlow	DE	6'4"	215	24		
Sid Fournet	LB-DE	6'	238	23	1	
Art Hauser	DT	6'	230	25		
Bud McFadin	DT	6'3"	250	28		9
Ken Panfil	OT-DT	6'6"	255	25		
Jack Ellena	LB	6'1"	223	24		
Bob Griffin	LB	6'3"	243	27		
Larry Morris	LB	6'2"	212	22		
Hugh Pitts	LB	6'2"	220	22	3	
Les Richter	LB	6'3"	243	25		60
Don Burroughs	DB	6'4"	173	25	2	
Jim Cason	DB	6'	175	29	4	
Jesse Castete (from Chi B)	DB	5'11"	175	21	2	
Will Sherman	DB	6'2"	197	27	4	12
Ray Shiver	DB	6'	190	24	1	
Jesse Whittenton	DB	6'	182	22	3	6
Rudy Bukich	QB	6'1"	190	25		
Norm Van Brocklin	QB	6'1"	200	30		6
Billy Wade	QB	6'2"	190	25		18
Ron Waller	HB	5'11"	190	23		6
Tom Wilson	HB	6'	197	23		6
Joe Marconi	FB	6'2"	220	22		42
Brad Myers	FB	6'1"	196	26		
Tank Younger	FB	6'3"	226	28		18
Bob Boyd	OE	6'3"	203	28		42
Bob Carey	OE	6'5"	220	28		6
Leon Clarke	OE	6'4"	220	23		24
Tom Fears	OE	6'2"	207	32		
Crazy Legs Hirsch	OE	6'2"	190	32		36
Ron Miller	OE	6'4"	200	23		

CHICAGO BEARS

RUSHING

Last Name	No.	Yds	Avg	TD
Casares	234	1126	4.8	12
Jeter	60	316	5.3	2
Watkins	68	276	4.1	2
Jo. Hoffman	56	272	4.9	2
Brown	40	164	4.1	1
Caroline	34	141	4.1	2
Carl	29	66	2.3	1
Blanda	6	47	7.8	0
Bingham	7	36	5.1	0
Hill	2	24	12.0	0

RECEIVING

Last Name	No.	Yds	Avg	TD
Hill	47	1128	24	11
McColl	24	322	13	4
Casares	23	203	9	2
Schroeder	20	315	16	1
Jo. Hoffman	7	85	12	0
Jeter	5	52	10	0
Dooley	4	47	12	0
Carl	2	31	16	0
Watkins	2	3	2	1
Bingham	1	7	7	0

PUNT RETURNS

Last Name	No.	Yds	Avg	TD
Jeter	6	66	11	1
Smith	6	65	11	0
Moore	3	28	9	0
Caroline	2	29	15	0
Bingham	13	7	1	0

KICKOFF RETURNS

Last Name	No.	Yds	Avg	TD
Bingham	17	444	26	1
Jeter	5	105	21	0
Carl	4	102	26	0
Casares	3	95	32	0
Caroline	2	32	16	0
Moore	1	19	19	0
Smith	1	16	16	0
Wallace	1	13	13	0
McColl	2	4	2	0
Atkins	1	0	0	0

PASSING – PUNTING – KICKING

PASSING	Att	Comp	%	Yds	Yd/Att	TD	Int–%	RK
Brown	168	96	57	1667	9.9	11	12– 7	1
Blanda	69	37	54	439	6.4	7	4– 6	
Haluska	4	1	25	8	2.0	0	0– 0	
McColl	4	1	25	79	19.8	1	2– 50	
Casares	3	0	0	0	0.0	0	1– 33	
Hill	1	0	0	0	0.0	0	0– 0	
Jeter	1	0	0	0	0.0	0	0– 0	

PUNTING	No	Avg
Brown	42	39.1
Blanda	1	33.0
Casares	1	51.0

KICKING	XP	Att	%	FG	Att	%
Blanda	45	47	96	12	28	43

DETROIT LIONS

RUSHING

Last Name	No.	Yds	Avg	TD
Gedman	135	479	3.5	7
Cassady	97	413	4.3	0
McIlhenny	87	372	4.3	3
Hart	76	348	4.6	5
Layne	46	169	3.7	5
Bowman	20	84	4.2	1
Girard	17	67	3.9	0
Tracy	12	32	2.7	0
Gilmer	8	19	2.4	0
Lary	1	10	10.0	0
Middleton	3	9	3.0	0
Dibble	1	8	8.0	0
Reichow	1	1	1.0	0
Stits	3	0	0.0	0

RECEIVING

Last Name	No.	Yds	Avg	TD
Middleton	39	606	16	5
Dibble	32	597	19	2
Doran	25	448	18	0
Gedman	15	142	9	1
Hart	14	116	8	1
Cassady	9	83	9	0
McIlhenny	8	70	9	2
Bowman	5	34	7	1
Reichow	4	63	16	1
Stits	3	52	17	0
Girard	3	33	11	0
Tracy	3	6	2	0

PUNT RETURNS

Last Name	No.	Yds	Avg	TD
Cassady	13	83	6	0
Christiansen	6	73	12	1
Lary	22	70	3	0
Girard	2	7	4	0

KICKOFF RETURNS

Last Name	No.	Yds	Avg	TD
Cassady	16	382	24	0
Christiansen	6	116	19	0
Lary	4	76	19	0
Stits	3	48	16	0
Bowman	1	24	24	0
Ane	1	19	19	0
Salsbury	1	13	13	0
Reichow	1	9	9	0

PASSING – PUNTING – KICKING

PASSING	Att	Comp	%	Yds	Yd/Att	TD	Int–%	RK
Layne	244	129	53	1909	7.8	9	17– 7	5
Gilmer	46	27	59	303	6.6	4	3– 7	
Reichow	6	3	50	19	3.2	0	1– 17	
Cassady	2	0	0	0	0.0	0	1– 50	
Girard	1	1	100	19	19.0	0	0– 0	
McIlhenny	1	0	0	0	0.0	0	0– 0	
Stits	1	0	0	0	0.0	0	1–100	

PUNTING	No	Avg
Lary	42	40.4
Girard	10	44.8

KICKING	XP	Att	%	FG	Att	%
Layne	33	33	100	12	15	80
Martin	3	3	100	4	10	40

SAN FRANCISCO FORTY NINERS

RUSHING

Last Name	No.	Yds	Avg	TD
McElhenny	185	916	5.0	8
Perry	115	520	4.5	3
J.H. Johnson	80	301	3.8	2
Tittle	24	67	2.8	4
Moegle	7	18	2.6	0
Morrall	6	10	1.7	0
McCormick	2	4	2.0	0

RECEIVING

Last Name	No.	Yds	Avg	TD
Wilson	60	889	15	5
Conner	22	362	16	1
Soltau	18	299	17	1
Perry	18	104	6	0
McElhenny	16	193	12	0
Arenas	14	226	16	1
J.H. Johnson	8	90	11	0
Moegle	3	79	26	0
Jessup	2	7	4	0

PUNT RETURNS

Last Name	No.	Yds	Avg	TD
Arenas	19	117	6	1
McElhenny	15	38	3	0
Moegle	1	5	5	0

KICKOFF RETURNS

Last Name	No.	Yds	Avg	TD
Arenas	27	801	30	1
McElhenny	13	300	23	0
Moegle	2	39	20	0
J.H. Johnson	1	23	23	0
Maderos	2	21	11	0
Goad	1	18	18	0
McCormick	1	18	18	0
Carr	1	11	11	0
Gonzaga	1	6	6	0
Herschman	1	6	6	0

PASSING – PUNTING – KICKING

PASSING	Att	Comp	%	Yds	Yd/Att	TD	Int–%	RK
Tittle	218	124	57	1641	7.5	7	12– 6	8
Morrall	78	38	49	621	8.0	1	6– 8	
McElhenny	1	0	0	0	0.0	0	1–100	

PUNTING	No	Avg
Morrall	45	37.9
Jessup	14	40.2

KICKING	XP	Att	%	FG	Att	%
Soltau	26	28	93	13	20	65

BALTIMORE COLTS

RUSHING

Last Name	No.	Yds	Avg	TD
Ameche	178	858	4.8	8
Moore	86	649	7.5	8
Vessels	44	215	4.9	2
Dupre	49	182	3.7	2
Unitas	28	155	5.5	1
Womble	20	72	3.6	0
Shaw	20	63	3.2	0
Young	5	7	1.4	0
Taseff	1	2	2.0	0
Rechichar	1	0	0.0	0

RECEIVING

Last Name	No.	Yds	Avg	TD
Mutscheller	44	715	16	6
Berry	37	601	16	2
Ameche	26	189	7	0
Dupre	16	216	14	2
Vessels	11	177	16	1
Moore	11	102	9	1
Womble	9	180	20	2
Colteryahn	3	29	10	0
Unitas	1	1	1	0

PUNT RETURNS

Last Name	No.	Yds	Avg	TD
Taseff	27	233	9	1
Moore	8	38	5	0
Nyers	2	16	8	0
Rechichar	5	10	2	0
Hermann	1	0	0	0

KICKOFF RETURNS

Last Name	No.	Yds	Avg	TD
Vessels	16	379	24	0
Taseff	9	206	23	0
Dupre	7	148	21	0
Moore	10	129	13	0
Nyers	3	69	23	0
Young	3	40	13	0
Ameche	2	38	19	0
Sandusky	1	24	24	0
Hermann	1	17	17	0
Spinney	1	10	10	0
Pellington	1	0	0	0
Shula	1	0	0	0

PASSING – PUNTING – KICKING

PASSING	Att	Comp	%	Yds	Yd/Att	TD	Int–%	RK
Unitas	198	110	56	1498	7.6	9	10– 5	2
Shaw	75	45	60	645	8.6	3	7– 9	
Moore	4	1	25	8	2.0	1	1– 25	
Kerkorian	2	2	100	59	29.5	1	0– 0	

PUNTING	No	Avg
Rechichar	33	38.7
Dupre	25	38.1

KICKING	XP	Att	%	FG	Att	%
Feamster	24	26	92	0	3	0
Rechichar	8	10	80	3	13	23
Kerkorian	1	2	50	0	0	0

GREEN BAY PACKERS

RUSHING

Last Name	No.	Yds	Avg	TD
Rote	84	398	4.7	11
Ferguson	99	367	3.7	0
Cone	49	211	4.3	2
Carmichael	32	199	6.2	0
Johnson	35	129	3.7	0
Losch	19	43	2.3	0
Reid	14	39	2.8	0
Starr	5	35	7.0	0

RECEIVING

Last Name	No.	Yds	Avg	TD
Howton	55	1188	22	12
Knafelc	30	418	14	6
Johnson	28	258	9	0
Ferguson	22	214	10	0
Carmichael	13	180	14	1
Cone	12	218	18	2
Losch	7	85	12	0
Reid	3	16	5	0
Roberts	1	14	14	0
Smith	1	13	13	0

PUNT RETURNS

Last Name	No.	Yds	Avg	TD
Carmichael	21	165	8	0
Losch	8	74	9	0
Reid	1	0	0	0

KICKOFF RETURNS

Last Name	No.	Yds	Avg	TD
Carmichael	33	927	28	1
Losch	15	390	26	0
Ferguson	5	83	17	0
Forester	4	36	9	0
Smith	1	14	14	0
Gremminger	1	6	6	0
Borden	1	0	0	0

PASSING – PUNTING – KICKING

PASSING	Att	Comp	%	Yds	Yd/Att	TD	Int–%	RK
Rote	308	146	47	2203	7.1	18	15– 5	3
Starr	44	24	55	325	7.4	2	3– 7	
Losch	1	1	100	63	63.0	1	0– 0	

PUNTING	No	Avg
Deschaine	62	42.7

KICKING	XP	Att	%	FG	Att	%
Cone	33	35	94	5	8	63

LOS ANGELES RAMS

RUSHING

Last Name	No.	Yds	Avg	TD
Waller	83	543	6.5	1
Younger	114	518	4.5	3
Wilson	64	470	7.3	0
Marconi	75	298	4.0	7
Wade	26	93	3.6	3
Myers	6	33	5.5	0
Bukich	1	8	8.0	0
Van Brocklin	4	1	0.3	1
Boyd	1	–7	–7.0	0

RECEIVING

Last Name	No.	Yds	Avg	TD
Clarke	36	650	18	4
Hirsch	35	603	17	6
Boyd	30	586	20	7
Younger	18	268	15	0
Marconi	12	70	6	0
R. Miller	11	129	12	0
Waller	9	76	8	0
Wilson	6	86	14	0
Carey	5	60	12	1
Fears	5	49	10	0

PUNT RETURNS

Last Name	No.	Yds	Avg	TD
Sherman	12	100	8	1
Waller	14	65	5	0
Myers	1	26	26	0
Whittenton	10	21	2	0
Wilson	2	0	0	0

KICKOFF RETURNS

Last Name	No.	Yds	Avg	TD
Wilson	15	477	32	1
Waller	11	276	25	0
Whittenton	4	85	21	0
Boyd	4	62	16	0
Myers	3	57	19	0
Toogood	1	13	13	0
Richter	1	4	4	0
Panfil	1	0	0	0
Putnam	1	0	0	0

PASSING – PUNTING – KICKING

PASSING	Att	Comp	%	Yds	Yd/Att	TD	Int–%	RK
Wade	178	91	51	1461	8.2	10	13– 7	6
Van Brocklin	124	68	55	966	7.8	7	12– 10	9
Bukich	23	10	43	130	5.7	1	3– 13	
Waller	3	1	33	44	14.7	0	0– 0	
Wilson	1	0	0	0	0.0	0	0– 0	

PUNTING	No	Avg
Van Brocklin	48	43.1

KICKING	XP	Att	%	FG	Att	%
Richter	36	38	95	8	15	53
McFadin	0	0	0	1	4	25

1957 No Ticket, No Television

When the NFL championship game at Detroit was sold out weeks in advance, Commissioner Bert Bell resisted popular pressure for him to relax the home-game blackout rule and allow local television coverage in the Motor City. "It's not honest," he said, "to sell tickets to thousands of people on the basis of no television and then, afterward, when all the tickets are gone to give the game away on television." The game stayed blacked out in Detroit, and Lion fans in the city had to follow the game on radio.

But regardless of the merits of this one case, attendance figures backed up the blackout rule. Attendance had been growing each year, but with CBS broadcasts of road games whetting the fans' interest in their home team, total league attendance bounced a robust 11 percent up to 2,836,318, setting a new record for the eighth year in a row. With sell-out crowds happening more often, such as the record 102,368 who watched the '49ers and Rams play in Los Angeles on November 10, Bell and the team owners had to wonder where the boom would level off.

The individual fan who followed the teams on TV and in the ballpark (when he could get a ticket) was learning a new football term—the flanker back. More and more of the NFL coaches began stationing one halfback out beyond an end and close to the line of scrimmage, thus creating in effect a third pass receiving end. Offenses now took on the look of the modern pro set, with two running backs behind the quarterback, a tight end lined up next to a tackle, and a split end and flanker set wide toward the sidelines as primary pass receivers.

EASTERN CONFERENCE

Cleveland Browns—Paul Brown had hoped to pick quarterback Len Dawson in the college draft, but when Pittsburgh chose him first, Brown instead selected fullback Jimmy Brown from Syracuse. From the start of training camp, coach Brown knew he had something special. Here was the consummate ball-carrier, so heavily muscled as to be impossible for one tackler to bring down, yet fast enough to outrun defensive backs and shifty enough to slip tackles with straight-arms and sidesteps. Young Brown could not block like Marion Motley, Cleveland's great fullback of the Otto Graham era, but he made up for it by running inside, running outside, and catching passes. Coach Brown immediately centered the offense around his young star, with occasional passes from Tom O'Connell and Milt Plum to divert the enemy—as Jimmy Brown captured his first rushing title and the Browns recaptured the Eastern crown.

New York Giants—From the first time the Giants played Cleveland with its star rookie runner, Jimmy Brown, the New Yorkers assigned middle linebacker Sam Huff to tail him wherever he went. The results of their meetings would be the same for years. Brown often would gain his yardage but would have a tougher time against the Giants than any other team. Opening day pitted the Giants against the Browns, and while the New York defense bottled up young Brown in his pro debut, Cleveland still won 6-3. After that, both clubs battled through the autumn for the Eastern lead until the Giants folded in their final three games.

Pittsburgh Steelers—Coach Walt Kiesling passed over Jimmy Brown to choose quarterback Len Dawson in the collegiate draft and counted on the rookie to take charge of the offense. However, by the end of the exhibition season, Kiesling was out as coach, with Buddy Parker coming over from Detroit to take command of the Steelers. Parker decided against going into the season with only rookies Dawson and Jack Kemp at quarterback, so he engineered a trade with San Francisco for second-year man Earl Morrall. The price was hard for some to swallow, as Parker handed over two first draft picks plus linebacker Marv Matuszak to the '49ers for Morrall and rookie lineman Mike Sandusky. But even with Morrall at quarterback and the blooming of Jack McClairen into a fine receiver, the Steelers still had problems scoring points.

Washington Redskins—For a second straight year, tragedy touched the Washington training camp when defensive back Roy Barni was shot to death in a barroom brawl. The Redskins trudged listlessly through most of the season, losing some close games and some runaways, until a surprising late-season turn-about. The defense jelled into a solid unit in the last three games as it allowed the Bears, Eagles, and Steelers a total of only 13 points.

Philadelphia Eagles—Rookies Clarence Peaks and Billy Barnes, a pair of strong runners, broke into the starting lineup immediately, while passer Sonny Jurgensen and receiver Tommy McDonald sat and learned for future seasons. But no newcomers helped out up front, where only Buck Lansford earned high grades, or at end, where Bill Stribling and Bobby Walston showed good hands but no speed. Quarterback Adrian Burk had retired, leaving long-time partner Bobby Thomason in charge of an offense without a breakaway threat among the runners or receivers. The defense held its own, even with the transfer of Chuck Bednarik to offense, but it could not save head coach Hugh Devore from getting the ax.

Chicago Cardinals—The Cards' plunge to last place was swift and complete, as an offensive collapse saddled the team with seven losses in its last eight games. Shining through the gloom was Ollie Matson, still one of the NFL's blue-chip halfbacks, but none of his mates could draw the defense's attention away from him. The plodding Cards gave fans very little to cheer about, and the deteriorating neighborhood around Comiskey Park discouraged paying customers from coming to the games. It was a bad situation that called for a new deal, but the only change made was to fire head coach Ray Richards.

WESTERN CONFERENCE

Detroit Lions—Two days before the first pre-season game, coach Buddy Parker stood to address the Detroit Boosters' banquet. "This team of ours has been the worst I've ever seen in training," he said, leaving his audience openmouthed in shock. "I don't want to get involved in another losing season, so I'm leaving Detroit. As a matter of fact, I'm leaving tonight." With those words, Parker had quit as coach, leaving assistant George Wilson in charge of the talented but listless squad. Shaken into action by Parker's resignation, the Lions battled the Colts and Bears all through the season for the Western crown. One innovation in the offense was a two-quarterback system, with Bobby Layne sharing the job with ex-Packer Tobin Rote. Neither man was pleased with the arrangement, but the depth at the spot came in handy when Layne broke his leg in a late-season game and Rote led the Lions to victories in the last two games to tie the '49ers for the conference crown.

San Francisco '49ers—After a three-game losing streak in mid-season slowed them up, the '49ers finished in a hurry, winning their last three games by close scores and deadlocking the Lions for first place as the season ended. Starring on the road to this finish were passer Y. A. Tittle, runner Hugh McElhenny, receivers Billy Wilson and R. C. Owens, and defenders Leo Nomellini and Marv Matuszak, a pre-season pick-up from Pittsburgh. In the playoff game for the Western title, Tittle had a hot first half and carved out a 27-7 San Francisco lead at halftime, only to have the Lions storm back in the second half for a 31-27 Detroit victory.

Baltimore Colts—Undefeated after three games, the Colts blew a 10-point lead with three minutes left to bow 31-27 in a rematch with the Lions. After two more losses the Colts regained their touch and regained the conference lead down the stretch. With a one-game lead over the '49ers and Lions with two games left, the Colts headed for California. In San Francisco, a Unitas-to-Lenny Moore touchdown pass put the Colts in front 13-10 with two minutes left in the game, only to have the '49ers come back to win on a Hugh McElhenny touchdown. Then, needing a win to tie for the crown, the Colts played the Rams and came away 37-21 losers.

Los Angeles Rams—The passing attack, the Rams' long suit since heading West, suddenly looked a little threadbare. The great receivers weren't around any longer, as Tom Fears had retired and Crazy Legs Hirsch had lost his game-breaking speed, and quarterbacks Norm Van Brocklin and Billy Wade weren't frightening defenses as the old Ram teams did. Coach Sid Gillman did find some strong runners to lug the ball, as second-year men Tom Wilson and Joe Marconi and veteran Tank Younger punched out hard yardage regularly. But even with impressive wins over the Packers and Colts to end the season, the Rams were still in the midst of a rebuilding program.

Chicago Bears—With rookie Willie Galimore, billed as the league's next great breakaway runner, and promising quarterback Zeke Bratkowski to bolster the offense, the Bears expected to improve on last year's title winning record. Instead, the Packers, Colts, and '49ers all beat them in the first three weeks of the season, and the Bears never did put more than two wins together in a row. The defense took no blame for the slump, as it actually allowed fewer points than last year, but all accusing fingers tabbed the offense as the culprit.

Green Bay Packers—It looked as though the Packers had signed a Heisman Trophy winner without a position when Paul Hornung, the golden-haired All-American from Notre Dame, bounced around the Green Bay backfield like a pinball. Coach Lisle Blackbourn first tried him at quarterback, but the rookie didn't have the arm for the position. Then came a trial at fullback, but Hornung had neither the bulk nor the inclination to be a work-horse power runner. The Packers had evidently chosen another lemon as their first draft choice, bringing a new round of calls for coach Blackbourn's firing. Another rookie, end Ron Kramer, made a good showing, while Bart Starr showed promise in replacing the traded Tobin Rote. But the season as a whole was a dismal way in which to open Green Bay's new football stadium and to end Blackbourn's three-year reign.

FINAL TEAM STATISTICS

OFFENSE

	BALT.	CHI.B.	CHI.C.	CLEVE.	DET.	G.BAY	L.A.	N.Y.	PHIL.	PITT.	S.F.	WASH.
FIRST DOWNS:												
Total	222	188	174	180	221	179	235	216	149	159	223	197
by Rushing	91	82	77	93	103	72	112	95	80	59	92	107
by Passing	117	92	75	76	105	90	104	103	51	92	115	78
by Penalty	14	14	22	11	13	17	19	18	18	8	16	12
RUSHING:												
Number	434	457	365	501	409	380	474	441	424	390	377	500
Yards	1735	1686	1442	1958	1811	1441	2142	1649	1582	1174	1622	1873
Average Yards	4.0	3.7	4.0	3.9	4.4	3.8	4.5	3.7	3.7	3.0	4.3	3.7
Touchdowns	12	15	12	19	12	13	15	13	9	7	15	17
PASSING:												
Attempts	314	286	271	195	361	325	296	269	204	312	305	201
Completions	177	130	111	108	163	157	144	147	99	149	191	109
Completion Percentage	56.4	45.5	41.0	55.4	45.2	48.3	48.6	54.6	48.5	47.8	62.6	54.2
Gross Yards	2608	1945	1969	1873	2239	2157	2256	2158	1379	2013	2407	1741
Yards Lost Passing	220	177	194	161	210	366	255	58	224	297	371	120
Net Yards	2388	1768	1775	1712	2029	1791	2001	2100	1155	1716	2036	1621
Avg. Yards per Attempt (Gross)	8.3	6.8	7.3	9.6	6.2	6.6	7.6	8.0	6.8	6.5	7.9	8.7
Avg. Yards per Comp. (Gross)	14.7	15.0	17.7	17.3	13.7	13.7	15.7	14.7	13.9	13.5	12.6	16.0
Touchdowns	25	7	12	12	17	12	21	15	10	11	17	11
Interceptions	19	28	22	14	22	23	23	12	23	14	18	13
Percent Intercepted	6.1	9.8	8.1	7.2	6.1	7.1	7.8	4.5	11.3	4.5	5.9	6.5
PUNTS:												
Number	55	63	59	61	54	63	56	60	68	70	57	50
Average Distance	34.5	38.8	42.5	39.3	39.9	42.0	44.4	44.6	41.1	40.1	44.7	42.8
PUNT RETURNS:												
Number	33	43	40	48	41	36	36	43	37	51	37	44
Yards	133	146	258	231	200	256	198	180	199	276	122	460
Average Yards	4.0	3.4	6.5	4.8	4.9	7.1	5.5	4.2	5.4	5.4	3.3	10.5
Touchdowns	0	0	0	0	0	0	0	0	0	0	0	2
KICKOFF RETURNS:												
Number	42	39	47	33	37	58	49	42	41	25	42	38
Yards	948	836	1167	686	747	1261	1150	976	838	581	1096	874
Average Yards	22.6	21.4	24.8	20.8	20.2	21.7	23.5	23.2	20.4	23.2	26.1	23.0
Touchdowns	1	0	0	0	0	0	1	0	0	1	0	0
INTERCEPTION RETURNS:												
Number	28	15	12	19	25	30	14	18	17	19	18	16
Yards	349	185	183	223	311	561	236	276	442	195	264	203
Average Yards	12.5	12.3	15.3	11.7	12.4	18.7	16.9	15.3	26.0	10.3	14.7	12.7
Touchdowns	2	0	0	0	1	1	1	3	2	0	1	0
PENALTIES:												
Number	67	63	51	66	65	43	60	66	75	48	66	31
Yards	712	614	468	597	673	516	580	597	654	405	629	321
FUMBLES:												
Number	22	25	22	19	29	28	24	36	25	39	22	30
Number Lost	12	15	15	10	13	18	14	20	16	18	14	17
POINTS:												
Total	303	203	200	269	251	218	307	254	173	161	260	251
PAT Attempts	41	23	26	32	30	26	39	32	21	20	33	30
PAT Made	36	23	24	32	30	26	38	32	20	15	33	29
FG Attempts	19	26	17	22	25	21	19	18	14	26	15	23
FG Made	7	14	6	15	13	12	11	10	9	8	9	14
Percent FG Made	36.8	53.8	35.3	68.2	52.0	57.1	57.9	55.6	64.3	30.8	60.0	60.9
Safeties	0	0	1	0	1	0	1	0	0	1	1	0

DEFENSE

	BALT.	CHI.B.	CHI.C.	CLEVE.	DET.	G.BAY	L.A.	N.Y.	PHIL.	PITT.	S.F.	WASH.
FIRST DOWNS:												
Total	204	185	208	164	198	226	216	174	199	156	239	174
by Rushing	69	68	120	79	81	117	96	92	83	69	107	82
by Passing	118	96	79	66	100	97	101	64	94	77	117	89
by Penalty	17	21	9	19	17	12	19	18	22	10	15	3
RUSHING:												
Number	375	419	521	396	406	462	440	442	451	412	434	394
Yards	1174	1383	2201	1502	1521	2159	1845	1777	1714	1425	1847	1567
Average Yards	3.1	3.3	4.2	3.8	3.7	4.7	4.2	4.0	3.8	3.5	4.3	4.0
Touchdowns	10	10	19	11	13	18	15	12	15	7	18	11
PASSING:												
Attempts	342	306	233	242	290	314	301	226	257	234	332	262
Completions	175	153	117	105	163	153	153	104	133	112	182	135
Completion Percentage	51.2	50.0	50.2	43.4	56.2	48.7	50.8	46.0	51.8	47.9	54.8	51.5
Gross Yards	2548	2212	2027	1511	2099	2185	2186	1596	2083	1523	2582	2193
Yards Lost Passing	316	479	120	211	255	147	306	202	114	157	181	165
Net Yards	2232	1733	1907	1300	1844	2038	1880	1394	1969	1366	2401	2028
Avg. Yards per Attempt (Gross)	7.5	7.2	8.7	6.2	7.2	7.0	7.3	7.1	8.1	6.5	7.8	8.4
Avg. Yards per Comp. (Gross)	14.6	14.4	17.3	14.4	12.9	14.3	14.3	15.3	15.7	13.6	14.2	16.2
Touchdowns	19	15	17	8	15	18	15	10	10	12	13	18
Interceptions	28	15	12	19	25	30	14	18	17	19	18	16
Percent Intercepted	8.2	4.9	5.2	7.9	8.6	9.6	4.7	8.0	6.6	8.1	5.4	6.1
PUNTS:												
Number	56	76	60	72	55	50	61	60	58	62	47	59
Average Distance	42.5	42.0	39.7	41.8	40.9	43.0	40.2	38.8	44.3	42.7	40.3	39.6
PUNT RETURNS:												
Number	34	47	46	47	33	40	37	45	45	45	35	35
Yards	109	244	266	315	54	149	229	325	351	324	205	88
Average Yards	3.2	5.2	5.8	6.7	1.6	3.7	6.2	7.2	7.8	7.2	5.9	2.5
Touchdowns	0	0	0	1	0	0	0	1	0	0	0	0
KICKOFF RETURNS:												
Number	49	33	31	42	47	42	53	42	31	35	45	43
Yards	1120	860	783	917	1044	897	1268	964	737	704	928	938
Average Yards	22.9	26.1	25.3	21.8	22.2	21.4	23.9	23.0	23.8	20.1	20.6	21.8
Touchdowns	0	1	1	0	0	0	1	0	0	0	0	0
INTERCEPTION RETURNS:												
Number	19	28	22	14	22	23	23	12	23	14	18	13
Yards	180	574	340	141	292	252	381	190	340	230	336	172
Average Yards	9.5	20.5	15.5	10.1	13.3	11.0	16.6	15.8	14.8	16.4	18.7	13.2
Touchdowns	0	2	0	1	1	2	1	1	1	1	1	0
PENALTIES:												
Number	60	65	68	42	65	75	49	49	65	43	55	65
Yards	546	744	726	412	577	709	516	423	642	370	502	599
FUMBLES:												
Number	29	22	27	20	28	26	24	34	26	39	25	21
Number Lost	12	15	13	12	18	17	11	14	19	23	16	12
POINTS:												
Total	235	211	299	172	231	311	278	211	230	178	264	230
PAT Attempts	29	29	37	22	29	39	33	25	27	21	32	30
PAT Made	29	25	35	19	27	39	33	25	26	20	31	29
FG Attempts	21	19	23	14	17	22	26	17	29	19	24	14
FG Made	10	4	14	7	10	12	15	12	14	10	13	7
Percent FG Made	47.6	21.1	60.9	50.0	58.8	54.5	57.7	70.6	48.3	52.6	54.2	50.0
Safeties	1	0	0	0	0	1	1	0	0	1	1	0

1957 CHAMPIONSHIP GAME

December 29, at Detroit
(Attendance 55,263)

Parker and the Unsleeping Lions

The Detroit Lions entered the championship game against the Cleveland Browns with at least three strikes against them. Their star field general, Bobby Layne, was out with a broken ankle; Charlie Ane, one of the league's best tackles, was hampered by a bad ankle; and head coach George Wilson found himself in a peculiar position. He had replaced Buddy Parker in training camp after Parker publicly denounced the team and walked out before the first exhibition game. To say the least, it seemed as if the Lions were in for a long afternoon. But Tobin Rote, who had filled in admirably after Layne's injury, and the Detroit team in general were prepared to cap the season successfully, to prove to Parker and their fans that they were not deadbeats nor an uncoachable football team. By the time the first half ended, the throng in Briggs Stadium were in near hysteria with the scoreboard reading Lions 31, Browns 7. In the third quarter, Cleveland put a little fear in the crown as they marched 80 yards in ten plays to make the score 31-14. But then, after the Lions had returned the kickoff to their own 22-yard line, Rote uncorked a 78-yard bomb to Jim Doran to give Detroit, after the conversion, a 38-14 lead. Before the quarter ended, Rote struck again to put the game out of reach. On the first play of the final quarter, Jerry Perry recovered a fumble on the Cleveland 32, and Rote and Co. returned to the field. A Rote-to-Dave Middleton pass pushed the score to 52-14 after Jim Martin's conversion. The final Cleveland embarrassment and Detroit vindication came when Jerry Reichow, in relief of Rote, capped a 56-yard drive by drilling a 16-yard pass to Hopalong Cassady, which, following Martin's eighth extra-point conversion, ran the score to 59-14—the second biggest championship-game drubbing ever.

SCORING

DETROIT	17	14	14	14–59
CLEVELAND	0	7	7	0–14

First Quarter

Det.	Martin, 31 yard Field goal	7:36
Det.	Rote, 1 yard rush PAT – Martin (kick)	11:04
Det.	Gedman, 1 yard rush PAT – Martin (kick)	13:52

Second Quarter

Cle.	Brown, 29 yard rush PAT – Groza (kick)	0:10
Det.	Junker, 26 yard pass from Rote PAT – Martin (kick)	7:41
Det.	Barr, 19 yard interception return (by O'Connell) PAT – Martin (kick)	11:36

Third Quarter

Cle.	L. Carpenter, 5 yard rush PAT – Groza (kick)	7:59
Det.	Doran, 78 yard pass from Rote PAT – Martin (kick)	8:43
Det.	Junker, 23 yard pass from Rote PAT – Martin (kick)	13:21

Fourth Quarter

Det.	Middleton, 32 yard pass from Rote PAT – Martin (kick)	0:07
Det.	Cassady, 16 yard pass from Richlow PAT – Martin (kick)	12:40

TEAM STATISTICS

DET.		CLE.
22	First Downs – Totals	17
9	First Downs – Rushing	11
10	First Downs – Passing	5
3	First Downs – Penalty	1
4	Fumbles – Number	2
1	Fumbles – Lost Ball	2
6	Penalties – Number	5
52	Yards – Penalized	64
1	Field Goals Missed	0

INDIVIDUAL STATISTICS

DETROIT	No.	Yds.	Avg.	CLEVELAND	No.	Yds.	Avg.
RUSHING							
Cassady	8	48	6.0	L. Carpenter	14	82	5.9
Johnson	8	40	5.0	Brown	20	69	3.5
Rote	7	27	3.9	Plum	3	46	15.3
Redman	12	27	2.3	Renfro	1	21	21.0
Reichlow	1	0	0.0		38	218	5.7
	36	142	3.9				
RECEIVING							
Junker	5	109	21.8	P. Carpenter	4	43	10.8
Doran	3	101	33.7	Brewster	3	52	17.3
Cassady	2	22	11.0	Renfro	1	9	9.0
Middleton	1	32	32.0	L. Carpenter	1	8	8.0
Johnson	1	16	16.0		9	112	12.4
Tracy	1	16	16.0				
	13	296	22.8				
PUNTING							
Lary	4		36.3	Konz	4		35.5
PUNT RETURNS							
Lary	1	12	12.0	Reynolds	2	1	0.5
Barr	1	1	1.0				
	2	13	6.5				
KICKOFF RETURNS							
Lary	3	85	28.3	Brown	4	106	26.5
				Reynolds	3	58	19.3
				Campbell	1	19	19.0
					8	183	22.9
INTERCEPTION RETURNS							
Barr	1	19	19.0	None			
Long	1	17	17.0				
Schmidt	1	2	2.0				
David	1	0	0.0				
Perry	1	0	0.0				
	5	38	7.6				

PASSING

	Att.	Comp.	Comp Pct.	Yds.	Int.	Yds/ Att.	Yds/ Comp.	Yards Lost Tackled
DETROIT								
Rote	19	12	63.2	280	0	14.7	23.3	0
Reichlow	3	1	33.3	16	0	5.3	16.0	0
	22	13	59.1	296	0	13.5	22.8	0– 0
CLEVELAND								
Plum	13	5	38.5	51	2	3.9	10.2	1–10
O'Connell	8	4	50.0	61	2	7.6	15.3	0
Hanulak	1	0	0.0	0	1	–	–	1– 7
	22	9	40.9	112	5	5.1	12.4	2–17

1957 N.F.L. — Eastern Conference

CLEVELAND BROWNS 9-2-1 Paul Brown

Scores of Each Game		
6	NEW YORK	3
23	Pittsburgh	12
24	PHILADELPHIA	7
7	Philadelphia	17
17	Chic. Cards	7
21	WASHINGTON	17
24	PITTSBURGH	0
30	Washington	30
45	LOS ANGELES	31
31	CHIC. CARDS	0
7	Detroit	20
34	New York	28

Use Name	Pos.	Hgt	Wgt	Age	Int	Pts
Lou Groza	OT	6'3"	248	33		77
Mike McCormack	OT	6'4"	247	30		
Herschel Forester	OG	6'	230	27		
Fred Robinson	OG	6'1"	242	27		
Stan Sheriff (from SF)	OG	6'1"	225	26		
Jim Ray Smith	OG	6'3"	240	26		
Joe Amstutz	C	6'5"	264	23		
Art Hunter	C	6'4"	242	24		
Len Ford	DE	6'4"	258	31		
Bill Quinlan	DE	6'3"	245	25		
Paul Wiggin	DE	6'3"	237	23		
Don Colo	DT	6'3"	250	32		
Bob Gain	DT	6'3"	260	29		
Henry Jordan	DT	6'3"	242	23		
Tom Catlin	LB	6'1"	210	26		
Vince Costello	LB	6'	224	25	2	
Galen Fiss	LB	6'	227	27	1	
Walt Michaels	LB	6'	237	28	1	
Chuck Noll	LB	6'1"	210	25		
Bobby Freeman	DB	6'1"	200	24	3	
Kenny Konz	DB	5'10"	187	29	4	
Warren Lahr	DB	5'11"	192	33	2	
Don Paul	DB	6'	192	31	4	6
Junior Wren	DB	6'	188	27	2	
John Borton	QB	6'	208	25		
Tom O'Connell	QB	5'11"	195	25		6
Milt Plum	QB	6'1"	205	23		
Milt Campbell	HB	6'3"	217	24		6
Lew Carpenter	HB	6'1"	205	25		24
Chet Hanulak	HB	5'10"	190	24		18
Billy Reynolds	HB	5'10"	195	25		6
Jimmy Brown	FB	6'2"	228	21		60
Ed Modzelewski	FB	6'	222	28		
Darrell Brewster	OE	6'3"	210	27		12
Preston Carpenter	OE	6'2"	192	23		18
Frank Clarke	OE	6'	207	24		
Ray Renfro	FL	6'1"	190	26		36

NEW YORK GIANTS 7-5-0 Jim Lee Howell

Scores of Each Game		
3	Cleveland	6
24	Philadelphia	20
24	Washington	20
35	PITTSBURGH	0
14	WASHINGTON	31
31	Green Bay	17
27	CHIC. CARDS	14
13	PHILADELPHIA	0
28	Chic. Cards	21
17	SAN FRANCISCO	27
10	Pittsburgh	21
28	CLEVELAND	34

Use Name	Pos.	Hgt	Wgt	Age	Int	Pts
Rosey Brown	OT	6'3"	245	24		
Dick Yelvington	OT	6'2"	235	30		
Bill Austin	OG	6'1"	225	28		
Ray Beck	OG	6'2"	225	25		
Jack Spinks	OT-OG	6'	235	27		
Jack Stroud	OT-OG	6'1"	235	28		
Ray Wietecha	C	6'1"	225	28		
Andy Robustelli	DE	6'1"	235	31		
Walt Yowarsky	OT-DE	6'3"	235	29		
John Martinkovic	DT-DE	6'3"	245	30		
Jim Katkavage	DT	6'3"	235	22		
Dick Modzelewski	DT	6'	260	26		
Sam Huff	LB	6'1"	230	22	1	6
Cliff Livingston	LB	6'3"	210	27		
Bill Svoboda	LB	6'	210	30	2	
Harland Svare	LB-DT	6'	215	26	1	
Johnny Bookman	DB	5'11"	175	22	3	6
Ed Crawford	OE-DB	6'3"	185	23	1	
Ed Hughes	DB	6'1"	185	29		
Dick Nolan	DB	6'1"	185	25	1	
Jimmy Patton	DB	6'	180	25	3	6
Em Tunnell	DB	6'1"	200	35	6	6
Bobby Clatterbuck	QB	6'3"	195	25		
Chuck Conerly	QB	6'1"	185	33		6
Don Heinrich	QB	6'	180	25		12
Don Chandler	HB	6'2"	205	22		
Gene Filipski	HB	5'11"	185	26		
Frank Gifford	HB	6'1"	205	27		54
Alex Webster	HB	6'3"	210	26		36
Bobby Epps	FB	5'9"	205	25		
Mel Triplett	FB	6'1"	215	25		
Ken MacAfee	OE	6'2"	215	27		12
Kyle Rote	OE	6'	205	28		18
Bob Schnelker	OE	6'3"	215	27		30
Ben Agajanian	K	6'	215	38		62

Jerry Huth – Military Service
Rosey Grier – Military Service

PITTSBURGH STEELERS 6-6-0 Buddy Parker

Scores of Each Game		
28	WASHINGTON	7
12	CLEVELAND	23
29	CHIC. CARDS	20
0	New York	35
6	PHILADELPHIA	0
19	Baltimore	13
0	Cleveland	24
10	GREEN BAY	27
6	Philadelphia	7
21	NEW YORK	10
3	Washington	10
27	Chic. Cards	2

Use Name	Pos.	Hgt	Wgt	Age	Int	Pts
Jerry Leahy	OT	6'2"	220	23		
Frank Varrichione	OT	6'1"	230	25		
Willie McClung	DT-OT	6'2"	250	28		
Sid Fournet	OG	6'	215	24		
Herm Lee	OG	6'4"	220	26		
Bill Michael	OG	6'2"	240	23		
John Nisby	OG	6'1"	230	24		
Bob O'Neil	OG	6'1"	230	24		
Mike Sandusky	OG	6'	235	24		
Ed Beatty	C	6'3"	230	25		
Bill McPeak	DE	6'1"	220	32		2
George Tarasovic	LB-DE	6'4"	250	28	2	
Joe Krupa	DT	6'2"	240	24		
Dave Liddick	DT	6'2"	240	23		
Ernie Stautner	DE-DT	6'1"	230	32		
Dale Dodrill	LB	6'1"	215	32	2	
Bill Priatko	LB	6'2"	220	26		
John Reger	LB	6'	220	26		6
Aubrey Rozelle	LB	6'2"	215	24	1	
Dick Alban	DB	6'	195	28	1	
Fred Bruney	DB	5'10"	180	26	1	
Jack Butler	DB	6'	195	29	10	
Gene Cichowski	DB	6'	195	23		
Gary Glick	DB	6'2"	190	26	2	25
Richie McCabe	DB	6'1"	185	23		
Len Dawson	QB	6'	195	23		
Jack Kemp	QB	6'1"	200	23		
Earl Morrall	QB	6'1"	205	23		12
Dick Hughes	HB	5'9"	185	25		
Sid Watson	HB	5'11"	185	24		
Billy Wells (from WAS)	HB	5'9"	170	25		6
Dean Derby	DB-HB	6'	185	23		21
Ray Mathews	OE-HB	6'	195	28		24
Bill Bowman	FB	6'2"	220	26		
Fran Rogel	FB	5'11"	205	30		6
Dick Young	FB	5'11"	210	26		12
Bob Gunderman	OE	6'2"	195	23		
Jug Girard	OE	5'11"	185	30		29
Jack McClairen	OE	6'4"	215	26		12
Elbie Nickel	OE	6'1"	205	34		6
Perry Richards	OE	6'2"	205	23		

Lynn Chandnois – Injury
Lowell Perry – Injury

WASHINGTON REDSKINS 5-6-1 Joe Kuharich

Scores of Each Game		
7	Pittsburgh	28
37	Chic. Cards	14
20	NEW YORK	24
14	CHIC. CARDS	44
31	New York	14
17	Cleveland	21
17	BALTIMORE	21
30	CLEVELAND	30
12	Philadelphia	21
14	Chic. Bears	3
42	PHILADELPHIA	7
10	PITTSBURGH	3

Use Name	Pos.	Hgt	Wgt	Age	Int	Pts
Don Boll	OT	6'2"	266	30		
Ray Lemek	OT	6'	232	23		
Ed Khayat	DT-OT	6'3"	220	22		
Dick Stanfel	OG	6'3"	230	30		
Red Stephens	OG	6'	230	27		
Ed Voytek	OG	6'2"	230	22		
Bill Fulcher	LB-OG	6'1"	190	23		
Johnny Allen	C	6'2"	228	25		
Jim Schrader	C	6'2"	232	25		
Gene Brito	DE	6'1"	230	32		
Chet Ostrowski	DE	6'1"	235	27		
Bob Dee	DT-DE	6'3"	225	24		
Don Owens	DT	6'5"	258	25		
Volney Peters	DT	6'4"	240	29		
Will Renfro	DT	6'5"	230	25		
Chuck Drazenovich	LB	6'1"	222	30	2	
Ralph Felton	LB	5'11"	200	25	1	
Lavern Torgeson	LB	6'	217	28	1	
Norb Hecker	DB	6'2"	200	30	3	
Don Shula	DB	5'11"	190	27	3	
Bert Zagers	DB	5'10"	185	24	2	12
Dick James	HB-DB	5'9"	180	23	2	
Scooter Scudero	HB-DB	5'10"	170	27		
Rudy Bukich	QB	6'1"	200	26		
Eddie LeBaron	QB	5'9"	165	27		
Jim Podoley	HB	6'2"	190	24		36
Tom Runnels	HB	5'10"	190	23		
Ed Sutton	DB-HB	6'1"	202	22	1	36
Sam Baker	FB	6'2"	217	25		77
Don Bosseler	FB	6'1"	212	21		42
Leo Elter	FB	5'10"	200	28		18
Tom Braatz	OE	6'1"	213	24		
Johnny Carson	OE	6'3"	202	27		18
Steve Meilinger	OE	6'2"	223	27		12
Joe Walton	DE-OE	5'11"	205	22	1	

J. D. Kimmel – Injury
Ralph Gugliemi – Military Service
Johnny Miller – Military Service
John Paluck – Military Service
Roy Barni – Shot to death Aug. 1957

PHILADELPHIA EAGLES 4-8-0 Hugh Devore

Scores of Each Game		
13	Los Angeles	17
20	NEW YORK	24
7	Cleveland	24
17	CLEVELAND	7
0	Pittsburgh	6
38	Chic. Cards	21
16	DETROIT	27
0	New York	13
21	WASHINGTON	12
7	PITTSBURGH	6
7	Washington	42
27	CHIC. CARDS	31

Use Name	Pos.	Hgt	Wgt	Age	Int	Pts
Bob Gaona	OT	6'3"	240	27		
Buck Lansford	OT	6'2"	232	24		
Len Szafaryn	OT	6'2"	225	29		
Abe Gibron	OG	5'11"	260	31		
Ken Huxhold	OG	6'1"	235	28		
Menil Mavraides	OG	6'1"	235	23		
John Simerson	C	6'3"	258	22		
Tom Scott	DE	6'2"	220	27		
Norm Willey	DE	6'2"	235	30		
Marion Campbell	DT	6'3"	255	28		
Tom Saidock	DT	6'5"	263	25		
Jim Weatherall	DT	6'4"	252	27		
Frank Wydo	DT	6'4"	232	33	1	
Sid Youngelman	DT	6'3"	255	25		
Chuck Bednarik	C-LB	6'3"	235	32	3	
Bill Koman	LB	6'2"	223	23		
Bob Hudson	DB-LB	6'4"	230	27		
Eddie Bell	DB	6'1"	215	26	2	
Tom Brookshier	DB	6'	198	25	4	
Jimmy Harris	DB	6'1"	180	22	3	6
Jerry Norton	DB	5'11"	195	27	4	6
Al Dorow	QB	6'	190	27		12
Sonny Jurgensen	QB	5'11"	200	23		12
Bobby Thomason	QB	6'1"	197	28		18
Billy Barnes	HB	5'11"	202	22		12
Ken Keller	HB	5'11"	185	23		
Rocky Ryan	OE-HB	6'1"	202	25		12
Tommy McDonald	FL-HB	5'10"	182	23		18
Clarence Peaks	FB	6'1"	218	21		6
Neil Worden	FB	5'10"	205	27		
Dick Bielski	OE	6'1"	236	25		12
Hank Burnine	OE	6'2"	190	25		
Bill Stribling	OE	6'1"	210	30		6
Bobby Walston	OE	6'	190	28		53
Pete Retzlaff	FL	6'1"	209	27		

Jess Richardson – Injury
Lum Snyder – Military Service

CHICAGO CARDINALS 3-9-0 Ray Richards

Scores of Each Game		
20	San Francisco	10
14	WASHINGTON	37
20	Pittsburgh	29
44	Washington	14
7	CLEVELAND	17
21	PHILADELPHIA	38
14	New York	27
21	NEW YORK	28
0	Cleveland	31
6	CHIC. BEARS	14
31	Philadelphia	27
2	PITTSBURGH	27

Use Name	Pos.	Hgt	Wgt	Age	Int	Pts
Jack Jennings	OT	6'4"	245	30		
Dave Lunceford	OT	6'4"	240	23		
Charlie Toogood	OG-OT	6'	230	29		
Doug Hogland	OG	6'3"	245	26		
Bob Konovsky	OG	6'2"	245	23		
Earl Putnam	C	6'6"	308	25		
Jim Taylor	LB-C	6'2"	235	23		
Stan West	C-DG	6'2"	235	30		
Leo Sugar	DE	6'1"	210	28		12
Pat Summerall	DE	6'4"	230	27		42
Chuck Weber	LB-DE	6'1"	225	28		
Wayne Bock	DT	6'4"	250	23		
Tom Finnin	DT	6'2"	270	29		
Len Teeuws	DT	6'4"	245	30		
Chuck Ulrich	DT	6'4"	250	26		
Carl Brettschneider	LB	6'1"	200	25		
Ed Husmann	OG-LB	6'	225	26		
Leo Sanford	C-LB	6'1"	230	28	1	
Jerry Tubbs	C-LB	6'2"	216	22		
Tony Pasquesi	DT-LB	6'4"	250	23		
Jimmy Carr	DB	6'1"	200	24		
Lindon Crow	DB	6'1"	187	24	1	
Jimmy Hill	DB	6'2"	190	28	3	
Night Train Lane	DB	6'1"	190	29	2	
Floyd Sagely	DB	6'1"	190	25	1	
Frank Bernardi	HB-DB	5'9"	180	24	2	
Paul Larson	QB	5'11"	185	25		
Ted Marchibroda	QB	5'10"	180	26		
Lamar McHan	QB	6'1"	197	25		12
Joe Childress	HB	6'	200	23		6
Ollie Matson	HB	6'2"	210	27		54
Jimmy Sears	HB	5'11"	180	26		6
Dave Mann	OE-HB	6'1"	190	24		
Mal Hammack	FB	6'2"	200	24		
Johnny Olszewski	FB	5'11"	196	26		12
Max Boydston	OE	6'2"	207	24		
Dick Brubaker	OE	6'	205	25		
Gern Nagler	OE	6'2"	190	24		24
Woodley Lewis	DB-OE	6'	195	32	2	30

John Dittrich – Military Service
John Roach – Military Service

CLEVELAND BROWNS

RUSHING

Last Name	No.	Yds	Avg	TD
Brown	202	942	4.7	9
Hanulak	125	375	3.0	3
L. Carpenter	83	315	3.8	4
Plum	26	118	4.5	0
P. Carpenter	3	86	28.7	1
Reynolds	29	57	2.0	1
Campbell	7	23	3.3	0
Renfro	2	22	11.0	0
Modzelewski	10	21	2.1	0
McCormack	0	4	0.0	0
O'Connell	14	−5	−0.4	1

RECEIVING

Last Name	No.	Yds	Avg	TD
Brewster	30	614	21	2
P. Carpenter	27	398	15	2
Renfro	21	589	28	6
Brown	16	55	3	1
L. Carpenter	5	65	13	0
Clarke	4	77	19	0
Hanulak	3	38	13	0
Campbell	1	25	25	1
Reynolds	1	12	12	0

PUNT RETURNS

Last Name	No.	Yds	Avg	TD
Reynolds	24	114	5	0
Paul	9	75	8	0
Hanulak	11	29	3	0
Konz	3	13	4	0
Robinson	1	0	0	0

KICKOFF RETURNS

Last Name	No.	Yds	Avg	TD
Campbell	11	263	24	0
Reynolds	7	152	22	0
Brown	6	136	23	0
Modzelewski	5	74	15	0
L. Carpenter	1	24	24	0
Clarke	2	22	11	0
Freeman	1	15	15	0

PASSING – PUNTING – KICKING

PASSING	Att	Comp	%	Yds	Yd/Att	TD	Int–%	RK
O'Connell	110	63	57	1229	11.2	9	8– 7	5
Plum	76	41	54	590	7.8	2	5– 7	
Borton	6	3	50	22	3.7	0	1– 17	
Hanulak	2	1	50	32	16.0	1	0– 0	
Campbell	1	0	0	0	0.0	0	0– 0	

PUNTING	No	Avg
Konz	61	39.3

KICKING	XP	Att	%	FG	Att	%
Groza	32	32	100	15	22	68

NEW YORK GIANTS

RUSHING

Last Name	No.	Yds	Avg	TD
Gifford	136	528	3.9	5
Webster	135	478	3.5	5
Epps	63	286	4.5	0
Triplett	61	216	3.5	0
Filipski	22	89	4.0	0
Conerly	15	24	1.6	1
Rote	1	13	13.0	0
Heinrich	4	10	2.5	2
Clatterbuck	3	3	1.0	0
Chandler	1	2	2.0	0

RECEIVING

Last Name	No.	Yds	Avg	TD
Gifford	41	588	14	4
Webster	30	330	11	1
Rote	25	358	14	3
Schnelker	20	450	23	5
MacAfee	16	229	14	2
Epps	8	81	10	0
Triplett	4	75	19	0
Crawford	2	40	20	0
Filipski	1	7	7	0

PUNT RETURNS

Last Name	No.	Yds	Avg	TD
Filipski	20	91	5	0
Tunnell	12	60	5	0
Patton	11	29	3	0

KICKOFF RETURNS

Last Name	No.	Yds	Avg	TD
Filipski	26	613	24	0
Patton	10	223	22	0
Bookman	4	102	26	0
Crawford	2	38	19	0

PASSING – PUNTING – KICKING

PASSING	Att	Comp	%	Yds	Yd/Att	TD	Int–%	RK
Conerly	232	128	55	1712	7.4	11	11– 5	4
Heinrich	26	11	42	224	8.6	1	1– 4	
Gifford	6	4	67	143	23.8	2	0– 0	
Chandler	2	2	100	40	20.0	0	0– 0	
Clatterbuck	2	2	100	39	19.5	1	0– 0	
Epps	1	0	0	0	0.0	0	0– 0	

PUNTING	No	Avg
Chandler	60	44.6

KICKING	XP	Att	%	FG	Att	%
Agajanian	32	32	100	10	18	56

PITTSBURGH STEELERS

RUSHING

Last Name	No.	Yds	Avg	TD
Wells	154	532	3.5	0
Rogel	68	232	3.4	1
Young	56	153	2.7	2
Morrall	41	81	2.0	2
Bowman	28	76	2.7	0
Derby	18	49	2.7	2
Dawson	3	31	10.3	0
Watson	12	21	1.8	0
Hughes	2	6	3.0	0
Kemp	3	−1	−0.3	0
Mathews	3	−1	−0.3	0
Girard	1	−5	−2.5	0

RECEIVING

Last Name	No.	Yds	Avg	TD
McClairen	46	630	14	2
Girard	21	419	20	4
Rogel	20	128	6	0
Mathews	15	369	25	4
Wells	14	89	6	0
Bowman	11	107	10	0
Nickel	10	115	12	1
Derby	4	79	20	0
Young	4	38	10	0
Watson	3	24	8	0
Richards	1	15	15	0

PUNT RETURNS

Last Name	No.	Yds	Avg	TD
Wells	21	143	7	0
Bruney	17	86	5	0
Derby	9	32	4	0
Butler	1	10	10	0
Hughes	1	5	5	0
Glick	1	0	0	0
Rozelle	1	0	0	0

KICKOFF RETURNS

Last Name	No.	Yds	Avg	TD
Wells	12	325	27	1
Derby	6	137	23	0
Bruney	5	101	20	0
Alban	2	33	17	0
Rogel	1	4	4	0

PASSING – PUNTING – KICKING

PASSING	Att	Comp	%	Yds	Yd/Att	TD	Int–%	RK
Morrall	289	139	48	1900	6.6	11	12– 4	6
Kemp	18	8	44	88	4.9	0	2– 11	
Dawson	4	2	50	25	6.3	0	0– 0	
Girard	1	0	0	0	0.0	0	0– 0	

PUNTING	No	Avg
Girard	68	40.5
Kemp	2	27.5

KICKING	XP	Att	%	FG	Att	%
Glick	10	12	83	5	18	28
Derby	3	3	100	2	4	50
Girard	2	3	67	1	3	33
Dawson	0	2	0	0	1	0

WASHINGTON REDSKINS

RUSHING

Last Name	No.	Yds	Avg	TD
Bosseler	167	673	4.0	7
Podoley	114	442	3.9	2
Sutton	108	407	3.8	5
Elter	45	211	3.8	2
Scudero	9	60	6.7	0
Runnels	20	52	2.6	0
Baker	2	23	11.5	1
James	7	19	2.7	0
Bukich	8	−2	−0.2	0
LeBaron	20	−12	−0.6	0

RECEIVING

Last Name	No.	Yds	Avg	TD
Carson	34	583	17	3
Podoley	27	554	21	4
Bosseler	19	152	8	0
Meilinger	13	183	14	2
Elter	6	94	16	1
Walton	3	57	19	0
Braatz	2	52	26	0
Sutton	2	32	16	1
Scudero	2	30	15	0
Runnels	1	4	4	0

PUNT RETURNS

Last Name	No.	Yds	Avg	TD
Zagers	14	217	16	2
Scudero	9	84	9	0
James	11	83	8	0
Runnels	10	76	8	0

KICKOFF RETURNS

Last Name	No.	Yds	Avg	TD
Zagers	15	348	23	0
James	12	259	22	0
Scudero	3	95	32	0
Runnels	2	66	33	0
Podoley	3	56	19	0
Sutton	1	19	19	0
Khayat	1	12	12	0

PASSING – PUNTING – KICKING

PASSING	Att	Comp	%	Yds	Yd/Att	TD	Int–%	RK
LeBaron	167	99	59	1508	9.0	11	10– 6	3
Bukich	28	6	21	103	3.7	0	3– 11	
Sutton	5	3	60	95	19.0	0	0– 0	
Runnels	1	1	100	35	35.0	0	0– 0	

PUNTING	No	Avg
Baker	50	42.8

KICKING	XP	Att	%	FG	Att	%
Baker	29	30	97	14	23	61

PHILADELPHIA EAGLES

RUSHING

Last Name	No.	Yds	Avg	TD
Barnes	143	529	3.7	1
Peaks	125	495	4.0	1
Keller	57	195	3.4	0
Worden	42	133	3.2	0
Norton	2	73	36.5	0
Thomason	15	62	4.1	3
Dorow	17	52	3.1	2
McDonald	12	36	3.0	0
Walston	1	7	7.0	0
Youngelman	0	3	0.0	0
Jurgensen	10	−3	−0.3	2

RECEIVING

Last Name	No.	Yds	Avg	TD
Barnes	19	212	11	1
Stribling	14	194	14	1
Walston	11	266	24	1
Peaks	11	99	9	0
Retzlaff	10	120	12	0
McDonald	9	228	25	3
Bielski	8	81	10	2
Burnine	7	63	9	0
Ryan	4	91	23	2
Keller	4	31	8	0
Worden	1	3	3	0
Gaona	1	−9	0	0

PUNT RETURNS

Last Name	No.	Yds	Avg	TD
McDonald	26	127	5	0
Keller	9	59	7	0
Norton	1	13	13	0
Harris	1	0	0	0

KICKOFF RETURNS

Last Name	No.	Yds	Avg	TD
Keller	15	320	21	0
McDonald	11	304	28	0
Peaks	5	98	20	0
Worden	4	63	16	0
Norton	2	33	17	0
Bielski	2	11	6	0
Bell	1	7	7	0
Wydo	1	2	2	0

PASSING – PUNTING – KICKING

PASSING	Att	Comp	%	Yds	Yd/Att	TD	Int–%	RK
Thomason	92	46	50	630	6.9	4	10– 11	
Jurgensen	70	33	47	470	6.7	5	8– 11	
Dorow	36	17	47	212	5.9	1	4– 11	
Peaks	3	2	67	56	18.7	0	1– 33	
Barnes	1	0	0	0	0.0	0	0– 0	
McDonald	1	1	100	11	11.0	0	0– 0	
Norton	1	0	0	0	0.0	0	0– 0	

PUNTING	No	Avg
Norton	68	41.4

KICKING	XP	Att	%	FG	Att	%
Walston	20	21	95	9	12	75
Bielski	0	0	0	0	2	0

CHICAGO CARDINALS

RUSHING

Last Name	No.	Yds	Avg	TD
Matson	134	577	4.3	6
Olszewski	83	271	3.3	2
Childress	41	168	4.1	1
Hammack	30	158	5.3	0
Mann	22	92	4.2	0
McHan	25	82	3.3	2
Sears	17	68	4.0	1
Larson	8	12	1.5	0
Marchibroda	4	10	2.5	0
Bernardi	1	4	4.0	0

RECEIVING

Last Name	No.	Yds	Avg	TD
Nagler	27	475	18	4
Lewis	21	424	20	5
Matson	20	451	23	3
Boydston	14	193	14	0
Childress	10	146	15	0
Mann	8	137	17	0
Sears	5	66	13	0
Olszewski	3	36	12	0
Hammack	1	14	14	0
Sugar	1	14	14	0
Bernardi	1	13	13	0

PUNT RETURNS

Last Name	No.	Yds	Avg	TD
Lewis	24	175	7	0
Matson	10	54	5	0
Bernardi	2	12	6	0
Hill	1	9	9	0
Lane	1	8	8	0
Mann	1	0	0	0
Sears	1	0	0	0

KICKOFF RETURNS

Last Name	No.	Yds	Avg	TD
Lewis	26	682	26	0
Sears	8	220	28	0
Matson	7	154	22	0
Carr	2	39	20	0
Hammack	2	33	17	0
Mann	1	23	23	0
Summerall	1	3	3	0
Olszewski	0	13	0	0

PASSING – PUNTING – KICKING

PASSING	Att	Comp	%	Yds	Yd/Att	TD	Int–%	RK
McHan	200	87	44	1568	7.8	10	15– 8	9
Marchibroda	45	15	33	238	5.3	1	5– 11	
Larson	14	6	43	61	4.4	0	1– 7	
Matson	5	2	40	59	11.8	0	0– 0	
Sears	3	0	0	0	0.0	0	0– 0	
Childress	2	1	50	43	21.5	0	1– 50	
Bernardi	1	0	0	0	0.0	0	0– 0	
Mann	1	0	0	0	0.0	0	0– 0	

PUNTING	No	Avg
Mann	59	42.5

KICKING	XP	Att	%	FG	Att	%
Summerall	24	26	92	6	17	35

DETROIT LIONS 8-4-0 George Wilson

Scores of Each Game		
14	Baltimore	34
24	Green Bay	14
10	LOS ANGELES	7
31	BALTIMORE	27
17	Los Angeles	35
31	San Francisco	35
27	Philadelphia	16
31	SAN FRANCISCO	10
7	CHIC. BEARS	27
18	GREEN BAY	6
20	CLEVELAND	7
21	Chic. Bears	13
	Playoff	
31	San Francisco	27

Use Name	Pos.	Hgt	Wgt	Age	Int	Pts
Charlie Ane	OT	6'2"	265	26		
Ken Russell	OT	6'3"	255	21		
Lou Creekmur	OG-OT	6'4"	254	30		
Stan Campbell	OG	6'	228	27		
Harley Sewell	OG	6'1"	226	26		
John Gordy	OT-OG	6'3"	238	21		
Frank Gatski	C	6'3"	240	35		
Gene Cronin	OG-DE	6'2"	228	24		
Gil Mains	DT-DE	6'2"	255	27		
Darris McCord	DT-DE	6'4"	245	24		
Ray Krouse	DT	6'3"	275	30		
Bob Miller	DT	6'3"	255	27		
Jerry Perry	DT	6'4"	237	26		2
Bob Long	LB	6'3"	230	23	1	
Jim Martin	LB	6'2"	223	33	1	26
Joe Schmidt	LB	6'1"	222	25	1	
Roger Zatkoff	LB	6'2"	220	26		
Terry Barr	DB	6'	185	22	1	
Jack Christiansen	DB	6'1"	196	28	10	6
Jim David	DB	5'11"	185	30	3	
Carl Karilivacz	DB	6'	190	26	5	
Gary Lowe (from WAS)	DB	5'11"	195	23	1	
Yale Lary	DB	6'	186	26	2	
Sonny Gandee — Injury						
Bobby Layne	QB	6'1"	208	30		43
Tobin Rote	QB	6'3"	215	29		6
Marv Brown	HB	5'8"	150	25		
Hopalong Cassady	HB	5'10"	180	23		36
Gene Gedman	HB	5'11"	196	25		18
John Henry Johnson	FB	6'2"	207	27		30
Tom Tracy	FB	5'9"	205	25		
Leon Hart	OE-FB	6'5"	250	28		
Dorne Dibble	OE	6'2"	197	28		
Jim Doran	OE	6'2"	202	29		30
Steve Junker	OE	6'3"	218	22		24
Dave Middleton	OE	6'1"	195	24		12
Jerry Reichow	QB-OE	6'2"	210	22		18

SAN FRANCISCO FORTY NINERS 8-4-0 Frankie Albert

Scores of Each Game		
10	CHIC. CARDS	20
23	LOS ANGELES	20
21	Chic. Bears	17
24	Green Bay	14
21	CHIC. BEARS	17
35	DETROIT	31
24	Los Angeles	37
10	Detroit	31
21	Baltimore	27
27	New York	17
17	BALTIMORE	13
27	GREEN BAY	20
	Playoff	
27	DETROIT	31

Use Name	Pos.	Hgt	Wgt	Age	Int	Pts
Bob Cross	OT	6'4"	250	26		
Tom Dahms	OT	6'5"	250	29		
John Gonzaga	OT	6'3"	240	24		
Bob St. Clair	OT	6'9"	263	26		
Bruce Bosley	OG	6'2"	240	23		
Ted Connolly	OG	6'3"	240	25		
Lou Palatella	OG	6'2"	230	24		
Frank Morze	C	6'4"	280	23		
Ed Henke	LB-DE	6'3"	227	29		
Charley Powell	OE-LB-DE	6'2"	225	25		
Bill Herchman	DT	6'2"	240	24	1	6
Leo Nomellini	DT	6'3"	255	32		2
Bob Toneff	DT	6'3"	255	27		
Matt Hazeltine	LB	6'1"	205	24	2	
Marv Matuszak	LB	6'3"	235	26		
Karl Rubke	C-LB	6'4"	235	21	1	
Paul Carr	DB-LB	6'	205	25		
Bob Holladay	DB	5'11"	175	24		
Jimmy Ridlon	DB	6'1"	195	22		
J. D. Smith	DB	6'1"	200	24	2	
Julian Spence	DB	5'11"	175	28		
Bill Stits	DB	6'	195	26	2	
Val Joe Walker	DB	6'1"	178	26	2	
Dick Moegle	HB-DB	6'	195	23	8	6
John Brodie	QB	6'1"	195	22		
Y. A. Tittle	QB	6'	195	30		36
Joe Arenas	HB	5'11"	180	31		6
Hugh McElhenny	HB	6'1"	198	28		18
Gene Babb	FB	6'3"	207	22		18
Larry Barnes	FB	6'1"	225	24		
Joe Perry	FB	6'	210	30		18
Clyde Conner	OE	6'2"	195	24		24
Gordie Soltau	OE	6'2"	195	32		60
Billy Wilson	OE	6'3"	190	30		36
Bill Jessup	OE-FL	6'1"	195	28		
R. C. Owens	OE-FL	6'3"	205	22		30

BALTIMORE COLTS 7-5-0 Weeb Ewbank

Scores of Each Game		
34	DETROIT	14
21	CHIC. BEARS	10
45	Green Bay	17
27	Detroit	31
21	GREEN BAY	24
13	PITTSBURGH	19
21	Washington	17
29	Chic. Bears	14
27	SAN FRANCISCO	21
31	LOS ANGELES	14
13	San Francisco	17
21	Los Angeles	37

Use Name	Pos.	Hgt	Wgt	Age	Int	Pts
Luke Owens	OT	6'2"	242	24		
Jim Parker	OT	6'3"	262	23		
Ken Jackson	OG-OT	6'2"	235	28		
Alex Sandusky	OG	6'1"	235	25		
Art Spinney	OG	6'	228	30		
George Preas	OT-LB-OG	6'2"	230	25		
Buzz Nutter	C	6'4"	225	26		
Dick Szymanski	LB-C	6'3"	228	25		
Ordell Braase	DE	6'4"	215	25		
Don Joyce	DE	6'3"	250	27	1	
Gino Marchetti	DE	6'4"	240	31		6
Art Donovan	DT	6'2"	265	32		
Big Daddy Lipscomb	DT	6'6"	282	26		
Joe Campanella	LB	6'2"	235	26		
Doug Eggers	LB	6'	214	27		
Jack Patera	LB	6'1"	225	25	1	
Bill Pellington	LB	6'2"	228	28		
Don Shinnick	LB	6'	230	22	2	
Steve Myhra	OG-LB	6'1"	235	23		26
Milt Davis	DB	6'1"	190	28	10	12
Art DeCarlo (from WAS)	DB	6'2"	195	27	1	
Henry Moore	DB	6'1"	195	23	1	
Andy Nelson	DB	6'1"	180	24	5	
Dick Nyers	DB	5'11"	175	23		
Bert Rechichar	DB	6'1"	210	27	5	31
Carl Taseff	DB	5'11"	190	28	1	
Jesse Thomas	DB	5'10"	180	28	1	
Cotton Davidson	QB	6'1"	185	25		
George Shaw	QB	6'1"	190	24		6
Johnny Unitas	QB	6'1"	190	24		6
Jack Call	HB	6'1"	200	22		
L. G. Dupre	HB	5'11"	190	25		24
Lenny Moore	HB	6'1"	190	24		66
Royce Womble	HB	6'	185	25		
Alan Ameche	FB	6'	217	24		42
Billy Pricer	FB	5'10"	195	22		
Ray Berry	OE	6'2"	190	24		36
Jim Mutscheller	OE	6'1"	215	27		48

LOS ANGELES RAMS 6-6-0 Sid Gillman

Scores of Each Game		
17	PHILADELPHIA	13
20	San Francisco	23
7	Detroit	10
26	Chic. Bears	34
35	DETROIT	17
10	CHIC. BEARS	16
37	SAN FRANCISCO	24
31	Green Bay	27
31	Cleveland	45
14	Baltimore	31
42	GREEN BAY	17
37	BALTIMORE	21

Use Name	Pos.	Hgt	Wgt	Age	Int	Pts
Bob Fry	OT	6'4"	238	26		
Glenn Holtzman	DE-OT	6'3"	254	27		
Ken Panfil	DT-OT	6'6"	268	26		
John Hock	OG	6'2"	234	29		
Duane Putnam	OG	6'	230	29		
John Houser	OG-C	6'3"	237	21		
Bob Griffin	LB-C	6'3"	250	28		
Paul Miller	DE	6'2"	220	25		
Billy Ray Smith	DE	6'4"	227	22		
Lamar Lundy	OE-DE	6'7"	235	22		18
Frank Fuller	DT	6'4"	243	28		
Art Hauser	DT	6'	246	26		6
George Strugar	DT	6'5"	258	22		
Dick Daugherty	LB	6'1"	223	28	1	8
Bob Dougherty	LB	6'	234	23	1	
Larry Morris	LB	6'2"	220	23	1	
Jack Pardee	LB	6'2"	215	21		
Les Richter	LB	6'3"	248	26	4	
Alex Bravo	DB	6'1"	190	25		
Don Burroughs	DB	6'4"	186	26	3	
Jesse Castete	DB	5'11"	180	22		
Will Sherman	DB	6'2"	197	28	1	
Del Shofner	DB	6'3"	185	21	2	
Corky Taylor	DB	5'10"	185	23		
Jesse Whittenton	DB	6'	190	23	1	
John Morrow — Military Service						
Norm Van Brocklin	QB	6'1"	202	31		24
Billy Wade	QB	6'2"	203	26		
Jon Arnett	HB	5'11"	194	22		36
Ron Waller	HB	5'11"	180	24		
Tom Wilson	HB	6'	204	24		24
Joe Marconi	FB	6'2"	230	23		24
Tank Younger	FB	6'3"	226	29		18
Bob Boyd	OE	6'2"	203	29		18
Leon Clarke	OE	6'4"	230	24		24
Crazy Legs Hirsch	OE	6'2"	190	33		36
Paige Cothren	K	5'11"	212	22		71

CHICAGO BEARS 5-7-0 Paddy Driscoll

Scores of Each Game		
17	Green Bay	21
10	Baltimore	21
17	SAN FRANCISCO	21
34	LOS ANGELES	26
17	San Francisco	21
16	Los Angeles	10
21	GREEN BAY	14
14	BALTIMORE	29
27	Detroit	7
3	WASHINGTON	14
14	Chic. Cards	6
13	DETROIT	21

Use Name	Pos.	Hgt	Wgt	Age	Int	Pts
Kline Gilbert	OT	6'2"	235	26		
Bob Kilcullen	OT	6'3"	245	21		
Bill Wightkin	OT	6'3"	235	30		
Herman Clark	OG	6'3"	255	26		
Stan Jones	OG	6'1"	255	26		
Tom Roggeman	OG	6'	235	26		
Larry Strickland	C	6'4"	245	26		
John Damore	OG-C	6'	228	24		
Doug Atkins	DE	6'8"	255	27		
Jack Hoffman	DE	6'5"	235	28		
Ed Meadows	DE	6'2"	220	25		
Bill Bishop	DT	6'4"	245	26		
Earl Leggett	DT	6'3"	250	23		
Fred Williams	DT	6'4"	245	27		
M. L. Brackett	DE-DT	6'5"	248	24		
Bill George	LB	6'2"	235	26		
Wayne Hansen	LB	6'2"	228	29	1	
Joe Fortunato	FB-LB	6'	225	27		6
Jack Johnson	DB	6'3"	198	23	4	
McNeil Moore	DB	6'	185	24	2	
Stan Wallace	DB	6'3"	210	25	2	
Vic Zucco	DB	6'	187	22	3	6
J. C. Caroline	HB-DB	6'1"	190	24	2	
Ray Gene Smith	HB-DB	5'10"	185	27	1	
John Mellekas — Military Service						
Charlie Sumner — Military Service						
George Blanda	QB	6'1"	207	29		71
Zeke Bratkowski	QB	6'2"	203	25		
Ed Brown	QB	6'2"	205	28		6
Ronnie Knox	QB	6'1"	198	23		
Ron Drzewiecki	HB	5'11"	185	25		
Willie Galimore	HB	6'1"	188	22		42
Perry Jeter	HB	5'7"	178	23		
Bobby Watkins	HB	5'10"	197	25		12
Rick Casares	FB	6'2"	224	26		36
Jim Dooley	OE	6'4"	198	27		6
Harlon Hill	OE	6'3"	198	25		12
Bill McColl	OE	6'4"	230	27		6
Gene Schroeder	OE	6'3"	195	28		

GREEN BAY PACKERS 3-9-0 Lisle Blackbourn

Scores of Each Game		
21	CHIC. BEARS	17
14	DETROIT	24
17	BALTIMORE	45
14	SAN FRANCISCO	24
24	Baltimore	21
17	NEW YORK	31
14	Chic. Bears	21
27	LOS ANGELES	31
27	Pittsburgh	10
6	Detroit	18
17	Los Angeles	42
20	San Francisco	27

Use Name	Pos.	Hgt	Wgt	Age	Int	Pts
Norm Masters	OT	6'2"	240	24		
Ollie Spencer	OT	6'2"	250	26		
Carl Vereen	OT	6'2"	247	21		
Norm Amundsen	OG	5'11"	245	24		
Al Barry	OG	6'2"	230	26		
Jim Salsbury	OG	6'1"	235	25		
Larry Lauer	C	6'3"	235	28		
Jim Ringo	C	6'1"	230	26		
Nate Borden	DE	6'	235	25		
Carlton Massey	DE	6'2"	225	28		
Jim Temp	DE	6'4"	230	24		
Dave Hanner	DT	6'2"	250	28		
Jerry Helluin	DT	6'2"	265	27	1	
Tom Bettis	LB	6'2"	235	24		
Ernie Danjean	LB	6'	230	23		
Bill Forester	LB	6'3"	235	26	4	
Sam Palumbo	LB	6'2"	230	26	1	
Bobby Dillon	DB	6'1"	180	27	9	6
Hank Gremminger	DB	6'1"	195	24	5	
Billy Kinard	DB	6'	185	23		
Johnny Petitbon	DB	5'11"	190	26	1	
Johnny Symank	DB	5'11"	180	22	9	
Hank Bullough — Military Service						
Forrest Gregg — Military Service						
Doyle Nix — Military Service						
Bob Skoronski — Military Service						
Babe Parilli	QB	6'1"	190	27		12
Bart Starr	QB	6'1"	200	24		18
Al Carmichael	HB	6'1"	190	27		6
Joe Johnson	HB	6'	180	27		6
Don McIlhenny	HB	6'	200	22		18
Paul Hornung	FB-HB	6'2"	215	21		18
Fred Cone	FB	5'11"	205	31		74
Howie Ferguson	FB	6'2"	220	27		12
Frank Purnell	FB	5'11"	230	24		
Billy Howton	OE	6'2"	190	27		30
Gary Knafelc	OE	6'4"	215	25		12
Ron Kramer	OE	6'3"	220	22		
Max McGee	OE	6'3"	205	25		6
Dick Deschaine	K	6'	215	27		

DETROIT LIONS

RUSHING

Last Name	No.	Yds	Avg	TD
Johnson	129	621	4.8	5
Rote	70	366	5.2	1
Gedman	67	278	4.1	3
Cassady	73	250	3.4	3
Hart	24	99	4.1	0
Layne	24	99	4.1	0
Tracy	16	46	2.9	0
Lary	1	32	32.0	0
Reichow	2	9	4.5	0
Brown	2	6	3.0	0
Dibble	1	5	5.0	0

RECEIVING

Last Name	No.	Yds	Avg	TD
Doran	33	624	19	5
Cassady	25	325	13	3
Junker	22	305	14	4
Johnson	20	141	7	0
Middleton	18	294	16	2
Reichow	17	215	13	3
Gedman	10	135	14	0
Dibble	8	121	15	0
Tracy	6	24	4	0
Hart	4	55	14	0

PUNT RETURNS

Last Name	No.	Yds	Avg	TD
Lary	25	139	6	0
Barr	9	33	4	0
Brown	3	16	5	0
Christiansen	3	12	4	0
Karilivacz	1	0	0	0

KICKOFF RETURNS

Last Name	No.	Yds	Avg	TD
Cassady	10	232	23	0
Gedman	6	158	26	0
Barr	9	153	17	0
Brown	6	106	18	0
Christiansen	4	80	20	0
Perry	1	18	18	0
Cronin	1	0	0	0

PASSING – PUNTING – KICKING

PASSING	Att	Comp	%	Yds	Yd/Att	TD	Int–%	RK
Layne	179	87	49	1169	6.5	6	12– 7	11
Rote	177	76	42	1070	6.1	11	10– 6	9
Gedman	2	0	0	0	0.0	0	0– 0	
Reichow	2	0	0	0	0.0	0	0– 0	
Lary	1	0	0	0	0.0	0	0– 0	

PUNTING	No	Avg
Lary	54	39.9

KICKING	XP	Att	%	FG	Att	%
Layne	25	25	100	6	11	55
Martin	5	5	100	7	14	50

SAN FRANCISCO FORTY NINERS

RUSHING

Last Name	No.	Yds	Avg	TD
McElhenny	102	478	4.7	1
Perry	97	454	4.7	3
Babb	102	330	3.2	3
Tittle	40	220	5.5	6
Barnes	20	78	3.9	0
Moegle	9	48	5.3	1
Arenas	5	14	2.8	1
Brodie	2	0	0.0	0

RECEIVING

Last Name	No.	Yds	Avg	TD
Wilson	52	757	15	6
McElhenny	37	458	12	2
Conner	30	412	14	4
Owens	27	395	15	5
Babb	20	141	7	0
Perry	15	130	9	0
Soltau	5	47	9	0
Jessup	2	29	15	0
Powell	1	27	27	0
Arenas	1	10	10	0
Barnes	1	1	1	0

PUNT RETURNS

Last Name	No.	Yds	Avg	TD
Arenas	25	80	3	0
McElhenny	10	41	4	0
Hazeltine	1	1	1	0
Moegle	1	0	0	0

KICKOFF RETURNS

Last Name	No.	Yds	Avg	TD
Arenas	24	657	27	0
Smith	14	368	26	0
Hazeltine	1	23	23	0
Carr	1	10	10	0
Jessup	1	8	8	0
Babb	1	0	0	0
Palatella	0	30	0	0

PASSING – PUNTING – KICKING

PASSING	Att	Comp	%	Yds	Yd/Att	TD	Int–%	RK
Tittle	279	176	63	2157	7.7	13	15– 5	2
Brodie	21	11	52	160	7.6	2	3– 14	
Arenas	3	3	100	92	30.7	2	0– 0	
Barnes	1	1	100	–2	–2.0	0	0– 0	
Perry	1	0	0	0	0.0	0	0– 0	

PUNTING	No	Avg
Jessup	38	43.6
Barnes	19	47.1

KICKING	XP	Att	%	FG	Att	%
Soltau	33	33	100	9	15	60

BALTIMORE COLTS

RUSHING

Last Name	No.	Yds	Avg	TD
Ameche	144	493	3.4	5
L. Moore	98	488	5.0	3
Dupre	101	375	3.7	2
Unitas	42	171	4.1	1
Call	33	145	4.4	0
Shaw	5	30	6.0	1
Pricer	2	18	9.0	0
Womble	7	18	2.6	0
Myhra	1	1	1.0	0
Nyers	1	–4	–4.0	0

RECEIVING

Last Name	No.	Yds	Avg	TD
Berry	47	800	17	6
L. Moore	40	687	17	7
Mutscheller	32	558	17	8
Dupre	32	339	11	2
Ameche	15	137	9	2
Womble	7	69	10	0
Call	4	18	5	0

PUNT RETURNS

Last Name	No.	Yds	Avg	TD
Rechichar	22	71	3	0
Taseff	7	60	9	0
Shinnick	1	2	2	0
L. Moore	2	0	0	0
Davis	1	0	0	0

KICKOFF RETURNS

Last Name	No.	Yds	Avg	TD
Nyers	17	350	21	0
Call	14	329	24	0
Moore*	1	108	–	1
Davidson	5	79	16	0
Pricer	2	40	20	0
Owens	1	23	23	0
Myhra	1	19	19	0
Rechichar	1	0	0	0

*TD on 92 yard lateral, also has a 16 yd return.

PASSING – PUNTING – KICKING

PASSING	Att	Comp	%	Yds	Yd/Att	TD	Int–%	RK
Unitas	301	172	57	2550	8.5	24	17– 6	1
Shaw	9	5	56	58	6.4	1	1– 11	
Davidson	2	0	0	0	0.0	0	1– 50	
L. Moore	2	0	0	0	0.0	0	0– 0	

PUNTING	No	Avg
Davidson	47	35.4
Rechichar	5	31.4
Dupre	3	25.0

KICKING	XP	Att	%	FG	Att	%
Rechichar	22	25	88	3	13	23
Myhra	14	16	88	4	6	67

LOS ANGELES RAMS

RUSHING

Last Name	No.	Yds	Avg	TD
Wilson	127	616	4.9	3
Marconi	104	481	4.6	3
Younger	96	401	4.2	3
Arnett	86	347	4.0	2
Waller	48	292	6.1	0
Hirsch	1	8	8.0	0
Wade	1	5	5.0	0
Clarke	1	–4	–4.0	0
Van Brocklin	10	–4	–0.4	4

RECEIVING

Last Name	No.	Yds	Avg	TD
Hirsch	32	477	15	6
Boyd	29	534	18	3
Clarke	23	442	19	4
Arnett	18	322	18	3
Marconi	16	171	11	1
Younger	8	61	8	0
Wilson	7	95	14	1
Lundy	6	114	19	3
Waller	5	40	8	0

PUNT RETURNS

Last Name	No.	Yds	Avg	TD
Arnett	14	85	6	0
Taylor	3	41	14	0
Waller	16	33	2	0
Wilson	1	28	28	0
Burroughs	1	11	11	0
Sherman	1	0	0	0

KICKOFF RETURNS

Last Name	No.	Yds	Avg	TD
Arnett	18	504	28	1
Wilson	11	290	26	0
Waller	13	289	22	0
Taylor	1	35	35	0
Pardee	3	21	7	0
Putnam	2	11	6	0
Lundy	1	0	0	0

PASSING – PUNTING – KICKING

PASSING	Att	Comp	%	Yds	Yd/Att	TD	Int–%	RK
Van Brocklin	265	132	50	2105	7.9	20	21– 8	6
Wade	24	10	42	116	4.8	1	1– 4	
Waller	6	2	33	35	5.8	0	0– 0	
Younger	1	0	0	0	0.0	0	1–100	

PUNTING	No	Avg
Van Brocklin	54	44.3
Shofner	2	48.5

KICKING	XP	Att	%	FG	Att	%
Cothren	38	38	100	11	19	58

CHICAGO BEARS

RUSHING

Last Name	No.	Yds	Avg	TD
Casares	204	700	3.4	6
Galimore	127	538	4.2	5
Watkins	57	212	3.7	1
Brown	31	129	4.2	1
Bratkowski	12	83	6.9	0
Drzewiecki	5	11	2.2	0
Jeter	10	11	1.1	0
Smith	1	8	8.0	0
Hill	2	7	3.5	0
Caroline	1	1	1.0	0
Blanda	5	5	–1.0	1
Fortunato	2	–9	–4.5	1

RECEIVING

Last Name	No.	Yds	Avg	TD
Dooley	37	530	14	1
Casares	25	225	9	0
Hill	21	483	23	2
McColl	19	282	15	1
Galimore	15	201	13	2
Watkins	3	90	30	1
Schroeder	3	48	16	0
Smith	3	37	12	0
Jeter	2	9	5	0
Caroline	1	33	33	0
Drzewiecki	1	7	7	0

PUNT RETURNS

Last Name	No.	Yds	Avg	TD
Drzewiecki	22	64	3	0
Zucco	11	58	5	0
Caroline	6	20	3	0
Jeter	2	3	2	0
Smith	2	1	1	0

KICKOFF RETURNS

Last Name	No.	Yds	Avg	TD
Drzewiecki	13	315	24	0
Zucco	8	224	28	0
Galimore	5	140	28	0
Caroline	4	77	19	0
Jeter	3	62	21	0
Damore	1	7	7	0
Williams	1	6	6	0
Brackett	3	5	2	0
Casares	1	0	0	0

PASSING – PUNTING – KICKING

PASSING	Att	Comp	%	Yds	Yd/Att	TD	Int–%	RK
Brown	185	84	45	1321	7.1	6	16– 9	12
Bratkowski	80	37	46	527	6.6	1	9– 11	
Blanda	19	8	42	65	3.4	0	3– 16	
Casares	2	1	50	32	16.0	0	0– 0	

PUNTING	No	Avg
Brown	34	40.1
Bratkowski	16	38.6
Johnson	11	36.2
Casares	2	33.5

KICKING	XP	Att	%	FG	Att	%
Blanda	23	23	100	14	26	53

GREEN BAY PACKERS

RUSHING

Last Name	No.	Yds	Avg	TD
McIlhenny	100	384	3.8	1
Hornung	60	319	5.3	3
Ferguson	59	216	3.7	1
Cone	53	135	2.5	2
Carmichael	37	118	3.2	1
Starr	31	98	3.2	3
Parilli	24	83	3.5	2
McGee	5	40	8.0	0
Purnell	5	22	4.4	0
Howton	4	20	5.0	0
Johnson	2	6	3.0	0

RECEIVING

Last Name	No.	Yds	Avg	TD
Howton	38	727	19	5
Kramer	28	337	12	0
McIlhenny	18	210	12	2
McGee	17	273	16	1
Ferguson	15	107	7	1
Carmichael	13	184	14	0
Knafelc	9	164	18	2
Johnson	7	75	11	1
Hornung	6	34	6	0
Cone	4	30	8	0
Purnell	2	16	8	0

PUNT RETURNS

Last Name	No.	Yds	Avg	TD
Carmichael	25	190	8	0
Johnson	4	39	10	0
Kinard	3	19	6	0
Dillon	1	8	8	0
Symank	3	0	0	0

KICKOFF RETURNS

Last Name	No.	Yds	Avg	TD
Carmichael	31	690	22	0
McIlhenny	14	362	26	0
Cone	5	83	17	0
McGee	4	69	17	0
Forester	4	57	14	0

PASSING – PUNTING – KICKING

PASSING	Att	Comp	%	Yds	Yd/Att	TD	Int–%	RK
Starr	215	117	54	1489	6.9	8	10– 5	8
Parilli	102	39	38	669	6.6	4	12– 12	13
Hornung	6	1	17	–1	–0.2	0	0– 0	
Ferguson	1	0	0	0	0.0	0	0– 0	
Kramer	1	0	0	0	0.0	0	1–100	

PUNTING	No	Avg
Deschaine	63	42.0

KICKING	XP	Att	%	FG	Att	%
Cone	26	26	100	12	17	71
Hornung	0	0	0	0	4	0

1958 Recognition in Overtime

By putting in a few minutes of overtime, the NFL reaped a multitude of favorable comment from fans, reporters, and television executives. The championship game between the Baltimore Colts and the New York Giants in Yankee Stadium on December 28 was a hard-fought, entertaining contest all afternoon, but when the final gun sounded with the score tied, this match transcended any previous football game. Sudden-death overtime, on the books since 1955 for post-season action, was being played for the first time, with 64,185 paid customers and many millions of television viewers riding the fine edge of tantalizing suspense. With the rule declaring the first team to score the winner, Baltimore's touchdown after eight minutes and fifteen seconds of overtime play gave them the NFL championship, but the league itself won the most, in publicity, in fan approval, and in the television industry's realization of the gem that pro football could be on the tube.

EASTERN CONFERENCE

New York Giants—Needing to win their two final games to tie the Cleveland Browns for the Eastern crown, the Giants trailed Detroit 17-12 at the start of the fourth quarter. With the ball at mid-field, Lions punter Yale Lary faked the kick and tried to run for the first down, only to be collared short of the needed yards. Chuck Conerly then drove his offense to the end zone in five plays, and the defense protected the 19-17 lead to the end. Then came the do-or-die battle with the Browns in New York. With Jimmy Brown running 65 yards for a touchdown on the first play of the game, Cleveland led 10-3 in the fourth quarter until a Conerly TD pass tied the score late in the game. Then, with snow falling and less than a minute left in the game, Pat Summerall drove a 49-yard field goal to win the game 13-10 and force a playoff.

Cleveland Browns—While people last year said that Jimmy Brown could be the greatest runner in football history, Brown this year proved that he already was. Brown shattered Steve Van Buren's old season's rushing mark, establishing a new standard of 1,527 yards. With defenses around the league looking for a way to stop him, only the gang-tackling Giants had any success in stopping Brown and in stopping the Browns. With Milt Plum clicking on short passes and Bobby Mitchell loosening defenses with his outside running, the Browns lost only to the Giants and Lions before meeting the Giants again on the last Sunday of the season. Needing only a tie to clinch the Eastern crown, the Browns lost. In the playoff game the next week in New York, Brown could gain only 8 yards in a 10-0 defeat.

Pittsburgh Steelers—Coach Buddy Parker had won three divisional titles at Detroit with Bobby Layne as his quarterback, so Parker jumped at the chance to get Layne from the Lions two weeks into the regular season. Traded for Earl Morrall and two draft choices, Layne immedicately took over at quarterback and took the winless Steelers to a 24-3 victory over the Philadelphia Eagles. Losses to Cleveland and New York followed, but then the Steelers hit their stride. Over the last seven weeks the Steelers won six and tied one to rush into third place in the East. Tom Tracy, a powerful halfback who also came to Pittsburgh from the Lions, handled the heavy-duty running chores, while Layne quickly hooked up with rookie end Jimmy Orr to form a productive passing combination.

Washington Redskins—With his four-year record at Washington under .500, coach Joe Kuharich needed a winning season to stay on owner George Marshall's payroll. But the club he was running had added no major new talent in years and was sliding from mediocrity into the ranks of the cellar dwellers. Of their last five first draft choices, only fullback Don Bosseler was playing regularly; Steve Meilinger, Ralph Guglielmi, Ed Vereb, and Mike Sommer were either riding the bench or playing elsewhere. Marshall's policy of not signing black players also was hampering the team from getting needed new blood. Another losing season just underlined the need for new players. Marshall responded by firing Kuharich.

Chicago Cardinals—With Pop Ivy the new head coach, the Cards scored more points but kept on losing. Ivy emphasized the offense, often using a double-wing T formation which fostered a pass-oriented attack. Ollie Matson still led the club in ground gaining, but a rookie halfback, John David Crow, showed promise. At quarterback, Ivy alternated Lamar McHan and M. C. Reynolds, while first draft choice King Hill did more watching than playing. The most surprising offensive star was thirty-two-year-old Woodley Lewis, who had become the team's leading receiver after spending most of his career as a defensive back with the Rams.

Philadelphia Eagles—When Buck Shaw, the genial ex-coach of the San Francisco '49ers, took over as the Eagles' new head coach, he immediately went into the market for an experienced quarterback. He came up with a fine passer and strong leader in Norm Van Brocklin, for whom he had to send tackle Buck Lansford, defensive back Jimmy Harris, and a first draft choice to the Los Angeles Rams. Van Brocklin gave the offense a boost with his passing, finding a pair of congenial young receivers in Pete Retzlaff and swift Tommy McDonald, but he needed better blocking from his linemen before he could consistently put points on the scoreboard. The defense also needed redoing, with Jess Richardson, Bob Pellegrini, and Tom Brookshier the only regulars destined to last through 1960 with the club.

WESTERN CONFERENCE

Baltimore Colts—With Baltimore fans packing Municipal Stadium for every game and fanatically cheering their team on, the Colts stormed out to a large lead in the West by winning their first six decisions handily. But in the sixth game, a 56-0 rout of the Packers, a hard tackle by Green Bay's Johnny Symank put quarterback Johnny Unitas in the hospital with three broken ribs and a punctured lung. With Unitas out indefinitely, George Shaw took over at quarterback and threw three touchdown passes in New York, although the Giants won the game 24-21. Then the Colts shut out the Bears 17-0 and swamped the Rams 34-7, a game in which Unitas returned to action briefly. The next week, with Unitas at the helm, the Colts fought back from a 27-7 halftime deficit to beat the '49ers 35-27 and clinch the crown.

Chicago Bears—After last year's 5-7-0 record, owner George Halas threw aside his past promises to hire a younger coach and again took up the coaching reigns, saying, "There's some new stuff I have in mind that I would like to try." The Bears didn't show much new stuff, but they did carry out their assignments with the hard-hitting precision of earlier Halas teams. The defense, staffed with the likes of Bill George, Doug Atkins, and Joe Fortunato, turned in ten good performances, falling down only in early-season losses to Baltimore and Los Angeles. And even without a full recovery by injured receiver Harlon Hill, the attack showed new life and muscle in moving the ball. The Bears had a chance to pull within one game of the top by beating the Colts late in the season, but the Baltimore defense knocked the Bears out of contention by shutting them out.

Los Angeles Rams—Sid Gillman made three moves which jazzed up the Ram offense and made the team interesting to watch: He junked the two-quarterback system, he put Jon Arnett into the starting backfield, and he shifted Del Shofner from defense to offense. Gillman installed young Billy Wade as his full-time quarterback, dealing veteran Norm Van Brocklin off to the Eagles, and Wade responded with a fine season. Given a starting halfback job in addition to his kick-return duties, Arnett rocketed to stardom with his jackrabbit quickness, using his speed and moves best on end runs and on screen passes. And Shofner turned out to be a worthy successor to the retired Crazy Legs Hirsch, shifting from the defensive backfield to become one of the league's top deep receiving threats.

San Francisco '49ers—The '49ers had entertained fans for years with their wide-open offensive style, but as the decade began to reach the end of the string, so were many of the '49er players. A lifeless break-even season underlined the advancing age of Y. A. Tittle, Joe Perry, Hugh McElhenny, Billy Wilson and Leo Nomellini. Coach Frankie Albert started easing some young talent into the lineup, as John Brodie often spelled Tittle at quarterback, J.D. Smith saw action at halfback, Clyde Connor and R.C. Owens were starting receivers, and rookie Abe Woodson filled a defensive secondary spot in addition to running back kicks.

Detroit Lions—After two games of this year, the Lions closed out an era in their history by trading quarterback Bobby Layne, ring leader of the champions of the early 1950s, to the Pittsburgh Steelers. Coach George Wilson was protected at quarterback with Tobin Rote, but injuries decimated the ranks at other positions to turn the season into a dragging catastrophe. A slow start of three losses and a tie in the first four contests wiped out any dreams of another championship, and a mid-season drive for a .500 season was stymied by close losses on the last two Sundays of the season.

Green Bay Packers—Bart Starr, Jim Taylor, and Paul Hornung were in the backfield, Jim Ringo, Jerry Kramer, and Forrest Gregg held jobs in the offensive line, and Ray Nitschke, Jess Whittenton, Dan Currie, and Bill Forester played on defense. But these were not the championship Packers of Vince Lombardi that would take the league by storm in the early 1960s; these were the pitiful Packers of Ray McLean, a team that would win only one game in a brutally demoralizing season. Although Taylor, Kramer, Nitschke, and Currie were rookies, the Packer fans saw no hope at all in this abject squad, and the executive committee went hunting for a new head coach after the season.

FINAL TEAM STATISTICS

OFFENSE

	BALT.	CHI.B.	CHI.C.	CLEVE.	DET.	G.BAY	L.A.	N.Y.	PHIL.	PITT.	S.F.	WASH.
FIRST DOWNS:												
Total	253	202	219	206	195	177	209	191	222	202	237	213
by Rushing	117	95	80	127	89	76	93	93	72	77	93	111
by Passing	120	94	124	71	95	87	104	83	125	107	126	90
by Penalty	16	13	15	8	11	14	12	15	25	18	18	12
RUSHING:												
Number	456	437	366	475	364	345	345	450	334	394	359	480
Yards	2127	1770	1456	2526	1360	1421	1734	1725	1093	1521	1628	1977
Average Yards	4.7	4.1	4.0	5.3	3.7	4.1	5.0	3.8	3.3	3.9	4.5	4.1
Touchdowns	24	15	9	24	9	7	18	14	13	14	18	11
PASSING:												
Attempts	354	321	407	206	319	348	358	266	402	336	383	251
Completions	178	146	198	110	141	161	186	119	214	156	223	121
Completion Percentage	50.3	45.5	48.6	53.4	44.2	46.3	52.0	44.7	53.2	46.4	58.2	48.2
Gross Yards	2537	2021	2735	1758	2148	2118	2909	1718	2772	2895	2691	1989
Yards Lost Passing	125	210	161	177	279	298	237	113	75	143	208	293
Net Yards	2412	1811	2574	1581	1869	1820	2672	1605	2697	2752	2483	1696
Avg. Yards per Attempt (Grs)	7.2	6.3	6.7	8.5	6.7	6.1	8.1	6.5	6.9	8.6	7.0	7.9
Avg. Yards per Comp. (Gross)	14.3	13.8	13.8	16.0	15.2	11.4	15.6	14.4	13.0	18.6	12.1	16.4
Touchdowns	26	18	23	12	20	15	19	15	18	16	15	14
Interceptions	11	24	27	14	14	27	26	12	21	21	29	17
Percent Intercepted	3.1	7.5	6.6	6.8	4.4	7.8	7.3	4.5	5.2	6.3	7.6	6.8
PUNTS:												
Number	62	59	57	51	60	62	51	65	54	51	48	48
Average Distance	36.7	39.4	37.8	41.2	42.5	42.3	40.9	44.0	41.2	39.7	38.3	45.4
PUNT RETURNS:												
Number	39	38	39	39	41	33	41	42	47	45	35	32
Yards	237	156	259	318	223	179	239	168	333	301	146	143
Average Yards	6.1	4.1	6.6	8.2	5.4	5.4	5.8	4.0	7.1	6.7	4.2	4.5
Touchdowns	0	0	0	1	1	0	0	0	0	0	0	0
KICKOFF RETURNS:												
Number	34	37	61	38	39	60	43	34	45	36	39	40
Yards	864	954	1532	908	839	1309	835	700	900	774	790	891
Average Yards	25.4	25.8	25.1	23.9	21.5	21.8	19.4	20.6	20.0	21.5	20.3	22.3
Touchdowns	2	1	2	2	1	0	0	0	0	0	0	0
INTERCEPTION RETURNS:												
Number	35	22	15	16	22	13	28	21	15	24	16	16
Yards	514	221	121	285	328	174	490	294	206	248	114	191
Average Yards	14.7	10.0	8.1	17.8	14.9	13.4	17.5	14.0	13.7	10.3	7.1	11.9
Touchdowns	1	1	0	1	1	1	5	0	0	0	1	0
PENALTIES:												
Number	55	76	71	59	52	52	67	44	55	78	58	40
Yards	518	742	615	554	513	545	636	379	570	875	619	365
FUMBLES:												
Number	26	29	37	14	36	26	34	29	41	32	31	18
Number Lost	11	19	22	8	19	17	23	14	22	21	11	16
POINTS:												
Total	381	298	261	302	261	193	344	246	235	261	257	214
PAT Attempts	52	38	35	40	32	23	42	30	31	31	33	25
PAT Made	48	37	33	38	30	22	42	28	31	31	29	25
FG Attempts	14	23	17	19	23	21	25	23	14	28	21	26
FG Made	5	11	6	8	11	11	14	12	6	14	8	13
Percent FG Made	35.7	47.8	35.3	42.1	47.8	52.4	56.0	52.2	42.9	50.0	38.1	50.0
Safeties	0	0	0	0	0	0	1	1	0	1	0	0

DEFENSE

	BALT.	CHI.B.	CHI.C.	CLEVE.	DET.	G.BAY	L.A.	N.Y.	PHIL.	PITT.	S.F.	WASH.
FIRST DOWNS:												
Total	188	168	253	201	199	236	235	170	225	209	227	215
by Rushing	70	67	121	82	94	109	109	83	101	81	106	100
by Passing	106	84	114	104	95	111	110	80	100	114	106	102
by Penalty	12	17	18	15	10	16	16	7	24	14	15	13
RUSHING:												
Number	331	351	449	369	407	427	405	399	488	403	380	396
Yards	1291	1297	2133	1448	1720	2040	1777	1440	1929	1491	2038	1734
Average Yards	3.9	3.7	4.8	3.9	4.2	4.8	4.4	3.6	4.0	3.7	5.4	4.4
Touchdowns	13	12	26	6	19	24	12	7	15	14	15	13
PASSING:												
Attempts	363	327	337	312	320	336	381	311	289	334	341	300
Completions	168	153	171	162	167	175	188	142	138	173	163	153
Completion Percentage	46.3	46.8	50.7	51.9	52.2	52.1	49.3	45.7	47.8	51.8	47.8	51.0
Gross Yards	2248	2142	2793	2387	2255	2653	2303	2130	2244	2136	2218	2782
Yards Lost Passing	255	373	166	175	138	78	252	152	126	244	246	114
Net Yards	1993	1769	2627	2212	2117	2575	2051	1978	2118	1892	1972	2668
Avg. Yards per Attempt (Grs)	6.2	6.6	8.3	7.7	7.0	7.9	6.0	6.8	7.8	6.4	6.5	9.3
Avg. Yards per Comp. (Gross)	13.4	14.0	16.3	14.7	13.5	15.2	12.3	15.0	16.3	12.3	13.6	18.2
Touchdowns	9	14	18	20	15	24	21	11	22	11	25	21
Interceptions	35	22	15	16	22	13	28	21	15	24	16	16
Percent Intercepted	9.6	6.7	4.5	5.1	6.9	3.9	7.3	6.8	5.2	7.2	4.7	5.3
PUNTS:												
Number	62	73	54	55	55	42	65	56	53	62	49	42
Average Distance	44.1	37.5	41.2	42.7	40.2	41.6	37.9	41.7	43.1	42.0	40.7	36.8
PUNT RETURNS:												
Number	40	36	35	38	44	46	33	51	41	38	36	33
Yards	176	376	154	95	151	268	143	376	363	233	132	235
Average Yards	4.4	10.4	4.4	2.5	3.4	5.8	4.3	7.4	8.9	6.1	3.7	7.1
Touchdowns	1	0	0	0	0	0	0	0	1	0	0	0
KICKOFF RETURNS:												
Number	43	48	41	48	33	32	53	40	40	50	42	36
Yards	1241	1072	933	1045	683	710	1116	889	961	1115	739	792
Average Yards	28.9	22.3	22.8	21.8	20.7	22.2	21.1	22.2	24.0	22.3	17.6	22.0
Touchdowns	1	1	1	0	0	0	1	0	1	2	0	1
INTERCEPTION RETURNS:												
Number	11	24	27	14	14	27	26	12	21	21	29	17
Yards	169	380	210	134	193	371	316	123	242	330	448	270
Average Yards	15.4	15.8	7.8	9.6	13.8	13.7	12.2	10.3	11.5	15.7	15.4	15.9
Touchdowns	3	1	0	0	1	1	2	1	0	0	2	0
PENALTIES:												
Number	60	77	68	37	52	72	47	45	74	62	52	61
Yards	555	832	696	347	458	657	476	451	722	585	510	642
FUMBLES:												
Number	31	34	29	27	27	31	22	35	18	34	32	33
Number Lost	17	18	16	18	16	19	13	19	12	18	15	22
POINTS:												
Total	203	230	356	217	276	382	278	183	306	230	324	268
PAT Attempts	26	28	46	26	35	49	37	22	39	28	41	35
PAT Made	23	26	44	26	34	46	35	21	39	26	40	34
FG Attempts	17	24	25	23	19	25	21	19	23	20	17	21
FG Made	6	12	12	11	8	12	7	10	11	12	10	8
Percent FG Made	35.3	50.0	48.0	47.8	42.1	48.0	30.0	52.6	47.8	60.0	58.8	38.1
Safeties	0	0	0	1	1	1	0	0	0	0	1	0

1958 CHAMPIONSHIP GAME

December 28, at New York
(Attendance 64,185)

One for the Books

When the game began it was simply a showdown for the championship of professional football between the Baltimore Colts and New York Giants. When the game ended it became the kind of contest which inspires folklore as well as finding a special place in the history books. The action began on a Johnny Unitas to Lenny Moore 60-yard pass play. That quick drive soon ended in a Steve Myhra 27-yard field-goal attempt that was blocked by Sam Huff. Before the first quarter was over, Frank Gifford took the ball 38 yards on an end sweep to put the Giants on the Colts' 27-yard line. Pat Summerall then sent the ball 36 yards for a 3-0 Giant lead. In the second quarter Gifford fumbled on the Giants' 20, and five plays later Alan Ameche went over for the score. Several plays later, on another Gifford fumble, the Colts marched downfield, Unitas passed 15 yards to Ray Berry, and Myhra converted to make it 14-3. In the third period the Giants tallied to make the score 14-10. In the beginning of the fourth quarter Chuck Conerly fired to Gifford to put the Giants in front, after the extra point, 17-14. Then, with less than two minutes to go, Unitas moved the ball to the New York 13, and with seven seconds remaining Myhra booted the tying field goal. It was now sudden death and the Giants got the ball, but they were unable to reach the scoreboard. The Colts then moved from their own 20 and, 12 plays later, including a 33-yard pass from Unitas to Berry, reached the Giants' one-yard line, where Ameche went over at 8:15 to give the Colts the historic 23-17 victory.

SCORING

NEW YORK	3	0	7	7	0–17
BALTIMORE	0	14	0	3	6–23

First Quarter
N. Y. — Summerall, 36 yard field goal — 12:58

Second Quarter
Balt. — Ameche, 2 yard rush — 2:26
PAT – Myhra (kick)
Balt. — Berry, 15 yard pass from Unitas — 13:40
PAT – Myhra (kick)

Third Quarter
N. Y. — Triplett, 1 yard rush — 11:14
PAT – Summerall (kick)

Fourth Quarter
N.Y. — Gifford, 15 yard pass from Conerly — 0:53
PAT – Summerall (kick)
Balt. — Myhra, 20 yard field goal — 14:53

Sudden Death
Balt. — Ameche, 1 yard rush — 8:15
No PAT Attempt made

TEAM STATISTICS

N. Y.		BALT.
10	First Downs – Total	27
3	First Downs – Rushing	10
7	First Downs – Passing	17
0	First Downs – Penalty	0
6	Fumbles – Number	2
4	Fumbles – Lost Ball	2
2	Penalties – Number	3
22	Yards Penalized	15
0	Field Goals Missed	2
4	Giveaways	3
3	Takeaways	4
–1	Difference	+1

INDIVIDUAL STATISTICS

NEW YORK	No.	Yds	Avg.	BALTIMORE	No.	Yds	Avg.
RUSHING							
Gifford	12	60	5.0	Ameche	14	59	4.2
Webster	9	24	2.7	Dupre	11	30	2.7
Triplett	5	12	2.4	Unitas	4	26	6.5
Conerly	2	5	2.5	Moore	9	24	2.7
King	3	–13	–4.3		38	139	3.7
	31	88	2.8				
RECEIVING							
Gifford	3	14	4.7	Berry	12	178	14.8
Rote	2	76	38.0	Moore	5	99	19.8
Schnelker	2	63	31.5	Mutscheller	4	63	15.8
Webster	2	17	8.5	Ameche	3	14	4.7
Triplett	2	15	7.5	Dupre	2	7	3.5
McAfee	1	15	15.0		26	361	13.9
	12	200	16.7				
PUNTING							
Chandler	6		45.6	Brown	4		50.8
PUNT RETURNS							
Maynard	2	13	6.5	Taseff	2	8	4.0
Patton	1	14	14.0	Simpson	1	0	0.0
Crow	1	0	0.0		3	8	2.7
	4	27	6.8				
KICKOFF RETURNS							
Maynard	2	28	14.0	Lyle	2	38	19.0
Brown	1	0	0.0	Simpson	1	23	23.0
Triplett	Lat	18	–		3	61	20.3
	3	46	15.3				
INTERCEPTION RETURNS							
Crow	1	5	5.0	None			

PASSING

NEW YORK	Att	Comp	Comp Pct.	Yds	Int	Yds/ Att.	Yds/ Comp	Yards Lost Tackled
Conerly	14	10	71.4	187	0	13.4	18.7	3–30
Heinrich	4	2	50.0	13	0	3.3	6.5	0
	18	12	66.7	200	0	11.1	16.7	3–30
BALTIMORE								
Unitas	40	26	65.0	361	1	9.0	13.9	5–38

NEW YORK GIANTS 9-3-0 Jim Lee Howell

Scores of Each Game		
37	Chic. Cards	7
24	Philadelphia	27
21	Washington	14
6	CHIC. CARDS	23
17	PITTSBURGH	6
21	Cleveland	17
24	BALTIMORE	21
10	Pittsburgh	31
30	WASHINGTON	0
24	PHILADELPHIA	10
19	Detroit	17
13	CLEVELAND	10
	Playoff	
10	CLEVELAND	0

Use Name	Pos.	Hgt	Wgt	Age	Int	Pts
Rosey Brown	OT	6'3"	245	25		
Frank Youso	OT	6'4"	260	22		
Al Barry	OG	6'2"	230	27		
Buzz Guy	OG	6'3"	248	23		
Jon Jelacic	OG	6'3"	230	21		
Bob Mischak	OG	6'	240	25		
Jack Stroud	OG	6'1"	235	29		
Ray Wietecha	C	6'1"	225	29		
Jim Katkavage	DE	6'3"	235	23		2
Andy Robustelli	DE	6'1"	235	32		
Pat Summerall	DE	6'4"	230	28		64
Rosey Grier	DT	6'5"	275	25		
Dick Modzelewski	DT	6'	260	27		
M. L. Brackett	DE-DT	6'5"	248	25		
Sam Huff	LB	6'1"	230	23	2	
Cliff Livingston	LB	6'3"	210	28		
Harland Svare	LB	6'	215	27	1	
Bill Svoboda	LB	6'	210	31		
Lindon Crow	DB	6'1"	187	25	3	
Ed Hughes	DB	6'1"	185	30		
Carl Karilivacz	DB	6'	190	27	3	6
Jimmy Patton	DB	6'	180	26	11	
Em Tunnell	DB	6'1"	200	36	1	
Billy Lott	HB-DB	6'	195	23		
Chuck Conerly	QB	6'1"	185	34		
Tom Dublinski	QB	6'2"	208	28		
Don Heinrich	QB	6'	180	26		6
Don Chandler	HB	6'2"	205	23		
Frank Gifford	HB	6'1"	205	28		60
Don Maynard	HB	6'	178	22		
Alex Webster	HB	6'3"	210	27		36
Phil King	FB-HB	6'4"	225	22		6
Mel Triplett	FB	6'1"	215	26		6
Ken MacAfee	OE	6'2"	215	28		12
Kyle Rote	OE	6'	205	29		18
Bob Schnelker	OE	6'3"	215	28		30

Jerry Huth – Military Service

CLEVELAND BROWNS 9-3-0 Paul Brown

Scores of Each Game		
30	Los Angeles	27
45	Pittsburgh	12
35	CHIC. CARDS	28
27	PITTSBURGH	10
38	Chic. Cards	24
17	NEW YORK	21
10	DETROIT	30
20	Washington	10
28	PHILADELPHIA	14
21	WASHINGTON	14
21	Philadelphia	14
10	New York	13
	Playoff	
0	New York	10

Use Name	Pos.	Hgt	Wgt	Age	Int	Pts
Lou Groza	OT	6'3"	248	34		60
Mike McCormack	OT	6'4"	247	31		
Willie McClung	DT-OT	6'2"	260	29		
Gene Hickerson	OG	6'3"	242	23		
Jim Ray Smith	OG	6'3"	242	27		
Chuck Noll	C-OG	6'1"	224	26		
Art Hunter	C	6'4"	242	25		
Bill Quinlan	DE	6'3"	250	26		
Paul Wiggin	DE	6'3"	237	24		
Willie Davis	OT-DE	6'3"	240	25		
Con Colo	DT	6'3"	254	33		
Bob Gain	DT	6'3"	260	30		
Henry Jordan	DT	6'3"	247	23		
Tom Catlin	LB	6'1"	213	27		
Vince Costello	LB	6'	224	26		
Galen Fiss	LB	6'	227	28		
Walt Michaels	LB	6'	230	29		
Kenny Konz	DB	5'10"	187	30	4	6
Warren Lahr	DB	5'11"	192	34	1	
Don Paul	DB	6'	192	32	4	
Jim Shofner	DB	6'2"	196	22	1	
Junior Wren	DB	6'	192	28	3	
Bobby Freeman	HB-DB	6'1"	205	25	3	
Jim Ninowski	QB	6'1"	210	22		
Milt Plum	QB	6'1"	205	24		26
Leroy Bolden	HB	5'8"	170	25		6
Lew Carpenter	HB	6'1"	210	26		12
Bobby Mitchell	HB	6'	188	23		36
Jimmy Brown	FB	6'2"	228	22		108
Ed Modzelewski	FB	6'	222	29		
Ray Renfro	HB-FL	6'1"	190	27		36
Darrell Brewster	OE	6'3"	210	28		6
Preston Carpenter	OE	6'2"	192	24		6
Frank Clarke	OE	6'	207	25		
Dick Deschaine	K	6'	210	28		

PITTSBURGH STEELERS 7-4-1 Buddy Parker

Scores of Each Game		
20	San Francisco	23
12	CLEVELAND	45
24	PHILADELPHIA	3
10	Cleveland	27
6	New York	17
24	WASHINGTON	16
31	Philadelphia	24
31	NEW YORK	10
27	Chic. Cards	20
24	CHIC. BEARS	10
14	Washington	14
38	CHIC. CARDS	21

Use Name	Pos.	Hgt	Wgt	Age	Int	Pts
Darrell Dess	OT	6'	235	22		
Frank Varrichione	OT	6'1"	230	26		
Ted Karras	LB-OT	6'1"	235	25		
Billy Krisher	OG	6'1"	230	22		
John Nisby	OG	6'1"	230	25		
Mike Sandusky	OG	6'	230	25		
Ed Beatty	C	6'3"	225	26		
Billy Ray Smith	DE	6'4"	230	23		
George Tarasovic	DE	6'4"	245	29		
Joe Krupa	DT	6'2"	225	25		
Joe Lewis	DT	6'2"	260	23	1	
Ernie Stautner	DE-DT	6'1"	230	33		2
Dick Campbell	LB	6'1"	225	22	1	
Dale Dodrill	LB	6'1"	215	33	1	
Bob Dougherty	LB	6'	235	24		
Dick Lasse	LB	6'2"	220	22		
John Reger	LB	6'	230	27	1	
Dick Alban	DB	6'	195	29	5	
Jack Butler	DB	6'	195	30	9	
Dean Derby	DB	6'	185	24	4	
Gary Glick	DB	6'2"	190	27	2	6
Richie McCabe	DB	6'1"	185	24		
Len Dawson	QB	6'	180	24		
Bobby Layne (from DET)	QB	6'1"	208	31		19
Dick Christy	HB	5'10"	180	22		
Billy Reynolds	HB	5'10"	200	26		6
Tom Tracy	HB	5'9"	205	26		54
Leo Elter	FB	5'10"	205	29		12
Larry Krutko	FB	6'	220	23		
Tank Younger	FB	6'3"	230	30		18
Don Bishop	HB-FL	6'2"	210	23		
Joe Evans	OE	6'4"	205	22		
Dick Lucas	OE	6'2"	210	24		
Jack McClairen	OE	6'4"	210	27		6
Jimmy Orr	OE	5'11"	195	22		42
Ray Mathews	HB-OE	6'	195	29		24
Tom Miner	K	6'4"	235	28		73

WASHINGTON REDSKINS 4-7-1 Joe Kuharich

Scores of Each Game		
24	Philadelphia	14
10	Chic. Cards	37
14	NEW YORK	21
37	GREEN BAY	21
10	Baltimore	35
16	Pittsburgh	24
45	CHIC. CARDS	31
10	CLEVELAND	20
0	New York	30
14	Cleveland	21
14	PITTSBURGH	14
20	PHILADELPHIA	0

Use Name	Pos.	Hgt	Wgt	Age	Int	Pts
Don Boll	OT	6'2"	272	31		
Ray Lemek	OT	6'	237	24		
Will Renfro	DT-OT	6'5"	240	26		
Dick Stanfel	OG	6'3"	230	31		
Red Stephens	OG	6'	232	28		
Ed Voytek	OG	6'2"	240	23		
Jim Schrader	C	6'2"	236	26		
Johnny Allen	LB-C	6'2"	227	26		
Gene Brito	DE	6'1"	230	33		
Bob Dee	DE	6'3"	230	25		
Chet Ostrowski	DT-DE	6'1"	235	28		
Jim Weatherall	DT	6'4"	245	28		
Johnny Miller	OT-DT	6'5"	250	24		
Charlie Brueckman	LB	6'2"	220	22		
Chuck Drazenovich	LB	6'1"	230	31	2	
Ralph Felton	LB	5'11"	210	26		
Bill Fulcher	LB	6'	200	24		
Frank Kuchta	LB	6'2"	220	22		
Gene Cichowski	DB	6'	195	24		
Dick Lynch	DB	6'1"	200	22	2	
Doyle Nix	DB	6'1"	188	25	3	
Mike Sommer	DB	5'11"	187	23		
Les Walters	DB	6'	185	21	1	
Dick James	HB-DB	5'9"	180	24	4	6
Scooter Scudero	HB-DB	5'10"	174	28	2	
Rudy Bukich (to Chi B)	QB	6'1"	200	27		
Ralph Guglielmi	QB	6'1"	195	25		
Eddie LeBaron	QB	5'9"	165	28		
Jim Podoley	HB	6'2"	200	25		24
Ed Sutton	HB	6'1"	207	23		18
Sid Watson	HB	5'11"	194	25		6
Bert Zagers	DB-HB	5'10"	185	25	2	6
Don Bosseler	FB	6'1"	207	22		24
Johnny Olszewski	FB	5'11"	202	27		12
Bill Anderson	OE	6'3"	195	22		12
Tom Braatz (from LA)	OE	6'1"	215	25		
Johnny Carson	OE	6'3"	200	28		12
Joe Walton	OE	5'11"	205	23		30
Sam Baker	K	6'2"	217	26		64

John Paluck – Military Service

CHICAGO CARDINALS 2-9-1 Pop Ivy

Scores of Each Game		
7	NEW YORK	37
37	WASHINGTON	10
28	Cleveland	35
23	New York	6
24	CLEVELAND	38
21	PHILADELPHIA	21
31	Washington	45
21	Philadelphia	49
20	PITTSBURGH	27
14	LOS ANGELES	20
14	Chic. Bears	30
21	Pittsburgh	38

Use Name	Pos.	Hgt	Wgt	Age	Int	Pts
Ed Cook	OT	6'2"	250	26		
Bob Cross	OT	6'4"	250	27		
Jim McCusker	OT	6'2"	245	22		
Bob Konovsky	OG	6'2"	245	24		
Dale Meinert	OT-OG	6'4"	218	25		
Ed Husmann	DE-LB-OG	6'	230	27		
Don Gillis	C	6'3"	240	23		
Jim Taylor	LB-C	6'2"	230	24	1	
Leo Sugar	DE	6'1"	210	29		
Luke Owens	DT-DE	6'2"	255	25		
Ed Culpepper	DT	6'1"	255	24		
Chuck Ulrich	DT	6'4"	250	27		
Carl Brettschneider	LB	6'1"	220	26		
Doug Eggers	LB	6'	215	28		
Ken Gray	LB	6'2"	235	22		
Jack Patera	LB	6'1"	225	26		
Jerry Tubbs (to SF)	LB	6'2"	216	23		
Chuck Weber	LB	6'1"	225	29		
Bobby Joe Conrad	DB	6'	180	23	4	51
Bobby Gordon	DB	6'	195	22	2	
Charlie Jackson	DB	5'11"	180	22	1	
Lowell Lander	DB	6'	195	25		
Night Train Lane	DB	6'1"	190	30	2	
Dick Nolan	DB	6'1"	185	26	5	
King Hill	QB	6'3"	207	22		
Lamar McHan	QB	6'1"	200	26		6
M. C. Reynolds	QB	6'	190	23		
Joe Childress	HB	6'	200	24		24
Ollie Matson	HB	6'2"	210	28		60
Jimmy Sears	HB	5'11"	185	27		12
Bobby Watkins	HB	5'10"	195	26		6
Mal Hammack	FB	6'2"	205	25		6
Dean Philpott	FB	6'	200	23		
John David Crow	HB-FB	6'2"	215	23		36
Max Boydston	OE	6'2"	207	25		6
Woodley Lewis	OE	6'	195	33		24
Gern Nagler	OE	6'2"	190	25		30

Jimmy Hill – Arm Injury

John Roach – Military Service
John Dittrich – Military Service

PHILADELPHIA EAGLES 2-9-1 Buck Shaw

Scores of Each Game		
14	WASHINGTON	24
27	NEW YORK	24
3	Pittsburgh	24
24	SAN FRANCISCO	30
35	Green Bay	38
21	Chic. Cards	21
24	PITTSBURGH	31
49	CHIC. CARDS	21
14	Cleveland	28
10	New York	24
14	CLEVELAND	21
0	Washington	20

Use Name	Pos.	Hgt	Wgt	Age	Int	Pts
Proverb Jacobs	OT	6'4"	255	23		
Lum Snyder	OT	6'5"	230	28		
Len Szafaryn	OT	6'2"	230	30		
Harold Bradley	OG	6'2"	230	29		
Ken Huxhold	OG	6'1"	235	29		
Galen Laack*	OG	6'	230	26		
Chuck Bednarik	C	6'3"	235	33		
John Simerson (to PIT)	C	6'3"	258	23		
Marion Campbell	DE	6'3"	255	29		
Ed Cooke (from Chi B)	DE	6'4"	238	23		
Ed Meadows	DE	6'2"	225	26		
Ed Khayat	DT	6'3"	225	23		
Don Owens	DT	6'5"	250	26		
Jess Richardson	DT	6'2"	272	28		
Sid Youngelman	DT	6'3"	255	26		
Volney Peters	DE-DT	6'4"	245	30		
Bill Koman	LB	6'2"	235	24	1	
Bob Pellegrini	LB	6'2"	225	23	4	
Tom Scott	LB	6'2"	220	28	2	
Tom Louderback	OG-C-LB	6'2"	234	24		
Eddie Bell	DB	6'1"	212	27	2	
Tom Brookshier	DB	6'	198	26	1	
Jerry Norton	DB	5'11"	195	28	1	
Lee Riley	DB	6'1"	190	26	1	
Bob Hudson	LB-DB	6'4"	230	28	1	
Sonny Jurgensen	QB	5'11"	200	24		
Norm Van Brocklin	QB	6'1"	202	32		6
Billy Barnes	HB	5'11"	202	23		42
Billy Wells	HB	5'9"	178	26		6
Brad Myers	DB-OE-HB	6'1"	195	28		
Clarence Peaks	FB	6'1"	218	22		30
Walt Kowalczyk	DB-FB	6'	205	23	1	6
Tommy McDonald	FL	5'10"	182	24		54
Pete Retzlaff	FL-OE	6'1"	210	27		12
Dick Bielski	OE	6'1"	218	26		6
Gene Mitcham	OE	6'2"	206	26		6
Andy Nacrelli	OE	6'1"	190	25		
Bobby Walston	OE	6'	190	29		67

Ken Keller – Military Service
Ton Saidock – Military Service

*Laack – died 1/1/59 – Auto Accident

NEW YORK GIANTS

RUSHING

Last Name	No.	Yds	Avg	TD
Gifford	115	468	4.1	8
Triplett	118	466	3.9	1
Webster	100	398	4.0	3
King	83	316	3.8	1
Maynard	12	45	3.8	0
Lott	4	30	7.5	0
Chandler	1	15	15.0	0
Heinrich	5	4	0.8	1
Conerly	12	−17	−1.4	0

RECEIVING

Last Name	No.	Yds	Avg	TD
Gifford	29	330	11	2
Webster	25	279	11	3
Schnelker	24	460	19	5
Rote	12	244	20	3
King	11	132	12	0
Triplett	7	110	16	0
Maynard	5	84	17	0
MacAfee	5	52	10	2
Mischak	1	27	27	0

PUNT RETURNS

Last Name	No.	Yds	Avg	TD
Maynard	24	117	5	0
Crow	11	46	4	0
Patton	1	5	5	0
Tunnell	6	0	0	0

KICKOFF RETURNS

Last Name	No.	Yds	Avg	TD
Maynard	11	284	26	0
King	13	279	21	0
Lott	5	78	16	0
Triplett	4	59	15	0
Brown	1	0	0	0

PASSING – PUNTING – KICKING

PASSING	Att	Comp	%	Yds	Yd/Att	TD	Int–%	RK
Conerly	184	88	48	1199	6.0	10	9– 5	11
Heinrich	68	26	38	369	5.4	4	2– 3	
Gifford	10	3	30	109	10.9	1	1– 10	
Dublinski	3	1	33	14	4.7	0	0– 0	
Chandler	1	1	100	27	27.0	0	0– 0	

PUNTING	No	Avg
Chandler	65	44.0

KICKING	XP	Att	%	FG	Att	%
Summerall	28	30	93	12	23	52

CLEVELAND BROWNS

RUSHING

Last Name	No.	Yds	Avg	TD
Brown	**257**	**1527**	5.9	**17**
Mitchell	80	500	6.3	1
L. Carpenter	73	308	4.2	2
Plum	37	107	2.8	4
Bolden	15	55	3.7	0
Renfro	3	17	5.7	0
Modzelewski	3	8	2.7	0
P. Carpenter	3	2	0.7	0
Freeman	2	1	0.5	0
Ninowski	1	1	0.5	0

RECEIVING

Last Name	No.	Yds	Avg	TD
P. Carpenter	29	474	16	1
Renfro	24	573	24	6
Brewster	16	294	18	1
Brown	16	138	9	1
Mitchell	16	131	8	3
L. Carpenter	5	47	9	0
Clarke	3	91	30	0
Modzelewski	1	10	10	0

PUNT RETURNS

Last Name	No.	Yds	Avg	TD
Mitchell	14	165	9	**1**
Konz	18	143	8	0
Shofner	4	10	3	0
Paul	2	0	0	0
Wren	1	0	0	0

KICKOFF RETURNS

Last Name	No.	Yds	Avg	TD
Mitchell	18	454	25	1
Bolden	14	362	26	1
Brown	3	74	25	0
L. Carpenter	1	18	18	0
McClung	1	0	0	0
Paul	1	0	0	0

PASSING – PUNTING – KICKING

PASSING	Att	Comp	%	Yds	Yd/Att	TD	Int–%	RK
Plum	189	102	54	1619	8.6	11	11– 6	2
Ninowski	17	8	47	139	8.2	1	3– 18	

PUNTING	No	Avg
Deschaine	50	41.3
Wren	1	38.0

KICKING	XP	Att	%	FG	Att	%
Groza	36	38	94	8	19	42
Plum	2	2	100	0	0	0

PITTSBURGH STEELERS

RUSHING

Last Name	No.	Yds	Avg	TD
Tracy	169	714	4.2	5
Younger	88	344	3.9	3
Layne	40	154	3.9	3
Elter	37	104	2.8	2
Christy	38	101	2.7	0
Reynolds	10	29	2.9	1
Mathews	4	24	6.0	0
Orr	1	8	8.0	0
Krutko	4	6	1.5	0
Dawson	2	−1	−0.5	0

RECEIVING

Last Name	No.	Yds	Avg	TD
Orr	33	910	**28**	7
Tracy	32	535	17	4
McClairen	29	491	17	1
Mathews	25	525	21	4
Younger	16	188	12	0
Christy	7	73	10	0
Elter	6	68	11	0
Lucas	4	47	12	0
Bishop	3	57	19	0
Reynolds	1	1	1	0

PUNT RETURNS

Last Name	No.	Yds	Avg	TD
Christy	17	153	9	0
Reynolds	25	143	6	0
Dodrill	1	5	5	0
Glick	2	0	0	0

KICKOFF RETURNS

Last Name	No.	Yds	Avg	TD
Christy	16	384	24	0
Reynolds	15	346	23	0
Varrichione	3	38	13	0
Karras	1	6	6	0
McClairen	1	0	0	0

PASSING – PUNTING – KICKING

PASSING	Att	Comp	%	Yds	Yd/Att	TD	Int–%	RK
Layne	294	145	49	2510	8.5	14	12– 4	2
Tracy	16	6	38	270	16.9	2	2– 12	
Dawson	6	1	17	11	1.8	0	2– 33	

PUNTING	No	Avg
Orr	61	39.7

KICKING	XP	Att	%	FG	Att	%
Miner	31	31	100	**14**	**28**	50
Layne	1	3	33	0	0	0

WASHINGTON REDSKINS

RUSHING

Last Name	No.	Yds	Avg	TD
Olszewski	98	505	5.2	2
Bosseler	109	475	4.4	4
Sutton	93	335	3.6	3
Podoley	48	169	3.5	0
Watson	46	166	3.6	0
James	24	88	3.7	1
Zagers	27	82	3.0	1
Guglielmi	17	74	4.4	0
Scudero	5	30	6.0	0
LeBaron	12	30	2.5	0
Bukich	2	16	8.0	0

RECEIVING

Last Name	No.	Yds	Avg	TD
Walton	32	532	17	5
Anderson	18	396	22	2
Podoley	16	381	24	4
Carson	14	244	17	2
Bosseler	14	101	7	0
Olszewski	11	102	9	0
Sutton	6	112	19	0
Watson	5	38	8	1
Zagers	3	50	17	0
James	2	33	17	0

PUNT RETURNS

Last Name	No.	Yds	Avg	TD
Zagers	7	41	6	0
James	6	37	6	0
Scudero	8	27	3	0
Watson	4	21	5	0
Nix	1	12	12	0
Sommer	3	3	1	0
Bosseler	1	2	2	0
Olszewski	2	0	0	0

KICKOFF RETURNS

Last Name	No.	Yds	Avg	TD
Watson	19	443	23	0
James	9	212	24	0
Scudero	4	122	31	0
Sommer	4	77	19	0
Miller	1	15	15	0
Renfro	1	12	12	0
Braatz	1	8	8	0
Olszewski	1	2	2	0

PASSING – PUNTING – KICKING

PASSING	Att	Comp	%	Yds	Yd/Att	TD	Int–%	RK
LeBaron	145	79	54	1365	**9.4**	11	10– 7	5
Guglielmi	81	34	42	458	5.7	2	6– 7	
Bukich	23	8	35	166	7.2	1	1– 4	
Sutton	3	0	0	0	0.0	0	0– 0	

PUNTING	No	Avg
Baker	48	**45.4**

KICKING	XP	Att	%	FG	Att	%
Baker	25	25	100	13	26	50

CHICAGO CARDINALS

RUSHING

Last Name	No.	Yds	Avg	TD
Matson	129	505	3.9	5
Reynolds	48	252	5.3	0
Crow	52	221	4.3	2
Childress	50	170	3.4	0
Hammack	35	121	3.5	1
McHan	17	65	3.8	1
Sears	17	51	3.0	0
Philpott	12	44	3.7	0
Watkins	3	17	5.7	0
Gordon	2	10	5.0	0
Hill	1	0	0.0	0

RECEIVING

Last Name	No.	Yds	Avg	TD
Lewis	46	690	15	4
Nagler	36	469	13	5
Childress	35	406	12	4
Matson	33	465	14	3
Crow	20	362	18	3
Sears	13	187	14	2
Watkins	4	62	16	1
Philpott	4	30	8	0
Boydston	3	42	14	1
Hammack	3	11	4	0
Lane	1	10	10	0
McHan	0	1	0	0

PUNT RETURNS

Last Name	No.	Yds	Avg	TD
Conrad	19	129	7	0
Sears	14	94	7	0
Lewis	2	12	6	0
Gordon	1	12	12	0
Jackson	2	10	5	0
Nolan	1	2	2	0

KICKOFF RETURNS

Last Name	No.	Yds	Avg	TD
Sears	**32**	**756**	24	0
Matson	14	497	**36**	**2**
Crow	6	145	24	0
Lewis	2	46	23	0
Conrad	1	33	33	0
Watkins	1	24	24	0
Philpott	3	18	6	0
Tubbs	1	11	11	0
Weber	1	2	2	0

PASSING – PUNTING – KICKING

PASSING	Att	Comp	%	Yds	Yd/Att	TD	Int–%	RK
McHan	198	91	46	1291	6.5	12	13– 7	11
Reynolds	195	105	54	1422	7.3	11	11– 6	
Hill	9	1	11	18	2.0	0	2– 22	
Matson	2	1	50	4	2.0	0	0– 0	
Childress	1	0	0	0	0.0	0	0– 0	
Crow	1	0	0	0	0.0	0	1–100	
Sears	1	0	0	0	0.0	0	0– 0	

PUNTING	No	Avg
Gordon	55	38.0
McHan	2	32.5

KICKING	XP	Att	%	FG	Att	%
Conrad	33	35	94	6	17	35

PHILADELPHIA EAGLES

RUSHING

Last Name	No.	Yds	Avg	TD
Barnes	156	551	3.5	7
Peaks	115	386	3.4	3
Wells	24	92	3.8	1
Kowalczyk	17	43	2.5	1
Myers	9	23	2.6	0
Van Brocklin	8	5	0.6	1
Jurgensen	1	1	1.0	0
Retzlaff	1	−4	−4.0	0
McDonald	3	−4	−1.3	0

RECEIVING

Last Name	No.	Yds	Avg	TD
Retzlaff	**56**	766	14	2
Barnes	35	423	12	0
McDonald	29	603	21	9
Peaks	29	248	9	2
Bielski	23	234	10	1
Walston	21	298	14	3
Kowalczyk	8	72	9	0
Wells	4	49	12	0
Myers	4	25	6	0
Mitcham	3	39	13	1
Nacrelli	2	15	8	0

PUNT RETURNS

Last Name	No.	Yds	Avg	TD
Wells	19	158	8	0
McDonald	18	135	8	0
Riley	7	27	4	0
Norton	1	8	8	0
Koman	1	5	5	0

KICKOFF RETURNS

Last Name	No.	Yds	Avg	TD
Wells	14	336	24	0
McDonald	14	262	19	0
Riley	9	205	23	0
Bielski	5	66	13	0
Jacobs	2	24	12	0
Koman	1	7	7	0

PASSING – PUNTING – KICKING

PASSING	Att	Comp	%	Yds	Yd/Att	TD	Int–%	RK
Van Brocklin	**374**	**198**	53	2409	6.4	15	20– 5	7
Jurgensen	22	12	55	259	11.8	0	1– 5	
Barnes	6	4	67	104	17.3	3	0– 0	

PUNTING	No	Avg
Van Brocklin	54	41.2

KICKING	XP	Att	%	FG	Att	%
Walston	31	31	100	6	14	43

1958 N.F.L. — Western Conference

BALTIMORE COLTS 9-3-0 Weeb Ewbank

Scores of Each Game		
28	DETROIT	15
51	CHIC. BEARS	38
24	Green Bay	17
40	Detroit	14
35	WASHINGTON	10
56	GREEN BAY	0
21	New York	24
17	Chic. Bears	0
34	LOS ANGELES	7
35	SAN FRANCISCO	27
28	Los Angeles	30
12	San Francisco	21

Use Name	Pos.	Hgt	Wgt	Age	Int	Pts
Jim Parker	OT	6'3"	270	24		
Sherman Plunkett	OT	6'4"	265	24		
George Preas	OT	6'2"	245	26		
Alex Sandusky	OG	6'1"	235	26		
Art Spinney	OG	6'	230	31		
Fuzzy Thurston	OG	6'1"	245	25		
Buzz Nutter	C	6'4"	235	27		
Ordell Braase	DE	6'4"	235	26		
Don Joyce	DE	6'3"	255	28		
Gino Marchetti	DE	6'4"	240	32		
Art Donovan	DT	6'2"	270	33		
Big Daddy Lipscomb	DT	6'6"	288	27		
Ray Krouse	DE-DT	6'3"	275	31		
Bill Pellington	LB	6'2"	230	29	4	
Leo Sanford	LB	6'1"	230	29	1	
Don Shinnick	LB	6'	230	23	3	
Steve Myhra	OG-LB	6'1"	235	24		60
Dick Szymanski	C-LB	6'3"	230	26		
Bert Rechichar	OE-LB	6'1"	210	28		9
Milt Davis	DB	6'1"	190	29	4	
Andy Nelson	DB	6'1"	180	25	8	6
Johnny Sample	DB	6'1"	203	21		
Jackie Simpson	DB	5'10"	180	24		
Carl Taseff	DB	5'11"	190	29	7	
Ray Brown	QB-DB	6'2"	195	22	8	
Art DeCarlo	OE-DB	6'2"	196	28		
Dick Horn	QB	6'1"	195	28		
George Shaw	QB	6'1"	190	25		6
Johnny Unitas	QB	6'1"	190	25		18
Jack Call	HB	6'1"	200	23		
L. G. Dupre	HB	5'11"	190	26		18
Lenny Moore	HB	6'1"	190	25		84
Avatus Stone	HB	6'1"	195	27		
Lenny Lyles	DB-HB	6'2"	198	22		24
Alan Ameche	FB	6'	220	25		54
Billy Pricer	FB	5'10"	210	23		6
Ray Berry	OE	6'2"	190	25		54
Jim Mutscheller	OE	6'1"	215	28		42

CHICAGO BEARS 8-4-0 George Halas

Scores of Each Game		
34	Green Bay	20
38	Baltimore	51
28	SAN FRANCISCO	6
31	LOS ANGELES	10
27	San Francisco	14
35	Los Angeles	41
24	GREEN BAY	10
0	BALTIMORE	17
20	Detroit	7
10	Pittsburgh	24
30	CHIC. CARDS	14
21	DETROIT	16

Use Name	Pos.	Hgt	Wgt	Age	Int	Pts
Bob Kilcullen	OT	6'3"	245	22		
Dick Klein	OT	6'4"	255	24		
Herm Lee	OT	6'4"	248	27		
Abe Gibron	OG	5'11"	250	32		
Don Healy	OG	6'3"	250	22		
Stan Jones	OG	6'1"	250	27		
John Mellekas	C	6'3"	255	25		
Larry Strickland	C	6'4"	245	27		
Doug Atkins	DE	6'8"	255	28		
Jack Hoffman	DE	6'5"	235	29	1	
Bill Bishop	DT	6'4"	248	27		6
Earl Leggett	DT	6'3"	250	24		
Fred Williams	DT	6'4"	248	28		
Joe Fortunato	LB	6'	225	28	1	
Bill George	LB	6'2"	235	27	1	1
Wayne Hansen	LB	6'2"	228	30	1	
Chuck Howley	LB	6'3"	228	22	1	
Bill Raehnelt	LB	6'1"	225	22		
Erich Barnes	DB	6'2"	198	23	4	12
Jack Johnson	DB	6'3"	198	24	1	
Charlie Sumner	DB	6'1"	195	28	6	6
Stan Wallace	DB	6'3"	205	26	3	
Vic Zucco	DB	6'	187	23	3	
Rocky Ryan (from PHI)	OE-DB	6'1"	202	26	1	
George Blanda	QB	6'1"	208	30		69
Zeke Bratkowski	QB	6'2"	203	26		
Ed Brown	QB	6'2"	208	29		18
Willie Galimore	HB	6'1"	187	23		72
Johnny Morris	HB	5'10"	180	23		12
J. C. Caroline	DB-HB	6'1"	190	25		6
Rick Casares	FB	6'2"	225	27		18
Merrill Douglas	HB-FB	6'	204	22		
Ralph Anderson	OE	6'4"	220	21		6
Bob Carey	OE	6'5"	224	30		
Harlon Hill	OE	6'3"	200	26		18
Bob Jewett	OE	6'2"	198	24		6
Bill McColl	OE	6'4"	230	28		48

Jim Dooley – Broken Ankle

LOS ANGELES RAMS 8-4-0 Sid Gillman

Scores of Each Game		
27	CLEVELAND	30
33	San Francisco	3
42	Detroit	28
10	Chic. Bears	31
24	DETROIT	41
41	CHIC. BEARS	35
56	SAN FRANCISCO	7
20	Green Bay	7
7	Baltimore	34
20	Chic. Cards	14
30	BALTIMORE	28
34	GREEN BAY	20

Use Name	Pos.	Hgt	Wgt	Age	Int	Pts
John Baker	OT	6'6"	290	23		
Charlie Bradshaw	OT	6'6"	240	22		
Bob Fry	OT	6'4"	238	27		
Buck Lansford	OG	6'2"	235	25		
Duane Putnam	OG	6'	230	30		
John Houser	C-OG	6'3"	237	22		
John Morrow	C	6'3"	235	25		
Glenn Holtzman	DE	6'3"	254	28		2
Lou Michaels	DE	6'2"	238	22	2	6
Roy Wilkins	LB-DE	6'3"	220	24		
Frank Fuller	DT	6'4"	243	29		
George Strugar	DT	6'5"	258	23		
Ken Panfil	OT-DT	6'6"	268	27		
Dick Daugherty	LB	6'1"	223	29	1	6
Bill Jobko	LB	6'2"	220	22		
Jack Pardee	LB	6'2"	215	22		
Les Richter	LB	6'3"	248	27	3	
Alex Bravo	DB	6'	190	26		
Fred Bruney	DB	5'10"	180	27		
Don Burroughs	DB	6'4"	186	27	7	
Jimmy Harris	DB	6'1"	176	23	4	
Floyd Iglehart	DB	6'4"	197	23		
Jim Jones	DB	6'1"	196	22		
Jack Morris	DB	6'	188	26	6	6
Will Sherman	DB	6'2"	197	29	5	12
Clendon Thomas	DB	6'2"	190	21		
Frank Ryan	QB	6'3"	190	22		
Billy Wade	QB	6'2"	203	27		12
Jon Arnett	HB	5'11"	194	23		42
Ron Waller	HB	5'11"	180	25		
Tom Wilson	HB	6'	204	25		60
Joe Marconi	FB	6'2"	230	24		6
Leon Clarke	OE	6'4"	230	25		30
Jim Phillips	OE	6'1"	200	21		12
Del Shofner	OE	6'3"	185	22		48
Lamar Lundy	DE-OE	6'7"	235	23		18
Paige Cothren	K	5'11"	195	23		84

SAN FRANCISCO FORTY NINERS 6-6-0 Frankie Albert

Scores of Each Game		
23	PITTSBURGH	20
3	LOS ANGELES	33
6	Chic. Bears	28
30	Philadelphia	24
14	CHIC. BEARS	27
24	DETROIT	21
7	Los Angeles	56
21	Detroit	35
33	Green Bay	12
27	Baltimore	35
48	GREEN BAY	21
21	BALTIMORE	12

Use Name	Pos.	Hgt	Wgt	Age	Int	Pts
John Gonzaga	OT	6'3"	245	25		
Bob St. Clair	OT	6'9"	265	27		
John Thomas	OT	6'4"	237	23		
Bruce Bosley	OG	6'2"	244	24		
Ted Connolly	OG	6'3"	245	26		
Lou Palatella	OG	6'2"	230	25		
John Wittenborn	OG	6'2"	233	22		
Frank Morze	C	6'4"	270	24		
Ed Henke	DE	6'3"	230	30		
Bob Toneff	DE	6'3"	260	28	1	
Walt Yowarsky	DE	6'2"	235	30		
Bill Herchman	DT	6'2"	245	25		
Leo Nomellini	DT	6'3"	255	33		
Matt Hazeltine	LB	6'1"	215	25	3	6
Marv Matuszak (to GB)	LB	6'3"	235	27	1	
Dennit Morris	LB	6'1"	230	22		
Karl Rubke	C-LB	6'4"	240	22		
Billy Atkins	DB	6'1"	200	23	1	
Jerry Mertens	DB	6'	185	22	2	
Dick Moegle	DB	6'	190	24		
Jimmy Ridlon	DB	6'1"	180	23	4	
Bill Stits	DB	6'	195	27	3	
Abe Woodson	HB-DB	5'11"	188	23	1	
John Brodie	QB	6'1"	195	23		6
Y. A. Tittle	QB	6'	195	31		12
Hugh McElhenny	HB	6'1"	198	29		48
Jim Pace	HB	6'	195	22		12
Tony Teresa	HB	5'9"	190	23		
J. D. Smith	FB-HB	6'1"	210	25		18
Gene Babb	FB	6'3"	215	23		
Joe Perry	FB	6'	197	31		30
R. C. Owens	OE-FL	6'3"	207	23		6
Bill Jessup	OE-FL	6'1"	195	29		6
Clyde Conner	OE	6'2"	202	25		30
Fred Dugan	OE	6'3"	195	24		
Gordie Soltau	OE	6'2"	195	33		53
Billy Wilson	OE	6'3"	190	31		30

DETROIT LIONS 4-7-1 George Wilson

Scores of Each Game		
15	Baltimore	28
13	Green Bay	13
28	LOS ANGELES	42
14	BALTIMORE	40
41	Los Angeles	24
21	San Francisco	24
30	Cleveland	10
35	SAN FRANCISCO	21
7	CHIC. BEARS	20
24	GREEN BAY	14
17	NEW YORK	19
16	Chic. Bears	21

Use Name	Pos.	Hgt	Wgt	Age	Int	Pts
Ken Russell	OT	6'3"	250	22		
Lou Creekmur	OG-OT	6'4"	254	31		
Stan Campbell	OG	6'	228	28		
Doug Hogland (from Chi C)	OG	6'3"	240	27		
Karl Koepfer	OG	6'2"	230	22		
Harley Sewell	OG	6'1"	233	27		
Charlie Ane	OT-C	6'2"	260	27		
Bill Glass	OT-C	6'5"	236	22		
Gene Cronin	DE	6'2"	230	25		
Darris McCord	DE	6'4"	240	25		
Jerry Perry	DT-DE	6'4"	235	27		13
Alex Karras	DT	6'2"	254	22		
Gil Mains	DT	6'2"	250	28		
Bob Miller	DT	6'3"	257	28		
Bob Long	LB	6'3"	234	24	2	
Jim Martin	LB	6'2"	230	34		49
Joe Schmidt	LB	6'1"	217	26	6	
Wayne Walker	LB	6'2"	220	21	1	12
Roger Zatkoff	LB	6'2"	217	27		
Terry Barr	DB	6'	190	23	3	6
Jack Christiansen	DB	6'1"	196	29	1	
Jim David	DB	5'11"	185	31	3	
Gary Lowe	DB	5'11"	195	24	2	
Dave Whitsell	DB	6'	184	22	1	
Yale Lary	DB	6'	190	27	3	6
Earl Morrall (from PIT)	QB	6'1"	200	24		
Tobin Rote	QB	6'3"	212	30		18
Hopalong Cassady	HB	5'10"	180	24		42
Gene Gedman	HB	5'11"	196	26		42
Dan Lewis	HB	6'1"	197	22		
Ken Webb	FB-HB	5'11"	208	23		18
John Henry Johnson	FB	6'2"	213	28		
Jim Doran	OE	6'2"	200	30		24
Jim Gibbons	OE	6'2"	215	22		12
Dave Middleton	OE	6'1"	195	25		18
Perry Richards	OE	6'2"	205	24		
Tom Rychlec	OE	6'3"	215	24		

John Gordy – Voluntarily Retired
Steve Junker – Knee Injury

Jerry Reichow – Knee Injury

GREEN BAY PACKERS 1-10-1 Ray McLean

Scores of Each Game		
20	CHIC. BEARS	34
13	DETROIT	13
17	BALTIMORE	24
21	Washington	37
38	PHILADELPHIA	35
0	Baltimore	56
10	Chic. Bears	24
7	LOS ANGELES	20
12	SAN FRANCISCO	33
14	Detroit	24
21	San Francisco	48
20	Los Angeles	34

Use Name	Pos.	Hgt	Wgt	Age	Int	Pts
Norm Masters	OT	6'2"	250	25		
Ollie Spencer	OT	6'2"	245	27		
Forrest Gregg	OG-DT-OT	6'4"	245	25		
Hank Bullough	OG	6'	240	24		
Jerry Kramer	OG	6'3"	235	23		
Jim Salsbury	OG	6'1"	240	26		
Jim Ringo	C	6'1"	236	27		
Nate Borden	DE	6'	240	26		
Len Ford	DE	6'4"	250	32		
Carlton Massey	DE	6'2"	226	29		
Jim Temp	DE	6'4"	250	25		
Dave Hanner	DT	6'2"	266	29		
J. D. Kimmel	DT	6'4"	250	29		
Tom Bettis	LB	6'2"	225	25		
Dan Currie	LB	6'3"	235	24		
Bill Forester	LB	6'3"	240	27		
Ray Nitschke	LB	6'3"	220	22	1	
Bobby Dillon	DB	6'1"	190	28	6	6
Hank Gremminger	DB	6'1"	200	25	3	
Johnny Symank	DB	5'11"	180	23	1	
Jesse Whittenton	DB	6'	195	24	1	
Billy Kinard	HB-DB	6'	202	24		
Al Romine	HB-DB	6'2"	184	25	1	
Babe Parilli	QB	6'1"	196	28		
Bart Starr	QB	6'1"	200	25		6
Joe Francis	HB-QB	6'1"	194	23		6
Al Carmichael	HB	6'1"	195	28		6
Paul Hornung	HB	6'2"	211	22		67
Joe Johnson	FL	6'	188	28		6
Don McIlhenny	HB	6'	200	23		12
Jim Shanley	HB	5'9"	174	22		
Howie Ferguson	FB	6'2"	213	28		6
Jim Taylor	FB	6'	205	23		12
Billy Howton	OE	6'2"	195	28		12
Gary Knafelc	OE	6'4"	217	26		6
Max McGee	OE	6'3"	196	26		42
Steve Meilinger	OE	6'2"	230	28		6

Ron Kramer – Military Service
Bob Skoronski – Military Service

BALTIMORE COLTS

RUSHING Last Name	No.	Yds	Avg	TD
Ameche	171	791	4.6	8
Moore	82	598	7.3	7
Dupre	95	390	4.1	3
Call	37	154	4.2	0
Unitas	33	139	4.2	3
Lyles	22	41	1.9	1
Pricer	10	26	2.6	1
Shaw	5	–3	–0.6	1
Brown	1	–9	–9.0	0

RECEIVING Last Name	No.	Yds	Avg	TD
Berry	56	794	14	9
Moore	50	938	19	7
Mutscheller	28	504	18	7
Dupre	13	111	9	0
Ameche	13	81	6	1
Lyles	5	24	5	1
Rechichar	4	34	9	1
Call	4	28	7	0
Pricer	3	14	5	0
DeCarlo	1	10	10	0
Pellington	1	–1	–1	0

PUNT RETURNS Last Name	No.	Yds	Avg	TD
Taseff	29	196	7	0
Rechichar	7	29	4	0
Moore	2	11	6	0
Simpson	1	1	1	0

KICKOFF RETURNS Last Name	No.	Yds	Avg	TD
Lyles	11	398	36	2
Pricer	9	168	19	0
Moore	4	91	23	0
Simpson	3	59	20	0
Rechichar	3	50	17	0
Taseff	1	50	50	0
Call	2	48	24	0
DeCarlo	1	0	0	0

PASSING	Att	Comp	%	Yds	Yd/Att	TD	Int–%	RK
Unitas	263	136	52	2007	7.6	19	7– 3	1
Shaw	89	41	46	531	6.0	7	4– 4	
Brown	2	1	50	–1	–0.5	0	0– 0	

PUNTING	No	Avg
Brown	41	39.9
Horn	19	34.1
Stone	1	28.0
Dupre	1	0.0

KICKING	XP	Att	%	FG	Att	%
Myhra	48	51	94	4	10	40
Rechichar	0	0	0	1	4	25
Shaw	0	1	0	0	0	0

CHICAGO BEARS

RUSHING Last Name	No.	Yds	Avg	TD
Casares	176	651	3.7	2
Galimore	130	619	4.8	8
Morris	52	239	4.6	2
Caroline	33	121	3.7	0
Brown	32	94	2.9	3
Douglas	10	53	5.3	0
Bratkowski	3	0	0.0	0

RECEIVING Last Name	No.	Yds	Avg	TD
McColl	35	517	15	8
Casares	32	290	9	1
Hill	27	365	14	3
Jewett	15	192	13	1
Anderson	11	177	16	1
Morris	11	170	15	0
Galimore	8	151	19	3
Caroline	5	78	16	1
Ryan	1	66	66	0
Carey	1	15	15	0

PUNT RETURNS Last Name	No.	Yds	Avg	TD
Morris	14	96	7	0
Zucco	15	35	2	0
Sumner	9	25	3	0
Ryan	1	0	0	0

KICKOFF RETURNS Last Name	No.	Yds	Avg	TD
Morris	16	399	25	0
Galimore	9	338	38	1
Caroline	6	123	21	0
Zucco	3	63	21	0
Sumner	1	19	19	0
Gibron	1	12	12	0
Barnes	1	0	0	0

PASSING	Att	Comp	%	Yds	Yd/Att	TD	Int–%	RK
Brown	218	102	47	1418	6.5	10	17– 8	13
Bratkowski	90	41	46	571	6.3	7	6– 7	
Blanda	7	2	29	19	2.7	0	0– 0	
Casares	4	1	25	13	3.3	1	0– 0	
Galimore	1	0	0	0	0.0	0	1–100	

PUNTING	No	Avg
Brown	27	42.2
Johnson	18	34.8
Bratkowski	14	39.6

KICKING	XP	Att	%	FG	Att	%
Blanda	36	37	97	11	23	48
George	1	1	100	0	0	0

LOS ANGELES RAMS

RUSHING Last Name	No.	Yds	Avg	TD
Arnett	133	683	5.1	6
Wilson	73	475	6.5	9
Marconi	89	428	4.8	1
Wade	42	90	2.1	2
Ryan	5	45	9.0	0
Waller	3	13	4.3	0

RECEIVING Last Name	No.	Yds	Avg	TD
Shofner	51	1097	22	8
Phillips	35	524	15	2
Arnett	35	494	14	1
Lundy	25	396	16	3
Clarke	18	135	8	4
Marconi	10	87	9	0
Wilson	9	101	11	1
Waller	3	75	25	0

PUNT RETURNS Last Name	No.	Yds	Avg	TD
Arnett	18	223	12	0
Morris	8	9	1	0
Waller	13	7	1	0
Sherman	1	0	0	0
Wilkins	1	0	0	0

KICKOFF RETURNS Last Name	No.	Yds	Avg	TD
Arnett	16	331	21	0
Wilson	16	324	20	0
Waller	7	120	17	0
Morris	2	37	19	0
Fry	2	23	12	0

PASSING	Att	Comp	%	Yds	Yd/Att	TD	Int–%	RK
Wade	341	181	53	2875	8.4	18	22– 6	2
Ryan	14	5	36	34	2.4	1	3– 2	
Arnett	1	0	0	0	0.0	0	0– 0	
Shofner	1	0	0	0	0.0	0	0– 0	
Wilson	1	0	0	0	0.0	0	1–100	

PUNTING	No	Avg
Shofner	49	41.2
Thomas	2	33.0

KICKING	XP	Att	%	FG	Att	%
Cothren	42	42	100	14	25	56

SAN FRANCISCO FORTY NINERS

RUSHING Last Name	No.	Yds	Avg	TD
Perry	125	758	6.1	4
McElhenny	113	451	4.0	6
Smith	26	209	8.0	3
Pace	52	161	3.1	2
Tittle	22	35	1.6	2
Woodson	2	12	6.0	0
Babb	7	9	1.3	0
Atkins	1	5	5.0	0
Brodie	11	–12	–1.1	1

RECEIVING Last Name	No.	Yds	Avg	TD
Conner	49	512	10	5
Wilson	43	592	14	5
Owens	40	620	16	1
McElhenny	31	366	12	2
Perry	23	218	9	1
Pace	10	59	6	0
Dugan	9	122	14	0
Soltau	7	77	11	0
Smith	6	59	10	0
Jessup	5	66	13	1

PUNT RETURNS Last Name	No.	Yds	Avg	TD
McElhenny	24	93	4	0
Woodson	7	53	8	0
Jessup	2	0	0	0
Pace	2	0	0	0

KICKOFF RETURNS Last Name	No.	Yds	Avg	TD
Smith	15	356	24	0
Woodson	11	239	22	0
Pace	8	134	17	0
McElhenny	2	31	16	0
Babb	2	30	15	0
Connolly	1	0	0	0

PASSING	Att	Comp	%	Yds	Yd/Att	TD	Int–%	RK
Tittle	208	120	58	1467	7.1	9	15– 7	9
Brodie	172	103	60	1224	7.1	6	13– 8	9
McElhenny	2	0	0	0	0.0	0	0– 0	
Jessup	1	0	0	0	0.0	0	1–100	

PUNTING	No	Avg
Atkins	25	39.3
Jessup	23	37.2

KICKING	XP	Att	%	FG	Att	%
Soltau	29	33	88	8	21	38

DETROIT LIONS

RUSHING Last Name	No.	Yds	Avg	TD
Rote	77	351	4.6	3
Johnson	56	254	4.5	0
Gedman	92	209	2.3	4
Cassady	45	198	4.4	0
Webb	56	172	3.1	2
Lewis	25	131	5.2	0
Morrall	11	80	7.3	0
Lary	1	2	2.0	0
Middleton	2	1	0.5	0

RECEIVING Last Name	No.	Yds	Avg	TD
Middleton	29	506	17	3
Gibbons	25	367	15	2
Cassady	23	406	18	7
Doran	22	495	23	4
Gedman	14	106	8	3
Webb	11	85	8	1
Richards	7	90	13	0
Johnson	7	60	9	0
Rychlec	2	21	11	0
Lewis	1	12	12	0

PUNT RETURNS Last Name	No.	Yds	Avg	TD
Lary	27	196	7	1
Barr	11	23	2	0
Cassady	3	4	1	0

KICKOFF RETURNS Last Name	No.	Yds	Avg	TD
Barr	4	197	49	1
Webb	7	154	22	0
Gedman	7	131	19	0
Cassady	6	126	21	0
Lewis	6	110	18	0
Whitsell	3	63	21	0
Creekmur	2	23	12	0
Karras	1	16	16	0
Middleton	1	15	15	0
Gibbons	1	4	4	0
Rychlec	1	0	0	0

PASSING	Att	Comp	%	Yds	Yd/Att	TD	Int–%	RK
Rote	257	118	46	1678	6.5	14	10– 4	8
Morrall	78	25	32	463	5.9	5	9– 12	
Gedman	3	2	67	111	37.0	1	0– 0	
Lary	1	0	0	0	0.0	0	0– 0	

PUNTING	No	Avg
Lary	59	42.8
Morrall	1	25.0

KICKING	XP	Att	%	FG	Att	%
Martin	28	28	100	7	19	37
Perry	1	1	100	4	4	100

GREEN BAY PACKERS

RUSHING Last Name	No.	Yds	Avg	TD
Hornung	69	310	4.5	2
Ferguson	59	268	4.5	1
Taylor	52	247	4.8	1
McIlhenny	74	239	3.2	1
Francis	24	153	6.4	1
Starr	25	113	4.5	1
Shanley	23	30	1.3	0
Carmichael	9	21	2.3	0
Parilli	8	15	1.9	0
Ringo	0	13	0.0	0
McGee	1	9	9.0	0
Salsbury	0	3	0.0	0
Romine	1	0	0.0	0

RECEIVING Last Name	No.	Yds	Avg	TD
McGee	37	655	18	7
Howton	36	507	14	2
McIlhenny	20	154	8	1
Hornung	15	137	9	0
Meilinger	13	139	11	1
Ferguson	12	121	10	0
Johnson	10	176	18	1
Knafelc	8	118	15	1
Taylor	4	72	18	1
Carmichael	3	26	9	1
Shanley	3	13	4	0

PUNT RETURNS Last Name	No.	Yds	Avg	TD
Shanley	14	105	8	0
Carmichael	15	67	4	0
Romine	2	7	4	0
McIlhenny	1	0	0	0
Symank	1	0	0	0

KICKOFF RETURNS Last Name	No.	Yds	Avg	TD
Carmichael	29	700	24	0
Hornung	10	248	25	0
Taylor	7	185	26	0
McIlhenny	7	146	21	0
Currie	2	14	7	0
Massey	1	10	10	0
Forester	1	6	6	0
Kramer	1	0	0	0
Nitschke	1	0	0	0
Temp	1	0	0	0

PASSING	Att	Comp	%	Yds	Yd/Att	TD	Int–%	RK
Parilli	157	68	43	1068	6.8	10	13– 8	14
Starr	157	78	50	875	5.6	3	12– 8	15
Francis	31	15	48	175	5.7	2	2– 6	
Ferguson	1	0	0	0	0.0	0	0– 0	
Hornung	1	0	0	0	0.0	0	0– 0	
McGee	1	0	0	0	0.0	0	0– 0	

PUNTING	No	Avg
McGee	62	42.3

KICKING	XP	Att	%	FG	Att	%
Hornung	22	23	96	11	21	52

1959 The Passing of Greatness

While the Philadelphia Eagles and Pittsburgh Steelers were battling on the turf at Franklin Field on October 11, Commissioner Bert Bell collapsed and died of a heart attack in the grandstand while watching the two clubs he had once owned and coached. The league mourned him both as a kind friend and a wise leader, a man who had led the NFL from the backwoods to center stage in the sporting world. Since becoming commissioner in 1946, Bell had successfully ended the war with the All-American Football Conference, had firmly upheld the game's honesty in the 1946 championship-game gambling affair, had used television to promote the game rather than give it away, and had administered the league office in truly big-league fashion. Bell was the second NFL pioneer to die this year, as New York Giant founder Tim Mara had passed on in February after a long illness.

League treasurer Austin Gunsel assumed Bell's duties until a new commissioner could be named by the owners. The new man would have to be a strong leader, since a new threat to the NFL was gathering in the wilderness. Organized by rich Texans Lamar Hunt and Bud Adams, the American Football League announced plans to operate an eight-team circuit starting next fall. With Houston, Dallas, New York, Los Angeles, Boston, Buffalo, Denver, and Minneapolis–St. Paul lined up as AFL franchises, the now established NFL was not quaking in its boots but could not afford to snear at this newcomer on the block.

EASTERN CONFERENCE

New York Giants—Heroics by the defense and by quarterback Chuck Conerly flavored the Giants' drive to the top of the East. After getting burned by the Eagles 49-21 the week before, the Giant defense vindicated itself on October 12 by shutting down Jimmy Brown and the Browns for a 10-6 victory. Two weeks later, this defense passed the supreme test in Pittsburgh. With New York leading 21-16, the Steelers recovered Joe Morrison's fumble on the Giant 16-yard line with 1:30 left in the game. Two plays took the Steelers to the 6½-yard line, but the Giant front wall held firm, twice stopping Tom Tracy from plunging for the first down. Then came Conerly's turn to shine. After missing two mid-season games with a bad leg, old Chuck limped into the lineup and passed the Giants to a 30-20 victory over the Cards. The next Sunday was officially celebrated as Chuck Conerly Day, with the guest of honor celebrating by leading his club to a 45-14 triumph over Washington.

Cleveland Browns—The Browns ran even with the Giants at the head of the East for eight weeks until bad luck and a bad day did them in. On the last two weeks of November, they lost a pair of 21-20 heartbreakers to Pittsburgh and San Francisco: On the first Sunday of December, they got the worst beating in the club's history. After being stopped in the first period, Jimmy Brown had to sit out the second quarter after being kicked in the head, and Chuck Conerly led the Giants to a 48-0 lead through three quarters, settling for a final 48-7 score. With Cleveland's sound defense and Jimmy Brown at fullback, fans now wondered out loud why Paul Brown couldn't win the Eastern title with this team. The Giants, though, had discovered how to shut the door on the Browns: Intimidate quarterback Milt Plum with a stiff pass rush and assign a watchdog named Sam Huff to stick with Brown like flypaper.

Philadelphia Eagles—With the interior line made up of Chuck Bednarik and four newcomers, giving him good protection, Norm Van Brocklin passed the Eagles to a 49-21 upset of the Giants in an early-October contest. After that, the young Eagles believed in themselves, driving to a second-place finish in the East and their first winning season in five years. Old pro Van Brocklin led by example, zipping passes to Tommy McDonald, Pete Retzlaff, and Bobby Walston and inspiring his mates with his own determination to win. Three pro-football greats blessed the Philadelphia offensive huddles, with Van Brocklin, center Bednarik, and tight end Bobby Walston all veterans at the top of their game. Another old pro, Tom Brookshier, helped glue the young defense together.

Pittsburgh Steelers—When the Steelers beat the Browns 17-7 to open the season, they ran their unbeaten streak to eight regular-season games. The Redskins ended the string a week later, and the Steelers would not come close to running off another long streak this year. But even with the Steelers' mediocre final record of 6-5-1, quarterback Bobby Layne showed Pittsburgh fans their first great T-formation quarterback. He wisely deployed a strong but slow corps of runners, using Tom Tracy to pick up vital short yardage, while his passes moved the ball in large bites. Jimmy Orr kept up his good work on short and medium passes, but rookie Buddy Dial, a pre-season cut by the Giants, won the headlines with his speed on long downfield passes.

Washington Redskins—After a 49-21 trouncing at the hands of the Cardinals on opening day, the Redskins seemed to hit their stride by beating the Steelers and the Cards on the next two weekends. But the victories were a false alarm, as the Skins dropped eight of their last nine contests to sink to fifth place in the East. Mike Nixon, an assistant under Joe Kuharich, was promoted to head coach to head up a new rebuilding program, but he had hoped to win more than three games this season.

Chicago Cardinals—With John David Crow developing into a top runner, the Cards decided to trade star Ollie Matson to get help at the other positions. Eight players and a draft choice came over from the Rams, with offensive tackle Ken Panfil and defensive tackle Frank Fuller the gems in the bunch. The Cards could hardly do worse than their recent seasons with Matson, but they actually did lose one more game than last year. By and large, the Cards were a dismal outfit on the field, and general manager Walter Wolfner was looking to get a fresh start for the team away from Chicago. So the Cardinals, one of the NFL's charter members, fled to St. Louis for the start of the new decade.

WESTERN CONFERENCE

Baltimore Colts—With their defense showing signs of creeping old age, the Colts trailed the San Francisco '49ers by two games in the West with only five weeks left to play. Even during this slow start, Johnny Unitas had kept the attack moving at a high clip, and now he shifted the offense into top speed for the final five games. Scoring an average of 37 points per game during this final stretch, the Colts swept all five games, twice beating the fading '49ers by scores of 45-14 and 34-14 to clear a path to the top of the conference. The Colts moved best through the air, with all the parts needed for a top-flight passing attack. Unitas set a league record of thirty-two touchdown passes, aided by superb pass blocking from linemen like Jim Parker and Art Spinney, and by a collection of receivers featuring swift Lenny Moore, sure-handed Ray Berry, and hard-working Jim Mutscheller.

Chicago Bears—With four losses in their first five games, the Bears found themselves mired in fifth place in the Western Conference. But George Halas' team was just a little slow out of the starting gate, as both the offensive and defensive platoons came alive for the last seven games. As the Bears began winning, they quickly passed the Rams and Packers on the way to the top and closed in on the '49ers and Colts. On the morning of the final Sunday of the season, the Colts held a one-game lead over the '49ers and Bears for the Western title. San Francisco, fading since early November, dropped out of contention by losing to Green Bay, while the Bears kept their chances alive by beating Detroit. But the late drive fell short, as the Colts beat Los Angeles to make that one-game margin permanent.

Green Bay Packers—Vince Lombardi's first statements in Green Bay made his position perfectly clear. To the executive committee he said, "Let's get one thing straight right now: I'm in complete command here." To his players he said, "Gentlemen, I've never been associated with a losing team. I do not intend to start now." The Packers took him at his word and gave their coach a winning season, a complete turn-around from last year's fiasco. Three quick wins began the Lombardi era with a flourish as halfback Paul Hornung responded to the coach's confidence in him by developing into a marvelous all-purpose halfback. When a five-game losing streak in mid-season threatened to drag this new coach under into losing waters, Lombardi came up with a master stroke: He replaced quarterback Lamar McHan with Bart Starr and won the last four games of this year.

San Francisco '49ers—A revitalized offense and rebuilt defense got the '49ers off winging to six wins in their first seven starts. New coach Red Hickey had promoted J. D. Smith to starting halfback, and Smith rewarded the coach with strong running week after week. Another Hickey project was the defensive secondary, where second-year men Abe Woodson and Jerry Mertens and rookies Eddie Dove and Dave Baker effectively shut off enemy passing attacks over the first half of the season. Over the final month of the season, however, the high-flying '49ers fell into a nose dive and the club blew a two-game lead with five games left by winning only once.

Detroit Lions—Even with a fine rookie fullback in Nick Pietrosante, the Detroit offense looked very tired most of the time. Age had caught up with the front line, as Lou Creekmur, Harley Sewell, and Charlie Ane could no longer play up to their earlier standards, and quarterback Tobin Rote now had as many bad days as good days. While ends Jim Gibbons and Dave Middleton weren't old, their speed was nothing to write home about. With the defense being rebuilt around Alex Karras, Joe Schmidt, and Yale Lary, the Lions dropped thier first four games before upsetting the Rams.

Los Angeles Rams—General manager Pete Rozelle had built a surefire championship club by trading for runner Ollie Matson and defensive end Gene Brito over the summer. Matson had cost the Rams eight players and a draft choice but was expected to join Billy Wade, Jon Arnett, and Del Shofner in an unstoppable offense, while Brito was to fit into the Les Richter-led defense. The Rams were favored to beat the New York Giants on opening day, but 71,000 fans in the Coliseum saw them bow 23-21. After the '49ers shellacked them 34-0 the next week, the dreams of glory began to fade.

FINAL TEAM STATISTICS

OFFENSE

	BALT.	CHI.B	CHI.C	CLEVE.	DET.	G.BAY	L.A.	N.Y.	PHIL.	PITT.	S.F.	WASH.
FIRST DOWNS:												
Total	267	190	179	234	198	212	232	198	211	207	182	193
by Rushing	95	69	85	118	90	109	101	82	78	82	93	94
by Passing	148	110	80	109	87	87	116	106	120	103	76	80
by Penalty	24	11	14	7	21	16	15	10	13	22	13	19
RUSHING:												
Number	435	392	367	457	399	421	371	433	391	406	407	422
Yards	1705	1438	1613	2149	1792	1907	1778	1646	1315	1543	1839	1964
Average Yards	3.9	3.7	4.4	4.7	4.5	4.5	4.8	3.8	3.4	3.8	4.5	4.7
Touchdowns	13	14	10	20	13	15	15	11	13	10	16	9
PASSING:												
Attempts	375	310	280	276	328	268	356	302	352	319	264	284
Completions	196	156	125	159	136	128	196	165	194	150	132	121
Completion Percentage	52.3	50.3	44.6	57.6	41.5	47.8	55.1	54.6	55.1	47.0	50.0	42.6
Gross Yards	2938	2284	1766	2033	2131	1963	2723	2633	2644	2298	1685	1824
Yards Lost Passing	185	211	207	167	467	131	241	106	72	246	136	301
Net Yards	2753	2073	1559	1866	1664	1832	2482	2527	2572	2052	1549	1523
Avg. Yards per Attempt (Gross)	7.8	7.4	6.3	7.4	6.5	7.3	7.6	8.7	7.5	7.2	6.4	6.4
Avg. Yards per Comp. (Gross)	15.0	14.6	14.1	12.8	15.7	15.3	13.9	16.0	13.6	15.3	12.8	15.1
Touchdowns	33	15	14	14	10	16	16	18	17	21	12	13
Interceptions	14	16	19	9	27	17	22	13	16	23	22	23
Percent Intercepted	3.7	5.2	6.8	3.3	8.2	6.3	6.2	4.3	4.5	7.2	8.3	8.1
PUNTS:												
Number	53	68	62	50	56	64	50	55	54	71	59	49
Average Distance	42.1	41.3	44.6	37.1	46.5	42.4	41.7	46.6	42.7	40.4	45.7	45.5
PUNT RETURNS:												
Number	38	26	56	26	50	33	36	50	36	38	37	30
Yards	233	243	548	211	197	316	251	164	239	152	269	119
Average Yards	6.1	9.3	9.8	8.1	3.9	9.6	7.0	3.3	6.6	4.0	7.3	4.0
Touchdowns	0	1	5	1	0	1	1	0	2	0	0	0
KICKOFF RETURNS:												
Number	38	33	52	29	42	43	43	31	42	30	41	50
Yards	792	735	1080	551	846	949	1054	703	842	613	980	1006
Average Yards	20.8	22.3	20.8	19.0	20.1	22.1	24.5	22.7	20.0	20.4	23.9	20.1
Touchdowns	0	0	0	0	0	0	0	0	0	0	1	0
INTERCEPTION RETURNS:												
Number	40	22	15	18	14	14	7	22	20	22	14	13
Yards	577	199	301	242	216	231	5	288	167	363	189	147
Average Yards	14.4	9.0	20.1	13.4	15.4	16.5	0.7	13.1	8.4	16.5	13.5	11.3
Touchdowns	4	1	1	1	0	0	0	2	0	0	1	0
PENALTIES:												
Number	56	66	44	36	65	49	51	54	52	60	57	51
Yards	634	597	431	329	496	435	465	480	501	532	489	453
FUMBLES:												
Number	22	26	48	8	36	24	34	30	26	22	24	25
Number Lost	9	15	36	5	19	16	19	20	9	10	10	17
POINTS:												
Total	374	252	234	270	203	248	242	284	268	257	255	185
PAT Attempts	51	32	31	37	25	32	29	32	35	32	31	22
PAT Made	50	28	30	33	23	31	27	32	34	32	31	21
FG Attempts	18	19	9	16	23	17	26	30	24	18	26	22
FG Made	6	10	6	5	10	7	11	20	8	11	12	10
Percent FG Made	33.3	52.6	66.7	31.3	43.5	41.2	42.3	66.7	33.3	61.1	46.2	45.5
Safeties	0	1	0	0	0	2	1	0	0	0	1	1

DEFENSE

	BALT.	CHI.B.	CHI.C.	CLEVE.	DET.	G.BAY	L.A.	N.Y.	PHIL.	PITT.	S.F.	WASH.
FIRST DOWNS:												
Total	195	208	212	205	196	215	216	167	220	179	238	252
by Rushing	65	95	99	75	79	101	96	66	103	85	123	109
by Passing	118	91	100	115	103	102	100	85	101	80	102	125
by Penalty	12	22	13	15	14	12	20	16	16	14	13	18
RUSHING:												
Number	325	429	477	360	403	430	427	379	429	405	433	404
Yards	1557	1783	1874	1422	1562	1770	1704	1261	2068	1500	1974	2214
Average Yards	4.8	4.2	3.9	4.0	3.9	4.1	4.0	3.3	4.8	3.7	4.6	5.5
Touchdowns	16	11	15	9	13	14	15	6	15	10	16	19
PASSING:												
Attempts	351	333	266	319	288	329	287	304	292	285	341	319
Completions	171	144	138	168	147	169	151	137	144	128	176	185
Completion Percentage	48.7	43.2	51.9	52.7	51.0	51.4	52.6	45.1	49.3	44.9	51.6	58.0
Gross Yards	2497	2147	2359	2457	2340	2030	2315	1811	2074	2014	2272	2606
Yards Lost Passing	155	254	218	115	246	248	225	229	204	172	228	176
Net Yards	2342	1893	2141	2342	2094	1782	2090	1582	1870	1842	2044	2430
Avg. Yards per Attempt (Gross)	7.1	6.4	8.9	7.7	8.1	6.2	8.1	6.0	7.1	7.1	6.7	8.2
Avg. Yards per Comp. (Gross)	14.6	14.9	17.1	14.6	15.9	12.0	13.7	13.2	14.4	15.7	12.9	14.1
Touchdowns	13	14	22	17	19	14	17	11	17	12	15	26
Interceptions	40	22	15	18	14	14	7	22	20	22	14	13
Percent Intercepted	11.4	6.6	5.6	5.6	4.9	4.3	2.4	7.2	6.8	7.7	4.1	4.1
PUNTS:												
Number	50	61	67	50	69	56	60	72	48	59	57	42
Average Distance	44.7	42.3	41.3	42.4	43.7	44.3	44.1	42.7	41.1	46.5	41.6	40.8
PUNT RETURNS:												
Number	33	46	39	32	36	40	30	38	40	49	35	38
Yards	120	360	181	39	230	291	205	527	312	418	186	73
Average Yards	3.6	7.8	4.6	1.2	6.4	7.3	6.8	13.9	7.8	8.5	5.3	1.9
Touchdowns	0	1	0	0	0	1	1	4	1	3	0	0
KICKOFF RETURNS:												
Number	46	38	33	38	37	40	42	52	37	43	40	28
Yards	950	754	692	734	774	917	980	1229	819	753	924	625
Average Yards	20.7	19.8	21.0	19.3	20.9	22.9	23.3	23.6	22.1	17.5	23.1	22.3
Touchdowns	0	0	0	0	0	0	1	0	0	0	0	0
INTERCEPTION RETURNS:												
Number	14	16	19	9	27	17	22	13	16	23	22	23
Yards	199	96	158	139	370	227	305	173	360	287	272	339
Average Yards	14.2	6.0	8.3	15.4	13.7	13.4	13.9	13.3	22.5	12.5	12.4	14.7
Touchdowns	2	0	1	1	1	1	1	0	2	0	1	0
PENALTIES:												
Number	65	62	61	32	64	51	60	40	47	55	45	59
Yards	610	553	528	285	603	450	562	324	457	483	417	570
FUMBLES:												
Number	18	38	25	20	31	28	25	29	28	22	34	27
Number Lost	9	17	15	12	19	15	14	16	20	12	22	14
POINTS:												
Total	251	196	324	214	275	246	315	170	278	216	237	350
PAT Attempts	31	26	41	28	34	30	38	22	36	26	31	46
PAT Made	29	26	40	28	34	28	36	20	35	24	28	44
FG Attempts	22	17	22	13	21	22	31	16	20	32	13	19
FG Made	12	4	12	6	11	12	17	6	9	12	5	10
Percent FG Made	54.5	23.5	54.5	46.2	52.4	54.5	54.8	37.5	45.0	37.5	38.5	52.6
Safeties	0	1	1	0	2	1	0	0	0	0	1	0

1959 CHAMPIONSHIP GAME

December 27, at Baltimore
(Attendance 57,545)

Convincingly If Not Easily

Meeting in a rematch of the famous 1958 sudden-death overtime confrontation, the Baltimore Colts and New York Giants gave fans an exciting but anticlimactic finish to one of the most thrilling championship matchups in NFL history. Although Baltimore drew first blood by driving 80 yards in six plays, capped by a 60-yard pass from Johnny Unitas to Lenny Moore, the Giants responded three times on Pat Summerall's toe to move in front 9-7 by the time the third quarter drew to a close. Unfortunately for the Giants, they entered the second half without the services of their star end Kyle Rote, the victim of a concussion, and safety Jimmy Patton, who injured his foot late in the second period and had to leave the game. Yet beyond the injuries, which surely hurt the Giants in the final and all-important fourth quarter, the turning point of the game came in the third quarter, when, with New York in front 9-7, the ball was on the Colts' 28-yard line with fourth down and inches to go. The Giants decided to go for the first down behind Alex Webster only to meet a stone-wall defense led by Gino Marchetti. The backfired strategy changed the momentum of the game, as the Colts scored four times in the fourth period, three on touchdowns, with one coming off an interception and the last on a field goal by Steve Myhra to bring the score to 31-9 before New York finally struck pay dirt with thirty-two seconds remaining to make the final count a little more respectable. The game was best summed up by Colt general manager Don Kellert, who said, "We didn't win easily, but we won convincingly."

SCORING

BALTIMORE	7	0	0	24–	31
NEW YORK	3	3	3	7–	16

First Quarter

Bal.	Moore, 60 yard pass from Unitas PAT – Myhra (kick)	4:55
N. Y.	Summerall, 23 yard field goal	13:16

Second Quarter

N. Y.	Summerall, 37 yard field goal	14:49

Third Quarter

N. Y.	Summerall, 23 yard field goal	5:45

Fourth Quarter

Bal.	Unitas, 4 yard rush PAT – Myhra (kick)	2:42
Bal.	Richardson, 12 yard pass from Unitas PAT – Myhra (kick)	7:21
Bal.	Sample, 42 yard interception return PAT – Myhra (kick)	9:31
Bal.	Myhra, 25 yard field goal	12:40
N. Y.	Schnelker, 32 yard pass from Conerly PAT – Summerall (kick)	14:28

TEAM STATISTICS

BAL.		N. Y.
12	First Downs – Total	17
3	First Downs – Rushing	4
9	First Downs – Passing	12
0	First Downs – Penalty	1
1	Fumbles – Number	1
0	Fumbles – Lost Ball	0
4	Penalties – Number	3
20	Yards Penalized	23
1	Field Goals Missed	0

INDIVIDUAL STATISTICS

BALTIMORE	No.	Yds.	Avg.	NEW YORK	No.	Yds.	Avg.
RUSHING							
Ameche	9	30	3.3	Gifford	9	50	5.6
Sommer	6	15	2.5	Triplett	6	39	6.5
Pricer	4	14	3.5	Webster	8	25	3.1
Moore	4	8	2.0	King	2	4	2.0
Unitas	2	6	3.0		25	118	4.7
	25	73	2.9				
RECEIVING							
Berry	5	68	13.6	Schnelker	9	178	19.8
Mutsch'ler	5	40	8.0	King	4	17	4.3
Moore	3	127	42.3	Rote	2	41	20.5
Price	2	6	3.0	Gifford	1	19	19.0
Ameche	1	13	13.0	Triplett	1	–2	–2.0
Richardson	1	12	12.0		17	253	14.9
Sommer	1	–1	–1.0				
	18	265	14.7				
PUNTING							
Sherer	6		37.9	Chandler	6		47.9
PUNT RETURNS							
Sample	2	23	11.5	Morrison	1	5	5.0
Taseff	1	10	10.0	King	1	2	2.0
	3	33	11.0		2	7	3.5
KICKOFF RETURNS							
Hawkins	2	63	31.5	King	2	52	26.0
Myhra	1	31	31.0	Morrison	2	43	21.5
Sample	1	8	8.0	Triplett	1	21	21.0
	4	102	25.5		5	116	23.2
INTERCEPTION RETURNS							
Sample	2	76	38.0	None			
Nelson	1	17	17.0				
	3	93	31.0				

PASSING

BALTIMORE	Att	Comp	Comp Pct.	Yds	Int	Yds/ Att.	Yds/ Comp	Yards Lost Tackled
Unitas	29	18	62.1	265	0	9.1	14.7	7-58
NEW YORK								
Conerly	35	16	45.7	234	2	6.7	14.6	5–47
Gifford	2	1	50.0	19	1	9.5	19.0	0– 0
King	1	0	0.0	0	0	–	–	0– 0
	38	17	44.7	253	3	6.7	14.9	5–47

NEW YORK GIANTS 10-2-0 Jim Lee Howell

Scores of Each Game		
23	Los Angeles	21
21	Philadelphia	49
10	Cleveland	6
24	PHILADELPHIA	7
21	Pittsburgh	16
20	GREEN BAY	3
9	CHIC. CARDS	3
9	PITTSBURGH	14
30	Chic. Cards	20
45	WASHINGTON	14
48	CLEVELAND	7
24	Washington	10

Use Name	Pos.	Hgt	Wgt	Age	Int	Pts
Rosey Brown	OT	6'3"	245	26		
Frank Youso	OT	6'4"	260	23		
Bob Schmidt	C-OT	6'4"	245	23		
Al Barry	OG	6'2"	230	28		
Darrell Dess	OG	6'	235	23		
Ellison Kelly	OG	6'1"	235	23		
Jack Stroud	OG	6'1"	235	30		
Buzz Guy	OT-DT-OG	6'3"	248	24		
Ray Wietecha	C	6'1"	225	30		
Jim Katcavage	DE	6'3"	230	24		
Andy Robustelli	DE	6'1"	230	33		
Rosey Grier	DT	6'5"	285	26		
Art Hauser (from Chi C)	DT	6'	235	28		
Dick Modzelewski	DT	6'	260	28		
Sam Huff	LB	6'1"	230	24	1	6
Cliff Livingston	LB	6'3"	215	29	2	
Harland Svare	LB	6'	215	28	3	6
Tom Scott	DE-LB	6'2"	220	29		
Lindon Crow	DB	6'1"	200	26	5	6
Dick Lynch	DB	6'1"	200	23	1	
Dick Nolan	DB	6'1"	185	27	5	
Jimmy Patton	DB	6'	180	27	5	
Bill Stits (from WAS)	DB	6'	195	28		
Chuck Conerly	QB	6'1"	185	35		6
Don Heinrich	QB	6'	180	27		
George Shaw	QB	6'1"	180	26		
Don Chandler	HB	6'2"	205	24		2
Frank Gifford	HB	6'1"	205	29		42
George Scott	HB	6'1"	180	21		
Alex Webster	HB	6'3"	225	28		42
Joe Morrison	DB-HB	6'1"	195	21		12
Mel Triplett	FB	6'1"	215	27		6
Phil King	HB-FB	6'4"	225	23		6
Joe Biscaha	OE	6'1"	190	22		
Bill Kimber	OE	6'2"	195	23		
Kyle Rote	OE	6'	200	30		24
Bob Schnelker	OE	6'3"	215	29		36
Pat Summerall	OE	6'4"	235	29		90

CLEVELAND BROWNS 7-5-0 Paul Brown

Scores of Each Game		
7	Pittsburgh	17
34	Chic. Cards	7
6	NEW YORK	10
17	CHIC. CARDS	7
34	WASHINGTON	7
38	Baltimore	31
28	PHILADELPHIA	7
31	Washington	17
20	PITTSBURGH	21
20	SAN FRANCISCO	21
7	New York	48
28	Philadelphia	21

Use Name	Pos.	Hgt	Wgt	Age	Int	Pts
Lou Groza	OT	6'3"	248	35		48
Mike McCormack	OT	6'4"	247	32		
Fran O'Brien	DE-OT	6'1"	235	24		
Gene Hickerson	OG	6'3"	242	24		
Jim Ray Smith	OG	6'3"	242	28		
John Wooten	OG	6'2"	235	24		
Dick Schafrath	DE-OG	6'3"	230	23		
Art Hunter	C	6'4"	242	26		
Bob Gain	DE	6'3"	260	31		
Paul Wiggin	DE	6'3"	237	25		
Willie Davis	OT-DE	6'3"	240	26		
Willie McClung	DT	6'2"	260	30		
Floyd Peters	DT	6'4"	250	24		
Sid Youngelman	DT	6'3"	262	27		
Vince Costello	LB	6'	225	27		
Galen Fiss	LB	6'	227	29	1	
Walt Michaels	LB	6'	237	30	1	
Chuck Noll	OG-LB	6'1"	224	27	2	
Dave Lloyd	C-LB	6'3"	240	23		
Kenny Konz	DB	5'10"	187	31	1	
Warren Lahr	DB	5'11"	192	35	1	
Bernie Parrish	DB	5'11"	190	24	5	6
Jim Shofner	DB	6'2"	187	23	2	
Junior Wren	DB	6'	192	29	5	6
Jim Ninowski	QB	6'1"	210	23		
Milt Plum	QB	6'1"	205	25		6
Bob Ptacek	QB	6'1"	205	23		
Leroy Bolden	HB	5'8"	170	26		
Bobby Mitchell	HB	6'	180	24		60
Jimmy Brown	FB	6'2"	228	23		84
Ed Modzelewski	FB	6'	222	30		6
Ray Renfro	FL	6'1"	190	28		36
Preston Carpenter	OE	6'2"	195	25		12
Frank Clarke	OE	6'	207	26		
Billy Howton	OE	6'2"	195	29		6
Rich Kreitling	OE	6'2"	205	24		

PHILADELPHIA EAGLES 7-5-0 Buck Shaw

Scores of Each Game		
14	San Francisco	24
49	NEW YORK	21
28	PITTSBURGH	24
7	New York	24
28	Chic. Cards	24
30	WASHINGTON	23
7	Cleveland	28
27	CHIC. CARDS	17
23	LOS ANGELES	20
0	Pittsburgh	31
34	Washington	14
21	CLEVELAND	28

Use Name	Pos.	Hgt	Wgt	Age	Int	Pts
Jerry DeLucca	OT	6'3"	245	23		
Jim McCusker	OT	6'2"	245	23		
J. D. Smith	OT	6'5"	250	23		
Darrell Aschbacher	OG	6'1"	220	24		
Stan Campbell	OG	6'	230	29		
Jerry Huth	OG	6'	228	26		6
Bill Striegel	OG	6'2"	230	23		
Chuck Bednarik	C	6'3"	235	34		
Ed Khayat	DE	6'3"	225	24	1	
Joe Robb	DE	6'3"	225	22		
Jerry Wilson	DE	6'3"	240	22		
Jess Richardson	DT	6'2"	262	29		
Don Owens	OT-DT	6'5"	255	27		6
Marion Campbell	DE-DT	6'3"	250	30	1	
Tom Catlin	LB	6'1"	220	28		
John Nocera	LB	6'1"	215	25		
Bob Pellegrini	LB	6'2"	235	24	3	
Chuck Weber	LB	6'1"	235	30	2	6
Tom Louderback	C-LB	6'3"	234	25		
Tom Brookshier	DB	6'	198	27	3	
Jimmy Carr	DB	6'1"	198	26	5	
Gene Johnson	DB	6'	190	24	1	
Art Powell	DB	6'3"	200	22	3	6
Lee Riley	DB	6'1"	190	27	1	
Sonny Jurgensen	QB	5'11"	200	25		
Norm Van Brocklin	QB	6'1"	202	33		12
Billy Barnes	HB	5'11"	202	24		54
Theron Sapp	HB	6'1"	200	24		6
Walt Kowalczyk	FB	6'	205	24		
Joe Pagliei	FB	6'	220	25		
Clarence Peaks	FB	6'1"	220	23		18
Tommy McDonald	FL	5'10"	182	25		66
Dick Bielski	OE	6'1"	218	27		6
Pete Retzlaff	OE	6'1"	210	28		6
Bobby Walston	OE	6'	190	30		51
Paige Cothren	K	5'11"	195	24		25

PITTSBURGH STEELERS 6-5-1 Buddy Parker

Scores of Each Game		
17	CLEVELAND	7
17	WASHINGTON	23
24	Philadelphia	28
27	Washington	6
16	NEW YORK	21
24	Chic. Cards	45
10	DETROIT	10
14	New York	9
21	Cleveland	20
31	PHILADELPHIA	0
21	Chic. Bears	27
35	CHIC. CARDS	20

Use Name	Pos.	Hgt	Wgt	Age	Int	Pts
Frank Varrichione	OT	6'1"	230	27		
Ray Fisher	OG-DT-OT	6'	230	25		
John Nisby	OG	6'1"	230	26		
Mike Sandusky	OG	6'	230	26		
Ted Karras	OT-OG	6'1"	235	26		
Ed Beatty	C	6'3"	225	27		
Billy Ray Smith	DE	6'4"	230	24		
George Tarasovic	C-DE	6'4"	245	30		6
Joe Krupa	DT	6'2"	240	26		
Joe Lewis	DT	6'2"	260	24		
Byron Beams	OT-DT	6'6"	250	25		
Ernie Stautner	DE-DT	6'1"	230	34		
Dick Campbell	LB	6'1"	230	23	1	
Dale Dodrill	LB	6'1"	215	34		
Rudy Hayes	LB	6'	220	24		
Mike Henry	LB	6'2"	230	23	2	
Dick Lasse	LB	6'2"	215	23		
John Reger	LB	6'	230	28		
Dick Alban	DB	6'	195	30	6	
Don Bishop (to Chi B)	DB	6'2"	210	24		
Jack Butler	DB	6'	195	31	2	
Dean Derby	DB	6'	185	25	7	
Ron Hall	DB	6'	190	22	1	
Bobby Luna	DB	5'11"	190	26	3	
Don Sutherin (from NY)	DB	5'10"	195	23		
Len Dawson	QB	6'	180	25		
Bobby Layne	QB	6'1"	208	32		77
Jack Call	HB	6'1"	200	24		
Tom Tracy	HB	5'9"	210	27		48
Tom Barnett	DB-HB	5'11"	190	22		12
Leo Elter	FB	5'10"	205	30		
Larry Krutko	FB	6'	215	24		24
Ray Mathews	FL	6'	190	30		
Buddy Dial	OE-FL	6'1"	185	22		36
Darrell Brewster	OE	6'3"	215	29		12
Jack McClairen	OE	6'4"	210	28		
Gern Nagler	OE	6'2"	190	26		12
Jimmy Orr	OE	5'11"	195	23		30

WASHINGTON REDSKINS 3-9-0 Mike Nixon

Scores of Each Game		
21	Chic. Cards	49
23	Pittsburgh	17
23	CHIC. CARDS	14
6	PITTSBURGH	27
7	Cleveland	34
23	Philadelphia	30
27	BALTIMORE	24
17	CLEVELAND	31
0	Green Bay	21
14	New York	45
14	PHILADELPHIA	34
10	NEW YORK	24

Use Name	Pos.	Hgt	Wgt	Age	Int	Pts
Ray Lemek	OT	6'	237	25		
Don Boll	OG-OT	6'2"	282	32		
Johnny Miller	DT-OT	6'5"	260	25		
Don Lawrence	OG	6'1"	245	22		
Red Stephens	OG	6'	232	29		
Frank Kuchta	C	6'2"	220	23		
Jim Schrader	C	6'2"	250	27		
Art Gob	DE	6'4"	230	22		2
Ed Meadows	DE	6'2"	225	27		
John Paluck	DE	6'2"	235	26		
Chet Ostrowski	DT-DE	6'1"	235	29		
Don Churchwell	DT	6'1"	250	22		
Will Renfro	DT	6'5"	240	27		
Bob Toneff	DT	6'3"	250	29		
Tom Braatz	LB	6'1"	215	26	1	
Chuck Drazenovich	LB	6'1"	224	32	1	
Ralph Felton	LB	5'11"	210	27	2	
Emil Karas	DE-LB	6'3"	227	25	1	
Bob Hudson	DB-LB	6'4"	230	29		
Gene Cichowski	DB	6'	195	25		
Gary Glick (from PIT)	DB	6'2"	190	28	2	
Richie McCabe	DB	6'1"	182	25	1	
Doyle Nix	DB	6'1"	188	26	1	
Ben Scotti	DB	6'1"	185	22		
Eagle Day	QB	6'	180	27		
Ralph Guglielmi	QB	6'1"	200	26		
Eddie LeBaron	QB	5'9"	167	29		
Jim Podoley	HB	6'2"	205	26		12
Ed Sutton	HB	6'1"	205	24		6
Dick James	DB-HB	5'9"	175	25	3	24
Dick Haley	DB-OE-HB	5'10"	190	22	1	6
Sam Baker	FB	6'2"	217	27		51
Don Bosseler	FB	6'1"	215	23		18
Johnny Olszewski	HB-FB	5'11"	202	28		6
Bill Anderson	OE	6'3"	211	23		36
Johnny Carson	OE	6'3"	205	29		
Ken MacAfee (from PHI)	OE	6'2"	215	29		6
Joe Walton	OE	5'11"	200	24		18

CHICAGO CARDINALS 2-10-0 Pop Ivy

Scores of Each Game		
49	WASHINGTON	21
7	CLEVELAND	34
14	Washington	23
7	Cleveland	17
24	PHILADELPHIA	28
45	PITTSBURGH	24
3	New York	9
17	Philadelphia	27
20	NEW YORK	30
7	CHIC. BEARS	31
21	Detroit	45
20	Pittsburgh	35

Use Name	Pos.	Hgt	Wgt	Age	Int	Pts
Bob Cross	OT	6'4"	250	28		
Ken Panfil	OT	6'6"	265	28		
Ed Cook	OG-OT	6'2"	237	27		
Ken Gray	OG	6'2"	235	23		
Dale Meinert	OG	6'2"	218	26		
Dale Memmelaar	OT-OG	6'2"	230	22		
Don Gillis	C	6'3"	240	24		
Mac Lewis	OT-C	6'6"	290	22		
Leo Sugar	DE	6'1"	210	30		
Luke Owens	DT-DE	6'2"	255	26		
Maury Schleicher	LB-DE	6'3"	232	22		
Ed Culpepper	DT	6'1"	255	25		
Frank Fuller	DT	6'4"	245	30		
Ed Husmann	DT	6'	230	28		
Ted Bates	LB	6'3"	215	22		
Carl Brettschneider	LB	6'1"	220	27	1	
Bill Koman	LB	6'2"	230	25		
Jack Patera	LB	6'1"	235	27	1	
Marion Rushing	LB	6'2"	210	22		
Freddy Glick	DB	6'1"	185	22		
Jimmy Hill	DB	6'2"	190	30	2	6
Night Train Lane	DB	6'1"	190	31	3	6
Jerry Norton	DB	5'11"	195	29	3	
Billy Stacy	DB	6'1"	190	23	5	12
Jim Wagstaff	DB	6'2"	195	23		
King Hill	QB	6'3"	207	23		30
M. C. Reynolds	QB	6'	190	24		
John Roach	DB-QB	6'4"	195	26		
Joe Childress	HB	6'	200	25		6
Bobby Joe Conrad	HB	6'	195	24		84
Ken Hall	HB	6'1"	205	23		12
Mal Hammack	FB	6'2"	205	26		6
Larry Hickman	FB	6'2"	223	23		
John David Crow	HB-FB	6'2"	215	24		42
Woodley Lewis	OE	6'	195	34		18
Sonny Randle	OE	6'2"	187	23		6
Perry Richards	OE	6'2"	205	25		6
John Tracey	OE	6'3"	218	25		

NEW YORK GIANTS

RUSHING

Last Name	No.	Yds	Avg	TD
Gifford	106	540	5.1	3
Triplett	91	381	4.2	1
Webster	79	250	3.2	5
King	72	232	3.2	0
Morrison	62	165	2.7	1
Conerly	15	38	2.5	1
Chandler	1	24	24.0	0
Scott	2	10	5.0	0
Heinrich	2	3	1.5	0
Shaw	3	3	1.0	0

RECEIVING

Last Name	No.	Yds	Avg	TD
Gifford	42	768	18	4
Schnelker	37	714	19	6
Webster	27	381	14	2
Rote	25	362	14	4
Morrison	17	183	11	1
King	7	98	14	1
Triplett	6	78	13	0
Summerall	2	32	16	0
Scott	1	12	12	0
Biscaha	1	5	5	0

PUNT RETURNS

Last Name	No.	Yds	Avg	TD
Crow	11	66	6	0
Morrison	15	51	3	0
Patton	8	23	3	0
Scott	12	17	1	0
Stits	4	7	2	0

KICKOFF RETURNS

Last Name	No.	Yds	Avg	TD
Morrison	15	345	23	0
Scott	10	253	25	0
King	4	84	21	0
Brown	1	18	18	0
Summerall	1	3	3	0

PASSING – PUNTING – KICKING

PASSING	Att	Comp	%	Yds	Yd/Att	TD	Int–%	RK
Conerly	194	113	58	1706	8.8	14	4– 2	1
Heinrich	58	22	38	329	5.7	1	6– 10	
Shaw	36	24	67	433	12.0	1	1– 3	
Gifford	11	5	45	151	13.7	2	2– 18	
Morrison	2	1	50	14	7.0	0	0– 0	
Webster	1	0	0	0	0.0	0	0– 0	

PUNTING	No	Avg
Chandler	55	46.6

KICKING	XP	Att	%	FG	Att	%
Summerall	30	30	100	20	29	69
Chandler	2	2	100	0	1	0

CLEVELAND BROWNS

RUSHING

Last Name	No.	Yds	Avg	TD
Brown	290	1329	4.6	14
Mitchell	131	743	5.7	5
Plum	21	20	1.0	1
Modzelewski	6	18	3.0	0
Ptacek	3	13	4.3	0
Bolden	4	11	2.8	0
Ninowski	1	11	11.0	0
Carpenter	1	4	4.0	0

RECEIVING

Last Name	No.	Yds	Avg	TD
Howton	39	510	13	1
Mitchell	35	351	10	4
Renfro	30	528	18	6
Carpenter	24	372	16	2
Brown	24	190	8	0
Clarke	3	44	15	0
Modzelewski	3	18	6	1
Plum	1	20	20	0

PUNT RETURNS

Last Name	No.	Yds	Avg	TD
Mitchell	17	177	10	1
Konz	9	34	4	0

KICKOFF RETURNS

Last Name	No.	Yds	Avg	TD
Mitchell	11	236	21	0
Bolden	9	170	19	0
Brown	4	88	22	0
Modzelewski	4	37	9	0
Noll	1	20	20	0

PASSING – PUNTING – KICKING

PASSING	Att	Comp	%	Yds	Yd/Att	TD	Int–%	RK
Plum	266	156	59	1992	7.5	14	8– 3	3
Ninowski	10	3	33	41	4.1	0	1– 10	

PUNTING	No	Avg
Wren	27	36.9
Shofner	23	37.4

KICKING	XP	Att	%	FG	Att	%
Groza	33	37	89	5	16	31

PHILADELPHIA EAGLES

RUSHING

Last Name	No.	Yds	Avg	TD
Barnes	181	687	3.8	7
Peaks	124	451	3.6	3
Sapp	41	145	3.5	1
Kowalczyk	26	37	1.4	0
Van Brocklin	11	13	1.2	2
Walston	2	8	4.0	0
Pagliei	2	–5	–2.5	0
McDonald	2	–10	–5.0	0
Retzlaff	2	–11	–5.5	0

RECEIVING

Last Name	No.	Yds	Avg	TD
McDonald	47	846	18	10
Retzlaff	34	595	18	1
Barnes	32	314	10	2
Peaks	28	209	7	0
Walston	16	279	17	3
Bielski	15	264	18	1
Kowalczyk	9	33	4	0
Sapp	6	47	8	0
Pagliei	2	9	5	0

PUNT RETURNS

Last Name	No.	Yds	Avg	TD
Powell	15	124	8	1
Mcdonald	21	115	5	1

KICKOFF RETURNS

Last Name	No.	Yds	Avg	TD
McDonald	24	444	19	0
Powell	14	379	27	0
Nocera	1	15	15	0
Wilson	2	4	2	0
DeLucca	1	0	0	0

PASSING – PUNTING – KICKING

PASSING	Att	Comp	%	Yds	Yd/Att	TD	Int–%	RK
Van Brocklin	340	191	56	2617	7.7	16	14– 4	4
Barnes	7	0	0	0	0.0	0	2– 29	
Jurgensen	5	3	60	27	5.4	1	0– 0	

PUNTING	No	Avg
Van Brocklin	53	42.7
Pagliei	1	45.0

KICKING	XP	Att	%	FG	Att	%
Walston	33	34	97	0	1	0
Cothren	1	1	100	8	18	44
Bielski	0	0	0	0	5	0

PITTSBURGH STEELERS

RUSHING

Last Name	No.	Yds	Avg	TD
Tracy	199	794	4.0	3
Barnett	75	238	3.2	1
Krutko	75	226	3.0	4
Layne	33	181	5.5	2
Orr	5	43	8.6	0
Elter	8	25	3.1	0
Dawson	4	20	5.0	0
Call	3	9	3.0	0
Mathews	1	4	4.0	0
Luna	3	3	1.0	0

RECEIVING

Last Name	No.	Yds	Avg	TD
Orr	35	604	17	5
Tracy	23	273	12	5
Brewster	22	360	16	2
Dial	16	428	27	6
Nagler	14	222	16	2
Mathews	13	182	14	0
Krutko	13	100	8	0
Barnett	7	52	7	1
McClairen	3	46	15	0
Elter	3	31	10	0
Call	1	0	0	0

PUNT RETURNS

Last Name	No.	Yds	Avg	TD
Sutherin	12	68	6	0
Hall	5	23	5	0
Mathews	2	17	9	0
Derby	9	16	2	0
Luna	2	13	7	0
Bishop	4	10	3	0
Tracy	4	5	1	0

KICKOFF RETURNS

Last Name	No.	Yds	Avg	TD
Sutherin	11	225	20	0
Call	6	146	24	0
Tracy	7	145	21	0
Derby	2	32	16	0
Barnett	2	24	12	0
Hall	1	22	22	0
Hayes	1	19	19	0

PASSING – PUNTING – KICKING

PASSING	Att	Comp	%	Yds	Yd/Att	TD	Int–%	RK
Layne	297	142	48	1986	6.7	20	21– 7	8
Tracy	12	3	25	159	13.3	0	2– 17	
Dawson	7	3	43	60	8.6	1	0– 0	
Luna	1	1	100	55	55.0	0	0– 0	
Mathews	1	1	100	38	38.0	0	0– 0	
Orr	1	0	0	0	0.0	0	0– 0	

PUNTING	No	Avg
Luna	63	40.7
Orr	8	37.8

KICKING	XP	Att	%	FG	Att	%
Layne	32	32	100	11	17	65
Sutherin	0	0	0	0	1	0

WASHINGTON REDSKINS

RUSHING

Last Name	No.	Yds	Avg	TD
Bosseler	119	644	5.4	3
Olszewski	65	432	6.6	1
James	100	384	3.8	3
Sutton	61	232	3.8	1
Guglielmi	26	97	3.7	0
Podoley	18	83	4.6	0
Haley	14	51	3.6	1
Day	3	27	9.0	0
LeBaron	13	7	0.5	0
Baker	2	3	1.5	0

RECEIVING

Last Name	No.	Yds	Avg	TD
Anderson	35	734	21	6
Walton	21	317	15	3
Podoley	18	282	16	2
James	13	192	15	1
Bosseler	11	47	4	0
MacAfee	9	87	10	1
Olszewski	7	62	9	0
Carson	6	74	12	0
Sutton	4	63	16	0
Haley	2	14	7	0

PUNT RETURNS

Last Name	No.	Yds	Avg	TD
James	21	95	5	0
Haley	7	15	2	0
Glick	1	9	9	0
Olszewski	1	0	0	0

KICKOFF RETURNS

Last Name	No.	Yds	Avg	TD
James	23	503	22	0
Haley	17	346	20	0
Podoley	5	126	25	0
MacAfee	1	12	12	0
Gob	1	0	0	0
Renfro	1	0	0	0
Scotti	1	0	0	0

PASSING – PUNTING – KICKING

PASSING	Att	Comp	%	Yds	Yd/Att	TD	Int–%	RK
LeBaron	173	77	45	1077	6.2	8	11– 6	11
Guglielmi	89	36	40	617	6.9	4	11– 12	
Day	13	6	46	79	6.1	0	1– 8	
Sutton	7	2	29	51	7.3	1	0– 0	
Bosseler	1	0	0	0	0.0	0	0– 0	
Podoley	1	0	0	0	0.0	0	0– 0	

PUNTING	No	Avg
Baker	49	45.5

KICKING	XP	Att	%	FG	Att	%
Baker	21	22	95	10	22	45

CHICAGO CARDINALS

RUSHING

Last Name	No.	Yds	Avg	TD
Crow	140	666	4.8	3
Conrad	74	328	4.4	2
Hammack	49	237	4.8	0
K. Hill	39	167	4.3	5
Hall	14	81	5.8	0
Childress	30	59	2.0	0
Norton	2	41	20.5	0
Roach	9	20	2.2	0
Hickman	5	18	3.6	0
Reynolds	5	–4	–0.8	0

RECEIVING

Last Name	No.	Yds	Avg	TD
Lewis	34	534	16	3
Crow	27	328	12	4
Tracey	17	258	15	0
Randle	15	202	13	1
Conrad	14	142	10	3
Richards	5	89	18	1
Childress	4	73	18	1
Hammack	4	69	17	0
Hall	4	60	15	1
Hickman	1	11	11	0

PUNT RETURNS

Last Name	No.	Yds	Avg	TD
Stacy	29	281	10	2
Conrad	16	133	8	1
Hall	3	91	30	1
Richards	3	22	7	0
Norton	3	4	1	0
J. Hill	1	0	0	0
Sugar	1	0	0	0
Hammack	0	17	0	1

KICKOFF RETURNS

Last Name	No.	Yds	Avg	TD
Conrad	18	388	22	0
Stacy	12	280	23	0
Crow	5	185	37	0
Hall	6	99	17	0
Norton	3	70	23	0
Randle	2	33	17	0
Tracey	1	14	14	0
Gray	1	11	11	0
Cross	1	0	0	0
Hammack	1	0	0	0
Panfil	1	0	0	0
Patera	1	0	0	0

PASSING – PUNTING – KICKING

PASSING	Att	Comp	%	Yds	Yd/Att	TD	Int–%	RK
K. Hill	181	82	45	1015	5.6	7	13– 7	14
Roach	57	22	39	340	6.0	2	4– 7	
Reynolds	37	19	49	329	8.4	4	1– 3	
Conrad	3	2	67	82	27.3	1	1– 33	

PUNTING	No	Avg
Norton	59	44.9
K. Hill	3	39.3

KICKING	XP	Att	%	FG	Att	%
Conrad	30	31	97	6	9	67

1959 N.F.L. — Western Conference

BALTIMORE COLTS 9-3-0 Weeb Ewbank

Scores of Each Game		
21	DETROIT	9
21	CHIC. BEARS	26
31	Detroit	24
21	Chic. Bears	7
38	GREEN BAY	21
31	CLEVELAND	38
24	Washington	27
28	Green Bay	24
45	SAN FRANCISCO	14
35	LOS ANGELES	21
34	San Francisco	14
45	Los Angeles	26

Use Name	Pos.	Hgt	Wgt	Age	Int	Pts
Jim Parker	OT	6'3"	270	25		
Sherman Plunkett	OT	6'4"	265	25		
George Preas	OT	6'2"	245	27		
Steve Myhra	OG	6'1"	235	25		68
Alex Sandusky	OG	6'1"	235	27		
Art Spinney	OG	6'	230	32		
Buzz Nutter	C	6'4"	235	28		
Ordell Braase	DE	6'4"	242	27		
Gino Marchetti	DE	6'4"	240	33	1	
Don Joyce	DT-DE	6'3"	255	29		
Art Donovan	DT	6'2"	270	34		
Big Daddy Lipscomb	DT	6'6"	288	28	1	
Ray Krouse	DE-DT	6'3"	275	32		
Marv Matuszak	LB	6'3"	232	28	1	
Bill Pellington	LB	6'2"	230	30	4	6
Bert Rechichar	LB	6'1"	210	29		
Don Shinnick	LB	6'	230	24	7	
Dick Szymanski	LB	6'3"	230	27	5	6
Milt Davis	DB	6'1"	190	30	7	6
Andy Nelson	DB	6'1"	180	26	6	6
Johnny Sample	DB	6'1"	203	22	1	
Jackie Simpson	DB	5'10"	180	25		
Carl Taseff	DB	5'11"	190	30	2	6
Ray Brown	QB-DB	6'2"	195	23	5	
Art DeCarlo	OE-DB	6'2"	196	29		
Johnny Unitas	QB	6'1"	190	26		12
L. G. Dupre	HB	5'11"	190	27		6
Alex Hawkins	HB	6'1"	190	22		
Lenny Moore	HB	6'1"	190	26		48
Mike Sommer (from WAS)	HB	5'11"	190	24		12
Harold Lewis	DB-HB	6'	195	23		
Alan Ameche	FB	6'	217	26		48
Billy Pricer	FB	5'10"	210	24		
Jerry Richardson	FL	6'3"	185	23		18
Ray Berry	OE	6'2"	190	26		84
Jim Mutscheller	OE	6'1"	215	29		48
Dave Sherer	OE	6'3"	210	22		

CHICAGO BEARS 8-4-0 George Halas

Scores of Each Game		
6	Green Bay	9
26	Baltimore	21
21	LOS ANGELES	28
7	BALTIMORE	21
17	San Francisco	20
26	Los Angeles	21
28	GREEN BAY	17
14	SAN FRANCISCO	3
24	Detroit	14
31	Chic. Cards	7
27	PITTSBURGH	21
25	DETROIT	14

Use Name	Pos.	Hgt	Wgt	Age	Int	Pts
Dick Klein	OT	6'4"	255	25		
Herm Lee	OT	6'4"	247	28		
Ed Nickla	OT	6'3"	240	26		
Abe Gibron	OG	5'11"	248	33		
Don Healy	OG	6'3"	255	23		
Stan Jones	OG	6'1"	250	28		
John Damore	C-OG	6'	228	26		
John Mellekas	C	6'3"	255	26		
Larry Strickland	C	6'4"	245	28		
Doug Atkins	DE	6'8"	255	29		
Earl Leggett	DT-DE	6'3"	250	25		2
Bill Bishop	DT	6'4"	248	28		
Fred Williams	DT	6'4"	248	29		
Joe Fortunato	LB	6'	225	29	2	
Bill George	LB	6'2"	235	28	2	
Chuck Howley	LB	6'3"	228	23		
Larry Morris	LB	6'2"	230	24	1	6
Bill Roehnelt	LB	6'1"	225	23		
Erich Barnes	DB	6'2"	198	24	5	
J. C. Caroline	DB	6'1"	190	26	5	
Jack Johnson	DB	6'3"	198	25	1	
Pete Johnson	DB	6'2"	200	22		
Richie Petitbon	DB	6'3"	205	21	3	6
Charlie Sumner	DB	6'1"	195	29	3	
Vic Zucco	DB	6'	187	24		
Zeke Bratkowski	QB	6'2"	203	27		
Ed Brown	QB	6'2"	208	30		6
Rudy Bukich	QB	6'1"	200	28		
Willie Galimore	HB	6'1"	187	24		18
Johnny Morris	HB	5'10"	180	24		18
John Adams	FB	6'3"	235	22		
Rick Casares	FB	6'2"	225	28		72
Merrill Douglas	FB	6'	204	23		12
Jim Dooley	FL	6'4"	198	29		18
Lionel Taylor	FL	6'2"	215	23		
Willard Dewveall	OE	6'4"	218	22		18
Harlon Hill	OE	6'3"	200	27		18
Bill McColl	OE	6'4"	230	29		
John Aveni	K	6'3"	210	24		58

Bob Kilcullen – Military Service

GREEN BAY PACKERS 7-5-0 Vince Lombardi

Scores of Each Game		
9	CHIC. BEARS	6
28	DETROIT	10
21	SAN FRANCISCO	20
6	LOS ANGELES	45
21	Baltimore	38
3	New York	20
17	Chic. Bears	28
24	BALTIMORE	28
21	WASHINGTON	0
24	Detroit	17
38	Los Angeles	20
36	San Francisco	14

Use Name	Pos.	Hgt	Wgt	Age	Int	Pts
Forrest Gregg	OT	6'4"	245	26		
Norm Masters	OT	6'2"	250	26		
Bob Skoronski	OT	6'3"	250	26		
John Dittrich	OG	6'1"	235	26		
Jerry Kramer	OG	6'3"	245	24		
Fuzzy Thurston	OG	6'1"	245	26		
Jim Ringo	C	6'1"	230	28		
Nate Borden	DE	6'	240	27		
Bill Quinlan	DE	6'3"	250	27	1	
Jim Temp	DE	6'4"	250	26	1	
Ken Beck	DT	6'2"	240	24		
Dave Hanner	DT	6'2"	260	30		2
Henry Jordan	DT	6'3"	250	24		
Tom Bettis	LB	6'2"	225	26	1	
Dan Currie	LB	6'3"	235	25	1	
Bill Forester	LB	6'3"	240	28	2	2
Ray Nitschke	LB	6'3"	230	23		
Bobby Dillon	DB	6'1"	180	29	1	
Bobby Freeman	DB	6'1"	205	26	2	
Hank Gremminger	DB	6'1"	205	26	1	
Johnny Symank	DB	5'11"	180	24	2	
Em Tunnell	DB	6'1"	215	37	2	
Jesse Whittenton	DB	6'	195	25		
Joe Francis	QB	6'1"	195	24		
Lamar McHan	QB	6'1"	205	27		
Bart Starr	QB	6'1"	200	26		
Timmy Brown	HB	5'10"	195	22		
Bill Butler	HB	5'10"	180	22		6
Paul Hornung	HB	6'2"	215	23		94
Don McIlhenny	HB	6'	200	24		12
Lew Carpenter	FB-HB	6'1"	210	27		6
Jim Taylor	FB	6'	212	24		48
Boyd Dowler	OE	6'5"	225	22		24
Gary Knafelc	OE	6'4"	220	27		24
Ron Kramer	OE	6'3"	230	24		
Max McGee	OE	6'3"	205	27		30
A. D. Williams	OE	6'2"	210	26		

Steve Meilinger – Broken Arm

SAN FRANCISCO FORTY NINERS 7-5-0 Red Hickey

Scores of Each Game		
24	PHILADELPHIA	14
34	LOS ANGELES	0
20	Green Bay	21
34	Detroit	13
20	CHIC. BEARS	17
33	DETROIT	7
24	Los Angeles	16
3	Chic. Bears	14
14	Baltimore	45
21	Cleveland	20
14	BALTIMORE	34
14	GREEN BAY	36

Use Name	Pos.	Hgt	Wgt	Age	Int	Pts
John Gonzaga	OT	6'3"	245	26		
Bob St. Clair	OT	6'9"	265	28		
John Thomas	OT	6'4"	243	24		
Bruce Bosley	OG	6'2"	237	25		
Ted Connolly	OG	6'3"	240	27		
John Wittenborn	OG	6'2"	233	23		
Frank Morze	DT-C	6'4"	275	25		
Charlie Krueger	DE	6'4"	245	23		2
Monte Clark	DT-DE	6'6"	255	22		
Ed Henke	LB-DE	6'3"	227	31		
Bill Herchman	DT	6'2"	245	26		
Leo Nomellini	DT	6'3"	255	34		
Henry Schmidt	DT	6'4"	245	22		
Bob Harrison	LB	6'2"	227	22		
Matt Hazeltine	LB	6'1"	220	26		6
Clancy Osborne	LB	6'3"	220	24		
Jerry Tubbs	LB	6'2"	220	24	2	
Karl Rubke	C-LB	6'4"	248	23		
Billy Atkins	DB	6'1"	192	24		
Dave Baker	DB	6'	190	22	5	
Eddie Dove	DB	6'2"	183	22	1	
Jerry Mertens	DB	6'	187	23	2	6
Jimmy Ridlon	DB	6'1"	186	24		
Abe Woodson	DB	5'11"	188	24	4	6
John Brodie	QB	6'1"	192	24		
Y. A. Tittle	QB	6'	195	32		
Lenny Lyles	HB	6'2"	198	23		6
Hugh McElhenny	HB	6'1"	198	30		24
Dick Moegle	HB	6'	190	25		
J. D. Smith	FB-HB	6'1"	210	26		66
Joe Perry	FB	6'	197	32		18
C. R. Roberts	FB	6'3"	215	23		6
R. C. Owens	OE-FL	6'3"	196	24		18
Clyde Conner	OE	6'2"	193	26		6
Fred Dugan	OE	6'3"	197	25		
Billy Wilson	FL-OE	6'3"	190	32		24
Tommy Davis	K	6'	212	24		67

Jim Pace – Injury

DETROIT LIONS 3-8-1 George Wilson

Scores of Each Game		
9	Baltimore	21
10	Green Bay	28
24	BALTIMORE	31
13	SAN FRANCISCO	34
17	Los Angeles	7
7	San Francisco	33
10	Pittsburgh	10
23	LOS ANGELES	17
14	CHIC. BEARS	24
17	GREEN BAY	24
45	CHIC. CARDS	21
14	Chic. Bears	25

Use Name	Pos.	Hgt	Wgt	Age	Int	Pts
Lou Creekmur	OT	6'4"	250	32		
Ken Russell	OT	6'3"	250	23		
Ollie Spencer	OT	6'2"	250	28		
Bob Grottkau	OG	6'4"	220	22		
Mike Rabold	OG	6'2"	235	22		
Harley Sewell	OG	6'1"	233	28		
John Gordy	OT-OG	6'3"	240	23		
Charlie Ane	OT-C	6'2"	260	28		
Gene Cronin	DE	6'2"	227	26		
Bill Glass	DE	6'5"	236	23		
Darris McCord	DE	6'4"	240	26		
Alex Karras	DT	6'2"	254	23		
Gil Mains	DT	6'2"	242	29		
Ben Paolucci	DT	6'2"	240	22		
Jerry Perry	DT	6'4"	234	28		27
Jim Weatherall	DT	6'4"	245	29		
Bob Long	LB	6'3"	234	25		
Jim Martin	LB	6'3"	230	35	2	21
Joe Schmidt	LB	6'1"	217	27	1	
Wayne Walker	LB	6'2"	220	22		5
Jim David	DB	5'10"	178	32	2	
Dick LeBeau	DB	6'1"	187	22		
Gary Lowe	DB	5'11"	197	25	5	
Jim Steffen	DB	6'	195	22		
Dave Whitsell	DB	6'	185	23		
Terry Barr	HB-DB	6'	190	24	1	6
Yale Lary	DB	6'	185	28	3	6
Earl Morrall	QB	6'1"	200	25		
Tobin Rote	QB	6'3"	220	31		12
Jerry Reichow	OE-QB	6'2"	215	24		6
Hopalong Cassady	HB	5'10"	182	25		30
Dan Lewis	HB	6'1"	197	23		12
Ken Webb	FB-HB	5'11"	208	24		12
John Henry Johnson	FB	6'2"	213	29		18
Nick Pietrosante	FB	6'2"	225	22		18
Gene Cook	OE	6'3"	215	25		
Jim Doran	OE	6'2"	200	31		12
Jim Gibbons	OE	6'2"	212	23		6
Steve Junker	-OE	6'3"	215	24		
Dave Middleton	OE	6'1"	196	26		12

Gene Gedman – Knee Injury

LOS ANGELES RAMS 2-10-0 Sid Gillman

Scores of Each Game		
21	NEW YORK	23
0	San Francisco	34
28	Chic. Bears	21
45	Green Bay	6
7	DETROIT	17
21	CHIC. BEARS	26
16	SAN FRANCISCO	24
17	Detroit	23
20	Philadelphia	23
21	Baltimore	35
20	GREEN BAY	38
26	BALTIMORE	45

Use Name	Pos.	Hgt	Wgt	Age	Int	Pts
Charlie Bradshaw	OT	6'6"	255	23		
Paul Dickson	OT	6'5"	245	22		
Gene Selawski	OT	6'4"	252	23		
Bob Fry	OG	6'4"	238	28		
Buck Lansford	OG	6'2"	232	26		
Duane Putnam	OG	6'	230	31		
John Morrow	C	6'3"	236	26		
John Houser	OG-C	6'3"	240	23		
Gene Brito	DE	6'1"	230	34		
Lou Michaels	DE	6'2"	238	23		36
Lamar Lundy	OE-DE	6'7"	240	24		
Sam Williams	OE-DE	6'5"	225	28		2
John Baker	DT	6'6"	290	24		
John Lovetere	DT	6'4"	266	23		
George Strugar	DT	6'5"	258	24		
John Guzik	LB	6'3"	230	22		
Bill Jobko	LB	6'2"	218	23	1	
Jack Pardee	LB	6'2"	215	23		
Les Richter	LB	6'3"	232	28		
Roy Wilkins	LB	6'3"	223	25		
Don Burroughs	DB	6'4"	186	28		
Tom Franckhauser	DB	6'	192	22	3	
Carl Karilivacz	DB	6'	190	28		
Ed Meador	DB	5'11"	185	22	3	
Jack Morris	DB	6'	188	27		24
Will Sherman	DB	6'2"	197	30		
Buddy Humphrey	QB	6'1"	190	23		
Frank Ryan	QB	6'3"	190	23		6
Billy Wade	QB	6'2"	203	28		12
Tom Wilson	HB	6'	204	26		6
Joe Marconi	FB-HB	6'2"	225	25		30
Jon Arnett	FL-OE-HB	5'11"	193	24		24
Ollie Matson	FB	6'2"	210	29		36
Clendon Thomas	DB-OE-FL	6'2"	190	22		
Leon Clarke	OE	6'4"	230	26		
Jim Phillips	OE	6'1"	200	22		24
Del Shofner	OE	6'3"	185	23		42

Ron Waller – Knee Injury

BALTIMORE COLTS

RUSHING

Last Name	No.	Yds	Avg	TD
Ameche	178	679	3.8	7
Moore	92	422	4.6	2
Sommer	62	231	3.7	2
Unitas	29	145	5.0	2
Pricer	34	128	3.8	0
Dupre	23	54	2.3	0
Hawkins	12	44	3.7	0
Brown	2	4	2.0	0
Lewis	4	2	0.5	0

RECEIVING

Last Name	No.	Yds	Avg	TD
Berry	66	959	15	14
Moore	47	846	18	6
Mutscheller	44	699	16	8
Ameche	13	129	10	1
Sommer	7	111	16	0
Richardson	7	81	12	3
Dupre	6	47	8	1
Lewis	3	54	18	0
Pricer	2	3	2	0
Sherer	1	9	9	0

PUNT RETURNS

Last Name	No.	Yds	Avg	TD
Sample	22	129	6	0
Taseff	15	104	7	0
Shinnick	1	0	0	0

KICKOFF RETURNS

Last Name	No.	Yds	Avg	TD
Sample	17	457	27	0
Sommer	9	185	21	0
Pricer	6	66	11	0
Rechichar	2	39	20	0
Lewis	2	31	16	0
Hawkins	1	21	21	0
Plunkett	1	12	12	0
Davis	1	0	0	0

PASSING – PUNTING – KICKING

PASSING	Att	Comp	%	Yds	Yd/Att	TD	Int–%	RK
Unitas	367	193	53	2899	7.9	32	14– 4	2
Brown	4	1	25	14	3.5	0	0– 0	
Moore	3	2	67	25	8.3	1	0– 0	
Dupre	1	0	0	0	0.0	0	0– 0	

PUNTING	No	Avg
Sherer	51	41.8
Brown	2	44.5

KICKING	XP	Att	%	FG	Att	%
Myhra	50	51	98	6	17	35
Rechichar	0	0	0	0	1	0

CHICAGO BEARS

RUSHING

Last Name	No.	Yds	Avg	TD
Casares	177	699	3.9	10
J. Morris	87	312	3.6	0
Galimore	58	199	3.4	1
Brown	33	108	3.3	1
Bratkowski	7	86	12.3	0
Douglas	24	47	2.0	2
Bukich	1	0	0.0	0
Hill	1	0	0.0	0
Adams	4	–13	–3.2	0

RECEIVING

Last Name	No.	Yds	Avg	TD
Dooley	41	580	14	3
Hill	36	578	16	3
Casares	27	273	10	2
Dewveall	20	420	21	3
J. Morris	13	197	15	2
Galimore	10	125	13	2
McColl	8	94	12	0
Douglas	1	17	17	0

PUNT RETURNS

Last Name	No.	Yds	Avg	TD
J. Morris	14	171	12	1
Petitbon	11	72	7	0
Zucco	1	0	0	0

KICKOFF RETURNS

Last Name	No.	Yds	Avg	TD
J. Morris	17	438	26	0
Galimore	11	229	21	0
Petitbon	4	68	17	0
Roehnelt	1	0	0	0

PASSING – PUNTING – KICKING

PASSING	Att	Comp	%	Yds	Yd/Att	TD	Int–%	RK
Brown	247	125	51	1881	7.6	13	10– 4	6
Bratkowski	62	31	50	403	6.5	2	5– 8	
Casares	1	0	0	0	0.0	0	1–100	

PUNTING	No	Avg
Brown	64	41.2
Casares	3	46.3
J. Johnson	1	32.0

KICKING	XP	Att	%	FG	Att	%
Aveni	28	32	88	10	19	53

GREEN BAY PACKERS

RUSHING

Last Name	No.	Yds	Avg	TD
Hornung	152	681	4.5	7
Taylor	120	452	3.8	6
Carpenter	60	322	5.4	1
McIlhenny	47	231	4.9	1
Starr	16	83	5.2	0
McHan	16	64	4.0	0
Butler	7	49	7.0	0
Dowler	1	20	20.0	0
Francis	2	5	2.5	0

RECEIVING

Last Name	No.	Yds	Avg	TD
Dowler	32	549	17	4
McGee	30	695	23	5
Knafelc	27	384	14	4
Hornung	15	113	8	0
Taylor	9	71	8	2
McIlhenny	8	95	12	1
Carpenter	5	47	9	0
Williams	1	11	11	0
Butler	1	–2	–2	0

PUNT RETURNS

Last Name	No.	Yds	Avg	TD
Butler	18	163	9	1
Carpenter	13	150	12	0
Tunnell	1	3	3	0
Symank	1	0	0	0

KICKOFF RETURNS

Last Name	No.	Yds	Avg	TD
Butler	21	472	22	0
Symank	14	338	24	0
Francis	2	52	26	0
McIlhenny	3	50	17	0
Carpenter	1	24	24	0
Nitschke	2	13	7	0

PASSING – PUNTING – KICKING

PASSING	Att	Comp	%	Yds	Yd/Att	TD	Int–%	RK
Starr	134	70	52	972	7.3	6	7– 5	9
McHan	108	48	44	805	7.5	8	9– 8	13
Francis	18	5	28	91	5.1	0	1– 6	
Hornung	8	5	63	95	11.9	2	0– 0	

PUNTING	No	Avg
McGee	64	42.4

KICKING	XP	Att	%	FG	Att	%
Hornung	31	32	97	7	17	41

SAN FRANCISCO FORTY NINERS

RUSHING

Last Name	No.	Yds	Avg	TD
Smith	207	1036	5.0	10
Perry	139	602	4.4	3
McElhenny	18	67	3.7	1
Roberts	10	67	6.7	1
Lyles	13	28	2.2	1
Tittle	11	24	2.2	0
Moegle	3	9	3.0	0
Brodie	5	6	1.2	0
Owens	1	0	0.0	0

RECEIVING

Last Name	No.	Yds	Avg	TD
Wilson	44	540	12	4
McElhenny	22	329	15	3
Owens	17	347	20	3
Conner	13	162	12	1
Smith	13	133	10	1
Perry	12	53	4	0
Dugan	6	72	12	0
Lyles	3	33	11	0
Moegle	1	12	12	0
Tittle	1	4	4	0

PUNT RETURNS

Last Name	No.	Yds	Avg	TD
Woodson	15	143	10	0
Dove	22	126	6	0

KICKOFF RETURNS

Last Name	No.	Yds	Avg	TD
Lyles	25	565	23	0
Woodson	13	382	29	1
Hazeltine	2	26	13	0
Herchman	1	7	7	0

PASSING – PUNTING – KICKING

PASSING	Att	Comp	%	Yds	Yd/Att	TD	Int–%	RK
Tittle	199	102	51	1331	6.7	10	15– 8	10
Brodie	64	30	47	354	5.5	2	7– 11	
Moegle	1	0	0	0	0.0	0	0– 0	

PUNTING	No	Avg
Davis	59	45.7

KICKING	XP	Att	%	FG	Att	%
Davis	31	31	100	12	26	46

DETROIT LIONS

RUSHING

Last Name	No.	Yds	Avg	TD
Pietrosante	76	447	5.9	3
Johnson	82	270	3.3	2
Webb	60	222	3.7	2
Cassady	52	203	3.9	1
Lewis	49	199	4.1	2
Rote	35	156	4.5	2
Morrall	26	112	4.3	0
Reichow	13	98	7.5	0
Barr	5	57	11.4	1
Lary	1	18	18.0	0
Ane	0	10	–	0

RECEIVING

Last Name	No.	Yds	Avg	TD
Gibbons	31	431	14	1
Middleton	18	402	22	2
Pietrosante	16	140	9	0
Cassady	15	316	21	4
Doran	14	191	14	1
Webb	12	201	17	0
Barr	10	180	18	0
Reichow	7	118	17	1
Johnson	7	34	5	1
Lewis	5	75	15	0
Cook	1	43	43	0

PUNT RETURNS

Last Name	No.	Yds	Avg	TD
Barr	16	102	6	0
Lary	21	43	2	0
Middleton	3	30	10	0
Cassady	1	14	14	0
Lowe	6	8	1	0
Steffens	3	0	0	0

KICKOFF RETURNS

Last Name	No.	Yds	Avg	TD
Webb	16	352	22	0
Barr	9	224	25	0
Cassady	8	163	20	0
Pietrosante	5	98	20	0
Lewis	1	9	9	0
Martin	1	0	0	0
Rabold	1	0	0	0
Russell	1	0	0	0

PASSING – PUNTING – KICKING

PASSING	Att	Comp	%	Yds	Yd/Att	TD	Int–%	RK
Rote	162	62	38	861	5.3	5	19– 11	12
Morrall	137	65	47	1102	8.0	5	6– 4	7
Reichow	27	9	33	168	6.2	0	2– 11	
Barr	1	0	0	0	0.0	0	0– 0	
Lary	1	0	0	0	0.0	0	0– 0	

PUNTING	No	Avg
Lary	45	47.1
Morrall	11	43.7

KICKING	XP	Att	%	FG	Att	%
Perry	18	18	100	3	6	50
Martin	0	1	0	7	17	41
Walker	5	6	83	0	0	0

LOS ANGELES RAMS

RUSHING

Last Name	No.	Yds	Avg	TD
Matson	161	863	5.4	6
Arnett	73	371	5.1	2
Wilson	40	210	5.3	0
Marconi	52	176	3.4	4
Wade	25	95	3.8	2
Ryan	19	57	3.0	1
Shofner	1	6	6.0	0

RECEIVING

Last Name	No.	Yds	Avg	TD
Shofner	47	936	20	7
Arnett	38	419	11	1
Phillips	37	541	15	4
Clarke	20	453	16	0
Matson	18	130	7	0
Wilson	12	83	7	0
Marconi	10	81	8	1
Lundy	4	74	19	0
Thomas	1	6	6	0

PUNT RETURNS

Last Name	No.	Yds	Avg	TD
Arnett	17	184	11	1
Matson	14	61	4	0
Thomas	3	6	2	0
Burroughs	1	0	0	0
Meador	1	0	0	0

KICKOFF RETURNS

Last Name	No.	Yds	Avg	TD
Matson	16	367	23	0
Arnett	14	320	23	0
Wilson	7	243	35	0
Thomas	3	95	32	0
Wilkins	2	29	15	0
Dickson	1	0	0	0

PASSING – PUNTING – KICKING

PASSING	Att	Comp	%	Yds	Yd/Att	TD	Int–%	RK
Wade	261	153	59	2001	7.7	12	17– 7	5
Ryan	89	42	47	709	8.0	2	4– 4	
Arnett	5	1	20	13	2.6	0	0– 0	
Matson	1	0	0	0	0.0	0	1–100	

PUNTING	No	Avg
Shofner	48	41.8
Marconi	2	40.5

KICKING	XP	Att	%	FG	Att	%
Michaels	12	14	86	8	17	47
Morris	15	15	100	3	8	38
Richter	0	0	0	0	1	0

Use Name (Nicknames) – Positions	Team by Year	See Section	Hgt	Wgt	College	Int	Pts
Abbey, Joe OE-DE	48-49ChiB 49NYB	2	6'1"	202	North Texas State		
Abbruzzi, Lou HB-DB	46Bos		5'10"	175	Rhode Island		
Aberson, Cliff TB-DB	46GB	12	6'	195	none	3	
47-49 played major league baseball							
Adamle, Tony LB-FB	47-49CleAA 50-51Cle 52-53VR 54Cle	2	6'	215	Ohio State	7	12
Adams, John T	45-49Was		6'7"	242	Notre Dame		
Addams, Abe DE	49Det		6'2"	220	Indiana		
Adducci, Nick LB	54-55Was		5'10"	207	Nebraska		
Afflis, Dick OT-DG-OG	51-54GB		6'	251	Nevada	1	
Agajanian, Ben (The Toeless Wonder) K	45Phi 45Pit 47-48LA-AA 49NYG 53LA 54-57NYG 60LA-A 61DalA 61GB 62OakA 64SDA	5	6'	215	New Mexico		655
Agase, Alex LB-G	47LA-AA 47ChiAA 48-49CleAA 50-51Cle 53Bal		5'10"	212	Illinois	8	
Agler, Bob HB-DB-FB-LB	48-49LA		6'1"	208	Otterbein		
Akins, Al DB-HB	46CleAA 47-48BknAA 48BufAA		6'1"	199	Washington, Washington State	2	18
Alban, Dick DB	56-59Pit		6'	193	Northwestern	30	
Albert, Frankie QB-DB	46-49SF-AA 50-52,HC56-58SF	12 4	5'10"	166	Stanford		169
Albright, Bill OG-OT-DT	51-54NYG 55CFL		6'1"	233	Wisconsin		6
Alderton, John DE	53Pit		6'1"	200	Maryland		
Aldridge, Ben DB-HB	50-51NYY 52SF 53GB	2	6'	195	Oklahoma State	11	6
Alford, Bruce OE-DB	46-49NY-AA 50-51NYY	2	6'	190	Texas Christian	1	72
Allen, Carl DB-WB	48BknAA		6'	175	Ouachita Baptist	2	6
Allen, Eddie FB-LB	47ChiB		6'1"	200	Pennsylvania		
Allen, Ermal DB-QB	47CleAA		5'11"	165	Kentucky	4	
Allen, Johnny C-LB	55-58Was		6'2"	224	Purdue		
Allen, Lou OT	50-51Pit		6'3"	215	Duke		
Amberg, John DB-HB	51-52NYG		5'11"	195	Kansas	5	
Ameche, Alan (The Horse) FB	55-60Bal	2	6'	218	Wisconsin		264
Amstutz, Joe C	57Cle		6'5"	264	Indiana		
Amundsen, Norm OG	57GB		5'11"	245	Wisconsin		
Andabaker, Rudy OG	52Pit 53MS 54Pit		6'	208	Pittsburgh		
Anderson, Billy HB-DB	53-54ChiB		6'	198	Compton J.C.		
Anderson, Charlie DE-OE	56ChiC		6'	230	Louisiana Tech		
Anderson, Cliff OE	52-53ChiC 53NYG	2	6'2"	215	Indiana		12
Anderson, Ezz (Sugarfoot) OE-DE	47LA-AA 48CFL	2	6'4"	215	Kentucky State		6
Andros, Plato G-OT	47-50ChiC		6'	240	Oklahoma		
Ane, Charlie OT-C	53-59Det		6'2"	260	Southern Calif.		
Angsman, Elmer HB	46-52ChiC	2	5'11"	200	Notre Dame		192
Apolskis, Ray LB-OG-C	41-42ChiC 43-44MS 45-50ChiC		5'11"	206	Marquette	6	
Arenas, Joe HB-DB	51-57SF	23	5'11"	180	Nebraska-Omaha	6	108
Arms, Lloyd G	46-48ChiC		6'1"	215	Oklahoma State		
Armstrong, Charlie DB-TB	46BknAA		5'10"	180	Mississippi Coll.	2	
Armstrong, Graham T	41Cle 42-44MS 45Cle 47-48BufAA	5	6'4"	230	John Carroll		23
Armstrong, Neill OE-DB	47-51Phi 52CFL	2	6'2"	189	Oklahoma State	9	66
Arterburn, Elmer DB	54ChiC		5'10"	175	Texas Tech		
Aschbacher, Darrell OG	59Phi		6'1"	220	Oregon		
Aschenbrenner, Frank FB	49ChiAA		5'10"	188	Northwestern		
Atkeson, Dale FB	54-56Was	23	6'2"	211	none		36
Atkins, George OG	55Det		6'1"	210	Auburn		
Atwood, John HB-WB-DB	48NYG	2	5'11"	185	Wisconsin	1	6
Audet, Earl T	45Was 46-48LA-AA		6'2"	252	Southern Calif.		
Austin, Bill OG-T	49-50NYG 51-52MS 53-57NYG HC66-68Pit HC70Was		6'1"	223	Oregon State	1	
Autrey, Billy C	53ChiB		6'3"	220	Austin		
Averno, Sisto OG-LB	50Bal 51NYY 52Dal 53-54Bal		5'11"	237	Muhlenberg		
Avery, Don T	46-47Was 48LA-AA		6'4"	254	Southern Calif.		
Avinger, Clarence FB	53NYG	4	6'1"	215	Alabama		
Babcock, Harry OE-DE	53-55SF	2	6'2"	193	Georgia		
Badaczewski, John OG-DG	46-48Bos 48ChiC 49-51 Was 53ChiB		6'1"	239	Case Reserve		
Bagarus, Steve HB-DB	45-46Was 47LA 48Was	23	6'	173	Notre Dame	5	60
Bagdon, Ed OG-LB	50-51ChiC 52Was		5'10"	204	Michigan State		7
Baggett, Billy HB-DB	52Dal		5'11"	175	Louisiana State	1	6
Bahnsen, Ken FB	53SF		5'10"	200	North Texas State		
Bailey, Byron HB	52-53Det 53GB	2	5'10"	192	Washington State		12
Bailey, Jim G	49ChiAA		6'2"	215	West Virginia St.		
Bailey, Sam DE-OE	46Bos		6'2"	195	Georgia		
Baker, Jon LB-OG	49-52NYG		6'2"	214	California		
Balatti, Ed OE-DB-DE	46-48SF-AA 48NY-AA 48BufAA	2	6'1"	195	none		21
Baldacci, Lou HB	56Pit	2 4	6'2"	200	Michigan		
Baldwin, Al OE-DB	47-49BufAA 50GB	2	6'2"	201	Arkansas	7	150
Baldwin, Burr OE-DE	47-49LA-AA	2	6'1"	197	U.C.L.A.	2	6
Baldwin, Jack C-LB	46-47NY-AA 47SF-AA 48BufAA		6'3"	223	Centenary		
Ball, Herman	HC49-51Was				Davis & Elkins		
Balog, Bob C-LB	49-50Pit		6'2"	225	Denver		
Banducci, Bruno OG-DG	44-45Phi 46-49SF-AA 50-54SF		5'11"	216	Stanford		6
Banonis, Vince C-LB	42ChiC 43MS 44C-P 46-50ChiC 51-53Det		6'1"	230	Detroit	14	12
Banta, Jack HB-DB	41Phi 42-43MS 44-45Phi 46-48LA	2 4	5'11"	191	Southern Calif.	5	42
Barbolak, Pete T	49Pit		6'3"	235	Purdue		
Barfield, Ken OT-DT	54Was		6'2"	238	Mississippi		
Barker, Ed OE	53Pit 54Was	2	6'3"	196	Washington State		24
Barnes, Emery DE	56GB		6'6"	235	Oregon		
Barnes, Larry FB-DE	57SF 60OakA	5	6'1"	228	Colorado State		55
Barnes, Walt (Piggy) OG-DG	48-51Phi		6'1"	238	Louisiana State		2
Barnett, Tom HB-DB	59-60Pit	2	5'11"	190	Purdue		12
Barni, Roy DB	52-53ChiC 54-55Phi 55-56Was		5'11"	185	San Francisco	11	6
Shot and killed – August 57							
Barry, Al OG	54GB 55-56MS 57GB 58-59NYG 60LA-A		6'2"	230	Southern Calif.		
Barry, Paul HB	50LA 51MS 52LA 53Was 54ChiC	2	6'	208	Tulsa		18
Barton, Don HB-DB	53GB		5'11"	175	Texas		6
Bartos, Joe HB	50Was		6'2"	194	Navy		
Barwegan, Dick OG-DG-LB	47NY-AA 48-49BalAA 50-52ChiB 53-54Bal		6'1"	227	Purdue	1	
Barzilauskas, Fritz OG-DG-LB	47-48Bos 49NYB 51NYG		6'1"	230	Yale		
Bass, Bill HB-DB	47ChiAA 48CFL	2	5'10"	180	Nevada	2	12
Bassett, Mo FB	54-56Cle	2	6'1"	231	Langston		66
Batorski, John OE-DE	46BufAA		6'2"	238	Colgate		
Bauer, John OG	54NYG		6'3"	235	Illinois		
Bauman, Alf DT-OT	47ChiAA 47Phi 48-50ChiB		6'2"	228	Northwestern		
Baumgartner, Bill OE-DE	47BalAA		6'3"	202	Minnesota		
Bawel, Bibbles DB-OE	52Phi 53-54MS 55-56Phi 56-57CFL	3	6'1"	185	Evansville	18	18
Baxter, Lloyd C	48GB		6'2"	210	S.M.U.		
Beals, Alyn OE-DB	46-49SF-AA 50-51SF	2	6'	188	Santa Clara	1	296

Use Name (Nicknames) – Positions	Team by Year	See Section	Hgt	Wgt	College	Int	Pts
Beatty, Ed C	55-56SF 57-61Pit 61Was		6'3"	229	Mississippi		
Bechtol, Hub DE-OE	47-49BalAA	2	6'3"	202	Texas	2	6
Beck, Ken DT-DE	59-60GB		6'2"	245	Texas A&M		
Beck, Ray OG-DG	52NYG 53-54MS 55-57NYG		6'2"	224	Georgia Tech	1	
Bednarik, Chuck LB-C	49-62Phi		6'3"	233	Pennsylvania	20	6
Beil, Larry T	48NYG		6'2"	235	Portland		
Bell, Ed G-T	46MiaAA 47-49GB		6'1"	227	Indiana		
Bell, Eddie DB	55-58Phi 59CFL 60NY-A		6'1"	212	Pennsylvania	11	6
Benners, Fred QB	52NYG	1	6'3"	195	S.M.U.		
Bennett, Earl G-LB	46GB		5'8"	188	Hardin-Simmons		
Benson, George HB-DB	47BknAA		6'1"	205	Northwestern		
Bentz,Roman G-T	46-48NY-AA 48SF-AA		6'2"	230	Tulane		
Berezney, Pete T	47LA-AA 48BalAA		6'2"	240	Notre Dame		
Bernardi, Frank DB-HB	55-57ChiC 60DenA	3	5'9"	181	Colorado	4	12
Bernet, Ed OE	55Pit 60DalA	2	6'3"	203	S.M.U.		6
Bernhardt, George G	46-48BknAA 48ChiAA		5'10"	213	Illinois		
Berrang, Ed DE-OE	49-51Was 51Det 52Was		6'2"	205	Villanova	3	
Berry, Rex DB-HB	51-56SF		5'11"	181	Brigham Young	22	18
Berry, Wayne HB-DB	54NYG		6'	175	Washington State		
Berschet, Marv OG-DE	54-55Was		6'2"	220	Illinois		
Bertelli, Angelo (The Springfield Rifle) QB	46LA-AA 47-48ChiAA	1	6'1"	190	Notre Dame		6
Berzinski, Will HB	56Phi		6'2"	195	Wis. St.–La Crosse		
Beson, Warren C	49BalAA		6'	205	Minnesota		
Bettis, Tom LB	55-61GB 62Pit 63ChiB		6'2"	228	Purdue	1	
Bielski, Dick OE-FB	55-59Phi 60-61Dal 62-63Bal	2 5	6'1"	224	Maryland		208
Bienemann, Tom DE-OE	51-56ChiC		6'3"	221	Drake	4	
Bighead, Jack DE-OE	54Bal 55LA		6'3"	215	Pepperdine		
Billman, John G-LB	46BknAA 47ChiAA		6'1"	202	Minnesota		
Bingaman, Les DG-OG	48-54Det		6'3"	272	Illinois	2	
Bingham, Don HB	56ChiB		6'	185	Sul Ross State		6
Biscaha, Joe OE	59NYG 60BosA		6'1"	190	Richmond		
Bishop, Bill DT-OT	52-60ChiB 61Min		6'4"	248	North Texas State	2	6
Black, Blondy DB-HB-FB	46BufAA 47BalAA		5'11"	195	Mississippi State	1	
Blackbourn, Lisle	HC54-57GB				Lawrence		
Blackburn, Bill LB-C	46-50ChiC	4	6'6"	228	Rice	11	26
Blake, Tom T	49NYB		6'2"	220	Cincinnati		
Blandin, Ernie DT-OT	46-47CleAA 48-49BalAA 50,53Bal		6'4"	248	Tulane		
Blount, Lamar OE-DB-HB	46MiaAA 47BufAA 47BalAA	2	6'1"	190	Mississippi State		6
Blumenstock, Jim FB-DB	47NYG	2	5'11"	190	Fordham		12
Bock, Wayne DT	57ChiC		6'4"	250	Illinois		
Boedecker, Bill HB-DB	46ChiAA 47-49CleAA 50GB 50Phi	2	5'11"	192	DePaul	1	84
Boensch, Fred G-LB	47-48Was		6'4"	228	Stanford	1	
Boggan, Rex DT	55NYG		6'3"	245	Mississippi		
Boland, Pat	HC46ChiAA				Minnesota		
Bolden, Leroy HB	58-59Cle		5'8"	170	Michigan State		6
Bolkovac, Nick DT-OT	53-54Pit	5	6'1'	230	Pittsburgh		57
Boll, Don OT-OG	53-59Was 60NYG		6'2"	270	Nebraska		
Bookout, Billy DB	55-56GB		5'11"	180	Austin	3	
Boone, J. R. HB-DB	48-51ChiB 52SF 53GB	23	5'8"	162	Tulsa	2	72
Borden, Nate DE	55-59GB 60-61Dal 62BufA		6'	234	Indiana		
Borton, John QB	57Cle		6'	208	Ohio State		
Bouley, Gil DT-OT	45Cle 46-50LA		6'2"	235	Boston College		6
Bowers, Bill DB	54LA		6'	198	Southern Calif.		
Bowman, Bill FB	54Det 55MS 56Det 57Pit	2	6'2"	215	William & Mary		42
Box, Cloyce OE-HB	49-50Det 51MS 52-54Det	2	6'4"	220	West Texas State		192
Boyd, Bob OE-DB	50-51LA 52MS 53-57LA	2	6'2"	201	Loyola (L.A.)	3	168
Boyda, Mike LB-FB	49NYB	4	6'1"	205	Wash. & Lee	1	
Boydston, Max OE	55-58ChiC 60-61DalA 62OakA	2	6'2"	210	Oklahoma		48
Braatz, Tom LB-OE	57Was 58LA 58-59Was 60Dal		6'1"	216	Marquette	2	
Brackett, M. L. DE-DT-LB	56-57ChiB 58NYG		6'5"	248	Auburn	1	
Brackins, Charlie QB	55GB		6'2"	202	Prairie View		
Bradley, Ed OG-DE	50,52ChiB 53CFL		6'	212	Wake Forest		
Bradley, Harold OG	54-56Cle 58Phi		6'2"	230	Iowa		
Brady, Pat QB-K	52-54Pit	4	6'1"	195	Bradley, Nevada		
Brancato, George HB-DB	54ChiC		5'9"	177	Louisiana State		
Brandau, Art C-LB	45-46Pit		6'2"	210	Tennessee		
Brandt, John HB-DB	52-54Pit	2	6'1"	200	St. Thomas		24
Bray, Ray OG-DG	39-42ChiB 43-45MS 46-51ChiB 52GB		6'	237	Western Michigan		
Brazinsky, Sam C-LB	46BufAA		6'1"	215	Villanova	2	
Bredde, Bill HB-DB	54ChiC		6'1"	195	Oklahoma State	2	6
Bredice, John OE	56Phi	2	6'1"	213	Boston U.		6
Brethauer, Monte DB-OE	53Bal 54MS 55Bal	2 4	6'1"	178	Oregon	1	
Brettschneider, Carl LB	56-59ChiC 60-63Det		6'1"	223	Iowa State	3	
Brewer, John FB	52-53Phi	2	6'4"	230	Louisville		18
Brewster, Darrell (Pete) OE	52-58Cle 59-60Pit	2	6'3"	210	Purdue		126
Briggs, Paul T	48Det		6'4"	248	Colorado		
Brink, Larry DE-OE	48-53LA 54ChiB		6'5"	235	Northern Illinois		8
Brito, Gene DE-OE	51-53Was 54CFL 55-58Was 59-60LA	2	6'1"	226	Loyola (L.A.)	1	12
Britt, Oscar G	46Was		5'11"	193	Mississippi		
Brookshier, Tom DB	53Phi 54-55MS 56-61Phi		6'	196	Colorado	20	
Brosky, Al DB	54ChiC		5'11"	175	Illinois	2	
Broussard, Fred C	55Pit 55NYG		6'3"	235	Texas A & M, NW State-La.		
Brown, Buddy OG	51-52Was 53-56GB		6'1"	220	Arkansas		
Brown, Dan DE	50Was		6'1"	200	Villanova		
Brown, Dave DB-WB	43NYG 44-45MS 46-47NYG	2	5'11"	190	Alabama	6	
Brown, Ed QB-DB	54-61ChiB 62-65Pit 65Bal	12 4	6'2"	209	San Francisco		94
Brown, George OG-DG	49NY-AA 50NYY		6'2"	222	Texas Christian		
Brown, Hardy LB-DB-FB	48BknAA 49ChiAA 50Bal 50Was 51-56SF 56ChiC 60DenA	5	6'	193	Tulsa	13	43
Brown, Howie OG-DG-OT-DT	48-50Det		5'11"	215	Indiana		
Brown, John LB-C	47-49LA-AA		6'4"	230	N.Car. Central	5	12
Brown, Marv HB	57Det		5'8"	150	East Texas State		
Brown, Paul	HC46-49CleAA HC50-62Cle HC68-69CinA HC70-73Cin				Miami–Ohio		
Brown, Pete C-LB	53-54SF	4	6'2"	210	Georgia Tech	1	
Brown, Ray DB-QB	58-60Bal	4	6'2"	195	Mississippi	13	
Brown, Rosey OT	53-65NYG		6'3"	249	Morgan State		
Browning, Greg OE	47NYG		6'	190	Denver		
Brubaker, Dick OE-DE	55,57ChiC 60BufA	2	6'	202	Ohio State		6

Use Name (Nicknames) – Positions	Team by Year	See Section	Hgt	Wgt	College	Int	Pts
Bruce Gail, DE-OE	48-49SF-AA 50-51SF		6'1"	206	Washington	2	1
Brueckman, Charlie LB	58Was 60LA-A		6'2"	223	Pittsburgh		
Brumfield, Jack DE	54SF		6'2"	215	Southern Miss.		
Brundage, Dewey DE	54Pit		6'3"	210	Brigham Young		
Bruney, Fred DB	53SF 54-55MS 56SF 56-57Pit 58LA 60-62BosA	3	5'10"	184	Ohio State	15	6
Brutz, Jim T	46,48ChiAA		6'	230	Notre Dame		
Bryant, Bob T	46-49SF-AA		6'3"	226	Texas Tech		
Bryant, Walter DB-HB	55Bal		6'1"	185	Texas Tech	1	
Bucek, Ray G-LB	46Pit		6'	186	Texas A & M		
Buffington, Harry G-LB-BB	42NYG 43-45MS 46-48BknAA		6'	206	Oklahoma State	1	
Buksar, George LB-FB	49ChiAA 50Bal 51-52Was	2 5	6'	206	Purdue	7	30
Bulger, Chet OT-DT	42-43ChiC 44C-P 45-49ChiC 50Det		6'3"	239	Auburn		7
Bullough, Hank OG-LB	55GB 56-57MS 58GB		6'	230	Michigan State		
Bumgardner, Max DE	48Det		6'2"	190	Texas		
Bumgardner, Rex HB-DB	48-49BufAA 50-52Cle	23	5'11"	193	West Virginia	4	72
Burk, Adrian QB	50Bal 51-56Phi	12 4	6'2"	190	Baylor		42
Burke, Don LB-OG	50-54SF		6'	235	Southern Calif.	1	6
Burkett, Jeff OE-DB killed in plane crash October 24, 1947	47ChiC		6'1"	190	Louisiana State	1	6
Burl, Alex HB	56ChiC		5'10"	165	Colorado State		6
Burnine, Hank OE	56NYG 56-57Phi	2	6'2"	188	Missouri		12
Burris, Buddy LB-OG	49-51GB		5'11"	215	Oklahoma	1	
Burrus, Harry DB-OE-WB	46-47NY-AA 48ChiAA 48BknAA	2	6'1"	195	Hardin-Simmons	6	26
Butkus, Carl T	48Was 48NY-AA 49NYG		6'1"	245	George Washington		
Butler, Jack DB-OE	51-59Pit		6'	195	St. Bonaventure	52	54
Byler, Joe T	46NYG		6'5"	240	Nebraska		
Cain, Jim DE-OE	49ChiC 50Det 51-52MS 53-55Det		6'1"	202	Alabama		6
Calacagni, Ralph T	46Bos 47Pit		6'3"	230	Pennsylvania		2
Call, Jack HB	57-58Bal 59Pit	2	6'1"	200	Colgate		
Callahan, Bob C-LB	48BufAA		6'	205	Michigan		
Callahan, Jim TB-DB	46Det	12	5'11"	185	Texas	2	12
Calvin, Tom HB	52-54Pit	2	6'	200	Alabama		
Cameron, Paul DB	54Pit 55-56MS		6'	185	U. C. L. A.	7	
Camp, Jim WB-DB	48BknAA		6'	170	North Carolina	1	
Campana, Al HB-DB	50-52ChiB 53ChiC	2	5'11"	181	Youngstown	1	6
Campanella, Joe LB-DT-OT	52Dal 53-57Bal		6'2"	242	Ohio State	3	
Campbell, Bill LB-C-DB	45-49ChiC 49NYB		6'	195	Oklahoma		
Campbell, Dick LB	58-60Pit		6'1"	227	Marquette	3	
Campbell, Leon FB	50Bal 52-54ChiB 55Pit	23	6'	199	Arkansas		6
Campbell, Marion DT-DE-OT	54-55SF 56-61Phi		6'3"	250	Georgia	3	
Campbell, Milt HB	57Cle		6'3"	217	Indiana		6
Campbell, Stan OG	52Det 53-54MS 55-58Det 59-61Phi 62OakA		6'	226	Iowa State		
Campion, T.G. T	47Phi		6'2"	235	Southeastern La.		
Campora, Don DT	50,52SF 53Was		6'3"	268	U. of Pacific		
Canadeo, Tony (The Gray Ghost of Gonzaga HB-DB-TB-FB	41-44GB 45MS 46-52GB	1234	5'11"	190	Gonzaga	9	186
Canady, Jim DB-HB	48-49ChiB 49NYB	2	5'10"	178	Texas	5	
Cannady, John LB-C-BB	47-54NYG		6'2"	227	Indiana	14	
Cannamela, Pat LB	52Dal	5	6'	195	Southern Calif.		8
Cannava, Tony HB-DB	50GB		5'10"	180	Boston College		
Capuzzi, Jim DBD-QB	55-56GB		6'	190	Cincinnati	2	
Carapella, Al DT-OT	51-55SF		6'	235	Miami(Fla.)	3	
Cardinal, Fred LB	47NY-AA		5'11"	220	Baldwin-Wallace		
Carey, Bob OE	52LA 53MS 54,56LA 58ChiB	2	6'5"	219	Michigan State		23
Carl, Harland HB	56ChiB	2	6'	195	Wisconsin		6
Carmichael, Al HB	53-58GB 60-61DenA	23	6'1"	192	Southern Calif.		84
Carpenter, Jack T	47-49BufAA 49SF-AA 50CFL		6'	240	Missouri, Michigan		
Carpenter, Ken HB-OE	50-53Cle 60DenA	23	6'	195	Oregon State		108
Carpenter, Lew HB-FB-FL-OE-DB	53-55Det 56MS 57-58Cle 59-63GB	23	6'1"	209	Arkansas	1	126
Carr, Ed DB-HB	47-49SF-AA	2	6'	185	none	16	54
Carr, Paul DB-LB	55-57SF		6'	205	Houston	3	
Carroccio, Russ OG-OT-DG-DT	54-55NYG 55Phi		6'1"	235	Virginia	1	
Carson, Johnny OE	54-59Was 60HouA	2	6'3"	202	Georgia		90
Carter, Willie HB-DB	53ChiC		5'11"	198	Tennessee State		
Casanega, Ken DB-HB	46,48SF-AA	2	5'11"	175	Santa Clara	8	12
Case, Ernie DB-QB	47BalAA		5'10"	170	U. C. L. A.	2	4
Casey, Tom TB-DB	48NY-AA		5'11"	175	Hampton Institute		6
Casner, Ken DT	52LA		6'2"	245	Baylor		6
Cason, Jim DB-HB	48-49SF-AA 50-52SF 53CFL 54SF 55-56LA	23	6'	171	Louisiana State	34	60
Cassady, Hopalong HB-FL	56-61Det 62Cle 62Phi 63Det	23	5'10"	183	Ohio State		144
Cassara, Frank FB-LB	54SF		6'	215	St. Mary's		
Castete, Jesse DB	56ChiB 56-57LA		5'11"	178	McNeese State	2	
Castiglia, Jim FB-LB 42 played major league baseball	41Phi 42-44MS 45-46Phi 47BalAA 47-48Was	2	5'11"	208	Georgetown	1	78
Cathcart, Royal HB	50SF		6'	185	Cal.-Santa Barbara		
Cathcart, Sam DB-HB	49SFAA 50,52SF	23	6'	175	Cal.-Santa Barbara	7	6
Catlin, Tom LB-C	53-54Cle 55-56MS 57-58Cle 59Phi		6'1"	213	Oklahoma	2	
Cato, Daryl C-LB	46MiaAA		6'2"	195	Arkansas	1	
Celeri, Bob QB	51NYY 52Dal	12 4	5'10"	180	California		12
Cenci, John C	56Pit		6'	215	Pittsburgh		
Chambers, Bill T-G	48-49NY-AA		6'2"	230	Alabama, Georgia Tech, U. C. L. A.		
Champagne, Ed DT-OT	47-50LA		6'3"	236	Louisiana State		6
Champion, Jim OT-DT-LB	50-51NYY		6'	238	Mississippi State		2
Chandnois, Lynn HB-TB	50-56Pit	123	6'2"	198	Michigan State		162
Chappuis, Bob TB-DB	48BknAA 49ChiAA	12	6'	190	Michigan		6
Chase, Ben G	47Det		6'3"	235	Navy		
Cheatham, Ernie DT	54Pit 54Bal		6'4"	245	Loyola(L.A.)		
Cheatham, Lloyd BB-LB-DB-WB	42ChiC 43-45MS 46-48NY-AA	2	6'2"	211	Auburn	2	24
Cheroke, George G	46CleAA		5'9"	195	Ohio State		
Cheverko, George DB-WB-HB	47NYG 48Was 48NYG	2	6'1"	195	Fordham	9	18
Chickillo, Nick LB-OG	53ChiC		5'11"	220	Miami (Fla.)		
Chipley, Bill OE-DB	47-48Bos 49NYB	2	6'3"	199	Wash. & Lee	3	30
Chorovich, Dick OT	55-56Bal 60LA-A		6'4"	260	Miami-Ohio		
Christensen, Erik DE	56Was		6'3"	235	Richmond		
Christiansen, Jack DB-HB	51-58Det HC63-67SF	3	6'1"	190	Colorado State	46	78
Christman, Paul (Pitchin' Paul) QB	45-49ChiC 50GB	12	6'	210	Missouri		48
Churchwell, Don OT-DT	59Was 60OakA		6'1"	253	Mississippi		
Cichowski, Gene DB	57Pit 58-59Was		6'	195	Indiana		
Cifelli, Gus OT	50-52Det 53GB 54Phi 54Pit		6'4"	244	Notre Dame		
Cifers, Bob HB-DB-BB	46Det 47-48Pit 49GB	2 4	5'11"	201	Tennessee	1	30
Cifers, Ed OE-DE	41-42Was 43-45MS 46 Was 47-48ChiB	2	6'2"	227	Tennessee	1	36
Clark, Don LB-G	48-49SF-AA		5'11"	197	Southern Calif.	2	
Clark, Herman OG-LB	52ChiB 53MS 54-57ChiB		6'3"	256	Oregon State	1	
Clark, Jim OG-OT-DT-LB	52-53Was		6'1"	230	Oregon State		
Clarke, Leon OE-FL	56-59LA 60-62Cle 63Min	2	6'4"	232	Southern Calif.		114
Clarkson, Stu LB-C	42ChiB 43-MS 46-51ChiB 52CFL		6'2"	217	Texas A & I	10	6
Clatt, Corwin DB-FB	48-49ChiC		6'	210	Notre Dame	3	
Clatterbuck, Bobby QB	54-57NYG 60LA-A	12	6'3"	195	Houston		6
Clay, Randy HB-DB	50NYG 51-52MS 53NYG	2 5	6'	188	Texas	4	47
Clay, Walt DB-HB-TB	46-47ChiAA 47-49LA-AA	12	5'11"	196	Colorado	9	30
Cleary, Paul DE-OE	48NY-AA 49ChiAA		6'1"	196	Southern Calif.		
Clemens, Bob FB	55GB		6'2"	200	Georgia		
Clement, Johnny TB-DB	41ChiC 42-45MS 46-48Pit 49ChiAA	12	6'	189	S. M. U.		78
Clemons, Ray G	47GB		5'10"	220	St. Mary's		
Cline, Ollie FB-LB	48CleAA 49BufAA 50-53Det	2	6'	200	Ohio State		42
Cloud, Jack (Flying) FB-LB	50-51GB 52-53Was	2	5'10"	220	William & Mary	2	36
Clowes, John DT-OT-OG	48BknAA 49ChiAA 50-51NYY 51Det		6'1"	240	William & Mary		
Coates, Ray HB-DB	48-49NYG	2	6'1"	195	Louisiana State	1	24
Cochran, Red DB-HB-FB	47-50ChiC	234	6'	193	Wake Forest	15	36
Cochran, Tom FB	49Was	2	6'	209	Auburn		6
Cody, Ed DB-FB	47-48GB 49-50ChiB	2 5	5'10"	191	Purdue	2	29
Cole, Emerson FB-DB-LB	50-52Cle 52ChiB	2	6'2"	215	Toledo		6
Coleman, Herb C-LB	46-48ChiAA 48BalAA		6'	200	Notre Dame	1	
Colhouer, Jake G	46-48ChiC 49NYG		6'1"	211	Oklahoma State		
Collier, Bobby OT-DT	51LA		6'3"	230	S. M. U.		
Collier, Floyd T	48SF-AA		6'1"	215	San Jose State		
Collins, Bill G	47Bos		5'8"	195	Texas		
Collins, Ray DT-OT	50-52SF 54NYG 55-59CFL 60-61DalA		5'11"	238	Louisiana State		
Collins, Rip HB-FB	49ChiAA 50Bal 51GB	2 4	6'	190	Louisiana State	4	
Colmer, Mickey FB-LB-BB	46-48BknAA 49NY-AA	2 4	6'2"	219	Miramonte J.C.	1	126
Colo, Don DT	50Bal 51NYY 52Dal 53-58Cle		6'3"	252	Brown	2	
Colteryahn, Lloyd OE	54-56Bal	2	6'2"	220	Maryland		18
Comer, Marty DE-OE	46-48BufAA		6'	203	Tulane		18
Comp, Irv DB-TB-QB	43-49GB	12	6'2"	204	St. Benedict's	33	66
Compagno, Tony FB-DB	46-48Pit	2	5'11"	199	St. Mary's	12	42
Compton, Ogden QB	55ChiC	1	6'1"	180	Hardin-Simmons		
Cone, Fred FB-K	51-57GB 60 Dal	2 5	5'11"	199	Clemson		494
Conerly, Chuck QB	48-61NYG	12 4	6'1"	185	Mississippi		64
Conger, Mel DE-OE	46NY-AA 47BknAA		6'2"	225	Georgia		
Conner, Clyde OE	56-63SF	2	6'2"	193	U. of Pacific		108
Connolly, Harry TB-DB	46BknAA		5'11"	190	Boston College		
Connolly, Ted OG	54SF 55MS 56-62SF 63Cle		6'3"	240	Tulsa, Santa Clara		
Connor, George OT-LB-DT-OG	48-55ChiB		6'3"	240	Notre Dame	7	6
Conoly, Bill G	46ChiC		6'	227	Texas		
Cook, Gene OE	59Det		6'3"	215	Toledo		
Cook, Ted OE-DB	47Det 48-50GB	2	6'2"	195	Alabama	13	30
Coomer, Joe T	41Pit 42-44MS 45-46Pit 47-49ChiC		6'6"	281	Austin		
Cooper, Jim C-LB	48BknAA		6'	205	North Texas State		
Cooper, Ken OG-DG	49BalAA 50Bal		6'1"	205	Vanderbilt		
Corbitt, Don C-LB	48Was		6'4"	224	Arizona		
Corley, Bert C-LB	47BufAA 48BalAA		6'2"	210	Mississippi State	1	
Corn, Joe HB-DB	48LA		5'6"	168	none		
Cothren, Paige K	57-58BLA 59Phi	5	5'11"	201	Mississippi		180
Coulter, Tex OT-DT-C-OE	46-49,51-52NYG 53 CFL		6'4"	250	Army		6
Couppee, Al G-FB	46Was		6'	225	Iowa		
Coutre, Larry HB	50GB 51-52MS 53GB 53Bal	2	5'10"	175	Notre Dame		18
Cowan, Bob HB-DB	47-48CleAA 49BalAA	2	5'11"	185	Michigan	3	48
Cowan, Les DT-DE	51ChiB		6'5"	235	McMurry		
Cowhig, Gerry LB-FB-DB	47-49LA 50ChiC 51Phi	2	6'2"	215	Notre Dame	6	30
Cox, Billy DB-HB-OE	51-52Was 53-54MS 55Was	4	6'3"	189	Duke	5	
Cox, Jim G-LB	48SF-AA		6'1"	208	Stanford		
Cox, Norm QB-TB	46-47ChiAA		6'2"	210	Texas Christian		
Craft, Russ DB-HB	46-53Phi 54Pit	23	5'9"	174	Alabama	22	42
Crawford, Denver T	48NY-AA		6'	210	Tennessee		
Crawford, Ed DB-OE	57NYG		6'3"	185	Mississippi	1	
Creekmur, Lou OT-OG-DT-DG	50-59Det		6'4"	246	William & Mary		
Cregar, Bill G-LB	47-48Pit		5'11"	195	Holy Cross		
Cremer, Ted DE-OE	46-47Det 48GB	2	6'2"	209	Auburn		6
Crisler, Hal OE-DE-DB	46-47Bos 48-49Was 50Bal	2	6'4"	213	San Jose State	2	132
Crittendon, Jack OE	54ChiC		6'1"	190	Wayne State		
Cronin, Gene DE-OG-LB	56-59Det 60Dal 61-62Was		6'2"	229	U. of Pacific	1	
Cross, Billy HB	51-53ChiC	23	5'6"	151	West Texas State		72
Cross, Bob OT-DT	52ChiB 53MS 54-55LA 56-57SF 58-59ChiC 60BosA		6'4"	248	Kilgore J. C.		
Crow, Lindon DB	55-57ChiC 58-60NYG 61-64LA	3	6'1"	195	Southern Calif.	38	20
Crowe, Clem	HC49 BufAA HC50Bal				Notre Dame		
Crowe, Paul DB-HB-FB	48-49SF-AA 49LA-AA 51NYY		6'1"	195	St. Mary's	9	18
Crowell, Odis T	47SF-AA		6'2"	220	Hardin-Simmons		
Crowley, Jim (Sleepy Jim) TB-DB	25GB 25Prov HC47ChiAA		5'9"	165	Notre Dame		
Cullom, Jim OG	51NYY		5'11"	235	California		
Cunningham, Leon LB-C	55Det		6'2"	215	South Carolina		
Curcillo, Tony DB-HB	53ChiC		6'1"	200	Ohio State	2	
Cure, Armand HB-DB 46-47 played in B.A.A.	47BalAA		6'4"	198	Rhode Island		
Currivan, Don OE-DB-DE	43ChiC 44C-P 45-48Bos 48-49LA	2	6'	193	Boston College	6	162
Czarobski, Ziggy T	48-49ChiAA		6'	230	Notre Dame		
Daffer, Ted DE	54ChiB		6'	198	Tennessee		
D'Agostino, Frank OG-OT	56Phi 60NY-A		6'1"	245	Auburn		
Dahms, Tom OT	51-54LA 55GB 56ChiC 57SF		6'5"	242	San Diego State		
Dale, Roland DE	50Was		6'3"	210	Mississippi		
Daley, Bill FB-DB-LB	46BknAA 46MiaAA 47ChiAA 48NY-AA	2	6'2"	210	Minnesota, Michigan		30
D'Alonzo, Pete FB	51-52Det		5'10"	210	Villanova		
Damore, John C-OG	57,59ChiB		6'	228	Northwestern		
Danahe, Dick T-C	47-48LA-AA		6'2"	235	Southern Calif.		
Dancewicz, Boley QB-DB	46-48Bos	12	5'10"	187	Notre Dame	1	12
Danjean, Ernie LB	57GB		6'	230	Auburn		
Daugherty, Dick OG-LB-C	51-53LA 54-55MS 56-58LA		6'1"	219	Oregon	2	14
Daukas, Lou LB-C	47BknAA		6'	203	Cornell	1	
Daukas, Nick T	46-47BknAA		6'4"	225	Dartmouth	1	
David, Bob G-LB	47-48LA-AA 48ChiAA		6'	219	Villanova		

Use Name (Nicknames) – Positions	Team by Year	See Section	Hgt	Wgt	College	Int	Pts
David, Jim DB	52-59Det		5'11"	178	Colorado State	36	
Davis, Andy DB	52Was		6'	188	George Wash.		
Davis, Art OT-DT	53ChiB		6'2"	235	Alabama State		
Davis, Art HB-DB	56Pit		6'1"	195	Mississippi State		
Davis, Bob T	48Bos		6'4"	235	Georgia Tech		
Davis, Bob DE-OE	46-50Pit		5'11"	192	Penn State		6
Davis, Fred OT-DT	41-42Was 43-44MS 45Was 46-51ChiB		6'3"	244	Alabama		
Davis, Glenn HB	50-51LA	2	5'11"	170	Army		54
Davis, Harper DB-HB	49LA-AA 50ChiB 51GB		5'11"	173	Mississippi State	11	12
Davis, Jerry DB-HB	48-51ChiC 52Dal	3	5'10"	178	Southeastern La.	24	24
Davis, Joe OE-DE	46BknAA	2	6'2"	195	Southern Calif.		7
Davis, Lamar (Racehorse) OE-DB	46MiaAA 47-49BalAA	2	6'1"	185	Georgia	11	72
Davis, Milt DB	57-60Bal		6'1"	188	U. C. L. A.	27	18
Davis, Paul FB-DB	47-48Pit		6'1"	188	Otterbein	1	
Davis, Ralph G	47-48GB		5'11"	205	Wisconsin		
Davis, Van DE-OE	47-49NY-AA	2	6'2"	215	Georgia	1	6
Davlin, Mike OT	55Was		6'1"	230	Notre Dame, San Francisco		
Dawson, Gib HB	53GB		5'11"	180	Texas		6
Dawson, Red	HC46-49 BufAA				Tulane		
Dean, Hal G-LB	47-49LA		6'	205	Ohio State	1	
Dean, Tom T	46-47Bos		6'2"	248	S. M. U.		
DeCarlo, Art DB-OE	53Pit 54-55MS 56-57Was 57-60Bal		6'2"	196	Georgia	7	
deCorrevont, Bill DB-HB-TB-WB	45Was 46Det 47ChiC 48-49ChiB	23	6'	186	Northwestern	10	18
Deeks, Don T-G	45-47Bos 47Was 48GB		6'4"	238	Washington		
Dees, Bob OT-DT	52GB		6'4"	245	SW Missouri St.		
DeFruiter, Bob DB-HB	45-47Was 47Det 48LA		6'	190	Nebraska	3	
DeGroot, Dud	HC44-45Was HC46-47LA-AA				Stanford		
Dekdebrun, Al TB-QB-DB	46BufAA 47ChiAA 48NY-AA 48Bos 49CFL	12	5'11"	182	Cornell	4	
Dekker, Paul OE	53Was 54CFL	2	6'5"	220	Michigan State		6
deLauer, Bob C-LB	45Cle 46LA		6'1"	218	Southern Calif.		
Del Bello, Jack QB	53Bal	1	6'1"	190	Miami (Fla.)		
Delevan, Burt OT	55-56ChiC		6'2"	236	U. of Pacific		
Dellerba, Spiro LB-FB	47CleAA 48-49BalAA	2	5'11"	200	Ohio State	2	6
DeMao, Al C-LB	45-53Was		6'2"	214	Duquesne	8	
DeMarco, Mario G-LB	49Det		5'11"	200	Miami (Fla.)		
DeMoss, Bob QB	49NYB		6'2"	185	Purdue		
Dempsey, Frank OG-LB-OT	50-53ChiB 54CFL		6'3"	235	Florida	1	
Derby, Dean DB-HB	57-61Pit 61-62Min		6'	187	Washington	21	21
DeRogatis, Al DT	49-52NYG		6'4"	239	Duke		12
Deschaine, Dick K	55-57GB 58Cle	4	6'	206	none		
DeShane, Chuck G-LB-BB-DB	45-49Det	5	6'1"	212	Alabama	5	22
Devore, Hugh	HC53GB HC56-57Phi				Notre Dame		
Dewar, Jim DB-HB-WB	47CleAA 48BknAA		6'1"	190	Indiana	1	6
Dewell, Bill OE-DE	40-41ChiC 42-44MS 45-49ChiC	2	6'4"	208	S. M. U.		102
Dibble, Dorne OE-DB	51Det 52MS 53-57Det	2	6'2"	195	Michigan State	1	114
Dillon, Bobby DB	52-59GB		6'1"	182	Texas	52	30
Dimancheff, Babe HB-DB	45-46Bos 47-50ChiC 52ChiB	23	5'11"	178	Purdue, Butler	2	90
Dimmick, Tom C-OT-LB	56Phi 60DalA		6'6"	253	Houston		
DiPierro, Ray OG	50-51GB		5'11"	210	Ohio State		
Dittrich, John OG	56ChiC 57-58MS 59GB 60OakA 61BufA		6'1"	236	Wisconsin		
Dobbs, Glenn TB-DB	46-47BknAA 47-49LA-AA 50CFL	1234	6'4"	211	Tulsa	8	90
Dobelstein, Bob G-LB	46-48NYG 49LA-AA		5'11"	214	Tennessee	1	6
Dodrill, Dale LB	51-59Pit		6'1"	211	Colorado State	10	12
Doherty, George G-T	44Bkn 45Bos 46NY-AA 46-47BufAA		6'1"	218	Louisiana Tech		
Doll, Don DB-HB	49-52Det 53Was 54LA	3	5'10"	185	Southern Calif.	41	18
Domnanovich, Joe C-LB	46-48Bos 49NYB 50-51NYY		6'1"	213	Alabama	3	
Donaldson, Gene OG	53Cle		5'9"	215	Kentucky		
Donaldson, John DB-TB	49LA-AA 49ChiAA		5'10"	180	Georgia		
Donovan, Art DT-OT	50Bal 51NYY 52Dal 53-61Bal		6'2"	263	Boston College		2
Doolan, Jack DB-WB-OE	45Was 45-46NYG 47-48ChiC	2	6'1"	191	Georgetown		
Dooley, Jim OE-FL-HB-DB	52-54ChiB 55MS 56-57ChiB 58BN 59-62,HC68-71ChiB	2	6'4"	198	Miami (Fla.)	5	96
Doran, Jim OE-DE	51-59Det 60-61Dal	2	6'2"	201	Iowa State	1	150
Dorow, Al QB	54-56Was 57Phi 58-59CFL 60-61NY-A 62BufA	12	6'	193	Michigan State		96
Doss, Noble HB-DB	47-48Phi 49NY-AA	2	6'	186	Texas	2	
Dottley, Kayo FB	51-53ChiB	2	6'1"	200	Mississippi		54
Douglas, Everett OT	53NYG		6'3"	240	Florida		
Douglas, Otis T	46-49Phi		6'1"	224	William & Mary		
Dove, Bob DE-OE	PC46,47ChiAA 48-53ChiC 53-54Det	2	6'2"	222	Notre Dame	1	12
Dow, Harley OG-OT	50SF		6'2"	220	San Jose State		
Dowda, Harry DB-HB	49-53Was 54-55Phi	2	6'2"	199	Wake Forest	16	36
Dowden, Steve OT	52GB		6'2"	235	Baylor		
Downs, Bob OG	51SF		5'10"	210	Southern Calif.		
Doyle, Dick DB	55Pit 60DenA		6'	193	Ohio State	2	
Drazenovich, Chuck LB-FB	50-59Was	2	6'1"	225	Penn State	15	48
Dreyer, Wally HB-DB	49ChiB 50GB	2	5'10"	170	Wisconsin	5	6
Driscoll, Paddy TB-DB 17 played major league baseball	20Det 20,PC21-22,23-25ChiC 26-29,HC56-57ChiB		5'8"	155	Northwestern		
Driskill, Walt	HC49BalAA				Maryland		
Drulis, Al LB-FB-BB	45-46ChiC 47Pit		5'10"	193	Temple		
Drulis, Chuck LB-G	42ChiB 43-44MS 45-49ChiB 50GB HC61StL		5'10"	216	Temple	4	
Drzewiecki, Ron HB-DB	55ChiB 56MS 57ChiB	3	5'11"	185	Marquette		6
Dublinski, Tom QB	52-54Det 55-57CFL 58NYG 60DenA	12	6'2"	197	Utah		6
Duckworth, Joe OE-DE	47Was	2	6'2"	220	Colgate		18
Duden, Dick DE-OE	49NYG		6'3"	212	Navy		
Dudish, Andy HB-DB	46BufAA 47BalAA 48Det	2	5'11"	182	Georgia		12
Dudley, Bill (Bullet Bill) HB-TB-DB-WB	42Pit 43-44MS 45-46Pit 47-49Det 50-51Was 52VR 53Was	12345	5'10"	175	Virginia	23	484
Dugger, Jack T-DE-OE	46BufAA 47-48Det 49ChiB		6'3"	230	Ohio State	1	6
Duke, Paul C-LB	47NY-AA		6'1"	210	Georgia Tech		
Duncan, Jim DE	50-53NYG		6'2"	205	Duke, Wake Forest	7	
Duncan, Maury QB	54-55SF	1	6'1"	185	San Fran. State		
Dupre, L. G. (Long Gone) HB	55-59Bal 60-61Dal	2 4	5'11"	190	Baylor		108
Durdan, Don HB-DB	46-47SF-AA	2	5'9"	175	Oregon State	2	6
Durishan, Jack T-G	47NY-AA		6'2"	230	Pittsburgh		
Durkota, Jeff FB-LB	48LA-AA		6'	205	Penn State	1	
Dutton, Bill HB-DB	46Pit	2	5'10"	180	Pittsburgh		12
Dworsky, Dan LB-BB	49LA-AA		6'	211	Michigan	1	
Dwyer, Jack DB	51Was 52-54LA		5'11"	175	Loyola (L.A.)	11	24

Use Name (Nicknames) – Positions	Team by Year	See Section	Hgt	Wgt	College	Int	Pts
Earhart, Ralph HB-DB	48-49GB	23	5'10"	165	Texas Tech		24
Earon, Blaine DE	52-53Det		6'1"	195	Duke		
Eason, Roger G-T	45Cle 46-48LA 49GB		6'2"	227	Oklahoma		
Eaton, Vic QB-DB	55Pit	4	6'2"	200	Missouri		
Ebli, Ray DE-OE	42ChiC 43-45MS 46BufAA 47ChiAA	2	6'2"	210	Notre Dame		12
Ecker, Ed OT-DT	47ChiB 48ChiAA 50-51GB 52Was		6'7"	276	John Carroll		
Ecklund, Brad C-LB	49NY-AA 50-51NYY 52Dal 53Bal		6'3"	215	Oregon		
Edwards, Dan OE-DE	48BknAA 49ChiAA 50-51NYY 52Dal 53-54Bal	2	6'1"	197	Georgia		102
Edwards, Weldon T	48Was		6'	225	Texas Christian		
Ehrhardt, Clyde C-LB	46,48-49Was		6'1"	232	Georgia	3	
Eikenberg, Charley QB	48ChiC		6'2"	205	Rice		
Eggers, Doug LB	54-57Bal 58ChiC		6'	213	S. Dakota State	4	
Ellena, Jack OG-LB	55-56LA		6'1"	225	U. C. L. A.		
Ellenson, Gene T	46MiaAA		6'1"	210	Georgia		
Elliott, Carl OE-DE	51-54GB	2	6'4"	220	Virginia		42
Elliott, Charlie T	47NY-AA 48ChiAA 48SF-AA		6'2"	240	Oregon		
Ellis, Herb C-LB	49NYB		6'2"	205	Texas A & M		
Ellis, Larry LB	48Det		6'1"	204	Syracuse		
Elsey, Earl HB-DB	46LA-AA	2	5'8	175	Loyola (L.A.)	2	
Elston, Art LB-C-G-BB	42Cle 43-45MS 46-48SF-AA	2	5'11"	191	South Carolina	4	
Elter, Leo FB-HB	53-54Pit 55-57Was 58-59Pit	2	5'10"	201	Villanova Duquesne		66
Embree, Mel OE	53Bal 54ChiC	2	6'3"	190	Pepperdine		6
Endriss, Al DE-OE	52SF		6'2"	200	San Fran. State		
Enke, Fred QB-HB	48-51Det 52Phi 53-54Bal	12	6'1"	201	Arizona		6
Epps, Bobby FB	54-55,57NYG	2	5'9"	198	Pittsburgh		12
Erickson, Bill G-LB	48NYG 49NY-AA		6'2"	210	Mississippi		
Eshmont, Len HB-DB-FB	41NYG 42-45MS 46-49SF-AA	2	5'11"	179	Fordham	10	90
Esser, Clarence DE-T	47ChiC		6'	190	Wisconsin		
Ethridge, Joe T	49GB		6'	230	S. M. U.		4
Ettinger, Don LB-OG	48-50NYG		6'2"	213	Kansas	4	
Evans, Fred HB-DB	46CleAA 47BufAA 47-48ChiAA 48ChiB	2	5'11"	185	Notre Dame	1	24
Evans, Jon OE	58Pit		6'4"	205	Oklahoma State		
Evans, Ray TB-DB	48Pit	12	6'1"	195	Kansas		12
Evans, Ray OG-OT-DT	48SF-AA 50SF		6'1"	225	Texas-El Paso		
Evansen, Paul G	48SF-AA		6'3"	240	Oregon State		
Ewart, Charley	HC49NYB				Yale		
Faircloth, Art DB-QB-HB	47-48 NYG		6'	190	N. Carolina State	3	
Fanucchi, Ledio OT-DT	54ChiC		6'2"	225	Fresno State		
Farmer, Tom HB-DB	46LA 47-48Was	2	5'11"	190	Iowa	6	30
Farragut, Ken C-LB	51-54Phi		6'4"	240	Mississippi		
Farris, Tom QB-DB	46-47ChiB 48ChiAA	12	6'1"	185	Wisconsin	5	
Faverty, Hal LB-DE-C	52GB		6'2"	220	Wisconsin		
Feamster, Tom OT-DE	56Bal	5	6'7"	260	Florida State		24
Fears, Tom OE-DB	48-56LA HC67-70NO	2 5	6'2"	213	U. C. L. A.	2	249
Feher, Nick OG	51-54SF 55Pit		6'1"	224	Georgia		
Fekete, Gene FB-LB	46CleAA	2	6'	195	Ohio State		6
Fekete, John HB-DB	46BufAA		5'11"	200	Ohio U.		
Felker, Art DE	51GB		6'3"	205	Marquette		
Felker, Gene OE	52Dal		6'1"	198	Wisconsin		6
Felton, Ralph LB-FB	54-60Was 61-62BufA	5	5'11"	210	Maryland	7	19
Fenenbock, Chuck TB-HB-DB-WB	43Det 44MS 45Det 46-48LA-AA 48ChiAA	1234	5'9"	174	U. C. L. A.	2	84
Fenimore, Bob HB-DB	47ChiB	2	6'1"	195	Oklahoma State	2	18
Fennema, Carl C-LB	48-49NYG		6'2"	210	Washington		6
Ferguson, Howie FB	53-58GB 60LA-A	2	6'2"	214	none		78
Ferrante, Jack OE-DE	41,44-50Phi	2	6'1"	197	none	1	186
Ferris, Neil DB-HB	51-52Was 52Phi 53LA		5'11"	181	Loyola (L.A.)		6
Ferry, Lou DT-OT	49GB 51ChiC 52-55Pit		6'2"	244	Villanova		8
Fichman, Leon T	46-47Det		6'1"	215	Alabama		
Figner, George DB	53ChiB		6'	185	Colorado	1	
Filipski, Gene HB	56-57NYG	23	5'11"	185	Army, Villanova		6
Finks, Jim QB-TB-DB	49-55Pit	12	6'	175	Tulsa	4	84
Finlay, Jack OG-LB	47-51LA		6'1"	217	U. C. L. A.		
Finnin, Tom DT	53-56Bal 57ChiC		6'2"	262	Detroit		2
Fiorentino, Ed DE	47Bos		6'1"	210	Boston College		
Fischer, Bill OT-OG-DT	49-53ChiC		6'2"	248	Notre Dame	1	
Fischer, Clete HB-DB	49NYG	2	5'9"	170	Nebraska	2	6
Fisher, Ray DT-OT-OG	59Pit 60JJ		6'	230	Eastern Illinois		
Flagerman, Jack C-LB	48LA-AA		6'	218	St. Mary's		
Flanagan, Dick LB-OG-C-HB-DB-DG-FB	48-49ChiB 50-52Det 53-55Pit		6'	216	Ohio State	8	
Fletcher, Ollie OG-LB-DG	49LA-AA 50Bal		6'3"	210	Southern Calif.		
Flowers, Bernie OE	56Bal		6'2"	190	Purdue		
Flowers, Bob C-LB	42-49GB		6'1"	210	Texas Tech	6	
Flowers, Dick QB	53Bal		6'	190	Northwestern		
Flowers, Keith C-LB	52Dal		6'	211	Texas Christian	1	3
Floyd, Bobby Jack FB	52GB 53ChiB	2	6'	210	Texas Christian		6
Foldberg, Hank OE-DE	48BknAA 49ChiAA	2	6'1"	203	Army		6
Ford, Henry HB-DB	55Cle 56Pit	3	6'	180	Pittsburgh	1	12
Ford, Len DE-OE	48-49LA-AA 50-57Cle 58GB	2	6'4	245	Michigan	3	56
Forester, Bill LB-DT	53-63GB		6'3"	237	S. M. U.	21	2
Forester, Herschel OG	54-57Cle		6'	230	S. M. U.		
Forkovitch, Nick FB-LB	48BknAA		5'11"	195	William & Mary		
Forrest, Ed G-LB	46-47SF-AA		5'11"	210	Santa Clara		
Forte, Bob HB-DB-LB	46-50GB 51MS 52-53GB	2	6'	199	Arkansas	22	24
Fowler, Aubrey DB-HB	48BalAA		5'10"	160	Arkansas	3	
Franceschi, Pete HB-DB	46SF-AA		5'9"	170	San Francisco		12
Francis, Joe QB-HB	58-59GB	12	6'1"	195	Oregon State		6
Frankowski, Ray G	45GB 46-48LA-AA		5'11"	223	Washington		6
Freeman, Jack G	46BknAA		6'	198	Texas		
Freitas, Jess QB-DB	46-47SF-AA 48ChiAA 49BufAA	12	5'10"	170	Santa Clara	3	
French, Barry OG-DG-OT	47,49BalAA 48JJ 50Bal 51Det		6'	225	Purdue		
Friedlund, Bob DE-OE	46Phi		6'3"	210	Michigan State		
Fritsch, Ted FB-LB 44-45,46-47 played in N.B.L.	42-50GB	23 5	5'10"	210	Wis. State — Stevens Point	10	380
Fry, Bob OT-OG	53LA 54-55MS 56-59LA 60-64Dal		6'4"	235	Kentucky		
Fucci, Dom DB	55Det		5'11"	190	Kentucky		
Fugler, Dick OT-DT	52Pit 53MS 54ChiC		6'2"	238	Tulane		
Fulcher, Bill LB-OG	56-58Was		6'	193	Georgia Tech	1	
Fuller, Frank DT-OG-C-DE	53,55,57-58LA 59ChiC 60-62StL 63Phi		6'4"	244	Kentucky		2
Fullerton, Ed DB	53Pit		5'10"	190	Maryland		

Use Name (Nickname)-Positions	Team by Year	See Section	Hgt	Wgt	College	Int	Pts
Gaffney, Jim HB-DB	45-46Was	2	6'1"	204	Tennessee		6
Gafford, Monk DB-HB-TB-WB	46MiaAA 46-48BknAA	123	5'11"	195	Auburn	7	66
Gage, Bob TB-DB	49-50Pit	123	5'11"	175	Clemson	9	48
Gain, Bob DT-DE-DG-OT-LB	52Cle 53MS 54-64Cle		6'3"	256	Kentucky	1	9
Galiffa, Arnie QB	53NYG 54SF	1	6'2"	193	Army		
Gallagher, Bernie G	47LA-AA		6'	234	Pennsylvania		
Galvin, John QB	47BalAA	4	5'10"	170	Purdue		
Gambino, Lu FB-LB	48-49BalAA	2	6'1"	205	Maryland		12
Gambold, Bob QB	53Phi		6'4"	215	Washington State		
Gandee, Sonny DE-LB	52Dal 52-56Det 57JJ		6'1"	216	Ohio State	4	8
Gaona, Bob OT-DT	53-56Pit 57Phi		6'3"	243	Wake Forest		
Garlin, Don HB-DB	49SF-AA 50SF		5'11"	188	Southern Calif.	1	6
Garnaas, Bill WB-BB-LB	46-48Pit		5'11"	187	Minnesota		18
Garrett, Bill DG-OG-DT	48-49BalAA 50 ChiB		6'1"	237	Mississippi State		6
Garrett, Bob QB	54GB	1	6'1"	198	Stanford		
Garrett, Thurman C-G	47-48ChiB		6'3"	268	Oklahoma State	1	
Garza, Dan OE	49NY-AA 51NYY	2	6'3"	203	Oregon		24
Garzoni, Mike G	47Was 48NYG 48NY-AA		5'11"	218	Southern Calif.		
Gasparella, Joe BB-LB	48,50-51Pit 51ChiC	1	6'4"	222	Notre Dame		
Gatewood, Les C-LB	46-47GB		6'2"	198	Baylor		
Gatski, Frank C-LB	46-49CleAA 50-56Cle 57Det		6'3"	233	Marshall	3	6
Gaudio, Bob OG-LB-DG	47-49CleAA 51Cle		5'10"	219	Ohio State		
Gaul, Frank T	49NYB		6'	200	Notre Dame		
Gay, Billy DB	51-52ChiC		5'11"	180	Notre Dame		
Gedman, Gene HB	53Det 54-55MS 56-58Det 59KJ	2	5'11"	195	Indiana		126
Gehrke, Bruce OE-DB	48NYG		6'2"	190	Columbia		6
Gehrke, Fred HB-DB-TB	40Cle 41-44MS 45Cle 46-49LA	23	5'11"	189	Utah	13	154
	50SF 50ChiC						
Gentry, Dale OE-DE	46-48LA-AA	2	6'3"	223	Washington State		42
George, Bill LB-OG-DT	52-65ChiB 66LA	5	6'2"	237	Wake Forest	18	26
Geri, Joe TB-HB	49-51Pit 52ChiC	12 45	5'10"	185	Georgia		198
Getchell, Gorham OE-DE	47BalAA		6'4"	225	Temple		
Giancanelli, Skippy HB	53-56Phi	23	5'10"	177	Loyola (L.A.)		84
Giannelli, Mario DG-OG	48-51Phi		6'	265	Boston College		2
Gibron, Abe OG-DG	49BufAA 50-56Cle 56-57Phi		5'11"	243	Purdue		
	58-59,HC72-73ChiB						
Gibson, Paul OE-DB-DE	47-49BufAA	2	6'2"	195	N. Carolina State	1	
Gifford, Frank HB-FL-DB	52-60NYG 61VR 62-64NYG	123 5	6'1"	197	Southern Calif.	2	484
Gilbert, Kline OT-OG	53-57ChiB		6'2"	233	Mississippi		
Gilchrist, George DT-DG	53ChiC		6'	260	Tennessee State		
Gillom, Horace DE-OE	47-49CleAA 50-56Cle	2 4	6'1"	221	Nevada	1	24
Gillette, Jim HB-DB-TB	40Cle 41-43MS 44-45CLe 46Bos	2	6'1"	185	Virginia	14	36
	47GB 48Det						
Gilmer, Harry QB-HB-DB	48-52Was 53JJ 54Was	12	6'	169	Alabama	5	12
	55-56,HC65-66Det						
Girard, Jug HB-OE-DB-QB	48-51GB 52-56Det 57Pit	1234	5'11"	176	Wisconsin	8	113
Gladchuck, Chet C-DT-LB	41NYG 42-45MS 46-47NYG		6'4"	248	Boston College	1	
Glamp, Joe HR-DB	47-49Pit	2 5	5'11'.	185	Louisiana State		125
Glatz, Fred OE	56Pit	4	6'1"	200	Pittsburgh		
Glick, Gary DB-HB	56-59Pit 59-61Was 61Bal 63SD-A	5	6'2"	195	Colorado State	14	65
Goad, Paul FB	56SF		6'	195	Abilene Christian		
Gob, Art DE	59-60Was 60LA-A		6'4"	230	Pittsburgh		2
Goble, Les HB-DB	54-55ChiC	23	5'11"	158	Alfred	1	18
Godwin, Bill C-LB	47-48Bos		6'3"	241	Georgia	2	
Golding, Joe DB-HB	47-48Bos 49NYB 50-51NYY	23	6'	184	Oklahoma	19	84
Goldman, Sam DE-OE	44Bos 45MS 46-47Bos 48ChiC 49Det	2	6'3"	228	Howard (Ala.)		
Goldsberry, John DT-OT	49-50ChiC		6'2"	245	Indiana	1	
Goldston, Ralph HB-DB	52Phi 53BL 54-55Phi 56CFL	2	5'11"	195	Youngstown		18
Gompers, Bill HB-DB	48BufAA	2	6'1"	185	Notre Dame	2	6
Goode, Rob FB-HB-LB-DB	49-51,54-55Was 52-53MS 55Phi	2	6'4"	222	Texas A&M	4	108
Goodnight, Clyde OE-DB	45-48GB 49-50Was	2	6'1"	196	Tulsa		90
Gordon, Bobby DB	58ChiC 60HouA	4	6'	195	Tennessee	5	
Gorgal, Ken DB	50Cle 51-52MS 53-54Cle 55-56ChiB 56GB		6'2"	200	Purdue	19	6
Gorgone, Pete BB-LB	46NYG		6'	220	Muhlenberg		
Gorinski, Walt FB-DB	46Pit		6'1"	207	Louisiana State		
Goss, Don OT-DT	56Cle		6'5"	260	S. M. U.		
Governali, Paul (Pitching Paul) QB	46-47Bos 47-48NYG	12	5'11"	193	Columbia		24
Graham, Mike FB-LB	48LA-AA		6'	200	Cincinnati		6
Graham Otto QB-DB	46-49CleAA 50-55Cle HC66-68Was	12	6'1"	196	Northwestern	7	276
45-46 played in N.B.L.							
Grain, Ed G	47NY-AA 47-48BalAA		6'	230	Pennsylvania		
Grandelius, Sonny HB	53NYG	2	6'	195	Michigan State		6
Grant, Bud OE-DE	51-52Phi 53CFL HC67-73Min	2	6'3"	199	Minnesota		42
49-51 played in N.B.A.							
Gray, Bill G	47-48Was		5'11"	210	Oregon State		
Gray, Sam DE-OE	46-47 Pit		6'	195	Tulsa		
Green, John DE-OE	47-51Phi		6'1"	192	Tulsa		6
Greene, John OE-DE-DB-BB	44-50-Det	2	6'	210	Michigan	5	164
Greene, Nelson T	48NY-AA		6'2"	235	Tulsa		
Greenhalgh, Bob FB	49NYG	2	6'1"	200	San Francisco		
Greenwood, Don DB-HB-FB-LB	45Cle 46-47CleAA	2	6'	195	Missouri,	6	60
					Illinois		
Gregory Garland G-LB	46-47SF-AA		5'11"	185	Louisiana Tech		
Grgich, Visco OG-LB-DG-OT-DT	46-49SF-AA 50-52SF		5'11"	217	Santa Clara	1	
Griffin, Bob LB-C	53-57LA 61DenA 61StL		6'3"	235	Arkansas	1	2
Griffin, Bobby DB	51NYY		6'	180	Baylor	4	
Griffin, Don HB-DB	46ChiAA	2	5'11"	195	Illinois	1	
Griffith, Forrest HB	50-51NYG	2	5'11"	190	Kansas		12
Grigg, Chubby DT-OT	46BufAA 47ChiAA 48-49CleAA	5	6'2"	294	Tulsa		21
	50-51Cle 52Dal						
Grimes, Billy HB	49LA-AA 50-52GB	23	6'1"	195	Oklahoma State		96
Grimes, George DB-WB	48Det	4	5'11"	190	Virginia	1	6
Groom Jerry DT-C-LB	51-55ChiC		6'3"	236	Notre Dame		
Groomes, Mel DB-WB-HB	48-49Det		6'	178	Indiana	1	6
Grossman, Rex LB-FB-K	48-49BalAA 50Bal 50Det	45	6'1"	215	Indiana	2	126
Groves, George G-LB	47BufAA 48BalAA		5'11"	195	Marquette		
Groza, Lou (The Toe) OT-DT-K	46-49CleAA 50-59Cle 60VR	5	6'3"	240	Ohio State		1608
	61-67Cle						
Gude, Henry C-G	46Phi		6'1"	225	Vanderbilt		
Gulyanics, George HB-DB	47-52ChiB	2 4	6'	198	Ellisville J.C.	2	126
Gunderman, Bob OE	57Pit		6'2"	195	Virginia		
Gustafson, Ed C-LB	47-48BknAA		6'3"	205	George Washington		
Guy, Buzz OG-DT-OT	58-59NYG 60Dal 61HouA 61DenA		6'3"	248	Duke		
Hachten, Bill G-LB	47NYG		6'	210	Stanford		
Hafen Bernie OE-DE	49-50Det		6'2"	195	Utah		

Use Name (Nicknames)-Positions	Team by Year	See Section	Hgt	Wgt	College	Int	Pts
Hall, Forrest HB	48SF-AA	2	5'8"	155	Duquesne,		12
					San Francisco		
Hall, John DE	55NYG		6'1"	220	Iowa		
Halliday, Jack OT-DT	51LA		6'3"	238	S. M. U.		
Haluska, Jim QB	56ChiB		6'	190	Wisconsin		
Handley, Dick C-LB	47BalAA		6'1"	215	Fresno State		
Hanley, Dick B	24Rac HC46ChiAA				Washington State		
Hanlon, Bob DB-HB	48ChiC 49Pit		6'1"	195	Notre Dame,	4	
					Loras		
Hannah, Herb OT	51NYG		6'3"	220	Alabama		
Hanner, Dave DT	52-64GB		6'2"	257	Arkansas	4	2
Hansen, Dale T-DE	44,48Det		6'3"	223	Michigan State		
Hansen, Ron G-LB	54Was		6'	220	Minnesota		
Hansen, Roscoe OT-DT	51Phi 52-53MS		6'3"	215	North Carolina		
Hansen, Wayne LB-C-OG-OT-DT	50-58ChiB 60Dal		6'2"	231	Texas-El Paso	6	6
Hantla, Bob OG-LB-DE	54-55SF		6'1"	220	Kansas		
Hanulak, Chet HB	54Cle 55-56MS 57Cle	23	5'10"	185	Maryland		42
Harder, Pat FB-LB	46-50ChiC 51-53Det	2 5	5'11"	203	Wisconsin		531
Harding, Roger C-LB	45Cle 46LA 47Phi 48Det 49NYB		6'2"	211	California	3	
	49GB						
Hardy, Carroll HB	55SF	2	6'	185	Colorado		24
58-64,67 played major league baseball							
Hardy, Jim QB-DB	46-48LA 49-51ChiC 52Det	12 4	6'	180	Southern Calif.		13
Harkey, Lem FB	55Pit 55SF		6'1"	205	Coll. of Emporia		
Harmon, Tommy HB-DB	46-47LA	23	6'1"	199	Michigan	11	54
Harness, Jim DB	56Bal		5'11"	180	Mississippi State		
Harrington, John OE-DE	46CleAA 47ChiAA	2	6'3"	198	Marquette		18
Harris, Amos G	47-48BknAA		6'	210	Mississippi State		
Harris, Elmore HB	47BknAA		5'11"	175	Morgan State		
Harris, Hank G-T	47-48Was		6'	265	Texas		
Harris, Jimmy DB	57Phi 58LA 60DalA 61Dal		6'1"	178	Oklahoma	11	6
Hart, Leon OE-FB	50-57Det	2	6'5"	257	Notre Dame	2	192
Hartley, Howard DB-HB-WB	48Was 49-52Pit	3	6'	185	Duke	28	6
Hartman, Fred T	47ChiB 48Phi		6'1"	229	Rice	1	6
Hartshorn, Larry OG	55ChiC		6'	225	Kansas State		
Hatley, John OG-DT	53ChiB 54-55ChiC 60DenA		6'3"	249	Sul Ross State		
Hauser, Art DT-OG	54-57LA 59ChiC 59NYG 60BosA 61DenA		6'	237	Xavier-Ohio		6
Haynes, Hall DB-HB	50Was 51-52MS 53Was 54-55LA		6'	187	Santa Clara	5	6
Haynes, Joe C-G	47BufAA		6'3"	225	Tulsa		
Hays, George DE-DT	50-52Pit 53GB		6'2"	211	St. Bonaventure	1	12
Hazelhurst, Bob HB-DB	48Ros		6'	188	Denver		
Hazelwood, Ted OT-DT	49ChiAA 53Was		6'1"	235	North Carolina		
Heap, Joe HB	55NYG		5'11"	185	Notre Dame		
Heap, Walt DB-BB	47-48LA-AA		6'1"	210	Texas	10	18
Heath, Leon FB	51-53Was	2	6'1"	203	Oklahoma		42
Heath, Stan QB	49GB 50CFL	1	6'1"	190	Nevada		6
Hecht, Al G	47ChiAA		6'	235	Alabama		
Heck, Bob DE	49ChiAA		6'3"	207	Purdue		
Hecker, Norb DB-OE	51-53LA 54CFL 55-57Was HC66-68Atl		6'2"	193	Baldwin-Wallace	28	20
Hein, Bob DE-OE	47BknAA		6'3"	220	Kent State		
Hegarty, Bill DE-OT	53Pit 53Was		6'4"	240	Georgia,		
					Villanova		
Heinrich, Don QB	54-59NYG 60Dal 62OakA	2	6'	182	Washington		30
Hekkers, George T	46MiaAA 47BalAA 47-49Det		6'4"	229	Wisconsin		
Held, Paul QB	54Pit 55GB	1 5	6'2"	195	San Jose State		23
Helluin, Jerry DT	52-53Cle 54-57GB 60HouA		6'2"	272	Tulane	1	6
Helms, Jack DE	46Det		6'4"	215	Georgia Tech		13
Helwig, John LB-DE	53-56ChiB		6'2"	208	Notre Dame	3	
Hendley, Dick BB	51Pit		6'	198	Clemson		
Hendren, Bob OT-DT-DE	49-51Was		6'8"	244	Southern Calif.		
Henke, Ed DE-LB-OG-DG-OT-DT	49LA-AA 51-52SF 53-54MS		6'3"	227	Southern Calif.		
	55CFL 56-60SF 61-63StL						
Hennessey, Jerry DE	50-51ChiC 52-53Was		6'2"	219	Sant Clara		2
Hensley, Dick OE-DE	49NYG 50-51MS 52Pit 53ChiB	2	6'4"	213	Kentucky		14
Herchman, Bill DT	56-59SF 60-61Dal 62HouA		6'2"	246	Texas Tech	1	6
Hermann, John DB	56NYG 56Bal		6'1"	180	U. C. L. A.		
Herring, Hal LB-C	49BufAA 50-52Cle		6'1"	211	Auburn	4	
Heywood, Ralph OE-DE	46ChiAA 47-48Det 48Bos 49NYB	2 4	6'2"	203	Southern Calif.		78
Hickey, Red OE-DE	41Cle 42-44MS 45Cle 46-48LA	2	6'2"	204	Arkansas		96
	HC59-63SF						
Higgins, Luke G	47BalAA		6'	210	Notre Dame		
Higgins, Tom OT-OG-DT	53ChiC 54-55Phi		6'2"	230	North Carolina		
Hill, Harlon OE-DB	54-61ChiB 62Pit 62Det	2	6'3"	199	Florence State	3	240
Hill, Jim DB	51-52Det 53-54MS 55Pit		6'	188	Tennessee	2	
Hillenbrand, Billy HB-DB	46ChiAA 47-48BalAA	23	6'	188	Indiana	4	186
Hillman, Bill FB-LB	47Det		5'11"	200	Tennessee		
Hipps, Claude DB	52-53Pitt		6'1"	189	Georgia	5	
Hirsch, Buckets LB-FB	47-49BufAA 50CFL		5'10"	207	Northwestern	3	6
Hirsch, Crazy Legs OE-HB-DB	46-48ChiAA 49-57LA	2 5	6'2"	190	Wisconsin	15	405
Hix, Billy OE	50Phi		6'2"	215	Arkansas		
Hobbs, Homer OG-DG	49SF-AA 50SF		5'11"	210	Georgia		
Hock, John OG-OT	50ChiC 51-52MS 53,55-57LA		6'2"	230	Santa Clara		
Hodell, Merwin FB	53NYG		6'2"	205	Colorado		
Hoerner, Dick FB-LB-DB	47-51LA 52Dal		6'4"	219	Iowa	1	204
Hoernschemeyer, Bob (Hunchy) HB-TB-DB-WB	46-47ChiAA	123	5'11"	194	Indiana	2	234
	47-48BknAA 49ChiAA 50-55Det						
Hoffman, Bob LB-FB-BB	40-41Was 42-45MS 46-49LA	2	6'1"	208	Southern Calif.	2	66
Hoffman, Jack DE-OE	52ChiB 53-54MS 55-58ChiB		6'5"	234	Xavier-Ohio	2	
Hoffman, John FB-OE-LB-HB-DE	49-56ChiB	2	6'2"	215	Arkansas	4	104
Hogan, Darrell LB-OG	49-53Pit		5'10"	210	Trinity(Texas)	7	6
Hogland, Doug OG-OT	53-55SF 56-58ChiC 58Det		6'3"	239	Oregon State		
Holder, Lew OE	49LA-AA		6'	191	Texas		
Holladay, Bob DB	56LA 56-57SF		5'11"	175	Tulsa	1	
Hollar, John FB-LB	48Was 49Det 49Was		6'	223	Appalachian State		12
Holley, Ken QB	46MiaAA		5'10"	185	Holy Cross		
Hollingsworth, Joe FB	49-51Pit		6'	200	Eastern Kentucky		
Holovak, Mike FB-LB	46LA 47-48ChiB HC61-68BosA	2	6'1"	213	Boston College	1	36
Holtzman, Glenn OT-DE	55-58LA		6'3"	250	North Texas State		2
Horn, Dick QB	58Bal		6'1"	195	Stanford		
Horne, Dick DE-OE	41NYG 42-45MS 46MiaAA 47SF-AA		6'2"	214	Oregon		
Hornick, Bill T	47Pit		6'1"	207	Tulane		
Horrell, Bill OG	52Phi 53-54MS		5'11"	222	Michigan State		
Horvath, Les HB-DB	47-48LA 49CleAA	2	5'10"	173	Ohio State	4	24
Houghton, Jerry LB-DT-OT	50Was 51ChiC		6'2"	226	Washington State		
Houston, Lin OG-DG	46-49CleAA 50-53Cle		6'	213	Ohio State		

Use Name (Nicknames)-Positions	Team by Year	See Section	Hgt	Wgt	College	Int	Pts
Houston, Walt OG	55Was		6'	217	Purdue		
Howard, Sherman HB-DB	49NY-AA 50-51NYY 52-53Cle	2	5'11"	193	Iowa, Nevada	2	132
Howell, Clarence OE-DE	48SF-AA		6'1"	188	Texas A&M	1	
Howell, Earl HB	49LA-AA	2	5'10"	189	Mississippi		12
Howton, Billy OE	52-58GB 59Cle 60-63Dal	2	6'2"	191	Rice		366
Hubbell, Frank DE-OE	47-49LA	2	6'2"	222	Tennessee	1	24
Hubka, Gene TB-DB	47Pit		5'10"	175	Bucknell		
Hudson, Bob LB-DB-OE	51-52NYG 53-55Phi 56VR 57-58Phi 59Was 60DalA 60-61DenA		6'4"	225	Clemson	19	
Huffman, Dick OT-DT	47-50LA 51CFL		6'2"	255	Tennessee		6
Hugasian, Harry HB-DB	55Bal 55ChiB		6'1"	192	Stanford		
Hughes, Dick HB	57Pit		5'9"	185	Tulsa		
Hughes, Ed DB	54-55LA 56-58NYG HC71Hou		6'1"	184	Tulsa	3	
Hughes, George OT-OG	50-54Pit		6'1"	225	William & Mary		
Humbert, Dick OE-DB	41Phi 42-44MS 45-49Phi	2	6'1"	179	Richmond	14	36
Humble, Weldon OG-LB	47-49CleAA 50Cle 52Dal		6'1"	221	Rice	5	
Huneke, Charlie T	46-47ChiAA 47-48BknAA		6'3"	225	St. Benedict's		
Hunsinger, Chuck HB	50-52ChiB 53CFL	23	6'	188	Florida		48
Hust, Al DE-OE	46ChiC		6'1"	220	Tennessee		
Hutchinson, Ralph T	49NYG		6'2"	230	Tenn.-Chattanooga		
Huxhold, Ken OG	54-58Phi		6'1"	226	Wisconsin		
Huzvar, John FB	52Phi 53-54Bal	2	6'4"	247	N. Carolina State, Pittsburgh		42
Iglehart, Floyd DB	58LA		6'4"	197	Wiley		
Irvin, Willie DE-OE	53Phi		6'3"	203	Florida A&M		
Iverson, Duke DB-WB-HB-BB-LB	47NYG 48-49NY-AA 50-51NYY		6'2"	200	Oregon	5	8
Ivory, Bob G	47Det		6'2"	212	Detroit		
Jackson, Bob FB	50-51NYG		5'11"	210	N. Carolina A&T		12
Jackson, Charlie DB	58ChiC 60DalA		5'11"	180	S. M. U.	1	
Jackson, Ken OT-OG	52Dal 53-57Bal		6'2"	236	Texas		
Jacobs, Jack (Indian Jack) QB-DB-TB-HB	42Cle 43-44MS 45Cle 46Was 47-49GB 50CFL	12 4	6'1"	186	Oklahoma	12	18
Jacobs, Marv T	48ChiC		6'2"	235	none		
Jaffurs, John G	46Was		5'10"	200	Penn State		
Jagade, Chick FB-LB	49BalAA 50BF 51-53Cle 54-55ChiB	2	6'	213	Indiana		84
James, Tommy DB-HB	47Det 48-49CleAA 50-55Cle 56Bal		5'10"	184	Ohio State	34	12
Jankovich, Keever LB-DE	52Dal 53ChiC		6'	215	U. of Pacific		
Janowicz, Vic HB	54-55Was	2 5	5'9"	187	Ohio State		109
	56 brain injury in auto accident						
	53-54 played major league baseball						
Jansante, Val OE-DE	46-50Pit 51GB	2	6'1"	190	Duquesne		86
Jarmoluk, Mike DT-OT-DE-DG-OE	46-47ChiB 48Bos 49NYB 49-55Phi		6'5"	252	Temple	7	18
Jaszewski, Floyd OT	50-51Det		6'4"	230	Minnesota		
Jecha, Ralph OG-LB	55ChiB 56Pit		6'2"	235	Northwestern		
Jeffers, Ed G	47BknAA		6'3"	215	Oklahoma State		
Jelley, Tom OE	51Pit		6'5"	225	Miami (Fla)		
Jenkins, Jack FB-LB	43Was 44-45MS 46-47Was	2	6'1"	206	Vanderbilt	4	7
Jenkins, Jon OT-DT	49BalAA 50Bal 50NYY		6'2"	225	Dartmouth		
Jenkins, Walt DE-DT	55Det		6'1"	223	Wayne State		
Jennings, Jack OT-DT	50-57ChiC		6'4"	245	Ohio State		
Jennings, Jim DE-OE	55GB		6'3"	195	Missouri		
Jensen, Bob DE-OE	48-49ChiAA 50Bal	2	6'2"	218	Iowa State		6
Jessup, Bill OE-FL	51-52SF 53MS 54SF 55HJ 56-58SF 60DenA	2 4	6'1"	195	Southern Calif.		42
Jeter, Perry HB	56-57ChiB	2	5'7"	178	Cal. St. Polytech		18
Jewett, Bob OE	58ChiB	2	6'2"	198	Michigan State		6
Joe, Larry HB	49BufAA		5'9"	190	Penn State		
Johnson, Al DB	48Phi		6'	175	Hardin-Simmons		
Johnson, Bill G-LB	47ChiB		6'	210	S. M. U.		
Johnson, Bill C-LB	48-49SF-AA 50-56SF		6'3"	228	Tyler J. C.	2	6
Johnson, Clyde T	46-47LA 48LA-AA		6'6"	269	Kentucky		
Johnson, Don HB	53-55Phi	2	6'	187	California		42
Johnson, Farnham DE	48ChiAA		6'	210	Wisconsin, Michigan		2
Johnson, Gil QB	49NY-AA	1	5'11"	195	S. M. U.		
Johnson, Glenn T	48NY-AA 49GB		6'4"	263	Arizona State		6
Johnson, Harvey LB-BB-FB-G	46-49NY-AA 51NYY HC68BufA HC71Buf	5	5'11"	212	William & Mary	1	262
Johnson, Herb HB	54NYG	2	5'10"	172	Washington		12
Johnson, Jack DB	57-59ChiB 60-61BufA 61DalA	4	6'3"	198	Miami (Fla.)	8	
Johnson, Joe WB-DB	48NYG	2	6'2"	195	Mississippi		12
Johnson, Joe HB-OE-FL	54-58GB 60-61BosA	2	6'	185	Boston College		48
Johnson, Marvin DB-HB	51-52LA 52-53GB		5'11"	183	San Jose State	6	
Johnson, Nate DT-OT	46-47NY-AA 48-49ChiAA 50NYY		6'3"	244	Illinois		
Johnson, Pete DB	59ChiB		6'2"	200	V.M.I.		
Johnson, Tom DT	52GB		6'2"	230	Michigan		
Johnston, Pres FB-LB	46MiaAA 46BufAA	2 4	6'	205	S. M. U.	1	19
Jones, Billy G	47BknAA		6'	220	West Va. Wesleyan		
Jones, Charlie OE	55Was		6'1"	202	George Washington		
Jones, Dub HB-DB-WB-TB	46MiaAA 46-47BknAA 48-49CleAA 50-55Cle	2	6'4"	202	Tulane, Louisiana State	2	246
Jones, Elmer G-LB	46BufAA 47-48Det		6'	224	Wake Forest		2
Jones, Jim DB-FB	58LA 61OakA		6'1"	204	Washington		
Jones, Jim (Casey) TB-DB	46Det		6'	180	Union (Tenn.)		
Jones, Ralph OE-DE	46Det 47BalAA		6'3"	200	Alabama		
Jones, Special Delivery HB-DB	45ChiB 46-49CleAA 50CFL	2	5'10"	193	Pittsburgh	2	174
Jones, Tom DT-OT	55Cle		6'2"	255	Miami—Ohio		
Joyce, Don DE-DT	51-53ChiC 54-60Bal 61Min 62DenA		6'3"	253	Tulane	1	
Judd, Saxon OE	46-48BknAA	2	6'1"	190	Tulsa		48
Jungmichel, Hal G	46MiaAA		5'9"	200	Texas	1	
Jurkiewicz, Walt C-LB	46Det		6'1"	220	Indiana		
Juster, Rube T	46Bos		6'2"	230	Minnesota		
Justice, Choo-Choo HB	50Was 51MS 52-54Was	2 4	5'10	176	North Carolina		60
Juzwik, Steve HB-DB-FB	42Was 43-45MS 46-47BufAA 48ChiAA	2 5	5'8"	186	Notre Dame	5	102
Kalmanir, Tommy HB	49-51LA 53Bal	23	5'8"	171	Nevada		36
Kapter, Alex G	46CleAA		6'	205	Northwestern		
Karilivacz, Carl DB	53-57Det 58NYG 59-60LA		6'	188	Syracuse	13	12
Karmazin, Mike G	46NY-AA		5'11"	210	Duke		
Karnofsky, Sonny HB-DB	45Phi 46Bos	23	5'10"	175	Arizona	1	30
Karras, Johnny HB	52ChiC		5'11"	187	Illinois		6
Karras, Lou DT	50-52Was		6'4"	241	Purdue		
Karstens, George C	49Det		6'4"	205	Indiana		
Kasap, Mike T	47BalAA		6'2"	255	Illinois, Purdue		
Katrishen, Mike G	48-49Was		6'1"	214	Souther Miss.		
Kavanaugh, Ken OE-DE	40-41ChiB 42-44MS 45-50ChiB	2	6'3"	207	Louisiana State	1	313
Keane, Jim OE-DE	46-51ChiB 52GB	2	6'4"	217	Iowa		144
Keane, Tom DB-OE-HB	48-51LA 52Dal 53-54Bal 55ChiC	2	6'1"	192	West Virginia	40	18
Kearns, Tom T	45NYG 46ChiC		6'4"	247	Miami (Fla.)		
Kekeris, Jim T	47Phi 48GB		6'1"	266	Missouri		2
Kellagher, Bill FB-LB-DB	46-48ChiAA	2	5'11"	205	Fordham	6	24
Keller, Ken HB	56-57Phi 58JJ	23	5'11"	185	North Carolina		24
Kelley, Bill OE	49GB	2	6'2"	195	Texas Tech		6
Kelley, Bob C	55-56Phi		6'2"	232	West Texas State		
Kelley, Ed T	49LA-AA		6'4"	230	Texas		
Kelly, Bob DB-HB	47-48LA-AA 49BalAA	2	5'10"	192	Notre Dame	8	18
Kelly, Ellison OG	59NYG		6'1"	235	Michigan State		
Kennard, George OG	52-55NYG		6'	210	Kansas		
Kennedy, Bill DE-G	42Det 43-46MS 47Bos		5'11"	200	Michigan State		
Kennedy, Bob FB-DB-LB-HB	46-49NY-AA 50NYY	2	5'11"	195	Washington State	12	60
Kennedy, Bob DB-HB	49LA-AA		6'	178	North Carolina	1	
Kercher, Dick HB-DB	54Det		6'2"	205	Tulsa		
Kerkorian, Gary QB	52Pit 54-56Bal	12 5	5'11"	185	Stanford		89
Kerns, John T	47-49BufAA 50CFL		6'3"	243	Ohio U.		
Kerr, Bill OE-DE	46LA-AA		6'	220	Notre Dame	1	
Kershaw, George DE	49NYG		6'4"	210	Colgate		
Keuper, Ken DB-BB-HB-DE45	45-47GB 48NYG		6'	207	Georgia	6	
Kielbasa, Max HB-DB	46Pit		6'1"	185	Duquesne		
Kilroy, Bucko DG-OT-DG-OG	43P-P 44-55Phi		6'2"	243	Temple	5	
Kimbrough, John (Jarrin' John) FB-LB	46-48LA-AA	2	6'2"	210	Texas A&M		138
Kimmel, J. D. DT	55-56Was 57BL 58GB		6'4"	248	Army, Houston		
Kinard, Billy DB-HB	56Cle 57-58GB 60BufA		6'	189	Mississippi	4	6
Kincaid, Jim DB	54Was		5'11"	180	South Carolina		1
Kindt, Don DB-FB-HB-LB	47-55ChiB	2	6'1"	207	Wisconsin	21	50
Kinek, George DB-OE	54ChiC		6'2"	190	Tulane	2	
King, Don OT-DT	54Cle 56Phi 56GB 60DenA		6'3"	260	Kentucky	2	
King, Ed OG-DE-DG	48-49BufAA 50Bal		6'	217	Boston College		
King, Emmett HB	54ChiC	2	5'9"	195	none		6
King, Fay (Dolly) OE	46-47BufAA 48-49ChiAA	2	6'3"	195	Georgia		120
Kingery, Ellsworth DB	54ChiC		5'11"	180	Tulane	1	
Kingery, Wayne HB-DB	49BalAA		5'11"	175	Louisiana State	1	
Kirby, Jack HB-DB	49GB		5'11"	185	Southern Calif.		
Kisiday, George OE-DE	48BufAA		6'1"	220	Duquesne, Columbia		
Kissell, Ed DB	52Pit 53MS 54Pit		6'1"	193	Wake Forest	6	14
Kissell, John DT-OT	48-49BufAA 50-52,54-56Cle 53CFL		6'3"	245	Boston College		2
Kissell, Vito LB-FB	49BufAA 50Bal 51NYY	5	5'10"	205	Holy Cross	3	11
Klapstein, Earl T	46Pit		6'	220	U. of Pacific		
Klasnic, John WB-DB	48BknAA		6'	185	none		
Klawitter, Dick C	56ChiB		6'7"	270	S. Dakota State		
Klenk, Quentin T	46BufAA 46ChiAA		6'2"	225	Southern Calif.		
Klimek, Tony DE	51-52ChiC		5'11"	200	Illinois	5	
Klosterman, Don QB	52LA 53-54MS		5'10"	180	Loyola (L.A.)		
Klug, Al G-T	46BufAA 47-48BalAA		6'1"	215	Marquette		
Klutka, Nick OE-DE	46BufAA		5'11"	200	Florida		
Kmetovic, Pete HB-DB	46Phi 47Det	2	5'9"	175	Stanford		12
Knafelc, Gary OE	54ChiC 54-62GB 63SF	2	6'4"	217	Colorado		138
Knight, Pat LB-DE-BB	52NYG 53MS 54-55NYG		6'2"	207	S.M.U.	5	
Knox, Ronnie QB	57ChiB		6'1"	198	U. C. L. A.		
Knutson, Gene DE	54GB 55MS 56GB		6'2"	218	Michigan		
Koch, George HB-DB	45Cle 47BufAA	2	6'	200	Baylor, St. Mary's (Tex.)	3	6
Kodba, Joe C-LB	47BalAA		5'11"	190	Purdue	1	
Koepfer, Karl OG	58Det		6'2"	230	Bowling Green		
Kolesar, Bob G	46CleAA		5'10"	200	Michigan		
Koniszewski, John T	45-46, 48Was		6'3"	243	George Washington		2
Konovsky, Bob OG-DE-OT	56-58ChiC 60ChiB 61DenA		6'2"	246	Wisconsin		
Konz, Kenny DB	53-59Cle	34	5'10"	184	Louisiana State	30	33
Kosikowski, Frank DE	48CleAA		6'1"	200	Marquette, Notre Dame		
Koslowski, Stan FB-LB	46MiaAA		6'1"	200	Holy Cross		
Kovatch, John DE-OE	42Was 43-45MS 46Was 47GB	2	6'3"	197	Notre Dame		6
Kowalski, Adolph BB-DB	47BknAA		6'3"	205	Tulsa		
Kozel, Chet G-T	47-48BufAA 48ChiAA		6'2"	211	Mississippi		
Kraemer, Eldred OG	55SF		6'2"	225	Pittsburgh		
Krall, Gerry HB-DB	50Det		5'10"	185	Ohio State		
Kramer, Jack T	46BufAA		6'	220	Marquette		
Kranz, Ken DB	49GB		5'10"	190	Wis.—Milwaukee		
Kreamcheck, John DT	53-55ChiB		6'5"	255	William & Mary		
Krivonak, Joe G	46MiaAA		6'2"	230	South Carolina		
Krouse, Ray DT-DE-OT	51-55NYG 56-57Det 58-59Bal 60Was		6'3"	263	Maryland		
Krutko, Larry FB	58-60Pit	2	6'	220	West Virginia		24
Ksionzyk, John QB	47LA		5'10"	190	St. Bonaventure		
Kuchta, Frank C-LB	58-59Was 60DenA		6'2"	225	Notre Dame		
Kuffell, Ray DE-OE	47BufAA 48-49ChiAA	2	6'3"	213	Marquette		18
Kulbitski, Vic FB-LB	46-48BufAA	2 5	5'11	205	Minnesota, Notre Dame	2	57
Kurrasch, Roy DE-OE	47NY-AA 48Pit		6'2"	195	U.C.L.A.		
Kusserow, Lou FB-LB	49NY-AA 50NYY 51CFL	2	6'1"	200	Columbia		
Kutner, Mal OE-DB	46-50ChiC	2	6'2"	197	Texas	12	198
Kuzman, John T	41ChiC 42-45MS 46SF-AA 47ChiAA		6'1"	232	Fordham		6
Laack, Galen OG	58Phi		6'	230	U. of Pacific		
	Killed in auto accident – Jan. 1, 1959						
Lach, Steve FB-DB-WB	42ChiC 43-45MS 46-47Pit	2 4	6'2"	207	Duke	5	109
Ladd, Jim OE	54ChiC	2	6'4"	205	Bowling Green		
Ladygo, Pete OG-LB	52Pit 53JJ 54Pit		6'2"	218	Maryland		
Lagod, Chet OG	53NYG		6'2"	220	Tenn-Chattanooga		
Lahar, Hal G	41ChiB 42-45MS 46-48BufAA		6'	221	Oklahoma		4
Lahey, Tom OE-DE	46-47ChiAA	2	6'2"	218	John Carroll	1	
Lahr, Warren DB-HB	48JJ 49CleAA 50-59Cle		5'11"	189	Case Reserve	44	36
Lamana, Pete LB-C-FB	46-48ChiAA		5'11"	210	Boston U.	2	6
Lamb, Walt DE-OE	46ChiB		6'1"	195	Oklahoma		
Land, Fed T-G	48SF-AA		6'1"	220	Louisiana State		
Lander, Lowell DB	58ChiC		6'	195	Westminster		
Landrigan, Jim T	47BalAA		6'4"	235	Holy Cross, Dartmouth		
Landry, Tom DB-HB-QB	49NY-AA 50-55NYG HC60-73Dal	12 4	6'1	195	Texas	32	36
Lane, Clayton T	48NY-AA		6'	215	New Hampshire		

Use Name (Nicknames) – Positions	Team by Year	See Section	Hgt	Wgt	College	Int	Pts
Lane, Night Train DB-OE	52-53LA 54-59ChiC 60-65Det		6'1"	194	Scottsbluff J.C.	68	50
Langas, Bob DE	54Bal		6'4"	230	Wayne State		
Lange, Bill OG-LB	51-52LA 53Bal 54-55ChiC		6'1"	239	Dayton		
Lansford, Buck OG-OT	55-57Phi 58-60LA		6'2"	232	Texas		
Lansford, Jim OT	52Dal		6'3"	235	Texas		
Larson, Paul QB	57ChiC 60OakA		5'11"	183	California		
Lary, Yale DB	52-53Det 54-55MS 56-64Det	34	6'	187	Texas A&M	50	36
Lattner, Johnny HB	54Pit 55-56MS	2	6'1"	195	Notre Dame		42
Lauer, Larry C	56-57GB		6'3"	235	Alabama		
Laughlin, Bud FB	55SF		6'1"	200	Kansas		
Lauricella, Hank HB	52Dal	4	5'11"	175	Tennessee		
Laurinaitis, Frank LB	47BknAA		5'10"	200	Richmond		
Lauro, Lindy DB	51ChiC		5'10"	195	Pittsburgh		
Lavelli, Dante OE	46-49CleAA 50-56Cle	2	6"	191	Ohio State		372
Lawler, Al HB-DB	48ChiB		5'10"	175	Texas		6
Layden, Pete DB-TB-HB	48-49NY-AA 50NYY	1234	5'11"	192	Texas	13	27
48 played major league baseball							
Layne, Bobby QB	48ChiB 49NYB 50-58Det 58-62Pit	12 5	6'1"	201	Texas		372
Lazetich, Mike OG-LB	45Cle 46-50LA		6'1"	211	Michigan	2	
Lea, Paul DT-OT	51Pit		6'2"	240	Tulane		
Leahy, Jerry OT	57Pit		6'2"	220	Colorado		
Lear, Les G-LB	44-45Cle 46LA 47Det 48CFL		5'11"	225	Manitoba	1	
LeBaron, Eddie QB	52-53Was 54CFL 55-59Was 60-63Dal	12 4	5'9"	166	U. of Pacific		60
Leberman, Bob DB	54Bal		6'1"	180	Syracuse	2	
Lecture, Jim G	46BufAA		5'10"	220	Northwestern		
Ledbetter, Toy HB-DB	50Phi 51-52MS 53-55Phi	2	5'10"	198	Oklahoma State		66
Ledyard, Hal QB	53SF		6'	185	Tenn.–Chattanooga		
Lee, Gene C-LB	46Bos		6'3"	226	Florida	1	
LeForce, Clyde QB-DB-WB	47-49Det	12	5'11"	176	Tulsa	4	36
Leggett, Dave QB-DB	55ChiC		6'2"	198	Ohio State		
Leicht, Jake DB-HB	48-49BalAA	2	5'9"	170	Oregon	6	12
Lennan, Reid G	47LA-AA		6'	232	none		
Leonard, Bill DE	49BalAA		6'2"	200	Notre Dame	1	
Leonetti, Bob G	48BufAA 48BknAA		6'	230	Wake Forest		
Lesane, Jimmy DB-HB	52ChiB 53MS 54ChiB 54Bal		5'10"	176	Virginia		
Levanti, Lou C-OG-LB	51-52Pit		6'1"	215	Illinois		
Levy, Len G-T	45Cle 46LA 47-48LA-AA		6'	256	Minnesota		6
Lewis, Cliff DB-QB	46-49CleAA 50-51Cle	123	5'11"	167	Duke	30	6
Lewis, Ernie FB-LB	46-49ChiAA	2 4	6'1"	211	Colorado	1	12
Lewis, Mac OT-C	59ChiC		6'6"	290	Iowa		
Lewis, Woodley DB-OE-HB	50-55LA 56-59ChiC 60Dal	23	6'	193	Oregon	26	108
Liddick, Dave OT	57Pit		6'2"	240	George Washington		
Lillywhite, Verl HB-DB	48-49SF-AA 50-51SF 52-55MS	2 4	5'10"	185	Southern Calif.	8	54
Lindskog, Vic C-LB	44-51Phi		6'1"	203	Stanford	4	6
Lininger, Ray LB-C	50-51Det		5'11"	217	Ohio State	3	
Lipinski, Jim OT-DT	50ChiC		6'4"	238	Fairmont State		
Lipscomb, Big Daddy DT-DE	53-55LA 56-60Bal 61-62Pit		6'6"	284	none	1	2
died May 10, 1963							
Lipscomb, Paul DT-OT	45-49GB 50-54Was 54ChiB		6'5"	246	Tennessee	2	
Listopad, Ed OG	52ChiC		6'2"	230	Wake Forest		
Little, Jack OT	53-54Bal		6'4"	235	Texas A&M		
Livingston, Howie DB-FB-WB-HB	44-47NYG 48-50Was 50SF 53ChiB	2	6'1"	193	Fullerton J.C.	29	108
Livingstone, Bob DB-HB	48-49ChiAA 49BufAA 50Bal	2	6'	173	Notre Dame	4	18
Loepfe, Dick T	48-49ChiC		6'2"	230	Wisconsin		
Logan, Dick OG-DT	52-53GB		6'2"	228	Ohio State		
Logel, Bob DE	49BufAA		6'3"	210	none		
Lolotai, Al G-T	45Was 46-49LA-AA		6'	224	Weber State	1	
Long, Bill OE-DE	49-50Pit	4	6'1"	200	Oklahoma State		
Long, Bob HB-DB	47Bos		5'10"	190	Tennessee		
Long, Bob LB-DE	55-59Det 60-61LA 62Dal		6'3"	232	U.C.L.A.	7	2
Long, Cutter HB-DB-OE	53-55NYG	2	6'1"	193	Florida	3	32
Lookabaugh, John OE-DE	46-47Was	2	6'4"	216	Maryland		6
Loomis, Ace DB-HB	51-53GB		6'1"	190	Wis. St.–LaCrosse	12	6
Losch, Jack HB	56GB		6'1"	205	Miami (Fla.)		
LoVuolo, Frank OE-DE	49NYG		6'2"	210	St. Bonaventure		6
Lowe, Lloyd DB-HB	53-54ChiB		5'10"	155	North Texas State	1	
Loyd, Alex OE	50SF	2	6'4"	198	Oklahoma State		
Lucky, Bill DT	55GB		6'3"	250	Baylor		
Luft, Don DE-OE	54Phi		6'5"	220	Indiana		
Luhn, Nolan OE-DE	45-49GB	2	6'3"	200	Tulsa		80
Lujack, Johnny QB-DB	48-51ChiB 52SJ	12 5	6'	186	Notre Dame	12	268
Lukens, Jim OE	49BufAA	2	6'4"	205	Washington & Lee		12
Luna, Bobby DB	55SF 59Pit	4	5'11"	187	Alabama	5	
Lunceford, Dave OT	57ChiC		6'4"	240	Baylor		
Lund, Bill HB-DB	46-47CleAA	2	5'10"	180	Case Reserve	3	36
Lusk, Bob C	56Det		6'1"	222	William & Mary		
Lynch, Lynn OG	51ChiC		6'2"	225	Illinois		
Maack, Herb T	46BknAA		6'2"	210	Columbia		
MacAfee, Ken OE	54-58NYG 59Phi 59Was	2	6'2"	212	Alabama		108
MacDowell, Jay DT-OT-DE-OE	46-51Phi		6'2"	217	Washington		2
Maceau, Mel C-LB	46-48CleAA		6'	203	Marquette		
Macerelli, John OG-OT	56Cle		6'2"	230	St. Vincent's		
Macioszczyk, Art FB-LB	44Phi 45-46MS 47Phi 48Was	2	5'9"	208	Western Michigan		
Mackrides, Bill QB	47-51Phi 53Pit 53NYG	12	5'11"	182	Nevada		18
Macon, Eddie HB-DB	52-53ChiB 54-59CFL 60OakA	2	6'	177	U. of Pacific	9	36
Madar, Elmer OE-DB	47BalAA		5'11"	185	Michigan		
Madarik, Tippy DB-HB-WB-TB	45-47Det 48Was	2	5'11"	200	Detroit	4	6
Maderos, George DB	55-56SF		6'1"	187	Chico State	4	
Magee, John (Maggie) OG-DG-LB	48-55Phi		5'10"	220	Rice		
Maggioli, Chick DB-HB	48BufAA 49Det 50Bal		5'11"	178	Illinois, Notre Dame	12	6
Magliolo, Joe LB	48NY-AA		6'	210	Texas	1	
Magnani, Dante HB-DB-WB	40-42Cle 43ChiB 44-45MS 46ChiB 47-48LA 49ChiB 50Det	23	5'10"	182	St. Mary's	5	90
Mains, Gil DT-DE	54-61Det		6'2"	243	Murray State		6
Maley, Howie QB-HB-DB	46-47Bos	2 4	5'11"	187	S.M.U.		
Malinowski, Gene TB-DB	48Bos	1	6'1"	210	Detroit	1	
Mallouf, Ray QB-DB-TB	41ChiC 42-45MS 46-48ChiC 49NYG	12 4	5'11"	180	S.M.U.	2	6
Maloney, Norm OE-DE	48-49SF-AA		6'1"	190	Purdue		7
Mancha, Vaughn C-LB	48Bos		6'1"	230	Alabama		
Mangum, Pete LB	54NYG 60DenA		6'	219	Mississippi		
Manley, Jack C-LB	53SF		6'3"	215	Mississippi State		

Use Name (Nicknames) – Positions	Team by Year	See Section	Hgt	Wgt	College	Int	Pts
Manley, Willie OG-OT	50-51GB		6'2"	218	Oklahoma		
Mann, Bob OE	48-49Det 50-53GB	2	5'11"	172	Michigan		144
Mann, Dave HB-OE	55-57ChiC 58CFL	2 4	6'1"	190	Oregon State		39
Marchetti, Gino DE-DT-OT	52Dal53-64Bal 65VR 66Bal		6'4"	244	San Francisco	1	20
Marchibroda, Ted QB	54-56Pit 57ChiC	12	5'10"	178	St. Bonaventure, Detroit		18
Marciniak, Ron OG	55Was		6'1"	218	Kansas State		
Marcolini, Hugo WB-DB	48BknAA		6'	203	St. Bonaventure		
Margucci, Joe WB-QB-HB-DB	47-48Det	12	5'10"	182	Southern Calif.		42
Marino, Vic G	47BalAA		5'8"	205	Ohio State		
Maronic, Duke OG-DG-LB	44-50Phi 51NYG		5'9"	209	none	2	
Martin, Caleb T	47ChiC		6'4"	245	Louisiana Tech		
Martin, Jack C-LB	47-49LA		6'3"	238	Navy	1	
Martin, Jim LB-OG-DE-OT-K	50Cle 51-61Det 62VR 63Bal 64Was	5	6'2"	227	Notre Dame	6	434
Martin, Pepper (The Wild Hoss of the Osage) K	48BknAA		5'8"	183	none		
28, 30-40, 44 played major league baseball							
Martinelli, John C-LB	46BufAA		6'	227	Scranton	1	
Martinkovic, John DE-DT	51-56GB 57NYG		6'3"	241	Xavier–Ohio		12
Martinovich, Phil G	39Det 40ChiB 42-45MS 46-47BknAA	5	5'10"	220	U. of Pacific		82
Masini, Len FB-LB	47-48SF-AA 48LA-AA	2	6'	225	Fresno State	1	12
Maskas, John G-T	47,49BufAA		5'11"	212	Virginia Tech		
Massey, Carlton DE	54-56Cle 57-58GB		6'2"	221	Texas	1	
Mastrangelo, John OG-DG-LB-OT-DT	47-48Pit 49NY-AA 50NYG		6'1"	228	Notre Dame		6
Matesic, Joe OT-DT	54Pit		6'4"	250	Arizona State		
Mathews, Ray HB-OE-FL-DB	51-59Pit 60Dal	123	5'9"	190	Clemson	2	261
Matson, Ollie HB-FB-DB-FL	52ChiC 53MS 54-58ChiC 59-62LA 63Det 64-66Phi	23	6'2"	210	San Francisco	3	438
Matthews, Clay DE-DT	50SF 51-52MS 53-55SF		6'3"	219	Georgia Tech	1	
Mattingly, Fran G-LB	47ChiAA		5'11"	215	Texas A&I	1	
Mattioli, Frank G-LB	46Pit		6'	210	Pittsburgh		
Matuszak, Marv LB-OG	53Pit 54MS 55-56Pit 57-58SF 58GB 59-61Bal 62-63BufA 64DenA		6'3"	232	Tulsa	14	
Mauldin, Stan T	46-48ChiC		6'2"	225	Texas	1	
died Sept. 24, 1948 – heart attack							
Maves, Earl WB-DB	48Det		5'9"	180	Wisconsin		
Mavraides, Menil OG	54Phi 55-56MS 57Phi		6'1"	235	Notre Dame		
Mayes, Carl HB	52LA		6'	190	Texas		
Mayne, Lew HB-TB-DB	46BknAA 47CleAA 48BalAA	12	6'1"	190	Texas		30
Maznicki, Frank HB-DB	42ChiB 43-45MS 46ChiB 47Bos	2 5	5'9"	181	Boston College	10	119
Mazza, Vince DE-OE	45-46Det 47-49BufAA 50CFL		6'1"	216	none	1	6
Mazzanti, Gino HB	50Bal		5'11"	190	Arkansas		6
McAfee, George HB-DB	40-41ChiB 42-44MS 45-50ChiB	234	6'	178	Duke	21	234
McCabe, Richie DB	55Pit 56MS 57-58Pit 59Was 60-61BufA		6'1"	185	Pittsburgh	9	6
McCafferty, Don OE-DE	46NYG HC70-72Bal HC73Det		6'4"	220	Ohio State		6
McCaffray, Art T	46Pit		5'11"	190	U. of Pacific		
McCain, Bob OE-DE	46BknAA		5'11"	195	Mississippi		
McCarthy, Jim OE-DE	46-47BknAA 48-49ChiAA	2 5	6'1"	205	Illinois	1	89
McChesney, Bob OE	50-52NYG	2	6'2"	190	Hardin-Simmons		84
McClairen, Jack OE	55-60Pit	2	6'4"	213	Bethune-Cookman		18
McClung, Willie OT-DT	55-57Pit 58-59Cle 60-61Det		6'2"	250	Florida A&M		
McClure, Bob G	47-48Bos		6'1"	224	Nevada		
McColl, Bill OE	52-59ChiB	2	6'4"	230	Stanford		156
McCollum, Harley T	46NY-AA 47ChiAA		6'4"	245	Tulane		
McConnell, Dewey DB-OE	54Pit		6'	190	Wyoming	3	
McCormack, Mike OT-DG-DT	51NYY 52-53MS 54-62Cle HC73Phi		6'4"	246	Kansas	1	
McCormick, Len C-LB	48BalAA		6'3"	232	Baylor	1	
McCormick, Tom HB	53-55LA 56SF	2	5'11"	185	U. of Pacific		6
McCormick, Walt C-LB	48SF-AA		6'1"	215	Southern Calif.		
McCoy, Joel TB-DB	46Det		5'10"	170	Alabama		
McDermott, Lloyd DT	50Det 50-51ChiC		6'2"	240	Kentucky	1	
McDonald, Walt BB-DB-QB	46MiaAA 46-48BknAA 49ChiAA	2	6'1"	210	Tulane	5	6
McDonough, Bob G	46Phi		5'11"	205	Duke		
McDougal, Bob LB-FB	47GB		6'2"	205	Miami (Fla.)		
McElhenny, Hugh (Hurryin' Hugh, The King) HB	52-60SF 61-62Min 63NYG 64Det	23	6'1"	197	Washington		360
McElroy, Bucky HB	54ChiB		5'11"	195	Southern Miss.		
McFadden, Marv OG	53Pit 54-55MS 56Pit		6'	223	Michigan State		
McGeary, Clarence DT	50GB		6'5"	250	N. Dakota State		
McGraw, Thurman DT-OT	50-54Det		6'5"	235	Colorado State	2	
McHan, Lamar QB	54-58ChiC 59-60GB 61-63Bal 63SF 64CFL	12	6'1"	201	Arkansas		72
McHugh, Pat DB-HB	47-51Phi	23	5'11"	165	Georgia Tech	16	18
McIlhenny, Don HB	56Det 57-59GB 60-61Dal 61SF	23	6'	197	S.M.U.		84
McKee, Paul OE-DE	47-48Was	2	6'3"	217	Syracuse		12
McKeever, Ed	HC48ChiAA				Texas Tech		
McKissack, Dick DB	52Dal		6'2"	208	S.M.U.		
McLaughlin, Leon C	51-55LA		6'2"	228	U.C.L.A.		
McMillan, Bo BB-DB	22-23Mil 23Cle HC48-50Det HC51Phi				Centre		
McMillan, Chuck DB	54Bal		6'3"	175	John Carroll		
McPeak, Bill DE	49-57Pit HC61-65Was		6'1"	206	Pittsburgh		6
McPhail, Buck FB	53Bal	2 5	6'1"	195	Oklahoma		27
McPhee, Frank DB-OE	55ChiC		6'3"	195	Princeton		
McQuary, John HB-DB	46LA-AA		6'1"	208	California		
McWilliams, Tom DB-TB-HB	49LA-AA 50Pit		5'11"	183	Mississippi State	4	
Mead, Jack OE-DB-DE	46-47NYG		6'3"	213	Wisconsin	1	
Meadows, Ed DE	54ChiB 55Pit 56-57ChiB 58Phi 59Was		6'2"	221	Duke		
Meagher, Jack	HC46MiaAA				Notre Dame		
Meeks, Bryant C-LB	47-48Pit		6'2"	193	South Carolina		
Mehelich, Charlie DE-OE	46-51Pit	2	6'1"	199	Duquesne		2
Meilinger, Steve OE	56-57Was 58GB 59BA 60GB 61Pit 61StL	2	6'2"	227	Kentucky		48
Meisenheimer, Darrell DB	51NYY		5'10"	195	Oklahoma State	3	
Mello, Jim DB-FB-LB	47Bos 48LA 48ChiAA 49Det	2	5'10"	190	Notre Dame	4	6
Menasco, Don DB	52-53NYG 54Was		6'	185	Texas	5	
Mergen, Mike DT	52ChiC		6'5"	245	San Francisco		
Mertes, Buzz FB-HB-DB	46ChiC 46LA-AA 47-49BalAA 49NYG	2	6'	201	Iowa	1	48
Meyer, Gil DE-OE	47BalAA		6'2"	200	Wake Forest		
Meyers, Bob FB	52SF		6'2"	184	Stanford		
Michael, Bill OG	57Pit		6'2"	240	Ohio State		
Michaels, Walt LB	51GB 52-61Cle 63NY-A		6'	231	Washington & Lee	11	12
Michalik, Art LB-OG	53-54SF 55-56Pit	5	6'2"	229	St. Ambrose		12
Michelosen, John	HC48-51Pit				Pittsburgh		
Michels, John OG	53Phi		5'11"	200	Tennessee		
Micka, Mike DB-HB-FB-LB	44-45Was 45-48Bos	2	6'	188	Colgate	9	6

Use Name (Nicknames) – Positions	Team by Year	See Section	Hgt	Wgt	College	Int	Pts
Middleton, Dave OE-HB-FL	55-60Det 61Min	2	6'1"	194	Auburn		
Mieszkowski, Ed T	46-47BknAA		6'2"	220	Notre Dame		
Mihajlovich, Lou OE	48LA-AA		5'11"	175	Indiana		
Mike, Bob T	48-49SF-AA		6'1"	220	U. C. L. A.		
Miketa, Andy C	54-55Det		6'2"	210	North Carolina		
Miklich, Bill LB-BB-G	47-48NYG 48Det		6'	208	Idaho		
Mikula, Tom FB-LB	48BknAA		5'10"	200	William & Mary		
Miles, Leo DB	53NYG		6'	200	Virginia State		
Miller, Bob DT-OT	52-58Det		6'3"	242	Virginia	1	
Miller, Don DB	54GB 54Phi		6'2"	195	S. M. U.		
Miller, Fred OT	55Was		6'3"	225	U. of Pacific		
Miller, Hal OT	53SF		6'4"	230	Georgia Tech		
Miller, Johnny OT-DT-DE	56Was 57MS 58-59Was 60GB		6'5"	253	Boston College		2
Miller, Paul DE-C	54-57LA 60-61DalA 62SD-A		6'2"	226	Louisiana State	1	
Miller, Ron OE	56LA	2	6'4"	200	Southern Calif.		
Milner, Bill LB-OG-DE	47-49ChiB 50NYG		6'1"	217	Duke	1	
Minarik, Henry OE	51Pit	2	6'2"	200	Michigan State		6
Miner, Tom K	58Pit	5	6'4"	235	Tulsa		
Minini, Frank HB-BB-DB	47-48ChiB 49Pit	23	6'1"	209	San Jose State	1	42
Minisi, Skippy HB-DB	48NYG	2	5'11"	190	Pennsylvania	2	12
Mioduszewski, Ed QB-DB	53Bal	1	5'10"	185	William & Mary	1	
Mitcham, Gene OE	58Phi		6'2"	206	Arizona State		6
Mitchell, Bob DB-HB-BB-QB	46-48LA-AA	2	5'11"	195	Stanford	6	6
Mitchell, Charlie DB	45ChiB 46GB		6'	188	Tulsa	1	
Mitchell, Fondren HB-DB	46MiaAA		6'	185	Florida	1	
Mitchell, Hal OT-OG	52NYG		6'1"	225	U. C. L. A.		
Mitchell, Paul DT-OT	46-48LA-AA 48-49NY-AA 50-51NYY		6'3"	235	Minnesota		
Mixon, Billy HB-DB	53-54SF	2	5'11"	191	Georgia	2	6
Mobley, Rudy (Little Doc) HB-DB	47BalAA	2	5'7"	155	Hardin-Simmons	2	12
Modzelewski, Dick (Little Mo) DT	53-54Was 55Pit		6'	258	Maryland		4
	56-63NYG 64-66Cle						
Modzelewski, Ed (Big Mo) FB	52Cle 53-54MS 55-59Cle	2	6'	217	Maryland		84
Moegle, Dick DB-HB	55-59SF 60Pit 61Dal	2	6'	190	Rice	28	42
Moje, Dick OE	51GB		6'2"	210	Loyola (L. A.)		
Momsen, Bob OG-LB	51Det 52SF		6'3"	225	Ohio State		2
Momsen, Tony C	51Pit 52Was		6'1"	215	Michigan		
Monachino, Jim HB-FB-DB	51,53SF 55Was	2	5'10"	187	California		24
Mont, Tommy QB-DB-HB	47-49Was	12	6'	194	Maryland	3	18
Montgomery, Bill FB-LB	46ChiC		6'	205	Louisiana State		
Montgomery, Jim T	46Det		6'4"	235	Texas A & M		
Moore, Bill G	47-49Pit		5'11"	218	Penn State		
Moore, Henry DB-HB	56NYG 57Bal		6'1"	195	Arkansas	1	
Moore, McNeil DB	54ChiB 55MS 56-57ChiB		6'	185	Sam Houston St.	8	
Morales, Gonzales TB-DB	47-48Pit	12	6'	188	St. Mary's	2	6
Morgan, Bob DT-OT	54ChiC 54Was		6'	235	Maryland		
Morgan, Joe T	49SF-AA		6'1"	245	Southern Miss.		
Morley, Sam OE	54Was		6'2"	182	Stanford		
Morris, George C-LB	56SF		6'2"	220	Georgia Tech		
Morris, Jack DB	58-60LA 60Pit 61Min	5	6'	189	Oregon	8	30
Morris, Max OE-DE	46-47ChiAA 48BknAA	2	6'2"	200	Illinois, Northwestern		18
46-49 played in N. B. L., 49-50, 56-57 played in N. B. A.							
Morrison, Curley FB-HB	50-53ChiB 54-56Cle	2345	6'2"	215	Ohio State		84
Morrow, Russ LB-C-DE-OE	46-47BknAA		6'7"	205	Tennessee		12
Morton, John OE-DE-DB	45ChiB 46LA-AA 47BufAA		6'	197	Missouri, Purdue	1	6
Morton, John LB	53SF		6'2"	220	Texas Christian	2	
Moselle, Dom DB-HB	50Cle 51-52GB 54Phi	23	6'	192	Wis. St.-Superior	4	36
Moser, Bob C	51-53ChiB		6'3"	238	U. of Pacific		
Mosley, Henry HB	55ChiB		6'2"	210	Morris Brown		
Mosley, Norm TB-DB	48Pit		5'9"	185	Alabama		6
Moss, Joe OT	52Was		6'1"	221	Maryland		
Moss, Perry QB	48GB		5'10"	170	Illinois		
Mote, Kelley OE-DE-DB	47-49Det 50-52NYG	2	6'2"	189	Duke	2	36
Motl, Bob OE-DE	46ChiAA		6'3"	195	Northwestern		6
Motley, Marion FB-LB	46-49CleAA 50-53Cle 55Pit	23	6'1"	232	Nevada	2	234
Mrkonic, George OT-DT	53Phi		6'2"	225	Kansas		
Muehlheuser, Frank FB-LB	48Bos 49NYB	2	6'2"	218	Colgate		12
Muha, Joe LB-FB	46-50Phi	2 4	6'1"	205	V. M. I.	5	38
Mullins, Noah DB-HB	46-48ChiB 49NYG	2	5'11"	182	Kentucky	19	42
Mulready, Jerry OE-DE	47ChiAA		6'1"	205	N. Dakota State		
Murakowski, Art FB-LB	51Det		6'	195	Northwestern		
Murley, Dick OT	56Pit 56Phi		6'	247	Purdue		
Murphy, George BB	49LA-AA		6'	200	Southern Calif.		
Murray, Earl OG	50Bal 51NYG 52Pit		6'2"	240	Purdue		
Mutryn, Chet HB-DB	46-49BufAA 50Bal	23	5'9"	179	Xavier-Ohio	1	253
Mutscheller, Jim OE-DE	54-61Bal	2	6'1"	213	Notre Dame		240
Myers, Bob DT	55Bal		6'	260	Ohio State		
Myers, Brad HB-FB-OE-DB	53LA 54-55MS 56LA 58Phi	2	6'1"	197	Bucknell		18
Myers, Jack FB-LB	48-50Phi 52LA	2	6'2"	200	U. C. L. A.	2	18
Myhra, Steve OG-LB	57-61Bal	5	6'1"	237	North Dakota		312
Nabors, Roland LB-C	48NY-AA		6'2"	200	Texas Tech	1	
Nacrelli, Andy OE	58Phi		6'1"	190	Fordham		
Nagel, Ray QB	53ChiC	1	5'11"	177	U. C. L. A.		
Nagel, Ross DT-OT	42ChiC 51NYY		6'4"	234	St. Louis	1	
Nagler, Gern OE	53ChiC 54MS 55-58ChiC 59Pit 60-61Cle	2	6'2"	190	Santa Clara		168
Naumetz, Fred C-LB	46-50LA		6'1"	222	Boston College	7	
Naumu, John HB	48LA-AA		5'8"	175	Southern Calif.		
Neal, Ed OG-DT-OT-OG-C	45-51GB 51ChiB		6'4"	285	Tulane, Louisiana State		6
Neale, Greasy	HC41-42Phi HC43P-P HC44-50Phi				West Va. Wesleyan		
16-22, 24 played major league baseball							
Negus, Fred LB-C	47-49ChiAA 50ChiB		6'1"	208	Wisconsin	7	12
Nelson, Bob C-LB-OT-DT-DE	41Det 42-44MS 45Det	5	6'1"	214	Baylor	6	67
	46-49LA-AA 50Bal						
Nelson, Frank DB-HB-TB	48Bos 49NYB	2	5'9"	167	Utah	2	
Nelson, Herb DE-OE-T	46BufAA 47-48BknAA		6'4"	219	Pennsylvania		
Nelson, Jimmy HB-QB-DB	46MiaAA	2	5'11"	180	Alabama	2	12
Nelson, Reed C-LB	47Det		6'	230	Brigham Young		
Nemeth, Steve QB-TB-DB	45Cle 46ChiAA 47BalAA	1 5	5'10"	174	Notre Dame		60
Nichols, Ham OG-LB	47-49ChiC 51GB		5'11"	209	Rice	1	
Nickel, Elbie OE-DE	47-57Pit	2	6'1"	196	Cincinnati		222
Nickla, Ed OT	59ChiB		6'3"	240	Maryland, Tennessee		
Nicksich, George LB-OG	50Pit		6'	225	St. Bonaventure	3	

Use Name (Nicknames) – Positions	Team by Year	See Section	Hgt	Wgt	College	Int	Pts
Niedziela, Bruno T	47ChiAA		6'2"	225	Iowa		
Niemi, Laurie OT-DT	49-53Was		6'1"	251	Washington State		6
Niles, Jerry QB	47NYG	1	6'1"	195	Iowa		
Nipp, Maury OG	52-53Phi 54-55MS 56Phi		6'	219	Loyola (L. A.)		
Nix, Doyle DB	55GB 56-57MS 58-59Was 60LA-A 61DalA		6'1"	191	S. M. U.	16	6
Nix, Jack OE	50SF		6'2"	200	Southern Calif.		1
Nobile, Leo G-LB	48-49Pit		5'10"	213	Penn State	1	
Nolan, Dick DB	54-57NYG 58ChiC 59-61NYG 62Dal		6'1"	185	Maryland	23	2
	HC68-73SF						
Nolan, John OT-DT	48Bos 49NYB 50NYY		6'2"	232	Penn State		
Nolander, Don C-LB	46LA-AA		6'1"	210	Minnesota	1	
Noll, Chuck LB-OG-C	53-59Cle HC69-73Pit		6'1"	218	Dayton	8	14
Nomellini, Leo (The Lion) DT-OT	50-63SF		6'3"	259	Minnesota		10
Norberg, Hank DE-OE	46-47SF-AA 48ChiB		6'2"	225	Stanford	1	
Norman, Jim DT-OT	55Was		6'2"	248	none		
Norris, Hal LB-DB	55-56Was		5'11"	194	California		
North, John OE-DB	48-49BalAA 50Bal HC73NO	2	6'2"	199	Vanderbilt	1	36
Norton, Jerry DB-HB	54-58Phi 59ChiC 60-61StL 62Dal	234	5'11"	195	S. M. U.	35	42
	63-64GB						
Nowaskey, Bob DE-OE	40-42ChiB 43-45MS 46-48LA-AA	2	6'	205	George Washington	4	49
	48-49BalAA 50Bal						
Nussbaumer, Bob DB-HB	46GB 47-48Was 49-50ChiC 51GB	2	5'11"	172	Michigan	16	30
Nutter, Buzz C-LB	54-60Bal 61-64Pit 65Bal		6'4"	230	Virginia Tech		
Nuzum, Jerry HB-DB	48-51Pit	2	6'1"	199	New Mexico State	1	60
Nyers, Dick DB-HB	56-57Bal		5'11"	177	Indiana Central		
Nygren, Bernie HB-DB	46LA-AA 47BknAA	2	5'9"	193	San Jose State	2	6
Oakley, Charley DB	54ChiC		5'10"	170	Louisiana State		
Obeck, Vic G	45ChiC 46BknAA		6'	225	Springfield		
O'Brien, Bill HB-DB	47Det		6'	180	none		
O'Brien, Jack OE-DE	54-56Pit	2	6'2"	213	Florida		12
O'Connell, Tom QB	53ChiB 54-55MS 56-57Cle 60-61BufA	12	5'11"	187	Illinois		26
O'Connor, Bill OE-DE	48BufAA 49CleAA 51NYY	2	6'4"	220	Notre Dame		12
O'Donahue, Pat DE	52SF 53-54MS 55GB		6'1"	208	Wisconsin		7
Odson, Urban T	46-49GB		6'3"	251	Minnesota		2
Olenski, Mitch T	46MiaAA 47Det		6'3"	222	Alabama		
Olsen, Ralph DE	49GB		6'4"	220	Utah		
Olsonoski, Larry G	48-49GB 49NYB		6'2"	214	Minnesota		
Olszewski, Johnny (Johnny O) FB-HB	53-57ChiC 58-60Was	2	5'11"	200	California		114
	61Det 62DenA						
O'Malley, Joe DE	55-56Pit		6'2"	218	Georgia		6
O'Malley, Tom QB	50GB		5'11"	185	Cincinnati		
O'Neal, Jim G	46-47ChiAA		6'1"	230	Texas Christian		
O'Neil, Bob OG-DE	56-57Pit 61NY-A		6'1"	229	Notre Dame		
Oniskey, Dick OG	55Pit		6'2"	225	Tenn.-Chattanooga		
O'Quinn, Red DB-OE-DE	50-51ChiB 51Phi 52CFL		6'2"	195	Wake Forest	3	6
Oristaglio, Bob DE-OE	49BufAA 50Bal 51Cle 52Phi	2	6'2"	214	Pennsylvania		6
Orlich, Dan DE-OE	49-51GB		6'5"	215	Nevada	1	6
Ormsbee, Elliott HB-DB	46Phi		5'11"	185	Bradley		
O'Rourke, Charlie QB-DB-TB	42ChiB 43-45MS 46-47LA-AA	12 4	5'11"	175	Boston College	3	24
	48-49BalAA						
Ortmann, Chuck TB-DB-QB	51Pit 52Dal	12	6'1"	190	Michigan	1	
Osmanski, Joe FB-LB	46-49ChiB 49NYB	2	6'2"	218	Holy Cross		36
Ossowski, Ted T	47NY-AA		6'	218	Oregon State		
Ostendarp, Jim HB	50-51NYG		5'8"	178	Bucknell		12
Ostrowski, Chet DE-DT	54-59Was		6'1"	232	Notre Dame	2	
Ottele, Dick BB-DB	48LA-AA		6'3"	210	Washington		
Owens, Ike DE	48ChiAA		6'1"	190	Illinois		
Owens, Jim OE-DE	50Bal	2	6'3"	205	Oklahoma	1	6
Pace, Jim HB	58SF 59JJ 60CFL	2	6'	195	Michigan		12
Pacewic, Vince HB-DB	47Was		6'1"	205	San Francisco		
Paffrath, Bob HB-DB-BB	46BknAA 46MinAA 47CFL	2	5'8"	190	Minnesota		12
Page, Paul HB-DB	49BalAA	2	6'	180	S. M. U.		
Paine, Homer T	49ChiAA		6'	235	Oklahoma		
Palatella, Lou OG-LB	55-58SF		6'2"	230	Pittsburgh		
Palazzi, Lou C-LB	46-47NYG		6'	198	Penn State		
Palmer, Darrell DT-OT	46-48NY-AA 49CleAA 50-53Cle		6'2"	240	Texas Christian		
Palmer, Les DB-HB	48Phi		6'	180	N. Carolina State		
Palmer, Tom DT	53-54Pit		6'2"	240	Wake Forest		
Palumbo, Sam LB-C	55-56Cle 57GB 60BufA		6'2"	226	Notre Dame	1	
Panciera, Don QB-DB	49NY-AA 50Det 52ChiC	1	6'1"	192	San Francisco	1	
Panelli, John LB-FB	49-50Det 51-53ChiC	2	5'11"	200	Notre Dame	5	
Panfil, Ken OT-DT	56-58LA 59ChiC 60-62StL		6'6"	262	Purdue		
Paolucci, Ben DT	59Det		6'2"	240	Wayne State		
Papach, George FB-DB	48-49Pit	2	6'2"	208	Purdue		18
Papit, Johnny HB	51-53Was 53GB	2	6'	190	Virginia		12
Parker, Howie BB-LB	48NY-AA		6'2"	220	S. M. U.		
Parker, Joe DE-OE	46-47ChiC		6'1"	220	Texas		
Parmer, Jim HB-FB-DB	48-56Phi	2	6'	193	Oklahoma State	3	126
Parseghian, Ara HB-DB	48-49CleAA	2	5'10"	194	Miami-Ohio	1	12
Parsons, Earle HB-DB	46-47SF-AA	23	6'	180	Southern Calif.		24
Paschka, Gordon FB-LB-G	43P-P 47NYG	2	6'	213	Minnesota		14
Pasquariello, Ralph FB	50LA 51-52ChiC 53JJ	2	6'2"	237	Villanova		12
Pasquesi, Tony DT-LB	55-57ChiC		6'4"	245	Notre Dame		
Patanelli, Mike DE	47BknAA		6'2"	215	Ball State		
Patera, Jack LB-OG	55-57Bal 58-59ChiC 60-61Dal		6'1"	234	Oregon	6	
Patterson, Paul WB-DB	49ChiAA	2	5'9"	185	Illinois	3	24
Patton, Bob OG	52NYG		6'	226	Clemson		
Patton, Cliff OG-DG-LB	46-50Phi 51ChiC	5	6'2"	243	Texas Christian	3	278
Paul, Don LB-C	48-55LA		6'1"	228	U. C. L. A.	11	
Paul, Don DB-HB	50-53ChiC 54-58Cle	23	6'	187	Washington State	34	84
Pavlich, Charlie G	46SF-AA		6'2"	210	none		
Pearcy, Jim G	46-49ChiAA		5'11"	210	Marshall		
Pearson, Lindy HB	50-52Det 52GB	2	6'	198	Oklahoma		12
Peebles, Jim DE-OE-OT	46-49, 51Was	2	6'4"	231	Vanderbilt		7
Pelfrey, Ray OE-HB	51GB 52Dal 52ChiC 53NYG	2	6'	190	Eastern Kentucky		
Pellington, Bill LB-OG	53-64Bal		6'2"	234	Rutgers	21	6
Pepper, Gene OG-OT-DT-LB-DG	50-53Was 54Bal		6'2"	239	Missouri		
Perantoni, Frank C	48-49NY-AA		6'	220	Princeton		
Perina, Bob DB-TB-HB	46NY-AA 47BknAA 48ChiAA 49ChiB	12	6'1"	205	Princeton	18	30
	50Bal						
Perini, Pete FB-LB	54-55ChiB 55Cle		6'	225	Ohio State		1
Perko, John G	46BufAA		6'1"	225	Minnesota		
Perpich, George T	46BknAA 47BalAA		6'2"	233	Georgetown		
Perotti, Mike T	48-49LA-AA		6'3"	243	Cincinnati		

Use Name (Nicknames) – Positions	Team by Year	See Section	Hgt	Wgt	College	Int	Pts
Perry, Jerry DT-DE-OT-OG	54Det 55MS 56-59Det 60-62StL	5	6'4"	237	California		190
Perry, Joe FB-DB	48-49SF-AA 50-60SF 61-62Bal 63SF	23	6'	203	Compton J.C.	1	513
Perry, Lowell OE-HB	56Pit	2	6'	195	Michigan		12
Peters, Volney DT-OT-DE	52-53ChiC 54-57Was 58Phi 60LA-A 61OakA		6'4"	237	Southern Calif.		6
Peterson, Jerry (The Heap) DT	56Bal		6'3"	290	Texas		
Petitbon, Johnny DB-HB	52Dal 53-54MS 55-56Cle 57GB		5'11"	186	Notre Dame	8	
Petrovich, George OG-OT-DT	49-50ChiC		6'2"	225	Texas		
Peviani, Bob LB	53NYG		6'1"	210	Southern Calif.		
Pfohl, Bob HB-DB	48-49BalAA	2	6'	200	Purdue		48
Phelan, Jimmy	HC48-49LA-AA HC52Dal				Notre Dame		
Phelps, Don HB-DB	50-52Cle	2	5'11"	185	Kentucky	1	24
Phillips, Mike C-LB	47BalAA		6'	208	Western Maryland		
Philpott, Dean FB	58ChiC		6'	200	Fresno State		
Pifferini, Bob LB-C	49Det		6'	210	San Jose State	3	
Piggott, Bert HB-DB	47LA-AA	2	6'2"	195	Illinois	1	6
Pihos, Pete OE-DE	47-55Phi	2	6'1"	211	Indiana	2	378
Pipkin, Joyce OE-DE-BB	48NYG 49LA-AA		6'1"	204	Arkansas		
Pirro, Rocco G-BB-LB-DB-HB	40-41Pit 42-45MS 46-49BufAA		6'	226	Catholic	1	
Piskor, Roman T	46NY-AA 47CleAA 48ChiAA		6'	245	Niagara		
Pitts, Hugh LB	56LA 60HouA		6'2"	223	Texas Christian	3	
Planutis, Jerry HB	56Was		5'9"	175	Michigan State		
Podoley, Jim HB-OE	57-60Was 61JJ	2	6'2"	200	Central Michigan		78
Poillon, Dick HB-DB-TB	42Was 43-45MS 46-49Was	2 45	6'	193	Canisius	2	247
Polanski, John FB-LB	42Det 43-45MS 46LA-AA	2	6'2"	211	Wake Forest	2	12
Pollard, Al HB-FB-DB	51NYY 51-53Phi	23	6'	196	Army, Loyola (L.A.)		7
Polofsky, Gordon OG-LB	52-54ChiC		6'1"	219	Tennessee		
Polsfoot, Fran OE	50-52ChiC 53Was	2 4	6'3"	203	Washington State		60
Poole, Barney DE-OE	49NY-AA 50-51NYY 52Dal 53Bal 54NYG	2	6'2"	231	Army, Mississippi	1	6
Poole, Ollie DE-OE	47NY-AA 48BalAA 49Det		6'3"	220	Mississippi		
Poole, Ray DE-OE	47-52NYG 53CFL	2 5	6'2"	215	Mississippi	3	223
Popa, Eli LB	52ChiC		5'10"	202	Illinois		
Poto, John HB-DB	47-48Bos	2	5'10"	194	none		6
Powell, Charley DE-LB-OE	52-53SF 54MS 55-57SF 58-59 retired for pro boxing career 60-61OakA		6'2"	226	none		2
Powers, Jim DB-QB LB	50-53SF	1 4	6'	185	Southern Calif.	11	
Prchlik, John DT-OT	49-53Det		6'4"	234	Yale		2
Pregulman, Merv C-LB	46GB 47-48Det 49NYB	5	6'3"	215	Michigan	3	32
Prescott, Hal OE-DB	46GB 47-49Phi 49NYB	2	6'2"	199	Hardin-Simmons	3	6
Preston, Pat G-LB	46-49ChiB		6'2"	216	Wake Forest		
Prewitt, Felto LB-C	46-48BufAA 49BalAA		5'11"	207	Tulsa	6	
Priatko, Bill LB	57Pit		6'2"	220	Pittsburgh		
Price, Eddie FB	50-55NYG	2	5'11	190	Tulane		144
Pricer, Billy FB	57-60Bal 61DalA	2	5'10"	208	Oklahoma		18
Pritchard, Bosh HB-DB	42Cle 42Phi 43-45MS 46-49Phi 50JJ 51Phi 51NYG	234	5'11"	164	V.M.I.	7	150
Pritko, Steve OE-DE	43NYG 44-45Cle 46-47LA 48Bos 49NYB 49-50GB	2	6'2"	209	Villanova	1	90
Proctor, Dewey FB-LB	46-47NY-AA 48ChiAA 49NY-AA	2	5'11"	215	Furman	1	24
Proctor, Rex DB	53ChiB		5'10"	180	Rice	1	
Prokop, Eddie FB-DB-HB-LB	46-47NY-AA 48ChiAA 49NY-AA	23	5'11"	200	Georgia Tech	4	84
Prokop, Joe HB-DB	48ChiAA		6'2"	170	Bradley		
Provo, Fred HB-DB	48GB	2	5'9"	185	Washington		
Psaltis, Jim DB	53ChiC 54GB 55ChiC		6'1"	190	Southern Calif.	6	6
Ptacek, Bob QB	59Cle		6'1"	205	Michigan		
Pucci, Ben T	46BufAA 47ChiAA 48CleAA		6'4"	255	none		
Puddy, Hal T	48SF-AA		6'3"	220	Oregon State		
Purdin, Cal WB-DB-HB	43ChiC 44-45MS 46BknAA 46MiaAA	2	6'2"	188	Tulsa		
Purnell, Frank FB	57GB		5'11"	230	Alcorn A&M		
Putman, Earl C	57ChiC		6'6"	308	Arizona State		
Putnam, Duane OG-LB	52-59LA 60Dal 61Cle 62LA		6'	228	U. of Pacific		
Quillen, Frank OE-DE	46-47ChiAA	2	6'5"	225	Pennsylvania	1	18
Quilter, Charley OT-DT	49SF-AA 50SF		6'1"	240	Tyler J.C.		
Quinlan, Skeets HB	52-56LA 56Cle	23	5'11"	173	San Diego State		96
Quirk, Ed FB-LB-C	48-51Was	2	6'1"	231	Missouri	2	30
Radosevich, George C-OT	54-56Bal		6'2"	228	Pittsburgh		
Ragunas, Vince LB	49Pit		5'11"	200	V.M.I.		
Raimondi, Ben TB	47NY-AA		5'10"	175	Indiana		
Ramona, Joe LB-OG	53NYG		6'1"	210	Santa Clara		
Ramsey, Buster OG-LB	46-51ChiC HC60-61BufA		6'1"	219	William & Mary	7	2
Ramsey, Knox OG-LB-DG	48-49LA-AA 50-51ChiC 52Phi 52-53Was		6'1"	216	William & Mary		
Ramsey, Ray DB-OE-WB-HB	47ChiAA 48BknAA 49ChiAA 47-49 played in B. A. A. 50-53ChiC	23	6'2"	166	Bradley	35	108
Rapacz, John C-LB	48-49ChiAA 50-54NYG		6'4"	252	Oklahoma		
Ratterman, George QB	47-49BufAA 50-51NYY 52-56Cle	12	6'1"	182	Notre Dame		84
Rauch, Johnny QB-DB	49NYB 50-51NYY 51Phi HC66-68OakA HC69BufA HC70Buf	1	6'	197	Georgia	2	6
Ravensburg, Bob OE-DB	48-49ChiC	2	6'	190	Indiana	1	18
Reader, Russ DR	47ChiB		6'	185	Michigan State		
Reagan, Frank DB-FB-QB-HB	41NYG 42-45MS 46-48NYG 49-51Phi	1234	5'11"	182	Pennsylvania	35	48
Rechichar, Bert DB-LB-HB-OE	52Cle 53-59Bal 60Pit 61NY-A	345	6'1"	209	Tennessee	31	179
Reece, Don FB-LB-T	46MiaAA	2	6'1"	230	Missouri	1	12
Reese, Ken HB-DB	47Det		5'11"	175	Alabama		
Reese, Lloyd FB-LB	46ChiB		6'2"	240	Tennessee		12
Reichardt, Bill FB	52GB	2 5	5'11"	210	Iowa		26
Reid, Breezy HB	50ChiB 50-56GB	2	5'10"	187	Georgia		108
Reid, Joe LB-C-DG	51LA 52Dal		6'3"	225	Louisiana State	1	
Reinhard, Bill DB-TB-HB	47-48LA-AA		5'10"	168	California	5	18
Reinhard, Bob DT-FB-OT	46-49LA-AA 50LA	2 4	6'4"	234	California	1	18
Remington, Bill C-LB	46SF-AA		6'1"	185	Washington State		
Renfro, Dean HB	55Bal		5'11"	180	North Texas State		
Renfro, Dick FB-LB	46SF-AA		5'10"	200	Washington State		18
Renfro, Ray FL-HB	52-63Cle	23	6'1"	190	North Texas State		330
Renfro, Will DT-DE-OT	57-59Was 60Pit 61Phi		6'5"	233	Memphis State		
Repko, Joe T	46-47Pit 48-49LA		6'	236	Boston College		6
Restic, Joe DB	52Phi		6'2"	180	Villanova		
Reynolds, Billy HB	53-54Cle 55-56MS 57Cle 58Pit 60OakA	23	5'10"	195	Pittsburgh		42
Reynolds, Jim FB-LB	46MiaAA	2	6'1"	190	Auburn	2	
Reynolds, Jim DB	46Pit		6'	193	Oklahoma State		
Rhodemyre, Jay C-LB	48-49, 51-52GB		6'1"	210	Kentucky	5	
Ricca, Jim OT-DG-DT	51-54Was 55Det 55-56Phi		6'4"	270	Georgetown	1	8
Rich, Herb DB-HB	50Bal 51-53LA 54-56NYG		5'11"	181	Vanderbilt	29	24

Use Name (Nicknames) – Positions	Team by Year	See Section	Hgt	Wgt	College	Int	Pts
Richardson, Jess DT	53-56Phi 57JJ 58-61Phi 62-64BosA		6'2"	261	Alabama	1	
Richeson, Roy G	49ChiAA		6'	235	Alabama		
Richter, Les LB	54-62LA	5	6'3"	238	California	16	193
Rickards, Paul QB	48LA		6'1"	190	Pittsburgh		
Rifenburg, Dick OE	50Det	2	6'3"	195	Michigan		6
Riffle, Charley G-LB	44Cle 45MS 46-48NY-AA		6'	212	Notre Dame	1	
Riley, Lee DB	55Det 56,58-59Phi 60NYG 61-62NY-A	3	6'1"	192	Detroit	23	
Roberts, Bill HB	56GB		6'	200	Dartmouth		
Roberts, Choo-Choo HB-FB-DB	47-50NYG 51CFL	2	5'11"	188	Tenn.-Chattanooga		158
Robinson, Bill HB	52GB		6"	195	Lincoln (Pa.)		
Robinson, Charley OG-LB	54Bal		6'	240	Morgan State		6
Robinson, Fred OG	57Cle		6'1"	242	Washington		
Robinson, Wayne LB-C	52-56Phi		6'2"	225	Minnesota	5	
Robison, George OG	52Dal		6'2"	215	V.M.I.		
Robnett, Ed FB-LB	47SF-AA		5'8"	205	Texas Tech		
Robustelli, Andy DE	51-55LA 56-64NYG		6'1"	230	Arnold	2	32
Rodgers, Hosea FB	49LA-AA	2	6'1"	192	North Carolina		30
Rodgers, Tom T	47Bos		6'	248	Bucknell		
Roffler, Bud DB	54Phi		6'1"	200	Washington State		
Rogas, Dan OG-DT-OT	51Det 52Phi		6'1"	228	Tulane		
Rogel, Fran FB	50-57Pit	2	5'11"	203	Penn State		114
Rogers, Cullen HB-DB	46Pit		5'10"	178	Texas A&M		
Roggeman, Tom OG	56-57ChiB		6'	235	Purdue		
Rohrig, Herm (Stumpy) DB-HB-TB	41GB 42-45MS 46-47GB	23	5'8"	190	Nebraska	11	4
Rokisky, John DE-OE	46CleAA 47ChiAA 48NY-AA	5	6'2"	202	Duquesne		46
Roman, George DT-OT	48Bos 49NYB 50NYG		6'4"	242	Case Reserve		
Romanik, Steve QB	50-53ChiB 53-54ChiC	12	6'1"	190	Villanova		18
Romboli, Rudy FB-LB	46-48Bos	2	5'10"	213	none	2	6
Romero, Ray OG	51Phi 52-53MS		5'11"	213	Kansas State		
Romine, Al DB-HB	55,58GB 60DenA 61BosA		6'2"	191	Florence State	4	
Root, Jim QB	53ChiC 54-55MS 56ChiC	12	6'1"	185	Miami-Ohio		18
Rosato, Sal FB-LB	45-47Was	2	6'1"	228	Villanova		30
Roskie, Ken FB-LB	46SF-AA 48GB 48Det		6'1"	225	South Carolina	1	6
Rosso, George DB	54Was		5'11"	177	Ohio State	4	
Rote, Kyle OE-HB	51-61NYG	2	6'	199	S.M.U.		312
Rote, Tobin QB	50-56GB 57-59Det 60-62CFL 63-64SD-A 66DenA	12	6'3"	211	Rice		228
Rothrock, Cliff C-LB	47ChiAA		5'10"	198	N. Dakota State		
Roussos, Mike T	48-49Was 49Det		6'3"	238	Pittsburgh		
Rowe, Harmon DB-HB-WB	47-49NY-AA 50-52NYG		6'	182	San Francisco	11	2
Rowland, Brad HB	51ChiB		6'1"	190	McMurry		
Royston, Ed G	48-49NYG		6'1"	220	Wake Forest		
Rozelle, Aubrey LB	57Pit		6'2"	215	Delta State	1	
Ruby, Martin DT-OT	46-48BknAA 49NY-AA 50NYY 51CFL		6'4"	249	Texas A & M	1	8
Rucka, Leo LB	56SF		6'3"	212	Rice		
Ruetz, Howie DT	51-53GB		6'3"	257	Loras	1	
Ruetz, Joe G-LB	46,48ChiAA		6'	200	Notre Dame	2	
Runnels, Tom HB	56-57Was	2	5'10"	187	North Texas State		6
Rush, Clive OE	53GB HC69BosA HC70Bos	2 4	6'2"	197	Miami-Ohio		
Ruskusky, Ray DE	47NY-AA		6'3"	200	St. Mary's	1	
Russas, Al T-DE	49Det		6'2"	210	Tennessee		
Russell, Jack OE-DE-DB	46-49NY-AA 50NYY 51CFL	2	6'1"	215	Baylor	3	108
Russell, Ken OT	57-59Det		6'3"	252	Bowling Green		
Ruthstrom, Ralph LB-FB	45Cle 46LA 47Was 49BalAA		6'5"	212	S.M.U.	2	
Ruzich, Steve OG-LB-OT-DT	52-54GB		6'2"	228	Ohio State		
Ryan, Dave TB-DB-HB	45-46Det 48Bos	12	5'10"	190	Hardin-Simmons	7	27
Ryan, Ed DE	48Pit		6'2"	200	St. Mary's		
Ryan, Rocky OE-DB-HB	56-58Phi 58ChiB		6'1"	202	Illinois	2	12
Rykovich, Julie HB-DB	47-48BufAA 48ChiAA 49-51ChiB 52-53Was	2	6'2"	204	Illinois, Notre Dame	5	193
Rymkus, Lou OT-DT	43Was 44-45MS 46-49CleAA 50-51Cle HC60HouA		6'4"	231	Notre Dame	1	12
Saban, Lou LB-FB	46-49CleAA HC60-61BosA HC62-65BufA HC67-69DenA HC70-71Den HC72Buf	5	6'	202	Indiana	13	27
Sabasteanski, Joe G-LB-C	47-48Bos 49NYB		6'	207	Fordham	3	
Sabuco, Tino C	49SF-AA		6'1"	206	San Francisco		
Sacrinty, Nick QB-DB	47ChiB	1	5'11"	185	Wake Forest	1	
Saenz, Eddie HB-DB	46-51Was	23	5'11"	169	Southern Calif.	3	72
Sagely, Floyd DB-OE	54,56SF 57ChiC		6'1"	191	Arkansas	1	
St. Clair, Bob OT	53-63SF 64JJ		6'9"	263	Tulsa, San Francisco		
St. John, Herb G	48BknAA 49ChiAA		5'10"	215	Georgia		
Salata, Paul OE	49-50SF-AA 50Bal	2	6'2"	191	Southern Calif.		48
Salem, Ed QB-DB	51Was		5'11"	193	Alabama	5	
Salsbury, Jim OG-OT	55-56Det 57-58GB		6'1"	233	U. C. L. A.		
Salschneider, Jack HB	49NYG	2	5'10"	185	St. Thomas		6
Samuel, Don DB-HB	49-50Pit	2	5'11"	190	Oregon State	1	6
Samuelson, Carl DT-OT	48-51Pit		6'4"	250	Nebraska	1	8
Sanchez, John OT-DT	47ChiAA 47Det 47-49Was 49-50NYG		6'3"	239	San Francisco	1	
Sanders, Spec TB-DB-WB-HB	46-48NY-AA 49KJ 50NYY	1234	6'1"	196	Texas	19	240
Sandifer, Dan DB-HB	48-49Was 50SF 50-51Phi 52-53GB 53ChiC	23	6'1"	190	Louisiana State	23	54
Sandusky, John OT-DT	50-55Cle 56GB		6'1"	251	Villanova		
Sanford, Leo LB-C-OG	51-57ChiC 58Bal		6'1"	224	Louisiana Tech	17	12
Sarratt, Charley, QB-DB	48Det		6'1"	185	Oklahoma		
Sarringhaus, Paul HB-DB	46ChiC 48Det		6'	185	Ohio State		
Satterfield, Al T	47SF-AA		6'3"	225	Vanderbilt		
Savitsky, George T	48-49Phi		6'2"	244	Pennsylvania		
Sazio, Ralph T	48BknAA 49CFL		6'1"	220	William & Mary		
Scalissi, Ted HB-DB	47ChiAA	2	5'8"	173	Ripon		12
Scarbath, Jack QB	53-54Was 56Pit	12	6'2"	206	Maryland		
Schabarum, Pete HB-DB	51SF 52MS 53-54SF	2	5'11"	185	California	1	18
Schaefer, Don FB	56Phi	2	6'	210	Notre Dame		12
Schilling, Ralph DE-OE	46Was 46BufAA		6'3"	218	Oklahoma City		
Schleich, Vic T	47NY-AA		6'3"	240	Nebraska		
Schlinkman, Walt FB	46-49GB	2	5'8"	191	Texas Tech		48
Schmidt, George DE-C-LB	52GB 53ChiC		6'2"	230	Lewis		2
Schmidt, Joe LB	53-65,HC67-72Det		6'1"	220	Pittsburgh	24	18
Schneider, Don HB	48BufAA		5'9"	170	Pennsylvania		
Schneider, Leroy T	47BknAA		5'11"	237	Tulane		
Schnelker, Bob OE	53Phi 54-60NYG 61Min 61Pit	2	6'3"	214	Bowling Green		204
Schnellbacher, Otto (The Claw) DB-OE	48-49NY-AA 48-49 played in B. A. A. 50-51NYG		6'2"	188	Kansas	34	18

Use Name (Nicknames) – Positions	Team by Year	See Section	Hgt	Wgt	College	Int	Pts
Schottel, Ivan BB-DB-DE	46,48Det		6'2"	204	NW Missouri St.		
Schrader, Jim C-OT	54Was 55MS 56-61Was 62-64Phi		6'2"	244	Notre Dame		
Schroeder, Bill DB-HB-TB	46-47ChiAA		6'	190	Wisconsin	5	18
Schroeder, Gene OE-DB	51-52ChiB 53MS 54-57ChiB	2	6'3"	192	Virginia	5	78
Schroll, Bill LB-FB	49BufAA 50Det 51GB		6'	214	Louisiana State	3	
Schuette, Carl LB-C-DB	48-49BufAA 50-51GB		6'1"	206	Marquette	5	6
Schuler, Bill T	47-48NYG		6'	215	Yale		
Schwall, Vic HB	47-50ChiC	2	5'8"	188	Northwestern		18
Schweder, John OG-LB	50Bal 51-55Pit		6'1"	224	Pennsylvania	1	
Schwenk, Bud QB-TB-DB	42ChiC 43-45MS 46CleAA 47BalAA 48NY-AA	12	6'2"	201	Washington-St. L.	1	24
Scollard, Nick DE-OE	46-48Bos 49NYB	2 5	6'4"	217	St. Joseph's-Ind.	1	91
Scott, Clyde (Smackover) HB-DB	49-52Phi 52Det	2	6'	174	Navy, Arkansas	1	42
Scott, George HB	59NYG		6'1"	180	Miami-Ohio		
Scott, Joe HB-DB-OE	48-53NYG	23	6'1"	198	San Francisco	6	132
Scott, Prince OE-DB	46MiaAA	2	6'1"	190	Texas Tech	1	12
Scott, Tom LB-DE	53-58Phi 59-64NYG		6'2"	219	Virginia	8	18
Scott, Vin G	47-48BufAA 49CFL		5'8"	215	Notre Dame		
Scruggs, Ed OE-DE	47-48BknAA		6'1"	195	Rice		
Scudero, Scooter DB-HB	54-58Was 60Pit	23	5'10"	173	San Francisco	10	18
Seabright, Charlie BB-LB	41Cle 42-45MS 46-50Pit	2	6'2"	204	West Virginia	5	24
Sears, Jimmy HB-DB	54ChiC 55-56MS 57-58ChiC 60LA-A	23	5'11"	183	Southern Calif.	2	18
Sears, Vic DT-OT	41-42Phi 43P-P 44BN 45-53Phi		6'3"	223	Oregon State	1	12
Sebek, Nick QB	50Was		6'1"	194	Indiana		
Self, Clarence DB-HB	49ChiC 50-51Det 52GB 53MS 54-55GB		5'8"	181	Wisconsin	7	6
Seno, Frank DB-HB-WB	43-44Was 45-46ChiC 47-48Bos 49Was	23	6'	191	George Wash.	19	54
Sensenbaugher, Dean HB-DB	48CleAA 49NYB	2	5'9"	190	Ohio State		12
Serini, Wash OG-DG-DT	48-51ChiB 52GB		6'2"	236	Kentucky		2
Sewell, Harley OG-LB	53-62Det 63LA		6'1"	230	Texas	1	6
Sexton, Lin HB-DB	48LA-AA		6'	180	Wichita State	1	
Shanley, Jim HB	58GB		5'9"	174	Oregon		
Sharkey, Ed OG-LB-OT-DG	47-49NY-AA 50NYY 52Cle 53Bal 54-55Phi 55-56SF		6'3"	229	Nevada, Duke	4	
Shaughnessy, Clark	HC48-49LA				Minnesota		
Shaw, Bob OE-DE	45Cle 46,49LA 50ChiC 51CFL	2	6'4"	226	Ohio State		126
45-47 played in N.B.L.							
Shaw, Buck	HC46-49SF-AA HC50-54SF HC58-60Phi				Notre Dame		
Shaw, Charlie OG	50SF		6'2"	220	Oklahoma State		
Shaw, George QB	55-58Bal 59-60NYG 61Min 62DenA	12	6'1"	183	Oregon		30
Shepard, Charlie HB-DB	56Pit 57CFL	2 4	6'2"	215	North Texas State		
Sheriff, Stan LB-OG-C	54Pit 55MS 56-57SF 57Cle		6'1"	224	Cal. St. Polytech	1	
Sherman, Will DB-HB	52Dal 54-60LA 61Min		6'2"	197	St. Mary's	29	24
Sherrod, Horace OE-DE	52NYG		6'	190	Tennessee		6
Shields, Burrell HB-DB	54Pit 55Bal		6'2"	203	John Carroll	1	
Shipkey, Jerry FB-DB-LB	48-52Pit 53ChiB	2	6'1"	213	U. C. L. A.	13	102
Shipkey, Ted	HC47LA-AA				Stanford		
Shipp, Billy DT	54NYG 55CFL		6'5"	275	Alabama		
Shirley, Marion T	48-49NY-AA		6'4"	260	Oklahoma City		
Shiver, Ray DB	56LA		6'	190	Miami (Fla.)	1	
Shoener, Hal OE-DE	48-49SF-AA 50SF	2	6'3"	200	Iowa	1	18
Shoener, Herb DE	48-49Was		6'3"	205	Iowa		6
Shoults, Paul HB	49NYB	2	5'11"	178	Miami-Ohio		
Shula, Don DB-HB	51-52Cle 53-56Bal 57Was HC63-69Bal HC70-73Mia		5'11"	190	John Carroll	21	
Shurnas, Marshall OE-DE	47CleAA		6'1"	205	Missouri		
Shurtz, Hubert T	48Pit		6'3"	235	Louisiana State		
Sidorik, Alex T	47Bos 48-49BalAA		6'	248	Mississippi State		
Siegert, Herb OG-LB	49-51Was		6'3"	216	Illinois	2	
Siegert, Wayne OT-LB-OG	51NYY		6'3"	225	Illinois		
Siegle, Jules FB-LB	48NYG		6'	210	Northwestern		
Sieradzki, Steve DB	48NY-AA		6'	194	Michigan State		
Sierocinski, Steve T	46Bos		6'3"	245	none		
Signiago, Joe OG-DG	48-49NY-AA 50NYY		6'1"	220	Notre Dame		
Sigurdson, Sig OE-DE	47Bal AA		6'2"	206	Pacific Lutheran		
Sikora, Mike OG	52ChiC		6'2"	230	Oregon		
Simensen, Don OT	51-52LA		6'2"	220	St. Thomas		
Simerson, John C-OT	57-58Phi 58Pit 60HouA 61BosA		6'3"	257	Purdue		
Simmons, Floyd HB-DB	48ChiAA	2	6'1"	200	Notre Dame		12
Simmons, Jack C-G-T	48BalAA 49-50Det 51-56 ChiC		6'4"	236	Detroit		
Simonetti, Len (Meatball) T	47-48CleAA		5'11"	225	Tennessee	1	
Sims, George DB	49-50LA		5'11"	170	Baylor	10	6
Sinkovitz, Frank LB-C	47-52Pit		6'1"	218	Duke	10	6
Sitko, Emil (Red, 6-Yard) HB	50SF 51-52ChiC	2	5'8"	183	Notre Dame		18
Skibinski, Joe OG	52Cle 53-54MS 55-56GB		5'11"	226	Purdue		
Skladany, Leo DE	49Phi 50NYG		6'1"	208	Pittsburgh		
Skoglund, Bob DE	47GB		6'1"	198	Notre Dame		
Skorich, Nick G-LB	46-48Pit HC61-63Phi HC71-72Cle		5'9"	197	Cincinnati		
Slater, Walt TB-DB	47Pit	123	5'11"	187	Tennessee	4	
Slosburg, Phil DB-HB-TB	48Bos 49NYB	2	5'10"	170	Temple	1	6
Smith, Allen DE-OE	47-48ChiB		6'2"	218	Mississippi		
Smith, Bill T	48ChiAA 48LA-AA		6'2"	250	North Carolina		
Smith, Bob FB	53-54Det		6'	205	Texas A&M		
Smith, Bob HB	55-56Cle 56Phi	2	5'10"	195	Nebraska		6
Smith, Bruce HB-DB-TB	45-48GB 48LA	2	6'	197	Minnesota	2	14
Smith, Charlie HB-DB	47ChiC		5'11"	170	Georgia	1	
Smith, Charlie DE	56SF		6'2"	205	Abilene Christian	1	
Smith, Clipper	HC47-48Bos				Notre Dame		
Smith, Ernie DB-HB	55-56SF		6'3"	190	Compton J.C.		
Smith, Jerry OG-LB	52-53SF 54-55MS 56SF 56GB		6'1"	230	Wisconsin		
Smith, Jim T	47LA-AA		6'4"	270	Colorado		
Smith, Jim DB-HB-WB	48BufAA 48BknAA 49ChiAA 49-53Det	2 4	6'1"	191	Iowa	33	18
Smith, Joe OE-DB	48BalAA		6'1"	183	Texas Tech	1	6
Smith, Oscar HB-DB	48-49GB 49NYB	2	6'	185	Texas-El Paso	2	
Smith, Ray Gene DB-HB	54-57ChiB	3	5'10"	187	Midwestern	9	
Smith, Truett BB	50-51Pit		6'2"	208	Wyoming, Mississippi St.		
Smith, Vitamin HB	49-53LA	23	5'8"	179	Abilene Christian		138
Smyth, Bill DE-OE-T	47-50LA	2	6'3"	243	Cincinnati		6
Snyder, Lum OT	52-55Phi 56-57MS 58Phi		6'5"	228	Georgia Tech		
Soboleski, Joe OG-OT-DT-DG	49ChiAA 49Was 50Det 52Dal		6'	213	Michigan		
Soltau, Gordie OE	50-58SF	2 5	6'2"	195	Minnesota		644
Sommers, Jack C-LB	47Was		6'3"	232	U. C. L. A.		

Use Name (Nicknames) – Positions	Team by Year	See Section	Hgt	Wgt	College	Int	Pts
Sossamon, Lou C-LB	46-48NY-AA		6'1"	207	South Carolina		6
Souders, Cecil DE-OE-T	47-49Det	2	6'1"	210	Ohio State		6
Spangler, Gene WB-DB	46Det		5'10"	195	Tulsa		
Spaniel, Frank HB	50Bal 50Was		5'10"	185	Notre Dame		12
Sparkman, Al T	48-49LA		6'6"	253	Texas A & M		
Sparks, Dave OG-OT	51SF 52-53MS 54Was		6'1"	229	South Carolina		
died of heart attack Dec. 5, 1954							
Sparlis, Al G-LB	46GB		5'11"	185	U. C. L. A.		
Spavital, Jimmie FB-LB	49LA-AA 50Bal	2	6'1"	210	Oklahoma State	4	18
Speedie, Mac OE-DE	46-49CleAA 50-52Cle 53CFL	2	6'3"	203	Utah		205
Spencer, Joe DT-OT	48BknAA 49CleAA 50-51GB		6'3"	239	Oklahoma State	1	
Spencer, Ollie OT-OG-C	53Det 54-55MS 56Det 57-58GB 59-61Det 63OakA		6'2"	245	Kansas		
Spinks, Jack OG-FB-OT	52Pit 53ChiC 55-56GB 56-57NYG	2	6'	236	Alcorn A & M		
Spinney, Art OG-DE-OE	50Bal 51-52MS 53-60Bal		6'	230	Boston College		
Sponaugle, Bob OE-DE	49NYB		6'1"	203	Pennsylvania		
Sprinkle, Ed DE-OE-OG-LB	44-55ChiB	2	6'1"	206	Hardin-Simmons	4	62
Spruill, Jim T	48-49BalAA		6'3"	225	Rice		
Stacco, Ed T	47Det 48Was		6'2"	261	Colgate		
Standlee, Norm FB-LB	41ChiB 42-45MS 46-49SF-AA 50-52SF	2	6'2"	238	Stanford	2	138
Stanfel, Dick OG	52-55Det 56-58Was		6'3"	236	San Francisco		
Stanley, C. B. T	46BufAA		6'4"	225	Tulsa		
Stansauk,Don DT	50-51GB		6'1"	255	Denver		
Stanton, Bill DE	49BufAA		6'2"	210	N. Carolina State		
Stanton, Henry DE-OE	46-47NY-AA		6'2"	200	Arizona		
Stasica, Stan HB-DB	46MiaAA		5'10"	175	South Carolina		
Staton, Jim DT	51Was		6'4"	246	Wake Forest		
Statuto, Art C	48-49BufAA 50LA		6'2"	221	Notre Dame		
Stautner, Ernie DT-DE-OG	50-63Pit		6'1"	230	Boston College	2	6
Stautzenberger, Odell G	49BufAA		6'	218	Texas A & M		
Steber, John OG-DG	46-50Was		6'	225	Georgia Tech		
Steere, Dick OG	51Phi		6'4"	240	Drake		
Stefik, Bob OE	48BufAA		5'11"	180	Niagara		
Steinbrunner, Don DT	53Cle		6'3"	220	Washington State		
Steiner, Rebel DB	50-51GB		6'	185	Alabama	10	6
Steinke, Gil HB-DB	45-48Phi	2	6'	175	Texas A & I	7	36
Stenn (born Stenko), Paul OT-DT	42NYG 43-45MS 46Was 47Pit 48-51ChiB		6'2"	242	Villanova		
Stephens, Red OG	55-60Was		6'	230	San Francisco		
Stephenson, Dave OG-C-DG	51-55GB		6'2"	232	West Virginia		
Steuber, Bob FB-HB-LB-DB	43ChiB 44-45MS 46CleAA 47LA-AA 48RufAA	2 5	6'2"	200	Missouri	1	41
Stevens, Don HB-DB	52,54Phi	2	5'9"	176	Illinois		6
Stevens, Mal	HC46BknAA				Yale		
Stewart, Ralph C-LB	47-48NY-AA 48BalAA		6'	205	Missouri, Notre Dame		
Stickel, Walt DT-OT	46-49ChiB 50-51Phi		6'3"	247	Pennsylvania		2
Still, Jim QB-DB	48-49BufAA	1 4	6'3"	193	Georgia Tech	1	
Stits, Bill DB-HB	54-56Det 57-58SF 59Was 59-61NYG	23	6'	194	U. C. L. A.	15	6
Stock, John OE	56Pit		6'2"	210	Pittsburgh		
Stofer, Ken QB-DB	46BufAA	1	5'9"	188	Cornell		
Stolhandske, Tom LB-DE	55SF		6'2"	210	Texas	1	
Stone, Avatus HB	58Bal		6'1"	195	Syracuse		
Stone, Billy HB-DB	49-50BalAA 51-54ChiB	23	6'	191	Bradley	11	186
Stonesifer, Don OE	51-56ChiC	2	6'	200	Northwestern		84
Stout, Pete FB-LB	49-50Was	2	6'	201	Texas Christian	2	36
Stoutberg, Jerry OG-LB	51ChiB		6'2"	228	Cincinnati		
Stovall, Dick LB-G-C	47-48Det 49Was		6'	202	Abilene Christian	1	
Strader, Red B	27ChiC HC48-49NY-AA HC50-51NYY HC55SF				St. Mary's		
Strausbaugh, Jim HB-DB	46ChiC	2	5'9"	180	Ohio State		18
Stribling, Bill OE	51-53NYG 55-57Phi 58CFL	2	6'1"	206	Mississippi		84
Strickland, Bishop FB	51SF	2	5'10"	195	South Carolina		
Strickland, Larry C	54-59ChiB		6'4"	248	North Texas State		
Striegel, Bill OG-OT-LB	59PHI 60BosA 60OakA		6'2"	235	U. of Pacific		
Stringer, Bob LB-FB	52-53Phi		6'1"	197	Tulsa	2	
Strode, Woody OE-DE	46LA 47CFL		6'3"	205	U. C. L. A.		
Strohmeyer, George LB-C	48BknAA 49ChiAA		5'10"	205	Notre Dame	7	
Stroschein, Breck DE	51NYY		6'1"	205	U. C. L. A.		
Stroud, Jack OG-OT	53-64NYG		6'1"	235	Tennessee		
Strzykalski, Johnny (Strike) HB-DB	46-49SF-AA 50-52SF	23	5'9"	190	Marquette	8	186
Sucic, Steve FB-LB	46LA 47Bos 47-48Det		6'	207	Illinois		
Sugar, Leo DE	54-59ChiC 60StL 61Phi 62Det		6'1"	214	Purdue	1	18
Suhey, Steve G	48-49Pit		5'11"	215	Penn State		
Sulatis, Joe BB-DE-LB-OG-QB-FB-WB	43-45NYG 46Bos 47-53NYG	12	6'2"	212	none	2	12
Sulima, George OE	52-54Pit	2	6'2"	200	Boston U.		12
Sullivan, Bob HB-TB-DB-LB-FB	47Pit 48BknAA		5'9"	191	Holy Cross, Iowa		12
Sullivan, Bob HB-DB	48SF-AA	2	5'10"	190	Holy Cross	1	6
Sullivan, George DE-OE	48Bos		6'2"	205	Notre Dame		
Suminski, Dave OG	53Was 53ChiC 54CFL		5'11"	230	Wisconsin		
Summerall, Pat DE-OE-K	52Det 53-57ChiC 58-61NYG	5	6'4"	228	Arkansas		563
Summerhays, Bob LB-FB	49-51GB	2	6'1"	210	Utah	3	6
Sumner, Charlie DB	55ChiB 56-57MS 58-60ChiB 61-62Min		6'1"	194	William & Mary	21	6
Sumpter, Tony G	46-47ChiAA		6'1"	215	Cameron State		
Susoeff, Nick OE-DE	46-49SF-AA	2	6'1"	211	Washington State		24
Susteric, Ed FB-LB	49CleAA		6'	205	Findlay		6
Sutch, George HB-DB	46ChiC				Temple		
Sutherin, Don DB	59NYG 59-60Pit		5'10"	193	Ohio State	1	
Sutton, Ed HB-DB	57-59Was 60NYG	2	6'1"	205	North Carolina	1	60
Sutton, Joe DB-HB	49BufAA 50-52Phi		5'11"	180	Temple	13	6
Svare, Harland (Swede) LB-DT	53-54LA 55-60NYG HC62-65LA HC71-72SD		6'	214	Washington State	9	6
Svoboda, Bill LB-FB	50-53ChiC 54-58NYG		6'	210	Tulane	9	
Sweiger, Bob BB-LB-DB-WB	46-48NY-AA 49ChiAA	2	6'	209	Minnesota	7	18
Swiacki, Bill OE	48-50NYG 51-52Det	2	6'2"	195	Columbia		108
Swistowicz, Mike DB	50NYY 50ChiC		5'10"	185	Notre Dame		
Switzer, Veryl HB-DB	54-55GB	23	5'11"	190	Kansas State		30
Sykes, Bob FB	52Was		6'1"	218	San Jose State		
Sylvester, John DB-HB	47NY-AA 48BalAA		6'	183	Temple	1	
Szafaryn, Len OT-OG-LB-DT	49Was 50GB 51-52MS 53-56GB 57-58Phi		6'2"	226	North Carolina		6
Szot, Walt DT-OT	46-48ChiC 49-50Pit		6'1"	222	Bucknell		
Szymanski, Frank C-LB	45-47Det 48Phi 49ChiB		6'	220	Notre Dame	1	

Use Name (Nicknames) – Positions	Team By Year	See Section	Hgt	Wgt	College	Int	Pts
Tackett, Doyle BB-DB-WB	46-48BknAA	2	6'	205	none	2	12
Tait, Art DE	51NYY 52Dal		5'11"	205	Mississippi State		12
Talcott, Dan T	47Phi		6'2"	235	Nevada		
Taliaferro, George HB-QB-TB-DB	49LA-AA 50-51NYY 52Dal 53-54Bal 55Phi	1234	5'11"	196	Indiana	4	168
Tamburo, Sam DE	49NYB		6'2"	200	Penn State		
Tanner, Hamp OT-DT	51SF 52Dal		6'2"	280	Georgia		2
Tarrant, Jim QB	46MiaAA		5'9"	160	Howard (Ala.), Tennessee		
Taseff, Carl DB-HB	51Cle 52MS 53-61Bal 61Phi 62BufA	23	5'11"	192	John Carroll	20	48
Tassos, Damon G-LB	45-46Det 47-49GB		6'1"	224	Texas A&M	5	3
Tavener, John C-LB	46MiaAA		6'	225	Indiana		
Taylor, Charlie G	46MiaAA		5'11"	205	Stanford		
Taylor, Corky DB-HB	55,57LA	2	5'10"	189	Kansas State	2	12
Taylor, Hugh (Bones) OE	47-54Was HC65HouA	2	6'4"	194	Oklahoma City		348
Taylor, Jim C-LB	56Pit 57-58ChiC		6'2"	232	Baylor	1	
Teeuws, Len DT-OT	52-53LA 54-57ChiC		6'4"	242	Tulane		
Temp, Jim DE	57-60GB		6'4"	245	Wisconsin	1	
Tepe, Lou C-LB	53-55Pit		6'2"	208	Duke	3	
Tereshinski, Joe DE-OE-LB	47-54Was	2	6'2"	215	Georgia	1	24
Terlep, George QB-DB	46-48BufAA 48CleAA	12	5'10"	180	Notre Dame	1	6
Terrell, Ray HB-DB	46CleAA 47BalAA 47CleAA	2	6'	185	Mississippi	4	6
Teteak, Deral LB-OG	52-56GB		5'10"	210	Wisconsin	6	
Tevis, Lee FB-LB	47-48BknAA		5'11"	190	Miami-Ohio, Washington-St.L.		
Tew, Lowell FB	48-49NY-AA	2	5'11"	195	Alabama		36
Thibaut, Jim FB-LB	46BufAA		5'11"	205	Tulane		6
Thomas, George HB-DB	50-51Was 52NYG	2	6'1"	183	Oklahoma		12
Thomas, Jesse DB	55-57Bal 60LA-A		5'10"	180	Michigan State	4	6
Thomas, Ralph OE-DE	52ChiC 53-54MS 55-56Was		5'11"	190	San Francisco		18
Thomas, Russ T	46-49Det		6'3"	237	Ohio State	1	
Thomason, Bobby QB	49LA 51GB 52-57Phi	12	6'1"	196	V. M. I.		36
Thompson, Hal OE-DE	47-48BknAA	2	6'1"	205	Delaware		6
Thompson, Harry OG-DE-LB-DG	50-54LA 55ChiC		6'2"	226	U. C. L. A.		
Thompson, Tommy QB-DB-TB-HB	40Pit 41-42Phi 43-44MS 45-50Phi	12	6'1"	192	Tulsa	9	42
Thompson, Tommy LB-C	49CleAA 50-53Cle		6'1"	221	William & Mary	6	
Thornton, Bob G-T	46-47SF-AA		5'10"	205	Santa Clara		
Thrower, Willie QB	53ChiB		5'11"	182	Michigan State		
Tidwell, Billy HB-DB	54SF		5'9"	178	Texas A&M		
Tidwell, Travis QB	50-51NYG	12	5'10"	185	Auburn		12
Tillman, Al C-LB	49BalAA		6'	210	Oklahoma		
Timberlake, George LB-OG	55GB		6'1"	220	Southern Calif.		
Timmons, Charlie FB-LB	46BknAA		5'10"	210	Clemson		
Tinsley, Buddy T	49LA-AA 50CFL		6'4"	245	Baylor		
Tittle, Y. A. (Ya-Ya, The Bald Eagle) QB	48-49BalAA 50Bal 51-60SF 61-64NYG	12	6'	192	Louisiana State		
Titus, George C-LB	46Pit		5'10"	185	Holy Cross		
Tobin, George G-LB	47NYG		5'10"	205	Notre Dame		
Tomasetti, Lou HB-DB-TB-WB	39-40Pit 41Phi 42Det 43-45MS 46-49BufAA	12	6'	198	Bucknell	4	120
Tomlinson, Dick OG	50-51Pit		6'1"	205	Kansas		
Toneff, Bob DT-DG-DE-OT-OG	52SF 53MS 54-58SF 59-64Was		6'2"	260	Notre Dame	2	
Tonnemaker, Clayton LB-C	50GB 51-52MS 53-54GB		6'2"	237	Minnesota	2	1
Toogood, Charlie DT-OT-OG	51-56LA 57ChiC		6'	232	Nebraska	3	
Topor, Ted LB	55Det		6'1"	210	Michigan		
Topp, Bob OE	54NYG		6'2"	190	Michigan		18
Torgeson, Lavern (Torgy) LB-C	51-54Det 55-57Was		6'	215	Washington State	18	6
Toth, Zollie FB	50-51NYY 52Dal 53KJ 54Bal	2	6'2"	219	Louisiana State		102
Towler, Dan (Deacon Dan) FB	50-55LA	2	6'2"	225	Wash. & Jefferson		264
Treadway, John T	48NYG 49Det		6'5"	258	Hardin-Simmons		
Trigillo, Frank FB-LB	46LA-AA 46MiaAA	2	5'11"	200	Alfred, Vermont, Indiana		6
Trimble, Jim	HC52-55Phi						
Triplett, Mel FB	55-60NYG 61-62Min	2	6'1"	215	Toledo		108
Triplett, Wally HB	49-50Det 51MS 52-53ChiC	23	5'10"	175	Penn State		24
Trippi, Charlie HB-DB-QB	47-55ChiC	1234	6'	186	Georgia	4	222
Tunnell, Em (Emlen the Gremlin) DB-HB	48-58NYG 59-61GB	3	6'1"	193	Iowa	79	60
Turley, Doug DE-OE	44-48Was	2	6'2"	215	Scranton		24
Turner, Bulldog C-LB-OG-OT-HB	40-52ChiB HC62NY-A		6'1"	237	Hardin-Simmons	16	24
Turner, Hal DE	54Det		6'2"	235	Tennessee State		
Tyree, Jim OE-DE	48Bos	2	6'3"	204	Oklahoma		6
Tyrrell, Joe OG	52 Phi		5'11"	216	Temple		
Ulinski, Ed G	46-49CleAA		5'11"	203	Marshall		
Ulinski, Harry C	50-51Was 52MS 53-56Was		6'4"	229	Kentucky		
Ulrich, Chuck DT	54-58ChiC		6'4"	243	Illinois		
Ulrich, Hub OE-DE	46MiaAA		6'	205	Kansas		6
Urban, Gasper G-LB	48ChiAA		6'1"	215	Notre Dame	1	
Vacanti, Sam QB	47-48ChiAA 48-49BalAA	12	5'11"	203	Nebraska, Iowa		21
Van Brocklin, Norm (The Dutchman) QB	49-57LA 58-60Phi HC61-66Min HC68-73Atl	12 4	6'1"	199	Oregon		66
Van Buren, Ebert LB-FB-HB	51-53Phi		6'2"	210	Louisiana State	2	8
Van Buren, Steve HB-DB	44-51Phi 52KJ	23	6'	203	Louisiana State	9	464
Vandeweghe, Al OE-DE	46BufAA		5'11"	200	William & Mary		12
Van Doren, Bob DE	53SF		6'3"	215	Southern Calif.		
Vardian, John HB-DB	46MiaAA 47-48BalAA	2	5'8"	167	none	3	6
Vasicek, Vic OG-LB-DG	49BufAA 50LA		5'11"	223	Southern Calif., Texas	1	
Vaught, Ted DE-OE	55SF		6'	208	Texas Christian		
Venturelli, Fred K	48ChiB		5'11"	235	none		7
Venuto, Sam HB	52Was		6'1"	195	Guilford		6
Vereen, Carl OT	57GB		6'2"	247	Georgia Tech		
Verry, Norm T	46-47ChiAA		6'1"	240	Southern Calif.		
Vessels, Billy HB	56Bal	2	6'	190	Oklahoma		18
Vetrano, Joe HB-DB	46-49SF-AA	2 5	5'9"	170	Southern Miss.	3	247
Vezmar, Walt G	46-47Det		5'11"	235	Michigan State		
Vinnola, Paul HB-DB	46LA-AA		5'10"	180	Santa Clara	1	
Vogds, Evan G	46-47ChiAA 48-49GB		5'10"	210	Wisconsin		
Vogelaar, Carroll DT-OT	47-48Bos 49NYB 50NYY		6'3"	253	San Francisco		
Volz, Wilbur HB-DB	49BufAA		6'	192	Missouri		6
Voyles, Carl	HC48BknAA				Oklahoma State		
Voytek, Ed OG	57-58Was		6'2"	235	Purdue		
Wade, Jim HB-DB	49NYB		5'11"	175	Oklahoma City	1	
Wagner, Lowell DB-WB-HB	46-48NY-AA 49SFAA 50-53SF 54CFL 55SF	2	6'	194	Southern Calif.	32	30
Walker, Doak HB-DB	50-55Det	2345	5'11"	173	S. M. U.	2	534

Use Name (Nicknames) – Positions	Team by Year	See Section	Hgt	Wgt	College	Int	Pts
Walker, Paul DB-OE	48NYG		6'3"	210	Yale	1	
Walker, Val Joe DB	53-56GB 57SF		6'1"	179	S. M. U.	17	6
Wallace, Bev QB	47-49SF-AA 51NYY	1	6'2"	180	Compton J.C.		6
Wallace, Stan DB	54ChiB 55MS 56-58ChiB		6'3"	208	Illinois	10	
Waller, Ron HB	55-58LA 59KJ 60LA-A HC73SD	23	5'11"	180	Maryland		54
Wallner, Fred LB-OG	51-52ChiC 53MS 54-55ChiC 60 HouA		6'2"	231	Notre Dame	3	
Walsh, Bill C	49-54Pit		6'2"	230	Notre Dame		
Walston, Bobby OE-FL-HB	51-62Phi	2 5	6'	190	Georgia		881
Walters, Les DB	58Was		6'	185	Penn State	1	
Ward, Bill G	46-47Was 47-49Det		6'	230	Washington State		
Wardlow, Duane DE	54LA 55MS 56LA		6'4"	215	Washington		
Warren, Morrie FB-LB	48BknAA		5'11"	208	Arizona State		
Warrington, Caleb C-G-LB	46-48BknAA		6'2"	210	William & Mary, Auburn		
Washington, Kenny HB-DB	46-48LA	2	6'1"	212	U. C. L. A.	2	54
Wasserbach, Lloyd T	46-47ChiAA		5'11"	205	Wisconsin	1	
Waterfield, Bob QB-DB	45Cle 46-52,HC60-62LA	12 45	6'1"	196	U. C. L. A.	20	573
Watford, Jerry OG-DE	53-54ChiC		6'3"	205	Alabama		
Watkins, Bobby HB	55-57ChiB 58ChiC	2	5'10"	196	Ohio State		84
Watson, Joe C-LB	50Det		6'3"	235	Rice	1	
Watson, Sid HB	55-57Pit 58Was	23 5	5'11"	187	Northeastern		49
Watt, Joe DB-HB	47Bos 47-48Det 49NYB	2	5'11"	184	Syracuse	7	12
Weatherall, Jim DT-OT	55-57Phi 58Was 59-60Det		6'4"	245	Oklahoma		
Weatherley, Jerry LB	50ChiB 51MS 52-54ChiB		6'5"	218	Rice	8	18
Weaver, John G	49NYB		6'2"	215	Miami-Ohio		
Weaver, Larry HB-DB	55NYG		5'11"	190	Fullerton J.C.		
Weber, Chuck LB-DE-OG	55-56Cle 56-58ChiC 59-61Phi		6'1"	229	West Chester St.	10	6
Webster, Alex (Big Red) HB-FB	55-64, HC69-73NYG	2	6'3"	218	N. Carolina State		336
Wedel, Dick G	48ChiC		5'11"	205	Wake Forest		
Wedemeyer, Herm HB-TB	48LA-AA 49BalAA	123	5'10"	178	St. Mary's		12
Weed, Tad K	55Pit	5	5'5"	140	Ohio State		21
Weedon, Don G	47Phi		5'11"	220	Texas		
Wegert, Ted HB	55-56Phi 60NY-A 60DenA 60BufA	2	5'11"	202	none		30
Weiner, Art OE-DE	50NYY	2	6'3"	212	North Carolina		36
Weinmeister, Arnie DT-OT	48-49NY-AA 50-53NYG 54CFL		6'4"	235	Washington		2
Wells, Billy HB	54Was 55MS 56-57Was 57Pit 58Phi 60BosA	23	5'9"	176	Michigan State		54
Wells, Don DE-OE	46-49GB		6'2"	200	Georgia		
Wendell, Marty G	49ChiAA		5'10"	215	Notre Dame		
Werder, Dick G	48NY-AA		5'9"	210	Georgetown		
West, Pat FB-LB	45Cle 46-48LA 48GB	2	6'	201	Southern Calif.	1	18
West, Stan DG-OG-C	56-57ChiC		6'2"	239	Oklahoma	3	
Wetz, Harlan T	47BknAA		6'5"	265	Texas		
Whalen, Jerry C-G	48BufAA		6'1"	235	Canisius		
Whaley, Ben G	49LA-AA		5'11"	210	Virginia State		
Wham, Tom DE-OE	49-51ChiC		6'2"	217	Furman	1	12
Whelchel, John	HC49Was				Navy		
White, Bob DB-HB	51-52SF 53-54MS 55Cle 55Bal	2	5'11"	176	Stanford	1	18
White, Gene G	46BufAA		6'	205	Indiana		
White, Gene DE	54GB		6'2"	205	Georgia	1	
White, Jim OT-DT	46-50NYG		6'2"	227	Notre Dame	1	18
White, Paul HB-DB	47Pit		6'1"	183	Michigan	2	
White, Wilford HB	51-52ChiB	23	5'9"	172	Arizona State		23
Whitlow, Ken LB-C	46MiaAA		6'1"	190	Rice	2	
Whitman, S. J. DB	51-53ChiC 53-54ChiB		5'11"	185	Tulsa	18	6
Wiese, Bob DB-HB-LB	47-48Det		6'3"	198	Michigan	5	
Wietecha, Ray C-LB	53-62NYG		6'1"	225	Northwestern	1	
Wightkin, Bill OT-OE-DE	50-57ChiB	2	6'3"	235	Notre Dame		24
Wilde, George HB-DB	47Was		6'1"	193	Texas A&M		6
Wildung, Dick DT-OT-OG-DG	46-51,53GB		6'	221	Minnesota		2
Willey, Jack OT-DT	46-50Pit		5'11"	208	Waynesburg		
Wilkins, Dick OE	49LA-AA 52Dal 54NYG	2	6'2"	194	Oregon		42
Wilkins, Roy LB-DE	58-59LA 60-61Was		6'3"	224	Georgia		
Wilkinson, Bob OE-DB-HB	51-52NYG	2	6'3"	215	U. C. L. A.	1	18
Willey, Norm (Wild Man) DE-OG-OE	50-57Phi		6'2"	224	Marshall	2	12
Williams, Bob QB	51-52ChiB 53-54MS 55ChiB	12	6'1"	197	Notre Dame		
Williams, Boyd C-LB	47Phi		6'3"	218	Syracuse		
Williams, Ellery OE	50NYG		6'	185	Santa Clara		
Williams, Frank FB-LB	48NYG		6'	212	Utah State		4
Williams, Fred DT-OG	52-63ChiB 64-65Was		6'4"	249	Arkansas	2	
Williams, Garland T	47-48BknAA		6'3"	220	Georgia		
Williams, Jerry HB-DB	49-52LA 53-54,HC69-71Phi	23	5'10"	175	Washington State	15	108
Williams, Joel C-LB	48SF-AA 50Bal		6'1"	220	Texas		6
Williams, Johnny DB-HB	52-53Was 54SF	3	5'11"	177	Southern Calif.	14	18
Williams, Stan DB-OE	52Dal 53CFL		6'2"	195	Baylor	5	6
Williams, Walt DB-TB-HB	46ChiAA 47Bos	1	6'1"	194	Boston U.	2	12
Williams, Win OE	48-49BalAA	2	6'2"	185	Rice		18
Williamson, Ernie T	47Was 48NYG 49LA-AA		6'4"	245	North Carolina		
Willis, Bill DG-OG	46-49CleAA 50-53Cle		6'2"	213	Ohio State	1	
Wilson, Billy OE-FL	51-60SF	2	6'3"	191	San Jose State		294
Wilson, Camp FB-LB	46-49Det	2	6'2"	201	Tulsa		36
Wilson, Gene DB-OE	47-48GB		5'10"	178	S. M. U.	2	
Wilson, Jack HB-DB	46-47LA		6'	200	Baylor	1	6
Wilson, Jerry LB-DE	59-60Phi 60SF		6'3"	238	Auburn		
Wilson, Tom (Touchdown Tommy) HB-FB	56-61LA 62Cle 63Min	23	6'	203	none		144
Wimberly, Ab DE-OE	49LA-AA 50-52GB		6'1"	213	Louisiana State	3	12
Wingate, Elmer DE	53Bal		6'3"	230	Maryland		
Winkler, Bernie T	48LA-AA		6'1"	232	Texas Tech		
Winkler, Jim DT-OG	51-52LA 53Bal		6'2"	250	Texas A&M		
Wissman, Pete C-LB	49SF-AA 50-52,54SF		6'	218	St. Louis	4	
Wistert, Al OT-DT-OG	43P-P 44-51Phi		6'1"	214	Michigan	1	
Witucki, Slug OG	50-51Was 52MS 53-56Was		5'11"	245	Indiana		
Wizbicki, Alex DB-HB	47-49BufAA 50GB		5'11"	188	Holy Cross	6	6
Woit, Dick DB	55Det		5'8"	175	Arkansas State		
Womack, Bruce OG	51Det		6'3"	210	West Texas State		
Womble, Royce HB-FL	54-57Bal 60LA-A	2	6'	185	North Texas State		54
Woodward, Dick C-LB	49LA-AA 50-51NYG 52Was 53NYG		6'2"	224	Iowa	6	12
Worden, Neil FB	54Phi 55-56MS 57Phi	2	5'10"	198	Notre Dame		6
Woudenberg, John T	40-42Pit 43-45MS 46-49SF-AA		6'3"	226	Denver		
Wozniak, John OG-LB	48BknAA 49NY-AA 50-51NYY 52Dal 53CFL		6'	218	Alabama	1	

Use Name (Nicknames) – Positions	Team by Year	See Section	Hgt	Wgt	College	Int	Pts
Wren, Junior DB	56-59Cle 60Pit 61NY-A	4	6'	192	Missouri	14	8
Wright, Jim G	47Bos		6'1"	222	S. M. U.		
Wright, John FB-LB	47BalAA	2	5'11"	225	Maryland	1	
Wyant, Fred QB	56Was		6'	200	West Virginia		
Wydo, Frank OT-DT	47-51Pit 52-57Phi		6'4"	225	Cornell	1	
Wyhonic, John G	46-47Phi 48-49BufAA		6'	213	Alabama		
Yablonski, Vinnie FB-LB	48-51ChiC	2 5	5'8"	195	Columbia		52
Yackanich, Joe G	46-48NY-AA		5'10"	205	Fordham		
Yagiello, Ray G-LB	48-49LA		6'	220	Catawba		
Yelvington, Dick OT	52-57NYG		6'2"	232	Georgia		
Yokas, Frank G	46LA-AA 47BalAA		5'11"	210	none		
Yonaker, John DE-OE-DT	46-49CleAA 50NYY 52Was	2	6'5"	222	Notre Dame	2	24
Yonamine, Wally HB-DB	47SF-AA		5'9"	180	none	1	
Youel, Jim QB-DB	46-47Was 48Bos 48Was	12	6'	175	Iowa	2	18
Young, Buddy HB-DB-FB	47-49NY-AA 50-51NYY 52Dal 53-54Bal	23	5'5"	173	Illinois		264
Young, Dick FB-HB	55-56Bal 57Pit	2	5'11"	210	Tenn.-Chattanooga		12
Young, George DE-OE	46-49CleAA 50-53Cle		6'3"	214	Georgia		14
Young, Glenn DB	56GB		6'2"	205	Purdue		
Youngelman, Sid DT-DE	55SF 56-58Phi 59Cle 60-61NY-A 62-63BufA		6'3"	257	Alabama		
Younger, Tank FB-HB-LB	49-57LA 58Pit	2	6'3"	225	Grambling	3	210
Yowarsky, Walt DE-OT	51Was 52-53MS 54Was 55Det 55-57NYG 58SF		6'2"	234	Kentucky		
Zagers, Bert HB-DB	55Was 56MS 57-58Was	23	5'10"	185	Michigan State	4	36
Zalejski, Ernie DB-HB	50Bal		6'	185	Notre Dame	2	12
Zatkoff, Roger LB-DE	53-56GB 57-58Det		6'2"	216	Michigan	4	
Ziegler, Frank HB-DB	49-53Phi	2	5'11"	175	Georgia Tech	1	90
Zilly, Jack DE-OE	47-51LA 52Phi	2	6'2"	212	Notre Dame		24
Zimny, Bob T	45-49ChiC		6'1"	233	Indiana		
Zombek, Joe OE	54Pit		6'1"	195	Pittsburgh		
Zucco, Vic DB	57-60ChiB	3	6'	187	Michigan State	8	6
Zupek, Al BB-DE	46GB		6'1"	205	Lawrence		

Lifetime Statistcis - 1946-1959 Players Section 1 - PASSING
(All men with 25 or more passing attempts)

Name	Years	Att.	Comp.	Comp Pct.	Yards	Yds./ Att.	TD	Int.	Pct. Int.
Cliff Aberson	46	41	14	34.1	184	4.5	0	5	12.2
Frankie Albert	46-52	1564	831	53.1	10795	6.9	115	98	6.3
Fred Benners	52	58	25	43.1	320	5.5	0	5	8.6
Angelo Bertelli	46-48	166	76	45.8	972	5.9	8	19	11.4
Ed Brown	54-65	1987	949	47.8	15600	7.9	102	138	6.9
Adrian Burk	50-56	1079	500	46.3	7001	6.5	61	89	8.2
Jim Callahan	46	68	22	32.4	359	5.3	2	7	10.3
Tony Canadeo	41-44,46-52	268	105	39.2	1642	6.1	16	20	7.5
Bob Celeri	51-52	313	133	42.5	2287	7.3	15	18	5.8
Lynn Chandnois	50-56	59	19	32.2	285	4.8	2	7	11.9
Bob Chappuis	48-49	227	102	44.9	1442	6.4	8	23	10.1
Paul Christman	45-50	1140	504	44.2	7294	6.4	58	76	6.7
Bobby Clatterbuck	54-57,60	149	77	51.7	1032	6.9	8	9	6.0
Walt Clay	46-49	28	13	46.4	148	5.3	2	3	10.7
Johnny Clement	41,46-49	442	192	43.4	3226	7.3	20	39	8.8
Irv Comp	43-49	519	213	41.0	3354	6.5	28	52	10.0
Ogden Compton	55	61	22	36.1	339	5.6	1	6	9.8
Chuck Conerly	48-61	2833	1418	50.1	19488	6.9	173	167	5.9
Boley Dancewicz	46-48	238	96	40.3	1651	6.9	12	28	11.8
Al Dekdebrun	46-48	164	84	51.2	1224	7.5	13	18	11.0
Jack Del Bello	53	61	27	44.3	229	3.8	1	5	8.2
Glenn Dobbs	46-49	934	446	47.8	5876	6.3	45	52	5.6
Al Dorow	54-57,60-62	1207	572	47.4	7708	6.4	64	93	7.7
Tom Dublinski	52-54,58,60	177	93	52.5	1300	7.3	8	13	7.3
Bill Dudley	42,45-51,53	222	81	36.5	985	4.4	6	17	7.7
Maury Duncan	54-55	26	8	30.8	122	4.7	0	2	7.7
Fred Enke	48-54	689	297	43.1	4169	6.1	31	53	7.7
Ray Evans	48	137	64	46.7	924	6.7	5	17	12.4
Tom Farris	46-48	32	11	34.4	132	4.1	1	6	18.8
Chuck Fenenbock	43,45-48	191	70	36.6	1233	6.5	12	23	12.0
Jim Finks	49-55	1382	661	47.8	8622	6.2	55	88	6.4
Joe Francis	58-59	49	20	40.8	266	5.4	2	3	6.1
Jess Freitas	46-49	253	123	48.6	1884	7.4	21	27	10.7
Monk Gafford	46-48	44	18	40.9	265	6.0	4	4	9.1
Bob Gage	49-50	94	38	40.4	623	6.6	3	9	9.6
Arnie Galiffa	53-54	25	7	28.0	183	7.3	1	5	20.0
Bob Garrett	54	30	15	50.0	143	4.8	0	1	3.3
Joe Gasparella	48,50-51	113	46	40.7	677	6.0	3	10	8.8
Joe Geri	49-52	280	101	36.1	1926	6.9	13	27	9.6
Frank Gifford	52-60,62-64	63	29	46.0	823	13.1	14	6	9.5
Harry Gilmer	48-52,54-56	579	263	45.4	3786	6.5	23	45	7.8
Jug Girard	48-57	197	67	34.0	1017	5.2	5	13	6.6
Paul Governali	46-48	500	218	43.6	3348	6.7	31	33	6.6
Otto Graham	46-55	2626	1464	55.8	23584	9.0	174	135	5.1
Jim Hardy	46-52	912	423	46.4	5690	6.2	53	73	8.0
Stan Heath	49	106	26	24.5	355	3.3	1	14	13.2
Don Heinrich	54-60,62	406	164	40.4	2287	5.6	17	23	5.7
Paul Held	54-55	77	26	33.8	332	4.3	1	6	7.8
Bob Hoernschemeyer	46-55	714	319	44.7	4302	6.0	42	56	7.8
Jack Jacobs	42,45-49	552	244	44.2	3268	5.9	27	49	8.9
Gil Johnson	49	36	12	33.3	179	5.0	0	5	13.9
Gary Kerkorian	52,54-56	259	139	53.7	1862	7.2	12	18	6.9
Tom Landry	49-55	47	11	23.4	172	3.7	1	7	14.9
Pete Layden	48-50	115	45	39.1	841	7.3	9	9	7.8
Bobby Layne	48-62	3700	1814	49.0	26768	7.2	196	243	6.6

Name	Years	Att.	Comp.	Comp. Pct.	Yards	Yds./ Att.	TD	Int.	Pct. Int.
Eddie LeBaron	52-53,55-63	1796	897	49.9	13399	7.5	104	141	7.9
Clyde LeForce	47-49	388	197	50.8	2961	7.6	25	37	9.5
Cliff Lewis	46-51	69	30	43.5	514	7.4	7	5	7.2
Johnny Lujack	48-51	808	404	50.0	6295	7.8	41	54	6.7
Bill Mackrides	47-51,53	315	131	41.6	1583	5.0	15	28	8.9
Gene Malinowski	48	54	15	27.8	218	4.0	3	7	13.0
Ray Mallouf	41,46-49	325	159	48.9	2504	7.7	20	16	4.9
Ted Marchibroda	53,55-57	385	172	44.7	2169	5.6	16	29	7.5
Joe Margucci	47-48	31	13	41.9	171	5.5	1	5	16.1
Ray Mathews	51-60	51	19	37.3	350	6.9	2	2	3.9
Lew Mayne	46-48	25	14	56.0	219	8.8	3	4	16.0
Lamar McHan	54-63	1351	610	45.2	9449	7.0	72	108	8.0
Ed Mioduszewski	53	30	11	36.7	113	3.8	2	2	6.7
Tommy Mont	47-49	35	15	42.9	201	5.7	2	2	5.7
Gonzales Morales	47-48	31	11	35.5	108	3.5	1	4	12.9
Ray Nagel	53	62	30	48.4	192	3.1	0	5	8.1
Steve Nemeth	45-47	30	7	23.3	86	2.9	0	2	6.7
Jerry Niles	47	57	19	33.3	269	4.7	1	7	12.3
Tom O'Connell	53,56-57,60-61	423	204	48.2	3261	7.7	21	34	8.0
Charlie O'Rourke	42,46-49	506	256	50.6	4039	8.0	39	51	10.1
Chuck Ortmann	51-52	154	61	39.6	744	4.8	3	14	9.1
Don Panciera	49-50,52	246	86	35.0	1383	5.6	10	25	10.2
Bob Perina	46-50	72	32	44.4	370	5.1	1	6	8.3
Jim Powers	50-53	70	31	44.3	367	5.2	1	4	5.7
George Ratterman	47-56	1396	737	52.8	10473	7.5	91	96	6.9
Johnny Rauch	49-51	170	70	41.2	959	5.6	8	9	5.3
Frank Reagan	41,46-51	37	16	43.2	239	6.5	1	2	5.4
Steve Romanik	50-54	433	179	41.3	2556	5.9	13	36	8.3
Jim Root	53,56	249	108	43.4	1482	6.0	11	16	6.4
Tobin Rote	50-59,63-64,66	2907	1329	45.7	18850	6.5	148	191	6.6
Dave Ryan	45-46,48	198	86	43.4	1296	6.5	9	27	13.6
Nick Sacrinty	47	48	15	31.3	299	6.2	5	3	6.2
Spec Sanders	46-48,50	421	206	48.9	2829	6.7	23	37	8.8
Jack Scarbath	53-54,56	279	101	36.2	1868	6.7	18	30	10.8
Bud Schwenk	42,46-48	662	315	47.6	3924	5.9	23	50	7.6
George Shaw	55-62	802	405	50.5	5829	7.3	41	63	7.9
Walt Slater	47	39	18	46.2	215	5.5	1	5	12.8
Jim Still	48-49	26	11	42.3	175	6.7	2	4	15.4
Ken Stofer	46	26	9	34.6	86	3.3	1	1	3.8
Joe Sulatis	43-53	31	11	35.5	179	5.8	1	4	12.9
George Taliaferro	49-55	284	92	32.4	1633	5.8	10	29	10.2
George Terlep	46-48	150	54	36.0	652	4.3	9	19	12.7
Bobby Thomason	49,51-57	1346	687	51.0	9480	7.0	68	90	6.7
Tommy Thompson	40-42,45-50	1424	732	51.4	10400	7.3	91	103	7.2
Travis Tidwell	50-51	76	33	43.4	493	6.5	5	7	9.2
Y. A. Tittle	48-64	4395	2427	55.2	33070	7.5	242	248	5.6
Lou Tomasetti	39-42,46-49	53	16	30.2	170	3.2	1	9	17.0
Charlie Trippi	47-55	434	205	47.2	2547	5.9	16	31	7.1
Sam Vacanti	47-49	368	154	41.8	2338	6.4	18	32	8.7
Norm Van Brocklin	49-60	2895	1553	53.6	23611	8.2	173	178	6.1
Bev Wallace	47-49,51	69	23	33.3	266	3.9	1	9	13.0
Bob Waterfield	45-52	1617	813	50.3	11849	7.3	98	127	7.9
Herm Wedemeyer	48-49	31	9	29.0	79	2.5	0	4	12.9
Bob Williams	51-52,55	160	74	46.3	981	6.1	10	12	7.5
Walt Williams	46-47	31	13	41.9	226	7.3	1	6	19.4
Jim Youel	46-48	146	50	34.2	849	5.8	7	10	6.8

Lifetime Statistics - 1946-1959 Players Section 2 - **RUSHING and RECEIVING**
(All men with 25 or more rushing attempts or 10 or more receptions)

Name	Years	RUSHING Att.	Yards	Avg.	TD	RECEIVING Rec.	Yards	Avg.	TD
Joe Abbey	48-49					13	177	13.6	0
Cliff Aberson	46	48	161	3.4	0				
Tony Adamle	47-51,54	60	255	4.3	2	2	35	17.5	0
Frankie Albert	46-52	329	1272	3.9	27	1	1	1.0	0
Ben Aldridge	50-53	29	105	3.6	0	8	78	9.8	1
Bruce Alford	46-51					81	1341	16.6	9
Alan Ameche	55-60	964	4045	4.2	40	101	733	7.3	4
Cliff Anderson	52-53					28	457	16.3	2
Ezz Anderson	47	3	24	8.0	0	11	126	11.5	1
Elmer Angsman	46-52	683	2908	4.3	27	41	654	16.0	5
Joe Arenas	51-57	203	987	4.9	10	46	675	14.7	6
Neill Armstrong	47-51					76	961	12.6	11
Dale Atkeson	54-56	208	639	3.1	4	19	184	9.7	1
John Atwood	48	9	6	0.7	0	10	141	14.1	1
Harry Babcock	53-55					16	181	11.3	0
Steve Bagarus	45-48	98	343	3.5	1	81	1055	13.0	9
Byron Bailey	52-53	32	103	3.2	2	10	147	14.7	0
Ed Balatti	46-48					12	113	9.4	1
Lou Baldacci	56	31	140	4.5	0	5	62	12.4	0
Al Baldwin	47-50	2	1	0.5	0	160	2658	16.6	25
Burr Baldwin	47-49	1	1	1.0	0	24	397	16.5	1
Jack Banta	41,44-48	198	847	4.3	6	30	373	12.4	1
Ed Barker	53-54					40	525	13.1	4
Tom Barnett	59-60	81	263	3.2	1	7	52	7.4	1
Paul Barry	50,52-54	158	604	3.8	2	24	264	11.0	1
Bill Bass	47	28	44	1.6	0	8	79	9.9	1
Mo Bassett	54-56	223	891	4.0	10	33	317	9.6	1
Alyn Beals	46-51	11	73	6.6	0	211	2951	14.0	49
Hub Bechtol	47-49	2	–1	–0.5	0	19	192	10.1	1
Ed Bernet	55-60					26	325	12.5	1
Dick Bielski	55-63	80	229	2.9	2	107	1305	12.2	10
Lamar Blount	46-47	4	5	1.3	0	21	366	17.4	1
Jim Blumenstock	47	54	168	3.1	2	4	15	3.8	0
Bill Boedecker	46-50	173	741	4.3	8	38	875	23.0	6
J. R. Boone	48-53	130	497	3.8	5	69	1251	18.1	7
Bill Bowman	54,56-57	144	557	3.9	3	50	429	8.6	3
Cloyce Box	49-50,52-54	31	82	2.6	0	129	2665	20.7	32
Bob Boyd	51-51,53-57	2	–9	–4.5	0	176	3611	20.5	28
Max Boydston	55-58,60-62					97	1328	13.7	8
Jim Brandt	52-54	61	188	3.1	4	3	24	8.0	0
John Bredice	56					10	146	14.6	1
Monte Brethauer	53,55					10	133	13.3	0
John Brewer	52-53	67	273	4.1	3	9	62	6.9	0
Darrell Brewster	52-60					210	3758	17.9	21
Gene Brito	51-53,55-60					47	618	13.1	2
Dave Brown	43,46-47	47	141	3.0	0	6	34	5.7	0
Ed Brown	54-65	265	920	3.6	14				
Dick Brubaker	55,57,60					13	200	15.4	1
George Buksar	49-52	28	63	2.3	1	4	5	1.3	0
Rex Bumgardner	48-52	236	868	3.7	4	22	404	18.4	6
Adrian Burk	50-56	122	324	2.7	7				
Hank Burnine	56-57					17	271	15.9	2
Harry Burrus	46-48	3	5	1.7	0	28	670	23.9	4
Jack Call	57-59	73	308	4.2	0	9	46	5.1	0
Jim Callahan	46	52	86	1.7	2				
Tom Calvin	52-54	32	136	4.3	0	7	51	7.3	0
Al Campana	50-53	58	146	2.5	1	6	61	10.2	0
Leon Campbell	50,52-55	102	379	3.7	0	20	156	7.8	0
Tony Canadeo	41-44,46-52	1025	4197	4.1	26	69	579	8.4	5
Jim Canady	48-49	25	99	4.0	0	5	80	16.0	0
Bob Carey	52-54,56,58					47	663	14.1	2
Harland Carl	56	29	66	2.3	1	2	31	15.5	0
Al Carmichael	53-58,60-61	222	947	4.3	4	112	1633	14.6	8
Ken Carpenter	50-53,60	242	1199	5.0	11	71	823	11.6	6
Lew Carpenter	53-55,57-63	468	2025	4.3	16	87	782	9.0	4
Ed Carr	47-49	44	283	6.4	3	14	246	17.6	3
Johnny Carson	54-60					173	2591	15.0	15
Ken Casanega	46,48	29	90	3.1	1	5	102	20.4	1
Jim Cason	48-56	82	351	4.3	4	40	519	13.0	4
Hopalong Cassady	56-63	316	1229	3.9	6	111	1601	14.4	18
Jim Castiglia	41,45-48	322	1073	3.3	10	34	246	7.2	2
Sam Cathcart	49-50,52	108	509	4.7	1	21	296	14.1	0
Bob Celeri	51-52	53	242	4.6	0	6	108	18.0	2
Lynn Chandnois	50-56	593	1934	3.3	16	163	2062	12.7	8
Bob Chappuis	48-49	56	323	5.8	1				
Lloyd Cheatham	42,46-48	7	2	0.3	0	21	283	13.5	4
George Cheverko	47-48	22	73	3.3	0	18	341	18.9	3
Bill Chipley	47-49	1	3	3.0	0	75	867	11.6	4
Paul Christman	45-50	85	–26	–0.3	8				
Bob Cifers	46-49	230	787	3.4	1	12	296	24.7	4
Ed Cifers	41-42,46-48	1	5	5.0	0	37	399	10.8	3
Leon Clarke	56-63	1	–4	–4.0	0	141	2215	15.7	18
Bobby Clatterbuck	54-57,60	29	–27	–0.9	1				
Randy Clay	50,53	90	280	3.1	2	12	120	10.0	1
Walt Clay	46-49	169	652	3.9	4	15	218	14.5	1
Johnny Clement	41,46-49	406	1473	3.6	13	2	28	14.0	0
Ollie Cline	48-53	281	1094	3.9	6	34	299	8.8	1
Jack Cloud	50-53	57	141	2.5	4	6	35	5.8	1
Ray Coates	48-49	77	231	3.0	3	8	152	19.0	1
Red Cochran	47-50	37	138	3.7	2	8	114	14.3	2
Tom Cochran	49	34	135	4.0	1	7	82	11.7	0
Ed Cody	47-50	93	346	3.7	2	1	2	2.0	0
Emerson Cole	50-52	72	357	5.0	1	4	30	7.5	0
Rip Collins	49-51	102	193	1.9	0	26	461	17.7	0
Mickey Colmer	46-49	398	1537	3.9	15	63	899	14.3	6

Name	Years	RUSHING Att.	Yards	Avg.	TD	RECEIVING Rec.	Yards	Avg.	TD
Lloyd Colteryahn	54-56					54	664	12.3	3
Irv Comp	43-49	255	502	2.0	7	3	66	22.0	2
Tony Campagno	46-48	125	444	3.6	3	17	271	15.9	1
Fred Cone	51-57,60	347	1156	3.3	12	75	852	11.4	4
Chuck Conerly	48-61	270	685	2.5	10				
Clyde Conner	56-63					203	2643	13.0	18
Ted Cook	47-50					61	891	14.6	5
Larry Coutre	50,53	63	322	5.1	1	18	202	11.2	2
Bob Cowan	47-49	72	280	3.9	3	21	351	16.7	5
Gerry Cowhig	47-51	81	342	4.2	3	3	18	6.0	0
Rus Craft	46-54	64	231	3.6	0	12	303	25.3	3
Ted Cremer	46-48					28	296	10.6	1
Hal Crisler	46-50	4	6	1.5	0	135	2042	15.1	22
Billy Cross	51-53	175	826	4.7	6	52	841	16.2	6
Don Currivan	43-49	1	–4	–4.0	0	78	1979	25.4	24
Bill Daley	46-48	175	612	3.5	5	18	142	7.9	0
Boley Dancewicz	46-48	65	229	3.5	2				
Glenn Davis	50-51	152	616	4.1	4	50	682	13.6	5
Joe Davis	46					22	337	15.3	1
Lamar Davis	46-49	17	78	4.6	0	147	2103	14.3	12
Van Davis	47-49					14	254	18.1	1
Bill deCorrevont	45-49	75	233	3.1	1	21	417	19.9	2
Al Dekdebrun	46-48	54	54	1.0	0				
Paul Dekker	53					14	182	13.0	1
Spiro Dellerba	47-49	31	176	5.7	0	1	14	14.0	0
Bill Dewell	40-41,45-49	1	–1	–1.0	0	178	2647	14.9	17
Dorne Dibble	51,53-57	2	13	6.5	0	146	2552	17.5	19
Babe Dimancheff	45-50,52	207	802	3.9	5	61	1086	17.8	10
Glen Dobbs	46-49	262	1039	4.0	12	5	27	5.4	0
Jack Doolan	45-48	22	59	2.7	0	10	95	9.5	0
Jim Dooley	52-54,56-57,59-62	1	0	0.0	0	211	3172	15.0	16
Jim Doran	51-61	3	59	19.7	0	212	3667	17.3	24
Al Dorow	54-57,60-62	282	864	3.1	16				
Noble Doss	47-49	78	253	3.2	0	10	113	11.3	0
Kayo Dottley	51-53	250	1122	4.5	7	28	359	12.8	2
Bob Dove	46-54	1	–2	–2.0	0	13	128	9.8	2
Harry Dowda	49-55	124	405	3.3	2	18	277	15.4	2
Chuck Drazenovich	50-59	117	330	2.8	8	10	139	13.9	0
Wally Dreyer	49-50	46	172	3.7	0	7	94	13.4	0
Tom Dublinski	52-54,58,60	28	118	4.2	1				
Joe Duckworth	47					14	250	17.9	3
Andy Dudish	46-48	59	141	2.4	1	9	163	18.1	1
Bill Dudley	42,45-51,53	765	3057	4.0	19	123	1383	11.2	18
L. G. Dupre	55-61	476	1761	3.7	11	104	1131	10.9	7
Don Durdan	46-47	33	134	4.1	0	2	27	13.5	1
Bill Dutton	46	53	169	3.2	2	2	68	34.0	0
Ralph Earhart	48-49	50	194	3.9	1	22	303	13.8	2
Ray Ebli	42,46-47					12	138	11.5	2
Dan Edwards	48-54					234	2898	12.4	16
Carl Elliott	51-54					60	581	9.7	6
Earl Elsey	46	47	165	3.5	0	14	179	12.8	0
Leo Elter	53-59	371	1380	3.7	9	46	556	12.1	2
Mel Embree	53-54					25	292	11.7	1
Fred Enke	48-54	170	640	3.8	1	4	39	9.8	0
Bobby Epps	54-55,57	188	771	4.1	2	18	109	6.1	0
Len Eshmont	41,46-49	282	1345	4.8	7	54	915	16.9	6
Fred Evans	46-48	49	166	3.4	1	7	89	12.7	1
Ray Evans	48	99	343	3.5	2	7	93	13.3	0
Tom Farmer	46-48	95	307	3.2	3	26	302	11.6	2
Tom Farris	46-48	27	19	0.7	0	1	16	16.0	0
Tom Fears	48-56	5	15	3.0	0	400	5397	13.5	38
Gene Fekete	46	26	106	4.1	1	1	2	2.0	0
Chuck Fenenbock	43,45-48	269	1102	4.1	7	45	523	11.6	4
Bob Fenimore	47	53	189	3.8	1	15	219	14.6	2
Howie Ferguson	53-58,60	670	2558	3.8	10	148	1247	8.4	3
Jack Ferrante	41,44-50					169	2894	17.1	31
Gene Filipski	56-57	35	174	5.0	1	4	44	11.0	0
Jim Finks	49-55	118	294	2.5	12	1	17	17.0	1
Clete Fischer	49	26	72	2.8	0	3	45	15.0	1
Bobby Jack Floyd	52-53	77	306	4.0	1	20	192	9.6	0
Hank Foldberg	48-49					31	331	10.7	0
Len Ford	48-58					67	1175	17.5	8
Bob Forte	46-50,52-53	101	331	3.3	0	24	242	10.1	3
Joe Francis	58-59	26	158	6.1	1				
Jess Freitas	46-49	39	8	0.2	0				
Ted Fritsch	42-50	619	2100	3.4	31	25	227	9.1	1
Jim Gaffney	45-46	26	90	3.5	0	7	85	12.1	1
Monk Gafford	46-48	100	349	3.5	3	37	657	17.8	8
Bob Gage	49-50	85	334	3.9	6	7	135	19.3	2
Lu Gambino	48-49	110	402	3.7	1	16	95	5.9	1
Dan Garza	49,51					40	663	16.6	4
Gene Gedman	53,56-58	377	1221	3.2	17	53	504	9.5	4
Fred Gehrke	40,45-50	343	1664	4.9	15	56	529	9.4	7
Dale Gentry	46-48	5	29	5.8	1	74	1001	13.5	5
Joe Geri	49-52	431	1550	3.6	10	3	42	14.0	1
Skippy Giancanelli	53-56	216	711	3.3	4	69	1024	14.8	10
Paul Gibson	47-49					22	402	18.3	0
Frank Gifford	52-60,62-64	840	3609	4.3	34	367	5434	14.8	43
Horace Gillom	47-56	3	–7	–2.3	0	74	1083	14.6	3
Jim Gillette	40,44-48	172	831	4.8	4	24	376	15.7	2
Harry Gilmer	48-52,54-56	201	923	4.6	1	20	220	11.0	1
Jug Girard	48-57	194	703	3.6	3	109	1838	16.9	15
Joe Glamp	47-49	32	161	5.0	1	10	152	15.2	2
Les Goble	54-55	37	53	1.4	1	1	–1	–1.0	0
Joe Golding	47-51	114	349	3.0	1	27	289	10.7	8

Lifetime Statistics - 1946-1959 Players Section 2 - **RUSHING and RECEIVING** (continued)
(All men with 25 or more rushing attempts or 10 or more receptions)

Name	Years	RUSHING Att.	Yards	Avg.	TD	RECEIVING Rec.	Yards	Avg.	TD
Sam Goldman	44,46-49	2	−3	−1.5	0	18	184	10.2	0
Ralph Goldston	52,54-55	79	203	2.6	3	4	20	5.0	0
Bill Gompers	48	48	219	4.6	1				
Rob Goode	49-51,54-55	596	2531	4.2	16	53	640	12.1	1
Clyde Goodnight	45-50	9	25	2.8	0	112	1967	17.6	15
Paul Governali	46-48	79	−84	−1.1	4				
Otto Graham	46-55	405	882	2.2	44				
Sonny Grandelius	53	108	278	2.6	1	15	80	5.3	0
Bud Grant	51-52					56	997	17.8	7
John Greene	44-50					173	2865	16.6	26
Bob Greenhalgh	49	62	188	3.0	0	3	23	7.7	0
Don Greenwood	45-47	196	744	3.8	10	12	121	10.1	0
Don Griffin	46	28	13	0.5	0	5	28	5.6	0
Forrest Griffith	50-51	99	277	2.8	2	3	45	15.0	0
Billy Grimes	49-52	228	1091	4.8	10	45	620	13.8	4
George Gulyanics	47-52	509	2081	4.1	19	52	600	11.5	2
Forrest Hall	48	66	413	6.3	2	4	87	21.8	0
Chet Hanulak	54,57	184	671	3.6	7	9	118	13.1	0
Pat Harder	46-53	740	3016	4.1	33	92	864	9.4	5
Carroll Hardy	55	15	37	2.5	0	12	338	28.2	4
Jim Hardy	46-52	52	72	1.4	2				
Tommy Harmon	46-47	107	542	5.1	3	15	288	19.2	3
John Harrington	46-47					25	369	14.8	3
Leon Hart	50-57	143	612	4.3	5	174	2499	14.4	26
Leon Heath	51-53	230	813	3.5	6	29	194	6.7	1
Don Heinrich	54-60,62	27	24	0.9	5				
Dick Hensley	49,52-53					19	358	18.8	2
Ralph Heywood	46-49	4	5	1.3	1	84	1192	14.2	10
Red Hickey	41,45-48	7	7	1.0	0	75	1288	17.2	16
Harlon Hill	54-62	12	103	8.6	0	233	4717	20.2	40
Billy Hillenbrand	46-48	216	889	4.1	11	110	1987	18.1	17
Crazy Legs Hirsch	46-57	207	687	3.3	4	387	7029	18.2	60
Dick Hoerner	47-52	506	2172	4.3	30	80	1180	14.8	4
Bob Hoernschemeyer	46-55	1059	4548	4.3	27	109	1139	10.4	11
Bob Hoffman	40-41,46-49	110	398	3.6	10	7	71	10.1	1
John Hoffman	49-56	317	1366	4.3	7	136	1870	13.8	9
Mike Holovak	46-48	136	720	5.3	6	13	155	11.9	0
Les Horvath	47-49	58	221	3.8	1	9	142	15.8	1
Sherman Howard	49-53	323	1301	4.0	10	45	968	21.5	11
Earl Howell	49	31	116	3.7	1	5	11	2.2	1
Billy Howton	52-63	5	29	5.8	0	503	8459	16.8	61
Frank Hubbell	47-49					15	226	15.1	3
Dick Humbert	41,45-49	1	2	2.0	0	68	731	10.8	6
Chuck Hunsinger	50-52	192	834	4.3	5	23	249	10.8	3
John Huzvar	52-54	243	893	3.7	6	19	92	4.8	1
Jack Jacobs	42,45-49	94	262	2.8	2	4	53	13.3	0
Chick Jagade	49,51-55	412	1728	4.2	13	68	628	9.2	1
Vic Janowicz	54-55	99	410	4.1	4	12	148	12.3	3
Val Jansante	46-51	3	2	0.7	0	55	2356	15.2	14
Jack Jenkins	43,46-47	84	274	3.3	1	7	123	17.6	0
Bob Jensen	48-50					22	290	13.2	1
Bill Jessup	51-52,54,56-58,60	1	−5	−5.0	0	61	994	16.3	7
Perry Jeter	56-57	70	327	4.7	2	7	61	8.7	0
Bob Jewett	58					15	192	12.8	1
Don Johnson	53-55	93	456	4.9	5	13	247	19.0	2
Herb Johnson	54	42	168	4.0	1	10	89	8.9	0
Joe Johnson	48					19	217	11.4	2
Joe Johnson	54-58,60-61	93	376	4.0	0	84	920	11.0	8
Pres Johnston	46	45	218	4.8	2	6	54	9.0	1
Dub Jones	46-55	540	2209	4.1	21	171	2874	16.8	20
Special Delivery Jones	45-49	297	1550	5.2	18	33	635	19.2	10
Saxon Judd	46-48					84	997	11.9	7
Choo-Choo Justice	50,52-54	266	1284	4.8	3	63	962	15.3	7
Steve Juzwik	42,46-48	125	679	5.4	5	29	397	13.7	4
Tommy Kalmanir	49-51,53	81	415	5.1	1	16	216	13.5	3
Sonny Karnofsky	45-46	77	218	2.8	3	13	252	19.4	1
Ken Kavanaugh	40-41,45-50					162	3622	22.4	50
Jim Keane	46-52					224	3222	14.4	24
Tom Keane	48-55	7	16	2.3	0	34	551	16.2	2
Bill Kellagher	46-48	124	518	4.2	4	5	58	11.6	0
Ken Keller	56-57	169	628	3.7	4	11	67	6.1	0
Bill Kelley	49					17	222	13.1	1
Bob Kelly	47-49	63	232	3.7	2	11	93	8.5	1
Bob Kennedy	46-50	253	1017	4.0	9	23	137	6.0	1
Gary Kerkorian	52,54-56	30	76	2.5	2				
John Kimbrough	46-48	329	1224	3.7	17	35	574	16.4	6
Don Kindt	47-55	172	586	3.4	4	43	506	11.8	2
Emmett King	54	57	167	2.9	0	6	43	7.2	1
Fay King	46-49					115	1583	13.8	20
Pete Kmetovic	46-47	19	53	2.8	0	10	211	21.1	2
Gary Knafelc	54-63					154	2162	14.0	23
George Koch	45,47	49	250	5.1	1	1	10	10.0	0
John Kovatch	42,46-47					18	157	8.7	1
Larry Krutko	58-60	96	331	3.4	4	14	108	7.7	0
Ray Kuffel	47-49					22	402	18.3	3
Vic Kulbitski	46-48	193	1006	5.2	3	13	154	11.8	4
Lou Kusserow	49-50	40	142	3.6	0				
Mal Kutner	46-50	11	59	5.4	1	145	3060	21.1	31
Steve Lach	42,46-47	192	580	3.0	13	31	349	11.3	5
Jim Ladd	54					22	254	11.5	0
Tom Lahey	46-47	1	−2	−2.0	0	30	351	11.7	0
Tom Landry	49-55	36	131	3.6	1	6	109	18.2	0
Johnny Lattner	54	69	237	3.4	5	25	305	12.2	2
Dante Lavelli	46-56	2	23	11.5	0	386	6488	16.8	62
Pete Layden	48-50	114	672	5.9	3	1	0	0.0	0

Name	Years	RUSHING Att.	Yards	Avg.	TD	RECEIVING Rec.	Yards	Avg.	TD
Bobby Layne	48-62	611	2451	4.0	25				
Eddie LeBaron	52-53,55-63	202	650	3.2	9				
Toy Ledbetter	50,53-55	210	729	3.5	3	39	498	12.8	8
Clyde LeForce	47-49	59	287	4.9	2	8	122	15.3	3
Jake Leicht	48-49	26	81	3.1	1	13	146	11.2	1
Cliff Lewis	46-51	54	48	0.9	1				
Ernie Lewis	46-49	94	308	3.3	2	3	32	10.7	0
Woodley Lewis	50-60	47	188	4.0	0	123	1885	15.3	12
Verl Lillywhite	48-51	196	1004	5.1	6	21	212	10.1	3
Howie Livingston	44-50,53	155	548	3.5	6	37	768	20.8	9
Bob Livingstone	48-50	57	171	3.0	0	18	320	17.8	2
Cutter Long	53-55	52	164	3.2	1	33	462	14.0	4
John Lookabaugh	46-47					12	145	12.1	1
Alex Loyd	50					32	402	12.6	0
Nolan Luhn	45-49					100	1525	15.3	13
Johnny Lujack	48-51	133	742	5.6	21	1	16	16.0	0
Jim Lukens	49					24	249	10.4	2
Bill Lund	46-47	37	177	4.8	2	10	174	17.4	3
Ken MacAfee	54-59					79	1160	14.7	18
Art Macioszczyk	44,47-48	46	159	3.5	0	6	48	8.0	0
Bill Mackrides	47-51,53	70	124	1.8	2				
Eddie Macon	52-53,60	70	324	4.6	2	14	49	3.5	2
Elmer Madarik	45-48	31	48	1.5	1	10	113	11.3	0
Dante Magnani	40-43,46-50	331	1475	4.5	3	79	942	11.9	10
Howie Maley	46-47	45	199	4.4	0	2	35	17.5	0
Ray Mallouf	41,46-49	66	139	2.1	1				
Bob Mann	48-53	8	55	6.9	0	208	3203	15.4	24
Dave Mann	55-57	154	544	3.5	4	37	444	12.0	2
Ted Marchibroda	53,55-57	50	176	3.5	3				
Joe Margucci	47-48	60	111	1.9	4	46	575	12.5	3
Len Masini	47-48	41	179	4.4	2	1	−1	−1.0	0
Ray Mathews	51-60	300	1057	3.5	5	233	3963	17.0	34
Ollie Matson	52,54-66	1170	5173	4.4	40	222	3285	14.8	23
Lew Mayne	46-48	125	292	2.3	1	13	280	21.5	3
Frank Maznicki	42,46-47	107	463	4.3	1	10	131	13.1	1
George McAfee	40-41,45-50	341	1685	4.9	22	85	1357	16.0	11
Jim McCarthy	46-49					28	531	19.0	3
Bob McChesney	50-52	2	2	1.0	0	54	1040	19.3	14
Jack McClairen	55-60					85	1253	14.7	3
Bill McColl	52-59					201	2815	14.0	25
Tom McCormick	53-56	86	272	3.2	1	11	129	11.7	0
Walt McDonald	46-49	12	5	0.4	0	22	197	9.0	1
Hugh McElhenny	52-64	1124	5281	4.7	38	264	3247	12.3	20
Lamar McHan	54-63	239	849	3.6	12	0	1	–	0
Pat McHugh	47-51	32	202	6.3	1	2	16	8.0	0
Don McIlhenny	56-61	414	1581	3.8	7	70	655	9.4	7
Paul McKee	47-48					30	413	13.8	2
Buck McPhail	53	53	138	2.6	0	10	38	3.8	0
Charlie Mehelich	46-51					15	172	11.5	0
Steve Meilinger	56-58,60-61	1	6	6.0	0	60	863	14.4	8
Jim Mello	47-49	90	308	3.4	1	6	81	13.5	0
Buzz Mertes	45-49	341	1273	3.7	6	19	182	9.6	2
Mike Micka	44-48	69	231	3.3	0	6	101	16.8	0
Dave Middleton	55-61	67	210	3.1	2	183	2966	16.2	17
Ron Miller	56					11	129	11.7	0
Henry Minarik	51					35	459	13.1	1
Frank Minini	47-49	51	216	4.2	4	3	37	12.3	1
Skippy Minisi	48	36	160	4.4	1	13	123	9.5	1
Bob Mitchell	46-48	42	71	1.7	0	4	37	9.3	1
Billy Mixon	53-54	32	195	6.1	1	1	7	7.0	0
Rudy Mobley	47	26	90	3.5	1	11	121	11.0	1
Ed Modzelewski	52,55-59	393	1292	3.3	11	38	277	7.3	3
Dick Moegle	55-61	60	310	5.2	6	8	185	23.1	0
Jim Monachino	51,53,55	71	291	4.1	4	11	89	8.1	0
Tommy Mont	47-49	26	185	7.1	1	10	119	11.9	2
Gonzales Morales	47-48	42	125	3.0	0				
Max Morris	46-48	1	20	20.0	0	53	677	12.8	2
Curley Morrison	50-56	578	2420	4.2	12	67	721	10.8	2
Dom Moselle	50-52,54	46	176	3.8	2	31	475	15.3	4
Kelley Mote	47-52					52	754	14.5	6
Marion Motley	46-53,55	828	4720	5.7	31	85	1107	13.0	7
Frank Muehlheuser	48-49	47	179	3.8	2	5	45	9.0	0
Joe Muha	46-50	67	257	3.8	2	4	42	10.5	0
Noah Mullins	46-49	67	377	5.6	1	12	176	14.7	5
Chet Mutryn	46-50	583	3031	5.2	27	121	1850	15.3	12
Jim Mutscheller	54-61					220	3684	16.7	40
Brad Myers	53,56,58	55	180	3.3	3	8	38	4.8	0
Jack Myers	48-50,52	125	541	4.3	3	28	360	12.9	0
Gern Nagler	53,55-61					196	3119	15.9	28
Frank Nelson	48-49	26	86	3.3	0	1	10	10.0	0
Jimmy Nelson	46	39	163	4.2	2	4	20	5.0	0
Elbie Nickel	47-57					329	5131	15.6	37
John North	48-50					38	784	20.6	5
Jerry Norton	54-64	47	341	7.3	1	11	125	11.4	1
Bob Nowaskey	40-42,46-50	8	26	3.3	0	51	767	15.0	6
Bob Nussbaumer	46-51	95	238	2.5	0	76	992	13.1	5
Jerry Nuzum	48-51	249	930	3.7	7	14	303	21.6	3
Bernie Nygren	46-47	26	111	4.3	0	13	170	13.1	1
Jack O'Brien	54-56					16	185	11.6	2
Tom O'Connell	53,56-57,60-61	67	27	0.4	4				
Bill O'Connor	48-49,51					45	493	11.0	2
Johnny Olszewski	53-62	837	3320	4.0	16	104	988	9.5	3
Bob Oristaglio	49-52	1	20	20.0	1	15	148	9.9	0
Charlie O'Rourke	43,46-49	96	103	1.1	4				
Chuck Ortmann	51-52	67	351	5.2	0	4	62	15.5	0

Lifetime Statistics - 1946-1959 Players Section 2 - **RUSHING and RECEIVING** (continued)
(All men with 25 or more rushing attempts or 10 or more receptions)

Name	Years	RUSHING Att.	Yards	Avg.	TD	RECEIVING Rec.	Yards	Avg.	TD
Joe Osmanski	46-49	274	1182	4.3	6	36	329	9.1	0
Jim Owens	50					19	188	9.9	0
Jim Pace	58	52	161	3.1	2	10	59	5.9	0
Bob Paffrath	46	31	100	3.2	2	4	−6	−1.5	0
Paul Page	49	25	81	3.2	0	4	62	15.5	0
John Panelli	49-53	55	157	2.9	0	4	27	6.8	0
George Papach	48-49	159	731	4.6	2	10	90	9.0	1
Johnny Papit	51-53	95	379	4.0	1	7	123	17.6	1
Jim Parmer	48-56	452	1636	3.6	20	53	351	6.6	1
Ara Parseghian	48-49	44	166	3.8	1	3	33	11.0	1
Earle Parsons	46-47	107	487	4.6	2	17	215	12.6	2
Gordon Paschka	43-47	48	143	3.0	2	1	−6	−6.0	0
Ralph Pasquariello	50-52	108	411	3.8	2	10	39	3.9	0
Paul Patterson	49	2	0	0.0	0	16	304	19.0	4
Don Paul	50-58	73	469	6.4	3	48	690	14.4	7
Lindy Pearson	50-52	58	172	3.0	2	7	63	9.0	0
Jim Peebles	46-49,51	1	−3	−3.0	0	13	190	14.6	1
Ray Pelfrey	51-53	3	44	14.7	0	75	959	12.8	10
Bob Perina	46-50	122	256	2.1	4	14	113	8.1	1
Joe Perry	48-63	1929	9723	5.0	71	260	2021	7.8	12
Lowell Perry	56	2	37	18.5	0	14	334	23.9	2
Bob Pfohl	48-49	174	660	3.8	6	20	196	9.8	1
Don Phelps	50-52	55	263	4.8	3	1	28	28.0	0
Bert Piggott	47	46	161	3.5	0	7	63	9.0	1
Pete Pihos	47-55	9	−4	−0.4	0	373	5619	15.1	61
Jim Podoley	57-60	209	746	3.6	2	78	1461	18.7	11
Dick Poillon	42,46-49	186	535	2.9	4	37	477	12.9	5
John Polanski	42,46	45	144	3.2	1	2	15	7.5	1
Al Pollard	51-53	104	351	3.4	1	18	127	7.1	0
Fran Polsfoot	50-53					106	1613	15.2	10
Barney Poole	49-54					12	188	15.5	1
Ray Poole	47-52					83	1164	14.0	8
John Poto	47-48	19	59	3.1	1	10	101	10.1	0
Hal Prescott	46-49					12	185	15.4	1
Eddie Price	50-55	846	3292	3.9	20	75	672	9.0	4
Billy Pricer	57-61	97	316	3.3	2	15	115	7.7	1
Bosh Pritchard	42,46-49,51	392	1730	4.4	11	75	1166	15.6	10
Steve Pritko	43-50					93	1114	12.0	13
Dewey Proctor	46-49	86	280	3.3	3	6	54	9.0	0
Eddie Prokop	46-49	226	935	4.1	8	16	361	22.6	5
Fred Provo	48	29	90	3.1	0	4	−9	−2.2	0
Cal Purdin	43,46	19	32	1.7	0	15	143	9.5	0
Frank Quillen	46-47					20	256	12.8	3
Skeets Quinlan	52-56	258	1514	5.9	9	75	1181	15.7	6
Ed Quirk	48-51	117	467	4.0	5	14	73	5.2	0
Ray Ramsey	47-53	124	524	4.2	2	88	1729	19.6	14
George Ratterman	47-56	106	49	0.5	14				
Bob Ravensburg	48-49	2	8	4.0	0	10	203	20.3	3
Frank Reagan	41,46-51	114	469	4.1	6	4	71	17.8	0
Don Reece	46	30	109	3.6	2	1	5	5.0	0
Bill Reichardt	52	39	121	3.1	1	5	18	3.6	0
Breezy Reid	50-56	459	1964	4.3	13	72	868	12.1	5
Bob Reinhard	46-50	43	141	3.3	0	9	101	11.2	2
Ray Renfro	52-63	137	682	5.0	4	281	5508	19.6	50
Billy Reynolds	53-54,57-58,60	176	585	3.3	7	24	252	10.5	0
Jim Reynolds	46	32	96	3.0	0	1	32	32.0	0
Dick Rifenburg	50					10	96	9.6	1
Choo-Choo Roberts	47-50	499	1904	3.8	14	64	1135	17.7	12
Hosea Rodgers	49	131	494	3.8	5	7	97	13.9	0
Fran Rogel	50-57	900	3271	3.6	17	150	1087	7.2	2
Herm Rohrig	41,46-47	43	1	0.0	0	13	88	6.8	0
Steve Romanik	50-54	27	35	1.3	3				
Rudy Romboli	46-48	49	137	2.8	1	12	107	8.9	0
Jim Root	53,56	43	57	1.3	3				
Sal Rosato	45-47	159	620	3.9	4	9	131	14.6	1
Kyle Rote	51-61	231	871	3.8	4	300	4797	16.0	48
Tobin Rote	50-59,63-64,66	635	3128	4.9	37	2	28	14.0	1
Tom Runnels	56-57	116	386	3.3	0	7	60	8.6	1
Clive Rush	53	1	−6	−6.0	0	14	190	13.6	0
Jack Russell	46-50					83	1331	16.0	15
Dave Ryan	45-46,48	110	159	1.4	2	3	62	20.7	1
Julie Rykovich	47-53	648	2584	4.0	28	75	1158	15.4	4
Eddie Saenz	46-51	190	619	3.3	2	84	1327	15.8	8
Paul Salata	49-50					74	907	12.3	8
Jack Salschneider	49	26	105	4.0	0	4	9	2.3	0
Don Samuel	49-50	39	163	4.2	1	1	2	2.0	0
Spec Sanders	46-48,50	540	2900	5.4	33	18	272	15.1	3
Don Sandifer	48-53	74	247	3.3	1	30	510	17.0	5
Ted Scalissi	47	35	37	1.1	0	5	67	13.4	2
Jack Scarbath	53-54,56	43	153	3.6	0				
Pete Schabarum	51,53-54	115	494	4.3	3	24	328	13.7	0
Don Schaefer	56	102	320	3.1	2	13	117	9.0	0
Walt Schlinkman	46-49	365	1455	4.0	8	3	−1	−0.3	0
Bob Schnelker	53-61					211	3667	17.4	33
Gene Schroeder	51-52,54-57	1	4	4.0	0	104	1870	18.0	13
Vic Schwall	47-50	56	301	5.4	1	6	28	4.7	2
Bud Schwenk	42,46-48	145	376	2.6	4				
Nick Scollard	46-49					14	200	14.3	3
Clyde Scott	49-52	100	400	4.0	2	19	381	20.1	4
Joe Scott	48-53	322	1218	3.8	14	79	1203	15.2	7
Prince Scott	46					13	180	13.8	2
Scooter Scudero	54-58,60	43	139	3.2	0	6	62	10.3	1
Charlie Seabright	41,46-50	1	4	4.0	0	31	241	7.8	3
Jimmy Sears	54,57-58,60-61	34	119	3.5	1	18	253	14.1	2
Frank Seno	43-49	364	1292	3.5	2	73	1034	14.2	5

Name	Years	RUSHING Att.	Yards	Avg.	TD	RECEIVING Rec.	Yards	Avg.	TD
Dean Sensenbaugher	48-49	38	95	2.5	2				
Bob Shaw	45-46,49-50					81	1569	19.4	20
George Shaw	55-62	130	431	3.3	5				
Charlie Shepard	6	30	91	3.0	0	1	31	31.0	0
Jerry Shipkey	48-53	109	310	2.8	16	12	138	11.5	0
Hal Shoener	48-50	1	1	1.0	0	22	160	7.3	3
Paul Shoults	49	46	124	2.7	0	10	124	12.4	0
Floyd Simmons	48	36	121	3.4	1	2	60	30.0	1
Emil Sitko	50-52	163	636	3.9	2	9	87	9.7	1
Walt Slater	47	46	167	3.6	0				
Phil Slosburg	48-49	69	210	3.0	1	6	40	6.7	0
Bob Smith	55-56	48	160	3.3	1	2	12	6.0	0
Bruce Smith	45-48	108	560	6.2	1	8	79	9.9	1
Jim Smith	48-53	37	181	4.9	0	5	76	15.2	0
Oscar Smith	48-49	43	109	2.5	0	12	121	10.1	0
Vitamin Smith	49-53	208	669	3.2	7	59	1025	17.4	12
Bill Smyth	47-50					13	123	9.5	1
Gordie Soltav	50-58	1	−4	−4.0	0	249	3487	14.0	25
Cecil Souders	47-49					17	203	11.9	1
Jimmie Spavital	49-50	73	290	4.0	2	22	237	10.8	1
Mac Speedie	46-52	2	0	0.0	0	349	5602	16.1	33
Jack Spinks	52-53,55-57	28	94	3.4	0	3	28	9.3	0
Ed Sprinkler	44-45	3	2	0.7	0	32	451	14.1	7
Norm Standlee	41,46-52	486	2244	4.6	23	7	15	2.1	0
Gil Steinke	45-48	66	267	4.0	2	11	209	19.0	3
Bob Steuber	46-48	79	461	5.8	3	3	23	7.7	0
Don Stevens	52,54	33	95	2.9	0	13	174	13.4	0
Bill Stits	54-61	49	165	3.4	0	8	69	8.6	0
Billy Stone	49-54	296	1112	3.8	11	143	2319	16.2	20
Don Stonesifer	51-56					231	2901	12.6	14
Pete Stout	49-50	71	298	4.2	4	10	117	11.7	2
Jim Strausbaugh	46	37	183	4.9	3	5	56	11.2	0
Bill Stribling	51-53,55-57					114	1573	13.8	14
Bishop Strickland	51	34	165	4.9	0				
Johnny Strzykalski	46-52	662	3415	5.2	19	93	1218	13.1	12
Joe Sulatis	43-53	39	141	3.6	1	48	469	9.8	1
George Sulima	52-54					49	746	15.2	2
Bob Sullivan	48	33	121	3.7	0	4	58	14.5	1
Bob Summerhays	49-51	29	101	3.5	0	1	34	34.0	0
Nick Susoeff	46-49					61	610	10.0	4
Ed Sutton	57-60	282	1109	3.9	9	14	237	16.9	1
Bob Sweiger	46-49	22	87	4.0	0	42	418	10.0	2
Bill Swiacki	48-52					139	1883	13.5	18
Veryl Switzer	54-55	31	160	5.2	0	31	269	8.7	3
Doyle Tackett	46-48	11	−6	−0.5	0	10	216	21.6	2
George Taliaferro	49-55	498	2266	4.6	15	95	1300	13.7	12
Carl Taseff	51,53-62	60	283	4.7	3	19	193	10.2	1
Corky Taylor	55,57	26	95	3.7	0	7	47	6.7	1
Hugh Taylor	47-54	1	7	7.0	0	272	5233	19.2	58
Joe Tereshinski	47-54					43	451	10.5	4
George Terlep	46-48	41	44	1.1	1				
Ray Terrell	46-47	65	165	2.5	0	10	42	4.2	0
Lowell Tew	48-49	38	160	4.2	6	7	97	13.9	0
George Thomas	50-52	68	189	2.8	0	10	208	20.8	2
Bobby Thomason	49,51-57	98	290	3.0	6				
Hal Thompson	47-48	1	4	4.0	0	19	187	9.8	1
Tommy Thompson	40-42,45-50	293	96	0.3	6	6	65	10.8	1
Travis Tidwell	50-51	40	147	3.7	2				
Y. A. Tittle	48-64	372	1245	3.3	39	1	4	4.0	0
Lou Tomasetti	39-42,46-49	501	1905	3.8	14	66	688	10.4	5
Zollie Toth	50-52,54	418	1589	3.8	14	49	394	8.0	3
Dan Towler	50-55	672	3493	5.2	43	62	665	10.7	1
Frank Trigillo	46	41	126	3.1	1				
Mel Triplett	55-62	685	2856	4.2	14	43	439	10.2	4
Wally Triplett	49-50,52-53	70	321	4.6	1	17	175	10.3	0
Charlie Trippi	47-55	687	3506	5.1	23	130	1321	10.2	11
Doug Turley	44-48					45	608	13.5	3
Jim Tyree	48					13	106	8.2	0
Sam Vacanti	47-49	25	8	0.3	3				
Norm Van Brocklin	49-60	102	40	0.4	11				
Steve Van Buren	44-51	1320	5860	4.4	68	45	503	11.2	4
John Vardian	46-48	46	62	1.3	0	26	414	15.9	1
Billy Vessels	56	44	215	4.9	2	11	177	16.1	1
Joe Vetrano	46-49	56	201	3.6	2	5	71	14.2	0
Lowell Wagner	46-53,55	21	55	2.6	0	20	281	14.1	3
Doak Walker	50-55	309	1520	4.9	12	152	2539	16.7	21
Ron Waller	55-58,60	294	1569	5.3	8	44	443	10.1	1
Bobby Walston	51-62	4	12	3.0	0	311	5363	17.2	46
Kenny Washington	46-48	140	859	6.1	8	15	227	15.1	1
Bob Waterfield	45-52	75	21	0.3	13	3	19	6.3	0
Bobby Watkins	55-58	238	1058	4.4	11	15	234	15.6	3
Sid Watson	55-58	199	516	2.6	4	39	423	10.8	2
Joe Watt	47-49	31	61	2.0	0	6	133	22.2	2
Alex Webster	55-64	1196	4638	3.9	39	240	2679	11.2	17
Herm Wedemeyer	48-49	143	540	3.8	0	46	442	9.6	2
Ted Wegert	55-56,60	109	408	3.7	4	14	131	9.4	1
Art Weiner	50					35	722	20.6	6
Billy Wells	54,56-58,60	361	1384	3.8	5	57	725	12.7	2
Pat West	45-48	105	457	4.4	3	4	35	8.8	0
Bob White	51-52,55	32	66	2.1	1	15	209	13.9	2
Wilford White	51-52	28	67	2.4	1	12	197	16.4	1
Bill Wightkin	50-57					13	213	16.4	2
Dick Wilkins	49,52,54	8	28	3.5	0	68	1050	15.4	7
Bob Wilkinson	51-52	26	26	1.0	0	17	330	19.4	3
Bob Williams	51-52,55	29	112	3.9	0				

Lifetime Statistics - 1946-1959 Players Section 2 - **RUSHING and RECEIVING** (continued)
(All men with 25 or more rushing attempts or 10 or more receptions)

Name	Years	RUSHING Att.	Yards	Avg.	TD	RECEIVING Rec.	Yards	Avg.	TD
Jerry Williams	49-54	172	910	5.3	10	91	1278	14.0	5
Win Williams	48-49					52	626	12.0	3
Billy Wilson	51-60					407	5902	14.5	49
Camp Wilson	46-49	378	1453	3.8	6	20	198	9.9	0
Tom Wilson	56-63	508	2553	5.0	18	61	617	10.1	5
Royce Womble	54-57,60	91	266	2.9	0	79	917	11.6	9
Neil Worden	54,57	100	261	2.6	1	8	66	8.3	0
John Wright	47	38	113	3.0	0				
Vinnie Yablonski	48-51	124	460	3.7	1	15	127	8.5	0
John Yonaker	46-50,52					18	220	12.2	4
Jim Youel	46-48	42	183	4.4	3	1	20	20.0	0
Buddy Young	47-55	597	2727	4.6	17	179	2711	15.1	21
Dick Young	55-57	78	199	2.6	2	6	53	8.8	0
Tank Younger	49-58	770	3640	4.7	34	100	1167	11.7	1
Bert Zagers	55,57-58	116	477	4.1	3	17	356	20.9	0
Frank Ziegler	49-53	519	1926	3.7	11	47	639	13.6	4
Jack Zilly	47-52					23	279	12.1	4

Section 3 - **PUNT RETURNS and KICKOFF RETURNS**
(All men with 25 or more Punt Returns or 25 or more Kickoff Returns)

Name	Years	PUNT RETURNS No.	Yards	Avg.	TD	KICKOFF RETURNS No.	Yards	Avg.	TD
Joe Arenas	51-57	124	774	6.2	1	139	3798	27.3	1
Dale Atkeson	54-56	5	41	8.2	0	29	754	26.0	1
Steve Bagarus	45-48	41	461	11.2	0	27	683	25.3	0
Bibbles Bawel	52,55-56	49	293	6.2	1	9	194	21.6	0
Frank Bernardi	55-57,60	39	392	10.1	1	4	101	25.3	0
J. R. Boone	48-53	72	725	10.1	0	2	31	15.5	0
Fred Bruney	53,56-58,60-62	53	265	5.0	0	18	421	23.4	0
Rex Bumgardner	48-52	24	395	16.5	2	26	468	18.0	0
Leon Campbell	50,52-55					28	771	27.5	1
Tony Canadeo	41-44,46-52	46	513	11.2	0	71	1626	22.9	0
Al Carmichael	53-58,60-61	122	912	7.5	0	191	4798	25.1	2
Ken Carpenter	50-53,60	34	370	10.9	1	41	895	21.8	0
Lew Carpenter	53-55,57-63	28	339	12.1	0	34	686	20.2	0
Jim Cason	48-52,54-56	67	948	14.1	0	33	703	21.3	0
Hopalong Cassady	56-63	43	341	7.9	0	77	1594	20.7	0
Sam Cathcart	49-50,52	35	514	14.7	0	21	469	22.3	0
Lynn Chandnois	50-56	66	312	4.7	0	92	2720	29.6	3
Jack Christiansen	51-58	85	1084	12.8	8	59	1329	22.5	0
Red Cochran	47-50	33	583	17.7	2	25	462	18.5	0
Russ Craft	46-54	32	247	7.7	0	17	484	28.5	1
Billy Cross	51.53	34	221	6.5	0	21	426	20.3	0
Lindon Crow	55-64	25	134	5.4	0				
Jerry Davis	48-52	25	398	15.9	2	18	462	25.7	0
Bill deCorrevont	45-49	21	248	11.8	0	34	655	19.3	0
Babe Dimancheff	45-50,52	16	197	12.3	0	31	670	21.6	0
Glenn Dobbs	46-49	26	361	13.9	1	19	371	19.5	0
Don Doll	49-54	17	164	9.6	0	32	808	25.3	0
Ron Drzewiecki	55,57	42	164	3.9	0	38	906	23.8	0
Bill Dudley	42,45-51,53	124	1515	12.2	3	78	1743	22.3	1
Ralph Earhart	48-49	25	298	11.9	1	13	238	18.3	0
Chuck Fenenbock	43.45-48	61	801	13.1	0	67	1658	24.7	1
Gene Filipski	56-57	21	116	5.5	0	45	1003	22.3	0
Henry Ford	55-56	29	160	5.5	0	6	135	22.5	0
Ted Fritsch	42-50	1	31	31.0	0	37	951	25.7	0
Monk Gafford	46-48	34	433	12.7	0	55	1469	26.7	0
Bob Gage	49-50	30	446	14.9	0	10	221	22.1	0
Fred Gehrke	40,45-50	44	552	12.5	1	38	909	23.9	1
Skippy Giancanelli	53-56	13	63	4.8	0	38	986	25.9	0
Frank Gifford	52-60,62-64	25	121	4.8	0	23	594	25.8	0
Jug Girard	48-57	41	219	5.3	0	34	738	21.7	0
Les Goble	54-55	22	51	2.3	0	35	909	26.0	2
Joe Golding	47-51	22	219	10.0	0	29	654	22.6	0
Billy Grimes	49-52	68	901	13.3	2	83	2015	24.3	0
Chet Hanulak	54,57	38	121	3.2	0	9	213	23.7	0
Tommy Harmon	46-47	32	449	14.0	1	15	342	22.8	0
Howard Hartley	48-52	35	341	9.7	0	6	122	20.3	0
Billy Hillenbrand	46-48	44	612	13.9	1	42	1042	24.8	2
Bob Hoernschemeyer	46-55	11	133	12.1	0	39	981	25.2	0
Chuck Hunsinger	50-52	2	11	5.5	0	31	717	23.1	0
Tommy Kalmanir	49-51,53	34	385	11.3	2	40	932	23.3	0
Sonny Karnofsky	45-46	9	141	15.7	0	27	763	28.3	1
Ken Keller	56-57	24	205	8.5	0	30	673	22.4	0
Kenny Konz	53-59	68	556	8.2	1	5	119	23.8	0
Yale Lary	52-53,56-64	126	758	6.0	3	22	495	22.5	0
Pete Layden	48-50	36	351	9.8	0	9	239	26.6	0
Cliff Lewis	46-51	77	710	9.2	0	14	288	20.6	0
Woodley Lewis	50-60	138	1026	7.4	3	137	3325	24.3	1
Dante Magnani	40-43,46-50	11	121	11.0	0	29	706	24.3	2
Ray Mathews	51-60	61	779	12.8	3	42	1069	25.5	0
Ollie Matson	52,54-66	65	595	9.2	3	144	3746	26.0	6
George McAfee	40-41,45-50	112	1431	12.8	2	11	265	24.1	2
Hugh McElhenny	52-64	126	920	7.3	2	83	1921	23.1	0
Pat McHugh	47-51	31	402	13.0	1	5	95	19.0	0
Don McIlhenny	56-61	1	0	0.0	0	30	747	24.9	0
Frank Minini	47-49					39	1021	26.2	1
Curley Morrison	50-56					33	723	21.9	0
Dom Moselle	50-52,54	23	283	12.3	0	37	886	23.9	0
Marion Motley	46-53,55	1	0	0.0	0	48	1122	23.3	0
Chet Mutryn	46-50	41	537	13.1	1	73	1902	26.1	1
Jerry Norton	54-64	46	147	3.2	0	14	415	29.6	1
Earle Parsons	46-47	25	304	12.2	0	8	193	24.1	0
Don Paul	50-58	113	902	8.0	2	57	1417	24.9	0
Joe Perry	48-63					33	758	23.0	1
Al Pollard	51-53	38	254	6.7	0	53	1293	24.4	0
Bosh Pritchard	42,46-49,51	95	1072	11.3	2	41	938	22.9	1
Eddie Prokop	46-49	17	274	16.1	1	27	620	23.0	0
Skeets Quinlan	52-56	30	276	9.2	1	35	803	22.9	0
Ray Ramsey	47-53	24	277	11.5	1	41	846	20.6	0
Frank Reagan	41,46-51	65	647	10.0	1	4	112	28.0	0
Bert Rechichar	52-61	85	311	3.7	0	23	448	19.5	0
Ray Renfro	52-63	40	225	5.6	0	9	154	17.1	0
Billy Reynolds	53-54,57-58,60	99	530	5.4	0	40	985	24.6	0
Lee Riley	55-56,58-61	48	249	5.2	0	32	764	23.9	0
Herm Rohrig	41,46-47	30	357	11.9	0	6	121	20.2	0
Eddie Saenz	46-51	59	643	10.9	0	93	2191	23.6	2
Spec Sanders	46-48,50	42	642	15.3	1	44	1205	27.4	2
Dan Sandifer	48-53	72	767	10.7	0	63	1367	21.7	1
Joe Scott	48-53	4	48	12.0	0	54	1467	27.2	1
Scooter Scudero	54-58,60	68	458	6.7	1	44	1143	26.0	1
Jimmy Sears	54,57-58,60-61	24	195	8.1	0	50	1169	23.4	0
Frank Seno	43-49	64	747	11.7	1	80	1916	24.0	1
Walt Slater	47	28	435	15.5	0	22	480	21.8	0
Ray Gene Smith	54-57	27	156	5.8	0	4	78	19.5	0
Vitamin Smith	49-53	75	814	10.9	1	57	1453	25.5	3
Bill Stits	54-61	40	305	7.6	0	27	621	23.0	0
Billy Stone	49-54	34	179	5.3	0	18	423	23.5	0
Johnny Strzykalski	46-52	26	316	12.2	0	24	508	21.2	0
Veryl Switzer	54-55	48	464	9.7	1	37	945	25.5	0
George Taliaferro	49-55	36	319	8.9	1	95	2035	21.4	0
Carl Taseff	51,53-62	117	850	7.3	2	45	1019	22.6	0
Wally Triplett	49-50,52-53	44	401	9.1	1	18	664	36.9	1
Charlie Trippi	47-55	63	864	13.7	2	66	1457	22.1	0
Em Tunnell	48-61	258	2209	8.6	5	46	1215	26.4	1
Steve Van Buren	44-51	34	473	13.9	2	76	2030	26.7	3
Doak Walker	50-55	18	284	15.8	1	38	968	25.5	0
Ron Waller	55-58,60	57	165	2.9	0	48	1146	23.9	0
Sid Watson	55-58	28	38	1.4	0	50	1269	25.4	0
Herm Wedemeyer	48-49	39	589	15.1	0	41	842	20.5	0
Billy Wells	54,56-58,60	57	427	7.5	0	55	1267	23.0	
Wilford White	51-52	37	248	6.7	0	5	134	26.8	0
Jerry Williams	49-54	51	277	5.4	0	20	476	23.8	0
Johnny Williams	52-54	42	538	12.8	2	29	710	24.5	0
Tom Wilson	56-63	3	28	9.3	0	62	1689	27.2	1
Buddy Young	47-55	67	698	10.4	2	125	3465	27.7	4
Bert Zagers	55,57-58	28	383	13.7	3	26	628	24.2	0
Vic Zucco	57-60	37	176	4.8	0	12	304	25.3	0

Section 4 - **PUNTING**
(All men with 25 or more punts)

Name	Years	No.	Avg.
Frankie Albert	46-52	299	43.0
Clarence Avinger	53	42	38.1
Lou Baldacci	56	26	38.8
Jack Banta	41,44-48	39	41.4
Bill Blackburn	46-50	36	41.3
Mike Boyda	49	56	44.2
Pat Brady	52-54	223	44.5
Monte Brethauer	53,55	55	39.3
Ed Brown	54-65	493	40.5
Pete Brown	53-54	49	37.5
Ray Brown	58-60	95	39.2
Adrian Burk	50-56	474	40.9
Tony Canadeo	41-44,46-52	45	37.1
Bob Celeri	51-52	26	42.3
Bob Cifers	46-49	161	41.4
Red Cochran	47-50	59	41.3
Rip Collins	49-51	45	42.2
Mickey Colmer	46-49	117	43.7
Chuck Conerly	48-61	130	38.9
Billy Cox	51-52,55	33	39.3
Dick Deschaine	55-58	231	42.3
Glenn Dobbs	46-49	231	46.4
Bill Dudley	42,45-51,53	191	38.2
L. G. Dupre	55-61	29	35.4
Vic Eaton	55	66	38.2
Chuck Fenenbock	43,45-48	33	38.3
John Galvin	47	66	36.0
Joe Geri	49-52	200	39.9
Horace Gillom	47-56	492	43.1
Jug Girard	48-57	397	40.1
Fred Glatz	56	25	39.4
Bobby Gordon	58-60	55	38.0
George Grimes	48	28	35.9
Rex Grossman	48-50	28	38.8
George Gulvanics	47-52	113	44.6
Jim Hardy	46-52	79	38.1
Ralph Heywood	46-49	68	37.1
Jack Jacobs	42,45-49	187	42.2
Bill Jessup	51-52,54,56-58,60	75	41.0
Jack Johnson	57-61	30	35.2
Pres Johnston	46	28	39.7
Choo-Choo Justice	50,52-54	94	40.4
Kenny Konz	53-59	61	39.3
Steve Lach	42,46-47	31	40.1
Tom Landry	49-55	389	40.9
Yale Lary	52-53,56-64	503	44.3
Hank Lauricella	52	58	35.1
Pete Layden	48-50	36	41.9
Eddie LeBaron	52-53,55-63	171	40.9
Ernie Lewis	46-49	191	41.9
Verl Lillywhite	48-51	53	40.4
Bill Long	49-50	30	37.6
Bobby Luna	55,59	126	40.7
Howie Maley	46-47	152	40.1
Ray Mallouf	41,46-49	188	38.7
Dave Mann	55-57	138	40.4
George McAfee	40-41,45-50	39	36.9
Curley Morrison	50-56	281	41.8
Joe Muha	46-50	179	42.9
Jerry Norton	54-64	358	43.8
Charlie O'Rourke	42,46-49	125	38.2
Dick Poillon	42,46-49	143	40.6
Fran Polsfoot	50-53	47	40.7
Jim Powers	50-53	42	40.6
Bosh Pritchard	42,46-51	28	34.5
Frank Reagan	41,46-51	227	40.9
Bert Rechichar	52-61	38	37.7
Bob Reinhard	46-50	78	44.6
Clive Rush	53	60	37.7
Spec Sanders	46-48,50	192	40.9
Charlie Shepard	56	26	36.6
Jim Smith	48-53	196	42.4
Jim Still	48-49	63	38.7
George Taliaferro	49-55	169	37.5
Charlie Trippi	47-55	196	40.4
Norm Van Brocklin	49-60	523	42.9
Doak Walker	50-55	50	39.1
Bob Waterfield	45-52	315	42.4
Junior Wren	56-61	36	36.3

Section 5 - **KICKING**
(All men with 10 or more PAT or Field Goal attempts)

Name	Years	PAT	PAT Att.	PAT Pct.	FG	FG Att.	FG Pct.
Ben Agajanian	45,47-49,53-57,60-62,64	343	351	98	104	204	51
Graham Armstrong	41,45,47-48	23	27	85	0	2	0
Larry Barnes	57,60	37	39	95	6	25	24
Dick Bielski	55-63	58	62	94	26	65	40
Nick Bolkovac	53-54	30	31	97	7	16	44
Hardy Brown	48-56,60	25	30	83	0	1	0
George Buksar	49-52	15	18	83	3	7	43
Pat Cannamela	52	8	10	80	0	1	0
Randy Clay	50,53	20	23	87	3	8	38
Ed Cody	47-50	11	13	85			
Fred Cone	51-57,60	221	237	93	59	102	58
Paige Cothren	57-59	81	81	100	33	62	53
Chuck DeShane	45-49	10	10	100	0	1	0
Bill Dudley	42,45-51,53	121	127	95	33	66	50
Tom Feamster	56	24	26	92	0	3	0
Tom Fears	48-56	12	14	86	1	4	25
Ralph Felton	54-62	16	17	94	1	2	50
Ted Fritsch	42-50	62	70	89	36	98	37
Bill George	52-66	14	15	93	4	8	50
Joe Geri	49-52	78	82	95	18	47	38
Frank Gifford	52-60,62-64	10	11	91	2	7	29
Joe Glamp	47-49	74	76	97	11	31	35
Gary Glick	56-61,63	26	29	90	9	25	36
Chubby Grigg	46-52	18	21	86	1	5	20
Rex Grossman	48-50	78	81	96	16	32	50
Lou Groza	46-59,61-67	810	834	97	264	481	55
Pat Harder	46-53	198	204	97	35	69	51
Paul Held	54-55	14	16	88	3	5	60
Crazy Legs Hirsch	46-57	9	12	75			
Vic Janowicz	54-55	37	40	93	10	28	36
Harvey Johnson	46-49,51	178	180	99	28	52	54
Steve Juzwik	42,46-48	36	40	90	2	3	67
Gary Kerkorian	52,54-56	47	55	85	10	21	48
Vito Kissell	49-51	11	11	100	0	1	0
Vic Kulbitski	46-48	9	11	82			
Bobby Layne	48-62	120	124	97	34	50	68
Johnny Lujack	48-51	130	136	96	4	9	44
Jim Martin	50-61,63-64	158	169	93	92	192	48
Phil Martinovich	39-40,46-47	43	47	91	13	38	34
Frank Maznicki	42,46-47	65	69	94	10	16	63
Jim McCarthy	46-49	47	51	92	8	17	47
Buck McPhail	53	21	23	91	2	5	40
Art Michalik	53-56	9	15	60	1	13	8
Tom Miner	58	31	31	100	14	28	50
Jack Morris	58-61	15	15	100	3	8	38
Steve Myhra	57-61	180	189	95	44	91	48
Bob Nelson	41,45-50	37	40	93	6	16	38
Steve Nemeth	45-47	33	34	97	9	13	69
Cliff Patton	46-51	179	185	97	33	69	48
Jerry Perry	54,56-62	92	96	96	32	58	55
Dick Poillon	42,46-49	127	139	91	20	38	53
Ray Poole	47-52	86	92	93	27	44	61
Merv Pregulman	46-49	26	27	96	2	6	33
Bert Rechichar	52-61	62	68	91	31	78	40
Bill Reichardt	52	5	5	100	5	20	25
Les Richter	54-62	106	109	97	29	55	53
John Rokisky	46-48	34	36	94	4	8	50
Lou Saban	46-49	21	22	95	0	2	0
Nick Scollard	46-49	49	55	89	6	18	33
Gordie Soltau	50-58	284	302	94	70	138	51
Bob Steuber	43,46-48	20	23	87	1	2	50
Pat Summerall	52-61	257	265	97	100	212	47
Joe Vetrano	46-49	187	203	92	16	34	47
Doak Walker	50-55	183	191	96	49	87	56
Bobby Walston	51-62	365	384	95	80	157	51
Bob Waterfield	45-52	315	336	94	60	110	55
Sid Watson	55-58	10	12	83	1	1	100
Tad Weed	55	12	12	100	3	6	50
Vinnie Yablonski	48-51	16	16	100	10	18	56

1960—1973
From 12 to 26, and Maybe More

The 1960s were the decade of expansion for pro football. In 1959 there were twelve teams; by 1969, the number swelled to twenty-six teams. This proliferation of teams came not from peace but from war. From 1960 to the spring of 1966, the National Football League and the new American Football League battled each other for franchise sites, players, and publicity. The two leagues battled by checkbook, offering young players coming out of college unheard-of pacts to sign contracts, and they battled by lawsuit, with the AFL hauling the NFL into court with an antitrust suit which eventually was dismissed.

The NFL had grown strong enough in recent years to have no worries about surviving the war, but it found the new AFL an itching annoyance. The new league drove the cost of new talent up and actually signed some All-Americans away, and it threatened to cut into NFL attendance in some cities.

At the outset of the decade, the NFL club owners picked Pete Rozelle, the thirty-three-year-old general manager of the Los Angeles Rams, to succeed the late Bert Bell as commissioner. Chosen as a compromise candidate, Rozelle gave the league an able administration and strong leadership both through the war and into the peace that followed.

To combat the new league and tap some of the football enthusiasm around the country, the NFL expanded to three new cities in the early 1960s. The Chicago Cardinals, an original member of the NFL, moved to St. Louis in 1960, while expansion clubs were placed in Dallas in 1960 and Minnesota in 1961. All three franchises were unqualified successes, with the Dallas franchise wiping away the embarrassing failure of the NFL there in 1952.

Cities without an NFL team could still watch games every weekend on the Columbia Broadcasting System. With CBS paying the NFL several million dollars each season, these telecasts attracted huge audiences and became prime targets for advertisers. The NFL tried to provide an attractive bundle of post-season action for both the live and television viewers. In addition to the NFL championship game and the Pro Bowl game, a Playoff Bowl pitted the runners-up in each conference against each other after each season from 1960 to 1969. The NFL provided the fans with another service by establishing a Hall of Fame in Canton, Ohio, in 1963.

The AFL, in its early years, had no players worthy of enshrinement in Canton, but the league did play entertaining football, with wild offensive battles standard fare in the first few seasons, along with the two-point conversion rule adding an extra twist. Although attendance was poor in the early years and the young league suffered in signing top players, lining up a sound ownership for the key New York franchise, and finding big-league stadiums to play in, a television contract with the American Broadcasting Company brought in additional revenues while helping to bring new fans over to the league's side.

With Joe Foss as commissioner, the league made gradual progress from its first shaky seasons, when various experts predicted an imminent collapse. Attendance climbed slowly, franchises were shifted from Los Angeles and Dallas to better sites in San Diego and Kansas City, most of the teams found good stadiums to play in, more young players began signing with the league, and the quality of play improved. But the most important development was the purchase of the New York franchise by a syndicate headed by Sonny Werblin—a move which began the AFL on the path to parity with the NFL in publicity. Werblin, with a long show-business background, moved the Jets in 1964 into spanking-new Shea Stadium, where the club immediately attracted record AFL crowds. Late in the year Werblin announced the signing of star college quarterbacks Joe Namath and John Huarte to the richest contracts ever offered to football players. The size of the contracts plus Namath's ensuing stardom blessed the Jets and the AFL with an abundance of publicity and gave the league a first-class image in the eyes of most fans. Finally, the league signed a multimillion-dollar contract with the National Broadcasting Company, and its survival was assured.

Although both leagues were spending over half a million dollars for top college prospects and many owners were considering an arrangement between the two factions, it was not until the NFL began pirating tactics that a merger was finally considered. After the 1965 season the Giants signed Pete Gogolak from the Buffalo Bills. The AFL then retaliated by naming aggressive young Al Davis as commissioner, and he soon began efforts to sign away leading NFL quarterbacks. The older league then decided that the time had come for peace, and a merger agreement was announced only two months after Davis had become AFL commissioner.

Starting with the 1966 season, both leagues would have a common draft of players, thus eliminating the expensive bidding between the leagues. An interleague championship game, dubbed the Super Bowl, was set up as a regular post-season event. By the end of the decade both leagues would merge into one giant league. Pete Rozelle was put in charge of both leagues as commissioner, and Al Davis returned to work for the AFL Oakland Raiders.

From 1966 to 1969 the two leagues operated separately under the direction of Rozelle. Both leagues added new members, with the NFL taking in Atlanta and New Orleans and the AFL admitting Miami and Cincinnati. The Super Bowl grew in stature to the level of the World Series and the Kentucky Derby, with millions around the country glued to their TV sets on that special Sunday in January. The NFL Green Bay Packers, under coach Vince Lombardi, took the first two championships, but the AFL captured the next two as the New York Jets and the Kansas City Chiefs upset highly favored NFL opponents.

Starting with the 1970 season, all the AFL teams became NFL teams, as the AFL was absorbed into the NFL with two thirteen-team conferences made possible by the Baltimore Colts, Pittsburgh Steelers, and Cleveland Browns joining the AFC. While the AFL no longer existed, all of its clubs had found a place in the NFL, unlike the All-American Football Conference of 1946-1949.

The crowds were larger than ever in the 1970s, but a gradual shift in tactics was occurring on the field of play. Pro football featured a lot of passing in the early 1960s, with quarterbacks like Johnny Unitas, Y.A. Tittle, and Sonny Jurgensen thrilling crowds with frequent long bombs. But with the refinement of zone defenses in the late 1960s, passers found the long pass denied to them. The Green Bay Packers set the standard for the decade with a conservative, ground-oriented attack, a rock-hard defense, and reliable field-goal kicking.

With the growing effectiveness of defenses, pro teams were more willing to settle for a three-point field goal than to risk going for a touchdown in certain situations. Place kickers like Lou Groza, Don Chandler, and Jim Bakken became essential parts of any winning team, and the arrival of Pete Gogolak in Buffalo in 1964 introduced the soccer-style kicker into pro ball. Following Gogolak, Jan Stenerud, Garo Yepremian, and other sidewinders brought added color to their specialty and furthered the trend to hard-fought defensive battles. But the future seemed to promise more than tight games when, in 1974, a new competitor, the World Football League, entered the pro-football arena with plans to try and capture some of the NFL marketplace.

1960–1973 SINGLE SEASON LEADERS

RUSHING

Most Yards Rushing

		Team	Year	Yds.
1	O.J. Simpson	Buf	1973	2003
2	Jimmy Brown	Cle-N	1963	1863
3	Jimmy Brown	Cle-N	1965	1544
4	Jim Taylor	GB-N	1962	1474
5	Jim Nance	Bos-A	1966	1458
6	Jimmy Brown	Cle-N	1964	1446
7	Jimmy Brown	Cle-N	1961	1408
8	Jim Taylor	GB-N	1961	1307
9	Jimmy Brown	Cle-N	1960	1257
10	O.J. Simpson	Buf	1972	1251

Most Rushing Attempts

		Team	Year	Att.
1	O.J. Simpson	Buf	1972	332
2	Jimmy Brown	Cle-N	1961	305
3	Jim Nance	Bos-A	1966	299
4	Ron Johnson	NYG	1972	298
5	O.J. Simpson	Buf	1972	292
6	Jimmy Brown	Cle-N	1963	291
7	Jimmy Brown	Cle-N	1965	289
8	Larry Brown	Was	1972	285
9	Floyd Little	Den	1971	284
10	Jimmy Brown	Cle-N	1964	280

Best Rushing Average
(Minimum 70 Attempts)

		Team	Year	Att.	Yds.	Avg.
1	Lenny Moore	Bal-N	1961	92	648	7.0
2	Bobby Douglass	Chi	1972	141	968	6.9
3	Greg Landry	Det	1972	81	524	6.5
4	Keith Lincoln	SD-A	1963	128	826	6.5
5	Mercury Morris	Mia	1973	149	954	6.4
6	Jimmy Brown	Cle-N	1963	291	1863	6.4
7	Paul Lowe	LA-A	1960	136	855	6.3
8	Dick Bass	LA-N	1961	98	608	6.2
9	Gale Sayers	Chi-N	1968	138	856	6.2
10	Ernie Green	Cle-N	1963	87	526	6.0

Most Touchdown Runs

		Team	Year	TD
1	Jim Taylor	GB-N	1962	19
2	Jimmy Brown	Cle-N	1965	17
3	Lenny Moore	Bal-N	1964	16
	Leroy Kelly	Cle-N	1968	16
5	Jim Taylor	GB-N	1961	15
	Leroy Kelly	Cle-N	1966	15
7	John David Crow	StL-N	1962	14
	Gale Sayers	Chi-N	1965	14
9	Paul Hornung	GB-N	1960	13
	Cookie Gilchrist	Buf-A	1962	13
	Abner Haynes	Dal-A	1962	13
	Jimmy Brown	Cle-N	1962	13

Most Yards Rushing per Game

		Team	Year	Yds/G
1	O.J. Simpson	Buf	1973	143
2	Jimmy Brown	Cle-N	1963	133
3	Jimmy Brown	Cle-N	1965	110
4	Jim Taylor	GB-N	1962	105
5	Jimmy Brown	Cle-N	1960	105
6	Jim Nance	Bos-A	1966	104
7	Jimmy Brown	Cle-N	1964	103
8	Jimmy Brown	Cle-N	1961	101
9	Jim Taylor	GB-N	1961	93
10	Jim Taylor	GB-N	1960	92

Best PUNT RETURN Average
(Minimum 14 Attempts)

		Team	Year	No.	Yds.	Avg.
1	Dick Christy	NYT-A	1961	18	383	21.3
2	Bob Hayes	Dal-N	1968	15	312	20.8
3	Floyd Little	Den-A	1967	16	270	16.9
4	Dick Christy	NYT-A	1962	15	250	16.7
5	Willie Wood	GB-N	1961	14	225	16.1
6	Pat Studstill	Det-N	1962	29	457	15.8
7	Leroy Kelly	Cle-N	1965	17	265	15.6
8	Speedy Duncan	SD-A	1965	30	464	15.5
9	Abner Haynes	Dal-A	1960	14	215	15.4
	Ken Ellis	GB	1972	14	215	15.4

Best KICKOFF RETURN Average
(Minimum 14 Attempts)

		Team	Year	No.	Yds.	Avg.
1	Travis Williams	GB-N	1967	18	729	41.1
2	Gale Sayers	Chi-N	1967	16	623	37.7
3	Jim Duncan	Bal	1970	20	707	35.4
4	Preston Pearson	Bal-N	1968	15	527	35.1
5	Tom Watkins	Det-N	1965	17	584	34.4
6	Bobby Williams	Det-N	1969	17	563	33.1
7	Abe Woodson	SF-N	1963	29	935	32.2
8	Gale Sayers	Chi-N	1965	21	660	31.4
9	Abe Woodson	SF-N	1962	37	1157	31.3

PASSING

Most Yards Passing

		Team	Year	Yds.
1	Joe Namath	NYJ-A	1967	4007
2	Sonny Jurgensen	Was-N	1967	3747
3	Sonny Jurgensen	Phi-N	1961	3723
4	Johnny Unitas	Bal-N	1963	3481
5	John Hadl	SD-A	1968	3473
6	Babe Parilli	Bos-A	1964	3465
7	Johnny Unitas	Bal-N	1967	3428
8	Norm Snead	Phi-N	1967	3399
9	Joe Namath	NYJ-A	1966	3379
10	George Blanda	Hou-A	1961	3330

Most Completed Passes

		Team	Year	Comp.
1	Sonny Jurgensen	Was-N	1967	288
2	Sonny Jurgensen	Was-N	1969	274
3	Roman Gabriel	Phi	1973	270
4	George Blanda	Hou-A	1964	262
5	Joe Namath	NYJ-A	1967	258
6	Johnny Unitas	Bal-N	1967	255
7	Sonny Jurgensen	Was-N	1966	254
8	Frank Tripucka	Den-A	1960	248
9	John Brodie	SF-N	1965	242
10	Frank Tripucka	Den-A	1962	240
	Norm Snead	Phi-N	1967	240

Best Completion Percentage
(Minimum 140 Attempts)

		Team	Year	Att.	Comp.	Pct.
1	Bart Starr	GB-N	1968	171	109	63.7
2	Ken Stabler	Oak	1973	260	163	62.7
3	Roger Staubach	Dal	1973	286	179	62.6
4	Bart Starr	GB-N	1962	285	178	62.4
5	Bart Starr	GB-N	1969	148	92	62.2
	Virgil Carter	Cin	1971	222	138	62.2
7	Bart Starr	GB-N	1966	251	156	62.2
8	Sonny Jurgensen	Was-N	1969	442	274	62.0
9	John Brodie	SF-N	1965	391	242	61.9
10	Rudy Bukich	Chi-N	1964	160	99	61.9

Most Touchdown Passes

		Team	Year	TD
1	George Blanda	Hou-A	1961	36
	Y. A. Tittle	NYG-N	1963	36
3	Daryle Lamonica	Oak-A	1969	34
4	Y. A. Tittle	NYG-N	1962	33
5	Sonny Jurgensen	Was-N	1961	32
6	Babe Parilli	Bos-A	1964	31
	Sonny Jurgensen	Was-N	1967	31
8	Len Dawson	KC-A	1964	30
	John Brodie	SF-N	1965	30
	Daryle Lamonica	Oak-A	1967	30

Most Yards Passing per Game

		Team	Year	Yds/G
1	Joe Namath	NYJ-A	1967	286
2	Sonny Jurgensen	Was-N	1967	268
3	Sonny Jurgensen	Phi-N	1961	266
4	Johnny Unitas	Bal-N	1960	258
5	Johnny Unitas	Bal-N	1963	249
6	John Hadl	SD-A	1968	247
7	Babe Parilli	Bos-A	1964	247
8	Johnny Unitas	Bal-N	1967	245
9	Norm Snead	Phi-N	1967	243
10	Joe Namath	NYJ-A	1966	241

Most Yards per Passing Attempt
(Minimum 140 Attempts)

		Team	Year	Att.	Yds.	Yds/Att
1	Bart Starr	GB-N	1968	171	1617	9.5
2	Len Dawson	KC-A	1968	224	2109	9.4
3	Greg Cook	Cin-A	1969	197	1854	9.4
4	Bob Berry	Atl-N	1968	153	1433	9.4
5	Johnny Unitas	Bal-N	1964	305	2824	9.3
6	George Blanda	Hou-A	1961	362	3330	9.2
7	Milt Plum	Cle-N	1960	250	2297	9.2
8	Earl Morrall	Bal-N	1968	317	2909	9.2
9	John Brodie	SF-N	1961	283	2588	9.1
10	Earl Morrall	Mia	1972	150	1360	9.1

Fewest Percent Intercepted
(Minimum 140 Attempts)

		Team	Year	Att.	Int.	% Int
1	Bart Starr	GB-N	1966	251	3	1.20
2	Bart Starr	GB-N	1964	272	4	1.47
3	Roman Gabriel	LA-N	1969	399	7	1.75
4	Roger Staubach	Dal	1971	211	4	1.90
5	Fran Tarkenton	NYG-N	1969	409	8	1.96
6	Johnny Unitas	Bal-N	1964	305	6	1.97
7	Milt Plum	Cle-N	1960	250	5	2.00
8	Gary Wood	SF-N	1964	143	3	2.10
9	Ken Anderson	Cin	1972	301	7	2.32
10	Edd Hargett	NO	1971	210	5	2.38

RECEIVING

Most Yards Receiving

		Team	Year	Yds.
1	Charley Hennigan	Hou-A	1961	1746
2	Lance Alworth	SD-A	1965	1602
3	Charley Hennigan	Hou-A	1964	1546
4	Bill Groman	Hou-A	1960	1473
5	Bobby Mitchell	Was-N	1963	1436
6	Don Maynard	NYJ-A	1967	1434
7	Bobby Mitchell	Was-N	1962	1384
8	Lance Alworth	SD-A	1965	1383
9	Art Powell	Oak-A	1964	1361
10	Dave Parks	SF-N	1965	1344

Most Receptions

		Team	Year	Rec.
1	Charley Hennigan	Hou-A	1964	101
2	Lionel Taylor	Den-A	1962	100
3	Johnny Morris	Chi-N	1964	93
4	Lionel Taylor	Den-A	1960	92
5	Lionel Taylor	Den-A	1965	85
6	Charley Hennigan	Hou-A	1961	82
7	Dave Parks	SF-N	1965	80
8	Jim Phillips	LA-N	1961	78
	Lionel Taylor	Den-A	1963	78
10	Bobby Joe Conrad	StL-N	1963	73

Most Yards per Reception
(Minimum 700 Yards)

		Team	Year	Rec.	Yds.	Avg.
1	Bucky Pope	LA-N	1964	25	786	31.4
2	Homer Jones	NYG-N	1965	26	709	27.3
3	El. Dubenion	Buf-A	1964	42	1139	27.1
4	Warren Wells	Oak-A	1969	47	1260	26.8
5	Jack Snow	LA-N	1967	28	735	26.3
6	Bob Hayes	Dal	1970	34	889	26.1
7	Ron Sellers	Bos-A	1969	27	705	26.1
8	Paul Warfied	Mia	1970	28	703	25.1
9	Homer Jones	NYG-N	1967	49	1209	24.7
10	Buddy Dial	Pit-N	1960	40	972	24.3

Most Touchdowns – Receiving

		Team	Year	TD
1	Bill Groman	Hou-A	1961	17
2	Art Powell	Oak-A	1963	16
3	Sonny Randle	StL-N	1960	15
4	Art Powell	NYT-A	1960	14
	Franke Clarke	Dal-N	1962	14
	Lance Alworth	SD-A	1965	14
	Don Maynard	NYJ-A	1965	14
	Warren Wells	Oak-A	1969	14

(10 tied with 13)

Most Yards Receiving per Game

		Team	Year	Yds/G
1	Charley Hennigan	Hou-A	1961	125
2	Lance Alworth	SD-A	1965	114
3	Charley Hennigan	Hou-A	1964	110
4	Ray Berry	Bal-N	1960	108
5	Bill Groman	Hou-A	1960	105
6	Bobby Mitchell	Was-N	1963	103
7	Don Maynard	NYJ-A	1967	102
8	Bobby Mitchell	Was-N	1962	99
9	Lance Alworth	SD-A	1965	99
10	Art Powell	Oak-A	1964	97

SCORING

Most Points

		Team	Year	TD	FG	PAT	Pts.
1	Paul Hornung	GB-N	1960	15	15	41	176
2	G. Cappelletti	Bos-A	1964	7	25	36	155
3	G. Cappelletti	Bos-A	1961	8	17	48	147
4	Paul Hornung	GB-N	1961	10	15	41	146
5	Jim Turner	NYJ-A	1968	0	34	43	145
6	Gene Mingo	Den-A	1962	4	27	32	137
7	G. Cappelletti	Bos-A	1965	9	17	27	132
	Gale Sayers	Chi-N	1965	22	0	0	132
9	David Ray	LA	1973	0	30	40	130
10	Jan Stenerud	KC-A	1968	0	30	39	129
	Jim Turner	NYJ-A	1969	0	32	33	129

Most Points per Game

		Team	Year	PPG
1	Paul Hornung	GB-N	1960	14.7
2	Gino Cappelletti	Bos-A	1964	11.1
3	Gino Cappelletti	Bos-A	1961	10.5
4	Paul Hornung	GB-N	1961	10.4
5	Jim Turner	NYJ-A	1968	10.4
6	Gene Mingo	Den-A	1962	9.8
7	Gino Cappelletti	Bos-A	1965	9.4
	Gale Sayers	Chi-N	1965	9.4
9	David Ray	LA	1973	9.3
10	Jan Stenerud	KC-A	1968	9.2
	Jim Turner	NYJ-A	1969	9.2

KICKING

Best Punting Average
(Minimum Punts)

		Team	Year	No.	Avg.
1	Yale Lary	Det-N	1963	35	48.9
2	Yale Lary	Det-N	1961	52	48.4
3	Bobby J. Green	Pit-N	1961	70	47.0
4	Gary Collins	Cle-N	1965	65	46.7
5	Bobby J. Green	Chi-N	1963	64	46.5
6	Bobby Walden	Min-N	1964	72	46.4
7	Yale Lary	Det-N	1964	67	46.3
8	Dave Lewis	Cin	1970	79	46.2
9	Jim Fraser	Den-A	1963	78	46.1
	Jerrel Wilson	KC-A	1965	68	46.1

Most Field Goals

		Team	Year	FG
1	Jim Turner	NYJ-A	1968	34
2	Chester Marcol	GB	1972	33
3	Jim Turner	NYJ-A	1969	32
4	Jan Stenerud	KC-A	1968	30
	Fred Cox	Min	1970	30
	Jan Stenerud	KC	1970	30
	David Ray	LA	1973	30
8	David Ray	LA	1970	29
	Curt Knight	Was	1971	29
	Roy Gerela	Pit	1973	29

Best Field Goal Percentage
(Minimum 14 Attempts)

		Team	Year	FG	Att.	Pct.
1	George Blair	SD-A	1962	17	20	85
2	Don Cockroft	Cle	1972	22	27	82
3	Bruce Gossett	SF	1973	26	33	79
4	Jan Stenerud	KC-A	1969	27	35	77
5	Garo Yepremian	Mia	1970	22	29	76
6	Jan Stenerud	KC-A	1968	30	40	75
7	Bruce Gossett	LA-N	1964	18	24	75
	Don Cockroft	Cle-N	1968	18	24	75
9	Curt Knight	Was	1970	20	27	74
	Jim Turner	NYJ-A	1968	34	46	74

Most Points after Touchdown

		Team	Year	PAT
1	George Blanda	Hou-A	1961	64
2	Danny Villanueva	Dal-N	1966	56
	George Blanda	Hou-A	1967	56
4	Mike Clark	Dal-N	1968	54
	George Blanda	Hou-A	1968	54
6	Lou Michaels	Bal-N	1964	53
7	Don Chandler	NYG-N	1963	52
	Tommy Davis	SF-N	1965	52
	Roger Le Clerc	Chi-N	1965	52
10	Sam Baker	Dal-N	1962	50

Most PAT – No Misses

		Team	Year	PAT
1	Danny Villanueva	Dal-N	1966	56
2	Mike Clark	Dal-N	1968	54
	George Blanda	Hou-A	1968	54
4	Roger Le Clerc	Chi-N	1965	52
5	Lou Michaels	Bal-N	1965	48
	Bruce Gossett	LA-N	1967	48
7	Mike Mercer	Oak-A	1963	47
	Mike Clark	Dal	1971	47
9	Pat Summerall	NYG-N	1961	46
	Tommy Brooker	KC-A	1964	46

INTERCEPTIONS

Most Passes Intercepted

		Team	Year	Int.
1	Freddy Glick	Hou-A	1963	12
	Paul Krause	Was-N	1964	12
	Dainard Paulson	NYJ-A	1964	12
4	Goose Gonsoulin	Den-A	1960	11
	Lee Riley	NYT-A	1962	11
	Ron Hall	Bos-A	1964	11
	Bill Bradley	Phi	1971	11

(15 tied with 10)

1960–1973 PERIOD LEADERS

PASSING

(All passers with at least 2000 attempts)

		Years	Att.	Comp.	Comp. Pct.	Yards	Yds/ Att.	TD	Int.	Pct. Int.
1	Sonny Jurgensen	1960-73	3998	2278	57.0	30283	7.6	238	175	4.4
2	Len Dawson	1960-73	3349	1899	56.7	25947	7.7	226	164	4.9
	Fran Tarkenton	*1961-73	**4449**	**2459**	55.3	**33248**	7.5	**249**	187	4.2
4	Bart Starr	1960-71	2599	1519	**58.4**	21057	**8.1**	133	106	4.1
5	Johnny Unitas	1960-73	4057	2219	54.7	31285	7.7	206	205	5.1
6	John Brodie	1960-73	4234	2325	54.9	29810	7.0	204	201	4.7
7	Roman Gabriel	*1962-73	3773	1975	52.3	25442	6.7	177	124	**3.3**
8	Earl Morrall	1960-73	2011	1059	52.7	16001	8.0	133	109	5.4
9	Frank Ryan	1960-70	2030	1043	51.4	15299	7.5	146	**104**	5.1
10	Don Meredith	*1960-68	2308	1170	50.7	17199	7.5	135	111	4.8
11	John Hadl	*1962-73	3899	1959	50.2	28946	7.4	223	222	5.7
12	Charley Johnson	*1961-73	3006	1536	51.1	21420	7.1	152	160	5.3
	Daryle Lamonica	*1963-73	2592	1285	49.6	19119	7.4	163	134	5.2
14	Norm Snead	*1961-73	3963	2049	51.7	28238	7.1	182	235	5.9
15	Joe Namath	*1965-73	2738	1374	50.2	21065	7.7	131	149	5.4
16	George Blanda	1960-73	3012	1464	48.6	20945	7.0	187	206	6.8
17	Babe Parilli	1960-69	2679	1270	47.4	18279	6.8	144	152	5.7
18	Jack Kemp	1960-67,69	2955	1429	48.4	21134	7.2	114	181	6.1

SCORING

		Years	TD-Rush	TD-Rec.	TD-Other	FG	PAT	2 Pt PAT	Points
1	George Blanda	1960-73	4	0	0	223	606	0	1299
2	Gino Cappelletti	*1960-70	0	42	2	172	342	4	1130
3	Fred Cox	*1963-73	0	0	0	230	384	0	1074
4	Jim Bakken	*1962-73	0	0	0	212	369	0	1005
5	Jim Turner	*1964-73	0	0	0	220	333	0	993
6	Bruce Gossett	*1964-73	0	0	0	208	349	0	973
7	Lou Michaels	1960-69,71	0	0	0	179	374	0	913
8	Pete Gogolak	*1964-73	0	0	0	163	323	0	812
9	Jan Stenerud	*1967-73	0	0	0	179	233	0	770
10	Mike Clark	*1963-71,73	0	0	0	133	325	0	724

RECEIVING

Most Receptions

		Years	Rec.
1	Don Maynard	1960-73	628
2	Lionel Taylor	1960-68	567
3	Lance Alworth	*1962-72	542
4	Charley Taylor	*1964-73	528
5	Art Powell	1960-68	479
6	Bobby Mitchell	1960-68	470
7	Boyd Dowler	1960-69,71	442
8	Carroll Dale	*1960-73	438
9	Jackie Smith	*1963-73	434
10	Mike Ditka	*1961-42	427

Most Yards

		Years	Yards
1	Don Maynard	1960-73	11750
2	Lance Alworth	*1962-72	10267
3	Carroll Dale	1960-73	8277
4	Art Powell	1960-68	8046
5	Bobby Mitchell	1960-68	7472
6	Charley Taylor	*1964-73	7470
7	Lionel Taylor	1960-68	7195
8	Jackie Smith	*1963-73	7188
9	Bob Hayes	*1965-73	7177
10	Paul Warfield	*1964-73	7165

Most Touchdowns

		Years	TD
1	Don Maynard	1960-73	88
2	Lance Alworth	*1962-72	85
3	Art Powell	1960-68	81
4	Paul Warfield	*1964-73	75
5	Gary Collins	*1962-71	70
	Bob Hayes	*1965-73	70
7	Charley Taylor	*1964-73	67
8	Sonny Randle	1960-68	64
9	Tommy McDonald	1960-68	62
10	Bobby Mitchell	1960-68	58

Most Yards Per Reception
(Minimum 100 Receptions)

		Years	Yds.	Rec.	Avg.
1	Warren Wells	*1964,67-70	3655	158	23.1
2	Homer Jones	*1964-70	4986	224	22.3
3	Paul Warfield	*1964-73	7165	344	20.8
4	Buddy Dial	1960-66	5008	245	20.4
5	Bob Hayes	*1965-73	7177	358	20.0
6	Bill Groman	*1960-65	3481	174	20.0
7	Jimmy Orr	1960-70	6400	332	19.3
8	John Gilliam	*1967-73	5276	274	19.3
9	Rich Caster	*1970-73	2273	119	19.1
10	Carroll Dale	1960-73	8277	438	18.9

RUSHING

Most Attempts

		Years	Att.
1	Jim Taylor	1960-67	1769
2	Leroy Kelly	*1964-73	1727
3	Bill Brown	*1961-73	1630
4	Jimmy Brown	1960-65	1610
5	Ken Willard	*1965-73	1582
6	Don Perkins	*1961-68	1500
7	Floyd Little	*1967-73	1399
8	Jim Nance	*1965-71,73	1341
9	Mike Garrett	*1966-73	1308
10	Dick Bass	*1960-69	1218

Most Yards

		Years	Yards
1	Jimmy Brown	1960-65	8514
2	Jim Taylor	1960-67	7898
3	Leroy Kelly	*1964-73	7274
4	Don Perkins	*1961-68	6217
5	Ken Willard	*1965-73	5930
6	Bill Brown	*1961-73	5797
7	Floyd Little	*1967-73	5566
8	Mike Garrett	*1966-73	5481
9	Dick Bass	*1960-69	5417
10	Jim Nance	*1965-71,73	5461

Most Touchdowns

		Years	TD
1	Jim Taylor	1960-67	76
2	Leroy Kelly	*1964-73	74
3	Jimmy Brown	1960-65	66
4	Bill Brown	*1961-73	52
5	Emerson Boozer	*1966-73	48
6	Abner Haynes	*1960-67	46
7	Tom Matte	*1961-72	45
	Jim Nance	*1965-71,73	45
	Ken Willard	*1965-73	45
10	Lenny Moore	1960-67	43

Most Yards per Attempt
(Minimum 500 Attempts)

		Years	Yds.	Att.	Avg.
1	Fran Tarkenton	*1961-73	3401	572	5.9
2	Jimmy Brown	1960-65	8514	1610	5.3
3	Gale Sayers	*1965-71	4956	1001	5.0
4	Paul Lowe	*1960-61,63-69	4995	1026	4.9
5	Marv Hubbard	*1969-73	3235	665	4.9
6	Larry Csonka	*1968-73	5151	1089	4.7
7	O.J. Simpson	*1969-73	5181	1108	4.7
8	Clem Daniels	*1960-68	5138	1146	4.5
9	Abner Haynes	*1960-67	4630	1036	4.5
10	Jim Taylor	1960-67	7898	1769	4.5

PUNT RETURNS

(Minimum 50 Returns)

		Years	Ret.	Yards	Avg.	TD
1	Claude Gibson	*1961-65	110	1381	12.6	3
2	Pat Studstill	*1961-62,64-72	59	716	12.1	0
3	Rodger Bird	*1966-68	94	1063	11.3	0
4	Bob Hayes	*1965-73	102	1147	11.2	3
5	Bill Thompson	*1969-73	111	1243	11.2	0
6	Floyd Little	*1967-73	77	859	11.2	2
7	Speedy Duncan	*1964-73	199	2182	11.0	4
8	Leroy Kelly	*1964-73	94	990	10.5	3
9	Bobby Jancik	*1962-67	67	695	10.4	1
10	Abner Haynes	*1960-67	96	970	10.1	3

KICKOFF RETURNS

(Minimum 50 Returns)

			Ret.	Yards	Avg.	TD
1	Gale Sayers	*1965-71	91	2781	30.6	6
2	Abe Woodson	1960-66	169	4917	29.1	4
3	Travis Williams	*1967-71	102	2801	27.5	6
4	Bobby Mitchell	1960-68	73	2000	27.4	4
5	Ike Thomas	*1971-73	51	1394	27.3	2
6	Rocky Thompson	*1971-73	65	1768	27.2	2
7	Gary Ballman	*1962-73	66	1754	26.6	1
8	Mercury Morris	*1969-73	111	2947	26.5	3
9	Bobby Jancik	*1962-67	158	4185	26.5	0
10	Mel Renfro	*1964-73	85	2246	26.4	2

INTERCEPTION RETURNS

(in Order by Returns)

			Int.	Yds.	Avg.	TD
1	Dick LeBeau	1960-72	62	762	12.3	3
	Paul Krause	*1964-73	62	836	13.5	3
3	Bobby Boyd	*1960-68	57	994	17.4	4
	Johnny Robinson	*1960-71	57	741	13.0	1
5	Larry Wilson	*1960-72	52	800	15.4	5
6	Dave Grayson	*1961-70	49	934	19.1	5
7	Willie Wood	*1960-71	48	699	14.6	2
	Herb Adderley	*1961-72	48	1046	21.8	7
9	Goose Gonsoulin	*1960-67	46	551	12.0	2
10	Jim Norton	*1960-68	45	592	13.2	1
	Dave Whitsell	1960-69	45	639	14.2	4
	Pat Fischer	*1961-73	45	847	18.8	4

PUNTING

(Minimum 200 Punts)

		Years	No.	Avg.
1	Tommy Davis	1960-69	452	44.57
2	Jerrel Wilson	*1963-73	725	44.53
3	Jerry Norton	1960-64	231	44.25
4	Bob Scarpitto	*1961-68	282	44.00
5	Dave Lewis	*1970-73	285	43.67
6	Jim Fraser	*1962-66,68	271	43.30
7	Don Chandler	1960-67	421	43.02
8	Bobby Walden	*1964-73	684	42.85
9	Danny Villanueva	*1960-67	488	42.75
10	Bill Van Heusen	*1968-73	405	42.73

KICKING

Most FIELD GOALS

			FG	Att.	Pct.
1	Fred Cox	*1963-73	230	370	62
2	George Blanda	1960-73	223	399	56
3	Jim Turner	*1964-73	220	356	62
4	Jim Bakken	*1962-73	212	336	63
5	Bruce Gossett	*1964-73	208	336	62
6	Lou Michaels	1960-69,71	179	324	55
	Jan Stenerud	*1967-73	179	271	66
8	Gino Cappelletti	*1960-70	172	333	52
9	Pete Gogolak	*1964-73	163	275	59
10	Mike Clark	*1963-71,73	133	232	57

Most Points After Touchdown

			PAT	Att.	Pct.
1	George Blanda	1960-73	606	613	98.9
2	Fred Cox	*1963-73	384	387	99.2
3	Lou Michaels	1960-69,71	374	388	96.4
4	Jim Bakken	*1962-73	369	375	98.4
5	Bruce Gossett	*1964-73	349	356	98.0
6	Gino Cappelletti	*1960-70	342	353	96.9
7	Sam Baker	1960-69	337	348	96.8
8	Jim Turner	*1964-73	333	337	98.8
9	Mike Clark	*1963-71,73	325	338	96.2
10	Pete Gogolak	*1964-73	323	331	97.6

* – Entire Career

1960 N.F.L. Mara's Compromise

After four days of meetings and twenty-one deadlocked ballots, the league owners had still not elected a new commissioner to succeed the late Bert Bell. With the older owners supporting acting commissioner Austin Gunsel and the young owners supporting San Francisco attorney Marshall Leahy, New York Giant vice-president Wellington Mara presented an acceptable compromise candidate. He nominated Pete Rozelle, thirty-three-year-old general manager of the Los Angeles Rams, and the other owners quickly confirmed the young man as commissioner. Like Bell, Rozelle faced the challenge of a new league, the American Football League, at the start of his administration, but the NFL was strong enough at this time also to expand, shifting the Cardinals to St. Louis, putting a new team in Dallas this year, and granting Minneapolis-St. Paul a franchise for 1961. The new league would drive player salaries up, but the NFL owners had no worries about their league surviving.

EASTERN CONFERENCE

Philadelphia Eagles—The Eagles hardly looked like champions when they lost to Cleveland on opening day and barely beat the new Dallas team 27-25 the next week. But the club slowly gained momentum and by mid-season was battling the Giants and Browns for the Eastern lead. They eliminated the Giants by beating them 17-10 and 31-23 in back-to-back games, while the Browns eliminated themselves with three mid-season losses. Quarterback Norm Van Brocklin moved the team with his passes, but reserve depth was the key to the title drive. When fullback Clarence Peaks was sidelined, rookie Ted Dean filled in splendidly, and when injuries depleted the linebacking corps, center Chuck Bednarik moved over to defense. The thirty-five-year-old Bednarik was the story of the year, playing most of the game while starring at center and middle linebacker.

Cleveland Browns—The Browns opened their year with an impressive 41-24 rout of the Eagles, but the Philadelphia club evened the score three weeks later with a 31-29 squeaker. Then, while the Eagles went on a hot streak, the Browns ran into trouble in mid-season. The Giants came to Cleveland in early November and held Jimmy Brown and Bobby Mitchell to a total of six yards rushing. The 17-13 New York victory was their sixth in a row over the Browns. After the Browns edged the Cards 28-27, a 14-10 loss to Pittsburgh and a 17-17 tie with the Cards put them too far behind the Eagles to catch up. But one element of satisfaction did come from the strong finale, a 48-34 victory over the Giants at Yankee Stadium.

New York Giants—A good early-season showing kept the Giants in the Eastern race into November, but the aging New York squad was barely holding together with paste and string. A bad knee sidelined Alex Webster for most of the year, elbow and leg troubles made Chuck Conerly's availability a week-to-week affair, and an injured shoulder put Jim Katcavage out of action for the last half of the season. The Eagles, holding a slim half-game lead, came to Yankee Stadium in mid-November and beat the New Yorkers 17-10. The biggest loss of the day, however, was halfback Frank Gifford, knocked unconscious with a concussion by Chuck Bednarik's vicious tackle. Another loss in Philadelphia made the Giants' chances slim, and a tie with the fledgling Cowboys ended their hopes completely.

St. Louis Cardinals—The team's move to St. Louis had an immediate effect, as the Cards beat the Rams 43-21 to open their new history. Long-time losers in Chicago, these new Cardinals moved up to fourth place in the East behind an improved defense and versatile offense. The defensive line, led by Frank Fuller, put strong pressure on enemy passers, while the mobile linebacking crew of Bill Koman, Dale Meinert, and Ted Bates improved with experience. In the secondary, Jerry Norton starred at safety, while rookie Larry Wilson broke into the lineup as a cornerback. John Roach was the third new starting quarterback in three years, but the main forces in the offensive resurgence were end Sonny Randle and halfback John David Crow.

Pittsburgh Steelers—After beating the new Dallas Cowboys to start the season, the Steelers won only once in their next seven games, with only a matching effort by the Redskins keeping them from dropping to the bottom of the East. Injuries plagued the Steelers along the way. Bobby Layne hurt his throwing hand, a bad leg slowed John Henry Johnson, and various physical ills bothered Jimmy Orr, Mike Sandusky, and Mike Henry. Flanker Buddy Dial stayed healthy and was the main offensive threat with his speed on long passes. The defense slacked off a bit, due partly to the retirement of All-Pro cornerback Jack Butler, but still was no pushover. Starting in late November, the Steelers drove back to respectabiltiy with a three-game win streak, crippling the Browns' title hopes 14-10, locking Washington into the basement 22-10, and ending the Eagles' nine-game win streak 27-21.

Washington Redskins—The Redskin defense sprang some major leaks in the secondary, but they were nothing compared to the leaks in the offensive line. Quarterback Ralph Guglielmi watched a flood of defensive linemen pour in on him every Sunday, forcing him either to hurry his pass or hang onto the ball and get smashed to the ground. The ends he was throwing to, Bill Anderson and Joe Walton, did not have good speed, and fullback Don Bosseler, the leading rusher, was no sprinter, so the Redskins scored 16 points or less in eight of their nine losses.

WESTERN CONFERENCE

Green Bay Packers—After a close five-team race, the Packers emerged from the fray with their first Western title since 1944. They did not back into the crown but won it by taking their last three contests, two of which included head-to-head victories over the Bears and the '49ers. The Packers again were national news, and their biggest star was halfback Paul Hornung, who grabbed headlines with his unprecedented point production. As a runner, he had a nose for the end zone; as a kicker, his toe churned out points with field goals and extra points. After twelve games Hornung had set a new season's scoring record of 176 points.

Detroit Lions—With their defense jelling into a top unit, the Lions won their last four games to capture second place in the West. Rookie tackle Roger Brown joined Alex Karras, Darris McCord, and Bill Glass in a powerful front line, while Carl Brettschneider came from the Cardinals to complete the linebacking trio with Joe Schmidt and Wayne Walker. Another ex-Card, Night Train Lane, tightened up a secondary that already featured Yale Lary, Dick LeBeau, and Gary Lowe. Newcomers also helped the offense, as ex-Cleveland quarterback Jim Ninowski and freshman end Gail Cogdill made the pass a vital weapon in the Detroit attack again.

San Francisco '49ers—In a turn-about in the club's image, the defense carried the '49ers through the season. The young secondary of Abe Woodson, Jerry Mertens, Eddie Dove, and Dave Baker had meshed into a fine unit, while veterans Matt Hazeltine and Leo Nomellini anchored the linebacking front line units. The offense, however, bucked and sputtered, relying more than usual on Tommy Davis' field goals to bail it out. Head coach Red Hickey did experiment with the shotgun formation, with both ends split, a flanker and two wingbacks up near the line of scrimmage, and a quarterback all alone in the backfield, five yards back from the center. With the mobile John Brodie beating out Y. A. Tittle for the quarterback slot, the new formation often caught enemy defenses by surprise.

Baltimore Colts—Playing with a fractured vertebra in his back, Johnny Unitas still had his Colts at the head of the West. In mid-November, Baltimore held a one-game lead over Green Bay and had just won three straight games, apparently on the way to a third straight Western title. But when a torn Achilles tendon ended fullback Alan Ameche's career in mid-season, the Colt running game withered away and died. With only Unitas' passing to Ray Berry and Lenny Moore to worry about, enemy defenses concentrated solely on rushing the fragile Unitas and blanketing his receivers.

Chicago Bears—Neither Zeke Bratkowski nor Ed Brown had impressed at quarterback, fullback Rick Casares was slowing up, and the ends had no speed, but the Bears had scrapped their way to a 5-3-1 record, a half game behind the first-place Colts, by late November. The defense, led by Bill George and Doug Atkins, had kept the Bears in the race with several strong efforts through the fall. But the visions of championships dancing in George Halas' head were just so many sugar plums. The Packers just about killed any Bear hopes with a 41-13 drubbing two weeks from the end of the year, and the last two games turned into a nightmare, with a 42-0 beating by Cleveland and a 36-0 loss to Detroit.

Los Angeles Rams—It would have made great newspaper copy for new head coach Bob Waterfield and new general manager Elroy "Crazy Legs" Hirsch, great players in the salad days of the early 1950s, to lead the Rams back to glory, but it wasn't to be. Four losses right at the start established the Rams as also-rans in the West and prompted Waterfield to shake his club up. Young Frank Ryan began sharing the quarterback job with Billy Wade, Ollie Matson was shifted to a flanker position where his main duties were blocking and receiving, and Del Shofner became a defensive back after losing his offensive end job to rookie Carroll Dale. Although the Rams did beat the Packers and Colts down the stretch, the season was a troubled one all around.

Dallas Cowboys—Former New York assistant Tom Landry came in as head coach and tried to combine young talent with a coating of experienced players. For quarterbacks, Landry traded for little Eddie LeBaron and got rookie Don Meredith in the expansion draft, but the offense they commanded was practically invisible. Of the other players, end Jim Doran and linebacker Jerry Tubbs showed the most, with the roster in general an arid stretch of mediocrity. A perfect record of losses seemed inevitable for the Cowboys until they visited New York in December and gained a 31-31 tie with the Giants.

FINAL TEAM STATISTICS

OFFENSE

	BALT.	CHI.	CLEVE.	DALL.	DET.	G.BAY	L.A.	N.Y.	PHIL.	PITT.	ST.L.	S.F.	WASH.
FIRST DOWNS:													
Total	227	183	219	180	192	**237**	194	202	190	198	229	201	166
by Rushing	64	83	107	57	89	**135**	76	81	54	81	127	90	83
by Passing	**143**	90	96	105	88	86	101	107	121	104	89	96	71
by Penalty	**20**	10	16	18	15	16	17	14	15	13	13	15	12
RUSHING:													
Number	345	373	383	312	392	463	343	406	351	411	**484**	413	415
Yards	1289	1639	1930	1049	1714	2150	1449	1440	1134	1623	**2356**	1681	1313
Average Yards	3.7	4.4	**5.0**	3.4	4.4	4.6	4.2	3.5	3.2	3.9	4.9	4.1	3.2
Touchdowns	10	11	18	6	19	**29**	9	10	9	9	13	9	9
PASSING:													
Attempts	**392**	324	264	354	333	279	335	322	331	285	285	336	274
Completions	**196**	146	160	163	166	137	177	156	177	139	126	174	147
Completion Pct.	50.0	45.1	**60.6**	46.0	49.8	49.1	52.8	48.4	53.5	48.8	44.2	51.8	53.6
Gross Yards	**3164**	2130	2343	2388	2022	1993	2188	2385	2957	2511	1990	1866	1816
Yards Lost Tackled	208	304	299	284	344	118	366	131	141	**89**	179	287	385
Net Yards	**2956**	1826	2044	2104	1678	1875	1822	2254	2816	2422	1811	1579	1431
Avg. Yds per Att (Gs)	8.1	6.6	8.9	6.7	6.1	7.1	6.5	7.4	**8.9**	8.8	7.0	5.6	6.6
Avg. Yds per Com (Gs)	16.1	14.6	14.6	14.7	12.2	14.5	12.4	15.3	16.7	**18.1**	15.8	10.7	12.4
Touchdowns	26	13	22	17	6	9	19	20	**29**	20	20	11	9
Interceptions	24	32	**5**	33	21	13	22	23	20	21	25	12	23
Percent Intercepted	6.1	9.9	**1.9**	9.3	6.3	4.7	6.6	7.1	6.0	7.4	8.8	3.6	8.4
PUNTING:													
Number	52	64	55	60	64	49	64	49	60	64	44	**65**	60
Average Distance	38.5	39.7	42.0	42.0	43.8	41.2	42.3	39.2	43.1	44.2	**44.9**	44.3	42.1
PUNT RETURNS:													
Number	23	27	21	23	**31**	26	25	**31**	28	30	30	24	15
Yards	127	182	208	175	227	172	129	209	119	183	**232**	217	65
Average Yards	5.5	6.7	**9.9**	7.6	7.3	6.6	5.2	6.7	4.3	6.1	7.7	9.0	4.3
Touchdowns	0	0	0	0	0	0	**1**	0	0	0	0	0	0
KICKOFF RETURNS:													
Number	47	47	45	**69**	43	35	40	41	52	44	45	43	62
Yards	1030	1055	900	1264	916	852	941	894	973	964	1045	1167	**1363**
Average Yards	21.9	22.4	20.0	18.3	21.3	24.3	23.5	21.8	18.7	21.9	23.2	**27.1**	22.0
Touchdowns	**1**	0	**1**	0	0	0	0	0	0	0	0	**1**	0
INTERCEPTION RETURNS:													
Number	30	10	**31**	15	19	22	23	22	30	16	21	20	15
Yards	297	111	**624**	97	365	358	362	294	341	130	178	141	189
Average Yards	9.9	11.1	**20.1**	6.5	19.2	16.3	15.7	13.4	11.4	8.1	8.5	7.1	12.6
Touchdowns	0	0	**6**	0	2	1	3	2	0	0	0	0	0
PENALTIES:													
Number	51	**83**	49	62	68	64	64	48	57	61	46	63	69
Yards	504	707	534	600	**726**	578	625	460	544	606	456	604	713
FUMBLES:													
Number	24	18	20	22	**13**	18	17	49	24	27	42	14	29
Number Lost	12	10	12	17	9	12	9	26	10	14	22	**4**	15
POINTS:													
Total	288	194	**362**	177	239	332	265	271	321	240	288	208	178
PAT Attempts	37	25	**46**	23	28	41	31	32	40	28	34	21	19
PAT Made	35	23	**44**	21	26	41	31	32	39	27	33	21	19
FG Attempts	19	16	20	13	24	28	22	26	20	19	25	**35**	23
FG Made	9	7	12	6	13	15	14	13	14	11	15	**19**	15
Percent FG Made	47.4	43.8	60.0	46.2	54.2	53.6	63.6	50.0	**70.0**	57.9	60.0	54.3	65.2
Safeties	2	0	0	0	3	0	0	1	0	0	**3**	2	0

DEFENSE

	BALT.	CHI.	CLEVE.	DALL.	DET.	G.BAY	L.A.	N.Y.	PHIL.	PITT.	ST.L.	S.F.	WASH.
FIRST DOWNS:													
Total	195	202	208	216	204	199	221	183	205	224	**158**	180	223
by Rushing	86	94	92	106	87	74	87	79	117	90	**56**	82	77
by Passing	98	84	102	97	94	110	114	89	**81**	120	93	89	126
by Penalty	11	24	14	13	23	15	20	15	**7**	14	9	9	20
RUSHING:													
Number	379	403	405	447	360	350	419	396	449	414	**344**	363	362
Yards	1591	1679	1643	2242	1348	1285	1718	1267	2200	1493	**1212**	1587	1502
Average Yards	4.2	4.2	4.1	5.0	3.7	3.7	4.1	**3.2**	4.9	3.6	3.5	4.4	4.1
Touchdowns	17	17	10	20	9	**7**	16	8	14	13	8	13	9
PASSING:													
Attempts	298	291	319	293	354	365	339	297	**283**	361	300	293	321
Completions	144	246	163	146	175	192	168	142	**139**	184	156	140	169
Completion Pct.	48.3	50.2	51.1	49.8	49.4	52.6	49.6	47.8	49.1	51.0	52.0	**47.8**	52.6
Gross Yards	2068	**1808**	2370	2305	2275	2432	2510	2010	1984	3075	2147	2001	2768
Yards Lost Tackled	342	**420**	207	175	226	275	155	177	157	284	330	183	204
Net Yards	1726	**1388**	2163	2130	2049	2157	2355	1833	1827	2791	1817	1818	2564
Avg. Yds per Att (Gs)	6.9	**6.2**	7.4	7.9	6.4	6.7	7.4	6.8	7.0	8.5	7.2	6.8	8.6
Avg. Yds per Com (Gs)	14.4	**12.4**	14.5	15.8	13.0	12.7	14.9	14.2	14.3	16.7	13.8	14.3	16.4
Touchdowns	**8**	14	15	22	17	19	18	19	14	20	20	11	24
Interceptions	30	10	**31**	15	19	22	23	22	30	16	21	20	15
Percent Intercepted	10.1	3.4	9.7	5.1	5.4	6.0	6.8	7.4	**10.6**	4.4	7.0	6.8	4.7
PUNTING:													
Number	54	**72**	46	50	69	66	50	66	48	54	63	62	50
Average Distance	46.4	41.3	45.5	42.1	**39.0**	39.4	43.8	40.8	43.6	43.4	44.3	41.2	39.5
PUNT RETURNS:													
Number	**15**	35	24	20	34	22	27	17	34	21	26	28	31
Yards	**48**	249	168	91	296	144	199	100	166	198	162	182	242
Average Yards	**3.2**	7.1	7.0	4.6	8.7	6.5	7.4	5.9	4.9	9.4	6.2	6.5	7.8
Touchdowns	**0**	1	**0**	**0**	**0**	**0**	**0**	**0**	**0**	**0**	**0**	**0**	**0**
KICKOFF RETURNS:													
Number	44	37	62	**31**	45	57	52	47	53	48	57	38	42
Yards	1253	1029	1177	803	979	1158	1083	995	1076	1078	1245	769	**719**
Average Yards	28.5	27.8	19.0	25.9	21.8	20.3	20.8	21.2	20.3	22.5	21.8	20.2	**17.1**
Touchdowns	1	1	**0**	1	**0**	**0**	**0**	**0**	**0**	**0**	**0**	**0**	**0**
INTERCEPTION RETURNS:													
Number	24	32	**5**	33	21	13	22	23	20	21	25	12	23
Yards	272	627	**58**	366	314	185	182	253	277	165	419	159	210
Average Yards	11.3	19.6	11.6	11.1	15.0	14.2	8.3	11.0	13.9	**7.9**	16.8	13.3	9.1
Touchdowns	1	4	1	2	2	**0**	**0**	2	1	**0**	**0**	**0**	1
PENALTIES:													
Number	59	**75**	48	72	60	61	59	55	54	58	52	64	68
Yards	538	**704**	526	671	637	636	517	532	597	565	500	580	654
FUMBLES:													
Number	20	13	27	21	19	23	29	28	31	25	**35**	15	31
Number Lost	9	9	14	11	11	15	13	12	15	13	**23**	8	19
POINTS:													
Total	234	299	217	369	212	209	297	261	246	275	230	**205**	309
PAT Attempts	27	38	26	45	28	**25**	35	32	27	33	30	**25**	34
PAT Made	27	37	25	44	27	24	34	31	24	33	29	**23**	34
FG Attempts	30	20	21	25	**12**	13	29	23	28	21	16	20	32
FG Made	15	8	12	17	**5**	9	17	12	16	14	7	10	21
Percent FG Made	50.0	**40.0**	57.1	68.0	41.7	69.2	58.6	52.2	57.1	66.7	43.8	50.0	65.6
Safeties	**0**	2	**0**	2	1	1	1	1	**0**	1	**0**	1	1

1960 NFL CHAMPIONSHIP GAME

December 26, at Philadelphia
(Attendance 67,325)

Start with Hornung, End with Dean

The Green Bay Packers, a tough, young team built by coach Vince Lombardi, came to Franklin Field to face the Eagles, a veteran team centering around Norm Van Brocklin and Chuck Bednarik, for the NFL title. The Packers got the first break of the game by recovering an Eagle fumble on the Philadelphia 14-yard line on the first play from scrimmage, but four Green Bay running plays gained only nine yards. The Eagles took the ball on downs but fumbled it away three plays later on the 22-yard line. Again the Packers couldn't move the ball, and they had to settle for a Paul Hornung field goal. The quarter ended with the score 3-0, as both defenses played well against the enemy's strength. The Eagles shut off the Green Bay running game; the Packers stopped Van Brocklin's passes. The halftime score was Philadelphia 10, Green Bay 6, and neither team scored in the third quarter. Within two minutes of the fourth period, however, Green Bay capped an 80-yard drive with a Bart Starr-to-Max McGee touchdown pass to give the Packers a 13-10 lead. On the kickoff following the touchdown, Ted Dean brought the Eagles back into the game by returning the ball to the Green Bay 39. Seven plays later, Dean carried the ball over from the 5-yard line. The Packers drove downfield in the waning minutes, but time ran out with the ball on the Philadelphia 9-yard line and the score 17-13 in favor of the Eagles.

SCORING

PHILADELPHIA	0	10	0	7	–17
GREEN BAY	3	3	0	7	–13

First Quarter

G. B.	Hornung, 20 yard field goal	6:20

Second Quarter

G. B.	Hornung, 23 yard field goal	1:44
PHI.	McDonald, 35 yard pass from Van Brocklin PAT – Walston (kick)	8:08
PHI.	Walston, 15 yard field goal	11:48

Fourth Quarter

G.B.	McGee, 7 yard pass from Starr PAT – Hornung (kick)	1:53
PHI.	Dean, 5 yard rush PAT – Walston (kick)	5:21

TEAM STATISTICS

PHI.		G.B.
13	First Downs – Total	22
5	First Downs – Rushing	14
6	First Downs – Passing	8
2	First Downs – Penalty	0
99	Rushing Yardage	223
20	Pass Attempts	35
9	Pass Completions	21
45.0	Completion Percentage	60.0
204	Passing Yardage	178
10.2	Avg. Yards per Attempt	5.1
22.7	Avg. Yards per Completion	8.5
7	Yards Lost Tackled	0
197	Net Passing Yardage	178
0	Interceptions By	1
0	Interception Return Yardage	0
3	Fumbles – Number	1
2	Fumbles – Lost Ball	1
0	Penalties – Number	4
0	Yards Penalized	27
0	Missed Field Goals	1

INDIVIDUAL STATISTICS

PHILADELPHIA	No.	Yds.	Avg.	GREEN BAY	No.	Yds.	Avg.
PUNTING							
Van Brocklin	6		39.5	McGee	5		45.2
PUNT RETURNS							
Dean	1	10	10.0	Wood	2	11	5.5
				Carpenter	2	7	3.5
					4	18	4.5
KICKOFF RETURNS							
Dean	1	58	58.0	Symank	2	49	24.5
Brown	1	20	20.0				
Lucas	1	9	9.0				
Robb	1	4	4.0				
	4	91	22.8				

1960 N.F.L. — Eastern Conference

PHILADELPHIA EAGLES 10-2-0 Buck Shaw

Scores of Each Game		
24	CLEVELAND	41
27	Dallas	25
31	ST. LOUIS	27
28	DETROIT	10
31	Cleveland	29
34	PITTSBURGH	7
19	WASHINGTON	13
17	New York	10
31	NEW YORK	23
20	St. Louis	6
21	Pittsburgh	27
38	Washington	28

Use Name	Pos.	Hgt	Wgt	Age	Int	Pts
Jim McCusker	OT	6'2"	245	24		
J. D. Smith	OT	6'5"	250	24		6
Howard Keys	C-OT	6'3"	235	25		
John Wilcox	DE-OT	6'5"	230	22		
Stan Campbell	OG	6'	230	30		
Jerry Huth	OG	6'	228	27		
John Wittenborn (from SF)	OG	6'2"	230	24		
Bill Lapham	C	6'3"	250	26		
Marion Campbell	DE	6'3"	250	31		
Joe Robb	LB-DE	6'3"	225	23		
Gene Gossage	DT-DE	6'3"	236	25		
Riley Gunnels	DT	6'3"	240	23		
Jess Richardson	DT	6'2"	262	30		
Ed Khayat	DE-DT	6'3"	240	25		
Maxie Baughan	LB	6'1"	220	22	3	
John Nocera	LB	6'1"	215	26		
Chuck Weber	LB	6'1"	235	31	6	
Bob Pellegrini	OG-LB	6'2"	235	25		
Chuck Bednarik	C-LB	6'3"	235	35	2	
Tom Brookshier	DB	6'	198	28	1	
Don Burroughs	DB	6'4"	186	29	9	
Jimmy Carr	DB	6'1"	198	27	2	6
Bobby Freeman	DB	6'1"	200	27	4	
Bobby Jackson	DB	6'1"	190	24		
Gene Johnson	DB	6'	190	25	3	
Sonny Jurgensen	QB	5'11"	200	26		
Norm Van Brocklin	QB	6'1"	202	34		
Jerry Reichow	OE-QB	6'2"	220	25		
Billy Barnes	HB	5'11"	198	25		36
Timmy Brown	HB	5'10"	195	23		24
Theron Sapp	HB	6'1"	200	25		
Ted Dean	FB-HB	6'2"	210	22		18
Clarence Peaks	FB	6'1"	220	24		18
Tommy McDonald	FL	5'10"	182	26		78
Dick Lucas	OE	6'2"	210	26		
Pete Retzlaff	OE	6'1"	210	29		30
Bobby Walston	FL-OE	6'	190	31		105

CLEVELAND BROWNS 8-3-1 Paul Brown

Scores of Each Game		
41	Philadelphia	24
28	PITTSBURGH	20
48	Dallas	7
29	PHILADELPHIA	31
31	Washington	10
13	NEW YORK	17
28	ST. LOUIS	27
10	Pittsburgh	14
17	St. Louis	17
27	WASHINGTON	16
42	CHICAGO	0
48	New York	34

Use Name	Pos.	Hgt	Wgt	Age	Int	Pts
Bob Denton	OT	6'4"	240	26		
Mike McCormack	OT	6'4"	247	33		
Dick Schafrath	OT	6'3"	245	24		
Gene Selawski	OT	6'4"	252	24		
Gene Hickerson	OG	6'3"	248	25		
Jim Ray Smith	OG	6'3"	245	29		
John Wooten	OG	6'2"	248	25		
John Morrow	C	6'3"	240	27		
Jim Houston	DE	6'2"	230	23		
Jim Marshall	DE	6'3"	220	23		
Paul Wiggin	DE	6'3"	240	26	1	6
Bob Gain	DT	6'3"	260	32	1	6
Floyd Peters	DT	6'4"	250	25		
Jim Prestel	DT	6'5"	250	23		
Larry Stephens	DT	6'4"	248	22	1	6
Vince Costello	LB	6'	225	28		
Galen Fiss	LB	6'	227	30	1	
Walt Michaels	LB	6'	237	31		
Dave Lloyd	C-LB	6'3"	248	24		
Ross Fichtner	DB	6'	185	22		
Don Fleming	DB	6'	185	23	5	
Bobby Franklin	DB	5'11"	180	24	8	12
Rich Mostardi	DB	5'11"	188	22		
Bernie Parrish	DB	5'11"	195	25	6	6
Jim Shofner	DB	6'2"	190	24	8	
Lou Groza — Voluntarily Retired						
Len Dawson	QB	6'	195	26		
Milt Plum	QB	6'1"	205	26		12
Prentice Gautt	HB	6'	195	22		6
Bobby Mitchell	HB	6'	188	25		72
Jamie Caleb	FB-HB	6'1"	210	23		6
Jimmy Brown	FB	6'2"	228	24		66
Ray Renfro	FL	6'1"	192	29		24
A. D. Williams	OE-FL	6'2"	210	27		
Leon Clarke	OE	6'4"	234	27		24
Rich Kreitling	OE	6'2"	208	25		18
Fred Murphy	OE	6'3"	205	22		
Gern Nagler	OE	6'2"	190	27		18
Sam Baker	K	6'2"	217	28		80

NEW YORK GIANTS 6-4-2 Jim Lee Howell

Scores of Each Game		
21	San Francisco	19
35	St. Louis	14
19	Pittsburgh	17
24	WASHINGTON	24
13	ST. LOUIS	20
17	Cleveland	13
27	PITTSBURGH	24
10	PHILADELPHIA	17
23	Philadelphia	31
31	DALLAS	31
17	Washington	3
34	CLEVELAND	48

Use Name	Pos.	Hgt	Wgt	Age	Int	Pts
Don Boll	OT	6'2"	270	33		
Rosey Brown	OT	6'3"	245	27		
Frank Youso	OT	6'4"	260	24		
Lou Cordileone	OG	6'	240	23		
Bill Crawford	OG	6'1"	235	23		
Darrell Dess	OG	6'	235	24		
Jack Stroud	OG	6'1"	235	31		
Ray Wietecha	C	6'1"	225	31		
Bob Schmidt	OT-OG-C	6'4"	245	24		
Jim Katcavage	DE	6'3"	230	25		
Andy Robustelli	DE	6'1"	230	34		
Tom Scott	LB-DE	6'2"	220	30	1	6
Rosey Grier	DT	6'5"	285	27		2
Proverb Jacobs	DT	6'4"	255	25		
Dick Modzelewski	DT	6'	260	29		
Sam Huff	LB	6'1"	230	25	3	
Jim Leo	LB	6'1"	215	22		
Cliff Livingston	LB	6'3"	215	30	1	
Harland Svare	LB	6'	215	29	1	
Lindon Crow	DB	6'1"	205	27	3	6
Dick Lynch	DB	6'1"	200	24	3	6
Dick Nolan	DB	6'1"	185	28	3	
Jimmy Patton	DB	6'	180	28	6	
Lee Riley	DB	6'1"	190	28	1	
Bill Stits	DB	6'	195	29		
Chuck Conerly	QB	6'1"	185	36		
Lee Grosscup	QB	6'1"	185	23		
George Shaw	QB	6'1"	180	27		
Don Chandler	HB	6'2"	205	25		
Frank Gifford	HB	6'1"	200	30		42
Joe Morrison	HB	6'1"	195	22		30
Ed Sutton	HB	6'1"	207	25		
Alex Webster	HB	6'3"	220	29		
Mel Triplett	FB	6'1"	215	28		36
Phil King	HB-FB	6'4"	225	24		
Bill Kimber	OE	6'2"	190	24		
Kyle Rote	OE	6'	200	31		60
Bob Schnelker	OE	6'3"	215	30		12
Pat Summerall	OE	6'4"	235	30		71
Bob Simms	DE-LB-OE	6'1"	210	22		

ST. LOUIS CARDINALS 6-5-1 Pop Ivy

Scores of Each Game		
43	Los Angeles	21
14	NEW YORK	35
27	Philadelphia	31
14	Pittsburgh	27
12	DALLAS	10
20	New York	13
44	WASHINGTON	7
27	Cleveland	28
26	Washington	14
17	CLEVELAND	17
6	PHILADELPHIA	20
38	PITTSBURGH	7

Use Name	Pos.	Hgt	Wgt	Age	Int	Pts
Ed Cook	OT	6'2"	245	28		
Dale Memmelaar	OT	6'2"	265	23		
Ken Panfil	OT	6'6"	265	29		
Tom Day	OG-OT	6'2"	240	25		
Ken Gray	OG	6'2"	245	24		
Mike McGee	OG	6'1"	230	22		
Mike Rabold	OG	6'2"	235	23		
Don Gillis	C	6'3"	250	25		
Ernie Fritsch	LB-C	6'	230	23		
Luke Owens	DE	6'2"	255	27		2
Jerry Perry	DE	6'4"	240	29		44
Leo Sugar	DE	6'1"	220	31		
Ed Culpepper	DT	6'1"	255	26		
Frank Fuller	DT	6'4"	245	31		2
Don Owens (from PHI)	DT	6'5"	255	28		
Tom Redmond	DT	6'5"	250	23		
Ted Bates	LB	6'3"	220	23		
Bill Koman	LB	6'2"	230	26	1	
Dale Meinert	LB	6'2"	218	27	3	
John Tracey	LB	6'3"	228	26	1	2
Charley Ellzey	C-LB	6'3"	245	22		
Joe Driskill	DB	6'1"	195	23		
Freddy Glick	DB	6'1"	185	23		
Jimmy Hill	DB	6'2"	190	31		
Billy Stacy	DB	6'1"	195	24	4	6
Larry Wilson	DB	6'	187	22	2	
Jerry Norton	DB	5'11"	195	30	10	
Bobby Towns	HB-OE-DB	6'1"	180	22		
King Hill	QB	6'3"	207	24		6
George Izo	QB	6'3"	230	23		
John Roach	QB	6'4"	195	27		6
Joe Childress	HB	6'	200	26		12
Bobby Joe Conrad	HB	6'	195	25		34
John David Crow	HB	6'2"	215	25		54
Willie West	HB	5'10"	185	22		
Mal Hammack	FB	6'2"	205	27		12
Frank Mestnik	FB	6'2"	200	22		18
Hugh McInnis	OE	6'3"	215	22		
Sonny Randle	OE	6'2"	187	24		90
Perry Richards	OE	6'2"	205	26		

PITTSBURGH STEELERS 5-6-1 Buddy Parker

Scores of Each Game		
35	Dallas	28
20	Cleveland	28
17	NEW YORK	19
27	ST. LOUIS	14
27	Washington	27
13	GREEN BAY	19
7	Philadelphia	34
24	New York	27
14	CLEVELAND	10
22	WASHINGTON	10
27	PHILADELPHIA	21
7	St. Louis	38

Use Name	Pos.	Hgt	Wgt	Age	Int	Pts
Byron Beams	OT	6'6"	248	26		
John Kapele	OT	6'	240	23		
Frank Varrichione	OT	6'1"	230	28		
Dan James	C-OT	6'4"	275	23		
John Nisby	OG	6'1"	230	27		
Mike Sandusky	OG	6'	230	27		
Ron Stehouwer	OT-OG	6'2"	240	23		
Ed Beatty	C	6'3"	225	28		
Billy Ray Smith	DE	6'4"	230	25		
George Tarasovic	DE	6'4"	245	31	1	
Ernie Stautner	DT-DE	6'1"	230	35		
Joe Krupa	DT	6'2"	225	27		
Joe Lewis	DT	6'2"	260	25		6
Ken Longenecker	DT	6'4"	285	22		
Will Renfro	DE-DT	6'5"	220	28		
Dick Campbell	LB	6'1"	225	24	1	
Rudy Hayes	LB	6'	215	25		
Mike Henry	LB	6'2"	215	24		
John Reger	LB	6'	230	29	1	
Dean Derby	DB	6'	185	26	3	
Dick Moegle	DB	6'	195	26	6	
Jack Morris (from LA)	DB	6'	190	28		
Bert Rechichar	DB	6'1"	210	30	1	15
Scooter Scudero	DB	5'10"	174	30		
Don Sutherin	DB	5'10"	190	24	1	
Fred Williamson	DB	6'2"	205	22		
Junior Wren	DB	6'	205	30	2	
Ron Hall — Military Service						
Rudy Bukich	QB	6'1"	200	29		
Bobby Layne	QB	6'1"	210	33		48
Rex Johnston	HB	6'1"	195	22		
Tom Tracy	FB-HB	5'9"	205	28		63
Tom Barnett	DB-HB	5'11"	190	23		
John Henry Johnson	FB	6'2"	215	30		18
Larry Krutko	FB	6'	225	25		
Charlie Scales	FB	5'11"	210	21		
Buddy Dial	FL	6'1"	195	23		54
Darrell Brewster	OE	6'3"	210	30		
Jack McClairen	OE	6'4"	215	29		
Preston Carpenter	HB-OE	6'2"	205	26		12
Jimmy Orr	FL-OE	5'11"	200	24		24
Bobby Joe Green	K	5'11"	175	22		

WASHINGTON REDSKINS 1-9-2 Mike Nixon

Scores of Each Game		
0	Baltimore	20
26	DALLAS	14
24	New York	24
27	PITTSBURGH	27
10	CLEVELAND	31
7	St. Louis	44
13	Philadelphia	19
14	ST. LOUIS	26
10	Pittsburgh	22
16	Cleveland	27
3	NEW YORK	17
28	PHILADELPHIA	38

Use Name	Pos.	Hgt	Wgt	Age	Int	Pts
Ray Lemek	OT	6'	240	26		
Don Lawrence	DT-OT	6'1"	245	23		
Don Stallings	DE-DT-OT	6'4"	250	21		
Fran O'Brien	OG	6'1"	240	25		
Vince Promuto	OG	6'1"	240	22		
Red Stephens	OG	6'	232	30		
Bob Whitlow	OG	6'1"	232	24		
Jim Schrader	C	6'2"	252	28		
Bob Khayat	OG-C	6'2"	230	22		64
John Paluck	DE	6'2"	235	27		
Art Gob (to LA-A)	DE	6'4"	230	23		
Andy Stynchula	C-DE	6'3"	255	21		
Ray Krouse	DT	6'3"	270	33		
Bob Toneff	DT	6'3"	265	30		
Rod Breedlove	LB	6'2"	220	22	3	
Ralph Felton	LB	5'11"	210	28		
Dick Lasse	LB	6'2"	225	24	3	
Bill Roehnelt	LB	6'1"	230	24		
Roy Wilkins	LB	6'3"	223	26		
Billy Brewer	DB	6'	190	25		
Jim Crotty	DB	5'11"	195	22	1	
Ben Scotti	DB	6'1"	185	23	4	
Jim Wulff	DB	5'11"	185	24		
Gary Glick	HB-DB	6'2"	200	29	3	6
Pat Heenan	OE-DB	6'1"	190	22	1	
Eagle Day	QB	6'	185	28		
Ralph Guglielmi	QB	6'1"	195	27		
M. C. Reynolds	QB	6'	195	25		
Dick Haley	HB	5'10"	195	23		
Ed Vereb	HB	6'	190	26		
Sam Horner	DB-HB	6'	195	22		
Dick James	DB-HB	5'9"	180	26		36
Jim Podoley	OE-HB	6'2"	205	27		6
Don Bosseler	FB	6'1"	212	24		12
Johnny Olszewski	FB	5'11"	202	29		18
Bill Anderson	OE	6'3"	210	24		18
Tom Osborne	OE	6'3"	190	23		
Joe Walton	OE	5'11"	205	25		18

PHILADELPHIA EAGLES

RUSHING

Last Name	No.	Yds	Avg	TD
Peaks	86	465	5.4	3
Barnes	117	315	2.7	4
Dean	113	304	2.7	0
Brown	9	35	3.2	2
Sapp	9	20	2.2	0
Jurgensen	4	5	1.3	0
Retzlaff	2	3	1.5	0
Van Brocklin	11	−13	−1.2	0

RECEIVING

Last Name	No.	Yds	Avg	TD
Retzlaff	46	826	18	5
McDonald	39	801	21	13
Walston	30	563	19	4
Barnes	19	132	7	2
Dean	15	218	15	3
Peaks	14	116	8	0
Brown	9	247	27	2
Lucas	3	34	11	0
Sapp	2	20	10	0

PUNT RETURNS

Last Name	No.	Yds	Avg	TD
Dean	16	65	4	0
Brown	10	47	5	0
Jackson	1	5	5	0
McDonald	1	2	2	0

KICKOFF RETURNS

Last Name	No.	Yds	Avg	TD
Dean	26	533	21	0
Brown	11	295	27	0
McDonald	2	45	23	0
Robb	4	44	11	0
Reichow	4	28	7	0
Baughan	2	18	9	0
Carr	1	5	5	0
Lucas	1	5	5	0

PASSING – PUNTING – KICKING Statistics

PASSING	Att	Comp	%	Yds	Yd/Att	TD	Int–%	RK
Van Brocklin	284	153	54	2471	8.7	24	17– 6	2
Jurgensen	44	24	55	486	11.0	5	1– 2	
Barnes	3	0	0	0	0.0	0	2– 67	

PUNTING	No	Avg
Van Brocklin	60	43.1

KICKING	XP	Att	%	FG	Att	%
Walston	39	40	98	14	20	70
Wittenborn	0	0	0	0	3	0

CLEVELAND BROWNS

RUSHING

Last Name	No.	Yds	Avg	TD
Brown	215	1257	5.8	9
Mitchell	111	506	4.6	5
Gautt	28	159	5.7	1
Caleb	8	60	7.5	1
Dawson	1	0	0.0	0
Baker	1	−11	−11.0	0
Kreitling	2	−17	−8.5	0
Plum	17	−24	−1.4	2

RECEIVING

Last Name	No.	Yds	Avg	TD
Mitchell	45	612	14	6
Nagler	36	616	17	3
Renfro	24	378	16	4
Brown	19	204	11	2
Kreitling	16	316	20	3
Clarke	11	184	17	4
Caleb	5	−18	−4	0
Murphy	2	36	18	0
Gautt	1	10	10	0
Williams	1	5	5	0

PUNT RETURNS

Last Name	No.	Yds	Avg	TD
Shofner	11	105	10	0
Mitchell	9	101	11	0
Franklin	1	2	2	0

KICKOFF RETURNS

Last Name	No.	Yds	Avg	TD
Mitchell	17	432	25	1
Brown	14	300	21	0
Caleb	5	90	18	0
Gautt	3	47	16	0
Franklin	1	23	23	0
Fleming	1	8	8	0
Parrish	2	0	0	0
Fichtner	1	0	0	0
Stephens	1	0	0	0

PASSING – PUNTING – KICKING Statistics

PASSING	Att	Comp	%	Yds	Yd/Att	TD	Int–%	RK
Plum	250	151	60	2297	9.2	21	5– 2	1
Dawson	13	8	62	23	1.8	0	0– 0	
Mitchell	1	1	100	23	23.0	1	0– 0	

PUNTING	No	Avg
Baker	55	42.0

KICKING	XP	Att	%	FG	Att	%
Baker	44	46	96	12	20	60

NEW YORK GIANTS

RUSHING

Last Name	No.	Yds	Avg	TD
Triplett	124	573	4.6	4
Morrison	103	346	3.4	2
Gifford	77	232	3.0	4
Sutton	20	135	6.8	0
King	26	97	3.7	0
Webster	22	48	2.2	0
Chandler	2	19	9.5	0
Conerly	14	1	0.1	0
Grosscup	3	1	0.3	0
Shaw	15	−12	−0.8	0

RECEIVING

Last Name	No.	Yds	Avg	TD
Rote	42	750	18	10
Schnelker	38	610	16	2
Morrison	29	367	13	3
Gifford	24	344	14	3
Webster	8	106	13	0
Triplett	5	48	10	2
King	3	6	2	0
Kimber	2	48	24	0
Sutton	2	30	15	0
Simms	1	58	58	0
Summerall	1	15	15	0
Dess	1	3	3	0

PUNT RETURNS

Last Name	No.	Yds	Avg	TD
Stits	18	166	9	0
Riley	10	42	4	0
Crow	2	1	1	0
Patton	1	0	0	0

KICKOFF RETURNS

Last Name	No.	Yds	Avg	TD
Stits	20	486	24	0
Sutton	12	223	19	0
King	2	73	37	0
Riley	3	67	22	0
Triplett	2	38	19	0
Youso	1	7	7	0
Brown	1	0	0	0

PASSING – PUNTING – KICKING Statistics

PASSING	Att	Comp	%	Yds	Yd/Att	TD	Int–%	RK
Shaw	155	76	49	1263	8.1	11	13– 8	9
Conerly	134	66	49	954	7.1	8	7– 5	7
Grosscup	25	11	44	144	5.8	1	1– 4	
Gifford	6	3	50	24	4.0	0	1– 17	
Morrison	1	0	0	0	0.0	0	1–100	
Summerall	1	0	0	0	0.0	0	0– 0	

PUNTING	No	Avg
Chandler	31	40.5
Conerly	18	36.9

KICKING	XP	Att	%	FG	Att	%
Summerall	32	32	100	13	26	50

ST. LOUIS CARDINALS

RUSHING

Last Name	No.	Yds	Avg	TD
Crow	183	1071	5.9	6
Mestnick	104	429	4.1	3
Hammack	96	347	3.6	2
Childress	34	240	7.5	0
Conrad	23	91	4.0	0
Hill	16	47	2.9	1
Norton	2	47	23.5	0
West	7	45	6.4	0
Roach	19	39	2.1	1

RECEIVING

Last Name	No.	Yds	Avg	TD
Randle	62	893	14	15
Crow	25	462	18	3
McInnis	13	260	20	0
Childress	11	202	18	2
Conrad	7	103	15	0
Hammack	4	36	9	0
Mestnick	3	24	8	0
Richards	1	10	10	0

PUNT RETURNS

Last Name	No.	Yds	Avg	TD
Conrad	8	86	11	0
Stacy	14	62	4	0
West	5	58	12	0
Wilson	3	26	9	0

KICKOFF RETURNS

Last Name	No.	Yds	Avg	TD
West	13	370	28	0
Conrad	12	338	28	0
Stacy	6	146	24	0
Wilson	6	115	19	0
Mestnick	3	39	13	0
Hammack	2	23	12	0
Memmelaar	1	8	8	0
Bates	1	6	6	0
Driskill	1	0	0	0

PASSING – PUNTING – KICKING Statistics

PASSING	Att	Comp	%	Yds	Yd/Att	TD	Int–%	RK
Roach	188	87	46	1423	7.6	17	19– 10	13
K. Hill	55	20	36	205	3.7	1	5– 9	
Izo	24	10	42	115	4.8	0	0– 0	
Crow	18	9	50	247	13.7	2	1– 6	

PUNTING	No	Avg
Norton	39	45.6
Hill	5	39.6

KICKING	XP	Att	%	FG	Att	%
Conrad	28	29	97	2	5	40
Perry	5	5	100	13	20	65

PITTSBURGH STEELERS

RUSHING

Last Name	No.	Yds	Avg	TD
Tracy	192	680	3.5	5
Johnson	118	621	5.3	2
Krutko	17	99	5.8	0
Scales	26	81	3.1	0
Orr	8	57	7.1	0
Carpenter	17	36	2.1	0
Barnett	6	25	4.2	0
Layne	19	12	0.6	2
Johnston	4	12	3.0	0
Dial	1	8	8.0	0
Bukich	3	−8	−2.7	0

RECEIVING

Last Name	No.	Yds	Avg	TD
Dial	40	972	24	9
Orr	29	541	19	4
Carpenter	29	495	17	2
Tracy	24	349	15	4
Johnson	12	112	9	1
Brewster	2	26	13	0
McClairen	1	17	17	0
Krutko	1	8	8	0
Scales	1	−2	−2	0
Varrichione	0	−7	0	0

PUNT RETURNS

Last Name	No.	Yds	Avg	TD
Carpenter	13	120	9	0
Johnston	12	45	4	0
Moegle	3	15	5	0
Scudero	2	3	2	0

KICKOFF RETURNS

Last Name	No.	Yds	Avg	TD
Johnston	18	393	22	0
Carpenter	10	255	26	0
Moegle	7	174	25	0
Scales	5	100	20	0
Tracy	1	30	30	0
Hayes	1	11	11	0
McClairen	1	1	1	0
Varrichione	1	0	0	0

PASSING – PUNTING – KICKING Statistics

PASSING	Att	Comp	%	Yds	Yd/Att	TD	Int–%	RK
Layne	209	103	49	1814	8.7	13	17– 8	6
Bukich	51	25	49	358	7.0	2	3– 6	
Tracy	22	9	41	322	14.6	4	1– 5	
Carpenter	2	1	50	2	1.0	0	0– 0	
Johnson	1	1	100	15	15.0	1	0– 0	

PUNTING	No	Avg
Green	64	44.2

KICKING	XP	Att	%	FG	Att	%
Layne	21	22	95	5	6	83
Rechichar	6	6	100	3	7	43
Tracy	0	0	0	3	6	50

WASHINGTON REDSKINS

RUSHING

Last Name	No.	Yds	Avg	TD
Bosseler	109	428	3.9	2
Guglielmi	79	247	3.1	0
Olszewski	75	227	3.0	3
James	73	199	2.7	4
Horner	22	80	3.6	0
Podoley	29	52	1.8	0
Vereb	19	38	2.0	0
Reynolds	4	20	5.0	0
Glick	1	15	15.0	0
Anderson	1	6	6.0	0
Day	3	1	0.3	0

RECEIVING

Last Name	No.	Yds	Avg	TD
Anderson	38	488	13	3
Walton	27	401	15	3
Podoley	17	244	14	1
James	16	243	15	2
Bosseler	13	86	7	0
Olszewski	10	62	6	0
Vereb	9	119	13	0
Horner	7	106	15	0
Osborne	7	46	7	0
Haley	3	21	7	0

PUNT RETURNS

Last Name	No.	Yds	Avg	TD
James	7	46	7	0
Horner	3	16	5	0
Podoley	3	3	1	0
Olszewski	1	0	0	0
Vereb	1	0	0	0

KICKOFF RETURNS

Last Name	No.	Yds	Avg	TD
Horner	24	511	21	0
James	19	458	24	0
Olszewski	5	119	24	0
Vereb	5	119	24	0
Podoley	4	87	22	0
Wilkins	2	24	12	0
Stallings	1	19	19	0
O'Brien	1	16	16	0
Lawrence	1	10	10	0

PASSING – PUNTING – KICKING Statistics

PASSING	Att	Comp	%	Yds	Yd/Att	TD	Int–%	RK
Guglielmi	223	125	56	1547	6.9	9	19– 9	9
Reynolds	30	13	44	154	5.1	0	3– 10	
Day	19	9	47	115	6.1	0	1– 5	
James	1	0	0	0	0.0	0	0– 0	
Vereb	1	0	0	0	0.0	0	0– 0	

PUNTING	No	Avg
Day	59	42.0
Horner	1	48.0

KICKING	XP	Att	%	FG	Att	%
Khayat	19	19	100	15	23	65

GREEN BAY PACKERS 8-4-0 Vince Lombardi

Scores of Each Game		
14	CHICAGO	17
28	DETROIT	9
35	BALTIMORE	21
41	SAN FRANCISCO	14
19	Pittsburgh	13
24	Baltimore	38
41	DALLAS	7
31	LOS ANGELES	33
10	Detroit	23
41	Chicago	13
13	San Francisco	0
35	Los Angeles	21

Use Name	Pos.	Hgt	Wgt	Age	Int	Pts
Forrest Gregg	OT	6'4"	250	27		
Norm Masters	OT	6'2"	250	27		
Bob Skoronski	OT	6'3"	250	27		
Andy Cvercko	OG	6'	240	23		
Jerry Kramer	OG	6'3"	250	25		
Fuzzy Thurston	OG	6'1"	250	27		
Ken Iman	C	6'1"	230	21		
Jim Ringo	C	6'1"	235	29		
Willie Davis	DE	6'3"	240	27		6
Bill Quinlan	DE	6'3"	250	28		
Jim Temp	DE	6'4"	250	27		
Dave Hanner	DT	6'2"	260	31		
Henry Jordan	DT	6'3"	250	25		
Ken Beck	DE-DT	6'2"	250	25		
Johnny Miller	DE-DT	6'5"	260	26		
Tom Bettis	LB	6'2"	225	27		
Dan Currie	LB	6'3"	240	26	4	
Bill Forester	LB	6'3"	240	29	2	
Ray Nitschke	LB	6'3"	235	24	3	6
Hank Gremminger	DB	6'1"	205	27	3	
Dale Hackbart	DB	6'3"	200	24		
Dick Pesonen	DB	6'	190	22		
Johnny Symank	DB	5'11"	180	25	1	
Em Tunnell	DB	6'1"	210	38	3	
Jesse Whittenton	DB	6'	195	26	6	
Willie Wood	DB	5'10"	185	24		
Lamar McHan	QB	6'1"	210	28		6
Bart Starr	QB	6'1"	200	27		
Paul Hornung	HB	6'2"	215	24		176
Tom Moore	HB	6'2"	215	22		30
Paul Winslow	HB	5'11"	200	22		6
Larry Hickman	FB	6'2"	230	24		
Jim Taylor	FB	6'	215	25		66
Boyd Dowler	FL	6'5"	220	23		12
Lew Carpenter	OE-FL	6'1"	215	28		
Gary Knafelc	OE	6'4"	220	28		
Ron Kramer	OE	6'3"	230	25		
Max McGee	OE	6'3"	205	28		24
Steve Meilinger	OE	6'2"	230	30		

DETROIT LIONS 7-5-0 George Wilson

Scores of Each Game		
9	Green Bay	28
10	SAN FRANCISCO	14
10	Philadelphia	28
30	BALTIMORE	17
35	Los Angeles	48
24	San Francisco	0
12	LOS ANGELES	10
7	Chicago	28
23	GREEN BAY	10
20	Baltimore	15
23	DALLAS	14
36	CHICAGO	0

Use Name	Pos.	Hgt	Wgt	Age	Int	Pts
Ollie Spencer	C-OT	6'2"	250	29		
John Gordy	OG-OT	6'3"	250	24		
Willie McClung	DT-OT	6'2"	260	31		
Grady Alderman	OG	6'2"	230	21		
Bob Grottkau	OG	6'4"	235	23		
Harley Sewell	OG	6'1"	230	29		
Bob Scholtz	C	6'4"	250	22		
Bill Glass	DE	6'5"	255	24		
Gil Mains	DE	6'2"	250	30		
Darris McCord	OT-DE	6'4"	250	27		
Sam Williams	LB-DE	6'5"	235	29		
Roger Brown	DT	6'5"	290	23		
Alex Karras	DT	6'2"	245	24		
Jim Weatherall	DT	6'4"	250	30		
Carl Brettschneider	LB	6'1"	225	28		
Jim Martin	LB	6'2"	230	36		65
Max Messner	LB	6'3"	225	22	1	
Joe Schmidt	LB	6'1"	220	28	2	12
Wayne Walker	LB	6'2"	225	23	1	2
Night Train Lane	DB	6'1"	195	32	5	6
Dick LeBeau	DB	6'1"	185	23	4	
Gary Lowe	DB	5'11"	195	26	2	
Bruce Maher	DB	5'11"	190	23	1	2
Jim Steffen	DB	6'	195	23		
Dave Whitsell	DB	6'	190	24		
Yale Lary	DB	6'	190	29	3	
Earl Morrall	QB	6'1"	206	26		6
Jim Ninowski	QB	6'1"	200	24		30
Warren Rabb	QB	6'1"	196	23		
Terry Barr	HB	6'	190	25		12
Dan Lewis	HB	6'1"	200	24		12
Ken Webb	FB-HB	5'11"	210	25		12
Nick Pietrosante	FB	6'2"	225	23		48
Hopalong Cassady	HB-FL	5'10"	185	26		12
Dave Middleton	OE-FL	6'1"	195	27		
Gail Cogdill	OE	6'2"	195	23		6
Glenn Davis	OE	6'	180	26		
Jim Gibbons	OE	6'2"	220	24		12
Steve Junker	OE	6'3"	220	25		

SAN FRANCISCO FORTY NINERS 7-5-0 Red Hickey

Scores of Each Game		
19	NEW YORK	21
13	LOS ANGELES	9
14	Detroit	10
10	Chicago	27
14	Green Bay	41
25	CHICAGO	7
0	DETROIT	24
26	Dallas	14
30	Baltimore	22
23	Los Angeles	7
0	GREEN BAY	13
34	BALTIMORE	10

Use Name	Pos.	Hgt	Wgt	Age	Int	Pts
Len Rohde	OT	6'4"	240	22		
Bob St. Clair	OT	6'9"	265	29		
John Thomas	OT	6'4"	246	25		
Bruce Bosley	OG	6'2"	240	26		
Ted Connolly	OG	6'3"	242	28		
Mike Magac	OG	6'3"	240	22		
Karl Rubke	C	6'4"	240	24		
Frank Morze	DT-C	6'4"	264	26		
Dan Colchico	DE	6'4"	236	23		
Ed Henke	DE	6'3"	227	32		
Charlie Krueger	DE	6'4"	245	24		2
Monte Clark	DT	6'6"	260	23		
Leo Nomellini	DT	6'3"	262	35		2
Henry Schmidt	DT	6'4"	260	23		
Bob Harrison	LB	6'2"	220	23	1	
Matt Hazeltine	LB	6'1"	220	27		
Gorden Kelley	LB	6'3"	230	22	2	
Clancy Osborne	LB	6'3"	218	25		
Jerry Wilson (from PHI)	LB	6'2"	235	23		
Dave Baker	DB	6'	193	23	10	
Eddie Dove	DB	6'2"	180	23	3	
Lenny Lyles	DB	6'2"	202	24		6
Jerry Mertens	DB	6'	183	24	2	
Jimmy Ridlon	DB	6'1"	177	25		
Abe Woodson	HB-DB	5'11"	188	25	2	
John Brodie	QB	6'1"	186	25		6
Y. A. Tittle	QB	6'	195	33		
Bob Waters	QB	6'2"	184	22		
Hugh McElhenny	HB	6'1"	198	31		6
Ray Norton	HB	6'2"	184	23		
J. D. Smith	FB-HB	6'1"	200	27		36
Joe Perry	FB	6'	206	33		6
C. R. Roberts	FB	6'3"	197	24		12
R. C. Owens	OE-FL	6'3"	190	25		36
Clyde Conner	OE	6'2"	190	27		12
Dee Mackey	OE	6'5"	236	24		
Monte Stickles	OE	6'4"	230	22		
Billy Wilson	FL-OE	6'3"	190	33		6
Tommy Davis	K	6'	212	25		78

BALTIMORE COLTS 6-6-0 Weeb Ewbank

Scores of Each Game		
20	WASHINGTON	0
42	CHICAGO	7
21	Green Bay	35
31	LOS ANGELES	17
17	DETROIT	30
45	Dallas	7
38	GREEN BAY	24
24	Chicago	20
22	SAN FRANCISCO	30
15	DETROIT	20
3	Los Angeles	10
10	San Francisco	34

Use Name	Pos.	Hgt	Wgt	Age	Int	Pts
Jim Parker	OT	6'3"	275	26		
Sherman Plunkett	OT	6'4"	270	26		
George Preas	OT	6'2"	255	28		
Lebrun Shields	DE-OT	6'4"	240	23		2
Steve Myhra	OG	6'1"	240	26		62
Palmer Pyle	OG	6'2"	240	23		
Alex Sandusky	OG	6'1"	238	28		
Art Spinney	OG	6'	236	33		
Buzz Nutter	C	6'4"	240	29		
Ordell Braase	DE	6'4"	242	28		
Gino Marchetti	DE	6'4"	245	34		
Jim Colvin	OG-DE	6'2"	240	23		
Don Joyce	DT-DE	6'3"	250	30		
Art Donovan	DT	6'2"	270	35		
Big Daddy Lipscomb	DT	6'6"	288	29		2
Marv Matuszak	LB	6'3"	228	29		
Bill Pellington	LB	6'2"	238	31	1	
Don Shinnick	LB	6'	235	25	5	
Dick Szymanski	LB	6'3"	235	28	1	
Zeke Smith	DE-LB	6'2"	230	24		
Bobby Boyd	DB	5'10"	190	22	7	
Milt Davis	DB	6'1"	180	31	6	
Andy Nelson	DB	6'1"	180	27	6	
Jackie Simpson	DB	5'10"	185	26		
Johnny Sample	HB-DB	6'1"	203	23	4	6
Carl Taseff	HB-DB	5'11"	194	31		
Ray Brown	QB	6'2"	195	24		
Johnny Unitas	QB	6'1"	194	27		
Alex Hawkins	HB	6'1"	190	23		30
Ed Kovac	HB	6'	197	22		
Lenny Moore	HB	6'1"	190	27		78
Mike Sommer	HB	5'11"	190	25		
Jim Welch	HB	6'	190	22		
Alan Ameche	FB	6'	220	27		18
Billy Pricer	FB	5'10"	210	25		12
Ray Berry	OE	6'2"	190	27		60
Jim Mutscheller	OE	6'1"	204	30		12
Art DeCarlo	DB-OE	6'2"	202	30		
Jerry Richardson	HB-OE	6'3"	185	24		6

CHICAGO BEARS 5-6-1 George Halas

Scores of Each Game		
17	Green Bay	14
7	Baltimore	42
34	LOS ANGELES	27
27	SAN FRANCISCO	10
24	Los Angeles	24
7	San Francisco	25
20	BALTIMORE	24
28	DETROIT	7
17	DALLAS	7
13	GREEN BAY	41
0	Cleveland	42
0	Detroit	36

Use Name	Pos.	Hgt	Wgt	Age	Int	Pts
Stan Fanning	OT	6'6"	252	22		
Bob Kilcullen	OT	6'3"	245	24		
Herm Lee	OT	6'4"	247	29		
Bob Wetoska	OT	6'3"	250	22		
Roger Davis	OG	6'3"	235	22		
Stan Jones	OG	6'1"	250	29		
Ted Karras	OG	6'1"	235	27		
Bob Konovsky	OG	6'2"	245	26		
John Mellekas	C	6'3"	255	27		
Doug Atkins	DE	6'8"	255	30		
Maury Youmans	OT-DE	6'6"	230	23		
Fred Williams	DT	6'4"	248	30		
Bill Bishop	OT-DT	6'4"	248	29		
Earl Leggett	DE-DT	6'3"	250	26	1	
Joe Fortunato	LB	6'	225	30		
Bill George	LB	6'2"	235	29	1	
Ken Kirk	LB	6'2"	230	22		
Larry Morris	LB	6'2"	230	25	1	
Roger LeClerc	C-DT-LB	6'3"	235	22		
Erich Barnes	DB	6'2"	198	25		
J. C. Caroline	DB	6'1"	190	27	3	6
Pete Manning	DB	6'3"	208	24		
Richie Petitbon	DB	6'3"	205	22	2	
Justin Rowland	DB	6'2"	188	22		
Charlie Sumner	DB	6'1"	195	30		
Vic Zucco	DB	6'	187	25	2	
Zeke Bratkowski	QB	6'2"	203	28		
Ed Brown	QB	6'2"	208	31		12
Charlie Bivins	HB	6'2"	212	21		
Willie Galimore	HB	6'1"	187	25		6
Johnny Morris	HB	5'10"	180	25		36
Glen Shaw	HB	6'1"	217	21		
John Adams	FB	6'3"	235	23		
Rick Casares	FB	6'2"	225	29		30
Merrill Douglas	FB	6'	204	24		
Angie Coia	OE	6'2"	211	22		24
Willard Dewveall	OE	6'4"	218	23		30
Jim Dooley	OE	6'4"	198	30		6
Bo Farrington	OE	6'3"	217	24		
Harlon Hill	OE	6'3"	200	28		
John Aveni	K	6'3"	210	25		44

LOS ANGELES RAMS 4-7-1 Bob Waterfield

Scores of Each Game		
21	ST. LOUIS	43
9	San Francisco	13
27	Chicago	34
17	Baltimore	31
24	CHICAGO	24
48	DETROIT	35
38	Dallas	13
10	Detroit	12
33	Green Bay	31
7	SAN FRANCISCO	23
10	BALTIMORE	3
21	GREEN BAY	35

Use Name	Pos.	Hgt	Wgt	Age	Int	Pts
Jim Boeke	OT	6'5"	230	21		
Charlie Bradshaw	OT	6'6"	255	24		
John Guzik	OG	6'3"	236	23		
Roy Hord	OG	6'4"	232	25		
Chuck Janerette	OG	6'3"	240	21		
Buck Lansford	OG	6'2"	232	27		
Art Hunter	C	6'4"	248	27		
Gene Brito	DE	6'1"	230	35		
Lamar Lundy	DE	6'7"	235	25	1	6
Lou Michaels	DE	6'2"	248	24		7
John Baker	DT-DE	6'6"	290	25	1	
John Lovetere	DT	6'4"	280	24		6
George Strugar	DT	6'5"	260	25		
John Kennerson	DE-DT	6'3"	255			
Bill Jobko	LB	6'2"	218	24	1	
Bob Long	LB	6'3"	234	26	1	
Jack Pardee	LB	6'2"	220	24	1	
Les Richter	LB	6'3"	232	29	2	2
Jerry Stalcup	OG-LB	6'	220	22	1	
Charley Britt	DB	6'2"	180	22	5	6
Don Ellersick	DB	6'1"	193	22	2	
Carl Karilivacz	DB	6'	190	29		
Ed Meador	DB	5'11"	185	23	4	6
Will Sherman	DB	6'2"	197	31	1	
Vern Valdez	DB	5'11"	190	24	1	
Buddy Humphrey	QB	6'1"	200	24		
Frank Ryan	QB	6'3"	195	24		12
Billy Wade	QB	6'2"	203	29		12
Jon Arnett	HB	5'11"	193	25		24
Dick Bass	HB	5'10"	190	23		
Tom Wilson	HB	6'	204	27		12
Clendon Thomas	DB-FL-HB	6'2"	190	23	1	12
Joe Marconi	FB	6'2"	220	26		18
Ollie Matson	FL-FB	6'2"	210	30		6
Carroll Dale	OE	6'1"	194	22		18
Jim Phillips	OE	6'1"	200	23		48
Del Shofner	DB-OE	6'3"	192	24	1	6
Danny Villanueva	K	5'11"	200	22		64

DALLAS COWBOYS 0-11-1 Tom Landry

Scores of Each Game		
28	PITTSBURGH	35
25	PHILADELPHIA	27
14	Washington	26
7	CLEVELAND	48
10	St. Louis	12
7	BALTIMORE	45
13	LOS ANGELES	38
7	Green Bay	41
14	SAN FRANCISCO	26
7	Chicago	17
31	New York	31
14	Detroit	23

Use Name	Pos.	Hgt	Wgt	Age	Int	Pts
Byron Bradfute	OT	6'3"	243	22		
Paul Dickson	OT	6'5"	250	23		
Bob Fry	OT	6'4"	240	29		
Dick Klein	OT	6'4"	255	26		
Mike Falls	OG	6'1"	240	26		
Buzz Guy	OG	6'3"	247	25		
Duane Putnam	OG	6'	233	32		
Mike Connelly	C	6'3"	235	24		
John Houser	C	6'3"	238	24		
Nate Borden	DE	6'	240	28		
Gene Cronin	DE	6'2"	232	27	1	
John Gonzaga	DE	6'3"	244	27		
Don Healy	DT	6'3"	264	24		
Bill Herchman	DT	6'2"	245	27		
Ed Husmann	DT	6'	238	29		
Tom Braatz	LB	6'1"	220	27	1	
Wayne Hansen	LB	6'2"	228	32	2	
Jack Patera	LB	6'1"	240	28	1	
Jerry Tubbs	LB	6'2"	220	25	1	
Bob Bercich	DB	6'1"	198	23	2	
Don Bishop	DB	6'2"	204	25	3	
Bill Butler	DB	5'10"	182	23	1	
Fred Doelling	DB	5'10"	190	21		
Tom Franckhauser	DB	6'	196	23	3	
Jim Mooty	DB	5'11"	177	22		
Gary Wisener	OE-DB	6'1"	206	22		
Don Heinrich	QB	6'	182	28		
Eddie LeBaron	QB	5'9"	166	30		6
Don Meredith	QB	6'2"	198	22		
L. G. Dupre	HB	5'11"	190	28		30
Don McIlhenny	HB	6'	204	25		12
Gene Babb	FB	6'3"	218	25		6
Mike Dowdle	FB	6'3"	210	22		
Walt Kowalczyk	FB	6'	205	25		12
Ray Mathews	FL	6'	200	31		
Dick Bielski	OE	6'1"	227	28		6
Frank Clarke	OE	6'	215	27		18
Jim Doran	OE	6'2"	211	32		18
Fred Dugan	OE	6'3"	200	26		6
Billy Howton	OE	6'2"	195	30		24
Woodley Lewis	OE	6'	195	35		
Dave Sherer	OE	6'3"	225	23		
Fred Cone	K	5'11"	198	34		39
Ray Fisher	— Injury					
Chuck Howley	— Injury					

GREEN BAY PACKERS

RUSHING

Last Name	No.	Yds	Avg	TD
Taylor	230	1101	4.8	11
Hornung	160	671	4.2	13
Moore	45	237	5.3	4
McHan	8	67	8.4	1
Carpenter	1	24	24.0	0
Hickman	7	22	3.1	0
Starr	7	12	1.7	0
McGee	2	11	5.5	0
Dowler	1	8	8.0	0
Winslow	2	−3	−1.5	0

RECEIVING

Last Name	No.	Yds	Avg	TD
McGee	38	787	21	4
Dowler	30	505	17	2
Hornung	28	257	9	2
Taylor	15	121	8	0
Knafelc	14	164	12	0
Moore	5	40	8	1
R. Kramer	4	55	14	0
Meilinger	2	43	22	0
Carpenter	1	21	21	0

PUNT RETURNS

Last Name	No.	Yds	Avg	TD
Wood	16	106	7	0
Carpenter	9	59	7	0
Forester	1	7	7	0

KICKOFF RETURNS

Last Name	No.	Yds	Avg	TD
Moore	12	397	33	0
Carpenter	12	249	21	0
Symank	4	103	26	0
Hickman	3	54	18	0
Nitschke	2	33	17	0
Temp	1	16	16	0
Meilinger	1	0	0	0

PASSING – PUNTING – KICKING

PASSING	Att	Comp	%	Yds	Yd/Att	TD	Int–%	RK
Starr	172	98	57	1358	7.9	4	8– 5	5
McHan	91	33	36	517	5.7	3	5– 5	
Hornung	16	6	38	118	7.4	2	0– 0	

PUNTING	No	Avg
McGee	31	41.6
Dowler	18	40.5

KICKING	XP	Att	%	FG	Att	%
Hornung	41	41	100	15	28	54

DETROIT LIONS

RUSHING

Last Name	No.	Yds	Avg	TD
Pietrosante	161	872	5.4	8
Lewis	92	438	4.8	1
Webb	59	166	2.8	2
Ninowski	32	81	2.5	5
Barr	17	74	4.4	1
Morrall	10	37	3.7	1
Cassady	17	28	1.6	1
Lary	1	19	19.0	0
Middleton	3	−1	−0.3	0

RECEIVING

Last Name	No.	Yds	Avg	TD
Gibbons	51	604	12	2
Cogdill	43	642	15	1
Cassady	20	238	12	1
Pietrosante	13	129	10	0
Lewis	12	192	16	1
Webb	10	68	7	0
Junker	6	55	9	0
Middleton	5	51	10	0
Barr	5	26	5	1
Davis	1	17	17	0

PUNT RETURNS

Last Name	No.	Yds	Avg	TD
Barr	14	104	7	0
Steffen	14	83	6	0
Cassady	1	25	25	0
Maher	1	10	10	0
Lary	1	5	5	0

KICKOFF RETURNS

Last Name	No.	Yds	Avg	TD
Steffen	8	225	28	0
Maher	10	214	21	0
Lewis	10	202	20	0
Cassady	4	82	21	0
Barr	4	81	20	0
Pietrosante	2	58	29	0
Webb	3	38	13	0
LeBeau	2	16	8	0

PASSING – PUNTING – KICKING

PASSING	Att	Comp	%	Yds	Yd/Att	TD	Int–%	RK
Ninowski	283	134	47	1599	5.7	2	18– 6	17
Morrall	49	32	65	423	8.6	4	3– 6	
Barr	1	0	0	0	0.0	0	0– 0	

PUNTING	No	Avg
Lary	64	43.8

KICKING	XP	Att	%	FG	Att	%
Martin	26	28	93	13	24	54

SAN FRANCISCO FORTY NINERS

RUSHING

Last Name	No.	Yds	Avg	TD
Smith	174	780	4.5	5
McElhenny	95	347	3.7	0
Roberts	73	213	2.9	2
Brodie	18	171	9.5	1
Perry	36	95	2.0	1
Tittle	10	61	6.1	0
Waters	1	8	8.0	0
Woodson	4	4	1.0	0
Norton	2	2	1.0	0

RECEIVING

Last Name	No.	Yds	Avg	TD
Connor	38	531	14	2
Owens	37	532	14	6
Smith	36	181	5	1
Stickles	22	252	11	0
McElhenny	14	114	8	1
Mackey	12	159	13	0
Roberts	9	49	5	0
Wilson	3	51	17	1
Perry	3	−3	−1	0

PUNT RETURNS

Last Name	No.	Yds	Avg	TD
Woodson	13	174	13	0
Dove	11	43	4	0

KICKOFF RETURNS

Last Name	No.	Yds	Avg	TD
Lyles	17	526	31	1
Woodson	17	498	29	0
Colchico	5	68	14	0
Roberts	3	60	20	0
Clark	1	15	15	0
J. Wilson	1	0	0	0

PASSING – PUNTING – KICKING

PASSING	Att	Comp	%	Yds	Yd/Att	TD	Int–%	RK
Brodie	207	103	50	1111	5.4	6	9– 4	12
Tittle	127	69	54	694	5.5	4	3– 2	8
Waters	2	2	100	61	30.5	1	0– 0	

PUNTING	No	Avg
Davis	62	44.1
Baker	3	47.7

KICKING	XP	Att	%	FG	Att	%
Davis	21	21	100	19	32	59

BALTIMORE COLTS

RUSHING

Last Name	No.	Yds	Avg	TD
Moore	91	374	4.1	4
Hawkins	76	267	3.5	2
Ameche	80	263	3.3	3
Unitas	36	195	5.4	0
Pricer	46	131	2.8	1
Brown	2	25	12.5	0
Welch	5	23	4.6	0
Sample	1	7	7.0	0
Taseff	4	3	0.8	0
Kovac	4	1	0.3	0

RECEIVING

Last Name	No.	Yds	Avg	TD
Berry	74	1298	18	10
Moore	45	936	21	9
Hawkins	25	280	11	3
Mutscheller	18	271	15	2
DeCarlo	8	116	15	0
Richardson	8	90	11	1
Pricer	8	77	10	1
Ameche	7	56	8	0
Kovac	2	27	14	0
Taseff	1	13	13	0

PUNT RETURNS

Last Name	No.	Yds	Avg	TD
Sample	14	101	7	0
Taseff	6	25	4	0
Nelson	3	1	0	0

KICKOFF RETURNS

Last Name	No.	Yds	Avg	TD
Sample	18	519	29	1
Taseff	14	291	21	0
Pricer	6	88	15	0
Welch	4	80	20	0
Moore	1	23	23	0
Pellington	2	11	6	0
Sommer	1	10	10	0
Kovac	1	8	8	0

PASSING – PUNTING – KICKING

PASSING	Att	Comp	%	Yds	Yd/Att	TD	Int–%	RK
Unitas	378	190	50	3099	8.2	25	24– 6	3
Brown	13	6	46	65	5.0	1	0– 0	
Moore	1	0	0	0	0.0	0	0– 0	

PUNTING	No	Avg
Brown	52	38.5

KICKING	XP	Att	%	FG	Att	%
Myhra	35	37	95	9	19	47

CHICAGO BEARS

RUSHING

Last Name	No.	Yds	Avg	TD
Casares	160	566	3.5	5
J. Morris	73	417	5.7	3
Galimore	74	368	5.0	1
Adams	23	114	5.0	0
Brown	19	89	4.7	2
Douglas	11	82	7.5	0
Bratkowski	8	20	2.5	0
Farrington	1	−2	−2.0	0
Coia	3	−4	−1.3	0
Bivens	1	−11	−11.0	0

RECEIVING

Last Name	No.	Yds	Avg	TD
Dewveall	43	804	19	5
Dooley	36	426	12	1
Coia	25	478	19	4
J. Morris	20	224	11	3
Casares	8	64	8	0
Hill	5	98	20	0
Galimore	3	35	12	0
Douglas	2	11	6	0
Adams	2	−20	−10	0
Lee	1	16	16	0
Brown	1	−6	0	0

PUNT RETURNS

Last Name	No.	Yds	Avg	TD
Zucco	10	83	8	0
J. Morris	13	75	6	0
Petitbon	2	22	11	0
Coia	2	2	1	0

KICKOFF RETURNS

Last Name	No.	Yds	Avg	TD
J. Morris	19	384	20	0
Bivens	15	362	24	0
Galimore	12	292	24	0
Zucco	1	17	17	0

PASSING – PUNTING – KICKING

PASSING	Att	Comp	%	Yds	Yd/Att	TD	Int–%	RK
Bratkowski	175	87	50	1051	6.0	6	21– 12	16
Brown	149	59	40	1079	7.2	7	11– 7	14

PUNTING	No	Avg
Brown	56	39.8
Bratkowski	7	36.0
Casares	1	60.0

KICKING	XP	Att	%	FG	Att	%
Aveni	23	25	92	7	16	44

LOS ANGELES RAMS

RUSHING

Last Name	No.	Yds	Avg	TD
Arnett	104	436	4.2	2
Marconi	42	240	5.7	3
Wade	26	171	6.6	2
Matson	61	170	2.9	1
Bass	31	153	4.9	0
Wilson	41	139	3.4	0
Ryan	19	85	4.5	1
Thomas	16	63	3.9	0
Humphrey	2	7	3.5	0
Shofner	1	−15	−15.0	0

RECEIVING

Last Name	No.	Yds	Avg	TD
Phillips	52	883	17	8
Arnett	29	226	8	2
Dale	19	336	18	3
Thomas	17	275	16	2
Matson	15	98	7	0
Bass	13	92	7	0
Shofner	12	122	10	1
Wilson	11	82	7	2
Marconi	9	32	4	0
Ryan	0	32	0	1
Wade	0	10	0	0

PUNT RETURNS

Last Name	No.	Yds	Avg	TD
Bass	11	62	6	0
Arnett	10	60	6	0
Lovetere	1	6	6	1
Sherman	1	1	1	0
Matson	1	0	0	0
Meador	1	0	0	0

KICKOFF RETURNS

Last Name	No.	Yds	Avg	TD
Arnett	17	416	24	0
Bass	11	246	22	0
Matson	9	216	24	0
Wilson	2	48	24	0
Michaels	1	15	15	0

PASSING – PUNTING – KICKING

PASSING	Att	Comp	%	Yds	Yd/Att	TD	Int–%	RK
Wade	182	106	58	1294	7.1	12	11– 6	4
Ryan	128	62	48	816	6.4	7	9– 7	14
Humphrey	24	9	38	78	3.3	0	2– 8	
Arnett	1	0	0	0	0.0	0	0– 0	

PUNTING	No	Avg
Shofner	54	42.6
Marconi	10	40.8

KICKING	XP	Att	%	FG	Att	%
Villaneuva	28	28	100	12	19	63
Richter	2	2	100	0	0	0
Michaels	1	1	100	2	3	67

DALLAS COWBOYS

RUSHING

Last Name	No.	Yds	Avg	TD
Dupre	104	362	3.5	3
McIlhenny	96	321	3.3	1
Kowalczyk	50	156	3.1	1
Babb	39	115	2.9	0
LeBaron	17	94	5.5	1
Meredith	3	4	1.3	0
Heinrich	2	3	1.5	0
Clarke	1	−6	−6.0	0

RECEIVING

Last Name	No.	Yds	Avg	TD
Doran	31	554	18	3
Dugan	29	461	16	1
Howton	23	363	16	4
Dupre	21	216	10	2
McIlhenny	15	120	8	1
Kowalczyk	14	143	10	1
Babb	13	140	11	1
Clarke	9	290	32	3
Bielski	4	38	10	1
Mathews	3	44	15	0
Lewis	1	19	19	0

PUNT RETURNS

Last Name	No.	Yds	Avg	TD
Butler	13	131	10	0
Mooty	8	37	5	0
Franckhauser	2	7	4	0

KICKOFF RETURNS

Last Name	No.	Yds	Avg	TD
Franckhauser	26	526	20	0
Butler	20	399	20	0
Mooty	12	210	18	0
Babb	3	46	15	0
Dupre	2	44	22	0
Dowdle	2	22	11	0
Putnam	1	13	13	0
Bielski	1	4	4	0
Kowalczyk	1	0	0	0
Sherer	1	0	0	0

PASSING – PUNTING – KICKING

PASSING	Att	Comp	%	Yds	Yd/Att	TD	Int–%	RK
LeBaron	225	111	49	1736	7.7	12	25– 11	9
Meredith	68	29	43	281	4.1	2	5– 7	
Heinrich	61	23	38	371	6.1	3	3– 5	

PUNTING	No	Avg
Sherer	57	42.5
LeBaron	3	33.0

KICKING	XP	Att	%	FG	Att	%
Cone	21	23	91	6	13	46

1960 A.F.L. A New Competitor

Even before the first game was played the new American Football League was a flurry of activity. Commissioner Joe Foss, the former South Dakota governor chosen by the team owners to run the league, faced a major problem when the Minneapolis owners quit the circuit in January to accept an NFL team in 1961. This strategic move by the NFL shut the new circuit out of the Midwest and almost killed it in the cradle, but the upstarts did not give up. After several days of discussion the league owners turned down a bid from an Atlanta group and instead granted the eighth franchise to a syndicate from Oakland, California. The AFL finally had its full contingent of cities—Boston, New York, Buffalo, Houston, Dallas, Denver, Los Angeles, and Oakland. In New York, Dallas, and Los Angeles, the new league would be bucking NFL teams. Oakland in reality would have to compete with the NFL San Francisco '49ers. Buffalo and Boston were both graveyards for previous pro-football failures, while Denver and Houston were virgin territory.

Work went on during the summer, when players had to be signed. The AFL honored existing NFL contracts with players and lured away no players from the established league. The new teams picked up experience by signing NFL rejects and oldsters. Most of the AFL quarterbacks had NFL credits, such as George Blanda, Jack Kemp, Babe Parilli, Tom O'Connell, Al Dorow, and Cotton Davidson. Some players from the Canadian League seized upon the AFL as a chance to play again in the United States. Frank Tripuka, Dave Kocourek, Goose Gonsoulin, Butch Songin, Al Jamison, and Sherrill Headrick all had been playing north of the border before signing with the AFL. And a flock of unknown rookies and free agents were signing, hard-working if unspectacular football players with a desire to play football for a living. Such unheralded names as Charley Hennigan, Abner Haynes, Jim Otto, and Larry Grantham went unnoticed by pro scouts until turning up in AFL training camps.

But the most spectacular aspect of the player recruiting was the bidding war with NFL teams over well-known college players. The new league wanted to build its image by signing the cream of the graduating college class, and some clubs engaged in financial combat with an NFL team to woo an All-American collegian. Some young men found this courtship so intoxicating that they signed contracts with both contestants. A series of court battles ensued that gave the AFL such dual signers as Heisman Trophy winner Billy Cannon, Johnny Robinson, and Charlie Flowers.

Another item on the agenda was finding a place to play. New York and Oakland fared the worst in the stadium hunt, with New York having to settle for the grimy old Polo Grounds, while Oakland had to play its home games in San Francisco because there was no stadium in Oakland. Houston played its games in a high-school facility and Denver used a minor-league baseball field.

A fourteen-game schedule was adopted for the league, and the two-point conversion rule, where the team may run or pass for two points after a touchdown, was put into effect for all games. But the most important move by Commissioner Foss was the signing of a national television contract with the American Broadcasting System which provided a needed $150,000 to each team.

After all this, play was ready to begin. Although average attendance per game was only 16,000, the AFL would survive 1960 and be back for more.

EASTERN DIVISION

Houston Oilers—The players came from all over, Billy Cannon, the Heisman Trophy halfback from Louisiana State, had signed a three-year contract for $100,000, one of the richest pacts in pro history. George Blanda had come out off a year's retirement after a ten-year career with the Chicago Bears. Charley Hennigan had been teaching high-school biology, and he taped his final paycheck from the school inside his helmet for inspiration in dull moments. Bill Groman was an unknown rookie from Heidelberg. Al Jamison came down from the Canadian League. Coach Lou Rymkus blended all the parts together into a high-scoring machine which took command in the Eastern Division right from the start. The Oilers at first relied on Blanda's long bombs to Groman and Hennigan, but Cannon recovered from a slow start to give the ground game some punch and the Oilers won the first AFL Eastern crown.

New York Titans—The drab old Polo Grounds, abandoned since 1957, was dusted off to serve as home for the Titans. While Titan games were played in virtual anonymity (with highly inflated announced attendance figures), the NFL Giants were playing to a packed house week after week within walking distance at Yankee Stadium. The Titans admittedly were no match for the Giants yet, but they did play interesting, wide-open football. Although fullback Bill Mathis showed promise as a runner after winning a job in mid-season, the attack lived on quarterback Al Dorow's scrambling runs and long passes to speedsters Art Powell and Don Maynard. The Titan defense was virtually nonexistent, although young Larry Grantham showed well at linebacker. The Titans won interesting games, as when they beat Denver 28-24 by blocking a punt with twenty seconds left in the game, and they lost interesting games, like a 50-43 shootout with the Chargers. But the death of guard Howard Glenn with a broken neck after the October 9 game with Houston and the dearth of paying fans cast a deep shadow over this debut season.

Buffalo Bills—The Bills were an early-AFL rarity, a team trying to live on its defense. They had two tough linemen in Lavern Torczon and Chuck McMurtry, a mobile, hard-hitting middle linebacker in Archie Matsos, and one of the league's better secondaries, headed by NFL veterans Richie McCabe and Jim Wagstaff. But the offense couldn't launch an effective passing attack, the staple of most AFL clubs this year. Tom O'Connell, the old Cleveland quarterback, could not hold the starting passer's job given to him at the outset of the season, and Penn State All-American Rickie Lucas flopped both at quarterback and halfback. Johnny Green, an unheralded rookie, eventually took charge of the offense, whose main weapons were runner Wray Carlton and flanker Elbert Dubenion. The high point of the year was a 32-3 upset of the Los Angeles Chargers, but the Buffalo attack stalled too often to do any better than third place in the East.

Boston Patriots—The AFL broke into the box scores in Boston on Friday night, September 9. A crowd of 21,597 fans turned out at Boston University Field to watch the first regular-season AFL game ever, between the Patriots and the Denver Broncos. The Patriots displayed their weak attack right from the start by losing 13-10 to the Broncos. Coach Lou Saban had little speed in an offense led by quarterback Butch Songin, a thirty-six-year-old veteran of the Canadian League who doubled as a local high-school coach, but the defense held together well around a nucleus of Bob Dee, Tom Addison, Fred Bruney, and Ross O'Hanley. With a 35-0 trouncing of the Chargers and a 42-14 beating of the Texans to their credit, the Patriots stayed at the break-even point until losing all four of their final games. In the season's finale, before a sell-out Boston crowd of 27,123, the Pats lost 37-21 to Houston. More importantly, coach Saban shifted Gino Cappelletti from defensive back to split end for this game and discovered Boston's top receiver for the next few years.

WESTERN DIVISION

Los Angeles Chargers—The eeriest sight in pro football was the Los Angeles Chargers playing to vast stretches of empty seats in the huge Memorial Coliseum. But despite the sparse fan support, coach Sid Gillman, who had coached the Rams last season, built a high-scoring outfit which took the Western Division crown in this first AFL season. The Chargers dropped three of their first five contests before hitting their stride, losing only once in their last nine games. The offense led this second-half charge, scoring 41 or more points in each of the last four games. Although the Chargers had shelled out a lot of money for Mississippi fullback Charlie Flowers, the offensive stars were quarterback Jack Kemp, rejected by the Steelers, Giants, and '49ers in the NFL; halfback Paul Lowe, an unknown rookie from Oregon State; and tackle Ron Mix, a first-draft choice of the NFL Colts. Tragedy hit the club when end Ralph Anderson, the team's leading receiver, died of a diabetes attack in November. But in general the Chargers were an artistic if not a financial success.

Dallas Texans—The Texans had the league's best runner, best defense, and worst luck. Halfback Abner Haynes, a speedster from North Texas State, was the AFL's first running star, carrying the ball for 875 yards, catching passes out of the backfield, and running back kicks with an exciting flair. The defense posted three shutouts and allowed a grand total of seven points in its last three games, the stingiest unit in this offense-oriented season. End Mel Branch, tackle Paul Rochester, middle linebacker Sherrill Headrick, and backs Dave Webster and Johnny Bookman were the main pillars of coach Hank Stram's defense. Only a couple of heartbreaking losses kept the Texans from challenging for the Western crown, as they lost 21-20 to the Chargers, 37-35 to the Titans, and 20-19 to the Raiders. But after the season the Texans could look back on a 17-0 victory over the Chargers and a 24-0 victory over the Oilers, shutouts over both divisional champions.

Oakland Raiders—Because of the problem of getting a late start, due to Oakland replacing Minneapolis as the eighth club in the new circuit, businessman Chet Soda, who headed the group granted the Oakland franchise, did not have an easy time when it came to signing players. But coach Ernie Erdelatz weeded through the available talent and built a surprisingly respectable team. He found two quarterbacks in rookie Tom Flores and NFL veteran Babe Parilli and three hard-working runners in Tony Teresa, Billy Lott, and Jack Larscheid. From this quickly organized squad, two players would stick with the Raiders through the entire ten-year life of the AFL—center Jim Otto and guard Wayne Hawkins.

Denver Broncos—With Gene Mingo returning a punt 76 yards for a touchdown, the Broncos beat the Boston Patriots 13-10 in the first regular-season AFL game. But Denver's main offensive weapon didn't join the team until the third week of the season. End Lionel Taylor, a slow-footed but sure-handed receiver, practiced with the Broncos for four days before catching eleven passes against the Titans on September 25, and he went on to catch enough passes in twelve games to lead the league in receiving. The Broncos lived on the pass, with thirty-two-year-old Frank Tripuka throwing 478 passes all year, including fifty-two against the Oilers on November 6. The airborne Denver attack boasted the league's top point producer in halfback and kicker Gene Mingo, but the defense leaked profusely despite fine seasons by tackle Bud McFadin and safety Goose Gonsoulin. With opposing teams scoring freely, the Broncos went winless in their last eight games, salvaging only a 38-38 tie with Boston by coming back from a 38-7 deficit in the third quarter.

FINAL TEAM STATISTICS

OFFENSE

	BOSTON	BUFFALO	DALLAS	DENVER	HOUSTON	L.A.	NEW YORK	OAKLAND
FIRST DOWNS:								
Total	234	211	272	248	262	263	286	254
by Rushing	86	77	119	84	83	96	111	98
by Passing	126	109	136	141	153	141	152	138
by Penalty	22	25	17	23	26	26	23	18
RUSHING:								
Number	401	462	483	440	474	437	485	475
Yards	1218	1211	1814	1195	1565	1536	1460	1785
Average Yards	3.0	2.6	3.8	2.7	3.3	3.5	3.0	3.7
Touchdowns	11	15	24	10	15	24	14	23
PASSING:								
Attempts	475	447	435	508	456	441	474	463
Completions	223	184	209	259	218	229	236	235
Completion Percentage	46.9	41.2	48.0	51.0	47.8	51.9	49.8	50.8
Yards	2865	2689	2831	3247	3371	3177	3334	2923
Average Yards per Attempt	6.0	6.0	6.5	6.4	7.4	7.2	7.0	6.3
Average Yards per Completion	12.8	14.6	13.5	12.5	15.5	13.9	14.1	12.4
Touchdowns	25	19	16	24	31	21	32	18
Interceptions	23	29	19	35	28	29	28	28
Percent Intercepted	4.8	6.5	4.4	6.9	6.1	6.6	5.9	6.0
PUNTING:								
Number	78	89	61	70	72	58	62	76
Average Distance	35.8	39.0	39.3	37.3	35.8	39.7	37.1	38.9
PUNT RETURNS:								
Number	28	27	33	29	15	32	17	26
Yards	203	185	496	261	208	301	120	151
Average Yards	7.3	6.9	15.0	9.0	13.9	9.4	7.1	5.8
Touchdowns	0	0	1	1	0	1	1	0
KICKOFF RETURNS:								
Number	60	47	40	67	48	58	62	63
Yards	1421	945	845	1547	1225	1213	1580	1504
Average Yards	23.7	20.1	21.1	23.1	25.5	20.9	25.5	23.9
Touchdowns	0	0	0	0	2	0	2	1
INTERCEPTION RETURNS:								
Number	25	33	32	27	25	28	24	25
Yards	312	356	410	417	190	317	201	278
Average Yards	12.5	10.8	12.8	15.4	7.6	11.3	8.4	11.1
Touchdowns	0	4	4	2	0	2	1	1
PENALTIES:								
Number	69	57	80	54	75	70	53	71
Yards	730.5	615	753	501	750	648	672	718
FUMBLES:								
Number	36	30	30	32	36	31	36	41
Number Lost	22	15	18	17	17	16	20	18
POINTS:								
Total	286	296	362	309	379	373	382	319
PAT (Kick) Attempts	32	34	44	36	47	47	50	39
PAT (Kick) Made	30	28	42	33	46	46	47	37
PAT (Rush or Pass) Attempts	5	3	2	1	0	0	1	4
PAT (Rush or Pass) Made	4	2	1	0	0	0	1	2
FG Attempts	23	26	34	28	34	24	21	25
FG Made	8	12	14	18	15	13	9	6
Percent FG Made	34.8	46.2	41.2	64.3	44.1	54.2	42.9	24.0
Safeties	1	0	0	0	0	0	0	1

DEFENSE

	BOSTON	BUFFALO	DALLAS	DENVER	HOUSTON	L.A.	NEW YORK	OAKLAND
FIRST DOWNS:								
Total	237	225	253	254	282	259	252	268
by Rushing	78	103	76	112	90	97	99	99
by Passing	135	109	148	123	164	138	133	146
by Penalty	24	13	29	19	28	24	20	23
RUSHING:								
Number	477	474	422	541	438	414	449	442
Yards	1513	1393	980	2145	1027	1750	1378	1598
Average Yards	3.2	2.9	2.3	4.0	2.3	4.2	3.1	3.6
Touchdowns	21	15	14	19	6	24	20	17
PASSING:								
Attempts	429	429	503	387	557	467	450	477
Completions	210	185	261	189	271	227	216	234
Completion Percentage	49.0	43.1	51.2	48.8	48.7	48.6	48.0	49.1
Yards	2958	2461	3002	2987	3874	2851	2919	3385
Average Yards per Attempt	6.9	5.7	6.0	7.7	7.0	6.1	6.5	7.1
Average Yards per Completion	14.1	13.3	11.5	15.8	14.3	12.6	13.5	14.5
Touchdowns	19	19	19	25	28	21	27	28
Interceptions	25	33	32	27	25	28	24	25
Percent Intercepted	5.8	7.7	6.4	7.0	4.5	6.0	5.3	5.2
PUNTING:								
Number	74	77	78	67	68	62	65	75
Average Distance	37.2	37.6	37.5	39.0	37.1	40.2	37.0	37.5
PUNT RETURNS:								
Number	21	33	27	20	28	17	31	30
Yards	361	232	157	149	258	197	342	229
Average Yards	17.2	7.0	5.8	7.5	9.2	11.6	11.0	7.6
Touchdowns	3	0	0	1	0	0	0	0
KICKOFF RETURNS:								
Number	50	55	57	54	46	70	70	43
Yards	1123	1402	1347	1087	1096	1481	1785	959
Average Yards	22.5	25.5	23.6	20.1	23.8	21.2	25.5	22.3
Touchdowns	1	0	1	1	0	0	1	1
INTERCEPTION RETURNS:								
Number	23	29	19	35	28	29	28	28
Yards	336	422	171	343	316	284	228	381
Average Yards	14.6	14.6	9.0	9.8	11.3	9.8	8.1	13.6
Touchdowns	3	2	0	3	2	1	0	3
PENALTIES:								
Number	77	62	59	62	74	59	77	59
Yards	825	608.5	579	633	664	569	911	598
FUMBLES:								
Number	41	27	34	26	42	39	27	36
Number Lost	20	16	16	17	26	17	16	15
POINTS:								
Total	349	303	253	393	285	336	399	388
PAT (Kick) Attempts								
PAT (Kick) Made	43	37	31	48	33	40	51	46
PAT (Rush or Pass) Attempts								
PAT (Rush or Pass) Made								
FG Attempts	27	27	23	28	27	28	25	30
FG Made	10	14	4	17	12	14	10	14
Percent FG Made	37.0	51.9	17.4	60.7	44.4	50.0	40.0	46.7
Safeties	0	1	0	0	0	1	0	0

1960 AFL CHAMPIONSHIP GAME

January 1, at Houston
(Attendance 32,183)

SCORING

HOUSTON	0	10	7	7–24
LOS ANGELES	6	3	7	0–16

First Quarter
- L.A. — Agajanian, 38 yard field goal — 4:02
- L.A. — Agajanian, 22 yard field goal — 8:16

Second Quarter
- Hous. — Smith, 17 yard pass from Blanda, PAT–Blanda (kick) — 3:51
- Hous. — Blanda, 18 yard field goal — 8:45
- L.A. — Agajanian, 27 yard field goal — 14:55

Third Quarter
- Hous. — Groman, 7 yard pass from Blanda, PAT–Blanda (kick)
- L.A. — Lowe, 2 yard rush, PAT–Agajanian (kick)

Fourth Quarter
- Hous. — Cannon, 88 yard pass from Blanda, PAT–Blanda (kick)

TEAM STATISTICS

HOUS.		L.A.
17	First Downs–Total	21
4	First Downs–Rushing	11
13	First Downs–Passing	9
0	First Downs–Penalty	1
0	Fumbles–Number	2
0	Fumbles–Lost Ball	0
4	Penalties–Number	3
54	Yards Penalized	15
0	Giveaways	2
2	Takeaways	0
+2	Difference	−2

Age and Blanda and a Crown

The Oilers and Chargers met on New Year's Day to decide the first AFL championship. Both clubs had high scoring offenses, but the defensive units turned in surprisingly strong performances. The only scoring of the first quarter came on a pair of field goals by Ben Agajanian, Los Angeles' forty-one-year-old kicking specialist. George Blanda, the old man in the Houston lineup, put the Oilers ahead early in the second period with a 17-yard touchdown pass to fullback Dave Smith and the successful conversion. Blanda and Agajanian both added three-pointers late in the quarter to make the score 10-9 Houston at the half. The offenses moved better in the second half, with the Oilers relying on Blanda's passing and the Chargers on Paul Lowe's running. Houston upped its lead to eight points with a seven-yard Blanda-to-Bill Groman touchdown pass, but the Chargers came right back on a long drive culminating in Lowe's two-yard dash into the end zone. Leading 17-16 after three quarters, the Oilers broke open a long pass play, a very common occurrence in the early AFL. Billy Cannon came out of the backfield and took a George Blanda pass 88 yards to a touchdown, with the extra point running the score to 24-16. The Oilers led by eight points, but the Chargers could tie the game in one swoop with a touchdown and a two-point conversion. Twice the Chargers drove deep into Houston territory only to lose the ball on downs on the 35-yard line and on the 22-yard line. The final Los Angeles drive died with one minute left, turning the ball and the league championship over to the Oilers.

INDIVIDUAL STATISTICS

HOUSTON	No.	Yds.	Avg.	LOS ANGELES	No.	Yds.	Avg.
RUSHING							
Cannon	18	50	2.8	Lowe	21	165	7.9
Smith	19	45	2.4	Ferguson	4	11	2.8
Hall	3	5	1.6	Ford	2	−5	−2.5
	40	100	2.5	Kemp	6	−9	−1.5
					33	162	4.9
RECEIVING							
Smith	5	52	10.4	Norton	6	55	9.2
Hennigan	4	71	17.8	Womble	6	29	4.8
Cannon	3	128	42.7	Kocourek	3	57	19.0
Groman	3	37	12.3	Lowe	3	5	1.7
Carson	1	13	13.0	Ferguson	2	19	9.5
	16	301	18.8	Flowers	1	6	6.0
					21	171	8.1
PUNTING							
Milstead	5		34.0	Laraba	4		41.0
PUNT RETURNS							
None				Harris	1	27	27.0
				Sears	1	15	15.0
					2	42	21.0
KICKOFF RETURNS							
Cannon	3	81	27.0	Lowe	4	101	25.3
Hall	2	47	23.5	Ford	1	22	22.0
	5	128	25.6		5	123	24.6
INTERCEPTION RETURNS							
Gordon	1	27	27.0	None			
Dukes	1	8	8.0				
	2	35	17.5				

PASSING

HOUSTON	Att.	Comp.	Comp. Pct.	Yds.	Int.	Yds/ Att.	Yds/ Comp.
Blanda	31	16	51.6	301	0	9.7	18.8
Cannon	1	0	0.0	0	0	–	–
	32	16	50.0	301	0	9.4	18.8
LOS ANGELES							
Kemp	41	21	51.2	171	2	4.2	8.1

1960 A.F.L. — Eastern Division

HOUSTON OILERS 10-4-0 Lou Rymkus

Scores of Each Game		
37	Oakland	22
38	LOS ANGELES	28
13	OAKLAND	14
27	NEW YORK	21
20	DALLAS	10
42	New York	28
24	Buffalo	25
45	Denver	25
21	Los Angeles	24
20	DENVER	10
24	Boston	10
0	Dallas	24
31	BUFFALO	23
37	BOSTON	21

Use Name	Pos.	Hgt	Wgt	Age	Int	Pts
Gary Greaves	OT	6'3"	235	24		
Al Jamison	OT	6'5"	240	23		
Rich Michael	OT	6'3"	230	21		
Fred Wallner	OG	6'2"	235	31		
Hogan Wharton	OG	6'2"	245	24		
Wahoo McDaniel	OG	6'	230	23		
Bob Talamini	OG	6'1"	230	21		
George Belotti	C	6'4"	255	25		
John Simerson	C	6'3"	255	25		
Dalva Allen	DE	6'5"	245	24	1	
Don Floyd	DE	6'4"	230	21		
Dan Lanphear	DE	6'2"	220	22		
Pete Davidson	DT	6'5"	255	26		
Jerry Helluin	DT	6'2"	260	30		
George Shirkey	DT	6'4"	260	23		
Orville Trask	DT	6'4"	260	25		
Mike Dukes	LB	6'3"	225	24	2	
Dennit Morris	LB	6'1"	225	24	4	
Phil Perlo	LB	6'	220	24		
Hugh Pitts	LB	6'2"	225	26		
Tony Banfield	DB	6'1"	185	21	3	
Bobby Gordon	DB	6'	195	24	3	
Mark Johnston	DB	6'	203	22	4	
Charlie Kendall	DB	6'2"	185	25	2	
Jim Norton	DB	6'3"	182	21	1	
Julian Spence	DB	5'11"	170	31	4	
George Blanda	QB	6'1"	210	32		115
Jacky Lee	QB	6'1"	185	21		
Charley Milstead	QB	6'2"	190	22		
Don Brown	HB	6'1"	205	23		
Billy Cannon	HB	6'1"	210	23		42
Ken Hall	HB	6'1"	200	24		6
Charley Tolar	HB	5'7"	195	22		18
Doug Cline	FB	6'2"	210	21		12
Dave Smith	FB	6'1"	205	23		42
Bob White	FB	6'2"	220	22		
Jack Atchason (from BOS)	OE	6'4"	215	23		6
Johnny Carson	OE	6'3"	205	30		24
Bill Groman	OE	6'	194	24		72
Charley Hennigan	OE	6'	190	24		36
John White	OE	6'4"	230	22		
Al Witcher	DE-OE	6'1"	200	23	1	6

NEW YORK TITANS 7-7-0 Sammy Baugh

Scores of Each Game		
27	BUFFALO	3
24	BOSTON	28
28	DENVER	24
37	Dallas	35
21	Houston	27
17	Buffalo	13
28	HOUSTON	42
27	OAKLAND	28
7	LOS ANGELES	21
21	Boston	38
41	DALLAS	35
30	Denver	27
31	Oakland	28
43	Los Angeles	50

Use Name	Pos.	Hgt	Wgt	Age	Int	Pts
Larry Baker	OT	6'2"	240	23		
Ernie Barnes	OT	6'3"	257	21		
Gene Cockrell	OT	6'3"	247	27		
Jack Klotz	OT	6'5"	260	26		
Dan Callahan	OG	6'	230	22		
Frank D'Agostino	OG	6'1"	245	26		
Howard Glenn (died Oct. 9)	OG	6'	235	25		
John McMullan	OG	6'	244	25		
Bob Mischak	OG	6'	238	27		
Mike Hudock	C	6'2"	245	25		
Ed Cooke	DE	6'4"	245	25		
Bob Reifsnyder	DE	6'2"	250	23		
Joe Ryan	DE	6'2"	235	26		
Nick Mumley	OT-DE	6'6"	245	24	1	6
Dick Guesman	DT	6'4"	255	24		
Joe Katchik	DT	6'9"	290	26		
Tom Saidock	DT	6'5"	260	28		
Sid Youngelman	DT	6'3"	265	28		
Leon Dumbrowski	LB	6'	215	22		
Roger Ellis	LB	6'3"	233	22	1	
Larry Grantham	LB	6'	195	21	5	
Bob Marques	LB	6'	220	23		
Hall Whitley	LB	6'2"	225	25		
Eddie Bell	DB	6'1"	215	29	2	
Roger Donnahoo	DB	6'	185	22	5	12
Charlie Dupre	DB	6'1"	195	24		
Dick Felt	DB	6'	180	27	2	
Fred Julian	DB	5'9"	185	22	6	
Corky Tharp	DB	5'10"	180	27	2	
Rick Sapienza	HB-DB	5'11"	185	24		
Al Dorow	QB	6'	195	30		42
Dick Jamieson	QB	6'1"	190	24		
Bob Scrabis	QB	6'3"	220	24		
Dewey Bohling	HB	5'11"	190	21		36
Leon Burton	HB	5'9"	172	25		18
Don Herndon	HB	6'	195	26		6
Bill Shockley	HB	6'	185	22		86
Pete Hart	FB	5'9"	190	22		
Bill Mathis	FB	6'1"	205	21		12
Joe Pagliei	FB	6'	220	26		6
Ken Campbell	OE	6'1"	213	21		
Don Maynard	OE	6'	185	24		36
Art Powell	OE	6'3"	210	23		84
Dave Ross	OE	6'3"	210	22		6
Thurlow Cooper	DE-OE	6'4"	228	27		20

BUFFALO BILLS 5-8-1 Buster Ramsey

Scores of Each Game		
3	New York	27
21	DENVER	27
13	Boston	0
10	LOS ANGELES	24
13	NEW YORK	17
38	OAKLAND	9
25	HOUSTON	24
28	DALLAS	45
7	Oakland	20
32	Los Angeles	3
38	Denver	38
38	BOSTON	14
23	Houston	31
7	Dallas	24

Use Name	Pos.	Hgt	Wgt	Age	Int	Pts
Tony Discenzo (from BOS)	OT	6'5"	240	24		
Ed Meyer	OT	6'2"	240	23		
Harold Olson	OT	6'3"	266	21		
Bob Sedlock	OT	6'4"	295	23		
Phil Blazer	OG	6'1"	235	24		
Don Chelf	OG	6'3"	235	25		
Ed Muelhaupt	OG	6'3"	230	24		
Dan McGrew	C	6'2"	250	22		
Leroy Moore	DE	6'	230	24		
Charlie Rutkowski	DE	6'3"	248	22		
Lavern Torczon	DE	6'2"	240	24		
Mack Yoho	DE	6'2"	240	24	1	12
Gene Grabosky	DT	6'5"	275	23		
Chuck McMurtry	DT	6'	310	22		
John Scott	DT	6'4"	260	24		
Jim Sorey	DT	6'4"	270	23		
Bernie Buzyniski	LB	6'3"	228	22	1	
Joe Hergert	LB	6'1"	217	24	1	12
Jack Laraway	LB	6'1"	220	24		
Archie Matsos	LB	6'	220	25	8	6
Sam Palumbo	LB	6'2"	230	29		
Dennis Remmert	LB	6'3"	215	21		
Joe Schaffer	LB	6'	210	22	1	
Jack Johnson	DB	6'3"	195	26	2	
Billy Kinard	DB	6'	185	26	4	
Richie McCabe	DB	6'1"	185	26	4	
Jim Wagstaff	DB	6'2"	190	24	6	6
Billy Atkins	HB-DB	6'1"	195	25	5	45
Bob Brodhead	QB	6'2"	207	23		2
Johnny Green	QB	6'3"	198	23		12
Tom O'Connell	QB	5'11"	190	28		8
Richie Lucas	HB-QB	6'	190	21		18
Elbert Dubenion	HB	6'	190	25		48
Willmer Fowler	HB	5'11"	185	23		6
Darrell Harper	HB	6'1"	195	21		7
Joe Kulbacki	HB	6'	185	22		6
Harold Lewis	HB	6'	200	24		
Wray Carlton	FB	6'2"	210	22		66
Carl Smith	FB	6'	200	25		6
Bob Barrett	OE	6'3"	200	24		
Dick Brubaker	OE	6'	195	28		6
Dan Chamberlain	OE	6'4"	200	23		24
Monte Crockett	OE	6'3"	210	21		6
Al Hoisington (from OAK)	OE	6'3"	200	25		12
Tom Rychlec	OE	6'3"	220	26		

BOSTON PATRIOTS 5-9-0 Lou Saban

Scores of Each Game		
10	DENVER	13
28	New York	24
0	BUFFALO	13
35	Los Angeles	0
14	Oakland	27
24	Denver	31
16	LOS ANGELES	45
34	OAKLAND	28
38	NEW YORK	21
42	DALLAS	14
10	HOUSTON	24
14	Buffalo	38
0	Dallas	34
21	Houston	37

Use Name	Pos.	Hgt	Wgt	Age	Int	Pts
Bob Cross	OT	6'4"	245	29		
Jerry DeLucca	OT	6'3"	250	24		
George McGee	OT	6'2"	255	24		
Abe Cohen	OG	5'11"	230	26		
Jack Davis	OG	6'	226	27		
Bob Lee	OG	6'1"	245	24		
Charlie Leo	OG	6'	233	25		
Walt Cudzik	C	6'2"	226	27		
Bill Danenhauer (from DEN)	DE	6'4"	245	25		
Bob Dee	DE	6'3"	234	27	1	
Harry Jacobs	DE	6'2"	235	23	4	
Don McComb	DE	6'4"	240	26		
Al Richardson	DE	6'3"	250	25		
Al Crow	DT	6'6"	260	27		
Art Hauser	DT	6'	243	29		
Jim Hunt	DT	5'11"	245	21		
Harry Jagielski	DT	6'	260	28		
Bob Yates	DT	6'3"	250	21		
Tom Addison	LB	6'3"	230	24		
Phil Bennett	LB	6'3"	225	24		
Bill Brown	LB	6'1"	230	23	1	
Jack Rudolph	LB	6'3"	225	22	2	
Tony Sardisco	LB	6'2"	225	27		
Fred Bruney	DB	5'10"	188	29	3	
Ross O'Hanley	DB	6'	185	21	3	
Chuck Shonta	DB	6'	190	22	2	6
Bob Soltis	DB	6'2"	205	23	2	
Clyde Washington	DB	6'	195	22	3	
Gino Capelletti	OE-DB	6'	190	26	4	60
Tom Dimitroff	QB	5'11"	200	25		
Tom Greene	QB	6'1"	190	22		
Butch Songin	QB	6'2"	190	36		12
Harvey White	QB	6'1"	190	22		
Walter Beach	HB	6'	180	25		6
Ron Burton	HB	5'10"	190	23		6
Dick Christy	HB	5'10"	192	24		36
Jake Crouthamel	HB	5'11"	195	22		
Larry Garron	HB	6'	185	23		
Jerry Green	HB	6'	190	23		
Walt Livingston	HB	6'	185	25		6
Ger Schwedes	HB	6'1"	205	21		
Billy Wells	HB	5'9"	175	28		6
Jim Crawford	FB	6'1"	205	24		14
Bill Larson	FB	5'10"	190	21		
Alan Miller	FB	6'	195	22		18
Joe Biscaha	OE	6'1"	190	23		
Jim Colclough	OE	6'	185	24		54
Joe Johnson	OE	6'	185	30		18
Oscar Lofton	OE	6'6"	218	22		24
Mike Long	OE	6'	188	21		
Tom Stephens	OE	6'1"	190	24		18

HOUSTON OILERS

RUSHING

Last Name	No.	Yds	Avg	TD
Cannon	152	644	4.2	1
Smith	154	643	4.2	5
Tolar	54	179	3.3	3
Hall	30	118	3.9	0
Cline	37	105	2.8	2
Talamini	0	14	0.0	0
Milstead	6	–21	–3.5	0
Lee	16	–57	–3.6	0
Blanda	25	–60	–2.4	4

RECEIVING

Last Name	No.	Yds	Avg	TD
Groman	72	1473	20	12
Carson	45	604	13	4
Hennigan	44	722	16	6
Smith	22	216	10	2
Cannon	15	187	12	5
Tolar	7	71	10	0
Atchason	5	48	10	1
Witcher	4	34	9	1
Cline	4	15	4	0
J. White	1	18	18	0
Norton	1	5	5	0

PUNT RETURNS

Last Name	No.	Yds	Avg	TD
Cannon	4	96	24	0
Hall	6	72	12	0
Tolar	5	40	8	0

KICKOFF RETURNS

Last Name	No.	Yds	Avg	TD
Hall	19	594	31	1
Cannon	8	266	33	1
Tolar	13	249	19	0
Dukes	4	58	15	0
Cline	3	42	14	0
Jamison	1	5	5	0
J. White	0	11	11	0

PASSING – PUNTING – KICKING

PASSING	Att	Comp	%	Yds	Yd/Att	TD	Int–%	RK
Blanda	363	169	47	2413	6.6	24	22– 6	5
Lee	77	41	53	842	10.9	5	6– 8	
Milstead	7	4	57	43	6.1	0	0– 0	
Smith	5	3	60	70	14.0	1	0– 0	
Cannon	3	0	0	0	0.0	0	0– 0	
Groman	1	1	100	3	3.0	1	0– 0	

PUNTING	No	Avg
Milstead	66	35.8
Hall	6	35.0

KICKING	XP	Att	%	FG	Att	%
Blanda	46	47	98	15	34	44

NEW YORK TITANS

RUSHING

Last Name	No.	Yds	Avg	TD
Bohling	123	431	3.5	2
Mathis	92	307	3.3	2
Dorow	124	167	1.3	7
Shockley	37	156	4.2	0
Burton	16	119	7.4	1
Hart	25	113	4.5	0
Pagliei	17	69	4.1	1
Jamieson	8	–61	–7.6	0

RECEIVING

Last Name	No.	Yds	Avg	TD
Maynard	72	1265	18	6
Powell	69	1167	17	14
Bohling	30	268	9	4
Mathis	18	103	6	0
Ross	10	122	12	1
Cooper	9	161	18	3
Shockley	8	69	9	2
Herndon	5	57	11	1
Hart	3	19	6	0
Burton	3	8	3	0
Pagliei	1	13	13	0
Sapienza	1	4	4	0
Klotz	0	5	0	0

PUNT RETURNS

Last Name	No.	Yds	Avg	TD
Burton	12	93	8	0
Donnahoo	1	15	15	1
Shockley	3	12	4	0
Tharp	1	0	0	0

KICKOFF RETURNS

Last Name	No.	Yds	Avg	TD
Burton	31	897	29	2
Shockley	17	411	24	0
Herndon	5	114	23	0
Powell	2	63	32	0
Maynard	3	59	20	0
Baker	1	18	18	0
Reifsnyder	1	16	16	0
Klotz	1	8	8	0
Cooper	1	0	0	0

PASSING – PUNTING – KICKING

PASSING	Att	Comp	%	Yds	Yd/Att	TD	Int–%	RK
Dorow	396	201	51	2748	6.9	26	26– 7	2
Jamieson	70	35	50	586	8.4	6	2– 3	
Bohling	5	0	0	0	0.0	0	0– 0	
Scrabis	3	0	0	0	0.0	0	0– 0	

PUNTING	No	Avg
Pagliei	48	37.1
Sapienza	8	32.4
Dorow	6	44.0

KICKING	XP	Att	%	FG	Att	%
Shockley	47	50	94	9	21	43

2 POINT XP
Cooper (1)

BUFFALO BILLS

RUSHING

Last Name	No.	Yds	Avg	TD
Carlton	137	533	3.9	7
Fowler	93	370	4.0	1
Kulbacki	41	108	2.6	1
Dubenion	16	94	5.9	1
Lucas	46	90	1.9	2
Smith	19	61	3.2	0
Atkins	2	47	23.5	0
Brodhead	21	45	2.1	0
Harper	1	3	3.0	0
O'Connell	22	–24	–1.0	1
Green	46	–156	–3.4	2

RECEIVING

Last Name	No.	Yds	Avg	TD
Rychlec	45	590	13	0
Dubenion	42	752	18	7
Carlton	29	477	16	4
Chamberlain	17	279	16	4
Crockett	14	173	12	1
Fowler	10	99	10	0
Hoisington	8	141	18	2
Smith	7	127	18	1
Brubaker	7	75	11	1
Lucas	5	58	12	1
Kulbacki	2	9	5	0
Green	1	0	0	0

PUNT RETURNS

Last Name	No.	Yds	Avg	TD
Kulbacki	12	100	8	0
Kinard	2	24	12	0
Matsos	1	20	20	0
Dubenion	2	6	3	0
Crockett	1	5	5	0
Lucas	4	3	1	0
Lewis	1	2	2	0

KICKOFF RETURNS

Last Name	No.	Yds	Avg	TD
Kulbacki	13	226	17	0
Fowler	12	201	17	0
Lewis	4	97	24	0
Smith	2	72	36	0
Dubenion	4	68	17	0
Kinard	1	39	39	0
Hoisington	2	25	13	0
Chamberlain	1	24	24	0
Rychlec	1	3	3	0

PASSING – PUNTING – KICKING

PASSING	Att	Comp	%	Yds	Yd/Att	TD	Int–%	RK
Green	228	89	39	1267	5.6	10	10– 4	8
O'Connell	145	65	45	1033	7.1	7	13– 9	8
Lucas	49	23	47	314	6.4	2	3– 6	
Brodhead	25	7	28	75	3.0	0	3– 12	

PUNTING	No	Avg
Atkins	89	39.0

KICKING	XP	Att	%	FG	Att	%
Atkins	27	32	84	6	13	46
Harper	1	2	50	2	3	67
Hergert	0	0	0	2	4	50
Yoho	0	0	0	2	5	40
O'Connell	0	0	0	0	1	0

2 POINT XP
Brodhead (1)
O'Connell (1)

BOSTON PATRIOTS

RUSHING

Last Name	No.	Yds	Avg	TD
Miller	101	416	4.2	1
Christy	78	363	4.7	4
Burton	66	280	4.3	1
Crawford	51	238	4.7	2
Wells	14	59	4.2	0
Garron	8	27	3.4	0
Crouthamel	4	16	4.0	0
Livingston	10	16	1.6	1
Washington	2	10	5.0	0
White	5	7	1.4	0
Beach	6	–4	–0.7	0
Dimitroff	2	–10	–5.0	0
Greene	16	–27	–1.7	0
Songin	36	–140	–3.9	2

RECEIVING

Last Name	No.	Yds	Avg	TD
Colclough	49	666	14	9
Miller	29	284	10	2
Christy	26	268	10	2
Stephens	22	320	15	3
Burton	21	196	9	0
Lofton	19	360	19	4
Wells	14	206	15	1
Johnson	11	186	17	3
Crawford	10	92	9	0
Beach	9	132	15	1
Green	3	52	17	0
White	2	24	12	0
Long	2	10	5	0
Cappelletti	1	28	28	0
Cudzik	1	11	11	0
Garron	1	8	8	0
Livingston	1	0	0	0

PUNT RETURNS

Last Name	No.	Yds	Avg	TD
Christy	8	73	9	0
Wells	12	66	6	0
Bruney	4	31	8	0
Beach	1	21	21	0
Cohen	1	9	9	0
Cappelletti	1	3	3	0
Burton	1	0	0	0

KICKOFF RETURNS

Last Name	No.	Yds	Avg	TD
Christy	24	617	26	0
Wells	11	275	25	0
Burton	4	161	40	0
Beach	7	146	21	0
Cappelletti	4	100	25	0
Bruney	2	39	20	0
Crouthamel	2	27	14	0
Garron	1	21	21	0
Hunt	1	8	8	0
Team	1	8	8	0
Greene	1	3	3	0
Livingston	1	3	3	0

PASSING – PUNTING – KICKING

PASSING	Att	Comp	%	Yds	Yd/Att	TD	Int–%	RK
Songin	392	187	48	2476	6.3	22	15– 4	4
Greene	63	27	43	251	4.0	1	6– 10	
Christy	11	6	55	94	8.5	2	2– 18	
White	7	3	43	44	6.3	0	0– 0	
Dimitroff	2	0	0	0	0.0	0	0– 0	

PUNTING	No	Avg
Greene	59	37.9
Washington	17	31.7

KICKING	XP	Att	%	FG	Att	%
Cappelletti	30	32	94	8	21	38
Crawford	0	0	0	0	1	0
Cudzik	0	0	0	0	1	0

2 POINT XP
Cappelletti (3)
Crawford (1)

LOS ANGELES 10-4-0 Sid Gillman

Scores of Each Game		
21	DALLAS	20
28	Houston	38
0	Dallas	17
24	Buffalo	10
0	BOSTON	35
23	Denver	19
45	Boston	16
21	New York	7
24	HOUSTON	21
3	BUFFALO	32
52	OAKLAND	28
41	Oakland	17
41	DENVER	33
50	NEW YORK	43

Use Name	Pos.	Hgt	Wgt	Age	Int	Pts
Dick Chorovich	OT	6'4"	260	27		
Sam DeLuca	OT	6'2"	245	24		
Ron Mix	OT	6'4"	245	22		
Ernie Wright	OT	6'4"	270	21		
Al Barry	OG	6'2"	235	29		
Fred Cole	OG	5'11"	226	23		
Orlando Ferrante	OG	6'	230	27		
Charlie Kempinski	OG	6'	235	21		
Don Rogers	C	6'2"	235	23		
Ben Donnell	DE	6'5"	248	23		
Art Gob (from WAS-N)	DE	6'4"	230	23		
Ron Nery	DE	6'6"	226	25		
Maury Schleicher	DE	6'3"	240	23	1	
Paul Maguire	OE-DE	6'	210	22	3	6
Gary Finneran	DT	6'3"	240	26		
John Kompara	DT	6'2"	245	23		
Volney Peters	DT	6'4"	240	31		
Al Bansavage	LB	6'2"	230	22		
Hubert Bobo	LB	6'1"	214	25		
Ron Botcham	LB	6'1"	238	25	2	
Charlie Brueckman	LB	6'2"	225	24		
Emil Karas	LB	6'3"	225	26		
Rommie Loudd	LB	6'3"	226	26	3	
Bob Garner	DB	5'10"	190	25	2	
Dick Harris	DB	5'11"	174	23	5	6
Charley McNeil	DB	5'11"	178	24	3	
Doyle Nix	DB	6'1"	195	27	4	6
Jesse Thomas	DB	5'10"	180	31		
Henry Wallace	DB	6'	195	22		
Bob Zeman	DB	6'1"	203	23	2	
Jimmy Sears	HB-DB	5'11"	187	29	2	
Bobby Clatterbuck	QB	6'3"	196	28		
Jack Kemp	QB	6'1"	200	26		48
Bob Laraba	LB-QB	6'3"	194	26	1	
Fred Ford (from BUF)	HB	5'8"	180	22		12
Paul Lowe	HB	6'	180	23		66
Ron Waller	HB	5'11"	184	27		
Howie Ferguson	FB	6'2"	217	30		36
Charlie Flowers	FB	6'1"	207	23		12
Blanche Martin (from NY)	FB	6'	195	23		6
Royce Womble	FL	6'	184	28		24
Ralph Anderson*	OE	6'4"	225	23		30
Howard Clark	OE	6'2"	204	25		
Dave Kocourek	OE	6'5"	225	23		6
Trusse Norris	OE	6'1"	190	23		
Don Norton	OE	6'1"	180	22		30
Ben Agajanian	K	6'	220	41		85

* died Nov. 26 of diabetes

DALLAS TEXANS 8-6-0 Hank Stram

Scores of Each Game		
20	Los Angeles	21
34	Oakland	16
17	LOS ANGELES	0
35	NEW YORK	37
19	OAKLAND	20
10	Houston	20
17	Denver	14
45	Buffalo	28
34	DENVER	7
14	Boston	42
35	New York	41
24	HOUSTON	0
34	BOSTON	0
24	BUFFALO	7

Use Name	Pos.	Hgt	Wgt	Age	Int	Pts
Jerry Cornelison	OT	6'3"	250	23		
Charley Diamond	OT	6'2"	235	24		
R. B. Nunnery	OT	6'4"	275	26		
Jack Stone	OT	6'2"	245	23		
Sid Fournet	OG	6'	235	27		
Billy Krisher	OG	6'1"	235	24		
Al Reynolds	OG	6'3"	225	22		
Marvin Terrell	OG	6'1"	235	22		
Jim Barton	C	6'5"	250	25		
Tom Dimmick	C	6'6"	255	29		
Mel Branch	DE	6'2"	220	23		
Dick Frey	DE	6'2"	230	29		
Paul Miller	DE	6'2"	235	28		
Ray Collins	DT	5'11"	250	32		
Rufus Granderson	DT	6'5"	277	23		
Walter Napier	DT	6'4"	280	24		
Paul Rochester	DT	6'2"	250	23		
Walt Corey	LB	6'	215	22	3	
Ted Greene	LB	6'1"	230	26	3	
Sherrill Headrick	LB	6'2"	215	23	2	
Bob Hudson (to DEN)	LB	6'4"	230	30	1	
Smokey Stover	LB	6'	215	21	1	
Johnny Bookman	DB	5'11"	185	25	4	
Don Flynn	DB	6'	205	25	3	6
Jimmy Harris	DB	6'1"	175	25	2	
Charlie Jackson	DB	5'11"	180	24		
Dave Webster	DB	6'4"	215	22	6	18
Duane Wood	DB	6'1"	190	24	4	6
Carroll Zaruba	DB	5'9"	210	26		
Clem Daniels	HB-DB	6'1"	220	23	3	
Cotton Davidson	QB	6'1"	180	28		17
Hunter Enis	QB	6'2"	190	23		18
Abner Haynes	HB	6'	185	22		72
Curley Johnson	HB	6'	215	25		14
Johnny Robinson	HB	6'	195	21		54
Jim Swink	HB	6'1"	185	24		
Bo Dickinson	FB	6'2"	220	25		6
Jack Spikes	FB	6'2"	220	22		103
Ed Bernet	OE	6'3"	205	27		
Max Boydston	OE	6'2"	215	27		18
Bob Bryant	OE	6'5"	230	23		
Chris Burford	OE	6'3"	210	22		30

OAKLAND RAIDERS 6-8-0 Eddie Erdalatz

Scores of Each Game		
22	HOUSTON	37
16	DALLAS	34
14	Houston	13
14	Denver	31
20	Dallas	19
27	BOSTON	14
9	Buffalo	38
28	New York	27
28	Boston	34
20	BUFFALO	7
28	Los Angeles	52
17	LOS ANGELES	41
28	NEW YORK	31
48	DENVER	10

Use Name	Pos.	Hgt	Wgt	Age	Int	Pts
Don Churchwell	OT	6'1"	255	23		
Bill Striegel (from BOS)	OT	6'2"	240	24		
Dalton Truax	OT	6'2"	235	25		
Don Deskins	OG	6'3"	240	27		
John Dittrich	OG	6'1"	240	27		
Wayne Hawkins	OG	6'	235	22		
Don Manoukian	OG	5'9"	242	25		
Ron Sabal	OG	6'2"	230	23		
Jim Otto	C	6'2"	227	22		
Larry Barnes	DE	6'1"	230	27		55
Carmen Cavalli	DE	6'4"	245	22		
George Fields	DE	6'3"	245	24	2	
Charley Powell	DE	6'2"	227	28		
Ray Armstrong	DT	6'1"	235	22		
Joe Barbee	DT	6'3"	250	25		
Paul Oglesby	DT	6'4"	235	20		
Ron Warzeka	DT	6'4"	250	29		
Bob Dougherty	LB	6'1"	240	26		
Billy Locklin	LB	6'2"	225	22		
Tom Louderback	LB	6'2"	235	26	2	
Riley Morris	LB	6'2"	230	23		
Alex Bravo	DB	6'	190	28	4	
Joe Cannavino	DB	5'11"	185	24	4	
Wayne Crow	DB	6'	205	22	4	
L. C. Joyner	DB	6'1"	187	25		
Eddie Macon	DB	6'	180	32	9	6
John Harris	HB-DB	6'1"	195	27		
Tom Flores	QB	6'1"	190	23		18
Paul Larson	QB	5'11"	180	28		
Babe Parilli	QB	6'1"	190	30		6
Bob Keyes	HB	5'10"	183	24		
Jack Larscheid	HB	5'6"	162	26		12
Nyle McFarlane	HB	6'2"	205	24		12
Billy Reynolds	HB	5'10"	200	28		
Tony Teresa	HB	5'9"	185	25		60
Billy Lott	FB	6'	205	25		38
J. D. Smith	FB	6'	220	25		50
Doug Asad	OE	6'3"	200	22		6
Al Goldstein	OE	6'	204	24		12
Charley Hardy	OE	6'	183	26		18
Gene Prebola	OE	6'3"	215	22		12

DENVER BRONCOS 4-9-1 Frankie Filchock

Scores of Each Game		
13	Boston	10
27	Buffalo	21
24	New York	28
31	OAKLAND	14
19	LOS ANGELES	23
31	BOSTON	24
14	DALLAS	17
25	HOUSTON	45
7	Dallas	34
10	Houston	20
38	BUFFALO	38
27	NEW YORK	30
33	Los Angeles	41
10	Oakland	48

Use Name	Pos.	Hgt	Wgt	Age	Int	Pts
Eldon Danenhauer	OT	6'4"	235	24		
Gordy Holz	OT	6'4"	270	26		
Willie Smith	OT	6'2"	255	22		
Ken Adamson	OG	6'2"	215	21		
Jack Davis	OG	6'2"	235	25		
Carl Larpenter	OG	6'4"	235	23		
Dave Strickland	OG	6'	220	28		
Frank Kuchta	C	6'2"	235	24		
Mike Nichols	C	6'3"	225	21		
Chuck Gavin	DE	6'1"	235	26		
Bill Yelverton	DE	6'4"	220	26	1	6
Joe Young	DE	6'3"	245	25		
John Hatley	DT	6'3"	260	29		
Bud McFadin	DT	6'3"	260	32		
Hal Smith (from BOS)	DT	6'5"	250	25		
Don King	OT-DT	6'3"	255	30	2	
Vaughan Alliston	LB	6'	218	26	1	
Hardy Brown	LB	6'	190	36		
Al Day	LB	6'2"	216	22		
Pete Mangum	LB	6'	220	28		
Frank Bernardi	DB	5'9"	185	27		
Dick Doyle	DB	6'	190	29	1	
Goose Gonsoulin	DB	6'3"	205	22	11	
John Pyeatt	DB	6'3"	204	26	4	6
Al Romine	DB	6'2"	195	27	3	
Bob McNamara	HB-DB	6'	188	26	4	12
Tom Dublinski	QB	6'2"	205	30		
George Herring	QB	6'2"	200	25		
Frank Tripucka	QB	6'2"	205	32		
Henry Bell	HB	5'10"	210	23		
Al Carmichael	HB	6'1"	195	30		42
Gene Mingo	HB	6'1"	200	21		123
Bob Stransky	HB	6'1"	180	24		
Ted Wegert (from NY-to BUF)	HB	5'11"	200	28		12
Don Allen	FB	6'	200	23		6
J. W. Brodnax	FB	6'	208	23		6
Dave Rolle	FB	6'	215	22		18
Don Carothers	OE	6'5"	225	24		
Pat Epperson	OE	6'3"	225	24		
Jim Greer	OE	6'3"	215	26		6
Bill Jessup	OE	6'1"	195	31		6
Lionel Taylor	OE	6'2"	214	24		72
Ken Carpenter	HB-OE	6'	212	34		6

LOS ANGELES CHARGERS

RUSHING

Last Name	No.	Yds	Avg	TD
Lowe	136	855	**6.3**	**9**
Ferguson	126	438	3.5	4
Ford	38	194	5.1	2
Flowers	39	161	4.1	1
Martin	18	58	3.2	0
Laraba	4	7	1.8	0
Waller	9	5	0.6	0
Norton	1	2	2.0	0
Clatterbuck	6	−6	−1.0	0
Kemp	90	−103	−1.1	8

RECEIVING

Last Name	No.	Yds	Avg	TD
Anderson	44	614	14	5
Kocourek	40	662	17	1
Womble	32	316	10	4
Clark	27	431	16	0
Norton	25	414	17	5
Lowe	23	377	16	2
Ferguson	21	168	8	2
Flowers	12	153	13	1
Martin	4	23	6	1
Waller	3	24	8	0
Ford	1	5	5	0

PUNT RETURNS

Last Name	No.	Yds	Avg	TD
Harris	13	105	8	0
Sears	9	101	11	0
Garner	6	85	14	0
Ford	2	6	3	0
Maguire	1	4	4	1
Lowe	1	0	0	0

KICKOFF RETURNS

Last Name	No.	Yds	Avg	TD
Lowe	28	611	22	0
Ford	18	400	22	0
Sears	8	155	19	0
Norton	8	153	19	0
DeLuca	1	0	0	0

PASSING – PUNTING – KICKING

PASSING	Att	Comp	%	Yds	Yd/Att	TD	Int–%	RK
Kemp	406	211	52	3018	**7.4**	20	25– 6	**1**
Clatterbuck	23	15	65	112	4.9	1	1– 4	
Laraba	7	2	29	23	3.3	0	2– 29	
Lowe	3	1	33	24	8.0	0	0– 0	
Ford	1	0	0	0	0.0	0	0– 0	
Waller	1	0	0	0	0.0	0	1–100	

PUNTING	No	Avg
Maguire	43	**40.5**
Laraba	15	37.2

KICKING	XP	Att	%	FG	Att	%
Agajanian	46	47	**98**	13	24	54

DALLAS TEXANS

RUSHING

Last Name	No.	Yds	Avg	TD
Haynes	**156**	**875**	5.6	**9**
Robinson	98	458	4.8	4
Spikes	115	457	4.0	5
Dickinson	35	143	4.1	1
Johnson	23	43	1.9	1
Swink	10	15	1.5	0
Daniels	1	−2	−2.0	0
Enis	12	−12	−1.0	3
Davidson	31	−122	−3.9	1

RECEIVING

Last Name	No.	Yds	Avg	TD
Haynes	55	576	10	3
Burford	46	789	17	5
Robinson	41	611	15	4
Boydston	29	357	12	3
Spikes	11	158	14	0
Johnson	10	174	17	1
Bryant	5	43	9	0
Bernet	4	49	12	0
Swink	4	37	9	0
Dickinson	3	38	13	0
Davidson	1	−1	−1	0

PUNT RETURNS

Last Name	No.	Yds	Avg	TD
Haynes	14	**215**	**15**	0
Robinson	14	207	15	1
Daniels	3	69	23	0
Harris	1	5	5	0
Rochester	1	0	0	0

KICKOFF RETURNS

Last Name	No.	Yds	Avg	TD
Haynes	19	434	23	0
Daniels	9	162	18	0
Harris	5	117	23	0
Robinson	3	54	18	0
Swink	1	36	36	0
Dickinson	2	29	15	0
Johnson	1	13	13	0

PASSING – PUNTING – KICKING

PASSING	Att	Comp	%	Yds	Yd/Att	TD	Int–%	RK
Davidson	379	179	47	2474	6.5	15	16– 4	5
Enis	54	30	56	357	6.6	1	2– 4	
Haynes	1	0	0	0	0.0	0	0– 0	
Robinson	1	0	0	0	0.0	0	1–100	

PUNTING	No	Avg
Davidson	58	39.4
Johnson	3	36.7

KICKING	XP	Att	%	FG	Att	%
Spikes	34	36	94	13	31	42
Davidson	8	8	100	1	1	100
Flynn	0	0	0	0	1	0
Johnson	0	0	0	0	1	0

2 POINT XP
Johnson (1)

OAKLAND RAIDERS

RUSHING

Last Name	No.	Yds	Avg	TD
Teresa	139	608	4.4	6
Lott	99	520	5.3	5
Larscheid	94	397	4.2	1
Smith	63	214	3.4	6
McFarlane	4	52	13.0	0
Parilli	32	25	0.8	1
Keyes	1	7	7.0	0
Reynolds	1	6	6.0	0
Goldstein	3	−2	−0.7	1
Flores	39	−42	−1.1	3

RECEIVING

Last Name	No.	Yds	Avg	TD
Lott	49	524	11	1
Teresa	35	393	11	4
Prebola	33	404	12	2
Goldstein	27	354	13	1
Hardy	24	423	18	3
Larscheid	22	187	9	1
Smith	17	194	11	1
Asad	14	197	14	1
McFarlane	5	89	18	2
Reynolds	3	43	14	0
Keyes	1	19	19	0
Parilli	1	0	0	0

PUNT RETURNS

Last Name	No.	Yds	Avg	TD
Larscheid	12	106	9	0
Reynolds	7	24	3	0
Teresa	5	12	2	0
Keyes	1	5	5	0
Cannavino	1	4	4	0

KICKOFF RETURNS

Last Name	No.	Yds	Avg	TD
Larscheid	30	852	28	0
Smith	14	373	27	1
McFarlane	5	71	14	0
Asad	3	66	22	0
Teresa	4	61	15	0
Harris	3	38	13	0
Deskins	1	15	15	0
Morris	1	3	3	0

PASSING – PUNTING – KICKING

PASSING	Att	Comp	%	Yds	Yd/Att	TD	Int–%	RK
Flores	252	136	**54**	1738	6.9	12	12– 5	2
Parilli	187	87	47	1003	5.4	5	11– 6	10
Teresa	18	9	50	111	6.2	1	3– 17	
Larscheid	6	3	50	71	11.8	0	2– 33	

PUNTING	No	Avg
Crow	76	38.9

KICKING	XP	Att	%	FG	Att	%
Barnes	37	39	95	6	25	24

2 POINT XP
Lott (1)
Smith(1)

DENVER BRONCOS

RUSHING

Last Name	No.	Yds	Avg	TD
Rolle	130	501	3.9	2
Mingo	83	323	3.9	4
Bell	43	238	5.5	0
Carmichael	41	211	5.1	2
Wegert	36	161	4.5	1
Stransky	28	78	2.8	0
McNamara	17	33	1.9	1
Brodnax	15	18	1.2	0
Allen	30	18	0.6	1
Carpenter	4	13	3.3	0
Nichols	0	3	0.0	0
Taylor	2	−6	−3.0	0
Herring	5	−46	−9.2	0
Tripucka	37	−226	−6.1	0

RECEIVING

Last Name	No.	Yds	Avg	TD
Taylor	**92**	**1235**	13	**12**
Carmichael	32	616	19	5
Carpenter	29	350	12	1
Greer	22	284	13	1
Rolle	21	122	6	1
Mingo	19	156	8	1
Epperson	11	99	9	0
Jessup	9	120	13	1
McNamara	7	143	20	1
Wegert	5	68	14	1
Brodnax	5	39	8	1
Allen	5	34	7	0
Stransky	3	11	4	0
Carothers	2	25	13	0
Bell	2	13	7	0

PUNT RETURNS

Last Name	No.	Yds	Avg	TD
Carmichael	**15**	101	7	0
Mingo	3	92	31	1
McNamara	11	68	6	0
Wegert	4	25	6	0

KICKOFF RETURNS

Last Name	No.	Yds	Avg	TD
Carmichael	22	581	26	0
Wegert	10	252	25	0
Mingo	9	209	23	0
McNamara	9	192	21	0
Stransky	7	153	22	0
Brodnax	5	117	23	0
Allen	5	72	14	0
Bell	2	60	30	0
W. Smith	1	13	13	0
Greer	1	11	11	0
Strickland	1	9	9	0

PASSING – PUNTING – KICKING

PASSING	Att	Comp	%	Yds	Yd/Att	TD	Int–%	RK
Tripucka	**478**	**248**	52	**3038**	6.4	24	34– 7	7
Herring	22	9	41	137	6.2	0	1– 5	
Mingo	7	1	14	46	6.6	0	0– 0	
Carmichael	1	1	100	26	26.0	0	0– 0	

PUNTING	No	Avg
Herring	70	37.3

KICKING	XP	Att	%	FG	Att	%
Mingo	33	36	92	**18**	28	**64**

1961 N.F.L. Bypassing the Crisis

For some teams, the forward pass became less important than the weekend pass. President Kennedy's activation of reserve units because of the Berlin crisis drafted many players into active military duty, among them Paul Hornung, Bobby Mitchell, Ray Nitschke, Boyd Dowler, Dick Schafrath, Bob DeMarco, John Gordy, and John Paluck. Since all of the reservists were stationed within the continental United States, most of the affected players could get back to their teams on a weekend pass, then return to their military base on Monday morning. Commissioner Pete Rozelle also had contact with the federal government, but not as a soldier. He successfully persuaded Congress to pass a bill officially exempting the NFL's package TV deal with CBS from anti-trust legislation.

EASTERN CONFERENCE

New York Giants—After the Giants lost to the Cards on opening day and looked sluggish in the first half against the Steelers, Giant coach Allie Sherman yanked quarterback Chuck Conerly and replaced him with newly acquired Y. A. Tittle. The bald-headed Tittle won the first-string job by pulling out a victory over the Steelers and flawlessly directed the New York attack through the season. With Del Shofner, Joe Walton, and Erich Barnes—all, like Tittle, acquired in off-season trades—blending in with the holdover Giant stars, New York climbed into a first-place tie with Philadelphia by beating the Eagles 38-21 in Yankee Stadium on November 12 and took sole possession of the top spot by knocking off the Eagles 28-24 in Philadelphia on December 10. Needing at least a tie to clinch the title, the Giants played Cleveland to a 7-7 deadlock to end the season.

Philadelphia Eagles—Starting with Timmy Brown's 105-yard kickoff return on the first play of the season, the Eagles displayed the league's most explosive offense. Sonny Jurgensen replaced the retired Norm Van Brocklin at quarterback and surpassed all expectations by throwing thirty-two touchdown passes in a superior air attack featuring receivers Tommy McDonald and Pete Retzlaff. But two flaws sabotaged the Eagles' title chances—a weak running game and a thin defensive secondary. Cornerback Tom Brookshier broke a leg in a 16-14 victory over the Bears, and the Giants exploited substitute Glen Amerson's inexperience the next week in a 38-21 New York win.

Cleveland Browns—Paul Brown may have been the coach of the 1950s, but a storm was gathering against him in the 1960s. Several Cleveland players, including Jimmy Brown, found the coach's stern way of dealing with his men increasingly hard to take, and quarterback Milt Plum was openly critical of Brown's system of sending every play in via alternating messenger guards. But despite the growing dissension and a disappointing defensive secondary, the Browns again were in the thick of the Eastern title chase. They trailed New York by only one game until a 37-21 Giant win on November 26 ended their hopes.

St. Louis Cardinals—Injuries crippled the Cardinal offense even before the season started. Halfback John David Crow broke an ankle, and quarterback Sam Etcheverry, debuting in the NFL after a great nine-year career in Canada, came up with a sore arm to put a dent in the running and passing attacks. Coach Pop Ivy kept his team together, throwing Prentice Gautt into Crow's spot and spelling Etcheverry with Ralph Guglielmi, and the Cards came up with upset wins over New York and Philadelphia. But more injuries, such as Ken Panfil's bad knee, dropped the club into the lower ranks in the East and prompted coach Ivy to resign with two games left.

Pittsburgh Steelers—Old age was catching up with the Steelers. Bobby Layne spent several weeks in drydock with a bad shoulder, ends Preston Carpenter and Bob Schnelker had lost their speed, and defensive linemen Ernie Stautner, Big Daddy Lipscomb, and Joe Krupa all were on the decline. With Layne out, Rudy Bukich, who had done more sitting than playing in his past six seasons, took over at quarterback and showed a good arm and no consistency. Only fullback John Henry Johnson, flanker Buddy Dial, defensive back Johnny Sample, and linebackers John Reger and Myron Pottios had top-notch seasons.

Dallas Cowboys—After going winless through their inaugural 1960 season, the Cowboys quickly picked up their first victory by beating Pittsburgh 27-24 on opening day. After four weeks, the Cowboys had also beaten Minnesota twice to climb to a 3-1 record before the league caught up with them. Two blue-chip rookies made the Cowboys a much improved team. Halfback Don Perkins, who missed the 1960 season with a broken foot, raced to 815 yards rushing with a fine showing late in the season. The defensive addition was Bob Lilly, a quick and strong defensive end who put heavy pressure on enemy passers. Veterans Eddie LeBaron and Billy Howton combined for many short pass completions, while Frank Clarke suddenly developed into a dangerous deep receiver.

Washington Redskins—Rookie head coach Bill McPeak and rookie quarterback Norm Snead both suffered through a frightening debut. McPeak found himself in charge of a club with no runners, no blockers, and a porous defensive secondary. Snead learned quickly how to throw under pressure, with his line giving him no protection from swarms of defenders clawing and thrashing him. After thirteen losses and heavy underdogs against the Dallas Cowboys, the Redskins won 34-24 to avert the stigma of a victoryless season.

WESTERN CONFERENCE

Green Bay Packers—Coach Vince Lombardi had built his team around good blocking and good tackling. His offense had the league's best running attack, with two superb guards in Jerry Kramer and Fuzzy Thurston escorting runners Jim Taylor, Paul Hornung, and Tommy Moore around end in the famous Green Bay power sweep. Against the run the Packers defense was murder, with a quick forward wall of Bill Quinlan, Henry Jordan, Dave Hanner, and Willie Davis perfectly complemented by smart linebackers Bill Forester, Ray Nitschke, and Dan Currie. The Packers were a brutally physical team, with quarterback Bart Starr directing the violence with pinpoint passing and a knack for picking apart enemy defenses. After losing to the Lions on opening day, Green Bay won its next six games and had the Western title sewed up with two weeks left in the season.

Detroit Lions—Detroit fans found it hard to believe that the Lions were NFL powers. Five times the Lions lost at home, with a 49-0 pasting by the '49ers the ultimate humiliation. But the Lions saved their best for the road by going undefeated. Coach George Wilson had built a defense to match Green Bay's, a unit with size, speed, and experience in all sectors. No other team could match tackles Alex Karras and Roger Brown, Joe Schmidt had no peer as a middle linebacker, and Yale Lary and Night Train Lane had a world of savvy in the secondary.

Baltimore Colts—Johnny Unitas' passes still packed the Baltimore attack with explosives, but the Colt defense no longer could defuse enemy offenses. With Big Daddy Lipscomb and Johnny Sample traded to Pittsburgh and Art Donovan at the end of his career, opponents found it easier to move the ball against the Colts than it had been in the late 1950s. A slow start of two wins in the first five games made any title hopes seem very slim, and even a 45-21 mid-season ambush of the Packers couldn't halt the Colts' decline into mediocrity. But the colts still showcased several fine individual performances, such as the explosive running and receiving of Lenny Moore, the continued superb pass-catching of Ray Berry, and All-Pro seasons from Jim Parker and Gino Marchetti.

Chicago Bears—First place in the West rode on the November 12 meeting of the Bears and Packers in Wrigley Field. Green Bay's record was 6-2, coming off a 45-21 pasting by the Colts; the Bears' record was 5-3, fresh from a close 16-14 loss to the Eagles. Although the Packers had shut the Bears out 24-0 in an earlier meeting, Chicago fans whipped themselves into a fury over the game. They saw a good game, as the Packers ran out to a 28-7 lead and then barely held on for a 31-28 triumph. The Bears did not recapture first place, but they did refurbish their passing attack this year. The main addition was rookie Mike Ditka, the first tight end to win a national following for his devastating blocking and effective receiving.

San Francisco '49ers—The shotgun formation burned the league up for five weeks. Using this pass-oriented formation, the '49ers won four of their first five games, including triumphs of 35-3 over Washington, 49-0 over Detroit, and 35-0 over Los Angeles. Coach Red Hickey was alternating John Brodie, rookie Bill Kilmer, and Bobby Waters at the quarterback slot on alternate plays, loading the shotgun with quarterback plunges, halfback reverses, and a spate of passes. But the dream ended on October 22 in Chicago. Knowing that a center could not block well while looking between his legs to hike a ball back to a tailback, Bear defensive coach Clark Shaughnessy put middle linebacker Bill George right over the center and had him charge straight through to the quarterback on every play. By halftime, the Bears had demoralized the '49ers; by the final gun, the Bears had won 31-0. Thus exposed, the shotgun never again exploded.

Los Angeles Rams—The Rams had a lot of offensive talent for a sixth-place team. Jon Arnett and Dick Bass were top-notch runners, Ollie Matson a multitalented back, and both Jim Phillips and Carroll Dale fine receivers. There was no fuse at quarterback, however, to start the machine rolling, as neither Zeke Bratkowski nor Frank Ryan showed any consistency in running the attack. The porous offensive line helped neither passers nor runners, and outside of rookie end Deacon Jones, bright spots were scarce for the defensive unit.

Minnesota Vikings—The Vikings, this year's expansion team, quickly surpassed Dallas' 1960 record as a new team by beating the Chicago Bears 37-13 in their first league game. The three wins the Vikes captured for the season surprised most experts and made Norm Van Brocklin's coaching debut a success. Van Brocklin stepped right from the playing ranks as quarterback with the Eagles into the head coach's job at Minnesota, and his quarterback was one with a style most unlike his own. While Van Brocklin was a pocket passer whom only a tidal wave could force to run, rookie Fran Tarkenton became the talk of the league with his scrambling.

FINAL STATISTICS

OFFENSE

	BALT.	CHI.	CLEVE.	DALLAS	DET.	G.BAY	L.A.	MINN.	N.Y.	PHIL.	PITT.	ST.L.	S.F.	WASH.
FIRST DOWNS:														
Total	274	239	246	239	233	274	236	236	**275**	252	239	202	258	193
by Rushing	124	103	116	100	96	**142**	109	104	99	78	102	83	116	55
by Passing	135	113	120	130	122	115	111	123	**160**	158	123	110	132	124
by Penalty	15	**23**	10	9	15	17	16	9	16	16	14	9	10	14
RUSHING:														
Number	456	436	476	416	439	474	415	419	464	373	**543**	386	448	361
Yards	2119	1890	2163	1819	1868	**2350**	1958	1897	1857	1507	1761	1405	2100	1072
Average Yards	4.6	4.3	4.5	4.4	4.3	**5.0**	4.7	4.5	4.0	4.0	3.2	3.6	4.7	3.0
Touchdowns	17	16	15	6	16	**27**	17	14	13	10	10	8	**27**	9
PASSING:														
Attempts	**438**	349	320	422	398	306	386	377	416	429	334	351	346	420
Completions	232	186	185	215	186	177	199	203	215	**241**	176	168	187	189
Completion Pct.	53.0	53.3	57.8	50.9	46.7	**57.8**	51.6	53.8	51.7	56.2	52.7	47.9	54.0	45.0
Passing Yards (Gross)	3018	3011	2538	2918	2830	2502	2709	2527	3035	**3824**	2622	2434	3057	2566
Yards Lost Tackled	215	339	164	257	286	**138**	372	538	295	219	290	461	253	391
Net Yards	2803	2672	2374	2661	2544	2364	2337	1989	2740	**3605**	2332	1973	2804	2175
Yds. per Att (Gross)	6.9	8.6	7.9	6.9	7.1	8.2	7.0	6.7	7.3	**8.9**	7.9	6.9	8.8	6.1
Yds. per Comp (Gross)	13.0	16.2	13.7	13.6	15.2	14.1	13.6	12.4	14.1	15.9	14.9	14.5	**16.3**	13.6
Touchdowns	17	26	20	23	14	18	13	22	27	**34**	23	21	15	12
Interceptions	29	24	**13**	27	27	16	21	22	23	26	34	23	19	28
Pct. Intercepted	6.6	6.9	**4.1**	6.4	6.8	5.2	5.4	5.8	5.5	6.1	10.2	6.6	5.5	6.7
PUNTING:														
Number	42	60	53	61	56	51	64	63	68	55	73	**85**	59	70
Average Distance	43.0	41.7	43.3	36.7	**47.6**	43.0	40.1	39.0	43.9	43.7	47.0	44.7	44.6	38.1
PUNT RETURNS:														
Number	33	27	28	23	38	20	14	23	**42**	34	40	26	24	28
Yards	269	170	283	103	357	355	184	309	289	353	**447**	236	232	197
Average Yards	8.2	6.3	10.1	4.5	9.4	**17.8**	13.1	13.4	6.9	10.4	11.2	9.1	9.7	7.0
Touchdowns	0	0	1	0	0	**2**	1	1	0	1	1	1	1	0
KICKOFF RETURNS:														
Number	53	51	50	64	50	41	56	**72**	38	53	49	47	49	64
Yards	1182	1247	1115	1345	1097	1077	1463	**1568**	850	1313	1020	992	1302	1661
Average Yards	22.3	24.5	22.3	21.0	21.9	26.3	26.1	21.8	22.4	24.8	20.8	21.1	**26.6**	26.0
Touchdowns	0	0	**1**	0	**1**	0	**1**	0	0	**1**	0	0	**1**	0
INTERCEPTION RETURNS:														
Number	16	24	20	25	29	29	23	22	**33**	17	25	24	19	26
Yards	123	371	160	374	312	446	277	356	**526**	239	498	459	322	325
Average Yards	7.7	15.5	8.0	15.0	10.8	15.4	12.0	16.2	15.9	14.1	**19.9**	19.1	16.9	12.5
Touchdowns	0	0	0	0	1	2	0	0	4	0	2	**5**	0	2
PENALTIES:														
Number	69	**81**	47	47	69	66	63	36	59	42	52	57	65	70
Yards	589	**719.5**	455	427	678	647	599	375	629	500	486	535	635	651
FUMBLES:														
Number	21	23	28	46	25	**18**	21	36	40	25	34	39	25	18
Number Lost	13	14	20	21	15	**10**	11	22	20	14	22	18	17	12
POINTS:														
Total	302	326	319	236	270	**391**	263	285	368	361	295	279	346	174
PAT Attempts	34	42	39	29	32	**49**	32	37	46	46	36	37	44	23
PAT Made	33	41	37	29	31	**49**	32	36	46	43	34	34	44	21
FG Attempts	**39**	27	23	24	33	24	27	21	34	25	28	17	22	28
FG Made	**21**	11	16	11	15	16	13	9	14	14	15	7	12	5
Percent FG Made	53.8	40.7	**69.6**	45.8	45.5	66.7	48.1	42.9	41.2	56.0	53.6	41.2	54.5	17.9
Safeties	1	0	0	0	1	0	0	0	**2**	0	0	1	1	0

DEFENSE

	BALT.	CHI.	CLEVE.	DALLAS	DET.	G. BAY	L.A.	MINN.	N.Y.	PHIL.	PITT.	ST.L.	S.F.	WASH.
FIRST DOWNS:														
Total	232	223	243	254	222	245	279	291	**212**	267	218	215	234	261
by Rushing	108	80	87	122	89	110	136	147	86	116	**71**	91	90	94
by Passing	**110**	124	146	120	121	117	121	132	**110**	145	132	112	132	154
by Penalty	14	19	10	12	12	18	22	12	16	**6**	15	12	12	13
RUSHING:														
Number	418	401	411	454	412	412	508	493	419	474	**396**	477	419	412
Yards	1869	1652	1605	2161	1520	1694	2440	2667	1761	2007	**1463**	1676	1701	1550
Average Yards	4.5	4.1	3.9	4.8	3.7	4.1	4.8	5.4	4.2	4.2	3.7	**3.5**	4.1	3.8
Touchdowns	17	10	16	20	14	12	26	29	**6**	12	11	9	13	10
PASSING:														
Attempts	351	398	358	**326**	385	414	328	365	386	383	420	389	380	409
Completions	**161**	209	200	168	203	218	184	194	176	224	201	187	196	238
Completion Pct.	45.9	52.5	55.9	51.5	52.7	52.7	56.1	53.2	**45.6**	58.5	47.9	48.1	51.6	58.2
Passing Yards (Gross)	**2320**	3164	2831	2635	2744	2630	2642	3051	2600	3183	2780	2644	2874	3493
Yards Lost Tackled	**407**	367	305	204	326	273	269	125	399	263	334	334	394	218
Net Yards	**1913**	2797	2526	2431	2418	2357	2373	2926	2201	2920	2446	2310	2480	3275
Yds. per Att (Gross)	6.6	7.9	7.9	8.1	7.1	**6.4**	8.1	8.4	6.7	8.3	6.6	6.8	7.6	8.5
Yds. per Comp (Gross)	14.4	15.1	14.2	15.7	13.5	**12.1**	14.4	15.7	14.8	14.2	13.8	14.1	14.7	14.7
Touchdowns	18	27	16	21	**11**	13	19	21	21	23	22	18	18	37
Interceptions	16	24	20	25	29	29	23	22	**33**	17	25	24	19	26
Pct. Intercepted	4.6	6.0	5.6	7.7	7.5	7.0	7.0	6.0	**8.5**	4.4	6.0	6.2	5.0	6.4
PUNTING:														
Number	64	66	54	43	67	49	51	46	83	64	**86**	67	62	58
Average Distance	41.4	42.7	42.9	45.5	43.0	**37.8**	43.3	41.4	42.4	41.8	43.8	42.0	44.0	44.2
PUNT RETURNS:														
Number	18	24	27	**17**	21	25	36	23	32	30	32	53	32	30
Yards	248	302	213	193	273	313	384	**138**	247	235	251	438	269	280
Average Yards	13.8	12.6	7.9	11.4	13.0	12.5	10.7	**6.0**	7.7	7.8	7.8	8.3	8.4	9.3
Touchdowns	1	1	**0**	**0**	1	1	**0**	**0**	**0**	1	1	1	1	1
KICKOFF RETURNS:														
Number	57	55	56	43	49	69	53	51	59	58	50	50	58	**29**
Yards	1552	1219	1465	978	1184	1597	1380	1148	1288	1224	1156	1007	1368	**666**
Average Yards	27.2	22.2	26.2	22.7	24.2	23.1	26.0	22.5	21.8	21.1	23.1	**20.1**	23.6	23.0
Touchdowns	**0**	1	1	**0**	2	**0**	**0**	**0**	**0**	1	**0**	**0**	**0**	**0**
INTERCEPTION RETURNS:														
Number	29	24	**13**	27	27	16	21	22	23	26	34	23	19	28
Yards	406	346	302	589	314	**238**	280	219	246	294	510	318	249	477
Average Yards	14.0	14.4	23.2	21.8	11.6	14.9	13.3	**10.0**	10.7	11.3	15.0	13.8	13.1	17.0
Touchdowns	1	**0**	1	6	**0**	**0**	**0**	2	1	1	2	**0**	**0**	2
PENALTIES:														
Number	66	**86**	38	38	39	52	75	65	67	62	57	59	56	63
Yards	547.5	**860**	367	362	381	609	662	638	677	684	533	546	456	603
FUMBLES:														
Number	19	22	23	30	21	30	27	31	**43**	27	36	36	21	33
Number Lost	8	13	18	18	12	17	16	**23**	21	16	20	20	12	15
POINTS:														
Total	307	302	270	380	258	223	333	407	**220**	297	287	267	272	392
PAT Attempts	37	39	34	49	28	**26**	45	52	29	38	37	30	32	50
PAT Made	37	36	33	44	28	**26**	45	50	29	36	35	30	32	49
FG Attempts	26	27	28	28	34	21	21	26	**20**	24	26	38	29	24
FG Made	16	10	11	14	20	13	6	15	**5**	11	10	19	16	13
Percent FG Made	61.5	37.0	39.3	50.0	58.8	61.9	28.6	57.7	**25.0**	45.8	38.5	50.0	55.2	54.2
Safeties	**0**	1	**0**	**0**	1	1	**0**	**0**	1	**0**	**0**	**0**	**0**	2

1961 NFL CHAMPIONSHIP GAME

December 31, at Green Bay
(Attendance 39,029)

New York's Cold Reception

Although the Packers had won five Western titles before this year, this was the first NFL championship game ever staged in Green Bay. The sub-freezing Wisconsin weather suited the Packers fine as they easily rolled over the Giants. The first quarter was scoreless, but New York's Kyle Rote dropped a sure touchdown pass deep in Green Bay territory. The Giants blew another touchdown in the second quarter when halfback Bob Gaiters overthrew Rote in the end zone. The Packers, meanwhile, took a comfortable lead by scoring three touchdowns in the quarter. Paul Hornung, on leave from the Army, scored from the 6-yard line after an 80-yard Packer drive, Boyd Dowler scored on a Bart Starr pass after a Ray Nitschke interception, and a Starr-to-Ron Kramer touchdown pass followed another Packer interception. Hornung added all the extra points and a 17-yard field goal to run the halftime score to 24-0. With their running game ineffective, the Giants turned to the pass, but Green Bay's Jess Whittenton blanketed top receiver Del Shofner like a shadow. While their defense continued to thwart the Giants, the Packers added ten more points in the third quarter to put the game on ice. The Packers turned a fumbled punt by Joe Morrison into a Hornung field goal, and another sustained drive resulted in Ron Kramer's second touchdown catch. A fourth-quarter Hornung field goal made the final score 37-0 and gave Hornung a record 19 points for the championship game.

SCORING

GREEN BAY	0	24	10	3	–37
NEW YORK	0	0	0	0	– 0

Second Quarter

G.B.	Hornung, 6 yard rush PAT – Hornung (kick)	0:04
G.B.	Dowler, 13 yard pass from Starr PAT – Hornung (kick)	4:19
G.B.	R. Kramer, 14 yard pass from Starr PAT – Hornung (kick)	10:04
G.B.	Hornung, 17 yard field goal	15:00

Third Quarter

G.B.	Hornung, 22 yard field goal	9:55
G.B.	R. Kramer, 13 yard pass from Starr PAT – Hornung (kick)	12:12

Fourth Quarter

G.B.	Hornung, 19 yard field goal	6:48

TEAM STATISTICS

G.B.		N.Y.
19	First Downs – Total	6
10	First Downs – Rushing	1
8	First Downs – Passing	4
1	First Downs – Penalty	1
1	Fumbles – Number	5
0	Fumbles – Number Lost	1
4	Penalties – Number	4
16	Yards Penalized	38
0	Giveaways	5
5	Takeaways	0
+5	Difference	–5

INDIVIDUAL STATISTICS

GREEN BAY	No	Yds	Avg.	NEW YORK	No	Yds	Avg.
RUSHING							
Hornung	20	89	4.5	Webster	7	19	2.7
Taylor	14	69	4.9	Wells	3	9	3.0
Moore	6	25	4.2	King	2	5	2.5
Roach	1	0	0.0	Gaiters	1	2	2.0
Pitts	3	–2	–0.7	Tittle	1	–4	–4.0
	44	181	4.1		14	31	2.2
RECEIVING							
R. Kramer	4	80	20.0	Rote	3	54	18.0
Hornung	3	47	15.7	Shofner	3	41	13.7
Dowler	3	37	12.3	Webster	3	5	1.7
	10	164	16.4	Walton	1	19	19.0
					10	119	11.9
PUNTING							
Dowler	5		42.0	Chandler	5		39.2
PUNT RETURNS							
Wood	1	4	4.0	Morrison	2	10	5.0
KICKOFF RETURNS							
Nitschke	1	18	18.0	Wells	5	98	19.6
				Gaiters	1	21	21.0
					6	119	19.8
INTERCEPTION RETURNS							
Adderley	1	14	14.0				
Gremminger	1	13	13.0	None			
Nitschke	1	9	9.0				
Whittenton	1	0	0.0				
	4	36	9.0				

PASSING

GREEN BAY	Att	Comp	Comp Pct.	Yds	Int	Yds/ Att.	Yds/ Comp	Yards Lost Tackled
Starr	17	10	58.8	164	0	9.6	16.4	0
Hornung	2	0	0.0	0	0	–	–	0
	19	10	52.6	164	0	8.6	16.4	0
NEW YORK								
Tittle	20	6	30.0	65	4	3.3	10.8	2–15
Conerly	8	4	50.0	54	0	6.8	13.5	1– 5
Gaiters	1	0	0.0	0	0	–	–	0
	29	10	34.5	119	4	4.1	11.9	3–20

NEW YORK GIANTS 10-3-1 Allie Sherman

Scores of Each Game		
10	ST. LOUIS	21
17	Pittsburgh	14
24	Washington	21
24	St. Louis	9
31	Dallas	10
24	LOS ANGELES	14
16	DALLAS	17
53	WASHINGTON	0
38	PHILADELPHIA	21
42	PITTSBURGH	21
37	Cleveland	21
17	GREEN BAY	20
28	Philadelphia	24
7	CLEVELAND	7

Use Name	Pos.	Hgt	Wgt	Age	Int	Pts
Rosey Brown	OT	6'3"	255	28		
Chuck Janerette	OT	6'3"	250	22		
Darrell Dess	OG	6'	245	25		
Zeke Smith	OG	6'2"	235	25		
Jack Stroud	OG	6'1"	250	32		
Mickey Walker	OG	6'	230	21		
Ray Wietecha	C	6'1"	230	32		
Greg Larson	OT-C	6'2"	245	22		
Jim Katcavage	DE	6'3"	240	26		2
Andy Robustelli	DE	6'1"	235	35		
Rosey Grier	OT	6'5"	290	28		
Dick Modzelewski	OT	6'	260	30		2
Frank Gifford – Voluntarily Retired						
Larry Hayes	LB	6'3"	230	26		6
Sam Huff	LB	6'1"	230	26	3	6
Cliff Livingston	LB	6'3"	215	31	3	
Tom Scott	LB	6'2"	220	31	1	6
Bob Simms	LB	6'1"	230	23		
Gene Johnson (from MIN)	DB	6'	180	26		
Dick Lynch	DB	6'1"	205	25	9	
Dick Nolan	DB	6'1"	185	29		
Jimmy Patton	DB	6'	185	29	8	6
Bill Stits	DB	6'	195	30		
Erich Barnes	HB-DB	6'2"	198	26	7	18
Allan Webb	HB-DB	5'11"	180	26		
Jim Podoley – Injury						
Chuck Conerly	QB	6'1"	185	37		
Lee Grosscup	QB	6'1"	185	24		
Y. A. Tittle	QB	6'	195	34		18
Don Chandler	HB	6'2"	210	26		
Bob Gaiters	HB	5'11"	210	23		42
Phil King	HB	6'4"	225	25		
Joel Wells	HB	6'1"	198	20		12
Joe Morrison	DB-HB	6'1"	212	23	2	12
Alex Webster	FB	6'3"	225	30		30
Pete Hall	OE	6'2"	200	23		
Kyle Rote	OE	6'	200	32		42
Del Shofner	OE	6'3"	185	25		66
Joe Walton	OE	5'11"	200	26		12
Pat Summerall	K	6'4"	235	31		88

PHILADELPHIA EAGLES 10-4-0 Nick Skorich

Scores of Each Game		
27	CLEVELAND	20
14	WASHINGTON	7
27	ST. LOUIS	30
21	PITTSBURGH	16
20	St. Louis	7
43	Dallas	7
27	Washington	24
16	CHICAGO	14
21	New York	38
24	Cleveland	45
35	DALLAS	13
35	Pittsburgh	24
24	NEW YORK	28
27	Detroit	24

Use Name	Pos.	Hgt	Wgt	Age	Int	Pts
Jim McCusker	OT	6'2"	245	25		
Don Oakes	OT	6'3"	245	23		
J. D. Smith	OT	6'5"	250	25		
Stan Campbell	OG	6'	230	31		
John Wittenborn	OG	6'2"	240	25		
Howard Keys	C	6'3"	240	26		
Gene Gossage	DE	6'3"	240	26		
Will Renfro	DE	6'5"	235	29		
Leo Sugar	DE	6'1"	230	32		
Marion Campbell	DT	6'3"	250	32		
Riley Gunnels	DT	6'3"	250	24		
Ed Khayat	DT	6'3"	248	26		
Jess Richardson	DT	6'2"	265	31		
Maxie Baughan	LB	6'1"	226	23	1	
Chuck Bednarik	LB	6'3"	235	36	2	
John Nocera	LB	6'1"	220	27		
Bob Pellegrini	LB	6'2"	225	26		
Chuck Weber	LB	6'1"	235	32	1	
Glen Amerson	DB	6'1"	186	22		
Tom Brookshier	DB	6'	198	29	2	
Don Burroughs	DB	6'4"	190	30	7	
Jimmy Carr	DB	6'1"	210	28	2	
Irv Cross	DB	6'1"	190	22	2	
Bobby Freeman	DB	6'1"	200	28		
King Hill	QB	6'3"	213	25		
Sonny Jurgensen	QB	5'11"	200	27		
Billy Barnes	HB	5'11"	202	26		24
Timmy Brown	HB	5'10"	190	24		30
Ted Dean	HB	6'2"	210	23		18
Clarence Peaks	FB	6'1"	220	25		30
Theron Sapp	FB	6'1"	205	26		6
Tommy McDonald	FL	5'10"	172	27		78
Dick Lucas	OE	6'2"	216	27		30
Pete Retzlaff	OE	6'1"	212	30		48
John Tracey	OE	6'3"	225	28		
Bobby Walston	OE	6'	195	32		97

CLEVELAND BROWNS 8-5-1 Paul Brown

Scores of Each Game		
20	Philadelphia	27
20	ST. LOUIS	17
25	DALLAS	7
31	WASHINGTON	7
17	GREEN BAY	49
30	Pittsburgh	28
21	St. Louis	10
13	PITTSBURGH	17
17	Washington	6
45	PHILADELPHIA	24
21	NEW YORK	37
38	Dallas	17
14	Chicago	17
7	New York	7

Use Name	Pos.	Hgt	Wgt	Age	Int	Pts
Lou Groza	OT	6'3"	248	37		85
Errol Linden	OT	6'5"	260	24		
Mike McCormack	OT	6'4"	250	34		
Ed Nutting	OT	6'4"	246	22		
Dick Schafrath	OT	6'3"	255	25		
Duane Putnam	OG	6'	233	33		
Jim Ray Smith	OG	6'3"	245	30		
John Wooten	OG	6'2"	250	26		
John Morrow	C	6'3"	248	28		
Jim Houston	DE	6'2"	235	24		
Paul Wiggin	DE	6'3"	245	27		
Johnny Brewer	OE-DE	6'4"	225	24		
Bob Gain	DT	6'3"	260	33		
Floyd Peters	DT	6'4"	255	26		
Larry Stephens	DT	6'4"	260	23		
Vince Costello	LB	6'	232	29		6
Galen Fiss	LB	6'	227	31	1	
Walt Michaels	LB	6'	237	32	2	
Dave Lloyd	C-LB	6'3"	248	25		
Ross Fichtner	DB	6'	185	23		
Don Fleming	DB	6'	188	24	3	
Bernie Parrish	DB	5'11"	195	26	7	6
Jim Shofner	DB	6'2"	190	25	5	
Bobby Franklin	HB-DB	5'11"	182	25	2	6
Gene Hickerson – Broken Leg						
Len Dawson	QB	6'	195	27		
Milt Plum	QB	6'1"	205	27		6
Bobby Mitchell	HB	6'	192	26		60
Tom Watkins	HB	6'1"	195	24		6
Jimmy Brown	FB	6'2"	228	25		60
Preston Powell	FB	6'2"	225	24		
Ray Renfro	FL	6'1"	192	30		36
Leon Clarke	OE	6'4"	235	28		12
Bob Crespino	OE	6'4"	217	23		6
Charley Ferguson	OE	6'5"	217	21		6
Rich Kreitling	OE	6'2"	208	26		18
Gern Nagler	OE	6'2"	190	28		6
Sam Baker	K	6'2"	217	29		

ST. LOUIS CARDINALS 7-7-0 Pop Ivy Chuck Drulis Ray Prochaska Ray Willsey

Scores of Each Game		
21	New York	10
17	Cleveland	20
30	Philadelphia	27
9	NEW YORK	24
7	PHILADELPHIA	20
24	Washington	0
10	CLEVELAND	21
31	Dallas	17
14	DETROIT	45
0	Baltimore	16
27	Pittsburgh	30
38	WASHINGTON	24
31	DALLAS	13
20	PITTSBURGH	0

Use Name	Pos.	Hgt	Wgt	Age	Int	Pts
Ed Cook	OT	6'2"	240	29		
Charley Granger (from DAL)	OT	6'2"	240	23		
Ernie McMillan	OT	6'6"	255	23		
Dale Memmelaar	OT	6'2"	245	24		
Ken Panfil	OT	6'6"	255	30		
Jerry Perry	OT	6'4"	240	30		51
Bob DeMarco	OG	6'3"	240	23		
Ken Gray	OG	6'2"	240	25		
Mike McGee	OG	6'1"	230	23		
Tom Redmond	OG	6'5"	240	24		
Charley Ellzey	C	6'3"	240	23		
Don Gillis	C	6'3"	250	26		
Bob Griffin (from DEN-A)	LB-C	6'3"	250	32		
Ed Henke	DE	6'3"	230	33		
Luke Owens	DE	6'2"	255	28		
Joe Robb	DE	6'3"	230	24	1	
Frank Fuller	DT	6'4"	245	32		
Ron McDole	DT	6'3"	250	21		
Don Owens	DT	6'5"	255	29		
Ted Bates	LB	6'3"	220	24		
Bill Koman	LB	6'2"	230	27	1	
Monte Lee	LB	6'4"	225	23	1	
Dale Meinert	LB	6'2"	220	28	2	
Joe Driskill	DB	6'1"	195	24		
Jimmy Hill	DB	6'2"	190	32	4	6
Jerry Norton	DB	5'11"	195	31	7	12
Willie West	DB	5'10"	185	23	1	6
Larry Willson	DB	6'	187	23	3	2
Pat Fischer	HB-DB	5'10"	165	21		
Billy Stacy	HB-DB	6'1"	190	25	4	24
Joe Childress – Injury						
Sam Etcheverry	QB	5'11"	190	31		
Ralph Guglielmi	QB	6'1"	195	28		6
Charley Johnson	QB	6'	190	24		
Bobby Joe Conrad	HB	6'	195	26		22
John David Crow	HB	6'2"	215	26		24
Prentice Gautt	HB	6'	200	23		36
Ken Hall (from HOU-A)	HB	6'1"	210	25		
Mal Hammack	FB	6'2"	205	28		6
Frank Mestnik	FB	6'2"	200	23		12
Taz Anderson	OE	6'2"	200	22		18
Dick Lage	OE	6'4"	228	21		
Hugh McInnis	OE	6'3"	220	23		
Sonny Randle	OE	6'2"	187	25		54

PITTSBURGH STEELERS 6-8-0 Buddy Parker

Scores of Each Game		
24	Dallas	27
14	NEW YORK	17
14	Los Angeles	24
16	Philadelphia	21
20	WASHINGTON	0
28	CLEVELAND	30
20	SAN FRANCISCO	10
17	Cleveland	13
37	DALLAS	7
21	New York	42
30	ST. LOUIS	27
24	PHILADELPHIA	35
30	Washington	14
0	St. Louis	20

Use Name	Pos.	Hgt	Wgt	Age	Int	Pts
Charlie Bradshaw	OT	6'6"	255	25		
Dan James	OT	6'4"	280	24		
Dick Klein (to BOS-A)	OT	6'4"	255	27		
John Nisby	OG	6'1"	230	28		
Mike Sandusky	OG	6'	230	28		
Ron Stehouwer	OG	6'2"	230	24		
Buzz Nutter	C	6'4"	230	30		
George Demko	DE	6'3"	240	26		
John Kapele	DE	6'	240	24		
Lou Michaels	DE	6'2"	235	25	1	72
Ernie Stautner	DT-DE	6'1"	230	36		
Joe Krupa	DT	6'2"	225	28		
Big Daddy Lipscomb	DT	6'6"	288	30		
Mike Henry	LB	6'2"	215	25	1	
Myron Pottios	LB	6'2"	240	22	2	
John Reger	LB	6'	230	30	1	
Bob Schmitz	LB	6'1"	235	23		
Wilbert Scott	LB	6'	215	22		
George Tarasovic	LB	6'4"	245	32	1	
Len Burnett	DB	6'1"	195	22		
Bill Butler	DB	5'10"	185	24	3	6
Willie Daniel	DB	5'11"	185	23	3	
Johnny Sample	DB	6'1"	200	24	8	12
Jackie Simpson	DB	5'10"	185	27	2	
Brady Keys	HB-DB	6'	185	25	2	
Dick Haley (from MIN)	FL-DB	5'10"	195	24	1	
Rudy Bukich	QB	6'1"	205	30		12
Bobby Layne	QB	6'1"	210	34		5
Terry Nofsinger	QB	6'4"	205	23		
Dick Hoak	HB	5'11"	190	22		
Jack Stanton	HB	6'1"	190	23		
Tom Tracy	HB	5'9"	205	29		20
John Henry Johnson	FB	6'2"	215	31		42
Charlie Scales	FB	5'11"	215	22		
Buddy Dial	FL	6'1"	195	24		72
Red Mack	HB-FL	5'10"	185	24		12
Preston Carpenter	OE	6'2"	190	27		24
Henry Clement	OE	6'2"	200	21		
Bob Coronado	OE	6'1"	195	25		
Steve Meilinger (to STL)	OE	6'2"	230	31		
Bob Schnelker (from MIN)	OE	6'3"	215	31		24
Bobby Joe Green	K	5'11"	175	23		

NEW YORK GIANTS

RUSHING

Last Name	No.	Yds	Avg	TD
Webster	196	928	4.7	2
Gaiters	116	460	4.0	6
Wells	65	216	3.3	1
Tittle	25	85	3.4	3
Webb	6	51	8.5	0
Morrison	33	48	1.5	1
Chandler	3	30	10.0	0
Conerly	13	16	1.2	0
Grosscup	2	10	5.0	0
King	4	7	1.8	0
Shofner	1	6	6.0	0

RECEIVING

Last Name	No.	Yds	Avg	TD
Shofner	68	1125	17	11
Rote	53	805	15	7
Walton	36	544	15	2
Webster	26	313	12	3
Morrison	11	67	6	1
Gaiters	11	54	5	1
Wells	6	31	5	1
Barnes	2	74	37	1
Hall	2	22	11	0

PUNT RETURNS

Last Name	No.	Yds	Avg	TD
Stits	17	132	8	0
Wells	17	90	5	0
Webb	5	61	12	0
Morrison	3	6	2	0

KICKOFF RETURNS

Last Name	No.	Yds	Avg	TD
Gaiters	11	288	26	0
Wells	12	273	23	0
Webb	8	156	20	0
Stits	4	87	22	0
Morrison	2	32	16	0
Simms	1	14	14	0

PASSING – PUNTING – KICKING Statistics

PASSING	Att	Comp	%	Yds	Yd/Att	TD	Int–	%	RK
Tittle	285	163	57	2272	8.0	17	12–	4	3
Conerly	106	44	42	634	6.0	7	8–	8	
Grosscup	22	5	23	87	4.0	1	3–	14	
Gaiters	3	3	100	42	14.0	2	0–	0	

PUNTING	No	Avg
Chandler	68	43.9

KICKING	XP	Att	%	FG	Att	%
Summerall	**46**	**46**	**100**	14	34	41

PHILADELPHIA EAGLES

RUSHING

Last Name	No.	Yds	Avg	TD
Peaks	135	471	3.5	5
Brown	50	338	6.8	1
Dean	66	321	4.9	2
Barnes	92	309	3.4	1
Jurgensen	20	27	1.4	0
Sapp	7	24	3.4	1
Hill	2	9	4.5	0
Retzlaff	1	8	8.0	0

RECEIVING

Last Name	No.	Yds	Avg	TD
McDonald	64	**1144**	18	**13**
Retzlaff	50	769	15	8
Walston	34	569	17	2
Peaks	32	472	15	0
Dean	21	335	16	1
Barnes	15	194	13	3
Brown	14	264	19	2
Lucas	8	67	8	5
Sapp	3	10	3	0

PUNT RETURNS

Last Name	No.	Yds	Avg	TD
Dean	18	140	8	0
Brown	8	125	16	1
Cross	7	77	11	0
Baughan	1	11	11	0

KICKOFF RETURNS

Last Name	No.	Yds	Avg	TD
Brown	**29**	**811**	28	1
Dean	21	462	22	0
Peaks	2	29	15	0
Cross	1	11	11	0

PASSING – PUNTING – KICKING Statistics

PASSING	Att	Comp	%	Yds	Yd/Att	TD	Int–	%	RK
Jurgensen	416	**235**	56	**3723**	8.9	**32**	24–	6	5
Hill	12	6	50	101	8.4	2	2–	17	
Peaks	1	0	0	0	0.0	0	0–	0	

PUNTING	No	Avg
Hill	55	43.7

KICKING	XP	Att	%	FG	Att	%
Walston	43	**46**	93	14	25	56

CLEVELAND BROWNS

RUSHING

Last Name	No.	Yds	Avg	TD
Brown	**305**	**1408**	4.6	8
Mitchell	101	548	5.4	5
Watkins	43	209	4.9	0
Franklin	1	12	12.0	1
Powell	1	5	5.0	0
Kreitling	0	4	0.0	0
McCormack	0	4	0.0	0
Dawson	1	–10	–10.0	0
Plum	24	–17	–0.7	1

RECEIVING

Last Name	No.	Yds	Avg	TD
Renfro	48	834	17	6
Brown	46	459	10	2
Mitchell	32	368	12	3
Kreitling	21	229	11	3
Nagler	19	241	13	1
Clarke	11	211	19	2
Watkins	4	66	17	1
Ferguson	2	68	34	1
Crespino	2	62	31	1

PUNT RETURNS

Last Name	No.	Yds	Avg	TD
Mitchell	14	164	12	1
Shofner	14	119	9	0

KICKOFF RETURNS

Last Name	No.	Yds	Avg	TD
Mitchell	16	428	27	1
Powell	16	321	20	0
Watkins	9	226	25	0
Baker	3	57	19	0
Brown	2	50	25	0
Stephens	1	15	15	0
Fichtner	1	11	11	0
Linden	1	5	5	0
Brewer	1	2	2	0

PASSING – PUNTING – KICKING Statistics

PASSING	Att	Comp	%	Yds	Yd/Att	TD	Int–	%	RK
Plum	302	177	**59**	2416	8.0	18	10–	**3**	**1**
Dawson	15	7	47	85	5.7	1	3–	20	
Brown	3	1	33	37	12.3	1	0–	0	

PUNTING	No	Avg
Baker	53	43.3

KICKING	XP	Att	%	FG	Att	%
Groza	37	38	97	16	23	**70**

ST. LOUIS CARDINALS

RUSHING

Last Name	No.	Yds	Avg	TD
Gautt	129	523	4.1	3
Mestnik	95	334	3.5	1
Crow	48	192	4.0	1
Guglielmi	22	101	4.6	1
Hammack	18	79	4.4	1
Etcheverry	33	73	2.2	0
Anderson	15	39	2.6	1
McInnis	4	30	7.5	0
Conrad	20	22	1.1	0
Norton	1	15	15.0	0
Johnson	1	–3	–3.0	0

RECEIVING

Last Name	No.	Yds	Avg	TD
Randle	44	591	13	9
Conrad	30	499	17	2
Anderson	22	399	18	2
Crow	20	306	15	3
Stacy	12	241	20	1
Gautt	12	132	11	3
Mestnik	12	29	2	1
McInnis	7	107	15	0
Hammack	5	70	14	0
Hall	3	38	13	0
Fischer	1	22	22	0

PUNT RETURNS

Last Name	No.	Yds	Avg	TD
Conrad	5	103	21	1
West	11	98	9	0
Fischer	4	18	5	0
Stacy	5	9	2	0
Driskill	1	8	8	0

KICKOFF RETURNS

Last Name	No.	Yds	Avg	TD
Fischer	17	426	25	0
West	16	340	21	0
Wilson	4	83	21	0
Stacy	3	60	20	0
Conrad	1	28	28	0
Mestnik	2	27	14	0
Lee	1	12	12	0
Driskill	2	8	4	0
Hammack	1	8	8	0

PASSING – PUNTING – KICKING Statistics

PASSING	Att	Comp	%	Yds	Yd/Att	TD	Int–	%	RK
Etcheverry	196	96	49	1275	6.5	14	11–	6	11
Guglielmi	116	56	48	927	8.0	5	8–	7	
Crow	14	4	29	76	5.4	1	1–	7	
Johnson	13	5	38	51	4.0	0	2–	15	
Gautt	11	6	55	100	9.1	1	1–	9	
Conrad	1	1	100	5	5.0	0	0–	0	

PUNTING	No	Avg
Norton	**85**	44.7

KICKING	XP	Att	%	FG	Att	%
Perry	30	33	91	7	16	44
Conrad	4	4	100	0	1	0

PITTSBURGH STEELERS

RUSHING

Last Name	No.	Yds	Avg	TD
Johnson	213	787	3.7	6
Tracy	147	402	2.7	2
Hoak	85	302	3.6	0
Scales	50	184	3.7	0
Green	2	37	18.5	0
Keys	6	14	2.3	0
Layne	8	11	1.4	0
Carpenter	7	9	1.3	0
Meilinger	1	6	6.0	0
Dial	3	6	2.0	0
Nofsinger	6	6	1.0	0
Bukich	14	4	0.3	2
Coronado	1	–7	–7.0	0

RECEIVING

Last Name	No.	Yds	Avg	TD
Dial	53	1047	20	12
Carpenter	33	460	14	4
Schnelker	24	401	17	4
Johnson	24	262	11	1
Tracy	14	133	10	1
Mack	8	128	16	2
Meilinger	8	103	13	0
Scales	7	43	6	0
Clement	5	65	13	0
Haley	3	43	14	0
Coronado	3	32	11	0
Hoak	3	18	6	0

PUNT RETURNS

Last Name	No.	Yds	Avg	TD
Sample	**26**	**283**	11	1
Keys	9	135	15	0
Carpenter	3	18	6	0
Butler	2	11	6	0

KICKOFF RETURNS

Last Name	No.	Yds	Avg	TD
Sample	23	532	23	0
Haley	13	278	21	0
Butler	6	117	20	0
Scales	3	41	14	0
Keys	2	41	21	0
Johnson	1	11	11	0
Schmitz	1	0	0	0

PASSING – PUNTING – KICKING Statistics

PASSING	Att	Comp	%	Yds	Yd/Att	TD	Int–	%	RK
Bukich	156	89	57	1253	8.0	11	16–	10	9
Layne	149	75	50	1205	8.1	11	16–	11	14
Tracy	12	4	33	73	6.1	0	0–	0	
Nofsinger	11	7	64	78	7.1	0	0–	0	
Hoak	3	1	33	13	4.3	1	1–	33	
Johnson	2	0	0	0	0.0	0	1–	50	
Green	1	0	0	0	0.0	0	0–	0	

PUNTING	No	Avg
Green	73	47.0

KICKING	XP	Att	%	FG	Att	%
Michaels	27	29	93	15	26	58
Layne	5	5	100	0	0	0
Tracy	2	2	100	0	1	0
Green	0	0	0	0	1	0

EASTERN CONFERENCE – Continued

DALLAS COWBOYS 4-9-1 Tom Landry

Scores of Each Game		
27	PITTSBURGH	24
21	MINNESOTA	7
7	Cleveland	25
28	Minnesota	0
10	NEW YORK	31
7	PHILADELPHIA	43
17	New York	16
17	ST. LOUIS	31
7	Pittsburgh	37
28	WASHINGTON	28
13	Philadelphia	35
17	CLEVELAND	38
13	St. Louis	31
24	Washington	34

Use Name	Pos.	Hgt	Wgt	Age	Int	Pts
Byron Bradfute	OT	6'3"	243	23		
Bob Fry	OT	6'4"	240	30		
Bob McCreary	OT	6'5"	256	22		
Andy Cvercko	OG	6'	240	24		
Mike Falls	OG	6'1"	240	27		
Bob Grottkau	OG	6'4"	230	24		
John Houser	OG	6'3"	242	25		
Mike Connelly	C	6'3"	235	25		
Nate Borden	DE	6'	240	29		
Bob Lilly	DE	6'4"	248	22		
Ken Frost	DT	6'4"	245	22	1	
Don Healy	DT	6'3"	264	25	1	
Bill Herchman	DT	6'2"	250	28		
Sonny Davis	LB	6'2"	220	22		
Mike Dowdle	LB	6'3"	210	23	1	
Chuck Howley	LB	6'3"	230	25	1	
Jack Patera	LB	6'1"	240	29		
Jerry Tubbs	LB	6'2"	220	26	3	
Gene Babb	FB-LB	6'3"	218	26		
Bob Bercich	DB	6'1"	198	24	3	
Don Bishop	DB	6'2"	204	26	8	
Tom Franckhauser	DB	6'	196	24	1	
Jimmy Harris	DB	6'1"	180	26	2	
Warren Livingston	DB	5'10"	180	23	1	
Dick Moegle	DB	6'	195	27	2	
Buddy Humphrey	QB	6'1"	200	25		
Eddie LeBaron	QB	5'9"	160	31		
Don Meredith	QB	6'2"	198	23		6
L. G. Dupre	HB	5'11"	190	29		
Don Perkins	HB	5'10"	198	23		30
J. W. Lockett (from SF)	FB	6'2"	230	24		18
Amos Marsh	FB	6'1"	208	22		18
Merrill Douglas	HB-FB	6'	204	25		
Dick Bielski	OE	6'1"	227	29		46
Frank Clarke	OE	6'	215	28		54
Jim Doran	OE	6'2"	211	33		12
Billy Howton	OE	6'2"	185	31		24
Lee Murchison	OE	6'3"	205	23		
Glynn Gregory	DB-OE	6'2"	200	22	1	
Allen Green	K	6'2"	215	23		34

WASHINGTON REDSKINS 1-12-1 Bill McPeak

Scores of Each Game		
3	San Francisco	35
7	Philadelphia	14
21	NEW YORK	24
7	Cleveland	31
0	Pittsburgh	20
0	ST. LOUIS	24
24	PHILADELPHIA	27
0	New York	53
6	CLEVELAND	17
28	Dallas	28
6	BALTIMORE	27
24	St. Louis	38
14	PITTSBURGH	30
34	DALLAS	24

Use Name	Pos.	Hgt	Wgt	Age	Int	Pts
Ray Lemek	OT	6'	240	27		
Riley Mattson	OT	6'4"	248	22		
Fran O'Brien	OT	6'1"	250	26		
Bernie Darre	OG	6'2"	230	21		
Vince Promuto	OG	6'1"	243	23		
Ed Beatty (from PIT)	C	6'3"	237	29		
Fred Hageman	C	6'4"	244	23		
Jim Schrader	C	6'2"	252	29		
John Paluck	DE	6'2"	240	28	1	
Andy Stynchula	DE	6'3"	250	22		
Gene Cronin	LB-DE	6'2"	228	28		
Don Lawrence	DT	6'1"	245	24		
Joe Rutgens	DT	6'2"	265	22		
Bob Toneff	DT	6'3"	270	31		
Rod Breedlove	LB	6'2"	225	23	2	
Dick Lasse	LB	6'2"	225	25		
Doyle Schick	LB	6'1"	210	22		
Roy Wilkins	LB	6'3"	228	27		
Jim Crotty (to BUF-A)	DB	5'11"	190	23		
Dale Hackbart	DB	6'3"	210	25	6	12
Jim Kerr	DB	6'	195	22	7	
Joe Krakoski	DB	6'2"	200	24	4	
Ben Scotti	DB	6'1"	186	24	1	
Jim Steffen (from DET)	DB	6'	195	24	1	
Jim Wulff	HB-DB	5'11"	184	25	3	
George Izo	QB	6'3"	214	24		
Norm Snead	QB	6'4"	215	21		18
Lew Luce	HB	6'	187	23		
Mike Sommer (from BAL)	HB	5'11"	190	26		
Sam Horner	DB-HB	6'	198	23		6
Dick James	DB-HB	5'9"	175	27	1	30
Don Bosseler	FB	6'1"	212	25		18
Jim Cunningham	FB	5'11"	220	22		12
Bill Anderson	OE	6'3"	214	25		
John Aveni	OE	6'3"	215	26		42
Fred Dugan	OE	6'3"	198	27		24
Steve Junker	OE	6'3"	217	26		
Tom Osborne	OE	6'3"	190	24		12

WESTERN CONFERENCE

GREEN BAY PACKERS 11-3-0 Vince Lombardi

Scores of Each Game		
13	DETROIT	17
30	SAN FRANCISCO	10
24	CHICAGO	0
45	BALTIMORE	7
49	Cleveland	17
33	Minnesota	7
28	MINNESOTA	10
21	Baltimore	45
31	Chicago	28
35	LOS ANGELES	17
17	Detroit	9
20	NEW YORK	17
21	San Francisco	22
24	Los Angeles	17

Use Name	Pos.	Hgt	Wgt	Age	Int	Pts
Forrest Gregg	OT	6'4"	250	28		
Norm Masters	OT	6'2"	250	28		
Bob Skoronski	OT	6'3"	250	28		
Jerry Kramer	OG	6'3"	250	26		
Fuzzy Thurston	OG	6'1"	250	28		
Ken Iman	C	6'1"	230	22		
Jim Ringo	C	6'1"	235	30		
Ben Davidson	DE	6'8"	275	21		
Willie Davis	DE	6'3"	240	28		
Lee Folkins	DE	6'5"	220	22		
Bill Quinlan	DE	6'3"	250	29		
Dave Hanner	DT	6'2"	260	32	1	
Henry Jordan	DT	6'3"	250	26		
Ron Kostelnik	DT	6'4"	260	21		
Tom Bettis	LB	6'2"	225	28		
Dan Currie	LB	6'3"	240	27	3	6
Bill Forester	LB	6'3"	240	30	2	
Ray Nitschke	LB	6'3"	235	25	2	
Nelson Toburen	LB	6'3"	235	22		
Herb Adderley	DB	6'1"	205	22	1	
Hank Gremminger	DB	6'1"	205	28	5	
Johnny Symank	DB	5'11"	180	26	5	
Em Tunnell	DB	6'1"	210	39		
Jesse Whittenton	DB	6'	195	27	5	6
Willie Wood	DB	5'10"	185	25	5	12
John Roach	QB	6'4"	200	28		6
Bart Starr	QB	6'1"	200	28		6
Lew Carpenter	HB	6'1"	215	29		
Paul Hornung	HB	6'2"	215	25		146
Tom Moore	HB	6'2"	215	23		12
Elijah Pitts	HB	6'1"	200	22		6
Jim Taylor	FB	6'	215	26		96
Boyd Dowler	FL	6'5"	220	24		18
Gary Knafelc	OE	6'4"	220	29		
Ron Kramer	OE	6'3"	230	26		24
Max McGee	OE	6'3"	205	29		42
Ben Agajanian (from DAL-A)	K	6'	220	42		11

DETROIT LIONS 8-5-1 George Wilson

Scores of Each Game		
17	Green Bay	13
16	Baltimore	15
0	SAN FRANCISCO	49
17	CHICAGO	31
14	LOS ANGELES	13
14	BALTIMORE	17
28	Los Angeles	10
20	San Francisco	20
45	St. Louis	14
37	Minnesota	10
9	GREEN BAY	17
16	Chicago	15
13	MINNESOTA	7
24	PHILADELPHIA	27

Use Name	Pos.	Hgt	Wgt	Age	Int	Pts
Dan LaRose	OT	6'5"	250	21		
Willie McClung	OT	6'2"	260	32		
Ollie Spencer	OG-OT	6'2"	250	30		
Harley Sewell	OG	6'1"	230	30		
Dick Mills	OG	6'3"	240	21		
John Gordy	OT-OG	6'3"	250	25		
Bob Scholtz	C	6'4"	250	23		
Bob Whitlow (from WAS)	OG-C	6'1"	236	25		
Bill Glass	DE	6'5"	255	25		
Darris McCord	DE	6'4"	250	28	1	
Sam Williams	OE-DE	6'5"	235	30		
Roger Brown	DT	6'5"	300	24	1	
John Gonzaga	DT	6'3"	250	28		
Alex Karras	DT	6'2"	245	25		
Gil Mains	DT	6'2"	250	31		
Paul Ward	DT	6'3"	247	24		
Carl Brettschneider	LB	6'1"	225	29		
Jim Martin	LB	6'2"	230	37		70
Max Messner	LB	6'3"	225	23		
Joe Schmidt	LB	6'1"	220	29	4	6
Wayne -Walker	LB	6'2"	225	24	2	6
Night Train Lane	DB	6'1"	200	33	6	
Dick LeBeau	DB	6'1"	185	24	3	
Gary Lowe	DB	5'11"	195	27	5	2
Bruce Maher	DB	5'11"	190	24	1	
Yale Lary	DB	6'	190	30	6	
Earl Morrall	QB	6'1"	206	27		
Jim Ninowski	QB	6'1"	200	25		30
Hopalong Cassady	HB	5'10"	185	27		12
Dan Lewis	HB	6'1"	200	25		24
Johnny Olszewski	FB	5'11"	202	30		
Nick Pietrosante	FB	6'2"	225	24		30
Ken Webb	FB	5'11"	205	26		6
Terry Barr	FL	6'	190	26		36
Pat Studstill	FL	6'1"	180	23		6
Gail Cogdill	OE	6'2"	195	24		36
Glenn Davis	OE	6'	180	27		
Jim Gibbons	OE	6'2"	220	25		6

BALTIMORE COLTS 8-6-0 Weeb Ewbank

Scores of Each Game		
27	LOS ANGELES	24
15	DETROIT	16
34	MINNESOTA	33
7	Green Bay	45
10	Chicago	24
17	Detroit	14
20	CHICAGO	21
45	GREEN BAY	21
20	Minnesota	28
16	ST. LOUIS	0
27	Washington	6
20	SAN FRANCISCO	17
17	Los Angeles	34
27	San Francisco	24

Use Name	Pos.	Hgt	Wgt	Age	Int	Pts
Tom Gilburg	OT	6'5"	245	22		
Jim Parker	OT	6'3"	275	27		
George Preas	OT	6'2"	250	29		
Wiley Feagin	OG	6'2"	235	24		
Alex Sandusky	OG	6'1"	242	29		
Palmer Pyle	OG	6'2"	250	24		
Dick Szymanski	C	6'3"	235	28		
Ordell Braase	DE	6'4"	242	29		
Gino Marchetti	DE	6'4"	245	35		2
John Diehl	DT	6'7"	285	25		
Art Donovan	DT	6'2"	265	36		
Joe Lewis	DT	6'2"	250	26		
Jim Colvin	DE-DT	6'2"	250	24		
Billy Ray Smith	DE-DT	6'4"	235	26		
Marv Matuszak	LB	6'3"	230	32		
Bill Pellington	LB	6'2"	238	32	3	
Don Shinnick	LB	6'	235	26	2	
Steve Myhra	OG-LB	6'1"	240	27		96
Jackie Burkett	C-LB	6'4"	230	24	1	
Bobby Boyd	DB	5'10"	190	23	2	
Gary Glick (from WAS)	DB	6'2"	200	30	4	
Bob Harrison	DB	5'11"	187	22	3	
Lenny Lyles	DB	6'2"	202	25		
Andy Nelson	DB	6'1"	180	28		
Carl Taseff (to PHI)	DB	5'11"	194	32	1	
Jim Welch	HB-DB	6'	190	23		6
Lamar McHan	QB	6'1"	205	29		
Johnny Unitas	QB	6'1"	194	28		12
Alex Hawkins	HB	6'1"	190	24		30
Jerry Hill	HB	5'11"	210	21		
Tom Matte	HB	6'	192	22		
Lenny Moore	HB	6'1"	190	28		90
Joe Perry	FB	6'	195	34		24
Mark Smolinski	FB	6'	222	22		6
Ray Berry	OE	6'2"	190	28		
Ken Gregory	OE	6'	190	24		
Aubrey Linne	OE	6'7"	235	22		
Dee Mackey	OE	6'5"	236	25		
Jim Mutscheller	OE	6'1"	205	31		12
Jimmy Orr	OE	5'11"	180	25		24

EASTERN CONFERENCE—Continued

DALLAS COWBOYS

RUSHING

Last Name	No.	Yds	Avg	TD
Perkins	200	815	4.1	4
Marsh	84	379	4.5	1
Lockett	77	298	3.9	1
Meredith	22	176	8.0	1
LeBaron	20	72	3.6	0
Dupre	16	60	3.8	0
Douglas	5	24	4.8	0
Howton	1	9	9.0	0

RECEIVING

Last Name	No.	Yds	Avg	TD
Howton	56	785	14	4
Clarke	41	919	22	9
Perkins	32	298	9	1
Bielski	26	377	15	3
Marsh	21	189	9	2
Lockett	19	149	8	2
Doran	13	153	12	2
Dupre	6	49	8	0
Gregory	3	30	10	0
Douglas	1	−2	−2	0

PUNT RETURNS

Last Name	No.	Yds	Avg	TD
Marsh	14	71	5	0
Livingston	6	20	3	0
Perkins	1	8	8	0
Dupre	2	4	2	0

KICKOFF RETURNS

Last Name	No.	Yds	Avg	TD
Marsh	26	667	26	0
Perkins	22	443	20	0
Dupre	6	110	18	0
Lockett	5	61	12	0
Babb	2	34	17	0
Dowdle	2	33	17	0
Douglas	1	12	12	0
Doran	1	0	0	0

PASSING – PUNTING – KICKING

PASSING	Att	Comp	%	Yds	Yd/Att	TD	Int–	%	RK
LeBaron	236	120	51	1741	7.4	14	16–	7	12
Meredith	182	94	52	1161	6.4	9	11–	6	15
Humphrey	2	1	50	16	8.0	0	0–	0	
Lockett	2	0	0	0	0.0	0	0–	0	

PUNTING	No	Avg
Green	61	36.7

KICKING	XP	Att	%	FG	Att	%
Green	19	19	100	5	15	33
Bielski	10	10	100	6	9	67

WASHINGTON REDSKINS

RUSHING

Last Name	No.	Yds	Avg	TD
James	71	374	5.3	3
Horner	96	275	2.9	0
Bosseler	77	220	2.9	2
Cunningham	69	160	2.3	1
Snead	34	47	1.4	3
Anderson	3	5	1.7	0
Luce	3	1	0.3	0
Sommer	11	1	0.9	0
Izo	3	−1	−0.3	0

RECEIVING

Last Name	No.	Yds	Avg	TD
Dugan	53	817	15	4
Anderson	40	637	16	0
Osborne	22	297	14	2
James	20	298	15	2
Bosseler	16	94	6	1
Cunningham	12	90	8	1
Horner	10	113	11	1
Junker	9	130	14	0
Aveni	6	84	14	1
Sommer	1	31	31	0
Wulff	1	6	6	0

PUNT RETURNS

Last Name	No.	Yds	Avg	TD
Steffen	19	153	8	0
James	12	90	8	0
Sommer	2	26	13	0
Kerr	5	23	5	0
Luce	1	0	0	0

KICKOFF RETURNS

Last Name	No.	Yds	Avg	TD
Steffen	29	691	24	0
James	21	617	29	0
Kerr	14	385	28	0
Sommer	4	98	25	0
Cunningham	4	80	20	0
Luce	4	77	19	0
Horner	4	75	19	0
Stynchula	2	73	37	0
Junker	1	0	0	0

PASSING – PUNTING – KICKING

PASSING	Att	Comp	%	Yds	Yd/Att	TD	Int–	%	RK
Snead	375	172	46	2337	6.2	11	22–	6	16
Izo	40	16	40	214	5.4	1	6–	15	
James	4	1	25	15	3.8	0	0–	0	
Aveni	1	0	0	0	0.0	0	0–	0	

PUNTING	No	Avg
Horner	63	38.2
James	6	35.0
Cunningham	1	46.0

KICKING	XP	Att	%	FG	Att	%
Aveni	21	23	91	5	28	18

WESTERN CONFERENCE

GREEN BAY PACKERS

RUSHING

Last Name	No.	Yds	Avg	TD
Taylor	243	1307	5.4	15
Hornung	127	597	4.7	8
Moore	61	302	5.0	1
Pitts	23	75	3.3	1
Starr	12	56	4.7	1
R. Kramer	5	13	2.6	0
Carpenter	1	5	5.0	0
Roach	2	−5	−2.5	1

RECEIVING

Last Name	No.	Yds	Avg	TD
McGee	51	883	17	7
Dowler	36	633	18	3
R. Kramer	35	559	16	4
Taylor	25	175	7	1
Hornung	15	145	10	2
Moore	8	41	5	1
Knafelc	3	32	11	0
Carpenter	3	29	10	0
Pitts	1	5	5	0

PUNT RETURNS

Last Name	No.	Yds	Avg	TD
Wood	14	225	16	2
Carpenter	6	130	22	0

KICKOFF RETURNS

Last Name	No.	Yds	Avg	TD
Adderley	18	478	27	0
Moore	15	409	27	0
Symank	4	121	30	0
Forester	3	55	18	0
Pitts	1	14	14	0

PASSING – PUNTING – KICKING

PASSING	Att	Comp	%	Yds	Yd/Att	TD	Int–	%	RK
Starr	295	172	58	2418	8.2	16	16–	5	3
Hornung	5	3	60	42	8.4	1	0–	0	
Roach	4	0	0	0	0.0	0	0–	0	
Moore	2	2	100	42	21.0	1	0–	0	

PUNTING	No	Avg
Dowler	38	44.1
McGee	13	40.0

KICKING	XP	Att	%	FG	Att	%
Hornung	41	41	100	15	22	68
Agajanian	8	8	100	1	2	50

DETROIT LIONS

RUSHING

Last Name	No.	Yds	Avg	TD
Pietrosante	201	841	4.2	5
Lewis	110	451	4.1	4
Ninowski	33	238	7.2	5
Cassady	31	131	4.2	1
Olszewski	30	109	3.6	0
Morrall	20	86	4.3	0
Lary	1	14	14.0	0
Webb	7	6	0.9	1
Barr	6	−8	−1.3	0

RECEIVING

Last Name	No.	Yds	Avg	TD
Cogdill	45	956	21	6
Gibbons	45	566	13	1
Barr	40	630	16	6
Peitrosante	26	315	12	0
Davis	9	115	13	0
Lewis	8	118	15	0
Studstill	5	54	11	0
Cassady	5	45	9	1
Olszewski	1	14	14	0
Williams	1	10	10	0
Webb	1	7	7	0

PUNT RETURNS

Last Name	No.	Yds	Avg	TD
Cassady	16	159	10	0
Studstill	8	75	9	0
Gibbons	1	14	14	0
Lary	1	8	8	0
Lane	1	6	6	0

KICKOFF RETURNS

Last Name	No.	Yds	Avg	TD
Studstill	16	448	28	1
Cassady	9	127	14	0
Olszewski	4	59	15	0
Maher	1	19	19	0
Williams	1	4	4	0
Webb	0	5	0	0

PASSING – PUNTING – KICKING

PASSING	Att	Comp	%	Yds	Yd/Att	TD	Int–	%	RK
Ninowski	247	117	47	1921	7.8	7	18–	7	17
Morrall	150	69	46	909	6.1	7	9–	6	18
Cassady	1	0	0	0	0.0	0	0–	0	

PUNTING	No	Avg
Lary	52	48.4
Morrall	3	37.7
Studstill	1	32.0

KICKING	XP	Att	%	FG	Att	%
Martin	25	26	96	15	30	50
Walker	6	6	100	0	3	0

BALTIMORE COLTS

RUSHING

Last Name	No.	Yds	Avg	TD
Perry	168	675	4.0	3
Moore	92	648	7.0	7
Hawkins	86	379	4.4	4
Unitas	54	190	3.5	2
Smolinski	31	98	3.2	0
Welch	1	60	60.0	1
Matte	13	54	4.2	0
Hill	1	4	4.0	0
McHan	4	1	0.3	0

RECEIVING

Last Name	No.	Yds	Avg	TD
Berry	75	873	12	0
Moore	49	728	15	8
Perry	34	322	9	1
Mutscheller	20	370	19	2
Hawkins	20	158	8	1
Orr	18	357	20	4
Smolinski	9	100	11	1
Mackey	4	66	17	0
Matte	1	8	8	0
Szymanski	1	5	5	0

PUNT RETURNS

Last Name	No.	Yds	Avg	TD
Boyd	18	173	10	0
Taseff	5	39	8	0
Hawkins	4	20	5	0
Nelson	4	19	5	0
Harrison	1	16	16	0
Smolinski	1	2	2	0

KICKOFF RETURNS

Last Name	No.	Yds	Avg	TD
Lyles	28	672	24	0
Harrison	11	250	23	0
Welch	5	146	29	0
Matte	2	50	25	0
Smolinski	3	27	9	0
Lewis	1	14	14	0
Matuszak	1	14	14	0
Mackey	1	6	6	0
Gregory	1	3	3	0

PASSING – PUNTING – KICKING

PASSING	Att	Comp	%	Yds	Yd/Att	TD	Int–	%	RK
Unitas	420	229	55	2990	7.1	16	24–	6	8
McHan	15	3	20	28	1.9	1	4–	27	
Moore	2	0	0	0	0.0	0	1–	50	
Boyd	1	0	0	0	0.0	0	0–	0	

PUNTING	No	Avg
Gilburg	42	43.0

KICKING	XP	Att	%	FG	Att	%
Myhra	33	34	97	21	39	54

WESTERN CONFERENCE – Continued

CHICAGO BEARS 8-6-0 George Halas

Scores of Each Game		
13	Minnesota	37
21	Los Angeles	17
0	Green Bay	24
31	Detroit	17
24	BALTIMORE	10
31	SAN FRANCISCO	0
21	Baltimore	20
14	Philadelphia	16
28	GREEN BAY	31
31	San Francisco	41
28	LOS ANGELES	24
15	DETROIT	16
17	CLEVELAND	14
52	MINNESOTA	35

Use Name	Pos.	Hgt	Wgt	Age	Int	Pts
Art Anderson	OT	6'3"	244	24		
Herm Lee	OT	6'4"	247	30		
Stan Fanning	OT	6'6"	270	23		
Roger Davis	OG	6'3"	235	23		
Stan Jones	OG	6'1"	250	30		
Ted Karras	OG	6'1"	243	28		
Bob Wetoska	OG	6'3"	240	23		
Roger LeClerc	C	6'3"	235	23		70
Mike Pyle	C	6'3"	240	22		
Doug Atkins	DE	6'8"	255	31		
Bob Kilcullen	DE	6'3"	245	25		
Maury Youmans	DE	6'6"	260	24		
John Mellekas	DT	6'3"	255	28		
Fred Williams	DT	6'4"	248	31		
Joe Fortunato	LB	6'	225	31	3	
Bill George	LB	6'2"	235	30	3	
Larry Morris	LB	6'2"	230	26	1	
Ken Kirk	C-LB	6'2"	230	23		
J.C. Caroline	DB	6'1"	190	28	3	
Bobby Jackson	DB	6'1"	190	25		
Pete Manning	DB	6'3"	208	25		
Don Mullins	DB	6'1"	195	22		
Richie Petitbon	DB	6'3"	205	23	5	
Rosey Taylor	DB	5'11"	186	22		
Dave Whitsell	DB	6'	190	25	6	
Ed Brown	QB	6'2"	210	32		4
Dick Norman	QB	6'3"	210	23		
Billy Wade	QB	6'2"	210	30		12
Charlie Bivins	HB	6'2"	212	22		6
Willie Galimore	HB	6'1"	187	26		42
J. D. Smith	HB	6'	210	26		
John Adams	FB	6'3"	235	24		6
Bill Brown	FB	5'11"	218	23		
Rick Casares	FB	6'2"	225	30		48
Johnny Morris	FL	5'10"	180	26		24
Angie Coia	OE	6'2"	202	23		18
Mike Ditka	OE	6'3"	230	21		72
Jim Dooley	OE	6'4"	198	31		
Bo Farrington	OE	6'3"	217	25		24
Harlon Hill	DB-OE	6'3"	200	29	3	

Earl Leggett – Knee Injury

SAN FRANCISCO FORTY NINERS 7-6-1 Red Hickey

Scores of Each Game		
35	WASHINGTON	3
10	Green Bay	30
49	Detroit	0
35	LOS ANGELES	0
38	Minnesota	24
0	Chicago	31
10	Pittsburgh	20
20	DETROIT	20
7	Los Angeles	17
41	CHICAGO	31
38	MINNESOTA	28
17	Baltimore	20
22	GREEN BAY	21
24	BALTIMORE	27

Use Name	Pos.	Hgt	Wgt	Age	Int	Pts
Len Rohde	OT	6'4"	240	23		
Bob St. Clair	OT	6'9"	265	30		
John Thomas	LB-OT	6'4"	246	26		
Bruce Bosley	OG	6'2"	240	27		
Ted Connolly	OG	6'3"	242	29		
Bill Lopasky	OG	6'2"	235	24		
Mike Magac	OG	6'3"	240	23		
Frank Morze	C	6'4"	264	27		
Dan Colchico	DE	6'4"	236	24		
Lou Cordileone	DE	6'	245	24		
Charlie Krueger	DE	6'4"	245	25		2
Roland Lakes	OT-DE	6'4"	247	21		
Monte Clark	DT	6'6"	260	24		
Leo Nomellini	DT	6'3"	262	36		
Bob Harrison	LB	6'2"	220	24	2	
Matt Hazeltine	LB	6'1"	220	28	1	
Carl Kammerer	LB	6'3"	237	24		
Gorden Kelley	LB	6'3"	230	23	1	
Dave Baker	DB	6'	193	24	6	
Eddie Dove	DB	6'2"	180	24	3	
Jim Johnson	DB	6'2"	190	23	5	
Jerry Mertens	DB	6'	183	25		
Jimmy Ridlon	DB	6'1"	177	26		
Abe Woodson	HB-DB	5'11"	188	26	1	12
John Brodie	QB	6'1"	186	26		12
Billy Kilmer	QB	6'	190	22		60
Bob Waters	QB	6'2"	184	23		18
Don McIlhenny	HB	6'	185	26		
Dale Messer	HB	5'10"	175	24		
Ray Norton	HB	6'2"	184	24		
J. D. Smith	FB-HB	6'1"	200	28		54
Bill Cooper	FB	6'1"	215	22		6
C. R. Roberts	FB	6'3"	197	25		6
Bernie Casey	OE	6'4"	215	22		6
Clyde Conner	OE	6'2"	190	28		6
R. C. Owens	OE	6'3"	195	26		36
Monte Stickles	OE	6'4"	230	23		30
Aaron Thomas	OE	6'3"	208	23		12
Tommy Davis	K	6'	212	26		80

LOS ANGELES RAMS 4-10-0 Bob Waterfield

Scores of Each Game		
24	Baltimore	27
17	CHICAGO	21
24	PITTSBURGH	14
0	San Francisco	35
13	Detroit	14
14	New York	24
10	DETROIT	28
31	MINNESOTA	17
17	SAN FRANCISCO	7
17	Green Bay	35
24	Chicago	28
21	Minnesota	42
34	BALTIMORE	17
17	GREEN BAY	24

Use Name	Pos.	Hgt	Wgt	Age	Int	Pts
Jim Boeke	OT	6'5"	245	22		
Willie Hector	OT	6'2"	220	21		
Frank Varrichione	OT	6'1"	235	29		
Charley Cowan	OG	6'4"	250	23		
Roy Hord	OG	6'4"	250	26		
Joe Scibelli	OG	6'1"	250	22		
Bruce Tarbox	OG	6'2"	230	22		
Art Hunter	C	6'4"	248	28		
Deacon Jones	DE	6'5"	240	22		
Lamar Lundy	DE	6'7"	235	26		
John Baker	DT-DE	6'6"	290	26		
Urban Henry	DT	6'4"	265	26		
John Lovetere	DT	6'4"	280	25		
George Strugar	DT	6'5"	258	26	1	
Bill Jobko	LB	6'2"	220	25	1	
Bob Long	LB	6'3"	235	27	1	
Marlin McKeever	LB	6'1"	230	21		
Jack Pardee	LB	6'2"	225	25	1	
Les Richter	LB	6'3"	235	30	4	
Charley Britt	DB	6'2"	185	23	5	
Ross Coyle	DB	6'2"	195	25		
Lindon Crow	DB	6'1"	200	28	6	
Alvin Hall	DB	6'	193	28		
Elbert Kimbrough	DB	5'11"	195	22		
Ed Meador	DB	5'11"	185	24	1	
Clendon Thomas	DB	6'2"	192	24	3	
Zeke Bratkowski	QB	6'2"	203	29		18
Frank Ryan	QB	6'3"	200	25		
Jon Arnett	HB	5'11"	194	26		30
Pervis Atkins	HB	6'1"	195	25		
Ollie Matson	HB	6'2"	210	31		30
Tom Wilson	HB	6'	204	28		6
Dick Bass	FB	5'10"	200	24		30
Joe Marconi	FB	6'2"	225	27		24
Frank Williams	FB	6'2"	215	29		
Duane Allen	OE	6'4"	210	23		12
Carroll Dale	OE	6'1"	195	23		12
Jim Phillips	OE	6'1"	198	24		30
Danny Villanueva	K	5'11"	200	23		71

MINNESOTA VIKINGS 3-11-0 Norm Van Brocklin

Scores of Each Game		
37	CHICAGO	13
7	Dallas	21
33	Baltimore	34
0	DALLAS	28
24	SAN FRANCISCO	38
7	GREEN BAY	33
10	Green Bay	28
17	Los Angeles	31
28	BALTIMORE	20
10	DETROIT	37
28	San Francisco	38
42	LOS ANGELES	21
7	Detroit	13
35	Chicago	52

Use Name	Pos.	Hgt	Wgt	Age	Int	Pts
Bob Denton	OT	6'4"	240	27		
Frank Youso	OT	6'4"	260	25		
Paul Dickson	DT-OT	6'5"	250	24		
Grady Alderman	OG	6'2"	235	22		
Jerry Huth	OG	6'	228	28		
Ken Petersen	OG	6'2"	235	22		
Mike Rabold	OG	6'2"	238	24		
Bill Lapham	C	6'3"	250	27		
Don Joyce	DE	6'3"	250	31		
Jim Leo	DE	6'1"	225	23		
Jim Marshall	DE	6'3"	230	24		
Lebron Shields	DE	6'4"	245	24		
Bill Bishop	DT	6'4"	248	30		
Ed Culpepper	DT	6'1"	255	27		
Jim Prestel	DT	6'5"	250	24		
Dick Grechi	LB	6'1"	230	23	1	
Rip Hawkins	LB	6'3"	230	22	5	
Clancy Osborne	LB	6'3"	217	26	4	
Karl Rubke	C-LB	6'4"	240	25	1	
Dean Derby (from PIT)	DB	6'	190	27	3	
Jack Morris	DB	6'	190	29	2	
Rich Mostardi	DB	5'11"	188	23	2	
Dick Pesonen	DB	6'	190	23	1	
Justin Rowland	DB	6'2"	188	23	1	
Charlie Sumner	DB	6'1"	195	31	2	
Will Sherman	HB-DB	6'2"	197	32		
George Shaw	QB	6'1"	180	28		
Fran Tarkenton	QB	6'1"	190	21		30
Jamie Caleb	HB	6'1"	210	24		
Billy Gault	HB	6'1"	185	24		
Tommy Mason	HB	6'	195	22		18
Hugh McElhenny	HB	6'1"	198	32		42
Ray Hayes	FB	6'3"	235	26		12
Doug Mayberry	FB	6'1"	225	24		
Mel Triplett	FB	6'1"	215	29		6
Dave Middleton	OE	6'1"	190	28		12
Fred Murphy	OE	6'3"	205	23		
Jerry Reichow	OE	6'2"	220	26		66
Gordon Smith	OE	6'2"	200	22		24
A. D. Williams	OE	6'2"	210	28		6
Mike Mercer	K	6'	220	25		63

WESTERN CONFERENCE – Continued

CHICAGO BEARS

RUSHING

Last Name	No.	Yds	Avg	TD
Galimore	153	707	4.6	4
Casares	135	588	4.4	8
Wade	45	255	5.7	2
Bivins	43	188	4.4	1
B. Brown	22	81	3.7	0
J. Morris	8	49	6.1	0
E. Brown	13	18	1.4	0
Smith	3	6	2.0	0
Adams	14	–2	–0.1	1

RECEIVING

Last Name	No.	Yds	Avg	TD
Ditka	56	1076	19	12
J. Morris	36	548	15	4
Galimore	33	502	15	3
Farrington	21	349	17	4
Coia	12	249	21	3
Casares	8	69	9	0
Dooley	6	90	15	0
Adams	5	80	16	0
Bivins	4	–9	–2	0
Hill	3	51	17	0
B. Brown	2	6	3	0

PUNT RETURNS

Last Name	No.	Yds	Avg	TD
J. Morris	23	155	7	0
Petitbon	2	9	5	0
Taylor	1	4	4	0
L. Morris	1	2	2	0

KICKOFF RETURNS

Last Name	No.	Yds	Avg	TD
Bivins	25	668	27	0
Taylor	14	379	27	0
Galimore	5	82	16	0
B. Brown	4	54	14	0
J. Morris	2	46	23	0
Smith	1	18	18	0

PASSING – PUNTING – KICKING

PASSING	Att	Comp	%	Yds	Yd/Att	TD	Int–	%	RK
Wade	250	139	56	2258	9.0	22	13–	5	2
E. Brown	98	46	47	742	7.6	4	11–	11	
Adams	1	1	100	11	11.0	0	0–	0	

PUNTING	No	Avg
E. Brown	58	42.2
Adams	2	28.0

KICKING	XP	Att	%	FG	Att	%
LeClerc	40	41	98	10	24	42
E. Brown	1	1	100	1	2	50
George	0	0	0	0	1	0

SAN FRANCISCO FORTY NINERS

RUSHING

Last Name	No.	Yds	Avg	TD
Smith	167	823	4.9	8
Kilmer	96	509	5.3	10
Roberts	63	338	5.4	1
Waters	47	233	5.0	3
Brodie	28	90	3.2	2
McIlhenny	10	34	3.4	0
Woodson	14	23	1.6	0
Cooper	8	17	2.1	1
Messer	3	13	4.3	0
Norton	2	–2	–1.0	0
A. Thomas	1	–15	–15.0	0
Owens	0	23	0.0	1

RECEIVING

Last Name	No.	Yds	Avg	TD
Owens	55	1032	19	5
Stickles	43	794	18	5
Smith	28	343	12	1
A. Thomas	15	301	20	2
Conner	11	177	16	1
Casey	10	185	19	1
Roberts	10	83	8	0
Woodson	8	74	9	0
Messer	3	33	11	0
McIlhenny	1	6	6	0

PUNT RETURNS

Last Name	No.	Yds	Avg	TD
Woodson	16	172	11	1
Dove	6	49	8	0
Messer	2	11	6	0

KICKOFF RETURNS

Last Name	No.	Yds	Avg	TD
Woodson	27	782	29	1
McIlhenny	6	189	32	0
Smith	7	158	23	0
Norton	1	60	60	0
Cooper	3	44	15	0
Messer	3	36	12	0
Kammerer	1	18	18	0

PASSING – PUNTING – KICKING

PASSING	Att	Comp	%	Yds	Yd/Att	TD	Int–	%	RK
Brodie	283	155	55	2588	9.1	14	12–	4	5
Kilmer	34	19	56	286	8.4	0	4–	12	
Waters	28	13	46	183	6.5	1	2–	7	
Smith	1	0	0	0	0.0	0	1–	100	

PUNTING	No	Avg
Davis	50	45.4
Kilmer	9	40.4

KICKING	XP	Att	%	FG	Att	%
Davis	44	44	100	12	22	55

LOS ANGELES RAMS

RUSHING

Last Name	No.	Yds	Avg	TD
Arnett	158	609	3.9	4
Bass	98	608	6.2	4
Wilson	44	220	5.0	1
Matson	24	181	7.5	2
Marconi	36	146	4.1	3
Ryan	38	139	3.7	0
Bratkowski	12	36	3.0	3
Atkins	5	19	3.8	0

RECEIVING

Last Name	No.	Yds	Avg	TD
Phillips	78	1092	14	5
Dale	35	561	16	2
Matson	29	537	19	3
Arnett	28	194	7	0
Bass	16	145	9	0
Atkins	5	67	13	0
Marconi	4	20	5	1
Allen	2	80	40	2
Wilson	1	12	12	0
Scibelli	1	1	1	0

PUNT RETURNS

Last Name	No.	Yds	Avg	TD
Bass	4	109	27	1
Arnett	10	75	8	0

KICKOFF RETURNS

Last Name	No.	Yds	Avg	TD
Bass	23	698	30	0
Arnett	25	653	26	1
Atkins	4	77	19	0
Varrichione	3	23	8	0
Jones	1	12	12	0

PASSING – PUNTING – KICKING

PASSING	Att	Comp	%	Yds	Yd/Att	TD	Int–	%	RK
Bratkowski	230	124	54	1547	6.7	8	13–	6	13
Ryan	142	72	51	1115	7.9	5	7–	5	10
Arnett	13	3	23	47	3.6	0	1–	8	
Villanueva	1	0	0	0	0.0	0	0–	0	

PUNTING	No	Avg
Villanueva	46	40.1
Bratkowski	12	38.2
Marconi	6	44.2

KICKING	XP	Att	%	FG	Att	%
Villanueva	32	32	100	13	27	48

MINNESOTA VIKINGS

RUSHING

Last Name	No.	Yds	Avg	TD
McElhenny	120	570	4.8	3
Triplett	80	407	5.1	1
Hayes	73	319	4.4	2
Tarkenton	56	308	5.5	5
Mason	60	226	3.8	3
Mayberry	13	40	3.1	0
Shaw	10	39	3.9	0
Caleb	3	11	3.7	0
Reichow	3	9	3.0	0
Mercer	1	–32	–32.0	0

RECEIVING

Last Name	No.	Yds	Avg	TD
Reichow	50	859	17	11
McElhenny	37	283	8	3
Middleton	30	444	15	2
Mason	20	122	6	0
Hayes	16	121	8	0
Williams	13	174	13	1
Smith	12	320	27	4
Triplett	10	41	4	0
Sherman	2	40	20	0
Mayberry	2	18	9	0
Caleb	2	–8	–4	0

PUNT RETURNS

Last Name	No.	Yds	Avg	TD
McElhenny	8	155	19	1
Mason	14	146	10	0
Caleb	1	8	8	0

KICKOFF RETURNS

Last Name	No.	Yds	Avg	TD
Mason	25	603	24	0
Caleb	22	504	23	0
Rowland	8	175	22	0
Pesonen	6	136	23	0
McElhenny	2	59	30	0
Triplett	3	41	14	0
Gault	2	41	21	0
Leo	3	9	3	0
Hayes	1	0	0	0

PASSING – PUNTING – KICKING

PASSING	Att	Comp	%	Yds	Yd/Att	TD	Int–	%	RK
Tarkenton	280	157	56	1997	7.1	18	17–	6	7
Shaw	91	46	51	530	5.8	4	4–	4	
Reichow	3	0	0	0	0.0	0	1–	33	
Caleb	1	0	0	0	0.0	0	0–	0	
Mason	1	0	0	0	0.0	0	0–	0	
McElhenny	1	0	0	0	0.0	0	0–	0	

PUNTING	No	Avg
Mercer	63	39.0

KICKING	XP	Att	%	FG	Att	%
Mercer	36	37	97	9	21	43

1961 A.F.L. The Feuding Ends at the Altar

Commissioner Joe Foss had enough problems to keep him busy this year. His authority to govern the league was actually at stake in one incident. To get a jump on the NFL in signing rookies, the team owners conducted a secret draft of college seniors in November, with each club taking six name players. Foss, who set the date for the draft in December, was not informed of this draft, and when he found out about it he declared it invalid. A potential revolt of the owners narrowed down to a public feud between Foss and New York Titan owner Harry Wismer. The Titans had selected Syracuse runner Ernie Davis in the November draft that Foss nullified, and when Buffalo picked Davis in the official December draft Wismer let loose his full vocal fury on Foss. Despite Wismer's calls for Foss's ouster, the commissioner stayed in office, directed the official draft, and won a five-year renewal of his contract from the owners when the season ended. The most amazing development came in the spring of 1962 when Foss was Wismer's best man at his wedding.

Attendance around the league also troubled Foss. League attendance rose a slight amount, up to 17,000, and Houston, Buffalo, Boston, and San Diego showed increases in home attendance. In these cases, though, it was generally a case of going from horrible to merely bad. The AFL was providing exciting, wide-open games for television, but fans did not yet think it reasonable to pay to see these new teams play.

The anti-trust suit filed by the AFL against the NFL was still going through the judicial process, so the main confrontation between the two leagues was still taking place at the box office and in the signing of rookie players. The NFL was winning on all fronts in the attendance war, and the old league also grabbed off the lion's share of graduating seniors from the class of 1961. With the element of surprise gone, the AFL signed only a handful of name collegians, among them Ken Rice, Art Baker, E. J. Holub, and Earl Faison.

The league also signed a new player from a different route, one who had played out his option in the NFL. Willard Dewveall, an offensive end with the Chicago Bears, played through 1960 without signing a new contract and agreed to terms with the Houston Oilers for the 1961 season. Dewveall thus became the first player to jump to the AFL from the active ranks of the NFL.

While new players were coming into the league, some of the old ones were lost to the federal activation of Reserve units in response to the Berlin crisis. The activated players all were stationed in the continental United States, and most were able to make the league games on weekend passes. These weekday soldiers and weekend football warriors included Ron Mix, Larry Grantham, Ross O'Hanley, Proverb Jacobs, Richie Lucas, Bill Roehnelt, George McGee, Oscar Lofton, John Jelacik, and Herm Urenda.

A new city also joined the circuit as owner Barron Hilton picked up his Los Angeles Chargers and transplanted them in the virgin soil of San Diego. Attendance in San Diego topped that of Los Angeles, but the Chargers still lost money while winning on the field.

One innovation by the league this season was the scheduling of an All-Star Game after the season to showcase the league's talent. Although some NFL boosters snickered at the contest, it provided one more television date for the league to win new fans.

EASTERN DIVISION

Houston Oilers—The Oilers were mired in last place with a 1-3-1 record when owner Bud Adams canned head coach Lou Rymkus and replaced him with assistant Wally Lemm. The club's fortunes immediately turned around, as the Oilers won all their remaining nine games with a blistering offensive blitzkrieg. Lemm gave the quarterback job back to George Blanda, whom Rymkus had benched in favor of Jacky Lee, and Blanda responded with a pro record of thirty-six touchdown passes, a pair of 400 passing-yards games, and reliable long-range place-kicking, including boots of 55 and 53 yards. Charley Hennigan and Bill Groman were Blanda's deep targets, while Billy Cannon and Charley Tolar punched out yardage on the ground at a steady clip. The Oilers took over first place by beating Boston 27-15 on November 12, and they kept on wining right to the end. Coach Lemm summed up his perfect relief job by saying, "I feel like someone who inherited a million dollars in tarnished silverware. All I did was polish it."

Boston Patriots—Like the Oilers, the Patriots profited from a mid-season switch in coaches. After Mike Holovak succeeded Lou Saban as head coach, the Patriots won seven of nine games to streak into first place, only to have the Oilers win nine out of nine over the same span to win the title. The Boston attack featured no stars but still was second in the league in points scored. Butch Songin and Babe Parilli, a pair of senior citizens, shared the quarterback job and found converted defensive back Gino Cappelletti their favorite receiver. Cappelletti's kicking, however, was the spearhead of the Boston attack and won him the AFL scoring title. The Pats lost only to Houston over the last eight games, but that one loss was enough to foil the late-season drive.

New York Titans—Owner Harry Wismer made news this year. He made news with his feud with coach Sammy Baugh. He made news by publicly calling for Commissioner Joe Foss's ouster and more news when they finally made up. And he made news by announcing that his losses for 1960 and 1961 totaled $1.2 million. Wismer made more news than his football team, which played its games in virtual privacy. Three wins in the first four games got the Titans out to an early lead in the East, but a rash of injuries plus hot streaks by Houston and Boston pushed New York back into third place. Although fullback Billy Mathis developed into a bruising runner, the Titans still relied on Al Dorow's passes to Don Maynard and Art Powell for most of the offense. But while the Titans moved well through the air, enemy passers found the New York secondary easy pickings in return.

Buffalo Bills—In a league not known for great quarterbacks, the Bills had the worst quarterback situation. Ex-Redskin M. C. Reynolds, sophomore Johnny Green, and ex-Lion Warren Raab were uniformly unimpressive, and the offense sputtered despite some fine rookies in the lineup. Fullback Art Baker contributed power running, end Glenn Bass injected speed into the attack after being cut by San Diego, and Al Bemiller, Billy Shaw, Stew Barber, and Ken Rice all won jobs in the offensive line. But without a competent quarterback, the Bills had to rely on the defense to stay competitive. Lavern Torczon, Chuck McMurtry, Archie Matsos, and Billy Atkins stood out as defenders, but the unbalanced team effort cost head coach Buster Ramsey his job at the end of the season.

WESTERN DIVISION

San Diego Chargers—The Chargers celebrated their move to San Diego by winning their first eleven games to make a shambles out of the Western Division race. Head coach and general manager Sid Gillman built his defensive unit into the league's best with the addition of three excellent rookies. End Earl Faison put steady pressure on enemy passers, tackle Ernie Ladd contributed 315 pounds of muscle to the center of the line, and middle linebacker Chuck Allen, a lightly regarded twenty-eighth draft choice, was a sensation until breaking his ankle late in the year. With Dick Harris and Charley McNeil heading up a solid secondary, the San Diego defense had no weak spots. The offense held up its end of the bargain, with Jack Kemp, Paul Lowe, Dave Kocourek, and Ron Mix starring. But the team's real star was Gillman, one of the few AFL general managers who was successfully signing most of the rookies on his draft list.

Dallas Texans—The Texans matched the Chargers in signing blue-chip rookies but fell farther behind them in the standings. Professional debuts by Jim Tyrer, Jerry Mays, E. J. Holub, and Dave Grayson did not prevent a slump by the defense and the team's dropping below .500 for the season. After winning three of their first four games, the Texans went into a six-game losing streak that ended the Western Division race. The team's passing attack did not live up to expectations, as quarterback Cotton Davidson was very erratic, but the running corps of Abner Haynes, Jack Spikes, Frank Jackson, and Bo Dickinson led the league in rushing yardage. Both lines had weak links, though, and suffered periodic breakdowns, throwing a mid-season monkey wrench into high pre-season hopes.

Denver Broncos—Without a balanced offensive diet, the Broncos grew weaker as the season progressed. The Denver running attack was dead last in the league, with the offense totally dependent on the passing of Frank Tripuka and George Herring. The Broncos threw the ball so often that split end Lionel Taylor set a new professional record with 100 catches for the season, not bad for a man the Chicago Bears had cut two years ago. Taylor's strong suit was his glue-fingered hands, but his lack of speed was underlined by his scoring only four touchdowns on the 100 receptions. After seven games, the Broncos had a respectable 3-4 record, but by then enemy defenses had wised up to the Denver air show. The Broncos lost their last seven games, and coach Frankie Filchock lost his job in the process.

Oakland Raiders—When the Raiders lost their first game 55-0 to Houston and their second game 44-0 to San Diego, the tone for a disastrous season was set. Coach Ernie Erdelatz was fired after the two opening massacres, but replacement Marty Feldman couldn't do much better with this squad. The Raiders scored the fewest points in the league, allowed the most points, and attracted minuscule crowds to their home games on the foreign turf of San Francisco's Candlestick Park. Not all the Raider players were inept, only most of them. Center Jim Otto won praise as the league's best at his position, Fred Williamson played well at cornerback, and halfback Clem Daniels showed promise after being picked up as a free agent. But a pair of mid-season victories over Denver and Buffalo was the best the Raiders could do as they lost their last six games of the season.

FINAL TEAM STATISTICS

OFFENSE

	BOSTON	BUFFALO	DALLAS	DENVER	HOUSTON	NEW YORK	OAKLAND	SAN DIEGO
FIRST DOWNS:								
Total	238	243	247	219	293	247	200	208
by Rushing	93	92	112	66	97	100	65	81
by Passing	120	128	122	127	182	126	116	110
by Penalty	25	23	13	26	14	21	19	17
RUSHING:								
Number	389	438	439	333	452	426	350	391
Yards	1675	1606	2183	1091	1896	1678	1234	1466
Average Yards	4.3	3.7	5.0	3.3	4.2	3.9	3.5	3.7
Touchdowns	15	18	23	11	15	17	10	24
PASSING:								
Attempts	420	439	399	568	498	460	423	423
Completions	206	194	177	265	254	204	209	190
Completion Percentage	49.0	44.2	44.4	46.7	51.0	44.3	49.4	44.9
Passing Yards	2795	2786	2815	3004	4568	2733	2514	3121
Average Yards per Attempt	6.7	6.3	7.1	5.3	9.2	5.9	5.9	7.4
Average Yards per Completion	13.6	14.4	15.9	11.3	18.0	13.4	12.0	16.4
Times Tackled Attempting to Pass	33	63	24	33	14	41	45	28
Yards Lost Attempting to Pass	256	442	239	284	176	346	463	274
Net Yards	2539	2344	2576	2720	4392	2387	2051	2847
Touchdowns	29	15	18	18	48	20	17	17
Interceptions	21	25	27	45	29	32	28	25
Percent Intercepted	5.0	5.7	6.8	7.9	5.8	7.0	6.6	5.9
PUNTING:								
Number	62	85	62	80	56	74	75	63
Average Distance	38.8	44.5	39.9	39.4	39.1	41.8	39.0	41.5
PUNT RETURNS:								
Number	35	19	26	33	19	26	15	29
Yards	288	187	219	369	118	463	117	458
Average Yards	8.2	9.8	8.4	11.2	6.2	17.8	7.8	15.8
Touchdowns	2	0	0	2	0	2	0	2
KICKOFF RETURNS:								
Number	49	57	53	66	43	66	68	39
Yards	1136	1208	1465	1501	940	1213	1383	642
Average Yards	23.2	21.2	27.6	22.7	21.9	18.4	20.3	16.5
Touchdowns	2	1	1	1	0	0	0	0
INTERCEPTION RETURNS:								
Number	22	29	25	26	33	25	23	49
Yards	326	311	418	355	528	315	285	929
Average Yards	14.8	10.7	16.7	13.7	16.0	12.6	12.4	19.0
Touchdowns	2	1	3	0	0	1	2	9
PENALTIES:								
Number	64	65	89	60	83	60	53	88
Yards	659	549	874.5	560	889	585	456	682.5
FUMBLES:								
Number	24	32	32	40	21	32	28	32
Number Lost	9	17	18	23	10	20	16	19
POINTS:								
Total	413	294	334	251	513	301	237	396
PAT (kick) Attempts	50	31	40	27	66	39	25	50
PAT (kick) Made	48	29	37	27	65	37	24	43
PAT (Rush or Pass) Attempts	2	7	4	5	0	1	4	2
PAT (Rush or Pass) Made	1	4	3	3	0	0	2	1
FG Attempts	32	26	24	25	26	23	26	27
FG Made	17	9	7	8	16	8	11	13
Percent FG Made	53.1	34.6	29.2	32.0	61.5	34.8	42.3	48.1
Safeties	0	1	0	1	2	0	1	0

DEFENSE

	BOSTON	BUFFALO	DALLAS	DENVER	HOUSTON	NEW YORK	OAKLAND	SAN DIEGO
FIRST DOWNS:								
Total	243	200	238	233	235	242	280	224
by Rushing	72	61	89	83	87	100	135	79
by Passing	151	124	129	127	126	121	129	124
by Penalty	20	15	20	23	22	21	16	21
RUSHING:								
Number	350	349	410	435	365	414	494	401
Yards	1041	1377	1525	1633	1634	1880	2382	1357
Average Yards	3.0	3.9	3.7	3.8	4.5	4.5	4.8	3.4
Touchdowns	9	9	18	17	17	20	36	7
PASSING:								
Attempts	479	430	439	433	493	462	409	485
Completions	241	206	219	194	212	211	192	224
Completion Percentage	50.3	47.9	49.9	44.8	43.0	45.7	46.9	46.2
Passing Yards	3490	3237	3077	3060	2750	3044	2942	2736
Average Yards per Attempt	7.3	7.5	7.0	7.1	5.6	6.6	7.2	5.6
Average Yards per Completion	14.5	15.7	14.1	15.8	13.0	14.4	15.3	12.2
Times Tackled Attempting to Pass	44	36	34	33	41	31	20	42
Yards Lost Attempting to Pass	408	350	300	275	359	247	168	373
Net Yards	3082	2887	2777	2785	2391	2797	2774	2363
Touchdowns	27	28	20	30	13	26	22	16
Interceptions	22	29	25	26	33	25	23	49
Percent Intercepted	4.6	6.7	5.7	6.0	6.7	5.4	5.6	10.1
PUNTING:								
Number	71	75	63	77	81	70	50	70
Average Distance	40.7	38.7	41.7	40.8	40.7	42.4	40.4	40.1
PUNT RETURNS:								
Number	15	45	20	26	20	20	34	22
Yards	245	291	216	368	271	284	352	192
Average Yards	16.3	6.5	10.8	14.2	13.6	14.2	10.4	8.7
Touchdowns	2	1	1	2	0	0	1	1
KICKOFF RETURNS:								
Number	53	54	65	42	66	51	45	65
Yards	1255	1112	1249	720	1481	1084	1066	1521
Average Yards	23.7	20.6	19.2	17.1	22.4	21.3	23.7	23.4
Touchdowns	1	1	1	0	1	1	0	0
INTERCEPTION RETURNS:								
Number	21	25	27	45	29	32	28	25
Yards	198	398	424	818	407	670	280	272
Average Yards	9.4	15.9	15.7	18.2	14.0	20.9	10.0	10.9
Touchdowns	1	4	1	5	2	3	1	1
PENALTIES:								
Number	67	76	62	98	57	86	62	54
Yards	661.5	693	619	799	588	869.5	524	501
FUMBLES:								
Number	36	20	31	25	31	36	29	33
Number Lost	20	15	18	14	15	21	12	17
POINTS:								
Total	313	342	343	432	242	390	458	219
PAT (kick) Attempts	40	42	38	55	26	48	53	26
PAT (kick) Made	40	41	37	51	22	46	50	23
PAT (Rush or Pass) Attempts	1	1	6	1	7	2	6	1
PAT (Rush or Pass) Made	0	1	3	1	2	1	5	1
FG Attempts	23	28	31	26	24	27	27	23
FG Made	9	13	12	13	6	14	12	10
Percent FG Made	39.1	46.4	38.7	50.0	25.0	51.9	44.4	43.5
Safeties	0	1	0	2	0	0	1	1

1961 AFL CHAMPIONSHIP GAME

December 24, at San Diego
(Attendance 29,556)

Oiling the Defense

For a second straight year, the defensive units excelled in the AFL championship game. The Chargers and Oilers, repeat winners of their divisional races, both found interceptions easy to come by, the Chargers picking off six passes and the Oilers four. Played on a sunny, 59-degree Christmas Eve, the game was a showcase for turnovers, with seven fumbles plus all the interceptions thwarting most offensive drives. Neither club generated much offense in the first half, with the only score coming on a 46-yard field goal by George Blanda late in the second quarter. The Oilers, who hadn't lost a game since Wally Lemm took over as head coach three months back, stubbornly defended their 3-0 lead throughout the third quarter and added to it late in the period. The Oilers had the ball on the San Diego 35-yard line with a third-and-five situation when a strong Charger pass rush forced Blanda out of his protective pocket. Rolling to his right, Blanda saw halfback Billy Cannon open down the middle and hit him with a pass on the 17-yard line. Cannon made a leaping catch, sidestepped a defender, and raced into the end zone. Blanda's extra point made the score 10-0 and put a heavy load of pressure on the San Diego offense. With Jack Kemp throwing freely, the Chargers broke the ice with a 12-yard George Blair field goal in the first minute of the fourth quarter, but a final San Diego bid fell short when Houston's Julian Spence picked off a Kemp pass on the Oiler 30-yard line with under two minutes left in the game.

SCORING

SAN DIEGO	0	0	0	3	– 3
HOUSTON	0	3	7	0	–10

Second Quarter

Hous.	Blanda, 46 yard field goal	8:06

Third Quarter

Hous.	Cannon, 35 yard pass from Blanda PAT–Blanda (kick)	11:39

Fourth Quarter

S.D.	Blair, 12 yard field goal	0:39

TEAM STATISTICS

S.D.		HOUS.
15	First Downs–Total	18
6	First Downs–Rushing	6
8	First Downs–Passing	8
1	First Downs–Penalty	4
2	Fumbles–Number	5
2	Fumbles–Number Lost	1
10	Penalties–Number	5
106	Yards Penalized	68
6	Giveaways	7
7	Takeaways	6
+1	Difference	–1

INDIVIDUAL STATISTICS

SAN DIEGO	No.	Yds.	Avg.	HOUSTON	No.	Yds.	Avg.
RUSHING							
Roberson	8	37	4.6	Tolar	16	52	3.3
Lowe	5	30	6.0	Cannon	15	48	3.2
Lincoln	3	7	2.3	Blanda	2	–4	–2.0
Kemp	4	5	1.3		33	96	2.9
	20	79	4.0				
RECEIVING							
Kocourek	7	123	17.6	Cannon	5	53	10.6
D. Norton	3	48	16.0	Hennigan	5	43	8.6
Flowers	2	17	8.5	Groman	3	32	10.7
Roberson	1	11	11.0	Dewveall	2	10	5.0
Lowe	1	10	10.0	Tolar	2	2	1.0
Scarpitto	1	9	9.0	McLeod	1	20	20.0
Hayes	1	5	5.0		18	160	8.9
Lincoln	1	3	3.0				
	17	226	13.3				
PUNTING							
Maguire	6		33.3	J. Norton	4		41.5
PUNT RETURNS							
Lincoln	1	16	16.0	None			
KICKOFF RETURNS							
Lowe	1	27	27.0	None			
Roberson	1	23	23.0				
	2	50	25.0				
INTERCEPTION RETURNS							
Whitehead	2	45	15.0	Cline	1	7	7.0
McNeil	2	15	7.5	Glick	1	0	0.0
Zeman	2	0	0.0	Johnston	1	0	0.0
	6	60	10.0	Spence	1	0	0.0
					4	7	1.8

PASSING

	Att.	Comp.	Comp. Pct.	Yds.	Int.	Yds/ Att.	Yds/ Comp.	Yards Lost Tackled
SAN DIEGO								
Kemp	32	17	53.1	226	4	7.1	13.3	6–49
HOUSTON								
Blanda	40	18	45.0	160	5	4.0	8.9	0
Gorman	1	0	0.0	0	1	–	–	0
	41	18	43.9	160	6	3.9	8.9	0

1961 A.F.L. — Eastern Division

HOUSTON OILERS 10-3-1 Lou Rymkus Wally Lemm

Scores of Each Game			Use Name	Pos.	Hgt	Wgt	Age	Int	Pts	Use Name	Pos.	Hgt	Wgt	Age	Int	Pts	Use Name	Pos.	Hgt	Wgt	Age	Int	Pts
55	OAKLAND	0	Al Jamison	OT	6'5"	245	24			Ron Botcham	LB	6'1"	230	26			George Blanda	QB	6'1"	210	33		112
24	San Diego	34	Bob Kelly	OT	6'3"	250	21			Doug Cline	LB	6'2"	220	22	1	12	Jacky Lee	QB	6'1"	185	22		
21	Dallas	26	Rich Michael	OT	6'3"	230	22			Mike Dukes	LB	6'3"	230	25	2		Billy Cannon	HB	6'1"	212	24		90
12	BUFFALO	22	Leo Reed (to DEN)	OG	6'4"	240	21			John Guzik	LB	6'3"	228	24			Ken Hall (to STL-N)	HB	6'1"	210	25		6
31	Boston	31	Bob Talamini	OG	6'1"	230	22			Gene Jones	LB	6'	200	24			Claude King	HB	5'11"	185	22		18
38	DALLAS	7	Hogan Wharton	OG	6'2"	245	25			Jack Laraway	LB	6'1"	215	25	1		Dave Smith	FB	6'1"	210	24		18
28	Buffalo	16	Bob Schmidt	C	6'4"	245	25			Dennit Morris	LB	6'1"	225	25	1		Charley Tolar	FB	5'7"	200	23		30
55	Denver	14	Dalva Allen	DE	6'5"	245	25			Tony Banfield	DB	6'1"	185	22	8		Charley Hennigan	FL	6'	185	25		72
27	BOSTON	15	Don Floyd	DE	6'4"	225	22			Freddy Glick	DB	6'1"	190	24	4		Willard Dewveall	OE	6'4"	220	24		18
49	NEW YORK	13	Dick Frey	OG-DE	6'2"	235	30			Mark Johnston	DB	6'	200	23	3	6	Bill Groman	OE	6'	195	25		108
45	DENVER	14	Byron Beams	DT	6'6"	250	27			Charley Milstead	DB	6'2"	190	23	2	1	Bob McLeod	OE	6'5"	225	22		12
33	SAN DIEGO	13	Ed Husmann	DT	6'	238	30			Jim Norton	DB	6'3"	190	22	9		John White	OE	6'4"	230	23		6
48	New York	21	George Shirkey	DT	6'4"	240	24			Gary Wisener	DB	6'1"	205	23									
47	Oakland	16	Orville Trask	DT	6'4"	260	26	1		Julian Spence	FL-DB	5'11"	158	32	1								

BOSTON PATRIOTS 9-4-1 Lou Saban Mike Holovak

Scores of Each Game			Use Name	Pos.	Hgt	Wgt	Age	Int	Pts	Use Name	Pos.	Hgt	Wgt	Age	Int	Pts	Use Name	Pos.	Hgt	Wgt	Age	Int	Pts
20	NEW YORK	21	Jerry DeLucca	OT	6'3"	250	25			Tom Addison	LB	6'3"	235	25	4		Babe Parilli	QB	6'1"	190	31		32
45	DENVER	17	Milt Graham	OT	6'6"	235	27			Harry Jacobs	LB	6'2"	235	24			Butch Songin	QB	6'2"	205	37		6
23	Buffalo	21	Dick Klein (from PIT-N)	OT	6'4"	255	27			Rommie Loudd	LB	6'3"	230	27	1		Tom Yewcic	HB-QB	5'11"	185	29		6
30	New York	37	Charley Long	OT	6'3"	240	23			Frank Robotti	LB	6'	220	22	2		Ron Burton	HB	5'10"	190	24		18
27	SAN DIEGO	38	John Simerson	OT	6'3"	255	26			Walter Beach	DB	6'	185	26	1		Larry Garron	HB	6'	200	24		36
31	HOUSTON	31	Charlie Leo	OG	6'	240	26			Fred Bruney	DB	5'10"	190	30	2		Ray Ratkowski	HB	6'	195	21		
52	BUFFALO	21	Willis Perkins (from HOU)	OG	6'	240	24			Ron Hall	DB	6'	190	24	2		Ger Schwedes	HB	6'1"	205	22		
18	Dallas	17	Tony Sardisco	OG	6'2"	235	28			Ross O'Hanley	DB	6'	175	22			Jim Crawford	FB	6'1"	205	25		
28	DALLAS	21	Walt Cudzik	C	6'2"	235	28			Al Romine	DB	6'2"	195	28			Billy Lott	FB	6'	205	26		66
15	Houston	27	Bob Yates	C	6'3"	230	22			Chuck Shonta	DB	6'	190	23	1		Gino Cappelletti	FL	6'	190	27		**147**
20	OAKLAND	17	Bob Dee	DE	6'3"	240	28			Bob Soltis	DB	6'2"	205	24			Jim Colclough	OE	6'	185	25		54
28	Denver	24	Larry Eisenhauer	DE	6'5"	235	21			Bobby Towns	DB	6'1"	180	23			Joe Johnson	OE	6'	195	31		6
35	Oakland	21	Leroy Moore	DE	6'	232	25			Don Webb	DB	5'10"	180	22	5	24	Bill Kimber	OE	6'2"	190	25		
41	San Diego	0	Houston Antwine	DT	6'	250	22			Clyde Washington	HB-DB	6'	195	23	4		Tom Stephens	OE	6'1"	195	25		18
			Jim Hunt	DT	5'11"	245	22																
			Paul Lindquist	DT	6'3"	265	23			Oscar Lofton – Military Service							George McGee – Military Service						

NEW YORK TITANS 7-7-0 Sammy Baugh

Scores of Each Game			Use Name	Pos.	Hgt	Wgt	Age	Int	Pts	Use Name	Pos.	Hgt	Wgt	Age	Int	Pts	Use Name	Pos.	Hgt	Wgt	Age	Int	Pts
21	Boston	20	Gene Cockrell	OT	6'3"	247	28			Hubert Bobo	LB	6'1"	218	26	4		Don Allard	QB	6'	190	25		
31	Buffalo	41	Moses Gray	OT	6'3"	260	23			Jerry Fields	LB	6'1"	222	22			Al Dorow	QB	6'	195	31		24
35	DENVER	28	Jack Klotz	OT	6'5"	260	27			Jim Furey	LB	6'	228	27			Dick Jamieson	QB	6'1"	192	25		
37	BOSTON	30	Ed Walsh	OT	6'4"	243	25			Larry Grantham	LB	6'	205	22	1		Bob Scrabis	QB	6'3"	225	25		6
10	SAN DIEGO	25	Tom Budrewicz	OG	6'2"	245	24			Johnny Bookman	DB	5'11"	185	26	6		Jim Apple	HB	6'	200	22		
10	Denver	27	John McMullan	OG	6'	244	26			Dick Felt	DB	6'	180	28	4	6	Dick Christy	HB	5'10"	195	25		30
14	Oakland	6	Bob Mischak	OG	6'	240	28			Don Flynn (from DAL)	DB	6'	205	26	2		Bob Renn	HB	6'	180	27		6
13	San Diego	48	Bob O'Neil	OG	6'1"	238	28			Paul Hynes (from DAL)	DB	6'1"	210	21			Bill Shockley (to BUF)	HB	6'	185	23		25
23	OAKLAND	12	Roger Ellis	C	6'3"	233	23			Dainard Paulson	DB	5'11"	190	24	1		Mel West (from BOS)	HB	5'9"	190	22		18
13	Houston	49	Mike Hudock	C	6'2"	245	26			Bert Rechichar	DB	6'1"	210	31			Bob Brooks	FB	6'	215	21		
21	BUFFALO	14	Ed Cooke	DE	6'4"	250	26	3		Lee Riley	DB	6'1"	190	29	4		Bill Mathis	FB	6'1"	220	22		48
28	DALLAS	7	Nick Mumley	DE	6'6"	255	25			Junior Wren	DB	6'	192	31	1		Don Maynard	FL	6'	185	25		48
21	HOUSTON	48	Bob Reifsnyder	DE	6'2"	260	24										Thurlow Cooper	OE	6'4"	228	28		24
24	Dallas	35	Dick Guesman	DT	6'4"	255	25		39								Curley Johnson	OE	6'	215	26		
			Proverb Jacobs	DT	6'4"	255	26										Art Powell	OE	6'3"	212	24		30
			Tom Saidock	DT	6'5"	260	29																
			Sid Youngelman	DE-DT	6'3"	265	29																

BUFFALO BILLS 6-8-0 Buster Ramsey

Scores of Each Game			Use Name	Pos.	Hgt	Wgt	Age	Int	Pts	Use Name	Pos.	Hgt	Wgt	Age	Int	Pts	Use Name	Pos.	Hgt	Wgt	Age	Int	Pts
10	DENVER	22	Don Chelf	OT	6'3"	235	26			Stew Barber	LB	6'3"	235	22	3	6	Johnny Green	QB	6'3"	198	24		6
41	NEW YORK	31	Harold Olson	OT	6'3"	260	22			Ralph Felton	LB	5'11"	210	29	2		Tom O'Connell	QB	5'11"	180	29		
21	BOSTON	23	Ken Rice	OT	6'2"	250	21			Joe Hergert	LB	6'1"	215	25	1	18	Warren Rabb	QB	6'1"	204	24		2
11	SAN DIEGO	19	John Dittrich	OG	6'1"	240	28			Cotton Letner	LB	6'1"	215	24			M. C. Reynolds	QB	6'	195	26		24
22	Houston	12	Ed Muelhaupt	OG	6'3"	230	25		6	Archie Matsos	LB	6'	215	26	2		Richie Lucas	DB-HB-QB	6'	190	22	2	12
27	DALLAS	24	Billy Shaw	OG	6'3"	240	21			Billy Atkins	DB	6'1"	195	26	10	41	Dewey Bohling (from NY)	HB	5'11"	190	22		18
21	Boston	52	Wayne Wolf	OG	6'2"	243	22			Jim Crotty (from WAS -N)	DB	5'11"	190	23	2		Fred Brown	HB	5'11"	187	21		12
16	HOUSTON	28	Al Bemiller	C	6'3"	225	22			Jack Johnson (to DAL)	DB	6'3"	200	27			Wray Carlton	HB	6'2"	210	23		24
22	OAKLAND	31	Lavern Torczon	DE	6'2"	235	25			Billy Majors	DB	6'	175	22			Dan Chamberlain	HB	6'4"	200	24		
30	Dallas	20	Mack Yoho	DE	6'2"	240	25	1		Richie McCabe	DB	6'1"	187	27	1		Elbert Dubenion	HB	6'	190	26		48
23	Denver	10	Tom Day	DT	6'2"	245	26			Don McDonald	DB	5'11"	185	24		6	Willmer Fowler	HB	5'11"	185	24		
14	New York	21	Chuck McMurtry	DT	6'	285	23			Vern Valdez	DB	5'11"	190	25	2		Art Baker	FB	6'	220	23		18
26	Oakland	21	John Scott	DT	6'4"	260	25			Jim Wagstaff	DB	6'2"	190	25	3		Glenn Bass	OE	6'2"	190	22		18
10	San Diego	28	Jim Sorey	DT	6'4"	280	24										Monte Crockett	OE	6'3"	210	22		
																	Perry Richards	OE	6'2"	205	27		18
																	Tom Rychlec	OE	6'3"	220	27		12

HOUSTON OILERS

RUSHING

Last Name	No.	Yds	Avg	TD
Cannon	200	948	4.7	6
Tolar	157	577	3.7	4
Smith	60	258	4.3	2
King	12	50	4.2	2
Lee	8	36	4.5	0
Hall	7	13	1.9	0
Blanda	7	12	1.7	0
Groman	1	2	2.0	1

RECEIVING

Last Name	No.	Yds	Avg	TD
Hennigan	82	1746	21	12
Groman	50	1175	24	17
Cannon	43	586	14	9
Tolar	24	219	9	1
McLeod	14	172	12	2
White	13	238	18	1
Dewveall	12	200	17	3
Smith	10	131	13	1
King	3	83	28	1
Hall	1	20	20	1
Spence	1	14	14	0
Blanda	1	−16	−16	0

PUNT RETURNS

Last Name	No.	Yds	Avg	TD
Cannon	9	70	8	0
King	7	32	5	0
Smith	1	15	15	0
Hall	2	1	1	0

KICKOFF RETURNS

Last Name	No.	Yds	Avg	TD
Cannon	18	439	24	0
King	8	190	24	0
Hall	6	140	23	0
Dukes	4	57	14	0
Tolar	2	42	21	0
Cline	1	24	24	0
Laraway	1	22	22	0
McLeod	1	13	13	0
Wharton	1	8	8	0
Smith	1	5	5	0

PASSING – PUNTING – KICKING Statistics

PASSING	Att	Comp	%	Yds	Yd/Att	TD	Int–%	RK
Blanda	362	187	52	3330	9.2	36	22– 6	1
Lee	127	66	52	1205	9.4	12	6– 5	
Cannon	5	0	0	0	0.0	0	1– 20	
Smith	2	1	50	33	16.5	0	0– 0	
Groman	1	0	0	0	0.0	0	0– 0	
Tolar	1	0	0	0	0.0	0	0– 0	

PUNTING	No	Avg
Norton	48	40.7
Hall	8	29.8

KICKING	XP	Att	%	FG	Att	%
Blanda	64	65	98	16	26	62
Milstead	1	1	100	0	0	0

BOSTON PATRIOTS

RUSHING

Last Name	No.	Yds	Avg	TD
Lott	100	461	4.7	5
Garron	69	389	5.6	2
Burton	82	260	3.2	2
Parilli	38	183	4.8	5
Crawford	41	148	3.6	0
Yewcic	11	51	4.6	1
Songin	8	39	4.9	0
Colclough	3	37	12.3	0
Schwedes	10	14	1.4	0
Washington	1	3	3.0	0

RECEIVING

Last Name	No.	Yds	Avg	TD
Cappelletti	45	768	17	8
Colclough	42	757	18	9
Lott	32	333	10	6
Garron	24	341	14	3
Stephens	19	186	10	2
Burton	13	115	9	0
Crawford	9	85	9	0
Johnson	9	82	9	1
Yewcic	6	56	9	0
Schwedes	1	21	21	0
Shonta	1	9	9	0

PUNT RETURNS

Last Name	No.	Yds	Avg	TD
Burton	8	128	16	0
Bruney	23	109	5	0
Klein	1	23	23	0
Webb	1	20	20	1
Lott	1	8	8	0
Moore	1	0	0	0

KICKOFF RETURNS

Last Name	No.	Yds	Avg	TD
Garron	16	438	27	1
Burton	15	401	27	1
Beach	2	38	19	0
Long	4	24	6	0
Webb	1	21	21	0
Ratkowski	1	17	17	0
Stephens	1	6	6	0
Schwedes	1	0	0	0
Cudzik	1	0	0	0

PASSING – PUNTING – KICKING Statistics

PASSING	Att	Comp	%	Yds	Yd/Att	TD	Int–%	RK
Songin	212	98	46	1429	6.7	14	9– 4	3
Parilli	198	104	53	1314	6.7	13	9– 5	2
Yewcic	8	3	38	25	3.1	1	2– 25	
Burton	1	0	0	0	0.0	0	1–100	
Cappelletti	1	1	100	27	27.0	1	0– 0	

PUNTING	No	Avg
Yewcic	62	38.8

KICKING	XP	Att	%	FG	Att	%
Cappelletti	48	50	96	17	32	53

2 POINT XP
Parilli (1)

NEW YORK TITANS

RUSHING

Last Name	No.	Yds	Avg	TD
Mathis	202	846	4.2	7
West	72	322	4.5	3
Dorow	54	317	5.9	4
Christy	81	180	2.2	2
Brooks	15	55	3.7	0
Renn	1	14	14.0	0
Shockley	5	9	1.8	0
Johnson	1	3	3.0	0
Apple	7	2	0.3	0
Scrabis	1	1	1.0	1

RECEIVING

Last Name	No.	Yds	Avg	TD
Powell	71	881	12	5
Maynard	43	629	15	8
Christy	29	521	18	1
Renn	18	268	15	1
Cooper	15	208	14	4
West	13	146	11	0
Mathis	12	42	4	1
Shockley	3	27	9	0
Johnson	1	32	32	0
O'Neil	1	−13	−13	0

PUNT RETURNS

Last Name	No.	Yds	Avg	TD
Christy	18	383	21	2
West	2	51	26	0
Apple	2	12	6	0
Maynard	1	9	9	0
Shockley	2	6	3	0
Cockrell	1	2	2	0

KICKOFF RETURNS

Last Name	No.	Yds	Avg	TD
Christy	15	360	24	0
West	13	306	24	0
Shockley	12	261	22	0
Renn	10	201	20	0
Brooks	8	111	14	0
Johnson	5	84	17	0
Hynes	2	45	23	0
Saidock	2	26	13	0
Ellis	3	25	8	0
Fields	1	19	19	0
Apple	1	16	16	0
Walsh	2	15	8	0
Budrewicz	1	0	0	0
Cooper	1	0	0	0

PASSING – PUNTING – KICKING Statistics

PASSING	Att	Comp	%	Yds	Yd/Att	TD	Int–%	RK
Dorow	438	197	45	2651	6.1	19	30– 7	7
Scrabis	21	7	33	82	3.9	1	2– 10	
Christy	1	0	0	0	0.0	0	0– 0	

PUNTING	No	Avg
Johnson	66	42.7
Wren	8	33.9

KICKING	XP	Att	%	FG	Att	%
Guesman	24	26	92	5	15	33
Shockley	13	13	100	4	9	44
Cooper	0	0	0	0	1	0

BUFFALO BILLS

RUSHING

Last Name	No.	Yds	Avg	TD
Baker	152	498	3.3	3
Carlton	101	311	3.1	4
Brown	53	192	3.6	1
Dubenion	17	173	10.2	2
Bohling	55	153	2.8	2
Reynolds	30	142	4.7	4
Atkins	2	87	43.5	1
Rabb	13	47	3.6	0
Lucas	10	15	1.5	0
Green	14	15	1.1	1
Bass	2	8	4.0	0
Fowler	1	2	2.0	0
Rychlec	1	−18	−18.0	0

RECEIVING

Last Name	No.	Yds	Avg	TD
Bass	50	765	15	3
Rychlec	33	405	12	2
Dubenion	31	461	15	6
Crockett	20	325	16	0
Richards	19	285	15	3
Carlton	17	193	11	0
Bohling	13	217	17	1
Baker	6	73	12	0
Lucas	6	69	12	0
Chamberlain	1	16	16	0
Brown	1	11	11	0

PUNT RETURNS

Last Name	No.	Yds	Avg	TD
Bass	8	75	9	0
Wagstaff	1	35	35	0
Valdez	1	30	30	0
Atkins	2	30	15	0
Brown	2	14	7	0
Dubenion	1	3	3	0
Bohling	4	0	0	0

KICKOFF RETURNS

Last Name	No.	Yds	Avg	TD
Dubenion	16	329	21	0
Baker	12	281	23	0
Bohling	10	246	25	0
Lucas	7	126	18	0
Brown	2	105	53	1
Carlton	4	60	15	0
Rice	2	13	7	0
Richards	1	10	10	0
Crockett	1	0	0	0

PASSING – PUNTING – KICKING Statistics

PASSING	Att	Comp	%	Yds	Yd/Att	TD	Int–%	RK
Reynolds	181	83	46	1004	5.6	2	13– 7	9
Green	126	56	44	903	7.2	6	5– 4	
Rabb	74	34	46	586	7.9	5	2– 3	
Lucas	50	20	40	282	5.6	2	4– 8	
O'Connell	5	1	20	11	2.2	0	1– 20	
Carlton	2	0	0	0	0.0	0	0– 0	
Bohling	1	0	0	0	0.0	0	0– 0	

PUNTING	No	Avg
Atkins	84	45.0

KICKING	XP	Att	%	FG	Att	%
Atkins	29	31	94	2	6	33
Hergert	0	0	0	6	14	43
Yoho	0	0	0	0	4	0

2 POINT XP
Lucas (3)
Rabb (1)

SAN DIEGO CHARGERS 12-2-0 Sid Gillman

Scores of Each Game		
26	Dallas	10
44	OAKLAND	0
34	HOUSTON	24
19	Buffalo	11
38	Boston	27
25	New York	10
41	Oakland	10
37	DENVER	0
48	NEW YORK	13
19	Denver	16
24	DALLAS	14
13	Houston	33
28	BUFFALO	10
0	BOSTON	41

Use Name	Pos.	Hgt	Wgt	Age	Int	Pts
Sam DeLuca	OT	6'2"	245	25		
Ron Mix	OT	6'4"	245	23		
Sherman Plunkett	OT	6'4"	285	27		
Ernie Wright	OT	6'4"	270	20		
Ernie Barnes	OG	6'3"	260	22		
Orlando Ferrante	OG	6'	230	28		
Gene Selawski	OT-OG	6'4"	252	25		
Geroge Belotti (from HOU)	C	6'4"	250	26		
Don Rogers	C	6'2"	250	24		
Earl Faison	DE	6'5"	256	22	2	
Ron Nery	DE	6'6"	230	26		
Bill Hudson	DT	6'4"	270	25	1	6
Ernie Ladd	DT	6'9"	315	22		
Henry Schmidt	DT	6'4"	260	24		
Chuck Allen	LB	6'1"	218	21	5	6
Emil Karas	LB	6'3"	230	27	3	
Paul Maguire	LB	6'	215	23	1	
Maury Schleicher	LB	6'3"	240	24		
Bob Laraba	HB-LB	6'3"	195	27	5	19
George Blair	DB	5'11"	190	23	2	81
Claude Gibson	DB	6'1"	190	22	5	2
Dick Harris	DB	5'11"	175	24	7	18
Charley McNeil	DB	5'11"	175	25	9	12
Bud Whitehead	DB	6'	180	22	1	
Bob Zeman	DB	6'1"	203	24	8	6
Hunter Enis	QB	6'2"	190	24		12
Jack Kemp	QB	6'1"	200	27		36
Keith Lincoln	HB	6'2"	205	22		18
Paul Lowe	HB	6'	180	24		54
Bo Roberson	HB	6'1"	185	26		18
Charlie Flowers	FB	6'1"	220	24		18
Bob Scarpitto	FL	5'11"	185	22		12
Howard Clark	OE	6'2"	215	26		
Luther Hayes	OE	6'4"	200	22		18
Dave Kocourek	OE	6'5"	230	24		24
Don Norton	OE	6'1"	185	23		36
Jacque Mackinnon	OG-OE	6'4"	240	22		

DALLAS TEXANS 6-8-0 Hank Stram

Scores of Each Game		
10	SAN DIEGO	26
42	Oakland	35
26	HOUSTON	21
19	Denver	12
24	Buffalo	27
7	Houston	38
17	BOSTON	18
21	Boston	28
20	BUFFALO	30
14	San Diego	24
43	OAKLAND	11
7	New York	28
49	DENVER	21
35	NEW YORK	24

Use Name	Pos.	Hgt	Wgt	Age	Int	Pts
Jerry Cornelison	OT	6'3"	250	24		
Charley Diamond	OT	6'2"	235	25		
Jim Tyrer	OT	6'6"	292	22		
John Cadwell	OG	6'3"	230	22		
Sid Fournet	OG	6'	240	28		
Billy Krisher	OG	6'1"	235	25		
Al Reynolds	OG	6'3"	235	23		
Marvin Terrell	OG	6'1"	235	23		
Jon Gilliam	C	6'2"	225	22		
Mel Branch	DE	6'2"	230	24		
Luther Jeralds	DE	6'3"	235	23		
Paul Miller	DE	6'2"	240	29		
Ray Collins	DT	5'11"	250	33		
Jerry Mays	DT	6'4"	245	21	1	
Walter Napier	DT	6'4"	270	25		
Paul Rochester	DT	6'2"	250	24		
Ted Greene	LB	6'1"	230	27	1	
Sherrill Headrick	LB	6'2"	215	24	2	12
E. J. Holub	LB	6'4"	230	23	1	
Smokey Stover	LB	6'	230	22	2	
Dave Grayson	DB	5'10"	180	22	4	6
Ed Kelley	DB	6'2"	195	26		
Doyle Nix	DB	6'1"	195	28	3	
Dave Webster	DB	6'4"	220	23	5	
Duane Wood	DB	6'1"	190	25	4	
Cotton Davidson	QB	6'1"	185	28		26
Randy Duncan	QB	6'	185	23		
Tom Greene	QB	6'1"	190	23		
Abner Haynes	HB	6'	180	23		78
Frank Jackson	HB	6'1"	182	21		30
Johnny Robinson	HB	6'	195	22		42
Bo Dickenson	FB	6'2"	210	26		34
Billy Pricer	FB	5'10"	215	26		
Jack Spikes	FB	6'2"	225	23		54
Charley Barnes	OE	6'5"	230	24		
Max Boydston	OE	6'2"	210	28		6
Chris Burford	OE	6'3"	210	23		30
Tony Romeo	OE	6'2"	215	22		
Ben Agajanian (to GB-N)	K	6'	220	42		16

DENVER BRONCOS 3-11-0 Frankie Filchock

Scores of Each Game		
22	Buffalo	10
17	Boston	45
28	New York	35
19	Oakland	33
12	DALLAS	19
27	OAKLAND	24
27	NEW YORK	10
0	San Diego	37
14	HOUSTON	55
16	SAN DIEGO	19
10	BUFFALO	23
14	Houston	45
24	BOSTON	28
21	Dallas	49

Use Name	Pos.	Hgt	Wgt	Age	Int	Pts
Eldon Danenhauer	OT	6'4"	235	25		
Jerry Sturm	FB-OT	6'3"	235	24		
Ken Adamson	OG	6'2"	225	22		
Buzz Guy (from HOU)	OG	6'3"	250	26		
Carl Larpenter	OG	6'4"	235	24		
Jim Barton	C	6'5"	250	26		
Mike Nichols	C	6'3"	225	22		
John Cash	DE	6'3"	230	25		
Chuck Gavin	DE	6'1"	240	27		6
Bob Konovsky	DE	6'2"	250	27		
Joe Young	DE	6'3"	245	26		
Art Hauser	DT	6'	240	30		
Gordy Holz	DT	6'4"	270	27		
Jack Mattox	DT	6'4"	240	22		
Bud McFadin	DT	6'3"	280	33		
Jim Eifrid	LB	6'1"	240	23		
Bob Griffin (to STL-N)	LB	6'3"	250	32		
Bob Hudson	LB	6'4"	235	31	3	
Pat Lamberti (from NY)	LB	6'2"	225	23	1	
Wahoo McDaniel	LB	6'	240	24		
Bill Roehnelt	LB	6'1"	225	25		
Jackie Simpson	LB	6'1"	230	24		
Jerry Stalcup	LB	6'	240	23		
Goose Gonsoulin	DB	6'3"	205	23	6	
Jim McMillin	DB	5'11"	180	23	5	
Bob McNamara	DB	6'	190	27	3	
Phil Nugent	DB	6'2"	195	22	7	
John Pyeatt	DB	6'3"	204	27		
Jimmy Sears	DB	5'11"	187	30		
Dan Smith	DB	5'10"	180	26		
George Herring	QB	6'2"	200	26		12
Frank Tripucka	QB	6'2"	205	33		
Buddy Allen	HB	5'10"	190	23		
Al Carmichael	HB	6'1"	195	31		
Dale Evans	HB	6'3"	210	22		
Al Frazier	HB	5'11"	180	26		50
Jack Hill	HB	6'1"	185	27		31
Gene Mingo	HB	6'1"	200	22		32
Donnie Stone	HB	6'2"	205	24		48
Jerry Traynham	HB	5'10"	190	22		
Dave Ames (from NY)	DB-HB	6'	185	24	1	
Fred Bukaty	FB	5'11"	195	22		32
Jim Stinnette	LB-FB	6'1"	230	23	1	6
Gene Prebola	OE	6'3"	215	23		8
Lionel Taylor	OE	6'2"	214	25		24

OAKLAND RAIDERS 2-12-0 Marty Feldman

Scores of Each Game		
0	Houston	55
0	San Diego	44
35	DALLAS	42
33	DENVER	19
24	Denver	27
10	SAN DIEGO	41
6	NEW YORK	14
31	Buffalo	22
12	New York	23
17	Boston	20
11	Dallas	43
21	BUFFALO	26
21	BOSTON	35
16	HOUSTON	47

Use Name	Pos.	Hgt	Wgt	Age	Int	Pts
Jim Brewington	OT	6'6"	280	22		
Cliff Roberts	OT	6'3"	260	26		
Ron Sabal	OT	6'2"	245	24		
Jack Stone	OT	6'2"	245	24		
Wayne Hawkins	OG	6'	235	23		
Herb Roedel	OG	6'3"	230	22		
Willie Smith	OG	6'2"	255	23		
Jim Otto	C	6'2"	240	23		
Jon Jelacic	DE	6'3"	255	24		
Charley Powell	DE	6'2"	245	29		
George Fields	DT	6'3"	245	25		
Gary Finneran	DT	6'3"	240	27		
Harry Jagielski (from BOS)	DT	6'	260	29	1	
Volney Peters	DT	6'4"	245	32		
Hal Smith	DT	6'5"	250	26		
Bob Voight	DT	6'5"	265	24		
Al Bansavage	LB	6'2"	220	23		
Bob Dougherty	LB	6'	240	27	2	
Tom Louderback	LB	6'2"	235	27	1	6
Riley Morris	LB	6'2"	230	24	3	6
Alex Bravo	DB	6'	190	29	2	
Joe Cannavino	DB	5'11"	185	25	5	
Bob Garner	DB	5'10"	190	26	2	
John Harris	DB	6'1"	195	28	3	
Fred Williamson	DB	6'2"	205	23	4	
Tom Flores	QB	6'1"	190	24		6
Nick Papac	QB	5'11"	190	26		6
Wayne Crow	HB	6'	205	23		14
Clem Daniels	HB	6'1"	220	24		12
George Fleming	HB	5'11"	188	22		63
Charley Fuller	HB	5'11"	176	22		12
Jack Larschied	HB	5'6"	162	27		
Jim Jones	FB	6'1"	212	25		
Walt Kowalczyk	FB	6'	216	26		
Alan Miller	FB	6'	197	23		42
Doug Asad	OE	6'3"	205	23		12
Jerry Burch	OE	6'1"	195	21		6
Bob Coolbaugh	OE	6'3"	200	21		26
Charley Hardy	OE	6'	185	27		24

SAN DIEGO CHARGERS

RUSHING

Last Name	No.	Yds	Avg	TD
Lowe	175	767	4.4	9
Roberson	58	275	4.7	3
Flowers	51	177	3.5	3
Lincoln	41	150	3.7	0
Kemp	43	105	2.4	6
Enis	16	13	0.8	2
Laraba	5	5	1.0	1

RECEIVING

Last Name	No.	Yds	Avg	TD
Kocourek	55	1055	19	4
Norton	47	816	17	6
Lowe	17	103	6	0
Flowers	16	175	11	0
Hayes	14	280	20	3
Lincoln	12	208	17	2
Clark	11	182	17	0
Scarpitto	9	163	18	2
Roberson	6	81	14	0
MacKinnon	3	58	19	0

PUNT RETURNS

Last Name	No.	Yds	Avg	TD
Gibson	14	209	15	0
Lincoln	7	150	21	1
Scarpitto	4	47	12	0
Zeman	2	47	24	1
Selawski	1	5	5	0
Lowe	1	0	0	0

KICKOFF RETURNS

Last Name	No.	Yds	Avg	TD
Lowe	10	240	24	0
Roberson	13	207	16	0
Lincoln	4	98	25	0
Scarpitto	3	50	17	0
Schmidt	1	22	22	0
Gibson	3	17	6	0
Karas	1	5	5	0
Blair	1	2	2	0
Selawski	1	1	1	0
Mix	1	0	0	0
Ferrante	1	0	0	0

PASSING – PUNTING – KICKING

PASSING	Att	Comp	%	Yds	Yd/Att	TD	Int–%	RK
Kemp	364	165	45	2686	7.4	15	22– 6	5
Enis	55	23	42	365	6.6	2	3– 5	
Lowe	4	2	50	70	17.5	0	0– 0	

PUNTING	No	Avg
Maguire	62	42.2

KICKING	XP	Att	%	FG	Att	%
Blair	42	47	89	13	27	48
Laraba	1	2	50	0	0	0
Lincoln	0	1	0	0	0	0

2 POINT XP
Gibson (1)

DALLAS TEXANS

RUSHING

Last Name	No.	Yds	Avg	TD
Haynes	179	841	4.7	9
Jackson	65	386	5.9	3
Spikes	39	334	8.6	5
Dickinson	71	263	3.7	3
Robinson	52	200	3.9	2
Davidson	21	123	5.9	1
Duncan	5	42	8.5	0
Pricer	5	13	2.6	0
Gilliam	1	–6	–6.0	0
Burford	1	–13	–13.0	0

RECEIVING

Last Name	No.	Yds	Avg	TD
Burford	51	850	17	5
Robinson	35	601	17	5
Haynes	34	558	16	3
Dickinson	14	209	15	2
Jackson	13	171	13	2
Boydston	12	167	14	1
Spikes	8	136	17	0
Romeo	7	89	13	0
Pricer	2	21	11	0
Barnes	1	13	13	0

PUNT RETURNS

Last Name	No.	Yds	Avg	TD
Haynes	19	196	10	0
Mays	1	12	12	0
Headrick	2	5	3	0
Robinson	2	4	2	0
Jackson	1	2	2	0
Miller	1	0	0	0

KICKOFF RETURNS

Last Name	No.	Yds	Avg	TD
Grayson	16	453	28	0
Jackson	24	645	27	0
Haynes	8	270	34	1
Gilliam	1	23	23	0
Pricer	1	19	19	0
Stover	1	15	15	0
Mays	1	13	13	0

PASSING – PUNTING – KICKING

PASSING	Att	Comp	%	Yds	Yd/Att	TD	Int–%	RK
Davidson	330	151	46	2445	7.4	17	23– 7	5
Duncan	67	25	37	361	5.4	1	3– 4	
Jackson	2	1	50	9	4.5	0	1– 50	

PUNTING	No	Avg
Davidson	61	40.6

KICKING	XP	Att	%	FG	Att	%
Davidson	20	20	100	0	2	0
Spikes	10	13	77	4	13	31
Agajanian	7	7	100	3	9	33

2 POINT XP
Dickinson (2)
Spikes (1)

DENVER BRONCOS

RUSHING

Last Name	No.	Yds	Avg	TD
Stone	127	505	4.0	4
Bukaty	76	187	2.5	5
Ames	19	114	6.0	0
Frazier	23	110	4.8	0
Herring	15	74	4.9	2
Mingo	18	51	2.8	0
Sturm	8	31	3.9	0
Carmichael	15	24	1.6	0
Traynham	6	12	2.0	0
Stinnette	19	8	0.4	0
Allen	3	–4	–1.3	0
Tripucka	4	–8	–2.0	0

RECEIVING

Last Name	No.	Yds	Avg	TD
Taylor	100	1176	13	4
Frazier	47	799	17	6
Stone	38	344	9	4
Prebola	29	349	12	1
Bukaty	14	94	7	0
Stinnette	11	58	5	1
Mingo	8	110	14	2
Ames	6	20	3	0
Carmichael	5	23	5	0
Hill	4	33	8	0
Sturm	2	–1	–1	0
Traynham	1	–1	–1	0

PUNT RETURNS

Last Name	No.	Yds	Avg	TD
Frazier	18	231	13	1
Carmichael	7	58	8	0
Gavin	1	45	45	1
McNamara	4	17	4	0
Ames	2	17	9	0
Mingo	1	1	1	0

KICKOFF RETURNS

Last Name	No.	Yds	Avg	TD
Frazier	18	504	28	1
Carmichael	16	310	19	0
Ames	12	240	20	0
Stone	9	215	24	0
Mingo	4	120	30	0
Bukaty	3	41	14	0
Gonsoulin	1	34	34	0
Hill	1	23	23	0
Prebola	1	8	8	0
Stinnette	1	6	6	0

PASSING – PUNTING – KICKING

PASSING	Att	Comp	%	Yds	Yd/Att	TD	Int–%	RK
Tripucka	344	167	49	1690	4.9	10	21– 6	8
Herring	211	93	44	1160	5.5	5	22– 10	10
Mingo	8	4	50	136	17.0	2	0– 0	
Stone	2	1	50	18	9.0	1	0– 0	
Taylor	2	0	0	0	0.0	0	1– 50	
Frazier	1	0	0	0	0.0	0	1–100	

PUNTING	No	Avg
Herring	80	39.4

KICKING	XP	Att	%	FG	Att	%
Hill	16	16	100	5	15	33
Mingo	11	11	100	3	10	30

2 POINT XP
Bukaty (1)
Frazier (1)
Prebola (1)

OAKLAND RAIDERS

RUSHING

Last Name	No.	Yds	Avg	TD
Crow	119	490	4.1	2
Miller	85	255	3.0	3
Daniels	31	154	5.1	2
Fuller	38	134	3.5	0
Fleming	31	112	3.6	1
Flores	23	36	1.6	1
Papac	6	28	4.7	1
Kowalczyk	10	28	2.8	0
Larschied	6	3	0.5	0

RECEIVING

Last Name	No.	Yds	Avg	TD
Asad	36	501	14	2
Miller	36	315	9	4
Coolbaugh	32	435	14	4
Hardy	24	337	14	4
Crow	23	196	9	0
Burch	18	235	13	1
Daniels	13	150	12	0
Fuller	12	277	23	2
Fleming	10	49	5	0
Kowalczyk	3	8	3	0
Larschied	2	11	6	0

PUNT RETURNS

Last Name	No.	Yds	Avg	TD
Fuller	4	52	13	0
Daniels	5	34	7	0
Fleming	3	24	8	0
Garner	2	5	3	0
H. Smith	1	2	2	0

KICKOFF RETURNS

Last Name	No.	Yds	Avg	TD
Fleming	29	588	20	0
Daniels	13	276	21	0
Larschied	9	254	28	0
Fuller	8	155	19	0
Miller	6	66	11	0
Kowalczyk	1	19	19	0
Coolbaugh	1	15	15	0
Asad	1	10	10	0

PASSING – PUNTING – KICKING

PASSING	Att	Comp	%	Yds	Yd/Att	TD	Int–%	RK
Flores	366	190	52	2176	6.0	15	19– 5	3
Papac	44	13	30	173	3.9	2	7– 16	
Crow	10	6	60	165	16.5	0	0– 0	
Fleming	1	0	0	0	0.0	0	1–100	
Fuller	1	0	0	0	0.0	0	0– 0	
Larschied	1	0	0	0	0.0	0	1–100	

PUNTING	No	Avg
Crow	61	42.8
Burch	11	28.6

KICKING	XP	Att	%	FG	Att	%
Fleming	24	25	96	11	26	42

2 POINT XP
Coolbaugh (1)
Crow (1)

1962 N.F.L. Millions from the Stay-at-Homes

It was a year of renewal, consolidation, innovation, and departures. Commissioner Pete Rozelle renewed the NFL's television contract with CBS at a new rate of $4.65 million per year, and the club owners rewarded Rozelle with a new five-year contract with a hefty raise. The consolidation took place in Los Angeles, where full control of the Rams was reacquired by Dan Reeves. After taking in Edwin Pauley and Fred Levy as partners, Reeves fell to feuding with his co-owners in recent years, so Rozelle arranged for the submission of secret bids for the controlling interest in the team, which Reeves won. Innovation brought the league a new rule against grabbing another player's face mask, ground-breaking for a Hall of Fame in Canton, Ohio, and a fabulously popular pre-season doubleheader in Cleveland. And leaving the NFL stage this year, by death, were Mrs. Violet Bidwill Wolfner and James Clark, owners of the Cardinals and Eagles, and, by pink slips, long-time coaches Paul Brown and Weeb Ewbank.

EASTERN CONFERENCE

New York Giants—After fourteen years of professional football, thirty-six-year-old Y. A. Tittle became an overnight sensation as the Giant quarterback. Tittle set a new NFL record of thirty-three touchdown passes in a season, including seven in one game against the Redskins, but his style captivated New York fans more than his passing. He would retreat to his protective pocket and calmly survey the field, a thin, middle-aged man defying the behemoths rushing at him. He would back-pedal with tacklers closing in on him and flip an unexpected screen pass to Alex Webster behind a covey of blockers. Near the goal line he often ran the ball in on the bootleg play, outsprinting the deceived defenders on his aged legs. With a strong cast of players surrounding Tittle, the Giants got to the championship game by winning their last nine games.

Pittsburgh Steelers—Bobby Layne had reason to smile after his final NFL season. He wound up his career with 196 touchdown passes, surpassing Sammy Baugh's old mark of 186, and he led the Steelers to three straight wins at the end of the year to capture second place in the East. Other oldsters besides Layne turned in key performances, such as John Henry Johnson, Ernie Stautner, and Big Daddy Lipscomb. Holdover receiver Buddy Dial starred as a deep threat, and newcomer Lou Michaels excelled as a place-kicker. Perhaps the most important job was coach Buddy Parker's patch-up of the defense after injuries wiped out all his linebackers and personal differences elbowed Johnny Sample into disfavor.

Cleveland Browns—The Paul Brown era crashed to an end in a year of disappointment and tragedy. Brown had traded fleet Bobby Mitchell to Washington for the draft rights to Heisman Trophy winner Ernie Davis of Syracuse. Davis, a powerful halfback, was expected to team with Jimmy Brown in a strong running duo, but leukemia struck the rookie down before he ever played a professional game. With no good running halfbacks to divert the enemy's forces, fullback Brown for the first time ever failed to win the league rushing crown. After a lackluster campaign in which the Browns were never contenders, owner Art Modell shocked the football world by firing the most successful coach in pro-football history.

Washington Redskins—The Redskins fielded their first black players this year in Bobby Mitchell, John Nisby, Leroy Jackson, and Ron Hatcher, and the club's fortunes immediately rocketed upward. Mitchell, obtained from Cleveland for the draft rights to Ernie Davis, set the league on fire with his spectacular receiving from his new flanker position, and with quarterback Norm Snead getting good protection from the bolstered offensive line, an all-out passing attack brought the Skins four wins and two ties in their first six contests before their running game and loose pass defense caught up with them.

Dallas Cowboys—Coach Tom Landry had been a great defensive player, but his coaching genius was in a different direction. The Dallas offense was the second best in the league, trailing only the Packers in points scored, but the Dallas defense was the second worst in the league, with only Minnesota allowing more points. Landry got good mileage out of quarterbacks Eddie LeBaron and Don Meredith by shuffling them in and out of the lineup on every play. But once LeBaron was injured in mid-season and Meredith had to go it alone at quarterback, the attack slipped and the Cowboys dropped five of their last six matches.

St. Louis Cardinals—Although Wally Lemm turned out a losing squad in his first year on the job, he did uncover a fine young passer in Charley Johnson. After sitting on the bench last year and beginning this season as Sam Etcheverry's back-up, Johnson won the quarterback job four games into the season. During the remaining stretch he learned by experience and threw a lot of passes to his complementary receivers, speedster Sonny Randle and sure-handed Bobby Joe Conrad. But even with strong running from John David Crow, the attack never caught fire, due to a mediocre line.

Philadelphia Eagles—The fair Philadelphia defense had sufficed when the offense was churning out points at a furious pace, but injuries this year crippled the attack and sent the Eagles tumbling into last place. Quarterback Sonny Jurgensen, still bothered by a shoulder separation suffered in last season's Playoff Bowl, found himself throwing the ball to a bunch of strangers. Only Tommy McDonald stayed healthy among the receivers, as Pete Retzlaff, Bobby Walston, and Dick Lucas all broke arms and Hopalong Cassady broke a leg, while runner Ted Dean joined the parade with a broken foot.

WESTERN CONFERENCE

Green Bay Packers—Even with Paul Hornung below par physically, the Packers overwhelmed the league with All-Pro performances. Fullback Jim Taylor, whose strong point was neither size nor speed but meanness, took the rushing title away from Jimmy Brown and also led the league in scoring with nineteen touchdowns. Bart Starr compiled the best passing record in the circuit, while Willie Wood intercepted the most aerials. The wire service All-Pro teams were overloaded with Packers as fullback Taylor, end Ron Kramer, offensive linemen Forrest Gregg, Jerry Kramer, Fuzzy Thurston, and Jim Ringo, defensive linemen Willie Davis and Henry Jordan, linebackers Bill Forester and Dan Currie, and cornerback Herb Adderley all won honors.

Detroit Lions—Eleven wins are usually good enough for a championship, but the Lions had to settle for second place in the West behind the stampeding Green Bay Packers. The Lions did expose Vince Lombardi's supermen as mere mortals, however, in their Thanksgiving Day meeting in Detroit. The unbeaten Packers that day ran up against a fired-up Detroit defense that turned in an almost perfect performance. Tackle Roger Brown constantly blasted into the Green Bay backfield, linebacker Joe Schmidt blitzed Packer quarterback Bart Starr into the ground, and the defensive unit kept the Packers scoreless until late in the 26-14 upset victory.

Chicago Bears—Like the Packers and Lions, the Bears had a tough defense at the core of the team. The front four and secondary were solid if not spectacular, but the linebacking corps of Joe Fortunato, Bill George, and Larry Morris ranked with the NFL's best. Offensively, coach George Halas had to scramble around for runners when injuries sidelined Rick Casares and Willie Galimore. Ex-Ram Joe Marconi did a yeoman's job at fullback, while freshman Ronnie Bull hustled enough to win Rookie of the Year honors. The air attack moved well on Billy Wade's passes to Mike Ditka and Johnny Morris, but the defense dominated the Bears, as a bruising 3-0 victory over the Lions to close the season underlined.

Baltimore Colts—The last few seasons had been lackluster, and a 7-7 record this season brought coach Weeb Ewbank's regime to an end. Quarterback Johnny Unitas still was the consummate passer and signal-caller, but his supporting cast was looking slightly worn. The running attack was weak, the offensive line was aging, and the place-kicking was unsure. Strong points included a competent defense and a pair of good receivers in Jimmy Orr and Ray Berry, but not enough to save coach Ewbank's job.

San Francisco '49ers—Before the season started, coach Red Hickey called this club the best football team he had ever coached. But once the schedule began, injuries turned the '49ers into a very ordinary team. Tackle Bob St. Clair, the team's best offensive lineman, went to the sidelines with an injured Achilles tendon, and halfback Billy Kilmer, an exciting runner, passer, and blocker missed the final three games after breaking a leg in a car accident. The defense also slipped a notch, as too much youth subverted the secondary and too much age cut down on tackle Leo Nomellini's quickness.

Minnesota Vikings—The Vikings couldn't match the three wins of their first campaign, but coach Norm Van Brocklin was gathering good young players who would later make Minnesota a title contender. Free agent Mick Tingelhoff won the center's job, rookie linebacker Roy Winston showed promise, and cornerback Ed Sharockman had a good NFL debut after missing 1961 with a broken leg. Aside from these three freshmen, improvement came from youngsters already on the roster, such as quarterback Fran Tarkenton, halfback Tommy Mason, tackle Grady Alderman, defensive end Jim Marshall, and middle linebacker Rip Hawkins.

Los Angeles Rams—Dan Reeves bought out partners Edwin Pauley and Fred Levy, thus ending the front-office bickering that had plagued the team in recent years. But while the ownership picture cleared up, the squad on the field collapsed in a wreck. The Rams won only one game all season, with their offense the worst in the league. Head coach Bob Waterfield tired of all the losing and quit after eight games, leaving the battered team to assistant Harland Svare. But even this season, the worst in Ram history, turned up two bright spots in rookies Merlin Olsen and Roman Gabriel.

FINAL TEAM STATISTICS

OFFENSE	BALT.	CHI.	CLEVE.	DALLAS	DET.	G.BAY	L.A.	MINN.	N.Y.	PHIL.	PITT.	ST.L.	S.F.	WASH.
FIRST DOWNS:														
Total	251	228	252	246	243	281	201	223	267	235	261	268	239	241
by Rushing	94	88	105	101	103	145	84	102	92	76	133	109	112	59
by Passing	145	128	133	136	124	120	107	107	150	146	112	138	112	156
by Penalty	12	12	14	9	16	16	10	14	25	13	16	21	15	26
RUSHING:														
Numbers	448	386	414	434	489	518	376	426	430	324	572	416	460	371
Yards	1601	1489	1772	2040	1922	2460	1689	1864	1698	1155	2333	1698	1873	1088
Average Yards	3.6	3.9	4.3	4.7	3.9	4.7	4.5	4.4	3.9	3.6	4.1	4.1	4.1	2.9
Touchdowns	9	17	18	16	14	36	10	7	11	13	17	20	15	10
PASSING:														
Attempts	423	430	370	380	379	311	372	348	411	428	319	434	323	428
Completions	237	229	200	200	211	187	189	170	215	228	160	220	185	223
Completion Pct.	56.0	53.3	54.1	52.6	55.7	60.1	50.8	48.9	52.3	53.3	50.2	50.7	57.3	52.1
Passing Yardage	3330	3286	2747	3115	2827	2621	2524	2699	3446	3632	2419	3388	2491	3532
Avg. Yds per Att.	7.9	7.6	7.4	8.2	7.5	8.4	6.8	7.8	8.4	8.5	7.6	7.8	7.7	8.3
Avg. Yds per Comp.	14.1	14.3	13.7	15.6	13.4	14.0	13.4	15.9	16.0	15.9	15.1	15.4	13.5	15.8
Yards Lost Tackled	265	226	213	243	246	290	348	483	139	247	350	288	423	309
Net Yards	3065	3060	2534	2872	2581	2331	2176	2216	3307	3385	2069	3100	2068	3223
Touchdowns	27	20	17	31	19	14	14	22	35	23	14	18	19	27
Interceptions	25	28	16	17	24	13	19	31	22	31	23	30	19	27
Pct. Intercepted	5.9	6.5	4.3	4.5	6.3	4.2	5.1	8.9	5.4	7.2	7.2	6.9	5.9	6.3
PUNTING:														
Number	58	69	45	57	53	50	87	65	55	64	60	59	48	63
Average Distance	41.5	43.7	42.8	45.4	45.3	40.9	45.5	40.3	40.6	42.9	40.0	38.3	45.6	34.5
PUNT RETURNS:														
Number	34	39	20	17	39	31	27	34	17	14	19	20	27	29
Yards	272	281	111	81	502	290	252	374	58	95	169	134	207	184
Average Yards	8.0	7.2	5.6	4.8	12.9	9.4	9.3	11.0	3.4	6.8	8.9	6.7	7.7	6.3
Touchdowns	0	1	0	0	0	0	0	0	0	0	0	0	1	0
KICKOFF RETURNS:														
Number	55	53	46	59	46	30	60	67	54	61	62	64	62	61
Yards	1263	1129	983	1207	1124	716	1447	1522	1405	1385	1350	1495	1739	1720
Average Yards	23.0	21.3	21.4	20.5	24.4	23.9	24.1	22.7	26.0	22.7	21.8	23.4	28.0	28.2
Touchdowns	0	0	0	1	0	1	0	0	1	1	0	0	0	1
INTERCEPTION RETURNS:														
Number	23	23	24	20	24	31	19	25	26	26	28	16	12	28
Yards	331	468	352	366	269	452	261	280	332	289	318	229	127	285
Average Yards	14.4	20.3	14.7	18.3	11.2	14.6	13.7	11.2	12.8	11.1	11.4	14.3	10.6	10.2
Touchdowns	0	2	0	1	2	1	2	1	0	0	2	1	0	0
PENALTIES:														
Number	63	69	56	62	62	59	71	44	62	58	45	56	63	62
Yards	675	776	600	639	624	617	704	447	601	619	427	655	636	663
FUMBLES:														
Number	26	29	24	32	26	29	26	37	24	25	24	36	24	31
Number Lost	19	16	17	19	18	15	16	23	14	13	13	21	14	17
POINTS:														
Total	293	321	291	398	315	415	220	254	398	282	312	287	282	305
PAT Attempts	37	41	36	51	38	53	27	31	49	38	33	39	36	39
PAT Made	31	36	33	50	37	52	26	31	47	36	32	38	36	38
FG Attempts	28	27	31	27	34	21	20	25	28	19	42	14	23	25
FG Made	12	13	14	14	14	15	10	11	19	6	26	5	10	11
Percent FG Made	42.9	48.1	45.2	51.9	41.2	71.4	50.0	44.0	67.9	31.6	61.9	35.7	43.5	44.0
Safeties	2	0	0	0	4	0	1	2	0	0	2	0	0	0

DEFENSE	BALT.	CHI.	CLEVE.	DALLAS	DET.	G.BAY	L.A.	MINN.	N.Y.	PHIL.	PITT.	ST.L.	S.F.	WASH.
FIRST DOWNS:														
Total	226	228	263	274	180	191	256	266	256	275	250	251	240	280
by Rushing	91	108	122	93	62	88	119	119	100	128	78	93	107	95
by Passing	119	101	125	166	105	94	124	139	136	129	157	141	113	165
by Penalty	16	19	16	15	13	9	13	8	20	18	15	17	20	20
RUSHING:														
Numbers	423	438	466	387	353	404	501	463	413	526	363	452	464	411
Yards	1504	2073	1940	1510	1231	1531	2092	1978	1677	2126	1419	1724	2241	1636
Average Yards	3.6	4.7	4.2	3.9	3.5	3.8	4.2	4.3	4.1	4.0	3.9	3.8	4.8	4.0
Touchdowns	17	17	17	17	6	4	14	20	13	23	13	18	22	12
PASSING:														
Attempts	381	363	341	437	367	355	379	397	450	363	438	377	296	412
Completions	206	170	189	233	187	187	217	214	223	198	223	196	164	247
Completion Pct.	54.1	46.8	55.4	53.3	51.0	52.7	57.3	53.9	49.6	54.5	50.9	52.0	55.4	60.0
Passing Yardage	2975	2460	2277	3904	2441	2084	3144	3365	3238	3023	3490	3302	2494	3860
Avg. Yds per Att.	7.8	6.8	6.7	8.9	6.7	5.9	8.3	8.5	7.2	8.3	8.0	8.8	8.4	9.4
Avg. Yds per Comp.	14.4	14.5	12.0	16.8	13.1	11.1	14.5	15.7	14.5	15.3	15.7	16.8	15.2	15.6
Yards Lost Tackled	356	386	293	230	455	338	255	242	369	103	284	315	186	258
Net Yards	2619	2074	1984	3674	1986	1746	2889	3123	2869	2920	3206	2987	2308	3602
Touchdowns	19	14	15	33	11	20	25	29	21	16	34	21	17	35
Interceptions	23	23	24	20	24	31	19	25	26	26	28	16	12	28
Pct. Intercepted	6.0	6.3	7.0	4.6	6.5	8.7	5.0	6.3	5.8	7.2	6.4	4.2	4.1	6.8
PUNTING:														
Number	67	71	56	63	70	58	56	52	65	42	62	61	61	49
Average Distance	42.7	41.8	40.6	40.6	44.1	43.2	45.5	43.3	38.8	38.2	40.7	40.6	44.6	42.4
PUNT RETURNS:														
Number	23	32	15	28	31	20	55	32	24	24	18	26	32	7
Yards	182	308	121	190	326	183	567	261	138	174	119	122	285	34
Average Yards	7.9	9.6	8.1	6.8	10.5	9.2	10.3	8.2	5.8	7.3	6.6	4.7	8.9	4.9
Touchdowns	0	0	0	0	0	1	1	0	0	0	0	0	0	0
KICKOFF RETURNS:														
Number	52	60	49	63	55	76	50	52	63	56	54	41	51	58
Yards	1433	1514	1098	1604	1379	1524	1211	1149	1700	1459	1151	870	1140	1253
Average Yards	27.6	25.2	22.4	25.5	25.1	20.1	24.2	22.1	27.0	26.1	21.3	21.2	22.4	21.6
Touchdowns	1	0	0	1	0	0	0	0	0	1	0	0	0	2
INTERCEPTION RETURNS:														
Number	25	28	16	17	24	13	19	31	22	31	23	30	19	27
Yards	386	328	161	263	352	122	293	445	182	555	257	389	334	292
Average Yards	15.4	11.7	10.1	15.5	14.7	9.4	15.4	14.4	8.3	17.9	11.2	13.0	17.6	10.8
Touchdowns	0	1	0	1	0	1	2	1	0	2	0	1	3	0
PENALTIES:														
Number	71	65	53	56	51	54	52	68	58	48	53	63	57	83
Yards	792	643	547	569	527	611	592	633	636	479	581	584	626	863
FUMBLES:														
Number	32	37	23	33	34	28	30	30	30	22	21	23	22	28
Number Lost	19	24	13	16	23	19	18	18	13	13	10	15	14	20
POINTS:														
Total	288	287	257	402	177	148	334	410	283	356	363	361	331	376
PAT Attempts	37	34	34	52	19	17	42	52	35	43	48	44	42	49
PAT Made	35	31	32	49	19	17	38	51	34	41	48	43	39	46
FG Attempts	22	31	14	25	25	22	33	30	27	37	19	33	20	26
FG Made	9	16	7	13	14	9	14	15	13	19	9	18	12	12
Percent FG Made	40.9	51.6	50.0	52.0	56.0	40.9	42.4	50.0	48.1	51.4	47.4	54.5	60.0	46.2
Safeties	2	2	0	1	1	1	1	1	0	0	0	0	2	0

1962 NFL
CHAMPIONSHIP GAME
December 30, at New York
(Attendance 64,892)

A Dismal Homecoming

A bone-chilling thirty-five-mile-per-hour wind lanced through Yankee Stadium, where the temperature was 20 degrees at game time and dropped steadily all afternoon. The Giants were out to avenge last year's loss to the Packers but fell short in a bitterly contested, hard-hitting ground game. The wind and cold made passing close to impossible, so the game was fought out primarily between the opposing lines and power runners. One particularly brutal pairing was Packer fullback Jim Taylor and Giant linebacker Sam Huff, the two of them butting heads constantly all game long. The Packers punched out yardage behind the crisp blocking of their offensive line and scored in the opening period on a 26-yard Jerry Kramer field goal. The Packers got a break in the second quarter when Dan Currie's hard tackle knocked the football loose from Phil King on the Giant 28-yard line. On the first play after the recovery, Paul Hornung passed 21 yards to Boyd Dowler on the halfback option, and Jim Taylor blasted through the line for the last seven yards on the next play. The Packers led 10-0 at halftime, but the Giants finally scored in the third period when Erich Barnes blocked Max McGee's punt and Jim Collier fell on it in the end zone for a touchdown. On the next series of downs, the Packers again punted, but New York's Sam Horner fumbled the ball and Green Bay recovered on the Giant 40-yard line. After that, the Packers never lost momentum, and two more Kramer field goals made the final score 16-7.

TEAM STATISTICS

N. Y.		G. B.
18	First Downs – Total	18
5	First Downs – Rushing	11
11	First Downs – Passing	6
2	First Downs – Penalty	1
7	Punts – Number	6
42.0	Punts – Average Distance	25.5
0	Punt Return Yardage	36
0	Interception Returns – Number	1
0	Interception Return – Yards	30
3	Fumbles – Number	2
2	Fumbles – Number Lost	0
4	Penalties – Number	5
62	Yards – Penalized	44
3	Giveaways	0
0	Takeaways	3
–3	Difference	+3

SCORING

NEW YORK	0	0	7	0– 7
GREEN BAY	3	7	3	3–16

First Quarter
G.B. J. Kramer, 26 yard field goal 7:11

Second Quarter
G.B. Taylor, 7 yard rush 12:21
PAT – J. Kramer (kick)

Third Quarter
N.Y. Collier, recovered blocked punt in the end zone. 7:26
PAT – Chandler (kick)
G.B. J. Kramer, 29 yard field goal 11:00

Fourth Quarter
G.B. J. Kramer, 30 yard field goal 13:10

INDIVIDUAL STATISTICS

RUSHING

NEW YORK	No	Yds	Avg.	GREEN BAY	No	Yds	Avg.
Webster	15	56	3.7	Taylor	31	85	2.7
King	11	38	3.5	Hornung	8	35	4.4
	26	94	3.6	Moore	6	24	4.0
				Starr	1	4	4.0
					46	148	3.2

RECEIVING

NEW YORK	No	Yds	Avg.	GREEN BAY	No	Yds	Avg.
Walton	5	75	15.0	Dowler	4	48	12.0
Shofner	5	69	13.8	Taylor	3	20	6.7
Gifford	4	34	8.5	R. Kramer	2	25	12.5
King	2	14	7.0	McGee	1	13	13.0
Webster	1	5	5.0		10	106	10.6
Morrison	1	0	0.0				
	18	197	10.9				

PASSING

	Att	Comp	Comp Pct.	Yds	Int	Yds/ Att.	Yds/ Comp
NEW YORK							
Tittle	41	18	43.9	197	1	4.8	10.9
GREEN BAY							
Starr	21	9	42.9	85	0	4.0	9.4
Hornung	1	1	100.0	21	0	21.0	21.0
	22	10	45.5	106	0	4.8	10.6

1962 N.F.L. — Eastern Conference

NEW YORK GIANTS 12-2-0 Allie Sherman

Scores of Each Game		
7	Cleveland	17
29	Philadelphia	13
31	Pittsburgh	27
31	St. Louis	14
17	PITTSBURGH	20
17	DETROIT	14
49	WASHINGTON	34
31	ST. LOUIS	28
41	Dallas	10
42	Washington	24
19	PHILADELPHIA	14
26	Chicago	24
17	CLEVELAND	13
41	DALLAS	31

Use Name	Pos.	Hgt	Wgt	Age	Int	Pts
Rosey Brown	OT	6'3"	255	29		
Jack Stroud	OT	6'1"	250	33		
Reed Bohovich	OG-OT	6'3"	260	21		
Bookie Bolin	OG	6'2"	235	22		
Darrell Dess	OG	6'	245	26		
Greg Larson	C-OG	6'2"	245	23		
Ray Wietecha	C	6'1"	230	33		
Ken Byers	DE	6'1"	240	22		
Jim Katcavage	DE	6'3"	240	27	1	
Andy Robustelli	DE	6'1"	235	36		
Rosey Grier	DT	6'5"	290	29		
Chuck Janerette	DT	6'3"	250	23		
Dick Modzelewski	DT	6'	260	31		
Sam Huff	LB	6'1"	230	27	1	
Dick Lasse	LB	6'2"	225	26		
Tom Scott	LB	6'2"	220	32	1	
Mickey Walker	LB	6'	230	22		
Bill Winter	LB	6'3"	220	22		
Erich Barnes	DB	6'2"	198	27	6	
Sam Horner	DB	6'	198	24		
Dick Lynch	DB	6'1"	205	26	5	12
Jimmy Patton	DB	6'	185	30	7	
Dick Pesonen	DB	6'	190	24	2	
Allan Webb	DB	5'11"	180	27	3	
Ralph Gugliemi	QB	6'1"	195	29		
Y. A. Tittle	QB	6'	195	35		12
Johnny Counts	HB	5'10"	170	23		6
Paul Dudley	HB	6'	185	22		6
Phil King	HB	6'4"	225	26		12
Joe Morrison	DB-HB	6'1"	212	24		18
Alex Webster	FB	6'3"	225	31		54
Frank Gifford	FL	6'1"	190	32		48
Jim Collier	OE	6'2"	195	23		
Del Shofner	OE	6'3"	185	26		72
Aaron Thomas (from SF)	OE	6'3"	208	24		
Joe Walton	OE	5'11"	200	27		54
Don Chandler	K	6'2"	210	27		104

PITTSBURGH STEELERS 9-5-0 Buddy Parker

Scores of Each Game		
7	Detroit	45
30	Dallas	28
27	NEW YORK	31
13	PHILADELPHIA	7
20	New York	17
27	DALLAS	42
14	CLEVELAND	41
39	MINNESOTA	31
26	St. Louis	17
23	WASHINGTON	21
14	Cleveland	35
19	ST. LOUIS	7
26	Philadelphia	17
27	Washington	24

Use Name	Pos.	Hgt	Wgt	Age	Int	Pts
Charlie Bradshaw	OT	6'6"	255	26		
Dan James	OT	6'4"	280	25		
Ray Lemek	OG	6'	240	28		
Mike Sandusky	OG	6'	230	29		
Ron Stehouwer	OG	6'2"	230	25		
Buzz Nutter	C	6'4"	230	31		
Lou Michaels	DE	6'2"	235	26		110
Ernie Stautner	DE	6'1"	230	37	1	2
John Kenerson (to NY-A)	DT	6'3"	255	23		
Joe Krupa	DT	6'2"	225	29		
Big Daddy Lipscomb	DT	6'6"	288	31		
George Strugar (to NY-A)	DT	6'5"	258	27		
Lou Cordileone (from LA)	DE-DT	6'	245	25		
Tom Bettis	LB	6'2"	225	29		
Rudy Hayes	LB	6'	215	27		
Ken Kirk	LB	6'2"	230	24		
John Reger	LB	6'	230	31	1	
Bob Schmitz	LB	6'1"	235	24	3	6
Bob Simms (from NY)	LB	6'1"	230	24		
George Tarasovic	LB	6'4"	245	33	4	
Willie Daniel	DB	5'11"	185	24	5	6
Glenn Glass	DB	6'	190	25		
Dick Haley	DB	5'10"	195	26	4	
Brady Keys	DB	6'	185	26	3	
Johnny Sample	DB	6'1"	200	25		
Jackie Simpson	DB	5'10"	185	28		
Clendon Thomas	DB	6'2"	192	25	7	
Ed Brown	QB	6'2"	210	33		
Bobby Layne	QB	6'1"	210	35		6
Terry Nofsinger	QB	6'4"	205	24		
Gary Ballman	HB	6'	190	22		
Dick Hoak	HB	5'11"	190	23		24
Tom Tracy	HB	5'9"	205	30		
Joe Womack	HB	5'9"	210	25		30
Bob Ferguson	FB	5'11"	220	21		
John Henry Johnson	FB	6'2"	215	32		54
Buddy Dial	FL	6'1"	195	25		36
Red Mack	FL	5'10"	185	25		12
John Burrell	OE	6'3"	188	22		
Preston Carpenter	OE	6'2"	190	28		24
Harlon Hill (to DET)	OE	6'3"	200	30		
John Powers	OE	6'2"	215	21		

Myron Pottios – Injury

CLEVELAND BROWNS 7-6-1 Paul Brown

Scores of Each Game		
17	NEW YORK	7
16	WASHINGTON	17
7	Philadelphia	35
19	DALLAS	10
14	BALTIMORE	36
34	St. Louis	7
41	Pittsburgh	14
14	PHILADELPHIA	14
9	Washington	17
38	ST. LOUIS	14
35	PITTSBURGH	14
21	Dallas	45
13	New York	17
13	San Francisco	10

Use Name	Pos.	Hgt	Wgt	Age	Int	Pts
John Brown	OT	6'2"	245	23		
Mike McCormack	OT	6'4"	250	35		
Dick Schafrath	OT	6'3"	255	26		
Gene Hickerson	OG	6'3"	248	27		
Jim Ray Smith	OG	6'3"	245	31		
John Wooten	OG	6'2"	250	27		
John Morrow	C	6'3"	248	29		
Frank Morze	C	6'4"	264	28		
Bill Glass	DE	6'5"	255	26		
Jim Houston	DE	6'2"	235	25		
Paul Wiggin	DE	6'3"	245	28		
Bob Gain	DT	6'3"	260	34		
Frank Parker	DT	6'5"	250	22		
Floyd Peters	DT	6'4"	255	27	1	
Vince Costello	LB	6'	232	30	3	6
Galen Fiss	LB	6'	227	32	4	
Mike Lucci	LB	6'2"	220	22		
Sam Tidmore	LB	6'1"	220	23		
Ross Fichtner	DB	6'	185	24	7	
Don Fleming	DB	6'	188	25	2	
Bobby Franklin	DB	5'11"	182	26	1	
Bernie Parrish	DB	5'11"	195	27	2	
Jim Shofner	DB	6'2"	190	26	4	
Jim Shorter	DB	5'11"	180	21		
John Furman	QB	6'4"	205	22		
Jim Ninowski	QB	6'1"	200	26		
Frank Ryan	QB	6'3"	200	26		6
Ernie Green	HB	6'2"	205	23		6
Charlie Scales	HB	5'11"	215	23		18
Tom Wilson	FB-HB	6'	204	29		6
Jimmy Brown	FB	6'2"	228	26		108
Ray Renfro	FL	6'1"	192	31		24
Johnny Brewer	OE	6'4"	225	25		12
Leon Clarke	OE	6'4"	235	29		
Gary Collins	OE	6'4"	208	21		12
Bob Crespino	OE	6'4"	217	24		
Rich Kreitling	OE	6'2"	208	27		18
Lou Groza	K	6'3"	248	38		75

WASHINGTON REDSKINS 5-7-2 Bill McPeak

Scores of Each Game		
35	Dallas	35
17	Cleveland	16
24	ST. LOUIS	14
20	LOS ANGELES	14
17	St. Louis	17
27	Philadelphia	21
34	New York	49
10	DALLAS	38
17	CLEVELAND	9
21	Pittsburgh	23
24	NEW YORK	42
14	PHILADELPHIA	37
21	Baltimore	34
24	PITTSBURGH	27

Use Name	Pos.	Hgt	Wgt	Age	Int	Pts
Fran O'Brien	OT	6'1"	250	27		
Riley Mattson	OT	6'4	248	23		
Bob Khayat	OG	6'2	230	24		71
Charlie Moore	OG	6'5"	230	22		
John Nisby	OG	6'1"	247	29		
Vince Promuto	OG	6'1"	243	24		
Fred Hageman	C	6'4"	244	24		
Gene Cronin	DE	6'2"	228	29		
Ed Khayat	DE	6'3"	248	27		
John Paluck	DE	6'2"	240	29		
Andy Stynchula	DE	6'3"	257	23		
Ben Davidson	DT	6'8"	275	22		
Joe Rutgens	DT	6'2"	265	23		
Bob Toneff	DT	6'3"	275	32		
Rod Breedlove	LB	6'2"	225	24	3	
Gorden Kelley	LB	6'3	230	24	2	
Al Miller	LB	6'	220	22		
Bob Pellegrini	LB	6'2"	225	27	4	
Claude Crabb	DB	6'	190	22	6	
Doug Elmore	DB	6'	188	22	2	
Bobby Freeman	DB	6'1"	200	29	3	
Dale Hackbart	DB	6'3"	210	26	3	
Jim Kerr	DB	6'	195	23	1	
Jim Steffen	DB	6'	195	25	4	6
Ron Hatcher	FB-DB	5'11"	215	23		
Galen Hall	QB	5'10"	205	23	6	
George Izo	QB	6'3	214	25		
Norm Snead	QB	6'4"	215	22		18
Billy Barnes	HB	5'11"	202	27		18
Leroy Jackson	HB	6'	190	22		6
Dick James	HB	5'9"	175	28		30
Don Bosseler	FB	6'1"	212	26		12
Jim Cunningham	FB	5'11"	220	23		12
Bobby Mitchell	FL	6'	192	27		72
Bill Anderson	OE	6'2"	214	26		12
Fred Dugan	OE	6'3"	198	28		30
Steve Junker	OE	6'3"	217	27		12
Hugh Smith	OE	6'4"	215	24		

DALLAS COWBOYS 5-8-1 Tom Landry

Scores of Each Game		
35	WASHINGTON	35
28	PITTSBURGH	30
27	Los Angeles	17
10	Cleveland	19
41	PHILADELPHIA	19
42	Pittsburgh	27
24	ST. LOUIS	28
38	Washington	10
10	NEW YORK	41
33	CHICAGO	34
14	Philadelphia	28
45	CLEVELAND	21
20	St. Louis	52
31	New York	41

Use Name	Pos.	Hgt	Wgt	Age	Int	Pts
Clyde Brock	OT	6'5"	268	22		
Monte Clark	OT	6'6"	260	25		
Bob Fry	OT	6'4"	240	31		
Dale Memmelaar	OT	6'2"	245	25		
Andy Cvercko	OG	6'	243	25		
Joe Bob Isbell	OG	6'1"	225	22		
Mike Connelly	C	6'3"	235	26		
Lynn Hoyem	C	6'4"	225	22		
George Andrie	DE	6'7"	247	22		
Bob Lilly	DE	6'4"	248	23		
Ken Frost	DT	6'4"	245	23		
John Meyers	DT	6'6"	267	22		
Guy Reese	DT	6'5"	238	22		
Mike Dowdle	LB	6'3"	210	24	1	
Chuck Howley	LB	6'3"	230	26	2	
Bob Lang	LB	6'3"	235	28		
Don Talbert	LB	6'5"	225	22		
Jerry Tubbs	LB	6'2"	220	27	4	
Don Bishop	DB	6'2"	204	27	6	6
Mike Gaechter	DB	6'	190	22	5	6
Cornell Green	DB	6'4"	210	22		
Warren Livingston	DB	5'10"	180	24		
Dick Nolan	DB	6'1"	185	30		
Jerry Norton	DB	5'11"	195	32	2	6
Buddy Humphrey	QB	6'1"	200	26		
Eddie LeBaron	QB	5'9"	160	32		
Don Meredith	QB	6'2"	198	24		
Amos Bullocks	HB	6'1"	197	23		18
Don Perkins	HB	5'10"	198	24		42
J. W. Lockett	FB	6'2"	230	25		18
Amos Marsh	FB	6'1"	208	23		54
Frank Clarke	FL	6'	215	29		84
Donnie Davis	FL	6'4"	214	22		
Lee Folkins	OE	6'5"	220	23		36
Billy Howton	OE	6'2"	194	32		36
Pettis Norman	OE	6'3"	215	22		
Glynn Gregory	DB-OE	6'2"	200	23		
Sam Baker	K	6'2"	217	30		92

John Houser – Injury
Ed Nutting – Injury

NEW YORK GIANTS

RUSHING

Last Name	No.	Yds	Avg	TD
Webster	207	743	3.6	5
King	108	460	4.3	2
Morrison	35	146	4.2	1
Tittle	17	108	6.4	2
Dudley	27	100	3.7	0
Counts	14	55	3.9	0
Guglielmi	11	40	3.6	0
Gifford	2	18	9.0	1
Shofner	1	4	4.0	0
Thomas	1	−9	−9.0	0
Chandler	1	−11	−11.0	0

RECEIVING

Last Name	No.	Yds	Avg	TD
Shofner	53	1133	21	12
Webster	47	477	10	4
Gifford	39	796	20	7
Walton	33	406	12	9
King	15	186	12	0
Dudley	9	112	12	1
Morrison	6	107	18	2
Thomas	4	80	20	0
Counts	4	62	16	0
Collier	1	27	27	0
Robustelli	1	26	26	0

PUNT RETURNS

Last Name	No.	Yds	Avg	TD
Counts	8	33	4	0
Morrison	5	22	4	0
Horner	3	3	1	0
Patton	1	0	0	0

KICKOFF RETURNS

Last Name	No.	Yds	Avg	TD
Counts	26	784	30	1
Horner	11	242	22	0
Dudley	8	229	29	0
Morrison	5	113	23	0
King	2	37	19	0
Collier	1	0	0	0
Walker	1	0	0	0

PASSING – PUNTING – KICKING

PASSING	Att	Comp	%	Yds	Yd/Att	TD	Int–	%	RK
Tittle	375	200	53	3224	8.6	33	20–	5	2
Guglielmi	31	14	45	210	6.8	2	1–	3	
Gifford	2	1	50	12	6.0	0	0–	0	
Dudley	1	0	0	0	0.0	0	1–	100	

PUNTING	No	Avg
Chandler	55	40.6

KICKING	XP	Att	%	FG	Att	%
Chandler	47	48	98	19	28	68

PITTSBURGH STEELERS

RUSHING

Last Name	No.	Yds	Avg	TD
Johnson	251	1141	4.5	7
Womack	128	468	3.7	5
Hoak	117	442	3.8	4
Tracy	20	116	5.8	0
Hill	7	72	10.3	0
Burrell	6	38	6.3	0
Ferguson	20	37	1.9	0
Layne	15	25	1.7	1
Ballman	3	7	2.3	0
Mack	2	−2	−1.0	0
Carpenter	1	−3	−3.0	0
Brown	2	−8	−4.0	0

RECEIVING

Last Name	No.	Yds	Avg	TD
Dial	50	981	20	6
Carpenter	36	492	14	4
Johnson	32	226	7	2
Hoak	9	133	15	0
Mack	8	203	25	2
Burrell	8	193	24	0
Hill	7	101	14	0
Womack	6	57	10	0
Tracy	2	11	6	0
Powers	1	16	16	0
Ferguson	1	6	6	0

PUNT RETURNS

Last Name	No.	Yds	Avg	TD
Carpenter	7	109	16	0
Keys	7	46	7	0
Haley	1	13	13	0
Sample	4	1	0	0

KICKOFF RETURNS

Last Name	No.	Yds	Avg	TD
Keys	28	667	24	0
Glass	16	396	25	0
Haley	7	105	15	0
Sample	2	52	26	0
Hoak	2	40	20	0
Ferguson	2	30	15	0
Carpenter	1	29	29	0
Womack	1	16	16	0
Michaels	2	15	8	0
Sandusky	1	0	0	0

PASSING – PUNTING – KICKING

PASSING	Att	Comp	%	Yds	Yd/Att	TD	Int–	%	RK
Layne	233	116	50	1686	7.2	9	17–	7	15
Brown	84	43	51	726	8.6	5	6–	7	
Hoak	1	0	0	0	0.0	0	0–	0	
Tracy	1	1	100	7	7.0	0	0–	0	

PUNTING	No	Avg
Brown	60	40.0

KICKING	XP	Att	%	FG	Att	%
Michaels	32	33	97	26	42	62

CLEVELAND BROWNS

RUSHING

Last Name	No.	Yds	Avg	TD
Jimmy Brown	230	996	4.3	13
Ryan	42	242	5.8	1
Scales	56	239	4.3	3
Wilson	46	141	3.1	1
Green	31	139	4.5	0
Ninowski	9	15	1.7	0

RECEIVING

Last Name	No.	Yds	Avg	TD
Jimmy Brown	47	517	11	5
Kreitling	44	659	15	3
Renfro	31	638	21	4
Brewer	22	290	13	2
Green	17	194	11	1
Collins	11	153	14	2
Clarke	10	106	11	0
Wilson	8	110	14	0
Scales	8	67	8	0
Crespino	2	13	7	0

PUNT RETURNS

Last Name	No.	Yds	Avg	TD
Shofner	8	33	4	0
Green	5	31	6	0

KICKOFF RETURNS

Last Name	No.	Yds	Avg	TD
Wilson	11	307	28	0
Green	13	250	19	0
Scales	9	154	17	0
Tidmore	2	39	20	0
Collins	1	0	0	0

PASSING – PUNTING – KICKING

PASSING	Att	Comp	%	Yds	Yd/Att	TD	Int–	%	RK
Ryan	194	112	58	1541	7.9	10	7–	4	4
Ninowski	173	87	50	1178	6.8	7	8–	5	14
Jimmy Brown	2	1	50	28	14.0	0	0–	0	
Scales	1	0	0	0	0.0	0	1–	100	

PUNTING	No	Avg
Collins	45	42.8

KICKING	XP	Att	%	FG	Att	%
Groza	33	35	94	14	31	45

WASHINGTON REDSKINS

RUSHING

Last Name	No.	Yds	Avg	TD
Barnes	159	492	3.1	3
Bosseler	93	336	3.6	2
Cunningham	35	144	4.1	1
Jackson	49	112	2.3	0
James	9	13	1.4	0
Snead	20	10	0.5	3
Mitchell	1	5	5.0	0
Hall	2	2	1.0	1
Izo	1	−3	−3.0	0
Dugan	1	−9	−9.0	0
Elmore	1	−14	−14	0

RECEIVING

Last Name	No.	Yds	Avg	TD
Mitchell	72	1384	19	11
Dugan	36	466	13	5
Bosseler	32	258	8	0
Anderson	23	386	17	2
James	19	373	20	5
Barnes	14	220	16	0
Junker	11	149	14	2
Jackson	10	253	25	1
Cunningham	6	43	7	1

PUNT RETURNS

Last Name	No.	Yds	Avg	TD
James	19	145	8	0
Steffen	6	30	5	0
Mitchell	3	7	2	0
Kerr	1	2	2	0

KICKOFF RETURNS

Last Name	No.	Yds	Avg	TD
James	32	889	28	0
Mitchell	12	398	33	1
Jackson	10	272	27	0
Steffen	4	107	27	0
Cunningham	2	54	27	0
Miller	1	0	0	0

PASSING – PUNTING – KICKING

PASSING	Att	Comp	%	Yds	Yd/Att	TD	Int–	%	RK
Snead	354	184	52	2926	8.3	22	22–	6	8
Izo	37	17	46	284	7.7	3	4–	11	
Hall	32	19	59	274	8.6	2	1–	3	
Barnes	4	3	75	48	12.0	0	0–	0	
Elmore	1	0	0	0	0.0	0	0–	0	

PUNTING	No	Avg
Elmore	54	34.4
Anderson	7	33.6
Hackbart	2	39.0

KICKING	XP	Att	%	FG	Att	%
B. Khayat	38	38	100	11	25	44

DALLAS COWBOYS

RUSHING

Last Name	No.	Yds	Avg	TD
Perkins	222	945	4.3	7
Marsh	144	802	5.6	6
Bullocks	33	196	5.9	2
Meredith	21	74	3.5	0
Lockett	8	24	3.0	1
LeBaron	6	−1	−0.2	0

RECEIVING

Last Name	No.	Yds	Avg	TD
Howton	49	706	14	6
Clarke	47	1043	22	14
Folkins	39	536	14	6
Marsh	35	467	13	2
Perkins	13	104	8	0
Lockett	7	78	11	2
Gregory	3	70	23	0
Bullocks	3	46	15	1
Norman	2	34	17	0
Davis	2	31	16	0

PUNT RETURNS

Last Name	No.	Yds	Avg	TD
Lockett	8	45	6	0
Gaechter	6	32	5	0
Marsh	3	4	1	0

KICKOFF RETURNS

Last Name	No.	Yds	Avg	TD
Marsh	29	725	25	1
Bullocks	14	265	19	0
Lockett	6	130	22	0
Davis	4	66	17	0
Gaechter	1	16	16	0
Norman	2	5	3	0
Cverko	1	0	0	0
Memmalaar	1	0	0	0
Talbert	1	0	0	0

PASSING – PUNTING – KICKING

PASSING	Att	Comp	%	Yds	Yd/Att	TD	Int–	%	RK
Meredith	212	105	50	1679	7.9	15	8–	4	10
LeBaron	166	95	57	1436	8.7	16	9–	5	3
Baker	1	0	0	0	0.0	0	0–	0	
Lockett	1	0	0	0	0.0	0	0–	0	

PUNTING	No	Avg
Baker	57	45.4

KICKING	XP	Att	%	FG	Att	%
Baker	50	51	98	14	27	52

EASTERN CONFERENCE – Continued

ST. LOUIS CARDINALS 4-9-1 Wally Lemm

Scores of Each Game		
27	Philadelphia	21
0	Green Bay	17
14	Washington	24
14	NEW YORK	31
17	WASHINGTON	17
7	CLEVELAND	34
28	Dallas	24
28	New York	31
17	PITTSBURGH	26
14	Cleveland	38
17	SAN FRANCISCO	24
7	Pittsburgh	19
52	DALLAS	20
45	PHILADELPHIA	35

Use Name	Pos.	Hgt	Wgt	Age	Int	Pts
Ed Cook	OT	6'2"	240	30		
Fate Echols	OT	6'1"	255	23		
Irv Goode	OT	6'4"	235	21		
Ernie McMillan	OT	6'6"	255	24		
Ken Panfil	OT	6'6"	255	31		
Ken Gray	OG	6'2"	240	26		
Mike McGee	OG	6'1"	230	24		
Jerry Perry	OG	6'4"	240	31		53
Tom Redmond	OG	6'5"	240	25		
Bob DeMarco	C	6'3"	240	24		
Ed Henke	DE	6'3"	230	34		
Luke Owens	DE	6'2"	255	29		
Joe Robb	DE	6'3"	230	25		
Frank Fuller	DT	6'4"	245	33		
George Hultz	DT	6'4"	250	23		
Don Owens	DT	6'5"	255	30		

Use Name	Pos.	Hgt	Wgt	Age	Int	Pts
Ted Bates	LB	6'3"	220	26		
Garland Boyette	LB	6'1"	225	22		
Bill Koman	LB	6'2"	230	28		
Dale Meinert	LB	6'2"	220	29	1	
Marion Rushing	LB	6'2"	210	25		
Roland Jackson	FB-LB	6'	210	22		
Norm Beal	DB	5'11"	170	22		
Pat Fischer	DB	5'10"	165	22	3	
Jimmy Hill	DB	6'2"	190	33	2	
Billy Stacy	DB	6'1"	190	26	6	
Larry Wilson	DB	6'	187	24	2	6

Don Gillis – Injury
Monte Lee – Military Service

Use Name	Pos.	Hgt	Wgt	Age	Int	Pts
Sam Etcheverry	QB	5'11"	190	32		
Charley Johnson	QB	6'	190	25		18
Joe Childress	HB	6'	200	28		6
John David Crow	HB	6'2"	215	27		102
Prentice Gautt	HB	6'	200	24		12
Bill Triplett	DB-HB	6'2"	212	23	1	
Mal Hammack	FB	6'2"	205	29		6
Bobby Joe Conrad	FL	6'	195	27		24
Taz Anderson	OE	6'2"	200	23		18
Chuck Bryant	OE	6'2"	220	21		
Jack Elwell	OE	6'3"	200	22		
Hugh McInnis	OE	6'3"	220	24		
Sonny Randle	OE	6'2"	187	26		42
Jim Bakken	K	6'	200	21		

PHILADELPHIA EAGLES 3-10-1 Nick Skorich

Scores of Each Game		
21	ST. LOUIS	27
13	NEW YORK	29
35	CLEVELAND	7
7	Pittsburgh	13
19	Dallas	41
21	WASHINGTON	27
21	Minnesota	31
14	Cleveland	14
0	GREEN BAY	49
14	New York	19
28	DALLAS	14
37	Washington	14
17	PITTSBURGH	26
35	St. Louis	45

Use Name	Pos.	Hgt	Wgt	Age	Int	Pts
Jim McCusker	OT	6'2"	245	26		
J. D. Smith	OT	6'5"	250	26		
Bob Butler	OG	6'1"	235	21		
Pete Case	OG	6'3"	230	21		
Roy Hord (from LA)	OG	6'4"	250	27		
John Wittenborn	OG	6'2"	240	26		6
Jim Schrader	C	6'2"	252	30		
Howard Keys	OT-OG-C	6'3"	240	27		
John Baker	DE	6'6"	290	27		
Bobby Richards	DE	6'2"	225	23		
Gene Gossage	OG-DE	6'3"	240	27		
Dick Stafford	DT-DE	6'4"	235	22		
Jim Beaver	DT	6'1"	235	23		
Riley Gunnels	DT	6'3"	250	25		
John Kapele (from PIT)	DT	6'	240	25		
Joe Lewis	DT	6'2"	250	27		
Dan Oakes	DT	6'3"	245	24		

Use Name	Pos.	Hgt	Wgt	Age	Int	Pts
Maxie Baughan	LB	6'1"	226	24	1	
Chuck Bednarik	LB	6'3"	235	37		
Bob Harrison	LB	6'2"	220	25	2	
John Nocera	LB	6'1"	220	28	1	
Mike Woulfe	LB	6'2"	225	23		
Don Burroughs	DB	6'4"	190	31	7	
Jimmy Carr	DB	6'1"	210	29	3	
Irv Cross	DB	6'1"	190	23	5	
Mike McClellan	DB	6'1"	185	23	3	
Ben Scotti	DB	6'1"	186	25	4	

Use Name	Pos.	Hgt	Wgt	Age	Int	Pts
King Hill	QB	6'3"	213	26		6
Sonny Jurgensen	QB	5'11"	200	28		12
Timmy Brown	HB	5'10"	190	25		78
Ted Dean	HB	6'2"	210	24		
Don Jonas	HB	5'11"	195	23		
Theron Sapp	HB	6'1"	205	27		12
Clarence Peaks	FB	6'1"	220	26		18
Merrill Douglas	HB-FB	6'	204	26		
Frank Budd	FL	5'10"	187	23		6
Hopalong Cassady (from CLE)	FL	5'10"	185	28		12
Tommy McDonald	FL	5'10"	172	28		60
Ken Gregory	OE	6'	190	25		
Dick Lucas	OE	6'2"	216	28		6
Pete Retzlaff	OE	6'1"	210	31		18
Ralph Smith	OE	6'2"	205	23		
Bobby Walston	OE	6'	195	33		48

WESTERN CONFERENCE

GREEN BAY PACKERS 13-1-0 Vince Lombardi

Scores of Each Game		
34	MINNESOTA	7
17	ST. LOUIS	0
49	CHICAGO	0
9	DETROIT	7
48	Minnesota	21
31	SAN FRANCISCO	13
17	Baltimore	6
38	Chicago	7
49	Philadelphia	0
17	BALTIMORE	13
14	Detroit	26
41	LOS ANGELES	10
31	San Francisco	21
20	Los Angeles	17

Use Name	Pos.	Hgt	Wgt	Age	Int	Pts
Forrest Gregg	OT	6'4"	250	29		
Norm Masters	OT	6'2"	250	29		
Bob Skoronski	OT	6'3"	250	29		
Ed Blaine	OG	6'2"	240	22		
Jerry Kramer	OG	6'3"	250	27		65
Fuzzy Thurston	OG	6'1"	250	29		
Ken Iman	C	6'1"	230	23		
Jim Ringo	C	6'1"	235	31		
Willie Davis	DE	6'3"	240	29		6
Bill Quinlan	DE	6'3"	250	30	1	
Ron Gassert	DT	6'3"	250	22		
Dave Hanner	DT	6'2"	260	33	1	
Henry Jordan	DT	6'3"	250	27	1	
Ron Kostelnik	DT	6'4"	260	22		

Use Name	Pos.	Hgt	Wgt	Age	Int	Pts
Dan Currie	LB	6'3"	240	28		
Bill Forester	LB	6'3"	240	31		
Ray Nitschke	LB	6'3"	235	26	4	
Nelson Toburen	LB	6'3"	235	23		
Herb Adderley	DB	6'1"	205	23	7	12
Hank Gremminger	DB	6'1"	205	29	5	
Johnny Symank	DB	5'11"	180	27		
Jesse Whittenton	DB	6'	195	28	3	
Howie Williams	DB	6'2"	190	25		
Willie Wood	DB	5'10"	185	26	9	

Use Name	Pos.	Hgt	Wgt	Age	Int	Pts
John Roach	QB	6'4"	200	29		
Bart Starr	QB	6'1"	200	29		6
Paul Hornung	HB	6'2"	215	26		74
Tom Moore	HB	6'2"	215	24		42
Elijah Pitts	HB	6'1"	200	23		12
Earl Gros	FB	6'3"	220	21		12
Jim Taylor	FB	6'	215	30		114
Lew Carpenter	FL	6'1"	215	30		
Boyd Dowler	FL	6'5"	220	25		12
Gary Barnes	OE	6'4"	210	27		
Gary Knafelc	OE	6'4"	220	30		
Ron Kramer	OE	6'3"	230	27		42
Max McGee	OE	6'3"	205	30		18

DETROIT LIONS 11-3-0 George Wilson

Scores of Each Game		
45	PITTSBURGH	7
45	SAN FRANCISCO	24
29	Baltimore	20
7	Green Bay	9
13	LOS ANGELES	10
14	New York	17
11	CHICAGO	3
12	Los Angeles	3
38	San Francisco	24
17	Minnesota	6
26	GREEN BAY	14
21	BALTIMORE	14
37	MINNESOTA	23
0	Chicago	3

Use Name	Pos.	Hgt	Wgt	Age	Int	Pts
Dan LaRose	OT	6'5"	250	22		
John Lomakoski	OT	6'4"	250	21		
Dick Mills	OG	6'3"	240	22		
Harley Sewell	OG	6'1"	230	31		
John Gordy	OT-OG	6'3"	250	26		
Bob Whitlow	C	6'1"	236	26		
Bob Scholtz	OT-C	6'4"	250	24		
Darris McCord	DE	6'4"	250	29		2
Leo Sugar	DE	6'1"	230	33		
Sam Williams	DE	6'5"	235	31	1	12
Roger Brown	DT	6'5"	300	25		4
Mike Bundra	DT	6'3"	250	23		
John Gonzaga	DT	6'3"	250	29		
Alex Karras	DT	6'2"	245	26	1	2
Paul Ward	DT	6'3"	247	25		

Use Name	Pos.	Hgt	Wgt	Age	Int	Pts
Carl Brettschneider	LB	6'1"	225	30	2	
Max Messner	LB	6'3"	225	24		
Joe Schmidt	LB	6'1"	220	30	1	
Wayne Walker	LB	6'2"	225	25	1	64
Dave Lloyd	C-LB	6'3"	248	26		
Night Train Lane	DB	6'1"	200	34	4	
Dick LeBeau	DB	6'1"	185	25	4	12
Gary Lowe	DB	5'11"	195	28	2	
Yale Lary	DB	6'	190	31	8	
Bruce Maner	HB-DB	5'11"	190	25		
Tom Hall	OE-DB	6'1"	195	21		

Jim Martin – Voluntarily Retired

Use Name	Pos.	Hgt	Wgt	Age	Int	Pts
Earl Morrall	QB	6'1"	206	28		6
Milt Plum	QB	6'1"	205	28		21
Dick Compton	HB	6'1"	190	22		
Dan Lewis	HB	6'1"	200	26		42
Tom Watkins	HB	6'1"	195	25		18
Nick Pietrosante	FB	6'2"	225	25		24
Ken Webb	FB	5'11"	205	27		6
Terry Barr	FL	6'	190	27		18
Pat Studstill	FL	6'1"	180	24		24
Gail Cogdill	OE	6'2"	195	25		48
Jim Gibbons	OE	6'2"	220	26		12
Larry Vargo	OE	6'3"	200	22		

CHICAGO BEARS 9-5-0 George Halas

Scores of Each Game		
30	San Francisco	14
27	Los Angeles	23
0	Green Bay	49
13	Minnesota	0
27	SAN FRANCISCO	34
35	BALTIMORE	15
3	Detroit	11
7	GREEN BAY	38
31	MINNESOTA	30
34	Dallas	33
57	Baltimore	0
24	NEW YORK	26
30	LOS ANGELES	14
3	DETROIT	0

Use Name	Pos.	Hgt	Wgt	Age	Int	Pts
Art Anderson	OT	6'3"	244	25		
Jim Cadile	OT	6'3"	230	21		
Herm Lee	OT	6'4"	247	31		
Bob Wetoska	OT	6'3"	240	24		
Roger Davis	OG	6'3"	235	24		
Stan Jones	OG	6'1"	250	31		
Ted Karras	OG	6'1"	243	29		
Mike Pyle	C	6'3"	240	23		
Doug Atkins	DE	6'8"	255	32		
Ed O'Bradovich	DE	6'3"	255	22		
Maury Youmans	DE	6'6"	260	25		
Stan Fanning	DT	6'6"	270	24		
Bob Kilcullen	DT	6'3"	245	26		
Earl Leggett	DT	6'3"	250	28		
Fred Williams	DT	6'4"	248	32		

Use Name	Pos.	Hgt	Wgt	Age	Int	Pts
Joe Fortunato	LB	6'	225	32	3	
Bill George	LB	6'2"	235	31	2	
Roger LeClerc	LB	6'3"	235	24		75
Larry Morris	LB	6'2"	230	27	2	
J. C. Caroline	DB	6'1"	190	29	2	
Bennie McRae	DB	6'1"	180	21	1	
Don Mullins	DB	6'1	195	23		
Tommy Neck	DB	5'11"	190	23		
Richie Petitbon	DB	6'3"	205	24	6	6
Rosey Taylor	DB	5'11"	186	23	2	12
Dave Whitsell	DB	6'	190	26	5	

Use Name	Pos.	Hgt	Wgt	Age	Int	Pts
Rudy Bukich	QB	6'1"	205	31		
Billy Wade	QB	6'2"	210	31		30
Charlie Bivins	HB	6'2"	212	23		6
Ronnie Bull	HB	6'	200	22		6
Willie Galimore	HB	6'1"	187	27		12
Billy Martin	HB	5'11"	197	24		6
Rick Casares	FB	6'2"	225	31		18
Joe Marconi	FB	6'2"	225	28		36
Johnny Morris	FL	5'10	180	27		30
John Adams	OE	6'3"	235	25		18
Angie Coia	OE	6'2"	202	24		24
Mike Ditka	OE	6'3"	230	22		36
Jim Dooley	OE	6'4"	198	32		
Bo Farrington	OE	6'3"	217	26		6
Bobby Joe Green	K	5'11"	175	24		

EASTERN CONFERENCE—Continued

ST. LOUIS CARDINALS

RUSHING

Last Name	No.	Yds	Avg	TD
Crow	192	751	3.9	14
Gautt	114	470	4.1	2
Childress	37	162	4.4	0
Hammack	38	160	4.2	1
Johnson	25	138	5.5	3
Triplett	2	12	6.0	0
Etcheverry	8	5	0.6	0

RECEIVING

Last Name	No.	Yds	Avg	TD
Randle	63	1158	18	7
Conrad	62	954	15	4
Anderson	35	535	15	3
Crow	23	246	11	3
Gautt	16	240	15	0
Childress	15	207	14	1
Hammack	4	27	7	0
Elwell	1	11	11	0
McInnis	1	10	10	0

PUNT RETURNS

Last Name	No.	Yds	Avg	TD
Beal	7	46	7	0
Fischer	4	37	9	0
Stacy	5	35	7	0
Conrad	2	10	5	0
Crow	2	6	3	0

KICKOFF RETURNS

Last Name	No.	Yds	Avg	TD
Triplett	24	608	25	0
Beal	16	394	25	0
Fischer	7	187	27	0
Gautt	6	124	21	0
Stacy	5	121	24	0
Hammack	2	36	18	0
Childress	3	19	6	0
Anderson	1	6	6	0

PASSING – PUNTING – KICKING

PASSING	Att	Comp	%	Yds	Yd/Att	TD	Int–	%	RK
Johnson	308	150	49	2440	7.9	16	20–	7	13
Etcheverry	106	58	55	707	6.7	2	10–	9	
Crow	20	12	60	241	12.1	0	0–	0	

PUNTING	No	Avg
Etcheverry	59	38.3

KICKING	XP	Att	%	FG	Att	%
Perry	38	39	97	5	12	42
Bakken	0	0	0	0	1	0
Conrad	0	0	0	0	1	0

PHILADELPHIA EAGLES

RUSHING

Last Name	No.	Yds	Avg	TD
Brown	137	545	4.0	5
Peaks	137	447	3.3	3
Sapp	23	53	2.3	2
Jurgensen	17	44	2.6	2
Hill	4	40	10.0	1
Smith	1	13	13.0	0
Douglas	4	7	1.8	0
Cassady	1	6	6.0	0

RECEIVING

Last Name	No.	Yds	Avg	TD
McDonald	58	1146	20	10
Brown	52	849	16	6
Peaks	39	347	9	0
Retzlaff	30	584	19	3
Lucas	19	236	12	1
Cassady	14	188	13	2
Sapp	6	80	13	0
Budd	5	130	26	1
Walston	4	43	11	0
Smith	1	29	29	0

PUNT RETURNS

Last Name	No.	Yds	Avg	TD
Brown	6	81	14	0
Cassady	8	49	6	0
McDonald	5	8	2	0
Cross	1	2	2	0
Smith	1	2	2	0

KICKOFF RETURNS

Last Name	No.	Yds	Avg	TD
Brown	30	831	28	1
Cassady	24	482	20	0
Douglas	6	136	23	0
Dean	4	83	21	0
Cross	2	72	36	0
Baughan	3	9	3	0
Woulfe	2	5	3	0

PASSING – PUNTING – KICKING

PASSING	Att	Comp	%	Yds	Yd/Att	TD	Int–	%	RK
Jurgensen	366	196	54	**3261**	**8.9**	22	26–	7	5
Hill	61	31	51	361	5.9	0	5–	8	
McDonald	1	1	100	10	10.0	1	0–	0	

PUNTING	No	Avg
Hill	64	42.9

KICKING	XP	Att	%	FG	Att	%
Walston	36	38	95	4	15	27
Wittenborn	0	0	0	2	4	50

WESTERN CONFERENCE

GREEN BAY PACKERS

RUSHING

Last Name	No.	Yds	Avg	TD
Taylor	**272**	**1474**	5.4	**19**
Moore	112	377	3.4	7
Hornung	57	219	3.8	5
Gros	29	155	5.3	2
Pitts	22	110	5.0	2
Starr	21	72	3.4	1
McGee	3	52	17.3	0
Roach	1	5	5.0	0
R. Kramer	1	–4	–4.0	0

RECEIVING

Last Name	No.	Yds	Avg	TD
McGee	49	820	17	3
Dowler	49	724	15	2
R. Kramer	37	555	15	7
Taylor	22	106	5	0
Moore	11	100	9	0
Hornung	9	168	19	2
Carpenter	7	104	15	0
Pitts	3	44	15	0

PUNT RETURNS

Last Name	No.	Yds	Avg	TD
Wood	23	273	12	0
Pitts	7	17	2	0
Kostelnik	1	0	0	0

KICKOFF RETURNS

Last Name	No.	Yds	Avg	TD
Adderley	15	418	28	1
Moore	13	284	22	0
Gros	1	7	7	0
Nitschke	1	7	7	0

PASSING – PUNTING – KICKING

PASSING	Att	Comp	%	Yds	Yd/Att	TD	Int–	%	RK
Starr	285	178	**62**	2438	8.6	12	9–	3	1
Roach	12	3	25	33	2.8	0	0–	0	
Hornung	6	4	67	80	13.3	0	2–	33	
Moore	5	2	40	70	14.0	2	1–	20	
Pitts	2	0	0	0	0.0	0	0–	0	
McGee	1	0	0	0	0.0	0	1–	100	

PUNTING	No	Avg
Dowler	36	43.1
McGee	14	35.4

KICKING	XP	Att	%	FG	Att	%
J. Kramer	38	39	97	9	11	82
Hornung	14	14	100	6	10	60

DETROIT LIONS

RUSHING

Last Name	No.	Yds	Avg	TD
Lewis	120	488	4.1	6
Watkins	113	485	4.3	3
Pietrosante	134	445	3.3	2
Webb	70	267	3.8	1
Plum	29	170	5.9	1
Morrall	17	65	3.8	1
Maher	3	8	2.7	0
Compton	1	3	3.0	0
Cogdill	1	2	2.0	0
Studstill	1	–11	–11.0	0

RECEIVING

Last Name	No.	Yds	Avg	TD
Cogdill	53	991	19	7
Studstill	36	479	13	4
Gibbons	33	318	10	2
Pietrosante	26	251	10	2
Barr	25	425	17	3
Lewis	16	158	10	1
Watkins	12	85	7	0
Webb	10	120	12	0

PUNT RETURNS

Last Name	No.	Yds	Avg	TD
Studstill	**29**	**457**	**16**	0
Watkins	8	42	5	0
Maher	2	3	2	0

KICKOFF RETURNS

Last Name	No.	Yds	Avg	TD
Studstill	20	511	26	0
Watkins	17	452	27	0
Maher	7	141	20	0
Hall	1	16	16	0
Cogdill	1	4	4	0

PASSING – PUNTING – KICKING

PASSING	Att	Comp	%	Yds	Yd/Att	TD	Int–	%	RK
Plum	325	179	55	2378	7.3	15	20–	6	11
Morrall	52	32	62	449	8.6	4	4–	8	
Lary	1	0	0	0	0.0	0	0–	0	
Lewis	1	0	0	0	0.0	0	0–	0	

PUNTING	No	Avg
Lary	52	45.3
Morrall	1	48.0

KICKING	XP	Att	%	FG	Att	%
Walker	37	37	100	9	22	41
Plum	0	0	0	5	12	42

CHICAGO BEARS

RUSHING

Last Name	No.	Yds	Avg	TD
Marconi	89	406	4.6	5
Bull	113	363	3.2	1
Casares	75	255	3.4	2
Galimore	43	233	5.4	2
Wade	40	146	3.7	5
Bivins	14	44	3.1	1
Martin	9	28	3.1	1
Anderson	1	7	7.0	0
J. Morris	2	7	3.5	0

RECEIVING

Last Name	No.	Yds	Avg	TD
Ditka	58	904	16	5
J. Morris	58	889	15	5
Bull	31	331	11	0
Marconi	23	306	13	1
Coia	22	361	16	4
Farrington	13	197	15	1
Casares	10	71	7	1
Adams	5	111	22	3
Galimore	5	56	11	0
Bivins	3	52	17	0
Martin	1	8	8	0

PUNT RETURNS

Last Name	No.	Yds	Avg	TD
J. Morris	20	208	10	0
Martin	17	62	4	0
Taylor	2	11	6	1

KICKOFF RETURNS

Last Name	No.	Yds	Avg	TD
Martin	25	515	21	0
Bivins	12	243	20	0
Bull	9	235	26	0
Taylor	4	98	25	0
Marconi	2	30	15	0
O'Bradovich	1	8	8	0

PASSING – PUNTING – KICKING

PASSING	Att	Comp	%	Yds	Yd/Att	TD	Int–	%	RK
Wade	**412**	**225**	55	3172	7.7	18	24–	6	9
Bukich	13	3	23	79	6.1	1	4–	31	
Bull	3	0	0	0	0.0	0	0–	0	
Casares	2	1	50	35	17.5	1	0–	0	

PUNTING	No	Avg
Green	69	43.7

KICKING	XP	Att	%	FG	Att	%
Leclerc	36	40	90	13	27	48

WESTERN CONFERENCE – Continued

BALTIMORE COLTS 7-7-0 Weeb Ewbank

Scores of Each Game		
30	LOS ANGELES	27
34	Minnesota	7
20	DETROIT	29
13	SAN FRANCISCO	21
36	Cleveland	14
15	Chicago	35
6	GREEN BAY	17
22	San Francisco	3
14	Los Angeles	2
13	Green Bay	17
0	CHICAGO	57
14	Detroit	21
34	WASHINGTON	21
42	MINNESOTA	17

Use Name	Pos.	Hgt	Wgt	Age	Int	Pts
Tom Gilburg	OT	6'5"	245	23		
George Preas	OT	6'2"	250	30		
Dan Sullivan	OT	6'3"	250	23		
Jim Parker	OG-OT	6'3"	275	28		
Wiley Feagin	OG	6'2"	235	25		
Bill Kirchiro	OG	6'1"	235	21		
Palmer Pyle	OG	6'2"	250	25		
Alex Sandusky	OG	6'1"	242	30		
Dick Szymanski	C	6'3"	235	30		
Ordell Braase	DE	6'4"	242	30		
Gino Marchetti	DE	6'4"	245	36		
Don Thompson	DE	6'4"	225	23		
Jim Colvin	DT	6'2"	250	25		
John Diehl	DT	6'7"	285	26		
Billy Ray Smith	DT	6'4"	235	27		
Jackie Burkett	LB	6'4"	230	25	2	
Bill Pellington	LB	6'2"	238	33	2	
Bill Saul	LB	6'4"	225	21		2
Don Shinnick	LB	6'	235	27	5	
Dave Yohn	LB	6'	220	24		
Wendell Harris	DB	5'11"	190	21	2	9
Lenny Lyles	DB	6'2"	202	26		
Andy Nelson	DB	6'1"	180	29	4	
Jim Welch	DB	6'	190	24	1	
Bobby Boyd	HB-DB	5'10"	190	24	7	
Lamar McHan	QB	6'1"	205	30		
Johnny Unitas	QB	6'1"	194	29		
Bob Clemens	HB	6'1"	208	23		
Alex Hawkins	HB	6'1"	190	25		24
Tom Matte	HB	6'	192	23		18
Lenny Moore	HB	6'1"	190	29		24
Joe Perry	FB	6'	195	35		
Mark Smolinski	FB	6'	222	23		12
Jimmy Orr	FL	5'11"	180	26		66
Bake Turner	FL	6'	180	22		6
Ray Berry	OE	6'2"	190	29		18
Dick Bielski	OE	6'1"	227	30		70
Dee Mackey	OE	6'5"	236	26		24
R. C. Owens	OE	6'3"	195	27		12

Jerry Hill – Injury

SAN FRANCISCO FORTY NINERS 6-8-0 Red Hickey

Scores of Each Game		
14	CHICAGO	30
24	Detroit	45
21	MINNESOTA	7
21	BALTIMORE	13
34	Chicago	27
13	Green Bay	31
14	LOS ANGELES	28
3	Baltimore	22
24	DETROIT	38
35	Los Angeles	17
24	St. Louis	17
24	Minnesota	12
21	GREEN BAY	31
10	CLEVELAND	13

Use Name	Pos.	Hgt	Wgt	Age	Int	Pts
Leon Donahue	OT	6'4"	245	23		
Roland Lakes	OT	6'4"	247	22		
Bob St. Clair	OT	6'9"	265	31		
John Sutro	OT	6'4"	245	21		
Bruce Bosley	OG	6'2"	240	28		
Ted Connolly	OG	6'3"	242	30		
Mike Magac	OG	6'3"	240	24		
John Mellekas	C	6'3"	255	29		
Dan Colchico	DE	6'4"	236	25		
Clark Miller	DE	6'5"	245	23		
Len Rohde	DE	6'4"	240	24		
Charlie Krueger	DT	6'4"	245	26		
Leo Nomellini	DT	6'3"	262	37		
Matt Hazeltine	LB	6'1"	220	29	2	
Carl Kammerer	LB	6'3"	237	25	1	
Ed Pine	LB	6'4"	230	22	2	
Karl Rubke	LB	6'4"	240	26		
John Thomas	LB	6'4"	246	27		
Eddie Dove	DB	6'2"	180	25	1	
Elbert Kimbrough	DB	5'11"	195	23		
Jerry Mertens	DB	6'	183	26	2	
Jimmy Ridlon	DB	6'1"	177	27	1	
Abe Woodson	DB	5'11"	188	27	2	12
John Brodie	QB	6'1"	186	27		24
Bob Waters	QB	6'2"	184	24		
Billy Kilmer	HB-QB	6'	190	23		36
Bob Gaiters (from NY)	HB	5'11"	210	24		
J. D. Smith	HB	6'1"	200	29		42
Dale Messer	DB-HB	5'10	175	25	1	
Bill Cooper	FB	6'1"	215	23		
C. R. Roberts	FB	6'3"	197	26		
Jim Vollenweider	FB	6"1"	210	22		
Lloyd Winston	FB	6'2"	215	22		
Bernie Casey	FL	6'4"	215	23		36
Jim Johnson	FL	6'2"	190	24		24
Kay McFarland	FL	6'2"	180	23		
Clyde Conner	OE	6'2"	190	29		24
Monte Stickles	OE	6'4"	230	24		18
Tommy Davis	K	6'	212	27		66

Dave Baker – Military Service

MINNESOTA VIKINGS 2-11-1 Norm Van Brocklin

Scores of Each Game		
7	Green Bay	34
7	BALTIMORE	34
7	San Francisco	21
0	CHICAGO	13
21	GREEN BAY	48
38	Los Angeles	14
31	PHILADELPHIA	21
31	Pittsburgh	39
30	Chicago	31
6	DETROIT	17
24	LOS ANGELES	24
12	SAN FRANCISCO	35
23	Detroit	37
17	Baltimore	42

Use Name	Pos.	Hgt	Wgt	Age	Int	Pts
Grady Alderman	OT	6'2"	235	23		
Errol Linden	OT	6'5"	260	25		
Frank Youso	OT	6'4"	260	26		
Larry Bowie	OG	6'2"	235	22		
Jerry Huth	OG	6'	228	29		
Mike Rabold	OG	6'2"	238	25		
Mick Tingelhoff	C	6'1"	230	22		
Bob Denton	DE	6'4"	240	28		
Jim Leo	DE	6'1"	225	24		2
Jim Marshall	DE	6'3"	230	25		
Paul Dickson	DT	6'5"	250	25		
Jim Prestel	DT	6'5"	250	25		
Jim Christopherson	LB	6'	215	24	1	61
Rip Hawkins	LB	6'3"	230	23	1	2
Cliff Livingston	LB	6'3"	215	32		
Clancy Osborne	LB	6'3"	217	27		
Roy Winston	LB	6'1"	225	22		
Bill Butler	DB	5'10"	194	25	5	6
Dean Derby	DB	6'	190	28	4	
Tom Franckhauser	DB	6'	196	25	4	
Chuck Lamson	DB	6'	185	23	1	
Ed Sharockman	DB	6'	195	22	6	6
Charlie Sumner	DB	6'1"	195	32	3	
John McCormick	QB	6'1"	210	26		
Fran Tarkenton	QB	6'1"	190	22		12
Tommy Mason	HB	6'	195	23		48
Hugh McElhenny	HB	6'1"	198	33		
Bob Reed	HB	5'11"	187	22		6
Bill Brown	FB	5'11"	218	24		6
Doug Mayberry	FB	6'1"	225	25		12
Mel Triplett	FB	6'1"	215	30		18
Oscar Donahue	FL	6'3"	195	24		6
Tom Adams	OE	6'5"	210	22		
Charley Ferguson	OE	6'5"	212	22		36
Jerry Reichow	OE	6'2"	220	27		18
Gordon Smith	OE	6'2"	200	23		6
Steve Stonebreaker	OE	6'3"	220	24		6
Mike Mercer	K	6'	220	26		3

LOS ANGELES RAMS 1-12-1 Bob Waterfield Harland Svare

Scores of Each Game		
27	Baltimore	30
23	CHICAGO	27
17	DALLAS	27
14	Washington	20
10	Detroit	13
14	MINNESOTA	38
28	San Francisco	14
3	DETROIT	12
2	BALTIMORE	14
17	SAN FRANCISCO	24
24	Minnesota	24
10	Green Bay	41
14	Chicago	30
17	GREEN BAY	20

Use Name	Pos.	Hgt	Wgt	Age	Int	Pts
Jim Boeke	OT	6'5"	245	23		
Joe Carollo	OT	6'2"	258	22		
Frank Varrichione	OT	6'1"	235	30		
Charley Cowan	OG	6'4"	250	24		
Duane Putnam	OG	6'	233	34		
Joe Scibelli	OG	6'1"	250	23		
Art Hunter	C	6'4"	248	29		
Deacon Jones	DE	6'5"	240	23		
Lamart Lundy	DE	6'7"	235	27		
Larry Stephens	DE	6'4"	260	24		
John Lovetere	DT	6'4"	280	26		
Merlin Olsen	DT	6'5"	265	21	1	6
Mike Henry	LB	6'2"	215	26	1	
Bill Jobko	LB	6'2"	220	26		
Marlin McKeever	LB	6'1"	230	22	2	
Jack Pardee	LB	6'2"	225	26		8
Les Richter	LB	6'3"	235	31		
Larry Hayes	C-LB	6'3"	230	27		
Charley Britt	DB	6'2"	185	24	3	
Lindon Crow	DB	6'1"	200	29	5	6
Alvin Hall	DB	6'	193	29	1	
Ed Meador	DB	5'11"	185	25	1	
Carver Shannon	DB	6'1"	198	24	4	
Bobby Smith	DB	6'	185	24	1	
Zeke Bratkowski	QB	6'2"	203	30		
Roman Gabriel	QB	6'4"	220	22		
Ron Miller	QB	6'	190	23		
Jon Arnett	HB	5'11"	194	27		12
Dick Bass	FB-HB	5'10"	200	25		48
Ollie Matson	FB	6'2"	210	32		6
Art Perkins	FB	6'	220	22		12
Glen Shaw	FB	6'1"	217	23		
Pervis Atkins	HB-FL	6'1"	195	26		6
Duane Allen	OE	6'4"	210	24		12
Carroll Dale	OE	6'1"	195	24		18
Karl Finch	OE	6'3"	195	23		
Jim Phillips	OE	6'1"	198	25		30
Danny Villanueva	K	5'11"	200	24		56

WESTERN CONFERENCE—Continued

BALTIMORE COLTS

RUSHING

Last Name	No.	Yds	Avg	TD
Moore	106	470	4.4	2
Perry	94	359	3.8	0
Smolinski	85	265	3.1	1
Matte	74	226	3.1	2
Unitas	50	137	2.7	0
Hawkins	29	87	3.0	4
Turner	1	17	17.0	0
Orr	1	14	14.0	0
Boyd	2	13	6.5	0
Clemens	2	9	4.5	0
McHan	4	4	1.0	0

RECEIVING

Last Name	No.	Yds	Avg	TD
Orr	55	974	18	11
Berry	51	687	13	3
Mackey	25	396	16	4
Owens	25	307	12	2
Perry	22	194	9	0
Moore	18	215	12	2
Bielski	15	200	13	2
Smolinski	13	128	10	1
Matte	8	81	10	1
Hawkins	4	37	9	0
Turner	1	*111	111	1

*Includes lateral

PUNT RETURNS

Last Name	No.	Yds	Avg	TD
Turner	10	95	10	0
Harris	8	61	8	0
Hawkins	11	42	4	0
Boyd	3	23	8	0
Nelson	2	22	11	0
Shinnick	0	29	0	0

KICKOFF RETURNS

Last Name	No.	Yds	Avg	TD
Matte	27	613	23	0
Turner	20	504	25	0
Harris	3	86	29	0
Hawkins	2	35	18	0
Smolinski	2	20	10	0
Diehl	1	5	5	0

PASSING – PUNTING – KICKING

PASSING	Att	Comp	%	Yds	Yd/Att	TD	Int–	%	RK
Unitas	389	222	57	2967	7.6	23	23–	6	7
McHan	20	10	50	278	13.9	3	2–	10	
Matte	13	5	38	85	6.5	1	0–	0	
Hawkins	1	0	0	0	0.0	0	0–	0	

PUNTING	No	Avg
Gilburg	57	41.8
McHan	1	22.0

KICKING	XP	Att	%	FG	Att	%
Bielski	25	28	89	11	25	44
Harris	6	9	67	1	3	33

SAN FRANCISCO FORTY NINERS

RUSHING

Last Name	No.	Yds	Avg	TD
Smith	258	907	3.5	6
Kilmer	93	478	5.1	5
Brodie	37	258	7.0	4
Gaiters	43	193	4.5	0
Waters	12	42	3.5	0
Vollenweider	11	37	3.4	0
Roberts	9	19	2.1	0
Cooper	2	−2	−1.0	0
Winston	1	−15	−15.0	0

RECEIVING

Last Name	No.	Yds	Avg	TD
Casey	53	819	15	6
Johnson	34	627	18	4
Conner	24	240	10	4
Stickles	22	366	17	3
Smith	21	197	9	1
Kilmer	16	152	10	1
Gaiters	5	47	9	0
Vollenweider	4	21	5	0
Messer	3	30	10	0
McFarland	3	24	8	0
Roberts	2	0	0	0
Winston	1	2	2	0

PUNT RETURNS

Last Name	No.	Yds	Avg	TD
Woodson	19	179	9	1
Dove	5	21	4	0
Messer	3	7	2	0

KICKOFF RETURNS

Last Name	No.	Yds	Avg	TD
Woodson	37	1157	31	0
Gaiters	11	273	25	0
Vollenweider	6	113	19	0
Messer	4	112	28	0
Winston	3	67	22	0
Cooper	1	17	17	0

PASSING – PUNTING – KICKING

PASSING	Att	Comp	%	Yds	Yd/Att	TD	Int–	%	RK
Brodie	304	175	58	2272	7.5	18	16–	5	6
Kilmer	13	8	62	191	14.7	1	3–	23	
Waters	6	2	33	28	4.7	0	0–	0	
Gaiters	2	0	0	0	0.0	0	0–	0	

PUNTING	No	Avg
Davis	48	45.6

KICKING	XP	Att	%	FG	Att	%
Davis	36	36	100	10	23	43

MINNESOTA VIKINGS

RUSHING

Last Name	No.	Yds	Avg	TD
Mason	167	740	4.4	2
Tarkenton	41	361	8.8	2
Mayberry	74	274	3.7	1
McElhenny	50	200	4.0	0
Triplett	52	160	3.1	2
Brown	34	103	3.0	0
Reed	6	22	3.7	0
McCormick	2	4	2.0	0

RECEIVING

Last Name	No.	Yds	Avg	TD
Reichow	39	561	14	3
Mason	36	603	17	6
Donahue	16	285	18	1
McElhenny	16	191	12	0
Ferguson	14	364	26	6
Stonebreaker	12	227	19	1
Mayberry	11	100	9	1
Brown	10	124	12	1
Smith	7	138	20	1
Reed	4	37	9	1
Adams	3	51	17	0
Triplett	2	30	15	1
Tarkenton	0	−12	0	0

PUNT RETURNS

Last Name	No.	Yds	Avg	TD
Butler	12	169	14	0
Reed	9	82	9	0
Mason	6	52	9	0
McElhenny	5	43	9	0
Sharockman	1	16	16	0
Franckhauser	1	12	12	0

KICKOFF RETURNS

Last Name	No.	Yds	Avg	TD
Butler	26	588	23	0
Reed	13	337	26	0
Mason	12	301	25	0
McElhenny	7	160	23	0
Sharockman	3	71	24	0
Prestel	2	29	15	0
Denton	1	17	17	0
Stonebreaker	1	12	12	0
Bowie	2	7	4	0

PASSING – PUNTING – KICKING

PASSING	Att	Comp	%	Yds	Yd/Att	TD	Int–	%	RK
Tarkenton	329	163	50	2595	7.9	22	25–	8	12
McCormick	18	7	39	104	5.8	0	5–	28	
Mason	1	0	0	0	0.0	0	1–	100	

PUNTING	No	Avg
McCormick	46	39.0
Mercer	19	43.5

KICKING	XP	Att	%	FG	Att	%
Christopherson	28	28	100	11	20	55
Mercer	3	3	100	0	5	0

LOS ANGELES RAMS

RUSHING

Last Name	No.	Yds	Avg	TD
Bass	196	1033	5.3	6
Arnett	76	238	3.1	2
Perkins	48	181	3.8	2
Gabriel	18	93	5.2	0
Shaw	18	76	4.2	0
Miller	3	27	9.0	0
Atkins	7	19	2.7	0
Bratkowski	7	14	2.0	0
Richter	0	8	0.0	0
Matson	3	0	0.0	0

RECEIVING

Last Name	No.	Yds	Avg	TD
Phillips	60	875	15	5
Atkins	35	393	11	1
Bass	30	262	9	2
Dale	29	584	20	3
Perkins	14	83	6	0
Arnett	12	137	11	0
Allen	3	90	30	2
Shaw	3	51	17	0
Matson	3	49	16	1

PUNT RETURNS

Last Name	No.	Yds	Avg	TD
Atkins	11	94	9	0
Bass	6	81	14	0
Arnett	5	49	10	0
Hall	4	21	5	0
Smith	1	7	7	0

KICKOFF RETURNS

Last Name	No.	Yds	Avg	TD
Atkins	28	676	24	0
Bass	19	446	23	0
Hall	8	178	22	0
Arnett	2	87	44	0
Smith	2	60	30	0
Jones	1	0	0	0

PASSING – PUNTING – KICKING

PASSING	Att	Comp	%	Yds	Yd/Att	TD	Int–	%	RK
Bratkowski	219	110	50	1541	7.0	9	16–	7	16
Gabriel	101	57	56	670	6.6	3	2–	2	
Miller	43	17	40	250	5.8	1	1–	2	
Arnett	5	3	60	28	5.6	1	0–	0	
Bass	3	1	33	22	7.3	0	0–	0	
Matson	1	1	100	13	13.0	0	0–	0	

PUNTING	No	Avg
Villanueva	87	45.5

KICKING	XP	Att	%	FG	Att	%
Villanueva	26	27	96	10	20	50

1962 A.F.L. Wismer's Rubbery Titans

The near collapse of the New York franchise was the league's biggest headache this year. A sports truism says that no circuit can be big league without a healthy New York franchise, but the media there had practically ignored the Titans. Owner Harry Wismer's boisterous outbursts against Commissioner Joe Foss, head coach Sammy Baugh, and the NFL Giants had stripped the club of most of its dignity and left it a local joke in New York. The Titans became a ghost team, playing its games before empty stands in the shadows of the old, decrepit Polo Grounds. But Wismer's verbal antics paled in the face of his financial ills, and the joke almost turned into an obituary. Wismer had been losing money in a steady outflow since the league began, and the till finally ran dry in November. When the players' paychecks bounced, the word was out that Wismer was broke. To keep the Titans going, Commissioner Foss stepped in and ran the club with league funds, thus averting the embarrassment of the New York franchise folding in mid-season. While league intervention kept the ship from sinking this year, new skippers for the franchise would be needed for next year.

Dallas owner Lamar Hunt was far from broke, but the situation in that city was a failing one for the AFL. Hunt had been an original founder of the new league when his bid for an NFL franchise for Dallas was turned down in the late 1950s. Once it was certain that the AFL would get off the ground, the NFL had put an expansion team in Dallas. Fans flocked to see the NFL Cowboys play, while the AFL Texans starved in a land full of football fans. Even with the team on the road to a championship this season, attendance stayed low, so Hunt started shopping around for a new place to settle his team.

But attendance in general around the circuit took a sharp turn upward. The number of paid fans at league games increased 20 percent over last year, filling both the stands and the team's coffers very pleasantly. Seats with fans in them looked much better than empty bleachers on ABC's national broadcasts, which still provided the league with enough money to keep the circuit solvent.

A less favorable development was the decision against the anti-trust suit against the NFL. The United States District Court in Baltimore ruled against the suit, and the team owners voted to appeal the decision and keep the legal process moving.

But fans are concerned less with lawsuits, attendance figures, and league maneuvering than with the playing on the field. The Dallas Texans blossomed into the league's top team, a colorful bunch of youngsters who swept through the league behind Len Dawson, a cool quarterback with six years of non-activity in the NFL behind him. The Eastern Division race came down to a tight struggle between the Houston Oilers and the Boston Patriots that kept interest in the league alive through the end of the schedule. The clubs in New York, Oakland, and Denver faired very poorly and definitely needed help to become competitive in the near future, but the level of competition in general was markedly improved over the past. The crowning achievement of the season was the championship game between the Texans and Oilers, played before a full house in Houston. The game ran into the second overtime period before Dallas' Tommy Brooker won it on a field goal. The longest game ever played up until then, this match kept television viewers glued to their TV sets well into the evening, convincing some of them that perhaps the AFL had something going for itself.

EASTERN DIVISION

Houston Oilers—When Oiler coach Wally Lemm resigned to head up the NFL St. Louis Cardinals, Houston owner Bud Adams replied by hiring deposed St. Louis coach Pop Ivy. Although Ivy was reputed to be an offensive genius, the Houston attack bogged down in the early part of the season. A bad back made Billy Cannon a shadow of his former self, quarterback George Blanda started serving up interceptions at a generous rate, and end Bill Groman suddenly wasn't getting open for passes any more. But like last year, the Oilers caught fire after a slow start. With squat Charley Tolar leading the way with his running, the Oilers won their last seven games, sweeping into first place by beating Boston on November 18 and winning every game the rest of the way.

Boston Patriots—Coach Mike Holovak's collection of unknown veterans and youngsters from local colleges battled Houston tooth and nail for the Eastern crown. The defense, led by Larry Eisenhauer, Houston Antwine, and rookie Nick Buoniconti, was more impressive as a unit than as individuals, while the offense scratched out points on Babe Parilli's passing, Ron Burton's running, and Gino Cappelletti's kicking. The Oilers recovered from a slow start to climb right behind the first-place Patriots, and the top spot rode on their November 18 meeting in Houston. Boston not only lost the game 21-17 and first place; they also lost quarterback Parilli with a broken collarbone. Reserve passer Tom Yewcic led the Pats to victories the rest of the way until stumbling 20-0 in the final game against Oakland and thus conceding the Eastern crown to Houston.

Buffalo Bills—The Bills had always had a tough defense, and now coach Lou Saban was building an offense that could score points. The main addition was fullback Cookie Gilchrist, a Canadian League veteran who turned out to be the best power runner in the league. Saban also picked up a fine quarterback when he claimed Jack Kemp off the San Diego waiver list. Kemp had a broken hand at the time, but Saban carried him on the roster until he healed in time to star in the last three games of the year. The defense also got an injection of new blood when rookies Tom Sestak, Mike Stratton, Ray Abruzzese, Booker Edgerson, and Carl Charon all won starting positions. The new players needed time to jell, as the Bills lost their first five games, but seven wins and a tie in the last nine games showed Buffalo fans and coach Saban that he had built a winner.

New York Titans—The front-office situation was so chaotic that the Titans were lucky to finish out the year. Owner Harry Wismer was broke by November, no longer able even to pay his players. With attendance microscopic, the team's image laughable, and the players clamoring for money, the league office stepped in and ran the team the rest of the year. The Titans stayed surprisingly competitive on the field through all the commotion. Coach Bulldog Turner discovered a good quarterback in ex-giant Lee Grosscup, and when injuries kayoed Grosscup, Turner came up with another passer in ex-Bill Johnny Green. Art Powell, Dick Christy, and Don Maynard were the principal targets for these passers, and with fullback Bill Mathis injured most of the season, the pass again was New York's sole offensive threat. Even with good seasons from Larry Grantham and Lee Riley, the defense leaked profusely and condemned the Titans to last place in the East.

WESTERN DIVISION

Dallas Texans—Hank Stram had coached Len Dawson when both were at Purdue, and when the Cleveland Browns cut the quarterback before the season started, Stram immediately invited him to join the Texans. Dawson made up for the six years he sat on NFL benches by passing for twenty-nine touchdowns and leading the Texans to the AFL championship. Runners-up to San Diego the past two years, the Texans dethroned the Chargers by adding Dawson and key rookies Curtis McClinton, Fred Arbanas, Bobby Hunt, Bill Hull, Bill Miller, Bobby Ply, and Tommy Brooker. Stram got All-Pro performances from holdovers Abner Haynes, Chris Burford, Jim Tyrer, Mel Branch, Jerry Mays, E. J. Holub, and Sherrill Headrick, and the Texans swept to the Western crown while the stands stayed clean of paying customers.

Denver Broncos—The Broncos put all their chips on their passing attack and got away with it for two months. With ancient quarterback Frank Tripuka throwing bushels of passes to Lionel Taylor, Bo Dickinson, Gene Prebola, and Bob Scarpitto, the Broncos won seven of their first nine contests to contend for the Western title for the first time ever. But since Denver had no running game and a mediocre defense, the rest of the league wised up to its unbalanced attack over the second half of the season. The Broncos lost their last five games and wound up at a 7-7 mark, but the season was an exciting one for Denver fans and new coach Jack Faulkner. Three of the Broncos won individual league titles, Lionel Taylor in receiving, Gene Mingo in scoring and field goals, and Jim Fraser in punting.

San Diego Chargers—After two years as champs in the West, the Chargers suddenly had problems fielding a healthy team. Linebacker Bob Laraba was killed in an off-season car accident, and an amazing string of injuries left the Chargers an empty shell of their winning teams. Halfback Paul Lowe started the parade by breaking his arm in a pre-season game, and a string of teammates fell in line behind him. Rookie flanker Lance Alworth, linebacker Chuck Allen, defensive back Charley McNeil, and center Wayne Frazier all missed large portions of the schedule with various ailments, and a total of eleven starters were knocked out for seven or more games. To make this season a total loss, quarterback Jack Kemp broke his hand, and when coach Sid Gillman tried to slip him through on waivers to the reserve list, Buffalo claimed him for the $100 waiver price. With rookies and substitutes playing out the schedule, the Chargers lost eight of their last nine games to sink out of contention in the West.

Oakland Raiders—The Raiders were no great football team, as the six-game losing streak left over from last year testified, but the lung infection that sidelined quarterback Tom Flores for the season left the Raiders in desperate straits. They began the year with M. C. Reynolds and Don Heinrich, a pair of old NFL rejects, as passers, but coach Marty Feldman decided to go shopping for another quarterback after only one game. He bought Cotton Davidson from Dallas, and Davidson played out the Oakland schedule with a bad shoulder. The rest of the Raider squad contained little quality outside of Jim Otto, Clem Daniels, and Fred Williamson, and the team proceeded to lose its first thirteen games to run its losing streak to a record nineteen games. On the last day of the season they treated their fans in Frank Youell Field, their temporary home in Oakland, to a 20-0 victory over Boston, their first triumph in over a year.

FINAL TEAM STATISTICS

OFFENSE

	BOSTON	BUFFALO	DALLAS	DENVER	HOUSTON	NEW YORK	OAKLAND	SAN DIEGO
FIRST DOWNS:								
Total	230	238	259	**270**	266	206	187	217
by Rushing	100	**119**	**119**	72	95	60	72	82
by Passing	114	96	125	**177**	157	131	100	113
by Penalty	16	**23**	15	21	14	15	15	22
RUSHING:								
Number	432	**501**	479	322	457	317	367	410
Yards	1970	**2480**	2407	1298	1742	1213	1392	1647
Average Yards	4.6	5.0	**5.0**	4.0	3.8	3.8	3.8	4.0
Touchdowns	11	20	**21**	12	15	9	14	13
PASSING:								
Attempts	382	351	322	**559**	475	505	446	416
Completions	195	150	195	**292**	227	242	175	168
Completion Percentage	51.0	42.7	**60.6**	52.2	47.8	47.9	39.2	40.4
Passing Yards	2930	2181	2824	**3739**	3323	3161	2671	2686
Average Yards per Attempt	7.7	6.2	**8.8**	6.7	7.0	6.3	6.0	6.5
Average Yards per Completion	15.0	14.5	14.5	12.8	14.6	13.1	15.3	**16.0**
Times Tackled Attempting to Pass	23	23	41	30	**11**	54	44	28
Yards Lost Attempting to Pass	164	197	369	335	**94**	419	376	252
Net Yards	2766	1984	2455	**3404**	3229	2742	2295	2434
Touchdowns	25	15	29	21	**32**	20	11	23
Interceptions	**13**	26	17	40	48	35	29	34
Percent Intercepted	**3.4**	7.4	5.3	7.2	10.1	6.9	6.5	8.2
PUNTING:								
Number	69	76	54	60	56	78	**83**	79
Average Distance	38.5	38.8	35.8	**42.9**	41.0	41.0	37.4	41.6
PUNT RETURNS:								
Number	26	28	27	19	28	25	**34**	29
Yards	138	196	236	128	**314**	308	257	278
Average Yards	5.3	7.0	8.7	6.7	11.2	**12.3**	7.6	9.6
Touchdowns	0	1	0	0	1	**3**	0	0
KICKOFF RETURNS:								
Number	53	52	37	57	48	**73**	65	67
Yards	1200	1176	955	1210	1245	1579	1425	**1585**
Average Yards	22.6	22.6	25.8	21.2	**25.9**	21.6	21.9	23.7
Touchdowns	1	**2**	0	0	0	0	1	1
INTERCEPTION RETURNS:								
Number	25	**36**	32	27	35	29	29	29
Yards	365	**505**	395	483	340	356	390	340
Average Yards	14.6	14.0	12.3	**17.9**	9.7	12.3	13.4	11.7
Touchdowns	3	3	0	**4**	2	1	1	1
PENALTIES:								
Number	52	74	66	64	63	84	69	**88**
Yards	456	**797**	644	613	633	771	695	768
FUMBLES:								
Number	37	27	26	28	**17**	35	31	24
Number Lost	20	12	14	14	**9**	20	20	14
POINTS:								
Total	346	309	**389**	353	387	278	213	314
PAT (kick) Attempts	40	40	**49**	36	**49**	32	23	35
PAT (kick) Made	38	34	47	34	**48**	31	20	31
PAT (Rush or Pass) Attempts	1	1	1	3	1	2	**4**	3
PAT (Rush or Pass) Made	1	1	0	1	1	1	**2**	**2**
FG Attempts	37	23	27	**39**	26	27	27	20
FG Made	20	9	14	**27**	11	13	9	17
Percent FG Made	54.1	39.1	51.9	69.2	42.3	48.1	33.3	**85.0**
Safeties	0	0	0	1	**2**	1	0	0

DEFENSE

	BOSTON	BUFFALO	DALLAS	DENVER	HOUSTON	NEW YORK	OAKLAND	SAN DIEGO
FIRST DOWNS:								
Total	220	229	234	234	**217**	253	233	248
by Rushing	**68**	89	76	88	75	103	115	105
by Passing	136	129	143	131	126	122	**106**	120
by Penalty	16	**11**	20	15	16	28	12	23
RUSHING:								
Number	393	373	**351**	439	362	453	477	437
Yards	1426	1687	**1250**	1868	1569	2049	2397	1903
Average Yards	3.6	4.5	**3.6**	4.3	4.3	4.5	5.0	5.0
Touchdowns	14	**10**	14	11	**10**	19	21	16
PASSING:								
Attempts	450	440	467	423	486	417	**371**	402
Completions	216	215	239	202	213	194	**169**	196
Completion Percentage	48.0	48.9	51.2	47.8	**43.8**	46.5	45.6	48.8
Passing Yards	3435	2996	2953	2894	2865	2929	**2517**	2926
Average Yards per Attempt	7.6	6.8	6.3	6.8	**5.9**	7.0	6.8	7.3
Average Yards per Completion	15.9	13.9	**12.4**	14.3	13.5	15.1	14.9	14.9
Times Tackled Attempting to Pass	34	32	28	25	32	36	23	**44**
Yards Lost Attempting to Pass	**327**	254	252	224	304	323	211	311
Net Yards	3108	2742	2701	2670	2561	2606	**2306**	2615
Touchdowns	19	24	**13**	24	18	28	21	29
Interceptions	25	**36**	32	27	35	29	29	29
Percent Intercepted	5.6	**8.2**	6.9	6.4	7.2	7.0	7.8	7.2
PUNTING:								
Number	**79**	70	63	66	72	70	67	68
Average Distance	38.5	38.1	41.2	41.5	38.9	**37.9**	40.9	40.7
PUNT RETURNS:								
Number	**11**	33	26	27	28	31	34	26
Yards	**54**	202	219	245	259	295	352	229
Average Yards	**4.9**	6.1	8.4	9.1	9.3	9.5	10.4	8.8
Touchdowns	**0**	**0**	1	**0**	2	**0**	1	1
KICKOFF RETURNS:								
Number	64	56	72	64	55	46	**39**	56
Yards	1697	1177	1559	1401	1155	1194	**961**	1231
Average Yards	26.5	21.0	21.7	21.9	**21.0**	26.0	24.6	22.0
Touchdowns	1	1	**0**	**0**	1	1	**0**	1
INTERCEPTION RETURNS:								
Number	**13**	26	17	40	48	35	29	34
Yards	**55**	299	113	421	725	544	509	508
Average Yards	**4.2**	11.5	6.6	10.5	15.1	15.5	17.6	14.9
Touchdowns	1	**0**	**0**	5	2	3	3	1
PENALTIES:								
Number	62	**80**	64	76	65	73	75	65
Yards	554	**786**	660	678	559	711	720	709
FUMBLES:								
Number	26	26	29	**34**	25	30	25	30
Number Lost	10	14	16	**19**	17	16	18	13
POINTS:								
Total	295	272	**233**	334	270	423	370	392
PAT (kick) Attempts	33	33	**27**	38	32	51	46	44
PAT (kick) Made	32	30	**24**	36	30	46	44	41
PAT (Rush or Pass) Attempts	3	2	2	3	1	1	**0**	4
PAT (Rush or Pass) Made	1	1	1	1	**0**	1	**0**	4
FG Attempts	26	**20**	28	27	31	31	32	31
FG Made	15	**10**	11	16	14	21	16	17
Percent FG Made	57.7	50.0	**39.3**	59.3	45.2	67.7	50.0	54.8
Safeties	**0**	**0**	**0**	1	**0**	**0**	1	2

1962 AFL CHAMPIONSHIP GAME

December 23, at Houston
(Attendance 37,981)

SCORING

HOUSTON	0	0	7	10	0	0–17
DALLAS	3	14	0	0	0	3–20

First Quarter

Dall.	Brooker, 16 yard field goal	10:32

Second Quarter

Dall.	Haynes, 28 yard pass from Dawson PAT–Brooker (kick)	0:27
Dall.	Haynes, 2 yard rush PAT–Brooker (kick)	11:21

Third Quarter

Hous.	Dewveall, 15 yard pass from Blanda PAT–Blanda (kick)	3:10

Fourth Quarter

Hous.	Blanda, 31 yard field goal	3:53
Hous.	Tolar, 1 yard rush PAT–Blanda (kick)	9:22

Second Overtime (Sixth Quarter)

Dall.	Brooker, 25 yard field goal	2:54

TEAM STATISTICS

DALLAS		HOUSTON
19	First Downs–Total	21
10	First Downs–Rushing	6
5	First Downs–Passing	15
4	First Downs–Penalty	0
2	Fumbles–Number	0
1	Fumbles–Number Lost	0
6	Penalties–Number	6
42	Yards Penalized	50
1	Giveaways	5
5	Takeaways	1
+4	Difference	–4

The Longest Afternoon

Houston had won its third straight Eastern title, but the Dallas Texans, making their first title-game appearance, almost blew the Oilers off the field in the first half, running up a 17-0 score on two Abner Haynes touchdowns and a Tommy Brooker field goal. The Oilers came out for the second half in top gear, however, and quickly fought back into the game. George Blanda passed to Willard Dewveall for 15 yards and Houston's first points early in the third quarter. With their backs against the wall, the Oilers rallied to tie the score in the fourth period. Blanda kicked a 31-yard field goal early in the period, and Charley Tolar scored on a one-yard plunge with five minutes left in the game. Blanda's extra point tied the score at 17-17, and regulation time ran out without any further scoring. As the teams readied for overtime, the captains met at mid-field for the coin toss for the next periods. Instructed to take advantage of the wind, Dallas' Abner Haynes blundered by electing to kick off, thus giving the Oilers the advantage of both receiving and having the wind at their backs. The Oilers couldn't score, however, and the Texans took the ball at mid-field near the end of the first overtime period on a Bill Hull interception. With Jack Spikes carrying and receiving the ball on key plays, the Texans moved down to the Houston 19-yard line. Tommy Brooker then booted a 25-yard field goal which ended Houston's championship reign and pro football's longest game.

INDIVIDUAL STATISTICS

HOUSTON	No.	Yds.	Avg.	DALLAS	No.	Yds.	Avg.
RUSHING							
Tolar	17	58	3.4	Spikes	11	77	7.0
Cannon	11	37	3.4	McClinton	24	70	2.9
Smith	2	3	1.5	Dawson	5	26	5.2
	30	98	3.3	Haynes	14	26	1.9
					54	199	3.7
RECEIVING							
Dewveall	6	95	15.8	Haynes	3	45	15.0
Cannon	6	54	9.0	Spikes	2	24	12.0
McLeod	5	70	14.0	Arbanas	2	21	10.5
Hennigan	3	37	11.3	McClinton	1	4	4.0
Tolar	1	8	8.0	Bishop	1	–6	–6.0
Smith	1	6	6.0		9	88	9.8
Jamison	1	–9	–9.0				
	23	261	11.3				
PUNTING							
Norton	3		39.3	Wilson	6		32.0
				Saxton	2		29.0
					8		31.2
PUNT RETURNS							
Jancik	1	0	0.0	Jackson	1	0	0.0
KICKOFF RETURNS							
Jancik	5	139	27.8	Grayson	3	64	21.3
				Haynes	1	22	22.0
					4	86	21.5
INTERCEPTION RETURNS							
None				Robinson	2	50	25.0
				Holub	1	43	43.0
				Hull	1	23	23.0
				Grayson	1	20	20.0
					5	136	27.2

PASSING

	Att.	Comp.	Comp. Pct.	Yds.	Int.	Yds/ Att.	Yds/ Comp.	Yards Lost Tackled
HOUSTON								
Blanda	46	23	50.0	261	5	5.7	11.3	0
DALLAS								
Dawson	14	9	64.3	88	0	6.3	9.8	6–50

HOUSTON OILERS 11-3-0 Pop Ivy

Scores of Each Game		
28	Buffalo	23
21	Boston	34
42	San Diego	17
17	BUFFALO	14
56	NEW YORK	17
10	Denver	20
7	DALLAS	31
14	Dallas	6
28	Oakland	20
21	BOSTON	17
33	SAN DIEGO	27
34	DENVER	17
32	OAKLAND	17
44	New York	10

Use Name	Pos.	Hgt	Wgt	Age	Int	Pts
Al Jamison	OT	6'5"	250	25		
Rich Michael	OT	6'3"	242	23		
Walt Suggs	OT	6'5"	245	23		
John Frongillo	OG	6'3"	250	22		
Bob Talamini	OG	6'1"	255	23		
Bill Wegener	OG	5'10"	245	21		
Hogan Wharton	OG	6'2"	250	26		
Bob Schmidt	C	6'4"	250	26		
Gary Cutsinger	DE	6'4"	240	21	1	
Don Floyd	DE	6'4"	247	23	4	6
Dan Lanphear	DE	6'2"	230	24		
Ron McDole	DE	6'3"	255	23		
Ed Culpepper	DT	6'1"	260	28		
Bill Herchman	DT	6'2"	255	29		
Ed Husmann	DT	6'	245	31		
Bob Kelly	DT	6'3"	250	22		
Bill Miller	DT	6'4"	270	24		
Doug Cline	LB	6'2"	230	23	2	
Mike Dukes	LB	6'3"	230	26	2	
Tom Goode	LB	6'3"	235	23		
Larry Onesti	LB	6'	205	23		
Gene Babb	FB-LB	6'3"	220	27	2	6
Tony Banfield	DB	6'1"	185	23	6	6
Freddy Glick	DB	6'1"	190	25	3	
Bobby Jancik	DB	5'11"	178	22	2	
Mark Johnston	DB	6'2"	200	24	4	
Jim Norton	DB	6'3"	195	23	8	
Bob Suci	DB	5'10"	178	24	1	
George Blanda	QB	6'1"	212	34		81
Jacky Lee	QB	6'1"	185	23		
Billy Cannon	HB	6'1"	215	25		80
Dave Smith	FB	6'1"	210	25		18
Charley Tolar	HB-FB	5'7"	198	24		48
Charley Hennigan	FL	6'	187	26		48
Willard Dewveall	OE	6'4"	230	25		30
Charley Frazier	OE	6'	160	23		6
Bill Groman	OE	6'	200	26		18
Bob McCleod	OE	6'5"	240	23		36

BOSTON PATRIOTS 9-4-1 Mike Holovak

Scores of Each Game		
28	Dallas	42
34	HOUSTON	21
41	DENVER	16
43	New York	14
7	DALLAS	27
24	SAN DIEGO	20
26	OAKLAND	16
28	Buffalo	28
33	Denver	29
17	Houston	21
21	BUFFALO	10
24	NEW YORK	17
20	San Diego	14
0	Oakland	20

Use Name	Pos.	Hgt	Wgt	Age	Int	Pts
Milt Graham	OT	6'6"	235	28		
Dick Klein	OT	6'4"	254	28		
Charley Long	OT	6'3"	230	24		
Charlie Leo	OG	6'	240	27		
Billy Neighbors	OG	5'11"	240	22		
Tony Sardisco	OG	6'2"	230	29		
Walt Cudzik	C	6'2"	235	29		
Bob Yates	C	6'3"	230	23		
Bob Dee	DE	6'3"	240	29		
Larry Eisenhauer	DE	6'5"	230	22		
Jim Hunt	DE	5'11"	245	23		
Houston Antwine	DT	6'	250	23		
Jess Richardson	DT	6'2"	265	32		
Tom Addison	LB	6'3"	230	26	5	6
Nick Buoniconti	LB	5'11"	220	21	2	
Harry Jacobs	LB	6'2"	235	25		
Rommie Loudd	LB	6'3"	225	28		
Jack Rudolph	LB	6'3"	230	24		
Fred Bruney	DB	5'10"	190	31	3	6
Dick Felt	DB	6'	185	29	5	
Ron Hall	DB	6'	190	25	3	6
Ross O'Hanley	DB	6'	185	23	5	
Chuck Shonta	DB	6'	190	24	2	
Don Webb	HB-DB	5'10"	200	23		
Don Allard	QB	6'	188	26		
Babe Parilli	QB	6'1"	190	32		12
Tom Yewcic	QB	5'11"	185	30		12
Ron Burton	HB	5'10"	190	25		42
Jim Crawford	HB	6'1"	200	26		26
Claude King	HB	5'11"	195	23		6
Larry Garron	FB	6'	215	25		36
Billy Lott	FB	6'	205	27		
Gino Capelletti	FL	6'	190	28		128
Jim Colclough	OE	6'	185	26		60
Tony Romeo	OE	6'2"	220	23		6
Tom Stephens	OE	6'1"	220	26		

Oscar Lofton – Military Service
George McGee – Military Service

BUFFALO BILLS 7-6-1 Lou Saban

Scores of Each Game		
23	HOUSTON	28
20	DENVER	23
6	NEW YORK	17
21	Dallas	41
14	Houston	17
35	SAN DIEGO	10
14	OAKLAND	6
45	Denver	38
28	BOSTON	28
40	San Diego	20
10	Oakland	6
10	Boston	21
23	DALLAS	14
20	New York	3

Use Name	Pos.	Hgt	Wgt	Age	Int	Pts
Stew Barbo	OT	6'3"	242	23		
Jerry DeLucca	OT	6'3"	250	26		
Harold Olson	OT	6'3"	258	23		
Tom Day	OG	6'2"	245	27		
George Flint	OG	6'4"	245	24		
Billy Shaw	OG	6'3"	240	22		
Al Bemiller	C	6'3"	238	23		
Frank Jackunas	C	6'3"	225	21		
Nate Borden	DE	6'	238	30		
Leroy Moore (from BOS)	DE	6'	232	26	1	6
Mack Yoho	DE	6'2"	238	26		23
Don Healy	DT	6'3"	264	26		
Tom Saidock	DT	6'5"	260	30		
Tom Sestak	DT	6'5"	267	26	1	6
Jim Sorey	DT	6'4"	285	25		
Sid Youngelman	DT	6'3"	256	30		
Ralph Felton	LB	5'11"	210	30		
Tom Louderback	LB	6'2"	235	28		
Archie Matsos	LB	6'	220	27		
Marv Matuszak	LB	6'3"	230	31	6	
Mike Stratton	LB	6'3"	225	20	6	
John Tracey	OE-LB	6'3"	225	28		
Ray Abruzzese	DB	6'1"	190	24	3	
Joe Cannavino	DB	5'11"	187	26	1	
Carl Charon	DB	5'10"	185	21	7	12
Jim Crotty	DB	5'11"	190	24		
Booker Edgerson	DB	5'10"	178	23	6	
Carl Taseff	DB	5'11"	193	33	2	
Willie West	DB	5'10"	193	24	3	
John Yaccino	DB	6'	190	24		
Al Dorow	QB	6'	195	32		
Jack Kemp (from SD)	QB	6'1"	205	28		12
Warren Rabb	QB	6'1"	205	25		20
Manch Wheeler	QB	6'	190	23		
Wayne Crow	HB	6'	205	24		12
Elbert Dubenion	HB	6'	197	27		36
Carey Henley	HB	5'10"	200	23		
Art Baker	FB	6'	220	24		6
Wray Carlton	FB	6'2"	220	24		12
Cookie Gilchrist	FB	6'3"	246	27		128
Willie Jones	FB	5'11"	208	22		
Glenn Bass	OE	6'2"	197	23		24
Monte Crockett	OE	6'3"	218	23		
Tom Rychlec	OE	6'3"	220	28		6
Ernie Warlick	OE	6'4"	235	30		12

Ken Rice – Injury

NEW YORK TITANS 5-9-0 Bulldog Turner

Scores of Each Game		
28	Oakland	17
14	San Diego	40
17	Buffalo	6
10	DENVER	32
14	BOSTON	43
17	Houston	56
17	Dallas	20
23	SAN DIEGO	3
31	OAKLAND	21
31	DALLAS	52
46	Denver	45
17	Boston	24
3	BUFFALO	20
10	HOUSTON	44

Use Name	Pos.	Hgt	Wgt	Age	Int	Pts
Fran Morelli	OT	6'2"	258	23		
Alex Kroll	C-OT	6'3"	230	24		
Moses Gray	DT-OT	6'3"	260	24		
Gene Cockrell	DE-OT	6'3"	247	29		
Sid Fournet	OG	6'	240	29		
Bob Mischak	OG	6'	240	29		
Mike Hudock	C	6'2"	245	27		
Karl Kaimer	DE	6'3"	230	23		
John Kenerson (from PIT-N)	DE	6'3"	255	23		
Nick Mumley	DE	6'6"	255	26		
Lavern Torczon (from BUF)	DE	6'2"	235	26		
Bob Watters	DE	6'4"	250	26		
Dick Guesman	DT	6'4"	255	26		2
Proverb Jacobs	DT	6'4"	260	27		
George Strugar (from PIT-N)	DT	6'5"	258	27		
Hubert Bobo	LB	6'1"	220	27	1	
Ed Cooke	LB	6'4"	250	27	1	6
Roger Ellis	LB	6'3"	233	24		
Jerry Fields	LB	6'1"	222	23		
Larry Grantham	LB	6'	200	23	2	6
Billy Atkins	DB	6'1"	196	27	4	
Wayne Fontes	DB	6'	190	22	4	6
Paul Hynes	DB	6'1"	210	22	2	
Dainard Paulson	DB	5'11"	190	25	3	
Lee Riley	DB	6'1"	195	30	11	
Ed Kovac	HB-DB	6'	200	24	1	
Johnny Green	QB	6'3"	208	25		18
Lee Grosscup	QB	6'1"	187	25		
Dean Look	QB	5'11"	185	25		
Bob Scrabis	QB	6'3"	225	26		
Butch Songin	QB	6'2"	205	38		
Harold Stephens	QB	5'11"	175	23		
Dick Christy	HB	5'10"	192	26		48
Curley Johnson	HB	6'	215	27		
Bill Shockley	HB	6'	185	24		68
Jim Tiller	HB	5'9"	165	23		
Mel West	HB	5'9"	190	23		
Charlie Flowers	FB	6'1"	217	25		
Bobby Fowler	FB	5'11"	212	26		
Bill Mathis	FB	6'1"	220	23		18
Don Maynard	FL	6'	185	26		48
Thurlow Cooper	OE	6'4"	228	29		8
Art Powell	OE	6'3"	212	25		48
Perry Richards	OE	6'2"	205	28		

HOUSTON OILERS

RUSHING

Last Name	No.	Yds	Avg	TD
Tolar	244	1012	4.1	7
Cannon	147	474	3.2	7
Smith	56	249	4.4	1
Blanda	3	6	2.0	0
Lee	4	1	0.3	0
Babb	3	0	0.0	0

RECEIVING

Last Name	No.	Yds	Avg	TD
Hennigan	54	867	16	8
McLeod	33	578	18	6
Dewveall	33	576	17	5
Cannon	32	451	14	6
Tolar	30	251	8	1
Groman	21	328	16	3
Smith	17	117	7	2
Frazier	7	155	22	1

PUNT RETURNS

Last Name	No.	Yds	Avg	TD
Jancik	14	164	12	0
Glick	12	79	7	0
Banfield	2	71	36	1

KICKOFF RETURNS

Last Name	No.	Yds	Avg	TD
Jancik	24	726	30	0
Cannon	18	442	25	0
Smith	2	37	19	0
Glick	1	22	22	0
Tolar	2	18	9	0
McLeod	1	0	0	0

PASSING – PUNTING – KICKING

PASSING	Att	Comp	%	Yds	Yd/Att	TD	Int–%	RK
Blanda	418	197	47	2810	6.7	27	42– 10	5
Lee	50	26	52	433	8.7	4	5– 10	
Cannon	3	2	67	46	15.3	1	0– 0	
Smith	3	2	67	34	11.3	0	0– 0	
Tolar	1	0	0	0	0.0	0	1–100	

PUNTING	No	Avg
Norton	55	41.7

KICKING	XP	Att	%	FG	Att	%
Blanda	48	49	98	11	26	42

2 POINT XP
Cannon (1)

BOSTON PATRIOTS

RUSHING

Last Name	No.	Yds	Avg	TD
Burton	134	548	4.0	2
Crawford	139	459	3.3	2
Garron	67	392	5.8	2
Yewcic	33	215	6.5	2
Parilli	28	169	6.0	2
King	21	144	6.8	1
Lott	8	34	4.2	0
Colclough	1	14	14.0	0
Cappelletti	1	–5	–5.0	0

RECEIVING

Last Name	No.	Yds	Avg	TD
Colclough	40	868	22	10
Burton	40	461	12	4
Romeo	34	608	18	1
Cappelletti	34	479	14	5
Crawford	22	224	10	2
Garron	18	236	8	3
King	5	42	8	0
Webb	1	11	11	0
Lott	1	1	1	0

PUNT RETURNS

Last Name	No.	Yds	Avg	TD
Burton	21	122	6	0
Bruney	3	8	3	0
Buoniconti	1	8	8	0
Hall	1	0	0	0

KICKOFF RETURNS

Last Name	No.	Yds	Avg	TD
Garron	24	686	29	1
Burton	13	238	18	0
King	9	177	20	0
Stephens	2	46	23	0
Crawford	2	24	12	0
Loudd	1	15	15	0
Dee	1	14	14	0
Jacobs	1	0	0	0

PASSING – PUNTING – KICKING

PASSING	Att	Comp	%	Yds	Yd/Att	TD	Int–%	RK
Parilli	253	140	55	1988	7.9	18	8– 3	2
Yewcic	126	54	43	903	7.2	7	5– 4	
Garron	3	1	33	39	13.0	0	0– 0	

PUNTING	No	Avg
Yewcic	68	38.7

KICKING	XP	Att	%	FG	Att	%
Cappelletti	38	40	95	20	37	54

2 POINT XP
Crawford (1)

BUFFALO BILLS

RUSHING

Last Name	No.	Yds	Avg	TD
Gilchrist	214	1096	5.1	13
Crow	110	589	5.4	1
Carlton	94	530	5.6	2
Kemp	20	84	4.2	2
Rabb	37	77	2.1	3
Dorow	15	57	3.8	0
Dubenion	7	40	5.7	0
Jones	4	17	4.2	0
Baker	2	9	4.5	0
Wheeler	3	7	2.3	0
Henley	3	2	0.6	0

RECEIVING

Last Name	No.	Yds	Avg	TD
Warlick	35	482	14	2
Dubenion	33	571	17	5
Bass	32	555	17	4
Gilchrist	24	319	13	2
Crow	8	80	10	1
Carlton	7	54	8	0
Rychlec	6	66	11	1
Baker	3	12	4	0
Tracey	1	28	28	0
Crockett	1	14	14	0

PUNT RETURNS

Last Name	No.	Yds	Avg	TD
West	14	112	8	0
Rychlec	1	24	24	0
Taseff	4	18	5	0
Abruzzese	3	17	6	0
Moore	2	12	6	0
Sestak	2	6	3	0
Cannavino	1	3	3	0
Edgerson	1	1	1	0
Charon	0	3	0	1

KICKOFF RETURNS

Last Name	No.	Yds	Avg	TD
Jones	14	287	21	0
Dubenion	7	231	33	1
Baker	7	220	31	1
Abruzzese	10	194	19	0
Gilchrist	7	150	21	0
Henley	5	90	18	0
Flint	1	4	4	0
DeLucca	1	0	0	0

PASSING – PUNTING – KICKING

PASSING	Att	Comp	%	Yds	Yd/Att	TD	Int–%	RK
Rabb	177	67	38	1196	6.8	10	14– 8	6
Kemp	139	64	46	928	6.7	5	6– 4	
Dorow	75	30	40	333	4.4	2	7– 9	
Crow	4	2	50	16	4.0	0	1– 25	
Taseff	1	0	0	0	0.0	0	0– 0	

PUNTING	No	Avg
Crow	75	39.0

KICKING	XP	Att	%	FG	Att	%
Yoho	20	24	83	1	3	33
Gilchrist	14	16	88	8	20	40

2 POINT XP
Rabb (1)

NEW YORK TITANS

RUSHING

Last Name	No.	Yds	Avg	TD
Christy	114	535	4.6	3
Mathis	71	245	3.4	3
Johnson	26	114	4.3	0
Flowers	21	78	3.7	0
Grosscup	8	62	7.7	0
Tiller	31	43	1.3	0
Green	17	35	2.1	3
Stephens	6	33	5.5	0
Fowler	5	27	5.4	0
West	9	16	1.7	0
Songin	4	11	2.7	0
Look	2	9	4.5	0
Kovac	3	5	1.6	0

RECEIVING

Last Name	No.	Yds	Avg	TD
Powell	64	1130	18	8
Christy	62	538	9	3
Maynard	56	1041	19	8
Johnson	14	62	4	0
Tiller	13	108	8	0
Cooper	12	122	10	1
Flowers	7	55	8	0
Richards	6	69	12	0
Mathis	6	32	5	0
Kovac	1	3	3	0
West	1	1	1	0

PUNT RETURNS

Last Name	No.	Yds	Avg	TD
Christy	15	250	17	2
Tiller	9	47	5	0
Cooke	1	11	11	1

KICKOFF RETURNS

Last Name	No.	Yds	Avg	TD
Christy	38	824	22	0
Tiller	22	462	21	0
West	3	131	44	0
Shockley	3	73	24	0
Kovac	4	72	18	0
Johnson	1	14	14	0
Cooper	1	3	3	0
Fournet	1	0	0	0

PASSING – PUNTING – KICKING

PASSING	Att	Comp	%	Yds	Yd/Att	TD	Int–%	RK
Green	258	128	50	1741	6.8	10	18– 7	4
Grosscup	126	57	45	855	6.8	8	8– 6	
Songin	90	42	47	442	4.9	2	7– 8	
Stephens	22	15	68	123	5.6	0	0– 0	
Christy	6	0	0	0	0.0	0	0– 0	
Scrabis	2	0	0	0	0.0	0	1– 50	
Look	1	0	0	0	0.0	0	1–100	

PUNTING	No	Avg
Johnson	50	39.9
Atkins	21	46.1
Green	3	40.3
Paulson	3	37.7

KICKING	XP	Att	%	FG	Att	%
Shockley	29	29	100	13	26	50
Guesman	2	3	67	0	1	0

2 POINT XP
Cooper (1)

DALLAS TEXANS 11-3-0 Hank Stram

Scores of Each Game		
42	BOSTON	28
26	Oakland	16
41	BUFFALO	21
28	San Diego	32
27	Boston	7
20	NEW YORK	17
31	Houston	7
6	HOUSTON	14
52	New York	31
24	Denver	3
35	OAKLAND	7
14	Buffalo	23
17	DENVER	10
26	SAN DIEGO	17

Use Name	Pos.	Hgt	Wgt	Age	Int	Pts
Jerry Cornelison	OT	6'3"	250	25		
Charley Diamond	OT	6'2"	262	26		
Jim Tyrer	OT	6'6"	290	23		
Carl Larpenter	OG-OT	6'4"	240	25		
Sonny Bishop	OG	6'2"	235	22		
Curt Merz	OG	6'4"	250	24		
Al Reynolds	OG	6'3"	235	24		
Marvin Terrell	OG	6'1"	235	24		
Jon Gilliam	C	6'2"	240	23		
Mel Branch	DE	6'2"	230	25		
Dick Davis	DE	6'2"	230	23		
Bill Hull	DE	6'6"	245	21		
Paul Rochester	DT	6'2"	260	25		
Jerry Mays	DE-DT	6'4"	247	22		
Walt Corey	LB	6'	220	24		
Ted Greene	LB	6'1"	230	28		
Sherrill Headrick	LB	6'2"	215	25	3	
Smokey Stover	LB	6'	235	23		
E. J. Holub	C-LB	6'4"	225	24	2	
Dave Grayson	DB	5'10"	180	23	4	
Bobby Hunt	DB	6'1"	180	22	8	
Ed Kelley	DB	6'2"	195	27		
Bobby Ply	DB	6'1"	190	21	7	
Duane Wood	DB	6'1"	200	26	4	
Johnny Robinson	HB-DB	6'	198	23	4	
Len Dawson	QB	6'	190	28		18
Eddie Wilson	QB	6'	190	22		
Abner Haynes	HB	6'	190	24		114
Frank Jackson	HB	6'1"	182	22		24
Jimmy Saxton	HB	5'11"	173	21		
Curtis McClinton	FB	6'3"	232	23		12
Jack Spikes	FB	6'2"	220	24		7
Fred Arbanas	OE	6'3"	236	23		36
Tommy Brooker	OE	6'2"	225	22		87
Chris Burford	OE	6'3"	215	24		72
Bill Miller	OE	6'	190	20		
Tom Pennington	K	6'2"	210	22		19

Dave Webster – Injury

DENVER BRONCOS 7-7-0 Jack Faulkner

Scores of Each Game		
30	SAN DIEGO	21
23	Buffalo	20
16	Boston	41
32	New York	10
44	OAKLAND	7
23	Oakland	6
20	HOUSTON	10
38	BUFFALO	45
23	San Diego	20
29	BOSTON	33
3	DALLAS	24
45	NEW YORK	46
17	Houston	34
10	Dallas	17

Use Name	Pos.	Hgt	Wgt	Age	Int	Pts
Eldon Danenhauer	OT	6'4"	245	26		
Jim Perkins	OT	6'5"	250	23		
Jerry Sturm	OT	6'3"	245	25		
Ken Adamson	OG	6'2"	225	23		
John Denvir	OG	6'4"	245	24		
Bob McCullough	OG	6'2"	240	21		
Jim Barton	C	6'5"	250	27		
John Cash	DE	6'3"	240	26	1	
Chuck Gavin	DE	6'1"	245	28	1	
Larry Jordan	DE	6'6"	230	24		
Don Joyce	DE	6'3"	260	32		
Gordy Holz	DT	6'4"	260	28		
Ike Lassiter	DE-DT	6'5"	270	21		
Tom Erlandson	LB	6'3"	220	22	1	
Jim Fraser	LB	6'3"	240	26	1	2
Wahoo McDaniel	LB	6'	240	25	4	
Bud McFadin	LB	6'3"	270	34		6
Bill Roehnelt	LB	6'1"	230	26		
Jerry Stalcup	LB	6'	230	24		
Goose Gonsoulin	DB	6'3"	210	24	7	6
Chuck Marshall	DB	6'	180	23		
John McGeever	DB	6'1"	195	23	2	6
Jim McMillin	DB	5'11"	190	24	4	12
Tom Minter (to BUF)	DB	5'10"	178	22		
Justin Rowland	DB	6'2"	190	24		
Bob Zeman	DB	6'1"	203	25	6	6
George Shaw	QB	6'1"	185	29		6
Frank Tripucka	QB	6'2"	208	34		6
Al Frazier	HB	5'11"	180	27		18
Gene Mingo	HB	6'1"	200	23		137
Donnie Stone	HB	6'2"	205	25		30
Jerry Tarr	HB	6'	190	22		12
Bo Dickinson	FB	6'2"	220	27		24
Johnny Olszewski	FB	5'11"	202	31		6
Jim Stinnette	FB	6'1"	230	24		6
Bob Scarpitto	FL	5'11"	195	23		36
Gene Prebola	OE	6'3"	225	24		8
Lionel Taylor	OE	6'2"	215	26		24

SAN DIEGO CHARGERS 4-10-0 Sid Gillman

Scores of Each Game		
21	Denver	30
40	NEW YORK	14
17	HOUSTON	42
42	Oakland	33
32	DALLAS	28
10	Buffalo	35
20	Boston	24
3	New York	23
20	DENVER	23
20	BUFFALO	40
27	Houston	33
31	OAKLAND	21
14	BOSTON	20
17	Dallas	26

Use Name	Pos.	Hgt	Wgt	Age	Int	Pts
Jack Klotz (from NY)	OT	6'5"	260	28		
Sherman Plunkett	OT	6'4"	297	28		
Ernie Wright	OT	6'4"	265	21		
Ron Mix	OG-OT	6'4"	245	24		
Ernie Barnes	OG	6'3"	247	23		
Pat Shea	OG	6'1"	230	23		
Dick Hudson	OT-OG	6'4"	260	22		
Sam Gruneisen	LB-OG	6'1"	232	21		
Don Rogers	OG-C	6'2"	250	25		
Wayne Frazier	LB-C	6'2"	235	22		
Earl Faison	DE	6'5"	256	23	1	
Paul Miller	DE	6'2"	240	30		
Ron Nery	DE	6'6"	244	27		
Bill Hudson	DT	6'4"	277	26		
Ernie Ladd	DT	6'9"	317	23		
Henry Schmidt	DE-DT	6'4"	246	25		
Chuck Allen	LB	6'1"	220	22	1	
Frank Buncom	LB	6'1"	225	22	4	
Emil Karas	LB	6'3"	230	28	2	
Paul Maguire	LB	6'	223	24	1	
Bob Mitinger	LB	6'2"	222	22		
Maury Schleicher	LB	6'3"	240	25		
Bob Bethune	DB	5'11"	190	23	3	
George Blair	DB	5'11"	197	24	2	82
Claude Gibson	DB	6'1"	193	23	8	6
Dick Harris	DB	5'11"	175	25	5	
Charley McNeil	DB	5'11"	180	26	1	
Bud Whitehead	DB	6'	180	23	1	
John Hadl	QB	6'2"	205	22		6
Val Keckin	QB	6'4"	215	25		
Dick Wood (to DEN)	QB	6'5"	200	26		
Keith Lincoln	HB	6'2"	205	23		24
Bert Coan	HB	6'4"	215	22		
Fred Gillett	HB	6'3"	225	24		
Hez Braxton	FB	6'2"	227	26		8
Bobby Jackson	FB	6'3"	227	22		42
Jacque Mackinnon	FB	6'4"	240	23		12
Gerry McDougall	FB	6'2"	225	27		18
Lance Alworth	OE	6'	183	22		18
Reg Carolan	OE	6'6"	225	22		6
Dave Kocourek	OE	6'5"	230	25		26
Don Norton	OE	6'1"	185	24		42
Jerry Robinson	OE	5'11"	190	23		18

Bob Laraba – died Feb. 16, 1962 – auto accident
Sam DeLuca – Voluntarily Retired
Paul Lowe – Broken Arm

OAKLAND RAIDERS 1-13-0 Marty Feldman Red Conkright

Scores of Each Game		
17	NEW YORK	28
16	DALLAS	26
33	SAN DIEGO	42
7	Denver	44
6	DENVER	23
6	Buffalo	14
16	Boston	26
21	New York	31
20	HOUSTON	28
6	BUFFALO	10
7	Dallas	35
21	San Diego	31
17	Houston	32
20	BOSTON	0

Use Name	Pos.	Hgt	Wgt	Age	Int	Pts
Charley Brown	OT	6'4"	245	25		
Pete Nicklas	OT	6'4"	240	22		
Jim Norris	OT	6'4"	235	22		
Jack Stone	OT	6'2"	245	25		
Stan Campbell	OG	6'	230	32		
Dan Ficca	OG	6'1"	230	23		
Wayne Hawkins	OG	6'	235	24		
Jim Otto	C	6'2"	240	24		
Dalva Allen	DE	6'5"	245	26		
Dan Birdwell	DE	6'4"	232	21		
Jon Jelacic	DE	6'3"	255	25	1	
Riley Morris	DE	6'2"	230	25		
Joe Novsek	DE	6'4"	237	22		
Chuck McMurtry	DT	6'	280	24		
George Shirkey	DT	6'4"	255	25		
Orville Trask	DT	6'4"	260	27		
Bob Dougherty	LB	6'	240	28		
Charley Rieves	LB	5'11"	215	23		
Jackie Simpson	LB	6'1"	225	25	3	15
George Boynton	DB	5'11"	190	24		
Bob Garner	DB	5'10"	175	27	3	
Mel Montalbo	DB	6'1"	190	23		
Tom Morrow	DB	5'11"	180	24	10	
Rich Mostardi	DB	5'11"	188	24		
Henry Rivera	DB	5'11"	180	22		
Vern Valdez	DB	5'11"	190	26	4	
Fred Williamson	DB	6'2"	208	24	8	6
Cotton Davidson (from DAL)	QB	6'1"	187	29		25
Hunter Enis (from DEN)	QB	6'2"	195	25		
Chan Gallegos	QB	5'9"	175	22		
Don Heinrich	QB	6'	180	30		
M. C. Reynolds	QB	6'	195	27		
Dobie Craig	HB	6'4"	200	23		24
Clem Daniels	HB	6'1"	220	25		48
Charley Fuller	HB	5'11"	175	23		
Harold Lewis	HB	6'	204	26		
Bo Roberson	HB	6'1"	197	27		44
Gene White	HB	6'1"	197	22		8
Alan Miller	FB	6'	205	24		6
Willie Simpson	FB	6'	218	23		
Max Boydston	OE	6'2"	220	29		
Dick Dorsey	OE	6'3"	200	24		12
Charley Hardy	OE	6'	185	28		
Ben Agajanian	K	6'	220	43		25

Tom Flores – Illness

DALLAS TEXANS

RUSHING

Last Name	No.	Yds	Avg	TD
Haynes	221	1049	4.7	13
McClinton	111	604	5.4	2
Dawson	38	252	6.6	3
Jackson	47	251	5.3	3
Spikes	57	232	4.0	0
Burford	1	13	13.0	0
Wilson	1	5	5.0	0
Saxton	3	1	0.3	0

RECEIVING

Last Name	No.	Yds	Avg	TD
Burford	45	645	14	12
Haynes	39	573	15	6
Arbanas	29	469	16	6
McClinton	29	333	11	0
Miller	23	277	12	0
Jackson	10	177	18	1
Spikes	10	132	13	1
Saxton	5	64	13	0
Brooker	4	138	35	3
Robinson	1	16	16	0

PUNT RETURNS

Last Name	No.	Yds	Avg	TD
Haynes	15	119	8	0
Jackson	11	117	11	0
Grayson	1	0	0	0

KICKOFF RETURNS

Last Name	No.	Yds	Avg	TD
Grayson	18	535	30	0
Jackson	10	254	25	0
Saxton	4	77	19	0
McClinton	2	32	16	0
Spikes	2	30	15	0
Haynes	1	27	27	0

PASSING – PUNTING – KICKING

PASSING	Att	Comp	%	Yds	Yd/Att	TD	Int–%	RK
Dawson	310	189	61	2759	8.9	29	17– 5	1
Wilson	11	6	55	65	5.9	0	0– 0	
Haynes	1	0	0	0	0.0	0	0– 0	

PUNTING	No	Avg
Wilson	47	35.8
Saxton	3	46.3

KICKING	XP	Att	%	FG	Att	%
Brooker	33	33	100	12	22	55
Pennington	13	15	87	2	5	40
Spikes	1	1	100	0	0	0

DENVER BRONCOS

RUSHING

Last Name	No.	Yds	Avg	TD
Stone	94	360	3.8	3
Mingo	43	287	5.3	4
Dickinson	73	247	3.3	0
Frazier	39	168	4.2	2
Olszewski	33	114	3.4	0
Stinnette	21	87	4.1	1
Taylor	2	26	13.0	0
Shaw	4	10	2.5	1
Tripucka	2	–1	–0.5	1

RECEIVING

Last Name	No.	Yds	Avg	TD
Taylor	77	908	12	4
Dickinson	60	554	9	4
Prebola	41	599	15	1
Scarpitto	35	667	19	6
Stone	20	223	11	2
Mingo	14	107	8	0
Olszewski	13	150	12	1
Stinnette	13	109	8	0
Frazier	11	211	19	1
Tarr	8	211	26	2

PUNT RETURNS

Last Name	No.	Yds	Avg	TD
Zeman	5	59	12	0
Mingo	7	36	5	0
Frazier	5	32	6	0
Minter	2	1	1	0

KICKOFF RETURNS

Last Name	No.	Yds	Avg	TD
Frazier	19	388	20	0
Minter	10	227	23	0
Tarr	8	217	27	0
McGeever	5	143	29	0
Mingo	6	99	17	0
Olszewski	3	66	22	0
Stinnette	2	27	14	0
Dickinson	2	26	13	0
Danenhauer	1	11	11	0
McMillin	1	6	6	0

PASSING – PUNTING – KICKING

PASSING	Att	Comp	%	Yds	YdTAtt	TD	Int–%	RK
Tripucka	440	240	55	2917	6.6	17	25– 6	3
Shaw	110	49	45	783	7.1	4	14– 13	
Stone	3	1	33	13	4.3	0	0– 0	
Mingo	2	1	50	18	9.0	0	1– 50	
Taylor	2	0	0	0	0.0	0	0– 0	

PUNTING	No	Avg
Fraser	54	44.4
McDaniel	5	34.6

KICKING	XP	Att	%	FG	Att	%
Mingo	32	34	94	27	39	69
Fraser	2	2	100	0	0	0

2 POINT XP
Prebola (1)

SAN DIEGO CHARGERS

RUSHING

Last Name	No.	Yds	Avg	TD
Lincoln	117	574	4.8	2
Jackson	106	411	3.8	5
MacKinnon	59	240	4.0	0
McDougall	43	197	4.5	3
Hadl	40	139	3.4	1
Braxton	17	35	2.1	1
Alworth	1	17	17.0	0
Robinson	2	10	5.0	0
Coan	12	10	0.8	0
Gillett	2	8	4.0	0
Keckin	1	3	3.0	0
Wood	1	0	0.0	0

RECEIVING

Last Name	No.	Yds	Avg	TD
Norton	48	771	16	7
Kocourek	39	688	18	4
Robinson	21	391	19	3
Lincoln	16	214	13	1
Jackson	13	136	10	2
Alworth	10	226	23	3
MacKinnon	9	125	14	2
McDougall	4	27	7	0
Braxton	4	17	4	0
Carolan	3	39	13	1
Coan	1	52	52	0

PUNT RETURNS

Last Name	No.	Yds	Avg	TD
Harris	7	95	14	0
Lincoln	11	94	9	0
Gibson	10	89	9	0
Braxton	1	0	0	0

KICKOFF RETURNS

Last Name	No.	Yds	Avg	TD
Robinson	32	748	23	0
Lincoln	14	398	28	1
Bethune	12	251	21	0
McDougall	3	71	24	0
Gibson	2	55	28	0
Coan	2	31	16	0
Jackson	1	16	16	0
Klotz	1	15	15	0

PASSING – PUNTING – KICKING

PASSING	Att	Comp	%	Yds	Yd/Att	TD	Int–%	RK
Hadl	260	107	41	1632	6.3	15	24– 9	7
Wood	97	41	42	655	6.8	4	7– 7	
Keckin	9	5	56	64	7.1	0	1– 11	
Lincoln	5	2	40	43	8.6	2	0– 0	

PUNTING	No	Avg
Maguire	79	41.6

KICKING	XP	Att	%	FG	Att	%
Blair	31	35	89	17	20	85

2 POINT XP
Braxton (1)
Kocourek (1)

OAKLAND RAIDERS

RUSHING

Last Name	No.	Yds	Avg	TD
Daniels	161	766	4.7	7
Roberson	89	270	3.0	3
Miller	65	182	2.8	1
Davidson	25	54	2.1	3
W. Simpson	10	32	3.2	0
Gallegos	3	25	8.3	0
Enis	2	24	12.0	0
Lewis	9	18	2.0	0
Reynolds	1	9	9.0	0
Craig	1	8	8.0	0
Heinrich	1	4	4.0	0

RECEIVING

Last Name	No.	Yds	Avg	TD
Boydston	30	374	12	0
Roberson	29	583	20	3
Craig	27	492	18	4
Daniels	24	318	13	1
Dorsey	21	344	16	2
Miller	20	259	13	0
Lewis	7	53	8	0
White	6	101	17	1
Hardy	6	80	13	0
Fuller	5	67	13	0

PUNT RETURNS

Last Name	No.	Yds	Avg	TD
Garner	20	162	8	0
Lewis	9	65	7	0
Valdez	2	14	7	0
Morrow	2	13	7	0
Williamson	1	3	3	0

KICKOFF RETURNS

Last Name	No.	Yds	Avg	TD
Roberson	27	748	28	1
Daniels	24	530	22	0
Lewis	3	65	22	0
Miller	6	45	8	0
Dougherty	1	20	20	0
Garner	1	8	8	0
W. Simpson	1	7	7	0
Norris	1	2	2	0
Novsek	1	0	0	0

PASSING – PUNTING – KICKING

PASSING	Att	Comp	%	Yds	Yd/Att	TD	Int–%	RK
Davidson	321	119	37	1977	6.2	7	23– 7	8
Enis	51	27	53	225	4.4	1	1– 2	
Gallegos	35	18	51	298	8.5	2	3– 9	
Heinrich	29	10	34	156	5.4	1	2– 7	
Roberson	6	0	0	0	0.0	0	0– 0	
Reynolds	5	2	40	23	4.6	0	0– 0	
Daniels	1	0	0	0	0.0	0	0– 0	

PUNTING	No	Avg
Morrow	45	36.7
Davidson	40	39.2

KICKING	XP	Att	%	FG	Att	%
Agajanian	10	11	91	5	14	36
J. Simpson	6	6	100	3	10	30
Davidson	4	5	80	1	2	50
Birdwell	0	0	0	0	1	0

2 POINTS XP
Roberson (1)
White (1)

1963 N.F.L. The Best Bet: No Bet

Commissioner Pete Rozelle dropped a bombshell when he announced that certain players had been betting on NFL games. Although none of the men had bet against their own teams, Rozelle decided that players must be above suspicion. Stars Paul Hornung of Green Bay and Alex Karras of Detroit were suspended indefinitely by Rozelle for placing a series of bets on league games, while five other members of the Detroit club were fined $2,000 apiece for betting on the championship game. Another touchy decision by Rozelle was to play the regular slate of games on November 24, a day of mourning for the assassinated President John F. Kennedy. Another tragedy was the death on May 10 of "Big Daddy" Lipscomb, one of the greatest defensive tackles of all time. He was found dead of an overdose of heroin, although many people believe that Lipscomb was drunk and was given the fatal dose after being knocked out in a robbery attempt. On the plus side, though, was the opening of the Hall of Fame in Canton, with seventeen charter members inducted.

EASTERN CONFERENCE

New York Giants—Two losses in the first five games created doubts over the aging Giants, but the team looked pleasantly ripe rather than overage by the end of the season. Winning nine of their last ten games, the Giants captured the Eastern crown for the third straight time. The New York offense, relying heavily on Y. A. Tittle's passes to split end Del Shofner, included such aged stars as Tittle, Frank Gifford, Rosey Brown, and Jack Stroud, while the defense numbered gaffers like Andy Robustelli, Dick Modzelewski, and Tom Scott as starters. But the Giants were old pros, winning all the games they needed to win and keeping their mistakes to a minimum.

Cleveland Browns—With Blanton Collier now the head coach, fullback Jimmy Brown came to camp in a much better state of mind. Brown ran wild once the regular season began, carrying the ball like a workhorse without ever looking tired. After eight games he was already over 1,000 yards for the campaign, and by the end of the season he had set a new record of 1,863 yards. Brown's running kept the Browns in the Eastern race until the Lions knocked them out one week from the end of the season. But in falling short of the title, the Browns did uncover in Frank Ryan their best quarterback since Otto Graham.

St. Louis Cardinals—Young Charley Johnson's passing was the spectacular element in the Cardinal attack, but the running game showed the greatest versatility and depth. Both John David Crow and Prentice Gautt went out with injuries, leaving the Cards without their regular running backs. To replace the injured men, coach Wally Lemm shifted Bill Triplett from defensive back to offensive halfback, and he promoted veteran Joe Childress to a starter's position after several seasons of sitting on the bench. Both runners placed in the top ten in the NFL rushing statistics and provided a fine complement to Johnson's passes to Sonny Randle and Bobby Joe Conrad.

Pittsburgh Steelers—The Steelers had played three ties during the season, so that they could win the title with the best percentage although winning fewer games than the Giants. This constitutional crisis of sorts was averted when the Giants crushed Pittsburgh 33-17. Still, the Steelers surprised most observers by getting as far as they did, relying on players whose futures seemed behind them. The attack depended on power running from John Henry Johnson and Dick Hoak, while the defense was a hardnosed outfit that compensated well for the absence of Big Daddy Lipscomb, who died tragically before the season began.

Dallas Cowboys—Although considered an outside contender for the Eastern crown, the Cowboys never got off the ground after losing their first two games. But although the defense still needed major work and the offensive line needed some shoring up, the Cowboys were still adding good young players to their core. Two rookies made good impressions, Lee Roy Jordan at outside linebacker and Tony Liscio at offensive tackle. In addition, Don Meredith assumed full-time duties at quarterback while Bob Lilly blossomed into a great defensive lineman after being shifted from end to tackle.

Washington Redskins—The long suit in the Redskin attack was the passing game, headed up by young quarterback Norm Snead. Better at the long pass than the short pass, Snead operated a long-range attack with passes to Bobby Mitchell, Fred Dugan, Bill Anderson, and rookie Pat Richter. Mitchell remained the star of the team, the most dangerous receiver in the league after he caught the ball. The running backs were slow and brittle, however, and the defense needed patching up.

Philadelphia Eagles—Winless in their last nine games, the Eagles did not even have injuries as an excuse for their last-place finish. What they could blame was poor morale on a team with better talent than the record indicated. The problems began in training camp when both Sonny Jurgensen and King Hill walked out in a joint holdout for more money. Left without a quarterback, the Eagles gave in to their demands, only to have Jurgensen bothered by various injuries during the season. Coach Nick Skorich got no production out of his fullbacks, had problems in the offensive line, and lost several mediocre defensive linemen with leg problems.

WESTERN CONFERENCE

Chicago Bears—A brutally effective defense brought coach George Halas his first championship in seventeen years. Assistant coach George Allen had installed a zone pass defense that made the Chicago unit the toughest in the league. Allowing only 10 points per game, the Bear defense grew famous around the league as it began to win games with minimal help from the offense. Doug Atkins, Ed O'Bradovich, Bill George, Joe Fortunato, Larry Morris, Richie Petitbon, and Rosey Taylor shone the brightest on defense, while the offense, led by Billy Wade, Johnny Morris, and Mike Ditka, was programmed to stick with safe running plays and short passes without any probability of interception.

Green Bay Packers—Paul Hornung was hardly missed, but the loss of quarterback Bart Starr for four games with a broken hand cost the Packers dearly. Tommy Moore and Elijah Pitts filled in admirably for Hornung at halfback, and guard Jerry Kramer handled the place-kicking duties with style. An opening 10-3 loss to the Bears was written off as a fluke, but when Chicago kept winning, first place in the West was on the line in the November 17 rematch at Chicago. By that time, however, Starr was out of action, and Zeke Bratkowski was running the Packer attack. The Bears swept the Pack out of Wrigley Field in taking a 26-7 victory, thus ending Green Bay domination.

Baltimore Colts—New coach Don Shula's regime began with five losses in the first eight games, hardly a reason for enthusiasm, but a fine stretch run served notice that the Colts were still title contenders. Shula had Johnny Unitas, Jim Parker, Ray Berry, Gino Marchetti, and some other veterans of the 1958-59 championship squads, but he also started blending in new talent of his own. Jerry Hill was promoted to starting fullback, and Tom Matte took over at halfback when Lenny Moore missed most the campaign with an appendectomy and a head injury. Two future stars joined the offensive line when tight end John Mackey and tackle Bob Vogel, both rookies, won starting jobs in the forward wall, and two more freshmen, Fred Miller and Johnny Logan, made the defensive unit.

Detroit Lions—The suspension of Alex Karras by Commissioner Rozelle sorely hurt the defensive line, and injuries further ripped up the once impregnable Detroit defense. Three starting defensive backs went out of the lineup with injuries, Yale Lary and Night Train Lane with bad knees and Gary Lowe with a sheared tendon, and Darris McCord and Joe Schmidt stayed on the field even though below par physically. The offense received an unexpected boost when Earl Morrall developed into a first-class quarterback in beating Milt Plum out of the starting job. But the Detroit attack was not strong enough to carry the club, while the defense was no longer healthy enough to lead the way.

Minnesota Vikings—The three-year-old Vikings were quickly losing their image as an expansion club as the young men in the lineup began maturing and blending together. The Vikings won five games and tied one, with the tie coming against the bruising Chicago Bears in a key December contest. Two other games resulted in near misses for the Vikings. They had the Packers beat with under two minutes left in the game, but a ten-yard field goal was blocked by Green Bay's Herb Adderley to thwart Minnesota's bid. The Vikings also had the Colts licked until Johnny Unitas drove his team 88 yards in forty-five seconds to a winning touchdown.

Los Angeles Rams—When the Rams dropped their first five games, fans expected a repeat of last year's disastrous season. Starting in mid-season, however, the team put together an improved offense with a sturdy defense to win five of its last nine games. The offensive upswing came from the confident play of quarterback Roman Gabriel, the fine running and blocking of rookie fullback Ben Wilson, and an improved offensive line. The defensive front four of Deacon Jones, Lamar Lundy, Merlin Olsen, and Roosevelt Grier combined size and quickness, while linebacker Jack Pardee and cornerback Eddie Meador held the back lines of the defense together.

San Francisco '49ers—Abe Woodson brought three kickoffs back for touchdowns and caused so much commotion with his speed that opposing teams resorted to squib kickoffs late in the year. Woodson was the only offense the '49ers had, as the attack lost quarterback John Brodie with a broken arm, leaving the signal-calling up to journeyman Lamar McHan. The defense also suffered losses, as Charlie Krueger, Jerry Mertens, Walt Rock, and Floyd Dean all missed most of the season with knee injuries. When the team went completely flat, dissension spread through the club, and coach Red Hickey was fired in mid-season in favor of the younger Jack Christiansen.

FINAL TEAM STATISTICS

OFFENSE

	BALT.	CHI.	CLEVE.	DALLAS	DET.	G.BAY	L.A.	MINN.	N.Y.	PHIL.	PITT.	ST.L.	S.F.	WASH.
FIRST DOWNS:														
Total	257	257	252	248	230	258	209	223	278	203	272	254	183	244
by Rushing	95	108	135	105	91	114	80	97	95	78	122	105	87	81
by Passing	149	117	100	132	124	126	117	112	164	114	129	134	87	140
by Penalty	13	32	17	11	15	18	12	14	19	11	21	15	9	23
RUSHING:														
Number	396	487	460	420	415	504	405	445	453	376	578	423	406	344
Yards	1642	1679	2639	1795	1601	2248	1393	1842	1777	1438	2136	1839	1454	1289
Average Yards	4.1	3.4	5.7	4.3	3.9	4.5	3.4	4.1	3.9	3.8	3.7	4.3	3.6	3.7
Touchdowns	11	15	15	18	11	22	14	17	12	8	14	10	8	15
PASSING:														
Attempts	433	404	322	375	406	345	384	355	426	380	368	438	349	430
Completions	248	221	164	200	202	179	186	197	243	193	170	228	156	204
Completion Pct.	57.3	54.7	50.9	53.3	49.8	51.9	48.4	55.5	57.0	50.8	46.2	52.1	44.7	47.4
Passing Yards	3605	2670	2449	2799	2997	2711	2558	2687	3558	2666	3028	3403	2090	3525
Avg. Yds per Att.	8.3	6.6	7.6	7.5	7.4	7.9	6.7	7.6	8.4	7.0	8.2	7.8	6.0	8.2
Avg. Yds. per Comp.	14.5	12.1	14.9	14.0	14.8	15.1	13.8	13.6	14.6	13.8	17.8	14.9	13.4	17.3
Times Tackled	44	20	25	43	33	20	59	51	35	27	30	40	35	43
Yds. Lost Tackled	309	177	232	331	274	178	481	518	311	252	251	372	263	391
Net Yards	3296	2493	2217	2468	2723	2533	2077	2169	3247	2414	2777	3031	1827	3134
Touchdowns	20	18	27	20	26	22	11	16	39	22	21	30	13	17
Interceptions	12	14	20	21	26	21	22	17	21	31	20	21	22	34
Pct. Intercepted	2.8	3.5	6.2	5.6	6.4	6.1	5.7	4.8	4.9	8.2	5.4	4.8	6.3	7.9
PUNTING:														
Number	56	64	54	71	66	51	85	70	59	69	59	65	73	53
Average Distance	41.0	46.5	40.0	44.2	44.6	44.7	44.7	38.7	44.9	43.1	39.4	40.7	45.4	41.7
PUNT RETURNS:														
Number	53	30	25	23	57	26	31	35	40	26	31	26	18	30
Yards	485	277	285	177	635	229	206	405	364	226	281	166	99	391
Average Yards	9.2	9.2	11.4	7.7	11.1	8.8	6.6	11.6	9.1	8.7	9.1	6.4	5.5	13.0
Touchdowns	0	0	0	0	1	0	0	1	0	0	0	0	0	0
KICKOFF RETURNS:														
Number	52	26	50	48	45	46	70	69	46	61	49	52	62	64
Yards	1114	424	1099	1100	949	1122	1651	1556	1018	1527	1312	1070	1659	1718
Average Yards	21.4	16.3	22.0	22.9	21.1	24.4	23.6	22.6	22.1	25.0	26.8	20.6	26.8	26.8
Touchdowns	0	0	0	0	0	1	1	1	0	1	1	0	3	1
INTERCEPTION RETURNS:														
Number	15	36	22	26	24	22	19	11	34	15	25	18	14	21
Yards	174	537	343	549	470	312	182	200	546	210	330	383	221	357
Average Yards	11.6	14.9	15.6	21.1	19.6	14.2	9.6	18.2	16.1	14.0	13.2	21.3	15.8	17.0
Touchdowns	2	4	1	0	3	0	0	2	5	1	1	2	0	2
PENALTIES:														
Number	77	92	52	67	60	53	70	58	67	53	51	69	51	74
Yards	823	804	609	627	531	517	788	627	755	558	495	692	439	736
FUMBLES:														
Number	35	16	25	29	26	30	30	45	28	30	25	29	25	32
Number Lost	25	11	17	15	14	20	17	18	13	16	13	18	8	19
POINTS:														
Total	316	301	343	305	326	369	210	309	448	242	321	341	198	279
PAT Attempts	35	37	43	40	42	46	26	39	57	32	37	44	24	35
PAT Made	32	35	40	38	42	43	25	39	52	29	34	44	24	33
FG Attempts	39	33	23	20	26	34	17	24	29	15	41	21	31	26
FG Made	24	14	15	9	10	16	9	12	18	7	21	11	10	12
Percent FG Made	61.5	42.4	65.2	45.0	38.5	47.1	52.9	50.0	62.1	46.7	51.2	52.4	32.3	46.2
Safeties	1	1	0	0	1	1	1	0	0	0	1	0	0	0

DEFENSE

	BALT.	CHI.	CLEVE.	DALLAS	DET.	G.BAY	L.A.	MINN.	N.Y.	PHIL.	PITT.	ST.L.	S.F.	WASH.
FIRST DOWNS:														
Total	228	196	242	266	194	193	244	258	213	266	244	235	304	285
by Rushing	89	82	99	114	74	92	100	103	89	125	90	105	121	110
by Passing	118	96	129	139	109	87	126	143	106	131	132	107	168	154
by Penalty	21	18	14	13	11	14	18	12	18	10	22	23	15	21
RUSHING:														
Number	434	412	423	455	405	428	431	410	411	466	419	461	488	469
Yards	1794	1442	1651	2094	1564	1586	1785	1733	1669	1985	1728	1802	2076	1863
Average Yards	4.1	3.5	3.9	4.6	3.9	3.7	4.1	4.2	4.1	4.3	4.1	3.9	4.3	4.0
Touchdowns	16	7	10	12	12	11	14	12	14	17	14	19	20	12
PASSING:														
Attempts	348	353	408	403	378	378	379	404	368	375	384	370	450	417
Completions	181	164	208	202	183	180	208	233	176	211	191	180	244	230
Completion Pct.	52.0	46.5	51.0	50.1	48.4	47.6	54.9	57.7	47.8	56.3	49.7	48.6	54.2	55.2
Passing Yards	2589	2045	2718	3392	2597	2340	3025	3362	2588	3106	3400	2519	3581	3484
Avg. Yds per Att.	7.4	5.8	6.7	8.4	6.9	6.2	8.0	8.3	7.0	8.3	8.9	6.8	8.0	8.4
Avg. Yds. per Comp.	14.3	12.5	13.1	16.8	14.2	13.0	14.5	14.4	14.7	14.7	17.8	14.0	14.7	15.1
Times Tackled	45	36	29	20	45	39	27	45	57	29	34	41	25	33
Yds. Lost Tackled	347	311	243	161	400	327	272	364	499	270	299	367	210	270
Net Yards	2242	1734	2475	3231	2197	2013	2753	2998	2089	2836	3101	2152	3371	3214
Touchdowns	19	10	16	31	17	9	25	31	22	28	21	13	27	33
Interceptions	15	36	22	26	24	22	19	11	34	15	25	18	14	21
Pct. Intercepted	4.3	10.2	5.4	6.5	6.3	5.8	5.0	2.7	9.2	4.0	6.5	4.9	3.1	5.0
PUNTING:														
Number	72	73	57	50	83	59	61	60	71	57	66	74	55	57
Average Distance	43.5	43.2	43.7	43.2	45.5	43.4	42.5	43.9	40.4	39.1	44.5	40.1	43.1	44.5
PUNT RETURNS:														
Number	19	34	22	36	29	29	60	27	32	34	29	25	50	25
Yards	119	277	216	176	319	220	681	155	283	451	287	294	587	161
Average Yards	6.3	8.1	9.8	4.9	11.0	7.6	11.4	5.7	8.8	13.3	9.9	11.8	11.7	6.4
Touchdowns	0	0	0	0	0	0	0	0	0	0	0	0	2	0
KICKOFF RETURNS:														
Number	66	52	58	47	56	69	44	48	69	31	53	51	37	59
Yards	1520	1261	1424	1125	1206	1331	1076	1342	1816	727	1133	1279	816	1263
Average Yards	23.0	24.3	24.6	23.9	21.5	19.3	24.5	28.0	26.3	23.5	21.4	25.1	22.1	21.4
Touchdowns	0	0	1	0	0	0	2	3	1	0	0	1	0	1
INTERCEPTION RETURNS:														
Number	12	14	20	21	26	21	22	17	21	31	20	21	22	34
Yards	161	216	317	437	393	297	369	168	379	516	316	284	283	678
Average Yards	13.4	15.4	15.9	20.8	15.1	14.1	16.8	9.9	18.0	16.6	15.8	13.5	12.9	19.9
Touchdowns	1	1	1	5	3	1	2	2	1	1	1	0	1	3
PENALTIES:														
Number	58	78	63	52	57	59	63	59	66	54	78	51	73	83
Yards	685	718	592	479	624	568	558	621	617	598	780	577	667	917
FUMBLES:														
Number	32	36	13	23	24	31	25	50	38	23	31	32	27	20
Number Lost	17	18	10	11	11	21	13	31	16	15	19	19	13	10
POINTS:														
Total	285	144	262	378	265	206	350	390	280	381	295	283	391	398
PAT Attempts	36	18	30	48	32	23	43	50	39	47	36	34	51	50
PAT Made	33	18	29	45	30	23	39	49	37	42	34	34	50	47
FG Attempts	27	17	35	33	24	33	35	22	14	31	22	26	27	33
FG Made	12	6	17	15	13	15	17	13	3	19	15	15	11	17
Percent FG Made	44.4	35.3	48.6	45.5	54.2	45.5	48.6	59.1	21.4	61.3	68.2	57.7	40.7	51.1
Safeties	0	0	1	0	2	0	1	1	0	0	0	0	1	0

1963 NFL CHAMPIONSHIP GAME

December 29, at Chicago
(Attendance 45,801)

Shofner's Hands and Tittle's Knee

The Bears and Giants, long-time rivals in the NFL, met in the eight-degree cold of Wrigley Field to decide the league championship. The two clubs played with contrasting styles, as the Giants depended heavily on Y. A. Tittle's passes, while the Bears relied on a fierce defense to force the enemy into mistakes. The Bears, however, made the first mistake when quarterback Billy Wade fumbled the ball away on the New York 17-yard line. The Giants then marched 83 yards, with a Tittle-to-Gifford pass counting for six points. After Don Chandler added the extra point, neither team could move the ball until Chicago's Willie Galimore fumbled on his own 31. On the next play, Del Shofner got free in the end zone but had a perfect Tittle pass bounce off his frigid hands. The Bear defense then took matters into hand, as Larry Morris picked off a Tittle screen pass and ran the ball back to the New York 5. Two plays later, Wade's quarterback sneak tied the score. The Giants added three points on a Chandler field goal to make the halftime score 10-7, New York. Tittle had twisted his knee in the second quarter, and he had trouble planting his feet while throwing after that. Late in the third period Ed O'Bradovich intercepted another Tittle screen pass, bringing it back to the New York 14. Three plays later, Wade snuck across the goal line to put the Bears ahead for the first time in the game. Tittle kept throwing the ball through the fourth quarter, but the Chicago defense intercepted two passes and protected the 14-10 margin of victory.

TEAM STATISTICS

CHIC.		N.Y.
14	First Downs – Total	17
6	First Downs – Rushing	8
7	First Downs – Passing	9
1	First Downs – Penalty	0
7	Punts – Number	4
41.0	Punts – Average Distance	43.3
5	Punt Return – Yards	21
5	Interception Returns – Number	0
71	Interception Return – Yards	0
2	Fumbles – Number	2
2	Fumbles – Lost Ball	1
5	Penalties – Number	3
35	Yards Penalized	25
2	Giveaways	6
6	Takeaways	2
+4	Difference	–4

SCORING

CHICAGO	7	0	7	0–14
NEW YORK	7	3	0	0–10

First Quarter
- N.Y. — Gifford, 14 yard pass from Tittle — 7:22
  PAT – Chandler (kick)
- CHI. — Wade, 2 yard rush — 14:44
  PAT – Jencks (kick)

Second Quarter
- N.Y. — Chandler, 13 yard field goal — 5:11

Third Quarter
- CHI. — Wade, 1 yard rush — 12:48
  PAT – Jencks (kick)

INDIVIDUAL STATISTICS

RUSHING

CHICAGO	No	Yds	Avg.	NEW YORK	No	Yds	Avg.
Bull	13	42	3.2	Morrison	18	61	3.4
Wade	8	34	4.5	King	9	39	4.3
Galimore	7	12	1.7	McElhenny	7	19	2.7
Marconi	3	5	1.7	Webster	3	7	2.3
	31	93	3.0	Tittle	1	2	2.0
					38	128	3.4

RECEIVING

CHICAGO	No	Yds	Avg.	NEW YORK	No	Yds	Avg.
Marconi	3	64	21.3	Gifford	3	45	15.0
Ditka	3	38	12.7	Morrison	3	18	6.0
J. Morris	2	19	9.5	Thomas	2	46	23.0
Coia	1	22	22.0	McElhenny	2	20	10.0
Bull	1	–5	–5.0	Webster	1	18	18.0
	10	138	13.8		11	147	13.4

PASSING

	Att	Comp	Comp Pct.	Yds	Int	Yds/ Att.	Yds/ Comp	Yards Lost Tackled
CHICAGO								
Wade	28	10	35.7	138	0	4.9	13.4	9
NEW YORK								
Tittle	29	11	37.9	147	5	5.1	13.4	7
Griffing	1	0	0.0	0	0	–	–	0
	30	11	36.7	147	5	4.9	13.4	7

NEW YORK GIANTS 11-3-0 Allie Sherman

Scores of Each Game		
37	Baltimore	28
0	Pittsburgh	31
37	Philadelphia	14
24	Washington	14
24	CLEVELAND	35
37	DALLAS	21
33	Cleveland	6
38	St. Louis	21
42	PHILADELPHIA	14
48	SAN FRANCISCO	14
17	ST. LOUIS	24
34	Dallas	27
44	WASHINGTON	14
33	PITTSBURGH	17

Use Name	Pos.	Hgt	Wgt	Age	Int	Pts
Rosey Brown	OT	6'3"	255	30		
Lou Kirouac	OT	6'3"	230	23		
Jack Stroud	OT	6'1"	250	34		
Lane Howell	DT-OT	6'5"	255	22		
Bookie Bolin	OG	6'2"	235	23		
Darrell Dess	OG	6'	245	27		
Ken Byers	DE-OG	6'1"	240	23		
Greg Larson	C	6'2"	245	24		
Jim Katcavage	DE	6'3"	240	28		6
Andy Robustelli	DE	6'1"	235	37		
John Lovetere	DT	6'4"	283	27		
Dick Modzelewski	DT	6'	260	32		
Bob Taylor	DE-DT	6'3"	235	23		
Al Gursky	LB	6'1"	210	22		
Jerry Hillebrand	LB	6'3"	240	23	5	6
Sam Huff	LB	6'1"	230	28	4	6
Tom Scott	LB	6'2"	220	33		
Mickey Walker	LB	6'	230	23		
Bill Winter	LB	6'3"	220	23	1	
Erich Barnes	DB	6'2"	198	28	3	
Eddie Dove (from SF)	DB	6'2"	180	26	2	
Dick Lynch	DB	6'1"	205	27	9	18
Jimmy Patton	DB	6'	185	31	6	
Dick Pesonen	DB	6'	190	25	1	
Allan Webb	DB	5'11"	180	28	3	
Louis Guy	FL-DB	6'	185	22		
Glynn Griffing	QB	6'1"	200	21		
Y. A. Tittle	QB	6'	195	36		12
Bob Anderson	HB	6'2"	210	26		
Johnny Counts	HB	5'10"	170	24		
Charlie Killett	HB	6'1"	205	22		
Phil King	HB	6'4"	225	27		48
Hugh McElhenny	HB	6'1"	190	34		12
Joe Morrison	FL-HB	6'1"	212	25		60
Alex Webster	FB	6'3"	225	32		24
Frank Gifford	FL	6'1"	190	33		42
Aaron Thomas	OE-FL	6'3"	208	25		18
Del Shofner	OE	6'3"	185	27		54
Joe Walton	OE	5'11"	200	28		36
Don Chandler	K	6'2"	210	28		106

CLEVELAND BROWNS 10-4-0 Blanton Collier

Scores of Each Game		
37	WASHINGTON	14
41	Dallas	24
20	LOS ANGELES	6
35	PITTSBURGH	23
35	New York	24
37	PHILADELPHIA	7
6	NEW YORK	33
23	Philadelphia	17
7	Pittsburgh	9
14	St. Louis	20
27	DALLAS	17
24	St. Louis	10
10	Detroit	38
27	Washington	20

Use Name	Pos.	Hgt	Wgt	Age	Int	Pts
John Brown	OT	6'2"	248	24		
Monte Clark	OT	6'6"	265	26		
Jim McCusker	OT	6'2"	245	27		
Dick Schafrath	OT	6'3"	255	27		
Roger Shoals	OT	6'4"	255	24		
Ted Connolly	OG	6'3"	242	31		
Gene Hickerson	OG	6'3"	248	28		
John Wooten	OG	6'2"	250	28		
John Morrow	C	6'3"	248	30		
Frank Morze	C	6'4"	280	29		
Bill Glass	DE	6'5"	255	27		
Paul Wiggin	DE	6'3"	245	29	1	
Bob Gain	DT	6'3"	260	35		
Jim Kanicki	DT	6'4"	270	21		
Frank Parker	DT	6'5"	255	23		
Vince Costello	LB	6'	228	31	7	
Galen Fiss	LB	6'	227	33	2	
Tom Goosby	LB	6'	235	24		
Jim Houston	LB	6'2"	240	26	1	
Mike Lucci	LB	6'2"	223	23		
Stan Sczurek	LB	5'11"	225	24		
Sam Tidmore	LB	6'1"	225	24		
Walter Beach	DB	6'	185	28		
Larry Benz	DB	5'11"	185	22	7	
Ross Fichtner	DB	6'	185	25	2	6
Bernie Parrish	DB	5'11"	195	28		
Jim Shofner	DB	6'2"	192	27		
Jim Shorter	DB	5'11"	186	22		
Bobby Franklin	HB-DB	5'11"	182	27	2	
Jim Ninowski	QB	6'1"	207	27		
Frank Ryan	QB	6'3"	200	27		12
Ernie Green	HB	6'2"	205	24		18
Charlie Scales	HB	5'11"	215	24		6
Ken Webb	HB	5'11"	205	28		
Jimmy Brown	FB	6'2"	228	27		90
Gary Collins	FL	6'4"	208	22		78
Ray Renfro	FL	6'1"	192	32		6
Johnny Brewer	OE	6'4"	235	26		
Bob Crespino	OE	6'4"	225	25		6
Tom Hutchinson	OE	6'1"	190	22		
Rich Kreitling	OE	6'2"	208	28		36
Lou Groza	K	6'3"	250	39		85

Don Fleming — killed in construction accident, June 4, 1963

ST. LOUIS CARDINALS 9-5-0 Wally Lemm

Scores of Each Game		
34	Dallas	7
28	Philadelphia	24
10	Pittsburgh	23
56	Minnesota	14
24	PITTSBURGH	23
7	GREEN BAY	30
21	Washington	7
21	NEW YORK	38
24	WASHINGTON	20
20	Cleveland	14
24	New York	17
10	CLEVELAND	24
38	PHILADELPHIA	14
24	DALLAS	28

Use Name	Pos.	Hgt	Wgt	Age	Int	Pts
Irv Goode	OT	6'4"	245	22		
Ernie McMillan	OT	6'6"	255	25		
Bob Reynolds	OT	6'6"	256	22		
Ed Cook	OG-OT	6'2"	240	31		
Ken Gray	OG	6'2"	240	27		
John Houser	OG	6'3"	242	27		
Bob DeMarco	C	6'3"	240	25		
Don Brumm	DE	6'3"	225	20		
Ed Henke	DE	6'3"	230	35		
Tom Redmond	DE	6'5"	240	26		
Joe Robb	DE	6'3"	230	26		
Fate Echols	DT	6'1"	260	24		
Don Owens	DT	6'5"	255	31		
Luke Owens	DT	6'2"	255	30		
Sam Silas	DT	6'4"	250	20		
Garland Boyette	LB	6'1"	225	23		
Bill Koman	LB	6'2"	230	29		
Dave Meggyesy	LB	6'1"	215	21		
Dale Meinert	LB	6'2"	220	30		
Marion Rushing	LB	6'2"	210	26		
Larry Stallings	LB	6'2"	225	21		
Jimmy Burson	DB	6'	180	21		
Pat Fischer	DB	5'10"	165	23	8	
Jimmy Hill	DB	6'2"	190	34	3	6
Billy Stacy	DB	6'1"	190	27	1	
Johnny Symank	DB	5'11"	180	28	1	6
Jerry Stovall	DB	6'2"	195	21	1	
Larry Wilson	DB	6'	185	25	4	12
Buddy Humphrey	QB	6'1"	197	27		
Charley Johnson	QB	6'	190	26		6
John David Crow	HB	6'2"	215	28		
Bob Paremore	HB	5'11"	190	23		12
Bill Triplett	HB	6'2"	210	24		48
Joe Childress	FB-HB	6'	200	29		24
Prentice Gautt	FB	6'	200	25		
Bill Thornton	FB	6'1"	205	23		6
Mal Hammack	OE-FB	6'2"	205	30		
Bobby Joe Conrad	FL	6'	195	28		60
Taz Anderson	OE	6'2"	200	24		
Billy Gambrell	OE	5'10"	175	21		
Sonny Randle	OE	6'2"	187	27		72
Jackie Smith	OE	6'4"	205	22		12
Jim Bakken	K	6'	200	22		77

John Wittenborn — Injury

PITTSBURGH STEELERS 7-4-3 Buddy Parker

Scores of Each Game		
21	Philadelphia	21
31	NEW YORK	0
23	ST. LOUIS	10
23	Cleveland	35
23	St. Louis	24
38	WASHINGTON	27
27	DALLAS	21
14	Green Bay	33
9	CLEVELAND	7
34	Washington	28
17	CHICAGO	17
20	PHILADELPHIA	20
24	Dallas	19
17	New York	33

Use Name	Pos.	Hgt	Wgt	Age	Int	Pts
Art Anderson	OT	6'3"	244	26		
Charlie Bradshaw	OT	6'6"	255	27		
Dan James	OT	6'4"	260	26		
Ray Lemek	OG	6'	240	29		
Mike Sandusky	OG	6'	230	30		
Ron Stehouwer	OG	6'2"	230	26		
Buzz Nutter	C	6'4"	230	32		
John Baker	DE	6'6"	270	28		
Lou Michaels	DE	6'2"	235	27	1	95
Ernie Stautner	DT-DE	6'1"	230	38		
Frank Atkinson	DT	6'3"	240	22		
Lou Cordileone	DT	6'	250	26		
Joe Krupa	DT	6'2"	235	30		
Myron Pottios	LB	6'2"	240	23	4	
John Reger	LB	6'	230	32	1	
Bob Rowley	LB	6'2"	225	21		
Andy Russell	LB	6'3"	210	21	3	
Bob Schmitz	LB	6'1"	230	25		2
George Tarasovic (to PHI)	LB	6'4"	245	34		
Jim Bradshaw	DB	6'1"	190	24	1	
Willie Daniel	DB	5'11"	185	25		
Glenn Glass	DB	6'	190	26	1	
Dick Haley	DB	5'10"	190	27	6	6
Brady Keys	DB	6'	185	27		
Clendon Thomas	DB	6'2"	195	26	8	
Ed Brown	QB	6'2"	210	34		12
Bill Nelsen	QB	6'	195	22		
Terry Nofsinger	QB	6'4"	205	25		
Dick Hoak	HB	5'11"	190	24		42
Theron Sapp (from PHI)	HB	6'1"	200	28		6
Tom Tracy (to WAS)	HB	5'9"	205	31		8
Bob Ferguson (to MIN)	FB	5'11"	220	22		6
John Henry Johnson	FB	6'2"	215	33		30
Gary Ballman	FL	6"	195	23		36
Roy Curry	FL	6'1"	195	23		6
John Burrell	OE	6'3"	188	23		
Preston Carpenter	OE	6'2"	190	29		6
Buddy Dial	OE	6'1"	195	26		54
Red Mack	OE	5'10"	185	26		18
John Powers	OE	6'2"	210	22		

Big Daddy Lipscomb — died May 10

DALLAS COWBOYS 4-10-0 Tom Landry

Scores of Each Game		
7	ST. LOUIS	34
24	CLEVELAND	41
17	Washington	21
21	Philadelphia	24
17	DETROIT	14
21	New York	37
21	Pittsburgh	27
35	WASHINGTON	20
24	San Francisco	31
27	PHILADELPHIA	20
17	Cleveland	27
27	NEW YORK	34
19	PITTSBURGH	24
28	St. Louis	24

Use Name	Pos.	Hgt	Wgt	Age	Int	Pts
Bob Fry	OT	6'4"	232	32		
Tony Liscio	OT	6'5"	240	23		
Ed Nutting	OT	6'4"	246	24		
Ray Schoenke	OT	6'3"	234	21		
Joe Bob Isbell	OG	6'1"	225	23		
Dale Memmelaar	OG	6'2"	245	26		
Lance Poimbeouf	OG	6'3"	225	23		
Jim Ray Smith	OT-OG	6'3"	245	32		
Mike Connelly	C	6'3"	242	27		
Lynn Hoyem	OG-C	6'4"	240	23		
George Andrie	DE	6'7"	248	23		
Larry Stephens	DE	6'4"	260	25		
Bob Lilly	DT-DE	6'4"	250	24		6
John Meyers	DT	6'6"	267	23		
Guy Reese	DT	6'5"	258	23		
Dave Edwards	LB	6'3"	215	24	1	
Harold Hays	LB	6'3"	235	22		
Chuck Howley	LB	6'3"	223	27	2	
Lee Roy Jordan	LB	6'2"	210	22	3	
Jerry Tubbs	LB	6'2"	215	28	2	
Don Bishop	DB	6'2"	210	28	5	
Mike Gaechter	DB	6'	196	23	3	
Cornell Green	DB	6'4"	216	23	7	6
Warren Livingston	DB	5'10"	185	25	3	
Jerry Overton	DB	6'2"	190	22		
Jimmy Ridlon	DB	6'1"	177	28		
Eddie LeBaron	QB	5'9"	170	33		
Don Meredith	QB	6'2"	200	25		18
Amos Bullocks	HB	6'1"	202	24		12
Wendell Hays	HB	6'2"	210	22		
Amos Marsh	HB	6'1"	223	24		30
Jim Stiger	HB	5'11"	190	22		6
Don Perkins	FB	5'10"	196	25		42
Frank Clarke	FL	6'	215	30		60
Gary Barnes	OE	6'4"	210	23		
Lee Folkins	OE	6'5"	220	24		24
Billy Howton	OE	6'2"	194	33		18
Pettis Norman	OE	6'3"	210	23		18
Sam Baker	K	6'2"	220	31		65

Maury Youmans — Injury
Dan Talbert — Military Service

NEW YORK GIANTS

RUSHING

Last Name	No.	Yds	Avg	TD
King	161	613	3.8	3
Morrison	119	568	4.8	3
Webster	75	255	3.4	4
McElhenny	55	175	3.2	0
Tittle	18	99	5.5	2
Killett	11	36	3.3	0
Griffing	5	20	4.0	0
Gifford	4	10	2.5	0
Chandler	1	0	0.0	0
Anderson	1	−2	−2.0	0

RECEIVING

Last Name	No.	Yds	Avg	TD
Shofner	64	1181	18	9
Gifford	42	657	16	7
King	32	377	12	5
Morrison	31	284	9	7
Walton	26	371	14	6
Thomas	22	469	21	3
Webster	15	128	9	0
McElhenny	11	91	8	2

PUNT RETURNS

Last Name	No.	Yds	Avg	TD
Dove	17	198	12	0
McElhenny	13	74	6	0
Pesonen	7	47	7	0
Webb	3	45	15	0

KICKOFF RETURNS

Last Name	No.	Yds	Avg	TD
Killett	14	332	24	0
Pesonen	8	197	25	0
McElhenny	6	136	23	0
Counts	5	107	21	0
Morrison	4	75	19	0
Webb	3	62	21	0
Dove	3	56	19	0
Guy	3	44	15	0
Scott	0	9	0	0

PASSING – PUNTING – KICKING

PASSING	Att	Comp	%	Yds	Yd/Att	TD	Int–	%	RK
Tittle	367	221	60	3145	8.6	36	14–	4	1
Griffing	40	16	40	306	7.7	3	4–	10	
Morrison	2	1	50	18	9.0	0	0–	0	

PUNTING	No	Avg
Chandler	59	44.9

KICKING	XP	Att	%	FG	Att	%
Chandler	52	56	93	18	29	62

CLEVELAND BROWNS

RUSHING

Last Name	No.	Yds	Avg	TD
Jim Brown	291	1863	6.4	12
Green	87	526	6.0	0
Ryan	62	224	3.6	2
Webb	12	58	4.8	0
Scales	2	−3	−1.5	1
Franklin	1	−10	−10.0	0
Ninowski	5	−19	−3.8	0

RECEIVING

Last Name	No.	Yds	Avg	TD
Collins	43	674	16	13
Brewer	29	454	16	0
Green	28	305	11	3
Jim Brown	24	268	11	3
Kreitling	22	386	18	6
Hutchinson	9	244	27	0
Renfro	4	82	21	1
Crespino	2	22	11	1
Webb	2	2	1	0
Scales	1	13	13	0
Ryan	0	−1	0	0

PUNT RETURNS

Last Name	No.	Yds	Avg	TD
Shorter	7	134	19	0
Green	6	79	13	0
Shofner	9	41	5	0
Parrish	3	31	10	0

KICKOFF RETURNS

Last Name	No.	Yds	Avg	TD
Scales	16	432	27	0
Green	18	394	22	0
Shorter	9	219	24	0
Franklin	2	33	17	0
Webb	1	12	12	0
Tidmore	1	5	5	0
Morrow	1	4	4	0
Benz	1	0	0	0
Shofner	1	0	0	0

PASSING – PUNTING – KICKING

PASSING	Att	Comp	%	Yds	Yd/Att	TD	Int–	%	RK
Ryan	256	135	53	2026	7.9	25	13–	5	4
Ninowski	61	29	48	423	6.9	2	6–	10	
Jim Brown	4	0	0	0	0.0	0	0–	0	
Groza	1	0	0	0	0.0	0	1–	100	

PUNTING	No	Avg
Collins	54	40.0

KICKING	XP	Att	%	FG	Att	%
Groza	40	43	93	15	23	65

ST. LOUIS CARDINALS

RUSHING

Last Name	No.	Yds	Avg	TD
Childress	174	701	4.0	2
Triplett	134	652	4.9	5
Johnson	41	143	3.5	1
Thornton	19	111	5.8	1
Paremore	36	107	3.0	0
Wilson	2	38	19.0	1
Crow	9	34	3.8	0
Stovall	1	32	32.0	0
Hammack	3	16	5.3	0
Gautt	3	5	1.7	0
Conrad	1	0	0.0	0

RECEIVING

Last Name	No.	Yds	Avg	TD
Conrad	73	967	13	10
Randle	51	1014	20	12
Triplett	31	396	13	3
Smith	28	445	16	2
Childress	25	354	14	2
Paremore	6	89	15	1
Anderson	5	47	9	0
Thornton	4	10	3	0
Gambrell	3	63	21	0
Hammack	1	15	15	0
Gautt	1	3	3	0

PUNT RETURNS

Last Name	No.	Yds	Avg	TD
Gambrell	11	111	10	0
Fischer	9	25	3	0
Paremore	4	23	6	0
Stacy	1	6	6	0
Conrad	1	1	1	0

KICKOFF RETURNS

Last Name	No.	Yds	Avg	TD
Stovall	15	419	28	0
Paremore	12	292	24	0
Triplett	14	229	16	0
Thornton	4	70	18	0
Hammack	4	60	15	0
Goode	1	0	0	0
Gray	1	0	0	0
Redmond	1	0	0	0

PASSING – PUNTING – KICKING

PASSING	Att	Comp	%	Yds	Yd/Att	TD	Int–	%	RK
Johnson	423	222	52	3280	7.8	28	21–	5	5
Humphrey	11	4	36	96	8.7	1	0–	0	
Crow	3	2	67	27	9.0	1	0–	0	
Gautt	1	0	0	0	0.0	0	0–	0	

PUNTING	No	Avg
Stovall	65	40.7

KICKING	XP	Att	%	FG	Att	%
Bakken	44	44	100	11	21	52

PITTSBURGH STEELERS

RUSHING

Last Name	No.	Yds	Avg	TD
Johnson	186	773	4.2	4
Hoak	216	679	3.1	6
Sapp	104	452	4.3	1
Ferguson	46	172	3.7	1
Tracy	29	61	2.1	1
Ballman	8	59	7.4	0
Brown	15	20	1.3	2
Mack	2	1	0.5	0
Carpenter	1	−3	−3.0	0
Nelsen	1	−6	−6.0	0

RECEIVING

Last Name	No.	Yds	Avg	TD
Dial	60	1295	22	9
Ballman	26	492	19	5
Mack	25	618	25	3
Johnson	21	145	7	1
Carpenter	17	233	14	1
Hoak	11	118	11	1
Tracy	7	112	16	0
Sapp	4	36	9	0
Ferguson	3	7	2	0
Burrell	2	27	14	0
Curry	1	31	31	1

PUNT RETURNS

Last Name	No.	Yds	Avg	TD
Keys	13	198	15	0
Haley	12	59	5	0
Thomas	6	24	4	0

KICKOFF RETURNS

Last Name	No.	Yds	Avg	TD
Ballman	22	698	32	1
Thomas	12	286	24	0
Keys	9	219	24	0
Sapp	5	58	12	0
Glass	2	46	23	0
Curry	1	27	27	0
Cordileone	1	18	18	0

PASSING – PUNTING – KICKING

PASSING	Att	Comp	%	Yds	Yd/Att	TD	Int–	%	RK
Brown	362	168	46	2982	8.2	21	20–	6	9
Tracy	4	1	25	23	5.8	0	0–	0	
Nofsinger	3	2	67	46	15.3	0	0–	0	
Nelsen	2	0	0	0	0.0	0	0–	0	

PUNTING	No	Avg
Brown	57	39.6
J. Bradshaw	2	35.0

KICKING	XP	Att	%	FG	Att	%
Michaels	32	35	91	21	41	51
Tracy	2	2	100	0	0	0

DALLAS COWBOYS

RUSHING

Last Name	No.	Yds	Avg	TD
Perkins	149	614	4.1	7
Marsh	99	483	4.9	5
Bullocks	96	341	3.6	2
Meredith	41	185	4.5	3
Stiger	31	140	4.5	1
Baker	1	15	15.0	0
Clarke	1	12	12.0	0
LeBaron	2	5	2.5	0

RECEIVING

Last Name	No.	Yds	Avg	TD
Clarke	43	833	19	10
Howton	33	514	16	3
Folkins	31	407	13	4
Marsh	26	224	9	0
Norman	18	341	19	3
Barnes	15	195	13	0
Perkins	14	84	6	0
Stiger	13	131	10	0
Bullocks	7	70	10	0

PUNT RETURNS

Last Name	No.	Yds	Avg	TD
Stiger	14	141	10	0
Overton	5	32	6	0
Gaechter	2	2	1	0
Howley	1	2	2	0
Norman	1	0	0	0

KICKOFF RETURNS

Last Name	No.	Yds	Avg	TD
Bullocks	19	453	24	0
Stiger	18	432	24	0
Marsh	9	167	19	0
Hays	2	48	24	0

PASSING – PUNTING – KICKING

PASSING	Att	Comp	%	Yds	Yd/Att	TD	Int–	%	RK
Meredith	310	167	54	2381	7.7	17	18–	6	10
LeBaron	65	33	51	418	6.4	3	3–	5	

PUNTING	No	Avg
Baker	71	44.2

KICKING	XP	Att	%	FG	Att	%
Baker	38	38	100	9	20	45

EASTERN CONFERENCE – Continued

WASHINGTON REDSKINS 3-11-0 Bill McPeak

Scores of Each Game			Use Name	Pos.	Hgt	Wgt	Age	Int	Pts
14	Cleveland	37	Fran O'Brien	OT	6'1"	260	28		
37	Los Angeles	14	Riley Mattson	OT	6'4"	257	24		
21	DALLAS	17	Andy Cvercko (from CLE)	OG	6'	243	26		
14	NEW YORK	24	Wiley Feagin	OG	6'2"	235	26		
24	PHILADELPHIA	37	John Nisby	OG	6'1"	247	30		
27	Pittsburgh	38	Vince Promuto	OG	6'1"	240	25		
7	ST. LOUIS	21	Fred Hageman	C	6'4"	242	25		
20	Dallas	35	John Paluck	DE	6'2"	252	30	1	
20	St. Louis	24	Ron Snidow	DE	6'4"	245	21		
28	PITTSBURGH	34	Andy Stynchula	DE	6'3"	257	24		
13	Philadelphia	10	Ben Davidson	DT	6'8"	275	23		
20	BALTIMORE	36	Ed Khayat	DT	6'3"	245	28		
14	New York	44	Joe Rutgens	DT	6'2"	265	24		
20	CLEVELAND	27	Bob Toneff	DT	6'3"	275	33		

Use Name	Pos.	Hgt	Wgt	Age	Int	Pts
Rod Breedlove	LB	6'2"	227	25	1	
Harry Butsko	LB	6'3"	220	22		
Carl Kammerer	LB	6'3"	237	26	2	
Gorden Kelley	LB	6'3"	230	25		
Al Miller	LB	6'	228	23		
Bob Pellegrini	LB	6'2"	235	28	2	
Claude Crabb	DB	6'	197	23	3	6
Dale Hackbart	DB	6'3"	208	27	1	
Ted Rzempoluch	DB	6'1"	195	22		
Johnny Sample	DB	6'1"	200	26	1	
Lonnie Sanders	DB	6'3"	200	21	3	
Jim Steffen	DB	6'	200	26	5	6

Use Name	Pos.	Hgt	Wgt	Age	Int	Pts
George Izo	QB	6'3"	214	26		
Norm Snead	QB	6'4"	215	23		12
Billy Barnes	HB	5'11"	195	28		36
Leroy Jackson	HB	6'	190	23		
Dick James	DB-HB	5'9"	180	29	2	36
Don Bosseler	FB	6'1"	212	27		12
Jim Cunningham	FB	5'11"	224	24		6
Dave Francis	FB	6'1"	210	22		
Frank Budd	FL	5'10"	187	24		
Bobby Mitchell	FL	6'	195	28		48
Bill Anderson	OE	6'3"	215	27		6
Jim Collier	OE	6'2"	195	24		
Fred Dugan	OE	6'3"	194	29		18
Pat Richter	OE	6'5"	230	22		18
Bob Khayat	K	6'2"	230	25		69

PHILADELPHIA EAGLES 2-10-2 Nick Skorich

Scores of Each Game			Use Name	Pos.	Hgt	Wgt	Age	Int	Pts
21	PITTSBURGH	21	Dave Graham	OT	6'3"	240	24		
24	ST. LOUIS	28	J. D. Smith	OT	6'5"	250	27		
14	NEW YORK	37	Howard Keys	OG-C-OT	6'3"	240	28		
24	DALLAS	21	Ed Blaine	OG	6'2"	240	23		
37	Washington	24	Bill Byrne	OG	6'	240	22		
7	Cleveland	37	Pete Case	OG	6'3"	237	22		
7	Chicago	16	Jim Skaggs	OG	6'2"	230	23		
17	CLEVELAND	23	Jim Schrader	C	6'2"	250	31		
14	New York	42	Jerry Mazzanti	DE	6'3"	240	23		
20	Dallas	27	Bill Quinlan	DE	6'3"	250	31		
10	WASHINGTON	13	Bobby Richards	DE	6'2"	240	24		
20	Pittsburgh	20	Dick Stafford	DE	6'4"	270	23		
14	St. Louis	38	Frank Fuller	DT	6'4"	250	34		
13	MINNESOTA	34	Riley Gunnels	DT	6'3"	250	26		
			Ray Mansfield	DT	6'3"	250	22		
			John Mellekas	DT	6'3"	255	30		

Use Name	Pos.	Hgt	Wgt	Age	Int	Pts
Maxie Baughan	LB	6'1"	226	25	1	
Lee Roy Caffey	LB	6'3"	230	23	1	6
Bob Harrison	LB	6'2"	220	26		
Ralph Heck	LB	6'2"	220	22		
Dave Lloyd	LB	6'3"	248	27	3	
Don Burroughs	DB	6'4"	190	32	4	
Jimmy Carr	DB	6'1"	205	30	1	
Irv Cross	DB	6'1"	192	24	2	
Mike McClellan	DB	6'1"	185	24	1	
Nate Ramsey	DB	6'1"	195	22	1	
Ben Scotti	DB	6'1"	186	26	1	

Mike Woulfe – Injury
Gene Gossage – Canadian Football League

Use Name	Pos.	Hgt	Wgt	Age	Int	Pts
Ralph Guglielmi (from NY)	QB	6'1"	195	30		
King Hill	QB	6'3"	213	27		
Sonny Jurgensen	QB	5'11"	200	29		6
Timmy Brown	HB	5'10"	190	26		66
Paul Dudley	HB	6'	185	23		
Tom Woodeshick	HB	6'	210	21		
Ted Dean	FB-HB	6'2"	210	25		
Clarence Peaks	FB	6'1"	220	27		12
Ron Goodwin	FL	6'	170	21		24
Tommy McDonald	FL	5'10"	172	29		48
Gary Henson	OE	6'3"	200	23		
Dick Lucas	OE	6'2"	215	29		
Pete Retzlaff	OE	6'1"	210	32		24
Ralph Smith	OE	6'2"	203	24		6
Mike Clark	K	6'1"	200	22		50

WESTERN CONFERENCE

CHICAGO BEARS 11-1-2 George Halas

Scores of Each Game			Use Name	Pos.	Hgt	Wgt	Age	Int	Pts
10	Green Bay	3	Steve Barnett	OT	6'1"	255	22		
28	Detroit	7	Herm Lee	OT	6'4"	247	32		
37	Minnesota	21	Bob Wetoska	OT	6'3"	240	25		
10	BALTIMORE	3	Jim Cadile	OG	6'3"	230	22		
52	Los Angeles	14	Roger Davis	OG	6'3"	235	25		
14	San Francisco	20	Ted Karras	OG	6'1"	243	30		
16	PHILADELPHIA	7	Mike Pyle	C	6'3"	245	24		
17	Baltimore	7	Doug Atkins	DE	6'8"	255	33	1	2
6	LOS ANGELES	0	Bob Kilcullen	DE	6'3"	245	27		
26	GREEN BAY	7	Ed O'Bradovich	DE	6'3"	255	23		
17	Pittsburgh	17	John Johnson	DT	6'5"	260	22		
17	MINNESOTA	17	Stan Jones	DT	6'1"	250	32		
27	SAN FRANCISCO	7	Earl Leggett	DT	6'3"	250	29		
24	DETROIT	14	Fred Williams	DT	6'4"	248	33		

Use Name	Pos.	Hgt	Wgt	Age	Int	Pts
Tom Bettis	LB	6'2"	235	30		
Joe Fortunato	LB	6'	225	33	2	
Bill George	LB	6'2"	235	32	1	
Roger LeClerc	LB	6'3"	235	25	1	39
Larry Morris	LB	6'2"	230	28		
J. C. Caroline	DB	6'1"	190	30	1	
Larry Glueck	DB	6'	190	21	1	
Bennie McRae	DB	6'1"	180	22	6	6
Richie Petitbon	DB	6'3"	205	25	8	6
Rosey Taylor	DB	5'11"	186	24	9	6
Dave Whitsell	HB-DB	6'	190	27	6	6

Use Name	Pos.	Hgt	Wgt	Age	Int	Pts
Rudy Bukich	QB	6'1"	205	32		6
Billy Wade	QB	6'2"	205	32		36
Charlie Bivins	HB	6'2"	212	24		
Ronnie Bull	HB	6'	200	23		18
Willie Galimore	HB	6'1"	187	28		30
Billy Martin	HB	5'11"	196	25		
Rick Casares	FB	6'2"	225	32		6
Joe Marconi	FB	6'2"	225	29		24
Johnny Morris	FL	5'10"	180	28		12
Angie Coia	OE	6'2"	202	25		6
Mike Ditka	OE	6'3"	230	23		48
Bo Farrington	OE	6'3"	217	27		12
Bob Jencks	OE	6'5"	227	22		38
Bobby Joe Green	K	5'11"	175	25		

GREEN BAY PACKERS 11-2-1 Vince Lombardi

Scores of Each Game			Use Name	Pos.	Hgt	Wgt	Age	Int	Pts
3	CHICAGO	10	Forrest Gregg	OT	6'4"	250	30		
31	DETROIT	10	Norm Masters	OT	6'2"	250	30		
31	BALTIMORE	20	Bob Skoronski	C-OT	6'3"	250	30		
42	LOS ANGELES	10	Dan Grimm	OG	6'3"	240	22		
37	Minnesota	28	Jerry Kramer	OG	6'3"	255	28		91
30	St. Louis	7	Fuzzy Thurston	OG	6'1"	250	30		
34	Baltimore	20	Ken Iman	C	6'1"	230	24		
33	PITTSBURGH	14	Jim Ringo	C	6'1"	235	32		
28	MINNESOTA	7	Lionel Aldridge	DE	6'4"	240	21		
7	Chicago	26	Willie Davis	DE	6'3"	240	30		2
28	SAN FRANCISCO	10	Urban Henry	DT-DE	6'4"	265	28		
13	Detroit	13	Dave Hanner	DT	6'2"	260	34	1	
31	Los Angeles	14	Ron Kostelnik	DT	6'4"	260	23		
21	San Francisco	17	Henry Jordan	DE-DT	6'3"	250	28		

Use Name	Pos.	Hgt	Wgt	Age	Int	Pts
Dan Currie	LB	6'3"	240	29	1	
Bill Forester	LB	6'3"	240	32	1	
Ed Holler	LB	6'2"	230	23		
Ray Nitschke	LB	6'3"	235	27	2	
Dave Robinson	LB	6'3"	240	22		
Herb Adderley	DB	6'1"	205	24	5	6
Hank Gremminger	DB	6'1"	205	30	3	6
Jerry Norton	DB	5'11"	195	33		
Jesse Whittenton	DB	6'	195	29	4	
Willie Wood	DB	5'10"	190	27	5	

Paul Hornung – Suspended by commissioner

Use Name	Pos.	Hgt	Wgt	Age	Int	Pts
John Roach	QB	6'4"	200	30		
Bart Starr	QB	6'1"	200	30		
Lew Carpenter	HB	6'1"	215	31		
Tom Moore	HB	6'2"	215	25		48
Elijah Pitts	HB	6'1"	200	24		36
Earl Gros	FB	6'3"	230	22		12
Frank Mestnik	FB	6'2"	220	25		
Jim Taylor	FB	6'	215	28		60
Boyd Dowler	FL	6'5"	225	26		36
Bob Jeter	FL	6'1"	190	25		
Jan Barrett (to OAK-A)	OE	6'3"	230	22		
Marv Fleming	OE	6'4"	225	21		12
Ron Kramer	OE	6'3"	240	28		24
Max McGee	OE	6'3"	205	31		36

BALTIMORE COLTS 8-6-0 Don Shula

Scores of Each Game			Use Name	Pos.	Hgt	Wgt	Age	Int	Pts
28	NEW YORK	37	Tom Gilburg	OT	6'5"	245	24		
20	San Francisco	14	George Preas	OT	6'2"	250	31		
20	Green Bay	31	Bob Vogel	OT	6'5"	232	21		
3	Chicago	10	Dan Sullivan	OG-OT	6'3"	250	24		
20	SAN FRANCISCO	3	Jim Parker	OG	6'3"	275	29		
25	Detroit	21	Palmer Pyle	OG	6'2"	250	26		
20	GREEN BAY	34	Alex Sandusky	OG	6'1"	242	31		
7	CHICAGO	17	Dick Szymanski	C	6'3"	235	31		
24	DETROIT	21	Ordell Braase	DE	6'4"	242	31		
37	Minnesota	34	Gino Marchetti	DE	6'4"	245	37		6
16	Los Angeles	17	Don Thompson	DE	6'4"	225	24		
36	Washington	20	Jim Colvin	DT	6'2"	255	26		2
41	MINNESOTA	10	John Diehl	DT	6'7"	285	27		
19	LOS ANGELES	16	Fred Miller	DT	6'3"	240	22		

Use Name	Pos.	Hgt	Wgt	Age	Int	Pts
Jackie Burkett	LB	6'4"	230	26		
Jim Maples	LB	6'4"	225	22		
Bill Pellington	LB	6'2"	238	34		
Bill Saul	LB	6'4"	225	22		
Don Shinnick	LB	6'	235	28	2	
Bobby Boyd	DB	5'10"	190	25	3	6
Wendell Harris	DB	5'11"	190	22		
Jerry Logan	DB	6'1"	185	22	1	
Lenny Lyles	DB	6'2"	202	27	2	6
Andy Nelson	DB	6'1"	180	30	3	6
Jim Welch	DB	6'	190	25	4	

Billy Ray Smith – Injury

Use Name	Pos.	Hgt	Wgt	Age	Int	Pts
Gary Cuozzo	QB	6'1"	190	22		
Johnny Unitas	QB	6'1"	194	30		
Tom Matte	HB	6'	195	24		30
Lenny Moore	HB	6'1"	190	30		24
Alex Hawkins	OE-HB	6'1"	190	26		
Nate Craddock	FB	6'	220	20		
Jerry Hill	FB	5'11"	210	23		36
J. W. Lockett	FB	6'2"	230	26		6
Jimmy Orr	FL	5'11"	175	27		30
Willie Richardson	FL	6'2"	198	23		
Ray Berry	OE	6'2"	190	30		18
Dick Bielski	OE	6'1"	225	31		
John Mackey	OE	6'3"	220	21		42
R. C. Owens	OE	6'3"	195	28		
Butch Wilson	OE	6'2"	210	21		
Jim Martin	K	6'2"	230	39		104

EASTERN CONFERENCE—Continued

WASHINGTON REDSKINS

RUSHING

Last Name	No.	Yds	Avg	TD
James	105	384	3.7	4
Barnes	93	374	4.0	5
Bosseler	79	290	3.7	2
Snead	23	100	4.3	2
Cunningham	16	33	2.1	1
Jackson	3	30	10.0	0
Mitchell	3	24	8.0	0
Izo	3	4	1.3	0

RECEIVING

Last Name	No.	Yds	Avg	TD
Mitchell	69	1436	21	7
Richter	27	383	14	3
Bosseler	25	289	12	0
Dugan	20	288	14	3
James	15	302	20	2
Barnes	15	256	17	1
Anderson	14	288	21	1
Cunningham	8	86	11	0
Budd	5	106	21	0

PUNT RETURNS

Last Name	No.	Yds	Avg	TD
James	16	214	13	0
Steffen	5	83	17	0
Mitchell	6	49	8	0
Sample	2	45	23	0
Barnes	1	0	0	0

KICKOFF RETURNS

Last Name	No.	Yds	Avg	TD
James	30	830	28	0
Mitchell	9	343	38	1
Budd	10	252	25	0
Jackson	5	113	23	0
Cunningham	6	96	16	0
Steffen	3	84	28	0
Snidow	1	0	0	

PASSING – PUNTING – KICKING

PASSING	Att	Comp	%	Yds	Yd/Att	TD	Int–	%	RK
Snead	363	175	48	3043	8.4	13	27–	7	11
Izo	58	25	43	378	6.5	3	6–	10	
Barnes	4	3	75	81	20.3	1	0–	0	
Anderson	1	0	0	0	0.0	0	1–	100	
James	1	0	0	0	0.0	0	0–	0	

PUNTING	No	Avg
Richter	53	41.7

KICKING	XP	Att	%	FG	Att	%
B. Khayat	33	35	94	12	26	46

PHILADELPHIA EAGLES

RUSHING

Last Name	No.	Yds	Avg	TD
Brown	192	841	4.4	6
Dean	79	268	3.4	0
Peaks	64	212	3.3	1
Jurgensen	13	38	2.9	1
Guglielmi	4	23	5.8	0
Dudley	11	21	1.9	0
Woodeshick	5	18	3.6	0
Hill	3	–1	–0.3	0

RECEIVING

Last Name	No.	Yds	Avg	TD
Retzlaff	57	895	16	4
McDonald	41	731	18	8
Brown	36	487	14	4
Peaks	22	167	8	1
Goodwin	15	215	14	4
Dean	14	108	8	0
R. Smith	5	63	13	1
Dudley	1	8	8	0
Woodeshick	1	–3	–3	0

PUNT RETURNS

Last Name	No.	Yds	Avg	TD
Brown	16	152	10	0
Dean	10	74	7	0

KICKOFF RETURNS

Last Name	No.	Yds	Avg	TD
Brown	33	945	29	1
Dean	16	425	27	0
Woodeshick	3	72	24	0
Henson	3	21	7	0
R. Smith	2	18	9	0
Caffey	1	6	6	0

PASSING – PUNTING – KICKING

PASSING	Att	Comp	%	Yds	Yd/Att	TD	Int–	%	RK
Hill	186	91	49	1213	6.5	10	17–	9	14
Jurgensen	184	99	54	1413	7.7	11	13–	7	12
Guglielmi	24	7	29	118	4.9	0	3–	13	
Brown	3	1	33	11	3.7	1	1–	33	

PUNTING	No	Avg
Hill	69	43.1

KICKING	XP	Att	%	FG	Att	%
Clark	29	32	91	7	15	47

WESTERN CONFERENCE

CHICAGO BEARS

RUSHING

Last Name	No.	Yds	Avg	TD
Marconi	118	446	3.8	2
Bull	117	404	3.5	1
Galimore	85	321	3.8	5
Casares	65	277	4.3	0
Wade	45	132	2.9	6
Bivins	44	104	2.4	0
J. Morris	1	10	10.0	0
Coia	2	2	1.0	0
Bukich	7	1	0.1	1
Whitsell	1	–8	–8.0	0
Green	2	–10	–5.0	0

RECEIVING

Last Name	No.	Yds	Avg	TD
Ditka	59	794	13	8
J. Morris	47	705	15	2
Marconi	28	335	12	2
Farrington	21	335	16	2
Bull	19	132	7	2
Casares	19	94	5	1
Galimore	13	131	10	0
Coia	11	116	11	1
Bivins	3	22	7	0
Jencks	1	6	6	0

PUNT RETURNS

Last Name	No.	Yds	Avg	TD
J. Morris	16	164	10	0
Martin	2	62	31	0
Taylor	12	51	4	0

KICKOFF RETURNS

Last Name	No.	Yds	Avg	TD
Taylor	6	118	20	0
Bull	7	105	15	0
Martin	4	99	25	0
Bivins	2	40	20	0
Galimore	1	19	19	0
Casares	2	18	9	0
Marconi	2	15	8	0
Johnson	1	10	10	0
Pyle	1	0	0	0

PASSING – PUNTING – KICKING

PASSING	Att	Comp	%	Yds	Yd/Att	TD	Int–	%	RK
Wade	356	192	54	2301	6.5	15	12–	3	8
Bukich	43	29	67	369	8.6	3	2–	5	
Bull	3	0	0	0	0.0	0	0–	0	
Green	1	0	0	0	0.0	0	0–	0	
LeClerc	1	0	0	0	0.0	0	0–	0	

PUNTING	No	Avg
Green	64	46.5

KICKING	XP	Att	%	FG	Att	%
Jencks	35	37	95	1	10	10
LeClerc	0	0	0	13	23	57

GREEN BAY PACKERS

RUSHING

Last Name	No.	Yds	Avg	TD
Taylor	248	1018	4.1	9
Moore	132	658	5.0	6
Pitts	54	212	3.9	5
Gros	48	203	4.2	2
Starr	13	116	8.9	0
Roach	3	31	10.3	0
Carpenter	2	8	4.0	0
Mestnik	1	4	4.0	0
Norton	2	0	0.0	0

RECEIVING

Last Name	No.	Yds	Avg	TD
Dowler	53	901	17	6
McGee	39	749	19	6
R. Kramer	32	537	17	4
Moore	23	237	10	2
Taylor	13	68	5	1
Pitts	9	54	6	1
Fleming	7	132	19	2
Gros	1	19	19	0
Carpenter	1	12	12	0
Jeter	1	2	2	0

PUNT RETURNS

Last Name	No.	Yds	Avg	TD
Wood	19	169	9	0
Pitts	7	60	9	0

KICKOFF RETURNS

Last Name	No.	Yds	Avg	TD
Adderley	20	597	30	1
Gros	17	430	25	0
Carpenter	5	75	15	0
Wood	1	20	20	0
Fleming	1	0	0	0
J. Kramer	1	0	0	0
Mestnik	1	0	0	0

PASSING – PUNTING – KICKING

PASSING	Att	Comp	%	Yds	Yd/Att	TD	Int–	%	RK
Starr	244	132	54	1855	7.6	15	10–	4	7
Roach	84	38	45	620	7.4	4	8–	10	
Moore	4	3	75	99	24.8	1	0–	0	
Pitts	2	2	100	41	20.5	1	0–	0	

PUNTING	No	Avg
Norton	51	44.7

KICKING	XP	Att	%	FG	Att	%
J. Kramer	43	46	93	16	34	47

BALTIMORE COLTS

RUSHING

Last Name	No.	Yds	Avg	TD
Matte	133	541	4.1	4
Hill	100	440	4.4	5
Lockett	81	273	3.4	0
Unitas	47	224	4.8	0
Moore	27	136	5.0	2
Cuozzo	3	26	8.7	0
Mackey	1	3	3.0	0
Craddock	1	1	1.0	0
Hawkins	3	–2	–0.7	0

RECEIVING

Last Name	No.	Yds	Avg	TD
Matte	48	466	10	1
Berry	44	703	16	3
Orr	41	708	17	5
Mackey	35	726	21	7
Hill	22	304	14	1
Moore	21	288	14	2
Richardson	17	204	12	0
Lockett	16	158	10	1
Hawkins	3	41	14	0
Owens	1	7	7	0

PUNT RETURNS

Last Name	No.	Yds	Avg	TD
Logan	28	279	10	0
Hawkins	17	156	9	0
Richardson	5	43	9	0
Moore	2	7	4	0
Hill	1	0	0	0

KICKOFF RETURNS

Last Name	No.	Yds	Avg	TD
Matte	16	331	21	0
Mackey	9	271	30	0
Harris	8	198	25	0
Logan	8	170	21	0
Lockett	3	52	17	0
Hill	2	32	16	0
Gilburg	3	29	10	0
Richardson	1	16	16	0
Parker	1	15	15	0
Bielski	1	0	0	0

PASSING – PUNTING – KICKING

PASSING	Att	Comp	%	Yds	Yd/Att	TD	Int–	%	RK
Unitas	410	237	58	3481	8.5	20	12–	3	2
Cuozzo	17	10	59	104	6.1	0	0–	0	
Matte	5	1	20	20	4.0	0	0–	0	

PUNTING	No	Avg
Gilburg	52	41.8
Logan	4	30.3

KICKING	XP	Att	%	FG	Att	%
Martin	32	35	91	24	39	62

WESTERN CONFERENCE – Continued

DETROIT LIONS 5-8-1 George Wilson

Det	Opponent	Opp
23	Los Angeles	2
10	Green Bay	31
21	CHICAGO	37
26	SAN FRANCISCO	3
14	Dallas	17
21	BALTIMORE	25
28	MINNESOTA	10
45	San Francisco	7
21	Baltimore	24
21	LOS ANGELES	28
31	Minnesota	34
13	GREEN BAY	13
38	CLEVELAND	10
14	Chicago	24

Use Name	Pos.	Hgt	Wgt	Age	Int	Pts
Daryl Sanders	OT	6'5"	240	21		
Lucien Reeberg	OT	6'4"	308	22		
Dan LaRose	OG-OT	6'5"	250	23		
John Gordy	OG	6'3"	250	27		
John Gonzaga	OT-OG	6'3"	250	30		
Bob Whitlow	C	6'1"	236	27		
Bob Scholtz	OT-C	6'4"	250	25		
Darris McCord	DE	6'4"	250	30	1	6
Sam Williams	DE	6'5"	235	32		
Jim Simon	LB-DE	6'5"	225	22		
Roger Brown	DT	6'5"	300	26	1	
Mike Bundra	DT	6'3"	260	24		
Floyd Peters	DT	6'4"	255	28		
Alex Karras – Suspended by commissioner						
Carl Brettschneider	LB	6'1"	225	31		
Ernie Clark	LB	6'1"	220	25		
Dennis Gaubatz	LB	6'2"	205	22	1	
Monte Lee	LB	6'4"	220	25		
Max Messner	LB	6'3"	225	25		
Joe Schmidt	LB	6'1"	220	31		
Wayne Walker	LB	6'2"	225	26	1	56
Larry Vargo	OE-LB	6'3"	215	23	1	6
Night Train Lane	DB	6'1"	200	35	5	
Dick LeBeau	DB	6'1"	185	26	5	6
Gary Lowe	DB	5'11"	195	29	2	
Bruce Maher	DB	5'11"	190	26	1	2
Dick Compton	HB-DB	6'1"	195	23	1	
Yale Lary	DB	6'	190	32	2	6
Tom Hall	OE-DB	6'1"	195	22	3	6
Earl Morrall	QB	6'1"	206	29		6
Milt Plum	QB	6'1"	205	29		16
Hopalong Cassady	HB	5'10"	185	29		
Larry Ferguson	HB	5'10"	185	22		
Dan Lewis	HB	6'1"	200	27		12
Tom Watkins	HB	6'1"	195	26		24
Nick Pietrosante	FB	6'2"	225	26		30
Nick Ryder	FB	6'	205	22		6
Ollie Matson	HB-FB	6'2"	210	33		
Terry Barr	FL	6'	190	28		78
Gail Cogdill	OE	6'2"	195	26		60
Jim Gibbons	OE	6'2"	220	27		6
Al Greer	OE	6'4"	190	22		
Pat Studstill – Injury						

MINNESOTA VIKINGS 5-8-1 Norm Van Brocklin

Min	Opponent	Opp
24	San Francisco	20
7	CHICAGO	28
45	SAN FRANCISCO	14
14	ST. LOUIS	56
28	GREEN BAY	37
24	Los Angeles	27
10	Detroit	28
21	LOS ANGELES	13
7	Green Bay	28
34	BALTIMORE	37
34	DETROIT	31
17	Chicago	17
10	Baltimore	41
34	Philadelphia	13

Use Name	Pos.	Hgt	Wgt	Age	Int	Pts
Grady Alderman	OT	6'2"	245	24		
Errol Linden	OT	6'5"	260	26		
Jim Battle	OG	6'1"	240	25		
Larry Bowie	OG	6'2"	245	23		
Jerry Huth	OG	6'	228	30		
Dave O'Brien	OG	6'3"	235	22		
Mick Tingelhoff	C	6'1"	235	23		
Bob Denton	DE	6'4"	240	29		
Don Hultz	DE	6'3"	220	22	1	6
Jim Marshall	DE	6'3"	235	26		6
Paul Dickson	DT	6'5"	255	26		
Jim Prestel	DT	6'5"	260	26		
Pat Russ	DT	6'4"	255	23		
John Campbell	LB	6'3"	215	24		
Rip Hawkins	LB	6'3"	230	24	1	
Bill Jobko	LB	6'2"	220	27		
Steve Stonebreaker	LN	6'3"	220	25		
Roy Winston	LB	6'1"	225	23	1	6
Lee Calland	DB	6'	190	22		
Terry Dillon*	DB	6'	193	22		
Tom Franckhauser	DB	6'	196	26	2	
Karl Kassulke	DB	6'	193	21		
Terry Kosens	DB	6'3"	195	21		
Chuck Lamson	DB	6'	185	24	1	
Ed Sharockman	DB	6'	200	23	5	6
Fran Tarkenton	QB	6'1"	190	23		6
Ron Vander Kelen	QB	6'1"	185	23		
Bill Butler	HB	5'10"	194	26		6
Tommy Mason	HB	6'	196	24		54
Bob Reed	HB	5'11"	187	23		
Tom Wilson	HB	6'	204	30		24
Bill Brown	FB	5'11"	218	25		48
Jim Boylan	FL	6'1"	185	24		6
Leon Clarke	FL	6'4"	235	30		
Ray Poage	FL	6'4"	203	22		12
Paul Flatley	OE	6'1"	187	22		24
Jerry Reichow	OE	6'2"	220	28		18
Gordon Smith	OE	6'2"	215	24		12
Fred Cox	K	5'10"	205	24		75

*Accidentally drowned

LOS ANGELES RAMS 5-9-0 Harland Svare

LA	Opponent	Opp
2	DETROIT	23
14	WASHINGTON	37
6	Cleveland	20
10	Green Bay	42
14	CHICAGO	52
27	MINNESOTA	24
28	SAN FRANCISCO	21
13	Minnesota	21
0	Chicago	6
28	Detroit	21
17	BALTIMORE	16
21	San Francisco	17
14	GREEN BAY	31
16	Baltimore	19

Use Name	Pos.	Hgt	Wgt	Age	Int	Pts
Jim Baeke	OT	6'5"	245	24		
Joe Carollo	OT	6'2"	260	23		
Frank Varrichione	OT	6'1"	237	31		
Don Chuy	OG	6'1"	255	22		
Charley Cowan	OG	6'4"	255	25		
Joe Scibelli	OG	6'1"	250	24		
Harley Sewell	OG	6'1"	230	32		
Larry Hayes	C	6'3"	230	28		
Art Hunter	C	6'4"	248	30		
Stan Fanning	DE	6'6"	270	25		
Deacon Jones	DE	6'5"	250	24	1	
Lamar Lundy	DE	6'7"	235	28		
Rosey Grier	DT	6'5"	290	30		
Merlin Olsen	DT	6'5"	265	22		
Mike Henry	LB	6'2"	220	27	5	
Cliff Livingston	LB	6'3"	215	33	1	
Jack Pardee	LB	6'2"	225	27	2	
Bill Swain	LB	6'2"	228	22		
Ken Kirk	C-LB	6'2"	225	25		
Charley Britt	DB	6'2"	185	25	1	
Lindon Crow	DB	6'1"	200	30		2
John Griffin	DB	6'1"	190	23		
Alvin Hall	DB	6'	198	30		
Bobby Smith	DB	6'	190	25	2	
Nat Whitmyer	DB	6'	183	22	1	
Ed Meador	DB	5'11"	193	26	6	
Carver Shannon	HB-DB	6'1"	198	25		6
Terry Baker	QB	6'3"	195	22		
Zeke Bratkowski (to GB)	QB	6'2"	203	31		
Roman Gabriel	QB	6'4"	255	23		18
Jon Arnett	HB	5'11"	194	28		12
Pervis Atkins	HB	6'1"	195	27		6
Dick Bass	HB	5'10"	200	26		30
Art Perkins	FB	6'	225	23		24
Ben Wilson	FB	6'	225	23		12
Jim Phillips	FL	6'1"	198	26		6
John Adams	OE	6'3"	235	26		
Duane Allen	OE	6'4"	225	25		
Carroll Dale	OE	6'1"	195	25		42
Marlin McKeever	OE	6'1"	235	23		
Danny Villanueva	K	5'11"	200	25		52

SAN FRANCISCO FORTY NINERS 2-12-0 Red Hickey Jack Christiansen

SF	Opponent	Opp
20	MINNESOTA	24
14	BALTIMORE	20
14	Minnesota	45
3	Detroit	26
3	Baltimore	20
20	CHICAGO	14
21	Los Angeles	28
7	DETROIT	45
31	DALLAS	24
14	New York	48
10	Green Bay	28
17	LOS ANGELES	21
7	Chicago	27
17	GREEN BAY	21

Use Name	Pos.	Hgt	Wgt	Age	Int	Pts
Clyde Brock (from DAL)	OT	6'5"	268	23		
Len Rohde	OT	6'4"	240	25		
Bob St. Clair	OT	6'9"	265	32		
Leon Donahue	OG	6'4"	245	24		
Mike Magac	OG	6'3"	240	25		
John Thomas	OG	6'4"	246	28		
Bruce Bosley	OG-C	6'2"	240	29		
Karl Rubke	DE-C	6'4"	240	27		
Clark Miller	DE	6'5"	245	24		
Dan Colchico	DE	6'4"	236	26		
Roland Lakes	DT-DE	6'4"	273	23		
Charlie Krueger	DT	6'4"	245	27		
Leo Nomellini	DT	6'3"	262	38		
Walt Rock	DT	6'3"	240	22		
Chuck Sieminski	DT	6'4"	245	23		
Roy Williams	DT	6'7"	265	25		
Bill Cooper	LB	6'1"	215	24		
Mike Dowdle	LB	6'3"	237	25	2	
Matt Hazeltine	LB	6'1"	220	30		
Ed Pine	LB	6'4"	230	23	1	
Kermit Alexander	DB	5'11"	186	22	5	
Elbert Kimbrough	DB	5'11"	190	24	1	
Howie Williams (from GB)	DB	6'2"	190	26		
Abe Woodson	DB	5'11"	188	28	3	18
Jim Johnson	FL-HB	6'2"	190	25	2	
Billy Kilmer – Injury						
Jerry Mertens – Injury						
Dave Baker – Military Service						
John Brodie	QB	6'1"	186	28		
Lamar McHan (from BAL)	QB	6'1"	205	31		
Bob Waters	QB	6'2"	184	25		
Don Lisbon	HB	6'	190	22		12
Dale Messer	HB	5'10"	175	26		
Jim Vollenweider	HB	6'1"	210	23		12
Mike Lind	FB	6'2"	215	23		
Joe Perry	FB	6'	200	36		
J. D. Smith	FB	6'1"	200	30		36
Lloyd Winston	FB	6'2"	215	23		6
Bernie Casey	FL	6'4"	215	24		42
Kay McFarland	FL	6'2"	180	24		6
Clyde Conner	OE	6'2"	190	30		
Gary Knafelc	OE	6'4"	220	31		12
Monte Stickles	OE	6'4"	230	25		
Tommy Davis	K	6'	212	28		54

WESTERN CONFERENCE—Continued

DETROIT LIONS

RUSHING

Last Name	No.	Yds	Avg	TD
Lewis	133	528	4.0	2
Watkins	97	423	4.4	2
Pietrosante	112	418	3.7	5
Morrall	26	105	4.0	1
Lary	1	26	26.0	0
Plum	9	26	2.9	0
Ryder	10	23	2.3	1
Ferguson	13	23	1.8	0
Matson	13	20	1.5	0
Barr	1	9	9.0	0

RECEIVING

Last Name	No.	Yds	Avg	TD
Barr	66	1086	16	13
Cogdill	48	945	20	10
Gibbons	32	412	13	1
Pietrosante	16	173	11	0
Watkins	16	168	11	1
Lewis	15	115	8	0
Hall	3	29	10	1
Compton	2	41	21	0
Matson	2	20	10	0
Ferguson	2	8	4	0

PUNT RETURNS

Last Name	No.	Yds	Avg	TD
Watkins	**32**	**399**	12	1
Ferguson	11	108	10	0
Hall	10	107	11	0
Compton	2	11	6	0
Cassady	1	7	7	0
Maher	1	3	3	0

KICKOFF RETURNS

Last Name	No.	Yds	Avg	TD
Watkins	21	447	21	0
Ferguson	9	231	26	0
Hall	6	143	24	0
Matson	3	61	20	0
Ryder	3	33	11	0
Clark	1	13	13	0
Compton	1	13	13	0
Vargo	1	8	8	0

PASSING – PUNTING – KICKING

PASSING	Att	Comp	%	Yds	Yd/Att	TD	Int–	%	RK
Morrall	328	174	53	2621	8.0	24	14–	4	3
Plum	77	27	35	339	4.4	2	12–	16	
Pietrosante	1	1	100	37	37.0	0	0–	0	

PUNTING	No	Avg
Lary	35	**48.9**
Morrall	29	39.4
Compton	2	42.5

KICKING	XP	Att	%	FG	Att	%
Walker	29	29	100	9	22	41
Plum	13	13	100	1	4	25

MINNESOTA VIKINGS

RUSHING

Last Name	No.	Yds	Avg	TD
Mason	166	763	4.6	7
Brown	128	445	3.5	5
Wilson	73	282	3.9	4
Tarkenton	28	162	5.8	1
Reed	21	88	4.2	0
Vander Kelen	8	65	8.1	0
Butler	17	48	2.8	0
Reichow	1	–12	–12.0	0

RECEIVING

Last Name	No.	Yds	Avg	TD
Flatley	51	867	17	4
Mason	40	365	9	2
Reichow	35	479	14	3
Brown	17	109	6	2
Poage	15	354	24	2
Reed	13	137	11	0
Wilson	7	48	7	0
Smith	6	177	30	2
Boylan	6	78	13	1
Butler	4	39	10	0
Clarke	3	34	11	0

PUNT RETURNS

Last Name	No.	Yds	Avg	TD
Butler	21	220	10	1
Reed	9	91	10	0
Mason	4	63	16	0
Kassulke	1	31	31	0

KICKOFF RETURNS

Last Name	No.	Yds	Avg	TD
Butler	**33**	**713**	22	0
Reed	13	367	28	0
Sharockman	7	139	20	0
Brown	3	105	35	1
Franckhauser	4	94	24	0
Mason	3	61	20	0
Calland	2	45	23	0
Smith	2	24	12	0
Campbell	1	8	8	0
Bowie	1	0	0	0

PASSING – PUNTING – KICKING

PASSING	Att	Comp	%	Yds	Yd/Att	TD	Int–	%	RK
Tarkenton	297	170	57	2311	7.8	15	15–	5	6
Vander Kelen	58	27	47	376	6.5	1	2–	3	

PUNTING	No	Avg
Cox	70	38.7

KICKING	XP	Att	%	FG	Att	%
Cox	39	39	100	12	24	50

LOS ANGELES RAMS

RUSHING

Last Name	No.	Yds	Avg	TD
Bass	143	520	3.6	5
Wilson	109	394	3.6	1
Arnett	58	208	3.6	1
Gabriel	39	132	3.4	3
Perkins	37	70	1.9	4
Baker	9	46	5.1	0
Dale	1	12	12.0	0
Atkins	5	11	2.2	0
Meador	1	1	1.0	0
Bratkowski	4	–3	–0.8	0

RECEIVING

Last Name	No.	Yds	Avg	TD
Phillips	54	793	15	1
Dale	34	638	19	7
Bass	30	348	12	0
Arnett	15	119	8	1
Atkins	14	174	12	1
McKeever	11	152	14	0
Wilson	9	173	19	1
Adams	9	93	10	0
Perkins	8	61	8	0
Shannon	2	7	4	0

PUNT RETURNS

Last Name	No.	Yds	Avg	TD
Shannon	15	132	9	0
Atkins	12	36	3	0
Smith	2	20	10	0
Bass	1	11	11	0
Arnett	1	7	7	0

KICKOFF RETURNS

Last Name	No.	Yds	Avg	TD
Shannon	28	823	29	1
Atkins	19	429	23	0
Arnett	12	279	23	0
Whitmyer	3	80	27	0
Wilson	1	17	17	0
Perkins	1	15	15	0
McKeever	2	8	4	0
Cowan	2	0	0	0
Hall	1	0	0	0
Olsen	1	0	0	0

PASSING – PUNTING – KICKING

PASSING	Att	Comp	%	Yds	Yd/Att	TD	Int–	%	RK
Gabriel	281	130	46	1947	6.9	8	11–	4	13
Bratkowski	93	49	53	567	6.1	4	9–	10	
Baker	19	11	58	140	7.4	0	4–	21	
Arnett	1	0	0	0	0.0	0	1–	100	
Bass	1	0	0	0	0.0	0	0–	0	

PUNTING	No	Avg
Villanueva	**81**	45.4
Adams	4	30.3

KICKING	XP	Att	%	FG	Att	%
Villanueva	25	26	96	9	17	53

SAN FRANCISCO FORTY NINERS

RUSHING

Last Name	No.	Yds	Avg	TD
Smith	162	560	3.5	5
Lisbon	109	399	3.7	0
Winston	27	127	4.7	1
Vollenweider	47	124	2.6	2
Perry	24	98	4.1	0
Brodie	7	63	9.0	0
McHan	17	59	3.5	0
Lind	8	26	3.3	0
Waters	5	–2	–0.4	0

RECEIVING

Last Name	No.	Yds	Avg	TD
Casey	47	762	16	7
Lisbon	21	259	12	2
Knafelc	18	221	12	2
Smith	17	196	12	1
Conner	16	247	15	0
Stickles	11	152	14	0
McFarland	11	126	11	1
Johnson	6	63	11	0
Perry	4	12	3	0
Lind	2	13	7	0
Winston	2	13	7	0
Vollenweider	1	26	26	0

PUNT RETURNS

Last Name	No.	Yds	Avg	TD
Woodson	13	95	7	0
Messer	5	4	1	0

KICKOFF RETURNS

Last Name	No.	Yds	Avg	TD
Woodson	29	935	**32**	3
Alexander	24	638	27	0
Vollenweider	4	75	19	0
Cooper	2	8	4	0
St. Clair	2	3	2	0
Stickles	1	0	0	0

PASSING – PUNTING – KICKING

PASSING	Att	Comp	%	Yds	Yd/Att	TD	Int–	%	RK
McHan	196	83	42	1243	6.3	8	11–	6	15
Waters	88	42	48	435	4.9	1	6–	7	
Brodie	61	30	49	367	6.0	3	4–	7	
Lisbon	2	1	50	45	22.5	1	0–	0	
Davis	1	0	0	0	0.0	0	0–	0	
Perry	1	0	0	0	0.0	0	0–	0	
Vollenweider	1	0	0	0	0.0	0	1–	100	

PUNTING	No	Avg
Davis	73	45.4

KICKING	XP	Att	%	FG	Att	%
Davis	24	24	100	10	31	32

1963 A.F.L. Approaching Pay Dirt

Three AFL franchises found secure footing this season after three years of tenuous existence. The Dallas Texans, the 1962 league champions, defended their title as the Kansas City Chiefs, as owner Lamar Hunt tired of losing money and playing second banana to the Cowboys in Dallas. With an attractive young team, the Chiefs sold 15,000 season tickets and made money in their first season in the Midwest. On the East Coast, the New York Titans became the New York Jets and left behind the laughable image of the Harry Wismer years. New owner Sonny Werblin and new coach Weeb Ewbank could not immediately produce a winning club, but they did give the AFL a major-league operation in New York. On the West Coast, young Al Davis took charge of the Oakland Raiders and built them from doormats into an exciting club that barely missed a divisional crown. All three of these clubs enjoyed big increases in attendance, and each of them would use their new revenues to sign top rookies for next year—a cycle that could only lead upward for the league.

EASTERN DIVISION

Boston Patriots—When the television coverage of the Eastern Division playoff between the Patriots and Bills began, viewers saw not players warming up but bulldozers scraping Buffalo's War Memorial Stadium clear of snow. The Patriots had made it to this frigid showdown with a solid defense, a scrappy offense, and a clutch field-goal kicker in Gino Cappelletti. Larry Eisenhauer, Houston Antwine, and Tom Addison steadied the defense, while middle linebacker Nick Buoniconti added the spice with his frequent blitzes. Don Webb, the team's best defensive back, sat out the whole season on the disabled list, but his platoon covered for him better than the offense covered for Ron Burton. With Burton sidelined for the entire schedule with a bad back, the Patriot attack lost most of its speed. But the collapse of the Oilers, the reorganization of the Jets, and the poor start by the Bills kept the Patriots in the divisional race all season. The Patriots and Bills finished in a tie for first place, and in the winter cold of Buffalo the Patriots' old pros won the title 26-8.

Buffalo Bills—Favored by many experts to win the Eastern Division, the Bills fell flat on their face in September. Their first four games netted them three losses and a tie, dropping them into last place before they finally jelled in the month of October. Showing an ability to win close games, the Bills then took seven of their last ten games to catch Boston in a tie for the Eastern title. Quarterback Jack Kemp hit Elbert Dubenion and Bill Miller with pinpoint passes, while Cookie Gilchrist carried the running chores without much help from the halfbacks. The two leading halfbacks were knocked out with hurts, Wray Carolton with a groin injury and Roger Kochman with a leg injury that ended his career after only eight professional games. Gilchrist kept plowing ahead despite little injuries, and he set a new record of 243 yards rushing in one game, on December 8 against New York. The defense was strong up front but vulnerable in the backfield.

Houston Oilers—After three years atop the Eastern Division, the Oilers learned the hard reality of how the other half lives by falling to third place. The defending champs lost their last four straight and five of their last six games, looking more often like a routed army than like a respected football team. Injuries took a hand in the collapse, as a bad back forced tackle Al Jamison into retirement, a pulled thigh muscle kept halfback Billy Cannon on the bench most of the season, and a broken jaw sidelined defensive end Don Floyd for half the schedule. Without Jamison and Cannon, the Houston pass blocking was atrocious, subjecting thirty-six-year-old George Blanda to a rush unfit for a man his age. Cannon's absence also put the whole rushing load on fullback Charley Tolar, who got little help from rookie halfback Bill Tobin. The defense put up no pass rush without Floyd, leaving enemy passers free to spot their receivers in leisure. With all their wounded, the Oilers still managed to stay in the Eastern race until the Patriots demolished them 45-3 on November 1.

New York Jets—New general manager and head coach Weeb Ewbank completely overhauled the team, shuffling players in and out of the pre-season training camp in a steady flow. Looking to shore up the barren New York roster, Ewbank signed free agents cut loose by NFL teams. He especially pounced on players cut from his old Baltimore team, picking up from this source Dee Mackey, Mark Smolinski, Bake Turner, Dave Yohn, and rookies Winston Hill and Bill Baird. For a quarterback, Ewbank discovered Dick Wood, a strong-armed young passer cut loose most recently by the Denver Broncos. Although Wood could throw perfect long passes, his bad knees made him totally immobile, so Ewbank tailored his blocking solely to protect his passer. Billy Mathis and Mark Smolinski won starting backfield jobs on their ability to block, and the offensive line, led by 297-pound Sherman Plunkett, shielded Wood from most enemy interference.

WESTERN DIVISION

San Diego Chargers—In winning their third Western title in four years, the Chargers fielded a backfield as exciting as any in pro football. They had a good veteran quarterback in Tobin Rote, back in the United States after three seasons in the Canadian League, and a good young quarterback in John Hadl. For runners they had Paul Lowe and Keith Lincoln, both quick, slashing runners who could get through the smallest openings in the line. The flanker was Lance Alworth, who came back from an injury-plagued rookie season to tantalize crowds with his leaping grabs and streaking deep patterns. With these talents operating behind a solid line, the San Diego offense put more points on the board than any other attack in the league, but coach Sid Gillman's riches did not end there. The defense also was both colorful and efficient, with Earl Faison, Ernie Ladd, Chuck Allen, and Dick Harris the stars of the unit. Avoiding the string of injuries that ruined the past season, the Chargers found their greatest challenge for the divisional crown not from the defending champion Kansas City team but instead from the surprising Oakland Raiders. Twice the Raiders beat the Chargers, pulling within one game of the top with a 41-27 victory with two weeks left in the season, but the Chargers won both their remaining contests to salt away the championship.

Oakland Raiders—Leaving a comfortable assistantship in San Diego to take over as head coach in Oakland, Al Davis blended holdovers from the disastrous 1962 season with free agents cut loose by other clubs and came up with an exciting team. Davis signed split end Art Powell, who had played out his option in New York, got Tom Flores back from illness, and coaxed several useful players away from other teams at a minimal cost. The offense relied on the passing of quarterbacks Flores and Cotton Davidson to receivers Powell and Bo Roberson and on the running of Clem Daniels to pile up points. Daniels combined speed and power to set a new AFL rushing record with 1,099 yards, and he was also a dangerous deep pass receiving threat coming out of the backfield. The defense had few recognizable names, but terrorized opponents with a dazzling array of blitzes. End Dalva Allen and rookie tackle Dave Costa anchored the forward wall, ex-Bill Archie Matsos starred at middle linebacker, and holdover backs Fred Williamson and Tom Morrow prospered in Davis' new setup. After starting out the season with two wins, the Raiders lost four straight games to Eastern opponents, but then the miracle began. Oakland started winning and never stopped, taking their last eight contests to finish one game behind the Chargers.

Kansas City Chiefs—A fatal injury to rookie Stone Johnson in a preseason game started the Chiefs' season on a foreboding note and dampened the club's enthusiasm. After beating Denver 59-7 to open the season, the Chiefs then won only once in their next ten games. The defense, bolstered by rookies Buck Buchanan and Bobby Bell, stayed tough, but a breakdown in blocking short-circuited the offense. Enemy defenses constantly rushed quarterback Len Dawson with blitzes that his blockers could not pick up, and backs Curtis McClinton and Abner Haynes both fell off from their 1963 performances. Haynes, the AFL's first star, slipped so much that he was restricted to returning kicks for a time. The mid-season drought ended any hopes of repeating as Western champions, and the Chiefs hit the bottom when the New York Jets shut them out 17-0 in a November meeting in New York. After that point, however, the Chiefs put the abundant talent on their roster to full use as they won their last three games.

Denver Broncos—When the Broncos at last uncovered a major-league runner, their passing attack fell apart. The Broncos had always lived and died on the passing of Frank Tripuka, relying on the air game to overcome the lack of any ground attack. Rookie fullback Billy Joe gave the club its first running threat, someone who could break tackles and pick up vital first-down yardage, but Tripuka's arm was no longer up to the weekly strain. After two games, both of which the Broncos lost, Tripuka quit, leaving rookie Mickey Slaughter the only quarterback on the roster. Coach Jack Faulkner then signed ex-Viking John McCormick, and after only four days of practice with the team McCormick led the Broncs to a 14-0 victory over Boston. Next came a 50-34 ambushing of the San Diego Chargers, in which McCormick directed the Denver offense with the precision of a surgeon. With better days obviously on the way, the Broncos suffered a loss from which they never recovered when the Houston Oilers tore up McCormick's knee on the way to a 33-24 victory.

FINAL TEAM STATISTICS

Note: Only offensive totals are available

	BOSTON	BUFFALO	DENVER	HOUSTON	KANSAS CITY	NEW YORK	OAKLAND	SAN DIEGO
FIRST DOWNS:								
by Rushing	100	107	84	68	94	52	85	112
by Passing	107	147	133	169	141	121	142	124
RUSHING:								
Number	437	455	384	341	400	306	359	395
Yards	1618	1838	1508	1209	1697	969	1595	2201
Average Yards	3.7	4.0	3.9	3.5	4.2	3.2	4.4	5.6
Touchdowns	17	21	10	11	12	8	11	20
PASSING:								
Attempts	410	457	453	501	439	480	442	358
Completions	184	228	217	261	231	209	191	202
Percentage	44.9	49.9	47.9	52.1	52.6	43.5	43.2	56.4
Net Yards	2547	3057	2487	3210	2651	2530	2926	2950
Touchdowns	17	16	23	26	30	21	31	28
Interceptions	29	24	28	33	22	29	24	24
Percent Intercepted	7.1	5.3	6.2	6.6	5.0	6.0	5.4	6.7
PUNTING:								
Number	75	62	81	65	62	72	76	61
Average Distance	38.4	40.2	44.3	42.9	43.1	42.1	39.5	37.9
PUNT RETURNS:								
Number	40	37	30	36	26	17	36	22
Yards	373	316	387	339	259	202	395	261
Average Yards	9.3	8.5	12.9	9.4	10.0	11.9	11.0	11.9
Touchdowns	0	0	0	0	0	1	2	0
KICKOFF RETURNS:								
Number	52	52	78	69	47	74	53	52
Yards	1109	1133	1801	1821	1172	1463	1008	1168
Average Yards	21.3	21.8	23.1	26.4	24.9	19.8	19.0	22.5
Touchdowns	0	0	1	0	1	0	0	0
INTERCEPTION RETURNS:								
Number	30	22	15	36	26	21	35	29
Yards	662	156	170	453	450	284	389	316
Average Yards	22.1	7.1	11.3	12.6	17.3	13.5	11.1	10.9
Touchdowns	3	1	1	2	1	0	2	1
POINTS:								
Total	327	304	301	302	347	249	363	399
PAT (kick) Attempts	36	37	35	39	44	30	47	48
PAT (kick) Made	35	32	35	39	43	30	47	44
PAT (2–pt) Attempts	1	2	1	0	1	2	1	2
PAT (2–pt) Made	0	2	1	0	1	0	0	2
FG Attempts	38	23	30	22	28	24	19	27
FG Made	22	10	16	9	8	9	8	17
Percent FG Made	57.9	43.5	53.3	40.9	28.6	37.5	42.1	63.0
Safeties	2	2	0	0	1	0	2	0

1963 AFL CHAMPIONSHIP GAME

January 5, at San Diego
(Attendance 30,127)

Boston's Buttery Defense

In the fourth AFL championship game, San Diego's famous offense made mincemeat out of Boston's heralded defense. On the second play from scrimmage of the game, Keith Lincoln took a handoff and burst through the middle of the Boston defense for a 56-yard gain; Tobin Rote's quarterback sneak seven plays later gave San Diego a quick 7-0 lead. As soon as the Chargers got the ball back, Lincoln headed around end for a 67-yard touchdown run, making the score 14-0. The Patriots came back with a quick touchdown, but a 58-yard touchdown run by Paul Lowe, the third long run of the first quarter for the Chargers, made the score 21-7. George Blair and Gino Cappelletti exchanged field goals early in the second quarter, but Don Norton scored on a 14-yard pass play to give the Chargers a 31-10 lead at halftime. The Patriot attack got nowhere in the second half, as the San Diego line rushed quarterback Babe Parilli ferociously every time he dropped back to pass. The Chargers, however, kept adding points against the Boston defense. Lance Alworth, the Chargers' chief pass receiver, scored in the third period on a 48-yard pass from Rote, and Lincoln added his third touchdown on a 25-yard pass from reserve quarterback John Hadl in the fourth quarter. Hadl then scored on a one-yard plunge with less than two minutes remaining in the game, and George Blair's kick made the final score a lopsided 51-10. Although not even close, the game helped the AFL by showcasing an exciting offensive team in the Chargers, a direct contrast with the defense-oriented NFL champions, the Chicago Bears.

SCORING

SAN DIEGO	21	10	7	13	–51
BOSTON	7	3	0	0	–10

First Quarter
- S.D. Rote, 2 yard rush
  PAT–Blair (kick)
- S.D. Lincoln, 67 yard rush
  PAT–Blair (kick)
- Bos. Garron, 7 yard rush
  PAT–Cappelletti (kick)
- S.D. Lowe, 58 yard rush
  PAT–Blair (kick)

Second Quarter
- S.D. Blair, 11 yard field goal
- Bos. Cappelletti, 15 yard field goal
- S.D. Norton, 14 yard pass from Rote
  PAT–Blair (kick)

Third Quarter
- S.D. Alworth, 48 yard pass from Rote
  PAT–Blair (kick)

Fourth Quarter
- S.D. Lincoln, 25 yard pass from Hadl
  PAT–Pass (No Good)
- S.D. Hadl, 1 yard rush
  PAT–Blair (kick)

TEAM STATISTICS

S.D.		BOS.
21	First Downs–Total	14
11	First Downs–Rushing	6
9	First Downs–Passing	8
1	First Downs–Penalty	0
1	Fumbles–Number	1
1	Fumbles–Lost Ball	0
6	Penalties–Number	1
30	Yards Penalized	18
1	Giveaways	2
2	Takeaways	1
+1	Difference	–1

INDIVIDUAL STATISTICS

SAN DIEGO	No	Yds	Avg.	BOSTON	No	Yds	Avg.
RUSHING							
Lincoln	13	206	15.8	Crump	7	18	2.6
Lowe	12	94	7.8	Garron	3	15	5.0
Rote	4	15	3.8	Lott	3	15	5.0
McDougall	1	2	2.0	Yewcic	1	14	14.0
Hadl	1	1	1.0	Parilli	1	10	10.0
Jackson	1	0	0.0	Burton	1	3	3.0
	32	218	6.8		16	75	4.7
RECEIVING							
Lincoln	7	123	17.6	Burton	4	12	3.0
Alworth	4	77	19.3	Colclough	3	26	8.7
MacKinnon	2	52	26.0	Cappelletti	2	72	36.0
Norton	2	44	22.0	Graham	2	68	34.0
Kocourek	1	5	5.0	Crump	2	28	14.0
McDougall	1	4	4.0	Lott	2	16	8.0
	17	305	17.9	Garron	2	6	3.0
					17	228	13.4
PUNTING							
Maguire	2		43.5	Yewcic	7		46.9
KICKOFF RETURNS							
Alworth	2	47	23.5	Crump	2	31	15.5
Lowe	1	23	23.0	Burton	2	27	13.5
	3	70	23.3	Garron	2	22	11.0
				Suci	1	18	18.0
				Romeo	1	9	9.0
				Yates	1	5	5.0
					9	112	12.4
INTERCEPTION RETURNS							
Maguire	1	10	10.0	None			
Mitinger	1	5	5.0				
	2	15	7.5				

PASSING

SAN DIEGO	Att.	Comp.	Comp. Pct.	Yds.	Int.	Yds/ Att.	Yds/ Comp.
Rote	15	10	66.7	173	0	11.5	17.3
Hadl	10	6	60.0	112	0	11.2	18.7
Lincoln	1	1	100.0	20	0	20.0	20.0
	26	17	65.4	305	0	11.7	17.9
BOSTON							
Parilli	29	14	48.3	189	1	6.5	13.5
Yewcic	8	3	37.5	39	1	4.9	13.0
	37	17	45.9	228	2	6.2	13.4

1963 A.F.L. — Eastern Division

BOSTON PATRIOTS 7-6-1 Mike Holovak

Scores of Each Game		
38	NEW YORK	14
13	San Diego	17
20	Oakland	14
10	Denver	14
24	New York	31
20	OAKLAND	14
40	DENVER	21
21	Buffalo	28
45	HOUSTON	3
6	SAN DIEGO	7
24	KANSAS CITY	24
17	BUFFALO	7
46	Houston	28
3	Kansas City	35
	EAST Playoff	
26	Buffalo	8

Use Name	Pos.	Hgt	Wgt	Age	Int	Pts
Don Oakes	OT	6'3"	255	25		
Bob Yates	OT	6'3"	230	24		
Charley Long	OG	6'3"	250	25		
Billy Neighbors	OG	5'11"	240	23		
Dave Watson	OG	6'1"	220	22		
Walt Cudzik	C	6'2"	235	30		
Bob Dee	DE	6'3"	240	30		
Larry Eisenhauer	DE	6'5"	245	23	1	
Jim Hunt	DE	5'11"	245	24	1	6
Houston Antwine	DT	6'	250	24		
Jerry DeLucca (from BUF)	DT	6'3"	250	27		
Milt Graham	DT	6'6"	235	29		
Bill Hudson	DT	6'4"	255	27		
Jess Richardson	DT	6'2"	265	33		
Tom Addison	LB	6'3"	230	27	4	
Nick Buoniconti	LB	5'11"	220	22	3	
Don McKinnon	LB	6'3"	215	21		
Jack Rudolph	LB	6'3"	230	25		
Dick Felt	DB	6'	185	30	3	
Ron Hall	DB	6'	190	26	3	
Ross O'Hanley	DB	6'	185	24	3	
Chuck Shonta	DB	6'	200	25	3	
Bob Suci	DB	5'10"	185	25	8	12
Tom Stephens	OE-DB	6'1"	215	27	1	
Don Webb – Injury						
Babe Parilli	QB	6'1"	190	33		30
Tom Yewcic	QB	5'11"	185	31		6
*Ron Burton	HB	5'10"	190	26		
Jim Crawford	HB	6'1"	200	27		6
Tom Neumann	HB	5'11"	205	22		6
Harry Crump	FB	6'	205	22		30
Larry Garron	FB	6'	215	26		24
Billy Lott	FB	6'	205	28		24
Jim Colclough	FL	6'	185	27		18
Gino Cappelletti	OE	6'	190	29		113
Art Graham	OE	6'1"	205	22		30
Tony Romeo	OE	6'2"	220	24		18

*Played only in playoffs

BUFFALO BILLS 7-6-1 Lou Saban

Scores of Each Game		
10	San Diego	14
17	Oakland	35
27	KANSAS CITY	27
20	HOUSTON	31
12	OAKLAND	0
35	Kansas City	26
14	Houston	28
28	BOSTON	21
30	Denver	28
27	DENVER	17
13	SAN DIEGO	23
7	Boston	17
45	NEW YORK	14
19	New York	10
	EAST Playoff	
8	BOSTON	26

Use Name	Pos.	Hgt	Wgt	Age	Int	Pts
Stew Barber	OT	6'3"	250	24		
Dave Behrman	OT	6'5"	260	21		
Ken Rice	OG-OT	6'2"	250	23		
Tom Day	OG	6'2"	262	28		
George Flint	OG	6'4"	246	25		
Dick Hudson	OG	6'4"	264	23		
Charlie Leo	OG	6'	240	28		
Billy Shaw	OG	6'3"	250	23		
Al Bemiller	C	6'3"	235	24		
Ron McDole	DE	6'3"	250	23		
Leroy Moore	DE	6'	232	27		
Mack Yoho	DE	6'2"	238	27		62
Jim Dunaway	DT	6'4"	270	21		
Tom Sestak	DT	6'5"	270	27		
Sid Youngelman	DT	6'3"	260	31		
Harry Jacobs	LB	6'2"	230	26	1	
Marv Matuszak	LB	6'3"	230	32		
Herb Paterra	LB	6'1"	222	22		
Mike Stratton	LB	6'3"	230	21	3	6
John Tracey	LB	6'3"	225	29	5	2
Ray Abruzzese	DB	6'1"	194	25	3	
Carl Charon	DB	5'10"	194	22		6
Booker Edgerson	DB	5'10"	177	24	1	
Henry Rivera	DB	5'11"	180	23		
Gene Sykes	DB	6'1"	200	22		
Willie West	DB	5'10"	193	25	5	
George Saimes	HB-DB	5'10"	192	21	4	
Jack Kemp	QB	6'1"	200	29		48
Daryle Lamonica	QB	6'2"	216	22		2
Glenn Bass	HB	6'2"	195	24		6
Hez Braxton	HB	6'2"	227	27		
Fred Brown	HB	5'11"	190	23		6
Wray Carlton	HB	6'2"	220	25		
Wayne Crow	HB	6'	205	25		
Roger Kochman	HB	6'2"	205	21		6
Ed Rutkowski	HB	6'1"	200	22		6
Cookie Gilchrist	FB	6'3"	250	28		84
Jesse Murdock (from OAK)	FB	6'2"	203	24		
Elbert Dubenion	FL	6'	188	28		24
Charley Ferguson	OE	6'5"	215	23		18
Bill Miller	OE	6'	200	21		18
Ernie Warlick	OE	6'4"	232	31		6

HOUSTON OILERS 6-8-0 Pop Ivy

Scores of Each Game		
13	OAKLAND	24
20	DENVER	14
17	New York	24
31	Buffalo	20
7	Kansas City	28
33	Denver	24
28	BUFFALO	14
28	KANSAS CITY	7
3	Boston	45
31	NEW YORK	27
0	San Diego	27
28	BOSTON	46
14	SAN DIEGO	20
49	Oakland	52

Use Name	Pos.	Hgt	Wgt	Age	Int	Pts
Bob Kelly	OT	6'3"	260	23		
Rich Michael	OT	6'3"	238	24		
Walt Suggs	OT	6'5"	255	24		
Bob Talamini	OG	6'1"	250	24		
Bill Wegener	OG	5'10"	245	22		
Hogan Wharton	OG	6'2"	250	27		
John Frongillo	C	6'3"	255	23		
Bob Schmidt	C	6'4"	250	27		
Gary Cutsinger	DE	6'4"	245	22		
Don Floyd	DE	6'4"	245	24		
Willis Perkins	DE	6'	260	26		
Ed Culpepper	DT	6'1"	250	29		
Ed Husmann	DT	6'	245	32		
Dudley Meridith	DT	6'4"	275	28		
Johnny Baker	LB	6'3"	220	22		
Danny Brabham	LB	6'4"	235	22	1	
Doug Cline	LB	6'2"	227	24	3	
Mike Dukes	LB	6'3"	230	27	1	
Tom Goode	LB	6'3"	235	24		
Larry Onesti	LB	6'	195	24		
Gene Babb	FB-LB	6'3"	220	28	2	
Tony Banfield	DB	6'1"	185	24	7	
Freddy Glick	DB	6'1"	190	26	12	6
Bobby Jancik	DB	5'11"	178	23	3	
Mark Johnston	DB	6'	200	25	1	6
Jim Norton	DB	6'3"	190	24	6	
George Blanda	QB	6'1"	215	35		64
Jacky Lee	QB	6'1"	187	24		
Bobby Brezina	HB	6'	200	21		
Billy Cannon	HB	6'1"	210	26		
Bill Tobin	HB	5'11"	210	21		32
Dave Smith	FB	6'1"	210	26		30
Charley Tolar	FB	5'7"	200	25		18
Charley Hennigan	FL	6'	187	27		60
Randy Kerbow	FL	6'1"	190	21		
Willard Dewveall	OE	6'4"	225	26		42
Charley Frazier	OE	6'	162	24		6
Bob McLeod	OE	6'5"	230	24		30

NEW YORK JETS 5-8-1 Weeb Ewbank

Scores of Each Game		
14	Boston	38
24	HOUSTON	17
10	OAKLAND	7
31	BOSTON	24
20	San Diego	24
26	Oakland	49
35	DENVER	35
7	SAN DIEGO	53
27	Houston	31
14	Denver	9
17	KANSAS CITY	0
14	Buffalo	45
10	BUFFALO	19
0	Kansas City	48

Use Name	Pos.	Hgt	Wgt	Age	Int	Pts
Winston Hill	OT	6'4"	275	21		
Jack Klotz	OT	6'5"	250	29		
Sherman Plunkett	OT	6'4"	297	29		
Bob Butler	OG	6'1"	230	22		
Dan Ficca	OG	6'1"	245	24		
Sid Fournet	OG	6'	240	30		
Roy Hord	OG	6'4"	245	28		
Pete Perreault	OG	6'3"	245	24		
Mike Hudock	C	6'2"	245	28		
Lavern Torczon	DE	6'2"	238	27	1	
Bob Watters	DE	6'4"	245	27		
Ed Cooke	LB-DE	6'4"	250	28		
Dick Guesman	DT	6'4"	255	27		57
Chuck Janerette	DT	6'3"	250	24	1	
Bob McAdams	DT	6'3"	250	23		
George Strugar	DT	6'5"	260	28		
Ted Bates	LB	6'3"	220	26		
Roger Ellis	LB	6'3"	233	25		
Larry Grantham	LB	6'	200	24	3	6
Walt Michaels	LB	6'	240	34		
Jim Price	LB	6'2"	225	22	1	
Dave Yohn	LB	6'	225	25		
Billy Atkins (to BUF)	DB	6'1"	196	28		
Bill Baird	DB	5'10"	182	24	6	6
Dainard Paulson	DB	5'11"	190	26	6	
Marsh Starks	DB	6'	190	24		6
Tony Stricker	DB	6'	185	22	1	
Clyde Washington	DB	6'	206	25	2	
Dave West	DB	6'3"	190	25		
Bill Wood	DB	5'11"	190	24		
Ed Chlebek	QB	5'11"	175	22		
Johnny Green	QB	6'3"	208	26		
Galen Hall	QB	5'10"	205	23		6
Dick Wood	QB	6'5"	205	27		6
Dick Christy	HB	5'10"	195	27		6
Bill Mathis	HB	6'1"	220	24		12
Bill Perkins	HB	6'2"	225	22		
Curley Johnson	FB	6'	210	28		
Mark Smolinski	FB	6'	222	24		30
Don Maynard	FL	6'	185	27		54
Ken Gregory	OE	6'	190	26		
Gene Heeter	OE	6'4"	235	22		6
Dee Mackey	OE	6'5"	236	27		18
Bake Turner	OE	6'	180	23		36

BOSTON PATRIOTS

RUSHING

Last Name	No.	Yds	Avg	TD
Garron	179	750	4.1	2
Crawford	71	233	3.3	1
Yewcic	22	161	7.3	1
Neumann	44	148	3.4	0
Parilli	36	126	3.5	5
Crump	49	120	2.5	5
Lott	35	78	2.2	3
Cappelletti	1	2	2.0	0

RECEIVING

Last Name	No.	Yds	Avg	TD
Colclough	42	793	19	3
Cappelletti	34	493	15	2
Romeo	31	438	14	3
Garron	26	418	16	2
A. Graham	21	550	26	5
Crawford	10	84	8	0
Neumann	10	48	5	1
Lott	3	61	20	1
Crump	3	19	6	0

PUNT RETURNS

Last Name	No.	Yds	Avg	TD
Suci	25	233	9	0
Stephens	14	117	8	0
Garron	1	23	23	0

KICKOFF RETURNS

Last Name	No.	Yds	Avg	TD
Garron	28	693	25	0
Suci	17	360	21	0
Crump	3	33	11	0
Romeo	1	9	9	0
Watson	1	9	9	0
Yates	2	5	3	0

PASSING – PUNTING – KICKING

PASSING	Att	Comp	%	Yds	Yd/Att	TD	Int–%	RK
Parilli	337	153	45	2335	6.9	13	24– 7	9
Yewcic	70	29	41	444	6.3	4	5– 7	
Crawford	2	2	100	27	13.5	0	0– 0	
Garron	1	0	0	0	0.0	0	0– 0	

PUNTING	No	Avg
Yewcic	73	39.4

KICKING	XP	Att	%	FG	Att	%
Cappelletti	35	36	97	22	38	58

BUFFALO BILLS

RUSHING

Last Name	No.	Yds	Avg	TD
Gilchrist	**232**	979	4.2	**12**
Kochman	47	232	4.9	0
Kemp	52	226	4.3	8
Rutowski	48	144	3.0	0
Carlton	29	125	4.3	0
Bass	14	59	4.2	0
Saimes	12	41	3.4	0
Brown	6	18	3.0	1
Lamonica	9	8	0.9	0
Crow	6	6	1.0	0

RECEIVING

Last Name	No.	Yds	Avg	TD
Miller	69	860	12	3
Dubenion	55	974	18	4
Warlick	24	479	20	1
Gilchrist	24	211	9	2
Rutkowski	19	264	14	1
Ferguson	9	181	20	3
Bass	9	153	17	1
Saimes	6	12	2	0
Crow	5	69	14	0
Kochman	4	148	37	1
Brown	2	7	4	0
Stratton	1	19	19	0
Carlton	1	9	9	0

PUNT RETURNS

Last Name	No.	Yds	Avg	TD
Abruzzese	17	152	9	0
West	11	86	8	0
Rutkowski	8	67	8	0
Kochman	1	11	11	0

KICKOFF RETURNS

Last Name	No.	Yds	Avg	TD
Rutkowski	13	396	30	0
Dubenion	13	333	26	0
Saimes	7	140	20	0
Abruzzese	6	118	20	0
West	6	56	9	0
Brown	2	40	20	0
Tracey	1	21	21	0
Rivera	1	20	20	0
Murdock	1	17	17	0
Barber	1	9	9	0
Paterra	1	0	0	0
Matuszak	1	17	17	0

PASSING – PUNTING – KICKING

PASSING	Att	Comp	%	Yds	Yd/Att	TD	Int–%	RK
Kemp	384	194	51	2914	7.5	13	20– 5	4
Lamonica	71	33	46	437	6.1	3	4– 6	
Gilchrist	1	1	100	35	35.0	0	0– 0	
Rutkowski	1	0	0	0	0.0	0	0– 0	

PUNTING	No	Avg
Lamonica	51	40.6
Crow	10	42.4

KICKING	XP	Att	%	FG	Att	%
Yoho	32	37	86	10	23	43

2 POINT XP
Lamonica
Tracey

HOUSTON OILERS

RUSHING

Last Name	No.	Yds	Avg	TD
Tolar	194	659	3.4	3
Tobin	75	270	3.6	4
Smith	50	202	4.0	3
Cannon	13	45	3.4	0
Norton	1	15	15.0	0
Lee	2	9	4.5	0
Babb	1	7	7.0	0
Blanda	4	1	0.2	0

RECEIVING

Last Name	No.	Yds	Avg	TD
Hennigan	61	1051	17	10
Dewveall	58	752	13	7
Tolar	41	275	7	0
McLeod	33	530	16	5
Smith	24	270	11	2
Frazier	16	269	17	1
Tobin	13	272	13	1
Kerbow	5	61	12	0
Cannon	5	39	8	0

PUNT RETURNS

Last Name	No.	Yds	Avg	TD
Glick	19	171	9	0
Jancik	13	145	11	0
Norton	4	23	6	0

KICKOFF RETURNS

Last Name	No.	Yds	Avg	TD
Jancik	**45**	**1317**	**29**	0
Glick	20	451	23	0
Cannon	2	39	20	0
Tobin	1	10	10	0
Tolar	1	4	4	0

PASSING – PUNTING – KICKING

PASSING	Att	Comp	%	Yds	Yd/Att	TD	Int–%	RK
Blanda	**423**	**224**	53	**3003**	7.0	24	25– 6	4
Lee	75	37	49	475	6.3	2	8–11	
Smith	2	0	0	0	0.0	0	0– 0	
Cannon	1	0	0	0	0.0	0	0– 0	

PUNTING	No	Avg
Norton	65	42.9

KICKING	XP	Att	%	FG	Att	%
Blanda	37	37	100	9	22	41

2 POINT XP
Tobin

NEW YORK JETS

RUSHING

Last Name	No.	Yds	Avg	TD
Smolinski	150	561	3.7	4
Mathis	107	268	2.5	1
Christy	26	88	3.4	1
Hall	9	24	2.7	1
D. Wood	7	17	2.4	1
Perkins	3	8	2.6	0
Maynard	2	6	3.0	0
Johnson	2	6	3.0	0

RECEIVING

Last Name	No.	Yds	Avg	TD
Turner	71	1007	14	6
Maynard	38	780	21	9
Smolinski	34	278	8	1
Mackey	23	263	11	3
Mathis	18	177	10	1
Gregory	9	90	10	0
Heeter	8	160	20	1
Christy	8	73	9	0

PUNT RETURNS

Last Name	No.	Yds	Avg	TD
Baird	4	143	36	1
Christy	9	46	5	0
Starks	3	7	2	0
Maynard	1	6	6	0

KICKOFF RETURNS

Last Name	No.	Yds	Avg	TD
Christy	24	585	24	0
Starks	19	336	18	0
Turner	14	299	21	0
Stricker	4	90	23	0
Johnson	6	77	13	0
Perkins	4	55	14	0
Mathis	1	11	11	0
Smolinski	1	10	10	0
Mackey	1	0	0	0

PASSING – PUNTING – KICKING

PASSING	Att	Comp	%	Yds	Yd/Att	TD	Int–%	RK
D. Wood	351	160	46	2202	6.3	18	18– 5	6
Hall	118	45	38	611	5.2	3	9– 8	
Green	6	2	33	10	1.7	0	1– 17	
Chlebek	4	2	50	5	1.3	0	0– 0	
Mathis	1	0	0	0	0.0	0	1–100	

PUNTING	No	Avg
Johnson	71	42.6

KICKING	XP	Att	%	FG	Att	%
Guesman	30	30	100	9	24	31

1963 A.F.L. — Western Division

SAN DIEGO CHARGERS 11-3-0 Sid Gillman

Scores of Each Game		
14	BUFFALO	10
17	BOSTON	14
24	KANSAS CITY	10
34	Denver	50
24	NEW YORK	20
38	Kansas City	17
33	OAKLAND	34
53	New York	7
7	Boston	6
23	Buffalo	13
27	HOUSTON	0
27	Oakland	41
20	Houston	14
58	DENVER	20

Use Name	Pos.	Hgt	Wgt	Age	Int	Pts
Ron Mix	OT	6'4"	250	25		
Ernie Park	OT	6'3"	240	21		
Ernie Wright	OT	6'4"	265	22		
Sam DeLuca	OG	6'2"	242	27		
Sam Gruneisen	OG	6'1"	252	22		
Pat Shea	OG	6'1"	243	24		
Walt Sweeney	OG	6'3"	260	22		
Don Rogers	C	6'2"	245	26		
Earl Faison	DE	6'5"	262	24		2
Bob Petrich	DE	6'4"	252	22		
George Gross	DT	6'3"	260	22		
Ernie Ladd	DT	6'9"	321	24		
Henry Schmidt	DT	6'4"	254	26		
Chuck Allen	LB	6'1"	225	23	5	6
Frank Buncom	LB	6'1"	235	23		
Emil Karas	LB	6'3"	235	29	2	
Bobby Layne	LB	6'2"	222	23		
Paul Maguire	LB	6'	225	25	4	
Bob Mitinger	LB	6'2"	235	23	3	
George Blair	DB	5'11"	195	25	1	95
Gary Glick	DB	6'2"	200	32	1	
Dick Harris	DB	5'11"	187	26	8	6
Charley McNeil	DB	5'11"	180	27	4	
Dick Westmoreland	DB	6'1"	180	22		
Bud Whitehead	DB	6'	185	24	1	
Keith Kinderman	FB-DB	6'	208	23		
John Hadl	QB	6'2"	205	23		
Tobin Rote	QB	6'3"	220	35		12
Paul Lowe	HB	6'	205	26		60
Bobby Jackson	FB	6'3"	238	23		24
Keith Lincoln	FB	6'2"	212	24		48
Gerry McDougall	FB	6'2"	225	28		6
Lance Alworth	FL	6'	185	23		66
Reg Carolan	OE	6'6"	235	23		
Dave Kocourek	OE	6'5"	245	26		32
Jacque MacKinnon	OE	6'4"	250	24		24
Don Norton	OE	6'1"	195	25		6
Jerry Robinson	OE	5'11"	190	24		12

OAKLAND RAIDERS 10-4-0 Al Davis

Scores of Each Game		
24	Houston	19
35	BUFFALO	17
14	BOSTON	20
7	New York	10
0	Buffalo	12
14	Boston	20
49	NEW YORK	26
34	San Diego	33
10	KANSAS CITY	7
22	Kansas City	7
26	Denver	10
41	SAN DIEGO	27
35	DENVER	31
52	HOUSTON	49

Use Name	Pos.	Hgt	Wgt	Age	Int	Pts
Proverb Jacobs	OT	6'4"	260	28		
Dick Klein	OT	6'4"	255	29		
Frank Youso	OT	6'4"	255	27		
Sonny Bishop	OG	6'2"	240	23		
Wayne Hawkins	OG	6'	240	25		
Ollie Spencer	OG	6'2"	240	32		
Bob Mischak	OE-OG	6'	240	30		
Jim Otto	C	6'2"	240	25		
Dalva Allen	DE	6'5"	240	27		
Dan Birdwell	DE	6'4"	240	22		
Jon Jelacic	DE	6'3"	255	26	1	12
Dave Costa	DT	6'3"	245	21		
Chuck McMurtry	DT	6'	270	25		
Jim Norris	DT	6'4"	235	23		
Bob Dougherty	LB	6'	240	29		
Archie Matsos	LB	6'	212	28	4	
Clancy Osborne	LB	6'3"	218	28	2	
Charley Rieves	LB	5'11"	218	24		
Jackie Simpson	LB	6'1"	225	26	2	
Claude Gibson	DB	6'1"	190	24	3	12
Joe Krakoski	DB	6'2"	195	26	4	
Jim McMillin	DB	5'11"	190	25	4	6
Tom Morrow	DB	5'11"	187	25	9	
Warren Powers	DB	6'	188	22		
Fred Williamson	DB	6'2"	215	25	6	
Herm Urenda	OE-DB	5'11"	170	23		
Cotton Devidson	QB	6'1"	180	30		24
Tom Flores	QB	6'1"	196	26		
Clem Daniels	HB	6'1"	220	26		48
Mike Somner	HB	5'11"	192	28		
Doug Mayberry	FB	6'1"	220	26		
Alan Miller	FB	6'	205	25		30
Glen Shaw	FB	6'1"	225	24		12
Bo Roberson	HB-FL	6'1"	197	28		18
Jan Barrett (from GB-N)	OE	6'3"	230	22		
Dobie Craig	OE	6'4"	200	24		12
Ken Herock	OE	6'2"	230	22		18
Art Powell	OE	6'3"	212	26		96
Mike Mercer	K	6'	200	27		71

KANSAS CITY CHIEFS 5-7-2 Hank Stram

Scores of Each Game		
59	Denver	7
27	Buffalo	27
10	San Diego	24
28	HOUSTON	7
26	BUFFALO	35
17	SAN DIEGO	38
7	Houston	28
7	Oakland	10
7	OAKLAND	22
24	Boston	24
0	New York	17
52	DENVER	21
35	BOSTON	3
48	NEW YORK	0

Use Name	Pos.	Hgt	Wgt	Age	Int	Pts
Charley Diamond	OT	6'2"	262	27		
Dave Hill	OT	6'5"	255	22		
Jim Tyrer	OT	6'6"	290	24		
Denny Biodrowski	OG	6'1"	255	23		
Ed Budde	OG	6'5"	260	22		
Bill Diamond	OG	6'	240	23		
Al Reynolds	OG	6'3"	235	25		
Marvin Terrell	OG	6'1"	240	25		
Jon Gilliam	C	6'2"	240	24		
Mel Branch	DE	6'2"	230	26		
Jerry Mays	DE	6'4"	247	23		6
Curt Merz	OG-DE	6'4"	250	25		
Buck Buchanan	DT	6'7"	276	23		
Curt Farrier	DT	6'6"	270	22		
Paul Rochester (to NY)	DT	6'2"	260	26		
Bobby Bell	LB	6'4"	228	23	1	
Walt Corey	LB	6'	220	25		
Sherrill Headrick	LB	6'2"	215	26	2	6
Smokey Stover	LB	6'	235	24		
E. J. Holub	C-LB	6'4"	225	25	5	
Dave Grayson	DB	5'10"	184	24	5	6
Bobby Hunt	DB	6'1"	180	23	6	
Bobby Ply	DB	6'1"	190	22		
Johnny Robinson	DB	6'	195	24	3	
Charley Warner	DB	5'11"	180	23	1	
Duane Wood	DB	6'1"	200	27	3	6
Len Dawson	QB	6'	190	29		12
Eddie Wilson	QB	6'	190	23		
Bert Coan	HB	6'4"	220	23		
Abner Haynes	HB	6'	190	25		36
Jerrel Wilson	LB-HB	6'4"	225	22		
Curtis McClinton	FB	6'3"	232	24		36
Jack Spikes	FB	6'2"	220	25		47
Frank Jackson	FL	6'1"	190	23		54
Fred Arbanas	OE	6'3"	240	24		36
Tommy Brooker	OE	6'2"	230	23		38
Chris Burford	OE	6'3"	210	25		56
Dick Johnson	OE	6'4"	220	24		6

DENVER BRONCOS 2-11-1 Jack Faulkner

Scores of Each Game		
7	KANSAS CITY	59
14	Houston	20
14	BOSTON	10
50	SAN DIEGO	34
24	HOUSTON	33
21	Boston	40
35	New York	35
28	BUFFALO	30
17	Buffalo	27
9	NEW YORK	14
10	OAKLAND	26
21	Kansas City	52
31	Oakland	35
20	San Diego	58

Use Name	Pos.	Hgt	Wgt	Age	Int	Pts
Eldon Danenhauer	OT	6'4"	245	27		
Harold Olson	OT	6'3"	255	24		
Jim Perkins	OT	6'5"	250	24		
Ernie Barnes	OG	6'3"	243	24		
Bob McCullough	OG	6'2"	245	22		
Tom Nomina	OG	6'5"	270	21		
Frank Jackunas	C	6'3"	225	22		
Jerry Sturm	C	6'3"	245	26		
Chuck Gavin	DE	6'1"	250	29		
Ray Jacobs	DE	6'3"	275	23		
Ike Lassiter	DE	6'5"	270	22		
Ron Nery (to HOU)	DE	6'6"	244	28		
Gordy Holz	DT	6'4"	260	29	1	
Bud McFadin	DT	6'3"	280	35		6
Anton Peters	DT	6'3"	250	21		
Tom Erlandson	LB	6'3"	235	23		
Jim Fraser	LB	6'3"	236	27		
Jerry Hopkins	LB	6'2"	235	22	1	
Wahoo McDaniel	LB	6'	238	26	2	
John Nocera	LB	6'1"	230	29		
Leon Simmons	LB	6'	225	24		
Willie Brown	DB	6'1"	190	22	1	
Goose Gonsoulin	DB	6'3"	210	25	6	6
Tom Janik	DB	6'3"	200	22	2	
John McGeever	DB	6'1"	195	24		
John Sklopan	DB	5'11"	190	22		
Bruce Starling	DB	6'1"	186	21		
Bob Zeman	DB	6'1"	203	26	1	
Don Breaux	QB	6'1"	205	23		
John McCormick	QB	6'1"	210	26		
Mickey Slaughter	QB	6'	190	21		6
Frank Tripucka	QB	6'2"	208	35		
Hewritt Dixon	HB	6'2"	215	23		12
Bob Gaiters	HB	5'11"	210	25		6
Gene Mingo	HB	6'1"	200	24		83
Donnie Stone	HB	6'2"	205	26		24
Clarence Walker	HB	6'1"	205	24		
Charley Mitchell	DB-HB	5'11"	185	23	1	6
Bo Dickinson (to HOU)	FB	6'2"	220	28		6
Billy Joe	FB	6'2"	250	22		30
Don Coffey	FL	6'3"	190	23		
Al Frazier	FL	5'11"	180	28		
Bill Groman	FL	6'	190	27		18
Bob Scarpitto	FL	5'11"	196	24		30
Gene Prebola	OE	6'3"	225	25		14
Tom Rychlec	OE	6'3"	225	29		
Lionel Taylor	OE	6'2"	215	27		60

SAN DIEGO CHARGERS

RUSHING

Last Name	No.	Yds	Avg	TD
Lowe	177	1010	5.7	8
Lincoln	128	826	6.5	5
McDougall	38	199	5.2	1
Jackson	18	64	3.6	4
Rote	24	62	2.6	2
Hadl	8	26	3.3	0
Alworth	2	14	7.0	0

RECEIVING

Last Name	No.	Yds	Avg	TD
Alworth	61	1206	20	11
Lowe	26	191	7	2
Lincoln	24	325	14	3
Kocourek	23	359	16	5
Norton	21	281	13	1
Robinson	18	315	18	1
MacKinnon	11	262	24	4
McDougall	10	115	12	0
Jackson	8	85	11	0

PUNT RETURNS

Last Name	No.	Yds	Avg	TD
Alworth	11	120	11	0
Lincoln	7	98	14	0
Harris	4	43	11	0

KICKOFF RETURNS

Last Name	No.	Yds	Avg	TD
Lincoln	17	439	26	0
Alworth	10	216	22	0
Westmoreland	10	204	20	0
Lowe	5	132	26	0
McDougall	3	77	26	0
Harris	2	34	17	0
Robinson	2	27	14	0
Sweeney	1	18	18	0
Jackson	1	16	16	0
Maguire	1	5	5	0

PASSING – PUNTING – KICKING

PASSING	Att	Comp.	%	Yds	Yd/Att	TD	Int–%	RK
Rote	286	170	59	2510	8.7	20	17– 6	1
Hadl	65	28	43	502	7.7	6	6– 9	
Lowe	4	2	50	100	25.0	1	1– 25	
Lincoln	1	0	0	0	0.0	0	0– 0	
McDougall	1	1	100	11	11.0	1	0– 0	
Norton	1	1	100	15	15.0	0	0– 0	

PUNTING	No	Avg.
Maguire	58	38.6
Hadl	2	37.5

KICKING	XP	Att	%	FG	Att	%
Blair	44	48	92	17	27	63

2 POINT XP
Faison
Kocourek

OAKLAND RAIDERS

RUSHING

Last Name	No.	Yds	Avg	TD
Daniels	214	1099	5.1	3
Miller	62	270	4.4	3
Davidson	26	115	4.4	4
Roberson	19	47	2.2	0
Shaw	20	46	2.3	1
Sommer	5	21	4.2	0
Flores	11	2	0.2	0
Mercer	1	–5	–5.0	0

RECEIVING

Last Name	No.	Yds	Avg	TD
Powell	73	1304	18	16
Miller	34	404	12	2
Daniels	30	685	23	5
Roberson	25	407	16	3
Herock	15	269	18	2
Craig	7	205	29	2
Shaw	2	64	32	1
Mischak	2	25	13	0
Sommer	1	24	24	0
Barrett	1	9	9	0

PUNT RETURNS

Last Name	No.	Yds	Avg	TD
Gibson	26	307	12	2
Sommer	4	44	11	0
Roberson	2	34	17	0
Krakoski	4	10	3	0

KICKOFF RETURNS

Last Name	No.	Yds	Avg	TD
Roberson	38	809	21	0
Sommer	5	102	20	0
McMillin	1	23	23	0
Shaw	2	19	10	0
Simpson	1	11	11	0
Gibson	2	10	5	0
Klein	1	7	7	0
Birdwell	1	7	7	0
Herock	1	3	3	0

PASSING – PUNTING – KICKING

PASSING	Att	Comp	%	Yds	Yd/Att	TD	Int–%	RK
Flores	247	113	46	2101	8.5	20	13– 5	2
Davidson	194	77	40	1276	6.5	11	10– 5	8
Daniels	1	1	100	10	10.0	0	0– 0	

PUNTING	No	Avg
Mercer	75	40.0

KICKING	XP	Att	%	FG	Att	%
Mercer	47	47	100	8	21	38

KANSAS CITY CHIEFS

RUSHING

Last Name	No.	Yds	Avg	TD
McClinton	142	568	4.0	3
Haynes	99	352	3.6	4
Dawson	37	272	7.4	2
Spikes	84	257	3.1	2
Coan	17	100	5.9	0
Jackson	3	52	17.3	1
E. Wilson	8	45	5.6	0
J. Wilson	9	41	4.6	0
Burford	1	10	10.0	0

RECEIVING

Last Name	No.	Yds	Avg	TD
Burford	68	824	12	9
Jackson	50	785	16	8
Arbanas	34	373	11	6
Haynes	33	470	14	2
McClinton	27	301	11	3
Spikes	11	125	11	1
Coan	2	35	18	0
Brooker	2	32	16	0
J. Wilson	2	21	11	0
Johnson	2	17	9	1

PUNT RETURNS

Last Name	No.	Yds	Avg	TD
Jackson	11	95	9	0
Haynes	6	57	10	0
Grayson	2	39	20	0
Warner	4	25	6	0
Wood	1	18	18	0
Robinson	1	16	16	0
Headrick	1	9	9	0

KICKOFF RETURNS

Last Name	No.	Yds	Avg	TD
Grayson	20	570	29	1
Haynes	12	317	26	0
Warner	9	215	24	0
Jackson	1	20	20	0
J. Wilson	1	20	20	0
Stover	2	18	9	0
Spikes	2	12	6	0

PASSING – PUNTING – KICKING

PASSING	Att	Comp	%	Yds	Yd/Att	TD	Int–%	RK
Dawson	352	190	54	2389	6.7	26	19– 5	3
E. Wilson	82	39	48	537	6.5	3	2– 2	
Haynes	2	1	50	24	12.0	0	0– 0	
McClinton	2	1	50	33	16.5	1	0– 0	
Spikes	1	0	0	0	0.0	0	1–100	

PUNTING	No	Avg
J. Wilson	60	43.8
E. Wilson	1	43.0

KICKING	XP	Att	%	FG	Att	%
Spikes	23	24	96	2	13	15
Brooker	20	20	100	6	15	40

2 POINT XP
Burford

DENVER BRONCOS

RUSHING

Last Name	No.	Yds	Avg	TD
Joe	154	649	4.2	4
Stone	96	382	3.9	3
Slaughter	32	124	3.9	1
Dixon	23	105	4.5	2
Mingo	24	90	3.7	0
Breaux	10	51	5.1	0
Mitchell	23	45	2.0	0
Dickinson	6	32	5.3	0
Gaiters	9	20	2.2	0
Walker	2	14	7.0	0
Barnes	0	2	0.0	0
McCormick	3	–5	–1.7	0

RECEIVING

Last Name	No.	Yds	Avg	TD
Taylor	78	1101	14	10
Prebola	30	471	16	2
Groman	27	437	16	3
Stone	22	208	9	1
Scarpitto	21	463	22	5
Joe	15	90	6	1
Dixon	10	132	13	0
Mitchell	8	71	9	0
Dickinson	6	57	10	0
Mingo	3	11	4	0
Gaiters	1	74	74	1
Rychlec	1	9	9	0

PUNT RETURNS

Last Name	No.	Yds	Avg	TD
Mitchell	12	141	12	0
Mingo	7	85	12	0
Dixon	3	58	19	0
Frazier	3	42	14	0
Zeman	2	32	16	0
Brown	3	29	10	0

KICKOFF RETURNS

Last Name	No.	Yds	Avg	TD
Mitchell	37	954	26	1
Gaiters	11	225	20	0
Dixon	9	195	22	0
Frazier	7	185	24	0
Mingo	7	151	22	0
Brown	3	70	23	0
Scarpitto	1	8	8	0
Olson	2	0	0	0
Fraser	1	0	0	0
Groman	0	9	0	0
Gonsoulin	0	4	0	0

PASSING – PUNTING – KICKING

PASSING	Att	Comp	%	Yds	Yd/Att	TD	Int–%	RK
Slaughter	223	112	50	1689	7.5	12	14– 6	7
Breaux	138	70	51	935	6.7	7	6– 4	
McCormick	72	28	39	417	5.7	4	3– 4	
Tripucka	15	7	47	31	2.1	0	5– 33	
Stone	3	0	0	0	0.0	0	0– 0	
Mingo	1	0	0	0	0.0	0	0– 0	
Taylor	1	0	0	0	0.0	0	0– 0	

PUNTING	No	Avg
Fraser	78	46.1

KICKING	XP	Att	%	FG	Att	%
Mingo	35	35	100	16	30	53

2 POINT XP
Prebola

1964 N.F.L. A Blue-Chip Business

The war between the leagues was going nicely for the NFL, as all but two NFL teams made a profit during 1964. Only St. Louis and Dallas lost money, and neither had the excuse of direct AFL competition. Franchises now were blue-chip investments, with price tags well into the millions of dollars. Two of the franchises changed hands this year: William Clay Ford purchased the Detroit Lions and Jerry Wolman headed a syndicate that bought the Philadelphia Eagles. The leagues were still at war, but the NFL owners worried very little at this point.

EASTERN CONFERENCE

Cleveland Browns—The Browns added a little variety to their attack to win their first conference title since 1957. Jimmy Brown still was the ultimate runner, but he got some help in the ball-carrying department from halfback Ernie Green. For the first time in years the Browns also launched a dangerous passing game, with Gary Collins and rookie Paul Warfield providing quarterback Frank Ryan with two fine receivers. Led by tackle Dick Schafrath, the offensive line both cleared paths for the runners and protected quarterback Ryan with equal expertise. The defense had problems defending against the pass, but ex-Giant Dick Modzelewski made the line very tough against the run.

St. Louis Cardinals—Coach Wally Lemm put together a marvelously balanced team, only to have it fall apart on three embarrassing occasions. In a four-week span in mid-season, the Cards lost 47-27 to Baltimore, dropped a 31-13 decision to Dallas, and were beaten 34-17 by the collapsing New York Giants. But before and after this cold spell, the Cardinals showed a versatile offense and spirited defense. Quarterback Charley Johnson had a propensity for throwing interceptions, but he usually made up for his errant tosses with long gainers. The strong offensive line cleared the way for runners John David Crow, Joe Childress, and Willie Crenshaw, while the defense combined a small but quick line with steady linebackers and an aggressive secondary featuring Pat Fischer and Larry Wilson.

Washington Redskins—Quarterback Sonny Jurgensen, obtained in a trade with the Eagles, had few peers as a passer, and receivers Bobby Mitchell, Angelo Coia, and Preston Carpenter gave him an abundance of open receivers. Rookie halfback Charley Taylor injected speed into the running attack. But the Washington offense also had a big hole at fullback and a spotty front line of blockers, making it difficult for Jurgensen, Taylor, and Mitchell to shine their brightest. Even with a defense bolstered by ex-Giant Sam Huff and rookie Paul Krause, the Redskins lost their first four games with poor offensive performances. But after rookies Len Hauss and George Seals were thrust into the offensive line, the Skins revived and won six of their next eight games.

Philadelphia Eagles—Joe Kuharich signed a fifteen-year contract as coach and general manager and immediately dived into the trading market to rebuild the Eagles. In a blinding series of deals, he obtained Norm Snead from Washington, Earl Gros and Jim Ringo from Green Bay, Ollie Matson and Floyd Peters from Detroit, Sam Baker from Dallas, and Ray Poage and Don Hultz from Minnesota. Add three good rookies in Bob Brown, Mike Morgan, and Joe Scarpati, and solid holdovers like Pete Retzlaff, Maxie Baughan, Don Burroughs, and Irv Cross, and the Eagles had the makings of a good football team.

Dallas Cowboys—Even after the Cowboys obtained star wide receivers Tommy McDonald and Buddy Dial, the offense had problems scoring points. One cause of the trouble was Don Meredith's leg injury, which had him hobbling through a sub-par season, and another was the erratic kicking of rookie Dick Van Raaphorst. Given the field-goal kicking job after Sam Baker was dealt to Philadelphia, Van Raaphorst cost the Cowboys several games by blowing easy kicks. Although Don Perkins and Frank Clarke kept up their good work, the Dallas offense fell off from its 1963 performance. The defense, however, suddenly blended together into a strong unit.

Pittsburgh Steelers—Coach Buddy Parker had an intricate plan to improve the Steelers this year. He drafted University of Pittsburgh star Paul Martha as a flanker, and then traded incumbent flanker Buddy Dial to Dallas for the draft rights to All-American defensive lineman Scott Appleton from the University of Texas. The whole maneuver failed miserably when Appleton signed with the AFL Houston Oilers, and Martha was a king-sized bust as a pass receiver. Rookies Ben McGee and Chuck Hinton took up the slack in the defensive line, but no one could fill Dial's vacated receiver spot opposite Gary Ballman.

New York Giants—The New York dynasty crashed heavily to pieces this season. Coach Allie Sherman had traded off Sam Huff and Dick Modzelewski during the off season, hoping to fill their spots with younger men, but none of the replacements came close to the steadiness of the two departed defenders. To add to Sherman's headaches, veterans Y. A. Tittle, Alex Webster, Frank Gifford, Del Shofner, Jack Stroud, and Andy Robustelli all showed signs of advanced old age.

WESTERN CONFERENCE

Baltimore Colts—Coach Don Shula had tried to trade Lenny Moore all summer but had found no takers. Moore had lost his halfback job to Tom Matte and was coming off two injury-plagued seasons which cut his market value down to nothing. Once the regular season started, though, Moore won back his job and set a new NFL record with twenty touchdowns. Moore, Tony Lorick, and Jerry Hill provided tough running, and the Baltimore passing attack was even more effective than usual. The defense responded to the offensive improvement by playing better than anyone could expect, with veterans Gino Marchetti, Bill Pellington, and Bob Boyd the core around which a group of average defenders clustered into a solid unit. With a proper mixture of veterans and youngsters, the Colts captured the conference crown.

Green Bay Packers—Paul Hornung rejoined the Packers after his year's suspension but left his kicking eye behind. The Pack lost three games because of easy kicks Hornung missed, such as the 21-20 loss to the Colts in which Hornung missed an extra point. Outside of this one serious flaw, the Packers still were a solid, precise football team. Bart Starr and Jim Taylor starred in the backfield, and the offensive line graded out well despite the trading of Jim Ringo to Philadelphia and the loss of Jerry Kramer to stomach surgery. No one moved the ball easily against the Green Bay defense, which boasted of four All-Pros in Willie Davis, Henry Jordan, Ray Nitschke, and Willie Wood.

Minnesota Vikings—With three straight wins to end the year, the Vikings jumped up into a second-place tie in the West with the Packers. The Vikings had caught up with Green Bay after only four years in existence, and the main stepladder to progress was the Minnesota offense. At quarterback the Vikings had Fran Tarkenton, the original and best scrambler in the league. The halfback was Tommy Mason, the team's breakaway threat, and the fullback was Bill Brown, a squat young man equally adept at running, receiving, and blocking. The offensive line was not spectacular but good enough to allow the backs to star, while the Minnesota defense was making slower but sure progress.

Detroit Lions—Age was cutting heavily into the vaunted Detroit defense. Night Train Lane was thirty-six and bothered by a bad knee, Yale Lary was thirty-three, Joe Schmidt was thirty-two with a bad shoulder, and Sam Williams was thirty-three. When all these veterans could play at top form, the Lion defense still was one of the league's best, but the days where one or more of them had to sit the game out were growing more frequent. The offense was still a rather plodding unit, with flanker Terry Barr the only speedster on the attack. With neither Milt Plum nor Earl Morrall able to take over at quarterback, the offense was far from ready to pick up the slack left by the aging defense.

Los Angeles Rams—Despite a late-season slump which saw them go winless in their last five games, the Rams developed two solid lines this year. The offensive line of Joe Wendryhoski, Joe Scibelli, Don Chuy, Joe Carollo, and Frank Varricheone was quietly efficient, while the defensive front four of Deacon Jones, Merlin Olsen, Roosevelt Grier, and Lamar Lundy won attention for their speed and violence. The backfields were less settled, as two rookies started in the defensive secondary and three freshman won jobs in the offensive backfield. Bucky Pope surprised everyone with his deep pass receiving as a flanker, and Les Josephson filled in well for the sore-kneed Dick Bass. Rookie Bill Munson won the quarterback job, giving the Rams a second good young quarterback to go along with Roman Gabriel.

Chicago Bears—The Chicago offense had been nothing to write home about last year, but when injuries cut the marvelous defense down to life size, the Bears plummeted into the depths of the Western Conference. When the Bears lost three of their first four games, one of them to the Colts by 52-0, hopes for a repeat championship fluttered away. To get some additional punch from the offense, which had been crippled by the pre-season deaths of Willie Galimore and Bo Farrington in an auto accident, coach George Halas used strong-armed Rudy Bukich more often at quarterback and geared his attack around passes to Johnny Morris and Mike Ditka. Although the passes were successful often enough to place Morris and Ditka one-two in the league receiving statistics and to give Morris a new NFL season's record of ninety-three receptions, the Bear season was a huge disappointment.

San Francisco '49ers—When all their running backs were knocked out with injuries, the '49ers couldn't find enough offensive dynamite in the rest of the lineup to ignite the attack. Although Bernie Casey, Monte Stickles, and rookie Dave Parks were a fine trio of receivers, quarterback John Brodie was not a great enough passer to overcome the lack of any ground attack. The defense gave up no easy yardage, with Charlie Krueger, Clark Miller, Matt Hazeltine, rookie Dave Wilcox, and converted flanker Jim Johnson the main ribs of the unit.

FINAL TEAM STATISTICS

OFFENSE

	BALT.	CHI.	CLEVE.	DALLAS	DET.	G.BAY	L.A.	MINN.	N.Y.	PHIL.	PITT.	ST.L.	S.F.	WASH.
FIRST DOWNS:														
Total	245	248	255	230	221	250	208	258	240	243	233	**275**	233	193
by Rushing	100	83	119	89	87	**133**	78	124	81	100	110	95	76	70
by Passing	129	141	118	119	115	106	104	115	140	126	105	**152**	136	116
by Penalty	16	24	18	22	19	11	26	19	19	17	18	**28**	21	7
RUSHING:														
Number	456	356	435	421	412	495	400	**519**	435	430	516	456	383	366
Yards	2007	1166	2163	1691	1414	**2276**	1629	2183	1404	1922	2102	1770	1332	1237
Average Yards	4.4	3.3	**5.0**	4.0	3.4	4.6	4.1	4.2	3.2	4.5	4.1	3.9	3.5	3.4
Touchdowns	**29**	5	14	15	7	23	11	14	12	16	14	12	11	11
PASSING:														
Attempts	345	**494**	344	404	386	321	368	326	431	397	323	422	461	415
Completions	176	**282**	181	192	206	186	173	179	217	199	141	223	225	214
Completion Pct.	51.0	57.1	52.6	47.5	53.4	**57.9**	47.0	54.9	50.3	50.1	43.7	52.8	48.8	51.6
Passing Yards	3045	3056	2542	2516	2890	2474	2769	2614	2848	2746	2308	3045	2990	**3071**
Avg. Yds per Att.	**8.8**	6.2	7.4	6.2	7.5	7.7	7.5	8.0	6.6	6.9	7.2	7.2	6.5	7.4
Avg. Yds per Comp.	**17.3**	10.8	14.0	13.1	14.0	13.3	16.0	14.6	13.1	13.8	16.4	13.7	13.3	14.4
Times Tackled	39	30	28	68	37	47	65	48	45	35	51	37	**27**	44
Yards Lost Tackled	273	**215**	219	503	332	369	490	491	373	268	450	298	249	350
Net Yards	2772	**2841**	2323	2013	2558	2105	2279	2123	2475	2478	1858	2747	2741	2721
Touchdowns	22	25	**28**	10	23	16	18	23	16	19	14	21	18	25
Interceptions	9	21	19	24	21	**6**	20	12	26	18	24	24	22	16
Pct. Intercepted	2.6	4.3	5.5	5.9	5.4	**1.9**	5.4	3.7	6.0	4.5	7.4	5.7	4.8	3.9
PUNTING:														
Number	59	71	49	78	68	56	82	72	74	73	62	56	79	**91**
Average Distance	41.8	44.5	41.9	38.9	45.7	42.2	44.1	**46.4**	45.4	41.7	43.2	40.9	45.6	41.2
PUNT RETURNS:														
Number	**48**	30	20	40	35	34	34	35	28	28	30	24	43	32
Yards	453	219	303	**459**	411	443	181	306	193	201	238	251	322	230
Average Yards	9.4	7.3	**15.2**	11.5	11.7	13.0	5.3	8.7	6.9	7.2	7.9	10.5	7.5	7.2
Touchdowns	0	0	1	1	**2**	1	0	0	0	0	0	1	1	0
KICKOFF RETURNS:														
Number	39	58	57	46	57	45	56	53	**67**	59	56	63	57	52
Yards	926	1314	1323	1102	1327	1160	1258	1130	**1688**	1365	1356	1424	1393	1097
Average Yards	23.7	22.7	23.2	24.0	23.3	**25.8**	22.5	21.3	25.2	23.1	24.2	22.6	24.4	21.1
Touchdowns	0	1	0	0	0	0	0	0	1	0	0	0	0	0
INTERCEPTION RETURNS:														
Number	23	10	19	18	22	16	17	19	15	17	12	25	15	**34**
Yards	366	258	444	316	267	263	**487**	224	179	272	96	388	155	317
Average Yards	15.9	25.8	23.4	17.6	12.1	16.4	**28.6**	11.8	11.9	16.0	8.0	15.5	10.3	9.3
Touchdowns	1	0	3	2	0	1	3	4	1	2	1	**5**	0	3
PENALTIES:														
Number	74	96	60	**97**	75	50	76	71	65	42	59	64	79	87
Yards	785	817	611	**952**	674	576	803	787	532	450	615	579	741	825
FUMBLES:														
Number	31	19	**15**	38	23	25	40	37	**44**	33	28	29	42	27
Number Lost	10	12	7	19	13	17	19	18	23	22	17	16	24	17
POINTS:														
Total	**428**	260	415	250	280	342	283	355	241	312	253	357	236	307
PAT Attempts	**54**	32	50	30	34	44	33	42	30	38	31	40	30	39
PAT Made	**53**	29	49	28	32	42	31	40	28	36	28	40	30	35
FG Attempts	35	23	33	29	25	**39**	24	33	20	26	25	38	25	28
FG Made	17	13	22	14	14	12	18	21	9	16	13	**25**	8	12
Pct. FG Made	48.6	56.5	66.7	48.3	56.0	30.8	**75.0**	63.6	45.0	61.5	52.0	65.8	32.0	42.9
Safeties	0	0	0	0	1	0	0	0	0	0	0	1	1	1

DEFENSE

	BALT.	CHI.	CLEVE.	DALLAS	DET.	G.BAY	L.A.	MINN.	N.Y.	PHIL.	PITT.	ST.L.	S.F.	WASH.
FIRST DOWNS:														
Total	242	248	275	211	241	**197**	235	216	247	234	253	235	255	243
by Rushing	93	99	119	**71**	92	95	92	94	101	93	109	96	90	101
by Passing	121	121	137	121	128	**91**	131	105	127	128	121	128	138	125
by Penalty	28	28	19	19	21	**11**	12	17	19	13	23	**11**	27	17
RUSHING:														
Number	422	436	465	439	429	417	419	**389**	468	445	454	414	443	440
Yards	1798	1863	2012	1504	1638	1532	**1501**	1616	1919	1746	1994	1800	1560	1813
Average Yards	4.3	4.3	4.3	**3.4**	3.8	3.7	3.6	4.2	4.1	3.9	4.4	4.0	3.5	4.1
Touchdowns	13	19	18	**6**	10	15	14	10	15	15	15	13	11	20
PASSING:														
Attempts	385	366	401	377	406	**318**	435	375	361	406	378	389	434	406
Completions	217	188	230	**172**	226	173	213	182	188	202	185	193	232	193
Completion Pct.	56.4	51.4	57.4	**45.6**	55.7	54.4	49.0	48.5	52.1	49.8	48.9	49.6	53.5	47.5
Passing Yards	2621	2897	2932	2571	2906	**1980**	3094	2993	2799	2950	2582	2848	3141	2600
Avg. Yds per Att.	6.8	7.9	7.3	6.8	7.2	**6.2**	7.1	8.0	7.8	7.3	6.8	7.3	7.2	6.4
Avg. Yds per Comp.	12.1	15.4	12.7	14.9	12.9	**11.4**	14.5	16.4	14.9	14.6	14.0	14.8	13.5	13.5
Times Tackled	**57**	30	28	45	50	45	49	36	44	47	42	42	43	43
Yards Lost Tackled	**489**	275	222	325	482	333	400	269	355	379	345	356	297	353
Net Yards	2132	2622	2710	2246	2424	**1647**	2694	2724	2444	2571	2237	2492	2844	2247
Touchdowns	14	27	18	22	14	**11**	27	23	28	18	16	21	23	16
Interceptions	23	10	19	18	22	16	17	19	15	17	12	25	15	**34**
Pct. Intercepted	6.0	2.7	4.7	4.8	5.4	5.0	3.9	5.1	4.2	4.2	3.2	6.4	3.5	**8.4**
PUNTING:														
Number	73	62	57	**80**	66	72	73	71	59	**80**	67	67	76	67
Average Distance	44.0	46.6	39.7	43.5	44.0	43.5	45.1	43.8	42.2	40.5	**39.5**	43.5	45.8	42.1
PUNT RETURNS:														
Number	25	35	20	**19**	33	31	43	30	40	35	24	26	50	50
Yards	175	436	183	**52**	243	397	360	247	559	333	172	151	540	362
Average Yards	7.0	12.5	15.3	**2.7**	7.4	12.8	8.4	8.2	14.0	9.5	7.2	5.8	10.8	7.2
Touchdowns	1	**0**	**0**	**0**	**0**	2	**0**	**0**	2	**0**	**0**	**0**	2	**0**
KICKOFF RETURNS:														
Number	70	47	75	50	48	60	58	57	45	55	40	63	**37**	60
Yards	1490	1183	1517	1090	1052	1320	1544	1324	990	1319	989	1663	**883**	1499
Average Yards	21.3	25.2	**20.2**	21.8	21.9	22.0	26.6	23.2	22.0	24.0	24.7	26.4	23.9	25.0
Touchdowns	**0**	**0**	**0**	**0**	**0**	**0**	**0**	2	**0**	**0**	**0**	**0**	**0**	**0**
INTERCEPTION RETURNS:														
Number	9	21	19	24	21	**6**	20	12	26	18	24	24	22	16
Yards	119	260	154	370	247	**58**	452	149	332	273	465	302	530	321
Average Yards	13.2	12.4	**8.1**	15.4	11.8	9.7	22.6	10.6	12.8	15.2	19.4	12.6	24.1	20.1
Touchdowns	**0**	1	**0**	4	3	**0**	2	**0**	2	3	6	**0**	2	3
PENALTIES:														
Number	59	**84**	64	75	83	56	70	70	75	71	81	71	76	60
Yards	641	743	643	781	**805**	521	675	708	674	748	706	695	783	624
FUMBLES:														
Number	28	32	30	26	29	34	28	32	**42**	27	24	24	33	**42**
Number Lost	18	20	21	20	8	**25**	13	16	18	12	14	14	14	21
POINTS:														
Total	**225**	379	293	289	260	245	339	296	399	313	315	331	330	305
PAT Attempts	**28**	47	36	34	29	30	44	36	49	40	39	36	40	39
PAT Made	**27**	46	32	32	29	29	42	33	46	40	36	34	39	36
FG Attempts	24	26	**23**	29	38	**23**	27	28	39	26	25	34	34	27
FG Made	**10**	17	15	17	19	12	11	13	19	11	15	27	17	11
Pct. FG Made	41.7	65.4	65.2	58.6	50.0	52.2	**40.7**	46.4	48.7	42.3	60.0	79.4	50.0	**40.7**
Safeties	**0**	**0**	**0**	1	**0**	**0**	**0**	1	1	**0**	**0**	**0**	**0**	1

1964 NFL CHAMPIONSHIP GAME
December 27, at Cleveland
(Attendance 79,544)

Whitewashing the Aerialists

The Colts came into the game as heavy favorites, but the Cleveland defense effectively shut off the famous Baltimore passing attack as the Browns themselves made several big plays through the air. Neither club scored in the first half, as quarterbacks Johnny Unitas and Frank Ryan both used conservative plays to feel out the enemy. Early in the third quarter, however, a 29-yard punt by Baltimore's Tom Gilburg gave the Browns good field position and led to Lou Groza's 43-yard field goal, which finally broke the scoreless deadlock. As soon as the Browns got the ball back, they sprang Jimmy Brown loose on a pitchout good for 46 yards; in short order, Ryan hit Gary Collins with an 18-yard scoring pass. Then, just before the end of the quarter, Ryan stunned the Colts by throwing a 42-yard bomb to Collins, which, along with the extra point, ran the score up to 17-0. The Colts, in a state of shock over this sudden Cleveland outburst, tried to fight their way back into the game but could make no headway against the charged-up Brown defense. The Browns added a nine-yard Groza field goal early in the final period to run their lead to 20-0, and Ryan threw a 51-yard scoring pass to Gary Collins, the third touchdown of the afternoon for the tall flanker, to make the final score a decisive 27-0 to give Cleveland their first championship since 1955.

TEAM STATISTICS

CLEVE.		BALT.
20	First Downs – Total	11
8	First Downs – Rushing	5
9	First Downs – Passing	4
3	First Downs – Penalty	2
3	Punts – Number	4
44.0	Punts – Average Distance	33.8
1	Punt Returns – Number	2
13	Punt Returns – Yards	18
2	Interception Returns – Number	1
10	Interception Returns – Yards	14
0	Fumbles – Number	2
0	Fumbles – Lost Ball	2
7	Penalties – Number	5
59	Yards Penalized	48
1	Giveaways	4
4	Takeaways	1
+3	Difference	–3

SCORING

CLEVELAND	0	0	17	10–27
BALTIMORE	0	0	0	0– 0

Third Quarter
Cle. Groza, 43 yard field goal
Cle. Collins, 18 yard pass from Ryan
PAT – Groza (kick)
Cle. Collins, 42 yard pass from Ryan
PAT – Groza (kick)

Fourth Quarter
Cle. Groza, 9 yard field goal
Cle. Collins, 51 yard pass from Ryan
PAT – Groza (kick)

INDIVIDUAL STATISTICS

CLEVELAND	No	Yds	Avg.	BALTIMORE	No	Yds	Avg.
RUSHING							
Brown	27	114	4.2	Moore	9	40	4.4
Green	10	29	2.9	Hill	9	31	3.4
Ryan	3	2	0.7	Unitas	6	30	5.0
Warfield	1	–3	–3.0	Boyd	1	–9	–9.0
	41	142	3.5		25	92	3.7
RECEIVING							
Collins	5	130	26.0	Berry	3	38	12.7
Brown	3	37	12.3	Lorick	3	18	6.0
Brewer	2	26	13.0	Orr	2	31	15.5
Warfield	1	13	13.0	Moore	2	4	2.0
	11	206	18.7	Mackey	1	2	2.0
				Hill	1	2	2.0
					12	95	7.9

PASSING

	Att	Comp	Comp Pct.	Yds	Int	Yds/ Att.	Yds/ Comp	Yards Lost Tackled
CLEVELAND								
Ryan	18	11	61.6	206	1	11.4	18.7	9
BALTIMORE								
Unitas	20	12	60.0	95	2	4.8	7.9	6

CLEVELAND BROWNS 10-3-1 Blanton Collier

Scores of Each Game		
27	Washington	13
33	ST. LOUIS	33
28	Philadelphia	20
27	DALLAS	6
7	PITTSBURGH	23
20	Dallas	16
42	NEW YORK	20
30	Pittsburgh	17
34	WASHINGTON	24
37	DETROIT	21
21	Green Bay	28
38	PHILADELPHIA	24
19	St. Louis	28
52	New York	20

Use Name	Pos.	Hgt	Wgt	Age	Int	Pts
John Brown	OT	6'2"	248	25		
Monte Clark	OT	6'6"	265	27		
Dick Schafrath	OT	6'3"	255	28		
Roger Shoals	OG-OT	6'4"	255	25		6
Gene Hickerson	OG	6'3"	248	29		
Dale Memmelaar	OG	6'2"	248	27		
John Wooten	OG	6'2"	250	29		
John Morrow	C	6'3"	248	31		
Bill Glass	DE	6'5"	255	28		
Paul Wiggin	DE	6'3"	245	30		6
Sid Williams	DE	6'2"	235	22		6
Mike Bundra (from MIN)	DT	6'3"	260	25		
Bob Gain	DT	6'3"	260	36		
Jim Kanicki	DT	6'4"	270	22		
Dick Modzelewski	DT	6'	260	33		
Frank Parker	DT	6'5"	255	24		
Ed Bettridge	LB	6'1"	235	24		
Vince Costello	LB	6'	228	32	2	
Galen Fiss	LB	6'	227	34	1	
Jim Houston	LB	6'2"	240	27	2	6
Mike Lucci	LB	6'2"	233	24		
Stan Sczurek	LB	5'11"	230	25		
Walter Beach	DB	6'	185	29	4	6
Larry Benz	DB	5'11"	185	23	4	
Lowell Caylor	DB	6'3"	205	23		
Ross Fichtner	DB	6'	185	26	2	
Bobby Franklin	DB	5'11"	182	28		
Bernie Parish	DB	5'11"	195	29	4	6
Dave Raimey	DB	5'10"	195	23		
Jim Ninowski	QB	6'1"	207	28		
Frank Ryan	QB	6'3"	200	28		6
Ernie Green	HB	6'2"	205	25		60
Leroy Kelly	HB	6'	195	22		6
Jimmy Brown	FB	6'2"	228	28		54
Charlie Scales	FB	5'11"	215	25		6
Gary Collins	FL	6'4"	208	23		48
Clifton McNeil	FL	6'2"	185	24		6
Walter Roberts	FL	5'10"	175	22		6
Johnny Brewer	OE	6'4"	235	27		18
Tom Hutchinson	OE	6'1"	190	23		
Paul Warfield	OE	6'	188	21		54
Lou Groza	K	6'3"	250	40		115

ST. LOUIS CARDINALS 9-3-2 Wally Lemm

Scores of Each Game		
16	Dallas	6
33	Cleveland	33
23	San Francisco	13
23	Washington	17
27	Baltimore	47
38	WASHINGTON	24
13	DALLAS	31
17	New York	34
34	PITTSBURGH	30
10	NEW YORK	10
38	Philadelphia	13
21	Pittsburgh	20
28	CLEVELAND	19
36	PHILADELPHIA	34

Use Name	Pos.	Hgt	Wgt	Age	Int	Pts
Ernie McMillan	OT	6'6"	255	26		
Bob Reynolds	OT	6'6"	265	23		
Ed Cook	OG-OT	6'2"	250	32		
Irv Goode	OG	6'4"	250	23		
Ken Gray	OG	6'2"	250	28		
Rick Sortun	OG	6'2"	225	21		
Herschel Turner	OT-OG	6'3"	230	22		
Bob DeMarco	C	6'3"	240	26		
Don Brumm	DE	6'3"	245	21		
Tom Redmond	DE	6'5"	240	27		
Joe Robb	DE	6'3"	245	27		
Chuck Walker	DE	6'2"	235	23		
Ken Kortas	DT	6'2"	290	22		
Luke Owens	DT	6'2"	260	31		
Sam Silas	DT	6'4"	250	21		
Bill Koman	LB	6'2"	230	30	2	
Dave Meggyesy	LB	6'1"	220	22		
Dale Meinert	LB	6'2"	220	31	2	6
Marion Rushing	LB	6'2"	230	27		2
Larry Stallings	LB	6'2"	230	22	2	
Monk Bailey	DB	6'	175	26		
Jimmy Burson	DB	6'	180	22	3	6
Pat Fischer	DB	5'10"	180	24	10	18
Jimmy Hill	DB	6'2"	195	35		
Jerry Stovall	DB	6'2"	205	22	3	6
Larry Wilson	DB	6'	190	26	3	6
Buddy Humphrey	QB	6'1"	200	28		
Charley Johnson	QB	6'	190	27		12
Joe Childress	HB	6'	210	30		12
Bob Paremore	HB	5'11"	190	24		
John David Crow	FB-HB	6'2"	220	29		48
Willie Crenshaw	FB	6'2"	215	23		6
Prentice Gautt	FB	6'	205	26		12
Bill Thornton	FB	6'1"	220	24		6
Bobby Joe Conrad	FL	6'	195	29		36
Taz Anderson	OE	6'2"	215	25		
Billy Gambrell	OE	5'10"	175	22		12
Sonny Randle	OE	6'2"	190	28		30
Jackie Smith	OE	6'4"	210	23		24
Mal Hammack	LB-OE	6'2"	210	31		
Jim Bakken	K	6'	200	23		115

Bill Triplett — Illness

PHILADELPHIA EAGLES 6-8-0 Joe Kuharich

Scores of Each Game		
38	NEW YORK	7
24	SAN FRANCISCO	28
20	CLEVELAND	28
21	PITTSBURGH	7
20	Washington	35
23	New York	17
34	Pittsburgh	10
10	WASHINGTON	21
10	Los Angeles	20
17	Dallas	14
13	ST. LOUIS	38
24	Cleveland	38
24	DALLAS	14
34	St. Louis	36

Use Name	Pos.	Hgt	Wgt	Age	Int	Pts
Bob Brown	OT	6'4"	280	21		
Dave Graham	OT	6'3"	250	25		
Jim Skaggs	OT	6'2"	230	24		
Ed Blaine	OG	6'2"	240	24		
Pete Case	OG	6'3"	243	23		
Lynn Hoyem	C	6'4"	240	24		
Jim Ringo	C	6'1"	230	33		
Jim Schrader	C	6'2"	250	32		
Riley Gunnels	DE	6'3"	253	27		
Don Hultz	DE	6'3"	235	23		
Bobby Richards	DE	6'2"	245	25		
George Tarasovic	DE	6'4"	245	35		
Don Thompson	DE	6'4"	240	25		
Ed Khayat	DT	6'3"	245	29		
John Meyers	DT	6'6"	267	24		
Floyd Peters	DT	6'4"	255	29		
Maxie Baughan	LB	6'1"	230	26		
Ralph Heck	LB	6'2"	224	23		
Dave Lloyd	LB	6'3"	248	28	3	
Mike Morgan	LB	6'4"	232	22		6
Don Burroughs	DB	6'4"	187	33	2	
Irv Cross	DB	6'1"	195	25	3	6
Glenn Glass	DB	6'	190	27	1	
Nate Ramsey	DB	6'1"	200	23	5	
Joe Scarpati	DB	5'10"	185	22	3	6
Claude Crabb	FL-DB	6'	197	24		
Jack Concannon	QB	6'3"	195	21		6
King Hill	QB	6'3"	213	28		
Norm Snead	QB	6'4"	215	24		12
Timmy Brown	HB	5'10"	200	27		60
Roger Gill	HB	6'1"	200	23		
Ollie Matson	HB	6'2"	210	34		30
Earl Gros	FB	6'3"	230	23		12
Izzy Lang	FB	6'1"	230	21		
Tom Woodeshick	FB	6'	205	22		12
Red Mack	FL	5'10"	185	27		6
Ron Goodwin	OE-FL	6'	184	22		18
Ray Poage	OE	6'4"	203	23		6
Pete Retzlaff	OE	6'1"	214	33		48
Ralph Smith	DB-OE	6'2"	213	25		
Sam Baker	K	6'2"	220	32		84

Jerry Mazzanti — Military Service
Mike McClellan — Military Service
Fate Echols — Canadian Football League

WASHINGTON REDSKINS 6-8-0 Bill McPeak

Scores of Each Game		
13	CLEVELAND	27
18	Dallas	24
10	New York	13
17	ST. LOUIS	23
35	PHILADELPHIA	20
24	St. Louis	38
27	CHICAGO	20
21	Philadelphia	10
24	Cleveland	34
30	Pittsburgh	0
28	DALLAS	16
36	NEW YORK	21
7	PITTSBURGH	14
17	Baltimore	45

Use Name	Pos.	Hgt	Wgt	Age	Int	Pts
Steve Barnett	OT	6'1"	255	23		
Riley Mattson	OT	6'4"	254	25		
Fran O'Brien	OT	6'1"	255	29		
John Nisby	OG	6'1"	238	31		
Vince Promuto	OG	6'1"	245	26		
George Seals	OG	6'2"	250	21		
Fred Hageman	C	6'4"	242	26		
Len Hauss	C	6'2"	220	23		
Carl Kammerer	DE	6'3"	237	27		
John Paluck	DE	6'2"	245	32		2
Ron Snidow	DE	6'4"	250	22		
Joe Rutgens	DT	6'2"	255	25		
Bob Toneff	DT	6'3"	257	34		
Fred Williams	DT	6'4"	248	34		
Rod Breedlove	LB	6'2"	227	26		
Jimmy Carr	LB	6'1"	210	31	2	
Sam Huff	LB	6'1"	230	29	4	
Bob Pellegrini	LB	6'2"	237	29		
John Reger	LB	6'	230	33	3	6
Paul Krause	DB	6'3"	198	22	12	6
Johnny Sample	DB	6'1"	200	27	4	6
Lonnie Sanders	DB	6'3"	210	22	2	
Jim Shorter	DB	5'11"	186	23	1	
Jim Steffen	DB	6'	196	27	4	
Tom Walters	DB	6'2"	195	22	2	
George Izo	QB	6'3"	218	27		
Sonny Jurgensen	QB	5'11"	200	30		18
Dick Shiner	QB	6'	190	22		
Pervis Atkins	HB	6'1"	217	28		6
Charley Taylor	HB	6'3"	215	23		60
Tom Tracy	HB	5'9"	205	32		6
Don Bosseler	FB	6'1"	214	28		
J.W. Lockett	FB	6'2"	226	27		18
Ozzie Clay	FL	6'	190	22		
Joe Hernandez	FL	6'2"	180	24		
Bobby Mitchell	FL	6'	196	29		60
Preston Carpenter	OE	6'2"	190	30		18
Angie Coia	OE	6'2"	202	26		30
Pat Richter	OE	6'5"	230	23		
Jim Martin	K	6'2"	238	40		71

DALLAS COWBOYS 5-8-1 Tom Landry

Scores of Each Game		
6	ST. LOUIS	16
24	WASHINGTON	18
17	Pittsburgh	23
6	Cleveland	27
13	NEW YORK	13
16	CLEVELAND	20
31	St. Louis	13
24	Chicago	10
31	New York	21
14	PHILADELPHIA	17
16	Washington	28
21	GREEN BAY	45
14	Philadelphia	24
17	PITTSBURGH	14

Use Name	Pos.	Hgt	Wgt	Age	Int	Pts
Jim Boeke	OT	6'5"	255	25		
Bill Frank	OT	6'5"	255	26		
Bob Fry	OT	6'4"	238	33		
Tony Liscio	OT	6'5"	240	24		
Ray Schoenke	OT	6'3"	234	22		
Jim Ray Smith	OG-OT	6'3"	245	33		
Joe Bob Isbell	OG	6'1"	250	24		
Jake Kupp	OG	6'3"	215	22		
Mike Connelly	C	6'3"	242	28		
Dave Manders	C	6'2"	240	22		
George Andrie	DE	6'7"	264	24		
Larry Stephens	DE	6'4"	260	26		
Maury Youmans	DE	6'6"	260	27		
Jim Colvin	DT	6'2"	253	27		
Bob Lilly	DT	6'4"	250	25		
Dave Edwards	LB	6'3"	213	25	1	
Harold Hays	LB	6'3"	235	23		
Chuck Howley	LB	6'3"	223	28	2	
Lee Roy Jordon	LB	6'2"	215	23	1	
Jerry Tubbs	LB	6'2"	215	29	2	
Don Bishop	DB	6'2"	215	29		
Mike Gaechter	DB	6'	196	24		
Cornell Green	DB	6'4"	220	24		
Warren Livingston	DB	5'10"	185	26	1	6
Mel Renfro	DB	6'	190	20	7	12
Jimmy Ridlon	DB	6'1"	180	29	4	12
Billy Lothridge	QB	6'1"	185	20		6
Don Meredith	QB	6'2"	205	26		24
John Roach	QB	6'4"	200	31		
Amos Bullocks	HB	6'1"	202	25		
Perry Lee Dunn	HB	6'2"	200	21		6
Amos Marsh	HB	6'1"	225	25		12
Jim Stiger	FB-HB	5'11"	190	23		12
Don Perkins	FB	5'10"	196	26		36
Frank Clarke	FL	6'	215	31		30
Buddy Dial	FL	6'1"	195	27		
Tommy McDonald	FL	5'10"	172	30		12
Lee Folkins	OE	6'5"	220	25		
Pete Gent	OE	6'4"	215	21		
Pettis Norman	OE	6'3"	223	24		12
Dick Van Raaphorst	K	5'11"	215	21		70

Jerry Overton — Off-season accident
Don Talbert — Military Service

CLEVELAND BROWNS

RUSHING

Last Name	No.	Yds	Avg	TD
Jimmy Brown	280	1446	5.2	7
Green	109	491	4.5	6
Ryan	37	217	5.9	1
Kelly	6	12	2.0	0
Scales	2	5	2.5	0
Ninowski	1	−8	−8.0	0

RECEIVING

Last Name	No.	Yds	Avg	TD
Warfield	52	920	18	9
Jimmy Brown	36	340	9	2
Collins	35	544	16	8
Brewer	25	338	14	3
Green	25	283	11	4
McNeil	4	69	17	1
Hutchinson	3	24	8	0
Roberts	1	24	24	1

PUNT RETURNS

Last Name	No.	Yds	Avg	TD
Kelly	9	171	19	1
Roberts	10	132	13	0
Williams	1	0	0	0

KICKOFF RETURNS

Last Name	No.	Yds	Avg	TD
Roberts	24	661	28	0
Kelly	24	582	24	0
Scales	5	75	15	0
Warfield	1	4	4	0
Franklin	1	1	1	0
Clark	1	0	0	0
Williams	1	0	0	0

PASSING – PUNTING – KICKING

PASSING	Att	Comp	%	Yds	Yd/Att	TD	Int–	%	RK
Ryan	334	174	52	2404	7.2	25	19–	6	6
Ninowski	9	6	67	125	13.9	2	0–	0	
Jimmy Brown	1	1	100	13	13.0	1	0–	0	

PUNTING	No	Avg
Collins	48	42.0
Franklin	1	36.0

KICKING	XP	Att	%	FG	Att	%
Groza	49	50	98	22	33	67

ST. LOUIS CARDINALS

RUSHING

Last Name	No.	Yds	Avg	TD
Crow	163	554	3.4	7
Childress	102	413	4.0	0
Crenshaw	60	297	5.0	1
Thornton	39	236	6.1	1
Gautt	59	191	3.2	1
Johnson	31	93	3.0	2
Wilson	2	−14	−7.0	0

RECEIVING

Last Name	No.	Yds	Avg	TD
Conrad	61	780	13	6
Smith	47	657	14	4
Randle	25	517	21	5
Gambrell	24	398	17	2
Crow	23	257	11	1
Childress	12	203	17	2
Gautt	9	72	8	1
Crenshaw	8	58	7	0
Anderson	7	60	9	0
Thornton	7	43	6	0

PUNT RETURNS

Last Name	No.	Yds	Avg	TD
Gambrell	12	126	11	0
Bruson	12	125	10	1

KICKOFF RETURNS

Last Name	No.	Yds	Avg	TD
Stovall	24	566	24	0
Crenshaw	13	340	26	0
Paremore	9	192	21	0
Gautt	5	104	21	0
Gambrell	4	92	23	0
Hammack	2	61	31	0
Burson	2	38	19	0
Conrad	1	26	26	0
Thornton	1	5	5	0
Gray	2	0	0	0

PASSING – PUNTING – KICKING

PASSING	Att	Comp	%	Yds	Yd/Att	TD	Int–	%	RK
Johnson	420	223	53	3045	7.3	21	24–	6	7
Crow	1	0	0	0	0.0	0	0–	0	
Humphrey	1	0	0	0	0.0	0.	0–	0	

PUNTING	No	Avg
Smith	41	40.4
Stovall	15	42.1

KICKING	XP	Att	%	FG	Att	%
Bakken	40	40	100	25	38	66

PHILADELPHIA EAGLES

RUSHING

Last Name	No.	Yds	Avg	TD
Gros	154	748	4.9	2
Matson	96	404	4.2	4
T. Brown	90	356	4.0	5
Woodeshick	37	180	4.9	2
Concannon	16	134	8.4	1
Snead	16	59	3.7	2
Lang	12	37	3.1	0
Hill	8	27	3.4	0
Goodwin	1	−23	−23.0	0

RECEIVING

Last Name	No.	Yds	Avg	TD
Retzlaff	51	855	17	8
Poage	37	479	13	1
Gros	29	234	8	0
Goodwin	23	335	15	3
Matson	17	242	14	1
T. Brown	15	244	16	5
Mack	8	169	21	1
Lang	6	69	12	0
Gill	4	58	15	0
Smith	4	35	9	0
Woodeshick	4	12	3	0
Crabb	1	14	14	0

PUNT RETURNS

Last Name	No.	Yds	Avg	TD
T. Brown	10	96	10	0
Gill	6	61	10	0
Lang	6	26	4	0
Matson	2	10	5	0
Scarpati	1	6	6	0
Hultz	1	2	2	0
Glass	1	0	0	0
Mack	1	0	0	0

KICKOFF RETURNS

Last Name	No.	Yds	Avg	TD
T. Brown	30	692	23	0
Lang	13	352	27	0
Gill	7	167	24	0
Matson	3	104	35	0
Gros	2	38	19	0
Glass	1	12	12	0
Morgan	2	0	0	0
Thompson	1	0	0	0

PASSING – PUNTING – KICKING

PASSING	Att	Comp	%	Yds	Yd/Att	TD	Int–	%	RK
Snead	283	138	49	1906	6.7	14	12–	4	11
Hill	88	49	56	641	7.3	3	4–	5	
Concannon	23	12	52	199	8.7	2	1–	4	
T. Brown	2	0	0	0	0.0	0	1–	50	
Gros	1	0	0	0	0.0	0	0–	0	

PUNTING	No	Avg
Baker	49	42.3
Hill	24	40.3

KICKING	XP	Att	%	FG	Att	%
Baker	36	37	97	16	26	62

WASHINGTON REDSKINS

RUSHING

Last Name	No.	Yds	Avg	TD
Taylor	199	755	3.8	5
Lockett	63	175	2.8	1
Atkins	25	98	3.9	1
Tracy	24	67	2.8	1
Jurgensen	27	57	2.1	3
Bosseler	22	46	2.1	0
Mitchell	2	33	16.5	0
Shiner	2	8	4.0	0
Carpenter	1	7	7.0	0
Richter	1	−9	−9.0	0

RECEIVING

Last Name	No.	Yds	Avg	TD
Mitchell	60	904	15	10
Taylor	53	814	15	5
Carpenter	31	466	15	3
Coia	29	500	17	5
Lockett	20	204	10	2
Atkins	8	35	4	0
Bosseler	6	56	9	0
Richter	4	49	12	0
Tracy	2	25	13	0
Hernandez	1	18	18	0

PUNT RETURNS

Last Name	No.	Yds	Avg	TD
Atkins	13	138	11	0
Hernandez	5	49	10	0
Shorter	6	19	3	0
Carpenter	2	19	10	0
Clay	4	5	1	0
Carr	1	0	0	0
Kammerer	1	0	0	0

KICKOFF RETURNS

Last Name	No.	Yds	Avg	TD
Clay	19	482	25	0
Atkins	14	319	23	0
Shorter	5	81	16	0
Lockett	3	72	24	0
Mitchell	3	58	19	0
Mattson	3	30	10	0
Taylor	1	20	20	0
Hernandez	1	19	19	0
Snidow	1	16	16	0
Carr	1	0	0	0
Pellegrini	1	0	0	0

PASSING – PUNTING – KICKING

PASSING	Att	Comp	%	Yds	Yd/Att	TD	Int–	%	RK
Jurgensen	385	207	54	2934	7.6	24	13–	3	3
Izo	18	5	28	83	4.6	1	2–	11	
Taylor	10	2	20	54	5.4	0	1–	10	
Carpenter	1	0	0	0	0.0	0	0–	0	
Shiner	1	0	0	0	0.0	0	0–	0	

PUNTING	No	Avg
Richter	91	41.2

KICKING	XP	Att	%	FG	Att	%
Martin	35	39	90	12	28	43

DALLAS COWBOYS

RUSHING

Last Name	No.	Yds	Avg	TD
Perkins	174	768	4.4	6
Marsh	100	401	4.0	2
Stiger	68	280	4.1	1
Dunn	26	103	4.0	1
Meredith	32	81	2.5	4
Clarke	10	46	4.6	0
Roach	8	9	1.1	0
Folkins	1	9	9.0	0
Lothridge	2	−6	−3.0	1

RECEIVING

Last Name	No.	Yds	Avg	TD
Clarke	65	973	15	5
McDonald	46	612	13	2
Norman	24	311	13	2
Perkins	15	155	10	0
Marsh	15	131	9	0
Dial	11	178	16	0
Stiger	9	85	9	1
Folkins	5	41	8	0
Dunn	2	30	15	0

PUNT RETURNS

Last Name	No.	Yds	Avg	TD
Renfro	32	418	13	1
Gaechter	5	24	5	0
McDonald	2	17	9	0
Stiger	1	0	0	0

KICKOFF RETURNS

Last Name	No.	Yds	Avg	TD
Renfro	40	1017	25	0
Dunn	2	333	17	0
Gaechter	1	31	31	0
Bullocks	1	19	19	0
Marsh	1	2	2	0
Folkins	1	0	0	0

PASSING – PUNTING – KICKING

PASSING	Att	Comp	%	Yds	Yd/Att	TD	Int–	%	RK
Meredith	323	158	49	2143	6.6	9	16–	5	15
Roach	68	32	47	349	5.1	1	6–	9	
Lothridge	9	2	22	24	2.7	0	2–	22	
Dunn	2	0	0	0	0.0	0	0–	0	
Clarke	1	0	0	0	0.0	0	0–	0	
Stiger	1	0	0	0	0.0	0	0–	0	

PUNTING	No	Avg
Lothridge	62	40.3
Folkins	15	33.1
Howley	1	37.0

KICKING	XP	Att	%	FG	Att	%
Van Raaphorst	28	29	97	14	29	48

EASTERN CONFERENCE – Continued

PITTSBURGH STEELERS 5-9-0 Buddy Parker

Scores of Each Game		
14	LOS ANGELES	26
27	NEW YORK	24
23	DALLAS	17
7	Philadelphia	21
23	Cleveland	7
10	Minnesota	30
10	PHILADELPHIA	34
17	CLEVELAND	30
30	St. Louis	34
0	WASHINGTON	30
44	New York	17
20	ST. LOUIS	21
14	Washington	7
14	Dallas	17

Use Name	Pos.	Hgt	Wgt	Age	Int	Pts
Charlie Bradshaw	OT	6'6"	255	28		
Dan James	OT	6'4"	250	27		
Ray Lemek	OG	6'	240	30		
Mike Sandusky	OG	6'	230	31		
Ron Stehouwer	OG	6'2"	230	27		
Buzz Nutter	C	6'4"	230	33		
John Baker	DE	6'6"	270	29		
Dan LaRose	DE	6'5"	250	24		
Ben McGee	DE	6'2"	250	22		
Urban Henry	DT	6'4"	265	29		
Chuck Hinton	DT	6'5"	235	25	1	6
Joe Krupa	DT	6'2"	235	31		
Ray Mansfield	DT	6'3"	255	23		
Bob Harrison	LB	6'2"	225	27		
Max Messner (from NY)	LB	6'3"	225	26		
Myron Pottios	LB	6'2"	240	24	1	
Bill Saul	LB	6'4"	225	23	1	
Bob Schmitz	LB	6'1"	230	26		
Bob Soleau	LB	6'2"	235	23		
Ed Holler	FB-LB	6'2"	235	24	1	
Jim Bradshaw	DB	6'1"	190	25	1	12
Willie Daniel	DB	5'11"	185	26	2	
Dick Haley	DB	5'10"	190	28	2	
Brady Keys	DB	6'	190	28	2	
Bob Sherman	DB	6'2"	195	22		
Ed Brown	QB	6'2"	210	35		12
Bill Nelsen	QB	6'	195	23		
Terry Nofsinger	QB	6'4"	205	26		
Tom Wade	QB	6'2"	195	22		
Dick Hoak	HB	5'11"	190	25		30
Phil King	HB	6'4"	218	28		12
Theron Sapp	HB	6'1"	200	29		
Marv Woodson	HB	6'	195	21		
John Henry Johnson	FB	6'2"	215	34		48
Clarence Peaks	FB	6'1"	212	28		12
Gary Ballman	OE-FL	6'	195	24		42
Paul Martha	OE-FL	6'	185	21		
John Burrell	OE	6'3"	190	24		
Jim Kelly	OE	6'2"	215	22		6
Chuck Logan	OE	6'4"	210	21		
John Powers	OE	6'2"	210	23		
Clendon Thomas	DB-OE	6'2"	195	27	1	6
Mike Clark	K	6'1"	200	23		67

Andy Russell – Military Service

NEW YORK GIANTS 2-10-2 Allie Sherman

Scores of Each Game		
7	Philadelphia	38
24	Pittsburgh	27
13	WASHINGTON	10
3	Detroit	26
13	Dallas	13
17	PHILADELPHIA	23
20	Cleveland	42
34	ST. LOUIS	17
21	DALLAS	31
10	St. Louis	10
17	PITTSBURGH	44
21	Washington	36
21	MINNESOTA	30
20	CLEVELAND	52

Use Name	Pos.	Hgt	Wgt	Age	Int	Pts
Roger Anderson	OT	6'5"	255	21		
Rosey Brown	OT	6'3"	255	31		
Lane Howell	OT	6'5"	255	23		
Frank Lasky	OT	6'2"	265	22		
Jack Stroud	OT	6'1"	250	35		
Bookie Bolin	OG	6'2"	240	24		
Ken Byers (to MIN)	OG	6'1"	240	24		
Darrell Dess	OG	6'	245	28		
Mickey Walker	C-OG	6'	235	24		
Greg Larson	C	6'2"	250	25		
Jim Katcavage	DE	6'3"	240	29		
Andy Robustelli	DE	6'1"	235	38		
Andy Stynchula	DE	6'3"	250	25		1
Bob Taylor	DE	6'3"	240	24		
John Contoulis	DT	6'4"	260	23		
John Lovetere	DT	6'4"	285	28		
Jim Moran	DT	6'5"	255	21		
Tom Costello	LB	6'3"	220	23		
Jerry Hillebrand	LB	6'3"	240	24	1	
Tom Scott	LB	6'2"	220	34	2	
Lou Slaby	LB	6'3"	235	22	2	
Bill Winter	LB	6'3"	220	24		
Erich Barnes	DB	6'2"	198	29	2	12
Dick Lynch	DB	6'1"	205	28	4	
Andy Nelson	DB	6'1"	180	31	1	
Jimmy Patton	DB	6'	185	32	2	
Dick Pesonen	DB	6'	190	26		
Allan Webb	DB	5'11"	180	29	1	
Y.A. Tittle	QB	6'	195	37		6
Gary Wood	QB	5'11"	188	21		18
Dick James	HB	5'9"	182	30		24
Steve Thurlow	HB	6'3"	210	21		6
Clarence Childs	DB-HB	6'	180	25		6
Alex Webster	FB	6'3"	220	33		18
Ernie Wheelwright	FB	6'3"	220	27		18
Frank Gifford	FL	6'1"	190	34		24
Homer Jones	FL	6'2"	205	23		
R. C. Owens	FL	6'3"	195	29		
Joe Morrison	HB-FL	6'1"	212	26		18
Bob Crespino	OE	6'4"	225	26		
Del Shofner	OE	6'3"	185	28		
Aaron Thomas	FL-OE	6'3"	210	26		36
Don Chandler	K	6'2"	210	29		54

Joe Walton – Injury

WESTERN CONFERENCE

BALTIMORE COLTS 12-2-0 Don Shula

Scores of Each Game		
24	Minnesota	34
21	Green Bay	20
52	CHICAGO	0
35	LOS ANGELES	20
47	ST. LOUIS	27
24	GREEN BAY	21
34	Detroit	0
37	SAN FRANCISCO	7
40	Chicago	24
17	MINNESOTA	14
24	Los Angeles	7
14	San Francisco	3
14	DETROIT	31
45	WASHINGTON	17

Use Name	Pos.	Hgt	Wgt	Age	Int	Pts
George Preas	OT	6'2"	250	32		
Tom Gilburg	OT	6'5"	245	25		
Lou Kirouac	OT	6'3"	240	24		
Bob Vogel	OT	6'5"	250	22		
Jim Parker	OG	6'3"	275	30		
Alex Sandusky	OG	6'1"	242	32		
Dan Sullivan	OT-OG	6'3"	250	25		
Dick Szymanski	C	6'3"	235	32		
Ordell Braase	DE	6'4"	242	32		
Gino Marchetti	DE	6'4"	245	38		
Lou Michaels	DE	6'2"	235	28		104
John Diehl	DT	6'7"	275	28		
Fred Miller	DT	6'3"	245	23		
Guy Reese	DT	6'5"	258	24		
Billy Ray Smith	DT	6'4"	240	29		
Jackie Burkett	LB	6'4"	228	27		
Ted Davis	LB	6'1"	225	22		
Bill Pellington	LB	6'2"	238	35	2	
Don Shinnick	LB	6'	235	29	3	
Steve Stonebreaker	LB	6'3"	220	26		6
Wendell Harris	DB	5'11"	190	23	1	
Alvin Haymond	DB	6'	190	22		
Jerry Logan	DB	6'1"	185	23	6	6
Lenny Lyles	DB	6'2"	202	28	2	
Jim Welch	DB	6'	190	26		
Bobby Boyd	HB-DB	5'10"	190	26	9	
Gary Cuozzo	QB	6'1"	195	23		
Johnny Unitas	QB	6'1"	194	31		12
Tom Matte	HB	6'	205	25		6
Lenny Moore	HB	6'1"	190	31		120
Jerry Hill	FB	5'11"	210	24		36
Joe Don Looney	FB	6'1"	230	21		12
Tony Lorick	FB	6'1"	203	22		24
Jimmy Orr	FL	5'11"	175	28		36
Willie Richardson	FL	6'2"	198	24		
Ray Berry	OE	6'2"	187	31		36
Alex Hawkins	OE	6'1"	190	27		6
John Mackey	OE	6'3"	217	22		12
Neal Petties	OE	6'2"	198	23		6
Butch Wilson	OE	6'2"	218	22		6

GREEN BAY PACKERS 8-5-1 Vince Lombardi

Scores of Each Game		
23	CHICAGO	12
20	BALTIMORE	21
14	Detroit	10
23	MINNESOTA	24
24	SAN FRANCISCO	14
21	Baltimore	24
17	LOS ANGELES	27
42	Minnesota	13
30	DETROIT	7
14	San Francisco	24
28	CLEVELAND	21
45	Dallas	21
17	Chicago	3
24	Los Angeles	24

Use Name	Pos.	Hgt	Wgt	Age	Int	Pts
Forrest Gregg	OT	6'4"	250	31		
Lloyd Voss	OT	6'4"	245	22		
Norm Masters	OT	6'2"	250	31		
Bob Skoronski	C-OT	6'3"	250	31		
Dan Grimm	OG	6'3"	245	23		
Fuzzy Thurston	OG	6'1"	245	31		
Jerry Kramer	OG	6'3"	245	29		
John McDowell	OT-OG	6'3"	260	21		
Ken Bowman	C	6'3"	230	21		
Lionel Aldridge	DE	6'4"	245	22		6
Willie Davis	DE	6'3"	245	31		
Steve Wright	DE	6'6'	250	22		
Dave Hanner	DT	6'2"	260	35		
Henry Jordan	DT	6'3"	250	29		6
Ron Kostelnik	DT	6'4"	260	24		
Gene Breen	LB	6'2"	225	23		
Lee Roy Caffey	LB	6'3"	240	24	1	
Dan Currie	LB	6'3"	240	30	2	
Ray Nitschke	LB	6'3"	240	28	2	
Dave Robinson	LB	6'3"	245	23		
Tommy Crutcher	FB-LB	6'3"	220	22		
Herb Adderley	DB	6'1"	210	25	4	
Tom Brown	DB	6'1"	190	23	1	
Hank Gremminger	DB	6'1"	200	31	1	
Doug Hart	DB	6'	190	25	1	
Jerry Norton	DB	5'11"	195	34		
Jesse Whittenton	DB	6'	195	30	1	
Willie Wood	DB	5'10"	190	28	3	7
Zeke Bratkowski	QB	6'2"	200	32		
Dennis Claridge	QB	6'3"	225	22		
Bart Starr	QB	6'1"	200	31		18
Paul Hornung	HB	6'2"	215	27		107
Tom Moore	HB	6'2"	210	26		24
Elijah Pitts	HB	6'1"	205	25		12
Jim Taylor	FB	6'	215	29		90
Boyd Dowler	FL	6'5"	225	27		30
Bob Long	FL	6'3"	190	23		
Bob Jeter	OE-FL	6'1"	205	26		
Marv Fleming	OE	6'4"	230	22		
Ron Kramer	OE	6'3"	240	29		
Max McGee	OE	6'3"	205	32		42

Ken Iman – Broken Hand

MINNESOTA VIKINGS 8-5-1 Norm Van Brocklin

Scores of Each Game		
34	BALTIMORE	24
28	CHICAGO	34
13	Los Angeles	22
24	Green Bay	23
20	DETROIT	24
30	PITTSBURGH	10
27	San Francisco	22
13	GREEN BAY	42
24	SAN FRANCISCO	7
14	Baltimore	17
23	Detroit	23
34	LOS ANGELES	13
30	New York	21
41	Chicago	14

Use Name	Pos.	Hgt	Wgt	Age	Int	Pts
Grady Alderman	OT	6'2"	245	25		
Errol Linden	OT	6'5"	260	27		
Larry Bowie	OG	6'2"	245	24		
Palmer Pyle	OG	6'2"	250	27		
Milt Sunde	OG	6'2"	222	21		
Mick Tingelhoff	C	6'1"	235	24		
Bob Denton	DE	6'4"	244	30		
Carl Eller	DE	6'6"	247	21		6
Jim Marshall	DE	6'3"	235	27		
Howard Simpson	DE	6'5"	230	21		
Paul Dickson	DT	6'5"	255	27		
Dave O'Brien	DT	6'3"	247	23		
Jim Prestel	DT	6'5"	275	27	1	6
John Campbell	LB	6'3"	215	25		
Rip Hawkins	LB	6'3"	230	25	2	12
Bill Jobko	LB	6'2"	225	28		
John Kirby	LB	6'3"	222	22		
Bill Swain	LB	6'2"	228	23		
Roy Winston	LB	6'1"	230	24	3	
Lee Calland	DB	6'	190	23		
Karl Kassulke	DB	6'	193	22	3	
George Rose	DB	5'11"	190	21	6	6
Ed Sharockman	DB	6'	200	24	1	
Bill Butler	HB-DB	5'10"	200	27	2	
Larry Vargo	OE-DB	6'3"	215	24	1	
Fran Tarkenton	QB	6'1"	190	24		12
Ron Vander Kelen	QB	6'1"	185	24		
Ted Dean	HB	6'2"	213	26		
Tommy Mason	HB	6'	196	25		30
Tom Michel	HB	6'	210	23		
Bill Brown	FB	5'11"	220	26		96
Darrell Lester	FB	6'2"	225	23		
Bill McWatters	FB	6'	225	22		6
Tom Hall	FL	6'1"	195	23		12
Hal Bedsole	OE	6'4"	230	22		30
Paul Flatley	OE	6'1"	187	23		18
Bob Lacey	OE	6'3"	205	22		
Jerry Reichow	OE	6'2"	220	29		12
Gordon Smith	OE	6'2"	220	25		6
Fred Cox	K	5'10"	200	25		103
Bobby Walden	K	6'	195	25		

Chuck Lamson – Injury

EASTERN CONFERENCE—Continued

PITTSBURGH STEELERS

RUSHING

Last Name	No.	Yds	Avg	TD
Johnson	235	1048	4.5	7
Peaks	118	503	4.3	2
Hoak	84	258	3.1	2
Brown	26	110	4.2	2
King	26	71	2.7	1
Ballman	11	43	3.9	0
Nelsen	3	17	5.7	0
Sapp	4	15	3.8	0
Martha	4	12	3.0	0
Powers	2	10	5.0	0
Holler	1	8	8.0	0
Thomas	2	7	3.5	0

RECEIVING

Last Name	No.	Yds	Avg	TD
Ballman	47	935	20	7
Thomas	17	334	20	1
Johnson	17	69	4	1
Hoak	12	137	11	3
Peaks	12	113	9	0
Kelly	10	186	19	1
Powers	8	193	24	0
Martha	6	145	24	0
Burrell	6	113	19	0
King	4	32	8	1
Sapp	1	44	44	0
Logan	1	7	7	0

PUNT RETURNS

Last Name	No.	Yds	Avg	TD
Keys	14	172	12	0
Martha	13	64	5	0
J. Bradshaw	1	2	2	0
Baker	1	0	0	0
Woodson	1	0	0	0

KICKOFF RETURNS

Last Name	No.	Yds	Avg	TD
Ballman	14	386	28	0
Peaks	12	326	27	0
Woodson	5	178	36	0
Thomas	7	171	24	0
Keys	7	168	24	0
Sapp	4	43	11	0
King	2	27	14	0
Martha	1	26	26	0
Lemek	1	19	19	0
Kelly	1	12	12	0
Burrell	2	0	0	0

PASSING – PUNTING – KICKING

PASSING	Att	Comp	%	Yds	Yd/Att	TD	Int–	%	RK
Brown	272	121	44	1990	7.3	12	19–	7	14
Nelsen	42	16	38	276	6.6	2	3–	7	
Nofsinger	4	3	75	35	8.8	0	1–	25	
Wade	3	1	33	7	2.3	0	0–	0	
Ballman	1	0	0	0	0.0	0	1–	100	
Hoak	1	0	0	0	0.0	0	0–	0	

PUNTING	No	Avg
Brown	31	43.4
Holler	31	43.0

KICKING	XP	Att	%	FG	Att	%
Clark	28	31	90	13	25	52

NEW YORK GIANTS

RUSHING

Last Name	No.	Yds	Avg	TD
Wheelwright	100	402	4.0	0
Webster	76	210	2.8	3
Thurlow	64	210	3.3	0
James	55	189	3.4	3
Wood	39	158	4.1	3
Morrison	45	138	3.1	1
Childs	40	102	2.6	0
Gifford	1	2	2.0	1
Tittle	15	–7	–0.5	1

RECEIVING

Last Name	No.	Yds	Avg	TD
Thomas	43	624	15	6
Morrison	40	505	13	2
Gifford	29	429	15	3
Shofner	22	323	15	0
Webster	19	199	10	0
Wheelwright	14	204	15	3
Crespino	12	165	14	0
James	12	101	8	1
Childs	11	97	9	0
Thurlow	7	74	11	1
Jones	4	82	21	0
Owens	4	45	11	0

PUNT RETURNS

Last Name	No.	Yds	Avg	TD
James	21	153	7	0
Childs	6	40	7	0
Barnes	1	0	0	0

KICKOFF RETURNS

Last Name	No.	Yds	Avg	TD
Childs	34	987	29	1
James	23	515	22	0
Jones	6	111	19	0
Morrison	4	75	19	0

PASSING – PUNTING – KICKING

PASSING	Att	Comp	%	Yds	Yd/Att	TD	Int–	%	RK
Tittle	281	147	52	1798	6.4	10	22–	8	16
Wood	143	66	46	952	6.7	6	3–	2	13
Thurlow	5	3	60	65	13.0	0	0–	0	
Gifford	1	1	100	33	33.0	0	0–	0	
James	1	0	0	0	0.0	0	1–	100	

PUNTING	No	Avg
Chandler	73	45.6
James	1	35.0

KICKING	XP	Att	%	FG	Att	%
Chandler	27	29	93	9	20	45
Stynchula	1	1	100	0	0	0

WESTERN CONFERENCE

BALTIMORE COLTS

RUSHING

Last Name	No.	Yds	Avg	TD
Moore	157	584	3.7	16
Lorick	100	513	5.1	4
Hill	88	384	4.4	5
Matte	42	215	5.1	1
Unitas	37	162	4.4	2
Looney	23	127	5.5	1
Boyd	1	25	25.0	0
Mackey	1	–1	–1.0	0
Cuozzo	7	–2	–0.3	0

RECEIVING

Last Name	No.	Yds	Avg	TD
Berry	43	663	15	6
Orr	40	867	22	6
Mackey	22	406	18	2
Moore	21	472	22	3
Hill	14	113	8	1
Lorick	11	164	15	0
Matte	10	169	17	0
Wilson	7	86	12	1
Richardson	3	42	14	0
Hawkins	2	42	21	1
Petties	2	20	10	1
Looney	1	1	1	1

PUNT RETURNS

Last Name	No.	Yds	Avg	TD
Harris	17	214	13	0
Hawkins	16	122	8	0
Logan	13	111	9	0
Haymond	1	6	6	0
Davis	1	0	0	0

KICKOFF RETURNS

Last Name	No.	Yds	Avg	TD
Lorick	13	385	30	0
Looney	14	345	25	0
Hill	4	85	21	0
Matte	3	71	24	0
Gilburg	1	19	19	0
Davis	1	12	12	0
Petties	1	9	9	0
Boyd	1	0	0	0
Haymond	1	0	0	0

PASSING – PUNTING – KICKING

PASSING	Att	Comp	%	Yds	Yd/Att	TD	Int–	%	RK
Unitas	305	158	52	2824	9.3	19	6–	2	4
Cuozzo	36	15	42	163	4.5	2	3–	8	
Matte	4	3	75	58	14.5	1	0–	0	

PUNTING	No	Avg
Looney	32	42.4
Gilburg	27	41.0

KICKING	XP	Att	%	FG	Att	%
Michaels	53	54	98	17	35	49

GREEN BAY PACKERS

RUSHING

Last Name	No.	Yds	Avg	TD
Taylor	235	1169	5.0	12
Hornung	103	415	4.0	5
Moore	102	371	3.6	2
Starr	24	165	6.9	3
Pitts	27	127	4.7	1
Norton	1	24	24.0	0
Crutcher	1	5	5.0	0
Bratkowski	2	0	0.0	0

RECEIVING

Last Name	No.	Yds	Avg	TD
Dowler	45	623	14	5
Taylor	38	354	9	3
R. Kramer	34	551	16	0
McGee	31	592	19	6
Moore	17	140	8	2
Hornung	9	98	11	0
Pitts	6	38	6	0
Fleming	4	36	9	0
Jeter	1	23	23	0
Long	1	19	19	0

PUNT RETURNS

Last Name	No.	Yds	Avg	TD
Wood	19	252	13	0
Pitts	15	191	13	1

KICKOFF RETURNS

Last Name	No.	Yds	Avg	TD
Adderly	19	508	27	0
Moore	16	431	27	0
Brown	7	167	24	0
Crutcher	2	54	27	0
Caffey	1	0	0	0

PASSING – PUNTING – KICKING

PASSING	Att	Comp	%	Yds	Yd/Att	TD	Int–	%	RK
Starr	272	163	60	2144	7.9	15	4–	1	1
Bratkowski	36	19	53	277	7.7	1	1–	3	
Hornung	10	3	30	25	2.5	0	1–	10	
Moore	3	1	33	28	9.3	0	0–	0	

PUNTING	No	Avg
Norton	56	42.2

KICKING	XP	Att	%	FG	Att	%
Hornung	41	43	95	12	38	32
Wood	1	1	100	0	1	0

MINNESOTA VIKINGS

RUSHING

Last Name	No.	Yds	Avg	TD
Brown	226	866	3.8	7
Mason	169	691	4.1	4
Tarkenton	50	330	6.6	2
Michel	39	129	3.3	0
McWatters	14	60	4.3	1
Dean	5	30	6.0	0
Lester	4	18	4.5	0
Walden	1	18	18.0	0
Butler	5	11	2.2	0
Vander Kelen	1	10	10.0	0
Smith	1	2	2.0	0
Hall	4	–4	–1.0	0
Alderman	0	22	0.0	0

RECEIVING

Last Name	No.	Yds	Avg	TD
Brown	48	703	15	9
Flatley	28	450	16	3
Mason	26	239	9	1
Hall	23	325	14	2
Reichow	20	284	14	2
Bedsole	18	295	16	5
Smith	10	211	21	1
McWatters	2	–1	–1	0
Butler	1	58	58	0
Dean	1	23	23	0
Michel	1	14	14	0
Vargo	1	13	13	0

PUNT RETURNS

Last Name	No.	Yds	Avg	TD
Butler	22	156	7	0
Mason	10	150	15	0
Dean	2	0	0	0
Kassulke	1	0	0	0

KICKOFF RETURNS

Last Name	No.	Yds	Avg	TD
Butler	26	597	23	0
Michel	8	192	24	0
Rose	8	180	23	0
Brown	5	68	14	0
Dean	3	50	17	0
Mason	2	36	18	0
McWatters	1	7	7	0

PASSING – PUNTING – KICKING

PASSING	Att	Comp	%	Yds	Yd/Att	TD	Int–	%	RK
Tarkenton	306	171	56	2506	8.2	22	11–	4	2
Vander Kelen	19	7	37	78	4.1	0	1–	5	
Mason	1	1	100	30	30.0	1	0–	0	

PUNTING	No	Avg
Walden	72	46.4

KICKING	XP	Att	%	FG	Att	%
Cox	40	42	95	21	33	64

WESTERN CONFERENCE—Continued

DETROIT LIONS 7-5-2 George Wilson

Scores of Each Game		
26	San Francisco	17
17	Los Angeles	17
10	GREEN BAY	14
26	NEW YORK	3
24	Minnesota	20
10	Chicago	0
0	BALTIMORE	34
37	LOS ANGELES	17
7	Green Bay	30
21	Cleveland	37
23	MINNESOTA	23
24	CHICAGO	27
31	Baltimore	14
24	SAN FRANCISCO	7

Use Name	Pos.	Hgt	Wgt	Age	Int	Pts
Daryl Sanders	OT	6'5"	250	22		
J. D. Smith	OT	6'5"	250	28		
John Gonzaga	OG-OT	6'3"	250	31		
John Gordy	OG	6'3"	250	28		
Jim Simon	OG	6'5"	235	23		
Wally Hilgenberg	LB-OG	6'3"	225	21		
Bob Whitlow	C	6'1"	236	28		
Bob Schlotz	OT-C	6'4"	250	26		
Darris McCord	DE	6'4"	250	31		
Bill Quinlan	DE	6'3"	240	32	1	
Sam Williams	DE	6'5"	235	33		6
Roger Brown	DT	6'5"	300	27		
Alex Karras	DT	6'2"	245	28	2	
Roger LaLonde	DT	6'3"	255	22		
Ernie Clark	LB	6'1"	220	26		
Dennis Gaubatz	LB	6'2"	220	23	1	2
Monte Lee	LB	6'4"	220	26		
Joe Schmidt	LB	6'1"	220	32		
Wayne Walker	LB	6'2"	225	27	1	74
Night Train Lane	DB	6'1"	200	36	1	
Dick LeBeau	DB	6'1"	185	27	5	
Bruce Maher	DB	5'11"	190	27	2	
Wayne Rasmussen	DB	6'2"	180	22		
Bobby Thompson	DB	5'10"	175	24	3	
Dick Compton	HB-DB	6'1"	195	24		
Yale Lary	DB	6'	190	33	6	
Gary Lowe	HB-DB	5'11"	195	30		
Sonny Gibbs	QB	6'7"	230	23		
Earl Morrall	QB	6'1"	206	30		
Milt Plum	QB	6'1"	205	30		6
Dan Lewis	HB	6'1"	200	28		12
Hugh McElhenny	HB	6'1"	190	35		
Tom Watkins	HB	6'1"	195	27		24
Pat Batten	FB	6'2"	225	22		
Nick Pietrosante	FB	6'2"	225	27		24
Nick Ryder	FB	6'	210	23		6
Terry Barr	FL	6'	190	29		54
Pat Studstill	FL	6'1"	175	26		6
Gail Cogdill	OE	6'2"	195	27		18
Jim Gibbons	OE	6'2"	220	28		48
Hugh McInnis	OE	6'3"	220	26		
Warren Wells	OE	6'1"	195	21		

Lucian Reeberg—Died Jan. 31, 1964 of Uremia

LOS ANGELES RAMS 5-7-2 Harland Svare

Scores of Each Game		
26	Pittsburgh	14
17	DETROIT	17
22	MINNESOTA	13
20	Baltimore	35
17	Chicago	38
42	SAN FRANCISCO	14
27	Green Bay	17
17	Detroit	37
20	PHILADELPHIA	10
24	CHICAGO	34
7	BALTIMORE	24
13	Minnesota	34
7	San Francisco	28
24	GREEN BAY	24

Use Name	Pos.	Hgt	Wgt	Age	Int	Pts
Joe Carollo	OT	6'2"	262	24		
Frank Varrichione	OT	6'1"	237	32		
Charley Cowan	OG-OT	6'4"	267	26		
Don Chuy	OG	6'1"	255	23		
Roger Davis	OG	6'3"	235	26		
Joe Scibelli	OG	6'1"	260	25		
Fred Whittingham	OG	6'1"	240	25		
Art Hunter	C	6'4"	248	31		
Joe Wendryhoski	C	6'2"	245	25		
Deacon Jones	DE	6'5"	267	25		
Lamar Lundy	DE	6'7"	250	29	1	6
Rosey Grier	DT	6'5"	290	31		
Gary Larsen	DT	6'5"	245	24		
Merlin Olsen	DT	6'5"	275	23		
Marv Harris	LB	6'1"	225	22		
Mike Henry	LB	6'2"	227	28		
Cliff Livingston	LB	6'3"	215	34		
Jack Pardee	LB	6'2"	230	28	1	
Andy Von Sonn	LB	6'2"	223	23		
Frank Budka	DB	6'	195	22	2	
Lindon Crow	DB	6'	200	31	1	
Aaron Martin	DB	6'	185	23	2	6
Ed Meador	DB	5'11"	198	27	3	
Jerry Richardson	DB	6'3"	190	21	5	
Bobby Smith	DB	6'	197	26	2	12
Roman Gabriel	QB	6'4"	220	24		6
Bill Munson	QB	6'2"	187	22		
Terry Baker	HB	6'3"	200	23		
Carver Shannon	HB	6'1"	206	26		
Ben Wilson	HB	6'	225	24		36
Dick Bass	FB	5'10"	200	27		12
Les Josephson	FB	6'	210	22		24
Willie Brown	FL	6'	186	21		
Jim Phillips	FL	6'1"	195	27		12
Duane Allen	OE	6'4"	225	26		6
Carroll Dale	OE	6'1"	195	26		12
Marlin McKeever	OE	6'1"	235	24		6
Bucky Pope	OE	6'5"	195	21		60
Billy Truax	OE	6'5"	240	21		
Bruce Gossett	K	6'2"	225	21		85
Danny Villanueva	K	5'11"	213	26		

CHICAGO BEARS 5-9-0 George Halas

Scores of Each Game		
12	Green Bay	23
34	Minnesota	28
0	Baltimore	52
21	San Francisco	31
38	LOS ANGELES	17
0	DETROIT	10
20	Washington	27
10	DALLAS	24
24	BALTIMORE	40
34	Los Angeles	24
23	SAN FRANCISCO	21
27	Detroit	24
3	GREEN BAY	17
14	MINNESOTA	41

Use Name	Pos.	Hgt	Wgt	Age	Int	Pts
George Burman	OT	6'3"	240	21		
Herm Lee	OT	6'4"	247	33		
Bob Wetoska	OT	6'3"	240	26		
Jim Cadile	OG	6'3"	240	23		
Dick Evey	OG	6'2"	225	23		
Ted Karras	OG	6'1"	243	31		
Mike Rabold	OG	6'2"	238	27		
Mike Pyle	C	6'3"	245	25		
Doug Atkins	DE	6'8"	255	34		
Bob Kilcullen	DE	6'3"	245	28		
Ed O'Bradovich	DE	6'3"	255	24		
John Johnson	DT	6'5"	260	23		
Stan Jones	DT	6'1"	250	33		
Earl Leggett	DT	6'3"	250	30		
Joe Fortunato	LB	6'	225	34		
Bill George	LB	6'2"	235	33	2	
Roger LeClerc	LB	6'3"	235	26		30
Larry Morris	LB	6'2"	230	29		
Jim Purnell	LB	6'2"	205	22		
Mike Reilly	LB	6'2"	210	21		
J. C. Caroline	DB	6'1"	190	31	2	
Larry Glueck	DB	6'	190	22		
Bennie McRae	DB	6'1"	180	23	2	
Richie Petitbon	DB	6'3"	205	26		
John Sisk	DB	6'3"	195	22		
Rosey Taylor	DB	5'11"	186	25	2	
Dave Whitsell	HB-DB	6'	190	28	2	
Rudy Bukich	QB	6'1"	205	33		
Larry Rakestraw	QB	6'2"	195	22		
Billy Wade	QB	6'2"	205	33		6
Jon Arnett	HB	5'11"	203	29		18
Charlie Bivins	HB	6'2"	212	25		6
Ronnie Bull	HB	6'	200	24		6
Andy Livingston	HB	6'	234	19		6
Billy Martin	HB	5'11"	196	26		
Rick Casares	FB	6'2"	225	33		12
Joe Marconi	FB	6'2"	225	30		30
Johnny Morris	FL	5'10"	180	29		60
Gary Barnes	OE-FL	6'4"	210	24		
Mike Ditka	OE	6'3"	230	24		36
Bob Jencks	OE	6'5"	227	23		38
Rich Kreitling	OE	6'2"	208	29		12
Bill Martin	OE	6'4"	240	21		
Bobby Joe Green	K	5'11"	175	26		

Bo Farrington, Willie Galimore } Died in auto accident during training camp.

SAN FRANCISCO FORTY NINERS 4-10-0 Jack Christiansen

Scores of Each Game		
17	DETROIT	26
28	Philadelphia	24
13	ST. LOUIS	23
31	CHICAGO	21
14	Green Bay	24
14	Los Angeles	42
22	MINNESOTA	27
7	Baltimore	37
7	Minnesota	24
24	GREEN BAY	14
21	Chicago	23
3	BALTIMORE	14
28	LOS ANGELES	7
7	Detroit	24

Use Name	Pos.	Hgt	Wgt	Age	Int	Pts
Walt Rock	OT	6'5"	245	23		
Len Rohde	OT	6'4"	240	26		
Leon Donahue	OG	6'4"	245	25		
Mike Magac	OG	6'3"	240	26		
Howard Mudd	OG	6'3"	240	22		
John Thomas	OG	6'4"	246	29		
Bruce Bosley	C	6'2"	240	30		
Frank Morze	C	6'4"	280	30		
Dan Colchico	DE	6'4"	245	27		
Clark Miller	DE	6'5"	245	25		
Karl Rubke	DE	6'4"	240	28		
Charlie Krueger	DT	6'4"	250	28		
Roland Lakes	DT	6'4"	263	24		
Chuck Sieminski	DT	6'4"	255	24		
Bill Cooper	LB	6'1"	215	25		
Floyd Dean	LB	6'4"	245	24		
Mike Dowdle	LB	6'3"	230	26	1	
Matt Hazeltine	LB	6'1"	230	31	1	
Ed Pine	LB	6'4"	235	24		
Dave Wilcox	LB	6'3"	230	21	1	
Kermit Alexander	DB	5'11"	186	23	5	6
Charley Britt (from MIN)	DB	6'2"	180	26		
Jim Johnson	DB	6'2"	190	26	3	
Elbert Kimbrough	DB	5'11"	190	25	2	
Jerry Mertens	DB	6'	185	28		
Ben Scotti	DB	6'1"	181	27		
Abe Woodson	DB	5'11"	188	29	2	
John Brodie	QB	6'1"	200	29		12
George Mira	QB	5'11"	183	22		
Billy Kilmer	HB-QB	6'	190	25		
Rudy Johnson	HB	5'1"	190	22		6
Dave Kopay	HB	6'2"	206	22		12
Don Lisbon	HB	6'	197	23		6
Gary Lewis	FB	6'3"	215	22		6
Mike Lind	FB	6'2"	215	24		42
J. D. Smith	FB	6'1"	210	31		
Bernie Casey	FL	6'4"	215	25		24
Dale Messer	FL	5'10"	175	27		
Kay McFarland	OE	6'2"	180	25		
Dave Parks	OE	6'2"	195	22		48
Bob Poole	OE	6'4"	216	22		
Monte Stickles	OE	6'4"	230	26		18
Tommy Davis	K	6'	212	29		54

Bob St. Clair – Injury

WESTERN CONFERENCE—Continued

DETROIT LIONS

RUSHING

Last Name	No.	Yds	Avg	TD
Pietrosante	147	536	3.6	4
Lewis	122	463	3.8	1
Watkins	80	218	2.7	1
Morrall	10	70	7.0	0
McElhenny	22	48	2.2	0
Barr	2	31	15.5	0
Plum	12	28	2.3	1
Lary	2	11	5.5	0
Ryder	11	11	1.0	0
Compton	3	2	0.7	0
Cogdill	1	–4	–4.0	0

RECEIVING

Last Name	No.	Yds	Avg	TD
Barr	57	1030	18	9
Cogdill	45	665	15	2
Gibbons	45	605	13	8
Pietrosante	19	152	8	0
Lewis	11	129	12	1
Watkins	10	125	13	1
Studstill	7	102	15	1
McElhenny	5	16	3	0
Ryder	4	30	8	1
Wells	2	21	11	0
McInnis	1	15	15	0

PUNT RETURNS

Last Name	No.	Yds	Avg	TD
Watkins	16	238	15	2
Studstill	17	137	8	0
Thompson	1	27	27	0
McElhenny	1	0	0	0
Maher	0	9	0	0

KICKOFF RETURNS

Last Name	No.	Yds	Avg	TD
Studstill	29	708	24	0
Watkins	16	368	23	0
McElhenny	3	72	24	0
Ryder	2	37	19	0
Clark	2	29	15	0
Lee	1	25	25	0
Thompson	1	24	24	0
Rasmussen	1	20	20	0
Hilgenberg	1	2	2	0
Simon	1	0	0	0
Compton	0	42	0	0

PASSING – PUNTING – KICKING

PASSING	Att	Comp	%	Yds	Yd/Att	TD	Int–	%	RK
Plum	287	154	54	2241	7.8	18	15–	5	5
Morrall	91	50	55	588	6.5	4	3–	3	
Gibbs	3	1	33	3	1.0	0	1–	33	
Barr	1	0	0	0	0.0	0	0–	0	
Lewis	1	0	0	0	0.0	0	0–	0	
Lowe	1	0	0	0	0.0	0	1–	100	
Pietrosante	1	0	0	0	0.0	0	1–	100	
Watkins	1	1	100	58	58.0	1	0–	0	

PUNTING	No	Avg
Lary	67	46.3
Morrall	1	8.0

KICKING	XP	Att	%	FG	Att	%
Walker	32	34	94	14	25	56

LOS ANGELES RAMS

RUSHING

Last Name	No.	Yds	Avg	TD
Wilson	159	553	3.5	5
Josephson	96	451	4.7	3
Bass	72	342	4.8	2
Munson	19	150	7.9	0
Baker	24	82	3.4	0
Shannon	17	35	2.1	0
Pope	2	11	5.5	0
Gabriel	11	5	0.5	1

RECEIVING

Last Name	No.	Yds	Avg	TD
McKeever	41	582	14	1
Dale	32	544	17	2
Pope	25	786	31	10
Josephson	21	269	13	1
Phillips	17	245	14	2
Wilson	15	116	8	1
Bass	9	83	9	0
Baker	8	92	12	0
Allen	2	29	15	1
Shannon	2	4	2	0
Brown	1	19	19	0

PUNT RETURNS

Last Name	No.	Yds	Avg	TD
Shannon	15	81	5	0
Smith	12	68	6	0
Brown	4	23	6	0
Meador	2	9	5	0
Bass	1	0	0	0

KICKOFF RETURNS

Last Name	No.	Yds	Avg	TD
Smith	20	489	24	0
Shannon	18	442	25	0
Meador	6	148	25	0
Brown	6	122	20	0
Bass	1	25	25	0
Martin	2	18	9	0
Larsen	2	14	7	0
Harris	1	0	0	0

PASSING – PUNTING – KICKING

PASSING	Att	Comp	%	Yds	Yd/Att	TD	Int–	%	RK
Munson	223	108	48	1533	6.9	9	15–	7	17
Gabriel	143	65	45	1236	8.6	9	5–	3	9
Baker	1	0	0	0	0.0	0	0–	0	
Meador	1	0	0	0	0.0	0	0–	0	

PUNTING	No	Avg
Villanueva	82	44.1

KICKING	XP	Att	%	FG	Att	%
Gossett	31	33	94	18	24	75

CHICAGO BEARS

RUSHING

Last Name	No.	Yds	Avg	TD
Arnett	119	400	3.4	1
Bull	86	320	3.7	1
Casares	35	123	3.5	0
Marconi	46	98	2.1	2
Wade	24	96	4.0	1
Bivins	29	92	3.2	0
Bukich	12	28	2.3	0
Whitsell	1	14	14.0	0
Green	2	–2	–1.0	0
Livingston	2	–3	–1.5	0

RECEIVING

Last Name	No.	Yds	Avg	TD
J. Morris	93	1200	13	10
Ditka	75	897	12	5
Arnett	25	223	9	2
Kreitling	20	185	9	2
Marconi	20	181	9	3
Bull	15	35	2	0
Casares	14	113	8	2
Bivins	11	59	5	1
Barnes	4	61	15	0
Bill Martin	3	93	31	0
Billy Martin	1	9	9	0
Livingston	1	0	0	0

PUNT RETURNS

Last Name	No.	Yds	Avg	TD
Arnett	19	188	10	0
Billy Martin	11	31	3	0

KICKOFF RETURNS

Last Name	No.	Yds	Avg	TD
Billy Martin	24	534	22	0
Arnett	15	331	22	0
Bivins	8	218	27	0
Livingston	6	167	28	1
Bull	2	44	22	0
Marconi	2	12	6	0
Purnell	1	8	8	0

PASSING – PUNTING – KICKING

PASSING	Att	Comp	%	Yds	Yd/Att	TD	Int–	%	RK
Wade	327	182	56	1944	5.9	13	14–	4	10
Bukich	160	99	62	1099	6.8	12	7–	4	8
Arnett	4	0	0	0	0.0	0	0–	0	
Bull	3	1	33	13	4.3	0	0–	0	

PUNTING	No	Avg
Green	71	44.5

KICKING	XP	Att	%	FG	Att	%
Jencks	29	32	91	3	7	43
LeClerc	0	0	0	10	16	63

SAN FRANCISCO FORTY NINERS

RUSHING

Last Name	No.	Yds	Avg	TD
Kopay	75	271	3.6	0
Lind	100	256	2.6	7
Mira	18	177	9.8	0
Lisbon	55	162	2.9	0
Brodie	27	135	5.0	2
Lewis	43	115	2.7	1
Kilmer	36	113	3.1	0
Smith	13	55	4.2	0
R. Johnson	16	48	3.0	1

RECEIVING

Last Name	No.	Yds	Avg	TD
Casey	58	808	14	4
Stickles	40	685	17	3
Parks	36	703	20	8
Lind	25	178	7	0
Kopay	20	135	7	2
Lisbon	13	104	8	1
Kilmer	11	136	12	0
Lewis	7	73	10	0
McFarland	5	67	13	0
R. Johnson	5	21	4	0
Messer	4	72	18	0
Poole	1	8	8	0

PUNT RETURNS

Last Name	No.	Yds	Avg	TD
Alexander	21	189	9	1
Woodson	22	133	6	0

KICKOFF RETURNS

Last Name	No.	Yds	Avg	TD
Woodson	32	880	28	0
Alexander	20	483	24	0
Kopay	2	30	15	0
Lewis	1	0	0	0
Pine	1	0	0	0
Thomas	1	0	0	0

PASSING – PUNTING – KICKING

PASSING	Att	Comp	%	Yds	Yd/Att	TD	Int–	%	RK
Brodie	392	193	49	2498	6.4	14	16–	4	12
Mira	53	23	43	331	6.3	2	5–	9	
Kilmer	14	8	57	92	6.6	1	1–	7	
Kopay	1	0	0	0	0.0	0	0–	0	
Lind	1	1	100	69	69.0	1	0–	0	

PUNTING	No	Avg
Davis	79	45.6

KICKING	XP	Att	%	FG	Att	%
Davis	30	30	100	8	25	32

1964 A.F.L. TV and New York, An Unbeatable Combination

"People have now stopped asking me if we are going to make it," said Commissioner Joe Foss after signing a new television contract with the National Broadcasting Company. Starting in 1965, NBC would handle the national TV coverage of AFL games and pay the league $36 million for five seasons from 1965 to 1969. With all clubs sharing equally in the television pot, Foss no longer had any worries about any teams going bankrupt. He also had no worries over job security, as the team owners extended him a new three-year contract with a sizable raise in salary.

One of the most gratifying developments for Foss was the sudden popularity of the New York Jets. Only two years before they were the bankrupt Titans, playing in an ancient ball park and living off league funds. Now they played in the new Shea Stadium, set a single-game attendance record three times during this season, and had solid ownership led by Sonny Werblin. With the New York team healthy and strong, the whole league found new respect coming from the East Coast media.

EASTERN DIVISION

Buffalo Bills—The heart of the Bills, the AFL's first great ball-control team, was a powerful fullback and a bruising defensive line. Cookie Gilchrist as usual took care of the heavy-duty running chores, leading the league in rushing despite the lack of an accomplished running mate at halfback. The Bills passed the ball less frequently than the other AFL clubs, as Jack Kemp ran the offense quite conservatively. But when the attack bogged down, coach Lou Saban could send young Daryle Lamonica in at quarterback. A second-year pro with a liking for the long pass, Lamonica relieved Kemp in several games and pulled out victories with deep bombs to Elbert Dubenion and Glenn Bass. Supporting the offense was a strong line featuring Billy Shaw and Stew Barber. The defensive unit also boasted of a strong line, as Ron McDole, Jim Dunaway, Tom Sestak, and Tom Day jelled into the league's best front four, and a tight group of linebackers and backs played well enough behind this line to make the Buffalo defense the stingiest in allowing points. The Bills won games by outplaying opponents in the line, by blocking and tackling better, and if the offense ever needed a three-point boost, coach Saban unveiled pro football's first soccer-style place-kicker in Pete Gogolak, a Hungarian refugee who kicked the ball sideways accurately enough to score 102 points. With a full pantry of hard-nosed ball players, the Bills swept their first nine games and put down a late Boston challenge to win the Eastern crown.

Boston Patriots—Closing with a rush, the Patriots just missed repeating as Eastern champion. Starting with a November 6 win over Houston, they won five straight games to pull within a half game of the first-place Bills before their season-closing showdown on December 20. The Pats had won last year's playoff game in frigid Buffalo, but the Bills turned the tables this year by winning this key game 24-14 in a snowstorm in Boston. The Patriots got as far as they did with little help from rookies, as coach Mike Holovak continued to depend on his shopworn veterans. Thirty-three-year-old Babe Parilli won his first All-Pro honors by passing for thirty-one touchdowns, while slow-footed Gino Cappelletti caught seven TD passes and scored a league-leading 155 points on his receiving and kicking. The defense was still the Patriots' long suit, bailing the team out in victories of 17-14 over Oakland and 12-7 over Denver. The front four of Larry Eisenhauer, Bob Dee, Houston Antwine, and Jim Hunt stood firm against enemy runners, while linebacker Nick Buoniconti blitzed opposing quarterbacks to distraction. But time was growing short for the Patriots, who would soon have to replace such oldsters as Parilli, Cappelletti, and Dee.

New York Jets—With their move into spanking new Shea Stadium, the Jets immediately became the attendance sensation of the league. Their first game in the new park drew an AFL record crowd of 45,665, the second game attracted 47,746, and the November 8 match with Buffalo brought out 60,300 fans. Several factors contributed to the Jets' sudden popularity, such as the new stadium, the scarcity of available tickets for Giant games, the scheduling of games on Saturday nights, and a close identification with the colorful baseball Mets. The fans who did come out saw a team rapidly improving with good young talent. This year's rich rookie class included Matt Snell, a talented all-around fullback; Gerry Philbin and Bert Wilder, a pair of strong defensive ends; Ralph Baker, who won a starting linebacker spot; John Schmitt and Dave Herman, two reserve offensive linemen who would star in later years; and place-kicker Jim Turner. Another newcomer won a large following, as middle linebacker Wahoo McDaniel became a folk hero with New York fans with his violent tackles. Holdovers such as Larry Grantham, Bill Mathis, Don Maynard, Bake Turner, Winston Hill, and Dainard Paulson formed the nucleus of a good club, but any championships would have to wait until a top quarterback was acquired.

Houston Oilers—Hopes that 1963 was just an isolated bad year for the Oilers faded as they lost nine straight games in the center of the schedule. Sammy Baugh was this year's head coach, with Pop Ivy disposed of for not winning a championship last season, and Baugh would get the ax after this losing campaign. The Oiler roster carried heavy doses of both rookies and aging veterans. Of the several freshmen to make the squad, Sid Blanks, Scott Appleton, Pete Jacquess, W. K. Hicks, Benny Nelson, and Willie Frazier saw considerable action. At the other end of the spectrum, thirty-six-year-old George Blanda, thirty-six-year-old Bud McFadin, and thirty-four-year-old Ed Hussman held down starting posts in the Houston lineup. In between the two extremes of age came players in their prime—Charley Hennigan, Freddy Glick, Bob Talamini, and Doug Cline. Hennigan, who was Blanda's favorite pass receiver, hauled in 101 passes to set a new professional record. But not enough Oiler players were at the peak of their powers, and the team hung all its hopes on this year's youngsters improving in the near future.

WESTERN DIVISION

San Diego Chargers—Tobin Rote's old arm had few passes left in it, so John Hadl assumed the bulk of the quarterbacking duties and took the Chargers back to the championship game. The road was a little rockier this year, though. After beating Houston to open the season, the Chargers lost to Boston and Buffalo and just managed a tie with New York. With none of the Western teams very hot in the early going, San Diego then rocketed out to a comfortable lead by winning their next six games. Even a late-season slump, in which they lost three of their last four games, could not bring the Chargers back to the pack. But despite their streaky play, the Chargers boasted of one of the deepest squads in the league. They had good runners in Keith Lincoln and Paul Lowe, pro football's most exciting receiver in Lance Alworth, fine offensive linemen in Ron Mix and Walt Sweeney, and good defenders in Earl Faison, Ernie Ladd, Chuck Allen, Frank Buncom, and Dick Westmoreland. The only thing missing from the San Diego arsenal was a consistent field-goal kicker. The Chargers tried Keith Lincoln, Herb Travenio, Ben Agajanian, and George Blair at the spot during the season. But that lack was not enough to keep the Chargers away from their fourth Western crown in five years.

Kansas City Chiefs—On paper, the Chiefs looked unbeatable; on the field, the Chiefs were a .500 club. They looked like the best team in the league when they beat the Chargers 49-6 and dismantled the Jets 24-7, but they looked like scrubs while losing 33-27 to the lowly Broncos. No one could figure out how a team with good offensive and defensive units could lose seven games, but the Chiefs complicated coach Hank Stram's life by doing that. Len Dawson sparked the attack with thirty touchdown passes despite a trio of slow receivers, while the Kansas City running corps was brimming with talent. Abner Haynes was less consistent but still dangerous at halfback, rookie Mack Lee Hill bulled his way into the starting lineup, and Curtis McClinton, Jack Spikes, and Bert Coan provided unheard-of depth. The defense was one of the league's best, with two superb linemen in Jerry Mays and Buck Buchanan, a trio of fine linebackers in E. J. Holub, Sherrill Headrick, and Bobby Bell, and top backs in Dave Grayson, Duane Wood, Bobby Hunt, and Johnny Robinson. But the Chiefs found ways to lose that defied the heavy weight of their roster.

Oakland Raiders—The miraculous finish of 1963 wore off as the Raiders lost their first five games, but Al Davis' men came back in the second half of the schedule to prove that they were indeed a solid football team. The final five games brought four wins and a tie to Oakland, and among the defeated teams were San Diego and Buffalo, the teams headed for the championship game. The Raiders no longer had the element of surprise on their side, as the rest of the league had seen their blitzes last year and no longer took them lightly, but they resorted to a more settled style of play with fine results in the back stretch. Clem Daniels got off to a slow start, but the powerful halfback recovered to star during the Raiders' late drive. Helping Daniels with strong blocking was Billy Cannon, obtained from Houston to fill the gap at fullback. The defense was strengthened by the addition of end Ben Davidson, a huge lineman cut by the NFL Washington Redskins, and rookie linebacker Dan Conners—and despite the disappointing third-place finish, coach Davis was happy about adding new talent to his future champions.

Denver Broncos—Coach Jack Faulkner resorted to lend lease to get himself a quarterback, sending defensive tackle Bud McFadin to Houston in exchange for quarterback Jacky Lee, who was to return to Houston after two seasons. The deal won press space but few ball games, as Lee was a distinct disappointment in leading the attack. The offensive line was a shambles, however, and few passers could have accomplished much behind it. The poor blocking wasted some good offensive talent, such as split end Lionel Taylor, tight end Hewritt Dixon, halfback Charley Mitchell, and fullback Billy Joe. The defense was easy to march through but did cause enemy quarterbacks some pain with a late-season blitzing campaign; the best performances were turned in by Ray Jacobs, Jerry Hopkins, Willie Brown, and Goose Gonsoulin. The Broncos went into the season with no title hopes, but when they were massacred in the first four games, coach Faulkner got the ax and assistant Mac Speedie took over as head man.

FINAL TEAM STATISTICS

OFFENSE

	BOSTON	BUFFALO	DENVER	HOUSTON	K. CITY	NEW YORK	OAKLAND	SAN DIEGO
FIRST DOWNS:								
Total	226	255	207	284	250	209	270	254
by Rushing	66	114	78	80	90	79	63	85
by Passing	144	130	116	186	148	108	186	156
by Penalty	16	11	13	18	12	22	21	13
RUSHING:								
Number	381	492	391	327	415	384	331	392
Yards	1361	2040	1311	1347	1825	1457	1480	1522
Average Yards	3.6	4.1	3.4	4.1	4.4	3.8	4.5	3.9
Touchdowns	9	25	10	14	14	11	9	14
PASSING:								
Attempts	476	397	456	592	412	451	521	445
Completions	229	174	230	299	228	201	253	224
Completion Percentage	48.1	43.8	50.4	50.5	55.3	44.6	48.6	50.3
Passing Yardage	3467	3422	2541	3734	3321	2694	3886	3363
Average Yards per Attempt	7.3	8.6	5.6	6.3	8.1	6.0	7.5	7.6
Average Yards per Completion	15.1	19.7	11.0	12.5	14.6	13.4	15.4	15.0
Times Tackled Attempting to Pass	29	35	61	23	44	27	56	22
Yards Lost Attempting to Pass	301	256	520	207	446	262	464	221
Net Yards	3166	3166	2021	3527	2875	2432	3422	3142
Touchdowns	31	19	14	19	32	19	28	28
Interceptions	27	34	32	29	21	33	33	30
Percent Intercepted	5.7	8.6	7.0	4.9	5.1	7.3	6.3	6.7
PUNTING:								
Number	78	65	83	55	79	79	59	63
Average Distance	38.0	42.7	43.4	41.2	42.5	41.3	41.5	39.3
PUNT RETURNS:								
Number	38	46	25	19	40	38	33	34
Yards	276	421	259	252	400	283	447	283
Average Yards	7.3	9.2	10.4	13.3	10.0	7.4	13.5	8.3
Touchdowns	0	1	1	1	0	0	0	0
KICKOFF RETURNS:								
Number	58	48	76	66	57	54	61	53
Yards	1167	1018	1758	1559	1261	1088	1525	1288
Average Yards	20.1	21.2	23.1	23.6	22.1	20.1	25.0	24.3
Touchdowns	0	0	0	1	0	0	0	0
INTERCEPTION RETURNS:								
Number	31	28	32	30	28	34	26	30
Yards	427	470	459	437	408	477	430	487
Average Yards	13.8	16.8	14.3	14.6	14.6	14.0	16.5	16.2
Touchdowns	1	2	1	3	1	4	0	2
PENALTIES:								
Number				Not Available				
Yards								
FUMBLES:								
Number	23	32	27	24	36	15	30	30
Number Lost	12	18	8	15	20	7	18	16
POINTS:								
Total	365	400	240	310	366	278	303	341
PAT (kick) Attempts	36	46	25	38	46	33	34	43
PAT (kick) Made	36	45	22	37	46	33	34	39
PAT (Rush or Pass) Attempts	5	2	3	1	3	1	2	1
PAT (Rush or Pass) Made	3	2	3	0	1	0	0	1
FG Attempts	39	29	34	29	17	27	24	26
FG Made	25	19	14	13	8	13	15	12
Percent FG Made	64.1	65.5	41.2	44.8	47.1	48.1	62.5	46.2
Safeties	1	3	1	0	0	1	1	0

DEFENSE

	BOSTON	BUFFALO	DENVER	HOUSTON	K. CITY	NEW YORK	OAKLAND	SAN DIEGO
FIRST DOWNS:								
Total	243	206	271	276	211	245	255	248
by Rushing	63	48	100	103	77	79	103	82
by Passing	165	145	148	159	124	152	134	147
by Penalty	15	13	23	14	10	14	18	19
RUSHING:								
Number	356	300	424	438	390	410	396	399
Yards	1143	913	2064	1961	1315	1675	1750	1522
Average Yards	3.2	3.0	4.9	4.5	3.4	4.1	4.4	3.8
Touchdowns	10	4	21	18	9	14	20	10
PASSING:								
Attempts	530	517	440	433	440	473	433	484
Completions	261	241	215	229	218	228	206	240
Completion Percentage	49.2	46.6	48.9	52.9	49.5	48.2	47.6	49.6
Passing Yardage	3645	3361	3353	3469	2910	3472	3292	2926
Average Yards per Attempt	6.9	6.5	7.6	8.0	6.6	7.3	7.6	6.0
Average Yards per Completion	14.0	13.9	15.6	15.1	13.3	15.2	16.0	12.2
Times Tackled Attempting to Pass	47	50	44	25	28	28	37	38
Yards Lost Attempting to Pass	428	396	447	189	279	231	299	408
Net Yards	3217	2965	2906	3280	2631	3241	2993	2518
Touchdowns	23	24	29	24	25	22	21	22
Interceptions	31	28	32	30	28	34	26	30
Percent Intercepted	5.8	5.4	7.3	6.9	6.4	7.2	6.0	6.2
PUNTING:								
Number	82	87	59	56	78	71	66	62
Average Distance	41.5	41.9	41.4	39.1	40.7	40.5	41.7	41.3
PUNT RETURNS:								
Number	24	24	40	33	36	43	41	32
Yards	185	250	526	295	251	426	272	416
Average Yards	7.7	10.4	13.2	8.9	7.0	9.9	6.6	13.0
Touchdowns	0	0	1	0	0	1	0	1
KICKOFF RETURNS:								
Number	70	59	44	53	64	53	64	66
Yards	1637	1385	1166	978	1459	1236	1239	1564
Average Yards	23.4	23.5	26.5	18.5	22.8	23.3	19.4	23.7
Touchdowns	1	0	0	0	0	0	0	0
INTERCEPTION RETURNS:								
Number	27	34	32	29	21	33	33	30
Yards	485	406	441	496	228	448	713	378
Average Yards	18.0	11.9	13.8	17.1	10.9	13.6	21.6	12.6
Touchdowns	1	0	1	3	3	1	4	1
PENALTIES:								
Number				Not Available				
Yards								
FUMBLES:								
Number	33	24	40	21	29	19	19	32
Number Lost	17	15	21	8	18	10	10	15
POINTS:								
Total	297	242	438	355	306	315	350	300
PAT (kick) Attempts	33	23	52	43	36	38	43	33
PAT (kick) Made	32	22	52	41	34	36	43	32
PAT (Rush or Pass) Attempts	3	5	0	2	2	1	2	3
PAT (Rush or Pass) Made	2	2	0	1	1	0	1	3
FG Attempts	27	27	25	30	20	27	34	32
FG Made	15	14	22	14	14	15	11	14
Percent FG Made	50.0	51.9	88.0	46.7	70.0	55.6	32.3	43.8
Safeties	0	0	4	0	0	0	1	2

1964 AFL CHAMPIONSHIP GAME

December 26, at Buffalo
(Attendance 40,242)

SCORING

BUFFALO	3	10	0	7	–20
SAN DIEGO	7	0	0	0	– 7

First Quarter
- S.D. Kocourek, 26 yard pass from Rote
  PAT–Lincoln (kick)
- BUF. Gogolak, 12 yard field goal

Second Quarter
- BUF. Carlton, 4 yard rush
  PAT–Gogolak (kick)
- BUF. Gogolak, 17 yard field goal

Fourth Quarter
- BUF. Kemp, 1 yard rush
  PAT–Gogolak (kick)

TEAM STATISTICS

BUFF.		S.D.
21	First Downs–Total	15
12	First Downs–Rushing	7
8	First Downs–Passing	7
1	First Downs–Penalty	1
0	Fumbles–Number	1
0	Fumbles–Number Lost	0
3	Penalties–Number	3
45	Yards Penalized	20
0	Missed Field Goals	0

Nò Instant Replay

The San Diego Chargers started fast in defending their AFL title, but the sturdy Buffalo defense caught up and turned the game around before the first half ended. The first time the Chargers got their hands on the ball they drove 80 yards in four plays; Keith Lincoln, the star of last year's championship game, ran 38 yards on one play, and Tobin Rote found Dave Kocourek with a pass good for 26 yards and the first touchdown of the game. Lincoln's extra point made the score 7-0, and some fans expected the Chargers to turn the game into a rout as they had the year before. On the Chargers' next drive, however, the Bills made the key play of the game. When Lincoln caught a short pass in the flat, Buffalo linebacker Mike Stratton leveled him with a crunching tackle that knocked the ball loose and broke one of Lincoln's ribs. With their star back out of action, the Chargers never again could move the ball against the Buffalo defense. Pete Gogolak scored the Bills' first three points on a 12-yard field goal, and 10 second-quarter points gave Buffalo a 13-7 lead at halftime. The third period was scoreless, but the differences in the teams showed through clearly. The San Diego running attack missed the injured Lincoln dearly, while Cookie Gilchrist blasted into the Chargers' line with jackhammer force and regularity. While the San Diego attack withered in the face of the Buffalo pass rush, the Bills added a final touchdown when a Jack Kemp-to-Glenn Bass pass covering 48 yards brought the ball down to the one-yard line before Kemp went over for the 20-7 victory and Buffalo's first major-league sports championship.

INDIVIDUAL STATISTICS

RUSHING

BUFFALO	No	Yds	Avg.	SAN DIEGO	No	Yds	Avg.
Gilchrist	16	122	7.6	Lincoln	3	47	15.7
Carlton	18	70	3.9	Lowe	7	34	4.9
Kemp	5	16	3.2	MacKinnon	1	17	17.0
Dubenion	1	9	9.0	Kinderman	4	14	3.5
Lamonica	1	2	2.0	Hadl	1	13	13.0
	41	219	5.3	Rote	1	6	6.0
				Norton	1	–7	–7.0
					18	124	6.9

RECEIVING

BUFFALO	No	Yds	Avg.	SAN DIEGO	No	Yds	Avg.
Dubenion	3	36	12.0	Linderman	4	52	13.0
Bass	2	70	35.0	MacKinnon	3	12	4.0
Warlick	2	41	20.5	Kocourek	2	52	26.0
Gilchrist	2	22	11.0	Lowe	2	9	4.5
Ross	1	–1	–1.0	Norton	1	13	13.0
	10	168	16.8	Lincoln	1	11	11.0
					13	149	11.5

PUNTING

BUFFALO	No	Yds	Avg.	SAN DIEGO	No	Yds	Avg.
Maguire	5		46.8	Hadl	5		36.4

PUNT RETURNS

BUFFALO	No	Yds	Avg.	SAN DIEGO	No	Yds	Avg.
Clarke	1	6	6.0	Robinson	1	30	30.0
				Duncan	1	28	28.0
					2	58	29.0

KICKOFF RETURNS

BUFFALO	No	Yds	Avg.	SAN DIEGO	No	Yds	Avg.
Rutkowski	1	27	27.0	Duncan	3	147	49.0
Warner	1	17	17.0	Warren	1	28	28.0
	2	44	22.0		4	175	43.8

INTERCEPTION RETURNS

BUFFALO	No	Yds	Avg.	SAN DIEGO	No	Yds	Avg.
Warner	1	8	8.0	None			
Byrd	1	0	0.0				
Stratton	1	0	0.0				
	3	8	2.7				

PASSING

	Att.	Comp.	Comp. Pct.	Yds.	Int.	Yds/ Att.	Yds/ Comp.
BUFFALO							
Kemp	20	10	50.0	168	0	8.4	16.8
SAN DIEGO							
Rote	26	10	38.5	118	2	4.5	11.8
Hadl	10	3	30.0	31	1	3.1	10.3
	36	13	36.1	149	3	4.1	11.5

1964 A.F.L. — Eastern Division

BUFFALO BILLS 12-2-0 Lou Saban

Scores of Each Game		
34	KANSAS CITY	17
30	DENVER	13
30	SAN DIEGO	3
23	OAKLAND	20
48	Houston	17
35	Kansas City	22
34	NEW YORK	24
24	HOUSTON	10
20	New York	7
28	BOSTON	36
27	San Diego	24
13	Oakland	16
30	Denver	19
24	Boston	14

Use Name	Pos.	Hgt	Wgt	Age	Int	Pts
Stew Barber	OT	6'3"	250	25		
Dick Hudson	OT	6'4"	272	24		
Joe O'Donnell	OT	6'2"	246	22		
Al Bemiller	OG	6'3"	260	25		
George Flint	OG	6'4"	244	26		
Billy Shaw	OG	6'3"	248	24		
Walt Cudzik	C	6'2"	240	31		
Tom Day	DE	6'2"	250	29		
Ron McDole	DE	6'3"	264	24	1	
Jim Dunaway	DT	6'4"	276	22		
Tom Keating	DT	6'3"	242	21		
Dudley Meredith	DT	6'4"	275	29		
Tom Sestak	DT	6'5"	270	28	1	6
Harry Jacobs	LB	6'2"	225	27	2	
Paul Maguire	LB	6'	220	26		
Mike Stratton	LB	6'3"	240	22	1	
John Tracey	LB	6'3"	225	30	3	
Ray Abbruzzese	DB	6'1"	194	26		
Butch Byrd	DB	6'	211	22	7	6
Hagood Clarke	DB	6'	188	22		6
Ollie Dobbins	DB	5'11"	185	22		
Booker Edgerson	DB	5'10"	180	25	4	
George Saimes	DB	5'10"	195	22	6	
Gene Sykes	DB	6'1"	195	23	2	
Charley Ferguson – Injury						
Jack Kemp	QB	6'1"	200	30		30
Daryle Lamonica	QB	6'2"	215	23		40
Joe Auer	HB	6'1"	205	22		18
Wray Carlton	HB	6'2"	216	26		6
Bobby Smith	HB	6'	203	22		24
Cookie Gilchrist	FB	6'3"	250	29		36
Willie Ross	FB	5'10"	200	23		6
Elbert Dubenion	FL	6'	187	29		60
Ed Rutkowski	FL	6'1"	208	23		6
Glenn Bass	OE	6'2"	206	25		42
Bill Groman	OE	6'	195	28		6
Ernie Warlick	OE	6'4"	235	32		
Pete Gogolak	K	6'2"	200	22		102

BOSTON PATRIOTS 10-3-1 Mike Holovak

Scores of Each Game		
17	Oakland	14
33	San Diego	28
26	NEW YORK	10
39	Denver	10
17	SAN DIEGO	26
43	OAKLAND	43
24	KANSAS CITY	7
14	New York	35
25	HOUSTON	24
36	Buffalo	28
12	DENVER	7
34	Houston	17
31	Kansas City	24
14	BUFFALO	24

Use Name	Pos.	Hgt	Wgt	Age	Int	Pts
Don Oakes	OT	6'3"	255	26		
Bob Schmidt	OT	6'4"	250	28		
Bob Yates	OT	6'3"	230	25		
Charley Long	OG	6'3"	250	26		
Billy Neighbors	OG	5'11"	240	24		
Dave Watson	OG	6'1"	230	23		
Jon Morris	C	6'4"	240	21		
Bob Dee	DE	6'3"	240	31		
Larry Eisenhauer	DE	6'5"	250	24		
Jim Hunt	DE-DT	5'11"	245	25		
Len St. Jean	DE	6'1"	240	22		
Houston Antwine	DT	6'	270	25		
Jerry DeLucca	DT	6'3"	250	28		
Jess Richardson	DT	6'2"	265	34		
Tom Addison	LB	6'3"	230	28	2	
Nick Buoniconti	LB	5'11"	220	23	5	
Mike Dukes	LB	6'3"	235	28	1	
Lonnie Farmer	LB	6'	220	23		
Jack Rudolph	LB	6'3"	230	26		
Don McKinnon	C-LB	6'3"	230	22		
Dave Cloutier	DB	6'	195	25		
Dick Felt	DB	6'	185	31	2	
Ron Hall	DB	6'	190	27	11	
Ross O'Hanley	DB	6'	185	25	3	6
Chuck Shonta	DB	6'	200	26	1	
Don Webb	DB	5'10"	200	25	6	
Tom Stephens	OE-DB	6'1"	215	28		
Babe Parilli	QB	6'1"	190	34		12
Tom Yewcic	QB	5'11"	185	32		
Ron Burton	HB	5'10"	190	27		30
J. D. Garrett	HB	5'11"	195	22		12
Jim Crawford	FB	6'1"	205	28		
Larry Garron	FB	6'	195	27		54
Jim Colclough	FL	6'	185	28		34
Al Snyder	FL	6'	195	22		
Gino Cappelletti	OE	6'	190	30		155
Art Graham	OE	6'1"	205	23		36
Tony Romeo	OE	6'2"	230	25		24

NEW YORK JETS 5-8-1 Weeb Ewbank

Scores of Each Game		
30	DENVER	6
10	Boston	26
17	SAN DIEGO	17
35	OAKLAND	13
24	HOUSTON	21
24	Buffalo	34
35	BOSTON	14
7	BUFFALO	20
16	Denver	20
26	Oakland	35
27	KANSAS CITY	14
3	San Diego	38
17	Houston	33
7	Kansas City	24

Use Name	Pos.	Hgt	Wgt	Age	Int	Pts
Winston Hill	OT	6'4"	275	22		
Jim McCusker	OT	6'2"	250	28		
Sherman Plunkett	OT	6'4"	295	30		
Sam DeLuca	OG	6'2"	250	28		
Dan Ficca	OG	6'1"	250	25		
Dave Herman	OG	6'2"	255	22		
Pete Perreault	OG	6'3"	245	25		
Mike Hudock	C	6'2"	245	29		
John Schmitt	C	6'4"	265	21		
Gerry Philbin	DE	6'2"	245	23		
Lavern Torczon	DE	6'2"	250	28	1	6
Bob Watters	DE	6'4"	245	28		
Bert Wilder	DE	6'3"	245	24		
Gordy Holz	DT	6'4"	260	30		
Bob McAdams	DT	6'3"	250	24		
Paul Rochester	DT	6'2"	250	27		
Ralph Baker	LB	6'3"	235	22	2	
Ed Cummings	LB	6'2"	232	23	1	
Larry Grantham	LB	6'	206	25	2	
Wahoo McDaniel	LB	6'	240	27	3	6
Bob Rowley	LB	6'2"	225	22		
Mark Johnston (from OAK)	DB	6'	200	26	1	
Bill Pashe	DB	5'11"	185	23		
Dainard Paulson	DB	5'11"	190	27	12	6
Bill Rademacher	DB	6'1"	190	22	1	
Marsh Starks	DB	6'	190	25	1	
Vince Turner	DB	5'11"	190	21	1	
Clyde Washington	DB	6'	206	26		
Bill Baird	HB-DB	5'10"	180	25	8	6
Mike Taliaferro	QB	6'2"	210	22		
Dick Wood	QB	6'5"	205	28		6
Pete Liske	DB-QB	6'2"	195	23		
Curley Johnson	HB	6'	215	29		
Bill Mathis	HB	6'1"	220	25		24
Mark Smolinski	FB	6'	215	25		6
Matt Snell	FB	6'2"	220	22		36
Jim Evans	FL	6'1"	190	24		
Al Lawson	FL	5'11"	190	22		
Don Maynard	FL	6'	185	28		48
Gene Heeter	OE	6'4"	235	23		6
Dee Mackey	OE	6'5"	225	28		
Bake Turner	OE	6'	185	24		54
Jim Turner	K	6'2"	205	23		72

HOUSTON OILERS 4-10-0 Sammy Baugh

Scores of Each Game		
21	San Diego	27
42	OAKLAND	28
38	Denver	17
7	Kansas City	28
17	BUFFALO	48
21	New York	24
17	SAN DIEGO	20
10	Buffalo	24
24	Boston	25
10	Oakland	20
19	KANSAS CITY	28
17	BOSTON	34
33	NEW YORK	17
34	DENVER	15

Use Name	Pos.	Hgt	Wgt	Age	Int	Pts
Staley Faulkner	OT	6'3"	245	23		
Jerry Fowler	OT	6'3"	255	23		
Bob Kelly	OT	6'3"	260	24		
Jack Klotz	OT	6'5"	250	30		
Walt Suggs	OT	6'5"	260	25		
Sonny Bishop	OG	6'2"	245	24		
John Frongillo	OG	6'3"	250	24		
Bob Talamini	OG	6'1"	255	25		
John Wittenborn	OG	6'2"	240	28		
Tom Goode	C	6'3"	250	25		
Gary Cutsinger	DE	6'4"	245	23		
Don Floyd	DE	6'4"	247	25		6
Scott Appleton	DT	6'3"	250	22	2	
Ed Husmann	DT	6'	245	34		
Bud McFadin	DT	6'3"	270	36		
Danny Brabham	LB	6'4"	240	23		
Doug Cline	LB	6'2"	230	25		
Sammy Odom	LB	6'2"	235	22	2	
Larry Onesti	LB	6'	200	25		
Charley Rieves	LB	5'11"	218	25	1	
Johnny Baker	OE-LB	6'3"	225	23	1	6
Freddy Glick	DB	6'1"	190	27	5	
W. K. Hicks	DB	6'1"	185	21	5	
Pete Jaquess	DB	6'	180	22	8	6
Benny Nelson	DB	6'	185	22	1	6
Jim Norton	DB	6'3"	190	25	2	
Bobby Jancik	FL-DB	5'11"	178	24	3	6
Rich Michael – Injury						
George Blanda	QB	6'1"	215	36		76
Don Trull	QB	6'1"	180	22		
Sid Blanks	HB	6'	198	23		42
Ode Burrell	HB	6'	185	24		6
Dalton Hoffman	FB	6'	207	22		6
Dave Smith	FB	6'1"	210	27		
Charley Tolar	FB	5'7"	200	26		24
Charley Hennigan	FL	6'	187	28		48
Dobie Craig	OE	6'4"	200	25		6
Willard Dewveall	OE	6'4"	230	27		24
Charley Frazier	OE	6'	175	25		12
Willie Frazier	OE	6'4"	225	21		6
Bob McLeod	OE	6'5"	230	25		12

BUFFALO BILLS

RUSHING

Last Name	No.	Yds	Avg	TD
Gilchrist	**230**	**981**	4.3	**6**
Smith	62	306	4.9	4
Lamonica	55	289	5.3	**6**
Auer	63	191	3.0	2
Kemp	37	124	3.4	5
Carlton	39	114	2.9	1
Dubenion	1	20	20.0	0
Ross	4	14	3.5	1
Hudson	1	1	1.0	0

RECEIVING

Last Name	No.	Yds	Avg	TD
Bass	43	897	21	7
Dubenion	42	1139	**27**	10
Gilchrist	30	345	12	0
Warlick	23	478	21	0
Rutkowski	13	234	18	1
Auer	11	166	15	0
Smith	6	72	12	0
Groman	4	68	17	1
Carlton	2	23	12	0

PUNT RETURNS

Last Name	No.	Yds	Avg	TD
Clarke	**33**	317	10	**1**
Rutkowski	8	45	6	0
Byrd	2	4	2	0

KICKOFF RETURNS

Last Name	No.	Yds	Avg	TD
Rutkowski	21	498	24	0
Clarke	16	330	21	0
Smith	3	68	23	0
Barber	2	0	0	0
Maguire	1	0	0	0
Auer	0	1	0	0

PASSING – PUNTING – KICKING

PASSING	Att	Comp	%	Yds	Yd/Att	TD	Int–%	RK
Kemp	269	119	44	2285	**8.5**	13	26– 10	6
Lamonica	128	55	43	1137	8.9	6	8– 6	

PUNTING	No	Avg
Maguire	65	42.7

KICKING	XP	Att	%	FG	Att	%
Gogolak	45	**46**	98	19	29	**66**

2 POINT XP
Lamonica (2)

BOSTON PATRIOTS

RUSHING

Last Name	No.	Yds	Avg	TD
Garron	183	585	3.2	2
Burton	102	340	3.3	3
Garrett	56	259	4.6	2
Parilli	34	168	4.9	2
Cappelletti	1	7	7.0	0
Yewcic	5	2	0.4	0

RECEIVING

Last Name	No.	Yds	Avg	TD
Cappelletti	49	865	18	7
Graham	45	720	16	6
Garron	40	350	9	7
Colclough	32	657	21	5
Burton	27	306	11	2
Romeo	26	445	17	4
Garrett	8	101	13	0
Snyder	1	12	12	0
Crawford	1	11	11	0

PUNT RETURNS

Last Name	No.	Yds	Avg	TD
Cloutier	20	136	7	0
Burton	11	78	7	0
Stephens	5	34	7	0
Garrett	2	28	14	0

KICKOFF RETURNS

Last Name	No.	Yds	Avg	TD
Garrett	32	749	23	0
Garron	10	198	20	0
Burton	7	131	19	0
Cloutier	1	46	46	0
Dukes	2	33	17	0
Stephens	2	5	3	0
Romeo	1	5	5	0
Oakes	1	0	0	0
Watson	1	0	0	0
Yates	1	0	0	0

PASSING – PUNTING – KICKING

PASSING	Att	Comp	%	Yds	Yd/Att	TD	Int–%	RK
Parilli	473	228	48	**3465**	7.3	**31**	**27–** **6**	**3**
Garron	2	0	0	0	0.0	0	0– 0	
Yewcic	1	1	100	2	2.0	0	0– 0	

PUNTING	No	Avg
Yewcic	72	38.7
Parilli	5	36.0

KICKING	XP	Att	%	FG	Att	%
Cappelletti	36	36	100	**25**	**39**	64

2 POINT XP
Cappelletti
Colclough (2)

NEW YORK JETS

RUSHING

Last Name	No.	Yds	Avg	TD
Snell	215	948	4.4	5
Mathis	105	305	2.9	4
Smolinski	34	117	3.4	1
Taliaferro	9	45	5.0	0
Johnson	6	22	3.7	0
Baird	1	8	8.0	0
Wood	9	6	0.7	1
Maynard	3	3	1.0	0
J. Turner	1	3	3.0	0
Liske	1	0	0.0	0

RECEIVING

Last Name	No.	Yds	Avg	TD
B. Turner	58	974	17	9
Snell	56	393	7	1
Maynard	46	847	18	8
Mackey	14	213	15	0
Heeter	13	153	12	1
Evans	7	56	8	0
Mathis	4	39	10	0
Smolinski	3	19	6	0

PUNT RETURNS

Last Name	No.	Yds	Avg	TD
Baird	18	170	9	0
Starks	5	36	7	0
Paulson	8	34	4	0
Pashe	4	28	7	0
Rademacher	1	3	3	0
V. Turner	2	2	1	0
Rowley	0	10	0	0

KICKOFF RETURNS

Last Name	No.	Yds	Avg	TD
Evans	13	259	20	0
Baird	11	240	22	0
Starks	7	183	26	0
Snell	7	158	23	0
Johnson	4	62	16	0
V. Turner	1	25	25	0
Smolinski	2	19	10	0
Heeter	1	0	0	0
Mathis	1	0	0	0
McCusker	1	0	0	0
Perreault	1	0	0	0

PASSING – PUNTING – KICKING

PASSING	Att	Comp	%	Yds	Yd/Att	TD	Int–%	RK
Wood	358	169	47	2298	6.4	17	25– 7	6
Taliaferro	73	23	32	341	4.7	2	5– 7	
Liske	18	9	50	55	3.1	0	2– 11	
Johnson	1	0	0	0	0.0	0	0– 0	
Snell	1	0	0	0	0.0	0	1–100	

PUNTING	No	Avg
Johnson	77	42.4

KICKING	XP	Att	%	FG	Att	%
J. Turner	33	33	100	13	27	48

HOUSTON OILERS

RUSHING

Last Name	No.	Yds	Avg	TD
Blanks	145	756	5.2	**6**
Tolar	139	515	3.7	4
Trull	12	42	3.5	0
Smith	8	16	2.0	0
Burrell	8	10	1.3	0
Hoffman	2	3	1.5	1
Blanda	4	–2	–0.5	0
C. Frazier	1	–4	–4.0	0

RECEIVING

Last Name	No.	Yds	Avg	TD
Hennigan	**101**	**1546**	15	8
Blanks	56	497	9	1
Dewveall	38	552	15	4
Tolar	35	244	7	0
C. Frazier	31	423	14	2
W. Frazier	9	208	23	1
McLeod	8	81	10	2
Smith	7	38	5	0
Burrell	5	73	15	0
Craig	4	46	12	1
Baker	2	18	9	0
Jancik	1	14	14	0
Hoffman	1	1	1	0
Bishop	1	0	0	0
Blanda	0	–7	0	0

PUNT RETURNS

Last Name	No.	Yds	Avg	TD
Jancik	12	220	**18**	**1**
Glick	6	32	5	0
Burrell	1	0	0	0

KICKOFF RETURNS

Last Name	No.	Yds	Avg	TD
Jancik	21	488	23	0
Burrell	17	449	26	1
Nelson	13	304	23	0
Blanks	9	207	23	0
Hoffman	2	52	26	0
Glick	1	27	27	0
W. Frazier	1	0	0	0

PASSING – PUNTING – KICKING

PASSING	Att	Comp	%	Yds	Yd/Att	TD	Int–%	RK
Blanda	**505**	**262**	52	3287	6.5	17	27– 5	3
Trull	86	36	42	439	5.1	1	2– 2	
Blanks	1	1	100	8	8.0	1	0– 0	

PUNTING	No	Avg
Norton	53	42.8

KICKING	XP	Att	%	FG	Att	%
Blanda	37	38	97	13	29	45

SAN DIEGO CHARGERS 8-5-1 Sid Gillman

Scores of Each Game		
27	HOUSTON	21
28	BOSTON	33
3	Buffalo	30
17	New York	17
26	Boston	17
42	DENVER	14
20	Houston	17
31	OAKLAND	17
31	Denver	20
28	Kansas City	14
24	BUFFALO	27
38	NEW YORK	3
6	KANSAS CITY	49
20	Oakland	21

Use Name	Pos.	Hgt	Wgt	Age	Int	Pts
Gary Kirner	OT	6'3"	245	22		
Ron Mix	OT	6'4"	250	26		
Ernie Park	OT	6'3"	253	22		
Ernie Wright	OT	6'4"	265	24		
Sam Gruneisen	OG	6'1"	255	23		
Lloyd McCoy	OG	6'1"	245	22		
Pat Shea	OG	6'1"	245	25		
Walt Sweeney	OG	6'3"	255	23		
Don Rogers	C	6'2"	245	27		
Earl Faison	DE	6'5"	270	25	1	6
Bob Mitinger	DE	6'2"	245	24		
Bob Petrich	DE	6'4"	257	23	1	
George Gross	DT	6'3"	270	23		
Ernie Ladd	DT	6'9"	295	25		
Fred Moore	DT	6'3"	255	24		
Henry Schmidt	DT	6'4"	270	27	1	6
Chuck Allen	LB	6'1"	225	24	4	
Frank Buncom	LB	6'1"	235	24	1	
Ron Carpenter	LB	6'2"	230	23	1	
Bob Horton	LB	6'2"	230	21		
Emil Karas	LB	6'3"	235	30		
Bobby Lane	LB	6'2"	222	24		
George Blair	DB	5'11"	195	26		14
Speedy Duncan	DB	5'10"	180	21	1	
Kenny Graham	DB	6'	200	22	4	
Dick Harris	DB	5'11"	187	27	3	
Charley McNeil	DB	5'11"	180	28	2	
Jimmy Warren	DB	5'11"	185	25	2	
Dick Westmoreland	DB	6'1"	190	23	6	
Bud Whitehead	FL-DB	6'	185	25	3	
John Hadl	QB	6'2"	210	24		6
Tobin Rote	QB	6'3"	220	36		
Paul Lowe	HB	6'	205	27		30
Mario Mendez	HB	5'11"	200	22		
Keith Kinderman	FB	6'	215	24		
Keith Lincoln	FB	6'2"	213	25		67
Gerry McDougall	FB	6'2"	225	29		14
Lance Alworth	FL	6'	185	24		90
Dave Kocourek	OE	6'5"	245	27		30
Don Norton	OE	6'1"	195	26		36
Jerry Robinson	OE	5'11"	200	25		
Jacque MacKinnon	FB-OE	6'4"	250	25		12
Ben Agajanian	K	6'	225	45		14
Herb Travenio	K	6'	218	33		16

KANSAS CITY CHIEFS 7-7-0 Hank Stram

Scores of Each Game		
17	Buffalo	34
21	Oakland	9
28	HOUSTON	7
27	Denver	33
22	BUFFALO	35
7	Boston	24
49	DENVER	39
42	OAKLAND	7
14	SAN DIEGO	28
28	Houston	19
14	New York	27
24	BOSTON	31
49	San Diego	6
24	NEW YORK	7

Use Name	Pos.	Hgt	Wgt	Age	Int	Pts
Jerry Cornelison	OT	6'3"	250	27		
Dave Hill	OT	6'5"	260	23		
Jim Tyrer	OT	6'6"	292	25		
Denny Biodrowski	OG	6'1"	255	24		
Ed Budd	OG	6'5"	260	23		
Curt Merz	OG	6'4"	250	26		
Al Reynolds	OG	6'3"	235	26		
Jon Gilliam	C	6'2"	240	25		
Mel Branch	DE	6'2"	230	27		
Ed Lothamer	DE	6'5"	240	21		
Jerry Kramer	DT-DE	6'4"	250	24		
Buck Buchanan	DT	6'7"	280	24		
Curt Farrier	DT	6'6"	245	23		
John Maczuzak	DT	6'5"	250	21		
Hatch Rosdahl (from BUF)	DT	6'5"	250	21		
Walt Corey	LB	6'	242	26	1	
Sherrill Headrick	LB	6'2"	215	27	1	
E. J. Holub	LB	6'4"	225	26		
Smokey Stover	LB	6'	232	25	2	
Bobby Bell	DE-LB	6'4"	228	24	1	6
Dave Grayson	DB	5'10"	184	25	7	
Bobby Hunt	DB	6'1"	190	24	7	6
Willie Mitchell	DB	6'1"	185	22	1	
Bobby Ply	DB	6'1"	190	23	1	
Johnny Robinson	DB	6'	195	25	2	
Charley Warner (to BUF)	DB	5'11"	180	24	1	
Duane Wood	DB	6'1"	200	28	5	
Pete Beathard	QB	6'2"	205	22		
Len Dawson	QB	6'	190	30		12
Eddie Wilson	QB	6'	190	24		6
Bert Coan	HB	6'4"	220	24		12
Abner Haynes	HB	6'	190	26		48
Jerrel Wilson	HB	6'4"	225	23		
Mack Lee Hill	FB	5'11"	225	22		36
Curtis McClinton	FB	6'3"	232	25		20
Jack Spikes (to SD)	FB	6'2"	220	26		
Frank Jackson	FL	6'1"	190	24		54
Fred Arbanas	OE	6'3"	240	25		48
Tommy Brooker	OE	6'2"	230	24		70
Chris Burford	OE	6'3"	210	26		42
Reg Carolan	OE	6'6"	232	24		6

OAKLAND RAIDERS 5-7-2 Al Davis

Scores of Each Game		
14	BOSTON	17
28	Houston	42
9	KANSAS CITY	21
20	Buffalo	23
13	New York	35
43	Boston	43
40	DENVER	7
17	San Diego	31
7	Kansas City	42
20	HOUSTON	10
35	NEW YORK	26
20	Denver	20
16	BUFFALO	13
21	SAN DIEGO	20

Use Name	Pos.	Hgt	Wgt	Age	Int	Pts
Proverb Jacobs	OT	6'4"	260	29		
Dick Klein	OT	6'4"	250	30		
Ken Rice	OT	6'2"	240	24		
Frank Youso	OT	6'4"	250	28		
Wayne Hawkins	OG	6'	240	26		
Bob Mischak	OG	6'	230	31		
Jim Otto	C	6'2"	240	26		
Dalva Allen	DE	6'5"	245	28		
Ben Davidson	DE	6'8"	265	24		
Jon Jelacic	DE	6'3"	255	27		
Dan Birdwell	DT	6'4"	250	23	2	
Doug Brown	DT	6'4"	250	24		
Dave Costa	DT	6'2"	250	22		
Rex Mirich	DT	6'4"	250	23		
Jim Norris	DT	6'4"	235	24	2	
Bill Budness	LB	6'1"	215	21	2	
Dan Conners	LB	6'1"	230	22		
Archie Matsos	LB	6'	212	29	2	
Clancy Osborne	LB	6'3"	220	29		
Jackie Simpson	LB	6'1"	225	27		
J. R. Williamson	LB	6'2"	220	22		
Claude Gibson	DB	6'1"	190	25	2	
Louis Guy	DB	6'	190	23		
Joe Krakoski	DB	6'2"	195	27		
Tom Morrow	DB	5'11"	187	26	4	
Warren Powers	DB	6'	185	23	5	
Howie Williams	DB	6'2"	185	27	1	
Fred Williamson	DB	6'2"	215	26	6	
Alan Miller – Injury						
Cotton Davidson	QB	6'1"	180	32		12
Tom Flores	QB	6'1"	190	27		
Billy Cannon	FB-HB	6'1"	225	27		48
Clem Daniels	HB	6'1"	220	27		48
Bo Dickinson	FB	6'2"	220	29		
Bobby Jackson (from HOU)	FB	6'3"	225	24		18
Glen Shaw	FB	6'1"	225	25		12
Bo Roberson	FL	6'1"	190	29		6
Jan Barrett	OE	6'3"	222	23		12
Fred Gillett	OE	6'3"	220	26		
Ken Herock	OE	6'2"	230	23		12
Bill Miller	OE	6'	190	22		
Art Powell	OE	6'3"	212	27		66
Mike Mercer	K	6'	200	28		79

DENVER BRONCOS 2-11-1 Jack Faulkner Mac Speedie

Scores of Each Game		
6	New York	30
13	Buffalo	30
17	HOUSTON	38
10	BOSTON	39
33	KANSAS CITY	27
14	San Diego	42
7	Oakland	40
39	Kansas City	49
20	SAN DIEGO	31
20	NEW YORK	16
7	Boston	12
20	OAKLAND	20
19	BUFFALO	30
15	Houston	34

Use Name	Pos.	Hgt	Wgt	Age	Int	Pts
Eldon Danenhauer	OT	6'4"	245	28		
Harold Olson	OT	6'3"	255	25		
Jim Perkins	OT	6'5"	250	25		
Ernie Barnes	OG	6'3"	243	25		
Bob McCullough	OG	6'2"	245	23		
Tom Nomina	OG	6'5"	270	22		
Don Shackleford	OG	6'4"	255	21		
Jerry Sturm	C-OG	6'3"	260	27		
Ray Kubala	C	6'4"	245	22		
Ed Cooke	DE	6'4"	250	29		6
Stan Fanning (from HOU)	DE	6'6"	270	26		
Ike Lassiter	DE	6'5"	270	23		
Leroy Moore	DE	6'	230	28	1	
Dick Guesman	DT	6'4"	255	28		31
Ray Jacobs	DT	6'3"	265	24		
Chuck Janerette	DT	6'3"	265	25		
Tom Erlandson	LB	6'3"	235	24		
Jim Fraser	LB	6'3"	236	28	1	
Jerry Hopkins	LB	6'2"	235	23	2	
Larry Jordan	LB	6'6"	230	26		
Marv Matuszak	LB	6'3"	240	33	2	
Jim Price	LB	6'2"	230	23		
Billy Atkins	DB	6'1"	195	29		
Norm Bass	DB	6'3"	210	25		
Willie Brown	DB	6'1"	190	23	9	
Goose Gonsoulin	DB	6'3"	210	26	7	
John Griffin	DB	6'1"	190	24		
Tom Janik	DB	6'3"	200	23	1	6
John McGeever	DB	6'1"	195	25	6	
Jim McMillin (from OAK)	DB	5'11"	195	26	1	6
Willie West (to NY)	DB	5'10"	193	26	2	
Jim Wright	DB	5'11"	190	25	1	
Jacky Lee	QB	6'1"	187	25		18
Mickey Slaughter	QB	6'	190	22		2
Gene Mingo (to OAK)	HB	6'1"	190	25		39
Charley Mitchell	HB	5'11"	185	24		36
Billy Joe	FB	6'2"	250	23		14
Donnie Stone	FB	6'2"	205	27		
Al Denson	FL	6'2"	208	22		8
Bob Scarpitto	FL	5'11"	196	25		24
Odell Barry	OE	5'10"	180	22		6
Matt Snorton	OE	6'5"	250	21		
Lionel Taylor	OE	6'2"	215	28		42
Hewritt Dixon	HB-OE	6'2"	217	24		6
John McCormick – Injury						
Bob Zeman – Injury						

SAN DIEGO CHARGERS

RUSHING

Last Name	No.	Yds	Avg	TD
Lincoln	155	632	4.1	4
Lowe	130	496	3.8	3
MacKinnon	24	124	5.2	2
Kinderman	24	111	4.6	0
McDougall	23	73	3.2	2
Hadl	20	70	3.5	1
Alworth	3	60	20.0	2
Robinson	1	10	10.0	0
Rote	10	–12	–1.2	0

RECEIVING

Last Name	No.	Yds	Avg	TD
Alworth	61	1235	20	13
Norton	49	669	14	6
Lincoln	34	302	9	2
Kocourek	33	593	18	5
Lowe	14	182	13	2
MacKinnon	10	177	18	0
Robinson	10	93	9	0
McDougall	8	106	13	0
Kinderman	3	21	7	0
Whitehead	1	–4	–4	0
Rote	1	–11	–11	0

PUNT RETURNS

Last Name	No.	Yds	Avg	TD
Alworth	18	189	11	0
Robinson	7	41	6	0
Graham	2	24	12	0
Duncan	4	19	5	0
Westmoreland	2	10	5	0
Warren	1	0	0	0

KICKOFF RETURNS

Last Name	No.	Yds	Avg	TD
Westmoreland	18	360	20	0
Warren	13	353	27	0
Duncan	9	318	35	0
Graham	7	172	25	0
Robinson	3	70	23	0
Carpenter	1	15	15	0
Norton	1	0	0	0
Wright	1	0	0	0

PASSING – PUNTING – KICKING

PASSING	Att	Comp	%	Yds	Yd/Att	TD	Int–%	RK
Hadl	274	147	54	2157	7.9	18	15– 6	2
Rote	163	74	45	1156	7.1	9	15– 9	11
Lincoln	4	2	50	61	15.3	1	0– 0	
Lowe	2	0	0	0	0.0	0	0– 0	
Alworth	1	1	100	–11	–11.0	0	0– 0	
Kinderman	1	0	0	0	0.0	0	0– 0	

PUNTING	No	Avg
Hadl	62	39.5
Whitehead	1	30.0

KICKING	XP	Att	%	FG	Att	%
Lincoln	16	17	94	5	12	42
Travenio	10	12	83	2	5	40
Agajanian	8	8	100	2	4	50
Blair	5	6	83	3	5	60

2 POINT XP
McDougall

KANSAS CITY CHIEFS

RUSHING

Last Name	No.	Yds	Avg	TD
Haynes	139	697	5.0	4
M. Hill	105	576	5.5	4
McClinton	73	252	3.5	1
Spikes	34	112	3.3	0
Dawson	40	89	2.2	0
Coan	11	56	5.1	2
Beathard	4	43	10.8	0
E. Wilson	6	5	0.8	1
Jackson	2	5	2.5	0
J. Wilson	1	–10	–10.0	0

RECEIVING

Last Name	No.	Yds	Avg	TD
Jackson	62	943	15	9
Burford	51	675	13	7
Haynes	38	562	15	3
Arbanas	34	686	20	8
M. Hill	19	144	8	2
McClinton	13	221	17	2
Spikes	5	17	3	0
Carolan	3	54	18	1
Coan	2	8	4	0
J. Wilson	1	11	11	0

PUNT RETURNS

Last Name	No.	Yds	Avg	TD
Warner	12	165	14	0
Mitchell	18	160	9	0
Jackson	11	103	9	0
Robinson	1	16	16	0
Haynes	1	11	11	0

KICKOFF RETURNS

Last Name	No.	Yds	Avg	TD
Grayson	30	679	23	0
Warner	12	301	25	0
Haynes	12	278	23	0
Coan	5	124	25	0
Lothamer	1	0	0	0
Rosdahl	1	0	0	0
Stover	1	0	0	0

PASSING – PUNTING – KICKING

PASSING	Att	Comp	%	Yds	Yd/Att	TD	Int–%	RK
Dawson	354	199	56	2879	8.1	30	18– 5	1
E. Wilson	47	25	53	392	8.3	1	1– 2	
Beathard	9	4	44	50	5.6	1	2– 22	
Haynes	1	0	0	0	0.0	0	0– 0	
Spikes	1	0	0	0	0.0	0	0– 0	

PUNTING	No	Avg
J. Wilson	78	42.6
E. Wilson	1	32.0

KICKING	XP	Att	%	FG	Att	%
Brooker	46	46	100	8	17	47

2 POINT XP
McClinton

OAKLAND RAIDERS

RUSHING

Last Name	No.	Yds	Avg	TD
Daniels	173	824	4.8	2
Cannon	89	338	3.8	3
C. Davidson	29	167	5.8	2
Jackson	23	64	2.8	3
Flores	11	64	5.8	0
Shaw	9	26	2.9	2
Dickinson	4	8	2.0	0
Roberson	1	–4	–4.0	0
Youso	0	4	0.0	0

RECEIVING

Last Name	No.	Yds	Avg	TD
Powell	76	1361	18	11
Roberson	44	624	14	1
Daniels	42	696	17	6
Cannon	37	454	12	5
Herock	23	360	16	2
Barrett	12	212	18	2
Jackson	10	81	8	0
Shaw	3	31	10	0
Dickinson	3	28	9	0
Miller	2	29	15	0

PUNT RETURNS

Last Name	No.	Yds	Avg	TD
Gibson	29	419	14	0
Roberson	1	20	20	0
Krakoski	1	8	8	0
Morrow	1	0	0	0

KICKOFF RETURNS

Last Name	No.	Yds	Avg	TD
Roberson	36	975	27	0
Cannon	21	518	25	0
Jackson	2	32	16	0
Daniels	1	32	32	0
Conners	1	0	0	0
Dickinson	1	0	0	0
Klein	1	0	0	0

PASSING – PUNTING – KICKING

PASSING	Att	Comp	%	Yds	Yd/Att	TD	Int–%	RK
C. Davidson	320	155	48	2497	7.8	21	19– 6	5
Flores	200	98	49	1389	7.0	7	14– 7	6
Daniels	1	0	0	0	0.0	0	0– 0	

PUNTING	No	Avg
Mercer	58	42.1

KICKING	XP	Att	%	FG	Att	%
Mercer	34	34	100	15	24	63

DENVER BRONCOS

RUSHING

Last Name	No.	Yds	Avg	TD
Mitchell	177	590	3.3	5
Joe	112	415	3.7	2
Lee	42	163	3.9	3
Slaughter	20	54	2.7	0
Stone	12	26	2.2	0
Mingo	6	26	4.3	0
Dixon	18	25	1.4	0
Barry	3	7	2.3	0
Scarpitto	1	5	5.0	0

RECEIVING

Last Name	No.	Yds	Avg	TD
Taylor	76	873	11	7
Dixon	38	585	15	1
Scarpitto	35	375	11	4
Mitchell	33	225	7	1
Denson	25	383	15	1
Joe	12	16	1	0
Stone	4	38	10	0
Barry	4	31	8	0
Mingo	4	25	6	1

PUNT RETURNS

Last Name	No.	Yds	Avg	TD
Barry	16	149	9	1
Mitchell	9	110	12	0

KICKOFF RETURNS

Last Name	No.	Yds	Avg	TD
Barry	47	1245	27	0
Mitchell	10	221	22	0
Mingo	8	163	20	0
West	5	142	28	0
Dixon	6	89	15	0
Olson	2	27	14	0
Shackleford	1	13	13	0
Jordan	1	0	0	0
Sturm	1	0	0	0

PASSING – PUNTING – KICKING

PASSING	Att	Comp	%	Yds	Yd/Att	TD	Int–%	RK
Lee	265	133	50	1611	6.1	11	20– 8	10
Slaughter	189	97	51	930	4.9	3	11– 6	9
Mitchell	1	0	0	0	0.0	0	0– 0	
Taylor	1	0	0	0	0.0	0	1–100	

PUNTING	No	Avg
Fraser	72	44.7
Janik	10	37.4

KICKING	XP	Att	%	FG	Att	%
Guesman	13	15	87	6	22	27
Mingo	9	10	90	8	12	67

2 POINT XP
Denson
Joe
Slaughter

1965 N.F.L. Passing Pioneers and Hello, Dixie

The league lost two long-standing members when Curly Lambeau and Jack Mara died in June. Lambeau had founded the Green Bay Packers in 1919 and coached them through 1949, molding them into NFL powers until a postwar slump set in. Mara had for years run the New York Giants, founded by his father Tim Mara, and his death put his younger brother Wellington at the head of the New York organization. But life went on as usual in the league, with a hot Western Division race, new stars in Gale Sayers, Bob Hayes, and Dick Butkus, and the usual assortment of injuries, errors, and great plays. To spread the riches around—and also rake in some more money—the league voted to expand into Atlanta starting in 1966, reaching into the Deep South for the first time.

EASTERN CONFERENCE

Cleveland Browns—Even with Paul Warfield sidelined for most of the year by a shoulder injury and the defense saddled with the weight of advancing years, the Browns still ran away with the Eastern crown. Coach Blanton Collier had some of the finest offensive assets in the division, including a solid line, a reliable flanker in Gary Collins, a steady quarterback in Frank Ryan, and the incomparable Jimmy Brown at fullback, and the patchwork defense held up well enough to win eleven games. The Browns counted their riches even in the specialists' department, with forty-one-year-old Lou Groza an accurate place-kicker, Leroy Kelly a good punt returner, Walter Roberts a dangerous kickoff returner, and Gary Collins a fine punter in addition to his pass-catching chores.

Dallas Cowboys—The Cowboys failed to break the .500 barrier, but they did uncover one of the league's most exciting performers in rookie end Bob Hayes. A world-record-holding sprinter, Hayes terrorized defensive backs with his pure speed, streaking away from them with no possibility of being caught from behind once in the clear. While Hayes scored thirteen touchdowns, tackle Ralph Neely went unnoticed by all but the coaches with a fine rookie season. Coach Tom Landry added several other freshmen who would contribute to the strong Dallas teams of the next few years in Dan Reeves, Jethro Pugh, Craig Morton, and Obert Logan.

New York Giants—After losing all five of their pre-season games, the Giants obtained quarterback Earl Morrall from Detroit and finished in a surprising tie for second place in the East. Morrall gave the team a steady hand at the head of the offense and threw for twenty-two touchdowns. Joining Morrall in the backfield was a collection of young runners known collectively in the press as the Baby Bulls. Tucker Frederickson, Steve Thurlow, Ernie Koy, and Chuck Mercein all ground out hard overland yardage despite a lack of speed, and split end Homer Jones gave the Giants all the speed they needed in a pass receiver. Even with only a faint knowledge of pass patterns, Jones picked up over 700 yards as a receiver on only twenty-six catches after breaking into the starting lineup in mid-season.

Washington Redskins—The Redskins lost their first five games with a poor offensive show that improved only a little over the season. The Washington running attack was the league's worst, as there still was no full-time fullback, and halfback Charley Taylor came nowhere near duplicating his fine rookie season. The passing offense also slumped, as Bobby Mitchell alone among the receivers consistently got open for Sonny Jurgensen's passes. The Washington defense was a competent unit but was hurt when cornerback Johnny Sample was suspended late in the season for insubordination.

Philadelphia Eagles—Joe Kuharich had traded the Eagles into respectability last year, but progress came more slowly this season. The big trouble spot was the defensive line, which put no pressure at all on enemy passers. The Eagles resorted to frequent blitzing to compensate for the weak line, but this just made them vulnerable to quick passes. The offense was sound throughout, starting with the Bob Brown-led line. Timmy Brown starred at halfback, using his quickness to best advantage on runs and passes, Earl Gros complemented Brown with his power at fullback, and Norm Snead showed progress at quarterback.

St. Louis Cardinals—Tied with the Browns for first place in the East on October 17, the Cards swan-dived out of contention by losing eight of the next nine games and their last six contests straight. Injuries to Charley Johnson, Larry Wilson, and Jerry Stovall contributed to the collapse, and the trading of John David Crow to San Francisco hurt the club more than had been expected. Crow had been a clutch runner, the man to give the ball to when vital yardage was needed, and his departure left the Cards without a leader in the backfield.

Pittsburgh Steelers—Head coach Buddy Parker quit two weeks before the season opener, saying, "I can't win with this bunch of stiffs." On that pleasant note, assistant Mike Nixon took over as head man for a brutal 2-12 season. Nixon benched veteran quarterback Ed Brown and replaced him with Bill Nelsen, who played most of the season on a bad knee, which made him a sitting duck for enemy pass-rushers. The running attack lost its best man when John Henry Johnson was sidelined by a bad knee, and the receiving corps was so thin that the starting split end, Clendon Thomas, was a converted defensive back. When Parker had quit as coach of the Detroit Lions before the 1957 season, the Lions went on to win the championship. This time, Parker knew what he was doing.

WESTERN CONFERENCE

Green Bay Packers—The return of guard Jerry Kramer from stomach surgery, the purchase of kicker Don Chandler from New York, and the development of Marv Fleming, Doug Hart, and Tom Brown into starters plastered over the few cracks in the Packers' solid front. After battling the Colts all season for the Western Conference lead, the Packers blew a chance to clinch the championship by managing only a tie with San Francisco in the final regular-season game. Baltimore and Green Bay finished with identical 10-3-1 records and squared off in a playoff for the Western crown. The Colts came into the playoff game with no experienced quarterback, but their fired-up defense knocked the ball loose from Bill Anderson on the first play from scrimmage, and Don Shinnick ran the fumble 25 yards for a Baltimore touchdown. Quarterback Bart Starr was shaken up on the play and missed most of the game, but the Packers fought back against the spirited Colts to tie the score at 10-10 with a Chandler field goal late in the game. For the second time in history, a pro-football game went into overtime, and another Chandler field goal, which the Colts and many observers claimed went wide, gave the Packers the victory after 13:39 of overtime play.

Baltimore Colts—Driving along to a repeat Western championship, the Colts suddenly lost both their quarterbacks, with Johnny Unitas ripping up a knee in the twelfth game and Gary Cuozzo dislocating a shoulder one week later. Coach Don Shula put halfback Tom Matte into the signal caller's spot, equiping him with a wrist band with some basic plays written on it. Relying on roll-out passes, quarterback keepers, pitchouts, and a fanatical defense, the Colts beat the Rams 20-17 in their final game to get into a Western Conference playoff with the Packers.

Chicago Bears—One of the Bears' three first-round draft picks, defensive end Steve DeLong got away to the AFL, but George Halas opened his wallet wide to sign the other two. Halfback Gale Sayers and linebacker Dick Butkus immediately rewarded Halas' genorosity with All-Pro rookie seasons. Sayers burst on the national consciousness like a comet, slamming through holes at top speed and eluding defensive backs by outdodging and outrunning them. Starring as a kick returner and pass receiver as well as a runner, Sayers scored a record twenty-two touchdowns in the season. While Sayers souped up the Bear offense, Butkus helped return the defense to a high peak with his ferocity at middle linebacker.

San Francisco '49ers—With John Brodie suddenly putting all his talent together in a marvelous season, the '49er offense suddenly blossomed into the league's most explosive. Wide receivers Bernie Casey and Dave Parks gave Brodie two fine targets to hit, and the offensive line gave him good protection against enemy pass rushes. The running game improved immensely over last year with the addition of two new hard-chargers, rookie fullback Ken Willand and ex-Cardinal halfback John David Crow. The defense, however, was as undistinguished as the attack was dynamic.

Minnesota Vikings— The Viking offense still put on a good show, but the defense failed to show the expected progress, seven times getting burned for 35 or more points. This so frustrated head coach Norm Van Brocklin that he resigned in mid-season, only to be talked out of it after a couple of days by the front office. One of Van Brocklin's biggest problems was a growing tension between himself and quarterback Fran Tarkenton. The coach kept trying to make a strict pocket passer out of Tarkenton, while the quarterback stuck to his free-wheeling, scrambling style.

Detroit Lions—Owner William Clay Ford started the year by firing all of head coach George Wilson's assistants, a warning to Wilson to win or face the same fate. Wilson throught it over for a couple of days and handed in his resignation. Harry Gilmer took over as head man and ran into a flood of injuries that weighted the club down in sixth place. One of Gilmer's first decisions was to rely on one quarterback, so he kept Milt Plum and traded Earl Morrall to New York. The only problem was, Plum had a poor year, while Morrall rejuvenated the Giants with his fine passing. With the offense erratic, the Detroit defense no longer was strong enough to carry the team.

Los Angeles Rams—The front four of Deacon Jones, Merlin Olsen, Rosie Grier, and Lamar Lundy became the league's most famous defensive line and often carried the rest of the Los Angeles defense, which was ladened with as many as five rookie starters at one point. The running attack was weak, but the blocking and receiving gave quarterbacks Bill Munson and Roman Gabriel something to work with. Munson started the first ten games and led the club to only one win despite frequent flashes of talent, and Gabriel headed the attack for the final four games after Munson hurt a knee.

FINAL TEAM STATISTICS

OFFENSE

	BALT.	CHI.	CLEVE.	DALLAS	DET.	G.BAY	L.A.	MINN.	N.Y.	PHIL.	PITT.	ST.L.	S.F.	WASH.
FIRST DOWNS:														
Total	266	257	257	211	204	201	251	277	230	267	194	251	**292**	210
by Rushing	94	132	**133**	87	93	85	76	130	91	94	71	90	97	69
by Passing	144	110	97	108	93	103	153	126	112	149	104	143	**172**	125
by Penalty	**28**	15	27	16	18	13	22	21	27	24	19	18	23	16
RUSHING:														
Number	445	479	476	416	453	432	378	**505**	423	404	407	431	428	354
Yards	1593	2131	**2331**	1608	1469	1488	1464	2278	1651	1824	1378	1619	1783	1037
Average Yards	3.6	4.4	**4.9**	3.9	3.2	3.4	3.9	4.5	3.9	4.5	3.4	3.8	4.2	2.9
Touchdowns	13	**27**	19	8	16	14	8	19	12	21	10	10	13	7
PASSING:														
Attempts	399	361	329	362	374	306	445	372	342	434	354	448	**454**	427
Completions	222	201	160	168	170	166	230	189	171	223	161	221	**272**	220
Completion Pct.	55.6	55.7	48.6	46.4	45.5	54.2	51.7	50.8	50.0	51.4	45.5	49.3	**59.9**	51.5
Passing Yards	3330	3020	2339	2756	2083	2508	3059	2861	2685	3442	2503	3222	**3633**	2908
Avg. Yds per Att.	8.3	**8.4**	7.1	7.6	5.6	8.2	6.9	7.7	7.9	7.9	7.1	7.2	8.0	6.8
Avg. Yds per Comp.	15.0	15.0	14.6	**16.4**	12.3	15.1	13.3	15.1	15.7	15.4	15.5	14.6	13.4	13.2
Tackled Att. to Pass	43	30	31	55	26	43	45	35	31	33	62	30	**19**	39
Yards Lost Tackled	325	254	272	369	249	395	344	315	255	254	527	279	**146**	337
Net Yards	3005	2766	2067	2387	1834	2113	2715	2546	2430	3188	1976	2943	**3487**	2571
Touchdowns	31	22	23	25	14	19	22	21	23	22	10	20	**35**	20
Interceptions	17	**12**	16	18	26	14	19	**12**	16	26	35	25	21	20
Pct. Intercepted	4.3	3.3	4.9	5.0	7.0	4.6	4.3	**3.2**	4.7	6.0	9.9	5.6	4.6	4.7
PUNTS:														
Number	56	58	69	73	**78**	74	66	51	61	56	**78**	67	54	70
Average Distance	39.6	42.7	45.7	41.3	42.8	42.9	39.7	42.1	41.6	42.2	45.1	40.4	**45.8**	42.1
PUNT RETURNS:														
Number	**45**	29	36	39	34	22	32	22	24	21	33	23	38	39
Yards	421	289	**427**	312	358	65	225	115	35	183	259	27	283	415
Average Yards	9.4	10.0	**11.9**	8.0	10.5	3.0	7.0	5.2	1.5	8.7	7.8	1.2	7.4	10.6
Touchdowns	0	1	**2**	0	0	0	0	1	0	1	0	0	0	1
KICKOFF RETURNS:														
Number	52	45	53	44	52	50	53	**67**	60	60	61	55	59	49
Yards	1242	1146	1209	1166	1416	1040	1351	**1524**	1303	1438	1238	1287	1276	1011
Average Yards	23.9	25.5	22.8	26.5	**27.2**	20.8	25.5	22.7	21.7	24.0	20.3	23.4	21.6	20.6
Touchdowns	0	**1**	0	**1**	0	0	0	**1**	0	0	0	0	0	0
INTERCEPTION RETURNS:														
Number	22	20	24	18	26	**27**	11	19	16	25	12	17	13	**27**
Yards	318	307	349	198	343	**561**	224	286	249	313	282	328	97	535
Average Yards	14.5	15.4	14.5	11.0	13.2	20.8	20.4	15.1	15.6	12.5	**23.5**	19.3	7.5	19.8
Touchdowns	**4**	2	1	2	3	**4**	1	2	1	3	2	1	0	2
PENALTIES:														
Number	69	**96**	84	68	77	48	61	76	61	61	40	45	79	81
Yards	616	826	**976**	710	767	529	560	771	618	686	326	458	785	692
FUMBLES:														
Number	31	33	20	31	27	18	40	41	31	21	42	**15**	33	41
Number Lost	19	16	9	17	15	12	22	25	14	10	22	**7**	19	21
POINTS:														
Total	389	409	363	325	257	316	269	383	270	363	202	296	**421**	257
PAT Attempts	48	**54**	45	40	33	38	32	44	37	48	25	33	53	33
PAT Made	48	**52**	45	37	33	37	30	44	34	45	19	33	**52**	29
FG Attempte	28	26	25	27	22	26	26	**35**	25	25	19	31	27	22
FG Made	17	11	16	16	8	17	15	**23**	4	10	11	21	17	10
Percent FG Made	60.7	42.3	64.0	59.3	36.4	65.4	57.7	65.7	16.0	40.0	57.9	**67.7**	63.0	45.5
Safeties	1	0	0	0	1	0	1	**3**	1	0	0	1	0	0

DEFENSE

	BALT.	CHI.	CLEVE.	DALLAS	DET.	G.BAY	L.A.	MINN.	N.Y.	PHIL.	PITT.	ST.L.	S.F.	WASH.
FIRST DOWNS:														
Total	233	244	265	240	210	240	**208**	242	266	243	243	238	259	237
by Rushing	**78**	87	104	80	84	115	82	99	108	100	122	89	94	100
by Passing	131	136	135	138	104	111	113	120	140	129	109	133	139	**101**
by Penalty	24	21	26	22	22	14	13	23	18	14	**12**	16	26	36
RUSHING:														
Number	410	**400**	412	422	409	480	417	408	447	419	483	433	405	486
Yards	1483	1530	1866	1444	1460	1988	**1409**	1755	1956	1582	2080	1813	1535	1753
Average Yards	3.6	3.8	4.5	3.4	3.6	4.1	**3.4**	4.3	4.4	3.8	4.3	4.2	3.8	3.6
Touchdowns	11	11	11	13	9	10	16	17	20	11	19	11	20	18
PASSING:														
Attempts	400	444	419	426	344	383	349	357	393	393	353	380	448	**318**
Completions	213	217	204	205	190	187	205	187	208	215	173	184	225	**161**
Completion Pct.	53.3	48.9	48.7	**48.1**	55.2	48.8	58.7	52.4	52.9	54.7	49.0	48.4	50.2	50.6
Passing Yards	2903	3086	3153	3063	2508	**2316**	2884	2692	3251	3123	2703	2826	3302	2539
Avg. Yds per Att.	7.3	7.0	7.5	7.2	7.3	**6.0**	8.3	7.5	8.3	7.9	7.7	7.4	7.4	8.0
Avg. Yds per Comp.	13.6	14.2	15.5	14.9	13.2	**12.4**	14.1	14.4	15.6	14.5	15.6	15.4	14.7	15.8
Tackled Att. to Pass	39	40	38	39	**49**	44	32	23	39	37	33	39	25	45
Yards Lost Tackled	341	348	307	315	411	335	270	199	294	287	253	342	197	**422**
Net Yards	2562	2738	2846	2748	2097	**1981**	2614	2493	2957	2836	2450	2484	3105	2117
Touchdowns	22	18	31	17	21	**11**	22	31	18	28	25	24	24	15
Interceptions	22	20	24	18	26	**27**	11	19	16	25	12	17	13	**27**
Pct. Intercepted	5.5	4.5	5.7	4.2	7.6	7.0	3.2	5.3	4.1	6.4	3.4	4.5	2.9	**8.5**
PUNTS:														
Number	71	65	69	71	74	60	66	64	45	54	**76**	65	62	69
Average Distance	43.9	42.3	41.1	42.9	42.9	42.1	45.4	**38.4**	42.7	41.8	42.2	43.3	41.9	43.4
PUNT RETURNS:														
Number	26	**22**	36	26	39	36	25	29	**22**	37	44	32	33	30
Yards	198	**123**	259	139	318	290	176	261	137	263	437	267	408	138
Average Yards	7.6	5.6	7.2	5.3	8.2	8.1	7.0	9.0	6.2	7.1	9.9	8.3	12.4	**4.6**
Touchdowns	**0**	**0**	0	1	1	**0**	1	**0**	**0**	**0**	2	**0**	1	**0**
KICKOFF RETURNS:														
Number	63	72	58	63	43	52	54	62	54	58	**30**	50	59	42
Yards	1346	1583	1334	1229	858	1216	1364	1557	1175	1531	**684**	1228	1566	976
Average Yards	21.4	22.0	23.0	**19.5**	20.0	23.4	25.3	25.1	21.8	26.4	22.8	24.6	26.5	23.2
Touchdowns	1	**0**	**0**	**0**	**0**	**0**	**0**	1	**0**	**0**	**0**	**0**	1	**0**
INTERCEPTION RETURNS:														
Number	17	**12**	16	18	26	14	19	**12**	16	26	35	25	21	20
Yards	341	219	275	268	515	209	**156**	215	182	476	646	465	232	191
Average Yards	20.1	18.3	17.2	14.9	19.8	14.9	**8.2**	17.9	11.4	18.3	18.5	18.6	11.0	9.6
Touchdowns	1	3	1	**0**	2	1	**0**	1	1	6	6	1	3	2
PENALTIES:														
Number	80	68	62	50	61	67	70	66	**83**	66	58	70	71	74
Yards	786	611	586	483	637	677	566	643	**848**	653	615	750	727	738
FUMBLES:														
Number	33	33	13	**37**	33	**37**	27	25	32	32	28	29	34	31
Number Lost	14	**24**	8	20	20	23	15	11	20	11	15	15	17	15
POINTS:														
Total	284	275	325	280	295	**224**	328	403	338	359	397	309	402	301
PAT Attempts	35	33	43	33	36	**22**	40	53	41	47	53	37	52	38
PAT Made	35	30	40	29	36	**22**	40	52	40	44	49	36	48	37
FG Attempte	23	24	**18**	30	22	33	32	20	29	26	26	32	27	22
FG Made	13	15	**9**	17	13	22	16	11	16	11	10	17	14	12
Percent FG Made	56.5	62.5	50.0	56.7	59.1	66.7	50.0	55.0	55.2	42.3	**38.5**	53.1	51.9	54.5
Safeties	**0**	1	**0**	1	2	2	**0**	**0**	2	**0**	**0**	**0**	**0**	**0**

1965 NFL CHAMPIONSHIP GAME

January 2, at Green Bay
(Attendance 50,777)

Bulldozing the Defense

After two years as Western Division runners-up, the Green Bay Packers returned to the NFL championship game they had won in 1961 and 1962. The Cleveland Browns, the defending NFL champions, came into Lambeau Field to furnish the opposition. The playing field was muddy and footing uncertain, making straight-ahead running plays the best bets of the afternoon. The Packer defense gave Green Bay a decisive edge by dogging Cleveland fullback Jimmy Brown all afternoon, while Packer runners Jim Taylor and Paul Hornung followed strong blocking to eat up yardage on the ground. Packer quarterback Bart Starr crossed up the Browns on the first series of downs by throwing the ball; he hit Carroll Dale with a long pass that gave the Packers a quick 7-0 lead. The Browns retaliated by moving steadily downfield and scoring on a Frank Ryan-to-Gary Collins pass. The extra point went awry, however, and the Packers still led 7-6. A Lou Groza field goal gave the Browns a 9-7 lead at the end of the first quarter, and three second-period field goals, one by Groza and two by Green Bay's Don Chandler, made the halftime score 13-12 in favor of the Packers. Coach Vince Lombardi stressed ball control to his players, and the Packer offense came out for the second half ready to grind out difficult yardage. Using off-tackle blasts and power sweeps with Taylor and Hornung carrying the ball, the Packers drove 90 yards on 11 plays in the third quarter, eating up seven minutes of the clock while putting seven more points on the scoreboard. Whenever the Browns got the ball in the second half, they couldn't move against the Green Bay defense; whenever the Packers had the ball, they would hold onto it for several precious minutes before giving it up. In all, the Green Bay offensive line contributed the most to the Packer victory by constantly knocking the Cleveland defenders back to make room for Taylor and Hornung in the 20-12 victory.

SCORING

GREEN BAY	7	6	7	3–23
CLEVELAND	9	3	0	0–12

First Quarter
- G.B. Dale, 47 yard pass from Starr
  PAT – Chandler (kick)
- Cle. Collins, 17 yard pass from Ryan
  PAT – No Good
- Cle. Groza, 24 yard field goal

Second Quarter
- G.B. Chandler, 15 yard field goal
- G.B. Chandler, 23 yard field goal
- Cle. Groza, 28 yard field goal

Third Quarter
- G.B. Hornung, 13 yard rush
  PAT – Chandler (kick)

Fourth Quarter
- G.B. Chandler, 29 yard field goal

TEAM STATISTICS

G.B.		CLEVE.
21	First Downs – Total	8
10	First Downs – Rushing	2
9	First Downs – Passing	5
2	First Downs – Penalty	1
3	Punts – Number	4
38.3	Punts – Average Distance	46.0
2	Punt Returns – Number	1
–10	Punt Returns – Yards	11
2	Interception Returns – Number	1
15	Interception Returns – Yards	0
0	Fumbles – Number	0
3	Penalties – Number	2
35	Yards Penalized	20
1	Giveaways	2
2	Takeaways	1
+1	Difference	–1

INDIVIDUAL STATISTICS

RUSHING

GREEN BAY	No.	Yds.	Avg.	CLEVELAND	No.	Yds.	Avg.
Hornung	18	105	5.8	Brown	12	50	4.2
Taylor	27	96	3.6	Ryan	3	9	3.0
Moore	2	3	1.5	Green	3	5	1.7
	47	204	4.3		18	64	3.6

RECEIVING

GREEN BAY	No.	Yds.	Avg.	CLEVELAND	No.	Yds.	Avg.
Dowler	5	59	11.8	Brown	3	44	14.7
Dale	2	60	30.0	Collins	3	41	13.7
Taylor	2	20	10.0	Warfield	2	30	15.0
Hornung	1	8	8.0		8	115	14.4
	10	147	14.7				

PASSING

	Att	Comp	Comp Pct.	Yds	Int	Yds/ Att.	Yds/ Comp	Yards Lost Tackled
GREEN BAY								
Starr	18	10	55.6	147	1	8.2	14.7	
Hornung	1	0	0.0	0	0	–	–	
	19	10	52.6	147	1	7.7	14.7	19
CLEVELAND								
Ryan	18	8	44.4	115	2	6.4	14.4	18

1965 N.F.L. — Eastern Conference

CLEVELAND BROWNS 11-3-0 Blanton Collier

Scores of Each Game		
17	Washington	7
13	ST. LOUIS	49
35	Philadelphia	17
24	PITTSBURGH	19
23	DALLAS	17
38	New York	14
17	MINNESOTA	27
38	PHILADELPHIA	34
34	NEW YORK	21
24	Dallas	17
42	Pittsburgh	21
24	WASHINGTON	16
7	Los Angeles	42
27	St. Louis	24

Use Name	Pos.	Hgt	Wgt	Age	Int	Pts
John Brown	OT	6'2"	248	26		
Monte Clark	OT	6'6"	265	28		
Dick Schafrath	OT	6'3"	255	29		
Gene Hickerson	OG	6'3"	248	30		
Dale Memmelaar	OG	6'2"	248	28		
John Wooten	OG	6'2"	250	30		
John Morrow	C	6'3"	248	32		
Jim Garcia	DE	6'4"	240	21		
Bill Glass	DE	6'5"	255	29	1	
Paul Wiggin	DE	6'3"	245	31		
Walter Johnson	DT	6'3"	265	22		
Jim Kanicki	DT	6'4"	270	23		
Dick Modzelewski	DT	6'	260	34		
Vince Costello	LB	6'	228	33	3	
Galen Fiss	LB	6'	227	35	1	
Jim Houston	LB	6'2"	240	28	2	
Dale Lindsey	LB	6'3"	220	22	1	
Stan Sczurek	LB	5'11"	230	26	1	
Sid Williams	LB	6'2"	235	23	1	
Erich Barnes	DB	6'2"	198	30	1	
Walter Beach	DB	6'	185	30		
Larry Benz	DB	5'11"	185	24	5	
Ross Fichtner	DB	6'	185	27	4	6
Bobby Franklin	DB	5'11"	182	29		
Mike Howell	DB	6'1"	187	22		
Bernie Parrish	DB	5'11"	195	30	4	
Jim Ninowski	QB	6'1"	207	29		
Frank Ryan	QB	6'3"	200	29		
Ernie Green	HB	6'2"	205	26		24
Leroy Kelly	HB	6'	195	23		12
Jimmy Brown	FB	6'2"	228	29		126
Jamie Caleb	FB	6'1"	210	28		
Charlie Scales	FB	5'11"	215	26		
Gary Collins	FL	6'4"	208	24		60
Clifton McNeil	FL	6'2"	185	25		
Johnny Brewer	TE	6'4"	235	28		6
Ralph Smith	TE	6'2"	215	26		
Tom Hutchinson	OE	6'1"	190	24		12
Walter Roberts	OE	5'10"	175	23		24
Paul Warfield	OE	6'	188	22		
Lou Groza	K	6'3"	250	41		93

Frank Parker – Operation

DALLAS COWBOYS 7-7-0 Tom Landry

Scores of Each Game		
31	NEW YORK	2
27	WASHINGTON	7
13	St. Louis	20
24	PHILADELPHIA	35
17	Cleveland	23
3	Green Bay	13
13	Pittsburgh	22
39	SAN FRANCISCO	31
24	PITTSBURGH	17
17	CLEVELAND	24
31	Washington	34
21	Philadelphia	19
27	ST. LOUIS	13
38	New York	20

Use Name	Pos.	Hgt	Wgt	Age	Int	Pts
Jim Boeke	OT	6'5"	255	26		
Ralph Neely	OT	6'5"	257	21		
Don Talbert	OT	6'5"	240	25		
Mike Connelly	OG	6'3"	248	29		
Leon Donahue (from SF)	OG	6'4"	245	26		
Mitch Johnson	OG	6'4"	245	23		
Jake Kupp	OG	6'3"	233	23		
Dave Manders	C	6'2"	240	23		
George Andrie	DE	6'7"	255	25		6
Garry Porterfield	DE	6'3"	223	22		
Jethro Pugh	DE	6'6"	255	21		
Maury Youmans	DE	6'6"	253	28		
Larry Stephens	DT-DE	6'4"	250	27		
Jim Colvin	DT	6'2"	255	28		
John Diehl (to OAK-A)	DT	6'7"	250	29		
Bob Lilly	DT	6'4"	255	26	1	6
Dave Edwards	LB	6'3"	226	26	2	
Harold Hays	LB	6'3"	223	24		
Chuck Howley	LB	6'3"	223	29		
Lee Roy Jordan	LB	6'2"	216	24		
Jerry Tubbs	LB	6'2"	222	30	2	
Russell Wayt	LB	6'4"	235	22		
Don Bishop	DB	6'2"	216	30		
Mike Gaechter	DB	6'	190	25	2	6
Cornell Green	DB	6'4"	215	25	3	6
Warren Livingston	DB	5'10"	190	27	3	
Obert Logan	DB	5'10"	180	23	3	6
Mel Renfro	HB-DB	6'	195	21	2	12
Don Meredith	QB	6'2"	206	27		6
Craig Morton	QB	6'4"	216	22		
Jerry Rhome	QB	6'	180	23		
Perry Lee Dunn	HB	6'2"	200	22		18
Dan Reeves	HB	6'1"	203	21		18
Don Perkins	FB	5'10"	206	27		
J. D. Smith	FB	6'1"	210	32		18
A. D. Whitfield	FB	5'10"	200	21		
Buddy Dial	FL	6'1"	195	28		6
Pete Gent	FL	6'4"	210	22		12
Pettis Norman	TE	6'3"	223	25		18
Frank Clarke	OE	6'	210	32		24
Bob Hayes	OE	6'	190	22		78
Colin Ridgway	K	6'5"	211	26		
Danny Villanueva	K	5'11"	200	27		85

Joe Bob Isbell – Injury
Tony Liscio – Injury

NEW YORK GIANTS 7-7-0 Allie Sherman

Scores of Each Game		
2	Dallas	31
16	Philadelphia	14
23	Pittsburgh	13
14	Minnesota	40
35	PHILADELPHIA	27
14	CLEVELAND	38
14	ST. LOUIS	10
7	WASHINGTON	23
21	Cleveland	34
28	St. Louis	15
14	CHICAGO	35
35	PITTSBURGH	10
27	Washington	10
20	DALLAS	38

Use Name	Pos.	Hgt	Wgt	Age	Int	Pts
Rosey Brown	OT	6'3"	255	32		
Frank Lasky	OT	6'2"	265	23		
John McDowell	OT	6'3"	260	22		
Bookie Bolin	OG	6'2"	240	25		
Pete Case	OG	6'3"	243	24		
Roger Davis	OG	6'3"	240	27		
Mickey Walker	OG	6'	235	25		
Greg Larson	C	6'2"	250	26		
Bob Scholtz	C	6'4"	250	27		
Glen Condren	DE	6'2"	225	23		
Rosey Davis	DE	6'5"	260	23		
Jim Katcavage	DE	6'3"	240	30		2
Andy Stynchula	DE	6'3"	250	26		21
Roger Anderson	DT	6'5"	265	22		
Mike Bundra (to BAL)	DT	6'3"	260	26		
Roger LaLonde	DT	6'3"	255	23		
John Lovetere	DT	6'4"	285	29		
Dave O'Brien	DT	6'3"	247	24		
Jim Carroll	LB	6'1"	225	22	1	
Tom Costello	LB	6'3"	220	24		
Jerry Hillebrand	LB	6'3"	240	25	2	6
Bill Swain	LB	6'2"	228	24		
Olen Underwood	LB	6'1"	210	23	1	
Lou Slaby	DT-LB	6'3"	235	23		
Henry Carr	DB	6'3"	205	22	2	
Clarence Childs	DB	6'	180	26		
Spider Lockhart	DB	6'2"	185	22	4	
Dick Lynch	DB	6'1"	198	29	4	6
Jimmy Patton	DB	6'	185	33	1	
Allan Webb	DB	5'11"	180	30		
Willie Williams	DB	6'	190	22	1	
Earl Morrall	QB	6'1"	206	31		
Bob Timberlake	QB	6'4"	220	22		24
Gary Wood	QB	5'11"	188	22		1
Tucker Frederickson	HB	6'3"	220	22		36
Ernie Koy	HB	6'2"	225	22		
Smith Reed	HB	6'	215	23		
Steve Thurlow	HB	6'3"	216	22		30
Chuck Mercein	FB	6'3"	230	22		12
Ernie Wheelwright	FB	6'3"	240	28		
Bob Crespino	TE	6'4"	225	27		24
Aaron Thomas	FL-TE	6'3"	210	27		30
Homer Jones	FL	6'2"	205	24		36
Joe Morrison	FL	6'1"	212	27		30
Bob Lacey	OE	6'3"	205	23		
Del Shofner	OE	6'3"	185	29		12

Jim Moran – Broken Leg

WASHINGTON REDSKINS 6-8-0 Bill McPeak

Scores of Each Game		
7	CLEVELAND	17
7	Dallas	27
10	Detroit	14
16	ST. LOUIS	37
7	BALTIMORE	38
24	St. Louis	20
23	PHILADELPHIA	21
23	New York	7
14	Philadelphia	21
31	Pittsburgh	3
34	DALLAS	31
16	Cleveland	24
10	NEW YORK	27
35	PITTSBURGH	14

Use Name	Pos.	Hgt	Wgt	Age	Int	Pts
Fran O'Brien	OT	6'1"	255	30		
Jim Snowden	DE-OT	6'3"	255	23		
Don Croftcheck	OG	6'1"	230	22		
Darrell Dess	OG	6'	245	29		
Vince Promuto	OG	6'1"	245	27		
Robert Reed	OG	6'1"	250	22		
Dave Crossan	C	6'3"	245	25		
Len Hauss	C	6'2"	235	24		
Carl Kammerer	DE	6'3"	243	28		
John Paluck	DE	6'2"	245	32		
Bill Quinlan	DE	6'3"	250	33		
Ron Snidow	DE	6'4"	250	23	1	
Joe Rutgens	DT	6'2"	255	26		
Fred Williams	DT	6'4"	256	35		
Willie Adams	LB	6'2"	235	23		
Jimmy Carr	LB	6'1"	225	32		
Chris Hanburger	LB	6'2"	218	24	1	
Sam Huff	LB	6'1"	230	30	2	
Bob Pellegrini	LB	6'2"	242	30		6
John Reger	LB	6'	220	34		
Rickie Harris	DB	6'	182	22	1	12
Johnny Sample	DB	6'1"	205	28	6	
Lonnie Sanders	DB	6'3"	207	23	4	
Jim Shorter	DB	5'11"	185	24	2	6
Jim Steffen	DB	6'	196	28	3	
Tom Walters	DB	6'2"	195	23	1	6
Paul Krause	FL-DB	6'3"	195	23	6	6
Sonny Jurgensen	QB	5'11"	205	31		12
Dick Shiner	QB	6'	197	23		
Pervis Atkins (to OAK-A)	HB	6'1"	210	29		
George Hughley	HB	6'2"	223	26		6
Dan Lewis	HB	6'1"	200	29		24
Charley Taylor	HB	6'3"	210	24		36
Bob Briggs	FB	6'1"	228	22		
Rick Casares	FB	6'2"	225	34		
Bobby Mitchell	FL	6'	196	30		36
Bill Hunter	DB-FL	6'1"	185	22		6
Fred Mazurek	DB-FL	5'11"	192	22		
Jerry Smith	TE	6'2"	208	22		12
Preston Carpenter	OE	6'2"	208	31		
Angie Coia	OE	6'2"	196	27		18
Bob Jencks	OE	6'5"	227	24		59
Pat Richter	OE	6'5"	230	24		12
John Seedborg	K	6'	227	22		

PHILADELPHIA EAGLES 5-9-0 Joe Kuharich

Scores of Each Game		
34	ST. LOUIS	27
14	NEW YORK	16
17	CLEVELAND	35
35	Dallas	24
27	New York	35
14	PITTSBURGH	20
21	Washington	23
34	Cleveland	38
21	WASHINGTON	14
24	Baltimore	34
28	St. Louis	24
19	DALLAS	21
47	Pittsburgh	13
28	DETROIT	35

Use Name	Pos.	Hgt	Wgt	Age	Int	Pts
Bob Brown	OT	6'4"	276	22		
Dave Graham	OT	6'3"	250	26		
Lane Howell	OT	6'5"	255	24		
Ed Blaine	OG	6'2"	240	25		
Jim Skaggs	OT-OG	6'2"	250	25		
Lynn Hoyem	C-OG	6'4"	253	25		
Dave Recher	C	6'1"	240	22		
Jim Ringo	C	6'1"	230	34		
Bobby Richards	DE	6'2"	245	26		
George Tarasovic	DE	6'4"	248	36	1	12
Don Hultz	LB-DE	6'3"	235	24	1	
Ed Khayat	DT	6'3"	250	30		
John Meyers	DT	6'6"	276	25	2	
Floyd Peters	DT	6'4"	255	30		
Erwin Will	DT	6'5"	270	22		
Maxie Baughan	LB	6'1"	227	27	1	6
Ralph Heck	LB	6'2"	230	24		
Dave Lloyd	LB	6'3"	248	29	2	10
Mike Morgan	LB	6'4"	242	23	1	
Harold Wells	LB	6'2"	223	26		
Irv Cross	DB	6'1"	190	26	3	
Al Nelson	DB	5'11"	180	21	2	
Jim Nettles	DB	5'9"	175	23	3	6
Nate Ramsey	DB	6'1"	200	24	6	
Bob Shann	DB	6'1"	187	22		6
Joe Scarpati	HB-DB	5'10"	185	23	3	
Claude Crabb	FL-DB	6'	190	25		
Jack Concannon	QB	6'3"	195	22		
King Hill	QB	6'3"	213	29		12
Norm Snead	QB	6'4"	205	25		18
Timmy Brown	HB	5'10"	198	28		54
Ollie Matson	HB	6'2"	210	35		18
Earl Gros	FB	6'3"	220	24		54
Izzy Lang	FB	6'1"	230	22		6
Tom Woodeshick	FB	6'	220	23		
Glenn Glass	FL	6'	203	28		
Ron Goodwin	OE-FL	6'	180	23		6
Roger Gill	TE	6'1"	200	24		
Bill Cronin	TE	6'4"	220	22		
Jim Kelly	TE	6'2"	215	23		
Pete Retzlaff	TE	6'1"	214	34		60
Fred Hill	OE	6'2"	215	22		
Ray Poage	OE	6'4"	200	24		30
Sam Baker	K	6'2"	218	33		65

Jerry Mazzanti – Military Service
Mike McClellan – Military Service

CLEVELAND BROWNS

RUSHING

Last Name	No.	Yds	Avg	TD
Jimmy Brown	289	1544	5.3	17
Green	111	436	3.9	2
Kelly	37	139	3.8	0
Ryan	19	72	3.8	0
Scales	11	59	5.4	0
Ninowski	4	46	11.5	0
Roberts	3	30	10.0	0
Collins	1	16	16.0	0
Franklin	1	−11	−11.0	0

RECEIVING

Last Name	No.	Yds	Avg	TD
Collins	50	884	18	10
Jimmy Brown	34	328	10	4
Green	25	298	12	2
Roberts	16	314	20	4
Brewer	13	174	13	1
Kelly	9	122	14	0
Hutchinson	6	113	19	2
McNeil	3	69	23	0
Warfield	3	30	10	0
Scales	1	7	7	0

PUNT RETURNS

Last Name	No.	Yds	Avg	TD
Kelly	17	265	16	2
Roberts	18	162	9	0
Scales	1	0	0	0

KICKOFF RETURNS

Last Name	No.	Yds	Avg	TD
Kelly	24	621	26	0
Roberts	18	493	27	0
Scales	4	88	22	0
Green	1	4	4	0
Howell	2	3	2	0
Hutchinson	2	0	0	0
Franklin	1	0	0	0
Lindsey	1	0	0	0

PASSING – PUNTING – KICKING

PASSING	Att	Comp	%	Yds	Yd/Att	TD	Int–%	RK
Ryan	243	119	49	1751	7.2	18	13– 5	12
Ninowski	83	40	48	549	6.6	4	3– 4	
Jimmy Brown	2	1	50	39	19.5	1	0– 0	
Groza	1	0	0	0	0.0	0	0– 0	

PASSING	No	Avg
Collins	65	46.7
Franklin	4	29.5

KICKING	XP	Att	%	FG	Att	%
Groza	45	45	100	16	25	64

DALLAS COWBOYS

RUSHING

Last Name	No.	Yds	Avg	TD
Perkins	177	690	3.9	0
Smith	86	295	3.4	2
Meredith	35	247	7.1	1
Dunn	54	171	3.2	2
Reeves	33	102	3.1	2
Clarke	8	58	7.3	0
Rhome	4	11	2.8	0
Whitfield	1	0	0.0	0
Hayes	4	−8	−2.0	1
Morton	3	−8	−2.7	0

RECEIVING

Last Name	No.	Yds	Avg	TD
Hayes	46	1003	22	12
Clarke	41	682	17	4
Dial	17	283	17	1
Gent	16	233	15	2
Perkins	14	142	10	0
Norman	11	110	10	3
Reeves	9	210	23	1
Dunn	8	74	9	1
Smith	5	10	2	1

PUNT RETURNS

Last Name	No.	Yds	Avg	TD
Hayes	12	153	13	0
Renfro	24	145	6	0

KICKOFF RETURNS

Last Name	No.	Yds	Avg	TD
Renfro	21	630	30	1
Hayes	17	450	26	0
Reeves	2	45	23	0
Neely	2	13	7	0

PASSING – PUNTING – KICKING

PASSING	Att	Comp	%	Yds	Yd/Att	TD	Int–%	RK
Meredith	305	141	46	2415	7.9	22	13– 4	8
Morton	34	17	50	173	5.1	2	4– 12	
Rhome	21	9	43	157	7.5	1	1– 5	
Reeves	2	1	50	11	5.5	0	0– 0	

PUNTING	No	Avg
Villanueva	60	41.8
Ridgway	13	39.2

KICKING	XP	Att	%	FG	Att	%
Villanueva	37	38	97	16	27	59

NEW YORK GIANTS

RUSHING

Last Name	No.	Yds	Avg	TD
Frederickson	195	659	3.4	5
Thurlow	106	440	4.2	4
Koy	35	174	5.0	0
Wheelwright	24	96	4.0	0
Reed	19	70	3.7	0
Wood	5	68	13.6	0
Mercein	18	55	3.1	2
Morrall	17	52	3.1	0
Morrison	3	20	6.7	1
Jones	1	17	17.0	0

RECEIVING

Last Name	No.	Yds	Avg	TD
Morrison	41	574	14	4
Thomas	27	631	23	5
Jones	26	709	27	6
Frederickson	24	177	7	1
Shofner	22	388	18	2
Thurlow	9	54	6	1
Crespino	7	57	8	4
Reed	6	42	7	0
Koy	4	22	6	0
Mercein	3	14	5	0
Wheelwright	2	17	9	0

PUNT RETURNS

Last Name	No.	Yds	Avg	TD
Williams	18	28	2	0
Carr	4	13	3	0
Lockhart	2	−6	−3	0

KICKOFF RETURNS

Last Name	No.	Yds	Avg	TD
Childs	29	718	25	0
Koy	21	401	19	0
Williams	5	113	23	0
Webb	2	48	24	0
Thurlow	1	19	19	0
Mercein	1	4	4	0
Brown	1	0	0	0

PASSING – PUNTING – KICKING

PASSING	Att	Comp	%	Yds	Yd/Att	TD	Int–%	RK
Morrall	302	155	51	2446	8.1	22	12– 4	5
Wood	36	15	42	190	5.3	1	2– 6	
Koy	2	0	0	0	0.0	0	1– 50	
Frederickson	1	0	0	0	0.0	0	1–100	
Thurlow	1	1	100	49	49.0	0	0– 0	

PUNTING	No	Avg
Koy	55	41.2
Lockhart	6	44.5

KICKING	XP	Att	%	FG	Att	%
Timberlake	21	22	95	1	15	7
Stynchula	12	13	92	3	7	43
Wood	1	1	100	0	0	0
Hillebrand	0	0	0	0	1	0
Mercein	0	0	0	0	2	0

WASHINGTON REDSKINS

RUSHING

Last Name	No.	Yds	Avg	TD
Taylor	145	402	2.8	3
Lewis	117	343	2.9	2
Hughley	37	175	4.7	0
Atkins	18	44	2.4	0
Shiner	12	35	2.9	0
Jurgensen	17	23	1.4	2
Briggs	6	10	1.7	0
Casares	2	5	2.5	0

RECEIVING

Last Name	No.	Yds	Avg	TD
Mitchell	60	867	14	6
Taylor	40	577	14	3
Lewis	25	276	11	2
Carpenter	23	298	13	0
Smith	19	257	14	2
Coia	18	240	13	3
Richter	16	189	12	2
Hughley	9	93	10	1
Briggs	3	40	13	0
Jencks	2	20	10	0
Krause	2	17	9	0
Hunter	1	29	29	1
Casares	1	5	5	0
Atkins	1	0	0	0

PUNT RETURNS

Last Name	No.	Yds	Avg	TD
Harris	31	377	12	1
Mitchell	1	15	15	0
Hughley	2	12	6	0
Atkins	3	11	4	0
Mazurek	1	0	0	0
Pellegrini	1	0	0	0

KICKOFF RETURNS

Last Name	No.	Yds	Avg	TD
Hunter	18	432	24	0
Hughley	13	295	23	0
Mitchell	5	106	21	0
Harris	5	96	19	0
Walters	2	30	15	0
Atkins	1	15	15	0
Taylor	1	15	15	0
Kammerer	1	14	14	0
Briggs	2	8	4	0
Hanburger	1	0	0	0

PASSING – PUNTING – KICKING

PASSING	Att	Comp	%	Yds	Yd/Att	TD	Int–%	RK
Jurgensen	356	190	53	2367	6.7	15	16– 5	10
Shiner	65	28	43	470	7.2	3	4– 6	
Taylor	4	1	25	45	11.3	1	0– 0	
Lewis	2	1	50	26	13.0	1	0– 0	

PUNTING	No	Avg
Richter	54	43.8
Snidow	9	37.3
Seedburg	7	35.3

KICKING	XP	Att	%	FG	Att	%
Jencks	29	33	88	10	22	46

PHILADELPHIA EAGLES

RUSHING

Last Name	No.	Yds	Avg	TD
T. Brown	158	861	5.4	6
Gros	145	479	3.3	7
Woodeshick	28	145	5.2	0
Concannon	9	104	11.6	0
Matson	22	103	4.7	2
Snead	24	81	3.4	3
Lang	10	25	2.5	1
K. Hill	7	20	2.9	2
Scarpati	1	6	6.0	0

RECEIVING

Last Name	No.	Yds	Avg	TD
Retzlaff	66	1190	18	10
T. Brown	50	682	14	3
Poage	31	612	20	5
Gros	29	271	9	2
Goodwin	18	252	14	1
Glass	15	201	13	0
Woodeshick	6	86	14	0
Crabb	2	41	21	0
Lang	2	30	15	0
Matson	2	29	15	1
Gill	1	27	27	0
F. Hill	1	21	21	0

PUNT RETURNS

Last Name	No.	Yds	Avg	TD
Cross	14	79	6	0
Shann	1	63	63	1
Gill	2	28	14	0
T. Brown	4	13	3	0

KICKOFF RETURNS

Last Name	No.	Yds	Avg	TD
Nelson	26	683	26	0
Cross	25	662	26	0
T. Brown	3	46	15	0
Lang	3	36	12	0
Wells	1	8	8	0
Morgan	1	3	3	0
Gill	1	0	0	0

PASSING – PUNTING – KICKING

PASSING	Att	Comp	%	Yds	Yd/Att	TD	Int–%	RK
Snead	288	150	52	2346	8.2	15	13– 5	7
K. Hill	113	60	53	857	7.6	5	10– 9	
Concannon	29	12	41	176	6.1	1	3– 10	
Gros	2	1	50	63	31.5	1	0– 0	
T. Brown	1	0	0	0	0.0	0	0– 0	
Poage	1	0	0	0	0.0	0	0– 0	

PUNTING	No	Avg
Baker	37	41.9
K. Hill	19	42.8

KICKING	XP	Att	%	FG	Att	%
Baker	38	40	95	9	23	39
Lloyd	7	7	100	1	2	50

EASTERN CONFERENCE – Continued

ST. LOUIS CARDINALS 5-9-0 Wally Lemm

Scores of Each Game		
27	Philadelphia	34
49	Cleveland	13
20	DALLAS	13
37	Washington	16
20	Pittsburgh	7
20	WASHINGTON	24
10	New York	14
21	PITTSBURGH	17
13	Chicago	34
15	NEW YORK	28
24	PHILADELPHIA	28
3	LOS ANGELES	27
13	Dallas	27
24	CLEVELAND	27

Use Name	Pos.	Hgt	Wgt	Age	Int	Pts
Ernie McMillan	OT	6'6"	260	27		
Bob Reynolds	OT	6'6"	265	24		
Ed Cook	OG-OT	6'2"	250	33		
Irv Goode	OG	6'4"	250	24		
Ken Gray	OG	6'2"	250	29		
Rick Sortun	OG	6'2"	235	22		
Herschel Turner	OT-OG	6'3"	230	23		
Mike Alford	C	6'3"	230	22		
Bob DeMarco	C	6'3"	240	27		
Don Brumm	DE	6'3"	245	22		6
Mike Melinkovich	DE	6'4"	240	23		
Tom Redmond	DE	6'5"	250	28		
Joe Robb	DE	6'3"	245	28		
Ed McQuarters	DT	6'1"	250	22		
Luke Owens	DT	6'2"	255	32		
Sam Silas	DT	6'4"	250	22		
Chuck Walker	DT	6'2"	245	24		
Bill Koman	LB	6'2"	230	31	1	
Dave Meggyesy	LB	6'1"	220	23		
Dale Meinert	LB	6'2"	220	32		
Marion Rushing	LB	6'2"	230	28		
Dave Simmons	LB	6'4"	245	22		
Larry Stallings	LB	6'2"	230	23		6
Monk Bailey	DB	6'	180	27		
Jimmy Burson	DB	6'	180	23	5	
Pat Fischer	DB	5'10"	170	25	3	
Carl Silvestri	DB	6'	195	22		
Jerry Stovall	DB	6'2"	205	23	2	
Larry Wilson	DB	6'	190	27	6	6
Abe Woodson	DB	5'11"	190	30		
Buddy Humphrey	QB	6'1"	200	29		
Charley Johnson	QB	6'	190	28		6
Terry Nofsinger	QB	6'4"	215	27		6
Prentice Gautt	HB	6'	210	27		12
Bill Triplett	HB	6'2"	210	26		42
Joe Childress	FB	6'	210	31		
Willie Crenshaw	FB	6'2"	230	24		6
Bill Thornton	FB	6'1"	215	25		
Bobby Joe Conrad	FL	6'	195	30		30
Mal Hammack	TE	6'2"	210	32		
Chuck Logan	TE	6'4"	210	22		
Jackie Smith	TE	6'4"	215	24		12
Billy Gambrell	OE	5'10"	175	23		12
Ray Ogden	OE	6'5"	225	22		
Sonny Randle	OE	6'2"	190	29		54
Jim Bakken	K	6'	200	24		96

PITTSBURGH STEELERS 2-12-0 Mike Nixon

Scores of Each Game		
9	GREEN BAY	41
17	San Francisco	27
13	NEW YORK	23
19	Cleveland	24
7	ST. LOUIS	20
20	Philadelphia	14
22	DALLAS	13
17	St. Louis	21
17	Dallas	24
3	WASHINGTON	31
21	CLEVELAND	42
10	New York	35
13	PHILADELPHIA	47
14	Washington	35

Use Name	Pos.	Hgt	Wgt	Age	Int	Pts
Charlie Bradshaw	OT	6'6"	260	29		
Dan James	OT	6'4"	250	28		
Bob Nichols	OT	6'3"	250	22		
Ray Lemek	OG	6'	240	31		
Mike Magac	OG	6'3"	240	27		
Mike Sandusky	OG	6'	235	32		
Ed Adamchik (from NY)	C	6'2"	235	23		
Ken Henson	C	6'6"	260	22		
Art Hunter	C	6'4"	247	32		
John Baker	DE	6'6"	270	30		
Ben McGee	DE	6'2"	225	23		
Fran Mallick	DT-DE	6'3"	245	24		
Riley Gunnels	DT	6'3"	253	28		
Chuck Hinton	DT	6'5"	260	26		
Ken Kortas	DT	6'2"	280	23		
Ray Mansfield	DT	6'3"	250	24		
Rod Breedlove	LB	6'2"	227	27		
Gene Breen	LB	6'2"	230	24		
John Campbell	LB	6'3"	225	26		6
Max Messner	LB	6'3"	225	27	1	
Ed Pine	LB	6'4"	235	25		
Myron Pottios	LB	6'2"	240	25		
Bob Schmitz	LB	6'1"	240	27		
Jim Bradshaw	DB	6'1"	205	26	5	6
Willie Daniel	DB	5'11"	185	27	1	6
Bob Hohn	DB	6'	190	24		
Brady Keys	DB	6'	198	29	1	
Bob Sherman	DB	6'2"	195	23	1	
Marv Woodson	DB	6'	195	22	3	6
Ed Brown (to BAL)	QB	6'2"	220	36		
Bill Nelsen	QB	6'	195	24		6
Tom Wade	QB	6'2"	195	23		
Cannonball Butler	HB	5'10"	195	22		6
Dick Hoak	HB	5'11"	190	26		36
John Henry Johnson	FB	6'2"	205	35		
Mike Lind	FB	6'2"	225	25		12
Clarence Peaks	FB	6'1"	215	29		
Theron Sapp	FB	6'1"	210	30		
Red Mack	FL	5'10"	185	28		
Paul Martha	HB-FL	6'	185	22		
Gary Ballman	OE-FL	6'	200	25		48
John Hilton	TE	6'5"	220	23		
John Powers	LB-TE	6'2"	210	24		
Duane Allen (to BAL)	OE	6'4"	225	27		
Lee Folkins	OE	6'5"	215	26		6
Roy Jefferson	OE	6'2"	195	21		6
Jerry Simmons	OE	6'1"	190	22		
Clendon Thomas	DB-OE	6'2"	205	28		6
Mike Clark	K	6'1"	205	24		52
Frank Lambert	K	6'3"	200	22		

Andy Russell – Military Service

WESTERN CONFERENCE

GREEN BAY PACKERS 10-3-1 Vince Lombardi

Scores of Each Game		
41	Pittsburgh	9
20	BALTIMORE	17
23	CHICAGO	14
27	SAN FRANCISCO	10
31	Detroit	21
13	DALLAS	3
10	Chicago	31
7	DETROIT	12
6	LOS ANGELES	3
38	Minnesota	13
10	Los Angeles	21
24	MINNESOTA	19
42	Baltimore	27
24	San Francisco	24
	Playoff	
13	BALTIMORE	10

Use Name	Pos.	Hgt	Wgt	Age	Int	Pts
Steve Wright	OT	6'6"	250	23		
Bob Skoronski	OT	6'3"	250	32		
Forrest Gregg	OG-OT	6'4"	250	32		
Dan Grimm	OG	6'3"	245	24		
Jerry Kramer	OG	6'3"	245	30		
Fuzzy Thurston	OG	6'1"	245	32		
Ken Bowman	C	6'3"	230	22		
Bill Curry	C	6'2"	235	22		
Lionel Aldridge	DE	6'4"	245	23		
Willie Davis	DE	6'3"	245	32	1	
Lloyd Voss	DE	6'4"	260	23		
Henry Jordan	DT	6'3"	250	30		
Ron Kostelnik	DT	6'4"	260	25		
Bud Marshall	DT	6'5"	270	23		
Lee Roy Caffey	LB	6'3"	250	25	1	6
Tommy Crutcher	LB	6'3"	230	23	1	
Ray Nitschke	LB	6'3"	240	29	1	
Dave Robinson	LB	6'3"	245	24	3	
Herb Adderley	DB	6'1"	210	26	6	18
Tom Brown	DB	6'1"	190	24	3	
Hank Gremminger	DB	6'1"	200	32		
Doug Hart	DB	6'	190	26	4	6
Bob Jeter	DB	6'1"	205	27	1	
Willie Wood	DB	5'10"	190	29	6	
Zeke Bratkowski	QB	6'2"	200	33		
Dennis Claridge	QB	6'3"	225	23		
Bart Starr	QB	6'1"	200	32		6
Junior Coffey	HB	6'1"	210	23		
Paul Hornung	HB	6'2"	215	28		48
Allen Jacobs	HB	6'1"	215	24		
Tom Moore	HB	6'2"	210	27		6
Elijah Pitts	HB	6'1"	205	26		30
Jim Taylor	FB	6'	215	30		24
Carroll Dale	FL	6'1"	200	27		12
Bob Long	FL	6'3"	190	24		24
Bill Anderson	TE	6'3"	215	29		6
Marv Fleming	TE	6'4"	235	23		12
Boyd Dowler	OE	6'5"	225	28		24
Max McGee	OE	6'3"	205	33		6
Don Chandler	K	6'2"	210	30		88

BALTIMORE COLTS 10-3-1 Don Shula

Scores of Each Game		
35	MINNESOTA	16
17	Green Bay	20
27	SAN FRANCISCO	24
31	DETROIT	7
38	Washington	7
35	LOS ANGELES	20
34	San Francisco	28
26	Chicago	21
41	Minnesota	21
34	PHILADELPHIA	24
24	Detroit	24
0	CHICAGO	13
27	GREEN BAY	42
20	Los Angeles	17
	Playoff	
10	Green Bay	13

Use Name	Pos.	Hgt	Wgt	Age	Int	Pts
Tom Gilburg	OT	6'5"	245	26		
George Preas	OT	6'2"	250	33		
Bob Vogel	OT	6'5"	250	23		
Jim Parker	OG	6'3"	275	31		
Alex Sandusky	OG	6'1"	242	33		
Dan Sullivan	OG	6'3"	250	26		
Buzz Nutter	C	6'4"	240	34		
Dick Szymanski	C	6'3"	235	33		
Ordell Braase	DE	6'4"	242	33		
Roy Hilton	DE	6'6"	225	20		
Lou Michaels	DE	6'2"	240	29		101
Fred Miller	DT	6'3"	245	24		
Guy Reese	DT	6'5"	260	25		
Billy Ray Smith	DT	6'4"	240	30	1	
Glenn Ressler	C-DT	6'3"	235	21		
Jackie Burkett	LB	6'4"	228	28		
Ted Davis	LB	6'1"	225	23		
Dennis Gaubatz	LB	6'2"	220	24	1	
Monte Lee	LB	6'4"	220	27		
Don Shinnick	LB	6'	235	30	1	
Steve Stonebreaker	LB	6'3"	222	27	1	
Mike Curtis	FB-LB	6'2"	225	21		
Bobby Boyd	DB	5'10"	190	27	9	6
Wendell Harris	DB	5'11"	185	24	3	
Alvin Haymond	DB	6'	190	23	3	6
Jerry Logan	DB	6'1"	185	24	2	12
Lenny Lyles	DB	6'2"	202	29	1	
Jim Welch	DB	6'	190	27		
Gary Cuozzo	QB	6'1"	195	24		
Johnny Unitas	QB	6'1"	194	32		6
Lenny Moore	HB	6'1"	190	32		48
Tom Matte	QB-HB	6'	205	26		6
Jerry Hill	FB	5'11"	210	25		30
Tony Lorick	FB	6'1"	215	23		18
Jimmy Orr	FL	5'11"	175	29		60
Willie Richardson	FL	6'2"	198	25		6
John Mackey	TE	6'3"	217	23		42
Butch Wilson	TE	6'2"	218	23		
Ray Berry	OE	6'2"	187	32		42
Alex Hawkins	FL-OE	6'1"	186	28		6
Neal Petties	FL-OE	6'2"	198	24		

Lou Kirouac – Injury

Gino Marchetti – Voluntarily Retired

CHICAGO BEARS 9-5-0 George Halas

Scores of Each Game		
24	San Francisco	52
28	Los Angeles	30
14	Green Bay	23
31	LOS ANGELES	6
45	Minnesota	37
38	DETROIT	10
31	GREEN BAY	10
21	BALTIMORE	26
34	ST. LOUIS	13
17	Detroit	10
35	New York	14
13	Baltimore	0
61	SAN FRANCISCO	20
17	MINNESOTA	24

Use Name	Pos.	Hgt	Wgt	Age	Int	Pts
Herm Lee	OT	6'4"	247	34		
Dick Leeuwenberg	OT	6'5"	242	21		
Bob Wetoska	OT	6'3"	240	27		
Jim Cadile	OG	6'3"	240	24		
Mike Rabold	OG	6'2"	238	28		
George Seals	DT-OG	6'2"	260	22		
Mike Pyle	C	6'3"	250	26		
Doug Atkins	DE	6'8"	255	35	1	
Dick Evey	DE	6'2"	225	24	1	
Bob Kilcullen	DE	6'3"	245	29		
Ed O'Bradovich	DE	6'3"	255	25		
John Johnson	DT	6'5"	260	24		
Stan Jones	DT	6'1"	250	34		
Earl Leggett	DT	6'3"	265	31		
Dennis Murphy	DT	6'1"	250	21		
Dick Butkus	LB	6'3"	240	21	5	
Joe Fortunato	LB	6'	225	35	2	
Bill George	LB	6'2"	235	34		
Roger LeClerc	LB	6'3"	235	27		85
Larry Morris	LB	6'2"	230	30		
Jim Purnell	LB	6'2"	205	23		
Mike Reilly	LB	6'2"	238	22		
J. C. Caroline	DB	6'1"	190	32		
Larry Glueck	DB	6'	190	23		
Bennie McRae	DB	6'1"	180	24	4	6
Richie Petitbon	DB	6'3"	205	27	2	
Ron Smith	DB	6'1"	185	22		
Rosey Taylor	DB	5'11"	186	26	1	6
Dave Whitsell	DB	6'	190	29	4	6
Rudy Bukich	QB	6'1"	205	34		18
Billy Wade	QB	6'2"	205	34		
Jon Arnett	HB	5'11"	203	30		30
Charlie Bivins	HB	6'2"	212	26		12
Ronnie Bull	HB	6'	200	25		24
Gale Sayers	HB	6'	198	22		132
Ralph Kurek	FB	6'2"	210	22		
Andy Livingston	FB	6'	234	20		12
Joe Marconi	FB	6'2"	225	31		
Johnny Morris	FL	5'10"	180	30		24
Mike Ditka	TE	6'3"	230	25		12
Billy Martin	TE	6'4"	240	22		
Dick Gordon	OE	5'11"	190	20		18
Jim Jones	OE	6'2"	187	21		24
Bobby Joe Green	K	5'11"	175	27		

Riley Mattson – Injury
Palmer Pyle – Injury

EASTERN CONFERENCE – Continued

ST. LOUIS CARDINALS

RUSHING

Last Name	No.	Yds	Avg	TD
Triplett	174	617	3.5	6
Crenshaw	127	437	3.4	0
Thornton	31	188	6.1	0
Gautt	44	175	4.0	2
Childress	19	94	4.9	0
Johnson	25	60	2.4	1
Bakken	1	28	28.0	0
Gambrell	4	15	3.8	0
Humphrey	2	4	2.0	0
Nofsinger	4	1	0.3	1

RECEIVING

Last Name	No.	Yds	Avg	TD
Conrad	58	909	16	5
Randle	51	845	17	9
Smith	41	648	16	2
Triplett	26	256	10	1
Crenshaw	23	232	10	1
Gambrell	9	171	19	2
Gautt	9	128	14	0
Childress	3	27	9	0
Thornton	1	6	6	0

PUNT RETURNS

Last Name	No.	Yds	Avg	TD
Silvestri	3	21	7	0
Woodson	18	7	0	0
Burson	1	0	0	0
Gambrell	1	–1	–1	0

KICKOFF RETURNS

Last Name	No.	Yds	Avg	TD
Woodson	27	665	25	0
Gambrell	9	216	24	0
Stovall	7	198	28	0
Silvestri	4	96	24	0
Ogden	2	55	28	0
Hammack	3	34	11	0
Crenshaw	2	23	12	0
Koman	1	0	0	0

PASSING – PUNTING – KICKING

PASSING	Att	Comp	%	Yds	Yd/Att	TD	Int–%	RK
Johnson	322	155	48	2439	7.6	18	15– 5	11
Humphrey	105	58	55	736	7.0	1	9– 9	
Nofsinger	20	8	40	47	2.4	1	1– 5	
Gautt	1	0	0	0	0.0	0	0– 0	

PUNTING	No	Avg
Smith	39	39.3
Bakken	26	42.2
Stovall	2	40.0

KICKING	XP	Att	%	FG	Att	%
Bakken	33	33	100	21	31	**68**

PITTSBURGH STEELERS

RUSHING

Last Name	No.	Yds	Avg	TD
Hoak	131	426	3.3	5
Lind	111	375	3.4	1
Peaks	47	230	4.9	0
Butler	46	108	2.3	0
Nelsen	26	84	3.2	1
Sapp	14	54	3.9	0
Ballman	17	46	2.7	3
Wade	8	43	5.4	0
Johnson	3	11	3.7	0
Martha	2	3	1.5	0
Jefferson	1	–1	–1.0	0
Brown	2	–3	–1.5	0

RECEIVING

Last Name	No.	Yds	Avg	TD
Ballman	40	859	21	5
Thomas	25	431	17	1
Lind	25	236	9	1
Hoak	19	228	12	1
Jefferson	13	287	22	1
Martha	11	171	16	0
Butler	9	117	13	1
Folkins	5	58	12	0
Hilton	4	32	8	0
Mack	3	41	14	0
Peaks	3	22	7	0
Simmons	2	16	8	0
Sapp	1	10	10	0
Nelsen	1	–5	–5	0

PUNT RETURNS

Last Name	No.	Yds	Avg	TD
Jefferson	13	100	8	0
Keys	10	77	8	0
J. Bradshaw	5	73	15	0
Thomas	5	9	2	0

KICKOFF RETURNS

Last Name	No.	Yds	Avg	TD
Butler	25	509	20	0
Peaks	20	429	21	0
Ballman	8	150	19	0
Sapp	5	77	15	0
Woodson	2	45	23	0
Simmons	1	28	28	0

PASSING – PUNTING – KICKING

PASSING	Att	Comp	%	Yds	Yd/Att	TD	Int–%	RK
Nelsen	270	121	45	1917	7.1	8	17– 6	15
Wade	66	33	50	463	7.0	2	13– 20	
Brown	23	10	44	204	8.9	1	5– 22	

PUNTING	No	Avg
Lambert	**78**	45.1
Brown	2	40.0

KICKING	XP	Att	%	FG	Att	%
Clark	19	24	79	11	19	58

WESTERN CONFERENCE

GREEN BAY PACKERS

RUSHING

Last Name	No.	Yds	Avg	TD
Taylor	207	734	3.5	4
Hornung	89	299	3.4	5
Starr	18	169	9.4	1
Moore	51	124	2.4	0
Pitts	54	122	2.3	4
Chandler	1	27	27.0	0
Coffey	3	12	4.0	0
Jacobs	3	5	1.7	0
Bratkowski	4	–1	–0.3	0
Claridge	2	–3	–1.5	0

RECEIVING

Last Name	No.	Yds	Avg	TD
Dowler	44	610	14	4
Dale	20	382	19	2
Taylor	20	207	10	0
Hornung	19	336	18	3
Fleming	14	141	10	2
Long	13	304	23	4
Pitts	11	182	17	1
McGee	10	154	15	1
Anderson	8	105	13	1
Moore	7	87	12	1

PUNT RETURNS

Last Name	No.	Yds	Avg	TD
Wood	13	38	3	0
Pitts	8	27	3	0
Adderley	1	0	0	0

KICKOFF RETURNS

Last Name	No.	Yds	Avg	TD
Pitts	20	396	20	0
Moore	15	361	24	0
Adderley	10	221	22	0
Crutcher	3	53	18	0
Coffey	1	9	9	0
Grimm	1	0	0	0

PASSING – PUNTING – KICKING

PASSING	Att	Comp	%	Yds	Yd/Att	TD	Int–%	RK
Starr	251	140	56	2055	8.2	16	9– 4	4
Bratkowski	48	21	44	348	7.3	3	4– 8	
Moore	2	2	100	22	11.0	0	0– 0	
Hornung	2	1	50	19	9.5	0	1– 50	
Pitts	2	1	50	51	25.5	0	0– 0	
Claridge	1	1	100	13	13.0	0	0– 0	

PUNTING	No	Avg
Chandler	74	42.9

KICKING	XP	Att	%	FG	Att	%
Chandler	37	38	97	17	26	65

BALTIMORE COLTS

RUSHING

Last Name	No.	Yds	Avg	TD
Hill	147	516	3.5	5
Moore	133	464	3.5	5
Lorick	63	296	4.7	1
Matte	69	235	3.4	1
Unitas	17	68	4.0	1
Cuozzo	6	8	1.3	0
Mackey	1	7	7.0	0
Curtis	6	1	0.2	0

RECEIVING

Last Name	No.	Yds	Avg	TD
Berry	58	739	13	7
Orr	45	847	19	10
Mackey	40	814	20	7
Moore	27	414	15	3
Hill	20	112	6	0
Lorick	15	184	12	2
Matte	12	131	11	0
Hawkins	2	32	16	1
Wilson	1	38	38	0
Richardson	1	14	14	1
Curtis	1	5	5	0

PUNT RETURNS

Last Name	No.	Yds	Avg	TD
Haymond	**41**	**403**	10	0
Hawkins	4	18	5	0

KICKOFF RETURNS

Last Name	No.	Yds	Avg	TD
Haymond	20	614	31	0
Lorick	9	211	23	0
Matte	8	211	26	0
Curtis	2	10	5	0
Hill	1	3	3	0
Hawkins	2	0	0	0

PASSING – PUNTING – KICKING

PASSING	Att	Comp	%	Yds	Yd/Att	TD	Int–%	RK
Unitas	282	164	58	2530	**9.0**	23	12– 4	2
Cuozzo	105	54	51	700	6.7	7	4– 4	
Matte	7	1	14	19	2.7	0	1– 14	

PUNTING	No	Avg
Gilburg	54	39.6

KICKING	XP	Att	%	FG	Att	%
Michaels	48	48	100	17	28	61

CHICAGO BEARS

RUSHING

Last Name	No.	Yds	Avg	TD
Sayers	166	867	5.2	14
Bull	91	417	4.6	3
Livingston	63	363	5.8	2
Arnett	102	363	3.6	5
Marconi	19	47	2.5	0
Bukich	28	33	1.2	3
Wade	5	18	3.6	0
J. Jones	2	13	6.5	0
Gordon	2	10	5.0	0
Kurek	1	0	0.0	0

RECEIVING

Last Name	No.	Yds	Avg	TD
J. Morris	53	846	16	4
Ditka	36	454	13	2
Sayers	29	507	17	6
J. Jones	21	350	17	4
Bull	16	186	12	1
Gordon	13	279	21	3
Livingston	12	134	11	0
Arnett	12	114	10	0
Bivins	4	108	27	2
Marconi	4	43	11	0
Martin	1	–1	–1	0

PUNT RETURNS

Last Name	No.	Yds	Avg	TD
Sayers	16	238	15	1
Arnett	11	52	5	0
Smith	1	2	2	0
Gordon	1	–3	–3	0

KICKOFF RETURNS

Last Name	No.	Yds	Avg	TD
Sayers	21	660	31	**1**
Gordon	14	242	17	0
Arnett	5	150	30	0
Livingston	2	66	33	0
Smith	1	17	17	0
Kurek	1	11	11	0
LeClerc	1	0	0	0

PASSING – PUNTING – KICKING

PASSING	Att	Comp	%	Yds	Yd/Att	TD	Int–%	RK
Bukich	312	176	56	2641	8.5	20	9– **3**	**1**
Wade	41	20	49	204	5.0	0	2– 5	
Bull	3	2	67	63	21.0	0	0– 0	
Sayers	3	2	67	53	17.7	1	1– 33	
Arnett	2	1	50	59	29.5	1	0– 0	

PUNTING	No	Avg
Green	58	42.7

KICKING	XP	Att	%	FG	Att	%
LeClerc	**52**	52	**100**	11	26	42

WESTERN CONFERENCE – Continued

SAN FRANCISCO FORTY NINERS 7-6-1 Jack Christiansen

Scores of Each Game		
52	CHICAGO	24
27	PITTSBURGH	17
24	Baltimore	27
10	Green Bay	27
45	Los Angeles	21
41	MINNESOTA	42
28	BALTIMORE	34
31	Dallas	39
27	Detroit	21
30	LOS ANGELES	27
45	Minnesota	24
17	DETROIT	14
20	Chicago	61
24	GREEN BAY	24

Use Name	Pos.	Hgt	Wgt	Age	Int	Pts
Jim Norton	OT	6'4"	255	22		
Walt Rock	OT	6'5"	245	24		
Len Rohde	OT	6'4"	245	27		
Howard Mudd	OG	6'3"	240	23		
John Thomas	OG	6'4"	246	30		
Jim Wilson	OG	6'3"	255	24		
Bruce Bosley	C	6'2"	240	31		
Joe Cerne	C	6'2"	235	22		
Dan Colchico	DE	6'4"	245	28		
Dan LaRose	DE	6'5"	250	25		
Clark Miller	DE	6'5"	245	26		6
Karl Rubke	DE	6'4"	240	29		
Charlie Krueger	DT	6'4"	254	29		6
Roland Lakes	DT	6'4"	263	25		
Chuck Sieminski	DT	6'4"	265	25		
Ed Beard	LB	6'2"	245	25		
Jack Chapple	LB	6'2"	227	22		6
Floyd Dean	LB	6'4"	245	25		
Mike Dowdle	LB	6'3"	235	27		
Bob Harrison	LB	6'2"	225	28		
Matt Hazeltine	LB	6'1"	230	32	1	
Dave Wilcox	LB	6'3"	230	22	1	6
Kermit Alexander	DB	5'11"	186	24	3	
George Donnelly	DB	6'3"	205	22		
Jim Johnson	DB	6'2"	190	27	6	
Elbert Kimbrough	DB	5'11"	190	26	2	
Jerry Mertens	DB	6'	185	29		
Wayne Swinford	DB	6'	190	22		
John Brodie	QB	6'1"	200	30		6
George Mira	QB	5'11"	190	23		
John David Crow	HB	6'2"	215	30		54
Rudy Johnson	HB	5'11"	190	23		
Dave Kopay	HB	6'2"	217	23		24
Gary Lewis	FB	6'3"	230	23		18
Ken Willard	FB	6'2"	230	22		54
Bernie Casey	FL	6'4"	215	26		48
Dale Messer	FL	5'10"	175	28		
Bob Poole	TE	6'4"	216	23		
Monte Stickles	TE	6'4"	230	27		6
Vern Burke	OE	6'4"	200	24		6
Kay McFarland	OE	6'2"	180	26		6
Dave Parks	OE	6'2"	195	23		72
Tommy Davis	K	6'	212	30		103

MINNESOTA VIKINGS 7-7-0 Norm Van Brocklin

Scores of Each Game		
16	Baltimore	35
29	DETROIT	31
38	Los Angeles	35
40	NEW YORK	14
37	CHICAGO	45
42	San Francisco	41
27	Cleveland	17
24	LOS ANGELES	13
21	BALTIMORE	41
13	GREEN BAY	38
24	SAN FRANCISCO	45
19	Green Bay	24
29	Detroit	7
24	Chicago	17

Use Name	Pos.	Hgt	Wgt	Age	Int	Pts
Grady Alderman	OT	6'2"	240	26		
Errol Linden	OT	6'5"	260	28		
Archie Sutton	OT	6'4"	262	22		
Larry Bowie	OG	6'2"	250	25		
Ken Byers	OG	6'1"	240	25		
Milt Sunde	C-OG	6'2"	234	22		
Mick Tingelhoff	C	6'1"	237	25		
Carl Eller	DE	6'6"	255	22		2
Jim Marshall	DE	6'3"	235	28		
Paul Dickson	DT	6'5"	255	28		
Gary Larsen	DT	6'5"	250	25		
Jim Prestel	DT	6'5"	275	28		2
Rip Hawkins	LB	6'3"	235	26	3	6
Bill Jobko	LB	6'2"	235	29		
John Kirby	LB	6'3"	222	23		
Lonnie Warwick	LB	6'3"	225	23		6
Roy Winston	LB	6'1"	230	25		
Lee Calland	DB	6'	190	24		
Gary Hill	DB	6'	200	21		
Jeff Jordan	DB	6'4"	190	21	4	
Karl Kassulke	DB	6'	193	23	2	
Earsell Mackbee	DB	6'1"	195	24		
George Rose	DB	5'11"	190	22	1	
Ed Sharockman	DB	6'	200	25	6	6
Larry Vargo	DB	6'3"	215	25	3	
Bob Berry	QB	5'11"	190	23		
Fran Tarkenton	QB	6'1"	190	25		6
Ron Vander Kelen	QB	6'1"	185	25		
Billy Barnes	HB	5'11"	202	30		
Dick James	HB	5'9"	185	31		
Phil King	HB	6'4"	220	29		6
Tommy Mason	HB	6'	196	26		66
Dave Osborn	HB	6'	205	22		12
Jim Young	HB	6'	205	22		
Bill Brown	FB	5'11"	230	27		42
Jim Phillips	FL	6'1"	195	28		6
Lance Rentzel	HB-FL	6'2"	210	21		6
Tom Hall	OE-FL	6'1"	195	24		12
Hal Bedsole	TE	6'4"	230	23		18
Paul Flatley	OE	6'1"	187	24		42
Gordon Smith	OE	6'2"	220	26		30
Fred Cox	K	5'10"	200	26		113
Bobby Walden	K	6'	195	26		

DETROIT LIONS 6-7-1 Harry Gilmer

Scores of Each Game		
20	LOS ANGELES	0
31	Minnesota	29
14	WASHINGTON	10
7	Baltimore	31
21	GREEN BAY	31
10	Chicago	38
31	Los Angeles	7
12	Green Bay	7
21	SAN FRANCISCO	27
10	CHICAGO	17
24	BALTIMORE	24
14	San Francisco	17
7	MINNESOTA	29
35	Philadelphia	28

Use Name	Pos.	Hgt	Wgt	Age	Int	Pts
Daryl Sanders	OT	6'5"	250	23		
Roger Shoals	OT	6'4"	255	26		
John Gonzaga	OG-OT	6'3"	250	32		
John Gordy	OG	6'3"	250	29		
Ted Karras	OG	6'1"	243	32		
Jim Simon	OG	6'5"	235	24		
Ed Flanagan	C	6'3"	250	21		
Bob Whitlow	C	6'1"	236	29		
Larry Hand	DE	6'4"	245	25		
Darris McCord	DE	6'4"	250	32		
Sam Williams	DE	6'5"	235	34		
Roger Brown	DT	6'5"	300	28		2
Alex Karras	DT	6'2"	245	29		
Jerry Rush	DT	6'4"	255	33		
Ernie Clark	LB	6'1"	220	27	1	
Wally Hilgenburg	LB	6'3"	225	22		
Mike Lucci	LB	6'2"	223	25		
Joe Schmidt	LB	6'1"	220	33	4	
Wayne Walker	LB	6'2"	225	28	2	57
Jimmy Hill	DB	6'2"	195	36	1	
Jim Kearney	DB	6'2"	200	22		
Night Train Lane	DB	6'1"	200	37		
Dick LeBeau	DB	6'1"	185	28	7	6
Bruce Maher	DB	5'11"	190	28	4	
Wayne Rasmussen	DB	6'2"	180	23	5	12
Bobby Thompson	DB	5'10"	175	25	2	
Tom Vaughn	DB	5'11"	195	22		
George Izo	QB	6'3"	218	28		
Tom Myers	QB	6'	188	21		
Milt Plum	QB	6'1"	205	31		18
Bobby Felts (from BAL)	HB	6'2"	205	22		
Joe Don Looney	HB	6'1"	230	22		36
Amos Marsh	HB	6'1"	220	26		48
Tom Watkins	HB	6'1"	195	28		
Tom Nowatzke	FB	6'3"	228	22		12
Nick Pietrosante	FB	6'2"	225	28		6
Terry Barr	FL	6'	190	30		18
Pat Studstill	FL	6'1"	175	27		18
Jim Gibbons	TE	6'2"	220	29		12
Ron Kramer	TE	6'3"	240	30		6
Gail Cogdill	OE	6'2"	195	28		
John Henderson	OE	6'3"	190	22		6

J. D. Smith – Injury
Warren Wells – Military Service

LOS ANGELES RAMS 4-10-0 Harland Svare

Scores of Each Game		
0	Detroit	20
30	CHICAGO	28
35	MINNESOTA	38
6	Chicago	31
21	SAN FRANCISCO	45
20	Baltimore	35
7	DETROIT	31
13	Minnesota	24
3	Green Bay	6
27	San Francisco	30
21	GREEN BAY	10
27	St. Louis	3
42	CLEVELAND	7
17	BALTIMORE	20

Use Name	Pos.	Hgt	Wgt	Age	Int	Pts
Joe Carollo	OT	6'2"	263	25		
Charley Cowan	OT	6'4"	275	27		
Roger Pillath	OT	6'4"	255	23		
Frank Varrichione	OT	6'1"	237	33		
Don Chuy	OG	6'1"	256	24		
Joe Scibelli	OG	6'1"	264	26		
Joe Wendryhoski	C-OG	6'2"	245	26		
Ken Iman	C	6'1"	235	26		
Frank Marchlewski	C	6'2"	226	21		
Deacon Jones	DE	6'5"	260	26		2
Lamar Lundy	DE	6'7"	260	30		
Tim Powell	DE	6'4"	248	21		
Rosey Grier	DT	6'5"	290	32		
Frank Molden	DT	6'5"	285	23	1	6
Merlin Olsen	DT	6'5"	276	24		
Fred Brown	LB	6'5"	223	22		
Mack Byrd	LB	6'	215	22		
Dan Currie	LB	6'3"	240	31		
Tony Guillory	LB	6'4"	220	22		
Cliff Livingston	LB	6'3"	212	35	1	
Mike Strofolino (to BAL)	LB	6'2"	240	21		
Doug Woodlief	LB	6'3"	235	21		
Chuck Lamson	DB	6'	190	26	2	
Aaron Martin	DB	6'	185	24	2	6
Dan McIlhany	DB	6'1"	195	22	2	
Jerry Richardson	DB	6'3"	190	22	1	
Bobby Smith (to DET)	DB	6'	197	27		
Ed Meador	DB	5'11"	203	28	2	6
Clancy Williams	HB-DB	6'2"	198	22		
Roman Gabriel	QB	6'4"	225	25		12
Bill Munson	QB	6'2"	197	23		6
Ron Smith	QB	6'5"	220	23		
Terry Baker	HB	6'3"	200	24		18
Les Josephson	HB	6'	210	23		
Willie Brown	FL-HB	6'	185	22		6
Dick Bass	FB	5'10"	198	28		24
Jim Stiger (from DAL)	FB	5'11"	214	24		
Ben Wilson	FB	6'	225	25		6
Tommy McDonald	FL	5'10"	175	31		54
Marlin McKeever	TE	6'1"	227	25		24
Billy Truax	TE	6'5"	240	22		6
Steve Heckard	OE	6'1"	195	22		
Jack Snow	OE	6'2"	210	22		18
Jon Kilgore	K	6'1"	200	21		
Bruce Gossett	K	6'2"	230	22		75
Billy Lothridge	K	6'1"	194	21		

Bucky Pope – Injury
Jack Pardee – Voluntarily Retired

WESTERN CONFERENCE – Continued

SAN FRANCISCO FORTY NINERS

RUSHING

Last Name	No.	Yds	Avg	TD
Willard	189	778	4.1	5
Crow	132	514	3.9	2
Lewis	52	256	4.9	3
Kopay	28	81	2.9	2
Mira	5	64	12.8	0
Brodie	15	60	4.0	1
Davis	1	21	21.0	0
R. Johnson	6	9	1.5	0

RECEIVING

Last Name	No.	Yds	Avg	TD
Parks	**80**	**1344**	17	**12**
Casey	59	765	13	8
Stickles	35	343	10	1
Willard	32	253	8	4
Crow	28	493	18	7
Kopay	11	147	13	1
Lewis	10	25	3	0
McFarland	8	106	13	1
R. Johnson	3	49	16	0
Messer	2	41	21	0
Burke	2	38	19	1
Poole	2	29	15	0

PUNT RETURNS

Last Name	No.	Yds	Avg	TD
Alexander	35	262	7	0
Swinford	2	18	9	0
Lewis	1	3	3	0

KICKOFF RETURNS

Last Name	No.	Yds	Avg	TD
Alexander	**32**	**741**	23	0
Lewis	15	355	24	0
R. Johnson	4	71	18	0
Swinford	4	61	15	0
Messer	1	27	27	0
Kopay	1	21	21	0
Cerne	1	0	0	0
Rubke	1	0	0	0

PASSING

Last Name	Att	Comp	%	Yds	Yd/Att	TD	Int–%	RK
Brodie	**391**	**242**	**62**	**3112**	8.0	**30**	16– 4	3
Mira	58	28	48	460	7.9	4	3– 5	
Crow	4	2	50	61	15.3	1	1– 25	
Willard	1	0	0	0	0.0	0	1–100	

PUNTING

Last Name	No	Avg
Davis	54	45.8

KICKING

Last Name	XP	Att	%	FG	Att	%
Davis	**52**	**53**	98	17	27	63

MINNESOTA VIKINGS

RUSHING

Last Name	No.	Yds	Avg	TD
Brown	160	699	4.4	6
Mason	141	597	4.2	10
Tarkenton	56	356	6.4	1
King	72	356	4.9	0
Barnes	48	148	3.1	0
Osborn	20	106	5.3	2
Vander Kelen	4	13	3.3	0
Young	3	4	1.3	0
Rentzel	1	–1	–1.0	0

RECEIVING

Last Name	No.	Yds	Avg	TD
Flatley	50	896	18	7
Brown	41	503	12	1
Smith	22	431	20	5
Mason	22	321	15	1
Hall	15	287	19	2
Phillips	15	185	12	1
King	12	96	8	1
Bedsole	8	123	15	3
Barnes	3	15	5	0
Osborn	1	4	4	0

PUNT RETURNS

Last Name	No.	Yds	Avg	TD
Mason	9	63	7	0
Hall	3	21	7	0
Warwick	1	10	10	1
Rentzel	4	9	2	0
Young	4	7	2	0
James	1	5	5	0

KICKOFF RETURNS

Last Name	No.	Yds	Avg	TD
Rentzel	23	602	26	**1**
Osborn	18	422	23	0
James	11	212	19	0
Hall	4	93	23	0
Young	4	78	20	0
Mason	3	66	22	0
Barnes	3	37	12	0
King	1	14	14	0

PASSING

Last Name	Att	Comp	%	Yds	Yd/Att	TD	Int–%	RK
Tarkenton	329	171	52	2609	7.9	19	11– 3	6
Vander Kelen	40	18	45	252	6.3	2	0– 0	
Berry	2	0	0	0	0.0	0	0– 0	
Mason	1	0	0	0	0.0	0	1–100	

PUNTING

Last Name	No	Avg
Walden	51	42.1

KICKING

Last Name	XP	Att	%	FG	Att	%
Cox	44	44	100	**23**	**35**	66

DETROIT LIONS

RUSHING

Last Name	No.	Yds	Avg	TD
Marsh	131	495	3.8	6
Pietrosante	107	374	3.5	1
Looney	114	356	3.1	5
Watkins	29	95	3.3	0
Nowatzke	27	73	2.7	1
Felts	22	58	2.6	0
Plum	21	37	1.8	3
Sanders	1	2	2.0	0
Studstill	1	–4	–4.0	0
Izo	1	–5	–5.0	0
Barr	1	–12	–12.0	0

RECEIVING

Last Name	No.	Yds	Avg	TD
Studstill	28	389	14	3
Barr	24	433	18	3
Cogdill	20	247	12	0
Kramer	18	206	11	1
Pietrosante	18	163	9	0
Marsh	17	159	9	2
Gibbons	12	111	9	2
Looney	12	109	9	1
Henderson	8	140	18	1
Watkins	5	53	11	0
Nowatzke	5	45	9	1
Felts	3	28	9	0

PUNT RETURNS

Last Name	No.	Yds	Avg	TD
Watkins	23	234	10	0
Vaughn	2	50	25	0
Studstill	5	47	9	0
Felts	3	27	9	0

KICKOFF RETURNS

Last Name	No.	Yds	Avg	TD
Watkins	17	584	**34**	0
Felts	18	422	23	0
Vaughn	13	316	24	0
Studstill	10	257	26	0
Nowatzke	2	12	6	0
Lucci	1	0	0	0

PASSING

Last Name	Att	Comp	%	Yds	Yd/Att	TD	Int–%	RK
Plum	308	143	46	1710	5.6	12	19– 6	14
Izo	59	24	41	357	6.1	2	6– 10	
Myers	5	3	60	16	3.2	0	1– 20	
Felts	1	0	0	0	0.0	0	0– 0	
Marsh	1	0	0	0	0.0	0	0– 0	

PUNTING

Last Name	No	Avg
Studstill	**78**	42.8

KICKING

Last Name	XP	Att	%	FG	Att	%
Walker	33	33	100	8	22	36

LOS ANGELES RAMS

RUSHING

Last Name	No.	Yds	Avg	TD
Bass	121	549	4.5	2
Josephson	71	225	3.2	0
Wilson	60	189	3.2	1
Munson	26	157	6.0	1
W. Brown	44	133	3.0	0
Baker	25	82	3.3	1
Gabriel	23	79	3.4	2
Stiger	14	62	4.4	0
Meador	2	35	17.5	1
Williams	3	3	1.0	0

RECEIVING

Last Name	No.	Yds	Avg	TD
McDonald	67	1036	15	9
McKeever	44	542	12	4
Snow	38	559	15	3
Baker	22	210	10	2
Bass	21	230	11	2
Josephson	18	169	9	0
Wilson	9	110	12	0
Truax	6	108	18	1
W. Brown	4	91	23	1
Stiger	1	9	9	0
Heckard	1	4	4	0

PUNT RETURNS

Last Name	No.	Yds	Avg	TD
Stiger	16	120	8	0
W. Brown	9	63	7	0
B. Smith	10	56	6	0
Bass	1	0	0	0

KICKOFF RETURNS

Last Name	No.	Yds	Avg	TD
W. Brown	24	615	26	0
B. Smith	18	475	26	0
Williams	9	213	24	0
Wilson	3	66	22	0
Stiger	2	28	14	0

PASSING

Last Name	Att	Comp	%	Yds	Yd/Att	TD	Int–%	RK
Munson	267	144	54	1701	6.4	10	14– 5	13
Gabriel	173	83	48	1321	7.6	11	5– 3	9
Josephson	2	1	50	15	7.5	1	0– 0	
Baker	1	1	100	14	14.0	0	0– 0	
Meador	1	0	0	0	0.0	0	0– 0	
Wilson	1	1	100	8	8.0	0	0– 0	

PUNTING

Last Name	No	Avg
Lothridge	42	38.5
Kilgore	24	41.6

KICKING

Last Name	XP	Att	%	FG	Att	%
Gossett	30	32	94	15	26	58

1965 A.F.L. Sonny and Joe and John

After years in show business, New York Jet owner Sonny Werblin was a firm believer in the star system, of the gate pull of a big-name star. Werblin set out with checkbook in hand and bagged two of college football's biggest names, Alabama's Joe Namath and Notre Dame's John Huarte, with astronomical contracts that dwarfed the pacts of even the biggest veteran stars. Some people talked about the two fine young quarterbacks Werblin had signed, some talked about the misplaced values of a society that rewarded football players with small fortunes while grossly underpaying schoolteachers, but the important thing was that they talked. They talked about Joe Namath, they talked about the New York Jets, and they talked about the AFL. They stopped talking about whether the AFL would survive; they talked more now of when the leagues would be on a par.

When the league schedule started, a lot of those talking people came out to the games. Opening day in Houston saw a crowd of 52,680 turn out to see the lowly Oilers beat the Jets, with Joe Namath glued to the bench all afternoon. One week later, 53,658 fans filled Shea Stadium in New York to welcome Namath to the big city. Namath's development into a fine passer by mid-season furthered his publicity value and made Werblin's move look like a stroke of genius.

The league was feeling confident enough to vote for expansion in 1966, setting up a new team in Miami, which had flopped as a pro-football town in 1946 but was now a fast-growing metropolis. Only a few years ago, the league had been more worried about franchises folding than in creating new outposts for the AFL.

EASTERN DIVISION

Buffalo Bills—The trade of Cookie Gilchrist to Denver took most of the punch out of the running game, and injuries to Elbert Dubenion and Glenn Bass robbed the team of its starting wide receivers, but the Bills coasted to another Eastern title on a stone-wall defense and Pete Gogolak's strong right leg. Anonymous people manned the defense, but although Ron McDole, Tom Day, Tom Sestak, Jim Dunaway, Mike Stratton, Harry Jacobs, John Tracey, Butch Byrd, Hagood Clarke, George Saimes, and Charley Warner were short on reputation as individuals, respect for them as a unit was universal. The offense began with a strong line but lacked the backs and ends to take full advantage of the blocking. Gilchrist had been dealt off because of recurring feuds with coach Lou Saban, but replacement Billy Joe was no match for Cookie as a runner, receiver, or blocker. The other runners—Wray Carlton, Bobby Smith, and Donnie Stone—were pedestrian pluggers. With Dubenion and Bass sidelined, journeymen Bo Roberson and Charley Ferguson filled the wide receiver spots, but quarterback Jack Kemp orchestrated this collection of odds and ends into a steady unit which headed for their third straight championship game in Lou Saban's last year before returning to college coaching.

New York Jets—Owner Sonny Werblin set the football world on its ear by signing the two most glamorous rookie quarterbacks to expensive contracts, Joe Namath to a $400,000 pact and Heisman Trophy winner John Huarte to a $200,000 pact. Huarte missed training camp because of the College All-Star Game and spent the year on the taxi squad, but Namath made a big splash right from the start. After sitting out the first few games, Namath took over the quarterback job and showed a quick release that triggered a strong passing arm. In addition, his sudden affluence and swinging bachelor's lifestyle made the newspapers constantly and proved to be a bonanza of publicity for the Jets and the AFL. But if Namath and Huarte attracted all the attention, other rookies made the Jets a stronger club down the second half of the season. George Sauer, playing tight end out of necessity, middle linebacker Al Atkinson, defensive end Verlon Biggs, defensive tackle Jim Harris, and defensive backs Jim Hudson and Cornell Gordon all put in solid freshman years for the improved New Yorkers who won five of their last eight games.

Boston Patriots—Head coach Mike Holovak had never paid much attention to pre-season games, expecting his team to start playing for real once the starting bell rang. The Patriots lost all five of their exhibition games this year, but then kept losing right into October. Winless in the first seven games, the Pats made a comeback in the second half of the schedule, but their horrid start killed any chances of challenging Buffalo for first place. Holovak had never gone all out to sign prestigious college seniors, relying instead on veterans and rookies from small and local schools, and now this policy was showing up in the deterioration of the team. The defense, long the club's strong point, began to creak with age, while the offense suffered because of Babe Parilli's off season. The thirty-four-year-old Parilli gave up twenty-six interceptions, a sign that his arm was losing its old zip. The Pats did sign two big-name rookie runners, Jim Nance and Joe Bellino, but neither had a good freshman season. Nance played overweight all year, while Bellino, making his pro debut after three years in the Navy, did not have the size to be a consistent ground-gainer.

Houston Oilers—With the exception of W. K. Hicks, the Oilers were using the same men in the defensive secondary that staffed the championship Houston teams in the early years of the AFL. Enemy passers burned the Oiler secondary for twenty-seven touchdown passes, a sign of the improvement in AFL play and of the lack of foresight in the Houston management. With the worst defense in the league, head coach Hugh Taylor was fortunate to pick up four wins in his year at the helm. The offense was in no shape to carry the team, as it had weaknesses in all sectors. The offensive line needed help, and the receiving fell off because of Charley Hennigan's bad knee. Halfback Sid Blanks missed the season with a knee injury, and fullback Charley Tolar had slowed up considerably, throwing the brunt of the running chores on 185-pound Ode Burrell. At quarterback, thirty-seven-year-old George Blanda was plagued with a flood of interceptions, but young Don Trull still saw little action. But even with all their problems, the Oilers did put together some good games, like a 19-17 upset of Buffalo and a 31-10 pasting of Boston.

WESTERN DIVISION

San Diego Chargers—Although the San Diego defense ranked with Buffalo's at the top of the league, the offense still won most of the headlines for the Chargers. The versatile attack boasted of stars in all quarters. Linemen Ron Mix and Walt Sweeney were among the AFL's best, and flanker Lance Alworth gained a phenomenal 1,602 yards with a variety of leaping, diving, and streaking catches which netted him fourteen touchdowns. Quarterback John Hadl developed into a top-flight pro as a passer and play-caller. Halfback Paul Lowe hustled his way to a new league rushing record of 1,121 yards, and Keith Lincoln combined with rookie Gene Foster to provide punch at the fullback slot. But the San Diego defense bailed out the offense on its rare off days, as in a 13-13 tie with Boston and a 10-10 tie with the Chiefs. Earl Faison and Ernie Ladd still stacked up runners and passers, but both star linemen expressed dissatisfaction with the organization and were playing out their option. Fitting right in with the veterans were several newcomers to the unit, rookies Rick Redman, Steve DeLong, Dick Degan, and Speedy Duncan—enough to give the Chargers their fifth Western crown in six years.

Oakland Raiders—Head coach and general manager Al Davis kept building the Raiders with top rookie talent. This year's batch of Oakland freshmen included wide receiver Fred Biletnikoff, cornerback Kent McCloughan, linebacker Gus Otto, and offensive tackles Bob Svihus and Harry Schuh. The Raiders now had sufficient depth to compensate for injuries, as Tom Flores and Dick Wood handled the quarterbacking in fine fashion with Cotton Davidson out for most of the year with an injury. The offense, with Clem Daniels and Art Powell the main guns, performed quite well, and the defense had two solid rookie starters in Otto and McCloughan and an All-Pro cornerback in Dave Grayson. An inability to beat San Diego and Buffalo killed the Oakland title chances, as the Raiders dropped all four of their contests with the divisional champions-to-be.

Kansas City Chiefs—With one of the deepest rosters in pro football, the Chiefs seemed to be playing in the shadow of an evil star. Since the team moved to Kansas City in 1963, serious injury or death struck four Chief players. Stone Johnson suffered a fatal neck injury in a 1963 pre-season game, Ed Budde almost died from a blow on the head when attacked on the street in 1964, Fred Arbanas lost most of the vision in his left eye from an off-the-field altercation, and fullback Mack Lee Hill died on the operating table of complications following knee surgery midway through this season. On the field, the Chiefs had a habit of winning some games in impressive fashion, then going flat and losing to a weaker team. The Kansas City offense still was a top-flight unit, with the receiving strengthened by rookie Otis Taylor and the running game weakened by the trade of Abner Haynes and the tragic death of Hill. The defense had no problems with men like Jerry Mays, Buck Buchanan, E. J. Holub, Sherrill Headrick, Bobby Bell, Fred Williamson, and Johnny Robinson in the lineup.

Denver Broncos—For the first time in their history, the Broncos relied on the running game as their main offensive threat. Trades brought fullback Cookie Gilchrist and halfback Abner Haynes, both legendary AFL runners, to Denver during the summer, and while Gilchrist still bulled over tackles at peak form, Haynes lost his starting job to rookie Wendell Hayes. At any rate, the depth in the running-back slots kept the attack alive despite severe uncertainty at quarterback. Coach Mac Speedie used John McCormick, Mickey Slaughter, and Jacky Lee in the passer's spot and was satisfied with none of them. Lionel Taylor got open for enough passes from the three quarterbacks to lead the league in receiving, his fifth pass-catching title in the AFL's six years of play, but none of the other receivers on the team made much of a dent on enemy defenses.

FINAL TEAM STATISTICS

OFFENSE

	BOSTON	BUFFALO	DENVER	HOUSTON	K. CITY	NEW YORK	OAKLAND	SAN DIEGO
FIRST DOWNS:								
Total	214	206	255	227	232	213	225	**268**
by Rushing	55	69	111	63	101	77	72	**127**
by Passing	130	119	117	**140**	121	121	134	127
by Penalty	**29**	18	27	24	10	15	19	14
RUSHING:								
Number	373	392	453	324	418	367	390	**486**
Yards	1117	1288	1829	1175	1752	1476	1538	**1998**
Average Yards	3.0	3.3	4.0	3.6	**4.2**	4.0	3.9	4.1
Touchdowns	8	**16**	14	10	15	11	8	13
PASSING:								
Attempts	473	461	482	**550**	395	459	431	401
Completions	193	208	222	**224**	199	209	195	203
Completion Percentage	40.8	45.1	46.1	40.7	50.4	45.5	45.2	**50.6**
Passing Yards	2854	2744	2848	3070	2894	2751	2713	**3379**
Average Yards Per Attempt	6.0	6.0	5.9	5.6	7.3	6.0	6.3	**8.4**
Average Yards Per Completion	14.8	13.2	12.8	13.7	14.5	13.2	13.9	**16.6**
Times Tackled Attempting to Pass	37	29	24	31	37	**17**	33	27
Yards Lost Attempting to Pass	347	283	208	257	351	**162**	253	276
Net Yards	2507	2461	2640	2813	2543	2589	2460	**3103**
Touchdowns	19	13	18	**25**	22	21	22	23
Interceptions	29	24	30	35	20	22	**17**	26
Percent Intercepted	6.1	5.2	6.2	6.4	5.1	4.8	**3.9**	6.5
PUNTING:								
Number	82	80	68	**85**	72	72	75	70
Average Distance	40.1	43.0	42.3	43.7	44.6	**45.3**	41.1	40.0
PUNT RETURNS:								
Number	27	36	37	28	**38**	29	34	**38**
Yards	152	389	355	189	419	166	365	**508**
Average Yards	5.6	10.8	9.6	6.8	11.0	5.7	10.7	**13.4**
Touchdowns	0	0	1	0	1	0	1	**2**
KICKOFF RETURNS:								
Number	60	45	71	**77**	48	54	46	50
Yards	1191	1022	**1731**	1669	1080	1107	990	1028
Average Yards	19.9	22.7	**24.4**	21.7	22.5	20.5	21.5	20.6
Touchdowns	0	**2**	0	0	0	0	0	0
INTERCEPTION RETURNS:								
Number	21	**32**	25	27	20	26	24	28
Yards	233	393	465	416	342	235	**482**	377
Average Yards	11.1	12.3	18.6	15.4	17.1	9.0	**20.1**	13.5
Touchdowns	0	1	3	0	2	0	**4**	3
PENALTIES:								
Number	58	78	69	76	70	58	69	**84**
Yards	537	685	750	856	744	684	661	**929**
FUMBLES:								
Number	24	28	29	23	34	27	**17**	22
Number Lost	12	14	16	11	20	18	**9**	13
POINTS:								
Total	244	313	303	298	322	285	298	**340**
PAT (Kick) Attempts	27	31	32	34	37	31	35	**40**
PAT (Kick) Made	27	31	32	34	37	31	35	**40**
PAT (Rush or Pass) Attempts	0	2	**6**	3	3	1	0	1
PAT (Rush or Pass) Made	0	0	2	2	**3**	1	0	0
FG Attempts	27	**46**	29	23	30	34	34	30
FG Made	17	**28**	13	12	13	20	17	18
Percent FG Made	**63.0**	60.9	44.8	52.2	43.3	58.8	50.0	60.0
Safeties	**2**	0	0	1	0	0	1	0

DEFENSE

	BOSTON	BUFFALO	DENVER	HOUSTON	K. CITY	NEW YORK	OAKLAND	SAN DIEGO
FIRST DOWNS:								
Total	232	226	244	271	207	235	235	**190**
by Rushing	92	65	87	132	69	85	90	**55**
by Passing	127	141	138	**111**	113	136	125	118
by Penalty	**13**	20	19	28	25	14	20	17
RUSHING:								
Number	425	360	384	508	381	432	407	**306**
Yards	1531	1114	1337	2683	1376	1551	1487	**1094**
Average Yards	3.6	**3.1**	3.5	5.3	3.6	3.6	3.7	3.6
Touchdowns	10	**5**	24	17	12	10	10	7
PASSING:								
Attempts	431	502	440	**416**	451	472	466	474
Completions	206	227	202	**177**	216	220	199	206
Completion Percentage	47.8	45.2	45.9	**42.5**	47.9	46.6	42.7	43.5
Passing Yards	2891	3416	3265	2643	2711	2900	2947	**2480**
Average Yards Per Attempt	6.7	6.8	7.4	6.4	6.0	6.1	6.3	**5.2**
Average Yards Per Completion	14.0	15.0	16.2	14.9	12.6	13.2	14.8	**12.0**
Times Tackled Attempting to Pass	30	28	26	22	**39**	22	30	38
Yards Lost Attempting to Pass	291	246	305	173	**326**	238	246	312
Net Yards	2600	3170	2960	2470	2385	2662	2701	**2168**
Touchdowns	**17**	19	23	27	18	22	27	**17**
Interceptions	21	**32**	25	27	20	26	24	28
Percent Intercepted	4.9	6.4	5.7	**6.5**	4.4	5.5	5.2	5.9
PUNTING:								
Number	78	76	73	59	**83**	78	77	80
Average Distance	42.1	40.2	45.9	42.5	44.1	**39.8**	42.1	43.4
PUNT RETURNS:								
Number	33	30	**26**	48	29	40	34	27
Yards	232	**222**	343	494	401	352	257	242
Average Yards	**7.0**	7.4	13.2	10.3	13.8	8.8	7.6	9.0
Touchdowns	**0**	**0**	1	2	2	**0**	**0**	**0**
KICKOFF RETURNS:								
Number	**41**	60	58	48	56	60	62	66
Yards	**946**	1449	1197	995	1173	1421	1227	1410
Average Yards	23.1	24.2	20.6	20.7	20.9	23.7	**19.8**	21.4
Touchdowns	1	**0**	**0**	**0**	**0**	1	**0**	**0**
INTERCEPTION RETURNS:								
Number	29	24	30	35	20	22	**17**	26
Yards	365	467	426	471	238	339	**186**	451
Average Yards	12.6	19.5	14.2	13.5	11.9	15.4	**10.9**	17.3
Touchdowns	4	1	2	3	**0**	2	**0**	1
PENALTIES:								
Number	72	69	**86**	67	60	77	69	62
Yards	658	832	836	701	623	**865**	666	665
FUMBLES:								
Number	17	**33**	27	31	24	25	23	24
Number Lost	9	**25**	14	13	13	12	14	13
POINTS:								
Total	302	**226**	392	429	285	303	239	227
PAT (Kick) Attempts	28	**21**	50	48	33	33	29	25
PAT (Kick) Made	28	**21**	50	48	33	33	29	25
PAT (Rush or Pass) Attempts	6	4	**0**	2	1	2	1	**0**
PAT (Rush or Pass) Made	2	4	**0**	2	**0**	**0**	**0**	**0**
FG Attempts	40	30	24	43	28	34	**20**	34
FG Made	22	15	14	25	16	20	**10**	16
Percent FG Made	55.0	50.0	58.3	58.1	57.1	58.8	50.0	**47.1**
Safeties	**0**	1	**0**	1	**0**	**0**	**0**	2

1965 AFL CHAMPIONSHIP GAME

December 26, at San Diego
(Attendance 30,361)

Stubbornly Brilliant

The San Diego weather was mild compared with last year's chill in Buffalo, but the Bills' defense played the same hard-hitting game and again would up as victors. Buffalo's strong front four and tight pass defense completely handcuffed the favored Chargers, as they never could get past the Buffalo 24-yard line. Through the first quarter and the first ten minutes of the second quarter, both defenses kept the scoreboard empty, but the Bills scored on a Jack Kemp-to-Ernie Warlick pass with five minutes left before intermission. The Chargers then punted the ball back to the Bills, and Butch Byrd returned the kick 74 yards down the sideline for another Buffalo score. The two quick touchdowns gave the Bills a 14-0 lead to take into the clubhouse at halftime, while the Chargers had to ponder on the goose egg on their side of the scoreboard. Going back to last year's championship game, the Chargers now were scoreless in their last five quarters against the Buffalo defense. The second half proved no more pleasant for the Chargers, as John Hadl, Keith Lincoln, Paul Lowe, and Lance Alworth could not get the ball across the Buffalo goal line. Jack Kemp, meanwhile, guided the Bills' offense steadily against the stubborn San Diego defense. Pete Gogolak booted a pair of field goals in the third quarter to give the Bills some breathing room, and his 32-yarder in the fourth quarter ran the final score to 23-0. Quarterback Kemp, a former Charger, won the game MVP award for his surgical precision in running the attack.

SCORING

SAN DIEGO	**0**	**0**	**0**	**0– 0**
BUFFALO	**0**	**14**	**6**	**3–23**

Second Quarter
- Buf. Warlick, 18 yard pass from Kemp
  PAT—Gogolak (kick)
- Buf. Byrd, 74 yard punt return
  PAT—Gogolak (kick)

Third Quarter
- Buf. Gogolak, 11 yard field goal
- Buf. Gogolak, 39 yard field goal

Fourth Quarter
- Buf. Gogolak, 32 yard field goal

TEAM STATISTICS

S.D.		BUF.
12	First Downs—Total	23
5	First Downs—Rushing	13
7	First Downs—Passing	9
0	First Downs—Penalty	1
7	Punts—Number	4
40.7	Punts—Average Distance	46.3
3	Penalties—Number	2
41	Yards—Penalized	21
2	Missed Field Goals	2

INDIVIDUAL STATISTICS

SAN DIEGO	No.	Yds.	Avg.	BUFFALO	No.	Yds.	Avg.
RUSHING							
Lowe	12	57	4.8	Carlton	16	63	3.9
Hadl	8	24	3.0	Joe	16	35	2.2
Lincoln	4	16	4.0	Stone	3	5	1.7
Foster	2	9	4.5	Smith	1	5	5.0
Breaux	1	−2	−2.0		36	108	3.0
	27	104	3.9				
RECEIVING							
Alworth	4	82	20.5	Roberson	3	88	29.3
Lowe	3	3	1.0	Warlick	3	35	11.7
Norton	1	35	35.0	Costa	2	32	16.0
Farr	1	24	24.0	Tracy	1	12	12.0
MacKinnon	1	10	10.0		9	167	18.6
Lincoln	1	7	7.0				
Kocourek	1	3	3.0				
	12	164	13.7				
PUNT RETURNS							
Duncan	1	12	12.0	Byrd	3	87	29.0
KICKOFF RETURNS							
Duncan	2	62	31.0	Warner	1	17	17.0
Farr	1	35	35.0				
	3	97	32.3				
INTERCEPTION RETURNS							
Warren	1	0	0.0	Byrd	1	24	24.0
				Jacobs	1	12	12.0
					2	36	18.0

PASSING

	Att.	Comp.	Comp. Pct.	Yds.	Int.	Yds/ Att.	Yds/ Comp.	Yards Lost Tackled
SAN DIEGO								
Hadl	23	11	47.8	140	2	6.1	12.7	
Breaux	2	1	50.0	24	0	12.0	24.0	
	25	12	48.0	164	2	6.6	13.7	45
BUFFALO								
Kemp	19	8	42.1	155	1	8.2	19.4	
Lamonica	1	1	100.0	12	0	12.0	12.0	
	20	9	45.0	167	1	8.4	18.6	15

1965 A.F.L. — Eastern Division

BUFFALO BILLS 10-3-1 Lou Saban

Scores of Each Game		
24	BOSTON	7
30	Denver	15
33	NEW YORK	21
17	OAKLAND	12
3	SAN DIEGO	34
23	Kansas City	7
31	DENVER	13
17	HOUSTON	19
23	Boston	7
17	Oakland	14
20	San Diego	20
29	Houston	18
34	KANSAS CITY	25
12	New York	14

Use Name	Pos.	Hgt	Wgt	Age	Int	Pts
Stew Barber	OT	6'3"	250	26		
Dick Hudson	OT	6'4"	272	25		
Joe O'Donnell	OT	6'2"	246	23		
Al Bemiller	OG	6'3"	260	26		
George Flint	OG	6'4"	244	27		
Billy Shaw	OG	6'3"	248	25		
Dave Behrman	C	6'5"	260	23		
Tom Day	DE	6'2"	250	30	1	
Ron McDole	DE	6'3"	264	25	1	
Jim Dunaway	DT	6'4"	276	23		
Tom Keating	DT	6'3"	242	22		
Dudley Meredith	DT	6'4"	275	30		
Henry Schmidt	DT	6'4"	270	28		
Tom Sestak	OT-DT	6'5"	270	29		
Harry Jacobs	LB	6'2"	225	28	1	
Bill Laskey	LB	6'2"	250	22		
Paul Maguire	LB	6'	220	27		
Marty Schottenheimer	LB	6'3"	225	22		
Mike Stratton	LB	6'3"	240	23	2	
John Tracey	OE-LB	6'3"	225	31	1	
Butch Byrd	DB	6'	211	23	5	
Hagood Clarke	DB	6'	188	23	7	
Booker Edgerson	DB	5'10"	180	26	5	
Tom Janik	DB	6'3"	200	24		
George Saimes	DB	5'10"	195	23	4	6
Gene Sykes	DB	6'1"	195	24		
Charley Warner	HB-DB	5'11"	180	25	5	24
Jack Kemp	QB	6'1"	200	31		24
Daryle Lamonica	QB	6'2"	215	24		6
Joe Auer	HB	6'1"	205	23		
Wray Carlton	HB	6'2"	216	27		42
Bobby Smith	HB	6'	203	24		6
Billy Joe	FB	6'2"	250	24		36
Donnie Stone	FB	6'2"	205	28		
Elbert Dubenion	FL	6'	187	30		6
Floyd Hudlow	FL	5'11"	185	21		
Bo Roberson (from OAK)	FL	6'1"	190	30		18
Ed Rutkowski	FL	6'1"	208	24		6
Glenn Bass	OE	6'2"	206	26		6
Paul Costa	OE	6'4"	240	23		
Charley Ferguson	OE	6'5"	215	25		12
Bill Groman	OE	6'	195	29		
Pete Mills	OE	5'11"	180	22		
Ernie Warlick	OE	6'4"	235	33		6
Pete Gogolak	K	6'2"	200	23		115

NEW YORK JETS 5-8-1 Weeb Ewbank

Scores of Each Game		
21	Houston	27
10	KANSAS CITY	14
21	Buffalo	33
13	Denver	16
24	OAKLAND	24
9	SAN DIEGO	34
45	DENVER	10
13	Kansas City	10
30	Boston	20
41	HOUSTON	14
23	BOSTON	27
7	San Diego	38
14	Oakland	24
14	BUFFALO	12

Use Name	Pos.	Hgt	Wgt	Age	Int	Pts
Nick DeFelice	OT	6'3"	250	25		
Winston Hill	OT	6'4"	275	23		
Sherman Plunkett	OT	6'4"	295	31		
Sam DeLuca	OG	6'2"	250	29		
Dan Ficca	OG	6'1"	250	26		
Dave Herman	OG	6'2"	255	23		
Pete Perreault	OG	6'3"	245	26		
Mike Hudock	C	6'2"	245	30		
John Schmitt	C	6'4"	265	22		
Gerry Philbin	DE	6'2"	245	24		
Lavern Torczon	DE	6'2"	250	29		
Bert Wilder	DE	6'3"	245	25		
Verlon Biggs	DT-DE	6'4"	250	22	1	
Jim Harris	DT	6'4"	265	21		
Paul Rochester	DT	6'2"	250	28		
Arnie Simkus	DT	6'4"	240	22		
Al Atkinson	LB	6'1"	225	22	1	
Ralph Baker	LB	6'3"	235	23	2	
Larry Grantham	LB	6'	206	26	1	
Wahoo McDaniel	LB	6'	240	28	1	
Jim O'Mahoney	LB	6'1"	233	24		
Ray Abbruzzese	DB	6'1"	200	27	2	
Bill Baird	DB	5'10"	180	26	3	
Cornell Gordon	DB	6'	185	24	2	
Dainard Paulson	DB	5'11"	190	28	7	
Bill Rademacher	DB	6'1"	190	23		
Clyde Washington	DB	6'	206	27		
Willie West	DB	5'10"	185	27	6	
Jim Hudson	HB-DB	6'2"	210	22		
Joe Namath	QB	6'2"	194	21		
Mike Taliaferro	QB	6'2"	210	23		
Charley Browning	HB	6'	220	22		
Kern Carson (from SD)	HB	6'	202	23		12
Cosmo Iacavazzi	HB	5'11"	200	22		
Curley Johnson	HB	6'	215	30		6
Bill Mathis	HB	6'1"	220	26		36
Bob Schweickert	HB	6'1"	195	22		
Mark Smolinski	FB	6'	215	26		
Matt Snell	FB	6'2"	220	23		24
Jim Evans	FL	6'1"	190	25		
Don Maynard	FL	6'	185	29		84
Gene Heeter	OE	6'4"	235	24		
Dee Mackey	OE	6'5"	225	29		8
Jerry Robinson	OE	5'11"	200	26		
George Sauer	OE	6'1"	206	21		12
Bake Turner	OE	6'	185	25		12
Jim Turner	K	6'2"	205	24		91

BOSTON PATRIOTS 4-8-2 Mike Holovak

Scores of Each Game		
7	Buffalo	24
10	Houston	31
10	DENVER	27
17	Kansas City	27
10	OAKLAND	24
13	SAN DIEGO	13
21	Oakland	30
22	San Diego	6
7	BUFFALO	23
20	NEW YORK	30
10	KANSAS CITY	10
27	New York	23
28	Denver	20
42	HOUSTON	14

Use Name	Pos.	Hgt	Wgt	Age	Int	Pts
Tom Neville	OT	6'4"	230	21		
Don Oakes	OT	6'3"	255	27		
Bob Schmidt	OT	6'4"	250	29		
Bob Yates	OT	6'3"	230	26		
Justin Canale	OG	6'2"	230	21		
Charley Long	OG	6'3"	250	27		
Billy Neighbors	OG	5'11"	240	25		
Jon Morris	C	6'4"	240	22		
Bob Dee	DE	6'3"	240	32		
Larry Eisenhauer	DE	6'5"	250	25		
Jim Hunt	DE	5'11"	245	26		
Len St. Jean	DE	6'1"	240	23		
Bill Dawson	OE-DE	6'3"	240	21		
Houston Antwine	DT	6'	270	26	1	
George Pyne	DT	6'4"	285	22		
Tom Addison	LB	6'3"	230	29	1	
Nick Buoniconti	LB	5'11"	220	24	3	
Mike Dukes (to NY)	LB	6'3"	235	29	1	
Lonnie Farmer	LB	6'	220	24	1	
Ed Meixler	LB	6'3"	245	22		
Jack Rudolph	LB	6'3"	230	27		
Jay Cunningham	DB	5'10"	180	22	2	
Dick Felt	DB	6'	185	32		
White Graves	DB	6'	185	22	2	
Ron Hall	DB	6'	190	28	3	
Tom Hennessey	DB	6'	180	25	2	
Ross O'Hanley	DB	6'	185	26	1	
Chuck Shonta	DB	6'	200	27	2	
Don Webb	DB	5'10"	200	26	2	
Babe Parilli	QB	6'1"	190	35		
Eddie Wilson	QB	6'	190	25		
Tom Yewcic	QB	5'11"	185	33		
Joe Bellino	HB	5'9"	187	27		
Ron Burton	HB	5'10"	190	28		18
J. D. Garrett	HB	5'11"	195	23		18
Larry Garron	FB	6'	195	28		12
Jim Nance	FB	6'1"	250	22		30
Jim Colclough	FL	6'	185	29		18
Ellis Johnson	HB-FL	6'2"	190	21		
Gino Cappelletti	OE	6'	190	31		**132**
Art Graham	OE	6'1"	205	24		
Tony Romeo	OE	6'2"	230	26		12
Jim Whalen	OE	6'2"	210	21		

HOUSTON OILERS 4-10-0 Hugh Taylor

Scores of Each Game		
27	NEW YORK	21
31	BOSTON	10
17	Oakland	21
14	San Diego	31
17	Denver	28
38	KANSAS CITY	36
19	Buffalo	17
21	OAKLAND	33
21	DENVER	31
14	New York	41
21	Kansas City	52
18	BUFFALO	29
26	SAN DIEGO	37
14	Boston	42

Use Name	Pos.	Hgt	Wgt	Age	Int	Pts
Norm Evans	OT	6'5"	235	23		
Rich Michael	OT	6'3"	245	26		
Walt Suggs	OT	6'5"	260	26		
Maxie Williams	OT	6'4"	242	25		
Sonny Bishop	OG	6'2"	245	25		
John Frongillo	OG	6'3"	250	25		
Bob Talamini	OG	6'1"	255	26		
John Wittenborn	OG	6'2"	240	29		
Wayne Frazier	C	6'2"	245	25		
Tom Goode	C	6'3"	250	26		
Gary Cutsinger	DE	6'4"	245	24	1	
Bob Evans	DE	6'3"	250	23		6
Don Floyd	DE	6'4"	247	26		
George Kinney	DE	6'4"	250	22		
Ray Straham	DE	6'6"	250	22		
Scott Appleton	DT	6'3"	250	23		
Jim Hayes	DT	6'4"	265	24		
Ed Husmann	DT	6'	245	34		
Bud McFadin	DT	6'3"	270	37		
Johnny Baker	LB	6'3"	225	24		
Danny Brabham	LB	6'4"	240	24		
Doug Cline	LB	6'2"	230	26		
Bobby Maples	LB	6'3"	230	22	1	
Larry Onesti	LB	6'	200	26		6
Charley Rieves	LB	5'11"	218	26		
Tony Banfield	DB	6'1"	185	26	3	
Freddy Glick	DB	6'1"	190	28	2	
W. K. Hicks	DB	6'1"	185	22	9	
Bobby Jancik	DB	5'11"	178	25	4	
Pete Jaquess	DB	6'	180	23		
Jim Norton	DB	6'3"	190	26	7	
George Blanda	QB	6'1"	215	37		61
Don Trull	QB	6'1"	180	23		12
Ode Burrell	HB	6'	185	25		46
B. W. Cheeks	HB	6'1"	230	23		
Dalton Hoffman	FB	6'	207	23		
Harry Hooligan	FB	6'2"	225	27		
Bobby Jackson	FB	6'3"	238	25		12
Keith Kinderman	FB	6'	215	25		
Jack Spikes	FB	6'2"	220	27		27
Charley Tolar	FB	5'7"	200	27		
Charley Hennigan	FL	6'	187	29		24
Sammy Weir	FL	5'9"	170	23		
Dick Compton	OE	6'1"	195	25		12
Charley Frazier	OE	6'	175	26		36
Willie Frazier	OE	6'4"	225	22		48
Bob McLeod	OE	6'5"	230	26		6

Sid Blanks – Knee Injury

BUFFALO BILLS

RUSHING

Last Name	No.	Yds	Avg	TD
Carlton	156	592	3.8	6
Joe	123	377	3.1	4
Smith	43	137	3.2	1
Stone	19	61	3.2	0
Kemp	36	49	1.4	4
Lamonica	10	30	3.0	1
Maguire	1	21	21.0	0
Auer	3	19	6.3	0
Warner	1	2	2.0	0
Roberson	1	–4	–4.0	0

RECEIVING

Last Name	No.	Yds	Avg	TD
Roberson	46	703	15	3
Joe	27	271	10	2
Carlton	24	196	8	1
Costa	21	401	19	0
Ferguson	21	262	12	2
Bass	18	299	17	1
Dubenion	18	281	16	1
Rutkowski	18	247	14	1
Smith	12	116	10	0
Warlick	8	112	14	1
Stone	6	29	5	0
Mills	1	43	43	0
Warner	1	11	11	1
Tracey	1	2	2	0
Kemp	1	–9	–9	0

PUNT RETURNS

Last Name	No.	Yds	Avg	TD
Byrd	22	220	10	0
Rutkowski	11	127	12	0
Warner	1	16	16	0
Clarke	1	13	13	0
Hudlow	1	12	12	0
Saimes	0	1	0	0

KICKOFF RETURNS

Last Name	No.	Yds	Avg	TD
Warner	32	825	26	2
Roberson	16	318	20	0
Rutkowski	5	97	19	0
Hudlow	2	36	18	0
Maguire	1	5	5	0
Dunaway	1	0	0	0

PASSING – PUNTING – KICKING

PASSING	Att	Comp	%	Yds	Yd/Att	TD	Int–%	RK
Kemp	391	179	46	2368	6.1	10	18– 5	6
Lamonica	70	29	41	376	5.4	3	6– 9	

PUNTING	No	Avg
Maguire	80	43.0

KICKING	XP	Att	%	FG	Att	%
Gogolak	31	31	100	28	46	61

NEW YORK JETS

RUSHING

Last Name	No.	Yds	Avg	TD
Snell	169	763	4.5	4
Mathis	147	604	4.1	5
Smolinski	24	59	2.5	0
Carson	7	25	3.6	2
Namath	8	19	2.4	0
McDaniel	1	13	13.0	0
Taliaferro	7	4	0.6	0
Johnson	2	3	1.5	0
Maynard	1	2	2.0	0

RECEIVING

Last Name	No.	Yds	Avg	TD
Maynard	68	1218	18	14
Snell	38	264	7	0
B. Turner	31	402	13	2
Sauer	29	301	10	2
Mathis	17	242	14	1
Mackey	16	255	16	1
Smolinski	6	25	4	0
Evans	2	24	12	0
Heeter	1	14	14	0
Johnson	1	6	6	1

PUNT RETURNS

Last Name	No.	Yds	Avg	TD
Baird	14	88	6	0
Robinson	3	36	12	0
West	10	34	3	0
Carson	1	7	7	0
B. Turner	1	1	1	0

KICKOFF RETURNS

Last Name	No.	Yds	Avg	TD
B. Turner	18	402	22	0
Carson	17	355	21	0
Robinson	7	164	23	0
Smolinski	6	98	16	0
Baird	2	50	25	0
Browning	1	31	31	0
Sauer	1	20	20	0
Abruzzese	1	16	16	0
O'Mahoney	1	15	15	0
DeFelice	1	0	0	0
Hudson	1	0	0	0
Paulson	1	0	0	0

PASSING – PUNTING – KICKING

PASSING	Att	Comp	%	Yds	Yd/Att	TD	Int–%	RK
Namath	340	164	48	2220	6.5	18	15– 4	3
Taliaferro	119	45	38	531	4.5	3	7– 6	

PUNTING	No	Avg
Johnson	72	45.3

KICKING	XP	Att	%	FG	Att	%
J. Turner	31	31	100	20	34	59

2 POINT XP
Mackey

BOSTON PATRIOTS

RUSHING

Last Name	No.	Yds	Avg	TD
Nance	111	321	2.9	5
Garron	74	259	3.5	1
Parilli	50	200	4.0	0
Garrett	42	147	3.5	1
Burton	45	108	2.4	1
Bellino	24	49	2.0	0
Johnson	19	29	1.5	0
Wilson	8	4	0.5	0

RECEIVING

Last Name	No.	Yds	Avg	TD
Colclough	40	677	17	3
Cappelletti	37	680	18	9
Graham	25	316	13	0
Whalen	222	381	17	0
Garron	15	222	15	1
Romeo	15	203	14	2
Nance	12	83	7	0
Burton	10	127	13	2
Garrett	7	49	7	2
Bellino	5	74	15	0
Johnson	4	29	7	0
Yewcic	1	13	13	0

PUNT RETURNS

Last Name	No.	Yds	Avg	TD
Burton	15	61	4	0
Cunningham	5	35	7	0
Hennessey	5	21	4	0
Garrett	1	19	19	0
Nance	1	16	16	0

KICKOFF RETURNS

Last Name	No.	Yds	Avg	TD
Cunningham	17	374	22	0
Garrett	12	232	19	0
Burton	7	188	27	0
Garron	5	141	28	0
Bellino	7	138	20	0
Dukes	3	45	15	0
Nance	3	40	13	0
Johnson	2	29	15	0
Rudolph	1	4	4	0
Canale	2	0	0	0
Pyne	1	0	0	0

PASSING – PUNTING – KICKING

PASSING	Att	Comp	%	Yds	Yd/Att	TD	Int–%	RK
Parilli	426	173	41	2597	6.1	18	26– 6	7
Wilson	46	20	44	257	5.6	1	3– 7	
Yewcic	1	0	0	0	0.0	0	0– 0	

PUNTING	No	Avg
Yewcic	74	41.8
E. Wilson	5	38.8

KICKING	XP	Att	%	FG	Att	%
Cappelletti	27	27	100	17	27	63

HOUSTON OILERS

RUSHING

Last Name	No.	Yds	Avg	TD
Burrell	130	528	4.1	3
Tolar	73	230	3.2	0
Spikes	47	173	3.7	3
Trull	29	145	5.0	2
Jackson	37	85	2.3	2
Hoffman	1	11	11.0	0
C. Frazier	1	10	10.0	0
Compton	1	2	2.0	0
Blanda	4	–6	–1.5	0

RECEIVING

Last Name	No.	Yds	Avg	TD
Burrell	55	650	12	4
Hennigan	41	578	14	4
C. Frazier	38	717	19	6
Wil. Frazier	37	521	14	8
Tolar	25	138	6	0
McLeod	15	226	15	1
Spikes	8	57	7	0
Compton	3	140	47	2
Jackson	1	31	31	0
Weir	1	12	12	0

PUNT RETURNS

Last Name	No.	Yds	Avg	TD
Jancik	12	85	7	0
Glick	7	44	6	0
Burrell	3	39	13	0
Jaquess	4	17	4	0
Hicks	1	4	4	0
Weir	1	0	0	0

KICKOFF RETURNS

Last Name	No.	Yds	Avg	TD
Jancik	18	430	24	0
Jaquess	13	280	22	0
Weir	10	215	22	0
Burrell	8	202	25	0
Hicks	7	181	26	0
Glick	4	84	21	0
Kinderman	4	72	18	0
Compton	4	68	17	0
Spikes	4	41	10	0
Jackson	2	39	20	0
Williams	1	23	23	0
Cheeks	1	19	19	0
Maples	1	15	15	0

PASSING – PUNTING – KICKING

PASSING	Att	Comp	%	Yds	Yd/Att	TD	Int–%	RK
Blanda	442	186	42	2542	5.8	20	30– 7	8
Trull	107	38	36	528	4.9	5	5– 5	
Tolar	1	0	0	0	0.0	0	0– 0	

PUNTING	No	Avg
Norton	84	44.2

KICKING	XP	Att	%	FG	Att	%
Blanda	28	28	100	11	21	52
Spikes	6	6	100	1	2	50

2 POINT XP
Burrell (2)

SAN DIEGO CHARGERS 9-2-3 Sid Gillman

Scores of Each Game		
34	DENVER	31
17	Oakland	6
10	KANSAS CITY	10
31	HOUSTON	14
34	Buffalo	3
13	Boston	13
34	New York	9
6	BOSTON	22
35	Denver	21
7	Kansas Ciry	31
20	BUFFALO	20
38	NEW YORK	7
37	Houston	26
24	OAKLAND	14

Use Name	Pos.	Hgt	Wgt	Age	Int	Pts
Gary Kirner	OT	6'3"	245	23		
Ron Mix	OT	6'4"	250	27		
Ernie Park	OT	6'3"	253	25		
Ernie Wright	OT	6'4"	265	26		
John Farris	OG	6'4"	245	24		
Ed Mitchell	OG	6'2"	265	23		
Pat Shea	OG	6'1"	245	26		
Walt Sweeney	OG	6'3"	255	24		
Sam Gruneisen	C	6'1"	255	24		
Steve DeLong	DE	6'3"	245	22		
Earl Faison	DE	6'5"	270	26	1	6
Howard Kindig	DE	6'6"	250	24		
Bob Petrich	DE	6'4"	257	24		
George Gross	DT	6'3"	270	24		
Ernie Ladd	DT	6'9"	295	26		
Fred Moore	DT	6'3"	255	25		
Chuck Allen	LB	6'1"	225	25	1	
Frank Buncom	LB	6'1"	235	25		
Ron Carpenter	LB	6'2"	230	24		
Dick Degen	LB	6'1"	225	23	2	
Bob Horton	LB	6'2"	230	22		
Rick Redman	LB	5'11"	220	22	1	
Speedy Duncan	DB	5'10"	180	22	4	12
Kenny Graham	DB	6'	200	23	5	6
Dick Harris	DB	5'11"	187	28	1	
Jack Jacobson	DB	6'2"	200	24		
Jimmy Warren	DB	5'11"	185	26	5	
Dick Westmoreland	DB	6'1"	190	24	1	
Bud Whitehead	DB	6'	185	26	7	6
Bob Zeman	DB	6'1"	195	28		
Don Breaux	QB	6'1"	200	25		
John Hadl	QB	6'2"	210	25		6
Steve Tensi	QB	6'5"	207	22		
Gene Foster	FB-HB	5'11"	200	22		12
Paul Lowe	HB	6'	205	28		48
Jim Allison	FB	6'	225	22		
Keith Lincoln	FB	6'2"	212	26		42
Lance Alworth	FL	6'	185	25		84
Sammy Taylor	FL	6'	190	25		
Dave Kocourek	OE	6'5"	245	28		12
Jacque MacKinnon	OE	6'4"	250	26		
Don Norton	OE	6'1"	195	27		12
Herb Travenio	K	6'	218	34		94

OAKLAND RAIDERS 8-5-1 Al Davis

Scores of Each Game		
37	KANSAS CITY	10
6	SAN DIEGO	17
21	HOUSTON	17
12	Buffalo	17
24	Boston	10
24	New York	24
30	BOSTON	21
7	Kansas City	14
33	Houston	21
14	BUFFALO	17
28	Denver	20
24	DENVER	13
24	NEW YORK	14
14	San Diego	24

Use Name	Pos.	Hgt	Wgt	Age	Int	Pts
Harry Schuh	OG-OT	6'2"	260	22		
Bob Svihus	OT	6'4"	245	22		
Frank Youso	OT	6'4"	250	29		
Rich Zecher	OT	6'2"	240	22		
Wayne Hawkins	OG	6'	240	27		
Marv Marinovich	OG	6'3"	250	26		
Bob Mischak	OG	6'	230	32		
Ken Rice	OG	6'2"	240	25		
Jim Otto	C	6'2"	240	27		
Ben Davidson	DE	6'8"	265	25		
Ike Lassiter	DE	6'5"	270	24		
Carleton Oats	DE	6'2"	235	22		
Dan Birdwell	DT	6'4"	250	24		
Dave Costa	DT	6'2"	250	23		
John Diehl (from DAL-N)	DT	6'7"	250	29		
Rex Mirich	DT	6'4"	250	24		
Bill Budness	LB	6'1"	215	22	1	
Dan Conners	LB	6'1"	230	23		
Dick Herman	LB	6'2"	215	22		
Archie Matsos	LB	6'	212	30	3	
Gus Otto	LB	6'2"	220	22	3	12
J. R. Williamson	LB	6'2"	220	23		
Dave Grayson	DB	5'10"	185	26	3	12
Claude Gibson	DB	6'1"	190	26	4	6
Joe Krakoski	DB	6'2"	195	28		
Kent McCloughan	DB	6'1"	190	22	3	
Warren Powers	DB	6'	185	24	5	
Howie Williams	DB	6'2"	185	28	2	
Cotton Davidson	QB	6'1"	180	33		
Tom Flores	QB	6'1"	190	28		
Dick Wood	QB	6'5"	200	29		6
Clem Daniels	HB	6'1"	220	28		72
Gene Mingo	HB	6'1"	190	26		24
Larry Todd	HB	6'1"	185	22		
Roger Hagberg	FB	6'2"	220	26		6
Alan Miller	FB	6'	210	27		24
Fred Biletnikoff	FL	6'1"	190	22		
Pervis Atkins (from WAS-N)	OE	6'1"	195	29		
Billy Cannon	OE	6'1"	225	28		
Ken Herock	OE	6'2"	230	24		
Art Powell	OE	6'3"	212	28		72
Mike Mercer	K	6'	200	29		62

KANSAS CITY CHIEFS 7-5-2 Hank Stram

Scores of Each Game		
10	Oakland	37
14	New York	10
10	San Diego	10
27	BOSTON	17
31	Denver	23
7	BUFFALO	23
36	Houston	38
14	OAKLAND	7
10	NEW YORK	13
31	SAN DIEGO	7
10	Boston	10
52	HOUSTON	21
25	Buffalo	34
45	DENVER	35

Use Name	Pos.	Hgt	Wgt	Age	Int	Pts
Jerry Cornelison	OT	6'3"	250	28		
Dave Hill	OT	6'5"	260	24		
Jim Tyrer	OT	6'6"	292	26		
Denny Biodrowski	OG	6'1"	255	25		
Ed Budde	OG	6'5"	260	24		
Curt Merz	OG	6'4"	250	27		
Al Reynolds	OG	6'3"	235	27		
Jon Gilliam	C	6'2"	240	26		
Mel Branch	DE	6'2"	230	28		
Chuck Hurston	DE	6'6"	227	22		
Ed Lothamer	DE	6'5"	240	22		
Buck Buchanan	DT	6'7"	280	25		
Al Dotson	DT	6'4"	255	22		
Curt Farrier	DT	6'6"	245	24		
Jerry Mays	DT	6'4"	250	25		
Hatch Rosdahl	DT	6'5"	250	22		
Ronnie Caveness	LB	6'1"	215	22		
Walt Corey	LB	6'	242	27		
Jim Fraser	LB	6'3"	236	29		
Sherrill Headrick	LB	6'2"	215	28	1	
E. J. Holub	LB	6'4"	225	27	1	
Smokey Stover	LB	6'	232	26		
Bobby Bell	DE-LB	6'4"	228	25	4	6
Bobby Hunt	DB	6'1"	190	25	1	
Willie Mitchell	DB	6'1"	185	23	2	12
Bobby Ply	DB	6'1"	190	24		
Johnny Robinson	DB	6'	195	26	5	
Fred Williamson	DB	6'2"	215	27	6	
Pete Beathard	QB	6'2"	205	23		26
Len Dawson	QB	6'	190	31		12
Soloman Brannan	HB	6'1"	188	23		
Bert Coan	HB	6'4"	220	25		18
*Mack Lee Hill	HB	5'11"	225	23		18
Jerrel Wilson	HB	6'4"	225	24		2
Curtis McClinton	FB	6'3"	232	26		54
Frank Jackson	FL	6'1"	190	25		6
Frank Pitts	FL	6'2"	190	21		
Fred Arbanas	OE	6'3"	240	26		24
Tommy Brooker	OE	6'2"	230	25		76
Chris Burford	OE	6'3"	210	27		36
Reg Carolan	OE	6'6"	232	25		2
Otis Taylor	OE	6'2"	215	22		30

*Died Dec. 14, 1965 after knee surgery

DENVER BRONCOS 4-10-0 Mac Speedie

Scores of Each Game		
31	San Diego	34
15	BUFFALO	30
27	Boston	10
16	NEW YORK	13
23	KANSAS CITY	31
28	HOUSTON	17
13	Buffalo	31
10	New York	45
21	SAN DIEGO	35
31	Houston	21
20	OAKLAND	28
13	Oakland	24
20	BOSTON	28
35	Kansas City	45

Use Name	Pos.	Hgt	Wgt	Age	Int	Pts
Lee Bernet	OT	6'2"	245	21		
Bob Breitenstein	OT	6'3"	250	22		
Eldon Danenhauer	OT	6'4"	245	29		
Jon Hohman	OG	6'1"	240	22		
Bob McCullough	OG	6'2"	245	24		
Tom Nomina	OG	6'5"	270	23		
Charlie Parker	OG	6'1"	245	23		
Jerry Sturm	OG	6'3"	260	28		
Ray Kubala	C	6'4"	245	23		
Ed Cooke	DE	6'4"	250	30	3	
Leroy Moore	DE	6'	230	29		
Ray Jacobs	DT	6'3"	265	25		
Chuck Janerette	DT	6'3"	265	26	1	
Max Leetzow	DT	6'4"	240	22		
Jim Thompson	DT	6'3"	255	24		
John Bramlett	LB	6'2"	210	24	1	12
Ed Cummings	LB	6'2"	228	24		
Tom Erlandson	LB	6'3"	235	25	1	
Jerry Hopkins	LB	6'2"	235	24	1	
Gene Jeter	LB	6'3"	230	23		
Jim Thibert	LB	6'3"	230	25		
Willie Brown	DB	6'1"	190	24	2	
Gerry Bussell	DB	6'	185	22		
Miller Farr (to SD)	DB	6'1"	188	22	2	
Goose Gonsoulin	DB	6'3"	210	27	6	2
John Griffin	DB	6'1"	190	25	4	12
Gary Kroner	DB	6'1"	200	24		71
John McGeever	DB	6'1"	195	26	1	
Jim McMillin	DB	5'11"	195	27		
Nemiah Wilson	DB	6'	180	22	3	6
Jacky Lee	QB	6'1"	187	26		
John McCormick	QB	6'1"	210	28		
Mickey Slaughter	QB	6'	190	23		
Paul Carmichael	HB	6'	200	20		
Wendell Hayes	HB	6'2"	195	24		44
Abner Haynes	HB	6'	190	27		36
Charley Mitchell	HB	5'11"	185	25		
Cookie Gilchrist	FB	6'3"	250	30		42
Darrell Lester	FB	6'2"	225	24		
Al Denson	FL	6'2"	208	23		
Bob Scarpitto	FL	5'11"	196	26		30
Odell Barry	OE	5'10"	180	23		
Hewritt Dixon	OE	6'2"	217	25		12
Lionel Taylor	OE	6'2"	215	29		36

SAN DIEGO CHARGERS

RUSHING

Last Name	No.	Yds	Avg	TD
Lowe	222	1121	5.1	7
Foster	121	469	3.9	2
Lincoln	75	302	4.1	3
Allison	29	100	3.5	0
Hadl	28	91	3.3	1
MacKinnon	3	17	5.7	0
Breaux	1	–1	–1.0	0
Shea	1	–5	–5.0	0
Norton	1	–5	–5.0	0
Alworth	3	–12	–4.0	0
Sweeney	0	8	0.0	0

RECEIVING

Last Name	No.	Yds	Avg	TD
Alworth	69	1602	23	14
Norton	34	485	14	2
Kocourek	28	363	13	2
Lincoln	23	376	16	4
Foster	17	199	12	0
Lowe	17	126	7	1
Allison	8	109	13	0
Mackinnon	6	106	18	0
Taylor	1	13	13	0

PUNT RETURNS

Last Name	No.	Yds	Avg	TD
Duncan	30	464	15	2
Graham	5	36	7	0
Harris	3	8	3	0

KICKOFF RETURNS

Last Name	No.	Yds	Avg	TD
Duncan	26	612	24	0
Foster	5	108	22	0
Allison	4	80	20	0
Lincoln	2	46	23	0
Harris	1	15	15	0
Kirner	1	0	0	0
Mackinnon	1	0	0	0

PASSING – PUNTING – KICKING

PASSING	Att	Comp	%	Yds	Yd/Att	TD	Int–%	RK
Hadl	348	174	50	2798	8.0	20	21– 6	2
Breaux	43	22	51	404	9.4	2	4– 9	
Lowe	4	3	75	81	20.3	0	0– 0	
Foster	3	2	67	31	10.3	0	0– 0	
Lincoln	3	2	67	65	21.7	1	1– 33	

PUNTING	No	Avg
Hadl	38	40.7
Redman	29	39.5
Allison	2	36.0
Whitehead	1	40.0

KICKING	XP	Att	%	FG	Att	%
Travenio	40	40	100	18	30	60

OAKLAND RAIDERS

RUSHING

Last Name	No.	Yds	Avg	TD
Daniels	219	884	4.0	5
Miller	73	272	3.7	1
Todd	32	183	5.7	0
Hagberg	48	171	3.6	1
Flores	11	32	2.9	0
Wood	4	16	4.0	1
Mercer	1	–1	–1.0	0

RECEIVING

Last Name	No.	Yds	Avg	TD
Powell	52	800	15	12
Daniels	36	568	16	7
Biletnikoff	24	331	14	0
Miller	21	208	10	3
Herock	18	221	12	0
Hagberg	12	121	10	0
Todd	8	106	13	0
Cannon	7	127	18	0
Atkins	1	6	6	0
Mingo	1	5	5	0

PUNT RETURNS

Last Name	No.	Yds	Avg	TD
Gibson	31	357	12	1
Krakoski	2	5	3	0
Hagberg	1	3	3	0

KICKOFF RETURNS

Last Name	No.	Yds	Avg	TD
Todd	20	461	23	0
Gibson	9	186	21	0
Hagberg	3	50	17	0
Grayson	1	34	34	0
Herman	1	0	0	0

PASSING – PUNTING – KICKING

PASSING	Att	Comp	%	Yds	Yd/Att	TD	Int–%	RK
Flores	269	122	45	1593	5.9	14	11– 4	5
Wood	157	69	44	1003	6.4	8	6– 4	4
Daniels	2	2	100	95	47.5	0	0– 0	
C. Davidson	1	1	100	8	8.0	0	0– 0	
Mercer	1	1	100	14	14.0	0	0– 0	
Todd	1	0	0	0	0.0	0	0– 0	

PUNTING	No	Avg
Mercer	75	41.1

KICKING	XP	Att	%	FG	Att	%
Mercer	35	35	100	9	15	60
Mingo	0	0	0	8	19	42

KANSAS CITY CHIEFS

RUSHING

Last Name	No.	Yds	Avg	TD
McClinton	175	661	3.8	6
M. Hill	125	627	5.0	2
Dawson	43	142	3.3	2
Beathard	25	138	5.5	4
Coan	45	137	3.0	1
Jackson	1	26	26.0	0
Taylor	2	17	8.5	0
Wilson	2	4	2.0	0

RECEIVING

Last Name	No.	Yds	Avg	TD
Burford	47	575	12	6
McClinton	37	590	16	3
Jackson	28	440	16	1
Taylor	26	446	17	5
Arbanas	24	418	17	4
M. Hill	21	264	13	1
Coan	9	85	9	2
Carolan	6	65	11	0
Pitts	1	11	11	0

PUNT RETURNS

Last Name	No.	Yds	Avg	TD
Mitchell	19	242	13	1
Jackson	13	163	13	0
Brannan	5	10	2	0
Pitts	1	4	4	0

KICKOFF RETURNS

Last Name	No.	Yds	Avg	TD
Coan	19	479	25	0
Jackson	9	260	29	0
Brannan	9	226	25	0
Pitts	5	100	20	0
Stover	3	7	2	0
Fraser	1	5	5	0
Mays	2	3	2	0

PASSING – PUNTING – KICKING

PASSING	Att	Comp	%	Yds	Yd/Att	TD	Int–%	RK
Dawson	305	163	53	2262	7.4	21	14– 5	1
Beathard	89	36	41	632	7.1	1	6– 7	
McClinton	1	0	0	0	0.0	0	0– 0	

PUNTING	No	Avg
Wilson	68	46.1
Fraser	3	27.0

KICKING	XP	Att	%	FG	Att	%
Brooker	37	37	100	13	30	43

2 POINT XP
Beathard
Carolan
Wilson

DENVER BRONCOS

RUSHING

Last Name	No.	Yds	Avg	TD
Gilchrist	252	954	3.8	6
Hayes	130	526	4.1	5
Haynes	41	166	4.1	3
Scarpitto	4	94	23.5	0
Slaughter	20	75	3.8	0
Barry	2	19	9.5	0
Lee	2	1	0.5	0
McCormick	1	–2	–2.0	0
Denson	1	–4	–4.0	0

RECEIVING

Last Name	No.	Yds	Avg	TD
Taylor	85	1131	13	6
Scarpitto	32	585	18	5
Haynes	26	216	8	2
Dixon	25	354	14	2
Hayes	24	294	12	2
Gilchrist	18	154	9	1
Denson	9	102	11	0
Barry	2	11	6	0
McCullough	1	1	1	0

PUNT RETURNS

Last Name	No.	Yds	Avg	TD
Barry	21	210	10	0
Haynes	14	121	9	1
Bussell	2	24	12	0

KICKOFF RETURNS

Last Name	No.	Yds	Avg	TD
Haynes	34	901	27	0
Barry	26	611	24	0
Farr	7	123	18	0
Bussell	5	103	21	0
Hayes	4	93	23	0
Carmichael	1	15	15	0
Dixon	1	8	8	0

PASSING – PUNTING – KICKING

PASSING	Att	Comp	%	Yds	Yd/Att	TD	Int–%	RK
McCormick	253	103	41	1292	5.1	7	14– 6	10
Slaughter	147	75	51	864	5.9	6	12– 8	9
Lee	80	44	55	692	8.7	5	3– 4	
Hayes	1	0	0	0	0.0	0	1–100	
Haynes	1	0	0	0	0.0	0	0– 0	

PUNTING	No	Avg
Scarpitto	67	42.3
McCormick	1	45.0

KICKING	XP	Att	%	FG	Att	%
Kroner	32	32	100	13	29	45

2 POINT XP
Gunsoulin
Hayes

1966 N.F.L. Closing the Checkbook

The war between the two leagues was getting very expensive. To sign heralded rookies Donny Anderson, Jim Grabowski, and Tommy Nobis, NFL clubs had to give each of them contracts more lucrative than that given to Joe Namath by the AFL Jets last year. But after the New York Giants signed kicker Pete Gogolak away from the AFL Buffalo Bills, the heat of battle became unbearable. Considering the signing of Gogolak as a direct slap, the AFL owners went all out to pirate away established NFL stars. With John Brodie, Roman Gabriel, and Mike Ditka on the verge of jumping and other NFL stars thinking it over, the established league sat down with the upstarts to discuss terms of peace. In June, officials of both leagues announced a merger that would change the organizational set-up of pro football. With Pete Rozelle as Commissioner over both leagues, the NFL and AFL would conduct a common draft of college players starting next year and would finish this season with the first Super Bowl between the two league champions.

EASTERN CONFERENCE

Dallas Cowboys—With Don Meredith at quarterback, the Dallas offense was the league's most versatile and explosive. Bob Hayes used his sprinter's speed to gain 1,232 yards on passes, while Dan Reeves succeeded at halfback despite his slowness afoot. Signed two years ago as a free agent, Reeves hustled his way to sixteen touchdowns, eight each by running and receiving, and was a threat to throw the option pass on sweeps. Ralph Neely led the blocking in a strong offensive line. The defense, loaded with quality players, led the league in sacking enemy quarterbacks and gave up yardage with extreme reluctance. Coach Tom Landry had been collecting talent for years, and now all the pieces had fit together.

Cleveland Browns—Jimmy Brown had retired to become an actor, but no one could blame replacement Leroy Kelly for Cleveland's slip to second place. Kelly had distinguished himself for two years as a kick returner, and when he was thrust into Brown's vacant shoes at fullback, he surprised the league by rushing for 1,141 yards, second only to Gale Sayers in the NFL. Kelly relied more on speed than did Brown, leaving the power running to Ernie Green. Paul Warfield returned from last year's shoulder injury to join Gary Collins in the wide receiving duo, and Frank Ryan found his targets often enough to throw for twenty-nine touchdowns. The Browns' fatal flaw this season was a slow start in which they lost two of their first three games.

Philadelphia Eagles—Despite a weak passing attack, the Eagles reached third place with their best record in five years. Behind a good offensive line, the running corps of Timmy Brown, Earl Gros, Tom Woodeshick, and Izzy Lang ate up large chunks of yardage, and Brown also doubled as the team's top kickoff returner, bringing two kickoffs back for touchdowns in one game against the Cowboys. The lack of quality receivers and Norm Snead's poor season hurt the attack, but the defense showed enough strength to carry the team.

St. Louis Cardinals—The Cards had a new coach in Charley Winner but the same old problem with injuries. Battling with Dallas for first place in the East, the Cards lost quarterback Charley Johnson with a knee injury and they scored only fifty-two points in their last five games, losing four of them, to fall to fourth place. Injuries also stripped end Sonny Randle, offensive linemen Bob DeMarco, Ken Gray, and Irv Goode, and cornerback Pat Fischer from the active rolls for varying lengths of time.

Washington Redskins—The Redskins brought former Cleveland great Otto Graham back to pro football as head coach, and Graham as expected put the emphasis in the Washington attack on the pass. The air game worked fine, with Sonny Jurgensen doing the pitching and Charley Taylor, converted from halfback to end in mid-season, Bobby Mitchell, and Jerry Smith doing most of the catching. Even without a legitimate running attack, the Redskins could put points on the scoreboard. But the defense needed time to jell, with seven new faces in the starting lineup.

Pittsburgh Steelers—Coach Bill Austin took the Steelers to five wins despite some severe problems on offense. The line blocked poorly, rookie Willie Asbury was the only effective runner, and the quarterback situation was unstable. Bill Nelsen hurt his knee in the second game of the year, and Ron Smith, let go by the Packers, filled in at quarterback for most of the season. The defense carried the club through the body of the schedule, but Nelsen returned to action for the last three games and beat New York 47-28 and Atlanta 57-33 to end the year.

Atlanta Falcons—The Falcons lost their first nine NFL games but came back to win three of their last five contests to escape the cellar in their first season in the league. Junior Coffey, obtained from Green Bay in the expansion draft, developed into a fine runner, but most of the impressive performances were turned in by rookies such as linebacker Tommy Nobis, quarterback Randy Johnson, and defensive backs Bob Riggle, Nick Rassas, and Ken Reaves.

New York Giants—With Tucker Frederickson out all year with a bad knee, Earl Morrall sidelined for the last half of the schedule with a broken wrist, and the defense a horrendous hodgepodge of journeymen and youth, the Giants suffered through the worst season in their history. They beat the Redskins 13-10 in mid-October for their only win of the year, and the rematch in late November resulted in a 72-41 embarrassment.

WESTERN CONFERENCE

Green Bay Packers—The Packers shelled out about $1,000,000 to sign All-American runners Donny Anderson and Jim Grabowski, but Vince Lombardi kept his Green Bay machine running with old pros and a few key replacement parts. With Paul Hornung bothered by a neck injury, Elijah Pitts did most of the playing at halfback, while ex-Ram Carroll Dale slipped past Max McGee into the starting lineup as a wide receiver. On defense, quick Bob Jeter switched from offensive end to capture a cornerback slot. The heart of the Packers, however, was still the troop of seasoned veterans who had grown used to the taste of winning, and that was good enough to bring the Packers home first in the West.

Baltimore Colts—The Colts lost the opening game of the season to the Packers and struggled futilely to catch up the rest of the year. With a veteran team that was approaching old age all at once, the Colts had solid units both on defense and offense. The defensive line relied on quickness and got some size late in the year when Gino Marchetti came out of retirement; the linebacking was strengthened by the conversion of Mike Curtis from fullback to a corner linebacker; and Bobby Boyd, Lenny Lyles, Alvin Haymond, Jerry Logan, and Jim Welch blanketed enemy pass receivers from their deep spots. The offense moved on the arm of Johnny Unitas, but the Colts lost twice to the Packers and had to settle for second place behind them.

Los Angeles Rams—The Rams had to go to court to get George Allen to be their head coach, but the results proved well worth the trouble. Allen rebuilt the Los Angeles defense into one of the league's best. He inherited a great front four in Deacon Jones, Lamar Lundy, Merlin Olsen, and Rosie Grier, but he completely overhauled the linebacking. He talked Jack Pardee out of retirement, signed Bill George as a free agent after the Bears cut him, and traded for Maxie Baughan from the Eagles and Myron Pottios from the Steelers. To tighten up the secondary, he brought in Irv Cross from Philadelphia. Although the offense lacked flair, the improved defense carried the club to its first winning season since 1958.

San Francisco '49ers—With the Houston Oilers trying to lure him into the AFL, John Brodie bargained himself into a multiyear contract worth over $900,000. With his financial future secure, Brodie did nothing to show that he could lead a team to a championship. With a good line, punishing runners in Ken Willard and John David Crow, and fine wide receivers like Bernie Casey and Dave Parks, the San Francisco attack ran in spurts, running up big scores against Detroit, Chicago, and Atlanta and losing 28-3 to Minnesota and 34-3 to Los Angeles.

Chicago Bears—With George Halas taking George Allen into court to keep him from resigning as an assistant coach, with Doug Atkins and Mike Ditka openly critical of Halas, with Rudy Bukich suffering through a miserable campaign, and with Johnny Morris sidelined with a bad knee, Bear fans found Gale Sayers' superb season a pleasant diversion from the Bears' problems. Sayers improved on his rookie season by leading the NFL in rushing, catching thirty-four passes and breaking off two touchdowns in pacing the league in kickoff returning. Adding together his rushing, receiving, and returning totals, Sayers gained 2,440 yards, a new record.

Detroit Lions—Problems at quarterback made the Detroit offense a plodding affair. Milt Plum began the year as signal-caller but went out of service with a mid-season injury. Karl Sweetan, who had spent last season with the semi-pro Pontiac Arrows, stepped in and did a creditable job as a passer but could not ignite the attack into steady fireworks. On one play, however, Sweetan got the offense moving, passing to Pat Studstill for a 99-yard touchdown against the Colts on October 16. Studstill was one of the league's sensations, developing into a dangerous pass receiver despite his small size and very ordinary speed. Another player to attract attention was Garo Yepremian, a soccer-style place-kicker from Cyprus who was signed in mid-season and booted a record six field goals against the Vikings on November 13.

Minnesota Vikings—Expecting to move up into championship status for the last few seasons, the Vikings simply were not improving with their current team. The defense was not getting much better, halfback Tommy Mason was spending more time hurt than healthy, and quarterback Fran Tarkenton was hardly on speaking terms with coach Norm Van Brocklin. Once in a while the potential would show through in big victories such as the 20-17 triumph over Green Bay, but this promising team kept losing without much promise of winning.

FINAL TEAM STATISTICS

OFFENSE

	ATL.	BALT.	CHI.	CLEV.	DALL.	DET.	G.B.	L.A.	MINN.	N.Y.	PHIL.	PITT.	ST.L.	S.F.	WASH.
FIRST DOWNS:															
Total	211	237	196	278	287	216	231	255	279	236	231	207	212	282	225
by Rushing	85	82	96	117	124	73	98	103	126	80	112	65	88	101	78
by Passing	104	142	85	142	139	126	115	133	132	129	104	117	108	153	130
by Penalty	22	13	15	19	24	17	18	19	21	27	15	25	16	28	17
RUSHING:															
Number	405	418	463	415	471	394	475	448	551	380	478	375	458	422	356
Yards	1519	1556	1927	2166	2122	1429	1673	1742	2091	1457	1859	1092	1601	1790	1377
Average Yards	3.8	3.7	4.2	5.2	4.5	3.6	3.5	3.9	3.8	3.8	3.9	2.9	3.5	4.2	3.9
Touchdowns	11	7	12	18	24	13	18	12	15	7	19	13	10	12	9
PASSING:															
Attempts	381	401	338	402	413	456	318	450	417	424	378	401	386	500	443
Completions	175	221	159	212	214	239	193	249	216	208	179	188	180	261	255
Completion Percentage	45.9	55.1	47.0	52.7	51.8	52.4	60.7	55.3	51.8	49.1	47.4	46.9	46.6	52.2	57.6
Passing Yards	2362	3172	2016	3142	3331	2752	2831	2891	2932	2999	2159	2877	2292	3239	3230
Average Yards per Attempt	6.2	7.9	5.0	7.8	8.1	6.0	8.9	6.4	7.0	7.1	5.7	7.2	5.9	6.5	7.3
Average Yards per Completion	13.5	14.4	12.7	14.8	15.6	11.5	14.7	11.6	13.6	14.4	12.1	15.3	12.7	12.4	12.7
Times Tackled Attempting to Pass	38	30	29	29	42	35	31	54	45	62	35	66	38	30	27
Yards Lost Tackled Attempting to Pass	345	242	244	237	308	328	229	351	384	524	259	523	352	247	216
Net Yards	2017	2930	1772	2905	3023	2424	2602	2540	2548	2475	1900	2354	1940	2992	3014
Touchdowns	14	26	10	33	27	8	18	12	18	20	14	18	13	21	28
Interceptions	27	27	23	15	14	28	5	17	22	31	22	22	19	26	20
Percent Intercepted	7.1	6.7	6.8	3.7	3.4	6.1	1.6	3.8	5.3	7.3	5.8	5.5	4.9	5.2	4.5
PUNTS:															
Number	73	49	80	57	65	72	62	71	60	53	65	78	81	70	68
Average Distance	40.7	45.6	42.0	39.0	39.2	41.1	41.0	42.8	41.1	38.9	39.8	42.1	35.6	40.6	42.4
PUNT RETURNS:															
Number	18	45	25	24	41	38	37	45	31	22	31	21	40	45	29
Yards	100	357	97	146	258	396	215	341	129	120	162	43	316	238	201
Average Yards	5.6	7.9	3.9	6.1	6.3	10.4	5.8	7.6	4.2	5.5	5.2	2.0	7.9	5.3	6.9
Touchdowns	0	0	0	0	0	1	1	0	0	0	1	0	1	1	1
KICKOFF RETURNS:															
Number	82	51	48	54	44	58	42	42	52	80	64	64	57	56	69
Yards	1737	1094	1341	1111	1006	1316	903	1015	987	1616	1419	1384	1348	1326	1435
Average	21.2	21.5	27.9	20.6	22.9	22.7	21.5	24.2	19.0	20.2	22.2	21.6	23.6	23.7	20.8
Touchdowns	0	0	2	0	1	0	0	0	0	1	2	1	1	0	0
INTERCEPTION RETURNS:															
Number	19	22	15	30	17	24	28	26	14	17	20	24	21	18	23
Yards	177	267	155	408	303	366	547	362	230	217	345	280	330	379	369
Average Yards	9.3	12.1	10.3	13.6	17.8	15.3	19.5	13.9	16.4	12.8	17.3	11.7	15.7	21.1	16.0
Touchdowns	1	2	0	1	3	1	6	4	1	2	1	2	3	3	1
PENALTIES:															
Number	79	64	80	69	83	82	57	72	67	57	63	75	67	86	64
Yards	753	617	714	747	824	931	544	651	787	602	666	768	586	819	591
FUMBLES:															
Number	30	19	26	17	23	33	23	25	33	29	32	34	26	26	27
Number Lost	17	12	12	10	10	21	19	12	14	13	17	17	18	12	15
POINTS:															
Total	204	314	234	403	445	206	335	289	292	263	326	316	264	320	351
PAT Attempts	26	36	26	54	56	23	43	29	34	31	39	36	28	39	41
PAT Made	21	35	24	52	56	23	41	29	34	29	38	35	27	38	39
FG Attempts	19	39	30	23	31	30	28	49	33	28	25	32	40	31	34
FG Made	9	21	18	9	17	15	12	28	18	16	18	21	23	16	22
Percent FG Made	47.4	53.8	60.0	39.1	54.8	50.0	42.9	57.1	54.5	57.1	72.0	65.6	57.5	51.6	64.7
Safeties	0	0	0	0	1	0	0	1	0	0	0	1	0	0	0

DEFENSE

	ATL.	BALT.	CHI.	CLEV.	DALL.	DET.	G.B.	L.A.	MINN.	N.Y.	PHIL.	PITT.	ST.L	S.F.	WASH.
FIRST DOWNS:															
Total	295	245	239	255	221	240	211	196	213	273	249	238	209	238	261
by Rushing	126	94	102	113	64	109	90	64	85	122	90	107	68	88	106
by Passing	151	134	116	124	140	108	106	114	116	137	139	105	109	126	134
by Penalty	18	17	21	18	17	23	15	18	12	14	20	26	32	24	21
RUSHING:															
Number	472	460	466	450	356	479	446	401	412	480	390	468	377	414	438
Yards	2172	1733	1604	1894	1176	2006	1644	1302	1686	2053	1693	1786	1192	1629	1831
Average Yards	4.6	3.8	3.4	4.2	3.3	4.2	3.7	3.2	4.1	4.3	4.3	3.8	3.2	3.9	4.2
Touchdowns	20	7	13	12	6	16	9	10	15	23	13	11	11	15	19
PASSING:															
Attempts	396	425	406	406	457	363	390	406	391	357	446	397	443	414	411
Completions	227	240	202	221	212	210	202	190	206	194	226	192	197	206	224
Completion Percentage	57.3	56.5	49.8	54.4	46.4	57.9	51.8	46.8	52.7	54.3	50.7	48.4	44.5	49.8	54.5
Passing Yards	3376	2759	2600	2650	2802	2702	2316	2830	2426	3086	2964	2849	2733	2895	3237
Average Yards per Attempt	8.5	6.5	6.4	6.5	6.1	7.4	5.9	7.0	6.2	8.6	6.6	7.2	6.2	7.0	7.9
Average Yards per Completion	14.9	11.5	12.9	12.0	13.2	12.9	11.5	14.9	11.8	15.9	13.1	14.8	13.9	14.1	14.5
Times Tackled Attempting to Pass	34	47	29	35	60	34	47	45	25	26	34	38	52	40	45
Yards Lost Tackled Attempting to Pass	276	401	233	278	420	294	357	361	190	194	287	344	433	345	376
Net Yards	3100	2358	2367	2372	2382	2408	1959	2469	2236	2892	2677	2505	2300	2550	2861
Touchdowns	26	14	13	14	17	19	7	13	13	36	23	27	15	22	21
Interceptions	19	22	15	30	17	24	28	26	14	17	20	24	21	18	23
Percent Intercepted	4.8	5.2	3.7	7.4	3.7	6.6	7.2	6.4	3.6	4.8	4.5	6.0	4.7	4.3	5.6
PUNTS:															
Number	38	71	71	56	79	71	69	73	72	58	60	64	85	76	61
Average Distance	38.6	40.6	42.4	39.7	42.4	41.1	41.3	43.8	40.6	39.8	39.9	37.8	40.7	41.2	38.4
PUNT RETURNS:															
Number	35	30	46	23	26	27	30	49	28	27	31	42	25	33	40
Yards	197	130	250	111	108	98	171	269	250	218	300	242	159	368	248
Average Yards	5.6	4.3	5.4	4.8	4.2	3.6	5.7	5.5	8.9	8.1	9.7	5.8	6.4	11.2	6.2
Touchdowns	1	0	1	0	1	0	0	0	0	1	1	0	0	1	0
KICKOFF RETURNS:															
Number	44	63	49	68	78	45	52	58	50	49	65	63	50	59	70
Yards	962	1320	1055	1501	1699	1004	1213	1329	1203	1085	1330	1485	1021	1343	1488
Average	21.9	21.0	21.5	22.1	21.8	22.3	23.3	22.9	24.1	22.1	20.5	23.6	20.4	22.8	21.3
Touchdowns	0	0	0	2	3	0	0	0	0	1	1	0	0	1	0
INTERCEPTION RETURNS:															
Number	27	27	23	15	14	28	5	17	22	31	22	22	19	26	20
Yards	385	438	426	68	274	409	75	338	337	465	380	319	236	334	251
Average Yards	14.3	16.2	18.5	4.5	19.6	14.7	15.0	19.9	15.3	15.0	17.3	14.5	12.4	12.8	12.6
Touchdowns	3	3	6	0	1	3	0	2	2	4	3	1	1	1	1
PENALTIES:															
Number	66	69	71	61	63	61	67	76	67	83	63	82	83	91	62
Yards	588	704	636	563	778	564	745	704	667	788	703	835	761	938	626
FUMBLES:															
Number	24	25	35	24	23	19	26	37	24	19	30	37	20	24	36
Number Lost	13	18	23	19	14	11	14	20	8	7	15	16	10	11	20
POINTS:															
Total	437	226	272	259	239	317	163	212	304	501	340	347	265	325	355
PAT Attempts	52	25	34	29	29	38	17	26	33	66	40	42	28	40	42
PAT Made	48	25	32	28	29	38	16	26	32	64	40	38	28	37	40
FG Attempts	41	33	29	28	31	31	27	22	41	23	30	33	41	31	31
FG Made	25	17	12	19	12	17	15	10	24	13	20	19	23	16	21
Percent FG Made	61.0	51.5	41.4	67.9	38.7	54.8	55.6	45.5	58.5	56.5	66.7	57.6	56.1	51.6	67.7
Safeties	1	0	0	0	0	0	0	0	1	1	0	0	0	0	0

Super-bound

A trip to the first Super Bowl awaited the winner of this NFL championship game, which featured the Packers and the Cowboys. The Packers took an early lead on a Bart Starr-to-Elijah Pitts touchdown pass and immediately added on another touchdown when Mel Renfro fumbled the kickoff and Jim Grabowski ran the recovery in from 17 yards out. The Cowboys, one of pro football's exciting young teams, came right back with two touchdowns to tie the score, 14-14, at the end of one quarter. The Packers scored in the second period on a long Bart Starr-to-Carroll Dale pass, while the Cowboys answered only with a Danny Villanueva field goal. Another Villanueva three-pointer lowered the Packer lead to 21-20 in the third quarter, but touchdown passes to Boyd Dowler and Max McGee ran the score to 34-20 and seemingly put the game on ice. The Cowboys fought back, however, scoring on a long pass from Don Meredith to Frank Clarke. In the final minutes, Dallas drove for the winning touchdown, only to fall short when Meredith's fourth-down pass was intercepted in the end zone by Tom Brown.

1966 NFL CHAMPIONSHIP GAME

January 1, at Dallas (Attendance 74,152)

SCORING

DALLAS	14	3	3	7–27
GREEN BAY	14	7	7	6–34

First Quarter
- GB Pitts, 17 yd pass by Starr (Chandler – kick)
- GB Grabowski, 18 yd Fumble recovery return (Chandler – kick)
- DA Reeves, 3 yd rush (Villanueva – kick)
- DA Perkins, 23 yd rush (Villanueva – kick)

Second Quarter
- GB Dale, 51 yd pass by Starr (Chandler – kick)
- DA Villanueva, 11 yd field goal

Third Quarter
- DA Villanueva, 32 yd field goal
- GB Dowler, 16 yd pass by Starr (Chandler – kick)

Fourth Quarter
- GB McGee, 28 yd pass by Starr (Kick Blocked)
- DA Clarke, 68 yd pass by Meredith (Villanueva – kick)

TEAM STATISTICS

DALL.		G. B.
23	First Downs – Total	19
12	First Downs – Rushing	3
10	First Downs – Passing	14
1	First Downs – Penalty	2
4	Punts – Number	4
32.2	Punts – Average Distance	40.0
3	Punt Returns – Number	0
–9	Punt Returns – Yards	0
0	Interception Ret – Number	1
0	Interception Ret – Yards	0
3	Fumbles – Number	1
1	Fumbles – Lost Ball	1
6	Penalties – Number	2
29	Yards Penalized	23
73	Offensive Plays	57
231	Net Yards	367
3.2	Average Gain	6.4
2	Giveaways	1
1	Takeaways	2
–1	Difference	+1

INDIVIDUAL STATISTICS

RUSHING

DALLAS	No	Yds	Avg.	GREEN BAY	No	Yds	Avg.
Perkins	17	108	6.4	Pitts	12	66	5.5
Reeves	17	47	2.8	Taylor	10	37	3.7
Meredith	4	22	5.5	Starr	2	–1	–0.5
Norman	2	10	5.0		24	102	4.3
	40	187	4.7				

RECEIVING

DALLAS	No	Yds	Avg.	GREEN BAY	No	Yds	Avg.
Reeves	4	77	19.3	Dale	5	128	25.6
Norman	4	30	7.5	Taylor	5	23	4.6
Clarke	3	102	34.0	Fleming	3	50	16.7
Gent	3	28	9.3	Dowler	3	49	16.3
Hayes	1	1	3.0	McGee	1	28	28.0
	15	238	15.9	Pitts	1	17	17.0
				Long	1	9	9.0
					19	304	16.0

PASSING

	Att	Comp	Comp Pct.	Yds	Int	Yds/ Att.	Yds/ Comp	Yds Lost Tackled
DALLAS								
Meredith	31	15	48.4	238	1	7.7	15.9	2– 7
GREEN BAY								
Starr	28	19	67.9	304	0	10.9	16.0	5–39

DALLAS COWBOYS 10-3-1 Tom Landry

Scores of Each Game		
52	NEW YORK	7
28	MINNESOTA	17
47	Atlanta	14
56	PHILADELPHIA	7
10	St. Louis	10
21	Clevleand	30
52	PITTSBURGH	21
23	Philadelphia	24
31	Washington	30
20	Pittsburgh	7
26	CLEVELAND	14
31	ST. LOUIS	17
31	WASHINGTON	34
17	New York	7

Use Name	Pos.	Hgt	Wgt	Age	Int	Pts
Jim Boeke	OT	6'5"	255	27		
Ralph Neely	OT	6'5"	257	22		
Tony Liscio	OG-OT	6'5"	255	26		
Leon Donahue	OG	6'4"	245	27		
John Niland	OG	6'4"	250	22		
Mike Connelly	OT-OG	6'3"	248	30		
Dave Manders	C	6'2"	240	24		
Malcolm Walker	OT-C	6'4"	245	23		
George Andrie	DE	6'7"	255	26	1	6
Larry Stephens	DE	6'4"	250	28		
Jethro Pugh	DT-DE	6'6"	250	22		
John Wilbur	DT-DE	6'3"	250	23		
Jim Colvin	DT	6'2"	255	29		
Bob Lilly	DT	6'4"	255	27		
Bill Sandeman	DT	6'6"	250	23		
Willie Townes	DE-DT	6'5"	265	23		2
Dave Edwards	LB	6'3"	226	27	1	
Harold Hays	LB	6'3"	223	25		
Chuck Howley	LB	6'3"	223	30		6
Lee Roy Jordan	LB	6'2"	216	25	1	6
Jerry Tubbs	LB	6'2"	222	31	1	
Dick Daniels	DB	5'9"	180	20		
Mike Gaechter	DB	6'	190	26	3	
Cornell Green	DB	6'4"	215	26	4	6
Mike Johnson	DB	5'10"	186	22		
Warren Livingston	DB	5'10"	190	28	2	
Obert Logan	DB	5'10"	180	24	2	
Mel Renfro	HB-DB	6'	195	22	2	6
Jim Steffen – Injury						
Don Meredith	QB	6'2"	206	28		30
Craig Morton	QB	6'4"	216	23		
Jerry Rhome	QB	6'	187	24		
Dan Reeves	HB	6'1"	203	22		96
Les Shy	HB	6'1"	210	22		6
Walt Garrison	FB-HB	6'	200	22		6
Don Perkins	FB	5'10"	206	28		48
J. D. Smith	FB	6'1"	210	33		6
Buddy Dial	FL	6'1"	195	29		6
Pete Gent	FL	6'4"	210	23		6
Frank Clarke	TE	6'	210	33		24
Pettis Norman	TE	6'3"	223	26		
Bob Hayes	OE	6'	190	23		78
Danny Villanueva	K	5'11"	200	28		107

CLEVELAND BROWNS 9-5-0 Blanton Collier

Scores of Each Game		
38	Washington	14
20	GREEN BAY	21
28	ST. LOUIS	34
28	New York	7
41	PITTSBURGH	10
30	DALLAS	21
49	Atlanta	17
6	Pittsburgh	16
27	PHILADELPHIA	7
14	WASHINGTON	3
14	Dallas	26
49	NEW YORK	40
21	Philadelphia	33
38	St. Louis	10

Use Name	Pos.	Hgt	Wgt	Age	Int	Pts
Jim Battle	OT	6'4"	235	25		
John Brown	OT	6'2"	248	27		
Monte Clark	OT	6'6"	265	29		
Dick Schafrath	OT	6'3"	255	30		
Gene Hickerson	OG	6'3"	248	31		
Joe Bob Isbell	OG	6'1"	250	26		
John Wooten	OG	6'2"	250	31		
Fred Hoaglin	C	6'4"	240	22		
John Morrow	C	6'3"	248	33		
Bill Glass	DE	6'5"	255	30		6
Paul Wiggin	DE	6'3"	245	32	1	
Walter Johnson	DT	6'3"	265	23		
Jim Kanicki	DT	6'4"	270	24		
Dick Modzelewski	DT	6'	260	35		
Frank Parker	DT	6'5"	270	26		
Johnny Brewer	LB	6'4"	235	29	1	
Vince Costello	LB	6'	228	34	1	
Galen Fiss	LB	6'	227	36		
Dale Lindsey	LB	6'3"	220	23		
Sid Williams	LB	6'2"	235	24		
Jim Houston	TE-LB	6'2"	240	29	2	7
Erich Barnes	DB	6'2"	198	31	4	
Walter Beach	DB	6'	185	31	1	
Ross Fichtner	DB	6'	185	28	8	6
Bobby Franklin	DB	5'11"	182	30		
Mike Howell	DB	6'1"	187	23	8	
Ernie Kellerman	DB	6'	183	22	3	
Bernie Parish (to HOU-A)	DB	5'11"	195	31	1	
Gary Lane	QB	6'1"	210	23		
Jim Ninowski	QB	6'1"	207	30		
Frank Ryan	QB	6'3"	200	30		
Leroy Kelly	HB	6'	195	24		96
Randy Schultz	FB-HB	5'11"	210	22		
Ernie Green	FB	6'2"	205	27		54
Charlie Harraway	FB	6'2"	230	21		
Nick Pietrosante	FB	6'2"	225	29		
Gary Collins	FL	6'4"	208	25		72
Clifton McNeil	FL	6'2"	185	26		12
Milt Morin	TE	6'4"	250	24		18
Ralph Smith	TE	6'2"	215	27		18
Paul Warfield	OE	6'	188	23		36
Walter Roberts	FL-OE	5'10"	163	24		
Lou Groza	K	6'3"	250	42		78

PHILADELPHIA EAGLES 9-5-0 Joe Kuharich

Scores of Each Game		
13	St. Louis	16
23	ATLANTA	10
35	NEW YORK	17
10	ST. LOUIS	41
7	Dallas	56
31	Pittsburgh	14
31	New York	3
13	WASHINGTON	27
24	DALLAS	23
7	Cleveland	27
35	San Francisco	34
27	PITTSBURGH	23
33	CLEVELAND	21
37	Washington	28

Use Name	Pos.	Hgt	Wgt	Age	Int	Pts
Bob Brown	OT	6'4"	276	23		
Dave Graham	OT	6'3"	250	27		
Lane Howell	OT	6'5"	270	25		
Ray Rissmiller	OT	6'4"	250	24		
Ed Blaine	OG	6'2"	240	26		
Jim Skaggs	OG	6'2"	250	26		
Bruce Van Dyke	OG	6'2"	235	22		
Lynn Hoyem	C-OG	6'4"	253	26		
Dave Recher	C	6'1"	245	23		
Jim Ringo	C	6'1"	230	35		
Randy Beisler	DE	6'4"	245	21		
Don Hultz	DE	6'3"	235	25		
Gary Pettigrew	DE	6'4"	245	21		
Dave Cahill	DT	6'3"	238	24		
John Meyers	DT	6'6"	276	26		
Floyd Peters	DT	6'4"	255	31		
Ike Kelley	LB	5'11"	225	22		
Dave Lloyd	LB	6'3"	248	30	3	
Mike Morgan	LB	6'4"	242	24	1	
Arunas Vasys	LB	6'2"	225	23		
Harold Wells	LB	6'2"	220	27	1	6
Fred Whittingham	LB	6'1"	240	27	1	
Aaron Martin	DB	6'	185	25	1	6
Ron Medved	DB	6'1"	210	22		
Al Nelson	DB	5'11"	186	22	1	6
Jim Nettles	DB	5'9"	180	24	3	6
Nate Ramsey	DB	6'1"	200	25	1	
Joe Scarpati	DB	5'10"	185	24	8	
Fred Brown – Injury						
Frank Molden – Injury						
Ray Poage – Injury						
Bob Shann – Injury						
Jack Concannon	QB	6'3"	195	23		12
King Hill	QB	6'3"	213	30		
Norm Snead	QB	6'4"	205	26		6
Timmy Brown	HB	5'10"	198	29		48
Ollie Matson	HB	6'2"	210	36		12
Earl Gros	FB	6'3"	220	25		54
Izzy Lang	FB	6'1"	230	23		6
Tom Woodeshick	HB-FB	6'	220	24		30
Willie Brown	FL	6'	185	23		
T.J. Jackson	FL	6'	180	23		
Ron Goodwin	OE-FL	6'	180	24		6
Pete Retzlaff	TE	6'1"	214	35		36
Dave Lince	TE	6'6"	250	22		
Fred Hill	OE	6'2"	215	23		
Ben Hawkins	FL-OE	6'	180	22		
Sam Baker	K	6'2"	218	34		92

ST. LOUIS CARDINALS 8-5-1 Charley Winner

Scores of Each Game		
16	PHILADELPHIA	13
23	WASHINGTON	7
34	Cleveland	28
41	Philadelphia	10
24	NEW YORK	19
10	DALLAS	10
20	Washington	26
24	CHICAGO	17
20	New York	17
9	Pittsburgh	30
6	PITTSBURGH	3
17	Dallas	31
10	Atlanta	16
10	CLEVELAND	38

Use Name	Pos.	Hgt	Wgt	Age	Int	Pts
John McDowell	OT	6'3"	260	23		
Ernie McMillan	OT	6'6"	260	28		
Bob Reynolds	OT	6'6"	265	25		
Dave O'Brien	OG-OT	6'3"	247	25		
Ken Gray	OG	6'2"	250	30		
Frank Roy	OG	6'2"	230	23		
Rick Sortun	OG	6'2"	235	23		
Irv Goode	C-OG	6'4"	250	25		
Bob DeMarco	C	6'3"	240	28		
Dick Kasperek	C	6'3"	225	22		
Don Brumm	DE	6'3"	245	23		
Mike Melinkovich	DE	6'4"	245	24		
Joe Robb	DE	6'3"	245	29		
Dave Long	DT-DE	6'4"	235	21		
Sam Silas	DT	6'4"	250	23		
Chuck Walker	DT	6'2"	245	25		
Fred Heron	DE-DT	6'4"	250	21		
Bill Koman	LB	6'2"	230	32		
Dave Meggyesy	LB	6'1"	220	24		
Dale Meinert	LB	6'2"	220	33		
Dave Simmons	LB	6'4"	245	23		
Larry Stallings	LB	6'2"	230	24	1	
Mike Strofolino	LB	6'2"	230	22		
Jimmy Burson	DB	6'	180	24	2	
Pat Fischer	DB	5'10"	170	26	1	
Jim Heidel	DB	6'1"	185	22		
Jerry Stovall	DB	6'2"	205	24	3	6
Bobby Williams	DB	6'1"	185	24		
Larry Wilson	DB	6'	190	28	10	12
Abe Woodson	DB	5'11"	190	31	4	
Bill Thornton – Injury						
Jim Hart	QB	6'2"	195	22		
Charley Johnson	QB	6'	190	29		12
Terry Nofsinger	QB	6'4"	215	28		12
Charlie Bryant	HB	6'1"	207	25		
Roy Shivers	HB	6'	200	24		6
Bill Triplett	HB	6'2"	210	27		
Johnny Roland	FB-HB	6'2"	207	23		36
Willie Crenshaw	FB	6'2"	230	25		
Prentice Gautt	HB-FB	6'	210	28		12
Bobby Joe Conrad	FL	6'	195	31		12
Mal Hammack	TE	6'2"	210	33		
Ray Ogden	TE	6'5"	225	23		
Jackie Smith	TE	6'4"	215	25		18
Sonny Randle	OE	6'2"	190	30		12
Billy Gambrell	FL-OE	5'10"	175	24		30
Jim Bakken	K	6'	200	25		96

WASHINGTON REDSKINS 7-7-0 Otto Graham

Scores of Each Game		
14	CLEVELAND	38
7	St. Louis	23
33	Pittsburgh	27
24	PITTSBURGH	10
33	ATLANTA	20
10	New York	13
26	ST. LOUIS	20
27	Philadelphia	13
10	Blatimore	37
30	DALLAS	31
3	Cleveland	14
72	NEW YORK	41
34	Dallas	31
28	PHILADELPHIA	37

Use Name	Pos.	Hgt	Wgt	Age	Int	Pts
Mitch Johnson	OT	6'4"	245	24		
John Kelly	OT	6'3"	256	22		
Jim Snowden	OT	6'3"	255	24		
Tom Goosby	OG	6'	235	27		
Jake Kupp	OG	6'3"	233	24		
Vince Promuto	OG	6'1"	245	28		
Ray Schoenke	OG	6'3"	234	24		
Don Croftcheck	LB-OG	6'1"	230	23		
Dave Crossan	C	6'3"	245	26		
Len Hauss	C	6'2"	235	25		
Willie Adams	DE	6'2"	235	24		
Bill Briggs	DE	6'3"	250	22		
Carl Kammerer	DE	6'3"	243	29		
Ron Snidow	DE	6'4"	250	24		
Walt Barnes	DT	6'3"	250	22		
Stan Jones	DT	6'1"	250	35		
Joe Rutgens	DT	6'2"	255	27		
Jim Carroll (from NY)	LB	6'1"	230	23	1	
Chris Hanburger	LB	6'2"	218	25	1	
Sam Huff	LB	6'1"	230	31	1	
Steve Jackson	LB	6'1"	225	23	1	
John Reger	LB	6'	220	35	3	6
Billy Clay	DB	6'1"	192	22	1	
Rickie Harris	DB	6'	182	23	1	6
Paul Krause	DB	6'3"	195	24	2	
Brig Owens	DB	5'11"	190	23	7	12
Lonnie Sanders	DB	6'3"	207	24		
Jim Shorter	DB	5'11"	185	25	5	
Tom Walters	DB	6'2"	195	24		
John Seedborg – Military Service						
Sonny Jurgensen	QB	5'11"	205	32		
Dick Shiner	QB	6'	197	24		
Ron Rector (to ATL)	HB	6'	200	22		
Steve Thurlow (from NY)	HB	6'3"	216	23		
Tom Barrington	FB-HB	6'1"	218	22		
Joe Kantor	FB	6'1"	217	23		
A. D. Whitfield	FB	5'10"	200	22		18
Joe Don Looney (fron DET)	HB-FB	6'1"	230	23		24
John Burrell	FL	6'3"	195	26		
Fred Mazurek	FL	5'11"	192	23		
Bobby Mitchell	FL	6'	196	31		60
Jim Avery	TE	6'2"	235	22		
Pat Richter	TE	6'5"	230	25		
Jerry Smith	TE	6'2"	208	23		36
Pat Hodgson	OE	6'2"	190	22		
Charley Taylor	HB-OE	6'3"	210	25		90
Charlie Gogolak	K	5'10"	165	21		105

DALLAS COWBOYS

RUSHING

Last Name	No.	Yds	Avg	TD
Reeves	175	757	4.3	8
Perkins	186	726	3.9	8
Meredith	38	242	6.4	5
Shy	17	118	6.9	1
Garrison	16	62	3.9	1
Renfro	8	52	6.5	0
Morton	7	50	7.1	0
Clarke	8	49	6.1	0
Rhome	7	37	5.3	0
Villanueva	1	23	23.0	0
Smith	7	7	1.0	1
Hayes	1	−1	−1.0	0

RECEIVING

Last Name	No.	Yds	Avg	TD
Hayes	64	1232	19	13
Reeves	41	557	14	8
Gent	27	474	18	1
Clarke	26	355	14	4
Perkins	23	231	10	0
Dial	14	252	18	1
Norman	12	144	12	0
Renfro	4	65	16	0
Garrison	2	18	9	0
Smith	1	3	3	0

PUNT RETURNS

Last Name	No.	Yds	Avg	TD
Renfro	21	123	6	0
Hayes	17	106	6	0
Howley	1	30	30	0
Reeves	2	−1	−1	0

KICKOFF RETURNS

Last Name	No.	Yds	Avg	TD
Renfro	19	487	26	1
Garrison	20	445	22	0
Reeves	3	56	19	0
Neely	2	18	9	0

PASSING – PUNTING – KICKING

PASSING	Att	Comp	%	Yds	Yd/Att	TD	Int–%	RK
Meredith	344	177	51	2805	8.2	24	12– 3	4
Rhome	36	21	58	253	7.0	0	1– 3	
Morton	27	13	48	225	8.3	3	1– 4	
Reeves	6	3	50	48	8.0	0	0– 0	

PUNTING	No	Avg
Villanueva	65	39.2

KICKING	XP	Att	%	FG	Att	%
Villanueva	56	56	100	17	31	55

CLEVELAND BROWNS

RUSHING

Last Name	No.	Yds	Avg	TD
Kelly	209	1141	5.5	15
Green	144	750	5.2	3
Ryan	36	156	4.3	0
Harraway	7	40	5.7	0
Collins	2	38	19.0	0
Schultz	7	32	4.6	0
Pietrosante	7	20	2.9	0
Ninowski	3	−11	−3.7	0

RECEIVING

Last Name	No.	Yds	Avg	TD
Collins	56	946	17	12
Green	45	445	10	6
Warfield	36	741	21	5
Kelly	32	366	11	1
Morin	23	333	14	3
Smith	13	183	14	3
McNeil	2	94	47	2
Roberts	2	19	10	0
Pietrosante	1	12	12	0
Houston	1	10	10	1
Costello	1	−7	−7	0

PUNT RETURNS

Last Name	No.	Yds	Avg	TD
Kelly	13	104	8	0
Roberts	11	42	4	0

KICKOFF RETURNS

Last Name	No.	Yds	Avg	TD
Roberts	20	454	23	0
Kelly	19	403	21	0
Harraway	9	193	21	0
Schultz	3	52	17	0
Pietrosante	2	9	5	0
Smith	1	0	0	0

PASSING – PUNTING – KICKING

PASSING	Att	Comp	%	Yds	Yd/Att	TD	Int–%	RK
Ryan	382	200	52	2974	7.8	29	14– 4	3
Ninowski	18	11	61	175	9.7	4	1– 6	
Groza	1	1	100	−7	−7.0	0	0– 0	
Kelly	1	0	0	0	0.0	0	0– 0	

PUNTING	No	Avg
Collins	57	39.0

KICKING	XP	Att	%	FG	Att	%
Groza	51	52	98	9	23	39
Houston	1	1	100	0	0	0

PHILADELPHIA EAGLES

RUSHING

Last Name	No.	Yds	Avg	TD
T. Brown	161	548	3.4	3
Gros	102	396	3.9	7
Woodeshick	85	330	3.9	4
Lang	52	239	4.6	1
Concannon	25	195	7.8	2
Matson	29	101	3.5	1
Snead	15	32	2.1	1
Baker	1	15	15.0	0
F. Hill	1	5	5.0	0
K. Hill	7	−2	−0.3	0

RECEIVING

Last Name	No.	Yds	Avg	TD
Retzlaff	40	653	16	6
T. Brown	33	371	11	3
F. Hill	29	304	10	0
Gros	18	214	12	2
Goodwin	16	212	13	1
Hawkins	14	143	10	0
Lang	12	107	9	0
Woodeshick	10	118	12	1
Matson	6	30	5	1
Concannon	1	7	7	0

PUNT RETURNS

Last Name	No.	Yds	Avg	TD
Martin	11	118	11	1
Hawkins	9	47	5	0
Concannon	2	3	2	0
Nelson	1	3	3	0
T. Brown	1	0	0	0
W. Brown	5	−1	0	0
Scarpati	2	−8	−4	0

KICKOFF RETURNS

Last Name	No.	Yds	Avg	TD
T. Brown	20	562	28	2
Matson	26	544	21	0
Martin	4	132	33	0
W. Brown	4	58	15	0
Nelson	2	34	17	0
Whittingham	2	33	17	0
Beisler	1	17	17	0
Jackson	1	16	16	0
Lince	1	13	13	0
Medved	2	10	5	0
Hawkins	1	0	0	0

PASSING – PUNTING – KICKING

PASSING	Att	Comp	%	Yds	Yd/Att	TD	Int–%	RK
Snead	226	103	46	1275	5.6	8	11– 5	16
K. Hill	97	53	55	571	5.9	5	7– 7	
Concannon	51	21	41	262	5.1	1	4– 8	
Lang	3	2	67	51	17.0	0	0– 0	
Gros	1	0	0	0	0.0	0	0– 0	

PUNTING	No	Avg
Baker	42	41.1
K. Hill	23	37.5

KICKING	XP	Att	%	FG	Att	%
Baker	38	39	97	18	25	72

ST. LOUIS CARDINALS

RUSHING

Last Name	No.	Yds	Avg	TD
Roland	192	695	3.6	5
Gautt	110	370	3.4	1
Crenshaw	94	360	3.8	0
Johnson	20	39	2.0	2
Bryant	5	31	6.2	0
Gambrell	3	26	8.7	0
Nofsinger	18	25	1.4	2
Triplett	13	25	1.9	0
Stovall	1	17	17.0	0
Smith	1	8	8.0	0
Shivers	1	5	5.0	0

RECEIVING

Last Name	No.	Yds	Avg	TD
Smith	45	810	18	3
Conrad	34	388	11	2
Gambrell	24	409	17	5
Roland	21	213	10	0
Randle	17	218	13	2
Gautt	16	114	7	1
Crenshaw	15	46	3	0
Shivers	5	81	16	0
Triplett	2	6	3	0
Sortun	1	7	7	0

PUNT RETURNS

Last Name	No.	Yds	Avg	TD
Roland	20	221	11	1
Shivers	16	49	3	0
Gambrell	4	46	12	0

KICKOFF RETURNS

Last Name	No.	Yds	Avg	TD
Shivers	27	762	28	1
Roland	15	347	23	0
Williams	7	132	19	0
Bryant	2	70	35	0
Gambrell	1	16	16	0
Roy	2	10	5	0
Long	1	9	9	0
Melinkovich	1	2	2	0
Ogden	1	0	0	0

PASSING – PUNTING – KICKING

PASSING	Att	Comp	%	Yds	Yd/Att	TD	Int–%	RK
Johnson	205	103	50	1334	6.5	10	11– 5	9
Nofsinger	162	68	42	799	4.9	2	8– 5	18
Hart	11	4	36	29	2.6	0	0– 0	
Roland	8	5	63	130	16.3	1	0– 0	

PUNTING	No	Avg
Smith	47	37.9
Bakken	29	33.1
Stovall	5	27.8

KICKING	XP	Att	%	FG	Att	%
Bakken	27	28	96	23	40	58

WASHINGTON REDSKINS

RUSHING

Last Name	No.	Yds	Avg	TD
Whitfield	93	472	5.1	2
Taylor	87	262	3.0	3
Thurlow	80	260	3.3	0
Looney	63	220	3.5	4
Mitchell	13	141	10.8	1
Rector	9	40	4.4	0
Barrington	10	37	3.7	0
Jurgensen	12	14	1.2	0
Shiner	1	10	10.0	0
Kantor	1	2	2.0	0

RECEIVING

Last Name	No.	Yds	Avg	TD
Taylor	72	1119	16	12
Mitchell	58	905	16	9
Smith	54	686	13	6
Thurlow	23	165	7	0
Whitfield	18	101	6	1
Looney	12	49	4	0
Richter	7	100	14	0
Kupp	4	28	7	0
Mazurek	2	28	14	0
Barrington	2	23	12	0
Rector	2	9	5	0
Burrell	1	9	9	0
Johnson	1	1	1	0

PUNT RETURNS

Last Name	No.	Yds	Avg	TD
Harris	18	108	6	1
Taylor	5	63	13	0
Mitchell	4	21	5	0
Mazurek	2	9	5	0

KICKOFF RETURNS

Last Name	No.	Yds	Avg	TD
Mazurek	21	505	24	0
Harris	20	405	20	0
Looney	13	265	20	0
Taylor	3	98	33	0
Rector	3	65	22	0
Barrington	2	39	20	0
Croftcheck	2	36	18	0
Kantor	2	35	18	0
Jackson	2	26	13	0
Johnson	2	22	11	0
Barnes	1	14	14	0
Goosby	1	0	0	0

PASSING – PUNTING – KICKING

PASSING	Att	Comp	%	Yds	Yd/Att	TD	Int–%	RK
Jurgensen	436	254	58	3209	7.4	28	19– 4	2
Shiner	5	0	0	0	0.0	0	1– 20	
Barrington	1	0	0	0	0.0	0	0– 0	
Mitchell	1	1	100	21	21.0	0	0– 0	

PUNTING	No	Avg
Richter	68	42.4

KICKING	XP	Att	%	FG	Att	%
Gogolak	39	41	95	22	34	65

EASTERN CONFERENCE – Continued

PITTSBURGH STEELERS 5-8-1 Bill Austin

Scores of Each Game		
34	NEW YORK	34
17	DETROIT	3
27	WASHINGTON	33
10	Washington	24
10	Cleveland	41
14	PHILADELPHIA	31
21	Dallas	52
16	CLEVELAND	6
30	ST. LOUIS	9
7	DALLAS	20
3	St. Louis	6
23	Philadelphia	27
47	New York	28
57	Atlanta	33

Use Name	Pos.	Hgt	Wgt	Age	Int	Pts
Charlie Bradshaw	OT	6'6"	260	30		
Dan James	OT	6'4"	250	29		
Fran O'Brien (from WAS)	OT	6'1"	255	30		
Roger Pillath	OT	6'4"	242	24		
Larry Gagner	OG	6'3"	240	22		
Mike Magac	OG	6'3"	240	28		
Eli Strand	OG	6'2"	250	23		
Ralph Wenzel	OG	6'3"	240	23		
Pat Killorin	C	6'2"	220	22		
Ray Mansfield	C	6'3"	250	25		
John Baker	DE	6'6"	270	31		
Ben McGee	DE	6'2"	225	24		
Tim Powell	DE	6'4"	248	22		
Riley Gunnels	DT	6'3"	253	29	1	
Chuck Hinton	DT	6'5"	260	27		
Ken Kortas	DT	6'2"	280	24		
Lloyd Voss	DT	6'4"	260	24		
Rod Breedlove	LB	6'2"	227	28	2	
Gene Breen	LB	6'2"	230	25		
John Campbell	LB	6'3"	225	27	2	
Andy Russell	LB	6'3"	215	24		7
Bill Saul	LB	6'4"	225	25	2	
Bob Schmitz (to MIN)	LB	6'1"	240	28		
Jim Bradshaw	DB	6'1"	205	27	4	6
Willie Daniel	DB	5'11"	185	28		
Bob Hohn	DB	6'	190	25		
Brady Keys	DB	6'	198	30	4	
Paul Martha	DB	6'	185	23	3	
Clendon Thomas	DB	6'2"	205	29	2	6
Marv Woodson	DB	6'	195	23	4	6
George Izo	QB	6'3"	218	29		
Ron Meyer	QB	6'4"	205	22		
Bill Nelsen	QB	6'	195	25		
Ron Smith	QB	6'5"	220	24		
Amos Bullocks	HB	6'1"	202	27		12
Cannonball Butler	HB	5'10"	185	23		24
Dick Hoak	HB	5'11"	190	27		6
Bobby Smith	HB	6'	203	24		
Dick Leftridge	FB	6'2"	240	21		12
Mike Lind	FB	6'2"	225	26		
Willie Asbury	FB	6'1"	230	23		54
Roy Jefferson	FL	6'2"	195	22		24
John Hilton	TE	6'5"	220	24		24
Tony Jeter	TE	6'3"	220	22		
Steve Smith	TE	6'5"	240	22		
Jerry Simmons	OE	6'1"	190	23		6
J. R. Wilburn	OE	6'2"	190	23		
Gary Ballman	FL-OE	6'	200	26		30
Mike Clark	K	6'1"	205	25		97
Frank Lambert	K	6'3"	200	23		

Theron Sapp – Injury

ATLANTA FALCONS 3-11-0 Norb Hecker

Scores of Each Game		
14	LOS ANGELES	19
10	Philadelphia	23
10	Detroit	28
14	DALLAS	47
20	Washington	33
7	SAN FRANCISCO	44
3	Green Bay	56
17	CLEVELAND	49
7	BALTIMORE	19
27	New York	16
6	Chicago	23
20	Minnesota	13
16	ST. LOUIS	10
33	PITTSBURGH	57

Use Name	Pos.	Hgt	Wgt	Age	Int	Pts
Rich Koeper	OT	6'4"	245	23		
Errol Linden	OT	6'5"	260	29		
Jim Simon	OT	6'5"	235	25		
Don Talbert	OT	6'5"	240	26		
Lou Kirouac	OG	6'3"	240	25		46
Ed Cook	OG	6'2"	250	34		
Dan Grimm	OG	6'3"	245	25		
Frank Marchlewski	C	6'2"	238	22		
Bob Whitlow	C	6'1"	236	30		
Bobby Richards	DE	6'2"	247	27		
Sam Williams	DE	6'5"	235	35		
Karl Rubke	DE	6'4"	244	30		
Jerry Jones	DT-DE	6'3"	277	22		
Bud Marshall (from WAS)	DT	6'5"	270	24		
Guy Reese	DT	6'5"	260	26		
Chuck Sieminski	DT	6'4"	265	26		
Joe Szczercko	DT	6'	245	24		
Ralph Heck	LB	6'2"	230	25		
Bill Jobko	LB	6'2"	235	30	2	
Larry Morris	LB	6'2"	230	31		
Tommy Nobis	LB	6'2"	230	22		
Marion Rushing	LB	6'2"	230	29	3	
Lee Calland	DB	6'	190	25	3	
Nick Rassas	DB	6'	190	22		
Ken Reaves	DB	6'3"	200	21	1	
Jerry Richardson	DB	6'3"	190	23	5	
Bob Riggle	DB	6'1"	200	22	3	6
Carl Silvestri	DB	6'	195	23		
Tommy Tolleson	DB	6'	185	23		
Ron Smith	HB-DB	6'1"	180	23	2	
Dennis Claridge	QB	6'3"	225	24		
Randy Johnson	QB	6'3"	195	22		24
Steve Sloan	QB	6'1"	185	22		
Junior Coffey	HB	6'1"	210	24		30
Perry Lee Dunn	HB	6'2"	200	23		
Rudy Johnson	HB	5'11"	190	24		
Preston Ridlehuber	HB	6'2"	215	22		12
Jimmy Sidle	TE-HB	6'2"	215	23		
Charlie Scales	FB	5'11"	215	27		
Ernie Wheelwright	FB	6'3"	240	29		36
Bill Wolski	FB	5'11"	203	22		
Glenn Glass (to DEN-A)	FL	6'	203	29		
Bob Sherlag	FL	6'	197	23		6
Gary Barnes	OE-FL	6'4"	210	26		6
Alex Hawkins	OE-FL	6'1"	186	29		12
Taz Anderson	TE	6'2"	215	27		18
Billy Martin	TE	6'4"	240	23		
Hugh McInnis	TE	6'3"	220	28		
Vern Burke	OE	6'4"	202	25		6
Angie Coia	OE	6'2"	196	28		
Tom Hutchinson	OE	6'1"	190	25		
Billy Lothridge	K	6'1"	194	22		
Wade Traynham	K	6'2"	218	24		2

NEW YORK GIANTS 1-12-1 Allie Sherman

Scores of Each Game		
34	Pittsburgh	34
7	Dallas	52
17	Philadelphia	35
7	CLEVELAND	28
19	St. Louis	24
13	WASHINGTON	10
3	PHILADELPHIA	31
17	ST. LOUIS	20
14	Los Angeles	55
16	ATLANTA	27
41	Washington	72
40	Cleveland	49
28	PITTSBURGH	47
7	DALLAS	17

Use Name	Pos.	Hgt	Wgt	Age	Int	Pts
Roger Davis	OT	6'3"	240	28		
Francis Peay	OT	6'5"	250	22		
Willie Young	OT	6'	247	23		
Bob Scholtz	C-OT	6'4"	250	28		
Bookie Bolin	OG	6'2"	240	26		
Pete Case	OG	6'3"	245	25		
Darrell Dess (from WAS)	OG	6'	245	30		
Charlie Harper	OG	6'2"	248	22		
Greg Larson	C	6'2"	250	27		
Joe Wellborn	C	6'2"	215	20		
Glen Condren	DE	6'2"	250	24		
Rosey Davis	DE	6'5"	260	24		
Jim Garcia	DE	6'4"	250	22		
Jim Katcavage	DE	6'3"	240	31		
Bill Matan	DE	6'4"	240	22		
Don Davis	DT	6'6"	260	22		
Jim Moran	DT	6'5"	270	23		
Jim Prestel	DT	6'5"	275	29		
Mike Ciccolella	LB	6'1"	235	22		
Jerry Hillebrand	LB	6'3"	240	26	1	6
Stan Sczurek	LB	5'11"	230	27		
Jeff Smith	LB	6'	237	22	1	
Larry Vargo	LB	6'3"	215	26	1	
Henry Carr	DB	6'3"	195	23	4	6
Clarence Childs	DB	6'	180	27	2	6
Phil Harris	DB	6'	195	21		
Wendell Harris	DB	5'11"	185	25	1	6
Spider Lockhart	DB	6'2"	175	23	6	
Dick Lynch	DB	6'1"	198	30		
Jimmy Patton	DB	6'	185	34	1	
Tom Kennedy	QB	6'1"	200	27		
Earl Morrall	QB	6'1"	206	32		
Gary Wood	QB	5'11"	188	23		18
Steve Bowman	HB	6'	195	21		
Allen Jacobs	HB	6'1"	215	25		6
Dan Lewis	HB	6'1"	200	30		6
Smith Reed	HB	6'	215	24		
Ernie Koy	FB-HB	6'2"	230	23		
Chuck Mercein	FB	6'3"	230	23		
Pep Menefee	FL	6'1"	198	24		
Joe Morrison	HB-FB-FL	6'1"	212	28		48
Bob Crespino	TE	6'4"	225	28		12
Aaron Thomas	TE	6'3"	210	28		24
Freeman White	LB-TE	6'5"	225	22		
Del Shofner	OE	6'3"	185	30		
Homer Jones	FL-OE	6'2"	205	25		48
Pete Gogolak	K	6'2"	200	24		77

Tucker Frederickson – Knee Injury
Bill Swain – Injury

WESTERN CONFERENCE

GREEN BAY PACKERS 12-2-0 Vince Lombardi

Scores of Each Game		
24	BALTIMORE	3
21	Cleveland	20
24	LOS ANGELES	13
23	DETROIT	14
20	San Francisco	21
17	Chicago	0
56	ATLANTA	3
31	Detroit	7
17	MINNESOTA	20
13	CHICAGO	6
28	Minnesota	16
20	SAN FRANCISCO	7
14	Baltimore	10
27	Los Angeles	23

Use Name	Pos.	Hgt	Wgt	Age	Int	Pts
Bob Skoronski	OT	6'3"	250	33		
Steve Wright	OT	6'6"	250	24		
Forrest Gregg	OG-OT	6'4"	250	33		
Gale Gillingham	OG	6'3"	250	22		
Jerry Kramer	OG	6'3"	245	31		
Fuzzy Thurston	OG	6'1"	245	33		
Ken Bowman	C	6'3"	230	23		
Bill Curry	C	6'2"	235	23		
Lionel Aldridge	DE	6'4"	245	24		
Bob Brown	DE	6'5"	270	25		
Willie Davis	DE	6'3"	245	33		
Henry Jordan	DT	6'3"	250	31		
Ron Kostelnik	DT	6'4"	260	26		
Jim Weatherwax	DT	6'7"	275	23		
Lee Roy Caffey	LB	6'3"	250	26	3	6
Tommy Crutcher	LB	6'3"	230	24	1	
Ray Nitschke	LB	6'3"	240	30	2	
Dave Robinson	LB	6'3"	245	25	5	
Phil Vandersea	LB	6'3"	225	23		
Herb Adderley	DB	6'1"	210	27	4	6
Tom Brown	DB	6'1"	190	25	4	
Doug Hart	DB	6'	190	27	1	6
Dave Hathcock	DB	6'	190	23		
Bob Jeter	DB	6'1"	205	28	5	12
Willie Wood	DB	5'10"	190	30	3	6
Zeke Bratkowski	QB	6'2"	200	34		
Bart Starr	QB	6'1"	200	33		12
Donny Anderson	HB	6'3"	220	23		18
Paul Hornung	HB	6'2"	215	29		30
Elijah Pitts	HB	6'1"	205	27		60
Jim Grabowski	FB	6'2"	225	22		6
Jim Taylor	FB	6'	215	31		36
Carroll Dale	FL	6'1"	200	28		42
Bob Long	FL	6'3"	190	25		
Red Mack (from ATL)	FL	5'10"	185	29		
Bill Anderson	TE	6'3"	216	30		
Allen Brown	TE	6'5"	240	23		
Marv Fleming	TE	6'4"	235	24		12
Boyd Dowler	OE	6'5"	225	29		
Max McGee	OE	6'3"	205	34		6
Don Chandler	K	6'2"	210	31		77

BALTIMORE COLTS 9-5-0 Don Shula

Scores of Each Game		
3	Green Bay	24
38	Minnesota	23
36	SAN FRANCISCO	14
17	Chicago	27
45	DETROIT	14
20	MINNESOTA	17
17	Los Angeles	3
37	WASHINGTON	10
19	Atlanta	7
14	Detroit	20
7	LOS ANGELES	23
21	CHICAGO	16
10	GREEN BAY	14
30	San Francisco	14

Use Name	Pos.	Hgt	Wgt	Age	Int	Pts
Sam Ball	OT	6'4"	240	22		
Jim Parker	OT	6'3"	275	32		
Bob Vogel	OT	6'5"	250	24		
Glenn Ressler	C-OT	6'3"	235	22		
Dale Memmelaar	OG	6'2"	248	29		
Alex Sandusky	OG	6'1"	242	34		
Dan Sullivan	OG	6'3"	250	27		
Dick Szymanski	C	6'3"	235	34		
Ordell Braase	DE	6'4"	242	34		
Roy Hilton	DE	6'6"	240	21		
Gino Marchetti	DE	6'4"	245	40		
Lou Michaels	DE	6'2"	250	30		98
Fred Miller	DT	6'3"	245	25		
Billy Ray Smith	DT	6'4"	250	31		
Andy Stynchula	DE-DT	6'3"	250	27		
Barry Brown	LB	6'3"	230	23	1	
Jackie Burkett	LB	6'4"	228	29		
Mike Curtis	LB	6'2"	232	22		6
Ted Davis	LB	6'1"	232	24	1	
Dennis Gaubatz	LB	6'2"	232	25	2	
Don Shinnick	LB	6'	228	31	3	
Steve Stonebreaker	LB	6'3"	228	28	1	
Tom Bleick	DB	6'2"	200	23		
Bobby Boyd	DB	5'10"	190	28	6	6
George Harold	DB	6'3"	205	24		
Alvin Haymond	DB	6'	190	24	4	6
Jerry Logan	DB	6'1"	185	25	3	
Lenny Lyles	DB	6'2"	202	30	1	
Jim Welch	DB	6'	190	28		
Gary Cuozzo	QB	6'1"	195	25		
Johnny Unitas	QB	6'1"	194	33		6
Jerry Allen	HB	6'1"	205	25		
Tom Matte	HB	6'	205	27		18
Lenny Moore	FL-HB	6'1"	190	33		18
Bob Baldwin	FB-HB	6'1"	225	23		
Jerry Hill	FB	5'11"	210	26		
Tony Lorick	FB	6'1"	215	24		18
Jimmy Orr	FL	5'11"	185	30		18
Willie Richardson	FL	6'2"	198	26		12
Al Snyder	FL	6'	195	24		
John Mackey	TE	6'3"	217	24		54
Butch Wilson	TE	6'2"	228	24		12
Ray Berry	OE	6'2"	187	33		42
Neal Petties	OE	6'2"	198	25		
David Lee	K	6'4"	215	22		

EASTERN CONFERENCE—Continued

PITTSBURGH STEELERS

RUSHING

Last Name	No.	Yds	Avg	TD
Asbury	169	544	3.2	7
Hoak	81	212	2.6	1
Butler	46	114	2.5	2
B. Smith	24	93	3.9	0
Bullocks	29	83	2.9	1
Jefferson	2	36	18.0	0
Nelsen	6	18	3.0	0
Leftridge	8	17	2.1	2
Lind	3	4	1.3	0
Meyer	1	–2	–2.0	0
R. Smith	4	–9	–2.3	0
Izo	2	–18	–9.0	0

RECEIVING

Last Name	No.	Yds	Avg	TD
Hilton	46	603	13	4
Ballman	41	663	16	5
Jefferson	32	772	24	4
Hoak	23	239	10	0
Asbury	19	228	12	2
Wilburn	7	103	15	0
Simmons	6	68	11	1
Bullocks	5	64	13	1
Butler	4	93	23	1
B. Smith	3	26	9	0
Jeter	2	18	9	0

PUNT RETURNS

Last Name	No.	Yds	Avg	TD
Jefferson	12	29	2	0
Keys	5	11	2	0
J. Bradshaw	2	3	2	0
Simmons	2	0	0	0

KICKOFF RETURNS

Last Name	No.	Yds	Avg	TD
Ballman	20	477	24	0
Butler	17	454	27	1
Simmons	10	196	20	0
Woodson	6	113	19	0
Martha	2	39	20	0
Saul	2	35	18	0
Keys	1	18	18	0
Campbell	1	15	15	0
Lind	1	15	15	0
Russell	2	12	6	0
Leftridge	1	10	10	0
Hilton	1	0	0	0

PASSING – PUNTING – KICKING

PASSING	Att	Comp	%	Yds	Yd/Att	TD	Int–%	RK
R. Smith	181	79	44	1249	6.9	8	12– 7	12
Nelsen	112	63	56	1122	10.0	7	1– 1	
Izo	81	35	43	360	4.4	2	8– 10	
Meyer	19	7	37	59	3.1	0	1– 5	
Hoak	6	4	67	87	14.5	1	0– 0	
Asbury	1	0	0	0	0.0	0	0– 0	
Bullocks	1	0	0	0	0.0	0	0– 0	

PUNTING	No	Avg
Lambert	78	42.1

KICKING	XP	Att	%	FG	Att	%
Clark	34	34	100	21	32	66
Russell	1	1	100	0	0	0

ATLANTA FALCONS

RUSHING

Last Name	No.	Yds	Avg	TD
Coffey	199	722	3.6	4
Wheelwright	121	458	3.8	3
Ran. Johnson	35	142	4.1	4
Dunn	22	52	2.4	0
Scales	10	38	3.8	0
Ridlehuber	4	23	5.8	0
Lothridge	1	22	22.0	0
Claridge	5	15	3.0	0
Sidle	1	12	12.0	0
Rud. Johnson	3	3	1.0	0

RECEIVING

Last Name	No.	Yds	Avg	TD
Hawkins	44	661	15	2
Martin	29	330	11	0
Burke	28	348	12	1
Coffey	15	182	12	1
Wheelwright	15	137	9	3
Barnes	12	173	14	1
Anderson	10	195	20	3
Dunn	5	45	9	0
Coia	4	93	23	0
Ridlehuber	4	84	21	2
Sherlag	4	53	13	1
Scales	3	16	5	0
Hutchinson	1	28	28	0
Sidle	1	16	16	0
Marchlewski	0	1	0	0

PUNT RETURNS

Last Name	No.	Yds	Avg	TD
Smith	11	80	7	0
Rassas	4	10	3	0
Sherlag	2	8	4	0
Reaves	1	2	2	0

KICKOFF RETURNS

Last Name	No.	Yds	Avg	TD
Smith	43	1013	24	0
Rassas	8	203	25	0
Sidle	6	117	20	0
Scales	5	101	20	0
Reaves	4	85	21	0
Rushing	2	52	26	0
Morris	5	50	10	0
Dunn	2	36	18	0
Hawkins	1	30	30	0
Wolski	1	21	21	0
Coffey	1	18	18	0
Glass	1	11	11	0
Heck	1	0	0	0
Martin	1	0	0	0
Sherlag	1	0	0	0

PASSING – PUNTING – KICKING

PASSING	Att	Comp	%	Yds	Yd/Att	TD	Int–%	RK
Ran. Johnson	295	129	44	1795	6.1	12	21– 7	17
Claridge	70	40	57	471	6.7	2	2– 3	
Sloan	13	6	46	96	7.4	0	2– 15	
Dunn	2	0	0	0	0.0	0	2–100	
Lothridge	1	0	0	0	0.0	0	0– 0	

PUNTING	No	Avg
Lothridge	73	40.7

KICKING	XP	Att	%	FG	Att	%
Kirouac	19	24	79	9	18	50
Traynham	2	2	100	0	1	0

NEW YORK GIANTS

RUSHING

Last Name	No.	Yds	Avg	TD
Mercein	94	327	3.5	0
Morrison	67	275	4.1	2
Jacobs	77	273	3.5	1
Wood	28	196	7.0	3
Lewis	32	164	5.1	1
Koy	66	146	2.2	0
Jones	5	43	8.6	0
Kennedy	5	16	3.2	0
Morrall	5	12	2.4	0
Larson	0	–2	0.0	0

RECEIVING

Last Name	No.	Yds	Avg	TD
Jones	48	1044	22	8
Morrison	46	724	16	6
Thomas	43	683	16	4
Mercein	27	152	6	0
Crespino	16	167	10	2
Jacobs	10	69	7	0
Koy	8	43	5	0
Lewis	6	87	15	0
Shofner	3	19	6	0
Menefee	1	11	11	0

PUNT RETURNS

Last Name	No.	Yds	Avg	TD
Lockhart	17	113	7	0
P. Harris	5	7	1	0

KICKOFF RETURNS

Last Name	No.	Yds	Avg	TD
Childs	34	855	25	1
P. Harris	22	480	22	0
Lewis	13	214	16	0
Koy	3	20	7	0
Jacobs	2	18	9	0
White	2	14	7	0
W. Harris	1	9	9	0
Young	2	6	3	0
Rog. Davis	1	0	0	0

PASSING – PUNTING – KICKING

PASSING	Att	Comp	%	Yds	Yd/Att	TD	Int–%	RK
Wood	170	81	48	1142	6.7	6	13– 8	15
Morrall	151	71	47	1105	7.3	7	12– 8	14
Kennedy	100	55	55	748	7.5	7	6– 6	
Koy	2	0	0	0	0.0	0	0– 0	
Lewis	1	1	100	4	4.0	0	0– 0	

PUNTING	No	Avg
Koy	49	39.4
Lockhart	4	32.8

KICKING	XP	Att	%	FG	Att	%
Gogolak	29	31	94	16	28	57

WESTERN CONFERENCE

GREEN BAY PACKERS

RUSHING

Last Name	No.	Yds	Avg	TD
Taylor	204	705	3.5	4
Pitts	115	393	3.4	7
Hornung	76	200	2.6	2
Grabowski	29	127	4.4	1
Starr	21	104	5.0	2
D. Anderson	25	104	4.2	2
Chandler	1	33	33.0	0
Bratkowski	4	7	1.8	0

RECEIVING

Last Name	No.	Yds	Avg	TD
Taylor	41	331	8	2
Dale	37	876	24	7
Fleming	31	361	12	2
Dowler	29	392	14	0
Pitts	26	460	18	3
Hornung	14	192	14	3
McGee	4	91	23	1
Grabowski	4	13	3	0
Long	3	68	23	0
D. Anderson	2	33	17	0
B. Anderson	2	14	7	0

PUNT RETURNS

Last Name	No.	Yds	Avg	TD
D. Anderson	6	124	21	1
Wood	22	82	4	0
Pitts	7	9	1	0
T. Brown	2	0	0	0

KICKOFF RETURNS

Last Name	No.	Yds	Avg	TD
D. Anderson	23	533	23	0
Adderley	14	320	23	0
Vandersea	3	50	17	0
Pitts	1	0	0	0
Wood	1	0	0	0

PASSING – PUNTING – KICKING

PASSING	Att	Comp	%	Yds	Yd/Att	TD	Int–%	RK
Starr	251	156	62	2257	9.0	14	3– 1	1
Bratkowski	64	36	56	569	8.9	4	2– 3	
Pitts	2	0	0	0	0.0	0	0– 0	
Hornung	1	1	100	5	5.0	0	0– 0	

PUNTING	No	Avg
Chandler	60	40.9
D. Anderson	2	44.5

KICKING	XP	Att	%	FG	Att	%
Chandler	41	43	95	12	28	43

BALTIMORE COLTS

RUSHING

Last Name	No.	Yds	Avg	TD
Lorick	143	524	3.7	3
Hill	104	395	3.8	0
Matte	86	381	4.4	0
Moore	63	209	3.3	3
Unitas	20	44	2.2	1
Cuozzo	1	9	9.0	0
Mackey	1	–6	–6.0	0

RECEIVING

Last Name	No.	Yds	Avg	TD
Berry	56	786	14	7
Mackey	50	829	17	9
Orr	37	618	17	3
Matte	23	307	13	3
Moore	21	260	12	0
Richardson	14	246	18	2
Lorick	12	81	7	0
Hill	5	18	4	0
Wilson	3	27	9	2

PUNT RETURNS

Last Name	No.	Yds	Avg	TD
Haymond	40	347	9	0
Davis	2	7	4	0
Logan	1	3	3	0
Allen	1	0	0	0
Matte	1	0	0	0

KICKOFF RETURNS

Last Name	No.	Yds	Avg	TD
Moore	18	453	25	0
Haymond	10	223	22	0
Lorick	10	214	21	0
Curtis	3	64	21	0
Matte	3	55	18	0
Allen	3	53	18	0
Baldwin	2	18	9	0
Brown	2	14	7	0

PASSING – PUNTING – KICKING

PASSING	Att	Comp	%	Yds	Yd/Att	TD	Int–%	RK
Unitas	348	195	56	2748	7.9	22	24– 7	5
Cuozzo	50	26	52	424	8.5	4	2– 4	
Matte	3	0	0	0	0.0	0	1– 33	

PUNTING	No	Avg
Lee	49	45.6

KICKING	XP	Att	%	FG	Att	%
Michaels	35	36	97	21	39	54

WESTERN CONFERENCE – Continued

LOS ANGELES RAMS 8-6-0 George Allen

Scores of Each Game		
19	Atlanta	14
31	CHICAGO	17
13	Green Bay	24
34	SAN FRANCISCO	3
14	Detroit	7
7	Minnesota	35
10	Chicago	17
3	BALTIMORE	17
13	San Francisco	21
55	NEW YORK	14
21	MINNESOTA	6
23	Baltimore	7
23	DETROIT	3
23	GREEN BAY	27

Use Name	Pos.	Hgt	Wgt	Age	Int	Pts
Joe Carollo	OT	6'2"	263	26		
Charley Cowan	OT	6'4"	275	28		
Bob Nichols	OT	6'3"	250	23		
Don Chuy	OG	6'1"	256	25		
Ted Karras	OG	6'1"	243	33		
Joe Scibelli	OG	6'1"	264	27		
Tom Mack	OG	6'3"	245	22		
Ken Iman	C	6'1"	235	27		
Joe Wendryhoski	C	6'2"	245	27		
Bruce Anderson	DE	6'4"	230	22		
Deacon Jones	DE	6'5"	260	27	1	
Lamar Lundy	DE	6'7"	260	31	1	6
Rosey Grier	DT	6'5"	290	33		2
Earl Leggett	DT	6'3"	265	32		
Merlin Olsen	DT	6'5"	276	25		

Use Name	Pos.	Hgt	Wgt	Age	Int	Pts
Maxie Baughan	LB	6'1"	227	28	2	
Dan Currie	LB	6'3"	240	32		
Bill George	LB	6'2"	235	35		
Jack Pardee	LB	6'2"	230	30	2	
Myron Pottios	LB	6'2"	240	26		
Doug Woodlief	LB	6'3"	235	22		
Irv Cross	DB	6'1"	190	27	1	6
Hank Gremminger	DB	6'1"	200	33	1	
Chuck Lamson	DB	6'	190	27	5	6
Clancy Williams	DB	6'2"	198	23	8	6
George Youngblood	DB	6'3"	200	21		
Ed Meador	DB	5'11"	203	29	5	
Claude Crabb	FL-DB	6'	190	26		

Tony Guillory – Injury

Use Name	Pos.	Hgt	Wgt	Age	Int	Pts
Roman Gabriel	QB	6'4"	225	26		18
Bill Munson	QB	6'2"	197	24		
Tom Moore	HB	6'	210	28		24
Les Josephson	HB	6'	210	24		6
Jim Stiger	FB-HB	5'11"	214	25		6
Dick Bass	FB	5'10"	198	29		48
Henry Dyer	FB	6'2"	225	21		
Tommy McDonald	FL	5'10"	175	32		12
Marlin McKeever	TE	6'1"	227	26		6
Dave Pivec	TE	6'3"	240	22		
Billy Truax	TE	6'5"	240	23		6
Steve Heckard	OE	6'1"	195	23		
Bucky Pope	OE	6'5"	195	22		6
Jack Snow	OE	6'2"	212	23		18
Bruce Gossett	K	6'2"	230	23		113
Jon Kilgore	K	6'1"	200	22		

SAN FRANCISCO FORTY NINERS 6-6-2 Jack Christiansen

Scores of Each Game		
20	MINNESOTA	20
14	Baltimore	36
3	Los Angeles	34
21	GREEN BAY	20
44	Atlanta	7
27	DETROIT	24
3	Minnesota	28
21	LOS ANGELES	13
30	Chicago	30
34	PHILADELPHIA	35
41	Detroit	14
7	Green Bay	20
41	CHICAGO	14
14	BALTIMORE	30

Use Name	Pos.	Hgt	Wgt	Age	Int	Pts
Dave McCormick	OT	6'6"	250	23		
Walt Rock	OT	6'5"	257	25		
Len Rohde	OT	6'4"	255	28		
Howard Mudd	OG	6'3"	263	24		
John Thomas	OG	6'4"	250	31		
Jim Wilson	OG	6'3"	255	25		
Bruce Bosley	C	6'2"	246	32		
Joe Cerne	C	6'2"	235	23		
Stan Hindman	DE	6'3"	232	22		
Clark Miller	DE	6'5"	245	27		
Jim Norton	DT-DE	6'4"	255	23		
Charlie Johnson	DT	6'2"	266	22		
Charlie Krueger	DT	6'4"	267	30		
Roland Lakes	DT	6'4"	285	26		

Use Name	Pos.	Hgt	Wgt	Age	Int	Pts
Ed Beard	LB	6'2"	225	26		
Mike Dowdle	LB	6'3"	248	28	1	6
Bob Harrison	LB	6'2"	225	29		
Matt Hazeltine	LB	6'1"	230	33	1	6
Dave Wilcox	LB	6'3"	234	23		
Kermit Alexander	DB	5'11"	186	25	4	12
George Donnelly	DB	6'3"	205	23	2	
Jim Johnson	DB	6'2"	187	28	4	6
Elbert Kimbrough	DB	5'11"	196	27	3	
Mel Phillips	DB	6'	188	24		
Al Randolph	DB	6'2"	190	22	3	6

Use Name	Pos.	Hgt	Wgt	Age	Int	Pts
John Brodie	QB	6'1"	210	31		18
Billy Kilmer	QB	6'	204	27		
George Mira	QB	5'11"	192	24		
John David Crow	HB	6'2"	224	31		24
Bob Daugherty	HB	6'2"	205	24		
Jim Jackson	HB	6'	180	22		6
Dave Kopay	HB	6'2"	225	24		12
Gary Lewis	FB	6'3"	230	24		18
Ken Willard	FB	6'2"	230	23		42
Bernie Casey	FL	6'4"	210	27		6
Kay McFarland	FL	6'2"	186	27		6
Dick Witcher	FL	6'3"	210	21		6
Kent Kramer	TE	6'5"	230	22		18
Monte Stickles	TE	6'4"	235	28		12
Dave Parks	OE	6'2"	207	24		30
Wayne Swinford	OE	6'	200	23		
Tommy Davis	K	6'	220	31		86

CHICAGO BEARS 5-7-2 George Halas

Scores of Each Game		
3	Detroit	14
17	Los Angeles	31
13	Minnesota	10
27	BALTIMORE	17
0	GREEN BAY	17
17	LOS ANGELES	10
17	St. Louis	24
10	DETROIT	10
30	SAN FRANCISCO	30
6	Green Bay	13
23	ATLANTA	6
16	Baltimore	21
14	San Francisco	41
41	MINNESOTA	28

Use Name	Pos.	Hgt	Wgt	Age	Int	Pts
Herm Lee	OT	6'4"	247	35		
Riley Mattson	OT	6'4"	255	27		
Bob Wetoska	OT	6'3"	240	28		
Jim Cadile	OG	6'3"	240	25		
Mike Rabold	OG	6'2"	238	29		
George Seals	OT-OG	6'2"	260	23		
Roger LeClerc	C	6'3"	235	28		78
Mike Pyle	C	6'3"	250	27		
Doug Atkins	DE	6'8"	255	36	1	
Ed O'Bradovich	DE	6'3"	255	26		6
Brian Schweda	DE	6'3"	240	23		
Frank Cornish	DT	6'6"	285	22		
Dick Evey	DT	6'2"	225	25		
John Johnson	DT	6'5"	260	25		
Bob Kilcullen	DT	6'3"	245	30		

Use Name	Pos.	Hgt	Wgt	Age	Int	Pts
Doug Buffone	LB	6'1"	218	22		
Dick Butkus	LB	6'3"	245	22	1	
Joe Fortunato	LB	6'	225	36	1	6
Jim Purnell	LB	6'2"	225	24		
Mike Reilly	LB	6'2"	238	23		
Charlie Brown	DB	6'1"	193	23		
Curtis Gentry	DB	6'	187	25	1	
Benny McRae	DB	6'1"	180	25	3	
Richie Petitbon	DB	6'3"	205	28	4	
Rosey Taylor	DB	5'11"	186	27	1	
Dave Whitsell	DB	6'	190	30	3	

Andy Livingston – Injury

Use Name	Pos.	Hgt	Wgt	Age	Int	Pts
Rudy Bukich	QB	6'1"	205	35		12
Larry Rakestraw	QB	6'2"	195	24		
Billy Wade	QB	6'2"	205	35		
Jon Arnett	HB	5'11"	203	31		6
Gale Sayers	HB	6'	198	23		72
Brian Piccolo	FB-HB	6'	205	22		
Ralph Kurek	FB	6'2"	210	23		6
Joe Marconi	FB	6'2"	225	32		
Ronnie Bull	HB-FB	6'	200	26		
Johnny Morris	FL	5'10"	180	31		
Duane Allen	TE	6'4"	225	28		
Charlie Bivins	TE	6'2"	212	27		
Mike Ditka	TE	6'3"	230	26		12
Dick Gordon	OE	5'11"	190	21		6
Jim Jones	OE	6'2"	187	22		30
Bobby Joe Green	K	5'11"	175	28		

DETROIT LIONS 4-9-1 Harry Gilmer

Scores of Each Game		
14	CHICAGO	3
3	Pittsburgh	17
28	ATLANTA	10
14	Green Bay	23
7	LOS ANGELES	14
14	Baltimore	45
24	San Francisco	27
7	GREEN BAY	31
10	Chicago	10
32	Minnesota	31
20	BALTIMORE	14
14	SAN FRANCISCO	41
3	Los Angeles	23
16	MINNESOTA	28

Use Name	Pos.	Hgt	Wgt	Age	Int	Pts
Daryl Sanders	OT	6'5"	250	24		
Roger Shoals	OT	6'4"	255	27		
J. D. Smith	OT	6'5"	250	30		
John Gordy	OG	6'3"	250	30		
Bob Kowalkowski	OG	6'3"	245	22		
Doug Van Horn	OG	6'2"	245	22		
Mike Alford	C	6'3"	235	23		
Ed Flanagan	C	6'3"	250	22		
Larry Hand	DE	6'4"	245	26		
Jerry Mazzanti	DE	6'3"	240	26		
Darris McCord	DE	6'4"	250	33		
Roger Brown	DT	6'5"	300	29		
Alex Karras	DT	6'2"	245	30		
Jerry Rush	DT	6'4"	270	24		

Use Name	Pos.	Hgt	Wgt	Age	Int	Pts
Ernie Clark	LB	6'1"	220	28	1	
Bill Cody	LB	6'1"	220	22		
Wally Hilgenberg	LB	6'3"	225	23		
Mike Lucci	LB	6'2"	223	26	5	6
Lou Slaby	LB	6'3"	235	24		
Wayne Walker	LB	6'2"	225	29	1	17
Jim Kearney	DB	6'2"	200	23		
Dick LeBeau	DB	6'1"	185	29	4	
Bruce Maher	DB	5'11"	190	29	5	
Wayne Rasmussen	DB	6'2"	180	24	3	
Bobby Smith	DB	6'	197	28		
Bobby Thompson	DB	5'10"	175	26	4	
Tom Vaughn	DB	5'11"	195	23	1	

Tom Watkins – Operation
Warren Wells – Military Service

Use Name	Pos.	Hgt	Wgt	Age	Int	Pts
Tom Myers	QB	6'	188	22		
Milt Plum	QB	6'1"	205	32		1
Karl Sweetan	QB	6'1"	210	23		6
Bobby Felts	HB	6'2"	202	23		12
Amos Marsh	HB	6'1"	220	27		18
Bruce McLenna	HB	6'3"	225	24		
Jim Todd	HB	5'11"	195	23		
Tom Nowatzke	FB	6'3"	233	23		42
Pat Studstill	FL	6'1"	175	28		30
Willie Walker	FL	6'3"	200	23		
Johnnie Robinson	DB-FL	6'3"	205	21		6
Jim Gibbons	TE	6'2"	220	30		6
Ron Kramer	TE	6'3"	240	31		
Gail Cogdill	OE	6'2"	195	29		6
Bill Malinchak	OE	6'1"	190	22		
John Henderson	FL-OE	6'3"	190	23		
Garo Yepremian	K	5'8"	160	22		50

MINNESOTA VIKINGS 4-9-1 Norm Van Brocklin

Scores of Each Game		
20	San Francisco	20
23	BALTIMORE	38
17	Dallas	28
10	CHICAGO	13
35	LOS ANGELES	7
17	Baltimore	20
28	SAN FRANCISCO	3
20	Green Bay	17
31	DETROIT	32
6	Los Angeles	21
16	GREEN BAY	28
13	ATLANTA	20
28	Detroit	16
28	Chicago	41

Use Name	Pos.	Hgt	Wgt	Age	Int	Pts
Doug Davis	OT	6'4"	240	22		
Chuck Arrobio	OT	6'4"	250	22		
Grady Alderman	OT	6'2"	240	27		
Archie Sutton	OT	6'4"	262	23		
Larry Bowie	OG	6'2"	250	26		
Milt Sunde	OG	6'2"	234	23		
Jim Vellone	OG	6'2"	255	22		
Mick Tinglehoff	C	6'1"	237	26		
Carl Eller	DE	6'6"	255	23		
Jim Marshall	DE	6'3"	235	29		
Paul Dickson	DT	6'5"	255	29		
Gary Larsen	DT	6'5"	250	26		
Jerry Shay	DT	6'3"	240	22		
Mike Tilleman	DT	6'5"	260	22		

Use Name	Pos.	Hgt	Wgt	Age	Int	Pts
Don Hansen	LB	6'3"	226	22		
John Kirby	LB	6'3"	222	24		
Dave Tobey	LB	6'3"	230	23		
Lonnie Warwick	LB	6'3"	225	24	2	
Roy Winston	LB	6'1"	230	26		
Mike Fitzgerald	DB	5'10"	180	25	1	
Dale Hackbart	DB	6'3"	210	30	5	6
Jeff Jordan	DB	6'4"	190	22		
Karl Kassulke	DB	6'	193	24	2	
Earsell Mackbee	DB	6'1"	195	25	2	
George Rose	DB	5'11"	190	23	1	
Ed Sharockman	DB	6'	200	26	1	

Ken Byers – Injury

Use Name	Pos.	Hgt	Wgt	Age	Int	Pts
Bob Berry	QB	5'11"	190	24		
Fran Tarkenton	QB	6'1"	190	26		24
Ron Vander Kelen	QB	6'1"	185	26		
Billy Barnes	HB	5'11"	202	31		6
Jim Lindsey	HB	6'2"	200	21		18
Tommy Mason	HB	6'	196	27		18
Dave Osborn	HB	6'	205	23		18
Jeff Williams	HB	6'1"	210	22		
Jim Young	HB	6'	205	23		
Bill Brown	FB	5'11"	230	28		36
Phil King	HB-FB	6'4"	220	30		6
Jim Phillips	FL	6'1"	195	29		18
Lance Rentzel	OE-FL	6'2"	210	22		
Hal Bedsole	TE	6'4"	230	24		
Preston Carpenter (from WAS)	TE	6'2"	208	32		24
John Powers	TE	6'2"	210	25		
Paul Flatley	OE	6'1"	187	25		18
Tom Hall	FL-OE	6'1"	195	25		12
Fred Cox	K	5'10"	200	27		88
Bobby Walden	K	6'	195	27		

WESTERN CONFERENCE – Continued

LOS ANGELES RAMS

RUSHING

Last Name	No.	Yds	Avg	TD
Bass	248	1090	4.4	8
Moore	104	272	2.6	1
Gabriel	52	176	3.4	3
Josephson	14	97	6.9	0
Stiger	24	95	4.0	0
Meador	1	7	7.0	0
Munson	4	3	0.8	0
Iman	1	2	2.0	0

RECEIVING

Last Name	No.	Yds	Avg	TD
Moore	60	433	7	3
McDonald	55	714	13	2
Snow	34	634	19	3
Bass	31	274	9	0
Truax	29	314	11	0
McKeever	23	277	12	1
Stiger	8	72	9	1
Heckard	5	102	20	0
Josephson	2	10	5	1
Crabb	1	47	47	0
Pope	1	14	14	1

PUNT RETURNS

Last Name	No.	Yds	Avg	TD
Stiger	33	259	8	0
Cross	12	82	7	0

KICKOFF RETURNS

Last Name	No.	Yds	Avg	TD
Williams	15	420	28	0
Cross	12	348	29	0
Stiger	7	150	21	0
Dyer	5	61	12	0
Currie	1	25	25	0
McKeever	1	8	8	0
Lamson	1	3	3	0

PASSING – PUNTING – KICKING

PASSING	Att	Comp	%	Yds	Yd/Att	TD	Int–%	RK
Gabriel	397	217	55	2540	6.4	10	16– 4	7
Munson	50	30	60	284	5.7	2	1– 2	
Kilgore	1	1	100	47	47.0	0	0– 0	
Meador	1	0	0	0	0.0	0	0– 0	
Moore	1	1	100	20	20.0	0	0– 0	

PUNTING	No	Avg
Kilgore	71	42.8

KICKING	XP	Att	%	FG	Att	%
Gossett	29	29	100	28	49	57

SAN FRANCISCO FORTY NINERS

RUSHING

Last Name	No.	Yds	Avg	TD
Willard	191	763	4.0	5
Crow	121	477	3.9	1
Kopay	47	204	4.3	1
Lewis	36	130	3.6	2
Mira	10	103	10.3	0
Davis	3	43	14.3	0
Casey	1	23	23.0	0
Kilmer	3	23	7.7	0
Brodie	5	18	3.6	3
Jackson	4	7	1.8	0
Parks	1	−1	−1.0	0

RECEIVING

Last Name	No.	Yds	Avg	TD
Parks	66	974	15	5
Casey	50	669	13	1
Willard	42	351	8	2
Crow	30	341	11	3
Stickles	27	315	12	2
McFarland	13	219	17	1
Witcher	10	115	12	1
Kopay	10	67	7	1
Lewis	7	44	6	1
Kramer	5	81	16	3
Jackson	1	63	63	1

PUNT RETURNS

Last Name	No.	Yds	Avg	TD
Alexander	30	198	7	1
Kopay	4	28	7	0
Swinford	8	12	2	0
Jackson	2	0	0	0
Donnelly	1	0	0	0

KICKOFF RETURNS

Last Name	No.	Yds	Avg	TD
Alexander	37	984	27	0
Jackson	8	162	20	0
Swinford	4	73	18	0
Lewis	3	65	22	0
Kopay	2	20	10	0
Phillips	1	20	20	0
Hindman	1	2	2	0

PASSING – PUNTING – KICKING

PASSING	Att	Comp	%	Yds	Yd/Att	TD	Int–%	RK
Brodie	427	232	54	2810	6.6	16	22– 5	8
Mira	53	22	42	284	5.4	5	2– 4	
Kilmer	16	5	31	84	5.3	0	1– 6	
Crow	4	2	50	61	15.3	0	1– 25	

PUNTING	No	Avg
Davis	63	41.4
Kilmer	7	33.4

KICKING	XP	Att	%	FG	Att	%
Davis	38	39	97	16	31	52

CHICAGO BEARS

RUSHING

Last Name	No.	Yds	Avg	TD
Sayers	229	**1231**	5.4	8
Bull	100	318	3.2	0
Kurek	52	179	3.4	1
Arnett	55	178	3.2	1
Bukich	18	14	0.8	2
Piccolo	3	12	4.0	0
Marconi	3	5	1.7	0
Gordon	1	2	2.0	0
Rakestraw	1	−5	−5.0	0
Jones	1	−7	−7.0	0

RECEIVING

Last Name	No.	Yds	Avg	TD
Sayers	34	447	13	2
Ditka	32	378	12	2
Jones	28	504	18	5
Bull	20	174	9	0
Gordon	15	210	14	1
Kurek	10	178	18	0
Arnett	10	42	4	0
Morris	5	49	10	0
Allen	3	28	9	0
Bivins	2	6	3	0

PUNT RETURNS

Last Name	No.	Yds	Avg	TD
Arnett	15	58	4	0
Sayers	6	44	7	0
Gordon	4	−5	−1	0

KICKOFF RETURNS

Last Name	No.	Yds	Avg	TD
Sayers	23	718	**31**	**2**
Gordon	19	521	27	0
Arnett	2	39	20	0
Butkus	3	32	11	0
Taylor	1	3	3	0
Brown	0	28	0	0

PASSING – PUNTING – KICKING

PASSING	Att	Comp	%	Yds	Yd/Att	TD	Int–%	RK
Bukich	309	147	48	1858	6.0	10	21– 7	13
Wade	21	9	43	79	3.8	0	1– 5	
Sayers	6	2	33	58	9.7	0	1– 17	
Arnett	1	0	0	0	0.0	0	0– 0	
Bull	1	1	100	21	21.0	0	0– 0	

PUNTING	No	Avg
Green	**80**	42.0

KICKING	XP	Att	%	FG	Att	%
Leclerc	24	25	96	18	30	60

DETROIT LIONS

RUSHING

Last Name	No.	Yds	Avg	TD
Nowatzke	151	512	3.4	6
Marsh	134	433	3.2	3
Sweetan	34	219	6.4	1
Felts	34	83	2.4	2
Plum	12	59	4.9	0
McLenna	16	51	3.2	0
Studstill	2	20	10.0	0
Todd	2	6	3.0	0
Wil. Walker	1	4	4.0	0

RECEIVING

Last Name	No.	Yds	Avg	TD
Studstill	67	**1266**	19	5
Nowatzke	54	316	6	1
Cogdill	47	411	9	1
Kramer	37	432	12	0
Marsh	12	111	9	0
Henderson	6	121	20	0
Malinchak	5	34	7	0
McLenna	3	13	4	0
Felts	2	1	1	0
Wil. Walker	1	21	21	0
Gibbons	1	2	2	1

PUNT RETURNS

Last Name	No.	Yds	Avg	TD
Robinson	13	185	14	1
Vaughn	18	179	10	0
Felts	2	20	10	0
Todd	5	12	2	0

KICKOFF RETURNS

Last Name	No.	Yds	Avg	TD
Vaughn	23	595	26	0
Felts	20	392	20	0
Robinson	6	127	21	0
Todd	3	105	35	0
Slaby	1	14	14	0
Mazzanti	1	8	8	0
Alford	1	0	0	0

PASSING – PUNTING – KICKING

PASSING	Att	Comp	%	Yds	Yd/Att	TD	Int–%	RK
Sweetan	309	157	51	1809	5.9	4	14– 5	11
Plum	146	82	56	943	6.5	4	13– 9	10
Myers	1	0	0	0	0.0	0	1–100	

PUNTING	No	Avg
Studstill	72	41.1

KICKING	XP	Att	%	FG	Att	%
Yepremian	11	11	100	13	22	59
Way. Walker	11	11	100	2	8	25
Plum	1	1	100	0	0	0

MINNESOTA VIKINGS

RUSHING

Last Name	No.	Yds	Avg	TD
Brown	**251**	829	3.3	6
Tarkenton	62	376	6.1	4
Osborn	87	344	4.0	1
Mason	58	235	4.1	2
Lindsey	57	146	2.6	1
Walden	5	82	16.4	0
King	17	40	2.4	0
Vender Kelen	4	19	4.8	0
Barnes	5	16	3.2	1
Berry	3	12	4.0	0
Williams	1	2	2.0	0
Carpenter	1	−10	−10.0	0

RECEIVING

Last Name	No.	Yds	Avg	TD
Flatley	50	777	16	3
Brown	37	359	10	0
Phillips	32	554	17	3
Carpenter	30	518	17	4
Hall	23	271	12	2
Lindsey	20	250	13	2
Osborn	15	141	9	2
Mason	7	39	6	1
King	2	24	12	1
Rentzel	2	10	5	0
Barnes	1	20	20	0

PUNT RETURNS

Last Name	No.	Yds	Avg	TD
Sharockman	9	95	11	0
Rentzel	11	16	1	0
Mason	3	9	3	0
Young	2	7	4	0
Lindsey	2	4	2	0
Williams	4	−2	−1	0

KICKOFF RETURNS

Last Name	No.	Yds	Avg	TD
Fitzgerald	14	301	22	0
Rentzel	9	181	20	0
Hall	7	141	20	0
Young	5	105	21	0
Lindsey	4	79	20	0
King	6	78	13	0
Williams	3	61	20	0
Rose	1	20	20	0
Osborn	1	19	19	0
Winston	1	2	2	0
Sunde	1	0	0	0

PASSING – PUNTING – KICKING

PASSING	Att	Comp	%	Yds	Yd/Att	TD	Int–%	RK
Tarkenton	358	192	54	2561	7.2	17	16– 4	6
Berry	37	13	35	215	5.8	1	5– 14	
Vander Kelen	20	10	50	147	7.4	0	1– 5	
Brown	1	0	0	0	0.0	0	0– 0	
King	1	1	100	9	9.0	0	0– 0	

PUNTING	No	Avg
Walden	60	41.1

KICKING	XP	Att	%	FG	Att	%
Cox	34	34	100	18	33	55

1966 A.F.L. Peace and the Super Bowl

After the New York Giants signed kicker Pete Gogolak away from the Buffalo Bills, the AFL owners decided to declare full-scale war against the NFL. Al Davis, the energetic young leader of the Oakland franchise, was put in charge of the war effort as Commissioner of the League, replacing Joe Foss in April, and an all-out effort was launched to steal star NFL players. Quarterbacks were special targets, with John Brodie and Roman Gabriel considered likely candidates to jump. With the bidding war for graduating collegians already costing clubs heavily, financial competition for established players would make bankruptcy a possibility for some teams. The two leagues sat down to put an end to the suicidal war, and the merger agreement was unveiled in June. Pete Rozelle became Commissioner over both leagues, the AFL agreed to pay reparations to the NFL teams, and a championship game—soon dubbed the Super Bowl—was arranged for the two league champions. By 1970, the AFL would be absorbed into the NFL, with all franchises to remain intact in their present locations. With peace at hand, Al Davis left the AFL office to return to Oakland as managing partner, just in time to preside over the opening of the new Oakland-Alameda County Coliseum. Milt Woodard took over as league president and would guide the league well up until its absorption into the NFL in 1970.

EASTERN DIVISION

Buffalo Bills—Head coach Lou Saban was looking for new challenges after winning two straight AFL championships, so he resigned to become top man at the University of Maryland. Assistant Coach Joe Collier took over the top spot and kept the Bills exactly as Saban had molded them, a tough defensive team with a ball-control offense. With a bad knee bothering Tom Sestak, Jim Dunaway and Ron McDole provided leadership in the defensive line, while the tight linebacking crew of Mike Stratton, Harry Jacobs, and John Tracey held the defense together. In the secondary, Butch Byrd, George Saimes, Hagood Clarke, and Tom Janik strangled enemy passing attacks. The Buffalo offense got help from rookies Bobby Burnett and Bobby Crockett. Burnett joined with Wray Carlton in providing the running necessary for the methodical Buffalo attack, while Crockett won the starting split-end job. The team surpassed last year's squad on paper, but lost twice to Boston during the season and headed into the final weekend a half game behind the Patriots. The Jets did their part by beating the Pats 38-28, and the Bills capitalized by defeating Denver to take their third straight Eastern title.

Boston Patriots—Jim Nance cut down on his weight and set the league on fire with his rushing in his second pro year. Using pure power plus surprising speed, Nance pounded away at defenses in work-horse fashion, gaining an AFL record 1,458 yards and eleven touchdowns for his troubles. Quarterback Babe Parilli used Nance to set up his passes, and receivers Art Graham, Gino Cappelletti, and Jim Whalen gave him targets to hit when not handing off to Nance. Parilli ran the attack so well that John Huarte, the Heisman Trophy winner obtained from the New York Jets, rarely took his warm-up wraps off. The Boston defense stuck to the same lines as in recent years, with a strong front four, a lot of blitzing from middle linebacker Nick Buoniconti, and a lukewarm secondary. With Cappelletti in top form as a place-kicker, the Pats had a final ace whenever their offense stalled in enemy territory. Coach Mike Holovak prepared his team well for the schedule, and the team twice beat the Bills during the year to take a slight lead into the final game of the year against New York, but dropped a 38-28 decision as Parilli passed for 379 yards.

New York Jets—With a wealth of young offensive talent, the Jets made an early run at the Eastern title with four straight wins to open the season. Joe Namath, Matt Snell, George Sauer, Emerson Boozer, Pete Lammons, Winston Hill, Dave Herman, and John Schmitt were all twenty-five years old or less, and veterans like Billy Mathis, Sherman Plunkett, Don Maynard, and Sam DeLuca added stability to this dynamic attack. The defense contained players of widely varied talents. Verlon Biggs, Gerry Philbin, and Al Atkinson were good young talents, but only Larry Grantham had a good season among the veterans. After the good start, several factors caught up with the Jets and dragged them back into third place. The defense had problems stopping enemy passers, Namath had problems with interceptions, and the Jets had problems winning away from Shea Stadium, beating only weak Denver and Miami teams on the road.

Houston Oilers—After losing his job with the St. Louis Cardinals, Wally Lemm returned to the Oilers as head coach for the second time. In his previous term in Texas he had taken the Oilers to a divisional crown in 1961 after being promoted to the top spot in mid-season. This year he went along mostly with the same veterans who had won for him five years ago, but the results were different, only three wins and a tie for fourth place with the fledgling Dolphins. George Blanda, Charley Hennigan, Rich Michael, Don Floyd, Freddy Glick, Bob McLeod, Jim Norton, and Bob Talamini started this year after starting for Lemm in his first regime. Veteran NFL players such as John Henry Johnson and Bernie Parrish further added to the age on the team but contributed little on the field. After opening the season with a 45-7 win over Denver and a 31-0 thumping of Oakland, the Oilers lost most of their games the rest of the way.

Miami Dolphins—The Dolphins had problems at almost every position in their first year, but nowhere more than at quarterback. Of the two passers taken in the expansion draft, Eddie Wilson hurt a knee in training camp and missed the season, while Dick Wood had very little left in his arm. Rookie Rick Norton went out with a fractured jaw in mid-season, leaving coach George Wilson with George Wilson, Jr., his son, as the starting quarterback. Not one to be accused of nepotism, coach Wilson promoted John Stofa from the North American Football League for the last few games, and Stofa came through with four touchdown passes in the season-ending victory over Houston. Stocked mostly with over-the-hill veterans, the Dolphins got their existence off to an auspicious start when Joe Auer returned the opening kickoff of their first game all the way for a touchdown.

WESTERN DIVISION

Kansas City Chiefs—The first AFL Super Bowl representatives swept through their schedule with a powerful offense and well-coordinated defense. The Chiefs had shelled out a lot of money to halfback Mike Garrett in a pre-merger signing, and the short halfback gave the Chiefs a dangerous breakaway runner in the backfield. Curtis McClinton and Bert Coan also pitched in with hard work as ball carriers, making it hard for defenses to watch for Len Dawson passes. Chris Burford continued to run his precise patterns from the split end position, and Otis Taylor provided a deep threat at flanker with a fine sophomore season. Jim Tyrer and Ed Budde starred in the offensive line, but their comrades there showed considerably less consistency. The attack got by on the brilliance of the backs and ends, but the defense got by with a few stars and some mediocre talents.

Oakland Raiders—During Al Davis' two-month term as AFL Commissioner, the Raiders hired Johnny Rauch as their new head coach, and when Davis returned to Oakland as managing partner, some observers expected a conflict between the two men. Davis and Rauch got along well, but the Raiders finished in second place for the third time in four years. The Raiders won four of six meetings with Western opponents but lost three times to Eastern teams to kill their title chances. Despite top performances from Clem Daniels and Art Powell, the attack was a mediocre unit, but the defense played consistently well with flashes of brilliance. Tom Keating, obtained from the Buffalo Bills, used his extraordinary quickness to put a strong rush on enemy passers, and defensive ends Ben Davidson and Ike Lassiter added size to the line. The linebacking showed improvement as the young starters gained experience. The secondary was perhaps the league's best, with Dave Grayson, Kent McCloughan, and Rodger Bird each an individual star. Still, the Raiders needed a little more experience on defense and a little more punch on offense.

San Diego Chargers—The Chargers underwent a lot of changes this year, including a drop out of first place. The team's ownership changed hands in August when Barron Hilton sold the club to a group headed by Eugene Klein and Sam Schulman, and head coach Sid Gillman also sent a group of veteran players into exile. Salary disputes sent defensive linemen Ernie Ladd to Houston and Earl Faison to Miami, and the expansion draft to stock the Dolphins siphoned off defensive backs Jim Warren and Dick Westmoreland. A broken ankle sidelined middle linebacker Chuck Allen for most of the campaign, making the defense a patchwork quilt. Two veterans on offense, halfback Paul Lowe and tackle Ron Mix, suffered through off seasons, but a strong passing attack kept the Chargers rolling. Rookie Gary Garrison joined flanker Lance Alworth in a devastating receiving combo, giving quarterback John Hadl many opportunities to throw the ball. Even with all their problems, the Chargers kept the winning habit by taking their first four games, but once enemy offenses learned they could run on the San Diego line, the Chargers limped home to third place.

Denver Broncos—The Broncos scored the fewest points of any team in pro football, with problems in all sectors of the offense. Quarterbacks came and went on the Denver roster all season. John McCormick started for most of the campaign but showed very little; Mickey Slaughter, an occasional starter for the last three years, rarely got off the bench; veteran Tobin Rote came out of retirement, threw eight passes, and went right back into retirement; and rookies Max Chaboian and Scotty Glacken got late-season starting shots. With the revolving door at quarterback, end Lionel Taylor's catches fell off to thirty-five, his lowest since the AFL began. The running corps was hurt by the absence of Cookie Gilchrist, who held out into the season and was dealt to Miami, and Eldon Danehauer's injury took the best blocker out of the line. The best offense on the Broncos this year came from the kick returners, as Goldie Sellers and Nemiah Wilson scored three times on kickoff returns and Abner Haynes had the second highest average in the league for punt returns. The defense changed personnel less often than the offense but got little better results. The whole situation prompted head coach Mac Speedie to quit after two games, and assistant Ray Malavasi guided the team the rest of the way.

FINAL TEAM STATISTICS

OFFENSE

	BOSTON	BUFFALO	DENVER	HOUSTON	K. CITY	MIAMI	NEW YORK	OAKLAND	SAN DIEGO
FIRST DOWNS:									
Total	243	255	171	246	266	200	254	226	230
by Rushing	100	110	61	76	106	75	81	70	77
by Passing	121	126	95	144	140	103	145	144	137
by Penalty	22	19	15	26	20	22	28	12	16
RUSHING:									
Number	471	455	376	413	439	394	376	363	361
Yards	1963	1892	1173	1515	2274	1410	1442	1427	1537
Average Yards	4.2	4.2	3.1	3.7	5.2	3.6	3.8	3.9	4.3
Touchdowns	17	19	6	11	19	5	15	13	9
PASSING:									
Attempts	393	473	402	485	377	454	514	450	434
Completions	186	199	166	226	199	179	251	212	224
Completion Percentage	47.3	42.1	41.3	46.6	52.8	39.4	48.8	47.1	51.6
Passing Yards	2784	3000	2351	3168	3123	2374	3556	3425	3347
Avg. Yards per Attempt	7.1	6.3	5.8	6.5	8.3	5.2	6.9	7.6	7.7
Avg. Yards per Completion	15.0	15.1	14.2	14.0	15.7	13.3	14.2	16.2	14.9
Times Tackled Att. to Pass	25	16	37	28	30	36	9	34	32
Yards Lost Tackled	211	144	356	271	283	326	92	281	331
Net Yards	2573	2856	1995	2897	2840	2048	3464	3144	3016
Touchdowns	20	15	12	29	31	16	21	26	29
Interceptions	21	21	30	28	15	32	29	26	15
Percent Intercepted	5.3	4.4	7.5	5.8	4.0	7.0	5.6	5.8	3.5
PUNTING:									
Number	76	69	77	69	62	82	62	74	66
Average Distance	36.5	41.2	45.2	42.2	43.8	39.4	42.5	41.6	37.0
PUNT RETURNS:									
Number	24	43	26	23	31	21	36	41	21
Yards	143	411	235	159	276	204	260	367	257
Average Yards	6.0	9.6	9.0	6.9	8.9	9.7	7.2	9.0	12.2
Touchdowns	0	2	0	0	2	0	0	0	1
KICKOFF RETURNS:									
Number	54	51	58	64	54	65	62	60	55
Yards	1145	1064	1558	1514	1148	1507	1300	1191	1282
Average Yards	21.2	20.9	26.9	23.7	21.3	23.2	21.0	19.9	23.3
Touchdowns	0	1	3	0	0	1	1	0	0
INTERCEPTION RETURNS:									
Number	22	29	13	18	33	31	21	23	27
Yards	348	472	109	259	408	522	218	380	359
Average Yards	15.8	16.3	8.4	14.4	12.4	16.8	10.4	16.5	13.3
Touchdowns	0	4	0	0	0	4	1	1	1
PENALTIES:									
Number	64	62	66	71	61	73	64	80	68
Yards	601	637	771	682	680	660	682	752	667
FUMBLES:									
Number	25	27	36	19	21	29	19	22	17
Number Lost	13	15	17	12	16	10	9	12	7
POINTS:									
Total	315	358	196	335	448	213	322	315	335
PAT (kick) Attempts	36	42	20	40	52	23	35	40	40
PAT (kick) Made	35	41	20	39	48	23	34	39	39
PAT (Rush or Pass) Attempts	2	1	2	1	3	3	3	0	1
PAT (Rush or Pass) Made	2	0	1	0	2	2	2	0	0
FG Attempts	32	38	25	30	28	22	35	30	31
FG Made	16	19	14	16	22	10	18	12	16
Percent FG Made	50.0	50.0	56.0	53.3	78.6	45.5	51.4	40.0	51.6
Safeties	0	1	0	1	0	0	1	0	1

DEFENSE

	BOSTON	BUFFALO	DENVER	HOUSTON	K.CITY	MIAMI	NEW YORK	OAKLAND	SAN DIEGO
FIRST DOWNS:									
Total	243	192	251	244	222	237	231	211	260
by Rushing	68	49	101	88	75	83	81	84	127
by Passing	153	131	122	131	125	140	131	106	116
by Penalty	22	12	28	25	22	14	19	21	17
RUSHING:									
Number	369	344	441	422	353	416	388	418	497
Yards	1135	1051	2029	1833	1356	1510	1524	1792	2403
Average Yards	3.1	3.1	4.6	4.3	3.8	3.6	3.9	4.3	4.8
Touchdowns	7	6	17	10	10	15	14	16	19
PASSING:									
Attempts	509	466	396	438	494	425	467	405	382
Completions	247	205	192	209	226	198	212	183	170
Completion Percentage	48.5	44.0	48.5	47.7	45.8	46.6	45.4	45.2	44.5
Passing Yards	3565	3307	2819	3390	2876	3281	3064	2440	2386
Avg. Yards per Attempt	7.0	7.1	7.1	7.7	5.8	7.7	6.6	6.0	6.2
Avg. Yards per Completion	14.4	16.1	14.7	16.2	12.7	16.6	14.5	13.3	14.0
Times Tackled Att. to Pass	22	32	33	21	26	16	35	36	26
Yards Lost Tackled	209	249	304	228	262	180	310	322	231
Net Yards	3356	3058	2515	3162	2614	3101	2754	2118	2155
Touchdowns	26	22	26	35	18	25	19	15	13
Interceptions	22	29	13	18	33	31	21	23	27
Percent Intercepted	4.3	6.2	3.3	4.1	6.7	7.3	4.5	5.7	7.1
PUNTING:									
Number	86	84	60	68	69	64	81	73	52
Average Distance	38.5	39.6	42.7	40.0	41.3	43.9	40.4	41.3	43.0
PUNT RETURNS:									
Number	20	20	38	37	36	40	24	35	16
Yards	127	301	296	269	359	412	121	343	84
Average Yards	6.4	15.1	7.8	7.3	10.0	10.3	5.0	9.8	5.3
Touchdowns	1	2	0	0	1	1	0	0	0
KICKOFF RETURNS:									
Number	46	65	43	60	84	46	57	56	66
Yards	988	1329	1000	1385	2045	939	1368	1268	1387
Average Yards	21.5	20.4	23.3	23.1	24.3	20.4	24.0	22.6	21.0
Touchdowns	0	0	0	2	1	1	1	1	0
INTERCEPTION RETURNS:									
Number	21	21	30	28	15	32	29	26	15
Yards	204	303	545	448	225	370	297	405	278
Average Yards	9.7	14.4	18.2	16.0	15.0	11.6	10.2	15.6	18.5
Touchdowns	2	1	2	3	2	1	2	0	0
PENALTIES:									
Number	76	55	75	69	56	79	85	54	60
Yards	757	546	576	725	592	852	883	614	527
FUMBLES:									
Number	30	19	35	25	21	25	15	28	17
Number Lost	15	9	18	13	8	15	8	17	8
POINTS:									
Total	283	225	381	396	276	362	312	288	284
PAT (kick) Attempts	36	28	46	49	28	42	36	31	32
PAT (kick) Made	34	28	46	49	28	38	34	30	31
PAT (Rush or Pass) Attempts	0	3	1	1	4	2	1	3	1
PAT (Rush or Pass) Made	0	1	1	1	1	1	1	2	1
FG Attempts	26	22	40	30	28	36	28	30	31
FG Made	11	13	17	15	18	18	18	16	17
Percent FG Made	42.3	59.1	42.5	50.0	64.3	50.0	64.3	53.3	54.8
Safeties	0	0	0	0	0	2	0	1	1

1966 AFL CHAMPIONSHIP GAME

January 1, at Buffalo
(Attendance 42,080)

SCORING

BUFFALO	7	0	0	0	– 7
KANSAS CITY	7	10	0	14	–31

First Quarter
K.C. Arbanas, 29 yard pass from Dawson
PAT – Mercer (kick)
BUFF. Dubenion, 69 yard pass from Kemp
PAT – Lusteg (kick)

Second Quarter
K.C. Taylor, 29 yard pass from Dawson
PAT – Mercer (kick)
K.C. Mercer, 32 yard Field goal

Fourth Quarter
K.C. Garrett, 1 yard rush
PAT – Mercer (kick)
K.C. Garrett, 18 yard rush
PAT – Mercer (kick)

TEAM STATISTICS

BUFF.		K.C.
9	First Downs – Total	14
2	First Downs – Rushing	6
7	First Downs – Passing	8
0	First Downs – Penalty	0
8	Punts – Number	6
39.3	Punts – Average Distance	42.3
3	Penalties – Number	4
23	Yards Penalized	40
0	Missed Field Goals	1

Super Reps

This year's AFL title was the most desirable in the league's short history, for this year's champion would get the chance to play the NFL champion in the first Super Bowl. The Buffalo Bills had won the last two AFL titles, but the Kansas City Chiefs solved the tough Buffalo defense and scored a decisive 31-7 victory. Len Dawson passed the Chiefs into a quick 7-0 lead with a 29-yard pass to Fred Arbanas early in the game. The Bills came back to tie the score on a surprise long pass to Elbert Dubenion from Jack Kemp, but the Chiefs moved ahead 14-7 with a second-quarter touchdown pass from Dawson to Otis Taylor. Toward the end of the first half Buffalo appeared on the verge of tying the game, but a key interception spelled disaster for the Bills. With Buffalo driving and but ten yards from a touchdown, Kemp's pass was intercepted in the end zone by Johnny Robinson, who ran the ball back 72 yards to set up a 32-yard field goal by Mike Mercer and run the score to 17-7 at halftime. The third quarter passed without any scoring, and the Chiefs put the game out of reach with a pair of fourth-quarter touchdowns. Mike Garrett, the star rookie halfback, scored from the one-yard line and the 18-yard line on running plays. The Bills remained scoreless and as a result of the Kansas City defense outshining the more famous Buffalo unit, the front four completely stifling the Bills' running game and putting a strong rush on Kemp when he dropped back to pass, the Chiefs became the AFL's first Super Bowl representatives.

INDIVIDUAL STATISTICS

BUFFALO	No	Yds	Avg.	KANSAS CITY	No	Yds	Avg.
RUSHING							
Carlton	9	31	3.4	Garrett	13	39	3.0
Burnett	3	6	2.0	McClinton	11	38	3.5
Kemp	1	3	3.0	Dawson	5	28	5.6
	13	40	3.1	Coan	2	6	3.0
				Eu. Thomas	2	2	1.0
					33	113	3.4
RECEIVING							
Burnett	6	127	21.2	Taylor	5	78	15.6
Dubenion	2	79	39.5	Burford	4	76	19.0
Bass	2	26	13.0	Garrett	4	16	4.0
Crockett	1	16	16.0	Arbanas	2	44	22.0
Carlton	1	5	5.0	McClinton	1	13	13.0
	12	253	21.1		16	227	14.2
PUNT RETURNS							
Byrd	3	0	0.0	Garrett	3	37	12.3
Rutkowski	2	16	8.0				
	5	16	3.2				
KICKOFF RETURNS							
Warner	5	91	18.2	Coan	1	35	35.0
Meredith	1	8	8.0	Garrett	1	3	3.0
	6	99	16.5		2	38	19.0
INTERCEPTION RETURNS							
None				Robinson	1	72	72.0
				Em. Thomas	1	26	26.0
					2	98	49.0

PASSING

	Att	Comp	Comp Pct.	Yds	Int	Yds/ Att.	Yds/ Comp	Yards Lost Tackled
BUFFALO								
Kemp	27	12	44.4	253	2	9.4	21.1	38
KANSAS CITY								
Dawson	24	16	66.7	227	0	9.5	14.2	63

1966 A.F.L. — Eastern Division

BUFFALO BILLS 9-4-1 Joe Collier

Scores of Each Game		
7	San Diego	27
20	KANSAS CITY	42
58	MIAMI	24
27	HOUSTON	20
29	Kansas City	14
10	BOSTON	20
17	SAN DIEGO	17
33	New York	23
29	Miami	0
14	NEW YORK	3
42	Houston	20
31	Oakland	10
3	Boston	14
38	DENVER	21

Use Name	Pos.	Hgt	Wgt	Age	Int	Pts
Stew Barber	OT	6'3"	250	27		
Wayne DeSutter	OT	6'4"	250	22		
Dick Hudson	OT	6'4"	265	26		
Joe O'Donnell	OG	6'2"	252	24		
Remi Prudhomme	OG	6'4"	240	24		
Billy Shaw	OG	6'3"	260	26		
Bob Schmidt	OT-C	6'4"	250	30		
Al Bemiller	OG-C	6'3"	240	27		
Tom Day	DE	6'2"	250	31		
Ron McDole	DE	6'3"	275	26	1	
Dave Costa	DT	6'2"	250	24		
Jim Dunaway	DT	6'4"	280	24		6
Dudley Meredith	DT	6'4"	285	31		
Tom Sestak	DT	6'5"	270	30		
Paul Guidry	LB	6'3"	225	22		
Harry Jacobs	LB	6'2"	226	29	2	
Paul Maguire	LB	6'	228	28		
Marty Schottenheimer	LB	6'3"	225	23	1	
Mike Stratton	LB	6'3"	235	24	3	6
John Tracey	LB	6'3"	228	32	1	
Butch Byrd	DB	6'	211	24	6	12
Hagood Clarke	DB	6'	203	24	5	6
Booker Edgerson	DB	5'10"	188	27		
Tom Janik	DB	6'3"	200	25	8	12
Charlie King	DB	6'	185	23	1	
George Saimes	DB	5'10"	185	24	1	
Charley Warner	DB	5'11"	170	26		6
Jack Kemp	QB	6'1"	200	32		30
Daryle Lamonica	QB	6'2"	218	25		6
Bobby Burnett	HB	6'2"	208	23		48
Allen Smith	HB	6'	200	23		
Wray Carlton	FB	6'2"	230	28		36
Doug Goodwin	FB	6'2"	228	24		
Jack Spikes	FB	6'2"	220	28		24
Elbert Dubenion	FL	6'	190	31		12
Paul Costa	TE	6'4"	255	24		18
Glenn Bass	OE	6'2"	206	27		
Bobby Crockett	OE	6'	195	23		18
Charley Ferguson	OE	6'5"	224	26		6
Pete Mills	OE	5'11"	180	23		
Ed Rutkowski	OE	6'1"	208	25		12
Booth Lusteg	K	5'11"	190	25		98

BOSTON PATRIOTS 8-4-2 Mike Holovak

Scores of Each Game		
0	San Diego	24
24	Denver	10
24	KANSAS CITY	43
24	NEW YORK	24
20	Buffalo	10
35	SAN DIEGO	17
24	OAKLAND	21
10	DENVER	17
27	HOUSTON	21
27	Kansas City	27
20	Miami	14
14	BUFFALO	3
38	Houston	14
28	New York	38

Use Name	Pos.	Hgt	Wgt	Age	Int	Pts
Tom Neville	OT	6'4"	230	22		
Don Oakes	OT	6'3"	255	28		
Karl Singer	OT	6'3"	245	22		
Justin Canale	OG	6'2"	230	22		
Charley Long	OG	6'3"	250	28		
Len St. Jean	OG	6'1"	240	24		
Joe Avezzano	C	6'2"	235	22		
Jon Morris	C	6'4"	240	23		
Jim Boudreaux	DE	6'4"	245	21		
Bob Dee	DE	6'3"	240	33		
Larry Eisenhauer	DE	6'5"	250	26		
Houstine Antwine	DT	6'	270	27		
Jim Hunt	DT	5'11"	245	27		6
Ed Khayat	DT	6'3"	250	31		
John Mangum	DT	6'3"	275	22		
Tom Addison	LB	6'3"	230	30		
Nick Buoniconti	LB	5'11"	220	25	4	
Lonnie Farmer	LB	6'	220	25		
Jim Fraser	LB	6'3"	235	30	1	
Doug Satcher	LB	6'	222	21		
Jay Cunningham	DB	5'10"	180	23		
Dick Felt	DB	6'	185	33	2	
White Graves	DB	6'	185	23	1	
Ron Hall	DB	6'	190	29	6	
Tom Hennessey	DB	6'	185	26	6	
Billy Johnson	DB	5'11"	180	23		
Vic Purvis	DB	5'11"	200	22		
Chuck Shonta	DB	6'	200	28	1	
Don Webb	DB	5'10"	200	27	1	
John Huarte	QB	6'	190	22		
Babe Parilli	QB	6'1"	190	36		6
Tom Yewcic	QB	5'11"	185	34		
J. D. Garrett	HB	5'11"	195	24		
Larry Garron	HB	6'	195	29		54
Bob Cappadonna	FB	6'1"	230	22		8
Jim Nance	FB	6'1"	235	23		66
Joe Bellino	FL	5'9"	185	28		6
Gino Cappelletti	FL	6'	190	32		**119**
Tony Romeo	TE	6'2"	230	27		2
Jim Whalen	TE	6'2"	210	22		24
Jim Colclough	OE	6'	185	30		
Art Graham	OE	6'1"	205	25		24
Ellis Johnson	OE	6'2"	190	22		

NEW YORK JETS 6-6-2 Weeb Ewbank

Scores of Each Game		
19	Miami	14
52	HOUSTON	13
16	Denver	7
24	Boston	24
17	SAN DIEGO	16
0	Houston	24
21	OAKLAND	24
23	BUFFALO	33
3	Buffalo	14
30	MIAMI	13
24	KANSAS CITY	32
28	Oakland	28
27	San Diego	42
38	BOSTON	28

Use Name	Pos.	Hgt	Wgt	Age	Int	Pts
Nick DeFelice	OT	6'3"	250	26		
Mitch Dudek	OT	6'4"	245	22		
Winston Hill	OT	6'4"	274	24		
Sherman Plunkett	OT	6'4"	300	32		
Steve Chomyszak	C-OT	6'5"	265	21		
Sam DeLuca	OG	6'2"	250	30		
Dan Ficca	OG	6'1"	245	27		
Dave Herman	OG	6'2"	255	24		
Pete Perreault	OG	6'3"	245	27		
John Schmitt	C	6'4"	265	23		
Jim Waskiewicz	C	6'4"	227	22		
Verlon Biggs	DE	6'4"	253	23		
Gerry Philbin	DE	6'2"	245	25		
Bill Yearby	DE	6'3"	235	22		
Bert Wilder	DT-DE	6'3"	245	26		
Bob Werl	OG-DE	6'3"	240	23		
Jim Harris	DT	6'4"	280	22		
Paul Rochester	DT	6'2"	250	29		
Henry Schmidt	DT	6'4"	255	29		
Al Atkinson	LB	6'1"	230	23	4	
Ralph Baker	LB	6'3"	228	24		
Paul Crane	LB	6'2"	205	22		
Larry Grantham	LB	6'	206	27	1	
Jim O'Mahoney	LB	6'1"	228	25		
Ray Abruzzese	DB	6'1"	194	28	2	
Bill Baird	DB	5'10"	180	27	5	6
Cornell Gordon	DB	6'	185	25		
Jim Gray	DB	6'	180	24		
Pat Gucciardo	DB	5'11"	185	22		
Sherman Lewis	DB	5'10"	180	24		
Dainard Paulson	DB	5'11"	190	29		
Johnny Sample	DB	6'1"	205	29	6	
Jim Hudson	HB-DB	6'2"	210	23	3	
Dee Mackey – Injury						
Joe Namath	QB	6'2"	190	22		12
Mike Taliaferro	QB	6'2"	205	24		2
Emerson Boozer	HB	5'11"	215	23		36
Earl Christy	HB	5'11"	190	23		
Bill Mathis	HB	6'1"	220	27		18
Allen Smith	HB	5'11"	195	22		
Mark Smolinski	FB	6'	215	27		18
Matt Snell	FB	6'2"	220	24		48
Don Maynard	FL	6'	180	30		30
Sammy Weir	FL	5'9"	170	24		
Pete Lammons	TE	6'3"	235	22		24
Bill Rademacher	OE	6'1"	190	24		
George Sauer	OE	6'1"	206	22		32
Bake Turner	OE	6'	180	26		
Curley Johnson	K	6'	215	31		6
Jim Turner	K	6'2"	205	25		88

HOUSTON OILERS 3-11-0 Wally Lemm

Scores of Each Game		
45	DENVER	7
31	OAKLAND	0
13	New York	52
20	Buffalo	27
38	Denver	40
24	NEW YORK	0
13	MIAMI	20
23	Kansas City	48
23	Oakland	38
21	Boston	27
20	BUFFALO	42
22	SAN DIEGO	28
14	BOSTON	38
28	Miami	29

Use Name	Pos.	Hgt	Wgt	Age	Int	Pts
George Allen	OT	6'7"	270	22		
Glen Ray Hines	OT	6'5"	255	22		
Rich Michael	OT	6'3"	242	27		
Walt Suggs	OT	6'5"	245	27		
Sonny Bishop	OG	6'2"	245	26		
Bob Talamini	OG	6'1"	255	27		
John Wittenborn	OG	6'2"	240	30		
John Frongillo	C	6'3"	255	26		
Gary Cutsinger	DE	6'4"	245	25		
Don Floyd	DE	6'4"	250	27		
Ed Scrutchins	DE	6'3"	260	25		
Scott Appleton	DT	6'3"	255	24		
Jim Hayes	DT	6'4"	260	25		
Pat Holmes	DT	6'5"	270	26		
Ernie Ladd	DT	6'9"	295	27		
George Rice	OG-DT	6'3"	267	22		
Johnny Baker	LB	6'3"	238	25	1	
Garland Boyette	LB	6'1"	238	26		
Danny Brabham	LB	6'4"	233	25		
John Carrell	LB	6'3"	227	23		
Ronnie Caveness	LB	6'1"	225	23	1	
Doug Cline (to SD)	LB	6'2"	230	27	1	6
Bobby Maples	LB	6'3"	245	23		
John Meyer	LB	6'1"	225	24		
Olen Underwood	LB	6'1"	230	24		
Freddy Glick	DB	6'1"	190	29	4	
W. K. Hicks	DB	6'1"	185	23	3	
Bobby Jancik	DB	5'11"	178	26	2	
Jim Norton	DB	6'3"	190	27	4	
Bernie Parrish	DB	5'11"	195	31	2	
Mickey Sutton	DB	6'	190	23		
Allen Trammell	DB	6'	190	24		
Theo Viltz	DB	6'2"	190	23		
George Blanda	QB	6'1"	220	38		87
Buddy Humphrey	QB	6'1"	200	30		
Jacky Lee	QB	6'1"	190	27		
Don Trull	QB	6'1"	190	24		42
Sid Blanks	HB	6'	205	25		12
Ode Burrell	HB	6'	185	26		30
Hoyle Granger	FB-HB	6'1"	225	22		12
John Henry Johnson	FB	6'2"	225	36		18
Donnie Stone	FB	6'2"	205	29		
Charley Tolar	FB	5'7"	200	28		
Larry Elkins	FL	6'1"	190	23		18
Charley Hennigan	FL	6'	187	30		18
Bob McLeod	TE	6'5"	230	27		18
Bob Poole	TE	6'4"	215	24		
Charley Frazier	OE	6'	175	27		72

MIAMI DOLPHINS 3-11-0 George Wilson

Scores of Each Game		
14	OAKLAND	23
14	NEW YORK	19
24	Buffalo	58
10	San Diego	44
10	Oakland	21
24	DENVER	7
20	Houston	13
0	BUFFALO	29
16	Kansas City	34
13	New York	30
14	BOSTON	20
7	Denver	17
18	KANSAS CITY	19
29	HOUSTON	28

Use Name	Pos.	Hgt	Wgt	Age	Int	Pts
Norm Evans	OT	6'5"	235	24		
Ernie Park	OT	6'3"	253	24		
Maxie Williams	OT	6'4"	240	26		
Billy Neighbors	OG	5'11"	245	26		
Ken Rice	OG	6'2"	240	26		
Jim Higgins	OT-OG	6'1"	250	24		
Tom Good	C	6'3"	240	27		
Mike Hudock	C	6'2"	245	31		
Mel Branch	DE	6'2"	230	29		
Whit Canale	DE	6'3"	245	24		
Ed Cooke	DE	6'4"	250	31		
Earl Faison (from SD)	DE	6'5"	265	27	1	
John Holmes	DE	6'2"	248	22		
Lavern Torczon	DE	6'2"	250	30		
Al Dotson	DT	6'4"	255	23		
Tom Nomina	DT	6'5"	270	24		
Rich Zecher	DT	6'2"	240	23		
Bob Bruggers	LB	6'1"	225	22		
Frank Emanuel	LB	6'3"	225	23	1	
Tom Erlandson	LB	6'3"	235	26	3	6
Wahoo McDaniel	LB	6'	230	29	2	
Jack Rudolph	LB	6'3"	225	28	1	
Jack Thornton	LB	6'1"	230	21		
Pete Jaquess	DB	6'	185	24	3	6
John McGeever	DB	6'1"	195	27	2	
Bob Neff	DB	6'1"	185	22	1	
Bob Petrella	DB	6'	185	21		
Hal Wantland	DB	6'	195	22		
Jimmy Warren	DB	5'11"	185	27	5	6
Willie West	DB	5'10"	187	28	8	
Dick Westmoreland	DB	6'1"	195	25	4	6
Ross O'Hanley – Injury						
Eddie Wilson – Knee Injury						
Rick Norton	QB	6'1"	198	22		
John Stofa	QB	6'3"	210	24		
George Wilson	QB	6'1"	190	23		2
Dick Wood	QB	6'5"	200	30		6
Joe Auer	HB	6'1"	200	24		54
Bill Hunter	HB	6'1"	180	23		
Gene Mingo	HB	6'1"	190	27		53
Sam Price	FB-HB	5'11"	215	22		
Rick Casares	FB	6'2"	233	35		6
George Chesser	FB	6'2"	225	23		
Cookie Gilchrist	FB	6'3"	250	31		6
Billy Joe	FB	6'2"	236	25		8
Frank Jackson	FL	6'1"	190	26		12
Bo Roberson	FL	6'1"	190	31		12
John Roderick	FL	6'1"	180	22		6
Bill Cronin	TE	6'4"	230	23		6
Dave Kocourek	TE	6'5"	240	29		12
Wes Mathews	OE	5'10"	180	22		
Stan Mitchell	OE	6'2"	220	22		
Doug Moreau	OE	6'2"	193	21		
Karl Noonan	OE	6'3"	185	22		6
Howard Twilley	OE	5'10"	180	22		

1966 A.F.L. — Eastern Division

BUFFALO BILLS

RUSHING

Last Name	No.	Yds	Avg	TD
Burnett	187	766	4.1	4
Carlton	156	696	4.5	6
Smith	31	148	4.8	0
Kemp	40	130	3.3	5
Spikes	28	119	4.3	3
Dubenion	3	16	5.3	0
Rutkowski	1	10	10.0	0
Lamonica	9	6	0.7	1
P. Costa	0	1	0.0	0

RECEIVING

Last Name	No.	Yds	Avg	TD
Dubenion	50	747	15	2
Burnett	34	419	12	4
Crockett	31	533	17	3
P. Costa	27	400	15	3
Carlton	21	280	13	0
Ferguson	16	293	18	1
Bass	10	130	13	0
Rutkowski	6	150	25	1
Spikes	2	45	23	1
O'Donnell	1	2	2	0
Smith	1	1	1	0

PUNT RETURNS

Last Name	No.	Yds	Avg	TD
Rutkowski	18	209	12	1
Byrd	23	186	8	1
Clarke	2	12	6	0
Stratton	0	4	0	0

KICKOFF RETURNS

Last Name	No.	Yds	Avg	TD
Warner	33	846	26	1
Rutkowski	6	121	20	0
Mills	4	76	19	0
Prudhomme	1	16	16	0
Schmidt	1	2	2	0
DeSutter	2	0	0	0
Ferguson	2	0	0	0
D. Costa	1	0	0	0
Maguire	1	0	0	0
O'Donnell	0	3	0	0

PASSING – PUNTING – KICKING Statistics

PASSING	Att	Comp	%	Yds	Yd/Att	TD	Int–%	RK
Kemp	389	166	43	2451	6.3	11	16– 4	7
Lamonica	84	33	39	549	6.5	4	5– 6	

PUNTING	No	Avg
Maguire	69	41.2

KICKING	XP	Att	%	FG	Att	%
Lusteg	41	42	98	19	38	50

BOSTON PATRIOTS

RUSHING

Last Name	No.	Yds	Avg	TD
Nance	**299**	**1458**	4.9	11
Garron	101	319	3.2	4
Cappadonna	22	88	4.0	1
Parilli	28	42	1.5	1
Huarte	7	40	5.7	0
Garrett	13	21	1.6	0
Yewcic	1	–5	–5.0	0

RECEIVING

Last Name	No.	Yds	Avg	TD
Graham	51	673	13	4
Cappelletti	43	676	16	6
Garron	30	416	14	5
Whalen	29	502	17	4
Colclough	16	284	18	0
Nance	8	103	13	0
Bellino	6	77	13	1
Romeo	2	46	23	0
Garrett	1	7	7	0

PUNT RETURNS

Last Name	No.	Yds	Avg	TD
Purvis	5	43	9	0
Hennessey	7	39	6	0
B. Johnson	7	37	5	0
Bellino	4	19	5	0
Graves	1	5	5	0

KICKOFF RETURNS

Last Name	No.	Yds	Avg	TD
Bellino	18	410	23	0
Cunningham	17	371	22	0
Purvis	8	185	23	0
Garron	2	49	25	0
Cappadonna	3	46	15	0
E. Johnson	2	45	23	0
Singer	1	27	27	0
Mangum	1	8	8	0
Colclough	1	2	2	0
B. Johnson	1	2	2	0

PASSING – PUNTING – KICKING Statistics

PASSING	Att	Comp	%	Yds	Yd/Att	TD	Int–%	RK
Parilli	382	181	47	2721	7.1	20	20– 5	6
Huarte	11	5	46	63	5.7	0	1– 9	

PUNTING	No	Avg
Fraser	53	38.6
Yewcic	20	36.6

KICKING	XP	Att	%	FG	Att	%
Cappelletti	35	36	97	16	32	50

2 POINT XP
Cappadonna
Romeo

NEW YORK JETS

RUSHING

Last Name	No.	Yds	Avg	TD
Snell	178	644	3.6	4
Boozer	97	455	4.7	5
Mathis	72	208	2.9	2
Smolinski	21	69	3.3	2
Namath	6	42	7.0	2
Johnson	2	24	12.0	0

RECEIVING

Last Name	No.	Yds	Avg	TD
Sauer	63	1079	17	5
Maynard	48	840	18	5
Snell	48	346	7	4
Lammons	31	565	14	4
Mathis	22	379	17	1
Smolinski	11	74	7	1
Boozer	8	133	17	0
B. Turner	7	115	16	0
Johnson	1	18	18	1
Weir	1	4	4	0
Rademacher	1	3	3	0

PUNT RETURNS

Last Name	No.	Yds	Avg	TD
Lewis	7	76	11	0
B. Turner	10	60	6	0
Weir	8	48	6	0
Baird	5	35	7	0
Christy	5	23	5	0
Hudson	1	18	18	0

KICKOFF RETURNS

Last Name	No.	Yds	Avg	TD
Boozer	26	659	25	1
Christy	10	203	20	0
Weir	6	121	20	0
Lewis	5	121	24	0
Gray	5	77	15	0
Smolinski	6	59	10	0
B. Turner	2	50	25	0
Wilder	1	6	6	0
Johnson	1	4	4	0

PASSING – PUNTING – KICKING Statistics

PASSING	Att	Comp	%	Yds	Yd/Att	TD	Int–%	RK
Namath	**471**	**232**	49	**3379**	7.2	19	27– 6	4
Taliaferro	41	19	46	177	4.3	2	2– 5	
Hudson	1	0	0	0	0.0	0	0– 0	
Snell	1	0	0	0	0.0	0	0– 0	

PUNTING	No	Avg
Johnson	62	42.5

KICKING	XP	Att	%	FG	Att	%
J. Turner	34	35	97	18	35	51

2 POINT XP
Sauer
Taliaferro

HOUSTON OILERS

RUSHING

Last Name	No.	Yds	Avg	TD
Burrell	122	406	3.3	0
Granger	56	388	6.9	1
Blanks	71	235	3.3	0
Johnson	70	226	3.2	3
Trull	38	139	3.7	7
Tolar	46	105	2.3	0
Stone	6	18	3.0	0
Blanda	3	1	0.3	0
Lee	1	–3	–3.0	0

RECEIVING

Last Name	No.	Yds	Avg	TD
Frazier	57	1129	20	12
Burrell	33	400	12	5
Hennigan	27	313	12	3
McLeod	23	339	15	3
Elkins	21	283	13	3
Blanks	19	234	12	2
Tolar	13	68	5	0
Poole	12	131	11	0
Granger	12	104	9	1
Johnson	8	150	19	0
Stone	1	17	17	0

PUNT RETURNS

Last Name	No.	Yds	Avg	TD
Burrell	8	78	10	0
Jancik	10	62	6	0
Trammell	5	19	4	0

KICKOFF RETURNS

Last Name	No.	Yds	Avg	TD
Jancik	**34**	**875**	26	0
Blanks	21	487	23	0
Trammell	3	63	21	0
Boyette	3	42	14	0
Hayes	2	31	16	0
Burrell	1	16	16	0

PASSING – PUNTING – KICKING Statistics

PASSING	Att	Comp	%	Yds	Yd/Att	TD	Int–%	RK
Blanda	271	122	45	1764	6.5	17	21– 8	9
Trull	172	84	49	1200	7.0	10	5– 3	4
Humphrey	32	15	47	168	5.3	2	1– 3	
Lee	8	4	50	27	3.4	0	1– 13	
Burrell	1	1	100	9	9.0	0	0– 0	
Tolar	1	0	0	0	0.0	0	0– 0	

PUNTING	No	Avg
Norton	69	42.2

KICKING	XP	Att	%	FG	Att	%
Blanda	39	40	98	16	30	53

MIAMI DOLPHINS

RUSHING

Last Name	No.	Yds	Avg	TD
Auer	121	416	3.4	4
Gilchrist	72	262	3.6	0
Joe	71	232	3.3	0
Wilson	27	137	5.1	0
Casares	43	135	3.1	0
Price	31	107	3.5	0
Chesser	16	74	4.6	0
Jackson	2	22	11.0	0
Stofa	3	17	5.7	0
Wood	5	6	1.2	1
Norton	3	2	0.7	0

RECEIVING

Last Name	No.	Yds	Avg	TD
Kocourek	27	320	12	2
Roberson	26	519	20	2
Auer	22	263	12	4
Noonan	17	224	13	1
Jackson	16	317	20	2
Joe	13	116	9	1
Gilchrist	13	110	8	1
Roderick	11	156	14	1
Twilley	10	128	13	0
Casares	8	45	6	1
Cronin	7	83	12	1
Mingo	3	40	13	0
Moreau	2	15	8	0
Price	2	14	7	0
Matthews	1	20	20	0
Chesser	1	4	4	0

PUNT RETURNS

Last Name	No.	Yds	Avg	TD
Auer	5	99	20	0
Neff	10	60	6	0
Matthews	4	38	10	0
Jackson	2	7	4	0

KICKOFF RETURNS

Last Name	No.	Yds	Avg	TD
Auer	28	698	25	1
Neff	15	376	25	0
Matthews	5	109	22	0
Jackson	4	105	26	0
Hunter	5	84	17	0
Jaquess	5	77	15	0
Roderick	1	17	17	0
Branch	1	15	15	0
Bruggers	1	3	3	0
Noonan	0	23	0	0

PASSING – PUNTING – KICKING Statistics

PASSING	Att	Comp	%	Yds	Yd/Att	TD	Int–%	RK
Wood	230	83	36	993	4.3	4	14– 6	10
Wilson	112	46	41	764	6.8	5	10– 9	
Stofa	57	29	51	425	7,5	4	2– 4	
Norton	55	21	38	192	3.5	3	6– 11	

PUNTING	No	Avg
Wilson	42	42.1
McDaniel	32	38.2
Chesser	7	33.3

KICKING	XP	Att	%	FG	Att	%
Mingo	23	23	100	10	22	46

2 POINT XP
Joe
Wilson

KANSAS CITY CHIEFS 11-2-1 Hank Stram

Scores of Each Game		
42	Buffalo	20
32	Oakland	10
43	Boston	24
14	BUFFALO	29
37	DENVER	10
13	OAKLAND	34
56	Denver	10
48	HOUSTON	23
24	SAN DIEGO	14
34	MIAMI	16
27	BOSTON	27
32	New York	24
19	Miami	18
27	San Diego	17

Use Name	Pos.	Hgt	Wgt	Age	Int	Pts
Tony DiMidio	OT	6'3"	250	24		
Dave Hill	OT	6'5"	254	25		
Jim Tyrer	OT	6'6"	292	27		
Denny Biodrowski	OG	6'1"	255	26		
Ed Budde	OG	6'5"	260	25		
Curt Merz	OG	6'4"	267	28		
Al Reynolds	OG	6'3"	250	28		
Hatch Rosdahl	OG	6'5"	250	23		
Wayne Frazier	C	6'2"	245	26		
Jon Gilliam	C	6'2"	240	27		
Aaron Brown	DE	6'5"	250	22		
Chuck Hurston	DE	6'6"	230	23		
Jerry Mays	DE	6'4"	252	26		
Buck Buchanan	DT	6'7"	287	26		
Ed Lothamer	DT	6'5"	270	23		
Andy Rice	DT	6'3"	266	24		
Bud Abell	LB	6'3"	220	25		
Bobby Bell	LB	6'4"	228	26	2	6
Walt Corey	LB	6'	233	28		
Sherrill Headrick	LB	6'2"	240	29	2	
E. J. Holub	LB	6'4"	236	28		
Smokey Stover	LB	6'	227	27	1	
Solomon Brannan	DB	6'1"	188	24		
Jimmy Hill	DB	6'2"	198	37		
Bobby Hunt	DB	6'1"	193	26	10	
Willie Mitchell	DB	6'1"	185	24	3	6
Bobby Ply	DB	6'1"	190	25	1	
Johnny Robinson	DB	6'	205	27	10	6
Fletcher Smith	DB	6'2"	188	22		2
Emmitt Thomas	DB	6'2"	190	23		
Fred Williamson	DB	6'2"	210	28	4	
Pete Beathard	QB	6'2"	210	24		6
Len Dawson	QB	6'	190	32		
Bert Coan	HB	6'4"	220	26		54
Mike Garrett	HB	5'9"	195	22		48
Gene Thomas	HB	6'1"	210	23		6
Curtis McClinton	FB	6'3"	227	28		54
Jerrel Wilson	FB	6'4"	222	25		2
Otis Taylor	FL	6'2"	211	23		48
Fred Arbanas	TE	6'3"	240	27		26
Chris Burford	OE	6'3"	210	28		48
Reg Carolan	OE	6'6"	238	26		18
Frank Pitts	OE	6'2"	190	22		6
Tommy Brooker	K	6'2"	235	26		19
Mike Mercer (from OAK)	K	6'	210	30		98

Curt Farrier – Injury

OAKLAND RAIDERS 8-5-1 Johnny Rauch

Scores of Each Game		
23	Miami	14
0	Houston	31
10	KANSAS CITY	32
20	SAN DIEGO	29
21	MIAMI	10
34	Kansas City	13
24	New York	21
21	Boston	24
38	HOUSTON	23
41	San Diego	19
17	Denver	3
10	BUFFALO	31
28	NEW YORK	28
28	DENVER	10

Use Name	Pos.	Hgt	Wgt	Age	Int	Pts
Jim Harvey	OT	6'5"	245	23		
Harry Schuh	OT	6'2"	260	23		
Bob Svihus	OT	6'4"	245	23		
Wayne Hawkins	OG	6'	240	28		
Palmer Pyle	OG	6'2"	245	29		
Dick Tyson	OG	6'2"	245	22		
Jim Otto	C	6'2"	240	28		
Ben Davidson	DE	6'8"	265	26		
Greg Kent	DE	6'6"	275	23		
Ike Lassiter	DE	6'5"	270	25	1	
Carleton Oats	DT-DE	6'2"	235	23		
Dan Birdwell	DT	6'4"	250	25	1	
Dave Daniels	DT	6'3"	245	25		
Tom Keating	DT	6'3"	247	23		
Rex Mirich	DT	6'4"	250	25		
Bill Budness	LB	6'1"	215	23		
Dan Conners	LB	6'1"	240	24	2	6
Rich Jackson	LB	6'2"	230	25		
Bill Laskey	LB	6'2"	240	23		
Gus Otto	LB	6'2"	220	23		
Ray Schmautz	LB	6'1"	225	23		
J. R. Williamson	LB	6'2"	220	24		
Rodger Bird	DB	5'11"	195	23	4	
Dave Grayson	DB	5'10"	185	27	3	
Joe Krakoski	DB	6'2"	195	29		
Kent McCloughan	DB	6'1"	190	23	4	
Warren Powers	DB	6'	190	25	5	
Howie Williams	DB	6'2"	187	29	3	
Willie Williams	DB	6'	190	23		
Cotton Davidson	QB	6'1"	180	34		
Tom Flores	QB	6'1"	190	29		6
Charlie Green	QB	6'	190	23		
Pervis Atkins	HB	6'1"	195	30		
Pete Banaszak	HB	5'11"	200	22		
Clem Daniels	HB	6'1"	218	29		60
Roger Hagberg	FB	6'2"	215	27		6
Hewritt Dixon	HB-FB	6'2"	225	26		54
Fred Biletnikoff	FL	6'1"	190	23		18
Billy Cannon	TE	6'1"	215	29		12
Tom Mitchell	TE	6'2"	235	22		6
Bill Miller	OE	6'	190	24		
Art Powell	OE	6'3"	212	29		66
Larry Todd	OE	6'1"	185	23		6
Mike Eischeid	K	6'	190	25		70

George Flint – Injury

SAN DIEGO CHARGERS 7-6-1 Sid Gillman

Scores of Each Game		
27	BUFFALO	7
24	BOSTON	0
29	Oakland	20
44	MIAMI	10
16	New York	17
17	Buffalo	17
17	Boston	35
24	DENVER	17
14	Kansas City	24
19	OAKLAND	41
17	Denver	20
28	Houston	22
42	NEW YORK	27
17	KANSAS CITY	27

Use Name	Pos.	Hgt	Wgt	Age	Int	Pts
Gary Kirner	OT	6'3"	248	24		
Ron Mix	OT	6'4"	250	28		
Terry Owens	OT	6'6"	240	22		
Ernie Wright	OT	6'4"	265	26		
Don Estes	OG	6'2"	250	23		
John Farris	OG	6'4"	245	25		
Ed Mitchell	OG	6'2"	280	24		
Walt Sweeney	OG	6'3"	250	25		
Sam Gruneisen	C	6'1"	240	25		
Paul Latzke	C	6'4"	245	24		
Jim Griffin	DE	6'3"	255	24		
Howard Kindig	DE	6'6"	255	25	1	
Fred Moore	DE	6'3"	255	26		
Bob Petrich	DE	6'4"	250	25		
Houston Ridge	DE	6'4"	232	22		
Steve DeLong	DT	6'3"	252	23		
George Gross	DT	6'3"	258	25		
Larry Martin	DT	6'2"	270	24		
Chuck Allen	LB	6'1"	225	26	1	
Frank Buncom	LB	6'1"	240	26		
Dick Degen	LB	6'1"	220	24	1	
Tom Good	LB	6'	230	22		
Emil Karas	LB	6'3"	230	32		
Mike London	LB	6'2"	230	21		
John Milks	LB	6'	222	22	1	
Bob Mitinger	LB	6'2"	230	26		
Rick Redman	LB	5'11"	225	23	2	6
Joe Beauchamp	DB	6'	185	22	2	
Speedy Duncan	DB	5'10"	175	23	7	6
Miller Farr	DB	6'1"	192	23	3	
Kenny Graham	DB	6'	195	24	5	6
Dave Plump	DB	6'1"	195	23		
Jim Tolbert	DB	6'3"	207	22	1	
Bud Whitehead	DB	6'	185	27	2	
Nat Whitmyer	DB	6'	180	25		
Bob Zeman	DB	6'1"	205	29		
John Hadl	QB	6'2"	215	26		12
Dan Henning	QB	6'	195	24		
Steve Tensi	QB	6'5"	215	23		
Paul Lowe	HB	6'	205	29		18
Gene Foster	FB-HB	5'11"	212	23		18
Jim Allison	FB	6'	220	23		12
Keith Lincoln	FB	6'2"	215	27		18
John Travis	FB	6'1"	216	23		
Lance Alworth	FL	6'	180	26		78
Willie Frazier	TE	6'4"	235	23		12
Jacque MacKinnon	TE	6'4"	250	27		36
Gary Garrison	OE	6'1"	195	22		24
Don Norton	OE	6'1"	195	28		
Dick Van Raaphorst	K	5'11"	215	23		87

Pat Shea – Injury

DENVER BRONCOS 4-10-0 Mac Speedie Ray Malavasi

Scores of Each Game		
7	Houston	45
10	BOSTON	24
7	NEW YORK	16
40	HOUSTON	38
10	Kansas City	37
7	Miami	24
10	KANSAS CITY	56
17	San Diego	24
17	Boston	10
3	OAKLAND	17
20	SAN DIEGO	17
17	MIAMI	7
10	Oakland	28
21	Buffalo	38

Use Name	Pos.	Hgt	Wgt	Age	Int	Pts
Lee Bernet	OT	6'2"	245	22		
Bob Breitenstein	OT	6'3"	270	23		
Sam Brunelli	OG	6'1"	240	23		
John Gonzaga	OG	6'3"	250	33		
Jon Hohman	OG	6'1"	245	23		
Bill Keating	OG	6'2"	236	21		
Pat Matson	OG	6'1"	250	22		
Jerry Sturm	OG	6'3"	260	29		
Larry Kaminski	C	6'2"	240	21		
Ray Kubala	C	6'4"	245	24		
Marvin Davis	DE	6'4"	252	22		
Dan LaRose	DE	6'5"	250	26		
Max Leetzow	DE	6'4"	240	23		
George Tarasovic	DE	6'4"	250	37		
Larry Cox	DT	6'2"	250	22		
Jerry Inman	DT	6'3"	255	26		
Ray Jacobs	DT	6'3"	275	26		
Bob Young	DT	6'2"	275	23		
John Bramlett	LB	6'2"	220	25	1	6
Don Gulseth	LB	6'1"	240	24		
Jerry Hopkins	LB	6'2"	235	25	2	
Gene Jeter	LB	6'3"	230	24		
Archie Matsos (to SD)	LB	6'	212	31	3	
Ron Sbranti	LB	6'2"	230	21		
Willie Brown	DB	6'1"	190	25	3	
Billy Fletcher	DB	5'10"	190	22		
Goose Gonsoulin	DB	6'3"	210	28		
John Griffin	DB	6'1"	190	26		
Bob Richardson	DB	6'1"	180	22		
Lew Scott	DB	5'10"	173	23		
Goldie Sellers	DB	6'2"	198	24	3	12
Nemiah Wilson	DB	6'	165	23	1	6
Lonnie Wright	DB	6'2"	205	22	1	
Eric Crabtree	OE-DB	5'11"	190	21		
Max Choboian	QB	6'4"	205	24		12
Scotty Glacken	QB	6'	190	21		
John McCormick	QB	6'1"	190	29		
Tobin Rote	QB	6'3"	220	38		
Mickey Slaughter	QB	6'	190	25		
Abner Haynes	HB	6'	190	28		18
Charley Mitchell	HB	5'11"	185	26		12
Mike Kellogg	FB	6'	220	23		
Darrell Lester	FB	6'2"	220	25		6
Wendell Hayes	HB-FB	6'2"	195	25		6
Bob Scarpitto	FL	5'11"	196	27		32
Al Denson	TE	6'2"	208	24		18
Max Wettstein	TE	6'3"	217	22		
Jason Franci	OE	6'1"	210	22		
Glenn Glass	OE	6'	203	29		
Lionel Taylor	OE	6'2"	215	30		6
Gary Kroner	K	6'1"	200	25		62

Eldon Danenhauer – Injury

KANSAS CITY CHIEFS

RUSHING

Last Name	No.	Yds	Avg	TD
Garrett	147	801	5.5	6
McClinton	140	540	3.9	4
Coan	96	521	5.4	7
Dawson	24	167	7.0	0
Beathard	20	152	7.6	1
G. Thomas	7	53	7.6	1
Taylor	2	33	16.5	0
Wilson	3	7	2.3	0

RECEIVING

Last Name	No.	Yds	Avg	TD
Taylor	58	1297	22	8
Burford	58	758	13	8
Arbanas	22	305	14	4
McClinton	19	285	15	5
Coan	18	131	7	2
Garrett	15	175	12	1
Carolan	7	154	22	3
Pitts	1	11	11	0
Wilson	1	7	7	0

PUNT RETURNS

Last Name	No.	Yds	Avg	TD
Garrett	17	139	8	1
E. Thomas	9	56	6	0
Brown	1	43	43	0
Pitts	1	21	21	1
Williamson	1	10	10	0
Mitchell	1	7	7	0
Ply	1	0	0	0

KICKOFF RETURNS

Last Name	No.	Yds	Avg	TD
E. Thomas	29	673	23	0
Garrett	14	323	23	0
G. Thomas	3	62	21	0
Brannan	1	24	24	0
Coan	1	22	22	0
Brown	1	6	6	0
Stover	3	0	0	0
Taylor	2	0	0	0
Pitts	0	38	0	0

PASSING – PUNTING – KICKING

PASSING	Att	Comp	%	Yds	Yd/Att	TD	Int–%	RK
Dawson	284	159	56	2527	8.9	26	10– 4	1
Beathard	90	39	43	578	6.4	4	4– 4	
Coan	1	1	100	18	18.0	1	0– 0	
Garrett	1	0	0	0	0.0	0	0– 0	
Taylor	1	0	0	0	0.0	0	1–100	

PUNTING	No	Avg
Wilson	61	44.5
Mercer	9	41.4

KICKING	XP	Att	%	FG	Att	%
Mercer	35	38	92	21	30	70
Brooker	13	13	100	2	2	100
Smith	2	4	50	0	0	0

2 POINT XP
Arbanas
Wilson

OAKLAND RAIDERS

RUSHING

Last Name	No.	Yds	Avg	TD
C. Daniels	204	801	3.9	7
Hagberg	62	282	4.6	0
Dixon	68	277	4.1	5
Flores	5	50	10.0	1
Banaszak	4	18	4.5	0
Atkins	14	10	0.7	0
C. Davidson	6	–11	–1.8	0

RECEIVING

Last Name	No.	Yds	Avg	TD
Powell	53	1026	19	11
C. Daniels	40	652	16	3
Dixon	29	345	12	4
Mitchell	23	301	13	1
Hagberg	21	248	12	1
Biletnikoff	17	272	16	3
Cannon	14	436	31	2
Todd	14	134	10	1
Banaszak	1	11	11	0

PUNT RETURNS

Last Name	No.	Yds	Avg	TD
Bird	37	323	9	0
Krakoski	2	19	10	0
Atkins	1	13	13	0
Cannon	1	12	12	0

KICKOFF RETURNS

Last Name	No.	Yds	Avg	TD
Atkins	29	608	21	0
Bird	19	390	21	0
Grayson	6	128	21	0
W. Williams	2	52	26	0
Hagberg	1	13	13	0
Mirich	2	0	0	0
Powers	1	0	0	0

PASSING – PUNTING – KICKING

PASSING	Att	Comp	%	Yds	Yd/Att	TD	Int–%	RK
Flores	306	151	49	2638	8.6	24	14– 5	3
C. Davidson	139	59	42	770	5.5	2	11– 8	
C. Daniels	3	0	0	0	0.0	0	1– 33	
Green	2	2	100	17	8.5	0	0– 0	

PUNTING	No	Avg
Eischeid	64	42.3

KICKING	XP	Att	%	FG	Att	%
Eischeid	37	37	100	11	26	42

SAN DIEGO CHARGERS

RUSHING

Last Name	No.	Yds	Avg	TD
Lowe	146	643	4.4	3
Foster	81	352	4.4	1
Lincoln	58	214	3.7	1
Allison	31	213	6.9	2
Hadl	38	95	2.5	2
Redman	2	14	7.0	0
Alworth	3	10	3.3	0
Tensi	1	–1	–1.0	0
Garrison	1	–3	–3.0	0

RECEIVING

Last Name	No.	Yds	Avg	TD
Alworth	73	1383	19	13
Garrison	46	642	14	4
MacKinnon	26	477	18	6
Foster	26	260	10	2
Lincoln	14	264	19	2
Allison	12	99	8	0
Lowe	12	41	3	0
Frazier	9	144	16	2
Norton	4	50	13	0
Hadl	2	–13	–7	0

PUNT RETURNS

Last Name	No.	Yds	Avg	TD
Duncan	18	238	13	1
Graham	2	15	8	0
Plump	1	4	4	0

KICKOFF RETURNS

Last Name	No.	Yds	Avg	TD
Duncan	25	642	26	0
Plump	15	345	23	0
Lowe	7	167	24	0
Beauchamp	4	64	16	0
Farr	2	54	27	0
Whitmyer	1	10	10	0
Gruneisen	1	0	0	0

PASSING – PUNTING – KICKING

PASSING	Att	Comp	%	Yds	Yd/Att	TD	Int–%	RK
Hadl	375	200	53	2846	7.6	23	14– 4	2
Tensi	52	21	40	405	7.8	5	1– 2	
Lincoln	4	2	50	71	17.8	1	0– 0	
Lowe	3	1	33	25	8.3	0	0– 0	

PUNTING	No	Avg
Redman	66	37.0

KICKING	XP	Att	%	FG	Att	%
Van Raaphorst	29	40	98	16	31	52

DENVER BRONCOS

RUSHING

Last Name	No.	Yds	Avg	TD
Hayes	105	417	4.0	1
Haynes	129	304	2.4	2
Mitchell	70	199	2.8	0
Scarpitto	4	110	27.5	1
Lester	34	84	2.5	0
Choboian	21	45	2.1	2
Slaughter	1	10	10.0	0
Kellogg	6	3	0.5	0
McCormick	4	2	0.5	0
Glacken	2	–1	–0.5	0

RECEIVING

Last Name	No.	Yds	Avg	TD
Haynes	46	480	10	1
Denson	36	725	20	3
Taylor	35	448	13	1
Scarpitto	21	335	16	4
Mitchell	14	239	17	2
Hayes	8	49	6	0
Lester	2	26	13	1
Crabtree	1	38	38	0
Franci	1	8	8	0
Kellogg	1	5	5	0
Wright	1	–2	–2	0

PUNT RETURNS

Last Name	No.	Yds	Avg	TD
Haynes	10	119	12	0
Scott	7	56	8	0
Sellers	6	49	8	0
Wilson	2	10	5	0
Lester	1	1	1	0

KICKOFF RETURNS

Last Name	No.	Yds	Avg	TD
Sellers	19	541	28	2
Wilson	10	309	31	1
Scott	9	282	31	0
Haynes	9	229	25	0
Crabtree	5	129	26	0
Mitchell	3	55	18	0
Lester	1	11	11	0
Sturm	1	2	2	0
Inman	1	0	0	0

PASSING – PUNTING – KICKING

PASSING	Att	Comp	%	Yds	Yd/Att	TD	Int–%	RK
McCormick	193	68	35	993	5.1	6	15– 8	11
Choboian	163	82	50	1110	6.8	4	12– 7	8
Slaughter	25	7	28	124	5.0	1	0– 0	
Glacken	11	6	55	84	7.6	1	0– 0	
Rote	8	3	38	40	5.0	0	1– 13	
Haynes	2	0	0	0	0.0	0	2–100	

PUNTING	No	Avg
Scarpitto	76	45.8

KICKING	XP	Att	%	FG	Att	%
Kroner	20	20	100	14	25	56

2 POINT XP
Scarpitto

Super Bowl I

January 15, at Los Angeles
(Attendance 61,946)

Thirty Minutes of Equality

It seemed somehow unreal. The Green Bay Packers and the Kansas City Chiefs had always been parts of different universes in the world of sports. But here they were, the champions of the NFL and the AFL, meeting on the field in a confrontation many thought was years away.

Until recently, the NFL had not even recognized that the AFL was there. The established league considered the newer league an inferior and annoying upstart, worthy only of contempt when it first began. But while AFL scores were never posted in NFL stadia, NFL owners felt the AFL's presence directly when the new league began signing a fair share of top players and driving player salaries up in general. Despite the icy external show, fans knew that the NFL people wanted nothing better than the death of the AFL.

The AFL people, however, had never denied the NFL's existence; in fact, they used the older league as an open measure of their own league. NFL games were reported right along with AFL games on the scoreboard, as if both belonged on an equal footing, and AFL clubs were measured by the hypothetical situation of how they would do against a good NFL team. Ultimate success for the AFL would be standing shoulder to shoulder with the NFL.

The war between the leagues had been fought in courtrooms and the press, with subpoenas and checkbooks. The NFL looked down on the new league with utter disdain at first, but as the rich men who owned AFL clubs bid up player salaries and threatened to lure away established NFL stars, the officials of the older league decided to swallow some pride and look for a way to end the war between the circuits.

Negotiations in the spring brought about a peace agreement between the leagues that changed the structure of pro football as it had been in the 1960s. The NFL and AFL agreed to end their financial war by holding a common draft of college seniors and respecting each other's player contracts, and although the AFL clubs had to pay reparations, the clubs of both leagues now were coequal members of a joint structure. By the end of the decade, the AFL would be absorbed completely into an expanded NFL.

But the biggest dividend for the football fan was the establishment of an NFL-AFL championship game between the two league champions. Unofficially dubbed "The Super Bowl" by the media, this game would bring together the top teams in two leagues which had never played each other. This year's game would be unprecedented.

Older fans, of course, remembered the startling entry of the Cleveland Browns into the NFL in 1950. The Browns had completely dominated the AAFC during its four-year existence, but many fans and reporters looked on that circuit as an inferior league. The Browns relished the chance to prove that *they* were not inferior, and they decisively defeated the defending champion Philadelphia Eagles in their first confrontation with NFL competition. The Browns went on to take the league title in that first season, and some fans liked the chances of the AFL team in the Super Bowl because of the Browns' example.

Emerging as the AFL champion and Super Bowl representative were the Kansas City Chiefs, a team which had played three years in Dallas before moving to Missouri. Owned by Lamar Hunt and coached from the beginning by Hank Stram, the Chiefs had compiled an 11-2-1 record during the season and dissected a strong Buffalo team in the AFL championship game. Len Dawson, who had been waived out of the NFL after five years of bench-sitting, had found himself as a quarterback in the AFL, excelling both as a passer and a play-caller. Otis Taylor, Mike Garrett, Ed Budde, Jim Tyrer, and Buck Buchanan were all talented young pros who obviously could make most teams in the NFL. For the rest of the Kansas City offense and most of the defense, a lingering doubt remained. How well would these men, all solid AFL players, make out against the best the NFL could offer?

That best, for the fourth time in the last six years, was the Green Bay Packers, that hard-hitting precision machine hand-built by coach Vince Lombardi. Although the parts were aging, Lombardi's machine still was a multifaceted wonder. His offensive line was quietly but constantly effective in moving people aside, and the running backs were the hard-nosed types who thrived on power sweeps and off-tackle smashes. At the heart of the attack was quarterback Bart Starr, a marvelous football tactician with a penchant for throwing very few interceptions. The Packer defense had set standards for all pro-football teams. Green Bay's mobile front four, big yet fast linebackers, and ball-hawking man-to-man pass defenders had written the book on modern defense. Presiding over it all and adding the special edge was coach Lombardi, the inspirational leader, the tough disciplinarian, the devout Catholic and family man, and a football theorist who set a tone for pro football which still is strong. Lombardi believed that the team that blocks and tackles best wins, and he drilled his teams to block crisply, to tackle hard, and to win.

So, on a warm January day in Los Angeles, the champions of two different leagues who played the same game but had never met came together on the same field. At first it was strange to see these two teams at the same time, but the fans and teams themselves soon settled into a very important football game for a lot of money plus the title of champion of all professional football.

The Chiefs fought the Packers to a standstill for most of the first period, but Green Bay got onto the scoreboard with a 37-yard pass from Bart Starr to Max McGee. Filling in for the injured Boyd Dowler, the thirty-four-year-old McGee would haul in seven passes today; eased out of the starting lineup this past season, he had caught only three passes during the regular campaign.

The Packers, however, were giving the Chiefs their first taste of what NFL teams had had to put up with for years. The only AFL fullback who had ever run with the ferocity of Jim Taylor was Cookie Gilchrist, who now was past his prime. The AFL had never produced as violent and perceptive a middle linebacker as Ray Nitschke, or as devastating a pair of corner linebackers as Dave Robinson and Lee Roy Caffey. The first quarter ended with the score only 7-0, but the Packers seemed to be on the verge of blowing the game wide open.

Far from folding, however, the Chiefs played their best football of the afternoon in the second period. Dawson's passes seemingly were finding gaps in the Packers' pass defense. Throwing both to his ends and backs, Dawson methodically moved the Chiefs downfield until they had the ball on the Green Bay seven-yard line. A short pass to fullback Curtis McClinton carried the ball into the end zone and marked the first time an AFL team had scored on an NFL team; some experts had freely predicted a Green Bay shutout in this contest. Seconds after the touchdown, Mike Mercer's extra-point kick knotted the score at 7-7.

With all expectations of an easy rout laid to rest, the Packers went to work on the next series of downs. Mixing passes and running plays, Starr drove the Packers deep into Kansas City territory, keying on several weak points he had discovered in the Chiefs' defense. He found that the Packers could run at end Chuck Hurston and tackle Andy Rice and throw against Sherrill Headrick, Fred Williamson, and Willie Mitchell; these men had held up against AFL competition but seemed out of their depth against the Packers. Green Bay especially enjoyed throwing against Williamson, since he had bragged that his hammer tackle, which was really only a forearm smash, would wreak havoc with the Packers. In the second half, Williamson himself would be carried from the field unconscious, the victim of a Green Bay "hammer tackle" of sorts.

Moving fairly easy through the Chiefs, the Packers scored their second touchdown on a 14-yard run by Jim Taylor, who simply ran over several Chiefs on the way to the end zone. Don Chandler's kick made the score 14-7, but the Chiefs were not yet ready to give up. Dawson responded with his own passing attack, and a 31-yard Mercer field goal cut the Green Bay lead to 14-10 at halftime.

The Chiefs had stayed surprisingly close to the Packers in the first half, and a good final thirty minutes of play could have brought them an upset victory. Beginning the second half with high hopes, the Chiefs quickly met with a misfortune which let all the air out of them. Dawson dropped back to pass but was surrounded by a strong Green Bay pass rush; instead of eating the ball and taking the loss, he heaved the ball downfield. Willie Wood of the Packers picked it off and brought it back all the way to the Kansas City five-yard line. Elijah Pitts carried it over from there, and the game was never the same afterward. The Packers oozed confidence the rest of the afternoon, while the Chiefs simply looked outmanned.

Dawson found it much harder to move the ball in the second half, and the Chiefs never threatened to score in the final two periods. The Packers, meanwhile, took firm control of the game with good blocking and tackling. Max McGee's second touchdown catch of the day built the Packer lead up to 28-10 after three quarters, and Elijah Pitts' second touchdown run made the final score 35-10.

The Chiefs came away beaten but not disgraced. Although the Green Bay steamroller eventually ground them down, the Chiefs never gave up, and their first-half showing proved that an AFL club could hold its own with a top NFL club—at least for thirty minutes. Coach Stram did learn from the game which of his players could be exploited by a strong club, and he was making plans to replace certain men before a week had passed after the game.

For Vince Lombardi and the Packers, the victory added one more trophy to their collection. Green Bay had won several NFL titles in the 1960s, and now they had won the Super Bowl, a distinct product of this decade.

Some people claimed that Super Bowl I proved the inferiority of the AFL. Probably closer to the truth was the statement that the Chiefs were not inferior to the NFL, only to the Green Bay Packers.

KANSAS CITY		GREEN BAY
	OFFENSE	
Burford	LE	Dale
Tyrer	LT	Skoronski
Budde	LG	Thurston
Frazier	C	Curry
Merz	RG	Kramer
Hill	RT	Gregg
Arbanas	RE	Fleming
Dawson	QB	Starr
O. Taylor	FL	Dowler
Garrett	HB	E. Pitts
McClinton	FB	J. Taylor
	DEFENSE	
Mays	LE	Davis
Rice	LT	Kostelnik
Buchanan	RT	Jordan
Hurston	RE	Aldridge
Bell	LLB	D. Robinson
Headrick	MLB	Nitschke
Holub	RLB	Coffey
Williamson	LCB	Adderley
Mitchell	RCB	Jeter
Hunt	LS	T. Brown
J. Robinson	RS	Wood

SUBSTITUTES

KANSAS CITY

Offense

Beathard	Gilliam
Biodrowski	F. Pitts
Carolan	Reynolds
Coan	G. Thomas
DiMidio	

Defense

Abell	Smith
A. Brown	Stover
Corey	E. Thomas
Ply	

Kickers

Mercer	Wilson

GREEN BAY

Offense

B. Anderson	Long
D. Anderson	Mack
Bowman	McGee
Bratkowski	Vandersea
Gillingham	Wright
Grabowski	

Defense

B. Brown	Heathcock
Crutcher	Weatherwax
Hart	

Kicker

Chandler

SCORING

KANSAS CITY	0	10	0	0—10
GREEN BAY	7	7	14	7—35

First Quarter
G.B. McGee, 37 yard pass from Starr
PAT – Chandler (kick)

Second Quarter
K.C. McClinton, 17 yard pass from Dawson PAT – Mercer (kick)
G.B. Taylor, 14 yard rush
PAT – Chandler (kick)
K.C. Mercer, 31 yard field goal

Third Quarter
G.B. Pitts, 5 yard rush
PAT – Chandler (kick)
G.B. McGee, 13 yard pass from Starr
PAT – Chandler (kick)

Fourth Quarter
G.B. Pitts, 1 yard rush
PAT – Chandler (kick)

TEAM STATISTICS

K. C.		G.B.
17	First Downs – Total	21
4	First Downs – Rushing	10
12	First Downs – Passing	11
1	First Downs – Penalty	0
1	Fumbles – Number	1
0	Fumbles – Lost Ball	0
4	Penalties – Number	4
26	Yards Penalized	40
64	Total Offensive Plays	64
239	Total Net Yards	358
3.7	Average Gain	5.6
1	Missed Field Goals	0
1	Giveaways	1
1	Takeaways	1
0	Difference	0

* includes Punts

INDIVIDUAL STATISTICS

KANSAS CITY	No	Yds	Avg.	GREEN BAY	No	Yds	Avg.
			RUSHING				
Dawson	3	24	8.0	Taylor	16	53	3.3
Garrett	6	17	2.8	Pitts	11	45	4.1
McClinton	6	16	2.7	D. Anderson	4	30	7.5
Beathard	1	14	14.0	Grabowski	2	2	1.0
Coan	3	1	0.3		33	130	3.9
	19	72	3.8				
			RECEIVING				
Burford	4	67	16.8	McGee	7	138	19.7
Taylor	4	57	14.3	Dale	4	59	14.8
Garrett	3	28	9.3	Pitts	2	32	16.0
McClinton	2	34	17.0	Fleming	2	22	11.0
Arbanas	2	30	15.0	Taylor	1	–1	–1.0
Carolan	1	7	7.0		16	250	15.6
Coan	1	5	5.0				
	17	228	13.4				
			PUNTING				
Wilson	7		45.3	Chandler	3		43.3
				D. Anderson	1		43.0
					4		43.3
			PUNT RETURNS				
Garrett	2	17	9.5	D. Anderson	3	25	8.3
E. Thomas	1	2	2.0	Wood	1	–2	–2.0
	3	19	6.3		4	23	5.8
			KICKOFF RETURNS				
Coan	4	87	21.8	Adderley	2	40	20.0
Garrett	2	43	21.5	D. Anderson	1	25	25.0
	6	130	21.7		3	65	21.7
			INTERCEPTION RETURNS				
Mitchell	1	0	0.0	Wood	1	50	50.0

PASSING

KANSAS CITY	Att	Comp	Comp Pct.	Yds	Int	Yds/ Att.	Yds/ Comp	Yards Lost Tackled
Dawson	27	16	59.3	211	1	7.8	13.2	43
Beathard	5	1	20.0	17	0	3.4	17.0	18
	32	17	53.1	228	1	7.1	13.4	6–61
GREEN BAY								
Starr	23	16	69.6	250	1	10.9	15.6	3–22
Bratkowski	1	0	0.0	0	0	–	–	0
	24	16	66.7	250	1	10.4	15.6	3–22

1967 N.F.L. Four Crowns and Then Some

With expansion to New Orleans bringing league membership to sixteen clubs, the NFL revamped its post-season playoff system by dividing the Eastern and Western conferences into four four-team divisions. The champions of the Coastal and Central divisions would meet for the Western crown, and the champions of the Capitol and Century divisions would meet for the Eastern crown; the winners of these matches then would clash for the NFL championship. This new arrangement expanded post-season title play to three weeks, with conference championships, the league championship, and the Super Bowl.

EASTERN CONFERENCE — CAPITOL DIVISION

Dallas Cowboys—Injuries to Don Meredith, Dan Reeves, and Dave Manders slowed the offense up, but the Cowboys still had more than enough power to take the Capitol Division crown. The Cowboys had depth few teams could match, so that coach Tom Landry could find adequate replacements for his wounded troops. When quarterback Meredith missed three games, young Craig Morton filled in well, and Mike Connelly took over for Manders at center. The Dallas defense kept its fine edge, with Bob Lilly, Chuck Howley, and Cornell Green winning All-Pro honors.

Philadelphia Eagles—A disappointing season had fans calling for coach Joe Kuharich's ouster at the end of the year. The Eagles hoped to challenge the Cowboys after obtaining receivers Gary Ballman and Mike Ditka, but with their rash of injuries the Eagles were lucky to hold onto second place. Timmy Brown, Bob Brown, Lane Howell, Al Nelson, Ditka, and Ballman all missed stretches of the schedule. Despite poor protection, quarterback Norm Snead had a good year, with flanker Ben Hawkins his chief pass receiver. The Eagle defense, however, could be blamed more on a lack of talent in the line than on injuries.

Washington Redskins—Three Redskin receivers finished in the top four in the receiving statistics, and Sonny Jurgensen won the league passing title, yet the Skins finished in third place in the Capitol Division. The running and kicking games gave the passing attack little support, so opposing defenses knew the Redskins would come out throwing. Coach Otto Graham thought he had found a good fullback in first-draft choice Ray McDonald, but the big freshman was a big disappointment.

New Orleans Saints—Coach Tom Fears stocked his team liberally with veterans, with Billy Kilmer, Jim Taylor, Ray Poage, Dough Atkins, Earl Leggett, Lou Cordileone, Jackie Burkett, and Dave Whitsell all key men. The Saints did uncover two good rookies in Dan Abramowicz, a slow-footed receiver with good moves, and defensive tackle Dave Rowe, but the team relied mostly on oldsters whose best days were behind them.

CENTURY DIVISION

Cleveland Browns—A bad arm troubled quarterback Frank Ryan, defensive ends Paul Wiggin and Bill Glass slumped off in their early thirties, Erich Barnes was slowing up at cornerback, and forty-three-year-old Lou Groza was not getting the old zip into his kicks. The Browns still had top performers in Leroy Kelly, Paul Warfield, Gary Collins, Dick Schafrath, Gene Hickerson, Jim Houston and other veterans at their peak, and with the other clubs in the Century Division experiencing problems, the Browns coasted to the title without much of a challenge.

New York Giants—The Giants sent a bundle of draft choices to Minnesota for quarterback Fran Tarkenton, and the scrambling quarterback immediately injected an element of excitement back into the team. Tarkenton found a kindred spirit in split end Homer Jones, a fast receiver who ran around until he got open rather than execute precise pass patterns; Tarkenton found Jones in the open often enough for Jones to gain 1,209 yards and score thirteen touchdowns.

St. Louis Cardinals—The Cards had some of the league's best talent, a flashy blitzing defense, and a top place-kicker in Jim Bakken, but head coach Charlie Winner had his hands full of problems this season. Before the regular season even started, quarterback Charley Johnson was drafted into the Army, leaving inexperienced Jim Hart at the throttle; the youngster showed a strong arm and a tendency to throw interceptions. By the end of the year, racial tension burst into the open, with black players claiming that not enough of them were used on defense.

Pittsburgh Steelers—Bill Nelsen's bad knees again forced the Steelers to field a substitute quarterback for part of the season, and this year's emergency passer was Kent Nix, former Green Bay taxi-squader. The Pittsburgh offense frightened few opponents, but the defense was a solid, hard-working unit that kept the Steelers in most of their games. The club won only four games, but their losses included a 27-24 decision to New York and a 15-10 defeat by Washington.

WESTERN CONFERENCE — CENTRAL DIVISION

Green Bay Packers—Coach Vince Lombardi thought he was well covered at running back despite the departure of both Jim Taylor and Paul Hornung from the roster, but injuries sent him scurrying in all directions for healthy ball-carriers. Elijah Pitts and Jim Grabowski missed the late-season games with physical ills, leaving Lombardi with only Donny Anderson from the regular runners. To flesh out the backfield, Lombardi picked up journeymen Ben Wilson and Chuck Mercein and started playing rookie Travis Williams at halfback. Williams was the talk of the league with his blistering kickoff returning, and now he combined with the other substitute Packer ball-carriers in a backfield that didn't look good but punched out the necessary yardage to win.

Chicago Bears—The Bear defense regularly held opponents under 20 points, but the offense rarely capitalized on this during the first half of the schedule. Over the last seven games, however, the offense generated enough points to win five and tie one. Gale Sayers shone as usual throughout the year, but other players helped him move the ball down the stretch. Jack Concannon, the scrambling quarterback obtained from Philadelphia for Mike Ditka, settled comfortably into the Chicago system after October, hustling Brian Piccolo provided a running threat besides Sayers, and Dick Gordon developed into a dangerous receiver. After this flourishing finish, seventy-three-year-old George Halas called it quits as a coach.

Detroit Lions—The team had problems in the passing and kicking departments, but two gilt-edge rookies entertained fans all season. Halfback Mel Farr ran for 860 yards to give the Lions their first running threat in years. In the defensive secondary, rookie Lem Barney covered the league's best receivers without giving anything away, and once he got his hands on an errant enemy pass he threatened to sprint away to a touchdown.

Minnesota Vikings—Gone were coach Norm Van Brocklin, Fran Tarkenton, and Tommy Mason, and coming down from Canada were new head coach Bud Grant and quarterback Joe Kapp. The trade of Tarkenton to New York gave the Vikings some extra high draft choices, so their rookie class was a rich one, including Alan Page, Gene Washington, Clint Jones, John Beasley, and Bob Grim.

COASTAL DIVISION

Los Angeles Rams—Myron Pottios took over for the retired Bill George at middle linebacker, and big Roger Brown was purchased from Detroit to replace the injured Rosie Grier, but the defense continued to play with an almost perfect teamwork. Quarterback Roman Gabriel ran a ball-control offense that scored enough points to win eleven games and lose only one during the season. The Baltimore Colts stayed right with the Rams in the standings, but Los Angeles took the Coastal title by outscoring Baltimore in their two meetings.

Baltimore Colts—Even while replacing some old veterans, the Colts still swept to a 11-1-2 record. Receivers Ray Berry and Jimmy Orr went out with injuries, and subs Willie Richardson and Alex Hawkins filled in in fine fashion. Offensive tackle Jim Parker retired in mid-season with physical ills, and Sam Ball effectively plugged the hole in the line. Two rookies, huge tackle Bubba Smith and safety Rick Volk, saved a lot of action on defense. But Johnny Unitas and the tough Colt defense kept the Colts strong during all the changes.

San Francisco '49ers—Quarterback John Brodie was inconsistent, split end Dave Parks was hurt, and the team lost three of four games with the Rams and Colts. The defense developed into a solid unit, with a strong pass rush, a top linebacker in Dave Wilcox, and two good cornerbacks in Jim Johnson and Kermit Alexander, but the offense lacked the firepower to move the club above the .500 mark.

Atlanta Falcons—The rookie crop brought little help, leaving the Falcons with the same top men as last year. Tommy Nobis, Randy Johnson, and Junior Coffey continued the strong play of their rookie seasons, but coach Norb Hecker could augment his squad only with castoffs from other clubs as defensive tackle Jim Norton, split end Jerry Simmons, and veteran flanker Tommy McDonald helped out among the bargain acquisitions.

FINAL TEAM STATISTICS

OFFENSE

	ATL.	BALT.	CHI.	CLEV.	DALL.	DET.	G.B.	L.A.	MINN.	N.O.	N.Y.	PHIL.	PITT.	ST.L.	S.F.	WASH.
FIRST DOWNS:																
Total	180	289	175	238	261	215	243	262	199	220	274	239	252	248	242	280
by Rushing	68	105	98	119	109	104	115	106	91	67	115	69	83	97	101	82
by Passing	95	159	62	102	141	92	112	133	85	135	135	146	145	131	121	177
by Penalty	17	25	15	17	11	19	16	23	23	18	24	24	24	20	20	21
RUSHING:																
Number	344	443	489	444	477	473	474	490	454	334	436	328	431	472	434	345
Yards	1303	1645	1852	2139	1900	1907	1915	1906	1811	1192	1864	1250	1397	1839	1764	1247
Average Yards	3.8	3.7	3.8	4.8	4.0	4.0	4.0	3.9	4.0	3.6	4.3	3.8	3.2	3.9	4.1	3.6
Touchdowns	6	21	12	15	13	14	18	16	10	9	16	12	13	15	16	13
PASSING:																
Attempts	370	457	268	333	417	351	331	390	336	478	406	445	442	431	469	527
Completions	179	265	131	160	210	160	182	206	150	237	221	244	214	204	228	301
Completion Percentage	48.4	58.0	48.9	48.0	50.4	45.6	55.0	52.8	44.6	49.6	54.4	54.8	48.4	47.3	48.6	57.1
Passing Yards	2144	3561	1673	2314	3093	1826	2758	2947	1951	2989	3382	3463	2781	3170	2862	3887
Average Yards per Attempt (Gross)	5.8	7.8	6.2	6.9	7.4	5.2	8.3	7.6	5.8	6.3	8.3	7.8	6.3	7.4	6.1	7.4
Average Yards per Completion (Gross)	12.0	13.4	12.8	14.5	14.7	11.4	15.2	14.3	13.0	12.6	15.3	14.2	13.0	15.5	12.6	12.9
Times Tackled Attempting to Pass	49	25	27	44	42	24	41	25	35	52	37	49	30	24	26	19
Yards Lost Tackled Attempting to Pass	434	198	232	372	294	195	394	213	284	391	342	369	270	229	208	157
Net Yards	1710	3363	1441	1942	2799	1631	2364	2734	1667	2598	3040	3094	2511	2941	2654	3730
Touchdowns	13	22	9	22	28	14	15	28	11	13	33	30	19	20	16	31
Interceptions	25	17	18	18	28	19	27	16	24	23	20	24	29	35	26	17
Percent Intercepted	6.8	3.7	6.7	5.4	6.7	5.4	8.2	4.1	7.1	4.8	4.9	5.4	6.6	8.1	5.5	3.2
PUNTS:																
Number	87	49	79	67	67	83	66	68	75	74	55	61	72	62	73	72
Average Distance	43.7	42.3	42.9	37.1	40.4	40.5	36.5	42.2	41.6	42.9	36.0	38.3	38.1	40.8	37.6	41.3
PUNT RETURNS:																
Number	25	42	22	35	33	34	39	50	35	23	22	29	30	34	35	34
Yards	94	323	194	357	320	97	157	328	107	79	102	158	143	198	314	203
Average Yards	3.8	7.7	8.8	10.2	9.7	2.9	4.0	6.6	3.1	3.4	4.6	5.4	4.8	5.8	9.0	6.0
Touchdowns	0	1	1	1	1	0	0	0	0	0	0	0	0	0	0	0
KICKOFF RETURNS:																
Number	69	42	47	55	48	50	46	43	53	72	69	62	58	66	56	61
Yards	1471	988	1157	1396	1014	1145	1241	1033	1215	1739	1363	1246	1221	1372	1326	1330
Average Yards	21.3	23.5	24.6	25.4	21.1	22.9	27.0	24.0	22.9	24.2	19.8	20.1	21.1	20.8	23.7	21.8
Touchdowns	1	0	3	1	0	0	4	0	1	2	0	0	0	0	0	1
INTERCEPTION RETURNS:																
Number	17	32	28	22	29	23	26	32	16	22	17	21	26	19	16	20
Yards	343	453	334	375	331	343	284	476	316	333	209	274	264	205	198	183
Average Yards	20.2	14.2	11.9	17.0	11.4	14.9	10.9	14.9	19.8	15.1	12.3	13.0	10.2	10.8	12.4	9.2
Touchdowns	2	3	2	3	3	6	2	4	2	2	0	2	1	1	0	1
PENALTIES:																
Number	88	52	98	72	81	65	48	85	100	76	80	77	68	65	89	67
Yards	866	458	953	773	785	712	531	854	1075	785	842	830	759	720	931	588
FUMBLES:																
Number	20	13	25	24	26	32	19	32	23	21	21	22	33	23	20	26
Number Lost	14	8	14	17	14	21	10	13	13	14	10	16	16	11	10	14
POINTS:																
Total	175	394	239	334	342	260	332	398	233	233	369	351	281	333	273	347
PAT Attempts	22	48	29	43	45	34	39	48	26	27	49	45	35	36	33	47
PAT Made	22	46	26	43	41	33	39	48	26	27	45	45	35	36	33	42
FG Attempts	18	37	26	23	23	21	29	43	33	32	21	19	22	39	33	26
FG Made	7	20	13	11	9	7	19	20	17	14	10	12	12	27	14	7
Percent FG Made	38.9	54.1	50.0	47.8	39.1	33.3	65.5	46.5	51.5	43.8	47.6	63.2	54.5	69.2	42.4	26.9
Safeties	0	0	0	0	2	1	1	1	0	1	0	0	0	0	0	1

DEFENSE

	ATL.	BALT.	CHI.	CLEV.	DALL.	DET.	G.B.	L.A.	MINN.	N.O.	N.Y.	PHIL.	PITT.	ST.L.	S.F.	WASH.
FIRST DOWNS:																
Total	294	208	215	281	236	205	183	200	217	276	261	286	228	216	237	274
by Rushing	124	78	91	115	64	98	98	75	105	114	113	105	80	79	92	98
by Passing	152	116	98	153	145	85	78	104	90	138	125	161	128	117	128	153
by Penalty	18	14	26	13	27	22	7	21	22	24	23	20	20	20	17	23
RUSHING:																
Number	504	387	419	459	339	471	443	361	500	469	416	434	418	410	407	431
Yards	2139	1411	1531	1767	1081	1795	1923	1119	2104	2092	1799	1741	1377	1502	1698	1852
Average Yards	4.2	3.6	3.7	3.8	3.2	3.8	4.3	3.1	4.2	4.5	4.3	4.0	3.3	3.7	4.2	4.3
Touchdowns	18	5	11	15	11	15	7	6	12	22	20	16	12	13	17	19
PASSING:																
Attempts	421	395	384	454	482	312	337	445	314	410	389	480	397	360	403	468
Completions	238	221	164	250	260	143	155	212	149	207	195	255	201	169	212	261
Completion Percentage	56.5	55.9	42.7	55.1	53.9	45.8	46.0	47.6	47.5	50.5	50.1	53.1	50.6	46.9	52.6	55.8
Passing Yards	3588	2678	2146	3231	3167	2089	1644	2694	2071	3035	2731	3382	2854	3023	2755	3713
Average Yards per Attempt (Gross)	8.5	6.8	5.6	7.1	6.6	6.7	4.9	6.1	6.6	7.4	7.0	7.0	7.2	8.4	6.8	7.9
Average Yards per Completion (Gross)	15.1	12.1	13.1	12.9	12.2	14.6	10.6	12.7	13.9	14.7	14.0	13.3	14.2	17.9	13.0	14.2
Times Tackled Attempting to Pass	21	36	30	41	45	39	29	43	36	23	31	23	29	37	48	38
Yards Lost Tackled Attempting to Pass	196	246	271	332	377	356	267	287	319	199	246	151	276	340	409	310
Net Yards	3392	2432	1875	2899	2790	1733	1377	2407	1752	2836	2485	3231	2578	2683	2346	3403
Touchdowns	31	13	14	19	21	11	13	14	17	25	25	29	22	26	19	25
Interceptions	17	32	28	22	29	23	26	32	16	22	17	21	26	19	16	20
Percent Intercepted	4.0	8.1	7.3	4.8	6.0	7.4	7.7	7.2	5.1	5.4	4.4	4.4	6.5	5.3	4.0	4.3
PUNTS:																
Number	49	69	77	62	72	79	75	86	79	63	56	50	70	81	70	72
Average Distance	39.9	39.4	41.3	39.9	42.5	39.3	41.6	40.8	38.9	39.9	39.7	38.8	38.9	39.0	43.8	40.1
PUNT RETURNS:																
Number	54	21	41	29	37	38	13	33	39	35	21	33	39	24	29	36
Yards	408	144	168	70	266	323	22	240	163	261	214	130	277	79	175	234
Average Yards	7.6	6.9	4.1	2.4	7.2	8.5	1.7	7.3	4.2	7.5	10.2	3.9	7.1	3.3	6.0	6.5
Touchdowns	0	0	0	0	0	1	0	0	0	0	0	0	1	1	1	0
KICKOFF RETURNS:																
Number	38	65	52	59	59	43	59	66	48	51	69	59	56	65	54	54
Yards	889	1483	1064	1288	1350	959	1276	1414	1076	1166	1511	1466	1300	1481	1311	1223
Average Yards	23.4	22.8	20.5	21.8	22.9	22.3	21.6	21.4	22.4	22.9	21.9	24.8	23.2	22.8	24.3	22.6
Touchdowns	0	1	0	2	0	1	0	2	0	0	1	2	1	1	1	1
INTERCEPTION RETURNS:																
Number	25	17	18	18	28	19	27	16	24	23	20	24	29	35	26	17
Yards	326	272	246	290	353	235	370	186	315	303	216	429	368	469	292	251
Average Yards	13.0	16.0	13.7	16.1	12.6	12.4	13.7	11.6	13.1	13.2	10.8	17.9	12.7	13.4	11.2	14.8
Touchdowns	4	2	1	1	3	2	3	0	4	0	1	3	1	5	3	1
PENALTIES:																
Number	87	82	82	57	64	73	55	91	90	83	68	67	73	89	64	86
Yards	853	927	782	655	717	822	482	912	906	824	774	715	833	782	596	882
FUMBLES:																
Number	26	17	23	28	27	13	23	18	38	21	28	28	26	19	24	21
Number Lost	10	8	16	14	19	10	14	13	19	10	15	14	13	13	13	14
POINTS:																
Total	422	198	218	297	268	259	209	196	294	379	379	409	320	356	337	353
PAT Attempts	53	21	27	37	35	32	24	23	34	48	48	52	39	46	41	46
PAT Made	52	21	26	36	34	31	23	22	34	46	47	52	36	42	40	45
FG Attempts	39	28	26	25	23	29	28	26	31	29	21	32	30	19	35	24
FG Made	16	17	10	13	8	12	14	12	18	15	14	15	16	12	17	10
Percent FG Made	41.0	60.7	38.5	52.0	34.8	41.4	50.0	46.2	58.1	51.7	66.7	46.9	53.3	63.2	48.6	41.7
Safeties	2	0	0	0	0	0	0	0	1	0	1	0	1	1	0	1

CONFERENCE PLAYOFFS

December 23, at Milwaukee (Attendance 49,861)

SCORING

GREEN BAY	0	14	7	7	–28
LOS ANGELES	7	0	0	0	– 7

First Quarter
L.A. Casey, 28 yard pass from Gabriel
PAT–Gossett (kick)

Second Quarter
G.B. Williams, 46 yard rush
PAT–Chandler (kick)
G.B. Dale, 18 yard pass from Starr
PAT–Chandler (kick)

Third Quarter
G.B. Mercein, 6 yard rush
PAT–Chandler (kick)

Fourth Quarter
G.B. Williams, 2 yard rush
PAT–Chandler (kick)

TEAM STATISTICS

G.B.		L.A.
20	First Downs–Total	12
11	First Downs–Rushing	2
8	First Downs–Passing	9
1	First Downs–Penalty	1
1	Times Tackled Passing	5
11	Yards Lost–Tackled	44
3	Fumbles–Number	0
3	Fumbles–Lost Ball	0
7	Penalties–Number	3
44	Yards Penalized	25
5	Punts–Number	6
32.6	Punts–Average Distance	39.3
3	Punt Returns–Number	1
44	Punt Returns–Yards	0
2	Kickoff Returns–Number	4
19	Kickoff Returns–Yards	80
1	Interception Returns–Number	1
20	Interception Returns–Yards	24
4	Giveaways	1
1	Takeaways	4
–3	Difference	+3

INDIVIDUAL STATISTICS

RUSHING

GREEN BAY	No	Yds	Avg.	LOS ANGELES	No	Yds	Avg.
Williams	18	88	4.9	Bass	14	40	2.9
Anderson	12	52	4.3	Jo'phson	9	16	1.8
Mercein	12	13	1.1	Gabriel	3	6	2.0
Starr	2	8	4.0	Mason	2	13	6.5
Wilson	1	2	2.0		28	75	2.7
	45	163	3.6				

RECEIVING

GREEN BAY	No	Yds	Avg.	LOS ANGELES	No	Yds	Avg.
Dale	6	109	18.2	Casey	5	82	16.4
Dowler	3	35	11.7	Traux	2	45	22.5
Fleming	3	30	10.0	Jo'phson	2	30	15.0
Anderson	2	30	15.0	Snow	1	17	17.0
Mercein	2	10	5.0	Pope	1	12	12.0
Williams	1	8	8.0		11	186	16.9
	17	222	13.1				

PASSING

	Att.	Cmp.	Comp. Pct.	Yds.	Int.	Yds/ Att.	Yds/ Comp.
G.B.							
Starr	23	17	73.9	222	1	9.7	13.1
L.A.							
Gabriel	31	11	35.5	186	1	6.0	16.9

December 24, at Dallas (Attendance 70,786)

SCORING

DALLAS	14	10	21	7	–52
CLEVELAND	0	7	0	7	–14

First Quarter
Dal. Baynham, 3 yard pass from Meredith
PAT–Villanueva (kick)
Dal. Perkins, 4 yard rush
PAT–Villanueva (kick)

Second Quarter
Dal. Hayes, 86 yard pass from Meredith
PAT–Villanueva (kick)
Dal. Villanueva, 10 yard field goal
Cle. Morin, 13 yard pass from Ryan
PAT–Groza (kick)

Third Quarter
Dal. Baynham, 1 yard rush
PAT–Villanueva (kick)
Dal. Perkins, 1 yard rush
PAT–Villanueva (kick)
Dal. Green, 60 yard interception return
PAT–Villanueva (kick)

Fourth Quarter
Dal. Baynham, 1 yard rush
PAT–Villanueva (kick)
Cle. Warfield, 75 yard pass from Ryan
PAT–Groza (kick)

TEAM STATISTICS

DAL.		CLE.
22	First Downs–Total	15
13	First Downs–Rushing	4
7	First Downs–Passing	10
2	First Downs–Penalty	1
1	Times Tackled Passing	5
2	Yards Lost Tackled	31
2	Fumbles–Number	0
1	Fumbles–Lost Ball	0
2	Penalties–Number	2
10	Yards Penalized	18
2	Punts–Number	7
44.5	Punts–Average Distance	39.8
4	Punt Returns–Number	2
155	Punt Returns–Yards	11
1	Kickoff Returns–Number	7
4	Kickoff Returns–Yards	112
1	Interception Returns–Number	1
60	Interception Returns–Yards	0
2	Giveaways	1
1	Takeaways	2
–1	Difference	+1

INDIVIDUAL STATISTICS

RUSHING

DALLAS	No	Yds	Avg.	CLEVELAND	No	Yds	Avg.
Perkins	18	74	4.1	Kelly	15	96	6.4
Baynham	13	50	3.8	Green	10	49	4.9
Garrison	9	33	3.6	Ryan	2	14	7.0
Clarke	1	8	8.0		27	159	5.9
Reeves	3	7	2.3				
Meredith	2	6	3.0				
	46	178	3.9				

RECEIVING

DALLAS	No	Yds	Avg.	CLEVELAND	No	Yds	Avg.
Hayes	5	144	28.8	Kelly	4	39	9.8
Rentzel	3	65	21.7	Warf'ld	3	99	33.9
Reeves	1	9	9.0	Marin	3	35	11.7
Perkins	1	4	4.0	Green	3	18	6.0
Baynham	1	3	3.0	Collins	1	3	3.0
	11	225	20.5		14	194	13.9

PASSING

	Att	Cmp	Pct	Yds	Int	Yd/A	Yd/C
DALL.							
Meredith	12	10	83.3	212	0	17.7	21.2
Morton	3	1	33.3	13	1	4.3	13.0
	15	11	73.3	225	1	15.0	20.5
CLEVE.							
Ryan	30	14	46.7	194	1	6.5	13.9

CAPITOL DIVISION

DALLAS COWBOYS 9-5-0 Tom Landry

Scores of Each Game		
21	Cleveland	14
38	NEW YORK	24
13	LOS ANGELES	35
17	Washington	14
14	NEW ORLEANS	10
24	Pittsburgh	21
14	Philadelphia	21
37	ATLANTA	7
27	New Orleans	10
20	WASHINGTON	27
46	ST. LOUIS	21
17	Baltimore	23
38	PHILADELPHIA	17
16	San Francisco	24

Use Name	Pos.	Hgt	Wgt	Age	Int	Pts
Jim Boeke	OT	6'5"	260	28		
Ralph Neely	OT	6'5"	265	23		
Tony Liscio	OT	6'5"	255	27		
Leon Donahue	OG	6'4"	245	28		
John Niland	OG	6'4"	245	23		
John Wilbur	OG	6'3"	240	24		
Mike Connelly	C	6'3"	248	31		
Malcolm Walker	OT-C	6'4"	250	24		
George Andrie	DE	6'7"	250	27		
Larry Stephens	DE	6'4"	250	29		
Willie Townes	DE	6'5"	260	24		
Ron East	DT	6'4"	242	24		
Bob Lilly	DT	6'4"	260	28		
Jethro Pugh	DT	6'6"	260	23		2
Dave Edwards	LB	6'3"	228	28	3	6
Harold Hays	LB	6'3"	225	26		
Chuck Howley	LB	6'3"	225	31	1	6
Lee Roy Jordan	LB	6'2"	225	26	3	8
Phil Clark	DB	6'2"	207	22	1	
Dick Daniels	DB	5'9"	180	21		
Mike Gaechter	DB	6'	190	27	2	
Cornell Green	DB	6'4"	208	27	7	
Mike Johnson	DB	5'10"	184	23	5	
Mel Renfro	DB	6'	190	23	7	
Buddy Dial — Injury						
Dave Manders — Injury						
Don Meredith	QB	6'2"	205	29		
Craig Morton	QB	6'4"	216	24		
Jerry Rhome	QB	6'	185	25		
Craig Baynham	HB	6'1"	200	23		6
Dan Reeves	HB	6'1"	200	23		66
Les Shy	HB	6'1"	200	23		
Don Perkins	FB	5'10"	200	29		36
Walt Garrison	HB-FB	6'	205	23		
Pete Gent	FL	6'4"	205	24		6
Lance Rentzel	OE-FL	6'2"	200	23		48
Frank Clarke	TE	6'	210	34		12
Pettis Norman	TE	6'3"	225	27		12
Rayfield Wright	TE	6'7"	235	22		
Bob Hayes	OE	6'	185	24		66
Sims Stokes	OE	6'1"	198	23		
Harold Deters	K	6'	200	23		12
Danny Villanueva	K	5'11"	200	29		56

PHILADELPHIA EAGLES 6-7-1 Joe Kuharich

Scores of Each Game		
35	WASHINGTON	24
6	BALTIMORE	38
34	PITTSBURGH	24
38	Atlanta	7
27	SAN FRANCISCO	28
14	St. Louis	48
21	DALLAS	14
24	New Orleans	31
17	Los Angeles	33
48	NEW ORLEANS	21
7	New York	44
35	Washington	35
17	Dallas	38
28	CLEVELAND	24

Use Name	Pos.	Hgt	Wgt	Age	Int	Pts
Bob Brown	OT	6'4"	295	24		
Lane Howell	OT	6'5"	272	26		
Randy Beisler	DE-OT	6'4"	245	22		
Dick Hart	OG	6'2"	250	24		
Jim Skaggs	OG	6'2"	252	27		
Bill Stetz	OG	6'3"	250	23		
Gordon Wright	OG	6'3"	245	23		
Lynn Hoyem	C-OG	6'4"	253	27		
Dave Recher	C	6'1"	246	24		
Jim Ringo	C	6'1"	230	36		
Don Hultz	DE	6'3"	242	26	1	6
Gary Pettigrew	DE	6'4"	245	22		
Mel Tom	DE	6'4"	243	26		
Dean Wink	DE	6'4"	246	22		
John Meyers	DT	6'6"	276	27		
Floyd Peters	DT	6'4"	255	32	1	
Fred Brown	LB	6'5"	232	24	2	
Ike Kelley	LB	5'11"	225	23	1	
Dave Lloyd	LB	6'3"	248	31	1	
Mike Morgan	LB	6'4"	242	25	1	
Arunas Vasys	LB	6'2"	235	24		
Harold Wells	LB	6'2"	220	28	1	
Jim Gray	DB	6'	182	25		
Aaron Martin	DB	6'	190	26	2	
Ron Medved	DB	6'1"	210	23	2	
Jim Nettles	DB	5'9"	177	25	4	6
Al Nelson	DB	5'11"	186	23		
Nate Ramsey	DB	6'1"	200	26		
Taft Reed	DB	6'2"	200	25		
Joe Scarpati	DB	5'10"	185	25	4	6
Bob Shann	DB	6'1"	190	24	1	
Dave Graham — Injury						
Frank Molden — Injury						
Benjy Dial	QB	6'1"	185	24		
King Hill	QB	6'3"	216	31		
Norm Snead	QB	6'4"	215	27		12
Timmy Brown	HB	5'10"	198	30		12
Harry Jones	HB	6'2"	205	22		
Harry Wilson	HB	5'11"	204	22		
Izzy Lang	FB	6'1"	232	24		30
Tom Woodeshick	HB-FB	6'	220	25		60
Chuck Hughes	FL	5'11"	172	24		
Ron Goodwin	OE-FL	6'	180	25		
Ben Hawkins	OE-FL	6'	180	23		60
Mike Ditka	TE	6'3"	235	27		12
Pete Emelianchik	TE	6'2"	220	24		
Jim Kelly	TE	6'2"	218	25		24
Dave Lince	TE	6'6"	265	23		
Fred Hill	OE	6'2"	215	24		
Gary Ballman	FL-OE	6'	205	27		42
Sam Baker	K	6'2"	218	35		81

WASHINGTON REDSKINS 5-6-3 Otto Graham

Scores of Each Game		
24	Philadelphia	35
30	New Orleans	10
38	NEW YORK	34
14	DALLAS	17
20	Atlanta	20
28	Los Angeles	28
13	BALTIMORE	17
21	ST. LOUIS	27
31	SAN FRANCISCO	28
27	Dallas	20
37	Cleveland	42
35	PHILADELPHIA	35
15	Pittsburgh	10
14	NEW ORLEANS	30

Use Name	Pos.	Hgt	Wgt	Age	Int	Pts
Mitch Johnson	OT	6'4"	250	25		
John Kelly	OT	6'3"	250	23		
Jim Snowden	OT	6'3"	255	25		
Don Bandy	OG	6'3"	250	22		
Vince Promuto	OG	6'1"	245	29		
Ray Schoenke	OG	6'3"	250	25		
Dave Crossan	C	6'3"	245	27		
Len Hauss	C	6'2"	235	26		
Heath Wingate	C	6'2"	240	22		
Bill Briggs	DE	6'3"	250	23		
Carl Kammerer	DE	6'3"	243	30		
Ron Snidow	DE	6'4"	250	25		
Walt Barnes	DT	6'3"	250	23		
Spain Musgrave	DT	6'4"	275	22		
Jim Prestel	DT	6'5"	275	30		
Joe Rutgens	DT	6'2"	255	28		
Ed Breding	LB	6'4"	235	22		2
Jim Carroll	LB	6'1"	230	24	1	
Chris Hanburger	LB	6'2"	218	26		
Larry Hendershot	LB	6'3"	240	22		
Sam Huff	LB	6'1"	230	32	2	
Steve Jackson	LB	6'1"	225	24		
Sid Williams	LB	6'2"	235	25		
Rickie Harris	DB	6'	182	24	1	
Paul Krause	DB	6'3"	195	25	8	
Brig Owens	DB	5'11"	190	24	1	8
Lonnie Sanders	DB	6'3"	207	25		
Jim Shorter	DB	5'11"	185	26	4	
Tom Walters	DB	6'2"	195	25		
Dick Smith	OE-DB	6'	205	23	3	
Sonny Jurgensen	QB	5'11"	203	33		12
Jim Ninowski	QB	6'1"	207	31		
Jerry Allen	HB	6'1"	205	26		24
Pete Larson	HB	6'1"	200	23		6
Steve Thurlow	HB	6'3"	222	24		
Joe Don Looney	FB-HB	6'1"	230	24		6
Ray McDonald	FB	6'4"	248	23		24
A. D. Whitfield	FB	5'10"	200	23		18
John Burrell	FL	6'3"	195	27		
T. J. Jackson	DB-FL	6'	180	24		
John Love	DB-FL	5'11"	185	23		34
Bobby Mitchell	HB-FL	6'	196	32		42
Pat Richter	TE	6'5"	230	26		
Jerry Smith	TE	6'2"	208	24		72
Charley Taylor	OE	6'3"	210	26		54
Bruce Alford	K	6'	185	22		3
Charlie Gogolak	K	5'10"	165	22		6
Gene Mingo (from MIA-A)	K	6'1"	190	28		32

NEW ORLEANS 3-11-0 Tom Fears

Scores of Each Game		
13	LOS ANGELES	27
10	WASHINGTON	30
7	CLEVELAND	42
21	New York	27
10	Dallas	14
13	San Francisco	27
10	PITTSBURGH	14
31	PHILADELPHIA	24
10	DALLAS	27
21	Philadelphia	48
27	ATLANTA	24
20	St. Louis	31
10	Baltimore	30
30	Washington	14

Use Name	Pos.	Hgt	Wgt	Age	Int	Pts
Dick Anderson	OT	6'5"	245	22		2
George Harvey	OT	6'4"	245	21		
Jerry Jones	OT	6'3"	270	23		
Dave McCormick	OT	6'6"	250	24		
Ray Rissmiller	OT	6'4"	250	25		
Jerry Sturm	OT	6'3"	260	30		
Roy Schmidt	OG	6'3"	250	25		
Eli Strand	OG	6'2"	250	24		
Del Williams	OG	6'2"	245	21		
Joe Wendryhoski	C	6'2"	245	28		
Doug Atkins	DE	6'8"	270	37		
Jim Garcia	DE	6'4"	250	23		
Brian Schweda	DE	6'3"	240	24		
Lou Cordileone	DT	6'	250	30		
Earl Leggett	DT	6'3"	265	33		
Dave Rowe	DT	6'6"	265	22		
Mike Tilleman	DT	6'5"	260	23		
Jackie Burkett	LB	6'4"	228	30	3	
Bill Cody	LB	6'1"	220	23		
Ted Davis	LB	6'1"	232	25		
Les Kelley	LB	6'3"	233	22		
Dave Simmons	LB	6'4"	245	24	1	
Steve Stonebreaker	LB	6'3"	228	29		
Phil Vandersea	LB	6'3"	225	24		
Fred Whittingham	LB	6'1"	240	28	1	
Bo Burris	DB	6'3"	195	22		
Bruce Cortez	DB	6'	175	21		
John Douglas	DB	6'1"	195	22	1	
Ben Hart	DB	6'2"	205	21	1	
Jim Heidel	DB	6'1"	185	23	1	
Obert Logan	DB	5'10"	180	25	3	
George Rose	DB	5'11"	190	24	1	
Dave Whitsell	DB	6'	190	31	10	12
Gary Cuozzo	QB	6'1"	195	26		6
Billy Kilmer	QB	6'	204	28		6
Gary Wood	QB	5'11"	188	24		
Tom Barrington	HB	6'1"	213	23		
Charlie Brown	HB	5'10"	187	21		12
John Gilliam	HB	6'1"	190	22		12
Jimmy Jordan	HB	6'1"	200	23		
Don McCall	HB	5'11"	195	22		12
Randy Schultz	FB-HB	5'11"	210	23		12
Jim Taylor	FB	6'	215	32		12
Ernie Wheelwright (from ATL)	FB	6'3"	236	30		6
Elijah Nevett	FL	6'	185	23		
Walter Roberts	FL	5'10"	163	25		30
Tom Hall	OE-FL	6'1"	195	26		
Vern Burke	TE	6'4"	202	26		
Jim Hester	TE	6'4"	225	22		
Kent Kramer	TE	6'5"	235	23		12
Dan Abramowicz	OE	6'1"	197	22		36
Ray Poage	OE	6'4"	205	26		
Charlie Durkee	K	5'11"	165	23		69
Tom McNeill	K	6'1"	195	25		

CAPITOL DIVISION

DALLAS COWBOYS

RUSHING

Last Name	No.	Yds	Avg	TD
Perkins	201	823	4.1	6
Reeves	173	603	3.5	5
Garrison	24	146	6.1	0
Norman	9	91	10.1	0
Meredith	28	84	3.0	0
Clarke	4	72	18.0	1
Shy	17	59	3.5	0
Morton	15	42	2.8	0
Baynham	3	6	2.0	1
Rhome	2	-11	-5.5	0
Villanueva	1	-15	-15.0	0

RECEIVING

Last Name	No.	Yds	Avg	TD
Rentzel	58	996	17	8
Hayes	49	998	20	10
Reeves	39	490	13	6
Norman	20	220	11	2
Perkins	18	116	6	0
Clarke	9	119	13	1
Gent	9	88	10	1
Shy	3	36	12	0
Baynham	3	13	4	0
Garrison	2	17	9	0

PUNT RETURNS

Last Name	No.	Yds	Avg	TD
Hayes	24	276	12	1
Rentzel	6	45	18	0
Renfro	3	-1	0	0

KICKOFF RETURNS

Last Name	No.	Yds	Avg	TD
Garrison	20	366	18	0
Baynham	12	331	28	0
Renfro	5	112	22	0
Shy	5	96	19	0
Stokes	4	92	23	0
Hayes	1	17	17	0
East	1	0	0	0

PASSING – PUNTING – KICKING

PASSING	Att	Comp	%	Yds	Yd/Att	TD	Int–%	RK
Meredith	255	128	50	1834	7.2	16	16– 6	8
Morton	137	69	50	978	7.1	10	10– 7	
Rhome	18	9	50	86	4.8	0	1– 6	
Reeves	7	4	57	195	27.9	2	1–14	

PUNTING	No	Avg
Villanueva	67	40.4

KICKING	XP	Att	%	FG	Att	%
Villanueva	32	34	94	8	19	42
Deters	9	10	90	1	4	25

PHILADELPHIA EAGLES

RUSHING

Last Name	No.	Yds	Avg	TD
Woodeshick	155	670	4.3	6
Lang	101	336	3.3	2
T. Brown	53	179	3.4	1
Snead	9	30	3.3	2
Jones	8	17	2.1	0
Ballman	1	17	17.0	1
Goodwin	1	1	1.0	0

RECEIVING

Last Name	No.	Yds	Avg	TD
Hawkins	59	1265	21	10
Ballman	36	524	15	6
Woodeshick	34	391	12	4
Ditka	26	274	11	2
Lang	26	201	8	3
T. Brown	22	202	9	1
Kelly	21	345	16	4
F. Hill	9	144	16	0
Goodwin	6	65	11	0
Jones	3	32	11	0
Wilson	2	20	10	0

PUNT RETURNS

Last Name	No.	Yds	Avg	TD
Martin	20	128	6	0
Shann	3	17	6	0
Hughes	3	11	4	0
Scarpati	1	2	2	0
Lince	1	0	0	0
Reed	1	0	0	0

KICKOFF RETURNS

Last Name	No.	Yds	Avg	TD
T. Brown	13	301	23	0
Hawkins	10	250	25	0
Wilson	7	150	21	0
Hughes	7	126	18	0
Shann	6	133	22	0
Reed	5	111	22	0
Lince	3	46	15	0
Ballman	2	43	22	0
Jones	2	32	16	0
Gray	1	30	30	0
F. Brown	1	17	17	0
Medved	1	7	7	0
Beisler	1	0	0	0
Kelley	1	0	0	0
Ramsey	1	0	0	0
Vasys	1	0	0	0

PASSING – PUNTING – KICKING

PASSING	Att	Comp	%	Yds	Yd/Att	TD	Int–%	RK
Snead	434	240	55	3399	7.8	29	24– 6	5
K. Hill	7	2	29	33	4.7	1	0– 0	
Dial	3	1	33	5	1.7	0	0– 0	
Lang	1	1	100	26	26.0	0	0– 0	

PUNTING	No	Avg
Baker	61	38.3

KICKING	XP	Att	%	FG	Att	%
Baker	45	45	100	12	19	63

WASHINGTON REDSKINS

RUSHING

Last Name	No.	Yds	Avg	TD
Whitfield	91	384	4.2	1
Allen	77	262	3.4	3
McDonald	52	223	4.3	4
Mitchell	61	189	3.1	1
Larson	25	84	3.4	1
Jurgensen	15	46	3.1	2
Thurlow	13	33	2.5	0
Looney	11	26	2.4	1

RECEIVING

Last Name	No.	Yds	Avg	TD
Taylor	70	990	14	9
J. Smith	67	849	13	12
Mitchell	60	866	14	6
Whitfield	36	494	14	2
Love	17	248	15	1
Allen	11	101	9	1
Thurlow	10	95	10	0
McDonald	10	60	6	0
Burrell	9	95	11	0
Larson	8	45	6	0
Richter	1	31	31	0
Looney	1	12	12	0
Hanburger	1	1	1	0

PUNT RETURNS

Last Name	No.	Yds	Avg	TD
Harris	23	208	9	0
Love	11	-5	-1	0

KICKOFF RETURNS

Last Name	No.	Yds	Avg	TD
Harris	25	580	23	0
Love	17	422	25	1
T. Jackson	7	131	19	0
D. Smith	4	120	30	0
Looney	2	42	21	0
Kelly	2	19	10	0
Allen	1	13	13	0
Burrell	1	2	2	0
Briggs	1	1	1	0
McDonald	1	0	0	0

PASSING – PUNTING – KICKING

PASSING	Att	Comp	%	Yds	Yd/Att	TD	Int–%	RK
Jurgenson	508	288	57	3747	7.4	31	16– 3	1
Ninowski	18	12	67	123	6.8	0	1– 6	
Mitchell	1	1	100	17	17.0	0	0– 0	

PUNTING	No	Avg
Richter	72	41.3

KICKING	XP	Att	%	FG	Att	%
Mingo	20	22	91	4	10	40
Love	10	11	91	2	7	29
Alford	3	4	75	0	2	0
Gogolak	3	3	100	1	4	25
Owens	2	3	67	0	2	0

NEW ORLEANS SAINTS

RUSHING

Last Name	No.	Yds	Avg	TD
Taylor	130	390	3.0	2
Wheelwright	80	241	3.0	1
Kilmer	20	142	7.1	1
Barrington	34	121	3.6	0
Schultz	32	117	3.7	2
McCall	21	86	4.1	1
Cuozzo	19	43	2.3	1
Gilliam	7	41	5.9	0
McNeill	4	38	9.5	0
Brown	8	16	2.0	2

RECEIVING

Last Name	No.	Yds	Avg	TD
Abramowicz	50	721	14	6
Taylor	38	251	7	0
Poage	24	380	16	0
Gilliam	22	264	12	1
Kramer	20	207	10	2
Hall	19	249	13	0
Roberts	17	384	23	3
Schultz	14	186	13	0
Wheelwright	13	107	8	0
Burke	8	84	11	0
McCall	4	75	19	1
Barrington	4	50	13	0
Brown	3	23	8	0
Hester	2	10	5	0

PUNT RETURNS

Last Name	No.	Yds	Avg	TD
Roberts	11	50	5	0
Douglas	2	15	8	0
Gilliam	7	13	2	0
Brown	3	1	0	0

KICKOFF RETURNS

Last Name	No.	Yds	Avg	TD
Roberts	28	737	26	1
Gilliam	16	481	30	1
McCall	7	198	28	0
Barrington	7	113	16	0
Brown	5	103	21	0
Jordan	3	56	19	0
Rose	1	21	21	0
Douglas	1	17	17	0
Vandersea	1	13	13	0
Logan	1	0	0	0
Nevett	1	0	0	0
Sturm	1	0	0	0

PASSING – PUNTING – KICKING

PASSING	Att	Comp	%	Yds	Yd/Att	TD	Int–%	RK
Cuozzo	260	134	52	1562	6.0	7	12– 5	9
Kilmer	204	97	48	1341	6.6	6	11– 5	15
Wood	11	5	46	62	5.6	0	0– 0	
Barrington	2	0	0	0	0.0	0	0– 0	
McNeill	1	1	100	24	24.0	0	0– 0	

PUNTING	No	Avg
McNeill	74	42.9

KICKING	XP	Att	%	FG	Att	%
Durkee	27	27	100	14	32	44

CENTURY DIVISION

CLEVELAND BROWNS 9-5-0 Blanton Collier

Scores of Each Game		
14	DALLAS	21
14	Detroit	31
42	New Orleans	7
21	PITTSBURGH	10
20	ST. LOUIS	16
24	CHICAGO	0
34	New York	38
34	Pittsburgh	14
7	Green Bay	55
14	MINNESOTA	10
42	WASHINGTON	37
24	NEW YORK	14
20	St. Louis	16
24	Philadelphia	28

Use Name	Pos.	Hgt	Wgt	Age	Int	Pts
Monte Clark	OT	6'6"	255	30		
John Demarie	OT	6'3"	250	22		
Dick Schafrath	OT	6'3"	255	31		
Jim Copeland	OG	6'2"	230	22		
Gene Hickerson	OG	6'3"	248	32		
Joe Taffoni	OG	6'3"	245	22		
John Wooten	OG	6'2"	250	32		
Fred Hoaglin	C	6'4"	240	23		
Bill Glass	DE	6'5"	255	31	1	
Jack Gregory	DE	6'6"	245	22		
Paul Wiggin	DE	6'3"	245	33		
Walter Johnson	DT	6'3"	270	24		
Jim Kanicki	DT	6'4"	270	25		
Frank Parker	DT	6'5"	270	27		
Billy Andrews	LB	6'	225	22		
Johnny Brewer	LB	6'4"	235	30	2	6
Jim Houston	LB	6'2"	245	30	3	12
Dale Lindsey	LB	6'3"	225	24	1	
Bob Matheson	LB	6'4"	240	22	1	
Erich Barnes	DB	6'2"	198	32	4	
Ben Davis	DB	5'11"	185	22	1	6
Ross Fichtner	DB	6'	185	29	4	
Mike Howell	DB	6'1"	187	24	3	
Ernie Kellerman	DB	6'	183	23	1	
Carl Ward	DB	5'9"	180	23	1	6
George Youngblood (to NO)	DB	6'3"	205	22		
Gary Lane	QB	6'1"	210	24		
Frank Ryan	QB	6'3"	200	31		
Dick Shiner	QB	6'	197	25		
Leroy Kelly	HB	6'	200	25		78
Larry Conjar	FB	6'	215	21		
Ernie Green	FB	6'2"	205	28		36
Charlie Harraway	FB	6'2"	230	22		
Nick Pietrosante	FB	6'2"	225	30		
Eppie Barney	FL	6'	198	23		
Gary Collins	FL	6'4"	215	26		42
Ron Green	FL	6'1"	200	23		
Clifton McNeil	FL	6'2"	185	27		12
Ron Duncan	TE	6'6"	255	24		
Milt Morin	TE	6'4"	250	25		
Ralph Smith	TE	6'2"	220	28		12
Paul Warfield	OE	6'	188	24		48
Lou Groza	K	6'3"	250	43		76

NEW YORK GIANTS 7-7-0 Allie Sherman

Scores of Each Game		
37	St. Louis	20
24	Dallas	38
34	Washington	38
27	NEW ORLEANS	21
27	Pittsburgh	24
21	GREEN BAY	48
38	CLEVELAND	34
24	Minnesota	27
7	Chicago	34
28	PITTSBURGH	20
44	PHILADELPHIA	7
14	Cleveland	24
7	DETROIT	30
37	ST. LOUIS	14

Use Name	Pos.	Hgt	Wgt	Age	Int	Pts
Francis Peay	OT	6'5"	250	23		
Willie Young	OT	6'	250	24		
Bookie Bolin	OG	6'2"	240	27		
Pete Case	OG	6'3"	245	26		
Darrell Dess	OG	6'	245	31		6
Andy Gross	OG	6'	230	21		
Charlie Harper	OG	6'2"	250	23		
Chuck Hinton	C	6'2"	235	24		
Greg Larson	C	6'2"	250	28		
Glen Condren	DE	6'2"	250	25		
Rosey Davis	DE	6'5"	260	25		
Jim Katcavage	DE	6'3"	240	32		
Randy Staten	DE	6'1"	225	23		
Bruce Anderson	DT	6'4"	250	23		
Roger Anderson	DT	6'5"	265	24		
Jim Colvin	DT	6'2"	245	30		
Bob Lurtsema	DT	6'6"	250	25		
Jim Moran	DT	6'5"	275	24		
Ken Avery	LB	6'1"	220	23		
Mike Ciccolella	LB	6'1"	235	23		
Vince Costello	LB	6'	228	35	4	
Dick Kotite	LB	6'3"	234	24		
Bill Swain	LB	6'2"	230	26	1	
Ed Weisacosky	LB	6'	236	23		
Freeman White	DB-LB	6'5"	225	23	2	
Henry Carr	DB	6'3"	195	24	1	
Clarence Childs	DB	6'	180	28		
Wendell Harris	DB	5'11"	185	26	1	2
Dave Hathcock	DB	6'	195	24		
Spider Lockhart	DB	6'2"	175	24	5	
Bobby Post	DB	6'1"	195	22		
Willie Williams	DB	6'	190	24	1	
Scott Eaton	FL-DB	6'3"	195	23	2	
Don Davis — Injury						
Tom Kennedy — Injury						
Earl Morrall	QB	6'1"	206	33		6
Fran Tarkenton	QB	6'1"	190	27		12
Allen Jacobs	HB	6'1"	215	26		
Randy Minniear	HB	6'	200	23		12
Bill Triplett	HB	6'2"	210	28		12
Ernie Koy	FB-HB	6'2"	230	24		30
Tucker Frederickson	FB	6'3"	230	24		12
Joe Morrison	HB-FB-FL	6'1"	212	29		54
Bob Crespino	TE	6'4"	225	29		6
Aaron Thomas	TE	6'3"	210	29		54
Del Shofner	OE	6'3"	190	31		6
Homer Jones	FL-OE	6'2"	215	26		84
Pete Gogolak	K	6'2"	200	25		46
Les Murdock	K	6'3"	245	23		25
Jeff Smith — Injury						
Larry Vargo — Injury						
Smith Reed — Military Service						

ST. LOUIS CARDINALS 6-7-1 Charlie Winner

Scores of Each Game		
20	NEW YORK	37
28	Pittsburgh	14
38	DETROIT	28
34	Minnesota	24
16	Cleveland	20
48	PHILADELPHIA	14
23	GREEN BAY	31
27	Washington	21
14	PITTSBURGH	14
3	Chicago	30
21	Dallas	46
31	NEW ORLEANS	20
16	CLEVELAND	20
14	New York	37

Use Name	Pos.	Hgt	Wgt	Age	Int	Pts
Ernie McMillan	OT	6'6"	260	29		
Bob Reynolds	OT	6'6"	265	26		
Clyde Williams	OT	6'2"	255	27		
Dave O'Brien	OG-OT	6'3"	245	26		
Ken Gray	OG	6'2"	250	31		
Ed Marcontell (to HOU-A)	OG	6'	260	23		
Rick Sortun	OG	6'2"	235	24		
Irv Goode	C-OG	6'4"	250	26		
Bob DeMarco	C	6'3"	240	29		
Dick Kasperek	C	6'3"	225	23		
Don Brumm	DE	6'3"	245	24		
Joe Robb	DE	6'3"	245	30		
Bob Rowe	DE	6'4"	255	22		
Dave Long	DT-DE	6'4"	235	22		
Sam Silas	DT	6'4"	250	24		
Chuck Walker	DT	6'2"	245	26		
Fred Heron	DE-DT	6'4"	250	22		
Jerry Hillebrand	LB	6'3"	240	27		
Bill Koman	LB	6'2"	230	33		
Dave Meggyesy	LB	6'1"	220	25		
Dale Meinert	LB	6'2"	220	34	1	
Larry Stallings	LB	6'2"	230	25		
Mike Strofolino	LB	6'2"	230	23		
Mike Barnes	DB	6'3"	205	22		
Jimmy Burson	DB	6'	180	25	2	
Pat Fischer	DB	5'10"	170	27	4	6
Chuck Latourette	DB	6'	190	22		
Phil Spiller	DB	6'	195	22	2	
Jerry Stovall	DB	6'2"	205	25	4	
Bobby Williams	DB	6'1"	185	25	2	
Larry Wilson	DB	6'	190	29	4	
Jim Hart	QB	6'2"	195	23		18
Charley Johnson	QB	6'	190	30		
Charlie Bryant	HB	6'1"	207	26		
Roy Shivers	HB	6'	200	25		6
Johnny Roland	FB-HB	6'2"	207	24		66
Willie Crenshaw	FB	6'2"	230	26		
Bill Thornton	FB	6'1"	215	27		
Prentice Gautt	HB-FB	6'	210	29		12
Bobby Joe Conrad	FL	6'	195	32		12
Dave Williams	FL	6'2"	205	22		30
Chuck Logan	TE	6'4"	220	24		
Jackie Smith	TE	6'4"	215	26		54
Ted Wheeler	TE	6'3"	230	21		
Billy Gambrell	FL-OE	5'10"	175	25		12
Jim Bakken	K	6'	200	26		117

PITTSBURGH STEELERS 4-9-1 Bill Austin

Scores of Each Game		
41	CHICAGO	13
14	ST. LOUIS	28
24	Philadelphia	34
10	Cleveland	21
24	NEW YORK	27
21	DALLAS	24
14	New Orleans	10
14	CLEVELAND	34
14	St. Louis	14
20	New York	28
27	MINNESOTA	41
24	Detroit	14
10	WASHINGTON	15
24	Green Bay	17

Use Name	Pos.	Hgt	Wgt	Age	Int	Pts
John Brown	OT	6'2"	248	28		
Mike Haggerty	OT	6'4"	230	21		
Fran O'Brien	OT	6'1"	265	31		
Larry Gagner	OG	6'3"	240	23		
Bruce Van Dyke	OG	6'2"	235	23		
Ralph Wenzel	OG	6'3"	240	24		
Sam Davis	OT-OG	6'1"	245	23		
Ray Mansfield	C	6'3"	250	26		
John Baker	DE	6'6"	270	32	1	
Jerry Mazzanti	DE	6'3"	240	27		
Ben McGee	DE	6'2"	260	25	1	6
Lloyd Voss	DE	6'4"	260	25	1	
Dick Arndt	DT	6'5"	265	23		
Chuck Hinton	DT	6'5"	260	28		6
Ken Kortas	DT	6'2"	280	25		6
Rod Breedlove	LB	6'2"	225	29		
John Campbell	LB	6'3"	225	28	2	
Ray May	LB	6'1"	230	22		
Andy Russell	LB	6'3"	215	25	3	
Bill Saul	LB	6'4"	225	26	1	
Jim Bradshaw	DB	6'1"	205	28		
John Foruria	DB	6'2"	205	22		
Bob Hohn	DB	6'	185	26	2	
Paul Martha	DB	6'	185	24	4	
Bobby Morgan	DB	6'	205	27		
Clendon Thomas	DB	6'2"	200	30	2	
Marv Woodson	DB	6'	195	24	7	
Wally Hilgenburg — Injury						
Rich Bader	QB	6'1"	190	24		
Bill Nelsen	QB	6'	195	26		
Kent Nix	QB	6'1"	195	23		12
Charlie Bivins (to BUF-A)	HB	6'2"	212	28		6
Cannonball Butler	HB	5'10"	185	24		
Dick Hoak	HB	5'11"	190	28		12
Don Shy	HB	6'1"	215	21		30
Willie Asbury	FB	6'1"	230	24		24
Earl Gros	FB	6'3"	230	26		6
Roy Jefferson	FL	6'2"	195	23		24
Jerry Marion	FL	5'10"	175	22		
Chet Anderson	TE	6'3"	245	22		12
John Hilton	TE	6'5"	220	25		30
Dick Compton	OE	6'1"	195	27		6
Marshall Cropper	OE	6'3"	210	23		
J. R. Wilburn	OE	6'2"	190	24		30
Mike Clark	K	6'1"	200	26		71
Jim Elliott	K	5'11"	184	24		

CENTURY DIVISION

CLEVELAND BROWNS

RUSHING

Last Name	No.	Yds	Avg	TD
Kelly	**235**	**1205**	**5.1**	**11**
E. Green	145	710	4.9	4
Conjar	20	78	3.9	0
Pietrosante	10	73	7.3	0
Ryan	22	57	2.6	0
Lane	2	21	10.5	0
Warfield	2	10	5.0	0
Collins	1	6	6.0	0
Shiner	2	−7	−3.5	0
Harraway	5	−14	−2.8	0

RECEIVING

Last Name	No.	Yds	Avg	TD
E. Green	39	369	9	2
Warfield	32	702	22	8
Collins	32	500	16	7
Kelly	20	282	14	2
Smith	14	211	15	1
Morin	7	90	13	0
Conjar	6	68	11	0
Pietrosante	6	56	9	0
McNeil	3	33	11	2
Barney	1	3	3	0

PUNT RETURNS

Last Name	No.	Yds	Avg	TD
Davis	18	229	**13**	**1**
Ward	6	62	10	0
Kelly	9	59	7	0
Harraway	1	7	7	0
Youngblood	1	0	0	0

KICKOFF RETURNS

Last Name	No.	Yds	Avg	TD
Davis	27	708	26	0
Ward	22	546	25	1
Kelly	5	131	26	0
Barney	1	11	11	0

PASSING – PUNTING – KICKING

PASSING	Att	Comp	%	Yds	Yd/Att	TD	Int–%	RK
Ryan	280	136	49	2026	7.2	20	16– 6	7
Lane	43	21	49	254	5.9	2	1– 2	
Shiner	9	3	33	34	3.8	0	1–11	
Kelly	1	0	0	0	0.0	0	0– 0	

PUNTING	No	Avg
Collins	57	36.5
Kelly	10	40.7

KICKING	XP	Att	%	FG	Att	%
Groza	43	43	100	11	23	48

NEW YORK GIANTS

RUSHING

Last Name	No.	Yds	Avg	TD
Koy	146	704	4.8	4
Frederickson	97	311	3.2	2
Tarkenton	44	306	7.0	2
Triplett	58	171	2.9	2
Morrison	36	161	4.5	2
Minniear	35	98	2.8	1
Jones	5	60	12.0	1
Jacobs	11	23	2.1	0
Morrall	4	11	2.8	1
Case	0	16	0.0	0
Young	0	2	0.0	0
Dess	0	1	0.0	1

RECEIVING

Last Name	No.	Yds	Avg	TD
Thomas	51	877	17	9
Jones	49	1209	**25**	**13**
Morrison	37	524	14	7
Koy	32	212	7	1
Frederickson	19	153	8	0
Crespino	10	125	13	1
Minniear	8	49	6	1
Shofner	7	146	21	1
Triplett	7	69	10	0
Eaton	1	18	18	0

PUNT RETURNS

Last Name	No.	Yds	Avg	TD
Lockhart	7	54	8	0
Williams	6	28	5	0
Minniear	4	13	3	0
Hathcock	3	7	2	0
Harris	2	0	0	0

KICKOFF RETURNS

Last Name	No.	Yds	Avg	TD
Childs	29	603	21	0
Hathcock	14	315	23	0
Triplett	7	139	20	0
Minniear	6	98	16	0
Jones	2	38	19	0
Frederickson	1	19	19	0
Koy	1	18	18	0
Crespino	1	7	7	0
Lurtsema	1	7	7	0
Post	1	0	0	0

PASSING – PUNTING – KICKING

PASSING	Att	Comp	%	Yds	Yd/Att	TD	Int–%	RK
Tarkenton	377	204	54	3088	8.2	29	19– 5	3
Morrall	24	13	54	181	7.5	3	1– 4	
Koy	4	3	75	101	25.3	1	0– 0	
Morrison	1	1	100	12	12.0	0	0– 0	

PUNTING	No	Avg
Koy	40	37.7
Morrall	15	31.5

KICKING	XP	Att	%	FG	Att	%
Gogolak	28	29	97	6	10	60
Murdock	13	15	87	4	9	44
Harris	2	2	100	0	1	0

ST. LOUIS CARDINALS

RUSHING

Last Name	No.	Yds	Avg	TD
Roland	234	876	3.7	10
Gautt	142	573	4.0	1
Crenshaw	44	149	3.4	0
Smith	9	86	9.6	0
Shivers	20	64	3.2	1
Hart	13	36	2.8	3
Latourette	2	23	11.5	0
Bryant	3	16	5.3	0
Thornton	4	9	2.3	0
D. Williams	1	7	7.0	0

RECEIVING

Last Name	No.	Yds	Avg	TD
Smith	56	1205	22	9
Conrad	47	637	14	2
D. Williams	28	405	14	5
Gambrell	28	398	14	2
Roland	20	269	13	1
Gautt	15	202	13	1
Crenshaw	6	30	5	0
Shivers	3	15	5	0
Thornton	1	9	9	0

PUNT RETURNS

Last Name	No.	Yds	Avg	TD
Spiller	15	124	8	0
Shivers	9	36	4	0
Latourette	6	21	4	0
Roland	3	17	6	0
C. Williams	1	0	0	0

KICKOFF RETURNS

Last Name	No.	Yds	Avg	TD
B. Williams	24	583	24	0
Bryant	14	324	23	0
Spiller	10	219	22	0
Shivers	9	160	18	0
Stallings	2	39	20	0
Roland	2	33	17	0
Crenshaw	2	14	7	0
Barnes	1	0	0	0
Fischer	1	0	0	0
Sortun	1	0	0	0

PASSING – PUNTING – KICKING

PASSING	Att	Comp	%	Yds	Yd/Att	TD	Int–%	RK
Hart	397	192	48	3008	7.6	19	30– 8	10
Johnson	29	12	41	162	5.6	1	3– 10	
Roland	4	0	0	0	0.0	0	1– 25	
Smith	1	0	0	0	0.0	0	1–100	

PUNTING	No	Avg
Latourette	62	40.8

KICKING	XP	Att	%	FG	Att	%
Bakken	36	36	100	**27**	39	**69**

PITTSBURGH STEELERS

RUSHING

Last Name	No.	Yds	Avg	TD
Shy	99	341	3.4	4
Asbury	80	315	3.9	4
Butler	90	293	3.3	0
Gros	72	252	3.5	1
Hoak	52	142	2.7	1
Nix	15	45	3.0	2
Bivins	7	23	3.3	1
Hilton	1	15	15.0	0
Compton	1	1	1.0	0
Jefferson	5	−11	−2.2	0
Nelsen	9	−19	−2.1	0

RECEIVING

Last Name	No.	Yds	Avg	TD
Wilburn	51	767	15	5
Compton	42	507	12	1
Jefferson	29	459	16	4
Hilton	26	343	13	5
Gros	19	175	9	0
Hoak	17	111	7	1
Shy	12	152	13	1
Anderson	8	141	18	2
Butler	4	23	6	0
Asbury	3	52	17	0
Bivins	1	24	24	0
Marion	1	16	16	0
Cropper	1	11	11	0

PUNT RETURNS

Last Name	No.	Yds	Avg	TD
Bradshaw	16	97	6	0
Thomas	9	34	4	0
Jefferson	1	10	10	0
Marion	1	2	2	0
Shy	1	−5	−5	0

KICKOFF RETURNS

Last Name	No.	Yds	Avg	TD
Shy	21	473	23	0
Martha	18	403	22	0
Butler	10	223	22	0
Russell	6	97	16	0
Campbell	1	25	25	0
Hilton	1	0	0	0
May	1	0	0	0

PASSING – PUNTING – KICKING

PASSING	Att	Comp	%	Yds	Yd/Att	TD	Int–%	RK
Nix	268	136	51	1587	5.9	8	19– 7	13
Nelsen	165	74	45	1125	6.8	10	9– 5	12
Hoak	8	4	50	69	8.6	1	1–13	
Clark	1	0	0	0	0.0	0	0– 0	

PUNTING	No	Avg
Elliott	72	38.1

KICKING	XP	Att	%	FG	Att	%
Clark	35	35	100	12	22	55

CENTRAL DIVISION

GREEN BAY PACKERS 9-4-1 Vince Lombardi

Scores of Each Game		
17	DETROIT	17
13	CHICAGO	10
23	ATLANTA	0
27	Detroit	17
7	MINNESOTA	10
48	New York	21
31	St. Louis	23
10	Baltimore	13
55	CLEVELAND	7
13	SAN FRANCISCO	0
17	Chicago	13
30	Minnesota	27
24	Los Angeles	27
17	PITTSBURGH	24

Use Name	Pos.	Hgt	Wgt	Age	Int	Pts
Forest Gregg	OT	6'4"	250	34		
Bob Skoronski	OT	6'3"	245	34		
Steve Wright	OT	6'6"	250	25		
Gale Gillingham	OG	6'3"	255	23		
Jerry Kramer	OG	6'3"	245	32		
Fuzzy Thurston	OG	6'1"	245	34		
Ken Bowman	C	6'3"	230	24		
Bob Hyland	OG-C	6'5"	250	22		
Lionel Aldridge	DE	6'4"	245	25		
Bob Brown	DE	6'5"	260	26		
Willie Davis	DE	6'3"	245	34		2
Henry Jordan	DT	6'3"	250	32		
Ron Kostelnik	DT	6'4"	260	27		
Jim Weatherwax	DT	6'7"	260	24		
Lee Roy Caffey	LB	6'3"	250	27	2	
Tommy Crutcher	LB	6'3"	230	25		
Jim Flanigan	LB	6'3"	230	22		
Ray Nitschke	LB	6'3"	240	31	3	6
Dave Robinson	LB	6'3"	240	26	4	
Herb Adderley	DB	6'1"	200	28	4	6
Tom Brown	DB	6'1"	190	26	1	
Doug Hart	DB	6'	190	28		
Bob Jeter	DB	6'1"	205	29	8	
John Rowser	DB	6'1"	180	23		
Willie Wood	DB	5'10"	190	31	4	
Zeke Bratkowski	QB	6'2"	210	35		
Don Horn	QB	6'2"	195	22		
Bart Starr	QB	6'1"	190	34		
Donny Anderson	HB	6'3"	210	24		54
Elijah Pitts	HB	6'1"	205	28		36
Travis Williams	HB	6'1"	210	21		36
Jim Grabowski	FB	6'2"	220	23		18
Chuck Mercein (from NY)	FB	6'3"	230	24		8
Ben Wilson	FB	6'	225	27		12
Carroll Dale	FL	6'1"	200	29		30
Bob Long	FL	6'3"	205	26		
Claudis James	HB-FL	6'2"	190	23		
Allen Brown	TE	6'5"	235	24		
Dick Capp	TE	6'3"	235	23		
Marv Fleming	TE	6'4"	235	25		6
Boyd Dowler	OE	6'5"	225	30		24
Max McGee	OE	6'3"	210	35		
Don Chandler	K	6'2"	210	32		96

CHICAGO BEARS 7-6-1 George Halas

Scores of Each Game		
13	Pittsburgh	41
10	Green Bay	13
17	Minnesota	7
3	BALTIMORE	24
14	DETROIT	3
0	Cleveland	24
17	LOS ANGELES	28
27	Detroit	13
34	NEW YORK	7
30	ST. LOUIS	3
13	GREEN BAY	17
28	San Francisco	14
10	MINNESOTA	10
23	Atlanta	14

Use Name	Pos.	Hgt	Wgt	Age	Int	Pts
Randy Jackson	OT	6'5"	245	23		
Dan James	OT	6'4"	250	30		
Bob Pickens	OT	6'4"	258	24		
George Seals	OT	6'2"	260	24		
Bob Wetoska	OT	6'3"	240	29		
Jim Cadile	OG	6'3"	240	26		
Don Croftcheck	OG	6'1"	230	24		
Doug Kriewald	OG	6'4"	245	23		
Mike Rabold	OG	6'2"	250	30		
Mike Pyle	C	6'3"	250	28		
Marty Amsler	DE	6'5"	260	24	1	
Ed O'Bradovich	DE	6'3"	255	27		
Loyd Phillips	DE	6'3"	230	22		
Frank Cornish	DT	6'6"	270	23	2	
Dick Evey	DT	6'2"	245	26		
John Johnson	DT	6'5"	260	26		
Frank McRae	DT	6'7"	270	23		
Doug Buffone	LB	6'1"	230	23	3	6
Dick Butkus	LB	6'3"	245	23	1	
Rudy Kuechenberg	LB	6'2"	215	24		
Jim Purnell	LB	6'2"	238	25		
Mike Reilly	LB	6'2"	230	24		
Charlie Brown	DB	6'1"	193	24	1	
Al Dodd	DB	6'	180	22		
Curtis Gentry	DB	6'	185	26	4	
Bennie McRae	DB	6'1"	180	26	5	12
Richie Petitbon	DB	6'3"	205	29	5	
Joe Taylor	DB	6'2"	195	26	1	
Rosey Taylor	DB	5'11"	186	28	5	6
Rudy Bukich	QB	6'1"	205	36		
Jack Concannon	QB	6'3"	205	24		18
Larry Rakestraw	QB	6'2"	195	25		12
Gale Sayers	HB	6'	198	24		72
Ronnie Bull	FB-HB	6'	200	27		6
Ralph Kurek	FB	6'2"	210	24		
Andy Livingston	FB	6'	234	22		
Brian Piccolo	HB-FB	6'	205	23		
Johnny Morris	FL	5'10"	180	32		6
Duane Allen	TE	6'4"	225	29		
Austin Denney	TE	6'2"	230	23		
Terry Stoepel	TE	6'4"	235	22		
Dick Gordon	OE	5'11"	190	22		30
Bob Jones	OE	6'4"	195	22		6
Jim Jones	OE	6'2"	187	23		
Bobby Joe Green	K	5'11"	175	29		
Mac Percival	K	6'4"	217	27		65

DETROIT LIONS 5-7-2 Joe Schmidt

Scores of Each Game		
17	Green Bay	17
31	CLEVELAND	14
28	St. Louis	38
17	GREEN BAY	27
3	Chicago	14
24	ATLANTA	3
45	San Francisco	3
13	CHICAGO	27
10	Minnesota	10
7	Baltimore	41
7	LOS ANGELES	31
14	PITTSBURGH	24
30	New York	7
14	MINNESOTA	3

Use Name	Pos.	Hgt	Wgt	Age	Int	Pts
Charlie Bradshaw	OT	6'6"	260	31		
Bill Cottrell	OT	6'3"	265	22		
Roger Shoals	OT	6'4"	255	28		
Randy Winkler	OT	6'5"	260	24		
Frank Gallagher	OG	6'2"	240	24		
John Gordy	OG	6'3"	250	31		
Bob Kowalkowski	OG	6'3"	245	23		
Chuck Walton	OG	6'3"	250	26		
Ed Flanagan	C	6'3"	250	23		
Larry Hand	DE	6'4"	245	27	2	12
Lew Kamanu	DE	6'4"	245	23		
John McCambridge	DE	6'4"	245	21		
Darris McCord	DE	6'4"	250	34	1	
Mike Melinkovich	DE	6'4"	245	25		
Alex Karras	DT	6'2"	245	31		
Denis Moore	DT	6'5"	230	23		
Jerry Rush	DT	6'4"	270	25		
Ernie Clark	LB	6'1"	220	29	1	
Ron Goovert	LB	5'11"	225	23		
Mike Lucci	LB	6'2"	230	27	2	6
Paul Naumoff	LB	6'1"	210	22		
Wayne Walker	LB	6'2"	225	30		26
Lem Barney	DB	6'	202	21	10	18
Mike Bass	DB	6'	190	22		
Dick LeBeau	DB	6'1"	185	30	4	
Bruce Maher	DB	5'11"	190	30	2	2
Wayne Rasmussen	DB	6'2"	180	25		
Bobby Thompson	DB	5'10"	175	27		
Tom Vaughn	DB	5'11"	195	24	1	
Mike Weger	DB	6'2"	195	21		
Johnnie Robinson — Injury						
Milt Plum	QB	6'1"	205	33		
Karl Sweetan	QB	6'1"	200	24		6
Mel Farr	HB	6'2"	208	22		36
Bobby Felts	HB	6'2"	202	24		
Tom Watkins	HB	6'1"	195	30		30
Amos Marsh	FB	6'1"	220	28		18
Tom Nowatzke	FB	6'3"	222	24		36
Pat Studstill	FL	6'1"	175	29		12
John Henderson	OE-FL	6'3"	190	24		
Jim Gibbons	TE	6'2"	220	31		
Ron Kramer	TE	6'3"	240	32		
Jerry Zawadzkas	TE	6'4"	220	20		
Gail Cogdill	OE	6'2"	195	30		6
Bill Malinchak	OE	6'1"	190	23		24
Garo Yepremian	K	5'8"	160	23		28

MINNESOTA VIKINGS 3-8-3 Bud Grant

Scores of Each Game		
21	SAN FRANCISCO	27
3	Los Angeles	39
7	CHICAGO	17
24	ST. LOUIS	34
10	Green Bay	7
20	BALTIMORE	20
20	Atlanta	21
27	NEW YORK	24
10	DETROIT	10
10	Cleveland	14
41	Pittsburgh	27
27	GREEN BAY	30
10	Chicago	10
3	Detroit	14

Use Name	Pos.	Hgt	Wgt	Age	Int	Pts
Grady Alderman	OT	6'2"	240	28		
Bob Breitenstein (from DEN)	OT	6'3"	267	24		
Doug Davis	OT	6'4"	250	23		
Archie Sutton	OT	6'4"	265	24		
Larry Bowie	OG	6'2"	255	27		
John Pentecost	OG	6'2"	250	23		
Milt Sunde	OG	6'2"	250	24		
Jim Vellone	OT-OG	6'2"	255	23		
Mick Tingelhoff	C	6'1"	237	27		
Carl Eller	DE	6'6"	265	24		
Jim Marshall	DE	6'3"	235	30		
Archie Simkus	DE	6'4"	250	24		
Paul Dickson	DT	6'5"	255	30		
Gary Larsen	DT	6'5"	255	27		
Alan Page	DT	6'5"	255	22		
Jerry Shay	DT	6'3"	245	23		
Paul Faust	LB	6'	220	23		
Don Hansen	LB	6'3"	228	23		
Jim Hargrave	LB	6'3"	230	22	1	6
John Kirby	LB	6'3"	235	25		
Dave Tobey	LB	6'3"	230	24		
Lonnie Warwick	LB	6'3"	235	25	2	
Roy Winston	LB	6'1"	230	27		
Al Coleman	DB	6'1"	195	22		
Mike Fitzgerald (to NY-ATL)	DB	5'10"	180	26		
Dale Hackbart	DB	6'3"	210	31	2	6
Jeff Jordan	DB	6'4"	190	23		
Karl Kassulke	DB	6'	195	25	2	
Brady Keys (from PIT)	DB	6'	185	31	3	
Earsell Mackbee	DB	6'1"	195	26	5	12
Ed Sharockman	DB	6'	200	27	3	
Bob Berry	QB	5'11"	190	25		
Joe Kapp	QB	6'2"	212	29		12
Ron Vander Kelen	QB	6'1"	190	27		6
Earl Denny	HB	6'1"	200	22		
Clint Jones	HB	6'	206	22		6
Jim Lindsey	HB	6'2"	200	22		
Dave Osborn	HB	6'	205	24		18
Pete Tatman	HB	6'1"	220	22		
Bill Brown	FB	5'11"	230	29		30
Jim Phillips	FL	6'1"	195	30		18
Bob Grim	DB-FL	6'	197	22		6
John Beasley	TE	6'3"	228	22		24
Marlin McKeever	TE	6'1"	235	27		
Paul Flatley	OE	6'1"	187	26		
Gene Washington	OE	6'3"	216	23		12
Fred Cox	K	5'10"	200	28		77
Bobby Walden	K	6'	190	28		

CENTRAL DIVISION

GREEN BAY PACKERS

RUSHING

Last Name	No.	Yds	Avg	TD
Grabowski	120	466	3.9	2
Wilson	103	453	4.4	2
Anderson	97	402	4.1	6
Pitts	77	247	3.2	6
Williams	35	188	5.4	1
Starr	21	90	4.3	0
Mercein	14	46	4.0	1
Dale	1	9	9.0	0
Bratkowski	5	6	1.2	0
Horn	1	−2	−2.0	0

RECEIVING

Last Name	No.	Yds	Avg	TD
Dowler	54	836	15	4
Dale	35	738	21	5
Anderson	22	331	15	3
Pitts	15	210	14	0
Wilson	14	88	6	0
Grabowski	12	171	14	1
Fleming	10	126	13	1
Long	8	96	12	0
Williams	5	80	16	1
A. Brown	3	43	14	0
McGee	3	33	11	0
Mercein	1	6	6	0

PUNT RETURNS

Last Name	No.	Yds	Avg	TD
Anderson	9	98	11	0
T. Brown	9	40	4	0
Pitts	9	16	2	0
Wood	12	3	0	0

KICKOFF RETURNS

Last Name	No.	Yds	Avg	TD
Williams	18	739	41	4
Anderson	11	226	21	0
Adderley	10	207	21	0
Crutcher	3	48	16	0
A. Brown	1	13	13	0
Hart	1	8	8	0
Robinson	1	0	0	0
Wood	1	0	0	0

PASSING – PUNTING – KICKING

PASSING	Att	Comp	%	Yds	Yd/Att	TD	Int–%	RK
Starr	210	115	55	1823	8.7	9	17– 8	6
Bratkowski	94	53	56	724	7.7	5	9–10	
Horn	24	12	50	171	7.1	1	1– 4	
Anderson	2	1	50	19	9.5	0	0– 0	
Pitts	1	1	100	21	21.0	0	0– 0	

PUNTING	No	Avg
Anderson	65	36.6
Chandler	1	31.0

KICKING	XP	Att	%	FG	Att	%
Chandler	39	39	100	19	29	66
Mercein	2	3	67	0	1	0

CHICAGO BEARS

RUSHING

Last Name	No.	Yds	Avg	TD
Sayers	186	880	4.7	7
Piccolo	87	317	3.6	0
Concannon	67	279	4.2	3
Bull	61	176	2.9	0
Kurek	37	112	3.0	0
Rakestraw	11	42	3.8	2
Livingston	28	41	1.5	0
J. Jones	4	19	4.8	0
Morris	1	6	6.0	0
Gordon	3	−7	−2.3	0
Bukich	4	−13	−3.3	0

RECEIVING

Last Name	No.	Yds	Avg	TD
Gordon	31	534	17	5
Morris	20	231	12	1
Bull	18	250	14	1
Sayers	16	126	8	1
Piccolo	13	103	8	0
Denny	12	113	9	0
J. Jones	7	138	20	0
Livingston	5	62	12	0
Kurek	5	30	6	0
B. Jones	3	80	27	1
Stoepel	1	6	6	0

PUNT RETURNS

Last Name	No.	Yds	Avg	TD
Gordon	12	82	7	0
Sayers	3	80	27	1
Morris	4	24	6	0
Dodd	3	8	3	0

KICKOFF RETURNS

Last Name	No.	Yds	Avg	TD
Sayers	16	603	38	3
Gordon	16	397	25	0
Kurek	5	81	16	0
Dodd	3	34	11	0
Brown	2	34	17	0
J. Taylor	1	8	8	0
Jackson	1	0	0	0
Kriewald	1	0	0	0
Kuechenberg	1	0	0	0
Stoepel	1	0	0	0

PASSING – PUNTING – KICKING

PASSING	Att	Comp	%	Yds	Yd/Att	TD	Int–%	RK
Concannon	186	92	49	1260	6.8	6	14– 8	17
Rakestraw	44	21	48	228	5.2	3	2– 5	
Bukich	33	18	55	185	5.6	0	2– 6	
Sayers	5	0	0	0	0.0	0	0– 0	

PUNTING	No	Avg
Green	79	42.9

KICKING	XP	Att	%	FG	Att	%
Percival	26	29	90	13	26	50

DETROIT LIONS

RUSHING

Last Name	No.	Yds	Avg	TD
Farr	206	860	4.2	3
Watkins	106	361	3.4	4
Nowatzke	70	288	4.1	4
Marsh	58	229	3.9	2
Sweetan	17	93	5.5	1
Felts	10	66	6.6	0
Plum	6	5	0.8	0
Flanagan	0	5	0.0	0

RECEIVING

Last Name	No.	Yds	Avg	TD
Farr	39	317	8	3
Malinchak	26	397	15	4
Cogdill	21	322	15	1
Nowatzke	21	145	7	2
Henderson	13	144	11	0
Studstill	10	162	16	2
Gibbons	10	107	11	0
Watkins	8	93	12	1
Marsh	7	103	15	1
Kramer	4	40	10	0
Walton	1	−4	−4	0

PUNT RETURNS

Last Name	No.	Yds	Avg	TD
Watkins	15	57	4	0
Thompson	9	20	2	0
Barney	4	14	4	0
Vaughn	4	7	2	0
Weger	1	0	0	0
Felts	1	−1	−1	0

KICKOFF RETURNS

Last Name	No.	Yds	Avg	TD
Vaughn	16	446	28	0
Watkins	20	411	21	0
Thompson	4	134	34	0
Barney	5	87	17	0
Goovert	2	40	20	0
Weger	2	27	14	0
Zawadzkas	1	0	0	0

PASSING – PUNTING – KICKING

PASSING	Att	Comp	%	Yds	Yd/Att	TD	Int–%	RK
Sweetan	177	74	42	901	5.1	10	11– 6	18
Plum	172	86	50	925	5.4	4	8– 5	14
Farr	2	0	0	0	0.0	0	0– 0	

PUNTING	No	Avg
Barney	47	37.4
Studstill	36	44.5

KICKING	XP	Att	%	FG	Att	%
Yepremian	22	23	96	2	6	33
Walker	11	11	100	5	15	33

MINNESOTA VIKINGS

RUSHING

Last Name	No.	Yds	Avg	TD
Osborn	215	972	4.5	2
Brown	185	610	3.3	5
Kapp	27	167	6.2	2
Jones	13	23	1.8	0
Grim	1	20	20.0	0
Lindsey	4	10	2.5	0
Vander Kelen	9	9	1.0	1

RECEIVING

Last Name	No.	Yds	Avg	TD
Osborn	34	272	8	1
Flatley	23	232	10	0
Brown	22	263	12	0
Phillips	21	352	17	3
McKeever	14	184	13	0
Washington	13	384	30	2
Beasley	13	120	9	4
Grim	6	108	18	1
Lindsey	4	36	9	0

PUNT RETURNS

Last Name	No.	Yds	Avg	TD
Grim	25	101	4	0
Keys	7	7	1	0
Fitzgerald	2	4	2	0
Sharockman	4	0	0	0

KICKOFF RETURNS

Last Name	No.	Yds	Avg	TD
Jones	25	597	24	1
Grim	22	493	22	0
Fitzgerald	12	240	20	0
Lindsey	3	71	24	0
Sharockman	1	22	22	0
Denny	1	18	18	0
Tatman	1	14	14	0

PASSING – PUNTING – KICKING

PASSING	Att	Comp	%	Yds	Yd/Att	TD	Int–%	RK
Kapp	214	102	48	1386	6.5	8	17– 8	19
Vander Kelen	115	45	39	522	4.5	3	7– 6	
Berry	7	3	43	43	6.1	0	0– 0	

PUNTING	No	Avg
Walden	75	41.6

KICKING	XP	Att	%	FG	Att	%
Cox	26	26	100	17	33	52

COASTAL DIVISION

LOS ANGELES RAMS 11-1-2 George Allen

Scores of Each Game		
27	New Orleans	13
39	MINNESOTA	3
35	Dallas	13
24	SAN FRANCISCO	27
24	Baltimore	24
28	WASHINGTON	28
28	Chicago	17
17	San Francisco	7
33	PHILADELPHIA	17
31	Atlanta	3
31	Detroit	7
20	ATLANTA	3
27	GREEN BAY	24
34	BALTIMORE	10

Use Name	Pos.	Hgt	Wgt	Age	Int	Pts
Joe Carollo	OT	6'2"	258	27		
Charley Cowan	OT	6'4"	265	29		
Bob Nichols	OT	6'3"	250	24		
Don Chuy	OG	6'1"	255	26		
Tom Mack	OG	6'3"	245	23		
Joe Scibelli	OG	6'1"	255	28		
Ken Iman	C	6'1"	240	28		
George Burman	OG-C	6'3"	255	24		
Deacon Jones	DE	6'5"	260	28		2
Lamar Lundy	DE	6'7"	260	32		
Gregg Schumacher	DE	6'2"	240	25		
Roger Brown	DT	6'5"	300	30		
Merlin Olsen	DT	6'5"	276	26		
Diron Talbert	DT	6'5"	238	23		
Dave Cahill	DE-DT	6'3"	238	25		

Use Name	Pos.	Hgt	Wgt	Age	Int	Pts
Maxie Baughan	LB	6'1"	230	29	4	
Gene Breen	LB	6'2"	230	26		
Tony Guillory	LB	6'4"	236	24		
Jack Pardee	LB	6'2"	230	31	6	12
Myron Pottios	LB	6'2"	240	27	1	
Doug Woodlief	LB	6'3"	230	23	2	
Claude Crabb	DB	6'	192	27	1	
Irv Cross	DB	6'1"	195	28	2	
Willie Daniel	DB	5'11"	190	29	2	
Chuck Lamson	DB	6'	195	28	2	
Ed Meador	DB	5'11"	200	30	8	12
Clancy Williams	DB	6'2"	198	24	4	
Kelton Winston	DB	6'	195	26		

Hal Bedsole — Injury
Henry Dyer — Injury
Rosey Grier — Injury

Use Name	Pos.	Hgt	Wgt	Age	Int	Pts
Roman Gabriel	QB	6'4"	230	27		36
Bill Munson	QB	6'2"	200	25		
Willie Ellison	HB	6'1"	207	22		
Les Josephson	HB	6'	220	25		48
Tommy Mason	HB	6'	190	28		
Dick Bass	FB	5'10"	195	30		42
Jim Stiger	FB	5'11"	214	26		
Bernie Casey	FL	6'4"	210	28		48
Billy Truax	TE	6'5"	235	24		24
Dave Pivec	LB-TE	6'3"	240	23		6
Bucky Pope	OE	6'5"	205	23		12
Jack Snow	OE	6'2"	195	24		48
Wendell Tucker	OE	5'10"	185	23		
Bruce Gossett	K	6'2"	230	24		108
Jon Kilgore	K	6'1"	205	23		

BALTIMORE COLTS 11-1-2 Don Shula

Scores of Each Game		
38	ATLANTA	31
38	Philadelphia	6
41	SAN FRANCISCO	7
24	Chicago	3
24	LOS ANGELES	24
20	Minnesota	20
17	Washington	13
13	GREEN BAY	10
49	Atlanta	7
41	DETROIT	7
26	San Francisco	9
23	DALLAS	17
30	NEW ORLEANS	10
10	Los Angeles	34

Use Name	Pos.	Hgt	Wgt	Age	Int	Pts
Sam Ball	OT	6'4"	240	23		
Jim Parker	OT	6'3"	275	33		
Bob Vogel	OT	6'5"	250	25		
Norman Davis	OG	6'3"	250	22		
Dale Memmelaar	OG	6'2"	246	30		
Glenn Ressler	OG	6'3"	250	23		
Dan Sullivan	OG	6'3"	250	28		
Dick Szymanski	C	6'3"	235	35		
Bill Curry	LB-C	6'2"	235	24		
Ordell Braase	DE	6'4"	245	35		6
Roy Hilton	DE	6'6"	240	22		
Lou Michaels	DE	6'2"	250	31		106
Bubba Smith	DE	6'7"	295	22		
Fred Miller	DT	6'3"	250	26		
Billy Ray Smith	DT	6'4"	250	32		
Andy Stynchula	DE-DT	6'3"	250	28		

Use Name	Pos.	Hgt	Wgt	Age	Int	Pts
Barry Brown	LB	6'3"	235	24		
Mike Curtis	LB	6'2"	232	23	1	
Dennis Gaubatz	LB	6'2"	232	26	2	
Ron Porter	LB	6'3"	232	22	1	
Don Shinnick	LB	6'	228	32	3	
Bobby Boyd	DB	5'10"	192	29	6	6
George Harold	DB	6'3"	194	25		
Alvin Haymond	DB	6'	194	25	2	
Jerry Logan	DB	6'1"	190	26	4	6
Lenny Lyles	DB	6'2"	204	31	5	6
Preston Pearson	DB	6'1"	190	22		
Charlie Stukes	DB	6'3"	212	23	2	
Rick Volk	DB	6'3"	195	22	6	6
Jim Welch	HB-DB	6'	196	29		

Use Name	Pos.	Hgt	Wgt	Age	Int	Pts
Johnny Unitas	QB	6'1"	196	34		
Jim Ward	QB	6'2"	195	23		
Tom Matte	HB	6'	214	28		72
Lenny Moore	HB	6'1"	198	34		24
Jerry Hill	FB	5'11"	215	27		12
Tony Lorick	FB	6'1"	217	25		36
Don Alley	FL	6'2"	200	21		
Jimmy Orr	FL	5'11"	185	31		6
Willie Richardson	FL	6'2"	198	27		48
John Mackey	TE	6'3"	224	25		18
Butch Wilson	TE	6'2"	228	25		
Ray Berry	OE	6'2"	190	34		6
Ray Perkins	OE	6'	183	25		12
Alex Hawkins (from ATL)	FL-OE	6'1"	186	30		24
David Lee	K	6'4"	215	23		

SAN FRANCISCO FORTY-NINERS 7-7-0 Jack Christiansen

Scores of Each Game		
27	Minnesota	21
38	ATLANTA	7
7	Baltimore	41
27	Los Angeles	24
28	Philadelphia	27
27	NEW ORLEANS	13
3	DETROIT	45
7	LOS ANGELES	17
28	Washington	31
0	Green Bay	13
9	BALTIMORE	26
14	CHICAGO	28
34	Atlanta	28
24	DALLAS	16

Use Name	Pos.	Hgt	Wgt	Age	Int	Pts
Dave Hettema	OT	6'4"	247	25		
Walt Rock	OT	6'5"	255	26		
Len Rohde	OT	6'4"	250	29		
Elmer Collett	OG	6'4"	230	22		
Howard Mudd	OG	6'3"	254	25		
Don Parker	OG	6'3"	235	22		
John Thomas	OG	6'4"	250	32		
Bruce Bosley	C	6'2"	244	33		
Joe Cerne	C	6'2"	240	24		
Stan Hindman	DE	6'3"	232	23		
Tom Holzer	DE	6'4"	250	22		
Walter Johnson	DE	6'4"	225	23		
Clark Miller	DE	6'5"	247	28	1	
Charlie Johnson	DT	6'2"	265	23		
Charlie Krueger	DT	6'4"	260	31		
Roland Lakes	DT	6'4"	280	27		

Use Name	Pos.	Hgt	Wgt	Age	Int	Pts
Ed Beard	LB	6'2"	226	27		
Bob Harrison	LB	6'2"	228	30		
Matt Hazeltine	LB	6'1"	230	34		
Frank Nunley	LB	6'2"	220	21	1	
Dave Wilcox	LB	6'3"	234	24	2	
Kermit Alexander	DB	5'11"	180	26	5	
George Donnelly	DB	6'3"	210	24		
Goose Gonsoulin	DB	6'3"	210	29	3	
Jim Jackson	DB	6'	193	23	1	
Jim Johnson	DB	6'2"	187	29	2	
Mel Phillips	DB	6'	192	25	1	
Al Randolph	DB	6'2"	192	23		
Wayne Trimble	DB	6'3"	203	21		

Kay McFarland — Injury

Use Name	Pos.	Hgt	Wgt	Age	Int	Pts
John Brodie	QB	6'1"	210	32		6
George Mira	QB	5'11"	190	25		
Steve Spurrier	QB	6'2"	203	22		
John David Crow	HB	6'2"	224	32		30
Doug Cunningham	HB	5'11"	185	21		12
Dave Kopay	HB	6'2"	218	25		
Bill Tucker	FB-HB	6'2"	222	23		
Gary Lewis	FB	6'3"	230	25		42
Ken Willard	FB	6'2"	230	24		36
Chip Myers	FL	6'4"	185	22		
Wayne Swinford	FL	6'	192	24		
Dick Witcher	TE-FL	6'3"	204	22		18
Dave Olerich	TE	6'1"	220	22		
Monte Stickles	TE	6'4"	235	29		
Bob Windsor	TE	6'4"	223	24		18
Dave Parks	OE	6'2"	207	25		12
Sonny Randle	OE	6'2"	190	31		24
Tommy Davis	K	6'	220	32		75

ATLANTA FALCONS 1-12-1 Norb Hecker

Scores of Each Game		
31	Baltimore	38
7	San Francisco	38
0	Green Bay	23
7	PHILADELPHIA	38
20	WASHINGTON	20
3	Detroit	24
21	MINNESOTA	20
7	Dallas	37
7	BALTIMORE	49
3	LOS ANGELES	31
24	New Orleans	27
3	Los Angeles	20
28	SAN FRANCISCO	34
14	CHICAGO	23

Use Name	Pos.	Hgt	Wgt	Age	Int	Pts
Errol Linden	OT	6'5"	260	30		
Bill Sandeman (from NO)	OT	6'6"	250	24		
Don Talbert	OT	6'5"	255	27		
Jim Simon	OG-OT	6'5"	240	26		
Ed Cook	OG	6'2"	250	35		
Dan Grimm	OG	6'3"	245	26		
Tom Harmon	OG	6'4"	238	25		
Lou Kirouac	OG	6'3"	240	26		
Jake Kupp (to NO)	OG	6'3"	233	25		
Jim Wilson	OG	6'3"	258	26		
Frank Marchlewski	C	6'2"	238	23		
Karl Rubke	DT-C	6'4"	244	31		
Bob Hughes	DE	6'4"	255	22		
Bobby Richards	DE	6'2"	245	28		
Sam Williams	DE	6'5"	245	36		
Bo Wood	DE	6'3"	225	21		
Jim Norton	DT	6'4"	254	24	1	
Chuck Sieminski	DT	6'4"	270	27		
Joe Szczecko	DT	6'	245	25		

Use Name	Pos.	Hgt	Wgt	Age	Int	Pts
Dick Absher (from WAS)	LB	6'4"	227	23		4
Andy Bowling	LB	6'3"	235	22		
Ralph Heck	LB	6'2"	230	26		
Tommy Nobis	LB	6'2"	235	23	3	6
Marion Rushing	LB	6'2"	230	30	1	
Bob Sanders	LB	6'3"	235	24		
Tom Bleick	DB	6'2"	200	24		
Lee Calland	DB	6'	190	26	3	6
Floyd Hudlow	DB	5'11"	195	23	2	
Nick Rassas	DB	6'	190	23		
Ken Reaves	DB	6'3"	205	22	7	
Jerry Richardson	DB	6'3"	190	24		
Bob Riggle	DB	6'1"	200	23		

Use Name	Pos.	Hgt	Wgt	Age	Int	Pts
Randy Johnson	QB	6'3"	196	23		6
Terry Nofsinger	QB	6'4"	215	29		
Steve Sloan	QB	6'	185	23		
Perry Lee Dunn	HB	6'2"	215	24		
Tom Moore	HB	6'2"	210	29		
Ron Rector	HB	6'	200	23		
Junior Coffey	FB	6'1"	210	25		30
Jim Mankins	FB	6'1"	235	23		
Tommy McDonald	FL	5'10"	175	33		24
Ron Smith	DB-FL	6'1"	192	24		6
Taz Anderson	TE	6'2"	215	28		6
Billy Martin	TE	6'4"	235	24		18
Ray Ogden (from NO)	TE	6'5"	225	24		6
Gary Barnes	OE	6'4"	210	27		6
Jerry Simmons (from NO)	OE	6'1"	190	24		12
Billy Lothridge	K	6'1"	195	23		
Wade Traynham	K	6'2"	218	25		43

COASTAL DIVISION

LOS ANGELES RAMS

RUSHING

Last Name	No.	Yds	Avg	TD
Josephson	178	800	4.5	4
Bass	187	627	3.4	6
Mason	63	213	3.4	0
Gabriel	43	198	4.6	6
Ellison	14	84	6.0	0
Stiger	3	6	2.0	0
Munson	2	−22	−11.0	0

RECEIVING

Last Name	No.	Yds	Avg	TD
Casey	53	871	16	8
Truax	37	487	13	4
Josephson	37	400	11	4
Snow	28	735	26	8
Bass	27	212	8	1
Mason	13	70	5	0
Pope	8	152	19	2
Pivec	2	2	1	1
Ellison	1	18	18	0

PUNT RETURNS

Last Name	No.	Yds	Avg	TD
Cross	17	136	8	0
Meador	21	131	6	0
Tucker	6	40	7	0
Winston	1	12	12	0
Stiger	4	9	2	0
Crabb	1	0	0	0

KICKOFF RETURNS

Last Name	No.	Yds	Avg	TD
Ellison	13	340	26	0
Tucker	11	242	22	0
Williams	7	161	23	0
Cross	4	134	34	0
Josephson	5	91	18	0
Winston	3	65	22	0

PASSING – PUNTING – KICKING

PASSING	Att	Comp	%	Yds	Yd/Att	TD	Int–%	RK
Gabriel	371	196	53	2779	7.5	25	13– 4	4
Munson	10	5	50	38	3.8	1	2–20	
Josephson	5	2	40	47	9.4	0	1–20	
Mason	3	2	67	65	21.7	1	0– 0	
Meador	1	1	100	18	18.0	1	0– 0	

PUNTING	No	Avg
Kilgore	68	42.2

KICKING	XP	Att	%	FG	Att	%
Gossett	48	48	100	20	43	47

BALTIMORE COLTS

RUSHING

Last Name	No.	Yds	Avg	TD
Matte	147	636	4.3	9
Lorick	133	436	3.3	6
Hill	90	311	3.5	2
Moore	42	132	3.1	4
Unitas	22	89	4.0	0
Ward	5	23	4.6	0
Hawkins	2	12	6.0	0
Welch	2	6	3.0	0

RECEIVING

Last Name	No.	Yds	Avg	TD
Richardson	63	860	14	8
Mackey	55	686	12	3
Matte	35	496	14	3
Hawkins	27	469	17	4
Lorick	22	189	9	0
Hill	19	156	8	0
Perkins	16	302	19	2
Moore	13	153	12	0
Berry	11	167	15	1
Orr	3	72	24	1
Alley	1	11	11	0

PUNT RETURNS

Last Name	No.	Yds	Avg	TD
Haymond	26	155	6	0
Volk	11	88	8	0
Logan	5	80	16	1

KICKOFF RETURNS

Last Name	No.	Yds	Avg	TD
Moore	16	392	25	0
Haymond	13	326	25	0
Lorick	8	212	27	0
Stukes	1	19	19	0
Logan	2	17	9	0
Matte	1	14	14	0
Davis	1	8	8	0

PASSING – PUNTING – KICKING

PASSING	Att	Comp	%	Yds	Yd/Att	TD	Int–%	RK
Unitas	436	255	58	3428	7.9	20	16– 4	2
Ward	16	9	56	115	7.2	2	1– 6	
Matte	5	1	20	18	3.6	0	0– 0	

PUNTING	No	Avg
Lee	49	42.3

KICKING	XP	Att	%	FG	Att	%
Michaels	46	48	96	20	37	54

SAN FRANCISCO FORTY NINERS

RUSHING

Last Name	No.	Yds	Avg	TD
Willard	169	510	3.0	5
Crow	113	479	4.2	2
Lewis	67	342	5.1	6
Cunningham	43	212	4.9	2
Brodie	20	147	7.4	1
Mira	7	23	3.3	0
Kopay	6	21	3.5	0
Spurrier	5	18	3.6	0
Windsor	1	7	7.0	0
Tucker	3	5	1.7	0

RECEIVING

Last Name	No.	Yds	Avg	TD
Witcher	46	705	15	3
Randle	33	502	15	4
Crow	31	373	12	3
Parks	26	313	12	2
Willard	23	242	11	1
Windsor	21	254	12	2
Lewis	21	218	10	1
Cunningham	13	121	9	0
Stickles	7	86	12	0
Tucker	2	22	11	0
Myers	2	13	7	0
Kopay	2	11	6	0
Olerich	1	2	2	0

PUNT RETURNS

Last Name	No.	Yds	Avg	TD
Cunningham	27	249	9	0
Alexander	6	64	11	0
Tucker	1	1	1	0
Gonsoulin	1	0	0	0

KICKOFF RETURNS

Last Name	No.	Yds	Avg	TD
Cunningham	31	826	27	0
Tucker	9	199	22	0
Lewis	9	190	21	0
Swinford	2	51	26	0
Kopay	1	21	21	0
Windsor	1	21	21	0
Alexander	1	18	18	0
Nunley	2	0	0	0

PASSING – PUNTING – KICKING

PASSING	Att	Comp	%	Yds	Yd/Att	TD	Int–%	RK
Brodie	349	168	48	2013	5.8	11	16– 5	11
Mira	65	35	54	592	9.1	5	3– 5	
Spurrier	50	23	46	211	4.2	0	7–14	
Crow	5	2	40	46	9.2	0	0– 0	

PUNTING	No	Avg
Spurrier	73	37.6

KICKING	XP	Att	%	FG	Att	%
Davis	33	33	100	14	33	42

ATLANTA FALCONS

RUSHING

Last Name	No.	Yds	Avg	TD
Coffey	180	722	4.0	4
Johnson	24	144	6.0	1
Rector	24	127	5.3	0
Moore	53	104	2.0	0
Dunn	27	63	2.3	0
Smith	8	42	5.3	0
Nofsinger	3	33	11.0	0
Lothridge	1	16	16.0	0
Mankins	2	7	3.5	0
Sloan	1	2	2.0	0

RECEIVING

Last Name	No.	Yds	Avg	TD
McDonald	33	436	13	4
Coffey	30	196	7	1
Simmons	23	312	14	2
Ogden	20	327	16	1
Martin	15	182	12	3
Dunn	13	111	9	0
Smith	11	227	21	0
Barnes	10	154	15	1
Moore	10	74	7	0
Anderson	8	99	12	1
Rector	4	13	3	0
Mankins	1	11	11	0

PUNT RETURNS

Last Name	No.	Yds	Avg	TD
Smith	20	92	5	0
Hudlow	1	2	2	0
Simmons	3	0	0	0

KICKOFF RETURNS

Last Name	No.	Yds	Avg	TD
Smith	39	976	25	1
Dunn	7	128	18	0
Hudlow	2	56	28	0
Rassas	2	51	26	0
Ogden	3	41	14	0
Simmons	2	38	19	0
Linden	3	37	12	0
Mankins	1	12	12	0
Wood	1	9	9	0
Talbert	1	2	2	0
Martin	1	0	0	0
Sandeman	1	0	0	0

PASSING – PUNTING – KICKING

PASSING	Att	Comp	%	Yds	Yd/Att	TD	Int–%	RK
Johnson	288	142	49	1620	5.6	10	21– 7	16
Nofsinger	60	30	50	352	5.9	1	2– 3	
Sloan	18	4	22	38	2.1	0	2–11	
Dunn	2	1	50	32	16.0	1	0– 0	
Moore	2	2	100	102	51.0	1	0– 0	

PUNTING	No	Avg
Lothridge	87	43.7

KICKING	XP	Att	%	FG	Att	%
Traynham	22	22	100	7	18	39
Absher	4	4	100	0	1	0

1967 A.F.L. Coming Up to Equal Footing

The AFL wasn't ready yet to win a Super Bowl, but the clubs in the newer league won some respect with their showing in interleague pre-season games. The games were far more competitive than had been expected, and the AFL drew first blood when the Denver Broncos beat the Detroit Lions 13-7 in the first interleague contest. The two leagues battled on even lines through the late-summer games, but the AFL administered the worst beating when the Chiefs, still smarting from their Super Bowl loss to Green Bay, crushed the Chicago Bears 66-27. The pre-season series seemed to prove that AFL teams could play on a par with average NFL teams but that time was needed to catch up with NFL powers like the Packers.

Time was on the AFL's side, however, as the common draft assured a steady flow of young talent into the league. Teams like Boston and Denver, which had never done well in signing its draft choices, now had an easier time coming to terms with graduating collegiate talent. The AFL teams also were moving into better stadia, with the San Diego Chargers this year setting up shop in a new municipal stadium.

EASTERN DIVISION

Houston Oilers—A 3-11 team only a year ago, the Oilers used a fine rookie class and a revitalized defense to capture their first divisional crown since 1962. Every adjustment head coach Wally Lemm made in the defense worked out splendidly; he moved veterans around and inserted rookies with the touch of a chess grandmaster. Pat Holmes, a disappointment last year as a tackle, caught fire as an end. Second-year man George Rice took over a tackle spot and drew compliments around the league. Rookie linebacker George Webster combined size, speed, and sound football sense in an All-Pro freshman season, and his linebacking mates were Garland Boyette, playing the middle for the first time, and Olen Underwood. W. K. Hicks and Jim Norton held onto their secondary posts, but joining them were newcomers Miller Farr, a quick cornerback picked up in a trade from San Diego, and rookie strong safety Ken Houston. This rebuilt unit allowed only eighteen touchdowns all year. The leading lights of the offense were fullback Hoyle Granger, quarterback Pete Beathard, who was picked up in mid-season from Kansas City, and star guard Bob Talamini.

New York Jets—As usual, the Jets looked like a sure title winner until December, and then, as usual, they fell apart. Ending November with a 7-2-1 record and a one-game lead over the coming Houston Oilers, the Jets started December by losing to Denver, Kansas City, and Oakland. They straightened out in time to beat San Diego in the season's finale, but by then the Oilers had locked up first place. The Jet pass defense contributed heavily to this year's late slump, as the line failed to rush enemy passers consistently and the secondary was not airtight. The Jets also had offensive problems, although Joe Namath and receivers George Sauer and Don Maynard bombed enemy defenses regularly. Fullback Matt Snell, the team's workhorse, ripped up a knee in the opening game and didn't return to action until mid-November; by then, halfback Emerson Boozer had gone out with an injured knee of his own.

Buffalo Bills—The Buffalo defensive unit stayed strong despite the loss of middle linebacker Harry Jacobs for the last seven games with a broken elbow, but the offense, never too robust to begin with, broke down completely under a rash of knee injuries. Bobby Crockett, last year's rookie receiving threat, sat out the entire year with a bad knee, while running back Bobby Burnett, veteran guard Billy Shaw, and split end Art Powell missed at least half the schedule with their knee injuries. Quarterback Jack Kemp's bad season further hurt the attack, and only newcomer Keith Lincoln, picked up in a swap with San Diego, kept the offense alive with his running and receiving. With all the injuries, the Bills scored more than 20 points in only three games all year—not nearly enough for a fourth straight championship.

Miami Dolphins—By mid-season rookie Bob Griese had taken over as the starting quarterback. Showing a strong arm and unshakable poise, Griese hooked up with rookie split end Jack Clancy in an effective passing combination. Outside of these two rookies, however, the Miami offense gave fans little to cheer about. Halfback Abner Haynes was long past his prime and was shipped out to New York before the year ended. The line had huge gaps, and flanker Howard Twilley had neither size nor speed. The defense, though not one of the league's best, did field several representative ball players.

Boston Patriots—Jim Nance still dominated the team with his powerful ball-carrying, but the supporting cast on the Patriots slipped, and they fell to last place in the East. With no speed at halfback or in the receivers, and with Babe Parilli showing advanced symptoms of old age, defenses waited for Nance's smashes into the line, yet the big fullback from Syracuse still bowled over the expectant defenders for 1,216 yards.

WESTERN DIVISION

Oakland Raiders—In a daring trade, the Raiders sent quarterback Tom Flores and split end Art Powell, both established starters, to Buffalo for quarterback Daryle Lamonica and Glenn Bass. Bass didn't make the team, but Lamonica developed into a fine long passer. End Bill Miller came from Buffalo at little cost and gave Lamonica a steady target. Willie Brown came over from Denver and beat All-Pro Dave Grayson out of a cornerback position. Thirty-nine-year-old George Blanda signed aboard after being released by Houston; the old-timer backed up Lamonica and led the league in scoring with his steady place-kicking. The rookie crop turned up guard Gene Upshaw, who immediately ranked among the league's best offensive linemen, and linebacker Duane Benson, who played on the special teams with zeal. Of course, the Raiders already had some top-notch players, with Billy Cannon, Jim Otto, Ben Davidson, Tom Keating, and Kent McCloughan winning All-League honors among the returning veterans. The Raiders' depth showed when halfback Clem Daniels broke his ankle late in the year and Pete Banaszak filled in with no noticeable drop in quality. Thus, the Raiders easily swept the Western Division title.

Kansas City Chiefs—AFL clubs learned well the lesson taught by the Green Bay Packers in the first Super Bowl. The Packers had singled out certain weak links in the Kansas City defense and ruthlessly exploited them, and now the AFL clubs found success in directing their attacks right at the same people. Enemy offenses singled out for special treatment, linebackers Chuck Hurston and Sherrill Headrick and cornerbacks Fred Williamson and Willie Mitchell, and by the time coach Hank Stram could readjust his defense the Chiefs had lost all four of their meetings with Oakland and San Diego and all chances for a repeat title in the West. But Stram did substitute some young talent into the lineup, and after Bud Abell, Emmitt Thomas, Fletcher Smith, and rookies Jim Lynch and Willie Lanier got their bearings, the Kansas City linebacking and secondary were a lot tougher. Aside from closing out the season with three straight wins, the high point of the year was the unveiling of two spectacular special team rookies: Norwegian place-kicker Jan Stenerud, and kick returner Noland Smith.

San Diego Chargers—The Chargers got off to a fast start and had high hopes of regaining the Western Division title, only to lose their last four games and slip back into a third-place finish. Coach Sid Gillman's biggest headache was his defense, which disintegrated down the stretch. Despite high-priced talents like Scott Appleton and Steve DeLong, the line put practically no pressure at all on enemy passers, and, given time, opposing quarterbacks found the San Diego secondary easy to pick apart. The offense kept the title drive alive until late in the season and kept the fans filing into the new San Diego Stadium. Enemy defenses had to worry first about flanker Lance Alworth, pro football's premier deep pass receiver, but if they paid too much attention to him, quarterback John Hadl simply threw to ends Gary Garrison and Willie Frazier, both fine pass catchers in their own right. The line was one of the best in pro football, especially at protecting the passer, and the San Diego running attack got a quick shot of energy in the form of Dickie Post and Brad Hubbert, a pair of rookie backs.

Denver Broncos—Lou Saban returned to pro football as head coach and general manager of the Broncos and immediately ripped the club apart to get a fresh start in building a winner. At times during the season Saban was starting fifteen rookies on the two platoons, a sign of his willingness to go with youth now to build a winner later. The team's biggest problems came in pass defense, where a rookie-laden secondary and linebacking corps could not handle good air attacks. The defensive line showed more stability as veteran Dave Costa, obtained from Buffalo for a draft pick, starred at a tackle post and youngsters Rich Jackson and Pete Duranko showed promise at the ends. Saban rebuilt the offense into a creditable unit, although the line was manned by and large with inexperienced or mediocre players. Saban got himself a quarterback by trading two first-round draft choices to San Diego for Steve Tensi, a promising young passer who learned as he played in Denver. Two fine wide receivers surfaced in Al Denson, last year's tight end, and Eric Crabtree, one of last year's bench warmers, while the running game improved immensely with the arrival of rookie halfback Floyd Little.

FINAL TEAM STATISTICS

OFFENSE

	BOSTON	BUFFALO	DENVER	HOUSTON	K.CITY	MIAMI	NEW YORK	OAKLAND	SAN DIEGO
FIRST DOWNS:									
Total	219	203	172	207	251	212	282	250	259
by Rushing	80	65	65	111	116	65	82	79	88
by Passing	120	119	91	86	117	123	180	154	150
by Penalty	19	19	16	10	18	24	20	17	21
RUSHING									
Number	391	371	420	476	462	326	389	458	417
Yards	1604	1271	1265	2122	2018	1323	1307	1928	1715
Average Yards	4.1	3.4	3.0	4.5	4.4	4.1	3.4	4.2	4.1
Touchdowns	10	9	10	12	18	10	17	19	14
PASSING:									
Attempts	434	434	374	332	382	480	515	464	463
Completions	191	183	150	143	213	229	271	236	230
Completion Percentage	44.0	42.2	40.1	43.1	55.8	47.7	52.6	50.9	49.7
Passing Yards	2784	2763	2190	1532	2773	2741	4128	3541	3517
Avg. Yards per Attempt	6.4	6.4	5.9	4.6	7.3	5.7	8.0	7.6	7.6
Avg. Yards per Completion	14.6	15.1	14.6	10.7	13.0	12.0	15.2	15.0	15.3
Time Tackled Att. to Pass	45	45	58	20	32	41	28	40	11
Yards Lost Tackled	361	446	508	151	301	405	283	353	107
Net Yards	2423	2317	1682	1381	2472	2336	3845	3188	3410
Touchdowns	20	14	17	11	26	16	27	33	26
Interceptions	32	34	18	20	19	28	29	23	24
Percent Intercepted	7.4	7.8	4.8	6.0	5.0	5.8	5.6	5.0	5.2
PUNTS:									
Number	65	77	105	71	61	70	65	76	63
Average Distance	40.5	43.1	44.9	42.6	41.3	41.6	42.1	44.3	37.5
PUNT RETURNS:									
Number	43	47	26	20	33	25	48	51	39
Yards	412	199	351	255	245	128	326	642	480
Average Yards	9.6	4.2	13.5	12.8	7.4	5.1	6.8	12.6	12.3
Touchdowns	0	0	1	0	0	0	0	0	0
KICKOFF RETURNS:									
Number	73	51	60	44	53	67	57	45	54
Yards	1436	1113	1518	1020	1245	1443	1144	962	1239
Average Yards	19.7	21.8	25.3	23.2	23.5	21.5	20.1	21.4	22.9
Touchdowns	0	0	0	1	1	0	0	0	0
INTERCEPTION RETURNS:									
Number	17	27	28	26	31	28	27	30	13
Yards	257	401	413	676	578	402	322	404	274
Average Yards	15.1	14.9	14.8	26.0	18.6	14.4	11.9	13.5	21.1
Touchdowns	2	3	3	6	4	1	1	4	2
PENALTIES:									
Number	59	74	48	61	68	53	64	71	72
Yards	520	828	512	698	680	490	691	768	817
FUMBLES:									
Number	37	32	30	17	28	36	15	19	18
Number Lost	22	13	12	7	8	16	8	13	10
POINTS:									
Total	280	237	256	258	408	219	371	468	360
PAT (kick) Attempts	31	26	30	30	45	28	40	57	45
PAT (kick) Made	30	25	28	30	45	27	36	56	45
PAT (2 Point) Attempts	2	1	1	1	4	0	6	1	0
PAT (2 Point) Made	0	1	1	0	2	0	4	1	0
FG Attempts	31	27	28	28	36	18	32	30	30
FG Made	16	16	12	14	21	8	17	20	15
Percent	51.6	59.3	42.9	50.0	58.3	44.4	53.1	66.7	50.0
Safeties	2	0	2	0	1	0	0	1	0

DEFENSE

	BOSTON	BUFFALO	DENVER	HOUSTON	K.CITY	MIAMI	NEW YORK	OAKLAND	SAN DIEGO
FIRST DOWNS:									
Total	219	201	276	233	221	269	203	182	251
by Rushing	61	73	115	86	73	115	80	60	88
by Passing	138	106	143	126	132	133	111	103	148
by Penalty	20	22	18	21	16	21	12	19	15
RUSHING									
Number	417	437	444	424	343	466	386	352	441
Yards	1350	1622	2076	1637	1408	2145	1633	1129	1553
Average Yards	3.2	3.7	4.7	3.9	4.1	4.6	4.2	3.2	3.5
Touchdowns	12	11	21	7	10	18	14	9	17
PASSING:									
Attempts	423	377	459	461	462	349	424	459	464
Completions	211	162	214	228	229	188	195	189	230
Completion Percentage	49.9	43.0	46.6	49.5	49.6	53.9	46.0	41.2	49.6
Passing Yards	3123	2191	3289	2619	2890	3082	2489	2831	3455
Avg. Yards per Attempt	7.4	5.8	7.2	5.7	6.3	8.8	5.9	6.2	7.5
Avg. Yards per Completion	14.8	13.5	15.4	11.5	12.6	16.4	12.8	15.0	15.0
Time Tackled Att. to Pass	31	43	18	25	38	28	39	67	31
Yards Lost Tackled	267	366	164	201	354	247	347	666	303
Net Yards	2856	1825	3125	2418	2536	2835	2142	2165	3152
Touchdowns	28	17	27	10	13	31	20	18	26
Interceptions	17	27	28	26	31	28	27	30	13
Percent Intercepted	4.0	7.2	6.1	5.6	6.7	8.0	6.4	6.5	2.8
PUNTS:									
Number	73	74	65	63	64	52	79	111	72
Average Distance	41.9	41.0	41.5	41.0	43.0	41.1	43.2	41.9	45.2
PUNT RETURNS:									
Number	31	33	61	41	31	41	36	37	21
Yards	252	301	718	383	331	268	311	250	224
Average Yards	8.1	9.1	11.8	9.3	10.7	6.5	8.6	6.8	10.7
Touchdowns	0	0	0	0	0	0	1	0	0
KICKOFF RETURNS:									
Number	45	56	42	51	55	46	64	82	63
Yards	946	1292	1046	950	1207	1079	1387	1707	1506
Average Yards	21.0	23.1	24.9	18.6	21.9	23.5	21.7	20.8	23.9
Touchdowns	0	0	1	0	1	0	0	0	0
INTERCEPTION RETURNS:									
Number	32	34	18	20	19	28	29	23	24
Yards	640	554	262	156	471	395	711	209	329
Average Yards	20.0	16.3	14.6	7.8	24.8	14.1	24.5	9.1	13.7
Touchdowns	7	2	2	1	5	3	5	0	1
PENALTIES:									
Number	70	51	58	59	76	59	67	69	61
Yards	722	507	628	614	757	691	717	702	666
FUMBLES:									
Number	26	26	23	29	34	19	24	29	22
Number Lost	17	9	13	13	18	8	6	15	10
POINTS:									
Total	389	285	409	199	254	407	329	233	352
PAT (kick) Attempts	46	33	50	14	28	50	40	27	44
PAT (kick) Made	44	32	48	14	28	47	39	26	44
PAT (2 Point) Attempts	2	0	2	4	2	3	1	2	0
PAT (2 Point) Made	0	0	2	3	1	0	1	2	0
FG Attempts	31	38	31	42	25	26	26	14	27
FG Made	19	17	15	23	14	14	14	9	14
Percent	61.3	44.7	48.4	54.8	56.0	53.8	53.8	64.3	51.9
Safeties	0	2	0	1	1	0	0	1	1

HOUSTON OILERS 9-4-1 Wally Lemm

Scores of Each Game		
20	KANSAS CITY	25
20	Buffalo	3
3	San Diego	13
10	DENVER	6
28	New York	28
24	Kansas City	19
10	BUFFALO	3
7	Boston	18
20	Denver	18
27	BOSTON	6
17	MIAMI	14
7	OAKLAND	19
24	SAN DIEGO	17
41	Miami	10

Use Name	Pos.	Hgt	Wgt	Age	Int	Pts
Glen Ray Hines	OT	6'5"	270	23		
Walt Suggs	OT	6'5"	265	28		
Sonny Bishop	OG	6'2"	245	27		
Ed Marcontell	OG	6'	260	23		
Tom Regner	OG	6'1"	255	23		
Bob Talamini	OG	6'1"	255	28		
Bobby Maples	C	6'3"	245	24		
Don Floyd	DE	6'4"	245	28		
Pat Holmes	DE	6'5"	260	27		
Willie Jones	DE	6'2"	260	25		
Carel Stith	DE	6'5"	270	22		
Bud Marshall	DT	6'5"	270	25		
Willie Parker	DT	6'2"	270	22		
Andy Rice (from KC)	DT	6'3"	266	25		
George Rice	DT	6'3"	260	23		
Pete Barnes	LB	6'3"	245	22		
Garland Boyette	LB	6'1"	240	27		
Danny Brabham	LB	6'4"	233	26		
Ronnie Caveness	LB	6'1"	225	24		
Olen Underwood	LB	6'1"	230	25	1	
George Webster	LB	6'4"	223	21	1	
Larry Carwell	DB	6'1"	187	23		
Miller Farr	DB	6'1"	188	24	10	18
W. K. Hicks	DB	6'1"	190	24	3	
Ken Houston	DB	6'3"	190	22	4	18
Bobby Jancik	DB	5'11"	178	27	1	
Pete Johns	DB	6'3"	188	22		
Zeke Moore	DB	6'2"	190	23		6
Jim Norton	DB	6'3"	180	28	6	6
Billy Anderson	QB	6'1"	195	26		
Pete Beathard (from KC)	QB	6'2"	210	25		6
Bob Davis	QB	6'3"	202	21		
Jacky Lee (to KC)	QB	6'1"	188	28		
Sid Blanks	HB	6'	208	26		12
Woody Campbell	HB	5'11"	205	22		36
Hoyle Granger	FB	6'1"	225	23		54
Roy Hopkins	FB	6'1"	227	22		
Glenn Bass	FL	6'2"	206	28		6
Ode Burrell	FL	6'	195	27		
Larry Elkins	FL	6'1"	195	24		
Bob Poole	TE	6'4"	215	25		
Alvin Reed	TE	6'5"	228	23		6
Charley Frazier	OE	6'	188	28		6
Lionel Taylor	OE	6'2"	215	31		6
John Wittenborn	K	6'2"	240	31		72

Gary Cutsinger – Injury

NEW YORK JETS 8-5-1 Weeb Ewbank

Scores of Each Game		
17	Buffalo	20
38	Denver	24
29	MIAMI	7
27	OAKLAND	14
28	HOUSTON	28
33	Miami	14
30	BOSTON	23
18	Kansas City	42
20	BUFFALO	10
29	Boston	24
24	DENVER	33
7	KANSAS CITY	21
29	Oakland	38
42	San Diego	31

Use Name	Pos.	Hgt	Wgt	Age	Int	Pts
Winston Hill	OT	6'4"	275	25		
Sherman Plunkett	OT	6'4"	330	33		
Jim Harris	OT	6'4"	280	23		
Paul Seiler	OG-OT	6'4"	255	21		
Dave Herman	OG	6'2"	255	25		
Pete Perreault	OG	6'3"	245	28		
Randy Rasmussen	OG	6'2"	255	22		
Jeff Richardson	OG	6'3"	260	22		
John Matlock	C	6'4"	246	22		
John Schmitt	C	6'4"	245	24		
Verlon Biggs	DE	6'4"	260	24		
Gerry Philbin	DE	6'2"	248	26		
Bert Wilder	DT-DE	6'3"	245	27		
Dennis Randall	DT	6'6"	245	21		
Paul Rochester	DT	6'2"	255	30		
John Elliott	DE-DT	6'4"	245	22		
Al Atkinson	LB	6'1"	228	24	5	
Ralph Baker	LB	6'3"	228	25	1	
Paul Crane	LB	6'2"	205	23		
Larry Grantham	LB	6'	206	28	5	
Carl McAdams	LB	6'3"	240	23		
Jim Waskiewicz	OT-LB	6'4"	235	23		
Bill Baird	DB	5'10"	180	28	3	
Randy Beverly	DB	5'11"	185	23	4	
Solomon Brannan	DB	6'1"	185	25		
Cornell Gordon	DB	6'	187	26	1	
Jim Hudson	DB	6'2"	210	24	4	
Henry King	DB	6'4"	205	22		
Sherman Lewis	DB	5'10"	180	25		
Bill Rademacher	DB	6'1"	190	25		
Johnny Sample	DB	6'1"	208	30	4	6
Joe Namath	QB	6'2"	195	23		6
Mike Taliaferro	QB	6'2"	205	25		
Jim Turner	QB	6'2"	205	26		87
Emerson Boozer	HB	5'11"	207	24		78
Earl Christy	HB	5'11"	195	24		
Bill Mathis	HB	6'1"	220	28		46
Billy Joe	FB	6'2"	236	26		12
Mark Smolinski	FB	6'	215	28		24
Matt Snell	FB	6'2"	220	25		
Don Maynard	FL	6'	180	31		62
Bob Schweickert	FL	6'1"	190	24		
Curley Johnson	TE	6'	215	32		
Pete Lammons	TE	6'3"	228	23		12
George Sauer	OE	6'1"	195	23		38
Bake Turner	OE	6'	180	27		

BUFFALO BILLS 4-10-0 Joe Collier

Scores of Each Game		
20	NEW YORK	17
3	HOUSTON	20
0	BOSTON	23
17	SAN DIEGO	37
17	Denver	16
20	OAKLAND	24
3	Houston	10
35	MIAMI	13
10	New York	20
20	DENVER	21
14	Miami	17
13	Kansas City	23
44	Boston	16
21	Oakland	28

Use Name	Pos.	Hgt	Wgt	Age	Int	Pts
Stew Barber	OT	6'3"	252	28		
Dick Cunningham	OT	6'2"	242	22		
Dick Hudson	OT	6'4"	265	27		
Gary Bugenhagen	OG	6'2"	248	22		
Joe O'Donnell	OG	6'2"	252	25		
Billy Shaw	OG	6'3"	258	27		
Al Bemiller	C	6'3"	246	28		
Bob Schmidt	C	6'4"	250	31		
Ron McDole	DE	6'4"	270	27	1	
Bob Petrich	DE	6'4"	250	26		
Remi Prudhomme	DE	6'4"	263	25		
Jim Dunaway	DT	6'4"	280	25	1	
Dudley Meredith	DT	6'4"	285	32	1	
Tom Sestak	DT	6'5"	260	31		6
Paul Guidry	LB	6'3"	234	23		
Harry Jacobs	LB	6'2"	244	30		
Jim LeMoine	LB	6'2"	245	22		
Paul Maguire	LB	6'	230	29		
Marty Schottenheimer	LB	6'3"	225	24	3	6
Mike Stratton	LB	6'3"	244	25	1	
John Tracey	TE-LB	6'3"	228	33	1	
Butch Byrd	DB	6'	208	25	5	
Hagood Clarke	DB	6'	195	25		
Booker Edgerson	DB	5'10"	183	28	2	
Tom Janik	DB	6'3"	190	26	10	12
Charlie King	DB	6'	185	24		
John Pitts	DB	6'4"	218	22		
George Saimes	DB	5'10"	188	25	2	
Tom Flores	QB	6'1"	200	30		
Jack Kemp	QB	6'1"	204	33		14
Teddy Bailey	HB	6'	220	23		
Charlie Bivins (from PIT-N)	HB	6'2"	212	28		
Bobby Burnett	HB	6'2"	208	24		
Gene Donaldson	HB	6'2"	225	25		
Allen Smith	HB	6'	200	24		
Keith Lincoln	FB-HB	6'2"	216	28		54
Jack Spikes	FB	6'2"	220	29		
Wray Carlton	HB-FB	6'2"	224	29		18
Elbert Dubenion	FL	6'	187	32		
Tony King	FL	6'1"	194	23		
Monte Ledbetter (from HOU)	FL	6'2"	185	24		12
Ed Rutkowski	FL	6'1"	198	26		
Paul Costa	TE	6'4"	246	25		12
Bill Masters	TE	6'5"	235	23		12
Art Powell	OE	6'3"	214	30		24
Mike Mercer	K	6'	217	31		73

Bobby Crockett – Knee Injury

Charley Ferguson – Injury
George Flint – Injury

MIAMI DOLPHINS 4-10-0 George Wilson

Scores of Each Game		
35	DENVER	21
0	KANSAS CITY	24
7	New York	29
0	Kansas City	41
10	Boston	41
14	NEW YORK	33
13	Buffalo	35
0	San Diego	24
17	Oakland	31
17	BUFFALO	14
14	Houston	17
41	SAN DIEGO	24
41	BOSTON	32
10	HOUSTON	41

Use Name	Pos.	Hgt	Wgt	Age	Int	Pts
Norm Evans	OT	6'5"	250	25		
Jack Pyburn	OT	6'6"	240	22		
Charlie Fowler	OG-OT	6'2"	260	23		
Billy Neighbors	OG	5'11"	250	27		
Ken Rice	OG	6'2"	240	27		
Freddie Woodson	OG	6'2"	250	23		
Maxie Williams	OT-OG	6'4"	250	27		
Tom Goode	C	6'3"	245	28		
Mel Branch	DE	6'2"	235	30		
Ed Cooke	DE	6'4"	250	32		
Jim Riley	DE	6'4"	240	22		
Claude Brownlee	DT	6'4"	265	23		
Ray Jacobs	DT	6'3"	285	27		
Tom Nomina	DT	6'5"	260	25		
John Richardson	DT	6'2"	250	22		
Rich Zecher (to BUF)	DT	6'2"	240	24		
John Bramlett	LB	6'2"	220	26	4	
Bob Bruggers	LB	6'1"	225	23	1	
Frank Emanuel	LB	6'3"	225	24	1	
Tom Erlandson	LB	6'3"	220	27	1	
Jerry Hopkins	LB	6'2"	235	26		
Wahoo McDaniel	LB	6'	230	30	1	
Pete Jaquess (to DEN)	DB	6'	184	25		
Mack Lamb	DB	6'1"	188	23		
Bob Neff	DB	6'	180	23	1	
Bob Petrella	DB	6'	185	22	3	
Jimmy Warren	DB	5'11"	175	28	4	6
Willie West	DB	5'10"	187	29	1	
Dick Westmoreland	DB	6'1"	190	26	10	6
Tom Beier	FL-DB	5'11"	198	22	1	
Bob Griese	QB	6'1"	190	22		6
Rick Norton	QB	6'1"	190	23		
Archie Roberts	QB	6'	193	24		
John Stofa	QB	6'3"	210	25		6
Joe Auer	HB	6'1"	205	25		18
Jack Harper	HB	5'11"	190	22		24
Abner Haynes (to NY)	HB	6'	190	29		12
Larry Seiple	HB	6'	200	22		
George Chesser	FB	6'2"	220	24		
Stan Mitchell	FB	6'2"	220	23		24
Sam Price	HB-FB	5'11"	215	23		12
Jack Clancy	FL	6'1"	195	23		12
Frank Jackson	FL	6'1"	185	27		6
John Roderick	FL	6'1"	180	23		
Preston Carpenter	TE	6'2"	208	33		
Doug Moreau	TE	6'2"	205	22		18
Karl Noonan	OE	6'3"	190	23		6
Howard Twilley	OE	5'10"	180	23		12
Booth Lusteg	K	5'11"	190	26		39
Gene Mingo (to WAS-N)	K	6'1"	190	28		12

BOSTON PATRIOTS 3-10-1 Mike Holovak

Scores of Each Game		
21	Denver	26
14	San Diego	28
7	Oakland	35
23	Buffalo	0
31	SAN DIEGO	31
41	MIAMI	10
14	OAKLAND	48
23	New York	30
18	HOUSTON	7
10	KANSAS CITY	33
24	NEW YORK	29
6	Houston	27
16	BUFFALO	44
32	Miami	41

Use Name	Pos.	Hgt	Wgt	Age	Int	Pts
Jim Boudreaux	OT	6'4"	245	22		
Tom Neville	OT	6'4"	255	23		
Don Oakes	OT	6'3"	255	29		
Karl Singer	OT	6'3"	250	23		
Justin Canale	OG	6'2"	250	23		1
Charley Long	OG	6'3"	250	29		
Len St. Jean	OG	6'1"	240	25		
Jon Morris	C	6'4"	240	24		
Bob Dee	DE	6'3"	250	34		
Larry Eisenhauer	DE	6'5"	255	27		
Tom Fussell	DE	6'3"	245	21		
Houston Antwine	DT	6'	270	28		
Jim Hunt	DT	5'11"	255	28		2
John Mangum	DT	6'3"	270	23		
Mel Witt	DT	6'3"	265	21		
Ed Toner	LB-DT	6'3"	250	22		
Tom Addison	LB	6'3"	230	31		
Nick Buoniconti	LB	5'11"	220	26	4	2
Ray Ilg	LB	6'1"	220	21		
Ed Philpott	LB	6'3"	240	21		
Doug Satcher	LB	6'	220	22		
John Charles	DB	6'1"	200	23	1	6
Jay Cunningham	DB	5'10"	180	24	1	6
White Graves	DB	6'	185	24		
Ron Hall	DB	6'	190	30	1	
Billy Johnson	DB	5'11"	175	24		
Leroy Mitchell	DB	6'2"	200	22	3	
Vic Purvis	DB	5'11"	200	23		
Chuck Shonta	DB	6'	200	29	3	
Don Webb	DB	5'10"	200	28	4	
John Huarte	QB	6'	190	23		
Babe Parilli	QB	6'1"	190	37		
Don Trull (from HOU)	QB	6'1"	190	25		18
Joe Bellino	HB	5'9"	185	29		
J. D. Garrett	HB	5'11"	195	25		6
Larry Garron	HB	6'	195	30		30
Bobby Leo	HB	5'10"	180	22		6
Jim Nance	FB	6'1"	240	24		48
Bob Cappadona	FB	6'1"	230	23		6
Gino Cappelletti	FL	6'	190	33		95
Bobby Nichols	TE	6'2"	220	23		
Tony Romeo	TE	6'2"	230	28		
Jim Whalen	TE	6'2"	210	23		30
Jim Colclough	OE	6'	185	31		
Art Graham	OE	6'1"	205	26		24
Terry Swanson	K	6'	210	22		

HOUSTON OILERS

RUSHING

Last Name	No.	Yds	Avg	TD
Granger	236	1194	5.1	6
Campbell	110	511	4.6	4
Blanks	66	206	3.1	1
Beathard	32	133	4.2	1
Hopkins	13	42	3.2	0
Davis	5	32	6.4	0
Elkins	2	19	9.5	0
Lee	6	-3	-0.5	0
Burrell	3	-3	-1.0	0
Norton	1	-7	-7.0	0

RECEIVING

Last Name	No.	Yds	Avg	TD
Granger	31	300	10	3
Frazier	23	253	11	1
Taylor	18	233	13	1
Campbell	17	136	8	2
Burrell	12	193	16	0
Reed	11	144	13	1
Blanks	11	93	8	1
Bass	5	42	8	1
Poole	4	55	14	0
Elkins	3	32	11	0
Hopkins	3	9	3	0
Lee	1	-1	-1	0

PUNT RETURNS

Last Name	No.	Yds	Avg	TD
Carwell	9	154	17	0
Moore	5	82	16	0
Jancik	6	19	3	0

KICKOFF RETURNS

Last Name	No.	Yds	Avg	TD
Moore	14	405	29	1
Jancik	16	349	22	0
Carwell	8	164	21	0
Houston	2	40	20	0
Hopkins	1	26	26	0
Campbell	1	19	19	0
Farr	1	17	17	0
Reed	1	0	0	0

PASSING – PUNTING – KICKING

PASSING	Att	Comp	%	Yds	Yd/Att	TD	Int–%	RK
Beathard	231	94	41	1114	4.8	9	14– 6	9
Lee	91	42	46	414	4.6	3	6– 7	
Davis	19	9	47	71	3.7	0	2–11	
Campbell	1	0	0	0	0.0	0	0– 0	

PUNTING	No	Avg
Norton	71	42.6

KICKING	XP	Att	%	FG	Att	%
Wittenborn	30	30	100	14	28	50

NEW YORK JETS

RUSHING

Last Name	No.	Yds	Avg	TD
Boozer	119	442	3.7	10
Mathis	78	243	3.1	4
Snell	61	207	3.4	0
Joe	37	154	4.2	2
Smolinski	64	139	2.2	1
Taliaferro	2	20	10.0	0
Maynard	4	18	4.5	0
Namath	6	14	2.3	0
Schweickert	1	1	1.0	0
Sauer	1	-3	-3.0	0

RECEIVING

Last Name	No.	Yds	Avg	TD
Sauer	75	1189	16	6
Maynard	71	1434	20	10
Lammons	45	515	11	2
Mathis	25	429	17	3
Smolinski	21	177	8	3
Boozer	12	205	17	3
Snell	11	54	5	0
Joe	8	85	11	0
B. Turner	3	40	13	0

PUNT RETURNS

Last Name	No.	Yds	Avg	TD
Baird	25	219	9	0
Christy	16	83	5	0
Lewis	7	24	3	0

KICKOFF RETURNS

Last Name	No.	Yds	Avg	TD
Christy	23	521	23	0
Boozer	11	213	19	0
Brannan	9	204	23	0
B. Turner	4	40	10	0
Lewis	1	22	22	0
McAdams	1	16	16	0
Smolinski	1	3	3	0
Waskiewicz	2	0	0	0
Wilder	1	0	0	0

PASSING – PUNTING – KICKING

PASSING	Att	Comp	%	Yds	Yd/Att	TD	Int–%	RK
Namath	491	258	53	4007	8.2	26	28– 6	3
Taliaferro	20	11	55	96	4.8	1	1– 5	
J. Turner	4	2	50	25	6.3	0	0– 0	

PUNTING	No	Avg
Johnson	65	42.1

KICKING	XP	Att	%	FG	Att	%
J. Turner	36	39	92	17	32	53

2 POINT XP

Mathis (2)
Maynard
Sauer

BUFFALO BILLS

RUSHING

Last Name	No.	Yds	Avg	TD
Lincoln	159	601	3.8	4
Carlton	107	467	4.4	3
Burnett	45	96	2.1	0
Bivins	15	58	3.9	0
Kemp	36	58	1.6	2
Spikes	4	9	2.3	0
Donaldson	3	-1	-0.3	0
Dubenion	2	-17	-8.5	0

RECEIVING

Last Name	No.	Yds	Avg	TD
Lincoln	41	558	14	5
Costa	39	726	19	2
Dubenion	25	384	15	0
Powell	20	346	17	4
Masters	20	274	14	2
Ledbetter	13	204	16	2
Burnett	11	114	10	0
Carlton	9	97	11	0
Rutkowski	6	59	10	0
Donaldson	1	20	20	0
Tracey	1	15	15	0
Spikes	1	9	9	0

PUNT RETURNS

Last Name	No.	Yds	Avg	TD
Byrd	30	142	5	0
Rutkowski	15	43	3	0
C. King	1	12	12	0
Edgerson	1	2	2	0

KICKOFF RETURNS

Last Name	No.	Yds	Avg	TD
Bivins	16	380	24	0
Smith	16	346	22	0
C. King	12	316	26	0
Rutkowski	3	71	24	0
Meredith	3	0	0	0
Guidry	1	0	0	0

PASSING – PUNTING – KICKING

PASSING	Att	Comp	%	Yds	Yd/Att	TD	Int–%	RK
Kemp	369	161	44	2503	6.8	14	26– 7	8
Flores	64	22	34	260	4.1	0	8–13	
Rutkowski	1	0	0	0	0.0	0	0– 0	

PUNTING	No	Avg
Maguire	77	43.1

KICKING	XP	Att	%	FG	Att	%
Mercer	25	25	100	16	27	59

2 POINT XP

Kemp

MIAMI DOLPHINS

RUSHING

Last Name	No.	Yds	Avg	TD
Haynes	72	346	4.8	2
Mitchell	83	269	3.2	3
Harper	41	197	4.8	1
Price	46	179	3.9	1
Griese	37	157	4.2	1
Auer	44	128	2.9	1
Seiple	3	58	19.3	0
Jackson	1	48	48.0	0
Norton	7	14	2.0	0
Chesser	2	3	1.5	0
Stofa	2	2	1.0	1
Moreau	1	-2	-2.0	0
Clancy	3	-4	-1.3	0

RECEIVING

Last Name	No.	Yds	Avg	TD
Clancy	67	868	13	2
Moreau	34	410	12	3
Twilley	24	314	13	2
Auer	18	218	12	2
Mitchell	18	133	7	1
Haynes	16	100	6	0
Noonan	12	141	12	1
Harper	11	212	19	3
Carpenter	10	127	13	0
Jackson	9	122	14	1
Price	8	56	7	1
Seiple	1	21	21	0
Beier	1	19	19	0

PUNT RETURNS

Last Name	No.	Yds	Avg	TD
Auer	9	42	5	0
Haynes	6	37	6	0
Neff	6	34	6	0
Harper	4	15	4	0

KICKOFF RETURNS

Last Name	No.	Yds	Avg	TD
Haynes	26	569	22	0
Auer	21	441	21	0
Neff	15	351	23	0
Carpenter	3	87	29	0
Roderick	4	63	16	0
Mitchell	2	57	29	0

PASSING – PUNTING – KICKING

PASSING	Att	Comp	%	Yds	Yd/Att	TD	Int–%	RK
Griese	331	166	50	2005	6.1	15	18– 5	5
Norton	133	53	40	596	4.5	1	9– 7	
Roberts	10	5	50	11	1.1	0	1–10	
Seiple	2	2	100	61	30.5	0	0– 0	
Stofa	2	2	100	51	25.5	0	0– 0	
Clancy	1	1	100	17	17.0	0	0– 0	
Lusteg	1	0	0	0	0.0	0	0– 0	

PUNTING	No	Avg
Seiple	70	41.6

KICKING	XP	Att	%	FG	Att	%
Lusteg	18	18	100	7	12	58
Mingo	9	9	100	1	6	17

BOSTON PATRIOTS

RUSHING

Last Name	No.	Yds	Avg	TD
Nance	269	1216	4.5	7
Garron	46	163	3.5	0
Cappadona	28	100	3.6	0
Parilli	14	61	4.4	0
Trull	22	30	1.4	3
Bellino	6	15	2.5	0
Garrett	5	7	1.4	0
Leo	1	7	7.0	0
Huarte	2	5	2.5	0
Graham	1	-5	-5.0	0

RECEIVING

Last Name	No.	Yds	Avg	TD
Graham	41	606	15	4
Whalen	39	651	17	5
Cappelletti	35	397	11	3
Garron	30	507	17	5
Nance	22	196	9	1
Colclough	14	263	19	0
Cappadona	6	104	17	1
Leo	1	25	25	1
Nichols	1	19	19	0
Garrett	1	12	12	0
Romeo	1	4	4	0

PUNT RETURNS

Last Name	No.	Yds	Avg	TD
Bellino	15	129	9	0
Johnson	6	124	21	0
Cunningham	17	105	6	0
Leo	5	54	11	0

KICKOFF RETURNS

Last Name	No.	Yds	Avg	TD
Cunningham	30	627	21	0
Bellino	18	357	20	0
Leo	11	232	21	0
Garrett	4	73	18	0
Garron	3	73	24	0
Singer	2	29	15	0
Cappadona	3	26	9	0
Ilg	1	10	10	0
Johnson	1	9	9	0

PASSING – PUNTING – KICKING

PASSING	Att	Comp	%	Yds	Yd/Att	TD	Int–%	RK
Parilli	344	161	47	2317	6.7	19	24– 7	6
Trull	92	31	34	480	5.2	1	7– 8	
Huarte	9	3	33	25	2.8	0	1–11	

PUNTING	No	Avg
Swanson	65	40.5

KICKING	XP	Att	%	FG	Att	%
Cappelletti	29	30	97	16	31	52
Canale	1	1	100	0	0	0

OAKLAND RAIDERS 13-1-0 Johnny Rauch

Scores of Each Game		
51	DENVER	0
35	BOSTON	7
23	KANSAS CITY	21
14	New York	27
24	Buffalo	20
48	Boston	14
51	SAN DIEGO	10
21	Denver	17
31	MIAMI	17
44	Kansas City	22
41	San Diego	21
19	Houston	7
38	NEW YORK	29
28	BUFFALO	21

Use Name	Pos.	Hgt	Wgt	Age	Int	Pts
Harry Schuh	OT	6'2"	260	24		
Bob Svihus	OT	6'4"	245	24		
Dan Archer	OG-OT	6'5"	245	22		
Jim Harvey	OG	6'5"	245	24		
Wayne Hawkins	OG	6'	240	29		
Bob Kruse	OG	6'2"	250	25		
Gene Upshaw	OT-OG	6'5"	255	22		
Jim Otto	C	6'2"	240	29		
Ben Davidson	DE	6'8"	265	27		
Ike Lassiter	DE	6'5"	270	26		
Carleton Oats	DE	6'2"	235	24		6
Dan Birdwell	DT	6'4"	250	26	1	2
Tom Keating	DT	6'3"	247	24		
Dick Sligh	DT	7'	300	22		
Duane Benson	LB	6'2"	215	22		
Bill Budness	LB	6'1"	215	24		
Dan Conners	LB	6'1"	230	25	3	12
Bill Fairband	LB	6'3"	228	21		
Bill Laskey	LB	6'2"	235	24		
Gus Otto	LB	6'2"	220	24	1	
J. R. Williamson	LB	6'2"	220	25	2	
Rodger Bird	DB	5'11"	195	24		
Willie Brown	DB	6'1"	190	26	7	6
Dave Grayson	DB	5'10"	185	28	4	
Kent McCloughan	DB	6'1"	190	24	2	
Warren Powers	DB	6'	190	26	6	12
Howie Williams	DB	6'2"	186	30	4	
George Blanda	QB	6'1"	215	39		116
Daryle Lamonica	QB	6'2"	215	26		24
Pete Banaszak	HB	5'11"	200	23		12
Estes Banks	HB	6'1"	200	22		
Clem Daniels	HB	6'1"	218	30		36
Larry Todd	HB	6'1"	185	24		12
Roger Hagberg	FB	6'2"	215	28		18
Hewritt Dixon	HB-FB	6'2"	220	27		42
Fred Biletnikoff	FL	6'1"	190	24		30
Rod Sherman	FL	6'	190	22		6
Billy Cannon	TE	6'1"	215	30		60
Dave Kocourek	TE	6'5"	240	30		2
Ken Herock	OE	6'2"	230	26		
Bill Miller	OE	6'	190	25		36
Warren Wells	OE	6'1"	190	24		36
Mike Eischeid	K	6'	190	26		

Charley Warner — Injury

KANSAS CITY CHIEFS 9-5-0 Hank Stram

Scores of Each Game		
25	Houston	20
24	Miami	0
21	Oakland	23
41	MIAMI	0
31	San Diego	45
19	HOUSTON	24
52	DENVER	9
42	NEW YORK	18
33	Boston	10
16	SAN DIEGO	17
22	OAKLAND	44
23	BUFFALO	13
21	New York	7
38	Denver	24

Use Name	Pos.	Hgt	Wgt	Age	Int	Pts
Dave Hill	OT	6'5"	260	26		
Bob Kelly	OT	6'3"	265	27		
Jim Tyrer	OT	6'6"	292	28		
Tony DiMidio	C-OT	6'3"	250	25		
Denny Biodrowski	OG	6'1"	255	27		
Ed Budde	OG	6'5"	260	26		
Curt Merz	OG	6'4"	267	29		
Al Reynolds	OG	6'3"	250	29		
Wayne Frazier (to BUF)	C	6'3"	245	27		
Jon Gilliam	C	6'2"	240	28		
Mike Hudock	C	6'2"	245	32		
Jerry Mays	DE	6'4"	252	27		
Gene Trosch	DT-DE	6'7"	277	22		
Buck Buchanan	DT	6'7"	287	27		
Ernie Ladd (from HOU)	DT	6'9"	292	28		
Ed Lothamer	DE-DT	6'5"	260	24		
Bud Abell	LB	6'3"	220	26		
Bobby Bell	LB	6'4"	228	27	4	6
Sherrill Headrick	LB	6'2"	240	30	1	
Chuck Hurston	LB	6'6"	240	24		
Willie Lanier	LB	6'1"	245	22		
Jim Lynch	LB	6'1"	235	22	1	
E. J. Holub	C-LB	6'4"	236	29		
Bobby Hunt	DB	6'1"	193	27	5	
Jim Kearney	DB	6'2"	206	24		
Sam Longmire	DB	6'3"	195	24		
Willie Mitchell	DB	6'1"	185	25	4	6
Johnny Robinson	DB	6'	205	28	5	
Fletcher Smith	DB	6'2"	188	23	6	
Emmitt Thomas	DB	6'2"	192	24	4	6
Fred Williamson	DB	6'2"	210	29	1	6
Len Dawson	QB	6'	190	33		
Bert Coan	HB	6'4"	220	27		24
Mike Garrett	HB	5'9"	200	23		60
Gene Thomas	HB	6'1"	210	24		18
Curtis McClinton	FB	6'3"	227	29		20
Jerrel Wilson	FB	6'4"	222	26		
Gloster Richardson	FL	6'	200	24		12
Noland Smith	FL	5'6"	154	23		6
Otis Taylor	FL	6'2"	215	24		72
Fred Arbanas	TE	6'3"	240	28		30
Reg Carolan	TE	6'6"	240	27		2
Chris Burford	OE	6'3"	210	29		18
Frank Pitts	OE	6'2"	200	23		12
Jan Stenerud	K	6'2"	187	24		108
Wayne Walker	K	6'2"	215	22		

Aaron Brown — Thigh Injury

SAN DIEGO CHARGERS 8-5-1 Sid Gillman

Scores of Each Game		
28	BOSTON	14
13	HOUSTON	3
37	Buffalo	17
31	Boston	31
45	KANSAS CITY	31
38	Denver	21
10	Oakland	51
24	MIAMI	0
17	Kansas City	16
24	DENVER	20
21	OAKLAND	41
24	Miami	41
17	Houston	24
31	NEW YORK	42

Use Name	Pos.	Hgt	Wgt	Age	Int	Pts
Harold Akin	OT	6'5"	262	22		
Gary Kirner	OT	6'3"	248	25		
Ron Mix	OT	6'4"	250	29		
Terry Owens	OT	6'6"	240	23		
Ernie Wright	OT	6'4"	265	27		
Ed Mitchell	OG	6'2"	280	25		
Walt Sweeney	OG	6'3"	255	26		
Larry Little	DT-OG	6'1"	265	21		
Sam Gruineisen	C	6'1"	240	26		
Paul Latzke	C	6'4"	240	25		
Tom Day	DE	6'2"	262	32		
Jim Griffin	DE	6'3"	255	25		
Howard Kindig (to BUF)	DE	6'6"	255	26		
Scott Appleton	DT	6'3"	256	25		6
Ron Billingsley	DT	6'8"	265	22		
Steve DeLong	DT	6'3"	252	24		
George Gross	DT	6'3"	258	26		
Houston Ridge	DT	6'4"	235	23		
Chuck Allen	LB	6'1"	225	27	2	
Johnny Baker	LB	6'3"	238	26		
Frank Buncom	LB	6'1"	240	27		
Bernie Erickson	LB	6'2"	238	22	1	
Ron McCall	LB	6'2"	245	22		
Bob Print	LB	6'	220	23		
Rick Redman	LB	5'11"	225	24	2	
Jeff Staggs	LB	6'2"	248	23		
Joe Beauchamp	DB	6'	185	23	3	
Speedy Duncan	DB	5'10"	175	24	2	18
Kenny Graham	DB	6'	195	25	2	6
Bob Howard	DB	6'1"	190	22		
Frank Marsh	DB	6'2"	205	26		
Jim Tolbert	DB	6'3"	207	23	1	
Bud Whitehead	HB-DB	6'	185	28		
John Hadl	QB	6'2"	215	27		18
Kay Stephenson	QB	6'1"	205	22		
Gene Foster	HB	5'11"	212	24		
Paul Lowe	HB	6'	205	30		6
Dickie Post	HB	5'9"	190	21		48
Jim Allison	FB	6'	220	24		
Brad Hubbert	FB	6'1"	227	26		24
Russ Smith	HB-FB	6'1"	225	23		6
Lance Alworth	FL	6'	180	27		54
Willie Frazier	TE	6'4"	225	24		60
Jacque MacKinnon	TE	6'4"	250	28		12
Ollie Cordill	OE	6'2"	180	24		
Gary Garrison	OE	6'1"	195	23		12
Steve Newell	OE	6'1"	186	22		
Dick Van Raaphorst	K	5'11"	215	24		90

Nat Whitmyer — Injury

DENVER BRONCOS 3-11-0 Lou Saban

Scores of Each Game		
26	BOSTON	21
0	Oakland	51
21	Miami	35
24	NEW YORK	38
6	Houston	10
16	BUFFALO	17
21	SAN DIEGO	38
9	Kansas City	52
17	OAKLAND	21
18	HOUSTON	20
21	Buffalo	20
20	San Diego	24
33	New York	24
24	KANSAS CITY	38

Use Name	Pos.	Hgt	Wgt	Age	Int	Pts
Dave Behrman	OT	6'5"	260	25		
Bob Breitenstein (to MIN-N)	OT	6'3"	267	24		
Sam Brunelli	OT	6'1"	255	24		
Tom Cichowski	OT	6'4"	250	22		
Mike Current (from MIA)	OT	6'4"	250	21		
Pat Matson	OG	6'1"	250	23		
Ernie Park	OG	6'3"	240	25		
Don Smith	OG	6'4"	240	24		
Dick Tyson	OG	6'2"	245	23		
Bob Young	OG	6'2"	260	24		
George Goeddeke	C-OG	6'3"	240	22		
Larry Kaminski	C	6'2"	240	22		
Ray Kubala	C	6'4"	245	25		
Roger LeClerc	C	6'3"	245	29		5
Pete Duranko	DE	6'3"	240	23		
Rich Jackson	DE	6'2"	255	26		2
Rex Mirich	DE	6'4"	250	26		
Dave Costa	DT	6'2"	265	25		
Larry Cox	DT	6'2"	250	23		
Jerry Inman	DT	6'3"	255	27		
Bill Keating (to MIA)	DT	6'2"	236	22		
Lou Andrus	LB	6'6"	255	24		
Carl Cunningham	LB	6'3"	240	23	1	
John Huard	LB	6'	220	23	2	
Gene Jeter	LB	6'3"	230	25		
Chip Myrtle	LB	6'2"	215	22	1	
Frank Richter	LB	6'3"	230	22	2	
Henry Sorrell	LB	6'1"	215	23		
Jack Lentz	DB	6'	195	22	4	
Bobby Ply (from KC-BUF)	DB	6'1"	190	26		
Errol Prisby	DB	5'10"	184	24		
Goldie Sellers	DB	6'2"	198	25	7	6
Jim Summers	DB	5'10"	175	21		
Gene Sykes	DB	6'1"	195	26	2	
Nemiah Wilson	DB	6'	165	24	4	12
Lonnie Wright	DB	6'2"	205	23	4	
Tom Cassese	HB-DB	6'1"	197	21	1	
Scotty Glacken	QB	6'	190	22		
Jim LeClair	QB	6'1"	208	23		6
Steve Tensi	QB	6'5"	215	24		
Floyd Little	HB	5'10"	195	25		12
Fran Lynch	HB	6'1"	210	21		
Charley Mitchell	HB	5'11"	185	27		
Cookie Gilchrist	FB	6'3"	250	32		
Wendell Hayes	FB	6'2"	220	26		26
Bo Hickey	FB	5'11"	225	21		30
Mike Kellogg	FB	6'	220	24		
Al Denson	FL	6'2"	208	25		66
Bob Scarpitto	FL	5'11"	196	28		
Tom Beer	TE	6'4"	235	22		
Andre White	TE	6'5"	225	22		2
Eric Crabtree	OE	5'11"	182	22		30
Neal Sweeney	OE	6'2"	170	22		
Rick Duncan	K	6'	208	26		9
Dick Humphreys	K	6'1"	240	27		39
Gary Kroner	K	6'1"	200	26		11

Max Leetzow — Injury

OAKLAND RAIDERS

RUSHING

Last Name	No.	Yds	Avg	TD
Daniels	130	575	4.4	4
Dixon	153	559	3.7	5
Banaszak	68	376	5.5	1
Hagberg	44	146	3.3	2
Todd	29	116	4.0	2
Lamonica	22	110	5.0	4
Banks	10	26	2.6	0
Sherman	1	13	13.0	1
Wells	1	7	7.0	0

RECEIVING

Last Name	No.	Yds	Avg	TD
Dixon	59	563	10	2
Biletnikoff	40	876	22	5
Miller	38	537	14	6
Cannon	32	629	20	10
Daniels	16	222	14	2
Banaszak	16	192	12	1
Wells	13	302	23	6
Hagberg	11	114	10	1
Sherman	5	61	12	0
Todd	4	42	11	0
Kocourek	1	4	4	0
Herock	1	–1	–1	0

PUNT RETURNS

Last Name	No.	Yds	Avg	TD
Bird	**46**	**612**	13	0
Powers	2	19	10	0
Grayson	3	11	4	0

KICKOFF RETURNS

Last Name	No.	Yds	Avg	TD
Grayson	19	405	21	0
Sherman	12	279	23	0
Bird	6	143	24	0
Todd	5	123	25	0
Hagberg	2	12	6	0
Benson	1	0	0	0

PASSING – PUNTING – KICKING

PASSING	Att	Comp	%	Yds	Yd/Att	TD	Int–%	RK
Lamonica	425	220	52	3228	7.6	**30**	20– 5	**1**
Blanda	38	15	39	285	7.5	3	3– 8	
Daniels	1	1	100	28	28.0	0	0– 0	

PUNTING	No	Avg
Eischeid	76	44.3

KICKING	XP	Att	%	FG	Att	%
Blanda	**56**	**57**	98	20	30	**67**

2 POINT XP
Kocourek

KANSAS CITY CHIEFS

RUSHING

Last Name	No.	Yds	Avg	TD
Garrett	236	1087	4.6	9
McClinton	97	392	4.0	2
Coan	63	275	4.4	4
G. Thomas	35	133	3.8	1
Dawson	20	68	3.4	0
Taylor	5	29	5.8	1
Pitts	3	19	6.3	1
Wilson	1	10	10.0	0
N. Smith	1	8	8.0	0

RECEIVING

Last Name	No.	Yds	Avg	TD
Taylor	59	958	16	**11**
Garrett	46	261	6	1
McClinton	26	219	8	1
Burford	25	389	16	3
Arbanas	20	295	15	5
G. Thomas	13	99	8	2
Richardson	12	312	26	2
Coan	5	41	8	0
Pitts	4	131	33	1
Carolan	2	26	13	0
N. Smith	1	42	42	0

PUNT RETURNS

Last Name	No.	Yds	Avg	TD
N. Smith	26	212	8	0
Garrett	4	22	6	0
E. Thomas	2	8	4	0
Robinson	1	3	3	0

KICKOFF RETURNS

Last Name	No.	Yds	Avg	TD
N. Smith	**41**	**1148**	28	**1**
G. Thomas	6	56	9	0
Coan	1	29	29	0
Carolan	1	2	2	0
Lanier	1	1	1	0
Buchanan	1	0	0	0
Hill	1	0	0	0
Lothamer	1	0	0	0
Pitts	0	9	0	0

PASSING – PUNTING – KICKING

PASSING	Att	Comp	%	Yds	Yd/Att	TD	Int–%	RK
Dawson	357	206	**58**	2651	7.4	24	17– 5	2
Garrett	4	1	25	17	4.3	1	0– 0	

PUNTING	No	Avg
Wilson	41	42.4
Walker	19	38.7
Carolan	1	42.0

KICKING	XP	Att	%	FG	Att	%
Stenerud	45	45	**100**	**21**	**36**	58

2 POINT XP
Carolan
McClinton

SAN DIEGO CHARGERS

RUSHING

Last Name	No.	Yds	Avg	TD
Post	161	663	4.1	7
Hubbert	116	643	**5.5**	2
Smith	22	115	5.2	1
Hadl	37	107	2.9	3
Foster	38	78	2.1	0
Lowe	28	71	2.5	1
Allison	10	34	3.4	0
Stephenson	2	11	5.5	0
Alworth	1	5	5.0	0
Garrison	1	1	1.0	0
Redman	1	–13	–13.0	0

RECEIVING

Last Name	No.	Yds	Avg	TD
Frazier	57	922	16	10
Alworth	52	1010	19	9
Garrison	44	772	18	2
Post	32	278	9	1
Hubbert	19	214	11	2
Foster	9	46	5	0
Mackinnon	7	176	25	2
Newell	7	68	10	0
Lowe	2	25	13	0
Smith	1	6	6	0

PUNT RETURNS

Last Name	No.	Yds	Avg	TD
Duncan	36	434	12	0
Graham	3	46	15	0

KICKOFF RETURNS

Last Name	No.	Yds	Avg	TD
Tolbert	18	441	25	0
Post	15	371	25	0
Duncan	9	231	26	0
Lowe	8	145	18	0
Smith	3	51	17	0
Erickson	1	0	0	0

PASSING – PUNTING – KICKING

PASSING	Att	Comp	%	Yds	Yd/Att	TD	Int–%	RK
Hadl	427	217	51	3365	7.9	24	22– 5	4
Stephenson	26	11	42	117	4.5	2	2– 8	
Post	6	1	17	9	1.5	0	0– 0	
Alworth	1	0	0	0	0.0	0	0– 0	
Foster	1	0	0	0	0.0	0	0– 0	
Lowe	1	1	100	26	26.0	0	0– 0	
Whitehead	1	0	0	0	0.0	0	0– 0	

PUNTING	No	Avg
Redman	58	37.0
Cordill	3	48.3
Hadl	2	35.0

KICKING	XP	Att	%	FG	Att	%
Van Raaphorst	45	45	**100**	15	30	50

DENVER BRONCOS

RUSHING

Last Name	No.	Yds	Avg	TD
Little	130	381	2.9	1
Mitchell	82	308	3.8	0
Hickey	73	263	3.6	4
Hayes	85	255	3.0	4
Gilchrist	10	21	2.1	0
Glacken	1	10	10.0	0
Lynch	2	7	3.5	0
LeClair	8	6	0.8	1
Cassese	1	5	5.0	0
Scarpitto	1	5	5.0	0
Tensi	24	4	0.2	0
Crabtree	2	2	1.0	0
Denson	1	–2	–2.0	0

RECEIVING

Last Name	No.	Yds	Avg	TD
Denson	46	899	20	**11**
Crabtree	46	716	16	5
Hayes	13	125	10	0
Beer	11	155	14	0
Hickey	7	36	5	1
Mitchell	7	15	2	0
Little	7	11	2	0
Sweeney	6	136	23	0
White	5	87	17	0
Scarpitto	1	14	14	0
Gilchrist	1	–4	–4	0

PUNT RETURNS

Last Name	No.	Yds	Avg	TD
Little	16	270	**17**	**1**
Sellers	4	24	6	0
Crabtree	2	24	12	0
Huard	1	19	19	0
Cassese	3	14	5	0

KICKOFF RETURNS

Last Name	No.	Yds	Avg	TD
Little	35	942	27	0
Mitchell	8	164	21	0
Sellers	6	120	20	0
Wilson	4	106	27	0
Hayes	3	104	35	0
Lynch	1	27	27	0
Crabtree	1	26	26	0
Cassese	1	19	19	0
Beer	1	10	10	0

PASSING – PUNTING – KICKING

PASSING	Att	Comp	%	Yds	Yd/Att	TD	Int–%	RK
Tensi	325	131	40	1915	5.9	16	17– 5	7
LeClair	45	19	42	275	6.1	1	1– 2	
Glacken	4	0	0	0	0.0	0	0– 0	

PUNTING	No	Avg
Scarpitto	**105**	**44.9**

KICKING	XP	Att	%	FG	Att	%
Humphreys	18	19	95	7	15	47
Kroner	5	6	83	2	2	100
Duncan	3	3	100	2	5	40
LeClerc	2	2	100	1	6	17

2 POINT XP
Hayes

NFL CHAMPIONSHIP GAME

December 31, at Green Bay
(Attendance 50,861)

SCORING

GREEN BAY	7	7	0	7–21
DALLAS	0	10	0	7–17

First Quarter
- G.B. Dowler, 8 yard pass from Starr
  PAT – Chandler (kick)

Second Quarter
- G.B. Dowler, 43 yard pass from Starr
  PAT – Chandler (kick)
- Dal. Andrie, 7 yard fumble return (by Starr)
  PAT – Villanueva (kick)
- Dal. Villanueva, 21 yard field goal

Fourth Quarter
- Dal. Rentzel, 50 yard pass from Reeves
  PAT – Villanueva (kick)
- G.B. Starr, 1 yard rush
  PAT – Chandler (kick)

TEAM STATISTICS

G. B.		DAL.
18	First Downs – Total	11
5	First Downs – Rushing	4
10	First Downs – Passing	6
3	First Downs – Penalty	1
1	Interception Returns – Number	0
15	Interception Returns – Yards	0
3	Fumbles – Number	3
2	Fumbles – Lost Ball	1
2	Penalties – Number	7
10	Yards Penalized	58
2	Giveaways	2
2	Takeaways	2
0	Difference	0

Green Bay's Golden Gamble

Last year's game between the Packers and Cowboys had been an NFL classic, but their rematch this season ranked among the most memorable football games of all time. Both clubs had won conference playoffs to get this far, with Green Bay beating the Rams 28-7 and Dallas clobbering the Browns 52-14, and they clashed for the NFL title in a titanic struggle under nightmarish conditions.

At game time the temperature in Green Bay was 13 degrees below zero, and a fifteen-mile-per-hour wind made it almost unbearable for player and spectator alike. Somewhat better acclimated to the cold than the Cowboys, the Packers mounted a 14-0 lead by early in the second quarter. The Dallas defense, however, took matters into its own hands. Willie Townes hit Starr attempting to pass, and when the ball squirted loose George Andrie picked it up and ran it into the end zone. When Willie Wood fumbled a punt a short time later, the Cowboys added a field goal to cut the score to 14-10 at halftime.

In the fourth period, the Cowboys went ahead on the first play when halfback Dan Reeves surprised the Packer secondary by throwing a long option pass to Lance Rentzel. With their backs to the wall, the Pack still trailed 17-14 when they took over the ball on their own 31-yard line with 4:50 left in the game. Mixing running plays and passes to his backs, Starr moved the Packers quickly downfield until they had a first down on the Dallas one-yard line with under a minute left on the clock. Twice Donny Anderson tried to run it in, twice he failed, and twice Starr called time out. With no time outs remaining and twenty seconds on the clock, the Packers snubbed a field-goal try and put all their chips on one last running play. At the snap, guard Jerry Kramer pushed Jethro Pugh out of the way, and Starr plunged through the gap for the winning touchdown.

INDIVIDUAL STATISTICS

GREEN BAY	No	Yds	Avg.	DALLAS	No	Yds	Avg.
				RUSHING			
Anderson	18	35	1.9	Perkins	17	51	3.0
Mercein	6	20	3.3	Reeves	13	42	3.2
Williams	4	13	3.3	Meredith	1	9	9.0
Wilson	3	11	3.7	Baynham	1	–2	–2.0
Starr	1	1	1.0	Clarke	1	–8	–8.0
	32	80	2.5		33	92	2.8
				RECEIVING			
Dowler	4	77	19.3	Hayes	3	16	5.3
Anderson	4	44	11.0	Reeves	3	11	3.7
Dale	3	44	14.7	Rentzel	2	61	30.5
Mercein	2	22	11.0	Clarke	2	24	12.0
Williams	1	4	4.0	Baynham	1	–3	–3.0
	14	191	13.6		11	109	9.9
				PUNTING			
Anderson	8		29.0	Villanueva	8		39.1
				PUNT RETURNS			
Wood	4	21	5.3	None			
Brown	1	–2	–2.0				
	5	19	3.8				
				KICKOFF RETURNS			
Caffey	1	7	7.0	Stevens	2	15	7.5
Crutcher	1	3	3.0	Stokes	1	28	28.0
Weatherwax	1	0	0.0		3	43	14.3
	3	10	3.3				

PASSING

	Att	Comp	Comp Pct.	Yds	Int	Yds/ Att.	Yds/ Comp	Yards Lost Tackled
GREEN BAY								
Starr	24	14	58.3	191	0	8.0	13.6	8–76
DALLAS								
Meredith	25	10	40.0	59	1	2.4	5.9	1– 9
Reeves	1	1	100.0	50	0	50.0	50.0	0– 0
	26	11	42.3	109	1	4.2	9.9	1– 9

AFL CHAMPIONSHIP GAME

December 31, at Oakland
(Attendance 53,330)

SCORING

OAKLAND	3	14	10	13–40
HOUSTON	0	0	0	7– 7

First Quarter
- Oak. Blanda, 37 yard field goal

Second Quarter
- Oak. Dixon, 69 yard rush
  PAT – Blanda (kick)
- Oak. Kocourek, 17 yard pass from Lamonica
  PAT – Blanda (kick)

Third Quarter
- Oak. Lamonica, 1 yard rush
  PAT – Blanda (kick)
- Oak. Blanda, 40 yard field goal

Fourth Quarter
- Oak. Blanda, 42 yard field goal
- Hous. Frazier, 5 yard pass from Beathard
  PAT – Wittenborn (kick)
- Oak. Blanda, 36 yard field goal
- Oak. Miller, 12 yard pass from Lamonica
  PAT – Blanda (kick)

TEAM STATISTICS

OAK.		HOUS.
18	First Downs – Total	11
11	First Downs – Rushing	4
6	First Downs – Passing	6
1	First Downs – Penalty	1
0	Fumbles – Number	4
0	Fumbles – Lost Ball	2
4	Penalties – Number	7
69	Yards Penalized	45
2	Missed Field Goals	0
0	Giveaways	3
3	Takeaways	0
+3	Difference	–3

Lamonica's Field-Goal Touchdown

The Oilers had won the Eastern Division title because of their strong defense, but the Raiders had no problems moving the ball in this championship game. With guard Gene Upshaw leading a fired-up Oakland offensive line, the Raiders attacked the Oilers on the ground, with Hewritt Dixon and Pete Banaszak steadily eating up the yardage all afternoon. George Blanda, whom the Oilers had put on waivers before the season, opened the scoring with a 37-yard field goal, and a 69-yard touchdown run around left end by Dixon gave Oakland more momentum. With eighteen seconds left in the half, the Raiders lined up for a close field-goal attempt, only to have holder Daryle Lamonica jump up and throw a touchdown pass to tight end Dave Kocourek.

Trailing 17-0 and getting nowhere against the Oakland defense, the Oilers needed some fireworks at the start of the second half to get back into the game. Instead, Zeke Moore fumbled the kickoff and gave the ball back to the Raiders deep in Houston territory. The Raiders needed seven plays to reach the end zone, with Lamonica sneaking over from the 1 for the score.

Once the score reached 24-0, all the steam leaked out of the Oilers. Fullback Hoyle Granger, the key to the Houston ground attack, never got untracked all day, and quarterback Pete Beathard had no success passing against the swarming Oakland secondary.

After three periods, the score had risen to 27-0, but the Oilers finally got on the scoreboard with a touchdown pass from Beathard to Charley Frazier plus John Whittenborn's extra point. That was the only Houston score of the day, however, and before the final gun sounded, the Raiders added ten points on a Blanda field goal and a scoring pass from Lamonica to Bill Miller. The 40-7 victory put the Raiders into the Super Bowl, but an Achilles tendon injury suffered by defensive tackle Tom Keating would hobble him for that upcoming match.

INDIVIDUAL STATISTICS

OAKLAND	No	Yds	Avg.	HOUSTON	No	Yds	Avg.
				RUSHING			
Dixon	21	144	6.9	Granger	14	19	1.4
Banaszak	15	116	7.7	Campbell	6	15	2.5
Lamonica	5	22	4.4	Blanks	1	6	6.0
Hagberg	2	–1	–0.5	Beathard	1	–2	–2.0
Todd	4	–8	–2.0		22	38	1.7
Biletnikoff	1	–10	–10.0				
	48	263	5.5				
				RECEIVING			
Miller	3	32	10.7	Frazier	7	81	11.6
Cannon	2	31	15.5	Reed	4	60	15.0
Biletnikoff	2	19	9.5	Campbell	2	5	2.5
Kocourek	1	17	17.0	Taylor	1	6	6.0
Dixon	1	8	8.0	Granger	1	–10	–10.0
Banaszak	1	4	4.0		15	142	9.5
	10	111	11.1				
				PUNTING			
Eischeid	4		44.3	Norton	11		38.5
				PUNT RETURNS			
Bird	5	49	9.8	None			
Sherman	1	–2	–2.0				
	6	47	7.8				
				KICKOFF RETURNS			
Grayson	1	47	47.0	Jancik	4	100	25.0
Todd	1	32	32.0	Moore	3	87	29.0
	2	79	39.5	Burrell	1	28	28.0
				Suggs	1	0	0.0
					9	215	23.9
				INTERCEPTION RETURNS			
Brown	1	2	2.0	None			

PASSING

	Att	Comp	Comp Pct.	Yds	Int	Yds/ Att.	Yds/ Comp	Yards Lost Tackled
OAKLAND								
Lamonica	24	10	41.7	111	0	4.6	11.1	
Blanda	2	0	0.0	0	0	–	–	
	26	10	38.5	111	0	4.3	11.1	10
HOUSTON								
Beathard	35	15	40.5	142	1	4.1	9.5	34

SUPER BOWL II
January 14, at Miami
(Attendance: 75,546)

The Errors of Youth

The Packers might naturally have suffered a mental letdown after their cliff-hanging NFL championship match with the Dallas Cowboys, but the knowledge that this was Vince Lombardi's last game as head coach gave the team all the incentive it needed against the AFL champion Oakland Raiders. In his nine seasons at Green Bay, Lombardi had turned the Packers from chronic losers to perennial champions, and his players were determined that he go out a winner.

The Oakland Raiders, on the other hand, had just won their first AFL crown by severely thrashing the Houston Oilers in the championship game. Like the Kansas City Chiefs last year, the Raiders had several players obviously good enough for any league, but other Oakland players would have to prove themselves against the Packers. They did, but what hurt the Raiders this day were mistakes, the sort of errors that plague young teams in any league.

The first quarter went fairly evenly, with the only scoring coming on Don Chandler's 39-yard field goal. Another Chandler three-pointer upped the score to 6-0 in the second quarter, and then the Raiders made their first costly mistake. The Packers had the ball on their own 38-yard line when Bart Starr dropped back to pass. Someone in the Raider secondary missed his assignment and left Boyd Dowler all alone downfield; Starr hit him with a perfect pass, which he carried to the end zone. With the extra point making the score 13-0, the Raiders seemed close to early death in this contest.

Daryle Lamonica revived his team's failing spirits, however, by driving the Raiders downfield and hitting Bill Miller with a 23-yard touchdown pass. The Oakland defense then stopped the Packer offense, but Rodger Bird, normally a sure-handed punt returner, called for a fair catch and fumbled the ball. The Packers recovered near mid-field and converted the break into another Chandler field goal and a 16-7 halftime lead.

Using their ball-control offense, the Packers nursed their lead through the second half and built it up to 33-14 on a Donny Anderson touchdown, a Chandler field goal, and Herb Adderley's return of an interception for a touchdown. Lamonica threw another touchdown pass to Miller in the fourth quarter, but that only made the final score a clear-cut 33-14. Vince Lombardi, retiring to the front office, was going out a winner.

GREEN BAY		OAKLAND
	OFFENSE	
Dowler	LE	Miller
Skoronski	LT	Svihus
Gillingham	LG	Upshaw
Bowman	C	J. Otto
Kramer	RG	Hawkins
Gregg	RT	Schuh
Fleming	RE	Cannon
Starr	QB	Lamonica
Dale	FL	Biletnikoff
Anderson	HB	Banaszak
Wilson	FB	Dixon
	DEFENSE	
Davis	LE	Lassiter
Kostelnik	LT	Birdwell
Jordan	RT	Keating
Aldridge	RE	Davidson
Robinson	LLB	Laskey
Nitschke	MLB	Connors
Caffey	RLB	G. Otto
Adderley	LCB	McCloughan
Jeter	RCB	W. Brown
T. Brown	LS	Powers
Wood	RS	H. Williams

SUBSTITUTES

GREEN BAY

Offense

Bratkowski	McGee
Capp	Mercein
Hyland	Thurston
Long	T. Williams

Defense

B. Brown	Hart
Crutcher	Rowser
Flanigan	Weatherwax

Kicker

Chandler

OAKLAND

Offense

Archer	Kocourek
Hagberg	Kruse
Harvey	Todd
Herock	Wells

Defense

Bird	Oates
Benson	Sligh
Budness	Williamson
Grayson	

Kickers

Blanda	Eischeid

SCORING

GREEN BAY	3	13	10	7	–33
OAKLAND	0	7	0	7	–14

First Quarter
- G.B. Chandler, 39 yard field goal

Second Quarter
- G.B. Chandler, 20 yard field goal
- G.B. Dowler, 62 yard pass from Starr PAT – Chandler (kick)
- Oak. Miller, 23 yard pass from Lamonica PAT – Blanda (kick)
- G.B. Chandler, 43 yard field goal

Third Quarter
- G.B. Anderson, 2 yard rush PAT – Chandler (kick)
- G.B. Chandler, 31 yard field goal

Fourth Quarter
- G.B. Adderley, 60 yard interception return PAT – Chandler (kick)
- Oak. Miller, 23 yard pass from Lamonica PAT – Blanda (kick)

TEAM STATISTICS

G. B.		OAK.
19	First Downs – Total	16
11	First Downs – Rushing	5
7	First Downs – Passing	10
1	First Downs – Penalties	1
0	Fumbles – Number	3
0	Fumbles – Lost Ball	2
1	Penalties – Number	4
12	Yards Penalized	31
69	Total Offensive Plays	57
322	Total Net Yards	293
4.7	Average Gain	5.1
0	Missed Field Goals	1
0	Giveaways	3
3	Takeaways	0
+3	Difference	–3

INDIVIDUAL STATISTICS

GREEN BAY	No	Yds	Avg.	OAKLAND	No	Yds	Avg.
			RUSHING				
Wilson	17	62	3.6	Dixon	12	54	4.5
Anderson	14	48	3.4	Todd	2	37	18.5
Williams	8	36	4.5	Banaszak	6	16	2.7
Starr	1	14	14.0		20	107	5.4
Mercein	1	0	0.0				
	41	160	3.9				
			RECEIVING				
Dale	4	43	10.8	Miller	5	84	16.8
Fleming	4	35	8.8	Banaszak	4	69	17.3
Dowler	2	71	35.5	Cannon	2	25	12.5
Anderson	2	18	9.0	Biletnikoff	2	10	5.0
McGee	1	35	35.0	Wells	1	17	17.0
	13	202	15.5	Dixon	1	3	3.0
					15	208	13.9
			PUNTING				
Anderson	6		39.0	Eischeid	6		44.0
			PUNT RETURNS				
Wood	5	35	7.0	Bird	2	12	6.0
			KICKOFF RETURNS				
Adderley	1	24	14.0	Todd	3	63	21.0
Williams	1	18	18.0	Grayson	2	61	30.5
Crutcher	1	7	7.0	Hawkins	1	3	3.0
	3	49	16.3	Kocourek	1	0	0.0
					7	127	18.1
			INTERCEPTION RETURNS				
Adderley	1	60	60.0	None			

PASSING

	Att	Comp	Comp Pct.	Yds	Int	Yds/ Att.	Yds/ Comp	Yards Lost Tackled
GREEN BAY								
Starr	24	13	54.2	202	0	8.4	15.5	4–30
OAKLAND								
Lamonica	34	15	44.1	208	1	6.1	13.9	3–22

1968 N.F.L. Eleven Missing Monuments

A lot of familiar faces were missing from NFL playing fields this season. Retired from active duty were Ray Berry, Jim Parker, Lenny Moore, Lou Groza, Sam Huff, Del Shofner, Jim Ringo, Jim Taylor, and Don Chandler, all of them top-notch performers in the league since the 1950s. Berry left with a record 631 lifetime receptions, Groza with records of twenty-one active professional seasons and 1,608 points scored, and Ringo left with an appearance record streak of 182 consecutive games, a streak still running at his retirement. Also tucked away in front-office positions out of the public's eye were George Halas and Vince Lombardi, two of the most famous coaches in pro-football history. Age prompted Halas to leave the sidelines, while Lombardi quit because he had accomplished everything in his nine years as Packer head coach.

EASTERN CONFERENCE — CAPITOL DIVISION

Dallas Cowboys—Depth was the key to the Cowboys' continued stay atop the Capitol Division. When quarterback Don Meredith needed a rest, young Craig Morton filled in and kept the offense rolling smoothly. When halfback Dan Reeves hurt his knee in the season's fourth game, substitute runners Craig Baynham and Walt Garrison filled the breach. Other top reserves on this team were Malcolm Walker, Rayfield Wright, Larry Cole, and Blaine Nye, each of whom could have started on most NFL teams.

New York Giants—The aerial circus of Fran Tarkenton to Homer Jones kept the attack alive, but the rest of the team needed shoring up. The running backs were slow, the defensive line couldn't mount an effective pass rush, and the linebacking was inexperienced and easily fooled. They did beat Dallas, but that was more a fluke than a true reading of the team.

Washington Redskins—Combined with the retirement of Sam Huff, a pair of decisions that backfired helped bring Otto Graham's pro coaching career to an end. Graham sent a first-draft pick to Los Angeles for rookie quarterback Gary Beban, last year's Heisman Trophy winner at UCLA. After signing with the Redskins for a lucrative salary, Beban flopped in training camp as a quarterback, spent most of the year on the taxi squad, and flopped late in the season as a running back. Another Graham move that didn't work out was the trading of safety Paul Krause to Minnesota.

Philadelphia Eagles—Norm Snead broke his leg in the first pre-season game, the Eagles lost their first eleven regular season games, owner Jerry Wolman went bankrupt, and coach Joe Kuharich heard hometown crowds screaming for his head. The Eagles ended their losing streak by beating Detroit 12-0 on four Sam Baker field goals, and a second win one week later gave the club some dignity but removed all chances of landing O. J. Simpson next year. At the end of the year, Leonard Tose bought the team from Wolman and canned Kuharich, fifteen-year contract and all.

CENTURY DIVISION

Cleveland Browns—When the Browns dropped two of their first three games with a meager offensive output, coach Blanton Collier benched quarterback Frank Ryan in favor of ex-Steeler Bill Nelsen. Playing behind the solid Cleveland line, Nelsen stayed healthy all season and put some life in the Browns' attack. With Nelsen, Leroy Kelly, and Paul Warfield leading the way, the Browns began an eight-game winning streak on October 20 by beating the undefeated Colts. The streak came to an end only on the final Sunday of the season, when a meaningless loss to St. Louis tightened the final standings.

St. Louis Cardinals—The Cards beat the Browns twice, but Cleveland finished ahead by half a game. With a strong, balanced squad, the Cards had severe problems with Western opponents, losing to the Rams, Colts, and 49ers and just barely beating the Falcons 17-12. Despite the near miss at the title, several developments pleased coach Charley Winner. Quarterback Jim Hart improved considerably in his second year at the helm, cutting his interceptions from 30 down to 18. The defense replaced retired linebackers Dale Meinert and Bill Koman without a hitch, and rookie Chuck Latourette put on a good show as a kick returner, punter and sometimes defensive back.

New Orleans Saints—Although the Saints won four games, their move up to third place was due more to the Steelers' deterioration than to their own improvement. Coach Tom Fears improved his offense by signing end Dave Parks after he played out his option at San Francisco. He had to pay a steep price, however, when Commissioner Pete Rozelle deemed rookie tackle Kevin Hardy and next year's number-one draft pick as San Francisco's just renumeration.

Pittsburgh Steelers—The Steelers combined a poor offense with a limp defense in an irresistible combination for defeat, and head coach Bill Austin found himself discharged after the debacle ended. Dick Hoak and Roy Jefferson turned in good offensive performances, but they were hardly noticeable admidst the mediocrity.

WESTERN CONFERENCE — CENTRAL DIVISION

Minnesota Vikings—The Vikings won the Central Division title with a defense as rugged as the Minnesota weather in December. The front line of Carl Eller, Jim Marshall, Alan Page, and Gary Larsen now ranked with Los Angeles' Fearsome Foursome as the top defensive lines in the league, and the linebacking and secondary were without weakness. The acquisition of safety Paul Krause from the Redskins was the knot that tied the Vikings' pass defense together. Although the offense ranked fourteenth in the league in total yardage and dead last in passing, quarterback Joe Kapp won as many headlines as the defensive people with his intense competitiveness and wobbling passes which often hit their mark in clutch situations.

Chicago Bears—Head coach Jim Dooley lost his first two games and then beat the Vikings at a terrible cost. In that game, Jack Concannon went out with a fractured collarbone and Rudy Bukich with a shoulder separation. After third-stringer Larry Rakestraw failed to move the team, Dooley gave rookie Virgil Carter a shot at quarterback. Carter drove the Bears to four straight wins before more injuries ended the team's title hopes. In the victory over San Francisco, a tackle by Kermit Alexander ripped ligaments and cartilage in Gale Sayers' right knee. One week later, a broken ankle ended Carter's fine rookie season.

Green Bay Packers—Vince Lombardi had quit as head coach, confining himself to the general manager's desk, and the Packers, under Phil Bengston, dropped to a 6-7-1 mark. Age was catching up on the players of the championship teams of the early 1960s, and replacements were not turning up. A bad arm kept quarterback Bart Starr out of action for almost half the season, and Don Chandler retired, leaving the Packers with no reliable place-kicker.

Detroit Lions—Last year's top newcomers had been Mel Farr and Lem Barney; this year's pair were wide receiver Earl McCullough and tight end Charlie Sanders. These two rookies joined with newcomers Bill Munson and Billy Gambrell to make the Detroit passing game a genuine threat to enemy defenses. Injuries plagued the running corps, however, and the reconstructed Lions needed more time together to play as a team.

COASTAL DIVISION

Baltimore Colts—A few weeks before their season's opener, the Colts had a solid team everywhere but at quarterback. Johnny Unitas was bothered by a bad elbow, so coach Don Shula sent a fourth-round draft pick and reserve end Butch Wilson to New York for journeyman quarterback Earl Morrall. Shula expected Morrall to fill in while Unitas recuperated, but while Unitas sat out most of the season, Morrall used his pinpoint passing and poised signal calling to lead the Colts to a 13-1 season. Morrall's job was made easier by the running of Tom Matte, the blocking and receiving of John Mackey, and the line play of Bob Vogel, while the defense made life miserable for heralded enemy quarterbacks.

Los Angeles Rams—Despite a string of injuries, the Rams fought their way to a 10-3-1 record. But after the season ended, owner Dan Reeves fired George Allen. Personality differences and Allen's practice of trading off draft picks for older pros convinced Reeves that he'd be better off with a different coach, but the Ram players immediately raised an outcry in favor of their deposed coach. The protests had some effect, because when Reeves held a press conference to name the new coach, he announced the return of Allen.

San Francisco '49ers—New head coach Dick Nolan took over a talent squad in his first head assignment, but he couldn't get his team past the Colts and Rams in the Coastal Division. With three losses and a tie against these two rivals, the '49ers had the misfortune of playing in pro football's strongest division. The '49ers did well against the rest of the league, with a steady attack their chief weapon. Bolstered by Nolan's confidence in him, quarterback John Brodie took firm charge of the offense, finding ex-Brown Clifton McNeil a most congenial pass receiver.

Atlanta Falcons—When the Falcons lost their first three games of the season, coach Norb Hecker was canned and ex-Viking head man Norm Van Brocklin given the job, and he tore the club apart in search of a winning combination. After a 30-7 loss to Cleveland, he put five starting players on waivers. He gave a starting safetyman's job to Billy Lothridge, a punting specialist with only one kidney. He dropped promising Randy Johnson from the starting lineup and promoted Bob Berry, whom he had coached in Minnesota to starting quarterback.

FINAL TEAM STATISTICS

OFFENSE

	ATL.	BALT.	CHI.	CLEV.	DALL.	DET.	G.B.	L.A.	MINN.	N.O.	N.Y.	PHIL.	PITT.	ST.L.	S.F.	WASH.
FIRST DOWNS:																
Total	174	258	219	248	297	221	240	245	223	224	256	197	245	245	260	223
by Rushing	71	110	121	104	135	87	96	111	114	80	119	78	91	117	98	67
by Passing	94	131	78	123	143	119	130	115	89	122	114	100	137	107	141	132
by Penalty	9	17	20	21	19	15	14	19	20	22	23	19	17	21	21	24
RUSHING:																
Number	366	463	500	447	480	433	450	503	500	409	474	369	399	463	443	360
Yards	1305	1809	2377	2031	2091	1702	1749	1932	1921	1527	1882	1411	1721	1996	1784	1164
Average Yards	3.6	3.9	4.8	4.5	4.4	3.9	3.9	3.8	3.8	3.7	4.0	3.8	4.3	4.3	4.0	3.2
Touchdowns	9	16	14	20	22	6	12	14	19	7	13	3	7	22	11	6
PASSING:																
Attempts	326	359	343	363	399	377	318	384	282	439	366	380	451	385	417	408
Completions	158	196	158	184	217	204	188	189	154	210	195	194	211	169	239	227
Completion Percentage	48.5	54.6	46.1	50.7	54.4	54.1	59.1	49.2	54.6	47.8	53.3	51.1	46.8	43.9	57.3	55.6
Passing Yards	2386	3094	1868	3039	3295	2649	2651	2413	1995	2549	2715	2357	2764	2389	3107	2824
Average Yards per Attempt	7.3	8.6	5.4	8.4	8.3	7.0	8.3	6.3	7.1	5.8	7.4	6.2	6.1	6.2	7.5	6.9
Average Yards per Completion	15.1	15.8	11.8	16.5	15.2	13.0	14.1	12.8	13.0	12.1	13.9	12.1	13.1	14.1	13.0	12.4
Times Tackled Attempting to Pass	70	29	24	21	34	45	41	28	35	33	30	26	41	23	27	37
Yards Lost Tackled Attempting to Pass	527	222	187	181	269	329	376	241	310	213	273	207	285	202	182	340
Net Yards	1859	2872	1681	2858	3026	2320	2275	2172	1685	2336	2442	2150	2479	2187	2925	2484
Touchdowns	9	28	10	27	25	17	21	20	11	17	21	16	22	16	24	23
Interceptions	24	22	21	16	18	15	15	17	17	29	17	29	26	20	23	18
Percent Intercepted	7.4	6.1	6.1	4.4	4.5	4.0	4.7	4.4	6.0	6.6	4.6	7.6	5.8	5.2	5.5	4.4
PUNTS:																
Number	75	49	66	63	59	71	59	81	61	75	57	60	68	65	68	76
Average Distance	44.3	39.5	38.0	37.3	40.9	40.4	40.0	39.6	39.3	37.6	36.0	41.3	40.4	41.6	39.0	43.3
PUNT RETURNS:																
Number	16	42	19	24	30	19	43	44	30	34	20	24	38	31	36	29
Yards	66	350	81	96	405	89	238	307	250	153	101	264	308	356	120	194
Average Yards	4.1	8.3	4.3	4.0	13.5	4.7	5.5	7.0	8.3	4.5	5.1	11.0	8.1	11.5	3.3	6.7
Touchdowns	0	0	0	0	2	0	1	0	1	1	0	1	1	1	0	0
KICKOFF RETURNS:																
Number	68	38	58	54	39	54	48	45	52	53	62	61	70	56	60	64
Yards	1273	1003	1370	974	841	1247	1007	1024	1049	1149	1110	1379	1502	1404	1064	1410
Average Yards	18.7	26.4	23.6	18.0	21.6	23.1	21.0	22.8	20.2	21.7	17.9	22.6	21.5	25.1	17.7	22.0
Touchdowns	0	2	0	0	0	1	0	1	0	0	0	1	0	0	0	0
INTERCEPTION RETURNS:																
Number	14	29	18	32	26	24	17	25	16	16	26	13	17	13	20	21
Yards	330	483	226	386	275	242	244	220	267	268	388	51	151	65	367	225
Average Yards	23.6	16.7	12.6	12.1	10.6	10.1	14.4	8.8	16.7	16.8	14.9	3.9	8.9	5.0	18.4	10.7
Touchdowns	2	4	1	2	3	1	0	2	1	1	2	0	1	0	3	1
PENALTIES:																
Number	63	75	113	74	77	70	64	74	65	82	67	63	46	66	90	65
Yards	659	655	1194	841	751	810	653	760	692	843	608	666	479	708	794	643
FUMBLES:																
Number	26	23	28	23	21	26	31	21	22	19	17	19	26	24	26	29
Number Lost	15	12	16	14	15	17	18	12	14	11	13	13	14	11	14	19
POINTS:																
Total	170	402	250	394	431	207	281	312	282	246	294	202	244	325	303	249
PAT Attempts	20	50	25	49	54	26	35	37	32	27	36	21	32	40	39	32
PAT Made	17	48	25	46	54	24	32	37	31	27	36	17	28	40	36	30
FG Attempts	21	28	36	24	29	29	29	31	29	37	24	30	21	24	24	19
FG Made	11	18	25	18	17	9	13	17	19	19	14	19	8	15	11	9
Percent FG Made	52.4	64.3	69.4	75.0	58.6	31.0	44.8	54.8	65.5	51.4	58.3	63.3	38.1	62.5	45.8	47.4
Safeties	0	0	0	0	1	0	0	1	1	0	0	1	0	0	0	0

DEFENSE

	ATL.	BALT.	CHI.	CLEV.	DALL.	DET.	G.B.	L.A.	MINN.	N.O.	N.Y.	PHIL.	PITT.	ST.L.	S.F.	WASH.
FIRST DOWNS:																
Total	302	207	240	259	202	214	213	190	210	228	263	256	244	238	250	259
by Rushing	129	71	102	110	61	92	105	66	98	97	125	128	92	90	111	122
by Passing	157	119	102	130	123	105	92	104	98	109	121	111	131	131	124	118
by Penalty	16	17	36	19	18	17	16	20	14	22	17	17	21	17	15	19
RUSHING:																
Number	518	375	427	423	369	457	476	397	432	439	425	515	441	423	445	497
Yards	3235	1339	1704	1842	1195	1680	1800	1305	1903	2105	2001	2141	1624	1558	1776	2194
Average Yards	4.3	3.6	4.0	4.4	3.2	3.7	3.8	3.3	4.4	4.8	4.7	4.2	3.7	3.7	4.0	4.4
Touchdowns	17	6	17	11	2	13	11	9	8	13	22	18	14	10	12	18
PASSING:																
Attempts	389	432	333	439	428	337	327	353	315	366	364	327	413	399	416	359
Completions	248	224	172	213	220	157	157	158	185	153	191	182	220	210	201	202
Completion Percentage	63.8	51.9	51.7	48.5	51.4	46.6	48.0	44.8	58.7	41.8	52.5	55.7	53.3	52.6	48.3	56.3
Passing Yards	3306	2405	2893	2447	2838	2448	2031	2196	2162	2483	2498	2557	3360	3261	2548	2662
Average Yards per Attempt	8.5	5.6	8.7	5.6	6.6	7.3	6.2	6.2	6.9	6.8	6.9	7.8	8.1	8.2	6.1	7.4
Average Yards per Completion	13.3	10.7	16.8	11.5	12.9	15.6	12.9	13.9	11.7	16.2	13.1	14.0	15.3	15.5	12.7	13.2
Times Tackled Attempting to Pass	29	45	30	26	51	36	28	51	44	34	21	21	28	44	35	21
Yards Lost Tackled Attempting to Pass	221	367	226	199	400	291	235	383	307	297	158	184	199	400	304	173
Net Yards	3085	2038	2667	2248	2438	2157	1796	1813	1855	2186	2340	2373	3161	2861	2244	2489
Touchdowns	30	9	25	19	20	12	14	12	16	25	18	20	29	23	19	16
Interceptions	14	29	18	32	26	24	17	25	16	16	26	13	17	13	20	21
Percent Intercepted	3.6	6.7	5.4	7.3	6.1	7.1	5.2	7.1	5.1	4.4	7.1	4.0	4.1	3.3	4.8	5.8
PUNTS:																
Number	45	78	66	60	77	66	77	88	64	69	47	55	66	70	68	57
Average Distance	41.5	40.8	40.1	39.9	40.4	40.7	39.6	40.0	38.4	40.8	40.0	38.9	40.0	38.1	40.9	39.6
PUNT RETURNS:																
Number	46	19	28	21	25	32	19	30	29	30	23	33	32	36	31	45
Yards	286	62	120	120	125	139	66	206	204	320	174	270	297	266	238	485
Average Yards	6.2	3.3	4.3	5.7	5.0	4.3	3.5	6.9	7.1	10.7	7.6	8.2	9.3	7.4	7.7	10.8
Touchdowns	0	0	0	0	0	0	0	1	0	1	1	0	2	1	0	2
KICKOFF RETURNS:																
Number	42	71	54	64	68	44	56	62	56	57	51	45	49	56	56	51
Yards	799	1391	968	1417	1326	1017	1211	1262	1291	1134	1344	1030	1154	1303	1163	996
Average Yards	19.0	19.6	17.9	22.1	19.5	23.1	21.6	20.4	23.1	19.9	26.4	22.9	23.6	23.3	20.8	19.5
Touchdowns	0	0	0	0	0	1	0	1	0	0	1	0	0	1	1	0
INTERCEPTION RETURNS:																
Number	24	22	21	16	18	15	15	17	17	29	17	29	26	20	23	18
Yards	326	192	260	152	331	150	150	286	360	294	120	408	404	173	390	192
Average Yards	13.6	8.7	12.4	9.5	18.4	10.0	10.0	16.8	21.2	10.1	7.1	14.1	15.5	8.7	17.0	10.7
Touchdowns	2	1	1	1	1	1	0	2	2	2	0	2	5	0	1	3
PENALTIES:																
Number	63	72	91	61	54	76	60	88	74	74	62	76	79	71	71	82
Yards	628	799	896	620	657	658	541	806	875	757	579	843	844	728	646	879
FUMBLES:																
Number	30	29	20	20	21	22	28	31	29	33	21	18	16	19	22	22
Number Lost	16	12	12	14	15	12	17	19	22	26	14	7	9	8	11	14
POINTS:																
Total	389	144	333	273	186	241	227	200	242	327	325	351	397	289	310	358
PAT Attempts	49	16	43	33	23	28	25	25	27	42	43	40	50	35	35	41
PAT Made	47	15	40	33	21	28	24	23	26	37	37	39	49	34	34	41
FG Attempts	30	19	31	26	22	29	26	17	27	27	23	35	26	33	32	32
FG Made	16	11	11	14	9	15	17	9	18	12	10	24	16	15	22	23
Percent FG Made	53.3	57.9	35.5	53.8	40.9	51.7	65.4	52.9	66.7	44.4	43.5	68.6	61.5	45.5	68.8	71.9
Safeties	0	0	1	0	0	0	1	0	0	1	0	0	0	0	0	1

CONFERENCE PLAYOFFS

EASTERN—December 21, at Cleveland (Attendance 81,497)

SCORING

CLEVELAND 3 7 14 7–31
DALLAS 7 3 3 7–20

First Quarter
Cle. Cockroft, 38 yard field goal
Dal. Howley, 44 yard fumble return
PAT – Clark (kick)
Second Quarter
Dal. Clark, 16 yard field goal
Cle. Kelly, 46 yard pass from Nelsen
PAT – Cockroft (kick)
Third Quarter
Cle. Lindsey, 27 yd interception return
PAT – Cockroft (kick)
Cle. Kelly, 35 yard run
PAT – Cockroft (kick)
Dal. Clark, 47 yard field goal
Fourth Quarter
Cle. E.Green, 2 yard rush
PAT – Cockroft (kick)
Dal. Garrison, 2 yard pass from Morton
PAT – Clark (kick)

TEAM STATISTICS

	CLE.	DAL.
First Downs – Total	12	13
First Downs – Rushing	4	5
First Downs – Passing	8	8
First Downs – Penalty	0	0
Times Tackled Passing	1	2
Yards Lost – Tackled	5	25
Fumbles – Number	1	1
Fumbles – Lost Ball	1	0
Penalties – Number	6	4
Yards Penalized	40	20
Punts – Number	7	5
Punts – Average Distance	36.1	41.0
Punt Returns – Number	3	0
Punt Returns – Yards	6	0
Kickoff Returns – Number	4	5
Kickoff Returns – Yards	67	72
Interception Returns – Number	4	1
Interception Returns – Yards	52	6
Missed Field Goals	0	2
Giveaways	2	4
Takeaways	4	2
Difference	+2	−2

INDIVIDUAL STATISTICS

RUSHING

CLEVELAND	No	Yds	Avg.	DALLAS	No	Yds	Avg.
Kelly	20	87	4.4	Perkins	14	51	3.6
Harraway	5	12	2.4	Morton	2	14	7.0
E.Green	3	5	1.7	Baynham	10	7	0.7
Nelsen	2	−2	−1.0	Garrison	1	6	6.0
	30	102	3.4	Meredith	1	5	5.0
				Shy	2	3	1.5
					30	86	2.9

RECEIVING

CLEVELAND	No	Yds	Avg.	DALLAS	No	Yds	Avg.
Warfield	4	86	21.5	Hayes	5	83	16.6
Morin	4	47	11.8	Rentzel	3	75	25.0
Kelly	2	46	23.0	Garrison	2	8	4.0
Collins	2	26	13.0	Baynham	1	34	34.0
Harraway	1	−2	−2.0	Norman	1	5	5.0
	13	203	15.6		12	205	17.1

PASSING

	Att	Cmp	Pct.	Yds	Int	Yd/A	Yd/C
Nelsen	25	13	52.0	203	1	8.1	15.6
Morton	23	9	39.1	163	1	7.1	18.1
Meredith	9	3	33.3	42	3	4.7	14.0
	32	12	37.5	205	4	6.4	17.1

WESTERN—December 22, at Baltimore (Attendance 60,238)

SCORING

BALTIMORE 0 7 14 3–24
MINNESOTA 0 0 0 14–14

Second Quarter
Bal. Mitchell, 3 yd pass from Morrall
PAT – Michaels (kick)

Third Quarter
Bal. Mackey, 49 yard pass from Morrall
PAT – Michaels (kick)
Bal. Curtis, 60 yard fumble return
PAT – Michaels (kick)

Fourth Quarter
Min. Martin, 1 yard pass from Kapp
PAT – Cox (kick)
Bal. Michaels, 33 yard field goal
Min. Brown, 7 yard pass from Kapp
PAT – Cox (kick)

TEAM STATISTICS

	BAL.	MIN.
First Downs – Total	15	22
First Downs – Rushing	2	4
First Downs – Passing	12	17
First Downs – Penalty	1	1
Times Tackled Passing	4	3
Yards Lost – Tackled	35	21
Fumbles – Number	1	2
Fumbles – Lost Ball	1	1
Penalties – Number	2	4
Yards Penalized	38	30
Punts – Number	5	6
Punts – Average Distance	40.4	39.6
Punt Returns – Number	2	3
Punt Returns – Yards	11	7
Kickoff Returns – Number	3	5
Kickoff Returns – Yards	54	113
Interception Returns – Number	2	1
Interception Returns – Yards	44	21
Missed Field Goals	1	0
Giveaways	2	3
Takeaways	3	2
Difference	+1	−1

INDIVIDUAL STATISTICS

RUSHING

BALTIMORE	No	Yds	Avg.	MINNESOTA	No	Yds	Avg.
Matte	14	31	2.2	Kapp	10	52	5.2
J. Hill	8	10	1.3	Brown	10	30	3.0
Mackey	1	9	9.0	Osborn	5	4	0.8
Pearson	4	0	0.0	Jones	2	0	0.0
	27	50	1.9	Lindsey	1	−1	−1.0
					28	85	3.0

RECEIVING

BALTIMORE	No	Yds	Avg.	MINNESOTA	No	Yds	Avg.
Rich'son	6	148	24.7	Brown	8	82	10.3
Mackey	2	92	46.0	Wash'ton	5	95	19.0
Orr	2	36	18.0	Beasley	5	69	13.8
Mitchell	1	3	3.0	Henderson	5	33	6.6
Pearson	1	1	1.0	Lindsey	1	9	9.0
	12	180	23.3	Martin	1	1	1.0
				Osborn	1	−2	−2.0
					26	287	11.0

PASSING

	Att	Cmp	Pct.	Yds	Int	Yd/A	Yd/C
Morrall	22	13	59.1	280	1	12.7	21.5
Kapp	44	26	59.1	287	2	6.5	11.0

CAPITOL DIVISION

DALLAS COWBOYS 12-2-0 Tom Landry

Scores of Each Game		
59	DETROIT	13
28	CLEVELAND	7
45	Philadelphia	13
27	St. Louis	10
34	PHILADELPHIA	14
20	Minnesota	7
17	GREEN BAY	28
17	New Orleans	3
21	NEW YORK	27
44	Washington	24
34	Chicago	3
29	WASHINGTON	20
28	PITTSBURGH	7
28	New York	10

Use Name	Pos.	Hgt	Wgt	Age	Int	Pts
Tony Liscio	OT	6'5"	255	28		
Ralph Neely	OT	6'5"	265	24		
Rayfield Wright	TE-OT	6'7"	243	23		6
John Niland	OG	6'4"	245	24		
Blaine Nye	OG	6'4"	255	22		
John Wilbur	OG	6'3"	240	25		
Dave Manders	C	6'2"	250	26		
Malcolm Walker	OT-C	6'4"	250	25		
George Andrie	DE	6'7"	250	28		
Larry Cole	DE	6'4"	230	21	1	12
Willie Townes	DE	6'5"	260	25		6
Andy Stynchula	DT-DE	6'3"	250	29		
Ron East	DT	6'4"	242	25		
Bob Lilly	DT	6'4"	260	29		
Jethro Pugh	DT	6'6'	260	24		2

Use Name	Pos.	Hgt	Wgt	Age	Int	Pts
Jackie Burkett	LB	6'4"	228	31		
Dave Edwards	LB	6'3"	228	29		
Chuck Howley	LB	6'3"	225	32	6	6
Lee Roy Jordan	LB	6'2"	225	27	3	
D. D. Lewis	LB	6'2"	210	22		
Dave Simmons	LB	6'4"	245	25	1	
Phil Clark	DB	6'2"	210	23		
Dick Daniels	DB	5'9"	180	22	2	
Mike Gaechter	DB	6'	190	28	3	
Cornell Green	DB	6'4"	208	28	4	6
Mike Johnson	DB	5'10"	184	24	3	
Mel Renfro	DB	6'	190	24	3	

Buddy Dial – Injury
Leon Donohue – Injury

Use Name	Pos.	Hgt	Wgt	Age	Int	Pts
Don Meredith	QB	6'2"	205	30		6
Craig Morton	QB	6'4"	216	25		12
Craig Baynham	HB	6'1"	206	24		48
Dan Reeves	HB	6'1"	200	24		30
Les Shy	HB	6'1"	200	24		6
Walt Garrison	FB	6'	205	24		30
Don Perkins	FB	5'10"	200	30		36
Bob Hayes	WR	6'	185	25		72
Dennis Homan	WR	6'1"	180	22		6
Dave McDaniels	WR	6'4"	200	23		
Sonny Randle (from SF)	WR	6'2"	190	32		6
Lance Rentzel	WR	6'2"	200	24		36
Pete Gent	TE	6'4"	205	25		
Pettis Norman	TE	6'3"	225	28		6
Mike Clark	K	6'1"	200	27		105
Ron Widby	K	6'4"	210	23		

NEW YORK GIANTS 7-7-0 Allie Sherman

Scores of Each Game		
34	Pittsburgh	20
34	Philadelphia	25
48	WASHINGTON	21
38	NEW ORLEANS	21
21	Atlanta	24
10	SAN FRANCISCO	26
13	Washington	10
0	BALTIMORE	26
27	Dallas	21
7	PHILADELPHIA	6
21	Los Angeles	24
10	Cleveland	45
21	ST. LOUIS	28
10	DALLAS	28

Use Name	Pos.	Hgt	Wgt	Age	Int	Pts
Rich Buzin	OT	6'4"	250	22		
Charlie Harper	OT	6'2"	250	24		
Steve Wright	OT	6'6"	250	26		
Willie Young	OT	6'	250	25		
Pete Case	OG	6'3"	245	27		
Darrell Dess	OG	6'	245	32		
Andy Gross	OG	6'	230	22		
Doug Van Horn	OG	6'2"	245	24		
Chuck Hinton	C	6'2"	235	25		
Greg Larson	C	6'2"	250	29		
Bruce Anderson	DE	6'4"	250	24		
McKinley Boston	DE	6'2"	245	22		
Jim Katcavage	DE	6'3"	240	33		
Roger Anderson	DT	6'5"	265	25	1	
Bob Lurtsema	DT	6'6"	250	26	1	
Sam Silas	DT	6'4"	250	25		

Use Name	Pos.	Hgt	Wgt	Age	Int	Pts
Ken Avery	LB	6'1"	220	24		
Barry Brown	LB	6'3"	235	25		
Mike Ciccolella	LB	6'1"	235	24	1	
Vince Costello	LB	6'	228	36		
Tommy Crutcher	LB	6'3"	230	26		
Henry Davis	LB	6'3"	235	25		
Scott Eaton	DB	6'3"	195	24	4	
Jim Holifield	DB	6'3"	195	22		
Spider Lockhart	DB	6'2"	175	25	8	12
Bruce Maher	DB	5'11"	190	31	1	
Willie Williams	DB	6'	190	25	10	
Freeman White	TE-DB	6'5"	225	24		

Smith Reed – Military Service

Use Name	Pos.	Hgt	Wgt	Age	Int	Pts
Gary Lane	QB	6'1"	210	25		
Fran Tarkenton	QB	6'1"	190	28		18
Gary Wood	QB	5'11"	188	25		
Ronnie Blye	HB	5'11"	185	24		6
Bobby Duhon	HB	6'	190	21		24
Randy Minniear	HB	6'	200	24		12
Ernie Kay	FB-HB	6'2"	230	25		24
Tucker Frederickson	FB	6'3"	230	25		18
Homer Jones	WR	6'2"	220	27		42
Joe Koontz	WR	6'1"	192	23		
Joe Morrison	WR	6'1"	212	30		36
Bob Crespino	TE-WR	6'4"	225	30		
Butch Wilson	TE	6'2"	228	26		
Aaron Thomas	WR-TE	6'3"	210	30		24
Pete Gogolak	K	6'2"	185	26		78

WASHINGTON REDSKINS 5-9-0 Otto Graham

Scores of Each Game		
38	Chicago	28
17	New Orleans	37
21	New York	48
17	PHILADELPHIA	14
16	PITTSBURGH	13
14	St. Louis	41
10	NEW YORK	13
14	Minnesota	27
16	Philadelphia	10
24	DALLAS	44
7	GREEN BAY	27
20	Dallas	29
21	CLEVELAND	24
14	DETROIT	3

Use Name	Pos.	Hgt	Wgt	Age	Int	Pts
Walt Rock	OT	6'5"	255	27		
Jim Snowden	OT	6'3"	255	26		
Fred Washington	OT	6'5"	268	23		
Ray Schoenke	OG-OT	6'3"	250	26		
Don Bandy	OG	6'3"	250	23		
Willie Banks	OG	6'2"	237	22		
Vince Promuto	OG	6'1"	245	30		
John Wooten	OG	6'2"	250	33		
Dave Crossan	C	6'3"	245	28		
Len Hauss	C	6'2"	235	27		
Carl Kammerer	DE	6'3"	243	31		
Spain Musgrove	DT-DE	6'4"	275	23		
Walt Barnes	DT	6'3"	250	24		
Frank Bosch	DT	6'4"	246	22		
Dennis Crane	DT	6'6"	260	23		
Joe Rutgens	DT	6'2"	255	29		

Use Name	Pos.	Hgt	Wgt	Age	Int	Pts
Ed Breding	LB	6'4"	235	23		
Jim Carroll	LB	6'1"	230	25		
Chris Hanburger	LB	6'2"	218	27	2	6
Mike Morgan	LB	6'4"	242	26	2	
Tom Roussel	LB	6'3"	235	23		
Pat Fischer	DB	5'10"	170	28	2	
George Harold	DB	6'3"	194	26		
Rickie Harris	DB	6'	182	25	2	
Aaron Martin	DB	6'	190	27	4	
Brig Owens	DB	5'11"	190	25	8	
Jim Smith	DB	6'3"	195	21		6
Dick Smith	HB-DB	6'	205	24	1	

John Love – Military Service
Sam Huff – Voluntarily Retired
Joe Don Looney – Military Service

Use Name	Pos.	Hgt	Wgt	Age	Int	Pts
Sonny Jurgensen	QB	5'11"	203	34		6
Jim Ninowski	QB	6'1"	207	32		
Harry Theofiledes	QB	5'10"	180	24		
Gary Beban	HB-QB	6'1"	195	22		
Jerry Allen	HB	6'1"	205	27		30
Bob Brunet	HB	6'1"	205	22		6
Pete Larson	HB	6'1"	200	24		12
Ray McDonald	FB	6'4"	248	24		
Steve Thurlow	FB	6'3"	222	25		
A. D. Whitfield	FB	5'10"	200	24		
Charley Taylor	WR	6'3"	210	27		30
Bobby Mitchell	WR	6'	196	33		
Jerry Smith	TE-WR	6'2"	208	25		36
Ken Barefoot	TE	6'5"	228	22		6
Marlin McKeever	TE	6'1"	235	28		
Pat Richter	TE	6'5"	230	27		54
Mike Bragg	K	5'11"	186	21		
Charlie Gogolak	K	5'10"	165	23		57

PHILADELPHIA EAGLES 2-12-0 Joe Kuharich

Scores of Each Game		
13	Green Bay	30
25	NEW YORK	34
13	DALLAS	45
14	Washington	17
14	Dallas	34
16	CHICAGO	29
3	Pittsburgh	6
17	ST. LOUIS	45
10	WASHINGTON	16
6	New York	7
13	Cleveland	47
12	Detroit	0
29	NEW ORLEANS	17
17	MINNESOTA	24

Use Name	Pos.	Hgt	Wgt	Age	Int	Pts
Bob Brown	OT	6'4"	295	25		
Dave Graham	OT	6'3"	250	29		
Lane Howell	OT	6'5"	272	27		
Mike Dirks	OG	6'2"	250	22		
Dick Hart	OG	6'2"	250	25		
Mark Nordquist	OG	6'4"	235	22		
Gene Ceppetelli	C	6'2"	247	26		
Mike Evans	C	6'5"	250	21		
Dave Recher	C	6'1"	246	25		
Don Hultz	DE	6'3"	242	27		
Gary Pettigrew	DE	6'4"	245	23		
Tim Rossovich	DE	6'4"	245	22		
Mel Tom	DE	6'4"	248	27		
Frank Molden	DT	6'5"	280	26		
Floyd Peters	DT	6'4"	255	33	1	
Dean Wink	DT	6'4"	246	23		
Randy Beisler	DE-DT	6'4"	245	23	1	

Use Name	Pos.	Hgt	Wgt	Age	Int	Pts
Fred Brown	LB	6'5"	232	25		
Wayne Colman	LB	6'1"	230	22		
Dave Lloyd	LB	6'3"	248	32		
Arunas Vasys	LB	6'2"	235	25		
Harold Wells	LB	6'2"	220	29	2	
Adrian Young	LB	6'1"	225	22		
Alvin Haymond	DB	6'	194	26	1	12
John Mallory	DB	6'	180	22		6
Ron Medved	DB	6'1"	210	24	1	
Al Nelson	DB	5'11"	186	24	3	
Jim Nettles	DB	5'9"	177	26		
Nate Ramsey	DB	6'1"	200	27	2	
Joe Scarpati	HB-DB	5'10"	185	26	2	

Ike Kelley – Injury
Jim Skaggs – Knee Injury
Harry Wilson – Injury

Use Name	Pos.	Hgt	Wgt	Age	Int	Pts
John Huarte	QB	6'	190	24		
Norm Snead	QB	6'4"	215	28		
Izzy Lang	HB	6'1"	232	25		6
Harry Jones	HB	6'2"	205	23		
Cyril Pinder	HB	6'2"	222	21		
Larry Conjar	FB	6'	214	22		2
Tom Woodeshick	FB	6'	220	26		18
Gary Ballman	WR	6'	205	28		24
Ron Goodwin	WR	6'	180	26		
Ben Hawkins	WR	6'	180	24		30
Chuck Hughes	WR	5'11"	170	25		
Mike Ditka	TE	6'3"	235	28		12
Fred Hill	TE	6'2"	215	25		18
Sam Baker	K	6'2"	218	36		74
Rick Duncan	K	6'	208	27		

CAPITOL DIVISION

DALLAS COWBOYS

RUSHING

Last Name	No.	Yds	Avg	TD
Perkins	191	836	4.4	4
Baynham	103	438	4.3	5
Garrison	45	271	6.0	5
Shy	64	179	2.8	1
Reeves	40	178	4.5	4
Meredith	22	123	5.6	1
Norman	4	51	12.8	0
Morton	4	28	7.0	2
Hayes	4	2	0.5	0
Gent	2	–5	–2.5	0
Wright	1	–10	–10.0	0

RECEIVING

Last Name	No.	Yds	Avg	TD
Rentzel	54	1009	19	6
Hayes	53	909	17	10
Baynham	29	380	13	3
Norman	18	204	11	1
Perkins	17	180	11	2
Gent	16	194	12	0
Shy	10	105	11	0
Garrison	7	111	16	0
Reeves	7	84	12	1
Homan	4	92	23	1
Randle	4	56	14	1
Wright	1	15	15	1

PUNT RETURNS

Last Name	No.	Yds	Avg	TD
Hayes	15	312	21	2
Rentzel	14	93	7	0
Homan	1	0	0	0

KICKOFF RETURNS

Last Name	No.	Yds	Avg	TD
Baynham	23	590	26	0
Daniels	9	193	21	0
Homan	2	21	11	0
Hayes	1	20	20	0
Neely	3	17	6	0
Norman	1	0	0	0

PASSING – PUNTING – KICKING

PASSING	Att	Comp	%	Yds	Yd/Att	TD	Int–	%	RK
Meredith	309	171	55	2500	8.1	21	12–	4	2
Morton	85	44	52	752	8.9	4	6–	7	
Reeves	4	2	50	43	10.8	0	0–	0	
Baynham	1	0	0	0	0.0	0	0–	0	

PUNTING	No	Avg
Widby	59	40.9

KICKING	XP	Att	%	FG	Att	%
M. Clark	54	54	100	17	29	59

NEW YORK GIANTS

RUSHING

Last Name	No.	Yds	Avg	TD
Frederickson	142	486	3.4	1
Koy	89	394	4.4	3
Duhon	101	362	3.6	3
Tarkenton	57	301	5.3	3
Blye	53	243	4.6	1
Minniear	14	38	2.7	2
Morrison	9	28	3.1	0
Jones	3	18	6.0	0
Thomas	2	14	7.0	0
Wood	2	0	0.0	0
Young	2	–2	–1.0	0

RECEIVING

Last Name	No.	Yds	Avg	TD
Jones	45	1057	23	7
Morrison	37	425	11	6
Duhon	37	373	10	1
Thomas	29	449	15	4
Koy	12	59	5	1
Blye	10	91	9	0
Frederickson	10	64	6	2
Crespino	7	130	19	0
Wilson	4	34	9	0
Minniear	4	32	8	0
Larson	0	1	0	0

PUNT RETURNS

Last Name	No.	Yds	Avg	TD
Lockhart	13	69	5	0
Duhon	7	32	5	0

KICKOFF RETURNS

Last Name	No.	Yds	Avg	TD
Blye	35	734	21	0
Duhon	13	214	16	0
Holifield	7	111	16	0
Frederickson	2	13	7	0
Koontz	1	13	13	0
Hinton	1	12	12	0
Lurtsema	1	11	11	0
Eaton	1	2	2	0
Williams	1	0	0	0

PASSING – PUNTING – KICKING

PASSING	Att	Comp	%	Yds	Yd/att	TD	Int–	%	RK
Tarkenton	337	182	54	2555	7.6	21	12–	4	5
Wood	24	9	38	123	5.1	0	5–	21	
Koy	3	2	67	13	4.3	0	0–	0	
Duhon	2	2	100	24	12.0	0	0–	0	

PUNTING	No	Avg
Koy	44	37.5
Williams	10	29.1
Lockhart	3	36.7

KICKING	XP	Att	%	FG	Att	%
Gogolak	36	36	100	14	24	58

WASHINGTON REDSKINS

RUSHING

Last Name	No.	Yds	Avg	TD
Allen	123	399	3.2	4
Brunet	71	227	3.2	0
Thurlow	51	184	3.6	0
Larson	44	132	3.0	1
Whitfield	37	125	3.4	0
Mitchell	10	46	4.6	0
Jurgensen	8	21	2.6	1
Beban	5	18	3.6	0
Ninowski	2	13	6.5	0
D. Smith	3	5	1.7	0
Theofiledes	3	0	0.0	0
Taylor	2	–3	–1.5	0
Bragg	1	–3	–3.0	0

RECEIVING

Last Name	No.	Yds	Avg	TD
Taylor	48	650	14	5
Jerry Smith	45	626	14	6
Richter	42	533	13	9
Allen	21	294	14	1
Brunet	18	160	9	1
Mitchell	14	130	9	0
Whitfield	13	107	8	0
Thurlow	12	151	13	0
Larson	12	146	12	1
D. Smith	1	15	15	0
Beban	1	12	12	0

PUNT RETURNS

Last Name	No.	Yds	Avg	TD
Harris	19	144	8	0
Jim Smith	6	38	6	0
Martin	2	12	6	0
Mitchell	1	0	0	0
Owens	1	0	0	0

KICKOFF RETURNS

Last Name	No.	Yds	Avg	TD
Harris	23	579	25	0
Mitchell	11	235	21	0
D. Smith	10	228	23	0
Larson	6	151	25	0
Martin	7	146	21	0
Jim Smith	3	61	20	0
Rock	2	10	5	0
Barnes	1	0	0	0
McKeever	1	0	0	0

PASSING – PUNTING – KICKING

PASSING	Att	Comp	%	Yds	Yd/Att	TD	Int–	%	RK
Jurgensen	292	167	57	1980	6.8	17	11–	4	8
Ninowski	95	49	52	633	6.7	4	6–	6	
Theofiledes	20	11	55	211	10.6	2	1–	5	
Beban	1	0	0	0	0.0	0	0–	0	

PUNTING	No	Avg
Bragg	76	43.3

KICKING	XP	Att	%	FG	Att	%
Gogolak	30	31	97	9	19	47

PHILADELPHIA EAGLES

RUSHING

Last Name	No.	Yds	Avg	TD
Woodeshick	217	947	4.4	3
Lang	69	235	3.4	0
Pinder	40	117	2.9	0
Ballman	1	30	30.0	0
Snead	9	27	3.0	0
Jones	22	24	1.1	0
Conjar	8	21	2.6	0
Huarte	2	9	4.5	0

RECEIVING

Last Name	No.	Yds	Avg	TD
Hawkins	42	707	17	5
Woodeshick	36	328	9	0
F. Hill	30	370	12	3
Ballman	30	341	11	4
Lang	17	147	9	1
Pinder	16	166	10	0
Ditka	13	111	9	2
Jones	5	87	17	0
Hughes	3	39	13	0
Mallory	1	58	58	1
Baker	1	3	3	0

PUNT RETURNS

Last Name	No.	Yds	Avg	TD
Haymond	15	201	13	1
Mallory	4	46	12	0
Scarpati	5	17	3	0

KICKOFF RETURNS

Last Name	No.	Yds	Avg	TD
Haymond	28	677	24	1
Nelson	11	308	28	0
Hawkins	12	254	21	0
Mallory	6	94	16	0
Rossovich	2	20	10	0
Jones	1	18	18	0
Graham	1	8	8	0

PASSING – PUNTING – KICKING

PASSING	Att	Comp	%	Yds	Yd/Att	TD	Int–	%	RK
Snead	291	152	52	1655	5.7	11	21–	7	15
Huarte	15	7	47	110	7.3	1	2–	13	
Scarpati	2	1	50	3	1.5	0	0–	0	
Baker	1	1	100	58	58.0	1	0–	0	

PUNTING	No	Avg
Baker	55	40.9
Duncan	5	45.6

KICKING	XP	Att	%	FG	Att	%
Baker	17	21	81	19	30	63

CENTURY DIVISION

CLEVELAND BROWNS 10-4-0 Blanton Collier

Scores of Each Game		
24	New Orleans	10
7	Dallas	28
6	LOS ANGELES	24
31	PITTSBURGH	24
21	ST. LOUIS	27
30	Baltimore	20
30	ATLANTA	7
33	San Francisco	21
35	NEW ORLEANS	17
45	Pittsburgh	24
47	PHILADELPHIA	13
45	NEW YORK	10
24	Washington	21
16	St. Louis	27

Use Name	Pos.	Hgt	Wgt	Age	Int	Pts
Monte Clark	OT	6'6"	255	31		
Dick Schafrath	OT	6'3"	255	32		
Joe Taffoni	OT	6'3"	250	23		
Jim Copeland	OG	6'2"	245	23		
John Demarie	OG	6'3"	255	23		
Gene Hickerson	OG	6'3"	248	33		
Fred Hoaglin	C	6'4"	240	24		
Bob Whitlow	C	6'1"	236	32		
Bill Glass	DE	6'5"	255	32	2	6
Jack Gregory	DE	6'6"	250	23		
Ron Snidow	DE	6'4"	250	26		
Marv Upshaw	DE	6'3"	245	21		
Walter Johnson	DT	6'3"	270	25		
Jim Kanicki	DT	6'4"	270	26		
Bill Sabatino	DT	6'3"	245	23		
Billy Andrews	LB	6'	225	23		
John Garlington	LB	6'1"	225	22	1	
Jim Houston	LB	6'2"	245	31	3	
Dale Lindsey	LB	6'3"	225	25	1	
Bob Matheson	LB	6'4"	240	23	2	
Wayne Meylan	LB	6'1"	240	22		
Erich Barnes	DB	6'2"	198	33	3	6
Ben Davis	DB	5'11"	185	23	8	
Mike Howell	DB	6'1"	187	25	6	
Nate James	DB	6'1"	195	23		
Ernie Kellerman	DB	6'	183	24	6	
Alvin Mitchell	DB	6'3"	195	24		
Carl Ward	DB	5'9"	180	24		
Bill Nelsen	QB	6'	195	27		6
Frank Ryan	QB	6'3"	200	32		
Leroy Kelly	HB	6'	200	26		120
Reece Morrison	HB	6'	205	22		12
Ernie Green	FB	6'2"	205	29		12
Charlie Harraway	FB	6'2"	230	23		6
Charlie Leigh	FB	5'11"	205	22		6
Eppie Barney	WR	6'	204	24		12
Gary Collins	WR	6'4"	215	27		
Ron Green	WR	6'1"	200	24		
Tommy McDonald	WR	5'10"	175	34		6
Paul Warfield	WR	6'	188	25		72
Milt Morin	TE	6'4"	250	26		30
Ralph Smith	TE	6'2"	220	29		
Don Cockroft	K	6'1"	185	23		100

ST. LOUIS CARDINALS 9-4-1 Charlie Winner

Scores of Each Game		
13	LOS ANGELES	24
17	San Francisco	35
21	New Orleans	20
10	DALLAS	27
27	Cleveland	21
41	WASHINGTON	14
31	NEW ORLEANS	17
45	Philadelphia	17
28	PITTSBURGH	28
0	Baltimore	27
17	ATLANTA	12
20	Pittsburgh	10
28	New York	21
27	CLEVELAND	16

Use Name	Pos.	Hgt	Wgt	Age	Int	Pts
Bob Duncum	OT	6'3"	250	24		
Ernie McMillan	OT	6'6"	260	30		
Bob Reynolds	OT	6'6"	265	27		
Clyde Williams	OG-OT	6'2"	255	28		
Ken Gray	OG	6'2"	250	32		
Rick Sortun	OG	6'2"	235	25		
Ted Wheeler	OG	6'3"	245	22		
Irv Goode	C-OG	6'4"	250	27		
Bob DeMarco	C	6'3"	240	30		
Dick Kasperek	C	6'3"	225	24		
Don Brumm	DE	6'3"	245	25		6
Dave Long	DE	6'4"	235	23		
Chuck Walker	DE	6'2"	245	27		
Fred Heron	DT	6'4"	250	23		
Bob Rowe	DT	6'4"	260	23		
Joe Schmiesing	DE-DT	6'4"	243	23		
Ernie Clark	LB	6'1"	230	30	1	
Dave Meggyesy	LB	6'1"	220	26		
Jamie Rivers	LB	6'2"	235	22	2	
Rocky Rosema	LB	6'2"	220	22		
Larry Stallings	LB	6'2"	230	26		
Mike Strofolino	LB	6'2"	230	24		
Bob Atkins	DB	6'3"	212	22	2	
Mike Barnes	DB	6'3"	205	23		
Brady Keys	DB	6'	185	32	1	
Chuck Latourette	DB	6'	190	23		6
Lonnie Sanders	DB	6'3"	207	26	3	
Mac Sauls	DB	6'	185	23		
Jerry Stovall	DB	6'2"	205	26		
Larry Wilson	DB	6'	190	30	4	
Jim Hart	QB	6'2"	195	24		36
Charley Johnson	QB	6'	190	31		
MacArthur Lane	HB	6'	220	26		
Johnny Roland	HB	6'2"	207	25		12
Roy Shivers	HB	6'	200	26		42
Willie Crenshaw	FB	6'2"	230	27		42
Cid Edwards	FB	6'2"	230	24		6
Bobby Joe Conrad	WR	6'	195	33		24
Jerry Daanen	WR	6'	190	23		
Freddie Hyatt	WR	6'3"	212	22		
Bob Lee	WR	6'3"	200	23		
Dave Williams	WR	6'2"	205	23		36
Chuck Logan	TE	6'4"	220	25		
Jackie Smith	TE	6'4"	215	27		30
Jim Bakken	K	6'	200	27		85

NEW ORLEANS SAINTS 4-9-1 Tom Fears

Scores of Each Game		
10	CLEVELAND	24
37	WASHINGTON	17
20	ST. LOUIS	21
21	New York	38
20	MINNESOTA	17
16	Pittsburgh	12
17	St. Louis	31
3	DALLAS	17
17	Cleveland	35
7	Green Bay	29
20	Detroit	20
17	CHICAGO	23
17	Philadelphia	29
24	PITTSBURGH	14

Use Name	Pos.	Hgt	Wgt	Age	Int	Pts
Jim Boeke	OT	6'5"	260	29		
Jerry Jones	OT	6'3"	265	24		
Dave McCormick	OT	6'6"	250	25		
Jerry Sturm	OT	6'3"	260	31		
Jake Kupp	OG	6'3"	233	26		
Ross Gwinn	OG	6'3"	273	24		
Roy Schmidt	OG	6'3"	250	26		
Del Williams	OG	6'2"	245	22		
Joe Wendryhoski	C	6'2"	245	29		
Doug Atkins	DE	6'8"	270	38		
Brian Schweda	DE	6'3"	240	25		
Tom Carr	DT	6'3"	267	26		
Lou Cordileone	DT	6'	250	31	1	
Earl Leggett	DT	6'3"	265	34		
Dave Rowe	DT	6'6"	265	23		
Mike Tilleman	DE-DT	6'5"	280	24		
Johnny Brewer	LB	6'4"	235	31		
Bill Cody	LB	6'1"	220	24		
Ted Davis	LB	6'1"	232	26		
Jim Ferguson	LB	6'4"	240	25		
Les Kelley	LB	6'3"	233	23	1	
Steve Stonebreaker	LB	6'3"	225	30		
Fred Whittingham	LB	6'1"	240	29	1	
Bo Burris	DB	6'3"	195	23	3	6
John Douglas	DB	6'1"	195	23		
Ross Fichtner	DB	6'	195	30		
Gene Howard	DB	6'	190	21	3	
Elbert Kimbrough	DB	5'11"	197	29	1	
Elijah Nevett	DB	6'	185	24		
Dave Whitsell	DB	6'	190	32	6	6
George Youngblood	DB	6'3"	205	23		
Billy Kilmer	QB	6'	204	29		12
Ronnie South	QB	6'1"	195	23		
Karl Sweetan	QB	6'1"	200	25		
Charlie Brown	HB	5'10"	187	22		6
Don McCall	HB	5'11"	195	23		36
Tom Barrington	FB-HB	6'1"	213	24		6
Tony Baker	FB	5'11"	230	23		
Tony Lorick	FB	6'1"	217	26		18
Ernie Wheelwright	FB	6'3"	236	31		6
Randy Schultz	HB-FB	5'11"	210	24		
Dan Abramowicz	WR	6'1"	195	23		42
John Gilliam	WR	6'1"	190	23		
Dave Parks	WR	6'2"	203	26		
Dave Szymakowski	WR	6'2"	198	22		
Jim Hester	TE	6'4"	225	23		12
Ray Poage	TE	6'4"	205	27		
Monte Stickles	TE	6'4"	235	30		12
Charlie Durkee	K	5'11"	165	24		84
Jim Fraser	K	6'3"	235	32		
Tom McNeill	K	6'1"	195	26		

PITTSBURGH STEELERS 2-11-1 Bill Austin

Scores of Each Game		
20	NEW YORK	34
10	Los Angeles	45
7	BALTIMORE	41
24	Cleveland	31
13	Washington	16
12	NEW ORLEANS	16
6	PHILADELPHIA	3
41	Atlanta	21
28	St. Louis	28
24	CLEVELAND	45
28	SAN FRANCISCO	45
10	ST. LOUIS	20
7	Dallas	28
14	New Orleans	24

Use Name	Pos.	Hgt	Wgt	Age	Int	Pts
John Brown	OT	6'2"	248	29		
Mike Haggerty	OT	6'4"	230	22		
Fran O'Brien	OT	6'1"	265	32		
Ernie Ruple	OT	6'4"	256	22		
Mike Taylor	OT	6'4"	247	23		
Sam Davis	OG	6'1"	245	24		
Larry Gagner	OG	6'3"	240	24		
Bruce Van Dyke	OG	6'2"	235	24		
Ralph Wenzel	OG	6'3"	240	25		
Mike Connelly	C	6'3"	248	32		
Ray Mansfield	C	6'3"	250	27		
Ben McGee	DE	6'2"	260	26		
Lloyd Voss	DE	6'4"	260	26		
Dick Arndt	DT	6'5"	265	24		
Chuck Hinton	DT	6'5"	260	29		
Ken Kortas	DT	6'2"	280	26		
Frank Parker	DT	6'5"	270	28		
John Campbell	LB	6'3"	225	29	1	
Dick Capp	LB	6'3"	235	24		
John Foruria	LB	6'2"	205	23		
Jerry Hillebrand	LB	6'3"	240	28	2	
Ray May	LB	6'1"	230	23	3	6
Andy Russell	LB	6'3"	215	26	2	
Bill Saul	LB	6'4"	225	27		
Lou Harris	DB	6'	180	22		
Bob Hohn	DB	6'	185	27		
Paul Martha	DB	6'	185	25	3	6
Clendon Thomas	DB	6'2"	200	31	3	
Bob Wade	DB	6'2"	200	23		
Marv Woodson	DB	6'	195	25	3	
Kent Nix	QB	6'1"	195	24		
Dick Shiner	QB	6'	197	26		
Rocky Bleier	HB	5'11"	190	22		
Dick Hoak	HB	5'11"	190	29		24
Don Shy	HB	6'1"	210	22		6
Tom Watkins	HB	6'1"	195	31		
Willie Asbury	FB	6'1"	230	25		
Earl Gros	FB	6'3"	230	27		36
Dick Compton	WR	6'1"	200	28		6
Marshall Cropper	WR	6'3"	210	24		
Ken Hebert	WR	6'	200	23		
Roy Jefferson	WR	6'2"	195	24		72
J. R. Wilburn	WR	6'2"	190	25		18
Jon Henderson	DB-WR	6'	195	23		
John Hilton	TE	6'5"	220	26		6
Tony Jeter	TE	6'3"	223	21		
Dick Kotite	TE	6'3"	235	25		12
Booth Lusteg	K	5'11"	190	27		50
Bill Shockley	K	6'	185	30		2
Bobby Walden	K	6'	190	29		

CENTURY DIVISION

CLEVELAND BROWNS

RUSHING

Last Name	No.	Yds	Avg	TD
Kelly	248	1239	5.0	16
Harraway	91	334	3.7	0
E. Green	41	152	3.7	0
Leigh	23	144	6.3	1
Ryan	11	64	5.8	0
Morrison	18	39	2.2	1
Nelsen	13	30	2.3	1
Smith	1	13	13.0	0
Morin	1	8	8.0	0
Barney	0	8	0.0	1

RECEIVING

Last Name	No.	Yds	Avg	TD
Warfield	50	1067	21	12
Morin	43	792	18	5
Kelly	22	297	14	4
Barney	18	189	11	1
E. Green	16	142	9	2
Harraway	12	162	14	1
Collins	9	230	26	0
McDonald	7	113	16	1
Leigh	3	−4	−1	0
Morrison	2	40	20	1
Smith	2	11	6	0

PUNT RETURNS

Last Name	No.	Yds	Avg	TD
Leigh	14	76	5	0
Davis	9	11	1	0
Kelly	1	9	9	0

KICKOFF RETURNS

Last Name	No.	Yds	Avg	TD
Leigh	14	322	23	0
Ward	13	236	18	0
James	8	166	21	0
Davis	8	152	19	0
Morrison	4	85	21	0
Kelly	1	10	10	0
Smith	1	3	3	0
Andrews	1	0	0	0
Barnes	1	0	0	0
Copeland	1	0	0	0
Houston	1	0	0	0
Howell	1	0	0	0

PASSING – PUNTING – KICKING

PASSING	Att	Comp	%	Yds	Yd/Att	TD	Int–	%	RK
Nelsen	293	152	52	2366	8.1	19	10–	3	6
Ryan	66	31	47	639	9.7	7	6–	9	
Kelly	4	1	25	34	8.5	1	0–	0	

PUNTING	No	Avg
Cockroft	61	37.7
Collins	2	26.0

KICKING	XP	Att	%	FG	Att	%
Cockroft	46	48	96	18	24	75

ST. LOUIS CARDINALS

RUSHING

Last Name	No.	Yds	Avg	TD
Crenshaw	203	813	4.0	6
Roland	121	455	3.8	2
Edwards	31	214	6.9	1
Shivers	44	184	4.2	4
Smith	12	163	13.6	3
Lane	23	74	3.2	0
D. Williams	3	47	15.7	0
Hart	19	20	1.1	6
Latourette	1	15	15.0	0
Wilson	1	12	12.0	0
Johnson	5	−1	−0.2	0

RECEIVING

Last Name	No.	Yds	Avg	TD
Smith	49	789	16	2
D. Williams	43	682	16	6
Conrad	32	449	14	4
Crenshaw	23	232	10	1
Shivers	9	103	11	3
Roland	8	97	12	0
Daanen	4	35	9	0
Edwards	1	2	2	0

PUNT RETURNS

Last Name	No.	Yds	Avg	TD
Latourette	28	345	12	1
Roland	3	11	4	0

KICKOFF RETURNS

Last Name	No.	Yds	Avg	TD
Latourette	46	1237	27	0
Crenshaw	6	104	17	0
Roland	3	63	21	0
Long	1	0	0	0

PASSING – PUNTING – KICKING

PASSING	Att	Comp	%	Yds	Yd/Att	TD	Int–	%	RK
Hart	316	140	44	2059	6.5	15	18–	6	14
Johnson	67	29	43	330	4.9	1	1–	1	
Latourette	1	0	0	0	0.0	0	0–	0	
Roland	1	0	0	0	0.0	0	1–	100	

PUNTING	No	Avg
Latourette	65	41.6

KICKING	XP	Att	%	FG	Att	%
Bakken	40	40	100	15	24	63

NEW ORLEANS SAINTS

RUSHING

Last Name	No.	Yds	Avg	TD
McCall	155	637	4.1	4
Lorick	104	344	3.3	0
Schultz	43	152	3.5	0
Barrington	45	111	2.5	0
Wheelwright	21	99	4.7	1
Kilmer	21	97	4.6	2
Gilliam	2	36	18.0	0
Abramowicz	2	27	13.5	0
Poage	1	22	22.0	0
South	4	5	1.3	0
Baker	4	2	0.5	0
McNeill	2	1	0.5	0
Whitsell	1	−1	−1.0	0
Sweetan	4	−5	−1.3	0

RECEIVING

Last Name	No.	Yds	Avg	TD
Abramowicz	54	890	16	7
Lorick	26	272	10	3
McCall	26	270	10	2
Parks	25	258	10	0
Gilliam	24	284	11	0
Hester	17	300	18	2
Stickles	15	206	14	2
Schultz	12	34	3	0
Barrington	9	33	4	1
Poage	1	11	11	0
Wheelwright	1	−9	−9	0

PUNT RETURNS

Last Name	No.	Yds	Avg	TD
Gilliam	15	60	4	0
Brown	8	60	8	1
Howard	8	42	5	0
Nevett	3	−9	−3	0

KICKOFF RETURNS

Last Name	No.	Yds	Avg	TD
Howard	23	533	23	0
Gilliam	15	328	22	0
Brown	8	137	17	0
Nevett	2	94	47	0
Stonebreaker	1	22	22	0
Kelley	1	20	20	0
Douglas	1	10	10	0
Jones	1	5	5	0
Whitsell	1	0	0	0

PASSING – PUNTING – KICKING

PASSING	Att	Comp	%	Yds	Yd/Att	TD	Int–	%	RK
Kilmer	315	167	53	2060	6.5	15	17–	5	10
Sweetan	78	27	35	318	4.1	1	9–	12	
South	38	14	37	129	3.4	1	3–	8	
Barrington	6	2	33	42	7.0	0	0–	0	
McCall	1	0	0	0	0.0	0	0–	0	
Parks	1	0	0	0	0.0	0	0–	0	

PUNTING	No	Avg
McNeill	49	41.0
South	14	27.6
Fraser	11	35.5
Lorick	1	36.0

KICKING	XP	Att	%	FG	Att	%
Durkee	27	27	100	19	37	51

PITTSBURGH STEELERS

RUSHING

Last Name	No.	Yds	Avg	TD
Hoak	175	858	4.9	3
Gros	151	579	3.8	3
Shy	35	106	3.0	1
Jefferson	6	57	9.5	0
Shiner	14	53	3.8	0
Bleier	6	39	6.5	0
Nix	6	15	2.5	0
Asbury	4	9	2.3	0
Walden	2	5	2.5	0

RECEIVING

Last Name	No.	Yds	Avg	TD
Jefferson	58	1074	19	11
Wilburn	39	514	13	3
Hoak	28	253	9	1
Gros	27	211	8	3
Hilton	20	285	14	1
Shy	13	106	8	0
Kotite	6	65	11	2
Compton	5	45	9	1
Cropper	4	54	14	0
Bleier	3	68	23	0
Asbury	3	27	9	0
Henderson	3	26	9	0
Hillebrand	1	27	27	0
Jeter	1	9	9	0

PUNT RETURNS

Last Name	No.	Yds	Avg	TD
Jefferson	28	274	10	1
Harris	6	21	4	0
Bleier	2	13	7	0
Watkins	2	0	0	0

KICKOFF RETURNS

Last Name	No.	Yds	Avg	TD
Shy	28	682	24	0
Henderson	29	589	20	0
Bleier	6	119	20	0
Cropper	3	53	8	0
Watkins	1	22	22	0
Harris	1	19	19	0
Hilton	1	9	9	0
Taylor	1	9	9	0

PASSING – PUNTING – KICKING

PASSING	Att	Comp	%	Yds	Yd/Att	TD	Int–	%	RK
Shiner	304	148	49	1856	6.1	18	17–	6	12
Nix	130	56	43	720	5.5	4	8–	6	
Hoak	16	7	44	188	11.8	0	1–	6	
Walden	1	0	0	0	0.0	0	0–	0	

PUNTING	No	Avg
Walden	68	40.4

KICKING	XP	Att	%	FG	Att	%
Lusteg	26	29	90	8	20	40
Shockley	2	3	67	0	1	0

1968 N.F.L. — Western Conference

CENTRAL DIVISION

MINNESOTA VIKINGS 8-6-0 Bud Grant

Scores of Each Game		
47	ATLANTA	7
26	Green Bay	13
17	CHICAGO	27
24	DETROIT	10
17	New Orleans	20
7	DALLAS	20
24	Chicago	26
27	WASHINGTON	14
14	GREEN BAY	10
13	Detroit	6
9	Baltimore	21
3	LOS ANGELES	31
30	San Francisco	20
24	Philadelphia	17

Use Name	Pos.	Hgt	Wgt	Age	Int	Pts
Grady Alderman	OT	6'2"	240	29		
Doug Davis	OT	6'4"	250	24		
Ron Yary	OT	6'6"	265	22		
Bookie Bolin	OG	6'2"	240	28		
Larry Bowie	OG	6'2"	255	28		
Milt Sunde	OG	6'2"	250	25		
Jim Vellone	OG	6'2"	255	24		
Mick Tingelhoff	C	6'1"	237	28		
Carl Eller	DE	6'6"	265	25		
Jim Marshall	DE	6'3"	235	31		2
Steve Smith	DE	6'5"	240	24		
Paul Dickson	DT	6'5"	255	31		
Gary Larsen	DT	6'5"	255	28		
Alan Page	DT	6'5"	265	23		
Jim Hargrove	LB	6'3"	230	22		
Wally Hilgenberg	LB	6'3"	225	25		
John Kirby	LB	6'3"	235	26		
Mike McGill	LB	6'2"	237	21		
Lonnie Warwick	LB	6'3"	235	26		
Roy Winston	LB	6'1"	230	28		
Bobby Bryant	DB	6'	175	24	2	6
Dale Hackbart	DB	6'3"	210	32		
Karl Kassulke	DB	6'	195	26	1	
Paul Krause	DB	6'3"	195	26	7	
Earsell Mackbee	DB	6'1"	195	27	2	
Ed Sharockman	DB	6'	200	28	4	
Charlie West	DB	6'1"	190	22		6
Gary Cuozzo	QB	6'1"	198	27		
King Hill (from PHI)	QB	6'3"	216	32		
Joe Kapp	QB	6'2"	212	30		18
Earl Denny	HB	6'1"	200	23		
Clint Jones	HB	6'	206	23		6
Dave Osborn	HB	6'	205	25		
Jim Lindsey	FB-HB	6'2"	200	23		24
Bill Brown	FB	5'11"	230	30		84
Oscar Reed	HB-FB	5'11"	220	24		
Bob Goodridge	WR	6'2"	202	22		
Bob Grim	WR	6'	197	23		
Tom Hall	WR	6'1"	195	27		6
John Henderson	WR	6'3"	190	25		
Art Powell	WR	6'3"	214	31		
Gene Washington	WR	6'3"	218	24		36
John Beasley	TE	6'3"	228	23		
Billy Martin	TE	6'4"	235	25		6
Fred Cox	K	5'10"	200	29		88

CHICAGO BEARS 7-7-0 Jim Dooley

Scores of Each Game		
28	WASHINGTON	38
0	Detroit	42
27	Minnesota	17
7	Baltimore	28
10	DETROIT	28
29	Philadelphia	16
26	MINNESOTA	24
13	Green Bay	10
27	SAN FRANCISCO	19
13	ATLANTA	16
3	DALLAS	34
23	New Orleans	17
17	Los Angeles	16
27	GREEN BAY	28

Use Name	Pos.	Hgt	Wgt	Age	Int	Pts
Randy Jackson	OT	6'5"	245	24		
Wayne Mass	OT	6'4"	245	22		
Bob Pickens	OT	6'4"	258	25		
Bob Wetoska	C-OT	6'3"	240	30		
Jim Cadile	OG	6'3"	240	27		
Doug Kriewald	OG	6'4"	245	23		
George Seals	OG	6'2"	260	25		
Mike Pyle	C	6'3"	250	29		
Ed O'Bradovich	DE	6'3"	255	28		
Loyd Phillips	DE	6'3"	240	23	2	
Willie Holman	DT-DE	6'4"	250	23		
Frank Cornish	DT	6'6"	285	24		
Dick Evey	DT	6'2"	245	27	1	
John Johnson	DT	6'5"	260	27		
Doug Buffone	LB	6'1"	230	24	1	
Dick Butkus	LB	6'3"	245	24	3	
Rudy Kuechenberg	LB	6'2"	215	25		
Dan Pride	LB	6'3"	225	26		
Jim Purnell	LB	6'2"	238	26		
Mike Reilly	LB	6'2"	230	25		
Clarence Childs	DB	6'	180	29		
Curtis Gentry	DB	6'	185	27	1	
Major Hazelton	DB	6'1"	185	23		
Bennie McRae	DB	6'1"	180	27	4	
Richie Petitbon	DB	6'3"	205	30	2	
Joe Taylor	DB	6'2"	200	27	1	
Rosey Taylor	DB	5'11"	186	29	3	6
Rudy Bukich	QB	6'1"	205	37		
Virgil Carter	QB	6'1"	185	22		24
Jack Concannon	QB	6'3"	205	25		12
Larry Rakestraw	QB	6'2"	195	26		
Garry Lyle	HB	6'2"	198	22		
Gale Sayers	HB	6'1"	205	25		12
Brian Piccolo	HB	6'	205	24		12
Ralph Kurek	FB	6'2"	210	25		6
Andy Livingston	FB	6'	234	23		
Ronnie Bull	HB-FB	6'	200	28		18
Mike Hull	TE-FB	6'3"	220	23		
Dick Gordon	WR	5'11"	190	23		24
Bob Jones	WR	6'4"	196	23		
Cecil Turner	WR	5'10"	170	24		12
Bob Wallace	WR	6'3"	211	22		12
Austin Denney	TE	6'2"	230	24		12
Emilio Vallez	TE	6'2"	210	22		
Bobby Joe Green	K	5'11"	175	30		
Jon Kilgore	K	6'1"	205	24		
Mac Percival	K	6'4"	217	28		100

Marty Amsler – Injury
Terry Stoepel – Military Service

GREEN BAY PACKERS 6-7-1 Phil Bengtson

Scores of Each Game		
30	PHILADELPHIA	13
13	MINNESOTA	26
17	DETROIT	23
38	Atlanta	7
14	LOS ANGELES	16
14	Detroit	14
28	Dallas	17
10	CHICAGO	13
10	Minnesota	14
29	NEW ORLEANS	7
27	Washington	7
20	San Francisco	27
3	BALTIMORE	16
28	Chicago	27

Use Name	Pos.	Hgt	Wgt	Age	Int	Pts
Forrest Gregg	OT	6'4"	250	35		
Dick Himes	OT	6'4"	244	22		
Francis Peay	OT	6'5"	250	24		
Bob Skoronski	OT	6'3"	245	35		
Gale Gillingham	OG	6'3"	255	24		
Jerry Kramer	OG	6'3"	245	33		21
Bill Lueck	OG	6'3"	235	22		
Ken Bowman	C	6'3"	230	25		
Bob Hyland	OG-C	6'5"	250	23		
Lionel Aldridge	DE	6'4"	245	26		
Leo Carroll	DE	6'7"	250	24		
Willie Davis	DE	6'3"	245	35		
Francis Winkler	DE	6'3"	230	21		
Leon Crenshaw	DT	6'6"	280	25		
Henry Jordan	DT	6'3"	250	33		
Ron Kostelnik	DT	6'4"	260	28		
Bob Brown	DE-DT	6'5"	260	27		
Lee Roy Caffey	LB	6'3"	250	28		
Fred Carr	LB	6'5"	238	22		
Jim Flanigan	LB	6'3"	240	23		
Ray Nitschke	LB	6'3"	240	32	2	
Dave Robinson	LB	6'3"	240	27	2	
Phil Vandersea	TE-LB	6'3"	225	25		
Herb Adderley	DB	6'1"	200	29	3	
Tom Brown	DB	6'1"	190	27	4	12
Doug Hart	DB	6'1"	190	29	1	
Bob Jeter	DB	6'1"	205	30	3	
John Rowser	DB	6'1"	180	24		
Gordon Rule	DB	6'2"	180	22		
Willie Wood	DB	5'10"	190	32	2	
Zeke Bratkowski	QB	6'2"	210	36		
Don Horn	QB	6'2"	195	23		
Bart Starr	QB	6'1"	190	34		6
Bill Stevens	QB	6'3"	195	23		
Donny Anderson	HB	6'3"	210	25		36
Elijah Pitts	HB	6'1"	205	29		12
Travis Williams	HB	6'1"	210	22		
Jim Grabowski	FB	6'2"	220	24		24
Chuck Mercein	FB	6'3"	230	25		19
Carroll Dale	WR	6'1"	200	30		48
Boyd Dowler	WR	6'5"	225	31		36
Claudis James	WR	6'2"	190	24		12
Bucky Pope	WR	6'5"	200	24		
Marv Fleming	TE	6'4"	235	26		18
Errol Mann	K	6'	203	27		4
Mike Mercer (from BUF-A)	K	6'	217	32		33

Jim Weatherwax – Knee Injury
Ben Wilson– Knee Injury

DETROIT LIONS 4-8-2 Joe Schmidt

Scores of Each Game		
13	Dallas	59
42	CHICAGO	0
23	Green Bay	17
10	Minnesota	24
28	Chicago	10
14	GREEN BAY	14
7	SAN FRANCISCO	14
7	Los Angeles	10
10	BALTIMORE	27
6	MINNESOTA	13
20	NEW ORLEANS	20
0	PHILADELPHIA	12
24	Atlanta	7
3	Washington	14

Use Name	Pos.	Hgt	Wgt	Age	Int	Pts
Charlie Bradshaw	OT	6'6"	260	32		
Bill Cottrell	OT	6'3"	250	23		
Rocky Freitas	OT	6'6"	258	22		
Greg Kent	OT	6'6"	265	25		
Roger Shoals	OT	6'4"	255	29		
Frank Gallagher	OG	6'2"	240	25		
Bob Kowalkowski	OG	6'3"	245	24		
Chuck Walton	OG	6'3"	250	27		
Ed Flanagan	C	6'3"	250	24		
John Baker	DE	6'6"	270	33		
Larry Hand	DE	6'4"	245	28		
Lew Kamanu	DE	6'4"	245	24		
Joe Robb	DE	6'3"	245	31		
Alex Karras	DT	6'2"	255	32		
Denis Moore	DT	6'5"	255	25		
Jerry Rush	DT	6'4"	260	26		
Chuck Sieminski	DT	6'4"	270	28		
Mike Lucci	LB	6'2"	230	28	1	
Ed Mooney	LB	6'2"	238	23		
Paul Naumoff	LB	6'1"	225	23	1	
Bill Swain	LB	6'2"	230	27	1	6
Wayne Walker	LB	6'2"	225	31	1	24
Lem Barney	DB	6'	185	22	7	12
Dick LeBeau	DB	6'1"	185	31	5	
Wayne Rasmussen	DB	6'2"	175	26		
Bobby Rasmussen	DB	5'10"	185	28		
Tom Vaughn	DB	5'11"	190	25	3	
Mike Weger	DB	6'2"	185	22	5	
Jim Welch	HB-DB	6'	196	30		
Greg Landry	QB	6'4"	205	21		6
Bill Munson	QB	6'2"	200	26		6
Mike Campbell	HB	5'11"	200	23		
Nick Eddy	HB	6'1"	205	24		
Mel Farr	HB	6'2"	205	23		42
Dave Kopay	FB-HB	6'2"	225	26		
Tom Nowatzke	FB	6'3"	230	25		6
Bill Triplett	HB-FB	6'2"	210	29		
Billy Gambrell	WR	5'10"	175	26		42
Bill Malinchak	WR	6'1"	200	24		
Earl McCullouch	WR	5'11"	172	22		30
Phil Odle	WR	5'11"	187	25		
Jim Gibbons	TE	6'2"	230	32		
Charlie Sanders	TE	6'4"	215	22		6
Jerry DePoyster	K	6'1"	200	22		27

CENTRAL DIVISION

MINNESOTA VIKINGS

RUSHING

Last Name	No.	Yds	Avg	TD
Brown	222	805	3.6	11
Jones	128	536	4.2	1
Kapp	50	269	5.4	3
Lindsey	53	152	2.9	4
Osborn	42	140	3.3	0
Denny	2	9	4.5	0
Reed	2	6	3.0	0
Cuozzo	1	4	4.0	0
Hill	1	1	1.0	0

RECEIVING

Last Name	No.	Yds	Avg	TD
Washington	46	756	16	6
Brown	31	329	11	3
Beasley	23	289	13	0
Hall	19	268	14	1
Lindsey	15	148	10	0
Martin	10	101	10	1
Henderson	4	42	11	0
Jones	4	26	7	0
Powell	1	31	31	0
Goodridge	1	5	5	0

PUNT RETURNS

Last Name	No.	Yds	Avg	TD
West	20	201	10	1
Bryant	10	49	5	0

KICKOFF RETURNS

Last Name	No.	Yds	Avg	TD
West	22	576	26	0
Bryant	19	373	20	0
Jones	4	60	15	0
Denny	3	19	6	0
Sharockman	1	14	14	0
Lindsey	1	7	7	0
Alderman	1	0	0	0
Martin	1	0	0	0

PASSING – PUNTING – KICKING

PASSING	Att	Comp	%	Yds	Yd/Att	TD	Int–	%	RK
Kapp	248	129	52	1695	6.8	10	17–	7	13
Hill	71	33	47	531	7.5	3	6–	8	
Cuozzo	33	24	73	297	9.0	1	0–	0	
Brown	1	1	100	3	3.0	0	0–	0	

PUNTING	No	Avg
Hill	33	41.0
Martin	28	37.4

KICKING	XP	Att	%	FG	Att	%
Cox	31	32	97	19	29	66

CHICAGO BEARS

RUSHING

Last Name	No.	Yds	Avg	TD
Sayers	138	856	6.2	2
Bull	107	472	4.4	3
Piccolo	123	450	3.7	2
Carter	48	265	5.5	4
Concannon	28	104	3.7	2
Kurek	17	95	5.6	1
Wallace	3	29	9.7	0
Lyle	4	28	7.0	0
Livingston	7	25	3.6	0
Hull	12	22	1.8	0
Turner	2	16	8.0	0
Rakestraw	9	12	1.3	0
Green	1	4	4.0	0
Denney	1	–1	–1.0	0

RECEIVING

Last Name	No.	Yds	Avg	TD
Gordon	29	477	16	4
Piccolo	28	291	10	0
Denney	23	247	11	2
Wallace	19	281	15	2
Bull	17	145	9	0
Sayers	15	117	8	0
Turner	14	208	15	2
Lyle	5	32	6	0
Kurek	4	50	13	0
Hull	4	20	5	0

PUNT RETURNS

Last Name	No.	Yds	Avg	TD
Sayers	2	29	15	0
Wallace	6	27	5	0
Turner	9	19	2	0
Gordon	1	5	5	0
Hazelton	1	1	1	0

KICKOFF RETURNS

Last Name	No.	Yds	Avg	TD
Sayers	17	461	27	0
Turner	20	363	18	0
Childs	8	291	36	0
Gordon	3	97	32	0
Wallace	3	80	27	0
Kurek	4	48	12	0
Butkus	2	30	15	0
Kuechenburg	1	0	0	0

PASSING – PUNTING – KICKING

PASSING	Att	Comp	%	Yds	Yd/Att	TD	Int–	%	RK
Concannon	143	71	50	715	5.0	5	9–	6	16
Carter	122	55	45	769	6.3	4	5–	4	
Rakestraw	67	30	45	361	5.4	1	7–	10	
Bukich	7	2	29	23	3.3	0	0–	0	
Sayers	2	0	0	0	0.0	0	0–	0	
Bull	1	0	0	0	0.0	0	0–	0	
Kilgore	1	0	0	0	0.0	0	0–	0	

PUNTING	No	Avg
Kilgore	35	35.2
Green	27	42.3
Lyle	4	33.5

KICKING	XP	Att	%	FG	Att	%
Percival	25	25	100	25	36	69

GREEN BAY PACKERS

RUSHING

Last Name	No.	Yds	Avg	TD
Anderson	170	761	4.5	5
Grabowski	135	518	3.8	3
Pitts	72	264	3.7	2
Williams	33	63	1.9	0
Starr	11	62	5.6	1
Mercein	17	49	2.9	1
Bratkowski	8	24	3.0	0
James	1	15	15.0	0
Horn	3	–7	–2.3	0

RECEIVING

Last Name	No.	Yds	Avg	TD
Dowler	45	668	15	6
Dale	42	818	19	8
Anderson	25	333	13	1
Fleming	25	278	11	3
Grabowski	18	210	12	0
Pitts	17	142	8	0
James	8	148	19	2
Williams	5	48	10	0
Mercein	3	6	2	0

PUNT RETURNS

Last Name	No.	Yds	Avg	TD
Wood	26	126	5	0
T. Brown	16	111	7	1
Pitts	1	1	1	0

KICKOFF RETURNS

Last Name	No.	Yds	Avg	TD
Williams	28	599	21	0
Adderley	14	331	24	0
Pitts	2	40	20	0
Robinson	2	29	15	0
Vandersea	1	8	8	0
Winkler	1	0	0	0

PASSING – PUNTING – KICKING

PASSING	Att	Comp	%	Yds	Yd/Att	TD	Int–	%	RK
Starr	171	109	64	1617	9.5	15	8–	5	4
Bratkowski	126	68	54	835	6.6	3	7–	6	
Horn	16	10	63	187	11.7	2	0–	0	
Anderson	3	1	33	12	4.0	1	0–	0	
Stevens	2	0	0	0	0.0	0	0–	0	

PUNTING	No	Avg
Anderson	59	40.0

KICKING	XP	Att	%	FG	Att	%
Mercer	12	14	86	7	12	58
Kramer	9	9	100	4	9	44
Mercein	7	7	100	2	5	40
Mann	4	4	100	0	3	0

DETROIT LIONS

RUSHING

Last Name	No.	Yds	Avg	TD
Farr	128	597	4.7	3
Triplett	120	384	3.2	0
Kopay	53	207	3.9	0
Eddy	48	176	3.7	0
Nowatzke	36	116	3.2	1
Munson	25	109	4.4	1
Landry	7	39	5.6	1
Campbell	7	24	3.4	0
DePoyster	1	20	20.0	0
Welch	3	14	4.7	0
McCullouch	3	13	4.3	0
Sanders	2	3	1.5	0

RECEIVING

Last Name	No.	Yds	Avg	TD
McCullouch	40	680	17	5
Sanders	40	533	13	1
Gambrell	28	492	18	7
Triplett	28	135	5	0
Farr	24	375	16	4
Kopay	18	130	7	0
Eddy	8	91	11	0
Odle	6	71	12	0
Nowatzke	4	6	2	0
Gibbons	2	38	19	0
Campbell	2	15	8	0
Malinchak	1	41	41	0

PUNT RETURNS

Last Name	No.	Yds	Avg	TD
Barney	13	79	6	0
Eddy	4	10	3	0
Vaughn	2	0	0	0

KICKOFF RETURNS

Last Name	No.	Yds	Avg	TD
Barney	25	670	27	1
Thompson	17	363	21	0
Vaughn	5	128	26	0
Nowatzke	3	34	11	0
Kopay	2	29	15	0
Gambrell	1	12	12	0
Mooney	1	11	11	0

PASSING – PUNTING – KICKING

PASSING	Att	Comp	%	Yds	Yd/Att	TD	Int–	%	RK
Munson	329	181	55	2311	7.0	15	8–	2	7
Landry	48	23	48	338	7.0	2	7–	15	

PUNTING	No	Avg
DePoyster	71	40.4

KICKING	XP	Att	%	FG	Att	%
DePoyster	18	20	90	3	15	20
Walker	6	6	100	6	14	43

COASTAL DIVISION

BALTIMORE COLTS 13-1-0 Don Shula

Scores of Each Game		
27	SAN FRANCISCO	10
28	Atlanta	20
41	Pittsburgh	7
28	CHICAGO	7
42	San Francisco	14
20	CLEVELAND	30
27	LOS ANGELES	10
26	New York	0
27	Detroit	10
27	ST. LOUIS	0
21	MINNESOTA	9
44	ATLANTA	0
16	Green Bay	3
28	Los Angeles	24

Use Name	Pos.	Hgt	Wgt	Age	Int	Pts
Sam Ball	OT	6'4"	240	24		
Bob Vogel	OT	6'5"	250	26		
Cornelius Johnson	OG	6'2"	245	25		
Glen Ressler	OG	6'3"	250	24		
Dan Sullivan	OG	6'3"	250	29		
Bill Curry	C	6'2"	235	25		
Dick Szymanski	C	6'3"	235	36		
Ordell Braase	DE	6'4"	245	36		
Roy Hilton	DE	6'6"	240	23	1	6
Lou Michaels	DE	6'2"	250	32		102
John Williams	DE	6'3"	256	22		
Fred Miller	DT	6'3"	250	27		
Billy Ray Smith	DT	6'4"	250	33		
Bubba Smith	DE-DT	6'7"	295	23		
Mike Curtis	LB	6'2"	232	24	2	6
Dennis Gaubatz	LB	6'2"	232	27	2	
Bob Grant	LB	6'2"	225	21		
Ron Porter	LB	6'3"	232	23		
Don Shinnick	LB	6'	228	33	1	
Sid Williams	LB	6'2"	235	26		
Ocie Austin	DB	6'3"	200	21		
Bobby Boyd	DB	5'10"	192	30	8	6
Jerry Logan	DB	6'1"	190	27	3	
Lenny Lyles	DB	6'2"	204	32	5	
Charlie Stukes	DB	6'3"	212	24	1	6
Rick Volk	DB	6'3"	195	23	6	
Earl Morrall	QB	6'1"	206	34		6
Johnny Unitas	QB	6'1"	196	35		
Jim Ward	QB	6'2"	195	24		
Timmy Brown	HB	5'10"	198	31		12
Tom Matte	HB	6'	214	29		60
Preston Pearson	HB	6'1"	190	23		24
Terry Cole	FB	6'1"	220	23		18
Jerry Hill	FB	5'11"	215	28		12
Gail Cogdill (from DET)	WR	6'2"	195	31		
Alex Hawkins	WR	6'1"	186	31		
Jimmy Orr	WR	5'11"	185	32		36
Ray Perkins	WR	6'	183	26		6
Willie Richardson	WR	6'2"	198	28		48
John Mackey	TE	6'3"	224	26		30
Tom Mitchell	TE	6'2"	215	24		24
David Lee	K	6'4"	215	24		

LOS ANGELES RAMS 10-3-1 George Allen

Scores of Each Game		
24	St. Louis	13
45	PITTSBURGH	10
24	Cleveland	6
24	SAN FRANCISCO	10
16	Green Bay	14
27	ATLANTA	14
10	Baltimore	27
10	DETROIT	7
17	Atlanta	10
20	San Francisco	20
24	NEW YORK	21
31	Minnesota	3
16	CHICAGO	17
24	BALTIMORE	28

Use Name	Pos.	Hgt	Wgt	Age	Int	Pts
Joe Carollo	OT	6'2"	258	28		
Charley Cowan	OT	6'4"	265	30		
Jim Wilson	OT	6'3"	258	27		
Don Chuy	OG	6'1"	255	27		
Tom Mack	OG	6'3"	250	24		
Joe Scibelli	OG	6'1"	255	29		
George Burman	C-OG	6'3"	255	25		
Ken Iman	C	6'1"	240	29		
Frank Marchlewski (from ATL)	C	6'2"	238	24		
Deacon Jones	DE	6'5"	260	29		
Lamar Lundy	DE	6'7"	260	33		
Gregg Schumacher	DE	6'2"	240	26		
Coy Bacon	DT	6'4"	270	26		
Roger Brown	DT	6'5"	300	31		
Merlin Olsen	DT	6'5"	276	27		
Diron Talbert	DT	6'5"	238	24		
Maxie Baughan	LB	6'1"	230	30	4	
Gene Breen	LB	6'2"	230	27		
Tony Guillory	LB	6'4"	236	25		
Dean Halverson	LB	6'2"	220	22		
Jack Pardee	LB	6'2"	230	32	2	12
Myron Pottios	LB	6'2"	235	28		
Doug Woodlief	LB	6'3"	230	24		
Claude Crabb	DB	6'	192	28		
Irv Cross	DB	6'1"	195	29	3	
Willie Daniel	DB	5'11"	190	30		
Ed Meador	DB	5'11"	200	31	6	
Ron Smith	DB	6'1"	192	25	3	6
Clancy Williams	DB	6'2"	203	25	7	
Kelton Winston	DB	6'	195	27		
Roman Gabriel	QB	6'4"	230	28		24
Milt Plum	QB	6'1"	205	34		
Mike Dennis	HB	6'1"	207	24		
Willie Ellison	HB	6'1"	207	23		42
Vilnis Ezerins	FB-HB	6'1"	217	23		
Tommy Mason	FB-HB	6'	200	29		18
Dick Bass	FB	5'10"	195	31		18
Henry Dyer	FB	6'2"	235	23		6
Bernie Casey	WR	6'4"	212	29		30
Harold Jackson	WR	5'10"	175	22		
Jack Snow	WR	6'2"	195	25		18
Pat Studstill	WR	6'1"	175	30		6
Wendell Tucker	WR	5'10"	185	24		24
Dave Pivic	TE	6'3"	240	24		2
Billy Truax	TE	6'5"	235	25		18
Bruce Gossett	K	6'2"	230	25		88

Dave Cahill – Knee Injury
Chuck Lamson – Injury
Les Josephson – Injury

SAN FRANCISCO FORTY NINERS 7-6-1 Dick Nolan

Scores of Each Game		
10	Baltimore	27
35	ST. LOUIS	17
28	ATLANTA	13
10	Los Angeles	24
14	BALTIMORE	42
26	New York	10
14	Detroit	7
21	CLEVELAND	33
19	Chicago	27
20	LOS ANGELES	20
45	Pittsburgh	28
27	GREEN BAY	20
20	MINNESOTA	30
14	Atlanta	12

Use Name	Pos.	Hgt	Wgt	Age	Int	Pts
Cas Banaszek	OT	6'3"	235	22		
Forrest Blue	OT	6'5"	248	22		
Lance Olssen	OT	6'5"	257	21		
Len Rohde	OT	6'4"	250	30		
Elmer Collett	OG	6'4"	244	23		
Howard Mudd	OG	6'3"	254	26		
Woody Peoples	OG	6'2"	247	25		
Bruce Bosley	C	6'2"	244	34		
Bill Belk	DE	6'3"	242	22	1	6
Stan Hindman	DE	6'3"	232	24	1	6
Clark Miller	DE	6'5"	247	29		
Charlie Johnson	DT	6'2"	265	24		
Charlie Krueger	DT	6'4"	260	32		
Roland Lakes	DT	6'4"	280	28		
Kevin Hardy	DE-DT	6'5"	287	23		
Ed Beard	LB	6'2"	226	28	2	
Tommy Hart	LB	6'3"	212	23		
Harold Hays	LB	6'3"	225	27		
Matt Hazeltine	LB	6'1"	230	35		
Frank Nunley	LB	6'2"	230	22		
Dave Wilcox	LB	6'3"	234	25		
Kermit Alexander	DB	5'11"	180	27	9	6
Johnny Fuller	DB	6'	175	22	2	
Jim Johnson	DB	6'2"	187	30	1	
Mel Phillips	DB	6'	192	26		
Al Randolph	DB	6'2"	192	24	4	
John Woitt	DB	5'11"	174	22		
John Brodie	QB	6'1"	210	33		
George Mira	QB	5'11"	190	26		
Steve Spurrier	QB	6'2"	203	23		
Doug Cunningham	HB	5'11"	193	22		
Clem Daniels	HB	6'1"	218	31		
Gary Lewis	FB	6'3"	230	26		24
Ken Willard	FB	6'2"	230	25		42
Bill Tucker	TE-FB	6'2"	220	24		42
Kay McFarland	WR	6'2"	186	29		6
Clifton McNeil	WR	6'2"	185	28		42
Dick Witcher	WR	6'3"	204	23		12
Dave Olerich	TE	6'1"	220	23		
Bob Windsor	TE	6'4"	224	25		12
John David Crow	HB-TE	6'2"	224	33		30
Tommy Davis	K	6'	220	33		53
Dennis Patera	K	6'	225	22		16

George Donnelly – Injury

Tom Holzer – Injury
George Rose – Injury
Don Parker – Knee Injury
John Thomas – Knee Injury
Dave Hettema – Military Service

ATLANTA FALCONS 2-12-0 Norb Hecker Norm Van Brocklin

Scores of Each Game		
7	Minnesota	47
20	BALTIMORE	28
13	San Francisco	28
7	GREEN BAY	38
24	NEW YORK	21
14	Los Angeles	27
7	Cleveland	30
21	PITTSBURGH	41
10	LOS ANGELES	17
16	Chicago	13
12	St. Louis	17
0	Baltimore	44
7	DETROIT	24
12	SAN FRANCISCO	14

Use Name	Pos.	Hgt	Wgt	Age	Int	Pts
Errol Linden	OT	6'5"	260	31		
Bill Sandeman	OT	6'6"	250	25		
Don Talbert	OT	6'5"	255	28		
Steve Duich	OG	6'3"	248	22		
Dan Grimm	OG	6'3"	245	27		
Jim Simon	OG	6'5"	240	27		
Randy Winkler	OT-OG	6'5"	255	25		
Joe Cerne	C	6'2"	240	25		
Phil Sobocinski	C	6'3"	235	22		
Rick Cash	DE	6'5"	260	23		
Claude Humphrey	DE	6'5"	255	24		
Jim Garcia	DT-DE	6'4"	250	24		
Carlton Dabney	DT	6'5"	250	21	1	
Jim Norton (to PHI)	DT	6'4"	254	25		
Jerry Shay	DT	6'3"	245	24		
Art Strahan	DT	6'5"	266	25		
Joe Szczecko	DT	6'	245	26		
Dick Absher	LB	6'4"	227	24		
Ron Acks	LB	6'2"	225	23		
Grady Allen	LB	6'3"	215	22		
Greg Brezina	LB	6'2"	220	22		
Ralph Heck	LB	6'2"	230	27	1	
Tommy Nobis	LB	6'2"	235	24	1	
Marion Rushing (to HOU-A)	LB	6'2"	230	31		
Jimmy Burson	DB	6'	185	26	4	6
Lee Calland	DB	6'	190	27	2	
Ollie Cordill	DB	6'2"	180	25		
Mike Freeman	DB	5'11"	190	24		
Floyd Hudlow	DB	5'11"	195	24		
Billy Lothridge	DB	6'1"	195	24	3	
Nick Rassas	DB	6'	190	24	1	
Ken Reaves	DB	6'3"	205	23	1	6
Phil Spiller (to CIN-A)	DB	6'	195	23		
Larry Suchy	DB	5'11"	180	22		
Bob Berry	QB	5'11"	190	26		12
Randy Johnson	QB	6'3"	196	24		6
Bruce Lemmerman	QB	6'1"	196	22		
Joe Auer	HB	6'1"	205	26		
Charlie Bryant	HB	6'1"	207	27		
Cannonball Butler	HB	5'10"	185	25		12
Perry Lee Dunn	HB	6'2"	215	25		18
Billy Harris	HB	6'	195	22		6
Dwight Lee (from SF)	HB	6'2"	198	22		
Doug Goodwin	FB	6'2"	228	26		
Brendan McCarthy (to DEN-A)	FB	6'3"	220	23		6
Harmon Wages	HB-FB	6'1"	210	22		6
Dave Dunaway (from GB)	WR	6'2"	205	23		
Rick Eber	WR	6'	173	23		
Paul Flatley	WR	6'1"	187	27		
Bob Long	WR	6'3"	205	27		24
Jerry Simmons	WR	6'1"	190	25		
John Wright	WR	6'	195	22		
Mike Donohoe	TE	6'3"	227	23		6
Ray Ogden	TE	6'5"	225	25		12
Bob Etter	K	5'11"	152	23		50

Junior Coffey – Knee Injury

Bob Sanders – Injury

COASTAL DIVISION

BALTIMORE COLTS

RUSHING

Last Name	No.	Yds	Avg	TD
Matte	183	662	3.6	9
Cole	104	418	4.0	3
Hill	91	360	4.0	1
Brown	39	159	4.1	2
MacKey	10	103	10.3	0
Pearson	19	78	4.1	0
Morrall	11	18	1.6	1
Lee	3	12	4.0	0
Unitas	3	−1	−0.3	0

RECEIVING

Last Name	No.	Yds	Avg	TD
Mackey	45	644	14	5
Richardson	37	698	19	8
Orr	29	743	26	6
Matte	25	275	11	1
Hill	18	161	9	1
Perkins	15	227	15	1
Cole	13	75	6	0
Mitchell	6	117	20	4
Brown	4	53	13	0
Cogdill	3	42	14	0
Pearson	2	70	35	2
Hawkins	2	31	16	0

PUNT RETURNS

Last Name	No.	Yds	Avg	TD
Volk	25	198	8	0
Brown	16	125	8	0
Logan	1	27	27	0

KICKOFF RETURNS

Last Name	No.	Yds	Avg	TD
Pearson	15	527	35	2
Brown	15	298	20	0
Cole	5	123	25	0
Matte	1	22	22	0
Porter	1	19	19	0
Logan	1	14	14	0

PASSING – PUNTING – KICKING

PASSING	Att	Comp	%	Yds	Yd/Att	TD	Int–	%	RK
Morrall	317	182	57	2909	9.2	26	17–	5	1
Unitas	32	11	34	139	4.3	2	4	13	
Ward	9	3	33	46	5.1	0	1–	11	
Matte	1	0	0	0	0.0	0	0–	0	

PUNTING	No	Avg
Lee	49	39.5

KICKING	XP	Att	%	FG	Att	%
Michaels	48	50	96	18	28	64

LOS ANGELES RAMS

RUSHING

Last Name	No.	Yds	Avg	TD
Ellison	151	616	4.1	5
Bass	121	494	4.1	1
Mason	108	395	3.7	3
Gabriel	34	139	4.1	4
Dennis	29	136	4.7	0
Dyer	55	136	2.5	1
Meador	1	11	11.0	0
Plum	2	3	1.5	0
Ezerins	2	2	1.0	0

RECEIVING

Last Name	No.	Yds	Avg	TD
Truax	35	417	12	3
Casey	29	565	19	5
Snow	29	500	17	3
Bass	27	195	7	2
Ellison	20	248	12	2
Mason	15	144	10	0
Dennis	8	53	7	0
Dyer	8	37	5	0
Tucker	7	124	18	4
Studstill	7	108	15	1
Pivec	3	27	9	0
Gabriel	1	−5	−5	0

PUNT RETURNS

Last Name	No.	Yds	Avg	TD
Smith	27	171	6	0
Meador	17	136	8	0

KICKOFF RETURNS

Last Name	No.	Yds	Avg	TD
Smith	26	718	28	1
Ellison	12	268	22	0
Meador	1	20	20	0
Williams	1	16	16	0
Dennis	2	2	1	0
Pivec	2	0	0	0
Ezerins	1	0	0	0

PASSING – PUNTING – KICKING

PASSING	Att	Comp	%	Yds	Yd/Att	TD	Int–	%	RK
Gabriel	366	184	50	2364	6.5	19	16–	4	9
Plum	12	5	42	49	4.1	1	1–	8	
Dennis	2	0	0	0	0.0	0	0–	0	
Mason	2	0	0	0	0.0	0	0–	0	
Ellison	1	0	0	0	0.0	0	0–	0	
Studstill	1	0	0	0	0.0	0	0–	0	

PUNTING	No	Avg
Studstill	81	39.6

KICKING	XP	Att	%	FG	Att	%
Gossett	37	37	100	17	31	55

SAN FRANCISCO FORTY NINERS

RUSHING

Last Name	No.	Yds	Avg	TD
Willard	227	967	4.3	7
Lewis	141	573	4.1	1
Tucker	30	135	4.5	3
Brodie	18	71	3.9	0
Daniels	12	37	3.1	0
Cunningham	6	7	1.2	0
Mira	1	5	5.0	0
Crow	4	4	1.0	0
McNeil	1	−1	−1.0	0
Spurrier	1	−15	−15.0	0

RECEIVING

Last Name	No.	Yds	Avg	TD
McNeil	71	994	14	7
Witcher	39	531	14	1
Willard	36	232	6	0
Crow	31	531	17	5
Lewis	27	244	9	3
Tucker	15	197	13	4
Windsor	8	146	18	2
McFarland	5	140	28	1
Cunningham	2	25	13	0
Daniels	2	23	12	0

PUNT RETURNS

Last Name	No.	Yds	Avg	TD
Alexander	24	87	4	0
Fuller	12	33	3	0

KICKOFF RETURNS

Last Name	No.	Yds	Avg	TD
Alexander	20	360	18	0
Cunningham	14	286	20	0
Daniels	10	206	21	0
Tucker	5	103	21	0
Fuller	1	23	23	0
Hays	2	21	11	0
Banaszek	1	15	15	0
Olerich	1	4	4	0
Hart	1	3	3	0
Nunley	2	0	0	0
Peoples	1	0	0	0

PASSING – PUNTING – KICKING

PASSING	Att	Comp	%	Yds	Yd/Att	TD	Int–	%	RK
Brodie	404	234	58	3020	7.5	22	21–	5	3
Mira	11	4	36	44	4.0	1	1–	9	
McNeil	2	1	50	43	21.5	1	1–	50	

PUNTING	No	Avg
Spurrier	68	39.0

KICKING	XP	Att	%	FG	Att	%
Davis	26	26	100	9	16	56
Patera	10	12	83	2	8	25

ATLANTA FALCONS

RUSHING

Last Name	No.	Yds	Avg	TD
Butler	94	365	3.9	2
Dunn	72	219	3.0	3
Wages	59	211	3.6	0
Harris	53	144	2.7	0
Berry	26	139	5.3	2
Johnson	11	97	8.8	1
McCarthy	31	86	2.8	1
Bryant	9	29	3.2	0
Auer	3	19	6.3	0
Ogden	1	12	12.0	0
Lee	6	7	1.2	0
Lemmerman	1	0	0.0	0
Simmons	1	−6	−6.0	0
Lothridge	1	−16	−16.0	0

RECEIVING

Last Name	No.	Yds	Avg	TD
Simmons	28	479	17	0
Ogden	25	452	18	2
Long	22	484	22	4
Flatley	20	305	15	0
Wages	16	121	8	1
Butler	15	127	8	0
McCarthy	13	119	9	0
Dunn	9	118	13	0
Donohoe	6	52	9	1
Harris	3	118	39	1
Bryant	1	11	11	0

PUNT RETURNS

Last Name	No.	Yds	Avg	TD
Burson	11	56	5	0
Rassas	4	10	3	0
Spiller	1	0	0	0

KICKOFF RETURNS

Last Name	No.	Yds	Avg	TD
Butler	37	799	22	0
Rassas	10	180	18	0
Bryant	5	112	22	0
Lee	3	63	21	0
Auer	2	31	16	0
Talbert	3	30	10	0
Wages	1	23	23	0
Donohoe	1	22	22	0
Szczecko	3	18	6	0
Spiller	1	18	18	0
Harris	1	16	16	0
Grimm	1	4	4	0
Allen	1	0	0	0
Cerne	1	0	0	0

PASSING – PUNTING – KICKING

PASSING	Att	Comp	%	Yds	Yd/Att	TD	Int–	%	RK
Johnson	156	73	47	892	5.7	2	10–	6	17
Berry	153	81	53	1433	9.4	7	13–	8	11
Lemmerman	15	3	20	40	2.7	0	1–	7	
Wages	2	1	50	21	10.5	0	0–	0	

PUNTING	No	Avg
Lothridge	75	44.3

KICKING	XP	Att	%	FG	Att	%
Etter	17	19	89	11	21	52

1968 A.F.L. The Jets, Heidi, and Howls

Heidi, the Swiss mountain girl from the storybooks, had football fans flooding telephone lines with cries of protest on November 17. With the Jets beating Oakland 32-29 with two minutes left in the game, NBC television was faced with a dilemma; it could either continue coverage of the football game to its conclusion or it could broadcast a special dramatization of "Heidi" at its scheduled hour and leave the football game before time ran out. NBC opted for "Heidi," and football fans poured calls of protest into the television station for taking the game off the air. To add fuel to the fire, the Raiders scored two touchdowns in those last minutes to take the game 43-32. NBC tried to make amends by showing films of the final two minutes of action on the late news shows, and the network promised never again to get burned with such a decision.

EASTERN DIVISION

New York Jets—There was no December collapse for the Jets this year, as they won their last three games from Miami, Cincinnati, and Miami, both easy marks. In first place heading into the final month, the Jets this year held onto the top spot right to the end. The New York offense was too much for the rest of the Eastern Division, with Joe Namath riding herd on one of pro football's most explosive attacks. Continuing to hit George Sauer and Don Maynard with bullet passes at regular intervals, Namath also blossomed into a top diagnostician, deftly sending runners Matt Snell and Emerson Boozer into the line at the right time more often than not. Much had been expected of the New York offense, and it delivered in style; but the New York defense, consistently downgraded by opponents and the press, hung together in a unit which jumped on every enemy mistake. Even place-kicker Jim Turner, aided by new holder Babe Parilli, had a good year. With the Eastern title in their pockets, the Jets headed for a post-season date with destiny.

Houston Oilers—The Oilers caught lightning in a bottle in their surprise 1967 Eastern title, but they dropped this year to a 7-7 mark more typical of a young club still in the midst of rebuilding. Paced by two of the league's top defensive players in George Webster and Miller Farr, the Oilers still surrendered points grudgingly, but the Houston attack frightened few opponents. Fullback Hoyle Granger ran well behind a strong line, but neither he nor Woody Campbell had game-breaking speed. The receiving was strengthened by rookies Mac Haik and Jim Beirne and the development of Alvin Reed into a top tight end, but quarterback problems made the Oiler passing game extremely erratic. Pete Beathard displayed a strong arm and periods of inaccuracy before an appendectomy shelved him late in the year, and Don Trull, picked up after the Patriots cut him, was not a permanent answer.

Miami Dolphins—Fullback Larry Csonka needed time to get used to pro football but showed unmistakable power as a runner. Catching on more quickly was halfback Jim Kiick, a fifth-round draft pick who was a reliable runner and receiver. The defense was shored up by freshmen Manny Fernandez and Dick Anderson; Fernandez, signed as a free agent, provided the team's only pass-rushing, while safetyman Anderson had a flair for both tackling and intercepting. Another rookie, tackle Doug Crusan, won a starting job in the offensive line. Of course, some of the veterans also turned in good performances, with quarterback Bob Griese leading the way. The second-year passer had a good season despite poor protection and the loss of Jack Clancy, his favorite receiver, to knee surgery. Split end Karl Noonan, a slow but meticulous receiver, filled in for Clancy and hauled in fifty-eight passes.

Boston Patriots—Coach Mike Holovak made a break with the past by trading veteran quarterback Babe Parilli to New York for young Mike Taliaferro, but the Boston attack suffered for the change. Taliaferro could not ignite the offense and lost his job to rookie Tom Sherman. Other veteran Patriot players endured poor seasons. A bad ankle robbed Jim Nance of much of his effectiveness, and bad knees put defensive end Larry Eisenhauer and middle linebacker Nick Buoniconti out of action for several games. Coach Holovak got good work from cornerback Leroy Mitchell, tight end Jim Whalen, center Jon Morris, and defensive tackle Houston Antwine, but the Patriots needed a complete overhauling.

Buffalo Bills—The Bills' quarterback ills started when veterans Jack Kemp and Tom Flores were both injured before the regular season began. Coach Joel Collier started the year with rookie Dan Darragh as the signal-caller, but with the offensive line thinned out by injuries and age, Darragh soon was racked up enough by enemy defenses that his knee gave out. Next on the firing line was Kay Stephenson, a young man picked up from San Diego, and he lasted a couple of games before going out with a broken collarbone. Ed Rutkowski, a veteran utility man who had last played quarterback at Notre Dame six years ago, then stepped in and stayed healthy while guiding the Bills to the end of the season. The team scored the least points in the league but did have the satisfaction of beating the Jets 37-35 for their only victory of the season. The Bills had been a championship team only two years before, so coach Collier paid with his head two games into the campaign.

WESTERN DIVISION

Oakland Raiders—The Raiders were hit with a long string of injuries, yet still charged to a 12-2 record and a tie for the Western title. Defensive tackle Tom Keating missed the entire season with an Achilles-tendon injury suffered in last year's AFL championship game, but Carleton Oats filled in competently and Dan Birdwell compensated with his best year ever. When linebacker Bill Laskey also hurt his Achilles tendon, rookie Chip Oliver stepped into the starting lineup with a fine performance. When a knee injury shelved cornerback Kent McCloughan in mid-season, the Raiders had an exciting substitute in rookie Butch Atkinson. The offense avoided injuries but found two new starters in wide receiver Warren Wells and halfback Charlie Smith. With the title on the line, Daryle Lamonica threw five touchdown passes to win the playoff game 41-6.

Kansas City Chiefs—The Chiefs came back from last year's poor season to tie for first place in the West with a 12-2 record. The Kansas City defense allowed the fewest points in the league, with top players in all departments. Jerry Mays and Buck Buchanan starred in the line, the linebacking trio of Bobby Bell, Willie Lanier, and Jim Lynch was tops in the league, and safety Johnny Robinson steadied a secondary with several new starters. The offense matched the defense in efficiency, although an injury to Otis Taylor put more emphasis on a ball-control attack. Rookie fullback Robert Holmes, an unknown fourteenth-round draft pick, surprised everyone with his dogged ball-carrying, while veterans Mike Garrett and Curtis McClinton were bothered by injuries.

San Diego Chargers—The Chargers made the Western pennant race a three-way affair until dropping three of their last four games. Before home-town audiences, the Chargers lost 37-15 to New York, 40-3 to Kansas City, and 34-27 to Oakland, shooting all their title hopes to pieces. The Chargers had to be ranked among the league powers, but they could not beat the other top teams like the Jets, Chiefs, and Raiders. The biggest problem for coach Sid Gillman was his defense. The front four of Steve DeLong, Scott Appleton, Russ Washington, and Houston Ridge had good college press clippings but rarely got to the enemy passer, the linebacking was no better than adequate, and the secondary was solid only at Kenny Graham's strong safety spot. The San Diego attack as always found ways to put points on the scoreboard regularly. Quarterback John Hadl, operating behind an excellent offensive line, kept receivers Lance Alworth and Gary Garrison busy catching passes, and although fullback Brad Hubbert missed most of the season with a knee injury, halfback Dickie Post kept up the fine running of his rookie year.

Denver Broncos—The Broncos embarrassed themselves by losing 24-10 to the new Cincinnati Bengals on opening day, but they jelled into a respectable team after losing their first three games. In a five-week stretch from October 6 to November 3, Denver beat the Bengals, Jets, Dolphins, and Patriots while losing only to the Chargers. The key to this hot streak was the heavy pressure put on opposing passers by the Bronco defensive line, with end Rich Jackson developing into an All-Pro performer and tackle Dave Costa providing steady play against the run. The linebacking and secondary still was in a state of flux, but the strong pressure exerted by the line prevented passers from exploiting these weak spots. The Denver attack moved the ball well until quarterback Steve Tensi and split end Al Denson both went out in mid-season with broken collarbones, but rookie Marlin Briscoe, the first black ever to play regularly at T-formation quarterback in the pro ranks, kept the club interesting to the end with his scrambling and clutch passing.

Cincinnati Bengals—Paul Brown had built the Cleveland Browns into a powerhouse by signing poised players returning from World War II, but he set a different course for the new Cincinnati Bengals. Brown threw his lineup open to rookies and young players who had not fit in elsewhere. With so many inexperienced players in the lineup, most clubs would have suffered through a dismal season of hard learning, but Brown drilled his young Bengals so that they learned and played competitive football right from the start.

FINAL TEAM STATISTICS

OFFENSE

	BOSTON	BUFFALO	CIN.	DENVER	HOUSTON	K.C.	MIAMI	N.Y.	OAKLAND	S.D.
FIRST DOWNS:										
Total	181	159	171	217	240	223	247	249	**287**	270
by Rushing	69	71	85	75	99	**123**	78	80	97	93
by Passing	94	72	73	124	128	89	144	144	162	**164**
by Penalty	18	16	13	18	13	11	25	25	**28**	13
RUSHING:										
Number	421	400	421	411	462	**537**	417	467	471	428
Yards	1362	1527	1807	1614	1804	**2227**	1704	1608	2168	1765
Average Yards	3.1	3.8	4.3	3.9	3.9	4.1	4.1	3.4	**4.6**	4.1
Touchdowns	8	9	14	11	16	16	12	**22**	16	12
PASSING:										
Attempts	409	405	313	427	414	270	423	436	468	**472**
Completions	160	168	167	179	191	156	216	217	**237**	225
Completion Percentage	39.1	41.5	53.4	41.9	46.1	**57.8**	51.1	49.8	50.6	47.7
Passing Yards	2121	1714	1896	2826	2864	2492	2843	3574	3771	**3813**
Average Yards per Att.	5.2	4.2	6.1	6.6	6.9	**9.2**	6.7	8.2	8.1	8.1
Average Yards per Comp.	13.3	10.2	11.4	15.8	15.0	16.0	13.2	16.5	15.9	**16.9**
Tackled Att. to pass	38	39	38	51	29	24	52	**18**	29	**18**
Yards Lost Tackled	356	371	277	469	316	216	441	**135**	243	190
Net Yards	1765	1343	1619	2357	2548	2276	2402	3439	3528	3623
Touchdowns	16	7	8	20	17	20	21	20	**31**	29
Interceptions	33	28	**11**	27	25	**11**	22	19	18	33
Percent Intercepted	8.1	6.9	**3.5**	6.3	6.0	4.1	5.2	4.4	3.8	7.0
PUNTS:										
Number	96	**100**	84	96	73	65	75	68	64	56
Average Distance	39.9	41.8	40.9	42.7	41.2	**45.3**	40.6	43.8	43.6	40.7
PUNT RETURNS:										
Number	37	44	30	38	52	31	28	36	**55**	39
Yards	197	301	196	332	443	450	205	286	**666**	292
Average Yards	5.3	6.8	6.5	8.7	8.5	**14.5**	7.3	7.9	12.1	7.5
Touchdowns	0	1	0	1	0	**2**	0	0	**2**	1
KICKOFF RETURNS:										
Number	**71**	69	54	60	53	38	50	46	49	51
Yards	1442	**1537**	1068	1361	1235	736	1134	995	1092	1065
Average Yards	20.3	22.3	19.8	22.7	**23.3**	19.9	22.7	21.6	22.3	20.9
Touchdowns	0	**1**	0	0	0	0	0	0	0	0
INTERCEPTION RETURNS:										
Number	23	22	10	20	20	**37**	22	28	25	20
Yards	220	**475**	144	165	396	469	386	456	424	275
Average Yards	9.6	**21.6**	14.4	8.3	19.8	12.7	17.5	16.3	17.0	13.8
Touchdowns	1	4	2	0	**5**	2	1	2	4	2
PENALTIES:										
Number	67	67	55	73	61	66	48	76	**81**	72
Yards	682	687	586	772	644	650	485	742	**958**	654
FUMBLES:										
Number	28	23	27	28	28	26	**17**	19	34	20
Number Lost	20	14	10	13	13	16	**8**	9	21	12
POINTS:										
Total	229	199	215	255	303	371	276	419	**453**	382
PAT (kick) Attempts	26	19	24	32	38	40	36	43	**54**	43
PAT (kick) Made	26	19	24	31	37	39	36	43	**54**	40
PAT (2-Point) Attempts	0	**3**	1	0	0	0	0	2	1	2
PAT (2-Point) Made	0	**2**	0	0	0	0	0	1	1	**2**
FG Attempts	27	28	27	23	29	40	19	**46**	34	32
FG Made	15	14	13	10	12	30	8	**34**	21	22
Percent FG Made	55.6	50.0	48.1	43.5	41.4	**75.0**	42.1	73.9	61.8	68.8
Safeties	1	1	1	1	1	1	0	1	**2**	1

DEFENSE

	BOSTON	BUFFALO	CIN.	DENVER	HOUSTON	K.C.	MIAMI	N.Y.	OAKLAND	S.D.
FIRST DOWNS:										
Total	237	210	275	251	198	215	240	**178**	215	225
by Rushing	86	85	116	94	89	**52**	116	59	83	90
by Passing	123	103	140	145	**96**	140	112	104	113	118
by Penalty	28	22	19	**12**	13	23	**12**	15	19	17
RUSHING:										
Number	479	505	473	457	462	**365**	445	368	442	439
Yards	1825	2021	2097	1861	1704	1266	2172	**1195**	1804	1641
Average Yards	3.8	4.0	4.4	4.1	3.7	3.5	4.9	**3.2**	4.1	3.7
Touchdowns	22	15	13	20	9	**4**	19	9	12	13
PASSING:										
Attempts	416	**340**	411	429	359	461	342	403	446	430
Completions	200	**143**	212	217	158	214	179	187	189	217
Completion Percentage	48.1	**42.1**	51.6	50.6	44.0	46.4	52.3	46.4	42.4	50.5
Passing Yards	2826	2477	2903	3419	**2003**	3262	2904	2567	2657	2896
Average Yards per Att.	6.8	7.3	7.1	8.0	**5.6**	7.1	8.5	6.4	6.0	6.7
Average Yards per Comp.	14.1	17.3	13.7	15.8	**12.7**	15.2	16.2	13.7	14.1	13.3
Tackled Att. to pass	27	31	32	31	33	45	21	43	**49**	24
Yards Lost Tackled	236	273	283	256	332	**439**	192	399	400	204
Net Yards	2590	2204	2620	3163	**1671**	2823	2712	2168	2257	2692
Touchdowns	20	19	25	25	**13**	14	23	17	**13**	20
Interceptions	23	22	10	20	20	**37**	22	28	25	20
Percent Intercepted	5.5	6.5	2.4	4.7	5.6	**8.0**	6.4	6.9	5.6	4.7
PUNTS:										
Number	81	75	63	76	88	73	55	**98**	94	74
Average Distance	40.5	39.7	44.2	43.0	44.1	42.8	43.4	**38.4**	42.3	42.3
PUNT RETURNS:										
Number	59	45	41	46	40	31	28	39	40	**21**
Yards	502	521	252	282	379	220	250	531	**211**	220
Average Yards	8.5	11.6	6.1	6.1	9.5	7.1	8.9	13.6	**5.3**	10.5
Touchdowns	1	1	**0**	**0**	1	**0**	**0**	3	**0**	1
KICKOFF RETURNS:										
Number	40	49	40	**29**	58	54	54	82	75	60
Yards	901	1062	977	**704**	1302	1044	1108	1664	1652	1251
Average Yards	22.5	21.7	24.4	24.3	22.4	**19.3**	20.5	20.3	22.0	20.9
Touchdowns	0	0	1	0	0	0	0	0	0	0
INTERCEPTION RETURNS:										
Number	33	28	**11**	27	25	**11**	22	19	18	33
Yards	510	472	**79**	328	326	119	432	455	155	534
Average Yards	15.5	16.9	**7.2**	12.1	13.0	10.8	19.6	23.9	8.6	16.2
Touchdowns	3	6	**0**	3	2	**0**	3	4	**0**	2
PENALTIES:										
Number	70	66	62	64	54	62	70	65	**90**	63
Yards	874	540	632	750	526	564	655	695	**932**	692
FUMBLES:										
Number	**37**	24	19	24	17	22	28	29	24	26
Number Lost	17	13	9	12	10	12	**18**	15	15	15
POINTS:										
Total	406	367	329	404	248	**170**	355	280	233	310
PAT (kick) Attempts	49	41	39	47	25	**18**	44	34	23	35
PAT (kick) Made	49	40	37	47	25	**18**	43	33	22	35
PAT (2-Point) Attempts	**0**	**0**	**0**	1	1	**0**	1	2	3	1
PAT (2-Point) Made	**0**	**0**	**0**	1	1	**0**	1	2	1	**0**
FG Attempts	31	48	35	34	30	27	24	**17**	28	31
FG Made	21	27	18	21	21	14	12	**9**	17	19
Percent FG Made	67.7	56.3	51.4	61.8	70.0	51.9	**50.0**	52.9	60.7	61.3
Safeties	**0**	**0**	2	2	1	1	2	**0**	1	1

WESTERN DIVISION PLAYOFF

December 22 at Oakland
(Attendance 53,605)

SCORING

OAKLAND	21	7	0	13–41
KANSAS CITY	0	6	0	0– 6

First Quarter
- Oak. Biletnikoff, 24 yard pass from Lamonica
  PAT–Blanda (kick)
- Oak. Wells, 23 yard pass from Lamonica
  PAT–Blanda (kick)
- Oak. Biletnikoff, 44 yard pass from Lamonica
  PAT–Blanda (kick)

Second Quarter
- K.C. Stenerud, 10 yard field goal
- K.C. Stenerud, 8 yard field goal
- Oak. Biletnikoff, 54 yard pass from Lamonica
  PAT–Blanda (kick)

Fourth Quarter
- Oak. Wells, 35 yard pass from Lamonica
  PAT–Blanda (kick)
- Oak. Blanda, 41 yard field goal
- Oak. Blanda, 40 yard field goal

TEAM STATISTICS

OAK.		K.C.
22	First Downs–Total	13
7	First Downs–Rushing	3
14	First Downs–Passing	9
1	First Downs–Penalty	1
1	Fumbles–Number	2
0	Fumbles–Lost Ball	0
1	Penalties–Number	2
2	Yards Penalized	20
0	Missed Field Goals	1
70	Offensive Plays–Total	61
454	Net Yards	312
6.5	Average Gain	5.1
0	Giveaways	4
4	Takeaways	0
+4	Difference	–4

INDIVIDUAL STATISTICS

OAKLAND	No.	Yds.	Avg.	KANSAS CITY	No.	Yds.	Avg.
RUSHING							
Smith	13	74	5.7	Holmes	13	46	3.5
Banaszak	3	19	6.3	Hayes	3	10	3.3
Dixon	10	13	1.3	Dawson	2	9	4.5
Hagberg	4	12	3.0	Garrett	6	5	0.8
	30	118	3.9		24	70	2.9
RECEIVING							
Biletnikoff	7	180	25.7	Pitts	5	56	11.2
Smith	5	52	10.4	Taylor	4	117	29.3
Wells	4	93	23.3	Garrett	4	31	7.8
Cannon	2	15	7.5	Richardson	3	57	19.0
Dixon	1	7	7.0	Holmes	1	–8	–8.0
	19	347	18.3		17	253	14.9
PUNTING							
Eischeid	5		45.4	Wilson	6		50.3
PUNT RETURNS							
Bird	3	29	9.7	Smith	2	–9	–4.5
KICKOFF RETURNS							
Atkinson	1	34	34.0	Smith	5	73	14.6
				Mitchell	2	46	23.0
				Lanier	1	0	0.0
					8	119	14.9
INTERCEPTION RETURNS							
Wilson	1	14	14.0	None			
Hopkins	1	7	7.0				
Connors	1	5	5.0				
Brown	1	0	0.0				
	4	26	6.5				

PASSING

OAKLAND	Att.	Comp.	Comp. Pct.	Yds.	Int.	Yds/ Att.	Yds/ Comp.	Yards Lost Tackled
Lamonica	39	19	48.7	347	0	8.9	18.3	1–11
KANSAS CITY								
Dawson	36	17	47.2	253	4	7.0	14.9	1–11

NEW YORK JETS 11-3-0 Weeb Ewbank

Scores of Each Game		
20	Kansas City	19
47	Boston	31
35	Buffalo	37
23	SAN DIEGO	20
13	DENVER	21
20	Houston	14
48	BOSTON	14
25	BUFFALO	21
26	HOUSTON	7
32	Oakland	43
37	San Diego	15
35	MIAMI	17
27	CINCINNATI	14
31	Miami	7

Use Name	Pos.	Hgt	Wgt	Age	Int	Pts
Winston Hill	OT	6'4"	280	26		
Sam Walton	OT	6'5"	270	25		
Jeff Richardson	C-OT	6'3"	250	23		
Randy Rasmussen	OG	6'2"	255	23		
Bob Talamini	OG	6'1"	255	29		
Dave Herman	OT-OG	6'2"	255	26		
John Schmitt	C	6'4"	245	25		
Paul Crane	LB-C	6'2"	205	24		2
Verlon Biggs	DE	6'4"	270	25		
Gerry Philbin	DE	6'2"	245	27		
Steve Thompson	DE	6'5"	245	23		
John Elliott	DT	6'4"	245	23		
Ray Hayes	DT	6'5"	245	21		
Karl Henke	DT	6'4"	245	23		
Paul Rochester	DT	6'2"	255	31		
Carl McAdams	DE-DT	6'3"	240	24		
Al Atkinson	LB	6'1"	230	25	2	
Ralph Baker	LB	6'3"	235	26	3	
Larry Grantham	LB	6'	210	29		
Mike Stromberg	LB	6'2"	235	23		
Bill Baird	DB	5'10"	180	29	4	
Randy Beverly	DB	5'11"	185	24	4	6
Earl Christy	DB	5'11"	195	25	1	
Mike D'Amato	DB	6'2"	204	25		
John Dockery	DB	6'	186	23		
Cornell Gordon	DB	6'	187	27	2	
Jim Hudson	DB	6'2"	210	25	5	
Jim Richards	DB	6'1"	180	21		
Johnny Sample	DB	6'1"	208	31	7	6
Paul Seiler — Military Service						
Joe Namath	QB	6'2"	195	24		12
Babe Parilli	QB	6'1"	190	38		6
Jim Turner	QB	6'2"	205	27		145
Emerson Boozer	HB	5'11"	204	25		30
Bill Mathis	HB	6'1"	220	29		38
Billy Joe	FB	6'2"	236	27		18
Matt Snell	FB	6'2"	220	26		42
Lee White	FB	6'4"	240	22		
Mark Smolinski	TE-FB	6'	215	29		6
Don Maynard	WR	6'	180	32		60
Harvey Nairn	WR	6'1"	178	22		
Bill Rademacher	WR	6'1"	190	26		
George Sauer	WR	6'1"	195	24		18
Bake Turner	WR	6'	180	28		12
Curley Johnson	TE	6'	215	33		
Pete Lammons	TE	6'3"	228	24		18

HOUSTON OILERS 7-7-0 Wally Lemm

Scores of Each Game		
21	KANSAS CITY	26
24	Miami	10
14	San Diego	30
15	OAKLAND	24
7	MIAMI	24
16	Boston	0
14	NEW YORK	20
30	Buffalo	7
27	Cincinnati	17
7	New York	26
38	DENVER	17
10	Kansas City	24
35	BUFFALO	6
45	BOSTON	17

Use Name	Pos.	Hgt	Wgt	Age	Int	Pts
Glen Ray Hines	OT	6'5"	265	24		
Bob Robertson	OT	6'4"	246	21		
Walt Suggs	OT	6'5"	265	29		
Sonny Bishop	OG	6'2"	245	28		
Tom Regner	OG	6'1"	255	24		
Dick Swatland	OG	6'3"	245	22		
Bobby Maples	C	6'3"	245	25		
Steve Quinn	C	6'1"	225	22		
Elvin Bethea	DE	6'3"	250	22		
Gary Cutsinger	DE	6'4"	245	27		
Pat Holmes	DE	6'5"	250	28		
Bud Marshall	DT	6'5"	275	26		
Dudley Meredith (from BUF)	DT	6'4"	285	33		
Willie Parker	DT	6'2"	265	23		
George Rice	DT	6'3"	260	24		
Carel Stith	DT	6'5"	265	23		
Tom Domres	DE-DT	6'3"	255	21		
Pete Barnes	LB	6'3"	245	23		
Garland Boyette	LB	6'1"	245	28	1	
Ronnie Caveness	LB	6'1"	225	25		
Marion Rushing (from ATL-N)	LB	6'2"	230	31		
Rich Stotter	LB	6'	225	23		
Olen Underwood	LB	6'1"	230	26	1	2
George Webster	LB	6'4"	223	22	1	
Larry Carwell	DB	6'1"	190	24	4	6
Miller Farr	DB	6'1"	190	25	3	12
W. K. Hicks	DB	6'1"	195	25	3	
Ken Houston	DB	6'3"	192	23	5	12
Pete Johns	DB	6'3"	190	23		
Zeke Moore	DB	6'2"	198	24		
Jim Norton	DB	6'3"	180	29	2	
Bob Smith	DB	6'	180	23		
Pete Beathard	QB	6'2"	207	26		12
Bob Davis	QB	6'3"	208	22		6
Don Trull	QB	6'1"	196	26		
Sid Blanks	HB	6'	210	27		
Ode Burrell	HB	6'	192	28		
Woody Campbell	HB	5'11"	202	23		36
Hoyle Granger	FB	6'1"	225	24		42
Roy Hopkins	FB	6'1"	225	23		
Glenn Bass	WR	6'2"	210	29		
Jim Beirne	WR	6'2"	196	21		24
Charley Frazier	WR	6'	184	29		
Mac Haik	WR	6'1"	196	22		48
Lionel Taylor	WR	6'2"	215	32		
Jim LeMoine	TE	6'2"	245	23		
Alvin Reed	TE	6'5"	230	24		30
Wayne Walker	K	6'2"	215	23		50
John Wittenborn	K	6'2"	240	32		23

MIAMI DOLPHINS 5-8-1 George Wilson

Scores of Each Game		
10	HOUSTON	24
21	OAKLAND	47
3	KANSAS CITY	48
24	Houston	7
14	BUFFALO	14
24	Cincinnati	22
14	Denver	21
28	San Diego	34
21	Buffalo	17
21	CINCINNATI	38
34	Boston	10
17	New York	35
38	BOSTON	7
7	NEW YORK	31

Use Name	Pos.	Hgt	Wgt	Age	Int	Pts
Doug Crusan	OT	6'5"	255	22		
Norm Evans	OT	6'5"	250	24		
Jack Pyburn	OT	6'6"	250	23		
Charlie Fowler	OG	6'2"	260	24		
Billy Neighbors	OG	5'11"	250	28		
Maxie Williams	OG	6'4"	250	28		
Freddie Woodson	DE-OG	6'2"	255	24		
Tom Goode	C	6'3"	250	29		
Mel Branch	DE	6'2"	235	31		
Manny Fernandez	DE	6'2"	250	22		
Bob Joswick	DE	6'5"	250	22		
Jim Riley	DE	6'4"	255	23		
Ray Jacobs	DT	6'3"	285	28		
Tom Nomina	DT	6'5"	260	26		
John Richardson	DT	6'2"	260	23		
Jim Urbanek	DT	6'4"	270	23		
Rudy Barber	LB	6'1"	255	23		
John Bramlett	LB	6'2"	210	27	2	
Bob Bruggers (to SD)	LB	6'1"	230	24		
Randy Edmunds	LB	6'2"	220	22	1	
Frank Emanuel	LB	6'3"	225	25	2	6
Jimmy Keyes	LB	6'2"	225	24		51
Wahoo McDaniel	LB	6'	230	31		
Ed Weisacosky	LB	6'	230	24		
Dick Anderson	DB	6'2"	205	22	8	6
Mack Lamb	DB	6'1"	188	24	1	
Bob Neff	DB	6'	180	24		
Bob Petrella	DB	6'	185	23	1	
Jimmy Warren	DB	5'11"	175	29	2	
Dick Washington	DB	6'1"	205	23		
Willie West	DB	5'10"	187	30	4	6
Dick Westmoreland	DB	6'1"	195	27	1	
Jack Clancy — Knee Injury						
Bob Griese	QB	6'1"	190	23		6
Kim Hammond	QB	6'1"	192	23		
Rick Norton	QB	6'1"	190	24		
Jack Harper	HB	5'11"	190	23		
Jim Kiick	HB	5'11"	215	22		24
Sam Price	HB	5'11"	215	24		
Gary Tucker	HB	5'11"	195	23		
Larry Seiple	TE-HB	6'	213	23		6
Larry Csonka	FB	6'3"	240	21		42
Stan Mitchell	HB-FB	6'2"	225	24		24
Bill Darnall	WR	6'2"	197	24		
Gene Milton	WR	5'10"	170	23		6
Karl Noonan	WR	6'3"	190	24		66
Howard Twilley	WR	5'10"	180	24		6
Jim Cox	TE	6'2"	227	24		
Doug Moreau	TE	6'2"	215	23		27

BOSTON PATRIOTS 4-10-0 Mike Holovak

Scores of Each Game		
16	Buffalo	7
31	NEW YORK	47
20	Denver	17
10	Oakland	41
0	HOUSTON	16
23	BUFFALO	6
14	New York	48
14	DENVER	35
17	SAN DIEGO	27
17	Kansas City	31
10	MIAMI	34
33	CINCINNATI	14
7	Miami	38
17	Houston	45

Use Name	Pos.	Hgt	Wgt	Age	Int	Pts
Jim Boudreaux	OT	6'4"	245	23		
Paul Feldhausen	OT	6'6"	270	22		
Tom Funchess	OT	6'5"	260	23		
Tom Neville	OT	6'4"	255	24		
Don Oakes	OT	6'3"	255	30		
Karl Singer	OT	6'3"	255	24		
Justin Canale	OG	6'2"	250	24		
Charley Long	OG	6'3"	250	30		
Len St. Jean	OG	6'1"	245	26		
Jon Morris	C	6'4"	240	25		
J. R. Williamson	LB-C	6'2"	220	26		
Dennis Byrd	DE	6'4"	260	21		
Larry Eisenhauer	DE	6'5"	255	28		
Mel Witt	DE	6'3"	265	22	1	6
Houston Antwine	DT	6'	270	29		
Whit Canale	DT	6'3"	245	26		
Jim Hunt	DT	5'11"	255	29		
Ed Toner	DT	6'3"	250	23		
Nick Buoniconti	LB	5'11"	220	27	3	
Jim Cheyunski	LB	6'2"	225	22	1	
Ray Ilg	LB	6'1"	220	22		
Ed Kocntz	LB	6'2"	230	21		
Ed Philpott	LB	6'3"	240	22	4	6
Doug Satcher	LB	6'	220	23	1	2
John Charles	DB	6'1"	200	24	1	
Billy Johnson	DB	5'11"	180	25	2	
Daryle Johnson	DB	5'11"	190	22	1	
Art McMahon	DB	5'11"	185	22	2	
Leroy Mitchell	DB	6'2"	190	23	7	
Willie Porter	DB	5'11"	195	22		
Don Webb	DB	5'10"	195	29		
Jim Corcoran	QB	6'	200	26		
Tom Sherman	QB	6'	190	22		
Mike Taliaferro	QB	6'2"	205	26		
Larry Garron	HB	6'	195	31		6
Gene Thomas (to OAK)	HB	6'1"	210	25		12
R. C. Gamble	FB-HB	6'3"	220	21		12
Preston Johnson	FB	6'2"	230	23		
Jim Nance	FB	6'1"	240	25		24
Gino Cappelletti	WR	6'	190	34		83
Jim Colclough	WR	6'	185	32		
Art Graham	WR	6'1"	205	27		6
Bobby Leo	WR	5'10"	180	23		
Aaron Marsh	WR	6'1"	190	23		24
Bill Murphy	WR	6'1"	185	21		
Bill Murphy	WR	5'11"	190	29		6
Bob Scarpitto	TE	6'2"	220	24		
Jim Whalen	TE	6'2"	210	24		42
Terry Swanson	K	6'	210	23		

BUFFALO BILLS 1-12-1 Joe Collier

Scores of Each Game		
7	BOSTON	16
6	OAKLAND	48
23	Cincinnati	34
37	NEW YORK	35
7	KANSAS CITY	18
14	Miami	14
6	Boston	23
7	HOUSTON	30
21	New York	25
17	MIAMI	21
6	SAN DIEGO	21
32	Denver	34
10	Oakland	13
6	Houston	35

Use Name	Pos.	Hgt	Wgt	Age	Int	Pts
Stew Barber	OT	6'3"	248	29		
Dick Cunningham	OT	6'2"	244	23		
Ray Rissmiller	OT	6'4"	250	26		
Mike McBath	DE-OT	6'4"	248	22		
George Flint	OG	6'4"	240	30		
Bob Kalsu	OG	6'3"	235	23		
Billy Shaw	OG	6'3"	252	28		
Al Bemiller	C	6'3"	243	29		
Jack Frantz	C	6'3"	230	21		
Tom Day	DE	6'2"	265	33		
Ron McDole	DE	6'3"	270	28	2	
Howard Kindig	C-DE	6'6"	264	27		
Jim Dunaway	DT	6'4"	282	26		
Tom Sestak	DT	6'5"	262	32		
Bob Tatarek	DT	6'4"	255	22		
Edgar Chandler	LB	6'3"	222	22		
Paul Guidry	LB	6'3"	228	24	1	
Harry Jacobs	LB	6'2"	226	31		
Paul Maguire	LB	6'	228	30		
Marty Schottenheimer	LB	6'3"	224	25	1	
Mike Stratton	LB	6'3"	230	26	1	
Butch Byrd	DB	6'	196	26	6	6
Hagood Clarke	DB	6'	192	26		6
Booker Edgerson	DB	5'10"	183	29	4	12
Tom Janik	DB	6'3"	195	27	3	6
Jerry Lawson	DB	5'11"	192	23		
John Pitts	DB	6'4"	215	23	2	
George Saimes	DB	5'10"	185	26	2	
Charlie Brown	HB-DB	6'1"	195	25		
Bobby Burnett — Injury						
Jack Kemp — Injury						
Joe O'Donnell — Injury						
Charley Ferguson — Injury						
Dan Darragh	QB	6'3"	196	21		
Tom Flores	QB	6'1"	202	31		
Benny Russell	QB	6'1"	190	24		
Kay Stephenson	QB	6'1"	210	23		
Ed Rutkowski	WR-QB	6'1"	200	27		6
Max Anderson	HB	5'8"	180	23		18
Gary McDermott	HB	6'1"	211	22		26
Charley Mitchell	HB	5'11"	185	28		
Ben Gregory	FB-HB	6'3"	220	21		6
Bob Cappadonna	FB	6'1"	230	24		20
Wayne Patrick	FB	6'2"	225	22		
Keith Lincoln (to SD)	HB-FB	6'2"	216	29		
Bobby Crockett	WR	6'	200	25		
Elbert Dubenion	WR	6'	187	33		
Monte Ledbetter	WR	6'2"	185	25		6
Haven Moses	WR	6'3"	200	22		12
Richard Trapp	WR	6'1"	174	21		
Bill Masters	TE	6'5"	225	24		
Paul Costa	OT-TE	6'4"	248	26		12
Bruce Alford	K	6'	185	23		57
Mike Mercer (to GB-N)	K	6'	217	32		4

NEW YORK JETS

RUSHING

Last Name	No.	Yds	Avg	TD
Snell	179	747	4.2	6
Boozer	143	441	3.1	5
Mathis	74	208	2.8	5
Joe	42	186	4.4	3
Sauer	2	21	10.5	0
Smolinski	12	15	1.3	0
Namath	5	11	2.2	2
Parilli	7	−2	−0.3	1
Johnson	2	−6	−3.0	0
Rademacher	1	−13	−13.0	0

RECEIVING

Last Name	No.	Yds	Avg	TD
Sauer	66	1141	17	3
Maynard	57	1297	23	10
Lammons	32	400	13	3
Snell	16	105	7	1
Boozer	12	101	8	0
B. Turner	10	241	24	2
Mathis	9	149	17	1
Smolinski	6	40	7	0
Johnson	5	78	16	0
Joe	2	11	6	0
Rademacher	2	11	6	0

PUNT RETURNS

Last Name	No.	Yds	Avg	TD
Christy	13	116	9	0
Baird	18	111	6	0
Richards	4	57	14	0
Philbin	1	2	2	0

KICKOFF RETURNS

Last Name	No.	Yds	Avg	TD
Christy	25	599	24	0
B. Turner	14	319	23	0
D'Amato	1	32	32	0
Snell	3	28	9	0
Smolinski	1	17	17	0
Rademacher	1	0	0	0

PASSING – PUNTING – KICKING

PASSING	Att	Comp	%	Yds	Yd/Att	TD	Int–%	RK
Namath	380	187	49	3147	8.3	15	17– 4	3
Parilli	55	29	53	401	7.3	5	2– 4	
Snell	1	1	100	26	26.0	0	0– 0	

PUNTING	No	Avg
Johnson	68	43.8

KICKING	XP	Att	%	FG	Att	%
J. Turner	43	43	100	34	46	74

2 POINT XP
Mathis

HOUSTON OILERS

RUSHING

Last Name	No.	Yds	Avg	TD
Granger	202	848	4.2	7
Campbell	115	436	3.8	6
Blanks	63	169	2.7	0
Hopkins	31	104	3.4	0
Davis	15	91	6.1	1
Beathard	18	79	4.4	2
Trull	14	47	3.4	0
Norton	1	20	20.0	0
Haik	2	7	3.5	0
Beirne	1	3	3.0	0

RECEIVING

Last Name	No.	Yds	Avg	TD
Reed	46	747	16	5
Haik	32	584	18	8
Beirne	31	474	15	4
Granger	26	361	14	0
Campbell	21	234	11	0
Blanks	13	184	14	0
Frazier	9	123	14	0
Taylor	6	90	15	0
Hopkins	4	40	10	0
Burrell	2	35	18	0
Wittenborn	1	−8	−8	0

PUNT RETURNS

Last Name	No.	Yds	Avg	TD
Carwell	27	227	8	0
Blanks	22	179	8	0
Burrell	2	26	13	0
Moore	1	11	11	0

KICKOFF RETURNS

Last Name	No.	Yds	Avg	TD
Moore	32	787	25	0
Carwell	15	335	22	0
Burrell	2	70	35	0
Hopkins	1	21	21	0
Houston	1	13	13	0
Robertson	2	9	5	0

PASSING – PUNTING – KICKING

PASSING	Att	Comp	%	Yds	Yd/Att	TD	Int–%	RK
Beathard	223	105	47	1559	7.0	7	16– 7	8
Trull	105	53	50	864	8.2	10	3– 3	
Davis	86	33	38	441	5.1	0	6– 7	

PUNTING	No	Avg
Norton	73	41.2

KICKING	XP	Att	%	FG	Att	%
Walker	26	26	100	8	16	50
Wittenborn	11	11	100	4	13	31

MIAMI DOLPHINS

RUSHING

Last Name	No.	Yds	Avg	TD
Kiick	165	621	3.8	4
Csonka	138	540	3.9	6
Griese	42	230	5.5	1
Mitchell	54	176	3.3	1
Milton	2	46	23.0	0
Seiple	5	42	8.4	0
Price	5	27	5.4	0
Tucker	4	13	3.3	0
Norton	1	9	9.0	0
Hammond	1	0	0.0	0

RECEIVING

Last Name	No.	Yds	Avg	TD
Noonan	58	760	13	11
Kiick	44	422	10	0
Twilley	39	604	15	1
Moreau	27	365	14	3
Cox	11	147	13	0
Csonka	11	118	11	1
Milton	9	143	16	1
Mitchell	8	190	24	3
Seiple	7	69	10	1
Darnell	2	25	13	0

PUNT RETURNS

Last Name	No.	Yds	Avg	TD
Neff	8	71	9	0
Milton	6	55	9	0
Tucker	5	40	8	0
Anderson	5	18	4	0
Washington	1	15	15	0
Harper	1	7	7	0
Warren	2	−1	−1	0

KICKOFF RETURNS

Last Name	No.	Yds	Avg	TD
Milton	18	408	23	0
Warren	10	227	23	0
Neff	5	190	38	0
Anderson	6	106	18	0
Tucker	3	54	18	0
Kiick	1	28	28	0
Price	1	22	22	0
Harper	1	18	18	0
Urbanek	2	15	8	0
Richardson	1	1	1	0
Woodson	1	0	0	0
Cox	0	41	0	0

PASSING – PUNTING – KICKING

PASSING	Att	Comp	%	Yds	Yd/Att	TD	Int–%	RK
Griese	355	186	52	2473	7.0	21	16– 5	4
Norton	41	17	41	254	6.2	0	4– 10	
Hammond	26	13	50	116	4.5	0	2– 8	
Kiick	1	0	0	0	0.0	0	0– 0	

PUNTING	No	Avg
Seiple	75	40.6

KICKING	XP	Att	%	FG	Att	%
Keyes	30	30	100	7	16	44
Moreau	6	6	100	1	3	33

BOSTON PATRIOTS

RUSHING

Last Name	No.	Yds	Avg	TD
Nance	177	593	3.4	4
Gamble	78	311	4.0	1
Thomas	88	215	2.4	2
Garron	36	97	2.7	1
Sherman	25	80	3.2	0
Taliaferro	8	51	6.4	0
Marsh	4	8	2.0	0
P. Johnson	2	6	3.0	0
Cappelletti	1	2	2.0	0
Whalen	1	0	0.0	0
Corcoran	1	−1	−1.0	0

RECEIVING

Last Name	No.	Yds	Avg	TD
Whalen	47	718	15	7
Marsh	19	331	17	4
Murphy	18	268	15	0
Graham	16	242	15	1
Nance	14	51	4	0
Cappelletti	13	182	14	2
Gamble	11	55	5	1
Thomas	10	85	9	0
Colclough	8	136	17	0
Scarpitto	2	49	25	1
Garron	1	4	4	0
J. Canale	1	0	0	0

PUNT RETURNS

Last Name	No.	Yds	Avg	TD
Porter	22	135	6	0
B. Johnson	10	34	3	0
Leo	2	12	6	0
Graham	2	11	6	0
D. Johnson	1	5	5	0

KICKOFF RETURNS

Last Name	No.	Yds	Avg	TD
Porter	36	812	23	0
B. Johnson	22	442	20	0
Marsh	4	74	19	0
D. Johnson	3	63	21	0
Thomas	1	22	22	0
Long	2	20	10	0
Graham	1	9	9	0
Cheyunski	1	0	0	0
Gamble	1	0	0	0

PASSING – PUNTING – KICKING

PASSING	Att	Comp	%	Yds	Yd/Att	TD	Int–%	RK
Sherman	226	90	40	1199	5.3	12	16– 7	9
Taliaferro	176	67	38	889	5.1	4	15– 9	11
Corcoran	7	3	43	33	4.7	0	2– 29	

PUNTING	No	Avg
Swanson	62	39.5
Scarpitto	34	40.6

KICKING	XP	Att	%	FG	Att	%
Cappelletti	26	26	100	15	27	56

BUFFALO BILLS

RUSHING

Last Name	No.	Yds	Avg	TD
Anderson	147	525	3.6	2
Gregory	52	283	5.4	1
Cappadona	73	272	3.7	1
McDermott	47	102	2.2	3
Rutkowski	20	96	4.8	1
Lincoln	26	84	3.2	0
Masters	6	70	11.7	0
Brown	3	39	13.0	0
Stephenson	4	30	7.5	0
Costa	2	11	5.5	1
Darragh	13	11	0.8	0
Maguire	1	6	6.0	0
Patrick	1	2	2.0	0
Moses	5	−4	−0.8	0

RECEIVING

Last Name	No.	Yds	Avg	TD
Moses	42	633	15	2
Trapp	24	235	10	0
Anderson	22	140	6	0
McDermott	20	115	6	1
Cappadona	18	92	5	2
Costa	15	172	11	1
Masters	8	101	13	0
Crockett	6	76	13	0
Gregory	5	21	4	0
Ledbetter	4	94	24	1
Rutkowski	1	27	27	0
Patrick	1	5	5	0
Lincoln	1	3	3	0
Bemiller	1	0	0	0

PUNT RETURNS

Last Name	No.	Yds	Avg	TD
Clarke	29	241	8	1
Trapp	5	26	5	0
Rutkowski	8	23	3	0
Byrd	2	11	6	0

KICKOFF RETURNS

Last Name	No.	Yds	Avg	TD
Anderson	39	971	25	1
Brown	12	274	23	0
Mitchell	5	98	20	0
Rutkowski	5	87	17	0
Costa	5	68	14	0
Lincoln	2	37	19	0
McDermott	1	16	16	0
Maguire	1	5	5	0
Barber	1	0	0	0
Ledbetter	0	18	0	0

PASSING – PUNTING – KICKING

PASSING	Att	Comp	%	Yds	Yd/Att	TD	Int–%	RK
Darragh	215	92	43	917	4.3	3	14– 7	10
Rutkowski	100	41	41	380	3.8	0	6– 6	
Stephenson	79	29	37	364	4.6	4	7– 9	
Flores	5	3	60	15	3.0	0	1– 20	
McDermott	3	2	67	35	11.7	0	0– 0	
Russell	2	1	50	3	1.5	0	0– 0	
Anderson	1	0	0	0	0.0	0	0– 0	

PUNTING	No	Avg
Maguire	100	41.8

KICKING	XP	Att	%	FG	Att	%
Alford	15	15	100	14	24	58
Mercer	4	4	100	0	4	0

2 POINT XP
Cappadona
McDermott

OAKLAND RAIDERS 12-2-0 Johnny Rauch

Scores of Each Game		
48	Buffalo	6
47	Miami	21
24	Houston	15
41	BOSTON	10
14	SAN DIEGO	23
10	Kansas City	24
31	CINCINNATI	10
38	KANSAS CITY	21
43	Denver	7
43	NEW YORK	32
34	Cincinnati	0
13	BUFFALO	10
33	DENVER	27
34	San Diego	27
	Playoff	
41	KANSAS CITY	6

Use Name	Pos.	Hgt	Wgt	Age	Int	Pts
Harry Schuh	OT	6'2"	260	25		
Art Shell	OT	6'5"	255	21		
Bob Svihus	OT	6'4"	245	25		
Jim Harvey	OG-OT	6'5"	245	25		
Wayne Hawkins	OG	6'	240	30		
Bob Kruse	OG	6'2"	250	26		
Gene Upshaw	OG	6'5"	255	23		
Jim Otto	C	6'2"	248	30		
Ben Davidson	DE	6'8"	275	28		
Ike Lassiter	DE	6'5"	270	27		
Carleton Oats	DE	6'2"	260	25		
Dan Birdwell	DT	6'4"	250	27		
Al Dotson	DT	6'4"	260	25		
Karl Rubke	C-DT	6'4"	234	32		
Duane Benson	LB	6'2"	215	23		
Bill Budness	LB	6'1"	215	25		
Dan Conners	LB	6'1"	230	26	2	
Bill Fairband	LB	6'3"	228	22		
Jerry Hopkins	LB	6'2"	238	27		
Dave Ogas	LB	6'3"	240	22		
Chip Oliver	LB	6'2"	220	22		
Gus Otto	LB	6'2"	220	25		
Butch Atkinson	DB	6'	180	21	4	18
Rodger Bird	DB	5'11"	195	25	3	6
Willie Brown	DB	6'1"	190	27	2	6
Dave Grayson	DB	5'10"	185	29	10	6
Kent McCloughan	DB	6'1"	190	25	1	
Warren Powers	DB	6'	190	27	1	
Howie Williams	DB	6'2"	190	31	2	
Nemiah Wilson	DB	6'	165	25		
George Blanda	QB	6'1"	215	40		117
Cotton Davidson	QB	6'1"	180	36		
Daryle Lamonica	QB	6'2"	215	27		6
Pete Banaszak	HB	5'11"	200	24		30
Preston Ridlehuber	HB	6'2"	215	24		6
Charlie Smith	HB	6'1"	205	22		42
Larry Todd	HB	6'1"	185	25		12
Hewritt Dixon	FB	6'2"	230	28		26
Roger Hagberg	FB	6'2"	215	29		12
Fred Biletnikoff	WR	6'1"	190	25		42
Eldridge Dickey	WR	6'2"	198	22		
John Eason	WR	6'2"	220	23		
Bill Miller	WR	6'	190	26		6
John Roderick	WR	6'1"	180	24		
Warren Wells	WR	6'1"	190	25		72
Billy Cannon	TE	6'1"	215	31		36
Dave Kocourek	TE	6'5"	235	31		6
Mike Eischeid	K	6'	190	27		

Tom Keating – Foot Injury
Bill Laskey – Foot Injury

KANSAS CITY CHIEFS 12-2-0 Hank Stram

Scores of Each Game		
26	Houston	21
19	NEW YORK	20
34	DENVER	2
48	Miami	3
18	Buffalo	7
13	CINCINNATI	3
24	OAKLAND	10
27	SAN DIEGO	20
21	Oakland	38
16	Cincinnati	9
31	BOSTON	17
24	HOUSTON	10
40	San Diego	3
30	Denver	7
	Playoff	
6	Oakland	41

Use Name	Pos.	Hgt	Wgt	Age	Int	Pts
Dave Hill	OT	6'5"	260	27		
Jim Tyrer	OT	6'6"	275	29		
Ed Budde	OG	6'5"	260	27		
George Daney	OG	6'3"	240	32		
Curt Merz	OG	6'4"	267	30		
Mo Moorman	OG	6'5"	252	24		
E. J. Holub	C	6'4"	236	30		
Aaron Brown	DE	6'5"	265	24		
Jerry Mays	DE	6'4"	252	28		
Remi Prudhomme	DT-DE	6'4"	250	26		
Buck Buchanan	DT	6'7"	287	28	1	2
Ernie Ladd	DT	6'9"	290	29	1	
Ed Lothamer	DT	6'5"	270	25		
Curley Culp	OG-DT	6'1"	265	22		
Bud Abell	LB	6'3"	220	27	2	
Bobby Bell	LB	6'4"	228	28	5	
Chuck Hurston	LB	6'6"	240	25		
Willie Lanier	LB	6'1"	245	23	4	6
Jim Lynch	LB	6'1"	235	23	3	6
Dave Martin	LB	6'	215	21		
Caesar Belser	DB	6'	212	23		
Jim Kearney	DB	6'2"	206	25	3	
Willie Mitchell	DB	6'1"	185	26	5	
Johnny Robinson	DB	6'	205	29	6	
Goldie Sellers	DB	6'2"	198	26	3	6
Emmitt Thomas	DB	6'2"	192	25	4	
Len Dawson	QB	6'	190	34		
Jacky Lee	QB	6'1"	185	29		
Mike Livingston	QB	6'3"	205	22		
Bert Coan	HB	6'4"	220	28		6
Mike Garrett	HB	5'9"	200	24		36
Paul Lowe (from SD)	HB	6'	205	31		
Wendell Hayes	FB-HB	6'2"	220	27		30
Robert Holmes	FB	5'9"	220	22		42
Curtis McClinton	FB	6'3"	227	30		
Jack Gehrke	WR	6'	178	22		
Sam Longmire	WR	6'3"	195	25		
Frank Pitts	WR	6'2"	200	24		36
Gloster Richardson	WR	6'	200	25		36
Noland Smith	WR	5'6"	154	24		6
Otis Taylor	WR	6'2"	215	25		30
Fred Arbanas	TE	6'3"	240	29		
Reg Carolan	TE	6'6"	240	28		
Jan Stenerud	K	6'2"	187	25		129
Jerrel Wilson	K	6'4"	222	27		

Gene Trosch – Injury

SAN DIEGO CHARGERS 9-5-0 Sid Gillman

Scores of Each Game		
29	CINCINNATI	13
30	HOUSTON	14
31	Cincinnati	10
20	New York	23
23	Oakland	14
55	DENVER	24
20	Kansas City	27
34	MIAMI	28
27	Boston	17
21	Buffalo	6
15	NEW YORK	37
47	Denver	23
3	KANSAS CITY	40
27	OAKLAND	34

Use Name	Pos.	Hgt	Wgt	Age	Int	Pts
Harold Akin	OT	6'5"	260	23		
Ron Mix	OT	6'4"	250	30		
Terry Owens	OT	6'6"	270	24		
Bob Wells	OT	6'4"	270	23		
Gary Kirner	OG	6'3"	255	26		
Larry Little	OG	6'1"	270	22		
Jim Schmedding	OG	6'2"	250	22		
Walt Sweeney	OG	6'3"	260	27		
Sam Gruneisen	C	6'1"	250	27		
Paul Latzke	C	6'4"	240	26		
Bill Lenkaitis	C	6'3"	250	22		
Marty Baccaglio (to CIN)	DE	6'3"	245	23		
Steve DeLong	DE	6'3"	252	25		
Houston Ridge	DE	6'4"	245	24		
Ron Billingsley	DT-DE	6'8"	265	23		
Scott Appleton	DT	6'3"	260	26		
Bob Briggs	DT	6'4"	270	23		
Russ Washington	DT	6'6"	290	21		
Chuck Allen	LB	6'1"	225	28	1	
Bernie Erickson (to CIN)	LB	6'2"	240	23		
Tom Erlandson	LB	6'3"	220	28	2	
Jim Fetherston	LB	6'2"	225	23	1	
Curtis Jones	LB	6'2"	245	25		
Ron McCall	LB	6'2"	245	23		
Bob Mitinger	LB	6'2"	230	28		
Bob Print	LB	6'	220	24		
Rick Redman	LB	5'11"	225	25		
Jeff Staggs	LB	6'2"	240	24	2	
Joe Beauchamp	DB	6'	185	24	5	12
Speedy Duncan	DB	5'10"	175	25	1	6
Dick Farley	DB	6'	185	22		
Kenny Graham	DB	6'	205	26	5	
Bob Howard	DB	6'1"	190	23	1	
Dick Speights	DB	5'11"	175	22		
Jim Tolbert	DB	6'3"	207	24	2	
Bud Whitehead	DB	6'	185	29		
Ken Dyer	WR-DB	6'3"	185	22		6
Jon Brittenum	QB	6'	185	24		
John Hadl	QB	6'2"	215	28		12
Dickie Post	HB	5'9"	190	22		18
Russ Smith	HB	6'1"	209	24		24
Jim Allison	FB	6'	215	25		
Gene Foster	FB	5'11"	220	25		6
Brad Hubbert	FB	6'1"	227	27		12
Gerry McDougall	FB	6'2"	225	33		
Lance Alworth	WR	6'	180	28		62
Lane Fenner	WR	6'5"	210	23		
Gary Garrison	WR	6'1"	195	24		60
Phil Tuckett	WR	6'	180	23		
Willie Frazier	TE	6'4"	235	25		18
Jacque MacKinnon	TE	6'4"	240	29		38
Andre White (from CIN)	TE	6'5"	225	23		
Dennis Partee	K	6'2"	208	22		106

DENVER BRONCOS 5-9-0 Lou Saban

Scores of Each Game		
10	Cincinnati	24
2	Kansas City	34
17	BOSTON	20
10	CINCINNATI	7
21	New York	13
24	San Diego	55
21	MIAMI	14
35	Boston	14
7	OAKLAND	43
17	Houston	38
34	BUFFALO	32
23	SAN DIEGO	47
27	Oakland	33
7	KANSAS CITY	30

Use Name	Pos.	Hgt	Wgt	Age	Int	Pts
Sam Brunelli	OT	6'1"	270	25		
Tom Cichowski	OT	6'4"	250	23		
Mike Current	OT	6'4"	260	22		
Wallace Dickey	OT	6'3"	260	27		
George Gaiser	OT	6'4"	255	23		
George Goeddeke	OG	6'3"	245	23		
Buzz Highsmith	OG	6'4"	230	25		
Bob Vaughn	OG	6'4"	240	23		
Bob Young	OG	6'2"	260	25		
Jay Bachman	C	6'3"	250	22		
Larry Kaminski	C	6'2"	245	23		
Pete Duranko	DE	6'2"	252	24		
Rich Jackson	DE	6'2"	255	27		
Paul Smith	DE	6'3"	245	23		
Dave Costa	DT	6'2"	265	26		
Larry Cox	DT	6'2"	250	24		
Jerry Inman	DT	6'3"	255	28		
Rex Mirich	DT	6'4"	250	27		
Carl Cunningham	LB	6'3"	240	24	1	
Fred Forsberg	LB	6'1"	235	24	1	
John Huard	LB	6'	220	24	2	
Gordon Lambert	LB	6'5"	245	23		
Frank Richter	LB	6'3"	230	23		
Dave Tobey	LB	6'3"	230	25		
Chip Myrtle	TE-LB	6'2"	225	23		2
Drake Garrett	DB	5'9"	183	23	2	
Charlie Greer	DB	6'	205	22	4	
Gus Holloman	DB	6'3"	195	22	1	
Pete Jaquess	DB	6'	182	26	5	
Jack Lentz	DB	6'	195	23	1	
Hal Lewis	DB	6'2"	188	25		
Tommy Luke	DB	6'	190	26		
Alex Moore	DB	6'	195	23		
Tom Oberg	DB	6'	185	23	3	
Jesse Stokes	DB	6'	190	24		
Marlin Briscoe	QB	5'10"	177	22		18
Joe DiVito	QB	6'2"	205	22		
Jim LeClair	QB	6'1"	208	24		
John McCormick	QB	6'1"	190	31		
Steve Tensi	QB	6'5"	215	25		
Terry Erwin	HB	6'	190	21		
Hub Lindsey	HB	5'11"	196	22		
Floyd Little	HB	5'10"	195	26		30
Fran Lynch	HB	6'1"	194	22		24
Garrett Ford	FB	6'2"	230	22		6
Brendan McCarthy (from ATL-N)	FB	6'3"	220	23		12
Eric Crabtree	WR	5'11"	182	23		30
Al Denson	WR	6'2"	208	26		30
Mike Haffner	WR	6'2"	205	26		6
Jim Jones	WR	6'2"	195	24		12
Bobby Moten	WR	6'4"	212	25		
Bill Van Heusen	WR	6'1"	200	22		18
Tom Beer	TE	6'4"	230	23		6
Dave Washington	TE	6'4"	228	27		
Bobby Howfield	K	5'9"	180	31		57
Bob Humphreys	K	6'1"	240	28		4

CINCINNATI BENGALS 3-11-0 Paul Brown

Scores of Each Game		
13	San Diego	29
24	DENVER	10
34	BUFFALO	23
10	SAN DIEGO	31
7	Denver	10
3	Kansas City	13
22	MIAMI	24
10	Oakland	31
17	HOUSTON	27
9	KANSAS CITY	16
38	Miami	21
0	OAKLAND	34
14	Boston	33
14	New York	27

Use Name	Pos.	Hgt	Wgt	Age	Int	Pts
Howard Fest	OT	6'6"	265	22		
Bob Kelly	OT	6'3"	270	28		
Ernie Wright	OT	6'4"	270	28		
Dan Archer	OG-OT	6'5"	245	23		
Pat Matson	OG	6'1"	245	24		
Dave Middendorf	OG	6'3"	260	22		
Pete Perreault	OG	6'3"	248	29		
Bob Johnson	C	6'5"	260	22		
John Matlock	OT-C	6'4"	255	23		
Jim Griffin	DE	6'3"	265	26		6
Harry Gunner	DE	6'6"	250	23	1	2
Willie Jones	DE	6'2"	260	26		
Dennis Randall	DE	6'6"	240	22		
Steve Chomyszak	DT	6'5"	280	23		
Bill Kindricks	DT	6'3"	268	22		
Andy Rice	DT	6'3"	268	26		
Bill Staley	DT	6'3"	250	21		
Al Beauchamp	LB	6'2"	236	24	2	6
Danny Brabham	LB	6'4"	233	27		
Frank Buncom	LB	6'1"	245	28		
Paul Elzey	LB	6'3"	235	22		
Sherrill Headrick	LB	6'2"	240	31	1	
Mike Hibler	LB	6'1"	235	22		
Wayne McClure	LB	6'1"	225	22		
John Neidert (to NY)	LB	6'2"	230	22		
Curt Frazier	DB	5'11"	193	23		
White Graves	DB	6'	185	25		
Rex Keeling	DB	6'3"	220	24		
Charlie King	DB	6'	184	25	1	6
Bill Scott	DB	6'	188	24		
Fletcher Smith	DB	6'2"	178	24	1	
Phil Spiller (from ATL-N)	DB	6'	195	23		
Bobby Hunt	HB-DB	6'1"	190	28	1	6
Jess Phillips	HB-DB	6'1"	205	21	3	
John Stofa	QB	6'3"	210	26		
Dewey Warren	QB	6'	205	23		
Sam Wyche	QB	6'4"	210	23		
Essex Johnson	HB	5'9"	190	21		18
Paul Robinson	HB	6'	200	23		54
Ted Washington	HB	5'11"	210	22		
Estes Banks	FB	6'1"	220	23		6
Ron Lamb (from DEN)	FB	6'2"	225	24		
Tom Smiley	FB	6'1"	235	24		6
Saint Saffold	WR	6'4"	202	24		
Rod Sherman	WR	6'	190	23		10
Monk Williams	WR	5'7"	155	23		
Warren McVea	HB-WR	5'10"	182	22		18
Ken Herock	TE	6'2"	230	27		
Bill Peterson	TE	6'3"	230	23		
Bob Trumpy	WR-TE	6'6"	220	23		18
Dale Livingston	K	6'	210	23		59

OAKLAND RAIDERS

RUSHING

Last Name	No.	Yds	Avg	TD
Dixon	206	865	4.2	2
Smith	95	504	3.6	5
Banaszak	91	362	4.0	4
Hagberg	39	164	4.2	1
Lamonica	19	98	5.2	1
Todd	13	89	6.8	2
Eischeid	2	41	20.5	0
Wells	2	38	19.0	1
Ridlehuber	4	7	1.8	0

RECEIVING

Last Name	No.	Yds	Avg	TD
Biletnikoff	61	1037	17	6
Wells	53	1137	21	11
Dixon	38	360	9	2
Cannon	23	360	16	6
Smith	22	321	15	2
Banaszak	15	182	12	1
Miller	9	176	20	1
Hagberg	8	78	10	1
Todd	4	40	10	0
Kocourek	3	46	15	1
Dickey	1	34	34	0

PUNT RETURNS

Last Name	No.	Yds	Avg	TD
Atkinson	**36**	**490**	14	**2**
Bird	11	128	12	0
Dickey	6	48	8	0
Shell	1	0	0	0
Wilson	1	0	0	0

KICKOFF RETURNS

Last Name	No.	Yds	Avg	TD
Atkinson	32	802	**25**	0
Smith	8	167	21	0
Wilson	4	84	21	0
Hagberg	1	21	21	0
Dickey	1	17	17	0
Kruse	1	1	1	0
Hopkins	1	0	0	0
G. Otto	1	0	0	0

PASSING – PUNTING – KICKING

PASSING	Att	Comp	%	Yds	Yd/Att	TD	Int–%	RK
Lamonica	416	206	50	3245	7.8	25	15– 4	2
Blanda	49	30	61	522	10.7	6	2– 4	
C. Davidson	2	1	50	4	2.0	0	0– 0	
Banaszak	1	0	0	0	0.0	0	1–100	

PUNTING	No	Avg
Eischeid	64	43.6

KICKING	XP	Att	%	FG	Att	%
Blanda	**54**	**54**	**100**	21	34	62

2 POINT XP
Dixon

KANSAS CITY CHIEFS

RUSHING

Last Name	No.	Yds	Avg	TD
Holmes	174	866	5.0	7
Garrett	164	564	3.4	3
Hayes	85	340	4.0	4
Coan	40	160	4.0	1
McClinton	24	107	4.5	0
Pitts	11	107	9.7	0
Taylor	5	41	8.2	1
Dawson	20	40	2.0	0
Arbanas	3	14	4.7	0
Livingston	2	2	1.0	0
Wilson	5	1	0.2	0
Lowe	2	−1	−0.5	0
Smith	2	−2	−1.0	0
Richardson	1	−3	−3.0	0

RECEIVING

Last Name	No.	Yds	Avg	TD
Garrett	33	359	11	3
Pitts	30	655	22	6
Richardson	22	494	22	6
Taylor	20	420	21	4
Holmes	19	201	11	0
Hayes	12	108	9	1
Arbanas	11	189	17	0
McClinton	3	−4	−1	0
Carolan	2	26	13	0
Coan	2	15	8	0
Smith	1	15	15	0
Wilson	1	14	14	0

PUNT RETURNS

Last Name	No.	Yds	Avg	TD
Smith	18	270	**15**	1
Sellers	7	129	18	1
Robinson	2	26	13	0
Mitchell	1	21	21	0
Garrett	2	4	2	0
Belser	1	0	0	0

KICKOFF RETURNS

Last Name	No.	Yds	Avg	TD
Smith	23	549	24	0
Coan	5	100	20	0
Sellers	2	40	20	0
Belser	4	38	10	0
Kearney	1	9	9	0
Abell	1	0	0	0
Daney	1	0	0	0
Prudhomme	1	0	0	0

PASSING – PUNTING – KICKING

PASSING	Att	Comp	%	Yds	Yd/Att	TD	Int–%	RK
Dawson	224	131	**59**	2109	**9.4**	17	9– 4	**1**
Lee	45	25	56	383	8.5	3	1– 2	
Garrett	1	0	0	0	0.0	0	1–100	

PUNTING	No	Avg
Wilson	63	**45.1**
Carolan	2	50.5

KICKING	XP	Att	%	FG	Att	%
Stenerud	39	40	98	30	40	**75**

SAN DIEGO CHARGERS

RUSHING

Last Name	No.	Yds	Avg	TD
Post	151	758	**5.0**	3
Smith	88	426	4.8	4
Foster	109	394	3.6	1
Hubbert	28	119	4.3	2
Allison	23	31	1.3	0
Alworth	3	18	6.0	0
Hadl	23	14	0.6	2
Brittenum	2	−4	−2.0	0

RECEIVING

Last Name	No.	Yds	Avg	TD
Alworth	**68**	**1312**	19	10
Garrison	52	1103	21	10
MacKinnon	33	646	20	6
Foster	23	224	10	0
Post	18	165	9	0
Frazier	16	237	15	3
Smith	7	71	10	0
Hubbert	5	11	2	0
Allison	2	22	11	0
White	2	18	9	0
Dyer	1	22	22	0

PUNT RETURNS

Last Name	No.	Yds	Avg	TD
Duncan	18	206	11	1
Graham	13	61	5	0
Smith	8	25	3	0

KICKOFF RETURNS

Last Name	No.	Yds	Avg	TD
Duncan	25	586	23	0
Post	10	199	20	0
Allison	7	121	17	0
Whitehead	2	81	41	0
Speights	1	21	21	0
Smith	1	20	20	0
Baccaglio	2	0	0	0
Latzke	1	0	0	0

PASSING – PUNTING – KICKING

PASSING	Att	Comp	%	Yds	Yd/Att	TD	Int–%	RK
Hadl	**440**	**208**	47	**3473**	7.9	**27**	32– 7	5
Brittenum	17	9	53	125	7.4	1	1– 6	
Foster	7	6	86	169	24.1	0	0– 0	
Post	4	1	25	23	5.8	0	0– 0	
Smith	3	0	0	0	0.0	1	0– 0	
Allison	1	1	100	23	23.0	1	0– 0	

PUNTING	No	Avg
Partee	56	40.7

KICKING	XP	Att	%	FG	Att	%
Partee	40	43	93	22	32	69

2 POINT XP
Alworth
MacKinnon

DENVER BRONCOS

RUSHING

Last Name	No.	Yds	Avg	TD
Little	158	584	3.7	3
Briscoe	41	308	7.5	3
Lynch	66	221	3.3	4
Ford	41	186	4.5	1
McCarthy	28	89	3.2	0
Erwin	24	76	3.2	0
LeClair	12	40	3.3	0
Moore	4	22	5.5	0
Lindsey	4	17	4.3	0
Van Heusen	1	6	6.0	0
Tensi	6	2	0.3	0
Haffner	2	2	1.0	0
DiVito	1	−1	−1.0	0
Jones	1	−1	−1.0	0

RECEIVING

Last Name	No.	Yds	Avg	TD
Crabtree	35	601	17	5
Denson	34	586	17	5
Beer	20	276	14	1
Van Heusen	19	353	19	3
Little	19	331	17	1
Jones	13	190	15	2
Haffner	12	232	19	1
McCarthy	7	69	10	2
Ford	6	40	7	0
Lynch	4	52	13	0
Moore	3	35	12	0
Erwin	2	21	11	0
Myrtle	1	18	18	0
Washington	1	12	12	0

PUNT RETURNS

Last Name	No.	Yds	Avg	TD
Little	24	261	11	1
Greer	9	53	6	0
Luke	3	13	4	0
Jaquess	2	5	3	0

KICKOFF RETURNS

Last Name	No.	Yds	Avg	TD
Little	26	649	25	0
Holloman	7	194	28	0
Stokes	5	106	21	0
Garrett	3	77	26	0
Moore	4	74	19	0
Lindsey	3	72	24	0
Erwin	3	55	18	0
Greer	2	41	21	0
Luke	2	34	17	0
Crabtree	1	30	30	0
Forsberg	2	16	8	0
Dickey	1	13	13	0
Jaquess	1	0	0	0

PASSING – PUNTING – KICKING

PASSING	Att	Comp	%	Yds	Yd/Att	TD	Int–%	RK
Briscoe	224	93	42	1589	7.1	14	13– 6	7
Tensi	119	48	40	709	6.0	5	8– 7	
LeClair	54	27	50	401	7.4	1	5– 9	
McCormick	19	8	42	89	4.7	0	1– 5	
DiVito	6	1	17	16	2.7	0	0– 0	
Little	2	0	0	0	0.0	0	0– 0	
Lynch	2	1	50	4	2.0	0	0– 0	
Haffner	1	1	100	18	18.0	0	0– 0	

PUNTING	No	Avg
Van Heusen	88	43.8
DiVito	8	30.3

KICKING	XP	Att	%	FG	Att	%
Howfield	30	30	100	9	18	50
Humphreys	1	1	100	1	5	20

CINCINNATI BENGALS

RUSHING

Last Name	No.	Yds	Avg	TD
Robinson	**238**	**1023**	4.3	8
E. Johnson	26	178	6.8	3
Smiley	63	146	2.3	1
McVea	9	133	14.8	1
Banks	34	131	3.9	0
Lamp	39	107	2.7	0
Wyche	12	74	6.2	0
Saffold	1	21	21.0	0
Warren	4	17	4.3	0
Livingston	1	11	11.0	0
Keeling	1	10	10.0	0
Phillips	1	7	7.0	0
Hunt	1	5	5.0	1
Washington	1	4	4.0	0
Sherman	1	3	3.0	0
Stofa	10	1	0.1	0
Trumpy	1	−1	−1.0	0

RECEIVING

Last Name	No.	Yds	Avg	TD
Trumpy	37	639	17	3
Sherman	31	374	12	1
Robinson	24	128	5	1
McVea	21	264	13	2
Smiley	19	86	5	0
Saffold	16	172	11	0
Lamb	7	87	12	0
Herock	6	75	13	0
Banks	4	15	4	1
E. Johnson	1	33	33	0
Peterson	1	10	10	0
Wyche	1	5	5	0

PUNT RETURNS

Last Name	No.	Yds	Avg	TD
E. Johnson	22	111	5	0
Spiller	2	51	26	0
Phillips	2	16	8	0
Williams	2	14	7	0
King	1	3	3	0
Robinson	1	1	1	0

KICKOFF RETURNS

Last Name	No.	Yds	Avg	TD
McVea	14	310	22	0
E. Johnson	14	266	19	0
Banks	6	106	18	0
Williams	5	112	22	0
Spiller	5	91	18	0
Peterson	3	80	27	0
Robinson	3	58	19	0
Lamb	1	24	24	0
Phillips	1	23	23	0
McClure	1	11	11	0
Randall	1	11	11	0
Neidert	1	0	0	0
Saffold	1	0	0	0

PASSING – PUNTING – KICKING

PASSING	Att	Comp	%	Yds	Yd/Att	TD	Int–%	RK
Stofa	177	85	48	896	5.1	5	5– **3**	6
Warren	80	47	59	506	6.3	1	4– 5	
Wyche	55	35	64	494	9.0	2	2– 4	
Keeling	1	0	0	0	0.0	0	0– 0	

PUNTING	No	Avg
Livingston	70	43.4
Smith	8	28.8
Keeling	6	28.3

KICKING	XP	Att	%	FG	Att	%
Livingston	20	20	100	13	26	50
Sherman	4	4	100	0	1	0

1968 Championship Games

NFL CHAMPIONSHIP GAME

December 29, at Cleveland
(Attendance 80,628)

SCORING

CLEVELAND	0	0	0	0– 0
BALTIMORE	0	17	7	10–34

Second Quarter
- Bal. Michaels, 28 yard field goal
- Bal. Matte, 1 yard rush
  PAT–Michaels (kick)
- Bal. Matte, 12 yard rush
  PAT–Michaels (kick)

Third Quarter
- Bal. Matte, 2 yard rush
  PAT–Michaels (kick)

Fourth Quarter
- Bal. Michaels, 10 yard field goal
- Bal. Brown, 4 yard run
  PAT–Michaels (Kick)

TEAM STATISTICS

CLE.		BAL.
12	First Downs–Total	22
2	First Downs–Rushing	13
8	First Downs–Passing	8
2	First Downs–Penalty	1
2	Fumbles–Number	2
1	Fumbles–Lost Ball	1
7	Penalties–Number	3
54	Yards Penalized	15
2	Missed Field Goals	0
3	Giveaways	2
2	Takeaways	3
–1	Difference	+1

Evening a Past Account

The conference playoffs had produced one expected result and one upset. The Baltimore Colts beat the Minnesota Vikings 24-14 as they had been picked to do, but the Cleveland Browns had surprised the Dallas Cowboys by knocking them off 31-20 in Don Meredith's playing farewell.

The Colts and Browns had met for the NFL title four years ago, with the Browns stunning Baltimore with a 27-0 upset. The Colts again were favored this year, but their stifling defense smothered the Cleveland attack and evened the score from 1964.

The Browns had the first scoring opportunity of the game when Don Cockroft attempted a 41-yard field goal, but Bubba Smith blocked the kick. With Bill Nelsen rushed incessantly and Leroy Kelly hounded every time he touched the ball, the Browns rarely crossed into Baltimore territory all afternoon.

The first period ended without a score, but a Lou Michaels field goal gave Baltimore a 3-0 lead early in the second period. With the Colt blockers beating the Cleveland front four regularly, the Colts put together a sixty-yard, ten-play drive which ended in Tom Matte's plunge into the end zone. When the Browns tried to come back with a pass, Mike Curtis intercepted and gave the ball to his offense on the Cleveland 33. Matte ran for twelve yards on the first play, then Jerry Hill carried for nine, and Matte finally covered the last twelve yards with a dodging run through the Cleveland secondary. The halftime score was 17-0, and the Browns looked like a beaten team.

The Colts stuck to the ground in the second half, eating up yardage and time with Matte and Hill running the ball. A time-consuming drive led to Matte's third touchdown of the day in the third quarter, and ten more points in the final period ran the final score up to 34-0. After this one-sided affair ended a quick survey of the press box uncovered not one writer who gave the New York Jets a chance against the Colts in the Super Bowl.

INDIVIDUAL STATISTICS

CLEVELAND	No	Yds	Avg.	BALTIMORE	No	Yds	Avg.
RUSHING							
Kelly	13	28	2.2	Matte	17	88	5.2
Harraway	6	26	4.3	Hill	11	60	5.5
Green	1	2	2.0	Brown	5	18	3.6
	20	56	2.8	Cole	3	14	4.7
				Mackey	2	4	2.0
				Morrall	1	0	0.0
					39	184	4.7
RECEIVING							
Harraway	4	40	10.0	Richardson	3	78	26.0
Morin	3	41	13.7	Mackey	2	34	17.0
Kelly	3	27	9.0	Orr	2	33	16.5
Warfield	2	30	15.0	Matte	2	15	7.5
Collins	1	13	13.0	Mitchell	1	7	7.0
	13	151	11.6	Cole	1	2	2.0
					11	169	15.4
PUNTING							
Cockroft	5		33.4	Lee	2		37.0
PUNT RETURNS							
Davis	1	4	4.0	Brown	1	0	0.0
KICKOFF RETURNS							
Morrison	3	51	19.0	Pearson	1	21	21.0
Davis	3	40	13.3				
	6	91	15.2				
INTERCEPTION RETURNS							
Davis	1	0	0.0	Volk	1	26	26.0
				Curtis	1	0	0.0
					2	26	13.0

PASSING

CLEVELAND	Att.	Comp.	Comp. Pct.	Yds.	Int.	Yds/ Att.	Yds/ Comp.	Yards Lost Tackled
Nelsen	26	11	42.3	132	2	5.1	12.0	
Ryan	6	2	33.3	19	0	3.3	8.5	
	32	13	40.6	151	2	4.7	11.6	4–34
BALTIMORE								
Morrall	25	11	44.4	169	1	6.8	15.4	0– 0

AFL CHAMPIONSHIP GAME

December 29, at New York
(Attendance 62,627)

SCORING

NEW YORK	10	3	7	7–27
OAKLAND	0	10	3	10–23

First Quarter
- N.Y. Maynard, 14 yard pass from Namath
  PAT–J. Turner (kick)
- N.Y. J. Turner, 33 yard field goal

Second Quarter
- Oak. Biletnikoff, 29 yard pass from Lamonica
  PAT–Blanda (kick)
- N.Y. J. Turner, 36 yard field goal
- Oak. Blanda, 26 yard field goal

Third Quarter
- Oak. Blanda, 9 yard field goal
- N.Y. Lammons, 20 yard pass from Namath
  PAT–J. Turner (kick)

Fourth Quarter
- Oak. Blanda, 20 yard field goal
- Oak. Banaszak, 4 yard rush
  PAT–Blanda (kick)
- N.Y. Maynard, 6 yard pass from Namath
  PAT–J. Turner (kick)

TEAM STATISTICS

N.Y.		OAK.
25	First Downs–Total	18
9	First Downs–Rushing	3
15	First Downs–Passing	14
1	First Downs–Penalty	1
1	Fumbles–Number	2
1	Fumbles–Lost Ball	0
4	Penalties–Number	2
26	Yards Penalized	23
1	Missed Field Goals	1
2	Giveaways	0
0	Takeaways	2
–2	Difference	+2

Down and Up, but Never Sideways

After beating the Chiefs in a Western Division playoff, the Oakland Raiders came to New York to face the brash, young New York Jets for the AFL title. Joe Namath came out throwing, and after only 3:39 of the opening period, the Jets had scored on a Namath-to-Don Maynard pass. Jim Turner later added a field goal to give the Jets a 10-0 lead after one quarter. Oakland wide receiver Fred Biletnikoff started getting open in the second quarter, however, and Daryle Lamonica hit him with a touchdown pass early in the period. Before the half ended, Jim Turner and George Blanda each kicked a three-pointer to make the score 13-10 in favor of the Jets.

Early in the second half, Lamonica's long bombs to Biletnikoff and Warren Wells gave the Raiders a first down on the New York 6-yard line. Three plays moved the ball only to the 1-yard line, so Blanda kicked a short field goal to knot the score at 13-13.

Late in the third period it was New York's turn to move. Namath mixed his plays well in driving the Jets 80 yards to a touchdown, with the final 20 yards coming on a pass to tight end Pete Lammons. Turner's kick made the count 20-13 with one period left.

The Raiders struck deep into New York territory early in the quarter, but had to settle for another Blanda field goal. Trailing 20-16, the Raiders turned the game around when George Atkinson picked off a Namath pass and returned it 32 yards to the New York 5. Pete Banaszak scored on the next play to put the Raiders ahead for the first time. Less than a minute later, a 52-yard pass play from Namath to Maynard brought the Jets into striking range of the Oakland end zone, and another pass to Maynard took the ball across the goal line and put New York on top 27-23. The Raiders drove right back into New York territory, but the Jets got the ball by recovering a loose lateral pass which the Raiders thought was an incomplete forward pass. After that, the Jets just hung on for their Super Bowl destiny.

INDIVIDUAL STATISTICS

NEW YORK	No	Yds	Avg.	OAKLAND	No	Yds	Avg.
RUSHING							
Snell	19	71	3.7	Dixon	8	42	5.3
Boozer	11	51	4.6	Banaszak	3	6	2.0
Namath	1	14	14.0	Lamonica	3	1	0.3
Mathis	3	8	2.7	Smith	5	1	0.2
	34	144	4.2		19	50	2.6
RECEIVING							
Sauer	7	70	10.0	Biletnikoff	7	190	11.2
Maynard	6	118	19.7	Dixon	5	48	9.6
Lammons	4	52	13.0	Cannon	4	69	17.3
Snell	1	15	15.0	Wells	3	83	27.7
Boozer	1	11	11.0	Banaszak	1	11	11.0
	19	266	14.0		20	401	20.1
PUNTING							
Johnson	10		41.5	Eischeid	7		42.7
PUNT RETURNS							
Baird	2	8	4.0	Atkinson	2	11	5.5
Christy	1	0	0.0	Bird	2	6	3.0
	3	8	2.7		4	17	4.3
KICKOFF RETURNS							
Christy	3	86	28.7	Atkinson	4	112	28.0
B. Turner	1	24	24.0	Smith	1	17	17.0
	4	110	27.5		5	129	25.8
INTERCEPTION RETURNS							
None				Atkinson	1	32	32.0

PASSING

NEW YORK	Att.	Comp.	Comp. Pct.	Yds.	Int.	Yds/ Att.	Yds/ Comp.	Yards Lost Tackled
Namath	49	19	38.8	266	1	5.4	14.0	10
OAKLAND								
Lamonica	47	20	42.6	401	0	8.5	20.1	8

SUPER BOWL III
January 12, at Miami
(Attendance 75,377)

The Ironclad Guarantee

When Joe Namath, three days before the game, said, "I think we'll win it; in fact, I'll guarantee it," people snickered. The New York Jets were close to three-touchdown underdogs against the Baltimore Colts, and everyone expected to see the Colts, an establishment NFL team, clobber the long-haired Jets and shut the mouth of their free-spirit quarterback. Coached by Don Shula, the Colts had a feared defense that mixed zone pass coverage and frequent blitzes and a poised offense led by quarterback Earl Morrall, who had substituted spectacularly during the season for the sore-armed Johnny Unitas.

On offense, the Colts did everything in the first half except score. They drove to the New York 20-yard line only to lose the ball on an interception. They recovered a fumble on the New York 12 only to have Lou Michaels miss a close-range field goal. They sprang Tom Matte loose on a 58-yard run only to suffer another interception to kill the drive. The play that typified the Colts' frustration the best came in the second quarter. On a razzle-dazzle play, Earl Morrall handed the ball off, got it back on a lateral, and looked downfield for a receiver. He never noticed Jimmy Orr free in the end zone, so alone that he was jumping up and down and waving his arms to get attention. Morrall instead threw the ball down the middle right into the arms of New York's Randy Beverly.

The Jets, meanwhile, unexpectedly used the off-tackle smash as their main offensive weapon. With Winston Hill leading the way, fullback Matt Snell repeatedly picked up five and six yards through the right side of the Colt line. Whenever the Colts threw their blitz at Namath, he somehow smelled it out and beat it by shooting a quick pass to George Sauer. Mixing his plays well, Namath led the Jets on an 80-yard drive in twelve plays, with Snell carrying the ball into the end zone from the four-yard line. At halftime, the Jets were ahead 7-0.

The script stayed the same in the second half. The Jets ground out the yardage slowly, scoring on three Jim Turner field goals, while Morrall could not get the Colts on the scoreboard. Johnny Unitas, sore arm and all, took over at quarterback in the final period, and although he drove the Colts to a touchdown, it was too little too late. The Jets had won the Super Bowl 16-7; the AFL had finally triumphed.

NEW YORK JETS		BALTIMORE
	OFFENSE	
Sauer	LE	Orr
W. Hill	LT	Vogel
Talamini	LG	Ressler
Schmitt	C	Curry
Rasmussen	RG	Sullivan
Herman	RT	Ball
Lammons	TE	Mackey
Namath	QB	Morrall
Maynard	FL	W. Richardson
Boozer	RB	Matte
Snell	RB	J. Hill
	DEFENSE	
Philbin	LE	B. Smith
Rochester	LT	B. R. Smith
Elliot	RT	Miller
Biggs	RE	Braase
Baker	LLB	Curtis
Atkinson	MLB	Gaubatz
Grantham	RLB	Shinnick
Sample	LHB	Boyd
Beverly	RHB	Lyles
Hudson	LS	Logan
Baird	FS	Volk

SUBSTITUTES

NEW YORK

Offense

Crane	J. Richardson
Mathis	Smolinski
Parilli	B. Turner
Rademacher	Walton

Defense

Christy	McAdams
D'Amato	Neidert
Dockery	Richards
Gordon	Thompson

Kickers

Johnson	J. Turner

BALTIMORE

Offense

Brown	Pearson
Cole	Perkins
Hawkins	Szymanski
Johnson	Unitas
Mitchell	J. Williams

Defense

Austin	Porter
Hilton	Stukes
Michaels	S. Williams

Kicker

Lee

SCORING

NEW YORK JETS	0	7	6	3–16
BALTIMORE	0	0	0	7– 7

Second Quarter

N.Y.	Snell, 4 yard rush	5:57
	PAT – Turner (kick)	

Third Quarter

N.Y.	Turner, 32 yd field goal	4:52
N.Y.	Turner, 30 yd field goal	11:02

Fourth Quarter

N.Y.	Turner, 9 yard field goal	1:34
Balt.	Hill, 1 yard rush	11:41
	PAT – Michaels (kick)	

TEAM STATISTICS

N. Y.		BALT.
21	First Downs – Total	18
10	First Downs – Rushing	7
10	First Downs – Passing	9
1	First Downs – Penalty	2
1	Fumbles – Number	1
1	Fumbles – Lost Ball	1
5	Penalties – Number	3
28	Yards Penalized	23
74	Total Offensive Plays	64
337	Total Net Yards	324
4.6	Average Gain	5.1
2	Field Goals Missed	2
1	Giveaways	5
5	Takeaways	1
+4	Difference	–4

INDIVIDUAL STATISTICS

NEW YORK JETS	No	Yds	Avg.	BALTIMORE	No	Yds	Avg.
RUSHING							
Swell	30	121	4.0	Matte	11	116	10.5
Boozer	10	19	1.9	Hill	9	29	3.2
Mathis	3	2	0.7	Unitas	1	0	0.0
	43	142	3.3	Morrall	2	–2	–1.0
					23	143	6.2
RECEIVING							
Sauer	8	133	16.6	Richardson	6	58	9.7
Snell	4	40	10.0	Orr	3	42	14.0
Mathis	3	20	6.7	Mackey	3	35	11.7
Lammons	2	13	6.5	Matte	2	30	15.0
	17	206	12.1	Hill	2	1	0.5
				Mitchell	1	15	15.0
					17	181	10.6
PUNTING							
Johnson	4		38.8	Lee	3		44.3
PUNT RETURNS							
Baird	1	0	0.0	Brown	4	34	8.5
KICKOFF RETURNS							
Christy	1	25	25.0	Pearson	2	59	29.5
				Brown	2	45	22.5
					4	104	26.0
INTERCEPTION RETURNS							
Beverly	2	0	0.0	None			
Hudson	1	9	9.0				
Sample	1	0	0.0				
	4	9	2.3				

PASSING

NEW YORK	Att	Comp	Comp Pct.	Yds	Int	Yds/ Att.	Yds/ Comp	Yards Lost Tackled
Namath	28	17	60.7	206	0	7.4	12.1	2–11
Parilli	1	0	0.0	0	0	–	–	0
	29	17	58.6	206	0	7.1	12.1	2–11
BALTIMORE								
Morrall	17	6	35.3	71	3	4.2	11.8	0
Unitas	24	11	45.8	110	1	4.6	10.0	0
	41	17	41.5	181	4	4.4	10.6	0

1969 N.F.L. Equalizing the Competition

It took a thirty-five-hour, forty-five minute meeting to do it, but the NFL came up with a blueprint for next year's merger of the two leagues. Commissioner Pete Rozelle announced on May 17 that both leagues would be part of the NFL next year and that the Baltimore Colts, Cleveland Browns, and Pittsburgh Steelers had agreed to join the present ten AFL clubs in the American Conference, while the thirteen remaining old-line NFL clubs would form the National Conference. Each conference would be parted into Eastern, Central, and Western divisions, and interconference play would begin in the regular season. In other words, this would be the last year in which the NFL and AFL would be separate, distinctive entries.

EASTERN CONFERENCE—CAPITAL DIVISION

Dallas Cowboys— Don Meredith and Don Perkins both retired this year, but the Cowboys came up with an entire new backfield and kept on winning without a hitch. Craig Morton moved up into the starting quarterback spot, Walt Garrison, a rodeo cowboy in the summer, took over at fullback, and rookie Calvin Hill, a product of the Ivy League, led the league in rushing all season only to lose the title when sidelined with an injury for the final game of the year. All the other parts of the Cowboy machine were in fine order. Bob Hayes and Lance Rentzel provided speed at wide receiver, the offensive line was both strong and deep, and the defense pressured quarterbacks unmercifully whenever they attempted to pass.

Washington Redskins—In search of new challenges, Vince Lombardi packed his bags and moved to Washington as the head coach and general manager of the Redskins. The results were immediate, as the Skins had their first winning season since 1955. Lombardi had a good passing attack left over from the previous regime, and he constructed a solid running game with rookie halfback Larry Brown and ex-Brown fullback Charlie Harraway. On defense, Lombardi concentrated on the pass defense, rigging up a tight secondary of Pat Fischer, Mike Bass, Brig Owens, and Rickie Harris.

New Orleans Saints—Billy Kilmer was no glamorous quarterback, but he was a fine leader who moved the team well. The strength of the attack was the stable of receivers; Dan Abramowicz, Al Dodd, and Dave Parks had few peers as a group. Coach Tom Fears added a running game to the offense by coming up with Andy Livingston and Tony Baker as his new running backs. Livingston came over from the Bears, and Baker came off of last year's taxi squad; both ran with power and speed. The defense was a trouble area, although tackles Dave Rowe and Mike Tilleman played well.

Philadelphia Eagles—The Eagles began a rebuilding program under the new leadership of general manager Pete Retzlaff and head coach Jerry Williams this year. The team still finished in last place, but emphasis was placed on developing young players for the future. Williams gave plenty of playing time to rookies Leroy Keyes, Ernie Calloway, and Bill Bradley, and young veterans like Ben Hawkins, Harold Jackson, Mike Evans, Gary Pettigrew, and Tim Rossovich all were handed full-time starting jobs.

CENTURY DIVISION

Cleveland Browns—The Browns were loaded with offensive talent, such as quarterback Bill Nelsen, runner Leroy Kelly, receivers Gary Collins, Paul Warfield, and Milt Morin, and blockers Dick Schafrath and Gene Hickerson. The defense, however, featured several young Turks amidst some overage and mediocre players. Jack Gregory developed into a strong pass-rusher toward the end of the season, rookie Walt Sumner filled in well for the injured Ben Davis at cornerback, and Ernie Kellerman kept up his good work at strong safety, but problems arose at middle linebacker, where Dale Lindsey was barely adequate, and cornerback, where thirty-four-year-old Erich Barnes was playing on borrowed time.

New York Giants—When the Giants lost all their pre-season games, owner Wellington Mara canned coach Allie Sherman, long-term contract and all, and elevated assistant Alex Webster. The Giants responded to the switch by beating the Vikings. Things leveled off after that, with the Giants winning some and losing some as befits a mediocre team. One of the biggest enigmas of the year was Homer Jones, who found his way into the end zone only once all year.

St. Louis Cardinals—Injuries to Jerry Stovall, Bob Atkins, and Jamie Rivers made the Cards vulnerable to the pass; the New Orleans Saints exploited this weakness to win a 52-41 decision. The offense could produce points in a hurry, with a good line, good receivers in John Gilliam, Dave Williams, and Jackie Smith and powerful runners in Cid Edwards and Johnny Roland. Charley Johnson and Jim Hart split the quarterbacking chores, but neither could provide leadership.

Pittsburgh Steelers—New head coach Chuck Noll won only one game all year but still felt that progress was made in several areas. The defensive line was upgraded by ferocious rookie tackle Joe Greene, the secondary found a hard-hitting safety in Chuck Beatty, and the offensive line improved with the development of young veterans Larry Gagner, Bruce Van Dyke, and Ray Mansfield. Noll also got good seasons out of veterans Roy Jefferson, Ben McGee, and Andy Russell but was disappointed by a poor rookie season for Terry Hanratty.

WESTERN CONFERENCE — CENTRAL DIVISION

Minnesota Vikings—Although the heart of the Vikings was their defense, the biggest star on the team was a quarterback who had problems passing. Joe Kapp, whose passes wobbled ominously but often found the mark, set the tone of the Vikings with actions, such as his scrambling runs which included hurdling over defenders and bulling through tacklers. The Viking attack was unrelenting but unspectacular, leading the league in points scored primarily because the defense kept giving it the ball.

Detroit Lions—Just as when he had played, coach Joe Schmidt's Lions relied on the defense to carry the club. The front four was anchored by Alex Karras, the linebacking trio of Paul Naumoff, Mike Lucci, and Wayne Walker combined mobility and strength, and cornerbacks Lem Barney and Dick LeBeau made passing a difficult task for enemy quarterbacks. The Lion quarterback situation was unsettled, however, as Bill Munson and Greg Landry split the job with indifferent results, and injuries to Mel Farr and Nick Eddy hurt the running game.

Green Bay Packers—The Packers remained a tough team despite several problems. Bart Starr missed the last four games with a shoulder injury, Jerry Kramer and Bob Skoronski retired, and age was creeping up on the defensive line. The most damaging deficiency, however, was the lack of a reliable place-kicker. Coach Phil Bengtson started the year with Mike Mercer, who hit on only five of seventeen field-goal attempts, and then switched to Booth Lusteg, whose one-for-five record was no improvement.

Chicago Bears—Gale Sayers recaptured his old form after a hesitant start and rocketed to the NFL rushing crown. Outside of that, the Bears endured a campaign of unbroken gloom. The team lost its first seven games, beat the just as miserable Pittsburgh Steelers, then went on to lose their last six games. Coach Jim Dooley juggled his quarterbacks to get some life into the passing attack, but all he got for his troubles were some unhappy passers. Jack Concannon started the year at the controls, but when he couldn't move the team, Dooley put rookie Bobby Douglass into the lineup.

COASTAL DIVISION

Los Angeles Rams—Old pros like Deacon Jones, Merlin Olsen, Jack Pardee, Maxie Baughan, Clancy Williams, and Eddie Meador made few errors on defense, the hallmark of a George Allen team, and the Roman Gabriel-led offense rarely turned the ball over without holding onto it for a stretch. Operating behind a superb line of Bob Brown, Charlie Cowan, Tom Mack, Joe Scibelli, and Ken Iman, Gabriel ground out yardage with handoffs to rookie Larry Smith, Les Josephson, and Tommy Mason and with quick passes to Jack Snow, Wendell Tucker, and Billy Truax. The Rams' ball-control tactics worked so well that they won their first eleven games.

Baltimore Colts—The ill omen of their Super Bowl defeat followed the Colts through this season. Ordell Braase, Don Shinnick, and Bobby Boyd retired after the loss to the Jets, and Jerry Hill, Terry Cole, Willie Richardson, John Mackey, Lou Michaels, Dennis Gaubatz, and Lenny Lyles suffered through sub-par seasons. Thus, one year after winning the NFL championship, the Colts had a completely different look. Ted Hendricks, Roy Hilton, Bob Grant, Charlie Stukes, and Tommy Maxwell were new starters on defense, with Mike Curtis having to learn the middle linebacker spot. Johnny Unitas reclaimed the quarterback position but showed little fire.

Atlanta Falcons—Coach Norm Van Brocklin fielded two strong defensive ends in Claude Humphrey and John Zook, a top cornerback in Ken Reaves, a good tight end in Jim Mitchell, and a potential All-Pro tackle in George Kunz. One of Van Brocklin's biggest problems, however, was that his offensive line, with four rookie starters, could not pass-block.

San Francisco '49ers—Injuries cut down Kevin Hardy, John Brodie, Stan Hindman, Ed Beard, and Johnny Fuller, retirement erased Matt Hazeltine, and the '49ers fell back into the basement in the Coastal Division. Coach Dick Nolan had veteran talent in such as Ken Willard, Elmer Collett, Charlie Krueger, Dave Wilcox, Jim Johnson, and mid-season pickup Rosey Taylor, and he had rookie talent in Gene Washington, Skip Vanderbundt, Ted Kwalick, and Earl Edwards, but the '49ers persisted as one of pro football's top enigmas.

FINAL TEAM STATISTICS

OFFENSE

	ATL.	BALT.	CHI.	CLEV.	DALL.	DET.	G.B.	L.A.	MINN.	N.O.	N.Y.	PHIL.	PITT.	ST.L.	S.F.	WASH.
FIRST DOWNS:																
Total	209	255	237	250	275	198	242	209	239	282	235	231	210	224	253	256
by Rushing	97	99	120	97	133	83	95	75	102	93	91	83	81	83	84	84
by Passing	89	140	97	138	125	93	122	114	117	158	133	132	115	125	153	149
by Penalty	23	16	20	15	17	22	25	20	20	31	11	16	14	16	16	23
RUSHING:																
Number	455	417	462	447	532	474	432	382	489	399	397	395	400	382	391	377
Yards	2058	1490	2078	1788	2276	1755	1692	1413	1850	1705	1593	1563	1542	1446	1536	1532
Average Yards	4.5	3.6	4.5	4.0	4.3	3.7	3.9	3.7	3.8	4.3	4.0	4.0	3.9	3.8	3.9	4.1
Touchdowns	9	16	14	17	17	11	11	8	15	12	8	10	8	17	13	11
PASSING:																
Attempts	282	429	384	378	355	329	319	416	346	453	435	458	391	430	496	444
Completions	149	225	193	199	189	165	182	222	176	245	234	216	176	216	278	275
Completion Percentage	52.8	52.4	50.3	52.6	53.2	50.2	57.1	53.4	50.9	54.1	53.8	47.2	45.0	50.2	56.0	61.9
Passing Yards	2230	3143	1929	2830	3212	1958	2678	2650	2498	3215	3076	3022	2458	2940	3379	3106
Average Yards per Attempt	7.9	7.3	5.0	7.5	9.0	6.0	8.4	6.4	7.2	7.1	7.1	6.6	6.3	6.8	6.8	7.0
Average Yards per Completion	15.0	14.0	10.0	14.2	17.0	11.9	14.7	11.9	14.2	13.1	13.1	14.0	14.0	13.6	12.2	11.3
Times Tackled Attempting to Pass	63	19	55	20	44	42	34	17	34	27	37	29	52	21	27	40
Yards Lost Tackled Attempting to Pass	477	156	439	190	366	358	302	129	252	241	301	240	374	201	221	322
Net Yards	1753	2987	1490	2640	2846	1600	2376	2521	2246	2974	2775	2782	2084	2739	3158	2784
Touchdowns	20	17	11	24	24	12	20	25	24	22	24	20	17	19	22	22
Interceptions	12	27	21	21	18	18	17	7	18	20	8	28	29	25	26	16
Percent Intercepted	4.3	6.3	5.5	5.6	5.1	5.5	5.3	1.7	5.2	4.4	1.8	6.1	7.4	5.8	5.2	3.6
PUNTS:																
Number	69	57	76	60	63	74	59	80	67	49	73	74	77	73	71	70
Average Distance	41.2	45.3	39.0	37.5	43.3	33.9	40.1	40.7	40.0	41.4	37.6	39.8	42.3	37.6	40.5	42.2
PUNT RETURNS:																
Number	26	37	30	32	38	21	32	58	45	30	15	36	37	38	22	26
Yards	82	192	164	183	273	230	287	556	266	217	50	219	165	201	63	190
Average Yards	3.2	5.2	5.5	5.7	7.2	11.0	9.0	9.6	5.9	7.2	3.3	6.1	4.5	5.3	2.9	7.3
Touchdowns	0	0	0	0	0	1	1	0	0	0	0	0	0	0	0	1
KICKOFF RETURNS:																
Number	52	51	52	46	36	42	50	53	33	62	56	63	60	68	47	60
Yards	1104	1290	1132	985	718	1017	1165	1107	774	1455	1075	1258	1241	1507	908	1268
Average Yards	21.2	25.3	21.8	21.4	19.9	24.2	23.3	20.9	23.5	23.5	19.2	20.0	20.7	22.2	19.3	21.1
Touchdowns	1	1	0	0	0	1	2	0	0	0	0	0	1	1	0	0
INTERCEPTION RETURNS:																
Number	19	15	16	19	24	21	19	26	30	12	19	15	25	15	20	16
Yards	200	106	132	217	339	207	428	424	459	73	221	179	257	245	194	246
Average Yards	10.5	7.1	8.3	11.4	14.1	9.9	22.5	16.3	15.3	6.1	11.6	11.9	10.3	16.3	9.7	15.4
Touchdowns	0	0	1	3	1	0	2	3	2	0	1	3	0	1	1	1
PENALTIES:																
Number	63	62	89	58	81	71	63	95	67	83	70	80	67	72	85	74
Yards	601	561	940	603	840	734	602	994	744	943	777	843	659	765	845	756
FUMBLES:																
Number	37	23	27	26	28	18	31	23	17	20	22	18	36	24	25	23
Number Lost	19	12	17	14	12	12	21	11	12	12	15	11	20	10	12	10
POINTS:																
Total	276	279	210	351	369	259	269	320	379	311	264	279	218	314	277	307
PAT Attempts	33	34	26	45	44	26	36	36	43	35	33	33	26	40	37	37
PAT Made	33	33	26	45	43	26	35	36	43	33	33	31	26	38	35	35
FG Attempts	30	31	21	23	36	37	22	34	37	41	21	30	26	24	21	27
FG Made	15	14	8	12	20	25	6	22	26	22	11	16	12	12	6	16
Percent FG Made	50.0	45.2	38.1	52.2	55.6	67.6	27.3	64.7	70.3	53.7	52.4	53.3	46.2	50.0	28.6	59.3
Safeties	0	0	2	0	1	1	0	1	0	1	0	1	0	0	1	1

DEFENSE

	ATL.	BALT.	CHI.	CLEV.	DALL.	DET.	G.B.	L.A.	MINN.	N.O.	N.Y.	PHIL.	PITT.	ST.L.	S.F.	WASH.
FIRST DOWNS:																
Total	254	256	208	257	203	182	224	242	158	242	243	268	260	289	242	277
by Rushing	120	70	89	120	52	64	103	84	55	88	120	111	101	83	91	149
by Passing	120	164	98	121	141	101	107	125	88	131	103	136	142	185	128	110
by Penalty	14	22	21	16	10	17	14	33	15	23	20	21	17	21	23	18
RUSHING:																
Number	475	399	440	417	313	372	485	415	337	419	466	467	455	438	422	511
Yards	2032	1400	1900	1990	1050	1223	1982	1475	1089	1835	2053	1909	1732	1644	1704	2299
Average Yards	4.3	3.5	4.3	4.8	3.4	3.3	4.1	3.6	3.2	4.4	4.4	4.1	3.8	3.8	4.0	4.5
Touchdowns	14	8	17	18	3	7	7	8	4	15	14	15	17	10	14	26
PASSING:																
Attempts	383	459	296	387	458	350	360	430	410	382	340	444	410	465	402	369
Completions	225	271	150	202	235	167	177	202	213	200	171	243	227	260	205	192
Completion Percentage	58.7	59.0	50.7	52.2	51.3	47.7	49.2	47.0	52.0	52.4	5.0	54.7	55.4	55.9	51.0	52.0
Passing Yards	2536	3499	2239	2787	3109	2238	2133	2919	2035	3382	2430	3250	2973	3752	2726	2316
Average Yards per Attempt	6.6	7.6	7.6	7.2	6.8	6.4	5.9	6.8	5.0	8.9	7.1	7.3	7.3	8.1	6.8	6.3
Average Yards per Completion	11.3	12.9	14.9	13.8	13.2	13.4	12.1	14.5	9.6	16.9	14.2	13.4	13.1	14.4	13.3	12.1
Times Tackled Attempting to Pass	30	33	33	37	55	46	36	50	49	21	32	25	33	33	30	18
Yards Lost Tackled Attempting to Pass	251	250	258	323	452	377	288	393	404	199	275	181	304	220	255	139
Net Yards	2285	3249	1981	2464	2657	1861	1845	2526	1631	3183	2155	3069	2669	3532	2471	2177
Touchdowns	13	20	23	19	23	15	13	18	8	32	18	23	27	38	22	11
Interceptions	19	15	16	19	24	21	19	26	30	12	19	15	25	15	20	16
Percent Intercepted	5.0	3.3	5.4	4.9	5.5	6.0	5.3	6.0	7.3	3.1	5.6	3.4	6.1	3.2	5.0	4.3
PUNTS:																
Number	56	69	63	64	82	70	72	77	100	58	53	69	65	67	65	62
Average Distance	38.8	38.4	41.4	40.5	42.2	40.0	39.7	41.0	36.8	41.6	38.9	40.9	40.1	40.4	40.4	40.7
PUNT RETURNS:																
Number	38	35	28	20	43	31	18	36	34	27	41	21	41	35	39	36
Yards	171	182	106	72	305	133	62	181	237	176	449	93	396	158	293	324
Average Yards	4.5	5.2	3.8	3.6	7.1	4.3	3.4	5.0	7.0	6.5	11.0	4.4	9.7	4.5	7.5	9.0
Touchdowns	0	0	0	0	0	0	0	0	0	0	2	0	1	0	0	0
KICKOFF RETURNS:																
Number	52	55	38	56	64	59	51	56	70	48	45	51	46	49	43	48
Yards	1132	1135	917	1166	1242	1242	1078	1208	1453	935	1100	1043	962	1007	1186	1198
Average Yards	21.8	20.6	24.1	20.8	19.4	21.1	21.1	21.6	20.8	19.5	24.4	20.5	20.9	20.6	27.6	25.0
Touchdowns	2	0	1	0	0	0	1	0	1	0	0	0	1	0	1	0
INTERCEPTION RETURNS:																
Number	12	27	21	21	18	18	17	7	18	20	8	28	29	25	26	16
Yards	233	394	271	275	167	168	256	40	208	265	78	343	535	202	304	188
Average Yards	19.4	14.6	12.9	13.1	9.3	9.3	15.1	5.7	11.6	13.3	9.8	12.3	18.4	8.1	11.7	11.8
Touchdowns	2	3	0	1	1	1	1	0	2	0	0	3	3	0	1	1
PENALTIES:																
Number	73	74	66	72	58	90	65	88	69	81	62	79	79	71	70	83
Yards	762	848	612	746	680	857	733	709	795	773	601	950	793	773	671	904
FUMBLES:																
Number	37	18	21	32	23	24	23	33	24	20	23	31	25	19	26	19
Number Lost	27	10	11	22	11	21	7	12	12	10	14	14	16	12	11	10
POINTS:																
Total	268	268	339	300	223	188	221	243	133	393	298	377	404	389	319	319
PAT Attempts	32	32	43	38	28	23	23	26	16	49	35	44	50	48	39	38
PAT Made	32	31	42	36	28	23	23	25	16	47	32	44	49	47	38	38
FG Attempts	27	34	31	22	25	29	34	26	18	29	29	37	26	31	36	27
FG Made	14	15	13	12	9	9	20	20	7	16	18	23	17	18	15	17
Percent FG Made	51.9	44.1	41.9	54.5	36.0	31.0	58.8	78.9	38.9	55.2	62.1	62.2	65.4	58.1	41.7	63.0
Safeties	1	0	0	0	0	0	0	1	0	2	1	0	2	0	1	1

CONFERENCE PLAYOFFS

December 27, at Bloomington (Attendance 47,900)

SCORING

MINNESOTA	7	0	7	9–23
LOS ANGELES	7	10	0	3–20

First Quarter
- LA Klein, 3 yard pass from Gabriel PAT–Gossett (kick)
- Mn. Osborn, 1 yard rush PAT–Cox (kick)

Second Quarter
- LA Gossett, 20 yard field goal
- LA Truax, 2 yard pass from Gabriel PAT–Gossett (kick)

Third Quarter
- Mn. Osborn, 1 yard rush PAT–Cox (kick)

Fourth Quarter
- LA Gossett, 27 yard field goal
- Mn. Kapp, 2 yard rush PAT–Cox (kick)
- Mn. Eller, Safety-tackled Gabriel in end zone.

TEAM STATISTICS

MINN.		L.A.
18	First Downs–Total	19
7	First Downs–Rushing	10
10	First Downs–Passing	9
1	First Downs–Penalty	0
2	Times Tackled Passing	3
18	Yards Lost–Tackled	21
3	Fumbles–Number	1
1	Fumbles–Lost Ball	0
4	Penalties–Number	4
36	Yards Penalized	37
3	Punts–Number	3
39.3	Punts–Average Distance	36.3
1	Punt Returns–Number	2
6	Punt Returns–Yards	8
6	Kickoff Returns–Number	4
111	Kickoff Returns–Yards	69
1	Interception Returns–Number	2
29	Interception Returns–Yards	19
0	Missed Field Goals	1
3	Giveaways	1
1	Takeaways	3
−2	Difference	+2

INDIVIDUAL STATISTICS

RUSHING

MINNESOTA	No	Yds	Avg.	LOS ANGELES	No	Yds	Avg.
Kapp	7	42	6.0	Smith	11	60	5.5
Osborn	13	30	2.3	Gabriel	4	26	6.5
Brown	8	22	2.8	Ellison	4	22	5.5
Reed	1	3	3.0	Josephson	10	16	1.6
	29	97	3.3	Mason	1	2	2.0
					30	126	4.2

RECEIVING

MINNESOTA	No	Yds	Avg.	LOS ANGELES	No	Yds	Avg.
Washington	4	90	22.5	Josephson	7	41	5.9
Henderson	4	68	17.0	Smith	6	36	6.0
Brown	2	20	10.0	Truax	5	47	9.4
Reed	2	18	9.0	Tucker	3	23	7.7
	12	196	16.3	Klein	1	3	3.0
					22	150	6.8

PASSING

	Att.	Cmp.	Pct.	Yds.	Int.	Yd/A	Yd/C
MINN.							
Kapp	19	12	63.2	196	2	10.3	16.3
L.A.							
Gabriel	32	22	62.5	150	1	4.7	6.8

December 28, at Dallas (Attendance 69,321)

SCORING

DALLAS	0	0	7	7–14
CLEVELAND	7	10	7	14–38

First Quarter
- Cle Scott, 2 yard rush PAT–Cockroft (kick)

Second Quarter
- Cle. Morin, 6 yard pass from Nelsen PAT–Cockroft (kick)
- Cle. Cockroft, 29 field goal

Third Quarter
- Cle. Scott, 2 yard rush PAT–Cockroft (kick)
- Dal. Morton, 2 yard rush PAT–Clark (kick)

Fourth Quarter
- Cle. Kelly, 1 yard rush PAT–Cockroft (kick)
- Cle. Sumner, 88 yard interception return PAT–Cockroft (kick)
- Dal. Rentzel, 5 yard pass from Staubach PAT–Clark (kick)

TEAM STATISTICS

DAL.		CLE.
17	First Downs–Total	22.
9	First Downs–Rushing	4
6	First Downs–Passing	17
2	First Downs–Penalty	1
3	Times Tackled Passing	1
19	Yards Lost–Tackled	7
2	Fumbles–Number	1
1	Fumbles–Lost Ball	0
6	Penalties–Number	6
51	Yards Penalized	50
5	Punts–Number	1
36.2	Punts–Average Distance	34.0
1	Punt Returns–Number	2
0	Punt Returns–Yards	11
5	Kickoff Returns–Number	3
106	Kickoff Returns–Yards	56
0	Interception Returns–Number	2
0	Interception Returns–Yards	123
0	Missed Field Goals	1
3	Giveaways	0
0	Takeaways	3
−3	Difference	+3

INDIVIDUAL

RUSHING

DALLAS				CLEVELAND			
Garrison	9	49	5.4	Kelly	19	66	3.5
Staubach	3	22	7.3	Scott	11	33	3.0
Hill	8	17	2.1	Morrison	2	3	1.5
Morton	4	12	3.0	Cockroft	1	0	0.0
Shy	1	0	0.0	Johnson	2	−5	−2.5
	25	100	4.0		35	97	2.8

RECEIVING

DALLAS				CLEVELAND			
Hayes	4	44	11.0	Warfield	8	99	11.4
Rentzel	3	41	13.7	Morin	4	52	13.0
Garrison	2	15	7.5	Scott	2	39	19.5
Norman	1	26	26.0	Collins	2	19	9.5
Hill	1	7	7.0	Kelly	2	10	5.0
Reeves	1	3	3.0	Morrison	1	18	18.0
	12	136	11.3	Jones	1	17	17.0
					20	254	12.7

PASSING

	Att.	Cmp.	Pct.	Yds.	Int.	Yd/A	Yd/C
DALLAS							
Morton	24	8	33.3	92	2	3.8	11.5
Staubach	5	4	80.0	44	0	8.8	11.0
	29	12	41.4	136	2	4.7	11.3
CLEVE.							
Nelsen	27	18	66.7	219	0	8.1	12.2
Rhome	2	2	100.0	35	0	17.5	17.5
	29	20	69.0	254	0	8.8	12.7

CAPITOL DIVISION

DALLAS COWBOYS 11-2-1 Tom Landry

Scores of Each Game		
24	ST. LOUIS	3
21	New Orleans	17
38	Philadelphia	7
24	Atlanta	17
49	PHILADELPHIA	14
25	NEW YORK	3
10	Cleveland	42
33	NEW ORLEANS	17
41	Washington	28
23	Los Angeles	24
24	SAN FRANCISCO	24
10	Pittsburgh	7
27	BALTIMORE	10
20	WASHINGTON	10

Use Name	Pos.	Hgt	Wgt	Age	Int	Pts
Tony Liscio	OT	6'5"	255	29		
Ralph Neely	OT	6'5"	265	25		
Rayfield Wright	TE-OT	6'7"	250	24		
John Niland	OG	6'4"	245	25		
Blaine Nye	OG	6'4"	250	23		
John Wilbur	OG	6'3"	240	26		
Dave Manders	C	6'2"	250	27		
Malcolm Walker	C	6'4"	250	26		
George Andrie	DE	6'7"	250	29		2
Larry Cole	DE	6'4"	255	22	1	6
Halvor Hagen	OT-DE	6'5"	250	22		
Ron East	DT	6'4"	242	26		
Bob Lilly	DT	6'4"	260	30		6
Jethro Pugh	DT	6'6"	260	25		
Jackie Burkett	LB	6'4"	228	32		
Dave Edwards	LB	6'3"	228	30	1	
Chuck Howley	LB	6'3"	225	33	2	
Lee Roy Jordan	LB	6'2"	220	28	2	
Tom Stincic	LB	6'2"	226	22		
Fred Whittingham	LB	6'1"	240	30		
Otto Brown	DB	6'1"	188	22	1	
Phil Clark	DB	6'2"	210	24	2	
Mike Gaechter	DB	6'	190	29	3	
Cornell Green	DB	6'4"	208	29	2	
Mike Johnson	DB	5'10"	184	25		
Mel Renfro	DB	6'	190	25	10	
Bob Belden	QB	6'2"	210	22		
Craig Morton	QB	6'4"	214	26		6
Roger Staubach	QB	6'2"	195	27		6
Craig Baynham	HB	6'1"	206	25		
Calvin Hill	HB	6'3"	230	22		48
Les Shy	HB	6'1"	200	25		12
Dan Reeves	FB-HB	6'1"	200	25		30
Walt Garrison	FB	6'	205	25		12
Claxton Welch	HB-FB	5'11"	200	22		
Bobby Joe Conrad	WR	6'	195	34		
Richmond Flowers	WR	6'	183	22		
Bob Hayes	WR	6'	185	26		24
Dennis Homan	WR	6'1"	180	23		
Lance Rentzel	WR	6'2"	202	25		78
Mike Ditka	TE	6'3"	225	29		18
Pettis Norman	TE	6'3"	220	29		18
Mike Clark	K	6'1"	205	28		103
Ron Widby	K	6'4"	210	24		

D. D. Lewis – Military Service
Willie Townes – Injury

WASHINGTON REDSKINS 7-5-2 Vince Lombardi

Scores of Each Game		
26	New Orleans	20
23	Cleveland	27
17	San Francisco	17
33	ST. LOUIS	17
20	NEW YORK	14
14	Pittsburgh	7
17	Baltimore	41
28	PHILADELPHIA	28
28	DALLAS	41
27	ATLANTA	20
13	LOS ANGELES	24
34	Philadelphia	29
17	NEW ORLEANS	14
10	Dallas	20

Use Name	Pos.	Hgt	Wgt	Age	Int	Pts
Walt Rock	OT	6'5"	255	28		
Jim Snowden	OT	6'3"	255	27		
Ray Schoenke	C-OT	6'3"	250	27		
Willie Banks	OG	6'2"	237	23		
Steve Duich	OG	6'3"	248	23		
Vince Promuto	OG	6'1"	245	31		
Dave Crossan	C	6'3"	245	29		
Len Hauss	C	6'2"	235	28		
Leo Carroll	DE	6'7"	250	25		
John Hoffman	DE	6'7"	260	26		6
Carl Kammerer	DE	6'3"	243	32		
Clark Miller	DE	6'5"	246	30		
Frank Bosch	DT	6'4"	246	23		
Dennis Crane	DT	6'6"	260	24		
Spain Musgrave	DT	6'4"	275	24		
Jim Norton	DT	6'4"	254	26		
Joe Rutgens	DT	6'2"	255	30		
Chris Hanburger	LB	6'2"	218	28		6
Sam Huff	LB	6'1"	230	34	3	6
Marlin McKeever	LB	6'1"	235	29	1	
Harold McLinton	LB	6'2"	235	22		
Tom Roussel	LB	6'3"	235	24		
John Didion	C-LB	6'4"	245	21		
Mike Bass	DB	6'	190	24	3	
Tom Brown	DB	6'1"	195	28		
Pat Fischer	DB	5'10"	170	29	2	
Rickie Harris	DB	6'	182	26	4	6
Brig Owens	DB	5'11"	190	26	3	
Ted Vactor	DB	6'	185	25		
Bob Wade	DB	6'2"	200	24		
Sonny Jurgensen	QB	5'11"	203	35		6
Frank Ryan	QB	6'3"	207	33		
Jerry Allen	HB	6'1"	200	28		
Larry Brown	HB	5'11"	195	21		24
Dave Kopay	FB-HB	6'2"	225	27		
Henry Dyer	FB	6'2"	230	24		6
Charlie Harraway	FB	6'2"	215	24		54
Chuck Mercein	FB	6'3"	220	26		
Gary Beban	WR	6'1"	195	23		
Bob Long	WR	6'3"	205	28		6
Walter Roberts	WR	5'10"	163	27		
Charley Taylor	WR	6'3"	210	28		48
Pat Richter	TE	6'5"	230	28		
Jerry Smith	TE	6'2"	208	26		54
Mike Bragg	K	5'11"	186	22		
Curt Knight	K	6'1"	190	26		83

NEW ORLEANS SAINTS 5-9-0 Tom Fears

Scores of Each Game		
20	WASHINGTON	26
17	DALLAS	21
17	Los Angeles	36
17	CLEVELAND	27
10	BALTIMORE	30
10	Philadelphia	13
51	St. Louis	42
17	Dallas	33
25	New York	24
43	SAN FRANCISCO	38
26	PHILADELPHIA	17
17	Atlanta	45
14	Washington	17
27	PITTSBURGH	24

Use Name	Pos.	Hgt	Wgt	Age	Int	Pts
Jerry Jones	OT	6'3"	265	25		
Errol Linden	OT	6'5"	250	32		
Don Talbert	OT	6'5"	255	29		
Norman Davis	OG	6'3"	245	24		
Jake Kupp	OG	6'3"	246	27		
John Shinners	OG	6'2"	254	22		
Del Williams	OG	6'2"	245	23		
Jerry Sturm	C	6'3"	265	32		
Doug Atkins	DE	6'8"	275	39		
Dan Colchico	DE	6'4"	245	32		
Dave Long	DE	6'4"	245	24		
Richard Neal	DE	6'3"	254	21		
Mike Rengel	DT	6'5"	260	22		
Dave Rowe	DT	6'6"	280	24		
Mike Tilleman	DT	6'5"	280	25		
Dick Absher	LB	6'4"	227	25	1	
Johnny Brewer	LB	6'4"	235	32		
Bill Cody	LB	6'1"	227	25		
Ted Davis	LB	6'1"	232	27		
Les Kelley	LB	6'3"	233	24		
Mike Morgan	LB	6'4"	242	27		
Bill Saul	LB	6'4"	225	28		
Bo Burris	DB	6'3"	195	24	1	
Ollie Cordill	DB	6'2"	180	26		
Gene Howard	DB	6'	190	22	2	
Elijah Nevett	DB	6'	185	25	3	
Steve Preece	DB	6'1"	195	22	1	6
Bobby Thompson	DB	5'10"	188	29	1	
Carl Ward	DB	5'9"	180	25		
Dave Whitsell	DB	6'	185	33	3	
Edd Hargett	QB	5'11"	186	22		
Billy Kilmer	QB	6'	204	30		
Jim Ninowski	QB	6'1"	207	33		
Joe Don Looney	HB	6'1"	230	26		
Don Shy	HB	6'1"	205	23		12
Tony Baker	FB-HB	5'11"	230	24		12
Tom Barrington	FB-HB	6'1"	213	25		6
Andy Livingston	FB	6'	234	24		48
Tony Lorick	FB	6'1"	217	27		
Ernie Wheelwright	FB	6'3"	236	32		30
Dan Abramowicz	WR	6'1"	195	24		42
Al Dodd	WR	6'	180	24		6
Dave Parks	TE-WR	6'2"	203	27		18
Jim Hester	TE	6'4"	250	24		6
Ray Poage	TE	6'4"	215	28		24
Tom Dempsey	K	6'1"	264	28		99
Tom McNeill	K	6'1"	195	27		

Lou Cordileone – Knee Injury

PHILADELPHIA EAGLES 4-9-1 Jerry Williams

Scores of Each Game		
20	CLEVELAND	27
41	PITTSBURGH	27
7	DALLAS	38
20	Baltimore	24
14	Dallas	49
13	NEW ORLEANS	10
23	New York	20
28	Washington	28
17	LOS ANGELES	23
34	St. Louis	30
17	New Orleans	26
29	WASHINGTON	34
3	ATLANTA	27
13	San Francisco	14

Use Name	Pos.	Hgt	Wgt	Age	Int	Pts
Joe Carollo	OT	6'2"	258	29		
Dave Graham	OT	6'3"	250	30		
Lane Howell	OT	6'5"	272	28		
Don Chuy	OG	6'1"	255	28		
Dick Hart	OG	6'2"	255	26		
Jim Skaggs	OG	6'2"	252	29		
Mark Nordquist	C-OG	6'4"	242	23		
Gene Ceppetelli (to NY)	C	6'2"	247	27		
Mike Evans	C	6'5"	250	22		
Don Hultz	DE	6'3"	242	28		
Tim Rossovich	DE	6'4"	260	23		
Mel Tom	DE	6'4"	250	28		2
Ernie Calloway	DT	6'6"	240	21		
Mike Dirks	DT	6'2"	246	23		
Floyd Peters	DT	6'4"	255	34		
Gary Pettigrew	DE-DT	6'4"	255	24		
Wayne Colman (to NO)	LB	6'1"	230	23	1	
Tony Guillory	LB	6'4"	235	26		
Bill Hobbs	LB	6'	213	23		
Jay Johnson	LB	6'3"	230	23		
Ike Kelley	LB	5'11"	222	25		
Dave Lloyd	LB	6'3"	248	33	2	
Ron Porter (from BAL)	LB	6'3"	232	24		
Adrian Young	LB	6'1"	225	23	1	
Bill Bradley	DB	5'11"	190	22	1	6
Irv Cross	DB	6'1"	195	30	1	
Ron Medved	DB	6'1"	195	25		
Al Nelson	DB	5'11"	186	25	3	
Nate Ramsey	DB	6'1"	200	28	2	6
Jimmy Raye	DB	6'	185	23		
Joe Scarpati	DB	5'10"	185	27	4	6
George Mira	QB	5'11"	190	27		
Norm Snead	QB	6'4"	215	29		12
Ronnie Blye	HB	5'11"	185	25		
Harry Jones	HB	6'2"	230	24		
Leroy Keyes	HB	6'3"	208	22		18
Harry Wilson	HB	5'11"	204	24		
Cyril Pinder	FB-HB	6'2"	222	22		6
Tom Woodeschick	FB	6'	225	27		24
Gary Ballman	WR	6'	205	29		12
Ben Hawkins	WR	6'	180	25		48
Chuck Hughes	WR	5'11"	175	26		
Harold Jackson	WR	5'10"	175	23		54
Kent Lawrence	WR	5'11"	175	22		
Fred Brown	TE	6'5"	237	26		
Fred Hill	TE	6'2"	215	26		6
Sam Baker	K	6'2"	218	37		79

CAPITOL DIVISION

DALLAS COWBOYS

RUSHING

Last Name	No.	Yds	Avg	TD
Hill	204	942	4.6	8
Garrison	176	818	4.6	2
Reeves	59	173	2.9	4
Shy	42	154	3.7	1
Morton	16	62	3.9	1
Staubach	15	60	4.0	1
Welch	6	21	3.5	0
Norman	5	20	4.0	0
Hayes	4	17	4.3	0
Rentzel	2	11	5.5	0
Baynham	3	−2	−0.7	0

RECEIVING

Last Name	No.	Yds	Avg	TD
Rentzel	43	960	22	12
Hayes	40	746	19	4
Hill	20	232	12	0
Reeves	18	187	10	1
Ditka	17	268	16	3
Norman	13	238	18	3
Garrison	13	131	10	0
Homan	12	240	20	0
Shy	8	124	16	1
Conrad	4	74	19	0
Wright	1	12	12	0

PUNT RETURNS

Last Name	No.	Yds	Avg	TD
Hayes	18	179	10	0
Renfro	15	80	5	0
Rentzel	4	14	4	0
Johnson	1	0	0	0

KICKOFF RETURNS

Last Name	No.	Yds	Avg	TD
Flowers	11	238	22	0
Hill	4	125	31	0
Baynham	6	114	19	0
Welch	5	112	22	0
Hayes	3	80	27	0
Shy	3	47	16	0
Garrison	1	2	2	0
Green	2	0	0	0
Johnson	1	0	0	0

PASSING – PUNTING – KICKING

PASSING	Att	Comp	%	Yds	Yd/Att	TD	Int–	%	RK
Morton	302	162	54	2619	8.7	21	15–	5	5
Staubach	47	23	49	421	9.0	1	2–	4	
Hill	3	3	100	137	45.7	2	0–	0	
Reeves	3	1	33	35	11.7	0	1–	33	

PUNTING	No	Avg
Widby	63	43.3

KICKING	XP	Att	%	FG	Att	%
M. Clark	43	44	98	20	36	56

WASHINGTON REDSKINS

RUSHING

Last Name	No.	Yds	Avg	TD
L. Brown	202	888	4.4	4
Harraway	141	428	3.0	6
Jurgensen	17	156	9.2	1
Taylor	3	24	8.0	0
Dyer	6	18	3.0	0
Smith	3	8	2.7	0
Kopay	3	4	1.3	0
Allen	1	3	3.0	0
Bragg	1	3	3.0	0

RECEIVING

Last Name	No.	Yds	Avg	TD
Taylor	71	883	12	8
Harraway	55	489	9	3
Smith	54	682	13	9
Long	48	533	11	1
L. Brown	34	302	9	0
Kopay	6	60	10	0
Roberts	4	66	17	0
Dyer	2	86	43	1
Allen	1	5	5	0

PUNT RETURNS

Last Name	No.	Yds	Avg	TD
Harris	14	158	11	1
Roberts	12	32	3	0

KICKOFF RETURNS

Last Name	No.	Yds	Avg	TD
Harris	19	458	24	0
Roberts	17	383	23	0
Dyer	11	207	19	0
Kopay	9	187	21	0
McKeever	2	31	16	0
Snowden	1	2	2	0
Richter	1	0	0	0

PASSING – PUNTING – KICKING

PASSING	Att	Comp	%	Yds	Yd/Att	TD	Int–%		RK
Jurgensen	442	274	62	3102	7.0	22	15–	3	1
Ryan	1	1	100	4	4.0	0	0–	0	
Knight	1	0	0	0	0.0	0	1–	100	

PUNTING	No	Avg
Bragg	70	42.2

KICKING	XP	Att	%	FG	Att	%
Knight	35	36	97	16	27	59

NEW ORLEANS SAINTS

RUSHING

Last Name	No.	Yds	Avg	TD
Livingston	181	761	4.2	5
Baker	134	642	4.8	1
Wheelwright	25	85	3.4	4
Shy	21	75	3.6	1
Abramowicz	3	61	20.3	0
Barrington	7	33	4.7	1
Kilmer	11	18	1.6	0
Hargett	5	15	3.0	0
Dodd	3	12	4.0	0
Lorick	5	11	2.2	0
Poage	1	−3	−3.0	0
Looney	3	−5	−1.7	0

RECEIVING

Last Name	No.	Yds	Avg	TD
Abramowicz	73	1015	14	7
Dodd	37	600	16	1
Baker	34	352	10	1
Parks	31	439	14	3
Livingston	28	278	10	3
Poage	18	236	13	4
Shy	9	141	16	1
Wheelwright	8	68	9	1
Barrington	4	42	11	0
Hester	3	44	15	1

PUNT RETURNS

Last Name	No.	Yds	Avg	TD
Dodd	15	106	7	0
Howard	9	73	8	0
Thompson	4	25	6	0
Barrington	1	8	8	0
Ward	1	5	5	0

KICKOFF RETURNS

Last Name	No.	Yds	Avg	TD
Shy	16	447	28	0
Barrington	17	394	23	0
Howard	9	227	25	0
Dodd	8	171	21	0
Thompson	5	101	20	0
Ward	3	58	19	0
Nevett	2	53	27	0
Hester	1	4	4	0
Preece	1	0	0	0

PASSING – PUNTING – KICKING

PASSING	Att	Comp	%	Yds	Yd/Att	TD	Int–	%	RK
Kilmer	360	193	54	2532	7.0	20	17–	5	8
Hargett	52	31	60	403	7.8	0	0–	0	
Ninowski	34	17	50	227	6.7	1	2–	6	
Livingston	4	3	75	38	9.5	1	1–	25	
Barrington	2	1	50	15	7.5	0	0–	0	
Looney	1	0	0	0	0.0	0	0–	0	

PUNTING	No	Avg
Cordill	42	40.9
McNeill	7	44.6

KICKING	XP	Att	%	FG	Att	%
Dempsey	33	35	94	22	41	54

PHILADELPHIA EAGLES

RUSHING

Last Name	No.	Yds	Avg	TD
Woodeshick	186	831	4.5	4
Keyes	121	361	3.0	3
Pinder	60	309	5.2	1
Blye	8	25	3.1	0
Mira	3	16	5.3	0
Jackson	2	10	5.0	0
Wilson	4	7	1.8	0
Bradley	1	5	5.0	0
Snead	8	2	0.3	2
Jones	1	0	0.0	0
Hawkins	1	−3	−3.0	0

RECEIVING

Last Name	No.	Yds	Avg	TD
Jackson	65	1116	17	9
Hawkins	43	761	18	8
Ballman	31	492	16	2
Keyes	29	276	10	0
Woodeshick	22	177	8	0
Pinder	12	77	6	0
Hill	6	64	11	1
Hughes	3	29	10	0
Blye	2	−6	−3	0
Brown	1	20	20	0
Lawrence	1	10	10	0
Wilson	1	6	6	0

PUNT RETURNS

Last Name	No.	Yds	Avg	TD
Bradley	28	181	6	0
Lawrence	2	26	13	0
Scarpati	4	6	2	0
Hawkins	1	6	6	0
Hughes	1	0	0	0

KICKOFF RETURNS

Last Name	No.	Yds	Avg	TD
Bradley	21	467	22	0
Blye	19	370	19	0
Keyes	9	200	22	0
Lawrence	5	97	19	0
Nelson	3	63	21	0
Pinder	4	56	14	0
Graham	2	5	3	0

PASSING – PUNTING – KICKING

PASSING	Att	Comp	%	Yds	Yd/Att	TD	Int–	%	RK
Snead	379	190	50	2768	7.3	19	23–	6	12
Mira	76	25	33	240	3.2	1	5–	7	
Keyes	2	1	50	14	7.0	0	0–	0	
Bradley	1	0	0	0	0.0	0	0–	0	

PUNTING	No	Avg
Bradley	74	39.8

KICKING	XP	Att	%	FG	Att	%
Baker	31	31	100	16	30	53

CENTURY DIVISION

CLEVELAND BROWNS 10-3-1 Blanton Collier

Scores of Each Game		
27	Philadelphia	20
27	WASHINGTON	23
21	DETROIT	28
27	New Orleans	17
42	PITTSBURGH	31
21	ST. LOUIS	21
42	DALLAS	10
3	Minnesota	51
24	Pittsburgh	3
28	NEW YORK	17
28	Chicago	24
20	GREEN BAY	7
27	St. Louis	21
14	New York	27

Use Name	Pos.	Hgt	Wgt	Age	Int	Pts
Monte Clark	OT	6'6"	250	32		
Bob Oliver	OT	6'3"	240	22		
Dick Schafrath	OT	6'3"	248	33		
Joe Taffoni	OT	6'3"	250	24		
Jim Copeland	OG	6'2"	245	24		
John Demarie	OG	6'3"	255	24		
Gene Hickerson	OG	6'3"	248	34		
Chuck Reynolds	OG	6'2"	240	22		
Fred Hoaglin	C	6'4"	250	25		
Jack Gregory	DE	6'6"	250	24	1	
Ron Snidow	DE	6'4"	250	27		
Marv Upshaw	DT-DE	6'3"	245	22	1	
Walter Johnson	DT	6'3"	275	26		6
Jim Kanicki	DT	6'4"	270	27		
Joe Righetti	DT	6'3"	253	21		
Al Jenkins	DE-DT	6'2"	255	23		

Use Name	Pos.	Hgt	Wgt	Age	Int	Pts
Billy Andrews	LB	6'	225	24		
John Garlington	LB	6'1"	225	23	2	
Jim Houston	LB	6'2"	240	32		
Dale Lindsey	LB	6'3"	225	26	1	
Bob Matheson	LB	6'4"	240	24		
Wayne Meylan	LB	6'1"	235	23		
Erich Barnes	DB	6'2"	212	34	1	6
Dean Brown	DB	5'10"	170	22		
Mike Howell	DB	6'1"	190	26	6	
Ernie Kellerman	DB	6'	185	25	3	6
Alvin Mitchell	DB	6'3"	195	25		
Freddie Summers	DB	6'1"	180	22		
Walt Sumner	DB	6'1"	180	22	4	6
Ben Davis – Injury						

Use Name	Pos.	Hgt	Wgt	Age	Int	Pts
Bill Nelsen	QB	6'	195	28		
Jerry Rhome	QB	6'	185	27		
Ron Johnson	HB	6'1"	205	21		42
Reece Morrison	HB	6'	205	23		6
Bo Scott	FB	6'3"	210	26		
Charlie Leigh	FB	5'11"	205	23		
Leroy Kelly	HB-FB	6'	200	27		60
Gary Collins	WR	6'4"	220	28		66
Fair Hooker	WR	6'1"	193	22		
Dave Jones	WR	6'2"	185	22		
Paul Warfield	WR	6'	188	26		60
Chip Glass	TE	6'4"	236	22		12
Milt Morin	TE	6'4"	250	27		
Don Cockroft	K	6'1"	185	24		81

NEW YORK GIANTS 6-8-0 Allie Sherman

Scores of Each Game		
24	MINNESOTA	23
0	Detroit	24
28	CHICAGO	24
10	PITTSBURGH	7
14	Washington	20
3	Dallas	25
20	PHILADELPHIA	23
17	St. Louis	42
24	NEW ORLEANS	25
17	Cleveland	28
10	Green Bay	20
49	ST. LOUIS	6
21	Pittsburgh	17
27	CLEVELAND	14

Use Name	Pos.	Hgt	Wgt	Age	Int	Pts
Rich Buzin	OT	6'4"	250	23		
Steve Wright	OT	6'6"	250	27		
Willie Young	OT	6'	265	26		
Pete Case	OG	6'3"	245	28		
Darrell Dess	OG	6'	245	33		
Doug Van Horn	OG	6'2"	245	25		
Charlie Harper	OT-OG	6'2"	250	25		
Chuck Hinton	C	6'2"	235	26		
Greg Larson	C	6'2"	250	30		
Bruce Anderson	DE	6'4"	250	25		
Fred Dryer	DE	6'6"	235	23		
John Johnson	DT	6'5"	260	28		
Tim McCann	DT	6'5"	265	22		
Frank Molden	DT	6'5"	280	27		
Frank Parker	DT	6'5"	270	29		
Joe Szczecko	DT	6'	245	27		
Bob Lurtsema	DE-DT	6'6"	250	27		

Use Name	Pos.	Hgt	Wgt	Age	Int	Pts
McKinley Boston	LB	6'2"	245	23		
Tommy Crutcher	LB	6'3"	230	27	1	
Henry Davis	LB	6'3"	235	26		
Ralph Heck	LB	6'2"	230	28	2	
Ray Hickl	LB	6'2"	210	22		
John Kirby (from MIN)	LB	6'3"	235	27		
Harold Wells	LB	6'2"	220	30		
Al Brenner	DB	6'1"	200	21		
Scott Eaton	DB	6'3"	195	25	2	6
Jim Holifield	DB	6'3"	195	23	1	
Spider Lockhart	DB	6'2"	175	26	2	
Tom Longo	DB	6'1"	198	25	2	
Bruce Maher	DB	5'11"	185	32	5	
Willie Williams	DB	6'	190	26	4	
Bobby Duhon – Injury						

Use Name	Pos.	Hgt	Wgt	Age	Int	Pts
Milt Plum	QB	6'1"	205	35		
Frank Tarkenton	QB	6'1"	190	29		
Gary Wood	QB	5'11"	188	26		
John Fuqua	HB	5'11"	200	22		
Randy Minniear	HB	6'	210	25		6
Ernie Koy	FB-HB	6'2"	230	26		36
Joe Morrison	WR-HB	6'1"	212	31		66
Junior Coffey (from ATL)	FB	6'1"	210	27		30
Tucker Frederickson	FB	6'3"	220	26		6
Dave Dunaway	WR	6'2"	205	24		
Don Herrman	WR	6'2"	195	22		30
Rich Houston	WR	6'2"	197	23		
Homer Jones	WR	6'2"	215	28		6
Dick Kotite	TE	6'3"	235	26		6
Freeman White	TE	6'5"	225	25		6
Butch Wilson	TE	6'2"	228	27		
Aaron Thomas	WR-TE	6'3"	210	31		18
Pete Gogolak	K	6'2"	185	27		66
Curley Johnson (from NY-A)	K	6'	215	34		

ST. LOUIS CARDINALS 4-9-1 Charlie Winner

Scores of Each Game		
3	Dallas	24
20	CHICAGO	17
27	Pittsburgh	14
17	Washington	33
10	MINNESOTA	27
21	Cleveland	21
42	NEW ORLEANS	51
42	NEW YORK	17
0	Detroit	20
30	PHILADELPHIA	34
47	PITTSBURGH	10
6	New York	49
21	CLEVELAND	27
28	Green Bay	45

Use Name	Pos.	Hgt	Wgt	Age	Int	Pts
Vern Emerson	OT	6'5"	260	23		
Ernie McMillan	OT	6'6"	260	31		
Bob Reynolds	OT	6'6"	265	28		
Clyde Williams	OT	6'2"	250	29		
Irv Goode	OG	6'4"	250	28		
Ken Gray	OG	6'2"	250	33		
Rick Sortun	OG	6'2"	240	26		
Bob DeMarco	C	6'3"	245	31		
Wayne Mulligan	C	6'2"	245	22		
Don Brumm	DE	6'3"	245	26		
Rolf Krueger	DE	6'4"	245	22		
Cal Snowden	DE	6'4"	235	22		
Chuck Walker	DE	6'2"	250	28		
Fred Heron	DT	6'4"	255	24		
Bob Rowe	DT	6'4"	255	24	2	6
Joe Schmiesing	DT	6'4"	245	24		

Use Name	Pos.	Hgt	Wgt	Age	Int	Pts
Chip Healy	LB	6'3"	230	22		
Dave Meggyesy	LB	6'1"	230	27		
Dave Olerich	LB	6'1"	220	24		
Jamie Rivers	LB	6'2"	235	23		
Rocky Rosema	LB	6'2"	230	23	1	
Larry Stallings	LB	6'2"	230	27		6
Bob Atkins	DB	6'3"	212	23	3	
Lonnie Sanders	DB	6'3"	205	27		
Mac Sauls	DB	6'	185	24		
Jerry Stovall	DB	6'2"	195	27	1	
Roger Wehrli	DB	6'1"	185	21	3	
Larry Wilson	DB	6'	190	31	2	6
Mike Wilson	DB	5'11"	185	22		
Terry Brown	WR-DB	6'1"	205	22	1	

Use Name	Pos.	Hgt	Wgt	Age	Int	Pts
Jim Hart	QB	6'2"	205	25		12
King Hill	QB	6'3"	216	33		
Charley Johnson	QB	6'	190	32		6
MacArthur Lane	HB	6'	220	27		6
Johnny Roland	HB	6'2"	215	26		36
Roy Shivers	HB	6'	200	27		18
Willie Crenshaw	FB	6'2"	230	28		18
Cid Edwards	FB	6'2"	230	25		18
Jerry Daanen	WR	6'	190	24		
John Gilliam	WR	6'1"	190	24		60
Freddie Hyatt	WR	6'3"	212	23		
Dave Williams	WR	6'2"	205	24		42
Bob Brown	TE	6'3"	225	26		
Jackie Smith	TE	6'4"	230	28		6
Jim Bakken	K	6'	200	28		74

PITTSBURGH STEELERS 1-13-0 Chuck Noll

Scores of Each Game		
16	DETROIT	13
27	Philadelphia	41
14	ST. LOUIS	27
7	New York	10
31	Cleveland	42
7	WASHINGTON	14
34	GREEN BAY	38
7	Chicago	38
3	CLEVELAND	24
14	Minnesota	52
10	St. Louis	47
7	DALLAS	10
17	NEW YORK	21
24	New Orleans	27

Use Name	Pos.	Hgt	Wgt	Age	Int	Pts
John Brown	OT	6'2"	255	30		
Mike Haggerty	OT	6'4"	240	23		
Mike Taylor (to NO)	OT	6'4"	245	24		
Sam Davis	OG	6'1"	245	25		
Larry Gagner	OG	6'3"	240	25		
Bruce Van Dyke	OG	6'2"	246	25		
Ralph Wenzel	OG	6'3"	236	26		
Jon Kolb	C	6'2"	220	22		
Ray Mansfield	C	6'3"	240	28		
L. C. Greenwood	DE	6'5"	240	22		
Ben McGee	DE	6'2"	250	27		
Lloyd Voss	DE	6'4"	256	27		
Dick Arndt	DT	6'5"	265	25		
Joe Greene	DT	6'4"	270	22		
Chuck Hinton	DT	6'5"	258	30	1	
Clarence Washington	DT	6'3"	265	22		

Use Name	Pos.	Hgt	Wgt	Age	Int	Pts
John Campbell (to BAL)	LB	6'3"	225	30		
Doug Fisher	LB	6'1"	225	22		
Jerry Hillebrand	LB	6'3"	240	29	1	
Ray May	LB	6'1"	230	24	2	
Andy Russell	LB	6'3"	225	27	2	
Brian Stenger	LB	6'4"	220	22	3	
Sid Williams	LB	6'2"	235	27		
Chuck Beatty	DB	6'2"	207	23		
Lee Calland (from CHI)	DB	6'	190	28	2	
Bob Hohn	DB	6'	185	28	5	
Paul Martha	DB	6'	187	26	5	
Clancy Oliver	DB	6'1"	180	21		
Jim Shorter	DB	5'11"	180	28	3	
Marv Woodson (to NO)	DB	6'	195	26	1	
Rocky Bleier – Military Service						

Use Name	Pos.	Hgt	Wgt	Age	Int	Pts
Terry Hanratty	QB	6'1"	200	21		
Kent Nix	QB	6'1"	195	25		
Dick Shiner	QB	6'	197	27		6
Bob Campbell	HB	6'	195	22		
Dick Hoak	HB	5'11"	195	30		18
Don McCall	HB	5'11"	195	24		6
Warren Bankston	FB	6'4"	226	22		6
Earl Gros	FB	6'3"	220	28		42
Don Alley	WR	6'2"	200	23		
Marshall Cropper	WR	6'3"	200	25		
Jon Henderson	WR	6'	195	24		18
Roy Jefferson	WR	6'2"	190	25		54
J. R. Wilburn	WR	6'2"	190	26		
Erwin Williams	WR	6'5"	215	22		6
Bob Adams	TE	6'2"	225	23		
John Hilton	TE	6'5"	222	27		
Gene Mingo	K	6'1"	216	30		62
Bobby Walden	K	6'	190	30		

CENTURY DIVISION

CLEVELAND BROWNS

RUSHING

Last Name	No.	Yds	Avg	TD
Kelly	196	817	4.2	9
R. Johnson	137	471	3.4	7
Morrison	60	301	5.0	1
Scott	44	157	3.6	0
Morin	2	30	15.0	0
Warfield	2	23	11.5	0
Rhome	1	0	0.0	0
Nelsen	5	–11	–2.2	0

RECEIVING

Last Name	No.	Yds	Avg	TD
Collins	54	786	15	11
Warfield	42	886	21	10
Morin	37	495	13	0
R. Johnson	24	164	7	0
Kelly	20	267	13	1
Morrison	6	71	12	0
Scott	6	25	4	0
Glass	4	91	23	2
Jones	2	33	17	0
Hooker	2	21	11	0
Leigh	2	–9	–5	0

PUNT RETURNS

Last Name	No.	Yds	Avg	TD
Sumner	9	88	10	0
Morrison	11	49	4	0
Kelly	7	28	4	0
Leigh	5	18	4	0

KICKOFF RETURNS

Last Name	No.	Yds	Avg	TD
Scott	25	722	29	0
Morrison	9	155	17	0
Brown	2	45	23	0
R. Johnson	1	31	31	0
Kelly	2	26	13	0
Leigh	2	6	3	0
Howell	1	0	0	0
Jenkins	1	0	0	0
Kanicki	1	0	0	0
Mathesen	1	0	0	0
Mitchell	1	0	0	0

PASSING – PUNTING – KICKING

PASSING	Att	Comp	%	Yds	Yd/Att	TD	Int–	%	RK
Nelson	352	190	54	2743	7.8	23	19–	5	6
Rhome	19	7	37	35	1.8	0	2–	11	
Kelly	5	1	20	36	7.2	1	0–	0	
Morrison	1	1	100	16	16.0	0	0–	0	
R. Johnson	1	0	0	0	0.0	0	0–	0	

PUNTING	No	Avg
Cockroft	57	37.5
Collins	3	37.3

KICKING	XP	Att	%	FG	Att	%
Cockroft	45	45	100	12	23	52

NEW YORK GIANTS

RUSHING

Last Name	No.	Yds	Avg	TD
Coffey	131	511	3.9	2
Morrison	107	387	3.6	4
Koy	76	300	3.9	2
Tarkenton	37	172	4.6	0
Minniear	35	141	4.0	1
Frederickson	33	136	4.1	0
Fuqua	20	89	4.5	0
Houston	1	11	11.0	0
Jones	3	8	2.7	0
Dunaway	1	4	4.0	0
Wood	1	3	3.0	0
Plum	1	–1	–1.0	0

RECEIVING

Last Name	No.	Yds	Avg	TD
Morrison	44	647	15	7
Jones	42	744	18	1
Herrmann	33	423	13	5
White	29	315	11	1
Thomas	22	348	16	3
Koy	19	152	8	4
Frederickson	14	95	7	1
Coffey	14	89	6	3
Wilson	10	132	13	0
Minniear	6	68	11	0
Fuqua	3	11	4	0
Houston	2	69	35	0
Dunaway	2	37	19	0
Young	1	8	8	0
Kotite	1	2	2	1

PUNT RETURNS

Last Name	No.	Yds	Avg	TD
Lockhart	10	29	3	0
Minniear	3	15	5	0
Brenner	2	6	3	0

KICKOFF RETURNS

Last Name	No.	Yds	Avg	TD
Fuqua	20	399	20	0
Houston	12	252	21	0
Holifield	8	156	20	0
Williams	6	96	16	0
Minniear	5	83	17	0
Brenner	2	39	20	0
Longo	2	31	16	0
Lockhart	1	19	19	0

PASSING – PUNTING – KICKING

PASSING	Att	Comp	%	Yds	Yd/Att	TD	Int–	%	RK
Tarkenton	409	220	54	2918	7.1	23	8–	2	3
Wood	16	10	63	106	6.6	1	0–	0	
Plum	9	3	33	37	4.1	0	0–	0	
Koy	1	1	100	15	15.0	0	0–	0	

PUNTING	No	Avg
Koy	26	35.9
C. Johnson	22	37.4
Dunaway	13	38.2
Gogolak	12	40.9

KICKING	XP	Att	%	FG	Att	%
Gogolak	33	33	100	11	21	52

ST. LOUIS CARDINALS

RUSHING

Last Name	No.	Yds	Avg	TD
Edwards	107	504	4.7	3
Roland	138	498	3.6	5
Crenshaw	55	172	3.1	3
Shivers	27	115	4.3	2
Lane	25	93	3.7	1
Johnson	17	51	3.0	1
Hart	7	16	2.3	2
D. Williams	1	1	1.0	0
Smith	4	0	0.0	0
Gilliam	1	–4	–4.0	0

RECEIVING

Last Name	No.	Yds	Avg	TD
D. Williams	56	702	13	7
Gilliam	52	997	19	9
Smith	43	561	13	1
Edwards	23	309	13	0
Roland	12	136	11	1
Crenshaw	11	94	9	0
Lane	9	61	7	0
Shivers	7	61	9	1
Daanen	2	12	6	0
T. Brown	1	7	7	0

PUNT RETURNS

Last Name	No.	Yds	Avg	TD
Wehrli	13	65	5	0
Roland	10	53	5	0
Shivers	9	44	5	0
T. Brown	6	39	7	0

KICKOFF RETURNS

Last Name	No.	Yds	Avg	TD
Lane	20	523	26	0
Gilliam	11	339	31	1
T. Brown	15	320	21	0
Shivers	10	205	21	0
M. Wilson	4	66	17	0
Crenshaw	4	34	9	0
Wehrli	1	18	18	0
Olerich	2	2	1	0
C. Williams	1	0	0	0

PASSING – PUNTING – KICKING

PASSING	Att	Comp	%	Yds	Yd/Att	TD	Int–	%	RK
Johnson	260	131	50	1847	7.1	13	13–	5	13
Hart	169	84	50	1086	6.4	6	12–	7	18
Hill	1	1	100	7	7.0	0	0–	0	

PUNTING	No	Avg
Hill	73	37.6

KICKING	XP	Att	%	FG	Att	%
Bakken	38	40	95	12	24	50

PITTSBURGH STEELERS

RUSHING

Last Name	No.	Yds	Avg	TD
Hoak	151	531	3.5	2
Gros	116	343	3.0	4
Bankston	62	259	4.2	1
Hanratty	10	106	10.6	0
McCall	30	98	3.3	0
Nix	10	70	7.0	0
Shiner	14	55	3.9	1
Jefferson	4	46	11.5	0
Wilburn	2	29	14.5	0
B. Campbell	1	5	5.0	0

RECEIVING

Last Name	No.	Yds	Avg	TD
Jefferson	67	1079	16	9
Wilburn	20	373	19	0
Hoak	20	190	10	1
Gros	17	131	8	3
Hilton	12	231	19	0
Henderson	12	188	16	3
Cropper	9	116	13	0
Adams	6	80	13	0
Bankston	6	6	1	0
E. Williams	3	14	5	1
McCall	2	2	1	0
B. Campbell	1	32	32	0
Alley	1	16	16	0

PUNT RETURNS

Last Name	No.	Yds	Avg	TD
B. Campbell	28	133	5	0
Jefferson	4	23	6	0
Hoak	1	9	9	0
Martha	3	0	0	0
Davis	1	0	0	0

KICKOFF RETURNS

Last Name	No.	Yds	Avg	TD
McCall	21	532	25	1
B. Campbell	26	522	20	0
Bankston	4	89	22	0
Jefferson	4	80	20	0
Woodson	1	18	18	0
Davis	3	0	0	0
Kolb	1	0	0	0

PASSING – PUNTING – KICKING

PASSING	Att	Comp	%	Yds	Yd/Att	TF	Int–	%	RK
Shiner	209	97	46	1422	6.8	7	10–	5	15
Hanratty	126	52	41	716	5.7	8	13–	10	
Nix	53	25	47	290	5.5	2	6–	11	
Hoak	3	2	67	30	10.0	0	0–	0	

PUNTING	No	Avg
Walden	77	42.3

KICKING	XP	Att	%	FG	Att	%
Mingo	26	26	100	12	26	46

CENTRAL DIVISION

MINNESOTA VIKINGS 12-2-0 Bud Grant

Scores of Each Game		
23	New York	24
52	BALTIMORE	14
19	GREEN BAY	7
31	Chicago	0
27	St. Louis	10
24	DETROIT	10
31	CHICAGO	14
51	CLEVELAND	3
9	Green Bay	7
52	PITTSBURGH	14
27	Detroit	0
20	Los Angeles	13
10	SAN FRANCISCO	7
3	Atlanta	10

Use Name	Pos.	Hgt	Wgt	Age	Int	Pts
Grady Alderman	OT	6'2"	242	30		
Doug Davis	OT	6'4"	255	25		
Ron Yary	OT	6'6"	265	23		
Bookie Bolin	OG	6'2"	250	29		
Milt Sunde	OG	6'2"	250	26		
Jim Vellone	OG	6'2"	255	25		
Ed White	OG	6'2"	252	22		
Mick Tingelhoff	C	6'1"	237	29		
Carl Eller	DE	6'6"	265	26		
Jim Marshall	DE	6'3"	260	32	1	
Steve Smith	DE	6'5"	240	25		
Paul Dickson	DT	6'5"	257	32		
Gary Larsen	DT	6'5"	260	29		
Alan Page	DT	6'5"	260	24		6
Jim Hargrove	LB	6'3"	232	24		
Wally Hilgenberg	LB	6'3"	235	26		
Mike McGill	LB	6'2"	237	22		
Mike Reilly	LB	6'2"	235	26		6
Lonnie Warwick	LB	6'3"	237	27	4	
Roy Winston	LB	6'1"	230	29	3	
Bobby Bryant	DB	6'	175	25	8	
Karl Kassulke	DB	6'	195	27	2	
Paul Krause	DB	6'3"	195	27	5	6
Earsell Mackbee	DB	6'1"	195	28	6	
Ed Sharockman	DB	6'	200	29	1	
Charlie West	DB	6'1"	190	23		
Dale Hackbart	LB-DB	6'3"	214	33		
Gary Cuozzo	QB	6'1"	195	28		
Joe Kapp	QB	6'2"	215	31		
Bob Lee	QB	6'2"	195	24		
Billy Harris	HB	6'	190	23		
Clint Jones	HB	6'	206	24		18
Dave Osborn	HB	6'	205	26		48
Bill Brown	FB	5'11"	230	31		18
Jim Lindsey	HB-FB	6'2"	212	24		12
Oscar Reed	HB-FB	5'11"	222	25		18
Bob Grim	WR	6'	197	24		6
Tom Hall	WR	6'1"	195	28		
John Henderson	WR	6'3"	190	26		30
Gene Washington	WR	6'3"	218	25		54
John Beasley	TE	6'3"	230	24		30
Kent Kramer	TE	6'5"	235	25		6
Fred Cox	K	5'10"	200	30		121

DETROIT LIONS 9-4-1 Joe Schmidt

Scores of Each Game		
13	Pittsburgh	16
24	NEW YORK	0
28	Cleveland	21
17	GREEN BAY	28
13	CHICAGO	7
10	Minnesota	24
26	San Francisco	14
27	ATLANTA	21
20	ST. LOUIS	0
16	Green Bay	10
0	MINNESOTA	27
17	Baltimore	17
28	LOS ANGELES	0
20	Chicago	3

Use Name	Pos.	Hgt	Wgt	Age	Int	Pts
Rocky Freitas	OT	6'6"	260	23		
Roger Shoals	OT	6'4"	255	30		
Jim Yarbrough	OT	6'6"	250	22		
Frank Gallagher	OG	6'2"	240	26		
Bob Kowalkowski	OG	6'3"	245	25		
Rocky Rasley	OG	6'3"	248	22		
Chuck Walton	OG	6'3"	250	28		
Ed Flanagan	C	6'3"	250	25		
Bill Cottrell	OG-C	6'3"	250	24		
Larry Hand	DE	6'4"	245	29		
Joe Robb	DE	6'3"	245	32		
Denis Moore	DT-DE	6'5"	255	25		
Alex Karras	DT	6'2"	255	33	1	
Jerry Rush	DT	6'4"	260	27		
Dan Goich	DE-DT	6'4"	265	25		
Mike Lucci	LB	6'2"	230	29		
Ed Mooney	LB	6'2"	240	24		
Paul Naumoff	LB	6'1"	225	24		
Tom Nowatzke	LB	6'3"	230	26		
Bill Swain	LB	6'2"	230	28		
Wayne Walker	LB	6'2"	225	32	1	
Lem Barney	DB	6'	185	23	8	6
Dick LeBeau	DB	6'1"	185	32	6	
Wayne Rasmussen	DB	6'2"	175	27		
Tom Vaughn	DB	5'11"	190	26	2	
Mike Weger	DB	6'2"	185	23	3	
Bobby Williams	DB	6'1"	205	27		6
Greg Barton	QB	6'2"	195	23		
Greg Landry	QB	6'4"	205	22		6
Bill Munson	QB	6'2"	200	27		
Nick Eddy	HB	6'1"	205	25		18
Mel Farr	HB	6'2"	205	24		24
Altie Taylor	HB	5'10"	196	21		
Bill Triplett	FB	6'2"	210	30		24
Larry Watkins	FB	6'2"	215	21		6
Bill Malinchak	WR	6'1"	200	25		
Earl McCullouch	WR	5'11"	180	23		30
Phil Odle	WR	5'11"	190	26		
Larry Walton	WR	5'11"	180	22		
John Wright	WR	6'	197	23		18
Craig Cotton	TE	6'4"	222	22		
Charlie Sanders	TE	6'4"	215	23		18
Rick Duncan	K	6'	208	28		
Errol Mann	K	6'	200	28		101

GREEN BAY PACKERS 8-6-0 Phil Bengtson

Scores of Each Game		
17	CHICAGO	0
14	SAN FRANCISCO	7
7	Minnesota	19
28	Detroit	17
21	Los Angeles	34
28	ATLANTA	10
38	Pittsburgh	34
6	Baltimore	14
7	MINNESOTA	9
10	DETROIT	16
20	NEW YORK	10
7	Cleveland	20
21	Chicago	3
45	ST. LOUIS	28

Use Name	Pos.	Hgt	Wgt	Age	Int	Pts
Forrest Gregg	OT	6'4"	250	36		
Bill Hayhoe	OT	6'8"	258	22		
Dick Himes	OT	6'4"	244	23		
Francis Peay	OT	6'5"	250	25		
Dave Bradley	OG	6'4"	245	22		
Gale Gillingham	OG	6'3"	255	25		
Bill Lueck	OG	6'3"	235	23		
Ken Bowman	C	6'3"	230	26		
Bob Hyland	OG-C	6'5"	250	24		
Lionel Aldridge	DE	6'4"	245	27		
Willie Davis	DE	6'3"	245	36	1	
Phil Vandersea	DE	6'3"	235	26		
Francis Winkler	DE	6'3"	230	22		
Bob Brown	DT	6'5"	260	28		
Henry Jordan	DT	6'3"	250	34		
Rich Moore	DT	6'6"	285	22		
Jim Weatherwax	DT	6'7"	260	26		
Lee Roy Caffey	LB	6'3"	250	29	2	
Fred Carr	LB	6'5"	238	23		
Jim Flanigan	LB	6'3"	240	24		
Ray Nitschke	LB	6'3"	235	33		2
Dave Robinson	LB	6'3"	240	28		
Herb Adderley	DB	6'1"	200	30	5	6
Doug Hart	DB	6'	190	30	3	6
Bob Jeter	DB	6'1"	205	31	3	
John Rowser	DB	6'1"	180	25		
Gordon Rule	DB	6'2"	180	23		
Willie Wood	DB	5'10"	190	33	3	
Don Horn	QB	6'2"	195	24		6
Bart Starr	QB	6'1"	190	36		
Bill Stevens	QB	6'3"	195	24		
Donny Anderson	HB	6'3"	210	26		12
Elijah Pitts	HB	6'1"	205	30		6
Travis Williams	HB	6'1"	210	23		54
Jim Grabowski	FB	6'2"	220	25		12
Perry Williams	FB	6'2"	220	22		
Dave Hampton	HB-FB	6'	210	22		42
Carroll Dale	WR	6'1"	200	31		36
Boyd Dowler	WR	6'5"	225	32		24
John Spilis	WR	6'3"	205	21		
Marv Fleming	TE	6'4"	235	27		12
Ron Jones	TE	6'3"	220	22		
Booth Lusteg	K	5'11"	190	28		15
Mike Mercer	K	6'	217	33		38

Zeke Bratkowski – Voluntarily Retired

CHICAGO BEARS 1-13-0 Jim Dooley

Scores of Each Game		
0	Green Bay	17
17	St. Louis	20
24	New York	28
0	MINNESOTA	31
7	Detroit	13
7	LOS ANGELES	9
14	Minnesota	31
38	PITTSBURGH	7
31	Atlanta	48
21	BALTIMORE	24
24	CLEVELAND	28
21	San Francisco	42
3	GREEN BAY	21
3	DETROIT	20

Use Name	Pos.	Hgt	Wgt	Age	Int	Pts
Randy Jackson	OT	6'5"	245	25		
Wayne Mass	OT	6'4"	245	23		
Rufus Mayes	OT	6'5"	255	21		
Bob Pickens	OT	6'4"	258	26		
Bob Wetoska	C-OT	6'3"	240	31		
Jim Cadile	OG	6'3"	240	28		
Howard Mudd (from SF)	OG	6'3"	252	27		
George Seals	OG	6'2"	260	26		
Jim Ferguson (from ATL)	C	6'4"	240	26		
Mike Pyle	C	6'3"	250	30		
Marty Amsler	DE	6'5"	255	26		
Dave Hale	DE	6'7"	230	22		
Willie Holman	DE	6'4"	250	24		
Ed O'Bradovich	DE	6'3"	255	29		2
Loyd Phillips	DE	6'3"	240	24		
Frank Cornish	DT	6'6"	300	25		
Dick Evey	DT	6'2"	245	28		2
Ken Kortas	DT	6'2"	280	27		
Doug Buffone	LB	6'1"	230	25	2	
Dick Butkus	LB	6'3"	245	25	2	2
Tim Casey (to DEN-A)	LB	6'1"	225	25		
Rudy Kuechenberg	LB	6'2"	215	26		
Dave Martin	LB	6'1"	225	22		
Dan Pride	LB	6'3"	225	27	1	
Dick Daniels	DB	5'9"	180	23	3	
Major Hazelton	DB	6'1"	185	24		
Bennie McRae	DB	6'1"	180	28	1	
Joe Taylor	DB	6'2"	200	28	3	
George Youngblood	DB	6'3"	205	24	3	6
Garry Lyle	HB-DB	6'2"	198	23	1	
Virgil Carter	QB	6'1"	185	23		
Jack Concannon	QB	6'3"	205	26		6
Bobby Douglass	QB	6'3"	215	22		12
Gale Sayers	HB	6'	198	26		48
Brian Piccolo	FB-HB	6'	205	25		18
Ronnie Bull	FB	6'	200	29		
Mike Hull	FB	6'3"	220	24		6
Ralph Kurek	FB	6'2"	210	26		
Ross Montgomery	FB	6'3"	220	22		
Ron Copeland	WR	6'4"	196	22		
Dick Gordon	WR	5'11"	190	24		24
Bob Jones	WR	6'4"	196	24		
Jerry Simmons (from ATL)	WR	6'1"	190	26		
Cecil Turner	WR	5'10"	170	25		
Bob Wallace	WR	6'3"	211	23		30
Austin Denney	TE	6'2"	230	25		6
Emilio Vallez	TE	6'2"	210	23		
Ray Odgen	WR-TE	6'5"	225	26		
Bobby Joe Green	K	5'11	175	31		
Mac Percival	K	6'4"	220	29		50

Terry Stoepel – Military Service

CENTRAL DIVISION

MINNESOTA VIKINGS

RUSHING

Last Name	No.	Yds	Avg	TD
Osborn	186	643	3.5	7
Brown	126	430	3.4	3
Reed	83	393	4.7	1
Jones	54	241	4.5	3
Kapp	22	104	4.7	0
Lindsey	6	21	3.5	1
Harris	6	13	2.2	0
Lee	3	9	3.0	0
Cuozzo	3	–4	–1.3	0

RECEIVING

Last Name	No.	Yds	Avg	TD
Washington	39	821	21	9
Henderson	34	553	16	5
Beasley	33	361	11	4
Osborn	22	236	11	1
Brown	21	183	9	0
Grim	10	155	16	1
Reed	7	59	8	2
Jones	3	23	8	0
Lindsey	2	45	23	1
Kramer	2	37	19	1
Harris	2	13	7	0
Hall	1	12	12	0

PUNT RETURNS

Last Name	No.	Yds	Avg	TD
West	39	245	6	0
Grim	4	12	3	0
Bryant	2	9	5	0

KICKOFF RETURNS

Last Name	No.	Yds	Avg	TD
Jones	17	444	26	0
West	9	240	27	0
Reed	1	38	38	0
Lindsey	2	26	13	0
Harris	1	23	23	0
Smith	1	3	3	0
Alderman	1	0	0	0
Sunde	1	0	0	0

PASSING – PUNTING – KICKING

PASSING	Att	Comp	%	Yds	Yd/Att	TD	Int–	%	RK
Kapp	237	120	51	1726	7.3	19	13–	5	10
Cuozzo	98	49	50	693	7.1	4	5–	5	
Lee	11	7	64	79	7.2	1	0–	0	

PUNTING	No	Avg
Lee	67	40.0

KICKING	XP	Att	%	FG	Att	%
Cox	43	43	100	26	37	70

DETROIT LIONS

RUSHING

Last Name	No.	Yds	Avg	TD
Triplett	111	377	3.4	3
Taylor	118	348	2.9	0
Eddy	78	272	3.5	2
Farr	58	245	4.2	4
Landry	33	243	7.4	1
Watkins	62	201	3.2	1
Barney	3	36	12.0	0
Munson	7	31	4.4	0
L. Walton	2	6	3.0	0
McCullouch	1	4	4.0	0
Sanders	1	–8	–8.0	0

RECEIVING

Last Name	No.	Yds	Avg	TD
Sanders	42	656	16	3
McCullouch	33	529	16	5
Triplett	13	141	11	1
Farr	13	94	7	0
Watkins	13	87	7	0
Taylor	13	86	7	0
Wright	12	130	11	2
L. Walton	12	109	9	0
Eddy	10	78	8	1
Malinchak	2	24	12	0
Odle	2	24	12	0

PUNT RETURNS

Last Name	No.	Yds	Avg	TD
Barney	9	191	21	1
L. Walton	9	24	3	0
Vaughn	2	10	5	0
Eddy	1	5	5	0

KICKOFF RETURNS

Last Name	No.	Yds	Avg	TD
Williams	17	563	33	1
L. Walton	12	230	19	0
Barney	7	154	22	0
Vaughn	2	44	22	0
Nowatzke	1	14	14	0
Mooney	2	12	6	0
Yarbrough	1	0	0	0

PASSING – PUNTING – KICKING

PASSING	Att	Comp	%	Yds	Yd/Att	TD	Int–	%	RK
Munson	166	84	51	1062	6.4	7	8–	5	14
Landry	160	80	50	853	5.3	4	10–	6	20
Barton	1	0	0	0	0.0	0	0–	0	
Farr	1	0	0	0	0.0	0	0–	0	
L. Walton	1	1	100	43	43.0	1	0–	0	

PUNTING	No	Avg
Barney	66	34.1
Malinchak	5	36.8
Duncan	3	25.7

KICKING	XP	Att	%	FG	Att	%
Mann	26	26	100	25	37	68

GREEN BAY PACKERS

RUSHING

Last Name	No.	Yds	Avg	TD
T. Williams	129	536	4.2	4
Hampton	80	365	4.6	4
Anderson	87	288	3.3	1
Grabowski	73	261	3.6	1
Pitts	35	134	3.8	0
Starr	7	60	8.6	0
P. Williams	18	55	3.1	0
Horn	3	–7	–2.3	1

RECEIVING

Last Name	No.	Yds	Avg	TD
Dale	45	879	20	6
Dowler	31	477	15	4
T. Williams	27	275	10	3
Fleming	18	226	13	2
Hampton	15	216	14	2
Anderson	14	308	22	1
Grabowski	12	98	8	1
Pitts	9	47	5	1
Spilis	7	89	13	0
P. Williams	4	63	16	0

PUNT RETURNS

Last Name	No.	Yds	Avg	TD
T. Williams	8	189	24	1
Pitts	16	60	4	0
Wood	8	38	5	0

KICKOFF RETURNS

Last Name	No.	Yds	Avg	TD
Hampton	22	582	26	1
T. Williams	21	517	25	1
Robinson	3	31	10	0
Pitts	1	22	22	0
Gillingham	1	13	13	0
Hyland	1	0	0	0
P. Williams	1	0	0	0

PASSING – PUNTING – KICKING

PASSING	Att	Comp	%	Yds	Yd/Att	TD	Int–	%	RK
Horn	168	89	53	1505	9.0	11	11–	7	11
Starr	148	92	62	1161	7.8	9	6–	4	2
Stevens	3	1	33	12	4.0	0	0–	0	

PUNTING	No	Avg
Anderson	58	40.2
Dowler	1	34.0

KICKING	XP	Att	%	FG	Att	%
Mercer	23	23	100	5	17	29
Lusteg	12	12	100	1	5	20

CHICAGO BEARS

RUSHING

Last Name	No.	Yds	Avg	TD
Sayers	236	1032	4.4	8
Douglass	51	408	8.0	2
Bull	44	187	4.3	0
Piccolo	45	148	3.3	2
Hull	29	81	2.8	1
Concannon	22	62	2.8	1
Montgomery	15	52	3.5	0
Gordon	2	28	14.0	0
Kurek	8	24	3.0	0
Carter	4	19	4.8	0
Green	1	17	17.0	0
Wallace	4	16	4.0	0
Denney	1	4	4.0	0

RECEIVING

Last Name	No.	Yds	Avg	TD
Wallace	47	553	12	5
Gordon	36	414	12	4
Denney	22	203	9	1
Piccolo	17	143	8	1
Sayers	17	116	7	0
Simmons	14	182	13	0
Bull	14	91	7	0
Hull	12	63	5	0
Ogden	7	100	14	0
Kurek	4	30	8	0
Montgomery	2	8	4	0
Turner	1	19	19	0
Lyle	1	11	11	0

PUNT RETURNS

Last Name	No.	Yds	Avg	TD
Lyle	12	78	7	0
Piccolo	9	43	5	0
Turner	8	32	4	0
Gordon	1	11	11	0

KICKOFF RETURNS

Last Name	No.	Yds	Avg	TD
Sayers	14	339	24	0
Turner	10	326	33	0
Lyle	11	248	23	0
Gordon	6	105	18	0
Kurek	4	66	17	0
Butkus	3	28	9	0
Seals	2	20	10	0
Holman	1	0	0	0
Kuechenberg	1	0	0	0

PASSING – PUNTING – KICKING

PASSING	Att	Comp	%	Yds	Yd/Att	TD	Int–	%	RK
Concannon	160	87	54	783	4.9	4	8–	5	16
Douglass	148	68	46	773	5.2	5	8–	5	19
Carter	71	36	51	343	4.8	2	5–	7	
Green	2	2	100	30	15.0	0	0–	0	
Sayers	2	0	0	0	0.0	0	0–	0	
Bull	1	0	0	0	0.0	0	0–	0	

PUNTING	No	Avg
Green	76	39.0

KICKING	XP	Att	%	FG	Att	%
Percival	26	26	100	8	21	38

COASTAL DIVISION

LOS ANGELES RAMS 11-3-0 George Allen

Scores of Each Game		
27	Baltimore	20
17	ATLANTA	7
36	NEW ORLEANS	17
27	San Francisco	21
34	GREEN BAY	21
9	Chicago	7
38	Atlanta	6
41	SAN FRANCISCO	30
23	Philadelphia	17
24	DALLAS	23
24	Washington	13
13	MINNESOTA	20
0	Detroit	28
7	BALTIMORE	13

Use Name	Pos.	Hgt	Wgt	Age	Int	Pts
Bob Brown	OT	6'4"	275	26		
Charley Cowan	OT	6'4"	265	31		
Mitch Johnson	OT	6'4"	250	27		
Mike LaHood	OG	6'3"	248	24		
Tom Mack	OG	6'3"	250	25		
Joe Scibelli	OG	6'1"	255	30		
George Burman	C-OG	6'3"	255	26		
Ken Iman	C	6'1"	240	30		
Frank Marchlewski	C	6'2"	240	25		
Rick Cash	DE	6'5"	260	24		
Deacon Jones	DE	6'5"	250	30		
Lamar Lundy	DE	6'7"	250	34		
Diron Talbert	DE	6'5"	245	25		
Coy Bacon	DT	6'4"	270	27		
Roger Brown	DT	6'5"	285	32		
Merlin Olsen	DT	6'5"	270	28		

Use Name	Pos.	Hgt	Wgt	Age	Int	Pts
Maxie Gaughan	LB	6'1"	230	31		
Jack Pardee	LB	6'2"	225	33	1	
John Pergine	LB	6'1"	225	22		
Myron Pottios	LB	6'2"	232	29	1	
Jim Purnell	LB	6'2"	238	27		
Doug Woodlief	LB	6'3"	225	25	4	
Willie Daniel	DB	5'11"	190	31	1	
Alvin Haymond	DB	6'	194	27		
Ed Meador	DB	5'11"	190	32	5	12
Jim Nettles	DB	5'9"	177	27	2	
Richie Petitbon	DB	6'3"	208	31	5	
Nate Shaw	DB	6'2"	205	24		
Ron Smith	DB	6'1"	192	26	3	6
Clancy Williams	DB	6'2"	194	26	4	

Jim Wilson – Injury

Use Name	Pos.	Hgt	Wgt	Age	Int	Pts
Roman Gabriel	QB	6'4"	220	29		30
Karl Sweetan	QB	6'1"	200	26		
Mike Dennis	HB	6'1"	207	25		
Willie Ellison	HB	6'1"	200	24		12
Larry Smith	HB	6'3"	220	21		18
Dick Bass	FB	5'10"	195	32		
Les Josephson	FB	6'	207	26		12
Izzy Lang	FB	6'1"	232	26		
Tommy Mason	HB-FB	6'	195	30		12
David Ray	WR	6'	195	24		
Jack Snow	WR	6'2"	190	26		36
Pat Studstill	WR	6'1"	175	31		
Wendell Tucker	WR	5'10"	185	25		42
Pat Curran	TE	6'3"	238	23		
Bob Klein	TE	6'5"	235	22		6
Billy Truax	TE	6'5"	235	26		30
Bruce Gossett	K	6'2"	230	26		102

BALTIMORE COLTS 8-5-1 Don Shula

Scores of Each Game		
20	LOS ANGELES	27
14	Minnesota	52
21	Atlanta	14
24	PHILADELPHIA	20
30	New Orleans	10
21	SAN FRANCISCO	24
41	WASHINGTON	17
14	GREEN BAY	6
17	San Francisco	20
24	Chicago	21
13	ATLANTA	6
17	DETROIT	17
10	Dallas	27
13	Los Angeles	7

Use Name	Pos.	Hgt	Wgt	Age	Int	Pts
Sam Ball	OT	6'4"	240	25		
Bob Vogel	OT	6'5"	250	27		
Dan Grimm (to WAS)	OG	6'3"	245	28		
Cornelius Johnson	OG	6'2"	245	26		
Glenn Ressler	OG	6'3"	250	25		
Dan Sullivan	OG	6'3"	250	30		
John Williams	OG	6'3"	256	23		
Bill Curry	C	6'2"	235	26		
Carl Mauck	C	6'3"	240	22		
Roy Hilton	DE	6'6"	240	24		
Lou Michaels	DE	6'2"	250	33		75
Bubba Smith	DE	6'7"	295	24		
Ron Kostelnik	DT	6'4"	260	29		
Fred Miller	DT	6'3"	250	28		
Billy Ray Smith	DT	6'4"	250	34		

Use Name	Pos.	Hgt	Wgt	Age	Int	Pts
Mike Curtis	LB	6'2"	232	25		
Dennis Gaubatz	LB	6'2"	232	28	1	
Bob Grant	LB	6'2"	225	23	3	
Ted Hendricks	LB	6'7"	215	21		
Butch Riley	LB	6'2"	220	22		
Don Shinnick	LB	6'	228	34		
Ocie Austin	DB	6'3"	200	22	2	
Jim Duncan	DB	6'2"	200	23		6
Jerry Logan	DB	6'1"	190	28	1	
Lenny Lyles	DB	6'2"	204	33		
Tommy Maxwell	DB	6'2"	195	22	3	
Charlie Stukes	DB	6'3"	212	25	1	
Rick Volk	DB	6'3"	195	24	4	

Use Name	Pos.	Hgt	Wgt	Age	Int	Pts
Earl Morrall	QB	6'1"	206	35		
Johnny Unitas	QB	6'1"	196	36		
Tom Matte	HB	6'	214	30		78
Preston Pearson	HB	6'1"	190	24		
Terry Cole	FB	6'1"	220	24		18
Larry Conjar	FB	6'	214	23		
Perry Lee Dunn	FB	6'2"	215	26		
Jerry Hill	FB	5'11"	215	29		12
Eddie Hinton	WR	6'	200	22		6
Jimmy Orr	WR	5'11"	185	33		12
Ray Perkins	WR	6'	183	27		18
Willie Richardson	WR	6'2"	198	29		18
Sam Havrilak	DB-WR	6'2"	195	21		6
John Mackey	TE	6'3"	224	27		12
Tom Mitchell	TE	6'2"	215	25		18
Roland Moss	TE	6'3"	215	22		
David Lee	K	6'4"	230	25		

ATLANTA FALCONS 6-8-0 Norm Van Brocklin

Scores of Each Game		
24	SAN FRANCISCO	12
7	Los Angeles	17
14	BALTIMORE	21
17	DALLAS	24
21	San Francsico	7
10	Green Bay	28
6	LOS ANGELES	38
21	Detroit	27
48	CHICAGO	31
20	Washington	27
6	Baltimore	13
45	NEW ORLEANS	17
27	Philadelphia	3
10	MINNESOTA	3

Use Name	Pos.	Hgt	Wgt	Age	Int	Pts
Bob Kelly	OT	6'3"	270	29		
George Kunz	OT	6'5"	245	22		
Bill Sandeman	OT	6'6"	250	26		
Bob Breitenstein	OG-OT	6'3"	267	26		
Dick Enderle	OG	6'1"	247	21		
Mal Snider	OG	6'4"	235	22		6
Roy Schmidt	OT-OG	6'3"	250	27		
Bruce Bosley	C	6'2"	244	35		
Jim Waskiewicz	C	6'4"	240	25		
Bob Hughes	DE	6'4"	250	24		
Claude Humphrey	DE	6'5"	255	25		6
John Zook	DE	6'5"	240	21	2	
Dave Cahill	DT	6'3"	245	27		
Glen Condren	DT	6'2"	250	27		
Bill Sabatino	DT	6'3"	245	24		
Jerry Shay	DT	6'3"	245	25		

Use Name	Pos.	Hgt	Wgt	Age	Int	Pts
Ron Acks	LB	6'2"	225	24		6
Grady Allen	LB	6'3"	225	23	1	
Greg Brezina	LB	6'2"	220	23	1	
Ted Cottrell	LB	6'1"	232	22		
Fritz Greenlee	LB	6'2"	230	25		
Don Hansen	LB	6'3"	228	25	2	
Tommy Nobis	LB	6'2"	235	25	1	
Jeff Van Note	LB	6'2"	230	23		
Mike Freeman	DB	5'11"	190	25		
Al Lavan	DB	6'1"	194	22	2	
John Mallory	DB	6'	190	23		6
Ken Reaves	DB	6'3"	205	24	3	
Rudy Redmond	DB	6'	185	22	5	
Jim Weatherford	DB	5'10"	180	23	1	6
Nate Wright (to STL)	DB	5'11"	180	22	2	

Randy Winkler – Military Service

Use Name	Pos.	Hgt	Wgt	Age	Int	Pts
Bob Berry	QB	5'11	190	27		
Randy Johnson	QB	6'3"	196	25		6
Bruce Lemmerman	QB	6'1"	196	23		6
Cannonball Butler	HB	5'10"	185	26		30
Gary McDermott	HB	6'1"	211	23		
Jeff Stanceil	HB	6'	192	22		
Paul Gipson	FB-HB	6'	205	23		6
Harmon Wages	FB	6'1"	210	23		18
Charlie Bryant	HB-FB	6'1"	207	28		
Gail Cogdill	WR	6'2"	200	32		30
Paul Flatley	WR	6'1"	187	28		36
Bob Lee	WR	6'3"	200	24		
Monte Ledbetter (From BUF-A)	WR	6'2"	185	26		
Tom McCauley	WR	6'3"	184	22		
Jim Mitchell	TE	6'2"	224	21		24
Ralph Smith	TE	6'2"	220	30		
Bob Etter	K	5'11"	152	24		78
Billy Lothridge	K	6'1"	190	25		

SAN FRANCISCO FORTY NINERS 4-8-2 Dick Nolan

Scores of Each Game		
12	Atlanta	24
7	Green Bay	14
17	WASHINGTON	17
21	LOS ANGELES	27
7	ATLANTA	21
24	Baltimore	21
14	DETROIT	26
30	Los Angeles	41
20	BALTIMORE	17
38	New Orleans	43
24	Dallas	24
42	CHICAGO	21
7	Minnesota	10
14	PHILADELPHIA	13

Use Name	Pos.	Hgt	Wgt	Age	Int	Pts
Cas Banaszek	OT	6'3"	240	23		
Lance Olssen	OT	6'5"	267	22		
Len Rohde	OT	6'4"	250	31		
Elmer Collett	OG	6'4"	244	24		
Woody Peoples	OG	6'2"	247	26		
Randy Beisler	OT-OG	6'4"	255	24		
Forrest Blue	C	6'5"	248	23		
Bill Belk	DE	6'3"	242	23		
Tommy Hart	DE	6'3"	235	24		
Stan Hindman	DE	6'3"	237	25		
Earl Edwards	DT-DE	6'6"	276	23		
Charlie Krueger	DT	6'4"	270	33	1	
Roland Lakes	DT	6'4"	265	29		6
Sam Silas	DE-DT	6'4"	255	26		

Use Name	Pos.	Hgt	Wgt	Age	Int	Pts
Ed Beard	LB	6'2"	220	29		
Harold Hays	LB	6'3"	225	28		
Frank Nunley	LB	6'2"	230	23	1	
Jim Sniadecki	LB	6'2"	220	22		
Skip Vanderbundt	LB	6'3"	240	22		
Dave Wilcox	LB	6'3"	237	26	2	
Kermit Alexander	DB	5'11"	186	28	5	
Johnny Fuller	DB	6'	175	23	1	
Jim Johnson	DB	6'2"	187	31	5	
Mel Phillips	DB	6'	192	27		
Al Randolph	DB	6'2"	204	25	2	
Rosey Taylor (from CHI)	DB	5'11"	186	30	2	
John Woitt	DB	5'11"	170	23	1	6

Kevin Hardy – Knee Injury
Dave Hettema – Military Service
Matt Hazeltine – Voluntary Retirement

Use Name	Pos.	Hgt	Wgt	Age	Int	Pts
John Brodie	QB	6'1"	204	34		
Steve Spurrier	QB	6'2"	203	24		
Doug Cunningham	HB	5'11"	190	23		18
Gene Moore	HB	6'	208	22		
Noland Smith (From KC-A)	HB	5'6"	156	25		
Jimmy Thomas	HB	6'1"	216	22		36
Gary Lewis	FB-HB	6'3"	230	27		
Ken Willard	FB	6'2"	225	26		60
Bill Tucker	FB	6'2"	226	25		24
Lee Johnson	WR	6'1"	204	24		
Clifton McNeil	WR	6'2"	185	29		18
Gene Washington	WR	6'1"	186	22		18
Dick Witcher	WR	6'3"	204	24		18
Bill Wondolowski	WR	5'10"	168	22		
Ted Kwalick	TE	6'4"	230	22		6
Bob Windsor	TE	6'4"	230	26		12
Tommy Davis	K	6'	225	34		22
Momcilo Gavric	K	5'10"	167	31		31
Jon Kilgore	K	6'1"	205	25		

COASTAL DIVISION

LOS ANGELES RAMS

RUSHING

Last Name	No.	Yds	Avg	TD
L. Smith	166	599	3.6	1
Josephson	124	461	3.7	0
Gabriel	35	156	4.5	5
Mason	33	135	4.1	1
Ellison	20	56	2.8	1
Meador	1	5	5.0	0
Bass	1	1	1.0	0
Lang	1	1	1.0	0
Sweetan	1	–1	–1.0	0

RECEIVING

Last Name	No.	Yds	Avg	TD
Snow	49	734	15	6
L. Smith	46	300	7	2
Tucker	38	629	17	7
Truax	37	431	12	5
Josephson	32	295	9	2
Mason	11	185	17	1
Ellison	4	31	8	1
Studstill	3	28	9	0
Klein	2	17	9	1

PUNT RETURNS

Last Name	No.	Yds	Avg	TD
Haymond	33	435	13	0
R. Smith	23	122	5	0
Pergine	1	0	0	0
Meador	1	–1	–1	0

KICKOFF RETURNS

Last Name	No.	Yds	Avg	TD
R. Smith	27	585	22	0
Haymond	16	375	23	0
Lang	4	70	18	0
Ellison	2	38	19	0
Curran	2	28	14	0
Burman	1	11	11	0
Klein	1	0	0	0

PASSING – PUNTING – KICKING

PASSING	Att	Comp	%	Yds	Yd/Att	TD	Int–	%	RK
Gabriel	399	217	54	2549	6.4	24	7–	2	4
Sweetan	13	5	38	101	7.8	1	0–	0	
Ellison	2	0	0	0	0.0	0	0–	0	
Meador	1	0	0	0	0.0	0	0–	0	
L. Smith	1	0	0	0	0.0	0	0–	0	

PUNTING	No	Avg
Studstill	80	40.7

KICKING	XP	Att	%	FG	Att	%
Gossett	36	36	100	22	34	65

BALTIMORE COLTS

RUSHING

Last Name	No.	Yds	Avg	TD
Matte	235	909	3.9	11
Cole	73	204	2.8	2
Hill	49	143	2.9	2
Pearson	24	81	3.4	0
Havrilak	5	49	9.8	1
Dunn	13	45	3.5	0
Perkins	3	36	12.0	0
Unitas	11	23	2.1	0
Mackey	2	3	1.5	0
Conjar	1	0	0.0	0
Hinton	1	–3	–3.0	0

RECEIVING

Last Name	No.	Yds	Avg	TD
Richardson	43	646	15	3
Matte	43	513	12	2
Mackey	34	443	13	2
Perkins	28	391	14	3
Orr	25	474	19	2
Hinton	13	269	21	1
Hill	11	44	4	0
Mitchell	9	199	22	3
Cole	9	65	7	1
Dunn	5	30	6	0
Pearson	4	64	16	0
Havrilak	1	5	5	0

PUNT RETURNS

Last Name	No.	Yds	Avg	TD
Volk	10	58	6	0
Havrilak	13	56	4	0
Logan	8	41	5	0
Pearson	6	37	6	0

KICKOFF RETURNS

Last Name	No.	Yds	Avg	TD
Pearson	31	706	23	0
Duncan	19	560	29	1
Hinton	1	24	24	0

PASSING – PUNTING – KICKING

PASSING	Att	Comp	%	Yds	Yd/Att	TD	Int–	%	RK
Unitas	327	178	54	2342	7.2	12	20–	6	9
Morrall	99	46	46	755	7.6	5	7–	7	
Matte	3	1	33	46	15.3	0	0–	0	

PUNTING	No	Avg
Lee	57	45.3

KICKING	XP	Att	%	FG	Att	%
Michaels	33	34	97	14	31	45

ATLANTA FALCONS

RUSHING

Last Name	No.	Yds	Avg	TD
Butler	163	655	4.0	3
Wages	72	375	5.2	2
Gipson	62	303	4.9	1
Bryant	50	246	4.9	0
Mitchell	5	77	15.4	0
Berry	20	68	3.4	0
Lemmerman	10	57	5.7	1
Johnson	11	55	5.0	1
McCauley	2	49	24.5	0
McDermott	7	6	0.9	0
Stanceil	4	–1	–0.3	0

RECEIVING

Last Name	No.	Yds	Avg	TD
Flatley	45	834	19	6
Cogdill	24	374	16	5
Mitchell	22	339	15	4
Wages	22	228	10	1
Butler	17	297	17	2
Gipson	4	33	8	0
Smith	2	17	9	0
Bryant	2	15	8	0
Ledbetter	1	16	16	0
Brezina	1	9	9	0

PUNT RETURNS

Last Name	No.	Yds	Avg	TD
Mallory	13	42	3	0
Freeman	4	30	8	0
Wright	4	21	5	0
Cahill	1	0	0	0
McCauley	4	–11	–3	0

KICKOFF RETURNS

Last Name	No.	Yds	Avg	TD
Bryant	21	407	19	0
Butler	13	405	31	0
Gipson	9	145	16	0
Wages	6	76	13	0
Snider	1	48	48	1
Kunz	1	13	13	0
Stanceil	1	10	10	0

PASSING – PUNTING – KICKING

PASSING	Att	Comp	%	Yds	Yd/Att	TD	Int–	%	RK
Berry	124	71	57	1087	8.8	10	2–	2	
Johnson	93	51	55	788	8.5	8	5–	5	
Lemmerman	62	25	40	330	5.3	1	4–	6	
Gipson	1	0	0	0	0.0	0	1–	100	
Lothridge	1	1	100	9	9.0	0	0–	0	
Wages	1	1	100	16	16.0	1	0–	0	

PUNTING	No	Avg
Lothridge	69	41.2

KICKING	XP	Att	%	FG	Att	%
Etter	33	33	100	15	30	50

SAN FRANCISCO FORTY NINERS

RUSHING

Last Name	No.	Yds	Avg	TD
Willard	171	557	3.3	7
Cunningham	147	541	3.7	3
Thomas	23	190	8.3	1
Tucker	20	72	3.6	2
Brodie	11	62	5.6	0
Spurrier	5	49	9.8	0
Windsor	5	39	7.8	0
Davis	2	21	10.5	0
Lewis	4	5	1.3	0
Moore	2	4	2.0	0
Washington	1	–4	–4.0	0

RECEIVING

Last Name	No.	Yds	Avg	TD
Washington	51	711	14	3
Cunningham	51	484	9	0
Windsor	49	597	12	2
Willard	36	326	9	3
Witcher	33	435	13	3
Thomas	18	364	20	5
McNeil	17	255	15	3
Tucker	14	104	7	2
L. Johnson	4	42	11	0
Kwalick	2	32	16	1
Moore	2	28	14	0
Edwards	1	1	1	0

PUNT RETURNS

Last Name	No.	Yds	Avg	TD
Smith	10	46	5	0
Cunningham	3	23	8	0
Fuller	5	12	2	0
Alexander	4	–18	–5	0

KICKOFF RETURNS

Last Name	No.	Yds	Avg	TD
Smith	14	315	23	0
Cunningham	9	207	23	0
Fuller	8	155	19	0
Lewis	5	155	31	0
Alexander	3	47	16	0
Taylor	1	16	16	0
Wilcox	1	10	10	0
Edwards	3	3	1	0
Kwalick	1	0	0	0
Sniadecki	1	0	0	0
Tucker	1	0	0	0

PASSING – PUNTING – KICKING

PASSING	Att	Comp	%	Yds	Yd/Att	TD	Int–	%	RK
Brodie	347	194	56	2405	6.9	16	15–	4	7
Spurrier	146	81	55	926	6.3	5	11–	8	17
Cunningham	3	3	100	48	16.0	1	0–	0	

PUNTING	No	Avg
Kilgore	36	40.3
Davis	23	41.5
Spurrier	12	39.0

KICKING	XP	Att	%	FG	Att	%
Gavric	22	24	92	3	11	27
Davis	13	13	100	3	10	30

1969 A.F.L. Losing One Status to Gain Another

With the announcement of the realignment of pro football for 1970, the AFL learned that this was its last season in existence. None of the league officials grieved very heavily, since all ten clubs would be part of the NFL's American Conference next year, but some fans and players openly mourned the passing of the AFL as a separate organization. With two distinct leagues, the Super Bowl had much of the flavor of baseball's World Series, but some people expected the excitement to pale with the amalgamation into one league.

Twenty players from the premier season of 1960 still were active in 1969. George Blanda, Billy Cannon, Gino Cappelletti, Tom Flores, Larry Grantham, Wayne Hawkins, Jim Hunt, Harry Jacobs, Jack Kemp, Jacky Lee, Paul Lowe, Paul Maguire, Billy Mathis, Don Maynard, Ron Mix, Jim Otto, Babe Parilli, Johnny Robinson, Paul Rochester, and Ernie Wright all followed different paths into the new league, and each of them stuck around for ten years to watch the AFL progress from an inferior product in fancy settings to a top-notch league on a par with the long-established NFL.

The AFL went out not with a whisper but with the trumpets of victory. The Kansas City Chiefs, who won the league championship in a new playoff setup which pitted first- and second-place finishers in the opposite divisions against each other in an opening round before the championship game, won a final triumph for the AFL by beating the Minnesota Vikings 23-7 in the Super Bowl.

EASTERN DIVISION

New York Jets—The Jets coasted to another divisional title, beating every Eastern opponent they met during the season. Their four losses to Western teams, however, pointed out weak spots in the defending champions' club. The New York secondary folded against a good passing attack. Last year's starting cornerbacks, Johnny Sample and Randy Beverly, both fell out of favor with coach Weeb Ewbank, and the younger replacements couldn't handle top-notch receivers. A strong pass rush and good linebacking compensated for the leaky secondary to some extent, with Gerry Philbin, John Elliott, and Larry Grantham key men in the front lines. The Jet offense still put a lot of points on the scoreboard, with Joe Namath, Matt Snell, Emerson Boozer, Don Maynard, George Sauer, and Pete Lammons moving the ball against the best of defenses.

Houston Oilers—The Houston defense played so well that the team won half its games with little help from the offense. Elvin Bethea, George Webster, Miller Farr, and Ken Houston all ranked with the AFL's top defenders, and Zeke Moore, Garland Boyette, and W. K. Hicks were quality players who stood up to any attack in the league. Not even the absence of Leroy Mitchell, the fine cornerback obtained from Boston who suffered a broken neck in training camp, seriously hurt the Oilers' defense. The offense, however, creaked and groaned with pain in several spots. Hoyle Granger and Roy Hopkins, the starting runners, both were fullback types, strong on straight-ahead plays but not fast enough to make outside plays work. Pete Beathard compounded the unit's problems by failing to ignite an effective passing attack; after leading the club to a divisional crown in 1967, the twenty-seven-year-old passer had made little progress since.

Boston Patriots—New head coach Clive Rush found instant unpopularity with the fans and press when the Patriots lost their first seven games of the season, but his charges found themselves and won four of their next five matches. They shut out Houston 24-0, beat Cincinnati, Buffalo, and Miami, and lost to Miami 17-16 when Rush elected to gamble for a two-point conversion which failed. The Boston defense, stripped of stars Nick Buoniconti and Leroy Mitchell in off-season trades, had no charismatic players or exciting standouts, but the unit grew tighter with each game. The offense got a boost from rookies Carl Garrett, Ron Sellers, and Mike Montler and veterans Mike Taliaferro and Jim Nance, both rebounding from off-seasons.

Buffalo Bills—Head coach Johnny Rauch quit the Oakland Raiders to come to Buffalo, and he lost more games in this one year than he had in three years in Oakland. But the big story of the season was the arrival of O. J. Simpson. The Heisman Trophy winner from USC had openly expressed reluctance about playing in Buffalo, but once he signed with the Bills, he gave the team a much-needed running threat in the backfield. Simpson gained 697 yards rushing despite playing behind a porous line and under a head coach who built his offense around passing.

Miami Dolphins—The Dolphins slipped back into last place in the East, and head coach George Wilson paid for it with his job. Wilson, however, left behind a solid core of quality players for the next regime. Guard Larry Little and linebacker Nick Buoniconti had joined the team this year in trades which cost Miami very little, and rookies Lloyd Mumford, Bill Stanfill, and Mercury Morris further swelled the ranks of top players on the team. Already on the Miami scene were Bob Griese, Larry Csonka, Jim Kiick, Manny Fernandez, and Howard Twilley—enough talent to change Miami's future fortunes.

WESTERN DIVISION

Oakland Raiders—Throwing for thirty-four touchdowns, Lamonica won the league MVP award for the second time in the past three seasons. On the other end of Lamonica's passes were two complementary wide receivers, Warren Wells, whose strong point was speed, and Fred Biletnikoff, who relied on good moves and sure hands to make fifty-four catches. With the running attack a secondary feature, the offensive line spent most of its time expertly shielding Lamonica from enemy rushers. On defense, the Raiders got better the farther back you went. The line was adequate; Tom Keating recovered from his Achilles tendon injury, but Dan Birdwell missed most of the season with a bad knee. The linebacking corps of Dan Conners, Gus Otto, and Chip Oliver used the excellent mobility to fine advantage, and the secondary of Willie Brown, Nemiah Wilson, Dave Grayson, and George Atkinson had few peers in the pro ranks. With new coach John Madden blending all the pieces together into a harmonious whole, the Raiders edged the Chiefs out for first place in the West by beating them twice during the season.

Kansas City Chiefs—While the Raiders moved the ball primarily on passes, the Chiefs stuck to the ground on offense. Quarterbacks Len Dawson and Mike Livingston had a deep contingent of running backs to call on; Mike Garrett and Warren McVea provided speed from the halfback slot, and Robert Holmes and Wendell Hayes gave the Chiefs power at fullback. These four handled the running chores so well that coach Hank Stram moved Curtis McClinton to tight end and used rookie Ed Podolak exclusively as a kick returner. The Chiefs reversed Oakland's strategy and used the pass only to loosen enemy defenses for the run. The Kansas City defensive unit was brimming with talented players. Jerry Mays and Buck Buchanan had long starred in the line, and Aaron Brown and Curley Culp had fit in since the championship season of 1966. The linebacking trio of Bobby Bell, Willie Lanier, and Jim Lynch had everything. The secondary of Emmitt Thomas, rookie Jim Marsalis, Johnny Robinson, and Jim Kearney left few enemy receivers unattended.

San Diego Chargers—Five games from the end of the season, a bad case of ulcers forced Sid Gillman to give up the coaching reign and concentrate on his general manager's duties. Of course, the Chargers' 4-5-0 record at the time may have contributed to Gillman's decision and to his ulcers. Assistant Charlie Waller moved up to head coach, and after the Chargers lost their first game for him, the team won its last four outings. The talent on the roster was deep enough to make winning an expected event, not just a late-season occurrence. Halfback Dickie Post, receivers Lance Alworth and Gary Garrison, and guard Walt Sweeney all stood out for excellence, but the Chargers were let down by John Hadl's poor season and Ron Mix's injury-plagued campaign. The defense got good years out of Steve DeLong, Pete Barnes, Rick Redman, Jim Hill, Bob Howard, and Kenny Graham, but the rest of the unit needed patching up.

Denver Broncos—The Broncos began the season with impressive victories over the Patriots and Jets, but injuries took most of the steam out of the offense by mid-season. Quarterback Steve Tensi was bothered by a bad knee, receivers Mike Haffner and Bill Van Heusen missed the last month of the season with injured knees, and runner Floyd Little missed five games with shoulder and knee problems. Little's absence particularly hurt the team, as he had developed into a top runner before getting hurt. Inexperience rather than injuries troubled the defense, but this young unit came up with occasional sterling performances like a 13-0 shutout of the Chargers. The strength of the defense lay up front, where Rich Jackson and Dave Costa were two of the league's top linemen. The linebackers and deep backs all were young players, with speedy rookie cornerback Bill Thompson one of the most exciting newcomers in the AFL.

Cincinnati Bengals—Paul Brown's youth parade brought Greg Cook, Speedy Thomas, Horst Muhlmann, Bill Bergey, Royce Berry, and Ken Riley to Cincinnati as freshman starters this year, with Cook an immediate sensation at quarterback. After starring in the College All-Star game, the blond, handsome Cook reported to the Bengal's training camp and took right over as the offensive leader. On opening day, he threw two touchdown passes in leading the team to a victory over Miami. One week later, he threw three scoring passes and ran for another six points in engineering an upset over San Diego, and he helped beat the Chiefs in their third game. Cook then sat out a month of action with a sore passing arm, but he returned to beat Oakland.

FINAL TEAM STATISTICS

OFFENSE

	BOSTON	BUFFALO	CIN.	DENVER	HOUSTON	K.C.	MIAMI	NEW YORK	OAKLAND	S.D.
FIRST DOWNS:										
Total	166	224	172	243	256	258	224	252	261	275
by Rushing	64	83	66	87	95	129	73	98	84	119
by Passing	87	122	95	130	146	125	131	130	153	131
by Penalty	15	19	11	26	15	4	20	24	24	25
RUSHING:										
Number	367	384	363	394	440	522	401	469	459	455
Yards	1489	1522	1523	1637	1706	2220	1513	1782	1765	1985
Average Yards	4.1	4.0	4.2	4.2	3.9	4.3	3.8	3.8	3.8	4.4
Touchdowns	11	7	10	12	12	19	12	14	4	18
PASSING:										
Attempts	338	442	308	403	489	351	424	394	439	444
Completions	162	215	163	192	239	196	201	203	227	208
Completion Percentage	47.9	48.6	52.9	47.6	48.9	55.8	47.4	51.5	51.7	46.8
Passing Yards	2191	2716	2720	2835	3147	2638	2558	2939	3375	2927
Average Yards per Att.	6.5	6.1	8.8	7.0	6.4	7.5	6.0	7.5	7.7	6.6
Average Yards per Comp.	13.5	12.6	16.7	14.8	13.2	13.5	12.7	14.5	14.9	14.1
Tackled Att. to Pass	24	42	57	44	36	26	53	16	12	33
Yards Lost Tackled	261	371	375	311	322	251	481	138	104	301
Net Yards	1930	2345	2345	2524	2825	2387	2077	2801	3271	2626
Touchdowns	19	17	22	23	15	16	12	21	36	13
Interceptions	18	30	15	23	31	20	29	20	26	21
Percent Intercepted	5.3	6.8	4.9	5.7	6.3	5.7	6.8	5.1	5.9	4.7
PUNTS:										
Number	70	78	85	72	70	68	85	56	69	71
Average Distance	41.5	44.5	38.8	40.1	38.9	44.4	40.6	44.3	42.7	44.6
PUNT RETURNS:										
Number	23	31	23	37	43	32	45	39	39	31
Yards	212	187	135	450	391	251	266	256	225	300
Average Yards	9.2	6.0	5.9	12.2	9.1	7.8	5.9	6.6	5.8	9.7
Touchdowns	0	0	0	0	0	0	0	0	0	0
KICKOFF RETURNS:										
Number	54	62	55	56	49	41	60	46	42	39
Yards	1247	1475	1165	1323	1141	1090	1383	985	996	842
Average Yards	23.1	23.8	21.2	23.6	23.3	26.6	23.1	21.4	23.7	21.6
Touchdowns	0	0	0	0	0	1	1	0	0	0
INTERCEPTION RETURNS:										
Number	20	19	21	14	23	32	18	29	26	31
Yards	326	251	362	228	335	595	317	348	484	444
Average Yards	16.3	13.2	17.2	16.3	14.6	18.6	17.6	12.0	18.6	14.3
Touchdowns	1	1	1	2	2	2	2	1	4	3
PENALTIES:										
Number	77	67	50	80	70	62	53	61	100	63
Yards	837	632	556	753	730	757	631	725	1274	731
FUMBLES:										
Number	15	35	30	15	24	34	27	19	17	27
Number Lost	10	21	23	8	17	19	13	13	7	13
POINTS:										
Total	266	230	280	297	278	359	233	353	377	288
PAT (kick) Attempts	29	24	33	37	29	38	27	33	45	34
PAT (kick) Made	26	23	32	36	29	38	26	33	45	33
PAT (2–Point) Attempts	3	2	0	0	2	2	1	4	0	1
PAT (2–Point) Made	1	0	0	0	2	0	0	1	0	0
FG Attempts	34	26	24	29	40	35	22	47	37	28
FG Made	14	17	16	13	19	27	13	32	20	15
Percent FG Made	41.2	65.4	66.7	44.8	47.5	77.1	59.1	68.1	54.1	53.6
Safeties	2	0	1	0	1	0	0	0	1	0

DEFENSE

	BOSTON	BUFFALO	CIN.	DENVER	HOUSTON	K.C.	MIAMI	NEW YORK	OAKLAND	S.D.
FIRST DOWNS:										
Total	278	236	278	276	183	181	206	229	232	232
by Rushing	142	106	135	95	77	53	66	63	90	71
by Passing	115	118	130	151	93	111	126	151	107	148
by Penalty	21	12	13	30	13	17	14	15	35	13
RUSHING:										
Number	528	454	523	436	430	314	422	343	438	366
Yards	2359	1858	2651	1709	1556	1091	1489	1326	1661	1442
Average Yards	4.5	4.1	5.1	3.9	3.6	3.5	3.5	3.9	3.8	3.9
Touchdowns	18	17	13	15	10	6	9	7	13	11
PASSING:										
Attempts	348	368	396	437	371	426	404	437	422	423
Completions	203	175	205	223	167	200	196	232	164	241
Completion Percentage	58.3	47.6	51.8	51.0	45.0	46.9	48.5	53.1	38.9	57.0
Passing Yards	2610	2772	2866	3295	2495	2491	2845	3086	2511	3075
Average Yards per Att.	7.5	7.5	7.2	7.5	6.7	5.8	7.0	7.1	6.0	7.3
Average Yards per Comp.	12.9	15.8	14.0	14.8	14.9	12.5	14.5	13.3	15.3	12.8
Tackled Att. to Pass	22	31	16	45	32	48	25	42	47	35
Yards Lost Tackled	159	296	180	363	278	419	208	330	402	280
Net Yards	2451	2476	2686	2932	2217	2072	2637	2756	2109	2795
Touchdowns	18	21	24	19	18	10	25	22	15	22
Interceptions	20	19	21	14	23	32	18	29	26	31
Percent Intercepted	5.7	5.2	5.3	3.2	6.2	7.5	4.5	6.6	6.2	7.3
PUNTS:										
Number	55	62	55	71	85	84	80	69	87	76
Average Distance	38.6	42.7	41.4	43.1	43.1	43.0	44.1	39.8	41.8	40.3
PUNT RETURNS:										
Number	19	45	39	35	37	43	30	28	37	30
Yards	114	466	297	246	196	502	130	280	151	291
Average Yards	6.0	10.4	7.6	7.0	5.3	11.7	4.3	10.0	4.1	9.7
Touchdowns	0	0	0	0	0	0	0	0	0	0
KICKOFF RETURNS:										
Number	56	55	39	21	38	59	47	72	64	53
Yards	1068	1322	1065	471	792	1431	1073	1669	1518	1238
Average Yards	19.1	24.0	27.3	22.4	20.8	24.3	22.8	23.2	23.7	23.4
Touchdowns	0	0	1	1	0	0	0	0	0	0
INTERCEPTION RETURNS:										
Number	18	30	15	23	31	20	29	20	26	21
Yards	225	449	239	421	441	325	596	380	349	265
Average Yards	12.5	15.0	15.9	18.3	14.2	16.3	20.6	19.0	13.4	12.6
Touchdowns	1	2	0	4	3	3	3	2	1	0
PENALTIES:										
Number	69	71	72	84	61	39	66	69	81	71
Yards	810	719	824	901	592	443	840	788	918	791
FUMBLES:										
Number	33	25	19	24	27	25	27	25	25	13
Number Lost	14	18	15	14	17	15	13	16	16	6
POINTS:										
Total	316	359	367	344	279	177	332	269	242	276
PAT (kick) Attempts	38	40	42	38	33	17	33	28	27	33
PAT (kick) Made	37	39	41	38	33	16	32	28	26	31
PAT (2–Point) Attempts	0	0	0	2	0	2	4	4	2	1
PAT (2–Point) Made	0	0	0	0	0	0	1	2	0	1
FG Attempts	28	41	46	32	30	27	36	27	30	25
FG Made	17	26	24	22	16	15	24	15	14	13
Percent FG Made	60.7	63.4	52.2	68.8	53.3	55.6	66.7	55.6	46.7	52.0
Safeties	0	1	1	0	0	1	2	0	0	0

INTER–DIVISIONAL PLAYOFFS

December 20, at New York (Attendance 62,977)

SCORING

NEW YORK	3	0	0	3– 6
KANSAS CITY	0	3	3	7–13

First Quarter
N.Y. J. Turner, 27 yard field goal

Second Quarter
K.C. Stenerud, 23 yard field goal

Third Quarter
K.C. Stenerud, 25 yard field goal

Fourth Quarter
N.Y. J. Turner, 7 yard field goal
K.C. Richardson, 19 yard pass from Dawson PAT–Stenerud (kick)

TEAM STATISTICS

N.Y.		K.C.
19	First Downs–Total	14
5	First Downs–Rushing	3
11	First Downs–Passing	9
3	First Downs–Penalty	2
1	Fumbles–Number	0
1	Fumbles–Lost Ball	0
3	Penalties–Number	5
15	Yards Penalized	63
0	Missed Field Goals	3
64	Offensive Plays–Total	59
235	Net Yards	276
3.7	Average Gain	4.7
4	Giveaways	0
0	Takeaways	4
–4	Difference	+4

INDIVIDUAL STATISTICS

NEW YORK	No	Yds	Avg.	KANSAS CITY	No	Yds	Avg.
RUSHING							
Shell	12	61	5.1	Garrett	18	67	3.7
Boozer	3	14	4.7	Hayes	10	32	3.2
Mathis	6	11	1.8	Holmes	1	0	0.0
Namath	1	1	1.0	McVea	1	0	0.0
	22	87	4.0		30	99	3.3
RECEIVING							
Sauer	5	61	12.2	Hayes	5	46	9.2
Lammons	3	37	12.3	Taylor	2	74	37.0
B. Turner	2	25	12.5	Arbanas	2	39	19.5
Maynard	1	18	18.0	Holmes	1	29	29.0
Boozer	1	10	10.0	Richardson	1	19	19.0
Snell	1	9	9.0	Pitts	1	–6	–6.0
Mathis	1	4	4.0		12	201	16.8
	14	164	11.7				
PUNTING							
O'Neal	5		37.2	Wilson	6		33.5
PUNT RETURNS							
Battle	2	10	5.0	Garrett	1	10	10.0
				Mitchell	1	4	4.0
					2	14	7.0
KICKOFF RETURNS							
Battle	3	64	21.3	Holmes	2	33	16.5
Nock	1	33	33.0	Hayes	1	31	31.0
	4	97	24.3		3	64	21.3
INTERCEPTION RETURNS							
None				Marsalis	2	42	21.0
				Thomas	1	0	0.0
					3	42	14.0

PASSING

NEW YORK	Att.	Comp.	Comp. Pct.	Yds.	Int.	Yds/ Att.	Yds/ Comp.	Yds Lost Tkld.
Namath	40	14	35.0	164	3	4.1	11.7	2–16
KANSAS CITY								
Dawson	27	12	44.4	201	0	7.4	16.8	2–24

December 21, at Oakland (Attendance 53,539)

SCORING

OAKLAND	28	7	14	7–56
HOUSTON	0	0	0	7– 7

First Quarter
Oak. Biletnikoff, 13 yard pass from Lamonica PAT–Blanda (kick)
Oak. Atkinson, 57 yard interception return PAT–Blanda (kick)
Oak. Sherman, 24 yard pass from Lamonica PAT–Blanda (kick)
Oak. Biletnikoff, 31 yard pass from Lamonica PAT–Blanda (kick)

Second Quarter
Oak. Smith, 60 yard pass from Lamonica PAT–Blanda (kick)

Third Quarter
Oak. Sherman, 23 yard pass from Lamonica PAT–Blanda (kick)
Oak. Gannon, 3 yard pass from Lamonica PAT–Blanda (kick)

Fourth Quarter
Hou. Reed, 8 yard pass from Beathard PAT–Gerela (kick)
Oak. Hubbard, 4 yard rush PAT–Blanda (kick)

TEAM STATISTICS

OAK.		HOUS.
17	First Downs–Total	14
5	First Downs–Rushing	1
11	First Downs–Passing	10
1	First Downs–Penalty	3
3	Fumbles–Number	3
1	Fumbles–Lost Ball	2
7	Penalties–Number	3
63	Yards Penalized	48
0	Missed Field Goals	0
60	Offensive Plays–Total	71
412	Net Yards	197
6.9	Average Gain	2.8
4	Giveaways	5
5	Takeaways	4
+1	Difference	–1

INDIVIDUAL STATISTICS

OAKLAND	No	Yds	Avg.	HOUSTON	No	Yds	Avg.
RUSHING							
Dixon	13	48	3.7	Granger	14	29	2.1
Todd	8	31	3.9	LeVias	1	4	4.0
Hubbard	6	19	3.2	Campbell	1	0	0.0
Hagberg	2	9	4.5	Beathard	3	–5	–1.7
Smith	8	3	0.4		19	28	1.5
	37	110	3.0				
RECEIVING							
Smith	4	103	25.8	Reed	7	81	11.6
Sherman	4	60	15.0	Beirne	5	48	9.6
Biletnikoff	3	70	23.3	Granger	3	31	10.3
Todd	1	40	40.0	Haik	2	42	21.0
Hubbard	1	33	33.0	LeVias	1	7	7.0
Cannon	1	3	3.0		18	209	11.6
	14	309	22.1				
PUNTING							
Eischeid	5		42.0	Burrell	11		41.4
PUNT RETURNS							
Atkinson	2	19	9.5	LeVias	2	4	2.0
Sherman	1	8	8.0				
	3	27	9.0				
KICKOFF RETURNS							
Atkinson	1	38	38.0	LeVias	4	69	17.3
Sherman	1	26	26.0	Burrell	3	61	20.3
	2	64	32.0		7	130	18.6
INTERCEPTION RETURNS							
Atkinson	1	57	57.0	Farr	1	0	0.0
Brown	1	15	15.0	Moore	1	0	0.0
Wilson	1	0	0.0	Peacock	1	0	0.0
	3	72	24.0		3	0	0.0

PASSING

OAKLAND	Att.	Cmp.	Comp. Pct.	Yds.	Int.	Yds/ Att.	Yds/ Comp.	Lost Tkld.
Lamonica	17	13	76.5	276	1	16.2	21.2	
Blanda	5	1	20.0	33	2	6.6	33.0	
	22	14	63.6	309	3	14.0	22.1	1– 7
HOUSTON								
Beathard	46	18	39.1	209	3	4.5	11.6	6–40

NEW YORK JETS 10-4-0 Weeb Ewbank

Scores of Each Game		
33	Buffalo	19
19	Denver	21
27	San Diego	34
23	Boston	14
21	Cincinnati	7
26	HOUSTON	17
23	BOSTON	17
34	MIAMI	31
16	BUFFALO	6
16	KANSAS CITY	34
40	CINCINNATI	7
14	OAKLAND	27
34	Houston	26
27	Miami	9

Use Name	Pos.	Hgt	Wgt	Age	Int	Pts
Winston Hill	OT	6'4"	280	27		
Sam Walton	OT	6'5"	270	26		
Roger Finnie	OT	6'3"	245	22		
Paul Seiler	C-OT	6'4"	255	23		
Dave Herman	OG	6'2"	255	27		
Pete Perreault	OG	6'3"	248	30		
Randy Rasmussen	OG	6'2"	255	24		
Gordon Wright	OG	6'3"	245	25		
John Schmitt	C	6'4"	245	26		
Paul Crane	LB-C	6'2"	205	25	3	12
Verlon Biggs	DE	6'4"	270	26		
Jimmie Jones	DE	6'3"	215	22		
Gerry Philbin	DE	6'2"	245	28	1	
John Elliott	DT	6'4"	245	24		
Carl McAdams	DT	6'3"	240	25		
Paul Rochester	DT	6'2"	255	32		
Steve Thompson	DT	6'5"	245	24		
Al Atkinson	LB	6'1"	230	26	2	
Ralph Baker	LB	6'3"	235	27	1	
Jim Carroll	LB	6'1"	230	26		
Larry Grantham	LB	6'	210	30		
John Neidert	LB	6'2"	230	23		
Bill Baird	DB	5'10"	180	30	5	
Mike Battle	DB	6'1"	175	23	1	
Randy Beverly	DB	5'11"	185	25	2	
John Dockery	DB	6'	186	24	5	
Cornell Gordon	DB	6'	187	28	4	
Jim Hudson	DB	6'2"	210	26	2	
Cecil Leonard	DB	5'11"	170	23		
Jim Richards	DB	6'1"	180	22	3	
Harvey Nairn – Military Service						
Joe Namath	QB	6'2"	195	25		12
Babe Parilli	QB	6'1"	190	39		
Jim Turner	QB	6'2"	205	28		129
Al Woodall	QB	6'5"	210	23		
Emerson Boozer	HB	5'11"	204	26		24
Bill Mathis	HB	6'1"	220	30		30
George Nock	HB	5'10"	200	23		
Matt Snell	FB	6'2"	220	27		30
Lee White	FB	6'4"	240	23		
Don Maynard	WR	6'	180	33		38
Steve O'Neal	WR	6'3"	185	23		
George Sauer	WR	6'1"	195	25		48
Bake Turner	WR	6'	180	29		18
Curley Johnson (to NY-N)	TE	6'	215	34		
Pete Lammons	TE	6'3"	228	25		12
Wayne Stewart	TE	6'7"	202	22		

HOUSTON OILERS 6-6-2 Wally Lemm

Scores of Each Game		
17	Oakland	21
17	Buffalo	3
22	MIAMI	10
28	BUFFALO	14
0	Kansas City	24
17	New York	26
24	DENVER	21
0	Boston	24
31	CINCINNATI	31
20	Denver	20
32	Miami	7
17	SAN DIEGO	21
26	NEW YORK	34
27	BOSTON	23

Use Name	Pos.	Hgt	Wgt	Age	Int	Pts
Elbert Drungo	OT	6'5"	250	26		
Glen Ray Hines	OT	6'5"	265	25		
Walt Suggs	OT	6'5"	260	30		
Sonny Bishop	OG	6'2"	245	29		
Jim LeMoine	OG	6'2"	245	24		
Tom Regner	OG	6'1"	255	25		
Hank Autry	C	6'3"	230	22		
Bobby Maples	C	6'3"	245	26		
Elvin Bethea	DE	6'3"	250	23		2
Pat Holmes	DE	6'5"	250	29		
Glenn Woods	DE	6'4"	250	23		
Ben Mayes	DT-DE	6'5"	265	24		
Tom Domres	DT	6'3"	255	22		6
Willie Parker	DT	6'2"	265	24		
George Rice	DT	6'3"	260	25		
Carel Stith	DT	6'5"	265	24		
Garland Boyette	LB	6'1"	245	29		
Ron Pritchard	LB	6'1"	222	22		
Olen Underwood	LB	6'1"	230	27	1	
Loyd Wainscott	LB	6'1"	235	22		
Ed Watson	LB	6'2"	222	24		
George Webster	LB	6'4"	223	23	2	
John Douglas	DB	6'1"	195	24		
Miller Parr	DB	6'1"	190	26	6	
W. K. Hicks	DB	6'1"	195	26	4	
Ken Houston	DB	6'3"	192	24	4	6
Zeke Moore	DB	6'2"	198	25	4	6
Johnny Peacock	DB	6'2"	205	22	2	6
Leroy Mitchell – Broken Neck						
Pete Beathard	QB	6'2"	207	27		12
Bob Davis	QB	6'3"	208	23		
Don Trull	QB	6'1"	196	27		12
Ode Burrell	HB	6'	192	29		
Woody Campbell	HB	5'11"	202	24		6
Mike Richardson	HB	5'11"	185	22		2
Hoyle Granger	FB-HB	6'1"	225	25		24
Roy Hopkins	FB	6'1"	225	24		30
Rich Johnson	HB-FB	6'1"	210	22		6
Jim Beirne	WR	6'2"	196	22		26
Mac Haik	WR	6'1"	196	23		6
Charlie Joiner	WR	5'11"	185	21		
Jerry LeVias	WR	5'10"	175	22		30
Paul Zaeske	WR	6'2"	200	23		
Ed Carrington	TE	6'4"	225	25		
Alvin Reed	TE	6'5"	230	25		12
Roy Gerela	K	5'10"	185	21		86

BOSTON PATRIOTS 4-10-0 Clive Rush

Scores of Each Game		
7	Denver	35
0	KANSAS CITY	31
23	OAKLAND	38
14	NEW YORK	23
16	Buffalo	23
10	SAN DIEGO	13
17	New York	23
24	HOUSTON	0
16	MIAMI	17
25	Cincinnati	14
35	BUFFALO	21
38	Miami	23
18	San Diego	28
23	Houston	27

Use Name	Pos.	Hgt	Wgt	Age	Int	Pts
Tom Funchess	OT	6'5"	260	24		
Ezell Jones	OT	6'4"	255	22		2
Tom Neville	OT	6'4"	255	25		
Charley Long	OG	6'3"	250	31		
Len St. Jean	OG	6'1"	245	27		
Mike Montler	C-OG	6'4"	270	25		
Jon Morris	C	6'4"	240	26		
J. R. Williamson	LB-C	6'2"	220	27		
Ron Berger	DE	6'8"	275	25		
Johnny Cagle	DE	6'3"	260	22		
Larry Eisenhauer	DE	6'5"	255	29		
Mel Witt	DE	6'3"	265	23		
Karl Henke	DT-DE	6'4"	245	24		
Houston Antwine	DT	6'	270	30		
Jim Hunt	DT	5'11"	255	30		
Ray Jacobs	DT	6'3"	285	29		
Ed Toner	DT	6'3"	250	24		
John Bramlett	LB	6'2"	210	28	1	
Jim Cheyunski	LB	6'2"	220	23	1	
Ed Philpott	LB	6'3"	240	23	4	
Marty Schottenheimer	LB	6'3"	224	26	1	
Larry Carwell	DB	6'1"	190	25	4	
John Charles	DB	6'1"	200	25	4	6
Tom Janik	DB	6'3"	195	28	1	
Daryle Johnson	DB	5'11"	190	23	2	8
Art McMahon	DB	5'11"	185	23		
John Outlaw	DB	5'10"	180	24		
Clarence Scott	DB	6'2"	205	25		
Don Webb	DB	5'10"	195	30	2	
Kim Hammond	QB	6'1"	192	24		2
Mike Taliaferro	QB	6'2"	205	27		
Teddy Bailey	HB	6'	200	25		
Sid Blanks	HB	6'	210	28		
Carl Garrett	HB	5'11"	210	21		42
Bob Gladieux	HB	5'11"	190	22		
Jim Nance	FB	6'1"	240	26		36
R. C. Gamble	HB-FB	6'3"	220	22		
Gino Cappelletti	WR	6'	190	35		68
Charley Frazier	WR	6'	184	30		42
Aaron Marsh	WR	6'1"	190	24		
Bill Rademacher	WR	6'1"	190	27		18
Tom Richardson	WR	6'2"	195	24		
Ron Sellers	WR	6'4"	198	22		36
Ken Herock	TE	6'2"	230	28		
Jim Whalen	TE	6'2"	210	25		6
Barry Brown	LB-TE	6'3"	220	26		

BUFFALO BILLS 4-10-0 Johnny Rauch

Scores of Each Game		
19	NEW YORK	33
3	HOUSTON	17
41	DENVER	28
14	Houston	28
23	BOSTON	16
21	Oakland	50
6	Miami	24
7	KANSAS CITY	29
6	New York	16
28	MIAMI	3
21	Boston	35
16	CINCINNATI	13
19	Kansas City	22
6	San Diego	45

Use Name	Pos.	Hgt	Wgt	Age	Int	Pts
Stew Barber	OT	6'3"	248	30		
Paul Costa	OT	6'4"	248	27		
Howard Kindig	OT	6'6"	264	28		
Mike Richey	OT	6'5"	250	22		
George Flint	OG	6'4"	240	31		
Billy Shaw	OG	6'3"	252	29		
Angelo Loukas	OG	6'3"	250	22		
Joe O'Donnell	OG	6'2"	252	26		
Al Bemiller	C	6'3"	243	30		
Mike McBath	DE	6'4"	248	23		
Ron McDole	DE	6'3"	270	29		
Julian Nunamaker	DE	6'3"	250	23		
Chuck DeVleigher	DT	6'4"	265	22		
Jim Dunaway	DT	6'4"	282	27		
Waddey Harvey	DT	6'4"	270	22		
Bob Kruse	DT	6'2"	250	27		
Bob Tatarek	DT	6'4"	255	23		
Edgar Chandler	LB	6'3"	222	23		
Jerald Collins	LB	6'1"	220	22		
Paul Guidry	LB	6'3"	228	25	2	
Harry Jacobs	LB	6'2"	226	32	2	
Paul Maguire	LB	6'	228	31		
Dave Ogas	LB	6'3"	240	23		
Mike Stratton	LB	6'3"	230	27		
Butch Byrd	DB	6'	196	27	7	6
Hilton Crawford	DB	6'	198	24		
Booker Edgerson	DB	5'10"	183	30	1	6
John Pitts	DB	6'4"	215	24	2	
Pete Richardson	DB	6'1"	205	22	2	
George Saimes	DB	5'10"	185	27	3	
Bobby James	WR-DB	6'1"	177	22		
Bob Kalsu – Military Service						
Dan Darragh	QB	6'3"	196	22		
Jim Harris	QB	6'3"	215	22		
Jack Kemp	QB	6'1"	204	35		
Tom Sherman (from BOS)	QB	6'	190	23		
Max Anderson	HB	5'8"	180	24		6
Preston Ridlehuber	HB	6'2"	215	25		
O. J. Simpson	HB	6'2"	204	22		30
Bill Enyart	FB	6'4"	236	22		18
Wayne Patrick	FB	6'2"	225	23		18
Marlin Briscoe	WR	5'10"	177	23		30
Bobby Crockett	WR	6'	200	26		
Monte Ledbetter (to ATL-N)	WR	6'2"	185	26		
Haven Moses	WR	6'3"	200	23		30
Roy Reeves	WR	5'11"	182	23		
Bubba Thornton	WR	6'	175	22		
Charley Ferguson	TE	6'5"	224	29		
Willie Grate	TE	6'4"	225	23		6
Bill Masters	TE	6'5"	225	25		6
Bruce Alford	K	6'	185	24		74

MIAMI DOLPHINS 3-10-1 George Wilson

Scores of Each Game		
21	Cincinnati	27
17	Oakland	20
10	Houston	22
20	OAKLAND	20
14	SAN DIEGO	21
10	Kansas City	17
24	BUFFALO	6
31	New York	34
17	Boston	16
3	Buffalo	28
7	HOUSTON	32
23	BOSTON	38
27	DENVER	24
9	NEW YORK	27

Use Name	Pos.	Hgt	Wgt	Age	Int	Pts
John Boynton	OT	6'4"	255	23		
Doug Crusan	OT	6'5"	255	23		
Norm Evans	OT	6'5"	250	25		
Billy Neighbors	OG	5'11"	250	29		
Maxie Williams	OG	6'4"	250	29		
Larry Little	OT-OG	6'1"	270	23		
Tom Goode	C	6'3"	250	30		
Jeff Richardson	OT-C	6'3"	250	24		
Norm McBride	DE	6'3"	235	22		
Jim Riley	DE	6'4"	255	24		
Bill Stanfill	DE	6'5"	250	22	2	12
Bob Joswick	DT-DE	6'5"	250	23		
Manny Fernandez	DT	6'2"	250	23		
Bob Heinz	DT	6'6"	265	22		
John Richardson	DT	6'2"	260	24		
Freddie Woodson	OG-DT	6'2"	255	25		
Nick Buoniconti	LB	5'11"	220	28	3	
Randy Edmunds	LB	6'2"	220	23		
Frank Emanuel	LB	6'3"	225	26		
Jimmy Keyes	LB	6'2"	225	25		
Dale McCullers	LB	6'1"	215	21		
Jesse Powell	LB	6'1"	212	22		
Ed Weisacosky	LB	6'	230	25	3	
Dick Anderson	DB	6'2"	205	23	3	
Tom Beier	DB	5'11"	198	24	1	
Garry Grady	DB	5'11"	180	22		
Lloyd Mumphord	DB	5'11"	180	22	5	
Willie Pearson	DB	6'	190	22		
Bob Petrella	DB	6'	185	24	1	
Jimmy Warren	DB	5'11"	175	30		
Dick Westmoreland	DB	6'1"	195	28		
Bob Griese	QB	6'1"	190	24		
Rick Norton	QB	6'1"	190	25		
John Stofa (From CIN)	QB	6'3"	210	27		
Jim Kiick	HB	5'11"	215	23		60
Mercury Morris	HB	5'10"	185	22		12
Barry Pryor	HB	6'	215	23		
Larry Csonka	FB	6'3"	240	22		18
Stan Mitchell	FB	6'2"	225	25		
Jack Clancy	WR	6'1"	195	25		6
Bill Darnall	WR	6'2"	197	25		
Jimmy Hines	WR	6'	175	22		
Gene Milton	WR	5'10"	170	24		6
Karl Noonan	WR	6'3"	190	25		18
Howard Twilley	WR	5'10"	180	25		6
Tommy Boutwell	QB-WR	6'2"	205	22		
Jim Mertens	TE	6'3"	235	22		
Doug Moreau	TE	6'2"	215	24		
Larry Seiple	TE	6'	213	24		30
Karl Kremser	K	6'	180	24		65

NEW YORK JETS

RUSHING

Last Name	No.	Yds	Avg	TD
Snell	191	695	3.6	4
Boozer	130	604	4.6	4
Mathis	96	355	3.7	4
White	28	88	3.1	0
Namath	11	33	3.0	2
Woodall	4	13	3.3	0
Sauer	1	5	5.0	0
Parilli	3	4	1.3	0
B. Turner	1	–4	–4.0	0
Nock	3	–5	–1.7	0
Maynard	1	–6	–6.0	0

RECEIVING

Last Name	No.	Yds	Avg	TD
Maynard	47	938	20	6
Sauer	45	745	17	8
Lammons	33	400	12	2
Snell	22	187	9	1
Boozer	20	222	11	0
Mathis	18	183	10	1
B. Turner	11	221	20	3
Stewart	5	39	8	0
Dockery	1	6	6	0
White	1	–2	–2	0

PUNT RETURNS

Last Name	No.	Yds	Avg	TD
Battle	34	235	7	0
Baird	4	21	5	0
Leonard	1	0	0	0

KICKOFF RETURNS

Last Name	No.	Yds	Avg	TD
Battle	31	750	24	0
Leonard	7	120	17	0
B. Turner	3	74	25	0
Richards	2	36	18	0
White	1	5	5	0
Carroll	1	0	0	0
Sauer	1	0	0	0

PASSING – PUNTING – KICKING

PASSING	Att	Comp	%	Yds	Yd/Att	TD	Int–	%	RK
Namath	361	185	51	2734	7.6	19	17–	5	2
Parilli	24	14	58	138	5.8	2	1–	4	
Woodall	9	4	44	67	7.4	0	2–	22	

PUNTING	No	Avg
O'Neal	54	44.3
B. Turner	2	44.5

KICKING	XP	Att	%	FG	Att	%
J. Turner	33	33	100	32	47	68

2 POINT XP
Maynard

HOUSTON OILERS

RUSHING

Last Name	No.	Yds	Avg	TD
Granger	186	740	4.0	3
Hopkins	131	473	3.6	4
Burrell	41	147	3.6	0
Campbell	28	98	3.5	1
Beathard	19	89	4.7	2
Richardson	5	51	10.2	0
Johnson	11	42	3.8	0
Trull	8	25	3.1	2
Haik	2	21	10.5	0
LeVias	6	18	3.0	0
Davis	3	2	0.7	0

RECEIVING

Last Name	No.	Yds	Avg	TD
Reed	51	664	13	2
LeVias	42	696	17	5
Beirne	42	540	13	4
Hopkins	29	338	12	1
Haik	27	375	14	1
Granger	27	330	12	1
Campbell	7	82	12	0
Joiner	7	77	11	0
Burrell	5	28	6	0
Johnson	2	17	9	1

PUNT RETURNS

Last Name	No.	Yds	Avg	TD
LeVias	35	292	8	0
Richardson	7	93	13	0
Burrell	1	6	6	0

KICKOFF RETURNS

Last Name	No.	Yds	Avg	TD
LeVias	38	940	25	0
Burrell	5	101	20	0
Joiner	3	73	24	0
Reed	3	0	0	0
Houston	0	27	0	0

PASSING – PUNTING – KICKING

PASSING	Att	Comp	%	Yds	Yd/Att	TD	Int–	%	RK
Beathard	370	180	49	2455	6.6	10	21–	6	8
Trull	75	34	45	469	6.3	3	6–	8	
Davis	42	25	60	223	5.3	2	4–	10	
LeVias	2	0	0	0	0.0	0	0–	0	

PUNTING	No	Avg
Gerela	41	40.4
Burrell	29	36.8

KICKING	XP	Att	%	FG	Att	%
Gerela	29	29	100	19	40	48

2 POINT XP
Beirne
Richardson

BOSTON PATRIOTS

RUSHING

Last Name	No.	Yds	Avg	TD
Nance	193	750	3.9	6
Garrett	137	691	5.0	5
Gamble	16	35	2.2	0
Blanks	7	30	4.3	0
Frazier	2	–1	–0.5	0
Taliaferro	12	–16	–1.3	0

RECEIVING

Last Name	No.	Yds	Avg	TD
Garrett	29	267	9	2
Nance	29	168	6	0
Sellers	27	705	26	6
Frazier	19	306	16	7
Rademacher	17	217	13	3
Whalen	16	235	15	1
Marsh	8	108	14	0
Gamble	7	74	11	0
Brown	6	69	12	0
Blanks	2	16	8	0
Cappelletti	1	21	21	0
Richardson	1	5	5	0

PUNT RETURNS

Last Name	No.	Yds	Avg	TD
Garrett	12	159	13	0
Carwell	5	43	9	0
Blanks	5	10	2	0
Janik	1	0	0	0

KICKOFF RETURNS

Last Name	No.	Yds	Avg	TD
Garrett	28	792	28	0
Marsh	6	136	23	0
Blanks	6	131	22	0
Gladieux	4	61	15	0
Scott	6	43	7	0
Carwell	1	28	28	0
Gamble	1	23	23	0
Berger	1	20	20	0
Schott'nhmer	1	13	13	0

PASSING – PUNTING – KICKING

PASSING	Att	Comp	%	Yds	Yd/Att	TD	Int–	%	RK
Taliaferro	331	160	48	2160	6.5	19	18–	5	11
Hammond	6	2	33	31	5.2	0	0–	0	
Garrett	1	0	0	0	0.0	0	0–	0	

PUNTING	No	Avg
Janik	70	41.5

KICKING	XP	Att	%	FG	Att	%
Cappelletti	26	27	96	14	34	41

2 POINT XP
Hammond

BUFFALO BILLS

RUSHING

Last Name	No.	Yds	Avg	TD
Simpson	181	697	3.9	2
Patrick	83	361	4.3	3
Enyart	47	191	4.1	1
Kemp	37	124	3.4	0
Anderson	13	74	5.7	1
Ridlehuber	4	25	6.3	0
Harris	10	25	2.5	0
Sherman	2	14	7.0	0
Darragh	6	14	2.3	0
Masters	1	–3	–3.0	0

RECEIVING

Last Name	No.	Yds	Avg	TD
Moses	39	752	19	5
Patrick	35	229	7	0
Masters	33	387	12	1
Briscoe	32	532	17	5
Simpson	30	343	11	3
Enyart	19	186	10	2
Thornton	14	134	10	0
Anderson	7	65	9	0
Crockett	4	50	13	0
Grate	1	19	19	1
James	1	19	19	0

PUNT RETURNS

Last Name	No.	Yds	Avg	TD
Anderson	19	142	7	0
Byrd	7	37	5	0
Reeves	2	3	2	0
Ridlehuber	1	3	3	0
James	1	2	2	0
Richardson	1	0	0	0

KICKOFF RETURNS

Last Name	No.	Yds	Avg	TD
Thornton	30	749	25	0
Simpson	21	529	25	0
Anderson	4	86	22	0
Crawford	3	74	25	0
Collins	2	14	7	0
Enyart	1	12	12	0
Harvey	1	11	11	0

PASSING – PUNTING – KICKING

PASSING	Att	Comp	%	Yds	Yd/Att	TD	Int–	%	RK
Kemp	344	170	49	1981	5.8	13	22–	6	9
Darragh	52	24	46	365	7.0	1	6–	12	
Harris	36	15	42	270	7.5	1	1–	3	
Sherman	2	2	100	20	10.0	1	0–	0	
Briscoe	1	0	0	0	0.0	0	1–	100	
Maguire	1	1	100	19	19.0	0	0–	0	
Ridlehuber	1	1	100	45	45.0	1	0–	0	

PUNTING	No	Avg
Maguire	78	44.5

KICKING	XP	Att	%	FG	Att	%
Alford	23	24	96	17	26	65

MIAMI DOLPHINS

RUSHING

Last Name	No.	Yds	Avg	TD
Kiick	180	575	3.2	9
Csonka	131	566	4.3	2
Morris	23	110	4.8	1
Griese	21	102	4.9	0
Mitchell	28	80	2.9	0
Milton	7	62	8.9	0
Norton	8	16	2.0	0
Hines	1	7	7.0	0
Seiple	1	6	6.0	0
Noonan	1	–11	–11.0	0

RECEIVING

Last Name	No.	Yds	Avg	TD
Seiple	41	577	14	5
Kiick	29	443	15	1
Noonan	29	307	11	3
Clancy	21	289	14	1
Csonka	21	183	9	1
Milton	12	179	15	0
Twilley	10	158	16	1
Mitchell	10	125	13	0
Moreau	10	136	14	0
Morris	6	65	11	0
Boutwell	4	29	7	0
Mertens	2	26	13	0
Hines	2	23	12	0
Pryor	2	–3	–2	0
Darnall	1	13	13	0
Anderson	1	8	8	0

PUNT RETURNS

Last Name	No.	Yds	Avg	TD
Morris	25	172	7	0
Anderson	12	82	7	0
Beier	5	8	2	0
Milton	1	4	4	0
McCullers	1	0	0	0
Twilley	1	0	0	0

KICKOFF RETURNS

Last Name	No.	Yds	Avg	TD
Morris	43	1136	26	1
Milton	8	166	21	0
Beier	4	58	15	0
Hines	1	22	22	0
Mertens	2	1	1	0
Mumphord	1	0	0	0
Warren	1	0	0	0

PASSING – PUNTING – KICKING

PASSING	Att	Comp	%	Yds	Yd/Att	TD	Int–	%	RK
Griese	252	121	48	1695	6.7	10	16–	6	10
Norton	148	65	44	709	4.8	2	11–	7	12
Stofa	23	14	61	146	6.4	0	2–	9	
Seiple	1	1	100	8	8.0	0	0–	0	

PUNTING	No	Avg
Seiple	80	40.8
Anderson	5	37.6

KICKING	XP	Att	%	FG	Att	%
Kremser	26	27	96	13	22	59

OAKLAND RAIDERS 12-1-1 John Madden

Scores of Each Game		
21	HOUSTON	17
20	MIAMI	17
38	Boston	23
20	Miami	20
24	Denver	14
50	BUFFALO	21
24	San Diego	12
17	Cincinnati	31
41	DENVER	10
21	SAN DIEGO	16
27	Kansas City	24
27	New York	14
37	CINCINNATI	17
10	KANSAS CITY	6

Use Name	Pos.	Hgt	Wgt	Age	Int	Pts
Harry Schuh	OT	6'2"	260	26		
Art Shell	OT	6'5"	255	22		
Bob Svihus	OT	6'4"	245	26		
George Buehler	OG	6'2"	260	22		
Jim Harvey	OG	6'5"	245	26		
Wayne Hawkins	OG	6'	240	31		
Gene Upshaw	OG	6'5"	255	24		
Jim Otto	C	6'2"	248	31		
Ben Davidson	DE	6'8"	275	29		
Ike Lassiter	DE	6'5"	270	28		
Carleton Oats	DT-DE	6'2"	260	26		
Dan Birdwell	DT	6'4"	250	28		
Al Dotson	DT	6'4"	260	26		2
Tom Keating	DT	6'3"	247	26		
Art Thoms	DT	6'5"	250	22		
Duane Benson	LB	6'2"	215	24		
Bill Budness	LB	6'1"	215	26		
Dan Conners	LB	6'1	230	27	1	12
Bill Laskey	LB	6'2"	235	26	3	
Chip Oliver	LB	6'2"	220	23	1	6
Gus Otto	LB	6'2"	220	26	2	
Jackie Allen	DB	6'1"	187	21		
Butch Atkinson	DB	6'	180	22	2	6
Willie Brown	DB	6'1"	190	28	5	
Dave Grayson	DB	5'10"	185	30	8	6
Kent McCloughan	DB	6'1"	190	26		
Howie Williams	DB	6'2"	190	32	2	
Nemiah Wilson	DB	6'	165	26	2	
George Blanda	QB	6'1"	215	41		105
Daryle Lamonica	QB	6'2"	215	28		6
Charlie Smith	HB	6'1"	205	23		24
Larry Todd	HB	6'1"	185	26		12
Pete Banaszak	FB-HB	5'11"	200	25		18
Hewritt Dixon	FB	6'2"	230	29		6
Marv Hubbard	FB	6'1"	215	23		
Fred Biletnikoff	WR	6'1"	190	26		72
Drew Buie	WR	6'2"	178	22		
Rod Sherman	WR	6'	190	24		
Warren Wells	WR	6'1"	190	26		84
Billy Cannon	TE	6'1"	215	32		12
Lloyd Edwards	TE	6'3"	248	22		
Roger Hagberg	TE	6'2"	215	30		6
Mike Eischeid	K	6'	190	28		

KANSAS CITY CHIEFS 11-2-0 Hank Stram

Scores of Each Game		
27	San Diego	9
31	Boston	0
19	Cincinnati	24
26	Denver	13
24	HOUSTON	0
17	MIAMI	10
42	CINCINNATI	22
29	Buffalo	7
27	SAN DIEGO	3
34	New York	16
24	OAKLAND	27
31	DENVER	17
22	BUFFALO	19
6	Oakland	10

Use Name	Pos.	Hgt	Wgt	Age	Int	Pts
Dave Hill	OT	6'5"	260	28		
Jim Tyrer	OT	6'6"	275	30		
Ed Budde	OG	6'5"	260	28		
George Daney	OG	6'3"	240	22		6
Mo Moorman	OG	6'5"	252	25		
E. J. Holub	C	6'4"	236	31		
Remi Prudhomme	C	6'4"	250	27		
Aaron Brown	DE	6'5"	265	25		
Jerry Mays	DE	6'4"	252	29		
Gene Trosch	DE	6'7"	277	24		
Buck Buchanan	DT	6'7"	287	29		
Curley Culp	DT	6'1"	265	23		
Ed Lothamer	DT	6'5"	270	26		
Bobby Bell	LB	6'4"	228	29		6
Chuck Hurston	LB	6'6"	240	26		
Willie Lanier	LB	6'1"	245	24	4	
Jim Lynch	LB	6'1"	235	24	3	
Bob Stein	LB	6'2"	235	21		
Caesar Belser	DB	6'	212	24		
Jim Kearney	DB	6'2"	206	26	5	6
Jim Marsalis	DB	5'11"	194	23	2	
Willie Mitchell	DB	6'1"	185	27	1	
Johnny Robinson	DB	6'	205	30	8	
Goldie Sellers	DB	6'2"	198	27		6
Emmitt Thomas	DB	6'2"	192	26	9	6
Len Dawson	QB	6'	190	35		
Tom Flores (from BUF)	QB	6'1"	202	32		
Jacky Lee	QB	6'1"	185	30		
Mike Livingston	QB	6'3"	205	23		
Mike Garrett	HB	5'9"	200	25		48
Paul Lowe	HB	6'	205	32		
Warren McVea	HB	5'10"	182	23		42
Ed Podolak	HB	6'1"	204	22		
Noland Smith (to SF-N)	HB	5'6"	156	25		
Wendell Hayes	FB	6'2"	220	28		24
Robert Holmes	FB	5'9"	220	23		30
Frank Pitts	WR	6'2"	200	25		12
Gloster Richardson	WR	6'	200	26		12
Otis Taylor	WR	6'2"	215	26		42
Mickey McCarty	TE	6'5"	255	22		
Curtis McClinton	TE	6'3"	227	31		
Morris Stroud	TE	6'10"	235	23		
Fred Arbanas	OT-TE	6'3"	240	30		
Jan Stenerud	K	6'2"	187	26		119
Jerrel Wilson	K	6'4"	222	28		

SAN DIEGO CHARGERS 8-6-0 Sid Gillman Charlie Waller

Scores of Each Game		
9	KANSAS CITY	27
20	Cincinnati	34
34	NEW YORK	27
21	CINCINNATI	14
21	Miami	14
13	Boston	10
12	OAKLAND	24
0	Denver	13
3	Kansas City	27
16	Oakland	21
45	DENVER	24
21	Houston	17
28	BOSTON	18
45	BUFFALO	6

Use Name	Pos.	Hgt	Wgt	Age	Int	Pts
Gene Ferguson	OT	6'7"	306	21		6
Ron Mix	OT	6'4"	250	31		
Terry Owens	OT	6'6"	270	25		
Bob Wells	OT	6'4"	270	24		
Gary Kirner	OG	6'3"	255	27		
Jim Schmedding	OG	6'2"	250	23		
Walt Sweeney	OG	6'3"	260	28		
Sam Gruneisen	C	6'1"	250	28		
Bill Lenkaitis	OG-C	6'3"	250	23		
Ron Billingsley	DE	6'8"	265	24		
Steve DeLong	DE	6'3"	252	26		
Houston Ridge	DE	6'4"	245	25		
Bob Briggs	DT	6'4"	270	24		
Levert Carr	DT	6'5"	250	25		
Dan Sartin	DT	6'1"	245	23		
Russ Washington	DT	6'6"	290	22		
Chuck Allen	LB	6'1"	225	29		
Pete Barnes	LB	6'3"	245	24	5	
Bob Bruggers	LB	6'1"	230	25	1	
Jim Campbell	LB	6'3"	218	23	1	
Jim Fetherston	LB	6'2"	225	24		
Rick Redman	LB	5'11"	225	26	1	
Jeff Staggs	LB	6'2"	240	25		
Joe Beauchamp	DB	6'	185	25		
Speedy Duncan	DB	5'10"	175	26	6	6
Dick Farley	DB	6'	185	23		
Kenny Graham	DB	6'	205	27	4	12
Jim Hill	DB	6'2"	192	22	7	
Bob Howard	DB	6'1"	190	24	6	
Gene Huey	DB	5'11"	190	22		
Larry Rentz	DB	6'1"	170	22		
Jim Tolbert	DB	6'3"	207	25		
Marty Domres	QB	6'3"	212	22		24
John Hadl	QB	6'2"	215	29		12
Dickie Post	HB	5'9"	190	23		36
Ron Sayers	HB	6'1"	202	22		
Russ Smith	FB-HB	6'1"	209	25		12
Gene Foster	FB	5'11"	220	26		6
Brad Hubbert	FB	6'1"	227	28		24
Lance Alworth	WR	6'	180	29		24
Rick Eber	WR	6'	185	24		6
Gary Garrison	WR	6'1"	195	25		42
Richard Trapp	WR	6'1"	174	22		
Willie Frazier	TE	6'4"	235	26		
Jacque MacKinnon	TE	6'4"	240	30		
Jeff Queen	TE	6'1"	230	23		
Dennis Partee	K	6'2"	208	23		78

DENVER BRONCOS 5-8-1 Lou Saban

Scores of Each Game		
35	BOSTON	7
21	NEW YORK	19
28	Buffalo	41
13	KANSAS CITY	26
14	OAKLAND	24
30	Cincinnati	23
21	Houston	24
13	SAN DIEGO	0
10	Oakland	41
20	HOUSTON	20
24	San Diego	45
17	Kansas City	31
24	Miami	27
27	CINCINNATI	16

Use Name	Pos.	Hgt	Wgt	Age	Int	Pts
Sam Brunelli	OT	6'1"	270	26		
Mike Current	OT	6'4"	260	23		
Wallace Dickey	OT	6'3"	260	28		
George Goeddeke	OG	6'3"	253	24		
Buzz Highsmith	OG	6'4"	230	26		
Mike Schnitker	OG	6'3"	235	22		
Bob Young	OG	6'2"	260	26		
Jay Bachman	C	6'3"	250	23		
Larry Kaminski	C	6'2"	245	24		
Walt Barnes	DE	6'3"	250	25		
Pete Duranko	DE	6'2"	252	25		
Rich Jackson	DE	6'2"	255	28		
Dave Costa	DT	6'2"	265	27		
Jerry Inman	DT	6'3"	255	29		
Rex Mirich	DT	6'4"	250	28		
Paul Smith	DT	6'3"	245	24		
Tim Casey (from CHI-N)	LB	6'1"	225	25		
Gary Crane	LB	6'4"	230	22		
Ken Criter	LB	5'11"	223	22		
Carl Cunningham	LB	6'3"	240	25	2	
John Huard	LB	6'	220	25	2	
Gordon Lambert	LB	6'5"	245	24		
Chip Myrtle	LB	6'2"	225	24		
Frank Richter	LB	6'3"	230	24		
Phil Brady	DB	6'2"	211	26		
George Burrell	DB	5'10"	180	21	2	6
Grady Cavness	DB	5'11"	187	22	2	
Charlie Greer	DB	6'	205	23	2	
Gus Holloman	DB	6'3"	195	23	1	
Pete Jaquess	DB	6'	182	27		
Tom Oberg	DB	6'	185	24		
Jimmy Smith	DB	6'3"	190	24		
Bill Thompson	DB	6'1"	200	22	3	6
Ted Alfen	HB-DB	6'	195	22		
Pete Liske	QB	6'2"	185	28		
Al Pastrana	QB	6'1"	190	24		
Steve Tensi	QB	6'5"	215	26		
Bobby Burnett	HB	6'2"	208	26		
Floyd Little	HB	5'10"	195	27		42
Frank Quayle	HB	5'10"	195	22		
Wandy Williams	HB	6'1"	193	23		6
Henry Jones	FB	6'2"	235	23		
Brendan McCarthy	FB	6'3"	220	24		
Tom Smiley	FB	6'1"	235	25		24
Fran Lynch	HB-FB	6'1"	194	23		12
Al Denson	WR	6'2"	208	27		60
John Embree	WR	6'4"	207	25		30
Mike Haffner	WR	6'2"	205	27		30
Bill Van Heusen	WR	6'1"	200	23		
Tom Beer	TE	6'4"	230	24		
Tom Buckman	TE	6'4"	230	22		6
Dave Pivec	TE	6'3"	240	25		
Bobby Howfield	K	5'9"	180	32		75

CINCINNATI BENGALS 4-9-1 Paul Brown

Scores of Each Game		
27	MIAMI	21
34	SAN DIEGO	20
24	KANSAS CITY	19
14	San Diego	21
7	NEW YORK	21
23	DENVER	30
22	Kansas City	42
31	OAKLAND	17
31	Houston	31
14	BOSTON	25
7	New York	40
13	Buffalo	16
17	Oakland	37
16	Denver	27

Use Name	Pos.	Hgt	Wgt	Age	Int	Pts
Howard Fest	OT	6'6"	265	23		
Frank Peters	OT	6'4"	250	21		
Ernie Wright	OT	6'4"	270	29		
Ernie Park	OG-OT	6'3"	240	27		
Justin Canale	OG	6'2"	250	25		
Guy Dennis	OG	6'2"	255	22		
Pat Matson	OG	6'1"	245	25		
Dave Middendorf	OG	6'3"	260	23		
Mike Wilson	OG	6'1"	240	21		
Bob Johnson	C	6'5"	260	23		
Marty Baccaglio	DE	6'3"	245	24		
Royce Berry	DE	6'3"	242	23		
Harry Gunner	DE	6'6"	250	24	1	6
Steve Chomyszak	DT	6'5"	280	24		
Andy Rice	DT	6'3"	268	27		
Bill Staley	DT	6'3"	250	22		
Ken Avery	LB	6'1"	225	25		
Al Beauchamp	LB	6'2"	236	25	1	
Bill Bergey	LB	6'2"	240	24	2	
Tim Buchanan	LB	6'	233	23		
Ed Harmon	LB	6'4"	230	22		
Bill Peterson	LB	6'3"	230	24	4	
Al Coleman	DB	6'1"	183	24		
Ken Dyer	DB	6'3"	185	23		
John Guillory	DB	5'10"	190	24	1	
Bobby Hunt	DB	6'1"	190	29	4	
Charlie King	DB	6'	184	26		
Ken Riley	DB	6'	182	22	4	
Fletcher Smith	DB	6'2"	178	25	4	
Jim Williams	DB	6'1"	190	23		
Greg Cook	QB	6'3"	212	22		6
Sam Wyche	QB	6'4"	210	24		6
Essex Johnson	HB	5'9"	190	22		
Paul Robinson	HB	6'	200	24		24
Ron Lamb	FB	6'2"	225	25		
Clem Turner	FB	6'1"	245	24		
Jess Phillips	HB-FB	6'1"	205	22		18
Eric Crabtree	WR	5'11"	182	24		42
Jack Gehrke	WR	6'	178	23		
Chip Myers	WR	6'4"	200	24		12
Tommie Smith	WR	6'4"	190	25		
Speedy Thomas	WR	6'1"	175	22		24
Bruce Coslet	TE	6'3"	225	23		6
Bob Trumpy	WR-TE	6'6"	220	24		54
Dale Livingston	K	6'	210	24		
Horst Muhlman	K	6'1"	210	29		80
Terry Swanson	K	6'	210	24		

Frank Buncom —Died Sept. 14, 1969 from pulmonary embolism

OAKLAND RAIDERS

RUSHING

Last Name	No.	Yds	Avg	TD
Smith	177	600	3.4	2
Dixon	107	398	3.7	0
Banaszak	88	377	4.3	0
Todd	47	198	4.2	1
Hubbard	21	119	5.7	0
Lamonica	13	36	2.8	1
Wells	3	24	8.0	0
Eischeid	1	10	10.0	0
Hagberg	1	3	3.0	0
Blanda	1	0	0.0	0

RECEIVING

Last Name	No.	Yds	Avg	TD
Biletnikoff	54	837	15	12
Wells	47	1260	27	14
Dixon	33	275	8	1
Smith	30	322	11	2
Cannon	21	262	12	2
Banaszak	17	119	7	3
Todd	16	149	9	1
Hagberg	6	84	14	1
Hubbard	2	30	15	0
Buie	1	37	37	0

PUNT RETURNS

Last Name	No.	Yds	Avg	TD
Atkinson	25	153	6	0
Sherman	9	46	5	0
Grayson	4	28	7	0
Allen	1	−2	−2	0

KICKOFF RETURNS

Last Name	No.	Yds	Avg	TD
Atkinson	16	382	24	0
Sherman	12	300	25	0
Smith	10	247	25	0
Allen	3	67	22	0
Benson	1	0	0	0

PASSING – PUNTING – KICKING

PASSING	Att	Comp	%	Yds	Yd/Att	TD	Int–	%	RK
Lamonica	426	221	52	3302	7.8	34	25–	6	3
Blanda	13	6	46	73	5.6	2	1–	8	

PUNTING	No	Avg
Eischeid	69	42.7

KICKING	XP	Att	%	FG	Att	%
Blanda	45	45	100	20	37	54

KANSAS CITY CHIEFS

RUSHING

Last Name	No.	Yds	Avg	TD
Garrett	168	732	4.4	6
Holmes	150	612	4.1	2
McVea	106	500	4.7	7
Hayes	62	208	3.4	4
Livingston	15	102	6.8	0
Lowe	10	33	3.3	0
Pitts	5	28	5.6	0
Dawson	1	3	3.0	0
Lee	1	3	3.0	0
Arbanas	1	1	1.0	0
Flores	1	0	0.0	0
Taylor	2	−2	−1.0	0

RECEIVING

Last Name	No.	Yds	Avg	TD
Garrett	43	432	10	2
Taylor	41	696	17	7
Pitts	31	470	15	2
Holmes	26	266	10	3
Richardson	23	381	17	2
Arbanas	16	258	16	0
Hayes	9	64	7	0
McVea	7	71	10	0

PUNT RETURNS

Last Name	No.	Yds	Avg	TD
Smith	9	107	12	0
Mitchell	13	101	8	0
Garrett	8	28	4	0
Sellers	2	15	8	0

KICKOFF RETURNS

Last Name	No.	Yds	Avg	TD
McVea	13	318	24	0
Mitchell	7	178	25	0
Podolak	7	165	24	0
Smith	4	125	31	0
Lowe	5	116	23	0
Hayes	2	81	41	0
Holmes	2	54	27	0
Bell	1	53	53	1

PASSING – PUNTING – KICKING

PASSING	Att	Comp	%	Yds	Yd/Att	TD	Int–	%	RK
Dawson	166	98	59	1323	8.0	9	13–	8	6
Livingston	161	84	52	1123	7.0	4	6–	4	4
Lee	20	12	60	109	5.5	1	1–	5	
Flores	6	3	50	49	8.2	1	0–	0	
McVea	3	1	33	50	16.7	1	0–	0	

PUNTING	No	Avg
Wilson	68	44.4

KICKING	XP	Att	%	FG	Att	%
Stenerud	38	38	100	27	35	77

SAN DIEGO CHARGERS

RUSHING

Last Name	No.	Yds	Avg	TD
Post	182	873	4.8	6
Hubbert	94	333	3.5	4
Foster	64	236	3.7	0
Smith	51	211	4.1	2
Domres	19	145	7.6	4
Hadl	26	109	4.2	2
Sayers	14	53	3.8	0
Alworth	5	25	5.0	0

RECEIVING

Last Name	No.	Yds	Avg	TD
Alworth	64	1003	16	4
Garrison	40	804	20	7
Post	24	235	10	0
Frazier	17	205	12	0
Foster	14	83	6	1
Hubbert	11	43	4	0
Queen	10	148	15	0
Smith	10	144	14	0
Eber	9	141	16	1
MacKinnon	7	82	12	0
Trapp	2	39	20	0

PUNT RETURNS

Last Name	No.	Yds	Avg	TD
Duncan	27	280	10	0
Graham	3	15	5	0
Smith	1	5	5	0

KICKOFF RETURNS

Last Name	No.	Yds	Avg	TD
Duncan	21	587	28	0
Smith	6	138	23	0
Post	4	74	19	0
Sayers	2	42	21	0
Foster	1	1	1	0
Fetherston	3	0	0	0
Briggs	1	0	0	0
Huey	1	0	0	0

PASSING – PUNTING – KICKING

PASSING	Att	Comp	%	Yds	Yd/Att	TD	Int–	%	RK
Hadl	324	158	49	2253	7.0	10	11–	3	5
Domres	112	47	42	631	5.6	2	10–	9	
Foster	5	2	40	39	7.8	1	0–	0	
Post	2	1	50	4	2.0	0	0–	0	
Hubbert	1	0	0	0	0.0	0	0–	0	

PUNTING	No	Avg
Partee	71	44.6

KICKING	XP	Att	%	FG	Att	%
Partee	33	33	100	15	28	54

DENVER BRONCOS

RUSHING

Last Name	No.	Yds	Avg	TD
Little	146	729	5.0	6
Lynch	96	407	4.2	2
Quayle	57	183	3.2	0
Smiley	56	166	3.0	3
Tensi	12	63	5.3	0
Liske	10	50	5.0	0
Williams	10	18	1.8	1
Denson	1	9	9.0	0
Burnett	5	9	1.8	0
Jones	1	3	3.0	0

RECEIVING

Last Name	No.	Yds	Avg	TD
Denson	53	809	15	10
Haffner	35	563	16	5
Embree	29	469	16	5
Little	19	218	11	1
Quayle	11	167	15	0
Beer	9	200	22	0
Pivic	9	117	13	0
Lynch	9	86	10	0
Williams	5	56	11	0
Smiley	5	23	5	1
Buckman	4	48	12	1
Van Heusen	3	64	21	0
Pastrana	1	15	15	0

PUNT RETURNS

Last Name	No.	Yds	Avg	TD
Thompson	25	288	12	0
Little	6	70	12	0
Burrell	5	56	11	0
Greer	1	36	36	0

KICKOFF RETURNS

Last Name	No.	Yds	Avg	TD
Williams	23	574	25	0
Thompson	18	513	29	0
Burrell	6	108	18	0
Little	3	81	27	0
Criter	3	31	10	0
Barnes	1	16	16	0
Hollomon	1	0	0	0
Myrtle	1	0	0	0

PASSING – PUNTING – KICKING

PASSING	Att	Comp	%	Yds	Yd/Att	TD	Int–	%	RK
Tensi	286	131	46	1990	7.0	14	12–	4	7
Liske	115	61	53	845	7.4	9	11–	10	
Little	2	0	0	0	0.0	0	0–	0	

PUNTING	No	Avg
Holloman	47	39.7
Van Heusen	25	40.8

KICKING	XP	Att	%	FG	Att	%
Howfield	36	37	97	13	29	45

CINCINNATI BENGALS

RUSHING

Last Name	No.	Yds	Avg	TD
Phillips	118	578	4.9	3
Robinson	160	489	3.1	4
Cook	25	148	5.9	1
Wyche	12	107	8.9	1
Turner	23	105	4.6	0
E. Johnson	15	54	3.6	0
Livingston	1	18	18.0	0
Thomas	4	16	4.0	1
Lamb	5	8	1.6	0

RECEIVING

Last Name	No.	Yds	Avg	TD
Crabtree	40	855	21	7
Trumpy	37	835	23	9
Thomas	33	481	15	3
Robinson	20	104	5	0
Phillips	13	128	10	0
Myers	10	205	21	2
Turner	5	14	3	0
Riley	2	15	8	0
T. Smith	1	41	41	0
Coslet	1	39	39	1
E. Johnson	1	3	3	0

PUNT RETURNS

Last Name	No.	Yds	Avg	TD
E. Johnson	17	85	5	0
Thomas	4	15	4	0
Coleman	1	0	0	0
Guillory	1	0	0	0
King	0	35	0	0

KICKOFF RETURNS

Last Name	No.	Yds	Avg	TD
E. Johnson	16	362	23	0
Riley	14	334	24	0
Guillory	8	170	21	0
Robinson	5	168	34	0
Lamb	5	64	13	0
Phillips	3	52	17	0
Turner	3	15	15	0
Gunner	1	0	0	0

PASSING – PUNTING – KICKING

PASSING	Att	Comp	%	Yds	Yd/Att	TD	Int–	%	RK
Cook	197	106	54	1854	9.4	15	11–	6	1
Wyche	108	54	50	838	7.8	7	4–	4	
Livingston	2	2	100	15	7.5	0	0–	0	
Gehrke	1	1	100	13	13.0	0	0–	0	

PUNTING	No	Avg
Livingston	70	39.6
Swanson	12	38.3
Muhlmann	2	19.0
Lamb	1	29.0

KICKING	XP	Att	%	FG	Att	%
Muhlmann	32	33	97	16	24	67

1969 NFL CHAMPIONSHIP GAME

January 4, 1970 at Minnesota
(Attendance 46,503)

SCORING

MINNESOTA	14	10	3	0–27
CLEVELAND	0	0	0	7– 7

First Quarter			
	Min.	Kapp, 7 yard rush PAT–Cox (kick)	3:48
	Min.	Washington, 75 yard pass from Kapp PAT–Cox (kick)	7:07
Second Quarter			
	Min.	Cox, 30 yard field goal	1:07
	Min.	Osborn, 20 yard rush PAT–Cox (kick)	10:15
Third Quarter			
	Min.	Cox, 32 yard field goal	11:18
Fourth Quarter			
	Cle.	Collins, 3 yard pass from Nelsen PAT–Cockroft (kick)	1:24

TEAM STATISTICS

MINN.		CLEVE.
18	First Downs–Total	14
13	First Downs–Rushing	4
5	First Downs–Passing	10
0	First Downs–Penalty	0
0	Fumbles–Number	2
0	Fumbles–Lost Ball	1
3	Penalties–Number	1
33	Yards Penalized	5
0	Giveaways	3
3	Takeaways	0
+3	Difference	–3

Viking Heat

The Browns had beaten the Cowboys 38-14 in the first round of the playoffs with a tight pass defense and sharp passing by Bill Nelsen, and they hoped to pull another upset over the Vikings in the NFL title match. The Vikings had crushed the Browns 51-3 in a regular-season meeting and had disposed of the powerful Los Angeles Rams 23-20 with a fourth-quarter rally in last week's opening playoff game, and their superb defense made them favorites for this game.

Conditions for the game were typical of Minnesota in January. Snow ringed the field, and 8-degree temperature chilled the spectators through their layers of clothing. The Browns suffered from the cold, resorting to heaters and special footgear to combat it, but the Vikings used no heaters at all. Coach Bud Grant said, "we generate our own heat."

On the first series of the game, the Browns showed their discomfort in this weather. Cornerback Walt Sumner slipped and fell while covering Viking receiver Gene Washington, and Joe Kapp hit his man with a pass good for 33 yards down to the Cleveland 24-yard line. The Vikings moved down to the 7-yard line, and Kapp scored on a play characteristic of his rough style. He bumped into fullback Bill Brown in his backfield, then stormed straight ahead and broke several tackles on his way to the end zone. Several minutes later, Cleveland cornerback Erich Barnes lost his footing and fell while covering Washington, and Kapp whipped a pass which the end carried 75 yards for a second Minnesota touchdown. Trailing 14-0 and fully aware that the Minnesota defense allowed its opponents an average of only ten points a game, the Browns looked like a beaten team before the first quarter had ended. With the Viking defense keeping the Cleveland attack bottled up all afternoon, Minnesota won the game 27-7 and the NFL championship in the team's ninth year of operation.

INDIVIDUAL STATISTICS

MINNESOTA	No	Yds	Avg.	CLEVELAND	No	Yds	Avg.
RUSHING							
Osborn	18	108	6.0	Kelly	15	80	5.3
Kapp	8	57	7.1	Scott	6	17	2.8
Brown	12	43	3.6		21	97	4.6
Reed	5	7	1.4				
Jones	2	7	3.5				
	45	222	4.9				
RECEIVING							
Washington	3	120	40.0	Scott	5	56	11.2
Henderson	2	17	8.5	Collins	5	43	8.6
Brown	1	20	20.0	Warfield	4	47	11.8
Beasley	1	12	12.0	Kelly	2	17	8.5
	7	169	24.1	Morin	1	18	18.0
					17	181	10.6
PUNTING							
Lee	3		41.0	Cockroft	3		33.0
PUNT RETURNS							
West	1	1	1.0	Kelly	2	10	5.0
				Morrison	1	11	11.0
					3	21	7.0
KICKOFF RETURNS							
West	1	22	22.0	Scott	4	60	15.0
Jones	1	20	20.0	Morrison	1	23	23.0
	2	42	21.0		5	83	16.6
INTERCEPTION RETURNS							
Hilgenberg	1	0	0.0	None			
Krause	1	0	0.0				
	2	0	0.0				

PASSING

	Att.	Comp.	Comp. Pct.	Yds.	Int.	Yds/ Att.	Yds/ Comp.	Yards Lost Tackled
MINNESOTA								
Kapp	13	7	53.8	169	0	13.0	24.1	1– 8
CLEVELAND								
Nelsen	33	17	51.5	181	2	5.5	10.6	2–10

1969 AFL CHAMPIONSHIP GAME

January 4, 1970 at Oakland
(Attendance 53,564)

SCORING

OAKLAND	7	0	0	0– 7
KANSAS CITY	0	7	7	3–17

First Quarter			
	Oak.	Smith, 3 yard rush PAT–Blanda (kick)	14:14
Second Quarter			
	K.C.	Hayes, 1 yard rush PAT–Stenerud (kick)	13:10
Third Quarter			
	K.C.	Holmes, 5 yard rush PAT–Stenerud (kick)	11:17
Fourth Quarter			
	K.C.	Stenerud, 22 yard field goal	10:12

TEAM STATISTICS

OAK.		K.C.
18	First Downs–Total	13
6	First Downs–Rushing	5
10	First Downs–Passing	6
2	First Downs–Penalty	2
1	Fumbles–Number	5
0	Fumbles–Lost Ball	4
5	Penalties–Number	5
45	Yards Penalized	43
4	Giveaways	4
4	Takeaways	4
0	Difference	0

Finishing First When It Counts

The AFL installed a new playoff system for its final season, pitting the first-place finishers against the runners-up in the opposite division, with the winners playing for the league crown. The result was that two Western clubs met in the title game, as the first-place Raiders clobbered Houston 56-7 while the second-place Chiefs upset the New York Jets 13-6.

While the Raiders took a 7-0 lead on Charlie Smith's touchdown late in the first period, Kansas City passer Len Dawson found the Oakland defense hard to crack, as he missed on seven straight passes. Late in the second quarter, however, he hit Frank Pitts with a 41-yard bomb which brought the ball to the Oakland 1-yard line. From there, Wendell Hayes smashed over, and the Chiefs took a 7-7 tie into the locker room at halftime.

Early in the second half, Lamonica hurt his passing hand against the helmet of Aaron Brown and could not grip the ball properly the rest of the game. George Blanda relieved Lamonica at quarterback but had no miracles up his sleeve today. In addition to missing three field-goal attempts, he could not stand up under the Kansas City pass rush and saw one of his passes intercepted in the end zone. After intercepting Blanda's pass, Emmitt Thomas had run it out to the 6-yard line. Dawson then moved his team downfield through the air. Otis Taylor and Robert Holmes caught passes for long gains, and a pass interference penalty on the Raiders gave the Chiefs a first down on the Oakland 7. Holmes carried the ball three straight times to reach the end zone and put the Chiefs ahead 14-7.

Sore hand and all, Lamonica returned to the lineup in the final period, but three of his crippled passes were picked off by the Chiefs, who won the game 17-7 and headed off to the Super Bowl despite finishing second behind the Raiders in the regular season.

INDIVIDUAL STATISTICS

OAKLAND	No	Yds	Avg.	KANSAS CITY	No	Yds	Avg.
RUSHING							
Dixon	12	36	3.0	Hayes	8	35	4.4
Smith	12	31	2.6	Garrett	7	19	2.7
Banaszak	2	8	4.0	Holmes	18	14	0.8
Todd	2	4	2.0	McVea	3	13	4.3
	28	79	2.8	Dawson	3	5	1.7
					39	86	2.2
RECEIVING							
Smith	8	86	10.8	Taylor	3	62	20.7
Sherman	3	45	15.0	Holmes	2	16	8.0
Cannon	2	22	11.0	Pitts	1	41	41.0
Banaszak	2	13	6.5	Arbanas	1	10	10.0
Wells	1	24	24.0		7	129	18.4
Dixon	1	1	1.0				
	17	191	11.2				
PUNTING							
Eischeid	6		48.5	Wilson	8		42.9
PUNT RETURNS							
Atkinson	2	–1	–0.5	Garrett	4	9	2.3
KICKOFF RETURNS							
Atkinson	3	95	31.7	Holmes	1	26	26.0
Sherman	1	17	17.0	Hill	1	0	0.0
	4	112	28.0	Hayes	Lat	17	–
					2	43	21.5
INTERCEPTION RETURNS							
None				Thomas	2	69	34.5
				Marsalis	1	23	23.0
				Kearney	1	17	17.0
					4	109	27.3

PASSING

	Att.	Comp.	Comp. Pct.	Yds.	Int.	Yds/ Att.	Yds/ Comp.	Yards Lost Tackled
OAKLAND								
Lamonica	39	15	38.5	167	3	4.3	11.1	
Blanda	6	2	33.3	24	1	4.0	12.0	
	45	17	37.8	191	4	4.2	11.2	4–37
KANSAS CITY								
Dawson	17	7	41.2	129	0	7.6	18.4	1– 8

SUPER BOWL IV

January 11, at New Orleans
(Attendance 80,562)

An Upsetting Farewell

All of the Kansas City Chiefs wore a patch on their jerseys saying "AFL-10." This referred to the ten-year existence of the AFL, which would fade into oblivion after this game and the AFL All-Star Game a week later. As things turned out, the Chiefs took the AFL out in style by handily beating the NFL champion Minnesota Vikings.

It didn't figure. The Vikings had bullied their way through the NFL with a frightening defense, led by the front four of Jim Marshall, Carl Eller, Alan Page, and Gary Larsen and a ball-control attack paced by tough quarterback Joe Kapp. Odds-makers branded the Vikings as two-touchdown favorites to return the Super Bowl title to the NFL after a year in the possession of the AFL New York Jets.

The Chiefs had been to the Super Bowl before, however, and knew how to prepare better for the fanfare. While the Vikings were awed by the hubbub in New Orleans during the week before the game, the Chiefs seriously set about to avenge their loss to Green Bay in Super Bowl I.

The "I" formation that Kansas City used, concealing the position of their backs until the last moment before the play, gave the Minnesota defense some problems right from the start. The Chiefs assigned two men each to block Marshall and Eller, and this move gave the Kansas City backs room to run. Quarterback Len Dawson also found the Viking zone pass coverage less difficult than had been imagined, and he would complete twelve of seventeen passes through the afternoon.

The Kansas City defensive linemen, meanwhile, were putting hot pressure on Joe Kapp, forcing him to hurry his passes. While the defense harassed Kapp in the first period, the Chiefs got close enough to the goal line for Jan Stenerud to boot a 32-yard field goal to put the Chiefs ahead 3-0.

The second quarter went no better for the Viking attack as the Chiefs scored 13 points to break the game open. Stenerud kicked another field goal, Mike Garrett scored a touchdown after the Vikings had fumbled deep in their own territory, and Stenerud's third field goal made the score 16-0 at halftime.

The Vikings came out for the second half ready to climb back into the game, and Kapp immediately led them on a 69-yard drive that led to the Vikings' first touchdown. But the Vikes could not score again, and Otis Taylor's brilliant 46-yard run with a short pass made the final score only a little worse, 23-7, in favor of the Chiefs and, for the final time, the AFL.

KANSAS CITY		MINNESOTA
	OFFENSE	
Pitts	WR	Washington
Tyrer	LT	Alderman
Budde	LG	Vellone
Holub	C	Tingelhoff
Moorman	RG	Sunde
Hill	RT	Yary
Arbanas	TE	Beasley
Taylor	WR	Henderson
Dawson	QB	Kapp
Garrett	RB	Osborn
Holmes	RB	B. Brown
	DEFENSE	
Mays	LE	Eller
Culp	LT	Larsen
Buchanan	RT	Page
A. Brown	RE	Marshall
Bell	LLB	Winston
Lanier	MLB	Warwick
Lynch	RLB	Hilgenberg
Marsalis	LCB	Mackbee
Thomas	RCB	Sharockman
Kearney	LS	Kassulke
Robinson	RS	Krause

SUBSTITUTES

KANSAS CITY

Offense
Daney, McVea, Hayes, Podolak, Livingston, Prudhomme, McClinton, Richardson

Defense
Belser, Sellers, Hurston, Stein, Lothamer, Trosch, Mitchell

Kickers
Stenerud, Wilson

MINNESOTA

Offense
Cuozzo, Lee, Grim, Lindsey, Harris, Reed, Jones, Smith, Kramer, White

Defense
Dickson, McGill, Hackbart, West, Hargrove

Kicker
Cox

SCORING

KANSAS CITY	3	13	7	0–23
MINNESOTA	0	0	7	0– 7

First Quarter
K.C. Stenerud, 48 yard field goal

Second Quarter
K.C. Stenerud, 32 yard field goal
K.C. Stenerud, 25 yard field goal
K.C. Garrett, 5 yard rush
PAT – Stenerud (kick)

Third Quarter
Minn. Osborn, 4 yard rush
PAT – Cox (kick)
K.C. Taylor, 46 yard pass from Dawson
PAT – Stenerud (kick)

TEAM STATISTICS

K. C.		MINN.
18	First Downs – Total	13
8	First Downs – Rushing	2
7	First Downs – Passing	10
3	First Downs – Penalty	1
0	Fumbles – Number	3
0	Fumbles – Lost Ball	2
4	Penalties – Number	6
47	Yards Penalized	67
62	Total Offensive Plays	50
273	Total Net Yards	239
4.4	Average Gain	4.8
0	Missed Field Goals	1
1	Giveaways	5
5	Takeaways	1
+4	Difference	–4

INDIVIDUAL STATISTICS

KANSAS CITY	No	Yds	Avg.	MINNESOTA	No	Yds	Avg.
			RUSHING				
Garrett	11	39	3.5	Brown	6	26	4.3
Pitts	3	37	12.3	Reed	4	17	4.3
Hayes	8	31	3.9	Osborn	7	15	2.1
McVea	12	26	2.2	Kapp	2	9	4.5
Dawson	3	11	3.7		19	67	3.5
Holmes	5	7	1.4				
	42	151	3.6				
			RECEIVING				
Taylor	6	81	13.5	Henderson	7	111	15.9
Pitts	3	33	11.0	Brown	3	11	3.7
Garrett	2	25	12.5	Beasley	2	41	20.5
Hayes	1	3	3.0	Reed	2	16	8.0
	12	142	11.8	Osborn	2	11	5.5
				Washington	1	9	9.0
					17	199	11.7
			PUNTING				
Wilson	4		48.5	Lee	3		37.0
			PUNT RETURNS				
Garrett	1	0	0.0	West	2	18	9.0
			KICKOFF RETURNS				
Hayes	2	36	18.0	West	3	46	15.3
				Jones	1	33	33.0
					4	79	19.8
			INTERCEPTION RETURNS				
Lanier	1	9	9.0	Krause	1	0	0.0
Robinson	1	9	9.0				
Thomas	1	6	6.0				
	3	24	8.0				

PASSING

KANSAS CITY	Att	Comp	Comp Pct.	Yds	Int	Yds/ Att.	Yds/ Comp	Yards Lost Tackled
Dawson	17	12	70.6	142	1	8.4	11.8	3–20
MINNESOTA								
Kapp	25	16	64.0	183	2	7.3	11.4	
Cuozzo	3	1	33.3	16	1	5.3	16.0	
	28	17	60.7	199	3	7.1	11.7	3–27

N.F.C. 1970 The Monday-Night Circus

The TV gridiron fan found a new addiction this season: Monday-night football. The American Broadcasting Company telecast a game every Monday night of the season, with Howard Cosell, Don Meredith and Keith Jackson the men behind the mikes. For the first time ever, the game itself became secondary to the show put on by the announcers in the press box. Cosell, the verbose ex-labor lawyer who had built a reputation by being highly critical of almost everything, commented on each game in highly dramatic tones, while ex-Dallas Cowboy quarterback Don Meredith, dubbed "Dandy Don" by Cosell, mixed his analysis with homespun country witticisms. The interplay between these two, sometimes veering off into mutual needling, delighted some and drove others to turn the sound off on their sets. Jackson, the member of the trio who concentrated on reporting the game, was rewarded after the season by being dropped from the series.

EASTERN DIVISION

Dallas Cowboys—The Cowboys had so much talent, some coaches would have been delighted to trade their starters for the Dallas second-stringers. With two good running backs already in the fold in Calvin Hill and Walt Garrison, the Cowboys this year added rookie Duane Thomas, an uncommunicative man who did his talking by running over people while carrying a football. Herb Adderley was obtained from Green Bay to further strengthen the secondary, and when Lance Rentzel sat out the last weeks of the season with personal problems, rookie Reggie Rucker filled in capably. Although the offensive line had always been strong, Dave Manders, Blaine Nye, and Rayfield Wright all rose up from the second string to win starting jobs. Even at quarterback, coach Tom Landry had his pick of a good pocket passer in Craig Morton or a top roll-out passer in Roger Staubach.

New York Giants—Quarterback Fran Tarkenton ran the attack with imagination, Ron Johnson developed into a superb runner and receiver after coming over from Cleveland, Tucker Frederickson shook the injury hex for this year, Clifton McNeil grabbed Tarkenton's passes, and the offensive line matured into a sturdy unit. The defense was less impressive, but aces Fred Dryer, Jim Files, and Spider Lockhart held the platoon together. After beating St. Louis one week from the end, the Giants held a share of first place with Dallas heading into their final game before losing 31-3 to the Rams.

St. Louis Cardinals—The Cards sailed into December with an 8-2-1 record and first place in the East was theirs for the taking. Twice during the year the Cards had beaten the Cowboys, laying a 38-0 drubbing on them in their meeting in Dallas. MacArthur Lane, Ernie McMillan, Larry Stallings, Roger Wehrli, and Larry Wilson all turned in All-Pro performances, while a host of other Cards all enjoyed good seasons. But just when the team seemed about to capture its first title since moving to St. Louis in 1960, the roof caved in. First the Detroit Lions beat them, then the New York Giants clubbed them 34-17 to knock them out of first place. Then, with the title a fleeting dream, the Cards dropped their finale 28-27 to the Redskins.

Washington Redskins—When training camp opened, head coach Vince Lombardi wasn't there; he was in the hospital, terminally ill with cancer. Assistant Bill Austin took over as head man until Lombardi got out of the hospital, but the all-time great coach died on September 3, two weeks before the start of the regular season. Austin guided the club through the season, but the team never really recovered from Lombardi's death. The only bright spot of the year was the development of runner Larry Brown into a star. Using his blockers well and fighting for every yard, Brown became the first Redskin to rush 1,000 yards.

Philadelphia Eagles—A flabby defense and an injury to fullback Tom Woodeshick shackled the Eagles into last place in the Eastern Division, but the team did have talent in several areas. The trio of Gary Ballman, Harold Jackson, and Ben Hawkins provided top-notch receiving, and Cyril Pinder ran well at halfback. The linebacking corps had three solid players in Adrian Young, Tim Rossovich, and Ron Porter; Rossovich had other skills in addition to his talents on the field. The curly-haired, mustachioed Rossovich would occasionally do unusual things, such as walking into a party with his hair on fire.

CENTRAL DIVISION

Minnesota Vikings—The Vikings still had that marvelous defense, but they lacked that extra inspirational spark when quarterback Joe Kapp sat out the early games over a salary dispute and then was sold to Boston. Carl Eller, Alan Page, Paul Krause, and the other members of the defense smothered enough enemy offenses to win twelve games, while the offense operated just enough under Gary Cuozzo to make it back to first place this year. Place kicker Fred Cox could be counted on to make good on three-pointers within the 40-yard line to bail out the offense. But although Cuozzo passed the ball better than Kapp, the fanatical leadership Kapp provided was missing.

Detroit Lions—Even without a clear-cut starter at quarterback, the Lion attack still blossomed into a steady point-producing outfit. Bill Munson and Greg Landry split the passer's spot, although Landry played more as the season went on, and both found good runners in Mel Farr and Altie Taylor and good receivers in Earl McCullough, Larry Walton, and Charlie Sanders. The line gave both quarterbacks good protection and figured highly in the offense's performance. On defense, the linebacking and secondary corps were full with top players, with Dick LeBeau and Paul Naumoff of All-Pro quality, but the front four needed some new blood, as Alex Karras no longer was rushing quarterbacks as he once had.

Chicago Bears—Gale Sayers, the once incomparable runner, hurt his knee and went out of action early in the season for surgery. Brian Piccolo fell fatally ill with cancer. Quarterback Bobby Douglass threw four touchdown passes in his first starting assignment of the year, but broke his wrist late in the game and missed the rest of the year. Pre-season trades for Elijah Pitts, Lee Roy Caffey, and Craig Baynham didn't work out. But the Bears did win six games, and did uncover an exciting player in little Cecil Turner, who returned four kickoffs all the way to tie the NFL record.

Green Bay Packers—The Packers kept dropping veterans of the Lombardi years and suffered through another losing season. Willie Davis, Henry Jordan, and Boyd Dowler all retired, Elijah Pitts, Lee Roy Caffey, and Bob Hyland were dealt to Chicago, and Herb Adderley and Marv Fleming went to Dallas and Miami in trades. Of those staying on the scene, a sore arm hampered quarterback Bart Starr, a torn Achilles tendon sidelined linebacker Dave Robinson, and age started catching up on middle linebacker Ray Nitschke.

WESTERN DIVISION

San Francisco '49ers—After years of near misses and disappointing finishes, the '49ers finally put everything together and won the Western crown. The offense, always respected, blossomed into one of pro football's best with fine seasons from John Brodie, Gene Washington, Forrest Blue, and Cas Banaszek. The entire front line had a good year, allowing Brodie to be dropped only eight times all season. The defense, however, surprised most experts by turning in a superb performance. Coach Dick Nolan rotated the front four spots and thus kept fresh men in the game at all times. Dave Wilcox starred at linebacker, and the secondary of Jim Johnson, rookie Bruce Taylor, Rosey Taylor, and Al Randolph discouraged enemy passers. The acquisition of place kicker Bruce Gossett from Los Angeles nicely rounded out the picture.

Los Angeles Rams—Coach George Allen kept adding veterans to the squad, this year bringing in Kermit Alexander, but the Rams fell just short of the Western title. The defense as usual made life difficult for enemy offenses, and the Los Angeles attack again moved slowly but surely under the direction of Roman Gabriel. The rise of the '49ers gave the Rams competition for the divisional crown, however, and a 28-23 loss to Detroit on the final Monday-night game of the year knocked the Rams out of first place for good. The team recovered to beat New York to end the season, but that was to be George Allen's last game with the Rams. Owner Dan Reeves, already dying with cancer, fired Allen after the season despite his 49-17-4 record.

Atlanta Falcons—After improving for several seasons, the Falcons fell back for the first time under coach Norm Van Brocklin's regime. One weight on the team's progress was a remarkably unexciting offense, with an unsettled quarterback situation, no speed in the running back and receiving spots, and chaos in the front line. The defense had three star players in end Claude Humphrey, middle linebacker Tommy Nobis, and cornerback Ken Reaves, but most of the other positions lacked a quality occupant.

New Orleans Saints—The Saints' roster was like a revolving door, with players joining and leaving the squad in steady flows all season. Head coach Tom Fears was one of the mid-season departures, with J. D. Roberts promoted from a minor-league team to take charge of the Saints. The Saints had a few good players who put out consistently good performances, but they were almost buried amidst the chaos and mediocrity which ruined the season for the team. Flanker Dan Abramowicz and defensive tackle Dave Rowe played well, but the hero of the club was place kicker Tom Dempsey, a man born without a right hand and without toes on his right foot. Using a special kicking shoe, Dempsey was an erratic kicker but made the record books by booting a 63-yard three-pointer to beat the Detroit Lions.

FINAL TEAM STATISTICS

OFFENSE

	ATL.	CHI.	DALL.	DET.	G.B.	L.A.	MINN.	N.O.	N.Y.G.	PHIL.	ST.L.	S.F.	WASH.
FIRST DOWNS:													
Total	199	179	229	243	194	224	225	183	257	229	226	237	249
by Rushing	76	55	119	113	69	93	98	55	94	81	110	86	122
by Passing	110	104	95	107	110	120	111	112	150	126	104	125	100
by Penalty	13	20	15	23	15	11	16	16	13	22	12	26	27
RUSHING:													
Number	431	353	522	514	453	430	508	371	465	450	429	471	444
Yards	1600	1092	2300	2127	1595	1763	1634	1215	1799	1539	1998	1580	2021
Average Yards	3.7	3.1	4.4	4.1	3.5	4.1	3.2	3.3	3.9	3.4	4.7	3.4	4.6
Touchdowns	4	3	16	16	8	12	16	4	11	11	18	13	11
PASSING:													
Attempts	342	422	297	294	351	426	344	415	403	410	390	383	342
Completions	197	210	149	167	177	218	173	213	230	218	178	226	203
Completion Percentage	57.6	49.8	50.2	56.8	50.4	51.2	50.3	51.3	57.1	53.2	45.6	59.0	59.4
Passing Yards	2262	2431	2445	2121	2196	2658	2378	2690	2892	2651	2689	2990	2357
Avg. Yards per Attempt	6.6	5.8	8.2	7.2	6.3	6.2	6.9	6.5	7.2	6.5	6.9	7.8	6.9
Avg. Yards per Complet.	11.5	11.6	16.4	12.7	12.4	12.2	13.7	12.6	12.6	12.2	15.1	13.2	11.6
Times Tackled Passing	53	33	39	36	43	23	29	28	37	23	26	8	29
Yards Lost Tackled	431	258	296	264	382	150	197	232	258	200	216	67	249
Net Yards	1831	2173	2149	1857	1814	2508	2181	2458	2634	2451	2473	2923	2108
Touchdowns	18	21	18	19	11	17	12	11	19	16	16	25	23
Interceptions	21	22	16	12	24	13	15	22	12	23	19	10	10
Percent Intercepted	6.1	5.2	5.4	4.1	6.8	3.1	4.4	5.3	3.0	5.6	4.9	2.6	2.9
PUNTS:													
Number	76	84	69	62	87	67	61	77	54	71	65	75	61
Average Distance	38.7	40.8	41.3	40.0	40.2	39.1	37.9	42.5	38.3	36.6	40.9	38.4	40.9
PUNT RETURNS:													
Number	34	57	32	34	25	62	35	29	29	32	41	48	27
Yards	356	246	237	306	98	418	216	214	193	100	315	550	45
Average Yards	10.5	4.3	7.4	9.0	3.9	6.7	6.2	7.4	6.7	3.1	7.7	11.5	1.7
Touchdowns	2	0	0	1	0	0	0	0	1	0	1	0	0
KICKOFF RETURNS:													
Number	47	56	37	43	63	47	36	53	52	59	47	49	61
Yards	916	1472	888	959	1422	1236	842	1044	1157	1252	926	967	1223
Average Yards	19.5	26.3	24.0	22.3	22.6	26.3	23.4	19.7	22.3	21.2	19.7	19.7	20.0
Touchdowns	0	4	1	1	2	1	0	0	0	0	0	0	0
INTERCEPTION RETURNS:													
Number	19	17	24	28	20	19	28	22	17	10	21	22	15
Yards	191	129	307	417	398	280	412	260	223	102	255	308	240
Average Yards	10.1	7.6	12.8	14.9	19.9	14.7	14.7	11.8	13.1	10.2	12.1	14.0	16.0
Touchdowns	0	0	0	4	1	2	2	0	0	0	2	2	0
PENALTIES:													
Number	76	94	87	58	76	88	60	91	71	73	84	88	65
Yards	807	853	934	659	691	959	631	1029	641	799	896	997	613
FUMBLES:													
Number	24	29	29	26	34	27	25	27	29	26	24	24	26
Number Lost	17	13	12	15	17	17	16	18	14	16	14	15	14
POINTS:													
Total	206	256	299	347	196	325	335	172	301	241	325	352	297
PAT Attempts	26	28	35	41	22	34	35	17	32	29	38	41	34
PAT Made	23	28	35	41	19	34	35	16	32	25	37	39	33
FG Attempts	25	34	27	29	28	45	46	34	41	25	32	31	27
FG Made	9	20	18	20	15	29	30	18	25	14	20	21	20
Percent FG Made	36.0	58.8	66.7	69.0	53.6	64.4	65.2	52.9	61.0	56.0	62.5	67.7	74.1
Safeties	0	0	0	0	0	0	0	0	1	0	0	2	0

DEFENSE

	ATL.	CHI.	DALL.	DET.	G.B.	L.A.	MINN.	N.O.	N.Y.G.	PHIL.	ST.L.	S.F.	WASH.
FIRST DOWNS:													
Total	211	234	205	186	202	195	168	263	223	213	242	213	266
by Rushing	93	83	87	61	88	64	68	100	98	102	96	81	125
by Passing	98	133	105	112	102	113	89	150	110	95	116	110	125
by Penalty	20	18	13	13	12	18	11	13	15	16	30	22	16
RUSHING:													
Number	479	459	415	362	453	395	398	469	419	457	472	425	468
Yards	1722	1471	1656	1152	1829	1359	1365	1891	1692	2064	1762	1799	2068
Average Yards	3.6	3.2	4.0	3.2	4.0	3.4	3.4	4.0	4.0	4.5	3.7	4.2	4.4
Touchdowns	14	11	10	7	14	6	4	15	11	16	10	12	19
PASSING:													
Attempts	348	394	399	371	369	378	367	430	364	313	382	384	374
Completions	191	233	193	194	177	196	195	238	186	161	183	185	205
Completion Percentage	54.9	59.1	48.4	52.3	48.0	51.9	53.1	55.3	51.1	51.4	47.9	48.2	54.8
Passing Yards	2397	2925	2226	2491	2496	2615	1798	3197	2650	2176	2416	2434	2434
Avg. Yards per Attempt	6.9	7.4	5.6	6.7	6.8	6.9	4.9	7.4	7.3	7.0	6.3	6.3	6.5
Avg. Yards per Complet.	12.5	12.6	11.5	12.8	14.1	13.3	9.2	13.4	14.2	13.5	13.2	13.2	11.9
Times Tackled Passing	30	42	41	23	32	53	49	17	35	34	40	30	24
Yards Lost Tackled	243	329	313	195	270	426	360	136	279	287	309	261	169
Net Yards	2154	2596	1913	2296	2226	2189	1438	3061	2371	1889	2107	2173	2265
Touchdowns	11	18	10	14	13	15	6	19	19	16	16	19	14
Interceptions	19	17	24	28	20	19	28	22	17	10	21	22	15
Percent Intercepted	5.5	4.3	6.0	7.5	5.4	5.0	7.6	5.1	4.7	3.2	5.5	5.7	4.0
PUNTS:													
Number	60	87	74	70	71	88	84	56	62	62	80	82	56
Average Distance	41.2	37.6	41.1	39.1	40.1	37.8	37.5	40.4	39.7	39.1	40.0	40.4	39.3
PUNT RETURNS:													
Number	40	40	38	29	40	32	38	41	21	22	26	38	35
Yards	267	268	281	113	338	181	322	434	61	163	90	180	259
Average Yards	6.7	6.7	7.4	3.9	8.5	5.7	8.5	10.6	2.9	7.4	3.5	4.7	7.4
Touchdowns	0	0	1	0	0	0	1	1	0	1	0	0	0
KICKOFF RETURNS:													
Number	41	47	60	67	36	71	69	35	57	50	54	58	49
Yards	983	935	1142	1427	888	1278	1514	735	1359	1030	1262	1362	1181
Average Yards	24.0	19.9	19.0	21.3	24.7	18.0	21.9	21.0	23.8	20.6	23.4	23.5	24.1
Touchdowns	1	0	0	0	0	0	3	0	1	1	1	0	1
INTERCEPTION RETURNS:													
Number	21	22	16	12	24	13	15	22	12	23	19	10	10
Yards	283	251	259	174	421	92	175	256	172	461	276	95	181
Average Yards	13.5	11.4	16.2	14.5	17.5	7.1	11.7	11.6	14.3	20.0	14.5	9.5	18.1
Touchdowns	1	1	1	1	3	0	0	1	0	2	0	0	1
PENALTIES:													
Number	93	76	70	90	63	77	58	79	71	90	68	87	87
Yards	897	826	732	805	686	825	586	875	675	991	659	965	930
FUMBLES:													
Number	22	27	25	30	29	28	27	26	31	25	20	35	22
Number Lost	16	14	15	16	17	16	16	16	13	18	14	20	13
POINTS:													
Total	261	261	221	202	293	202	143	347	270	332	228	267	314
PAT Attempts	29	31	24	22	30	22	14	40	32	36	27	32	37
PAT Made	27	27	24	22	29	22	14	38	30	35	27	30	36
FG Attempts	40	29	26	26	42	25	27	34	29	39	26	24	26
FG Made	20	16	17	16	28	16	15	23	16	27	13	15	18
Percent FG Made	50.0	55.2	65.4	61.5	66.7	64.0	55.6	67.6	55.2	69.2	50.0	62.5	69.2
Safeties	0	0	1	0	0	0	0	0	0	0	0	0	1

CONFERENCE PLAYOFFS

December 26, at Dallas
(Attendance 69,613)

SCORING

DALLAS	3	0	0	2–5
DETROIT	0	0	0	0–0

First Quarter
Dal. Clark, 26 yard field goal

Fourth Quarter
Dal. Andrie, Safety-tackled Landry

TEAM STATISTICS

DALLAS		DETR.
19	First Downs–Total	7
11	First Downs–Rushing	2
8	First Downs–Passing	5
0	First Downs–Penalty	0
0	Fumbles–Number	3
0	Fumbles–Lost Ball	2
6	Penalties–Number	0
47	Yards Penalized	0
0	Missed Field Goals	0
69	Offensive Plays–Total	50
231	Net Yards	156
3.3	Average Gain	3.1
1	Giveaways	3
3	Takeaways	1
+2	Difference	–2

INDIVIDUAL STATISTICS

DALLAS	No.	Yds.	Avg.	DETROIT	No.	Yds.	Avg.
RUSHING							
Thomas	30	135	4.5	Farr	12	31	2.6
Garrison	17	72	4.2	Taylor	9	16	1.8
Morton	3	2	0.7	Landry	3	15	5.0
	50	209	4.2	Owens	2	9	4.5
				Walton	1	5	5.0
					27	76	2.8
RECEIVING							
Garrison	2	8	4.0	Walton	3	39	13.0
Hayes	1	20	20.0	Taylor	2	7	3.5
Norman	1	10	10.0	McCullough	1	39	39.0
	4	38	9.5	Owens	1	7	7.0
					7	92	13.1
PUNTING							
Widby	8		44.7	Weaver	8		48.8
PUNT RETURNS							
Renfro	4	23	5.8	Barney	5	20	4.0
				Vaughan	1	1	1.0
					6	21	3.5
KICKOFF RETURNS							
Hayes	1	16	16.0	Williams	1	24	24.0
Waters	1	9	9.0	Maxwell	1	13	13.0
	2	25	12.5		2	37	18.5
INTERCEPTION RETURNS							
Renfro	1	13	13.0	Weger	1	31	31.0

PASSING

	Att.	Comp.	Comp. Pct.	Yds.	Int.	Yds/ Att.	Yds/ Comp.	Yds Lost Tkld.
DALLAS								
Morton	18	4	22.2	38	1	2.1	9.5	1–16
DETROIT								
Landry	12	5	41.7	48	0	4.0	9.6	
Munson	8	2	25.0	44	1	5.5	22.0	
	20	7	35.0	92	1	4.8	13.1	3–12

December 27, at Bloomington
(Attendance 45,103)

SCORING

MINNESOTA	7	0	0	7–14
SAN FRANCISCO	7	3	0	7–17

First Quarter
Min. Krause, 22 yard fumble return
PAT–Cox (kick)
S.F. Witcher, 24 yard pass from Brodie
PAT–Gossett (kick)

Second Quarter
S.F. Gossett, 40 yard field goal

Fourth Quarter
S.F. Brodie, 1 yard rush
PAT–Gossett (kick)
Min. Washington, 24 yard pass from Cuozzo
PAT–Cox (kick)

TEAM STATISTICS

MINN.		S.F.
14	First Downs–Total	14
7	First Downs–Rushing	5
6	First Downs–Passing	8
1	First Downs–Penalty	1
3	Fumbles–Number	5
2	Fumbles–Lost Ball	3
1	Penalties–Number	3
5	Yards Penalized	37
2	Missed Field Goals	1
60	Offensive Plays–Total	71
241	Net Yards	289
4.1	Average Gain	4.1
4	Giveaways	3
3	Takeaways	4
–1	Difference	+1

INDIVIDUAL STATISTICS

MINNESOTA	No.	Yds.	Avg.	SAN FRANCISCO	No	Yds	Avg.
RUSHING							
Jones	15	60	4.0	Willard	27	85	3.1
Osborn	12	41	3.4	Tucker	7	5	0.7
Cuozzo	1	11	11.0	Brodie	2	3	1.5
Brown	2	5	2.5	Kwalick	1	2	2.0
	30	117	3.9	Cunningham	1	0	0.0
					38	95	2.5
RECEIVING							
Henderson	5	80	16.0	Tucker	6	48	8.0
Grim	2	37	18.5	Witcher	4	45	11.3
Washington	1	24	24.0	Kwalick	3	45	15.0
Jones	1	5	5.0	Washington	2	45	22.5
	9	146	16.2	Willard	1	18	18.0
					16	201	12.6
PUNTING							
McNeil	7		39.4	Spurrier	8		33.8
PUNT RETURNS							
None				B. Taylor	5	69	13.8
KICKOFF RETURNS							
Jones	3	49	16.3	Beard	1	17	17.0
Brown	1	23	23.0	Tucker	1	13	13.0
	4	72	18.0	Hoskins	1	0	0.0
					3	30	10.0
INTERCEPTION RETURNS							
None				Sniadecki	1	5	5.0
				B. Taylor	1	0	0.0
					2	5	2.5

PASSING

	Att.	Comp.	Comp. Pct.	Yds.	Int.	Yds/ Att.	Yds/ Comp.	Yds Lost Tkld.
MINNESOTA								
Cuozzo	27	9	33.3	146	2	5.4	16.2	3–22
SAN FRANCISCO								
Brodie	32	16	50.0	201	0	6.3	12.6	1– 8

DALLAS COWBOYS 10-4-0 Tom Landry

Scores of Each Game		
17	Philadelphia	7
28	N. Y. GIANTS	10
7	St. Louis	20
13	ATLANTA	0
13	Minnesota	54
27	Kansas City	16
21	PHILADELPHIA	17
20	N. Y. Giants	23
0	ST. LOUIS	38
45	Washington	21
16	GREEN BAY	3
34	WASHINGTON	0
6	Cleveland	2
52	HOUSTON	10

Use Name	Pos.	Hgt	Wgt	Age	Int	Pts
Bob Asher	OT	6'5"	250	22		
Tony Liscio	OT	6'5"	255	30		
Ralph Neely	OT	6'5"	265	26		
Rayfield Wright	OT	6'7"	255	25		
John Niland	OG	6'4"	245	26		
Blaine Nye	OG	6'4"	250	24		
Halvor Hagen	C-OG	6'5"	253	23		
Dave Manders	C	6'2"	250	28		
George Andrie	DE	6'7"	250	30		
Larry Cole	DE	6'4"	255	23		
Pat Toomay	DE	6'5"	244	25		
Ron East	DT	6'4"	242	27		
Bob Lilly	DT	6'4"	260	31		
Jethro Pugh	DT	6'6"	260	26	1	
Dave Edwards	LB	6'3"	225	31	2	
Chuck Howley	LB	6'3"	225	34	2	
Lee Roy Jordan	LB	6'2"	220	29	1	
Steve Kiner	LB	6'	218	23	1	
D. D. Lewis	LB	6'2"	225	24		
Tom Stincic	LB	6'2"	230	23	1	
Herb Adderley	DB	6'1"	200	31	3	
Richmond Flowers	DB	6'	180	23		
Cornell Green	DB	6'4"	208	30	1	
Cliff Harris	DB	6'	184	21	2	
Mel Renfro	DB	6'	190	26	4	
Mark Washington	DB	5'10"	188	22	1	6
Charlie Waters	DB	6'1"	193	21	5	
Bob Belden	QB	6'2"	205	23		
Craig Morton	QB	6'4"	214	27		
Roger Staubach	QB	6'2"	197	28		
Dan Reeves	HB	6'1"	200	26		12
Claxton Welch	HB	5'11"	203	23		6
Calvin Hill	FB-HB	6'3"	227	23		24
Duane Thomas	FB-HB	6'1"	220	23		30
Walt Garrison	FB	6'	205	26		30
Margene Atkins	WR	5'10"	183	23		
Bob Hayes	WR	6'	185	27		66
Dennis Homan	WR	6'1"	180	24		
Lance Rentzel	WR	6'2"	202	26		30
Reggie Rucker	WR	6'2"	190	22		6
Mike Ditka	TE	6'3"	225	30		
Pettis Norman	TE	6'3"	220	30		
Mike Clark	K	6'1"	205	29		89
Ron Widby	K	6'4"	210	25		

NEW YORK GIANTS 9-5-0 Alex Webster

Scores of Each Game		
16	CHICAGO	24
10	Dallas	28
10	New Orleans	14
30	PHILADELPHIA	23
16	Boston	0
35	ST. LOUIS	17
22	N. Y. Jets	10
23	DALLAS	20
35	WASHINGTON	33
20	Philadelphia	23
27	Washington	24
20	BUFFALO	6
34	St. Louis	17
3	LOS ANGELES	31

Use Name	Pos.	Hgt	Wgt	Age	Int	Pts
Rich Buzin	OT	6'4"	250	24		
Dennis Crane	OT	6'6"	260	25		
Willie Young	OT	6'	265	27		
Charlie Harper	OG-OT	6'2"	250	26		
Willie Banks	OG	6'2"	237	24		
Pete Case	OG	6'3"	245	29		
Doug Van Horn	OG	6'2"	245	26		
Len Johnson	C-OG	6'2"	250	24		
Pat Hughes	C	6'2"	240	23		
Greg Larson	C	6'2"	250	31		
John Baker	DE	6'5"	260	28		
Fred Dryer	DE	6'6"	240	24		
Bob Lurtsema	DE	6'6"	250	28		
Jim Kanicki	DT	6'4"	270	28		
Jim Norton	DT	6'4"	254	27		
Jerry Shay	DT	6'3"	245	26		
John Douglas	LB	6'2"	225	25		
Jim Files	LB	6'4"	240	22	1	2
Matt Hazeltine	LB	6'1"	225	37	1	
Ralph Heck	LB	6'2"	230	29	1	
Ray Hickl	LB	6'2"	220	23		
John Kirby	LB	6'3"	232	28		
Al Brenner	DB	6'1"	200	22		
Otto Brown	DB	6'1"	188	23		
Scott Eaton	DB	6'3"	205	26	2	
Joe Green	DB	5'11"	195	23		
Spider Lockhart	DB	6'2"	175	27	4	
Tom Longo	DB	6'1"	200	26	2	
Kenny Parker	DB	6'1"	190	24		
Willie Williams	DB	6'	190	27	6	
Dick Shiner	QB	6'	197	28		
Fran Tarkenton	QB	6'1"	190	30		12
Bobby Duhon	HB	6'	195	23		6
Ron Johnson	HB	6'1"	205	22		72
Les Shy	HB	6'1"	200	26		
Joe Morrison	FB-WR-HB	6'1"	212	32		
Tucker Frederickson	FB	6'3"	220	27		24
Ernie Koy	HB-FB	6'2"	225	27		
Don Herrmann	WR	6'2"	195	23		12
Rich Houston	WR	6'2"	197	24		
Clifton McNeil	WR	6'2"	187	30		30
Bob Tucker	TE	6'3"	230	25		30
Aaron Thomas	WR-TE	6'3"	210	32		6
Pete Gogolak	K	6'2"	190	28		107
Bill Johnson	K	6'2"	208	26		

Junior Coffey – Knee Injury
Tommy Crutcher – Knee Injury

ST. LOUIS CARDINALS 8-5-1 Charlie Winner

Scores of Each Game		
13	Los Angeles	34
27	WASHINGTON	17
20	DALLAS	7
24	NEW ORLEANS	17
35	Philadelphia	20
17	N. Y. Giants	35
44	HOUSTON	0
31	BOSTON	0
38	Dallas	0
6	Kansas City	6
23	PHILADELPHIA	14
3	Detroit	16
17	N. Y. GIANTS	34
27	Washington	28

Use Name	Pos.	Hgt	Wgt	Age	Int	Pts
Vern Emerson	OT	6'5"	260	24		
Ernie McMillan	OT	6'6"	255	32		
Bob Reynolds	OT	6'6"	265	29		
Clyde Williams	OG-OT	6'2"	250	30		
Irv Goode	OG	6'4"	255	29		
Chuck Hutchison	OG	6'3"	240	21		
Mike LaHood	OG	6'3"	250	25		
Wayne Mulligan	C	6'2"	245	23		
Rolf Krueger	DE	6'4"	250	23		
Cal Snowden	DE	6'4"	250	23		
Chuck Walker	DE	6'2"	250	29		
Joe Schmiesing	DT-DE	6'4"	250	25		
Fred Heron	DT	6'4"	260	25		
Bob Rowe	DT	6'4"	255	25		
Mike Siwok	DT	6'3"	260	22		
Chip Healy	LB	6'3"	235	23		
Dave Olerich	LB	6'1"	225	25		
Don Parish	LB	6'1"	220	22	1	6
Jamie Rivers	LB	6'2"	235	24		
Rocky Romesa	LB	6'2"	230	24		
Larry Stallings	LB	6'2"	230	28	1	
Terry Brown	DB	6'1"	210	23		
Miller Farr	DB	6'1"	190	27	5	6
Chuck Latourette	DB	6'	190	25		6
Tony Plummer	DB	5'11"	190	23		
Jerry Stovall	DB	6'2"	195	28	2	
Roger Wehrli	DB	6'1"	195	22	6	
Larry Wilson	DB	6'	195	32	5	
Nate Wright	DB	5'11"	180	23	1	
Pete Beathard	QB	6'2"	210	28		
Jim Hart	QB	6'2"	205	26		
Charlie Pittman	HB	6'1"	200	22		
Roy Shivers	HB	6'	200	28		12
Paul White	HB	6'	200	22		
MacArthur Lane	FB-HB	6'	220	28		78
Cid Edwards	FB	6'2"	230	26		12
Johnny Roland	HB-FB	6'2"	215	27		30
Jerry Daanen	WR	6'	190	25		
John Gilliam	WR	6'1"	195	25		36
Freddie Hyatt	WR	6'3"	210	24		
Dave Williams	WR	6'2"	210	25		18
Bob Brown	TE	6'3"	225	27		
Jim McFarland	TE	6'5"	225	22		
Jackie Smith	TE	6'4"	235	29		24
Jim Bakken	K	6'	195	29		97

WASHINGTON REDSKINS 6-8-0 Bill Austin

Scores of Each Game		
17	San Francisco	26
17	St. Louis	27
33	Philadelphia	21
31	DETROIT	10
20	Oakland	34
20	CINCINNATI	0
19	Denver	3
10	MINNESOTA	19
33	N. Y. Giants	35
21	DALLAS	45
24	N. Y. GIANTS	27
0	Dallas	34
24	PHILADELPHIA	6
28	ST. LOUIS	27

Use Name	Pos.	Hgt	Wgt	Age	Int	Pts
Walt Rock	OT	6'5"	255	29		
Jim Snowden	OT	6'3"	255	28		
Steve Wright	OT	6'6"	250	28		
Paul Laaveg	OG	6'4"	245	21		
Vince Promuto	OG	6'1"	245	32		
Roy Schmidt	OG	6'3"	250	28		
Ray Schoenke	OG	6'3"	250	28		
Gene Hamlin	C	6'3"	245	24		
Len Hauss	C	6'2"	235	29		
Bruce Anderson	DE	6'4"	250	26		
Bill Brundige	DE	6'5"	270	21		
Leo Carroll	DE	6'7"	250	26		
Terry Hermeling	DE	6'5"	255	24		
John Hoffman	DE	6'7"	260	27		
Frank Bosch	DT	6'4"	246	24		
Floyd Peters	DT	6'4"	255	35		
Manny Sistrunk	DT	6'5"	265	23		
Chris Hanburger	LB	6'2"	218	29	1	
Marlin McKeever	LB	6'1"	235	30		
Harold McLinton	LB	6'2"	235	23		
Tom Roussel	LB	6'3"	235	25		
Russ Tillman	LB	6'2"	230	24		
John Didion	C-LB	6'4"	245	22		
Mike Bass	DB	6'	190	25	4	
Pat Fischer	DB	5'10"	170	30	2	
Jim Harris	DB	5'11"	173	24		
Rickie Harris	DB	6'	182	27	3	
Jon Jaqua	DB	6'	190	22	1	
Brig Owens	DB	5'11"	190	27	4	
Ted Vactor	DB	6'	185	26		
Sonny Jurgensen	QB	5'11"	203	36		6
Frank Ryan	QB	6'3"	207	34		
Larry Brown	HB	5'11"	195	22		42
Bob Brunet	HB	6'1"	205	24		
Danny Pierce	FB-HB	6'3"	216	22		
Henry Dyer	FB	6'2"	230	25		
Charlie Harraway	FB	6'2"	215	25		30
Dave Kopay	HB-FB	6'2"	225	28		
Jon Henderson	WR	6'	200	25		18
Bill Malinchak	WR	6'1"	200	26		
Walter Roberts	WR	5'10"	163	28		6
Charley Taylor	WR	6'3"	210	29		48
Mack Alston	TE	6'2"	230	23		
Pat Richter	TE	6'5"	230	29		
Jerry Smith	TE	6'2"	208	27		54
Mike Bragg	K	5'11"	186	23		
Curt Knight	K	6'1"	190	27		93

PHILADELPHIA EAGLES 3-10-1 Jerry Williams

Scores of Each Game		
7	DALLAS	17
16	Chicago	20
21	WASHINGTON	33
23	N. Y. Giants	30
20	ST. LOUIS	35
17	Green Bay	30
17	Dallas	21
24	MIAMI	17
13	ATLANTA	13
23	N. Y. GIANTS	20
14	St. Louis	23
10	Baltimore	29
6	Washington	24
30	PITTSBURGH	20

Use Name	Pos.	Hgt	Wgt	Age	Int	Pts
Joe Carollo	OT	6'2"	265	30		
Wade Key	OT	6'4"	245	23		
Dick Stevens	OT	6'4"	240	22		
Norman Davis	OG	6'3"	245	25		
Dick Hart	OG	6'2"	250	27		
Jim Skaggs	OG	6'2"	250	30		
Mark Nordquist	C-OG	6'4"	246	24		
Mike Evans	C	6'5"	250	23		
Calvin Hunt	C	6'3"	243	22		
Don Brumm	DE	6'3"	245	27		
Ernie Calloway	DE	6'6"	240	22		
Mel Tom	DE	6'4"	250	29		
Mike Dirks	DT	6'2"	246	24		6
Gary Pettigrew	DT	6'4"	255	25		
Don Hultz	DE-DT	6'3"	240	29		
Carl Gersbach	LB	6'1"	230	23		
Bill Hobbs	LB	6'	220	24		
Jay Johnson	LB	6'3"	230	24		
Ike Kelley	LB	5'11"	224	26		
Dave Lloyd	LB	6'3"	248	34		
Ron Porter	LB	6'3"	232	25		
Tim Rossovich	LB	6'4"	250	24		
Adrian Young	LB	6'1"	232	24	2	
Bill Bradley	DB	5'11"	190	23		
Richard Harvey	DB	6'2"	190	24		
Ed Hayes	DB	6'1"	185	24	1	
Ray Jones	DB	6'	187	22	2	
Ron Medved	DB	6'1"	200	26		
Al Nelson	DB	5'11"	186	26	2	
Steve Preece	DB	6'1"	195	23	2	6
Nate Ramsey	DB	6'1"	200	29	1	
Jim Throner	DB	6'2"	194	21		
Rick Arrington	QB	6'2"	185	23		6
Norm Snead	QB	6'4"	215	30		18
Harry Jones	HB	6'2"	205	25		
Leroy Keyes	HB	6'3"	208	23		
Cyril Pinder	HB	6'2"	222	23		12
Larry Watkins	FB-HB	6'2"	215	22		6
Lee Bouggess	FB	6'2"	210	22		24
Tom Woodeshick	FB	6'	222	28		12
Ben Hawkins	WR	6'	180	26		24
Harold Jackson	WR	5'10"	175	24		30
Billy Walik	WR	5'11"	180	22		
Steve Zabel	TE	6'4"	235	22		6
Gary Ballman	WR-TE	6'	205	30		18
Fred Hill	WR-TE	6'2"	215	27		6
Mark Moseley	K	5'11"	182	22		67

Dave Graham – Injury

DALLAS COWBOYS

RUSHING

Last Name	No.	Yds	Avg	TD
Thomas	151	803	5.3	5
Hill	153	577	3.8	4
Garrison	126	507	4.0	3
Staubach	27	221	8.2	0
Reeves	35	84	2.4	2
Morton	16	37	2.3	0
Hayes	4	34	8.5	1
Norman	2	16	8.0	0
Welch	5	13	2.6	1
Rentzel	1	11	11.0	0
Homan	2	–3	–1.5	0

RECEIVING

Last Name	No.	Yds	Avg	TD
Hayes	34	889	26	10
Rentzel	28	556	20	5
Garrison	21	205	10	2
Hill	13	95	7	0
Reeves	12	140	12	0
Thomas	10	73	7	0
Rucker	9	200	22	1
Ditka	8	98	12	0
Homan	7	105	15	0
Norman	6	70	12	0
Kiner	1	14	14	0

PUNT RETURNS

Last Name	No.	Yds	Avg	TD
Hayes	15	116	8	0
Renfro	13	77	6	0
Adkins	4	44	11	0

KICKOFF RETURNS

Last Name	No.	Yds	Avg	TD
Thomas	19	416	22	0
Washington	5	242	48	1
Adkins	7	149	21	0
Kiner	3	50	17	0
Harris	1	22	22	0
Waters	1	6	6	0
Flowers	1	3	3	0

PASSING – PUNTING – KICKING

PASSING	Att	Comp	%	Yds	Yd/Att	TD	Int–	%	RK
Morton	207	102	49	1819	8.8	15	7–	3	5
Staubach	82	44	54	542	6.6	2	8–	10	
Hill	4	1	25	12	3.0	0	0–	0	
Reeves	3	1	33	14	4.7	0	1–	33	
Rentzel	1	1	100	58	58.0	1	0–	0	

PUNTING	No	Avg
Widby	69	41.3

KICKING	XP	Att	%	FG	Att	%
Clark	35	35	100	18	27	67

NEW YORK GIANTS

RUSHING

Last Name	No.	Yds	Avg	TD
R. Johnson	263	1027	3.9	8
Frederickson	120	375	3.1	1
Tarkenton	43	236	5.5	2
Duhon	18	111	6.2	0
Morrison	11	25	2.3	0
Shy	4	13	3.3	0
McNeil	4	7	1.8	0
Koy	2	5	2.5	0

RECEIVING

Last Name	No.	Yds	Avg	TD
McNeil	50	764	15	4
R. Johnson	48	487	10	4
Tucker	40	571	14	5
Frederickson	40	408	10	3
Herrmann	24	290	12	2
Morrison	11	136	12	0
Thomas	6	92	15	1
Houston	4	68	17	0
Duhon	4	58	15	0
Shy	2	8	4	0
Koy	1	10	10	0

PUNT RETURNS

Last Name	No.	Yds	Avg	TD
Duhon	19	157	8	1
Lockhart	9	31	3	0
Brenner	1	5	5	0

KICKOFF RETURNS

Last Name	No.	Yds	Avg	TD
Shy	21	544	26	0
Duhon	14	255	18	0
Houston	8	173	22	0
R. Johnson	5	140	28	0
Green	2	26	13	0
Douglas	1	16	16	0
Hughes	1	3	3	0

PASSING – PUNTING – KICKING

PASSING	Att	Comp	%	Yds	Yd/Att	TD	Int–	%	RK
Tarkenton	389	219	56	2777	7.1	19	12–	3	3
Shiner	12	9	75	87	7.3	0	0–	0	
Duhon	2	2	100	28	14.0	0	0–	0	

PUNTING	No	Avg
B. Johnson	43	39.5
Koy	11	33.5

KICKING	XP	Att	%	FG	Att	%
Gogalak	32	32	100	25	41	61

ST. LOUIS CARDINALS

RUSHING

Last Name	No.	Yds	Avg	TD
Lane	206	977	4.7	11
Roland	94	392	4.2	3
Edwards	70	350	5.0	1
Shivers	24	98	4.1	2
Gilliam	5	68	13.6	1
Smith	5	43	8.6	0
Latourette	2	38	19.0	0
Hart	18	18	1.0	0
B. Brown	1	8	8.0	0
Pittman	2	4	2.0	0
Beathard	2	2	1.0	0

RECEIVING

Last Name	No.	Yds	Avg	TD
Gilliam	45	952	21	5
Smith	37	687	19	4
Lane	32	365	11	2
D. Williams	23	364	16	3
Edwards	19	150	8	1
Roland	17	96	6	1
Shivers	3	44	15	0
Daanen	2	31	16	0

PUNT RETURNS

Last Name	No.	Yds	Avg	TD
Latourette	30	171	6	0
Roland	10	140	14	1
Wehrli	1	4	4	0

KICKOFF RETURNS

Last Name	No.	Yds	Avg	TD
Latourette	13	254	20	0
Pittman	10	237	24	0
Wright	8	156	20	0
Gilliam	5	107	21	0
White	3	65	22	0
Roland	3	40	13	0
Shivers	2	35	18	0
T. Brown	2	32	16	0
Wilson	1	0	0	0

PASSING – PUNTING – KICKING

PASSING	Att	Comp	%	Yds	Yd/Att	TD	Int–	%	RK
Hart	373	171	46	2575	6.9	14	18–	5	9
Beathard	17	7	41	114	6.7	2	1–	6	

PUNTING	No	Avg
Latourette	65	40.9

KICKING	XP	Att	%	FG	Att	%
Bakken	37	38	97	20	32	63

WASHINGTON REDSKINS

RUSHING

Last Name	No.	Yds	Avg	TD
Brown	237	1125	4.7	5
Harraway	146	577	4.0	5
Dyer	21	102	4.9	0
Kopay	13	49	3.8	0
Jurgensen	6	39	6.5	1
Brunet	9	37	4.1	0
Smith	2	29	14.5	0
Bragg	2	25	12.5	0
Taylor	1	17	17.0	0
Roberts	2	15	7.5	0
Pierce	5	6	1.2	0

RECEIVING

Last Name	No.	Yds	Avg	TD
Smith	43	575	13	9
Taylor	42	593	14	8
Brown	37	341	9	2
Roberts	27	411	15	1
Harraway	24	136	6	0
Henderson	13	176	14	3
Kopay	7	24	3	0
Dyer	4	37	9	0
Brunet	3	28	9	0
Richter	2	30	15	0
Pierce	1	6	6	0

PUNT RETURNS

Last Name	No.	Yds	Avg	TD
Roberts	10	28	3	0
R. Harris	14	10	1	0
Vactor	2	7	4	0
Kopay	1	0	0	0

KICKOFF RETURNS

Last Name	No.	Yds	Avg	TD
Vactor	28	700	25	0
R. Harris	10	208	21	0
J. Harris	9	172	19	0
Dyer	5	78	16	0
Hanburger	2	33	17	0
McKeever	1	21	21	0
Tillman	1	10	10	0
Brundige	1	1	1	0
Richter	2	0	0	0
Bass	1	0	0	0
Henderson	1	0	0	0

PASSING – PUNTING – KICKING

PASSING	Att	Comp	%	Yds	Yd/Att	TD	Int–	%	RK
Jurgensen	337	202	60	2354	7.0	23	10–	3	2
Ryan	4	1	25	3	0.8	0	0–	0	
Bragg	1	0	0	0	0.0	0	0–	0	

PUNTING	No	Avg
Bragg	61	40.9

KICKING	XP	Att	%	FG	Att	%
Knight	33	34	97	20	27	74

PHILADELPHIA EAGLES

RUSHING

Last Name	No.	Yds	Avg	TD
Pinder	166	657	4.0	2
Bouggess	159	401	2.5	2
Woodeshick	52	254	4.9	2
Watkins	32	96	3.0	1
H. Jones	13	44	3.4	0
Snead	18	35	1.9	3
Arrington	4	33	8.3	1
Bradley	1	14	14.0	0
Keyes	2	7	3.5	0
Hawkins	2	3	1.5	0
Jackson	1	–5	–5.0	0

RECEIVING

Last Name	No.	Yds	Avg	TD
Bouggess	50	401	8	2
Ballman	47	601	13	3
Jackson	41	613	15	5
Hawkins	30	612	20	4
Pinder	28	249	9	0
Zabel	8	119	15	1
Woodeshick	6	28	5	0
Hill	3	10	3	1
Watkins	3	6	2	0
H. Jones	1	12	12	0
Walik	1	0	0	0

PUNT RETURNS

Last Name	No.	Yds	Avg	TD
Walik	20	78	4	0
Hawkins	10	16	2	0
Hayes	2	6	3	0

KICKOFF RETURNS

Last Name	No.	Yds	Avg	TD
Walik	32	805	25	0
Nelson	10	187	19	0
Hayes	6	107	18	0
R. Jones	6	97	16	0
H. Jones	2	23	12	0
Rossovich	1	22	22	0
Pettigrew	1	11	11	0
Hawkins	1	0	0	0

PASSING – PUNTING – KICKING

PASSING	Att	Comp	%	Yds	Yd/Att	TD	Int–	%	RK
Snead	335	181	54	2323	6.9	15	20–	6	7
Arrington	73	37	51	328	4.5	1	3–	4	
Ballman	1	0	0	0	0.0	0	0–	0	
Bouggess	1	0	0	0	0.0	0	0–	0	

PUNTING	No	Avg
Bradley	61	36.8
Moseley	10	35.0

KICKING	XP	Att	%	FG	Att	%
Moseley	25	28	89	14	25	56

MINNESOTA VIKINGS 12-2-0 Bud Grant

Scores of Each Game		
27	KANSAS CITY	10
26	NEW ORLEANS	0
10	Green Bay	13
24	Chicago	0
54	DALLAS	13
13	LOS ANGELES	3
30	Detroit	17
19	Washington	10
24	DETROIT	20
10	GREEN BAY	3
10	N. Y. Jets	20
16	CHICAGO	13
35	Boston	14
37	Atlanta	7

Use Name	Pos.	Hgt	Wgt	Age	Int	Pts
Grady Alderman	OT	6'2"	245	31		
Doug Davis	OT	6'4"	255	26		
Steve Smith	OT	6'5"	250	26		
Ron Yary	OT	6'6"	255	24		
Milt Sunde	OG	6'2"	250	27		
Jim Vellone	OG	6'2"	255	26		
Ed White	OG	6'2"	260	23		
Mick Tingelhoff	C	6'1"	237	30		
Carl Eller	DE	6'6"	250	27		
Jim Marshall	DE	6'3"	248	33		
John Ward	DE	6'4"	260	22		
Paul Dickson	DT	6'5"	250	33		
Gary Larsen	DT	6'5"	260	30		
Alan Page	DT	6'5"	245	25	1	6
Jim Hargrove	LB	6'3"	235	25		
Wally Hilgenberg	LB	6'3"	230	27	2	
Mike McGill	LB	6'2"	235	23		6
Wayne Meylan	LB	6'1"	235	24		
Lonnie Warwick	LB	6'3"	237	28	3	
Roy Winston	LB	6'1"	228	30	1	6
Bobby Bryant	DB	6'	170	26	3	6
John Charles	DB	6'1"	200	26	1	
Dale Hackbart	DB	6'3"	205	34		
Karl Kassulke	DB	6'	195	28	3	
Paul Krause	DB	6'3"	188	28	6	
Ted Provost	DB	6'2"	195	22		
Ed Sharockman	DB	6'	200	30	7	18
Charlie West	DB	6'1"	190	24	1	
Bill Cappleman	QB	6'3"	210	23		
Gary Cuozzo	QB	6'1"	195	29		
Bob Lee	QB	6'2"	195	25		6
Clint Jones	HB	6'	206	25		54
Dave Osborn	HB	6'	205	27		36
Bill Brown	FB	5'11"	230	32		12
Jim Lindsey	HB-FB	6'2"	210	25		6
Oscar Reed	HB-FB	5'11"	222	26		6
Bob Grim	WR	6'	200	25		
John Henderson	WR	6'3"	190	27		12
Gene Washington	WR	6'3"	208	26		24
John Beasley	TE	6'3"	233	25		12
Kent Kramer	TE	6'5"	235	26		
Stu Voigt	TE	6'1"	220	22		
Fred Cox	K	5'10"	200	31		125
Tom McNeill	K	6'1"	195	28		

Billy Harris – Injury

DETROIT LIONS 10-4-0 Joe Schmidt

Scores of Each Game		
40	Green Bay	0
38	CINCINNATI	3
28	CHICAGO	14
10	Washington	31
41	Cleveland	24
16	Chicago	10
17	MINNESOTA	30
17	New Orleans	19
20	Minnesota	24
28	SAN FRANCISCO	7
28	OAKLAND	14
16	ST. LOUIS	3
28	Los Angeles	23
20	GREEN BAY	0

Use Name	Pos.	Hgt	Wgt	Age	Int	Pts
Rocky Freitas	OT	6'6"	280	24		
Roger Shoals	OT	6'4"	260	31		
Jim Yarbrough	OT	6'6"	250	23		
Frank Gallagher	OG	6'2"	245	27		
Bob Kowalkowski	OG	6'3"	240	26		
Rocky Rasley	OG	6'3"	250	23		
Chuck Walton	OG	6'3"	255	29		
Bill Cottrell	C	6'3"	255	25		
Ed Flanagan	C	6'3"	245	26		
Larry Hand	DE	6'4"	250	30	1	6
Jim Mitchell	DE	6'3"	245	21		
Joe Robb	DE	6'3"	245	33		
Dan Goich	DT	6'4"	265	26		
Dave Haverdick	DT	6'4"	245	22		
Alex Karras	DT	6'2"	245	34		
Jerry Rush	DT	6'4"	265	28		
Mike Lucci	LB	6'2"	230	30	2	
Ed Mooney	LB	6'2"	225	25		
Paul Naumoff	LB	6'1"	215	25		
Bill Saul	LB	6'4"	225	29		
Wayne Walker	LB	6'2"	228	33		
Lem Barney	DB	6'	188	24	7	18
Dick LeBeau	DB	6'1"	185	33	9	
Wayne Rasmussen	DB	6'2"	180	28	2	
Tom Vaughn	DB	5'11"	190	27	1	
Mike Weger	DB	6'2"	200	24	5	6
Bobby Williams	DB	6'1"	200	28	1	6
Greg Landry	QB	6'4"	205	23		6
Bill Munson	QB	6'2"	210	28		
Nick Eddy	HB	6'1"	207	26		6
Altie Taylor	HB	5'10"	196	22		24
Mel Farr	FB-HB	6'2"	210	25		66
Steve Owens	FB	6'2"	220	22		12
Bill Triplett	FB	6'2"	215	31		6
Bruce Maxwell	HB-FB	6'1"	220	23		
Charlie Brown	WR	6'2"	195	21		
Chuck Hughes	WR	5'11"	175	27		
Earl McCullouch	WR	5'11"	175	24		24
Phil Odle	WR	5'11"	195	27		
Larry Walton	WR	5'11"	180	23		30
John Wright	WR	6'	197	23		
Craig Cotton	TE	6'4"	222	23		
Charlie Sanders	TE	6'4"	235	24		36
Errol Mann	K	6'	200	29		101
Herman Weaver	K	6'4"	210	21		

CHICAGO BEARS 6-8-0 Jim Dooley

Scores of Each Game		
24	N. Y. Giants	16
20	PHILADELPHIA	16
14	Detroit	28
0	MINNESOTA	24
7	SAN DIEGO	20
10	DETROIT	16
23	Atlanta	14
16	SAN FRANCISCO	37
19	Green Bay	20
31	BUFFALO	13
20	Baltimore	21
13	Minnesota	16
35	GREEN BAY	17
24	New Orleans	3

Use Name	Pos.	Hgt	Wgt	Age	Int	Pts
Jeff Curchin	OT	6'6"	265	22		
Randy Jackson	OT	6'5"	245	26		
Wayne Mass	OT	6'4"	240	24		
Jim Cadile	OG	6'3"	240	29		
Glenn Holloway	OG	6'3"	245	21		
Howard Mudd	OG	6'3"	252	28		
Ted Wheeler	OG	6'3"	245	24		
Bob Hyland	C	6'5"	250	25		
Harry Gunner	DE	6'6"	250	25		
Ed O'Bradovich	DE	6'3"	255	26		
Willie Holman	DT-DE	6'4"	250	25		
Dave Hale	DT	6'7"	260	23		
George Seals	DT	6'2"	260	27	1	
Bill Staley	DT	6'3"	248	23		
Ross Brupbacher	LB	6'3"	215	22	2	
Doug Buffone	LB	6'1"	225	26	4	
Dick Butkus	LB	6'3"	245	26	3	
Lee Roy Caffey	LB	6'3"	250	30		
Jimmy Gunn	LB	6'1"	220	21		
John Neidert	LB	6'2"	230	24		
Phil Clark	DB	6'2"	208	25	1	
Dick Daniels	DB	5'9"	180	24	2	
Butch Davis	DB	5'11"	183	22	1	
Bennie McRae	DB	6'1"	180	29	1	
Ron Smith	DB	6'1"	192	27		
Joe Tayler	DB	6'2"	200	29	2	
Garry Lyle	HB-DB	6'2"	198	24		
Jack Concannon	QB	6'3"	205	27		12
Bobby Douglass	QB	6'3"	215	23		
Kent Nix	QB	6'1"	195	26		
Craig Baynham	HB	6'1"	203	26		
Gale Sayers	HB	6'	198	27		
Don Shy (from NO)	HB	6'1"	205	24		6
Ronnie Bull	FB-HB	6'	200	30		
Mike Hull	FB	6'3"	220	25		
Ralph Kurek	FB	6'2"	210	27		
Ross Montgomery	FB	6'3"	220	23		
Linzy Cole	WR	5'11"	170	22		
George Farmer	WR	6'4"	210	22		12
Dick Gordon	WR	5'11"	190	25		78
Jim Seymour	WR	6'4"	210	23		24
Cecil Turner	WR	5'10"	170	26		24
Jim Hester	TE	6'4"	250	25		
Ray Ogden	TE	6'5"	225	27		6
Bob Wallace	TE	6'3"	211	24		
Rich Coady	C-TE	6'3"	238	25		6
Bobby Joe Green	K	5'11'	175	32		
Mac Percival	K	6'4"	220	30		88

Brian Piccolo – Died 6-16-70 – cancer

GREEN BAY PACKERS 6-8-0 Phil Bengtson

Scores of Each Game		
0	DETROIT	40
27	ATLANTA	24
13	MINNESOTA	10
22	San Diego	20
21	LOS ANGELES	31
30	PHILADELPHIA	17
10	San Francisco	26
10	BALTIMORE	13
20	CHICAGO	19
3	Minnesota	10
3	Dallas	16
20	Pittsburgh	12
17	Chicago	35
0	Detroit	20

Use Name	Pos.	Hgt	Wgt	Age	Int	Pts
Forrest Gregg	OT	6'4"	250	37		
Bill Hayhoe	OT	6'8"	258	23		
Dick Himes	OT	6'4"	244	24		
Francis Peay	OT	6'5"	250	26		
Dave Bradley	OG	6'4"	245	23		
Gale Gillingham	OG	6'3"	255	26		
Bill Lueck	OG	6'3"	235	24		
Ken Bowman	C	6'3"	230	27		
Malcolm Walker	OT-C	6'4"	250	27		
Lionel Aldridge	DE	6'4"	245	28		
Marty Amsler	DE	6'5"	255	27		
Bob Brown	DE	6'5"	260	29		
Clarence Williams	DE	6'5"	255	23		
Kevin Hardy	DT	6'5"	260	25		
Mike McCoy	DT	6'5"	284	21		
Rich Moore	DT	6'6"	285	23		
Fred Carr	LB	6'5"	238	24	2	
Jim Carter	LB	6'3"	235	21		
Jim Flanigan	LB	6'3"	240	25		
Rudy Kuechenberg	LB	6'2"	215	27		
Ray Nitschke	LB	6'3"	235	34		
Dave Robinson	LB	6'3"	240	29	2	
Cleo Walker	C-LB	6'3"	220	22		
Ken Ellis	DB	5'10"	190	22	3	
Lee Harden	DB	5'11"	195	23		
Doug Hart	DB	6'	190	31	3	6
Ervin Hunt	DB	6'2"	190	23		
Bob Jeter	DB	6'1"	205	32	3	
Al Matthews	DB	5'11"	190	22		
Willie Wood	DB	5'10"	190	34	7	
Don Horn	QB	6'2"	195	25		
Rick Norton	QB	6'1"	190	26		
Frank Patrick	QB	6'7"	225	23		
Bart Starr	QB	6'1"	190	37		6
Donny Anderson	HB	6'3"	210	27		30
Larry Krause	HB	6'	208	22		6
Travis Williams	HB	6'1"	210	24		12
Jim Grabowski	FB	6'2"	220	26		6
Perry Williams	FB	6'2"	220	23		
Dave Hampton	HB-FB	6'	210	23		6
Mike Carter	WR	6'1"	210	22		
Jack Clancy	WR	6'1"	195	26		12
Carroll Dale	WR	6'1"	200	32		12
John Spilis	WR	6'3"	205	22		
John Hilton	TE	6'5"	225	28		24
Rich McGeorge	TE	6'4"	235	21		12
Dale Livingston	K	6'	210	25		64

Zeke Bratkowski – Voluntarily Retired
Boyd Dowler – Voluntarily Retired

MINNESOTA VIKINGS

RUSHING

Last Name	No.	Yds	Avg	TD
Osborn	207	681	3.3	5
Jones	120	369	3.1	9
Brown	101	324	3.2	0
Reed	42	132	3.1	1
Cuozzo	17	61	3.6	0
Lindsey	11	47	4.3	0
Lee	10	20	2.0	1

RECEIVING

Last Name	No.	Yds	Avg	TD
Washington	44	702	16	4
Henderson	31	527	17	2
Grim	23	287	12	0
Osborn	23	202	9	1
Beasley	17	237	14	2
Brown	15	149	10	2
Jones	9	117	13	0
Reed	6	53	9	0
Lindsey	4	94	24	1
Kramer	1	10	10	0

PUNT RETURNS

Last Name	No.	Yds	Avg	TD
West	29	169	6	0
Grim	5	46	9	0
Dickson	1	1	1	0

KICKOFF RETURNS

Last Name	No.	Yds	Avg	TD
Jones	19	452	24	0
West	11	319	29	0
Reed	5	71	14	0
Smith	1	0	0	0

PASSING – PUNTING – KICKING

PASSING	Att	Comp	%	Yds	Yd/Att	TD	Int–	%	RK
Cuozzo	257	128	50	1720	6.7	7	10–	4	9
Lee	79	40	51	610	7.7	5	5–	6	
Cappleman	7	4	57	49	7.0	0	0–	0	
Cox	1	1	100	–1	–1.0	0	0–	0	

PUNTING	No	Avg
McNeill	61	37.9

KICKING	XP	Att	%	FG	Att	%
Cox	35	35	100	30	46	65

DETROIT LIONS

RUSHING

Last Name	No.	Yds	Avg	TD
Farr	166	717	4.3	9
Taylor	198	666	3.4	2
Landry	35	350	10.0	1
Triplett	48	156	3.3	1
Owens	36	122	3.4	2
Eddy	18	47	2.6	1
Munson	9	33	3.7	0
L. Walton	2	20	10.0	0
Maxwell	1	9	9.0	0
McCullouch	1	7	7.0	0

RECEIVING

Last Name	No.	Yds	Avg	TD
Sanders	40	544	14	6
L. Walton	30	532	18	5
Farr	29	213	7	2
Taylor	27	261	10	2
McCullouch	15	278	19	4
Hughes	8	162	20	0
Triplett	6	52	9	0
Eddy	4	22	6	0
Owens	4	21	5	0
Brown	2	38	19	0
Cotton	1	6	6	0
Freitas	1	–8	–8	0

PUNT RETURNS

Last Name	No.	Yds	Avg	TD
Barney	25	259	10	1
Eddy	4	25	6	0
Vaughn	3	22	7	0
L. Walton	2	0	0	0

KICKOFF RETURNS

Last Name	No.	Yds	Avg	TD
Williams	25	544	22	1
Eddy	7	168	24	0
Barney	2	96	48	0
Vaughn	3	66	22	0
Owens	1	26	26	0
L. Walton	1	21	21	0
Maxwell	1	20	20	0
Mooney	1	12	12	0
Naumoff	2	6	3	0

PASSING – PUNTING – KICKING

PASSING	Att	Comp	%	Yds	Yd/Att	TD	Int–	%	RK
Munson	158	84	53	1049	6.6	10	7–	4	8
Landry	136	83	61	1072	7.9	9	5–	4	

PUNTING	No	Avg
Weaver	62	40.0

KICKING	XP	Att	%	FG	Att	%
Mann	41	41	100	20	29	69

CHICAGO BEARS

RUSHING

Last Name	No.	Yds	Avg	TD
Montgomery	62	229	3.7	0
Shy	79	227	2.9	1
Bull	68	214	3.1	0
Concannon	42	136	3.2	2
Hull	32	99	3.1	0
Baynham	26	68	2.6	0
Sayers	23	52	2.3	0
Kurek	6	24	4.0	0
Douglass	7	22	3.1	0
Gordon	4	17	4.3	0
Green	1	7	7.0	0
Turner	3	–3	–1.0	0

RECEIVING

Last Name	No.	Yds	Avg	TD
Gordon	71	1026	14	13
Farmer	31	496	16	2
Wallace	15	160	11	0
Montgomery	14	75	5	0
Bull	13	60	5	0
Hull	13	44	3	0
Baynham	12	43	4	0
Shy	10	149	15	0
Hester	7	54	8	0
Seymour	6	145	24	4
Coady	6	44	7	1
Cole	3	47	16	0
Kurek	3	11	4	0
Turner	2	53	27	0
Percival	1	19	19	0
Ogden	1	6	6	1
Lyle	1	5	5	0
Sayers	1	–6	–6	0

PUNT RETURNS

Last Name	No.	Yds	Avg	TD
Smith	33	126	4	0
Cole	14	83	6	0
Lyle	9	37	4	0
Turner	1	0	0	0

KICKOFF RETURNS

Last Name	No.	Yds	Avg	TD
Turner	23	752	33	4
Smith	28	651	23	0
Montgomery	4	69	17	0
Butkus	1	0	0	0

PASSING – PUNTING – KICKING

PASSING	Att	Comp	%	Yds	Yd/Att	TD	Int–	%	RK
Concannon	385	194	50	2130	5.5	16	18–	5	9
Douglass	30	12	40	218	7.3	4	3–	10	
Bull	4	2	50	46	11.5	1	1–	25	
Green	2	2	100	37	18.5	0	0–	0	
Nix	1	0	0	0	0.0	0	0–	0	

PUNTING	No	Avg
Green	83	40.9
Lyle	1	29.0

KICKING	XP	Att	%	FG	Att	%
Percival	28	28	100	20	34	59

GREEN BAY PACKERS

RUSHING

Last Name	No.	Yds	Avg	TD
Anderson	222	853	3.8	5
T. Williams	74	276	3.7	1
Grabowski	67	210	3.1	1
Hampton	48	115	2.4	0
Starr	12	62	5.2	1
P. Williams	17	44	2.6	0
Krause	2	13	6.5	0
Dale	2	9	4.5	0
Patrick	2	5	2.5	0
Horn	5	4	0.8	0
McGeorge	1	3	3.0	0
Livingston	1	1	1.0	0

RECEIVING

Last Name	No.	Yds	Avg	TD
Dale	49	814	17	2
Anderson	36	414	12	0
Hilton	25	350	14	4
Grabowski	19	83	4	0
Clancy	16	244	15	2
T. Williams	12	127	11	1
Hampton	7	23	3	0
Spilis	6	76	13	0
P. Williams	3	11	4	0
McGeorge	2	32	16	2
Krause	2	22	11	0

PUNT RETURNS

Last Name	No.	Yds	Avg	TD
Wood	11	58	5	0
Ellis	7	27	4	0
T. Williams	4	20	5	0
C. Williams	1	0	0	0
Harden	2	–7	–4	0

KICKOFF RETURNS

Last Name	No.	Yds	Avg	TD
Krause	18	513	29	1
Ellis	22	451	21	0
T. Williams	10	203	20	0
Hampton	6	188	31	1
McCoy	3	22	7	0
Gregg	2	21	11	0
P. Williams	1	20	20	0
Himes	1	4	4	0

PASSING – PUNTING – KICKING

PASSING	Att	Comp	%	Yds	Yd/Att	TD	Int–	%	RK
Starr	255	140	55	1645	6.5	8	13–	5	1
Horn	76	28	37	428	5.6	2	10–	13	
Patrick	14	6	43	59	4.2	0	1–	7	
Norton	5	3	60	64	12.8	1	0–	0	
Anderson	1	0	0	0	0.0	0	0–	0	

PUNTING	No	Avg
Anderson	81	40.8
Livingston	6	33.2

KICKING	XP	Att	%	FG	Att	%
Livingston	19	21	90	15	28	54

SAN FRANCISCO FORTY NINERS 10-3-1 Dick Nolan

Scores of Each Game		
26	WASHINGTON	17
34	CLEVELAND	31
20	Atlanta	21
20	Los Angeles	6
20	NEW ORLEANS	20
19	DENVER	14
26	GREEN BAY	10
37	Chicago	16
30	Houston	20
7	Detroit	28
13	LOS ANGELES	30
24	ATLANTA	20
38	New Orleans	27
38	Oakland	7

Use Name	Pos.	Hgt	Wgt	Age	Int	Pts
Cas Banaszek	OT	6'3"	250	24		
Len Rohde	OT	6'4"	250	32		
Randy Beisler	OG-OT	6'4"	255	25		
Elmer Collett	OG	6'4"	240	25		
Bob Hoskins	OG	6'2"	235	24		
Woody Peoples	OG	6'2"	247	27		
Forrest Blue	C	6'5"	260	24		
Bill Belk	DE	6'3"	254	24		
Cedrick Hardman	DE	6'3"	255	21		
Tommy Hart	DE	6'3"	250	25	1	
Stan Hindman	DE	6'3"	235	26		
Earl Edwards	DT	6'6"	265	24		
Charlie Krueger	DT	6'4"	270	34		
Roland Lakes	DT	6'4"	268	30		
Sam Silas	DE-DT	6'4"	255	27		
Ed Beard	LB	6'2"	220	30		
Carter Campbell	LB	6'3"	214	22		
Frank Nunley	LB	6'2"	230	24	3	
Jim Sniadecki	LB	6'2"	220	23		
Skip Vanderbundt	LB	6'3"	234	23	3	
Dave Wilcox	LB	6'3"	237	27	2	
Johnny Fuller	DB	6'	175	24	1	
Jim Johnson	DB	6'2"	184	32	2	8
Mel Phillips	DB	6'	192	28	3	6
Al Randolph	DB	6'2"	200	26	1	2
Mike Simpson	DB	5'11"	175	23		
Bruce Taylor	DB	6'	180	22	3	6
Rosey Taylor	DB	5'11"	186	31	3	
John Brodie	QB	6'1"	203	35		12
Steve Spurrier	QB	6'2"	203	25		
Doug Cunningham	HB	5'11"	190	24		18
John Isenbarger	HB	6'3"	205	22		6
Jim Strong	HB	6'1"	204	23		
Jimmy Thomas	WR-HB	6'1"	216	23		18
Ken Willard	FB	6'2"	225	27		60
Bill Tucker	HB-FB	6'2"	216	26		12
Lee Johnson	WR	6'1"	204	25		
Preston Riley	WR	6'	180	22		
Gene Washington	WR	6'1"	186	23		72
Dick Witcher	WR	6'3"	204	25		12
Ted Kwalick	TE	6'4"	230	23		6
Bob Windsor	TE	6'4"	230	27		12
Bruce Gossett	K	6'2"	225	27		102

LOS ANGELES RAMS 9-4-1 George Allen

Scores of Each Game		
34	ST. LOUIS	13
19	Buffalo	0
37	SAN DIEGO	10
6	SAN FRANCISCO	20
31	Green Bay	21
3	Minnesota	13
30	New Orleans	17
10	ATLANTA	10
20	N.Y. JETS	31
17	Atlanta	7
30	San Francisco	13
34	NEW ORLEANS	16
23	DETROIT	28
31	N.Y. Giants	3

Use Name	Pos.	Hgt	Wgt	Age	Int	Pts
Bob Brown	OT	6'4"	290	27		
Charley Cowan	OT	6'4"	265	32		
Mitch Johnson	OT	6'4"	250	28		
Tom Mack	OG	6'3"	250	26		
Joe Scibelli	OG	6'1"	255	31		
John Wilbur	OG	6'3"	240	27		
Ken Iman	C	6'1"	240	31		
George Burman	OG-C	6'3"	255	27		
Coy Bacon	DE	6'4"	270	28		6
Rick Cash	DE	6'5"	260	25		
Deacon Jones	DE	6'5"	250	31		
Clark Miller	DE	6'5"	246	31		
Dick Evey	DT	6'2"	245	29		
Merlin Olsen	DT	6'5"	270	29		
Diron Talbert	DT	6'5"	255	26		
Maxie Baughan	LB	6'1"	230	32	1	
Jack Pardee	LB	6'2"	225	34	1	
John Pergine	LB	6'1"	225	23		
Myron Pottios	LB	6'2"	232	30	2	
Jim Purnell	LB	6'2"	238	28		
Jack Reynolds	LB	6'1"	232	22		
Rich Saul	LB	6'3"	235	22		
Kermit Alexander	DB	5'11"	186	29	4	6
Alvin Haymond	DB	6'	194	28		6
Ed Meador	DB	5'11"	190	33	2	
Jim Nettles	DB	5'9"	177	28	3	
Richie Petitbon	DB	6'3"	208	32	1	
Nate Shaw	DB	6'2"	205	25		
Clancy Williams	DB	6'2"	194	27	5	6
Roman Gabriel	QB	6'4"	220	30		6
Karl Sweetan	QB	6'1"	205	27		
Willie Ellison	HB	6'1"	200	25		42
Larry Smith	HB	6'3"	220	22		12
Tommy Mason	FB-HB	6'	195	31		6
Pat Curran	FB	6'3"	238	24		6
Les Josephson	FB	6'	207	27		30
Jeff Jordan	HB-FB	6'1"	215	25		
Bob Long	WR	6'3"	205	29		6
David Ray	WR	6'	195	25		121
Jack Snow	WR	6'2"	190	27		42
Pat Studstill	WR	6'1"	175	32		12
Wendell Tucker	WR	5'10"	185	26		
Donnie Williams	WR	6'3"	210	22		
Bob Klein	TE	6'5"	235	23		
Billy Truax	TE	6'5"	235	27		18

Doug Woodlief — Injury
Jim Wilson — Injury

ATLANTA FALCONS 4-8-2 Norm Van Brocklin

Scores of Each Game		
14	New Orleans	3
24	Green Bay	27
21	SAN FRANCISCO	20
0	Dallas	13
10	Denver	24
32	NEW ORLEANS	14
14	CHICAGO	23
10	Los Angeles	10
13	Philadelphia	13
7	LOS ANGELES	17
7	MIAMI	20
20	San Francisco	24
27	PITTSBURGH	16
7	MINNESOTA	37

Use Name	Pos.	Hgt	Wgt	Age	Int	Pts
Dave Hettema	OT	6'4"	250	28		
George Kunz	OT	6'5"	245	23		
Bill Sandeman	OT	6'6"	260	27		
Mal Snider	OT	6'4"	250	23		
Dick Enderle	OG	6'1"	258	22		
Andy Mauer	OG	6'3"	257	21		
Gary Roberts	OG	6'2"	242	23		
Bob Breitenstein	OT-OG	6'3"	267	27		
John Matlock	C	6'4"	250	25		
Jeff Van Note	C	6'2"	244	24		
Claude Humphrey	DE	6'5"	244	26	1	
Randy Marshall	DE	6'5"	237	23		6
John Rook	DE	6'5"	240	22	1	
Glen Condren	DT	6'2"	247	28		
Greg Lens	DT	6'5"	260	25		
Jim Sullivan	DE-DT	6'4"	240	26		
Ron Acks	LB	6'2"	225	25		
Grady Allen	LB	6'3"	230	24	1	
Ted Cottrell	LB	6'1"	233	23		
Dean Halverson	LB	6'2"	220	24		
Don Hansen	LB	6'3"	220	26	1	
Tommy Nobis	LB	6'2"	237	26	2	
John Small	LB	6'5"	254	23		
Grady Cavness	DB	5'11"	192	23		
Mike Freeman	DB	5'11"	180	26	1	
Al Lavan	DB	6'1"	194	23	3	
John Mallory	DB	6'	198	24	1	12
Tom McCauley	DB	6'3"	184	23	1	6
Ken Reaves	DB	6'3"	202	25	6	
Rudy Redmond	DB	6'	190	23	1	
Bob Berry	QB	5'11"	190	28		
Randy Johnson	QB	6'3"	210	26		
Cannonball Butler	HB	5'10"	195	27		6
Sonny Campbell	HB	5'11"	192	22		12
Paul Gipson	FB-HB	6'	205	24		18
Harmon Wages	FB	6'1"	215	24		18
Art Malone	HB-FB	5'11"	209	22		6
Mike Brunson	WR	6'1"	187	23		
Gail Cogdill	WR	6'2"	200	33		6
Paul Flatley	WR	6'1"	190	29		6
Kent Lawrence	WR	5'11"	175	23		
Todd Snyder	WR	6'2"	184	21		12
Mike Donohoe	TE	6'3"	227	25		6
Jim Mitchell	TE	6'2"	235	22		42
Billy Lothridge	K	6'1"	190	26		
Kenny Vinyard	K	5'10"	190	23		50

Greg Brezina — Injury

Carlton Dabney — Back Injury
Randy Winkler — Military Service

NEW ORLEANS SAINTS 2-11-1 Tom Fears J. D. Roberts

Scores of Each Game		
3	ATLANTA	14
0	Minnesota	26
14	N.Y. GIANTS	10
17	St. Louis	24
20	San Francisco	20
14	Atlanta	32
17	LOS ANGELES	30
19	DETROIT	17
10	Miami	21
6	DENVER	31
6	Cincinnati	26
16	Los Angeles	34
27	SAN FRANCISCO	38
3	CHICAGO	24

Use Name	Pos.	Hgt	Wgt	Age	Int	Pts
Errol Linden	OT	6'5"	250	33		
Mike Richey	OT	6'5"	263	23		
Don Talbert	OT	6'5"	255	30		
Mike Taylor	OT	6'4"	245	25		
Jake Kupp	OG	6'3"	248	28		
John Shinners	OG	6'2"	254	23		
Doug Sutherland	OG	6'3"	250	22		
Jerry Sturm	C-OT-OG	6'3"	265	33		
Del Williams	C	6'2"	240	24		
Larry Estes	DE	6'6"	260	23		
Dave Long	DE	6'4"	245	25		
Richard Neal	DE	6'3"	254	22		
Willie Townes	DT-DE	6'5"	265	27		
Dave Rowe	DT	6'6"	280	25		
Clovis Swinney	DT	6'3"	240	25		
Mike Tilleman	DT	6'5"	280	26		
Dick Absher	LB	6'4"	235	26		
Johnny Brewer	LB	6'4"	235	33		
Jackie Burkett	LB	6'4"	228	33	4	
Bill Cody	LB	6'1"	230	26		
Wayne Colman	LB	6'1"	230	24		
Frank Emanuel	LB	6'3"	225	27		
Hap Farber (from MIN)	LB	6'1"	220	22		
Harry Jacobs	LB	6'2"	226	33		
Mike Morgan	LB	6'4"	242	28	1	6
Major Hazelton	DB	6'1"	185	25		
Hugo Hollas	DB	6'1"	190	25	5	
Gene Howard	DB	6'	190	23		
Delles Howell	DB	6'3"	195	23	3	
Dicky Lyons	DB	6'	190	23	1	
Elijah Nevett	DB	6'	185	26	3	
Joe Scarpati	DB	5'10"	185	28	1	
Doug Wyatt	DB	6'1"	195	23	4	
Edd Hargett	QB	5'11"	185	23		
Billy Kilmer	QB	6'	204	31		
Steve Ramsey	QB	6'2"	210	22		
Bill Dusenbery	HB	6'2"	198	21		
Don McCall	HB	5'11"	195	25		6
Vic Nyvall	HB	5'10"	185	22		
Elijah Pitts (from LA)	HB	6'1"	205	31		
Tony Baker	FB-HB	5'11"	225	25		6
Tom Barrington	FB-HB	6'1"	213	26		12
Dick Davis (from DEN)	FB-HB	5'11"	215	23		
Earl Gros	FB	6'3"	220	29		
Andy Livingston	FB	6'	235	25		
Jim Otis	FB	6'	220	22		
Ernie Wheelwright	FB	6'3"	235	33		
Gary Lewis	HB-FB	6'3"	230	28		
Dan Abramowicz	WR	6'1"	195	25		30
Ken Burrough	WR	6'4"	212	22		12
Al Dodd	WR	6'	180	25		12
Bob Shaw	WR	6'	194	21		
Dave Parks	TE	6'2"	203	28		12
Ray Poage	TE	6'4"	215	29		6
Tom Dempsey	K	6'1"	264	29		70
Julian Fagan	K	6'3"	205	22		

Mike Rengel — Injury

SAN FRANCISCO FORTY NINERS

RUSHING

Last Name	No.	Yds	Avg	TD
Willard	236	789	3.3	7
Cunningham	128	443	3.5	3
Tucker	42	137	3.3	1
Thomas	31	89	2.9	0
Kwalick	3	65	21.7	0
Isenbarger	18	43	2.4	0
Brodie	9	29	3.2	2
Strong	2	3	1.5	0
Spurrier	2	–18	–9.0	0

RECEIVING

Last Name	No.	Yds	Avg	TD
Washington	53	1100	21	12
Cunningham	35	209	6	0
Windsor	31	363	12	2
Willard	31	259	8	3
Witcher	22	288	13	2
Tucker	17	108	6	1
Thomas	12	221	18	3
Kwalick	10	148	15	1
Isenbarger	8	158	20	1
Riley	7	136	19	0

PUNT RETURNS

Last Name	No.	Yds	Avg	TD
B. Taylor	43	516	12	0
Fuller	4	29	7	0
Riley	1	5	5	0

KICKOFF RETURNS

Last Name	No.	Yds	Avg	TD
Tucker	25	577	23	0
B. Taylor	12	190	16	0
Thomas	6	177	30	0
Beard	2	8	4	0
Fuller	1	8	8	0
Belk	1	7	7	0
Riley	1	0	0	0
Windsor	1	0	0	0

PASSING – PUNTING – KICKING

PASSING	Att	Comp	%	Yds	Yd/Att	TD	Int–	%	RK
Brodie	378	223	59	2941	7.8	24	10–	3	1
Spurrier	4	3	75	49	12.3	1	0–	0	
Isenbarger	1	0	0	0	0.0	0	0–	0	

PUNTING	No	Avg
Spurrier	75	38.4

KICKING	XP	Att	%	FG	Att	%
Gossett	39	41	95	21	31	68

LOS ANGELES RAMS

RUSHING

Last Name	No.	Yds	Avg	TD
Josephson	150	640	4.3	5
Ellison	90	381	4.2	5
Smith	77	338	4.4	1
Mason	44	123	2.8	0
Gabriel	28	104	3.7	1
Curran	25	92	3.7	0
Jordan	10	50	5.0	0
Studstill	1	23	23.0	0
Petitbon	1	3	3.0	0
Johnson	1	1	1.0	0

RECEIVING

Last Name	No.	Yds	Avg	TD
Snow	51	859	17	7
Josephson	44	427	10	0
Truax	36	420	12	3
Smith	24	164	7	1
Studstill	18	252	14	2
Tucker	12	230	19	0
Mason	12	127	11	1
Ellison	10	84	8	2
Long	3	35	12	1
Curran	3	25	8	0
Klein	2	20	10	0
Ray	1	11	11	0
D. Williams	1	9	9	0
Jordan	1	–5	–5	0

PUNT RETURNS

Last Name	No.	Yds	Avg	TD
Haymond	53	376	7	0
Alexander	7	38	5	0
Nettles	2	4	2	0

KICKOFF RETURNS

Last Name	No.	Yds	Avg	TD
Haymond	35	1022	29	1
Alexander	7	126	18	0
Curran	3	51	17	0
Ellison	1	20	20	0
Johnson	1	17	17	0

PASSING – PUNTING – KICKING

PASSING	Att	Comp	%	Yds	Yd/Att	TD	Int–	%	RK
Gabriel	407	211	52	2552	6.3	16	12–	3	6
Sweetan	13	6	46	81	6.2	1	0–	0	
Curran	2	0	0	0	0.0	0	1–	50	
Smith	2	0	0	0	0.0	0	0–	0	
Josephson	1	1	100	25	25.0	0	0–	0	
Studstill	1	0	0	0	0.0	0	0–	0	

PUNTING	No	Avg
Studstill	67	39.1

KICKING	XP	Att	%	FG	Att	%
Ray	34	34	100	29	45	64

ATLANTA FALCONS

RUSHING

Last Name	No.	Yds	Avg	TD
Butler	166	636	3.8	0
Wages	119	422	3.5	1
Gipson	52	177	3.4	0
Malone	40	136	3.4	0
Campbell	28	116	4.1	2
Berry	13	60	4.6	0
Mitchell	5	23	4.6	1
Johnson	7	21	3.0	0
Brunson	1	9	9.0	0

RECEIVING

Last Name	No.	Yds	Avg	TD
Mitchell	44	650	15	6
Flatley	39	544	14	1
Wages	26	153	6	2
Butler	24	151	6	1
Snyder	23	311	14	2
Gipson	16	186	12	3
Malone	9	38	4	1
Cogdill	7	101	14	1
Campbell	7	92	13	0
Donohoe	2	36	18	1

PUNT RETURNS

Last Name	No.	Yds	Avg	TD
Mallory	17	203	12	1
McCauley	14	138	10	1
Freeman	3	15	5	0

KICKOFF RETURNS

Last Name	No.	Yds	Avg	TD
Butler	14	284	20	0
Campbell	10	230	23	0
Gipson	8	189	24	0
Malone	5	66	13	0
Cavness	3	61	20	0
Brunson	4	54	14	0
Wages	1	22	22	0
Lavan	1	10	10	0
Freeman	1	0	0	0

PASSING – PUNTING – KICKING

PASSING	Att	Comp	%	Yds	Yd/Att	TD	Int–	%	RK
Berry	269	156	58	1806	6.7	16	13–	5	4
Johnson	72	40	56	443	6.2	2	8–	11	
Wages	1	1	100	13	13.0	0	0–	0	

PUNTING	No	Avg
Lothridge	76	38.7

KICKING	XP	Att	%	FG	Att	%
Vinyard	23	26	88	9	25	36

NEW ORLEANS SAINTS

RUSHING

Last Name	No.	Yds	Avg	TD
Baker	82	337	4.1	1
Barrington	72	228	3.2	2
Otis	71	211	3.0	0
Pitts	35	104	3.0	0
Davis	27	94	3.5	0
McCall	23	63	2.7	1
Wheelwright	16	45	2.8	0
Kilmer	12	42	3.5	0
Dodd	5	31	6.2	0
Livingston	10	29	2.9	0
Poage	1	13	13.0	0
Abramowicz	1	7	7.0	0
Hargett	4	7	1.8	0
Dusenbery	4	6	1.5	0
Nyvall	5	6	1.2	0
Burrough	1	4	4.0	0
Gros	4	2	0.5	0
Fagan	1	–6	–6.0	0

RECEIVING

Last Name	No.	Yds	Avg	TD
Abramowicz	55	906	16	5
Dodd	28	484	17	1
Parks	26	447	17	2
Barrington	22	130	6	0
Otis	20	124	6	0
Poage	15	166	11	1
Burrough	13	196	15	2
Baker	12	47	4	0
Pitts	7	63	9	0
McCall	5	43	9	0
Davis	4	29	7	0
Gros	2	0	0	0
Nyvall	2	–1	–1	0
Shaw	1	49	49	0
Wheelwright	1	7	7	0

PUNT RETURNS

Last Name	No.	Yds	Avg	TD
Dodd	14	129	9	0
Lyons	5	34	7	0
Hollas	4	22	6	0
Wyatt	1	15	15	0
Howard	5	14	3	0

KICKOFF RETURNS

Last Name	No.	Yds	Avg	TD
Dodd	15	319	21	0
Burrough	15	298	20	0
Dusenbery	10	183	18	0
Barrington	6	129	22	0
McCall	1	26	26	0
Otis	2	22	11	0
Pitts	1	22	22	0
Lyons	1	20	20	0
Lewis	1	19	19	0
Poage	1	6	6	0

PASSING – PUNTING – KICKING

PASSING	Att	Comp	%	Yds	Yd/Att	TD	Int–	%	RK
Kilmer	237	135	57	1557	6.6	6	17–	7	12
Hargett	175	78	45	1133	6.5	5	5–	3	12
Ramsey	2	0	0	0	0.0	0	0–	0	
Dodd	1	0	0	0	0.0	0	0–	0	

PUNTING	No	Avg
Fagan	77	42.5

KICKING	XP	Att	%	FG	Att	%
Dempsey	16	17	94	18	34	53

1970 A.F.C. New League, Old Faces

In their first season in the NFL, the old AFL clubs found things rougher than they expected. In interconference games, the NFC came out on top in two thirds of them. An AFC team did win the Super Bowl, but that was the Baltimore Colts, an old-line NFL club which had moved over to the AFC this season along with Cleveland and Pittsburgh. Nevertheless, the ten clubs which had made up the AFL placed a good share of players on all All-Pro teams, and the two expansion teams which came out of the AFL gave good reason for the former members to be proud. The Miami Dolphins and Cincinnati Bengals, both created in the mid 1960s, each made the playoffs. The Atlanta Falcons and New Orleans Saints, NFL expansion teams from the same period, came nowhere near matching the record of these two.

EASTERN DIVISION

Baltimore Colts—Soft-Spoken Don McCafferty took over as head coach after Don Shula quit to go to Miami, and the Colts rewarded him with a championship in his first season on the job. The Baltimore offense scored the most points in the conference, yet went through some mid-season changes. John Williams moved into the starting lineup at guard after an embarrassing 44-24 loss to Kansas City, hustling Tom Nowatzke filled in as running back when injuries kayoed Tom Matte, and oldsters Johnny Unitas and Earl Morrall occasionally relieved each other at quarterback. The defense, however, was a picture of stability, with stars Bubba Smith, Mike Curtis, Ted Hendricks, Rick Volk, and Jerry Logan leading a quick and mobile unit.

Miami Dolphins—The Dolphins had to pay highly to get Don Shula, including a first-draft choice which went to Baltimore as compensation, but the results proved the new coach's worth. Under Shula's direction, Bob Griese matured as a quarterback, Larry Csonka, Jim Kiick, and Mercury Morris developed into top runners, and the offensive line meshed into a fine unit, with Larry Little blossoming into a star. On defense, however, Shula did his best job, turning an indifferent unit into the conference's best. Five rookies started on defense, Mike Kolen, Doug Swift, Tim Foley, Curtis Johnson, and Jake Scott. The veteran pillars on the platoon were Manny Fernandez, Nick Buoniconti, and Dick Anderson.

New York Jets—Injuries destroyed the Jets' chances of defending their divisional title. Joe Namath's broken wrist robbed the offense of its leader, and a torn Achilles tendon took fullback Matt Snell out of the lineup just when he was running better than at any time in his career. Emerson Boozer, Don Maynard, and Roger Finnie also missed a lot of time in sick bay, forcing wholesale replacements on the offensive unit. Although Al Woodall, George Nock, and Rich Caster were capable substitutes, they could not replace the firepower lost in Namath, Snell, and Maynard. Injuries also hurt the defense, with Steve Thompson and Jim Hudson the major casualties, but that unit held together well and kept the Jets respectable in their worst moments.

Buffalo Bills—Rookie Dennis Shaw won the starting quarterback job and showed the potential to become a fine passer, while receiver Marlin Briscoe caught enough Shaw passes to lead the league in receiving. On the defensive unit, Al Cowlings, Edgar Chandler, and Bobby James showed talent and enthusiasm to make up for their inexperience. Unfortunate events of the year included O. J. Simpson's knee injury which sidelined him for the second half of the season, Mike Stratton's Achilles tendon injury, and Wayne Patrick's separated shoulder.

Boston Patriots—The Patriots shelled out a bundle to pick up quarterback Joe Kapp from Minnesota in mid-season, but Kapp was out of shape and unfamiliar with the Boston system; the result was a season in which he threw three touchdown passes and seventeen interceptions. Kapp's poor season fit in well with the entire situation on the Patriots. Running backs Jim Nance and Carl Garrett seemed apathetic at times, Gino Cappelletti continued to regress as a place kicker, the offensive line never lived up to its potential, and the defense lost Jim Cheyunski and rookie Phil Olsen to injuries. By mid-season, John Mazur had replaced Clive Rush as head coach.

CENTRAL DIVISION

Cincinnati Bengals—Even with quarterback Greg Cook out of action with a bad shoulder, the Bengals still stormed into the playoffs and delighted coach 'Paul Brown by beating the Browns out for first place in the Central Division. The Cincinnati defense had been strengthened by rookies Mike Reid, Ron Carpenter, and Lemar Parrish, but the offense started out slowly under new quarterback Virgil Carter. After losing six of their first seven games, the Bengals suddenly jelled; they beat Buffalo, Cleveland, Pittsburgh, and their other four remaining opponents to streak past the rival Browns from upstate. Starring along the way were runners Jess Phillips and Paul Robinson, receiver Chip Myers, center Bob Johnson, kicker Horst Muhlmann, linebacker Bill Bergey, and rookies Reid, Carpenter, and Parrish.

Cleveland Browns—Aside from Leroy Kelly's bad season and a chaotic linebacking situation, two off-season trades contributed the most to Cleveland's slump this year. With Bill Nelsen's bad knees making him a constant question mark, the Browns traded star receiver Paul Warfield to Miami for their first-draft pick, which Cleveland used to take Purdue quarterback Mike Phipps. Then the Browns shipped Ron Johnson, Jim Kanicki, and Wayne Meylan to New York for receiver Homer Jones. While Warfield and Johnson starred in their new surroundings, Phipps showed that he needed plenty more seasoning and Jones failed to even win a starting job.

Pittsburgh Steelers—Even with Terry Bradshaw not delivering as expected, the Steelers did make a mid-season run at the Central Division crown before slumping off into five losses in their last six games. The big improvement in the Steelers came on defense, where Mean Joe Greene and Andy Russell stood out on a unit with eleven solid starters. Less impressive was the offense, where coach Chuck Noll fielded a complete new set of runners and receivers to go with his rookie quarterback.

Houston Oilers—Coach Wally Lemm announced before the season that this was his final year with the Oilers, but his team gave him very little in the way of a going-away gift, as they dropped into last place in the AFC Central Division. Injuries hurt the team, as quarterback Charley Johnson, newly acquired from St. Louis, linebacker George Webster, guard Tom Regner, and fullback Hoyle Granger all suffered disabling wounds. But even without the injuries, the Oilers had too few good players to challenge seriously for the title in their weak division.

WESTERN DIVISION

Oakland Raiders—Old George Blanda, playing his twenty-first season of pro football, made a specialty out of pulling games out of the fire at the last second as he saved five games in a row with late heroics. He filled in for the injured Daryle Lamonica and threw a pair of touchdown passes to beat Pittsburgh 31-14, he kicked a 48-yard field goal with three seconds left to tie Kansas City 17-17, he kicked a 52-yarder to beat Cleveland 23-20 in the last three seconds, he came off the bench to drive the Raiders to the winning touchdown in a 24-19 victory over Denver, and he kicked a field goal with four seconds left to beat San Diego 20-17—all of which helped Oakland to take first place in the West.

Kansas City Chiefs—The spark which had moved the club last year was missing, especially on offense; the Kansas City attack virtually ignored long-gaining plays and confined itself to short passes and inside running plays. The overconservative offense wasted the talents of Otis Taylor, who scored only three touchdowns all year, and Ed Podolak, who scored only four times after breaking into the starting lineup. Coach Hank Stram made only two substitutions in last year's lineup, replacing Mike Garrett at halfback with Podolak and promoting Jack Rudnay to starting center over sore-kneed E. J. Holub.

San Diego Chargers—With a flabby pass rush and a secondary that picked off only five enemy passes all year, the defense gave head coach Charlie Walker his biggest headache in his first full season on the job. The front four contained heralded ex-collegians in Steve DeLong, Ron Billingsley, and Gene Ferguson, but the best work came from unknown rookie Joe Owens. While Pete Barnes and Bob Babich solidified the linebacking, the secondary of Bob Howard, Joe Beauchamp, Jim Hill, and Jim Tolbert was remarkably undistinguished. Injuries to Dickie Post and Brad Hubbert hurt the running attack, but a strong passing game kept the offense in business.

Denver Broncos—The Broncos charged out of the starting gate with a 4-1 record, but problems at quarterback eventually caught up with the team. Steve Tensi missed most of the campaign with injuries and Pete Liske played quarterback most of the way. Although Liske had leadership ability and skill at reading defenses, the ex-Canadian League star did not have a strong enough arm to hold the job. By the end of the year, coach Lou Saban was playing rookie Al Pastrana at the spot with dismal results. The high point of the season for Saban was the development of Floyd Little into an All-Pro workhorse runner and the good showing of rookie Bobby Anderson.

FINAL TEAM STATISTICS

OFFENSE

	BALT.	BOS.	BUFF.	CIN.	CLEV.	DENV.	HOUS.	K.C.	MIAMI	N.Y.J.	OAK.	PITT.	S.D.
FIRST DOWNS:													
Total	242	184	203	210	239	217	232	183	228	230	270	206	231
by Rushing	70	63	71	100	87	84	88	83	106	90	107	84	83
by Passing	148	98	120	97	134	112	126	86	100	122	139	97	119
by Penalty	24	23	12	13	18	21	18	14	22	18	24	25	29
RUSHING:													
Number	411	334	367	461	462	436	419	448	492	463	471	432	395
Yards	1336	1040	1465	2057	1579	1802	1556	1858	2082	1653	1964	1715	1450
Average Yards	3.3	3.1	4.0	4.5	3.4	4.1	3.7	4.1	4.2	3.6	4.2	4.0	3.7
Touchdowns	9	11	8	16	14	17	10	11	14	11	7	13	9
PASSING:													
Attempts	416	392	402	339	392	403	470	289	299	386	418	384	387
Completions	219	176	213	172	190	183	238	154	159	193	210	150	192
Completion Percentage	52.6	44.9	53.0	50.7	48.5	45.4	50.6	53.3	53.2	50.0	50.2	39.1	49.6
Passing Yards	3087	1975	2916	2097	2752	2358	2768	2038	2284	2592	3029	2312	2936
Avg. Yards per Attempt	7.4	5.0	7.3	6.2	7.0	5.9	5.9	7.1	7.6	6.7	7.2	6.0	7.6
Avg. Yards per Complet.	14.1	11.2	13.7	12.2	14.5	12.9	11.6	13.2	14.4	13.4	14.4	15.4	15.3
Times Tackled Passing	33	42	53	31	16	44	33	38	36	35	19	28	57
Yards Lost Tackled	289	389	486	227	170	333	262	319	327	285	164	275	433
Net Yards	2798	1586	2430	1870	2582	2025	2506	1719	1957	2307	2865	2037	2503
Touchdowns	23	7	13	12	17	11	12	13	15	14	28	12	24
Interceptions	22	28	26	11	24	28	23	16	19	22	21	32	19
Percent Intercepted	5.3	7.1	6.5	3.2	6.1	6.9	4.9	5.5	6.4	5.7	5.0	8.3	4.9
PUNTS:													
Number	63	86	83	79	71	87	84	76	58	73	79	78	74
Average Distance	44.7	39.1	38.9	46.2	42.6	42.9	42.4	44.9	41.2	40.1	39.5	44.2	42.8
PUNT RETURNS:													
Number	36	32	45	37	34	63	41	31	30	26	37	51	31
Yards	351	305	298	327	236	556	257	371	295	150	308	281	173
Average Yards	9.8	9.5	6.6	8.8	6.9	8.8	6.3	12.0	9.8	5.8	8.3	5.5	5.6
Touchdowns	1	0	0	1	0	0	0	0	1	0	1	0	0
KICKOFF RETURNS:													
Number	45	62	62	39	44	49	55	44	48	56	44	40	42
Yards	1161	1275	1244	1002	1001	1114	1168	997	1036	1106	1017	997	813
Average Yards	25.8	20.6	20.1	25.7	22.8	22.7	21.2	22.7	21.6	19.8	23.1	24.9	19.4
Touchdowns	1	0	2	1	1	0	0	0	1	0	0	0	0
INTERCEPTION RETURNS:													
Number	25	8	11	23	19	16	18	31	23	23	19	23	9
Yards	408	184	179	180	324	220	242	395	414	281	112	266	90
Average Yards	16.3	23.0	16.3	7.8	17.1	13.8	13.4	12.7	18.0	12.2	5.9	11.6	10.0
Touchdowns	3	0	2	0	3	0	0	1	1	2	0	1	0
PENALTIES:													
Number	71	88	99	71	65	94	78	83	77	88	92	82	79
Yards	708	849	1108	831	634	887	833	888	834	1022	1021	835	852
FUMBLES:													
Number	25	18	37	22	24	23	26	26	24	20	21	30	19
Number Lost	14	13	26	12	14	13	15	15	11	11	9	16	6
POINTS:													
Total	321	149	204	312	286	253	217	272	297	255	300	210	282
PAT Attempts	38	18	25	34	35	28	23	26	33	28	36	26	35
PAT Made	36	17	24	33	34	27	23	26	33	28	36	24	34
FG Attempts	34	22	19	37	22	32	32	42	30	35	29	28	19
FG Made	19	8	10	25	12	18	18	30	22	19	16	10	12
Percent FG Made	55.9	36.4	52.6	67.6	54.5	56.3	56.3	71.4	73.3	54.3	55.2	35.7	63.2
Safeties	0	0	0	0	3	2	1	0	0	1	0	0	1

DEFENSE

	BALT.	BOS.	BUFF.	CIN.	CLEVE	DENV.	HOUS.	K.C.	MIAMI	N.Y.J.	OAK.	PITT.	S.D.
FIRST DOWNS:													
Total	214	242	213	236	236	199	227	226	226	216	223	225	245
by Rushing	79	115	87	87	104	67	85	83	82	65	90	91	106
by Passing	120	105	103	131	120	118	115	111	128	122	104	120	117
by Penalty	15	22	23	18	12	14	27	32	16	29	29	14	22
RUSHING:													
Number	390	503	484	418	451	409	466	418	387	408	460	487	480
Yards	1439	2074	1718	1543	2006	1351	1793	1657	1453	1283	2027	1679	1967
Average Yards	3.7	4.1	3.5	3.7	4.4	3.3	3.8	4.0	3.8	3.1	4.4	3.4	4.1
Touchdowns	6	20	16	11	10	7	16	10	8	7	10	8	15
PASSING:													
Attempts	452	334	338	428	357	379	344	408	403	383	339	393	365
Completions	238	177	157	209	186	191	164	195	234	165	157	191	207
Completion Percentage	52.7	53.0	46.4	48.8	52.1	50.4	47.7	47.8	58.1	43.1	46.3	48.6	56.7
Passing Yards	2780	2430	2334	2885	2528	2810	2851	2280	2708	2680	2386	2555	2422
Avg. Yards per Attempt	6.2	7.3	6.9	6.7	7.1	7.4	8.3	5.6	6.7	7.0	7.0	6.5	6.6
Avg. Yards per Complet.	11.7	13.7	14.9	13.8	13.6	14.7	17.4	11.7	11.6	16.2	15.2	13.4	11.7
Times Tackled Passing	41	28	31	28	34	50	30	35	18	35	39	26	27
Yards Lost Tackled	374	243	246	250	290	456	246	270	157	308	297	238	207
Net Yards	2406	2187	2088	2635	2238	2354	2605	2010	2551	2372	2089	2317	2215
Touchdowns	16	19	15	18	16	20	25	15	17	20	22	21	13
Interceptions	25	8	11	23	19	16	18	31	23	23	19	23	9
Percent Intercepted	5.5	2.4	3.3	5.4	5.3	4.2	5.2	7.6	5.7	6.0	5.6	5.9	2.5
PUNTS:													
Number	78	63	76	80	66	89	77	79	63	68	80	85	64
Average Distance	38.4	43.8	44.0	43.8	42.4	44.9	44.4	43.4	41.7	38.9	41.6	41.9	44.1
PUNT RETURNS:													
Number	38	42	42	48	23	56	52	51	20	42	40	51	34
Yards	365	303	291	392	83	416	441	414	241	380	303	304	312
Average Yards	9.6	7.2	6.9	8.2	3.6	7.4	8.5	8.1	12.1	9.0	7.6	6.0	9.2
Touchdowns	1	1	2	2	0	0	0	0	1	1	0	1	0
KICKOFF RETURNS:													
Number	58	41	46	33	39	24	32	45	55	58	54	49	52
Yards	1237	841	1112	774	956	544	741	1128	1142	1210	1233	1068	1153
Average Yards	21.3	20.5	24.2	23.5	24.5	22.7	23.2	25.1	20.8	20.9	22.8	21.8	22.2
Touchdowns	0	2	1	0	0	0	0	0	1	2	0	1	0
INTERCEPTION RETURNS:													
Number	22	28	26	11	24	28	23	16	19	22	21	32	19
Yards	283	302	334	150	399	213	334	195	258	397	303	318	235
Average Yards	12.9	10.8	12.8	13.6	16.6	7.6	14.5	12.2	13.6	18.0	14.4	9.9	12.4
Touchdowns	1	2	0	0	4	0	2	0	1	3	1	1	0
PENALTIES:													
Number	101	101	73	81	88	82	76	77	68	70	87	76	89
Yards	1032	1096	814	784	871	817	833	817	704	655	1148	790	998
FUMBLES:													
Number	14	33	23	28	28	35	22	22	24	22	17	29	21
Number Lost	9	17	15	16	12	16	8	12	15	11	8	15	15
POINTS:													
Total	234	361	337	255	265	264	352	244	228	286	293	272	278
PAT Attempts	25	44	35	31	32	28	44	26	28	33	33	32	30
PAT Made	25	44	35	31	31	27	44	25	27	32	32	29	29
FG Attempts	37	28	46	24	26	36	30	28	22	32	31	32	40
FG Made	19	17	30	12	14	23	14	21	11	18	21	15	23
Percent FG Made	51.4	60.7	65.2	50.0	53.8	63.9	46.7	75.0	50.0	56.3	67.7	46.9	57.5
Safeties	1	1	1	1	0	0	1	0	0	1	0	3	0

CONFERENCE PLAYOFFS

December 27, at Oakland
(Attendance 52,594)

SCORING

OAKLAND	0	7	7	7–21
MIAMI	0	7	0	7–14

Second Quarter
Mia. Warfield, 16 yard pass from Griese
PAT–Yepremian (kick)
Oak. Biletnikoff, 22 yard pass from Lamonica
PAT–Blanda (kick)

Third Quarter
Oak. Brown, 50 yard interception return
PAT–Blanda (kick)

Fourth Quarter
Oak. Sherman, 82 yard pass from Lamonica
PAT–Blanda (kick)
Mia. Richardson, 7 yard pass from Griese
PAT–Yepremian (kick)

TEAM STATISTICS

OAK.		MIAMI
12	First Downs–Total	16
5	First Downs–Rushing	5
7	First Downs–Passing	9
0	First Downs–Penalty	2
4	Fumbles–Number	2
2	Fumbles–Lost Ball	0
4	Penalties–Number	0
30	Yards Penalized	0
1	Missed Field Goals	2
52	Offensive Plays–Total	63
301	Net Yards	242
5.8	Average Gain	3.8
2	Giveaways	1
1	Takeaways	2
–1	Difference	+1

INDIVIDUAL STATISTICS

OAKLAND	No.	Yds.	Avg.	MIAMI	No.	Yds.	Avg.
RUSHING							
Hubbard	18	58	3.2	Kiick	14	64	6.0
Smith	9	37	4.1	Morris	8	29	3.6
Dixon	8	31	3.9	Csonka	10	23	2.3
Banaszak	1	–6	–6.0	Griese	1	2	2.0
	36	120	3.3		33	118	3.6
RECEIVING							
Biletnikoff	3	46	15.3	Warfield	4	62	15.5
Chester	2	47	23.5	Kiick	4	34	8.5
Sherman	1	82	82.0	Richardson	2	30	15.0
Smith	1	9	9.0	Morris	2	15	7.5
Dixon	1	3	3.0	Twilley	1	14	14.0
	8	187	23.4		13	155	11.9
PUNTING							
Eischeid	4		32.2	Seiple	5		39.2
PUNT RETURNS							
Atkinson	1	–1	–1.0	Scott	1	–1	–1.0
				Anderson	1	–4	–4.0
					2	–5	–2.5
KICKOFF RETURNS							
Sherman	1	22	22.0	Ginn	2	27	13.5
Atkinson	1	19	19.0	Morris	1	21	21.0
Budness	1	0	0.0	Seiple	1	8	8.0
	3	41	13.7		4	56	14.0

PASSING

OAKLAND	Att.	Comp.	Comp. Pct.	Yds.	Int.	Yds/ Att.	Yds/ Comp.	Yards Lost Tkld.
Lamonica	16	8	50.0	187	0	11.7	23.4	0– 0
MIAMI								
Griese	27	13	48.1	155	1	5.7	11.9	3–31

December 26, at Baltimore
(Attendance 49,694)

SCORING

BALTIMORE	7	3	0	7–17
CINCINNATI	0	0	0	0– 0

First Quarter
Bal. Jefferson, 45 yard pass from Unitas
PAT–O'Brien (kick)

Second Quarter
Bal. O'Brien, 44 yard field goal

Fourth Quarter
Bal. Hinton, 53 yard pass from Unitas
PAT–O'Brien (kick)

TEAM STATISTICS

BALT.		CIN.
15	First Downs–Total	7
12	First Downs–Rushing	2
3	First Downs–Passing	5
0	First Downs–Penalty	0
0	Fumbles–Number	1
0	Fumbles–Lost Ball	0
6	Penalties–Number	1
63	Yards Penalized	5
2	Missed Field Goals	1
66	Offensive Plays–Total	46
299	Net Yards	139
4.5	Average Gain	3.0
0	Giveaways	1
1	Takeaways	0
+1	Difference	–1

INDIVIDUAL STATISTICS

BALTIMORE	No.	Yds.	Avg.	CINCINNATI	No.	Yds.	Avg.
RUSHING							
Bulaich	25	116	4.6	Robinson	5	25	5.0
Nowatzke	10	25	2.5	Carter	2	16	8.0
Unitas	2	18	9.0	Phillips	10	12	1.2
Hill	3	11	3.7	Lewis	3	10	3.3
Jefferson	3	5	1.7	Johnson	2	0	0.0
Havrilak	3	0	0.0		22	63	2.9
Hinton	1	–5	–5.0				
	47	170	3.6				
RECEIVING							
Hinton	3	86	28.7	Myers	4	66	16.5
Jefferson	2	51	25.5	Phillips	2	12	6.0
Mackey	1	8	8.0	Thomas	1	9	9.0
	6	145	24.2	Johnson	1	6	6.0
					8	93	11.6
PUNTING							
Lee	6		38.3	Lewis	8		39.1
PUNT RETURNS							
Gardin	7	28	4.0	Parrish	2	6	3.0
KICKOFF RETURNS							
Nowatzke	1	0	0.0	Robinson	2	29	14.5
				Lamb	1	17	17.0
					3	46	15.3
INTERCEPTION RETURNS							
M. Curtis	1	0	0.0	None			

PASSING

BALTIMORE	Att.	Comp.	Comp. Pct.	Yds.	Int.	Yds/ Att.	Yds/ Comp.	Yds Lost Tkld
Unitas	17	6	35.3	145	0	8.5	24.2	2–16
CINCINNATI								
Carter	20	7	35.0	64	1	3.2	9.1	
Wyche	1	1	100.0	29	0	29.0	29.0	
	21	8	38.1	93	1	4.4	11.6	3–17

BALTIMORE COLTS 11-2-1 Don McCafferty

Scores of Each Game		
16	San Diego	14
24	KANSAS CITY	44
14	Boston	6
24	Houston	20
29	N.Y. Jets	22
27	BOSTON	3
35	MIAMI	0
13	Green Bay	10
17	BUFFALO	17
17	Miami	34
21	CHICAGO	20
29	PHILADELPHIA	10
20	Buffalo	14
35	N.Y. JETS	20

Use Name	Pos.	Hgt	Wgt	Age	Int	Pts
Sam Ball	OT	6'4"	240	26		
Dennis Nelson	OT	6'5"	260	24		
Bob Vogel	OT	6'5"	250	28		
Cornelius Johnson	OG	6'2"	245	27		
Glenn Ressler	OG	6'3"	250	26		
Dan Sullivan	OG	6'3"	250	31		
John Williams	OG	6'3"	256	24		
Bill Curry	C	6'2"	235	27		
Tom Goode	C	6'3"	245	31		
Roy Hilton	DE	6'6"	240	25		
Billy Newsome	DE	6'4"	240	22		
Bubba Smith	DE	6'7"	295	25		
Jim Bailey	DT	6'4"	245	22		
Fred Miller	DT	6'3"	250	29		
Billy Ray Smith	DT	6'4"	250	35		
George Wright	DT	6'3"	260	23		
Mike Curtis	LB	6'2"	232	26	5	
Bob Grant	LB	6'2"	225	24	2	6
Ted Hendricks	LB	6'7"	215	22	1	6
Ray May	LB	6'1"	230	25	1	
Robbie Nichols	LB	6'3"	220	23		
Tom Curtis	DB	6'1"	196	22	1	
Jim Duncan	DB	6'2"	220	24	2	6
Ron Gardin	DB	5'11"	180	25		6
Jerry Logan	DB	6'1"	190	29	6	12
Tommy Maxwell	DB	6'2"	195	23		
Charlie Stukes	DB	6'3"	212	26	3	
Rick Volk	DB	6'3"	195	25	4	
Earl Morrall	QB	6'1"	206	36		
Johnny Unitas	QB	6'1"	196	37		
Sam Havrilak	HB	6'2"	195	22		
Jack Maitland	HB	6'1"	210	22		12
Tom Matte	HB	6'	214	31		
Norm Bulaich	FB-HB	6'1"	218	23		18
Larry Conjar	FB	6'	214	24		
Jerry Hill	FB	5'11"	217	30		12
Tom Nowatzke	FB	6'3"	230	27		6
Eddie Hinton	WR	6'	200	23		42
Roy Jefferson	WR	6'2"	190	26		42
Jim O'Brien	WR	6'	195	23		93
Jimmy Orr	WR	5'11"	185	34		12
Ray Perkins	WR	6'	183	28		6
John Mackey	TE	6'3"	224	28		18
Tom Mitchell	TE	6'2"	215	26		24
David Lee	K	6'4"	230	26		

MIAMI DOLPHINS 10-4-0 Don Shula

Scores of Each Game		
14	Boston	27
20	Houston	10
20	OAKLAND	13
20	N.Y. Jets	6
33	Buffalo	14
0	CLEVELAND	28
0	Baltimore	35
17	Philadelphia	24
21	NEW ORLEANS	10
34	BALTIMORE	17
20	Atlanta	7
37	BOSTON	20
16	N.Y. JETS	10
45	BUFFALO	7

Use Name	Pos.	Hgt	Wgt	Age	Int	Pts
Doug Crusan	OT	6'5"	260	24		
Norm Evans	OT	6'5"	250	26		
Wayne Moore	OT	6'6"	265	25		
Bob Kuechenberg	OG	6'3"	255	22		
Jim Langer	OG	6'2"	240	23		
Larry Little	OG	6'1"	270	24		
Maxie Williams	OG	6'4"	250	30		
Bob DeMarco	C	6'3"	245	32		
Carl Mauck	C	6'3"	240	23		
Norm McBride	DE	6'3"	245	23		
Jim Riley	DE	6'4"	260	25		
Bill Stanfill	DE	6'5"	250	23		
Frank Cornish (from CHI)	DT	6'6"	285	26		
Manny Fernandez	DT	6'2"	250	24		
Bob Heinz	DT	6'6"	290	23		
John Richardson	DT	6'2"	260	25		
Nick Buoniconti	LB	5'11"	220	29		
Ted Davis	LB	6'1"	232	28	1	
Mike Kolen	LB	6'2"	215	21		
Dick Palmer	LB	6'2"	220	22		
Jesse Powell	LB	6'1"	215	23		
Doug Swift	LB	6'3"	230	21		
Ed Weisacosky	LB	6'	230	26		
Dick Anderson	DB	6'2"	200	24	8	
Dean Brown	DB	5'10"	170	23	1	
Tim Foley	DB	6'	195	22		
Curtis Johnson	DB	6'2"	200	22	3	
Lloyd Mumphord	DB	5'11"	180	23	5	12
Bob Petrella	DB	6'	185	25		
Jake Scott	DB	6'	188	24	5	6
Bill Darnall—Injury						
Bob Griese	QB	6'1"	190	25		12
John Stofa	QB	6'3"	210	28		
Hubert Ginn	HB	5'11"	190	23		
Jim Kiick	HB	5'11"	220	24		36
Mercury Morris	HB	5'10"	190	23		6
Barry Pryor	HB	6'	215	24		
Larry Csonka	FB	6'3"	250	23		36
Stan Mitchell	FB	6'2"	210	26		6
Karl Noonan	WR	6'3"	205	26		6
Willie Richardson	WR	6'2"	198	30		6
Howard Twilley	WR	5'10"	180	26		30
Paul Warfield	WR	6'	190	27		36
Marv Fleming	TE	6'4"	235	28		
Jim Mandich	TE	6'3"	225	21		6
Larry Seiple	TE	6'	220	25		
Karl Kremser	K	6'	175	25		2
Garo Yepremian	K	5'8"	172	26		97

NEW YORK JETS 4-10-0 Weeb Ewbank

Scores of Each Game		
21	Cleveland	31
31	Boston	21
31	Buffalo	34
6	MIAMI	20
22	BALTIMORE	29
6	BUFFALO	10
10	N.Y. GIANTS	22
17	Pittsburgh	21
31	Los Angeles	20
17	BOSTON	3
20	MINNESOTA	10
13	OAKLAND	14
10	Miami	16
20	Baltimore	35

Use Name	Pos.	Hgt	Wgt	Age	Int	Pts
Dave Foley	OT	6'5"	255	22		
Winston Hill	OT	6'4"	285	28		
Roger Finnie	OG-OT	6'3"	245	23		
Tom Bayless	OG	6'3"	240	22		
Dave Herman	OG	6'2"	255	28		
Dave Middendorf	OG	6'3"	260	24		
Randy Rasmussen	OG	6'2"	255	25		
Pete Perreault	OT-OG	6'3"	248	31		
John Schmitt	C	6'4"	250	27		
Paul Crane	LB-C	6'2"	212	26		
Verlon Biggs	DE	6'4"	270	27		
Jimmie Jones	DE	6'3"	215	23		
Gerry Philbin	DE	6'2"	245	29		
Mark Lomas	DT-DE	6'4"	230	22		
John Elliott	DT	6'4"	244	25		2
John Little	DE-DT	6'3"	220	23		
Steve Thompson	DE-DT	6'5"	245	25		
Al Atkinson	LB	6'1"	230	27	3	
Ralph Baker	LB	6'3"	235	28	2	
John Ebersole	LB	6'3"	240	21		
Larry Grantham	LB	6'	210	31	3	6
Dennis Onkotz	LB	6'1"	220	22		
Mike Battle	DB	6'1"	175	24		
John Dockery	DB	6'	186	25		
W.K. Hicks	DB	6'1"	195	27	8	
Gus Holloman	DB	6'3"	195	24	3	
Jim Hudson	DB	6'2"	210	27		
Cecil Leonard	DB	5'11"	160	24		
Steve Tannen	DB	6'1"	194	22	2	6
Earlie Thomas	DB	6'1"	190	24	2	6
Jim Richards—Military Service						
Paul Seiler—Injury						
Bob Davis	QB	6'3"	205	25		
Joe Namath	QB	6'2"	200	26		
Jim Turner	QB	6'2"	215	29		85
Al Woodall	QB	6'5"	205	24		
Emerson Boozer	HB	5'11"	195	27		30
Cliff McClain	HB	6'	217	22		
George Nock	HB	5'10"	200	24		36
Chuck Mercein	FB	6'3"	222	27		6
Matt Snell	FB	6'2"	220	28		6
Lee White	FB	6'4"	235	24		6
Eddie Bell	WR	5'10"	160	22		12
Rich Caster	WR	6'5"	222	21		18
Don Maynard	WR	6'	180	34		
Steve O'Neal	WR	6'3"	185	24		
George Sauer	WR	6'1"	195	26		24
Gary Arthur	TE	6'5"	230	22		
Pete Lammons	TE	6'3"	230	26		12
Wayne Stewart	TE	6'7"	213	23		

BUFFALO BILLS 3-10-1 Johnny Rauch

Scores of Each Game		
10	DENVER	25
0	LOS ANGELES	19
34	N.Y. JETS	31
10	Pittsburgh	23
14	MIAMI	33
10	N.Y. Jets	6
45	Boston	10
14	CINCINNATI	43
17	Baltimore	17
13	Chicago	31
10	BOSTON	14
6	N.Y. Giants	20
14	BALTIMORE	20
7	Miami	45

Use Name	Pos.	Hgt	Wgt	Age	Int	Pts
Levert Carr	OT	6'5"	260	26		
Paul Costa	OT	6'4"	255	28		
Jerry Gantt	OT	6'4"	266	21		
Art Laster	OT	6'4"	280	22		
Howard Kindig	C-OT	6'6"	264	29		
Richard Cheek	OG	6'3"	266	22		
Joe O'Donnell	OG	6'2"	262	27		
Jim Reilly	OG	6'2"	260	22		
Wayne Fowler	C	6'3"	260	21		
Frank Marchlewski	C	6'2"	240	26		
Al Cowlings	DE	6'5"	258	23		
Mike McBath	DE	6'4"	248	24		
Ron McDole	DE	6'3"	288	30		
Jim Dunaway	DT	6'4"	277	28		
Waddey Harvey	DT	6'4"	282	23		
Julian Nunamaker	DT	6'3"	252	24		
Bob Tatarek	DT	6'4"	260	24		
Al Andrews	LB	6'3"	216	26		
Edgar Chandler	LB	6'3"	235	24	1	6
Jerald Collins	LB	6'1"	220	23		
Dick Cunningham	LB	6'2"	244	25		
Paul Guidry	LB	6'3"	233	26		
Mike McCaffrey	LB	6'3"	235	24		
Mike Stratton	LB	6'3"	240	28		
Jackie Allen	DB	6'1"	187	22		
Butch Byrd	DB	6'	196	28	4	6
Ike Hill	DB	5'10"	180	23		
Bobby James	DB	6'1"	177	23		
Tommy Pharr	DB	5'10"	187	23		
John Pitts	DB	6'4"	223	25	1	
Pete Richardson	DB	6'1"	193	23	5	
Max Anderson—Injury						
Dan Darragh	QB	6'3"	196	23		
Jim Harris	QB	6'3"	215	23		
Dennis Shaw	QB	6'2"	210	23		
Greg Jones	HB	6'1"	200	22		12
Lloyd Pate	HB	6'1"	205	24		6
O. J. Simpson	HB	6'2"	204	23		36
Bill Enyart	FB	6'4"	236	23		6
Wayne Patrick	FB	6'2"	254	24		6
Glenn Alexander	WR	6'3"	205	23		
Marlin Briscoe	WR	5'10"	177	24		48
Clyde Glosson	WR	5'11"	175	23		
Haven Moses	WR	6'3"	205	24		12
Austin Denney	TE	6'2"	230	26		
Willie Grate	TE	6'4"	225	24		12
Roland Moss (from SD)	HB-TE	6'3"	215	23		
Grant Guthrie	K	6'	210	22		54
Paul Maguire	K	6'	232	32		

BOSTON PATRIOTS 2-12-0 Clive Rush John Mazur

Scores of Each Game		
27	MIAMI	14
21	N.Y. JETS	31
6	Baltimore	14
10	Kansas City	23
0	N.Y. GIANTS	16
3	BALTIMORE	27
10	BUFFALO	45
0	St. Louis	31
14	SAN DIEGO	16
3	N.Y. Jets	17
14	Buffalo	10
20	Miami	37
14	MINNESOTA	35
7	Cincinnati	45

Use Name	Pos.	Hgt	Wgt	Age	Int	Pts
Tom Funchess	OT	6'5"	260	25		
Ezell Jones	OT	6'4"	255	23		
Tom Neville	OT	6'4"	255	26		
Len St. Jean	OG	6'1"	245	28		
Gary Bugenhagen	OT-OG	6'2"	250	25		
Angelo Loukas	OT-OG	6'3"	250	23		
Jon Morris	C	6'4"	255	27		
Mike Montler	OG-C	6'4"	270	26		
Ron Berger	DE	6'8"	275	26		
Ike Lassiter	DE	6'5"	270	29		
Dennis Wirgowski	DE	6'5"	255	22		
Mel Witt	DE	6'3"	250	24		
Houston Antwine	DT	6'	270	31		
Jim Hunt	DT	5'11"	255	31		
Rex Mirich	DT	6'4"	258	29		
Mike Ballou	LB	6'3"	235	22		
John Bramlett	LB	6'2"	220	29	1	
Jim Cheyunski	LB	6'2"	220	24		
Ed Philpott	LB	6'3"	240	24	1	
Marty Schottenheimer	LB	6'3"	225	27		
Fred Whittingham	LB	6'1"	240	31		
J.R. Williamson	LB	6'2"	220	28	1	
Randy Beverly	DB	5'11"	185	26		
Larry Carwell	DB	6'1"	190	26		
Tom Janik	DB	6'3"	200	29		
Daryle Johnson	DB	5'11"	190	24	2	
Art McMahon	DB	5'11"	190	24	1	
John Outlaw	DB	5'10"	180	25		
Clarence Scott	DB	6'2"	205	26	1	
Don Webb	DB	5'10"	195	31	1	
Ed Toner — Injury						
Joe Kapp	QB	6'2"	215	32		
Mike Taliaferro	QB	6'2"	205	28		
Sid Blanks	HB	6'	205	29		
Carl Garrett	HB	5'11"	210	22		24
Bob Gladieux (to BUF)	HB	5'11"	190	23		
Odell Lawson	HB	6'2"	218	22		
Jim Nance	FB	6'1"	240	27		42
Eddie Ray	TE-FB	6'1"	230	23		
Ginn Cappelletti	WR	6'	190	36		30
Charley Frazier	WR	6'	190	31		
Gayle Knief	WR	6'3"	205	23		6
Bill Rademacher	WR	6'1"	190	28		
Tom Richardson	WR	6'2"	195	25		
Ron Sellers	WR	6'4"	195	23		24
Bake Turner	WR	6'	180	30		12
Tom Beer	TE	6'4"	228	25		
Barry Brown	TE	6'3"	220	27		
Charlie Gogolak	K	5'10"	170	25		11

BALTIMORE COLTS

RUSHING

Last Name	No.	Yds	Avg	TD
Bulaich	139	426	3.1	3
Nowatzke	73	248	3.4	1
Maitland	74	209	2.8	1
Havrilak	54	159	2.9	0
Hill	36	115	3.2	2
Hinton	5	58	11.6	2
Jefferson	4	47	11.8	0
Matte	12	43	3.6	0
Unitas	9	16	1.8	0
Morrall	2	6	3.0	0
Perkins	2	6	3.0	0
Conjar	1	3	3.0	0

RECEIVING

Last Name	No.	Yds	Avg	TD
Hinton	47	733	16	5
Jefferson	44	749	17	7
Mackey	28	435	16	3
Mitchell	20	261	13	4
Nowatzke	16	93	6	0
Havrilak	14	141	10	0
Bulaich	11	123	11	0
Orr	10	199	20	2
Perkins	10	194	19	1
Maitland	9	67	7	1
Hill	8	62	8	0
O'Brien	1	28	28	0
Matte	1	2	2	0

PUNT RETURNS

Last Name	No.	Yds	Avg	TD
Gardin	28	330	12	1
Volk	3	15	5	0
Logan	2	4	2	0
T. Curtis	3	2	1	0

KICKOFF RETURNS

Last Name	No.	Yds	Avg	TD
Duncan	20	707	35	1
Gardin	11	265	24	0
Nowatzke	7	93	13	0
Havrilak	2	36	18	0
Maitland	1	28	28	0
Grant	1	21	21	0
Jefferson	1	11	11	0
Newsome	1	0	0	0
Stukes	1	0	0	0

PASSING – PUNTING – KICKING

PASSING	Att	Comp	%	Yds	Yd/Att	TD	Int–	%	RK
Unitas	321	166	52	2213	6.9	14	18–	6	6
Morrall	93	51	55	792	8.5	9	4–	4	
Havrilak	2	2	100	82	41.0	0	0–	0	

PUNTING	No	Avg
Lee	63	44.7

KICKING	XP	Att	%	FG	Att	%
O'Brien	36	38	95	19	34	56

MIAMI DOLPHINS

RUSHING

Last Name	No.	Yds	Avg	TD
Csonka	193	874	4.5	6
Kiick	191	658	3.4	6
Morris	60	409	6.8	0
Griese	26	89	3.4	2
Mitchell	8	23	2.9	0
Seiple	2	21	10.5	0
Warfield	2	13	6.5	0
Stofa	2	5	2.5	0
Pryor	2	0	0.0	0
Ginn	5	−1	−0.2	0
Noonan	1	−9	−9.0	0

RECEIVING

Last Name	No.	Yds	Avg	TD
Kiick	42	497	12	0
Warfield	28	703	25	6
Twilley	22	281	13	5
Fleming	18	205	11	0
Morris	12	149	12	0
Csonka	11	94	9	0
Noonan	10	186	19	1
W. Richardson	7	67	10	1
Mitchell	6	85	14	1
Seiple	2	14	7	0
Mandich	1	3	3	1

PUNT RETURNS

Last Name	No.	Yds	Avg	TD
Scott	27	290	11	1
Anderson	1	6	6	0
Morris	2	−1	−1	0

KICKOFF RETURNS

Last Name	No.	Yds	Avg	TD
Morris	28	812	29	1
Scott	4	117	29	0
Ginn	5	59	12	0
Mitchell	4	35	9	0
Anderson	1	8	8	0
Seiple	2	5	3	0
Mandich	2	0	0	0
Brown	1	0	0	0
Foley	1	0	0	0

PASSING – PUNTING – KICKING

PASSING	Att	Comp	%	Yds	Yd/Att	TD	Int–	%	RK
Griese	245	142	58	2019	8.2	12	17–	7	4
Stofa	53	16	30	240	4.5	3	2–	4	
Kiick	1	1	100	25	25.0	0	0–	0	

PUNTING	No	Avg
Seiple	58	41.2

KICKING	XP	Att	%	FG	Att	%
Yepremian	31	31	100	22	29	76
Kremser	2	2	100	0	1	0

NEW YORK JETS

RUSHING

Last Name	No.	Yds	Avg	TD
Boozer	139	581	4.2	5
Nock	135	402	3.0	5
Snell	64	281	4.4	1
White	70	215	3.1	0
Woodall	28	110	3.9	0
Mercein	20	44	2.2	0
O'Neal	1	16	16.0	0
Davis	2	11	5.5	0
Turner	1	1	1.0	0
Namath	1	−1	−1.0	0
Bell	2	−7	−3.5	0

RECEIVING

Last Name	No.	Yds	Avg	TD
Maynard	31	525	17	0
Sauer	31	510	16	4
Boozer	28	258	9	0
Lammons	25	316	13	2
Bell	21	246	12	2
Caster	19	393	21	3
Nock	18	146	8	1
White	12	125	10	1
Mercein	3	27	9	1
Snell	2	26	13	0
McClain	1	11	11	0
Stewart	1	7	7	0
Battle	1	2	2	0

PUNT RETURNS

Last Name	No.	Yds	Avg	TD
Battle	19	117	6	0
Bell	7	33	5	0

KICKOFF RETURNS

Last Name	No.	Yds	Avg	TD
Battle	40	891	22	0
McClain	4	70	18	0
Bell	3	61	20	0
Leonard	1	35	35	0
Mercein	4	32	8	0
Nock	1	18	18	0
Caster	1	0	0	0
Onkotz	1	0	0	0
Tannen	1	−1	−1	0

PASSING – PUNTING – KICKING

PASSING	Att	Comp	%	Yds	Yd/Att	TD	Int–	%	RK
Woodall	188	96	51	1265	6.7	9	9–	5	9
Namath	179	90	50	1259	7.0	5	12–	7	13
Davis	17	6	35	66	3.9	0	0–	0	
Bell	1	0	0	0	0.0	0	1–	100	
O'Neal	1	1	100	2	2.0	0	0–	0	

PUNTING	No	Avg
O'Neal	73	40.1

KICKING	XP	Att	%	FG	Att	%
Turner	28	28	100	19	35	54

BUFFALO BILLS

RUSHING

Last Name	No.	Yds	Avg	TD
Simpson	120	488	4.1	5
Patrick	66	259	3.9	1
Shaw	39	210	5.4	0
Enyart	58	196	3.4	0
Pate	46	162	3.5	1
Jones	31	113	3.6	1
Darragh	1	26	26.0	0
Briscoe	3	19	6.3	0
Harris	3	−8	−2.7	0

RECEIVING

Last Name	No.	Yds	Avg	TD
Briscoe	57	1036	18	8
Moses	39	726	19	2
Enyart	35	235	7	1
Pate	19	103	5	0
Patrick	16	142	9	0
Denney	14	201	14	0
Simpson	10	139	14	0
Jones	8	89	11	0
Grate	7	147	21	2
Alexander	4	51	13	0
Moss	2	31	16	0
Glosson	2	16	8	0

PUNT RETURNS

Last Name	No.	Yds	Avg	TD
Pharr	23	184	8	0
Hill	19	102	5	0
Allen	2	10	5	0
Alexander	1	2	2	0

KICKOFF RETURNS

Last Name	No.	Yds	Avg	TD
Simpson	7	333	48	1
Alexander	12	204	17	0
Hill	9	165	18	0
Jones	7	162	23	1
Moss	7	131	19	0
Glosson	4	61	15	0
Enyart	3	60	20	0
Patrick	3	38	13	0
Pate	1	21	21	0
Collins	2	17	9	0
Andrews	1	16	16	0
McCaffrey	2	15	8	0
Laster	2	8	4	0
McBath	1	7	7	0
Pharr	1	6	6	0
Costa	1	0	0	0

PASSING – PUNTING – KICKING

PASSING	Att	Comp	%	Yds	Yd/Att	TD	Int–	%	RK
Shaw	321	178	55	2507	7.8	10	20–	6	4
Harris	50	24	48	338	6.8	3	4–	8	
Darragh	29	11	38	71	2.5	0	2–	7	
Simpson	2	0	0	0	0.0	0	0–	0	

PUNTING	No	Avg
Maguire	83	38.9

KICKING	XP	Att	%	FG	Att	%
Guthrie	24	25	96	10	19	53

BOSTON PATRIOTS

RUSHING

Last Name	No.	Yds	Avg	TD
Nance	145	522	3.6	7
Garrett	88	272	3.1	4
Lawson	56	99	1.8	0
Kapp	20	71	3.6	0
Blanks	13	44	3.4	0
Ray	5	13	2.6	0
Taliaferro	3	11	3.7	0
Gladieux	4	8	2.0	0

RECEIVING

Last Name	No.	Yds	Avg	TD
Sellers	38	550	14	4
Turner	28	428	15	2
Garrett	26	216	8	0
Nance	26	148	6	0
Brown	15	145	10	0
Beer	11	150	14	0
Lawson	11	113	10	0
Frazier	9	86	10	0
Blanks	5	49	10	0
Rademacher	4	51	13	0
Knief	3	39	13	1

PUNT RETURNS

Last Name	No.	Yds	Avg	TD
Garrett	17	168	10	0
Blanks	9	83	9	0
Carwell	3	48	16	0
Johnson	2	6	3	0
Lawson	1	0	0	0

KICKOFF RETURNS

Last Name	No.	Yds	Avg	TD
Lawson	25	546	22	0
Garrett	24	511	21	0
Blanks	7	152	22	0
Carwell	1	30	30	0
Whittingham	1	24	24	0
Schottenheimer	1	8	8	0
Beer	1	4	4	0
Beverly	1	0	0	0
Brown	1	0	0	0

PASSING – PUNTING – KICKING

PASSING	Att	Comp	%	Yds	Yd/Att	TD	Int–	%	RK
Kapp	219	98	45	1104	5.0	3	17–	8	17
Taliaferro	173	78	45	871	5.0	4	11–	6	16

PUNTING	No	Avg
Janik	86	39.1

KICKING	XP	Att	%	FG	Att	%
Cappelletti	12	13	92	6	15	40
Gogolak	5	5	100	2	7	29

CINCINNATI BENGALS 8-6-0 Paul Brown

Scores of Each Game		
31	OAKLAND	21
3	Detroit	38
13	HOUSTON	20
27	Cleveland	30
19	KANSAS CITY	27
0	Washington	20
10	Pittsburgh	21
43	Buffalo	14
14	CLEVELAND	10
34	PITTSBURGH	7
26	NEW ORLEANS	6
17	San Diego	14
30	Houston	20
45	BOSTON	7

Use Name	Pos.	Hgt	Wgt	Age	Int	Pts
Howard Fest	OT	6'6"	268	24		
Rufus Mayes	OT	6'5"	255	22		
Ernie Wright	OT	6'4"	270	30		
Guy Dennis	OG	6'2"	255	23		
Pat Matson	OG	6'1"	245	26		
Mike Wilson	OT-OG	6'1"	240	22		
Bob Johnson	C	6'5"	265	24		
Marty Baccaglio	DE	6'3"	245	25		
Royce Berry	DE	6'3"	248	24		12
Ron Carpenter	DE	6'4"	260	22		
Nick Roman	DE	6'3"	230	22		
Steve Chomyszak	DT	6'5"	265	25		
Willie Jones	DT	6'2"	260	28		
Mike Reid	DT	6'3"	258	23		
Ken Avery	LB	6'1"	225	26	1	
Al Beauchamp	LB	6'2"	236	26	1	6
Bill Bergey	LB	6'2"	240	25	3	
Larry Ely	LB	6'1"	230	22		
Wayne McClure	LB	6'1"	225	24		
Bill Peterson	LB	6'3"	230	25		
Al Coleman	DB	6'1"	183	25		
Sandy Durko	DB	6'1"	185	22		
Ken Dyer	DB	6'3"	186	24	3	
Kenny Graham (to PIT)	DB	6'	205	28	3	
John Guillory	DB	5'10"	190	25		
Lemar Parrish	DB	5'11"	185	22	5	18
Ken Riley	DB	6'	184	23	4	
Fletcher Smith	DB	6'2"	180	26	3	
Greg Cook—Shoulder Injury						
Virgil Carter	QB	6'1"	200	24		12
Dave Lewis	QB	6'2"	210	24		
Sam Wyche	QB	6'4"	210	25		12
Essex Johnson	HB	5'9"	200	23		24
Paul Robinson	HB	6'	200	25		42
Paul Dunn	FB-HB	6'	210	22		
Doug Dressler	FB	6'3"	220	22		
Ron Lamb	FB	6'2"	230	26		
Jess Phillips	HB-FB	6'1"	210	23		30
Eric Crabtree	WR	5'11"	182	25		12
Chip Myers	WR	6'4"	200	25		6
Speedy Thomas	WR	6'1"	178	23		12
Bruce Coslet	TE	6'3"	230	24		6
Mike Kelly	TE	6'4"	215	22		
Bob Trumpy	TE	6'6"	225	25		12
Horst Muhlmann	K	6'1"	210	30		108

CLEVELAND BROWNS 7-7-0 Blanton Collier

Scores of Each Game		
31	N.Y. JETS	21
31	San Francisco	34
15	PITTSBURGH	7
30	CINCINNATI	27
24	DETROIT	41
28	Miami	0
10	SAN DIEGO	27
20	Oakland	23
10	Cincinnati	14
28	HOUSTON	14
9	Pittsburgh	28
21	Houston	10
2	DALLAS	6
27	Denver	13

Use Name	Pos.	Hgt	Wgt	Age	Int	Pts
Al Jenkins	OT	6'2"	255	24		
Bob McKay	OT	6'5"	260	22		
Dick Schafrath	OT	6'3"	258	34		
Joe Taffoni	OT	6'3"	250	25		
Jim Copeland	OG	6'2"	245	25		
John Demarie	OG	6'3"	255	25		
Gene Hickerson	OG	6'3"	248	35		
Fred Hoaglin	C	6'4"	250	26		
Chuck Reynolds	C	6'2"	240	23		2
Jack Gregory	DE	6'6"	250	25		
Joe Jones	DE	6'6"	246	22		
Ron Snidow	DE	6'4"	250	28		2
Walter Johnson	DT	6'3"	275	27	1	2
Joel Righetti	DT	6'3"	253	22		
Jerry Sherk	DT	6'4"	253	22		
Bill Yanchar	DT	6'3"	250	22		
Billy Andrews	LB	6'	225	25	1	6
Tom Beutler	LB	6'1"	232	23		
John Garlington	LB	6'1"	225	24	1	
Jim Houston	LB	6'2"	240	33	1	
Dale Lindsey	LB	6'3"	225	27	2	6
Bob Matheson	LB	6'4"	240	25	1	
Erich Barnes	DB	6'2"	212	35	5	6
Ben Davis	DB	5'11"	185	25	1	
Mike Howell	DB	6'1"	190	27	1	
Ernie Kellerman	DB	6'	185	26	1	
Tom Schoen	DB	5'11"	185	24		
Rickey Stevenson	DB	5'11"	188	22		
Freddie Summers	DB	6'1"	180	23		
Walt Sumner	DB	6'1"	180	23	4	
Don Gault	QB	6'2"	190	24		
Bill Nelsen	QB	6'	195	29		
Mike Phipps	QB	6'2"	207	22		
Ken Brown	HB	5'10"	205	24		
Leroy Kelly	HB	6'	200	28		48
Randy Minniear	HB	6'	210	26		6
Reece Morrison	HB	6'	205	24		6
Bo Scott	FB	6'3"	210	27		66
Steve Engel	HB-FB	6'1"	218	22		
Gary Collins	WR	6'4"	210	29		24
Fair Hooker	WR	6'1"	193	23		12
Dave Jones	WR	6'2"	185	23		
Homer Jones	WR	6'2"	215	29		12
Chip Glass	TE	6'4"	236	23		12
Milt Morin	TE	6'4"	240	28		6
Don Cockroft	K	6'1"	190	25		70

PITTSBURGH STEELERS 5-9-0 Chuck Noll

Scores of Each Game		
7	HOUSTON	19
13	Denver	16
7	Cleveland	15
23	BUFFALO	10
7	Houston	3
14	Oakland	31
21	CINCINNATI	10
21	N.Y. JETS	17
14	KANSAS CITY	31
7	Cincinnati	34
28	CLEVELAND	9
12	GREEN BAY	20
16	Atlanta	27
20	Philadelphia	30

Use Name	Pos.	Hgt	Wgt	Age	Int	Pts
John Brown	OT	6'2"	255	31		
Mike Haggerty	OT	6'4"	240	24		
Rick Sharp	OT	6'3"	262	22		
Sam Davis	OG	6'1"	245	26		
Bruce Van Dyke	OG	6'2"	225	26		
Ralph Wenzel	OG	6'3"	250	27		
Ray Mansfield	C	6'3"	240	29		
Jon Kolb	OT-C	6'2"	220	23		
L. C. Greenwood	DE	6'5"	240	23		
Ben McGee	DE	6'2"	250	28		
Lloyd Voss	DE	6'4"	256	28		
Dick Arndt	DT	6'5"	265	26		
Joe Greene	DT	6'4"	270	23		
Chuck Hinton	DT	6'5"	248	31		
Clarence Washington	DT	6'3"	265	23		
Rocky Bleier – Injury						
Chuck Allen	LB	6'1"	225	30	4	
Carl Crennel	LB	6'1"	230	21		
Henry Davis	LB	6'3"	235	27		
Doug Fisher	LB	6'1"	225	23		
Jerry Hillebrand	LB	6'3"	240	30	2	
Andy Russell	LB	6'3"	225	28	3	
Brian Stenger	LB	6'4"	220	23		
Ocie Austin	DB	6'3"	200	23	1	
Fred Barry	DB	5'10"	184	22		
Chuck Beatty	DB	6'2"	200	24	2	6
Mel Blount	DB	6'3"	205	22	1	
Lee Calland	DB	6'	190	29	7	
Clancy Oliver	DB	6'1"	180	22		
John Rowser	DB	6'1"	180	26	3	
John Sodaski	DB	6'1"	197	22		
Larry Gagner—Injury						
Terry Bradshaw	QB	6'3"	218	21		6
Terry Hanratty	QB	6'1"	200	22		
Dick Hoak	HB	5'11"	190	31		6
Preston Pearson	HB	6'1"	190	25		12
John Fugua	FB-HB	5'11"	200	23		54
Warren Bankston	FB	6'4"	225	23		12
Terry Cole	FB	6'1"	220	25		
Hubie Bryant	WR	5'10"	175	24		
Dave Kalina	WR	6'3"	205	23		
Ron Shanklin	WR	6'1"	180	23		24
Dave Smith	WR	6'2"	205	23		12
Jon Staggers	WR	5'10"	186	21		6
J. R. Wilburn	WR	6'2"	190	27		
Bob Adams	TE	6'2"	225	24		
Dennis Hughes	TE	6'1"	220	22		18
Gene Mingo	K	6'1"	210	31		32
Bobby Walden	K	6'	190	31		
Allen Watson	K	5'10"	165	25		22

HOUSTON OILERS 3-10-1 Wally Lemm

Scores of Each Game		
19	Pittsburgh	7
10	MIAMI	20
20	Cincinnati	13
20	BALTIMORE	24
3	PITTSBURGH	7
31	San Diego	31
0	St. Louis	44
9	Kansas City	24
20	SAN FRANCISCO	30
14	Cleveland	28
31	DENVER	21
10	CLEVELAND	21
20	CINCINNATI	30
10	Dallas	52

Use Name	Pos.	Hgt	Wgt	Age	Int	Pts
Elbert Drungo	OT	6'5"	250	27		
Glen Ray Hines	OT	6'5"	265	26		
Walt Suggs	OT	6'5"	260	31		
Ken Gray	OG	6'2"	250	34		
Tom Regner	OG	6'1"	255	26		
Ron Saul	OG	6'2"	255	22		
Doug Wilkerson	OG	6'2"	245	23		
Hank Autry	C	6'3"	235	23		
Bobby Maples	C	6'3"	245	27		
Elvin Bethea	DE	6'3"	255	24		
Pat Holmes	DE	6'5"	250	30		
Spain Musgrove	DT-DE	6'4"	275	25		
Lee Brooks	DT	6'5"	266	22		
Tom Domres	DT	6'3"	255	23		
Willie Parker	DT	6'2"	265	25		
Garland Boyette	LB	6'1"	245	30	1	
Claude Harvey	LB	6'4"	225	22		
Jess Lewis	LB	6'1"	230	23		
Ron Pritchard	LB	6'1"	235	23	2	2
Olen Underwood	LB	6'1'	220	28		
Loyd Wainscott	LB	6'1"	235	23		
George Webster	LB	6'4"	223	24		
Bob Atkins	DB	6'3"	215	24	1	
Ken Houston	DB	6'3"	195	25	3	
Benny Johnson	DB	5'11"	178	22		
Leroy Mitchell	DB	6'2"	190	25	2	
Zeke Moore	DB	6'2"	198	26	6	
Johnny Peacock	DB	6'2"	200	23	3	6
John Douglas—Injury						
Charley Johnson	QB	6'	190	33		
Bob Naponic	QB	6'	190	23		
Jerry Rhome	QB	6'	188	28		6
Woody Campbell	HB	5'11"	208	25		6
Mike Richardson	HB	5'11"	198	23		18
Joe Dawkins	FB-HB	5'11"	220	22		12
Hoyle Granger	FB	6'1"	225	26		6
Roy Hopkins	FB	6'1"	215	25		18
Tom Smiley	FB	6'1"	235	26		
Jim Beirne	WR	6'2"	196	23		6
Mac Haik	WR	6'1"	196	24		
Charlie Joiner	WR	5'11"	185	22		18
Jerry LeVias	WR	5'10"	175	23		30
Paul Zaeske	WR	6'2"	200	24		
Donnie Davis	TE	6'4"	225	30		
Alvin Reed	TE	6'5"	230	26		12
Terry Stoepel	TE	6'4"	235	25		
Roy Gerela	K	5'10"	185	22		77
Spike Jones	K	6'2"	190	23		

CINCINNATI BENGALS

RUSHING

Last Name	No.	Yds	Avg	TD
Phillips	163	648	4.0	4
Robinson	149	622	4.2	6
E. Johnson	65	273	4.2	2
Carter	34	246	7.2	2
Wyche	19	118	6.2	2
Dressler	18	77	4.3	0
Lamb	6	35	5.8	0
Crabtree	3	23	7.7	0
Lewis	2	8	4.0	0
Thomas	2	7	3.5	0

RECEIVING

Last Name	No.	Yds	Avg	TD
Myers	32	542	17	1
Phillips	31	124	4	1
Trumpy	29	480	17	2
Thomas	21	257	12	2
Crabtree	19	231	12	2
Robinson	17	175	10	1
E. Johnson	15	190	13	2
Coslet	8	98	12	1

PUNT RETURNS

Last Name	No.	Yds	Avg	TD
Parrish	23	194	8	1
E. Johnson	7	72	10	0
Graham	1	41	41	0
Thomas	4	20	5	0
Robinson	1	0	0	0
Smith	1	0	0	0

KICKOFF RETURNS

Last Name	No.	Yds	Avg	TD
Parrish	16	482	30	1
Robinson	14	363	26	0
E. Johnson	3	68	23	0
Dressler	4	48	12	0
Lamb	2	41	21	0

PASSING – PUNTING – KICKING

PASSING	Att	Comp	%	Yds	Yd/Att	TD	Int–	%	RK
Carter	278	143	51	1647	5.9	9	9–	3	7
Wyche	57	26	46	411	7.2	3	2–	4	
Lewis	4	3	75	39	9.8	0	0–	0	

PUNTING	No	Avg
Lewis	79	46.2

KICKING	XP	Att	%	FG	ATT	%
Muhlman	33	33	100	25	37	68

CLEVELAND BROWNS

RUSHING

Last Name	No.	Yds	Avg	TD
Kelly	206	656	3.2	6
Scott	151	625	4.1	7
Morrison	73	175	2.4	0
Phipps	11	94	8.5	0
Minniear	12	39	3.3	1
Morin	1	2	2.0	0
Nelsen	7	–4	–0.6	0
Brown	1	–8	–8.0	0

RECEIVING

Last Name	No.	Yds	Avg	TD
Scott	40	351	9	4
Morin	37	611	17	1
Hooker	28	490	18	2
Collins	26	351	14	4
Kelly	24	311	13	2
Glass	19	403	21	2
H. Jones	10	141	14	1
Morrison	5	95	19	1
Minniear	1	–1	–1	0

PUNT RETURNS

Last Name	No.	Yds	Avg	TD
Morrison	15	133	9	0
Sumner	8	70	9	0
Schoen	8	18	2	0
Kelly	2	15	8	0
Jenkins	1	0	0	0

KICKOFF RETURNS

Last Name	No.	Yds	Avg	TD
H. Jones	29	739	25	1
Morrison	7	153	22	0
Brown	2	44	22	0
Schoen	1	27	27	0
Matheson	2	21	11	0
Righetti	1	17	17	0
Glass	1	0	0	0
Morin	1	0	0	0

PASSING – PUNTING – KICKING

PASSING	Att	Comp	%	Yds	Yd/Att	TD	Int–	%	RK
Nelsen	313	159	51	2156	6.9	16	16–	5	8
Phipps	60	29	48	529	8.8	1	5–	8	
Gault	19	2	11	67	3.5	0	3–	16	

PUNTING	No	Avg
Cockroft	71	42.6

KICKING	XP	Att	%	FG	Att	%
Cockroft	34	35	97	12	22	55

PITTSBURGH STEELERS

RUSHING

Last Name	No.	Yds	Avg	TD
Fuqua	138	691	5.0	7
Pearson	173	503	2.9	2
Bradshaw	32	233	7.3	1
Bankston	26	122	4.7	2
Hoak	40	115	2.9	1
Bryant	3	25	8.3	0
Wilburn	5	25	5.0	0
Cole	9	8	0.9	0
Smith	1	6	6.0	0
Hanratty	4	–5	–1.3	0
Hughes	1	–8	–8.0	0

RECEIVING

Last Name	No.	Yds	Avg	TD
Shanklin	30	691	23	4
Smith	30	458	15	2
Hughes	24	332	14	3
Fuqua	23	289	13	2
Bryant	8	154	19	0
Bankston	7	30	4	0
Staggers	6	118	20	1
Wilburn	6	77	13	0
Pearson	6	71	12	0
Hoak	4	25	6	0
Adams	3	36	12	0
Cole	3	31	10	0

PUNT RETURNS

Last Name	No.	Yds	Avg	TD
Bryant	37	159	4	0
Staggers	13	70	5	0
Blount	1	52	52	0

KICKOFF RETURNS

Last Name	No.	Yds	Avg	TD
Blount	18	535	30	0
Staggers	14	333	24	0
Pearson	4	114	29	0
Sharp	1	9	9	0
Wenzel	1	6	6	0
Calland	1	0	0	0
Washington	1	0	0	0

PASSING – PUNTING – KICKING

PASSING	Att	Comp	%	Yds	Yd/Att	TD	Int–	%	RK
Bradshaw	218	83	38	1410	6.5	6	24–	11	15
Hanratty	163	64	39	842	5.2	5	8–	5	14
Hoak	2	2	100	40	20.0	1	0–	0	
Walden	1	1	100	20	20.0	0	0–	0	

PUNTING	No	Avg
Walden	75	45.2
Bradshaw	3	17.3

KICKING	XP	Att	%	FG	Att	%
Mingo	17	17	100	5	18	28
Watson	7	8	88	5	10	50

HOUSTON OILERS

RUSHING

Last Name	No.	Yds	Avg	TD
Dawkins	124	517	4.2	2
Richardson	103	368	3.6	2
Hopkins	57	207	3.6	3
Campbell	59	189	3.2	1
Granger	51	169	3.3	1
Rhome	9	54	6.0	1
LeVias	7	37	5.3	0
Naponic	3	12	4.0	0
C. Johnson	5	3	0.6	0
Smiley	1	0	0.0	0

RECEIVING

Last Name	No.	Yds	Avg	TD
Reed	47	604	13	2
LeVias	41	529	13	5
Richardson	34	381	11	1
Joiner	28	416	15	3
Haik	17	190	11	0
Beirne	16	216	14	1
Dawkins	15	94	6	0
Campbell	15	78	5	0
Hopkins	14	142	10	0
Granger	11	118	11	0

PUNT RETURNS

Last Name	No.	Yds	Avg	TD
LeVias	25	213	9	0
Richardson	10	30	3	0
Houston	4	13	3	0
Beirne	1	1	1	0
Dawkins	1	0	0	0

KICKOFF RETURNS

Last Name	No.	Yds	Avg	TD
LeVias	26	598	23	0
B. Johnson	15	320	21	0
Moore	7	190	27	0
Drungo	1	25	25	0
Hopkins	1	20	20	0
Lewis	1	15	15	0
Davis	2	0	0	0
Granger	1	0	0	0
Reed	1	0	0	0

PASSING – PUNTING – KICKING

PASSING	Att	Comp	%	Yds	Yd/Att	TD	Int–	%	RK
C. Johnson	281	144	51	1652	5.9	7	12–	4	10
Rhome	168	88	52	1031	6.1	5	8–	5	11
Naponic	20	6	30	85	4.3	0	2–	10	
LeVias	1	0	0	0	0.0	0	1–	100	

PUNTING	No	Avg
Jones	84	42.4

KICKING	XP	Att	%	FG	Att	%
Gerela	23	23	100	18	32	56

OAKLAND RAIDERS 8-4-2 John Madden

Scores of Each Game		
21	Cincinnati	31
27	San Diego	27
13	Miami	20
35	DENVER	23
34	WASHINGTON	20
31	PITTSBURGH	14
17	Kansas City	17
23	CLEVELAND	20
24	Denver	19
20	SAN DIEGO	17
14	Detroit	28
14	N.Y. Jets	13
20	KANSAS CITY	6
7	SAN FRANCISCO	38

Use Name	Pos.	Hgt	Wgt	Age	Int	Pts
Harry Schuh	OT	6'2"	260	27		
Art Shell	OT	6'5"	255	23		
Bob Svihus	OT	6'4"	245	27		
George Buehler	OG	6'2"	260	23		
Jim Harvey	OG	6'5"	250	27		
Gene Upshaw	OG	6'5"	255	25		
Jim Otto	C	6'2"	248	32		
Tony Cline	DE	6'2"	230	22	1	
Ben Davidson	DE	6'8"	280	30		
Carleton Oats	DT-DE	6'2"	260	27		
Al Dotson	DT	6'4"	260	27		
Tom Keating	DT	6'3"	247	27		
Art Thoms	DT	6'5"	250	23		
Duane Benson	LB	6'2"	215	25	1	
Bill Budness	LB	6'1"	215	27		
Dan Conners	LB	6'1"	230	28		
Gerald Irons	LB	6'2"	230	23		
Bill Laskey	LB	6'2"	235	27	1	
Gus Otto	LB	6'2"	220	27		
Carl Weathers	LB	6'2"	220	22		
Butch Atkinson	DB	6'	180	23	3	
Willie Brown	DB	6'1"	190	29	3	
Dave Grayson	DB	5'10"	187	31	1	
Kent McCloughan	DB	6'1"	190	27	5	
Jimmy Warren	DB	5'11"	175	31	2	
Nemiah Wilson	DB	6'	160	27	2	
Alvin Wyatt	DB	5'10"	185	22		6
George Blanda	QB	6'1"	215	42		84
Daryle Lamonica	QB	6'2"	215	29		
Ken Stabler	QB	6'3"	194	24		
Pete Banaszak	HB	5'11"	200	26		12
Don Highsmith	HB	6'	200	22		
Charlie Smith	HB	6'1"	205	24		30
Larry Todd	HB	6'1"	185	27		
Hewritt Dixon	FB	6'2"	230	30		12
Marv Hubbard	FB	6'1"	215	24		6
Fred Biletnikoff	WR	6'1"	190	27		42
Drew Buie	WR	6'2"	178	23		
Rod Sherman	WR	6'	190	25		
Warren Wells	WR	6'1"	190	27		66
Ray Chester	TE	6'3"	220	22		42
Ted Koy	TE	6'1"	210	22		
Jacque MacKinnon	TE	6'4"	240	31		
Mike Eischeid	K	6'	190	29		

KANSAS CITY CHIEFS 7-5-2 Hank Stram

Scores of Each Game		
10	Minnesota	27
44	Baltimore	24
13	Denver	26
23	BOSTON	10
27	Cincinnati	19
16	DALLAS	27
17	OAKLAND	17
24	HOUSTON	9
31	Pittsburgh	14
6	ST. LOUIS	6
26	SAN DIEGO	14
16	DENVER	0
6	Oakland	20
13	San Diego	31

Use Name	Pos.	Hgt	Wgt	Age	Int	Pts
Dave Hill	OT	6'5"	260	29		
Sid Smith	OT	6'4"	260	22		
Jim Tyrer	OT	6'6"	270	31		
Ed Budde	OG	6'5"	260	29		
George Daney	OG	6'3"	240	23		
Mo Moorman	OG	6'5"	252	26		
E. J. Holub	C	6'4"	236	32		
Mike Oriard	C	6'4"	223	22		
Jack Rudnay	C	6'3"	240	22		
Aaron Brown	DE	6'5"	265	26		
Jerry Mays	DE	6'4"	250	30		
Marv Upshaw	DE	6'3"	245	23		
Buck Buchanan	DT	6'7"	275	30		
Curley Culp	DT	6'1"	265	24		
Bob Liggett	DT	6'2"	255	23		
Bobby Bell	LB	6'4"	228	30	3	6
Chuck Hurston	LB	6'6"	240	27		
Willie Lanier	LB	6'1"	245	25	2	
Jim Lynch	LB	6'1"	235	25	3	
Bob Stein	LB	6'2"	235	22		
Clyde Werner	LB	6'4"	225	22		
Ceasar Belser	DB	6'	212	25		
Dave Hadley	DB	5'9"	186	21		
Jim Kearney	DB	6'2"	206	27	4	
Jim Marsalis	DB	5'11"	194	24	4	
Willie Mitchell	DB	6'1"	185	28		
Johnny Robinson	DB	6'	205	31	10	6
Emmitt Thomas	DB	6'2"	192	27	5	
Len Dawson	QB	6'	190	36		
John Huarte	QB	6'	185	26		
Mike Livingston	QB	6'3"	212	24		
Warren McVea	HB	5'10"	182	24		
Ed Podolak	HB	6'1"	204	23		24
Wendell Hayes	FB	6'2"	220	29		30
Robert Holmes	FB	5'9"	220	24		24
Frank Pitts	WR	6'2"	200	26		12
Otis Taylor	WR	6'2"	215	27		18
Lewis Porter	WR	5'11"	178	23		
Gloster Richardson	WR	6'	200	27		12
Fred Arbanas	TE	6'3"	245	31		6
Billy Cannon	TE	6'1"	215	33		12
Morris Stroud	TE	6'10"	245	24		6
Jan Stenerud	K	6'2"	187	27		116
Jerrel Wilson	K	6'4"	222	29		

Remi Prudhomme–Injury
Goldie Sellers–Injury
Gene Trosch–Injury

SAN DIEGO CHARGERS 5-6-3 Charlie Waller

Scores of Each Game		
14	BALTIMORE	16
27	OAKLAND	27
10	Los Angeles	37
20	GREEN BAY	22
20	Chicago	7
31	HOUSTON	31
27	Cleveland	10
24	DENVER	21
16	Boston	14
17	Oakland	20
14	Kansas City	26
14	CINCINNATI	17
17	Denver	17
31	KANSAS CITY	13

Use Name	Pos.	Hgt	Wgt	Age	Int	Pts
Terry Owens	OT	6'6"	275	26		
Russ Washington	OT	6'6"	295	23		
Bob Wells	OT	6'4"	280	25		
Ira Gordon	OG	6'3"	268	22		
Bill Lenkaitis	OG	6'3"	265	24		
Jim Schmedding	OG	6'2"	250	24		
Walt Sweeney	OG	6'3"	256	29		
Sam Gruneisen	C	6'1"	250	29		
Cal Withrow	C	6'	240	25		
Bob Briggs	DE	6'4"	276	25		
Joe Owens	DE	6'2"	235	22		2
Jeff Staggs	DE	6'2"	246	26		
Ron Billingsley	DT	6'8"	290	25		
Steve DeLong	DT	6'3"	252	27	1	
Gene Ferguson	DT	6'7"	300	22		
Andy Rice	DT	6'3"	268	28		
Tom Williams	DT	6'4"	250	22		
Bob Babich	LB	6'2"	230	23		
Pete Barnes	LB	6'3"	247	25	3	
Bob Bruggers	LB	6'1"	224	26		
Jack Protz	LB	6'1"	218	22		
Rick Redman	LB	5'11"	230	27		
Joe Beauchamp	DB	6'	185	26	1	
Chuck Detwiler	DB	6'	185	23		6
Speedy Duncan	DB	5'10"	175	27		
Chris Fletcher	DB	5'11"	185	21		
Jim Hill	DB	6'2"	190	23		
Bob Howard	DB	6'1"	190	25	2	
Jim Tolbert	DB	6'3"	207	26	2	
Wayne Clark	QB	6'2"	200	23		
Marty Domres	QB	6'3"	215	23		
John Hadl	QB	6'2"	218	30		6
Mike Garrett (from KC)	HB	5'9"	200	26		12
Dickie Post	HB	5'9"	190	24		6
Dave Smith	HB	6'1"	210	22		
Russ Smith	FB-HB	6'1"	212	26		18
Brad Hubbert	FB	6'1"	240	29		6
Jeff Queen	FB	6'1"	220	24		12
Gene Foster	HB-FB	5'11"	220	27		
Lance Alworth	WR	6'	180	30		24
Rick Eber	WR	6'	185	25		
Gary Garrison	WR	6'1"	193	26		72
Walker Gillette	WR	6'5"	198	23		
Willie Frazier	TE	6'4"	250	27		48
Art Strozier	TE	6'2"	220	24		
Mike Mercer	K	6'	215	34		70
Dennis Partee	K	6'2"	218	24		

Ron Mix– Voluntarily Retired
Houston Ridge– Injury

DENVER BRONCOS 5-8-1 Lou Saban

Scores of Each Game		
25	Buffalo	10
16	PITTSBURGH	13
26	KANSAS CITY	13
23	Oakland	35
24	ATLANTA	10
14	San Francisco	19
3	WASHINGTON	19
21	San Diego	24
19	OAKLAND	24
31	New Orleans	6
21	Houston	31
0	Kansas City	16
17	SAN DIEGO	17
13	CLEVELAND	27

Use Name	Pos.	Hgt	Wgt	Age	Int	Pts
Sam Brunelli	OT	6'1"	270	27		
Mike Current	OT	6'4"	274	24		
Steve Alexakos	OG	6'2"	260	23		
George Goeddeke	OG	6'3"	253	25		
Mike Schnitker	OG	6'3"	245	23		
Bob Young	OG	6'2"	256	27		
Jay Bachman	C	6'3"	250	24		
Larry Kaminski	C	6'2"	245	25		
Walt Barnes	DE	6'3"	250	26		
Pete Duranko	DE	6'2"	250	26		
Rich Jackson	DE	6'2"	255	29		
Alden Roche	DE	6'4"	255	25		
Dave Costa	DT	6'2"	260	28		
Jerry Inman	DT	6'3"	256	30		
Paul Smith	DT	6'3"	256	25		
Bill Butler	LB	6'4"	226	26		
Ken Criter	LB	5'11"	223	23		
Carl Cunningham	LB	6'3"	240	26		
Fred Forsberg	LB	6'1"	235	26		
Bill McKoy	LB	6'3"	235	22		
Chip Myrtle	LB	6'2"	225	25		
Dave Washington	LB	6'5"	215	22		2
Booker Edgerson	DB	5'10"	183	31		
Drake Garrett	DB	5'9"	183	24		
Cornell Gordon	DB	6'	187	29	3	
Charlie Greer	DB	6'	205	24	4	
Pete Jaquess	DB	6'	182	28		
Paul Martha	DB	6'	187	27	6	
George Saimes	DB	5'10"	185	28		
Bill Thompson	DB	6'1"	200	23	2	
Bob Wade	DB	6'2"	200	25	1	
Alvin Mitchell	WR-DB	6'3"	195	26		
Pete Liske	QB	6'2"	206	29		6
Al Pastrana	QB	6'1"	190	25		6
Steve Tensi	QB	6'5"	210	27		
Floyd Little	HB	5'10"	196	28		18
Wandy Williams	HB	6'1"	190	24		
Bobby Anderson	FB-HB	6'	208	22		24
Willie Crenshaw	FB	6'2"	230	29		36
Clem Turner	FB	6'1"	236	25		12
Fran Lynch	HB-FB	6'1"	205	24		6
Al Denson	WR	6'2"	208	28		12
John Embree	WR	6'4"	194	26		
Mike Haffner	WR	6'2"	205	28		6
Jerry Hendren	WR	6'2"	187	22		
Bill Van Heusen	WR	6'1"	200	24		12
Bill Masters	TE	6'5"	240	26		12
Jim Whalen	TE	6'2"	210	26		18
Bobby Howfield	K	5'9"	180	33		81

John Huard–Injury

OAKLAND RAIDERS

RUSHING

Last Name	No.	Yds	Avg	TD
Dixon	197	861	4.4	1
Smith	168	681	4.1	3
Hubbard	51	246	4.8	1
Banaszak	21	75	3.6	2
Todd	17	39	2.3	0
Wells	3	34	11.3	0
Lamonica	8	24	3.0	0
Blanda	2	4	2.0	0
Sherman	1	2	2.0	0
Highsmith	2	2	1.0	0
Stabler	1	–4	–4.0	0

RECEIVING

Last Name	No.	Yds	Avg	TD
Biletnikoff	45	768	17	7
Wells	43	935	22	11
Chester	42	556	13	7
Dixon	31	207	7	1
Smith	23	173	8	2
Sherman	18	285	16	0
Todd	5	51	10	0
Buie	2	52	26	0
Banaszak	1	2	2	0

PUNT RETURNS

Last Name	No.	Yds	Avg	TD
Wyatt	25	231	9	1
Sherman	8	65	8	0
Atkinson	4	12	3	0

KICKOFF RETURNS

Last Name	No.	Yds	Avg	TD
Atkinson	23	574	25	0
Wyatt	13	286	22	0
Warren	2	47	24	0
Hubbard	2	41	21	0
Sherman	2	39	20	0
Thoms	2	30	15	0

PASSING – PUNTING – KICKING

PASSING	Att	Comp	%	Yds	Yd/Att	TD	Int–	%	RK
Lamonica	356	179	50	2516	7.1	22	15–	4	1
Blanda	55	29	53	461	8.4	6	5–	9	
Stabler	7	2	29	52	7.4	0	1–	14	

PUNTING	No	Avg
Eischeid	79	39.5

KICKING	XP	Att	%	FG	Att	%
Blanda	36	36	100	16	29	55

KANSAS CITY CHIEFS

RUSHING

Last Name	No.	Yds	Avg	TD
Podolak	168	749	4.5	3
Hayes	109	381	3.5	5
McVea	61	260	4.3	0
Holmes	63	206	3.3	3
Pitts	5	84	16.8	0
Dawson	11	46	4.2	0
Livingston	3	26	8.7	0
Porter	2	21	10.5	0
Taylor	3	13	4.3	0
Cannon	1	6	6.0	0
Richardson	1	4	4.0	0

RECEIVING

Last Name	No.	Yds	Avg	TD
Taylor	34	618	18	3
Podolak	26	307	12	1
Hayes	26	219	8	0
Holmes	23	173	8	1
Pitts	11	172	16	2
Arbanas	8	108	14	1
Cannon	7	125	18	2
Richardson	5	171	34	2
McVea	5	26	5	0
Stroud	4	86	22	1
Porter	1	29	29	0

PUNT RETURNS

Last Name	No.	Yds	Avg	TD
Podolak	23	311	14	0
Mitchell	4	33	8	0
Porter	1	–3	–3	0

KICKOFF RETURNS

Last Name	No.	Yds	Avg	TD
Holmes	19	535	28	0
Podolak	17	348	20	0
McVea	3	57	19	0
Stein	3	23	8	0
Porter	1	22	22	0
Smith	1	12	12	0

PASSING – PUNTING – KICKING

PASSING	Att	Comp	%	Yds	Yd/Att	TD	Int–	%	RK
Dawson	262	141	54	1876	7.2	13	14–	5	3
Livingston	22	11	50	122	5.6	0	1–	5	
Huarte	2	0	0	0	0.0	0	1–	50	
Podolak	2	2	100	40	20.0	0	0–	0	
McVea	1	0	0	0	0.0	0	0–	0	

PUNTING	No	Avg
Wilson	76	44.9

KICKING	XP	Att	%	FG	Att	%
Stenerud	26	26	100	30	42	71

SAN DIEGO CHARGERS

RUSHING

Last Name	No.	Yds	Avg	TD
Queen	77	261	3.4	1
Post	74	225	3.0	1
Garrett	67	208	3.1	1
Hadl	28	188	6.7	1
Hubbert	49	175	3.6	1
R. Smith	52	163	3.1	3
Frazier	5	120	24.0	1
Foster	32	84	2.6	0
D. Smith	14	42	3.0	0
Domres	14	39	2.8	0
Garrison	4	7	1.8	0

RECEIVING

Last Name	No.	Yds	Avg	TD
Garrison	44	1006	23	12
Frazier	38	497	13	6
Alworth	35	608	17	4
Queen	20	236	12	1
Garrett	14	131	9	1
Post	13	113	9	0
Foster	10	92	9	0
Hubbert	7	44	6	0
R. Smith	5	44	9	0
D. Smith	4	65	16	0
Eber	2	43	22	0
Strozier	2	40	20	0
Gillette	2	21	11	0

PUNT RETURNS

Last Name	No.	Yds	Avg	TD
Fletcher	16	137	9	0
R. Smith	9	31	3	0
Garrett	3	30	10	0
Duncan	5	10	2	0
Detwiler	1	–5	–5	0

KICKOFF RETURNS

Last Name	No.	Yds	Avg	TD
Duncan	19	410	22	0
Fletcher	17	382	22	0
Queen	1	12	12	0
R. Smith	1	9	9	0
Beauchamp	1	0	0	0
Hill	1	0	0	0
T. Owens	1	0	0	0

PASSING – PUNTING – KICKING

PASSING	Att	Comp	%	Yds	Yd/Att	TD	Int–	%	RK
Hadl	327	162	50	2388	7.3	22	15–	5	2
Domres	55	28	51	491	8.9	2	4–	7	
Foster	3	1	33	9	3.0	0	0–	0	
Clark	2	1	50	48	24.0	0	0–	0	

PUNTING	No	Avg
Partee	65	43.9
Mercer	8	35.4
Hadl	1	30.0

KICKING	XP	Att	%	FG	Att	%
Mercer	34	35	97	12	19	63

DENVER BRONCOS

RUSHING

Last Name	No.	Yds	Avg	TD
Little	209	901	4.3	3
Anderson	83	368	4.4	4
Crenshaw	69	200	2.9	5
Turner	29	106	3.7	2
Pastrana	14	89	6.4	1
Lynch	20	81	4.1	1
Liske	7	42	6.0	1
Tensi	4	14	3.5	0
Haffner	1	1	1.0	0

RECEIVING

Last Name	No.	Yds	Avg	TD
Denson	47	646	14	2
Whalen	36	503	14	3
Crenshaw	18	105	6	1
Little	17	161	9	0
Van Heusen	16	382	24	2
Haffner	12	196	16	1
Anderson	9	140	16	0
Masters	9	83	9	2
Turner	8	23	3	0
Lynch	7	69	10	0
Embree	4	50	13	0

PUNT RETURNS

Last Name	No.	Yds	Avg	TD
Thompson	23	233	10	0
Little	22	187	9	0
Greer	14	123	9	0
Jaquess	4	13	3	0

KICKOFF RETURNS

Last Name	No.	Yds	Avg	TD
Anderson	21	520	25	0
Hendren	8	197	25	0
Thompson	9	188	21	0
Little	6	126	21	0
Turner	1	31	31	0
Criter	2	20	10	0
Washington	1	20	20	0
Myrtle	1	1	1	0
Lynch	0	11	0	0

PASSING – PUNTING – KICKING

PASSING	Att	Comp	%	Yds	Yd/Att	TD	Int–	%	RK
Liske	238	112	47	1340	5.6	7	11–	5	12
Tensi	80	38	48	539	6.7	3	8–	10	
Pastrana	75	29	39	420	5.6	1	9–	12	
Anderson	7	4	57	59	8.4	0	0–	0	
Little	2	0	0	0	0.0	0	0–	0	
Van Heusen	1	0	0	0	0.0	0	0–	0	

PUNTING	No	Avg
Van Heusen	87	42.9

KICKING	XP	Att	%	FG	Att	%
Howfield	27	28	96	18	32	56

1970 Championship Games

NFC CHAMPIONSHIP GAME

January 3, at San Francisco
(Attendance 59,364)

Two Interceptions Too Many

SCORING

SAN FRANCISCO	3	0	7	0–10
DALLAS	0	3	14	0–17

First Quarter
S.F. Gossett, 16 yard field goal

Second Quarter
Dal. Clark, 21 yard field goal

Third Quarter
Dal. Thomas, 13 yard rush
PAT–Clark (kick)
Dal. Garrison, 5 yard pass from Morton
PAT–Clark (kick)
S.F. Witcher, 26 yard pass from Brodie
PAT–Gossett (kick)

TEAM STATISTICS

S.F.		DALLAS
15	First Downs–Total	22
2	First Downs–Rushing	16
12	First Downs–Passing	5
1	First Downs–Penalty	1
1	Fumbles–Number	4
0	Fumbles–Lost Ball	1
5	Penalties–Number	7
51	Yards Penalized	75
1	Missed Field Goals	2
61	Offensive Plays–Total	75
307	Net Yards	319
5.0	Average Gain	4.3
2	Giveaways	1
1	Takeaways	2
–1	Difference	+1

The opening round of the first NFC playoffs had produced two interesting games, as the Cowboys had beaten the Lions 5-0 on a field as muddy as a pigsty and the '49ers had edged the tough Vikings 17-14. In the conference championship, the Cowboys and '49ers would use different offensive styles with different results.

Dallas quarterback Carl Morton had a sore arm and could not match the passing ability of San Francisco's John Brodie, but the Cowboys did have two strong runners in rookie Duane Thomas and Walt Garrison, plus a top-notch offensive line to block for them. Neither offense did much in the first quarter, as Bruce Gossett of San Francisco booted a 16-yard field goal while Dallas' Mike Clark missed from the 40. The defensive deadlock continued into the second period, with Clark hitting on a 21-yard field goal to knot the first half score at 3-3.

The Cowboys got the first big break of the game in the third period. With Dallas end Larry Cole putting heavy pressure on him, Brodie rushed a pass over the middle which Lee Roy Jordan picked off at the San Francisco 13-yard line. Duane Thomas covered the ground to the end zone on the very next play, and Clark's extra point made the score 10-3. The '49ers drove right back into Dallas territory, but Mel Renfro intercepted a Brodie pass on the 18-yard line to extinguish that threat. The Cowboys then pounded their way downfield on the running of Thomas and Garrison, with a swing pass from Morton to Garrison covering the final five yards to the goal line.

Brodie then led his team on a 73-yard drive capped by a 26-yard scoring pitch to Dick Witcher; with Gossett's extra point, the '49ers trailed 17-10 with fifteen minutes left to play. The Dallas defense stood firm for the rest of the day, however, and the Cowboys headed off to the Super Bowl after failing in four previous playoff tries.

INDIVIDUAL STATISTICS

SAN FRANCISCO	No	Yds	Avg.	DALLAS	No	Yds	Avg.
				RUSHING			
Willard	13	42	3.2	Thomas	27	143	5.3
Cunningham	5	14	2.8	Garrison	17	71	4.2
Thomas	1	5	5.0	Welch	5	27	5.4
	19	61	3.2	Reeves	2	–12	–6.0
					51	229	4.5
				RECEIVING			
Washington	6	88	14.7	Garrison	3	51	17.0
Cunningham	4	34	8.5	Thomas	2	24	12.0
Windsor	3	70	23.3	Rucker	1	21	21.0
Witcher	3	41	13.7	Ditka	1	5	5.0
Willard	2	22	11.0		7	101	14.4
Kwalick	1	7	7.0				
	19	262	13.8				
				PUNTING			
Spurrier	5		41.0	Widby	6		40.2
				PUNT RETURNS			
B. Taylor	2	5	2.5	Hayes	1	8	8.0
				Reeves	1	0	0.0
					2	8	4.0
				KICKOFF RETURNS			
Thomas	3	66	22.0	Washington	1	20	20.0
Tucker	1	23	23.0	Waters	1	16	16.0
	4	89	22.3	Kiner	1	10	10.0
					3	46	15.3
				INTERCEPTION RETURNS			
None				Renfro	1	19	19.0
				Jordan	1	4	4.0
					2	23	11.5

PASSING

SAN FRANCISCO	Att.	Comp.	Comp. Pct.	Yds.	Int.	Yds/ Att.	Yds/ Comp.	Yards Lost Tackled
Brodie	30	19	47.5	262	2	6.6	13.8	2–16
DALLAS								
Morton	22	7	31.8	101	0	4.6	14.4	2–11

AFC CHAMPIONSHIP GAME

January 3, at Baltimore
(Attendance 54,799)

Two Old Men and One Crown

SCORING

BALTIMORE	3	7	10	7–27
OAKLAND	0	3	7	7–17

First Quarter
Balt. O'Brien, 16 yard field goal

Second Quarter
Balt. Bulaich, 2 yard rush
PAT–O'Brien (kick)
Oak. Blanda, 48 yard field goal

Third Quarter
Oak. Biletnikoff, 38 yard pass from Blanda
PAT–Blanda (kick)
Balt. O'Brien, 23 yard field goal
Balt. Bulaich, 11 yard rush
PAT–O'Brien (kick)

Fourth Quarter
Oak. Wells, 15 yard pass from Blanda
PAT–Blanda (kick)
Balt. Perkins, 68 yard pass from Unitas
PAT–O'Brien (kick)

TEAM STATISTICS

BALT.		OAK.
18	First Downs–Total	16
7	First Downs–Rushing	5
11	First Downs–Passing	10
0	First Downs–Penalty	1
0	Fumbles–Number	1
0	Fumbles–Lost Ball	1
2	Penalties–Number	2
10	Yards Penalized	20
2	Missed Field Goals	0
71	Offensive Plays–Total	63
363	Net Yards	336
5.1	Average Gain	5.3
0	Giveaways	4
4	Takeaways	0
+4	Difference	–4

One old AFL team and one old NFL team squared off in the first AFC championship match. The Oakland Raiders got this far by beating the upcoming Miami Dolphins 21-14 in the first playoff round, while the Baltimore Colts arrived at this game fresh from a 17-0 whitewash of the Cincinnati Bengals. Before the game was over, it had developed into a duel of two of pro football's oldest quarterbacks, Johnny Unitas and George Blanda.

Baltimore scored the only points of the first quarter on Jim O'Brien's 16-yard field goal, as neither Unitas nor Oakland's Daryle Lamonica could spark the offense. Early in the second quarter, however, Lamonica pulled a thigh muscle when hit by Bubba Smith, so the forty-three-year-old Blanda had to take over at quarterback. By the time he entered the game, Baltimore had run its lead to 10-0 on a Norm Bulaich touchdown that Unitas had set up with a key pass to Eddie Hinton. When Blanda could drive his team only to the Baltimore 40-yard line, he simply kicked a field goal to net three points and drop the halftime score to 10-3.

The Raiders tied the score in the third quarter when Blanda hit Fred Biletnikoff with a 38-yard touchdown pass. Coolly directing his offense, Unitas brought the Colts back close enough for O'Brien to kick a field goal, and he engineered another long drive late in the period which Bulaich capped with his second touchdown.

Blanda responded in the final period by driving the Raiders 80 yards, with the final 15 yards coming on a pass to Warren Wells. The Raiders now trailed 20-17, but the Baltimore defense came through with clutch plays when needed. The Raiders twice were in scoring range of the Baltimore goal line, but both drives ended with Blanda passes getting intercepted in the end zone. The Colts finally iced the victory away when Unitas hit Ray Perkins, one of four wide receivers in on the play, with a 68-yard scoring pass which lengthened the final score to 27-17.

INDIVIDUAL STATISTICS

BALTIMORE	No	Yds	Avg.	OAKLAND	No	Yds	Avg.
				RUSHING			
Bulaich	22	71	3.2	Dixon	10	51	5.1
Nowatzke	8	32	4.0	Smith	9	44	4.9
Hill	5	12	2.4	Hubbard	3	12	4.0
Unitas	2	9	4.5		22	107	4.9
Havrilak	1	2	2.0				
	38	126	3.3				
				RECEIVING			
Hinton	5	115	23.0	Wells	5	108	21.6
Jefferson	3	36	12.0	Biletnikoff	5	92	18.4
Perkins	2	80	40.0	Dixon	3	15	5.0
Mackey	1	14	14.0	Chester	2	36	18.0
	11	245	22.3	Smith	2	21	10.5
				Hubbard	1	5	5.0
					18	277	15.4
				PUNTING			
Lee	6		45.3	Eischeid	5		40.0
				PUNT RETURNS			
Gardin	2	1	0.5	Atkinson	2	10	5.0
				KICKOFF RETURNS			
Duncan	4	105	26.3	Atkinson	2	37	18.5
				Sherman	1	23	23.0
					3	60	20.0
				INTERCEPTION RETURNS			
Logan	1	16	16.0	None			
May	1	0	0.0				
Volk	1	0	0.0				
	3	16	5.3				

PASSING

BALTIMORE	Att.	Comp.	Comp. Pct.	Yds.	Int.	Yds/ Att.	Yds/ Comp.	Yards Lost Tackled
Unitas	30	11	36.7	245	0	8.2	22.3	3– 8
OAKLAND								
Blanda	32	17	53.0	271	3	8.5	15.9	
Lamonica	4	1	25.0	6	0	1.5	6.0	
	36	18	50.0	277	3	7.7	15.4	5–48

SUPER BOWL V

January 17, at Miami

(Attendance 80.055)

Follow the Bouncing Ball

The first Super Bowl under the new merger arrangement ended in high drama after being, for most of the afternoon, a comedy of errors. Both the Dallas Cowboys and Baltimore Colts took turns giving the game away, but neither team would take it until the final seconds of play.

The strong defenses of both clubs dominated the first-quarter action, although the Cowboys did score on a 14-yard Mike Clark field goal. Another Clark field goal made the score 6-0 in the second quarter when the Colts tied the score on a fluke play. Baltimore quarterback Johnny Unitas threw a long pass down the center of the field to wide receiver Eddie Hinton; the ball bounced off Hinton's hands, back up into the air, grazed the fingertips of Dallas cornerback Mel Renfro, and came right down to the surprised John Mackey. Taking the ball around mid-field, Mackey sprinted the rest of the way to the end zone. The Cowboys blocked the Baltimore extra point, however, so the score remained tied at 6-6.

On the next Baltimore offensive series, a hard tackle by George Andrie forced Unitas to fumble the ball on his own 29-yard line and sent him out of the game with bruised ribs. Cowboy quarterback Craig Morton, operating with a sore arm, then moved his team down to the 7-yard line, from where a short pass to Duane Thomas scored the only Dallas touchdown of the day. Clark's conversion ran the score to 13-6, and neither offense could score again before the end of the half.

The Colts kept up the parade of mistakes when Jim Duncan fumbled the opening kickoff deep in Baltimore territory. The Cowboys then drove from the 31-yard line to the two-yard line on five plays, with Thomas' hard running the key element. With the ball in the shadows of the goal posts, Thomas took a handoff and fumbled the ball, the Colts recovering on the one-foot line.

With the threat erased, the third quarter settled into a pattern of offensive futility, with neither Morton nor Earl Morrall, filling in for the injured Unitas, able to ignite an attack. With only eight minutes left in the game, the Cowboys still clung to their 13-6 lead.

At that point, however, a Morton pass bounced off the fingers of fullback Walt Garrison into the hands of Colt safety Rick Volk, who returned the ball 17 yards to the Dallas three-yard line. In short order, Tom Nowatzke smashed over for the touchdown, and Jim O'Brien added the tying extra point.

Overtime seemed imminent late in the final quarter, but another Morton pass was intercepted with 1:09 left in the game. Mike Curtis stole the pass on the Dallas 41 and returned it to the 28. Two running plays ran the clock down, and then Jim O'Brien, Baltimore's rookie kicker, booted a 32-yard three-pointer to give the Colts an artistically flawed but nonetheless satisfying 16-13 victory.

BALTIMORE		DALLAS
	OFFENSE	
Hinton	WR	Hayes
Vogel	LT	Neely
Ressler	LG	Niland
Curry	C	Manders
Williams	RG	Nye
Sullivan	RT	Wright
Mackey	TE	Norman
Jefferson	WR	Rucker
Unitas	QB	Morton
Bulaich	RB	Thomas
Nowatzke	RB	Garrison
	DEFENSE	
Bubba Smith	LE	Cole
B. R. Smith	LT	Pugh
Miller	RT	Lilly
Hilton	RE	Andrie
May	LLB	Edwards
Curtis	MLB	Jordan
Hendricks	RLB	Howley
Stukes	LCB	Adderley
Duncan	RCB	Renfro
Logan	LS	Green
Volk	RS	Waters

SUBSTITUTES

BALTIMORE

Offense

Ball	Maitland
Goode	Mitchell
Havrilak	Morrall
J. Hill	Perkins
Johnson	

Defense

Gardin	Newsome
Grant	Nichols
Maxwell	

Kickers

O'Brien	Lee

DALLAS

Offense

Asher	Homan
Ditka	Reeves
C. Hill	Welch

Defense

East	Lewis
Flowers	Stincic
Harris	Toomay
Kiner	Washington

Kickers

Clark	Widby

SCORING

	1	2	3	4	Total
BALTIMORE	0	6	0	10	16
DALLAS	3	10	0	0	13

First Quarter

Dall.	Clark, 14 yard field goal

Second Quarter

Dall.	Clark, 30 yard field goal
Balt.	Mackey, 75 yard pass from Unitas
	PAT – O'Brien (kick–blocked)
Dall.	Thomas, 7 yard pass from Morton
	PAT – Clark (kick)

Fourth Quarter

Balt.	Nowatzke, 2 yard rush
	PAT – O'Brien (kick)
Balt.	O'Brien, 32 yard field goal

TEAM STATISTICS

BALT.		DALLAS
14	First Downs – Total	10
4	First Downs – Rushing	4
6	First Downs – Passing	5
4	First Downs – Penalty	1
5	Fumbles – Number	1
3	Fumbles – Lost Ball	1
4	Penalties – Number	10
31	Yards Penalized	133
1	Missed Field Goals	0
56	Offensive Plays	59
329	Net Yards	215
5.9	Average Gain	3.7
6	Giveaways	4
4	Takeaways	6
–2	Difference	+2

INDIVIDUAL STATISTICS

BALTIMORE	No	Yds	Avg.	DALLAS	No	Yds	Avg.
RUSHING							
Nowatzke	10	33	3.3	Garrison	12	65	5.4
Bulaich	18	28	1.6	Thomas	18	35	1.9
Unitas	1	4	4.0	Morton	1	2	2.0
Havrilak	1	3	3.0		31	102	3.3
Morrall	1	1	1.0				
	31	69	2.2				
RECEIVING							
Jefferson	3	52	17.3	Reeves	5	46	9.2
Mackey	2	80	40.0	Thomas	4	21	5.3
Hinton	2	51	25.5	Garrison	2	19	9.5
Havrilak	2	27	13.5	Hayes	1	41	41.0
Nowatzke	1	45	45.0		12	127	10.6
Bulaich	1	5	5.0				
	11	260	23.6				
PUNTING							
Lee	4		41.5	Widby	9		41.9
PUNT RETURNS							
Gardin	4	4	1.0	Hayes	3	9	3.0
Logan	1	8	8.0				
	5	12	2.4				
KICKOFF RETURNS							
Duncan	4	90	22.5	Harris	1	18	18.0
				Hill	1	14	14.0
				Lewis	1	2	2.0
					3	34	11.1
INTERCEPTION RETURNS							
Volk	1	30	30.0	Howley	2	22	11.0
Logan	1	14	14.0	Renfro	1	0	0.0
Curtis	1	13	13.0		3	22	7.3
	3	57	19.0				

PASSING

BALTIMORE	Att	Comp	Comp Pct.	Yds.	Int	Yds/ Att.	Yds/ Comp	Yards Lost Tackled
Morrall	15	7	46.7	147	1	9.8	21.0	0– 0
Unitas	9	3	33.3	88	2	9.8	29.3	0– 0
Havrilak	1	1	100.0	25	0	25.0	25.0	0– 0
	25	11	44.0	260	3	10.4	23.6	0– 0
DALLAS								
Morton	26	12	46.2	127	3	4.9	10.6	2–14

1971 N.F.C. With a Little Offensive Help

The long bomb and frequent passing had enlivened the game ever since Don Hutson and Sammy Baugh made their debuts in the 1930s and had become a way of offensive life since the days of Otto Graham and Bob Waterfield in the late 1940s. This year, however, defense had caught up. With most teams rigging up complex zone defenses which rendered long-passing quarterbacks impotent, scoring dropped and the field-goal kicker replaced the deep receiver as pro football's glamorous point producer. To counter the new defenses, pro offenses employed big, strong running backs and quarterbacks who could throw on the roll-out play and carry the ball occasionally. But a rule of thumb for this season was that the team with the better defense usually won; indeed, all four teams which made the playoffs had outstanding defenses which often overshadowed their offensive platoons.

EASTERN DIVISION

Dallas Cowboys—For the first half of the season, coach Tom Landry alternated Craig Morton and Roger Staubach at quarterback; the Cowboys won four games and lost three. But starting with the eighth game, Landry gave the job full time to Staubach, and the team won its last seven games to move past the Redskins into first place. Both Dallas quarterbacks were fine passers, but Staubach gave the defense something extra to worry about by often running with the ball. By mid-season, defenses also had to worry about Duane Thomas running the ball. After sitting out the early games over a salary dispute, Thomas returned to the team in a sullen mood, but his ball-carrying fit right into the Dallas scheme of things.

Washington Redskins—When George Allen was hired as head coach he immediately set out to trade for veteran players who would make no mistakes on the field. The resulting collection of football oldsters became known as the Over the Hill Gang. In a dazzling array of trades, Allen picked up Billy Kilmer, Roy Jefferson, Boyd Dowler, Clifton McNeil, Ron McDole, Verlon Biggs, Diron Talbert, Jack Pardee, Myron Pottios, Richie Petitbon, John Wilbur, and Speedy Duncan. Allen rigged together a defense which indeed made no errors, which delighted in forcing enemy offenses into fumbles and interceptions. The Washington attack started out fast but slumped when injuries erased Sonny Jurgensen, Charley Taylor, and Jerry Smith from the lineup and cut down on Larry Brown's effectiveness.

Philadelphia Eagles—Apparently on the way to another dismal season after losing their first three games, the Eagles fired head coach Jerry Williams and replaced him with young Ed Khayat. The Eagles lost their first two games under Khayat, but then went on to a 7-2 record. The defense triggered the reversal by jelling into one of the league's top units. On this surprising platoon, only Tim Rossovich and Bill Bradley had recognizable names; the others were parts of a nameless horde which swarmed over enemy players. The Eagles' offense, on the other hand, was feeble.

St. Louis Cardinals—Bob Hollway's first season as head coach flattened out into a 4-9-1 record and a disappointing fourth-place finish in the East. Hollway had coached the magnificent Viking defense as an assistant at Minnesota, but the St. Louis defense this season suffered from a variety of injuries and a slow adjustment to Hollway's new system. The Cardinal offense also sputtered, with neither Jim Hart nor Pete Beathard taking charge at quarterback.

New York Giants—The Giants had the worst defense in the NFC, totally unable to put pressure on enemy passers, while the secondary suffered from injuries and Bennie McRae's advanced years. Ron Johnson's knee injury ripped the heart out of the Giant running attack. In the passing department, quarterback Fran Tarkenton found tight end Bob Tucker a congenial target, but there was no deep threat to replace the traded Homer Jones.

CENTRAL DIVISION

Minnesota Vikings—The Vikings' great defense again won first place in the Central Division, but the Minnesota offense just didn't have the power or direction to make the Vikings a complete team. At the quarterback spot, Gary Cuozzo, Bob Lee, and Norm Snead all rotated without any of them igniting a spark in the attack. Injuries to receivers Gene Washington and John Beasley also hurt the passing game, although Bob Grim rebounded from years of injuries to become a legitimate deep threat. Clint Jones, Dave Osborn, Jim Lindsey, Oscar Reed, and Bill Brown all were short-yardage runners, adept at grinding out yards behind the strong Viking front wall.

Detroit Lions—Blossoming into stardom in his fourth pro season was quarterback Greg Landry, a man with a strong passing arm plus the size and strength of a fullback in carrying the ball. Landry set a record for quarterbacks this season with 530 yards rushing. Second in the entire NFC in rushing yardage was Lion fullback Steve Owens, the powerful Heisman Trophy winner who had suffered through an injury-ruined rookie season last year. With Altie Taylor also picking up yardage on the ground, the Lions had the best running attack in the conference. The defense held the Lions back this season, with the front four unable to mount a pass rush now that Alex Karras had passed his prime and was cut loose before the season started. One tragic note of the season was the death of Chuck Hughes, who collapsed of a heart attack on the field in full view of millions.

Chicago Bears—Even with Gale Sayers still out with his bad knee, the Bears got off to a strong start. Middle linebacker Dick Butkus held the defense together with his outstanding play, and reserve quarterback Kent Nix was the offensive hero in the early going. After mid-season, however, both Nix and Jack Concannon were injured, leaving the entire quarterbacking load on Bobby Douglass' shoulders. The Bears dropped six of their last seven, and coach Jim Dooley got the ax at the end of the season.

Green Bay Packers—Dan Devine, who left the University of Missouri to take over as head coach in Green Bay, suffered through a trying professional debut as his Packers blew an early lead and lost to the Giants 42-40 on opening day. To make matters worse, several players smashed into Devine on an out-of-bounds play and broke his leg. Getting through the rest of the season with the help of a crutch, Devine found little pleasing in the Packers' drop to last place in the Central Division. His hardest decision was to bench all-time great Ray Nitschke, and his greatest pleasure was the play of rookie fullback John Brockington, who led the NFC in rushing 1,105 yards.

WESTERN DIVISION

San Francisco '49ers—Even with John Brodie suffering through an erratic season, the '49ers still had enough talent on both platoons to beat out the surprising Los Angeles Rams for first place in the West. Operating behind a top-notch offensive line, the '49ers running game prospered with Ken Willard's good year and a fine rookie performance from speedster Vic Washington. This took the pressure off Brodie, who still had Gene Washington, Ted Kwalick, and Dick Witcher to throw to. On defense, coach Dick Nolan stuck with one set of linemen and was rewarded with excellent seasons from Cedrick Hardman, Charlie Krueger, Earl Edwards, and Tommy Hart.

Los Angeles Rams—Long-time UCLA coach Tommy Prothro moved into the professional ranks by rebuilding the Rams and almost winning a divisional title. Prothro traded away Diron Talbert, Jack Pardee, Myron Pottios, Maxie Baughan, Richie Petitbon, Tommy Mason, Bob Brown, Wendell Tucker, and Billy Truax from last year's team and replaced them with younger players. The defense had eight new starters, with only Deacon Jones, Merlin Olsen, and Coy Bacon returning, but the new unit hung together well. On the offense, key new starters were Willie Ellison, who ran for a record 247 yards against New Orleans on December 5, Lance Rentzel, Bob Klein, and Harry Schuh.

Atlanta Falcons—The Falcons enjoyed their first season ever with an aggressive defense and a patchwork offense. The front four fielded two top linemen in Claude Humphrey and John Zook, linebacker Don Hansen's fine season made up for the loss of Tommy Nobis to a knee injury, and Ken Reaves starred in an underrated secondary which allowed the least passing yards in the Conference. On offense, the line improved into a good unit, with George Kunz and Mal Snider the top performers. The running attack lost its speed when a knee injury sidelined rookie Joe Profit, but Cannonball Butler, Art Malone, Harmon Wages, and free agent rookie Willie Belton ground out the yardage with straight-ahead power plays. Both of the wide receivers were rookies, Ken Burrow and Wes Chesson, but at quarterback the Falcons could field only journeymen Bob Berry and Dick Shiner.

New Orleans Saints—Rookie quarterback Archie Manning made a fine professional debut by scoring a touchdown on the last play of the game to beat the Rams 24-20 on opening day. Foot and leg problems kept him on the bench for much of the campaign, but Manning did show a strong arm and a talent for running with the ball. With Manning or Ed Hargett at quarterback, the New Orleans offense showed new punch. The line was improved with the addition of Glen Ray Hines, Don Morrison, and John Didion, and the receiving corps had always been the Saints' strongest department. At running back, second-year man Jim Strong, picked up from San Francisco, and rookies Bob Gresham and Jamie Ford handled most of the running chores.

FINAL TEAM STATISTICS

OFFENSE

	ATL.	CHI.	DALL.	DET.	G.B.	L.A.	MINN.	N.O.	N.Y.G.	PHIL.	ST.L.	S.F.	WASH.
FIRST DOWNS:													
Total	221	189	288	269	208	234	198	242	236	201	212	257	212
by Rushing	99	75	135	131	115	105	89	105	86	65	86	113	77
by Passing	108	99	144	104	87	111	95	106	140	119	109	122	112
by Penalty	14	15	9	34	6	18	14	31	10	17	17	22	23
RUSHING:													
Number	494	365	512	532	500	460	484	452	394	407	417	498	477
Yards	1703	1434	2249	2376	2229	2139	1695	1711	1461	1248	1530	2129	1757
Average Yards	3.4	3.9	4.4	4.5	4.5	4.7	3.5	3.8	3.7	3.1	3.7	4.3	3.7
Touchdowns	12	6	25	15	18	15	14	18	11	6	8	12	8
PASSING:													
Attempts	285	443	361	299	254	370	334	387	462	390	385	391	334
Completions	167	186	206	157	121	185	157	182	268	200	170	209	182
Completion Percentage	58.6	42.0	57.1	52.5	47.6	50.0	47.0	47.0	58.0	51.3	44.2	53.5	54.5
Passing Yards	2495	2294	3037	2453	1842	2304	1910	2355	3062	2552	2656	2688	2391
Avg. Yards per Attempt	8.8	5.4	8.4	8.2	7.3	6.2	5.7	6.1	6.6	6.5	6.9	6.9	7.2
Avg. Yards per Complet.	14.9	12.3	14.7	15.6	15.2	12.5	12.2	12.9	11.4	12.8	15.6	12.9	13.1
Times Tackled Passing	31	49	32	31	18	26	28	50	40	26	19	11	17
Yards Lost Tackled	239	392	251	252	157	210	255	400	348	229	185	111	118
Net Yards	2256	1902	2786	2201	1685	2094	1655	1955	2714	2323	2471	2577	2273
Touchdowns	16	12	22	17	12	18	9	12	14	13	14	18	13
Interceptions	21	28	14	14	24	11	18	14	25	20	26	24	15
Percent Intercepted	7.4	6.3	3.9	4.7	9.4	3.0	5.4	3.6	5.4	5.1	6.8	6.1	4.5
PUNTS:													
Number	60	77	56	42	56	70	89	77	66	75	61	51	58
Average Distance	36.9	40.2	41.6	41.7	40.0	41.4	39.5	41.4	40.6	41.9	38.8	38.7	40.5
PUNT RETURNS:													
Number	37	36	31	23	38	35	27	16	19	24	30	39	45
Yards	174	262	248	194	177	172	164	100	122	172	234	268	427
Average Yards	4.7	7.3	8.0	8.4	4.7	4.9	6.1	6.3	6.4	7.2	7.8	6.9	9.5
Touchdowns	0	0	0	0	0	0	0	0	0	0	0	0	0
KICKOFF RETURNS:													
Number	59	59	50	51	58	54	41	56	63	49	58	46	43
Yards	1477	1325	1376	1233	1546	1322	960	1143	1416	1183	1363	1075	913
Average Yards	25.0	22.5	27.5	24.2	26.7	24.5	23.4	20.4	22.5	24.1	23.5	23.4	21.2
Touchdowns	0	0	2	2	1	1	0	0	1	0	1	0	0
INTERCEPTION RETURNS:													
Number	20	22	26	22	16	27	27	20	15	22	17	14	29
Yards	180	267	402	295	205	452	572	342	227	374	191	186	480
Average Yards	9.0	12.1	15.5	13.4	12.8	16.7	21.2	17.1	15.1	17.0	11.2	13.3	16.6
Touchdowns	1	0	0	3	0	2	1	1	1	1	1	0	5
PENALTIES:													
Number	79	78	94	69	61	79	70	85	77	81	66	88	80
Yards	723	746	952	738	568	642	661	869	640	838	643	961	801
FUMBLES:													
Number	39	28	30	35	29	32	25	29	37	21	35	33	32
Number Lost	15	18	21	19	20	18	12	11	20	15	20	18	20
POINTS:													
Total	274	185	406	341	274	313	245	266	228	221	231	300	276
PAT Attempts	34	20	50	39	33	37	25	31	30	24	24	33	27
PAT Made	29	20	50	39	32	37	25	29	30	23	24	33	27
FG Attempts	21	33	33	37	26	29	32	28	17	37	32	36	49
FG Made	13	15	18	22	14	18	22	17	6	18	21	23	29
Percent FG Made	61.9	45.5	54.5	59.5	53.8	62.1	68.8	60.7	35.3	48.6	65.6	63.9	59.2
Safeties	1	0	1	1	1	0	2	0	0	0	0	0	0

DEFENSE

	ATL.	CHI.	DALL.	DET.	G.B.	L.A.	MINN.	N.O.	N.Y.G.	PHIL.	ST.L.	S.F.	WASH.
FIRST DOWNS:													
Total	237	234	200	210	230	239	194	260	228	251	244	199	213
by Rushing	114	99	59	97	104	91	88	129	104	104	109	80	73
by Passing	106	117	125	99	110	129	88	110	112	129	120	96	119
by Penalty	17	18	16	14	16	19	18	21	12	18	15	23	21
RUSHING:													
Number	500	509	353	432	489	455	447	495	449	450	486	408	408
Yards	2149	2116	1144	1842	1707	1658	1600	2200	2059	1962	1985	1668	1396
Average Yards	4.3	4.2	3.2	4.3	3.5	3.6	3.6	4.4	4.6	4.4	4.1	4.1	3.4
Touchdowns	19	14	8	15	7	11	2	18	12	16	10	4	7
PASSING:													
Attempts	343	362	421	306	353	387	405	333	333	407	375	341	411
Completions	164	192	209	163	186	200	206	175	173	220	212	152	191
Completion Percentage	47.8	53.0	49.6	53.3	52.7	51.7	50.9	52.6	52.0	54.1	56.5	44.6	46.5
Passing Yards	1895	2607	2660	2163	2469	2693	2022	2472	2458	2971	2546	2309	2448
Avg. Yards per Attempt	5.5	7.2	6.3	7.1	7.0	7.0	5.0	7.4	7.4	7.3	6.8	6.8	6.0
Avg. Yards per Complet.	11.6	13.6	12.7	13.3	13.3	13.5	9.8	14.1	14.2	13.5	12.0	15.2	12.8
Times Tackled Passing	31	28	43	18	19	37	27	24	18	32	20	38	36
Yards Lost Tackled	257	203	336	146	168	314	216	234	151	311	166	298	321
Net Yards	1638	2404	2324	2017	2301	2379	1806	2238	2307	2660	2380	2011	2127
Touchdowns	9	12	15	17	21	15	10	20	25	16	12	17	11
Interceptions	20	22	26	22	16	27	27	20	15	22	17	14	29
Percent Intercepted	5.8	6.1	6.2	7.2	4.5	7.0	6.7	6.1	4.5	5.4	4.5	4.1	7.1
PUNTS:													
Number	63	67	65	58	61	66	78	50	61	57	58	73	77
Average Distance	41.4	40.2	41.5	41.2	40.1	39.4	40.0	41.2	39.8	40.5	40.4	39.7	41.2
PUNT RETURNS:													
Number	26	31	26	18	23	27	47	43	50	40	24	19	17
Yards	117	172	231	111	169	67	336	251	319	372	160	44	87
Average Yards	4.5	5.5	8.9	6.2	7.3	2.5	7.1	5.8	6.4	9.3	6.7	2.3	5.1
Touchdowns	0	0	0	0	0	0	0	0	0	0	1	0	0
KICKOFF RETURNS:													
Number	52	32	70	70	56	57	49	54	45	48	54	61	61
Yards	1228	817	1681	1627	1248	1176	1077	1326	1063	1101	1318	1467	1066
Average Yards	23.6	25.5	24.0	23.2	22.3	20.6	22.0	24.6	23.6	22.9	24.4	24.0	17.5
Touchdowns	1	1	0	0	0	1	0	2	0	1	1	0	0
INTERCEPTION RETURNS:													
Number	21	28	14	14	24	11	18	14	25	20	26	24	15
Yards	242	465	304	207	449	83	204	171	377	359	358	385	284
Average Yards	11.5	16.6	21.7	14.8	18.7	7.5	11.3	12.2	15.1	18.0	13.8	16.0	18.9
Touchdowns	0	1	1	1	2	1	1	1	4	1	0	1	1
PENALTIES:													
Number	61	78	61	97	60	62	57	98	69	94	79	75	93
Yards	614	819	647	942	514	665	615	967	730	908	831	610	720
FUMBLES:													
Number	32	36	40	23	33	22	34	39	29	34	28	31	22
Number Lost	18	23	25	11	16	7	18	25	15	25	16	16	12
POINTS:													
Total	277	276	222	286	298	260	139	347	362	302	279	216	190
PAT Attempts	31	29	25	35	34	30	14	44	42	36	29	23	20
PAT Made	31	28	24	35	32	29	13	44	42	35	28	21	19
FG Attempts	23	41	25	25	37	32	32	26	32	33	39	33	33
FG Made	20	24	16	13	20	17	14	13	22	17	25	19	17
Percent FG Made	87.0	58.5	64.0	52.0	54.1	53.1	43.8	50.0	68.8	51.5	64.1	57.6	51.5
Safeties	0	1	0	1	1	0	0	0	1	0	1	0	0

CONFERENCE PLAYOFFS

December 25 at Bloomington
(Attendance 47,307)

SCORING

MINNESOTA	0	3	0	9	–12
DALLAS	3	3	14	0	–20

First Quarter
Dal. Clark, 26 yard field goal

Second Quarter
Min. Cox, 27 yard field goal
Dal. Clark, 44 yard field goal

Third Quarter
Dal. Thomas, 13 yard rush
PAT–Clark (kick)
Dal. Hayes, 9 yard pass from Staubach
PAT–Clark (kick)

Fourth Quarter
Min. Page, safety tackled Staubach in end zone
Min. Voigt, 6 yard pass from Cuozzo
PAT–Cox (kick)

TEAM STATISTICS

MINN.		DALLAS
17	First Downs–Total	10
5	First Downs–Rushing	5
12	First Downs–Passing	5
0	First Downs–Penalty	0
1	Fumbles–Number	0
1	Fumbles–Lost Ball	0
2	Penalties–Number	2
18	Yards Penalized	10
2	Missed Field Goals	0
64	Offensive Plays–Total	55
311	Net Yards	183
4.9	Average Gain	3.3
5	Giveaways	0
0	Takeaways	5
–5	Difference	+5

INDIVIDUAL STATISTICS

MINNESOTA	No.	Yds.	Avg.	DALLAS	No.	Yds.	Avg.
RUSHING							
Jones	15	52	3.5	D. Thomas	21	66	3.1
Lee	3	28	9.3	Hill	14	28	2.0
Osborn	6	13	2.2	Garrison	2	2	1.0
Lindsey	1	6	6.0	Staubach	2	2	1.0
Grim	1	2	2.0		39	98	2.5
	26	101	3.9				
RECEIVING							
Washington	5	70	14.0	Hayes	3	31	10.3
Grim	4	74	18.5	Alworth	2	33	16.5
Voigt	4	46	11.5	Ditka	2	18	9.0
Reed	4	–3	–0.8	Hill	2	14	7.0
Lindsey	1	25	25.0	D. Thomas	1	3	3.0
White	1	–2	–2.0		10	99	9.9
	19	210	11.1				
PUNTING							
Lee	4		43.5	Widby	7		37.0
PUNT RETURNS							
West	2	6	3.0	Waters	2	37	18.5
KICKOFF RETURNS							
Jones	2	75	37.5	I. Thomas	2	31	15.5
West	2	74	37.0	Harris	1	21	21.0
Bryant	1	22	22.0		3	52	17.3
Brown	1	17	17.0				
	6	188	31.3				
INTERCEPTION RETURNS							
None				Harris	1	30	30.0
				Howley	1	26	26.0
				Adderly	1	8	8.0
				Jordan	1	5	5.0
					4	69	17.3

PASSING

MINNESOTA	Att.	Comp.	Comp. Pct.	Yds.	Int.	Yds/ Att.	Yds/ Comp.	Yds. Lost Tkld.
Cuozzo	22	12	54.5	124	2	5.6	10.3	0– 0
Lee	16	7	43.8	86	2	5.4	12.3	0– 0
	38	19	50.0	210	4	5.5	11.1	0– 0
DALLAS								
Staubach	14	10	71.4	99	0	7.1	9.9	2–14

December 26, at San Francisco
(Attendance 45,327)

SCORING

SAN FRANCISCO	0	3	14	7	–24
WASHINGTON	7	3	3	7	–20

First Quarter
Was. Smith, 5 yard pass from Kilmer
PAT–Knight (kick)

Second Quarter
S.F. Gossett, 23 yard field goal
Was. Knight, 40 yard field goal

Third Quarter
S.F. G. Washington, 78 yard pass from Brodie PAT–Gossett (kick)
S.F. Windsor, 2 yard pass from Brodie
PAT–Gossett (kick)
Was. Knight, 36 yard field goal

Fourth Quarter
S.F. Hoskins, recovered fumble in end zone
PAT–Gossett (kick)
Was. Brown, 16 yard pass from Kilmer
PAT–Knight (kick)

TEAM STATISTICS

S.F.		WASH.
11	First Downs–Total	13
2	First Downs–Rushing	6
9	First Downs–Passing	5
0	First Downs–Penalty	2
0	Fumbles – Number	3
0	Fumbles–Lost Ball	2
3	Penalties–Number	4
41	Yards Penalized	55
0	Missed Field Goals	1
59	Offensive Plays–Total	67
285	Net Yards	192
4.8	Average Gain	2.9
0	Giveaways	3
3	Takeaways	0
+3	Difference	–3

INDIVIDUAL STATISTICS

SAN FRANCISCO	No.	Yds.	Avg.	WASHINGTON	No.	Yds.	Avg.
RUSHING							
V. Washington	16	59	3.7	Brown	27	84	3.1
Willard	19	46	2.4	Harraway	10	28	2.8
Schreiber	4	7	1.8	Kilmer	1	0	0.0
	39	112	2.8	Jefferson	1	–13	–13.0
					39	99	2.5
RECEIVING							
Kwalick	3	26	8.7	Brown	6	62	10.3
Witcher	2	28	14.0	Smith	3	32	10.7
G. Washington	1	78	78.0	Mason	1	8	8.0
Schreiber	1	22	22.0	Harraway	1	4	4.0
V. Washington	1	10	10.0		11	106	9.6
Willard	1	10	10.0				
Windsor	1	2	2.0				
	10	176	17.6				
PUNTING							
Spurrier	10		33.7	Bragg	5		46.0
PUNT RETURNS							
Fuller	1	8	8.0	Duncan	2	11	5.5
Simpson	1	4	4.0	Vactor	1	47	47.0
B. Taylor	1	1	1.0		3	58	19.3
	3	13	4.3				
KICKOFF RETURNS							
V. Washington	4	79	19.8	Duncan	3	170	56.7
Cunningham	1	0	0.0	McLinton	1	19	19.0
	5	79	15.8		4	189	47.3
INTERCEPTION RETURNS							
R. Taylor	1	17	17.0	None			

PASSING

SAN FRANCISCO	Att.	Cmp.	Comp. Pct.	Yds.	Int.	Yds/ Att.	Yds/ Comp.	Yds Lost Tkld.
Brodie	19	10	52.6	176	0	9.3	17.6	1– 3
WASHINGTON								
Kilmer	27	11	40.7	106	1	3.9	9.6	1–13

DALLAS COWBOYS 11-3-0 Tom Landry

Scores of Each Game		
49	Buffalo	37
42	Philadelphia	7
16	WASHINGTON	20
20	N.Y. GIANTS	13
14	New Orleans	24
44	NEW ENGLAND	21
19	Chicago	23
16	St. Louis	13
20	PHILADELPHIA	7
13	Washington	0
28	LOS ANGELES	21
52	N.Y. JETS	10
42	N.Y. Giants	14
31	ST. LOUIS	12

Use Name	Pos.	Hgt	Wgt	Age	Int	Pts
Forrest Gregg	OT	6'4"	250	38		
Tony Liscio	OT	6'5"	255	31		
Ralph Neely	OT	6'5"	265	27		
Don Talbert	OT	6'5"	255	31		
Rayfield Wright	OT	6'7"	255	26		
John Niland	OG	6'4"	245	27		
Blaine Nye	OG	6'4"	250	25		
Rodney Wallace	OG	6'5"	255	22		
John Fitzgerald	C	6'5"	250	23		
Dave Manders	C	6'2"	250	29		
George Andrie	DE	6'7"	250	31		
Larry Cole	DE	6'4"	255	24		
Tody Smith	DE	6'5"	245	22		
Pat Toomay	DE	6'5"	244	26		
Bill Gregory	DT	6'5"	255	21		
Bob Lilly	DT	6'4"	260	32		6
Jethro Pugh	DT	6'6"	260	27		
Lee Roy Caffey	LB	6'3"	250	31		
Dave Edwards	LB	6'3"	225	32	2	
Chuck Howley	LB	6'3"	225	35	5	
Lee Roy Jordan	LB	6'2"	220	30	2	
D. D. Lewis	LB	6'2"	225	25	1	
Tom Stincic	LB	6'2"	230	24		
Herb Adderley	DB	6'1"	200	32	6	
Cornell Green	DB	6'4"	208	31	2	
Cliff Harris	DB	6'	184	22	2	
Mel Renfro	DB	6'	190	27	4	
Ike Thomas	DB	6'2"	193	23		12
Mark Washington	DB	5'10"	183	23		
Charlie Waters	DB	6'1"	193	22	2	
Bob Asher – Injury						
Craig Morton	QB	6'4"	214	28		6
Roger Staubach	QB	6'2"	197	29		12
Dan Reeves	HB	6'1"	200	27		1
Claxton Welch	HB	5'11"	203	24		8
Joe Williams	HB	6'	195	24		6
Calvin Hill	FB-HB	6'3"	235	24		66
Duane Thomas	FB-HB	6'1"	210	24		78
Walt Garrison	FB	6'	205	27		12
Margene Adkins	WR	5'10"	183	24		
Lance Alworth	WR	6'	180	31		12
Bob Hayes	WR	6'	185	28		48
Gloster Richardson	WR	6'	200	28		18
Mike Ditka	TE	6'3"	225	31		6
Billy Truax	TE	6'5"	235	28		6
Mike Clark	K	6'1"	205	30		86
Toni Fritsch	K	5'7"	185	26		17
Ron Widby	K	6'4"	210	26		

WASHINGTON REDSKINS 9-4-1 George Allen

Scores of Each Game		
24	ST. LOUIS	17
30	N.Y. Giants	3
20	Dallas	16
22	HOUSTON	13
20	ST. LOUIS	0
20	Kansas City	27
24	NEW ORLEANS	14
7	PHILADELPHIA	7
15	Chicago	16
0	DALLAS	13
20	Philadelphia	13
23	N.Y. GIANTS	7
38	Los Angeles	24
13	CLEVELAND	20

Use Name	Pos.	Hgt	Wgt	Age	Int	Pts
Terry Hermeling	OT	6'5"	255	25		
Walt Rock	OT	6'5"	255	30		
Jim Snowden	OT	6'3"	255	29		
Mike Taylor	OT	6'4"	245	26		
Paul Laaveg	OG	6'4"	245	22		
Ray Schoenke	OG	6'3"	250	29		
John Wilbur	OG	6'3"	250	28		
George Burman	C-OG	6'3"	255	28		
Len Hauss	C	6'2"	235	30		
Verlon Biggs	DE	6'4"	270	28		
Jimmie Jones	DE	6'3"	215	24		
Ron McDole	DE	6'3"	288	31	3	6
Bill Brundige	DT	6'5"	270	22		
Manny Sistrunk	DT	6'5"	265	24		
Diron Talbert	DT	6'5"	255	27		
Bob Grant	LB	6'2"	225	25		
Chris Hanburger	LB	6'2"	218	30	1	6
Harold McLinton	LB	6'2"	235	24		
Jack Pardee	LB	6'2"	225	35	5	6
Myron Pottios	LB	6'2"	232	31	1	
Russ Tillman	LB	6'2"	230	25		
Mike Bass	DB	6'	190	26	8	6
Speedy Duncan	DB	5'10"	175	28	1	6
Pat Fischer	DB	5'10"	170	31	3	6
Jon Jaqua	DB	6'	190	23		
Brig Owens	DB	5'11"	190	28	2	
Richie Petitbon	DB	6'3"	208	33	5	
Ted Vactor	DB	6'	185	27		
Sonny Jurgensen	QB	5'11"	203	37		
Billy Kilmer	QB	6'	204	32		12
Sam Wyche	QB	6'4"	210	26		
Larry Brown	HB	5'11"	195	23		36
Bob Brunet	HB	6'1"	205	25		
Tommy Mason	FB-HB	6'	195	32		
Charlie Harraway	FB	6'2"	215	26		12
Mike Hull	FB	6'3"	220	26		
Jeff Jordan	HB-FB	6'1"	215	26		
Boyd Dowler	WR	6'5"	225	34		
Roy Jefferson	WR	6'2"	195	27		24
Bill Malinchak	WR	6'1"	200	27		
Clifton McNeil (from NYG)	WR	6'2"	187	31		18
Charley Taylor	WR	6'3"	210	30		24
Mack Alston	TE	6'2"	230	24		
Jerry Smith	TE	6'2"	208	28		6
Mike Bragg	K	5'11"	186	24		
Curt Knight	K	6'1"	190	28		114

PHILADELPHIA EAGLES 6-7-1 Jerry Williams Ed Khayat

Scores of Each Game		
14	Cincinnati	37
7	DALLAS	42
3	SAN FRANCISCO	31
0	MINNESOTA	13
10	Oakland	34
23	N.Y. GIANTS	7
17	DENVER	16
7	Washington	7
7	Dallas	20
37	St. Louis	20
13	WASHINGTON	20
23	Detroit	20
19	ST. LOUIS	7
41	N.Y. Giants	28

Use Name	Pos.	Hgt	Wgt	Age	Int	Pts
Wayde Key	OT	6'4"	245	24		
Steve Smith	OT	6'5"	250	27		6
Dick Stevens	OT	6'4"	240	23		
Henry Allison	OG	6'2"	255	24		
Jim Skaggs	OG	6'2"	250	31		
Tuufuli Uperesa	OG	6'3"	255	23		
Mike Evans	C	6'5"	250	24		
Mark Nordquist	OG-C	6'4"	245	25		
Don Brumm	DE	6'3"	245	28		
Richard Harris	DE	6'4"	260	23		
Mel Tom	DE	6'4"	250	30		
Mike Dirks	DT	6'2"	245	25		
Don Hultz	DT	6'3"	240	30	1	
Gary Pettigrew	DT	6'4"	255	26		
Ernie Calloway	DE-DT	6'6"	240	23		
Dick Hart – Injury						
Harry Jones – Injury						
Bob Creech	LB	6'3"	222	22		
Bill Hobbs	LB	6'	220	25		6
Ike Kelley	LB	5'11"	224	27		
Ron Porter	LB	6'3"	232	26		
Tim Rossovich	LB	6'4"	240	25	1	
Fred Whittingham	LB	6'1"	240	32		
Adrian Young	LB	6'1"	232	25		
Steve Zabel	TE-LB	6'4"	235	23	1	12
Bill Bradley	DB	5'11"	190	24	11	
Vern Davis	DB	6'4"	208	21		
Leroy Keyes	DB	6'3"	208	24	6	
Al Nelson	DB	5'11"	186	27	2	12
Steve Preece	DB	6'1"	195	24		
Nate Ramsey	DB	6'1"	200	30		
Jack Smith	DB	6'4"	204	23		
Jim Thrower	DB	6'2"	194	22		
Greg Barton – Canadian Football League						
Rich Arrington	QB	6'2"	190	24		
Pete Liske	QB	6'2"	200	30		6
Jim Ward	QB	6'2"	200	27		
Tom Bailey	HB	6'2"	211	22		6
Ronnie Bull	FB-HB	6'	200	31		6
Sonny Davis	FB-HB	5'11"	215	23		6
Larry Watkins	FB-HB	6'2"	215	23		6
Lee Bouggess	FB	6'2"	210	23		18
Tom Woodeshick	FB	6'	222	29		6
Tony Baker (from NO)	FB	5'11"	225	26		6
Harold Carmichael	WR	6'7"	225	21		
Ben Hawkins	WR	6'	180	27		30
Harold Jackson	WR	5'10"	175	25		18
Billy Walik	WR	5'11"	180	23		
Kent Kramer	TE	6'5"	235	27		6
Gary Ballman	WR-TE	6'	210	31		
Fred Hill	WR-TE	6'2"	215	28		
Tom Dempsey	K	6'1"	264	30		49
Happy Feller	K	5'11"	185	22		28
Tom McNeill	K	6'1"	195	29		

ST. LOUIS CARDINALS 4-9-1 Bob Hollway

Scores of Each Game		
17	WASHINGTON	24
17	N.Y. JETS	10
20	N.Y. GIANTS	21
26	Atlanta	9
0	Washington	20
14	SAN FRANCISCO	26
28	Buffalo	23
13	DALLAS	16
17	San Diego	20
20	PHILADELPHIA	37
24	N.Y. Giants	7
16	GREEN BAY	16
7	Philadelphia	19
12	Dallas	31

Use Name	Pos.	Hgt	Wgt	Age	Int	Pts
Vern Emerson	OT	6'5"	260	25		
Ernie McMillan	OT	6'6"	255	33		
Bob Reynolds	OT	6'6"	265	30		
Dan Dierdorf	OG-OT	6'4"	265	22		
Irv Goode	OG	6'4"	255	30		
Chuck Hutchison	OG	6'3"	240	22		
Clyde Williams	OG	6'2"	250	31		
Tom Banks	C	6'1"	240	23		
Wayne Mulligan	C	6'2"	245	24		
Joe Schmiesing	DE	6'4"	260	26		
Chuck Walker	DE	6'2"	250	30		
Ron Yankowski	DE	6'5"	225	24		
Rolf Krueger	DT-DE	6'4"	250	24		
Paul Dickson	DT	6'5"	250	34		
Fred Heron	DT	6'4"	260	26		
Bob Rowe	DT	6'4"	260	26		
Terry Brown – Injury						
Jim Hargrove	LB	6'3"	223	26		
Mike McGill	LB	6'2"	235	24	1	
Terry Miller	LB	6'2"	225	25		
Rick Ogle	LB	6'3"	230	22		
Jamie Rivers	LB	6'2"	235	25		
Rocky Rosema	LB	6'2"	230	25		
Larry Stallings	LB	6'2"	230	29	1	6
Jeff Allen	DB	5'11"	190	23		
Miller Farr	DB	6'1"	190	28	2	
Dale Hackbart	DB	6'3"	220	35	1	
George Haey	DB	5'10"	170	24		6
Tom Longo	DB	6'1"	200	27		
Ted Provost	DB	6'2"	195	23		
Jerry Stovall	DB	6'2"	195	29	2	
Norm Thompson	DB	6'1"	175	23	4	
Roger Wehrli	DB	6'1"	195	23	2	
Larry Willingham	DB	6'1"	190	22		
Larry Wilson	DB	6'	195	33	4	
Pete Beathard	QB	6'2"	200	29		
Jim Hart	QB	6'2"	200	27		
Roy Shivers	HB	6'	200	29		6
Larry Stegent	HB	6'1"	200	23		
Paul White	HB	6'	200	23		
MacArthur Lane	FB-HB	6'	220	29		18
Cid Edwards	FB	6'2"	230	27		24
Johnny Roland	HB-FB	6'2"	215	28		
John Gilliam	WR	6'1"	195	26		18
Mel Gray	WR	5'9"	170	22		24
Freddie Hyatt	WR	6'3"	200	25		
Chuck Latourette	WR	6'	190	26		
Dave Williams	WR	6'2"	210	26		6
Jim McFarland	TE	6'5"	225	23		12
Jackie Smith	TE	6'4"	235	30		24
Jim Bakken	K	6'	195	30		87

NEW YORK GIANTS 4-10-0 Alex Webster

Scores of Each Game		
42	Green Bay	40
3	WASHINGTON	30
21	St. Louis	20
13	Dallas	20
7	BALTIMORE	31
7	Philadelphia	23
10	MINNESOTA	17
35	SAN DIEGO	17
21	Atlanta	17
13	Pittsburg	17
7	ST. LOUIS	24
7	Washington	23
14	DALLAS	42
28	PHILADELPHIA	41

Use Name	Pos.	Hgt	Wgt	Age	Int	Pts
Willie Young	OT	6'	265	28		
Charlie Harper	OG-OT	6'2"	250	27		
Bob Hyland	OG-OT	6'5"	250	26		
Steve Alexakos	OG	6'2"	260	24		
Doug Van Horn	OG	6'2"	245	27		
Wayne Walton	OG	6'5"	245	22		
Greg Larson	C	6'2"	250	32		
Fred Dryer	DE	6'6"	240	25		
Bob Lurtsema	DE	6'6"	250	29		
Henry Reed	DE	6'3"	230	22	1	
Dave Tipton	DE	6'6"	240	22		
Dick Hanson	DT	6'6"	280	22		
Jim Kanicki	DT	6'4"	270	29		
Roland Lakes	DT	6'4"	263	31		
Dave Roller	DT	6'2"	240	21		
Jerry Shay	DT	6'3"	245	27		
Vern Vanoy	DT	6'8"	270	25		
John Douglas	LB	6'2"	225	26		
Jim Files	LB	6'4"	240	23	1	
Ralph Heck	LB	6'2"	230	30	1	6
Ron Hornsby	LB	6'3"	232	22		
Pat Hughes	LB	6'2"	240	24		
Pete Athas	DB	5'11"	185	25	2	6
Otto Brown	DB	6'1"	183	24		6
Scott Eaton	DB	6'3"	205	27	1	
Richmond Flowers (from DAL)	DB	6'	180	24	1	
Joe Green	DB	5'11"	195	24		6
Spider Lockhart	DB	6'2"	175	28	3	
Bennie McRae	DB	6'1"	180	30		
Willie Williams	DB	6'	190	28		5
Randy Johnson	QB	6'3"	205	27		
Fran Tarkenton	QB	6'1"	190	31		18
Bobby Duhon	HB	6'	195	24		6
Ron Johnson	HB	6'1"	205	23		6
Rocky Thompson	HB	5'11"	200	23		12
Charlie Evans	FB	6'1"	215	23		30
Tucker Frederickson	FB	6'3"	220	28		6
Junior Coffey	HB-FB	6'1"	215	29		
Don Herrmann	WR	6'2"	195	24		6
Rich Houston	WR	6'2"	197	25		24
Coleman Zeno	WR	6'4"	210	24		
Joe Morrison	HB-FB-WR	6'1"	212	33		6
Dick Kotite	TE	6'3"	230	28		12
Bob Tucker	TE	6'3"	230	26		24
Tom Blanchard	K	6'	190	23		
Pete Gogolak	K	6'2"	190	29		48

DALLAS COWBOYS

RUSHING

Last Name	No.	Yds	Avg	TD
D. Thomas	175	793	4.5	11
Hill	106	468	4.4	8
Garrison	127	429	3.4	1
Staubach	41	343	8.4	2
Reeves	17	79	4.6	0
Williams	21	67	3.2	1
Welch	14	51	3.6	1
Hayes	3	18	6.0	0
Morton	4	9	2.3	1
Ditka	2	2	1.0	0
Alworth	2	−10	−5.0	0

RECEIVING

Last Name	No.	Yds	Avg	TD
Garrison	40	396	10	1
Hayes	35	840	24	8
Alworth	34	487	14	2
Ditka	30	360	12	1
Hill	19	244	13	3
Truax	15	232	15	1
D. Thomas	13	153	12	2
Richardson	8	170	21	3
Adkins	4	53	13	0
Williams	3	59	20	0
Reeves	3	25	8	0
Welch	1	−1	−1	0

PUNT RETURNS

Last Name	No.	Yds	Avg	TD
Harris	17	129	8	0
Waters	9	109	12	0
Adkins	4	5	1	0
Hayes	1	5	5	0

KICKOFF RETURNS

Last Name	No.	Yds	Avg	TD
Harris	29	823	28	0
I. Thomas	7	295	42	2
Welch	4	105	26	0
D. Thomas	2	64	32	0
Ditka	3	30	10	0
Waters	1	18	18	0
Lewis	1	15	15	0
Hayes	1	14	14	0
Williams	1	12	12	0
Green	1	0	0	0

PASSING

Last Name	Att	Comp	%	Yds	Yd/Att	TD	Int– %	RK
Staubach	211	126	60	1882	8.9	15	4– 2	1
Morton	143	76	55	1131	7.9	7	8– 6	7
Reeves	5	2	40	24	4.8	0	1– 20	
Hill	1	0	0	0	0.0	0	1–100	
D. Thomas	1	0	0	0	0.0	0	0– 0	

PUNTING

Last Name	No	Avg
Widby	56	41.6

KICKING

Last Name	XP	Att	%	FG	Att	%
Clark	47	47	100	13	25	52
Fritsch	2	2	100	5	8	63
Reeves	1	1	100	0	0	0

WASHINGTON REDSKINS

RUSHING

Last Name	No.	Yds	Avg	TD
Brown	253	948	3.7	4
Harraway	156	635	4.1	2
Mason	31	85	2.7	0
Jurgensen	3	29	9.7	0
Brunet	10	27	2.7	0
Jefferson	2	13	6.5	0
Hull	2	8	4.0	0
Kilmer	17	5	0.3	2
Smith	1	5	5.0	0
Wyche	1	4	4.0	0
Petitbon	1	−2	−2.0	0

RECEIVING

Last Name	No.	Yds	Avg	TD
Jefferson	47	701	15	4
McNeil	30	453	15	3
Dowler	26	352	14	0
C. Taylor	24	370	15	4
Harraway	20	121	6	0
Smith	16	227	14	1
Brown	16	176	11	2
Mason	12	109	9	0
Alston	5	87	17	0
Brunet	2	4	2	0

PUNT RETURNS

Last Name	No.	Yds	Avg	TD
Duncan	22	233	11	0
Vactor	23	194	8	0

KICKOFF RETURNS

Last Name	No.	Yds	Avg	TD
Duncan	27	724	27	0
Jaqua	6	78	13	0
Bass	4	61	15	0
McLinton	5	46	9	0
Tillman	1	4	4	0

PASSING

Last Name	Att	Comp	%	Yds	Yd/Att	TD	Int– %	RK
Kilmer	306	166	54	2221	7.3	13	13– 4	3
Jurgensen	28	16	57	170	7.1	0	2– 7	

PUNTING

Last Name	No	Avg
Bragg	58	40.5

KICKING

Last Name	XP	Att	%	FG	Att	%
Knight	27	27	100	29	49	59

PHILADELPHIA EAGLES

RUSHING

Last Name	No.	Yds	Avg	TD
Bull	94	351	3.7	0
Bouggess	97	262	2.7	2
Woodeshick	66	188	2.8	0
Baker	46	174	3.8	0
S. Davis	47	163	3.5	1
Watkins	35	98	2.8	1
Bailey	5	41	1.8	1
Jackson	23	41	8.2	0
Liske	13	29	2.2	1
Arrington	5	23	4.6	0
Hawkins	4	8	2.0	0
Zabel	1	−5	−5.0	0

RECEIVING

Last Name	No.	Yds	Avg	TD
Jackson	47	716	15	3
Hawkins	37	650	18	4
Bouggess	24	170	7	1
Carmichael	20	288	14	0
Ballman	13	238	18	0
S. Davis	11	46	4	0
Baker	10	80	8	1
Bull	9	75	8	1
Hill	7	92	13	0
Bailey	7	55	8	0
Kramer	6	65	11	1
Watkins	6	40	7	0
Woodeshick	6	36	6	1
Zabel	2	4	2	2

PUNT RETURNS

Last Name	No.	Yds	Avg	TD
Bradley	18	118	7	0
Walik	5	48	10	0
Hawkins	1	6	6	0

KICKOFF RETURNS

Last Name	No.	Yds	Avg	TD
Walik	14	369	26	0
Nelson	13	358	28	0
Thrower	12	299	25	0
Jackson	2	48	24	0
S. Davis	2	44	22	0
Pettigrew	2	37	19	0
Harris	2	28	14	0
Kramer	1	0	0	0
Zabel	1	0	0	0

PASSING

Last Name	Att	Comp	%	Yds	Yd/Att	TD	Int– %	RK
Liske	269	143	53	1957	7.3	11	15– 6	9
Arrington	118	55	47	576	4.9	2	5– 4	
Bull	1	1	100	15	15.0	0	0– 0	
S. Davis	1	0	0	0	0.0	0	0– 0	
Ward	1	1	100	4	4.0	0	0– 0	

PUNTING

Last Name	No	Avg
McNeill	73	42.0
Bradley	2	38.0

KICKING

Last Name	XP	Att	%	FG	Att	%
Dempsey	13	14	93	12	17	71
Feller	10	10	100	6	20	30

ST. LOUIS CARDINALS

RUSHING

Last Name	No.	Yds	Avg	TD
Lane	150	592	3.9	3
Edwards	108	316	2.9	4
Roland	78	278	3.6	0
Shivers	55	202	3.7	1
Gray	2	56	28.0	0
Beathard	4	29	7.3	0
Latourette	3	19	6.3	0
Gilliam	2	16	8.0	0
Smith	1	10	10.0	0
Hart	13	9	0.7	0
White	1	3	3.0	0

RECEIVING

Last Name	No.	Yds	Avg	TD
Gilliam	42	837	20	3
Lane	29	298	10	0
Smith	21	379	18	4
Gray	18	534	30	4
Roland	15	108	7	0
D. Williams	12	182	15	1
Edwards	12	122	10	0
Shivers	10	76	8	0
McFarland	5	54	11	2
Hyatt	4	58	15	0
Stegent	1	12	12	0
Reynolds	1	−4	−4	0

PUNT RETURNS

Last Name	No.	Yds	Avg	TD
Willingham	10	84	8	0
Wehrli	9	84	9	0
Thompson	5	27	5	0
Gilliam	1	21	21	0
Roland	3	10	3	0
Stallings	1	8	8	0
Dickson	1	0	0	0

KICKOFF RETURNS

Last Name	No.	Yds	Avg	TD
Gray	30	740	25	0
Hoey	9	251	28	1
Thompson	7	182	26	0
Willingham	6	125	21	0
Edwards	2	41	21	0
Roland	2	24	12	0
Dierdorf	1	0	0	0
Stegent	1	0	0	0

PASSING

Last Name	Att	Comp	%	Yds	Yd/Att	TD	Int– %	RK
Hart	243	110	45	1626	6.7	8	14– 6	13
Beathard	141	60	43	1030	7.3	6	12– 9	15
Shivers	1	0	0	0	0.0	0	0– 0	

PUNTING

Last Name	No	Avg
Latourette	56	38.5
Bakken	5	41.4

KICKING

Last Name	XP	Att	%	FG	Att	%
Bakken	24	24	100	21	32	66

NEW YORK GIANTS

RUSHING

Last Name	No.	Yds	Avg	TD
Duhon	93	344	3.7	1
Frederickson	64	242	3.8	0
Thompson	54	177	3.3	1
Evans	48	171	3.6	5
Ron Johnson	32	156	4.9	1
Morrison	38	131	3.4	0
Tarkenton	30	111	3.7	3
Coffey	22	70	3.2	0
Randy Johnson	6	29	4.8	0
Zeno	2	10	5.0	0
Athas	1	3	3.0	0
Houston	2	2	1.0	0
Tucker	1	1	1.0	0

RECEIVING

Last Name	No.	Yds	Avg	TD
Tucker	59	791	13	4
Morrison	40	411	10	1
Herrmann	27	297	11	1
Duhon	25	266	11	0
Houston	24	426	18	4
Frederickson	21	114	5	1
Thompson	16	85	5	0
Evans	13	144	11	0
Kotite	10	146	15	2
Ron Johnson	6	47	8	0
Zeno	5	97	19	0
Coffey	5	20	4	0

PUNT RETURNS

Last Name	No.	Yds	Avg	TD
Duhon	12	77	6	0
Lockhart	4	24	6	0
Athas	3	21	7	0

KICKOFF RETURNS

Last Name	No.	Yds	Avg	TD
Thompson	36	947	26	1
Duhon	11	200	18	0
Flowers	8	156	20	0
Green	5	106	21	0
Douglas	1	7	7	0
Dryer	1	0	0	0
Walton	1	0	0	0

PASSING

Last Name	Att	Comp	%	Yds	Yd/Att	TD	Int– %	RK
Tarkenton	386	226	59	2567	6.7	11	21– 5	8
Ran. Johnson	74	41	55	477	6.5	3	3– 4	
Blanchard	1	1	100	18	18.0	0	0– 0	
Duhon	1	0	0	0	0.0	0	1–100	

PUNTING

Last Name	No	Avg
Blanchard	66	40.6

KICKING

Last Name	XP	Att	%	FG	Att	%
Gogolak	30	30	100	6	17	35

MINNESOTA VIKINGS 11-3-0 Bud Grant

Scores of Each Game		
16	Detroit	13
17	CHICAGO	20
19	BUFFALO	0
13	Philadelphia	0
24	Green Bay	13
10	BALTIMORE	3
17	N.Y. Giants	10
9	SAN FRANCISCO	13
3	GREEN BAY	0
23	New Orleans	10
24	ATLANTA	7
14	San Diego	30
29	DETROIT	10
27	Chicago	10

Use Name	Pos.	Hgt	Wgt	Age	Int	Pts
Grady Alderman	OT	6'2"	247	32		
Doug Davis	OT	6'4"	250	27		
Ron Yary	OT	6'6"	255	25		
Pete Perreault	OG-OT	6'3"	248	32		
Roy Schmidt	OG	6'3"	250	29		
Milt Sunde	OG	6'2"	250	28		
Doug Sutherland	OG	6'3"	250	23		
Ed White	OG	6'2"	262	24		
Mick Tingelhoff	C	6'1"	237	31		
Godfrey Zaunbrecher	C	6'2"	235	23		
Carl Eller	DE	6'6"	247	28		
Jim Marshall	DE	6'3"	248	34		
John Ward	DE	6'4"	260	23		
Gary Larsen	DT	6'5"	260	31		
Alan Page	DT	6'5"	245	26		
Jerry Patton	DT	6'3"	260	25		
Carl Gersbach	LB	6'1"	230	24		
Wally Hilgenberg	LB	6'3"	230	28	2	
Noel Jenke	LB	6'1"	218	24		
Lonnie Warwick	LB	6'3"	238	29		
Carl Winfrey	LB	6'	230	22		
Roy Winston	LB	6'1"	222	31	1	6
Bobby Bryant	DB	6'	170	27	3	
Karl Kassulke	DB	6'	195	29	2	
Paul Krause	DB	6'3"	200	29	6	
Ed Sharockman	DB	6'	200	31	6	
Charlie West	DB	6'1"	197	25	7	
Jeff Wright	DB	5'11"	190	22		
Nate Wright	DB	5'11"	180	24		
John Beasley – Injury						
Gary Cuozzo	QB	6'1"	195	30		
Bob Lee	QB	6'2"	195	26		6
Norm Snead	QB	6'4"	215	31		6
Clint Jones	HB	6'	205	26		24
Dave Osborn	HB	6'	208	28		36
Bill Brown	FB	5'11"	230	33		12
Leo Hayden	HB-FB	6'	212	23		
Jim Lindsey	HB-FB	6'2"	210	26		6
Oscar Reed	HB-FB	5'11"	222	27		6
Al Denson	WR	6'2"	208	29		
Bob Grim	WR	6'	195	26		42
John Henderson	WR	6'3"	195	28		
Gene Washington	WR	6'3"	208	27		
Bob Brown	TE	6'3"	225	28		
John Hilton	TE	6'5"	225	29		
Stu Voigt	TE	6'1"	220	23		6
Fred Cox	K	5'10"	200	32		91

DETROIT LIONS 7-6-1 Joe Schmidt

Scores of Each Game		
13	MINNESOTA	16
34	New England	7
41	ATLANTA	38
31	GREEN BAY	28
31	Houston	7
23	CHICAGO	28
14	Green Bay	14
24	Denver	20
13	LOS ANGELES	21
28	Chicago	3
32	KANSAS CITY	21
20	PHILADELPHIA	23
10	Minnesota	29
27	San Francisco	31

Use Name	Pos.	Hgt	Wgt	Age	Int	Pts
Rocky Freitas	OT	6'6"	280	25		
Ray Parson	OT	6'4"	250	24		
Jim Yarbrough	OT	6'6"	250	24		
Frank Gallagher	OG	6'2"	245	28		
Bob Kowalkowski	OG	6'3"	240	27		
Chuck Walton	OG	6'3"	255	30		
Dave Thompson	C-OG	6'4"	275	22		
Ed Flanagan	C	6'3"	245	27		
Larry Hand	DE	6'4"	250	31		
Jim Mitchell	DE	6'3"	245	22		
Joe Robb	DE	6'3"	245	34		
Bob Bell	DT	6'4"	250	23		6
Dick Evey	DT	6'2"	245	30		
Jerry Rush	DT	6'4"	265	29		
Larry Woods	DT	6'6"	260	23		
Ken Lee	LB	6'4"	230	22		
Mike Lucci	LB	6'2"	230	31	5	12
Ed Mooney	LB	6'2"	225	26		
Paul Naumoff	LB	6'1"	215	26		
Wayne Walker	LB	6'2"	228	34	2	2
Charlie Weaver	LB	6'2"	218	22		
Lem Barney	DB	6'	188	25	3	6
Al Clark	DB	6'	180	23		
Dick LeBeau	DB	6'1"	185	34	6	
Wayne Rasmussen	DB	6'2"	180	29	4	
Tom Vaughn	DB	5'11"	190	28	1	
Mike Weger	DB	6'2"	200	25	1	6
Bobby Williams	DB	6'1"	200	29		
Charlie Brown – Injury						
Bill Cottrell – Injury						
Nick Eddy – Injury						
Greg Landry	QB	6'4"	205	24		18
Bill Munson	QB	6'2"	210	29		
Altie Taylor	HB	5'10"	196	23		30
Mickey Zofko	HB	6'3"	195	21		
Mel Farr	FB-HB	6'2"	210	26		6
Paul Gipson	FB-HB	6'	210	25		
Steve Owens	FB	6'2"	220	23		60
Bill Triplett	FB	6'2"	215	32		
*Chuck Hughes	WR	5'11"	175	28		
Ron Jessie	WR	6'	183	22		14
Earl McCullouch	WR	5'11"	175	25		18
Larry Walton	WR	5'11"	180	24		30
Craig Cotton	TE	6'4"	222	24		
Charlie Sanders	TE	6'4"	235	25		30
Errol Mann	K	6'	200	30		103
Herman Weaver	K	6'4"	210	22		

*Died Oct. 24, 1971 – Heart Attack

CHICAGO BEARS 6-8-0 Jim Dooley

Scores of Each Game		
17	PITTSBURGH	15
20	Minnesota	17
3	Los Angeles	17
35	NEW ORLEANS	14
0	San Francisco	13
28	Detroit	23
23	DALLAS	19
14	GREEN BAY	17
16	WASHINGTON	15
3	DETROIT	28
3	Miami	34
3	Denver	6
10	Green Bay	31
10	MINNESOTA	27

Use Name	Pos.	Hgt	Wgt	Age	Int	Pts
Jeff Curchin	OT	6'6"	255	23		
Randy Jackson	OT	6'5"	245	27		
Steve Wright	OT	6'6"	250	29		
Jim Cadile	OG	6'3"	240	30		
Glenn Holloway	OG	6'3"	245	22		
Bob Newton	OT-OG	6'4"	250	21		
Rich Coady	C	6'3"	238	26		
Gene Hamlin	C	6'3"	245	25		
John Hoffman	DE	6'7"	260	28		
Willie Holman	DE	6'4"	250	26		
Tony McGee	DE	6'4"	250	22		
Ed O'Bradovich	DE	6'3"	255	31		
Dave Hale	DT	6'7"	260	24		
George Seals	DT	6'2"	260	28		6
Bill Staley	DT	6'3"	248	24		
Ross Brupbacher	LB	6'3"	215	23	2	6
Doug Buffone	LB	6'1"	225	27	2	
Dick Butkus	LB	6'3"	245	27	4	1
Jimmy Gunn	LB	6'1"	215	22	1	
Larry Rowden	LB	6'2"	220	21		
Charlie Ford	DB	6'3"	185	22	5	
Cliff Hardy	DB	6'	187	24		
Bob Jeter	DB	6'1"	205	33	1	
Garry Lyle	DB	6'2"	198	25	1	
Jerry Moore	DB	6'3"	208	21		
Ron Smith	DB	6'1"	192	28	3	
Joe Taylor	DB	6'2"	200	30	3	
Craig Baynham – Injury						
Jack Concannon	QB	6'3"	205	28		
Bobby Douglass	QB	6'3"	215	24		19
Kent Nix	QB	6'1"	195	27		
Joe Moore	HB	6'1"	205	22		
Cyril Pinder	HB	6'2"	222	24		6
Gale Sayers	HB	6'	198	28		
Don Shy	HB	6'1"	210	27		12
Jim Grabowski	FB	6'2"	220	27		
Jim Harrison	FB	6'4"	235	22		
Bill Tucker	FB	6'2"	220	27		
George Farmer	WR	6'4"	210	23		30
Dick Gordon	WR	5'11"	190	26		30
Jim Seymour	WR	6'4"	210	24		
Cecil Turner	WR	5'10"	170	27		
Ray Ogden	TE	6'5"	225	28		
Earl Thomas	TE	6'3"	224	22		
Bob Wallace	TE	6'3"	211	25		12
Bobby Joe Green	K	5'11"	175	33		
Mac Percival	K	6'4"	220	31		63

GREEN BAY PACKERS 4-8-2 Dan Devine

Scores of Each Game		
40	N.Y. GIANTS	42
34	DENVER	13
20	CINCINNATI	17
28	Detroit	31
13	MINNESOTA	24
13	Los Angeles	30
14	DETROIT	14
17	Chicago	14
0	Minnesota	3
21	Atlanta	28
21	NEW ORLEANS	29
16	St. Louis	16
31	CHICAGO	10
6	Miami	27

Use Name	Pos.	Hgt	Wgt	Age	Int	Pts
Bill Hayhoe	OT	6'8"	258	24		
Dick Himes	OT	6'4"	244	25		
Francis Peay	OT	6'5"	250	27		
Dave Bradley	OG	6'4"	245	24		
Gale Gillingham	OG	6'3"	255	27		
Bill Lueck	OG	6'3"	235	25		
Randy Winkler	OG	6'5"	260	28		
Ken Bowman	C	6'3"	230	28		
Wimpy Winther	C	6'4"	260	23		
Cal Withrow	C	6'	240	26		
Lionel Aldridge	DE	6'4"	245	29		
Alden Roche	DE	6'4"	255	26		
Donnell Smith	DE	6'4"	245	22		
Clarence Williams	DE	6'5"	255	24		
Bob Brown	DT	6'5"	260	30		
Jim DeLisle	DT	6'4"	254	22		
Mike McCoy	DT	6'5"	284	22		
Fred Carr	LB	6'5"	238	25		
Jim Carter	LB	6'3"	235	22	1	
Tommy Crutcher	LB	6'3"	235	29		
Ray Nitschke	LB	6'3"	235	35	1	
Dave Robinson	LB	6'3"	245	30	3	
Ken Ellis	DB	5'10"	190	23	6	6
Charlie Hall	DB	6'1"	195	22		
Doug Hart	DB	6'	190	32	2	8
Al Matthews	DB	5'11"	190	23	1	
Al Randolph	DB	6'2"	196	27	1	
Willie Wood	DB	5'10"	190	35	1	
Zeke Bratkowski	QB	6'2"	215	39		6
Scott Hunter	QB	6'2"	205	23		24
Frank Patrick	QB	6'7"	225	24		
Bart Starr	QB	6'1"	190	38		6
Donny Anderson	HB	6'3"	210	28		36
Larry Krause	HB	6'	208	23		
Elijah Pitts	HB	6'1"	210	32		
Dave Hampton	FB-HB	6'	210	24		30
John Brockington	FB	6'	225	22		30
Perry Williams	FB	6'2"	220	24		
Carroll Dale	WR	6'1"	200	33		24
Dave Davis	WR	6'	175	23		
John Spilis	WR	6'3"	205	23		6
Len Garrett	TE	6'3"	230	22		
Rich McGeorge	TE	6'4"	235	22		24
Dave Conway	K	6'	195	25		5
Ken Duncan	K	6'2"	210	26		
Lou Michaels	K	6'2"	250	35		43
Tim Webster	K	6'	195	21		26

MINNESOTA VIKINGS

RUSHING Last Name	No.	Yds	Avg	TD
Jones	180	675	3.8	4
Osborn	123	349	2.8	5
Lindsey	46	182	4.0	0
Reed	50	182	3.6	1
Bill Brown	46	136	3.0	2
Grim	6	127	21.2	0
Cuozzo	15	24	1.6	0
Lee	11	14	1.3	1
Snead	6	6	1.0	1
Denson	1	0	0.0	0

RECEIVING Last Name	No.	Yds	Avg	TD
Grim	45	691	15	7
Osborn	25	195	8	1
Voigt	15	214	14	1
Reed	15	138	9	0
Washington	12	165	14	0
Denson	10	125	13	0
Bill Brown	10	94	9	0
Jones	9	98	11	0
Lindsey	8	31	4	0
Bob Brown	6	141	24	0
Henderson	2	18	9	0

PUNT RETURNS Last Name	No.	Yds	Avg	TD
West	18	94	5	0
Grim	7	44	6	0
Bryant	2	26	13	0

KICKOFF RETURNS Last Name	No.	Yds	Avg	TD
West	24	556	23	0
Jones	12	329	27	0
Grim	3	52	17	0
Bryant	1	23	23	0
Voigt	1	0	0	0

PASSING	Att	Comp	%	Yds	Yd/Att	TD	Int– %	RK
Cuozzo	168	75	45	842	5.0	6	8– 5	14
Lee	90	45	50	598	6.6	2	4– 4	
Snead	75	37	49	470	6.3	1	6– 8	
Grim	1	0	0	0	0.0	0	0– 0	

PUNTING	No	Avg
Lee	89	39.5

KICKING	XP	Att	%	FG	Att	%
Cox	25	25	100	22	32	69

DETROIT LIONS

RUSHING Last Name	No.	Yds	Avg	TD
Owens	246	1035	4.2	8
Taylor	174	736	4.2	4
Landry	76	530	7.0	3
Farr	22	64	2.9	0
Gipson	4	12	3.0	0
Munson	3	9	3.0	0
Triplett	4	4	1.0	0
Jessie	1	0	0.0	0
McCullouch	1	–7	–7.0	0
L. Walton	1	–7	–7.0	0

RECEIVING Last Name	No.	Yds	Avg	TD
Owens	32	350	11	2
Sanders	31	502	16	5
L. Walton	30	491	16	5
Taylor	26	270	10	1
McCullouch	21	552	26	3
Cotton	6	88	15	0
Farr	5	60	12	1
Jessie	4	87	22	0
Hughes	1	32	32	0
Gipson	1	21	21	0

PUNT RETURNS Last Name	No.	Yds	Avg	TD
Barney	14	122	9	0
L. Walton	6	38	6	0
Vaughn	2	30	15	0
Thompson	1	4	4	0

KICKOFF RETURNS Last Name	No.	Yds	Avg	TD
Jessie	16	470	29	2
Barney	9	222	25	0
Clark	8	216	27	0
Williams	4	112	28	0
Gipson	5	105	21	0
Triplett	3	70	23	0
Parson	2	26	13	0
Mooney	2	8	4	0
Cotton	1	4	4	0
Rasmussen	1	0	0	0

PASSING	Att	Comp	%	Yds	Yd/Att	TD	Int– %	RK
Landry	261	136	52	2237	8.6	16	13– 5	2
Munson	38	21	55	216	5.7	1	1– 3	

PUNTING	No	Avg
H. Weaver	42	41.7

KICKING	XP	Att	%	FG	Att	%
Mann	37	37	100	22	37	60
Walker	2	2	100	0	0	0

CHICAGO BEARS

RUSHING Last Name	No.	Yds	Avg	TD
Shy	116	420	3.6	2
Pinder	63	311	4.9	1
Douglass	39	284	7.3	3
Grabowski	51	149	2.9	0
Joe Moore	29	90	3.1	0
Tucker	32	82	2.6	0
Sayers	13	38	2.9	0
Buffone	1	19	19.0	0
Harrison	5	13	2.6	0
Nix	9	12	1.3	0
Farmer	1	11	11.0	0
Concannon	5	5	1.0	0
Wallace	1	0	0.0	0

RECEIVING Last Name	No.	Yds	Avg	TD
Farmer	46	737	16	5
Gordon	43	610	14	5
Wallace	27	400	15	2
Shy	19	163	9	0
Grabowski	17	100	6	0
Tucker	11	65	6	0
Pinder	10	51	5	0
Seymour	5	75	15	0
Thomas	3	40	13	0
Joe Moore	2	22	11	0
Harrison	2	18	9	0
Turner	1	13	13	0

PUNT RETURNS Last Name	No.	Yds	Avg	TD
Smith	26	194	7	0
Turner	9	63	7	0
Lyle	1	5	5	0

KICKOFF RETURNS Last Name	No.	Yds	Avg	TD
Smith	26	671	26	0
Turner	31	639	21	0
Butkus	2	15	8	0

PASSING	Att	Comp	%	Yds	Yd/Att	TD	Int– %	RK
Douglass	225	91	40	1164	5.2	5	15– 7	16
Nix	137	51	37	760	5.6	6	10– 7	
Concannon	77	42	55	334	4.3	0	3– 4	
Green	2	1	50	13	6.5	0	0– 0	
Shy	1	1	100	23	23.0	1	0– 0	
Wallace	1	0	0	0	0.0	0	0– 0	

PUNTING	No	Avg
Green	77	40.2

KICKING	XP	Att	%	FG	Att	%
Percival	18	18	100	15	33	46
Butkus	1	1	100	0	0	0
Douglass	1	1	100	0	0	0

GREEN BAY PACKERS

RUSHING Last Name	No.	Yds	Avg	TD
Brockington	216	1105	5.1	4
Anderson	186	757	4.1	5
Hampton	67	307	4.6	3
Hunter	21	50	2.4	4
Starr	3	11	3.7	1
P. Williams	3	4	1.3	0
Bratkowski	1	1	1.0	1
Krause	3	–6	–2.0	0

RECEIVING Last Name	No.	Yds	Avg	TD
Dale	31	598	19	4
McGeorge	27	463	17	4
Anderson	26	306	12	1
Spilis	14	281	20	1
Brockington	14	98	7	1
Davis	6	59	10	0
Hampton	3	37	12	1

PUNT RETURNS Last Name	No.	Yds	Avg	TD
Ellis	22	107	5	0
Davis	6	36	6	0
Wood	4	21	5	0
Pitts	5	13	3	0
Randolph	1	0	0	0

KICKOFF RETURNS Last Name	No.	Yds	Avg	TD
Hampton	46	1314	29	1
Krause	5	101	20	0
Pitts	2	41	21	0
P. Williams	2	41	21	0
Davis	1	22	22	0
Ellis	1	22	22	0
Carter	1	5	5	0

PASSING	Att	Comp	%	Yds	Yd/Att	TD	Int– %	RK
Hunter	163	75	46	1210	7.4	7	17– 10	11
Starr	45	24	53	286	6.4	0	3– 7	
Bratkowski	37	19	51	298	8.1	4	3– 8	
Patrick	5	1	20	39	7.8	0	1– 20	
Anderson	4	2	50	9	2.3	1	0– 0	

PUNTING	No	Avg
Anderson	50	40.4
Duncan	6	36.0

KICKING	XP	Att	%	FG	Att	%
Michaels	19	20	95	8	14	57
Webster	8	8	100	6	11	55
Conway	5	5	100	0	1	0

SAN FRANCISCO FORTY NINERS 9-5-0 Dick Nolan

Scores of Each Game		
17	Atlanta	20
38	New Orleans	20
31	Philadelphia	3
13	LOS ANGELES	20
13	CHICAGO	0
26	St. Louis	14
27	NEW ENGLAND	10
13	Minnesota	9
20	NEW ORLEANS	26
6	Los Angeles	17
24	N.Y. Jets	21
17	KANSAS CITY	26
24	ATLANTA	3
31	DETROIT	27

Use Name	Pos.	Hgt	Wgt	Age	Int	Pts
Cas Banaszek	OT	6'3"	250	25		
Len Rohde	OT	6'4"	250	33		
John Watson	OT	6'4"	248	22		
Randy Beisler	OG	6'4"	255	26		
Elmer Collett	OG	6'4"	240	26		
Bob Hoskins	OG	6'2"	235	25		
Woody Peoples	OG	6'2"	247	28		
Forrest Blue	C	6'5"	260	25		6
Bill Belk	DE	6'3"	258	25		
Cedrick Hardman	DE	6'3"	255	22		
Tommy Hart	DE	6'3"	257	26		6
Earl Edwards	DT	6'6"	272	25		
Charlie Krueger	DT	6'4"	260	35		
Stan Hindman	DE-DT	6'3"	235	27		
Ed Beard	LB	6'2"	220	31		
Frank Nunley	LB	6'2"	232	25	1	
Jim Sniadecki	LB	6'2"	220	24		
Skip Vanderbundt	LB	6'3"	230	24	1	
Dave Wilcox	LB	6'3"	235	28		
Johnny Fuller	DB	6'	185	25	2	
Tony Harris	DB	6'2"	190	22		
Jim Johnson	DB	6'2"	185	33	3	
Mel Phillips	DB	6'	196	29		
Mike Simpson	DB	5'11"	175	24	1	
Bruce Taylor	DB	6'	180	23	3	6
Rosey Taylor	DB	5'11"	186	32	3	
John Brodie	QB	6'1"	203	36		18
Steve Spurrier	QB	6'2"	200	26		
Doug Cunningham	HB	5'11"	192	25		6
John Isenbarger	HB	6'3"	205	23		
Vic Washington	HB	5'10"	196	25		42
Ken Willard	FB	6'2"	225	28		30
Larry Schreiber	HB-FB	6'	200	24		7
Preston Riley	WR	6'	180	23		
Gene Washington	WR	6'1"	185	24		24
Dick Witcher	WR	6'3"	204	26		18
Jimmy Thomas	HB-WR	6'1"	214	24		6
Ted Kwalick	TE	6'4"	220	24		30
Bob Windsor	TE	6'4"	230	28		
Bruce Gossett	K	6'2"	235	28		101
Jim McCann	K	6'2"	170	22		

LOS ANGELES RAMS 8-5-1 Tommy Prothro

Scores of Each Game		
20	New Orleans	24
20	ATLANTA	20
17	CHICAGO	3
20	San Francisco	13
24	Atlanta	16
30	GREEN BAY	13
14	MIAMI	20
17	Baltimore	24
21	Detroit	13
17	SAN FRANSCISCO	6
21	Dallas	28
45	NEW ORLEANS	28
24	WASHINGTON	38
23	Pittsburgh	14

Use Name	Pos.	Hgt	Wgt	Age	Int	Pts
Rich Buzin	OT	6'4"	250	25		
Joe Carollo	OT	6'2"	265	31		
Charley Cowan	OT	6'4"	265	33		
Harry Schuh	OT	6'2"	260	28		
Mike LaHood	OG	6'3"	250	26		
Tom Mack	OG	6'3"	250	27		
Joe Scibelli	OG	6'1"	255	32		
Ken Iman	C	6'1"	240	32		
Rich Saul	OG-C	6'3"	235	23		
Deacon Jones	DE	6'5"	250	32		
Jack Youngblood	DE	6'4"	248	21		
Coy Bacon	DT-DE	6'4"	270	29	1	
Bill Nelson	DT	6'7"	270	23		
Merlin Olsen	DT	6'5"	270	30		
Phil Olsen	DT	6'5"	265	23		
Greg Wojcik	DT	6'6"	268	25		
Ken Geddes	LB	6'3"	235	24		
Dean Halverson	LB	6'2"	212	25		
Marlin McKeever	LB	6'1"	235	31	4	
Don Parish (from STL)	LB	6'1"	220	23		
John Pergine	LB	6'1"	225	24		
Jim Purnell	LB	6'2"	238	29	2	
Jack Reynolds	LB	6'1"	232	23		
Isiah Robertson	LB	6'3"	225	22	4	
Kermit Alexander	DB	5'11"	186	30	3	6
Dave Elmendorf	DB	6'1"	195	22	2	
Alvin Haymond	DB	6'	194	29		
Gene Howard	DB	6'	190	24	6	6
Jim Nettles	DB	5'9"	177	29	5	6
Clancy Williams	DB	6'2"	194	28		
Jim Wilson – Injury						
Jim Ferguson – Injury						
Roman Gabriel	QB	6'4"	220	31		12
Jerry Rhome	QB	6'	188	29		
Willie Ellison	HB	6'1"	200	26		24
Larry Smith	HB	6'3"	220	23		30
Bob Thomas	HB	5'10"	200	22		
Travis Williams	HB	6'1"	210	25		6
Les Josephson	FB	6'	207	28		30
Lee White	FB	6'4"	235	25		
Matt Maslowski	WR	6'3"	210	21		6
David Ray	WR	6'	195	26		91
Lance Rentzel	WR	6'2"	202	27		36
Jack Snow	WR	6'2"	190	28		30
Pat Studstill	WR	6'1"	175	33		
Roger Williams	WR	5'10"	180	25		
Pat Curran	TE	6'3"	238	25		6
Bob Klein	TE	6'5"	235	24		24

ATLANTA FALCONS 7-6-1 Norm Van Bracklin

Scores of Each Game		
20	SAN FRANCISCO	17
20	Los Angeles	20
38	Detroit	41
9	ST. LOUIS	26
16	LOS ANGELES	24
28	NEW ORLEANS	6
31	Cleveland	14
9	Cincinnati	6
17	N.Y. GIANTS	21
28	GREEN BAY	21
7	Minnesota	24
24	OAKLAND	13
3	San Francisco	24
24	New Orleans	20

Use Name	Pos.	Hgt	Wgt	Age	Int	Pts
George Kunz	OT	6'5"	256	24		
Bill Sandeman	OT	6'6"	256	28		
Mal Snider	OT	6'4"	252	24		
Dick Enderle	OG	6'1"	248	23		
Andy Mauer	OG	6'3"	257	22		
Jim Miller	OG	6'3"	240	22		
John Matlock	C	6'4"	250	26		
Jeff Van Note	C	6'2"	244	25		
Claude Humphrey	DE	6'5"	248	27		
Mike Lewis	DE	6'3"	223	22		
Randy Marshall	DE	6'5"	237	24		
John Zook	DE	6'5"	248	23		2
Glen Condren	DT	6'2"	250	29		
Greg Lens	DT	6'5"	260	26		
John Small	LB-DT	6'5"	254	24		
Ron Acks	LB	6'2"	220	26	1	
Grady Allen	LB	6'3"	230	25		
John Bramlett	LB	6'2"	220	30		
Greg Brezina	LB	6'2"	226	25	3	
Don Hansen	LB	6'3"	220	27	3	6
Rudy Kuechenberg	LB	6'2"	215	28		
Tommy Nobis	LB	6'2"	237	27		
Cleo Walker	LB	6'3"	220	23		
Ray Brown	DB	6'2"	198	22	3	
Tom Hayes	DB	6'1"	193	25	3	18
John Mallory	DB	6'	184	25		6
Tom McCauley	DB	6'3"	193	24	1	
Tony Plummer	DB	5'11"	190	24		
Ken Reaves	DB	6'3"	203	26	6	
Rudy Redmond	DB	6'	190	24		
Larry Shears	DB	5'10"	185	22		
Bob Berry	QB	5'11"	190	29		
Leo Hart	QB	6'4"	203	22		
Dick Shiner	QB	6'	195	29		6
Willie Belton	HB	5'11"	196	22		6
Cannonball Butler	HB	5'10"	200	28		24
Sonny Campbell	HB	5'11"	192	23		
Joe Profit	HB	6'	204	22		6
Art Malone	FB	5'11"	209	23		48
Harmon Wages	FB	6'1"	222	25		12
Ken Burrow	WR	6'	190	23		36
Wes Chesson	WR	6'2"	190	22		
Ray Jarvis	WR	5'11"	193	22		
Todd Snyder	WR	6'2"	184	22		
Mike Donohoe	TE	6'3"	228	26		
Jim Mitchell	TE	6'2"	225	23		36
Ray Poage	TE	6'4"	215	30		
Bill Bell	K	6'1"	190	23		68
Billy Lothridge	K	6'1"	200	27		

NEW ORLEANS SAINTS 4-8-2 J. D. Roberts

Scores of Each Game		
24	LOS ANGELES	20
20	SAN FRANCISCO	38
13	Houston	13
14	Chicago	35
24	DALLAS	14
6	Atlanta	28
14	Washington	24
21	OAKLAND	21
26	San Francisco	20
10	MINNESOTA	23
29	Green Bay	21
28	Los Angeles	45
17	CLEVELAND	21
20	ATLANTA	24

Use Name	Pos.	Hgt	Wgt	Age	Int	Pts
Glen Ray Hines	OT	6'5"	265	27		
Sam Holden	OT	6'3"	258	24		
Don Morrison	OT	6'5"	255	21		
Jake Kupp	OG	6'3"	248	29		
John Shinners	OG	6'2"	254	24		
Remi Pudhomme	C-OG	6'4"	250	29		
John Didion	C	6'4"	245	23		
Del Williams	C	6'2"	240	25		
Larry Estes	DE	6'6"	260	24		
Richard Neal	DE	6'3"	254	23		
Joe Owens	DE	6'2"	235	23		
Mike Walker	DE	6'4"	235	21		
Dan Goich	DT	6'4"	265	27		
Dave Long	DT	6'4"	245	26		
Bob Pollard	DT	6'3"	245	22		
Doug Mooers	DE-DT	6'6"	265	24		
Dick Absher	LB	6'4"	235	27	1	
Wayne Colman	LB	6'1"	230	25	1	
Carl Cunningham	LB	6'3"	240	27		
Jim Flanigan	LB	6'3"	240	26	1	
Ray Hester	LB	6'2"	215	22		
Tom Roussel	LB	6'3"	235	26		
Richard Harvey	DB	6'2"	190	25		
Hugo Hollas	DB	6'1"	190	26	5	
Delles Howell	DB	6'3"	195	24	5	
Bivian Lee	DB	6'3"	200	23		
Dee Martin	DB	6'1"	190	22	3	
Reynaud Moore	DB	6'2"	190	21		
Doug Wyatt	DB	6'1"	195	24	4	6
Leo Carroll – Injury						
John Huard – Injury						
Mike Morgan – Injury						
Joe Scarpati – Injury						
Edd Hargett	QB	5'11"	185	24		6
Archie Manning	QB	6'3"	204	22		24
Bob Gresham	HB	5'11"	193	23		36
Billy Harris	HB	6'	204	25		
Virgil Robinson	HB	5'11"	195	23		12
Jamie Ford	FB-HB	6'	205	21		12
Hoyle Granger	FB	6'1"	225	27		6
Dave Kopay	HB-FB	6'2"	218	29		
Jim Strong	HB-FB	6'1"	204	24		18
Dan Abramowicz	WR	6'1"	195	26		30
Al Dodd	WR	6'	185	26		
Bob Newland	WR	6'2"	190	22		
Carlos Bell	TE	6'5"	238	22		
Don Burchfield	TE	6'2"	227	22		
Dave Parks	TE	6'2"	203	29		30
Skip Butler (to NYG)	K	6'2"	200	24		8
Charlie Durkee	K	5'11"	165	27		72
Julian Fagan	K	6'3"	205	23		

SAN FRANCISCO FORTY NINERS

RUSHING

Last Name	No.	Yds	Avg	TD
Willard	216	855	4.0	4
V. Washington	191	811	4.2	3
Schreiber	34	180	5.3	0
Cunningham	25	98	3.9	1
Kwalick	6	62	10.3	0
Brodie	14	45	3.2	3
Thomas	3	36	12.0	1
Isenbarger	5	34	6.8	0
Windsor	1	21	21.0	0
Spurrier	1	2	2.0	0
McCann	2	−15	−7.5	0

RECEIVING

Last Name	No.	Yds	Avg	TD
Kwalick	52	664	13	5
G. Wash'gton	46	884	19	4
V. Wash'gton	36	317	9	4
Willard	27	202	7	1
Cunningham	19	188	10	0
Witcher	18	250	14	3
Schreiber	3	79	26	1
Riley	3	39	13	0
Thomas	3	33	11	0
Windsor	2	32	16	0

PUNT RETURNS

Last Name	No.	Yds	Avg	TD
B. Taylor	34	235	7	0
Fuller	3	31	10	0
Riley	1	2	2	0
Vanderbundt	1	0	0	0

KICKOFF RETURNS

Last Name	No.	Yds	Avg	TD
V. Wash'gton	33	858	26	0
Cunningham	6	121	20	0
Windsor	4	66	17	0
Beard	1	21	21	0
Kwalick	2	9	5	0

PASSING – PUNTING – KICKING

PASSING	Att	Comp	%	Yds	Yd/Att	TD	Int–	%	RK
Brodie	387	208	54	2642	6.8	18	24–	6	6
Spurrier	4	1	25	46	11.5	0	0–	0	

PUNTING	No	Avg
McCann	49	38.7
Spurrier	2	38.5

KICKING	XP	Att	%	FG	Att	%
Gossett	32	32	100	23	36	64
Schreiber	1	1	100	0	0	0

LOS ANGELES RAMS

RUSHING

Last Name	No.	Yds	Avg	TD
Ellison	211	1000	4.7	4
Josephson	99	449	4.5	3
Smith	91	404	4.4	5
Rentzel	14	113	8.1	1
T. Williams	18	103	5.7	0
Gabriel	18	48	2.7	2
Klein	3	21	7.0	0
White	2	11	5.5	0
Rhome	3	0	0.0	0
Snow	1	−10	−10.0	0

RECEIVING

Last Name	No.	Yds	Avg	TD
Rentzel	38	534	14	5
Snow	37	666	18	5
Ellison	32	238	7	0
Smith	31	324	10	0
Josephson	26	230	9	2
Klein	14	160	11	4
Maslowski	3	82	27	1
T. Williams	3	68	23	0
Curran	1	2	2	1

PUNT RETURNS

Last Name	No.	Yds	Avg	TD
Haymond	24	123	5	0
Rentzel	9	40	4	0
Alexander	1	5	5	0
T. Williams	1	4	4	0

KICKOFF RETURNS

Last Name	No.	Yds	Avg	TD
T. Williams	25	743	30	1
Haymond	9	207	23	0
Howard	7	164	23	0
R. Williams	4	100	25	0
Youngblood	2	36	18	0
Curran	3	35	12	0
LaHood	1	25	25	0
Thomas	1	12	12	0
Josephson	1	0	0	0
Saul	1	0	0	0

PASSING – PUNTING – KICKING

PASSING	Att	Comp	%	Yds	Yd/Att	TD	Int–	%	RK
Gabriel	352	180	51	2238	6.4	17	10–	3	5
Rhome	18	5	28	66	5.6	1	1–	6	

PUNTING	No	Avg
Studstill	70	41.4

KICKING	XP	Att	%	FG	Att	%
Ray	37	37	100	18	29	62

ATLANTA FALCONS

RUSHING

Last Name	No.	Yds	Avg	TD
Butler	186	594	3.2	2
Malone	120	438	3.7	6
Wages	64	266	4.2	1
Belton	56	237	4.2	1
Campbell	29	79	2.7	0
Berry	19	31	1.6	0
Mitchell	4	25	6.3	0
Jarvis	1	13	13.0	0
Profit	3	10	3.3	1
Shiner	10	9	0.9	1
Burrow	1	5	5.0	0
Chesson	1	−4	−4.0	0

RECEIVING

Last Name	No.	Yds	Avg	TD
Malone	34	380	11	2
Burrow	33	741	22	6
Mitchell	33	593	18	5
Chesson	20	224	11	0
Wages	19	249	13	1
Butler	15	143	10	2
Poage	4	71	18	0
Campbell	3	40	13	0
Belton	3	22	7	0
Mallory	1	27	27	0
Brezina	1	3	3	0
Kunz	1	2	2	0

PUNT RETURNS

Last Name	No.	Yds	Avg	TD
Belton	30	163	5	0
McCauley	1	8	8	0
Mallory	5	3	1	0
Brown	1	0	0	0

KICKOFF RETURNS

Last Name	No.	Yds	Avg	TD
Belton	28	706	25	0
Butler	13	372	29	0
Profit	10	247	25	0
Campbell	4	95	24	0
Wages	1	21	21	0
Enderle	1	20	20	0
Small	1	12	12	0
Matlock	1	4	4	0

PASSING – PUNTING – KICKING

PASSING	Att	Comp	%	Yds	Yd/Att	TD	Int–	%	RK
Berry	226	136	60	2005	8.9	11	16–	7	4
Shiner	57	30	53	463	8.1	5	5–	9	
Hart	1	0	0	0	0.0	0	0–	0	
Lothridge	1	1	100	27	27.0	0	0–	0	

PUNTING	No	Avg
Lothridge	44	37.3
Bell	16	36.1

KICKING	XP	Att	%	FG	Att	%
Bell	29	33	88	13	21	62

NEW ORLEANS SAINTS

RUSHING

Last Name	No.	Yds	Avg	TD
Strong	95	404	4.3	3
Gresham	127	383	3.0	6
Ford	93	379	4.1	2
Manning	33	172	5.2	4
Granger	32	139	4.3	1
Robinson	29	96	3.3	1
Hargett	9	24	2.7	1
Dodd	1	7	7.0	0
Harris	1	1	1.0	0
Parks	2	−2	−1.0	0
Fagan	1	−17	−17.0	0

RECEIVING

Last Name	No.	Yds	Avg	TD
Abramowicz	37	657	18	5
Parks	35	568	16	5
Newland	21	319	15	0
Gresham	17	203	12	0
Strong	16	78	5	0
Dodd	15	298	20	0
Robinson	12	53	4	1
Granger	12	52	4	0
Ford	7	54	8	0
Burchfield	3	36	12	0
Manning	1	−7	−7	0

PUNT RETURNS

Last Name	No.	Yds	Avg	TD
Dodd	13	88	7	0
Moore	2	12	6	0
Abramowicz	1	0	0	0

KICKOFF RETURNS

Last Name	No.	Yds	Avg	TD
Robinson	19	443	23	0
Dodd	12	252	21	0
Moore	11	246	22	0
Strong	9	134	15	0
Gresham	3	60	20	0
Burchfield	1	5	5	0
Absher	1	3	3	0

PASSING – PUNTING – KICKING

PASSING	Att	Comp	%	Yds	Yd/Att	TD	Int–	%	RK
Hargett	210	96	46	1191	5.7	6	5–	2	10
Manning	177	86	49	1164	6.6	6	9–	5	11

PUNTING	No	Avg
Fagan	77	41.4

KICKING	XP	Att	%	FG	Att	%
Durkee	24	25	96	16	23	70
Butler	5	6	83	1	5	20

1971 A.F.C. Aerial Oneupmanship

The old American Football League had never had an abundant supply of good quarterbacks, but the AFC now held the edge in that department over the NFC. The AFC had good veterans like Johnny Unitas and Len Dawson, men in their peak years like Joe Namath, John Hadl, Bob Griese, and Daryle Lamonica, and promising young passers like Jim Plunkett, Terry Bradshaw, Mike Phipps, and Dan Pastorini. After five years of the common draft, the AFC had picked the quarterback plums from the college crop, while the only exciting young passers in the NFC were Roger Staubach, Greg Landry, and Archie Manning.

EASTERN DIVISION

Miami Dolphins— Although the Miami defense played surprisingly strong, the pride of the Dolphins was their versatile offense. Enemy defenses had to contend with an unheralded but solid line, a great deep receiver in Paul Warfield, a good short receiver in Howard Twilley, two relentless runners in Larry Csonka and Jim Kiick, a breakaway runner in Mercury Morris, and an enormously resourceful quarterback in young Bob Griese. Whenever the attack stalled, place kicker Garo Yepremian was deadly within the 50-yard line. With all this offensive firepower, the Dolphins raced evenly with the Colts through most of the season. Although assured of at least a wild-card berth in the playoffs, the Dolphins seemed to have conceded first place by losing to Baltimore on the next to last weekend, but a victory over Green Bay, plus the Colts' upset loss to New England, let the Dolphins slip into first place on the final day of the season.

Baltimore Colts—The Colts won the wild-card playoff spot on the strength of the conference's best defense and a strong offense. The defense had some problems at one cornerback slot, but the presence of stars Bubba Smith, Ted Hendricks, Mike Curtis, Ray May, Charlie Stukes, Rick Volk, and Jerry Logan glossed over any shortcomings in the other positions. The offense went with Earl Morrall at quarterback for the first half of the schedule, but Johnny Unitas recovered from an off-season Achilles tendon injury to reclaim the starting spot down the stretch. Although his arm was not what it once had been, Unitas still had enough guile to maneuver his way througl the best defenses in the league.

New England Patriots—The Patriots had a brand-new name, a brand-new stadium in Foxboro, Massachusetts, to play in, and a talented new quarterback in rookie Jim Plunkett. In his professional debut, Plunkett threw two touchdown passes in leading the Patriots to a 20-6 upset victory over the Oakland Raiders, and the big rookie continued to impress friend and foe alike all season with his arm and poise. To catch Plunkett's passes, the Patriots signed little Randy Vataha, Plunkett's college teammate who had been cut by the Rams early in training camp. Other newcomers who made a good impression were rookie defensive tackle Julius Adams and ex-Dallas linebacker Steve Kiner.

New York Jets—The Jets again went through the season with many of their regulars missing from action. Injuries sidelined Joe Namath, Matt Snell, Gerry Philbin, and John Elliott for long stretches of time, George Sauer and Steve Thompson both quit football at their physical prime for other interests, and Verlon Biggs played out his option and signed with the Washington Redskins. Injuries so decimated the defensive line that coach Weeb Ewbank at one point talked Clovis Swinney out of his job selling cars to help the Jets out.

Buffalo Bills—For the second time in the last four years, scout Harvey Johnson stepped in as interim head coach under dismal conditions. This year, Johnny Rauch was canned even before the season began, leaving Johnson to guide the dispirited Bills through a horrendous 1-13-0 campaign. Major problems during the year were injuries in the offensive line, where Johnson was forced to start five rookies and a second-year man, quarterback Dennis Shaw's serious regression from his good rookie showing, and a disorganized defense.

CENTRAL DIVISION

Cleveland Browns—With Mike Phipps still not ready to take over as starting quarterback, Bill Nelsen took his aching knees into battle once more and took the Browns to the championship of the NFL's weakest division. The road to first place was a rocky one, with the Browns losing four straight mid-season games before going on a five-game winning streak. On paper, the Browns looked like a team evenly balanced between strengths and weaknesses. Leroy Kelly, Bo Scott, Milt Morin, Clarence Scott, Jack Gregory, and Walter Johnson fit comfortably into the asset column, but under the deficit heading were listed disorganization in the linebacking and secondary, advanced age in several offensive linemen, and the lack of a clutch wide receiver.

Pittsburgh Steelers—Dave Smith won a place on the roster of famous bloopers with his bonehead play of October 18. Sprinting to the end zone with a pass, Smith mistook the 5-yard line for the goal line and slammed the ball down on the ground, thinking that he had scored a touchdown. The referee noticed full well that Smith had never carried the ball across the goal line, and when the ball rolled through the end zone, he ruled it a touchback, gave the ball to Kansas City, and erased six points that Smith and the Steelers were already counting. But aside from that play, Smith enjoyed a fine season, as did fellow wide receiver Ron Shanklin and quarterback Terry Bradshaw.

Houston Oilers—Owner Bud Adams hired Ed Hughes, a man highly respected around the league, as his new head coach, but Adams quickly lost confidence in the coach and put him on the spot by firing one of his assistants in mid-season with no notice. The players rallied around Hughes late in the year and won their final three games after a very slow start. One of Hughes' moves during the season was to bench quarterback Charley Johnson and try rookies Lynn Dickey and Dan Pastorini at the position. Pastorini finally nailed down the starting job, showing good potential despite taking a steady pounding from defenders who sliced right through the porous Houston front wall.

Cincinnati Bengals—The Bengals slumped back into last place in the Central Division. Six of those losses, however, were by four points or less, so the Bengals were not nearly as lame as their record indicated. The Cincinnati attack again relied heavily on the run, with rookie Fred Willis and Essex Johnson taking over from Jess Phillips and Paul Robinson as the heavy-duty ball carriers. The need for a strong ground game was underlined by the weakened situation at quarterback. Greg Cook, the rookie marvel of 1970, still was out of action with a bad shoulder, and Virgil Carter missed several games with injuries.

WESTERN DIVISION

Kansas City Chiefs—The Chiefs opened up their offense and won first place in the Western Division. Morris Stroud and rookie Elmo Wright developed into good receivers, giving Len Dawson two new targets to throw at and also taking some of the defense's attention away from Otis Taylor. No longer the only receiving threat on the team, Taylor enjoyed his best year as a pro, leading the NFL in yards gained on receptions. Ed Podolak spearheaded the running game and also contributed in the receiving and kick-returning departments. On defense, Jerry Mays' retirement weakened the front four, but the linebacking trio of Bobby Bell, Willie Lanier, and Jim Lynch plus the talented secondary kept the unit in fine condition.

Oakland Raiders—The Raiders finished out of first place for the first time in five years, but they still compiled a winning record despite several sizable difficulties. First of all, Warren Wells, who was Daryle Lamonica's favorite deep receiver, ran afoul of the law and had to sit the season out. Then Hewritt Dixon and Charlie Smith, both starting running backs, went out of action with injuries, and the advancing years started cutting down in Tom Keating's and Ben Davidson's effectiveness in the defensive line. To remedy all these problems, Madden inserted rookie receiver Mike Siani into the lineup to team up with Fred Biletnikoff on the flanks, he promoted subs Marv Hubbard and Pete Banaszak to starters with fine results, and he rejuvenated the defense by giving lots of playing time to youngsters Tony Cline, Art Thoms, Harold Rice, Horace Jones, and Phil Villapiano.

San Diego Chargers—The San Diego management had a new look at the start of the season as Sid Gillman decided to resume his coaching duties and Harland Svare came in as general manager. By mid-season, however, Gillman got into a disagreement with owner Eugene Klein and found himself out of work. Svare, meanwhile, found himself back on the field as head coach for the final four games. As usual, the San Diego defense leaked profusely, while the offense cranked out points at a rapid clip. The trade of Lance Alworth to Dallas gave the attack a new look, with rookie Billy Parks filling in with great results until he broke his arm late in the year.

Denver Broncos—Floyd Little's strong running cheered Lou Saban somewhat, but assorted other troubles made the coach's final half season a vexing one. Injuries erased starters Rich Jackson, Pete Duranko, Larry Kaminski, and Sam Brunelli and exposed the thinness of the Denver bench. None of the wide receivers on the team took up the slack left by the trade of Al Denson to Minnesota, and the quarterback situation was a highly unhealthy one. After several injury-filled seasons, quarterback Steve Tensi packed it all in, leaving ex-Packer Don Horn at the starting quarterback. After a lackluster first half, Horn went out with an injury, leaving only inexperienced Steve Ramsey as a passer. Nine games were enough for Saban this year, and assistant Jerry Smith took over as head man for the final five games.

FINAL TEAM STATISTICS

OFFENSE

	BALT.	BUFF.	CIN.	CLEV.	DENV.	HOUS.	K.C.	MIAMI	N.ENG.	N.Y.J.	OAK.	PITT.	S.D.
FIRST DOWNS:													
Total	242	185	236	231	217	201	240	232	190	202	258	226	**264**
by Rushing	123	68	109	89	102	62	108	121	85	115	**128**	98	86
by Passing	104	96	115	127	105	117	119	94	94	67	110	111	**147**
by Penalty	15	21	12	15	10	22	13	17	11	20	20	17	**31**
RUSHING:													
Number	**512**	320	462	461	**512**	361	487	486	419	485	473	416	390
Yards	2149	1337	2142	1558	2093	1106	1843	**2429**	1669	1888	2130	1758	1604
Average Yards	4.2	4.2	4.6	3.4	4.1	3.1	3.8	**5.0**	4.0	3.9	4.5	4.2	4.1
Touchdowns	**23**	6	14	19	9	10	14	11	7	12	19	10	11
PASSING:													
Attempts	344	401	365	376	358	423	337	293	330	278	348	414	**450**
Completions	176	202	214	188	175	194	183	156	159	119	174	214	**244**
Completion Percentage	51.2	50.4	**58.6**	50.0	48.9	45.9	54.3	53.2	48.2	42.8	50.0	51.7	54.2
Passing Yards	2152	2410	2427	2521	2243	2643	2694	2248	2206	1556	2363	2446	**3305**
Avg. Yards per Attempt	6.3	6.0	6.6	6.7	6.3	6.2	**8.0**	7.7	6.7	5.6	6.8	5.9	7.3
Avg. Yards per Complet.	12.2	11.9	11.3	13.4	12.8	13.6	**14.7**	14.4	13.9	13.1	13.6	11.4	13.5
Times Tackled Passing	27	49	40	22	22	31	35	25	36	23	24	37	**19**
Yards Lost Tackled	230	421	303	222	178	234	347	265	319	177	235	322	**171**
Net Yards	1922	1989	2124	2299	2065	2409	2347	1983	1887	1379	2128	2124	**3134**
Touchdowns	10	12	15	14	8	12	15	20	19	15	21	15	**23**
Interceptions	21	32	11	27	27	37	13	**10**	16	16	26	26	28
Percent Intercepted	6.1	8.0	**3.0**	7.2	7.5	8.7	3.9	3.4	4.8	5.8	7.5	6.3	6.2
PUNTS:													
Number	62	75	73	67	76	75	64	52	**87**	78	62	79	55
Average Distance	41.0	40.9	44.7	39.9	41.8	40.6	**44.8**	40.1	37.3	38.8	39.9	43.7	43.5
PUNT RETURNS:													
Number	43	**44**	25	40	41	32	33	41	31	25	29	35	37
Yards	351	343	145	359	320	198	150	**432**	181	155	182	264	215
Average Yards	8.2	7.8	5.8	9.0	7.8	6.2	4.5	**10.5**	5.8	6.2	6.3	7.5	5.8
Touchdowns	0	**2**	0	0	0	0	0	0	0	0	0	1	0
KICKOFF RETURNS:													
Number	32	**74**	43	46	44	59	47	32	64	55	54	49	49
Yards	679	**1673**	863	1065	960	1409	1031	806	1354	1168	1234	1120	1000
Average Yards	21.2	22.6	20.1	23.2	21.8	23.9	21.9	**25.2**	21.2	21.2	22.9	22.9	20.4
Touchdowns	0	0	0	0	0	0	0	**1**	0	0	0	0	0
INTERCEPTION RETURNS:													
Number	**28**	11	27	24	20	23	27	17	15	13	23	17	22
Yards	367	93	273	283	288	**456**	403	143	229	136	453	246	317
Average Yards	13.1	8.5	10.1	11.8	14.4	**19.8**	14.9	8.4	15.3	10.5	19.7	14.5	14.4
Touchdowns	1	0	2	0	1	**5**	3	0	2	0	2	1	2
PENALTIES:													
Number	57	74	82	68	67	**91**	72	65	67	70	81	88	81
Yards	529	691	**921**	612	781	856	734	632	657	672	869	898	895
FUMBLES:													
Number	26	33	29	29	25	24	23	**22**	26	30	26	37	30
Number Lost	11	16	12	18	12	14	13	13	16	**10**	13	16	15
POINTS:													
Total	313	184	284	285	203	251	302	315	238	212	**344**	246	311
PAT Attempts	36	21	32	34	18	29	32	33	29	27	**43**	28	37
PAT Made	35	20	32	34	18	26	32	33	28	26	**41**	27	36
FG Attempts	29	25	36	28	38	28	**45**	40	21	19	22	27	29
FG Made	20	12	20	15	25	17	26	**28**	12	8	15	17	17
Percent FG Made	69.0	48.0	55.6	53.6	65.8	60.7	57.8	**70.0**	57.1	42.1	68.2	63.0	58.6
Safeties	**1**	**1**	0	**1**	**1**	0	0	0	0	0	0	0	**1**

DEFENSE

	BALT.	BUFF.	CIN.	CLEV.	DENV.	HOUS.	K.C.	MIAMI	N.ENG.	N.Y.J.	OAK.	PITT.	S.D.
FIRST DOWNS:													
Total	**166**	250	213	232	206	237	223	214	237	235	242	225	272
by Rushing	**60**	135	93	115	90	117	73	93	106	118	100	81	143
by Passing	95	101	102	100	**91**	97	125	111	111	101	122	132	114
by Penalty	11	14	18	17	25	23	25	**10**	20	16	20	12	15
RUSHING:													
Number	**352**	562	446	484	426	489	367	403	481	472	480	440	493
Yards	**1113**	2496	1778	2227	1834	1723	1300	1661	1918	2302	1751	1482	2296
Average Yards	**3.2**	4.4	4.0	4.6	4.3	3.5	3.5	4.1	4.0	4.9	3.6	3.4	4.7
Touchdowns	**8**	21	11	14	11	22	9	10	14	18	14	13	25
PASSING:													
Attempts	361	**303**	335	339	356	354	418	363	350	342	359	408	347
Completions	185	157	157	156	**150**	180	209	206	170	163	184	235	193
Completion Percentage	51.2	51.8	46.9	46.0	**42.1**	50.8	50.0	56.7	48.6	47.7	51.3	57.6	55.6
Passing Yards	**2027**	2333	2382	2170	2420	2416	2703	2293	2403	2285	2609	3060	2439
Avg. Yards per Attempt	**5.6**	7.7	7.1	6.4	6.8	6.8	6.5	6.3	6.9	6.7	7.3	7.5	7.0
Avg. Yards per Complet.	**11.0**	14.9	15.2	13.9	16.1	13.4	12.9	11.1	14.1	14.0	14.2	13.0	12.6
Times Tackled Passing	33	30	30	25	**44**	37	28	34	25	27	32	33	19
Yards Lost Tackled	288	225	254	203	**435**	344	235	293	249	230	223	294	177
Net Yards	**1739**	2108	2128	1967	1985	2072	2468	2000	2154	2055	2386	2766	2262
Touchdowns	**9**	20	19	12	18	11	11	10	16	17	15	16	15
Interceptions	**28**	11	27	24	20	23	27	17	15	13	23	17	22
Percent Intercepted	7.8	3.6	**8.1**	7.1	5.6	6.5	6.5	4.7	4.3	3.8	6.4	4.2	6.3
PUNTS:													
Number	**88**	66	73	66	67	76	67	72	66	65	59	77	67
Average Distance	38.9	39.0	40.9	42.4	45.7	42.2	40.7	40.7	38.8	**38.1**	41.7	41.5	43.7
PUNT RETURNS:													
Number	40	40	41	26	45	39	40	26	36	41	26	45	**20**
Yards	267	446	304	227	468	304	286	106	279	359	168	319	**40**
Average Yards	6.7	11.2	7.4	8.7	10.4	7.8	7.2	4.1	7.8	8.8	6.5	7.1	**2.0**
Touchdowns	0	0	1	0	0	0	0	0	1	0	0	0	0
KICKOFF RETURNS:													
Number	62	42	39	55	43	41	47	59	49	**34**	55	45	55
Yards	1345	971	1024	1252	1059	**862**	1071	1180	1427	906	1155	1002	1245
Average Yards	21.7	23.1	26.3	22.8	24.6	20.8	22.8	**20.0**	29.1	26.6	21.0	22.3	22.6
Touchdowns	0	0	0	0	0	0	0	0	1	1	0	0	**0**
INTERCEPTION RETURNS:													
Number	21	32	11	27	27	37	13	**10**	16	16	26	26	28
Yards	220	418	219	453	432	505	167	166	**157**	279	267	350	339
Average Yards	10.5	13.1	19.9	16.8	16.0	13.6	12.8	16.6	**9.8**	17.4	10.3	13.5	12.1
Touchdowns	1	3	1	2	2	3	**0**	1	1	1	**0**	1	4
PENALTIES:													
Number	67	**89**	72	86	78	75	71	62	60	81	80	81	84
Yards	687	883	722	772	771	**916**	751	569	559	814	832	784	887
FUMBLES:													
Number	22	17	21	31	36	31	16	**38**	35	35	26	27	27
Number Lost	13	11	12	16	**20**	14	6	14	14	14	17	18	10
POINTS:													
Total	**140**	394	265	273	275	330	208	174	325	299	278	292	341
PAT Attempts	**18**	45	32	30	32	37	21	21	35	37	30	32	44
PAT Made	**17**	45	31	30	32	36	20	21	34	35	30	30	44
FG Attempts	**18**	38	22	31	35	35	32	21	36	25	34	35	24
FG Made	**5**	25	14	21	17	24	20	9	27	14	22	22	11
Percent FG Made	**27.8**	65.8	63.6	67.7	48.6	68.9	62.5	42.9	75.0	56.0	64.7	62.9	45.8
Safeties	**0**	2	**0**	**0**	**0**	**0**	1	**0**	**0**	**0**	1	2	**0**

CONFERENCE PLAYOFFS

December 25, at Kansas City
(Attendance 45,822)

SCORING

KANSAS CITY	10	0	7	7	0	0–24
MIAMI	0	10	7	7	0	3–27

First Quarter
- K.C. Stenerud, 24 yard field goal
- K.C. Podolak, 7 yard pass from Dawson
  PAT–Stenerud (kick)

Second Quarter
- Mia. Csonka, 1 yard rush
  PAT–Yepremian (kick)
- Mia. Yepremian, 14 yard field goal

Third Quarter
- K.C. Otis, 1 yard rush
  PAT–Stenerud (kick)
- Mia. Kiick, 1 yard rush
  PAT–Yepremian (kick)

Fourth Quarter
- K.C. Podolak, 3 yard rush
  PAT–Stenerud (kick)
- Mia. Fleming, 5 yard pass from Griese
  PAT–Yepremian (kick)

Second Overtime Period
- Mia. Yepremian, 37 yard field goal 7:40

TEAM STATISTICS

K.C.		MIAMI
23	First Downs–Total	22
13	First Downs–Rushing	6
10	First Downs–Passing	14
0	First Downs–Penalty	2
2	Fumbles–Number	0
2	Fumbles–Lost Ball	0
6	Penalties–Number	5
44	Yards Penalized	26
3	Missed Field Goals	1
71	Offensive Plays–Total	78
451	Net Yards	407
6.4	Average Gain	5.2
4	Giveaways	2
2	Takeaways	4
–2	Difference	+2

INDIVIDUAL STATISTICS

KANSAS CITY	No.	Yds.	Avg.	MIAMI	No.	Yds.	Avg.
RUSHING							
Hayes	22	100	4.5	Csonka	24	86	3.6
Podolak	17	85	5.0	Kiick	15	56	3.7
Wright	2	15	7.5	Griese	2	9	4.5
Otis	3	13	4.3	Warfield	2	–7	–3.5
	44	213	4.8		43	144	3.3
RECEIVING							
Podolak	8	110	13.8	Warfield	7	140	20.0
Wright	3	104	34.7	Twilley	5	58	11.6
Taylor	3	12	4.0	Fleming	4	37	9.3
Hayes	3	6	2.0	Kiick	3	24	8.0
Frazier	1	14	14.0	Mandich	1	4	4.0
	18	246	13.7		20	263	13.2
PUNTING							
Wilson	2		51.0	Seiple	6		40.0
PUNT RETURNS							
Podolak	2	1	0.5	Scott	1	18	18.0
KICKOFF RETURNS							
Podolak	3	154	52.0	Morris	2	61	30.5
INTERCEPTION RETURNS							
Lanier	1	17	17.0	Scott	1	13	13.0
Lynch	1	0	0.0	Johnson	1	0	0.0
	2	17	8.5		2	13	6.5

PASSING

KANSAS CITY	Att.	Comp.	Comp. Pct.	Yds.	Int.	Yds/ Att.	Yds/ Comp.	Yds Lost Tkld.
Dawson	26	18	69.2	246	2	9.5	13.7	1–8
Podolak	1	0	0.0	0	0	–	–	
	27	18	66.7	246	2	9.1	13.7	1–8
MIAMI								
Griese	35	20	57.1	263	2	7.5	13.2	0–0

December 26, at Cleveland
(Attendance 70,734)

SCORING

CLEVELAND	0	0	3	0– 3
BALTIMORE	0	14	3	3–20

Second Quarter
- Balt. Nottingham, 1 yard rush
  PAT–O'Brien (kick)
- Balt. Nottingham, 7 yard rush
  PAT–O'Brien (kick)

Third Quarter
- Cle. Cockroft, 14 yard field goal
- Balt. O'Brien, 42 yard field goal

Fourth Quarter
- Balt. O'Brien, 15 yard field goal

TEAM STATISTICS

CLE.		BALT.
11	First Downs–Total	16
5	First Downs–Rushing	7
5	First Downs–Passing	8
1	First Downs–Penalty	1
6	Fumbles–Number	2
2	Fumbles–Lost Ball	2
3	Penalties–Number	5
16	Yards Penalized	43
2	Missed Field Goals	0
56	Offensive Plays–Total	64
165	Net Yards	271
2.9	Average Gain	4.2
5	Giveaways	3
3	Takeaways	5
–2	Difference	+2

INDIVIDUAL STATISTICS

CLEVELAND	No.	Yds.	Avg.	BALTIMORE	No.	Yds.	Avg.
RUSHING							
Kelly	14	49	3.5	Nottingham	23	92	4.0
Bo Scott	8	25	3.1	Matte	16	26	1.6
Nelsen	2	–5	–2.5	McCauley	3	9	3.0
	24	69	2.9	Nowatzke	1	1	1.0
					43	128	3.0
RECEIVING							
Bo Scott	5	41	8.2	Mitchell	5	73	14.6
Kelly	4	24	6.0	Matte	3	22	7.3
Hooker	1	39	39.0	Hinton	2	30	15.0
Morin	1	16	16.0	Perkins	1	10	10.0
Glass	1	11	11.0	Nottingham	1	5	5.0
	12	131	10.9	Havrilak	1	3	3.0
					13	143	11.0
PUNTING							
Cockroft	5		40.8	Lee	6		37.2
PUNT RETURNS							
Kelly	3	71	23.7	Volk	4	27	6.8
D. Jones	1	3	3.0				
	4	74	18.5				
KICKOFF RETURNS							
S. Brown	2	34	17.0	Pittman	1	25	25.0
Bo Scott	1	30	30.0				
Morrison	1	19	19.0				
Dieken	1	15	15.0				
	5	98	19.6				
INTERCEPTION RETURNS							
Snidow	1	1	1.0	Volk	2	56	28.0
C. Scott	Lat	22	–	Stukes	1	23	23.0
	1	23	23.0		3	89	29.7

PASSING

CLEVE.	Att.	Cmp.	Pct.	Yds.	Int.	Yd/A	Yd/C	Tkld
Nelsen	21	9	42.9	104	3	5.0	11.6	
Phipps	6	3	50.0	27	0	4.5	9.0	
	27	12	44.4	131	3	4.9	10.9	5–35
BALT.								
Unitas	21	13	61.9	143	1	6.8	11.0	0– 0

MIAMI DOLPHINS 10-3-1 Don Shula

Scores of Each Game		
10	Denver	10
29	Buffalo	14
10	N.Y. JETS	14
23	Cincinnati	13
41	NEW ENGLAND	3
30	N.Y. Jets	14
20	Los Angeles	14
34	BUFFALO	0
24	PITTSBURGH	21
17	BALTIMORE	14
34	CHICAGO	3
13	New England	34
3	Baltimore	14
27	GREEN BAY	6

Use Name	Pos.	Hgt	Wgt	Age	Int	Pts
Doug Crusan	OT	6'5"	250	25		
Norm Evans	OT	6'5"	252	27		
Wayne Mass	OT	6'4"	240	25		
Bob Kuechenberg	CG	6'3"	247	23		
Jim Langer	OG	6'2"	250	24		
Larry Little	OG	6'1"	265	25		
Bob DeMarco	C	6'3"	250	33		
Vern Den Herder	DE	6'6"	250	22		
Jim Riley	DE	6'4"	250	26		
Bill Stanfill	DE	6'5"	250	24		
Frank Cornish	DT	6'6"	285	27		
Manny Fernandez	DT	6'2"	248	25		
John Richardson	DT	6'2"	248	26		
Bob Heinz	DE-DT	6'6"	270	24		
Nick Buoniconti	LB	5'11"	220	30	1	
Dale Farley	LB	6'3"	235	22		
Mike Kolen	LB	6'2"	220	22		
Bob Matheson	LB	6'4"	240	26		
Jesse Powell	LB	6'1"	215	24		
Doug Swift	LB	6'3"	228	22	1	
Dick Anderson	DB	6'2"	196	25	2	
Tim Foley	DB	6'	194	23	4	
Curtis Johnson	DB	6'2"	196	23	2	6
Ray Jones	DB	6'	187	23		
Lloyd Mumphord	DB	5'11"	180	24		
Bob Petrella	DB	6'	190	26		
Jake Scott	DB	6'	188	25	7	
Bob Griese	QB	6'1"	190	26		
George Mira	QB	5'11"	192	29		
Hubert Ginn	HB	5'11"	188	24		
Jim Kiick	HB	5'11"	215	25		18
Mercury Morris	HB	5'10"	190	24		12
Terry Cole	FB	6'1"	220	26		
Larry Csonka	FB	6'3"	237	24		48
Charlie Leigh	FB	5'11"	205	25		
Karl Noonan	WR	6'3"	198	27		
Otto Stowe	WR	6'2"	188	22		6
Howard Twilley	WR	5'10"	185	27		24
Paul Warfield	WR	6'	185	28		66
Marv Fleming	TE	6'4"	235	29		12
Jim Mandich	TE	6'3"	224	22		6
Larry Seiple	TE	6'	215	26		
Garo Yepremian	K	5'8"	165	27		117

Dick Palmer–Injury

Dean Brown–Injury
Dick Daniels–Injury
Stan Mitchell–Injury

BALTIMORE COLTS 10-4-0 Don McCafferty

Scores of Each Game		
22	N.Y. JETS	0
13	CLEVELAND	14
23	New England	3
43	Buffalo	0
31	N.Y. Giants	7
3	Minnesota	10
34	PITTSBURGH	21
24	LOS ANGELES	17
14	N.Y. Jets	13
14	Miami	17
37	Oakland	14
24	BUFFALO	0
14	MIAMI	3
17	NEW ENGLAND	21

Use Name	Pos.	Hgt	Wgt	Age	Int	Pts
Lynn Larson	OT	6'4"	254	23		
Dennis Nelson	OT	6'5"	260	25		
Bob Vogel	OT	6'5"	250	29		
Cornelius Johnson	OG	6'2"	245	28		
Glenn Ressler	OG	6'3"	250	27		
Dan Sullivan	OG	6'3"	250	32		
John Williams	OG	6'3"	256	25		
Bill Curry	C	6'2"	236	28		
Ken Mendenhall	C	6'3"	235	23		
Roy Hilton	DE	6'6"	240	26		
Billy Newsome	DE	6'4"	240	23	2	6
Bubba Smith	DE	6'7"	295	26		
Jim Bailey	DT	6'4"	245	23		
Rusty Ganas	DT	6'4"	257	21		
Fred Miller	DT	6'3"	250	30		
George Wright	DT	6'3"	260	24		
Tom Beutler	LB	6'1"	232	24		
Mike Curtis	LB	6'2"	232	27	3	
Ted Hendricks	LB	6'7"	215	23	5	6
Bill Laskey	LB	6'2"	235	28		
Ray May	LB	6'1"	230	26	1	
Robbie Nichols	LB	6'3"	220	24		
Tom Nowatzke	FB-LB	6'3"	230	28	1	
Tom Curtis	DB	6'1"	196	23		
Jim Duncan	DB	6'2"	200	25		
Lenny Dunlap	DB	6'1"	195	22		
Lonnie Hepburn	DB	5'11"	185	22		
Rex Kern	DB	5'11"	190	22		
Jerry Logan	DB	6'1"	190	30	4	
Charlie Stukes	DB	6'3"	212	27	8	
Rick Volk	DB	6'3"	195	26	4	
Earl Morrall	QB	6'1"	206	37		
Johnny Unitas	QB	6'1"	196	38		
Tom Matte	HB	6'	214	32		48
Don McCauley	HB	6'1"	207	22		12
Charlie Pittman	HB	6'1"	200	23		
Don Nottingham	FB	5'10"	210	22		36
Norm Bulaich	HB-FB	6'1"	218	24		60
Sam Havrilak	WR	6'2"	195	23		
Eddie Hinton	WR	6'	200	24		12
Jim O'Brien	WR	6'	195	24		95
Ray Perkins	WR	6'	183	29		24
Willie Richardson	WR	6'2"	198	31		12
John Mackey	TE	6'3"	224	29		
Tom Mitchell	TE	6'2"	215	27		
David Lee	K	6'4"	230	27		

NEW ENGLAND PATRIOTS 6-8-0 John Mazur

Scores of Each Game		
20	OAKLAND	6
7	DETROIT	34
3	BALTIMORE	23
20	N.Y. JETS	0
3	Miami	41
21	Dallas	44
10	San Francisco	27
28	HOUSTON	20
38	BUFFALO	33
7	Cleveland	27
20	Buffalo	27
34	MIAMI	13
6	N.Y. Jets	13
21	Baltimore	17

Use Name	Pos.	Hgt	Wgt	Age	Int	Pts
Mike Haggerty	OT	6'4"	250	25		
Mike Montler	OT	6'4"	270	27		
Tom Neville	OT	6'4"	255	27		
Bill Lenkaitis	OG	6'3"	265	25		
Len St. Jean	OG	6'1"	245	29		
Halvor Hagen	C-OG	6'5"	253	24		
Jon Morris	C	6'4"	255	28		
Ike Lassiter	DE	6'5"	270	30		
Art May	DE	6'3"	245	22		
Dennis Wirgowski	DE	6'5"	255	23		
Ron Berger	DT-DE	6'8"	275	27		
Julius Adams	DT	6'3"	258	23		
Houston Antwine	DT	6'	270	32		
Dave Rowe	DT	6'6"	280	26		
Bill Atessis	DE-DT	6'3"	240	22		
Jim Cheyunski	LB	6'2"	220	25	1	
Dennis Coleman	LB	6'3"	225	22		
Randy Edmunds	LB	6'2"	225	25		
Steve Kiner	LB	6'	219	24	4	
Ed Philpott	LB	6'3"	240	25		
Ed Weisacosky	LB	6'	220	27		
Randy Beverly	DB	5'11"	205	27	2	
Larry Carwell	DB	6'1"	200	27	5	6
Phil Clark	DB	6'2"	208	26		
Rickie Harris	DB	6'	182	28		
Tom Janik	DB	6'3"	200	30		
Irv Mallory	DB	6'1"	196	22		
John Outlaw	DB	5'10"	175	26	3	6
Perry Pruett	DB	6'1"	190	22		
Clarence Scott	DB	6'2"	205	27		
Don Webb	DB	5'10"	185	32		
Ron Gardin (from BAL)	WR-DB	5'11"	180	26		
Jim Plunkett	QB	6'3"	220	23		
Mike Taliaferro	QB	6'2"	205	29		
Carl Garrett	HB	5'11"	210	23		12
Bob Gladieux	HB	5'11"	190	24		
Jack Maitland	HB	6'1"	210	23		6
Odell Lawson	FB	6'2"	218	23		
Jim Nance	FB	6'1"	240	28		30
Hubie Bryant	WR	5'10"	168	25		6
Eric Crabtree (from CIN)	WR	5'11"	185	26		18
Reggie Rucker (from DAL-NYG)	WR	6'2"	190	23		6
Ron Sellers	WR	6'4"	195	24		18
Eric Stolberg	WR	6'2"	180	22		
Al Sykes	WR	6'3"	180	24		
Randy Vataha	WR	5'10"	180	22		54
Roland Moss	TE	6'3"	215	24		12
Tom Beer	OG-TE	6'4"	235	26		18
Charlie Gogolak	K	5'10"	170	26		64

Rick Cash–Injury
Joe Kapp–Holdout
J. R. Williamson–Injury

NEW YORK JETS 6-8-0 Weeb Ewbank

Scores of Each Game		
0	Baltimore	22
10	St. Louis	17
14	Miami	10
0	New England	20
28	BUFFALO	17
14	MIAMI	30
21	San Diego	49
13	KANSAS CITY	10
13	BALTIMORE	14
20	Buffalo	7
21	SAN FRANCISCO	24
10	Dallas	52
13	NEW ENGLAND	6
35	CINCINNATI	21

Use Name	Pos.	Hgt	Wgt	Age	Int	Pts
Winston Hill	OT	6'4"	285	29		
John Mooring	OT	6'6"	255	24		
Bob Svihus	OT	6'4"	245	28		
Dave Foley	C-OT	6'5"	255	23		
Dave Herman	OG	6'2"	255	29		
Roy Kirksey	OG	6'1"	255	23		
Randy Rasmussen	OG	6'2"	255	26		
John Schmitt	C	6'4"	250	28		
Paul Crane	LB-C	6'2"	212	27	1	
Mark Lomas	DE	6'4"	230	23		
Gerry Philbin	DE	6'2"	245	30		
John Little	DT-DE	6'3"	220	24		
Steve Thompson	DT-DE	6'5"	245	25		
John Elliott	DT	6'4"	244	26		
Roger Finnie	DT	6'3"	245	24		
Chuck Hinton (from PIT)	DT	6'5"	264	32		
Scott Palmer	DT	6'3"	245	23		
Clovis Swinney	DT	6'3"	240	26		
Al Atkinson	LB	6'1"	230	28	2	
Ralph Baker	LB	6'3"	235	29		1
Larry Grantham	LB	6'	210	32	1	
John Ebersole	LB	6'3"	240	22		
Bill Zapalac	DE-LB	6'4"	225	23		
John Dockery	DB	6'	186	26	2	
Chris Farasopoulos	DB	5'11"	190	22		
W.K. Hicks	DB	6'1"	195	28		4
Gus Holloman	DB	6'3"	195	25	2	
Rich Sowells	DB	6'	175	22		
Steve Tannen	DB	6'1"	194	23		
Earlie Thomas	DB	6'1"	190	25		
Phil Wise	DB	6'	190	22	1	
Bob Davis	QB	6'3"	205	26		6
Joe Namath	QB	6'2"	200	27		
Al Woodall	QB	6'5"	205	25		
Emerson Boozer	HB	5'11"	195	28		36
George Nock	HB	5'10"	200	25		30
Cliff McClain	FB-HB	6'	217	23		12
John Riggins	FB	6'2"	237	22		18
Matt Snell	FB	6'2"	220	29		
Steve Harkey	HB-FB	6'	215	22		
Eddie Bell	WR	5'10"	160	23		6
Rich Caster	WR	6'5"	222	22		36
Don Maynard	WR	6'	180	35		12
Steve O'Neal	WR	6'3"	185	25		
Vern Studdard	WR	5'11"	175	23		
Gary Arthur	TE	6'5"	230	23		
Pete Lammons	TE	6'3"	230	27		6
Wayne Stewart	TE	6'7"	213	24		
Bobby Howfield	K	5'9"	180	34		49

Jim Richards–Military Service

BUFFALO BILLS 1-13-0 Harvey Johnson

Scores of Each Game		
37	DALLAS	49
14	MIAMI	29
0	Minnesota	19
0	BALTIMORE	43
17	N.Y. Jets	28
3	San Diego	20
23	ST. LOUIS	28
0	Miami	34
33	New England	38
7	N.Y. JETS	20
27	NEW ENGLAND	20
0	Baltimore	24
14	HOUSTON	20
9	Kansas City	22

Use Name	Pos.	Hgt	Wgt	Age	Int	Pts
Paul Costa	OT	6'4"	255	29		
Donnie Green	OT	6'7"	270	23		
Willie Young	OT	6'4"	270	23		
Bob Hews	DE-OT	6'5"	240	22		
Joe O'Donnell	OG	6'2"	262	28		
Mike Wilson	OG	6'1"	240	23		
Levert Carr	OT-OG	6'5"	260	27		
Bruce Jarvis	C	6'7"	246	22		
Howard Kindig	OT-C	6'6"	265	30		
Mike McBath	DE	6'4"	248	25		
Al Cowlings	DE	6'5"	258	24		
Louis Ross	DE	6'6"	238	24		
Cal Snowden	DE	6'4"	242	24		
Bill McKinley	LB-DE	6'3"	240	22		
Jim Dunaway	DT	6'4"	277	29		
Bob Tatarek	DT	6'4"	260	25		
Al Andrews	LB	6'3"	216	27	1	
Edgar Chandler	LB	6'3"	235	25	1	2
Jerald Collins	LB	6'1"	220	24		
Dick Cunningham	LB	6'2"	232	26		
Paul Guidry	LB	6'3"	233	27	1	
Mike Stratton	LB	6'3"	240	29		
Chuck Hurston	LB	6'6"	240	28		
Jackie Allen	DB	6'1"	187	23		
Tim Beamer	DB	5'11"	185	23		
Tony Greene	DB	5'10"	170	21		
Bobby James	DB	6'1"	185	24	4	6
John Pitts	DB	6'4"	223	26	2	
Pete Richardson	DB	6'1"	193	24	1	
Alvin Wyatt	DB	5'10"	185	23	1	6
Jim Harris	QB	6'3"	215	24		
Dennis Shaw	QB	6'2"	210	24		
Max Anderson	HB	5'8"	180	26		
Greg Jones	HB	6'1"	200	23		6
O.J. Simpson	HB	6'2"	214	24		30
Jim Braxton	FB	6'2"	226	22		
Wayne Patrick	FB	6'2"	254	25		6
Marlin Briscoe	WR	5'10"	178	25		30
Bob Chandler	WR	6'	180	22		
J.D. Hill	WR	6'1"	193	22		12
Haven Moses	WR	6'3"	205	25		12
Ike Hill	DB-WR	5'10"	180	24		12
Austin Denney	TE	6'2"	230	27		
Ted Koy	TE	6'1"	210	23		6
Jan White	TE	6'2"	215	22		
Dave Chapple	K	6'	180	24		
Grant Guthrie	K	6'	210	23		17
Spike Jones	K	6'2"	190	24		
John Leypoldt	K	6'2"	224	25		39

Richard Cheek – Injury
Julian Nunamaker – Injury
Jim Reilly – Illness

MIAMI DOLPHINS

RUSHING

Last Name	No.	Yds	Avg	TD
Csonka	195	1051	**5.4**	7
Kiick	162	738	4.6	3
Morris	57	315	5.5	1
Warfield	9	115	12.8	0
Ginn	22	97	4.4	0
Griese	26	82	3.2	0
Leigh	5	15	3.0	0
Seiple	1	14	14.0	0
Cole	3	11	3.7	0
Mira	6	–9	–1.5	0

RECEIVING

Last Name	No.	Yds	Avg	TD
Warfield	43	996	**23**	**11**
Kiick	40	338	8	0
Twilley	23	349	15	4
Fleming	13	137	11	2
Csonka	13	113	9	1
Noonan	10	180	18	0
Stowe	5	68	14	1
Morris	5	16	3	0
Mandich	3	19	6	1
Seiple	1	32	32	0

PUNT RETURNS

Last Name	No.	Yds	Avg	TD
Scott	33	318	10	0
Anderson	8	114	14	0

KICKOFF RETURNS

Last Name	No.	Yds	Avg	TD
Morris	15	423	28	1
Ginn	10	252	25	0
Leigh	4	99	25	0
Matheson	3	32	11	0

PASSING – PUNTING – KICKING

PASSING	Att	Comp	%	Yds	Yd/Att	TD	Int–	%	RK
Griese	263	145	55	2089	7.9	19	9–	3	1
Mira	30	11	37	158	5.3	1	1–	3	

PUNTING	No	Avg
Seiple	52	40.1

KICKING	XP	Att	%	FG	Att	%
Yepremian	33	33	100	**28**	40	**70**

BALTIMORE COLTS

RUSHING

Last Name	No.	Yds	Avg	TD
Bulaich	152	741	4.9	8
Matte	173	607	3.5	8
Nottingham	95	388	4.1	5
McCauley	58	246	4.2	2
Hinton	4	56	14.0	0
Perkins	5	35	7.0	0
Richardson	2	27	13.5	0
Mackey	3	18	6.0	0
Morrall	6	13	2.2	0
Mitchell	2	9	4.5	0
Unitas	9	5	0.6	0
Pittman	2	3	1.5	0
Nowatzke	1	1	1.0	0

RECEIVING

Last Name	No.	Yds	Avg	TD
Mitchell	33	402	12	0
Matte	29	239	8	0
Hinton	25	436	17	2
Bulaich	25	229	9	2
Perkins	24	424	18	4
Nottingham	15	88	6	0
Mackey	11	143	13	0
Richardson	10	173	17	2
McCauley	3	6	2	0
Havrilak	1	12	12	0

PUNT RETURNS

Last Name	No.	Yds	Avg	TD
Volk	22	118	5	0
Dunlap	8	112	14	0
Kern	3	19	6	0
T. Curtis	7	15	2	0
Logan	1	12	12	0

KICKOFF RETURNS

Last Name	No.	Yds	Avg	TD
Pittman	14	330	24	0
McCauley	8	194	24	0
Duncan	3	102	34	0
Dunlap	1	28	28	0
Logan	1	16	16	0
Stukes	1	8	8	0
Nowatzke	1	1	1	0
T. Curtis	1	0	0	0
Matte	1	0	0	0
Mitchell	1	0	0	0

PASSING – PUNTING – KICKING

PASSING	Att	Comp	%	Yds	Yd/Att	TD	Int–	%	RK
Unitas	176	92	52	942	5.4	3	9–	5	10
Morrall	167	84	50	1210	7.3	7	12–	7	9
Matte	1	0	0	0	0.0	0	0–	0	

PUNTING	No	Avg
Lee	62	41.0

KICKING	XP	Att	%	FG	Att	%
O'Brien	35	36	97	20	29	69

NEW ENGLAND PATRIOTS

RUSHING

Last Name	No.	Yds	Avg	TD
Garrett	181	784	4.3	1
Nance	129	463	3.6	5
Plunkett	45	210	4.7	0
Gladieux	37	175	4.7	0
Maitland	13	25	1.9	1
Crabtree	3	12	4.0	0
Lawson	8	8	1.0	0
Bryant	4	1	0.3	0
Rucker	1	14	14.0	0
Neville	0	–8	0.0	0

RECEIVING

Last Name	No.	Yds	Avg	TD
Vataha	51	872	17	9
Crabtree	23	222	10	3
Garrett	22	265	12	1
Nance	18	95	5	0
Sellers	14	222	16	3
Bryant	14	212	15	1
Beer	12	191	16	3
Moss	9	124	14	1
Gladieux	6	60	10	0
Rucker	4	52	13	1
Sykes	1	15	15	0
Maitland	1	6	6	0

PUNT RETURNS

Last Name	No.	Yds	Avg	TD
Garrett	8	124	16	0
Gardin	6	89	15	0
Bryant	10	24	2	0
Harris	5	19	4	0
Gladieux	4	0	0	0

KICKOFF RETURNS

Last Name	No.	Yds	Avg	TD
Garrett	24	538	22	0
Gardin	14	321	23	0
Bryant	10	252	25	0
Gladieux	6	85	14	0
Lawson	2	47	24	0
Rucker	2	45	23	0
Maitland	2	40	20	0
Mallory	1	19	19	0
Hagen	1	7	7	0
Janik	1	0	0	0
Webb	1	0	0	0

PASSING – PUNTING – KICKING

PASSING	Att	Comp	%	Yds	Yd/Att	TD	Int–	%	RK
Plunkett	328	158	48	2158	6.6	19	16–	5	5
Gladieux	2	1	50	48	24.0	0	0–	0	

PUNTING	No	Avg
Janik	**87**	37.3

KICKING	XP	Att	%	FG	Att	%
Gogolak	28	28	100	12	21	57

NEW YORK JETS

RUSHING

Last Name	No.	Yds	Avg	TD
Riggins	180	769	4.3	1
Boozer	188	618	3.3	5
Davis	18	154	8.6	1
Nock	48	137	2.9	3
McClain	12	108	9.0	2
Harkey	20	62	3.1	0
Woodall	13	26	2.0	0
Caster	2	10	5.0	0
Maynard	1	2	2.0	0
Namath	3	–1	–0.3	0
Lammons	0	3	0.0	0

RECEIVING

Last Name	No.	Yds	Avg	TD
Riggins	36	231	6	2
Caster	26	454	17	6
Maynard	21	408	19	2
Boozer	11	120	11	1
Lammons	8	149	19	1
Nock	6	44	7	2
Bell	5	110	22	1
Harkey	5	28	6	0
Arthur	1	12	12	0

PUNT RETURNS

Last Name	No.	Yds	Avg	TD
Farasopoulos	19	155	8	0
Studdard	4	3	1	0
Hicks	1	0	0	0
Bell	1	–3	–3	0

KICKOFF RETURNS

Last Name	No.	Yds	Avg	TD
Farasopoulos	25	545	22	0
Studdard	15	329	22	0
Wise	8	210	26	0
Nock	5	71	14	0
McClain	1	11	11	0
Harkey	1	2	2	0

PASSING – PUNTING – KICKING

PASSING	Att	Comp	%	Yds	Yd/Att	TD	Int–	%	RK
Davis	121	49	40	624	5.2	10	8–	7	
Woodall	97	42	43	395	4.1	0	2–	2	
Namath	59	28	47	537	9.1	5	6–	10	
O'Neal	1	0	0	0	0.0	0	0–	0	

PUNTING	No	Avg
O'Neal	78	38.8

KICKING	XP	Att	%	FG	Att	%
Howfield	25	26	96	8	19	42
Baker	1	1	100	0	0	0

BUFFALO BILLS

RUSHING

Last Name	No.	Yds	Avg	TD
Simpson	183	742	4.1	5
Patrick	79	332	4.2	1
Braxton	21	84	4.0	0
Shaw	14	82	5.9	0
G. Jones	16	53	3.3	0
Harris	6	42	7.0	0
J. D. Hill	1	2	2.0	0

RECEIVING

Last Name	No.	Yds	Avg	TD
Briscoe	44	603	14	5
Patrick	36	327	9	0
Moses	23	470	20	2
Simpson	21	162	8	0
Braxton	18	141	8	0
G. Jones	16	113	7	1
White	13	130	10	0
J. D. Hill	11	216	20	2
Koy	10	133	13	1
B. Chandler	5	60	12	0
I. Hill	5	55	11	1

PUNT RETURNS

Last Name	No.	Yds	Avg	TD
Wyatt	23	188	8	1
I. Hill	14	133	10	1
Beamer	7	22	3	0

KICKOFF RETURNS

Last Name	No.	Yds	Avg	TD
Wyatt	30	762	25	0
Beamer	20	394	20	0
I. Hill	12	280	23	0
Simpson	4	107	27	0
Braxton	5	90	18	0
G. Jones	1	24	24	0
Kindig	2	16	8	0

PASSING – PUNTING – KICKING

PASSING	Att	Comp	%	Yds	Yd/Att	TD	Int–	%	RK
Shaw	291	149	51	1813	6.2	11	26–	9	11
Harris	103	51	50	512	5.0	1	6–	6	
Braxton	3	1	33	49	16.3	0	0–	0	
Briscoe	2	1	50	36	18.0	0	0–	0	
Simpson	2	0	0	0	0.0	0	0–	0	

PUNTING	No	Avg
S. Jones	72	41.2
Chapple	3	33.7

KICKING	XP	Att	%	FG	Att	%
Leypoldt	12	12	100	9	15	60
Guthrie	8	9	89	3	10	30

1971 A.F.C. — Central Division

CLEVELAND BROWNS 9-5-0 Nick Skorich

Scores of Each Game		
31	HOUSTON	0
14	Baltimore	13
20	OAKLAND	34
27	PITTSBURG	17
27	Cincinnati	24
0	DENVER	27
14	ATLANTA	31
9	Pittsburgh	26
7	Kansas City	13
27	NEW ENGLAND	7
37	Houston	24
31	CINCINNATI	27
21	New Orleans	17
20	Washington	13

Use Name	Pos.	Hgt	Wgt	Age	Int	Pts
Doug Dieken	OT	6'5"	237	22		2
Mitch Johnson	OT	6'4"	250	29		
Bob McKay	OT	6'5"	260	23		
Dick Schrafrath	OT	6'3"	258	35		
Jim Copeland	OG	6'2"	245	26		
John Demarie	OG	6'3"	255	26		
Gene Hickerson	OG	6'3"	248	36		
Mike Sikich	OG	6'2"	243	22		
Fred Hoaglin	C	6'4"	250	27		
Jack Gregory	DE	6'6"	250	26		
Joe Jones	DE	6'6'	246	23		
Bob Briggs	DT-DE	6'4"	276	26		
Walter Johnson	DT	6'3"	275	28		6
Jerry Sherk	DT	6'4"	253	23	2	
Ron Snidow	DT	6'4"	250	29		

Use Name	Pos.	Hgt	Wgt	Age	Int	Pts
Billy Andrews	LB	6'	225	26	3	
John Garlington	LB	6'1"	225	25	1	
Charlie Hall	LB	6'3"	215	22		
Jim Houston	LB	6'2"	240	34		
Rick Kingrea	LB	6'1"	233	22		
Dale Lindsey	LB	6'3"	225	28	2	
Erich Barnes	DB	6'2"	212	36		
Ben Davis	DB	5'11"	186	26	2	
Mike Howell	DB	6'1"	190	28	2	
Ernie Kellerman	DB	6'	185	27	3	
Clarence Scott	DB	6'	175	22	4	
Freddie Summers	DB	6'1"	180	24		
Walt Sumner	DB	6'1"	180	24	5	

Use Name	Pos.	Hgt	Wgt	Age	Int	Pts
Bill Nelson	QB	6'	195	30		
Mike Phipps	QB	6'2"	207	23		
Ken Brown	HB	5'10"	205	25		
Leroy Kelly	HB	6'	200	29		72
Reece Morrison	HB	6'	205	25		
Bo Scott	FB	6'3"	210	28		60
Bo Cornell	FB	6'1"	217	22		
Stan Brown	WR	5'9"	184	22		
Gary Collins	WR	6'4"	210	30		18
Fair Hooker	WR	6'1"	193	24		6
Dave Jones	WR	6'2"	185	24		
Frank Pitts	WR	6'2"	200	27		24
Chip Glass	TE	6'4"	236	24		6
Milt Morin	TE	6'4"	240	29		12
Don Cockroft	K	6'1"	190	26		79

PITTSBURGH STEELERS 6-8-0 Chuck Noll

Scores of Each Game		
15	Chicago	17
21	CINCINNATI	10
21	SAN DIEGO	17
17	Cleveland	27
16	Kansas Ctiy	38
23	HOUSTON	16
21	Baltimore	34
26	CLEVELAND	9
21	Miami	24
17	N.Y. GIANTS	13
10	DENVER	22
3	Houston	29
21	Cincinnati	13
14	LOS ANGELES	23

Use Name	Pos.	Hgt	Wgt	Age	Int	Pts
John Brown	OT	6'2"	255	32		
Rick Sharp	OT	6'3"	265	23		
Jon Kolb	C-OT	6'2"	262	24		
Sam Davis	OG	6'1"	255	27		
Mel Holmes	OG	6'3"	250	21		
Gerry Mullins	OG	6'3"	235	22		
Bruce Van Dyke	OG	6'2"	255	27		
Jim Clack	C	6'3"	250	23		
Ray Mansfield	C	6'3"	255	30		
Bobby Maples	C	6'3"	245	28		
Bert Askon	DE	6'3"	220	25		
L.C. Greenwood	DE	6'5"	240	24		
Dwight Write	DE	6'4"	250	22		
Ben McGee	DT-DE	6'2"	260	29		
Joe Greene	DT	6'4"	280	24		
Lloyd Voss	DT	6'4"	255	29		

Use Name	Pos.	Hgt	Wgt	Age	Int	Pts
Chuck Allen	LB	6'1"	227	31	3	
Henry Davis	LB	6'3"	235	28		
Jack Ham	LB	6'3"	220	22	2	
Andy Russell	LB	6'3"	225	29		
Brian Stenger	LB	6'4"	230	24		
Ralph Anderson	DB	6'2"	180	22	1	
Ocie Austin	DB	6'3"	200	24		
Chuck Beatty	DB	6'2"	200	25		
Mel Blount	DB	6'3"	205	23	2	
Lee Calland	DB	6'	190	30	2	
Glen Edwards	DB	6'	185	24	1	
John Rowser	DB	6'1"	185	27	4	6
Mike Wagner	DB	6'1"	196	22	2	

Clarence Washington—Injury

Use Name	Pos.	Hgt	Wgt	Age	Int	Pts
Terry Bradshaw	QB	6'3"	218	22		30
Terry Hanratty	QB	6'1"	210	23		6
Bob Leahy	QB	6'2"	205	25		
Rocky Bleier	HB	5'11"	205	25		
Jim Brumfield	HB	6'1"	195	24		
Preston Pearson	HB	6'1"	190	26		18
John Fuqua	FB-HB	5'11"	200	24		30
Warren Bankston	FB	6'4"	230	24		
Frank Lewis	WR	6'1"	196	24		
Ron Shanklin	WR	6'1"	180	24		36
Dave Smith	WR	6'2"	205	24		30
Jon Staggers	WR	5'10"	186	22		6
Al Young	WR	6'1"	195	22		
Bob Adams	TE	6'2"	225	25		
Larry Brown	TE	6'4"	225	22		6
Dennis Hughes	TE	6'1"	220	23		
Roy Gerela	K	5'10"	185	23		78
Bobby Walden	K	6'	190	32		

HOUSTON OILERS 4-9-1 Ed Hughes

Scores of Each Game		
0	Cleveland	31
16	KANSAS CITY	20
13	NEW ORLEANS	13
13	Washington	22
7	DETROIT	31
16	Pittsburgh	23
10	CINCINNATI	6
20	New England	28
21	Oakland	41
13	Cincinnati	28
24	CLEVELAND	37
29	PITTSBURGH	3
20	Buffalo	14
49	SAN DIEGO	33

Use Name	Pos.	Hgt	Wgt	Age	Int	Pts
Tom Funchess	OT	6'5"	260	26		
Sam Walton	OT	6'5"	270	28		
Gene Ferguson	OT	6'7"	300	23		
Walt Suggs	C-OT	6'5"	250	32		
Elbert Drungo	OG	6'5"	250	28		
Tom Regner	OG	6'1"	255	27		
Ron Saul	OG	6'2"	255	23		
Bob Young	OG	6'2"	256	28		
Jerry Sturm	C	6'3"	265	34		
Allen Aldridge	DE	6'6"	260	26		
Elvin Bethea	DE	6'3"	262	25		
Pat Holmes	DE	6'5"	250	31		
Scott Lewis	DE	6'6"	260	21		
Ron Billingsley	DT	6'8"	290	26		
Lee Brooks	DT	6'5"	266	23	1	
Tom Domres (to DEN)	DT	6'3"	260	24		
Mike Tilleman	DT	6'5"	280	27		

Use Name	Pos.	Hgt	Wgt	Age	Int	Pts
Garland Boyette	LB	6'1"	235	31		6
Phil Croyle	LB	6'3"	220	23		
Dave Olerich	LB	6'1"	225	26		
Ron Pritchard	LB	6'1"	235	24		
George Webster	LB	6'4"	223	25		
Willie Alexander	DB	6'2"	195	22	4	
Bob Atkins	DB	6'3"	210	25	1	6
John Charles	DB	6'1"	200	27	5	
Ken Houston	DB	6'3"	196	26	9	30
Leroy Howard	DB	5'11"	175	22		
Benny Johnson	DB	5'11"	178	23		
Zeke Moore	DB	6'2"	196	27	3	

Roy Hopkins – Injury

Use Name	Pos.	Hgt	Wgt	Age	Int	Pts
Lynn Dickey	QB	6'4"	218	21		
Charley Johnson	QB	6'	190	34		
Dan Pastorini	QB	6'3"	220	22		18
Woody Campbell	HB	5'11"	208	26		6
Andy Hopkins	HB	5'10"	187	22		
Dickie Post (from DEN)	HB	5'9"	190	25		6
Mike Richardson	HB	5'11"	196	24		
Ward Walsh	HB	6'	215	22		6
Robert Holmes (from KC)	FB	5'9"	220	25		24
Leroy Sledge	FB	6'2"	230	25		6
Joe Dawkins (to DEN)	HB-FB	5'11"	222	23		12
Jim Beirne	WR	6'2"	196	24		6
Ken Burrough	WR	6'4"	210	23		6
Linzy Cole	WR	5'11"	170	23		
Mac Haik	WR	6'1"	195	25		
Charlie Joiner	WR	5'11"	188	23		42
Alvin Reed	TE	6'5"	230	27		6
Floyd Rice	TE	6'3"	220	22		
Braden Beck	K	6'2"	200	27		4
Mark Moseley	K	5'11"	182	23		73

CINCINNATI BENGALS 4-10-0 Paul Brown

Scores of Each Game		
37	PHILADELPHIA	14
10	Pittsburgh	21
17	Green Bay	20
13	MIAMI	23
24	CLEVELAND	27
27	Oakland	31
6	Houston	10
6	ATLANTA	9
24	Denver	10
28	HOUSTON	13
31	SAN DIEGO	0
27	Cleveland	31
13	PITTSBURGH	21
21	N.Y. JETS	35

Use Name	Pos.	Hgt	Wgt	Age	Int	Pts
Howard Fest	OT	6'6"	268	25		
Vern Holland	OT	6'5"	270	23		
Rufus Mayes	OT	6'5"	255	23		
Ernie Wright	OT	6'4"	270	31		
Guy Dennis	OG	6'2"	255	24		
Steve Lawson	OG	6'3"	265	22		
Pat Matson	OG	6'1"	245	27		
Bob Johnson	C	6'5"	265	25		
Royce Berry	DE	6'3"	248	25		
Ron Carpenter	DE	6'4"	260	23		
Ken Johnson	DE	6'5"	262	23		
Nick Roman	DE	6'3"	230	23		
Steve Chomyszak	DT	6'5"	265	26		
Willie Jones	DT	6'2"	260	29		
Mike Reid	DT	6'3"	258	24		

Use Name	Pos.	Hgt	Wgt	Age	Int	Pts
Doug Adams	LB	6'	223	22		
Ken Avery	LB	6'1"	225	27		
Al Beauchamp	LB	6'2"	236	27	6	6
Bill Bergey	LB	6'2"	240	26	1	
Larry Ely	LB	6'1"	230	23		
Bill Peterson	LB	6'3"	230	26	1	
Al Coleman	DB	6'1"	183	26	1	
Neal Craig	DB	6'1"	185	23	1	
Sandy Durko	DB	6'1"	185	23	4	
Ken Dyer	DB	6'3"	190	25		
Jim Harris	DB	5'11"	173	25		
Lemar Parrish	DB	5'11"	185	23	7	12
Ken Riley	DB	6'	184	24	5	
Fletcher Smith	DB	6'2"	180	27	1	

Greg Cook—Shoulder Injury

Use Name	Pos.	Hgt	Wgt	Age	Int	Pts
Ken Anderson	QB	6'1"	202	22		6
Virgil Carter	QB	6'1"	200	25		1
Dave Lewis	QB	6'2"	210	25		
Essex Johnson	HB	5'9"	195	24		36
Paul Robinson	HB	6'	200	26		6
Jess Phillips	HB	6'1"	210	24		6
Doug Dressler	FB	6'3"	220	23		6
Ron Lamb	FB	6'2"	230	27		
Fred Willis	FB	6'	215	23		42
Mike Haffner	WR	6'2"	205	29		
Ed Marshall	WR	6'5"	200	23		
Chip Myers	WR	6'4"	200	26		6
Speedy Thomas	WR	6'1"	178	24		12
Bruce Coslet	TE	6'3"	230	25		24
Mike Kelley	TE	6'4"	215	23		
Bob Trumpy	TE	6'6"	225	26		18
Horst Muhlmann	K	6'1"	210	31		91

CLEVELAND BROWNS

RUSHING

Last Name	No.	Yds	Avg	TD
Kelley	234	865	3.7	10
B. Scott	179	606	3.4	9
K. Brown	11	47	4.3	0
Phipps	6	35	5.8	0
Cornell	11	12	1.1	0
Cockroft	1	12	12.0	0
Morin	1	1	1.0	0
Morrison	5	−2	−0.4	0
Nelsen	13	−18	−1.4	0

RECEIVING

Last Name	No.	Yds	Avg	TD
Hooker	45	649	14	1
Morin	40	581	15	2
B. Scott	30	233	8	1
Pitts	27	487	18	4
Kelly	25	252	10	2
Collins	15	231	15	3
D. Jones	4	66	17	0
Cornell	1	18	18	0
Glass	1	4	4	1

PUNT RETURNS

Last Name	No.	Yds	Avg	TD
Kelly	30	292	10	0
D. Jones	9	63	7	0
Kellerman	1	4	4	0

KICKOFF RETURNS

Last Name	No.	Yds	Avg	TD
K. Brown	15	330	22	0
Morrison	9	267	30	0
Pitts	9	238	26	0
S. Brown	7	157	22	0
Houston	1	21	21	0
Cornell	1	19	19	0
Dieken	1	16	16	0
Kelly	1	11	11	0
Kellerman	1	5	5	0
Glass	1	1	1	0

PASSING – PUNTING – KICKING

PASSING	Att	Comp	%	Yds	Yd/Att	TD	Int–	%	RK
Nelsen	325	174	54	2319	7.1	13	23–	7	5
Phipps	47	13	28	179	3.8	1	4	9	
Kelly	4	1	25	23	5.8	0	0–	0	

PUNTING	No	Avg
Cockroft	62	40.5
Collins	5	32.4

KICKING	XP	Att	%	FG	Att	%
Cockroft	34	34	100	15	28	54

PITTSBURGH STEELERS

RUSHING

Last Name	No.	Yds	Avg	TD
Fuqua	155	625	4.0	4
Pearson	131	605	4.6	0
Bankston	70	274	3.9	0
Bradshaw	53	247	4.7	5
Walden	1	14	14.0	0
Staggers	1	5	5.0	0
Hanratty	1	3	3.0	1
Shanklin	2	1	0.5	0
Leahy	1	−6	−6.0	0
Smith	1	−10	−10.0	0

RECEIVING

Last Name	No.	Yds	Avg	TD
Shanklin	49	652	13	6
Fuqua	49	427	9	1
Smith	47	663	14	5
Pearson	20	246	12	2
Adams	20	160	8	0
Bankston	17	148	9	0
Staggers	8	103	13	0
Lewis	3	44	15	0
L. Brown	1	3	3	1

PUNT RETURNS

Last Name	No.	Yds	Avg	TD
Staggers	31	262	8	1
Wagner	2	2	1	0
Edwards	1	0	0	0
Fuqua	1	0	0	0

KICKOFF RETURNS

Last Name	No.	Yds	Avg	TD
Brumfield	12	271	23	0
Staggers	10	261	26	0
Pearson	7	205	29	0
Edwards	9	198	22	0
Bankston	5	76	15	0
Blount	4	76	19	0
Bleier	1	21	21	0
Clack	1	12	12	0

PASSING – PUNTING – KICKING

PASSING	Att	Comp	%	Yds	Yd/Att	TD	Int–	%	RK
Bradshaw	373	203	54	2259	6.1	13	22–	6	8
Hanratty	29	7	24	159	5.5	2	3–	10	
Leahy	11	3	27	18	1.6	0	1–	9	
Walden	1	1	100	10	10.0	0	0–	0	

PUNTING	No	Avg
Walden	79	43.7

KICKING	XP	Att	%	FG	Att	%
Gerela	27	27	100	17	27	63

HOUSTON OILERS

RUSHING

Last Name	No.	Yds	Avg	TD
R. Holmes	112	323	2.9	4
Campbell	96	259	2.7	1
Pastorini	26	140	5.4	3
Dawkins	42	135	3.2	2
Walsh	38	129	3.4	0
Post	40	86	2.2	0
Sledge	24	74	3.1	0
Richardson	17	33	1.9	0
Dickey	1	4	4.0	0
Hopkins	2	2	1.0	0
C. Johnson	2	0	0.0	0

RECEIVING

Last Name	No.	Yds	Avg	TD
Beirne	38	550	14	1
Joiner	31	681	22	7
Reed	25	408	16	1
Burrough	25	370	15	1
Campbell	20	179	9	0
R. Holmes	19	154	8	0
Post	9	112	12	1
Dawkins	9	53	6	0
Walsh	6	36	6	1
Sledge	6	32	5	1
Richardson	4	17	4	0

PUNT RETURNS

Last Name	No.	Yds	Avg	TD
Cole	14	107	8	0
Houston	16	91	6	0
Rice	2	0	0	0

KICKOFF RETURNS

Last Name	No.	Yds	Avg	TD
Cole	32	834	26	0
R. Holmes	12	300	25	0
Moore	10	214	21	0
Burrough	8	157	20	0
Post	5	116	23	0
Dawkins	2	34	17	0
Richardson	1	26	26	0
Joiner	1	25	25	0
Walsh	1	24	24	0
Rice	1	0	0	0

PASSING – PUNTING – KICKING

PASSING	Att	Comp	%	Yds	Yd/Att	TD	Int–	%	RK
Pastorini	270	127	47	1702	6.3	7	21–	8	12
C. Johnson	94	46	49	592	6.3	3	7–	7	
Dickey	57	19	33	315	5.5	0	9–	16	
Campbell	2	2	100	34	17.0	2	0–	0	

PUNTING	No	Avg
Pastorini	75	40.6

KICKING	XP	Att	%	FG	Att	%
Moseley	25	27	93	16	26	62
Beck	1	2	50	1	2	50

CINCINNATI BENGALS

RUSHING

Last Name	No.	Yds	Avg	TD
Willis	135	590	4.4	7
E. Johnson	85	522	6.1	4
Phillips	94	420	4.5	0
Robinson	49	213	4.3	1
Dressler	54	204	3.8	1
Anderson	22	125	5.7	1
Carter	8	42	5.3	0
Lamb	5	13	2.6	0
Durko	1	7	7.0	0
Lewis	6	6	1.0	0
Thomas	2	−1	−0.5	0

RECEIVING

Last Name	No.	Yds	Avg	TD
Trumpy	40	531	13	3
Myers	27	286	11	1
Willis	24	223	9	0
Thomas	22	327	15	2
Phillips	22	125	6	1
Coslet	21	356	17	4
Dressler	19	145	8	0
E. Johnson	14	258	18	2
Robinson	8	47	6	0
Marshall	2	18	9	0
Kelly	1	9	9	0

PUNT RETURNS

Last Name	No.	Yds	Avg	TD
Parrish	12	93	8	0
E. Johnson	3	28	9	0
Durko	6	14	2	0
Thomas	4	10	3	0

KICKOFF RETURNS

Last Name	No.	Yds	Avg	TD
Robinson	18	335	19	0
Parrish	13	296	23	0
Willis	4	81	20	0
Phillips	2	49	25	0
Lamb	2	42	21	0
E. Johnson	2	40	20	0
Dressler	1	20	20	0
Kelly	1	0	0	0

PASSING – PUNTING – KICKING

PASSING	Att	Comp	%	Yds	Yd/Att	TD	Int–	%	RK
Carter	222	138	62	1624	7.3	10	7–	3	3
Anderson	131	72	55	777	5.9	5	4–	3	
Lewis	10	3	30	18	1.8	0	0–	0	
Willis	2	1	50	8	4.0	0	0–	0	

PUNTING	No	Avg
Lewis	72	44.8
Dressler	1	34.0

KICKING	XP	Att	%	FG	Att	%
Muhlmann	31	31	100	20	36	56
Carter	1	1	100	0	0	0

KANSAS CITY CHIEFS 10-3-1 Hank Stram

Scores of Each Game		
14	San Diego	21
20	Houston	16
16	Denver	3
31	SAN DIEGO	10
38	PITTSBURGH	16
27	WASHINGTON	20
20	Oakland	20
10	N.Y. Jets	13
13	CLEVELAND	7
28	DENVER	10
21	Detroit	32
26	San Francisco	17
16	OAKLAND	14
22	BUFFALO	9

Use Name	Pos.	Hgt	Wgt	Age	Int	Pts
Dave Hill	OT	6'5"	260	30		
Sid Smith	OT	6'4"	260	23		
Jim Tyrer	OT	6'6"	270	32		
Ed Budde	OG	6'5"	260	30		
George Daney	OG	6'3"	240	24		
Mo Moorman	OG	6'5"	252	27		
Mike Oriard	C	6'4"	223	23		
Jack Rudnay	C	6'3"	240	[illegible]		
Bruce Bergey	DE	6'4"	240	24		
Aaron Brown	DE	6'5"	265	27	1	6
Marv Upshaw	DE	6'3"	245	24		
Buck Buchanan	DT	6'7"	275	31	1	
Curley Culp	DT	6'1"	265	25		
Ed Lothamer	DT	6'5"	270	28		
Wilbur Young	DT	6'6"	305	22	1	

Use Name	Pos.	Hgt	Wgt	Age	Int	Pts
Bobby Bell	LB	6'4"	228	31	1	6
Willie Lanier	LB	6'1"	245	26	2	
Jim Lynch	LB	6'1"	235	26	1	
Bob Stein	DE-LB	6'2"	235	23	1	
Nate Allen	DB	5'10"	170	23		
Caesar Belser	DB	6'	212	26		
Dave Hadley	DB	5'9"	186	22	1	
Jim Kearney	DB	6'2"	206	28	3	
Jim Marsalis	DB	5'11"	194	25	3	
Kerry Reardon	DB	5'11"	180	22		
Johnny Robinson	DB	6'	205	32	4	
Mike Sensibaugh	DB	5'11"	192	22		
Emmitt Thomas	DB	6'2"	192	28	8	6

Clyde Werner—Knee Injury

Use Name	Pos.	Hgt	Wgt	Age	Int	Pts
Len Dawson	QB	6'	190	37		
John Huarte	QB	6'	185	27		
Mike Livingston	QB	6'3"	212	25		
Mike Adamle	HB	5'9"	197	21		6
Warren McVea	HB	5'10"	182	25		18
Ed Podolak	HB	6'1"	202	24		54
Glenn Ellison	HB-FB	6'1"	215	22		
Wendell Hayes	FB	6'2"	220	30		12
Jim Otis	WR	6'	220	23		12
Dennis Homan	WR	6'1"	180	25		
Bruce Jankowski	WR	5'11"	185	22		
Otis Taylor	WR	6'2"	215	28		48
Elmo Wright	WR	6'	190	22		18
Willie Frazier (from HOU)	TE	6'4"	250	28		
Morris Stroud	TE	6'10"	255	25		6
Jan Stenerud	K	6'2"	187	28		110
Jerrel Wilson	K	6'4"	222	30		

OAKLAND RAIDERS 8-4-2 John Madden

Scores of Each Game		
6	New England	20
34	San Diego	0
34	Cleveland	20
27	Denver	16
34	PHILADELPHIA	10
31	CINCINNATI	27
20	KANSAS CITY	20
21	New Orleans	21
41	HOUSTON	21
34	SAN DIEGO	33
14	BALTIMORE	37
13	Atlanta	24
14	Kansas City	16
21	DENVER	13

Use Name	Pos.	Hgt	Wgt	Age	Int	Pts
Bob Brown	OT	6'4"	290	28		
Ron Mix	OT	6'4"	250	33		
Art Shell	OT	6'5"	255	24		
Paul Seiler	C-OT	6'4"	260	25		
George Buehler	OG	6'2"	260	24		
Jim Harvey	OG	6'5"	250	28		
Gene Upshaw	OG	6'5"	255	26		
Warren Koegel	C	6'3"	250	21		
Jim Otto	C	6'2"	248	33		
Tony Cline	DE	6'2"	230	31		
Ben Davidson	DE	6'8"	280	31		
Horace Jones	DE	6'3"	240	22		
Harold Rice	DE	6'2"	230	26		
Tom Gibson	DT	6'6"	290	23		
Tom Keating	DT	6'3"	247	28		
Carleton Oats	DT	6'2"	260	28		
Art Thomas	DT	6'5"	250	24		

Use Name	Pos.	Hgt	Wgt	Age	Int	Pts
Duane Benson	LB	6'2"	215	26		
Dan Conners	LB	6'1"	230	29	3	
Gerald Irons	LB	6'2"	230	24		
Terry Mendenhall	LB	6'1"	210	22		
Gus Otto	LB	6'2"	220	28		
Greg Slough	LB	6'3"	230	23		
Phil Villapiano	LB	6'1"	210	22	2	
Carl Weathers	LB	6'2"	220	23		
Butch Atkinson	DB	6'	180	24	4	6
Willie Brown	DB	6'1"	190	30	2	
Tommy Maxwell	DB	6'2"	195	24		
Jack Tatum	DB	5'10"	200	22	4	
Jimmy Warren	DB	5'11"	175	32	2	12
Nemiah Wilson	DB	6'	160	28	5	

Hewitt Dixon – Injury
Warren Wells – Legal probation – ineligible to play pro football.

Use Name	Pos.	Hgt	Wgt	Age	Int	Pts
George Blanda	QB	6'1"	215	43		86
Daryle Lamonica	QB	6'2"	215	30		
Ken Stabler	QB	6'3"	194	25		12
Clarence Davis	HB	5'10"	190	22		12
Don Highsmith	HB	6'	200	23		6
Charlie Smith	HB	6'1"	205	25		6
Pete Banaszak	FB-HB	5'11"	210	27		48
Bill Enyart	FB	6'4"	235	24		
Marv Hubbard	FB	6'1"	215	25		36
Fred Biletnikoff	WR	6'1"	190	28		54
Drew Buie	WR	6'2"	178	24		12
Eldridge Dickey	WR	6'2"	198	25		6
Rod Sherman	WR	6'	190	26		6
Ray Chester	TE	6'3"	220	23		42
Bob Moore	TE	6'3"	220	22		
Jerry DePoyster	K	6'1"	205	25		
Mike Eischeid	K	6'	190	30		

SAN DIEGO CHARGERS 6-8-0 Sid Gillman Harland Svare

Scores of Each Game		
21	KANSAS CITY	14
0	OAKLAND	34
17	Pittsburg	21
10	Kansas City	31
16	Denver	20
20	BUFFALO	3
49	N.Y. JETS	21
17	N.Y. Giants	35
20	St. LOUIS	17
33	Oakland	34
0	Cincinnati	31
30	MINNESOTA	14
45	DENVER	17
33	Houston	49

Use Name	Pos.	Hgt	Wgt	Age	Int	Pts
Terry Owens	OT	6'6"	275	27		
Russ Washington	OT	6'6"	295	24		
Ira Gordon	OG-OT	6'3"	268	23		
Harris Jones	OG	6'4"	233	26		
Walt Sweeney	OG	6'3"	256	30		
Doug Wilkerson	OG	6'2"	245	24		
Sam Gruneisen	C	6'1"	250	30		
Carl Mauck	C	6'3"	234	24		
Jack Porter	C	6'4"	255	23		
West Grant (from BUF)	DE	6'3"	245	24		
Jeff Staggs	DE	6'2"	246	27		
Lee Thomas	DE	6'5"	246	24		
Steve DeLong	DT-DE	6'3"	252	28		
Ron East	DT	6'4"	242	28		
Kevin Hardy	DT	6'5"	260	26		
Andy Rice	DT	6'3"	268	29		
Gary Nowak	DT	6'5"	247	22		
Tom Williams	DT	6'4"	250	23		

Use Name	Pos.	Hgt	Wgt	Age	Int	Pts
Bob Babich	LB	6'2"	230	24		6
Pete Barnes	LB	6'3"	247	26	2	6
Bob Bruggers	LB	6'1"	224	27		
Rick Redman	LB	5'11"	230	28	1	
Mel Rogers	LB	6'2"	230	23		
John Tanner	LB	6'4"	222	26		
Ray White	LB	6'1"	225	21		2
Joe Beauchamp	DB	6'	185	27	4	
Chuck Detwiler	DB	6'	185	24		
Chris Fletcher	DB	5'11"	185	22	3	6
Jim Hill	DB	6'2"	190	24	2	
Bob Howard	DB	6'1"	190	26	4	
Bryant Salter	DB	6'4"	200	21	6	
Jim Tolbert	DB	6'3"	207	27		

Rick Eber—Injury

Use Name	Pos.	Hgt	Wgt	Age	Int	Pts
Marty Domres	QB	6'3"	215	24		
John Hadl	QB	6'2"	218	31		6
Mike Garrett	HB	5'9"	200	27		42
Mike Montgomery	HB	6'2"	202	22		18
Leon Burns	FB	6'2"	223	26		6
Jeff Queen	FB	6'1"	220	25		42
Eddie Ray	FB	6'1"	230	24		
Chuck Dicus	WR	6'	172	22		6
Gary Garrison	WR	6'1"	193	27		36
Walker Gillette	WR	6'5"	198	24		12
Jerry LeVias	WR	5'10"	178	24		6
Billy Parks	WR	6'1"	185	23		24
Pettis Norman	TE	6'3"	220	31		6
Art Strozier	TE	6'2"	220	25		
Dennis Partee	K	6'2"	218	25		87

DENVER BRONCOS 4-9-1 Lou Saban Jerry Smith

Scores of Each Game		
10	MIAMI	10
13	Green Bay	34
3	KANSAS CITY	16
16	OAKLAND	27
20	SAN DIEGO	16
27	Cleveland	0
16	Philadelphia	17
20	DETROIT	24
10	CINCINNATI	24
10	Kansas City	28
22	Pittsburg	10
6	CHICAGO	3
17	San Diego	45
13	Oakland	21

Use Name	Pos.	Hgt	Wgt	Age	Int	Pts
Sam Brunelli	OT	6'1"	270	28		
Mike Current	OT	6'4"	274	25		
Marv Montgomery	OT	6'6"	255	23		
Roger Shoals	OT	6'4"	260	32		
George Goeddeke	OG	6'3"	253	26		
Mike Schitkner	OG	6'3"	245	24		
Larron Jackson	OT-OG	6'3"	270	22		
Jay Bachman	C	6'3"	250	25		
Larry Kaminski	C	6'2"	245	26		
Tommy Lyons	C	6'2"	228	23		
Lyle Alzado	DE	6'3"	252	22		
Walt Barnes	DE	6'3"	250	27		
Rich Jackson	DE	6'2"	255	30		
Dave Costa	DT	6'2"	260	29		
Jerry Inman	DT	6'3"	256	31		
Paul Smith	DT	6'3"	256	26		

Use Name	Pos.	Hgt	Wgt	Age	Int	Pts
Carter Campbell	LB	6'3"	232	23		
Ken Criter	LB	5'11"	223	24		
Fred Forsberg	LB	6'1"	235	27	3	6
Bill McKoy	LB	6'3"	235	23		
Chip Myrtle	LB	6'2"	225	26	3	
Olen Underwood	LB	6'1"	220	29	1	
Dave Washington	LB	6'5"	215	23	1	
Butch Byrd	DB	6'	196	29		
Cornell Gordon	DB	6'	187	30	2	
Charlie Greer	DB	6'	205	25	3	
Leroy Mitchell	DB	6'2"	190	26	2	
Randy Montgomery	DB	5'11"	182	24		
George Saimes	DB	5'10"	183	29		
Bill Thompson	DB	6'1"	200	24	5	

Tom Buckman – Injury
Pete Duranko – Injury

Use Name	Pos.	Hgt	Wgt	Age	Int	Pts
Don Horn	QB	6'2"	195	26		
Steve Ramsey	QB	6'2"	210	23		
Floyd Little	HB	5'10"	196	29		36
Fran Lynch	FB-HB	6'1"	205	25		8
Clem Turner	FB	6'1"	236	26		6
Bobby Anderson	HB-FB	6'	208	23		24
Gordon Bowdell	WR	6'2"	203	22		
Jack Gehrke	WR	6'	178	25		
Dwight Harrison	WR	6'1"	178	22		12
Jerry Simmons	WR	6'1"	190	28		6
Bill Van Huesen	WR	6'1"	200	25		
Bill Masters	TE	6'5"	240	27		6
John Mosier	TE	6'3"	220	23		
Jim Whalen (to PHI)	TE	6'2"	210	27		
Jim Turner	K	6'2"	205	30		93

John Embree—Injury

KANSAS CITY CHIEFS

RUSHING

Last Name	No.	Yds	Avg	TD
Podolak	184	708	3.8	9
Hayes	132	537	4.1	1
McVea	68	288	4.2	3
Otis	49	184	3.8	0
Adamle	13	43	3.3	0
Taylor	1	25	25.0	1
Dawson	12	24	2.0	0
Livingston	5	11	2.2	0
Frazier	1	−2	−2.0	0
Wright	1	−10	−10.0	0

RECEIVING

Last Name	No.	Yds	Avg	TD
Taylor	57	**1110**	19	7
Podolak	36	252	7	0
Wright	26	528	20	3
Stroud	22	454	21	1
Hayes	16	150	9	1
Otis	13	81	6	2
Frazier	10	154	15	0
McVea	5	−3	−1	0
Homan	2	47	24	0
Smith	1	12	12	0
Adamle	1	6	6	1

PUNT RETURNS

Last Name	No.	Yds	Avg	TD
Podolak	14	84	6	0
Homan	10	61	6	0
Reardon	3	5	2	0
Belser	1	2	2	0
Sensibaugh	5	−2	0	0

KICKOFF RETURNS

Last Name	No.	Yds	Avg	TD
Reardon	12	308	26	0
McVea	9	177	20	0
Adamle	7	149	21	0
Hayes	4	75	19	0
Sensibaugh	4	71	18	0
Podolak	3	65	22	0
Bergey	1	15	15	0

PASSING – PUNTING – KICKING

PASSING	Att	Comp	%	Yds	Yd/Att	TD	Int–	%	RK
Dawson	301	167	55	2504	**8.3**	15	13–	4	2
Livingston	28	12	43	130	4.6	0	0–	0	
Huarte	6	2	33	18	3.0	0	0–	0	
Podolak	2	2	100	42	21.0	0	0–	0	

PUNTING	No	Avg
Wilson	64	44.8

KICKING	XP	Att	%	FG	Att	%
Stenerud	32	32	100	26	**44**	59
Stein	0	0	0	0	1	0

OAKLAND RAIDERS

RUSHING

Last Name	No.	Yds	Avg	TD
Hubbard	181	867	4.8	5
Banaszak	137	563	4.1	8
Davis	54	321	5.9	2
Highsmith	76	307	4.0	1
Buie	2	32	16.0	0
Stabler	4	29	7.3	2
Lamonica	4	16	4.0	0
Chester	3	5	1.7	0
Smith	11	4	0.4	1
DePoyster	1	−14	−14.0	0

RECEIVING

Last Name	No.	Yds	Avg	TD
Biletnikoff	**61**	929	15	9
Chester	28	442	16	7
Hubbard	22	167	8	1
Davis	15	97	6	0
Banaszak	13	128	10	0
Sherman	12	187	16	1
Highsmith	10	109	11	0
Buie	5	133	27	2
Dickey	4	78	20	1
Smith	2	67	34	0
Moore	2	26	13	0

PUNT RETURNS

Last Name	No.	Yds	Avg	TD
Atkinson	20	159	8	0
Maxwell	6	21	4	0
Sherman	2	2	1	0
Highsmith	1	0	0	0

KICKOFF RETURNS

Last Name	No.	Yds	Avg	TD
Davis	27	734	27	0
Highsmith	21	454	22	0
Hubbard	3	46	15	0
Banaszak	1	0	0	0
Seiler	1	0	0	0
Smith	1	0	0	0

PASSING – PUNTING – KICKING

PASSING	Att	Comp	%	Yds	Yd/Att	TD	Int–	%	RK
Lamonica	242	118	49	1717	7.1	16	16–	7	7
Blanda	58	32	55	378	6.5	4	6–	10	
Stabler	48	24	50	268	5.6	1	4	8	

PUNTING	No	Avg
DePoyster	51	39.5
Eischeid	11	41.9

KICKING	XP	Att	%	FG	Att	%
Blanda	**41**	**42**	98	15	22	68

SAN DIEGO CHARGERS

RUSHING

Last Name	No.	Yds	Avg	TD
Garrett	140	591	4.2	4
Queen	95	318	3.3	4
Montgomery	60	226	3.8	1
Burns	61	223	3.7	1
Parks	5	77	15.4	0
Hadl	18	75	4.2	1
LeVias	4	73	18.3	0
Ray	2	15	7.5	0
Partee	1	7	7.0	0
Norman	1	1	1.0	0
Domres	1	0	0.0	0
Garrison	1	0	0.0	0
Dicus	1	−2	−2.0	0

RECEIVING

Last Name	No.	Yds	Avg	TD
Garrison	42	889	21	6
Parks	41	609	15	4
Garrett	41	283	7	3
Montgomery	28	361	13	2
Norman	27	358	13	1
Queen	23	270	12	3
LeVias	21	265	13	1
Gillette	10	147	15	2
Dicus	6	89	15	1
Burns	3	22	7	0
Strozier	1	6	6	0
Tanner	1	6	6	0

PUNT RETURNS

Last Name	No.	Yds	Avg	TD
LeVias	22	145	7	0
Fletcher	12	68	6	0
Garrett	3	2	1	0

KICKOFF RETURNS

Last Name	No.	Yds	Avg	TD
LeVias	24	559	23	0
Fletcher	11	217	20	0
Salter	8	172	22	0
Rogers	1	20	20	0
Burns	2	19	10	0
Sweeney	1	13	13	0
Thomas	1	0	0	0
Wilkerson	1	0	0	0

PASSING – PUNTING – KICKING

PASSING	Att	Comp	%	Yds	Yd/Att	TD	Int–	%	RK
Hadl	**431**	**233**	54	**3075**	7.1	**21**	25–	6	4
Domres	12	7	58	97	8.1	1	3–	25	
Montgomery	6	3	50	80	13.3	1	0–	0	
Garrett	1	1	100	53	53.0	0	0–	0	

PUNTING	No	Avg
Partee	55	43.5

KICKING	XP	Att	%	FG	Att	%
Partee	36	37	97	17	29	59

DENVER BRONCOS

RUSHING

Last Name	No.	Yds	Avg	TD
Little	**284**	**1133**	4.0	6
Anderson	139	533	3.8	3
Lynch	26	162	6.2	0
Masters	7	71	10.1	0
C. Turner	17	43	2.5	0
Harrison	5	36	7.2	0
Mosier	4	31	7.8	0
Horn	6	15	2.5	0
Van Heusen	1	10	10.0	0
Simmons	1	7	7.0	0
Ramsey	3	6	2.0	0
Gehrke	1	2	2.0	0

RECEIVING

Last Name	No.	Yds	Avg	TD
Anderson	37	353	10	1
Masters	27	382	14	1
Little	26	255	10	0
Simmons	25	403	16	1
Harrison	19	265	14	2
Gehrke	14	254	18	0
Whalen	8	165	21	0
C. Turner	7	65	9	1
Mosier	3	36	12	0
Lynch	2	42	21	1
Bowdell	1	19	19	0
Van Heusen	1	10	10	0
Washington	1	0	0	0
Schnitker	1	−11	−11	0

PUNT RETURNS

Last Name	No.	Yds	Avg	TD
Thompson	29	274	9	0
Greer	11	46	4	0
Mitchell	1	0	0	0

KICKOFF RETURNS

Last Name	No.	Yds	Avg	TD
Little	7	199	28	0
Anderson	8	187	23	0
Thompson	5	105	21	0
C. Turner	5	100	20	0
Criter	5	81	16	0
R. Montgomery	4	80	20	0
Bachman	2	20	10	0
Forsberg	1	19	19	0
Lynch	0	19	0	0

PASSING – PUNTING – KICKING

PASSING	Att	Comp	%	Yds	Yd/Att	TD	Int–	%	RK
Ramsey	178	84	47	1120	6.3	15	13–	7	13
Horn	173	89	51	1056	6.1	3	14–	8	14
Anderson	3	1	33	48	16.0	0	0–	0	
Gehrke	2	1	50	19	9.5	0	0–	0	
Little	1	0	0	0	0.0	0	0–	0	
Van Heusen	1	0	0	0	0.0	0	0–	0	

PUNTING	No	Avg
Van Heusen	76	41.8

KICKING	XP	Att	%	FG	Att	%
J. Turner	18	18	100	25	38	66

1971 Championship Games

NFC CHAMPIONSHIP GAME

January 2, at Dallas
(Attendance 63,409)

Brodie's Mistake and Dallas' Defense

The Cowboys and '49ers both won a return trip to the conference title game on the strength of a strong defense. Dallas had beaten the Vikings 20-12 to begin the playoffs, while the '49ers topped Washington 24-20 in the opening round, and the defensive units would decide the game today as they had last week.

Quarterbacks Roger Staubach and John Brodie made no headway against the psyched-up defenses in the first quarter. In the second period, however, Brodie committed a fatal error that the Cowboys capitalized on. Deep in his own territory, Brodie aimed a short screen pass to fullback Ken Willard without noticing Dallas' George Andrie lurking ominously on the scene. Once the ball was in the air, Andrie stepped in front of Willard, grabbed it, and lumbered down to the 1-yard line before being stopped. Calvin Hill carried the ball in, and Mike Clark's kick gave the Cowboys a 7-0 lead. Bruce Gossett put the '49ers on the scoreboard with a 28-yard field goal late in the period that cut the halftime Dallas lead down to 7-3.

The defensive units continued to dominate in the third period, and the slender Dallas lead looked as though it might hold up. In the fourth quarter, however, Roger Staubach went to work on some insurance points. Taking over on their own 20-yard line, the Cowboys drove downfield in a drive in which they converted four third-down situations into first downs. Staubach kept the drive alive with his scrambling, often creating time for his receivers to get open or finding room to run the ball himself. One key third-down play saw coach Tom Landry send tight end Mike Ditka into the lineup after '49er safety Mel Phillips was injured; Ditka promptly caught a clutch third-down pass against substitute safety Johnny Fuller. Duane Thomas sprinted around end for the final two yards, and the Dallas defense never let up for a second in preserving the 14-3 victory.

SCORING

DALLAS	0	7	0	7–14
SAN FRANCISCO	0	0	3	0– 3

Second Quarter
Dall. — Hill, 1 yard rush
PAT—Clark (kick)

Third Quarter
S.F. — Gossett, 28 yard field goal

Fourth Quarter
Dall. — D. Thomas, 2 yard rush
PAT—Clark (kick)

TEAM STATISTICS

DALLAS		S.F.
16	First Downs–Total	9
9	First Downs–Rushing	2
7	First Downs–Passing	7
0	First Downs–Penalty	0
2	Fumbles–Number	0
1	Fumbles–Lost Ball	0
2	Penalties–Number	1
30	Yards Penalized	12
3	Missed Field Goals	1
70	Offensive Plays–Total	47
244	Net Yards	239
3.5	Average Gain	5.1
1	Giveaways	3
3	Takeaways	1
+2	Difference	–2

INDIVIDUAL STATISTICS

DALLAS	No	Yds	Avg.	SAN FRANCISCO	No	Yds	Avg.
RUSHING							
Staubach	8	55	6.9	V. Washington	10	58	5.8
Garrison	14	52	3.7	Willard	6	3	0.5
D. Thomas	15	44	2.9		16	61	3.8
Hill	9	21	2.3				
	46	172	3.7				
RECEIVING							
Truax	2	43	21.5	G. Washington	4	88	22.0
Hayes	2	22	11.0	Kwalick	4	52	13.0
Alworth	1	17	17.0	V. Washington	3	28	9.3
Reeves	1	17	17.0	Willard	1	6	6.0
D. Thomas	1	7	7.0	Witcher	1	6	6.0
Ditka	1	5	5.0	Cunningham	1	4	4.0
Garrison	1	–8	–8.0		14	184	13.1
	9	103	11.4				
PUNTING							
Widby	6		45.0	Spurrier	6		38.2
PUNT RETURNS							
Hayes	1	3	3.0	Fuller	2	10	5.0
Harris	1	1	1.0	Taylor	1	0	0.0
	2	4	2.0		3	10	3.3
KICKOFF RETURNS							
Harris	1	19	19.0	V. Washington	2	35	17.5
				Cunningham	1	21	21.0
					3	56	18.7
INTERCEPTION RETURNS							
Jordan	1	23	23.0	None			
Andrie	1	7	7.0				
Harris	1	2	2.0				
	3	32	10.7				

PASSING

	Att.	Comp.	Comp. Pct.	Yds.	Int.	Yds/ Att.	Yds/ Comp.	Yards Lost Tackled
DALLAS								
Staubach	18	9	50.0	103	0	5.7	11.4	6–31
SAN FRANCISCO								
Brodie	30	14	46.7	184	3	6.1	13.1	1– 6

AFC CHAMPIONSHIP GAME

January 2, at Miami
(Attendance 76,622)

Good Strategy, Wrong Target

The Dolphins had to guard against a letdown in this game as they were coming off an exhausting victory in the opening round of the playoffs. The Chiefs and Dolphins had battled back and forth all afternoon, with regulation time ending in a 24-24 tie. The two clubs fought through almost eighteen minutes of overtime before Garo Yepremian ended football's longest game with a 37-yard field goal.

The Colts, on the other hand, were coming off an easy 20-3 triumph over the Browns, so they were well rested physically and emotionally. Coach Don McCafferty planned to use a ball-control offense and a tight defense to defeat the Dolphins, but a 75-yard touchdown pass from Bob Griese to Paul Warfield early in the first quarter put Miami ahead 7-0 and put the pressure on Johnny Unitas and the Baltimore offense. But with starting backs Tom Matte and Norm Bulaich out of action with injuries, the Colts could not grind the yardage out against the quick Miami defense. The Colt defense also held up after the early Miami touchdown, and the half ended with the score 7-0.

With their ground attack getting no place against the Miami defense, the Colts went to the air in the third period. But while Griese had scored on a long bomb in the opening period, Unitas met disaster when he went for the bomb in the third quarter. Throwing deep for Eddie Hinton, Unitas undershot his man and instead hit Miami safety Dick Anderson. With his mates throwing blocks like experienced offensive players, Anderson weaved 62 yards with the ball for the second Miami touchdown.

Unitas had no luck crossing the Miami goal line for the rest of the afternoon, while the Dolphins scored a third touchdown on Larry Csonka's five-yard run which had been set up by a 50-yard pass to Warfield.

SCORING

MIAMI	7	0	7	7–21
BALTIMORE	0	0	0	0– 0

First Quarter
Miami — Warfield, 75 yard pass from Griese
PAT—Yepremian (kick)

Third Quarter
Miami — Anderson, 62 yard interception return
PAT—Yepremian (kick)

Fourth Quarter
Miami — Csonka, 5 yard rush
PAT—Yepremian (kick)

TEAM STATISTICS

MIAMI		BALT.
13	First Downs–Total	16
8	First Downs–Rushing	6
4	First Downs–Passing	10
1	First Downs–Penalty	0
0	Fumbles–Number	1
0	Fumbles–Lost Ball	0
1	Penalties–Number	2
12	Yards Penalized	20
0	Missed Field Goals	3
45	Offensive Plays–Total	68
286	Net Yards	302
6.4	Average Gain	4.4
1	Giveaways	3
3	Takeaways	1
+2	Difference	–2

INDIVIDUAL STATISTICS

MIAMI	No	Yds	Avg.	BALTIMORE	No	Yds	Avg.
RUSHING							
Kiick	18	66	3.7	McCauley	15	50	3.3
Csonka	15	63	4.2	Nottingham	11	33	3.0
Griese	1	12	12.0	Nowatzke	2	5	2.5
Morris	1	3	3.0	Unitas	1	5	5.0
	35	144	4.1		29	93	3.2
RECEIVING							
Warfield	2	125	62.5	Hinton	6	98	16.3
Twilley	2	33	16.5	Nottingham	4	26	6.5
	4	158	39.5	Perkins	3	19	6.3
				Havrilak	2	31	15.5
				McCauley	2	24	12.0
				Mitchell	1	14	14.0
				Mackey	1	6	6.0
				Matte	1	6	6.0
					20	224	11.2
PUNTING							
Seiple	6		42.7	Lee	3		45.3
PUNT RETURNS							
Scott	2	20	10.0	Volk	5	20	4.0
KICKOFF RETURNS							
Morris	1	22	22.0	Pittman	2	58	29.0
INTERCEPTION RETURNS							
Anderson	1	62	62.0	Logan	1	0	0.0
Kolen	1	11	11.0				
Scott	1	0	0.0				
	3	73	24.3				

PASSING

	Att.	Comp.	Comp. Pct.	Yds.	Int.	Yds/ Att.	Yds/ Comp.	Yards Lost Tackled
MIAMI								
Griese	8	4	50.0	158	1	19.8	39.5	2–16
BALTIMORE								
Unitas	36	20	55.6	224	3	6.3	11.2	3–15

January 16, at New Orleans
(Attendance 80,591)

Finally Lassoing the Championship

The Cowboys had ended every season since 1966 with a loss in the playoffs, before finally losing last year in the Super Bowl to Baltimore. But now they were hopeful of kicking that habit with a new quarterback in charge of the offense. Since Roger Staubach had replaced Craig Morton as the starting passer halfway through the season, the Cowboys had won seven straight regular-season games and two playoff games. To end the doubts about their ability to win the big games, the Cowboys would have to beat the Miami Dolphins, an up-and-coming young team masterfully built by head coach Don Shula.

The young Dolphins made their first mistake in the opening period when fullback Larry Csonka muffed a handoff from quarterback Bob Griese on the Dallas 48-yard line. After Dallas recovered the fumble, Staubach led the Cowboys deep into Miami territory before settling for a Mike Clark field goal.

Even in the first quarter, Dallas consistently ate up yardage on the ground, with Duane Thomas and Walt Garrison carrying the ball through gaping holes cut open by Cowboy linemen. The Dallas defense, meanwhile, completely shut off the Miami running attack of Csonka and Jim Kiick. The Cowboys also mixed passes into their attack, and a seven-yard touchdown pass from Staubach to Lance Alworth capped a long Dallas drive in the second period. Although the Dolphins scored on a Garo Yepremian field goal, the Cowboys dominated the first half and took a 10-3 lead into the clubhouse at halftime.

After taking the second-half kickoff, the Cowboys ate up five minutes of the clock with a ball-control drive that featured strong running by Duane Thomas. A pitchout to Thomas for three yards scored the touchdown and opened the Dallas lead to 17-3.

Trailing by two touchdowns after three periods, the Dolphins desperately needed some offensive fireworks in the fourth quarter. Instead, they ran into disaster. With his team finally on the march, Griese lashed a pass at Kiick at mid-field. Cowboy linebacker Chuck Howley had been knocked down when the pass was thrown, but he jumped up and picked it off in front of Kiick. With a convoy of blockers in front of him, Howley chugged downfield with the ball before running out of gas on the Miami 9. Two running plays moved the ball to the 7, and then Staubach hit Mike Ditka in the end zone with a pass to put the game out of reach for the Dolphins. Mike Clark's extra point made the score 24-3, and although the Dolphins launched a drive deep into Dallas territory, a fumble by Griese ended the last Miami scoring threat of the day.

DALLAS	OFFENSE	MIAMI
Hayes	WR	Warfield
Liscio	LT	Crusan
Niland	LG	Kuechenberg
Manders	C	DeMarco
Nye	RG	Little
Wright	RT	Evans
Ditka	TE	Fleming
Alworth	WR	Twilley
Staubach	QB	Griese
D. Thomas	RB	Kiick
Garrison	RB	Csonka
	DEFENSE	
L. Cole	LE	Riley
Pugh	LT	Fernandez
Lillie	RT	Heinz
Andrie	RE	Stanfill
Edwards	LLB	Swift
Jordan	MLB	Buoniconti
Howley	RLB	Kolen
Adderley	LCB	Foley
Renfro	RCB	Johnson
Green	LS	Anderson
Harris	RS	Scott

SUBSTITUTES

DALLAS

Offense
Fitzgerald Truax
Hill Welch
Reeves Williams

Defense
Gregory I. Thomas
Lewis Toomay
Smith Waters
Stincic

Kickers
Clark Widby

MIAMI

Offense
T. Cole Moore
Ginn Morris
Langer Noonan
Mandich Stowe

Defense
Cornish Mumphord
Den Herder Petrella
Matheson Powell

Kickers
Yepremian Seiple

SCORING

DALLAS	3	7	7	7–24
MIAMI	0	3	0	0– 3

First Quarter
Dallas Clark, 9 yard field goal

Second Quarter
Dallas Alworth, 7 yard pass from Staubach PAT – Clark (kick)
Miami Yepremian, 31 yard field goal

Third Quarter
Dallas D. Thomas, 3 yard rush PAT – Clark (kick)

Fourth Quarter
Dallas Ditka, 7 yard pass from Staubach PAT – Clark (kick)

TEAM STATISTICS

DALLAS		MIAMI
23	First Downs – Total	10
15	First Downs – Rushing	3
8	First Downs – Passing	7
0	First Downs – Penalty	0
1	Fumbles – Number	2
1	Fumbles – Lost Ball	2
3	Penalties – Number	0
15	Yards Penalized	0
0	Missed Field Goals	1
69	Offensive Plays	44
352	Net Yards	185
5.1	Average Gain	4.2
1	Giveaways	3
3	Takeaways	1
+2	Difference	–2

INDIVIDUAL STATISTICS

DALLAS	No	Yds	Avg.	MIAMI	No	Yds	Avg.
RUSHING							
D. Thomas	19	95	5.0	Csonka	9	40	4.4
Garrison	14	74	5.3	Kiick	10	40	4.0
Hill	7	25	3.6	Griese	1	0	0.0
Staubach	5	18	3.6		20	80	4.0
Ditka	1	17	17.0				
Hayes	1	16	16.0				
Reeves	1	7	7.0				
	48	252	5.3				
RECEIVING							
D. Thomas	3	17	5.7	Warfield	4	39	9.8
Alworth	2	28	14.0	Kiick	3	21	7.0
Ditka	2	28	14.0	Csonka	2	18	9.0
Hayes	2	23	11.5	Fleming	1	27	27.0
Garrison	2	11	5.5	Twilley	1	20	20.0
Hill	1	12	12.0	Mandich	1	9	9.0
	12	119	9.9		12	134	11.2
PUNTING							
Widby	5		37.2	Seiple	5		40.0
PUNT RETURNS							
Hayes	1	–1	–1.0	Scott	1	21	21.0
KICKOFF RETURNS							
I. Thomas	1	32	32.0	Morris	4	90	22.5
Waters	1	11	11.0	Ginn	1	32	32.0
	2	43	21.5		5	122	24.4
INTERCEPTION RETURNS							
Howley	1	41	41.0	None			

PASSING

DALLAS	Att	Comp	Comp Pct.	Yds	Int	Yds/ Att.	Yds/ Comp	Yards Lost Tackled
Staubach	19	12	63.2	119	0	6.3	9.9	2–19
MIAMI								
Griese	23	12	52.2	134	1	5.8	11.2	1–29

1972 N.F.C. Grounded but Not Stopped

In modern offensive football, the wide receiver was fast becoming an ornamental decoy, while the quarterback's main function was no longer passing the ball but handing it off. A record number of ten rushers carried the ball for 1,000 yards this year as the running back now was pro football's chief offensive weapon. The development of zone pass defenses had cut down on the air game's potency, so clubs more and more decided to move the ball on the ground in three- and four-yard chunks rather than going for twenty or thirty yards at a time with pass plays. An ever-increasing number of teams found that the best offense against a zone defense was two strong running backs and a strong-legged place kicker. Fading away into history were the days when long bombers like Van Brocklin, Unitas, and Lamonica captivated crowds and captured headlines with spectacular heaves.

EASTERN DIVISION

Washington Redskins—George Allen's collection of misfits and rejects, known collectively as the Over the Hill Gang, stayed at a high level of enthusiasm all season and knocked the Dallas Cowboys out of first place in the Eastern Division for the first time since 1965. Allen's pride and joy was his defensive unit, which allowed the fewest points of any defense in the conference. The offense moved the ball well despite the absence of Sonny Jurgensen for most of the season with injuries; most of the time, substitute quarterback Bill Kilmer had only to hand off to halfback Larry Brown to keep the Skins on the march. Running at top speed and using his blockers well, Brown piled up a conference-leading total of 1,216 yards rushing despite sitting out the last two games of the season with an injury.

Dallas Cowboys—The Cowboys still had one of the deepest rosters in the NFL, but they dropped to second place in the East because they lacked the fine competitive edge they had last year. They lost to the Packers, Redskins, and '49ers during the season, and with a chance to take first place on the final day of the season they lost a listless 23-3 decision to New York and settled for the wild-card spot in the playoffs. The Cowboys did have several personnel problems. Duane Thomas' non-relations with his teammates forced the team to trade him to San Diego, a shoulder injury sidelined quarterback Roger Staubach for most of the season, a bad back took George Andrie out of the defensive line, and Bob Lilly's back hurt him all through the season.

New York Giants—Comebackers and newcomers led the Giants to a surprising winning season. The chief comeback was by halfback Ron Johnson, rebounding from a 1971 knee injury to carry the ball with his old authority and flair. Kicker Pete Gogolak also came back from a poor 1971 season to give the Giants a consistent three-point threat within the 40-yard line. Newcomers to the New York squad more than made up for the traded Fran Tarkenton and Fred Dryer. Quarterback Norm Snead led the NFC in passing statistics, but his main value was as a steady leader on offense. The defensive line improved immensely with the addition of end Jack Gregory from the Browns and rookie tackles John Mendenhall and Larry Jacobson.

St. Louis Cardinals—Despite top talent in some positions, the Cards stumbled through a season in which Gary Cuozzo, Tim Van Galder, and Jim Hart took turns as the starting quarterback, in which the defensive line had problems rushing opposing passers, and in which injuries sidelined linebackers Jamie Rivers, Jeff Staggs, and Mike McGill. Even though the Cards won their final two games, coach Bob Holloway got the ax after the season; departing of his own accord was safety Larry Wilson, retiring after a great thirteen-year pro career.

Philadelphia Eagles—The tough defense coach Ed Khayat had built last year was weakened by the trade of Tim Rossovich to San Diego because of a personality clash with the coach and by injuries to Ernie Calloway and Steve Zabel. The offensive had great receivers in Harold Jackson, Ben Hawkins, and Harold Carmichael but didn't have a quarterback who could consistently get the ball to them. Veteran Pete Liske had all the qualifications except a strong arm, while rookie John Reaves had a great arm but also the chronic rookie problem of inexperience. Rookie Po James played well at halfback, but the Eagles lacked the great back necessary in this era of running football.

CENTRAL DIVISION

Green Bay Packers—In his second year as coach, Dan Devine took the Packers back to the top in the Central Division with a grinding defense and a methodical ball-control offense. The pride of the defense was the secondary of Ken Ellis, rookie Willie Buchanon, Jim Hill, and Al Matthews, four young speedsters who minimized the effect of Willie Wood's retirement. The Packers didn't have any stars like Willie Davis or Henry Jordan or a younger Ray Nitschke in the front lines, but the rebuilt front four and linebacking constantly frustrated enemy running attacks. Bart Starr's retirement left Scott Hunter in charge of the offense, although Starr remained as an assistant coach and called all the plays for Hunter. Even though his arm was not strong, Hunter kept the attack moving simply by handing off to backs John Brockington and MacArthur Lane.

Detroit Lions—The Detroit offense steadily turned out points, ranking second in the league in point production, but the defense could not compete with the other units in Green Bay and Minnesota. Coach Joe Schmidt was swimming in offensive talents—a fine quarterback in Greg Landry, good runners in Steve Owens and Altie Taylor, a star receiver in Charlie Sanders, and one of the best offensive lines in the NFL. The chief defensive shortcoming was the lack of a strong pass rush. Despite taking defensive linemen Bob Bell and Herb Orvis as their first draft choices the last two years, the Lions had not rebuilt their line into a top unit. At the end of the year coach Schmidt resigned and defensive stars Wayne Walker and Dick LeBeau retired.

Minnesota Vikings—The Vikings solved their quarterback problems by getting Fran Tarkenton back from the Giants in a trade, but the defense slumped off from the super level it had been playing at. Injuries nagged Carl Eller, Alan Page, and Gary Larsen and made the Minnesota front four less fearsome than usual. Middle linebacker Lonnie Warwick missed eight games on the disabled list, and rookie Jeff Siemon showed much promise and made many mistakes. On offense, Tarkenton gave the team a major-league passer, but the receiving corps suffered because of Gene Washington's second straight injury-plagued season. The Viking running backs were all good for sure short yardage, but none of them ever threatened to break loose a long run.

Chicago Bears—The Bears had a completely schizophrenic offense, first in the NFL in rushing, last in passing. Quarterback Bobby Douglass was a big, strong lad who set a new record of 968 yards gained rushing by a quarterback, but his passes came infrequently and often shot wide of the intended receiver. Douglass, fullback Jim Harrison, and halfbacks Don Shy and Cyril Pinder moved the ball well on the ground, but enemy defenses paid a minimum of attention to the Chicago air game. For a while the all-out running attack worked, but once opposing teams got wise to the Bear game plan, Chicago lost six of their last seven games. Coach Abe Gibron's first year on the job saw Gale Sayers retire with a bad knee and Dick Butkus continue to play up to All-Pro standards with a knee that hurt him more and more with each game.

WESTERN DIVISION

San Francisco '49ers—Heisman Trophy winner Steve Spurrier had done little else but punt in his past five seasons as a pro, but he stepped in for the injured John Brodie in mid-season and quarterbacked the '49ers to first place in the West. With a solid line to protect him and two great receivers in Gene Washington and Ted Kwalick to throw to, Spurrier engineered five San Francisco victories in the final six games, reaching his personal peak with five touchdown passes on November 19 against the Bears. On defense, the '49ers launched a ferocious pass rush despite disabling injuries to Cedrick Hardman and Earl Edwards; Tommy Hart and Charley Krueger responded with superior seasons to pick up the slack. The '49er playoff hopes soared in their final game when Brodie returned from the injured list to spark the team to a 20-17 victory over Minnesota.

Atlanta Falcons—The Falcons were strong at every position except quarterback, kicker, and defensive tackle, but these flaws kept the club from doing better than second place in the West. Quarterback Bob Berry had made the best of his limited talent, but coach Norm Van Brocklin had lost confidence in his ability to lead the Falcons to a title. Neither did kicker Bill Bell nor defensive tackles Glen Condren and Mike Lewis satisfy the coach. The Falcons did have a liberal supply of All-Stars in Claude Humphrey, John Zook, Tommy Nobis, Ken Reaves, George Kunz, Jim Mitchell, and Dave Hampton. Picked up from Green Bay, Hampton gained his 1,000th yard rushing of the year late in the final game. The game was stopped and the ball presented to Hampton. On his next carry Hampton lost five yards to finish at 995 yards for the year. Hampton, however, kept the ball.

Los Angeles Rams—With the death of owner Dan Reeves in April 1971, his family operated the club for a year and then sold the Rams to Robert Irsay. Before the 1972 season began, however, Irsay traded the Rams to Carroll Rosenbloom for his ownership of the Colts. Rosenbloom had grown accustomed to excellence from his Colt teams, but his first Ram squad disappointed him by finishing below .500 and in third place. Coach Tommy Prothro had daringly traded off Deacon Jones during the summer and replaced him with ex-Giant Fred Dryer, but leaks in the secondary hurt the defense more than the rebuilt front four. Quarterback Roman Gabriel's sore arm put a crimp in the offense, and five losses in the last six games cost Prothro his job.

New Orleans Saints—While the mid-1960s expansion teams in Atlanta, Miami, and Cincinnati had all achieved respectability, the Saints still had a look of a patchwork team created out of odds and ends. Coach J.D. Roberts had some topnotch players in quarterback Archie Manning, receiver Danny Abramowicz, tackle Glen Ray Hines, and rookie middle linebacker Joe Federspiel, but most of the roster was made up of journeymen and inexperienced youngsters. The distinguishing marks of the Saints this year were an uncanny ability to lose the ball on fumbles and interceptions and a morale problem in which the players expected one another to make errors and lose games.

FINAL TEAM STATISTICS

OFFENSE

	ATL.	CHI.	DALL.	DET.	G.B.	L.A.	MINN.	N.O.	N.Y.	PHIL.	ST.L.	S.F.	WASH.
FIRST DOWNS:													
Total	231	190	256	240	195	238	235	226	**265**	203	181	234	235
by Rushing	113	**124**	118	120	109	113	95	83	120	78	68	87	110
by Passing	101	54	126	97	72	108	127	123	124	110	102	**129**	106
by Penalty	17	12	12	**23**	14	17	13	20	21	15	11	18	19
RUSHING:													
Number	500	536	499	473	**544**	472	472	337	524	398	361	445	513
Yards	2092	**2360**	2124	2021	2127	2209	1740	1230	2022	1393	1229	1616	2082
Average Yards	4.2	4.4	4.3	4.3	3.9	**4.7**	3.7	3.6	3.9	3.5	3.4	3.6	4.1
Touchdowns	16	15	17	**20**	17	17	11	5	16	2	9	11	17
PASSING:													
Attempts	296	205	367	305	237	371	385	**449**	344	375	363	380	284
Completions	157	78	196	155	101	184	218	**230**	206	184	171	217	159
Completion Percentage	53.0	38.0	53.4	50.8	42.6	49.6	56.6	51.2	**59.9**	49.1	47.1	57.1	56.0
Passing Yards	2202	1283	2580	2283	1536	2282	2726	2781	2537	2527	2259	**2888**	2281
Avg. Yards per Attempt	7.4	6.3	7.0	7.5	6.5	6.2	7.1	6.2	7.4	6.7	6.2	7.6	**8.0**
Avg. Yards per Complet.	14.0	**16.4**	13.2	14.7	15.2	12.4	12.5	12.1	12.3	13.7	13.2	13.3	14.3
Times Tackled Passing	41	32	31	26	17	16	26	43	**10**	53	30	22	11
Yards Lost Tackled	283	175	238	149	124	136	203	347	**76**	457	221	153	88
Net Yards	1919	1108	2342	2134	1412	2146	2523	2434	2461	2070	2038	**2735**	2193
Touchdowns	13	9	16	19	7	13	19	18	20	10	11	**27**	21
Interceptions	15	13	23	18	**9**	22	13	21	15	20	23	24	15
Percent Intercepted	5.1	4.3	6.3	5.9	3.8	5.9	**3.4**	4.7	4.4	5.3	6.3	6.3	5.3
PUNTS:													
Number	61	67	51	43	65	53	62	71	47	63	**73**	64	59
Average Distance	42.8	41.2	38.2	40.3	41.8	**44.2**	42.8	40.8	42.7	40.3	39.4	39.7	38.5
PUNT RETURNS:													
Number	27	28	28	18	25	33	26	16	18	27	16	**44**	34
Yards	194	178	134	100	364	347	159	43	125	179	61	**373**	159
Average Yards	7.2	6.4	4.8	5.6	**14.6**	10.5	6.1	2.7	6.9	6.6	3.8	8.5	4.7
Touchdowns	0	0	0	0	**2**	0	0	0	0	0	0	0	0
KICKOFF RETURNS:													
Number	52	52	50	52	49	56	42	**62**	50	59	53	44	48
Yards	1039	**1528**	1080	1304	1141	1287	989	1312	1262	1375	1152	1041	1133
Average Yards	20.0	**29.4**	21.6	25.1	23.3	23.0	23.5	21.2	25.2	23.3	21.7	23.7	23.6
Touchdowns	0	**2**	0	0	0	0	0	0	1	0	0	1	0
INTERCEPTION RETURNS:													
Number	18	21	16	12	17	16	**26**	14	23	19	11	19	17
Yards	205	193	213	184	223	251	365	141	205	164	118	146	287
Average Yards	11.4	9.2	13.3	15.3	13.1	15.7	14.0	10.1	8.9	8.6	10.7	7.7	**16.9**
Touchdowns	1	0	1	1	1	1	2	0	2	0	0	**3**	1
PENALTIES:													
Number	73	74	**90**	48	63	78	51	69	57	76	64	73	78
Yards	650	574	**841**	417	610	648	440	585	512	690	582	664	721
FUMBLES: Number	42	40	27	**17**	22	24	32	33	32	37	43	30	27
Number Lost	19	22	15	**7**	10	9	19	16	14	18	16	13	11
POINTS:													
Total	269	225	319	339	304	291	301	215	331	145	193	**353**	336
PAT Attempts	31	27	36	40	29	31	34	26	39	12	22	**43**	42
PAT Made	31	27	36	39	29	31	34	24	34	11	19	**41**	40
FG Attempts	30	24	36	29	**48**	41	33	25	31	35	22	29	30
FG Made	16	12	21	20	**33**	24	21	11	21	20	14	18	14
Percent FG Made	53.3	50.0	58.3	**69.0**	68.8	58.5	63.6	44.0	67.7	57.1	63.6	62.1	46.7
Safeties	**2**	0	**2**	0	1	1	0	1	0	1	0	0	1

DEFENSE

	ATL.	CHI.	DALL.	DET.	G.B.	L.A.	MINN.	N.O.	N.Y.	PHIL.	ST.L.	S.F.	WASH.
FIRST DOWNS:													
Total	221	224	217	239	209	235	**200**	251	218	268	276	221	223
by Rushing	122	96	**81**	126	85	101	103	107	101	137	119	96	95
by Passing	83	108	113	103	109	110	**82**	129	111	117	138	105	108
by Penalty	16	20	23	10	15	24	15	15	**6**	14	19	20	20
RUSHING:													
Number	504	476	428	491	443	438	454	482	**402**	544	548	446	427
Yards	2063	1751	**1515**	2204	1517	1762	2002	2089	1855	2266	2189	1847	1733
Average Yards	4.1	3.7	3.5	4.5	**3.4**	4.0	4.4	4.3	4.6	4.2	4.0	4.1	4.1
Touchdowns	16	11	**7**	14	14	9	13	15	9	22	11	12	12
PASSING:													
Attempts	**301**	342	382	312	340	363	331	367	333	318	365	366	367
Completions	**137**	180	187	171	174	181	169	213	182	175	221	169	186
Completion Percentage	**45.5**	52.6	49.0	54.8	51.2	49.9	51.1	58.0	54.7	55.0	60.5	46.2	50.7
Passing Yards	1911	2345	2508	2146	2209	2472	**1791**	2596	2571	2615	2733	2582	2130
Avg. Yards per Attempt	6.3	6.9	6.6	6.9	6.5	6.8	**5.4**	7.1	7.7	8.2	7.5	7.1	5.8
Avg. Yards per Complet.	13.9	13.0	13.4	12.5	12.7	13.7	**10.6**	12.2	14.1	14.9	12.4	15.3	11.5
Times Tackled Passing	24	23	32	21	29	42	21	24	37	17	22	**46**	35
Yards Lost Tackled	207	173	268	142	252	327	92	194	232	143	183	**403**	268
Net Yards	1704	2172	2240	2004	1957	2145	**1699**	2402	2339	2472	2550	2179	1862
Touchdowns	13	16	18	18	**7**	20	13	21	19	20	15	14	10
Interceptions	18	21	16	12	17	16	**26**	14	23	19	11	19	17
Percent Intercepted	6.0	6.1	4.2	3.8	5.0	4.4	**7.9**	3.8	6.9	6.0	3.0	5.2	4.6
PUNTS:													
Number	56	62	65	46	66	71	62	52	47	54	48	**72**	69
Average Distance	41.8	43.0	40.6	38.8	41.4	41.2	41.5	39.3	**38.1**	40.5	39.4	43.4	40.1
PUNT RETURNS:													
Number	30	24	**15**	26	32	22	35	36	27	26	37	20	19
Yards	239	126	41	321	225	54	317	281	171	137	144	70	**39**
Average Yards	8.0	5.3	2.7	12.3	7.0	2.5	9.1	7.8	6.3	5.3	3.9	3.5	**2.1**
Touchdowns	0	0	0	1	0	0	0	0	0	0	0	0	0
KICKOFF RETURNS:													
Number	48	42	52	68	46	54	62	50	63	41	**40**	66	53
Yards	1076	1025	1272	1593	932	999	1373	1129	1516	**886**	1037	1530	1191
Average Yards	22.4	24.4	24.5	23.4	20.3	**18.5**	22.1	22.6	24.1	21.6	25.9	23.2	22.5
Touchdowns	1	0	0	1	0	0	0	0	0	0	1	0	0
INTERCEPTION RETURNS:													
Number	15	13	23	23	**9**	22	13	21	15	20	23	24	15
Yards	206	104	302	294	**69**	439	116	349	192	198	289	240	160
Average Yards	13.7	8.0	13.1	16.3	**7.7**	20.0	8.9	16.6	12.8	9.9	12.6	10.0	10.7
Touchdowns	1	1	1	**0**	2	3	**0**	1	**0**	**0**	3	1	1
PENALTIES:													
Number	61	69	59	**86**	50	60	47	78	66	72	68	81	64
Yards	555	644	586	703	446	553	490	**711**	641	637	645	677	568
FUMBLES: Number	23	37	**40**	32	35	25	27	27	31	30	31	**40**	28
Number Lost	15	14	17	15	**19**	11	14	13	15	8	16	17	15
POINTS:													
Total	274	275	240	290	226	286	252	361	247	352	303	249	**218**
PAT Attempts	32	31	28	34	26	34	27	38	28	43	31	28	**23**
PAT Made	31	30	27	32	25	32	24	38	25	42	31	28	**23**
FG Attempts	31	27	34	34	27	30	35	43	29	**25**	47	29	33
FG Made	17	19	**15**	18	**15**	16	22	31	18	16	28	17	19
Percent FG Made	54.8	70.4	**44.1**	52.9	55.6	53.3	62.9	72.1	62.1	64.0	59.6	58.6	57.6
Safeties	**0**	1	**0**	**0**	**0**	1	**0**	1	**0**	2	1	1	**0**

CONFERENCE PLAYOFFS

December 23, at San Francisco (Attendance 59,746)

SCORING

SAN FRANCISCO	**7**	**14**	**7**	**0–28**
DALLAS	**3**	**10**	**0**	**17–30**

First Quarter
- S.F. V. Washington, 97 yard kickoff return–PAT–Gossett (kick)
- DAL. Fritsch, 37 yard field goal

Second Quarter
- S.F. Schreiber, 1 yard rush PAT–Gossett (kick)
- S.F. Schreiber, 1 yard rush PAT–Gossett (kick)
- DAL. Fritsch, 45 yard field goal
- DAL. Alworth, 28 yard pass from Morton–PAT–Fritsch (kick)

Third Quarter
- S.F. Schreiber, 1 yard rush PAT–Gossett (kick)

Fourth Quarter
- DAL. Fritsch, 27 yard field goal
- DAL. Parks, 20 yard pass from Staubach–PAT–Fritsch (kick)
- DAL. Sellers, 10 yard pass from Staubach–PAT–Fritsch (kick)

TEAM STATISTICS

S.F.		DAL.
13	First Downs–Total	22
7	First Downs–Rushing	5
6	First Downs–Passing	15
0	First Downs–Penalty	2
5	Fumbles–Number	4
1	Fumbles–Lost Ball	3
7	Penalties–Number	3
56	Yards Penalized	35
2	Missed Field Goals	0
59	Offensive Plays	77
261	Net Yards	402
4.4	Average Gain	5.2
3	Giveaways	5
5	Takeaways	3
+2	Difference	–2

INDIVIDUAL STATISTICS

SAN FRANCISCO	No.	Yds.	Avg.	DALLAS	No.	Yds.	Avg.
RUSHING							
V. Washington	10	56	5.6	Hill	18	125	6.9
Schreiber	26	52	2.0	Staubach	3	23	7.7
Thomas	1	3	3.0	Garrison	9	15	1.7
	37	111	3.0	Morton	1	2	2.0
					31	165	5.3
RECEIVING							
Riley	4	41	10.3	Parks	7	125	16.9
G. Washington	3	76	25.3	Garrison	3	24	8.0
Schreiber	3	20	6.7	Alworth	2	50	25.0
V. Washington	1	8	8.0	Sellers	2	21	10.5
Kwalick	1	5	5.0	Montgomery	2	19	9.5
	12	150	12.5	Hayes	1	13	13.0
				Ditka	1	9	9.0
				Hill	1	6	6.0
				Truax	1	3	3.0
					20	270	13.5
PUNTING							
McCann	6		37.3	Bateman	6		41.8
PUNT RETURNS							
Taylor	1	5	5.0	Waters	1	2	2.0
KICKOFF RETURNS							
V. Washington	3	136	45.3	Harris	3	83	27.7
Beard	1	5	5.0				
McGill	1	5	5.0				
	5	146	29.2				
INTERCEPTION RETURNS							
Vanderbundt	2	4	2.0	Waters	2	12	6.0

PASSING

SAN FRANCISCO	Att.	Comp.	Comp. Pct.	Yds.	Int.	Yds/ Att.	Yds/ Comp.	Yards Lost Tackled
Brodie	22	12	54.5	150	2	6.8	12.5	0– 0
DALLAS								
Morton	21	8	38.1	96	2	4.6	12.0	
Staubach	20	12	60.0	174	0	8.7	14.5	
	41	20	48.8	270	2	6.6	13.5	5–33

December 24, at Washington (Attendance 52,321)

SCORING

WASHINGTON	**0**	**10**	**0**	**6–16**
GREEN BAY	**0**	**3**	**0**	**0– 3**

Second Quarter
- G.B. Marcol, 17 yard field goal
- WASH. Jefferson, 32 yard pass from Kilmer–PAT–Knight (kick)
- WASH. Knight, 42 yard field goal

Fourth Quarter
- WASH. Knight, 35 yard field goal
- WASH. Knight, 46 yard field goal

TEAM STATISTICS

WASH.		G.B.
13	First Downs–Total	10
6	First Downs–Rushing	2
4	First Downs–Passing	8
3	First Downs–Penalty	0
1	Fumbles–Number	0
1	Fumbles–Lost Ball	0
4	Penalties–Number	6
39	Yards Penalized	54
0	Missed Field Goals	1
51	Offensive Plays	55
232	Net Yards	211
4.5	Average Gain	3.8
1	Giveaways	1
1	Takeaways	1
0	Difference	0

INDIVIDUAL STATISTICS

WASHINGTON	No.	Yds.	Avg.	GREEN BAY	No.	Yds.	Avg.
RUSHING							
Brown	25	101	4.0	Lane	14	56	4.0
Harraway	10	34	3.4	Hunter	2	13	6.5
Kilmer	1	3	3.0	Brockington	13	9	0.7
	36	138	3.8		29	78	2.7
RECEIVING							
Jefferson	5	84	16.8	Lane	4	42	10.5
Taylor	2	16	8.0	Dale	2	28	14.0
	7	100	14.3	Glass	2	23	11.5
				Brockington	2	17	8.5
				Staggers	1	23	23.0
				Garrett	1	17	17.0
					12	150	12.5
PUNTING							
Bragg	6		46.5	Widby	8		36.6
PUNT RETURNS							
Haymond	2	4	2.0	Staggers	3	20	6.7
Vactor	1	15	15.0	Ellis	1	13	13.0
	3	19	6.3		4	33	8.3
KICKOFF RETURNS							
Mul-Key	2	60	30.0	Thomas	3	50	16.7
				Hudson	1	12	12.0
					4	62	15.5
INTERCEPTION RETURNS							
Hanburger	1	15	15.0	None			

PASSING

WASHINGTON	Att.	Comp.	Comp. Pct.	Yds.	Int.	Yds/ Att.	Yds/ Comp.	Yards Lost Tackled
Kilmer	14	7	50.0	100	0	7.1	14.3	1– 6
GREEN BAY								
Hunter	24	12	50.0	150	1	6.3	12.5	2–17

WASHINGTON REDSKINS 11-3-0 George Allen

Scores of Each Game		
24	Minnesota	21
24	ST. LOUIS	10
23	New England	24
14	PHILADELPHIA	0
33	St. Louis	3
24	DALLAS	20
23	N.Y. Giants	16
35	N.Y. Jets	17
27	N.Y. GIANTS	13
24	ATLANTA	13
21	GREEN BAY	16
23	Philadelphia	7
24	Dallas	34
17	BUFFALO	24

Use Name	Pos.	Hgt	Wgt	Age	Int	Pts
Terry Hermeling	OT	6'5"	255	26		
Mitch Johnson	OT	6'4"	250	30		
Walt Rock	OT	6'5"	255	31		
Paul Laaveg	OG	6'4"	245	23		
John Wilbur	OG	6'3"	250	29		
Ray Schoenke	OT-OG	6'3"	250	30		
Len Hauss	C	6'2"	235	31		
George Burman	OG-C	6'3"	255	29		
Verlon Biggs	DE	6'4"	275	29		6
Mike Fanucci	DE	6'4"	225	22		
Jimmie Jones	DE	6'3"	215	25		
Ron McDole	DT-DE	6'3"	265	32		
Bill Brundige	DT	6'5"	270	23		
Manny Sistrunk	DT	6'5"	265	25		
Diron Talbert	DT	6'5"	255	28		
Chris Hamburger	LB	6'2"	218	31	4	6
Harold McLinton	LB	6'2"	235	25	2	
Jack Pardee	LB	6'2"	225	36		
Myron Pottios	LB	6'2"	232	32		
Russ Tillman	LB	6'2"	230	26		
Mike Bass	DB	6'	190	27	3	6
Speedy Duncan	DB	5'10"	180	29	1	
Pat Fischer	DB	5'10"	170	32	4	
Alvin Haymond	DB	6'	194	30		
Jon Jaqua	DB	6'	190	24		
Brig Owens	DB	5'11"	190	29	1	
Richie Petitbon	DB	6'3"	208	34		
Jeff Severson	DB	6'1"	180	22		
Rosey Taylor	DB	5'11"	186	33	1	
Ted Vactor	DB	6'	185	28	1	
Sonny Jurgensen	QB	5'11"	203	38		
Billy Kilmer	QB	6'	204	33		
Sam Wyche	QB	6'4"	218	27		
Larry Brown	HB	5'11"	195	24		72
Bob Brunet	HB	6'1"	205	26		12
Herb Mul–Key	HB	6'	190	22		6
George Nock	HB	5'10"	200	26		
Charlie Harraway	FB	6'2"	215	27		36
Mike Hull	FB	6'3"	220	27		
Jeff Jordan	HB-FB	6'1"	215	27		
Roy Jefferson	WR	6'2"	195	28		18
Bill Malinchak	WR	6'1"	200	28		8
Clifton McNeil	WR	6'2"	187	32		
Charley Taylor	WR	6'3"	210	31		42
Mack Alston	TE	6'2"	230	25		
Jerry Smith	TE	6'2"	208	29		42
Mike Bragg	K	5'11"	186	25		
Curt Knight	K	6'1"	190	29		82

Jim Snowden – Injury

Tommy Mason – Injury

DALLAS COWBOYS 10-4-0 Tom Landry

Scores of Each Game		
28	PHILADELPHIA	6
23	N.Y. Giants	14
13	Green Bay	16
17	PITTSBURGH	13
21	Baltimore	0
20	Washington	24
28	DETROIT	24
34	San Diego	28
33	ST. LOUIS	24
28	Philadelphia	7
10	SAN FRANCISCO	31
27	St. Louis	6
34	WASHINGTON	24
3	N.Y. GIANTS	23

Use Name	Pos.	Hgt	Wgt	Age	Int	Pts
Ralph Neely	OT	6'5"	265	28		
Rayfield Wright	OT	6'7"	255	27		
Rodney Wallace	OG-OT	6'5"	255	23		
John Niland	OG	6'4"	245	28		6
Blaine Nye	OG	6'4"	250	26		
John Fitzgerald	C-OG	6'5"	250	24		
Dave Manders	C	6'2"	250	30		
George Andrie	DE	6'7"	250	32		
Larry Cole	DE	6'4"	250	25		
Tody Smith	DE	6'5"	245	23		
Pat Toomay	DE	6'5"	244	27		
Bill Gregory	DT	6'5"	255	22		
Bob Lilly	DT	6'4"	260	33		
Jethro Pugh	DT	6'6"	260	28		
John Babinecz	LB	6'1"	222	22		
Ralph Coleman	LB	6'4"	216	22		
Dave Edwards	LB	6'3"	225	33		
Chuck Howley	LB	6'3"	225	36	1	
Lee Roy Jordan	LB	6'2"	220	31	2	
Mike Keller	LB	6'4"	220	21		
D. D. Lewis	LB	6'2"	225	26	1	
Herb Adderly	DB	6'1"	200	33		
Benny Barnes	DB	6'1"	190	21		
Cornell Green	DB	6'4"	208	32	2	
Cliff Harris	DB	6'	184	23	3	
Mel Renfro	DB	6'	190	28	1	
Mark Washington	DB	5'10"	188	24		2
Charlie Waters	DB	6'1"	193	23	6	6
Craig Morton	QB	6'4"	214	29		12
Roger Staubach	QB	6'2"	197	30		
Mike Montgomery	HB	6'2"	210	23		18
Dan Reeves	HB	6'1"	200	28		
Calvin Hill	FB-HB	6'3"	227	25		54
Robert Newhouse	FB-HB	5'10"	202	22		6
Walt Garrison	FB	6'	205	28		60
Bill Thomas	FB	6'2"	225	22		
Lance Alworth	WR	6'	180	32		12
Bob Hayes	WR	6'	185	29		
Billy Parks	WR	6'1"	185	24		6
Ron Sellers	WR	6'4"	195	25		30
Mike Ditka	TE	6'3"	225	32		6
Jean Fugett	TE	6'3"	220	20		
Billy Truax	TE	6'5"	240	29		
Marv Bateman	K	6'4"	213	22		
Toni Fritsch	K	5'7"	185	27		99

NEW YORK GIANTS 8-6-0 Alex Webster

Scores of Each Game		
16	Detroit	30
14	DALLAS	23
27	Philadelphia	12
45	NEW ORLEANS	21
23	San Francisco	17
27	ST. LOUIS	21
16	WASHINGTON	23
29	DENVER	17
13	Washington	27
13	St. Louis	7
62	PHILADELPHIA	10
10	Cincinnati	13
13	MIAMI	23
23	Dallas	3

Use Name	Pos.	Hgt	Wgt	Age	Int	Pts
Joe Taffoni	OT	6'3"	255	27		
Willie Young	OT	6'	265	29		
John Hill	C-OT	6'2"	245	22		
Mark Ellison	OG	6'2"	250	23		
Dick Enderle	OG	6'1"	250	24		
Doug Van Horn	OG	6'2"	245	28		
Bob Hyland	C-OT-OG	6'5"	255	27		
Greg Larson	C	6'2"	250	33		
Jack Gregory	DE	6'6"	250	27		
Henry Reed	DE	6'3"	230	23		
Larry Jacobsen	DT-DE	6'6"	260	22		
Dan Goich	DT	6'4"	250	28		
John Mendenhall	DT	6'1"	255	23		
Charlie Harper	DT	6'2"	250	28		
Dave Tipton	DE-DT	6'	240	23		
Carter Campbell	LB	6'3"	240	24		
John Douglas	LB	6'2"	228	27	1	
Jim Files	LB	6'4"	240	24	2	6
Ron Hornsby	LB	6'3"	232	23		
Pat Hughes	LB	6'2"	240	25	2	
Pete Athas	DB	5'11"	185	26	4	
Otto Brown	DB	6'1"	188	25	1	
Chuck Crist	DB	6'2"	205	21	1	
Richmond Flowers	DB	6'	180	25	4	
Spider Lockhart	DB	6'2"	175	29	4	6
Eldridge Small	DB	6'1"	190	22		
Willie Williams	DB	6'	190	29	4	
Randy Johnson	QB	6'3"	205	28		6
Norm Snead	QB	6'4"	215	32		
Bobby Duhon	HB	6'	195	25		
Ron Johnson	HB	6'1"	205	24		84
Rocky Thompson	HB	5'11"	200	24		6
Vin Clements	FB	6'3"	210	23		
Charlie Evans	FB	6'1"	220	24		30
Joe Orduna	HB-FB	6'	195	24		12
Bob Grim	WR	6'	200	27		6
Don Herrmann	WR	6'2"	205	25		30
Rich Houston	WR	6'2"	195	26		18
Joe Morrison	HB-FB-WR	6'1"	212	34		
Dick Kotite	TE	6'3"	230	29		
Bob Tucker	TE	6'3"	230	27		30
Tom Gatewood	WR-TE	6'3"	215	21		
Tom Blanchard	K	6'	190	24		
Pete Gogolak	K	6'2"	190	30		97

Scott Eaton – Injury

Jim Kanicki – Knee Injury

ST. LOUIS CARDINALS 4-9-1 Bob Holloway

Scores of Each Game		
10	Baltimore	3
10	Washington	24
19	PITTSBURGH	25
19	Minnesota	17
3	WASHINGTON	33
21	N.Y. Giants	27
10	CHICAGO	27
6	Philadelphia	6
24	Dallas	33
7	N.Y. GIANTS	13
10	Miami	31
6	DALLAS	27
24	LOS ANGELES	14
24	PHILADELPHIA	23

Use Name	Pos.	Hgt	Wgt	Age	Int	Pts
Ernie McMillan	OT	6'6"	255	34		
Steve Wright	OT	6'6"	250	30		
Dan Dierdorf	OG-OT	6'4"	265	23		
Dave Bradley	OG	6'4"	245	25		
Conrad Dobler	OG	6'3"	250	21		
Chuck Hutchison	OG	6'3"	240	23		
Bob Young	OG	6'2"	260	29		
Wayne Mulligan	C	6'2"	245	25		
Tom Banks	OG-C	6'1"	240	24		
Tom Beckman	DE	6'5"	250	21		
Don Brumm	DE	6'3"	245	29		
Martin Imhof	DE	6'6"	255	22		
Ron Yankowski	DE	6'5"	225	25		
Fred Heron	DT	6'4"	240	27		
Scott Palmer	DT	6'3"	245	24		
John Richardson	DT	6'2"	250	28		
Bob Rowe	DT	6'4"	260	27		
Mark Arneson	LB	6'2"	220	22		
Steve Conley (from CIN)	LB	6'2"	225	23		
Jim Hargrove	LB	6'3"	225	27		
Mike McGill	LB	6'2"	235	25	2	
Terry Miller	LB	6'2"	225	26		
Jamie Rivers	LB	6'2"	235	26		
Jeff Staggs	LB	6'2"	240	28	1	
Larry Stallings	LB	6'2"	230	30		
Miller Farr	DB	6'1"	190	29	3	
Dale Hackbart	DB	6'3"	210	36	1	
Norm Thompson	DB	6'1"	175	24	1	12
Eric Washington	DB	6'2"	190	22		
Roger Wehrli	DB	6'1"	195	24		
Larry Willingham	DB	6'1"	190	23		
Larry Wilson	DB	6'	195	34	3	
Gary Cuozzo	QB	6'1"	195	31		
Jim Hart	QB	6'2"	200	28		
Tim Van Galder	QB	6'1"	190	28		
Danny Anderson	HB	6'3"	210	29		36
Craig Baynham	HB	6'1"	205	28		
Cannonball Butler	HB	5'10"	200	29		
Roy Shivers	HB	6'	200	30		
Leo Hayden	FB-HB	6'	210	24		6
Don Heater	FB-HB	6'2"	205	22		
Leon Burns	FB	6'2"	235	27		12
Tom Woodeshick	FB	6'	222	30		
Johnny Roland	HB-FB	6'2"	215	29		24
Walker Gillette	WR	6'5"	200	25		12
Mel Gray	WR	5'9"	170	23		
Freddie Hyatt	WR	6'3"	200	26		
Bobby Moore	WR	6'2"	210	22		18
Bob Wicks	WR	6'3"	195	22		
Jim McFarland	TE	6'5"	225	24		
Ara Person	TE	6'2"	220	23		
Jackie Smith	TE	6'4"	235	31		12
Jim Bakken	K	6'	195	31		61

Jeff Allen – Injury

Larry Stegent – Injury

PHILADELPHIA EAGLES 2-11-1 Ed Khayat

Scores of Each Game		
6	Dallas	28
17	CLEVELAND	27
12	N.Y. GIANTS	27
0	Washington	14
3	LOS ANGELES	34
21	Kansas City	20
3	New Orleans	21
6	ST. LOUIS	6
18	Houston	17
7	DALLAS	28
10	N.Y. Giants	62
7	WASHINGTON	23
12	CHICAGO	21
23	St. Louis	24

Use Name	Pos.	Hgt	Wgt	Age	Int	Pts
Wade Key	OT	6'4"	245	25		
Wayne Mass (from NE)	OT	6'4"	245	26		
Steve Smith	OT	6'5"	250	28		
Dick Stevens	OT	6'4"	240	24		
Henry Allison	OG	6'2"	255	25		
Tom Luken	OG	6'3"	253	22		
Jim Skaggs	OG	6'2"	250	32		
Vern Winfield	OG	6'2"	248	23		
Mark Nordquist	C-OG	6'4"	246	26		
Mike Evans	C	6'5"	250	26		
Jerry Sturm	C	6'3"	260	35		
Larry Estes	DE	6'6"	250	25		
Richard Harris	DE	6'4"	260	24		
Mel Tom	DE	6'4"	250	31		
Houston Antwine	DT	6'	270	33		
Don Hultz	DT	6'3"	240	31		
Gary Pettigrew	DT	6'4"	255	27		
Ernie Calloway	DE-DT	6'6"	255	24		
Dick Absher	LB	6'4"	235	28	1	
Chuck Allen	LB	6'1"	225	32	1	
John Bunting	LB	6'1"	220	22	1	
Bill Cody	LB	6'1"	230	28		
Bob Creech	LB	6'3"	228	23		
Bill Overmeyer	LB	6'3"	220	23		
Ron Porter	LB	6'3"	232	27	2	
John Sodaski	LB	6'2"	222	24		
Steve Zabel	LB	6'4"	235	24		
Kermit Alexander	DB	5'11"	186	31		
Jackie Allen	DB	6'1"	187	24		
Bill Bradley	DB	5'11"	190	25	9	
Al Coleman	DB	6'1"	183	27		2
Pat Gibbs	DB	5'10"	188	22		
Leroy Keyes	DB	6'3"	208	25	2	
Al Nelson	DB	5'11"	186	28		
Nate Ramsey	DB	6'1"	200	31	3	
Jim Thrower	DB	6'2"	194	23		
Rick Arrington	QB	6'2"	185	25		
Pete Liske	QB	6'2"	200	31		
John Reaves	QB	6'3"	210	22		6
Larry Crowe	HB	6'1"	198	22		
Po James	HB	6'1"	202	23		6
Tom Sullivan	HB	6'	190	22		
Sonny Davis	FB-HB	5'11"	215	24		
Tony Baker	FB	5'11"	225	27		
Larry Watkins	FB	6'2"	230	24		6
Tom Bailey	HB-FB	6'2"	211	23		
Harold Carmichael	WR	6'7"	225	22		12
Ben Hawkins	WR	6'	180	28		6
Harold Jackson	WR	5'10"	175	26		24
Billy Walik	WR	5'11"	180	24		6
Clark Hoss	TE	6'8"	235	23		
Kent Kramer	TE	6'5"	235	28		6
Gary Ballman	WR-TE	6'	215	32		
Tom Dempsey	K	6'1"	255	31		71
Tom McNeil	K	6'1"	195	30		

Lee Bouggess – Injury

Ike Kelly – Injury

WASHINGTON REDSKINS

RUSHING

Last Name	No.	Yds	Avg	TD
Brown	265	1216	4.3	8
Harraway	148	567	3.8	6
Mul-Key	33	155	4.7	1
Brunet	30	82	2.7	2
C. Taylor	3	39	13.0	0
Nock	6	22	3.7	0
Smith	1	9	9.0	0
Kilmer	3	–3	–1.0	0
Jurgensen	4	–5	–1.3	0

RECEIVING

Last Name	No.	Yds	Avg	TD
C. Taylor	49	673	14	7
Jefferson	35	550	16	3
Brown	32	473	15	4
Smith	21	353	17	7
Harraway	15	105	7	0
Mul-Key	4	66	17	0
Alston	2	53	27	0
Brunet	1	8	8	0

PUNT RETURNS

Last Name	No.	Yds	Avg	TD
Vactor	17	88	5	0
Duncan	11	70	6	0
Haymond	6	1	0	0

KICKOFF RETURNS

Last Name	No.	Yds	Avg	TD
Duncan	15	364	24	0
Haymond	10	291	29	0
Mul-Key	8	209	26	0
Brunet	8	190	24	0
Bass	2	22	11	0
Vactor	1	21	21	0
Fanucci	1	15	15	0
McLinton	1	15	15	0
Tillman	2	6	3	0

PASSING – PUNTING – KICKING

PASSING	Att	Comp	%	Yds	Yd/Att	TD	Int–	%	RK
Kilmer	225	120	53	1648	7.3	19	11–	5	4
Jurgensen	59	39	66	633	10.7	2	4–	7	

PUNTING	No	Avg
Bragg	59	38.5

KICKING	XP	Att	%	FG	Att	%
Knight	40	41	98	14	30	47

DALLAS COWBOYS

RUSHING

Last Name	No.	Yds	Avg	TD
Hill	245	1036	4.2	6
Garrison	167	784	4.7	7
Newhouse	28	116	4.1	1
Montgomery	35	81	2.3	1
Staubach	6	45	7.5	0
Morton	8	26	3.3	2
Reeves	3	14	4.7	0
Neely	1	10	10.0	0
Hayes	2	8	4.0	0
Alworth	1	2	2.0	0
Fugett	3	2	0.7	0

RECEIVING

Last Name	No.	Yds	Avg	TD
Hill	43	364	8	3
Garrison	37	390	11	3
Sellers	31	653	21	5
Parks	18	298	17	1
Ditka	17	198	12	1
Hayes	15	200	13	0
Alworth	15	195	13	2
Montgomery	8	131	16	1
Fugett	7	94	13	0
Truax	4	49	12	0
Newhouse	1	8	8	0

PUNT RETURNS

Last Name	No.	Yds	Avg	TD
Harris	19	78	4	0
Waters	9	56	6	0

KICKOFF RETURNS

Last Name	No.	Yds	Avg	TD
Harris	26	615	24	0
Newhouse	18	382	21	0
Thomas	2	50	25	0
Waters	2	18	9	0
Montgomery	1	15	15	0
Fugett	1	0	0	0

PASSING – PUNTING – KICKING

PASSING	Att	Comp	%	Yds	Yd/Att	TD	Int–	%	RK
Morton	339	185	55	2396	7.1	15	21–	6	8
Staubach	20	9	45	98	4.9	0	2–	10	
Hill	3	1	33	55	18.3	1	0–	0	
Montgomery	3	1	33	31	10.3	0	0–	0	
Reeves	2	0	0	0	0.0	0	0–	0	

PUNTING	No	Avg
Bateman	51	38.2

KICKING	XP	Att	%	FG	Att	%
Fritsch	36	36	100	21	36	58

NEW YORK GIANTS

RUSHING

Last Name	No.	Yds	Avg	TD
Ron Johnson	298	1182	4.0	9
Evans	91	317	3.5	4
Clements	46	221	4.8	0
Orduna	36	129	3.6	1
Morrison	9	36	4.0	0
Thompson	9	35	3.9	0
Randy Johnson	9	26	2.9	1
Duhon	9	23	2.6	0
Snead	10	21	2.1	0
Blanchard	1	17	17.0	0
Herrmann	3	9	3.0	0
Tucker	3	6	2.0	1

RECEIVING

Last Name	No.	Yds	Avg	TD
Tucker	55	764	14	4
Ron Johnson	45	451	10	5
Herrmann	28	422	15	5
Houston	27	468	17	3
Evans	26	182	7	1
Clements	9	118	13	0
Grim	5	67	13	1
Morrison	5	39	8	0
Orduna	4	6	2	1
Duhon	2	20	10	0

PUNT RETURNS

Last Name	No.	Yds	Avg	TD
Athas	8	95	12	0
Duhon	2	20	10	0
Grim	7	10	1	0
Mendenhall	1	0	0	0

KICKOFF RETURNS

Last Name	No.	Yds	Avg	TD
Thompson	29	821	28	1
Orduna	12	244	20	0
Small	1	100	100	0
Duhon	2	47	24	0
Douglas	4	43	11	0
Crist	1	7	7	0
Enderle	1	0	0	0

PASSING – PUNTING – KICKING

PASSING	Att	Comp	%	Yds	Yd/Att	TD	Int–	%	RK
Snead	325	196	60	2307	7.1	17	12–	4	2
Ran Johnson	17	10	59	230	13.5	3	3–	18	
Blanchard	1	0	0	0	0.0	0	0–	0	
Ron Johnson	1	0	0	0	0.0	0	0–	0	

PUNTING	No	Avg
Blanchard	47	42.7

KICKING	XP	Att	%	FG	Att	%
Gogolak	34	38	89	21	31	68

ST. LOUIS CARDINALS

RUSHING

Last Name	No.	Yds	Avg	TD
Anderson	153	536	3.5	4
Roland	105	414	3.9	2
Burns	26	69	2.7	2
Moore	9	44	4.9	0
Baynham	17	43	2.5	0
Smith	5	31	6.2	0
Van Galder	9	28	3.1	0
Hart	9	17	1.9	0
Woodeshick	5	14	2.8	0
Shivers	5	12	2.4	0
Hayden	8	11	1.4	1
Cuozzo	4	7	1.8	0
Butler	6	3	0.5	0
Conley	3	8	2.7	0

RECEIVING

Last Name	No.	Yds	Avg	TD
Roland	38	321	8	2
Gillette	33	550	17	2
Moore	29	500	17	3
Anderson	28	298	11	2
Smith	26	407	16	2
Burns	6	24	4	0
Gray	3	62	21	0
Hyatt	2	32	16	0
Shivers	1	20	20	0
Hayden	1	17	17	0
Baynham	1	10	10	0
Butler	1	8	8	0
Wicks	1	8	8	0
Woodeshick	1	2	2	0

PUNT RETURNS

Last Name	No.	Yds	Avg	TD
Willingham	9	41	5	0
Wehrli	5	24	5	0
Gray	2	–4	–2	0

KICKOFF RETURNS

Last Name	No.	Yds	Avg	TD
Moore	20	437	22	0
Gray	17	378	22	0
Willingham	9	194	22	0
Butler	4	85	21	0
Hyatt	1	41	41	0
Wehrli	1	10	10	0
Burns	1	7	7	0

PASSING – PUNTING – KICKING

PASSING	Att	Comp	%	Yds	Yd/Att	TD	Int–	%	RK
Cuozzo	158	69	44	897	5.7	5	11–	7	13
Hart	119	60	50	857	7.2	5	5–	4	
Van Galder	79	40	51	434	5.5	1	7–	9	
Anderson	3	2	67	71	23.7	0	0–	0	
Smith	2	0	0	0	0.0	0	0–	0	
Wilson	2	0	0	0	0.0	0	0–	0	

PUNTING	No	Avg
Anderson	72	39.5
Bakken	1	26.0

KICKING	XP	Att	%	FG	Att	%
Bakken	19	21	90	14	22	64

PHILADELPHIA EAGLES

RUSHING

Last Name	No.	Yds	Avg	TD
James	182	565	3.1	0
Baker	90	322	3.6	0
Watkins	67	262	3.9	1
Reaves	18	109	6.1	1
Jackson	9	76	8.4	0
Bailey	7	22	3.1	0
Liske	7	20	2.9	0
Sullivan	13	13	1.0	0
Arrington	1	2	2.0	0
Crowe	1	2	2.0	0
Hawkins	3	0	0.0	0

RECEIVING

Last Name	No.	Yds	Avg	TD
Jackson	62	1048	17	4
Hawkins	30	512	17	1
Carmichael	20	276	14	2
James	20	156	8	1
Baker	16	114	7	0
Kramer	11	176	16	1
Ballman	9	183	20	0
Watkins	6	–2	0	0
Bailey	5	32	6	0
Sullivan	4	17	4	0
Walik	1	15	15	1

PUNT RETURNS

Last Name	No.	Yds	Avg	TD
Bradley	22	155	7	0
Winfield	1	12	12	0
Gibbs	1	8	8	0
Walik	3	4	1	0

KICKOFF RETURNS

Last Name	No.	Yds	Avg	TD
Nelson	25	728	29	0
Walik	21	466	22	0
Sullivan	3	72	24	0
Gibbs	3	61	20	0
Bradley	2	22	11	0
Pettigrew	1	17	17	0
Winfield	3	9	3	0
Overmyer	1	0	0	0

PASSING – PUNTING – KICKING

PASSING	Att	Comp	%	Yds	Yd/Att	TD	Int–	%	RK
Reaves	224	108	48	1508	6.7	7	12–	5	10
Liske	138	71	51	973	7.1	3	7–	5	
Arrington	13	5	38	46	3.5	0	1–	8	

PUNTING	No	Avg
Bradley	56	40.2
McNeill	7	41.4

KICKING	XP	Att	%	FG	Att	%
Dempsey	11	12	92	20	35	57

GREEN BAY PACKERS 10-4-0 Dan Devine

Scores of Each Game		
26	Cleveland	10
14	OAKLAND	20
16	DALLAS	13
20	CHICAGO	17
24	Detroit	23
9	ATLANTA	10
13	MINNESOTA	27
34	SAN FRANCISCO	24
23	Chicago	17
23	Houston	10
16	Washington	21
33	DETROIT	7
23	Minnesota	7
30	New Orleans	20

Use Name	Pos.	Hgt	Wgt	Age	Int	Pts
Bill Hayhoe	OT	6'8"	258	25		
Dick Himes	OT	6'4"	244	26		
Kevin Hunt	OT	6'5"	260	24		
Francis Peay	OT	6'5"	250	28		
Bill Lueck	OG	6'3"	235	26		
Mal Snider	OG	6'4"	250	25		
Keith Wortman	OG	6'2"	245	22		
Ken Bowman	C	6'3"	230	29		
Cal Withrow	C	6'	240	27		
Dave Pureifory	DE	6'1"	260	22		
Alden Roche	DE	6'4"	255	27		
Clarence Williams	DE	6'5"	255	25		6
Bob Brown	DE	6'5"	260	31		2
Gale Gillingham	DT	6'3"	255	28		
Mike McCoy	DT	6'5"	284	23		
Vern Vanoy	DT	6'8"	270	26		

Use Name	Pos.	Hgt	Wgt	Age	Int	Pts
Fred Carr	LB	6'5"	238	26		
Jim Carter	LB	6'3"	235	23	1	
Tommy Crutcher	LB	6'3"	230	30		
Larry Hefner	LB	6'2"	215	23		
Ray Nitschke	LB	6'3"	235	36		
Dave Robinson	LB	6'3"	245	31	2	
Willie Buchanon	DB	6'	190	22	4	6
Ken Ellis	DB	5'10"	190	24	4	12
Paul Gibson	DB	6'2"	195	24		
Charlie Hall	DB	6'1"	195	23		
Jim Hill	DB	6'2"	190	25	4	
Bob Kroll	DB	6'1"	195	22		
Al Matthews	DB	5'11"	190	24	2	
Ike Thomas	DB	6'2"	193	24		

Larry Krause – Injury

Use Name	Pos.	Hgt	Wgt	Age	Int	Pts
Scott Hunter	QB	6'2"	205	24		30
Frank Patrick	QB	6'7"	225	25		
Jerry Tagge	QB	6'2"	220	22		6
Bob Hudson	HB	5'11"	210	24		
MacArthur Lane	HB	6'	220	30		18
Dave Kopay	FB-HB	6'2"	218	30		
John Brockington	FB	6'1"	225	23		54
Perry Williams	FB	6'2"	220	25		
Carroll Dale	WR	6'1"	200	34		6
Dave Davis	WR	6'	175	24		6
Leland Glass	WR	6'	185	22		6
Jon Staggers	WR	5'10"	186	23		12
Len Garrett	TE	6'3"	230	23		
Pete Lammons	TE	6'3"	228	28		
Rich McGeorge	TE	6'4"	235	23		12
Chester Marcol	K	6'	190	23		128
Ron Widby	K	6'4"	210	27		

DETROIT LIONS 8-5-1 Joe Schmidt

Scores of Each Game		
30	N.Y. GIANTS	16
10	MINNESOTA	34
38	Chicago	24
26	Atlanta	23
23	GREEN BAY	24
34	SAN DIEGO	20
24	Dallas	28
14	CHICAGO	0
14	Minnesota	16
27	NEW ORLEANS	14
37	N.Y. JETS	20
7	Green Bay	33
21	Buffalo	21
34	Los Angeles	17

Use Name	Pos.	Hgt	Wgt	Age	Int	Pts
Rocky Freitas	OT	6'6"	270	26		
Gordon Jolley	OT	6'5"	230	23		
Jim Yarbrough	OT	6'6"	265	25		
Frank Gallagher	OG	6'2"	245	29		
Bob Kowalkowski	OG	6'3"	240	28		
Rocky Rasley	OG	6'3"	250	25		
Chuck Walton	OG	6'3"	255	31		
Ed Flanagan	C	6'3"	245	28		
Dave Thompson	OT-C	6'4"	275	23		
Gene Hamlin	C	6'3"	245	26		
Larry Hand	DE	6'4"	250	32		
Jim Mitchell	DE	6'3"	245	23	1	
Herb Orvis	DE	6'5"	240	25		
Ken Sanders	DE	6'5"	225	22		
Bob Bell	DT	6'4"	250	24		
John Gordon	DT	6'6"	260	24		
Joe Schmiesing	DT	6'4"	260	27		
Bob Tatarek (from BUF)	DT	6'4"	270	26		
Larry Woods	DT	6'6"	260	24		

Use Name	Pos.	Hgt	Wgt	Age	Int	Pts
Mike Lucci	LB	6'2"	230	32	2	
Paul Naumoff	LB	6'1"	215	27	1	
Rick Ogle	LB	6'3"	230	23		
Wayne Walker	LB	6'2"	228	35		
Charlie Weaver	LB	6'2"	218	23	1	
Adrian Young (from PHI)	LB	6'1"	232	26		
Lem Barney	DB	6'	188	26	3	
Leon Jenkins	DB	5'11"	165	22		
Dick LeBeau	DB	6'1"	185	35		
Charlie Potts	DB	6'3"	210	23		
Al Randolph	DB	6'2"	205	28		
Wayne Rasmussen	DB	6'2"	180	30	2	
Rudy Redmond	DB	6'	195	25	2	6
Mike Weger	DB	6'2"	200	26		

Sonny Campbell – Injury
Ed Mooney – Injury

Use Name	Pos.	Hgt	Wgt	Age	Int	Pts
Greg Landry	QB	6'4"	210	25		54
Bill Munson	QB	6'2"	210	30		
Nick Eddy	HB	6'1"	210	28		6
Mel Farr	HB	6'2"	210	27		18
Altie Taylor	HB	5'10"	200	24		36
Mickey Zofko	HB	6'3"	195	22		1
Steve Owens	FB	6'2"	215	24		24
Bill Triplett	FB	6'2"	215	33		
Al Barnes	WR	6'1"	170	23		6
Ron Jessie	WR	6'	183	23		24
Earl McCullouch	WR	5'11"	175	26		6
Larry Walton	WR	5'11"	180	25		36
Craig Cotton	TE	6'4"	222	25		6
John Hilton	TE	6'5"	225	30		6
Charlie Sanders	TE	6'4"	225	26		12
Errol Mann	K	6'	200	31		98
Herman Weaver	K	6'4"	210	23		

MINNESOTA VIKINGS 7-7-0 Bud Grant

Scores of Each Game		
21	WASHINGTON	24
34	Detroit	10
14	MIAMI	16
17	ST. LOUIS	19
23	Denver	20
10	Chicago	13
27	Green Bay	13
37	NEW ORLEANS	6
16	DETROIT	14
45	Los Angeles	41
10	Pittsburgh	23
23	CHICAGO	10
7	GREEN BAY	23
17	San Francisco	20

Use Name	Pos.	Hgt	Wgt	Age	Int	Pts
Grady Alderman	OT	6'2"	247	33		
Doug Davis	OT	6'4"	250	28		
Ron Yary	OT	6'6"	255	26		
Ed White	OG	6'2"	262	25		
Milt Sunde	C-OG	6'2"	250	29		
John Ward	DE-OG	6'4"	250	24		
Mick Tingelhoff	C	6'1"	237	32		
Godfrey Zaunbrecher	C	6'2"	240	24		
Carl Eller	DE	6'6"	247	29		
Jim Marshall	DE	6'3"	248	35		
Bob Lurtsema	DT-DE	6'6"	250	30		
Gary Larsen	DT	6'5"	260	32		
Alan Page	DT	6'5"	245	27		
Doug Sutherland	DE-DT	6'3"	250	24		

Use Name	Pos.	Hgt	Wgt	Age	Int	Pts
Carl Gersbach	LB	6'1"	230	25		
Wally Hilgenberg	LB	6'3"	230	29	1	6
Amos Martin	LB	6'3"	228	23		
Jeff Siemon	LB	6'2"	230	22	2	
Lonnie Warwick	LB	6'3"	238	30	1	
Roy Winston	LB	6'1"	222	32	3	
Terry Brown	DB	6'1"	205	25		
Bobby Bryant	DB	6'	170	28	4	6
Karl Kassulke	DB	6'	195	30	2	
Paul Krause	DB	6'3"	200	30	6	12
Ed Sharockman	DB	6'	200	32		
Charlie West	DB	6'1"	197	26	3	
Jeff Wright	DB	5'11"	190	23	2	
Nate Wright	DB	5'11"	180	25	2	

Use Name	Pos.	Hgt	Wgt	Age	Int	Pts
Bob Lee	QB	6'2"	195	27		
Fran Tarkenton	QB	6'1"	190	32		
Clint Jones	HB	6'	205	27		12
Dave Osborn	HB	6'	208	29		18
Ed Marinaro	FB-HB	6'2"	212	22		6
Bill Brown	FB	5'11"	228	34		48
Oscar Reed	HB-FB	5'11"	222	28		12
Jim Lindsey	HB-FB	6'2"	210	27		
Calvin Demery	WR	6'1"	190	22		
John Gilliam	WR	6'	195	27		42
John Henderson	WR	6'3"	195	29		12
Gene Washington	WR	6'3"	208	28		12
John Beasley	TE	6'3"	228	27		6
Stu Voigt	TE	6'1"	220	24		12
Fred Cox	K	5'10"	200	33		97
Mike Eischeid	K	6'	190	31		

CHICAGO BEARS 4-9-1 Abe Gibron

Scores of Each Game		
21	ATLANTA	37
13	LOS ANGELES	13
24	DETROIT	38
17	Green Bay	20
17	Cleveland	0
13	MINNESOTA	10
27	St. Louis	10
0	Detroit	14
17	GREEN BAY	23
21	SAN FRANCISCO	34
3	CINCINNATI	13
10	Minnesota	23
21	Philadelphia	12
21	Oakland	28

Use Name	Pos.	Hgt	Wgt	Age	Int	Pts
Lionel Antoine	OT	6'6"	255	22		
Rich Buzin	OT	6'4"	250	26		
Randy Jackson	OT	6'5"	250	28		
Bob Asher	OG-OT	6'5"	250	24		
Jim Cadile	OG	6'3"	250	31		
Glen Holloway	OG	6'3"	250	23		
Ernie Janet	OG	6'4"	250	23		
Bob Newton	OG	6'4"	250	22		
Rich Coady	C	6'3"	245	27		
Steve DeLong	DE	6'3"	254	29		
Willie Holman	DE	6'4"	250	27		
Larry Horton	DT-DE	6'4"	248	23		
Bill Line	DT	6'7"	260	23		
Jim Osborne	DT	6'3"	250	22		
Andy Rice	DT	6'3"	268	30		
Bill Staley	DT	6'3"	250	25		
Tony McGee	DE-DT	6'4"	250	23		

Use Name	Pos.	Hgt	Wgt	Age	Int	Pts
Ross Brupbacher	LB	6'3"	215	24	1	6
Doug Buffone	LB	6'1"	230	28	1	
Jimmy Gunn	LB	6'1"	220	23		
Bill McKinney	LB	6'1"	226	27		
Bob Pifferini	LB	6'2"	226	22		
Larry Rowden	LB	6'2"	220	22		
Dick Butkus	C-LB	6'3"	245	28	2	1
Craig Clemons	DB	5'11"	187	23		
Charlie Ford	DB	6'3"	185	23	7	
Bob Jeter	DB	6'1"	200	34	2	
Garry Lyle	DB	6'2"	198	26	2	
Jerry Moore	DB	6'3"	208	22	1	
Ron Smith	DB	6'1"	195	29	1	6
Joe Taylor	DB	6'2"	200	31	4	

Joe Moore – Injury
Dave Hale – Injury

Use Name	Pos.	Hgt	Wgt	Age	Int	Pts
Bobby Douglass	QB	6'3"	225	25		48
John Huarte	QB	6'	185	28		
Cyril Pinder	HB	6'2"	210	25		18
Gary Kosins	FB-HB	6'1"	215	23		6
Don Shy	FB-HB	6'1"	210	26		6
Jim Harrison	FB	6'4"	235	23		18
Roger Lawson	HB-FB	6'2"	215	22		6
George Farmer	WR	6'4"	214	24		12
Jim Seymour	WR	6'4"	210	25		6
Cecil Turner	WR	5'10"	176	28		
Bob Parsons	TE	6'4"	234	22		6
Earl Thomas	TE	6'3"	224	23		24
Bob Wallace	TE	6'3"	220	26		
Bobby Joe Green	K	5'11"	175	34		
Mac Percival	K	6'4"	220	32		62

GREEN BAY PACKERS

RUSHING

Last Name	No.	Yds	Avg	TD
Brockington	274	1027	3.7	8
Lane	177	821	4.6	3
P. Williams	33	139	4.2	0
Hudson	15	62	4.1	0
Kopay	10	39	3.9	0
Hunter	22	37	1.7	5
Glass	2	13	6.5	0
Davis	2	0	0.0	0
Tagge	8	–3	–0.4	1
Staggers	1	–8	–8.0	0

RECEIVING

Last Name	No.	Yds	Avg	TD
Lane	26	285	11	0
Brockington	19	243	13	1
Dale	16	317	20	1
Glass	15	261	17	1
Staggers	8	123	15	1
Davis	4	119	30	1
Garrett	4	66	17	0
McGeorge	4	50	13	2
Kopay	3	19	6	0
Nitschke	1	34	34	0
Lammons	1	19	19	0

PUNT RETURNS

Last Name	No.	Yds	Avg	TD
Ellis	14	215	15	1
Staggers	9	148	16	1
Glass	1	1	1	0
Hudson	1	0	0	0

KICKOFF RETURNS

Last Name	No.	Yds	Avg	TD
Thomas	21	572	27	0
Staggers	11	260	24	0
Hudson	11	247	22	0
Kroll	1	23	23	0
Robinson	1	20	20	0
Ellis	1	10	10	0
P. Williams	1	9	9	0
Garrett	1	0	0	0
Wortman	1	0	0	0

PASSING – PUNTING – KICKING

PASSING	Att	Comp	%	Yds	Yd/Att	TD	Int–	%	RK
Hunter	199	86	43	1252	6.3	6	9–	5	10
Tagge	29	10	34	154	5.3	0	0–	0	
Patrick	4	1	25	9	2.3	0	0–	0	
Lane	2	2	100	19	9.5	0	0–	0	
Widby	2	2	100	102	51.0	1	0–	0	
Staggers	1	0	0	0	0.0	0	0–	0	

PUNTING	No	Avg
Widby	65	41.8

KICKING	XP	Att	%	FG	Att	%
Marcol	29	29	100	33	48	69

PASSING	Att	Comp	%	Yds	Yd/Att	TD	Int–	%	RK

DETROIT LIONS

RUSHING

Last Name	No.	Yds	Avg	TD
Taylor	154	658	4.3	4
Landry	81	524	6.5	9
Owens	143	519	3.6	4
Farr	62	216	3.5	3
Triplett	17	48	2.8	0
Zofko	7	28	4.0	0
Eddy	8	28	3.5	0
Munson	1	0	0.0	0

RECEIVING

Last Name	No.	Yds	Avg	TD
Taylor	29	250	9	2
C. Sanders	27	416	15	2
L. Walton	24	485	20	6
Jessie	24	424	18	4
Owens	15	100	7	0
Farr	10	132	13	0
Cotton	8	129	16	1
Hilton	5	133	27	1
McCullouch	5	96	19	1
Barnes	4	58	15	1
Eddy	2	46	23	1
Zofko	2	14	7	0

PUNT RETURNS

Last Name	No.	Yds	Avg	TD
Barney	15	108	7	0
L. Walton	3	–8	–3	0

KICKOFF RETURNS

Last Name	No.	Yds	Avg	TD
Zofko	26	616	24	0
Jessie	23	558	24	0
Barney	1	17	17	0
Triplett	1	12	12	0
Orvis	1	5	5	0
L. Walton	0	96	0	0

PASSING – PUNTING – KICKING

PASSING	Att	Comp	%	Yds	Yd/Att	TD	Int–	%	RK
Landry	268	134	50	2066	7.7	18	17–	6	6
Munson	35	20	57	194	5.5	1	1–	3	
Jessie	1	0	0	0	0.0	0	0–	0	
McCullouch	1	1	100	23	23.0	0	0–	0	

PUNTING	No	Avg
H. Weaver	43	40.3

KICKING	XP	Att	%	FG	Att	%
Mann	38	39	97	20	29	69
Zofko	1	1	100	0	0	0

MINNESOTA VIKINGS

RUSHING

Last Name	No.	Yds	Avg	TD
Reed	151	639	4.2	2
Bill Brown	82	263	3.2	4
Osborn	82	261	3.2	2
Marinaro	66	223	3.4	0
Tarkenton	27	180	6.7	0
Jones	52	164	3.2	2
Gilliam	8	14	1.8	0
Lindsey	1	8	8.0	0
Voigt	1	1	1.0	1
Krause	1	0	0.0	0
Eischeid	1	–13	–13.0	0

RECEIVING

Last Name	No.	Yds	Avg	TD
Gilliam	47	1035	22	7
Reed	30	205	7	0
Beasley	28	232	8	1
Marinaro	28	218	8	1
Bill Brown	22	298	14	4
Osborn	20	166	8	1
Washington	18	259	14	2
Henderson	10	190	19	2
Voigt	6	50	8	1
Jones	6	42	7	0
Lindsey	3	28	9	0
White	0	3	0	0

PUNT RETURNS

Last Name	No.	Yds	Avg	TD
West	16	111	7	0
Bryant	10	48	5	0

KICKOFF RETURNS

Last Name	No.	Yds	Avg	TD
Gilliam	14	369	26	0
Jones	12	327	27	0
West	9	196	22	0
Bryant	2	41	21	0
Bill Brown	3	37	12	0
Lindsey	1	17	17	0
Voigt	1	2	2	0

PASSING – PUNTING – KICKING

PASSING	Att	Comp	%	Yds	Yd/Att	TD	Int–	%	RK
Tarkenton	378	215	57	2651	7.0	18	13–	3	1
Lee	6	3	50	75	12.5	1	0–	0	
Krause	1	0	0	0	0.0	0	0–	0	

PUNTING	No	Avg
Eischeid	62	42.8

KICKING	XP	Att	%	FG	Att	%
Cox	34	34	100	21	33	64

CHICAGO BEARS

RUSHING

Last Name	No.	Yds	Avg	TD
Douglass	141	968	6.9	8
Harrison	167	622	3.7	2
Shy	91	342	3.8	1
Pinder	87	300	3.4	3
Lawson	33	106	3.2	1
Butkus	1	28	28.0	0
Thomas	5	13	2.6	0
Kosins	3	5	1.7	0
Parsons	1	0	0.0	0
Turner	3	0	0.0	0
Huarte	1	–2	–2.0	0
Seymour	1	–9	–9.0	0
Farmer	2	–13	–6.5	0

RECEIVING

Last Name	No.	Yds	Avg	TD
Thomas	20	365	18	3
Farmer	14	380	27	2
Seymour	10	165	17	1
Shy	10	109	11	0
Lawson	8	120	15	0
Harrison	8	30	4	1
Turner	3	71	24	0
Kosins	2	15	8	1
Pinder	1	13	13	0
Wallace	1	9	9	0
Parsons	1	6	6	1

PUNT RETURNS

Last Name	No.	Yds	Avg	TD
Smith	26	163	6	0
Clemons	2	15	8	0

KICKOFF RETURNS

Last Name	No.	Yds	Avg	TD
Smith	30	924	31	1
Turner	16	409	26	0
Clemons	2	53	27	0
Holloway	1	28	28	0
Butkus	1	15	15	0
Pinder	1	14	14	0
Horton	1	3	3	0
Thomas	0	82	0	1

PASSING – PUNTING – KICKING

PASSING	Att	Comp	%	Yds	Yd/Att	TD	Int–	%	RK
Douglass	198	75	38	1246	6.3	9	12–	6	12
Huarte	5	2	40	14	2.8	0	0–	0	
Green	2	1	50	23	11.5	0	1–	50	

PUNTING	No	Avg
Green	67	41.2

KICKING	XP	Att	%	FG	Att	%
Percival	26	26	100	12	24	50
Butkus	1	1	100	0	0	0

SAN FRANCISCO FORTY NINERS 8-5-1 Dick Nolan

Scores of Each Game		
34	SAN DIEGO	3
20	Buffalo	27
37	New Orleans	2
7	Los Angeles	31
17	N.Y. GIANTS	23
20	NEW ORLEANS	20
49	Atlanta	14
24	Green Bay	34
24	BALTIMORE	21
34	Chicago	21
31	Dallas	10
16	LOS ANGELES	26
20	ATLANTA	0
20	MINNESOTA	17

Use Name	Pos.	Hgt	Wgt	Age	Int	Pts
Len Rohde	OT	6'4"	248	34		
John Watson	OT	6'4"	248	23		
Cas Banaszek	C-OT	6'3"	250	26		
Randy Beisler	OG	6'4"	250	27		
Elmer Collett	OG	6'4"	240	27		
Woody Peoples	OG	6'2"	258	29		
Forrest Blue	C	6'5"	260	26		
Bill Belk	DE	6'3"	253	26		
Cedrick Hardman	DE	6'3"	255	23		
Tommy Hart	DE	6'3"	248	27	1	
Rolf Krueger	DT-DE	6'4"	253	25		
Earl Edwards	DT	6'6"	262	26		
Bob Hoskins	DT	6'2"	253	26		
Charlie Krueger	DT	6'4"	268	36		

Use Name	Pos.	Hgt	Wgt	Age	Int	Pts
Ed Beard	LB	6'2"	220	32	1	
Marty Huff	LB	6'2"	234	23		
Frank Nunley	LB	6'2"	230	26	1	
Dave Olerich	LB	6'1"	220	27		
Jim Sniadecki	LB	6'2"	230	25		
Skip Vanderbundt	LB	6'3"	224	25	2	18
Dave Wilcox	LB	6'3"	240	29	3	
Johnny Fuller	DB	6'	185	26	1	
Windlan Hall	DB	5'11"	178	22	1	
Jim Johnson	DB	6'2"	187	34	4	
Ralph McGill	DB	5'11"	183	22		
Mel Phillips	DB	6'	194	30	1	
Mike Simpson	DB	5'11"	168	25	2	6
Bruce Taylor	DB	6'	187	24	2	

Use Name	Pos.	Hgt	Wgt	Age	Int	Pts
John Brodie	QB	6'1"	203	37		6
Joe Reed	QB	6'1"	195	24		
Steve Spurrier	QB	6'2"	203	27		
John Isenbarger	HB	6'3"	205	24		6
Doug Cunningham	HB	5'11"	190	26		
Jimmy Thomas	HB	6'1"	214	25		6
Vic Washington	HB	5'10"	196	26		30
Ken Willard	FB	6'2"	216	29		30
Larry Schreiber	HB-FB	6'	200	25		18
Terry Beasley	WR	5'10"	184	21		
Preston Riley	WR	6'	180	24		6
Gene Washington	WR	6'1"	185	25		72
Ted Kwalick	TE	6'4"	223	25		54
Dick Witcher	TE	6'3"	204	27		6
Bruce Gossett	K	6'2"	228	29		95
Jim McCann	K	6'2"	163	23		

ATLANTA FALCONS 7-7-0 Norm Van Brocklin

Scores of Each Game		
37	Chicago	21
20	New England	21
31	LOS ANGELES	3
23	DETROIT	26
21	New Orleans	14
10	Green Bay	9
14	SAN FRANCISCO	49
7	Los Angeles	20
36	NEW ORLEANS	20
13	Washington	24
23	DENVER	20
20	HOUSTON	10
0	San Francisco	20
14	KANSAS CITY	17

Use Name	Pos.	Hgt	Wgt	Age	Int	Pts
Len Gotshalk	OT	6'4"	244	22		
George Kunz	OT	6'5"	257	25		
Bill Sandeman	OT	6'6"	252	29		
Dennis Havig	OG	6'2"	245	23		
Andy Mauer	OG	6'3"	265	23		
Jim Miller	OG	6'3"	240	23		
Ted Fritsch	C	6'2"	240	22		
Jeff Van Note	OG-C	6'2"	243	26		
Claude Humphrey	DE	6'5"	252	28		2
John Zook	DE	6'5"	243	24		6
Chuck Walker (from STL)	DT-DE	6'2"	250	31		
Glen Condren	DT	6'2"	250	30		
Rosie Manning	DT	6'5"	256	22		
John Small	DT	6'5"	270	25		
Mike Lewis	DE-DT	6'3"	244	23	1	2

Use Name	Pos.	Hgt	Wgt	Age	Int	Pts
Grady Allen	LB	6'3"	230	26		
Duane Benson	LB	6'2"	215	27		
Greg Brezina	LB	6'2"	226	26		
Don Hansen	LB	6'3"	235	28	1	
Noel Jenke	LB	6'1"	220	25		
Tommy Nobis	LB	6'2"	240	28	3	6
Ray Brown	DB	6'2"	208	23	2	
Ray Easterling	DB	6'	195	22		
Clarence Ellis	DB	5'11"	193	22	3	
Willie Germany	DB	6'	192	24		
Tom Hayes	DB	6'1"	200	26	5	
Tony Plummer	DB	5'11"	188	25		
Ken Reaves	DB	6'3"	210	77	3	
Larry Shears	DB	5'10"	185	23		

Harmon Wages — Knee Injury

Use Name	Pos.	Hgt	Wgt	Age	Int	Pts
Bob Berry	QB	5'11"	185	30		12
Pat Sullivan	QB	6'0"	198	22		
Willie Belton	HB	5'11"	207	23		
Dave Hampton	HB	6'	210	25		42
Joe Profit	HB	6'	213	23		
Ron Lamb	FB	6'2"	225	28		
Art Malone	FB	5'11"	211	24		60
Eddie Ray	FB	6'1"	240	25		
Ken Burrow	WR	6'	190	24		30
Wes Chesson	WR	6'2"	195	23		6
Ray Jarvis	WR	5'11"	200	23		
Todd Snyder	WR	6'2"	194	23		
Larry Mialik	TE	6'2"	226	22		
Jim Mitchell	TE	6'2"	234	24		24
Bill Bell	K	6'1"	192	24		79
John James	K	6'3"	197	23		

LOS ANGELES RAMS 6-7-1 Tommy Prothro

Scores of Each Game		
34	NEW ORLEANS	14
13	Chicago	13
3	Atlanta	31
31	SAN FRANCISCO	7
34	Philadelphia	3
15	CINCINNATI	12
17	Oakland	45
20	ATLANTA	7
10	DENVER	16
41	MINNESOTA	45
16	New Orleans	19
26	San Francisco	16
14	St. Louis	24
17	DETROIT	34

Use Name	Pos.	Hgt	Wgt	Age	Int	Pts
Charley Cowan	OT	6'4"	250	23		
Harry Schuh	OT	6'2"	260	29		
John Williams	OG-OT	6'3"	256	26		
Mike LaHood	OG	6'3"	250	27		
Tom Mack	OG	6'3"	250	28		
Joe Scibelli	OG	6'1"	255	33		
Ken Iman	C	6'1"	240	33		
Rich Saul	OG-C	6'3"	235	24		
Coy Bacon	DE	6'4"	270	30		
Fred Dryer	DE	6'6"	240	26		
Jack Youngblood	DE	6'4"	250	22		
Larry Brooks	DT	6'3"	255	22		
Bill Nelson	DT	6'7"	270	24		
Merlin Olsen	DT	6'5"	270	31		
Phil Olsen	DT	6'5"	265	24		

Use Name	Pos.	Hgt	Wgt	Age	Int	Pts
Ken Geddes	LB	6'3"	235	25		
Dean Halverson	LB	6'2"	212	26		
Marlin McKeever	LB	6'1"	235	32	2	
John Pergine	LB	6'1"	225	25		
Jim Purnell	LB	6'2"	238	30	1	
Jack Reynolds	LB	6'1"	232	24		
Isiah Robertson	LB	6'3"	225	23		
Al Clark	DB	6'	180	24	1	
Dave Elmendorf	DB	6'1"	195	23	3	
Gene Howard	DB	6'	190	25	3	6
Jim Nettles	DB	5'9"	177	30	6	
Clancy Williams	DB	6'2"	194	29		
Roger Williams	DB	5'10"	180	26		

Travis Williams — Knee Injury

Use Name	Pos.	Hgt	Wgt	Age	Int	Pts
Pete Beathard	QB	6'2"	200	30		
Roman Gabriel	QB	6'4"	220	32		6
Jim Bertelsen	HB	5'11"	205	22		36
Larry McCutcheon	HB	6'1"	205	22		
Larry Smith	HB	6'3"	220	24		18
Bob Thomas	HB	5'10"	200	23		18
Les Josephson	FB	6'	207	29		6
Willie Ellison	HB-FB	6'1"	200	27		36
Dick Gordon	WR	5'11"	190	27		6
John Love	WR	5'11"	185	28		6
David Ray	WR	6'	195	27		103
Lance Rentzel	WR	6'2"	202	28		12
Jack Snow	WR	6'2"	190	29		24
Joe Sweet	WR	6'2"	196	24		8
Pat Curran	TE	6'3"	238	26		
Bob Klein	TE	6'5"	235	25		6
Dave Chapple	K	6'	180	25		

NEW ORLEANS SAINTS 2-11-1 J. D. Roberts

Scores of Each Game		
14	Los Angeles	34
17	KANSAS CITY	20
2	SAN FRANCISCO	37
21	N.Y. Giants	45
14	ATLANTA	21
20	San Francisco	20
21	PHILADELPHIA	3
6	Minnesota	37
20	Atlanta	36
14	Detroit	27
19	LOS ANGELES	16
17	N.Y. Jets	18
10	NEW ENGLAND	17
20	GREEN BAY	30

Use Name	Pos.	Hgt	Wgt	Age	Int	Pts
Glen Ray Hines	OT	6'5"	265	28		
Don Morrison	OT	6'5"	255	22		
Craig Robinson	OT	6'4"	250	23		
Carl Johnson	OG-OT	6'3"	240	22		
Jake Kupp	OG	6'3"	248	30		
Royce Smith	OG	6'3"	245	23		
Del Williams	OG	6'2"	240	26		
John Didion	C	6'4"	245	24		
Bob Kuziel	C	6'4"	255	22		
Wimpy Winther	C	6'4"	260	24		
Mike Crangle	DE	6'4"	243	25		
Richard Neal	DE	6'3"	254	24		6
Joe Owens	DE	6'2"	245	24		2
Faddie Tillman	DT-DE	6'5"	230	23		
Dave Long	DT	6'4"	245	27		
Doug Mooers	DT	6'6"	265	25		
Bob Pollard	DT	6'3"	245	23		

Use Name	Pos.	Hgt	Wgt	Age	Int	Pts
Wayne Coleman	LB	6'1"	230	26		
Joe Federspiel	LB	6'1"	225	22		
Willie Hall	LB	6'2"	217	22		
Ray Hester	LB	6'2"	215	23		
Bill Hobbs	LB	6'	220	26		
Dick Palmer (from BUF)	LB	6'2"	232	24		
Tom Roussel	LB	6'3"	235	27	2	
Tom Stincic	LB	6'2"	230	25		
Billy Hayes	DB	6'1"	175	25		
Hugo Hollas	DB	6'1"	190	27	1	
Delles Howell	DB	6'3"	202	25	1	
Ernie Jackson	DB	5'10"	173	22	3	6
Bivian Lee	DB	6'3"	200	24	4	
Tom Myers	DB	5'11"	184	21	3	
Doug Wyatt	DB	6'1"	195	25		6

Carlos Bell — Injury
Al Dodd — Injury
Dee Martin — Injury

Use Name	Pos.	Hgt	Wgt	Age	Int	Pts
Edd Hargett	QB	5'11"	190	25		
Archie Manning	QB	6'3"	204	23		12
Bob Gresham	HB	5'11"	195	24		18
Virgil Robinson	HB	5'11"	195	24		
Joe Williams	HB	6'	193	25		
Jamie Ford	FB-HB	6'	200	22		
Bill Butler	FB	6'	218	22		12
Jim Strong	FB	6'1"	204	25		
Arthur Green	HB-FB	5'11"	198	24		
Dan Abramowicz	WR	6'1"	195	27		42
Margene Adkins	WR	5'10"	183	25		
Bob Newland	WR	6'2"	190	23		12
Cephus Weatherspoon	WR	6'1"	182	24		
Creston Whitaker	WR	6'2"	187	24		
Bob Brown	TE	6'3"	225	29		6
Dave Parks	TE	6'2"	203	30		36
Charlie Durkee	K	5'11"	165	28		18
Julian Fagan	K	6'3"	205	24		
Happy Feller	K	5'11"	185	23		28
Toni Linhart	K	6'	170	30		11

SAN FRANCISCO FORTY NINERS

RUSHING

Last Name	No.	Yds	Avg	TD
V. Washington	141	468	3.3	3
Schreiber	118	420	3.6	2
Willard	100	345	3.5	4
Thomas	52	250	4.8	1
Spurrier	11	51	4.6	0
Cunningham	8	32	4.0	0
Reed	4	22	5.5	0
Kwalick	5	11	2.2	0
Isenbarger	3	9	3.0	0
Brodie	3	8	2.7	1

RECEIVING

Last Name	No.	Yds	Avg	TD
G. Wash'gton	46	918	20	12
V. Wash'gton	43	393	9	1
Kwalick	40	751	19	9
Schreiber	31	283	9	1
Willard	24	131	5	1
Thomas	15	148	10	0
Riley	11	156	14	1
Isenbarger	3	66	22	1
Witcher	3	22	7	1
Beasley	1	20	20	0

PUNT RETURNS

Last Name	No.	Yds	Avg	TD
McGill	22	219	10	0
Taylor	21	145	7	0
Fuller	1	9	9	0

KICKOFF RETURNS

Last Name	No.	Yds	Avg	TD
V. Washington	27	771	29	1
McGill	10	192	19	0
Schreiber	2	41	21	0
Nunley	1	21	21	0
Hoskins	2	17	9	0
Beard	2	–1	–1	0

PASSING – PUNTING – KICKING

PASSING	Att	Comp	%	Yds	Yd/Att	TD	Int–	%	RK
Spurrier	269	147	55	1983	7.4	18	16–	6	4
Brodie	110	70	64	905	8.2	9	8–	7	
Isenbarger	1	0	0	0	0.0	0	0–	0	

PUNTING	No	Avg
McCann	64	39.7

KICKING	XP	Att	%	FG	Att	%
Gossett	41	42	98	18	29	62

ATLANTA FALCONS

RUSHING

Last Name	No.	Yds	Avg	TD
Hampton	230	995	4.3	6
Malone	180	798	4.4	8
Profit	40	132	3.3	0
Berry	24	86	3.6	2
Ray	8	34	4.3	0
Belton	10	20	2.0	0
Mitchell	2	19	9.5	0
Sullivan	2	8	4.0	0
Burrow	3	3	1.0	0
Bell	1	–3	–3.0	0

RECEIVING

Last Name	No.	Yds	Avg	TD
Malone	50	585	12	2
Burrow	29	492	17	5
Mitchell	28	470	17	4
Hampton	23	244	11	1
Chesson	18	338	19	1
Profit	3	22	7	0
Snyder	1	19	19	0
Jarvis	1	18	18	0
Ray	1	14	14	0
Lamb	1	10	10	0
Belton	1	–1	–1	0
Berry	1	–9	–9	0

PUNT RETURNS

Last Name	No.	Yds	Avg	TD
Belton	17	110	6	0
Brown	8	71	9	0
Ellis	1	13	13	0
Small	1	0	0	0

KICKOFF RETURNS

Last Name	No.	Yds	Avg	TD
Hampton	25	535	21	0
Belton	21	441	21	0
Malone	2	37	19	0
Plummer	1	21	21	0
Germany	2	5	3	0
Chesson	1	0	0	0

PASSING – PUNTING – KICKING

PASSING	Att	Comp	%	Yds	Yd/Att	TD	Int–	%	RK
Berry	277	154	56	2158	7.8	13	12–	4	3
Sullivan	19	3	16	44	2.3	0	3–	16	

PUNTING	No	Avg
James	61	42.8

KICKING	XP	Att	%	FG	Att	%
Bell	31	31	100	16	30	53

LOS ANGELES RAMS

RUSHING

Last Name	No.	Yds	Avg	TD
Ellison	170	764	4.5	5
Bertelsen	123	581	4.7	5
Thomas	77	433	5.6	3
Smith	60	276	4.6	2
Josephson	18	75	4.2	0
Rentzel	7	71	10.1	1
Gabriel	14	16	1.1	1
Sweet	1	1	1.0	0
Beathard	1	–1	–1.0	0
Klein	1	–7	–7.0	0

RECEIVING

Last Name	No.	Yds	Avg	TD
Snow	30	590	20	4
Bertelsen	29	331	11	1
Klein	29	330	11	1
Rentzel	27	365	14	1
Ellison	23	141	6	1
Smith	15	186	12	1
Josephson	14	170	12	1
Thomas	11	95	9	0
Gordon	3	29	10	1
Sweet	2	26	13	1
Love	1	19	19	1

PUNT RETURNS

Last Name	No.	Yds	Avg	TD
Bertelson	16	232	15	0
Elmendorf	3	56	19	0
Love	10	39	4	0
Gordon	4	20	5	0

KICKOFF RETURNS

Last Name	No.	Yds	Avg	TD
Ellison	14	345	25	0
Thomas	8	212	27	0
Love	8	167	21	0
R. Williams	6	141	24	0
Gordon	4	141	35	0
Bertelsen	4	88	22	0
Clark	3	59	20	0
Howard	2	51	26	0
Pergine	3	46	15	0
Curran	4	37	9	0

PASSING – PUNTING – KICKING

PASSING	Att	Comp	%	Yds	Yd/Att	TD	Int–	%	RK
Gabriel	323	165	51	2027	6.3	12	15–	5	9
Beathard	48	19	40	255	5.3	1	7–	15	

PUNTING	No	Avg
Chapple	53	44.2

KICKING	XP	Att	%	FG	Att	%
Ray	31	31	100	24	41	59

NEW ORLEANS SAINTS

RUSHING

Last Name	No.	Yds	Avg	TD
Gresham	121	381	3.1	3
Manning	63	351	5.6	2
Butler	54	233	4.3	0
Strong	37	120	3.2	0
J. Williams	31	72	2.3	0
Green	14	51	3.6	0
Ford	11	28	2.5	0
V. Robinson	5	1	0.2	0
Parks	1	–7	–7.0	0

RECEIVING

Last Name	No.	Yds	Avg	TD
Newland	47	579	12	2
Abramowicz	38	668	18	7
Parks	32	542	17	6
Gresham	29	192	7	0
Butler	25	226	9	2
J. Williams	16	116	7	0
Strong	14	123	9	0
Brown	11	175	16	1
Adkins	9	96	11	0
Green	7	49	7	0
Ford	1	9	9	0
Whitaker	1	6	6	0

PUNT RETURNS

Last Name	No.	Yds	Avg	TD
Myers	9	43	5	0
Adkins	7	0	0	0

KICKOFF RETURNS

Last Name	No.	Yds	Avg	TD
Adkins	43	1020	24	0
Green	8	187	23	0
Strong	4	53	13	0
J. Williams	2	23	12	0
Butler	1	14	14	0
Hollas	2	9	5	0
Newland	1	6	6	0

PASSING – PUNTING – KICKING

PASSING	Att	Comp	%	Yds	Yd/Att	TD	Int–	%	RK
Manning	448	230	51	2781	6.2	18	21–	5	7
Gresham	1	0	0	0	0.0	0	0–	0	

PUNTING	No	Avg
Fagan	71	40.8

KICKING	XP	Att	%	FG	Att	%
Feller	10	11	91	6	11	55
Durkee	9	9	100	3	9	33
Linhart	5	5	100	2	5	40

1972 A.F.C. Perfect From Start to Finish

Vince Lombardi's Packers had never done it. George Halas' Chicago Bears had come close but always fallen short. But Don Shula's Miami Dolphins did it; they went through the season unbeaten and untied and won three more games in the playoffs to finish with a perfect 17-0-0 record. The Bears had finished the 1934 and 1942 regular seasons with unblemished records, but both squads lost in the NFL championship game. Before the NFL split up into divisions, the Canton Bulldogs had gone undefeated in 1922 and 1923 and the Green Bay Packers in 1929, but each of those teams had been tied during the season. Paul Brown's Cleveland Browns breezed through the 1948 AAFC season without a loss or tie, but they had not been able to repeat that achievement after coming over to the NFL. The Dolphins were the first NFL team to compile an absolutely perfect record for a season, and they were a young team which had still not reached full development.

EASTERN DIVISION

Miami Dolphins—Seven years ago the Dolphins had been created out of castoffs from the eight AFL teams; four years ago, they had finished on the bottom of the AFL's Eastern Division. But since Don Shula had taken over as coach in 1970, he had rebuilt, reorganized, and psyched the Dolphins into a powerhouse which rolled undefeated and untied through the 1973 season. The Miami defense was known as the "No-Name Defense," but those anonymous defenders allowed the fewest points in the NFL. After Bob Griese went out with an ankle injury in mid-season, veteran Earl Morrall stepped in at quarterback and kept the offense moving. The five Miami interior linemen—Norm Evans, Wayne Moore, Bob Keuchenberg, Larry Little, and Jim Langer—had all been cut loose by other pro teams, but the Dolphin blocking protected Morrall and cleared the way for runners Larry Csonka, Mercury Morris, and Jim Kiick. Csonka and Morris became the first teammates ever to gain 1,000 yards each in one season.

New York Jets—Quarterback Joe Namath stayed healthy all year and again wreaked havoc on defensive backs with his bullet passing, but the Jets nevertheless finished with a 7-7 record and out of the playoffs. The Jet defense unfortunately allowed points as readily as Namath and the offense could score them. None of the deep backs had a good year, while the front line was hurt by Gerry Philbin's disenchantment with coach Weeb Ewbank and John Elliott's slow recovery from knee surgery. The New York offensive cupboard was full. Running behind a line that was growing shopworn, John Riggins and Emerson Boozer balanced Namath's passing with consistently strong ball-carrying. But when Riggins and Boozer both went out of action late in the year with injuries, the Jet attack lost most of its spark.

Baltimore Colts—New owner Bob Irsay installed Joe Thomas as his general manager, and Thomas began ripping the team apart after it fell out of contention with four losses in the first five games. He fired coach Don McCafferty, ordered interim coach John Sandusky to bench veteran quarterback John Unitas in favor of younger Marty Domres, and one by one disposed of Baltimore veterans who had starred in the late 1960s and early 1970s. Before next season would begin, Thomas had traded off Unitas, Tom Matte, Dan Sullivan, Bill Curry, Bubba Smith, Fred Miller, Jerry Logan, Billy Newsome, Tom Nowatzke, and Norm Bulaich, and Bob Vogel retired.

Buffalo Bills—By the end of the opening game, starting offensive linemen Bruce Jarvis and Jim Reilly were out for the season with injuries. More blockers went onto the disabled list as the season progressed, and the Bills scoured the country for healthy offensive linemen to fill the breach. But even with the patchwork line, O. J. Simpson blossomed into stardom by running for 1,251 yards, the most in the NFL. Helping O. J. to prominence was head coach Lou Saban, who returned to the Bills with an offensive plan of going to Simpson twice as often as he had been used. Saban had quit the Bills after leading them to the AFL championship in 1965, but victories came harder with this Buffalo squad as only Walt Patulski, Don Croft, and Bobby James caused any excitement in the defensive platoon.

New England Patriots—General manager Upton Bell and head coach John Mazur battled with each other all season over how to build the Patriots. When the team won only three games all year, both Bell and Mazur were out of work by the end of the year. The biggest offensive problem was a deteriorating offensive line which exposed quarterback Jim Plunkett to severe punishment from enemy linemen. On defense, only Julius Adams and Jim Cheyunski provided any stability in the line and linebacking. Several veteran Patriots were lopped from the squad this year, as Jim Nance, Houston Antwine, Ron Sellers, and Don Webb all were casualties of a rebuilding program cursed with two dissenting architects. Before the season was over, coach Mazur had quit. In an unusual move to end an unusual season, the San Diego Chargers lent scout Phil Bengtson to the Patriots as interim head coach for the rest of the year.

CENTRAL DIVISION

Pittsburgh Steelers—Pittsburgh fans thoroughly enjoyed the Steelers' drive to their first title of any sort. One group of fans dubbed themselves "Franco's Army" and adopted rookie fullback Franco Harris as their favorite. Harris' power running had given the Pittsburgh attack a new dimension. Another group of fans, known as "Gerela's Gorillas," took place-kicker Roy Gerela as their idol. Appreciated by all Steeler fans were quarterback Terry Bradshaw and the very strong defensive unit. With both platoons playing well, the Steelers held a share of first place until December 3, when a 30-0 thumping of the Browns gave the teams complete possession of the top rung in the division.

Cleveland Browns—The Browns' greatest asset was their ability to stay cool in pressure situations. Despite injuries in the defensive line, a chaotic linebacking situation, and problems in the offensive line, the Browns calmly beat the Bengals and Jets in the final two games to win the AFC wild-card berth in the playoffs. The partial retirement of Bill Nelsen put the quarterbacking burden squarely on Mike Phipps' shoulders, and the young passer responded with a season of steady progress as a leader. The Browns had strength at running back, with Leroy Kelly and Bo Scott, and in the secondary, where youngsters Clarence Scott and Tom Darden had become instant stars.

Cincinnati Bengals—The Bengals' season unfolded in three separate stages. First came the good start of four wins in the opening five games, then a mid-season slump of four losses in five games, and finally a late spurt of three wins in the last four games. Playing consistently well throughout the season was the Cincinnati defense, a unit strengthened by the addition of two top rookies in Sherman White and Tommy Casanova. Veteran Bengal defenders Mike Reid, Ron Carpenter, Bill Bergey, and Lemar Parrish shared with the rookies a wealth of talent, but the offense lacked the polished excellence of the defense; too many holes remained to be filled in this platoon. The Bengals needed a powerful running back and a speedy wide receiver, but few people bet against Paul Brown finding them in next year's draft as he had found his defense.

Houston Oilers—Owner Bud Adams used a long-term contract to lure head coach Bill Peterson away from Rice, but the new coach could not stop the deterioration of the Oilers. Outside of an early-season upset of the Jets, the Oilers served as the NFL's punching bag. Mid-season trades brought Fred Willis, Paul Robinson, and Dave Smith to Houston, but they could not help an offensive plagued with a porous line. On defense, the team's two best linemen, Elvin Bethea and Mike Tilleman, demanded to be traded; two starting linebackers, George Webster and Ron Pritchard, were traded in mid-season.

WESTERN DIVISION

Oakland Raiders—The Raiders had a knack for slipping new talent into the lineup while continuing to win without interruption. The defensive line, for instance, had been completely rebuilt in the last two seasons. Veterans like Ben Davidson, Tom Keating, and Carleton Oates had been eased aside in favor of youngsters Horace Jones, Art Thoms, Otis Sistrunk, and Tony Cline. The defense, meanwhile, suffered no letdown at all in stopping the run or pressuring the passer. At linebacker, the Raiders surrounded veteran Dan Conners with young outside men Phil Villipiano and Gerald Irons, and the secondary had veteran cornerbacks in Willie Brown and Nemiah Wilson and young safeties in George Atkinson and Jack Tatum. The offense had the same mixture of experience and youth, while the specialists ranged from rookie punt returner Cliff Branch to forty-four-year-old place-kicker George Blanda.

Kansas City Chiefs—Unable to win regularly at home, the Chiefs thus gave the Raiders only a weak challenge for the Western Division title. After years as an AFC power, the team was starting to crack under the weight of time. Safety Johnny Robinson retired, offensive linemen Ed Budde, Jim Tyrer, and Dave Hill were slowing down, and quarterback Len Dawson needed more rest. Other trouble spots for coach Hank Stram were receiver Elmo Wright's injury, a mediocre showing by the defensive ends, and a disappointing showing by rookie runner Jeff Kinney.

Denver Broncos—The Broncos followed the trend to hiring college coaches by signing John Ralston away from Stanford, but Ralston went out and traded for a veteran quarterback to lead the young Broncos on the field. Charley Johnson came over from Houston and gave the club a top passer and a poised offensive leader. With the Denver passing attack in good order, Floyd Little carried less of the offensive burden but still picked up 859 yards on the ground. Ralston traded away veteran defensive linemen Richard Jackson and Dave Costa, but the new unit of Lyle Alzado, Paul Smith, Pete Duranko, and Lloyd Voss kept pressure on opposing quarterbacks as the Broncos had their highest finish in ten years.

San Diego Chargers—Coach Harland Svare traded for some of the league's most famous oldsters and malcontents, bringing John Mackey, Deacon Jones, Lionel Aldridge, Dave Costa, Cid Edwards, Tim Rossovich, and Duane Thomas to San Diego. The Thomas deal was a complete washout, as Thomas' personal problems put him in no mood to play football. Injuries bothered Rossovich, and age had cut down on Mackey's skills, but the other acquisitions enjoyed good seasons in their new home. The defense suffered, however, when injuries decimated the secondary, and the offense was hurt by a difference in philosophy between quarterback John Hadl and offensive coach Bob Schnelker. Whereas Hadl had always run a wide-open passing attack, Schnelker insisted on a ball-control offense.

FINAL TEAM STATISTICS

OFFENSE

	BALT.	BUFF.	CIN	CLEV.	DENV.	HOUS.	K.C.	MIAMI	N.ENG.	N.Y.	OAK.	PITT.	S.D.
FIRST DOWNS:													
Total	251	221	255	215	237	183	245	291	236	250	**297**	228	262
by Rushing	97	104	112	102	87	80	118	**170**	86	106	145	131	123
by Passing	124	98	122	101	**132**	88	116	102	126	117	122	79	116
by Penalty	**30**	19	21	12	18	15	11	19	24	27	**30**	18	23
RUSHING:													
Number	462	512	491	453	409	397	476	**613**	386	461	521	497	504
Yards	1894	2132	1996	1793	1838	1518	1915	**2960**	1532	2010	2376	2520	1995
Average Yards	4.1	4.2	4.1	4.0	4.5	3.8	4.0	4.8	4.0	4.4	4.6	**5.1**	4.0
Touchdowns	10	11	16	13	17	7	6	**26**	13	18	20	22	12
PASSING:													
Attempts	381	316	384	337	384	375	384	259	**412**	347	370	324	377
Completions	203	164	**219**	158	201	181	217	144	198	172	198	156	192
Completion Percentage	53.3	51.9	**57.0**	46.9	52.3	48.3	56.5	55.6	48.1	49.6	53.5	48.1	50.9
Passing Yards	2503	2012	2513	2135	2900	2045	2335	2235	2579	**2930**	2599	1958	2516
Avg. Yards per Attempt	6.6	6.4	6.5	6.3	7.6	5.5	6.1	**8.6**	6.3	8.4	7.0	6.0	6.7
Avg. Yards per Complet.	12.3	12.3	11.5	13.5	14.4	11.3	10.8	15.5	13.0	**17.0**	13.1	12.6	13.1
Time Tackled Passing	25	49	24	27	38	45	34	21	44	**17**	24	32	23
Yards Lost Tackled	210	411	192	219	266	372	297	159	452	**153**	230	247	212
Net Yards	2293	1601	2321	1916	2634	1673	2038	2076	2127	**2777**	2369	1711	2304
Touchdowns	15	16	10	13	19	10	20	17	10	21	**23**	12	15
Interceptions	12	24	**11**	19	23	23	20	12	28	22	15	12	28
Percent Intercepted	3.1	7.6	**2.9**	5.6	6.0	6.1	5.2	4.6	6.8	6.3	7.6	3.7	7.4
PUNTS:													
Number	57	80	66	81	60	**85**	66	44	75	51	55	66	45
Average Distance	42.1	38.8	42.1	43.2	40.1	41.0	**44.8**	39.4	38.1	39.3	36.9	43.6	40.3
PUNT RETURNS:													
Number	43	25	**47**	37	28	34	29	40	17	25	24	30	23
Yards	348	164	**437**	211	310	163	126	329	37	242	66	262	185
Average Yards	8.1	6.6	9.3	5.7	**11.1**	4.8	4.3	8.2	2.2	9.7	2.8	8.7	8.0
Touchdowns	0	0	**2**	0	1	0	0	0	0	1	0	0	0
KICKOFF RETURNS:													
Number	47	**60**	46	41	55	54	46	24	55	56	38	33	**60**
Yards	**1321**	1389	1018	933	1256	1093	1057	546	1293	1218	813	760	1273
Average Yards	**28.1**	23.2	22.1	22.8	22.8	20.2	23.0	22.8	23.5	21.8	21.4	23.0	21.2
Touchdowns	**1**	0	0	0	**1**	0	0	0	0	0	0	0	0
INTERCEPTION RETURNS:													
Number	23	23	20	13	10	6	24	26	10	19	25	**28**	24
Yards	331	369	326	154	109	93	**396**	286	223	282	328	395	310
Average Yards	14.4	16.0	16.3	11.8	10.9	15.5	16.5	11.0	**22.3**	14.8	13.1	14.1	12.9
Touchdowns	1	3	3	1	0	0	**5**	1	0	0	1	1	1
PENALTIES:													
Number	58	87	76	57	**89**	66	69	68	66	74	84	81	87
Yards	605	**900**	738	536	827	581	653	714	761	719	757	728	789
FUMBLES:													
Number	37	29	28	**21**	25	30	23	25	26	**21**	31	27	40
Number Lost	22	15	18	**9**	11	10	12	16	10	**9**	17	14	20
POINTS:													
Total	235	257	299	268	325	164	287	**385**	192	367	365	343	264
PAT Attempts	28	30	31	29	38	18	32	**45**	24	41	**45**	37	30
PAT Made	28	29	30	28	37	17	32	43	24	40	**44**	35	28
FG Attempts	39	24	40	27	29	21	36	37	16	37	26	**41**	31
FG Made	13	16	27	22	20	13	21	24	8	27	17	**28**	18
Percent FG Made	33.3	66.7	67.5	**81.5**	69.0	61.9	58.3	64.9	50.0	73.0	65.4	68.3	58.1
Safeties	0	0	1	0	0	0	0	0	0	0	0	**1**	**1**

DEFENSE

	BALT.	BUFF.	CIN.	CLEV.	DENV.	HOUS.	K.C.	MIAMI	N.ENG.	N.Y.	OAK.	PITT.	S.D.
FIRST DOWNS:													
Total	233	249	207	240	251	263	227	**186**	288	255	227	228	244
by Rushing	111	125	98	130	102	147	93	**76**	143	121	97	88	99
by Passing	109	95	92	**89**	123	100	116	96	124	118	104	116	124
by Penalty	**13**	29	17	21	26	16	18	14	21	16	26	24	21
RUSHING:													
Number	515	532	406	520	439	546	453	**389**	548	476	469	445	435
Yards	1989	2241	1815	2333	1668	2591	1805	**1548**	2717	2072	1764	1715	1673
Average Yards	3.9	4.2	4.5	4.5	3.8	4.7	4.0	4.0	5.0	4.4	**3.8**	3.9	3.8
Touchdowns	15	26	11	13	15	23	12	8	27	16	9	**6**	18
PASSING:													
Attempts	313	**308**	350	310	397	324	368	348	326	363	348	411	358
Completions	178	**131**	167	160	206	174	186	178	175	186	166	206	201
Completion Percentage	56.9	**42.5**	47.7	51.6	51.9	53.7	50.5	51.1	53.7	51.2	47.7	50.1	56.1
Passing Yards	2555	2148	2033	**1994**	2540	2315	2483	2029	2634	2888	2363	2393	2441
Avg. Yards per Attempt	8.2	7.0	**5.8**	6.4	6.4	7.1	6.7	5.8	8.1	8.0	6.8	5.8	6.8
Avg. Yards per Complet.	14.4	16.4	12.2	12.5	12.3	13.3	13.3	**11.4**	15.1	15.5	14.2	11.6	12.1
Time Tackled Passing	25	22	38	38	**41**	24	32	33	15	27	27	40	26
Yards Lost Tackled	232	197	296	258	**357**	172	261	280	101	251	211	337	233
Net Yards	2323	1951	1737	**1736**	2183	2143	2222	1749	2533	2637	2152	2056	2208
Touchdowns	15	19	11	14	19	12	17	10	24	18	14	**9**	18
Interceptions	23	23	20	13	10	6	24	26	10	19	25	**28**	24
Percent Intercepted	7.3	**7.5**	5.7	4.2	2.5	1.9	6.5	7.5	3.1	5.2	7.2	6.8	6.7
PUNTS:													
Number	71	65	**84**	74	66	61	61	68	48	56	56	74	56
Average Distance	39.0	39.5	42.4	40.9	45.2	42.1	40.3	41.1	40.4	39.4	42.5	40.3	**38.4**
PUNT RETURNS:													
Number	29	39	26	46	28	31	38	**17**	34	23	28	37	**17**
Yards	204	329	152	357	249	299	328	**67**	366	239	215	169	157
Average Yards	7.0	8.4	5.8	7.8	8.9	9.6	8.6	**3.9**	10.8	10.4	7.7	4.6	9.2
Touchdowns	**0**	1	**0**	**0**	1	1	**0**	**0**	1	**0**	**0**	**0**	1
KICKOFF RETURNS:													
Number	50	29	44	50	54	**28**	43	56	32	47	59	54	53
Yards	1091	644	984	1198	1246	**547**	1083	1283	784	1386	1393	1190	1225
Average Yards	21.8	22.2	22.4	24.0	23.1	**19.5**	25.2	22.9	24.5	29.5	23.6	22.0	23.1
Touchdowns	**0**	**0**	**0**	**0**	**0**	**0**	**0**	**0**	**0**	1	1	**0**	1
INTERCEPTION RETURNS:													
Number	12	24	**11**	19	23	23	20	12	28	22	15	12	28
Yards	169	305	**70**	145	441	319	278	249	490	271	178	195	229
Average Yards	14.1	12.7	**6.4**	7.6	19.2	13.9	13.9	20.8	17.5	12.3	11.9	16.3	8.2
Touchdowns	**0**	1	**0**	**0**	6	3	**0**	2	2	1	**0**	1	**0**
PENALTIES:													
Number	84	72	69	63	83	79	66	70	**88**	86	83	77	75
Yards	826	685	581	557	784	741	643	659	**862**	856	801	712	679
FUMBLES:													
Number	22	**20**	30	39	27	29	35	32	23	21	22	37	26
Number Lost	13	8	9	16	12	18	19	**20**	14	12	12	**20**	10
POINTS:													
Total	252	377	229	249	350	380	254	**171**	446	324	248	175	344
PAT Attempts	30	47	24	27	41	40	30	21	54	37	27	**18**	41
PAT Made	27	47	23	27	39	39	29	18	54	36	26	**17**	41
FG Attempts	24	27	29	29	33	40	31	**19**	36	33	37	27	28
FG Made	15	16	20	20	21	33	15	**9**	22	22	20	16	19
Percent FG Made	62.5	59.3	69.0	69.0	63.6	82.5	48.4	**47.4**	61.1	66.7	54.1	59.3	67.9
Safeties	**0**	**0**	1	**0**	1	1	**0**	**0**	1	**0**	**0**	1	**0**

CONFERENCE PLAYOFFS

December 23, at Pittsburgh (Attendance 50,327)

SCORING

PITTSBURGH	0	0	3	10–13
OAKLAND	0	0	0	7– 7

Third Quarter
PIT. Gerela, 18 yard field goal

Fourth Quarter
PIT. Gerela, 29 yard field goal
OAK. Stabler, 30 yard rush
PAT–Blanda (kick)
PIT. Harris, 60 yard pass from Bradshaw PAT–Gerela (kick)

TEAM STATISTICS

PITT.		OAK.
13	First Downs–Total	13
7	First Downs–Rushing	9
6	First Downs–Passing	4
0	First Downs–Penalty	0
0	Fumbles–Number	3
0	Fumbles–Lost Ball	2
1	Penalties–Number	2
5	Yards Penalized	15
1	Missed Field Goals	0
64	Offensive Plays	65
252	Net Yards	216
3.9	Average Gain	3.3
1	Giveaways	4
4	Takeaways	1
+3	Difference	–3

INDIVIDUAL STATISTICS

PITTSBURGH	No.	Yds.	Avg.	OAKLAND	No.	Yds.	Avg.
RUSHING							
Harris	18	64	3.6	Smith	14	57	4.1
Fuqua	16	25	1.6	Hubbard	14	44	3.1
Bradshaw	2	19	9.5	Stabler	1	30	30.0
	36	108	3.0	Davis	2	7	3.5
					31	138	4.5
RECEIVING							
Harris	5	96	19.2	Chester	3	40	13.3
Shanklin	3	55	18.3	Biletnikoff	3	28	9.3
Fuqua	1	11	11.0	Smith	2	8	4.0
McMakin	1	9	9.0	Banaszek	1	12	12.0
Young	1	4	4.0	Siani	1	7	7.0
	11	175	15.9	Otto	1	5	5.0
				Hubbard	1	2	2.0
					12	102	8.5
PUNTING							
Walden	6		48.2	DePoyster	7		45.1
PUNT RETURNS							
Edwards	3	39	13.0	Atkinson	1	37	37.0
KICKOFF RETURNS							
Pearson	1	21	21.0	Davis	1	26	26.0
INTERCEPTION RETURNS							
Ham	1	0	0.0	Wilson	1	7	7.0
Russell	1	0	0.0				
	2	0	0.0				

PASSING

PITTSBURGH	Att.	Comp.	Comp. Pct.	Yds.	Int.	Yds/ Att.	Yds/ Comp.	Yards Lost Tackled
Bradshaw	25	11	44.0	175	1	7.0	15.9	3–31
OAKLAND								
Lamonica	18	6	33.0	45	2	2.5	7.5	
Stabler	12	6	50.0	57	0	4.8	9.5	
	30	12	40.0	102	2	3.4	8.5	4–24

December 24, at Miami (Attendance 78,916)

SCORING

MIAMI	10	0	0	10–20
CLEVELAND	0	0	7	7–14

First Quarter
MIA. Babb, 6 yard return of blocked punt PAT–Yepremiam (kick)
MIA. Yepremiam, 40 yard field goal

Third Quarter
CLE. Phipps, 5 yard rush
PAT – Cockroft (kick)

Fourth Quarter
MIA. Yepremiam, 46 yard field goal
CLE. Hooker, 27 yard pass from Phipps PAT–Cockroft (kick)
MIA. Kiick, 8 yard rush
PAT–Yepremiam (kick)

TEAM STATISTICS

MIAMI		CLEVE.
17	First Downs–Total	15
11	First Downs–Rushing	9
4	First Downs–Passing	6
2	First Downs–Penalty	0
2	Fumbles–Number	2
2	Fumbles–Lost Ball	0
3	Penalties–Number	3
25	Yards Penalized	25
2	Missed Field Goals	0
64	Offensive Plays	57
272	Net Yards	283
4.3	Average Gain	5.0
2	Giveaways	5
5	Takeaways	2
+3	Difference	–3

INDIVIDUAL STATISTICS

MIAMI	No.	Yds.	Avg.	CLEVELAND	No.	Yds.	Avg.
RUSHING							
Morris	15	72	4.8	Scott	16	94	5.9
Kiick	14	50	3.6	Phipps	8	47	5.9
Warfield	2	41	20.5	Brown	4	13	3.3
Csonka	12	32	2.7	Kelly	4	11	2.8
Morrall	4	3	0.8		32	165	5.2
	47	198	4.2				
RECEIVING							
Twilley	3	33	11.0	Scott	4	30	7.5
Warfield	2	50	25.0	Hooker	3	53	17.7
Kiick	1	5	5.0	Kelly	1	27	27.0
	6	88	14.7	Morin	1	21	21.0
					9	131	14.6
PUNTING							
Seiple	5		42.0	Cockroft	6		34.7
PUNT RETURNS							
Scott	1	1	1.0	Darden	1	38	38.0
				Kelley	1	8	8.0
					2	46	23.0
KICKOFF RETURNS							
None				Lefear	3	56	18.7
INTERCEPTION RETURNS							
Swift	2	19	9.5	None			
Anderson	2	12	6.0				
Johnson	1	33	33.0				
	5	64	12.8				

PASSING

MIAMI	Att.	Comp.	Comp. Pct.	Yds.	Int.	Yds/ Att.	Yds/ Comp.	Yards Lost Tackled
Morrall	13	6	46.2	88	0	6.8	14.7	4–14
CLEVELAND								
Phipps	23	9	39.1	131	5	5.7	14.6	2–13

MIAMI DOLPHINS 14-0-0 Don Shula

Scores of Each Game		
20	Kansas City	10
34	HOUSTON	13
16	Minnesota	14
27	N.Y. Jets	17
24	SAN DIEGO	10
24	BUFFALO	23
23	Baltimore	0
30	Buffalo	16
52	NEW ENGLAND	0
28	N.Y. JETS	24
31	ST. LOUIS	10
37	New England	21
23	N.Y. Giants	13
16	BALTIMORE	0

Use Name	Pos.	Hgt	Wgt	Age	Int	Pts
Doug Crusan	OT	6'5"	250	26		
Norm Evans	OT	6'5"	252	28		
Wayne Moore	OT	6'6"	265	27		
Bob Kuechenberg	OG	6'3"	247	24		
Larry Little	OG	6'1"	265	26		
Al Jenkins	OT-OG	6'2"	245	26		
Jim Langer	C	6'2"	250	25		
Howard Kindig	OT-C	6'6"	260	31		
Vern Den Herder	DE	6'6"	250	23	1	
Bill Stanfill	DE	6'5"	250	25		
Bob Matheson	LB-DE	6'4"	240	27		
Jim Dunaway	DT	6'4"	277	30		
Manny Fernandez	DT	6'2"	248	26		
Baldy Moore	DT	6'5"	265	26		
Bob Heinz	DE-DT	6'6"	270	25		

Use Name	Pos.	Hgt	Wgt	Age	Int	Pts
Larry Ball	LB	6'6"	225	23		
Nick Buoniconti	LB	5'11'	220	31	2	
Mike Kolen	LB	6'2"	220	23	1	
Jesse Powell	LB	6'1"	215	25		
Doug Swift	LB	6'3"	228	23	3	
Dick Anderson	DB	6'2"	196	26	3	6
Charlie Babb	DB	6'	190	22	1	
Tim Foley	DB	6'	194	24	3	
Curtis Johnson	DB	6'2"	196	24	3	
Lloyd Mumphford	DB	5'11"	180	25	4	6
Jake Scott	DB	6'	188	26	5	

Karl Noonan – Knee Injury
Jim Riley – Knee Injury

Use Name	Pos.	Hgt	Wgt	Age	Int	Pts
Jim Del Gaizo	QB	6'1"	198	25		
Bob Griese	QB	6'1"	190	27		6
Earl Morrall	QB	6'1"	206	38		6
Hubert Ginn	HB	5'11"	188	25		6
Ed Jenkins	HB	6'2"	210	22		
Jim Kiick	HB	5'11"	215	26		36
Mercury Morris	HB	5'10"	190	25		72
Larry Csonka	FB	6'3"	237	25		36
Charlie Leigh	FB	5'11"	205	26		
Marlin Briscoe	WR	5'10"	178	26		24
Otto Stowe	WR	6'2"	188	23		12
Howard Twilley	WR	5'10"	185	28		18
Paul Warfield	WR	6'	185	29		18
Marv Fleming	TE	6'4"	235	30		6
Jim Mandich	TE	6'3"	224	23		18
Larry Seiple	TE	6'	215	27		
Billy Lothridge	K	6'1"	200	28		
Garo Yepremian	K	5'8"	172	28		115

NEW YORK JETS 7-7-0 Weeb Ewbank

Scores of Each Game		
41	Buffalo	24
44	Baltimore	34
20	Houston	26
17	MIAMI	27
41	New England	13
24	BALTIMORE	20
34	NEW ENGLAND	10
17	WASHINGTON	35
41	BUFFALO	3
24	Miami	28
20	Detroit	37
18	NEW ORLEANS	17
16	Oakland	24
10	CLEVELAND	26

Use Name	Pos.	Hgt	Wgt	Age	Int	Pts
Winston Hill	OT	6'4"	270	30		
Bob Svihus	OT	6'4"	245	29		
John Mooring	C-OT	6'6"	255	25		
Roger Finnie	OG	6'3"	245	25		
Dave Herman	OG	6'2"	255	30		
Randy Rasmussen	OG	6'2"	255	27		6
Roy Kirksey	DT-OG	6'1"	265	24		
John Schmitt	C	6'4"	250	29		
Gerry Philbin	DE	6'2"	245	31		
Joey Jackson	DT-DE	6'4"	257	23		
Mark Lomas	DT-DE	6'4"	245	24		
John Elliott	DT	6'4"	244	27		
John Little	DT	6'3"	235	25		
Steve Thompson	DT	6'5"	237	27		
Ed Galigher	DE-DT	6'4"	255	21		

Use Name	Pos.	Hgt	Wgt	Age	Int	Pts
Al Atkinson	LB	6'1"	230	29	1	
Ralph Baker	LB	6'3"	228	30	2	
John Ebersole	LB	6'3"	227	23		
Larry Grantham	LB	6'	210	33		
Mike Taylor	LB	6'1"	230	22	1	
Paul Crane	C-LB	6'2"	212	28	1	
Bill Zapalac	DE-LB	6'4"	225	24		
Chris Farasopoulos	DB	5'11"	190	23	2	6
W. K. Hicks	DB	6'1"	195	29	1	
Gus Holloman	DB	6'3"	195	26	1	
Rich Sowells	DB	6'	175	23	2	
Steve Tannen	DB	6'1"	194	24	7	
Earlie Thomas	DB	6'1"	190	26	1	
Phil Wise	DB	6'	190	23		

Al Woodall – Injury

Use Name	Pos.	Hgt	Wgt	Age	Int	Pts
Bob Davis	QB	6'3"	205	27		
Joe Namath	QB	6'2"	200	28		
Hank Bjorkland	BH	6'1"	200	22		
Emerson Boozer	HB	5'11"	195	29		84
Cliff McClain	HB	6'	217	24		
John Riggins	FB	6'2"	233	23		48
Matt Snell	FB	6'2"	220	30		
Steve Harkey	HB-FB	6'	215	23		
Jerome Barkum	WR	6'3"	215	22		12
Eddie Bell	WR	5'10"	160	24		12
Don Maynard	WR	6'	180	36		12
Rocky Turner	WR	6'	190	22		
Rich Caster	TE	6'5"	228	23		60
Wayne Stewart	TE	6'7"	213	25		6
Bobby Howfield	K	5'9"	180	35		121
Steve O'Neal	K	6'3"	185	26		

BALTIMORE COLTS 5-9-0 Don McCafferty John Sandusky

Scores of Each Game		
3	ST. LOUIS	10
34	N.Y. JETS	44
17	Buffalo	0
20	SAN DIEGO	23
0	DALLAS	21
20	N.Y. Jets	24
0	MIAMI	23
24	New England	17
21	San Francisco	24
20	Cincinnati	19
31	NEW ENGLAND	0
35	BUFFALO	7
10	Kansas City	24
0	Miami	16

Use Name	Pos.	Hgt	Wgt	Age	Int	Pts
Tom Drougas	OT	6'4"	257	22		
Dennis Nelson	OT	6'5"	260	26		
Bob Vogel	OT	6'5"	250	30		
Cornelius Johnson	OG	6'2"	245	29		
Glenn Ressler	OG	6'3"	250	28		
John Shinners	OG	6'2"	254	25		
Dan Sullivan	OG	6'3"	250	33		
Bill Curry	C	6'2"	236	29		
Ken Mendenhall	C	6'3"	235	24		
Dick Amman	DE	6'5"	234	21		
Roy Hilton	DE	6'6"	240	27		
Billy Newsome	DE	6'4"	250	24		
Chuck Hinton	DT	6'5"	264	33		
Fred Miller	DT	6'3"	250	31		
Jim Bailey	DE-DT	6'4"	255	24		

Use Name	Pos.	Hgt	Wgt	Age	Int	Pts
Mike Curtis	LB	6'2"	232	28	4	6
Randy Edmunds	LB	6'2"	225	26		
Ted Hendricks	LB	6'7"	220	24	2	
Bill Laskey	LB	6'2"	235	29		
Ray May	LB	6'1"	230	27	2	
Stan White	LB	6'1"	225	22		
Lonnie Hepburn	DB	5'11"	180	23	1	
Rex Kern	DB	5'11"	190	23		
Bruce Laird	DB	6'	185	22	1	
Jerry Logan	DB	6'1"	190	31	4	
Jack Mildren	DB	6'1"	200	22		
Nelson Munsey	DB	6'1"	185	24		6
Charlie Stukes	DB	6'3"	212	28	5	
Rick Volk	DB	6'3"	195	27	4	

Bubba Smith – Injury

Use Name	Pos.	Hgt	Wgt	Age	Int	Pts
Marty Domres	QB	6'3"	220	25		6
Johnny Unitas	QB	6'1"	196	39		
Tom Matte	HB	6'	214	33		6
Don McCauley	HB	6'1"	207	23		30
Lydell Mitchell	HB	5'11"	204	23		12
Don Nottingham	FB	5'10"	210	23		18
Tom Nowatzke	FB	6'3"	230	29		
Norm Bulaich	HB-FB	6'1"	218	25		6
Glenn Doughty	WR	6'2"	204	22		
Willie Franklin	WR	6'2"	194	22		
Sam Havrilak	WR	6'2"	195	24		36
Eddie Hinton	WR	6'	200	25		6
Jim O'Brien	WR	6'	195	25		75
Cotton Speyrer	WR	6'	175	23		
Tom Mitchell	TE	6'2"	215	28		24
John Mosier	TE	6'3"	220	24		
David Lee	K	6'4"	230	28		
Boris Shlapak	K	6'	165	22		4

BUFFALO BILLS 4-9-1 Lou Saban

Scores of Each Game		
24	N.Y. JETS	41
27	SAN FRANCISCO	20
0	BALTIMORE	17
38	NEW ENGLAND	14
16	Oakland	28
23	Miami	24
21	PITTSBURGH	38
16	MIAMI	30
3	N.Y. Jets	41
27	New England	24
10	Cleveland	27
7	Baltimore	35
21	DETROIT	21
24	Washington	17

Use Name	Pos.	Hgt	Wgt	Age	Int	Pts
Paul Costa	OT	6'4"	268	30		
Dave Foley	OT	6'5"	255	24		
Donnie Green	OT	6'7"	285	24		
Willie Young	OT	6'4"	270	24		
Bill Adams	OG	6'2"	250	22		
Dick Hart	OG	6'2"	250	29		
Reggie McKenzie	OG	6'4"	235	22		
Jeff Curchin	OT-OG	6'6"	255	24		
Remi Prudhomme (from NO)	C-OG	6'4"	250	30		
Tom Beard	C	6'6"	280	23		
Bruce Jarvis	C	6'7"	245	23		
John Matlock	C	6'4"	250	27		
Bobby Penchion	OG-C	6'5"	255	23		
Walt Patulski	DE	6'6"	252	22		
Louis Ross	DE	6'6"	242	25		
Al Cowlings	DT-DE	6'5"	250	25		
Frank Cornish	DT	6'6"	285	28		
Don Croft	DT	6'3"	252	23		
Steve Okoniewski	DT	6'3"	247	23		
Jerry Patton	DT	6'3"	250	26		
Mike McBath	DE-DT	6'4"	250	26		

Use Name	Pos.	Hgt	Wgt	Age	Int	Pts
Edgar Chandler	LB	6'3"	225	26		
Dick Cunningham	LB	6'2"	232	27		
Dale Farley	LB	6'3"	235	23	1	
Paul Guidry	LB	6'3"	233	28	1	
Ken Lee	LB	6'4"	232	23	6	6
Jeff Lyman	LB	6'2"	230	22		
Andy Selfridge	LB	6'4"	218	23		
Mike Stratton	LB	6'3"	240	30	1	
Dave Washington	TE-LB	6'5"	220	24	1	
Leon Garror	DB	6'	180	24		
Tony Greene	DB	5'10"	170	22	3	6
Bobby James	DB	6'1"	185	25	1	
John Pitts	DB	6'4"	215	27	1	
John Saunders	DB	6'3"	202	22		
Maurice Tyler	DB	6'	188	22	4	
Alvin Wyatt	DB	5'10"	180	24	4	6

Mike Clark – Injury
Irv Goode – Injury

Use Name	Pos.	Hgt	Wgt	Age	Int	Pts
Leo Hart	QB	6'4"	203	23		
Dennis Shaw	QB	6'2"	215	25		
Mike Taliaferro	QB	6'2"	205	30		
Randy Jackson	HB	6'	220	23		6
O. J. Simpson	HB	6'2"	214	25		36
Ted Koy	FB-HB	6'1"	215	24		
Jim Braxton	FB	6'2"	226	23		36
Wayne Patrick	FB	6'2"	245	26		6
Bob Chandler	WR	6'	180	23		30
Linzy Cole (from HOU)	WR	5'11"	170	24		
Dwight Harrison (from DEN)	WR	6'1"	178	23		
J. D. Hill	WR	6'1"	193	23		30
Bob Christiansen	TE	6'4"	230	23		
Jan White	TE	6'2"	216	23		12
Spike Jones	K	6'2"	190	25		
John Leypoldt	K	6'2"	224	26		77

Bill McKinley – Injury
Jim Reilly – Illness

NEW ENGLAND PATRIOTS 3-11-0 John Mazur Phil Bengtson

Scores of Each Game		
7	CINCINNATI	31
21	ATLANTA	20
24	WASHINGTON	23
14	Buffalo	38
13	N.Y. JETS	41
3	Pittsburgh	33
10	N.Y. Jets	34
17	BALTIMORE	24
0	Miami	52
24	BUFFALO	27
0	Baltimore	31
21	MIAMI	37
17	New Orleans	10
21	Denver	45

Use Name	Pos.	Hgt	Wgt	Age	Int	Pts
Mike Montler	OT	6'4"	255	28		
Tom Neville	OT	6'4"	255	28		
Bob Reynolds	OT	6'6"	265	31		
Sam Adams	OG	6'3"	252	23		
Halvor Hagen	OG	6'5"	253	25		
Len St. Jean	OG	6'1"	250	30		
Bill Lenkaitis	C-OG	6'3"	260	26		
Jon Morris	C	6'4"	254	29		
Ron Berger	DE	6'8"	285	28		
Jim White	DE	6'3"	256	22		
Dennis Wirgowski	DT-DE	6'5"	250	24		
Rick Cash	DT	6'5"	260	26		
Dave Rowe	DT	6'6"	280	27		
Julius Adams	DE-DT	6'3"	260	24		

Use Name	Pos.	Hgt	Wgt	Age	Int	Pts
Ron Acks	LB	6'2"	220	27		
Dick Blanchard	LB	6'3"	225	23	1	
Jim Cheyunski	LB	6'2"	225	26		
Ralph Cindrich	LB	6'1"	228	22		
Ron Kadziel	LB	6'4"	230	23		
Ed Weisacosky	LB	6'	220	28		
Ron Bolton	DB	6'2"	180	22		
Larry Carwell	DB	6'1"	190	28	1	6
Rickie Harris	DB	6'	182	29	3	
George Haey	DB	5'10"	170	25	1	
Honor Jackson	DB	6'1"	195	23	4	
Art McMahon	DB	5'11"	190	26		
John Outlaw	DB	5'10"	180	27		
Clarence Scott	DB	6'2"	200	28		

Use Name	Pos.	Hgt	Wgt	Age	Int	Pts
Brian Dowling	QB	6'2"	210	25		18
Jim Plunkett	QB	6'3"	220	24		6
Carl Garrett	HB	5'11"	215	24		30
Bob Gladieux	HB	5'11"	195	25		
Jack Maitland	HB	6'1"	210	24		
Henry Matthews	HB	6'3"	203	23		
John Tarver	FB	6'3"	227	23		12
Josh Ashton	HB-FB	6'1"	205	23		24
Hubie Bryant	WR	5'10"	168	26		
Tom Reynolds	WR	6'3"	200	23		12
Reggie Rucker	WR	6'2"	190	24		18
Pat Studstill	WR	6'1"	175	34		
Randy Vataha	WR	5'10"	175	23		12
Tom Beer	TE	6'4"	235	27		
Bob Windsor	TE	6'4"	226	29		6
Charlie Gogolak	K	5'10"	170	27		27
Mike Walker	K	6'	190	22		21

MIAMI DOLPHINS

RUSHING

Last Name	No.	Yds	Avg	TD
Csonka	213	1117	5.2	6
Morris	190	1000	5.3	12
Kiick	137	521	3.8	5
Ginn	27	142	5.3	1
Leigh	21	79	3.8	0
Morrall	17	67	3.9	1
Warfield	4	23	5.8	0
Griese	3	11	3.7	1
DelGaizo	1	0	0.0	0

RECEIVING

Last Name	No.	Yds	Avg	TD
Warfield	29	606	21	3
Kiick	21	147	7	1
Twilley	20	364	18	3
Briscoe	16	279	17	4
Morris	15	168	11	0
Stowe	13	276	21	2
Fleming	13	156	12	1
Mandich	11	168	15	3
Csonka	5	48	10	0
Ginn	1	23	23	0

PUNT RETURNS

Last Name	No.	Yds	Avg	TD
Leigh	22	210	10	0
Scott	13	100	8	0
Anderson	5	19	4	0

KICKOFF RETURNS

Last Name	No.	Yds	Avg	TD
Morris	14	334	24	0
Leigh	6	153	26	0
Matheson	2	34	17	0
Ginn	1	25	25	0
Briscoe	1	0	0	0

PASSING – PUNTING – KICKING Statistics

PASSING	Att	Comp	%	Yds	Yd/Att	TD	Int- %	RK
Morrall	150	83	55	1360	9.1	11	7- 5	1
Griese	97	53	55	638	6.6	4	4- 4	
DelGaizo	9	5	56	165	18.3	2	1- 11	
Briscoe	3	3	100	72	24.0	0	0- 0	

PUNTING	No	Avg
Seiple	36	39.9
Lothridge	4	37.5
Anderson	4	36.8

KICKING	XP	Att	%	FG	Att	%
Yepremian	43	45	96	24	37	65

NEW YORK JETS

RUSHING

Last Name	No.	Yds	Avg	TD
Riggins	207	944	4.6	7
Boozer	120	549	4.6	11
McClain	59	305	5.2	0
Harkey	45	129	2.9	0
Bjorklund	15	42	2.8	0
Davis	6	32	5.3	0
Namath	6	8	1.3	0
Caster	2	6	3.0	0
Bell	1	−5	−5.0	0

RECEIVING

Last Name	No.	Yds	Avg	TD
Caster	39	833	21	10
Bell	35	629	18	2
Maynard	29	510	18	2
Riggins	21	230	11	1
Barkum	16	304	19	2
Boozer	11	142	13	3
Harkey	9	114	13	0
McClain	6	88	15	0
Bjorklund	4	54	14	0
Stewart	2	26	13	1

PUNT RETURNS

Last Name	No.	Yds	Avg	TD
Farasopoulos	17	179	11	1
Turner	5	38	8	0
Hicks	3	25	8	0

KICKOFF RETURNS

Last Name	No.	Yds	Avg	TD
Farasopoulos	26	627	24	0
Wise	9	211	23	0
Bjorklund	7	150	21	0
Hicks	4	73	24	0
Turner	3	57	19	0
McClain	2	45	23	0
Kirksey	2	33	17	0
Snell	1	14	14	0
Zapalac	1	8	8	0
Barkum	1	0	0	0

PASSING – PUNTING – KICKING Statistics

PASSING	Att	Comp	%	Yds	Yd/Att	TD	Int- %	RK
Namath	324	162	50	2816	8.7	19	21- 6	8
Davis	22	10	46	114	5.2	2	1- 5	
McClain	1	0	0	0	0.0	0	0- 0	

PUNTING	No	Avg
O'Neal	51	39.3

KICKING	XP	Att	%	FG	Att	%
Howfield	40	41	98	27	37	73

BALTIMORE COLTS

RUSHING

Last Name	No.	Yds	Avg	TD
McCauley	178	675	3.8	2
Nottingham	123	466	3.8	3
L. Mitchell	45	215	4.8	1
Matte	33	137	4.2	0
Domres	30	137	4.6	1
Bulaich	27	109	4.0	1
Havrilak	12	72	6.0	2
Doughty	2	33	16.5	0
Unitas	3	15	5.0	0
Nowatzke	3	11	3.7	0
O'Brien	3	9	3.0	0
Mildren	3	8	2.7	0
T. Mitchell	0	7	0.0	0

RECEIVING

Last Name	No.	Yds	Avg	TD
T. Mitchell	40	494	12	4
Havrilak	33	571	17	4
McCauley	30	256	9	2
Nottingham	25	191	7	0
L. Mitchell	18	147	8	1
Matte	14	182	13	1
O'Brien	11	263	24	2
Hinton	11	146	13	1
Bulaich	9	55	6	0
Speyrer	8	114	14	0
Doughty	3	31	10	0
Mosier	1	53	53	0

PUNT RETURNS

Last Name	No.	Yds	Avg	TD
Laird	34	303	9	0
Volk	5	25	5	0
Logan	4	20	5	0

KICKOFF RETURNS

Last Name	No.	Yds	Avg	TD
Laird	29	843	29	0
McCauley	13	377	29	1
Bulaich	1	62	62	0
Nottingham	2	38	19	0
Mildren	1	1	1	0
Hendricks	1	0	0	0

PASSING – PUNTING – KICKING Statistics

PASSING	Att	Comp	%	Yds	Yd/Att	TD	Int- %	RK
Domres	222	115	52	1392	6.3	11	6- 3	6
Unitas	157	88	56	1111	7.1	4	6- 4	4
Havrilak	1	0	0	0	0.0	0	0- 0	
Mildren	1	0	0	0	0.0	0	0- 0	

PUNTING	No	Avg
Lee	57	42.1

KICKING	XP	Att	%	FG	Att	%
O'Brien	24	24	100	13	31	42
Shlapak	4	4	100	0	8	0

BUFFALO BILLS

RUSHING

Last Name	No.	Yds	Avg	TD
Simpson	29	1251	4.3	6
Braxton	116	453	3.9	5
Shaw	35	138	3.9	0
Patrick	35	130	3.7	0
Jackson	17	57	3.4	0
B. Chandler	3	27	9.0	0
L. Hart	5	19	3.8	0
Taliaferro	5	19	3.8	0
Jones	2	18	9.0	0
Hill	1	11	11.0	0
Harrison	1	9	9.0	0
Koy	1	9	9.0	0

RECEIVING

Last Name	No.	Yds	Avg	TD
Hill	52	754	15	5
B. Chandler	33	528	16	5
Simpson	27	198	7	0
Braxton	24	232	10	1
White	12	148	12	2
Patrick	8	42	5	1
Jackson	2	21	11	1
Harrison	1	16	16	0
Koy	1	9	9	0
Washington	1	4	4	0

PUNT RETURNS

Last Name	No.	Yds	Avg	TD
Wyatt	11	85	8	0
Cole	7	35	5	0
Hill	4	24	6	0
Greene	2	18	9	0
Harrison	1	2	2	0

KICKOFF RETURNS

Last Name	No.	Yds	Avg	TD
Cole	18	456	25	0
Wyatt	17	432	25	0
Greene	15	378	25	0
Koy	5	63	13	0
Selfridge	3	36	12	0
Hill	2	32	16	0
Simpson	1	21	21	0
Braxton	1	12	12	0
Prudhomme	1	0	0	0

PASSING – PUNTING – KICKING Statistics

PASSING	Att	Comp	%	Yds	Yd/Att	TD	Int- %	RK
Shaw	258	136	53	1666	6.5	14	17- 7	9
Taliaferro	33	16	48	176	5.3	1	4- 12	
L. Hart	15	6	40	53	3.5	0	3- 20	
Simpson	8	5	63	113	14.1	1	0- 0	
Jones	2	1	50	4	2.0	0	0- 0	

PUNTING	No	Avg
Jones	80	38.8

KICKING	XP	Att	%	FG	Att	%
Leypoldt	29	30	97	16	24	67

NEW ENGLAND PATRIOTS

RUSHING

Last Name	No.	Yds	Avg	TD
Ashton	128	546	4.3	3
Garrett	131	488	3.7	5
Plunkett	36	230	6.4	1
Tarver	42	132	3.1	1
Gladieux	24	56	2.3	0
Dowling	7	35	5.0	3
Maitland	13	33	2.5	0
Studstill	1	11	11.0	0
Rucker	3	5	1.7	0
Windsor	1	−4	−4.0	0

RECEIVING

Last Name	No.	Yds	Avg	TD
Rucker	44	681	15	3
Windsor	33	383	12	1
Garrett	30	410	14	0
Vataha	25	369	15	2
Ashton	22	207	9	1
Gladieux	19	192	10	0
Tarver	11	112	10	1
T. Reynolds	8	152	19	2
Maitland	4	33	8	0
Beer	2	40	20	0

PUNT RETURNS

Last Name	No.	Yds	Avg	TD
Garrett	6	36	6	0
Harris	4	5	1	0
Carwell	5	2	0	0
Gladieux	2	−6	−3	0

KICKOFF RETURNS

Last Name	No.	Yds	Avg	TD
Garrett	16	410	26	0
Ashton	15	309	21	0
Rucker	8	227	28	0
Hoey	9	210	23	0
Matthews	3	74	25	0
Maitland	3	48	16	0
Beer	1	15	15	0

PASSING – PUNTING – KICKING Statistics

PASSING	Att	Comp	%	Yds	Yd/Att	TD	Int- %	RK
Plunkett	355	169	48	2196	6.2	8	25- 7	14
Dowling	54	29	54	383	7.1	2	1- 2	
Garrett	1	0	0	0	0.0	0	1-100	
Gladieux	1	0	0	0	0.0	0	1-100	
Studstill	1	0	0	0	0.0	0	0- 0	

PUNTING	No	Avg
Studstill	75	38.1

KICKING	XP	Att	%	FG	Att	%
Walker	15	15	100	2	8	25
Gogolak	9	9	100	6	8	75

1972 A.F.C. — Central Division

PITTSBURGH STEELERS 11-3-0 Chuck Noll

Scores of Each Game		
34	OAKLAND	28
10	Cincinnati	15
25	St. Louis	19
13	Dallas	17
24	HOUSTON	7
33	NEW ENGLAND	3
38	Buffalo	21
40	CINCINNATI	17
16	KANSAS CITY	7
24	Cleveland	26
23	MINNESOTA	10
30	CLEVELAND	0
9	Houston	3
24	San Diego	2

Use Name	Pos.	Hgt	Wgt	Age	Int	Pts
Gordon Gravelle	OT	6'5"	250	23		
Jon Kolb	OT	6'2"	262	25		
Gerry Mullins	OG-OT	6'3"	235	23		6
Sam Davis	OG	6'1"	255	28		
Bruce Van Dyke	OG	6'2"	255	28		
Mel Holmes	OT-OG	6'3"	250	22		
Jim Clack	C	6'3"	250	24		
Ray Mansfield	C	6'3"	255	31		
L.C. Greenwood	DE	6'5"	245	25		
Craig Hanneman	DE	6'3"	240	23		
Dwight White	DE	6'4"	250	23		
Steve Furness	DT	6'4"	255	21		
Joe Greene	DT	6'4"	270	25		
Ernie Holmes	DT	6'3"	260	24		
Ben McGee	DT	6'2"	260	30		

Bob Adams – Injury

Use Name	Pos.	Hgt	Wgt	Age	Int	Pts
Ed Bradley	LB	6'2"	240	22		
Henry Davis	LB	6'3"	235	29	2	6
Jack Ham	LB	6'3"	220	23	7	6
Andy Russell	LB	6'3"	225	30		
Brian Stenger	LB	6'4"	230	25		
George Webster (from HOU)	LB	6'4"	223	26		
Carl Winfrey	LB	6'	230	23		
Ralph Anderson	DB	6'2"	180	23	3	2
Chuck Beatty (to STL)	DB	6'2"	205	26	2	
Mel Blount	DB	6'3"	205	24	3	6
Lee Calland	DB	6'	190	31		
John Dockery	DB	6'	186	27		
Glen Edwards	DB	6'	185	25	1	
John Rowser	DB	6'1"	185	28	4	
Mike Wagner	DB	6'1"	196	23	6	

John Brown – Injury

Use Name	Pos.	Hgt	Wgt	Age	Int	Pts
Terry Bradshaw	QB	6'3"	218	23		42
Joe Gilliam	QB	6'2"	187	21		
Terry Hanratty	QB	6'1"	210	24		
Rocky Bleier	HB	5'11"	205	26		
Preston Pearson	HB	6'1"	205	27		
Franco Harris	FB-HB	6'2"	230	22		66
Warren Bankston	FB	6'4"	235	25		
Steve Davis	HB-FB	6'1"	218	22		6
John Fuqua	HB-FB	5'11"	200	25		24
Frank Lewis	WR	6'1"	196	25		30
Barry Pearson	WR	5'11"	185	22		
Ron Shanklin	WR	6'1"	180	25		18
Al Young	WR	6'1"	195	23		
Larry Brown	TE	6'4"	225	23		6
John McMakin	TE	6'3"	232	21		6
Roy Gerela	K	5'10"	185	24		119
Bobby Walden	K	6'	190	33		

CLEVELAND BROWNS 10-4-0 Nick Skorich

Scores of Each Game		
10	GREEN BAY	26
27	Philadelphia	17
27	CINCINNATI	6
7	KANSAS CITY	31
0	CHICAGO	17
23	HOUSTON	17
27	Denver	20
20	HOUSTON	0
21	San Diego	17
26	PITTSBURGH	24
27	BUFFALO	10
0	Pittsburgh	30
27	Cincinnati	24
26	N.Y. Jets	10

Use Name	Pos.	Hgt	Wgt	Age	Int	Pts
Joe Carollo	OT	6'2"	265	32		
Doug Dieken	OT	6'5"	237	23		
Bob McKay	OT	6'5"	260	24		
Chris Morris	OT	6'3"	250	22		
John Demarie	C-OG-OT	6'3"	246	27		
Gene Hickerson	OG	6'3"	252	37		
Bubba Pena	OG	6'2"	250	23		
Craig Wycinsky	OG	6'3"	243	24		
Jim Copeland	C-OG	6'2"	243	27		
Bob DeMarco	C	6'3"	248	34		
Fred Hoaglin	C	6'4"	246	28		
Wes Grant	DE	6'3"	245	25		
Rich Jackson (from DEN)	DE	6'2"	255	31		
Nick Roman	DE	6'3"	235	24	1	6
Ron Snidow	DE	6'4"	247	30		
Bob Briggs	DT-DE	6'4"	258	27	1	6
Cotton Fest	DT	6'2"	255	22		
Walter Johnson	DT	6'3"	263	29	1	
George Wright	DT	6'3"	265	25		
Jerry Sherk	DE-DT	6'4"	258	24		

Use Name	Pos.	Hgt	Wgt	Age	Int	Pts
Billy Andrews	LB	6'	220	27	1	
John Garlington	LB	6'1"	218	26	1	
Charlie Hall	LB	6'3"	220	23	1	
Rick Kingrea	LB	6'1"	233	23		
Dale Lindsey	LB	6'3"	225	29		
Mel Long	LB	6'	228	25		
Jim Houston	DE-LB	6'2"	236	35		
Cliff Brooks	DB	6'1"	190	23		
Tom Darden	DB	6'2"	195	22	3	
Ben Davis	DB	5'11"	180	27	3	
Mike Howell (to MIA)	DB	6'1"	190	29	1	
Bobby Majors	DB	6'1"	193	23		
Clarence Scott	DB	6'	180	23		6
Walt Sumner	DB	6'1"	195	25		

Joe Jones – Knee Injury

Use Name	Pos.	Hgt	Wgt	Age	Int	Pts
Don Horn	QB	6'2"	195	27		
Bill Nelsen	QB	6'	195	31		
Mike Phipps	QB	6'2"	208	24		30
Leroy Kelly	HB	6'	202	30		30
Bill LeFear	HB	5'11"	197	22		
Ken Brown	FB-HB	5'10"	203	26		12
Bo Cornell	FB	6'1"	215	23		
Bo Scott	FB	6'3"	215	29		12
Charlie Brinkman	WR	6'2"	208	23		
Fair Hooker	WR	6'1"	190	25		12
Frank Pitts	WR	6'2"	200	28		48
Gloster Richardson	WR	6'	200	29		
Paul Staroba	WR	6'3"	204	23		6
Chip Glass	TE	6'4"	235	25		
Milt Morin	TE	6'4"	236	30		6
Don Cockroft	K	6'1"	195	27		94

CINCINNATI BENGALS 8-6-0 Paul Brown

Scores of Each Game		
31	New England	7
15	PITTSBURGH	10
6	Cleveland	27
21	DENVER	10
23	Kansas City	16
12	Los Angeles	15
30	HOUSTON	7
17	Pittsburgh	40
14	OAKLAND	20
19	BALTIMORE	20
13	Chicago	3
13	N.Y. GIANTS	10
24	CLEVELAND	27
61	Houston	17

Use Name	Pos.	Hgt	Wgt	Age	Int	Pts
Vern Holland	OT	6'5"	270	24		
Stan Walters	OT	6'6"	270	23		
Rufus Mayes	OG-OT	6'5"	260	24		
Guy Dennis	OG	6'2"	255	25		
Steve Lawson	OG	6'3"	265	23		
Pat Matson	OG	6'1"	245	28		
Howard Fest	OT-OG	6'6"	262	26		
Tom DeLeone	C-OG	6'2"	252	22		
Bob Johnson	C	6'5"	260	26		
Royce Berry	DE	6'3"	250	26		
Ron Carpenter	DE	6'4"	260	24		
Sherman White	DE	6'5"	255	23		2
Steve Chomyszak	DT	6'5"	270	27		
Ken Johnson	DT	6'5"	265	24		
Mike Reid	DT	6'3"	250	25		

Use Name	Pos.	Hgt	Wgt	Age	Int	Pts
Doug Adams	LB	6'	227	23	3	
Ken Avery	LB	6'1"	230	28		
Al Beauchamp	LB	6'2"	237	28	1	
Bill Bergey	LB	6'2"	243	27		
Tim Kearney	LB	6'2"	227	23		
Jim LeClair	LB	6'2"	226	22		
Bill Peterson	LB	6'3"	226	27		
Ron Pritchard (from HOU)	LB	6'1"	235	25		
Tommy Casanova	DB	6'2"	202	21	5	6
Neal Craig	DB	6'1"	190	24	2	6
Bernie Jackson	DB	6'	173	22	1	
Ernie Kellerman	DB	6'	183	28		
Lemar Parrish	DB	5'11"	184	24	5	18
Ken Riley	DB	6'	180	25	3	

Greg Cook – Shoulder Injury
Sandy Durko – Injury

Use Name	Pos.	Hgt	Wgt	Age	Int	Pts
Ken Anderson	QB	6'1"	211	23		18
Virgil Carter	QB	6'1"	198	26		12
Dave Lewis	QB	6'2"	218	26		
Essex Johnson	HB	5'9"	197	25		36
Reece Morrison (from CLE)	HB	6'	207	26		
Doug Dressler	FB	6'3"	226	24		42
Jess Phillips	HB-FB	6'1"	205	25		6
Drew Buie	WR	6'2"	185	25		
Charlie Joiner (from HOU)	WR	5'11"	188	24		12
Chip Myers	WR	6'4"	210	27		18
Speedy Thomas	WR	6'1"	170	25		6
Bruce Coslet	TE	6'3"	220	26		6
Mike Kelly	TE	6'4"	222	24		
Bob Trumpy	TE	6'6"	228	27		12
Pete Watson	TE	6'1"	210	22		
Horst Muhlmann	K	6'1"	220	32		111

HOUSTON OILERS 1-13-0 Bill Peterson

Scores of Each Game		
17	Denver	30
13	Miami	34
26	N.Y. JETS	20
0	OAKLAND	34
7	Pittsburgh	24
17	CLEVELAND	23
7	Cincinnati	30
0	Cleveland	20
17	PHILADELPHIA	18
10	GREEN BAY	23
20	San Diego	34
10	Atlanta	20
3	PITTSBURGH	9
17	CINCINNATI	61

Use Name	Pos.	Hgt	Wgt	Age	Int	Pts
Lavert Carr	OT	6'5"	260	28		
Gene Ferguson	OT	6'7"	300	24		
Tom Funchess	OT	6'5"	265	27		
Buzz Highsmith	C-OT	6'4"	255	29		
Soloman Freelon	OG	6'2"	250	21		
Ralph Miller	OG	6'4"	260	23		
Tom Regner	OG	6'1"	255	28		
Ron Saul	OG	6'2"	255	24		
Calvin Hunt	C	6'3"	245	24		
Guy Murdock	C	6'2"	245	21		
Allen Aldridge	DE	6'6"	260	27		
Elvin Bethea	DE	6'3"	262	26		
Council Rudolph	DE	6'3"	260	21		
Pat Holmes	DT-DE	6'5"	250	32		
Ron Billingsley	DT	6'8"	290	27		
Lee Brooks	DT	6'5"	255	24		
Mike Tilleman	DT	6'5"	280	28		
Greg Sampson	DE-DT	6'6"	260	21		

Use Name	Pos.	Hgt	Wgt	Age	Int	Pts
Garland Boyette	LB	6'1"	235	32		
Phil Croyle	LB	6'3"	220	24		
Rich Lewis	LB	6'3"	220	22		
Floyd Rice	LB	6'3"	225	23		
Guy Roberts	LB	6'1"	215	21		
Willie Alexander	DB	6'2"	195	23	1	
Bob Atkins	DB	6'3"	210	26	2	
John Charles	DB	6'1"	192	28	2	
Ken Houston	DB	6'3"	195	27		
Benny Johnson	DB	5'11"	178	24	1	
Zeke Moore	DB	6'2"	196	28		
Jim Tolbert	DB	6'3"	202	28		

Lynn Dickey – Injury
Elbert Drungo – Injury

Use Name	Pos.	Hgt	Wgt	Age	Int	Pts
Ed Baker	QB	6'2"	198	23		
Kent Nix	QB	6'1"	195	28		
Dan Pastorini	QB	6'3"	215	23		12
Al Johnson	HB	6'	200	21		
Paul Robinson (from CIN)	HB	6'	198	27		18
Willie Rodgers	HB	6'	210	23		12
Ward Walsh (to GB)	HB	6'	210	23		6
Hoyle Granger	FB	6'1"	255	28		
Robert Holmes	FB	5'9"	220	26		
Fred Willis (from CIN)	FB	6'	212	24		12
Lewis Jolley	HB-FB	6'	210	22		
Ken Burrough	WR	6'4"	210	24		24
Rhett Dawson	WR	6'1"	185	23		6
Dave Smith (from PIT)	WR	6'2"	205	25		
Alvin Reed	TE	6'5"	235	28		
Jim Beirne	WR-TE	6'2"	196	25		6
Skip Butler	K	6'2"	200	25		51
Mark Moseley	K	5'11"	182	24		5

PITTSBURGH STEELERS

RUSHING

Last Name	No.	Yds	Avg	TD
Harris	188	1055	5.6	10
Fuqua	150	665	4.4	4
Bradshaw	58	346	6.0	7
P. Pearson	67	264	3.9	0
Steve Davis	20	85	4.3	1
Lewis	3	68	22.7	0
Bankston	7	20	2.9	0
Bleier	1	17	17.0	0
McMakin	1	0	0.0	0
Gilliam	2	0	0.0	0

RECEIVING

Last Name	No.	Yds	Avg	TD
Shanklin	38	669	18	3
Lewis	27	391	14	5
McMakin	21	277	13	1
Harris	21	180	9	1
Fuqua	18	152	8	0
P. Pearson	11	79	7	0
Young	6	86	14	0
Brown	1	13	13	1
Bankston	1	5	5	0
Steve Davis	1	5	5	0
Mullins	1	3	3	1

PUNT RETURNS

Last Name	No.	Yds	Avg	TD
Edwards	22	202	9	0
Lewis	5	56	11	0
Bleier	2	1	1	0
P. Pearson	1	3	3	0

KICKOFF RETURNS

Last Name	No.	Yds	Avg	TD
P. Pearson	13	292	22	0
Steve Davis	7	207	30	0
Harris	8	183	23	0
Bleier	2	40	20	0
Bankston	1	20	20	0
Edwards	1	18	18	0
McMakin	1	0	0	0

PASSING – PUNTING – KICKING

PASSING	Att	Comp	%	Yds	Yd/Att	TD	Int–	%	RK
Bradshaw	308	147	48	1887	6.1	12	12–	4	12
Gilliam	11	7	64	48	4.4	0	0–	0	
Hanratty	4	2	50	23	5.8	0	0–	0	
Walden	1	0	0	0	0.0	0	0–	0	

PUNTING	No	Avg
Walden	65	43.8
Gerela	1	29.0

KICKING	XP	Att	%	FG	Att	%
Gerela	35	36	97	28	41	68

CLEVELAND BROWNS

RUSHING

Last Name	No.	Yds	Avg	TD
Kelly	224	811	3.6	4
B. Scott	123	571	4.6	2
Phipps	60	256	4.3	5
Brown	32	114	3.6	2
Pitts	3	29	9.7	0
Cornell	7	8	1.1	0
Lefear	3	6	2.0	0
Nelsen	1	–2	–2.0	0

RECEIVING

Last Name	No.	Yds	Avg	TD
Pitts	36	620	17	8
Hooker	32	441	14	2
Morin	30	540	18	1
Kelly	23	204	9	1
B. Scott	23	172	8	0
Brown	5	64	13	0
Glass	5	61	12	0
Cornell	2	7	4	0
Staroba	1	19	19	1
Richardson	1	7	7	0

PUNT RETURNS

Last Name	No.	Yds	Avg	TD
Majors	16	96	6	0
Darden	15	61	4	0
Kelly	5	40	8	0
Sumner	1	14	14	0

KICKOFF RETURNS

Last Name	No.	Yds	Avg	TD
Brown	20	473	24	0
Majors	10	222	22	0
Lefear	6	138	23	0
Johnson	2	33	17	0

PASSING – PUNTING – KICKING

PASSING	Att	Comp	%	Yds	Yd/Att	TD	Int–	%	RK
Phipps	305	144	47	1994	6.5	13	16–	5	11
Nelsen	31	14	45	141	4.6	0	3–	10	
Kelly	1	0	0	0	0.0	0	0–	0	

PUNTING	No	Avg
Cockroft	81	43.2

KICKING	XP	Att	%	FG	Att	%
Cockroft	28	29	97	22	27	81

CINCINNATI BENGALS

RUSHING

Last Name	No.	Yds	Avg	TD
E. Johnson	212	825	3.9	4
Dressler	128	565	4.4	6
Phillips	48	207	4.3	1
Anderson	22	94	4.3	3
Carter	12	57	4.8	2
Lewis	1	15	15.0	0
Joiner	3	14	4.7	0
Morrison	1	2	2.0	0

RECEIVING

Last Name	No.	Yds	Avg	TD
Myers	57	792	14	3
Trumpy	44	500	11	2
Dressler	39	348	9	1
E. Johnson	29	420	14	2
Joiner	24	439	18	2
Thomas	17	171	10	1
Phillips	10	50	5	0
Coslet	5	48	10	1
Buie	1	5	5	0

PUNT RETURNS

Last Name	No.	Yds	Avg	TD
Casanova	30	289	10	1
Parrish	15	141	9	1
E. Johnson	2	7	4	0

KICKOFF RETURNS

Last Name	No.	Yds	Avg	TD
Jackson	21	509	24	0
Parrish	15	348	23	0
Joiner	5	88	18	0
Morrison	3	67	22	0
Casanova	1	34	34	0
Lewis	1	15	15	0
E. Johnson	1	13	13	0
Dennis	1	11	11	0
Kelly	1	0	0	0

PASSING – PUNTING – KICKING

PASSING	Att	Comp	%	Yds	Yd/Att	Td	Int–	%	RK
Anderson	301	171	57	1918	6.4	7	7–	2	5
Carter	82	47	57	579	7.1	3	4–	5	

PUNTING	No	Avg
Lewis	66	42.1

KICKING	XP	Att	%	FG	Att	%
Muhlmann	30	31	97	27	40	68

HOUSTON OILERS

RUSHING

Last Name	No.	Yds	Avg	TD
Willis	134	461	3.4	0
Robinson	107	449	4.2	3
Pastorini	38	205	5.4	2
Rodgers	71	204	2.9	2
Granger	42	175	4.2	0
Holmes	43	172	4.0	0
Walsh	8	36	4.5	0
A. Johnson	11	13	1.2	0
Baker	1	9	9.0	0
Nix	3	3	1.0	0

RECEIVING

Last Name	No.	Yds	Avg	TD
Willis	45	297	7	2
Smith	30	316	11	0
Burrough	26	521	20	4
Reed	19	251	13	0
Granger	15	74	5	0
Robinson	14	112	8	0
Beirne	7	95	14	1
Dawson	6	78	13	1
Rodgers	6	61	10	0
Holmes	6	32	5	0
A. Johnson	6	24	4	0
Walsh	4	22	6	0

PUNT RETURNS

Last Name	No.	Yds	Avg	TD
Houston	25	148	6	0
Moore	7	15	2	0
A. Johnson	2	0	0	0

KICKOFF RETURNS

Last Name	No.	Yds	Avg	TD
Rodgers	17	335	20	0
B. Johnson	13	230	18	0
Jolley	11	267	24	0
A. Johnson	7	154	22	0
Holmes	2	39	20	0
Moore	1	22	22	0
Granger	1	5	5	0

PASSING – PUNTING – KICKING

PASSING	Att	Comp	%	Yds	Yd/Att	Td	Int–	%	RK
Pastorini	299	144	48	1711	5.7	7	12–	4	13
Nix	63	33	52	287	4.6	3	6–	9	
Baker	10	4	40	47	4.7	0	4–	40	
Willis	4	1	25	16	4.0	0	1–	25	

PUNTING	No	Avg
Pastorini	82	41.2
Butler	3	35.0

KICKING	XP	Att	%	FG	Att	%
Butler	15	16	94	12	19	63
Moseley	2	2	100	1	2	50

OAKLAND RAIDERS 10-3-1 John Madden

Scores of Each Game		
28	Pittsburgh	34
20	Green Bay	14
17	SAN DIEGO	17
34	Houston	0
28	BUFFALO	16
23	DENVER	30
45	LOS ANGELES	17
14	Kansas City	27
20	Cincinnati	14
37	Denver	20
26	KANSAS CITY	3
21	San Diego	19
24	N.Y. JETS	16
28	CHICAGO	21

Use Name	Pos.	Hgt	Wgt	Age	Int	Pts
Bob Brown	OT	6'4"	280	29		
Art Shell	OT	6'5"	265	25		
Paul Seiler	C-OT	6'4"	260	26		
George Buehler	OG	6'2"	260	25		
Gene Upshaw	OG	6'5"	255	27		
John Vella	OG	6'4"	255	22		
Jim Otto	C	6'2"	255	34		
Dave Dalby	OG-C	6'2"	240	21		
Tony Cline	DE	6'2"	240	24	1	
Horace Jones	DE	6'3"	240	23		
Tom Keating	DT	6'3"	247	29		
Carleton Oats	DT	6'2"	260	29		
Art Thoms	DT	6'5"	250	25	1	
Otis Sistrunk	DE-DT	6'4"	255	25	1	
Joe Carroll	LB	6'1"	220	22		
Dan Conners	LB	6'1"	230	30	1	
Gerald Irons	LB	6'2"	230	25	2	
Terry Mendenhall	LB	6'1"	210	23		
Gus Otto	LB	6'2"	220	29		
Greg Slough	LB	6'3"	230	24		
Phil Villapiano	LB	6'1"	222	23	3	6
Butch Atkinson	DB	6'	180	25	4	
Willie Brown	DB	6'1"	190	31	4	
Tommy Maxwell	DB	6'2"	195	25		
Jack Tatum	DB	5'10"	200	23	4	6
Alonzo Thomas	DB	6'1"	205	22		
Jimmy Warren	DB	5'11"	175	33		
Nemiah Wilson	DB	6'	165	29	4	
George Blanda	QB	6'1"	215	44		95
Daryle Lamonica	QB	6'2"	215	31		
Ken Stabler	QB	6'3"	215	26		
Clarence Davis	HB	5'10"	190	23		36
Don Highsmith	HB	6'	200	24		6
Charlie Smith	HB	6'1"	205	26		60
Marv Hubbard	FB	6'1"	225	26		24
Peter Banaszak	HB-FB	5'11"	210	28		6
Jeff Queen	TE-FB	6'11"	220	26		
Fred Biletnikoff	WR	6'1"	190	29		42
Cliff Branch	WR	5'11"	170	24		
Mike Siani	WR	6'2"	195	22		30
Ray Chester	TE	6'3"	225	24		48
Bob Moore	TE	6'3"	220	23		6
Jerry DePoyster	K	6'1"	200	26		

Ben Davidson—Injury

Warren Koegel — Injury

KANSAS CITY CHIEFS 8-6-0 Hank Stram

Scores of Each Game		
10	MIAMI	20
20	New Orleans	17
45	Denver	24
31	Cleveland	7
16	CINCINNATI	23
20	PHILADELPHIA	21
26	San Diego	14
27	OAKLAND	14
7	Pittsburgh	16
17	SAN DIEGO	27
3	Oakland	26
24	DENVER	21
24	BALTIMORE	10
17	Atlanta	14

Use Name	Pos.	Hgt	Wgt	Age	Int	Pts
Dave Hill	OT	6'5"	260	31		
Sid Smith	OT	6'4"	260	24		
Jim Tyrer	OT	6'6"	280	33		
Ed Budde	OG	6'5"	265	31		
George Daney	OG	6'3"	240	25		
Larry Gagner	OG	6'3"	268	28		
Mo Moorman	OG	6'5"	252	28		
Mike Oriard	C	6'4"	223	24		
Jack Rudnay	C	6'3"	240	24		
Aaron Brown	DE	6'5"	255	28		
Marv Upshaw	DE	6'3"	260	25		
Wilbur Young	DT-DE	6'6"	285	23		
Buck Buchanan	DT	6'7"	270	32		
Curley Culp	DT	6'1"	265	26		
Ed Lothamer	DT	6'5"	270	29		
George Seals	DT	6'2"	260	29		
Bobby Bell	LB	6'4"	228	32	3	6
Keith Best	LB	6'3"	220	22		
Willie Lanier	LB	6'1"	245	27	2	
Jim Lynch	LB	6'1"	235	27		
Bob Stein	LB	6'2"	235	24		
Clyde Werner	LB	6'4"	225	24	1	
Nate Allen	DB	5'10"	170	24	1	
Jim Kearney	DB	6'2"	206	29	5	24
Jim Marsalis	DB	5'11"	194	26	2	
Larry Marshall	DB	5'10"	195	22		
Kerry Reardon	DB	5'11"	180	23		
Mike Sensibaugh	DB	5'11"	192	23	8	
Emmitt Thomas	DB	6'2"	192	29	2	
Len Dawson	QB	6'	190	38		
Mike Livingston	QB	6'3"	212	26		
Mike Adamle	HB	5'9"	197	22		6
Ed Podolak	HB	6'1"	204	25		36
Wendell Hayes	FB	6'2"	220	31		18
Jim Otis	FB	6'	220	24		
Jeff Kinney	HB-FB	6'2"	215	21		6
Dennis Homan	WR	6'1"	180	26		6
Bruce Jankowski	WR	5'11"	185	23		
Otis Taylor	WR	6'2"	215	29		36
Bob West	WR	6'4"	218	21		18
Elmo Wright	WR	6'	190	23		
Willie Frazier	TE	6'4"	234	29		30
Morris Stroud	TE	6'10"	255	26		6
Jan Stenerud	K	6'2"	187	29		95
Jerrel Wilson	K	6'4"	222	31		

Warren McVea—Knee Injury

DENVER BRONCOS 5-9-0 John Ralston

Scores of Each Game		
30	HOUSTON	17
14	San Diego	37
24	KANSAS CITY	45
10	Cincinnati	21
20	MINNESOTA	23
30	Oakland	23
20	CLEVELAND	27
17	N.Y. Giants	29
16	Los Angeles	10
20	OAKLAND	37
20	Atlanta	23
21	Kansas City	14
38	SAN DIEGO	13
45	NEW ENGLAND	21

Use Name	Pos.	Hgt	Wgt	Age	Int	Pts
Mike Current	OT	6'4"	274	26		
Marv Montgomery	OT	6'6"	255	24	1	
Rick Sharp	OT	6'3"	265	24		
George Goeddeke	OG-OT	6'3"	253	27		
Bill Cottrell	OG	6'3"	255	27		
Larron Jackson	OG	6'3"	270	23		
Mike Schnitker	OG	6'3"	245	25		
Tommy Lyons	C-OG	6'2"	228	24		
Larry Kaminski	C	6'2"	245	27		
Bobby Maples	C	6'3"	250	29		
Lyle Alzado	DE	6'3"	252	23		
John Hoffman (from STL)	DE	6'7"	260	29		
Lloyd Voss	DT-DE	6'4"	255	30		
Tom Domres	DT	6'3"	260	25		
Paul Smith	DT	6'3"	256	27		
Pete Duranko	DE-DT	6'2"	250	28		
Ken Criter	LB	5'11"	223	25		
Fred Forsberg	Lb	6'1"	235	28		
Bob Geddes	LB	6'2"	240	26		
Tom Graham	LB	6'2"	235	22	2	
Bill McKoy	LB	6'3"	235	24		
Chip Myrtle	LB	6'2"	225	27		
Don Parish	LB	6'1"	220	24		
Mike Simone	LB	6'	210	22		
Cornell Gordon	DB	6'	187	31		
Charlie Greer	DB	6'	205	26	2	6
Leroy Mitchell	DB	6'2"	190	27	3	
Randy Montgomery	DB	5'11"	182	25		6
Steve Preece (from PHI)	DB	6'1"	195	25	1	
George Saimes	DB	5'10"	188	30		
Bill Thompson	DB	6'1"	200	25	1	
Bill West	DB	5'10"	185	24		
Mike Ernst	QB	6'1"	190	21		
Charley Johnson	QB	6'	190	35		
Steve Ramsey	QB	6'2"	210	24		12
Floyd Little	HB	5'10"	196	30		78
Fran Lynch	FB-HB	6'1"	205	26		12
Clem Turner	FB	6'1"	236	27		
Bobby Anderson	HB-FB	6'	208	24		12
Joe Dawkins	HB-FB	5'11"	223	24		12
Jim Krieg	WR	5'9"	172	23		
Haven Moses (from BUF)	WR	6'3"	205	26		36
Rod Sherman	WR	6'	190	27		18
Jerry Simmons	WR	6'1"	190	29		12
Bill Van Heusen	WR	6'1"	200	26		6
Bill Masters	TE	6'5"	240	28		18
Riley Odoms	TE	6'4"	230	22		6
Jim Turner	K	6'2"	205	31		97

Walt Barnes — Injury

Sam Brunelli — Injury
Jack Gehrke — Injury

Jerry Inman — Injury

SAN DIEGO CHARGERS 4-9-1 Harland Svare

Scores of Each Game		
3	San Francisco	34
37	DENVER	14
17	Oakland	17
23	Baltimore	20
10	Miami	24
20	Detroit	34
14	KANSAS CITY	26
28	DALLAS	34
17	CLEVELAND	21
27	Kansas City	17
34	HOUSTON	20
19	OAKLAND	21
13	Denver	38
2	PITTSBURGH	24

Use Name	Pos.	Hgt	Wgt	Age	Int	Pts
Ira Gordon	OT	6'3"	268	24		
Terry Owens	OT	6'6"	268	28		
Russ Washington	OT	6'6"	294	25		
Ernie Wright	OT	6'4"	270	32		
Walt Sweeney	OG	6'3"	256	31		
Ralph Wenzel	OG	6'3"	250	29		
Doug Wilkerson	OG	6'2"	250	25		
Sam Gruneisen	C	6'1"	250	31		
Carl Mauck	C	6'3"	245	25		6
Lionel Aldridge	DE	6'4	245	30		
Deacon Jones	DE	6'5"	250	33		
Cal Snowden	DE	6'4"	253	25		
Lee Thomas	DE	6'5"	246	25		
Dave Costa	DT	6'2"	260	30		2
Ron East	DT	6'4"	236	29		
Kevin Hardy	DT	6'5"	276	27		
Greg Wojcik	DT	6'6"	268	26		
John Andrews	LB	6'3"	225	23		
Bob Babich	LB	6'2"	230	25	2	
Pete Barnes	LB	6'3"	240	27	1	
Lee Roy Caffey	LB	6'3"	250	32	1	
Pete Lazetich	LB	6'3"	245	22		
Rick Redman	LB	5'11"	222	29	1	
Tim Rossovich	LB	6'4"	240	26	1	
Ray White	LB	6'1"	242	22		
Joe Beauchamp	DB	6'	182	28	6	6
Reggie Berry	DB	6'	190	23		
Chuck Detwiler	DB	6'	185	24		
Lenny Dunlap	DB	6'1"	195	23	5	
Chris Fletcher	DB	5'11"	185	23		
Bob Howard	DB	6'1"	175	27		
Ray Jones	DB	6'	187	24		
Bryant Salter	DB	6'4"	194	22	7	
Wayne Clark	QB	6'2"	200	25		
John Hadl	QB	6'2"	214	32		6
Mike Garrett	HB	5'9"	200	28		42
John Sykes	HB	5'11"	195	23		
Jesse Taylor	HB	6'	200	24		6
Oscar Dragon	FB-HB	6'	214	22		
Cid Edwards	FB	6'2"	230	28		42
Lee White	FB	6'4"	240	26		
Mike Carter	WR	6'1"	210	24		
Chuck Dicus	WR	6'	176	23		12
Gary Garrison	WR	6'1"	193	28		42
Jerry LeVias	WR	5'10"	178	25		
Dave Williams	WR	6'2"	200	27		18
John Mackey	TE	6'3"	224	30		
Pettis Norman	TE	6'3"	220	32		
Bill McClard	K	5'10"	202	20		11
Dennis Partee	K	6'2"	230	26		71

Harris Jones — Injury
Mel Rodgers — Injury

Duane Thomas — Holdout

OAKLAND RAIDERS

RUSHING

Last Name	No.	Yds	Avg	TD
Hubbard	219	1100	5.0	4
Smith	170	686	4.0	8
Davis	71	363	5.1	6
Banaszak	30	138	4.6	1
Lamonica	10	33	3.3	0
Stabler	6	27	4.5	0
Highsmith	9	11	1.2	1
Queen	4	10	2.5	0
Branch	1	5	5.0	0
Chester	1	3	3.0	0

RECEIVING

Last Name	No.	Yds	Avg	TD
Biletnikoff	58	802	14	7
Chester	34	576	17	8
Siani	28	496	18	5
Smith	28	353	13	2
Hubbard	22	103	5	0
Banaszak	9	63	7	0
Davis	8	82	10	0
Moore	6	49	8	1
Branch	3	41	14	0
Highsmith	2	34	17	0

PUNT RETURNS

Last Name	No.	Yds	Avg	TD
Atkinson	10	33	3	0
Branch	12	21	2	0
Maxwell	2	12	6	0

KICKOFF RETURNS

Last Name	No.	Yds	Avg	TD
Davis	18	464	26	0
Branch	9	191	21	0
Atkinson	3	75	25	0
Warren	4	57	14	0
Maxwell	1	26	26	0
Seiler	1	0	0	0
Slough	1	0	0	0
Smith	1	0	0	0

PASSING – PUNTING – KICKING

PASSING	Att	Comp	%	Yds	Yd/Att	TD	Int–	%	RK
Lamonica	281	149	53	1998	7.1	18	12–	4	2
Stabler	74	44	60	524	7.1	4	3–	4	
Blanda	15	5	33	77	5.1	1	0–	0	

PUNTING	No.	Avg
DePoyster	55	36.9

KICKING	XP	Att	%	FG	Att	%
Blanda	44	44	100	17	26	65

KANSAS CITY CHIEFS

RUSHING

Last Name	No.	Yds	Avg	TD
Podolak	171	615	3.6	4
Hayes	128	536	4.2	0
Adamle	73	303	4.2	1
Livingston	14	133	9.5	0
Kinney	38	122	3.2	1
Otis	29	92	3.2	0
Dawson	15	75	5.0	0
Wright	1	24	24.0	0
Taylor	5	13	2.6	0
West	2	2	1.0	0

RECEIVING

Last Name	No.	Yds	Avg	TD
Taylor	57	821	14	6
Podolak	46	345	8	2
Hayes	31	295	9	3
Adamle	15	76	5	0
Frazier	13	172	13	5
Homan	12	135	11	1
Otis	12	76	6	0
Wright	11	81	7	0
West	9	165	18	2
Stroud	4	80	20	1
Kinney	4	45	11	0
Jankowski	2	24	12	0
Allen	1	20	20	0

PUNT RETURNS

Last Name	No.	Yds	Avg	TD
Marshall	18	103	8	0
Podolak	8	11	1	0
Homan	2	9	5	0
Reardon	1	3	3	0

KICKOFF RETURNS

Last Name	No.	Yds	Avg	TD
Marshall	23	651	28	0
Adamle	8	185	23	0
Podolak	7	119	17	0
Kinney	4	63	16	0
Reardon	2	35	18	0
Upshaw	1	4	4	0
Kearney	1	0	0	0

PASSING – PUNTING – KICKING

PASSING	Att	Comp	%	Yds	Yd/Att	TD	Int–	%	RK
Dawson	305	175	57	1835	6.0	13	12–	4	7
Livingston	78	41	53	480	6.2	7	8–	10	
Wilson	1	1	100	20	20.0	0	0–	0	

PUNTING	No	Avg
Wilson	66	44.8

KICKING	XP	Att	%	FG	Att	%
Stenerud	32	32	100	21	36	58

DENVER BRONCOS

RUSHING

Last Name	No.	Yds	Avg	TD
Little	216	859	4.0	9
Anderson	72	319	4.4	1
Dawkins	56	243	4.3	2
Lynch	34	164	4.8	2
Van Heusen	3	76	25.3	1
Odoms	5	72	14.4	0
Krieg	1	63	63.0	0
C. Turner	5	16	3.2	0
Ramsey	6	15	2.5	2
Moses	2	11	5.5	0
Ernst	1	4	4.0	0
Sherman	1	2	2.0	0
Johnson	3	0	0.0	0
Masters	3	–15	–5.0	0

RECEIVING

Last Name	No.	Yds	Avg	TD
Sherman	38	661	17	3
Little	28	367	13	4
Masters	25	393	16	3
Anderson	23	215	9	1
Odoms	21	320	15	1
Moses	18	284	16	6
Dawkins	18	242	13	0
Simmons	17	235	14	2
Lynch	7	75	11	0
Krieg	4	99	25	0
Van Heusen	4	59	15	0
C. Turner	1	10	10	0

PUNT RETURNS

Last Name	No.	Yds	Avg	TD
Sherman	10	89	9	0
Thomspson	4	82	21	0
Greer	4	67	17	1
Little	8	64	8	0
Simone	1	5	5	0
Krieg	1	3	3	0

KICKOFF RETURNS

Last Name	No.	Yds	Avg	TD
Montgomery	29	756	26	1
Dawkins	15	357	24	0
Little	3	48	16	0
Lynch	3	45	15	0
C. Turner	1	25	25	0
Krieg	1	18	18	0
Anderson	1	13	13	0
Simone	1	–6	–6	0
Preece	1	0	0	0

PASSING – PUNTING – KICKING

PASSING	Att	Comp	%	Yds	Yd/Att	TD	Int–	%	RK
Johnson	238	132	55	1783	7.5	14	14–	6	3
Ramsey	137	65	47	1050	7.7	3	9–	7	
Ernst	4	1	25	10	2.5	0	0–	0	
Anderson	3	1	33	14	4.7	1	0–	0	
Little	2	2	100	43	21.5	1	0–	0	

PUNTING	No	Avg
Van Heusen	60	40.1

KICKING	XP	Att	%	FG	Att	%
J Turner	37	37	100	20	29	69

SAN DIEGO CHARGERS

RUSHING

Last Name	No.	Yds	Avg	TD
Garrett	272	1031	3.8	6
Edwards	157	679	4.3	5
Hadl	22	99	4.5	1
L. White	23	75	3.3	0
Taylor	13	58	4.5	0
Dragon	9	30	3.3	0
Carter	1	25	25.0	0
Williams	1	14	14.0	0
Norman	1	9	9.0	0
Garrison	2	–6	–3.0	0
Clark	2	–8	–4.0	0
Dicus	1	–11	–11.0	0

RECEIVING

Last Name	No.	Yds	Avg	TD
Garrison	52	744	14	7
Edwards	40	557	14	2
Garrett	31	245	8	1
Norman	19	262	14	0
Dicus	18	227	13	2
Williams	14	315	23	3
Mackey	11	110	10	0
L. White	3	20	7	0
Carter	2	24	12	0
LeVias	1	8	8	0
Hadl	1	4	4	0

PUNT RETURNS

Last Name	No.	Yds	Avg	TD
Dunlap	19	179	9	0
Garrett	2	10	5	0
Taylor	1	0	0	0
LeVias	1	–4	–4	0

KICKOFF RETURNS

Last Name	No.	Yds	Avg	TD
Taylor	31	676	22	0
Dunlap	12	271	23	0
Berry	7	138	20	0
Detwiler	4	94	24	0
Sykes	2	44	22	0
R. Jones	3	41	14	0
Beauchamp	1	0	0	0
Williams	0	9	0	0

PASSING – PUNTING – KICKING

PASSING	Att	Comp	%	Yds	Yd/Att	TD	Int–	%	RK
Hadl	370	190	51	2449	6.6	15	26–	7	10
Clark	6	2	33	67	11.2	0	2–	33	
Garrett	1	0	0	0	0.0	0	0–	0	

PUNTING	No	Avg
Partee	45	40.3

KICKING	XP	Att	%	FG	Att	%
Partee	26	28	93	15	25	60
McClard	2	2	100	3	6	50

1972 Championship Games

NFC CHAMPIONSHIP GAME

December 31, at Washington
(Attendance 53,129)

No Stronger Than Its Weakest Link

SCORING

WASHINGTON	0	10	0	16–26
DALLAS	0	3	0	0– 3

Second Quarter
- Wash. — Knight, 18 yard field goal
- Wash. — Taylor, 15 yard pass from Kilmer; PAT–Knight (Kick)
- Dall. — Fritsch, 35 yard field goal

Fourth Quarter
- Wash. — Taylor, 45 yard pass from Kilmer; PAT–Knight (Kick)
- Wash. — Knight, 39 yard field goal
- Wash. — Knight, 46 yard field goal
- Wash. — Knight, 45 yard field goal

TEAM STATISTICS

WASH.		DALLAS
16	First Downs–Total	8
4	First Downs–Rushing	3
11	First Downs–Passing	3
1	First Downs–Penalty	2
2	Fumbles–Number	1
1	Fumbles–Lost Ball	1
4	Penalties–Number	4
38	Yards Penalized	30
0	Missed Field Goals	1
62	Offensive Plays–Total	45
316	Net Yards	169
5.1	Average Gain	3.8
1	Giveaways	1
1	Takeaways	1
0	Difference	0

The Cowboys and Redskins, arch-rivals in the Eastern Division, each made it to the NFC title game with a strong showing in the first round of the playoffs. The Redskins completely stifled the Packer running attack in a 16-3 triumph, while the Cowboys rallied in the fourth quarter to beat the '49ers 30-28. The two clubs had split their meetings during the regular season, and this match would decide the Super Bowl berth.

Roger Staubach, who had sat out most of the season with an injured shoulder but had returned to action in the come-from-behind victory over San Francisco the week before, started at quarterback for the Cowboys in place of Craig Morton. The Washington defense greeted him with a ferocious pass rush that kept him off balance all afternoon and prevented any second-half heroics.

The Washington offensive game plan called for attacking the Cowboys at their weak left cornerback spot, where Charley Waters, normally a safety, had beaten Herb Adderley out of a job. Leading 3-0 in the second quarter, the Redskins went to work on Waters. Charley Taylor beat him to haul in a 51-yard pass, and several plays later Kilmer hit Taylor with a 15-yard scoring pitch. The Cowboys answered with a drive deep into Washington territory, but when Calvin Hill overthrew Walt Garrison in the end zone on an option pass, they had to settle for a Toni Fritsch field goal.

Early in the third period Waters broke an arm, and coach Tom Landry put Mark Washington into the corner position and left the veteran Adderley on the bench. Taylor exploited Washington's inexperience in the fourth quarter by beating him for a 45-yard touchdown pass which gave the Redskins some breathing room. Forced to go to the air, the Cowboys could make no headway against the Redskin defense, and three Curt Knight field goals in the final quarter gave the Redskins a much savored 26-3 victory.

INDIVIDUAL STATISTICS

WASHINGTON	No	Yds	Avg.	DALLAS	No	Yds	Avg.
RUSHING							
Brown	30	88	2.9	Staubach	5	59	11.8
Harraway	11	19	1.7	Hill	9	22	2.4
Kilmer	3	15	5.0	Garrison	7	15	2.1
	44	122	2.8		21	96	4.6
RECEIVING							
Taylor	7	146	20.9	Sellers	2	29	14.5
Harraway	3	13	4.3	Garrison	2	18	9.0
Jefferson	2	19	9.5	Hill	2	11	5.5
Brown	2	16	8.0	Parks	1	21	21.0
	14	194	13.9	Alworth	1	15	15.0
				Ditka	1	4	4.0
					9	98	10.9
PUNTING							
Bragg	4		36.0	Bateman	7		43.1
PUNT RETURNS							
Haymond	4	10	2.5	Waters	3	–5	–1.7
KICKOFF RETURNS							
None				Harris	2	29	14.5
				Newhouse	1	25	25.0
					3	54	18.0

PASSING

WASHINGTON	Att.	Comp.	Comp. Pct.	Yds.	Int.	Yds/ Att.	Yds/ Comp.	Yards Lost Tackled
Kilmer	18	14	77.8	194	0	10.8	13.9	0– 0
DALLAS								
Staubach	20	9	45.0	98	0	4.9	10.9	3–25
Hill	1	0	0.0	0	0	–	–	
	21	9	42.9	98	0	4.7	10.9	3–25

AFC CHAMPIONSHIP GAME

December 31, at Pittsburgh
(Attendance 50,845)

Simply Not Enough of Bradshaw

SCORING

PITTSBURGH	7	0	3	7–17
MIAMI	0	7	7	7–21

First Quarter
- Pitt. — Mullins, Recovery of Pitt fumble in end zone; PAT–Gerela (kick)

Second Quarter
- Miami — Csonka, 9 yard pass from Morrall; PAT–Yepremian (kick)

Third Quarter
- Pitt. — Gerela, 14 yard field goal
- Miami — Kiick, 2 yard rush; PAT–Yepremian (kick)

Fourth Quarter
- Miami — Kiick, 3 yard rush; PAT–Yepremian (kick)
- Pitt. — Young, 12 yard pass from Bradshaw; PAT–Gerela (kick)

TEAM STATISTICS

PITT.		MIAMI
13	First Downs–Total	19
6	First Downs–Rushing	11
6	First Downs–Passing	6
1	First Downs–Penalty	2
2	Fumbles–Number	0
0	Fumbles–Lost Ball	0
4	Penalties–Number	2
30	Yards Penalized	19
1	Missed Field Goals	0
48	Offensive Plays–Total	65
250	Net Yards	314
5.2	Average Gain	4.8
2	Giveaways	1
1	Takeaways	2
–1	Difference	+1

The Dolphins came into this game after a miracle season, while the Steelers came in after a miracle play. By beating Cleveland 20-14 last week in the start of the playoffs, the Dolphins ran their record to 15-0 for the season. The Steelers had a less shining record, but their spirits were high after beating the Raiders 13-7 in the opening round of the playoffs. In that game the Steelers scored the winning touchdown with five seconds left on a deflected pass which Franco Harris snagged in mid-air and carried across the goal line.

In the first quarter, after an extended drive into Miami territory, Terry Bradshaw fumbled on the three-yard line and Gerry Mullins fell on the ball as it rolled into the end zone. Although the Steelers took a 7-0 lead, the play was costly, as Bradshaw was knocked dizzy and had to be relieved by Terry Hanratty.

An alert play by punter Larry Seiple helped the Dolphins tie the score in the second quarter. Noticing that all the Steelers had dropped back to block for the return, Seiple crossed the defense up and ran with the ball, gaining 37 yards to the Pittsburgh 12-yard line. Two plays later Morrall hit Csonka with a scoring pass, and Garo Yepremian added the extra point.

As the second half began, Miami coach Don Shula put Bob Griese, out since October with a broken leg, in at quarterback to shake up his offense. The Steelers went ahead 10-7 on a Roy Gerela field goal, but Griese hit Paul Warfield with a 52-yard pass play which put the Dolphins in striking distance. Six plays later, Jim Kiick carried the ball in, and another Kiick touchdown in the fourth quarter lengthened the Miami lead to 21-10. Bradshaw returned to action for the final seven minutes of the game, but after leading the Steelers to one touchdown, he suffered two interceptions in his final three passes.

INDIVIDUAL STATISTICS

PITTSBURGH	No	Yds	Avg.	MIAMI	No	Yds	Avg.
RUSHING							
Harris	16	76	4.8	Morris	16	76	4.8
Fuqua	8	47	5.9	Csonka	24	68	2.8
Bradshaw	2	5	2.5	Seiple	1	37	37.0
	26	128	4.9	Kiick	8	12	1.5
					49	193	3.9
RECEIVING							
Young	4	54	13.5	Fleming	5	50	10.0
Shanklin	2	49	24.5	Warfield	2	63	31.5
Harris	2	3	1.5	Csonka	1	9	9.0
McMakin	1	22	22.0	Mandich	1	5	5.0
Brown	1	9	9.0	Morris	1	–6	–6.0
	10	137	13.7		10	121	12.1
PUNTING							
Walden	4		51.3	Seiple	4		35.5
PUNT RETURNS							
Edwards	1	5	5.0	None			
KICKOFF RETURNS							
P. Pearson	2	63	31.5	Morris	1	23	23.0
S. Davis	1	22	22.0				
	3	85	28.3				
INTERCEPTION RETURNS							
Edwards	1	28	28.0	Buoniconti	1	6	6.0
				Kuler	1	5	5.0
					2	11	5.5

PASSING

PITTSBURGH	Att.	Comp.	Comp. Pct.	Yds.	Int.	Yds/ Att.	Yds/ Comp.	Yards Lost Tackled
Bradshaw	10	5	50.0	80	2	8.0	16.0	
Hanratty	10	5	50.0	57	0	5.7	11.4	
	20	10	50.0	137	2	6.9	13.7	2–15
MIAMI								
Morrall	11	7	63.6	51	1	4.6	7.3	
Griese	5	3	60.0	70	0	14.0	23.3	
	16	10	62.5	121	1	7.6	12.1	0– 0

SUPER BOWL VII

January 14, at Los Angeles
(Attendance 90,182)

Super Perfect

The contrasts were interesting. The Miami Dolphins had swept through fourteen regular-season games and two playoff games without a loss and now had a chance to compile a perfect 17-0 record for the year. Under the thorough leadership of head coach Don Shula, the Dolphins had rebounded from last year's Super Bowl loss to Dallas to become a cool, mature, precise club, with programmed brutality on both platoons.

The Washington Redskins had mostly veteran players, but their style was not one of coolness. Coach George Allen strove to whip his men into a frenzy before every game, and he put a fanatical emphasis on this game. A loss in this game would spoil the entire season, he said, and he drilled his troops in Spartan fashion to prepare them for the younger Dolphins.

The Miami defense scuttled the Washington running attack right from the start, a reversal from last year's dissection of the Dolphin front wall by the Cowboys. Larry Brown and Charley Harraway found Miami tackle Manny Fernandez forever in their path, and quarterback Bill Kilmer suffered through a bad afternoon with his passing. The Dolphins picked off three passes, with safety Jake Scott making two of the interceptions.

The Dolphin attack moved well against the heralded Redskin defense, but three penalties prevented any score until late in the period. Just before the end of the quarter Howard Twilley beat Pat Fischer to the outside and hauled in a 28-yard Bob Griese touchdown pass which he carried in from the 5. Leading 7-0, the Dolphins continued to paralyze the Redskin offense in the second period and scored again late in the period. One minute before halftime Jim Kiick capped a long Miami drive by going over from the one-yard line, giving the Dolphins a solid 14-0 lead at intermission.

The Redskins finally got their offense rolling after taking the second-half kickoff. With Brown gaining on the ground and Kilmer completing three passes, the Redskins drove into Miami territory before the drive stalled. Curt Knight then lined up a comparitively easy 32-yard field goal, but his kick sailed wide to the right and the Dolphins took possession.

The Miami defense re-established its superiority through the second half as the Dolphin offense held onto the ball long enough on each possession to eat up valuable time. With two minutes left in the game, Garo Yepremian attempted a 42-yard field goal, only to have it blocked. When the ball bounced back to him, he picked it up and started to run toward the sidelines. With no football experience except kicking, Yepremian then attempted to pass the ball, only to have it slip out of his hands right to Mike Bass of the Redskins. Bass ran 49 yards with the aborted pass for Washington's only score of the day, but the Dolphins hung onto the 14-7 lead the rest of the way and became the first NFL team ever to go through a complete season with all wins.

MIAMI		WASHINGTON
	OFFENSE	
Warfield	WR	C. Taylor
W. Moore	LT	Hermeling
Kuechenberg	LG	Laaveg
Langer	C	Hauss
Little	RG	Wilbur
Evans	RT	Rock
Fleming	TE	Smith
Twilley	WR	Jefferson
Griese	QB	Kilmer
Kiick	RB	Brown
Csonka	RB	Harraway
	DEFENSE	
Den Herder	LE	McDole
Fernandez	LT	Brundige
Heinz	RT	Talbert
Stanfill	RE	Biggs
Swift	LLB	Pardee
Bouniconti	MLB	Pottios
Kolen	RLB	Hanburger
Mumphord	LCB	Fischer
Johnson	RCB	Bass
Anderson	LS	Owens
Scott	RS	R. Taylor

SUBSTITUTES

MIAMI

Offense

Briscoe	Leigh
Crusan	Mandich
Ginn	Morrall
Jenkins	Morris
Kindig	

Defense

Babb	M. Moore
Ball	Powell
Matheson	Stuckey

Kickers

Seiple	Yepremian

WASHINGTON

Offense

Alston	McNeil
Brunet	Mul-Key
Burman	Wyche
Hull	

Defense

Fanucci	Severson
Haymond	Sistrunk
Jaqua	Tillman
McLinton	Vactor

Kickers

Bragg	Knight

SCORING

MIAMI	7	7	0	0–14
WASHINGTON	0	0	0	7– 7

First Quarter
Mia. Twilley, 28 yd pass from Griese
PAT – Yepremian (kick) 14:59

Second Quarter
Mia. Kiick, 1 yard rush
PAT – Yepremian (kick) 14:42

Fourth Quarter
Was. Bass, 49 yard fumble return
PAT – Knight 12:53

TEAM STATISTICS

MIAMI		WASH.
12	First Downs – Total	16
7	First Downs – Rushing	9
5	First Downs – Passing	7
0	First Downs – Penalty	0
2	Fumbles – Number	1
1	Fumbles – Lost Ball	0
3	Penalties – Number	3
35	Yards Penalized	25
50	Total Offensive Plays	66
253	Total Net Yards	228
5.1	Average Gain	3.5
1	Missed Field Goals	1
2	Giveaways	3
3	Takeaways	2
+1	Difference	–1

INDIVIDUAL STATISTICS

MIAMI	No	Yds	Avg.	WASHINGTON	No	Yds	Avg.
			RUSHING				
Csonka	15	112	7.5	Brown	22	72	3.3
Kiick	12	38	3.2	Harraway	10	37	3.7
Morris	10	34	3.4	Kilmer	2	18	9.0
	37	184	5.0	Taylor	1	8	8.0
				Smith	1	6	6.0
					36	141	3.9
			RECEIVING				
Warfield	3	36	12.0	Jefferson	5	50	10.0
Kiick	2	6	3.0	Brown	5	26	5.2
Twilley	1	28	28.0	Taylor	2	20	10.0
Mandich	1	19	19.0	Smith	1	11	11.0
Csonka	1	–1	–1.0	Harraway	1	–3	–3.0
	8	88	11.0		14	104	7.4
			PUNTING				
Seiple	7		43.0	Bragg	5		31.2
			PUNT RETURNS				
Scott	2	4	2.0	Haymond	4	9	2.3
			KICKOFF RETURNS				
Morris	2	33	16.5	Haymond	2	30	15.0
				Mul-Key	1	15	15.0
					3	45	15.0
			INTERCEPTION RETURNS				
Scott	2	63	31.5	Owens	1	0	0.0
Buoniconti	1	32	32.0				
	3	95	31.7				

PASSING

	Att	Comp	Comp Pct.	Yds	Int	Yds/ Att.	Yds/ Comp	Yards Lost Tackled
MIAMI								
Griese	11	8	72.7	88	1	8.0	11.0	2–19
WASHINGTON								
Kilmer	28	14	50.0	104	3	3.7	7.4	2–17

1973 N.F.C. Recession at the Concessions

When Congress passed a bill forbidding television blackouts of games sold out forty-eight hours ahead of time, the NFL reluctantly televised home games for the first time in years. This situation gave birth to a new football term, the "no-show," who was a fan holding a ticket for a sold-out game but instead watched it at home on TV. Ticket sales were not affected by the new ruling, but concession profits, fell in the parks on days when unpleasant weather made the television set a much more comfortable way to view the game.

EASTERN DIVISION

Dallas Cowboys—The Cowboys had injuries at several key positions but still made the playoffs. When newly acquired flanker Otto Stowe broke an ankle in mid-season, rookie Drew Pearson stepped into the starting lineup and began grabbing passes in all kinds of situations. A bad back made defensive tackle Bob Lilly's season a miserable one, but middle linebacker Lee Roy Jordan took charge of the defense with his first All-Pro season in an eleven-year pro career. Other added assets for coach Tom Landry were quarterback Roger Staubach's staying healthy for the entire season, Bob Hayes's recovery from an off-season to reclaim his starting wide-receiver job, and tight end Billy Joe DuPree's good rookie season.

Washington Redskins—The Over the Hill Gang was far from finished. Coach George Allen added Dave Robinson, Ken Houston, Alvin Reed, and Duane Thomas to his squad through a variety of trades. Robinson and Houston replaced the retired Jack Pardee and Roosevelt Taylor on the defensive unit, while Reed and Thomas gave the Skins all-star depth on offense. Thomas left his personal problems behind him when he reported to the Redskins, working hard to regain his top form of the 1971 season, but the superb running and blocking of backs Larry Brown and Charley Harraway kept Duane on the bench for most of the season. Veteran passing ace Sonny Jurgensen stayed healthy enough to share the quarterback job with Billy Kilmer, and their collective wisdom guided the Redskins attack

Philadelphia Eagles—New head coach Mike McCormack ripped the Eagles apart and started all over again from scratch. To run the offense, he paid a high price to the Rams for Roman Gabriel, a quarterback who was used to winning. Ex-Colt Norm Bulaich and second-year man Tom Sullivan started at running back, tall Harold Carmichael and rookie Don Zimmerman won the wide-receiver jobs, and rookie Charley Young was an instant All-Pro at tight end. Operating behind a line with two fine rookies in Jerry Sisemore and Guy Morriss, Gabriel picked enemy defenses apart with precision passing and sharp play-calling. Coach McCormack had less success in rebuilding the defense. End Mel Tom was traded to Chicago after an argument with an assistant coach, cornerback Nate Ramsey was cut in mid-season, linebacker Ron Porter was traded to Minnesota, and knee injuries kayoed linebacker Steve Zabel and cornerback Al Nelson.

St. Louis Cardinals—New head coach Don Coryell succeeded in building a fine passing attack, but injuries and a bad defense held the Cards under .500 for the third straight season. Quarterback Jim Hart won the starting position and developed into a top passer, hitting wide receivers Mel Gray and Ahmad Rashad (previously known as Bobby Moore) with long bombs which had grown infrequent in 1970s pro football. But the St. Louis defense had problems stopping even mediocre attacks, despite a good rookie season from massive end Dave Butz. Late-season injuries crippled both platoons, with Hart and most of the offensive line out for the last few games of the year.

New York Giants—A perfect 6-0 record in pre-season play inflated Giant hopes to a vibrating level, but the cruel reality which followed turned the season into a nightmare. After opening with a win and tie in Yankee Stadium, the Giants for all purposes became a road team for the rest of the season. Yankee Stadium was shut for repairs, so the Giants held their practices in Jersey City and played their "home" games in the Yale Bowl in New Haven. The gypsy life disheartened the players, and the team lost seven straight games after leaving the old ball park. Coach Alex Webster announced his resignation before the final game, not a totally unexpected move.

CENTRAL DIVISION

Minnesota Vikings—Fran Tarkenton finally began burying his image as a loser by leading the Vikings into the playoffs with a 12-2 record for the regular season. Aiding Tarkenton considerably was the front four of Carl Eller, Alan Page, Gary Larsen, and Jim Marshall, all of whom stayed healthy and gave the Minnesota defense its old devastating strength. The secondary lost safety Karl Kassulke when he was seriously hurt in a pre-season motorcycle accident, but the quartet of Bobby Bryant, Nate Wright, Paul Krause, and Jeff Wright threw an airtight cover on enemy receivers. The Viking offense had a new weapon in rookie Chuck Foreman, a slashing runner who also caught passes. At wide receiver, John Gilliam made fans forget the traded Gene Washington with his speed and sure hands. The Vikings had always had a defense, but now that they had an offense they outclassed their rivals in the Central Division.

Detroit Lions—High hopes for a divisional title flattened out into a disappointing second-place finish and bitter words from the owner and coach. The Lions compiled a 1-4-1 record in their first six games, with a 29-27 loss to Baltimore on October 21 the bitterest pill to swallow. Coach Don McCafferty said, "If we can't beat the Colts, we can't beat anybody." Owner William Clay Ford added, "I don't think they want to win—at least it doesn't look like it." The Lions responded with a 27-0 shutout of the Packers the next week, but a limp 20-0 loss to Washington on Thanksgiving Day brought another public blast from McCafferty. "We stunk out the joint," said the coach. We've got some losers on this ball club and they won't be around next year."

Green Bay Packers—The Packer defense had carried the team into the playoffs last year, but the one-dimensional Green Bay offense was too much of a load for the defense to carry this season. John Brockington and MacArthur Lane kept eating up the yardage on the ground, with Brockington gaining 1,000 yard for the third time in his three-year pro career. The Green Bay passing attack, however, was next to nonexistent. Coach Dan Devine gave youngsters Scott Hunter, Jim Del Gaizo, and Jerry Tagge each a shot at the quarterback job, but none of them took the pressure off the runners with a consistent passing game. The offensive line enjoyed its greatest success clearing the way for Brockington and Lane, with guard Gale Gillingham bouncing back from an injury-filled 1972 season to win All-Pro honors.

Chicago Bears—Dick Butkus scored the first touchdown of his pro career by falling on a Houston fumble in the end zone on October 28, but a bad knee made it increasingly hard for him to cover pass receivers coming out of the backfield. The problem with the Bears' offense had nothing to do with injuries; quarterback Bobby Douglass was a superior runner but simply could not pass well. Chicago fans singled Douglass out for insults whenever the Bears lost, calling on coach Abe Gibron to stick rookie quarterback Gary Huff into the lineup. Gibron stayed with Douglass until November 18, when he gave Huff his first extended chance. The inexperienced rookie threw four interceptions as the Lions crushed the Bears 30-7; the fans afterward booed Douglass but didn't call for Huff.

WESTERN DIVISION

Los Angeles Rams—Carroll Rosenbloom had given Weeb Ewbank, Don Shula, and Don McCafferty their first head coaching positions while he owned the Colts, and he struck gold again this year with the Rams by hiring Chuck Knox as the head man. Knox led a team supposedly in need of an overhauling to a runaway title in the Western Division and a berth in the playoffs. The Los Angeles passing attack profited from two new faces brought in by Knox. Quarterback John Hadl came over from San Diego and receiver Harold Jackson from Philadelphia in major trades, and both men starred in their new surroundings. Two strong young runners, Larry McCutcheon and Jim Bertelsen, made Hadl's signal-calling task easier, with the excellent offensive line laboring anonymously for both the runners and passers. The defensive unit played up to the standards set by George Allen, although Merlin Olsen was the only starter left from that era. With little expected of them, the Rams won their first six games of the year and ran away from the other teams in the division.

Atlanta Falcons—With solid starters at every position except quarterback, the Falcons opened the season with a smashing triumph over the Saints in which Dick Shiner masterfully engineered the Atlanta attack. Shiner soon regressed into the mediocre form he had shown all his career, and coach Norm Van Brocklin next turned to Bob Lee at the position. An ex-Viking with little experience, Lee sparked the Falcons to a 41-0 victory over San Diego and a mid-season winning streak which made the team a prime candidate for the wild-card spot in the playoffs. December, however, brought bad times to the Falcons, as they lost to Buffalo and St. Louis.

San Francisco '49ers—Disappointment colored the '49ers season as the team finished a distant third in the West. Fullback Ken Willard publicly expressed his disappointment when benched at the start of the season. Bad knees turned receiver Gene Washington and cornerback Jim Johnson into disappointing performers. Quarterback John Brodie endured the bitterest season of all, finding himself on the bench behind Steve Spurrier and Joe Reed after the team got off to a slow start. The thirty-eight-year-old Brodie announced in mid-season that this would be his last campaign, and coach Dick Nolan gave him the starting nod in the season's finale against the Steelers, but a sore arm sent him out of the game in the first half.

New Orleans Saints—John North replaced J. D. Roberts as head coach in training camp, taking over a club that looked like one of the worst in the league. An opening-day trouncing by the Falcons embarrassed the team, but North patiently developed his defense into a good unit. The Saints beat the Bears on October 7 for their first victory, and they won four other games during the season, including an upset of the Washington Redskins. Young veterans Billy Newsome, Joe Owens, Joe Federspiel, Ernie Jackson, and Bivian Lee starred on the improved defensive platoon, while quarterback Archie Manning got some help on offense from end John Beasley, runner Jess Phillips and receiver Jubilee Dunbar, all picked up in trades.

FINAL TEAM STATISTICS

(Other statistics not available at press time)

OFFENSE

	ATL.	CHI.	DALL.	DET.	G.B.	L.A.	MINN.	N.O.	N.Y.	PHIL.	ST.L.	S.F.	WASH.
FIRST DOWNS:													
Total	240	193	281	237	187	294	246	207	239	267	238	251	232
by Rushing	123	97	139	122	98	177	135	100	83	103	96	97	76
by Passing	100	77	127	104	72	101	99	88	141	147	111	127	131
by Penalty	17	19	15	11	17	16	12	19	15	17	31	27	25
RUSHING:													
Number	518	496	542	496	527	659	538	497	456	417	416	422	459
Yards	2037	1907	2418	2133	1973	2925	2275	1842	1478	1791	1671	1743	1439
Average Yards	3.9	3.8	4.5	4.3	3.7	4.4	4.2	3.7	3.2	4.3	4.0	4.1	3.1
Touchdowns	18	11	17	17	10	18	14	5	11	9	13	15	9
PASSING:													
Attempts	320	303	321	325	255	271	298	338	412	479	394	466	372
Completions	168	136	192	171	119	144	179	163	230	275	210	233	209
Completion Percentage	52.5	44.9	59.8	52.6	46.7	53.1	60.1	48.2	55.8	57.4	53.3	50.0	56.2
Passing Yards	2362	1617	2602	2105	1503	2107	2234	1901	2762	3236	2592	2645	2560
Avg. Yards per Attempt	7.4	5.3	8.1	6.4	5.9	7.8	7.5	5.6	6.7	6.8	6.6	5.7	6.9
Avg. Yards per Complet.	14.1	11.9	13.6	12.3	12.6	14.6	12.5	11.7	12.0	11.8	12.3	11.4	12.2
Times Tackled Passing	41	49	43	27	27	17	32	37	28	34	27	27	31
Yards Lost Tackled	361	395	269	192	220	126	278	242	201	238	209	164	202
Net Yards	2001	1222	2333	1913	1283	1981	1956	1659	2561	2998	2383	2481	2358
Touchdowns	14	8	26	12	7	22	16	11	14	23	16	9	20
Interceptions	12	16	16	19	17	11	9	17	30	13	15	25	14
Percent Intercepted	3.8	5.3	5.0	5.8	6.7	4.1	3.0	5.0	7.3	2.7	3.8	5.4	3.8
PUNTS:													
Number	63	86	59	54	68	51	66	81	68	64	66	79	64
Average Distance	42.6	39.8	41.5	43.2	41.0	40.8	39.8	41.7	38.8	40.9	37.5	43.7	40.3
PUNT RETURNS:													
Number	48	37	28	35	30	51	28	22	21	15	27	37	40
Yards	429	204	174	289	137	478	140	218	160	116	192	393	331
Average Yards	8.9	5.5	6.2	8.3	4.6	9.4	5.0	9.9	7.6	7.7	7.1	10.6	8.3
Touchdowns	0	1	0	0	0	0	0	0	0	0	0	0	0
KICKOFF RETURNS:													
Number	53	59	33	50	53	36	35	47	56	63	58	63	43
Yards	1107	1344	725	1061	1189	915	752	947	1198	1441	1369	1301	1118
Average Yards	20.9	22.8	22.0	21.2	22.4	25.4	21.5	20.1	21.4	22.9	23.6	20.7	26.0
Touchdowns	0	1	0	0	0	1	0	0	0	0	1	0	1
INTERCEPTION RETURNS:													
Number	22	14	18	22	15	20	21	16	20	15	10	17	26
Yards	528	176	300	522	220	300	263	126	214	120	71	134	598
Average Yards	24.0	12.6	16.7	23.7	14.7	15.0	12.5	7.9	10.7	8.0	7.1	7.9	23.0
Touchdowns	2	0	2	1	3	1	2	0	0	1	0	0	4
PENALTIES:													
Number	66	86	83	64	68	54	55	58	67	61	61	93	81
Yards	598	817	762	584	653	606	482	516	586	566	594	903	771
FUMBLES:													
Number	40	40	25	30	23	21	29	34	23	41	36	32	32
Number Lost	21	26	12	14	11	9	17	17	10	15	14	14	18
POINTS:													
Total	318	195	382	271	202	388	296	163	226	310	286	262	325
PAT Attempts	34	22	46	30	20	42	33	16	25	34	31	26	37
PAT Made	34	21	45	28	19	40	33	16	25	34	31	26	37
FG Attempts	38	24	30	33	35	47	35	36	28	40	32	33	42
FG Made	26	14	19	21	21	30	21	17	17	24	23	26	22
Percent FG Made	68.4	58.3	63.3	63.6	60.0	63.8	60.0	47.2	60.7	60.0	71.9	78.8	52.4
Safeties	1	0	2	0	0	3	1	0	0	0	0	1	0

DEFENSE

	ATL.	CHI.	DALL.	DET.	G.B.	L.A.	MINN.	N.O.	N.Y.	PHIL.	ST.L.	S.F.	WASH.
FIRST DOWNS:													
Total	212	247	208	245	230	173	220	271	240	286	307	242	233
by Rushing	104	138	83	127	114	71	105	131	126	136	135	112	89
by Passing	92	90	106	98	101	87	100	119	94	135	157	115	119
by Penalty	16	19	19	20	15	15	15	21	20	15	15	15	25
RUSHING:													
Number	520	563	435	501	506	366	450	556	497	513	504	513	480
Yards	2129	2509	1471	2117	1999	1270	1974	2402	2174	2423	2120	1963	1603
Average Yards	4.1	4.5	3.4	4.2	4.0	3.5	4.4	4.3	4.4	4.7	4.2	3.8	3.3
Touchdowns	12	19	5	10	13	5	5	17	21	22	16	11	8
PASSING:													
Attempts	324	303	352	332	327	328	377	337	275	370	417	383	406
Completions	151	156	187	173	180	179	198	176	161	219	252	194	203
Completion Percentage	46.6	51.5	53.1	52.1	55.0	54.6	52.5	52.2	58.5	59.2	60.4	50.7	50.0
Passing Yards	1619	1978	2301	2058	2050	2023	2124	2333	2252	2789	3226	2591	2531
Avg. Yards per Attempt	5.0	6.5	6.5	6.2	6.3	6.2	5.6	6.9	8.2	7.5	7.7	6.8	6.2
Avg. Yards per Complet.	10.7	12.7	12.3	11.9	11.4	11.3	10.7	13.3	14.0	12.7	12.8	13.4	12.5
Times Tackled Passing	29	32	40	33	25	45	30	24	35	21	29	32	53
Yards Lost Tackled	189	304	306	270	228	342	230	155	267	150	197	225	355
Net Yards	1430	1674	1995	1788	1822	1681	1894	2178	1985	2639	3029	2366	2176
Touchdowns	11	17	15	15	14	10	8	15	17	22	23	19	12
Interceptions	22	14	18	22	15	20	21	16	20	15	10	17	26
Percent Intercepted	6.8	4.6	5.1	6.6	4.6	6.1	5.6	4.7	7.3	4.1	2.4	4.4	6.4
PUNTS:													
Number													
Average Distance													
PUNT RETURNS:													
Number	30	40	29	30	41	24	41	49	32	35	23	46	14
Yards													
Average Yards	6.1	7.4	5.2	5.5	7.3	10.9	6.5	11.9	11.8	10.8	8.1	8.0	7.4
Touchdowns		0			0								
KICKOFF RETURNS:													
Number	58	33	53	59	40	68	58	33	43	55	57	52	62
Yards													
Average Yards	23.6	24.6	24.9	20.7	20.4	19.4	19.1	22.0	22.7	22.7	23.7	22.1	20.0
Touchdowns		0			0								
INTERCEPTION RETURNS:													
Number	12	16	16	19	17	11	9	17	30	13	15	25	14
Yards	83	335	151	171	256	103	88	280	525	287	267	379	173
Average Yards	6.9	20.9	9.4	9.0	15.1	9.4	9.8	16.5	17.5	22.1	17.8	15.2	12.4
Touchdowns	0	1	1	0	1	1	0	3	3	1	2	1	0
PENALTIES:													
Number													
Yards													
FUMBLES:													
Number													
Number Lost													
POINTS:													
Total	224	334	203	247	259	178	168	312	362	393	365	319	198
PAT Attempts	24	37	23	26	28	17	15	36	42	47	42	32	21
PAT Made													
FG Attempts													
FG Made													
Percent FG Made													
Safeties													

CONFERENCE PLAYOFFS

December 22, at Minnesota (Attendance 45,475)

SCORING

MINNESOTA	0	3	7	17	–27
WASHINGTON	0	7	3	10	–20

Second Quarter
- Minn. Cox, 19 yard field goal
- Wash. Brown, 3 yard rush PAT–Knight (kick)

Third Quarter
- Minn. Brown, 2 yard rush PAT–Cox (kick)
- Wash. Knight, 52 yard field goal

Fourth Quarter
- Wash. Knight, 42 yard field goal
- Minn. Gilliam, 28 yard pass from Tarkenton PAT–Cox (kick)
- Minn. Gilliam, 6 yard pass from Tarkenton PAT–Cox (kick)
- Wash. Jefferson, 28 yard pass from Kilmer PAT–Knight (kick)
- Minn. Cox, 30 yard field goal

TEAM STATISTICS

MINN.		WASH.
17	First Downs–Total	18
6	First Downs–Rushing	10
11	First Downs–Passing	7
0	First Downs–Penalty	1
2	Fumbles–Number	2
2	Fumbles–Lost Ball	1
2	Penalties–Number	0
9	Yards Penalized	0
0	Missed Field Goals	2
63	Offensive Plays	66
359	Net Yards	314
5.7	Average Gain	4.8
3	Giveaways	2
2	Takeaways	3
–1	Difference	+1

INDIVIDUAL STATISTICS

MINNESOTA	No.	Yds.	Avg.	WASHINGTON	No.	Yds.	Avg.
RUSHING							
Reed	17	95	5.6	Brown	29	115	4.0
Foreman	11	40	3.6	Harraway	13	40	3.1
Marinaro	1	3	3.0		42	155	3.7
Brown	1	2	2.0				
Tarkenton	4	1	0.3				
	34	141	4.1				
RECEIVING							
Reed	5	76	15.2	Jefferson	6	84	14.0
Voigt	3	39	13.0	Taylor	4	56	14.0
Foreman	3	23	7.7	Brown	2	13	6.5
Gilliam	2	36	18.0	Harraway	1	6	6.0
Dale	2	31	15.5		13	159	12.2
Lash	1	17	17.0				
	16	222	13.9				
PUNTING							
Eischeid	6		31.9	Bragg	4		37.3
PUNT RETURNS							
Bryant	2	3	1.5	Duncan	3	8	2.7
				Mul-Key	1	10	10.0
					4	18	4.5
KICKOFF RETURNS							
Gilliam	3	49	16.3	Mul-Key	3	69	23.0
West	2	78	39.0	Brunet	2	35	17.5
	5	127	25.4		5	104	20.8
INTERCEPTION RETURNS							
N. Wright	1	26	26.0	Bass	1	28	28.0

PASSING

	Att.	Comp.	Comp. Pct.	Yds.	Int.	Yds/ Att.	Yds/ Comp.	Yards Lost Tackled
MINNESOTA								
Tarkenton	28	16	57.1	222	1	7.9	13.9	1–4
WASHINGTON								
Kilmer	24	13	54.2	159	1	6.6	12.2	0–0

December 23, at Irving, Tex. (Attendance 64,291)

SCORING

DALLAS	14	3	0	10	–27
LOS ANGELES	0	6	0	10	–16

First Quarter
- Dall. Hill, 3 yard rush PAT–Fritsch (kick)
- Dall. Pearson, 4 yard pass from Staubach PAT–Fritsch (kick)

Second Quarter
- Dall. Fritsch, 39 yard field goal
- L.A. Ray, 33 yard field goal
- L.A. Ray, 37 yard field goal

Fourth Quarter
- L.A. Ray, 40 yard field goal
- L.A. Baker, 5 yard rush PAT–Ray (kick)
- Dall. Pearson, 83 yard pass from Staubach PAT–Fritsch (kick)
- Dall. Fritsch, 12 yard field goal

TEAM STATISTICS

DALL.		L.A.
15	First Downs–Total	11
11	First Downs–Rushing	5
4	First Downs–Passing	5
0	First Downs–Penalty	1
2	Fumbles–Number	2
2	Fumbles–Lost Ball	2
5	Penalties–Number	2
44	Yards Penalized	20
0	Missed Field Goals	3
68	Offensive Plays	58
298	Net Yards	192
4.4	Average Gain	3.3
4	Giveaways	3
3	Takeaways	4
–1	Difference	+1

INDIVIDUAL STATISTICS

DALLAS	No.	Yds.	Avg.	LOS ANGELES	No.	Yds.	Avg.
RUSHING							
Hill	25	97	3.9	McCutcheon	13	48	3.7
Staubach	4	30	7.5	Bertelsen	12	37	3.1
Garrison	10	30	3.0	Hadl	2	10	5.0
Newhouse	6	5	0.8	Baker	1	5	5.0
	45	162	3.6	Smith	2	–7	–3.5
					30	93	3.1
RECEIVING							
Pearson	2	87	43.5	Snow	3	77	25.7
Hill	2	21	10.5	Smith	2	13	6.5
Fuggett	1	38	38.0	Jackson	1	40	40.0
Hayes	1	29	29.0	McCutcheon	1	3	3.0
Garrison	1	3	3.0		7	133	19.0
DuPree	1	2	2.0				
	8	180	22.5				
PUNTING							
Bateman	7		46.7	Chapple	5		43.6
PUNT RETURNS							
Richards	2	3	1.5	Bertelsen	4	52	13.0
				Elmendorf	1	1	1.0
					5	53	10.6
KICKOFF RETURNS							
Waters	1	23	23.0	Scribner	4	106	26.5
Harris	1	19	19.0	Clark	2	49	24.5
	2	42	21.0		6	155	25.8
INTERCEPTION RETURNS							
Jordan	1	2	2.0	Reynolds	1	4	4.0
				Elmendorf	1	0	0.0
					2	4	2.0

PASSING

	Att.	Comp.	Comp. Pct.	Yds.	Int.	Yds/ Att.	Yds/ Comp.	Yards Lost Tackled
DALLAS								
Staubach	16	8	50.0	180	2	11.3	22.5	7–44
LOS ANGELES								
Hadl	23	7	30.4	133	1	5.8	19.0	5–34
McCutcheon	1	0	0.0	0	0	–	–	0– 0
	24	7	29.2	133	1	5.5	19.0	5–34

1973 N.F.C. — Eastern Division

DALLAS COWBOYS 10-4-0 Tom Landry

Scores of Each Game		
20	Chicago	17
40	NEW ORLEANS	3
45	ST. LOUIS	10
7	Washington	14
31	Los Angeles	37
45	N. Y. GIANTS	28
16	Philadelphia	30
38	CINCINNATI	10
23	N. Y. Giants	10
31	PHILADELPHIA	10
7	MIAMI	14
22	Denver	10
27	WASHINGTON	7
30	St. Louis	3

Use Name	Pos.	Hgt	Wgt	Age	Int	Pts
Ralph Neely	OT	6'5"	265	29		
Rodney Wallace	OT	6'5"	255	24		
Rayfield Wright	OT	6'7"	255	28		
John Niland	OG	6'4"	245	29		
Blaine Nye	OG	6'4"	250	27		
Jim Arneson	C-OG	6'3"	236	22		
Bruce Walton	C-OG	6'6"	250	22		
John Fitzgerald	C	6'5"	250	25		
Dave Manders	C	6'2"	250	31		
Larry Cole	DE	6'4"	250	26		
Harvey Martin	DE	6'5"	262	22		
Pat Toomay	DE	6'5"	244	28	1	
Bill Gregory	DT	6'5"	255	23		
Bob Lilly	DT	6'4"	260	34		
Jethro Puth	DT	6'6"	260	29		

Use Name	Pos.	Hgt	Wgt	Age	Int	Pts
John Babinecz	LB	6'1"	222	23		
Rodrigo Barnes	LB	6'1"	215	23		
Dave Edwards	LB	6'3"	225	34		
Chuck Howley	LB	6'3"	225	27		
Lee Roy Jordan	LB	6'2"	220	32	6	6
Mike Keller	LB	6'4"	220	22		
D. D. Lewis	LB	6'2"	225	27		6
Benny Barnes	DB	6'1"	190	22	1	4
Cornell Green	DB	6'4"	208	33		
Cliff Harris	DB	6'	184	24	2	
Mel Renfro	DB	6'	190	29	2	6
Mark Washington	DB	5'10"	188	25	1	
Charlie Waters	DB	6'1"	193	24	5	

Use Name	Pos.	Hgt	Wgt	Age	Int	Pts
Craig Morton	QB	6'4"	214	30		
Roger Staubach	QB	6'2"	197	31		18
Cyril Pinder	HB	6'2"	210	26		
Les Strayhorn	HB	5'10"	205	22		6
Calvin Hill	FB-HB	6'3"	227	26		36
Walt Garrison	FB	6'	205	29		48
Robert Newhouse	HB-FB	5'10"	202	23		12
Larry Robinson	HB-FB	6'4"	210	22		
Bob Hayes	WR	6'	185	30		18
Mike Montgomery	WR	6'2"	210	24		18
Drew Pearson	WR	6'	175	22		12
Golden Richards	WR	6'	172	23		6
Otto Stowe	WR	6'2"	188	24		36
Billy Joe DuPree	TE	6'4"	225	23		30
Jean Fugett	TE	6'3"	220	21		18
Billy Truax	TE	6'5"	240	30		
Marv Bateman	K	6'4"	213	23		1
Mike Clark	K	6'1"	205	32		4
Toni Fritsch	K	5'7"	185	28		97

WASHINGTON REDSKINS 10-4-0 George Allen

Scores of Each Game		
38	SAN DIEGO	0
27	St. Louis	34
28	Philadelphia	7
14	DALLAS	7
21	N. Y. Giants	3
31	ST. LOUIS	13
3	New Orleans	19
16	Pittsburgh	21
33	SAN FRANCISCO	9
22	BALTIMORE	14
20	Detroit	0
27	N. Y. GIANTS	24
7	Dallas	27
38	PHILADELPHIA	20

Use Name	Pos.	Hgt	Wgt	Age	Int	Pts
Terry Hermeling	OT	6'5"	255	27		
Walt Rock	OT	6'5"	255	32		
George Starke	OT	6'5"	250	24		
Paul Laaveg	OG	6'4"	245	24		
Ray Schoenke	OG	6'3"	250	31		
John Wilbur	OG	6'3"	250	30		
Len Hauss	C	6'2"	235	32		
Dan Ryczek	C	6'3"	250	24		
Verlon Biggs	DE	6'4"	275	30		6
Jimmie Jones	DE	6'3"	215	26		
Ron McDole	DE	6'3"	265	33		
Bill Brundige	DT	6'5"	270	24		
Manny Sistrunk	DT	6'5"	265	26		
Diron Talbert	DT	6'5"	255	29		

Jon Jaqua – Injury

Use Name	Pos.	Hgt	Wgt	Age	Int	Pts
Chris Hanburger	LB	6'2"	218	32	1	
Harold McLinton	LB	6'2"	235	26		
John Pergine	LB	6'1"	225	26		
Myron Pottios	LB	6'2"	232	33		
Dave Robinson	LB	6'3"	245	32	4	6
Russ Tillman	LB	6'2"	230	27		
Mike Bass	DB	6'	190	28	5	6
Speedy Duncan	DB	5'10"	180	30	1	
Pat Fischer	DB	5'10"	170	33	3	
Ken Houston	DB	6'3"	198	28	6	
Brig Owens	DB	5'11"	190	30	5	12
Richie Petitbon	DB	6'3"	208	35		
Ted Vactor	DB	6'	185	29	1	6
Larry Willis	DB	5'11"	170	24		

Rosey Taylor – Injury

Use Name	Pos.	Hgt	Wgt	Age	Int	Pts
Sonny Jurgensen	QB	5'11"	203	39		
Billy Kilmer	QB	6'	204	34		
Larry Brown	HB	5'11"	195	25		84
Bob Brunet	HB	6'1"	205	27		
Herb Mul-Key	HB	6'	190	23		6
Charlie Harraway	FB	6'2"	215	28		24
Mike Hull	FB	6'3"	220	28		
Duane Thomas	HB-FB	6'1"	215	26		
Frank Grant	WR	5'11"	180	23		6
Roy Jefferson	WR	6'2"	195	29		6
Bill Malinchak	WR	6'1"	200	29		
Charlie Taylor	WR	6'3"	210	32		42
Mike Hancock	TE	6'4"	220	23		12
Alvin Reed	TE	6'5"	235	29		
Jerry Smith	TE	6'2"	208	30		
Mike Bragg	K	5'11"	186	26		
Curt Knight	K	6'1"	190	30		103

PHILADELPHIA EAGLES 5-8-1 Mike McCormick

Scores of Each Game		
23	ST. LOUIS	34
23	N. Y. Giants	23
7	WASHINGTON	28
26	Buffalo	27
27	St. Louis	24
21	Minnesota	28
30	DALLAS	16
24	NEW ENGLAND	23
27	ATLANTA	44
10	Dallas	31
20	N. Y. GIANTS	16
28	San Francisco	38
24	N. Y. JETS	23
20	Washington	38

Use Name	Pos.	Hgt	Wgt	Age	Int	Pts
Jerry Sisemore	OT	6'4"	260	22		
Steve Smith	OT	6'5"	250	29		
Dick Stevens	OT	6'4"	240	25		
Wade Key	OG	6'4"	245	26		
Roy Kirksey	OG	6'1"	265	25		
Tom Luken	OG	6'3"	253	23		
Mark Nordquist	OG	6'4"	246	27		
Vern Winfield	OG	6'2"	248	24		
Mike Evans	C	6'5"	250	27		
Guy Morriss	C	6'4"	255	22		
Gerry Philbin	DE	6'2"	245	32		
Dennis Wirgowski	DE	6'5"	250	25	1	
Bill Wynn	DE	6'4"	240	23		6
Bill Dunstan	DT	6'4"	250	24		
Don Hultz	DT	6'3"	240	32		
Gary Pettigrew	DT	6'4"	255	28		
Richard Harris	DE-DT	6'4"	260	25		

Use Name	Pos.	Hgt	Wgt	Age	Int	Pts
John Bunting	LB	6'1"	220	23		
Dick Cunningham	LB	6'2"	238	28		
Dean Halverson	LB	6'2"	225	27		
Marlin McKeever	LB	6'1"	235	33		
Kevin Reilly	LB	6'2"	220	22		
Tom Roussel	LB	6'3"	235	28		
John Sodaski	LB	6'1"	222	25	1	
Steve Zabel	LB	6'4"	235	25	2	
Kermit Alexander	DB	5'11"	186	32		
Bill Bradley	DB	5'11"	190	26	4	
Al Coleman	DB	6'1"	183	28		
Joe Lavender	DB	6'4"	190	24		
Randy Logan	DB	6'1"	195	22	5	
Al Nelson	DB	5'11"	186	29		
John Outlaw	DB	5'10"	180	28	2	6

Use Name	Pos.	Hgt	Wgt	Age	Int	Pts
Roman Gabriel	QB	6'4"	220	33		6
John Reaves	QB	6'3"	210	23		
Po James	HB	6'1"	202	24		6
Greg Oliver	HB	6'	192	24		
Tom Sullivan	HB	6'	190	23		30
Tom Bailey	FB-HB	6'2"	211	24		6
Lee Bouggess	FB	6'2"	210	25		6
Norm Bulaich	HB-FB	6'1"	218	26		24
Harold Carmichael	WR	6'7"	225	23		54
Stan Davis	WR	5'10"	180	23		
Ben Hawkins	WR	6'	180	29		
Bob Picard	WR	6'1"	195	23		
Dan Zimmerman	WR	6'3"	195	23		18
Kent Kramer	TE	6'5"	235	29		
Charlie Young	TE	6'4"	230	22		42
Tom Dempsey	K	6'1"	255	32		106
Tom McNeill	K	6'1"	195	31		

ST. LOUIS CARDINALS 4-9-1 Don Coryell

Scores of Each Game		
34	Philadelphia	23
34	WASHINGTON	27
10	Dallas	45
10	OAKLAND	17
24	PHILADELPHIA	27
13	Washington	31
35	N. Y. GIANTS	27
17	DENVER	17
21	Green Bay	25
13	N. Y. Giants	24
24	Cincinnati	42
16	DETROIT	20
32	Atlanta	10
3	DALLAS	30

Use Name	Pos.	Hgt	Wgt	Age	Int	Pts
Dan Dierdorf	OT	6'4"	265	24		
Ernie McMillan	OT	6'6"	255	35		
Mike Taylor	OT	6'4"	255	28		
Tom Banks	OG	6'1"	240	25		
Ron Davis	OG	6'2"	235	22		
Conrad Dobler	OG	6'3"	250	22		
Roger Finnie	OG	6'3"	245	26		
Bob Young	OG	6'2"	260	30		
Tom Brahaney	C	6'2"	225	21		
Warren Koegel	C	6'3"	250	23		
Wayne Mulligan	C	6'2"	245	26		
Council Rudolph	DE	6'3"	260	22		
Ron Yankowski	DE	6'5"	240	26		
Dave Butz	DT-DE	6'7"	290	23		
Lee Brooks	DT	6'5"	265	25		
John Richardson	DT	6'2"	250	27		
Bob Rowe	DT	6'4"	260	28		
Bonnie Sloan	DT	6'5"	260	24		

Use Name	Pos.	Hgt	Wgt	Age	Int	Pts
Mark Arneson	LB	6'2"	220	23	1	
Pete Barnes	LB	6'3"	240	28	1	
Jack LeVeck	LB	6'	225	23		
Terry Miller	LB	6'2"	225	27		
Jamie Rivers	LB	6'2"	235	27	1	
Jeff Staggs	LB	6'2"	240	29		
Larry Stallings	LB	6'2"	230	31	1	
Dwayne Crump	DB	5'11"	180	23		
Chuck Detwiler	DB	6'	185	26	1	
Clarence Duren	DB	6'1"	190	22	2	
Norm Thompson	DB	6'1"	175	25		
Jim Tolbert	DB	6'3"	202	29	2	
Eric Washington	DB	6'2"	190	23		
Roger Wehrli	DB	6'1"	195	25	1	

Leon Burns – Injury

Use Name	Pos.	Hgt	Wgt	Age	Int	Pts
Jim Hart	QB	6'2"	215	29		
Gary Keithley	QB	6'3"	205	22		
Donny Anderson	HB	6'3"	210	30		78
Willie Belton	HB	5'11"	195	24		
Terry Metcalf	HB	5'10"	185	21		12
Eddie Moss	HB	6'	215	24		
Jim Otis	FB	6'	220	25		6
Leo Hayden	HB-FB	6'	210	25		
Don Shy	HB-FB	6'1"	210	27		12
Walker Gillette	WR	6'5"	200	26		6
Mel Gray	WR	5'9"	170	24		42
Don Maynard	WR	6'	180	37		
Marv Owens	WR	5'11"	205	23		
Ahmad Rashad	WR	6'2"	210	23		18
Gary Hammond	HB-WR	5'11"	180	24		
Jim McFarland	TE	6'5"	225	25		6
Jackie McFarland	TE	6'4"	235	32		6
Jim Bakken	K	6'	200	32		100

NEW YORK GIANTS 2-11-1 Alex Webster

Scores of Each Game		
34	HOUSTON	14
23	PHILADELPHIA	23
10	Cleveland	12
14	GREEN BAY	16
3	WASHINGTON	21
28	Dallas	45
27	St. Louis	35
0	Oakland	42
10	DALLAS	23
24	St. LOUIS	13
16	Philadelphia	20
24	Washington	27
6	Los Angeles	40
7	MINNESOTA	31

Use Name	Pos.	Hgt	Wgt	Age	Int	Pts
Bart Buetow	OT	6'5"	250	23		
John Hill	OT	6'2"	245	23		
Joe Taffoni	OT	6'3"	255	28		
Willie Young	OT	6'	265	30		
Mark Ellison	OG	6'2"	250	24		
Dick Enderle	OG	6'1"	250	25		
Doug Van Horn	OG	6'2"	245	29		
Bob Hyland	OT-C	6'5"	255	28		
Greg Larson	C	6'2"	250	34		
Carter Campbell	DE	6'3"	240	25		
Jack Gregory	DE	6'6"	250	28		
Dave Tipton	DE	6'6"	240	24		
Rich Glover	DT	6'1"	240	22		
Dan Goich	DT	6'4"	250	29		
Larry Jacobson	DT	6'6"	260	23		
John Mendenhall	DT	6'1"	255	24		

Use Name	Pos.	Hgt	Wgt	Age	Int	Pts
John Douglas	LB	6'2"	228	28	1	
Jim Files	LB	6'4"	240	25	1	
Ron Hornsby	LB	6'3"	232	24		
Pat Hughes	LB	6'2"	240	26	3	
Brian Kelley	LB	6'3"	222	22		
Henry Reed	LB	6'3"	230	24	1	
Brad Van Pelt	LB	6'5"	235	22		
Pete Athas	DB	5'11"	185	27	5	
Otto Brown	DB	6'1"	188	26		
Chuck Crist	DB	6'2"	205	22	2	
Richmond Flowers	DB	6'	180	26	1	
Spider Lockhart	DB	6'2"	175	30	2	
Ron Lumpkin	DB	6'2"	200	22		
Eldridge Small	DB	6'1"	190	23		
Willie Williams	DB	6'	190	30	4	

Use Name	Pos.	Hgt	Wgt	Age	Int	Pts
Randy Johnson	QB	6'3"	205	29		6
Norm Snead	QB	6'4"	215	33		
Ron Johnson	HB	6'1"	205	25		54
Jack Rizzo	HB	5'10"	195	24		
Rocky Thompson	HB	5'11"	200	25		
Joe Orduna	FB-HB	6'	195	25		6
Vin Clements	FB	6'3"	215	24		12
Charlie Evans	FB	6'1"	220	25		6
Johnny Roland	HB-FB	6'2"	220	30		12
Bob Grim	WR	6'	200	28		12
Don Herrmann	WR	6'2"	205	26		12
Rich Houston	WR	6'2"	195	27		
Walt Love	WR	5'9"	180	22		
Gary Ballman (to MIN)	TE	6'	215	33		
Tom Gatewood	TE	6'3"	215	22		
Bob Tucker	TE	6'3"	230	28		30
Tom Blanchard	K	6'	190	25		
Pete Gogolak	K	6'2"	190	31		76
Jim McCann	K	6'2"	163	24		

DALLAS COWBOYS

RUSHING

Last Name	No.	Yds	Avg	TD
Hill	273	1142	4.2	6
Garrison	105	440	4.2	6
Newhouse	84	436	5.2	1
Staubach	46	250	5.4	3
Strayhorn	11	62	5.6	1
Fugett	1	34	34.0	0
Stowe	3	28	9.3	0
Robinson	2	17	8.5	0
Pinder	12	15	1.3	0
Richards	1	2	2.0	0
DuPree	2	2	1.0	0
Morton	2	0	0.0	0
Montgomery	1	–10	–10.0	0

RECEIVING

Last Name	No.	Yds	Avg	TD
Hill	32	290	9	0
DuPree	29	392	14	5
Garrison	26	273	11	2
Stowe	23	389	17	6
Pearson	22	388	18	2
Hayes	22	360	16	3
Montgomery	14	164	12	3
Fugett	9	168	19	3
Newhouse	9	87	10	1
Richards	6	91	15	1

PUNT RETURNS

Last Name	No.	Yds	Avg	TD
Richards	21	139	7	0
Harris	3	20	7	0
Pearson	2	13	7	0
Montgomery	2	2	1	0

KICKOFF RETURNS

Last Name	No.	Yds	Avg	TD
Montgomery	6	175	29	0
Pearson	7	155	22	0
Harris	6	148	25	0
Robinson	4	86	22	0
Newhouse	3	62	21	0
Richards	3	44	15	0
Strayhorn	2	44	22	0
Walton	1	11	11	0
Washington	1	0	0	0

PASSING – PUNTING – KICKING

PASSING	Att	Comp	%	Yds	Yd/Att	TD	Int–%	RK
Staubach	286	179	63	2428	8.5	23	15– 5	2
Morton	32	13	41	174	5.4	3	1– 3	
Garrison	1	0	0	0	0.0	0	0– 0	
Hill	1	0	0	0	0.0	0	0– 0	
Montgomery	1	0	0	0	0.0	0	0– 0	

PUNTING	No	Avg
Bateman	55	41.6
Montgomery	4	39.5

KICKING	XP	Att	%	FG	Att	%
Fritsch	43	43	100	18	28	64
Clark	1	2	50	1	2	50
Bateman	1	1	100	0	0	0

WASHINGTON REDSKINS

RUSHING

Last Name	No.	Yds	Avg	TD
Brown	273	860	3.2	8
Harraway	128	452	3.5	1
Thomas	32	95	3.0	0
Mul-Key	8	20	2.5	0
Kilmer	9	10	1.1	0
Jurgensen	3	7	2.3	0
Brunet	2	4	2.0	0
Jefferson	1	1	1.0	0
Hull	2	–3	–1.5	0
C. Taylor	1	–7	–7.0	0

RECEIVING

Last Name	No.	Yds	Avg	TD
C. Taylor	59	801	14	7
Jefferson	41	595	15	1
Brown	40	482	12	6
Harraway	32	291	9	3
Smith	19	215	11	0
Reed	9	124	14	0
Thomas	5	40	8	0
Hancock	2	3	2	2
Grant	1	12	12	1
Jurgensen	1	–3	–3	0

PUNT RETURNS

Last Name	No.	Yds	Avg	TD
Duncan	28	228	8	0
Mul-Key	11	103	9	0
Smith	1	0	0	0

KICKOFF RETURNS

Last Name	No.	Yds	Avg	TD
Mul-Key	36	1011	28	1
Duncan	4	65	16	0
Tillman	3	42	14	0

PASSING – PUNTING – KICKING

PASSING	Att	Comp	%	Yds	Yd/Att	TD	Int–%	RK
Kilmer	227	122	54	1656	7.3	14	9 – 4	6
Jurgensen	145	87	60	904	6.2	6	5 – 3	

PUNTING	No	Avg
Bragg	64	40.3

KICKING	XP	Att	%	FG	Att	%
Knight	37	37	100	22	42	52

PHILADELPHIA EAGLES

RUSHING

Last Name	No.	Yds	Avg	TD
Sullivan	217	968	4.5	4
Bulaich	106	436	4.1	1
James	36	178	4.9	1
Bailey	20	91	4.6	0
Carmichael	3	42	14.0	0
Bouggess	15	34	2.3	1
Young	4	24	6.0	1
Gabriel	12	10	0.8	1
Oliver	1	6	6.0	0
Reaves	2	2	1.0	0
Bradley	1	0	0.0	0

RECEIVING

Last Name	No.	Yds	Avg	TD
Carmichael	67	1116	17	9
Young	55	854	16	6
Sullivan	50	322	6	1
Bulaich	42	403	10	3
Zimmerman	22	220	10	3
James	17	94	6	0
Bailey	10	80	8	1
Hawkins	6	114	19	0
Bouggess	4	18	5	0
Oliver	1	9	9	0
Davis	1	6	6	0

PUNT RETURNS

Last Name	No.	Yds	Avg	TD
Bradley	8	106	13	0
Alexander	5	10	2	0
Davis	2	0	0	0

KICKOFF RETURNS

Last Name	No.	Yds	Avg	TD
James	16	413	26	0
Sullivan	12	280	23	0
Nelson	11	264	24	0
Davis	10	236	24	0
Alexander	9	189	21	0
Coleman	2	24	12	0
Bailey	2	18	9	0
Oliver	1	17	17	0

PASSING – PUNTING – KICKING

PASSING	Att	Comp	%	Yds	Yd/Att	TD	Int–%	RK
Gabriel	460	270	59	3219	7.0	23	12– 3	1
Reaves	19	5	26	17	0.9	0	1– 5	

PUNTING	No	Avg
McNeill	46	40.9
Bradley	18	40.8

KICKING	XP	Att	%	FG	Att	%
Dempsey	34	34	100	24	40	60

ST. LOUIS CARDINALS

RUSHING

Last Name	No.	Yds	Avg	TD
Anderson	167	679	4.1	10
Metcalf	148	628	4.2	2
Otis	55	234	4.3	1
Shy	16	66	4.1	0
Moss	14	41	2.9	0
Keithley	8	29	3.6	0
Hammond	4	11	2.8	0
Hart	3	–3	–1.0	0
Smith	1	–14	–14.0	0

RECEIVING

Last Name	No.	Yds	Avg	TD
Smith	41	600	15	1
Anderson	41	409	10	3
Metcalf	37	316	9	0
Rashad	30	409	14	3
Gray	29	513	18	7
Gillette	20	244	12	1
Hammond	4	39	10	0
Shy	3	15	5	1
Otis	2	19	10	0
McFarland	2	10	5	0
Maynard	1	18	18	0

PUNT RETURNS

Last Name	No.	Yds	Avg	TD
Wehrli	9	92	10	0
Hammond	11	80	7	0
Thompson	6	18	3	0
Belton	1	2	2	0

KICKOFF RETURNS

Last Name	No.	Yds	Avg	TD
Shy	16	445	28	1
Hammond	12	314	26	0
Metcalf	4	124	31	0
Hayden	5	98	20	0
Belton	3	83	28	0
Moss	4	78	20	0
Gray	4	73	18	0
McFarland	3	57	19	0
Detwiler	3	55	18	0
Butz	1	23	23	0
Owens	1	19	19	0
Wehrli	2	0	0	0

PASSING – PUNTING – KICKING

PASSING	Att	Comp	%	Yds	Yd/Att	TD	Int–%	RK
Hart	320	178	56	2223	7.0	15	10– 3	4
Keithley	73	32	44	369	5.1	1	5 – 7	
Hammond	1	0	0	0	0.0	0	0 – 0	

PUNTING	No	Avg
Keithley	66	37.5

KICKING	XP	Att	%	FG	Att	%
Bakken	31	31	100	23	32	72

NEW YORK GIANTS

RUSHING

Last Name	No.	Yds	Avg	TD
Ron Johnson	260	902	3.5	6
Clements	57	214	3.8	1
Roland	53	142	2.7	1
Orduna	36	104	2.9	1
Evans	34	77	2.3	1
Randy Johnson	4	24	6.0	1
Snead	4	13	3.3	0
Thompson	5	5	1.0	0
Tucker	1	4	4.0	0
Rizzo	1	3	3.0	0
Grim	1	–10	–10.0	0

RECEIVING

Last Name	No.	Yds	Avg	TD
Tucker	50	681	14	5
Herrmann	43	520	12	2
Grim	37	593	16	2
Ron Johnson	32	377	12	3
Roland	22	190	9	1
Clements	15	129	9	1
Evans	13	100	8	0
Houston	8	90	11	0
Orduna	6	44	7	0
Ballman	3	38	13	0
Hyland	1	16	16	0
Rizzo	1	11	11	0
Young	1	–5	–5	0

PUNT RETURNS

Last Name	No.	Yds	Avg	TD
Athas	20	153	8	0
Crist	1	7	7	0

KICKOFF RETURNS

Last Name	No.	Yds	Avg	TD
Love	18	396	22	0
Houston	15	375	25	0
Small	11	207	19	0
Orduna	6	104	17	0
Rizzo	4	86	22	0
Kelley	2	30	15	0

PASSING – PUNTING – KICKING

PASSING	Att	Comp	%	Yds	Yd/Att	TD	Int–%	RK
Snead	235	131	56	1483	6.3	7	22– 9	11
Ran. Johnson	177	99	56	1279	7.2	7	8 – 5	

PUNTING	No	Avg
Blanchard	56	41.9
McCann	12	24.5

KICKING	XP	Att	%	FG	Att	%
Gogolak	25	25	100	17	28	61

MINNESOTA VIKINGS 12-2-0 Bud Grant

Scores of Each Game		
24	OAKLAND	16
22	Chicago	13
11	GREEN BAY	3
23	Detroit	9
17	San Francisco	13
28	PHILADELPHIA	21
10	LOS ANGELES	9
26	CLEVELAND	3
28	DETROIT	7
14	Atlanta	20
31	CHICAGO	13
0	Cincinnati	27
31	Green Bay	7
31	N. Y. Giants	7

Use Name	Pos.	Hgt	Wgt	Age	Int	Pts
Grady Alderman	OT	6'2"	247	34		
Ron Yary	OT	6'6"	255	27		
Charlie Goodrum	OG-OT	6'3"	256	23		
Frank Gallagher (from ATL)	OG	6'2"	245	30		
Steve Lawson	OG	6'3"	265	24		
Milt Sunde	OG	6'2"	250	30		
John Ward	OG	6'4"	260	25		
Ed White	OG	6'2"	262	26		
Mick Tingelhoff	C	6'1"	237	33		
Godfrey Zaunbrecher	C	6'2"	240	25		
Carl Eller	DE	6'6"	247	30		
Jim Marshall	DE	6'3"	248	36		
Bob Lurtsema	DT-DE	6'6"	250	31		
Gary Larsen	DT	6'5"	260	33		
Alan Page	DT	6'5"	245	28		
Doug Sutherland	DT	6'3"	250	25		
Wally Hilgenberg	LB	6'3"	230	30	1	6
Amos Martin	LB	6'3"	228	24		
Ron Porter	LB	6'3"	232	28		
Jeff Siemon	LB	6'2"	230	23	2	
Roy Winston	LB	6'1"	222	33		2
Terry Brown	DB	6'1"	205	26	1	6
Bobby Bryant	DB	6'	170	29	7	6
Paul Krause	DB	6'3"	200	31	4	
Al Randolph	DB	6'2"	205	29		
Charlie West	DB	6'1"	197	27		
Jeff Wright	DB	5'11"	190	24	3	
Nate Wright	DB	5'11"	180	26	3	
Bob Berry	QB	5'11"	185	31		
Fran Tarkenton	QB	6'1"	190	33		6
Brent McClanahan	HB	5'10"	202	22		
Dave Osborn	HB	6'	208	30		
Chuck Foreman	FB-HB	6'2"	216	23		36
Bill Brown	FB	5'11"	222	35		24
Ed Marinaro	HB-FB	6'2"	212	23		24
Oscar Reed	HB-FB	5'11"	222	29		18
Carroll Dale	WR	6'1"	200	35		
Rhett Dawson	WR	6'1"	185	24		
John Gilliam	WR	6'1"	195	28		54
Jim Lash	WR	6'2"	200	22		
Doug Kingswriter	TE	6'2"	222	23		
Stu Voigt	TE	6'1"	220	25		12
Fred Cox	K	5'10"	200	34		96
Mike Eischeid	K	6'	190	32		

Karl Kassulke – Paralyzed in motorcycle accident

DETROIT LIONS 6-7-1 Don McCafferty

Scores of Each Game		
10	Pittsburgh	24
13	Green Bay	13
31	ATLANTA	6
9	MINNESOTA	23
13	New Orleans	20
27	BALTIMORE	29
34	GREEN BAY	0
30	SAN FRANCISCO	20
7	Minnesota	28
30	Chicago	7
0	WASHINGTON	20
20	St. Louis	16
40	CHICAGO	7
7	Miami	34

Use Name	Pos.	Hgt	Wgt	Age	Int	Pts
Rocky Freitas	OT	6'6"	270	27		
Mike Haggerty	OT	6'4"	245	27		
Gordon Jolley	OT	6'5"	250	24		
Jim Yarbrough	OT	6'6"	265	26		
Guy Dennis	OG	6'2"	255	26		
Bob Kowalkowski	OG	6'3"	240	29		
Rocky Rasley	OG	6'3"	250	26		
Chuck Walton	OG	6'3"	255	32		
Ed Flanagan	C	6'3"	245	29		
Dave Thompson	OG-C	6'4"	275	24		
Larry Hand	DE	6'4"	250	33		
Jim Mitchell	DE	6'3"	245	24		
Ken Sanders	DE	6'5"	240	23		
Bob Bell	DT	6'4"	250	25		
Herb Orvis	DT	6'5"	240	26		
Ernie Price	DT	6'4"	255	22		
John Small	DT	6'5"	260	26		
Mike Hennigan	LB	6'2"	210	21		
Jim Laslavic	LB	6'2"	230	21		
Mike Lucci	LB	6'2"	230	33	4	
Paul Naumoff	LB	6'1"	215	28		
Jim Teal	LB	6'3"	225	23		
Charlie Weaver	LB	6'2"	218	24	2	
Lem Barney	DB	6'	188	27	4	
Miller Farr	DB	6'1"	190	30	1	
Willie Germany	DB	6'	192	25		
Dick Jauron	DB	6'	190	23	4	6
Levi Johnson	DB	6'3"	190	23	5	
Jim Thrower	DB	6'2"	194	24		
Mike Weger	DB	6'2"	200	27	2	
Doug Wyatt	DB	6'1"	195	26		
Bill Cappleman	QB	6'3"	210	26		
Greg Landry	QB	6'4"	210	26		12
Bill Munson	QB	6'2"	210	31		
Mel Farr	HB	6'2"	210	28		24
Altie Taylor	HB	5'10"	200	25		30
Mickey Zofko	HB	6'3"	195	23		
Leon Crosswhite	FB	6'2"	215	22		6
Jim Hooks	FB	5'11"	225	22		
Steve Owens	FB	6'2"	215	25		18
Al Barnes	WR	6'1"	170	24		6
Ron Jessie	WR	6'	183	24		24
Earl McCullouch	WR	5'11"	175	27		6
Jim O'Brien	WR	6'	195	26		38
Larry Walton	WR	5'11"	180	26		30
John Hilton	TE	6'5"	225	31		6
Charlie Sanders	TE	6'4"	225	27		12
Errol Mann	K	6'	200	32		53
Herman Weaver	K	6'4"	210	24		

Wayne Rasmussen – Injury
Rudy Redmond – Injury

GREEN BAY PACKERS 5-7-2 Dan Devine

Scores of Each Game		
23	N. Y. JETS	7
13	DETROIT	13
3	Minnesota	11
16	N. Y. Giants	14
10	KANSAS CITY	10
7	Los Angeles	24
0	Detroit	34
17	CHICAGO	31
25	ST. LOUIS	21
24	New England	33
6	San Francisco	20
30	NEW ORLEANS	10
7	MINNESOTA	31
21	Chicago	0

Use Name	Pos.	Hgt	Wgt	Age	Int	Pts
Kent Branstetter	OT	6'3"	260	24		
Bill Hayhoe	OT	6'8"	258	26		
Dick Himes	OT	6'4"	244	27		
Mal Snider	OG-OT	6'4"	250	26		
Gale Gillingham	OG	6'3"	255	29		
Bill Lueck	OG	6'3"	235	27		
Keith Wortman	OG	6'2"	245	23		
Ken Bowman	C	6'3"	230	30		
Larry McCarren	C	6'3"	240	22		
Cal Withrow	C	6'	240	28		
Aaron Brown	DE	6'5"	270	29		
Dave Pureifory	DE	6'1"	260	23		
Alden Roche	DE	6'4"	255	28		
Clarence Williams	DE	6'5"	255	26		
Bob Brown	DT	6'5"	260	32		
Mike McCoy	DT	6'5"	284	24		
Carleton Oats	DT	6'2"	260	30		
Fred Carr	LB	6'5"	238	27		
Jim Carter	LB	6'3"	235	24	3	6
Larry Hefner	LB	6'2"	230	24	1	
Noel Jenke	LB	6'1"	225	26		
Tom MacLeod	LB	6'3"	220	22	2	
Tom Toner	LB	6'3"	225	23	1	
Hise Austin	DB	6'4"	195	22		
Willie Buchanan	DB	6'	190	23		
Ken Ellis	DB	5'10"	190	25	3	6
Charlie Hall	DB	6'1"	195	24		
Jim Hill	DB	6'2"	190	26	3	
Al Matthews	DB	5'11"	190	25	2	6
Perry Smith	DB	6'1"	195	22		
Ike Thomas	WR-DB	6'2"	193	25		
Jim Del Gaizo	QB	6'1"	198	26		
Scott Hunter	QB	6'2"	205	25		6
Jerry Tagge	QB	6'2"	220	23		12
Don Highsmith	HB	6'	200	25		
Larry Krause	HB	6'	208	25		
MacArthur Lane	HB	6'	220	31		12
Ron McBride	HB	6'	200	24		
Les Goodman	FB-HB	5'11"	206	23		6
John Brockington	FB	6'1"	225	24		18
Perry Williams	FB	6'2"	220	26		6
Leland Glass	WR	6'	185	23		
Barry Smith	WR	6'1"	185	22		12
Jon Staggers	WR	5'10"	186	24		24
Paul Staroba	WR	6'3"	204	24		
Mike Donohoe	TE	6'3"	228	28		
Rich McGeorge	TE	6'4"	235	24		6
Chester Marcol	K	6'	190	24		82
Ron Widby	K	6'4"	220	28		

Bob Kroll – Injury

CHICAGO BEARS 3-11-0 Abe Gibron

Scores of Each Game		
17	DALLAS	20
13	MINNESOTA	22
33	Denver	14
16	New Orleans	21
6	Atlanta	46
10	NEW ENGLAND	13
35	HOUSTON	14
31	Green Bay	17
7	Kansas City	19
7	DETROIT	30
13	Minnesota	31
0	LOS ANGELES	26
7	Detroit	40
0	GREEN BAY	21

Use Name	Pos.	Hgt	Wgt	Age	Int	Pts
Lionel Antwine	OT	6'6"	255	23		
Bob Asher	OT	6'5"	250	25		
Randy Jackson	OT	6'5"	250	29		
Steve Kinney	OT	6'5"	255	24		
Glenn Holloway	OG	6'3"	255	24		
Ernie Janet	OG	6'4"	250	24		
Bob Newton	OG	6'4"	250	23		
Rich Coady	C	6'3"	235	28		
Willie Holman (to WAS)	DE	6'4"	250	28		
Gary Hrivnak	DE	6'5"	248	22		
Tony McGee	DE	6'4"	250	24		
Mel Tom (from PHI)	DE	6'4"	250	32		
Wally Chambers	DT	6'6"	250	22		
Dave Hale	DT	6'7"	255	26		
Jim Osborne	DT	6'3"	250	23		
Andy Rice	DT	6'3"	268	31		
Doug Buffone	LB	6'1"	225	29	3	
Dick Butkus	LB	6'3"	245	29	1	6
Gail Clark	LB	6'2"	227	22		
Jimmy Gunn	LB	6'1"	220	24		
Bob Pifferini	LB	6'2"	226	23		
Don Rives	LB	6'2"	215	22		
Adrian Young	LB	6'1"	232	27		
Craig Clemons	DB	5'11"	200	24	2	
Allan Ellis	DB	5'10"	185	21	1	
Charlie Ford	DB	6'3"	185	24	2	
Bob Jeter	DB	6'1"	200	35		
Garry Lyle	DB	6'2"	198	27	5	
Willie Roberts	DB	6'1"	190	25		
Joe Taylor	DB	6'2"	200	32		
Bobby Douglass	QB	6'3"	225	26		30
Gary Huff	QB	6'1"	200	22		
Carl Garrett	HB	5'11"	215	25		30
Joe Moore	HB	6'1"	205	24		
Reggie Sanderson	HB	5'10"	206	22		
Gary Kosins	FB-HB	6'1"	220	24		
Jim Harrison	FB	6'4"	235	24		18
Roger Lawson	HB-FB	6'2"	215	23		
George Farmer	WR	6'4"	214	25		6
Ike Hill	WR	5'10"	180	26		12
Dave Juenger	WR	6'1"	195	22		
Mike Reppond	WR	6'	180	22		
Tom Reynolds	WR	6'3"	200	24		
Cecil Turner	WR	5'10"	176	29		
Craig Cotton	TE	6'4"	222	26		
Bob Parsons	TE	6'4"	234	23		6
Earl Thomas	WR-TE	6'3"	215	24		24
Bobby Joe Green	K	5'11"	175	35		
Mac Percival	K	6'4"	220	33		28
Mirro Roder	K	6'1"	218	29		35

MINNESOTA VIKINGS

RUSHING

Last Name	No.	Yds	Avg	TD
Foreman	182	801	4.4	4
Reed	100	401	4.0	3
Marinaro	95	302	3.2	2
Osborn	48	216	4.5	0
B. Brown	47	206	4.4	3
Tarkenton	41	202	4.9	1
Gilliam	5	71	14.2	1
McClanahan	17	69	4.1	0
Berry	2	5	2.5	0
Voigt	1	2	2.0	0

RECEIVING

Last Name	No.	Yds	Avg	TD
Gilliam	42	907	22	8
Foreman	37	362	10	2
Marinaro	26	196	8	2
Voigt	23	318	14	2
Reed	19	122	6	0
Dale	14	192	14	0
B. Brown	5	22	4	1
Osborn	3	4	1	0
Lash	2	34	17	0
Kingsriter	2	27	14	0
Dawson	2	24	12	0
Ward	1	1	1	0

PUNT RETURNS

Last Name	No.	Yds	Avg	TD
Bryant	25	140	6	0
J. Wright	2	0	0	0
West	1	0	0	0

KICKOFF RETURNS

Last Name	No.	Yds	Avg	TD
McClanahan	16	410	26	0
Gilliam	10	174	17	0
West	3	104	35	0
B. Brown	3	35	12	0
Reed	2	29	15	0
J. Wright	1	0	0	0

PASSING – PUNTING – KICKING

PASSING	Att	Comp	%	Yds	Yd/Att	TD	Int–%	RK
Tarkenton	274	169	62	2113	7.7	15	7– 3	3
Berry	24	10	42	121	5.0	1	2– 8	

PUNTING	No	Avg
Eischeid	66	39.8

KICKING	XP	Att	%	FG	Att	%
Cox	33	33	100	21	35	60

DETROIT LIONS

RUSHING

Last Name	No.	Yds	Avg	TD
Taylor	176	719	4.1	5
Owens	113	401	3.5	3
Mel Farr	97	373	3.8	4
Landry	42	267	6.4	2
Hooks	19	110	5.8	0
L. Walton	4	74	18.5	1
Munson	10	33	3.3	0
Zofko	11	33	3.0	0
Jessie	5	31	6.2	1
Crosswhite	11	30	2.7	1
C. Walton	1	26	26.0	0
H. Weaver	1	18	18.0	0
McCullouch	2	12	6.0	0
Barney	2	9	4.5	0
C. Sanders	1	−1	−1.0	0
Cappleman	1	−2	−2.0	0

RECEIVING

Last Name	No.	Yds	Avg	TD
C. Sanders	28	433	15	2
Taylor	27	252	9	0
Mel Farr	26	183	7	0
Owens	24	232	10	0
L. Walton	21	302	14	4
Jessie	20	364	18	3
McCullouch	9	179	20	1
Hilton	6	70	12	1
Barnes	3	43	14	1
Zofko	2	16	8	0
O'Brien	2	14	7	0
C. Walton	1	7	7	0
Hooks	1	6	6	0
Crosswhite	1	4	4	0

PUNT RETURNS

Last Name	No.	Yds	Avg	TD
Barney	27	231	9	0
Jauron	6	49	8	0
L. Walton	1	9	9	0
Teal	1	0	0	0

KICKOFF RETURNS

Last Name	No.	Yds	Avg	TD
Jauron	17	405	24	0
Taylor	12	295	25	0
Jessie	6	154	26	0
Thrower	3	54	18	0
Hooks	2	52	26	0
Johnson	3	51	17	0
Barney	1	28	28	0
Jolley	1	15	15	0
Zofko	1	7	7	0
Barnes	1	0	0	0
Dennis	1	0	0	0
Germany	1	0	0	0
C. Weaver	1	0	0	0

PASSING – PUNTING – KICKING

PASSING	Att	Comp	%	Yds	Yd/Att	TD	Int–%	RK
Munson	187	95	51	1129	6.0	9	8– 4	12
Landry	128	70	55	908	7.1	3	10– 8	
Cappleman	11	5	45	33	3.0	0	1– 9	
Zofko	1	1	100	35	35.0	0	0– 0	

PUNTING	No	Avg
H. Weaver	54	43.2

KICKING	XP	Att	%	FG	Att	%
Mann	14	14	100	13	19	68
O'Brien	14	14	100	8	14	57

GREEN BAY PACKERS

RUSHING

Last Name	No.	Yds	Avg	TD
Brockington	265	**1144**	4.3	3
Lane	170	528	3.1	1
Goodman	18	88	4.9	1
P. Williams	32	87	2.7	1
Tagge	15	62	4.1	2
Staggers	4	33	8.3	1
Staroba	1	11	11.0	0
Krause	1	8	8.0	0
Highsmith	7	7	1.0	0
B. Smith	1	5	5.0	0
Hunter	8	3	0.4	1
Del Gaizo	4	1	0.3	0

RECEIVING

Last Name	No.	Yds	Avg	TD
Lane	27	255	9	1
Staggers	25	412	16	3
McGeorge	16	260	16	1
Brockington	16	128	8	0
B. Smith	15	233	16	2
Glass	11	119	11	0
P. Williams	5	44	9	0
Goodman	2	19	10	0
Staroba	1	23	23	0
Donohoe	1	10	10	0

PUNT RETURNS

Last Name	No.	Yds	Avg	TD
Staggers	19	90	5	0
Ellis	11	47	4	0

KICKOFF RETURNS

Last Name	No.	Yds	Avg	TD
Thomas	23	527	23	0
Ellis	12	319	27	0
Krause	11	244	22	0
Lane	2	31	16	0
P. Williams	1	24	24	0
A. Brown	2	19	10	0
Highsmith	1	18	18	0
B. Brown	1	7	7	0

PASSING – PUNTING – KICKING

PASSING	Att	Comp	%	Yds	Yd/Att	TD	Int–%	RK
Tagge	106	56	53	720	6.8	2	7– 7	
Hunter	84	35	42	442	5.3	2	4– 5	
Del Gaizo	62	27	44	318	5.1	2	6–10	
Lane	2	1	50	23	11.5	1	0– 0	
Brockington	1	0	0	0	0.0	0	0– 0	

PUNTING	No	Avg
Widby	56	43.1
Staroba	12	31.1

KICKING	XP	Att	%	FG	Att	%
Marcol	19	20	95	21	35	60

CHICAGO BEARS

RUSHING

Last Name	No.	Yds	Avg	TD
Garrett	175	655	3.7	5
Douglass	94	525	5.6	5
Harrison	100	374	3.7	1
Moore	58	191	3.3	0
Lawson	24	70	2.9	0
Kosins	24	65	2.7	0
Huff	11	22	2.0	0
Sanderson	3	8	2.7	0
Farmer	1	8	8.0	0
Thomas	1	5	5.0	0
Parsons	2	2	1.0	0
Hill	3	−14	−4.7	0

RECEIVING

Last Name	No.	Yds	Avg	TD
Thomas	24	343	14	4
Garrett	23	292	13	0
Harrison	21	200	10	2
Farmer	15	219	15	1
Cotton	13	186	14	0
Hill	10	119	12	0
Lawson	9	60	7	0
Reynolds	7	127	18	0
Sanderson	5	23	5	0
Kosins	4	8	2	0
Moore	3	17	6	0
Parsons	2	23	12	1

PUNT RETURNS

Last Name	No.	Yds	Avg	TD
Hill	36	204	6	**1**
Moore	1	0	0	0

KICKOFF RETURNS

Last Name	No.	Yds	Avg	TD
Hill	27	637	24	**1**
Garrett	16	486	**30**	0
Turner	8	127	16	0
Sanderson	2	44	22	0
Cotton	2	15	8	0
Parsons	2	15	8	0
Holloway	1	8	8	0
Osborne	1	0	0	0
Thomas	0	12	0	0

PASSING – PUNTING – KICKING

PASSING	Att	Comp	%	Yds	Yd/Att	TD	Int–%	RK
Douglass	174	81	47	1057	6.1	5	7– 4	13
Huff	126	54	43	525	4.2	3	8– 6	
Garrett	1	0	0	0	0.0	0	0– 0	
Hill	1	1	100	35	35.0	0	0– 0	
Thomas	1	0	0	0	0.0	0	1–100	

PUNTING	No	Avg
Green	**82**	40.5
Parsons	4	26.5

KICKING	XP	Att	%	FG	Att	%
Roder	11	12	92	8	16	50
Percival	10	10	100	6	8	75

LOS ANGELES RAMS 12-2-0 Chuck Knox

Scores of Each Game		
23	Kansas City	13
31	ATLANTA	0
40	San Francisco	20
31	Houston	26
37	DALLAS	31
24	GREEN BAY	7
9	Minnesota	10
13	Atlanta	15
29	NEW ORLEANS	7
31	SAN FRANCISCO	13
24	New Orleans	13
26	Chicago	0
40	N. Y. GIANTS	6
30	CLEVELAND	17

Use Name	Pos.	Hgt	Wgt	Age	Int	Pts
Charley Cowan	OT	6'4"	265	35		
Harry Schuh	OT	6'2"	260	30		
John Williams	OT	6'3"	256	27		
Tom Mack	OG	6'3"	250	29		
Joe Scibelli	OG	6'1"	255	34		
Rich Saul	C-OG	6'3"	235	25		
Ken Iman	C	6'1"	240	34		
Fred Dryer	DE	6'6"	240	27		
Jack Youngblood	DE	6'4"	250	23		
Larry Brooks	DT	6'3"	255	23		
Bill Nelson	DT	6'7"	270	25		
Merlin Olsen	DT	6'5"	270	32		
Phil Olsen	DT	6'5"	265	25		

Use Name	Pos.	Hgt	Wgt	Age	Int	Pts
Ken Geddes	LB	6'3"	235	26		
Rick Kay	LB	6'4"	235	23		
Jack Reynolds	LB	6'1"	232	25	2	
Isiah Robertson	LB	6'3"	225	24	3	6
Bob Stein	LB	6'2"	235	25	1	
Jim Youngblood	LB	6'3"	240	23	1	
Cullen Bryant	DB	6'1"	210	22		6
Al Clark	DB	6'	180	25	1	
Dave Elmendorf	DB	6'1"	195	24	1	
Eddie McMillan	DB	6'	180	21	4	
Steve Preece	DB	6'1"	195	26	2	6
Charlie Stukes	DB	6'3"	212	29	5	
Bill Drake	WR-DB	6'1"	195	23		

Use Name	Pos.	Hgt	Wgt	Age	Int	Pts
John Hadl	QB	6'2"	214	33		
Jim Harris	QB	6'3"	210	26		
Jim Bertelsen	HB	5'11"	205	23		30
Larry McCutcheon	HB	6'1"	205	23		30
Bob Scribner	HB	6'	200	22		
Larry Smith	HB	6'3"	220	25		12
Tony Baker	FB	5'11"	225	28		42
Les Josephson	FB	6'	207	30		12
Dick Gordon (to GB)	WR	5'11"	190	28		
Harold Jackson	WR	5'10"	175	27		78
David Ray	WR	6'	195	28		130
Rod Sherman	WR	6'	190	28		
Jack Snow	WR	6'2"	190	30		12
Joe Sweet	WR	6'2"	196	25		
Pat Curran	TE	6'3"	238	27		
Bob Klein	TE	6'5"	235	26		12
Dave Chapple	K	6'	180	26		

ATLANTA FALCONS 9-5-0 Norm Van Brocklin

Scores of Each Game		
62	New Orleans	7
0	Los Angeles	31
6	Detroit	31
9	SAN FRANCISCO	13
46	CHICAGO	6
41	San Diego	0
17	San Francisco	0
15	LOS ANGELES	13
44	Philadelphia	27
20	MINNESOTA	14
28	N. Y. Jets	20
6	BUFFALO	17
10	ST. LOUIS	32
14	NEW ORLEANS	10

Use Name	Pos.	Hgt	Wgt	Age	Int	Pts
Nick Bebout	OT	6'5"	260	22		
Len Gotshalk	OT	6'4"	260	23		
George Kunz	OT	6'5"	268	26		
Bill Sandeman	OT	6'6"	265	30		
Dennis Havig	OG	6'2"	256	24		
Andy Mauer	OG	6'3"	247	24		
Ted Fritsch	C	6'2"	240	23		
Jeff Van Note	C	6'2"	247	27		
Claude Humphrey	DE	6'5"	265	29	1	
Greg Marx	DE	6'4"	260	23		
John Zook	DE	6'5"	250	25		
Mike Lewis	DT	6'3"	260	24		
Rosie Manning	DT	6'5"	256	23		
Mike Tilleman	DT	6'5"	278	29		
Chuck Walker	DT	6'2"	260	32	1	

Use Name	Pos.	Hgt	Wgt	Age	Int	Pts
Duane Benson	LB	6'2"	215	28		
Greg Brezina	LB	6'2"	226	27	3	
Don Hansen	LB	6'3"	228	29	1	
Ken Mitchell	LB	6'1"	224	25		
Tommy Nobis	LB	6'2"	243	29		
Lonnie Warwick	LB	6'3"	240	31		
Ray Brown	DB	6'2"	202	24	6	
Ray Easterling	DB	6'	195	23		
Clarence Ellis	DB	5'11"	190	23	2	
Tom Hayes	DB	6'1"	198	27	4	12
Rolland Lawrence	DB	5'10"	180	22	1	
Tony Plummer	DB	5'11"	188	26	1	6
Ken Reaves	DB	6'3"	210	28	2	

Use Name	Pos.	Hgt	Wgt	Age	Int	Pts
Bob Lee	QB	6'2"	195	28		
Dick Shiner (to NE)	QB	6'	195	31		
Pat Sullivan	QB	6'	200	23		
Dave Hampton	HB	6'	210	26		30
Joe Washington	HB	5'9"	180	22		
Eddie Ray	FB	6'1"	240	26		66
Art Malone	FB	5'11"	216	25		18
Harmon Wages	FB	6'1"	212	27		6
Ken Burrow	WR	6'	190	25		42
Wes Chesson	WR	6'2"	195	24		6
Al Dodd	WR	6'	178	28		
Tom Geredine	WR	6'2"	195	23		6
Louis Neal	WR	6'4"	215	23		6
Larry Mialik	TE	6'2"	226	23		
Jim Mitchell	TE	6'2"	236	25		
John James	K	6'3"	197	24		
Nick Mike-Mayer	K	5'8"	186	23		112

SAN FRANCISCO FORTY-NINERS 5-9-0 Dick Nolan

Scores of Each Game		
13	Miami	21
36	Denver	34
20	LOS ANGELES	40
13	Atlanta	9
13	MINNESOTA	17
40	NEW ORLEANS	0
3	ATLANTA	17
20	Detroit	30
9	Washington	33
13	Los Angeles	31
20	GREEN BAY	6
38	PHILADELPHIA	28
10	New Orleans	16
14	PITTSBURGH	37

Use Name	Pos.	Hgt	Wgt	Age	Int	Pts
Cas Banaszek	OT	6'3"	250	27		
Len Rohde	OT	6'4"	248	35		
John Watson	OG-OT	6'4"	248	24		
Randy Beisler	OG	6'4"	244	28		
Ed Hardy	OG	6'4"	242	22		
Woody Peoples	OG	6'2"	250	30		
Forrest Blue	C	6'5"	260	27		
Jean Barrett	OT-C	6'6"	254	22		
Bill Belk	DE	6'3"	242	27		
Cedrick Hardman	DE	6'3"	255	24		2
Tommy Hart	DE	6'3"	248	28		
Bob Hoskins	DT	6'2"	250	27		
Charlie Krueger	DT	6'4"	254	37		
Rolf Krueger	DT	6'4"	253	26		

Use Name	Pos.	Hgt	Wgt	Age	Int	Pts
Willie Harper	LB	6'2"	215	23		
Charlie Hunt	LB	6'2"	212	22		
Frank Nunley	LB	6'2"	230	27	1	
Dave Olerich	LB	6'1"	220	28		
Jim Sniadecki	LB	6'2"	228	26	1	
Skip Vanderbundt	LB	6'3"	224	26	1	
Dave Wilcox	LB	6'3"	234	30	2	
Windlan Hall	DB	5'11"	175	23	1	12
Jim Johnson	DB	6'2"	188	35	4	
Ralph McGill	DB	5'11"	186	23		
Mel Phillips	DB	6'	190	31	1	
Mike Simpson	DB	5'11"	170	26		
Bruce Taylor	DB	6'	180	25	6	

Terry Beasley — Shoulder Injury

Use Name	Pos.	Hgt	Wgt	Age	Int	Pts
John Brodie	QB	6'1"	203	38		6
Joe Reed	QB	6'1"	192	25		
Steve Spurrier	QB	6'2"	200	28		12
Dave Atkins	HB	6'1"	202	24		6
Doug Cunningham	HB	5'11"	195	27		6
Jimmy Thomas	HB	6'1"	214	26		6
Vic Washington	HB	5'10"	196	27		48
Ken Willard	FB	6'2"	220	30		12
Randy Jackson	HB-FB	6'	220	24		
Larry Schreiber	HB-FB	6'	210	26		
Dan Abramowicz (from NO)	WR	6'1"	195	28		6
Ed Beverly	WR	5'11"	168	23		
John Isenbarger	WR	6'3"	196	25		
Gene Washington	WR	6'1"	185	26		12
Ted Kwalick	TE	6'4"	226	26		30
Dick Witcher	TE	6'3"	204	28		
Bruce Gossett	K	6'2"	228	30		104
Tom Wittum	K	6'1"	185	23		

NEW ORLEANS SAINTS 5-9-0 John North

Scores of Each Game		
7	ATLANTA	62
3	Dallas	40
10	Baltimore	14
21	CHICAGO	16
20	DETROIT	13
0	San Francisco	40
19	WASHINGTON	3
13	BUFFALO	0
7	Los Angeles	29
14	San Diego	17
13	LOS ANGELES	24
10	Green Bay	30
16	SAN FRANCISCO	10
10	Atlanta	14

Use Name	Pos.	Hgt	Wgt	Age	Int	Pts
Paul Ferson	OT	6'5"	260	23		
Carl Johnson	OT	6'3"	255	23		
Don Morrison	OT	6'5"	255	23		
Craig Robinson	OT	6'4"	250	24		
Jake Kupp	OG	6'3"	248	31		
Royce Smith	OG	6'3"	245	24		
Del Williams	OG	6'2"	240	27		
John Didion	C	6'4"	245	25		
Steve Baumgartner	DE	6'7"	260	22		
Andy Dorris	DE	6'4"	230	22		
Billy Newsome	DE	6'4"	250	25	1	
Joe Owens	DE	6'2"	245	25	1	
Derland Moore	DT	6'4"	260	21	1	
Bob Pollard	DT	6'3"	245	24		
Elex Price	DT	6'3"	260	23		

Use Name	Pos.	Hgt	Wgt	Age	Int	Pts
Wayne Colman	LB	6'1"	230	27		
Bob Creech	LB	6'3"	228	24		
Joe Federspiel	LB	6'1"	225	23	1	
Willie Hall	LB	6'2"	225	23		
Ray Hester	LB	6'2"	215	24		
Rick Kingrea	LB	6'1"	233	24		
Dale Lindsey	LB	6'3"	225	30		
Jim Merlo	LB	6'1"	220	21	3	
Dick Palmer	LB	6'2"	232	25		
Mike Fink	DB	5'11"	180	22		
Johnny Fuller	DB	6'	185	27	1	
Ernie Jackson	DB	5'10"	175	23	3	
Bivian Lee	DB	6'3"	200	25	3	
Jerry Moore	DB	6'3"	208	23		
Tom Myers	DB	5'11"	184	22	3	
Nate Ramsey	DB	6'1"	200	32		

Ron Billingsley — Injury
Hugo Hollas — Knee Injury

Use Name	Pos.	Hgt	Wgt	Age	Int	Pts
Bob Davis	QB	6'3"	205	27		
Archie Manning	QB	6'3"	215	24		12
Bobby Scott	QB	6'1"	200	24		
Henry Matthews	HB	6'3"	203	24		
Joe Profit (from ATL)	HB	6'	213	24		12
Howard Stevens	HB	5'10"	175	24		12
Jess Phillips	FB-HB	6'1"	210	26		
Bill Butler	FB	6'	210	23		18
Odell Lawson	FB	6'2"	205	25		
Lincoln Minor	HB-FB	6'2"	211	23		
Jubilee Dunbar	WR	6'	196	24		24
Freddie Hyatt	WR	6'3"	200	27		
Bob Newland	WR	6'2"	190	24		24
Preston Riley	WR	6'	180	25		
Speedy Thomas	WR	6'1"	170	26		
Doug Winslow	WR	5'11"	180	22		
Bert Askon	TE	6'3"	220	27		
John Beasley (from MIN)	TE	6'3"	228	28		12
Bob Brown	TE	6'3"	225	30		
Len Garrett (from GB)	TE	6'3"	230	24		
Mike Kelly	TE	6'4"	215	25		
Happy Feller	K	5'11"	185	24		19
Bill McClard	K	5'10"	202	21		48
Steve O'Neal	K	6'3"	185	27		

LOS ANGELES RAMS

RUSHING

Last Name	No.	Yds	Avg	TD
McCutcheon	210	1097	5.2	2
Bertelsen	206	854	4.1	4
Baker	85	344	4.0	7
Smith	79	291	3.7	2
Josephson	36	174	4.8	2
Scribner	20	109	5.5	0
Harris	4	29	7.3	0
Gordon	2	15	7.5	0
Preece	1	11	11.0	1
Hadl	14	5	0.4	0
Chapple	1	0	0.0	0
Jackson	2	–8	–4.0	0

RECEIVING

Last Name	No.	Yds	Avg	TD
Jackson	40	874	22	13
McCutcheon	30	289	10	3
Klein	21	277	13	2
Bertelsen	19	267	14	1
Snow	16	252	16	2
Smith	10	65	7	0
Curran	5	56	11	1
Scribner	2	19	10	0
Sherman	1	8	8	0

PUNT RETURNS

Last Name	No.	Yds	Avg	TD
Bertelsen	26	259	10	0
Elmendorf	22	187	9	0
Scribner	3	32	11	0

KICKOFF RETURNS

Last Name	No.	Yds	Avg	TD
Bryant	13	369	28	1
Scribner	11	314	29	0
Clark	2	80	40	0
Gordon	3	68	23	0
Curran	1	24	24	0
Elmendorf	2	23	12	0
Smith	1	16	16	0
Bertelsen	1	15	15	0
McCutcheon	1	6	6	0
Klein	1	0	0	0

PASSING – PUNTING – KICKING

PASSING	Att	Comp	%	Yds	Yd/Att	TD	Int–%	RK
Hadl	258	135	52	2008	7.8	22	11– 4	5
Harris	11	7	64	68	6.2	0	0– 0	
Smith	2	2	100	31	15.5	0	0– 0	

PUNTING	No	Avg
Chapple	51	40.8

KICKING	XP	Att	%	FG	Att	%
Ray	40	42	95	30	47	64

ATLANTA FALCONS

RUSHING

Last Name	No.	Yds	Avg	TD
Hampton	263	997	3.8	4
Ray	96	434	4.5	9
Malone	76	336	4.4	2
Lee	29	67	2.3	0
Wages	18	47	2.6	1
Washington	4	36	9.0	0
J. Mitchell	5	34	6.8	0
Sullivan	3	19	6.3	0
Burrow	2	17	8.5	0
Shiner	3	–2	–0.7	0
Geredine	1	–3	–3.0	0

RECEIVING

Last Name	No.	Yds	Avg	TD
J. Mitchell	32	420	13	0
Burrow	31	567	18	7
Hampton	25	273	11	1
Dodd	19	291	15	0
Ray	19	192	10	2
Malone	19	177	9	1
Geredine	12	231	19	1
Neal	5	131	26	1
Chesson	2	36	18	1
Mialik	2	30	15	0
Wages	2	14	7	0

PUNT RETURNS

Last Name	No.	Yds	Avg	TD
Brown	40	360	9	0
Dodd	8	69	9	0

KICKOFF RETURNS

Last Name	No.	Yds	Avg	TD
Washington	20	432	22	0
Hampton	11	258	23	0
Geredine	9	211	23	0
Plummer	5	115	23	0
Lawrence	3	71	24	0
Benson	3	20	7	0
Wages	1	0	0	0

PASSING – PUNTING – KICKING

PASSING	Att	Comp	%	Yds	Yd/Att	TD	Int–%	RK
Lee	230	120	52	1786	7.8	10	8– 3	7
Shiner	68	36	53	432	6.4	3	4– 6	
Sullivan	26	14	54	175	6.7	1	0– 0	

PUNTING	No	Avg
James	63	42.6

KICKING	XP	Att	%	FG	Att	%
Mike-Mayer	34	34	100	26	38	68

SAN FRANCISCO FORTY-NINERS

RUSHING

Last Name	No.	Yds	Avg	TD
V. Washington	151	543	3.5	8
Willard	83	366	4.4	1
Thomas	56	259	4.6	1
Cunningham	44	165	3.8	1
Schreiber	42	163	3.9	0
Reed	15	85	5.7	0
Wittum	1	63	63.0	0
Kwalick	5	37	7.4	0
Spurrier	9	32	3.6	2
Atkins	4	19	4.8	1
Brodie	5	16	3.2	1
Jackson	6	10	1.7	0
Isenbarger	1	–6	–6.0	0

RECEIVING

Last Name	No.	Yds	Avg	TD
Kwalick	47	729	16	5
G. Washington	37	606	16	2
Abramowicz	37	460	12	1
V. Washington	33	238	7	0
Willard	22	160	7	1
Thomas	19	157	8	0
Cunningham	15	118	8	0
Schreiber	12	98	8	0
Isenbarger	10	67	7	0
Jackson	1	20	20	0
Witcher	1	13	13	0
Atkins	1	–3	–3	0

PUNT RETURNS

Last Name	No.	Yds	Avg	TD
Taylor	15	207	14	0
McGill	22	186	8	0

KICKOFF RETURNS

Last Name	No.	Yds	Avg	TD
V. Washington	24	549	23	0
McGill	17	374	22	0
Cunningham	8	173	22	0
Atkins	3	93	31	0
Thomas	5	81	16	0
Olerich	2	17	9	0
Hall	1	14	14	0
Simpson	1	0	0	0
Sniadecki	1	0	0	0
Willard	1	0	0	0

PASSING – PUNTING – KICKING

PASSING	Att	Comp	%	Yds	Yd/Att	TD	Int–%	RK
Brodie	194	98	51	1126	5.8	3	12– 6	15
Spurrier	157	83	53	882	5.6	4	7– 4	14
Reed	114	51	45	589	5.2	2	6– 5	
Isenbarger	1	1	100	48	48.0	0	0– 0	

PUNTING	No	Avg
Wittum	79	43.7

KICKING	XP	Att	%	FG	Att	%
Gossett	26	26	100	26	33	79

NEW ORLEANS SAINTS

RUSHING

Last Name	No.	Yds	Avg	TD
Phillips	198	663	3.3	0
Butler	87	348	4.0	1
Profit	90	329	3.7	2
Manning	63	293	4.7	2
Stevens	45	183	4.1	2
Lawson	6	23	3.8	0
Scott	9	18	2.0	0
Davis	3	10	3.3	0
Minor	3	10	3.3	0
Myers	1	8	8.0	0
Newland	1	6	6.0	0
Matthews	4	4	1.0	0
Dunbar	3	3	1.0	0
O'Neal	2	–1	–0.5	0

RECEIVING

Last Name	No.	Yds	Avg	TD
Beasley	32	283	9	2
Newland	29	489	17	4
Dunbar	23	447	19	4
Phillips	22	169	8	0
Butler	19	125	7	2
Brown	11	132	12	0
Profit	11	108	10	0
Winslow	4	45	11	0
Stevens	4	39	10	0
Garrett	2	30	15	0
Matthews	2	19	10	0
Lawson	2	–5	–3	0
Minor	1	5	5	0

PUNT RETURNS

Last Name	No.	Yds	Avg	TD
Stevens	17	171	10	0
Winslow	5	47	9	0

KICKOFF RETURNS

Last Name	No.	Yds	Avg	TD
Stevens	26	590	23	0
Profit	8	144	18	0
Lawson	7	118	17	0
Fink	5	81	16	0
Moore	1	14	14	0
Jackson	1	0	0	0

PASSING – PUNTING – KICKING

PASSING	Att	Comp	%	Yds	Yd/Att	TD	Int–%	RK
Manning	267	140	52	1642	6.2	10	12– 4	10
Scott	54	18	33	245	4.5	1	3– 6	
Davis	17	5	29	14	0.8	0	2–12	

PUNTING	No	Avg
O'Neal	81	41.7

KICKING	XP	Att	%	FG	Att	%
McClard	9	9	100	13	24	54
Feller	7	7	100	4	12	33

1973 A.F.C. The Runningest Buffalo

Just as baseball fans had spent the year counting Hank Aaron's home runs as he closed in on Babe Ruth's one-year home run mark, football fans added up O. J. Simpson's rushing yardage week by week as he went after Jimmy Brown's one-year rushing mark of 1,863 yards. Simpson, the main ingredient in the Buffalo offense, excited the football world by running for a record 250 yards on opening day against New England. After seven games, he already had gained 1,000 yards, a goal coveted by runners for an entire season. With two games left on the schedule, O. J. had 1,584 yards and needed two good days to break the record. A good day of 219 yards against New England put him within shouting distance of the record. Needing 61 yards to set a new mark, Simpson quickly broke the record in the season's finale in cold, rainy New York. With a workhorse performance the rest of the day, he became the first runner ever to gain 2,000 yards in one season.

EASTERN DIVISION

Miami Dolphins—The Dolphins were aiming at a second perfect season, but a tough 12-7 loss to Oakland in their second game brought an end to those hopes. But the Dolphins still had the cold, hard precision and flawless execution which made them the class of professional football. The offense still had Griese, Csonka, Warfield, Little, Langer, and company; the defense boasted of Stanfill, Buoniconti, Anderson, Scott, and the rest of the No Name Defense. Coach Don Shula again made sure that his players were hungry, and except for the loss to Oakland and a 16-3 upset by the Colts after Miami had clinched the Eastern crown, the Dolphins came close to another flawless season.

Buffalo Bills—When O. J. Simpson faced the reporters after breaking Jimmy Brown's single-season rushing mark, he began the meeting by introducing the offensive linemen one by one. They included Bruce Jarvis, Reggie MacKenzie, Donnie Green, Dave Foley, and rookies Joe DeLamielleure and Paul Seymour. They were the reasons for O. J.'s success, so he figured they deserved to share in the glory. Simpson was not the entire story of the Bills' surge to a 9-5 record and second place in the East. Rookie quarterback Joe Ferguson played well, although his main task was handing off to Simpson. J. D. Hill and Bob Chandler gave the team a pair of fine wide receivers, and another receiver, Dwight Harrison, was converted into a starter in the secondary. Earl Edwards came from the '49ers in a trade and beefed up the front line of the defense.

New England Patriots—The defense could not stop a strong running attack, and good clubs simply cranked the yardage out against the Patriots on the ground. O. J. Simpson, for instance, enjoyed his two most productive days of his record season against New England. But even with the defensive problems, coach Chuck Fairbanks' first season was successful because of the fine rookie class the Patriots fielded. Guard John Hannah strengthened the blocking, Darryl Stingley won a starting wide-receiver job, Sam Cunningham added power to the running game, and little Mack Herron excited people on kick returns. Veteran receiver Reggie Rucker provided a bonus by developing into a star, but the kicking game still bothered the Pats, as rookie Jeff White booted a punt for -6 yards in one game and missed an extra point and an 18-yard field goal in a 24-23 loss to Philadelphia.

New York Jets—Weeb Ewbank's final year as head coach before retirement degenerated into a dismal 4-10 season. The defense played well through the campaign, but the offensive unit suffered from age, injury, and turmoil. Flanker Don Maynard was cut in the pre-season, while fullback John Riggins did not sign a contract until just before opening day and never did reach his best form. The offensive line slipped in its pass protection, exposing the Jet quarterbacks to enemy tacklers. Joe Namath went out of action with an injured shoulder against the Colts on September 23, and Al Woodall followed him onto the disabled list two weeks later to leave rookie free-agent Bill Demory as the team's only quarterback.

Baltimore Colts—A thorough housecleaning had swept out many veterans of recent years, as new head coach Howard Schnellenberger suffered through a 4-10 season in which few of his personnel shifts worked out very well. Second-year runner Lydell Mitchell did star in the backfield, but the offense was hurt by ex-Raider tight end Raymond Chester's poor showing and by a confused quarterback situation. Rookie Bert Jones began the year as the starter, but veteran Marty Domres took over the position over the back part of the schedule; neither name could ignite much of a passing attack. The Colts enjoyed one moment of glory by beating the Dolphins late in the year.

CENTRAL DIVISION

Cincinnati Bengals—The maturing of quarterback Ken Anderson and the addition of three talented rookies brought the Cincinnati offense up to the level of its topnotch defensive unit. With experience improving his poise, Anderson calmly executed the plays called by coach Paul Brown via messenger guards. Giving Brown and Anderson more to work with were rookies Isaac Curtis, Bobby Clark, and Lenvil Elliott, three swift and powerful freshmen. Curtis gave the Bengals a deep threat at wide receiver, while Clark provided power in the backfield to go along with the speed of veteran Eassex Johnson. When injuries slowed up these two runners late in the season, Elliott broke into the lineup with a flair. The Bengal defense had been solid all along, so the team stormed into first place with a strong finish.

Pittsburgh Steelers—The Pittsburgh offense kept raking in points despite constant injuries to key players. Fullback Franco Harris missed the early going with a bad knee, and by the time he got back into action, halfback Frenchy Fuqua went out with a broken collarbone. Quarterback Terry Bradshaw starred until he suffered a shoulder separation in mid-season; Terry Hanratty then stepped in and kept the attack rolling until injured ribs put him out of commission. With third-stringer Joe Gilliam at quarterback, the Steelers rose up and beat the Washington Redskins 21-16. The defense turned in strong performances week after week, with Joe Greene, L. C. Greenwood, Andy Russell, Jack Ham, and Mike Wagner all candidates for All-Pro honors as the Steelers again made it to the playoffs.

Cleveland Browns—Age had turned the Browns into a mediocre team that finished third in the AFC Central Division. The Cleveland offensive unit especially creaked, with the line laboring under the weight of three thirty-three-year-old members. Fullback Bo Scott's injury and quarterback Mike Phipps' slower-than-expected development further slowed the attack, and the Browns' two first-round draft picks were of very little help. Receiver Steve Holden spent most of the season on the bench, while guard Pete Adams passed his rookie season on the disabled list. The Cleveland defense, however, held together well, aided immensely by ex-Charger Bob Babich's work at middle linebacker, and the Browns posted a winning record.

Houston Oilers—The Oilers had given coach Bill Peterson what was described as a "lifetime" pact to join the team in 1972, but his lifetime as Houston head coach ran out after five games of this season. With Peterson's two-year record at 1-18 after five straight losses this year, general manager Sid Gillman stepped out of the front office to take over as head coach. Hoping to recapture the magic of his years at San Diego, Gillman headed the Oilers for the remainder of the season, but could only manage one victory.

WESTERN DIVISION

Oakland Raiders—The Raiders failed to score a touchdown in their first three games, so coach John Madden decided to bench quarterback Daryle Lamonica and replace him with lefty Ken Stabler. Whereas Lamonica excelled at throwing the long pass, Stabler thrived on running the ball-control offense preferred by coach Madden. With two strong runners in Marv Hubbard and Charlie Smith, two sure-handed receivers in Fred Biletnikoff and Mike Siani, and a superb front line, Stabler found many assets to manipulate in the Oakland attack. The defense had lots of old assets and one big addition in ex-Colt Bubba Smith. The Raider defense kept the team in the Western race early in the year, and the offense came through in victories over Kansas City and Denver in December to win first place and a playoff berth.

Denver Broncos—Bronco fans were amazed to find their club in the fight for first place all season long. In two years on the job, coach John Ralston had built a fine offense around the passing of veteran Charley Johnson and the running of star Floyd Little, with a solid line supporting both the air and ground games. The defense added two stand-out rookies in end Barney Chavous and cornerback Calvin Jones, and Veteran tackle Paul Smith sparked the squad with his All-Pro performance at rushing enemy passers. On the last day of the season the Broncos faced Oakland in a face-to-face duel for the Western title. Trailing 14-10 in the fourth quarter, the Broncos gambled on a fake punt play on fourth down. Bill Van Heusen did not gain the needed yards. The Raiders took the ball over and scored a touchdown as the Broncos had to settle for second place in their first winning season ever.

Kansas City Chiefs—After a poor pre-season, the Kansas City defense played with its accustomed vigor in the regular season, but the offense had problems generating any steam at all. Veteran quarterback Len Dawson suffered from a variety of small hurts which kept him out of the lineup much of the time, and substitute Pete Beathard, in his second tour of duty in Kansas City, could not get the attack moving in early season trials. Coach Hank Stram finally turned to Mickey Livingston, who brought the offense back to life, and the Chiefs suddenly were in first place in late November. A 14-10 loss to Denver, however, knocked them out of first place, and a 37-7 beating at the hands of the Raiders ended any playoffs hopes for this year.

San Diego Chargers—The Chargers' attempt to regain respectability by bringing in old, established players failed miserably this year. Quarterback Johnny Unitas had little zip left in his arm after seventeen years with the Colts, and he wound up on the bench watching rookie Dan Fouts lead the attack. An injury to receiver Gary Garrison further hurt the offense, and coach Harland Svare unexplainedly benched runner Mike Garrett early in the season. Morale on the club plunged, and when receiver Dave Williams was released in mid-season, he called the team "a zoo." Svare resigned as coach after eight games to concentrate on front-office duties as general manager, turning over the reigns to assistant Ron Waller.

FINAL TEAM STATISTICS

(Other statistics not available at press time)

OFFENSE

	BALT.	BUFF.	CIN.	CLEV.	DENV.	HOUS.	K.C.	MIAMI	N.ENG.	N.Y.	OAK.	PITT.	S.D.
FIRST DOWNS:													
Total	218	219	252	200	253	193	208	215	237	222	**288**	217	198
by Rushing	121	**152**	124	107	111	89	106	111	97	95	129	111	88
by Passing	79	60	108	79	127	93	93	91	122	109	**139**	89	93
by Penalty	18	7	**20**	14	15	11	9	13	18	18	**20**	17	17
RUSHING:													
Number	536	**605**	515	506	487	386	511	507	454	453	547	555	431
Yards	2031	**3088**	2236	1968	1954	1388	1793	2521	1612	1864	2510	2143	1814
Average Yards	3.8	**5.1**	4.3	3.9	4.0	3.6	3.5	5.0	3.6	4.1	4.6	3.9	4.2
Touchdowns	9	**20**	13	12	16	9	11	16	15	7	14	12	9
PASSING:													
Attempts	300	213	332	308	378	**411**	313	256	380	373	353	309	363
Completions	137	96	180	152	196	**225**	173	133	195	181	205	140	161
Completion Percentage	45.7	45.1	54.2	49.4	51.9	54.7	55.3	52.0	51.3	48.5	**58.1**	45.3	44.4
Passing Yards	1746	1236	2439	1741	**2706**	2370	2039	1675	2581	2353	2611	2157	2129
Avg. Yards per Attempt	5.8	5.8	7.3	5.7	7.2	5.8	6.5	6.5	6.8	6.3	**7.4**	7.0	5.9
Avg. Yards per Complet.	12.7	12.9	13.6	11.5	13.8	10.5	11.8	12.6	13.2	13.0	12.7	**15.4**	13.2
Times Tackled Passing	32	31	24	45	27	43	39	**13**	37	37	45	30	37
Yards Lost Tackled	271	239	163	368	187	451	296	**93**	350	297	348	230	321
Net Yards	1475	997	2276	1373	**2519**	1919	1743	1582	2231	2056	2263	1927	1808
Touchdowns	14	4	18	10	**22**	11	10	17	13	16	16	20	9
Interceptions	25	14	**12**	20	20	27	13	**12**	17	22	18	26	30
Percent Intercepted	8.3	6.6	**3.6**	6.5	5.3	6.6	4.2	4.7	4.5	5.9	5.1	8.4	8.3
PUNTS:													
Number	62	66	68	82	69	**85**	80	48	61	74	69	62	72
Average Distance	38.7	40.3	41.0	40.5	45.1	38.8	**45.5**	42.3	37.7	37.1	45.3	41.1	41.1
PUNT RETURNS:													
Number	24	32	45	36	40	30	42	37	33	27	46	**52**	33
Yards	129	279	333	308	404	227	279	382	324	165	344	**416**	408
Average Yards	5.4	8.7	7.4	8.6	10.1	7.6	6.6	10.3	9.8	6.1	7.5	8.0	**12.4**
Touchdowns	0	1	0	0	0	0	0	0	0	0	1	0	**2**
KICKOFF RETURNS:													
Number	60	42	39	49	36	**76**	31	24	57	52	39	40	70
Yards	1343	972	876	1084	793	**1799**	725	523	1372	1061	937	843	1597
Average Yards	22.4	23.1	22.5	22.1	22.0	23.7	23.4	21.8	**24.1**	20.4	24.0	21.1	22.8
Touchdowns	1	**2**	0	0	0	1	0	0	1	1	0	0	0
INTERCEPTION RETURNS:													
Number	15	14	18	12	14	17	21	21	13	19	17	**37**	16
Yards	116	224	166	202	220	298	328	335	105	288	162	**673**	205
Average Yards	7.7	16.0	9.2	16.8	15.7	17.5	15.6	16.0	8.1	15.2	9.5	**18.2**	12.8
Touchdowns	1	1	0	1	2	0	1	2	0	2	0	**3**	1
PENALTIES:													
Number	57	75	83	70	83	**95**	83	52	50	62	82	84	74
Yards	483	744	799	620	745	**900**	797	416	550	575	759	817	628
FUMBLES:													
Number	**16**	27	25	34	21	43	36	22	51	32	29	36	41
Number Lost	13	13	14	17	**9**	25	18	16	25	17	16	14	21
POINTS:													
Total	226	259	286	234	**354**	199	231	343	258	240	292	347	188
PAT Attempts	26	28	32	24	**41**	22	23	38	31	27	32	37	22
PAT Made	22	28	31	24	**40**	22	21	38	25	27	21	36	20
FG Attempts	28	30	31	31	33	24	38	37	29	24	33	**43**	27
FG Made	16	21	21	22	22	15	24	25	15	17	23	**29**	12
Percent FG Made	57.1	70.0	67.7	**71.0**	66.7	62.5	63.2	67.6	51.7	70.8	69.7	67.4	44.4
Safeties	0	0	0	0	1	0	0	1	1	0	0	1	0

DEFENSE

	BALT.	BUFF.	CIN.	CLEV.	DENV.	HOUS.	K.C.	MIAMI	N.ENG.	N.Y.	OAK.	PITT.	S.D.
FIRST DOWNS:													
Total	243	231	219	196	239	274	209	195	215	226	**194**	210	267
by Rushing	104	101	109	102	97	138	90	109	142	116	**88**	95	125
by Passing	123	112	97	79	121	114	95	78	**67**	101	92	91	124
by Penalty	16	18	13	15	21	22	24	8	**6**	9	14	24	18
RUSHING:													
Number	491	455	459	513	455	576	493	511	560	538	**435**	488	559
Yards	2089	1797	1807	2091	1795	2410	1956	1991	2850	2228	**1470**	1652	2264
Average Yards	4.3	3.9	3.9	4.1	3.9	4.2	4.0	3.9	5.1	4.1	**3.4**	3.4	4.1
Touchdowns	15	11	15	7	14	19	11	9	16	12	**5**	8	23
PASSING:													
Attempts	331	368	338	312	387	326	324	320	**240**	296	370	359	341
Completions	199	166	182	144	202	178	157	151	**134**	150	170	164	177
Completion Percentage	60.1	**45.1**	53.8	46.2	52.2	54.6	48.5	47.2	55.8	50.7	45.9	45.7	51.9
Passing Yards	2599	2394	2240	1984	2766	2466	1942	1604	**1600**	2148	1995	1923	2473
Avg. Yards per Attempt	7.9	6.5	6.6	6.4	7.1	7.6	6.0	**5.0**	6.7	7.3	5.4	5.4	7.3
Avg. Yards per Complet.	13.1	14.4	12.3	13.8	13.7	13.9	12.4	**10.6**	11.9	14.3	11.7	11.7	14.0
Times Tackled Passing	25	32	**43**	29	36	27	38	**45**	32	26	40	33	26
Yards Lost Tackled	200	276	**342**	248	326	229	323	314	262	198	305	251	219
Net Yards	2399	2118	1898	1736	2440	2237	1619	**1290**	1338	1950	1690	1672	2254
Touchdowns	16	12	9	16	15	26	11	**5**	11	18	12	11	18
Interceptions	15	14	18	12	14	17	21	21	13	19	17	**37**	16
Percent Intercepted	4.5	3.8	5.3	3.8	3.6	5.2	6.5	6.6	5.4	6.4	4.6	**10.3**	4.7
PUNTS:													
Number													
Average Distance													
PUNT RETURNS:													
Number	**27**	34	**27**	44	31	44	48	30	29	36	40	37	35
Yards													
Average Yards	10.4	9.2	**4.6**	6.1	8.3	7.8	9.5	6.1	5.2	11.3	7.3	8.3	7.4
Touchdowns													
KICKOFF RETURNS:													
Number	42	44	42	48	61	37	40	56	40	44	46	59	**35**
Yards													
Average Yards	22.6	21.2	27.9	24.3	**20.4**	21.9	25.8	21.5	24.1	23.2	21.4	23.0	24.6
Touchdowns													
INTERCEPTION RETURNS:													
Number	25	14	**12**	20	20	27	13	**12**	17	22	18	26	30
Yards	336	**149**	198	271	331	357	151	190	385	296	187	512	532
Average Yards	13.4	10.6	16.5	13.6	16.6	13.2	11.6	15.8	22.6	13.5	**10.4**	19.7	17.7
Touchdowns	4	**0**	1	**0**	1	4	**0**	**0**	1	2	1	2	**0**
PENALTIES:													
Number													
Yards													
FUMBLES:													
Number													
Number Lost													
POINTS:													
Total	341	230	231	255	296	467	192	**150**	300	306	175	210	386
PAT Attempts	39	25	27	23	31	53	22	**15**	32	34	19	22	46
PAT Made													
FG Attempts													
FG Made													
Percent FG Made													
Safeties													

CONFERENCE PLAYOFFS

December 22, at Oakland (Attendance 51,110)

SCORING

OAKLAND	7	3	13	10–33
PITTSBURGH	0	7	0	7–14

First Quarter
- Oak. Hubbard, 1 yard rush PAT–Blanda (kick)

Second Quarter
- Oak. Blanda, 25 yard field goal
- Pitt. B. Pearson, 4 yard pass from Bradshaw PAT–Gerela (kick)

Third Quarter
- Oak. Blanda, 31 yard field goal
- Oak. Blanda, 22 yard field goal
- Oak. W. Brown, 54 yard interception return PAT–Blanda (kick)

Fourth Quarter
- Oak. Blanda, 10 yard field goal
- Pitt. Lewis, 26 yard pass from Bradshaw PAT–Gerela (kick)
- Oak. Hubbard, 1 yard rush PAT–Blanda (kick)

TEAM STATISTICS

OAK.		PITT.
24	First Downs–Total	15
14	First Downs–Rushing	2
8	First Downs–Passing	10
2	First Downs–Penalty	3
0	Fumbles–Number	1
0	Fumbles–Lost Ball	0
9	Penalties–Number	4
75	Yards Penalized	60
1	Missed Field Goals	0
74	Offensive Plays	46
361	Net Yards	223
4.8	Average Gain	4.8
0	Giveaways	3
3	Takeaways	0
+3	Difference	–3

INDIVIDUAL STATISTICS

OAKLAND	No	Yds	Avg.	PITTSBURGH	No	Yds	Avg.
RUSHING							
Hubbard	20	91	4.6	Harris	10	29	2.9
C. Smith	17	73	4.3	P. Pearson	4	14	3.5
C. Davis	12	48	4.0	Fuqua	3	13	4.3
Banaszak	5	17	3.4	Bradshaw	3	9	3.0
Moore	1	3	3.0		20	65	3.2
	55	232	4.2				
RECEIVING							
Siani	5	68	13.6	Lewis	4	70	17.5
Moore	3	26	8.7	Fuqua	4	52	13.0
C. Smith	2	10	5.0	B. Pearson	2	7	3.5
Hubbard	1	17	17.0	P. Pearson	1	24	24.0
Biletnikoff	1	8	8.0	Williams	1	14	14.0
Banaszak	1	5	5.0		12	167	13.9
	13	134	10.3				
PUNTING							
Guy	2		39.0	Walden	5		41.6
PUNT RETURNS							
Atkinson	2	11	5.5	Edwards	1	20	20.0
KICKOFF RETURNS							
C. Davis	3	58	19.3	P. Pearson	4	79	19.8
				Steve Davis	3	77	25.7
					7	156	22.3
INTERCEPTION RETURNS							
W. Brown	1	54	54.0				
Atkinson	1	8	8.0	None			
Villapiano	1	0	0.0				
	3	62	20.7				

PASSING

OAKLAND	Att.	Comp.	Comp. Pct.	Yds.	Int.	Yds/ Att.	Yds/ Comp.	Yards Lost Tackled
Stabler	17	14	82.4	142	0	8.4	10.1	2–13
PITTSBURGH								
Bradshaw	25	12	48.0	167	3	6.7	13.9	1– 9

December 23, at Miami (Attendance 80,047)

SCORING

MIAMI	14	7	10	3–34
CINCINNATI	3	13	0	0–16

First Quarter
- Mia. Warfield, 13 yard pass from Griese PAT–Yepremian (kick)
- Cin. Muhlmann, 24 yard field goal
- Mia. Csonka, 1 yard rush PAT–Yepremian (kick)

Second Quarer
- Mia. Morris, 4 yard rush PAT–Yepremian (kick)
- Cin. Craig, 45 yard interception return PAT–Muhlmann (kick)
- Cin. Muhlmann, 46 yard field goal
- Cin. Muhlmann, 12 yard field goal

Third Quarter
- Mia. Mandich, 7 yard pass from Griese PAT–Yepremian (kick)
- Mia. Yepremian, 50 yard field goal

Fourth Quarter
- Mia. Yepremian, 46 yard field goal

TEAM STATISTICS

MIAMI		CIN.
27	First Downs–Total	11
18	First Downs–Rushing	5
9	First Downs–Passing	6
0	First Downs–Penalty	0
2	Fumbles–Number	0
1	Fumbles–Lost Ball	0
1	Penalties–Number	2
5	Yards Penalized	19
0	Missed Field Goals	0
71	Offensive Plays	50
400	Net Yards	194
5.6	Average Gain	3.9
3	Giveaways	1
1	Takeaways	3
–2	Difference	+2

INDIVIDUAL STATISTICS

MIAMI	No	Yds	Avg.	CINCINNATI	No	Yds	Avg.
RUSHING							
Morris	20	106	5.3	Clark	7	40	5.7
Csonka	20	71	3.6	Anderson	3	26	8.8
Kiick	10	51	5.1	E. Johnson	2	17	8.5
Leigh	1	8	8.0	Elliott	7	15	2.1
Nottingham	1	5	5.0	Curtis	1	–1	–1.0
	52	241	4.6		20	97	4.9
RECEIVING							
Warfield	4	95	23.8	Elliott	9	53	5.9
Mandich	3	28	9.3	Joiner	2	33	16.5
Kiick	3	19	6.3	Clark	2	18	9.0
Briscoe	1	17	17.0	Curtis	1	9	9.0
	11	159	14.5		14	113	8.1
PUNTING							
Seiple	2		49.0	Lewis	7		36.3
PUNT RETURNS							
Scott	1	4	4.0	Casanova	1	15	15.0
Anderson	1	2	2.0	Parrish	1	11	11.0
	2	6	3.0		2	26	13.0
KICKOFF RETURNS							
Anderson	1	14	14.0	Parrish	1	25	25.0
Morris	1	0	0.0	Jackson	1	17	17.0
	2	14	7.0		2	42	21.0
INTERCEPTION RETURNS							
Anderson	1	19	19.0	Craig	1	45	45.0
				Casanova	1	0	0.0
					2	45	22.5

PASSING

MIAMI	Att.	Comp.	Comp. Pct.	Yds.	Int.	Yds/ Att.	Yds/ Comp.	Yards Lost Tackled
Griese	18	11	61.1	159	1	8.8	14.5	
Briscoe	1	0	0.0	0	1	–	–	
	19	11	57.9	159	2	8.4	14.5	0– 0
CINCINNATI								
Anderson	27	14	51.9	113	1	4.2	8.1	3–16

MIAMI DOLPHINS 12-2 Don Shula

Scores of Each Game		
21	SAN FRANCISCO	13
7	Oakland	12
44	NEW ENGLAND	23
31	N. Y. JETS	3
17	Cleveland	9
27	BUFFALO	6
30	New England	14
14	N. Y. Jets	24
44	BALTIMORE	0
17	Buffalo	0
14	Dallas	7
30	PITTSBURGH	26
16	Baltimore	3
34	DETROIT	7

Use Name	Pos.	Hgt	Wgt	Age	Int	Pts
Doug Crusan	OT	6'5"	250	27		
Norm Evans	OT	6'5"	252	29		
Wayne Moore	OT	6'6"	265	28		
Willie Young	OT	6'4"	270	25		
Bob Kuchenberg	OG	6'3"	247	25		
Larry Little	OG	6'1"	265	27		
Ed Newman	OG	6'2"	245	22		
Jim Langer	C	6'2"	250	26		
Irv Goode	OG-C	6'4"	252	32		
Vern Den Herder	DE	6'6"	250	24		
Bill Stanfill	DE	6'5"	250	26		
Bob Heinz	DT-DE	6'6"	270	26		
Manny Fernandez	DT	6'2"	250	27		
Baldy Moore	DT	6'2"	265	27		
Larry Woods	DT	6'6"	260	25		
Larry Ball	LB	6'6"	225	24	1	
Bruce Bannon	LB	6'3"	225	22		
Nick Buoniconti	LB	5'11"	220	32		6
Mike Kolen	LB	6'2"	220	24	2	
Bob Matheson	LB-DE	6'4"	240	28		
Jesse Powell	LB	6'1"	215	26		
Doug Swift	LB	6'3"	228	24	1	
Dick Anderson	DB	6'2"	196	27	8	12
Charlie Babb	DB	6'	190	23		
Tim Foley	DB	6'	194	25	2	12
Curtis Johnson	DB	6'2"	196	25	2	2
Lloyd Mumphord	DB	5'11"	180	26		
Jake Scott	DB	6'	188	27	4	
Henry Stuckey	DB	6'1"	190	22	1	
Bob Griese	QB	6'1"	190	28		
Earl Morrall	QB	6'1"	206	39		
Jim Kiick	HB	5'11"	215	27		
Mercury Morris	HB	5'10"	190	26		60
Charlie Leigh	FB-HB	5'11"	205	27		6
Larry Csonka	FB	6'3"	237	26		30
Don Nottingham (from BAL)	FB	5'10"	210	24		6
Marlin Briscoe	WR	5'10"	178	27		12
Bo Rather	WR	6'1"	182	22		
Ron Sellers	WR	6'4"	195	26		
Howard Twilley	WR	5'10"	185	29		
Paul Warfield	WR	6'	185	30		66
Marv Fleming	TE	6'4"	235	31		
Jim Mandich	TE	6'3"	224	24		24
Larry Seiple	TE	6'	215	28		
Garo Yepremian	K	5'8"	175	29		113

Jim Dunaway – Injury
Howard Kindig – Injury

Ed Jenkins – Injury

BUFFALO BILLS 9-5 Lou Saban

Scores of Each Game		
31	New England	13
7	San Diego	34
9	N. Y. JETS	7
27	PHILADELPHIA	26
31	BALTIMORE	13
6	Miami	27
23	KANSAS CITY	14
0	New Orleans	13
13	CINCINNATI	16
0	MIAMI	17
24	Baltimore	17
17	Atlanta	6
37	NEW ENGLAND	13
34	N. Y. Jets	14

Use Name	Pos.	Hgt	Wgt	Age	Int	Pts
Dave Foley	OT	6'5"	255	25		
Donnie Green	OT	6'7"	272	25		
Mike Montler	C-OT	6'4"	255	29		
Joe DeLamielleure	OG	6'3"	254	22		
Reggie McKenzie	OG	6'4"	235	23		
Bobby Penchion	OG	6'5"	265	24		
Bruce Jarvis	C	6'7"	250	24		
Willie Parker	OG-C	6'3"	240	23		
Earl Edwards	DE	6'6"	262	27		
Halvor Hagen	DE	6'5"	245	26		
Walt Patulski	DE	6'6"	260	23		
Mike Kadish	DT	6'5"	265	23		
Bob Kampa	DT	6'4"	252	22		
Steve Okoniewski	DT	6'3"	247	24		
Jerry Patton	DT	6'3"	265	27		
Jeff Winans	DT	6'5"	265	21		
Jim Cheyunski	LB	6'2"	225	27	3	
Phil Croyle (from HOU)	LB	6'3"	220	25		
Dale Farley	LB	6'3"	235	24		
Fred Forsberg (from DEN)	LB	6'1"	235	29	1	
Merv Krakau	LB	6'1"	242	22		
Rich Lewis	LB	6'3"	220	23		
John Skorupan	LB	6'2"	214	22		
Bill Cahill	DB	5'11"	180	22		6
Leon Garror	DB	6'	180	25	1	
Tony Green	DB	5'10"	170	23	1	
Dwight Harrison	DB	6'1"	178	24	5	6
Bobby James	DB	6'1"	185	26	1	
Ernie Kellerman	DB	6'	183	29	2	
Ken Stone (to WAS)	DB	6'1"	180	22		6
Donnie Walker	DB	6'1"	185	22	1	
Joe Ferguson	QB	6'1"	190	22		12
Dennis Shaw	QB	6'2"	215	26		
Steve Jones	HB	6'	200	22		
O. J. Simpson	HB	6'2"	214	26		72
Pete Van Valkenberg	HB	6'2"	192	23		
Jim Braxton	FB	6'2"	243	24		24
Bo Cornell	FB	6'1"	215	24		
Larry Watkins	FB	6'2"	230	25		18
Bob Chandler	WR	6'	180	24		19
Wallace Francis	WR	5'11"	188	21		12
J. D. Hill	WR	6'1"	202	24		
Ray Jarvis	WR	5'11"	193	24		
Ted Koy	TE	6'1"	212	25		
Paul Seymour	TE	6'5"	260	23		
Dave Washington	TE	6'5"	220	25		
Spike Jones	K	6'2"	190	26		
John Leypoldt	K	6'2"	230	27		90

Don Croft – Knee Injury

NEW ENGLAND PATRIOTS 5-9 Chuck Fairbanks

Scores of Each Game		
13	BUFFALO	31
7	KANSAS CITY	10
23	Miami	44
24	BALTIMORE	16
7	N. Y. JETS	9
13	Chicago	10
14	MIAMI	30
23	Philadelphia	24
13	N. Y. Jets	33
33	GREEN BAY	24
32	Houston	0
30	SAN DIEGO	14
13	Buffalo	37
13	Baltimore	18

Use Name	Pos.	Hgt	Wgt	Age	Int	Pts
Tom Neville	OT	6'4"	255	29		
Bob Reynolds (to STL)	OT	6'6"	265	32		
Willie Banks	OG	6'2"	250	27		
Sam Adams	OG	6'3"	252	24		
John Hannah	OG	6'2"	265	22		
Bill Lenkaitis	OG	6'3"	260	27		
Len St. Jean	OG	6'1"	250	31		
Jon Morris	C	6'4"	254	30		
Doug Dumler	C	6'3"	242	23		
Nate Dorsey	DE	6'4"	240	23		
Ray Hamilton	DE	6'1"	232	22		
Donnell Smith	DE	6'4"	245	24		
Julius Adams	DT-DE	6'3"	257	25		
Rick Cash	DT	6'5"	260	27		
Leon Gray	DT	6'3"	256	22		
Mel Lunsford	DT	6'3"	250	23		
Art Moore	DT	6'5"	253	22		
Dave Rowe	DT	6'6"	280	26		
Ron Acks	LB	6'2"	200	28	1	
Edgar Chandler	LB	6'3"	225	27		
Will Foster	LB	6'2"	230	24		6
Bob Geddes	LB	6'2"	240	27		
Steve Kiner	LB	6'	218	26		2
Steve King	LB	6'4"	255	22		
Brian Stenger	LB	6'4"	230	26		
John Tanner	LB	6'4"	235	28		
Ralph Anderson	DB	6'2"	180	24	2	
Ron Bolton	DB	6'2"	180	23	6	
Greg Boyd	DB	6'2"	200	23		
Sandy Durko	DB	6'1"	185	25	3	
George Hoey	DB	5'10"	170	26		
Honor Jackson (to NYG)	DB	6'1"	195	24	1	
Don Martin	DB	5'11"	187	24		
Dave Mason	DB	6'	200	24		
Brian Dowling	QB	6'2"	200	26		
Jim Plunkett	QB	6'3"	220	25		30
Josh Ashton	HB	6'1"	205	24		
Mack Herron	HB	5'5"	170	25		24
Bob McCall	HB	6'	205	23		
Claxton Welch	HB	5'11"	203	26		
Paul Gipson	FB-HB	6'	210	26		
Sam Cunningham	FB	6'3"	215	23		30
John Tarver	FB	6'3"	227	24		24
Reggie Rucker	WR	6'2"	190	25		18
Darryl Stingley	WR	6'	190	22		12
Randy Vataha	WR	5'10"	175	24		12
Bob Adams	TE	6'2"	225	27		
John Mosier	TE	6'3"	220	25		
Bob Windsor	TE	6'4"	226	30		24
Bruce Barnes	K	5'11"	215	22		
Bill Bell	K	6'1"	192	25		7
Jeff White	K	5'11"	170	24		63

Wayne Patrick – Injury

NEW YORK JETS 4-10 Weeb Ewbank

Scores of Each Game		
7	Green Bay	23
34	Baltimore	10
7	Buffalo	9
3	Miami	31
9	New England	7
14	Pittsburgh	26
28	DENVER	40
24	MIAMI	14
33	NEW ENGLAND	13
14	Cincinnati	20
20	ATLANTA	28
20	BALTIMORE	17
23	Philadelphia	24
14	BUFFALO	34

Use Name	Pos.	Hgt	Wgt	Age	Int	Pts
Winston Hill	OT	6'4"	280	31		
Bob Svihus	OT	6'4"	245	30		
Bob Woods	OT	6'3"	255	23		
John Mooring	C-OT	6'6"	255	26		
Dave Herman	OG	6'2"	255	31		
Randy Rasmussen	OG	6'2"	255	28		
Garry Puetz	OT-OG	6'3"	255	21		
Rick Harrell	C	6'3"	238	22		
John Schmitt	C	6'4"	250	30		
Ed Galigher	DE	6'4"	255	22		
Mark Lomas	DE	6'4"	250	25		
Joey Jackson	DT-DE	6'4"	270	24		
Richard Neal	DT-DE	6'3"	254	25		
John Little	DT	6'3"	250	26		
Steve Thompson	DT	6'5"	250	28		
John Elliott	DE-DT	6'4"	244	28		
Al Atkinson	LB	6'1"	230	30	1	
Ralph Baker	LB	6'3"	228	31	4	6
John Ebersole	LB	6'3"	235	24	1	
Bill Ferguson	LB	6'3"	225	22		
Rob Spicer	LB	6'4"	227	22		
Mike Taylor	LB	6'1"	230	23		
Bill Zapalac	LB	6'4"	225	25		
Chris Farasopoulos	DB	5'11"	190	24	1	
Delles Howell	DB	6'3"	200	26	4	
Burgess Owens	DB	6'2"	200	22	1	6
Rich Sowells	DB	6'	175	24	3	6
Steve Tannen	DB	6'1"	194	25	1	
Earlie Thomas	DB	6'1"	190	27	2	
Phil Wise	DB	6'	190	24		6
Bill Demory	QB	6'2"	195	22		
Joe Namath	QB	6'2"	200	29		
Al Woodall	QB	6'5"	194	27		
Mike Adamle	HB	5'9"	197	23		
Hank Bjorklund	HB	6'1"	200	23		
Emerson Boozer	HB	5'11"	205	30		36
Cliff McClain	HB	6'	217	25		
Jim Nance	FB	6'1"	240	30		
John Riggins	FB	6'2"	230	24		24
Margene Adkins	WR	5'10"	183	26		
Jerome Barkum	WR	6'3"	215	23		36
Eddie Bell	WR	5'10"	160	25		12
Dave Knight	WR	6'1"	182	22		6
Rocky Turner	DB-WR	6'	200	23		
Dennis Cambal	TE	6'3"	228	24		
Rich Caster	TE	6'5"	228	24		24
Julian Fagan	K	6'3"	205	25		
Bobby Howfield	K	5'9"	180	36		78

BALTIMORE COLTS 4-10 Howard Schnellenberger

Scores of Each Game		
14	Cleveland	24
10	N. Y. JETS	34
14	NEW ORLEANS	10
16	New England	24
13	Buffalo	31
29	Detroit	27
21	OAKLAND	34
27	HOUSTON	31
0	Miami	44
14	Washington	22
24	BUFFALO	17
17	N. Y. Jets	20
16	MIAMI	3
18	NEW ENGLAND	13

Use Name	Pos.	Hgt	Wgt	Age	Int	Pts
Tom Drogas	OT	6'4"	257	23		
Dennis Nelson	OT	6'5"	260	27		
Dave Taylor	OT	6'4"	254	22		
Elmer Collett	OG	6'4"	240	28		
Cornelius Johnson	OG	6'2"	245	30		
Glenn Ressler	OG	6'3"	250	29		
Fred Hoaglin	C	6'4"	246	29		
Ken Mendenhall	C	6'3"	235	25		
Dan Neal	C	6'4"	240	21		
Mike Barnes	DE	6'6"	255	21		
Roy Hilton	DE	6'6"	240	28		
Dick Amman	DT-DE	6'5"	250	22		
Jim Bailey	DT	6'4"	255	25		
Joe Ehrmann	DT	6'5"	260	22		
Joe Schmiesing	DE-DT	6'4"	260	28		
Stan Cherry	LB	6'5"	200	22		
Mike Curtis	LB	6'2"	232	29	2	
Tom Hendricks	LB	6'7"	220	25	3	6
Mike Kaczmarek	LB	6'4"	235	22	1	
Ed Mooney	LB	6'2"	225	28		
Stan White	LB	6'1"	225	23	4	6
Brian Herosian	DB	6'3"	200	22		
Rex Kern	DB	5'11"	190	24	2	
Bruce Laird	DB	6'	185	23		
Jack Mildren	DB	6'1"	200	23		
Nelson Munsey	DB	6'1"	185	25		
Ray Oldham	DB	6'	200	22	2	
Rick Volk	DB	6'3"	195	28	1	
Marty Domres	QB	6'3"	220	26		12
Bert Jones	QB	6'3"	205	21		
Hubert Ginn (from MIA)	HB	5'11"	188	26		
Lydell Mitchell	HB	5'11"	204	24		12
Bill Olds	FB	6'1"	224	22		12
Don McCauley	HB-FB	6'1"	207	24		12
Glenn Doughty	WR	6'2"	204	23		24
Sam Havrilak	WR	6'2"	195	25		
Ollie Smith	WR	6'2"	195	23		
Cotton Speyrer	WR	6'	175	24		30
Tom Mitchell	TE-WR	6'2"	215	29		24
John Andrews	TE	6'3"	227	24		6
Ray Chester	TE	6'3"	235	25		6
George Hunt	K	6'1"	215	23		70
David Lee	K	6'4"	230	29		

MIAMI DOLPHINS

RUSHING

Last Name	No.	Yds	Avg	TD
Csonka	219	1003	4.6	5
Morris	149	954	6.4	10
Kiick	76	257	3.4	0
Nottingham	52	252	4.8	1
Leigh	22	134	6.1	1
Griese	13	20	1.5	0
Warfield	1	15	15.0	0
Morrall	1	9	9.0	0
Briscoe	2	–5	–2.5	0

RECEIVING

Last Name	No.	Yds	Avg	TD
Briscoe	30	447	15	2
Warfield	29	514	18	11
Kiick	27	208	8	0
Mandich	24	302	13	4
Csonka	7	22	3	0
Morris	4	51	13	0
Leigh	4	9	2	0
Nottingham	3	26	9	0
Fleming	3	22	7	0
Sellers	2	54	27	0
Twilley	2	30	15	0

PUNT RETURNS

Last Name	No.	Yds	Avg	TD
Scott	22	266	12	0
Leigh	9	64	7	0
Anderson	6	52	9	0

KICKOFF RETURNS

Last Name	No.	Yds	Avg	TD
Leigh	9	251	28	0
Morris	11	242	22	0
Scott	2	20	10	0
Nottingham	1	17	17	0
Bannon	1	10	10	0
Seiple	1	0	0	0

PASSING – PUNTING – KICKING

PASSING	Att	Comp	%	Yds	Yd/Att	TD	Int–%	RK
Griese	218	116	53	1422	6.5	17	8– 4	3
Morrall	38	17	45	253	6.7	0	4–11	

PUNTING	No.	Avg
Seiple	48	42.3

KICKING	XP	Att	%	FG	Att	%
Yepremian	38	38	100	25	37	68

BUFFALO BILLS

RUSHING

Last Name	No.	Yds	Avg	TD
Simpson	332	2003	6.0	12
Braxton	108	494	4.6	4
Watkins	98	414	4.2	2
Ferguson	48	147	3.1	2
Van Valkenberg	2	20	10.0	0
Cornell	4	13	3.3	0
Steve Jones	4	9	2.3	0
Shaw	4	2	0.5	0
Chandler	5	–14	–2.8	0

RECEIVING

Last Name	No.	Yds	Avg	TD
Chandler	30	427	14	3
Hill	29	422	15	0
Watkins	12	86	7	1
Seymour	10	114	11	0
Braxton	6	101	17	0
Simpson	6	70	12	0
R. Jarvis	1	12	12	0
Van Valkenberg	1	7	7	0
Ferguson	1	–3	–3	0

PUNT RETURNS

Last Name	No.	Yds	Avg	TD
Walker	25	210	8	0
Cahill	4	73	18	1
Chandler	2	5	3	0
Hill	1	–9	–9	0

KICKOFF RETURNS

Last Name	No.	Yds	Avg	TD
Francis	23	687	30	2
Jones	6	116	19	0
R. Jarvis	5	84	17	0
Cahill	2	42	21	0
Watkins	1	18	18	0
Parker	1	16	16	0
T. Greene	1	7	7	0
Cornell	1	2	2	0
Braxton	1	0	0	0
Van Valkenberg	1	0	0	0

PASSING – PUNTING – KICKING

PASSING	Att	Comp	%	Yds	Yd/Att	TD	Int–%	RK
Ferguson	164	73	45	939	5.7	4	10– 6	13
Shaw	46	22	48	300	6.5	0	4– 9	
Simpson	2	1	50	–3	–1.5	0	0– 0	
Chandler	1	0	0	0	0.0	0	0– 0	

PUNTING	No	Avg
Spike Jones	66	40.3

KICKING	XP	Att	%	FG	Att	%
Leypoldt	27	27	100	21	30	70
Chandler	1	1	100	0	0	0

NEW ENGLAND PATRIOTS

RUSHING

Last Name	No.	Yds	Avg	TD
Cunningham	155	516	3.3	4
Tarver	72	321	4.5	4
Ashton	93	305	3.3	0
Plunkett	44	209	4.8	5
Herron	61	200	3.3	2
Stingley	6	64	10.7	0
McCall	10	15	1.5	0
B. Adams	2	7	3.5	0
Gipson	5	–1	–0.2	0
Rucker	2	–1	–0.5	0
Welch	1	–2	–2.0	0
Windsor	1	–6	–6.0	0
Vataha	2	–15	–7.5	0

RECEIVING

Last Name	No.	Yds	Avg	TD
Rucker	53	743	14	3
Windsor	23	348	15	4
Stingley	23	339	15	2
Vataha	20	341	17	2
Herron	18	265	15	1
Cunningham	15	144	10	1
B. Adams	14	197	14	0
Ashton	11	113	10	0
Tarver	9	41	6	0
Welch	6	22	4	0
McCall	3	18	6	0

PUNT RETURNS

Last Name	No.	Yds	Avg	TD
Herron	27	282	10	0
Durko	3	21	7	0
Stingley	3	31	7	0

KICKOFF RETURNS

Last Name	No.	Yds	Avg	TD
Herron	41	1092	27	1
Stingley	6	143	24	0
Rucker	5	103	21	0
McCall	2	17	9	0
Tarver	1	17	17	0
Hannah	1	0	0	0
Windsor	1	0	0	0

PASSING – PUNTING – KICKING

PASSING	Att	Comp	%	Yds	Yd/Att	TD	Int–%	RK
Plunkett	376	193	51	2550	6.8	13	17– 5	5

PUNTING	No	Avg
Barnes	55	38.8
White	6	27.2

KICKING	XP	Att	%	FG	Att	%
White	21	25	84	14	25	56
Bell	4	5	80	1	4	25

NEW YORK JETS

RUSHING

Last Name	No.	Yds	Avg	TD
Boozer	182	831	4.6	3
Riggins	134	482	3.6	4
Adamle	67	264	3.9	0
Nance	18	78	4.3	0
Bjorkland	22	72	3.3	0
Woodall	13	68	5.2	0
Fagan	2	47	23.5	0
McClain	8	32	4.0	0
Barkum	1	2	2.0	0
Demory	4	–1	–0.3	0
Namath	1	–2	–2.0	0
Caster	1	–9	–9.0	0

RECEIVING

Last Name	No.	Yds	Avg	TD
Barkum	44	810	18	6
Caster	35	593	17	4
Bell	24	319	13	2
Riggins	23	158	7	0
Boozer	22	130	6	3
Adamle	9	63	7	0
Adkins	6	109	18	0
Knight	6	78	13	1
McClain	6	52	9	0
Nance	4	26	7	0
Bjorkland	2	15	8	0

PUNT RETURNS

Last Name	No.	Yds	Avg	TD
Farasopoulos	14	111	8	0
Turner	11	54	5	0
Tannen	2	0	0	0

KICKOFF RETURNS

Last Name	No.	Yds	Avg	TD
Adkins	31	615	20	0
Bjorkland	9	175	19	0
Owens	2	103	52	1
McClain	5	89	18	0
Adamle	5	79	16	0

PASSING – PUNTING – KICKING

PASSING	Att	Comp	%	Yds	Yd/Att	TD	Int–%	RK
Woodall	201	101	50	1228	6.1	9	8– 4	6
Namath	133	68	51	966	7.3	5	6– 5	
Demory	39	12	31	159	4.1	2	8–21	

PUNTING	No	Avg
Fagan	74	37.1

KICKING	XP	Att	%	FG	Att	%
Howfield	27	27	100	17	24	71

BALTIMORE COLTS

RUSHING

Last Name	No.	Yds	Avg	TD
L. Mitchell	253	963	3.8	2
McCauley	144	514	3.6	2
Domres	32	126	3.9	2
Olds	26	100	3.8	2
Doughty	10	96	9.6	0
Jones	18	58	3.2	0
Ginn	16	47	2.9	0
Mildren	2	14	7.0	0
Havrilak	2	9	4.5	0
Chester	1	1	1.0	0
Speyrer	1	1	1.0	0
Smith	1	–3	–3.0	0
Lee	2	–16	–8.0	0
Nelson	0	3	0.0	0

RECEIVING

Last Name	No.	Yds	Avg	TD
Doughty	25	587	23	4
T. Mitchell	25	313	13	4
McCauley	25	186	7	0
Chester	18	181	10	1
Speyrer	17	311	18	4
L. Mitchell	17	113	7	0
Ginn	3	2	1	0
Olds	2	–4	–2	0
Smith	1	37	37	0
Havrilak	1	9	9	0
Andrews	1	1	1	1

PUNT RETURNS

Last Name	No.	Yds	Avg	TD
Laird	15	72	5	0
Volk	7	45	6	0
Kern	2	12	6	0

KICKOFF RETURNS

Last Name	No.	Yds	Avg	TD
Laird	24	547	23	0
Speyrer	17	496	29	1
Ginn	9	198	22	0
White	1	17	17	0
Volk	2	16	8	0
Olds	3	14	5	0
Andrews	1	13	13	0
Munsey	1	13	13	0
McCauley	1	12	12	0

PASSING – PUNTING – KICKING

PASSING	Att	Comp	%	Yds	Yd/Att	TD	Int–%	RK
Domres	191	93	49	1153	6.0	9	13– 7	11
Jones	108	43	40	539	5.0	4	12–11	
Speyrer	1	1	100	54	54.0	1	0– 0	

PUNTING	No	Avg
Lee	62	38.7

KICKING	XP	Att	%	FG	Att	%
Hunt	22	24	92	16	28	57

CINCINNATI BENGALS 10-4-0 Paul Brown

Score	Opponent	Opp.
10	Denver	28
24	HOUSTON	10
20	San Diego	13
10	CLEVELAND	17
9	PITTSBURGH	7
14	KANSAS CITY	6
13	Pittsburgh	20
10	Dallas	38
16	Buffalo	13
20	N. Y. JETS	14
42	ST. LOUIS	24
27	MINNESOTA	0
34	Cleveland	17
27	Houston	24

Use Name	Pos.	Hgt	Wgt	Age	Int	Pts
Vern Holland	OT	6'5"	270	25		
Rufus Mayes	OT	6'5"	260	25		
Stan Walters	OT	6'6"	270	24		
Howard Fest	OG-OT	6'6"	262	27		
Pat Matson	OG	6'1"	245	29		
John Shinners	OG	6'2"	254	26		
Tom DeLeone	C	6'2"	252	23		
Bob Johnson	C	6'5"	260	27		
Royce Berry	DE	6'3"	250	27		
Ken Johnson	DE	6'5"	265	25		
Lee Thomas	DE	6'5"	246	26		
Sherman White	DE	6'5"	255	24		
Ron Carpenter	DT	6'4"	260	25		
Steve Chomyszak	DT	6'5"	265	28		
Mike Reid	DT	6'3"	255	26		
Doug Adams	LB	6'	222	24		
Ken Avery	LB	6'1"	227	29	1	
Al Beauchamp	LB	6'2"	237	29	3	
Bill Bergey	LB	6'2"	243	28	3	
Tim Kearney	LB	6'2"	227	24		
Jim LeClair	LB	6'2"	226	23		
Ron Pritchard	LB	6'1"	235	26		
Lyle Blackwood	DB	6'	190	22		
Tommy Casanova	DB	6'2"	202	22	4	
Neal Craig	DB	6'1"	190	25	2	
Bernie Jackson	DB	6'	173	23	1	
Bob Jones	DB	6'1"	194	22		
Lemar Parrish	DB	5'11"	185	25	2	6
Ken Riley	DB	6'	180	26	2	
Ken Anderson	QB	6'1"	211	24		
Greg Cook	QB	6'3"	215	26		
Mike Ernst	QB	6'1"	190	22		
Lenvil Elliott	HB	6'	200	21		12
Essex Johnson	HB	5'9"	200	26		42
Reece Morrison	HB	6'	207	27		
Booby Clark	FB	6'2"	245	22		48
Joe Wilson	HB-FB	5'10"	210	22		
Isaac Curtis	WR	6'	190	22		54
Tim George	WR	6'5"	225	21		
Charlie Joiner	WR	5'11"	188	25		
Chip Myers	WR	6'4"	210	28		
Bruce Coslet	TE	6'3"	227	27		
Al Chandler	TE	6'2"	233	22		
Bob Trumpy	TE	6'6"	228	28		30
Dave Lewis	K	6'2"	225	27		
Horst Muhlmann	K	6'1"	220	33		94

Virgil Carter – Injury
Doug Dressler – Injury

PITTSBURGH STEELERS 10-4-0 Chuck Noll

Score	Opponent	Opp.
24	DETROIT	10
33	CLEVELAND	6
36	Houston	7
38	SAN DIEGO	21
7	Cincinnati	19
26	N. Y. JETS	14
20	CINCINNATI	13
21	WASHINGTON	16
17	Oakland	9
13	DENVER	23
16	Cleveland	21
26	Miami	30
33	HOUSTON	7
37	San Francisco	14

Use Name	Pos.	Hgt	Wgt	Age	Int	Pts
Gordon Gravelle	OT	6'5"	250	24		
Glen Ray Hines	OT	6'5"	265	29		
Jon Kolb	OT	6'2"	262	26		
Sam Davis	OG	6'1"	255	29		
Mel Holmes	OG	6'3"	250	23		
Bruce Van Dyke	OG	6'2"	255	29		
Gerry Mullins	OT-OG	6'3"	244	24		
Jim Clack	C	6'3"	250	25		
Ray Mansfield	C	6'3"	260	32		
L. C. Greenwood	DE	6'5"	245	26		
Dwight White	DE	6'4"	250	24	2	2
Steve Furness	DT-DE	6'4"	255	23		
Joe Green	DT	6'4"	275	26		
Craig Hanneman	DT	6'3"	240	24		
Ernie Holmes	DT	6'3"	260	25		
Tom Keating	DT	6'3"	247	30		
Ed Bradley	LB	6'2"	240	23		
Henry Davis	LB	6'3"	235	30	2	
Jack Ham	LB	6'3"	225	24	2	6
Andy Russell	LB	6'3"	225	31	3	6
Loren Toews	LB	6'3"	212	21	2	
George Webster	LB	6'4"	223	27		
Mel Blount	DB	6'3"	205	25	4	
John Dockery	DB	6'	186	28	1	
Glen Edwards	DB	6'	185	26	6	6
Dennis Meyer	DB	5'11"	186	22	6	6
John Rowser	DB	6'1"	185	29		
Jim Thomas	DB	6'2"	196	21	1	
Mike Wagner	DB	6'1"	196	24	8	6
Terry Bradshaw	QB	6'3"	218	24		18
Joe Gilliam	QB	6'2"	187	22		
Terry Hanratty	QB	6'1"	210	25		
Rocky Bleier	HB	5'11"	205	27		
Preston Pearson	HB	6'1"	205	28		24
Franco Harris	FB-HB	6'2"	230	23		18
Steve Davis	HB-FB	6'1"	218	23		18
John Fuqua	HB-FB	5'11"	205	26		12
Dave Davis	WR	6'	175	25		
Frank Lewis	WR	6'1"	196	26		18
Barry Pearson	WR	5'11"	185	23		18
Glenn Scolnik	WR	6'3"	190	22		
Ron Shanklin	WR	6'1"	180	26		60
Larry Brown	TE	6'4"	225	24		
John McMakin	TE	6'3"	232	22		6
Roy Gerela	K	5'10"	185	25		123
Bobby Walden	K	6'	190	34		

Al Young – Illness

CLEVELAND BROWNS 7-5-2 Nick Skorich

Score	Opponent	Opp.
24	BALTIMORE	14
6	Pittsburgh	33
12	N. Y. GIANTS	10
17	Cincinnati	10
9	MIAMI	17
42	HOUSTON	13
16	SAN DIEGO	16
3	Minnesota	26
23	Houston	13
7	Oakland	3
21	PITTSBURGH	16
20	Kansas City	20
17	CINCINNATI	34
17	Los Angeles	30

Use Name	Pos.	Hgt	Wgt	Age	Int	Pts
Joe Carollo	OT	6'2"	265	33		
Doug Dieken	OT	6'5"	254	24		
Bob McKay	OT	6'5"	260	25		
Chris Morris	OT	6'3"	250	23		
John Demarie	OG	6'3"	246	28		
Chuck Hutchison	OG	6'3"	240	24		
Gene Hickerson	OG	6'3"	252	38		
Jim Copeland	C-OG	6'3"	243	28		
Bob DeMarco	C	6'3"	248	35		
Bob Briggs	DE	6'4"	258	28		
Joe Jones	DE	6'6"	250	25		
Nick Roman	DE	6'3"	244	25		
Carl Barisich	DT	6'4"	255	22		
Walter Johnson	DT	6'3"	265	30		
Jerry Sherk	DT	6'4"	255	25		
Billy Andrews	LB	6'	220	28		
Bob Babich	LB	6'2"	230	26	1	
John Garlington	LB	6'1"	218	27	1	
Charlie Hall	LB	6'3"	225	24		
Mel Long	LB	6'	228	26		
Jim Romaniszyn	LB	6'2"	214	22		
Cliff Brooks	DB	6'1"	190	24		
Tom Darden	DB	6'2"	195	23	1	
Ben Davis	DB	5'11"	180	28	2	
Van Green	DB	6'1"	192	22		6
Clarence Scott	DB	6'	180	24	5	6
Jim Stienke	DB	5'11"	188	22		
Walt Sumner	DB	6'1"	195	26	2	
Don Horn	QB	6'2"	195	28		
Mike Phipps	QB	6'2"	205	25		30
Leroy Kelly	HB	6'	202	31		18
Billy LeFear	HB	5'11"	197	23		
Greg Pruitt	HB	5'10"	186	22		30
Hugh McKinnis	FB	6'	225	25		
Bo Scott	FB	6'3"	215	30		6
Ken Brown	HB-FB	5'10"	203	27		
Steve Holden	WR	6'	192	22		
Fair Hooker	WR	6'1"	195	26		12
Frank Pitts	WR	6'2"	200	29		24
Gloster Richardson	WR	6'	200	30		6
Dave Sullivan	WR	5'11"	185	22		
Chip Glass	TE	6'4"	235	26		
Milt Morin	TE	6'4"	236	31		6
Ken Smith	TE	6'4"	225	22		
Don Cockroft	K	6'1"	195	28		90

Bubba Pena – Knee Injury

HOUSTON OILERS 1-13-0 Bill Peterson Sid Gillman

Score	Opponent	Opp.
14	N. Y. Giants	34
10	Cincinnati	24
7	PITTSBURGH	36
26	LOS ANGELES	31
20	DENVER	48
13	Cleveland	42
14	Chicago	35
31	Baltimore	27
13	CLEVELAND	23
14	Kansas City	38
0	NEW ENGLAND	32
6	OAKLAND	17
7	Pittsburgh	33
24	CINCINNATI	27

Use Name	Pos.	Hgt	Wgt	Age	Int	Pts
Levert Carr	OT	6'5"	260	29		
Elbert Drungo	OT	6'5"	265	30		
Tom Funchess	OT	6'5"	270	28		
Kevin Hunt (from NE)	OT	6'5"	260	25		
Soloman Freelon	OG	6'2"	250	22		
Brian Goodman	OG	6'2"	250	24		
Al Jenkins	OG	6'2"	245	27		
Harris Jones	OG	6'4"	245	28		
Ralph Miller	OG	6'4"	260	24		
Ron Saul	OG	6'2"	255	25		
Bill Curry	C	6'2"	236	30		
Sam Gruneisen	C	6'1"	250	32		
Calvin Hunt	C	6'3"	245	25		
Ron Lou	C	6'2"	235	22		
Elvin Bethea	DE	6'3"	262	27		
Mike Fanucci	DE	6'4"	240	23		
Tody Smith	DE	6'5"	245	24		
Wes Grant	DT-DE	6'3"	245	26		
Al Cowlings	DT	6'5"	255	26		
John Matuszak	DT	6'8"	290	23		
Greg Sampson	DT	6'6"	260	22		
Greg Bingham	LB	6'1"	227	22	2	
Ralph Cindrich	LB	6'1"	228	23		
Paul Guidry	LB	6'3"	233	29		
Brian McConnell	LB	6'4"	207	23		
Guy Roberts	LB	6'1"	215	22	4	
Ted Washington	LB	6'1"	240	23		
Willie Alexander	DB	6'2"	195	24	3	
Bob Atkins	DB	6'3"	210	27		
Joe Blahak	DB	5'9"	182	22	2	
John Charles	DB	6'1"	200	29		
Larry Eaglin	DB	6'3"	195	22		6
Alvin Haymond	DB	6'	194	31		
Benny Johnson	DB	5'11"	178	25		
Zeke Moore	DB	6'2"	196	29		
Jeff Severson	DB	6'1"	180	23	4	
Alvin Wyatt	DB	5'10"	180	25		
Lynn Dickey	QB	6'4"	218	21		1
Edd Hargett	QB	5'11"	190	26		
Dan Pastorini	QB	6'3"	215	24		
Bob Gresham	HB	5'11"	195	25		24
Al Johnson	HB	6'	200	22		
Paul Robinson	HB	6'	195	28		12
George Amundson	FB-HB	6'3"	215	21		
Lewis Jolley	FB-HB	6'	210	23		
Bill Thomas	FB	6'2"	225	23		
Fred Willis	FB	6'	212	25		30
Jim Beirne	WR	6'2"	196	26		
Ken Burrough	WR	6'4"	210	25		18
Eddie Hinton	WR	6'	200	26		
Clifton McNeil	WR	6'2"	187	33		
Billy Parks	WR	6'1"	185	25		6
Dave Parks	TE	6'2"	203	31		6
Mack Alston	TE	6'2"	230	26		24
Ron Mayo	TE	6'3"	223	23		
Skip Butler	K	6'2"	200	26		66
Dave Green (to CIN)	K	5'11"	200	23		

Willie Rodgers – Injury
Sid Smith – Injury

CINCINNATI BENGALS

RUSHING

Last Name	No.	Yds	Avg	TD
E. Johnson	195	997	5.1	4
Clark	254	988	3.9	8
Elliott	22	122	5.5	1
Anderson	26	97	3.7	0
Wilson	10	39	3.9	0
Morrison	3	11	3.7	0
Lewis	3	-7	-2.3	0
Curtis	2	-11	-5.5	0

RECEIVING

Last Name	No.	Yds	Avg	TD
Curtis	45	**843**	**19**	9
Clark	45	347	8	0
Trumpy	29	435	15	5
E. Johnson	28	356	13	3
Joiner	13	214	16	0
Coslet	9	123	14	0
Myers	7	77	11	0
George	2	28	14	0
Elliott	1	12	12	1
Morrison	1	4	4	0

PUNT RETURNS

Last Name	No.	Yds	Avg	TD
Parrish	25	200	8	0
Casanova	15	119	8	0
Blackwood	4	12	3	0
Lewis	1	2	2	0

KICKOFF RETURNS

Last Name	No.	Yds	Avg	TD
Jackson	21	520	25	0
Wilson	8	173	22	0
Parrish	7	143	20	0
Lewis	2	40	20	0
Coslet	1	0	0	0

PASSING – PUNTING – KICKING

PASSING	Att	Comp	%	Yds	Yd/Att	TD	Int–%	RK
Anderson	329	179	54	2428	7.4	18	12– **4**	**1**
Cook	3	1	33	11	3.7	0	0– 0	

PUNTING	No	Avg
Lewis	68	41.0

KICKING	XP	Att	%	FG	Att	%
Muhlmann	31	32	97	21	31	68

PITTSBURGH STEELERS

RUSHING

Last Name	No.	Yds	Avg	TD
Harris	188	698	3.7	3
P. Pearson	132	554	4.2	2
Fugua	117	457	3.9	2
Steve Davis	67	266	4.0	2
Bradshaw	34	145	4.3	3
Gilliam	6	23	3.8	0
Shanklin	3	1	0.3	0
Bleier	3	0	0.0	0
Hanratty	3	0	0.0	0
Walden	1	0	0.0	0
Lewis	1	-1	-1.0	0

RECEIVING

Last Name	No.	Yds	Avg	TD
Shanklin	30	711	24	10
Lewis	23	409	18	3
B. Pearson	23	317	14	3
Fugua	17	150	9	0
McMakin	13	195	15	1
P. Pearson	11	173	16	2
Harris	10	69	7	0
Steve Davis	7	31	4	1
Brown	5	88	18	0
D. Davis	1	14	14	0

PUNT RETURNS

Last Name	No.	Yds	Avg	TD
Edwards	34	336	10	0
Meyer	18	80	4	0

KICKOFF RETURNS

Last Name	No.	Yds	Avg	TD
Steve Davis	15	404	27	0
P. Pearson	16	308	19	0
Bleier	3	47	16	0
Harris	1	23	23	0
Fuqua	1	22	22	0
Hanneman	1	20	20	0
Edwards	1	10	10	0
Webster	1	9	9	0
Mansfield	1	0	0	0

PASSING – PUNTING – KICKING

PASSING	Att	Comp	%	Yds	Yd/Att	TD	Int–%	RK
Bradshaw	180	89	49	1183	6.6	10	15– 8	8
Hanratty	69	31	45	643	9.3	8	5– 7	
Gilliam	60	20	33	331	5.5	2	6–10	

PUNTING	No	Avg
Walden	62	41.1

KICKING	XP	Att	%	FG	Att	%
Gerela	36	37	97	**29**	**43**	67

CLEVELAND BROWNS

RUSHING

Last Name	No.	Yds	Avg	TD
Brown	161	537	3.3	0
Phipps	60	395	6.6	5
Kelly	132	389	2.9	3
Pruitt	61	369	6.0	4
LeFear	26	135	5.2	0
Bo Scott	34	79	2.3	0
McKinnis	28	77	2.8	0
Cockroft	1	-3	-3.0	0
Richardson	3	-10	-3.3	0

RECEIVING

Last Name	No.	Yds	Avg	TD
Pitts	31	317	10	4
Morin	26	417	16	1
Brown	22	187	9	0
Hooker	18	196	11	2
Kelly	15	180	12	0
Richardson	12	175	15	1
Pruitt	9	110	12	1
Bo Scott	6	23	4	1
LeFear	5	38	8	0
Holden	3	27	9	0
McKinnis	3	11	4	0
Glass	2	60	30	0

PUNT RETURNS

Last Name	No.	Yds	Avg	TD
Pruitt	16	180	11	0
Darden	9	51	6	0
LeFear	7	51	7	0
Holden	2	19	10	0
Kelly	1	7	7	0
Hall	1	0	0	0

KICKOFF RETURNS

Last Name	No.	Yds	Avg	TD
Pruitt	16	453	28	0
Le Fear	15	337	22	0
Holden	8	172	22	0
Long	6	87	15	0
Romaniszyn	2	21	11	0
Dieken	2	14	7	0

PASSING – PUNTING – KICKING

PASSING	Att	Comp	%	Yds	Yd/Att	TD	Int–%	RK
Phipps	299	148	49	1719	5.8	9	20– 7	9
Horn	8	4	50	22	2.8	1	0– 0	
Pruitt	1	0	0	0	0.0	0	0– 0	

PUNTING	No	Avg
Cockroft	**82**	40.5

KICKING	XP	Att	%	FG	Att	%
Cockroft	24	24	100	22	31	**71**

HOUSTON OILERS

RUSHING

Last Name	No.	Yds	Avg	TD
Willis	171	579	3.4	4
Gresham	104	400	3.8	2
Robinson	34	151	4.4	2
Pastorini	31	102	3.3	0
Amundson	15	56	3.7	0
Thomas	10	39	3.9	0
Burrough	5	38	7.6	1
Alston	1	13	13.0	0
Dickey	6	9	1.5	0
Jolley	7	6	0.9	0
Hinton	1	-2	-2.0	0
Johnson	1	-3	-3.0	0

RECEIVING

Last Name	No.	Yds	Avg	TD
Willis	**57**	371	7	1
B. Parks	43	581	14	1
Burrough	43	577	13	2
Gresham	28	244	9	1
Alston	19	195	10	4
Hinton	13	202	16	1
Amundson	7	60	9	0
Robinson	7	46	7	0
Jolley	3	56	19	0
D. Parks	3	31	10	1
Thomas	1	4	4	0
McNeil	1	3	3	0

PUNT RETURNS

Last Name	No.	Yds	Avg	TD
Severson	16	126	8	0
Haymond	14	101	7	0

KICKOFF RETURNS

Last Name	No.	Yds	Avg	TD
Gresham	27	723	27	0
Haymond	28	703	25	0
Hinton	8	141	18	0
Eaglin	3	76	25	0
Blahak	2	41	21	0
Jolley	2	41	21	0
Fanucci	3	40	13	0
Severson	1	17	17	0

PASSING – PUNTING – KICKING

PASSING	Att	Comp	%	Yds	Yd/Att	TD	Int–%	RK
Pastorini	290	154	53	1482	5.1	5	17– 6	10
Dickey	120	71	59	888	7.4	6	10– 8	
Willis	1	0	0	0	0.0	0	0– 0	

PUNTING	No	Avg
Butler	36	37.3
Pastorini	27	40.3
Green	22	39.5

KICKING	XP	Att	%	FG	Att	%
Butler	21	21	100	15	24	63
Dickey	1	1	100	0	0	0

OAKLAND RAIDERS 9-4-1 John Madden

Scores of Each Game		
16	Minnesota	24
12	MIAMI	7
3	Kansas City	16
17	St. Louis	10
27	SAN DIEGO	17
23	Denver	23
34	Baltimore	21
42	N. Y. GIANTS	0
9	PITTSBURGH	17
3	CLEVELAND	7
31	San Diego	3
17	Houston	6
37	KANSAS CITY	7
21	DENVER	7

Use Name	Pos.	Hgt	Wgt	Age	Int	Pts
Art Shell	OT	6'5"	265	26		
John Vella	OT	6'4"	255	23		
Bob Brown	OT	6'4"	280	30		
Paul Seiler	C-OT	6'4"	260	27		
George Buehler	OG	6'2"	260	26		
Gene Upshaw	OG	6'5"	255	28		
Dave Dalby	C-OG	6'2"	240	22		
Jim Otto	C	6'2"	255	35		
Tony Cline	DE	6'2"	240	25		
Horace Jones	DE	6'3"	255	24		
Bubba Smith	DE	6'7"	265	28		
Kelvin Korver	DT	6'6"	260	24	1	
Otis Sistrunk	DT	6'4"	255	26		
Art Thoms	DT	6'5"	250	26		

Use Name	Pos.	Hgt	Wgt	Age	Int	Pts
Joe Carroll	LB	6'1"	220	23		
Dan Conners	LB	6'1"	230	31		
Gerald Irons	LB	6'2"	230	26	2	
Monte Johnson	LB	6'4"	235	21		
Phil Villapiano	LB	6'1"	222	24	1	
Gary Weaver	LB	6'1"	224	24		
Butch Atkinson	DB	6'	180	25	3	12
Willie Brown	DB	6'1"	190	32	3	
Tommy Maxwell	DB	6'2"	195	26		
Jack Tatum	DB	5'10"	200	24	1	
Alonzo Thomas	DB	6'1"	205	23	2	
Jimmy Warren	DB	5'11"	175	34	1	
Nemiah Wilson	DB	6'	165	30	3	

Jackie Allen – Injury

Use Name	Pos.	Hgt	Wgt	Age	Int	Pts
George Blanda	QB	6'1"	215	45		100
Daryle Lamonica	QB	6'2"	215	32		
Ken Stabler	QB	6'3"	215	27		
Clarence Davis	HB	5'10"	190	24		24
Bob Hudson	HB	5'11"	205	25		
Charlie Smith	HB	6'1"	205	27		30
Marv Hubbard	FB	6'1"	225	27		36
Pete Banaszak	HB-FB	5'11"	210	29		
Jeff Queen	TE-FB	6'1"	220	27		
Fred Biletnikoff	WR	6'1"	190	30		24
Cliff Branch	WR	5'11"	170	25		18
Mike Siani	WR	6'2"	195	23		18
Steve Sweeney	WR	6'3"	205	22		6
Warren Bankston	TE	6'4"	235	26		
Bob Moore	TE	6'3"	220	24		24
Ray Guy	K	6'3"	190	23		

DENVER BRONCOS 7-5-2 John Ralston

Scores of Each Game		
28	CINCINNATI	10
34	SAN FRANCISCO	36
14	CHICAGO	33
14	Kansas City	16
48	Houston	20
23	OAKLAND	23
40	N. Y. Jets	28
17	St. Louis	17
30	SAN DIEGO	19
23	Pittsburgh	13
14	KANSAS CITY	10
10	DALLAS	22
42	San Diego	28
7	Oakland	21

Use Name	Pos.	Hgt	Wgt	Age	Int	Pts
Mike Askea	OT	6'4"	260	22		
Mike Current	OT	6'4"	274	27		
Larron Jackson	OT	6'3"	270	24		
Marv Montgomery	OT	6'6"	255	25		
Paul Howard	OG	6'3"	260	23		
Tommy Lyons	OG	6'2"	228	25		
Mike Schniter	OG	6'3"	245	26		
Larry Kaminski	C	6'2"	245	28		
Bobby Maples	C	6'3"	250	30		
Lyle Alzado	DE	6'3"	252	24		
Barney Chavous	DE	6'3"	252	26		
John Grant	DE	6'3"	235	23		
Ed Smith	DE	6'5"	240	23		
Pete Duranko	DT	6'2"	250	29		
Jerry Inman	DT	6'3"	256	33		
Paul Smith	DT	6'3"	256	28		

Use Name	Pos.	Hgt	Wgt	Age	Int	Pts
Ken Criter	LB	5'11"	223	26		2
Tom Graham	LB	6'2"	235	23		
Tom Jackson	LB	5'11"	220	22		
Bill Laskey	LB	6'2"	235	30	2	
Ray May (from BAL)	LB	6'1"	230	28	1	
Jim O'Malley	LB	6'1"	230	22		
Mike Simone	LB	6'	210	23		
Charlie Greer	DB	6'	205	27	1	
Dale Hackbart	DB	6'3"	210	37		
Calvin Jones	DB	5'7"	170	22	4	
Leroy Mitchell	DB	6'2"	190	28		
Randy Montgomery	DB	5'11"	182	26		
John Pitts	DB	6'4"	218	28		
Bill Thompson	DB	6'1"	200	26	3	12
Maurice Tyler	DB	6'	188	23		

Tom Domres – Injury
George Goeddeke – Injury
Chip Myrtle – Injury

Use Name	Pos.	Hgt	Wgt	Age	Int	Pts
Charley Johnson	QB	6'	190	36		
Steve Ramsey	QB	6'2"	210	25		
Bobby Anderson	HB	6'	208	25		6
Otis Armstrong	HB	5'10"	196	23		6
Floyd Little	HB	5'10"	196	31		78
Oliver Ross	FB-HB	6'	210	24		
Joe Dawkins	FB	5'11"	223	25		12
Fran Lynch	HB-FB	6'1"	205	27		
Haven Moses	WR	6'3"	205	27		54
Jerry Simmons	WR	6'1"	190	30		6
Bill Van Heusen	WR	6'1"	200	27		6
Gene Washington	WR	6'3"	205	29		18
Bill Masters	TE	6'5"	240	29		
Riley Odoms	TE	6'4"	230	23		42
Jim Turner	K	6'2"	205	32		106

KANSAS CITY CHIEFS 7-5-2 Hank Stram

Scores of Each Game		
13	LOS ANGELES	23
10	New England	7
16	OAKLAND	3
16	DENVER	14
10	Green Bay	10
6	Cincinnati	14
14	Buffalo	23
19	San Diego	0
19	CHICAGO	7
38	HOUSTON	14
10	Denver	14
20	CLEVELAND	20
7	Oakland	37
33	SAN DIEGO	6

Use Name	Pos.	Hgt	Wgt	Age	Int	Pts
Dave Hill	OT	6'5"	260	32		
Francis Peay	OT	6'5"	250	29		
Jim Tyrer	OT	6'6"	280	34		
Ed Budde	OG	6'5"	265	32		
George Daney	OG	6'3"	240	26		
Mo Moorman	OT-OG	6'5"	252	29		
Wayne Walton	OT-OG	6'5"	255	24		
Jack Rudnay	C	6'3"	240	25		
Mike Oriard	OG-C	6'4"	223	25		
Pat Holmes	DE	6'5"	250	33	1	
John Lohmeyer	DE	6'4"	230	21		6
Marv Upshaw	DE	6'3"	260	26		
Wilbur Young	DE	6'6"	285	24		
Buck Buchanan	DT	6'7"	270	33	1	
Curley Culp	DT	6'1"	265	27		
George Seals	DT	6'2"	260	30		

Use Name	Pos.	Hgt	Wgt	Age	Int	Pts
Bobby Bell	LB	6'4"	228	33	1	
Willie Lanier	LB	6'1"	245	28	3	6
Jim Lynch	LB	6'1"	235	28	1	
Al Palewicz	LB	6'1"	215	23		
Clyde Werner	LB	6'4"	225	25		
Nate Allen	DB	5'10"	170	25	1	
Doug Jones	DB	6'2"	202	22		
Jim Kearney	DB	6'2"	206	30	3	
Jim Marsalis	DB	5'11"	194	27	2	
Larry Marshall	DB	5'10"	195	23		
Kerry Reardon	DB	5'11"	180	24	2	
Mike Sensibaugh	DB	5'11"	192	24	3	
Emmitt Thomas	DB	6'2"	192	30	3	

Cannonball Butler – Injury
Ernie Calloway – Injury

Use Name	Pos.	Hgt	Wgt	Age	Int	Pts
Pete Beathard	QB	6'2"	200	31		6
Len Dawson	QB	6'	190	39		
Mike Livingston	QB	6'3"	212	27		12
Leroy Keyes	HB	6'3"	208	26		
Warren McVea	HB	5'10"	182	27		
Ed Podolak	HB	6'1"	205	26		18
Willie Ellison	FB-HB	6'1"	210	28		12
Wendell Hayes	FB	6'2"	220	32		12
Jeff Kinney	HB-FB	6'2"	215	22		6
Andy Hamilton	WR	6'3"	190	23		
Dan Kratzer	WR	6'3"	194	24		
Dave Smith	WR	6'2"	205	26		
Otis Taylor	WR	6'2"	215	30		24
Bob West	WR	6'4"	218	22		
Elmo Wright	WR	6'	190	24		12
Gary Butler	TE	6'3"	235	22		12
Morris Stroud	TE	6'10"	255	27		12
Jan Stenerud	K	6'2"	187	30		93
Jerrel Wilson	K	6'4"	222	32		

SAN DIEGO CHARGERS 2-11-1 Harland Svare Ron Waller

Scores of Each Game		
0	Washington	38
34	BUFFALO	7
13	CINCINNATI	20
21	Pittsburgh	38
17	Oakland	27
0	ATLANTA	41
16	Cleveland	16
0	KANSAS CITY	19
19	Denver	30
17	NEW ORLEANS	14
3	OAKLAND	31
14	New England	30
28	DENVER	42
6	Kansas City	33

Use Name	Pos.	Hgt	Wgt	Age	Int	Pts
Ira Gordon	OT	6'3"	268	25		
Terry Owens	OT	6'6"	268	29		
Russ Washington	OT	6'6"	290	26		
Al Dennis	OG	6'4"	250	22		
Walt Sweeney	OG	6'3"	256	32		
Ralph Wenzel	OG	6'3"	250	30		
Doug Wilkerson	OG	6'2"	256	26		
Jay Douglas	C	6'6"	242	23		
Carl Mauck	C	6'3"	243	26		
Lionel Aldridge	DE	6'4"	245	31		
Coy Bacon	DE	6'4"	270	31		6
Deacon Jones	DE	6'5"	250	34		
Pete Lazetich	DE	6'3"	225	23		
Cal Snowden	DE	6'4"	253	26		
Dave Costa	DT	6'2"	260	31		
Greg Wojcik	DT	6'4"	243	30		

Use Name	Pos.	Hgt	Wgt	Age	Int	Pts
Carl Gersbach	LB	6'1"	230	26	1	
Rick Redman	LB	5'11"	222	30	1	
Floyd Rice (from HOU)	LB	6'3"	223	24	1	6
Mel Rodgers	LB	6'2"	230	25	1	
Tim Rossovich	LB	6'4"	240	27	1	
Mike Stratton	LB	6'3"	240	31	3	
Joe Beauchamp	DB	6'	188	29		
Reggie Berry	DB	6'	190	24		
Lenny Dunlap	DB	6'1"	195	24		
Chris Fletcher	DB	5'11"	185	24		
Bob Howard	DB	6'1"	177	28	5	
Willie McGee	DB	5'11"	175	23		
Bryant Salter	DB	6'4"	196	23	1	
Ron Smith	DB	6'1"	195	30	1	12

Ray White – Injury

Use Name	Pos.	Hgt	Wgt	Age	Int	Pts
Wayne Clark	QB	6'2"	205	26		
Dan Fouts	QB	6'3"	193	22		
Johnny Unitas	QB	6'1"	196	40		
Mike Garrett	HB	5'9"	200	29		6
Clint Jones	HB	6'	205	28		6
Bob Thomas	HB	5'10"	200	24		6
Cid Edwards	FB	6'2"	230	29		6
Robert Holmes	FB	5'9"	220	27		42
Gary Garrison	WR	6'1"	193	29		12
Ron Holliday	WR	5'9"	168	25		1
Jerry LeVias	WR	5'10"	178	26		18
Dave Williams (to PIT)	WR	6'2"	200	28		
Pettis Norman	TE	6'3"	220	33		
Gary Parris	TE	6'2"	226	23		
Jim Thaxton	TE	6'2"	240	24		12
Dennis Partee	K	6'2"	230	27		7
Ray Wersching	K	5'11"	210	23		48

OAKLAND RAIDERS

RUSHING

Last Name	No.	Yds	Avg	TD
Hubbard	193	903	4.7	6
C. Smith	173	682	3.9	4
Davis	116	609	5.3	4
Banaszak	34	198	5.8	0
Stabler	21	101	4.8	0
Guy	1	21	21.0	0
Hudson	4	3	0.8	0
Lamonica	5	–7	–1.4	0

RECEIVING

Last Name	No.	Yds	Avg	TD
Biletnikoff	48	660	14	4
Siani	45	742	16	3
Moore	34	375	11	4
C. Smith	28	260	9	1
Branch	19	290	15	3
Hubbard	15	116	8	0
Davis	7	76	11	0
Banaszak	6	31	5	0
Sweeny	2	52	26	1
Hudson	1	9	9	0

PUNT RETURNS

Last Name	No.	Yds	Avg	TD
Atkinson	41	336	8	1
Maxwell	4	8	2	0
Warren	1	0	0	0

KICKOFF RETURNS

Last Name	No.	Yds	Avg	TD
Davis	19	504	27	0
Hudson	14	350	25	0
Banaszak	3	48	16	0
C. Smith	2	23	12	0
Bankston	1	12	12	0

PASSING – PUNTING – KICKING

PASSING	Att	Comp	%	Yds	Yd/Att	TD	Int–%	RK
Stabler	260	163	63	1997	7.7	14	10– 4	2
Lamonica	93	42	45	614	6.6	2	8– 9	

PUNTING	No	Avg
Guy	69	45.3

KICKING	XP	Att	%	FG	Att	%
Blanda	31	31	100	23	33	70

DENVER BRONCOS

RUSHING

Last Name	No.	Yds	Avg	TD
Little	256	979	3.8	12
Dawkins	160	706	4.4	2
Armstrong	26	90	3.5	0
Anderson	19	61	3.2	1
Odoms	5	53	10.6	0
Van Heusen	4	34	8.5	0
Moses	3	25	8.3	1
Ross	5	21	4.2	0
Johnson	7	–2	–0.3	0
Simmons	1	–4	–4.0	0
Masters	1	–9	–9.0	0

RECEIVING

Last Name	No.	Yds	Avg	TD
Odoms	43	629	15	7
Little	41	423	10	1
Dawkins	30	329	11	0
Moses	28	518	19	8
Anderson	15	153	10	0
Simmons	13	249	19	1
Washington	10	150	15	3
Van Heusen	8	149	19	1
Masters	5	65	13	0
Armstrong	2	43	22	1
Jackson	1	–2	–2	0

PUNT RETURNS

Last Name	No.	Yds	Avg	TD
Thompson	30	366	12	0
Tyler	4	20	5	0
Greer	3	11	4	0
Little	1	7	7	0
Criter	1	0	0	0
Mitchell	1	0	0	0

KICKOFF RETURNS

Last Name	No.	Yds	Avg	TD
Armstrong	20	472	24	0
Dawkins	10	222	22	0
Thompson	1	25	25	0
Tyler	1	23	23	0
Montgomery	1	22	22	0
Lynch	1	14	14	0
Forsberg	1	12	12	0
Simone	1	3	3	0

PASSING – PUNTING – KICKING

PASSING	Att	Comp	%	Yds	Yd/Att	TD	Int–%	RK
Johnson	346	184	53	2465	7.1	20	17– 5	3
Ramsey	27	10	37	194	7.2	2	2– 7	
Anderson	3	2	67	47	15.7	0	0– 0	
Turner	1	0	0	0	0.0	0	1–100	
Van Heusen	1	0	0	0	0.0	0	0– 0	

PUNTING	No	Avg
Van Heusen	69	45.1

KICKING	XP	Att	%	FG	Att	%
Turner	40	40	100	22	33	67

KANSAS CITY CHIEFS

RUSHING

Last Name	No.	Yds	Avg	TD
Podolak	210	721	3.4	3
Ellison	108	411	3.8	2
Hayes	95	352	3.7	2
Kinney	50	128	2.6	1
Livingston	19	94	4.9	2
Dawson	6	40	6.7	0
Wright	5	29	5.8	0
Beathard	6	16	2.7	1
Butler	2	10	5.0	0
McVea	4	5	1.3	0
Keyes	2	1	0.5	0
Taylor	4	–14	–3.5	0

RECEIVING

Last Name	No.	Yds	Avg	TD
Podolak	55	445	8	0
Taylor	34	565	17	4
Hayes	18	134	7	0
Wright	16	252	16	2
Stroud	12	216	18	2
Kinney	11	126	11	0
Ellison	9	64	7	0
Butler	8	124	16	2
West	4	65	16	0
Hamilton	2	35	18	0
Smith	2	20	10	0
Moorman	1	–1	–1	0
Keyes	1	–6	–6	0

PUNT RETURNS

Last Name	No.	Yds	Avg	TD
Marshall	29	180	6	0
Podolak	11	90	8	0
Reardon	2	9	5	0

KICKOFF RETURNS

Last Name	No.	Yds	Avg	TD
Marshall	14	391	28	0
McVea	8	146	18	0
Kinney	5	130	26	0
Reardon	2	45	23	0
Werner	1	13	13	0
West	1	0	0	0

PASSING – PUNTING – KICKING

PASSING	Att	Comp	%	Yds	Yd/Att	TD	Int–%	RK
Livingston	145	75	52	916	6.3	6	7– 5	7
Dawson	101	66	65	725	7.2	2	5– 5	
Beathard	64	31	48	389	6.1	2	1– 2	
Keyes	1	0	0	0	0.0	0	0– 0	
Podolak	1	0	0	0	0.0	0	0– 0	
Wilson	1	1	100	9	9.0	0	0– 0	

PUNTING	No	Avg
Wilson	80	45.5

KICKING	XP	Att	%	FG	Att	%
Stenerud	21	23	91	24	38	63

SAN DIEGO CHARGERS

RUSHING

Last Name	No.	Yds	Avg	TD
Edwards	133	609	4.6	1
Garrett	114	467	4.1	0
Holmes	78	289	3.7	7
C. Jones	55	170	3.1	1
Clark	13	86	6.6	0
Holliday	6	70	11.7	0
Thomas	22	48	2.2	0
LeVias	2	33	16.5	0
Fouts	7	32	4.6	0
Norman	1	10	10.0	0

RECEIVING

Last Name	No.	Yds	Avg	TD
LeVias	30	536	18	3
Edwards	25	164	7	0
Holmes	19	151	8	0
Garrett	15	124	8	1
Garrison	14	292	21	2
Holliday	14	182	13	0
Norman	13	200	15	0
C. Jones	7	126	18	0
Thaxton	7	119	17	2
Dave Williams	7	118	17	0
Thomas	7	51	7	1
McGee	3	67	22	0

PUNT RETURNS

Last Name	No.	Yds	Avg	TD
Smith	27	352	13	2
McGee	6	56	9	0

KICKOFF RETURNS

Last Name	No.	Yds	Avg	TD
Smith	36	947	26	0
McGee	20	423	21	0
C. Jones	10	217	22	0
Rice	2	17	9	0
East	1	8	8	0
Rogers	1	4	4	0
Douglas	1	0	0	0
Wenzel	1	0	0	0
Holliday	0	–2	0	0

PASSING – PUNTING – KICKING

PASSING	Att	Comp	%	Yds	Yd/Att	TD	Int–%	RK
Fouts	194	87	45	1126	5.8	6	13– 7	12
Clark	90	40	44	532	5.9	0	9–10	
Unitas	76	34	45	471	6.2	3	7– 9	
Holliday	2	0	0	0	0.0	0	1–50	
Garrett	1	0	0	0	0.0	0	0– 0	

PUNTING	No	Avg
Partee	72	41.1

KICKING	XP	Att	%	FG	Att	%
Wersching	15	17	88	11	25	44
Partee	4	4	100	1	2	50
Holliday	1	1	100	0	0	0

1973 Championship Games

NFC CHAMPIONSHIP GAME

December 30, at Irving, Texas
(Attendance 60,272)

SCORING

DALLAS	0	0	10	0–10
MINNESOTA	3	7	7	10–27

First Quarter
Minn. — Cox, 44 yard field goal

Second Quarter
Minn. — Foreman, 5 yard rush
PAT–Cox (kick)

Third Quarter
Dall. — Richards, 63 yard punt return
PAT–Fritsch (kick)
Minn. — Gilliam, 54 yard pass from Tarkenton
PAT–Cox (kick)
Dall. — Fritsch, 17 yard field goal

Fourth Quarter
Minn. — Bryant, 63 yard interception return
PAT–Cox (kick)
Minn. — Cox, 34 yard field goal

TEAM STATISTICS

DALLAS		MINN.
9	First Downs–Total	20
3	First Downs–Rushing	14
5	First Downs–Passing	6
1	First Downs–Penalty	0
2	Fumbles–Number	4
2	Fumbles–Lost Ball	3
2	Penalties–Number	3
20	Yards Penalized	33
0	Missed Field Goals	0
49	Offensive Plays	72
153	Net Yards	306
3.1	Average Gain	4.3
6	Giveaways	4
4	Takeaways	6
−2	Difference	+2

Tarkenton's Winning Formula

Fran Tarkenton was in his first playoffs in his thirteen-year career, and he celebrated last week by leading the Vikings to a 27-20 victory over the Redskins. Now he hoped to further destroy his image as a loser by beating the Cowboys, who had defeated the Rams 27-16 in the opening round of the playoffs.

The Vikings established a winning formula on offense in the first half by mixing unexpected passes with a strong running attack. The Minnesota blockers keyed on removing middle linebacker Lee Roy Jordan from all running plays, and with star tackle Bob Lilly out of action with a bad back, the Cowboys could not stop ball carriers Chuck Foreman and Oscar Reed. The Vikings controlled the ball for most of the first half, and their defense foiled the Cowboys whenever they got the ball.

Fred Cox scored Minnesota's first three points with a first-quarter field goal, and the Vikings added a touchdown in the second period on an 86-yard drive capped by Foreman's five-yard run.

The Dallas offense, playing without the injured Calvin Hill, could not crack the Minnesota defense until Golden Richards put the Cowboys on the scoreboard by returning a punt 63 yards for a touchdown. The Cowboys now had the momentum to take the lead, but Tarkenton deflated the Dallas hopes three plays later when he hit John Gilliam with a long bomb that went for a 54-yard touchdown. The Cowboys added a Toni Fritsch field goal late in the period to make the score 17-10 with fifteen minutes left.

Turnovers dominated the final period. The teams took turns giving the ball up until Bobby Bryant intercepted a Staubach pass and returned it 63 yards for a score. Another intercepted pass led to a Cox field goal which lengthened the Viking lead to 27-10. The Cowboys suffered the final indignity late in the game when Walt Garrison fumbled the ball away on the Minnesota two-yard line.

INDIVIDUAL STATISTICS

DALLAS	No	Yds	Avg.	MINNESOTA	No	Yds	Avg.
			RUSHING				
Newhouse	14	40	2.9	Foreman	19	76	4.0
Staubach	5	30	6.0	Reed	18	75	4.2
Garrison	5	9	1.8	Osborn	4	27	6.8
Fugett	1	1	1.0	Tarkenton	4	16	4.0
	25	80	3.2	Brown	2	9	4.5
					47	203	4.3
			RECEIVING				
Hayes	2	25	12.5	Foreman	4	28	7.0
Pearson	2	24	12.0	Gilliam	2	63	31.5
Montgomery	2	15	7.5	Voigt	2	23	11.5
DuPree	1	20	20.0	Lash	1	11	11.0
Garrison	1	10	10.0	Reed	1	8	8.0
Fugett	1	−1	−1.0		10	133	13.3
Newhouse	1	−4	−4.0				
	10	89	8.9				
			PUNTING				
Bateman	4		39.5	Eischeid	3		43.3
			PUNT RETURNS				
Richards	1	63	63.0	Bryant	1	0	0.0
			KICKOFF RETURNS				
Harris	2	54	27.0	West	2	45	22.5
Waters	1	18	18.0	Gilliam	1	21	21.0
	3	72	24.0		3	66	22.0
			INTERCEPTION RETURNS				
Waters	1	1	1.0	Bryant	2	63	31.5
				J. Wright	1	13	13.0
				Siemon	1	0	0.0
					4	76	19.0

PASSING

	Att.	Comp.	Comp. Pct.	Yds.	Int.	Yds/ Att.	Yds/ Comp.	Yards Lost Tackled
DALLAS								
Staubach	21	10	47.6	89	4	4.2	8.9	2–26
MINNESOTA								
Tarkenton	21	10	47.6	133	1	6.3	13.3	4–30

AFC CHAMPIONSHIP GAME

December 30, at Miami
(Attendance 75,105)

SCORING

MIAMI	7	7	3	10–27
OAKLAND	0	0	10	0–10

First Quarter
Miami — Csonka, 11 yard rush
PAT–Yepremian (kick)

Second Quarter
Miami — Csonka, 2 yard rush
PAT–Yepremian (kick)

Third Quarter
Oak. — Blanda, 21 yard field goal
Miami — Yepremian, 42 yard field goal
Oak. — Siani, 25 yard pass from Stabler
PAT–Blanda (kick)

Fourth Quarter
Miami — Yepremian, 26 yard field goal
Miami — Csonka, 2 yard rush
PAT–Yepremian (kick)

TEAM STATISTICS

MIAMI		OAK.
21	First Downs–Total	15
18	First Downs–Rushing	4
2	First Downs–Passing	8
1	First Downs–Penalty	2
1	Fumbles–Number	1
0	Fumbles–Lost Ball	0
3	Penalties–Number	3
26	Yards Penalized	35
0	Missed Field Goals	1
60	Offensive Plays	49
292	Net Yards	236
4.9	Average Gain	4.8
1	Giveaways	1
1	Takeaways	1
0	Difference	0

Bringing the Raiders Down to Earth

The Raiders had used a powerful running attack to beat the Steelers 33-14 in the AFC semifinal match, but the Dolphins, coming off a 34-16 victory over the Bengals, taught the Raiders a lesson about ball control in this AFC title match. Dolphin quarterback Bob Griese passed the ball only six times all game, relying instead on his powerful running backs to grind out the yardage. Larry Csonka and Mercury Morris plowed through gaping holes cut in the Oakland defense by the Miami blockers, and the Dolphins succeeded in eating up both yardage and the clock.

On the first series of the day, the Dolphins drove 64 yards to a touchdown, with the key play of the drive a 27-yard scramble by Griese on third-and-11 on the Oakland 38-yard line. Larry Csonka plowed over from the 11-yard line for the score.

The Raiders threatened in the first period when Ken Stabler hit Mike Siani with a pass deep in Miami territory, but a holding penalty nullified the play and extinguished the threat. The Dolphins, meanwhile, put together another long drive late in the half, and Csonka scored from the 2 after Griese had frozen the Raiders by faking a roll-out.

George Blanda put the Raiders on the scoreboard early in the second half with a 21-yard field goal, but Charley Leigh's 52-yard return of the kickoff led to Garo Yepremian's 42-yard three-pointer to make the score 17-3. Stabler started clicking on short passes late in the period, and his 25-yard scoring pitch to Siani narrowed the Miami lead to 17-10.

The Dolphins gave themselves some breathing room five minutes into the fourth quarter with a Yepremian field goal, and when the defensive unit stopped the Raiders on a fourth-and-inches try, the Miami attack ground out a final touchdown to run the winning margin to 27-10.

INDIVIDUAL STATISTICS

MIAMI	No	Yds	Avg.	OAKLAND	No	Yds	Avg.
			RUSHING				
Csonka	29	117	4.0	Hubbard	10	54	5.4
Morris	14	86	6.1	C. Smith	10	35	3.5
Griese	3	39	13.0	C. Davis	4	15	3.8
Kiick	6	12	2.0	Banaszak	2	3	1.5
Nottingham	1	12	12.0		26	107	4.1
	53	266	5.0				
			RECEIVING				
Warfield	1	27	27.0	C. Smith	5	43	8.6
Briscoe	1	6	6.0	Siani	3	45	15.0
Kiick	1	1	1.0	Biletnikoff	2	15	7.5
	3	34	11.3	Hubbard	2	11	5.5
				Moore	1	9	4.5
				C. Davis	1	6	6.0
					15	129	8.6
			PUNTING				
Seiple	1		39.0	Guy	2		51.0
			PUNT RETURNS				
Scott	2	10	5.0	Atkinson	1	0	0.0
			KICKOFF RETURNS				
Leigh	1	52	52.0	C. Davis	3	68	22.7
Morris	1	19	19.0	C. Smith	1	21	21.0
Nottingham	1	19	19.0		4	89	22.3
	3	90	30.0				
			INTERCEPTION RETURNS				
Matheson	1	29	29.0	W. Brown	1	0	0.0

PASSING

	Att.	Comp.	Comp. Pct.	Yds.	Int.	Yds/ Att.	Yds/ Comp.	Yards Lost Tackled
MIAMI								
Griese	6	3	50.0	34	1	5.7	11.3	1–8
OAKLAND								
Stabler	23	15	65.2	129	1	5.6	8.6	0–0

SUPER BOWL VIII

January 13, at Houston

(Attendance 68,142)

Dolphin Defense and Csonka Crashes

The Dolphins did not enjoy a perfect season this year, but they did play an almost perfect game against the Vikings in the Super Bowl. After receiving the opening kickoff, the Dolphins immediately set the tone of the day with a crunching 62-yard drive. With the Miami line ripping the famous Minnesota front four to shreds, Larry Csonka repeatedly burst through the middle for good yardage. On the tenth play of the drive, Csonka bulled into the end zone from five yards out; the Dolphins now had a 7-0 lead to nurse.

Viking quarterback Fran Tarkenton, a man eager to erase his image as a loser, could make no progress against the swarming Miami defense. The Dolphin line smothered the Minnesota running game, and the Dolphin zone defense made passing a very risky proposition. Tarkenton tried every play in the Viking playbook to no avail.

The Dolphins, meanwhile, did not stop with their seven-point lead. With Bob Griese passing very rarely, the Miami attack continued to move the ball on the ground. The Dolphin linemen habitually beat the Viking front four off the ball, slamming into them before they could react; Minnesota ends Carl Eller and Jim Marshall were taken out of almost every play. The second Dolphin touchdown came late in the opening quarter on a plunge by Jim Kiick, who had not scored all season. Garo Yepremian added the extra point, and the 14-0 lead looked close to impregnable.

Yepremian added a field goal in the second quarter to give the Dolphins a 17-0 halftime edge that understated the one-sidedness of the first half. The Vikings were not making out-and-out blunders; they simply were being beaten by better blocking and tackling. They did make a mistake on the second-half kickoff when a clipping penalty called back a long return by John Gilliam. The momentum which the return had given to the Vikings immediately shifted back to the Dolphins, and within seven minutes Csonka drove into the end zone for the third Miami touchdown.

With the decision no longer in doubt, the Vikings got onto the scoreboard in the fourth quarter on a touchdown run by Tarkenton. After Cox booted the extra point, the Vikings shocked Miami by recovering an on-side kick; once again, however, a penalty nullified the play and nipped a Minnesota rally before it could begin.

By the end of the day, the Dolphins again were undisputed champions of pro football, and Larry Csonka had set a Super Bowl rushing record with 145 hard-fought yards. With two straight championships to their credit, the Dolphins now drew comparisons with the Packers of Vince Lombardi's era. Although Marv Fleming, who played on both clubs, said, "This is the greatest team ever," the question joined the ranks of unanswerable sports fantasies.

LINEUPS

MIAMI		MINNESOTA
	OFFENSE	
Warfield	WR	Dale
W. Moore	LT	Alderman
Kuechenberg	LG	White
Langer	C	Tinglehoff
Little	RG	Gallagher
Evans	RT	Yary
Mandich	TE	Voigt
Briscoe	WR	Gilliam
Griese	QB	Tarkenton
Morris	RB	Foreman
Csonka	RB	Reed
	DEFENSE	
Den Herder	LE	Eller
Fernandez	LT	Larsen
Heinz	RT	Page
Stanfill	RE	Marshall
Swift	LLB	Winston
Buoniconti	MLB	Siemon
Kolen	RLB	Hilgenberg
Mumphord	LCB	N. Wright
Johnson	RCB	Bryant
Anderson	LS	J. Wright
Scott	RS	Krause

SUBSTITUTES

MIAMI

OFFENSE	
Crusan	Morrall
Fleming	Newman
Goode	Nottingham
Kiick	Twilley
DEFENSE	
Babb	Matheson
Ball	M. Moore
Bannon	Stuckey
Foley	
KICKERS	
Seiple	Yepremian

MINNESOTA

OFFENSE	
B. Brown	Lash
Goodrum	Marinaro
Kingsriter	Osborn
DEFENSE	
T. Brown	Porter
Lurtsema	Sutherland
Martin	West
KICKERS	
Cox	Eischeid

SCORING

MIAMI	14	3	7	0	–24
MINNESOTA	0	0	0	7	– 7

First Quarter
- Mia. Csonka, 5 yard rush 9:33 — PAT – Yepremian (kick)
- Mia. Kiick, 1 yard rush 13:38 — PAT – Yepremian (kick)

Second Quarter
- Mia. Yepremian, 28 yard field goal 8:58

Third Quarter
- Mia. Csonka, 2 yard rush 6:16 — PAT – Yepremian (kick)

Fourth Quarter
- Minn. Tarkenton, 4 yard rush 1:35 — PAT – Cox (kick)

TEAM STATISTICS

MIAMI		MINN.
21	First Downs – Total	14
13	First Downs – Rushing	5
4	First Downs – Passing	8
4	First Downs – Penalty	1
1	Fumbles – Number	2
0	Fumbles – Lost Ball	1
1	Penalties – Number	7
4	Yards Penalized	65
0	Missed Field Goals	0
61	Offensive Plays	54
259	Net Yards	238
4.2	Average Gain	4.4
0	Giveaways	2
2	Takeaways	0
+2	Difference	–2

INDIVIDUAL STATISTICS

MIAMI	No	Yds	Avg.	MINNESOTA	No	Yds	Avg.
				RUSHING			
Csonka	33	145	4.4	Reed	11	32	2.9
Morris	11	34	3.1	Foreman	7	18	2.6
Kiick	7	10	1.4	Tarkenton	4	17	4.3
Griese	2	7	3.5	Marinaro	1	3	3.0
	53	196	3.7	B. Brown	1	2	2.0
					24	72	3.0
				RECEIVING			
Warfield	2	33	16.5	Foreman	5	27	5.4
Mandich	2	21	10.5	Gilliam	4	44	11.0
Briscoe	2	19	9.5	Voigt	3	46	15.3
	6	73	12.2	Marinaro	2	39	19.5
				B. Brown	1	9	9.0
				Kingsriter	1	9	9.0
				Lash	1	9	9.0
				Reed	1	–1	–1.0
					18	182	10.1
				PUNTING			
Seiple	3		39.6	Eischeid	5		42.2
				PUNT RETURNS			
Scott	3	20	6.7				
				KICKOFF RETURNS			
Scott	2	47	23.5	Gilliam	2	41	20.5
				West	2	28	14.0
					4	69	17.3
				INTERCEPTION RETURNS			
Johnson	1	10	10.0	None			

PASSING

	Att	Comp	Comp Pct.	Yds	Int	Yds/ Att.	Yds/ Comp	Yards Lost Tackled
MIAMI								
Griese	7	6	85.7	73	0	10.4	12.2	1–10
MINNESOTA								
Tarkenton	28	18	64.3	182	1	6.5	10.1	2–16

Use Name (Nicknames) – Positions	Team by Year	See Section	Hgt	Wgt	College	Int	Pts
Abell, Bud LB	66-68KC-A		6'3"	220	Missouri	2	
Abramowicz, Dan WR-OE	67-73NO 73SF	2	6'1"	195	Xavier-Ohio		228
Abruzzese, Ray DB	62-64BufA 65-66NY-A		6'1"	194	Alabama	10	
Absher, Dick LB	67Was 67-68Atl 69-71NO 72Phi		6'4"	231	Maryland	3	4
Acks, Ron LB	68-71Atl 72-73NE		6'2"	223	Illinois	2	6
Adamchik, Ed C	65NYG 65Pit		6'2"	235	Pittsburgh		
Adamle, Mike HB	71-72KC 73NYJ	2	5'9"	197	Northwestern		12
Adams, Bill OG	72Buf		6'2"	250	Holy Cross		
Adams, Bob TE	69-71Pit 72JJ 73NE	2	6'2"	225	U. of Pacific		
Adams, Doug LB	71-73Cin		6'	224	Ohio State	3	
Adams, John FB-OE	59-62ChiB 63LA	2	6'3"	235	Los Angeles State		24
Adams, Julius DT-DE	71-73NE		6'3"	258	Texas Southern		
Adams, Sam OG	72-73NE		6'3"	252	Prairie View		
Adams, Tom OE	62Min		6'5"	210	Minnesota-Duluth		
Adams, Willie LB-DE	65-66Was		6'2"	235	New Mexico State		
Adamson, Ken OG	60-62DenA		6'2"	222	Notre Dame		
Adderly, Herb DB	61-69GB 70-72Dal	3	6'1"	204	Michigan State	48	54
Addison, Tom LB	60-67BosA		6'3"	231	South Carolina	16	6
Adkins, Margene WR	70-71Dal 72NO 73NYJ	23	5'10"	183	Henderson J. C.		
Akin, Harold OT	67-68SD-A		6'5"	261	Oklahoma State		
Alderman, Grady OT-OG	60Det 61-73Min		6'2"	241	Detroit		
Aldridge, Allen DE	71-72Hou		6'6"	260	Prairie View		
Aldridge, Lionel DE	63-71GB 72-73SD		6'4"	245	Utah State		6
Alexakos, Steve OG	70Den 71NYG		6'2"	260	San Diego State		
Alexander, Glenn WR	70Buf		6'3"	205	Grambling		
Alexander, Kermit DB	63-69SF 70-71LA 72-73Phi	3	5'11"	185	U. C. L. A.	43	36
Alexander, Willie DB	71-73Hou		6'2"	195	Alcorn A&M	8	
Alfen, Ted DB-HB	69DenA		6'	195	Springfield		
Alford, Bruce K	67Was 68-69BufA	5	6'	185	Texas Christian		134
Alford, Mike C	65StL 66Det		6'3"	233	Auburn		
Allard, Don QB	61NY-A 62BosA		6'	189	Boston College		
Allen, Buddy HB	61DenA		5'10"	190	Utah State		
Allen, Chuck LB	61-69SD-A 70-71Pit 72Phi		6'1"	224	Washington	28	12
Allen, Dalva DE	60-61HouA 62-64OakA		6'5"	244	Houston	1	
Allen, Don FB	60DenA	2	6'	200	Texas		6
Allen, Duane OE-TE	61-64LA 65Pit 65Bal 66-67ChiB	2	6'4"	221	Santa Ana J. C.		30
Allen, George OT	66HouA		6'7"	270	West Texas State		
Allen, George	HC66-70LA HC71-73Was				Michigan		
Allen, Grady LB	68-72Atl		6'3"	226	Texas A&M	2	
Allen, Jackie DB	69OakA 70-71Buf 72Phi 73JJ		6'1"	187	Baylor		
Allen, Jeff DB	71StL 72JJ		5'11"	190	Iowa State		
Allen, Jerry HB	66Bal 67-69Was	2	6'1"	204	Nebraska-Omaha		54
Allen, Nate DB	71-73KC		5'10"	170	Texas Southern	2	
Alley, Don WR-FL	67Bal 69Pit		6'2"	200	Adams State		
Allison, Henry OG	71-72Phi		6'2"	255	San Diego State		
Allison, Jim FB	65-68SD-A	2	6'	220	San Diego State		12
Alliston, Vaughan LB	60DenA		6'	218	Mississippi	1	
Alston, Mack TE	70-72Was 73Hou	2	6'2"	230	Md. Eastern Shore		
Alworth, Lance FL-WR-OE	62-70SD-A 71-72Dal	23	6'	182	Arkansas		524
Alzado, Lyle DE	71-73Den		6'3"	252	Yankton		
Amerson, Glen DB	61Phi		6'1"	186	Texas Tech		
Ames, Dave HB-DB	61NY-A 61DenA		6'	185	Richmond	1	
Amman, Dick DE-DT	72-73Bal		6'5"	242	Florida State		
Amsler, Marty DE	67ChiB 68JJ 69ChiB 70GB		6'5"	257	Indiana, Evansville	1	
Amundson, George HB-FB	73Hou		6'3"	215	Iowa State		
Anderson, Art OT	61-62ChiB 63Pit		6'3"	244	Idaho		
Anderson, Bill OE-TE	58-63Was 65-66GB	2	6'3"	211	Tennessee		90
Anderson, Billy QB	67HouA		6'1"	195	Tulsa		
Anderson, Bob HB	63NYG		6'2"	210	Army		
Anderson, Bobby HB-FB	70-73Den	23	6'	208	Colorado		66
Anderson, Bruce DE-DT	66LA 67-69NYG 70Was		6'4"	246	Willamette		
Anderson, Chet TE	67Pit		6'3"	245	Minnesota		12
Anderson, Dick OT	67NO		6'5"	245	Ohio State		2
Anderson, Dick DB	68-73MiaA	3	6'2"	200	Colorado	32	24
Anderson, Donny HB	66-71GB 72-73StL	234	6'3"	211	Texas Tech		300
Anderson, Ken QB	71-73Cin	12	6'1"	208	Augustana		24
Anderson, Max HB	68-69BufA 70JJ 71Buf	23	5'8"	180	Arizona State		24
Anderson, Ralph OE	58ChiB 60LA-A	2	6'4"	223	Los Angeles State		36
died Nov. 26, 1960—diabetes							
Anderson, Ralph DB	71-72Pit 73NE		6'2"	180	West Texas State	6	2
Anderson, Roger DT-OT	64-65NYG 66CFL 67-68NYG		6'5"	263	Virginia Union	1	
Anderson, Taz OE-TE	61-64StL 66-67Atl	2	6'2"	208	Georgia Tech		60
Andrews, Al LB	70-71Buf		6'3"	216	New Mexico State	1	
Andrews, Billy LB	67-73Cle		6'	224	Southeastern La.	5	6
Andrews, John LB-TE	72SD 73Bal		6'3"	226	Indiana		6
Andrie, George DE	62-72Dal		6'7"	252	Marquette	1	14
Andrus, Lou LB	67DenA		6'6"	255	Brigham Young		
Antoine, Lionel OT	72-73ChiB		6'6"	255	Southern Illinois		
Antwine, Houston DT	61-69BosA 70Bos 71NE 72Phi		6'	265	Southern Illinois	1	
Apple, Jim HB	61NY-A		6'	200	Upsala		
Appleton, Scott DT	64-66HouA 67-68SD-A		6'3"	254	Texas	2	6
Arbanas, Fred TE-OE	61XJ 62DalA 63-69KC-A 70KC	2	6'3"	240	Michigan State		206
Archer, Dan OG-OT	67OakA 68CinA		6'5"	245	Oregon		
Armstrong, Otis HB	73Den	2	5'10"	196	Purdue		6
Armstrong, Ray DT	60OakA		6'1"	235	Texas Christian		
Arndt, Dick DT	67-70Pit		6'5"	265	Idaho		
Arneson, Jim OG-C	73Dal		6'3"	236	Arizona		
Arneson, Mark LB	72-73StL		6'2"	220	Arizona	1	
Arnett, Jon HB-FL-OE	57-63LA 64-66ChiB	123	5'11"	197	Southern Calif.		234
Arrington, Rick QB	70-72Phi	1	6'2"	187	Tulsa		6
Arrobio, Chuck OT	66Min		6'4"	250	Southern Calif.		
Arthur, Gary TE	70-71NYJ		6'5"	230	Miami—Ohio		
Asad, Doug OE	60-61OakA	2	6'3"	203	Northwestern		18
Asbury, Willie FB	66-68Pit	2	6'1"	230	Kent State		78
Asher, Bob OT-OG	70Dal 71JJ 72-73ChiB		6'5"	250	Vanderbilt		
Ashton, Josh HB-FB	72-73NE	2	6'1"	205	Tulsa		24
Askea, Mike OT	73Den		6'4"	260	Stanford		
Askon, Bert DE-TE	71Pit 73NO		6'3"	220	Texas Southern		
Atchason, Jack OE	60BosA 60HouA		6'4"	215	Western Illinois		6
Atessis, Bill DT-DE	71NE		6'3"	240	Texas		

Use Name (Nicknames) – Positions	Team by Year	See Section	Hgt	Wgt	College	Int	Pts
Athas, Pete DB	71-73NYG	3	5'11"	196	Tennessee	11	6
Atkins, Billy DB-HB	58-59SF 60-61BufA 62-63NY-A 63BufA 64DenA	45	6'1"	196	Auburn	20	86
Atkins, Bob DB	68-69StL 70-73Hou		6'3"	212	Grambling	9	6
Atkins, Dave HB	73SF		6'1"	202	Texas—El Paso		6
Atkins, Doug DE	53-54Cle 55-66ChiB 67-69NO		6'8"	257	Tennessee	3	2
Atkins, Pervis HB-FL-OE	61-63LA 64-65Was 65-66OakA	23	6'1"	200	New Mexico State		18
Atkinson, Al LB	65-69NY-A 70-73NYJ		6'1"	229	Villanova	21	
Atkinson, Butch DB	68-69OakA 70-73Oak	3	6'	180	Morris Brown	20	42
Atkinson, Frank DT	63Pit		6'3"	240	Stanford		
Auer, Joe HB	64-65BufA 66-67MiaA 68Atl	23	6'1"	204	Georgia Tech		90
Austin, Hise DB	73GB		6'4"	195	Prairie View		
Austin, Ocie DB	70-71Pit		6'3"	200	Utah State	3	
Autry, Hank C	69HouA 70Hou		6'3"	233	Southern Miss.		
Aveni, John OE-K	59-60ChiB 61Was	5	6'3"	212	Indiana		144
Avery, Jim TE	66Was		6'2"	235	Northern Illinois		
Avery Ken LB	67-68NYG 69CinA 70-73Cin		6'1"	225	Southern Miss.	2	
Avezzano, Joe C	66BosA		6'2"	235	Florida State		
Babb, Charlie DB	72-73Mia		6'	190	Memphis State	1	
Babb, Gene FB-LB	57-58SF 60-61Dal 62-63HouA	2	6'3"	216	Austin	4	30
Babich, Bob LB	70-72SD 73Cle		6'2"	230	Miami (Fla.)	3	6
Babinecz, John LB	72-73Dal		6'1"	222	Villanova		
Baccaglio, Marty DE	68SD-A 68-69CinA 70Cin		6'3"	245	San Jose State		
Bachman, Jay C	68-69DenA 70-71Den		6'3"	250	Cincinnati		
Bacon, Coy DE-DT	68-72LA 73SD		6'4"	270	Jackson State	2	6
Badar, Rich QB	67Pit		6'1"	190	Indiana		
Bailey, Jim DT-DE	70-73Bal		6'4"	250	Kansas		
Bailey, Monk DB	64-65StL		6'	178	Utah		
Bailey, Teddy HB	67BufA 69BosA		6'	210	Cincinnati		
Bailey, Tom HB-FB	71-73Phi	2	6'2"	211	Florida State		12
Baird, Bill DB-HB	63-69NY-A	3	5'10"	180	San Fran. State	34	18
Baker, Art FB	61-62BufA	2	6'	220	Syracuse		24
Baker, Dave DB	59-61SF 62-63MS		6'	192	Oklahoma	21	
Baker, Ed QB	72Hou		6'2"	198	Lafayette		
Baker, John DE-DT-OT	58-61LA 62Phi 63-67Pit 68Det		6'6"	279	N. Car. Central	2	
Baker, John DE	70NYG		6'5"	260	Norfolk State		
Baker, Johnny LB-OE	63-66HouA 67SD-A		6'3"	229	Mississippi State	2	6
Baker, Larry OT	60NY-A		6'2"	240	Bowling Green		
Baker, Ralph LB	64-69NY-A 70-73NYJ		6'3"	232	Penn State	17	7
Baker, Sam FB-K	53Was 54-55MS 56-59Was 60-61Cle 62-63Dal 64-69Phi	2 45	6'2"	217	Oregon State		977
Baker, Terry HB-QB	63-65LA	2	6'3"	198	Oregon State		18
Baker, Tony FB-HB	68-71NO 71-72Phi 73LA	2	5'11"	227	Iowa State		66
Bakken, Jim K	62-73StL	45	6'	199	Wisconsin		1005
Baldwin, Bob HB-FB	66Bal		6'1"	225	Clemson		
Ball, Larry LB	72-73Mia		6'6"	225	Louisville	1	
Ball, Sam OT	66-70Bal		6'4"	240	Kentucky		
Ballman, Gary WR-FL-OE-TE-HB	62-66Pit 67-72Phi 73NYG 73Min	23	6'	203	Michigan State		252
Ballou, Mike LB	70Bos		6'3"	235	U. C. L. A.		
Banaszak, Pete HB-FB	66-69OakA 70-73Oak	2	5'11"	204	Miami (Fla.)		126
Banaszek, Cas OT	67NJ 68-73SF		6'3"	246	Northwestern		
Bandy, Don OG	67-68Was		6'3"	250	Tulsa		
Banfield, Tony DB	60-63, 65HouA		6'1"	185	Oklahoma State	27	6
Banks, Estes FB-HB	67OakA 68CinA	2	6'1"	210	Colorado		6
Banks, Tom C-OG	71-73StL		6'1"	240	Auburn		
Banks, Willie OG	68-69Was 70NYG 73NE		6'2"	240	Alcorn A&M		
Bankston, Warren FB-TE	69-72Pit 73Oak	2	6'4"	230	Tulane		18
Bannon, Bruce LB	73Mia		6'3"	225	Penn State		
Bansavage, Al LB	60LA-A 61OakA		6'2"	225	Southern Calif.		
Barbee, Joe DT	60OakA		6'3"	250	Kent State		
Barber, Rudy LB	68MiaA		6'1"	255	Bethune-Cookman		
Barber,Stew OT-LB	61-69BufA		6'3"	247	Penn State	3	6
Barefoot, Ken TE	68Was		6'5"	228	Virginia Tech		6
Barisich, Carl DT	73Cle		6'4"	255	Princeton		
Barkum, Jerome WR	72-73NYJ	2	6'3"	215	Jackson State		48
Barnes, Al WR	72-73Det		6'1"	170	New Mexico State		12
Barnes, Benny DB	72-73Dal		6'1"	190	Stanford	1	4
Barnes, Billy HB	57-61Phi 62-63Was 65-66Min	12	5'11"	201	Wake Forest		228
Barnes, Bruce K	73NE	4	5'11"	215	U. C. L. A		
Barnes, Charlie OE	61DalA		6'5"	230	Northeast La.		
Barnes, Erich DB	58-60ChiB 61-64NYG 65-71Cle		6'2"	201	Purdue	45	60
Barnes, Ernie OG-OT	60NY-A 61-62SD-A 63-64DenA		6'3"	250	N. Car. Central		
Barnes, Gary OE-FL	62GB 63Dal 64ChiB 66-67Atl	2	6'4"	210	Clemson		12
Barnes, Mike DE	73Bal		6'6"	255	Miami (Fla.)		
Barnes, Mike DB	67-68StL		6'3"	205	Texas-Arlington		
Barnes, Pete LB	67-68HouA 69SD-A 70-72SD 73StL		6'3"	244	Southern U.	12	6
Barnes, Rodrigo LB	73Dal		6'1"	215	Rice		
Barnes, Walt DE-DT	66-68Was 69DenA 70-71Den 72JJ		6'3"	250	Nebraska		
Barnett, Steve OT	63ChiB 64Was		6'1"	255	Oregon		
Barney, Eppie WR-FL	67-68Cle	2	6'	201	Iowa State		12
Barney, Lem DB	67-73Det	34	6'	189	Jackson State	42	60
Barr, Terry, FL-DB-HB	57-65Det	23	6'	189	Michigan	5	228
Barrett, Bob OE	60BufA		6'3"	200	Baldwin-Wallace		
Barrett, Jan OE	63GB 63-64OakA	2	6'3"	226	Fresno State		12
Barrett, Jean OT-C	73SF		6'6"	254	Tulsa		
Barrington, Tom HB-FB	66Was 67-70NO	23	6'1"	214	Ohio State		24
Barry, Fred DB	70Pit		5'10"	184	Boston U.		
Barry, Odell OE	64-65DenA	3	5'10"	180	Findlay		6
Barton, Greg QB	69Det 71CFL		6'2"	195	Tulsa		
Barton, Jim C	60DalA 61-62DenA		6'5"	250	Marshall		
Bass, Dick FB-HB	60-69LA	23	5'10"	197	U. of Pacific		252
Bass, Glenn OE-HB-FL-WR	61-66BufA 67-68HouA	2	6'2"	202	East Carolina		102
Bass, Mike DB	67Det 69-73Was		6'	190	Michigan	23	18
Bass, Norm DB	64DenA		6'3"	210	U. of Pacific		
61-63 played major league baseball							
Bateman, Marv K	72-73DAl	4	6'4"	213	Utah		1
Bates, Ted LB	59ChiC 60-62StL 63NY-A		6'3"	219	Oregon State		
Batten, Pat FB	64Det		6'2"	225	Hardin-Simmons		
Battle, Jim OG	63Min		6'1"	240	Southern Illinois		
Battle, Jim OT	66Cle		6'4"	235	Southern U.		
Battle, Mike DB	69NY-A 70NYJ	3	6'1"	175	Southern Calif.	1	

Use Name (Nicknames) – Positions	Team by Year	See Section	Hgt	Wgt	College	Int	Pts
Baughan, Maxie LB	60-65Phi 66-70LA		6'1"	227	Georgia Tech	18	6
Baumgartner, Steve DE	73NO		6'7"	260	Purdue		
Bayless, Tom OG	70NYJ		6'3"	240	Purdue		
Baynham, Craig HB	67-69Dal 70ChiB 71JJ 72StL	23	6'1"	204	Georgia Tech		54
Beach, Walter DB	60-61BosA 63-66Cle		6'	184	Central Michigan	6	12
Beal, Norm DB	62StL		5'11"	170	Missouri		
Beamer, Tim DB	71Buf		5'11"	185	Johnson C. Smith		
Beams, Byron OT-DT	59-60Pit 61HouA		6'6"	249	Notre Dame		
Beard, Ed LB	65-72SF		6'2"	225	Tennessee	3	
Beard, Tom C	72Buf		6'6"	280	Michigan State		
Beasley, John TE	67-70Min 71JJ 72-73Min 73NO	2	6'3"	229	California		84
Beasley, Terry WR	72SF 73SJ		5'10"	184	Auburn		
Beathard, Pete QB	64-67KC-A 67-69HouA 70-71StL 72LA 73KC	12	6'2"	205	Southern Calif.		68
Beatty, Chuck DB	69-72Pit 72StL		6'2"	203	North Texas State	4	6
Beauchamp, Al LB	68-69CinA 70-73Cin		6'2"	236	Southern U.	14	18
Beauchamp, Joe DB	66-69SD-A 70-73SD		6'	185	Iowa State	21	18
Beaver, Jim DT	62Phi		6'1"	235	Florida		
Beban, Gary QB-HB-WR	68-69Was		6'1"	195	U. C. L. A.		
Bebout, Nick OT	73Atl		6'5"	260	Wyoming		
Beck, Braden K	71Hou		6'2"	200	Stanford		4
Beckman, Tom DE	72StL		6'5"	250	Michigan		
Bedsole, Hal TE-OE	64-66Min 67JJ	2	6'4"	230	Southern Calif.		48
Beer, Tom TE-OG	67-69DenA 70Bos 71-72NE	2	6'4"	232	Houston		24
Behrman, Dave OT-C	63,65BufA 67DenA		6'5"	260	Michigan State		
Beier, Tom DB-FL	67,69MiaA		5'11"	198	Georgia Tech	2	
Beirne, Jim WR-TE	68-69HouA 70-73Hou	2	6'2"	196	Purdue		68
Beisler, Randy OG-DE-OT-DT	66-68Phi 69-73SF		6'4"	249	Indiana	1	
Belden, Bob QB	69-70Dal		6'2"	208	Notre Dame		
Belk, Bill DE	68-73SF		6'3"	249	Md. Eastern Shore	1	6
Bell, Bill K	71-72Atl 73NE	5	6'1"	191	Kansas		154
Bell, Bob DT	71-73Det		6'4"	250	Cincinnati		6
Bell, Bobby LB-DE	63-69KC-A 70-73KC		6'4"	228	Minnesota	25	48
Bell, Carlos TE	71NO 72JJ		6'5"	238	Houston		
Bell, Eddie WR	70-73NYJ	2	5'10"	160	Idaho State		42
Bell, Henry HB	60DenA	2	5'10"	210	none		
Bellino, Joe HB-FL	65-67BosA	23	5'9"	186	Navy		6
Belotti, George C	60-61HouA 61SD-A		6'4"	253	Southern Calif.		
Belser, Caesar DB	68-69KC-A 70-71KC		6'	212	Ark.-Pine Bluff		
Belton, Willie HB	71-72Atl 73StL	23	5'11"	199	Md. Eastern Shore		6
Bemiller, Al C-OG	61-69BufA		6'3"	243	Syracuse		
Bengtson, Phil	HC68-70GB				Minnesota		
Bennett, Phil LB	60BosA		6'3"	225	Miami (Fla.)		
Benson, Duane LB	67-69OakA 70-71Oak 72-73Atl		6'2"	215	Hamline	1	
Benz, Larry DB	63-65Cle		5'11"	185	Northwestern	16	
Bercich, Bob DB	60-61Dal		6'1"	198	Michigan State	5	
Berger, Ron DE-DT	69BosA 70Bos 71-72NE		6'8"	278	Wayne State		
Bergey, Bill LB	69CinA 70-73Cin		6'2"	241	Arkansas State	9	
Bergey, Bruce DE	71KC		6'4"	240	U. C. L. A.		
Bernet, Lee OT	65-66DenA		6'2"	245	Wisconsin		
Berry, Bob QB	65-67Min 68-72Atl 73Min	12	5'11"	189	Oregon		24
Berry, Ray OE	55-67Bal	2	6'2"	189	S. M. U.		408
Berry, Reggie DB	72-73SD		6'	190	Long Beach State		
Berry, Royce DE	69CinA 70-73Cin		6'3"	248	Houston		12
Bertelsen, Jim HB	72-73LA	23	5'11"	205	Texas		66
Best, Keith LB	72KC		6'3"	220	Kansas State		
Bethea, Elvin DE	68-69HouA 70-73Hou		6'3"	257	N. Carolina A&T		2
Bethune, Bob DB	62SD-A		5'11"	190	Mississippi State	3	
Bettridge, Ed LB	64Cle		6'1"	235	Bowling Green		
Beutler, Tom LB	70Cle 71Bal		6'1"	232	Toledo		
Beverly, Ed WR	73SF		5'11"	168	Arizona State		
Beverly, Randy DB	67-69NY-A 70Bos 71NE		5'11"	189	Colorado State	12	6
Biggs, Verlon DE-DT	65-69NY-A 70NYG 71-73Was		6'4"	266	Jackson State	1	12
Biletnikoff, Fred WR-FL	65-69OakA 70-73Oak	2	6'1"	190	Florida State		324
Billingsley, Ron DT-DE	67-69SD-A 70SD 71-72Hou 73JJ		6'8"	278	Wyoming		
Bingham, Greg LB	73Hou		6'1"	227	Purdue	2	
Biodrowski, Denny OG	63-67KC-A		6'1"	255	Memphis State		
Bird, Rodger DB	66-68OakA	3	5'11"	195	Kentucky	7	6
Birdwell, Dan DT-DE	62-69OakA		6'4"	247	Houston	4	2
Bishop, Don DB-FL-HB	58-59Pit 59ChiB 60-65Dal		6'2"	209	Los Ang. City C.	22	6
Bishop, Sonny OG	62DalA 63OakA 64-69HouA		6'2"	243	Fresno State		
Bivins, Charlie HB-TE	60-66ChiB 67Pit 67BufA	23	6'2"	212	Morris Brown		36
Bjorkland, Hank HB	72-73NYJ	2	6'1"	200	Princeton		
Blackwood, Lyle DB	73Cin		6'	190	Texas Christian		
Blahak, Joe DB	73Hou		5'9"	182	Nebraska		2
Blaine, Ed OG	62GB 63-66Phi		6'2"	240	Missouri		
Blair, George DB	61-64SD-A	5	5'11"	194	Mississippi	5	272
Blanchard, Dick LB	72NE		6'3"	225	Tulsa	1	
Blanchard, Tom K	71-73NYG	4	6'	190	Oregon		
Blanda, George QB-DB-LB	49-58ChiB 60-66HouA 67-69OakA 70-73Oak	12 5	6'1"	210	Kentucky	1	1840
Blanks, Sid HB	64HouA 65KJ 66-68HouA 69BosA 70Bos	23	6'	206	Texas A&I		66
Blazer, Phil OG	60BufA		6'1"	235	North Carolina		
Bleick, Tom DB	66Bal 67Atl		6'2"	200	Georgia Tech		
Bleier, Rocky HB	68Pit 69MS 70 – inj. from MS 71-73Pit		5'11"	201	Notre Dame		
Blount, Mel DB	70-73Pit		6'3"	205	Southern U.	10	6
Blue, Forrest C-OT	68-73SF		6'5"	256	Auburn		6
Blye, Ronnie HB	68NYG 69Phi	23	5'11"	185	Notre Dame, Florida A & M		6
Bobo, Hubert LB	60LA-A 61-62NY-A		6'1"	217	Ohio State	5	
Boeke, Jim OT	60-63LA 64-67Dal 68NO		6'5"	250	Heidelberg		
Bohling, Dewey HB	60-61NY-A 61BufA	2	5'11"	190	Hardin-Simmons		54
Bohovich, Reed OG-OT	62NYG		6'3"	260	Lehigh		
Bolin, Bookie OG	62-67NYG 68-69Min		6'2"	240	Mississippi		
Bolton, Ron DB	72-73NE		6'2"	180	Virginia State	6	
Bookman, Johnny DB	57NYG 60DalA 61NY-A		5'11"	182	Miami (Fla.)	13	6
Boozer, Emerson HB	66-69NY-A 70-73NYJ	23	5'11"	203	Md. Eastern Shore		354
Bosch, Frank DT	68-70Was		6'4"	246	Colorado		
Bosley, Bruce OG-C-DE	56-68SF 69Atl		6'2"	241	West Virginia		
Bosseler, Don FB	57-64Was	2	6'1"	212	Miami (Fla.)		138
Boston, McKinley DE-LB	68-69NYG		6'2"	245	Minnesota		

Use Name (Nicknames) – Positions	Team by Year	See Section	Hgt	Wgt	College	Int	Pts
Botchan, Ron LB	60LA-A 61HouA		6'1"	234	Occidental	2	
Boudreaux, Jim OT-DE	66-68BosA		6'4"	245	Louisiana Tech		
Bouggess, Lee FB	70-71Phi 72JJ 73Phi	2	6'2"	210	Louisville		48
Boutwell, Tommy WR-QB	69MiaA		6'2"	205	Southern Miss.		
Bowdell, Gordon WR	71Den		6'2"	203	Michigan		
Bowie, Larry OG	62-68Min		6'2"	247	Purdue		
Bowling, Andy LB	67Atl		6'3"	235	Virginia Tech		
Bowman, Ken C	64-73GB		6'3"	230	Wisconsin		
Bowman, Steve HB	66NYG		6'	195	Alabama		
Boyd, Bobby DB-HB	60-68Bal		5'10"	190	Oklahoma	57	30
Boyd, Greg DB	73NE		6'2"	200	Arizona		
Boyette, Garland LB	62-63StL 66-69HouA 70-72Hou		6'1"	237	Grambling	2	6
Boylan, Jim FL	63Min		6'1"	185	Washington State		6
Boynton, George DB	62OakA		5'11"	190	East Texas State		
Boynton, John OT	69MiaA		6'4"	255	Tennessee		
Brase, Ordell DE	57-68Bal		6'4"	240	South Dakota		12
Brabham, Danny LB	63-67HouA 68CinA		6'4"	236	Arkansas	1	
Bradfute, Byron OT	60-61Dal		6'3"	243	Southern Miss.		
Bradley, Bill DB	69-73Phi	34	5'11"	190	Texas	25	6
Bradley, Dave OG	69-71GB 72StL		6'4"	245	Penn State		
Bradley, Ed LB	72-73Pit		6'2"	240	Wake Forest		
Bradshaw, Charlie OT	58-60LA 61-66Pit 67-68Det		6'6"	255	Baylor		
Bradshaw, Jim DB	63-67Pit		6'1"	199	Tenn.-Chattanooga	11	24
Bradshaw, Terry QB	70-73Pit	12	6'3"	218	Louisiana Tech		96
Brady, Phil DB	69DenA		6'2"	211	Brigham Young		
Bragg, Mike K	68-73Was	4	5'11"	186	Richmond		
Brahaney, Tom C	73StL		6'2"	225	Oklahoma		
Bramlett, John LB	65-66DenA 67-68MiaA 69BosA 70Bos 71Atl		6'2"	216	Memphis State	10	18
Branch, Cliff WR	72-73Oak	2	5'11"	170	Colorado		18
Branch, Mel DE	60-62DalA 63-65KC-A 66-68MiaA		6'2"	231	Louisiana State		
Brannan, Solomon DB-HB	65-66KC-A 67NY-A		6'1"	188	Morris Brown		
Branstetter, Kent OT	73GB		6'3"	260	Houston		
Bratkowski, Zeke QB	54ChiB 55-56MS 57-60ChiB 61-63LA 64-68GB 69-70VR 71GB	12 4	6'2"	204	Georgia		30
Bravo, Alex DB	57-58LA 60-61OakA		6'	190	Cal. St. Polytech	6	
Braxton, Hez FB-HB	62SD-A 63BufA		6'2"	227	Virginia Union		8
Braxton, Jim FB	71-73Buf	2	6'2"	232	West Virginia		60
Breaux, Don QB	63DenA 65SD-A	1	6'1"	203	McNeese State		
Breding, Ed LB	67-68Was		6'4"	235	Texas A&M		2
Breedlove, Rod LB	65-67Pit		6'2"	225	Maryland	11	
Breen, Gene LB	64GB 65-66Pit 67-68LA		6'2"	229	Virginia Tech		
Breitenstein, Bob OT-OG	65-67DenA 67Min 69-70Atl		6'3"	264	Tulsa		
Brenner, Al DB	69-70NYG		6'1"	200	Michigan State		
Brewer, Billy DB	60Was		6'	190	Mississippi		
Brewer, Johnny LB-OE-TE-DE	61-67Cle 68-70NO	2	6'4"	233	Mississippi	3	42
Brewington, Jim OT	61OakA		6'6"	280	N. Car. Central		
Brezina, Bobby HB	63HouA		6'	200	Houston		
Brezina, Greg LB	68-69Atl 70JJ 71-73Atl		6'2"	224	Houston	7	
Briggs, Bill DE	66-67Was		6'3"	250	Iowa		
Briggs, Bob FB	65Was		6'1"	228	Central St.-Okla.		
Briggs, Bob DE-DT	68-70SD-A 71-73Cle		6'4"	268	Heidelberg	1	12
Brinkman, Charlie WR	72Cle		6'2"	208	Louisville		
Briscoe, Marlin WR-QB	68DenA 69BufA 70-71Buf 72-73Mia	12	5'10"	178	Nebraska-Omaha		162
Britt, Charley DB	60-63LA 64Min 64SF		6'2"	183	Georgia	14	6
Brittenum, Jon QB	68SD-A		6'	185	Arkansas		
Brock, Clyde OT	62-63Dal 63SF		6'5"	268	Utah State		
Brockington, John FB	71-73GB	2	6'1"	225	Ohio State		102
Brodhead, Bob QB	60BufA	1	6'2"	207	Duke		2
Brodie, John QB	57-73SF	12	6'1"	198	Stanford		132
Brodnax, J. W. FB	60DenA		6'	208	Louisiana State		6
Brooker, Tommy OE-K	62DalA 63-66KC-A	5	6'2"	230	Alabama		290
Brooks, Bob FB	61NY-A		6'	215	Ohio U.		
Brooks, Cliff DB	72-73Cle		6'1"	190	Tennessee State		
Brooks, Larry DT	72-73LA		6'3"	255	Virginia State		
Brooks, Lee DT	70-72Hou 73StL		6'5"	263	Texas	1	
Brown, Aaron DE	66KC-A 67LJ 68-69KC-A 70-72KC 73GB		6'5"	262	Minnesota	1	6
Brown, Allen TE	66-67GB		6'5"	238	Mississippi		
Brown, Barry LB-TE	66-67Bal 68NYG 69BosA 70Bos	2	6'3"	228	Florida	1	
Brown, Bill LB	60BosA		6'1"	230	Syracuse	1	
Brown, Bill FB	61ChiB 62-73Min	2	5'11"	226	Illinois		456
Brown, Bob TE	69-70StL 71Min 72-73NO	2	6'3"	225	Alcorn A&M		6
Brown, Bob DT-DE	66-73GB		6'5"	261	Ark.-Pine Bluff		2
Brown, Bob OT	64-68Phi 69-70LA 71-73Oak		6'4"	284	Nebraska		
Brown, Charley OT	62OakA		6'4"	245	Houston		
Brown, Charlie DB-HB	66-67ChiB 68BufA		6'1"	194	Syracuse	1	
Brown, Charlie HB	67-68NO		5'10"	187	Missouri		18
Brown, Charlie WR	70Det 71JJ		6'2"	195	Northern Arizona		
Brown, Dean DB	69Cle 70Mia 71JJ		5'10"	170	Fort Valley St.	1	
Brown, Don HB	60HouA		6'1"	205	Houston		
Brown, Doug DT	64OakA		6'4"	250	Fresno State		
Brown, Fred HB	61,63BufA	2	5'11"	189	Georgia		18
Brown, Fred LB-TE	65LA 66JJ 67-69Phi		6'5"	231	Miami (Fla.)	2	
Brown, Jimmy FB	57-65Cle	23	6'2"	228	Syracuse		756
Brown, John OT	62-66Cle 67-71Pit 72JJ		6'2"	250	Syracuse		
Brown, Ken HB-FB	70-73Cle	23	5'10"	204	none		12
Brown, Larry TE	71-73Pit		6'4"	225	Kansas		12
Brown, Larry HB	69-73Was	2	5'11"	195	Kansas State		258
Brown, Otto DB	69Dal 70-73NYG		6'1"	187	Prairie View	2	6
Brown, Ray DB	71-73Atl	3	6'2"	203	West Texas State	11	
Brown, Roger DT	60-66Det 67-69LA		6'5"	298	Md. Eastern Shore	2	6
Brown, Stan WR	71Cle		5'9"	184	Purdue		
Brown, Terry DB-WR	69-70StL 71JJ 72-73Min		6'1"	206	Oklahoma State	2	6
Brown, Timmy HB	59GB 60-67Phi 68Bal	23	5'10"	195	Ball State		384
Brown, Tom DB	64-68GB 69Was	3	6'1"	191	Maryland	13	12
63 played major league baseball							
Brown, Willie FL-HB	64-65LA 66Phi	23	6'	185	Southern Calif.		6
Brown, Willie DB	63-66DenA 67-69OakA 70-73Oak		6'1"	190	Grambling	41	12
Browning, Charley HB	65NY-A		6'	220	Washington		
Brownlee, Claude DT	67MiaA		6'4"	265	Benedict		
Bruggers, Bob LB	66-68MiaA 68-69SD-A 70-71SD		6'1"	226	Minnesota	2	
Brumfield, Jim HB	71Pit		6'1"	195	Indiana State		

Use Name (Nicknames) – Positions	Team by Year	See Section	Hgt	Wgt	College	Int	Pts
Brumm, Don DE	63-69StL 70-71Phi 72StL		6'3"	243	Purdue		12
Brundige, Bill DT-DE	70-73Was		6'5"	270	Colorado		
Brunelli, Sam OT-OG	66-69DenA 70-71Den 72JJ		6'1"	263	Colorado State		
Brunet, Bob HB	68,70-73Was	2	6'1"	205	Louisiana Tech		18
Brunson, Mike WR	70Atl		6'1"	187	Arizona State		
Brupbacher, Ross LB	70-72ChiB		6'3"	215	Texas A&M	5	12
Bryant, Bob OE	60DalA		6'5"	230	Texas		
Bryant, Bobby DB	68-73Min	3	6'	172	South Carolina	27	24
Bryant, Charlie HB-FB	66-67StL 68-69Atl	23	6'1"	207	Allen		
Bryant, Chuck OE	62StL		6'2"	220	Ohio State		
Bryant, Cullen DB	73LA		6'1"	210	Colorado		6
Bryant, Hubie WR	70Pit 71-72NE	23	5'10"	170	Minnesota		6
Buchanan, Buck DT	63-69KC-A 70-73KC		6'7"	279	Grambling	3	2
Buchanan, Tim LB	69CinA		6'	233	Hawaii		
Buchanon, Willie DB	72-73GB		6'	190	San Diego State	4	6
Buckman, Tom TE	69DenA 71JJ		6'4"	230	Texas A&M		6
Budd, Frank FL	62Phi 63Was	2	5'10"	187	Villanova		6
Budde, Ed OG	63-69KC-A 70-73KC		6'5"	261	Michigan State		
Budka, Frank DB	64LA		6'	195	Notre Dame	2	
Budness, Bill LB	64-69OakA 70Oak		6'1"	215	Boston U.	3	
Budrewicz, Tom OG	61NY-A		6'2"	245	Brown		
Buehler, George OG	69OakA 70-73Oak		6'2"	260	Stanford		
Buetow, Bart OT	73NYG		6'5"	250	Minnesota		
Buffone, Doug LB	66-73ChiB		6'1"	227	Louisville	16	6
Bugenhagen, Gary OG-OT	67BufA 70Bos		6'2"	249	Syracuse		
Buie, Drew WR	69OakA 70-71Oak 72Cin		6'2"	180	Catawba		12
Bukaty, Fred FB	61DenA	2	5'11"	195	Kansas		32
Bukich, Rudy QB	53LA 54-55MS 56LA 57-58Was 58-59ChiB 60-61Pit 62-68ChiB	12	6'1"	202	Southern Calif.		54
Bulaich, Norm HB-FB	70-72Bal 73Phi	2	6'1"	218	Texas Christian		108
Bull, Ronnie HB-FB	62-70ChiB 71Phi	2	6'	200	Baylor		84
Bullocks, Amos HB	62-64Dal 66Pit	23	6'1"	201	Southern Illinois		42
Buncom, Frank LB	62-67SD-A 68CinA		6'1"	236	Southern Calif.	5	
died Sept. 14, 1969 – pulmonary embolism							
Bundra, Mike DT	62-63Det 64Min 64Cle 65NYG 65Bal		6'3"	258	Southern Calif.		
Bunting, John LB	72-73Phi		6'1"	220	North Carolina	1	
Buoniconti, Nick LB	62-68BosA 69MiaA 70-73Mia		5'11"	220	Notre Dame	30	8
Burch, Jerry OE	61OakA	2	6'1"	195	Georgia Tech		6
Burchfield, Don TE	71NO	2	6'2"	227	Ball State		
Burford, Chris OE	60-62DalA 63-67KC-A	2	6'3"	211	Stanford		332
Burke, Vern OE-TE	65SF 66Atl 67NO	2	6'4"	201	Oregon State		12
Burkett, Jackie LB-C	61-66Bal 67NO 68-69Dal 70NO		6'4"	229	Auburn	10	
Burman, George C-OG-OT	64ChiB 67-70LA 71-72Was		6'3"	253	Northwestern		
Burnett, Bobby HB	66-67BufA 68JJ 69DenA	2	6'2"	208	Arkansas		48
Burnett, Len DB	61Pit		6'1"	195	Oregon		
Burns, Leon FB	71SD 72StL 73JJ	2	6'2"	229	Long Beach State		18
Burrell, George DB	69DenA		5'10"	180	Pennsylvania	2	6
Burrell, John OE-FL	62-64Pit 66-67Was	2	6'3"	191	Rice		
Burrell, Ode HB-FL	64-69HouA	234	6'	189	Mississippi State		82
Burris, Bo DB	67-69NO		6'3"	195	Houston	4	6
Burrough, Ken WR	70NO 71-73Hou	2	6'4"	211	Texas Southern		60
Burroughs, Don DB	55-59LA 60-64Phi		6'4"	185	Colorado State	50	
Burrow, Ken WR	71-73Atl	2	6'	190	San Diego State		108
Burson, Jimmy DB	63-67StL 68Atl		6'	181	Auburn	16	12
Burton, Leon HB	60NY-A	3	5'9"	172	Arizona State		18
Burton, Ron HB	60-65BosA	23	5'10"	190	Northwestern		114
Bussell, Gerry DB	65DenA		6'	185	Georgia Tech		
Butkus, Dick LB-C	65-73ChiB		6'3"	244	Illinois	22	10
Butler, Bill FB	72-73NO	2	6'	214	Kansas State		30
Butler, Bill DB-HB	59GB 60Dal 61Pit 62-64Min	23	5'10"	189	Tenn.-Chattanooga	11	24
Butler, Bill LB	70Den		6'4"	226	San Fern. Valley		
Butler, Bob OG	62Phi 63NY-A		6'1"	233	Kentucky		
Butler, Cannonball HB	65-67Pit 68-71Atl 72StL 73JJ	23	5'10"	191	Edward Waters		102
Butler, Gary TE	73KC		6'3"	235	Rice		12
Butler, Skip K	71NO 71NYG 72-73Hou	45	6'2"	200	Texas-Arlington		125
Butsko, Harry LB	63Was		6'3"	220	Maryland		
Butz, Dave DE-DT	73StL		6'7"	290	Purdue		
Buzin, Rich OT	68-70NYG 71LA 72ChiB		6'4"	250	Penn State		
Buzyniski, Bernie LB	60BufA		6'3"	228	Holy Cross	1	
Byers, Ken OG-DE	62-63NYG 64-65Min 66JJ		6'1"	240	Cincinnati		
Byrd, Butch DB	63-69BufA 70Buf 71Den	3	6'	203	Boston U.	40	36
Byrd, Dennis DE	68BosA		6'4"	260	N. Carolina State		
Byrd, Mack LB	65LA		6'	215	Southern Calif.		
Byrne, Bill OG	63Phi		6'	240	Boston College		
Cadile, Jim OG-OT	62-72ChiB		6'3"	239	San Jose State		
Cadwell, John OG	61DalA		6'3"	230	Oregon State		
Caffey, Lee Roy LB	63Phi 64-69GB 70ChiB 71Dal 72SD		6'3"	247	Texas A & M	11	18
Cagle, Johnny DE	69BosA		6'3"	260	Clemson		
Cahill, Bill DB	73Buf		5'11"	180	Washington		6
Cahill, Dave DT-DE	66Phi 67LA 68KJ 69Atl		6'3"	240	Arizona State		
Caleb, Jamie HB-FB	60Cle 61Min 65Cle	3	6'1"	210	Grambling		6
Callahan, Dan OG	60NY-A		6'	230	Wooster		
Calland, Lee DB	63-65Min 66-68Atl 69ChiB 69-72Pit		6'	190	Louisville	19	6
Calloway, Ernie DT-DE	69-72Phi 73JJ		6'6"	244	Texas Southern		
Cambal, Dennis TE	73NYJ		6'3"	228	William & Mary		
Campbell, Bob HB	69Pit	3	6'	195	Penn State		
Campbell, Carter LB-DE	70SF 71Den 72-73NYG		6'3"	232	Weber State		
Campbell, Jim LB	69SD-A		6'3"	218	West Texas State	1	
Campbell, John LB	63-64Min 65-69Pit 69Bal		6'3"	222	Minnesota	5	6
Campbell, Ken OE	60NY-A		6'1"	213	West Chester St.		
Campbell, Mike HB	68Det		5'11"	200	Lenoir Rhyne		
Campbell, Sonny HB	70-71Atl 72JJ	2	5'11"	192	Northern Arizona		12
Campbell, Woody HB	67-69HouA 70-71Hou	2	5'11"	205	Northwestern		90
Canale, Justin OG	65-68BosA 69CinA		6'2"	242	Mississippi State		1
Canale, Whit DE-DT	66MiaA 68BosA		6'3"	245	Tennessee		
Cannavino, Joe DB	60-61OakA 62BufA		5'11"	186	Ohio State	10	
Cannon, Billy TE-HB-FB-OE	60-63HouA 64-69OakA 70KC	23	6'1"	216	Louisiana State		392
Capp, Dick LB-TE	67GB 68Pit		6'3"	235	Boston College		
Cappadonna, Bob FB	66-67BosA 68BufA	2	6'1"	230	Northeastern		34
Cappelletti, Gino FL-WR-OE-DB	60-69BosA 70Bos	2 5	6'	190	Minnesota	4	1130
Cappleman, Bill QB	70Min 73Det		6'3"	210	Florida State		

Use Name (Nicknames) – Positions	Team by Year	See Section	Hgt	Wgt	College	Int	Pts
Carlton, Wray HB-FB	60-67BufA	2	6'2"	218	Duke		204
Carmichael, Harold WR	71-73Phi	2	6'7"	225	Southern U.		66
Carmichael, Paul HB	65DenA		6'	200	El Camino J.C.		
Carolan, Reg OE-TE	62-63SD-A 64-68KC-A	2	6'6"	235	Toledo		34
Caroline, J. C. DB-HB	56-65ChiB	2	6'1"	190	Illinois	24	36
Carollo, Joe OT	62-68LA 69-70Phi 71LA 72-73Cle		6'2"	262	Notre Dame		
Carothers, Don OE	60DenA		6'5"	225	Bradley		
Carpenter, Preston OE-TE-HB	56-59Cle 60-63Pit 64-66Was 66Min 67MiaA	23	6'2"	197	Arkansas		144
Carpenter, Ron DE-DT	70-73Cin		6'4"	260	N. Carolina State		
Carpenter, Ron LB	64-65SD-A		6'2"	230	Texas A&M	1	
Carr, Fred LB	68-73GB		6'5"	238	Texas-El Paso	2	
Carr, Henry DB	65-67NYG		6'3"	198	Arizona State	7	6
Carr, Jimmy DB-LB-HB	55,57ChiC 59-63Phi 64-65Was	2	6'1"	206	Morris Harvey	15	6
Carr, Levert OT-DT-OG	69SD-A 70-71Buf 72-73Hou		6'5"	258	North Central		
Carr, Tom DT	68NO		6'3"	267	Morgan State		
Carrell, John LB	66HouA		6'3"	227	Texas Tech		
Carrington, Ed TE	68KJ 69HouA		6'4"	225	Virginia		
Carroll, Jim LB	65-66NYG 66-68Was 69NY-A		6'1"	229	Notre Dame	3	
Carroll, Joe LB	72-73Oak		6'1"	220	Pittsburgh		
Carroll, Leo DE	67KJ 68GB 69-70Was 71JJ		6'7"	250	San Diego State		
Carson, Kern HB	65SD-A 65NY-A		6'	202	San Diego State		12
Carter, Jim LB	70-73GB		6'3"	235	Minnesota	5	6
Carter, Mike WR	70GB 72SD		6'1"	210	Sacramento State		
Carter, Virgil QB	68-69ChiB 70-72Cin 73BC	12	6'1"	194	Brigham Young		49
Carwell, Larry DB	67-68HouA 69BosA 70Bos 71-72NE	3	6'1"	191	Iowa State	14	18
Casanova, Tommy DB	72-73Cin	3	6'2"	202	Louisiana State	9	6
Casares, Rick FB	55-64ChiB 65Was 66MiaA	2	6'2"	226	Florida		360
Case, Pete OG	62-64Phi 65-70NYG		6'3"	242	Georgia		
Casey, Bernie FL-WR-OE	61-66SF 67-68LA	2	6'4"	213	Bowling Green		240
Casey, Tim LB	69ChiB 69DenA		6'1"	225	Oregon		
Cash, John DE	61-62DenA		6'3"	235	Allen	1	
Cash, Rick DE-DT	68Atl 69-70LA 71JJ 72-73NE		6'5"	260	NE Missouri St.		
Cassese, Tom DB-HB	67DenA		6'1"	197	C.W. Post	1	
Caster, Rich TE-WR	70-73NYJ	2	6'5"	225	Jackson State		138
Cavalli, Carmen DE	60OakA		6'4"	245	Richmond		
Caveness, Ronnie LB	65KC-A 66-68HouA		6'1"	223	Arkansas	1	
Cavness, Grady DB	69DenA 70Atl		5'11"	190	Texas-El Paso	2	
Caylor, Lowell DB	64Cle		6'3"	205	Miami-Ohio		
Ceppetelli, Gene C	68-69Phi 69NYG		6'2"	247	Villanova		
Cernel, Joe C	65-67SF 68Atl		6'2"	238	Northwestern		
Chamberlain, Dan OE-HB	60-61BufA	2	6'4"	200	Sacramento State		24
Chambers, Wally DT	73ChiB		6'6"	250	Eastern Kentucky		
Chandler, Al TE	73Cin		6'2"	233	Oklahoma		
Chandler, Bob WR	71-73Buf	2	6'	180	Southern Calif.		49
Chandler, Don HB-K	56-64NYG 65-67GB	45	6'2"	208	Florida		530
Chandler, Edgar LB	68-69BufA 70-72Buf 73NE		6'3"	227	Georgia	2	8
Chapple, Dave K	71Buf 72-73LA	4	6'	180	Cal.-Santa Barbara		
Chapple, Jack LB	65SF		6'2"	227	Stanford		6
Charles, John DB	67-69BosA 70Min 71-73Hou		6'1"	199	Purdue	16	12
Charon, Carl DB	62-63BufA		5'10"	190	Michigan State	7	18
Chavous, Barney DE	73Den		6'3"	252	S. Carolina State		
Cheek, Richard OG	70Buf 71JJ		6'3"	266	Auburn		
Cheeks, B. W. HB	65HouA		6'1"	230	Texas Southern		
Chelf, Don OG-OT	60-61BufA		6'3"	235	Iowa		
Cherry, Stan LB	73Bal		6'5"	200	Morgan State		
Chesser, George FB	66-67MiaA		6'2"	223	Delta Stata		
Chesson, Wes WR	71-73Atl	2	6'2"	193	Duke		12
Chester, Ray TE	70-72Oak 73Bal	2	6'3"	225	Morgan State		138
Cheyunski, Jim LB	68-69BosA 70Bos 71-72NE 73Buf		6'2"	223	Syracuse	6	
Childress, Joe HB-FB	56-59ChiC 60StL 61JJ 62-65StL	2	6'	202	Auburn		96
Childs, Clarence DB-HB	64-67NYG 68ChiB	23	6'	180	Florida A&M	2	12
Chlebek, Ed QB	63NY-A		5'11"	175	Western Michigan		
Choboian, Max QB	66DenA	1	6'4"	205	San Fran. State		12
Chomyszak, Steve DT-C-OT	66NY-A 68-69CinA 70-73Cin		6'5"	270	Syracuse		
Christiansen, Bob TE	72Buf		6'4"	230	U. C. L. A.		
Christopherson, Jim LB	62Min	5	6'	215	Concordia-Moor.	1	61
Christy, Dick HB	58Pit 60BosA 61-63NY-A	23	5'10"	191	N. Carolina State		120
Christy, Earl HB-DB	66-68NY-A		5'11"	193	Md. Eastern Shore	1	1
Chuy, Don OG	63-68LA 69Phi		6'1"	255	Clemson		
Ciccolella, Mike LB	66-68NYG		6'1"	235	Dayton	1	
Cichowski, Tom OT	67-68DenA		6'4"	250	Maryland		
Cindrich, Ralph LB	72NE 73Hou		6'1"	228	Pittsburgh		
Clack, Jim C	71-73Pit		6'3"	250	Wake Forest		
Clancy, Jack WR-FL	67MiaA 68KJ 69MiaA 70GB	2	6'1"	195	Michigan		30
Claridge, Dennis QB	64-65GB 66Atl	1	6'3"	225	Nebraska		
Clark, Al DB	71Det 72-73LA		6'	180	Eastern Michigan	2	
Clark, Booby FB	73Cin	2	6'2"	245	Bethune-Cookman		48
Clark, Ernie LB	63-67Det 68StL		6'1"	222	Michigan State	4	
Clark, Gail LB	73ChiB		6'2"	227	Michigan State		
Clark, Howard OE	60LA-A 61SD-A	2	6'2"	210	Tenn.-Chattanooga		
Clark, Mike K	63Phi 64-67Pit 68-71Dal 72JJ 73Dal	5	6'1"	203	Texas A & M		724
Clark, Monte OT-DT-DE	59-61SF 62Dal 63-69Cle		6'6"	260	Southern Calif.		
Clark, Phil DB	67-69Dal 70ChiB 71NE		6'2"	209	Northwestern	4	
Clark, Wayne QB	70,72-73SD	1	6'2"	203	U.S. International		
Clarke, Frank OE-FL-TE	57-59Cle 60-67Dal	2	6'	211	Colorado		306
Clarke, Hagood DB	64-68BufA	3	6'	193	Florida	12	18
Clay, Billy DB	66Was		6'1"	192	Mississippi	1	
Clay, Ozzie FL	64Was		6'	190	Iowa State		
Clemens, Bob HB	62Bal		6'1"	208	Pittsburgh		
Clement, Henry OE	61Pit		6'2"	200	North Carolina		
Clements, Vin FB	72-73NYG	2	6'3"	213	Connecticut		12
Clemons, Craig DB	72-73ChiB		5'11"	194	Iowa	2	
Cline, Doug LB-FB	60-66HouA 66SD-A	2	6'2"	225	Clemson	7	30
Cline, Tony DE	70-73Oak		6'2"	235	Miami (Fla.)	3	
Cloutier, Dave DB	64BosA		6'	195	Maine		
Coady, Rich C-TE	70-73ChiB		6'3"	239	Memphis State		6
Coan, Bert HB	62SD-A 63-68KC-A	23	6'4"	219	Kansas		114
Cockrell, Gene OT-DE	60-62NY-A		6'3"	247	Hardin-Simmons		
Cockroft, Don K	68-73Cle	45	6'1"	190	Adams State		514

Use Name (Nicknames) – Positions	Team by Year	See Section	Hgt	Wgt	College	Int	Pts
Cody, Bill LB	66Det 67-70NO 72Phi		6'1"	225	Auburn		
Coffey, Don FL	63DenA		6'3"	190	Memphis State		
Coffey, Junior FB-HB	65GB 66-67Atl 68KJ 69Atl 69NY 70KJ 71NYG	2	6'1"	211	Washington		90
Cogdill, Gail OE-WR	60-68Det 68Bal 69-70Atl	2	6'2"	196	Washington State		216
Cohen, Abe OG	60BosA		5'11"	230	Tenn.-Chattanooga		
Coia, Angie OE	60-63ChiB 64-65Was 66Atl	2	6'2"	202	Southern Calif.		120
Colchico, Dan DE	60-65SF 69NO		6'4"	240	San Jose State		
Colclough, Jim OE-FL-WR	60-68BosA	2	6'	185	Boston College		238
Cole, Fred OG	60LA-A		5'11"	226	Maryland		
Cole, Larry DE	68-73Dal		6'4"	249	Hawaii	2	18
Cole, Linzy WR	70ChiB 71-72Hou 72Buf	3	5'11"	170	Texas Christian		
Cole, Terry FB	68-69Bal 70Pit 71Mia	2	6'1"	220	Indiana		36
Coleman, Al DB	67Min 69CinA 70-71Cin 72-73Phi		6'1"	185	Tennessee State	1	2
Coleman, Dennis LB	71NE		6'3"	225	Mississippi		
Coleman, Ralph LB	72Dal		6'4"	216	N. Carolina A & T		
Collett, Elmer OG	67-72SF 73Bal		6'4"	240	San Fran. State		
Collier, Blanton	HC63-70Cle				Georgetown (Ky.)		
Collier, Jim OE	62NYG 63Was		6'2"	195	Arkansas		
Collier, Joel	HC66-68BufA				Northwestern		
Collins, Gary FL-WR-OE	62-71Cle	2 4	6'4"	211	Maryland		420
Collins, Jerald LB	69BufA 70-71Buf		6'1"	220	Western Michigan		
Colman, Wayne LB	68-69Phi 69-73NO		6'1"	230	Temple	2	
Colvin, Jim DT-DE-OG	60-63Bal 64-66Dal 67NYG		6'2"	250	Houston		2
Compton, Dick OE-DB-HB-WR	62-64Det 65HouA 67-68Pit	2	6'1"	195	McMurry	1	24
Concannon, Jack QB	64-66Phi 67-71ChiB	12	6'3"	201	Boston College		66
Condren, Glen DT-DE	65-67NYG 69-72Atl		6'2"	246	Oklahoma		
Conjar, Larry FB	67Cle 68Phi 69-70Bal	2	6'	214	Notre Dame		2
Conley, Steve LB	72Cin 72StL		6'2"	225	Kansas		
Connelly, Mike C-OG-OT	60-67Dal 68Pit		6'3"	242	Utah State		
Conners, Dan LB	64-69OakA 70-73Oak		6'1"	231	Miami (Fla.)	12	30
Conrad, Bobby Joe FL-HB-WR-DB	58-59ChiC 60-68StL 69Dal	3 5	6'	194	Texas A & M	4	389
Contoulis, John DT	64NYG		6'4"	260	Connecticut		
Conway, Dave K	71GB		6'	195	Texas		5
Cook, Ed OT-OG	58-59ChiC 60-65StL 66-67Atl		6'2"	245	Notre Dame		
Cook, Greg QB	69CinA 70-72SJ 73Cin	12	6'3"	214	Cincinnati		6
Cooke, Ed DE-LB	58ChiB 58Phi 60-63NY-A 64-65DenA 66-67MiaA		6'4"	248	Maryland	7	12
Coolbaugh, Bob OE	61OakA	2	6'3"	200	Richmond		26
Cooper, Bill FB-LB	61-64SF		6'1"	215	Muskingum		6
Cooper, Thurlow OE-DE	60-62NY-A	2	6'4"	228	Maine		52
Copeland, Jim OG-C	67-73Cle		6'2"	242	Virginia		
Copeland, Ron WR	69ChiB		6'4"	196	U. C. L. A.		
Corcoran, Jim QB	68BosA		6'	200	Maryland		
Cordileone, Lou DT-DE-OG	60NYG 61SF 62LA 62-63Pit 67-68NO 69KJ		6'	247	Clemson	1	
Cordill, Ollie DB-OE	67SD-A 68Atl 69NO	4	6'2"	180	Memphis State		
Corey, Walt LB	60,62DalA 63-66KC-A		6'	229	Miami (Fla.)	4	
Cornelison, Jerry OT	60-62DalA 64-65KC-A		6'3"	250	S. M. U.		
Cornell, Bo FB	71-72Cle 73Buf		6'1"	216	Washington		
Cornish, Frank DT	66-70ChiB 70-71Mia 72Buf		6'6"	285	Grambling	2	
Coronado, Bob OE	61Pit		6'1"	195	U. of Pacific		
Cortez, Bruce DB	67NO		6'	175	Parsons		
Coryell, Don	HC73StL				Washington		
Coslet, Bruce TE	69CinA 70-73Cin	2	6'3"	226	U. of Pacific		42
Costa, Dave DT	63-65OakA 66BufA 67-69DenA 70-71Den 72-73SD		6'2"	257	Utah		2
Costa, Paul OT-TE-OE	65-69BufA 70-72Buf	2	6'4"	252	Notre Dame		42
Costello, Tom LB	64-65NYG		6'3"	220	Dayton		
Costello, Vince LB	57-66Cle 67-68NYG		6'	228	Ohio U.	22	12
Cotton, Craig TE	69-72Det 73ChiB	2	6'4"	222	Youngstown		6
Cottrell, Bill OT-C-OG	67-70Det 71JJ 72Den		6'3"	255	Delaware Valley		
Cottrell, Ted LB	69-70Atl		6'1"	233	Delaware Valley		
Counts, Johnny HB	62-63NYG	3	5'10"	170	Illinois		6
Cowan, Charley OT-OG	61-73LA		6'4"	264	N. Mex. Highlands		
Cowlings, Al DE-DT	70-72Buf 73Hou		6'5"	255	Southern Calif.		
Cox, Fred K	63-73Min	45	5'10"	200	Pittsburgh		1074
Cox, Jim TE	68MiaA	2	6'2"	227	Miami (Fla.)		
Cox, Larry DT	66-68DenA		6'2"	250	Abilene Christian		
Coyle, Russ DB	61LA		6'2"	195	Oklahoma		
Crabb, Claude DB-FL	62-63Was 64-65Phi 66-68LA		6'	193	Colorado	10	6
Crabtree, Eric WR-OE-DB	66-68DenA 69CinA 70-71Cin 71NE	2	5'11"	184	Pittsburgh		132
Craddock, Nate FB	63Bal		6'	220	Parsons		
Craig, Dobie OE-HB	62-63OakA 64HouA	2	6'4"	200	Howard Payne		42
Craig, Neal DB	71-73Cin		6'1"	188	Fisk	5	6
Crane, Dennis DT-OT	68-69Was 70NYG		6'6"	260	Southern Calif.		
Crane, Gary LB	69DenA		6'4"	230	Arkansas State		
Crane, Paul LB-C	66-69NY-A 70-72NYJ		6'2"	208	Alabama	5	14
Crangle, Mike DE	72NO		6'4"	243	Tennessee-Martin		
Crawford, Bill OG	60NYG		6'1"	235	British Columbia		
Crawford, Hilton DB	69BufA		6'	198	Grambling		
Crawford, Jim FB-HB	60-64BosA	2	6'1"	203	Wyoming		46
Creech, Bob LB	71-72Phi 73NO		6'3"	226	Texas Christian		
Crennel, Carl LB	70Pit		6'1"	230	West Virginia		
Crenshaw, Leon DT	68GB		6'6"	280	Tuskegee		
Crenshaw, Willie FB	64-69StL 70Den	23	6'2"	228	Kansas State		108
Crespino, Bob OE-TE-WR	61-63Cle 64-68NYG	2	6'4"	223	Mississippi		54
Crist, Chuck DB	72-73NYG		6'2"	205	Penn State	3	
Criter, Ken LB	69DenA 70-73Den		5'11"	223	Wisconsin		2
Crockett, Bobby WR-OE	66BufA 67KJ 68-69BufA	2	6'	198	Arkansas		18
Crockett, Monte OE	60-62BufA	2	6'3"	213	N. Mex. Highlands		6
Croft, Don DT	72Buf 73KJ		6'3"	252	Texas-El Paso		
Croftcheck, Don OG-LB	65-66Was 67ChiB		6'1"	230	Indiana		
Cronin, Bill TE	65Phi 66MiaA		6'4"	225	Boston College		6
Cropper, Marshall WR-OE	67-69Pit	2	6'3"	207	Md. Eastern Shore		
Cross, Irv DB	61-65Phi 66-68LA 69Phi	3	6'1"	192	Northwestern	22	12
Crossan, Dave C	65-69Was		6'3"	245	Maryland		
Crosswhite, Leon FB	73Det		6'2"	215	Oklahoma		6
Crotty, Jim DB	60-61Was 61-62BufA		5'11"	192	Notre Dame	3	
Crouthamel, Jake HB	60BosA		5'11"	195	Dartmouth		
Crow, Al DT	60BosA		6'6"	260	William & Mary		
Crow, John David HB-FB-TE	58-59ChiC 60-64StL 65-68SF	12	6'2"	218	Texas A & M		444
Crow, Wayne HB-DB	60-61OakA 62-63BufA	2 4	6'	205	California	4	26
Crowe, Larry HB	72Phi		6'1"	198	Texas Southern		
Croyle, Phil LB	71-73Hou 73Buf		6'3"	220	California		
Crump, Dwayne DB	73StL		5'11"	180	Fresno State		
Crump, Harry FB	63BosA	2	6'	205	Boston College		30
Crusan, Doug OT	68-69MiaA 70-73Mia		6'5"	253	Indiana		
Crutcher, Tommy LB-FB	64-67GB 68-69NYG 70KJ 71-72GB		6'3"	229	Texas Christian	3	
Csonka, Larry FB	68-69MiaA 70-73Mia	2	6'3"	240	Syracuse		210
Cudzik, Walt C-LB	54Was 60-63BosA 64BufA		6'2"	231	Purdue		
Culp, Curley DT-OG	68-69KC-A 70-73KC		6'1"	265	Arizona State		
Culpepper, Ed DT	58-59ChiC 60StL 61Min 62-63HouA		6'1"	255	Alabama		
Cummings, Ed LB	64NY-A 65DenA		6'2"	230	Stanford	1	
Cunningham, Carl LB	67-69DenA 70Den 71NO		6'3"	240	Houston	4	
Cunningham, Dick LB-OT	67-69BufA 70-72Buf 73Phi		6'2"	239	Arkansas		
Cunningham, Doug HB	67-73SF	23	5'11"	191	Mississippi		60
Cunningham, Jay DB	65-67BosA	3	5'10"	180	Bowling Green	3	6
Cunningham, Jim FB	61-63Was	2	5'11"	221	Pittsburgh		30
Cunningham, Sam FB	73NE	2	6'3"	215	Southern Calif.		30
Cuozzo, Gary QB	63-66Bal 67NO 68-71Min 72StL	12	6'1"	195	Virginia		6
Curchin, Jeff OT-OG	70-71ChiB 72Buf		6'6"	258	Florida State		
Curran, Pat TE-FB	69-73LA	2	6'3"	238	Lakeland		18
Current, Mike OT	67MiaA 67-69DenA 70-73Den		6'4"	267	Ohio State		
Currie, Dan LB	58-64GB 65-66LA		6'3"	239	Michigan State	11	6
Curry, Bill C-LB	65-66GB 67-72Bal 73Hou		6'2"	235	Georgia Tech		
Curry, Ray FL	63Pit		6'1"	195	Jackson State		6
Curtis, Isaac WR	73Cin	2	6'	190	San Diego State		54
Curtis, Mike LB-FB	65-73Bal		6'2"	231	Duke	17	18
Curtis, Tom DB	70-71Bal		6'1"	196	Michigan		
Cutsinger, Gary DE	62-66HouA 67JJ 68HouA		6'4"	244	Oklahoma State		
Cvercko, Andy OG	60GB 61-62Dal 63Cle 63Was		6'	242	Northwestern		
Daanen, Jerry WR	68-70StL		6'	190	Miami (Fla.)		
Dabney, Carlton DT	68Atl 69-70XJ		6'5"	250	Morgan State	1	
Dalby, Dave C-OG	72-73Oak		6'2"	240	U. C. L. A.		
Dale, Carroll WR-OE-FL	60-64LA 65-72GB 73Min	2	6'1"	198	Virginia Tech		312
D'Amato, Mike DB	68NY-A		6'2"	204	Hofstra		
Danenhauer, Bill DE	60DenA 60BosA		6'4"	245	Kansas St. Teach.		
Danenhauer, Eldon OT	60-65DenA 66KJ		6'4"	242	Kansas State C.		
Daney, George OG	68-69KC-A 70-73KC		6'3"	240	Texas-El Paso		6
Daniel, Willie DB	61-66Pit 67-69LA		5'11"	187	Mississippi State	14	12
Daniels, Clem HB-DB	60DalA 61-67OakA 68SF	23	6'1"	219	Prairie View	3	324
Daniels, Dave DT	66OakA		6'3"	245	Florida A & M		
Daniels, Dick DB	66-68Dal 69-70ChiB 71JJ		5'9"	180	Pacific (Ore.)	7	
Darden, Tom DB	72-73Cle		6'2"	195	Michigan	4	
Darnall, Bill WR	68-69Mia 70JJ		6'2"	197	North Carolina		
Darragh, Dan QB	68-69BufA 70Buf	1	6'3"	196	William & Mary		
Darre, Bernie OG	61Was		6'2"	230	Tulane		
Daugherty, Bob HB	66SF		6'2"	205	Tulsa		
Davidson, Ben DE-DT	61GB 62-63Was 64-69OakA 70-71Oak 72JJ		6'8"	272	Washington		
Davidson, Cotton QB	54Bal 55-56MS 57Bal 58CFL 60-62DalA 62-66OakA 67JJ 68OakA	12 45	6'1"	182	Baylor		104
Davidson, Pete DT	60HouA		6'5"	255	The Citadel		
Davis, Al	HC63-65OakA				Syracuse		
Davis, Ben DB	67-68Cle 69JJ 70-73Cle	3	5'11"	184	Defiance	17	6
Davis, Bob QB	67-69HouA 70-72NYJ 73NO	12	6'3"	205	Virginia		12
Davis, Butch DB	70ChiB		5'11"	183	Missouri	1	
Davis, Clarence HB	71-73Oak	23	5'10"	190	Southern Calif.		72
Davis, Dave WR	71-72GB 73Pit	2	6'	175	Tennessee State		6
Davis, Dick DE	62DalA		6'2"	230	Kansas		
Davis, Dick HB-FB	70Den 70NO	2	5'11"	215	Nebraska		
Davis, Don DT	66NYG 67JJ		6'6"	260	Los Angeles State		
Davis, Donnie FL-TE	62Dal 70Hou		6'4"	220	Southern U.		
Davis, Doug OT	66-72Min		6'4"	250	Kentucky		
Davis, Glenn OE	60-61Det	2	6'	180	Ohio State		
Davis, Henry LB	68-69NYG 70-73Pit		6'3"	235	Grambling	4	6
Davis, Jack OG	60BosA		6'	226	Maryland		
Davis, Jack OG	60DenA		6'2"	235	Arizona		
Davis, Marvin DE	66DenA		6'4"	252	Wichita State		
Davis, Norman OG	67Bal 69NO 70Phi		6'3"	247	Grambling		
Davis, Roger OG-OT	60-63ChiB 64LA 65-66NYG		6'3"	236	Syracuse		
Davis, Ron OG	73StL		6'2"	235	Virginia State		
Davis, Rosey DE	65-67NYG		6'5"	260	Tennessee State		
Davis, Sam OG-OT	67-73Pit		6'1"	249	Allen		
Davis, Sonny HB-FB	71-72Phi	2	5'11"	215	Tennessee State		6
Davis, Sonny LB	61Dal		6'2"	220	Baylor		
Davis, Stan WR	73Phi		5'10"	180	Memphis State		
Davis, Steve HB-FB	72-73Pit	2	6'1"	218	Delaware State		24
Davis, Ted LB	64-66Bal 67-69NO 70Mia		6'1"	230	Georgia Tech	2	
Davis, Tommy K	59-69SF	45	6'	215	Louisiana State		738
Davis, Vern DB	71Phi		6'4"	208	Western Michigan		
Davis, Willie DE-OT	58-59Cle 60-69GB		6'3"	243	Grambling	2	16
Dawkins, Joe HB-FB	70-71Hou 71-73Den	23	5'11"	222	Wisconsin		48
Dawson, Bill DE-OE	65BosA		6'3"	240	Florida State		
Dawson, Len QB	57-59Pit 60-61Cle 62DalA 63-69KC-A 70-73KC	12	6'	190	Purdue		54
Dawson, Rhett WR	72Hou 73Min		6'1"	185	Florida State		6
Day, Al LB	60DenA		6'2"	216	Eastern Michigan		
Day, Eagle QB	59-60Was	1 4	6'	183	Mississippi		
Day, Tom DE-OG-DT-OT	60StL 61-66BufA 67SD-A 68BufA		6'2"	252	N. Carolina A & T	1	
Dean, Floyd LB	64-65SF		6'4"	245	Florida		
Dean, Ted HB-FB	60-63Phi 64Min	23	6'2"	211	Wichita State		36
Dee, Bob DE-DT	57-58Was 60-67BosA		6'3"	248	Holy Cross	1	
DeFelice, Nick OT	65-66NY-A		6'3"	250	Southern Conn. St.		
Degen, Dick LB	65-66SD-A		6'1"	223	Long Beach State	3	
DeLamielleure, Joe OG	73Buf		6'3"	254	Michigan State		
DeLeone, Tom C-OG	72-73Cin		6'2"	252	Ohio State		
Del Gaizo, Jim QB	72Mia 73GB	1	6'1"	198	Tampa		
DeLisle, Jim DT	71GB		6'4"	254	Wisconsin		
DeLong, Steve DT-DE	65-69SD-A 70-71SD 72ChiB		6'3"	251	Tennessee	1	
DeLuca, Sam OG-OT	60LA-A 61SD-A 62VR 63SD-A 64-66NY-A		6'2"	247	South Carolina		

Use Name (Nicknames) – Positions	Team by Year		Hgt	Wgt	College	Int	Pts
DeLucca, Jerry OT-DT	59Phi 60-61BosA 62-63BufA 63-64BosA		6'3"	249	Middle Tennessee		
DeMarco, Bob C-OG	61-69StL 70-71Mia 72-73Cle		6'3"	243	Dayton		
Demarie, John OG-OT-C	67-73Cle		6'3"	252	S. M. U.		
Demery, Calvin WR	72Min		6'	190	Arizona State		
Demko, George DE	61Pit		6'3"	240	Appalachian State		
Demory, Bill QB	73NYJ	1	6'2"	195	Arizona		
Dempsey, Tom K	69-70NO 71-73Phi	5	6'1"	260	Palomar J.C.		395
Den Herder, Vern DE	71-73Mia		6'6"	250	Central (Iowa)	1	
Denney, Austin TE	67-69ChiB 70-71Buf	2	6'2"	230	Tennessee		18
Dennis, Al OG	73SD		6'4"	250	Grambling		
Dennis, Guy OG	69CinA 70-72Cin 73Det		6'2"	255	Florida		
Dennis, Mike HB	68-69LA	2	6'1"	207	Mississippi		
Denny, Earl HB	67-68Min		6'1"	200	Missouri		
Denson, Al WR-FL-TE	64-69DenA 70Den 71Min	2	6'2"	208	Florida A & M		194
Denton, Bob DE-OT	60Cle 61-64Min		6'4"	241	U. of Pacific		
Denvir, John OG	62DenA		6'4"	245	Colorado		
DePoyster, Jerry K	68Det 71-72Oak	45	6'1"	202	Wyoming		27
Deskins, Don OG	60OakA		6'3"	240	Michigan		
Dess, Darrell OG-OT	58Pit 59-64NYG 65-66Was 66-69NYG		6'	243	N. Carolina State		6
DeSutter, Wayne OT	66BufA		6'4"	250	Western Illinois		
Deters, Harold K	67Dal	5	6'	200	N. Carolina State		12
Detwiller, Chuck DB	70-72SD 73StL		6'	185	Utah State	1	6
Devine, Dan	HC71-73GB				Minnesota-Duluth		
DeVleigher, Chuck DT	69BufA		6'4"	265	Memphis State		
Dewveall, Willard OE	59-60ChiB 61-64HouA	2	6'4"	224	S. M. U.		162
Dial, Benjy QB	67Phi		6'1"	185	Eastern New Mex.		
Dial, Buddy FL-OE	59-63Pit 64-66Dal 67-68JJ	2	6'1"	194	Rice		264
Diamond, Bill OG	63KC-A		6'	240	Miami (Fla.)		
Diamond, Charley OT	60-62DalA 63KC-A		6'2"	249	Miami (Fla.)		
Dickey, Eldridge WR	68OakA 71Oak		6'2"	198	Tennessee State		6
Dickey, Lynn QB	71Hou 72JJ 73Hou	1	6'4"	214	Kansas State		1
Dickey, Wallace OT	68-69DenA		6'3"	260	SW Texas State		
Dickinson, Bo FB	60-61DalA 62-63DenA 63HouA 64OakA	2	6'2"	218	Southern Miss.		70
Dickson, Paul DT-OT	59LA 60Dal 61-70Min 71StL		6'5"	252	Baylor		
Dicus, Chuck WR	71-72SD	2	6'	174	Arkansas		18
Didion, John C-LB	69-70Was 71-73NO		6'4"	245	Oregon State		
Diehl, John DT	61-64Bal 65Dal 65OakA		6'7"	276	Virginia		
Dieken, Doug OT	71-73Cle		6'5"	243	Illinois		2
Dierdorf, Dan OG-OT	71-73StL		6'4"	265	Michigan		
Dillon, Terry DB	63Min		6'	193	Montana		
died in 1963 - accidental drowning							
DiMidio, Tony OT-C	66-67KC-A		6'3"	250	West Chester St.		
Dimitroff, Tom QB	60BosA		5'11"	200	Miami-Ohio		
Dirks, Mike DT-OG	68-71Phi		6'2"	247	Wyoming		6
Discenzo, Tony OT	60BosA 60BufA		6'5"	240	Michigan State		
Ditka, Mike TE-OE	61-66ChiB 67-68Phi 69-72Dal	2	6'3"	229	Pittsburgh		270
DiVito, Joe QB	68DenA		6'2"	205	Boston College		
Dixon, Hewritt FB-HB-OE	63-65DenA 66-69OakA 70Oak 71JJ	2	6'2"	223	Florida A & M		170
Dobbins, Ollie DB	64BufA		5'11"	185	Morgan State		
Dobler, Conrad OG	72-73StL		6'3"	250	Wyoming		
Dockery, John DB	68-69NY-A 70-71NYJ 72-73Pit		6'	186	Harvard	8	
Dodd, Al WR-DB	67ChiB 69-71NO 72JJ 73Atl	23	6'	181	NW State-La.		18
Doelling, Fred DB	60Dal		5'10"	190	Pennsylvania		
Domres, Marty QB	69SD-A 70-71SD 72-73Bal	12	6'3"	216	Columbia		42
Domres, Tom DT-DE	68-69HouA 70-71Hou 71-72Den 73JJ		6'3"	257	Wisconsin		6
Donahue, Oscar FL	62Min	2	6'3"	195	San Jose State		6
Donaldson, Gene FB	67BufA		6'2"	225	Purdue		
Donnahoo, Roger DB	60NY-A		6'	185	Michigan State	5	12
Donnell, Ben DE	60LA-A		6'5"	248	Vanderbilt		
Donnelly, George DB	65-67SF 68JJ		6'3"	207	Illinois	2	
Donohue, Leon OG-OT	62-65SF 65-67Dal 68JJ		6'4"	245	San Jose State		
Donohue, Mike TE	68,70-71Atl 73GB		6'3"	228	San Fran. State		12
Dorris, Andy DE	73NO		6'4"	230	New Mexico State		
Dorsey, Dick OE	62OakA	2	6'3"	200	Southern Calif., Oklahoma		12
Dorsey, Nate DE	73NE		6'4"	240	Miss. Valley St.		
Dotson, Al DT	65KC-A 66MiaA 68-69OakA 70Oak		6'4"	258	Grambling		2
Dougherty, Bob LB	57LA 58Pit 60-63OakA		6'	238	Cincinnati, Kentucky	3	
Doughty, Glenn WB	72-73Bal	2	6'2"	204	Michigan		24
Douglas, Jay C	73SD		6'6"	242	Memphis State		
Douglas, John LB	70-73NYG		6'2"	227	Missouri	2	
Douglas, John DB	67-68NO 69HouA 70JJ		6'1"	195	Texas Southern	1	
Douglas, Merrill FB-HB	58-60ChiB 61Dal 62Phi	2	6'	204	Utah		12
Douglass, Bobby QB	69-73ChiB	12	6'3"	219	Kansas		109
Dove, Eddie DB	59-63SF 63NYG	3	6'2"	181	Colorado	10	
Dowdle, Mike LB-FB	60-62Dal 63-66SF		6'3"	226	Texas	6	6
Dowler, Boyd FL-OE-WR	59-69GB 70VR 71Was	2 4	6'5"	224	Colorado		240
Dowling, Brian QB	72-73NE	1	6'2"	205	Yale		18
Dragon, Oscar HB-FB	72SD		6'	214	Arizona State		
Drake, Bill DB-WB	73LA		6'1"	195	Oregon		
Dressler, Doug FB	70-72Cin 73JJ	2	6'3"	222	Chico State		48
Driskill, Joe DB	60-61StL		6'1"	195	Northeast La.		
Drougas, Tom OT	72-73Bal		6'4"	257	Oregon		
Drungo, Elbert OT-OG	69HouA 70-71Hou 72JJ 73Hou		6'5"	254	Tennessee State		
Dryer, Fred DE	69-71NYG 72-73LA		6'6"	239	San Diego State		4
Dubenion, Elbert FL-HB-WR	60-68BufA	23	6'	189	Bluffton		234
Dudek, Mitch OT	66NY-A		6'4"	245	Xavier-Ohio		
Dudley, Paul HB	62NYG 63Phi	2	6'	185	Arkansas		6
Dugan, Fred OE	58-59SF 60Dal 61-63Was	2	6'3"	197	Dayton		78
Duhon, Bobby HB	68NYG 69JJ 70-72NYG	23	6'	194	Tulane		
Duich, Steve OG	68Atl 69Was		6'3"	248	San Diego State		36
Dukes, Mike LB	60-63HouA 64-65BosA 65NY-A		6'3"	231	Clemson	9	
Dumbrowski, Leon LB	60NY-A		6'	215	Delaware		
Dumler, Doug C	73NE		6'3"	242	Nebraska		
Dunaway, Dave WR	68GB 68Atl 69NYG		6'2"	205	Duke		
Dunaway, Jim DT	63-69BufA 70-71Buf 72Mia 73JJ		6'4"	278	Mississippi	1	6
Dunbar, Jubilee WR	73NO	2	6'	196	Southern U.		24
Duncan, Jim DB	69-71Bal	3	6'2"	200	Md. Eastern Shore	2	12
Duncan, Ken K	71GB		6'2"	210	Tulsa		

Use Name (Nicknames) – Positions	Team by Year		Hgt	Wgt	College	Int	Pts
Duncan, Randy QB	61DalA	1	6'	185	Iowa		
Duncan, Rick K	67DenA 68Phi 69Det		6'	208	Eastern Montana		9
Duncan, Ron TE	67Cle		6'6"	255	Wittenberg		
Duncan, Speedy DB	64-69SD-A 70SD 71-73Was	3	5'10"	177	Jackson State	24	54
Duncum, Bob OT	68StL		6'3"	250	West Texas State		
Dunlap, Lenny DB	71Bal 72-73SD	3	6'1"	195	North Texas State	5	
Dunn, Paul HB-FB	70Cin		6'	210	U.S. International		
Dunn, Perry Lee HB-FB	64-65Dal 66-68Atl 69Bal	2	6'2"	208	Mississippi		42
Dunstan, Bill DT	73Phi		6'4"	250	Utah State		
Dupre, Charlie DB	60NY-A		6'1"	195	Baylor		
DuPree, Billy Joe TE	73Dal	2	6'4"	225	Michigan State		30
Duranko, Pete DE-DT	67-69DenA 70Den 71JJ 72-73Den		6'2"	249	Notre Dame		
Duren, Clarence DB	73StL		6'1"	190	California	2	
Durkee, Charlie K	67-68, 71-72NO	5	5'11"	165	Oklahoma State		243
Durko, Sandy DB	70-71Cin 72JJ 73NE		6'1"	185	Southern Calif.	7	
Dusenbery, Bill HB	70NO		6'2"	198	Johnson C. Smith		
Dyer, Henry FB	66LA 67JJ 68LA 69-70Was	2	6'2"	230	Grambling		12
Dyer, Ken DB-WR	68SD-A 69CinA 70-71Cin		6'3"	187	Arizona State	3	6
Eaglin, Larry DB	73Hou		6'3"	195	S.F. Austin State		6
Eason, John WR	68OakA		6'2"	220	Florida A & M		
East, Ron DT	67-70Dal 71-73SD		6'4"	241	Montana State		
Easterling, Ray DB	72-73Atl		6'	195	Richmond		
Eaton, Scott DB-FL	67-71NYG 72JJ		6'3"	199	Oregon State	11	6
Eber, Rick WR	68Atl 69SD-A 70SD 71JJ	2	6'	181	Tulsa		6
Ebersole, John LB	70-73NYJ		6'3"	236	Penn State	1	
Echols, Fate OT-DT	62-63StL 64CFL		6'1"	258	Northwestern		
Eddy, Nick HB	67JJ 68-70Det 71KJ 72Det	2	6'1"	207	Notre Dame		30
Edgerson, Booker DB	62-69BufA 70Den		5'10"	182	Western Illinois	23	2
Edmunds, Randy LB	68-69MiaA 71NE 72Bal		6'2"	223	Georgia Tech	1	
Edwards, Cid FB	68-71StL 72-73SD	2	6'2"	230	Tennessee State		108
Edwards, Dave LB	63-73Dal		6'3"	224	Auburn	13	6
Edwards, Earl DT-DE	69-72SF 73Buf		6'6"	267	Wichita State		
Edwards, Glen DB	71-73Pit	3	6'	185	Florida A & M	8	6
Edwards, Lloyd TE	69OakA		6'3"	248	San Diego State		
Ehrmann, Joe DT	73Bal		6'5"	260	Syracuse		
Eifrid, Jim LB	61DenA		6'1"	240	Colorado State		
Eischeid, Mike K	66-69OakA 70-71Oak 72-73Min	45	6'	190	Upper Iowa		70
Eisenhauer, Larry DE	61-69BosA		6'5"	247	Boston College	1	
Elkins, Larry FL	66-67HouA 69JJ	2	6'1"	193	Baylor		18
Eller, Carl DE	64-73Min		6'6"	254	Minnesota		8
Ellersick, Don DB	60LA		6'1"	193	Washington State	2	
Elliott, Jim K	67Pit	4	5'11"	184	Presbyterian		
Elliott, John DT-DE	67-69NY-A 70-73NYJ		6'4"	244	Texas		2
Elliott, Lenvil HB	73Cin		6'	200	NE Missouri St.		12
Ellis, Allan DB	73ChiB		5'10"	185	U. C. L. A.	1	
Ellis, Clarence DB	72-73Atl		5'11"	192	Notre Dame	5	
Ellis, Ken DB	70-73GB	3	5'10"	190	Southern U.	16	24
Ellis, Roger LB-C	60-63NY-A		6'3"	233	Maine	1	
Ellison, Glenn HB-FB	71Oak		6'1"	215	Arkansas		
Ellison, Mark OG	72-73NYG		6'2"	250	Dayton		
Ellison, Willie HB-FB	67-72LA 73KC	23	6'1"	203	Texas Southern		168
Ellzey, Charley C-LB	60-61StL		6'3"	243	Southern Miss.		
Elmendorf, Dave DB	71-73LA	3	6'1"	195	Texas A & M	6	
Elmore, Doug DB	62Was	4	6'	188	Mississippi	2	
Elwell, Jack OE	62StL		6'3"	200	Purdue		
Ely, Larry LB	70-71Cin		6'1"	230	Iowa		
Elzey, Paul LB	68CinA		6'3"	235	Toledo		
Emanuel, Frank LB	66-69MiaA 70NO		6'3"	225	Tennessee	4	6
Embree, John WR	69DenA 70Den 71JJ	2	6'4"	201	Compton J.C.		30
Emelianchik, Pete TE	67Phi		6'2"	220	Richmond		
Emerson, Vern OT	69-71StL		6'5"	260	Minnesota-Duluth		
Enderle, Dick OG	69-71Atl 72-73NYG		6'1"	251	Minnesota		
Engel, Steve HB-FB	70Cle		6'1"	218	Colorado		
Enis, Hunter QB	60DalA 61SD-A 62DenA 62OakA	12	6'2"	192	Texas Christian		30
Enyart, Bill FB	69BufA 70Buf 71Oak 72KJ	2	6'4"	236	Oregon State		24
Epperson, Pat OE	60DenA	2	6'3"	225	Adams State		
Erdelatz, Eddie	HC60OakA				St. Mary's		
Erickson, Bernie LB	67-68SD-A 68CinA		6'2"	239	Abilene Christian	1	
Erlandson, Tom LB	62-65DenA 66-67MiaA 68SD-A		6'3"	229	Washington State	8	6
Ernst, Mike QB	72Den 73Cin		6'1"	190	Fullerton State		
Erwin, Terry HB	68DenA		6'	190	Boston College		
Estes, Don OG	66SD-A		6'2"	250	Louisiana State		
Estes, Larry DE	70-71NO 72Phi		6'6"	257	Alcorn A & M		
Etcheverry, Sam QB	61-62StL	12 4	5'11"	190	Denver		
Etter, Bob K	68-69Atl	5	5'11"	152	Georgia		128
Evans, Bob DE	65HouA		6'3"	250	Texas A & M		
Evans, Charlie FB	71-73NYG	2	6'1"	218	Southern Calif.		66
Evans, Dale HB	61DenA		6'3"	210	Kansas State		
Evans, Jim FL	64-65NY-A		6'1"	190	Texas-El Paso		
Evans, Mike C	68-73Phi		6'5"	250	Boston College		
Evans, Norm OT	65HouA 66-68MiaA 69MiaA 70-73Mia		6'5"	247	Texas Christian		6
Evey, Dick DT-DE-OG	64-69ChiB 70LA 71Det		6'2"	238	Tennessee	2	
Ewbank, Weeb	HC54-62Bal HC63-69NY-A HC70-73NYJ				Miami-Ohio		
Ezerins, Vilnis HB-FB	68LA		6'1"	217	Whitewater		
Fagan, Julian K	70-72NO 73NYJ	4	6'3"	205	Mississippi		
Fairband, Bill LB	67-68OakA		6'3"	228	Colorado		
Fairbanks, Chuck	HC73NE				Michigan State		
Faison, Earl DE	61-66SD-A 66MiaA		6'5"	263	Indiana	6	14
Falls, Mike OG	60-61Dal		6'1"	240	Minnesota		
Fanning, Stan OT-DE-DT	60-62ChiB 63LA 64HouA 64DenA		6'6"	267	Idaho		
Fanucci, Mike DE	72Was 73Hou		6'4"	233	Arizona State		
Farasopoulos, Chris DB	71-73NYJ	3	5'11"	190	Brigham Young	3	6
Farber, Hap LB	70Min 70NO		6'1"	220	Mississippi		
Farley, Dale LB	71Mia 72-73Buf		6'3"	235	West Virginia		
Farley, Dick DB	68-69SD-A		6'	185	Boston U.		
Farmer, George WR	70-73ChiB	2	6'4"	212	U. C. L. A.		60
Farmer, Lonnie LB	64-66BosA		6'	220	Tenn.-Chattanooga	1	
Farr, Mel HB-FB	67-73Det	2	6'2"	208	U. C. L. A.		216

Use Name (Nicknames) - Positions	Team by Year	See Section	Hgt	Wgt	College	Int	Pts
Farr, Miller DB	65DenA 65-66SD-A 67-69HouA 70-72StL 73Det		6'1"	190	Wichita	35	36
Farrier, Curt DT	63-65KC-A 66JJ		6'6"	253	Montana State		
Farrington, Bo OE	60-63ChiB	2	6'3"	217	Prairie View		42
killed in auto accident at 1964 training camp							
Farris, John OG	65-66SD-A		6'4"	245	San Diego State		
Faulkner, Jack	HC62-64DenA				Miami (Fla.)		
Faulkner, Staley OT	64HouA		6'3"	245	Texas		
Faust, Paul LB	67Min		6'	220	Minnesota		
Feagin, Wiley OG	61-62Bal 63Was		6'2"	235	Houston		
Federspiel, Joe LB	72-73NO		6'1	225	Kentucky	1	
Feldhausen, Paul OT	68BosA		6'6"	270	Northland		
Feldman, Marty	HC61-62OakA				Stanford		
Feller, Happy K	71Phi 72-73NO	5	5'11"	185	Texas		75
Felt, Dick DB	60-61NY-A 62-66BosA		6'	184	Brigham Young	18	6
Felts, Bobby HB	65Bal 65-67Det	23	6'2"	203	Florida A&M		12
Fenner, Lane WR	68SD-A		6'5"	210	Florida State		
Ferguson, Bill LB	73NYJ		6'3"	225	San Diego State		
Ferguson, Bob FB	62-63Pit 63Min	2	5'11"	220	Ohio State		6
Ferguson, Charley OE-TE	61Cle 62Min 63BufA 64JJ 65-66BufA 67-68JJ 69BufA	2	6'5"	218	Tennessee State		78
Ferguson, Gene OT-DT	69SD-A 70SD 71-72Hou		6'7"	302	Norfolk State		
Ferguson, Jim C-LB	68NO 69Atl 69ChiB 71JJ		6'4"	240	Southern Calif.		
Ferguson, Joe QB	73Buf	12	6'1"	190	Arkansas		12
Ferguson, Larry HB	63Det		5'10"	185	Iowa		
Fernandez, Manny DT-DE	68-69MiaA 70-73Mia		6'2"	249	Utah		
Ferrante, Orlando OG	60LA-A 61SD-A		6'	230	Southern Calif.		
Fersen, Paul OT	73NO		6'5"	260	Georgia		
Fest, Cotton DT	72Cle		6'2"	255	Dayton		
Fest, Howard OT-OG	68-69CinA 70-73Cin		6'6"	265	Texas		
Fetherston, Jim LB	68-69SD-A		6'2"	225	California	1	
Ficca, Dan OG	62OakA 63-66NY-A		6'1"	244	Southern Calif.		
Fichtner, Ross DB	60-67Cle 68NO		6'	186	Purdue	27	18
Fields, George DE-DT	60-61OakA		6'3"	245	Cal. St.-Bakersf.	2	
Fields, Jerry LB	61-62NY-A		6'1"	222	Ohio State		
Files, Jim LB	70-73NYG		6'4"	240	Oklahoma	5	8
Finch, Karl OE	62LA		6'3"	195	Cal. St. Polytech		
Fink, Mike DB	73NO		5'11"	180	Missouri		
Finneran, Gary DT	60LA-A 61OakA		6'3"	240	Southern Calif.		
Finnie, Roger OG-OT-DT	69NY-A 70-72NYJ 73StL		6'3"	245	Florida A&M		
Fischer, Pat DB-HB	61-67StL 68-73Was	3	5'10"	170	Nebraska	45	30
Fisher, Doug LB	69-70Pit		6'1"	225	San Diego State		
Fiss, Galen LB	56-66Cle		6'	226	Kansas	13	
Fitzgerald, John C-OG	71-73Dal		6'5"	250	Boston College		
Fitzgerald, Mike DB	66-67Min 67NYG 67Atl	3	5'10	180	Iowa State	1	
Flanagan, Ed C	65-73Det		6'3"	248	Purdue		
Flanigan, Jim LB	67-70GB 71NO		6'3"	238	Pittsburgh	1	
Flatley, Paul OE-WR	63-67Min 68-70Atl	2	6'1"	187	Northwestern		144
Fleming, Don DB	60-62Cle		6'	187	Florida	10	
died June 4, 1963 – construction accident							
Fleming, George HB	61OakA	23 5	5'11"	188	Washington		63
Fleming, Marv TE-OE	63-69GB 70-73Mia	2	6'4"	234	Utah		90
Fletcher, Billy DB	66DenA		5'10"	190	Memphis State		
Fletcher, Chris DB	70-73SD	3	5'11"	185	Temple	3	6
Flint, George OG	62-65BufA 66JJ 67-69BufA		6'4"	243	Arizona State		
Flores, Tom QB	60-61OakA 62IL 63-66OakA 67-69BufA 69KC-A	12	6'1"	194	U. of Pacific		30
Flowers, Charlie FB	60LA-A 61SD-A 62NY-A	2	6'1"	215	Mississippi		30
Flowers, Richmond DB-WR	69-71Dal 71-73NYG		6'	181	Tennessee	6	
Floyd, Don DE	60-67HouA		6'4"	242	Texas Christian	4	12
Flynn, Don DB	60-61DalA 61NY-A		6'	205	Houston	5	6
Foley, Dave OT-C	70-71NYJ 72-73Buf		6'5"	255	Ohio State		
Foley, Tim DB	70-73Mia		6'	194	Purdue	9	12
Folkins, Lee OE-DE	61GB 62-64Dal 65Pit	2	6'5"	219	Washington		66
Fontes, Wayne DB	62NY-A		6'	190	Michigan State	4	6
Ford, Charlie DB	71-73ChiB		6'3"	185	Houston		14
Ford, Fred HB	60BufA 60LA-A	2	5'8"	180	Cal. St. Polytech		12
Ford, Garrett FB	68DenA	2	6'2"	230	West Virginia		6
Ford, Jamie HB-FB	71-72NO	2	6'	203	Texas Southern		12
Foreman, Chuck HB-FB	73Min	2	6'2"	216	Miami (Fla.)		36
Forsberg, Fred LB	68, 70-73DenA 73BufA		6'1"	235	Washington	5	6
Fortunato, Joe LB-FB	55-66ChiB		6'	225	Mississippi State	16	18
Foruria, John DB-LB	67-68Pit		6'2"	205	Idaho		
Foster, Gene FB-HB	65-69SD-A 70SD	2	5'11"	214	Arizona State		42
Foster, Will LB	73NE		6'2"	230	Eastern Michigan		6
Fournet, Sid OG-LB-DE	55-56LA 57Pit 60-61DalA 62-63NY-A		6'	235	Louisiana State	1	
Fouts, Dan QB	73SD	1	6'3"	193	Oregon		
Fowler, Bobby FB	62NY-A		5'11"	212	Martin J.C.		
Fowler, Charlie OG-OT	67-68MiaA		6'2"	260	Houston		
Fowler, Jerry OT	64HouA		6'3"	255	NW State-La.		
Fowler, Wayne C	70Buf		6'3"	260	Richmond		
Fowler, Willmer HB	60-61BufA	2	5'11"	185	Northwestern		6
Franci, Jason OE	66DenA		6'1"	210	Cal.-Santa Barbara		
Francis, Dave FB	63Was		6'1"	210	Ohio State		
Francis, Wallace WR	73Buf		5'11"	188	Ark.-Pine Bluff		12
Franckhauser, Tom DB	59LA 60-61Dal 62-63Min	3	6'	195	Purdue	13	
Frank, Bill OT	64Dal		6'5"	255	Colorado		
Franklin, Bobby DB-HB	60-66Cle		5'11"	182	Mississippi	13	18
Franklin, Willie WR	72Bal		6'2"	195	Oklahoma		
Frantz, Jack C	68BufA		6'3"	230	California		
Fraser, Jim LB-K	62-64DenA 65KC-A 66BosA 68NO	4	6'3"	236	Wisconsin	3	2
Frazier, Al HB-FL	61-63DenA	23	5'11"	180	Florida A&M		68
Frazier, Charley OE-WR	62-68HouA 69BosA 70Bos	2	6'	177	Texas Southern		180
Frazier, Curt DB	68CinA		5'11"	193	Fresno State		
Frazier, Wayne C-LB	62SD-A 65HouA 66-67KC-A 67BufA		6'2"	243	Auburn		
Frazier, Willie TE-OE	64-65HouA 66-69SD-A 70SD 71Hou 71-72KC	2	6'4"	235	Ark.-Pine Bluff		222
Frederickson, Tucker FB-HB	65NYG 66KJ 67-71NYG	2	6'3"	223	Auburn		102
Freelon, Soloman OG	72-73Hou		6'2"	250	Grambling		
Freeman, Bobby DB-HB	57-58Cle 59GB 60-61Phi 62Was		6'1"	202	Auburn	15	
Freeman, Mike DB	68-70Alt		5'11"	187	Fresno State	1	
Freitas, Rocky OT	68-73Det		6'6"	271	Oregon State		
Frey, Dick DE-OG	60DalA 61HouA		6'2"	233	Texas A&M		

Use Name (Nicknames) - Positions	Team by Year	See Section	Hgt	Wgt	College	Int	Pts
Fritsch, Ernie C-LB	60StL		6'	230	Detroit		
Fritsch, Ted C	72-73Atl		6'2"	240	St. Norbert		
Fritsch, Toni K	71-73Dal	5	5'7"	185	none		213
Frongillo, John OG-C	62-66HouA		6'3"	252	Baylor		
Frost, Ken DT	61-62Dal		6'4"	245	Tennessee	1	
Fugett, Jean TE	72-73Dal	2	6'3"	220	Amherst		18
Fuller, Charley HB	61-62OakA	2	5'11"	176	San Fran. State		12
Fuller, Johnny DB	68-72SF 73NO	3	6'	180	Lamar Tech	7	
Funchess, Tom OT	68-69BosA 70Bos 71-73Hou		6'5"	263	Jackson State		
Fuqua, John (Frenchy) HB-FB	69NYG 70-73Pit	2	5'11"	201	Morgan State		120
Furey, Jim LB	61NY-A		6'	228	Kansas State		
Furman, John QB	62Cle		6'4"	205	Texas-El Paso		
Furness, Steve DT-DE	72-73Pit		6'4"	255	Rhode Island		
Fussell, Tom DE	67BosA		6'3"	245	Louisiana State		
Gabriell, Roman QB	62-72LA 73Phi	12	6'4"	225	N. Carolina State		174
Gaechter, Mike DB	62-69Dal		6'	192	Oregon	21	12
Gagner, Larry OG	66-69Pit 70JJ 72KC		6'3"	246	Florida		
Gaiser, George OT	68DenA		6'4"	255	S. M. U.		
Gaiters, Bob HB	61-62NYG 62SF 63DenA	23	5'11"	210	New Mexico State		48
Galigher, Ed DE-DT	72-73NYJ		6'4"	255	U. C. L. A.		
Galimore, Willie HB	57-63ChiB	23	6'1"	187	Florida A&M		222
killed in auto accident at 1964 training camp							
Gallagher, Frank OG	67-72Det 73Atl 73Min		6'2"	243	North Carolina		
Gallegos, Chan QB	62OakA	1	5'9"	175	San Jose State		
Gamble, R.C. HB-FB	68-69BosA	2	6'3"	220	S. Carolina State		12
Gambrell, Billy OE-FL-WR	63-67StL 68Det	23	5'10"	175	South Carolina		108
Ganas, Rusty DT	71Bal		6'4"	257	South Carolina		
Gantt, Jerry OT	70Buf		6'4"	266	N. Car. Central		
Garcia, Jim DE-DT	65Cle 66NYG 67NO 68Atl		6'4"	248	Purdue		
Gardin, Ron DB-WR	70-71Bal 71NE	3	5'11"	180	Arizona		6
Garlington, John LB	68-73Cle		6'1"	223	Louisiana State	7	
Garner, Bob DB	60LA-A 61-62OakA	3	5'10"	185	Fresno State	7	
Garrett, Carl HB	69BosA 70Bos 71-72NE 73ChiB	23	5'11"	212	N. Mex. Highlands		138
Garrett, Drake DB	68DenA 70Den		5'9"	183	Michigan State	2	
Garrett, J. D. HB	64-67BosA	23	5'11"	195	Grambling		36
Garrett, Len TE	71-73GB 73NO		6'3"	230	N. Mex. Highlands		
Garrett, Mike HB	66-69KC-A 70KC 70-73SD	23	5'9"	199	Southern Calif.		294
Garrison, Gary WR-OE	66-69SD-A 70-73SD	2	6'1"	194	San Diego State		300
Garrison, Walt FB-HB	66-73Dal	23	6'	204	Oklahoma State		198
Garron, Larry HB-FB	60-68BosA	23	6'	199	Western Illinois		252
Garror, Leon DB	72-73Buf		6'	180	Alcorn A & M	1	
Gassert, Ron DT	62GB		6'3"	250	Virginia		
Gatewood, Tom TE-WR	72-73NYG		6'3"	215	Notre Dame		
Gaubatz, Dennis LB	63-64Det 65-69Bal		6'2"	225	Louisiana State	10	2
Gault, Billy HB	61Min		6'1"	185	Texas Christian		
Gault, Don QB	70Cle		6'2"	190	Hofstra		
Gault, Prentice HB-FB	60Cle 61-67StL	2	6'	204	Oklahoma		102
Gavin, Chuck DE	60-63DenA		6'1"	243	Tennessee State	1	6
Gavric, Momcilo K	69SF	5	5'10"	167	none		31
Geddes, Bob LB	72Den 73NE		6'2"	240	U. C. L. A.		
Geddes, Ken LB	71-73LA		6'3"	235	Nebraska		
Gehrke, Jack WR	68KC-A 69CinA 71Den 72JJ	2	6'	178	Utah		
Gent, Pete FL-TE-OE	64-68Dal	2	6'4"	209	Michigan State		24
Gentry, Curtis DB	66-68ChiB		6'	186	Md. Eastern Shore	6	
George, Tim WR	73Cin		6'5"	225	Whittier		
Geredine, Tom WR	73Atl		6'2"	195	NE Missouri St.		6
Gerela, Roy K	69HouA 70Hou 71-73Pit	45	5'10"	185	New Mexico State		483
Germany, Willie DB	72Atl 73Det		6'	192	Morgan State		
Gersbach, Carl LB	70Phi 71-72Min 73SD		6'1"	230	West Chester St.	1	
Gibbons, Jim OE-TE	58-68Det	2	6'2"	220	Iowa		120
Gibbs, Pat DB	72Phi		5'10"	188	Lamar Tech		
Gibbs, Sonny QB	64Det		6'7"	230	Texas Christian		
Gibson, Claude DB	61-62SD-A 63-65OakA	3	6'1"	191	N. Carolina State	22	26
Gibson, Paul DB	72GB		6'2"	195	Texas-El Paso		
Gibson, Tom DT	71Oak		6'6"	290	Texas-El Paso		
Gilburg, Tom OT	61-65Bal	4	6'5"	245	Syracuse		
Gilchrist, Cookie FB	62-64BufA 65DenA 66MiaA 67DenA	2 5	6'3"	249	none		296
Gill, Roger HB-TE	64-65Phi		6'1"	200	Texas Tech		
Gillett, Fred HB-OE	62SD-A 64OakA		6'3"	223	Los Angeles State		
Gillette, Walker WR	70-71SD 72-73StL	2	6'5"	199	Richmond		30
Gilliam, Joe QB	72-73Pit	1	6'2"	187	Tennessee State		
Gilliam, John WR-HB	67-68NO 69-71 StL 72-73Min	23	6'1"	193	S. Carolina State		222
Gilliam, Jon C	61-62DalA 63-67KC-A		6'2"	238	East Texas State		
Gillingham, Gale OG-DT	66-73GB		6'3"	254	Minnesota		
Gillis, Don C	58-59ChiC 60-61StL 62JJ		6'3"	245	Rice		
Gillman, Sid	HC55-59LA HC60LA-A HC61-69SD-A HC71SD HC73Hou				Ohio State		
Ginn, Hubert HB	70-73Mia 73Bal	23	5'11"	189	Florida A&M		6
Gipson, Paul HB-FB	69-70Atl 71Det 73NE	2	6'	208	Houston		24
Glacken, Scotty QB	66-67DenA		6'	190	Duke		
Gladieux, Bob HB	69BosA 70Bos 70Buf 71-72NE	2	5'11"	191	Notre Dame		
Glass, Bill DE-C-OT	58-61Det 62-68Cle		6'5"	250	Baylor	4	12
Glass, Chip TE	69-73Cle	2	6'4"	236	Florida State		30
Glass, Glenn DB-FL-OE	62-63Pit 64-65Phi 66Alt 66DenA	2	6'	197	Tennessee	2	
Glass, Leland WR	72-73GB	2	6'	185	Oregon		6
Glenn, Howard OG	60NY-A		6'	235	Linfield		
died Oct. 9, 1960 – broken neck							
Glick, Freddy DB	59ChiC 60StL 61-66HouA	3	6'1"	189	Colorado State	31	6
Glosson, Clyde WR	70Buf		5'11"	175	Texas-El Paso		
Glover, Rich DT	73NYG		6'1"	240	Nebraska		
Glueck, Larry DB	63-65ChiB		6'	190	Villanova	1	
Goeddeke, George OG-OT-C	67-69DenA 70-72Den 73JJ		6'3"	250	Notre Dame		
Gogolak, Charlie K	66-68Was 70Bos 71-72NE	5	5'10"	168	Princeton		270
Gogolak, Pete K	64-65BufA 66-73NYG	5	6'2"	193	Cornell		812
Goich, Dan DT-DE	69-70Det 71NO 72-73NYG		6'4"	259	California		
Goldstein, Al OE	60OakA	2	6'	204	North Carolina		12
Gonsoulin, Goose DB	60-66DenA 67SF		6'3"	209	Baylor	46	14
Gonzaga, John OT-OG-DT-DE	56-59SF 60Dal 61-65Det 66DenA		6'3"	247	none		
Good, Tom LB	66SD-A		6'	230	Marshall		
Goode, Irv OG-OT-C	62-71StL 72JJ 73Mia		6'4"	249	Kentucky		
Goode, Tom C-LB	62-65HouA 66-69MiaA 70Bal		6'3"	244	Mississippi State		

Use Name (Nicknames) – Positions	Team by Year		Hgt	Wgt	College	Int	Pts
Goodman, Brian OG	73Hou		6'2"	250	U. C. L. A.		
Goodman, Les HB-FB	73GB		5'11"	206	Yankton		6
Goodridge, Bob WR	68Min		6'2"	202	Vanderbilt		
Goodrum, Charlie OT-OG	73Min		6'3"	256	Florida A & M		
Goodwin, Doug FB	65KJ 66BufA 68Atl		6'2"	228	Md. Eastern Shore		
Goodwin, Ron OE-FL-WR	63-68Phi	2	6'	180	Baylor		54
Goosby, Tom OG-LB	63Cle 66Was		6'	235	Baldwin-Wallace		
Goovert, Ron LB	67Det		5'11"	225	Michigan State		
Gordon, Cornell DB	65-69NY-A 70-72Den		6'	187	N. Carolina A & T	14	
Gordon, Dick WR-OE	65-71ChiB 72-73LA 73GB	23	5'11"	190	Michigan State		216
Gordon, Ira OT-OG	70-73SD		6'3"	268	Kansas State		
Gordon, John DT	72Det		6'6"	260	Hawaii		
Gordy, John OG-OT	57Det 58VR 59-67Det		6'3"	248	Tennessee		
Gossage, Gene DE-OG-DT	60-62Phi 63CFL		6'3"	239	Northwestern		
Gossett, Bruce K	64-69LA 70-73SF	5	6'2"	229	Richmond		973
Gotshalk, Len OT	72-73Atl		6'4"	252	Humboldt State		
Grabosky, Gene DT	60BufA		6'5"	275	Syracuse		
Grabowski, Jim FB	66-70GB 71ChiB	2	6'2"	221	Illinois		66
Grady, Garry DB	69MiaA		5'11"	180	Eastern Michigan		
Graham, Art OE-WR	63-68BosA	2	6'1"	205	Boston College		120
Graham, Dave OT	63-66Phi 67JJ 68-69Phi 70JJ		6'3"	248	Virginia		
Graham, Kenny DB	64-69SD-A 70Cin 70Pit	3	6'	201	Washington State	28	30
Graham, Milt OT-DT	61-63BosA		6'6"	235	Colgate		
Graham, Tom LB	72-73Den		6'2"	235	Oregon	2	
Granderson, Rufus DT	60DalA		6'5"	277	Prairie View		
Granger, Charley OT	61Dal 61StL		6'2"	240	Southern U.		
Granger, Hoyle FB-HB	66-69HouA 70Hou 71NO 72Hou	2	6'1"	225	Mississippi State		144
Grant, Bob LB	68-70Bal 71Was		6'2"	225	Wake Forest	5	6
Grant, Frank WR	73Was		5'11"	180	S. Colorado State		6
Grant, John DE	73Den		6'3"	235	Southern Calif.		
Grant, Wes DE-DT	70JJ 71Buf 71SD 72Cle 73Hou		6'3"	245	U. C. L. A.		
Grantham, Larry LB	60-69NY-A 70-73NYJ		6'	204	Mississippi	24	18
Grate, Willie TE	69BufA 70Buf		6'4"	225	S. Carolina State		18
Gravelle, Gordon OT	72-73Pit		6'5"	250	Brigham Young		
Graves, White DB	65-67BosA 68CinA		6'	185	Louisiana State	3	
Gray, Jim DB	66NY-A 67Phi		6'	181	Toledo		
Gray, Ken OG-LB	58-59ChiC 60-69StL 70Hou		6'2"	245	Howard Payne		
Gray, Leon DT	73NE		6'3"	256	Jackson State		
Gray, Mel WR	71-73StL	23	5'9"	170	Missouri		66
Gray, Moses OT-DT	61-62NY-A		6'3"	260	Indiana		
Grayson, Dave DB	61-62DalA 63-64KC-A 65-69OakA 70Oak	3	5'10"	184	Oregon	49	36
Greaves, Gary OT	60HouA		6'3"	235	Miami (Fla.)		
Grecni, Dick LB	61Min		6'1"	230	Ohio U.	1	
Green, Allen K	61Dal	45	6'2"	215	Mississippi		34
Green, Arthur HB-FB	72NO		5'11"	198	Albany State		
Green, Bobby Joe K	60-61Pit 62-73ChiB	4	5'11"	175	Florida		
Green, Charlie QB	66OakA		6'	190	Wittenberg		
Green, Cornell DB	62-73Dal		6'4"	211	Utah State	32	24
Green, Dave K	73Hou 73Cin		5'11"	200	Ohio U.		
Green, Donnie OT	71-73Buf		6'7"	276	Purdue		
Green, Ernie HB-FB	62-68Cle	23	6'2"	205	Louisville		210
Green, Jerry HB	60BosA		6'	190	Georgia Tech		
Green, Joe DB	70-71NYG		5'11"	195	Bowling Green		6
Green, Johnny QB	60-61BufA 62-63NY-A	12	6'3"	203	Tenn.-Chattanooga		36
Green, Ron FL-WR	67-68Cle		6'1"	200	North Dakota		
Green, Van DB	73Cle		6'1"	192	Shaw		6
Greene, Joe (Mean Joe) DT	69-73Pit		6'4"	273	North Texas State		
Greene, Ted LB	60-62DalA		6'1"	230	Tampa	4	
Greene, Tom QB	60BosA 61DalA	12 4	6'1"	190	Holy Cross		
Greene, Tony DB	71-73Buf		5'10"	170	Maryland	4	6
Greenlee, Fritz LB	69SF		6'2"	230	Arizona State		
Greenwood, L. C. DE	69-73Pit		6'5"	242	Ark.-Pine Bluff		
Greer, Al OE	63Det		6'4"	190	Jackson State		
Greer, Charlie DB	68-69DenA 70-73Den	3	6'	205	Colorado	16	1
Greer, Jim OE	60DenA	2	6'3"	215	Elizabeth City St.		6
Gregg, Forrest OT-OG-DT	56GB 57MS 58-70GB 71Dal		6'4"	249	S. M. U.		
Gregory, Ben HB-FB	68BufA	2	6'3"	220	Nebraska		6
Gregory, Bill DT	71-73Dal		6'5"	255	Wisconsin		
Gregory, Glynn OE-DB	61-62Dal		6'2"	200	S. M. U.	1	
Gregory, Jack DE	67-71Cle 72-73NYG		6'6"	249	Tenn.-Chattanooga, Delta State	1	
Gregory, Ken OE	61Bal 62Phi 63NY-A		6'	190	Whittier		
Gremminger, Hank DB	56-65GB 66LA		6'1"	201	Baylor	29	6
Gresham, Bob HB	71-72NO 73Hou	23	5'11"	194	West Virginia		78
Grier, Rosey DT	55-56NYG 57MS 58-62NYG 63-66LA 67JJ		6'5"	284	Penn State		4
Griese, Bob QB	67-69MiaA 70-73Mia	12	6'1"	190	Purdue		30
Griffin, Jim DE	66-67SD-A 68CinA		6'3"	258	Grambling		6
Griffin, John DB	63LA 64-66DenA		6'1"	190	Memphis State	4	12
Griffing, Glynn QB	63NYG	1	6'1"	200	Mississippi		
Grim, Bob WR-DB-FL	72-73NYG	23	6'	198	Oregon State		72
Grimm, Dan OG	63-65GB 66-68Atl 69Bal 69Was		6'3"	244	Colorado		
Groman, Bill OE-FL	60-62HouA 63DenA 64-65BufA	2	6'	195	Heidelberg		222
Gros, Earl FB	62-63GB 64-66Phi 67-69Pit 70NO	2	6'3"	224	Louisiana State		228
Gross, Andy OG	67-68NYG		6'	230	Auburn		
Gross, George DT	63-67SD-A		6'3"	263	Auburn		
Grosscup, Lee QB	60-61NYG 62NY-A	1	6'1"	186	Utah		
Grottkau, Bob OG	59-60Det 61Dal		6'4"	228	Oregon		
Gruneisen, Sam C-OG-LB	62-69SD-A 70-72SD 73Hou		6'1"	248	Villanova		
Gucciardo, Pat DB	66NY-A		5'11"	185	Kent State		
Guesman, Dick DT	60-63NY-A 64DenA	5	6'4"	255	West Virginia		129
Gugliemi, Ralph QB	55Was 56-57MS 58-60Was 61StL 62-63NYG 63Phi	12	6'1"	196	Notre Dame		12
Guidry, Paul LB	66-69BufA 70-72Buf 73Hou		6'3"	229	McNeese State	5	
Guillory, John DB	69CinA 70Cin		5'10"	190	Stanford	1	
Guillory, Tony LB	65LA 66JJ 67-68LA 69Phi		6'4"	232	Nebraska, Lamar Tech		
Gulseth, Don LB	66DenA		6'1"	240	North Dakota		
Gunn, Jimmy LB	70-73ChiB		6'1"	219	Southern Calif.	1	
Gunnels, Riley DT-DE	60-64Phi 65-66Pit		6'3"	250	Georgia	1	
Gunner, Harry DE	68-69CinA 70ChiB		6'6"	250	Oregon State	2	8
Gursky, Al LB	63NYG		6'1"	210	Penn State		
Guthrie, Grant K	70-71Buf	5	6'	210	Florida State		71

Use Name (Nicknames) – Positions	Team by Year		Hgt	Wgt	College	Int	Pts
Guy, Louis DB-FL	63NYG 64OakA		6'	188	Mississippi		
Guy, Ray K	73Oak	4	6'3"	190	Southern Miss.		
Guzik, John LB-OG	59-60LA 61HouA		6'3"	231	Pittsburgh		
Gwinn, Ross OG	68NO		6'3"	273	NW State-La.		
Hackbart, Dale DB	60GB 61-63Was 66-70Min 71-72StL 73Den		6'3"	210	Wisconsin	19	24
Hadl, John QB	62-69SD-A 70-72SD 73LA	12 4	6'2"	212	Kansas		90
Hadley, Dave DB	70-71KC		5'9"	186	Alcorn A & M	1	
Haffner, Mike WR	68-69DenA 70Den 71Cin	2	6'2"	205	U. C. L. A.		42
Hagberg FB-TE	65-69OakA	2	6'2"	216	Minnesota		48
Hageman, Fred C	61-64Was		6'4"	243	Kansas		
Hagen, Halvor C-OG-DE-OT	69-70Dal 71-72NE 73Buf		6'5"	251	Weber State		
Haggerty, Mike OT	67-70Pit 71NE 73Det		6'4"	239	Miami (Fla.)		
Haik, Mac WR	68-69HouA 70-71Hou	2	6'1"	196	Mississippi		54
Hale, Dave DT-DE	69-71ChiB 72JJ 73ChiB		6'7"	251	Ottawa (Kan.)		
Haley, Dick DB-HB-FL-OE	59-60Was 61Min 61-64Pit	3	5'10"	193	Pittsburgh	14	12
Hall, Alvin DB	61-63LA		6'	195	none	1	
Hall, Charlie LB	71-73Cle		6'3"	220	Houston		
Hall, Charlie DB	71-73GB		6'1"	195	Pittsburgh		
Hall, Galen QB	62Was 63NY-A	1	5'10"	200	Penn State		12
Hall, Ken HB	59ChiC 60-61HouA 61StL	23	6'1"	205	Texas A & M		24
Hall, Pete OE	61NYG		6'2"	200	Marquette		
Hall, Ron DB	59Pit 60MS 61-67BosA		6'	190	Missouri Valley	30	6
Hall, Tom FL-OE-WR-DB	62-63Det 64-66Min 67NO 68-69Min	2	6'1"	195	Minnesota	3	48
Hall, Willie LB	72-73NO		6'2"	221	Southern Calif.		
Hall, Windlan DB	72-73SF		5'11"	177	Arizona State	2	12
Halverson, Dean LB	68LA 70Atl 71-72LA 73Phi		6'2"	218	Washington		
Ham, Jack LB	71-73Pit		6'3"	222	Penn State	11	12
Hamilton, Andy WR	73KC		6'3"	190	Louisiana State		
Hamilton, Ray DE	73NE		6'1"	232	Oklahoma		
Hamlin, Gene C	70Was 71ChiB 72Det		6'3"	245	Western Michigan		
Hammack, Mal FB-OE-TE-LB	55,57-59ChiC 56MS 60-66StL	2	6'2"	205	Florida		48
Hammond, Gary WR-HB	73StL		5'11"	180	S. M.U.		
Hammond, Kim QB	68MiaA 69BosA	1	6'1"	192	Florida State		2
Hampton, Dave HB-FB	69-71GB 72-73Atl	23	6'	210	Wyoming		150
Hanburger, Chris LB	65-73Was		6'2"	218	North Carolina	11	24
Hancock, Mike TE	73Was		6'4"	220	Idaho State		12
Hand, Larry DE	65-73Det		6'4"	247	Appalachian State	3	18
Hannah, John OG	73NE		6'2"	265	Alabama		
Hanneman, Craig DT-DE	72-73Pit		6'3"	240	Oregon State		
Hanratty, Terry QB	69-73Pit	1	6'1"	206	Notre Dame		6
Hansen, Don LB	66-67Min 69-73Atl		6'3"	226	Illinois	8	6
Hanson, Dick DT	71NYG		6'6"	280	N. Dakota State		
Harden, Lee DB	70GB		5'11"	195	Texas-El Paso		
Hardman, Cedrick DE	70-73SF		6'3"	255	North Texas State		2
Hardy, Charley OE	62-62OakA	2	6'	184	San Jose State		42
Hardy, Cliff DB	71ChiB		6'	187	Michigan State		
Hardy, Ed OG	73SF		6'4"	242	Jackson State		
Hardy, Kevin DT-DE	68SF 69KJ 70GB 71-72SD		6'5"	271	Notre Dame		
Hargett, Edd QB	69-72NO 73Hou	1	5'11"	187	Texas A & M		6
Hargrove, Jim LB	67Min 68MS 69-70Min 71-72StL		6'3"	229	Howard Payne	1	6
Harkey, Steve HB-FB	71-72NYJ	2	6'	215	Georgia Tech		
Harmon, Ed LB	69CinA		6'4"	230	Louisville		
Harmon, Tom OG	67Atl		6'4"	238	Gustavus Adolphus		
Harold, George DB	66-67Bal 68Was		6'3"	198	Allen		
Harper, Charlie OG-OT-DT	66-72NYG		6'2"	250	Oklahoma State		
Harper, Darrell HB	60BufA		6'1"	195	Michigan		7
Harper, Jack HB	67-68MiaA	2	5'11"	190	Florida		24
Harper, Willie LB	73SF		6'2"	215	Nebraska		
Harraway, Charlie FB	66-68Cle 69-73Was	2	6'2"	221	San Jose State		
Harrell, Rick C	73NYJ		6'3"	238	Clemson		162
Harris, Billy HB	68Atl 69Min 70JJ 71NO	2	6'	196	Colorado		6
Harris, Cliff DB	70-73Dal	3	6'	184	Ouachita Baptist	9	
Harris, Dick DB	60LA-A 61-65SD-A	3	5'11"	181	McNeese State	29	30
Harris, Franco HB-FB	72-73Pit	2	6'2"	230	Penn State		84
Harris, Jim DB	70Was 71Cin		5'11"	173	Howard Payne		
Harris, Jim DT	65-67NY-A		6'4"	275	Utah State		
Harris, Jim QB	69-71,73BufA	1	6'3"	214	Grambling		
Harris, John DB-HB	60-61OakA		6'1"	195	Santa Monica J.C.	3	
Harris, Lou DB	68Pit		6'	180	Kent State		
Harris, Marv LB	64LA		6'1"	225	Stanford		
Harris, Phil DB	66NYG		6'	195	Texas		
Harris, Richard DE-DT	71-73Phi		6'4"	260	Grambling		
Harris, Rickie DB	65-70Was 71-72NE	3	6'	182	Arizona	15	24
Harris, Tony DB	71SF		6'2"	190	Toledo		
Harris, Wendell DB	62-65Bal 66-67NYG	3 5	5'11"	188	Louisiana State	8	17
Harrison, Bob LB	59-61SF 62-63Phi 64Pit 65-67SF		6'2"	223	Oklahoma	5	
Harrison, Bob DB	61Bal		5'11"	187	Ohio U.	3	
Harrison, Dwight WR-DB	71-72Den 72-73Buf	2	6'1"	178	Texas A & I	5	18
Harrison, Jim FB	71-73ChiB	2	6'4"	235	Missouri		36
Hart, Ben DB	67NO		6'2"	205	Oklahoma		1
Hart, Dick OG	67-70Phi 71JJ 72Buf		6'2"	250	none		
Hart, Doug DB	64-71GB		6'	190	Texas-Arlington	15	32
Hart, Jim QB	66-73StL	12	6'2"	201	Southern Illinois		66
Hart, Leo QB	71Atl 72Buf		6'4"	203	Duke		
Hart, Pete FB	60NY-A	2	5'9"	190	Hardin-Simmons		
Hart, Tommy DE-LB	68-73SF		6'3"	242	Morris Brown	2	6
Harvey, Claude LB	70Hou		6'4"	225	Prairie View		
Harvey, George OT	67NO		6'4"	245	Kansas		
Harvey, Jim OG-OT	66-69OakA 70-71Oak		6'5"	247	Mississippi		
Harvey, Richard DB	70Phi 71NO		6'2"	190	Jackson State		
Harvey, Waddey DT	69BufA 70Buf		6'4"	276	Virginia Tech		
Hatcher, Ron DB-FB	62Was		5'11"	215	Michigan State		
Hathcock, Dave DB	66GB 67NYG		6'	193	Memphis State		
Hauss, Len C	64-73Was		6'2"	234	Georgia		
Haverdick, Dave DT	70Det		6'4"	245	Morehead State		
Havig, Dennis OG	72-73Atl		6'2"	250	Colorado		
Havrilak, Sam WR-HB-DB	69-73Bal	2	6'2"	195	Bucknell		42
Hawkins, Alex HB-OE-FL-WR	59-65Bal 66-67Atl 67-68Bal	23	6'1"	188	South Carolina		132
Hawkins, Ben WR-FL-OE	66-73Phi	2	6'	180	Arizona State		198
Hawkins, Rip LB	61-65Min		6'3"	231	North Carolina	12	20

Use Name (Nicknames) – Positions	Team by Year	See Section	Hgt	Wgh	College	Int	Pts
Hawkins, Wayne OG	60-69OakA		6'	239	U. of Pacific		
Hayden, Leo HB-FB	71Min 72-73StL		6'	211	Ohio State		6
Hayes, Billy DB	72NO		6'1"	175	San Diego State		
Hayes, Bob WR-OE	65-73Dal	23	6'	186	Florida A & M		450
Hayes, Ed DB	70Phi		6'1"	185	Morgan State	1	
Hayes, Jim DT	65-66HouA		6'4"	263	Jackson State		
Hayes, Larry C-LB	61NYG 62-63LA		6'3"	230	Vanderbilt		6
Hayes, Luther OE	61SD-A	2	6'4"	200	Southern Calif.		18
Hayes, Ray FB	61Min	2	6'3"	235	Central St.-Okla.		12
Hayes, Ray DT	68NY-A		6'5"	248	Toledo		
Hayes, Rudy LB	59-60,62Pit		6'	217	Clemson		
Hayes, Tom DB	71-73Atl		6'1"	197	San Diego State	12	30
Hayes, Wendell FB-HB	63Dal 65-67DenA 68-69KC-A 70-73KC	2	6'2"	214	Humboldt State		202
Hayhoe, Bill OT	69-73GB		6'8"	258	Southern Calif.		
Haymond, Alvin DB	64-67Bal 68Phi 69-71LA 72Was 73Hou	3	6'	193	Southern U.	10	30
Haynes, Abner HB	60-62DalA 63-64KC-A 65-66DenA 67MiaA 67NY-A	23	6'	188	North Texas State		414
Hays, Harold LB	68-69SF		6'3"	227	Southern Miss.		
Hazeltine, Matt LB	55-68SF 69VR 70NYG		6'1"	220	California	13	18
Hazelton, Major DB	68-69ChiB 70NO		6'1"	185	Florida A & M		
Headrick, Sherrill LB	60-62DalA 63-67KC-A 68CinA		6'2"	223	Texas Christian	15	18
Healy, Chip LB	69-70StL		6'3"	233	Vanderbilt		
Healy, Don DT-OG	58-59ChiB 60-61Dal 62BufA		6'3"	259	Maryland	1	
Heater, Don HB	72StL		6'2"	205	Montana State		
Hebert, Ken WR	68Pit		6'	200	Houston		
Heck, Ralph LB	63-65Phi 66-68Atl 69-71NYG		6'2"	228	Colorado	5	6
Heckard, Steve OE	65-66LA		6'1"	195	Davidson		
Hector, Willie OT	61LA		6'2"	220	U. of Pacific		
Heenan, Pat DB-OE	60Was		6'1"	190	Notre Dame	1	
Heeter, Gene OE	63-65NY-A	2	6'4"	235	West Virginia		12
Hefner, Larry LB	72-73GB		6'2"	223	Clemson	1	
Heidel, Jim DB	66StL 67NO		6'1"	185	Mississippi	1	
Heinz, Bob DT-DE	69MiaA 70-73Mia		6'6"	273	U. of Pacific		
Hendershot, Larry LB	67Was		6'3"	240	Arizona State		
Henderson, John WR-OE-FL	65-67Det 68-72Min	2	6'3"	191	Michigan		60
Henderson, Jon WR-DB	68-69Pit 70Was	23	6'	198	Colorado State		36
Hendren, Jerry WR	70Den		6'2"	187	Idaho		
Hendricks, Ted LB	69-73Bal		6'7"	217	Miami (Fla.)	11	18
Henke, Karl DT-DE	68NY-A 69BosA		6'4"	245	Tulsa		
Henley, Carey HB	62RufA		5'10"	200	Tenn.-Chattanooga		
Hennessey, Tom DB	65-66BosA		6'	183	Holy Cross	8	
Hennigan, Charley FL-OE	60-66HouA	2	6'	187	NW State-La.		306
Hennigan, Mike LB	73Det		6'2"	210	Tennessee Tech		
Henning, Dan QB	66SD-A		6'	195	William & Mary		
Henry, Mike LB	59-61Pit 62-64LA		6'2"	220	Southern Calif.	9	
Henry, Urban DT-DE	61LA 63GB 64Pit		6'4"	265	Georgia Tech		
Henson, Gary OE	63Phi		6'3"	200	Colorado		
Henson, Ken C	65Pit		6'6"	260	Texas Christian		
Hepburn, Lonnie DB	71-72Bal		5'11"	183	Texas Southern	1	
Hergert, Joe LB	60-61BufA	5	6'1"	216	Florida	2	30
Herman, Dave OG-OT	64-69NY-A 70-73NYJ		6'2"	255	Michigan State		
Herman, Dick LB	65OakA		6'2"	215	Florida State		
Hermeling, Terry OT-DE	70-73Was		6'5"	255	Nevada		
Hernandez, Joe FL	64Was		6'2"	180	Arizona		
Herndon, Don HB	60NY-A		6'	195	Tampa		6
Herock, Ken OE-TE	63-65,67OakA 68CinA 69BosA	2	6'2"	230	West Virginia		30
Heron, Fred DT-DE	66-72StL		6'4"	255	San Jose State		
Herosian, Brian DB	73Bal		6'3"	200	Connecticut		
Herring, George QB	60-61DenA	1 4	6'2"	200	Southern Miss.		12
Herrmann, Don WR	69-73NYG	2	6'2"	199	Waynesburg		90
Herron, Mack HB	73NE	23	5'5"	170	Kansas State		24
Hester, Jim TE	67-69NO 70ChiB		6'4"	238	North Dakota		18
Hester, Ray LB	71-73NO		6'2"	215	Tulane		
Hettema, Dave OT	67SF 68-69MS 70Atl		6'4"	249	New Mexico		
Hews, Bob OT-DE	71Buf		6'5"	240	Princeton		
Hibler, Mike LB	68CinA		6'1"	235	Stanford		
Hickerson, Gene OG	58-60Cle 61BL 62-73Cle		6'3"	248	Mississippi		
Hickey, Bo FB	67DenA	2	5'11"	225	Maryland		30
Hickl, Ray LB	69-70NYG		6'2"	215	Texas A & I		
Hickman, Larry FB	59ChiC 60GB		6'2"	227	Baylor		
Hicks, W. K. DB	64-69HouA 70-72NYJ		6'1"	191	Texas Southern	40	
Higgins, Jim OG-OT	66MiaA		6'1"	250	Xavier-Ohio		
Highsmith, Buzz OG-OT-C	68-69DenA 72Hou		6'4"	238	Florida A & M		
Highsmith, Don HB	70-72Oak 73GB	2	6'	200	Michigan State		12
Hilgenberg, Wally LB-OG	64-66Det 67JJ 68-73Min		6'3"	228	Iowa	6	12
Hill, Calvin HB-FB	69-73Dal	2	6'3"	229	Yale		228
Hill, Dave OT	63-69KC-A 70-73KC		6'5"	259	Auburn		
Hill, Fred TE-OE-WR	65-71Phi	2	6'2"	215	Southern Calif.		30
Hill, Gary DB	65Min		6'	200	Southern Calif.		
Hill, Ike WR-DB	70-71Buf 73ChiB	23	5'10"	180	Catawba		24
Hill, Jack HB	61DenA	5	6'1"	185	Utah State		31
Hill, J. D. WR	71-73Buf	2	6'1"	196	Arizona State		42
Hill, Jerry FB-HB	61Bal 62JJ 63-70Bal	2	5'11"	212	Wyoming		150
Hill, Jim DB	68KJ 69SD-A 70-71SD 72-73GB		6'2"	190	Texas A & I	16	
Hill, Jimmy DB	55-57ChiC 58AJ 59ChiC 60-64StL 65Det 66KC-A		6'2"	192	Sam Houston St.	20	18
Hill, John OT-C	72-73NYG		6'2"	245	Lehigh		
Hill, King QB	58-59ChiC 60StL 61-68Phi 68Min 69StL	12 4	6'3"	212	Rice		54
Hill, Mack Lee HB-FB	64-65KC-A	2	5'11"	225	Southern U.		54
died Dec. 14, 1965 after knee surgery							
Hill, Winston OT	63-69NY-A 70-73NYJ		6'4"	278	Texas Southern		
Hillebrand, Jerry LB	63-66NYG 67StL 68-70Pit		6'3"	240	Colorado	14	18
Hilton, John TE	65-69Pit 70GB 71Min 72-73Det	2	6'5"	222	Richmond		96
Hilton, Roy DE	65-73Bal		6'6"	238	Jackson State	1	6
Himes, Dick OT	68-73GB		6'4"	244	Ohio State		
Hindman, Stan DE-DT	66-71SF		6'3"	234	Mississippi	1	6
Hines, Glen Ray OT	66-69HouA 70Hou 71-72NO 73Pit		6'5"	264	Arkansas		
Hines, Jimmy WR	69MiaA		6'	175	Texas Southern		
Hinton, Chuck DT	64-71Pit 71NYJ 72Bal		6'5"	257	N. Car. Central	2	12
Hinton, Chuck C	67-69NYG		6'2"	235	Mississippi		
Hinton, Eddie WR	69-72Bal 73Hou	2	6'	200	Oklahoma		72

Use Name (Nicknames) – Positions	Team by Year	See Section	Hgt	Wgt	College	Int	Pts
Hoaglin, Fred C	66-72Cle 73Bal		6'4"	245	Pittsburgh		
Hoak, Dick HB	61-70Pit	12	5'11"	191	Penn State		198
Hobbs, Bill LB	69-71Phi 72NO		6'	218	Texas A & M		6
Hodgson, Pat OE	66Was		6'2"	190	Georgia		
Hoey, George DB	71StL 72-73NE		5'10"	170	Michigan	1	6
Hoffman, Dalton FB	64-65HouA		6'	207	Baylor		6
Hoffman, John DE	69-70Was 71ChiB 72StL 72Den		6'7"	260	Hawaii		6
Hohman, John OG	65-66DenA		6'1"	243	Wisconsin		
Hohn, Bob DB	65-69Pit		6'	187	Nebraska	7	
Hoisington, Al OE	60OakA 60BufA		6'3"	200	Pasadena City		12
Holden, Sam OT	71NO		6'3"	258	Grambling		
Holden, Steve WR	73Cle		6'	192	Arizona State		
Holifield, Jim DB	68-69NYG		6'3"	195	Jackson State	1	
Holland, Vern OT	71-73Cin		6'5"	270	Tennessee State		
Hollas, Hugo DB	70-72NO 73KJ		6'1"	190	Rice	11	
Holler, Ed LB-FB	63GB 64Pit	4	6'2"	233	South Carolina	1	
Holliday, Ron WR	73SD	2	5'9"	168	Pittsburgh		1
Holloman, Gus DB	68-69DenA 70-72NYJ	4	6'3"	195	Houston	8	
Holloway, Glenn OG	70-73ChiB		6'3"	249	North Texas State		
Hollway, Bob	HC71-72StL				Michigan		
Holman, Willie DE-DT	68-73ChiB 73Was		6'4"	250	S. Carolina State		
Holmes, Ernie DT	72-73Pit		6'3"	260	Texas Southern		
Holmes, John DE	66MiaA		6'2"	248	Florida A & M		
Holmes, Mel OG-OT	71-73Pit		6'3"	250	N. Carolina A & T		
Holmes, Pat DE-DT	66-69HouA 70-72Hou 73KC		6'5"	254	Texas Tech	1	
Holmes, Robert FB	68-69KC-A 70-71KC 71-72Hou 73SD	23	5'9"	220	Southern U.		162
Holub, E. J. LB-C	61-62DalA 63-69KC-A 70KC		6'4"	231	Texas Tech	9	
Holz, Gordy DT-OT	60-63DenA 64NY-A		6'4"	264	Minnesota	1	
Holzer, Tom DE	67SF 68JJ		6'4"	250	Louisville		
Homan, Dennis WR	68-70Dal 71-72KC	2	6'1"	180	Alabama		12
Hooker, Fair WR	69-73Cle	2	6'1"	193	Arizona State		42
Hooks, Jim FB	73Det		5'11"	225	Central St.-Okla.		
Hooligan, Harry FB	65HouA		6'2"	225	Bishop		
Hopkins, Andy HB	71Hou		5'10"	187	S. F. Austin St.		
Hopkins, Jerry LB	63-66DenA 67MiaA 68OOakA		6'2"	236	Texas A & M	6	
Hopkins, Roy FB	67-69HouA 70Hou 71JJ	2	6'1"	223	Texas Southern		48
Hord, Roy OG	60-62LA 62Phi 63NY-A		6'4"	244	Duke		
Horn, Don QB	67-70GB 71Den 72-73Cle	1	6'2"	195	San Diego State		6
Horner, Sam HB-DB	60-61Was 62NYG	234	6'	197	V. M. I.		6
Hornsby, Ron LB	71-73NYG		6'3"	232	Southeastern La.		
Hornung, Paul (The Golden Boy) HB-FB	57-62GB 63SL 64-66GB	12 5	6'2"	215	Notre Dame		760
Horton, Bob LB	64-65SD-A		6'2"	230	Boston U.		
Horton, Larry DE-DT	72ChiB		6'4"	248	Iowa		
Hoskins, Bob DT-OG	70-73SF		6'2"	243	Wichita State		
Hoss, Clark TE	72Phi		6'8"	235	Oregon State		
Houser, John OG-C	57-59LA 60-61Dal 62JJ 63StL		6'3"	239	Redlands		
Houston, Jim LB-DE-TE	60-72Cle		6'2"	239	Ohio State	14	25
Houston, Ken DB	67-69HouA 70-72Hou 73Was	3	6'3"	194	Prairie View	31	66
Houston, Rich WR	69-73NYG	23	6'2"	196	East Texas State		42
Howard, Bob DB	67-69SD-A 70-73SD		6'1"	186	San Diego State	18	
Howard, Gene DB	68-70NO 71-72LA	3	6'	190	Langston	14	12
Howard, Leroy DB	71Hou		5'11"	175	Bishop		
Howard, Paul OG	73Den		6'3"	260	Brigham Young		
Howell, Delles DB	70-72NO 73NYJ		6'3"	198	Grambling	13	
Howell, Lane OT-DT	63-64NYG 65-69Phi		6'5"	264	Grambling		
Howell, Mike DB	65-72Cle 72Mia		6'1"	189	Grambling	27	
Howfield, Bobby K	68-69DenA 70Den 71-73NYJ	5	5'9"	180	none		461
Howley, Chuck LB	58-59ChiB 60JJ 61-73Dal		6'3"	228	West Virginia	25	
Hoyem, Lynn C-OG	62-63Dal 64-67Phi		6'4"	244	Long Beach State		
Hrivnak, Gary DE	73ChiB		6'5"	248	Purdue		
Huard, John LB	67-69DenA 70-71JJ		6'	220	Maine	6	
Huarte, John QB	66-67BosA 68Phi 70-71KC 72ChiB	1	6'	188	Notre Dame		
Hubbard, Marv FB	69OakA 70-73Oak	2	6'1"	221	Colgate		102
Hubbert, Brad FB	67-69SD-A 70SD	2	6'1"	230	Arizona		66
Hudlow, Floyd DB-FL	65BufA 67-68Atl		5'11"	192	Arizona	2	
Hudock, Mike C	60-65NY-A 66MiaA 67KC-A		6'2"	245	Miami (Fla.)		
Hudson, Bill DT	61-62SD-A 63BosA		6'4"	267	Clemson	1	6
Hudson, Bob HB	72GB 73Oak	3	5'11"	208	Northeast La.		
Hudson, Dick OT-OG	62SD-A 63-67BufA		6'4"	266	Memphis State		
Hudson, Jim DB-HB	65-69NY-A 70NYJ		6'2"	210	Texas	14	
Huey, Gene DB	69SD-A		5'11"	190	Wyoming		
Huff, Gary QB	73ChiB	1	6'1"	200	Florida State		
Huff, Marty LB	72SF		6'2"	234	Michigan		
Huff, Sam LB	56-63NYG 64-67Was 68VR 69Was		6'1"	230	West Virginia	30	30
Hughes, Bob DE	67,69Atl		6'4"	253	Jackson State		
Hughes, Chuck WR	67-69Phi 70-71Det	2	5'11"	173	Texas-El Paso		
died Oct. 24, 1971 – heart attack							
Hughes, Dennis TE	70-71Pit	2	6'1"	220	Georgia		18
Hughes, Pat LB-C	70-73NYG		6'2"	240	Boston U.	5	
Hughley, George HB	65Was	2	6'2"	223	Central St.-Okla.		6
Hull, Bill DE	62DalA		6'6"	245	Wake Forest		
Hull, Mike FB-TE	68-70ChiB 71-73Was	2	6'3"	220	Southern Calif.		6
Hultz, Don DE-DT-LB	63Min 64-73Phi		6'3"	237	Southern Miss.	4	12
Hultz, George DT	62StL		6'4"	250	Southern Miss.		
Humphrey, Buddy QB	59-60LA 61-62Dal 63-65StL 66HouA	1	6'1"	198	Baylor		
Humphrey, Claude DE	68-73Atl		6'5"	253	Tennessee State	2	8
Humphreys, Bob K	67-68DenA	5	6'1"	240	Wichita State		43
Hunt, Bobby DB-HB	62DalA 63-67KC-A 68-69CinA		6'1"	188	Auburn	42	12
Hunt, Calvin C	70Phi 72-73Hou		6'3"	244	Baylor		
Hunt, Charlie LB	73SF		6'2"	212	Florida State		
Hunt, Ervin DB	70GB		6'2"	190	Fresno State		
Hunt, George K	73Bal	5	6'1"	215	Tennessee		70
Hunt, Jim (Earthquake) DT-DE	60-69BosA 70Bos		5'11"	249	Prairie View	1	14
Hunt, Kevin OT	72GB 73NE 73Hou		6'5"	260	Doane		
Hunter, Art C-OT-DT-DE	54GB 55MS 56-59Cle 60-64LA 65Pit		6'4"	243	Notre Dame		
Hunter, Bill FL-HB-DB	65Was 66MiaA		6'1"	183	Syracuse		6
Hunter, Scott QB	71-73GB	12	6'2"	205	Alabama		60
Hurston, Chuck LB-DE	65-69KC-A 70KC 71Buf		6'6"	237	Auburn		

Use Name (Nicknames) – Positions	Team by Year	See Section	Hgt	Wgt	College	Int	Pts
Husmann, Ed DT-OG-LB-DE	53ChiC 54-55MS 56-59ChiC		6'	235	Nebraska		
	60Dal 61-65HouA						
Hutchinson, Tom OE	63-65Cle 66Atl	2	6'1"	190	Kentucky		12
Hutchison, Chuck OG	70-72StL 73Cle		6'3"	240	Ohio State		
Huth, Jerry OG	56NYG 57-58MS 59-60Phi 61-63Min		6'	226	Wake Forest		6
Hyatt, Freddie WR	68-72StL 73NO		6'3"	207	Auburn		
Hyland, Bob C-OG-OT	67-69GB 70ChiB 71-73NYG		6'5"	251	Boston College		
Hynes, Paul DB	61DalA 61-62NY-A		6'1"	210	Louisiana Tech	2	
Iacavazzi, Cosmo HB	65NY-A		5'11"	200	Princeton		
Ilg, Ray LB	67-68BosA		6'1"	220	Colgate		
Iman, Ken C	60-63GB 64BH 65-73LA		6'1"	236	SE Missouri St.		
Imhof, Martin DE	72StL		6'6"	255	San Diego State		
Inman, Jerry DT	66-69DenA 70-71Den 72JJ 73Den		6'3"	255	Oregon		
Irons, Gerald LB	70-73Oak		6'2"	230	Md. Eastern Shore	4	
Isbell, Joe Bob OG	62-64Dal 65JJ 66Cle		6'1"	238	Houston		
Isenbarger, John HB-WR	70-73SF	2	6'3"	203	Indiana		12
Izo, George QB	60StL 61-64Was 65Det 66Pit	1	6'3"	218	Notre Dame		
Jackson, Bernie DB	72-73Cin	3	6'	173	Washington State	2	
Jackson, Bobby DB	60Phi 61ChiB		6'1"	190	Alabama		
Jackson, Bobby FB	62-63SD-A 64HouA 64OakA 65HouA	2	6'3"	232	New Mexico State		96
Jackson, Ernie DB	72-73NO		5'10"	174	Duke	6	6
Jackson, Frank FL-HB	61-62DalA 63-65KC-A 66-67MiaA	23	6'1"	187	S.M.U.		186
Jackson, Harold WR	68LA 69-72Phi 73LA	2	5'10"	175	Jackson State		204
Jackson, Honor DB	72-73NE 73NYG		6'1"	195	U. of Pacific	5	
Jackson, Jim DB-HB	66-67SF		6'	187	Western Illinois	1	6
Jackson, Joey DE-DT	72-73NYJ		6'4"	264	New Mexico State		
Jackson, Larron OG-OT	71-73Den		6'3"	270	Missouri		
Jackson, Leroy HB	62-63Was	2	6'	190	Western Illinois		6
Jackson, Randy OT	67-73ChiB		6'5"	246	Florida		
Jackson, Randy HB-FB	72Buf 73SF		6'	220	Wichita State		6
Jackson, Rich DE-LB	66OakA 67-69DenA 70-72Den 72Cle		6'2"	252	Southern U.		2
Jackson, Roland FB-LB	62StL		6'	210	Rice		
Jackson, Steve LB	66-67Was		6'1"	225	Texas-Arlington	1	
Jackson, T. J. FL-DB	66Phi 67Was		6'	180	none		
Jackson, Tom LB	73Den		5'11"	220	Louisville		
Jackunas, Frank C	62BufA 63DenA		6'3"	225	Detroit		
Jacobs, Allen HB	65GB 66-67NYG	2	6'1"	215	Utah		6
Jacobs, Harry LB-DE	60-62BosA 63-69BufA 70NO		6'2"	228	Bradley	12	
Jacobs, Proverb DT-OT	58Phi 60NYG 61-62NY-A 63-64OakA		6'4"	258	California		
Jacobs, Ray DT-DE	63-66DenA 67-68MiaA 69BosA		6'3"	276	Howard Payne		
Jacobson, Jack DB	65SD-A		6'2"	200	Oklahoma State		
Jacobson, Larry DT-DE	72-73NYG		6'6"	260	Nebraska		
Jagielski, Harry DT-OT	56ChiC 56Was 60-61BosA 61OakA		6'	257	Indiana	1	
James, Bobby DB-WR	69BufA 70-73Buf		6'1"	182	Fisk	6	6
James, Claudis WR-HB-FL	67-68GB		6'2"	190	Jackson State		
James, Dan OT-C	60-66Pit 67ChiB		6'4"	262	Ohio State		
James, Dick HB-DB	56-63Was 64NYG 65Min	23	5'9"	179	Oregon	12	204
James, John K	72-73Atl	4	6'3"	197	Florida		
James, Nate DB	68Cle		6'1"	195	Florida A&M		
James, Po HB	72-73Phi	2	6'1"	202	New Mexico State		12
Jamieson, Dick QB	60-61NY-A	1	6'1"	191	Bradley		
Jamison, Al OT	60-62HouA		6'5"	245	Colgate		
Jancik, Bobby DB-FL	62-67HouA	3	5'11"	178	Lamar Tech	15	6
Janerette, Chuck DT-OT-OG	60LA 61-62NYG 63NY-A		6'3"	253	Penn State	2	
	64-65DenA						
Janet, Ernie OG	72-73ChiB		6'4"	250	Washington		
Janik, Tom DB	63-64DenA 65-68BufA 69BosA 70Bos 71NE	4	6'3"	198	Texas A&I	25	36
Jankowski, Bruce WR	71-72KC		5'11"	185	Ohio State		
Jaqua, Jon DB	70-72Was 73JJ		6'	190	Lewis & Clark	1	
Jaquess, Pete DB	64-65HouA 66-67MiaA 67-69DenA 70Den		6'	182	Eastern New Mex.	16	12
Jarvis, Bruce C	71-73Buf		6'7"	247	Washington		
Jarvis, Ray WR	71-72Atl 73Buf		5'11"	195	Norfolk State		
Jauron, Dick DB	73Det		6'	190	Yale	4	6
Jefferson, Roy WR-FL-OE	65-69Pit 70Bal 71-73Was	23	6'2"	194	Utah		270
Jelacic, Jon DE-OG	58NYG 61-64OakA		6'3"	250	Minnesota	2	12
Jencks, Bob OE	63-64ChiB 65Was	5	6'5"	227	Miami-Ohio		135
Jenke, Noel LB	71Min 72Atl 73GB		6'1"	221	Minnesota		
Jenkins, Al OG-OT-DE-DT	69-70Cle 72Mia 73Hou		6'2"	250	Tulsa		
Jenkins, Ed HB	72Mia 73JJ		6'2"	210	Holy Cross		
Jenkins, Leon DB	72Det		5'11"	165	West Virginia		
Jeralds, Luther DE	61DalA		6'3"	235	N. Car. Central		
Jessie, Ron WR	71-73Det	23	6'	183	Kansas		62
Jeter, Bob DB-FL-OE	63-70GB 71-73ChiB		6'1"	203	Iowa	26	12
Jeter, Gene LB	65-67DenA		6'3"	230	Ark.-Pine Bluff		
Jeter, Tony TE	66,68Pit		6'3"	222	Nebraska		
Jobko, Bill LB	58-62LA 63-65Min 66Atl		6'2"	224	Ohio State	5	
Joe, Billy FB	63-64DenA 65BufA 66MiaA 67-68NY-A	2	6'2"	243	Villanova		118
Johns, Pete DB	67-68HouA		6'3"	189	Tulane		
Johnson, Al HB	72-73Hou		6'	200	Cincinnati		
Johnson, Benny DB	70-73Hou	3	5'11'	178	Johnson C. Smith	1	
Johnson, Bill K	70NYG	4	6'2"	208	Livingston		
Johnson, Billy DB	66-68BosA		5'11'	178	Nebraska	2	
Johnson, Bob C	68-69CinA 70-73Cin		6'5"	262	Tennessee		
Johnson, Carl OT-OG	72-73NO		6'3"	248	Nebraska		
Johnson, Charley QB	61-69StL 70-71Hou 72-73Den	12	6'	190	New Mexico State		60
Johnson, Charlie DT	66-68SF		6'2"	265	Louisville		
Johnson, Cornelius OG	68-73Bal		6'2"	245	Virginia Union		
Johnson, Curley HB-TE-OE-FB-K	60DalA 61-69NY-A 69NYG	2 4	6'	215	Houston		26
Johnson, Curtis DB	70-73Mia		6'2"	197	Toledo	10	8
Johnson, Daryle DB	68-69BosA 70Bos		5'11'	190	Morgan State	5	8
Johnson, Dick OE	63KC-A		6'4"	220	Minnesota		6
Johnson, Ellis HB-FL-OE	65-66BosA		6'2"	190	Southeastern La		
Johnson, Essex HB	68-69CinA 70-73Cin	23	5'9"	195	Grambling		156
Johnson, Gene DB	59-60Phi 61Min 61NYG		6'	187	Cincinnati	4	
Johnson, Jay LB	69-70Phi		6'3"	230	East Texas State		
Johnson, Jim DB-FL	61-73SF	2	6'2"	188	U.C.L.A.	41	38
Johnson, John DT	63-68ChiB 69NYG		6'5"	260	Indiana		
Johnson, John Henry FB-HB-DB	54-56SF 57-59Det	2	6'2"	210	St. Mary's		330
	60-65Pit 66HouA				Arizona State		
Johnson, Ken DE-DT	71-73Cin		6'5"	264	Indiana		

Use Name (Nicknames) – Positions	Team by Year	See Section	Hgt	Wgt	College	Int	Pts
Johnson, Lee WR	69-70SF		6'1"	204	Tennessee State		
Johnson, Len C-OG	70NYG		6'2"	250	St. Cloud State		
Johnson, Levi DB	73Det		6'3"	190	Texas A&I	5	
Johnson, Mike DB	66-69Dal		5'10"	185	Kansas	8	
Johnson, Mitch OT-OG	65Dal 66-67Was 69-70LA 71Cle		6'4"	249	U.C.L.A.		
	72Was						
Johnson, Monte LB	73Oak		6'4"	235	Nebraska		
Johnson, Preston FB	68BosA		6'2"	230	Florida A&M		
Johnson, Randy QB	66-70Atl 71-73NYG	12	6'3"	201	Texas A&I		54
Johnson, Rich HB-FB	69HouA		6'1"	210	Illinois		6
Johnson, Ron HB	69Cle 70-73NYG	2	6'1"	205	Michigan		258
Johnson, Rudy HB	64-65SF 66Atl	2	5'11"	190	Nebraska		6
Johnson, Walter DT	65-73Cle		6'3"	269	Los Angeles State	2	14
Johnson, Walter DE	67SF		6'4"	225	Tuskegee		
Johnston, Mark DB	60-63HouA 64OakA 64NY-A		6'	201	Northwestern	13	12
Johnston, Rex HB	60Pit		6'1"	195	Southern Calif.		
64 played major league baseball							
Joiner, Charlie WR	69HouA 70-72Hou 72-73Cin	2	5'11"	187	Grambling		72
Jolley, Gordon OT	72-73Det		6'5"	240	Utah		
Jolley, Lewis HB-FB	72-73Hou		6'	210	North Carolina		
Jonas, Don HB	62Phi		5'11"	195	Penn State		
Jones, Bert QB	73Bal	1	6'3"	205	Louisiana State		
Jones, Bob WR-OE	67-69ChiB		6'4"	196	San Diego State		6
Jones, Bob DB	73Cin		6'1"	194	Virginia Union		
Jones, Calvin DB	73Den		5'7"	170	Washington	4	
Jones, Clint HB	67-72Min 73SD	23	6'	206	Michigan State		126
Jones, Curtis LB	68SD-A		6'2"	245	Missouri		
Jones, Dave WR	69-71Cle		6'2"	185	Kansas State		
Jones, Deacon DE	61-71LA 72-73SD		6'5"	253	S. Carolina State	2	2
Jones, Doug DB	73KC		6'2"	202	San Fern. Valley		
Jones, Ezell OT	69BosA 70Bos		6'4"	255	Minnesota		
Jones, Gene LB	61HouA		6'	200	Rice		
Jones, Greg HB	70-71Buf	2	6'1"	200	U.C.L.A.		18
Jones, Harris OG	71SD 72JJ 73Hou		6'4"	239	Johnson C. Smith		
Jones, Harry HB	67-70Phi 71JJ	2	6'2"	205	Arkansas		
Jones, Henry FB	69DenA		6'2"	235	Grambling		
Jones, Homer WR-FL-OE	64-69NYG 70Cle	23	6'2"	211	Texas Southern		228
Jones, Horace DE	71-73Oak		6'3"	245	Louisville		
Jones, Jerry OT-DT-DE	66Atl 67-69NO		6'3"	269	Bowling Green		
Jones, Jim OE-WR	65-67ChiB 68DenA	2	6'2"	189	Wisconsin		66
Jones, Jimmie DE	69NY-A 70NYJ 71-73Was		6'3"	215	Wichita State		
Jones, Joe (Turkey) DE	70-71Cle 72KJ 73Cle		6'6"	247	Tennessee State		
Jones, Ray DB	70Phi 71Mia 72SD		6'	187	Southern U.	2	
Jones, Ron TE	69GB		6'3"	220	Texas-El Paso		
Jones, Spike K	70Hou 71-73Buf	4	6'2"	190	Georgia		
Jones, Stan OG-DT-OT	54-65ChiB 66Was		6'1"	252	Maryland		
Jones, Steve HB	73Buf		6'	200	Duke		
Jones, Willie FB	62BufA		5'11"	208	Purdue		
Jones, Willie DT-DE	67HouA 68CinA 70-71Cin		6'2"	260	Kansas State		
Jordan, Henry DT-DE	57-58Cle 59-69GB		6'3"	249	Virginia	1	6
Jordan, Jeff DB	65-67Min		6'4"	190	Tulsa	4	
Jordan, Jeff HB-FB	67-69JJ 70LA 71-72Was		6'1"	215	Washington		
Jordan, Jimmy HB	67NO		6'1"	200	Florida		
Jordan, Larry LB-DE	62,64DenA		6'6"	230	Youngstown		
Jordan, Lee Roy LB	63-73Dal		6'2"	219	Alabama	24	20
Josephson, Les FB-HB	64-67LA 68JJ 69-73LA	2	6'	209	Augustana (S. D.)		168
Joswick, Bob DE-DT	68-69MiaA		6'5"	250	Tulsa		
Joyner, L. C. DB	60OakA		6'1"	187	none		
Juenger, Dave WR	73ChiB		6'1"	195	Ohio U.		
Julian, Fred DB	60NY-A		5'9"	185	Michigan	6	
Junker, Steve OE	57Det 58KJ 59-60Det 61-62Was	2	6'3"	217	Xavier-Ohio		36
Jurgensen, Sonny QB	57-63Phi 64-73Was	12	5'11"	202	Duke		90
Kaczmarek, Mike LB	73Bal		6'4"	235	Southern Illinois	1	
Kadish, Mike DT	73Buf		6'5"	265	Notre Dame		
Kadziel, Ron LB	72NE		6'4"	230	Stanford		
Kaimer, Karl DE	62NY-A		6'3"	230	Boston U.		
Kalina, Dave WR	70Pit		6'3"	205	Miami (Fla.)		
Kalsu, Bob OG	68BufA 69MS		6'3"	235	Oklahoma		
Kamanu, Lew DE	67-68Det		6'4"	245	Weber State		
Kaminski, Larry C	66-69DenA 70-73Den		6'2"	244	Purdue		
Kammerer, Carl DE-LB	61-62SF 63-69Was		6'3"	240	U. of Pacific	3	
Kampa, Bob DT	73Buf		6'4"	252	California		
Kanicki, Jim DT	63-69Cle 70-71NYG 72KJ		6'4"	270	Michigan State		
Kantor, Joe FB	66Was		6'1"	217	Notre Dame		
Kapele, John DE-OT-DT	60-62Pit 62Phi		6'	240	Brigham Young		
Kapp, Joe QB	67-69Min 70Bos 71HO	12	6'2"	214	California		30
Karas, Emil LB-DE	59Was 60LA-A 61-64,66SD-A		6'3"	230	Dayton	8	
Karras, Alex DT	58-62Det 63SL 64-70Det		6'2"	248	Iowa	4	2
Karras, Ted OG-OT-LB	58-59Pit 60-64ChiB 65Det 66LA		6'1"	240	Indiana		
Kasperek, Dick C	66-68StL		6'3"	225	Iowa State		
Kassulke, Karl DB	63-72Min		6'	194	Drake	19	
1973 paralyzed in motorcycle accident							
Katcavage, Jim DE-DT	56-68NYG		6'3"	237	Dayton	1	12
Katcik, Joe DT	60NY-A		6'9"	290	Notre Dame		
Kay, Rick LB	73LA		6'4"	235	Colorado		
Kearney, Jim DB	65-66Det 67-69KC-A 70-73KC		6'2"	205	Prairie View	23	30
Kearney, Tim LB	72-73Cin		6'2"	227	Northern Michigan		
Keating, Bill OG-DT	66-67DenA 67MiaA		6'2"	236	Michigan		
Keating, Tom DT	64-65BufA 66-67OakA 68FJ 69OakA		6'3"	246	Michigan		
	70-72Oak73Pit						
Keckin, Val QB	62SD-A		6'4"	215	Southern Miss.		
Keeling, Rex DB	68CinA		6'3"	220	Samford		
Keithley, Gary QB	73StL	1 4	6'3"	205	Texas-El Paso		
Keller, Mike LB	72-73Dal		6'4"	220	Michigan		
Kellerman, Ernie DB	66-71Cle 72Cin 73Buf		6'	184	Miami-Ohio	19	6
Kelley, Brian LB	73NYG		6'3"	222	Calif. Lutheran		
Kelley, Ed DB	61-62DalA		6'2"	195	Texas		
Kelley, Gordon LB	60-61SF 62-63Was		6'3"	230	Georgia	5	
Kelley, Ike LB	66-67Phi 68JJ 69-71Phi 72JJ		5'11'	224	Ohio State	1	
Kelley, Les LB	67-69NO		6'3"	233	Alabama	1	
Kellogg, Mike FB	66-67DenA		6'	220	Santa Clara		
Kelly, Bob OT-DT	61-64HouA 67KC-A 68CinA 69Atl		6'3"	261	New Mexico State		

Use Name (Nickname) – Positions	Team by Year	See Section	Hgt	Wgt	College	Int	Pts
Kelly, Jim TE-OE	64Pit 65,67Phi	2	6'2"	216	Notre Dame		30
Kelly, John OT	66-67Was		6'3"	253	Florida A&M		
Kelly, Leroy HB-FB	64-73Cle	23	6'	199	Morgan State		540
Kelly, Mike TE	70-72Cin 73NO		6'4"	217	Davidson		
Kemp, Jack QB	57Pit 58CFL 60LA-A 61-62SD-A 62-67BufA 68JJ 69BufA	12	6'1"	201	Occidental		242
Kempinski, Charlie OG	60LA-A		6'	235	Mississippi		
Kendall, Charlie DB	60HouA		6'2"	185	U.C.L.A.	2	
Kenerson, John DE-DT	60LA 62Pit 62NY-A		6'3"	255	Kentucky State		
Kennedy, Tom QB	66NYG 67JJ	1	6'1"	200	Los Angeles State		
Kent, Greg OT-DE	66OakA 67CFL 68Det		6'6"	270	Utah		
Kerbow, Randy FL	63HouA		6'1"	190	Rice		
Kern, Rex DB	71-73Bal		5'11"	190	Ohio State	2	
Kerr, Jim DB	61-62Was		6'	195	Penn State	8	
Key, Wade OT-OG	70-73Phi		6'4"	245	SW Texas State		
Keyes, Bob HB	60OakA		5'10"	183	San Diego		
Keyes, Jimmy LB	68-69MiaA	5	6'2"	225	Mississippi		51
Keyes, Leroy HB-DB	69-72Phi 73KC	2	6'3"	208	Purdue	8	18
Keys, Brady DB-HB	61-67Pit 67Min 68StL	3	6'	189	Colorado State	16	
Keys, Howard C-OT-OG	60-63Phi		6'3"	239	Oklahoma State		
Khayat, Bob OG-C-K	60,62-63Was	5	6'2"	230	Mississippi		204
Khayat, Ed DT-DE-OT	57Was 58-61Phi 62-63Was 64-65Phi 66BosA HC71-71Phi		6'3"	240	Tulane	1	
Kiick, Jim HB	68-69MiaA 70-73Mia	2	5'11"	216	Wyoming		174
Kilcullen, Bob DE-OT-DT	57-58ChiB 59MS 60-66ChiB		6'3"	245	Texas Tech		
Kilgore, Jon K	65-67LA 68ChiB 69SF	4	6'1"	203	Auburn		
Killett, Charlie HB	63NYG		6'1"	205	Memphis State		
Killorin, Pat C	66Pit		6'2"	220	Syracuse		
Kilmer, Billy QB-HB	61-62SF 63JJ 64,66SF 67-70NO 71-73Was	12	6'	200	U.C.L.A.		126
Kimber, Bill OE	59-60NYG 61BosA		6'2"	192	Florida State		
Kimbrough, Elbert DB	61LA 62-66SF 68NO		5'11"	193	Northwestern	9	
Kinderman, Keith FB-DB	63-64SD-A 65HouA		6'	213	Florida State		
Kindig, Howard DE-OT-C	65-67SD-A 67-69BufA 70-71Buf 72Mia 73JJ		6'6"	260	Los Angeles State	1	
Kindricks, Bill DT	68CinA		6'3"	268	Alabama A&M		
Kiner, Steve LB	70Dal 71,73NE		6'	218	Tennessee	5	2
King, Charlie DB	66-67BufA 68-69CinA		6'	185	Purdue	2	6
King, Claude HB	61HouA 62Bos A	2	5'11"	190	Houston		24
King, Henry DB	67NY-A		6'4"	205	Utah State		
King, Phil (Chief) HB-FB	58-63NYG 64Pit 65-66Min	23	6'4"	223	Vanderbilt		96
King, Steve LB	73NE		6'4"	255	Tulsa		
King, Tony FL	67BufA		6'1"	194	Findlay		
Kingrea, Rick LB	71-72Cle 73NO		6'1"	233	Tulane		
Kingsriter, Doug TE	73Min		6'2"	222	Minnesota		
Kinney, George DE	65HouA		6'4"	250	Wiley		
Kinney, Jeff HB-FB	72-73KC	2	6'2"	215	Nebraska		12
Kinney, Steve OT	73ChiB		6'5"	255	Utah State		
Kirby, John LB	64-69Min 69-70NYG		6'3"	229	Nebraska		
Kirchiro, Bill OG	62Bal		6'1"	235	Maryland		
Kirk, Ken LB-C	60-61ChiB 62Pit 63LA		6'2"	229	Mississippi		
Kirksey, Roy OG-DT	71-72NYJ 73Phi		6'1"	265	Md. Eastern Shore		
Kirner, Gary OT-OG	64-69SD-A		6'3"	249	Southern Calif.		
Kirouac, Lou OG-OT	63NYG 64Bal 65JJ 66-67Atl	5	6'3"	238	Boston College		46
Klein, Bob TE	69-73LA	2	6'5"	235	Southern Calif.		48
Klein, Dick OT	58-59ChiB 60Dal 61Pit 61-62BosA 63-64OakA		6'4"	254	Iowa		
Klotz, Jack OT	60-62NY-A 62SD-A 63NY-A 64HouA		6'5"	256	PMC Colleges		
Knief, Gayle WR	70Bos		6'3"	205	Morningside		6
Knight, Curt K	69-73Was	5	6'1"	190	Coast Guard		475
Knight, Dave WR	73NYJ		6'1"	182	William & Mary		6
Knox, Chuck	HC73LA				Juniata		
Kochman, Roger HB	63BufA	2	6'2"	205	Penn State		6
Kocourek, Dave OE-TE	60LA-A 61-65SD-A 66MiaA 67-68OakA	2	6'5"	237	Wisconsin		150
Koegel, Warren C	71Oak 72JJ 73StL		6'3"	250	Penn State		
Koeper, Rich OT	66Atl		6'4"	245	Oregon State		
Kolb, Jon OT-C	69-73Pit		6'2"	245	Oklahoma State		
Kolen, Mike LB	70-73Mia		6'2"	219	Auburn	3	
Koman, Bill LB	56Bal 57-58Phi 59ChiC 60-67StL		6'2"	229	North Carolina	7	
Kompara, John DT	60LA-A		6'2"	245	South Carolina		
Koontz, Ed LB	68BosA		6'2"	230	Catawba		
Koontz, Joe WR	68NYG		6'1"	192	San Fran. State		
Kopay, Dave HB-FB	64-67SF 68Det 69-70Was 71NO 72GB	2	6'2"	220	Washington		48
Kortas, Ken DT	64StL 65-68Pit 69ChiB		6'2"	282	Louisville		6
Korver, Kelvin DT	73Oak		6'6"	260	Northwestern, Iowa	1	
Kosens, Terry DB	63Min		6'3"	195	Hofstra		
Kosins, Gary HB-FB	72-73ChiB	2	6'1"	218	Dayton		6
Kostelnik, Ron DT	61-68GB 69Bal		6'4"	260	Cincinnati		
Kotite, Dick TE-LB	67NYG 68Pit 69,71-72NYG	2	6'3"	233	Wagner		30
Kovac, Ed HB-DB	60Bal 62NY-A		6'	199	Cincinnati	1	
Kowalczyk, Walt FB-DB	58-59Phi 60Dal 61OakA	2	6'	208	Michigan State	1	18
Kowalkowski, Bob OG	66-73Det		6'3"	243	Virginia		
Koy, Ernie HB-FB	65-70NYG	234	6'2"	228	Texas		90
Koy, Ted TE-HB-FB	70Oak 71-73Buf	2	6'1"	212	Texas		6
Krakau, Merv LB	73Buf		6'1"	242	Iowa State		
Krakoski, Joe DB	61Was 63-66OakA		6'2"	196	Illinois	8	
Kramer, Jerry OG	58-68GB	5	6'3"	246	Idaho		177
Kramer, Kent TE	66SF 67NO 69-70Min 71-73Phi	2	6'5"	234	Minnesota		48
Kramer, Ron OE-TE	57GB 58MS 59-64GB 65-67Det	2	6'3"	234	Michigan		96
Kratzer, Dan WR	73KC		6'3"	194	Missouri Valley		
Krause, Larry HB	70-71GB 72JJ 73GB	3	6'	208	St. Norbert		6
Krause, Paul DB-FL	64-67Was 68-73Min		6'3"	196	Iowa	62	30
Kreitling, Rich OE	59-63Cle 64ChiB	2	6'2"	208	Illinois		102
Kremser, Karl K	69MiaA 70Mia	5	6'	178	Army, Tennessee		67
Krieg, Jim WR	72Den		5'9"	172	Washington		
Kriewald, Doug OG	67-68ChiB		6'4"	245	West Texas State		
Krisher, Billy OG	58Pit 60-61DalA		6'1"	233	Oklahoma		
Kroll, Alex C-OT	62NY-A		6'3"	230	Rutgers		
Kroll, Bob DB	72GB 73JJ		6'1"	195	Northern Michigan		
Kroner, Gary DB-K	65-67DenA	5	6'1"	200	Wisconsin		144
Krueger, Charlie DT-DE	59-73SF		6'4"	256	Texas A&M	1	12
Krueger, Rolf DE-DT	69-71StL 72-73SF		6'4"	250	Texas A&M		

Use Name (Nicknames) – Positions	Team by Year	See Section	Hgt	Wgt	College	Int	Pts
Krupa, Joe DT	56-64Pit		6'2"	232	Purdue		
Kruse, Bob OG-DT	67-68OakA 69BufA		6'2"	250	Colorado State, Wayne State-Neb.		
Kubala, Ray C	64-67DenA		6'4"	245	Texas A&M		
Kuechenberg, Bob OG	70-73Mia		6'3"	249	Notre Dame		
Kuechenberg, Rudy L	67-69ChiB 70GB 71Atl		6'2"	215	Indiana		
Kulbacki, Joe HB	60BufA	2	6'	185	Purdue		6
Kunz, George OT	69-73Atl		6'5"	254	Notre Dame		
Kupp, Jake OG	64-65Dal 66Was 67Atl 67-73NO		6'3"	239	Washington		
Kurek, Ralph FB	65-70ChiB	2	6'2"	210	Wisconsin		12
Kuziel, Bob C	72NO		6'4"	255	Pittsburgh		
Kwalick, Ted TE	69-73SF	2	6'4"	226	Penn State		126
Laaveg, Paul OG	70-73Was		6'4"	245	Iowa		
Lacey, Bob OE	64Min 65NYG		6'3"	205	North Carolina		
Ladd, Ernie DT	61-65SD-A 66-67HouA 67-68KC-A		6'9"	302	Grambling	1	
Lage, Dick OE	61StL		6'4"	228	Lenoir Rhyne		
LaHood, Mike OG	69LA 70StL 71-72LA		6'3"	250	Wyoming		
Laird, Bruce DB	72-73Bal	3	6'	185	American Inter.	1	
Lakes, Roland DT-OT-DE	61-70SF 71NYG		6'4"	267	Wichita State		6
LaLonde, Roger DT	64Det 65NYG		6'3"	255	Muskingum		
Lamb, Mack DB	67-68MiaA		6'1"	188	Tennessee State	1	
Lamb, Ron FB	68DenA 68-69CinA 70-71Cin 72Atl	2	6'2"	227	South Carolina		
Lambert, Frank K	65-66Pit	4	6'3"	200	Mississippi		
Lambert, Gordon LB	68-69DenA		6'5"	245	West Virginia, Tennessee-Martin		
Lamberti, Pat LB	61NY-A 61DenA		6'2"	225	Richmond	1	
Lammons, Pete TE	67-69NY-A 70-71NYJ 72GB	2	6'3"	229	Texas		84
Lamonica, Daryle QB	63-66BufA 67-69OakA 70-73Oak	12 4	6'2"	215	Notre Dame		90
Lamson, Chuck DB	62-63Min 64JJ 65-67LA 68JJ		6'	189	Wyoming	11	6
Landry, Greg QB	68-73Det	12	6'4"	207	Massachusetts		102
Lane, Bobby LB	63-64SD-A		6'2"	222	Baylor		
Lane, Gary QB	66-67Cle 68NYG	1	6'1"	210	Missouri		
Lane, MacArthur HB-FB	68-71StL 72-73GB	2	6'	220	Utah State		132
Lang, Izzy FB-HB	64-68Phi 69LA	2	6'1"	231	Tennessee State		48
Langer, Jim C-OG	70-73Mia		6'2"	248	S. Dakota State		
Lanier, Willie LB	67-69KC-A 70-73KC		6'1"	245	Morgan State	17	12
Lanphear, Dan DE	60,62HouA		6'2"	225	Wisconsin		
Lapham, Bill C	60Phi 61Min		6'3"	250	Iowa		
Laraba, Bob LB-QB-HB	60LO-A 61SD-A		6'3"	195	Texas-El Paso	6	19
died Feb. 16, 1962 – auto accident							
Laraway, Jack LB	60BufA 61HouA		6'1"	218	Purdue	1	
LaRose, Dan DE-OT-OG	61-63Det 64Pit 65SF 66DenA		6'5"	250	Missouri		
Larpenter, Carl OG-OT	60-61DenA 62DalA		6'4"	237	Texas		
Larscheid, Jack HB	60-61OakA	23	5'6"	162	U. of Pacific		12
Larsen, Gary DT	64LA 65-73Min		6'5"	256	Concordia-Moor.		
Larson, Bill FB	60BosA		5'10"	190	Illinois Wesleyan		
Larson, Greg C-OG-OT	61-73NYG		6'2"	249	Minnesota		
Larson, Lynn OT	71Bal		6'4"	254	Kansas State		
Larson, Pete HB	67-68Was	2	6'1"	200	Cornell		18
Lash, Jim WR	73Min		6'2"	200	Northwestern		
Laskey, Bill LB	65BufA 66-67OakA 68FJ 69OakA 70Oak 71-71Bal 73Den		6'2"	238	Michigan	6	
Lasky, Frank OT	64-65NYG		6'2"	265	Florida		
Laslavic, Jim LB	73Det		6'2"	230	Penn State		
Lasse, Dick LB	58-59Pit 60-61Was 62NYG		6'2"	222	Syracuse	3	
Lassiter, Ike DE-DT	62-64DenA 65-69OakA 70Bos 71NE		6'5"	270	St. Augustine	1	
Laster, Art OT	70Buf		6'4"	280	Md. Eastern Shore		
Latourette, Chuck DB-WR	67-68, 70-71StL	34	6'	190	Rice		12
Latzke, Paul C	66-68SD-A		6'4"	240	U. of Pacific		
Lavan, Al DB	69-70Atl		6'1"	194	Colorado State	5	
Lavender, Joe DB	73Phi		6'4"	190	San Diego State		
Lawrence, Don DT-OG-OT	59-61Was		6'1"	245	Notre Dame		
Lawrence, Kent WR	69Phi 70Atl		5'11"	175	Georgia		
Lawrence, Roll and DB	73Atl		5'10"	180	Tabor	1	
Lawson, Al FL	64NY-A		5'11"	190	Delaware State		
Lawson, Jerry DB	68BufA		5'11"	192	Utah		
Lawson, Odell FB-HB	70Bos 71NE 73NO	23	6'2"	214	Langston		
Lawson, Roger HB-FB	72-73ChiB	2	6'2"	215	Western Michigan		6
Lawson, Steve OG	71-72Cin 73Min		6'3"	265	Kansas		
Lazetich, Pete DE-LB	72-73SD		6'3"	235	Stanford		
Leahy, Bob QB	71Pit		6'2"	205	Coll. of Emporia		
LeBeau, Dick DB	59-72Det		6'1"	185	Ohio State	62	14
LeClair, Jim QB	67-68DenA	1	6'1"	208	C.W. Post		6
LeClair, Jim LB	72-73Cin		6'2"	226	North Dakota		
LeClerc, Roger LB-C-DT	60-66ChiB 67DenA	5	6'3"	236	Trinity (Conn.)		382
Ledbetter, Monte WR-FL	67HouA 67-69BufA 69Atl	2	6'2"	185	NW State-La.		18
Lee, Bivian DB	71-73NO		6'3"	200	Prairie View	7	
Lee, Bob WR	68StL 69Atl		6'3"	200	Minnesota		
Lee, Bob OG	60BosA		6'1"	245	Missouri		
Lee, Bob QB	69-72Min 73Atl	12 4	6'2"	195	U. of Pacific		12
Lee, David K	66-73Bal	4	6'4"	224	Louisiana Tech		
Lee, Dwight HB	68SF 68Atl		6'2"	198	Michigan State		
Lee, Herm OT-OG	57Pit 58-66ChiB		6'4"	244	Florida A&M		
Lee, Jacky QB	60-63HouA 64-65DenA 66-67HouA 67-69KC-A	12	6'1"	186	Cincinnati		18
Lee, Ken LB	71Det 72Buf		6'4"	231	Washington	6	6
Lee, Monte LB	61StL 62MS 63-64Det 65Bal		6'4"	221	Texas	1	
Leetzow, Max DE-DT	65-66DenA 67JJ		6'4"	240	Idaho		
Leeuwenberg, Dick OT	65ChiB		6'5"	242	Stanford		
LeFear, Billy HB	72-73Cle	2	5'11"	197	Henderson State		
Leftridge, Dick FB	66Pit		6'2"	240	West Virginia		12
Leggett, Earl DT-DE	57-60ChiB 61KJ 62-65ChiB 66LA 67-68NO		6'3"	254	Louisiana State	1	2
Leigh, Charlie FB-HB	68-69Cle 71-73Mia	23	5'11"	205	none		12
Lemek, Ray OT-OG	57-61Was 62-65Pit		6'	238	Notre Dame		
Lemm, Wally	HC61HouA HC62-65StL HC66-69HouA HC70Hou				Carroll (Wis.)		
Lemmerman, Bruce QB	68-69Atl	1	6'1"	196	San Fern. Valley		
LeMoine, Jim OG-LB-TE	67BufA 68-69HouA		6'2"	245	Utah State		
Lenkaitis, Bill OG-C	68-69SD-A 70SD 71-73NE		6'3"	258	Penn State		
Lens, Greg DT	70-71Atl		6'5"	260	Trinity (Texas)		
Lentz, Jack DB	67-68DenA		6'	195	Holy Cross	5	
Leo, Bobby HB-WR	67-68BosA		5'10"	180	Harvard		6
Leo, Charlie OG	60-62BosA 63BufA		6'	238	Indiana		

Use Name (Nicknames) – Positions	Team by Year	See Section	Hgt	Wgt	College	Int	Pts
Leo, Jim DE-LB	60NYG 61-62Min		6'1"	222	Cincinnati		2
Leonard, Cecil DB	69NY-A 70NYJ		5'11"	165	Tuskegee		
Lester, Darrell FB	64Min 65-66DenA	2	6'2"	223	McNeese State		6
Letner, Cotton LB	61BufA		6'1"	215	Tennessee		
LeVeck, Jack LB	73StL		6'	225	Ohio U.		
LeVias, Jerry WR	69HouA 70Hou 71-73SD	23	5'10"	177	S. M. U.		84
Lewis, Dan HB	58-64Det 65Was 66NYG	23	6'1"	199	Wisconsin		144
Lewis, Dave QB-K	70-73Cin	4	6'2"	216	Stanford		
Lewis, D. D. LB	68Dal 69MS 70-73Dal		6'2"	222	Mississippi State	2	6
Lewis, Frank WR	71-73Pit	2	6'1"	196	Grambling		48
Lewis, Gary FB-HB	64-69SF 70NO	23	6'3"	228	Arizona State		108
Lewis, Hal DB	68DenA		6'2"	188	Arizona State		
Lewis, Harold HB-DB	59Bal 60BufA 62OakA		6'	200	Houston		
Lewis, Jess LB	70Hou		6'1"	230	Oregon State		
Lewis, Joe DT	58-60Pit 61Bal 62Phi		6'2"	256	Compton J.C.	1	6
Lewis, Mike DT-DE	71-73Atl		6'3"	242	Ark.-Pine Bluff	1	2
Lewis, Rich LB	72Hou 73Buf		6'3"	220	Portland State		
Lewis, Scott DE	71Hou		6'6"	260	Grambling		
Lewis, Sherman DB	66-67NY-A		5'10"	180	Michigan State		
Leypoldt, John K	71-73Buf	5	6'2"	226	none		206
Liggett, Bob DT	70KC		6'2"	255	Nebraska		
Lilly, Bob DT-DE	61-73Dal		6'4"	256	Texas Christian	1	24
Lince, Dave TE	66-67Phi		6'6"	258	North Dakota		
Lincoln, Keith HB-FB	61-66SD-A 67-68BufA 68SD-A	23 5	6'2"	212	Washington State		271
Lind, Mike FB	63-64SF 65-66Pit	2	6'2"	220	Notre Dame		54
Linden, Errol OT	61Cle 62-65Min 66-68Atl 69-70NO		6'5"	258	Houston		
Lindquist, Paul DT	61BosA		6'3"	265	New Hampshire		
Lindsey, Dale LB	65-72Cle 73NO		6'3"	224	Western Kentucky	8	6
Lindsey, Hub HB	68DenA		5'11"	196	Wyoming		
Lindsey, Jim HB-FB	66-72Min	2	6'2"	206	Arkansas		66
Line, Bill DT	72ChiB		6'7"	260	S. M. U.		
Linhart, Toni K	72NO		6'	170	none		11
Linne, Aubrey OE	61Bal		6'7"	235	Texas Christian		
Lisbon, Don HB	63-64SF	2	6'	194	Bowling Green		18
Liscio, Tony OT-OG	63-64Dal 65JJ 66-71Dal		6'5"	251	Tulsa		
Liske, Pete QB	64NY-A 69DenA 70Den 71-72Phi	12	6'2"	199	Penn State		12
Little, Floyd HB	67-69DenA 70-73Den	23	5'10"	196	Syracuse		294
Little, John DT-DE	70-73NYJ		6'3"	231	Oklahoma State		
Little, Larry OG-DT-OT	67-68SD-A 69MiaA 70-73Mia		6'1"	267	Bethune-Cookman		
Livingston, Andy FB-HB	64-65ChiB 66JJ 67-68ChiB 69-70NO	2	6'	234	none		66
Livingston, Cliff LB-DE	54-61NYG 62Min 63-65LA		6'3"	212	U. C. L. A.	8	6
Livingston, Dale K	68-69CinA 70GB	45	6'	210	Western Michigan		123
Livingston, Mike QB	68-69KC-A 70-73KC	12	6'3"	210	S. M. U.		12
Livingston, Walt HB	60BosA		6'	185	Heidelberg		
Livingston, Warren DB	61-66Dal		5'10"	185	Arizona	10	6
Lloyd, Dave LB-C	59-61Cle 62Det 63-70Phi		6'3"	247	Georgia	14	10
Lockett, J. W. FB	61SF 61-62Dal 63Bal 64Was	2	6'2"	229	Central St.-Okla.		60
Lockhart, Spider DB	65-73NYG	3	6'2"	176	North Texas State	38	18
Locklin, Billy LB	60OakA		6'2"	225	New Mexico State		
Lofton, Oscar OE	60BosA 61-62MS	2	6'6"	218	Southeastern La.		24
Logan, Chuck TE-OE	64Pit 65, 67-68StL		6'4"	215	Northwestern		
Logan, Jerry DB	63-72Bal	3	6'1"	188	West Texas State	34	36
Logan, Obert DB	65-66Dal 67NO		5'10"	180	Trinity (Texas)	8	6
Logan, Randy DB	73Phi		6'1"	195	Michigan	5	
Lohmeyer, John DE	73KC		6'4"	230	Kansas St. Teach.		6
Lomakoski, John OT	62Det		6'4"	250	Western Michigan		
Lomas, Mark DE-DT	70-73NYG		6'4"	239	Northern Arizona		
Lombardi, Vince died Sept. 3, 1970 - cancer	HC59-67GB HC69-70Was				Fordham		
London, Mike LB	66SD-A		6'2"	230	Wisconsin		
Long, Bob FL-WR	64-67GB 68Atl 69Was 70LA	2	6'3"	199	Wichita State		60
Long, Charley OG-OT	61-69BosA		6'3"	247	Tenn.-Chattanooga		
Long, Dave DE-DT	66-68StL 69-72NO		6'4"	241	Iowa		
Long, Mel LB	72-73Cle		6'	228	Toledo		
Long, Mike OE	60BosA		6'	188	Brandeis		
Longenecker, Ken DT	60Pit		6'4"	285	Lebanon Valley		
Longmire, Sam DB-WR	67-68KC-A		6'3"	195	Purdue		
Longo, Tom DB	69-70NYG 71StL		6'1"	199	Notre Dame	4	
Look, Dean QB 61 played major league baseball	62NY-A		5'11"	185	Michigan State		
Looney, Joe Don FB-HB	64Bal 65-66Det 66-67Was 68MS 69NO	234	6'1"	230	Oklahoma		78
Lopasky, Bill OG	61SF		6'2"	235	West Virginia		
Lorick, Tony FB	64-67Bal 68-69NO	23	6'1"	214	Arizona State		114
Lothamer, Ed DT DE	64-69KC-A 71-72KC		6'5"	261	Michigan State		
Lothridge, Billy QB-DB-K	64Dal 65LA 66-71Atl 72Mia	4	6'1"	194	Georgia Tech	3	6
Lott, Billy FB-HB-DB	58NYG 60OakA 61-63BosA	2	6'	203	Mississippi		128
Lou, Ron C	73Hou		6'2"	235	Arizona State		
Loudd, Rommie LB	60LA-A 61-62BosA		6'3"	227	U. C. L. A.	4	
Louderback, Tom LB-C-OG	58-59Phi 60-61OakA 62BufA		6'2"	235	San Jose State	3	6
Loukas, Angelo OG-OT	69BufA 70Bos		6'3"	250	Northwestern		
Love, John FL-WR-DB	67Was 68MS 72LA	23 5	5'11"	185	North Texas State		40
Love, Walt WR	73NYG		5'9"	180	Westminster (Utah)		
Lovetere, John DT	59-62LA 63-65NYG		6'4"	280	Compton J. C.		6
Lowe, Gary DB-HB	56-57Was 57-64Det		5'11"	196	Michigan State	20	2
Lowe, Paul HB	60LA-A 61SD-A 62BA 63-67SD-A 68-69KC-A	23	6'	200	Oregon State		282
Lucas, Dick OE	58Pit 60-63Phi	2	6'2"	213	Boston College		36
Lucas, Richie QB-HB-DB	60-61BufA	12	6'	190	Penn State	2	30
Lucci, Mike LB	62-64Cle 65-73Det		6'2"	230	Tennessee	21	24
Luce, Lew HB	61Was		6'	187	Penn State		
Lueck, Bill OG	68-73GB		6'3"	235	Arizona		
Luke, Tommy DB	68DenA		6'	190	Mississippi		
Luken, Tom OG	72-73Phi		6'3"	253	Purdue		
Lumpkin, Ron DB	73NYG		6'2"	200	Arizona State		
Lundy, Lamar DE-OE	57-69LA	2	6'7"	245	Purdue	3	54
Lunsford, Mel DT	73NE		6'3"	250	Central St.-Okla.		
Lurtsema, Bob DE-DT	67-71NYG 72-73Min		6'6"	250	Western Michigan	1	
Lusteg, Booth K	66BufA 67MiaA 68Pit 69GB	5	5'11"	190	Connecticut		202
Lyle, Garry DB-HB	68-73ChiB		6'2"	198	George Washington	9	
Lyles, Lenny DB-HB	58Bal 59-60SF 61-69Bal	23	6'2"	202	Louisville	16	48
Lyman, Jeff LB	72Buf		6'2"	230	Brigham Young		
Lynch, Dick DB	58Was 59-66NYG		6'1"	202	Notre Dame	37	42
Lynch, Fran HB-FB	67-69DenA 70-73Den	2	6'1"	203	Hofstra		62
Lynch, Jim LB	67-69KC-A 70-73KC		6'1"	235	Notre Dame	12	6
Lyons, Dicky DB	70NO		6'	190	Kentucky	1	
Lyons, Tommy C-OG	71-73Den		6'2"	228	Georgia		
Mack, Red FL-OE-HB	61-63Pit 64Phi 65Pit 66Atl 66GB	2	5'10"	185	Notre Dame		48
Mack, Tom OG	66-73LA		6'3"	249	Michigan		
Mackbee, Earsell DB	65-69Min		6'1"	195	Utah State	15	12
Mackey, Dee OE	60SF 61-62Bal 63-66NY-A	2	6'5"	232	East Texas State		50
Mackey, John TE-OE	63-71Bal 72SD	2	6'3"	222	Syracuse		228
MacKinnon, Jacque TE-OE-FB-OG	61-69SD-A 70Oak	2	6'4"	245	Colgate		134
MacLeod, Tom LB	73GB		6'3"	220	Minnesota	2	
Maczuzak, John DT	64KC-A		6'5"	250	Pittsburgh		
Madden, Johnny	HC69OakA HC70-73Oak				Cal. St. Polytech		
Magac, Mike OG	60-64SF 65-66Pit		6'3"	240	Missouri		
Maguire, Paul LB-DE-OE-K	60LA-A 61-63SD-A 64-69BufA 70Buf	4	6'	224	The Citadel	9	6
Maher, Bruce DB-HB	60-67Det 68-69NYG		5'11"	190	Detroit	22	6
Maitland, Jack HB	70Bal 71-72NE	2	6'1"	210	Williams		18
Majors, Billy DB	61BufA		6'	175	Tennessee		
Majors, Bobby DB	72Cle		6'1"	193	Tennessee		
Malavasi, Ray	HC66DenA				Army, Mississippi State		
Malinchak, Bill WR-OE	66-69Det 70-73Was	2	6'1"	198	Indiana		32
Mallick, Fran DE-DT	65Pit		6'3"	245	none		
Mallory, Irvin DB	71NE		6'1"	196	Virginia Union		
Mallory, John DB	68Phi 69-71Atl	3	6'	188	West Virginia	2	24
Malone, Art FB-HB	70-73Atl	2	5'11"	211	Arizona State		132
Manders, Dave C	64-66Dal 67JJ 68-73Dal		6'2"	247	Michigan State		
Mandich, Jim TE	70-73Mia	2	6'3"	224	Michigan		54
Mangum, John DT	66-67BosA		6'3"	273	Southern Miss.		
Mankins, Jim FB	67Atl		6'1"	235	Florida State		
Mann, Errol K	68GB 69-73Det	5	6'	201	Notre Dame		460
Manning, Archie QB	71-73NO	12	6'3"	208	Mississippi		48
Manning, Pete DB	60-61ChiB		6'3"	208	Wake Forest		
Manning, Rosie DT	72-73Atl		6'5"	256	NE State-Okla.		
Manoukian, Don OG	60OakA		5'9"	242	Stanford		
Mansfield, Ray C-DT	64-73Pit		6'3"	250	Washington		
Maples, Bobby C-LB	65-69HouA 70Hou 71Pit 72-73Den		6'3"	244	Baylor	1	
Maples, Jim LB	63Bal		6'4"	225	Baylor		
Marchlewski, Frank C	65LA 66-68Atl 68-69LA 70Buf		6'2"	237	Minnesota		
Marcol, Chester K	72-73GB	5	6'	190	Hillsdale		210
Marconi, Joe FB-HB	56-61LA 62-66ChiB	2	6'2"	225	West Virginia		234
Marcontell, Ed OG	67StL 67HouA		6'	260	Lamar Tech		
Marinaro, Ed HB-FB	72-73Min	2	6'2"	212	Cornell		30
Marinovich, Marv OG	65OakA		6'3"	250	Southern Calif		
Marion, Jerry FL	67Pit		5'10"	175	Wyoming		
Marques, Bob LB	60NY-A		6'	220	Boston U.		
Marsalis, Jim DB	69KC-A 70-73KC		5'11"	194	Tennessee State	13	
Marsh, Aaron WR	68-69BosA	2	6'	190	Eastern Kentucky		24
Marsh, Amos HB-FB	61-64Dal 65-67Det	23	6'	218	Oregon State		198
Marsh, Frank DB	67SD-A		6'2"	205	Oregon State		
Marshall, Bud DT	65GB 66Was 66Atl 67-68HouA		6'5"	271	S. F. Austin St.		
Marshall, Chuck DB	62DenA		6'	180	Oregon State		
Marshall, Ed WR	71Cin		6'5"	200	Cameron State		
Marshall, Jim DE	60Cle 61-73Min		6'3"	239	Ohio State	1	8
Marshall, Larry DB	72-73KC	3	5'10"	195	Md. Eastern Shore		
Marshall, Randy DE	70-71Atl		6'5"	237	Linfield		6
Martha, Paul DB-FL-OE-HB	64-69Pit 70Den	2	6'	186	Pittsburgh	21	6
Martin, Aaron DB	64-65LA 66-67Phi 68Was	3	6'	187	N. Car. Central	11	18
Martin, Amos LB	72-73Min		6'3"	228	Louisville		
Martin, Billy (Bill) TE-OE	64-65ChiB 66-67Atl 68Min	2 4	6'4"	238	Georgia Tech		24
Martin, Billy HB	62-64ChiB	3	5'11"	196	Minnesota		6
Martin, Blanche FB	60NY-A 60LA-A		6'	195	Michigan State		6
Martin, Dave LB	68KC-A 69ChiB		6'	220	Notre Dame		
Martin, Dee DB	71NO 72JJ		6'1"	190	Kentucky State	3	
Martin, Don DB	73NE		5'11"	187	Yale		
Martin, Harvey DE	73Dal		6'5"	262	East Texas State		
Martin, Larry DT	66SD-A		6'2"	270	San Diego State		
Marx, Greg DE	73Atl		6'4"	260	Notre Dame		
Maslowski, Matt WR	71LA		6'3"	210	San Diego		6
Mason, Dave DB	73NE		6'	200	Nebraska		
Mason, Tommy HB-FB	61-66Min 67-70LA 71Was 72JJ	23	6'	195	Tulane		270
Mass, Wayne OT	68-70ChiB 71Mia 72NE 72Phi		6'4"	243	Clemson		
Masters, Bill TE	67-69BufA 70-73Den	2	6'5"	235	Louisiana State		54
Masters, Norm OT	57-64GB		6'2"	249	Michigan State		
Matan, Bill DE	66NYG		6'4"	240	Kansas State		
Matheson, Bob LB-DE	67-70Cle 71-73Mia		6'4"	240	Duke	4	
Mathis, Bill HB-FB	60-69NY-A	2	6'1"	219	Clemson		282
Matlock, John C-OT	67NY-A 68CinA 70-71Atl 72Buf		6'4"	250	Miami (Fla.)		
Matson, Pat OG	66-67DenA 68-69CinA 70-73Cin		6'1"	246	Oregon		
Matsos, Archie LB	60-62BufA 63-65OakA 66DenA 66SD-A		6'	215	Michigan State	22	6
Matte, Tom HB-QB	61-72Bal	123	6'	207	Ohio State		342
Matthews, Al DB	70-73GB		5'11"	190	Texas A&I	5	6
Matthews, Henry HB	72NE-73NO		6'3"	203	Michigan State		
Matthews, Wes OE	66MiaA		5'10"	180	NE State-Okla.		
Mattox, Jack DT	61DenA		6'4"	240	Fresno State		
Mattson, Riley OT	61-64Was 65JJ 66ChiB		6'4"	252	Oregon		
Matuszak, John DT	73Hou		6'8"	290	Tampa		
Mauck, Carl C	69Bal 70Mia 71-73SD		6'3"	240	Southern Illinois		6
Mauer, Andy OG	70-73Atl		6'3"	257	Oregon		
Maxwell, Bruce HB-FB	70Det		6'1"	220	Arkansas		
Maxwell, Tommy DB	69-70Bal 71-73Oak		6'2"	195	Texas A&M	3	
May, Art DE	71NE		6'3"	245	Tuskègee		
May, Ray LB	67-69Pit 70-73Bal 73Den		6'1"	230	Southern Calif.	10	6
Mayberry, Doug FB	61-62Min 6300akA	2	6'1"	223	Utah State		12
Mayes, Ben DE-DT	69HouA		6'5"	265	Drake		
Mayes, Rufus OT-OG	69ChiB 70-73Cin		6'5"	257	Ohio State		
Maynard, Don FL-WR-OE-HB	58NYG 60-69NY-A 70-72NYG 73StL	23	6'	180	Texas-El Paso		532

Use Name (Nicknames) – Positions	Team by Year	See Section	Hgt	Wgt	College	Int	Pts
Mayo, Ron TE	73Hou		6'3"	223	Morgan State		
Mays, Jerry DE-DT	61-62DalA 63-69KC-A 70KC		6'4"	250	S. M. U.	1	6
Mazur, John	HC70Bos HC71-72NE				Notre Dame		
Mazurek, Fred FL-DB	65-66Was		5'11"	192	Pittsburgh		
Mazzanti, Jerry DE	63Phi 64-65MS 66Det 67Pit		6'3"	240	Arkansas		
McAdams, Bob DT	63-64NY-A		6'3"	250	N. Car. Central		
McAdams, Carl LB-DT-DE	66BN 67-69NY-A		6'3"	240	Oklahoma		
McBath, Mike DE-OT-DT	68-69BufA 70-72Buf		6'4"	248	Penn State		
McBride, Norm DE	69MiaA 70Mia		6'3"	240	Utah		
McBride, Ron HB	73GB		6'	200	Missouri		
McCaffrey, Mike LB	70Buf		6'3"	235	California		
McCall, Bob HB	73NE		6'	205	Arizona		
McCall, Don HB	67-68NO 69Pit 70NO	23	5'11"	195	Southern Calif.		60
McCall, Ron LB	67-68SD-A		6'2"	245	Weber State		
McCambridge, John DE	67Det		6'4"	245	Northwestern		
McCann, Jim K	71-72SF 73NYG	4	6'2"	165	Arizona State		
McCann, Tim DT	69NYG		6'5"	265	Princeton		
McCarren, Larry C	73GB		6'3"	240	Illinois		
McCarthy, Brendan FB	68Atl 68-69DenA	2	6'3"	220	Boston College		18
McCarty, Mickey TE	69KC-A		6'5"	255	Texas Christian		
McCauley, Don HB-FB	71-73Bal	2	6'1"	207	North Carolina		54
McCauley, Tom DB-WR	69-71Atl		6'3"	187	Wisconsin	2	6
McClain, Cliff HB-FB	70-73NYJ	2	6'	217	S. Carolina State		12
McClanahan, Brent HB	73Min		5'10"	202	Arizona State		
McClard, Bill K	72SD 73NO	5	5'10"	202	Arkansas		59
McClellan, Mike DB	62-63Phi 64-65MS		6'1"	185	Oklahoma	4	
McClinton, Curtis FB-TE	62DalA 63-69KC-A	2	6'3"	230	Kansas		196
McCloughan, Kent DB	65-69OakA 70Oak		6'1"	190	Nebraska	15	
McClure, Wayne LB	68CinA 70Cin		6'1"	225	Mississippi		
McComb, Don DE	60BosA		6'4"	240	Villanova		
McConnell, Brian LB	73Hou		6'4"	207	Michigan State		
McCord, Darris DE-DT-OT	55-67Det		6'4"	247	Tennessee	3	8
McCormick, Dave OT	66SF 67-68NO		6'6"	250	Louisiana State		
McCormick, John QB	62Min 63DenA 64JJ 65-66,68DenA	1 4	6'1"	201	Massachusetts		
McCoy, Lloyd OG	64SD-A		6'1"	245	San Diego State		
McCoy, Mike DT	70-73GB		6'5"	284	Notre Dame		
McCreary, Bob OT	61Dal		6'5"	256	Wake Forest		
McCullers, Dale LB	69MiaA		6'1"	215	Florida State		
McCullouch, Earl WR	68-73Det	2	5'11"	175	Southern Calif.		114
McCullough, Bob OG	62-65DenA		6'5"	244	Colorado		
McCusker, Jim OT	58ChiC 59-62Phi 63Cle 64NY-A		6'2"	246	Pittsburgh		
McCutcheon, Larry HB	72-73LA	2	6'1"	205	Colorado State		30
McDaniel, Wahoo LB-OG	60HouA 61-63 DenA 64-65NY-A 66-68MiaA	4	6'	235	Oklahoma	13	6
McDaniels, Dave WR	68Dal		6'4"	200	Miss. Valley St.		
McDermott, Gary HB	68BufA 69Atl	2	6'1"	211	Tulsa		26
McDole, Ron DE-DT	61StL 62HouA 63-69BufA 70Buf 71-73Was		6'3"	267	Nebraska	9	6
McDonald, Don DB	61BufA		5'11"	185	Houston		
McDonald, Ray FB	67-68Was	2	6'4"	248	Idaho		24
McDonald, Tommy FL-HB-WR	57-63Phi 64Dal 65-66LA 67Atl 68Cle	23	5'10"	176	Oklahoma		510
McDougall, Gerry FB	62-64,68SD-A	2	6'2"	225	U. C. L. A.		38
McDowell, John OT-OG	64GB 65NYG 66StL		6'3"	260	St. John's-Minn.		
McFadin, Bud DT-LB-OG	52-56LA 60-63DenA 64-65HouA		6'3"	260	Texas	1	24
McFarland, Jim TE	70-73StL		6'5"	225	Nebraska		18
McFarland, Kay FL-OE-WR	62-66SF 67JJ 68SF	2	6'2"	182	Colorado State		24
McFarlane, Nyle HB	60OakA		6'2"	205	Brigham Young		12
McGee, Ben DE-DT	64-72Pit		6'2"	259	Jackson State	1	6
McGee, George OT	60BosA 61-62MS		6'2"	255	Southern U.		
McGee, Max OE	54GB 55-56MS 57-67GB	2 4	6'3"	205	Tulane		306
McGee, Mike OG	60-62StL		6'1"	230	Duke		
McGee, Tony DE-DT	71-73ChiB		6'4"	250	Bishop		
McGee, Willie DB	73SD		5'11"	175	Alcorn A & M		
McGeever, John DB	62-65DenA 66MiaA		6'1"	195	Auburn	11	6
McGeorge, Rich TE	70-73G B		6'4"	235	Elon		54
McGill, Mike LB	68-70Min 71-72StL		6'2"	236	Notre Dame	3	6
McGill, Ralph DB	72-73SF	3	5'11"	185	Tulsa		
McGrew, Dan C	60BufA		6'2"	250	Purdue		
McIlhany, Dan DB	65LA		6'1"	195	Texas A & M	2	
McInnis, Hugh OE-TE	60-62StL 64Det 66Atl	2	6'3"	219	Southern Miss.		
McKay, Bob OT	70-73Cle		6'5"	260	Texas		
McKeever, Marlin LB-TE-OE	61-66LA 67Min 68-70Was 71-72LA 73Phi	2	6'1"	233	Southern Calif.	9	36
McKenzie, Reggie OG	72-73Buf		6'4"	235	Michigan		
McKinley, Bill DE-LB	71Buf 72JJ		6'3"	240	Arizona		
McKinney, Bill LB	72ChiB		6'1"	226	West Texas State		
McKinnis, Hugh FB	73Cle	2	6'	225	Arizona State		
McKinnon, Don LB-C	63-64BosA		6'3"	223	Dartmouth		
McKoy, Bill LB	70-72Den		6'3"	235	Purdue		
McLenna, Bruce HB	66Det		6'3"	225	Hillsdale		
McLeod, Bob OE-TE	61-66HouA	2	6'5"	231	Abilene Christian		114
McLinton, Harold LB	69-73Was		6'2"	235	Southern U.	2	
McMahon, Art DB	68-69BosA 70Bos 72NE		5'11"	188	N. Carolina State	3	
McMakin, John TE	72-73Pit	2	6'3"	232	Clemson		12
McMillan, Eddie DB	73LA		6'	180	Florida State	4	
McMillan, Ernie OT	61-73StL		6'6"	257	Illinois		
McMillan, Jim DB	61-62DenA 63-64OakA 64-65DenA		5'11"	190	Colorado State	14	24
McMullan, John OG	60-61NY-A		6'	244	Notre Dame		
McMurtry, Chuck DT	60-61BufA 62-63OakA		6'	286	Whittier		
McNamara, Bob DB-HB	60-61DenA		6'	189	Minnesota	7	12
McNeil, Charley DB	60LA-A 61-64SD-A		5'11"	179	Compton J.C.	19	12
McNeil, Clifton WR-FL	64-67Cle 68-69SF 70-71NYG 71-72Was 73Hou	2	6'2"	186	Grambling		138
McNeill, Tom K	67-69NO 70Min 71-73Phi	4	6'1"	195	S.F. Austin St.		
McQuarters, Ed DT	65StL		6'1"	250	Oklahoma		
McRae, Bennie DB	62-70ChiB 71NYG		6'1"	180	Michigan	27	24
McRae, Frank DT	67ChiB		6'7"	270	Tennessee State		
McVea, Warren HB-WR	68CinA 69KC-A 70-71KC 72KJ 73KC	23	5'10"	182	Houston		78
McWatters, Bill FB	64Min		6'	225	North Texas State		
Meador, Ed DB	59-70LA	3	5'11"	193	Arkansas Tech	46	36
Medved, Ron DB	66-70Phi		6'1"	205	Washington	3	

Use Name (Nicknames) – Positions	Team by Year	See Section	Hgt	Wgt	College	Int	Pts
Meggyesy, Dave LB	63-69StL		6'1"	221	Syracuse		
Meinert, Dale LB-OG-OT	58-59ChiC 60-67Stl		6'2"	219	Oklahoma State	9	6
Meixler, Ed LB	65BosA		6'3"	245	Boston U.		
Melinkovich, Mike DE	65-66StL 67Det		6'4"	243	Grays Harbor J. C.		
Mellekas, John C-DT-OT	56ChiB 57MS 58-61ChiB 62SF 63Phi		6'3"	255	Arizona		
Memmelaar, Dale OG-OT	59ChiC 60-61StL 62-63Dal 64-65Cle 66-67Bal		6'2"	247	Wyoming		
Mendenhall, John DT	72-73NYG		6'1"	255	Grambling		
Mendenhall, Ken C	72-73Bal		6'3"	235	Oklahoma		
Mendenhall, Terry LB	71-72Oak		6'1"	210	San Diego State		
Mendez, Mario HB	64SD-A		5'11"	200	San Diego State		
Menefee, Pep FL	66NYG		6'1"	198	New Mexico State		
Mercein, Chuck FB	65-67NYG 67-68GB 69Was 70NYJ	2 5	6'3"	227	Yale		45
Mercer, Mike K	61-62Min 63-66OakA 66KC-A 67-68BufA 68-69GB 70SD	45	6'	208	Arizona State		594
Meredith, Don (Dandy Don) QB	60-68Dal	12	6'2"	202	S. M. U.		
Meredith, Dudley DT	63HouA 64-68BufA 68HouA		6'4"	280	Lamar Tech	1	
Merlo, Jim LB	73NO		6'1"	220	Stanford	3	
Mertens, Jerry DB	58-62SF 63JJ 64-65SF		6'	184	Drake	8	6
Mertens, Jim TE	69MiaA		6'3"	235	Fairmont State		
Merz, Curt OG-DE	62DalA 63-68KC-A		6'4"	257	Iowa		
Messer, Dale HB-FL-DB	61-65SF	2	5'10"	175	Fresno State	1	
Messner, Max LB	60-63Det 64NYG 64-65Pit		6'3"	225	Cincinnati	2	
Mestnik, Frank FB	60-61StL 63GB	2	6'2"	200	Marquette		30
Metcalf, Terry HB	73StL	2	5'10"	185	Long Beach State		12
Meyer, Dennis DB	73Pit		5'11"	186	Arkansas State		
Meyer, Ed OT	60BufA		6'2"	240	West Texas State		
Meyer, John LB	66HouA		6'1"	225	Notre Dame		
Meyer, Ron QB	66Pit		6'4"	205	S. Dakota State		
Meyers, John DT	62-63Dal 64-67Phi		6'6"	272	Washington	2	
Meylan, Wayne LB	68-69Cle 70Min		6'1"	237	Nebraska		
Mialik, Larry TE	72-73Atl		6'2"	226	Wisconsin		
Michael, Rich OT	60-63HouA 64JJ 65-66HouA		6'3"	238	Ohio State		
Michaels, Lou DE-K	58-60LA 61-63Pit 64-69Bal 71GB	5	6'2"	243	Kentucky		955
Michel, Tom HB	64Min	2	6'	210	East Carolina		
Middendorf, Dave OG	68-69CinA 70NYJ		6'3"	260	Washington State		
Mike-Mayer, Nick K	73Atl	5	5'8"	186	Temple		112
Mildren, Jack DB	72-73Bal		6'1"	200	Oklahoma		
Milks, John LB	66SD-A		6'	222	San Diego State	1	
Miller, Al LB	62-63Was		6'	224	Ohio U.		
Miller, Alan FB	60BosA 61-63OakA 64JJ 65OakA	2	6'	202	Boston College		120
Miller, Bill DT	62HouA		6'4"	270	N. Mex. Highlands		
Miller, Bill OE-WR	62DalA 63BufA 64,66-68OakA	2	6'	192	Miami (Fla.)		60
Miller, Clark DE	62-68SF 69Was 70LA		6'5"	246	Utah State	1	6
Miller, Fred DT	63-72Bal		6'3"	248	Louisiana State		
Miller, Jim OG	71-72Atl		6'3"	240	Iowa		
Miller, Ralph OG	72-73Hou		6'4"	260	Alabama State		
Miller, Ron QB	62LA	1	6'	190	Wisconsin		
Miller, Terry LB	71-73StL		6'2"	225	Illinois		
Mills, Dick OG	61-62Det		6'3"	240	Pittsburgh		
Mills, Pete OE	65-66BufA		5'11"	180	Wichita State		
Milstead, Charley QB-DB	60-61HouA	4	6'2"	190	Texas A & M	2	1
Milton, Gene WR	68-69MiaA	23	5'10"	170	Florida A & M		12
Mingo, Gene HB-K	60-63DenA 64-65OakA 66-67MiaA 67Was 69-70Pit	23 5	6'1"	199	none		629
Minniear, Randy HB	66BL 67-69NYG 70Cle	2	6'	205	Purdue		36
Minor, Lincoln HB-FB	73NO		6'2"	211	New Mexico State		
Minter, Tom DB	62DenA 62BufA		5'10"	178	Baylor		
Mira, George QB	64-68SF 69Phi 71Mia	12	5'11"	190	Miami (Fla.)		
Mirich, Rex DT-DE	64-66OakA 67-69DenA 70Bos		6'4"	251	Arizona State		
Mischak, Bob OG	58NYG 60-62NY-A 63-65OakA		6'	237	Army		
Mitchell, Alvin DB-WR	68-69Cle 70Den		6'3"	195	Morgan State		
Mitchell, Bobby FL-HB-WR	58-61Cle 62-68Was	23	6'	192	Illinois		546
Mitchell, Charley HB-DB	63-67DenA 68BufA	23	5'11"	185	Washington	1	54
Mitchell, Ed OG	65-67SD-A		6'2"	275	Southern U.		
Mitchell, Jim TE	69-73Atl	2	6'2"	231	Prairie View		126
Mitchell, Jim DE	70-73Det		6'3"	245	Virginia State	1	
Mitchell, Ken LB	73Atl		6'1"	224	Nevada-Las Vegas		
Mitchell, Leroy DB	67-68BosA 69BQ 70Hou 71-73Den		6'2"	192	Texas Southern	19	6
Mitchell, Lydell HB	72-73Bal	2	5'11"	204	Penn State		24
Mitchell, Stan FB-HB-OE	66-69MiaA 70Mia 71JJ	2	6'2"	220	Tennessee		54
Mitchell, Tom TE-WR	66OakA 68-73Bal	2	6'2"	218	Bucknell		120
Mitchell, Willie DB	64-69KC-A 70KC	3	6'1"	185	Tennessee State	16	24
Mitinger, Bob LB-DE	62-64,66,68SD-A		6'2"	232	Penn State	3	
Mix, Ron OT-OG	60LA-A 61-69SD-A 70VR 71Oak		6'4"	249	Southern Calif.		
Molden, Frank DT	65LA 66-67JJ 68Phi 69NYG		6'5"	282	Jackson State	1	6
Montalbo, Mel DB	62OakA		6'1"	190	Utah State		
Montgomery, Marv OT	71-73Den		6'6"	255	Southern Calif.	1	
Montgomery, Mike HB-WR	71SD 72-73Dal	2	6'2"	207	Kansas State		54
Montgomery, Randy DB	71-73Den	3	5'11"	182	Weber State		6
Montgomery, Ross FB	69-70ChiB	2	6'3"	220	Texas Christian		
Montler, Mike OT-OG-C	69BosA 70Bos 71-72NE 73Buf		6'4"	264	Colorado		
Mooers, Doug DT-DE	71-72NO		6'6"	265	Whittier		
Mooney, Ed LB	68-71Det 72JJ 73Bal		6'2"	231	Texas Tech		
Moore, Alex DB	68DenA		6'	195	Norfolk State		
Moore, Art DT	73NE		6'5"	253	Tulsa		
Moore, Baldy DT	72-73Mia		6'5"	265	Bethune-Cookman		
Moore, Bob TE	71-73Oak	2	6'3"	220	Stanford		30
Moore, Charlie OG	62Was		6'5"	230	Arkansas		
Moore, Denis DT-DE	67-69Det		6'5"	247	Southern Calif.		
Moore, Derland DT	73NO		6'4"	260	Oklahoma	1	
Moore, Fred DT-DE	64-66SD-A		6'3"	255	Memphis State		
Moore, Gene HB	69SF		6'	208	Occidental		
Moore, Jerry DB	71-72ChiB 73NO		6'3"	208	Arkansas	1	
Moore, Joe HB	71ChiB 72JJ 73ChiB	2	6'1"	205	Missouri		
Moore, Lenny HB-FL	56-67Bal	23	6'1"	191	Penn State		678
Moore, Leroy DE	60BufA 61-62BosA 62-63BufA 64-65DenA		6'	231	Ft. Valley State	2	6
Moore, Reynaud DB	71NO		6'2"	190	U. C. L. A.		
Moore, Rich DT	69-70GB		6'6"	285	Villanova		
Moore, Tom HB	60-65GB 66LA 67Atl	23	6'2"	213	Vanderbilt		186
Moore, Wayne OT	70,72-73Mia		6'6"	265	Lamar Tech		

Use Name (Nicknames) – Positions	Team by Year			Hgt	Wgt	College	Int	Pts
Moore, Zeke DB	67-69HouA 70-73Hou	3		6'2"	196	Lincoln (Mo.)	13	12
Mooring, John OT-C	71-73NYJ			6'6"	255	Tampa		
Moorman, Mo OG-OT	68-69KC-A 70-73KC			6'5"	252	Texas A&M		
Mooty, Jim DB	60Dal			5'11"	177	Arkansas		
Moran, Jim DT	64NYG 65BL 66-67NYG			6'5"	260	Idaho		
Moreau, Doug TE-OE	66-69MiaA	2		6'2"	207	Louisiana State		45
Morelli, Fran OT	62NY-A			6'2"	258	Colgate		
Morgan, Bobby DB	67Pit			6'	205	New Mexico		
Morgan, Mike LB	64-67Phi 68Was 69-70NO 71JJ			6'4"	241	Louisiana State	6	12
Morin, Milt TE	66-73Cle	2		6'4"	244	Massachusetts		78
Morrall, Earl QB	56SF 57-58Pit 59-64Det 65-67NYG	12	4	6'1"	204	Michigan State		48
	68-71Bal 72-73Mia							
Morris, Chris OT	72-73Cle			6'3"	250	Indiana		
Morris, Dennit LB	58SF 60-61HouA			6'1"	228	Oklahoma	5	
Morris, Johnny FL-HB	58-67ChiB	23		5'10"	180	Cal.-Santa Barbara		222
Morris, Jon C	64-69BosA 70Bos 71-73NE			6'4"	246	Holy Cross		
Morris, Larry LB-HB	55-57LA 59-65ChiB 66Atl	2		6'2"	226	Georgia Tech	6	12
Morris, Mercury HB	69MiaA 70-73Mia	23		5'10"	189	West Texas State		162
Morris, Riley LB-DE	60-62OakA			6'2"	230	Florida A&M	3	6
Morrison, Don OT	71-73NO			6'5"	255	Texas-Arlington		
Morrison, Joe HB-FL-WR-FB-DB	59-72NYG	23		6'1"	210	Cincinnati		390
Morrison, Reece HB	68-72Cle 72-73Cin	23		6'	206	SW Texas State		24
Morriss, Guy C	73Phi			6'4"	255	Texas Christian		
Morrow, John C-OG-DE	56LA 57MS 58-59LA 60-66Cle			6'3"	244	Michigan		
Morrow, Tom DB	62-64OakA		4	5'11	185	Southern Miss.	23	
Morton, Craig QB	65-73Dal	12		6'4"	215	California		36
Morze, Frank C-DT	57-61SF 62-63Cle 64SF			6'4"	272	Boston College		
Moseley, Mark K	70Phi 71-72Hou		5	5'11	182	S. F. Austin St.		145
Moses, Haven WR	68-69BufA 70-72Buf 72-73Den	2		6'3"	203	San Diego State		156
Mosier, John TE	71Den 72Bal 73NE			6'3"	220	Kansas		
Moss, Eddie HB	73StL			6'	215	SE Missouri St.		
Moss, Roland TE-FB	69Bal 70SD 70Buf 71NE	2		6'3"	215	Toledo		12
Mostardi, Rich DB	60Cle 61Min 62OakA			5'11"	188	Kent State	2	
Moten, Bobby WR	68DenA			6'4"	212	Bishop		
Mudd, Howard OG	64-69SF 69-70ChiB			6'3"	251	Hillsdale		
Muelhaupt, Ed OG	60-61BufA			6'3"	230	Iowa State		6
Muhlmann, Horst K	69CinA 70-73Cin		5	6'1"	214	none		484
Mul-Key, Herb HB	72-73Was	23		6'	190	none		12
Mulligan, Wayne C	69-73StL			6'2"	245	Clemson		
Mullins, Don DB	61-62ChiB			6'1"	195	Houston		
Mullins, Gerry OG-OT	71-73Pit			6'3"	238	Southern Calif.		6
Mumley, Nick DE-OT	60-62NY-A			6'6"	252	Purdue	1	6
Mumphord, Lloyd DB	69MiaA 70-73Mia			5'11"	180	Texas Southern	14	18
Munsey, Nelson DB	72-73Bal			6'1"	185	Wyoming		6
Munson, Bill QB	64-67LA 68-73Det	12		6'2"	202	Utah State		12
Murchison, Lee OE	61Dal			6'3"	205	U. of Pacific		
Murdock, Guy C	72Hou			6'2"	245	Michigan		
Murdock, Jesse HB-FB	63OakA 63BufA			6'2"	203	Calif. Western		
Murdock, Les K	67NYG		5	6'3"	245	Florida State		25
Murphy, Bill WR	68BosA	2		6'1"	185	Cornell		
Murphy, Dennis DT	65ChiB			6'1"	250	Florida		
Murphy, Fred OE	60Cle 61Min			6'3"	205	Georgia Tech		
Musgrove, Spain DT-DE	67-69Was 70Hou			6'4"	275	Utah State		
Myers, Chip WR-FL	67SF 69CinA 70-73Cin	2		6'4"	201	NW State-Okla.		42
Myers, Tom DB	72-73NO			5'11"	184	Syracuse	6	
Myers, Tom QB	65-66Det			6'	188	Northwestern		
Myrtle, Chip LB-TE	67-69DenA 70-72Den 73JJ			6'2"	223	Maryland	4	2
Nairn, Harvey WR	68NY-A 69MS			6'1"	178	Southern U.		
Namath, Joe QB	65-69NY-A 70-73NYJ	12		6'2"	197	Alabama		42
Nance, Jim FB	65-69BosA 70Bos 71NE 73NYJ	2		6'1"	241	Syracuse		276
Napier, Walter DT	60-61DalA			6'4"	275	Paul Quinn		
Naponic, Bob QB	70Hou			6'	190	Illinois		
Naumoff, Paul LB	67-73Det			6'1"	217	Tennessee	2	
Neal, Dan C	73Bal			6'4"	240	Kentucky		
Neal, Louis WR	73Atl			6'4"	215	Prairie View		6
Neal, Richard DE-DT	69-72NO 73NYJ			6'3"	254	Southern U.		6
Neck, Tommy DB	62ChiB			5'11"	190	Louisiana State		
Neely, Ralph OT	65-73Dal			6'5"	263	Oklahoma		
Neff, Bob DB	66-68MiaA		3	6'	182	S. F. Austin St.	2	
Neidert, John (J. T.) LB	68CinA 68-69NY-A 70ChiB			6'2"	230	Louisville		
Neighbors, Billy OG	62-65BosA 66-69MiaA			5'11	244	Alabama		
Nelsen, Bill QB	63-67Pit 68-72Cle	12		6'	195	Southern Calif.		12
Nelson, Al DB	65-73Phi		3	5'11"	185	Cincinnati	13	18
Nelson, Andy (Bones) DB	57-63Bal 64NYG			6'1"	180	Memphis State	33	18
Nelson, Benny DB	64HouA			6'	185	Alabama	1	6
Nelson, Bill DT	71-73LA			6'7"	270	Oregon State		
Nelson, Dennis OT	70-73Bal			6'5"	260	Illinois State		
Nery, Ron DE	60LA-A 61-62SD-A 63DenA 63HouA			6'6"	236	Kansas State		
Nettles, Jim DB	65-68Phi 69-72LA			5'9"	177	Wisconsin	26	24
Neumann, Tom HB	63BosA	2		5'11"	205	Northern Michigan		6
Nevett, Elijah DB-FL	67-70NO			6'	185	Clark-Ga.	6	
Neville, Tom OT	65-69BosA 70Bos 71-73NE			6'4"	249	Mississippi State		
Newell, Steve OE	67SD-A			6'1"	186	Long Beach State		
Newhouse, Robert HB-FB	72-73Dal	2		5'10"	202	Houston		18
Newland, Bob WR	71-73NO	2		6'2"	190	Oregon		36
Newman, Ed OG	73Mia			6'2"	245	Duke		
Newsome, Billy DE	70-72Bal 73NO			6'4"	245	Grambling	3	6
Newton, Bob OG-OT	71-73ChiB			6'4"	250	Nebraska		
Nichols, Bob OT	65Pit 66-67LA			6'3"	250	Stanford		
Nichols, Bobby TE	66-67BosA			6'2"	220	Boston U.		
Nichols, Mike C	60-61DenA			6'3"	225	ARk.-Pine Bluff		
Nichols, Robbie LB	70-71Bal			6'3"	220	Tulsa		
Nicklas, Pete OT	62OakA			6'4"	240	Baylor		
Niland, John OG	66-73Dal			6'4"	246	Iowa		6
Ninowski, Jim QB	58-59Cle 60-61Det 62-66Cle 67-68Was	12		6'1"	206	Michigan State		60
	69NO							
Nisby, John OG	57-61Pit 62-64Was			6'1"	235	Pacific (Ore.)		
Nitschke, Ray LB	58-72GB			6'3"	235	Illinois	25	12
Nix, Kent QB	67-69Pit 70-71ChiB 72Hou	12		6'1"	195	Texas Christian		12
Nobis, Tommy LB	66-73Atl			6'2"	237	Texas	10	12

Use Name (Nicknames) – Positions	Team by Year			Hgt	Wgt	College	Int	Pts
Nocera, John LB	59-62Phi 63DenA			6'1"	220	Iowa	1	
Nock, George HB	69-71NYJ 72Was	2		5'10"	200	Morgan State		66
Nofsinger, Terry QB	61-64Pit 65-66StL 67Atl	12		6'4"	209	Utah		18
Nomina, Tom DT-OG	63-65DenA 66-68MiaA			6'5"	267	Miami-Ohio		
Noonan, Karl WR-OE	66-69MiaA 70-71Mia 72KJ	2		6'3"	193	Iowa		102
Nordquist, Mark OG-C	68-73Phi			6'4"	243	U. of Pacific		
Norman, Dick QB	61ChiB			6'3"	210	Stanford		
Norman, Pettis TE-OE	62-70Dal 71-73SD	2		6'3"	220	Johnson C. Smith		90
Norris, Jim DT-OT	62-64OakA			6'4"	235	Houston	2	
Norris, Trusse OE	69LA-A			6'1"	190	U. C. L. A.		
Norton, Don OE	60LA-A 61-66SD-A	2		6'1"	190	Iowa		162
Norton, Jim DB	60-68HouA		4	6'3"	187	Idaho	45	
Norton, Jim DT-OT-DE	65-66SF 67-68Atl 68Phi 69Was			6'4"	254	Washington	1	
	70NYG							
Norton, Ray HB	60-61SF			6'2"	184	San Jose State		
Norton, Rick QB	66-69MiaA 70GB	1		6'1"	192	Kentucky		
Nottingham, Don FB	71-73Bal 73Mia	2		5'10"	210	Kent State		60
Novsek, Joe DE	62OakA			6'4"	237	Tulsa		
Nowak, Gary DT	71SD			6'5"	247	Michigan State		
Nowatzke, Tom FB-LB	65-69Det 70-72Bal	2		6'3"	229	Indiana	1	102
Nugent, Phil DB	61DenA			6'2"	195	Tulane	7	
Nunamaker, Julian DE-DT	69BufA 70Buf 71JJ			6'3"	251	Tennessee-Martin		
Nunley, Frank LB	67-73SF			6'2"	229	Michigan	8	
Nunnery, R. B. OT	60DalA			6'4"	275	Louisiana State		
Nutting, Ed OT	61Cle 62JJ 63Dal			6'4"	246	Georgia Tech		
Nye, Blaine OG	68-73Dal			6'4"	251	Stanford		
Nyvall, Vic HB	70NO			5'10"	185	NW State-La.		
Oakes, Don OT-DT	61-62Phi 63-68BosA			6'3"	253	Virginia Tech		
Oates, Carleton DE-DT	65-69OakA 70-72Oak 73GB			6'2"	252	Florida A&M		6
Oberg, Tom DB	68-69DenA			6'	185	Portland State	3	
O'Bradovich, Ed DE	62-71ChiB			6'3"	255	Illinois		8
O'Brien, Dave DT-OT-OG	63-64Min 65NYG 66-67StL			6'3"	244	Boston College		
O'Brien, Fran OT-OG-DE	59Cle 60-66Was 66-68Pit			6'1"	253	Michigan State		
O'Brien, Jim WR	70-72Bal 73Det	2	5	6'	195	Cincinnati		301
Odle, Phil WR	68-70Det			5'11"	191	Brigham Young		
Odom, Sammy LB	64HouA			6'2"	235	NW State-La.	2	
Odoms, Riley TE	72-73Den	2		6'4"	230	Houston		48
O'Donnell, Joe OG-OT	64-67BufA 68JJ 69BufA 70-71Buf			6'2"	253	Michigan		
Ogas, Dave LB	68OakA 69BufA			6'3"	240	San Diego State		
Ogden Ray TE-WR-OE	65-66StL 67NO 67-68Atl 69-71ChiB	2		6'5"	225	Alabama		24
Ogle, Rick LB	71StL 72Det			6'3"	230	Colorado		
Oglesby, Paul DT	60OakA			6'4"	235	U. C. L. A.		
O'Hanley, Ross DB	60-65BosA 66JJ			6'	183	Boston College	15	6
Okoniewski, Steve DT	72-73Buf			6'3"	247	Montana		
Oldham, Ray DB	73Bal			6'	200	Middle Tennessee	2	
Olds, Bill FB	73Bal	2		6'1"	224	Nebraska		12
Olerich, Dave LB-TE	67-68SF 69-70StL 71Hou 72-73SF			6'1"	221	San Fran. State		
Oliver, Bob OT	69Cle			6'3"	240	Abilene Christian		
Oliver, Chip LB	68-69OakA			6'2"	220	Southern Calif.	1	6
Oliver, Clancy DB	69-70Pit			6'1"	180	San Diego State		
Oliver, Greg HB	73Phi			6'	192	Trinity (Texas)		
Olsen, Merlin DT	62-73LA			6'5"	272	Utah State	1	6
Olsen, Phil DT	71-73LA			6'5"	265	Utah State		
Olson, Harold OT	60-62BufA 63-64DenA			6'3"	259	Clemson		
Olssen, Lance OT	68-69SF			6'5"	262	Purdue		
O'Mahoney, Jim LB	65-66NY-A			6'1"	231	Miami (Fla.)		
O'Malley, Jim LB	73Den			6'1"	230	Notre Dame		
O'Neal, Steve WR-K	69NY-A 70-72NYJ 73NO		4	6'3"	185	Texas A&M		
Onesti, Larry LB	62-65HouA			6'	200	Northwestern		6
Onkotz, Dennis LB	70NYJ			6'1"	220	Penn State		
Orduna, Joe HB-FB	72-73NYG	2		6'	195	Nebraska		18
Oriard, Mike C-OG	70-73KC			6'4"	223	Notre Dame		
Orr, Jimmy FL-OE-WR	58-60Pit 61-70Bal	2	4	5'11"	185	Georgia		396
Orvis, Herb DE-DT	72-73Det			6'5"	240	Colorado		
Osborn, Dave HB	65-73Min	2		6'	206	North Dakota		186
Osborne, Clancy LB	59-60SF 61-62Min 63-64OakA			6'3"	218	Arizona State	6	
Osborne, Jim DT	72-73ChiB			6'3"	250	Southern U.		
Osborne, Tom OE	60-61Was	2		6'3"	190	Hastings		12
Otis, Jim FB	70NO 71-72KC 73StL	2		6'	220	Ohio State		18
Otto, Gus LB	65-69OakA 70-73Oak			6'2"	220	Missouri	6	12
Otto, Jim C	60-69OakA 70-73Oak			6'2"	244	Miami (Fla.)		
Outlaw, John DB	68JJ 69BosA 70Bos 71-72NE 73Phi			5'10"	179	Jackson State	5	12
Overmeyer, Bill LB	72Phi			6'3"	220	Ashland		
Overton, Jerry DB	63Dal			6'2"	190	Utah		
injured in accident before 1964 season								
Owens, Brig DB	66-73Was			5'11"	190	Cincinnati	31	32
Owens, Burgess DB	73NYJ			6'2"	200	Miami (Fla.)	1	6
Owens, Don DT-OT	57Was 58-60Phi 60-63StL			6'5"	255	Southern Miss.		6
Owens, Joe DE	70SD 71-73NO			6'2"	240	Alcorn A&M	1	4
Owens, Luke DE-DT-OT	57Bal 58-59ChiC 60-65StL			6'2"	254	Kent State		2
Owens, Marv WR	73StL			5'11"	205	San Diego State		
Owens, R. C. (Alley Oop) OE-FL	57-61SF 62-63Bal 64NYG	2		6'3"	197	Coll. of Idaho		138
Owens, Steve FB	70-73Det	2		6'2"	218	Oklahoma		114
Owens, Terry OT	66-69SD-A 70-73SD			6'6"	263	Jacksonville St.		
Page, Alan DT	67-73Min			6'5"	251	Notre Dame	1	16
Pagliei, Joe FB	59Phi 60NY-A		4	6'	220	Clemson		6
Palewicz, Al LB	73KC			6'1"	215	Miami (Fla.)		
Palmer, Dick LB	70Mia 71JJ 72Buf 72-73NO			6'2"	228	Kentucky		
Palmer, Scott DT	71NYJ 72StL			6'3"	245	Texas		
Paluck, John DE-DT	56Was 57-58MS 59-65Was			6'2"	241	Pittsburgh	2	8
Papac, Nick QB	61OakA	1		5'11"	190	Fresno State		6
Pardee, Jack LB	57-64LA 65VR 66-70LA 71-72Was			6'2"	224	Texas A&M	22	38
Paremore, Bob HB	63-64StL	2		5'11"	190	Florida A&M		12
Parilli, Babe QB	52-53GB 54-55MS 56Cle 57-58GB 59CFL	12		6'1"	190	Kentucky		146
	60OakA 61-67BosA 68-69NY-A							
Parish, Don LB	70-71StL 71LA 72Den			6'1"	220	Stanford	1	6
Park, Ernie OT-OG	63-65SD-A 66MiaA 67DenA 69CinA			6'3"	247	McMurry		
Parker, Charlie OG	65DenA			6'1"	245	Southern Miss.		
Parker, Don OG	67SF 68KJ			6'3"	235	Virginia		
Parker, Frank DT	62-64Cle 65IL 66-67Cle 68Pit 69NYG			6'5"	263	Oklahoma State		
Parker, Jim OT-OG	57-67Bal			6'3"	273	Ohio State		

Use Name (Nicknames) – Positions	Team by Year	See Section	Hgt	Wgt	College	Int	Pts
Parker, Kenny DB	70NYG		6'1"	190	Fordham		
Parker, Willie DT	66-69HouA 70Hou		6'2"	266	Ark.-Pine Bluff		
Parker, Willie C-OG	73Buf		6'3"	240	North Texas State		
Parks, Billy WR	71SD 72Dal 73Hou	2	6'1"	185	Long Beach State		36
Parks, Dave OE-TE-WR	64-67SF 68-72NO 73Hou	2	6'2"	202	Texas Tech		264
Parris, Gary TE	73SD		6'2"	226	Florida State		
Parrish, Bernie DB	59-66Cle 66HouA		5'11"	194	Florida	31	24
Parrish, Lemar DB	70-73Cin	3	5'11"	185	Lincoln (Mo.)	19	54
Parson, Ray OT	71Det		6'4"	250	Minnesota		
Parsons, Bob TE	72-73ChiB		6'4"	234	Penn State		12
Partee, Dennis K	68-69SD-A 70-73SD	45	6'2"	219	S. M. U.		349
Pashe, Bill DB	64NY-A		5'11"	185	George Washington		
Pastorini, Dan (Dante) QB	71-73Hou	12 4	6'3"	217	Santa Clara		30
Pastrana, Al QB	69DenA 70Den	1	6'1"	190	Maryland		6
Pate, Lloyd HB	70Buf	2	6'1"	205	Cincinnati		6
Patera, Dennis K	68SF	5	6'	225	Brigham Young		16
Patera, Herb LB	63BufA		6'1"	222	Michigan State		
Patrick, Frank QB	70-72GB		6'7"	225	Nebraska		
Patrick, Wayne FB	68-69BufA 70-72Buf 73JJ	2	6'2"	241	Louisville		36
Patton, Jerry DT	71Min 72-73Buf		6'3"	258	Nebraska		
Patton, Jimmy DB	55-66NYG	3	6'	183	Mississippi	52	24
Patulski, Walt DE	72-73Buf		6'6"	256	Notre Dame		
Paulson, Dainard DB	61-66NY-A		5'11"	190	Oregon State	29	6
Peacock, Johnny DB	69HouA 70Hou		6'2"	203	Houston	5	12
Peaks, Clarence FB	57-63Phi 64-65Pit	23	6'1"	218	Michigan State		144
Pearson, Barry WR	72-73Pit	2	5'11"	185	Northwestern		18
Pearson, Drew WR	73Dal	2	6'	175	Tulsa		12
Pearson, Preston HB-DB	70-73Pit	23	6'1"	194	Illinois		78
Pearson, Willie DB	69MiaA		6'	190	N. Carolina A & T		
Peay, Francis OT	66-67NYG 68-72GB 73KC		6'5"	250	Missouri		
Pellegrini, Bob LB-OG	56,58-61Phi 62-65Was		6'2"	233	Maryland	13	6
Pena, Bubba OG	72Cle 73KJ		6'2"	250	Massachusetts		
Penchion, Bobby OG-C	72-73Buf		6'5"	260	Alcorn A & M		
Pennington, Tom K	62DalA	5	6'2"	210	Georgia		19
Pentecost, John OG	67Min		6'2"	250	U. C. L. A.		
Peoples, Woody OG	68-73SF		6'2"	249	Grambling		
Percival, Mac K	67-73ChiB	5	6'4"	219	Texas Tech		456
Pergine, John LB	69-72LA 73Was		6'1"	225	Notre Dame		
Perkins, Art FB	62-63LA	2	6'	223	North Texas State		36
Perkins, Bill HB	63NY-A		6'2"	225	Iowa		
Perkins, Don FB-HB	61-68Dal	2	5'10"	200	New Mexico		270
Perkins, Jim OT	62-64DenA		6'5"	250	Colorado		
Perkins, Ray WR-OE	67-71Bal	2	6'	183	Alabama		66
Perkins, Willis OG-DE	61HouA 61BosA 63HouA		6'	250	Texas Southern		
Perlo, Phil LB	60HouA		6'	220	Maryland		
Perreault, Pete OG-OT	63-67NY-A 68CinA 69NY-A 70NYJ 71Min		6'3"	246	Boston U.		
Person, Ara TE	72StL		6'2"	220	Morgan State		
Pesonen, Dick DB	60GB 61Min 62-64NYG		6'	190	Minnesota-Duluth	4	
Peters, Anton DT	63DenA		6'3"	250	Florida		
Peters, Floyd DT	59-62Cle 63Det 64-69Phi 70Was		6'4"	254	San Fran. State	3	
Peters, Frank OT	69CinA		6'4"	250	Ohio U.		
Petersen, Ken OG	61Min		6'2"	235	Utah		
Peterson, Bill	HC72-73Hou				Ohio Northern		
Peterson, Bill LB-TE	68-69CinA 70-72Cin		6'3"	229	San Jose State	5	
Petitbon, Richie DB	59-68ChiB 69-70LA 71-73Was		6'3"	206	Tulane	48	18
Petrella, Bob DB	66-69MiaA 70-71Mia		6'	186	Tennessee	5	
Petrich, Bob DE	63-66SD-A 67BufA		6'4"	253	West Texas State	1	
Petties, Neal OE-FL	64-66Bal		6'2"	198	San Diego State		6
Pettigrew, Gary DT-DE	66-73Phi		6'4"	251	Stanford		
Pharr, Tommy DB	70Buf		5'10"	187	Mississippi State		
Philbin, Gerry DE	64-69NY-A 70-72NYJ 73Phi		6'2"	245	Buffalo	1	
Phillips, Jess HB-FB-DB	68-69CinA 70-72Cin 73NO	2	6'1"	208	Michigan State	3	60
Phillips, Jim (Red) OE-FL	58-64LA 65-67Min	2	6'1"	197	Auburn		204
Phillips, Loyd DE	67-69ChiB		6'3"	237	Arkansas	2	
Phillips, Mel DB	66-73SF		6'	192	N. Carolina A & T	6	6
Philpott, Ed LB	67-69BosA 70Bos 71NE		6'3"	240	Miami-Ohio	9	6
Phipps, Mike QB	70-73Cle	12	6'2"	207	Purdue		60
Picard, Bob WR	73Phi		6'1"	195	Eastern Wash. St.		
Piccolo, Brian HB-FB	66-69ChiB	2	6'	205	Wake Forest		30
died June 16, 1970 - cancer							
Pickens, Bob OT	67-69ChiB		6'4"	258	Nebraska		
Pierce, Danny HB-FB	70Was		6'3"	216	Memphis State		
Pietrosante, Nick FB	59-65Det 66-67Cle	2	6'2"	225	Notre Dame		180
Pifferini, Bob LB	72-73ChiB		6'2"	226	U. C. L. A.		
Pillath, Roger OT	65LA 66Pit		6'4"	249	Wisconsin		
Pinder, Cyril HB-FB	68-70Phi 71-72ChiB 73Dal	2	6'2"	218	Illinois		42
Pine, Ed LB	62-64SF 65Pit		6'4"	233	Utah	3	
Pittman, Charlie HB	70StL 71Bal		6'1"	200	Penn State		
Pitts, Elijah HB	61-69GB 70LA 70NO 71GB	23	6'1"	204	Philander Smith		210
Pitts, Frank WR-OE-FL	65-69KC-A 70KC 71-73Cle	2	6'2"	198	Southern U.		174
Pitts, John DB	67-69BufA 70-72Buf 73Den		6'4"	218	Arizona State	8	
Pivec, Dave TE-LB	66-68LA 69DenA	2	6'3"	240	Notre Dame		8
Plum, Milt QB	57-61Cle 62-67Det 68LA 69NYG	12 5	6'1"	205	Penn State		112
Plummer, Tony DB	70StL 71-73Atl		5'11"	189	U. of Pacific	1	6
Plump, Dave DB	66SD-A		6'1"	195	Fresno State		
Plunkett, Jim QB	71-73NE	12	6'3"	220	Stanford		36
Plunkett, Sherman (Tank) OT	58-60Bal 61-62SD-A 63-67NY-A		6'4"	290	Md. Eastern Shore		
Ply, Bobby DB	62DalA 63-67KC-A 67BufA 67DenA		6'1"	190	Baylor	9	
Poage, Ray TE-OE-FL	63Min 64-65Phi 66JJ 67-70NO 71Atl	2	6'4"	208	Texas		78
Podolak, Ed HB	69KC-A 70-73KC	23	6'1"	204	Iowa		132
Poimbeouf, Lance OG	63Dal		6'3"	225	Southwestern La.		
Pollard, Bob DT	71-73NO		6'3"	245	Weber State		
Poole, Bob TE-OE	64-65SF 66-67HouA	2	6'4"	216	Clemson		
Pope, Bucky OE-WR	64LA 65JJ 66-67LA 68GB	2	6'5"	199	Catawba		78
Porter, Jack C	71SD		6'4"	255	Oklahoma		
Porter, Lewis WR	70KC		5'11"	178	Southern U.		
Porter, Ron LB	67-69Bal 69-72Phi 73Min		6'3"	232	Idaho	3	
Porter, Willie DB	68BosA	3	5'11"	195	Texas Southern		
Porterfield, Garry DE	65Dal		6'3"	223	Tulsa		

Use Name (Nicknames) – Positions	Team by Year	See Section	Hgt	Wgt	College	Int	Pts
Post, Bobby DB	67NYG		6'1"	195	Kings Point		
Post, Dickie HB	67-69SD-A 70SD 71Den 71Hou	23	5'9"	190	Houston		114
Pottios, Myron LB	61Pit 62JJ 63-65Pit 66-70LA 71-73Was		6'2"	236	Notre Dame	12	
Potts, Charlie DB	72Det		6'3"	210	Purdue		
Powell, Art OE-DB-WR	59Phi 60-62NY-A 63-66OakA 67BufA 68Min	2	6'3"	211	San Jose State	3	492
Powell, Jessee LB	69MiaA 70-73Mia		6'1"	214	West Texas State		
Powell, Preston FB	61Cle		6'2"	225	Grambling		
Powell, Tim DE	65LA 66Pit		6'4"	248	Northwestern		
Powers, John OE-TE-LB	62-65Pit 66Min		6'2"	211	Notre Dame		
Powers, Warren DB	63-68OakA		6'	188	Nebraska	22	12
Preas, George OT-OG-LB	55-65Bal		6'2"	244	Virginia Tech		
Prebola, Gene OE	60OakA 61-63DenA	2	6'3"	220	Boston U.		42
Preece, Steve DB	69NO 70-72Phi 72Den 73LA		6'1"	195	Oregon State	6	18
Prestel, Jim DT	60Cle 61-65Min 66NYG 67Was		6'5"	264	Idaho	1	8
Price, Elex DT	73NO		6'3"	260	Alcorn A & M		
Price, Ernie DT	73Det		6'4"	255	Texas A & I		
Price, Jim LB	63NY-A 64DenA		6'2"	228	Auburn	1	
Price, Sam HB-FB	66-68MiaA	2	5'11"	215	Illinois		12
Pride, Dan LB	68-69ChiB		6'3"	225	Jackson State	1	
Print, Bob LB	67-68SD-A		6'	220	Dayton		
Prisby, Errol DB	67DenA		5'10"	184	Cincinnati		
Pritchard, Ron LB	69HouA 70-72Hou 72-73Cin		6'1"	232	Arizona State	2	2
Profit, Joe HB	71-73Atl 73NO	2	6'	210	Northeast La.		18
Promuto, Vince OG	60-70Was		6'1"	244	Holy Cross		
Prothro, Tommy	HC71-72LA				Duke		
Protz, Jack LB	70SD		6'1"	218	Syracuse		
Provost, Ted DB	70Min 71StL		6'2"	195	Ohio State		
Prudhomme, Remi C-OG-DE-DT	66-67BufA 68-69KC-A 70JJ 71-72NO 72Buf		6'4"	251	Louisiana State		
Pruett, Perry DB	71NE		6'1"	190	North Texas State		
Pruitt, Greg HB	73Cle	2	5'10"	186	Oklahoma		30
Pryor, Barry HB	69MiaA 70Mia		6'	215	Boston U.		
Puetz, Garry OG-OT	73NYJ		6'3"	255	Valparaiso		
Pugh, Jethro DT-DE	65-73Dal		6'6"	258	Elizabeth City St.	1	4
Pureifory, Dave DE	72-73GB		6'1"	260	Eastern Michigan		
Purnell, Jim LB	64-68ChiB 69-72LA		6'2"	229	Wisconsin	3	
Purvis, Vic DB	66-67BosA		5'11"	200	Southern Miss.		
Pyburn, Jack OT	67-68MiaA		6'6"	245	Texas A & M		
Pyeatt, John DB	60-61DenA		6'3"	204	none	4	6
Pyle, Mike C	61-69ChiB		6'3"	247	Yale		
Pyle, Palmer OG	60-63Bal 64Min 65JJ 66OakA		6'2"	248	Michigan State		
Pyne, George DT	65BosA		6'4"	285	Olivet		
Quayle, Frank HB	69DenA	2	5'10"	195	Virginia		
Queen, Jeff FB-TE	69SD-A 70-71SD 72-73Oak	2	6'1"	222	Morgan State		54
Quinlan, Bill DE	57-58Cle 59-62GB 63Phi 64Det 65Was		6'3"	248	Michigan	3	
Quinn, Steve C	68HouA		6'1"	225	Notre Dame		
Rabb, Warren QB	60Det 61-62BufA	12	6'1"	202	Louisiana State		22
Rabold, Mike OG	59Det 60StL 61-62Min 64-67ChiB		6'2"	239	Indiana		
Rademacher, Bill WR-DB-OE	64-68NY-A 69BosA 70Bos	2	6'1"	190	Northern Michigan	1	18
Raimey, Dave DB	64Cle		5'10"	195	Michigan		
Rakestraw, Larry QB	64,66-68ChiB	1	6'2"	195	Georgia		12
Ralston, John	HC72Den				California		
Ramsey, Nate DB	63-72Phi 73NO		6'1"	200	Indiana	21	6
Ramsey, Steve QB	70NO 71-73Den	1	6'2"	210	North Texas State		12
Randall, Dennis DE-DT	67NY-A 68CinA		6'6"	243	Oklahoma State		
Randle, Sonny OE-WR	59ChiC 60-66StL 67-68SF 68Dal	2	6'2"	189	Virginia		390
Randolph, Al DB	66-70SF 71GB 72Det 73Min		6'2"	198	Iowa	11	8
Rashad, Ahmad WR 72 played as Bobby Moore	72-73StL	2	6'2"	210	Oregon		36
Rasley, Rocky OG	69-70,72-73Det		6'3"	250	Oregon State		
Rasmussen, Randy OG	67-69NY-A 70-73NYJ		6'2"	255	Kearney State		6
Rasmussen, Wayne DB	64-72Det 73JJ		6'2"	179	S. Dakota State	16	12
Rassas, Nick DB	66-68Atl		6'	190	Notre Dame	1	
Rather, Bo WR	73Mia		6'1"	182	Michigan		
Ratkowski, Ray HB	61BosA		6'	195	Notre Dame		
Ray, David WR	69-73LA	5	6'	195	Alabama		445
Ray, Eddie FB-TE	70Bos 71SD 72-73Atl	2	6'1"	235	Louisiana State		66
Raye, Jimmy DB	69Phi		6'	185	Michigan State		
Reardon, Kerry DB	71-73KC		5'11"	180	Iowa	2	
Reaves, John QB	72-73Phi	1	6'3"	210	Florida		
Reaves, Ken DB	66-73Atl		6'3"	205	Norfolk State	29	6
Recher, Dave C	65-68Phi		6'1"	244	Iowa		
Rector, Ron HB	66Was 66-67Atl	2	6'	200	Northwestern		
Redman, Rick LB	65-69SD-A 70-73SD	4	5'11"	225	Washington	9	6
Redmond, Rudy DB	69-71Atl 72Det 73JJ		6'	190	U. of Pacific	8	6
Redmond, Tom DE-OG-DT	60-65StL		6'5"	243	Vanderbilt		
Reeberg, Lucian OT	63Det		6'4"	308	Hampton Institute		
died Jan. 31, 1964 - uremia							
Reed, Alvin TE	67-69HouA 70-72Hou 73Was	2	6'5"	231	Prairie View		66
Reed, Bob HB	62-63Min	23	5'11"	187	U. of Pacific		6
Reed, Henry DE-LB	71-73NYG		6'3"	230	Weber State	2	
Reed, Joe QB	72-73SF	1	6'1"	194	Mississippi State		
Reed, Leo OG-OT	61HouA 61DenA		6'4"	240	Colorado State		
Reed, Oscar HB-FB	68-73Min	2	5'11"	222	Colorado State		60
Reed, Robert OG	65Was		6'1"	250	Tennessee State		
Reed, Smith HB	65-66NYG 67-68MS		6'	215	Alcorn A & M		
Reed, Taft DB	67Phi		6'2"	200	Jackson State		
Reese, Guy DT	62-63Dal 64-65Bal 66Atl		6'5"	255	S. M. U.		
Reeves, Dan HB-FB	65-72Dal	12	6'1"	201	South Carolina		253
Reeves, Roy WR	69BufA		5'11"	182	South Carolina		
Reger, John LB-OG	55-63Pit 64-66Was		6'	225	Pittsburgh	15	18
Regner, Tom OG	67-69HouA 70-72Hou		6'1"	255	Notre Dame		
Reichow, Jerry OE-QB	56-57Det 58KJ 59Det 60Phi 61-64Min	12	6'2"	217	Iowa		144
Reid, Mike DT	70-73Cin		6'3"	255	Penn State		
Reifsnyder, Bob DE	60-61NY-A		6'2"	255	Navy		
Reilly, Jim OG	70-71Buf 72IL		6'2"	260	Notre Dame		
Reilly, Kevin LB	73Phi		6'2"	220	Villanova		
Reilly, Mike LB	64-68ChiB 69Min		6'2"	230	Iowa		6
Remmert, Dennis LB	60BufA		6'3"	215	Iowa State		
Renfro, Mel DB-HB	64-73Dal	3	6'	191	Oregon	42	36
Rengel, Mike DT	69NO 70JJ		6'5"	260	Hawaii		

Use Name (Nicknames) – Positions	Team by Year	See Section	Hgt	Wgt	College	Int	Pts
Renn, Bob HB	61NY-A	2	6'	180	Florida State		6
Rentz, Larry DB	69SD-A		6'1"	170	Florida		
Rentzel, Lance WR-FL-OE-HB	65-66Min 67-70Dal 71-72LA 73SL	23	6'2"	204	Oklahoma		246
Reppond, Mike WR	73ChiB		6'	180	Arkansas		
Ressler, Glenn OG-C-OT-DT	65-73Bal		6'3"	247	Penn State		
Retzlaff, Pete OE-TE-FL	56-66Phi	2	6'1"	211	S. Dakota State		282
Reynolds, Al OG	60-62DalA 63-67KC-A		6'3"	238	Tarkio		
Reynolds, Bob OT	63-71StL 72-73NE 73StL		6'6"	264	Bowling Green		
Reynolds, Chuck C-OG	69-70Cle		6'2"	240	Tulsa		2
Reynolds, Jack LB	70-73LA		6'1"	232	Tennessee	2	
Reynolds, M.C. (Chief) QB	58-59ChiC 60Was 61BufA 62OakA	12	6'	193	Louisiana State		24
Reynolds, Tom WR	72NE 73ChiB	2	6'3"	200	San Diego State		12
Rhome, Jerry QB	65-67Dal 69Cle 70Hou 71LA	12	6'	186	Tulsa		6
Rice, Andy DT	66-67KC-A 67HouA 68-69CinA 70-71SD 72-73ChiB		6'3"	268	Texas Southern		
Rice, Floyd LB-TE	71-73Hou 73SD		6'3"	223	Alcorn A & M	1	6
Rice, George DT-OG	66-69HouA		6'3"	262	Louisiana State		
Rice, Harold DE	71Oak		6'2"	230	Tennessee State		
Rice, Ken OG-OT	61BufA 62JJ 63BufA 64-65OakA 66-67MiaA		6'2"	243	Auburn		
Richards, Bobby DE	62-65Phi 66-67Atl		6'2"	241	Louisiana State		
Richards, Golden WR	73Dal		6'	172	Hawaii		6
Richards, Jim DB	68-69NY-A 70-71MS		6'1"	180	Virginia Tech	3	
Richards, Perry OE	57Pit 58Det 59ChiC 60StL 61BufA 62NY-A	2	6'2"	205	Detroit		24
Richardson, Al DE	60BosA		6'3"	250	Grambling		
Richardson, Bob (Red) DB	66DenA		6'1"	180	U. C. L. A.		
Richardson, Gloster WR-FL	67-69KC-A 70KC 71Dal 72-73Cle	2	6'	200	Jackson State		96
Richardson, Jeff OT-C-OG	67-68NY-A 69MiaA		6'3"	253	Michigan State		
Richardson, Jerry (The Razor) FL-OE-HB	59-60Bal	2	6'3"	185	Wofford		24
Richardson, Jerry DB	64-65LA 66-67Atl		6'3"	190	West Texas State	11	
Richardson, John DT	67-69MiaA 70-71Mia 72-73StL		6'2"	254	U. C. L. A.		
Richardson, Mike HB	69HouA 70-71Hou	2	5'11"	193	S. M. U.		20
Richardson, Pete DB	69BufA 70-71Buf		6'1"	197	Dayton	8	
Richardson, Tom WR	69BosA 70Bos		6'2"	195	Jackson State		
Richardson, Willie FL-WR	63-69Bal 70Mia 71Bal	2	6'2"	198	Jackson State		150
Richey, Mike OT	69BufA 70NO		6'5"	257	North Carolina		
Richter, Frank LB	67-69DenA		6'3"	230	Georgia	2	
Richter, Pat OE-TE	63-70Was	2 4	6'5"	230	Wisconsin		84
Ridge, Houston DE-DT	66-69SD-A 70JJ		6'4"	239	San Diego State		
Ridgway, Colin K	65Dal		6'5"	211	Lamar Tech		
Ridlehuber, Preston HB	66Atl 68OakA 69BufA		6'2"	215	Georgia		18
Ridlon, Jimmy DB	57-62SF 63-64Dal		6'1"	181	Syracuse	9	12
Rieves, Charley LB	62-63OakA 64-65HouA		5'11"	217	Houston	1	
Riggins, John FB	71-73NYJ	2	6'2"	233	Kansas State		90
Riggle, Bob DB	66-67Atl 68JJ		6'1"	200	Penn State	3	6
Righetti, Joe DT	69-70Cle		6'3"	253	Waynesburg		
Riley, Butch LB	69Bal		6'2"	220	Texas A & I		
Riley, Jim DE	67-69MiaA 70-71Mia 72KJ		6'4"	252	Oklahoma		
Riley, Ken DB	69CinA 70-73Cin		6'	182	Florida A & M	18	
Riley, Preston WR	70-72SF 73NO	2	6'	180	Memphis State		6
Ringo, Jim C	53-63GB 64-67Phi		6'1"	232	Syracuse		
Rissmiller, Ray OT	66Phi 67NO 68BufA		6'4"	250	Georgia		
Rivera, Henry DB	62OakA 63BufA		5'11"	180	Oregon State		
Rivers, Jamie LB	68-73StL		6'2"	235	Bowling Green	3	
Rives, Don LB	73ChiB		6'2"	215	Texas Tech		
Rizzo, Jack HB	73NYG		5'10"	195	Lehigh		
Roach, Johnny QB-DB	56ChiC 57-58MS 59ChiC 60StL 61-63GB 64Dal	12	6'4"	197	S. M. U.		12
Robb, Joe DE-LB	59-60Phi 61-67StL 68-71Det		6'3"	238	Texas Christian	1	
Roberson, Bo FL-HB	61SD-A 62-65OakA 65BufA 66MiaA	23	6'1"	192	Cornell		116
Roberts, Archie QB	67MiaA		6'	193	Columbia		
Roberts, Cliff OT	61OakA		6'3"	260	Illinois		
Roberts, C. R. FB	59-62SF	2	6'3"	202	Southern Calif.		24
Roberts, Gary OG	70Atl		6'2"	242	Purdue		
Roberts, Guy LB	72-73Hou		6'1"	215	Maryland	4	
Roberts, J. D.	HC70-72NO				Oklahoma		
Roberts, Walter (The Flea) FL-WR-OE	64-66Cle 67NO 69-70Was	23	5'10"	167	San Jose State		66
Roberts, Willie DB	73ChiB		6'1"	190	Houston		
Robertson, Bob OT	68HouA		6'4"	246	Illinois		
Robertson, Isiah LB	71-73LA		6'3"	225	Southern U.	7	6
Robinson, Craig OT	72-73NO		6'4"	250	Houston		
Robinson, Dave LB	63-72GB 73Was		6'3"	243	Penn State	25	6
Robinson, Jerry OE	62-64SD-A 65NY-A	23	5'11"	195	Grambling		30
Robinson, Johnnie DB-FL	66Det 67JJ		6'3"	205	Tennessee State		6
Robinson, Johnny DB-HB	60-62DalA 63-69KC-A 70-71KC	2	6'	200	Louisiana State	57	108
Robinson, Larry HB-FB	73Dal		6'4"	210	Tennessee		
Robinson, Paul HB	68-69CinA 70-72Cin 72-73Hou	23	6'	199	Arizona		156
Robinson, Virgil HB	71-72NO	2	5'11"	195	Grambling		12
Robotti, Frank LB	61BosA		6'	220	Boston College	2	
Roche, Alden DE	70Den 71-73GB		6'4"	255	Southern U.		
Rochester, Paul DT	60-62DalA 63KC-A 63-69NY-A		6'2"	254	Michigan State		
Rock, Walt OT-DT	63-67SF 68-73Was		6'5"	252	Maryland		
Roder, Mirro K	73ChiB	5	6'1"	218	none		35
Roderick, John FL-WR	66-67MiaA 68OakA	2	6'1"	180	S. M. U.		6
Rodgers, Willie HB	72Hou 73JJ	2	6'	210	Kentucky		12
Roedel, Herb OG	61OakA		6'3"	230	Marquette		
Roehnelt, Bill LB	58-59ChiB 60Was 61-62DenA		6'1"	227	Bradley		
Rogers, Don C-OG	60LA-A 61-64SD-A		6'2"	245	South Carolina		
Rogers, Mel LB	71SD 72JJ 73SD		6'2"	230	Florida A & M	1	
Rohde, Len OT-DE	60-73SF		6'4"	246	Utah State		
Roland, Johnny HB-FB	66-72StL 73NYG	23	6'2"	213	Missouri		216
Rolle, Dave FB	60DenA	2	6'	215	Oklahoma		18
Roller, Dave DT	71NYG		6'2"	240	Kentucky		
Roman, Nick DE	70-71Cin 72-73Cle		6'3"	235	Ohio State	1	6
Romaniszyn, Jim LB	73Cle		6'2"	214	Edinboro State		
Romeo, Tony OE-TE	61DalA 62-67BosA	2	6'2"	225	Florida State		62
Rosdahl, Hatch DT-OG-DE	64BufA 64-66KC-A		6'5"	250	Penn State		
Rose, George DB	64-66Min 67NO 68JJ		5'11"	190	Auburn	9	6
Rosema, Rocky LB	68-71StL		6'2"	228	Michigan	1	
Ross, Dave OE	60NY-A	2	6'3"	210	Los Angeles State		6

Use Name (Nicknames) – Positions	Team by Year	See Section	Hgt	Wgt	College	Int	Pts
Ross, Louis DE	71-72Buf		6'6"	240	S. Carolina State		
Ross, Oliver HB-FB	73Den		6'	210	Alcorn A & M		
Ross, Willie FB	64BufA		5'10"	200	Nebraska		6
Rossovich, Tim LB-DE	68-71Phi 72-73SD		6'4"	246	Southern Calif.	3	
Roussel, Tom LB	68-70Was 71-72NO 73Phi		6'3"	235	Southern Miss.	2	
Rowden, Larry LB	71-72ChiB		6'2"	220	Houston		
Rowe, Bob DT-DE	67-73StL		6'4"	258	Western Michigan	2	6
Rowe, Dave DT	67-70NO 71-73NE		6'6"	276	Penn State		
Rowland, Justin DB	60ChiB 61Min 62DenA		6'2"	189	Texas Christian	1	
Rowley, Bob LB	63Pit 64NY-A		6'2"	225	Virginia		
Rowser, John DB	67-69GB 70-73Pit		6'1"	182	Michigan	17	12
Roy, Frank OG	66StL		6'2"	230	Utah		
Rubke, Karl LB-DE-C-DT	57-60SF 61Min 62-65SF 66-67Atl 68OakA		6'4"	240	Southern Calif.	2	
Rucker, Reggie WR	70-71Dal 71NYG 71-73NE	2	6'2"	190	Boston U.		48
Rudnay, Jack C	70-73KC		6'3"	240	Northwestern		
Rudolph, Council DE	72Hou 73StL		6'3"	260	Kentucky State		
Rudolph, Jack LB	60,62-65BosA 66MiaA		6'3"	228	Georgia Tech	3	
Rule, Gordon DB	68-69GB		6'2"	180	Dartmouth		
Ruple, Ernie OT	68Pit		6'4"	256	Arkansas		
Rush, Jerry DT	65-71Det		6'4"	264	Michigan State		
Rushing, Marion LB	59ChiC 62-65StL 66-68Atl 68HouA		6'2"	223	Southern Illinois	4	2
Russ, Pat DT	63Min		6'4"	255	Purdue		
Russell, Andy LB	63Pit 64-65MS 66-73Pit		6'3"	220	Missouri	16	13
Russell, Benny QB	68BufA		6'1"	190	Louisville		
Rutgens, Joe DT	61-69Was		6'2"	258	Illinois		
Rutkowski, Charlie DE	60BufA		6'3"	248	Ripon		
Rutkowski, Ed FL-HB-OE-QB-WR	63-68BufA	123	6'1"	204	Notre Dame		36
Ryan, Frank QB	58-61LA 62-68Cle 69-70Was	12	6'3"	199	Rice		42
Ryan, Joe DE	60NY-A		6'2"	235	Villanova		
Rychlec, Tom OE	58Det 60-62BufA 63DenA	2	6'3"	220	American Inter.		18
Ryczek, Dan C	73Was		6'3"	250	Virginia		
Ryder, Nick FB	63-64Det		6'	208	Miami (Fla.)		12
Rzempolich, Ted DB	63Was		6'1"	195	Virginia		
Sabal, Ron OT-OG	60-61OakA		6'2"	238	Purdue		
Sabatino, Bill DT	68Cle 69Atl		6'3"	245	Colorado		
Saffold, Saint WR	68CinA	2	6'4"	202	San Jose State		
Saidock, Tom DT	57Phi 58JJ 60-61NY-A 62BufA		6'5"	261	Michigan State		
Saimes, George DB-HB	63-69BufA 70-72Den		5'10"	188	Michigan State	22	6
St. Jean, Len OG-DE	64-69BosA 70Bos 71-73NE		6'1"	244	Northern Michigan		
Salter, Bryant DB	71-73SD		6'4"	197	Pittsburgh	14	
Sample, Johnny DB-HB	58-60Bal 61-62Pit 63-65Was 66-68NY-A	3	6'1"	203	Md. Eastern Shore	41	36
Sampson, Greg DT-DE	72-73Hou		6'6"	260	Stanford		
Sandeman, Bill OT-DT	65KJ 66Dal 67NO 67-73Atl		6'6"	254	U. of Pacific		
Sanders, Bob LB	67Atl 68JJ		6'3"	235	North Texas State		
Sanders, Charlie TE	68-73Det	2	6'4"	225	Minnesota		114
Sanders, Daryl OT	63-66Det		6'5"	248	Ohio State		
Sanders, Ken DE	72-73Det		6'5"	233	Howard Payne		
Sanders, Lonnie DB	63-67Was 68-69StL		6'3"	206	Michigan State	12	
Sanderson, Reggie HB	73ChiB		5'10"	206	Stanford		
Sandusky, Alex OG	54-66Bal		6'1"	235	Clarion St. (Pa.)		
Sandusky, Mike OG	57-65Pit		6'	231	Maryland		
Sapienza, Rick DB-HB	60NY-A		5'11"	185	Villanova		
Sapp, Theron HB-FB	59-63Phi 63-65Pit 66JJ	2	6'1"	203	Georgia		30
Sardisco, Tony OG-LB	56Was 56SF 60-62BosA		6'2"	226	Tulane		
Sartin, Dan DT	69SD-A		6'1"	245	Mississippi		
Satcher, Doug LB	66-68BosA		6'	221	Southern Miss.	1	2
Sauer, George WR-OE	65-69NY-A 70NYJ	2	6'1"	199	Texas		172
Saul, Bill LB	62-63Bal 64,66-68Pit 69NO 70Det		6'4"	225	Penn State	4	2
Saul, Rich OG-C-LB-OT	70-73LA		6'3"	235	Michigan State		
Saul, Ron OG	70-73Hou		6'2"	255	Michigan State		
Sauls, Mac DB	68-69StL		6'	185	SW Texas State		
Saunders, John DB	72Buf		6'3"	202	Toledo		
Saxton, Jimmy HB	62DalA		5'11"	173	Texas		
Sayers, Gale HB	65-71ChiB	23	6'	199	Kansas		336
Sayers, Ron HB	69SD-A		6'1"	202	Nebraska-Omaha		
Sbranti, Ron LB	66DenA		6'2"	230	Utah State		
Scales, Charlie FB-HB	60-61Pit 62-65Cle 66Atl	23	5'11"	214	Indiana		30
Scarpati, Joe DB-HB	64-69Phi 70NO 71JJ		5'10"	185	N. Carolina State	25	18
Scarpitto, Bob FL-WR	61SD-A 62-67DenA 68BosA	2 4	5'11"	194	Notre Dame		170
Schaffer, Joe LB	60BufA		6'	210	Tennessee	1	
Schafrath, Dick OT-OG-DE	59-71Cle		6'3"	253	Ohio State		
Schick, Doyle LB	61Was		6'1"	210	Kansas		
Schleicher, Maury LB-DE	59ChiC 60LA-A 61-62SD-A		6'3"	238	Penn State	1	
Schmautz, Ray LB	66OakA		6'1"	225	San Diego State		
Schmedding, Jim OG	68-69SD-A 70SD		6'2"	250	Weber State		
Schmidt, Bob C-OT-OG	59-60NYG 61-63HouA 64-65BosA 66-67BufA		6'4"	248	Minnesota		
Schmidt, Henry DT-DE	59-60SF 61-64SD-A 65BufA 66NY-A		6'4"	258	Southern Calif., Trinity (Texas)	1	6
Schmidt, Roy OG-OT	67-68NO 69Atl 70Was 71Min		6'3"	250	Long Beach State		
Schmiesing, Joe DT-DE	68-71StL 72Det 73Bal		6'4"	253	New Mexico State		
Schmitt, John C	64-69NY-A 70-73NYJ		6'4"	253	Hofstra		
Schmitz, Bob LB	61-66Pit 66Min		6'1"	235	Montana State	3	8
Schnellenberger, Howard	HC73Bal				Kentucky		
Schnitker, Mike OG	69DenA 70-73Den		6'3"	243	Colorado		
Schoen, Tom DB	70Cle		5'11"	185	Notre Dame		
Schoenke, Ray OG-OT-C	63-64Dal 66-73Was		6'3"	245	S. M. U.		
Scholtz, Bob C-OT	60-64Det 65-66NYG		6'4"	250	Notre Dame		
Schottenheimer, Marty LB	65-68BufA 69BosA 70Bos		6'3"	225	Pittsburgh	6	6
Schreiber, Larry HB-FB	71-73SF	2	6'	203	Tennessee Tech		25
Schuh, Harry OT-OG	65-69OakA 70Oak 71-73LA		6'2"	260	Memphis State		
Schultz, Randy HB-FB	66Cle 67-68NO	2	5'11"	210	Iowa State		12
Schumacher, Gregg DE	67-68LA		6'2"	240	Illinois		
Schweda, Brian DE	65HJ 66ChiB 67-68NO		6'3"	240	Kansas		
Schwedes, Ger HB	60-61BosA		6'1"	205	Syracuse		
Schweickert, Bob HB-FL	65,67NY-A		6'1"	193	Virginia Tech		
Scibelli, Joe OG	61-73LA		6'1"	256	Notre Dame		
Scolnik, Glenn WR	73Pit		6'3"	190	Indiana		
Scott, Bill DB	68CinA		6'	188	Idaho		
Scott, Bo FB	69-73Cle	23	6'3"	212	Ohio State		144

Use Name (Nicknames) - Positions	Team by Year	See Section	Hgt.	Wgt	College	Int	Pts
Scott, Bobby QB	73NO	1	6'1"	200	Tennessee		
Scott, Clarence DB	71-73Cle		6'	178	Kansas State	9	12
Scott, Clarence DB	69BosA 70Bos 71-72NE		6'2"	204	Morgan State	1	
Scott, Jake DB	70-73Mia	3	6'	188	Georgia	21	6
Scott, John DT	60-61BufA		6'4"	260	Ohio State		
Scott, Lew DB	66DenA		5'10"	173	Oregon State		
Scott, Wilbert LB	61Pit		6'	215	Indiana		
Scotti, Ben DB	59-61Was 62-63Phi 64SF		6'1"	185	Maryland	10	
Scrabis, Bob QB	60-62NY-A	1	6'3"	223	Penn State		6
Scribner, Bob HB	73LA		6'	200	U. C. L. A.		
Scrutchins, Ed DE	66HouA		6'3"	260	Toledo		
Sczurek, Stan LB	63-65Cle 66NYG		5'11"	229	Purdue	1	
Seals, George DT-OG-OT	64Was 65-71ChiB 72-73KC		6'2"	259	Missouri	1	6
Sedlock, Bob OT	60BufA		6'4"	295	Georgia		
Seedborg, John K	65Was 66MS		6'	227	Arizona State		
Seiler, Paul OT-C	67NY-A 68MS 69NY-A 70JJ 71-73Oak		6'4"	258	Notre Dame		
Seiple, Larry TE-HB	67-69MiaA 70-73Mia	2 4	6'	213	Kentucky		36
Selawski, Gene OT-OG	59LA 60Cle 61SD-A		6'4"	252	Purdue		
Selfridge, Andy LB	72Buf		6'4"	218	Virginia		
Sellers, Goldie DB	66-67DenA 68-69KC-A 70JJ	3	6'2"	198	Grambling	13	30
Sellers, Ron WR	69BosA 70Bos 71NE 72Dal 73Mia	2	6'4"	196	Florida State		108
Sensibaugh, Mike DB	71-73KC		5'11"	192	Ohio State	11	
Sestak, Tom DT-OT	62-68BufA		6'5"	267	McNeese State	2	18
Severson, Jeff DB	72Was 73Hou		6'1"	180	Long Beach State	4	
Seymour, Jim WR	70-72ChiB	2	6'4"	210	Notre Dame		30
Seymour, Paul TE	73Buf	2	6'5"	260	Michigan		
Shackleford, Don OG	64DenA		6'4"	255	U. of Pacific		
Shanklin, Ron WR	70-73Pit	2	6'1"	180	North Texas State		138
Shann, Bob DB	65Phi 66JJ 67Phi		6'1"	189	Boston College	1	6
Shannon, Carver DB-HB	62-64LA	3	6'1"	201	Southern Illinois	4	6
Sharockman, Ed DB	61BN 62-72Min		6'	200	Pittsburgh	40	36
Sharp, Rick OT	70-71Pit 72Den		6'3"	264	Washington		
Shaw, Billy OG	61-69BufA		6'3"	250	Georgia Tech		
Shaw, Bob WR	70NO		6'	194	Winston-Salem St.		
Shaw, Dennis QB	70-73Buf	12	6'2"	213	San Diego State		
Shaw, Glen FB-HB	60ChiB 62LA 63-64OakA	2	6'1"	221	Kentucky		24
Shaw, Nate LB	69-70LA		6'2"	205	Southern Calif.		
Shay, Jerry DT	66-67Min 68-69Atl 70-71NYG		6'3"	244	Purdue		
Shea, Pat OG	62-65SD-A 66JJ		6'1"	241	Southern Calif.		
Shears, Larry DB	71-72Atl		5'10"	185	Lincoln (Mo.)		
Shell, Art OT	68-69OakA 70-73Oak		6'5"	258	Md. Eastern Shore		
Sherer, Dave OE	59Bal 60Dal	4	6'3"	218	S. M. U.		
Sherk, Jerry DT-DE	70-73Cle		6'4"	255	Oklahoma State	2	
Sherlag, Bob FL	66Atl		6'	197	Memphis State		6
Sherman, Bob DB	64-65Pit		6'2"	195	Iowa	1	
Sherman, Rod WR-FL	67OakA 68CinA 69OakA 70-71Oak 72Den 73LA	23	6'	190	Southern Calif.		40
Sherman, Tom QB	68-69BosA 69BufA	12	6'	190	Penn State		
Shields, Lebron DE-OT	60Bal 61Min		6'4"	243	Tennessee		2
Shiner, Dick QB	64-66Was 67Cle 68-69Pit 70NYG 71,73Atl 73NE	12	6'	196	Maryland		12
Shinners, John OG	69-71NO 72Bal 73Cin		6'2"	254	Xavier-Ohio		
Shinnick, Don LB	57-69Bal		6'	232	U. C. L. A.	37	
Shirkey, George DT	60-61HouA 62OakA		6'4"	252	Austin		
Shivers, Roy HB	66-72StL	23	6'	200	Utah State		90
Shlapak, Boris K	72Bal		6'	165	Michigan State		4
Shoals, Roger OT-OG	63-64Cle 65-70Det 71Den		6'4"	256	Maryland		6
Shockley, Bill HB-K	60-61NY-A 61BufA 62NY-A 68Pit	23 5	6'	185	West Chester St.		181
Shofner, Del OE-DB	57-60LA 61-67NYG	2 4	6'3"	186	Baylor	3	306
Shofner, Jim DB	58-63Cle	3	6'2"	191	Texas Christian	20	
Shonta, Chuck DB	60-67BosA		6'	196	Eastern Michigan	15	6
Shorter, Jim DB	62-63Cle 64-67Was 69Pit		5'11"	184	Detroit	15	6
Shy, Don HB-FB	67-68Pit 69-70NO 70-72ChiB 73StL	23	6'1"	209	San Diego State		84
Shy, Les HB	66-69Dal 70NYG	23	6'1"	202	Long Beach State		24
Siani, Mike WR	72-73Oak	2	6'2"	195	Villanova		48
Sidle, Jimmy TE-HB	66Atl		6'2"	215	Auburn		
Sieminski, Chuck DT	63-65SF 66-67Atl 68Det		6'4"	262	Penn State		
Siemon, Jeff LB	72-73Min		6'2"	230	Stanford	4	
Sikich, Mike OG	71Cle		6'2"	243	Northwestern		
Silas, Sam DT-DE	63-67StL 68NYG 69-70SF		6'4"	251	Southern Illinois		
Silvestri, Carl DB	65StL 66Atl		6'	195	Wisconsin		
Simkus, Arnie DT-DE	65NY-A 67Min		6'4"	245	Michigan		
Simmons, Dave LB	65-66StL 67NO 68Dal		6'4"	245	Georgia Tech	2	
Simmons, Jerry WR-OE	65-67Pit 67NO 67-69Atl 69ChiB 71-73Den	2	6'1"	190	Bethune-Cookman		42
Simmons, Leon LB	63DenA		6'	225	Grambling		
Simms, Bob LB-OE-DE	60-62NYG 62Pit		6'1"	223	Rutgers		
Simon, Jim OG-OT-DE-LB	63-65Det 66-68Atl		6'5"	235	Miami (Fla.)		
Simone, Mike LB	72-73Den		6'	210	Stanford		
Simpson, Howard DE	64Min		6'5"	230	Auburn		
Simpson, Jackie DB	58-60Bal 61-62Pit		5'10"	183	Florida	2	
Simpson, Jackie LB	61DenA 62-64OakA	5	6'1"	226	Mississippi	5	15
Simpson, Mike DB	70-73SF		5'11"	172	Houston	3	6
Simpson, O. J. HB	69BufA 70-73Buf	23	6'2"	210	Southern Calif.		204
Simpson, Willie FB	62OakA		6'	218	San Fran. State		
Singer, Karl OT	66-68BosA		6'3"	250	Purdue		
Sisemore, Jerry OT	73Phi		6'4"	260	Texas		
Sisk, John DB	64ChiB		6'3"	195	Miami (Fla.)		
Sistrunk, Manny DT	70-73Was		6'5"	265	Ark.-Pine Bluff		
Sistrunk, Otis DT-DE	72-73Oak		6'4"	255	none	1	
Siwek, Mike DT	70StL		6'3"	260	Western Michigan		
Skaggs, Jim OG-OT	62BN 63-67Phi 68KJ 69-72Phi		6'2"	246	Washington		
Sklopan, John DB	63DenA		5'11"	190	Southern Miss.		
Skoronski, Bob OT-C	56GB 57-58MS 59-68GB		6'3"	249	Indiana		
Skorupan, John LB	73Buf		6'2"	214	Penn State		
Slaby, Lou LB-DT	64-65NYG 66Det		6'3"	235	Pittsburgh		
Slaughter, Mickey QB	63-66DenA	12	6'	190	Louisiana Tech		8
Sledge, Leroy FB	71Hou		6'2"	230	Bakersfield J. C.		6
Sligh, Dick DT	67OakA		7'	300	N. Car. Central		
Sloan, Bonnie DT	73StL		6'5"	260	Austin Peay		
Sloan, Steve QB	66-67Atl	1	6'	185	Alabama		
Slough, Greg LB	71-72Oak		6'3"	230	Southern Calif.		
Small, Eldridge DB	72-73NYG		6'1"	190	Texas A&I		
Small, John DT-LB	70-72Atl 73Det		6'5"	260	The Citadel		
Smiley, Tom FB	68CinA 69DenA 70Hou	2	6'1"	235	Lamar Tech		30
Smith, Allen HB	66NY-A		5'11"	195	Findlay		
Smith, Allen HB	66-67BufA	2	6'	200	Ft. Valley State		
Smith, Barry WR	73GB	2	6'1"	185	Florida State		12
Smith, Billy Ray DT-DE	57LA 58-60Pit 61-62Bal 63JJ 64-70Bal		6'4"	240	Arkansas	1	
Smith, Bob DB	68HouA		6'	180	Miami-Ohio		
Smith, Bobby HB	64-65BufA 66Pit	2	6'	203	North Texas State		30
Smith, Bobby DB	62-65LA 65-66Det	3	6'	193	U. C. L. A.	5	12
Smith, Bubba DE-DT	67-71Bal 72JJ 73Oak		6'7"	290	Michigan State		
Smith, Carl FB	60BufA		6'	200	Tennessee		6
Smith, Charlie HB	68-69OakA 70-73Oak	2	6'1"	205	Utah		192
Smith, Dan DB	61DenA		5'10"	180	NE State-Okla.		
Smith, Dave WR	70-72Pit 72Hou 73KC	2	6'2"	205	Indiana State		42
Smith, Dave FB	60-64HouA	2	6'1"	209	Ripon		108
Smith, Dave HB	70SD		6'1"	210	Utah		
Smith, Dick DB-HB-OE	67-68Was		6'	205	Northwestern	4	
Smith, Don OG	67DenA		6'4"	240	Florida A&M		
Smith, Donnell DE	71GB 73NE		6'4"	245	Southern U.		
Smith, Ed DE	73Den		6'5"	240	Colorado College		
Smith, Fletcher DB	66-67KC-A 68-69CinA 70-71Cin		6'2"	182	Tennessee State	15	2
Smith, Gordon OE	61-65Min	2	6'2"	211	Missouri		78
Smith, Hal DT	60BosA 60DenA 61OakA		6'5"	250	U. C. L. A.		
Smith, Hugh OE	62Was		6'4"	215	Kansas		
Smith, Jack DB	71Phi		6'4"	204	Troy State		
Smith, Jackie TE-OE	63-73StL	2 4	6'4"	222	NW State-La.		222
Smith, J. D. FB-HB-DB	56ChiB 56-64SF 65-66Dal	2	6'1"	205	N. Carolina A&T	2	276
Smith, J. D. OT	59-63Phi 64Det 65JJ 66Det		6'5"	250	Rice		6
Smith, J. D. (Jet Stream) FB-HB	60OakA 61ChiB	2	6'	215	Compton J. C.		50
Smith, Jeff LB	66NYG 67JJ		6'	237	Southern Calif.	1	
Smith, Jerry TE-WR	65-73Was	2	6'2"	208	Arizona State		312
Smith, Jerry	HC71Den				Wisconsin		
Smith, Jim DB	68Was		6'3"	195	Oregon		6
Smith, Jimmy DB	69DenA		6'3"	190	Utah State		
Smith, Jim Ray OG-OT-DE	56-62Cle 63-64Dal		6'3"	241	Baylor		
Smith, Ken TE	73Cle		6'4"	225	New Mexico		
Smith, Larry HB	69-73LA	2	6'3"	220	Florida		90
Smith, Noland (Super Gnat) WR-FL-HB	67-69KC-A 69SF	3	5'6"	155	Tennessee State		12
Smith, Ollie WR	73Bal		6'2"	195	Tennessee		
Smith, Paul DT-DE	68-69DenA 70-73Den		6'3"	252	New Mexico		
Smith, Perry DB	73GB		6'1"	195	Colorado State		
Smith, Ralph (Catfish) TE-OE-DB	62-64Phi 65-68Cle 69Atl	2	6'2"	214	Mississippi		36
Smith, Ron QB	65LA 66Pit	1	6'5"	220	Richmond		
Smith, Ron DB-FL-HB	65ChiB 66-67Atl 68-69LA 70-72ChiB 73SD	23	6'1"	191	Wisconsin	13	36
Smith, Royce OG	72-73NO		6'3"	245	Georgia		
Smith, Russ HB-FB	67-69SD-A 70SD	2	6'1"	214	Miami (Fla.)		60
Smith, Sid OT	70-72KC 73JJ		6'4"	260	Southern Calif.		
Smith, Steve OT-DE-TE	66Pit 68-70Min 71-37Phi		6'5"	246	Michigan		6
Smith, Tody DE	71-72Dal 73Hou		6'5"	245	Southern Calif.		
Smith, Tommie WR	69CinA		6'4"	190	San Jose State		
Smith, Willie OG-OT	60DenA 61OakA		6'2"	255	Michigan		
Smith, Zeke OG-DE-LB	60Bal 61NYG		6'2"	233	Auburn		
Smolinski, Mark FB-TE	61-62Bal 63-68NY-A	2	6'	218	Wyoming		102
Snead, Norm QB	61-63Was 64-70Phi 71Min 72-73NYG	12	6'4"	215	Wake Forest		132
Snell, Matt FB	64-69NY-A 70-72NYJ	2	6'2"	220	Ohio State		186
Sniadecki, Jim LB	69-73SF		6'2"	224	Indiana	1	
Snider, Mal OG-OT	69-71Atl 72-73GB		6'4"	247	Stanford		6
Snidow, Ron DE-DT	63-67Was 68-72Cle		6'4"	249	Oregon	1	2
Snorton, Matt OE	64DenA		6'5"	250	Michigan State		
Snow, Jack WR-OE	65-73LA	2	6'2"	196	Notre Dame		246
Snowden, Cal DE	69-70StL 71Buf 72-73SD		6'4"	247	Indiana		
Snowden, Jim OT-DE	65-71Was 72JJ		6'3"	255	Notre Dame		
Snyder, Al FL	64BosA 66Bal		6'	195	Holy Cross		
Snyder, Todd WR	70-72Atl	2	6'2"	187	Ohio U.		12
Soborinski, Phil C	68Atl		6'3"	235	Wisconsin		
Sodaski, John LB-DB	70,72Pit 73Phi		6'1"	214	Villanova	1	
Soleau, Bob LB	64Pit		6'2"	235	William & Mary		
Soltis, Bob DB	60-61BosA		6'2"	205	Minnesota	2	
Sommer, Mike HB-DB	58-59Was 59-61Bal 61Was 63OakA	2	5'11"	190	George Washington		12
Songin, Butch QB	60-61BosA 62NY-A	12	6'2"	200	Boston College		18
Sorey, Jim DT	60-62BufA		6'4"	278	Texas Southern		
Sorrell, Henry LB	67DenA		6'1"	215	Tenn.-Chattanooga		
Sortun, Rick OG	64-69StL		6'2"	234	Washington		
South, Ronnie QB	68NO	1	6'1"	195	Arkansas		
Sowells, Rich DB	71-73NYJ		6'	175	Alcorn A&M	5	6
Speights, Dick DB	68SD-A		5'11"	175	Wyoming		
Spence, Julian (Sus) DB-FL	56ChiC 57SF 60-61HouA		5'11"	170	Sam Houston St.	6	
Speyrer, Cotton WR	72-73Bal	2	6'	175	Texas		30
Spicer, Bob LB	73NYJ		6'4"	227	Indiana		
Spikes, Jack FB	60-62DalA 63-64KC-A 64SD-A 65HouA 66-67BufA	2 5	6'2"	221	Texas Christian		262
Spilis, John WR	69-71GB	2	6'3"	205	Northern Illinois		6
Spiller, Phil DB	67StL 68Atl 68CinA		6'	195	Los Angeles State	2	
Spurrier, Steve QB	67-73SF	12 4	6'2"	202	Florida		12
Stabler, Ken QB	70-73Oak	12	6'3"	205	Alabama		12
Stacy, Billy DB-HB	59ChiC 60-63StL	23	6'1"	191	Mississippi State	20	42
Stafford, Dick DE-DT	62-63Phi		6'4"	253	Texas Tech		
Staggers, Jon WR	70-71Pit 72-73GB	23	5'10"	186	Missouri		48
Staggs, Jeff LB-DE	67-69SD-A 70-71SD 72-73StL		6'2"	242	San Diego State	3	
Stalcup, Jerry LB-OG	60LA 61-62DenA		6'	230	Wisconsin	1	
Staley, Bill DT	68-69CinA 70-72ChiB		6'3"	249	Utah State		
Stallings, Don DT-DE-OT	60Was		6'4"	250	North Carolina		
Stallings, Larry LB	63-73StL		6'2"	230	Georgia Tech	6	18
Stanceil, Jeff HB	69Atl		6'	192	Miss. Valley St.		
Stanfill, Bill DE	69MiaA 70-73Mia		6'5"	250	Georgia	2	12
Stanton, Jack HB	61Pit		6'1"	190	N. Carolina State		
Starks, Marsh DB	63-64NY-A	3	6'	190	Illinois	1	6

Use Name (Nicknames) – Positions	Team by Year	See Section	Hgt	Wgt	College	Int	Pts
Starling, Bruce DB	63DenA		6'1"	186	Florida		
Staroba, Paul WR	72Cle 73GB		6'3"	204	Michigan		6
Starke, George OT	73Was		6'5"	250	Columbia		
Starr, Bart QB	56-71GB	12	6'1"	197	Alabama		90
Staten, Randy DE	67NYG		6'1"	225	Minnesota		
Staubach, Roger (The Dodger) QB	69-73Dal	12	6'2"	197	Navy		36
Steffen, Jim DB	59-61Det 61-65Was 66JJ	3	6'	196	U. C. L. A.	17	12
Stegent, Larry HB	71StL 72JJ		6'1"	200	Texas A & M		
Stehouwer, Ron OG-OT	60-64Pit		6'2"	232	Colorado State		
Stein, Bob LB-DE	69KC-A 70-72KC 73LA		6'2"	235	Minnesota	2	
Stenerud, Jan K	67-69KC-A 70-73KC	5	6'2"	187	Montana State		770
Stenger, Brian LB	69-72Pit 73NE		6'4"	226	Notre Dame	3	
Stephens, Harold QB	62NY-A		5'11"	175	Hardin-Simmons		
Stephens, Larry DE-DT	60-61Cle 62LA 63-67Dal		6'4"	245	Texas	1	6
Stephens, Tom OE-DB	60-64BosA	2	6'1"	207	Syracuse	1	36
Stephenson, Kay QB	67SD-A 68BufA	1	6'1"	208	Florida		
Stetz, Bill OG	67Phi		6'3"	250	Boston College		
Stevens, Bill QB	68-69GB		6'3"	195	Texas-El Paso		
Stevens, Dick OT	70-73Phi		6'4"	240	Baylor		
Stevens, Howard HB	73NO	23	5'10"	175	Louisville		12
Stevenson, Rickey DB	70Cle		5'11"	188	Arizona		
Stewart, Wayne TE	69NY-A 70-72NYJ		6'7"	210	California		6
Stickles, Monte OE-TE	60-67SF 68NO	2	6'4"	232	Notre Dame		96
Stienke, Jim DB	73Cle		5'11"	188	SW Texas State		
Stiger, Jim HB-FB	63-65Dal 65-67LA	23	5'11"	204	Washington		24
Stincic, Tom LB	69-71Dal 72NO		6'2"	229	Michigan	1	
Stingley, Darryl WR	73NE	2	6'	190	Purdue		12
Stinnette, Jim FB-LB	61-62DenA	2	6'1"	230	Oregon State	1	12
Stith, Carel DT-DE	67-69HouA		6'5"	267	Nebraska		
Stoepel, Terry TE	67ChiB 68-69MS 70Hou		6'4"	235	Tulsa		
Stofa, John QB	66-67MiaA 68-69CinA 69MiaA 70Mia	1	6'3"	210	Buffalo		6
Stokes, Jesse DB	68DenA		6'	190	Corpus Christi		
Stokes, Sims OE	67Dal		6'1"	198	Northern Arizona		
Stolberg, Eric WR	71NE		6'2"	180	Indiana		
Stone, Donnie HB-FB	61-64DenA 65BufA 66HouA	2	6'2"	205	Arkansas		102
Stone, Jack OT	60DalA 61-62OakA		6'2"	245	Oregon		
Stone, Ken DB	73Buf 73Was		6'1"	180	Vanderbilt		6
Stonebraker, Steve LB-OE	62-63Min 64-66Bal 67-68NO	2	6'3"	223	Detroit	2	12
Stotter, Rich LB	68HouA		6'	225	Houston		
Stovall, Jerry DB	63-71StL	34	6'2"	201	Louisiana State	18	12
Stover, Smokey LB	60-62DalA 63-66KC-A		6'	229	Northeast La.	6	
Stowe, Otto WR	71-72Mia 73Dal	2	6'2"	188	Iowa State		54
Strahan, Art DT	68Atl		6'5"	266	Texas Southern		
Strahan, Ray DE	65HouA		6'6"	250	Texas Southern		
Stram, Hank	HC60-62DalA HC63-69KC-A HC70-73KC				Purdue		
Strand, Eli OG	66Pit 67NO		6'2"	250	Iowa State		
Stransky, Bob HB	60DenA	2	6'1"	180	Colorado		
Stratton, Mike LB	62-69BufA 70-72Buf 73SD		6'3"	236	Tennessee	21	12
Strayhorn, Les HB	73Dal		5'10"	205	East Carolina		6
Stricker, Tony DB	63NY-A		6'	185	Colorado	1	
Strickland, Dave OG	60DenA		6'	220	Memphis State		
Strofolino, Mike LB	65LA 65Bal 66-68StL		6'2"	233	Villanova		
Stromberg, Mike LB	68NY-A		6'2"	235	Temple		
Strong, Jim HB-FB	70SF 71-72NO	2	6'1"	204	Houston		18
Stroud, Morris TE	69KC-A 70-73KC	2	6'10"	249	Clark-Ga.		30
Strozier, Art TE	70-71SD		6'2"	220	Kansas State		
Strugar, George DT	57-61LA 62Pit 62-63NY-A		6'5"	259	Washington	1	
Stuckey, Henry DB	73Mia		6'1"	190	Missouri	1	
Studdard, Vern WR	71NYJ		5'11"	175	Mississippi		
Studstill, Pat FL-WR	61-62Det 63JJ 64-67Det 68-71LA 72NE	234	6'1"	176	Houston		114
Stukes, Charlie DB	67-72Bal 73LA		6'3"	212	Md. Eastern Shore	25	6
Sturm, Jerry C-OT-OG-FB	61-66DenA 67-70NO 71Hou 72Phi		6'3"	257	Illinois		
Stynchula, Andy DE-DT-C	60-63Was 64-65NYG 66-67Bal 68Dal	5	6'3"	252	Penn State		22
Suchy, Larry DB	68Atl		5'11"	180	Mississippi Coll.		
Suci, Bob DB	62HouA 63BosA	3	5'10"	182	Michigan State	9	12
Suggs, Walt OT-C	62-69HouA 70-71Hou		6'5"	257	Mississippi State		
Sullivan, Dan OG-OT	62-72Bal		6'3"	250	Boston College		
Sullivan, Dave WR	73Cle		5'11"	185	Virginia		
Sullivan, Jim DE-DT	70Atl		6'4"	240	Lincoln (Mo.)		
Sullivan, Pat QB	72-73Atl	1	6'	199	Auburn		
Sullivan, Tom HB	72-73Phi	2	6'	190	Miami (Fla.)		30
Summers, Freddie DB	69-71Cle		6'1"	180	Wake Forest		
Summers, Jim DB	67DenA		5'10"	175	Michigan State		
Sumner, Walt DB	69-73Cle		6'1"	186	Florida State	15	6
Sunde, Milt OG-C	64-73Min		6'2"	244	Minnesota		
Sutherland, Doug OG-DT-DE	70NO 71-73Min		6'3"	250	Wis. St.-Superior		
Sutro, John OT	62SF		6'4"	245	San Jose State		
Sutton, Archie OT	65-67Min		6'4"	263	Illinois		
Sutton, Mickey DB	66HouA		6'	190	Auburn		
Svihus, Bob OT-OG	65-69OakA 70Oak 71-73NYJ		6'4"	245	Southern Calif.		
Swain, Bill LB	63LA 64Min 65NYG 66JJ 67NYG 68-69Det		6'2"	229	Oregon	2	6
Swanson, Terry K	67-68BosA 69CinA	4	6'	210	Massachusetts		
Swatland, Dick OG	68HouA		6'3"	245	Notre Dame		
Sweeney, Neal OE	67DenA		6'2"	170	Tulsa		
Sweeney, Steve WR	73Oak		6'3"	205	California		
Sweeney, Walt OG	63-69SD-A 70-73SD		6'3"	256	Syracuse		
Sweet, Joe WR	72-73LA		6'2"	196	Tennessee State		8
Sweetan, Karl QB	66-67Det 68NO 69-70LA	12	6'1"	203	Wake Forest		12
Swift, Doug LB	70-73Mia		6'3"	229	Amherst	5	
Swinford, Wayne DB-OE-FL	65-67SF		6'	194	Georgia		
Swink, Jim HB	60DalA		6'1"	185	Texas Christian		
Swinney, Clovis DT	70NO 71NYJ		6'3"	240	Arkansas State		
Sykes, Al WR	71NE		6'3"	180	Florida A & M		
Sykes, Gene DB	63-65BufA 67DenA		6'1"	196	Louisiana State	4	
Sykes, John HB	72SD		5'11"	195	Morgan State		
Symank, Johnny DB	57-62GB 63StL		5'11"	180	Florida	19	6
Szczecko, Joe DT	66-68Atl 69NYG		6'	245	Northwestern		
Szymakowski, Dave WR	68NO		6'2"	198	West Texas State		
Szymanski, Dick C-LB	55Bal 56MS 57-68Bal		6'3"	233	Notre Dame	6	6

Use (Nicknames) – Positions	Team by Year	See Section	Hgt	Wgt	College	Int	Pts
Taffoni, Joe OT-OG	67-70Cle 72-73NYG		6'3"	251	West Virginia, Tennessee-Martin		
Tagge, Jerry QB	72-73GB	12	6'2"	220	Nebraska		18
Talamini, Bob OG	60-67HouA 68NY-A		6'1"	249	Kentucky		
Talbert, Diron DT-DE	67-70LA 71-73Was		6'5"	249	Texas		
Talbert, Don OT-LB	62Dal 63-64MS 65Dal 66-68Atl 69-70NO 71Dal		6'5"	248	Texas		
Taliaferro, Mike QB	64-67NY-A 68-69BosA 70Bos 71NE 72Buf	12	6'2"	206	Illinois		2
Tannen, Steve DB	70-73NYJ		6'1"	194	Florida	10	6
Tanner, John LB	71SD 73NE		6'4"	229	Tennessee Tech		
Tarasovic, George DE-LB-C	52-53Pit 54-55MS 56-63Pit 63-65Phi 66DenA		6'4"	245	Louisiana State	7	18
Tarbox, Bruce OG	61LA		6'2"	230	Syracuse		
Tarkenton, Fran QB	61-66Min 67-71NYG 72-73Min	12	6'1"	190	Georgia		156
Tarr, Jerry HB	62DenA		6'	190	Oregon		12
Tarver, John FB	72-73NE	2	6'3"	227	Colorado		36
Tatarek, Bob DT	68-69BufA 70-72Buf 72Det		6'4"	260	Miami (Fla.)		
Tatman, Pete HB	67Min		6'1"	220	Nebraska		
Tatum, Jack DB	71-73Oak		5'10"	200	Ohio State	9	6
Taylor, Altie HB	69-73Det	2	5'10"	198	Utah State		120
Taylor, Bob DE-DT	63-64NYG		6'3"	238	Md. Eastern Shore		
Taylor, Bruce DB	70-73SF	3	6'	182	Boston U.	14	12
Taylor, Charley WR-HB-OE	64-73Was	2	6'3"	211	Arizona State		474
Taylor, Dave OT	73Bal		6'4"	254	Catawba		
Taylor, Jesse HB	72SD	3	6'	200	Cincinnati		6
Taylor, Jim FB	58-66GB 67NO	2	6'	214	Louisiana State		558
Taylor, Joe DB	67-73ChiB		6'2"	199	N. Carolina A & T	14	
Taylor, Lionel OE-WR-FL	59ChiB 60-66DenA 67-68HouA	2	6'2"	215	N. Mex. Highlands		270
Taylor, Mike LB	72-73NYJ		6'1"	230	Michigan	1	
Taylor, Mike OT	68-69Pit 69-70NO 71Was 73StL		6'4"	247	Southern Calif.		
Taylor, Otis WR-FL-OE	65-69KC-A 70-73KC	2	6'2"	215	Prairie View		348
Taylor, Rosey DB	61-69ChiB 69-71SF 72Was 73JJ	3	5'11"	186	Grambling	32	36
Taylor, Sammy FL	65SD-A		6'	190	Grambling		
Teal, Jim LB	73Det		6'3"	225	Purdue		
Tensi, Steve QB	65-66SD-A 67-69DenA 70Den	12	6'5"	213	Florida State		
Teresa, Tony HB	58SF 60OakA	2	5'9"	188	San Jose State		60
Terrell, Marvin OG	60-62DalA 63KC-A		6'1"	236	Mississippi		
Tharp, Corky DB	60NY-A		5'10"	180	Alabama	2	
Thaxton, Jim TE	73SD		6'2"	240	Tennessee State		12
Theofiledes, Harry QB	68Was		5'10"	180	Waynesburg		
Thibert, Jim LB	65DenA		6'3"	230	Toledo		
Thomas, Aaron TE-OE-FL-WR	61-62SF 62-70NYG	2	6'3"	209	Oregon State		222
Thomas, Alonzo DB	72-73Oak		6'1"	205	Southern Calif.	2	
Thomas, Bill FB	72Dal 73Hou		6'2"	225	Boston College		
Thomas, Bob HB	71-72LA 73SD	2	5'10"	210	Arizona State		24
Thomas, Clendon DB-OE-FL-HB	58-61LA 62-68Pit	2	6'2"	196	Oklahoma	27	30
Thomas, Duane HB-FB	70-71Dal 72HO 73Was	2	6'1"	215	West Texas State		108
Thomas, Earl TE-WR	71-73ChiB	2	6'3"	221	Houston		48
Thomas, Earlie DB	70-73NYJ		6'1"	190	Colorado State	5	6
Thomas, Emmitt DB	66-69KC-A 70-73KC	3	6'2"	192	Bishop	35	18
Thomas, Gene HB	66-67KC-A 68BosA 68OakA	2	6'1"	210	Florida A & M		36
Thomas, Ike DB-WR	71Dal 72-73GB	3	6'2"	193	Bishop		12
Thomas, Jim DB	73Pit		6'2"	196	Florida State	1	
Thomas, Jimmy HB-WR	69-73SF	2	6'1"	215	Texas-Arlington		72
Thomas, John OG-OT-LB	58-67SF 68JJ		6'4"	246	U. of Pacific		
Thomas, Lee DE	71-72SD 73Cin		6'5"	246	Jackson State		
Thomas, Speedy WR	69CinA 70-72Cin 73NO	2	6'1"	174	Utah		54
Thompson, Bill DB	69DenA 70-73Den	3	6'1"	200	Md. Eastern Shore	14	18
Thompson, Bobby DB	64-68Det 69NO	3	5'10"	179	Arizona	10	
Thompson, Dave OG-C-OT	71-73Det		6'4"	275	Clemson		
Thompson, Don DE	62-63Bal 64Phi		6'4"	230	Richmond		
Thompson, Jim DT	65DenA		6'3"	255	Southern Illinois		
Thompson, Norm DB	71-73StL		6'1"	175	Utah	5	12
Thompson (born Symonds), Rocky HB	71-73NYG	23	5'11"	200	West Texas State		18
Thompson, Steve DT-DE	68-69NY-A 70NYJ 71VR 72-73NYJ		6'5"	244	Washington		
Thoms, Art DT	69OakA 70-73Oak		6'5"	250	Syracuse	1	
Thornton, Bill FB	63-65StL 66JJ 67StL	2	6'1"	214	Nebraska		12
Thornton, Bubba WR	69BufA	23	6'	175	Texas Christian		
Thornton, Jack LB	66MiaA		6'1"	230	Auburn		
Thrower, Jim DB	70-72Phi 73Det		6'2"	194	East Texas State		
Thurlow, Steve HB-FB	64-66NYG 66-68Was	2	6'3"	217	Stanford		36
Thurston, Fuzzy OG	58Bal 59-67GB		6'1"	247	Valparaiso		
Tidmore, Sam LB	62-63Cle		6'1"	223	Ohio State		
Tiller, Jim HB	62NY-A	2	5'9"	165	Purdue		
Tilleman, Mike DT-DE	66Min 67-70NO 71-72Hou 73Atl		6'5"	275	Montana		
Tillman, Faddie DE-DT	72NO		6'5"	230	Boise State		
Tillman, Russ LB	70-73Was		6'2"	230	Northern Arizona		
Timberlake, Bob QB	65NYG	5	6'4"	220	Michigan		24
Tingelhoff, Mick C	62-73Min		6'1"	236	Nebraska		
Tipton, Dave DE-DT	71-73NYG		6'6"	240	Stanford		
Tobey, Dave LB	66-67Min 68DenA		6'3"	230	Oregon		
Tobin, Bill HB	63HouA	2	5'11"	210	Missouri		32
Toburen, Nelson LB	61-62GB		6'3"	235	Wichita State		
Todd, Jim HB	66Det		5'11"	195	Ball State		
Todd, Larry HB	65-69OakA 70Oak	23	6'1"	185	Arizona State		42
Toews, Loren LB	73Pit		6'3"	212	California	2	
Tolar, Charley FB-HB	60-66HouA	2	5'7"	199	NW State-La.		138
Tolbert, Jim DB	66-69SD-A 70-71SD 72Hou 73StL		6'3"	206	Lincoln (Mo.)	8	
Tolleson, Tommy DB	66Atl		6'	185	Alabama		
Tom, Mel DE	67-73Phi 73ChiB		6'4"	249	Hawaii, San Jose State		2
Toner, Ed DT-LB	67-69BosA 70JJ		6'3"	250	Massachusetts		
Toner, Tom LB	73GB		6'3"	225	Idaho State	1	
Toomay, Pat DE	70-73Dal		6'5"	244	Vanderbilt	1	
Torczon, Lavern DE	60-62BufA 62-65NY-A 66MiaA		6'2"	243	Nebraska	2	6
Townes, Willie DE-DT	66-68Dal 69JJ 70NO		6'5"	263	Tulsa		8
Towns, Bobby DB-OE-HB	60StL 61BosA		6'1"	180	Georgia		
Tracey, John (Jack) LB-OE-TE	59ChiC 60StL 61Phi 62-67BufA	2	6'3"	225	Texas A & M	12	4
Tracy, Tom (Tom the Bomb) HB-FB	56-57Det 58-63Pit 63-64Was	12	5'9"	205	Tennessee		199

Use Name (Nicknames) – Positions	Team by Year	See Section	Hgt	Wgt	College	Int	Pts
Trammell, Allen DB	66HouA		6'	190	Florida		
Trapp, Richard WR	68BufA 69SD-A	2	6'1"	174	Florida		
Trask, Orville DT	60-61HouA 62OakA		6'4"	260	Rice	1	
Travenio, Herb K	64-65SD-A	5	6'	218	none		110
Travis, John FB	66SD-A		6'1"	216	San Jose State		
Traynham, Jerry HB	61DenA		5'10"	190	Southern Calif.		
Traynham, Wade K	66-67Atl	5	6'2"	218	Frederick		45
Trimble, Wayne DB	67SF		6'3"	203	Alabama		
Triplett, Bill HB-FB-DB	62-63StL 64IL 65-66StL 67NYG 68-72Det	23	6'2"	212	Miami-Ohio	1	132
Tripucka, Frank QB	49Det 50-52ChiC 52Dal 53-59CFL 60-63DenA	12 4	6'2"	192	Notre Dame		36
Trosch, Gene DE-DT	67KC-A 68JJ 69KC-A 70JJ		6'7"	277	Miami (Fla.)		
Truax, Billy TE-OE	64-70LA 71-73Dal	2	6'5"	238	Louisiana State		108
Truax, Dalton OT	60OakA		6'2"	235	Tulane		
Trull, Don QB	64-67HouA 67BosA 68-69HouA	12	6'1"	189	Baylor		84
Trumpy, Bob TE-WR	68-69CinA 70-73Cin	2	6'6"	225	Illinois, Utah		144
Tubbs, Jerry LB-C	57-58ChiC 58-59SF 60-66Dal		6'2"	221	Oklahoma	17	
Tucker, Bill FB-HB-TE	67-70SF 71ChiB	23	6'2"	221	Tennessee State		78
Tucker, Bob TE	70-73NYG	2	6'3"	230	Bloomsburg State		114
Tucker, Gary HB	68MiaA		5'11"	195	Tenn.-Chattanooga		
Tucker, Wendell WR-OE	67-70LA	2	5'10"	185	S. Carolina State		66
Tuckett, Phil WR	68SD-A		6'	180	Weber State		
Turner, Bake OE-WR-FL	62Bal 63-69NY-A 70Bos	23	6'	180	Texas Tech		150
Turner, Cecil WR	68-73ChiB	23	5'10"	172	Cal. St. Polytech		36
Turner, Clem FB	69CinA 70-72Den	2	6'1"	238	Cincinnati		18
Turner, Herschel OG-OT	64-65StL		6'3"	230	Kentucky		
Turner, Jim QB-K	64-69NY-A 70NYJ 71-73Den	5	6'2"	206	Utah State		993
Turner, Rocky WR-DB	72-73NYJ		6'	195	Tenn.-Chattanooga		
Turner, Vince DB	64NY-A		5'11"	190	Missouri	1	
Twilley, Howard WR-OE	66-69MiaA 70-73Mia	2	5'10"	182	Tulsa		96
Tyler, Maurice DB	72Buf 73Den		6'	188	Morgan State	4	
Tyrer, Jim OT	61-62DalA 63-69KC-A 70-73KC		6'6"	284	Ohio State		
Tyson, Dick OG	66OakA 67DenA		6'2"	245	Tulsa		
Underwood, Olen LB	65NYG 66-69HouA 70Hou 71Den		6'1"	224	Texas	5	2
Unitas, Johnny QB	56-72Bal 73SD	12	6'1"	194	Louisville		78
Uperesa, Tuufuli OG	71Phi		6'3"	255	Montana		
Upshaw, Gene OG-OT	67-69OakA 70-73Oak		6'5"	255	Texas A & I		
Upshaw, Mary DE-DT	68-69Cle 70-73KC		6'3"	250	Trinity (Texas)	1	
Urbanek, Jim DT	68MiaA		6'4"	270	Mississippi		
Urenda, Herm DB-OE	63OakA		5'11"	170	U. of Pacific		
Vactor, Ted DB	69-73Was	3	6'	185	Nebraska	2	6
Valdez, Vern DB	60LA 61BufA 62OakA		5'11"	190	San Diego	7	
Vallez, Emilio TE	68-69ChiB		6'2"	210	New Mexico		
Vanderbundt, Skip LB	69-73SF		6'3"	230	Oregon State	7	18
Vander Kelen, Ron QB	63-67Min	12	6'1"	186	Wisconsin		6
Vandersea, Phil LB-DE-TE	66GB 67NO 68-69GB		6'3"	228	Massachusetts		
Van Dyke, Bruce OG	66Phi 67-73Pit		6'2"	243	Missouri		
Van Galder, Tim QB	72StL	1	6'1"	190	Iowa State		
Van Heusen, Bill WR	68-69DenA 70-73Den	2 4	6'1"	200	Maryland		42
Van Horn, Doug OG	66Det 68-73NYG		6'2"	245	Ohio State		
Van Note, Jeff C-LB-OG	69-73Atl		6'2"	242	Kentucky		
Vanoy, Vern DT	71NYG 72GB		6'8"	270	Kansas		
Van Pelt, Brad LB	73NYG		6'5"	235	Michigan State		
Van Raaphorst, Dick K	64Dal 66-67SD-A	5	5'11"	215	Ohio State		247
Van Valkenberg, Pete HB	73Buf		6'2"	192	Brigham Young		
Vargo, Larry DB-OE-LB	62-63Det 64-65Min 66NYG 67JJ		6'3"	212	Detroit	6	6
Varrichione, Frank OT	55-60Pit 61-65LA		6'1"	234	Notre Dame		
Vasys, Arunas LB	66-68Phi		6'2"	232	Notre Dame		
Vataha, Randy WR	71-73NE	2	5'10"	177	Stanford		78
Vaughn, Bob OG	68DenA		6'4"	240	Mississippi		
Vaughn, Tom DB	65-71Det	3	5'11"	192	Iowa State	9	
Vella, John OT-OG	72-73Oak		6'4"	255	Southern Calif.		
Vellone, Jim OG-OT	66-70Min		6'2"	255	Southern Calif.		
Vereb, Ed HB	60Was		6'	190	Maryland		
Villanueva, Danny K	60-64LA 65-67Dal	45	5'11"	202	New Mexico State		491
Villapiano, Phil LB	71-73Oak		6'1"	218	Bowling Green	6	6
Viltz, Theo DB	66HouA		6'2"	190	Southern Calif.		
Vinyard, Kenny K	70Atl	5	5'10"	190	Texas Tech		50
Vogel, Bob OT	63-72Bal		6'5"	248	Ohio State		
Voight, Bob DT	61OakA		6'5"	265	Los Angeles State		
Voigt, Stu TE	70-73Min	2	6'1"	220	Wisconsin		30
Volk, Rick DB	67-73Bal	3	6'3"	195	Michigan	29	6
Vollenweider, Jim HB-FB	62-63SF	2	6'1"	210	Miami (Fla.)		12
Von Sonn, Andy LB	64LA		6'2"	223	U. C. L. A.		
Voss, Lloyd DE-DT-OT	64-65GB 66-71Pit 72Den		6'4"	256	Nebraska	1	
Wade, Billy QB	54-60LA 61-66ChiB	12	6'2"	204	Vanderbilt		144
Wade, Bob DB	68Pit 69Was 70Den		6'2"	200	Morgan State	1	
Wade, Tom QB	64-65Pit	1	6'2"	195	Texas		
Wages, Harmon FB-HB	68-71Atl 72KJ 73Atl	2	6'1"	214	Florida		60
Wagner, Mike DB	71-73Pit		6'1"	196	Western Illinois	16	6
Wagstaff, Jim DB	59ChiC 60-61BufA		6'2"	192	Idaho State	9	6
Wainscott, Loyd LB	69HouA 70Hou		6'1"	235	Texas-Austin		
Walden, Bobby K	64-67Min 68-73Pit	4	6'	192	Georgia		
Walik, Billy WR	70-72Phi	3	5'11"	180	Villanova		6
Walker, Chuck DT-DE	64-72StL 72-73Atl		6'2"	248	Duke	1	
Walker, Clarence HB	63DenA		6'1"	205	Southern Illinois		
Walker, Cleo LB-C	70GB 71Atl		6'3"	220	Louisville		
Walker, Donnie DB	73Buf	3	6'1"	185	Central St.-Ohio	1	
Walker, Malcolm C-OT	65KJ 66-69Dal 70GB		6'4"	249	Rice		
Walker, Mickey OG-LB-C	61-65NYG		6'	232	Michigan State		
Walker, Mike K	72NE	5	6'	190	none		21
Walker, Mike DE	71NO		6'4"	235	Tulane		
Walker, Wayne LB	58-72Det	5	6'2"	225	Idaho	14	345
Walker, Wayne K	67KC-A 68HouA	5	6'2"	215	NW State-La.		50
Walker, Willie FL	66Det		6'3"	200	Tennessee State		
Wallace, Bob TE-WR	68-72ChiB	2	6'3"	213	Texas-El Paso		54
Wallace, Henry DB	60LA-A		6'	195	U. of Pacific		
Wallace, Rodney OG-OT	71-73Dal		6'5"	255	New Mexico		
Waller, Charlie	HC69SD-A HC70SD				Georgia		

Use Name (Nicknames) – Positions	Team by Year	See Section	Hgt	Wgt	College	Int	Pts
Walsh, Ed OT	61NY-A		6'4"	243	PMC Colleges		
Walsh, Ward HB	71-72Hou 72GB	2	6'	213	Colorado		12
Walters, Stan OT	72-73Cin		6'6"	270	Syracuse		
Walters, Tom DB	64-67Was		6'2"	195	Southern Miss.	3	6
Walton, Bruce OG-C	73Dal		6'6"	250	U. C. L. A.		
Walton, Chuck OG	67-73Det		6'3"	253	Iowa State		
Walton, Joe OE-DE	57-60Was 61-63NYG 64XJ	2	5'11"	202	Pittsburgh	1	168
Walton, Larry WR	69-73Det	2	5'11"	180	Arizona State		126
Walton, Sam OT	68-69NY-A 71Hou		6'5"	270	East Texas State		
Walton, Wayne OG-OT	71NYG 73KC		6'5"	250	Abilene Christian		
Wantland, Hal DB	66MiaA		6'	195	Tennessee		
Ward, Carl DB	67-68Cle 69NO	3	5'9"	180	Michigan	1	6
Ward, Jim QB	67-68Bal 71Phi 72JJ	1	6'2"	197	Gettysburg		
Ward, John DE-OG	70-73Min		6'4"	258	Oklahoma State		
Ward, Paul DT	61-62Det		6'3"	247	Whitworth		
Warfield, Paul WR-OE	64-69Cle 70-73Mia	2	6'	187	Ohio State		456
Warlick, Ernie OE	62-65BufA	2	6'4"	234	N. Car. Central		24
Warner, Charley DB-HB	63-64KC-A 64-66BufA 67JJ	3	5'11"	178	Prairie View	7	30
Warren, Dewey QB	68CinA	1	6'	205	Tennessee		
Warren, Jimmy DB	64-65SD-A 66-69MiaA 70-73Oak	3	5'11"	178	Illinois	23	24
Warwick, Lonnie LB	65-72Min 73Atl		6'3"	234	Tennessee Tech	12	6
Warzeka, Ron DT	60OakA		6'4"	250	Montana State		
Washington, Clarence DT	69-70Pit 71JJ		6'3"	265	Ark.-Pine Bluff		
Washington, Clyde DB-HB	60-61BosA 63-65NY-A		6'	202	Purdue	9	
Washington, Dave LB-TE	70-71Den 72-73Buf		6'5"	218	Alcorn A & M	2	2
Washington, Dave TE	68DenA		6'4"	228	Southern Calif.		
Washington, Dick DB	68MiaA		6'1"	205	Bethune-Cookman		
Washington, Eric DB	72-73StL		6'2"	190	Texas-El Paso		
Washington, Fred OT	68Was		6'5"	268	North Texas State		
Washington, Gene WR-OE	67-72Min 73Den	2	6'3"	212	Michigan State		156
Washington, Gene WR	69-73SF	2	6'1"	185	Stanford		198
Washington, Joe HB	73Atl		5'9"	180	Illinois State		
Washington, Mark DB	70-73Dal		5'10"	187	Morgan State	2	8
Washington, Russ OT-DT	68-69SD-A 70-73SD		6'6"	292	Missouri		
Washington, Ted LB	73Hou		6'1"	240	Miss. Valley St.		
Washington, Ted HB	68CinA		5'11"	210	San Diego State		
Washington, Vic HB	71-73SF	23	5'10"	196	Wyoming		120
Waskiewicz, Jim C-OT-LB	66-67NY-A 69Atl		6'4"	237	Wichita State		
Waters, Bob QB	60-63SF	12	6'2"	184	Presbyterian		18
Waters, Charlie DB	70-73Dal		6'1"	193	Clemson	18	6
Watkins, Larry FB-HB	69Det 70-72Phi 73Buf	2	6'2"	221	Alcorn A & M		42
Watkins, Tom HB	61Cle 62-65Det 66JJ 67Det 68Pit	23	6'1"	195	Iowa State		102
Watson, Allen K	70Pit		5'10"	165	Newport-Wales		22
Watson, Dave OG	63-64BosA		6'1"	225	Georgia Tech		
Watson, Ed LB	69HouA		6'2"	222	Grambling		
Watson, John OT-OG	71-73SF		6'4"	248	Oklahoma		
Watson, Pete TE	72Cin		6'1"	210	Tufts		
Watters, Bob DE	62-64NY-A		6'4"	247	Lincoln (Mo.)		
Wayt, Russell LB	65Dal		6'4"	235	Rice		
Weatherford, Jim DB	69Atl		5'10"	180	Tennessee	1	6
Weathers, Carl LB	70-71Oak		6'2"	220	San Diego State		
Weatherspoon, Cephus WR	72NO		6'1"	182	Fort Lewis		
Weatherwax, Jim DT	66-67GB 68KJ 69GB		6'7"	265	Los Angeles State		
Weaver, Charlie LB	71-73Det		6'2"	218	Southern Calif.	3	
Weaver, Gary LB	73Oak	4	6'1"	224	Fresno State		
Weaver, Herman K	70-73Det		6'4"	210	Tennessee		
Webb, Allan DB-HB	61-65NYG		5'11"	180	Arnold	7	
Webb, Don DB-HB	61-62BosA 63JJ 64-69BosA 70Bos 71NE		5'10"	196	Iowa State	21	24
Webb, Ken HB-FB	58-62Det 63Cle	23	5'11"	207	Presbyterian		54
Webster, Dave DB	60-61DalA 62JJ		6'4"	218	Prairie View	11	18
Webster, George LB	67-69HouA 70-72Hou 72-73Pit		6'4"	223	Michigan State	4	
Webster, Tim K	71GB	5	6'	195	Arkansas		26
Wegener, Bill OG	62-63HouA		5'10"	245	Missouri		
Weger, Mike DB	67-73Det		6'2"	195	Bowling Green	16	12
Wehrli, Roger DB	69-73StL	3	6'1"	193	Missouri	12	
Weir, Sammy FL	65HouA 66NY-A		5'9"	170	Arkansas State		
Weisacosky, Ed LB	67NYG 68-69MiaA 70Mia 71-72NE		6'	228	Miami (Fla.)	3	
Welch, Claxton HB-FB	69-71Dal 73NE	2	5'11"	202	Oregon		14
Welch, Jim DB-HB	60-67Bal 68Det		6'	191	S. M. U.	5	6
Wellborn, Joe C	66NYG		6'2"	215	Texas A&M		
Wells, Bob OT	68-69SD-A 70SD		6'4"	273	Johnson C. Smith		
Wells, Harold LB	65-68Phi 69NYG		6'2"	221	Purdue	4	6
Wells, Joel HB	61NYG	2	6'1"	198	Clemson		12
Wells, Warren WR-OE	64Det 65-66MS 67-69OakA 70Oak	2	6'1"	191	Texas Southern		258
71 – Declared ineligible to play pro football							
Wendryhoski, Joe C-OG	64-66LA 67-68NO		6'2"	245	Illinois		
Wenzel, Ralph OG	66-70Pit 72-73SD		6'3"	244	San Diego State		
Werl, Bob OG-DE	66NY-A		6'3"	240	Miami (Fla.)		
Werner, Clyde LB	70KC 71KJ 72-73KC		6'4"	225	Washington	1	
Wersching, Ray K	73SD	5	5'11"	210	California		48
West, Bill DB	72Den		5'10"	185	Tennessee State		
West, Bob WR	72-73KC	2	6'4"	218	San Diego State		18
West, Charlie DB	68-73Min	3	6'1"	194	Texas-El Paso	11	6
West, Dave DB	63NY-A		6'3"	190	Central St.-Ohio		
West, Mel HB	61BosA 61-62NY-A	2	5'9"	190	Missouri		18
West, Willie DB-HB	60-61StL 62-63BufA 64DenA 64-65NY-A 66-68MiaA	3	5'10"	188	Oregon	30	12
Westmoreland, Dick DB	63-65SD-A 66-69MiaA	3	6'1"	191	N. Carolina A&T	22	12
Wetoska, Bob OT-OG-C	60-69ChiB		6'3"	241	Notre Dame		
Wettstein, Max TE	66DenA		6'3"	217	Florida State		
Whalen, Jim TE-OE	65-69BosA 70-71Den 71Phi	2	6'2"	210	Boston College		120
Wharton, Hogan OG	60-63HouA		6'2"	248	Houston		
Wheeler, Manch QB	62BufA		6'	190	Maine		
Wheeler, Ted OG-TE	67-68StL 70ChiB		6'3"	240	West Texas State		
Wheelwright, Ernie FB	64-65NYG 66-67Atl 67-70NO	2	6'3"	235	Southern Illinois		96
Whitaker, Creston WR	72NO		6'2"	187	North Texas State		
White, Andre TE	67DenA 68CinA 68SD-A		6'5"	225	Florida A&M		2
White, Bob FB	60HouA		6'2"	220	Ohio State		
White, Dwight DE	71-73Pit		6'4"	250	East Texas State	2	2
White, Ed OG	69-73Min		6'2"	260	California		

Use Name (Nicknames) – Positions	Team by Year	See Section	Hgt	Wgt	College	Int	Pts
White, Freeman TE-DB-LB	66-69NYG	2	6'5"	225	Nebraska	2	6
White, Gene HB	62OakA		6'1"	197	Florida A&M		8
White, Harvey QB	60BosA		6'1"	190	Clemson		
White, Jan TE	71-72Buf	2	6'2"	216	Ohio State		12
White, Jeff K	73NE	5	5'11"	170	Texas-El Paso		63
White, Jim DE	72NE		6'3"	256	Colorado State		
White, John OE	60-61HouA	2	6'4"	230	Texas Southern		6
White, Lee FB	68-69NY-A 70NYJ 71LA 72SD	2	6'4"	238	Weber State		6
White, Paul HB	70-71StL		6'	200	Texas-El Paso		
White, Ray LB	71-72SD 73JJ		6'1"	234	Syracuse		
White, Sherman DE	72-73Cin		6'5"	255	California		
White, Stan LB	72-73Bal		6'1"	225	Ohio State	4	6
Whitehead, Bud DB-FL-HB	61-68SD-A		6'	184	Florida State	15	6
Whitfield, A. D. FB	65Dal 66-68Was	2	5'10"	200	North Texas State		36
Whitley, Hall LB	60NY-A		6'2"	225	Texas A&I		
Whitlow, Bob C-OG	60-61Was 61-65Det 66Atl 68Cle		6'1"	236	Arizona		
Whitmyer, Nat DB	63LA 66SD-A 67JJ		6'	182	Washington	1	
Whitsell, Dave DB-HB	58-60Det 61-66ChiB 67-69NO		6'	189	Indiana	46	30
Whittenton, Jesse DB	56-57LA 58-64GB		6'	193	Texas-El Paso	24	12
Whittingham, Fred LB-OG	63JJ 64LA 66Phi 67-68NO 69Dal 70Bos 71Phi		6'1"	240	Cal. St. Polytech	3	
Wicks, Bob WR	72StL		6'3"	195	Utah State		
Widby, Ron K 67-68 played in A.B.A.	68-71Dal 72-73GB	4	6'4"	212	Tennessee		
Wiggin, Paul DE	57-67Cle		6'3"	242	Stanford	3	12
Wilbur, John OG-DE-DT	66-69Dal 70LA 71-73Was		6'3"	245	Stanford		
Wilburn, J. R. WR-OE	66-70Pit	2	6'2"	190	South Carolina		48
Wilcox, Dave LB	64-73SF		6'3"	235	Oregon	13	6
Wilcox, John OT-DE	60Phi		6'5"	230	Oregon		
Wilder, Bert DE-DT	64-67NY-A		6'3"	245	N. Carolina State		
Wilkerson, Doug OG	70Hou 71-73SD		6'2"	249	N. Car. Central		
Will, Erwin DT	65Phi		6'5"	270	Dayton		
Willard, Ken FB	65-73SF	2	6'2"	224	North Carolina		366
Williams, A. D. OE-FL	59GB 60Cle 61Min	2	6'2"	210	U. of Pacific		6
Williams, Bobby DB	66-67StL 69-71Det	3	6'1"	195	Central St.-Okla.	3	12
Williams, Clancy DB-HB	65-72LA	3	6'2"	197	Washington State	28	12
Williams, Clarence (Sweeny) DE	70-73GB		6'5"	255	Prairie View		6
Williams, Clyde OT-OG	67-71StL		6'2"	252	Southern U.		
Williams, Dave WR-FL	67-71StL 72-73SD 73Pit	2	6'2"	205	Washington		150
Williams, Del OG-C	67-73NO		6'2"	242	Florida State		
Williams, Donnie WR	70LA		6'3"	210	Prairie View		
Williams, Erwin WR	69Pit		6'5"	215	Md. Eastern Shore		6
Williams, Frank FB	61LA		6'2"	215	Pepperdine		
Williams, Howie DB	62-63GB 63SF 64-69OakA		6'2"	188	Howard-D.C.	14	
Williams, Jeff HB	66Min		6'1"	210	Oklahoma State		
Williams, Jim DB	69CinA		6'1"	190	Alcorn A&M		
Williams, Joe HB	71Dal 72NO	2	6'	194	Wyoming		6
Williams, John OG-OT-DE	68-71Bal 72-73LA		6'3"	256	Minnesota		
Williams, Maxie OG-OT	65HouA 66-69MiaA 70Mia		6'4"	247	Southeastern La.		
Williams, Monk WR	68CinA		5'7"	155	Ark.-Pine Bluff		
Williams, Perry FB	69-73GB	2	6'2"	220	Purdue		6
Williams, Roger DB-WR	71-72LA		5'10"	180	Grambling		
Williams, Roy DT	63SF		6'7"	265	U. of Pacific		
Williams, Sam DE-OE-LB	59LA 60-65Det 66-67Atl		6'5"	235	Michigan State	1	20
Williams, Sid LB-DE	64-66Cle 67Was 68Bal 69Pit		6'2"	235	Southern U.	1	6
Williams, Tom DT	70-71SD		6'4"	250	California-Davis		
Williams, Travis HB	67-70GB 71LA 72KJ	23	6'1"	210	Arizona State		108
Williams, Wandy HB	69DenA 70Den		6'1"	192	Kansas, Hofstra		6
Williams, Willie DB	65NYG 66OakA 67-73NYG		6'	190	Grambling	35	
Williamson, Fred (The Hammer) DB	60Pit 61-64OakA 65-67KC-A		6'2"	210	Northwestern	35	12
Williamson, J. R. LB-C	64-67OakA 68-69BosA 70Bos 71JJ		6'2"	220	Louisiana Tech	3	
Willingham, Larry DB	71-72StL		6'1"	190	Auburn		
Willis, Fred FB	71-72Cin 72-73Hou	2	6'	213	Boston College		
Willis, Larry DB	73Was		5'11"	170	Texas-El Paso		
Willsey, Ray	HC61StL				California		
Wilson, Ben FB-HB	63-65LA 67GB 68KJ	2	6'	225	Southern Calif.		66
Wilson, Butch TE-OE	63-67Bal 68-69NYG	2	6'2"	223	Alabama		18
Wilson, Eddie QB	62DalA 63-64KC-A 65BosA 66KJ	1 4	6'	190	Arizona		6
Wilson, George QB	66MiaA	12 4	6'1"	190	Xavier-Ohio		2
Wilson, Harry HB	67Phi 68JJ 69Phi		5'11"	204	Nebraska		
Wilson Jerrel HB-FB-LB-K	63-69KC-A 70-73KC	4	6'4"	223	Southern Miss.	4	
Wilson, Jim OG-OT	65-66SF 67Atl 68LA 69-71JJ		6'3"	257	Georgia		
Wilson, Joe HB-FB	73Cin		5'10"	210	Holy Cross		
Wilson, Larry DB	60-72StL		6'	190	Utah	52	50
Wilson, Mike OG-OT	69CinA 70Cin 71Buf		6'1"	240	Dayton		
Wilson, Mike DB	69StL		5'11"	185	Western Illinois		
Wilson, Nemiah DB	65-67DenA 68-69OakA 70-73Oak		6'	166	Grambling	24	24
Winans, Jeff DT	73Buf		6'5"	265	Southern Calif.		
Windsor, Bob TE	67-71SF 72-73NE	2	6'4"	227	Kentucky		84
Winfield, Vern OG	72-73Phi		6'2"	248	Minnesota		
Winfrey, Carl LB	71Min 72Pit		6'	230	Wisconsin		
Wingate, Heath C	67Was		6'2"	240	Bowling Green		
Wink, Dean DE-DT	67-68Phi		6'4"	246	Yankton		
Winkler, Francis DE	68-69GB		6'3"	230	Memphis State		
Winkler, Randy OG-OT	67Det 68Atl 69-70MS 71GB		6'5"	258	Tarleton State		
Winner, Charlie	HC66-70StL				SE Missouri St., Washington-St.L.		
Winslow, Doug WR	73NO		5'11"	180	Drake		
Winslow, Paul HB	60GB		5'11"	200	N. Car. Central		6
Winston, Kelton DB	67-68LA		6'	195	Wiley		
Winston, Lloyd FB	62-63SF	2	6'2"	215	Southern Calif.		6
Winston, Roy LB	62-73Min		6'1"	227	Louisiana State	12	20
Winter, Bill LB	62-64NYG		6'4"	220	St. Olaf		
Winther, Wimpy C	71GB 72NO		6'3"	260	Mississippi		
Wirgowski, Dennis DE-DT	70Bos 71-72NE 73Phi		6'5"	253	Purdue	1	
Wise, Phil DB	71-73NYJ		6'	200	Nebraska-Omaha	1	6
Wisener, Gary DB-OE	60Dal 61HouA		6'1"	206	Baylor		
Witcher, Al OE-DE	60HouA		6'1"	200	Baylor	1	6
Witcher, Dick WR-TE-FL	66-73SF	2	6'3"	205	U.C.L.A.		90
Withrow, Cal C	70SD 71-73GB		6'	240	Kentucky		
Witt, Mel DE-DT	67-69BosA 70Bos		6'3"	261	Texas-Arlington	1	6
Wittenborn, John OG-K	58-60SF 60-62Phi 63JJ 64-68HouA	5	6'2"	238	SE Missouri St.		101
Wittum, Tom K	73SF	4	6'1"	185	Northern Illinois		
Woitt, John DB	68-69SF		5'11"	172	Mississippi State	1	6
Wojcik, Greg DT	71LA 72-73SD		6'6"	268	Southern Calif.		
Wolff, Wayne OG	61BufA		6'2"	243	Wake Forest		
Wolski, Bill FB	66Atl		5'11"	203	Notre Dame		
Womack, Joe HB	62Pit	2	5'9"	210	Los Angeles State		30
Wondolowski, Bill WR	69SF		5'10"	168	Eastern Montana		
Wood, Bill DB	63NY-A		5'11"	190	West Va. Wesleyan		
Wood, Bo DE	67Atl		6'3"	225	North Carolina		
Wood, Dick QB	62SD-A 62DenA 63-64NY-A 65OakA 66MiaA	12	6'5"	202	Auburn		24
Wood, Duane DB	60-62DalA 63-64KC-A		6'1"	196	Oklahoma State	20	12
Wood, Gary QB	64-66NYG 67NO 68-69NYG	12	5'11"	188	Cornell		37
Wood, Willie DB	60-71GB	3	5'10"	189	Southern Calif.	48	25
Woodall, Al QB	69NY-A 70-71NYJ 72JJ 73NYJ	12	6'5"	204	Duke		
Woodeshick, Tom FB-HB	63-71Phi 72StL	2	6'	219	West Virginia		162
Woodlief, Doug LB	65-69LA 70JJ		6'3"	231	Memphis State	6	
Woods, Bob OT	73NYJ		6'3"	255	Tennessee State		
Woods, Glenn DE	69HouA		6'4"	250	Prairie View		
Woods, Larry DT	71-72Det 73Mia		6'6"	260	Tennessee State		
Woodson, Abe DB-HB	58-64SF 65-66StL	3	5'11"	188	Illinois	19	48
Woodson, Freddie OG-DE-DT	67-69MiaA		6'2"	253	Florida A&M		
Woodson, Marv DB-HB	64-69Pit 69NO		6'	195	Indiana	18	12
Wooten, John OG	59-67Cle 68Was		6'2"	248	Colorado		
Wortman, Keith OG	72-73GB		6'2"	245	Nebraska		
Woulfe, Mike LB	62Phi 63JJ		6'2"	225	Colorado		
Wright, Elmo WR	71-73KC	2	6'	190	Houston		30
Wright, Ernie OT	60LA-A 61-67SD-A 68-69CinA 70-71Cin 72SD		6'4"	268	Ohio State		
Wright, George DT	70-71Bal 72 Cle		6'3"	262	Sam Houston St.		
Wright, Gordon OG	67Phi 69NY-A		6'3"	245	Delaware State		
Wright, Jeff DB	71-73Min		5'11"	190	Minnesota	5	
Wright, Jim DB	64DenA		5'11"	190	Memphis State	1	
Wright, John WR	68Atl 69Det 70JJ	2	6'	196	Illinois		18
Wright, Lonnie DB 67-72 played in A.B.A.	66-67Den A		6'2"	205	Colorado State	5	
Wright, Nate DB	69Atl 69-70StL 71-73Min		5'11"	180	San Diego State	8	
Wright, Rayfield OT-TE	67-73Dal		6'7"	250	Ft. Valley State		6
Wright, Steve OT-DE	64-67GB 68-69NYG 70Was 71ChiB 72StL		6'6"	250	Alabama		
Wulff, Jim DB-HB	60-61Was		5'11"	185	Michigan State	3	
Wyatt, Alvin DB	70Oak 71-72Buf 73Hou	3	5'10"	183	Bethune-Cookman	5	18
Wyatt, Doug DB	70-72NO 73Det		6'1"	195	Tulsa	8	12
Wyche, Sam QB	68-69CinA 70Cin 71-72Was	12	6'4"	212	Furman		18
Wycinsky, Craig OG	72Cle		6'3"	243	Michigan		
Wynn, Bill DE	73Phi		6'4"	240	Tennessee State		6
Yaccino, John DB	62BufA		6'	190	Pittsburgh		
Yanchar, Bill DT	70Cle		6'3"	250	Purdue		
Yankowski, Ron DE	71-73StL		6'5"	230	Kansas State		
Yarbrough, Jim OT	69-73Det		6'6"	256	Florida		
Yary, Ron OT	68-73Min		6'6"	258	Southern Calif.		
Yates, Bob OT-C-DT	60-65BosA		6'3"	233	Syracuse		
Yearby, Bill DE	66NY-A		6'3"	235	Michigan		
Yelverton, Bill DE	60DenA		6'4"	220	Mississippi	1	6
Yepremian, Garo K	66-67Det 70-73Mia	5	5'8"	167	none		520
Yewcic, Tom QB-HB 57 played major league baseball	61-66BosA	12 4	5'11"	185	Michigan State		24
Yohn, Dave LB	62Bal 63NY-A		6'	223	Gettysburg		
Yoho, Mack DE	60-63BufA	5	6'2"	239	Miami-Ohio	2	97
Youmans, Maury DE-OT	60-62ChiB 63JJ 64-65Dal		6'6"	253	Syracuse		
Young, Adrian LB	68-72Phi 72Det 73ChiB		6'1"	230	Southern Calif.	3	
Young, Al WR	71-72Pit 73IL		6'1"	195	S. Carolina State		
Young, Bob OG-DT	66-69DenA 70Den 71Hou 72-73StL		6'2"	261	Texas, Howard Payne, SW Texas State		
Young, Charlie TE	73Phi	2	6'4"	230	Southern Calif.		42
Young, Jim HB	65-66Min		6'	205	Queens (Ont.)		
Young, Joe DE	60-61DenA		6'3"	245	Arizona		
Young, Wilbur DT-DE	71-73KC		6'6"	292	William Penn	1	
Young, Willie OT	71-72Buf 73Mia		6'4"	270	Alcorn A&M		
Young, Willie OT	66-73NYG		6'	259	Grambling		
Youngblood, George DB	66LA 67Cle 67-68NO 69ChiB		6'3"	204	Los Angeles State	3	6
Youngblood, Jack DE	71-73LA		6'4"	249	Florida		
Youngblood, Jim LB	73LA		6'3"	240	Tennessee Tech	1	
Youso, Frank OT	58-60NYG 61-62Min 63-65OakA		6'4"	257	Minnesota		
Zabel, Steve LB-TE	70-73Phi	2	6'4"	235	Oklahoma	3	18
Zaeske, Paul WR	69HouA 70Hou		6'2"	200	North Park		
Zapalac, Bill LB-DE	71-73NYJ		6'4"	225	Texas		
Zaruba, Carroll DB	60DalA		5'9"	210	Nebraska		
Zaunbrecher, Godfrey C	71-73Min		6'4"	238	Louisiana State		
Zawadzkas, Jerry TE	67Det		6'4"	220	Columbia		
Zecher, Rich DT-OT	65OakA 66-67MiaA 67BufA		6'2"	240	Utah State		
Zeman, Bob DB	60LA-A 61SD-A 62-63DenA 64JJ 65-66SD-A		6'1"	202	Wisconsin	17	12
Zeno, Coleman WR	71NYG		6'4"	210	Grambling		
Zimmerman, Dan WR	73Phi	2	6'3"	195	Northeast La.		18
Zofko, Mickey HB	71-73Det	3	6'3"	195	Auburn		1
Zook, John DE	69-73Atl		6'5"	244	Kansas	3	8

Lifetime Statistics - 1960-1973 Players Section 1 - **PASSING**
(All men with 25 or more passing attempts)

Name	Years	Att.	Comp.	Comp. Pct.	Yards	Yds./ Att.	TD	Int.	Pct. Int.
Ken Anderson	71-73	761	422	55.5	5123	6.7	30	23	3.0
Jon Arnett	57-66	33	8	24.2	147	4.5	2	2	6.1
Rick Arrington	70-72	204	97	47.5	950	4.7	3	9	4.4
Billy Barnes	57-63,65-66	25	10	40.0	233	9.3	4	4	16.0
Pete Beathard	64-73	1282	575	44.9	8176	6.4	43	84	6.6
Bob Berry	65-73	1119	624	55.8	8878	7.9	59	63	5.6
George Blanda	49-58,60-73	4000	1909	47.7	26881	6.7	235	276	6.9
Terry Bradshaw	70-73	1079	522	48.4	6739	6.2	41	73	6.8
Zeke Bratkowski	54,57-68,71	1484	762	51.3	10345	7.0	65	122	8.2
Don Breaux	63,65	181	92	50.8	1339	7.4	9	10	5.5
Marlin Briscoe	68-73	230	97	42.2	1697	7.4	14	14	6.1
Bob Brodhead	60	25	7	28.0	75	3.0	0	3	12.0
John Brodie	57-73	4491	2469	55.0	31548	7.0	214	224	5.0
Rudy Bukich	53,56-68	1190	626	52.6	8433	7.1	61	74	6.2
Virgil Carter	68-72	775	419	54.1	4962	6.4	28	30	3.9
Max Choboian	66	163	82	50.3	1110	6.8	4	12	7.4
Dennis Claridge	64-66	71	41	57.7	484	6.8	2	2	2.8
Wayne Clark	70,72-73	98	43	43.9	647	6.6	0	11	11.2
Jack Concannon	64-71	1054	531	50.4	5859	5.6	35	60	5.7
Greg Cook	69,73	200	107	53.5	1865	9.3	15	11	5.5
John David Crow	58-68	70	33	47.1	759	10.8	5	5	7.1
Gary Cuozzo	63-72	1182	584	49.4	7402	6.3	43	55	4.7
Dan Darragh	68-70	296	127	42.9	1352	4.6	4	22	7.4
Cotton Davidson	54,57,60-66,68	1752	770	43.9	11760	6.7	73	108	6.2
Bob Davis	67-73	324	137	42.3	1553	4.8	14	23	7.1
Len Dawson	57-73	3366	1905	56.6	26043	7.7	227	166	4.9
Eagle Day	59-60	32	15	46.9	194	6.1	0	2	6.2
Jim Del Gaizo	72-73	71	32	45.1	483	6.8	4	7	9.9
Bill Demory	73	39	12	30.8	159	4.1	2	8	20.5
Lynn Dickey	71,73	177	90	50.8	1203	6.8	6	19	10.7
Marty Domres	69-73	592	290	49.0	3764	6.4	25	36	6.1
Bobby Douglass	69-73	775	327	42.2	4458	5.8	28	45	5.8
Brian Dowling	72-73	54	29	53.7	383	7.1	2	1	1.9
Randy Duncan	61	67	25	37.3	361	5.4	1	3	4.5
Hunter Enis	60-62	160	80	50.0	947	5.9	4	6	3.7
Sam Etcheverry	61-62	302	154	51.0	1982	6.6	16	21	7.0
Joe Ferguson	73	164	73	44.5	939	5.7	4	10	6.1
Tom Flores	60-61,63-69	1715	838	48.9	11959	7.0	93	92	5.4
Dan Fouts	73	194	87	44.8	1126	5.8	6	13	6.7
Roman Gabriel	62-73	3773	1975	52.3	25442	6.7	177	124	3.3
Chan Galleaos	62	35	18	51.4	298	8.5	2	3	8.6
Joe Gilliam	72-73	71	27	38.0	379	5.3	2	6	8.5
Johnny Green	60-63	618	275	44.5	3921	6.3	26	34	5.5
Tom Greene	60-61	63	27	42.9	251	4.0	1	6	9.5
Bob Griese	67-73	1761	929	52.8	12341	7.0	98	88	5.0
Glynn Griffing	63	40	16	40.0	306	7.7	3	4	10.0
Lee Grosscup	60-62	173	73	42.2	1086	6.3	10	12	6.9
Ralph Gugliemi	55,58-63	626	292	46.6	4119	6.6	24	52	8.3
John Hadl	62-73	3899	1959	50.2	28946	7.4	223	222	5.7
Galen Hall	62-63	150	64	42.7	885	5.9	5	10	6.7
Kim Hammond	68-69	32	15	46.9	147	4.6	0	2	6.3
Terry Hanratty	69-73	391	156	39.9	2383	6.1	23	29	7.4
Edd Hargett	69-73	437	205	46.9	2727	6.2	11	10	2.3
Jim Harris	69-71,73	200	97	48.5	1188	5.9	5	11	5.5
Jim Hart	66-73	1948	939	48.2	13463	6.9	82	107	5.5
George Herring	60-61	233	102	43.8	1297	5.6	5	23	9.9
King Hill	58-69	881	429	48.7	5553	6.3	37	71	8.1
Dick Hoak	61-70	40	20	50.0	427	10.7	4	3	7.5
Don Horn	67-73	465	232	49.9	3369	7.2	20	36	7.7
Paul Hornung	57-62,64-66	55	24	43.6	383	7.0	5	4	7.3
John Huarte	66-68,70-72	48	19	39.6	230	4.8	1	5	10.4
Gary Huff	73	126	54	42.9	525	4.2	3	8	6.3
Buddy Humphrey	59-66	175	87	49.7	1094	6.3	4	12	6.9
Scott Hunter	71-73	446	196	43.9	2904	6.5	15	30	6.7
George Izo	60-66	317	132	41.6	1791	5.6	12	32	10.1
Dick Jamieson	60-61	70	35	50.0	586	8.4	6	2	2.9
Charley Johnson	61-73	3006	1536	51.1	21420	7.1	152	160	5.3
Randy Johnson	66-73	1172	585	49.9	7524	6.4	47	79	6.7
Bert Jones	73	108	43	39.8	539	5.0	4	12	11.1
Sonny Jurgensen	57-73	4095	2326	56.8	31039	7.6	244	184	4.5
Joe Kapp	67-70	918	449	48.9	5911	6.4	40	64	7.0
Gary Keithley	73	73	32	43.8	369	5.1	1	5	6.8
Jack Kemp	57,60-67,69	2973	1437	48.3	21222	7.1	114	183	6.2
Tom Kennedy	66	100	55	55.0	748	7.5	7	6	6.0
Billy Kilmer	61-62,64,66-73	1952	1040	53.3	13668	7.0	95	104	5.3
Daryle Lamonica	63-73	2592	1285	49.6	19119	7.4	163	134	5.2
Greg Landry	68-73	1001	526	52.5	7474	7.5	52	62	6.2
Gary Lane	66-68	43	21	48.8	254	5.9	2	1	2.3
Jim LeClair	67-68	99	46	46.5	678	6.8	2	6	6.1
Bob Lee	69-73	416	215	51.7	3148	7.6	19	17	4.1

Name	Years	Att.	Comp.	Comp. Pct.	Yards	Yds./ Att.	TD	Int.	Pct. Int.
Jacky Lee	60-69	838	430	51.3	6191	7.4	46	57	6.8
Bruce Lemmerman	68-69	77	28	36.4	370	4.8	1	5	6.5
Pete Liske	64,69-72	778	396	50.9	5170	6.6	30	46	5.9
Mike Livingston	68-73	434	223	51.4	2771	6.4	17	22	5.1
Richie Lucas	60-61	99	43	43.4	496	5.0	4	7	7.1
Archie Manning	71-73	892	456	51.1	5587	6.3	34	42	4.7
Tom Matte	61-72	42	12	28.6	246	5.9	2	2	4.8
John McCormick	62-63,65-66,68	555	214	38.6	2895	5.2	17	38	6.8
Don Meredith	60-68	2308	1170	50.7	17199	7.5	135	111	4.8
Ron Miller	62	43	17	39.5	250	5.8	1	1	2.3
George Mira	64-69,71	346	148	42.8	2110	6.1	19	20	5.8
Earl Morrall	56-73	2593	1326	51.1	20087	7.7	155	142	5.5
Craig Morton	65-73	1306	683	52.3	10267	7.9	80	73	5.6
Bill Munson	64-73	1463	772	52.8	9517	6.5	65	65	4.4
Joe Namath	65-73	2738	1374	50.2	21065	7.7	131	149	5.4
Bill Nelsen	63-72	1905	963	50.6	14165	7.4	98	101	5.3
Jim Ninowski	58-69	1048	513	49.0	7133	6.8	34	67	6.4
Kent Nix	67-72	652	301	46.2	3644	5.6	23	49	7.5
Terry Nofsinger	61-67	260	118	45.4	1357	5.2	4	12	4.6
Rick Norton	66-70	382	159	41.6	1815	4.8	7	30	7.9
Nick Papac	61	44	13	29.5	173	3.9	2	7	15.8
Babe Parilli	52-53,56-58,60-69	3330	1552	46.6	22671	6.8	178	220	6.6
Dan Pastorini	71-73	859	425	49.5	4895	5.7	19	50	5.8
Al Pastrana	69-70	75	29	38.7	420	5.6	1	9	12.0
Mike Phipps	70-73	711	334	47.0	4421	6.2	24	45	6.3
Milt Plum	57-69	2419	1306	54.0	17536	7.2	132	127	5.3
Jim Plunkett	71-73	1059	520	49.1	6904	6.5	40	58	5.5
Warren Rabb	60-62	251	101	40.2	1782	7.1	15	16	6.4
Larry Rakestraw	64,66-68	111	51	45.9	589	5.3	4	9	8.1
Steve Ramsey	70-73	344	159	46.2	2364	6.9	10	24	7.0
John Reaves	72-73	243	113	46.5	1525	6.3	7	13	5.3
Joe Reed	72-73	114	51	44.7	589	5.2	2	6	5.3
Dan Reeves	65-72	32	14	43.8	370	11.6	2	4	12.5
Jerry Reichow	56-57,59-64	38	12	31.6	187	4.9	0	4	10.5
M. C. Reynolds	58-62	450	222	49.3	2932	6.5	17	28	6.2
Jerry Rhome	65-67,69-71	280	139	49.6	1628	5.8	7	14	5.0
Johnny Roach	56,59-64	413	182	44.1	2765	6.7	24	37	9.0
Ed Rutkowski	63-68	102	41	40.2	380	3.7	0	6	5.9
Frank Ryan	58-70	2133	1090	51.1	16042	7.5	149	111	5.2
Bobby Scott	73	54	18	33.3	245	4.5	1	3	5.6
Bob Scrabis	60-62	26	7	26.9	82	3.2	1	3	11.5
Dennis Shaw	70-73	916	485	52.9	6286	6.9	35	67	7.3
Tom Sherman	68-69	228	92	40.4	1219	5.3	16	16	7.0
Dick Shiner	64-71,73	730	351	48.1	4764	6.5	36	42	5.8
Mickey Slaughter	63-66	584	291	49.8	3607	6.2	22	37	6.3
Steve Sloan	66-67	31	10	32.3	134	4.3	0	4	12.9
Ron Smith	65-66	181	79	43.6	1249	6.9	8	12	6.6
Norm Snead	61-73	3963	2049	51.7	28238	7.1	182	235	5.9
Butch Songin	60-62	694	327	47.1	4347	6.3	38	31	4.5
Ronnie South	68	38	14	36.8	129	3.4	1	3	7.9
Steve Sourrier	67-73	630	338	53.7	4097	6.5	28	41	6.5
Ken Stabler	70-73	389	233	59.9	2841	7.3	19	18	4.6
Bart Starr	56-71	3149	1808	57.4	24718	7.8	152	138	4.4
Roger Staubach	69-73	646	381	59.0	5371	8.3	41	31	4.8
Kay Stephenson	67-68	105	40	38.1	481	4.6	6	9	8.6
John Stofa	66-70	312	146	46.8	1758	5.6	12	11	3.5
Pat Sullivan	72-73	45	17	37.8	219	4.9	1	3	6.7
Karl Sweetan	66-70	590	269	45.6	3210	5.4	17	34	5.8
Jerry Tagge	72-73	135	66	48.9	874	6.5	2	7	5.2
Mike Taliaferro	64-72	966	419	43.4	5241	5.4	36	63	6.5
Fran Tarkenton	61-73	4449	2459	55.3	33248	7.5	249	187	4.2
Steve Tensi	65-70	862	369	42.8	5558	6.4	43	46	5.3
Tom Tracy	56-64	67	24	35.8	854	12.7	6	5	7.5
Frank Tripucka	49-52,60-63	1745	879	50.4	10282	5.9	59	124	7.1
Don Trull	64-69	617	276	44.7	3980	6.5	30	28	4.5
Johnny Unitas	56-73	5186	2830	54.6	40239	7.8	290	253	4.9
Ron Vander Kelen	63-67	252	107	42.5	1375	5.5	6	11	4.4
Tim Van Galder	72	79	40	50.6	434	5.5	1	7	8.9
Billy Wade	54-66	2523	1370	54.3	18530	7.3	124	134	5.3
Tom Wade	64-65	69	34	49.3	470	6.8	2	13	18.8
Jim Ward	67-68,71	26	13	50.0	165	6.3	2	2	7.7
Dewey Warren	68	80	47	58.8	506	6.3	1	4	5.0
Bob Waters	60-63	124	59	47.6	707	5.7	3	8	6.5
Eddie Wilson	62-65	186	90	48.4	1251	6.7	5	6	3.2
George Wilson	66	112	46	41.1	764	6.8	5	10	8.9
Dick Wood	62-66	1193	522	43.8	7151	6.0	51	70	5.9
Gary Wood	64-69	400	186	46.5	2575	6.4	14	23	5.7
Al Woodall	69-71,73	495	243	49.1	2955	6.0	18	21	4.2
Sam Wyche	68-72	220	115	52.3	1743	7.9	12	8	3.6
Tom Yewcic	61-66	206	87	42.2	1374	6.7	12	12	5.8

Lifetime Statistics - 1960-1973 Section 2 – **RUSHING and RECEIVING**
(All men with 25 or more rushing attempts or 10 or more receptions)

Name	Years	RUSHING Att.	Yards	Avg.	TD	RECEIVING Rec.	Yards	Avg.	TD
Dan Abramowicz	67-73	6	95	15.8	0	344	5317	15.5	38
Mike Adamle	71-73	153	610	4.0	1	25	145	5.8	1
Bob Adams	69-71,73	2	7	3.5	0	43	473	11.0	0
John Adams	59-63	41	99	2.4	1	21	264	12.6	3
Margene Adkins	70-73					19	258	13.6	0
Don Allen	60	30	18	0.6	1	5	34	6.8	0
Duane Allen	61-67					10	227	22.7	5
Jerry Allen	66-69	201	664	3.3	7	33	400	12.1	2
Jim Allison	65-68	93	378	4.1	2	22	230	10.5	0
Mack Alston	70-73	1	13	13.0	0	26	335	12.9	4
Lance Alworth	62-72	24	129	5.4	2	542	10267	18.9	85
Bill Anderson	58-63,65-66	4	11	2.8	0	168	3048	18.1	15
Bobby Anderson	70-73	313	1281	4.1	9	84	861	10.3	2
Donny Anderson	66-73	1107	4380	4.0	38	194	2432	12.5	11
Ken Anderson	71-73	70	316	4.5	4				
Max Anderson	68-69,71	160	599	3.7	3	29	205	7.1	0
Ralph Anderson	58,60					55	791	14.4	6
Taz Anderson	61-64,66-67					87	1335	15.3	9
Fred Arbanas	62-70	4	15	3.8	0	218	3101	14.2	34
Otis Armstrong	73	26	90	3.5	0	2	43	21.5	1
Jon Arnett	57-66	964	3833	4.0	26	222	2290	10.3	10
Doug Asad	60-61					50	698	14.0	3
Willie Asbury	66-68	253	868	3.4	11	25	307	12.2	2
Josh Ashton	72-73	221	851	3.9	3	33	320	9.7	1
Pervis Atkins	61-66	74	201	2.7	1	64	675	10.5	2
Joe Auer	64-68	234	773	3.3	7	51	647	12.7	6
Gene Babb	57-58,60-63	152	461	3.0	3	33	281	8.5	1
Tom Bailey	71-73	32	154	4.8	1	22	167	7.6	1
Art Baker	61-62	154	507	3.3	3	9	85	9.4	0
Sam Baker	53,56-69	49	234	4.8	2	7	59	8.4	0
Terry Baker	63-65	58	210	3.6	1	30	302	10.1	2
Tony Baker	68-73	441	1821	4.1	9	72	593	8.2	2
Gary Ballman	62-73	41	202	4.9	4	323	5366	16.6	37
Pete Banaszak	66-73	473	2107	4.5	16	78	728	9.3	5
Estes Banks	67-68	44	157	3.6	0	4	15	3.8	1
Warren Bankston	69-73	165	675	4.1	3	31	189	6.1	0
Jerome Barkum	72-73	1	2	2.0	0	60	1114	18.6	8
Billy Barnes	57-63,65-66	994	3421	3.4	29	153	1786	11.7	9
Gary Barnes	62-64,66-67					41	583	14.2	2
Eppie Barney	67-68	0	8	—	1	19	192	10.1	1
Terry Barr	57-65	32	151	4.7	2	227	3810	16.8	35
Jan Barrett	63-64					13	221	17.0	2
Tom Barrington	66-70	168	530	3.2	3	41	278	6.8	1
Dick Bass	60-69	1218	5417	4.4	34	204	1841	9.0	7
Glenn Bass	60-68	16	67	4.2	0	167	2841	17.0	17
Craig Baynham	67-70,72	152	553	3.6	6	45	466	10.4	3
John Beasley	67-70,72-73					146	1522	10.4	13
Pete Beathard	64-73	131	680	5.2	11				
Hal Bedsole	64-66					26	418	16.1	8
Tom Beer	67-72					65	1012	15.6	4
Jim Beirne	68-73	1	3	3.0	0	134	1875	14.0	11
Eddie Bell	70-73	3	−12	−4.0	0	85	1304	15.3	7
Henry Bell	60	42	238	5.5	0	2	13	6.5	0
Joe Bellino	65-67	30	64	2.1	0	11	153	13.9	1
Willie Belton	71-73	66	257	3.9	1	4	21	5.3	0
Bob Berry	65-73	107	401	3.7	4				
Ray Berry	55-67					631	9275	14.7	68
Jim Bertelsen	72-73	329	1435	4.4	9	48	598	12.5	2
Fred Biletnikoff	65-73					408	6512	16.0	53
Charlie Bivins	60-67	153	498	3.3	3	28	262	9.4	3
Hank Bjorkland	72-73	37	114	3.1	0	6	69	11.5	0
George Blanda	49-58,60-73	144	268	1.9	9	1	-16	-16.0	0
Sid Blanks	64-70	365	1440	3.9	7	106	1073	10.1	4
Ronnie Blye	68-69	61	268	4.4	1	12	85	7.1	0
Dewey Bohling	60-61	178	584	3.3	4	43	485	11.3	5
Emerson Boozer	66-73	1118	4521	4.0	48	124	1311	10.6	10
Don Bosseler	57-64	775	3112	4.0	22	136	1083	8.0	1
Lee Bouggess	70-71,73	271	697	2.6	5	78	589	7.6	3
Terry Bradshaw	70-73	177	971	5.5	16				
Cliff Branch	72-73	1	5	5.0	0	22	331	15.0	3
Zeke Bratkowski	54,57-68,71	92	308	3.3	5				
Jim Braxton	71-73	245	1031	4.2	9	48	474	9.9	1
Johnny Brewer	61-70					89	1256	14.1	6
Marlin Briscoe	68-73	46	322	7.0	3	179	2897	16.2	24
John Brockington	71-73	755	3276	4.3	15	49	469	9.6	2
John Brodie	57-73	235	1167	5.0	22				
Barry Brown	66-70					21	214	10.2	0
Bill Brown	61-73	1630	5797	3.6	52	281	3142	11.2	23
Bob Brown	69-73	1	8	8.0	0	28	448	16.0	1
Fred Brown	61,63	59	210	3.6	2	3	18	6.0	0
Jimmy Brown	57-65	2359	12312	5.2	106	262	2499	9.5	20
Ken Brown	70-73	205	690	3.4	2	27	251	9.3	0
Larry Brown	69-73	1250	5037	4.0	29	159	1774	11.2	14
Timmy Brown	59-68	889	3862	4.3	31	235	3399	14.5	26
Willie Brown	64-66	44	133	3.0	0	5	110	22.0	1
Bob Brunet	68,70-73	122	377	3.1	2	24	200	8.3	1
Charlie Bryant	66-69	67	322	4.8	0	3	26	8.7	0
Hubie Bryant	70-72	7	26	3.7	0	22	366	16.6	1
Frank Budd	62-63					10	236	23.6	1
Fred Bukaty	61	76	187	2.5	5	15	94	6.7	0
Rudy Bukich	53,56-68	112	109	1.0	9				
Norm Bulaich	70-73	424	1712	4.0	13	87	810	9.3	5
Ronnie Bull	62-71	881	3222	3.7	9	172	1479	8.6	5
Amos Bullocks	62-64,66	158	620	3.9	5	15	180	12.0	2
Jerry Burch	61					18	235	13.1	1

Name	Years	RUSHING Att.	Yards	Avg.	TD	RECEIVING Rec.	Yards	Avg.	TD
Chris Burford	60-67	3	10	3.3	0	391	5505	14.1	55
Vern Burke	65-67					38	470	12.4	2
Bobby Burnett	66-67,69	237	871	3.7	4	45	533	11.8	4
Leon Burns	71-72	87	292	3.4	3	9	44	4.9	0
John Burrell	62-64,66-67	6	38	6.3	0	26	437	16.8	0
Ode Burrell	64-69	304	1088	3.6	3	112	1379	12.3	9
Ken Burrough	70-73	6	42	7.0	1	107	1664	15.6	9
Ken Burrow	71-73	6	25	4.2	0	93	1800	19.4	18
Ron Burton	60-65	429	1536	3.6	9	111	1205	10.9	8
Bill Butler	72-73	141	581	4.1	1	44	351	8.0	4
Bill Butler	59-64	29	108	3.7	0	6	95	15.8	0
Cannonball Butler	65-72	797	2768	3.5	9	89	959	10.8	7
Sonny Campbell	70-71	57	195	3.4	2	10	132	13.2	0
Woody Campbell	67-71	408	1493	3.7	13	80	709	8.9	2
Billy Cannon	60-70	602	2455	4.1	17	236	3656	15.5	47
Bob Cappadonna	66-68	123	460	3.7	2	24	196	8.2	3
Gino Cappelletti	60-70	4	6	1.5	0	292	4589	15.7	42
Wray Carlton	60-67	819	3368	4.1	29	110	1329	12.1	5
Harold Carmichael	71-73	3	42	14.0	0	107	1680	15.7	11
Reg Carolan	62-68					23	364	15.8	5
J. C. Caroline	56-65	68	263	3.9	2	6	111	18.5	1
Preston Carpenter	56-67	223	884	4.0	1	305	4457	14.6	23
Jimmy Carr	55,57,59-65	30	115	3.8	0	9	157	17.4	0
Virgil Carter	68-72	106	629	5.9	8				
Rick Casares	55-66	1431	5787	4.0	49	191	1588	8.3	11
Bernie Casey	61-68	1	23	23.0	23	359	5444	15.2	40
Rich Caster	70-73	5	7	1.4	0	119	2273	19.1	23
Don Chamberlain	60-61					18	295	16.4	4
Bob Chandler	71-73	8	13	1.6	0	68	1015	14.9	8
Wes Chesson	71-73	1	−4	−4.0	0	40	598	15.0	2
Ray Chester	70-73	5	9	1.8	0	122	1755	14.4	23
Joe Childress	56-60,62-65	530	2210	4.2	3	121	1700	14.0	13
Clarence Childs	64-68	40	102	2.6	0	11	97	8.8	0
Dick Christy	58,60-63	337	1267	3.8	10	132	1473	11.2	6
Jack Clancy	67,69-70	3	-4	-1.3	0	104	1401	13.5	5
Boobie Clark	73	254	988	3.9	8	45	347	7.7	0
Howard Clark	60-61					38	613	16.1	0
Frank Clarke	57-67	32	231	7.2	1	291	5426	18.6	50
Vin Clements	72-73	103	435	4.2	1	24	247	10.3	1
Doug Cline	60-66	37	105	2.8	2	4	15	3.8	0
Bert Coan	62-68	284	1259	4.4	15	39	367	9.4	4
Junior Coffey	65-67,69,71	535	2037	3.8	10	64	487	7.6	5
Gail Gogdill	60-70	2	−2	−1.0	0	356	5696	16.0	34
Angie Coia	60-66	5	−2	−0.4	0	121	2037	16.8	20
Jim Colclough	60-68	4	51	12.8	0	283	5101	18.0	39
Terry Cole	68-71	189	641	3.4	5	25	171	6.8	1
Gary Collins	62-71	4	60	15.0	0	331	5299	16.0	70
Dick Compton	62-65,67-68	6	8	1.3	0	52	733	14.1	14
Jack Concannon	64-71	214	1019	4.8	11				
Larry Conjar	67-70	30	102	3.4	0	6	68	11.3	0
Bobby Joe Conrad	58-69	118	441	3.7	2	422	5902	14.0	38
Greg Cook	69,73	25	148	5.9	1				
Bob Coolbaugh	61					32	435	13.6	4
Thurlow Cooper	60-62					36	491	13.6	8
Bruce Coslet	69-73					44	664	15.1	7
Paul Costa	65-72	2	12	6.0	1	102	1699	16.7	6
Craig Cotton	69-73					28	409	14.6	1
Jim Cox	68					11	147	13.4	0
Eric Crabtree	66-71	8	37	4.6	0	164	2663	16.2	22
Dobie Craig	62-64	1	8	8.0	0	38	743	19.6	7
Jim Crawford	60-64	302	1078	3.6	5	52	496	9.5	2
Willie Crenshaw	64-70	652	2428	3.7	15	104	797	7.7	3
Bob Crespino	61-68					58	741	12.8	9
Bobby Crockett	66,68-69					41	659	16.1	3
Monte Crockett	60-62					35	512	14.6	1
Marshall Cropper	67-69					14	181	12.9	0
John David Crow	58-68	1157	4963	4.3	38	258	3699	14.3	35
Wayne Crow	60-63	235	1085	4.6	3	36	345	9.6	1
Harry Crump	63	49	120	2.5	5	3	19	6.3	0
Larry Csonka	68-73	1089	5151	4.7	32	68	578	8.5	3
Doug Cunningham	67-73	401	1498	3.7	10	135	1145	8.5	0
Jim Cunningham	61-63	120	337	2.8	3	26	219	8.4	2
Sam Cunningham	73	155	516	3.3	4	15	144	9.6	1
Gary Cuozzo	63-72	76	176	2.3	1				
Pat Curran	69-73	25	92	3.7	0	9	83	9.2	2
Isaac Curtis	73	2	−11	−5.5	0	45	843	18.7	9
Carroll Dale	60-73	4	30	7.5	0	438	8277	18.9	52
Clem Daniels	60-68	1146	5138	4.5	30	203	3314	16.3	24
Cotton Davidson	54,57,60-66,68	149	357	2.4	11				
Bob Davis	67-73	52	332	6.4	2				
Clarence Davis	71-73	241	1293	5.4	12	30	255	8.5	0
Dave Davis	71-73	2	0	0.0	0	11	192	17.5	1
Dick Davis	70	27	94	3.5	0	4	29	7.3	0
Glenn Davis	60-61					10	132	13.2	0
Sonny Davis	71-72	47	163	3.5	1	11	46	4.2	0
Steve Davis	72-73	87	351	4.0	3	8	36	4.5	1
Joe Dawkins	70-73	382	1601	4.2	8	72	718	10.0	0
Len Dawson	57-73	278	1258	4.5	9				
Ted Dean	60-64	263	923	3.5	2	51	684	13.4	4
Austin Denney	67-71	2	3	1.5	0	71	764	10.8	3
Mike Dennis	68-69	29	136	4.7	0	8	53	6.6	0
Al Denson	64-71	4	3	0.8	0	260	4275	16.4	32
Willard Dewveall	59-64					204	3304	16.2	27
Buddy Dial	59-66	4	14	3.5	0	261	5436	20.8	44
Bo Dickinson	60-64	189	693	3.7	4	86	886	10.3	6

(All men with 25 or more rushing attempts or 10 or more receptions)

Name	Years	RUSHING Att.	Yards	Avg.	TD	RECEIVING Rec.	Yards	Avg.	TD
Chuck Dicus	71-72	2	−13	−6.5	0	24	316	13.2	3
Mike Ditka	61-72	2	2	1.0	0	427	5812	13.6	43
Hewritt Dixon	63-70	772	3090	4.0	15	263	2821	10.7	13
Al Dodd	67,69-71,73	9	50	5.6	0	99	1673	16.9	2
Marty Domres	69-73	96	447	4.7	7				
Oscar Donahue	62					16	285	17.8	1
Dick Dorsey	62					21	344	16.4	2
Glenn Doughty	72-73	12	129	10.8	0	28	618	22.1	4
Merrill Douglas	58-62	54	213	3.9	2	4	26	6.5	0
Bobby Douglass	69-73	332	2207	6.6	18				
Boyd Dowler	59-69,71	2	28	14.0	0	474	7270	15.3	40
Doug Dressler	70-72	200	846	4.2	7	58	493	8.5	1
Elbert Dubenion	60-68	46	326	7.1	3	296	5309	17.9	35
Paul Dudley	62-63	38	121	3.2	0	10	120	12.0	1
Fred Dugan	58-63	1	−9	−9.0	0	153	2226	14.5	13
Bobby Duhon	68,70-72	221	840	3.8	4	68	717	10.5	1
Jubilee Dunbar	73	3	3	1.0	0	23	447	19.4	4
Perry Lee Dunn	64-69	214	653	3.1	6	42	408	9.7	1
Billy Joe DuPree	73	2	2	1.0	0	29	392	13.5	5
Henry Dyer	66,68-70	82	256	3.1	1	14	160	11.4	1
Rick Eber	68-70					11	184	16.7	1
Nick Eddy	68-70,72	152	523	3.4	3	24	237	9.9	2
Cid Edwards	68-73	606	2672	4.4	15	120	1304	10.9	3
Larry Elkins	66-67	2	19	9.5	0	24	315	13.1	3
Willie Ellison	67-73	764	3312	4.3	22	99	824	8.3	6
John Embree	69-70					33	519	15.7	5
Hunter Enis	60-62	30	25	0.8	5				
Bill Enyart	69-71	105	387	3.7	1	54	421	7.8	3
Pat Epperson	60					11	99	9.0	0
Sam Etcheverry	61-62	41	78	1.9	0				
Charlie Evans	71-73	173	565	3.3	10	52	426	8.2	1
George Farmer	70-73	4	6	1.5	0	106	1832	17.3	10
Mel Farr	67-73	739	3072	4.2	26	146	1374	9.4	10
Bo Farrington	60-63	1	−2	−2.0	0	55	881	16.0	7
Bobby Felts	65-67	66	207	3.1	2	5	29	5.8	0
Bob Ferguson	62-63	66	209	3.2	1	4	13	3.3	0
Charley Ferguson	61-63,65-66,68-69					62	1168	18.8	13
Joe Ferguson	73	48	147	3.1	2	1	−3	−3.0	0
Paul Flatley	63-70					306	4905	16.0	24
George Fleming	61	31	112	3.6	1	10	49	4.9	0
Marv Fleming	63-73					156	1820	11.7	15
Tom Flores	60-61,63-69	101	142	1.4	5				
Charlie Flowers	60-62	111	416	3.7	4	35	383	10.9	1
Lee Folkins	61-65	1	9	9.0	0	80	1042	13.0	10
Fred Ford	60	38	194	5.1	2	1	5	5.0	0
Garrett Ford	68	41	186	4.5	1	6	40	6.7	0
Jamie Ford	71-72	104	407	3.9	2	8	63	7.9	0
Chuck Foreman	73	182	801	4.4	4	37	362	9.8	2
Gene Foster	65-70	445	1613	3.6	4	99	904	9.1	3
Willmer Fowler	60-61	94	372	4.0	1	10	99	9.9	0
Al Frazier	61-63	62	278	4.5	2	58	1010	17.4	7
Charley Frazier	62-70	4	5	1.3	0	209	3461	16.6	30
Willie Frazier	64-72	6	118	19.7	1	206	3060	14.9	35
Tucker Frederickson	65,67-71	651	2209	3.4	9	128	1011	7.9	8
Jean Fugett	72-73	4	36	9.0	0	16	262	16.4	3
Charley Fuller	61-62	38	134	3.5	0	17	344	20.2	2
John Fuqua	69-73	580	2527	4.4	17	110	1029	9.4	3
Roman Gabriel	62-73	327	1156	3.5	29	1	−5	−5.0	0
Bob Gaiters	61-63	168	673	4.0	6	17	175	10.3	2
Willie Galimore	57-63	670	2985	4.5	26	87	1201	13.8	10
R. C. Gamble	68-69	94	346	3.7	1	18	129	7.2	1
Billy Gambrell	63-68	7	41	5.9	0	116	1931	16.6	18
Carl Garrett	69-73	712	2890	4.1	20	130	1450	11.2	3
J. D. Garrett	64-67	116	434	3.7	3	17	169	9.9	2
Mike Garrett	66-73	1308	5481	4.2	35	238	2010	8.4	13
Gary Garrison	66-73	9	−1	−0.1	0	334	6252	18.7	50
Walt Garrison	66-73	786	3457	4.4	25	148	1541	10.4	8
Larry Garron	60-68	763	2981	3.9	14	185	2502	13.5	26
Prentice Gautt	60-67	629	2466	3.9	11	79	901	11.4	6
Jack Gehrke	68-69,71-72	1	2	2.0	0	14	254	18.1	0
Pete Gent	64-68	2	−5	−2.5	0	68	989	14.5	4
Jim Gibbons	58-68					287	3561	12.4	20
Cookie Gilchrist	62-67	1010	4293	4.3	37	110	1135	10.3	6
Walker Gillette	70-73					65	962	14.8	5
John Gilliam	67-73	30	242	8.1	2	274	5276	19.3	33
Hubert Ginn	70-73	70	285	4.1	1	4	25	6.3	0
Paul Gipson	69-71,73	123	491	4.0	1	21	240	11.4	3
Bob Gladieux	69-72	65	239	3.7	0	25	252	10.1	0
Chip Glass	69-73					31	619	20.0	5
Glenn Glass	62-66					15	201	13.4	0
Leland Glass	72-73	2	13	6.5	0	26	380	14.6	1
Al Goldstein	60	3	−2	−0.7	1	27	354	13.1	1
Ron Goodwin	63-68	2	−22	−11.0	0	78	1079	13.8	9
Dick Gordon	65-73	14	65	4.6	0	241	3579	14.9	36
Jim Grabowski	66-71	475	1731	3.6	8	82	675	8.2	3
Art Graham	63-68	1	−5	−5.0	0	199	3107	15.6	20
Hoyle Granger	66-72	805	3653	4.5	19	134	1339	10.0	5
Mel Gray	71-73	2	56	28.0	0	50	1109	22.2	11
Ernie Green	62-68	668	3204	4.8	15	195	2036	10.4	20
Johnny Green	60-63	77	−106	−1.4	6	1	0	0.0	0
Tom Greene	60-61	16	−27	−1.7	0				
Jim Greer	60					22	284	12.9	1
Ben Gregory	68	52	283	5.4	1	5	21	4.2	0
Bob Gresham	71-73	352	1164	3.3	11	74	639	8.6	1
Bob Griese	67-73	168	691	4.1	5				

Name	Years	RUSHING Att.	Yards	Avg.	TD	RECEIVING Rec.	Yards	Avg.	TD
Bob Grim	67-73	8	137	17.1	0	126	1901	15.1	12
Bill Groman	60-65	1	2	2.0	1	174	3481	20.0	36
Earl Gros	62-70	821	3157	3.8	28	142	1255	8.8	10
Ralph Guglielmi	55,58-63	177	633	3.6	2				
John Hadl	62-73	302	1018	3.4	15	3	−9	−3.0	0
Mike Haffner	68-71	3	3	1.0	0	59	991	16.8	7
Roger Hagberg	65-69	194	766	3.9	4	58	645	11.1	4
Mac Haik	67-71	4	28	7.0	0	76	1149	15.1	9
Ken Hall	59-61	51	212	4.2	0	8	118	14.8	2
Tom Hall	62-69	4	−4	−1.0	0	103	1441	14.0	8
Mal Hammack	55,57-66	320	1278	4.0	7	27	255	9.4	0
Dave Hampton	69-73	688	2779	4.0	17	73	793	10.9	5
Charley Hardy	60-62					54	840	15.6	7
Steve Harkey	71-72	65	191	2.9	0	14	142	10.1	0
Jack Harper	67-68	41	197	4.8	1	11	212	19.3	3
Charlie Harraway	66-73	822	3019	3.7	20	158	1304	8.3	7
Billy Harris	68-69,71	60	158	2.6	0	5	131	26.2	1
Franco Harris	72-73	376	1753	4.7	13	31	249	8.0	1
Dwight Harrison	71-73	6	45	7.5	0	20	281	14.1	2
Jim Harrison	71-73	272	1009	3.7	3	31	248	8.0	3
Jim Hart	66-73	82	113	1.4	11				
Pete Hart	60	25	113	4.5	0	3	19	6.3	0
Sam Havrilak	69-73	73	289	4.0	3	50	738	14.8	4
Alex Hawkins	59-68	208	787	3.8	10	129	1751	13.6	12
Ben Hawkins	66-73	10	8	0.8	0	261	4764	18.3	32
Bob Hayes	65-73	22	70	3.2	2	358	7177	20.0	70
Luther Hayes	61					14	280	20.0	3
Ray Hayes	61	73	319	4.4	2	16	121	8.1	0
Wendell Hayes	63,65-73	931	3552	3.8	26	157	1438	9.2	7
Abner Haynes	60-67	1036	4630	4.5	46	287	3538	12.3	20
Gene Heeter	63-65					22	327	14.9	2
John Henderson	65-72					108	1735	16.1	10
Jon Henderson	68-70					28	390	13.9	6
Charley Hennigan	60-66					410	6823	16.6	51
Ken Herock	63-69					63	924	14.7	4
Don Herrmann	69-73	3	9	3.0	0	155	1952	12.6	15
Mack Herron	73	61	200	3.3	2	18	265	14.7	1
Bo Hickey	67	73	263	3.6	4	7	36	5.1	1
Don Highsmith	70-73	94	327	3.5	2	12	143	11.9	0
Calvin Hill	69-73	981	4165	4.2	32	127	1225	9.6	6
Fred Hill	65-71	1	5	5.0	0	85	1005	11.8	5
Ike Hill	70-71,73	3	−14	−4.7	0	15	174	11.6	1
J. D. Hill	71-73	2	13	6.5	0	92	1392	15.1	7
Jerry Hill	61,63-70	606	2668	4.4	22	117	970	8.3	3
King Hill	58-69	88	306	3.5	9				
Mack Lee Hill	64-65	230	1203	5.2	6	40	408	10.2	3
John Hilton	65-73	1	15	15.0	0	144	2047	14.2	16
Eddie Hinton	69-73	11	109	9.9	2	109	1786	16.4	10
Dick Hoak	61-70	1132	3965	3.5	25	146	1452	9.9	8
Ron Holliday	73	6	70	11.7	0	14	182	13.0	0
Robert Holmes	68-73	620	2468	4.0	23	112	977	8.7	4
Dennis Homan	68-72	2	−3	−1.5	0	37	619	16.7	2
Fair Hooker	69-73					125	1797	14.4	7
Roy Hopkins	67-70	232	826	3.6	7	50	529	10.6	1
Sam Horner	60-62	118	355	3.0	0	17	219	12.9	1
Paul Hornung	57-62,64-66	893	3711	4.2	50	130	1480	11.4	12
Rich Houston	69-73	3	13	4.3	0	65	1121	17.2	7
Marv Hubbard	69-73	665	3235	4.9	16	61	416	6.8	1
Brad Hubbert	67-70	287	1270	4.4	9	42	312	7.4	2
Chuck Hughes	67-71					15	262	17.5	0
Dennis Hughes	70-71	1	−8	−8.0	0	24	332	13.8	3
George Hughley	65	37	175	4.7	0	9	93	10.3	1
Mike Hull	68-73	77	207	2.7	1	29	127	4.4	0
Scott Hunter	71-73	51	90	1.8	10				
Tom Hutchinson	63-66					19	409	21.5	2
John Isenbarger	70-73	27	80	3.0	0	21	291	13.9	2
Bobby Jackson	62-65	184	624	3.4	14	32	333	10.4	2
Frank Jackson	61-67	121	790	6.5	7	188	2955	15.7	24
Harold Jackson	68-73	37	114	3.1	0	255	4367	17.1	34
Leroy Jackson	62-63	52	142	2.7	0	10	253	25.3	0
Allen Jacobs	65-67	91	301	3.3	1	10	69	6.9	0
Dick James	56-65	502	1930	3.8	19	104	1669	16.0	15
Po James	72-73	218	743	3.4	1	37	250	6.8	1
Roy Jefferson	65-73	25	188	7.5	0	366	6266	17.1	44
Ron Jessie	71-73	6	31	5.2	1	48	875	18.2	7
Billy Joe	63-68	539	2013	3.7	15	77	589	7.6	4
Charley Johnson	61-73	182	521	2.9	10				
Curley Johnson	60-69	64	209	3.3	1	32	370	11.6	3
Essex Johnson	68-73	598	2849	4.8	17	88	1260	14.3	9
Jim Johnson	61-73					40	690	17.3	4
John Henry Johnson	54-66	1571	6803	4.3	48	186	1478	7.9	7
Randy Johnson	66-73	107	538	5.0	9				
Ron Johnson	69-73	990	3738	3.8	31	155	1526	9.8	12
Rudy Johnson	64-66	25	60	2.4	1	8	70	8.8	0
Charlie Joiner	69-73	3	14	4.7	0	103	1827	17.7	12
Clint Jones	67-73	602	2178	3.6	20	38	431	11.3	0
Greg Jones	70-71	47	166	3.5	1	24	202	8.4	1
Harry Jones	67-70	44	85	1.9	0	9	131	14.6	0
Homer Jones	64-70	17	146	8.6	1	224	4986	22.3	36
Jim Jones	65-68	8	24	3.0	0	69	1182	17.1	11
Les Josephson	64-67,69-73	786	3372	4.3	17	194	1970	10.2	11
Steve Junker	57,59-62					48	639	13.3	6
Sonny Jurgensen	57-73	177	499	2.8	15	1	−3	−3.0	0
Joe Kapp	67-70	119	611	5.1	5				
Jim Kelly	64-65,67					31	531	17.1	5

Lifetime Statistics 1960-1973 Players Section 2 - **RUSHING and RECEIVING** (continued)
(All men with 25 or more rushing attempts or 10 or more receptions)

Name	Years	RUSHING Att.	Yards	Avg.	TD	RECEIVING Rec.	Yards	Avg.	TD
Leroy Kelly	64-73	1727	7274	4.2	74	190	2281	12.0	13
Jack Kemp	57,60-67,69	394	796	2.0	40				
Leroy Keyes	69-73	125	369	3.0	3	30	270	9.0	0
Jim Kiick	68-73	911	3370	3.7	27	203	2055	10.1	2
Billy Kilmer	61-62,64,66-73	321	1434	4.5	20	27	288	10.7	1
Claude King	61-62	33	194	5.9	3	8	125	15.6	1
Phil King	58-66	569	2192	3.9	7	86	951	11.1	9
Jeff Kinney	72-73	88	250	2.8	2	15	171	11.4	0
Bob Klein	69-73	4	14	3.5	0	68	804	11.8	8
Roger Kochman	63	47	232	4.9	0	4	148	37.0	1
Dave Kocourek	60-68					249	4090	16.4	24
Dave Kopay	64-72	235	876	3.7	3	77	593	7.7	4
Gary Kosins	72-73	27	70	2.6	0	6	23	3.8	1
Dick Kotite	67-69,71-72					17	213	12.5	5
Walt Kowalczyk	58-61	103	264	2.6	2	34	256	7.5	1
Ernie Koy	65-70	414	1723	4.2	9	76	498	6.6	6
Ted Koy	70-73	1	9	9.0	0	11	142	12.9	1
Kent Kramer	66-67,69-73					45	576	12.8	8
Ron Kramer	57,59-67	6	9	1.5	0	229	3272	14.3	16
Rich Kreitling	59-64	2	−13	−6.5	0	123	1775	14.4	17
Joe Kulbacki	60	41	108	2.6	1	2	9	4.5	0
Ralph Kurek	65-70	121	434	3.6	2	26	299	11.5	0
Ted Kwalick	69-73	19	175	9.2	0	151	2324	15.4	21
Ron Lamb	68-72	55	163	3.0	0	8	97	12.1	0
Pete Lammons	66-72	0	3	–	0	185	2364	12.8	14
Daryle Lamonica	63-73	164	643	3.9	14				
Greg Landry	68-73	274	1953	7.1	17				
MacArthur Lane	68-73	751	3085	4.1	19	123	1264	10.3	3
Izzy Lang	64-69	245	873	3.6	4	63	554	8.8	4
Jack Larscheid	60-61	100	400	4.0	1	24	198	8.3	1
Pete Larson	67-68	69	216	3.1	2	20	191	9.6	1
Odell Lawson	70-71,73	70	130	1.9	0	13	108	8.3	0
Roger Lawson	72-73	57	176	3.1	1	17	180	10.6	0
Monte Ledbetter	67-69					18	314	17.4	3
Bob Lee	69-73	53	110	2.1	2				
Jacky Lee	60-69	82	150	1.8	3	1	−1	−1.0	0
Billy LeFear	72-73	29	141	4.9	0	5	38	7.6	0
Charlie Leigh	68-69,71-73	71	372	5.2	2	9	−4	−0.4	0
Darrell Lester	64-66	38	102	2.7	0	2	26	13.0	1
Jerry LeVias	69-73	19	161	8.5	0	135	2034	15.1	14
Dan Lewis	58-66	800	3205	4.0	19	99	1162	11.7	5
Frank Lewis	71-73	4	67	16.8	0	53	844	15.9	8
Gary Lewis	64-70	343	1421	4.1	13	72	604	8.4	5
Keith Lincoln	61-68	759	3383	4.5	19	165	2250	13.6	19
Mike Lind	63-66	222	661	3.0	8	52	427	8.2	1
Jim Lindsey	66-72	178	566	3.2	6	56	632	11.3	4
Don Lisbon	63-64	164	561	3.4	0	34	363	10.7	3
Pete Liske	64,69-72	38	141	3.7	2				
Floyd Little	67-73	1399	5566	4.0	40	157	2060	13.1	7
Andy Livingston	64-65,67-70	291	1216	4.2	7	46	474	10.3	3
Mike Livingston	68-73	58	368	6.3	2				
J. W. Lockett	61-64	229	770	3.4	3	62	589	9.5	7
Oscar Lofton	60					19	360	18.9	4
Bob Long	64-70					98	1539	15.7	10
Joe Don Looney	64-67,69	214	724	3.4	11	26	171	6.6	2
Tony Lorick	64-69	548	2124	3.9	14	86	890	10.3	5
Billy Lott	58,60-63	246	1123	4.6	13	85	919	10.8	8
John Love	67,72					18	267	14.8	2
Paul Lowe	60-61,63-69	1026	4995	4.9	40	111	1045	9.4	7
Dick Lucas	58,60-63					34	384	11.3	6
Richie Lucas	60-61	56	105	1.9	2	11	127	11.5	1
Lamar Lundy	57-69					35	584	16.7	6
Lenny Lyles	58-69	35	69	2.0	2	8	57	7.1	1
Fran Lynch	67-73	244	1042	4.3	9	29	324	11.2	1
Red Mack	61-66	4	−1	−0.2	0	52	1159	22.3	8
Dee Mackey	60-65					94	1352	14.4	8
John Mackey	63-72	19	127	6.7	0	331	5236	15.8	38
Jacque Mackinnon	61-70	86	377	4.4	2	112	2109	18.8	20
Jack Maitland	70-72	100	267	2.7	2	14	106	7.6	1
Bill Malinchak	66-72					34	496	14.6	4
Art Malone	70-73	416	1708	4.1	16	112	1180	10.5	6
Jim Mandich	70-73					39	492	12.6	9
Joe Marconi	56-66	673	2771	4.1	30	136	1326	9.8	9
Ed Marinaro	72-73	161	525	3.3	0	54	414	7.7	3
Aaron Marsh	68-69	4	8	2.0	0	27	439	16.3	4
Amos Marsh	61-67	750	3222	4.3	25	133	1384	10.4	7
Paul Martha	64-70	6	15	2.5	0	17	316	18.6	0
Billy Martin	64-48					58	705	12.2	4
Tommy Mason	61-71	1040	4203	4.0	32	214	2324	10.9	13
Bill Masters	67-73	18	114	6.3	0	127	1685	13.3	9
Bill Mathis	60-69	1044	3589	3.4	37	149	1775	11.9	9
Tom Matte	61-72	1200	4646	3.9	45	249	2869	11.5	12
Doug Mayberry	61-63	87	314	3.6	1	13	118	9.1	1
Don Maynard	58, 60-73	24	70	2.9	0	633	11834	18,7	88
Don McCall	67-70	229	884	3.9	6	37	390	10.5	3
Brendan McCarthy	68-69	59	175	3.0	1	20	184	9.2	2
Don McCauley	71-73	430	1435	3.3	6	58	448	7.7	2
Cliff McClain	70-73	79	445	5.6	2	13	151	11.6	0
Curtis McClinton	62-69	762	3124	4.1	18	154	1945	12.6	14
Earl McCullouch	68-73	8	29	3.6	0	123	2314	18.8	19
Larry McCutcheon	72-73	210	1097	5.2	2	30	289	9.6	3
Gary McDermott	68-69	54	108	2.0	3	20	115	5.8	1
Ray McDonald	67-68	52	223	4.3	4	10	60	6.0	0
Tommy McDonald	57-68	17	22	1.3	0	495	8380	16.9	84
Gerry McDougall	62-64, 68	104	469	4.5	6	22	248	11.3	0
Kay McFarland	62-66,68					45	682	15.2	4
Max McGee	54,57-67	12	121	10.1	0	345	6346	18.4	50
Rich McGeorge	70-73	1	3	3.0	0	49	805	16.4	9
Hugh McInnis	60-62,64,66	4	30	7.5	0	22	392	17.8	0
Marlin McKeever	61-73					133	1737	13.1	6
Hugh McKinnis	73	28	77	2.8	0	3	11	3.7	0
Bob McLeod	61-66					126	1926	15.3	19
John McMakin	72-73	1	0	0.0	0	34	472	13.9	1
Clifton McNeil	64-73	5	6	1.2	0	181	2734	15.1	22
Warren McVea	68-71,73	248	1186	4.8	11	38	358	9.4	2
Chuck Mercein	65-70	163	531	3.3	4	37	205	5.5	1
Don Meredith	60-68	242	1216	5.0	15				
Dale Messer	61-65					12	176	14.7	0
Frank Mestnik	60-61,63	200	767	3.8	14	15	53	3.5	1
Terry Metcalf	73	148	628	4.2	2	37	316	8.5	0
Tom Michel	64	39	129	3.3	0	1	14	14.0	0
Alan Miller	60-63,65	386	1395	3.6	9	130	1470	11.3	11
Bill Miller	62-64,66-68					141	1879	13.3	10
Gene Milton	68-69	9	108	12.0	0	21	322	15.3	1
Gene Mingo	60-70	185	777	4.2	8	52	454	8.7	4
Randy Minniear	67-70	96	316	3.3	5	19	148	7.8	1
George Mira	64-69,71	50	379	7.6	0				
Bobby Mitchell	58-68	513	2735	5.3	18	521	7954	15.3	65
Charley Mitchell	63-68	352	1142	3.2	5	62	550	8.9	3
Jim Mitchell	69-73	21	178	8.5	1	159	2472	15.5	19
Lydell Mitchell	72-73	298	1178	4.0	3	35	260	7.4	1
Stan Mitchell	66-70	173	548	3.2	4	42	533	12.7	5
Tom Mitchell	66,68-73	2	16	8.0	0	156	2087	13.4	20
Mike Montgomery	71-73	96	297	3.1	2	50	656	13.1	6
Ross Montgomery	69-70	77	281	3.6	0	16	83	5.2	0
Bob Moore	71-73					42	450	10.7	5
Joe Moore	71,73	87	281	3.2	0	5	39	7.8	0
Lenny Moore	56-67	1069	5174	4.8	63	363	6039	16.6	48
Tom Moore	60-67	660	2445	3.7	21	141	1152	8.2	10
Doug Moreau	66-69	1	−2	−2.0	0	73	926	12.7	6
Milt Morin	66-73	5	41	8.2	0	243	3859	15.9	13
Earl Morrall	56-73	230	834	3.6	8				
Johnny Morris	58-67	224	1040	4.6	5	356	5059	14.2	31
Larry Morris	55-57,59-66	40	148	3.7	1				
Mercury Morris	69-73	479	2788	5.8	24	42	449	10.7	0
Joe Morrison	59-72	677	2474	3.7	18	395	4993	12.6	47
Reece Morrison	68-73	160	526	3.3	2	14	210	15.0	2
Craig Morton	65-73	74	246	3.3	6				
Haven Moses	68-73	10	32	3.2	1	189	3383	17.9	25
Roland Moss	69-71					11	155	14.1	1
Herb Mul-Key	72-73	41	175	4.3	1	4	66	16.5	0
Bill Munson	64-73	106	503	4.7	2				
Bill Murphy	68					18	268	14.9	0
Chip Myers	67,69-73					135	1915	14.2	7
Joe Namath	65-73	47	123	2.6	6				
Jim Nance	65-71,73	1341	5401	4.0	45	133	870	6.5	1
Bill Nelsen	63-72	84	89	1.1	2	1	−5	−5.0	0
Tom Neumann	63	44	148	3.4	0	10	48	4.8	0
Robert Newhouse	72-73	112	552	4.9	2	10	95	9.5	1
Bob Newland	71-73	1	6	6.0	0	97	1387	14.3	6
Jim Ninowski	58-69	92	367	4.0	10				
Kent Nix	67-72	43	145	3.4	2				
George Nock	69-72	192	556	2.9	8	24	190	7.9	3
Terry Nofsinger	61-67	31	65	2.1	3				
Karl Noonan	66-71	2	−20	−10.0	0	136	1798	13.2	17
Pettis Norman	62-73	23	198	8.6	0	183	2492	13.6	15
Don Norton	60-66	2	−3	−1.5	0	228	3486	15.3	27
Don Nottingham	71-73	270	1106	4.1	9	43	305	7.1	0
Tom Nowatzke	65-72	361	1249	3.5	13	100	605	6.1	4
Jim O'Brien	70-73	3	9	3.0	0	14	305	21.8	2
Riley Odoms	72-73	10	125	12.5	0	64	949	14.8	8
Ray Ogden	65-73	1	12	12.0	0	53	885	16.7	4
Bill Olds	73	26	100	3.8	2	2	−4	−2.0	0
Joe Orduna	72-73	72	233	3.2	2	10	50	5.0	1
Jimmy Orr	58-70	15	122	8.1	0	400	7914	19.8	66
Dave Osborn	65-73	1010	3712	3.7	24	143	1220	8.5	7
Tom Osborne	60-61					29	343	11.8	2
Jim Otis	70-73	204	721	3.5	1	47	300	6.4	2
R. C. Owens	57-64	1	23	23.0	1	206	3285	15.9	22
Steve Owens	70-73	538	2077	3.9	17	75	703	9.4	2
Bob Paremore	63-64	36	107	3.0	0	6	89	14.8	1
Babe Parilli	52-53, 56-58, 60-69	394	1416	3.6	24				
Billy Parks	71-73	5	77	15.4	0	102	1488	14.6	6
Dave Parks	64-73	4	-10	-2.5	0	360	5619	15.6	4
Dan Pastorini	71-73	95	447	4.7	5				
Lloyd Pate	70	46	162	3.5	1	19	103	5.4	0
Wayne Patrick	68-72	264	1084	4.1	5	96	745	7.8	1
Clarence Peaks	57-65	951	3660	3.8	21	190	1793	9.4	3
Barry Pearson	72-73					23	317	13.8	3
Drew Pearson	73					22	388	17.6	2
Preston Pearson	67-73	546	2085	3.8	4	54	703	13.0	6
Art Perkins	62-63	85	251	3.0	6	22	144	6.5	0
Don Perkins	61-68	1500	6217	4.1	42	146	1310	9.0	3
Ray Perkins	67-71	10	77	7.7	0	93	1538	16.5	11
Jess Phillips	68-73	622	2523	4.1	8	98	596	6.1	2
Jim Phillips	58-67					401	6044	15.1	34
Mike Phipps	70-73	137	780	5.7	10				
Brian Piccolo	66-69	258	927	3.6	4	58	537	9.3	
Nick Pietrosante	59-67	955	4026	4.2	28	131	1391	10.6	2
Cyril Pinder	68-73	428	1709	4.0	7	67	556	8.3	0

Lifetime Statistics 1960-1973 Players Section 2 - RUSHING and RECEIVING (continued)
(All men with 25 or more rushing attempts or 10 or more receptions)

Name	Years	RUSHING				RECEIVING			
		Att.	Yards	Avg.	TD	Rec.	Yards	Avg.	TD
Elijah Pitts	61-71	514	1788	3.5	28	104	1245	12.0	6
Frank Pitts	65-73	27	267	9.9	1	172	2874	16.7	27
Dave Pivec	66-69					14	146	10.4	1
Milt Plum	57-69	217	531	2.4	13	1	20	20.0	0
Jim Plunkett	71-73	125	649	5.2	6				
Ray Poage	63-65,67-71	3	32	10.7	0	145	2309	15.9	13
Ed Podolak	69-73	733	2793	3.8	19	163	1349	8.3	3
Bob Poole	64-67					19	223	11.7	0
Bucky Pope	64,66-68	2	11	5.5	0	34	952	28.0	13
Dickie Post	67-71	608	2605	4.3	17	96	903	9.4	2
Art Powell	59-68					479	8046	16.8	81
Gene Prebola	60-63					133	1823	13.7	6
Sam Price	66-68	82	313	3.8	1	10	70	7.0	1
Joe Profit	71-73	133	471	3.5	3	14	130	9.3	0
Greg Pruitt	73	61	369	6.0	4	9	110	12.2	1
Frank Quayle	69	57	183	3.2	0	11	167	15.2	0
Jeff Queen	69-73	176	589	3.3	5	53	654	12.3	4
Warren Rabb	60-62	50	124	2.5	3				
Bill Rademacher	64-70	1	−13	−13.0	0	24	282	11.8	3
Sonny Randle	59-68					365	5996	16.4	65
Ahmad Rashad	72-73	9	44	4.9	0	59	909	15.4	6
Eddie Ray	70-73	111	496	4.5	9	20	206	10.3	2
Ron Rector	66-67	33	167	5.1	0	6	22	3.7	0
Alvin Reed	67-73	1	0	0.0	0	208	2942	14.1	11
Bob Reed	62-63	27	110	4.1	0	17	174	10.2	1
Oscar Reed	68-73	428	1753	4.1	8	77	577	7.5	2
Dan Reeves	65-72	535	1990	3.7	25	129	1693	13.1	17
Jerry Reichow	56-57,59-64	20	105	5.3	0	172	2579	15.0	24
Bob Renn	61	1	14	14.0	0	18	268	14.9	1
Lance Rentzel	65-72	25	205	8.2	2	250	4430	17.7	37
Pete Retzlaff	56-66	6	−4	−0.7	0	452	7412	16.4	47
M. C. Reynolds	58-62	88	419	4.8	4				
Tom Reynolds	72-73					15	279	18.6	2
Jerry Rhome	65-67,69-71	26	91	3.5	1				
Perry Richards	57-62					39	558	14.3	4
Gloster Richardson	67-73	5	−9	−1.8	0	83	1710	20.6	16
Jerry Richardson	59-60					15	171	11.4	4
Mike Richardson	69-71	125	452	3.6	2	38	398	10.5	1
Willie Richardson	63-71	2	27	13.5	0	195	2950	15.1	25
Pat Richter	63-70	1	−9	−9.0	0	99	1315	13.3	14
John Riggins	71-73	521	2195	4.2	12	79	619	7.8	3
Preston Riley	70-72					21	331	15.8	1
Johnny Roach	56,59-64	42	99	2.4	2				
Bo Roberson	61-66	168	584	3.5	6	176	2917	16.6	12
C. R. Roberts	59-62	155	637	4.1	4	21	132	6.3	0
Walter Roberts	64-67,69-70	5	45	9.0	0	67	1218	18.2	9
Jerry Robinson	62-65	3	20	6.7	0	49	799	16.3	4
Johnny Robinson	60-71	150	658	4.4	6	77	1228	15.9	9
Paul Robinson	68-73	737	2947	4.0	24	90	612	6.8	2
Virgil Robinson	71-72	34	97	2.9	1	12	53	4.4	1
John Roderick	66-68					11	156	14.2	1
Willie Rodgers	72	71	204	2.9	2	6	61	10.2	0
Johnny Roland	66-73	1015	3750	3.7	28	153	1430	9.3	6
Dave Rolle	60	130	501	3.9	2	21	122	5.8	1
Tony Romeo	61-67					116	1833	15.8	10
Dave Ross	60					10	122	12.2	1
Reggie Rucker	70-73	6	18	3.0	0	110	1676	15.2	8
Ed Rutkowski	63-68	69	250	3.6	1	63	981	15.6	4
Frank Ryan	58-70	310	1358	4.4	6	0	31	—	1
Tom Rychlec	58,60-63	1	−18	−18.0	0	87	1091	12.5	3
Saint Saffold	68	1	21	21.0	0	16	172	10.8	0
Charlie Sanders	68-73	4	−6	−1.5	0	208	3084	14.8	19
Theron Sapp	59-65	202	763	3.8	5	23	247	10.7	0
George Sauer	65-70	4	23	5.8	0	309	4965	16.1	28
Gale Sayers	65-71	1001	4956	5.0	39	112	1307	11.7	9
Charlie Scales	60-66	157	603	3.8	4	21	144	6.9	0
Bob Scarpitto	61-68	10	214	21.4	1	156	2651	17.0	27
Larry Schreiber	71-73	194	763	3.9	2	46	460	10.0	2
Randy Schultz	66-68	82	301	3.7	2	26	220	8.5	0
Bo Scott	69-73	531	2038	3.8	18	105	804	7.7	6
Larry Seiple	67-73	11	127	11.5	0	52	713	13.7	6
Ron Sellers	69-73					112	2184	19.5	18
Jim Seymour	70-72	1	−9	−9.0	0	21	385	18.3	5
Paul Seymour	73					10	114	11.4	0
Ron Shanklin	70-73	5	2	0.4	0	147	2723	18.5	23
Dennis Shaw	70-73	92	432	4.7	0				
Glen Shaw	60,62-64	47	148	3.1	3	8	146	18.3	1
Rod Sherman	67-73	4	20	5.0	0	105	1576	15.0	5
Tom Sherman	68-69	27	94	3.5	0				
Dick Shiner	64-71,73	58	161	2.8	2				
Roy Shivers	66-72	176	680	3.9	10	38	400	10.5	4
Bill Shockley	60-62,68	42	165	3.9	0	11	96	8.7	2
Del Shofner	57-67	4	1	0.3	0	349	6470	18.5	51
Don Shy	67-73	457	1577	3.5	10	76	835	11.0	3
Les Shy	66-70	144	523	3.6	3	23	273	11.9	1
Mike Siani	72-73					73	1238	17.0	8
Jerry Simmons	65-69,71-73	3	−3	−1.0	0	128	1944	15.2	7
O. J. Simpson	69-73	1108	5181	4.7	30	94	912	9.7	3
Mickey Slaughter	63-66	73	263	3.6	1				
Tom Smiley	68-70	120	312	2.6	4	24	109	4.5	1
Allen Smith	66-67	31	148	4.8	0	1	1	1.0	0
Barry Smith	73	1	5	5.0	0	15	233	15.5	2
Bobby Smith	64-66	129	536	4.2	5	21	214	10.2	0
Charlie Smith	68-73	794	3157	4.0	23	133	1496	11.2	9
Dave Smith	60-64	328	1368	4.2	11	80	772	9.7	7

Name	Years	RUSHING				RECEIVING			
		Att.	Yards	Avg.	TD	Rec.	Yards	Avg.	TD
Dave Smith	70-73	2	−4	−2.0	0	109	1457	13.4	7
Gordon Smith	61-65	1	2	2.0	0	57	1277	22.4	13
Jackie Smith	63-73	38	327	8.6	3	434	7188	16.6	34
J. D. Smith	56-66	1100	4672	4.2	40	127	1122	8.8	6
J. D. Smith	60-61	66	220	3.3	6	17	194	11.4	1
Jerry Smith	65-73	7	51	7.3	0	338	4470	13.2	52
Larry Smith	69-73	473	1908	4.0	11	126	1039	8.2	4
Ralph Smith	62-69	2	26	13.0	0	41	549	13.4	5
Ron Smith	65-73	8	42	5.3	0	11	227	20.6	0
Russ Smith	67-70	213	915	4.3	10	23	265	11.5	0
Mark Smolinski	61-68	421	1323	3.1	9	103	841	8.2	7
Norm Snead	61-73	196	463	2.4	22				
Matt Snell	64-72	1057	4285	4.1	24	193	1375	7.1	7
Jack Snow	65-73	1	−10	−10.0	0	312	5529	17.7	41
Todd Snyder	70-72					24	330	13.8	2
Mike Sommer	58-61,63	78	253	3.2	2	9	166	18.4	0
Butch Songin	60-62	48	−90	−1.9	2				
Cotton Speyrer	72-73	1	1	1.0	0	25	425	17.0	4
Jack Spikes	60-67	408	1693	4.1	18	56	679	12.1	3
John Spilis	69-71					27	446	16.5	1
Steve Spurrier	67-73	34	119	3.5	2				
Ken Stabler	70-73	32	153	4.8	2				
Billy Stacy	59-63					12	241	20.1	1
Jon Staggers	70-73	6	30	5.0	1	47	756	16.1	5
Bart Starr	56-71	247	1308	5.3	15				
Roger Staubach	69-73	135	919	6.8	6				
Tom Stephens	60-64					41	506	12.3	5
Howard Stevens	73	45	183	4.1	2	4	39	9.8	0
Monte Stickles	60-68					222	3199	14.4	16
Jim Stiger	63-67	140	583	4.2	2	31	297	9.6	2
Darryl Stingley	73	6	64	10.7	0	23	339	14.7	2
Jim Stinnette	61-62	40	95	2.4	1	24	167	7.0	1
Donnie Stone	61-66	354	1352	3.8	10	91	859	9.4	7
Steve Stonebraker	62-68					12	227	18.9	1
Otto Stowe	71-73	3	28	9.3	0	41	733	17.9	9
Bob Stransky	60	28	78	2.8	0	3	11	3.7	0
Jim Strong	70-72	134	527	3.9	3	30	201	6.7	0
Morris Stroud	69-73					42	836	19.9	5
Pat Studstill	61-62,64-72	6	39	6.5	0	181	2840	15.7	18
Tom Sullivan	72-73	230	981	4.3	4	54	339	6.3	1
Karl Sweetan	66-70	56	307	5.5	2				
Jerry Tagge	72-73	23	59	2.6	3				
Mike Taliaferro	64-72	46	134	2.9	0				
Fran Tarkenton	61-73	572	3401	5.9	26	0	12	—	0
John Tarver	72-73	114	443	3.9	5	20	163	8.2	1
Altie Taylor	69-73	820	3127	3.8	15	122	1119	9.2	5
Charley Taylor	64-73	441	1489	3.4	11	528	7470	14.1	68
Jim Taylor	58-67	1941	8597	4.4	83	225	1756	7.8	10
Lionel Taylor	59-68	4	20	5.0	0	567	7195	12.7	45
Otis Taylor	65-73	29	155	5.3	3	386	6931	18.0	55
Steve Tensi	65-70	47	82	1.7	0				
Tony Teresa	58,60	139	608	4.4	6	35	393	11.2	4
Aaron Thomas	61-70	4	−10	−2.5	0	262	4554	17.4	37
Bob Thomas	71-73	99	481	4.9	3	18	146	8.1	1
Clendon Thomas	58-68	18	70	3.9	0	60	1046	17.4	4
Duane Thomas	70-71,73	358	1691	4.7	16	28	266	9.5	2
Earl Thomas	71-73	6	18	3.0	0	47	748	15.9	7
Gene Thomas	66-68	130	401	3.1	4	23	18.4	8.0	2
Jimmy Thomas	69-73	165	824	5.0	4	67	923	13.8	8
Speedy Thomas	69-72	8	22	2.8	1	93	1236	13.3	8
Rocky Thompson	71-73	68	217	3.2	1	16	85	5.3	0
Bill Thornton	63-65,67	93	544	5.8	2	13	68	5.2	0
Bubba Thornton	69					14	134	9.6	0
Steve Thurlow	64-68	314	1127	3.6	4	61	539	8.8	2
Jim Tiller	62	31	43	1.3	0	13	108	8.3	0
Bill Tobin	63	75	270	3.6	4	13	172	13.2	1
Larry Todd	65-70	138	625	4.5	5	51	522	10.2	2
Charley Tolar	60-66	907	3277	3.6	21	175	1266	7.2	2
John Tracey	59-67					20	303	15.2	0
Tom Tracy	56-64	808	2912	3.6	17	113	1468	13.0	14
Richard Trapp	68-69					26	274	10.5	0
Bill Triplett	62-63,65-72	681	2446	3.6	17	113	1055	9.3	5
Frank Tripucka	49-52,60-63	70	−125	−1.6	6				
Billy Truax	64-73					199	2458	12.4	17
Don Trull	64-69	123	428	3.5	14				
Bob Trumpy	68-73	1	−1	−1.0	0	216	3420	15.8	24
Bill Tucker	67-71	127	431	3.4	6	59	496	8.4	7
Bob Tucker	70-73	5	11	2.2	1	204	2807	13.8	18
Wendell Tucker	67-70					57	983	17.2	11
Bake Turner	62-70	2	13	6.5	0	220	3539	16.1	25
Cecil Turner	68-73	8	13	1.6	0	21	364	17.3	2
Clem Turner	69-72	74	270	3.6	2	21	114	5.4	1
Howard Twilley	66-73					150	2228	14.9	16
Johnny Unitas	56-73	450	1777	3.9	13	1	1	1.0	0
Ron Vander Kelen	63-67	26	116	4.5	1				
Bill Van Heusen	68-73	9	126	14.0	1	51	1017	19.9	6
Randy Vataha	71-73	2	−15	−7.5	0	96	1582	16.5	13
Stu Voigt	70-73	2	3	1.5	1	44	582	13.2	4
Jim Vollenweider	62-63	58	161	2.8	2	5	47	9.4	0
Billy Wade	54-66	318	1334	4.2	24	0	10	—	0
Harmon Wages	68-71,73	332	1321	4.0	5	85	765	9.0	5
Bob Wallace	68-72	8	45	5.6	0	109	1403	12.9	9
Ward Walsh	71-72	46	165	3.6	0	10	58	5.8	1
Joe Walton	57-63					178	2628	14.8	28
Larry Walton	69-73	9	93	10.3	1	117	1919	16.4	20

Lifetime Statistics – 1960-1973 Players   Section 2 – RUSHING and RECEIVING (continued)
(All men with 25 or more rushing attempts or 10 or more receptions)

Name	Years	Rushing Att.	Rushing Yards	Rushing Avg.	Rushing TD	Receiving Rec.	Receiving Yards	Receiving Avg.	Receiving TD
Paul Warfield	64-73	20	199	10.0	0	344	7165	20.8	75
Ernie Warlick	62-65					90	1551	17.2	4
Gene Washington	67-73					182	3237	17.8	26
Gene Washington	69-73	1	−4	−4.0	0	233	4219	18.1	33
Vic Washington	71-73	483	1813	3.8	14	112	948	8.5	5
Bob Waters	60-63	65	281	4.3	3				
Larry Watkins	69-73	294	1071	3.6	6	40	217	5.4	1
Tom Watkins	61-65,67-68	468	1791	3.8	10	55	590	10.7	4
Ken Webb	58-63	264	891	3.4	8	46	483	10.5	1
Claxton Welch	69-71,73	26	83	3.2	2	7	21	3.0	0
Joel Wells	61	65	216	3.3	1	6	31	5.2	1
Warren Wells	64,67-70	9	103	11.4	1	158	3655	23.1	42
Bob West	72-73	2	2	1.0	0	13	230	17.7	2
Mel West	61-62	81	338	4.2	3	14	147	10.5	0
Jim Whalen	65-71	1	0	0.0	0	197	3155	16.0	20
Ernie Wheelwright	64-70	387	1426	3.7	9	54	531	9.8	7
Freeman White	66-69					29	315	10.9	1
Jan White	71-72					25	278	11.1	2
John White	60-61					14	256	18.3	1
Lee White	68-72	123	389	3.2	0	16	143	8.9	1
A. D. Whitfield	65-68	222	981	4.4	3	67	702	10.5	3
J. R. Wilburn	66-70	7	54	7.7	0	123	1834	14.9	8
Ken Willard	65-73	1582	5930	3.7	45	273	2156	7.9	16
A. D. Williams	59-61					15	190	12.7	1
Dave Williams	67-73	6	69	11.5	0	183	2768	15.1	25
Joe Williams	71-72	52	139	2.7	1	19	175	9.2	0
Perry Williams	69-73	103	329	3.2	1	12	118	9.8	0
Travis Williams	67-71	289	1166	4.0	6	52	598	11.5	5
Fred Willis	71-73	440	1630	3.7	11	126	891	7.1	3
Ben Wilson	63-65,67	431	1589	3.7	9	47	487	10.4	2
Butch Wilson	63-69					25	317	12.7	3
George Wilson	66	27	137	5.1	0				
Bob Windsor	67-73	9	57	6.3	0	167	2123	12.7	13
Lloyd Winston	62-63	28	112	4.0	1	3	15	5.0	0
Dick Witcher	66-73					172	2359	13.7	14
Joe Womack	62	128	468	3.7	5	6	57	9.5	0
Dick Wood	62-66	26	45	1.7	4				
Gary Wood	64-69	75	419	5.6	6				
Al Woodall	69-71,73	58	217	3.7	0				
Tom Woodeshick	63-72	836	3577	4.3	21	126	1175	9.3	6
Elmo Wright	71-73	7	43	6.1	0	53	861	16.2	5
John Wright	68-69					12	130	10.8	2
Sam Wyche	68-72	44	303	6.9	3	1	5	5.0	0
Tom Yewcic	61-66	72	424	5.9	4	7	69	9.9	0
Charlie Young	73	4	24	6.0	1	55	854	15.5	6
Steve Zabel	70-73	1	−5	−5.0	0	10	123	12.3	3
Dan Zimmerman	73					22	220	10.0	3

Lifetime Statistics – 1960-1973 Players   Section 3– PUNT RETURNS and KICKOFF RETURNS
(All men with 25 or more Punt Returns or 25 or more Kickoff Returns)

Name	Years	Punt Returns No.	Punt Returns Yards	Punt Returns Avg.	Punt Returns TD	Kickoff Returns No.	Kickoff Returns Yards	Kickoff Returns Avg.	Kickoff Returns TD
Herb Adderley	61-72	1	0	0.0	0	120	3080	25.7	2
Margene Adkins	70-73	15	49	3.3	0	81	1784	22.0	0
Kermit Alexander	63-73	133	835	6.3	2	153	3586	23.4	0
Lance Alworth	62-72	29	309	10.7	0	10	216	21.6	0
Bobby Anderson	70-73					30	720	24.0	0
Dick Anderson	68-73	31	239	7.7	0	7	14	16.3	0
Donny Anderson	66-73	15	222	14.8	1	34	759	22.3	0
Max Anderson	68-69,71	19	142	7.5	0	43	1057	24.6	1
Jon Arnett	57-66	120	981	8.2	1	126	3110	24.7	2
Pete Athas	71-73	31	269	8.7	0				
Pervis Atkins	61-66	40	292	7.3	0	95	2124	22.4	0
Butch Atkinson	68-73	136	1183	8.7	3	74	1833	24.8	0
Joe Auer	64-68	14	141	10.1	0	51	1171	23.0	1
Bill Baird	63-69	88	787	8.9	1	13	290	22.3	0
Gary Ballman	62-73					66	1754	26.6	1
Lem Barney	67-73	107	1004	9.4	2	50	1274	25.5	1
Terry Barr	57-65	50	262	5.2	0	26	655	25.2	1
Tom Barrington	66-70	1	8	8.0	0	32	675	21.1	0
Odell Barry	64-65	37	359	9.7	1	73	1856	25.4	0
Dick Bass	60-69	24	263	11.0	1	54	1415	26.2	0
Mike Battle	69-70	53	352	6.6	0	71	1641	23.1	0
Craig Baynham	67-70,72					41	1035	25.2	0
Joe Bellino	65-67	19	148	7.8	0	43	905	21.0	0
Willie Belton	71-73	48	275	5.7	0	52	1230	23.7	0
Jim Bertelsen	72-73	42	491	11.7	0	5	103	20.6	0
Rodger Bird	66-68	94	1063	11.3	0	25	533	21.3	0
Charlie Bivins	60-67					78	1911	24.5	0
Sid Blanks	64-70	36	272	7.6	0	43	977	22.7	0
Ronnie Blye	68-69					54	1104	20.4	0
Emerson Boozer	66-73					37	872	23.6	1
Bill Bradley	69-73	76	560	7.4	0	23	489	21.3	0
Jimmy Brown	57-65					29	648	22.3	0
Ken Brown	70-73					37	847	22.9	0
Ray Brown	71-73	49	431	8.8	0				
Timmy Brown	59-68	71	639	9.0	1	184	4781	26.0	5
Tom Brown	64-69	27	151	5.6	1	7	167	23.9	0
Willie Brown	64-66	18	85	4.7	0	34	795	23.4	0
Bobby Bryant	68-73	49	272	5.6	0	22	437	19.9	0
Charlie Bryant	66-69					42	913	21.7	0
Hubie Bryant	70-72	47	183	3.9	0	10	252	25.2	0
Amos Bullocks	62-64,66					34	737	21.7	0
Ode Burrell	64-69	15	149	9.9	0	33	838	25.4	1
Leon Burton	60	12	93	7.8	0	31	897	28.9	2
Ron Burton	60-65	56	389	6.9	0	46	1119	24.3	1
Bill Butler	59-64	88	850	9.7	2	132	2886	21.9	0
Cannonball Butler	65-72					133	2931	22.0	1
Butch Byrd	64-71					86	600	7.0	1
Jamie Caleb	60-61,65	1	8	8.0	0	27	594	22.0	0
Bob Campbell	69	28	133	4.8	0	26	522	20.1	0
Billy Cannon	60-70	14	178	12.7	0	67	1704	25.4	1
Preston Carpenter	56-67	26	284	10.9	0	29	752	25.9	0
Larry Carwell	67-72	49	474	9.7	0	25	557	22.3	0
Tommy Casanova	72-73	45	408	9.1	1	1	34	34.0	0
Clarence Childs	64-68	6	40	6.7	0	134	3454	25.8	2
Dick Christy	58,60-63	67	905	13.5	4	117	2770	23.7	0
Earl Christy	66-68	34	222	6.5	0	58	1323	22.8	0
Hagood Clarke	64-68	65	583	9.0	2	16	330	20.6	0
Bert Coan	62-68					33	785	23.9	0
Linzy Cole	70-72	35	225	6.4	0	50	1290	25.8	0
Bobby Joe Conrad	58-69	51	462	9.1	2	33	813	24.6	0
Johnny Counts	62-63	8	33	4.1	0	31	891	28.7	1
Willie Crenshaw	64-70					27	515	19.1	0
Irv Cross	61-69	51	376	7.4	0	44	1227	27.9	0
Doug Cunningham	67-73	30	272	9.1	0	68	1613	23.7	0
Jay Cunningham	65-67	22	140	6.4	0	64	1372	21.4	0
Clem Daniels	60-68	8	103	12.9	0	57	1206	21.2	0
Ben Davis	67-68,70-73	27	240	8.9	1	35	860	24.6	0
Clarence Davis	71-73					45	1198	26.6	0
Joe Dawkins	70-73	1	0	0.0	0	27	613	22.7	0
Ted Dean	60-64	46	279	6.1	0	70	1553	22.2	0
Al Dodd	67,69-71,73	53	400	7.5	0	38	776	20.4	0
Eddie Dove	59-63	61	437	7.2	0	3	56	18.7	0
Elbert Dubenion	60-68	3	9	3.0	0	40	961	24.0	1
Bobby Duhon	68,70-72	40	286	7.2	1	40	716	17.9	0
Jim Duncan	69-71					42	1369	32.6	2
Speedy Duncan	64-73	199	2182	11.0	4	180	4539	25.2	0
Lenny Dunlap	71-73	27	291	10.8	0	13	299	23.0	0
Glen Edwards	71-73	57	538	9.4	0	11	226	20.5	0
Ken Ellis	70-73	54	396	7.3	1	36	802	22.3	0
Willie Ellison	67-73					42	1011	24.1	0
Dave Elmendorf	71-73	25	243	9.7	0	2	23	11.5	0
Chris Farasopoulos	71-73	50	445	8.9	1	51	1172	23.0	0
Bobby Felts	65-67	6	46	7.7	0	38	814	21.4	0
Pat Fischer	61-73	17	80	4.7	0	25	613	24.5	0
Mike Fitzgerald	66-67	2	4	2.0	0	26	541	20.8	0
George Fleming	61	3	24	8.0	0	29	588	20.3	0
Chris Fletcher	70-73	28	205	7.3	0	28	599	21.4	0
Tom Franckhauser	59-63	3	19	6.3	0	30	620	20.7	0
Al Frazier	61-63	26	305	11.7	1	44	1077	24.5	1
Johnny Fuller	68-73	25	114	4.6	0	10	186	18.6	0
Bob Gaiters	61-63					33	786	23.8	0
Willie Galimore	57-63					43	1100	25.6	1
Billy Gambrell	63-68	28	282	10.1	0	15	336	22.4	0
Ron Gardin	70-71	34	419	12.3	1	25	586	23.4	0
Bob Garner	60-63	28	252	9.0	0	1	8	8.0	0
Carl Garrett	69-73	43	487	11.3	0	108	2737	25.3	0
J. D. Garrett	64-67	3	47	15.7	0	48	1054	22.0	0
Mike Garrett	66-73	39	235	6.0	1	14	323	23.1	0
Walt Garrison	66-73					41	813	19.8	0
Larry Garron	60-68	1	23	23.0	0	89	2299	25.8	2
Claude Gibson	61-65	110	1381	12.6	3	17	268	15.8	0
John Gilliam	67-73	23	94	4.1	0	71	1798	25.3	2
Hubert Ginn	70-73					25	534	21.4	0
Freddy Glick	59-66	44	326	7.4	0	26	584	22.5	0
Dick Gordon	65-73	23	110	4.8	0	65	1571	24.2	0
Kenny Graham	64-70	29	238	8.2	0	7	172	24.6	0
Mel Gray	71-73	2	−4	−2.0	0	51	1191	23.4	0
Dave Grayson	61-70	10	78	7.8	0	110	2804	25.5	1
Ernie Green	62-68	11	110	10.0	0	32	648	20.3	0
Charlie Greer	68-73	42	336	8.0	1	2	41	20.5	0
Bob Gresham	71-73					30	783	26.1	1
Bob Grim	67-73	48	213	4.4	0	25	545	21.8	0
Dick Haley	59-64	20	87	4.4	0	37	729	19.7	0
Ken Hall	59-61	11	164	14.9	1	31	833	26.9	1
Dave Hampton	69-73					110	2877	26.2	3
Cliff Harris	70-73	39	227	5.8	0	62	1608	25.9	0
Dick Harris	60-65	27	251	9.3	0	3	49	16.3	0
Rickie Harris	65-72	128	1029	8.0	3	102	2326	22.8	0
Wendell Harris	62-67	27	275	10.2	0	12	293	24.4	0
Alex Hawkins	59-68	52	358	6.9	0	6	86	14.3	0

Lifetime Statistics - 1960-1973 Players Section 3 - **PUNT RETURNS and KICKOFF RETURNS** (continued)
(All men with 25 or more Punt Returns or 25 or more Kickoff Returns)

Name	Years	PUNT RETURNS No.	Yards	Avg.	TD	KICKOFF RETURNS No.	Yards	Avg.	TD
Bob Hayes	65-73	102	1147	11.2	3	23	581	25.3	0
Alvin Haymond	64-73	253	2148	8.5	1	170	4438	26.1	2
Abner Haynes	60-67	85	875	10.3	1	121	3025	25.0	1
Jon Henderson	68-70					30	589	19.6	0
Mack Herron	73	27	282	10.4	0	41	1092	26.6	1
Ike Hill	70-71,73	69	439	6.4	2	21	445	21.2	0
Robert Holmes	68-73					35	928	26.5	0
Sam Horner	60-62	6	19	3.2	0	39	828	21.2	0
Ken Houston	67-73	45	252	5.6	0	3	80	26.7	0
Rich Houston	69-73					35	800	22.9	0
Gene Howard	68-72	22	129	5.9	0	41	975	23.8	0
Bob Hudson	72-73	1	0	0.0	0	25	597	23.9	0
Bernie Jackson	72-73					42	1029	24.5	0
Frank Jackson	61-67	49	487	9.9	0	48	1284	26.8	0
Dick James	56-65	120	952	7.9	0	189	4676	24.7	0
Bobby Jancik	62-67	67	695	10.4	1	158	4185	26.5	0
Roy Jefferson	65-73	58	436	7.5	1	5	91	18.2	0
Ron Jessie	71-73					45	1182	26.3	2
Benny Johnson	70-73					28	550	19.6	0
Essex Johnson	68-73	51	303	5.9	0	36	749	20.8	0
Clint Jones	67-73					99	2426	24.5	1
Homer Jones	64-70					37	888	24.0	1
Leroy Kelly	64-73	94	990	10.5	3	76	1784	23.5	0
Brady Keys	61-68	65	646	9.9	0	47	1113	23.7	0
Phil King	58-66					30	592	19.7	0
Ernie Koy	65-70					25	439	17.6	0
Larry Krause	70-71,73					34	858	25.2	1
Bruce Laird	72-73	49	375	7.7	0	53	1390	26.2	0
Jack Larscheid	60-61	12	106	8.8	0	39	1106	28.4	0
Chuck Latourette	67-68,70-71	64	537	8.4	1	59	1491	25.3	0
Odell Lawson	70-71,73	1	0	0.0	0	27	593	22.0	0
Charlie Leigh	68-69,71-73	50	368	7.4	0	35	831	23.7	0
Jerry LeVias	69-73	83	646	7.8	0	88	2097	23.8	0
Dan Lewis	58-66					30	535	17.8	0
Gary Lewis	64-70	1	3	3.0	0	32	784	24.5	0
Keith Lincoln	61-68	25	342	13.7	1	39	1018	26.1	1
Floyd Little	67-73	77	859	11.2	2	80	2045	25.6	0
Spider Lockhart	65-73	62	314	5.1	0	1	19	19.0	0
Jerry Logan	63-72	62	577	9.3	1	12	217	18.1	0
Joe Don Looney	64-67,69					29	652	22.5	0
Tony Lorick	64-69					40	1022	25.6	0
John Love	67,72	21	34	1.6	0	25	589	23.6	1
Paul Lowe	60-61,63-69	2	0	0.0	0	63	1411	22.4	0
Lenny Lyles	58-69					81	2161	26.7	3
John Mallory	68-71	39	294	7.5	1	6	94	15.7	0
Amos Marsh	61-67	17	75	4.4	0	65	1561	24.0	1
Larry Marshall	72-73	47	283	6.0	0	37	1042	28.2	0
Aaron Martin	64-68	33	258	7.8	1	13	296	22.8	0
Billy Martin	62-64	30	155	5.2	0	53	1148	21.7	0
Tommy Mason	61-71	46	483	10.5	0	45	1067	23.7	0
Tom Matte	61-72	1	0	0.0	0	62	1367	22.0	0
Don Maynard	58,60-73	26	132	5.1	0	14	343	24.5	0
Don McCall	67-70					29	756	26.1	1
Tommy McDonald	57-68	73	404	5.5	1	51	1055	20.7	0
Ralph McGill	72-73	44	405	9.2	0	27	566	21.0	0
Warren McVea	68-71,73					47	1008	21.4	0
Ed Meador	59-70	43	275	6.4	0	7	168	24.0	0
Gene Milton	68-69	7	59	8.4	0	26	574	22.1	0
Gene Mingo	60-70	18	214	11.9	1	34	742	21.8	0
Bobby Mitchell	58-68	69	699	10.1	3	102	2690	26.4	5
Charley Mitchell	63-68	21	251	12.0	0	63	1492	23.7	1
Willie Mitchell	64-70	56	564	10.1	1	7	178	25.4	0
Randy Montgomery	71-73					33	836	25.3	1
Lenny Moore	56-67	14	56	4.0	0	49	1088	22.2	0
Tom Moore	60-67					71	1882	26.5	0
Zeke Moore	67-73	8	93	11.6	0	64	1618	25.3	1
Johnny Morris	58-67	104	893	8.6	1	54	1267	23.5	0
Mercury Morris	69-73	27	171	6.3	0	111	2947	26.5	3
Joe Morrison	56-67	23	79	3.4	0	30	640	21.3	0
Reece Morrison	60-67	26	182	7.0	0	32	727	22.7	0
Herb Mul-Key	72-73	11	103	9.4	0	44	1220	27.7	1
Bob Neff	66-68	24	165	6.9	0	35	917	26.2	0
Al Nelson	65-73	1	3	3.0	0	101	2625	26.0	0
Lemar Parrish	70-73	75	628	8.4	2	51	1269	24.9	1
Jimmy Patton	55-66	27	143	5.3	1	28	735	26.3	1
Clarence Peaks	57-65					39	882	22.6	0
Preston Pearson	67-73	7	40	5.7	0	86	2152	25.0	2
Elijah Pitts	61-71	75	394	5.3	1	28	535	19.1	0
Ed Podolak	69-73	56	496	8.9	0	34	697	20.5	0
Willie Porter	68	22	135	6.1	0	36	812	22.6	0
Dickie Post	67-71					34	760	22.4	0
Bob Reed	62-63	18	173	9.6	0	26	704	27.1	0
Mel Renfro	64-73	108	842	7.8	1	85	2246	26.4	2
Lance Rentzel	65-72	48	217	4.5	0	32	783	24.5	1
Bo Roberson	61-66	3	54	18.0	0	130	3057	23.5	1
Walter Roberts	54-67,69-70	72	446	6.2	0	107	2728	25.5	1
Jerry Robinson	62-65	10	77	7.7	0	44	1009	22.9	0
Paul Robinson	68-73	2	1	0.5	0	40	924	23.1	0
Johnny Roland	66-73	49	452	9.2	2	25	507	20.3	0
Ed Rutkowski	63-68	68	514	7.6	1	53	1270	24.0	0
Johnny Sample	58-68	68	559	8.2	1	60	1560	26.0	1
Gale Sayers	65-71	27	391	14.5	2	91	2781	30.6	6
Charlie Scales	60-66	1	0	0.0	0	46	991	21.5	0
Bo Scott	69-73					25	722	28.9	0
Jake Scott	70-73	95	974	10.3	1	6	137	22.8	0
Goldie Sellers	66-69	19	217	11.4	1	27	701	26.0	2
Carver Shannon	62-64	30	213	7.1	0	46	1265	27.5	1
Rod Sherman	67-73	29	202	7.0	0	26	618	23.8	0
Roy Shivers	66-72	34	129	3.8	0	48	1162	24.2	1
Bill Shockley	60-62,68	5	18	3.6	0	32	745	23.3	0
Jim Shofner	58-63	46	308	6.7	0	1	0	0.0	0
Don Shy	67-73	1	−5	−5.0	0	81	2047	25.3	1
Les Shy	66-70					29	687	23.7	0
O. J. Simpson	69-73					33	990	30.0	1
Bobby Smith	62-66	25	151	6.0	0	40	1024	25.6	0
Noland Smith	67-69	63	635	10.1	1	82	2137	26.1	1
Ron Smith	65-73	194	1302	6.7	2	256	6502	25.4	3
Billy Stacy	59-63	54	393	7.3	2	26	607	23.3	0
Jon Staggers	70-73	72	570	7.9	2	35	854	24.4	0
Marsh Starks	63-64	8	43	5.4	0	26	519	20.0	0
Jim Steffen	59-66	47	349	7.4	0	44	1107	25.2	0
Howard Stevens	73	17	171	10.1	0	26	590	22.7	0
Jim Stiger	63-67	68	529	7.8	0	27	610	22.6	0
Jerry Stovall	63-71					46	1183	25.7	0
Pat Studstill	61-62,64-72	59	716	12.1	0	75	1924	25.7	1
Bob Suci	62-63	25	233	9.3	0	17	360	21.2	0
Bruce Taylor	70-73	113	1103	9.8	0	12	190	15.8	0
Jesse Taylor	72	1	0	0.0	0	31	676	21.8	0
Rosey Taylor	61-72	15	66	4.4	1	26	614	23.6	0
Emmitt Thomas	66-73	11	64	5.8	0	29	673	23.2	0
Ike Thomas	71-73					51	1394	27.3	2
Bill Thompson	69-73	111	1243	11.2	0	33	831	25.2	0
Bobby Thompson	64-69	14	72	5.1	0	27	622	23.0	0
Rocky Thompson	71-73					65	1768	27.2	2
Bubba Thornton	69					30	749	25.0	0
Larry Todd	65-70					25	584	23.3	0
Bill Triplett	62-63,65-72					49	1058	21.6	0
Bill Tucker	67-71	1	1	1.0	0	40	879	22.0	0
Bake Turner	62-70	21	156	7.4	0	75	1688	22.5	0
Cecil Turner	68-73	27	114	4.2	0	108	2616	24.2	4
Ted Vactor	69-73	42	289	6.9	0	29	721	24.9	0
Tom Vaughn	65-71	33	298	9.0	0	62	1595	25.7	0
Rick Volk	67-73	83	547	5.6	0	2	16	8.0	0
Billy Walik	70-72	28	130	4.6	0	67	1640	24.5	0
Donnie Walker	73	25	210	8.4	0				
Carl Ward	67-69	7	67	9.6	0	38	840	22.1	1
Charley Warner	63-66	17	206	12.1	0	86	2187	25.4	3
Jimmy Warren	64-73	4	−1	−0.2	0	30	684	22.8	0
Vic Washington	71-73					84	2178	25.9	1
Tom Watkins	61-65,67-68	96	970	10.1	3	101	2510	24.9	0
Ken Webb	58-63					27	561	20.8	0
Roger Wehrli	69-73	37	269	7.3	0	4	28	7.0	0
Charlie West	68-73	123	820	6.7	1	78	1991	25.5	0
Willie West	60-68	51	388	7.6	0	40	908	22.7	0
Dick Westmoreland	63-69	2	10	5.0	0	28	564	20.1	0
Bobby Williams	66-67,69-71					77	1934	25.1	2
Clancy Williams	65-72					32	810	25.3	0
Travis Williams	67-71	13	213	11.8	1	102	2801	27.5	6
Willie Wood	60-71	187	1391	7.4	2	3	20	6.7	0
Abe Woodson	58-66	123	956	7.8	2	193	5538	28.7	5
Alvin Watt	70-73	59	594	8.5	2	60	1480	24.7	0
Mickey Zofko	71-73					27	623	23.1	0

Lifetime Statistics – 1960-1973 Players — Section 4 – PUNTING
(All men with 25 or more Punts)

Name	Years	No.	Avg.
Donny Anderson	66-73	387	39.6
Billy Atkins	58-64	219	42.0
Sam Baker	53,56-69	701	42.7
Jim Bakken	62-73	61	37.5
Bruce Barnes	73	55	38.8
Lem Barney	67-73	113	35.5
Marv Bateman	72-73	106	40.0
Tom Blanchard	71-73	169	41.6
Bill Bradley	69-73	211	39.1
Mike Bragg	68-73	388	41.1
Zeke Bratkowski	54,57-68,71	90	38.7
Ode Burrell	64-69	29	36.8
Skip Butler	71-73	39	37.2
Don Chandler	56-67	660	43.5
Dave Chapple	71-73	107	42.3
Don Cockroft	68-73	414	40.5
Gary Collins	62-71	336	41.0
Ollie Cordill	67-69	45	41.4
Fred Cox	63-73	70	38.7
Wayne Crow	60-63	222	40.2
Cotton Davidson	54,57,60-66,68	278	38.4
Tommy Davis	59-69	511	44.7
Eagle Day	59-60	59	42.0
Jerry DePoyster	68,71-72	106	38.2
Boyd Dowler	59-69,71	93	42.9
Mike Eischeid	66-73	491	42.1
Jim Elliott	67	72	38.1
Doug Elmore	62	54	34.4
Sam Etcheverry	61-62	59	38.3
Julian Fagan	70-73	299	40.5
Jim Fraser	62-66,68	271	43.3
Roy Gerela	69-73	42	40.1
Tom Gilburg	61-65	232	41.4
Allen Green	61	61	36.7
Bobby Joe Green	60-73	970	42.6

Name	Years	No.	Avg.
Tom Greene	60-61	59	37.9
Ray Guy	73	69	45.3
John Hadl	62-73	105	39.7
George Herring	60-61	150	38.4
King Hill	58-69	368	41.3
Ed Holler	63-64	31	43.0
Gus Holloman	68-72	47	39.7
Sam Horner	60-62	64	38.4
John James	72-73	124	42.7
Tom Janik	63-71	253	39.1
Bill Johnson	70	43	39.5
Curley Johnson	60-69	556	42.5
Spike Jones	70-73	302	40.4
Gary Keithley	73	66	37.5
Jon Kilgore	65-69	234	41.0
Ernie Koy	65-70	225	38.5
Frank Lambert	65-66	156	43.6
Daryle Lamonica	63-73	51	40.6
Chuck Latourette	67-68,70-71	248	40.5
Bob Lee	69-73	156	39.7
David Lee	66-73	448	42.4
Dave Lewis	70-73	285	43.7
Dave Livingston	68-70	146	41.1
Joe Don Looney	64-67,69	32	42.4
Billy Lothridge	64-72	532	41.0
Paul Maguire	60-70	794	41.7
Billy Martin	64-68	28	37.4
Jim McCann	71-73	125	37.9
John McCormick	62-63,65-66,68	47	39.1
Wahoo McDaniel	60-68	37	37.7
Max McGee	54,57-67	256	41.6
Tom McNeill	67-73	317	41.1
Mike Mercer	61-70	307	40.6
Charley Milstead	60-61	66	35.8
Earl Morrall	56-73	106	37.7

Name	Years	No.	Avg.
Tom Morrow	62-64	45	36.7
Jim Norton	60-68	518	42.4
Steve O'Neal	69-73	337	40.7
Jimmy Orr	58-70	59	39.4
Joe Pagliei	59-60	49	37.3
Dennis Partee	68-73	364	42.5
Dan Pastorini	71-73	184	40.8
Rick Redman	65-73	153	37.5
Pat Richter	63-70	338	42.0
Bob Scarpitto	61-68	282	44.0
Larry Seiple	67-73	419	41.0
Dave Sherer	59-60	102	42.2
Del Shofner	57-67	153	42.0
Jackie Smith	63-73	86	38.5
Steve Spurrier	67-73	230	38.3
Jerry Stovall	63-71	87	40.2
Pat Studstill	61-62,64-72	560	40.7
Terry Swanson	67-69	139	39.8
Frank Tripucka	49-52,60-63	93	38.8
Bill Van Heusen	68-73	405	42.7
Danny Villanueva	60-67	488	42.7
Bobby Walden	64-73	684	42.9
Herman Weaver	70-73	201	41.3
Ron Widby	68-73	368	42.0
Eddie Wilson	62-65	54	36.1
George Wilson	66	42	42.1
Jerrel Wilson	63-73	725	44.5
Tom Wittum	73	79	43.7
Tom Yewcic	61-66	369	39.4

Lifetime Statistics – 1960-1973 Players — Section 5 – KICKING
(All men with 10 or more PAT or Field Goal attempts)

Name	Years	PAT	PAT Att.	PAT Pct.	FG	FG Att.	FG Pct.
Bruce Alford	67-69	41	43	95	31	52	60
Billy Atkins	58-64	56	63	89	8	19	42
John Aveni	59-61	72	80	90	22	63	35
Sam Baker	53,56-69	428	444	96	179	316	57
Jim Bakken	62-73	369	375	98	212	336	63
Bill Bell	71-73	64	69	93	30	55	55
George Blair	61-64	122	136	90	50	79	63
George Blanda	49-58,60-73	853	863	99	311	600	52
Tommy Brooker	62-66	149	149	100	41	86	48
Skip Butler	71-73	41	43	95	28	52	54
Gino Cappelletti	60-70	342	353	97	172	333	52
Don Chandler	56-67	248	258	96	94	161	58
Jim Christopherson	62	28	28	100	11	20	55
Mike Clark	63-71,73	325	338	96	133	232	57
Don Cockroft	68-73	211	215	98	101	155	65
Bobby Joe Conrad	58-69	95	99	96	14	33	42
Fred Cox	63-73	384	387	99	230	370	62
Cotton Davidson	54,57,60-66,68	32	33	97	2	5	40
Tommy Davis	59-69	348	350	99	130	276	47
Tom Dempsey	69-73	107	112	96	96	167	57
Jerry DePoyster	68,71-72	18	20	90	3	15	20
Harold Deters	67	9	10	90	1	4	25
Charlie Durkee	67-68,71-72	87	88	99	52	101	51
Mike Eischeid	66-73	37	37	100	11	26	42
Bob Etter	68-69	50	52	96	26	51	51
Happy Feller	71-73	27	28	96	16	43	37
George Fleming	61	24	25	96	11	26	42
Toni Fritsch	71-73	81	81	100	44	72	61
Momcilo Gavric	69	22	24	92	3	11	27
Roy Gerela	69-73	150	152	99	111	183	61
Cookie Gilchrist	62-67	14	16	88	8	20	40
Charlie Gogolak	66-68,70-72	114	117	97	52	93	56
Pete Gogolak	64-73	323	331	98	163	275	59
Bruce Gossett	64-73	349	356	98	208	336	62
Allen Green	61	19	19	100	5	15	33
Dick Guesman	60-64	69	74	93	20	62	32
Grant Guthrie	70-71	32	34	94	13	29	45
Wendell Harris	62-67	8	11	73	1	4	25
Joe Hergert	60-61				8	18	44
Jack Hill	61	16	16	100	5	15	33
Paul Hornung	57-62,64-66	190	194	98	66	140	47
Bobby Howfield	68-73	185	189	98	92	159	58
Bob Humphreys	67-68	19	20	95	8	20	40
George Hunt	73	22	24	92	16	28	57
Bob Jencks	63-65	93	102	91	14	39	36
Jimmy Keyes	68-69	30	30	100	7	16	44
Bob Khayat	60,62-63	90	92	98	38	74	51
Lou Kirouac	63-64,66-67	19	24	79	9	18	50
Curt Knight	69-73	172	175	98	101	175	58
Jerry Kramer	58-68	90	94	96	29	54	54

Name	Years	PAT	PAT Att.	PAT Pct.	FG	FG Att.	FG Pct.
Karl Kremser	69-70	28	29	97	13	23	57
Gary Kroner	65-67	57	58	98	29	56	52
Roger LeClerc	60-67	154	160	96	76	152	50
John Leypoldt	71-73	68	69	99	46	69	67
Keith Lincoln	61-68	16	18	89	5	12	42
Dale Livingston	68-70	39	41	95	28	54	52
John Love	67,72	10	11	91	2	7	29
Booth Lusteg	66-69	97	101	96	35	75	47
Errol Mann	68-73	160	161	99	100	154	65
Chester Marcol	72-73	48	49	98	54	83	65
Bill McClard	72-73	11	11	100	16	30	53
Chuck Mercein	65-70	9	10	90	2	8	25
Mike Mercer	61-70	288	295	98	102	195	52
Lou Michaels	58-69,71	386	402	96	187	341	55
Nick Mike-Mayer	73	34	34	100	26	38	64
Gene Mingo	60-70	215	223	96	112	220	51
Mark Moseley	70-72	52	57	91	31	53	58
Horst Muhlmann	69-73	157	160	98	109	168	65
Les Murdock	67	13	15	87	4	9	44
Jim O'Brien	70-73	109	112	97	60	108	56
Dennis Partee	68-73	139	145	96	70	116	60
Dennis Patera	68	10	12	83	2	8	25
Tom Pennington	62	13	15	87	2	5	40
Mac Percival	67-73	159	162	98	99	182	54
Milt Plum	57-69	16	16	100	6	16	38
David Ray	69-73	142	144	99	101	162	62
Mirro Roder	73	11	12	92	8	16	50
Bill Shockley	60-62,68	91	95	96	26	57	46
Jackie Simpson	61-64	6	6	100	3	10	30
Jack Spikes	60-67	74	80	93	20	59	34
Jan Stenerud	67-73	233	236	99	179	271	66
Andy Stynchula	60-68	13	14	93	3	7	43
Bob Timberlake	65	21	22	95	1	15	17
Herb Travenio	64-65	50	52	96	20	35	57
Wade Traynham	66-67	24	24	100	7	19	37
Jim Turner	64-73	333	337	99	220	356	62
Dick Van Raaphorst	64,66-67	112	114	98	45	90	50
Danny Villanueva	60-67	236	241	98	85	160	53
Kenny Vinyard	70	23	26	88	9	25	36
Mike Walker	72	15	15	100	2	8	25
Wayne Walker	67-68	26	26	100	8	16	50
Wayne Walker	58-72	172	175	98	53	131	40
Tim Webster	71	8	8	100	6	11	55
Ray Wersching	73	15	17	88	11	25	44
Jeff White	73	21	25	84	14	25	56
John Wittenborn	58-62,64-68	41	41	100	20	45	44
Garo Yepremian	66-67,70-73	178	181	98	114	171	67
Mack Yoho	60-63	52	61	85	13	35	37

Leaders and Features

The mention of any sport brings certain images to mind. When it comes to pro football the pictures are vivid and swift. Mostly though it is an extreme of functions. For those in love with risk and the dramatics of suddenness, there is nothing more serene than the aerial ballet of a 50-yard pass play. And for those who like to chew their fantasy in small, but certain chunks of yardage, there is nothing more pleasurable than the fullback who eludes a mammoth of flesh in search of four yards of daylight. Yet these two simplified illustrations have not always held true for pro football. If nothing else, football is a game of constant change. Unlike any other major sport, there is no way to compare the football athletes of today's two platoon game with those men who needed a double set of talents in which to sustain their playing careers. This point, for example, could not be any sharper than when one considers Joe Namath attempting to play in the 1940s. But fortunately for Namath, and perhaps even the fans of today who would have been denied the excitement of his precision arm, football is no longer a game of one man for sixty minutes.

It is for this reason that many of the records which appear on the following pages have no continuity with the players of yesteryear and those of the modern game. Field goals, for example, are a modern phenomenon and Lou Groza (who revolutionized the kicking game), is the only pre-1960 player to appear on the list of the top 56 single-season leaders. Yet, on the other hand, in the category of punters, Yale Lary, with a 48.9 average, is the only post-1960 player to make the top ten in the single-season leaders. Of course, the changing hash marks and goal post positions are greatly responsible for these records.

Yet beyond the comparison of any era, more important are the achievements of the men who made up their time, and the fact that whatever the criteria, each contributed the fullest and best of his talents. It is on this basis that each must be measured and appreciated in the light of pro football's changing game.

Section Explanations

The following is an explanation of certain statistical matter which may appear unfamiliar:

Yards per Game — In the category of Yards per Game for individuals, "per game" refers to games played by the team as there is no available statistical information of the games played by the individual.

Passing Ranks — These ranks are determined by the formula used by the National Football League for its official rankings from 1960 to 1971. Each passer who qualifies by having a minimum number of passing attempts is ranked in four categories: Percent Completed, Percent Intercepted, Average Yards per Attempt, and Touchdowns. The four ranks are then added for each passer and the totals are then ranked. This ranking of the sum of the four ranks is the passer's rank.

Active Players — On certain of the lifetime categories, active players who are approaching the minimum needed to qualify for that category may be included. This does not mean that the ranking listed for the active player is truly his lifetime ranking in that category.

YEARLY CHAMPIONSHIP GAMES

NATIONAL FOOTBALL LEAGUE (CONFERENCE)

Year	Winner (Share)	Loser (Share)	Score
1933	CHICAGO BEARS ($210.34)	New York Giants ($140.22)	23–21
1934	NEW YORK GIANTS ($621)	Chicago Bears ($414.02)	30–13
1935	DETROIT LIONS ($313.35)	New York Giants ($200.20)	26–7
1936	Green Bay Packers ($250) (At New York)	Boston Redskins ($180)	21–6
1937	Washington Redskins ($225.90)	CHICAGO BEARS ($127.78)	28–21
1938	NEW YORK GIANTS ($504.45)	Green Bay Packers ($368.81)	23–17
1939	GREEN BAY PACKERS ($703.97) (at Milwaukee)	New York Giants ($455.57)	27–0
1940	Chicago Bears ($873)	WASHINGTON REDSKINS ($606)	73–0
1941	CHICAGO BEARS ($430)	New York Giants ($288)	37–9
1942	WASHINGTON REDSKINS ($965)	Chicago Bears ($637)	14–6
1943	CHICAGO BEARS ($1,146)	Washington Redskins ($765)	41–21
1944	Green Bay Packers ($1,449)	NEW YORK GIANTS ($814)	14–7
1945	CLEVELAND RAMS ($1,469)	Washington Redskins ($902)	15–14
1946	Chicago Bears ($1,975)	NEW YORK GIANTS ($1,295)	24–14
1947	CHICAGO CARDINALS ($1,132)	Philadelphia Eagles ($754)	28–21
1948	PHILADELPHIA EAGLES ($1,540)	Chicago Cardinals ($874)	7–0
1949	Philadelphia Eagles ($1,094)	LOS ANGELES RAMS ($739)	14–0
1950	CLEVELAND BROWNS ($1,113)	Los Angeles Rams ($686)	30–28
1951	LOS ANGELES RAMS ($2,108)	Cleveland Browns ($1,483)	24–17
1952	Detroit Lions ($2,274)	CLEVELAND BROWNS ($1,712)	17–7
1953	DETROIT LIONS ($2,424)	Cleveland Browns ($1,654)	17–16
1954	CLEVELAND BROWNS ($2,478)	Detroit Lions ($1,585)	56–10
1955	Cleveland Browns ($3,508)	LOS ANGELES RAMS ($2,316)	38–14
1956	NEW YORK GIANTS ($3,779)	Chicago Bears ($2,485)	47–7
1957	DETROIT LIONS ($4,295)	Cleveland Browns ($2,750)	59–14
1958	Baltimore Colts ($4,718)	NEW YORK GIANTS ($3,111)	*23–17
1959	BALTIMORE COLTS ($4,674)	New York Giants ($3,083)	31–16
1960	PHILADELPHIA EAGLES ($5,116)	Green Bay Packers ($3,105)	17–13
1961	GREEN BAY PACKERS ($5,195)	New York Giants ($3,339)	37–0
1962	Green Bay Packers ($5,888)	NEW YORK GIANTS ($4,166)	16–7
1963	CHICAGO BEARS ($5,899)	New York Giants ($4,218)	14–10
1964	CLEVELAND BROWNS ($8,052)	Baltimore Colts ($5,571)	27–0
1965	GREEN BAY PACKERS ($7,819)	Cleveland Browns ($5,288)	23–12
1966	Green Bay Packers ($9,813)	DALLAS COWBOYS ($6,527)	34–27
1967	GREEN BAY PACKERS ($7,950)	Dallas Cowboys ($5,299)	21–17
1968	Baltimore Colts ($9,306)	CLEVELAND BROWNS ($5,963)	34–0
1969	MINNESOTA VIKINGS ($7,930)	Cleveland Browns ($5,118)	27–7
1970	Dallas Cowboys ($8,500)	SAN FRANCISCO 49ers ($5,500)	17–10
1971	DALLAS COWBOYS ($8,500)	San Francisco 49ers ($5,500)	14–3
1972	WASHINGTON REDSKINS ($8,500)	Dallas Cowboys ($5,500)	26–3
1973	Minnesota Vikings ($8,500)	DALLAS COWBOYS ($5,500)	27–10

Note: Home Team in Upper Case.

* – Sudden Death game

ALL-AMERICAN FOOTBALL CONFERENCE

Year	Winner (Share)	Loser (Share)	Score
1946	CLEVELAND BROWNS ($931.57)	New York Yankees ($645.88)	14–9
1947	Cleveland Browns ($1,191.99)	NEW YORK YANKEES ($794.66)	14–3
1948	CLEVELAND BROWNS ($594.18)	Buffalo Bills ($386.22)	49–7
1949	CLEVELAND BROWNS ($266.11)	San Francisco 49ers ($172.61)	21–7

AMERICAN FOOTBALL LEAGUE (CONFERENCE)

Year	Winner (Share)	Loser (Share)	Score
1960	HOUSTON OILERS ($1,025)	Los Angeles Chargers ($718)	24–16
1961	Houston Oilers ($1,792)	SAN DIEGO CHARGERS ($1,111)	10–3
1962	Dallas Chiefs ($2,206)	HOUSTON OILERS ($1,471)	*21–17
1963	SAN DIEGO CHARGERS ($2,498)	Boston Patroits ($1,596)	51–10
1964	BUFFALO BILLS ($2,668)	San Diego Chargers ($1,738)	20–7
1965	Buffalo Bills ($5,189)	SAN DIEGO CHARGERS($3,447)	23–0
1966	Kansas City Chiefs ($5,309)	BUFFALO BILLS ($3,799)	31–7
1967	OAKLAND RAIDERS ($6,321)	Houston Oilers ($4,996)	40–7
1968	NEW YORK JETS ($7,007)	Oakland Raiders ($5,349)	27–23
1969	Kansas City Chiefs ($7,755)	OAKLAND RAIDERS ($6,252)	17–7
1970	BALTIMORE COLTS ($8,500)	Oakland Raiders ($5,5000)	27–17
1971	MIAMI DOLPHINS ($8,500)	Baltimore Colts ($5,500)	21–0
1972	Miami Dolphins ($8,500)	PITTSBURGH STEELERS ($5,500)	21–17
1973	MIAMI DOLPHINS ($8,500)	Oakland Raiders ($5,500)	27–10

COMPOSITE STANDINGS
(All Leagues)

Team	Games	Wins	Losses	Pct.	Total Share
Chiefs	3	3	0	1.000	$15,270
Dolphins	3	3	0	1.000	25,500
Vikings	2	2	0	1.000	16,430
Jets	1	1	0	1.000	7,007
Packers	10	8	2	.800	42,541.78
Lions	5	4	1	.800	10,891.35
Eagles	4	3	1	.750	8,504
Colts	6	4	2	.667	38,169
Bills (AFL)	3	2	1	.667	11,656
Bears	10	6	4	.600	14,197.14
Browns	15	8	7	.533	42,102.85
Oilers	4	2	2	.500	9,284
Cardinals	2	1	1	.500	2,006
Redskins	7	3	4	.429	12,143.90
Rams	5	2	3	.400	7,318
Cowboys	6	2	4	.333	39,826
Giants	14	3	11	.214	26,014.44
Chargers	5	1	4	.200	9,512
Raiders	5	1	4	.200	28,922
49ers	3	0	3	.000	11,172.61
Yankees (AAFC)	2	0	2	.000	1,440.54
Bills (AAFC)	1	0	1	.000	386.22
Patriots	1	0	1	.000	1,596
Steelers	1	0	1	.000	5,500

YEARLY TEAM LEADERS

OFFENSE

YEAR	LGUE	POINTS – PTS/G	FIRST DOWNS	RUSH YARDS YDS/GAME	RUSH AVERAGE	RUSH TD	PASS COMPLETION PERCENTAGE	PASS YARDS YDS/GAME	PASS YARDS/ ATTEMPT	PASS TD	FEWEST INT.	LEAST INT. %	PUNTING AVERAGE	PUNT RETURN AVERAGE	KICKOFF RETURN AVERAGE	YEAR	LGUE
1933	NFL	NYG 244 17.4					Bkn. 46.7									1933	NFL
1934	NFL	ChiB 286 22.0					NYG 40.9									1934	NFL
1935	NFL	ChiB 192 16.0	ChiB 140	ChiB 2096 175		Det. 15	NYG 44.8	G.B. 1545 129	G.B. 6.72	ChiB 13						1935	NFL
1936	NFL	G.B. 248 20.7	Det. 170	Det. 2883 240	Det. 4.73	Det. 22	G.B. 42.4	G.B. 1629 136	ChiB 6.46	ChiB 17 G.B. 17						1936	NFL
1937	NFL	G.B. 220 20.0	Was. 149	Det. 2074 189	Det. 4.30	Det. 12	Was. 44.6	G.B. 1397 127	ChiB 6.97	ChiB 16 G.B. 16	NYG 11	NYG 5.42				1937	NFL
1938	NFL	G.B. 223 20.7	Was. 147	Det. 1893 172	Det. 4.01	NYG 12	NYG 48.9	Was. 1536 140	G.B. 6.98	G.B. 20	Bkn. 8	Bkn. 4.73				1938	NFL
1939	NFL	ChiB 298 27.1	G.B. 149	ChiB 2043 186	ChiB 4.66	ChiB 21	Was. 58.2	ChiB 1965 179	Was. 8.93	Was. 18	NYG 11	NYG 6.21				1939	NFL
1940	NFL	Was. 245 22.2	G.B. 154	ChiB 1818 165	Bkn. 3.92	ChiB 16	Was. 59.0	Was. 1887 172	ChiB 8.19	G.B. 18 Was. 18	Bkn. 13	Phi. 5.52				1940	NFL
1941	NFL	ChiB 396 36.0	ChiB 181	ChiB 2290 208	ChiB 4.63	ChiB 30	G.B. 52.6	ChiB 2002 182	**ChiB 10.21**	ChiB 19	ChiB 11	G.B. 5.14	Was. 45.9	**ChiB 20.2**	Det. 26.5	1941	NFL
1942	NFL	ChiB 376 34.2	G.B. 176	ChiB 1911 174	ChiB 4.07	ChiB 23	Was. 53.3	G.B. 2407 219	ChiB 10.18	G.B. 28	Pit. 11	G.B. 5.45	Was. 44.3	Pit. 15.4	Was. 27.8	1942	NFL
1943	NFL	ChiB 303 30.3	ChiB 161	P-P 1730 173	ChiB 3.89	P-P 18	Was. 54.7	ChiB 2310 231	ChiB 10.09	ChiB 28	NYG 9	NYG 6.04	Was. 43.1	Det. 13.6	Det. 24.9	1943	NFL
1944	NFL	Phi. 267 26.7	G.B. 147	Phi. 1661 166	Phi. 3.92	Phi. 23	Was. 56.9	Was. 2021 202	ChiB 7.45	ChiB 21	Phi. 12	Was. 5.69	Det. 40.5	Det. 14.2	NYG 27.4	1944	NFL
1945	NFL	Phi. 272 27.2	ChiB 164	Cle. 1714 171	Cle. 4.61	Phi. 26	**Was. 64.0**	ChiB 1857 186	Cle. 8.88	Cle. 16	Was. 11	Was. 4.82	Was. 43.3	Det. 14.4	Phi. 24.5	1945	NFL
1946	NFL	ChiB 289 26.3	L.A. 214	G.B. 1765 160	L.A. 4.17	ChiB 19	Phi. 53.5	L.A. 2080 189	ChiB 7.71	L.A. 19	Pit. 13	L.A. 7.36	L.A. 44.4	Pit. 13.5	NYG 26.0	1946	NFL
1946	AAFC	Cle. 423 30.2	L.A. 183	S.F. 2175 155	Buf. 4.08	Cle. 27	L.A. 54.7	Cle. 2266 162	Cle. 9.56	Cle. 22	Cle. 7	Cle. 2.95	Bkn. 46.5	N.Y. 15.3	Chi. 24.5	1946	AAFC
1947	NFL	ChiB 363 30.3	ChiB 263	L.A. 2171 181	L.A. 4.73	ChiB 21 Phi. 21	Was. 55.5	Was. 3336 278	ChiB 8.18	ChiB 29	Was. 18	Was. 4.33	G.B. 43.6	Bos. 15.1	Was. 22.1	1947	NFL
1947	AAFC	Cle. 410 29.8	S.F. 218	N.Y. 2930 209	N.Y. 5.49	N.Y. 27	Cle. 58.8	Cle. 2990 214	Cle. 10.10	Cle. 26	Cle. 12	Cle. 4.05	L.A. 45.0	Bal. 16.5	Buf. 25.6	1947	AAFC
1948	NFL	ChiC 395 32.9	ChiB 242	ChiC 2560 213	ChiC 4.82	ChiC 25	Was. 56.1	Was. 2861 238	Was. 7.95	L.A. 28	ChiC 12	ChiC 4.21	Phi. 45.9	ChiC 19.1	ChiB 25.9	1948	NFL
1948	AAFC	S.F. 495 35.4	Cle. 243	**S.F. 3663 262**	**S.F. 6.07**	S.F. 35	S.F. 56.3	Bal. 2899 207	Bal. 8.53	S.F. 30	Bal. 13	Bal. 3.82	L.A. 47.2	Buf. 16.9	S.F. 24.4	1948	AAFC
1949	NFL	Phi. 364 30.3	ChiB 248	Phi. 2607 217	ChiC 4.56	Phi. 25	L.A. 52.5	ChiB 3055 255	ChiB 7.94	ChiB 24	Phi. 14	Phi. 5.56	L.A. 44.4	ChiC 18.2	NYG 26.0	1949	NFL
1949	AAFC	S.F. 416 34.7	Buf. 184	S.F. 2798 233	S.F. 5.53	S.F. 26	Buf. 57.1	Cle. 2929 244	Cle. 9.90	S.F. 28	Cle. 12	Cle. 4.05	S.F. 45.5	S.F. 15.5	L.A. 23.7	1949	AAFC
1950	NFL	**L.A. 466 38.8**	L.A. 278	NYG 2336 195	NYY 4.56	L.A. 28	L.A. 55.8	L.A. 3709 309	L.A. 8.19	L.A. 31	NYG 10	NYG 5.35	Cle. 43.2	G.B. 16.6	Det. 26.7	1950	NFL
1951	NFL	L.A. 392 32.7	L.A. 272	ChiB 2408 201	L.A. 5.19	ChiB 24	Cle. 55.7	L.A. 3296 275	L.A. 8.84	Det. 29	Cle 7	L.A. 5.90	Cle. 45.5	Det. 15.1	NYG 25.9	1951	NFL
1952	NFL	L.A. 349 29.1	Cle. 228	S.F. 1905 159	Cle. 4.53	L.A. 17	S.F. 51.8	Cle. 2839 237	G.B. 7.98	G.B. 26	Phi. 19	Phi. 5.26	Cle. 45.7	Det. 14.9	Pit. 28.9	1952	NFL
1953	NFL	S.F. 372 31.0	Phi. 256	S.F. 2230 186	L.A. 5.04	S.F. 26	Cle. 63.0	Phi. 3357 280	Cle. 10.10	Phi. 25	Cle. 9	Cle. 2.97	Pit. 46.9	G.B. 8.9	NYG 26.3	1953	NFL
1954	NFL	Det. 337 28.1	L.A. 255	S.F. 2498 208	S.F. 5.65	S.F. 28	Cle. 59.0	ChiB 3299 275	L.A. 9.91	Phi. 33	S.F. 12	S.F. 3.53	Pit. 43.2	G.B. 9.9	Cle. 25.3	1954	NFL
1955	NFL	Cle. 349 29.1	ChiB 235	ChiB 2388 199	ChiB 4.90	Cle. 20	Cle. 55.6	Phi. 2696 225	Cle. 9.51	Cle. 21	Cle. 11	Cle. 4.70	L.A. 44.6	ChiC 12.0	Pit. 26.3	1955	NFL
1956	NFL	ChiB 363 30.3	Det. 247	ChiB 2468 206	L.A. 5.15	ChiB 22	Bal. 56.6	L.A. 2601 217	ChiB 8.77	G.B. 21	ChiC 14	NYG 5.09	L.A. 43.1	ChiC 9.5	Pit. 26.1	1956	NFL
1957	NFL	L.A. 307 25.6	L.A. 235	L.A. 2142 179	L.A. 4.52	Cle. 19	S.F. 62.6	Bal. 2608 217	Cle. 9.61	Bal. 25	NYG 12	NYG 4.46	S.F. 44.7	Was. 10.5	S.F. 26.1	1957	NFL
1958	NFL	Bal. 381 31.8	Bal. 253	Cle. 2526 211	Cle. 5.32	Bal. 24 Cle. 24	S.F. 58.2	L.A. 2909 242	Pit. 8.62	Bal. 26	Bal. 11	Bal. 3.11	Was. 45.4	Cle. 8.2	ChiB 25.8	1958	NFL
1959	NFL	Bal. 374 31.2	Bal. 267	Cle. 2149 179	L.A. 4.79	Cle. 20	Cle. 57.6	Bal. 2938 245	NYG 8.72	Bal. 33	Cle. 9	Cle. 3.26	NYG 46.6	ChiC 9.8	L.A. 24.5	1959	NFL
1960	NFL	Cle. 362 30.2	G.B. 237	StL. 2356 196	Cle. 5.04	G.B. 29	Cle. 60.6	Bal. 3164 264	Phi. 8.93	Phi. 29	**Cle. 5**	Cle. 1.89	StL. 44.9	Cle. 9.9	S.F. 27.1	1960	NFL
1960	AFL	N.Y. 382 27.3	N.Y. 286	Dal. 1814 130	Dal. 3.76	Dal. 24	L.A. 51.9	Hou. 3371 241	Hou. 7.39	NYT 32	Dal. 19	Dal. 4.37	L.A. 39.7	Dal. 15.0	Hou. 25.5	1960	AFL
1961	NFL	G.B. 391 27.9	NYG 275	G.B. 2350 168	G.B. 4.96	G.B. 27 S.F. 27	G.B. 57.8	Phi. 3824 273	Phi. 8.91	Phi. 34	Cle. 13	Cle. 4.06	**Det. 47.6**	G.B. 17.8	S.F. 26.6	1961	NFL
1961	AFL	**Hou. 513** 36.6	Hou. 293	Dal. 2183 156	Dal. 4.97	S.D. 24	Hou. 51.0	**Hou. 4568 326**	Hou. 9.17	**Hou. 48**	Bos. 21	Bos. 5.00	Buf. 44.5	N.Y. 17.8	Dal. 27.6	1961	AFL
1962	AFL	G.B. 415 29.6	G.B. 281	G.B. 2460 176	G.B. 4.75	**G.B. 36**	G.B. 60.1	Phi. 3632 259	Phi. 8.49	NYG 35	G.B. 13	G.B. 4.18	S.F. 45.6	Det. 12.9	Was. 28.2	1962	NFL
1962	AFL	Dal. 389 27.8	Den. 270	Buf. 2480 177	Buf. 4.95	Dal. 21	Dal. 60.6	Den. 3739 267	Dal. 8.77	Hou. 32	Bos. 13	Bos. 3.40	Den. 42.9	N.Y. 12.3	Hou. 25.9	1962	AFL
1963	NFL	NYG 448 32.0	NYG 278	Cle. 2639 189	Cle. 5.74	G.B. 22	Bal. 57.3	Bal. 3605 258	NYG 8.35	NYG 39	Bal. 12	Bal. 2.77	Chi. 46.5	Was. 13.0	Was. 26.8	1963	NFL
1963	AFL	S.D. 399 28.5	N/A	S.D. 2201 157	S.D. 5.57	Buf. 21	S.D. 56.4	Hou. 3478 248	Oak. 7.69	Oak. 31	K.C. 22	K.C. 5.01	Den. 44.3	Den. 12.9	Hou. 26.4	1963	AFL
1964	NFL	Bal. 428 30.6	StL. 275	G.B. 2276 163	Cle. 4.97	Bal. 29	G.B. 57.9	Was. 3071 219	Bal. 8.83	Cle. 28	G.B. 6	G.B. 1.87	Min. 46.4	Cle. 15.2	G.B. 25.8	1964	NFL
1964	AFL	Buf. 400 28.6	Hou. 284	Buf. 2040 146	Oak. 4.47	Buf. 25	K.C. 55.3	Oak. 3886 276	Buf. 8.62	K.C. 32	K.C. 21	Hou. 4.90	Den. 43.4	Oak. 13.5	Oak. 25.0	1964	AFL
1965	NFL	S.F. 421 30.1	S.F. 292	Cle. 2331 167	Cle. 4.90	ChiB 27	S.F. 59.9	S.F. 3633 260	Chi. 8.37	S.F. 35	Min. 12	Min. 3.23	S.F. 45.8	Cle. 11.9	Det. 27.2	1965	NFL
1965	AFL	S.D. 340 24.3	S.D. 268	S.D. 1998 143	K.C. 4.19	Buf. 16	S.D. 50.6	S.D. 3379 241	S.D. 8.43	Hou. 25	Oak. 17	Oak. 3.94	NYJ 45.3	S.D. 13.4	Den. 23.4	1965	AFL
1966	NFL	Dal. 445 31.8	Dal. 287	Cle. 2166 155	Cle. 5.22	Dal. 24	G.B. 60.7	Dal. 3331 238	G.B. 8.90	Cle. 33	**G.B. 5**	**G.B. 1.57**	Bal. 45.6	Det. 10.4	Chi. 27.9	1966	NFL
1966	AFL	K.C. 448 32.0	K.C. 266	K.C. 2274 162	K.C. 5.18	Buf. 19 K.C. 19	K.C. 52.8	NYJ 3556 254	K.C. 8.28	K.C. 31	K.C. 15 S.D. 15	S.D. 3.46	Den. 45.2	S.D. 12.2	Den. 26.9	1966	AFL
1967	NFL	L.A. 398 28.4	Bal. 289	Cle. 2139 153	Cle. 4.82	Bal. 21	Bal. 58.0	Was. 3887 278	G.B. 8.33	NYG 33	L.A. 16	Was. 3.23	Atl. 43.7	Cle. 10.2	G.B. 27.0	1967	NFL
1967	AFL	Oak. 468 33.4	NYJ 282	Hou. 2122·152	Hou. 4.46	Oak. 19	K.C. 55.8	NYJ 4128 295	NYJ 8.02	Oak. 33	Den. 18	Den. 4.81	Den. 44.9	Den. 13.5	Den. 25.3	1967	AFL
1968	NFL	Dal. 431 30.8	**Dal. 297**	Chi. 2377 170	Chi. 4.75	Dal. 22	G.B. 59.1	Dal. 3295 235	Bal. 8.62	Bal. 28	Det. 15 G.B. 15	Det. 3.98	Atl. 44.3	Dal. 13.5	Bal. 26.4	1968	NFL
1968	AFL	Oak. 453 32.4	Oak. 287	K.C. 2227 159	Oak. 4.64	NYJ 22	K.C. 57.8	S.D. 3813 272	K.C. 9.23	Oak. 31	Cin. 11	Cin. 3.51	K.C. 45.3	K.C. 14.5	Hou. 23.3	1968	AFL
1969	NFL	Min. 379 27.1	N.O. 282	Dal. 2276 163	Atl. 4.52	Cle. 17 Dal. 17 StL. 17	Was. 61.9	S.F. 3379 241	Dal. 9.05	L.A. 25	L.A. 7	L.A. 1.68	Bal. 45.3	Det. 11.0	Bal. 25.3	1969	NFL
1969	AFL	Oak. 377 26.9	S.D. 275	K.C. 2220 159	S.D. 4.36	K.C. 19	K.C. 55.8	Oak. 3375 241	Cin. 8.83	Oak. 36	Cin. 15	S.D. 4.73	S.D. 44.6	Den. 12.2	K.C. 26.6	1969	AFL
1970	NFC	S.F. 352 25.1	NYG 257	Dal. 2300 164	StL. 4.66	StL. 18	Was. 59.4	S.F. 2990 214	Dal. 8.23	S.F. 25	S.F. 10	S.F. 2.61	N.O. 42.5	S.F. 11.5	L.A. 26.3	1970	NFC
1970	AFC	Bal. 321 22.9	Oak. 270	Mia. 2082 149	Cin. 4.46	Den. 17	K.C. 53.3	Bal. 3087 221	Mia. 7.64	Oak. 28	Cin. 11	Cin. 3.24	Cin. 46.2	K.C. 12.0	Bal. 25.8	1970	AFC
1971	NFC	Dal. 406 29.0	Dal. 288	Det. 2376 170	L.A. 4.65	Dal. 25	Atl. 58.6	NYG 3062 219	Atl. 8.75	Dal. 22	L.A. 11	L.A. 2.97	Phi. 41.9	Was. 9.5	Dal. 27.5	1971	NFC
1971	AFC	Oak. 344 24.6	S.D. 264	Mia. 2429 174	Mia. 5.00	Bal. 23	Cin. 58.6	S.D. 3305 236	K.C. 7.99	S.D. 23	Mia. 10	Cin. 3.01	K.C. 44.8	Mia. 10.5	Mia. 25.2	1971	AFC
1972	NFC	S.F. 353 25.2	NYG 265	Chi. 2360 169	L.A. 4.68	Det. 20	NYG 59.9	S.F. 2888 206	Was. 8.03	S.F. 27	G.B. 9	Min. 3.37	L.A. 44.2	G.B. 14.6	**Chi. 29.4**	1972	NFC
1972	AFC	Mia. 385 27.5	**Oak. 297**	Mia. 2960 211	Pit. 5.07	Mia. 26	Cin. 57.0	NYJ 2930 209	Mia. 8.63	Oak. 23	Cin. 11	Cin. 2.86	K.C. 44.8	Den. 11.1	Bal. 28.1	1972	AFC
1973	NFC	L.A. 388 27.7	L.A. 294	L.A. 2925 209	Dal. 4.46	Atl+LA18	Min. 60.1	Phi. 3236 231	L.A. 6.88	Dal. 26	Min. 9	Phi. 2.71	S.F. 43.8	S.F. 10.6	Was. 26.0	1973	NFC
1973	AFC	Den. 354 25.3	Oak. 288	Buf. 3088 221	Buf. 5.10	Buf. 20	Oak. 58.1	Den. 2706 193	Cin. 6.39	Den. 22	Cin. 12 Mia. 12	Cin. 3.61	K.C. 45.6	S.D. 12.4	N.E. 24.1	1973	AFC

Bold – designates all time leader

YEARLY TEAM LEADERS
DEFENSE

TEAM	LGUE	POINTS–PTS/G	FIRST DOWNS	RUSH YARDS/ YARDS GAME	RUSH AVERAGE	RUSH TD	PASS COMPLETION PERCENTAGE	PASS YARDS/ YARDS GAME	PASS YARDS/ ATTEMPT	PASS TD	MOST INT.	HIGHEST INT. %	PUNT RETURN AVERAGE	KICKOFF RETURN AVERAGE	TEAM	LGUE
1933	NFL	**Bkn. 54** 5.4													1933	NFL
1934	NFL	Det. 59 **4.5**													1934	NFL
1935	NFL	G.B. 96 8.0 NYG 96 8.0					**ChiB 30.4**				**ChiB 37**	**ChiB 19.1**			1935	NFL
1936	NFL	ChiB 94 7.8					Bos. 31.5				ChiB 35	ChiB 15.4			1936	NFL
1937	NFL	ChiB 100 9.1					Pit. 32.4				NYG 30	NYG 16.5			1937	NFL
1938	NFL	NYG 79 7.2					NYG 34.1				NYG 34	NYG 15.0			1938	NFL
1939	NFL	NYG 85 7.7					Was. 37.0				NYG 35	NYG 15.8			1939	NFL
1940	NFL	Bkn. 120 10.9					ChiC 37.1				G.B. 40	Det. 16.4			1940	NFL
1941	NFL	NYG 114 10.3	Bkn. 110 ChiC 110	ChiB 1076 98	Was. 2.71	Bkn. 6 ChiB 6	ChiB 40.0	Pit. 1168 106	ChiB 5.5	Bkn. 6 NYG 6	ChiB 34	NYG 13.3	Cle. 8.2	Was. 19.4	1941	NFL
1942	NFL	ChiB 84 7.6	ChiB 98	ChiB 519 **47**	ChiB 1.77	ChiB 3	Was. 37.5	Was. 1093 99	**ChiB 4.2**	NYG 4	ChiB 33 G.B. 33	G.B. 13.6	Det. 10.2	Pit. 18.5	1942	NFL
1943	NFL	Was. 137 13.7	P-P 96	P-P 793 79	P-P 2.54	NYG 8	ChiB 31.5	ChiB 980 98	ChiB 4.8	ChiB 8	G.B. 42	G.B. 17.4	Was. 9.5	NYG 19.3	1943	NFL
1944	NFL	NYG 75 7.5	**Phi. 86**	**Phi. 558** 56	**Phi. 1.74**	NYG 6	ChiB 33.2	ChiB 1052 105	NYG 5.0	**NYG 3**	NYG 34	Phi. 14.3	C-P 9.9	Phi. 18.0	1944	NFL
1945	NFL	Was. 121 12.1	Phi. 104	Phi. 817 82	Det. 2.56	Det. 7	Cle. 39.1	Was. 1121 112	Was. 5.4	NYG 6	Bos. 30	Bos. 13.2	Det. 9.8	Det. 16.6	1945	NFL
1946	NFL	Pit. 117 10.6	ChiB 138	ChiB 1044 95	Phi. 2.69	Pit. 9	Pit. 39.5	**Pit. 939 85**	Pit. 5.8	G.B. 6 Pit. 6	ChiB 27	Phi. 11.8	Pit. 7.7	**ChiB 16.0**	1946	NFL
1946	AAFC	Cle. 137 9.8	N.Y. 119	S.F. 873 62	S.F. 2.05	S.F. 7	Cle. 41.8	Cle. 1317 94	Cle. 4.4	Cle. 8	Cle. 41	Cle. 13.7	N.Y. 10.8	Mia. 18.5	1946	AAFC
1947	NFL	G.B. 210 17.5	Pit. 170	Phi. 1329 111	L.A. 3.41	ChiB 6	Pit. 40.2	G.B. 1790 149	G.B. 6.5	G.B. 14 L.A. 14	G.B. 30	G.B. 10.8	ChiC 9.4	ChiB 17.5	1947	NFL
1947	AAFC	Cle. 185 13.2	N.Y. 140	N.Y. 1237 88	N.Y. 3.33	L.A. 9	Cle. 42.6	Cle. 1707 122	Cle. 5.6	Cle. 11	Cle. 32	Cle. 10.6	L.A. 10.8	Bal. 17.0	1947	AAFC
1948	NFL	ChiB 151 12.6	Phi. 158	Phi. 1209 101	Phi. 3.22	Phi. 5	Phi. 41.1	G.B. 1626 135	ChiB 4.9	ChiB 12	NYG 39	NYG 12.5	ChiB 9.2	Pit. 17.8	1948	NFL
1948	AAFC	Cle. 190 13.6	Cle. 171	Cle. 1519 108	Cle. 3.48	Cle. 10	Cle. 44.9	Bkn. 1985 142	Cle. 5.9	Cle. 14	S.F. 32	S.F. 8.6	Bal. 10.3	Chi. 17.5	1948	AAFC
1949	NFL	Phi. 134 11.2	Phi. 148	ChiB 1196 100	ChiB 2.79	Phi. 5	Phi. 39.9	Phi. 1607 134	Phi. 5.3	Pit. 9	ChiC 33	Det. 10.3	L.A. 8.3	Det. 18.7	1949	NFL
1949	AAFC	Cle. 171 14.2	N.Y. 129	N.Y. 1134 94	N.Y. 3.15	N.Y. 8	Cle. 39.5	Cle. 1677 140	Cle. 5.5	Cle. 9	S.F. 32	S.F. 10.1	N.Y. 11.0	L.A. 19.2	1949	AAFC
1950	NFL	Phi. 141 11.7	Phi. 141	Det. 1367 114	NYG 2.93	Phi. 5	Phi. 36.8	Cle. 1581 132	Cle. 5.4	Cle. 8	Bal. 34	Phi. 11.2	Cle. 6.6	Pit. 19.2	1950	NFL
1951	NFL	Cle. 152 12.7	NYG 174	NYG 913 76	NYG 2.33	Cle. 8 NYG 8	Phi. 41.5	Pit. 1687 141	Cle. 6.0	Cle. 10	NYG 41	NYG 10.9	S.F. 6.7	G.B. 18.5	1951	NFL
1952	NFL	Det. 192 16.0	S.F. 167	Det. 1145 95	NYG 3.23	ChiC 8 Det. 8 NYG 8 Pit. 8	Cle. 40.5	Was. 1817 151	S.F. 5.6	Was. 12	L.A. 38	L.A. 10.6	NYG 6.7	Pit. 18.3	1952	NFL
1953	NFL	Cle. 162 13.5	Pit. 184	Phi. 1117 93	Pit. 3.07	Phi. 6	Cle. 42.2	Was. 1950 162	Was. 5.6	Was. 8	Det. 38	Det. 10.7	ChiC 1.5	Pit. 16.3	1953	NFL
1954	NFL	Cle. 162 13.5	Cle. 147	Cle. 1050 88	Cle. 2.82	Cle. 4	Phi. 41.4	Cle. 1784 149	Phi. 5.9	Det. 10	NYG 33	Pit. 10.2	**ChiC 1.2**	G.B. 18.5	1954	NFL
1955	NFL	Cle. 218 18.2	Cle. 171	Cle. 1189 99	Was. 3.26	Was. 8	Cle. 39.0	Pit. 1530 127	Cle. 5.5	S.F. 10	G.B. 31 L.A. 31	G.B. 12.0	Bal. 1.9	L.A. 19.7	1955	NFL
1956	NFL	Cle. 177 14.7	Pit. 167	NYG 1443 120	NYG 3.48	Det. 9	ChiC 44.9	Cle. 1215 101	Cle. 5.4	Cle. 7	ChiC 33	ChiC 11.5	S.F. 3.5	Pit. 19.0	1956	NFL
1957	NFL	Cle. 172 14.3	Pit. 156	Bal. 1174 98	Bal. 3.13	Pit. 7	Cle. 43.4	Cle. 1511 126	Cle. 6.2	Cle. 8	G.B. 30	G.B. 9.6	Det. 1.6	Pit. 20.1	1957	NFL
1958	NFL	NYG 183 15.2	ChiB 168	Bal. 1291 108	NYG 3.61	Cle. 6	NYG 45.7	NYG 2130 177	L.A. 6.0	Bal. 9	Bal. 35	Bal. 9.6	Cle. 2.5	S.F. 17.6	1958	NFL
1959	NFL	NYG 170 14.2	NYG 167	NYG 1261 105	NYG 3.33	NYG 6	Pit. 44.9	NYG 1811 151	NYG 6.0	NYG 11	Bal. 40	Bal. 11.4	**Cle. 1.2**	Pit. 17.5	1959	NFL
1960	NFL	S.F. 205 17.1	StL. 158	StL 1212 101	NYG 3.20	G.B. 7	S.F. 47.8	Chi. 1808 151	Chi. 6.2	Bal. 8	Cle. 31	Phi. 10.6	Bal. 3.2	Was. 17.1	1960	NFL
1960	AFL	Da. 253 18.1	Buf. 225	Dal. 980 70	Dal. 2.32	Hou. 6	Buf. 43.1	Buf. 2461 176	Buf. 5.7	Bos. 19 Buf. 19 Dal. 19	Buf. 33	Buf. 7.7	Dal. 5.8	Den. 20.1	1960	AFL
1961	NFL	NYG 220 15.7	NYG 212	Pit. 1463 104	StL. 3.51	NYG 6	NYG 45.6	Bal. 2320 166	G.B. 6.4	Det. 11	NYG 33	NYG 8.5	Min. 6.0	StL. 20.1	1961	NFL
1961	AFL	S.D. 219 15.6	Buf. 200	Bos. 1041 74	Bos. 2.97	S.D. 7	Hou. 43.0	S.D. 2736 195	Hou. 5.6	Hou. 13	**S.D. 49**	S.D. 10.1	Buf. 6.5	Den. 17.1	1961	AFL
1962	NFL	G.B. 148 10.6	Det. 180	Det. 1231 88	Det. 3.51	G.B. 4	Chi. 46.8	G.B. 2084 149	G.B. 5.9	G.B. 10	G.B. 31	G.B. 8.7	StL. 4.7	G.B. 20.1	1962	NFL
1962	AFL	Dal. 233 16.6	Hou. 217	Dal. 1250 89	Dal. 3.56	Buf. 10	Hou. 43.8	Oak. 2517 180	Hou. 5.9	Dal. 13	Buf. 36	Buf. 8.2	Bos. 4.9	Hou. 21.0	1962	AFL
1963	NFL	Chi. 144 10.3	G.B. 193	Chi. 1442 103	Chi. 3.50	Chi. 7	Chi. 46.5	Chi. 2045 146	Chi. 5.8	G.B. 9	ChiB 36	ChiB 10.2	Dal. 4.9	G.B. 19.3	1963	NFL
1963	AFL	S.D. 256 18.3	N/A	N/A	N/A	N/A	N/A	N/A	N/A	N/A	N/A	N/A	N/A	N/A	1963	NFL
1964	NFL	Bal. 225 16.1	G.B. 197	L.A. 1501 107	Dal. 3.43	Dal. 6	Dal. 45.6	G.B. 1980 141	G.B. 6.2	G.B. 11	Was. 34	Was. 8.4	Dal. 2.7	Cle. 20.2	1964	NFL
1964	AFL	Buf. 242 17.3	Buf. 206	Buf. 913 65	Buf. 3.04	Buf. 4	Buf. 46.6	K.C. 2910 208	S.D. 6.0	Oak. 21	NYT 34	Den. 7.3	Oak. 6.6	Hou. 18.5	1964	AFL
1965	NFL	L.A. 224 16.0	L.A. 208	L.A. 1409 101	L.A. 3.38	Det. 9	Dal. 48.1	G.B. 2316 165	G.B. 6.0	G.B. 11	G.B. 27 Was. 27	Was. 8.5	Was. 4.6	Dal. 19.5	1965	NFL
1965	AFL	Buf. 226 16.1	S.D. 190	S.D. 1094 78	Buf. 3.09	Buf. 5	Hou. 42.5	S.D. 2480 177	S.D. 5.2	Bos. 17	Buf. 32	Hou. 6.5	Bos. 7.0	Oak. 19.8	1965	AFL
1966	NFL	G.B. 163 11.6	L.A. 196	Dal. 1176 84	StL. 3.16	Dal. 6	StL. 44.5	G.B. 2316 165	G.B. 5.9	G.B. 7	Cle. 30	Cle. 7.4	Det. 3.6	StL. 20.4	1966	NFL
1966	AFL	Buf. 255 18.2	Buf. 192	Buf. 1051 75	Buf. 3.06	Buf. 6	Buf. 44.0	S.D. 2386 170	K.C. 5.8	S.D. 13	K.C. 33	Mia. 7.3	NYJ 5.0	Mia. 20.4	1966	AFL
1967	NFL	L.A. 196 14.0	G.B. 183	Dal. 1081 77	L.A. 3.10	Bal. 5	Chi. 42.7	G.B. 1644 117	G.B. 4.9	Det. 11	Bal. 32 L.A. 32	Bal. 8.1	G.B. 1.7	Chi. 20.5	1967	NFL
1967	AFL	Hou. 199 14.2	Oak. 182	Oak. 1129 81	Oak. 3.21	Hou. 7	Oak. 41.2	Buf. 2191 156	Hou. 5.7	Hou. 10	K.C. 31	Mia. 8.0	Mia. 6.5	Hou. 18.6	1967	AFL
1968	NFL	Bal. 144 10.3	L.A. 190	Dal. 1195 85	Dal. 3.24	**Dal. 2**	N.O. 41.8	G.B. 2031 145	Bal. 5.6	Bal. 9	Cle. 32	Cle. 7.3	Bal. 3.3	Chi. 17.9	1968	NFL
1968	AFL	K.C. 170 12.1	N.Y. 178	NYJ 1195 85	NYJ 3.25	K.C. 4	Buf. 42.1	Hou. 2003 143	Hou. 5.6	Hou. 13	K.C. 37	K.C. 8.0	Oak. 5.3	K.C. 19.3	1968	AFL
1969	NFL	Min. 133 9.5	Min. 158	Dal. 1050 75	Min. 3.23	Dal. 3	L.A. 47.0	Min. 2035 145	Min. 5.0	Min. 8	Min. 30	Min. 7.3	G.B. 3.4	Dal. 19.4	1969	NFL
1969	AFL	K.C. 177 12.6	K.C. 181	K.C. 1091 78	K.C. 3.47	K.C. 6	Oak. 38.9	K.C. 2491 178	K.C. 5.8	K.C. 10	K.C. 32	K.C. 7.5	Oak. 4.1	Bos. 19.1	1969	AFL
1970	NFC	Min. 143 10.2	Min. 168	Det. 1152 82	Det. 3.18	Min. 4	StL. 47.9	Min. 1798 128	Min. 4.9	Min. 6	Det. 28 Min. 28	Min. 7.6	NYG 2.9	L.A. 18.1	1970	NFC
1970	AFC	Mia. 228 16.3	Den. 199	NYJ 1283 92	NYJ 3.14	Bal. 6	NYJ 43.1	K.C. 2280 163	K.C. 5.6	S.D. 13	K.C. 31	K.C. 7.6	Cle. 3.6	Bos. 20.5	1970	AFC
1971	NFC	Min. 139 9.9	Min. 194	Dal. 1144 82	Dal. 3.24	**Min. 2**	S.F. 44.6	Atl. 1895 135	Min. 5.0	Atl. 9	Was. 29	Det. 7.2	S.F. 2.3	Was. 17.5	1971	NFC
1971	AFC	Bal. 140 10.0	Bal. 196	Bal. 1113 80	Bal. 3.16	Bal. 8	Den. 42.1	Bal. 2027 145	Bal. 5.6	Bal. 9	Bal. 28	Cin. 8.1	S.D. 2.0	Mia. 20.0	1971	AFC
1972	NFC	Was. 218 15.6	Min. 200	Dal. 1515 108	G.B. 3.42	Dal. 7	Atl. 45.5	Min. 1791 128	Min. 5.4	G.B. 7	Min. 26	Min. 7.9	Was. 2.1	L.A. 18.5	1972	NFC
1972	AFC	Mia. 171 12.2	Mia. 186	Mia. 1548 111	Oak. 3.76	Pit. 6	Buf. 42.5	Cle. 1994 142	Cin. 5.8	Pit. 9	Pit. 28	Buf. 7.5	Mia. 3.9	Hou. 19.5	1972	AFC
1973	BFC	Min. 168 12.0	L.A. 173	Dal. 1471 105	Was. 3.34	Dal. 5 L.A. 5 Min. 5	Atl. 46.6	Atl. 1619 116	Atl. 5.0	Min. 8	Was. 26	NYG 7.3	Dal. 5.2	Min. 19.1	1973	NFC
1973	AFC	Mia. 150 10.7	Min. 168	Oak. 1470 105	Oak. 3.38	Oak. 5	Buf. 45.1	N.E. 1600 114	Mia. 5.0	Mia. 6	Pit. 37	Pit. 10.3	Cin. 4.6	Den. 20.4	1973	AFC

Bold – designates All-Time Leader

YEARLY PASSING LEADERS

		RANK		YARDS			COMPLETIONS			COMP. PCT.			TOUCHDOWNS			YARDS/ATT.			FEWEST PCT. INT.				
YEAR	LGUE	NAME	TEAM	NAME	TEAM		NAME	TEAM		NAME	TEAM		TEAM	NAME		NAME	TEAM		NAME	TEAM		YEAR	LGUE
1933	NFL	Friedman	Bkn.	Newman	NY G	973	Newman	NY G	53	Friedman	Bkn.	52.5	Newman	NY G	9	Molesworth	ChiB.	8.4	Monnett	G.B.	6.5	1933	NFL
1934	NFL	Herber	G.B.	Herber	G.B.	799	Herber	G.B.	42	Clark	Det.	46.9	Herber	G.B.	8	Clark	Det.	7.8	Newman	NY G	5.5	1934	NFL
1935	NFL	Danowski	NY G	Danowski	NY G	795	Danowski	NY G	57	Danowski	NY G	50.4	Danowski	NY G	11	Masterson	ChiB.	10.4	Not Available			1935	NFL
1936	NFL	Herber	G.B.	Herber	G.B.	1239	Herber	G.B.	77	Clark	Det.	53.5	Herber	G.B.	11	Herber	G.B.	7.2	Monnett	G.B.	3.8	1936	NFL
1937	NFL	Monnett	G.B.	Baugh	Was.	1127	Baugh	Was.	81	Monnett	G.B.	50.7	Monnett	G.B.	9	Masterson	ChiB.	8.5	Danowski	NY G	3.7	1937	NFL
1938	NFL	Monnett	G.B.	Parker	Bkn.	865	Danowski	NY G	70	Monnett	G.B	54.4	Monnett	G.B.	9	Monnett	G.B.	8.2	Parker	Bkn.	4.7	1938	NFL
1939	NFL	Filchock	Was.	O'Brien	Phi.	1324	Hall	Cle.	106	Filchock	Was.	61.8	Filchock	Was.	11	Filchock	Was.	12.3	Sloan	Det.	2.8	1939	NFL
1940	NFL	Baugh	Was.	Baugh	Was.	1367	O'Brien	Phi.	124	Baugh	Was.	62.7	Baugh	Was.	12	Luckman	ChiB.	9.0	Watkins	Phi.	3.5	1940	NFL
1941	NFL	Luckman	ChiB.	Isbell	G.B.	1479	Isbell	G.B.	117	Luckman	ChiB.	57.1	Isbell	G.B.	15	Luckman	ChiB.	9.9	Mallouf	ChiC.	4.2	1941	NFL
1942	NFL	Baugh	Was.	Isbell	G.B.	2021	Isbell	G.B.	146	Baugh	Was.	58.7	Isbell	G.B.	24	O'Rourke	ChiB.	10.8	Baugh	Was.	4.9	1942	NFL
1943	NFL	Luckman	ChiB.	Luckman	ChiB.	2194	Baugh	Was.	133	Baugh	Was.	56.2	Luckman	ChiB.	28	Luckman	ChiB.	10.9	Comp	G.B.	4.3	1943	NFL
1944	NFL	Filchock	Was.	Comp	G.B.	1159	Filchock	Was.	84	Filchock	Was.	57.1	Filchock	Was.	13	Ronzani	ChiB.	8.0	Baugh	Was.	5.5	1944	NFL
1945	NFL	Baugh	Was.	Luckman	ChiB.	1725	Baugh	Was.	128	Baugh	Was.	70.3	Luckman	ChiB.	14	Waterfield	Cle.	9.4	Baugh	Was.	2.2	1945	NFL
													Waterfield	Cle.	14								
1946	NFL	Luckman	ChiB.	Luckman	ChiB.	1826	Waterfield	L.A.	127	Thompson	Phi.	55.3	Waterfield	L.A.	18	Luckman	ChiB.	8.0	Governali	Bos.	5.2	1946	NFL
1946	AAFC	Graham	Cle.	Dobbs	Bkn.	1886	Dobbs	Bkn.	135	O'Rourke	L.A.	57.7	Graham	Cle.	17.	Graham	Cle.	10.5	Parker	N.Y.	2.6	1946	AAFC
1947	NFL	Baugh	Was.	Baugh	Was.	2938	Baugh	Was.	210	Baugh	Was.	59.3	Baugh	Was.	25	Luckman	ChiB.	8.4	Baugh	Was.	4.2	1947	NFL
1947	AAFC	Graham	Cle.	Graham	Cle.	2753	Schwenk	Bal.	168	Graham	Cle.	60.6	Graham	Cle.	25	Graham	Cle.	10.2	Graham	Cle.	4.1	1947	AAFC
1948	NFL	Baugh	Was.	Baugh	Was.	2599	Baugh	Was.	185	Baugh	Was.	58.7	Thompson	Phi.	25	LeForce	Det.	9.0	Hardy	L.A.	3.3	1948	NFL
1948	AAFC	Tittle	Bal.	Graham	Cle.	2713	Dobbs	L.A.	185	Albert	S.F.	58.3	Albert	S.F.	29	Tittle	Bal.	8.7	Tittle	Bal.	3.1	1948	AAFC
1949	NFL	Baugh	Was.	Lujack	ChiB.	2658	Lujack	ChiB.	162	Baugh	Was.	56.9	Lujack	ChiB.	23	Lujack	ChiB.	8.2	Enke	Det.	3.5	1949	NFL
1949	AAFC	Graham	Cle.	Graham	Cle.	2785	Graham	Cle.	161	Ratterman	Buf.	57.9	Albert	S.F.	27	Graham	Cle.	9.8	Graham	Cle.	3.5	1949	AAFC
1950	NFL	Van Brocklin	L.A.	Layne	Det.	2323	Tittle	Bal.	161	Waterfield	L.A.	57.3	Ratterman	NY Y	22	Van Brocklin	L.A.	8.8	Conerly	NY G	5.3	1950	NFL
1951	NFL	Graham	Cle.	Layne	Det.	2403	Layne	Det.	152	Thomason	G.B.	56.6	Layne	Det.	26	Waterfield	L.A.	8.9	Thomason	G.B.	4.1	1951	NFL
1952	NFL	Rote	G.B.	Graham	Cle.	2816	Graham	Cle.	181	Van Brocklin	L.A.	55.1	Finks	Pit.	20	Van Brocklin	L.A.	8.5	Thomason	Phi.	4.2	1952	NFL
													Graham	Cle.	20								
1953	NFL	Graham	Cle.	Graham	Cle.	2722	Blanda	ChiB.	169	Graham	Cle.	64.7	Thomason	Phi.	21	Graham	Cle.	10.6	Graham	Cle.	3.5	1953	NFL
1954	NFL	Layne	Det.	Van Brocklin	L.A.	2637	Rote	G.B.	180	Graham	Cle.	59.2	Burk	Phi.	23	Van Brocklin	L.A.	10.1	Tittle	S.F.	3.1	1954	NFL
1955	NFL	Graham	Cle.	Finks	Pit.	2270	Finks	Pit.	165	Graham	Cle.	53.0	Rote	G.B.	17	Graham	Cle.	9.3	Gilmer	Det.	3.3	1955	NFL
													Tittle	S.F.	17								
1956	NFL	Brown	ChiB.	Rote	G.B.	2203	Rote	G.B.	146	Brown	ChiB.	57.1	Rote	G.B.	18	Brown	ChiB.	9.9	Conerly	NY G	4.0	1956	NFL
1957	NFL	Unitas	Bal.	Unitas	Bal.	2550	Tittle	S.F.	176	Tittle	S.F.	63.1	Unitas	Bal.	24	O'Connell	Cle.	11.2	Morrall	Pit.	4.2	1957	NFL
1958	NFL	Unitas	Bal.	Wade	L.A.	2875	Van Brocklin	Phi.	198	Brodie	S.F.	59.9	Unitas	Bal.	19	Le Baron	Was.	9.4	Unitas	Bal.	2.7	1958	NFL
1959	NFL	Conerly	NY G	Unitas	Bal.	2899	Unitas	Bal.	193	Wade	L.A.	58.6	Unitas	Bal.	32	Conerly	NY G	8.8	Conerly	NY G	2.1	1959	NFL
1960	NFL	Plum	Cle.	Unitas	Bal.	3099	Unitas	Bal.	190	Plum	Cle.	60.4	Unitas	Bal.	25	Plum	Cle.	9.2	Plum	Cle.	2.0	1960	NFL
1960	AFL	Kemp	L.A.	Tripucka	Den.	3038	Tripucka	Den.	248	Flores	Oak.	54.0	Dorow	NY T	26	Kemp	L.A.	7.4	Songin	Bos.	3.8	1960	AFL
1961	NFL	Plum	Cle.	Jurgensen	Phi.	3723	Jurgensen	Phi.	235	Plum	Cle.	58.6	Jurgensen	Phi.	32	Brodie	S.F.	9.1	Plum	Cle.	3.3	1961	NFL
1961	AFL	Blanda	Hou.	Blanda	Hou.	3330	Dorow	NY T	197	Parilli	Bos.	52.5	Blanda	Hou.	36	Blanda	Hou.	9.2	Songin	Bos.	4.3	1961	AFL
1962	NFL	Starr	G.B.	Jurgensen	Phi.	3261	Wade	Chi.	225	Starr	G.B.	62.4	Tittle	NY G	33	Jurgensen	Phi.	8.9	Starr	G.B.	3.2	1962	NFL
1962	AFL	Dawson	Dal.	Tripuka	Den.	2917	Tripucka	Den.	240	Dawson	Dal.	61.0	Dawson	Dal.	29	Dawson	Dal.	8.9	Parilli	Bos.	3.2	1962	AFL
1963	NFL	Tittle	NY G	Unitas	Bal.	3481	Unitas	Bal.	237	Tittle	NY G	60.2	Tittle	NY G	36	Tittle	NY G	8.6	Unitas	Bal.	2.9	1963	NFL
1963	AFL	Rote	S.D.	Blanda	Hou.	3003	Blanda	Hou.	224	Rote	S.D.	59.4	Dawson	Dal.	26	Rote	S.D.	8.7	Wood	NY T	5.1	1963	AFL
1964	NFL	Starr	G.B.	Johnson	StL.	3045	Johnson	StL.	223	Bukich	Chi.	61.9	Ryan	Cle.	25	Unitas	Bal.	9.3	Starr	G.B.	1.5	1964	NFL
1964	AFL	Dawson	K.C.	Parilli	Bos.	3465	Blanda	Hou.	262	Dawson	K.C.	56.2	Parilli	Bos.	31	Kemp	Buf.	8.5	Dawson	K.C.	5.1	1964	AFL
1965	NFL	Bukich	ChiB.	Brodie	S.F.	3112	Brodie	S.F.	242	Brodie	S.F.	61.9	Brodie	S.F.	30	Unitas	Bal.	9.0	Bukich	Chi.	2.9	1965	NFL
1965	AFL	Dawson	K.C.	Hadl	S.D.	2798	Blanda	Hou.	186	Dawson	K.C.	53.4	Dawson	K.C.	21	Hadl	S.D.	8.0	Wood	Oak.	3.8	1965	AFL
1966	NFL	Starr	G.B.	Jurgensen	Was.	3209	Jurgensen	Was.	254	Starr	G.B.	62.2	Ryan	Cle.	29	Starr	G.B.	9.0	Starr	G.B.	1.2	1966	NFL
1966	AFL	Dawson	K.C.	Namath	NY J	3379	Namath	NY J	232	Dawson	K.C.	56.0	Dawson	K.C.	26	Dawson	K.C.	8.9	Trull	Hou.	2.9	1966	AFL
1967	NFL	Jurgensen	Was.	Jurgensen	Was.	3747	Jurgensen	Was.	288	Unitas	Bal.	58.5	Jurgensen	Was.	31	Starr	G.B.	8.7	Jurgensen	Was.	3.2	1967	NFL
1967	AFL	Lamonica	Oak.	Namath	NY J	4007	Namath	NY J	258	Dawson	K.C.	57.7	Lamonica	Oak.	30	Namath	NY J	8.2	Lamonica	Oak.	4.7	1967	AFL
1968	NFL	Morrall	Bal.	Brodie	S.F.	3020	Brodie	S.F.	234	Starr	G.B.	63.7	Morrall	Bal.	26	Starr	G.B.	9.5	Munson	Det.	2.4	1968	NFL
1968	AFL	Dawson	K.C.	Hadl	S.D.	3473	Hadl	S.D.	208	Dawson	K.C.	58.5	Hadl	S.D.	27	Dawson	K.C.	9.4	Stofa	Cin.	2.8	1968	AFL
1969	NFL	Jurgensen	Was.	Jurgensen	Was.	3102	Jurgensen	Was.	274	Starr	G.B.	62.2	Gabriel	L.A.	24	Horn	G.B.	9.0	Gabriel	L.A.	1.8	1969	NFL
1969	AFL	Cook	Cin.	Lamonica	Oak.	3302	Lamonica	Oak.	221	Dawson	K.C.	59.0	Lamonica	Oak.	34	Cook	Cin.	9.4	Hadl	S.D.	3.4	1969	AFL
1970	NFC	Brodie	S.F.	Brodie	S.F.	2941	Brodie	S.F.	223	Jurgensen	Was.	59.9	Brodie	S.F.	24	Morton	Dal.	8.8	Brodie	S.F.	2.7	1970	NFC
1970	AFC	Lamonica	Oak.	Lamonica	Oak.	2516	Lamonica	Oak.	179	Griese	Mia.	58.0	Hadl	S.D.	22	Griese	Mia.	8.2	Carter	Cin.	3.2	1970	AFC
													Lamonica	Oak.	22								
1971	NFC	Staubach	Dal.	Brodie	S.F.	2642	Tarkenton	NY G	226	Berry	Atl.	60.2	Brodie	S.F.	18	Staubach	Dal.	8.9	Staubach	Dal.	1.9	1971	NFC
1971	AFC	Griese	Mia.	Hadl	S.D.	3075	Hadl	S.D.	233	Carter	Cin.	62.2	Hadl	S.D.	21	Dawson	K.C.	8.3	Carter	Cin.	3.2	1971	AFC
1972	NFC	Tarkenton	Min.	Manning	N.O.	2781	Manning	N.O.	230	Snead	NY G	60.3	Kilmer	Was.	19	Berry	Atl.	7.8	Tarkenton	Min.	3.4	1972	NFC
1972	AFC	Morrall	Mia.	Namath	NY J	2816	Hadl	S.D.	190	Dawson	K.C.	57.4	Namath	NY J	19	Morrall	Mia.	9.1	Anderson	Cin.	2.3	1972	AFC
1973	NFC	Gabriel	Phi.	Gabriel	Phi.	3219	Gabriel	Phi.	270	Staubach	Dal.	62.6	Gabriel	Phi.	23	Staubach	Dal.	8.5	Tarkenton	Min.	2.6	1973	NFC
													Staubach	Dal.	23								
1973	AFC	Anderson	Cin.	Plunkett	N.E.	2550	Plunkett	N.E.	193	Stabler	Oak.	62.7	Johnson	Den.	20	Stabler	Oak.	7.7	Anderson	Cin.	3.6	1973	AFC

YEARLY RUSHING LEADERS

YEAR	LGUE	ATTEMPTS NAME	TEAM		YARDS NAME	TEAM		AVERAGE YARDS NAME	TEAM		TOUCHDOWNS NAME	TEAM		YEAR	LGUE
1933	NFL	Jim Musick	Bos.	173	Jim Musick	Bos.	809	Kink Richards	NY G	6.2	Glenn Presnell	Det.	6	1933	NFL
1934	NFL	Swede Hanson	Phi.	147	Beattie Feathers	ChiB.	1004	Beattie Feathers	ChiB.	9.9	Dutch Clark	Det.	8	1934	NFL
											Beattie Feathers	ChiB.	8		
1935	NFL	Kink Richards	NY G.	149	Doug Russell	ChiC.	499	Ernie Caddel	Det.	5.2	Ernie Caddel	Det.	6	1935	NFL
1936	NFL	Tuffy Leemans	NY G.	206	Tuffy Leemans	NY G.	830	Ernie Caddel	Det.	6.4	Dutch Clark	Det.	7	1936	NFL
1937	NFL	Cliff Battles	Was.	216	Cliff Battles	Was.	874	Ernie Caddel	Det.	5.6	Cliff Battles	Was.	5	1937	NFL
											Dutch Clark	Det.	5		
											Clark Hinkle	G.B.	5		
1938	NFL	Whizzer White	Pit.	152	Whizzer White	Pit.	567	Cecil Isbell	G.B.	5.2	Andy Farkas	Was.	6	1938	NFL
1939	NFL	Andy Farkas	Was.	139	Bill Osmanski	ChiB.	699	Joe Maniaci	ChiB.	7.1	Johnny Drake	Cle.	9	1939	NFL
1940	NFL	Whizzer White	Det.	146	Whizzer White	Det.	514	Banks McFadden	Bkn.	6.3	Johnny Drake	Cle.	9	1940	NFL
1941	NFL	Clarke Hinkle	G.B.	129	Pug Manders	Bkn.	486	George McAfee	ChiB.	7.3	Hugh Gallarneau	ChiB.	8	1941	NFL
1942	NFL	Bill Dudley	Pit.	162	Bill Dudley	Pit.	696	Frank Maznicki	ChiB.	6.4	Gary Famiglietti	ChiB.	8	1942	NFL
1943	NFL	Bill Paschal	NY G.	147	Bill Paschal	NY G.	572	Ward Cuff	NY G.	6.5	Bill Paschal	NY G.	10	1943	NFL
1944	NFL	Bill Paschal	NY G.	196	Bill Paschal	NY G.	737	Al Grygo	ChiB.	6.1	Bill Paschal	NY G.	9	1944	NFL
1945	NFL	Frank Akins	Was.	147	Steve Van Buren	Phi.	832	Fred Gehrke	Cle.	6.3	Steve Van Buren	Phi.	15	1945	NFL
1946	NFL	Bill Dudley	Pit.	146	Bill Dudley	Pit.	604	Elmer Angsman	ChiC.	6.8	Ted Fritsch	G.B.	9	1946	NFL
1946	AAFC	Spec Sanders	N.Y.	140	Spec Sanders	N.Y.	709	Chuck Fenenbock	L.A.	8.4	Len Eshmont	S.F.	6	1946	AAFC
											Don Greenwood	Cle.	6		
											John Kimbrough	L.A.	6		
											Spec Sanders	N.Y.	6		
1947	NFL	Steve Van Buren	Phi.	217	Steve Van Buren	Phi.	1008	Kenny Washington	L.A.	7.4	Steve Van Buren	Phi.	13	1947	NFL
1947	AAFC	Spec Sanders	N.Y.	231	Spec Sanders	N.Y.	1432	Special Delivery Jones	Cle.	7.0	Spec Sanders	N.Y.	18	1947	AAFC
1948	NFL	Steve Van Buren	Phi.	201	Steve Van Buren	Phi.	945	Charlie Trippi	ChiC.	5.4	Steve Van Buren	Phi.	10	1948	NFL
1948	AAFC	Spec Sanders	N.Y.	169	Marion Motley	Cle.	964	Joe Perry	S.F.	7.3	Chet Mutryn	Buf.	10	1948	AAFC
											Joe Perry	S.F.	10		
1949	NFL	Steve Van Buren	Phi.	263	Steve Van Buren	Phi.	1146	Bosh Pritchard	Phi.	6.0	Steve Van Buren	Phi.	11	1949	NFL
1949	AAFC	Bob Hoernschemeyer	Chi.	133	Joe Perry	S.F.	783	Frankie Albert	S.F.	7.1	Marion Motley	Cle.	8	1949	AAFC
											Joe Perry	S.F.	8		
1950	NFL	Joe Geri	Pit.	188	Marion Motley	Cle.	810	Johnny Lujack	ChiB.	6.3	Johnny Lujack	ChiB.	11	1950	NFL
		Steve Van Buren	Phi.	188											
1951	NFL	Eddie Price	NY G.	271	Eddie Price	NY G.	971	Tobin Rote	G.B.	6.9	Rob Goode	Was.	9	1951	NFL
1952	NFL	Eddie Price	NY G.	183	Dan Towler	L.A.	894	Hugh McElhenny	S.F.	7.0	Dan Towler	L.A.	10	1952	NFL
1953	NFL	Joe Perry	S.F.	192	Joe Perry	S.F.	1018	Skeets Quinlan	L.A.	7.3	Joe Perry	S.F.	10	1953	NFL
1954	NFL	Joe Perry	S.F.	173	Joe Perry	S.F.	1049	Hugh McElhenny	S.F.	8.0	Dan Towler	L.A.	11	1954	NFL
1955	NFL	Alan Ameche	Bal.	213	Alan Ameche	Bal.	961	Rick Casares	ChiB.	5.4	Alan Ameche	Bal.	9	1955	NFL
1956	NFL	Rick Casares	ChiB.	234	Rick Casares	ChiB.	1126	Lenny Moore	Bal.	7.5	Rick Casares	ChiB.	12	1956	NFL
1957	NFL	Rick Casares	ChiB.	204	Jimmy Brown	Cle.	942	Lenny Moore	Bal.	5.0	Jimmy Brown	Cle.	9	1957	NFL
1958	NFL	Jimmy Brown	Cle.	257	Jimmy Brown	Cle.	1527	Lenny Moore	Bal.	7.3	Jimmy Brown	Cle.	17	1958	NFL
1959	NFL	Jimmy Brown	Cle.	290	Jimmy Brown	Cle.	1329	Johnny Olszewski	Was.	6.6	Jimmy Brown	Cle.	14	1959	NFL
1960	NFL	Jim Taylor	G.B.	230	Jimmy Brown	Cle.	1257	John David Crow	StL.	5.9	Paul Hornung	G.B.	13	1960	NFL
1960	AFL	Abner Haynes	Dal.	156	Abner Haynes	Dal.	875	Paul Lowe	L.A.	6.3	Abner Haynes	Dal.	9	1960	AFL
											Paul Lowe	L.A.	9		
1961	NFL	Jimmy Brown	Cle.	305	Jimmy Brown	Cle.	1408	Lenny Moore	Bal.	7.0	Jim Taylor	G.B.	15	1961	NFL
1961	AFL	Bill Mathis	NY T.	202	Billy Cannon	Hou.	948	Jack Spikes	Dal.	8.6	Abner Haynes	Dal.	9	1961	AFL
											Paul Lowe	L.A.	9		
1962	NFL	Jim Taylor	G.B.	272	Jim Taylor	G.B.	1474	Amos Marsh	Dal.	5.6	Jim Taylor	G.B.	19	1962	NFL
1962	AFL	Charley Tolar	Hou.	244	Cookie Gilchrist	Buf.	1096	Len Dawson	Dal.	6.6	Cookie Gilchrist	Buf.	13	1962	AFL
											Abner Haynes	Dal.	13		
1963	NFL	Jimmy Brown	Cle.	291	Jimmy Brown	Cle.	1863	Jimmy Brown	Cle.	6.4	Jimmy Brown	Cle.	12	1963	NFL
1963	AFL	Cookie Gilchrist	Buf.	232	Clem Daniels	Oak.	1099	Keith Lincoln	S.D.	6.5	Cookie Gilchrist	Buf.	12	1963	AFL
1964	NFL	Jimmy Brown	Cle.	280	Jimmy Brown	Cle.	1446	Jimmy Brown	Cle.	5.2	Lenny Moore	Bal.	16	1964	NFL
1964	AFL	Cookie Gilchrist	Buf.	230	Cookie Gilchrist	Buf.	981	Mack Lee Hill	K.C.	5.5	Sid Blanks	Hou.	6	1964	AFL
											Cookie Gilchrist	Buf.	6		
											Daryle Lamonica	Buf.	6		
1965	NFL	Jimmy Brown	Cle.	289	Jimmy Brown	Cle.	1544	Timmy Brown	Phi.	5.4	Jimmy Brown	Cle	17	1965	NFL
1965	AFL	Cookie Gilchrist	Buf.	252	Paul Lowe	S.D.	1121	Paul Lowe	S.D.	5.1	Paul Lowe	S.D.	7	1965	AFL
1966	NFL	Bill Brown	Min.	251	Gale Sayers	Chi.	1231	Leroy Kelly	Cle.	5.5	Leroy Kelly	Cle.	15	1966	NFL
1966	AFL	Jim Nance	Bos.	299	Jim Nance	Bos.	1458	Mike Garrett	K.C.	5.5	Jim Nance	Bos.	11	1966	AFL
1967	NFL	Leroy Kelly	Cle.	235	Leroy Kelly	Cle.	1205	Leroy Kelly	Cle.	5.1	Leroy Kelly	Cle.	11	1967	NFL
1967	AFL	Jim Nance	Bos.	269	Jim Nance	Bos.	1216	Brad Hubbert	S.D.	5.5	Emerson Boozer	NY J.	10	1967	AFL
1968	NFL	Leroy Kelly	Cle.	248	Leroy Kelly	Cle.	1239	Gale Sayers	Chi.	6.2	Leroy Kelly	Cle.	16	1968	NFL
1968	AFL	Paul Robinson	Cin.	238	Paul Robinson	Cin.	1023	Dickie Post	S.D.	5.0	Paul Robinson	Cin.	8	1968	AFL
1969	NFL	Gale Sayers	Chi.	236	Gale Sayers	Chi.	1032	Tony Baker	N.O.	4.8	Tom Matte	Bal.	11	1969	NFL
1969	AFL	Jim Nance	Bos.	193	Dickie Post	S.D.	873	Carl Garrett	Bos.	5.0	Jim Kiick	Mia.	9	1969	AFL
1970	NFC	Ron Johnson	NY G.	263	Larry Brown	Was.	1125	Duane Thomas	Dal.	5.3	MacArthur Lane	StL.	11	1970	NFC
1970	AFC	Floyd Little	Den.	209	Floyd Little	Den.	901	John Fuqua	Pit.	5.0	John Fuqua	Pit.	7	1970	AFC
											Jim Nance	Bos.	7		
											Bo Scott	Cle.	7		
1971	NFC	Larry Brown	Was.	253	John Brockington	G.B.	1105	John Brockington	G.B.	5.1	Duane Thomas	Dal.	11	1971	NFC
1971	AFC	Floyd Little	Den.	284	Floyd Little	Den.	1133	Larry Csonka	Mia.	5.4	Leroy Kelly	Cle.	10	1971	AFC
1972	NFC	Ron Johnson	NY G.	298	Larry Brown	Was.	1216	Bobby Douglass	Chi.	6.9	Ron Johnson	NY G.	9	1972	NFC
											Greg Landry	Det.	9		
1972	AFC	O. J. Simpson	Buf.	292	O. J. Simpson	Buf.	1251	Franco Harris	Pit.	5.6	Mercury Morris	Mia.	12	1972	AFC
1973	NFC	Calvin Hill	Dal.	273	John Brockington	G.B.	1144	Bobby Douglass	Chi.	5.6	Donny Anderson	StL.	10	1973	NFC
1973	AFC	O. J. Simpson	Buf.	332	O. J. Simpson	Buf.	2003	Mercury Morris	Mia.	6.4	Floyd Little	Den.	12	1973	AFC
											O. J. Simpson	Buf.	12		

YEARLY LEADERS

RECEIVING | INTERCEPTION RETURNS

YEAR	LGUE	RECEPTIONS NAME	TEAM		YARDS NAME	TEAM		AVERAGE YARDS NAME	TEAM		TOUCHDOWNS NAME	TEAM		INTERCEPTION RETURNS NAME	TEAM		YEAR	LGUE
1933	NFL	Shipwreck Kelly	Bkn.	22	Paul Moss	Pit.	383	Paul Moss	Pit.	29.5	5 tied with 3 each						1933	NFL
1934	NFL	Red Badgro	NY G	16	Harry Ebding	Det.	257	Harry Ebding	Det.	28.6	Bill Hewitt	Chi B	5				1934	NFL
		Joe Carter	Phi.	16														
1935	NFL	Tod Goodwin	NY G	26	Charley Malone	Bos.	433	Joe Carter	Phi.	23.6	Don Hutson	G.B.	7				1935	NFL
1936	NFL	Don Hutson	G.B.	34	Don Hutson	G.B.	526	Bill Hewitt	Chi B	23.9	Don Hutson	G.B.	8				1936	NFL
1937	NFL	Don Hutson	G.B.	41	Gaynell Tinsley	Chi C	675	Jeff Barrett	Bkn.	23.1	Don Hutson	G.B.	7				1937	NFL
1938	NFL	Gaynell Tinsley	Chi C	41	Don Hutson	G.B.	548	Jim Benton	Cle.	19.9	Don Hutson	G.B.	9				1938	NFL
1939	NFL	Don Hutson	G.B.	34	Don Hutson	G.B.	846	Andy Farkas	Was.	27.3	Jim Benton	Cle.	7				1939	NFL
1940	NFL	Don Looney	Phi.	58	Don Looney	Phi.	707	Paul McDonough	Cle.	26.3	Don Hutson	G.B.	7	Don Hutson	G.B.	6	1940	NFL
														Ace Parker	Bkn.	6		
														Rip Ryan	Det.	6		
1941	NFL	Don Hutson	G.B.	58	Don Hutson	G.B.	738	Ken Kavanaugh	Chi B	28.5	Don Hutson	G.B.	10	Marshall Goldberg	Chi C	7	1941	NFL
														Art Jones	Pit.	7		
1942	NFL	Don Hutson	G.B.	74	Don Hutson	G.B.	1211	Ray McLean	Chi B	30.1	Don Hutson	G.B.	17	Bulldog Turner	Chi B	8	1942	NFL
1943	NFL	Don Hutson	G.B.	47	Don Hutson	G.B.	776	Tony Bova	P–P	24.6	Don Hutson	G.B.	11	Sammy Baugh	Was.	11	1943	NFL
1944	NFL	Don Hutson	G.B.	58	Don Hutson	G.B.	866	Mel Bleeker	Phi.	37.4	Don Hutson	G.B.	9	Howie Livingston	NY G	9	1944	NFL
1945	NFL	Don Hutson	G.B.	47	Jim Benton	Cle.	1067	Frank Liebel	NY G	27.0	Frank Liebel	NY G	10	Roy Zimmerman	Phi.	7	1945	NFL
1946	NFL	Jim Benton	L.A.	63	Jim Benton	L.A.	981	Bill Dewell	Chi C	23.8	Bill Dewell	Chi C	7	Bill Dudley	Pit.	10	1946	NFL
1946	AAFC	Alyn Beals	S.F.	40	Dante Lavelli	Cle.	843	Jim McCarthy	Bkn.	26.9	Alyn Beals	S.F.	10	Tom Colella	Cle.	10	1946	AAFC
		Dante Lavelli	Cle.	40														
1947	NFL	Jim Keane	Chi B	64	Mal Kutner	Chi C	944	Dan Currivan	Bos.	32.6	Ken Kavanaugh	Chi B	13	Frank Reagan	NY G	10	1947	NFL
														Frank Seno	Bos.	10		
1947	AAFC	Mac Speedie	Cle.	67	Mac Speedie	Cle.	1146	Crazy Legs Hirsch	Chi.	28.2	Alyn Beals	S.F.	10	Tom Colella	Cle.	6	1947	AAFC
														Len Eshmont	S.F.	6		
														Bill Killagher	Chi.	6		
1948	NFL	Tom Fears	L.A.	51	Mal Kutner	Chi.C	943	Frank Seno	Bos.	24.8	Mal Kutner	Chi C	14	Dan Sandifer	Was.	13	1948	NFL
1948	AAFC	Mac Speedie	Cle.	58	Billy Hillenbrand	Bal.	970	John North	Bal.	26.0	Alyn Beals	S.F.	14	Otto Schnellbacher	N.Y.	11	1948	AAFC
1949	NFL	Tom Fears	L.A.	77	Bob Mann	Det.	1014	Elbie Nickel	Pit.	24.3	Tom Fears	L.A.	9	Bob Nussbaumer	Chi C	12	1949	NFL
											Ken Kavanaugh	Chi B	9					
											Hugh Taylor	Was.	9					
1949	AAFC	Mac Speedie	Cle.	62	Mac Speedie	Cle.	1028	Bill Boedecker	Cle.	33.7	Alyn Beals	S.F.	12	Jim Cason	S.F.	9	1949	AAFC
1950	NFL	Tom Fears	L.A.	84	Tom Fears	L.A.	1116	Hugh Taylor	Was.	21.4	Bob Shaw	Chi C	12	Spec Sanders	NY Y	13	1950	NFL
1951	NFL	Crazy Legs Hirsch	L.A.	66	Crazy Legs Hirsch	L.A.	1495	Crazy Legs Hirsch	L.A.	22.7	Crazy Legs Hirsch	L.A.	17	Otto Schnellbacher	NY G	11	1951	NFL
1952	NFL	Mac Speedie	Cle.	62	Billy Howton	G.B.	1231	Hugh Taylor	Was.	23.4	Cloyce Box	Det.	15	Night Train Lane	L.A.	14	1952	NFL
1953	NFL	Pete Pihos	Phi.	63	Pete Pihos	Phi.	1049	Bob Boyd	L.A.	22.8	Pete Pihos	Phi.	10	Jack Christiansen	Det.	12	1953	NFL
											Billy Wilson	S.F.	10					
1954	NFL	Pete Pihos	Phi.	60	Bob Boyd	L.A.	1212	Harlon Hill	Chi B	25.0	Harlon Hill	Chi B	12	Night Train Lane	Chi C	10	1954	NFL
		Billy Wilson	S.F.	60														
1955	NFL	Pete Pihos	Phi.	62	Pete Pihos	Phi.	864	Ray Renfro	Cle.	20.8	Harlon Hill	Chi B	9	Will Sherman	L.A.	11	1955	NFL
1956	NFL	Billy Wilson	S.F.	60	Billy Howton	G.B.	1188	Harlon Hill	Chi B	24.0	Billy Howton	G.B.	12	Linden Crow	Chi C	11	1956	NFL
1957	NFL	Billy Wilson	S.F.	52	Ray Berry	Bal.	800	Ray Renfro	Cle.	28.0	Jim Mutscheller	Bal.	8	Jack Butler	Pit.	10	1957	NFL
														Jack Christiansen	Det.	10		
														Milt Davis	Bal.	10		
1958	NFL	Ray Berry	Bal.	56	Del Shofner	L.A.	1097	Jimmy Orr	Pit.	27.6	Ray Berry	Bal.	9	Jimmy Patton	NY G	11	1958	NFL
		Pete Retzlaff	Phi.	56							Tommy McDonald	Phi.	9					
1959	NFL	Ray Berry	Bal.	66	Ray Berry	Bal.	959	Max McGee	G.B.	23.2	Ray Berry	Bal.	14	Milt Davis	Bal.	7	1959	NFL
														Dean Derby	Pit.	7		
														Don Shinnick	Bal.	7		
1960	NFL	Ray Berry	Bal.	74	Ray Berry	Bal.	1298	Buddy Dial	Pit.	24.3	Sonny Randle	St L.	15	Dave Baker	S.F.	10	1960	NFL
														Jerry Norton	St L.	10		
1960	AFL	Lionel Taylor	Den.	92	Bill Groman	Hou.	1473	Bill Groman	Hou.	20.5	Art Powell	NY T	14	Goose Gonsoulin	Den.	11	1960	AFL
1961	NFL	Jim Phillips	L.A.	78	Tommy McDonald	Phi.	1144	Franke Clarke	Dal.	22.4	Tommy McDonald	Phi.	13	Dick Lynch	NY G	9	1961	NFL
1961	AFL	Lionel Taylor	Den.	100	Charley Hennigan	Hou.	1746	Bill Groman	Hou.	23.5	Bill Groman	Hou.	17	Billy Atkins	Buf.	10	1961	AFL
1962	NFL	Bobby Mitchell	Was.	72	Bobby Mitchell	Was.	1384	Frank Clarke	Dal.	22.2	Frank Clarke	Dal.	14	Willie Wood	G.B.	9	1962	NFL
1962	AFL	Lionel Taylor	Den.	77	Art Powell	NY T	1130	Jim Colclough	Bos.	21.7	Chris Burford	Dal.	12	Lee Riley	NY T	11	1962	AFL
1963	NFL	Bobby Joe Conrad	St L.	73	Bobby Mitchell	Was.	1436	Buddy Dial	Pit.	21.6	Terry Barr	Det.	13	Dick Lynch	NY G	9	1963	NFL
											Gary Collins	Cle.	13	Rosey Taylor	Chi B	9		
1963	AFL	Lionel Taylor	Den.	78	Art Powell	Oak.	1304	Clem Daniels	Oak.	22.8	Art Powell	Oak.	16	Freddy Glick	Hou.	12	1963	AFL
1964	NFL	Johnny Morris	Chi.	93	Johnny Morris	Chi.	1200	Gary Ballman	Pit.	19.9	Bobby Mitchell	Was.	10	Paul Krause	Was.	12	1964	NFL
											Johnny Morris	Chi B	10					
											Bucky Pope	L.A.	10					
1964	AFL	Charley Hennigan	Hou.	101	Charley Hennigan	Hou.	1546	Elbert Dubenion	Buf.	27.1	Lance Alworth	S.D.	13	Dainard Paulson	NY T	12	1964	AFL
1965	NFL	Dave Parks	S.F.	80	Dave Parks	S.F.	1344	Bob Hayes	Dal.	21.8	Bob Hayes	Dal.	12	Bobby Boyd	Bal.	9	1965	NFL
											Dave Parks	S.F.	12					
1965	AFL	Lionel Taylor	Den.	85	Lance Alworth	S.D.	1602	Lance Alworth	S.D.	23.2	Lance Alworth	S.D.	14	W. K. Hicks	Hou.	9	1965	AFL
											Don Maynard	NY J	14					
1966	NFL	Charley Taylor	Was.	72	Pat Studstill	Det.	1266	Homer Jones	NY G	21.8	Bob Hayes	Dal.	13	Larry Wilson	St L.	10	1966	NFL
1966	AFL	Lance Alworth	S.D.	73	Lance Alworth	S.D.	1383	Otis Taylor	K.C.	22.4	Lance Alworth	S.D.	13	Bobby Hunt	K.C.	10	1966	AFL
														Johnny Robinson	K.C.	10		
1967	NFL	Charley Taylor	Was.	70	Ben Hawkins	Phi.	1265	Homer Jones	NY G	24.7	Homer Jones	NY G	13	Lem Barney	Det.	10	1967	NFL
														Dave Whitsell	N.O.	10		
1967	AFL	George Sauer	NY J	75	Don Maynard	NY J	1434	Don Maynard	NY J	20.2	Al Denson	Den.	11	Miller Farr	Hou.	10	1967	AFL
											Otis Taylor	K.C.	11	Tom Janik	Buf.	10		
														Dick Westmoreland	Mia.	10		
1968	NFL	Clifton McNeil	S.F.	71	Roy Jefferson	Pit.	1074	Homer Jones	NY G	23.5	Paul Warfield	Cle.	12	Willie Williams	NY G	10	1968	NFL
1968	AFL	Lance Alworth	S.D.	68	Lance Alworth	S.D.	1312	Don Maynard	NY J	22.8	Warren Wells	Oak.	11	Dave Grayson	Oak.	10	1968	AFL
1969	NFL	Dan Abramowicz	N.O.	73	Harold Jackson	Phi.	1116	Lance Rentzel	Dal.	22.3	Lance Rentzel	Dal.	12	Mel Renfro	Dal.	10	1969	NFL
1969	AFL	Lance Alworth	S.D.	64	Warren Wells	Oak.	1260	Warren Wells	Oak.	26.8	Warren Wells	Oak.	14	Emmitt Thomas	K.C.	9	1969	AFL
1970	NFC	Dick Gordon	Chi B	71	Gene Washington	S.F.	1100	John Gilliam	St L.	21.2	Dick Gordon	Chi B	13	Dick LeBeau	Det.	9	1970	NFC
1970	AFC	Marlon Briscoe	Buf.	57	Marlon Briscoe	Buf.	1036	Gary Garrison	S.D.	22.9	Gary Garrison	S.D.	12	Johnny Robinson	K.C.	10	1970	AFC
1971	NFC	Bob Tucker	NY G	59	Gene Washington	S.F.	884	Bob Hayes	Dal.	24.0	Bob Hayes	Dal.	8	Bill Bradley	Phi.	11	1971	NFC
1971	AFC	Fred Biletnikoff	Oak.	61	Otis Taylor	K.C.	1110	Paul Warfield	Mia.	23.2	Paul Warfield	Mia.	11	Ken Houston	Hou.	9	1971	AFC
1972	NFC	Harold Jackson	Phi.	62	Harold Jackson	Phi.	1048	John Gilliam	Min.	22.0	Gene Washington	S.F.	12	Bill Bradley	Phi.	9	1972	NFC
1972	AFC	Fred Biletnikoff	Oak.	58	Rich Caster	NY J	833	Rich Caster	NY J	21.4	Rich Caster	NY J	10	Mike Sensibaugh	K.C.	8	1972	AFC
1973	NFC	Harold Carmichael	Phi.	67	Harold Carmichael	Phi.	1116	Harold Jackson	L.A.	21.9	Harold Jackson	L.A.	13	Bobby Bryant	Min.	7	1973	NFC
1973	AFC	Fred Willis	Hou.	57	Issac Curtis	Cin.	843	Issac Curtis	Cin.	18.7	Paul Warfield	Mia.	11	Dick Anderson	Mia.	8	1973	AFC
														Mike Wagner	Pit.	8		

YEARLY RETURN LEADERS

		PUNT RETURNS: RETURNS			PUNT RETURNS: YARDS			PUNT RETURNS: AVERAGE YARDS			KICKOFF RETURNS: RETURNS			KICKOFF RETURNS: YARDS			KICKOFF RETURNS: AVERAGE YARDS				
YEAR	LGUE	NAME	TEAM		NAME	TEAM		NAME	TEAM		NAME	TEAM		NAME	TEAM		NAME	TEAM		YEAR	LGUE
1941	NFL	Whizzer White	Det.	19	Whizzer White	Det.	262													1941	NFL
1942	NFL	Merl Condit	Bkn.	21	Bill Dudley	Pit.	271	Ernie Steele	Phi.	26.4	Marshall Golberg	ChiC	15	Marshall Goldberg	ChiC	393	Bill Dudley	Pit.	27.1	1942	NFL
1943	NFL	Andy Farkas	Was.	15	Frankie Sinkwich	Det.	228	Frankie Sinkwich	Det.	20.7	Ken Heineman	Bkn.	16	Ken Heineman	Bkn.	442	Ned Mathews	Det.	35.1	1943	NFL
1944	NFL	Bob Davis	Bos.	22	Bob Davis	Bos.	271	Ernie Steele	Phi.	16.5	John Grigas	C–P	23	John Grigas	C–P	471	Steve Van Buren	Phi.	33.3	1944	NFL
1945	NFL	Steve Bagarus	Was.	21	Steve Bagarus	Was.	251	Fred Gehrke	Cle.	15.0	Frank Seno	ChiC	19	Frank Seno	ChiC	408	Ted Fritsch	G.B.	34.9	1945	NFL
1946	NFL	Bill Dudley	Pit.	27	Bill Dudley	Pit.	385	Gil Steinke	Phi.	14.5	Sonny Karnofsky	Bos.	21	Sonny Karnofsky	Bos.	599	Frank Seno	ChiC	31.4	1946	NFL
1946	AAFC	Ken Casanega	S.F.	18	Chuck Fenenbock	L.A.	299	Chuck Fenenbock	L.A.	18.7	Steve Juzwik	Buf.	21	Chuck Fenenbock	L.A.	479	Monk Gafford	Bkn–Mia	31.4	1946	AAFC
		Bob Seymour	L.A.	18																	
1947	NFL	Walt Slater	Pit.	28	Walt Slater	Pit.	435	Frank Seno	Bos.	17.8	Eddie Saenz	Was.	29	Eddie Saenz	Was.	797	Steve Van Buren	Phi.	29.4	1947	NFL
1947	AAFC	Glenn Dobbs	Bkn–L.A.	19	Glenn Dobbs	Bkn–L.A.	215	Spec Sanders	N.Y.	27.3	Spec Sanders	N.Y.	22	Chet Mutryn	Buf.	691	Chet Mutryn	Buf.	32.9	1947	AAFC
1948	NFL	George McAfee	ChiB	30	George McAfee	ChiB	417	Jerry Davis	ChiC	20.9	Dan Sandifer	Was.	26	Dan Sandifer	Was.	594	Frank Minini	G.B.	30.8	1948	NFL
1948	AAFC	Cliff Lewis	Cle.	26	Herm Wedemeyer	L.A.	368	Tom Casey	N.Y.	25.4	Monk Gafford	Bkn.	23	Monk Gafford	Bkn.	559	Forrest Hall	S.F.	28.4	1948	AAFC
1949	NFL	Vitamin Smith	L.A.	27	Vitamin Smith	L.A.	427	Red Cochran	ChiC	20.9	Eddie Saenz	Was.	24	Don Doll	Det.	536	J. Salschneider	NY G	31.6	1949	NFL
											Dan Sandifer	Was.	24								
1949	AAFC	Pete Layden	N.Y.	29	Jim Cason	S.F.	351	Buddy Young	N.Y.	19.0	Herm Wedemeyer	Bal.	30	Herm Wedemeyer	Bal.	602	Ray Ramsey	Chi.	29.2	1949	AAFC
1950	NFL	George McAfee	ChiB	33	Billy Grimes	G.B.	555	Herb Rich	Bal.	23.0	Don Paul	ChiC	28	Vitamin Smith	L.A.	742	Vitamin Smith	L.A.	33.7	1950	NFL
1951	NFL	Em Tunnell	NY G	34	Em Tunnell	NY G	489	Buddy Young	NY Y	19.3	George Taliaferro	NY Y	27	George Taliaferro	NY Y	622	Lynn Chadnois	Pit.	32.5	1951	NFL
1952	NFL	Bibbles Bawel	Phi.	34	Em Tunnell	NY G	411	J. Christiansen	Det.	21.5	Billy Baggett	Dal.	23	Buddy Young	Dal.	643	Lynn Chadnois	Pit.	35.2	1952	NFL
											Buddy Young	Dal.	23								
1953	NFL	Em Tunnell	NY G	38	Woodley Lewis	L.A.	267	Charlie Trippi	ChiC	11.4	Woodley Lewis	L.A.	32	Woodley Lewis	L.A.	830	Joe Arenas	S.F.	34.4	1953	NFL
1954	NFL	Chet Hanulak	Cle.	27	Veryl Switzer	G.B.	306	Veryl Switzer	G.B.	12.8	Woodley Lewis	L.A.	34	Woodley Lewis	L.A.	836	Billy Reynolds	Cle.	29.5	1954	NFL
1955	NFL	Bert Rechichar	Bal.	30	Ollie Matson	ChiC	245	Ollie Matson	ChiC	18.8	Sid Watson	Pit.	27	Sid Watson	Pit.	716	Al Carmichael	G.B.	29.9	1955	NFL
1956	NFL	Carl Taseff	Bal.	27	Carl Taseff	Bal.	233	Kenny Konz	Cle.	14.4	Al Carmichael	G.B.	33	Al Carmichael	G.B.	927	Tom Wilson	L.A.	31.8	1956	NFL
1957	NFL	Tommy McDonald	Phi.	26	Bert Zagers	Was.	217	Bert Zagers	Was.	15.5	Al Carmichael	G.B.	31	Al Carmichael	G.B.	690	Jon Arnett	L.A.	28.0	1957	NFL
1958	NFL	Carl Taseff	Bal.	29	Jon Arnett	L.A.	223	Jon Arnett	L.A.	12.4	Jimmy Sears	ChiC	32	Jimmy Sears	ChiC	756	Ollie Matson	ChiC	35.5	1958	NFL
1959	NFL	Bill Stacy	ChiC	29	Bill Stacy	ChiC	281	Johnny Morris	ChiB	12.2	Lenny Lyles	S.F.	25	Lenny Lyles	S.F.	565	Abe Woodson	S.F.	29.4	1959	NFL
1960	NFL	Bill Stits	NY G	18	Abe Woodson	S.F.	174	Abe Woodson	S.F.	13.4	Ted Dean	Phi.	26	Ted Dean	Phi.	533	Tom Moore	G.B.	33.1	1960	NFL
											Tom Frankhouser	Dal.	26								
1960	AFL	Al Carmichael	Den.	15	Abner Haynes	Dal.	215	Abner Haynes	Dal.	15.4	Leon Burton	NY T	31	Leon Burton	NY T	897	Ken Hall	Hou.	31.3	1960	AFL
1961	NFL	Johnny Sample	Pit.	26	Johnny Sample	Pit.	283	Willie Wood	G.B.	16.1	Timmy Brown	Phi.	29	Timmy Brown	Phi.	811	Dick Bass	L.A.	30.3	1961	NFL
											Jim Steffen	Was.	29								
1961	AFL	Fred Bruney	Bos.	23	Dick Christy	NY T	383	Dick Christy	NY T	21.3	George Fleming	Oak.	29	Frank Jackson	Dal.	645	Dave Grayson	Oak.	28.3	1961	AFL
1962	NFL	Pat Studstill	Det.	29	Pat Studstill	Det.	457	Pat Studstill	Det.	15.8	Abe Woodson	S.F.	37	Abe Woodson	S.F.	1157	Abe Woodson	S.F.	31.3	1962	NFL
1962	AFL	Leon Burton	Bos.	21	Dick Christy	NY T	250	Dick Christy	NY T	16.7	Dick Christy	NY T	38	Dick Christy	NY T	824	Bobby Jancik	Hou.	30.3	1962	AFL
1963	NFL	Tom Watkins	Det.	32	Tom Watkins	Det.	399	Dick James	Was.	13.4	Timmy Brown	Phi.	33	Timmy Brown	Phi.	945	Abe Woodson	S.F.	32.2	1963	NFL
											Bill Butler	Min.	33								
1963	AFL	Claude Gibson	Oak.	26	Claude Gibson	Oak.	307	Claude Gibson	Oak.	11.8	Bobby Jancik	Hou.	45	Bobby Jancik	Hou.	1317	Bobby Jancik	Hou.	29.3	1963	AFL
1964	NFL	Mel Renfro	Dal.	32	Mel Renfro	Dal.	418	Tom Watkins	Det.	14.9	Mel Renfro	Dal.	40	Mel Renfro	Dal.	1017	Clarence Childs	NY G	29.0	1964	NFL
1964	AFL	Hagood Clarke	Buf.	33	Claude Gibson	Oak.	419	Bobby Jancik	Hou.	18.3	Odell Barry	Den.	47	Odel Barry	Den.	1245	Bo Roberson	Oak.	27.1	1964	AFL
1965	NFL	Alvin Haymond	Bal.	41	Alvin Haymond	Bal.	403	Leroy Kelly	Cle.	15.6	Kermit Alexander	S.F.	32	Kermit Alexander	S.F.	741	Tom Watkins	Det.	34.4	1965	AFL
1965	AFL	Claude Gibson	Oak.	31	Speedy Duncan	S.D.	464	Speedy Duncan	S.D.	15.5	Abner Haynes	Den.	34	Abner Haynes	Den.	901	Abner Haynes	Den.	26.5	1965	AFL
1966	NFL	Alvin Haymond	Bal.	40	Alvin Haymond	Bal.	347	Johnny Roland	StL.	11.1	Ron Smith	Atl.	43	Ron Smith	Atl.	1013	Gale Sayers	Chi.	31.2	1966	NFL
1966	AFL	Rodger Bird	Oak.	37	Rodger Bird	Oak.	323	Speedy Duncan	S.D.	13.2	Bobby Jancik	Hou.	34	Bobby Jancik	Hou.	875	Goldie Sellers	Den.	28.5	1966	AFL
1967	NFL	Doug Cunningham	S.F.	27	Bob Hayes	Dal.	276	Ben Davis	Cle.	12.7	Ron Smith	Atl.	39	Ron Smith	Atl.	976	Travis Williams	G.B.	41.1	1967	NFL
1967	AFL	Rodger Bird	Oak.	46	Rodger Bird	Oak.	612	Floyd Little	Den.	16.9	Noland Smith	K.C.	41	Noland Smith	K.C.	1148	Zeke Moore	Hou.	28.9	1967	AFL
1968	NFL	Roy Jefferson	Pit.	28	Chuck Latourette	StL.	345	Bob Hayes	Dal.	20.8	Chuck Latourette	StL.	46	Chuck Latourette	StL.	1237	Preston Pearson	Bal.	35.1	1968	NFL
		Chuck Latourette	StL.	28																	
1968	AFL	Butch Atkinson	Oak.	36	Butch Atkinson	Oak.	490	Noland Smith	K.C.	15.0	Max Anderson	Buf.	39	Max Anderson	Buf.	971	Butch Atkinson	Oak.	25.1	1968	AFL
1969	NFL	Charlie West	Min.	39	Alvin Haymond	L.A.	435	Alvin Haymond	L.A.	13.2	Preston Pearson	Bal.	31	Bo Scott	Cle.	722	Bobby Williams	Det.	33.1	1969	NFL
1969	AFL	Jerry LeVias	Hou.	35	Jerry LeVias	Hou.	292	Bill Thompson	Den.	11.5	Mercury Morris	Mia.	43	Mercury Morris	Mia.	1136	Bill Thompson	Den.	28.5	1969	AFL
1970	NFC	Alvin Haymond	L.A.	53	Bruce Taylor	S.F.	516	Bruce Taylor	S.F.	12.0	Alvin Haymond	L.A.	35	Alvin Haymond	L.A.	1022	Cecil Turner	Chi.	32.7	1970	NFC
1970	AFC	Hubie Bryant	Pit.	37	Ron Gardin	Bal.	330	Ed Podolak	K.C.	13.5	Mike Battle	NY J	40	Mike Battle	NY J	891	Jim Duncan	Bal.	35.4	1970	AFC
1971	NFC	Bruce Taylor	S.F.	34	Bruce Taylor	S.F.	235	Speedy Duncan	Was.	10.6	Dave Hampton	G.B.	46	Dave Hampton	G.B.	1314	Travis Williams	L.A.	29.7	1971	NFC
1971	AFC	Jake Scott	Mia.	33	Jake Scott	Mia.	318	Leroy Kelly	Cle.	9.7	Linzy Cole	Hou.	32	Linzy Cole	Hou.	834	Mercury Morris	Mia.	28.2	1971	AFC
1972	NFC	Ron Smith	Chi.	26	Jim Bertelsen	L.A.	232	Ken Ellis	G.B.	15.4	Margene Adkins	N.O.	43	Margene Adkins	N.O.	1020	Ron Smith	Chi.	30.8	1972	NFC
1972	AFC	Bruce Laird	Bal.	34	Bruce Laird	Bal.	303	C. Farasopoulos	NY J	10.5	Jesse Taylor	S.D.	31	Bruce Laird	Bal.	843	Bruce Laird	Bal.	29.1	1972	AFC
1973	NFC	Ray Brown	Atl.	40	Ray Brown	Atl.	360	Bruce Taylor	S.F.	13.8	Herb Mul-Key	Was.	36	Herb Mul-Key	Was.	1011	Carl Garrett	Chi.	30.4	1973	NFC
1973	AFC	Butch Atkinson	Oak.	41	Bill Thompson	Den.	366	Ron Smith	S.D.	13.0	Mack Herron	N.E.	41	Mack Herron	N.E.	1092	Wallace Francis	Buf.	29.9	1973	AFC

YEARLY LEADERS

		PUNTING			FIELD GOALS													
		AVERAGE			MADE			PERCENTAGE			PAT'S MADE			POINTS SCORED				
YEAR	LGUE	NAME	TEAM		NAME	TEAM		NAME	TEAM		NAME	TEAM		NAME	TEAM		YEAR	LGUE
1933	NFL				Jack Manders	Chi B	5				Jack Manders	Chi B	14	Glenn Pressnell	Det.	63	1933	NFL
					Glenn Pressnell	Det.	5				Ken Strong	NY G	14					
					Ken Strong	NY G	5											
1934	NFL				Jack Manders	Chi B	10				Jack Manders	Chi B	31	Jack Manders	Chi B	79	1934	NFL
1935	NFL				Armand Niccolai	Pit.	6				Dutch Clark	Det.	16	Dutch Clark	Det.	55	1935	NFL
					Bill Smith	Chi C	6				Jack Manders	Chi B	16					
1936	NFL				Jack Manders	Chi B	7				Dutch Clark	Det.	19	Dutch Clark	Det.	73	1936	NFL
					Armand Niccolai	Pit.	7											
1937	NFL				Jack Manders	Chi B	8				Riley Smith	Was.	22	Jack Manders	Chi B	69	1937	NFL
1938	NFL				Ward Cuff	NY G	5	Regis Monahan	Det.	80	Ward Cuff	NY G	18	Clarke Hinkle	G.B.	58	1938	NFL
					Ralph Kercheval	Bkn.	5											
1939	NFL	George Faust	Chi C	44	Ward Cuff	NY G	7	Chuck Hanneman	Det.	80	Tiny Engebretsen	G.B.	18	Andy Farkas	Was.	68	1939	NFL
		Sid Luckman	Chi B	44														
1940	NFL	Sammy Baugh	Was.	51.3	Clarke Hinkle	G.B.	9	Clarke Hinkle	G.B.	64	Ace Parker	Bkn.	19	Don Hutson	G.B.	57	1940	NFL
1941	NFL	Sammy Baugh	Was.	48.7	Clarke Hinkle	G.B.	6	Andy Marefos	NY G	80	Don Hutson	G.B.	20	Don Hutson	G.B.	95	1941	NFL
											Bob Snyder	Chi B	20					
1942	NFL	Sammy Baugh	Was.	46.6	Bill Daddio	Chi C	5	Ted Fritsch	G.B.	80	Don Hutson	G.B.	33	Don Hutson	G.B.	138	1942	NFL
								Frank Maznicki	Chi B	80								
1943	NFL	Sammy Baugh	Was.	45.9	Ward Cuff	NY G	3	Don Hutson	G.B.	60	Bob Snyder	Chi B	39	Don Hutson	G.B.	117	1943	NFL
					Don Hutson	G.B.	3											
1944	NFL	Cecil Johnson	Bkn.	42.6	Ken Strong	NY G	6	Ken Strong	NY G	50	Pete Gudauskas	Chi B	36	Don Hutson	G.B.	85	1944	NFL
1945	NFL	Sammy Baugh	Was.	43.3	Joe Aguirre	Was.	7	Ben Agajanian	Phi. + Pit.	100	Don Hutson	G.B.	31	Steve Van Buren	Phi.	110	1945	NFL
											Bob Waterfield	Cle.	31					
1946	NFL	Bob Cifers	Det.	45.6	Ted Fritsch	G.B.	9	Bob Waterfield	L.A.	67	Bob Waterfield	L.A.	37	Ted Fritsch	G.B.	100	1946	NFL
1946	AAFC	Glenn Dobbs	Bkn.	47.8	Lou Groza	Cle.	13	Steve Nemeth	Chi.	75	Lou Groza	Cle.	45	Lou Groza	Cle.	84	1946	AAFC
1947	NFL	George Gulyanics	Chi B	44.8	Ward Cuff	G.B.	7	Pat Harder	Chi C	70	Ray McLean	Chi B	44	Pat Harder	Chi C	102	1947	NFL
					Pat Harder	Chi C	7											
					Bob Waterfield	L.A.	7											
1947	AAFC	Bob Reinhard	L.A.	45.7	Ben Agajanian	L.A.	15	Harvey Johnson	N.Y.	88	Harvey Johnson	N.Y.	49	Spec Sanders	N.Y.	114	1947	AAFC
1948	NFL	Joe Muha	Phi.	47.2	Cliff Patton	Phi.	8	Dick Poillon	Was.	71	Pat Harder	Chi C	53	Pat Harder	Chi C	110	1948	NFL
1948	AAFC	Glenn Dobbs	L.A.	49.1	Rex Grossman	Bal.	10	Joe Vetrano	S.F.	63	Joe Vetrano	S.F.	62	Chet Mutryn	BUF.	96	1948	AAFC
1949	NFL	George Gulyanics	Chi B	47.2	Cliff Patton	Phi.	9	Vinnie Yablonski	Chi C	83	Pat Harder	Chi C	45	Pat Harder	Chi C	102	1949	NFL
					Bob Waterfield	L.A.	9							Choo-Choo Roberts	NY G	102		
1949	AAFC	Frankie Albert	S.F.	48.2	Harvey Johnson	N.Y.	7	Rex Grossman	Bal.	55	Joe Vetrano	S.F.	56	Alyn Beals	S.F.	73	1949	AAFC
1950	NFL	Curley Morrison	Chi B	43.3	Lou Groza	Cle.	13	Lou Groza	Cle.	68	Bob Waterfield	L.A.	54	Doak Walker	Det.	128	1950	NFL
1951	NFL	Horace Gillom	Cle.	45.5	Bob Waterfield	L.A.	13	Bill Dudley	Was.	77	Lou Groza	Cle.	43	Crazy Legs Hirsch	L.A.	102	1951	NFL
											Doak Walker	Det.	43					
1952	NFL	Horace Gillom	Cle.	45.7	Lou Groza	Cle.	19	Bob Waterfield	L.A.	61	Bob Waterfield	L.A.	44	Gordie Soltau	S.F.	94	1952	NFL
1953	NFL	Pat Brady	Pit.	46.9	Lou Groza	Cle.	23	Lou Groza	Cle.	88	Gordie Soltau	S.F.	48	Gordie Soltau	S.F.	114	1953	NFL
1954	NFL	Pat Brady	Pit.	43.2	Lou Groza	Cle.	16	Lou Groza	Cle.	67	Doak Walker	Det.	43	Bobby Walston	Phi.	114	1954	NFL
1955	NFL	Norm Van Brocklin	L.A.	44.6	Fred Cone	G.B.	16	Fred Cone	G.B.	67	Lou Groza	Cle.	44	Doak Walker	Det.	96	1955	NFL
1956	NFL	Norm Van Brocklin	L.A.	43.1	Sam Baker	Was.	17	Bobby Layne	Det.	80	George Blanda	Chi B	45	Bobby Layne	Det.	99	1956	NFL
1957	NFL	Don Chandler	NY G	44.6	Lou Groza	Cle.	15	Bobby Walston	Phi.	75	Paige Cothren	L.A.	38	Sam Baker	Was.	77	1957	NFL
1958	NFL	Sam Baker	Was.	45.4	Paige Cothren	L.A.	14	Paige Cothren	L.A.	56	Steve Myhra	Bal.	48	Jimmy Brown	Cle.	108	1958	NFL
					Tom Miner	Pit.	14											
1959	NFL	Yale Lary	Det.	47.1	Pat Summerall	NY G	20	Pat Summerall	NY G	69	Steve Myhra	Bal.	50	Paul Hornung	G.B.	94	1959	NFL
1960	NFL	Jerry Norton	St L.	45.6	Tommy Davis	S.F.	19	Bobby Walston	Phi.	70	Sam Baker	Cle.	44	Paul Hornung	G.B.	176	1960	NFL
1960	AFL	Paul Maguire	L.A.	40.5	Gene Mingo	Den.	18	Gene Mingo	Den.	64	Bill Shockley	NY T	47	Gene Mingo	Den.	123	1960	AFL
1961	NFL	Yale Lary	Det.	48.4	Steve Myhra	Bal.	21	Lou Groza	Cle.	70	Pat Summerall	NY G	46	Paul Hornung	G.B.	146	1961	NFL
1961	AFL	Billy Atkins	Buf.	45.0	Gino Cappelletti	Bos.	17	George Blanda	Hou.	62	George Blanda	Hou.	64	Gino Cappelletti	Bos.	147	1961	AFL
1962	NFL	Tommy Davis	S.F.	45.6	Lou Michaels	Pitt.	26	Don Chandler	NY G	68	Sam Baker	Dal.	50	Jim Taylor	G.B.	114	1962	NFL
1962	AFL	Jim Fraser	Den.	44.4	Gene Mingo	Den.	27	George Blair	S.D.	85	George Blanda	Hou.	48	Gene Mingo	Den.	137	1962	AFL
1963	NFL	Yale Lary	Det.	48.9	Jim Martin	Bal.	24	Lou Groza	Cle.	65	Don Chandler	NY G	52	Don Chandler	NY G	106	1963	NFL
1963	AFL	Jim Fraser	Den.	46.1	Gino Cappelletti	Bos.	22	George Blair	S.D.	63	Mike Mercer	Oak.	47	Gino Cappelletti	Bos.	113	1963	AFL
1964	NFL	Bobby Walden	Min.	46.4	Jim Bakken	StL.	25	Bruce Gossett	L.A.	75	Lou Michaels	Bal.	53	Lenny Moore	Bal.	120	1964	NFL
1964	AFL	Jim Fraser	Den.	44.7	Gino Cappelletti	Bos.	25	Pete Gogolak	Buf.	66	Tommy Brooker	K.C.	46	Gino Cappelletti	Bos.	155	1964	AFL
1965	NFL	Gary Collins	Cle.	46.7	Fred Cox	Min.	23	Jim Bakken	StL.	68	Tommy Davis	S.F.	52	Gale Sayers	Chi B	132	1965	NFL
											Roger Le Clerc	Chi B	52					
1965	AFL	Jerrel Wilson	K.C.	46.1	Pete Gogolak	Buf.	28	Gino Cappelletti	Bos.	63	Herb Travenio	S.D.	40	Gino Cappelletti	Bos.	132	1965	AFL
1966	NFL	David Lee	Bal.	45.6	Bruce Gossett	L.A.	28	Sam Baker	Phi.	72	Danny Villanueva	Dal.	56	Bruce Gossett	L.A.	113	1966	NFL
1966	AFL	Bob Scarpitto	Den.	45.8	Mike Mercer	Oak. + KC	21	Mike Mercer	Oak + KC	70	Booth Lusteg	Buf.	41	Gino Cappelletti	Bos.	119	1966	AFL
1967	NFL	Billy Lothridge	Atl.	43.7	Jim Bakken	StL.	27	Jim Bakken	StL.	69	Bruce Gossett	L.A.	48	Jim Bakken	StL.	117	1967	NFL
1967	AFL	Bob Scarpitto	Den.	44.9	Jan Stenerud	K.C.	21	George Blanda	Hou.	67	George Blanda	Hou.	56	George Blanda	Hou.	116	1967	AFL
1968	NFL	Billy Lothridge	Atl.	44.3	Mac Percival	Chi.	25	Don Cockroft	Cle.	75	Mike Clark	Dal.	54	Leroy Kelly	Cle.	120	1968	NFL
1968	AFL	Jerrel Wilson	K.C.	45.1	Jim Turner	NY J	34	Jan Stenerud	K.C.	75	George Blanda	Hou.	54	Jim Turner	NY J	145	1968	AFL
1969	NFL	David Lee	Bal.	45.3	Fred Cox	Min.	26	Fred Cox	Min.	70	Don Cockroft	Cle.	45	Fred Cox	Min.	121	1969	NFL
1969	AFL	Dennis Partee	S.D.	44.6	Jim Turner	NY J	32	Jan Stenerud	K.C.	77	George Blanda	Oak.	45	Jim Turner	NY J	129	1969	AFL
1970	NFC	Julian Fagan	N.O.	42.5	Fred Cox	Min.	30	Curt Knight	Was.	74	Errol Mann	Det.	41	Fred Cox	Min.	125	1970	NFC
1970	AFC	Dave Lewis	Cin.	46.2	Jan Stenerud	K.C.	30	Garo Yepremian	Mia.	76	George Blanda	Oak.	36	Jan Stenerud	K.C.	116	1970	AFC
											Jim O'Brien	Bal.	36					
1971	NFC	Tom McNeill	Phi.	42.0	Curt Knight	Was.	29	Tom Dempsey	Phi.	71	Mike Clark	Dal.	47	Curt Knight	Was.	114	1971	NFC
1971	AFC	Dave Lewis	Cin.	44.8	Garo Yepremian	Mia.	28	Garo Yepremian	Mia.	70	George Blanda	Oak.	41	Garo Yepremain	Mia.	117	1971	AFC
1972	NFC	Dave Chapple	L.A.	44.2	Chester Marcol	G.B.	33	Errol Mann	Det.	69	Bruce Gossett	S.F.	41	Chester Marcol	G.B.	128	1972	NFC
1972	AFC	Jerrel Wilson	K.C.	44.8	Roy Gerela	Pit.	28	Don Cockroft	Cle.	82	George Blanda	Oak.	44	Bobby Howfield	NY J	121	1972	AFC
1973	NFC	Tom Wittum	S.F.	43.7	David Ray	L.A.	30	Bruce Gossett	S.F.	79	Toni Fritsch	Dal.	43	David Ray	L.A.	130	1973	NFC
1973	AFC	Jerrel Wilson	K.C.	45.5	Roy Gerela	Pit.	29	Don Cockroft	Cle.	71	Jim Turner	Den.	40	Roy Gerela	Pit.	123	1973	AFC

SINGLE SEASON LEADERS

PASSING

Note: (For all single season leaders) Number after individual name indicates the number of times that individual appears within a specific category; the bold indicates the individual appearing most within a specific category.

COMPLETIONS

	Name	Team	League	Year	Comp
1	Sonny Jurgensen–1	Was.	NFL	67	288
2	Sonny Jurgensen–2	Was.	NFL	69	274
3	Roman Gabriel–1	Phi.	NFC	73	270
4	George Blanda–1	Hou.	AFL	64	262
5	Joe Namath–1	NY J	AFL	67	258
6	Johnny Unitas–1	Bal.	NFL	67	255
7	Sonny Jurgensen–3	Was.	NFL	66	254
8	Frank Tripucka–1	Den.	AFL	60	248
9	John Brodie–1	S.F.	NFL	65	242
10	Frank Tripucka–2	Den.	AFL	62	240
	Norm Snead–1	Phi.	NFL	67	240
12	Johnny Unitas–2	Bal.	NFL	63	237
13	Sonny Jurgensen–4	Phi.	NFL	61	235
14	John Brodie–2	S.F.	NFL	68	234
15	John Hadl–1	S.D.	AFC	71	233
16	John Brodie–3	S.F.	NFL	66	332
	Joe Namath–2	NY J	AFL	66	232
18	Archie Manning	N.O.	NFC	72	230
19	Johnny Unitas–3	Bal.	NFL	61	229
20	Babe Parilli	Bos.	AFL	64	228
21	Fran Tarkenton–1	NY G	NFC	71	226
22	Billy Wade	Chi.	NFL	62	225
23	George Blanda–2	Hou.	AFL	63	224
24	Charley Johnson–1	StL.	NFL	64	223
	John Brodie–4	S.F.	NFC	70	223
26	Johnny Unitas–4	Bal.	NFL	62	222
	Charley Johnson–2	St.L.	NFL	63	222
28	Y.A. Tittle–1	NY G	NFL	63	221
	Daryle Lamonica–1	Oak.	AFL	69	221
30	Daryle Lamonica–2	Oak.	AFL	67	220
	Fran Tarkenton–1	NY G	NFL	69	220
32	Fran Tarkenton–2	NY G	NFC	70	219
33	Roman Gabriel–2	L.A.	NFL	66	217
	John Hadl–2	S.D.	AFL	67	217
	Roman Gabriel–3	L.A.	NFL	69	217
36	Fran Tarkenton–3	Min.	NFC	72	215
37	Jack Kemp	L.A.	AFL	60	211
	Roman Gabriel–4	L.A.	NFC	70	211
39	Sammy Baugh	Was.	NFL	47	210
40	John Hadl–3	S.D.	AFL	68	208
	John Brodie–5	S.F.	NFC	71	208
42	Sonny Jurgensen–5	Was.	NFL	64	207
43	Len Dawson–1	K.C.	AFL	67	206
	Daryle Lamonica–3	Oak.	AFL	68	206
45	Fran Tarkenton–4	NY G	NFL	67	204
46	Terry Bradshaw	Pit.	AFC	71	203
47	Sonny Jurgensen–6	Was.	NFC	71	202
48	Al Dorow–1	NY T	AFL	60	201
49	Y.A. Tittle–2	NY G	NFL	62	200
	Frank Ryan	Cle.	NFL	66	200
	John Hadl–4	S.D.	AFL	66	200
52	Len Dawson–2	K.C.	AFL	64	199
53	Norm Van Brocklin	Phi.	NFL	58	198
54	Al Dorow–2	NY T	AFL	61	197
	George Blanda–3	Hou	AFL	62	197
56	Sonny Jurgensen–7	Phi.	NFL	62	196
	Roman Gabriel–5	L.A.	NFL	67	196
	Norm Snead	NY G	NFC	72	196
59	Johnny Unitas–5	Bal.	NFL	66	195

COMPLETION PERCENTAGE
(Minimum 100 Attempts)

	Name	Team	League	Year	Att	Comp	Pct.
1	Sammy Baugh–1	Was.	NFL	45	182	128	70.3
2	Len Dawson–1	K.C.	AFC	73	101	66	65.3
3	Otto Graham–1	Cle.	NFL	53	258	167	64.7
4	Bart Starr–1	G.B.	NFL	68	171	109	63.7
5	John Brodie–1	S.F.	NFC	72	110	70	63.6
6	Y. A. Tittle–1	S.F.	NFL	57	279	176	63.1
7	Sammy Baugh–2	Was.	NFL	40	177	111	62.7
8	Ken Stabler	Oak.	AFC	73	260	163	62.7
9	Roger Staubach–1	Dal.	NFC	73	286	179	62.6
10	Bart Starr–2	G.B.	NFL	62	285	178	62.5
11	Bart Starr–3	G.B.	NFL	69	148	92	62.2
	Virgil Carter	Cin.	AFC	71	222	138	62.2
13	Bart Starr–4	G.B.	NFL	66	251	156	62.2
14	Sonny Jurgensen–1	Was.	NFL	69	442	274	62.0
15	John Brodie–2	S.F.	NFL	65	391	242	61.9
16	Rudy Bukich	Chi.	NFL	64	160	99	61.9
17	Fran Tarkenton–1	Min.	NFC	73	274	169	61.7
18	Len Dawson–2	Dal.	AFL	62	310	189	61.0
19	Otto Graham–2	Cle.	AAFC	47	269	163	60.6
20	Milt Plum–1	Cle.	NFL	60	250	151	60.4
21	Norm Snead	NY G	NFC	72	325	196	60.3
22	Y. A. Tittle–2	NY G	NFL	63	367	221	60.2
23	Bob Berry–1	Atl.	NFC	71	226	136	60.2
24	Sonny Jurgensen–2	Was.	NFC	73	145	87	60.0
25	Sonny Jurgensen–3	Was.	NFC	70	337	202	59.9
26	Bart Starr–5	G.B.	NFL	64	272	163	59.9
27	John Brodie–3	S.F.	NFL	58	172	103	59.9
28	Roger Staubach–2	Dal.	NFC	71	211	126	59.7
29	Tobin Rote	S.D.	AFL	63	286	170	59.4
30	Sammy Baugh–3	Was.	NFL	47	354	210	59.3
31	Eddie LeBaron	Was.	NFL	57	167	99	59.3
32	Otto Graham–3	Cle.	NFL	54	240	142	59.2
	Lynn Dickey	Hou.	AFC	73	120	71	59.2
34	Len Dawson–3	K.C.	AFL	69	166	98	59.0
35	John Brodie–4	S.F.	NFC	70	378	223	59.0
36	Sammy Baugh–4	Was.	NFL	48	315	185	58.7
37	Roman Gabriel	Phi.	NFC	73	460	270	58.7
38	Sammy Baugh–5	Was.	NFL	42	225	132	58.7
39	Milt Plum–2	Cle.	NFL	59	266	156	58.6
40	Billy Wade–1	L.A.	NFL	59	261	153	58.6
41	Milt Plum–3	Cle.	NFL	61	302	177	58.6
42	Fran Tarkenton–2	NY G	NFC	71	386	226	58.5
43	Johnny Unitas–1	Bal.	NFL	67	436	255	58.5
44	Len Dawson–4	K.C.	AFL	68	224	131	58.5
45	Frankie Albert	S.F.	AAFC	48	264	154	58.3
46	Bart Starr–6	G.B.	NFL	61	295	172	58.3
47	Sonny Jurgensen–4	Was.	NFL	66	436	254	58.3
48	Charlie Conerly	NY G	NFL	59	194	113	58.2
49	Billy Wade–2	L.A.	NFL	60	182	106	58.2
50	Johnny Unitas–2	Bal.	NFL	65	282	164	58.2
51	Bob Berry–2	Atl.	NFC	70	269	156	58.0
52	Bob Griese	Mia.	AFC	70	245	142	58.0
53	George Ratterman	Buf.	AAFC	49	252	146	57.9
54	John Brodie–5	S.F.	NFL	68	404	234	57.9
55	Johnny Unitas–3	Bal.	NFL	63	410	237	57.8
56	Frank Ryan	Cle.	NFL	62	194	112	57.7
57	Len Dawson–5	K.C.	AFL	67	357	206	57.7
58	Y. A. Tittle–3	S.F.	NFL	58	208	120	57.7
59	Y. A. Tittle–4	S.F.	NFL	54	295	170	57.6
60	John Brodie–6	S.F.	NFL	62	304	175	57.6
61	Y. A. Tittle–5	S.F.	NFL	53	259	149	57.5

PASSING YARDS

	Name	Team	League	Year	Yards
1	Joe Namath–1	NY J	AFL	67	4007
2	Sonny Jurgensen–1	Was.	NFL	67	3747
3	Sonny Jurgensen–2	Phi.	NFL	61	3723
4	Johnny Unitas–1	Bal.	NFL	63	3481
5	John Hadl–1	S.D.	AFL	68	3473
6	Babe Parilli	Bos.	AFL	64	3465
7	Johnny Unitas–2	Bal.	NFL	67	3428
8	Norm Snead–1	Phi.	NFL	67	3399
9	Joe Namath–2	NY J	AFL	66	3379
10	John Hadl–2	S.D.	AFL	67	3365
11	George Blanda–1	Hou.	AFL	61	3330
12	Daryle Lamonica–1	Oak.	AFL	69	3302
13	George Blanda–2	Hou.	AFL	64	3287
14	Charley Johnson–1	StL.	NFL	63	3280
15	Sonny Jurgensen	Phi.	NFL	62	3261
16	Daryle Lamonica–2	Oak.	AFL	68	3245
17	Daryle Lamonica–3	Oak.	AFL	67	3228
18	Y. A. Tittle–1	NY G	NFL	62	3224
19	Roman Gabriel–1	Phi.	NFC	73	3219
20	Sonny Jurgensen–4	Was.	NFL	66	3209
21	Billy Wade–1	Chi.	NFL	62	3172
22	Joe Namath–3	NY J	AFL	68	3147
23	Y. A. Tittle–2	NY G	NFL	63	3145
24	John Brodie–1	S.F.	NFL	65	3112
25	Sonny Jurgensen–5	Was.	NFL	69	3102
26	Johnny Unitas–3	Bal.	NFL	60	3099
27	Fran Tarkenton–1	NY G	NFL	67	3088
28	John Hadl–3	S.D.	AFC	71	3075
29	Charley Johnson–2	StL.	NFL	64	3045
30	Norm Snead–2	Was.	NFL	63	3043
31	Frank Tripucka–1	Den.	AFL	60	3038
32	John Brodie–2	S.F.	NFL	68	3020
33	Jack Kemp–1	L.A.	AFL	60	3018
34	Jim Hart	StL.	NFL	67	3008
35	George Blanda–3	Hou.	AFL	63	3003
36	Johnny Unitas–4	Bal.	NFL	61	2990
37	Ed Brown	Pit.	NFL	63	2982
38	Frank Ryan	Cle.	NFL	66	2974
39	Johnny Unitas–5	Bal.	NFL	62	2967
40	John Brodie–3	S.F.	NFC	70	2941
41	Sammy Baugh	Was.	NFL	47	2938
42	Sonny Jurgensen–6	Was.	NFL	64	2934
43	Norm Snead–3	Was.	NFL	62	2926
44	Fran Tarkenton–2	NY G	NFL	69	2918
45	Frank Tripucka–2	Den.	AFL	62	2917
46	Jack Kemp–2	Buf.	AFL	63	2914
47	Earl Morrall	Bal.	NFL	68	2909
48	Johnny Unitas–6	Bal.	NFL	59	2899
49	Len Dawson–1	K.C.	AFL	64	2879
50	Billy Wade–2	L.A.	NFL	58	2875
51	John Hadl–3	S.D.	AFL	66	2846
52	Johnny Unitas–7	Bal.	NFL	64	2824
53	Otto Graham–1	Cle.	NFL	52	2816
	Joe Namath–4	NYJ	AFC	72	2816
55	George Blanda–4	Hou.	AFL	62	2810
	John Brodie–4	S.F.	NFL	66	2810
57	Don Meredith	Dal.	NFL	66	2805
58	John Hadl–4	S.D.	AFL	65	2798
59	Otto Graham–2	Cle.	AAFC	49	2785
60	Roman Gabriel–2	L.A.	NFL	67	2779
61	Norm Snead–4	Phi.	NFL	69	2768
62	Len Dawson–2	Dal.	AFL	62	2759
63	Otto Graham–3	Cle.	AAFC	47	2753

PASSING YARDS PER SCHEDULED GAME

	Name	Team	League	Year	Yds/Game
1	Joe Namath–1	NY J	AFL	67	286
2	Sonny Jurgensen–1	Was.	NFL	67	268
3	Sonny Jurgensen–2	Phi.	NFL	61	266
4	Johnny Unitas–1	Bal.	NFL	60	258
5	Johnny Unitas–2	Bal.	NFL	63	249
6	John Hadl–1	S.D.	AFL	68	241
7	Babe Parilli	Bos.	AFL	64	248
8	Sammy Baugh	Was.	NFL	47	245
9	Johnny Unitas–3	Bal.	NFL	67	245
10	Norm Snead–1	Phi.	NFL	67	243
11	Johnny Unitas–4	Bal.	NFL	59	242
12	Joe Namath–2	NY J	AFL	66	241
13	John Hadl–2	S.D.	AFL	67	240
14	Billy Wade–1	L.A.	NFL	58	240
15	George Blanda–1	Hou.	AFL	61	238
16	Daryle Lamonica–1	Oak.	AFL	69	236
17	George Blanda–2	Hou.	AFL	64	235
18	Otto Graham–1	Cle.	NFL	52	235
19	Charley Johnson–1	StL.	NFL	63	234
20	Sonny Jurgensen–3	Phi.	NFL	62	233
21	Daryle Lamonica–2	Oak.	AFL	68	232
22	Daryle Lamonica–3	Oak.	AFL	67	231
23	Y. A. Tittle–1	NY G	NFL	62	230
24	Roman Gabriel	Phi.	NFC	73	230
25	Sonny Jurgensen–4	Was.	NFL	66	229
26	Otto Graham–2	Cle.	NFL	53	227
27	Billy Wade–2	Chi.	NFL	62	227
28	Sid Luckman–1	ChiB	NFL	47	226
29	Joe Namath–3	NY J	AFL	68	225
30	Y. A. Tittle–2	NY G	NFL	63	225
31	John Brodie–1	S.F.	NFL	65	222
32	Johnny Lujak	ChiB	NFL	49	222
33	Sonny Jurgensen–5	Was	NFL	69	222
34	Fran Tarkenton–1	NY G	NFL	67	221
35	Norm Van Brocklin–1	L.A.	NFL	54	220
36	John Hadl–3	S.D.	AFC	71	220
37	Sid Luckman–2	ChiB	NFL	43	219
38	Norm Van Brocklin–2	Phi.	NFL	59	218
39	Charley Johnson–2	StL.	NFL	64	218
40	Norm Snead–2	Was.	NFL	63	217
41	Sammy Baugh–2	Was.	NFL	48	217
	Frank Tripucka–1	Den.	AFL	60	217
43	John Brodie–2	S.F.	NFL	68	216
44	Jack Kemp–1	L.A.	AFL	60	216
45	Jim Hart	St.L.	NFL	67	215
46	George Blanda–3	Hou.	AFL	63	215
47	Johnny Unitas–5	Bal.	NFL	61	214
48	Ed Brown	Pit.	NFL	63	213
49	Johnny Unitas–6	Bal.	NFL	57	213
50	Frank Ryan	Cle.	NFL	66	212
51	Johnny Unitas–7	Bal.	NFL	62	212
52	John Brodie–3	S.F.	NFC	70	210
53	Sonny Jurgensen–6	Was.	NFL	64	210
54	Bobby Lane–1	Pit.	NFL	58	209
55	Norm Snead–3	Was.	NFL	62	209
56	Fran Tarkenton–2	NY G	NFL	69	208
57	Frank Tripucka–2	Den.	AFL	62	208
58	Jack Kemp–2	Buf.	AFL	63	208
59	Earl Morrall	Bal.	NFL	68	208
60	Norm Van Brocklin–3	Phi.	NFL	60	206
61	Len Dawson	K.C.	AFL	64	206
62	Bobby Thomason	Phi.	NFL	53	205
63	John Hadl–4	S.D.	AFL	66	203
64	Johnny Unitas–8	Bal.	NFL	64	202
65	Joe Namath–4	NY J	AFC	72	201
66	Norm Van Brocklin–4	Phi.	NFL	58	201
67	George Blanda–4	Hou.	AFL	62	201
	John Brodie–4	S.F.	NFL	66	201
69	Don Meredith	Dal.	NFL	66	200
70	Bobby Layne–2	Det.	NFL	51	200

YARDS PER ATTEMPT
(Minimum 100 Attempts)

	Name	Team	League	Year	Att	Yds.	Yd/A
1	Tom O'Connell	Cle.	NFL	57	110	1229	11.2
2	Sid Luckman	ChiB	NFL	43	202	2194	10.9
3	Otto Graham–1	Cle.	NFL	53	258	2722	10.6
4	Otto Graham–2	Cle.	AAFC	46	174	1834	10.5
5	Otto Graham–3	Cle.	AAFC	47	269	2753	10.2
6	Norm Van Brocklin	L.A.	NFL	54	260	2637	10.1
7	Sid Luckman–2	ChiB	NFL	41	119	1181	9.9
8	Ed Brown	ChiB	NFL	56	168	1667	9.9
9	Otto Graham–4	Cle.	AAFC	49	285	2785	9.8
10	Sid Luckman–3	ChiB	NFL	42	105	1023	9.7
11	Bart Starr–1	G.B.	NFL	68	171	1617	9.5
12	Len Dawson	K.C.	AFL	68	224	2109	9.4
13	Eddie LeBaron–1	Was.	NFL	58	145	1365	9.4
14	Greg Cook	Cin.	AFL	69	197	1854	9.4
15	Bob Waterfield	Cle.	NFL	45	171	1609	9.4
16	Bob Berry	Atl.	NFL	68	153	1433	9.4
17	Otto Graham–5	Cle.	NFL	55	185	1721	9.3
18	Johnny Unitas–1	Bal.	NFL	64	305	2824	9.3
19	George Blanda	Hou.	AFL	61	362	3330	9.2
20	Milt Plum	Cle.	NFL	60	250	2297	9.2
21	Earl Morrall–1	Bal.	NFL	68	317	2909	9.2
22	Sammy Baugh	Was	NFL	45	182	1669	9.2
23	John Brodie	S.F.	NFL	61	283	2588	9.1
24	Earl Morrall–2	Mia.	AFC	72	150	1360	9.1
25	Billy Wade	Chi.	NFL	61	250	2258	9.0
26	Eddie LeBaron–2	Was.	NFL	57	167	1508	9.0
27	Clyde LeForce	Det.	NFL	48	101	912	9.0
28	Bart Starr–2	G.B.	NFL	66	251	2257	9.0
29	Johnny Unitas–2	Bal.	NFL	65	282	2530	9.0
30	Sid Luckman–4	ChiB	NFL	40	105	941	9.0
31	Don Horn	G.B.	NFL	69	168	1505	9.0

TOUCHDOWN PASSES

	Name	Team	League	Year	TD
1	George Blanda–1	Hou.	AFL	61	36
	Y. A. Tittle–1	NY G	NFL	63	36
3	Daryle Lamonica–1	Oak.	AFL	69	34
4	Y. A. Tittle–2	NY G	NFL	62	33
5	Johnny Unitas–1	Bal.	NFL	59	32
6	Babe Parilli	Bos.	AFL	64	31
	Sonny Jurgensen–1	Was.	NFL	67	31
8	Len Dawson–1	K.C.	AFL	64	30
	John Brodie–1	S.F.	NFL	65	30
	Daryle Lamonica–2	Oak.	AFL	67	30
11	Frankie Albert–1	S.F.	AAFC	48	29
	Len Dawson–2	Dal.	AFL	62	29
	Frank Ryan–1	Cle.	NFL	66	29
	Fran Tarkenton	NY G	NFL	67	29
	Norm Snead	Phi.	NFL	67	29
16	Sid Luckman–1	ChiB	NFL	43	28
	Charley Johnson	StL.	NFL	63	28
	Sonny Jurgensen–2	Was.	NFL	66	28
19	Frankie Albert–2	S.F.	AAFC	49	27
	George Blanda–2	Hou.	AFL	62	27
	John Hadl–1	S.D.	AFL	68	27
22	Bobby Layne	Det.	NFL	51	26
	Al Dorow	NYT	AFL	60	26
	Len Dawson–3	K.C.	AFL	63	26
	Len Dawson–4	K.C.	AFL	66	26
	Joe Namath	NY J	AFL	67	26
	Earl Morrall–1	Bal.	NFL	68	26
28	Sammy Baugh	Was.	NFL	47	25
	Otto Graham–1	Cle.	AAFC	47	25
	Tommy Thompson	Phi.	NFL	48	25
	Otto Graham–2	Cle.	AAFC	48	25
	Johnny Unitas–2	Bal.	NFL	60	25
	Frank Ryan–2	Cle.	NFL	63	25
	Frank Ryan–3	Cle.	NFL	64	25
	Roman Gabriel–1	L.A.	NFL	67	25
	Daryle Lamonica–3	Oak.	AFL	68	25
37	Cecil Isbell	G.B.	NFL	42	24
	Sid Luckman–2	ChiB	NFL	47	24
	Johnny Unitas–3	Bal.	NFL	57	24
	Norm Van Brocklin	Phi.	NFL	60	24
	Frank Tripucka	Den.	AFL	60	24
	George Blanda–3	Hou.	AFL	60	24
	Sonny Jurgensen–3	Phi.	NFL	61	24
	Johnny Unitas–4	Bal.	NFL	61	24
	Earl Morrall–2	Det.	NFL	63	24
	George Blanda–4	Hou.	AFL	63	24
	Sonny Jurgensen–4	Was.	NFL	64	24
	Don Meredith	Dal.	NFL	66	24
	Tom Flores	Oak.	AFL	66	24
	Len Dawson–5	K.C.	AFL	67	24
	John Hadl–2	S.D.	AFL	67	24
	Roman Gabriel–2	L.A.	NFL	69	24
	John Brodie–2	S.F.	NFC	70	24

SINGLE SEASON LEADERS

LOWEST PASS INTERCEPTION PERCENTAGE

(Minimum 100 Attempts)

					Att	Int	Pct.
1	Bart Starr–1	G.B.	NFL	66	251	3	1.195
2	Bart Starr–2	G.B.	NFL	64	272	4	1.471
3	Bob Berry	Atl.	NFL	69	124	2	1.612
4	Roman Gabriel–1	L.A.	NFL	69	399	7	1.754
5	Roger Staubach	Dal.	NFC	71	211	4	1.895
6	Fran Tarkenton–1	NY G	NFL	69	409	8	1.955
7	Johnny Unitas–1	Bal.	NFL	64	305	6	1.967
8	Milt Plum	Cle.	NFL	60	250	5	2.000
9	Chuck Conerly	NY G	NFL	59	194	4	2.062
10	Gary Wood	NY G	NFL	64	143	3	2.098
11	Sammy Baugh	Was.	NFL	45	182	4	2.198
12	Ken Anderson	Cin.	AFC	72	301	7	2.325
13	Y. A. Tittle	S.F.	NFL	60	127	3	2.362
14	Ed Hargett–1	N.O.	NFC	71	210	5	2.380
15	Bill Munson	Det.	NFL	68	329	8	2.431
16	Fran Tarkenton–2	Min.	NFC	73	274	7	2.554
17	Ace Parker	N.Y.	AAFC	46	115	3	2.608
18	Roman Gabriel–2	Phi.	NFC	73	460	12	2.609
19	John Brodie	S.F.	NFC	70	378	10	2.645
20	Johnny Unitas–2	Bal.	NFL	58	263	7	2.662
21	Marty Domres	Bal.	AFC	72	222	6	2.702
22	Dwight Sloan	Det.	NFL	39	107	3	2.803
23	John Stofa	Cin.	AFL	68	177	5	2.824
24	Roman Gabriel–3	L.A.	NFC	71	352	10	2.840
25	Don Trull–1	Hou.	AFL	68	105	3	2.857
	Ed Hargett–2	N.O.	NFC	70	175	5	2.857
27	Otto Graham	Cle.	AAFC	46	174	5	2.873
28	Rudy Bukich	Chi.	NFL	65	312	9	2.885
29	Roman Gabriel–4	L.A.	NFL	65	173	5	2.890
30	Don Trull–2	Hou.	AFL	66	172	5	2.907
31	Johnny Unitas–3	Bal.	NFL	63	410	12	2.927
32	Roman Gabriel–5	L.A.	NFC	70	407	12	2.948
33	Sonny Jurgensen	Was.	NFC	70	337	10	2.967

RUSHING

ATTEMPTS

1	O.J. Simpson–1	Buf.	AFC	73	332
2	Jimmy Brown–1	Cle.	NFL	61	305
3	Jim Nance–1	Bos.	AFL	66	299
4	Ron Johnson–1	NY G	NFC	72	298
5	O.J. Simpson–2	Buf.	AFC	72	292
6	Jimmy Brown–2	Cle.	NFL	63	291
7	Jimmy Brown–3	Cle.	NFL	59	290
8	Jimmy Brown–4	Cle.	NFL	65	289
9	Larry Brown–1	Was.	NFC	72	285
10	Floyd Little–1	Den.	AFC	71	284
11	Jimmy Brown–5	Cle.	NFL	64	280
12	John Brockington–1	G.B.	NFC	72	274
13	Calvin Hill–1	Dal.	NFC	73	273
	Larry Brown–2	Was.	NFC	73	273
15	Jim Taylor–1	G.B.	NFL	62	272
	Mike Garrett–1	S.D.	AFC	72	272
17	Eddie Price	NY G	NFL	51	271
18	Jim Nance–2	Bos.	AFL	67	269
19	John Brockington–2	G.B.	NFC	73	265
20	Steve Van Buren	Phi.	NFL	49	263
	Ron Johnson–2	NY G	NFC	70	263
	Dave Hampton–1	Atl.	NFC	73	263
23	Ron Johnson–3	NY G	NFC	73	260
24	J. D. Smith	S.F.	NFL	62	258
25	Jimmy Brown–6	Cle.	NFL	58	257
26	Floyd Little–2	Den.	AFC	73	256
27	Boobie Clark	Cin.	AFC	73	254
28	Larry Brown–3	Was.	NFC	71	253
	Lydell Mitchell	Bal.	AFC	73	253
30	Cookie Gilchrist–1	Den.	AFL	65	252
31	Bill Brown–1	Min.	NFL	66	251
	John Henry Johnson–1	Pit.	NFL	62	251
33	Jim Taylor–2	G.B.	NFL	63	248
	Dick Bass	L.A.	NFL	66	248
	Leroy Kelly–1	Cle.	NFL	68	248
36	Steve Owens	Det.	NFC	71	246
37	Calvin Hill–2	Dal.	NFC	72	245
38	Charley Tolar	Hou.	AFL	62	244
39	Jim Taylor–3	G.B.	NFL	61	243
40	Paul Robinson	Cin.	AFL	68	238
41	Larry Brown–4	Was.	NFC	70	237
42	Hoyle Granger	Hou.	AFL	67	236
	Mike Garrett–2	K.C.	AFL	67	236
	Gale Sayers–1	Chi.	NFL	69	236
	Ken Willard–1	S.F.	NFC	70	236
46	Jim Taylor–4	G.B.	NFL	64	235
	John Henry Johnson–2	Pit.	NFL	64	235
	Leroy Kelly–2	Cle.	NFL	67	235
	Tom Matte	Bal.	NFL	69	235
50	Rick Casares	ChiB	NFL	56	234
	Johnny Roland	StL.	NFL	67	234
	Leroy Kelly–3	Cle.	AFC	71	234
53	Cookie Gilchrist–2	Buf.	AFL	63	232
54	Spec Sanders	N.Y.	AAFC	47	231
55	Jim Taylor–5	G.B.	NFL	60	230
	Jimmy Brown–7	Cle.	NFL	62	230
	Cookie Gilchrist–3	Buf.	AFL	64	230
	Dave Hampton–2	Atl.	NFC	72	230
59	Gale Sayers–2	Chi.	NFL	66	229
60	Ken Willard–2	S.F.	NFL	68	227
61	Bill Brown–2	Min.	NFL	64	226

YARDS

1	O.J. Simpson–1	Buf.	AFC	73	2003
2	Jimmy Brown–1	Cle.	NFL	63	1863
3	Jimmy Brown–2	Cle.	NFL	65	1544
4	Jimmy Brown–3	Cle.	NFL	58	1527
5	Jim Taylor–1	G.B.	NFL	62	1474
6	Jim Nance–1	Bos.	AFL	66	1458
7	Jimmy Brown–4	Cle.	NFL	64	1446
8	Spec Sanders	N.Y.	AAFC	47	1432
9	Jimmy Brown–5	Cle.	NFL	61	1408
10	Jimmy Brown–6	Cle.	NFL	59	1329
11	Jim Taylor–2	G.B.	NFL	61	1307
12	Jimmy Brown–7	Cle.	NFL	60	1257
13	O.J. Simpson–2	Buf.	AFC	72	1251
14	Leroy Kelly–1	Cle.	NFL	68	1239
15	Gale Sayers–1	Chi.	NFL	66	1231
16	Jim Nance–2	Bos.	AFL	67	1216
	Larry Brown–1	Was.	NFC	72	1216
18	Leroy Kelly–2	Cle.	NFL	67	1205
19	Hoyle Granger	Hou.	AFL	67	1195
20	Ron Johnson–1	NY G	NFC	72	1182
21	Jim Taylor–3	G.B.	NFL	64	1169
22	Steve Van Buren–1	Phi.	NFL	49	1146
23	John Brockington–1	G.B.	NFC	73	1144
24	Calvin Hill–1	Dal.	NFC	73	1142
25	John Henry Johnson–1	Pit.	NFL	62	1141
	Leroy Kelly–3	Cle.	NFL	66	1141
27	Floyd Little	Den.	AFC	71	1133
28	Rick Casares	ChiB	NFL	56	1126
29	Larry Brown–2	Was.	NFC	70	1125
30	Paul Lowe–1	S.D.	AFL	65	1121
31	Larry Csonka–1	Mia.	AFC	72	1117
32	John Brockington–2	G.B.	NFC	71	1105
33	Jim Taylor–4	G.B.	NFL	60	1101
34	Marv Hubbard	Oak.	AFC	72	1100
35	Clem Daniels	Oak.	AFL	63	1099
36	Larry McCutcheon	L.A.	NFC	73	1097
37	Cookie Gilchrist	Buf.	AFL	62	1096
38	Dick Bass–1	L.A.	NFL	66	1090
39	Mike Garrett–1	K.C.	AFL	67	1087
40	John David Crow	StL.	NFL	60	1071
41	Franco Harris	Pit.	AFC	72	1055
42	Tony Canadeo	G.B.	NFL	49	1052
43	Larry Csonka–2	Mia.	AFC	71	1051
44	Joe Perry–1	S.F.	NFL	54	1049
	Abner Haynes	Dal.	AFL	62	1049
46	John Henry Johnson–2	Pit.	NFL	64	1048
47	J. D. Smith	S.F.	NFL	59	1036
	Calvin Hill–2	Dal.	NFC	72	1036
49	Steve Owens	Det.	NFC	71	1035
50	Dick Bass–2	L.A.	NFL	62	1033
51	Gale Sayers–2	Chi.	NFL	69	1032
52	Mike Garrett–2	S.D.	AFC	72	1031
53	Ron Johnson–2	NYG	NFC	70	1027
	John Brockington–3	G.B.	NFC	72	1027
55	Paul Robinson	Cin.	AFL	68	1023
56	Jim Taylor–5	G.B.	NFL	63	1018
	Joe Perry–2	S.F.	NFL	53	1018
58	Charley Tolar	Hou.	AFL	62	1012
59	Paul Lowe–2	S.D.	AFL	63	1010
60	Steve Van Buren–2	Phi.	NFL	47	1008
61	Beattie Feathers	ChiB	NFL	34	1004
62	Larry Csonka–3	Mia.	AFC	73	1003
63	Willie Ellison	L.A.	NFC	71	1000
	Mercury Morris	Mia.	AFC	72	1000

YARDS PER SCHEDULED GAMES

1	O.J. Simpson–1	Buf.	AFC	73	143
2	Jimmy Brown–1	Cle.	NFL	63	133
3	Jimmy Brown–2	Cle.	NFL	58	127
4	Jimmy Brown–3	Cle.	NFL	59	111
5	Jimmy Brown–4	Cle.	NFL	65	110
6	Jim Taylor–1	G.B.	NFL	62	105
7	Jimmy Brown–5	Cle.	NFL	60	105
8	Jim Nance–1	Bos.	AFL	66	104
9	Jimmy Brown–6	Cle.	NFL	64	103
10	Spec Sanders	N.Y.	AAFC	47	102
11	Jimmy Brown–7	Cle.	NFL	61	101
12	Steve Van Buren	Phi.	NFL	49	96
13	Rick Casares	ChiB	NFL	56	94
14	Jim Taylor–2	G.B.	NFL	61	93
15	O.J. Simpson–2	Buf.	AFC	72	89
16	Leroy Kelly–1	Cle.	NFL	68	89
17	Gale Sayers	ChiB	NFL	66	88
18	Tony Canadeo	G.B.	NFL	49	88
19	Joe Perry–1	S.F.	NFL	54	87
20	Jim Nance–2	Bos.	AFL	67	87
	Larry Brown	Was.	NFC	72	87
22	J. D. Smith	S.F.	NFL	59	86
23	Leroy Kelly–2	Cle.	NFL	67	86
24	Hoyle Granger	Hou.	AFL	67	85
25	Joe Perry–2	S.F.	NFL	53	85

AVERAGE YARDS

(Minimum 100 rushes)

					Att	Yards	Avg.
1	Beattie Feathers	ChiB	NFL	34	101	1004	9.94
2	Bobby Douglass	Chi.	NFC	72	141	968	6.87
3	Joe Perry–1	S.F.	AAFC	49	115	783	6.81
4	Dan Towler–1	L.A.	NFL	51	126	854	6.78
5	John Strzykalski–1	S.F.	AAFC	48	141	915	6.49
6	Keith Lincoln	S.D.	AFL	63	128	826	6.45
7	Mercury Morris	Mia.	AFC	73	149	954	6.40
8	Jimmy Brown–1	Cle.	NFL	63	291	1863	6.40
9	John Strzykalski–2	S.F.	AAFC	47	143	906	6.34
10	Paul Lowe–1	L.A.	AFL	60	136	855	6.29
11	Dutch Clark	Det.	NFL	34	122	763	6.25
12	Gale Sayers	Chi.	NFL	68	138	856	6.20
13	Chet Mutryn–1	Buf.	AAFC	47	140	868	6.20
14	Spec Sanders	N.Y.	AAFC	47	231	1432	6.20
15	Marion Motley–1	Cle.	AAFC	48	157	964	6.14
16	Buddy Young	N.Y.	AAFC	47	116	712	6.14
17	Marion Motley–2	Cle.	AAFC	47	146	889	6.09
18	Joe Perry–2	S.F.	NFL	58	125	758	6.06
19	Joe Perry–3	S.F.	NFL	54	173	1049	6.06
20	O.J. Simpson	Buf.	AFC	73	332	2003	6.03
21	Jimmy Brown–2	Cle.	NFL	58	257	1527	5.94
22	John David Crow	StL.	NFL	60	183	1071	5.85
23	Jimmy Brown–3	Cle.	NFL	60	215	1257	5.85
24	Steve Van Buren	Phi.	NFL	45	143	832	5.82
25	Marion Motley–3	Cle.	NFL	50	140	810	5.79
26	Dan Towler–2	L.A.	NFL	53	152	879	5.78
27	Bill Osmanski	ChiB	NFL	39	121	699	5.78
28	Dan Towler–3	L.A.	NFL	52	156	894	5.73
29	Paul Lowe–2	S.D.	AFL	63	177	1010	5.71
30	Bobby Mitchell–1	Cle.	NFL	59	131	743	5.67
31	Franco Harris	Pit.	AFC	72	188	1055	5.61
32	Abner Haynes	Dal.	AFL	60	156	875	5.61
33	Chet Mutryn–2	Buf.	AAFC	48	147	823	5.60
34	Eddie Price	NY G	NFL	50	126	703	5.58
35	Amos Marsh	Dal.	NFL	62	144	802	5.57
36	Brad Hubbert	S.D.	AFL	67	116	643	5.54
37	Mack Lee Hill	K.C.	AFL	64	105	576	5.49
38	Swede Hanson	Phi.	NFL	34	147	805	5.48
39	Leroy Kelly	Cle.	NFL	66	209	1141	5.46
40	Timmy Brown	Phi.	NFL	65	158	861	5.45
41	Mike Garrett	K.C.	AFL	66	147	801	5.45
42	Curtis McClinton	Dal.	AFL	62	111	604	5.44
43	Bobby Mitchell–2	Cle.	NFL	61	101	548	5.43
44	Frank Akins	Was.	NFL	45	147	797	5.42
45	Nick Pietrosante	Det.	NFL	60	161	872	5.42
46	Don Bosseler	Was.	NFL	59	119	644	5.41
	Jim Taylor	G.B.	NFL	62	272	1472	5.41

TOUCHDOWNS

1	Jim Taylor–1	G.B.	NFL	62	19
2	Spec Sanders	N.Y.	AAFC	47	18
3	Jimmy Brown–1	Cle.	NFL	58	17
	Jimmy Brown–2	Cle.	NFL	65	17
5	Lenny Moore	Bal.	NFL	64	16
	Leroy Kelly–1	Cle.	NFL	68	16
7	Steve Van Buren–1	Phi.	NFL	45	15
	Jim Taylor–2	G.B.	NFL	61	15
	Leroy Kelly–2	Cle.	NFL	66	15
10	Jimmy Brown–3	Cle.	NFL	59	14
	John David Crow	StL.	NFL	62	14
	Gale Sayers	Chi.	NFL	65	14
13	Steve Van Buren–2	Phi.	NFL	47	13
	Paul Hornung	G.B.	NFL	60	13
	Jimmy Brown–4	Cle.	NFL	62	13
	Abner Haynes	Dal.	AFL	62	13
	Cookie Gilchrist–1	Buf.	AFL	62	13
18	Rick Casares	ChiB	NFL	56	12
	Jim Taylor–3	G.B.	NFL	64	12
	Jimmy Brown–5	Cle.	NFL	63	12
	Cookie Gilchrist–2	Buf.	AFL	63	12
	Mercury Morris	Mia.	AFC	72	12
	Floyd Little	Den.	AFC	73	12
	O.J. Simpson	Buf.	AFC	73	12
25	Steve Van Buren–3	Phi.	NFL	49	11
	Johnny Lujack	ChiB	NFL	50	11
	Dan Towler	L.A.	NFL	54	11
	Tobin Rote	G.B.	NFL	56	11
	Jim Taylor–4	G.B.	NFL	60	11
	Jim Nance	Bos.	AFL	66	11
	Leroy Kelly–3	Cle.	NFL	67	11
	Bill Brown	Min.	NFL	68	11
	Tom Matte	Bal.	NFL	69	11
	MacArthur Lane	St.L.	NFC	70	11
	Duane Thomas	Dal.	NFC	71	11
	Emerson Boozer	NY J	AFC	72	11

SINGLE SEASON LEADERS

RECEIVING

RECEPTIONS

1	Charley Hennigan–1	Hou.	AFL	64	101
2	Lionel Taylor–1	Den.	AFL	61	100
3	Johnny Morris	Chi.	NFL	64	93
4	Lionel Taylor–2	Den.	AFL	60	92
5	Lionel Taylor–3	Den.	AFL	65	85
6	Tom Fears–1	L.A.	NFL	50	84
7	Charley Hennigan–2	Hou.	AFL	61	82
8	Dave Parks–1	S.F.	NFL	65	80
9	Jim Phillips	L.A.	NFL	61	78
	Lionel Taylor–4	Den.	AFL	63	78
11	Tom Fears–2	L.A.	NFL	49	77
	Lionel Taylor–5	Den.	AFL	62	77
13	Art Powell–1	Oak.	AFL	64	76
	Lionel Taylor–6	Den.	AFL	64	76
15	Ray Berry–1	Bal.	NFL	61	75
	Mike Ditka	Chi.	NFL	64	75
	George Sauer–1	NYJ	AFL	67	75
18	Don Hutson	G.B.	NFL	42	74
	Ray Berry–2	Bal.	NFL	60	74
20	Bobby Joe Conrad	StL.	NFL	63	73
	Art Powell–2	NYT	AFL	63	73
	Lance Alworth–1	S.D.	AFL	66	73
	Dan Abramowicz	N.O.	NFL	69	73
24	Bill Groman	Hou.	AFL	60	72
	Don Maynard–1	NYT	AFL	60	72
	Bobby Mitchell–1	Was.	NFL	62	72
	Charley Taylor–1	Was.	NFL	66	72
28	Art Powell–3	NYT	AFL	61	71
	Bake Turner	NYT	AFL	63	71
	Don Maynard–2	NY J	AFL	67	71
	Clifton McNeill	S.F.	NFL	68	71
	Charley Taylor–2	Was.	NFL	69	71
	Dick Gordon	Chi.	NFC	70	71
34	Charley Taylor–3	Was.	NFL	67	70
35	Art Powell–4	NYT	AFL	60	69
	Bobby Mitchell–2	Was.	NFL	63	69
	Bill Miller	Buf.	AFL	63	69
	Lance Alworth–2	S.D.	AFL	65	69
39	Del Shofner	NYG	NFL	61	68
	Chris Burford	K.C.	AFL	63	68
	Don Maynard–3	NYJ	AFL	65	68
	Lance Alworth–3	S.D.	AFL	68	68
43	Mac Speedie	Cle.	AAFC	47	67
	Tommy McDonald	L.A.	NFL	65	67
	Pat Studstill	Det.	NFL	66	67
	Jerry Smith	Was.	NFL	67	67
	Jack Clancy	Mia.	AFL	67	67
	Roy Jefferson	Pit.	NFL	69	67
	Harold Carmichael	Phi.	NFC	73	67
50	Bob Mann	Det.	NFL	49	66
	Crazy Legs Hirsch	L.A.	NFL	51	66
	Ray Berry–3	Bal.	NFL	59	66
	Terry Barr	Det.	NFL	63	66
	Pete Retzlaff	Phi.	NFL	65	66
	Dave Parks	S.F.	NFL	66	66
	George Sauer–2	NYJ	AFL	68	66
57	Frank Clark	Dal.	NFL	64	65
	Harold Jackson	Phi.	NFL	69	65

YARDS

1	Charley Hennigan–1	Hou.	AFL	61	1746
2	Lance Alworth–1	S.D.	AFL	65	1602
3	Charley Hennigan–2	Hou.	AFL	64	1546
4	Crazy Legs Hirsch	L.A.	NFL	51	1495
5	Bill Groman–1	Hou.	AFL	60	1473
6	Bobby Mitchell–1	Was.	NFL	63	1436
7	Don Maynard–1	NYJ	AFL	67	1434
8	Bobby Mitchell–2	Was.	NFL	62	1384
9	Lance Alworth–2	S.D.	AFL	66	1383
10	Art Powell–1	Oak.	AFL	64	1361
11	Dave Parks	S.F.	NFL	65	1344
12	Lance Alworth–3	S.D.	AFL	68	1312
13	Art Powell–2	NYT	AFL	63	1304
14	Ray Berry	Bal.	NFL	60	1298
15	Otis Taylor–1	K.C.	AFL	66	1297
	Don Maynard–2	NYJ	AFL	68	1297
17	Buddy Dial	Pit.	NFL	63	1295
18	Pat Studstill	Det.	NFL	66	1266
19	Don Maynard–3	NYT	AFL	60	1265
	Ben Hawkins	Phi.	NFL	67	1265
21	Warren Wells–1	Oak.	AFL	69	1260
22	Lionel Taylor–1	Den.	AFL	60	1235
	Lance Alworth–4	S.D.	AFL	64	1235
24	Bob Hayes	Dal.	NFL	66	1232
25	Billy Howton–1	G.B.	NFL	52	1231
26	Don Maynard–4	NYJ	AFL	65	1218
27	Bob Boyd	L.A.	NFL	54	1212
28	Don Hutson	G.B.	NFL	42	1211
29	Homer Jones	NYG	NFL	67	1209
30	Lance Alworth–5	S.D.	AFL	63	1206
31	Jackie Smith	StL.	NFL	67	1205
32	Johnny Morris	Chi.	NFL	64	1200
33	Pete Retzlaff	Phi.	NFL	65	1190
34	George Sauer–1	NYJ	AFL	67	1189
35	Billy Howton–2	G.B.	NFL	56	1188
36	Del Shofner–1	NYG	NFL	63	1181
37	Lionel Taylor–2	Den.	AFL	61	1176
38	Bill Groman–2	Hou.	AFL	61	1175
39	Art Powell–3	NYT	AFL	60	1167
40	Sonny Randle	StL.	NFL	62	1158
41	Mac Speedie	Cle.	AAFC	47	1146
	Tommy McDonald–1	Phi.	NFL	62	1146
43	Tommy McDonald–2	Phi.	NFL	61	1144
44	George Sauer–2	NYJ	AFL	68	1141
45	Elbert Dubenion	Buf.	AFL	64	1139
46	Warren Wells–2	Oak.	AFL	68	1137
47	Del Shofner–2	NYG	NFL	62	1133
48	Lionel Taylor–3	Den	AFL	65	1131
49	Art Powell–4	NYT	AFL	62	1130
50	Charley Frazier	Hou.	AFL	66	1129
51	Harlon Hill–1	ChiB	NFL	56	1128
52	Del Shofner–3	NYG	NFL	61	1125
53	Harlon Hill–2	ChiB	NFL	54	1124
54	Charley Taylor	Was.	NFL	66	1119
55	Tom Fears	L.A.	NFL	50	1116
	Harold Jackson	Phi.	NFL	69	1116
	Harold Carmichael	Phi.	NFC	73	1116.
58	Otis Taylor–2	K.C.	AFC	71	1110
59	Gary Garrison	S.D.	AFL	68	1103
60	Lionel Taylor–4	Den.	AFL	63	1101
61	Gene Washington	S.F.	NFC	70	1100

YARDS PER SCHEDULED GAME

1	Charley Hennigan–1	Hou.	AFL	61	125
2	Crazy Legs Hirsch	L.A.	NFL	51	125
3	Lance Alworth–1	S.D.	AFL	65	114
4	Charley Hennigan–2	Hou.	AFL	64	110
5	Don Hutson–1	G.B.	NFL	42	110
6	Ray Berry	Bal.	NFL	60	108
7	Jim Benton–1	Cle.	NFL	45	107
8	Bill Groman–1	Hou.	AFL	60	105
9	Billy Howton–1	G.B.	NFL	52	103
10	Bobby Mitchell–1	Was.	NFL	63	103
11	Don Maynard–1	NYJ	AFL	67	102
12	Bob Boyd	L.A.	NFL	54	101
13	Billy Howton–2	G.B.	NFL	56	99
14	Bobby Mitchell–2	Was.	NFL	62	99
15	Lance Alworth–2	S.D.	AFL	66	99
16	Art Powell–1	Oak.	AFL	64	97
17	Dave Parks	S.F.	NFL	65	96
18	Harlon Hill–1	ChiB	NFL	56	94
19	Lance Alworth–3	S.D.	AFL	68	94
20	Harlon Hill–2	ChiB	NFL	54	94
21	Art Powell–2	NYT	AFL	63	93
22	Tom Fears–1	L.A.	NFL	50	93
23	Otis Taylor	K.C.	AFL	66	93
24	Don Maynard–2	NYJ	AFL	68	93
25	Buddy Dial	Pit.	NFL	63	93
26	Del Shofner–1	L.A.	NFL	58	91
27	Pat Studstill	Det.	NFL	66	90
28	Don Maynard–3	NYT	AFL	60	90
29	Ben Hawkins	Phi.	NFL	67	90
30	Warren Wells	Oak.	AFL	69	90
31	Jim Benton–2	L.A.	NFL	46	89
32	Lionel Taylor–1	Den.	AFL	60	88
33	Lance Alworth–4	S.D.	AFL	64	88
34	Bob Hayes	Dal.	NFL	66	88
35	Pete Pihos	Phi.	NFL	53	87
36	Don Hutson–2	G.B.	NFL	44	87
37	Don Maynard–4	NYJ	AFL	65	87
38	Homer Jones	NYG	NFL	67	86
39	Lance Alworth–5	S.D.	AFL	63	86
40	Jackie Smith	StL.	NFL	67	86
41	Johnnie Morris	Chi.	NFL	64	86
42	Mac Speedie	Cle.	AAFC	49	86
43	Pete Retzlaff	Phi.	NFL	65	85
44	George Sauer	NYJ	AFL	67	85
45	Bob Mann	Det.	NFL	49	85
46	Tom Fears–2	L.A.	NFL	49	84
47	Del Shofner–2	NYG	NFL	63	84
48	Cloyce Box	Det.	NFL	50	84
49	Lionel Taylor–2	Den.	AFL	61	84
50	Bill Groman–2	Hou.	AFL	61	84
51	Art Powell–3	NYT	AFL	60	83
52	Harry Grant	Phi.	NFL	52	83
53	Don Hutson–3	G.B.	NFL	45	83
54	Sonny Randle	StL.	NFL	62	83

AVERAGE YARDS

(Minimum 400 Yards)

					Rec	Yards	Avg.
1	Don Currivan	Bos.	NFL	47	24	782	32.6
2	Bucky Pope	L.A.	NFL	64	25	786	31.4
3	Billy Cannon	Oak.	AFL	66	14	436	31.1
4	Ray McLean–1	ChiB	NFL	42	19	571	30.1
5	Mel Gray	StL.	NFC	71	18	534	29.7
6	Ray Renfro	Cle.	NFL	57	21	589	28.0
7	Jimmy Orr–1	Pit.	NFL	58	33	910	27.6
8	Homer Jones–1	NY G	NFL	65	26	709	27.3
9	Elbert Dubenion	Buf.	AFL	64	42	1139	27.1
10	Frank Liebel	NY G	NFL	45	22	593	27.0
11	Warren Wells	Oak.	AFL	69	47	1260	26.8
12	Buddy Dial–1	Pit.	NFL	59	16	428	26.8
13	Earl McCullough	Det.	NFC	71	21	552	26.3
14	Jack Snow	L.A.	NFL	67	28	735	26.3
15	Art Graham	Bos.	AFL	63	21	550	26.2
16	Bob Hayes–1	Dal.	NFC	70	34	889	26.2
17	Ron Sellers	Bos.	NFL	69	27	705	26.1
18	Jimmy Orr–2	Bal.	NFL	68	29	743	25.6
19	Ken Kavanaugh	ChiB	NFL	47	32	818	25.6
20	Paul Warfield	Mia.	AFC	70	28	703	25.1
21	Harlon Hill–1	ChiB	NFL	54	45	1124	25.0
22	Don Hutson	G.B.	NFL	39	34	846	24.9
23	Red Mack	Pit.	NFL	63	25	618	24.7
24	Homer Jones–2	NY G	NFL	67	49	1209	24.7
25	Tony Bova	P-P.	NFL	43	17	419	24.6
26	Elbert Wickel–1	Pit.	NFL	49	26	633	24.3
27	Buddy Dial–2	Pit.	NFL	60	40	972	24.3
28	Ray McLean–2	ChiB	NFL	43	18	435	24.2
29	Roy Jefferson	Pit.	NFL	62	32	772	24.1
30	Harlon Hill–2	ChiB	NFL	56	47	1128	24.0
	Bob Hayes–2	Dal.	NFC	71	35	840	24.0
32	Elbert Nickel–2	Pit.	NFL	50	22	527	24.0

TOUCHDOWNS

1	Don Hutson	G.B.	NFL	42	17
	Crazy Legs Hirsch	L.A.	NFL	51	17
	Bill Groman–1	Hou.	AFL	61	17
4	Art Powell–1	NYT	AFL	63	16
5	Cloyce Box	Det.	NFL	52	15
	Sonny Randle–1	StL.	NFL	60	15
7	Mal Kutner	ChiC	NFL	48	14
	Alyn Beals–1	S.F.	AAFC	48	14
	Ray Berry	Bal.	NFL	59	14
	Art Powell–2	NYT	AFL	60	14
	Frank Clarke	Dal.	NFL	62	14
	Lance Alworth–1	S.D.	AFL	65	14
	Don Maynard	NYJ	AFL	65	14
	Warren Wells	Oak.	AFL	69	14
15	Ken Kavanaugh	ChiB	NFL	47	13
	Billy Howton–1	G.B.	NFL	52	13
	Tommy McDonald–1	Phi.	NFL	60	13
	Tommy McDonald–2	Phi.	NFL	61	13
	Terry Barr	Det.	NFL	63	13
	Gary Collins–1	Cle.	NFL	63	13
	Lance Alworth–2	S.D.	AFL	64	13
	Lance Alworth–3	S.D.	AFL	66	13
	Bob Hayes–1	Dal.	NFL	66	13
	Homer Jones	NYG	NFL	67	13
	Dick Gordon	ChiC	NFC	70	13
	Harold Johnson	L.A.	NFC	73	13
27	Alyn Beals–2	S.F.	AAFC	49	12
	Bob Shaw	ChiC	NFL	50	12
	Leon Hart	Det.	NFL	51	12
	Hugh Taylor	Was.	NFL	52	12
	Harlon Hill	ChiB	NFL	54	12
	Billy Howton–2	G.B.	NFL	56	12
	Bill Groman–2	Hou.	AFL	60	12
	Lionel Taylor	Den.	AFL	60	12
	Buddy Dial	Pit.	NFL	61	12
	Mike Ditka	Chi.	NFL	61	12
	Charley Hennigan	Hou.	AFL	61	12
	Chris Burford	Dal.	AFL	62	12
	Del Shofner	NYG	NFL	62	12
	Sonny Randle–2	StL.	NFL	63	12
	Bob Hayes–2	Dal.	NFL	65	12
	Dave Parks	S.F.	NFL	65	12
	Art Powell–3	Oak.	AFL	65	12
	Gary Collins–2	Cle.	NFL	66	12
	Charley Frazier	Hou.	AFL	66	12
	Charley Taylor	Was.	NFL	66	12
	Jerry Smith	Was.	NFL	67	12
	Paul Warfield	Cle.	NFL	68	12
	Fred Biletnikoff	Oak.	AFL	69	12
	Lance Rentzel	Dal.	NFL	69	12
	Gary Garrison	S.D.	AFC	70	12
	Gene Washington–1	S.F.	NFC	70	12
	Gene Washington–2	S.F.	NFC	72	12

INTERCEPTION RETURNS

1	Night Train Lane–1	L.A.	NFL	52	14
2	Dan Sandifer	Was.	NFL	48	13
	Spec Sanders	NYY	NFL	50	13
4	Bob Nussbaumer	ChiC	NFL	49	12
	Don Doll–1	Det.	NFL	50	12
	Woodley Lewis	L.A.	NFL	50	12
	Fred Glick	Hou.	AFL	63	12
	Paul Krause	Min.	NFL	64	12
	Dainard Paulson	NYJ	AFL	64	12
10	Sammy Baugh	Was.	NFL	43	11
	Otto Schnellbacher–1	N.Y.	AAFC	48	11
	Don Doll–2	Det.	NFL	49	11
	Otto Schnellbacher–2	NYG	NFL	51	11
	Tom Keane–1	Bal.	NFL	53	11
	Will Sherman	L.A.	NFL	55	11
	Lindon Crow	ChiC	NFL	56	11
	Jimmy Patton	NYG	NFL	58	11
	Goose Gonsoulin	Den.	AFL	60	11
	Lee Riley	NYT	AFL	62	11
	Ron Hall	Bos.	AFL	63	11
	Bill Bradley	Phi.	NFC	71	11
22	Irv Comp	G.B.	NFL	43	10
	Bill Dudley	Pit.	NFL	46	10
	Tom Colella	Cle.	AAFC	46	10
	Frank Seno	Bos.	NFL	47	10
	Frank Reagan	NYG	NFL	47	10
	Em Tunnell	NYG	NFL	49	10
	Howard Hartley	Pit	NFL	51	10
	Tom Keane–2	Dal.	NFL	52	10
	Don Doll–3	Was.	NFL	53	10
	Ray Ramsey	ChiC	NFL	53	10
	Night Train Lane–2	ChiC	NFL	54	10
	Jack Butler	Pit.	NFL	57	10
	Jack Christiansen	Det.	NFL	57	10
	Milt Davis	Bal.	NFL	57	10
	Dave Baker	S.F.	NFL	60	10
	Jerry Norton	StL.	NFL	60	10
	Billy Atkins	Buf.	AFL	61	10
	Tommy Morrow	Oak.	AFL	62	10
	Pat Fischer	StL.	NFL	64	10
	Larry Wilson	StL.	NFL	66	10
	Bobby Hunt	K.C.	AFL	66	10
	Johnny Robinson–1	K.C.	AFL	66	10
	Lem Barney	Det.	NFL	67	10
	Dave Whitsell	N.O.	NFL	67	10
	Miller Farr	Hou.	AFL	67	10
	Tom Janik	Buf.	AFL	67	10
	Dick Westmoreland	Mia.	AFL	67	10
	Willie Williams	NYG	NFL	68	10
	Dave Grayson	Oak.	AFL	68	10
	Mel Renfro	Dal.	NFL	69	10
	Johnny Robinson–2	K.C.	AFC	70	10

SINGLE SEASON LEADERS

POINTS

Rank	Player	Team	League	Year	Points
1	Paul Hornung–1	G.B.	NFL	60	176
2	Gino Cappelletti–1	Bos.	AFL	64	155
3	Gino Cappelletti–2	Bos.	AFL	61	147
4	Paul Hornung–2	G.B.	NFL	61	146
5	Jim Turner–1	NYJ	AFL	68	145
6	Don Hutson–1	G.B.	NFL	42	138
7	Gene Mingo–1	Den.	AFL	62	137
8	Gale Sayers	Chi.	NFL	65	132
	Gino Cappelletti–3	Bos.	AFL	65	132
10	Dave Ray–1	L.A.	NFC	73	130
11	Jan Stenerud–1	K.C.	AFL	68	129
	Jim Turner–2	NYJ	AFL	69	129
13	Doak Walker	Det.	NFL	50	128
	Gino Cappelletti–4	Bos.	AFL	62	128
	Cookie Gilchrist	Buf.	AFL	62	128
	Chester Marcol	G.B.	NFC	72	128
17	Jimmy Brown	Cle.	NFL	65	126
18	Fred Cox–1	Min.	NFC	70	125
19	Gene Mingo–2	Den.	AFL	60	123
	Roy Gerela–1	Pit.	AFC	73	123
21	Fred Cox–2	Min.	NFL	69	121
	Dave Ray–2	L.A.	NFC	70	121
	Bobby Howfield	NYJ	AFC	72	121
24	Lenny Moore	Bal.	NFL	64	120
	Leroy Kelly	Cle.	NFL	68	120
26	Gino Cappelletti–5	Bos.	AFL	66	119
	Jan Stenerud–2	K.C.	AFL	69	119
	Roy Gerela–2	Pit.	AFC	72	119
29	Don Hutson–2	G.B.	NFL	43	117
	Jim Bakken–1	StL.	NFL	67	117
	George Blanda–1	Oak.	AFL	68	117
	Garo Yepremian–1	Mia.	AFC	71	117
33	George Blanda–2	Oak.	AFL	67	116
	Jan Stenerud–3	K.C.	AFC	70	116
35	George Blanda–3	Hou.	AFL	60	115
	Jim Bakken–2	StL.	NFL	64	115
	Lou Groza	Cle.	NFL	64	115
	Pete Gogolak	Buf.	AFL	65	115
	Garo Yepremian–2	Mia.	AFC	72	115
40	Spec Sanders	N.Y.	AAFC	47	114
	Gordon Soltau	S.F.	NFL	53	114
	Bobby Walston	Phi.	NFL	54	114
	Jim Taylor	G.B.	NFL	62	114
	Abner Haynes	Dal.	AFL	62	114
	Curt Knight	Was.	NFC	71	114
46	Gino Cappelletti–6	Bos.	AFL	63	113
	Fred Cox–3	Min.	NFL	65	113
	Bruce Gossett	L.A.	NFL	66	113
	Garo Yepremian–3	Mia.	AFC	73	113
50	George Blanda–4	Hou.	AFL	61	112
	Nick Mike-Mayer	Atl.	NFC	73	112
52	Horst Muhlmann	Cin.	AFC	72	111
53	Steve Van Buren	Phi.	NFL	45	110
	Pat Harder	ChiC	NFL	48	110
	Lou Michaels	Pit.	NFL	62	110
	Jan Stenerud–4	K.C.	AFC	71	110

POINTS PER SCHEDULED GAME

Rank	Player	Team	League	Year	Avg.
1	Paul Hornung–1	G.B.	NFL	60	14.7
2	Don Hutson–1	G.B.	NFL	42	12.5
3	Don Hutson–2	G.B.	NFL	43	11.7
4	Gino Cappelletti–1	Bos.	AFL	64	11.1
5	Steve Van Buren	Phi.	NFL	45	11.0
6	Doak Walker–1	Det.	NFL	50	10.7
7	Gino Cappelletti–2	Bos.	AFL	61	10.5
8	Paul Hornung–2	G.B.	NFL	61	10.4
9	Jim Turner–1	NYJ	AFL	68	10.4
10	Gene Mingo–1	Den.	AFL	62	9.8
11	Don Hutson–3	G.B.	NFL	45	9.7
12	Gordon Soltau	S.F.	NFL	53	9.5
	Bobby Walston–1	Phi.	NFL	54	9.5
14	Gale Sayers	Chi.	NFL	65	9.4
	Gino Cappelletti–3	Bos.	AFL	65	9.4
16	Dave Ray–1	L.A.	NFC	73	9.3
17	Jan Stenerud–1	K.C.	AFC	68	9.2
	Jim Turner–2	NYJ	AFL	69	9.2
19	Pat Harder–1	ChiC	NFL	48	9.2
20	Gino Cappelletti–4	Bos.	AFL	62	9.1
	Cookie Gilchrist	Buf.	AFL	62	9.1
	Chester Marcol	G.B.	NFC	72	9.1
23	Johnny Lujack	ChiB	NFL	50	9.1
24	Lou Groza–1	Cle.	NFL	53	9.0
	Jimmy Brown–1	Cle.	NFL	58	9.0
	Jimmy Brown–2	Cle.	NFL	65	9.0
27	Fred Cox–1	Min.	NFC	70	8.9
28	Doak Walker–2	Det.	NFL	54	8.8
29	Gene Mingo–2	Den.	AFL	60	8.8
	Roy Gerela–1	Pit.	AFC	70	8.8
31	Bobby Walston–2	Phi.	NFL	60	8.8
32	Fred Cox–2	Min.	NFL	69	8.6
	Dave Ray–2	L.A.	NFC	70	8.6
	Bobby Howfield	NYJ	AFC	72	8.6
35	Don Hutston–4	G.B.	NFL	41	8.6
36	Lenny Moore	Bal.	NFL	64	8.6
	Leroy Kelly	Cle.	NFL	68	8.6
38	Don Hutson–5	G.B.	NFL	44	8.5
	Pat Harder–2	ChiC	NFL	47	8.5
	Pat Harder–3	ChiC	NFL	49	8.5
	Choo-Choo Roberts	NYG	NFL	49	8.5
	Crazy Legs Hirsch	L.A.	NFL	51	8.5
	Gino Cappelletti–5	Bos.	AFL	66	8.5
	Jan Stenerud–2	K.C.	AFL	69	8.5
	Roy Gerela–2	Pit.	AFC	72	8.5
46	Jim Bakken–1	StL.	NFL	67	8.4
	George Blanda–1	Oak.	AFL	68	8.4
	Garo Yepremian–1	Mia.	AFC	71	8.4
49	Ted Fritsch	G.B.	NFL	46	8.3
50	George Blanda–2	Oak.	AFL	67	8.3
	Jan Stenerud–3	K.C.	AFC	70	8.3
52	Bobby Layne	Det.	NFL	56	8.3
53	George Blanda–3	Hou.	AFL	60	8.2
	Jim Bakken–2	StL.	NFL	64	8.2
	Lou Groza–2	Cle.	NFL	64	8.2
	Pete Gogolak	Buf.	AFL	65	8.2
	Garo Yepremian–2	Mia.	AFC	72	8.2
58	Bob Waterfield	L.A.	NFL	51	8.2
59	Spec Sanders	N.Y.	AAFC	47	8.1
	Jim Taylor	G.B.	NFL	62	8.1
	Abner Haynes	Dal.	AFL	62	8.1
	Curt Knight	Was.	NFC	71	8.1
63	Doak Walker–3	Det.	NFL	51	8.1
64	Gino Cappelletti–6	Bos.	AFL	63	8.1
	Fred Cox–3	Min.	NFL	65	8.1
	Bruce Gossett	L.A.	NFL	66	8.1
	Garo Yepremian–3	Mia.	AFC	73	8.1
68	Doak Walker–4	Det.	NFL	55	8.0
	George Blanda–4	Hou.	AFL	61	8.0
	Nick Mike-Mayer	Atl.	NFC	73	8.0

FIELD GOALS

Rank	Player	Team	League	Year	FG
1	Jim Turner–1	NYJ	AFL	68	34
2	Chester Marcol	G.B.	NFC	72	33
3	Jim Turner–2	NYJ	AFL	69	32
4	Jan Stenerud–1	K.C.	AFL	68	30
	Jan Stenerud–2	K.C.	AFC	70	30
	Fred Cox–1	Min.	NFC	70	30
	Dave Ray–1	L.A.	NFC	73	30
8	Dave Ray–2	L.A.	NFC	70	29
	Curt Knight–1	Was.	NFC	71	29
	Roy Gerela–1	Pit.	AFC	73	29
11	Pete Gogolak–1	Buf.	AFL	65	28
	Bruce Gossett–1	L.A.	NFL	66	28
	Garo Yepremian–1	Mia.	AFC	71	28
	Roy Gerela–2	Pit.	AFC	72	28
15	Gene Mingo	Den.	AFL	62	27
	Jim Bakken–1	StL.	NFL	67	27
	Jan Stenerud–3	K.C.	AFL	69	27
	Bobby Howfield	NYJ	AFC	72	27
	Horst Muhlmann–1	Cin.	AFC	72	27
20	Lou Michaels	Pit.	NFL	62	26
	Fred Cox–2	Min.	NFL	69	26
	Jan Stenerud–4	K.C.	AFC	71	26
	Bruce Gossett–2	S.F.	NFC	73	26
	Nick Mike-Mayer	Atl.	NFC	73	26
25	Jim Bakken–2	StL.	NFL	64	25
	Gino Cappelletti–1	Bos.	AFL	65	25
	Mac Percival	Chi.	NFL	68	25
	Errol Mann–1	Det.	NFL	69	25
	Pete Gogolak–2	NYG	NFC	70	25
	Horst Muhlmann–2	Cin.	AFC	70	25
	Jim Turner–3	Den.	AFC	71	25
	Garo Yepremian–2	Mia.	AFC	73	25
33	Jim Martin	Bal.	NFL	63	24
	Dave Ray–3	L.A.	NFC	72	24
	Garo Yepremian–3	Mia.	AFC	72	24
	Tom Dempsey–1	Phi.	NFC	73	24
	Jan Stenerud–5	K.C.	AFC	73	24
38	Lou Groza–1	Cle.	NFL	53	23
	Fred Cox–3	Min.	NFL	65	23
	Jim Bakken–3	StL.	NFL	66	23
	Bruce Gossett–3	S.F.	NFC	71	23
	Jim Bakken–4	StL.	NFC	73	23
	George Blanda	Oak.	AFC	73	23
44	Gino Cappelletti–2	Bos.	AFL	63	22
	Lou Groza–2	Cle.	NFL	64	22
	Charlie Gogolak	Was.	NFL	66	22
	Dennis Partee	S.D.	AFL	68	22
	Tom Dempsey–2	N.O.	NFL	69	22
	Bruce Gossett–4	L.A.	NFL	69	22
	Garo Yepremian–4	Mia.	AFC	70	22
	Fred Cox–4	Min.	NFC	71	22
	Errol Mann–2	Det.	NFC	71	22
	Don Cockroft–1	Cle.	AFC	72	22
	Don Cockroft–2	Cle.	AFC	73	22
	Curt Knight–2	Was.	NFC	73	22
	Jim Turner–4	Den.	AFC	73	22

PERCENTAGE–FIELD GOALS MADE

(Minimum Attempts: To 1949=5, 50-59=10, 1960 + up = 20)

Rank	Player	Team	League	Year	Made	Att	Pct.
1	Lou Groza	Cle.	NFL	53	23	26	88.5
2	Jack Manders	ChiB	NFL	36	7	8	87.5
3	Don Cockroft-1	Cle.	AFC	72	22	27	81.5
4	Bobby Layne	Det.	NFL	56	12	15	80.0
	Regis Monahan	Det.	NFL	38	4	5	80.0
	Chuck Hanneman	Det.	NFL	39	4	5	80.0
	Andy Marefos	NY G	NFL	41	4	5	80.0
	Ted Fritsch	G.B.	NFL	42	4	5	80.0
	Frank Maznicki	ChiB	NFL	42	4	5	80.0
10	Bruce Gossett–1	S.F.	NFC	73	26	33	78.8
11	Jan Stenerud–1	K.C.	AFL	69	27	35	77.1
12	Bill Dudley	Was.	NFL	51	10	13	76.9
13	Garo Yepremian–1	Mia.	AFC	70	22	29	75.9
14	Jan Stenerud–2	K.C.	AFL	67	30	40	75.0
	Bruce Gossett–2	L.A.	NFL	64	18	24	75.0
	Don Cockroft–2	Cle.	NFL	68	18	24	75.0
	Ray Poole	NY G	NFL	51	12	16	75.0
	Steve Nemeth	Chi.	AAFC	46	9	12	75.0
	Bobby Walston–1	Phi.	NFL	57	9	12	75.0
20	Curt Knight	Was.	NFC	70	20	27	74.1
21	Jim Turner	NY J	AFL	67	34	46	73.9
22	Bobby Howfield–1	NY J	AFC	72	27	37	73.0
23	Sam Baker	Phi.	NFL	66	18	25	72.0
24	Jim Baken	StL.	NFC	73	23	32	71.9
25	Jan Stenerud–3	K.C.	AFC	70	30	42	71.4
26	Don Cockroft–3	Cle.	AFC	73	22	31	71.0
27	Bobby Howfield–2	NY J	AFC	73	17	24	70.8
28	Fred Cone	G.B.	NFL	57	12	17	70.6
29	Fred Cox	Min.	NFL	69	26	37	70.3
30	Garo Yepremian–2	Mia.	AFC	71	28	40	70.0
	Mike Mercer	Oak. - K.C.	AFL	66	21	30	70.0
	John Leypoldt	Buf.	AFC	73	21	30	70.0
	Bobby Walston–2	Phi.	NFL	60	14	20	70.0
	Pat Harder	ChiC	NFL	47	7	10	70.0

POINTS AFTER TOUCHDOWN

Rank	Player	Team	League	Year	PAT
1	George Blanda–1	Hou.	AFL	61	64
2	Joe Vetrano–1	S.F.	AAFC	48	62
3	Joe Vetrano–2	S.F.	AAFC	49	56
	Danny Villanueva	Dal.	NFL	66	56
	George Blanda–2	Oak.	AFL	67	56
6	Bob Waterfield	L.A.	NFL	50	54
	George Blanda–3	Oak.	AFL	68	54
	Mike Clark–1	Dal.	NFL	68	54
9	Pat Harder–1	ChiC	NFL	48	53
	Lou Michaels–1	Bal.	NFL	64	53
11	Don Chandler–1	NYG	NFL	63	52
	Tommy Davis	S.F.	NFL	65	52
	Rodger LeClerc	Chi.	NFL	65	52
14	Lou Groza–1	Cle.	AAFC	48	51
	Lou Groza–2	Cle.	NFL	66	51
16	Cliff Patton	Phi.	NFL	48	50
	Steve Myhra–1	Bal.	NFL	59	50
	Sam Baker–1	Dal.	NFL	62	50
19	Harvey Johnson	N.Y.	AAFC	47	49
	Lou Groza–3	Cle.	NFL	64	49
21	Gordie Soltau	S.F.	NFL	53	48
	Steve Myhra–2	Bal.	NFL	58	48
	Gino Cappelletti	Bos.	AFL	61	48
	George Blanda–4	Hou.	AFL	62	48
	Jim Bakken	StL.	NFL	65	48
	Bruce Gossett	L.A.	NFL	67	48
	Lou Michaels–2	Bal.	NFL	68	48
28	Bill Shockley	NYT	AFL	60	47
	Don Chandler–2	NYG	NFL	62	47
	Mike Mercer	Oak.	AFL	63	47
	Mike Clark–2	Dal.	NFC	71	47
32	Ben Agajanian	L.A.	AFL	60	46
	George Blanda–5	Hou.	AFL	60	46
	Pat Summerall	NYG	NFL	61	46
	Tommy Brooker	K.C.	AFL	64	46
	Pete Gogolak	Buf.	AFL	64	46
	Lou Michaels–3	Bal.	NFL	67	46
	Don Cockroft–1	Cle.	NFL	68	46
39	Lou Groza–4	Cle.	AAFC	46	45
	Pat Harder–2	ChiC	NFL	49	45
	Chet Adams	NYY	NFL	50	45
	Bobby Walston	Phi.	NFL	53	45
	George Blanda–6	ChiB	NFL	56	45
	Lou Groza–5	Cle.	NFL	65	45
	Sam Baker–2	Phi.	NFL	67	45
	Jan Stenerud	K.C.	AFL	67	45
	Dick Van Raaphorst	S.D.	AFL	67	45
	George Blanda–7	Oak.	AFL	69	45
	Don Cockroft–2	Cle.	NFL	69	45

MOST PAT'S – NO MISSES

Rank	Player	Team	League	Year	PAT
1	Joe Vetrano	S.F.	AAFC	49	56
	Danny Villanueva	Dal.	NFL	66	56
3	George Blanda–1	Oak.	AFL	68	54
	Mike Clark–1	Dal.	NFL	68	54
5	Pat Harder	ChiC	NFL	48	53
6	Rodger LeClerc	Chi.	NFL	65	52
7	Cliff Patton	Phi.	NFL	48	50
8	Jim Bakken–1	StL.	NFL	65	48
	Bruce Gossett–1	L.A.	NFL	67	48
10	Mike Mercer	Oak.	AFL	63	47
	Mike Clark–2	Dal.	NFC	71	47
12	Pat Summerall	NYG	NFL	61	46
	Tommy Brooker–1	K.C.	AFL	64	46
14	Lou Groza–1	Cle.	NFL	65	45
	Sam Baker–1	Phi.	NFL	67	45
	Jan Stenerud–1	K.C.	AFL	67	45
	Dick Van Raaphorst	S.D.	AFL	67	45
	George Blanda–2	Oak.	AFL	69	45
	Don Cockroft	Cle.	NFL	69	45
20	Tommy Davis	S.F.	NFL	61	44
	Jim Bakken–2	StL.	NFL	63	44
	Fred Cox–1	Min.	NFL	65	44
	George Blanda–3	Oak.	AFC	72	44
24	Rex Grossman	Bal.	AAFC	48	43
	Lou Groza–2	Cle.	NFL	51	43
	Doak Walker	Det.	NFL	54	43
	Lou Groza–3	Cle.	NFL	67	43
	Jim Turner–1	NYJ	AFL	68	43
	Fred Cox–2	Min.	NFL	69	43
	Toni Fritsch	Dal.	NFC	73	43
31	Paige Cothren–1	L.A.	NFL	58	42
32	Paul Hornung–1	G.B.	NFL	60	41
	Paul Hornung–2	G.B.	NFL	61	41
	Errol Mann–1	Det.	NFC	70	41
35	Jim Bakken–3	StL.	NFL	64	40
	Herb Traveno	S.D.	AFL	65	40
	Jim Bakken–4	StL.	NFL	68	40
	Jim Turner–2	Den.	AFC	73	40
39	Fred Cox–3	Min.	NFL	63	39
	Don Chandler	G.B.	NFL	67	39
41	Les Richter	L.A.	NFL	54	38
	Paige Cothren–2	L.A.	NFL	57	38
	Bob Khayat	Was.	NFL	62	38
	Sam Baker–2	Dal.	NFL	63	38
	Jan Stenerud–2	K.C.	AFL	69	38
	Garo Yepremian	Mia.	AFC	73	38
47	Bob Waterfield	L.A.	NFL	46	37
	Harvey Johnson	N.Y.	AAFC	48	37
	George Blanda–4	ChiB	NFL	55	37
	Wayne Walker	Det.	NFL	62	37
	George Blanda–5	Hou.	AFL	63	37
	Tommy Brooker–2	K.C.	AFL	65	37
	Mike Eischeid	Oak.	AFL	66	37
	Bruce Gossett–2	L.A.	NFL	68	37
	Errol Mann–2	Det.	NFC	71	37
	Dave Ray	L.A.	NFC	71	37
	Jim Turner–3	Den.	AFC	72	37
	Curt Knight	Was.	NFC	73	37

SINGLE SEASON LEADERS
PUNTING AVERAGE

(Minimum 30 Punts)

1	Sammy Baugh–1	Was.	NFL	40	51.3
2	Glenn Dobbs–1	L.A.	AAFC	48	49.1
3	Yale Lary–1	Det.	NFL	63	48.9
4	Sammy Baugh–2	Was.	NFL	41	48.7
5	Yale Lary–2	Det.	NFL	61	48.4
6	Frankie Albert	S.F.	AAFC	49	48.2
7	Glenn Dobbs–2	Bkn.	AAFC	46	47.8
8	Joe Muha	Phi.	NFL	48	47.2
9	Yale Lary–3	Det.	NFL	59	47.1
10	Bobby Joe Green–1	Pit.	NFL	61	47.0
11	Pat Brady	Pit.	NFL	53	46.9
12	Gary Collins	Cle.	NFL	65	46.7
13	Sammy Baugh–3	Was.	NFL	42	46.6
	Don Chandler–1	NYG	NFL	59	46.6
15	Bobby Joe Green–2	Chi.	NFL	63	46.5
16	Bobby Walden–1	Min.	NFL	64	46.4
17	Yale Lary–4	Det.	NFL	64	46.3
18	Dave Lewis	Cin.	AFL	70	46.2
19	Jim Fraser	Den.	AFL	63	46.1
	Jerrel Wilson–1	K.C.	AFL	65	46.1
21	Sammy Baugh–4	Was.	NFL	43	45.9
22	Tommy Davis–1	S.F.	NFL	65	45.8
	Bob Scarpitto	Den.	AFL	66	45.8
24	Horace Gillom–1	Cle.	NFL	52	45.7
	Tommy Davis–2	S.F.	NFL	59	45.7
26	Bob Cifers	Det.	NFL	46	45.6
	Jerry Norton	StL.	NFL	60	45.6
	Tommy Davis–3	S.F.	NFL	62	45.6
	Don Chandler–2	NYG	NFL	64	45.6
	Tommy Davis–4	S.F.	NFL	64	45.6
	David Lee–1	Bal.	NFL	66	45.6
32	Horace Gillom–2	Cle.	NFL	51	45.5
	Sam Baker–1	Was.	NFL	59	45.5
	Danny Villanueva–1	L.A.	NFL	62	45.5
	Jerrel Wilson–2	K.C.	AFC	73	45.5
36	Bob Reinhard	L.A.	AAFC	46	45.4
	Sam Baker–2	Was.	NFL	58	45.4
	Tommy Davis–5	S.F.	NFL	61	45.4
	Sam Baker–3	Dal.	NFL	62	45.4
	Danny Villanueva–2	L.A.	NFL	63	45.4
	Tommy Davis–6	S.F.	NFL	63	45.4
42	Yale Lary–5	Det.	NFL	62	45.3
	Curley Johnson	NYJ	AFL	65	45.3
	David Lee–2	Bal.	NFL	69	45.3
	Guy Ray	Oak.	AFC	73	45.3
46	Bobby Walden–2	Pit.	AFC	70	45.2
47	Sammy Baugh–5	Was.	NFL	46	45.1
	Frank Lambert	Pit.	NFC	65	45.1
	Jerrel Wilson–3	K.C.	AFL	68	45.1
	Billy Van Heusen	Den.	AFC	73	45.1
51	Billy Atkins	Buf.	AFL	61	45.0

PUNT RETURNS

1	Alvin Haymond–1	L.A.	NFC	70	53
2	Rodger Bird–1	Oak.	AFL	67	46
3	Bruce Taylor–1	S.F.	NFC	70	43
4	Alvin Haymond–2	Bal.	NFL	65	41
	Butch Atkinson–1	Oak.	AFC	73	41
6	Alvin Haymond–3	Bal.	NFL	66	40
	Ray Brown	Atl.	NFC	73	40
8	Charlie West	Min.	NFL	69	39
9	Em Tunnell–1	NYG	NFL	53	38
10	Rodger Bird–2	Oak.	AFL	66	37
	Hubie Bryant	Pit.	AFC	70	37
12	Speedy Duncan–1	S.D.	AFL	67	36
	Butch Atkinson–2	Oak.	AFL	68	36
	Ike Hill	Chi.	NFC	73	36
15	Woodley Lewis	L.A.	NFL	53	35
	Kermit Alexander–1	S.F.	NFL	65	35
	Jerry LeVias	Hou.	AFL	69	35
18	Em Tunnell–2	NYG	NFL	51	34
	Bibbles Bawel	Phi.	NFL	52	34
	Mike Battle	NYJ	AFL	69	34
	Bruce Taylor–2	S.F.	NFC	71	34
	Bruce Laird	Bal.	AFC	72	34
	Glenn Edwards	Pit.	AFC	72	34
24	George McAfee–1	ChiB	NFL	50	33
	Hagood Clarke	Buf.	AFL	64	33
	Jim Stiger	L.A.	NFL	66	33
	Alvin Haymond–4	L.A.	NFL	69	33
	Ron Smith	Chi.	NFC	70	33
	Jake Scott	Mia.	AFC	71	33
30	Tom Watkins	Det.	NFL	63	32
	Mel Renfro	Dal.	NFL	64	32
32	Em Tunnell–3	NYG	NFL	50	31
	Rickie Harris	Was.	NFL	65	31
	Claude Gibson	Oak.	AFL	65	31
	Jon Staggers	Pit.	AFC	71	31
36	George McAfee–2	ChiB	NFL	48	30
	Em Tunnell–4	NYG	NFL	51	30
	Bert Rechichar	Bal.	NFL	55	30
	Speedy Duncan–2	S.D.	AFL	65	30
	Kermit Alexander–2	S.F.	NFL	66	30
	Butch Byrd	Buf.	AFL	67	30
	Chuck Latourette	StL.	NFC	70	30
	Leroy Kelly	Cle.	AFC	71	30
	Willie Belton	Atl.	NFC	71	30
	Tommy Casanova	Cin.	AFC	72	30
	Bill Thompson	Den.	AFC	73	30

YARDS

1	Rodger Bird–1	Oak.	AFL	67	612
2	Billy Grimes	G.B.	NFL	50	555
3	Bruce Taylor	S.F.	NFC	70	516
4	Butch Atkinson–1	Oak.	AFL	68	490
5	Em Tunnell–1	NYG	NFL	51	489
6	Speedy Duncan–1	S.D.	AFL	65	464
7	Pat Studstill	Det.	NFL	62	457
8	Walt Slater	Pit.	NFL	47	435
	Alvin Haymond–1	L.A.	NFL	69	435
10	Speedy Duncan–2	S.D.	AFL	67	434
11	Vitamin Smith	L.A.	NFL	49	427
12	Claude Gibson–1	Oak.	AFL	64	419
13	Mel Renfro	Dal.	NFL	64	418
14	George McAfee	ChiB	NFL	48	417
15	Em Tunnell–2	NYG	NFL	52	411
16	Alvin Haymond–2	Bal.	NFL	65	403
17	Tom Watkins	Det.	NFL	63	399
18	Ray Mathews	Pit.	NFL	52	397
19	Tom Harmon	L.A.	NFL	47	392
20	Bill Dudley	Pit.	NFL	46	385
21	Dick Christy	NYT	AFL	61	383
22	Rickie Harris	Was.	NFL	65	377
23	Alvin Haymond–3	L.A.	NFC	70	376
24	Herm Wedemeyer	L.A.	AAFC	48	368
25	John Williams	Was.	NFL	52	366
	Bill Thompson	Den.	AFC	73	366
27	Ray Brown	Atl.	NFC	73	360
28	Claude Gibson–2	Oak.	AFL	65	357
29	Ron Smith	S.D.	AFC	73	352
30	Jim Cason–1	S.F.	AAFC	49	351
	Woodley Lewis	L.A.	NFL	52	351
32	Alvin Haymond–4	Bal.	NFL	66	347
33	Chuck Latourette	StL.	NFL	68	345
34	Jack Christiansen–1	Det.	NFL	51	343
35	Rex Baumgardner	Buf.	AAFC	48	336
	Butch Atkinson–2	Oak.	AFC	73	336
	Glen Edwards	Pit.	AFC	73	336
38	Jerome Davis	ChiC	NFL	48	334
39	Ron Gardin	Bal.	AFC	70	330
40	Rodger Bird–1	Oak.	AFL	66	323
41	Jack Christiansen–2	Det.	NFL	52	322
42	Jake Scott	Mia.	AFC	71	318
43	Hagood Clarke	Buf.	AFL	64	317
44	Em Tunnell–3	NYG	NFL	49	315
45	Red Cochran	ChiC	NFL	49	314
46	Bob Hayes	Dal.	NFL	68	312
47	Ed Podolak	K.C.	AFC	70	311
48	Jim Cason–2	S.F.	AAFC	48	309
49	Eddie Saenz	Was.	NFL	47	308
50	Claude Gibson–3	Oak.	AFL	63	307
51	Sam Cathcart	S.F.	AAFC	49	306
	Veryl Switzer	G.B.	NFL	54	306
53	Em Tunnell–4	NYG	NFL	50	305
54	Bruce Laird	Bal.	AFC	72	303

AVERAGE RETURN

(Minimum – 1 Return per Game)

					Ret.	Yds.	Avg.
1	Ernie Steele	Phi.	NFL	42	10	264	26.40
2	Herb Rich	Bal.	NFL	50	12	276	23.00
3	Jack Christianson–1	Det.	NFL	52	15	322	21.47
4	Dick Christy	NY T	AFL	61	18	383	21.28
5	Rex Baumgardner	Buf.	AAFC	48	16	336	21.00
6	Red Cochran	ChiC	NFL	49	15	314	20.93
7	Jerome Davis	ChiC	NFL	48	16	334	20.88
8	Bob Hayes	Dal.	NFL	68	15	312	20.80
9	Frankie Sinkwich	Det.	NFL	43	11	228	20.73
10	Buddy Young	NY Y	NFL	51	12	231	19.25
11	Billy Grimes	G.B.	NFL	50	29	555	19.14
12	Jack Christianson–2	Det.	NFL	51	18	343	19.06
13	Ollie Matson	ChiC	NFL	55	13	245	18.85
14	Chuck Fenenbock	L.A.	AAFC	46	16	299	18.69
15	Woodley Lewis	L.A.	NFL	52	19	351	18.47
16	Frank Seno	Bos.	NFL	47	12	213	17.75

KICKOFF RETURNS

1	Odell Barry	Den.	AFL	64	47
2	Chuck Latourette	StL.	NFL	68	46
	Dave Hampton	G.B.	NFC	71	46
4	Bobby Jancik–1	Hou.	AFL	63	45
5	Ron Smith–1	Atl.	NFL	66	43
	Mercury Morris	Mia.	AFL	69	43
	Margene Adkins	N.O.	NFC	72	43
8	Noland Smith	K.C.	AFL	67	41
	Mack Herron	N.E.	NFC	73	41
10	Mel Renfro	Dal.	NFL	64	40
	Mike Battle	NYJ	AFC	70	40
12	Ron Smith–2	Atl.	NFL	67	39
	Max Anderson	Buf.	AFL	68	39
14	Dick Christy	NYT	AFL	62	38
	Bo Roberson–1	Oak.	AFL	63	38
	Jerry LeVias	Hou.	AFL	69	38
17	Abe Woodson–1	S.F.	NFL	62	37
	Charley Mitchell	Den.	AFL	63	37
	Kermit Alexander–1	S.F.	NFL	66	37
	Cannonball Butler	Atl.	NFL	68	37
21	Bo Roberson–2	Oak.	AFL	64	36
	Willie Porter	Bos.	AFL	68	36
	Rocky Thompson	NYG	NFC	71	36
	Herb Mul-Key	Was.	NFC	73	36
	Ron Smith–3	S.D.	AFC	73	36
26	Floyd Little	Den.	AFL	67	35
	Ronnie Blye	NYG	NFL	68	35
	Alvin Haymond	L.A.	NFC	70	35
29	Woodley Lewis–1	L.A.	NFL	54	34
	Clarence Childs–1	NYG	NFL	64	34
	Abner Haynes	Den.	AFL	65	34
	Clarence Childs–2	NYG	NFL	66	34
	Bobby Jancik–2	Hou.	AFL	66	34
34	Al Carmichael	G.B.	NFL	56	33
	Timmy Brown	Phi.	NFL	63	33
	Bill Butler	Min.	NFL	63	33
	Charley Warner	Buf.	AFL	66	33
	Vic Washington	S.F.	NFC	71	33
39	Woodley Lewis–2	L.A.	NFL	53	32
	Jimmy Sears	ChiC	NFL	58	32
	Dick James	Was.	NFL	62	32
	Jerry Robinson	S.D.	AFL	62	32
	Abe Woodson–2	S.F.	NFL	64	32
	J. D. Garrett	Bos.	AFL	64	32
	Kermit Alexander–2	S.F.	NFL	65	32
	Charley Warner	Buf.	AFL	65	32
	Butch Atkinson	Oak.	AFL	68	32
	Zeke Moore	Hou.	AFL	68	32
	Billy Walik	Phi.	NFC	70	32
	Linzy Cole	Hou.	AFC	71	32

YARDS

1	Bobby Jancik–1	Hou.	AFL	63	1317
2	Dave Hampton	G.B.	NFC	71	1314
3	Odell Barry	Den.	AFL	64	1245
4	Chuck Latourette	StL.	NFL	68	1237
5	Abe Woodson–1	S.F.	NFL	62	1157
6	Noland Smith	K.C.	AFL	67	1148
7	Mercury Morris–1	Mia.	AFC	69	1136
8	Mack Herron	N.E.	AFC	73	1092
9	Alvin Haymond	L.A.	NFC	70	1022
10	Margene Adkins	N.O.	NFC	72	1020
11	Mel Renfro	Dal.	NFL	64	1017
12	Ron Smith–1	Atl.	NFL	66	1013
13	Herb Mul-Key	Was.	NFC	73	1011
14	Clarence Childs–1	NYG	NFL	64	987
15	Kermit Alexander	S.F.	NFL	66	984
16	Ron Smith–2	Atl.	NFL	67	976
17	Bo Roberson–1	Oak.	AFL	64	975
18	Max Anderson	Buf.	AFL	68	971
19	Charley Mitchell	Den.	AFL	63	954
20	Rocky Thompson–1	NYG	NFC	71	947
	Ron Smith–3	S.D.	AFC	73	947
22	Timmy Brown–1	Phi.	NFL	63	945
23	Floyd Little	Den.	AFL	67	942
24	Jerry LeVias	Hou.	AFL	69	940
25	Abe Woodson–2	S.F.	NFL	63	935
26	Al Carmichael	G.B.	NFL	56	927
27	Ron Smith–4	Chi.	NFC	72	924
28	Abner Haynes	Den.	AFL	65	901
29	Leon Burton	NYT	AFL	60	897
30	Mike Battle	NYJ	AFC	70	891
31	Dick James–1	Was.	NFL	62	889
32	Abe Woodson–3	S.F.	NFL	64	880
33	Bobby Jancik–2	Hou.	AFL	66	875
34	Vic Washington	S.F.	NFC	71	858
35	Clarence Childs–2	NYG	NFL	66	855
36	Jack Larscheid	Oak.	AFL	60	852
37	Charley Warner–1	Buf.	AFL	66	846
38	Bruce Laird	Bal.	AFC	72	843
39	Woodley Lewis–1	L.A.	NFL	54	836
40	Linzy Cole	Hou.	AFC	71	834
41	Timmy Brown–2	Phi.	NFL	62	831
42	Woodley Lewis–2	L.A.	NFL	53	830
	Dick James–2	Was.	NFL	63	830
44	Doug Cunningham	S.F.	NFL	67	826
45	Charley Warner–2	Buf.	AFL	65	825
46	Dick Christy	NYT	AFL	62	824
47	Carver Shannon	L.A.	NFL	63	823
	Cliff Harris	Dal.	NFC	71	823
49	Rocky Thompson–2	NYG	NFL	72	821
50	Willie Porter	Bos.	AFL	68	812
	Mercury Morris–2	Mia.	AFC	70	812
52	Timmy Brown–3	Phi.	NFL	61	811
53	Bo Roberson–2	Oak.	AFL	63	809
54	Billy Walik	Phi.	NFC	70	805
55	Butch Atkinson	Oak.	AFL	68	802
56	Joe Arenas	S.F.	NFL	56	801

AVERAGE RETURN

(Minimum – 1 Return per Game)

					Ret.	Yards	Avg.
1	Travis Williams	G.B.	NFL	67	18	739	41.06
2	Gale Sayers–1	Chi.	NFL	67	16	603	37.69
3	Ollie Matson–1	ChiC	NFL	58	14	497	35.50
4	Speedy Duncan	Bal.	AFC	70	20	707	35.35
5	Lynn Chadnois–1	Pit.	NFL	52	17	599	35.24
6	Preston Pearson	Bal.	NFL	68	15	527	35.13
7	Joe Arenas	S.F.	NFL	53	16	551	34.44
8	Tom Watkins	Det.	NFL	65	17	584	34.35
9	Vitamin Smith	L.A.	NFL	50	22	742	33.73
10	Bobby Williams	Det.	NFL	69	17	563	33.12
11	Tom Moore	G.B.	NFL	60	12	397	33.08
12	Chet Mutryn	Buf.	AAFC	47	21	691	32.90
13	Cecil Turner	Chi.	NFC	70	23	752	32.70
14	Lynn Chadnois–2	Pit.	NFL	51	12	390	32.50
15	Abe Woodson–1	S.F.	NFL	63	29	935	32.24
16	Tom Wilson	L.A.	NFL	56	15	477	31.80
17	Gary Ballman	Pit.	NFL	63	22	698	31.73
18	Jack Salscheider	NY G	NFL	49	15	474	31.60
19	Gale Sayers–2	Chi.	NFL	65	21	660	31.43
20	Frank Seno	ChiC	NFL	46	13	408	31.38
21	Abe Woodson–2	S.F.	NFL	62	37	1157	31.27
22	Ken Hall	Hou.	AFL	60	19	594	31.26
23	Gale Sayers–3	Chi.	NFL	66	23	718	31.22
24	Ollie Matson–2	ChiC	NFL	52	20	624	31.20
25	Lenny Lyles	S.F.	NFL	60	19	526	30.94
26	Frank Minini	ChiB	NFL	48	12	370	30.83
27	Ron Smith	Chi.	NFC	72	30	924	30.80
28	Alvin Haymond	Bal.	NFL	65	20	614	30.70
29	Buddy Young	NY Y	NFL	51	14	427	30.50
30	Carl Garrett	Chi.	NFC	73	16	486	30.38
31	Dick Bass	L.A.	NFL	61	23	698	30.35
32	Bobby Jancik	Hou.	AFL	62	24	726	30.25
33	Johnny Counts	NY G	NFL	62	26	784	30.15
34	Lamar Parish	Cin.	AFC	70	16	482	30.13
35	John Gilliam	N.O.	NFL	67	16	481	30.01
36	Mel Renfro	Dal.	NFL	65	21	630	30.00

LIFETIME LEADERS
PASSING

ATTEMPTS (1500)

Rank	Player	Years	Att.
1	**Johnny Unitas**	1956-	5186
2	John Brodie	1957-73	4491
3	**Fran Tarkenton**	1961-	4449
4	Y. A. Tittle	1948-64	4395
5	**Sonny Jurgenson**	1957-	4095
6	**George Blanda**	1949-58,60-	4000
7	**Norm Snead**	1961-	3963
8	**John Hadl**	1962-	3899
9	**Roman Gabriel**	1962-	3773
10	Bobby Layne	1948-62	3700
11	**Len Dawson**	1957-	3366
12	Babe Parilli	1952-53,56-68,60-69	3330
13	Bart Starr	1956-71	3149
14	**Charley Johnson**	1961-	3006
15	Sammy Baugh	1937-52	2995
16	Jack Kemp	1957,60-67,69	2973
17	Tobin Rote	1950-59,63-64,66	2907
18	Norm Van Brocklin	1949-60	2895
19	Chuck Conerly	1948-61	2833
20	**Joe Namath**	1965-	2738
21	Otto Graham	1946-55	2626
22	**Earl Morrall**	1956-	2593
23	**Daryle Lamonica**	1963-	2592
24	Billy Wade	1954-66	2523
25	Milt Plum	1957-69	2419
26	Don Meredith	1960-68	2308
27	Frank Ryan	1958-70	2133
28	Ed Brown	1954-65	1987
29	**Billy Kilmer**	1961-62,64,66-	1952
30	**Jim Hart**	1966-	1948
31	Bill Nelsen	1963-72	1905
32	Eddie LeBaron	1952,53,55-63	1796
33	**Bob Griese**	1967-	1761
34	Cotton Davidson	1954,57,60-66,68	1752
35	Frank Tripucka	1949-52,60-63	1745
36	Tom Flores	1960-61,63-69	1715
37	Sid Luckman	1939-50	1657
38	Bob Waterfield	1945-52	1617
39	Frankie Albert	1946-52	1564
	Bill Munson	1964-	1463
	Craig Morton	1965-	1306
	Pete Beathard	1964-	1282
	Randy Johnson	1966-	1172
	Bob Berry	1965-	1119

COMPLETIONS (1000)

1	**Johnny Unitas**	1956-	2830
2	John Brodie	1957-73	2469
3	**Fran Tarkenton**	1961-	2459
4	Y. A. Tittle	1948-64	2427
5	**Sonny Jurgensen**	1957-	2326
6	**Norm Snead**	1961-	2049
7	**Roman Gabriel**	1962-	1975
8	**John Hadl**	1962-	1959
9	**George Blanda**	1949-58,60-	1909
10	**Len Dawson**	1957-	1905
11	Bobby Layne	1948-62	1814
12	Bart Starr	1956-71	1808
13	Sammy Baugh	1937-52	1693
14	Norm Van Brocklin	1949-60	1553
15	Babe Parilli	1952-53,56-58,60-69	1552
16	**Charley Johnson**	1961-	1536
17	Otto Graham	1946-55	1464
18	Jack Kemp	1957,60-67,69	1437
19	Chuck Conerly	1948-61	1418
20	**Joe Namath**	1965-	1374
21	Billy Wade	1954-66	1370
22	Tobin Rote	1950-59,63-64,66	1329
23	**Earl Morrall**	1956-	1326
24	Milt Plum	1957-69	1306
25	**Daryle Lamonica**	1963-	1285
26	Don Meredith	1960-68	1170
27	Frank Ryan	1958-70	1090
28	**Billy Kilmer**	1961-62,64,66-	1040
	Jim Hart	1966-	939
	Bob Griese	1967-	929

COMPLETION PERCENT (50%)
(Minimum 1500 Attempts)

Rank	Player	Years	Att.	Comp.	Pct.
1	Bart Starr	1956-71	3149	1808	57.42
2	**Sonny Jurgensen**	1957-	4095	2326	56.80
3	**Len Dawson**	1957-	3366	1905	56.60
4	Sammy Baugh	1937-52	2995	1693	56.63
5	Otto Graham	1946-55	2626	1464	55.75
6	**Fran Tarkenton**	1961-	4449	2459	55.27
7	Y. A. Tittle	1948-64	4395	2427	55.22
8	John Brodie	1957-73	4491	2469	54.98
9	**Johnny Unitas**	1956-	5186	2830	54.57
10	Sid Luckman	1939-50	1657	904	54.56
11	Billy Wade	1954-66	2523	1370	54.30
12	Milt Plum	1957-69	2419	1306	54.99
13	Norm Van Brocklin	1949-60	2895	1553	53.64
14	**Billy Kilmer**	1961-62,64,66-	1952	1040	53.28
15	Frankie Albert	1946-52	1564	831	53.13
16	**Bob Griese**	1967-	1761	929	52.75
17	**Roman Gabriel**	1962-	3773	1975	52.35
18	**Norm Snead**	1961-	3963	2049	51.70
19	**Earl Morrall**	1956-	2593	1326	51.14
20	Frank Ryan	1958-70	2133	1090	51.10
21	**Charley Johnson**	1961-	3006	1536	51.10
22	Don Meredith	1960-68	2308	1170	50.69
23	Bill Nelsen	1963-72	1905	963	50.55
24	Frank Tripucka	1949-52,60-63	1745	879	50.37
25	Bob Waterfield	1945-52	1617	813	50.28
26	**John Hadl**	1962-	3899	1959	50.24
27	**Joe Namath**	1965-	2738	1374	50.18
28	Chuck Conerly	1948-61	2833	1418	50.05
	Bob Berry	1965-	1119	624	55.76
	Bill Munson	1964-	1463	772	52.77
	Craig Morton	1965-	1306	683	52.30
	Randy Johnson	1966-	1172	585	49.91
	Daryle Lamonica	1963-	2592	1285	49.58

YARDS (15,000)

Rank	Player	Years	Yards
1	**Johnny Unitas**	1956-	40239
2	**Fran Tarkenton**	1961-	33248
3	Y. A. Tittle	1948-64	33070
4	John Brodie	1957-73	31548
5	**Sonny Jurgenson**	1957-	31039
6	**John Hadl**	1962-	28946
7	**Norm Snead**	1961-	28238
8	**George Blanda**	1949-58,60-	26881
9	Bobby Layne	1948-62	26768
10	**Len Dawson**	1957-	26043
11	**Roman Gabriel**	1962-	25442
12	Bart Starr	1956-71	24718
13	Norm Van Brocklin	1949-60	23611
14	Otto Graham	1946-55	23584
15	Babe Parilli	1952-53,56-58,60-69	22671
16	Sammy Baugh	1937-52	21886
17	**Charley Johnson**	1961-	21420
18	Jack Kemp	1957,60-67,69	21222
19	**Joe Namath**	1965-	21065
20	**Earl Morrall**	1956-	20087
21	Chuck Conerly	1948-61	19488
22	**Daryle Lamonica**	1963-	19119
23	Tobin Rote	1950-59,63-64,66	18850
24	Billy Wade	1954-66	18530
25	Milt Plum	1957-69	17536
26	Don Meredith	1960-68	17199
27	Frank Ryan	1958-70	16042
28	Ed Brown	1954-65	15600
	Billy Kilmer	1961-62,64,66-	13668
	Jim Hart	1966-	13463
	Bob Griese	1967-	12341

YARDS PER ATTEMPT (7.0)
(Minimum 1500 Attempts)

Rank	Player	Years	Yards	Att.	Yd/A
1	Sid Luckman	1939-50	14683	1657	9.95
2	Otto Graham	1946-55	23584	2626	8.98
3	Norm Van Brocklin	1949-60	23611	2895	8.16
4	Ed Brown	1954-65	15600	1987	7.85
5	Bart Starr	1956-71	24718	3149	7.85
6	**Johnny Unitas**	1956-	40239	5186	7.76
7	**Earl Morrall**	1956-	20087	2593	7.75
8	**Len Dawson**	1957-	26043	3366	7.74
9	**Joe Namath**	1965-	21065	2738	7.69
10	**Sonny Jurgenson**	1957-	31039	4095	7.58
11	Y. A. Tittle	1948-64	33070	4395	7.52
12	Frank Ryan	1958-70	16042	2133	7.52
13	**Fran Tarkenton**	1961-	33248	4449	7.47
14	Eddie LeBaron	1952-53,55-63	13399	1796	7.46
15	Don Meredith	1960-68	17199	2308	7.45
16	Bill Nelsen	1963-72	14165	1905	7.44
17	John Hadl	1962-	28946	3899	7.42
18	**Daryle Lamonica**	1963-	19119	2592	7.38
19	Billy Wade	1954-66	18530	2523	7.34
20	Bob Waterfield	1945-52	11849	1617	7.33
21	Sammy Baugh	1937-52	21886	2995	7.31
22	Milt Plum	1957-69	17536	2419	7.25
23	Bobby Layne	1948-62	26768	3700	7.24
24	Jack Kemp	1957,60-67,69	21222	2973	7.14
25	**Charley Johnson**	1961-	21420	3006	7.13
26	**Norm Snead**	1961-	28238	3963	7.13
27	John Brodie	1957-73	31548	4491	7.03
28	**Bob Griese**	1967-	12341	1761	7.01
29	**Billy Kilmer**	1961-62,64,66-	13668	1952	7.00
	Craig Morton	1965-	10267	1306	7.86

TOUCHDOWN PASSES (100)

1	**Johnny Unitas**	1956-	290
2	**Fran Tarkenton**	1961-	249
3	**Sonny Jurgenson**	1957-	244
4	Y. A. Tittle	1948-64	242
5	**George Blanda**	1949-58,60-	235
6	**Len Dawson**	1957-	227
7	**John Hadl**	1962-	223
8	John Brodie	1957-73	214
9	Bobby Layne	1948-62	196
10	Sammy Baugh	1937-52	188
11	**Norm Snead**	1961-	182
12	Babe Parilli	1952-53,56-58,60-69	178
13	**Roman Gabriel**	1962-	177
14	Otto Graham	1946-55	174
15	Norm Van Brocklin	1949-60	173
	Chuck Conerly	1948-61	173
17	**Daryle Lamonica**	1963-	163
18	**Earl Morrall**	1956-	155
19	Bart Starr	1956-71	152
	Charley Johnson	1961-	152
21	Frank Ryan	1958-70	149
22	Tobin Rote	1950-59,63-64,66	148
23	Sid Luckman	1939-50	137
24	Don Meredith	1960-68	135
25	Milt Plum	1957-69	132
26	**Joe Namath**	1965-	131
27	Billy Wade	1954-66	124
28	Frankie Albert	1946-52	115
29	Jack Kemp	1957,60-67,69	114
30	Eddie LeBaron	1952-53,55-63	104
31	Ed Brown	1954-65	102
	Bob Griese	1967-	98
	Billy Kilmer	1961-62,64,66-	95
	Jim Hart	1966-	82
	Craig Martin	1965-	80

LEAST INTERCEPTED (140)
(Minimum 1500 Attempts)

1	**Bob Griese**	1967	88
2	Tom Flores	1960-61,63-69	92
3	Frankie Albert	1946-52	98
4	Bill Nelsen	1963-72	101
5	**Billy Kilmer**	1961-62,64,66-	104
6	**Jim Hart**	1966-	107
7	Cotton Davidson	1954,57,60-66,68	108
8	Frank Ryan	1958-70	111
	Don Meredith	1960-68	111
10	Frank Tripucka	1949-52,60-63	124
	Roman Gabriel	1962-	124
12	Bob Waterfield	1945-52	127
	Milt Plum	1957-69	127
14	Sid Luckman	1939-50	131
15	Billy Wade	1954-66	134
	Daryle Lamonica	1963-	134
17	Otto Graham	1946-55	135
18	Ed Brown	1954-65	138
	Bart Starr	1956-71	138
	Bill Munson	1964-	65
	Craig Morton	1965-	73

LOWEST PERCENT INTERCEPTED (6.0)
(Minimum 1500 Attempts)

Rank	Player	Years	Att.	Int.	Pct.
1	**Roman Gabriel**	1962-	3773	124	3.287
2	**Fran Tarkenton**	1961-	4449	187	4.203
3	Bart Starr	1956-71	3149	138	4.382
4	**Sonny Jurgenson**	1957-	4095	184	4.493
5	Don Meredith	1960-68	2308	111	4.809
6	**Johnny Unitas**	1956-	5186	253	4.879
7	**Len Dawson**	1957-	3366	166	4.932
8	John Brodie	1957-73	4491	224	4.988
9	**Bob Griese**	1967-	1761	88	4.997
10	Otto Graham	1946-55	2626	135	5.141
11	**Daryle Lamonica**	1963-	2592	134	5.170
12	Frank Ryan	1958-70	2133	111	5.204
13	Milt Plum	1957-69	2419	127	5.250
14	Bill Nelsen	1963-72	1905	101	5.302
15	Billy Wade	1954-66	2523	134	5.311
16	**Charley Johnson**	1961-	3006	160	5.323
17	**Billy Kilmer**	1961-62,64,66-	1952	104	5.328
18	Tom Flores	1960-61,63-69	1715	92	5.364
19	**Joe Namath**	1965-	2738	149	5.442
20	**Earl Morrall**	1956-	2593	142	5.476
21	**Jim Hart**	1966-	1948	107	5.493
22	Y. A. Tittle	1948-64	4395	242	5.506
23	**John Hadl**	1962-	3899	222	5.694
24	Chuck Conerly	1948-61	2822	167	5.895
25	**Norm Snead**	1961-	3963	235	5.930
	Bill Munson	1964-	1463	65	4.444
	Craig Morton	1965-	1306	73	5.590

RANK – all passers with over 1500 Attempts rated on Completion Pct., TD passes, Yards per Attempt, and Pct. intercepted.

1 **Jurgenson**	6 Graham	11 Ryan	16 Wade	21 **Namath**	26 **Kilmer**	31 **Blanda**	36 **Hart**
2 **Unitas**	7 Tittle	12 Meredith	Plum	22 **C. Johnson**	27 Conerly	32 LeBaron	37 Tripucka
3 **Tarkenton**	8 Brodie	**Gabriel**	18 **Hadl**	23 **Hart**	28 Albert	33 Parilli	38 Rote
4 **Dawson**	9 Van Brocklin	14 Baugh	19 **Lamonica**	**Griese**	Brown	34 Kemp	39 Davidson
5 Starr	10 **Morrall**	15 Luckman	20 **Snead**	25 Layne	30 Flores	35 Waterfield	

Players active at the end of 1973 are shown in **bold face.**

LIFETIME LEADERS
RUSHING

ATTEMPTS (1000)

Rank	Player	Years	Att.
1	Jimmy Brown	1957-65	2359
2	Jim Taylor	1958-67	1941
3	Joe Perry	1948-63	1929
4	**Leroy Kelly**	1964-	1727
5	**Bill Brown**	1961-	1630
6	**Ken Willard**	1965-	1582
7	John Henry Johnson	1954-66	1571
8	Don Perkins	1961-68	1500
9	Rick Casares	1955-66	1431
10	**Floyd Little**	1967-	1399
11	Jim Nance	1965-71,73	1341
12	Steve Van Buren	1944-51	1320
13	**Mike Garrett**	1966-	1308
14	**Larry Brown**	1969-	1250
15	Tom Matte	1961-71	1240
16	Dick Bass	1960-69	1218
17	Alex Webster	1955-64	1196
18	Ollie Matson	1952,54-66	1170
19	John David Crow	1958-68	1157
20	Clem Daniels	1960-68	1146
21	Dick Hoak	1961-70	1132
22	Hugh McElhenny	1952-64	1124
23	**Emerson Boozer**	1966-	1118
24	**O. J. Simpson**	1969-	1108
25	**Donny Anderson**	1966-	1107
26	J. D. Smith	1956-66	1100
27	**Larry Csonka**	1968-	1089
28	Lenny Moore	1956-67	1069
29	Bob Hoernschemeyer	1946-55	1059
30	Matt Snell	1964-72	1057
31	Bill Mathis	1960-69	1044
32	Clarke Hinkle	1933-41	1043
33	Tommy Mason	1961-71	1040
34	Abner Haynes	1960-67	1036
35	Paul Lowe	1960-61,63-69	1026
36	Tony Canadeo	1941-44,46-52	1025
37	**Johnny Roland**	1966-	1015
38	Cookie Gilchrist	1962-67	1010
	Dave Osborn	1965-	1010
40	Gale Sayers	1965-71	1001
	Ron Johnson	1969-	990
	Calvin Hill	1969-	981
	Wendell Hayes	1963,65-	931
	Jim Kiick	1968-	911
	Charlie Harraway	1966-	822
	Altie Taylor	1969-	820
	Charlie Smith	1968-	794
	Walt Garrison	1966-	786
	Les Josephson	1964-67,69-	786
	Willie Ellison	1967-	764
	John Brockington	1971-	755
	MacArthur Lane	1968-	751

YARDS (3500)

1	Jimmy Brown	1957-65	12312
2	Joe Perry	1948-63	9723
3	Jim Taylor	1958-67	8597
4	**Leroy Kelly**	1964-	7274
5	John Henry Johnson	1954-66	6803
6	Don Perkins	1961-68	6217
7	**Ken Willard**	1965-	5930
8	Steve Van Buren	1944-51	5860
9	**Bill Brown**	1961-	5797
10	Rick Casares	1955-66	5787
11	**Floyd Little**	1967-	5566
12	**Mike Garrett**	1966-	5481
13	Dick Bass	1960-69	5417
14	Jim Nance	1965-71,73	5401
15	Hugh McElhenny	1952-64	5281
16	**O. J. Simpson**	1969-	5181
17	Lenny Moore	1956-67	5174
18	Ollie Matson	1952,54-66	5173
19	**Larry Csonka**	1968-	5151
20	Clem Daniels	1960-68	5138
21	**Larry Brown**	1969-	5037
22	Paul Lowe	1960-61,63-69	4995
23	John David Crow	1958-68	4963
24	Gale Sayers	1965-71	4956
25	Marion Motley	1946-53,55	4720
26	J. D. Smith	1956-66	4672
27	Tom Matte	1961-72	4646
28	Alex Webster	1955-64	4638
29	Abner Haynes	1960-67	4630
30	Bob Hoernschemeyer	1946-55	4548
31	**Emerson Boozer**	1966-	4521
32	**Donny Anderson**	1966-	4380
33	Cookie Gilchrist	1962-67	4293
34	Matt Snell	1964-72	4285
35	Tommy Mason	1961-71	4203
36	Tony Canadeo	1941-44,46-52	4197
37	**Calvin Hill**	1969-	4165
38	Alan Ameche	1955-60	4045
39	Nick Pietrosante	1959-67	4026
40	Dick Hoak	1961-70	3965
41	Timmy Brown	1959-68	3862
42	Jon Arnett	1957-66	3833
43	**Johnny Roland**	1966-	3750
44	**Ron Johnson**	1969-	3738
45	**Dave Osborn**	1965-	3712
46	Paul Hornung	1957-62,64-66	3711
47	Clarence Peaks	1957-65	3660
48	Hoyle Granger	1966-72	3653
49	Tank Younger	1949-58	3640
50	Frank Gifford	1952-60,62-64	3609
51	Bill Mathis	1960-69	3589
52	Tom Woodeshick	1963-72	3577
53	**Wendell Hayes**	1963,65-	3552
54	Clarke Hinkle	1933-41	3519
55	Charley Trippi	1947-55	3506
	Walt Garrison	1966-	3457
	Fran Tarkenton	1961-	3401
	Les Josephson	1964-67,69-	3372
	Jim Kiick	1968-	3370
	Willie Ellison	1967-	3312
	John Brockington	1971-	3276
	Marv Hubbard	1969-	3235
	Charlie Smith	1968-	3157
	Alty Taylor	1969-	3127
	MacArthur Lane	1968-	3085
	Mel Farr	1967-	3072
	Charlie Harraway	1966-	3019
	Paul Robinson	1968-	2947
	Carl Garrett	1967-	2890
	Essex Johnson	1968-	2849
	Mercury Morris	1969-	2788
	Dave Hampton	1969-	2779

AVERAGE YARDS (4.0)
(Minimum 700 Rushes)

Rank	Player	Years	Att.	Yards	Avg.
1	Marion Motley	1946-53,55	828	4720	5.70
2	Jimmy Brown	1957-65	2359	12312	5.22
3	Joe Perry	1948-63	1929	9723	5.04
4	Gale Sayers	1965-71	1001	4956	4.95
5	Paul Lowe	1960-61,63-69	1026	4995	4.87
6	Lenny Moore	1956-67	1069	5174	4.84
7	**Larry Csonka**	1968-	1089	5151	4.73
8	Tank Younger	1949-58	770	3640	4.73
9	Hugh McElhenny	1952-64	1124	5281	4.70
10	**O. J. Simpson**	1969-	1108	5181	4.68
11	Hoyle Granger	1966-72	805	3653	4.54
12	Clem Daniels	1960-68	1146	5138	4.48
13	Abner Haynes	1960-67	1036	4630	4.47
14	Keith Lincoln	1961-68	759	3383	4.46
15	Dick Bass	1960-69	1218	5417	4.45
16	Steve Van Buren	1944-51	1320	5860	4.44
17	Jim Taylor	1958-67	1941	8597	4.43
18	Ollie Matson	1952,54-66	1170	5173	4.42
19	**Walt Garrison**	1966-	786	3457	4.40
20	Timmy Brown	1959-68	889	3862	4.34
21	**John Brockington**	1971-	755	3276	4.34
22	**Willie Ellison**	1967-	764	3312	4.34
23	John Henry Johnson	1954-66	1571	6803	4.33
24	Frank Gifford	1952-60,62-64	840	3609	4.30
25	Amos Marsh	1961-67	750	3222	4.30
26	Bob Hoernschemeyer	1946-55	1059	4548	4.29
27	**Les Josephson**	1964-67,69-	786	3372	4.29
28	John David Crow	1958-68	1157	4963	4.29
29	Tom Woodeshick	1963-72	836	3577	4.28
30	Cookie Gilchrist	1962-67	1010	4293	4.25
31	J. D. Smith	1956-66	1100	4672	4.25
32	**Calvin Hill**	1969-	981	4165	4.25
33	Nick Pietrosante	1959-67	955	4026	4.22
34	**Leroy Kelly**	1964-	1727	7274	4.21
35	Cliff Battles	1933-37	725	3046	4.20
36	Alan Ameche	1955-60	964	4045	4.20
37	**Mike Garrett**	1966-	1308	5481	4.19
38	**Mel Farr**	1967-	739	3072	4.16
39	Paul Hornung	1957-62,64-66	893	3711	4.16
40	Don Perkins	1961-68	1500	6217	4.14
41	Wray Carlton	1960-67	819	3368	4.11
42	**MacArthur Lane**	1968-	751	3085	4.11
43	Curtis McClinton	1962-69	762	3124	4.10
44	Tony Canadeo	1941-44,46-52	1025	4197	4.09
45	Pat Harder	1946-53	740	3016	4.08
46	**Carl Garrett**	1969-	712	2890	4.06
47	Matt Snell	1964-72	1057	4285	4.05
48	Rick Casares	1955-66	1431	5787	4.04
49	**Emerson Boozer**	1966-	1118	4521	4.04
50	Tommy Mason	1961-71	1040	4203	4.04
51	**Larry Brown**	1969-	1250	5037	4.03
52	Jim Nance	1965-71,73	1341	5401	4.03
53	Don Bosseler	1957-64	775	3112	4.02
54	Dan Lewis	1958-66	800	3205	4.01
55	Hewitt Dixon	1963-70	772	3090	4.00
56	**Paul Robinson**	1968-	737	2947	4.00
57	Bill Dudley	1942,45-51,53	765	3057	4.00
	Fran Tarkenton	1961-	572	3401	5.95
	Marv Hubbard	1969-	665	3235	4.87
	Essex Johnson	1968-	598	2849	4.76
	Cid Edwards	1968-	606	2672	4.41
	John Fugua	1969-	580	2527	4.36
	John Riggins	1971-	521	2195	4.21
	Jess Phillips	1968-	622	2523	4.06
	Dave Hampton	1969-	688	2779	4.04
	Robert Holmes	1968-	620	2468	3.98
	Floyd Little	1967-	1399	5566	3.98
	Charlie Smith	1968-	794	3157	3.98
	Donnie Anderson	1966-	1107	4380	3.96
	Wendell Hayes	1963,65-	931	3552	3.82
	Altie Taylor	1969-	820	3127	3.81
	Ed Podolak	1969-	733	2793	3.81
	Ron Johnson	1969-	990	3738	3.78

TOUCHDOWNS (35)

1	Jimmy Brown	1957-65	106
2	Jim Taylor	1958-67	83
3	**Leroy Kelly**	1964-	74
4	Joe Perry	1948-63	71
5	Steve Van Buren	1944-51	68
6	Lenny Moore	1956-67	63
7	**Bill Brown**	1961-	52
8	Paul Hornung	1957-62,64-66	50
9	Rick Casares	1955-66	49
10	John Henry Johnson	1954-66	48
	Emerson Boozer	1966-	48
12	Abner Haynes	1960-67	46
13	Tom Matte	1961-72	45
	Jim Nance	1965-71,73	45
	Ken Willard	1965-	45
16	Otto Graham	1946-55	44
17	Dan Towler	1950-55	43
18	Don Perkins	1961-68	42
19	Alan Ameche	1955-60	40
	Ollie Matson	1952,54-66	40
	J. D. Smith	1956-66	40
	Jack Kemp	1957,60-67,69	40
	Paul Lowe	1960-61,63-69	40
	Floyd Little	1967-	40
25	Y. A. Tittle	1948-64	39
	Alex Webster	1955-64	39
	Gale Sayers	1965-71	39
28	Hugh McElhenny	1952-64	38
	John David Crow	1958-68	38
	Donny Anderson	1966-	38
31	Tobin Rote	1950-59,63-64,66	37
	Bill Mathis	1960-69	37
	Cookie Gilchrist	1962-67	37
34	Pug Manders	1939-47	36
35	**Mike Garrett**	1966-	35
	Larry Csonka	1968-	32
	Calvin Hill	1969-	32
	Ron Johnson	1969-	31
	O. J. Simpson	1969-	30

POINTS
(400)

Rank	Player	Years	Points
1	**George Blanda**	1949-58,60-	1840
2	Lou Groza	1946-59,61-67	1608
3	Gino Cappelletti	1960-70	1130
4	**Fred Cox**	1963-	1074
5	**Jim Bakken**	1962-	1005
6	**Jim Turner**	1964-	993
7	Sam Baker	1953,56-69	977
8	**Bruce Gossett**	1964-	973
9	Lou Michaels	1958-69,71	955
10	Bobby Walston	1951-62	881
11	Don Hutson	1935-45	823
12	**Pete Gogolak**	1964-	812
13	**Jan Stenerud**	1967-	770
14	Paul Hornung	1957-62,64-66	760
15	Jimmy Brown	1957-65	756
16	Tommy Davis	1959-69	738
17	Lenny Moore	1956-67	678
18	Ben Agajanian	1945,47-49,53-57,60-62,64	655
19	Gordie Soltau	1950-58	644
20	Gene Mingo	1960-67,69-70	629
21	Mike Mercer	1961-70	594
22	Bob Waterfield	1945-52	573
23	Pat Summerall	1952-61	563
24	Jim Taylor	1958-67	558
25	Bobby Mitchell	1958-68	546
26	**Leroy Kelly**	1964-	540
27	Doak Walker	1950-55	534
28	**Don Maynard**	1958,60-	532
29	Pat Harder	1946-53	531
30	Lance Alworth	1962-72	524
31	**Garo Yepremian**	1966-	520
32	Joe Perry	1948-63	513
33	Tommy McDonald	1957-68	510
34	Fred Cone	1951-57,60	494
35	Art Powell	1959-67	492
36	Danny Villanueva	1960-67	491
37	Bill Dudley	1942,45-51,53	484
	Frank Gifford	1952-60,62-64	484
	Horst Muhlmann	1969-	484
40	**Roy Gerela**	1969-	483
41	**Curt Knight**	1969-	475
42	**Charley Taylor**	1964-	474
43	Steve Van Buren	1944-51	464
44	**Bobby Howfield**	1968-	461
45	**Errol Mann**	1968-	460
46	**Bill Brown**	1961-	456
	Paul Warfield	1964-	456
	Mac Percival	1967-	456
49	**Bob Hayes**	1965-	450
50	**David Ray**	1969-	445
51	Ollie Matson	1952,54-66	438
52	Jim Martin	1950-61,63-64	434
53	Gary Collins	1962-71	420
54	Abner Haynes	1960-67	414
55	Ray Berry	1955-67	408
56	Crazy Legs Hirsch	1946-57	405
	Tom Dempsey	1969-	395
	Ken Willard	1965-	366
	Emerson Boozer	1966-	354
	Dennis Partee	1968-	349
	Otis Taylor	1965-	348
	Fred Biletnikoff	1965-	324
	Jerry Smith	1965-	312
	Jim O'Brien	1970-	301
	Donny Anderson	1966-	300
	Gary Garrison	1966-	300

Players active at the end of 1973 are shown in **bold face.**

LIFETIME LEADERS
RECEIVING

RECEPTIONS (300)

Rank	Player	Years	No.
1	**Don Maynard**	1958,60-	633
2	Ray Berry	1955-67	631
3	Lionel Taylor	1959-68	567
4	Lance Alworth	1962-72	542
5	**Charley Taylor**	1964-	528
6	Bobby Mitchell	1958-68	521
7	Billy Howton	1952-63	503
8	Tommy McDonald	1957-68	495
9	Don Hutson	1935-45	488
10	Art Powell	1959-68	479
11	Boyd Dowler	1959-69,71	474
12	Pete Retzlaff	1956-66	452
13	**Carroll Dale**	1960-	438
14	**Jackie Smith**	1963-	434
15	Mike Ditka	1961-72	427
16	Bobby Joe Conrad	1958-59	422
17	Charley Hennigan	1960-66	410
18	**Fred Biletnikoff**	1965-	408
19	Billy Wilson	1951-60	407
20	Jim Phillips	1958-67	401
21	Tom Fears	1948-56	400
	Jimmy Orr	1958-70	400
23	Joe Morrison	1959-72	395
24	Chris Burford	1960-67	391
25	Crazy Legs Hirsch	1946-57	387
26	Dante Lavelli	1946-56	386
	Otis Taylor	1965-	386
28	Pete Pihos	1947-55	373
29	Frank Gifford	1952-60,62-64	367
30	**Roy Jefferson**	1965-	366
31	Sonny Randle	1959-68	365
32	Lenny Moore	1956-67	363
33	**Dave Parks**	1964-	360
34	Bernie Casey	1961-68	359
35	**Bob Hayes**	1965-	358
36	Johnny Morris	1958-67	356
	Gail Cogdill	1960-70	356
38	Mac Speedie	1946-52	349
	Del Shofner	1957-67	349
40	Max McGee	1954,57-67	345
41	**Paul Warfield**	1964-	344
	Dan Abramowicz	1967-	344
43	**Jerry Smith**	1965-	338
44	**Gary Garrison**	1966-	334
45	Gary Collins	1962-71	331
	John Mackey	1963-72	331
47	Elbie Nickel	1947-67	329
48	**Gary Ballman**	1962-	323
49	**Jack Snow**	1965-	312
40	Bobby Walston	1951-62	311
51	George Sauer	1965-70	309
52	Paul Flatley	1963-70	306
53	Preston Carpenter	1956-67	305
54	Kyle Rote	1951-61	300
	Bill Brown	1961-	281
	John Gilliam	1967-	274
	Ken Willard	1965-	273
	Ben Hawkins	1966-	261
	Harold Jackson	1968-	255
	Milt Morin	1966-	243
	Dick Gordon	1965-	241

YARDS (4500)

Rank	Player	Years	Yards
1	**Don Maynard**	1958,60-	11834
2	Lance Alworth	1962-72	10267
3	Ray Berry	1955-67	9275
4	Billy Howton	1952-63	8459
5	Tommy McDonald	1957-68	8380
6	**Carroll Dale**	1960-	8277
7	Art Powell	1959-68	8046
8	Don Hutson	1935-45	7981
9	Bobby Mitchell	1958-68	7954
10	Jimmy Orr	1958-70	7914
11	**Charley Taylor**	1964-	7470
12	Pete Retzlaff	1956-66	7412
13	Boyd Dowler	1959-69,71	7270
14	Lionel Taylor	1959-68	7195
15	**Jackie Smith**	1963-	7188
16	**Bob Hayes**	1965-	7177
17	**Paul Warfield**	1964-	7165
18	Crazy Legs Hirsch	1946-67	7029
19	**Otis Taylor**	1965-	6931
20	Charley Hennigan	1960-66	6823
21	**Fred Biletnikoff**	1965-	6512
22	Dante Lavelli	1946-56	6488
23	Del Shofner	1957-67	6470
24	Max McGee	1954,57-67	6346
25	**Roy Jefferson**	1965-	6266
26	**Gary Garrison**	1966-	6252
27	Jim Phillips	1958-67	6044
28	Lenny Moore	1956-67	6039
29	Sonny Randle	1959-68	5996
30	Billy Wilson	1951-60	5902
	Bobby Joe Conrad	1958-69	5902
32	Mike Ditka	1961-72	5812
33	Gail Cogdill	1960-70	5696
34	Pete Pihos	1947-55	5619
	Dave Parks	1964-	5619
36	Mac Speedie	1946-52	5602
37	**Jack Snow**	1965-	5529
38	Ray Renfro	1952-63	5508
39	Chris Burford	1960-67	5505
40	Buddy Dial	1959-66	5436
41	Frank Gifford	1952-60,62-64	5434
42	Frank Clarke	1957-67	5426
43	Tom Fears	1948-56	5397
44	**Gary Ballman**	1962-	5366
45	Bobby Walston	1951-62	5363
46	**Dan Abramowicz**	1967-	5317
47	Elbert Dubenion	1960-68	5309
48	Gary Collins	1962-71	5299
49	**John Gilliam**	1967-	5276
50	John Mackey	1963-72	5236
51	Hugh Taylor	1947-54	5233
52	Elbie Nickel	1947-57	5131
53	Jim Colclough	1960-68	5101
54	Johnny Morris	1958-67	5059
55	Joe Morrison	1959-72	4993
56	Homer Jones	1964-70	4986
57	George Sauer	1965-70	4965
58	Paul Flatley	1963-70	4905
59	Kyle Rote	1951-61	4797
60	**Ben Hawkins**	1966-	4764
61	Harlon Hill	1954-62	4717
62	Gino Cappelletti	1960-70	4589
63	Aaron Thomas	1961-70	4554
	Jerry Smith	1965-	4470
	Harold Jackson	1968-	4367
	Gene Washington	1969-	4219
	Dick Gordon	1965-	3579
	Bob Trumpy	1968-	3420

AVERAGE YARDS (16.0)
(Minimum 200 Receptions)

Rank	Player	Years	Rec.	Yards	Avg.
1	Homer Jones	1964-70	224	4986	22.26
2	**Paul Warfield**	1964-	344	7165	20.83
3	Buddy Dial	1959-66	261	5436	20.83
4	Harlon Hill	1954-62	233	4717	20.25
5	**Bob Hayes**	1965-	358	7177	20.05
6	Jimmy Orr	1958-70	400	7914	19.79
7	Ray Renfro	1952-63	281	5508	19.60
8	**John Gilliam**	1967-	274	5276	19.26
9	Hugh Taylor	1947-54	272	5233	19.24
10	Lance Alworth	1962-72	542	10267	18.94
11	**Carroll Dale**	1960-	438	8277	18.90
12	**Gary Garrison**	1966-	334	6252	18.72
13	**Don Maynard**	1958-60	633	11834	18.70
14	Franke Clarke	1957-67	291	5426	18.65
15	Del Shofner	1957-67	349	6470	18.54
16	Max McGee	1954,57-67	345	6346	18.39
17	**Ben Hawkins**	1966-	261	4764	18.25
18	Crazy Legs Hirsch	1946-57	387	7029	18.16
19	**Gene Washington**	1969-	233	4219	18.11
20	Jim Colclough	1960-68	283	5101	18.03
21	**Otis Taylor**	1965-	386	6931	17.96
22	Elbert Dubenion	1960-68	296	5309	17.94
23	Darrel Brewster	1952-60	210	3758	17.90
24	**Jack Snow**	1965-	312	5529	17.72
25	Lance Rentzel	1965-72	250	4430	17.72
26	Aaron Thomas	1961-70	262	4554	17.38
27	Bob Schnelker	1953-61	211	3667	17.38
28	Jim Doran	1951-61	212	3667	17.30
29	Bobby Walston	1951-62	311	5363	17.24
30	**Harold Jackson**	1968-	255	4367	17.13
31	**Roy Jefferson**	1965-	366	6266	17.12
32	Ray Mathews	1951-60	233	3963	17.01
33	Tommy McDonald	1957-68	495	8380	16.93
34	Billy Howton	1952-63	503	8459	16.82
35	Dante Lavelli	1946-56	386	6488	16.81
36	Art Powell	1959-68	479	8046	16.80
37	Terry Barr	1957-65	227	3810	16.78
38	Jim Mutscheller	1954-61	220	3684	16.75
39	Jim Benton	1938-40,42-47	288	4801	16.67
40	Charley Hennigan	1960-66	410	6823	16.64
41	Lenny Moore	1956-67	363	6039	16.64
42	**Gary Ballman**	1962-	323	5366	16.61
43	**Jackie Smith**	1963-	434	7188	16.56
44	Charley Frazier	1962-70	209	3461	16.56
45	Al Denson	1964-71	260	4275	16.44
46	Sonny Randle	1959-68	365	5996	16.43
47	Dave Kocourek	1960-68	249	4090	16.43
48	Pete Retzlaff	1956-66	452	7412	16.40
49	Don Hutson	1935-45	488	7981	16.36
50	Clem Daniels	1960-68	203	3314	16.33
51	Willard Dewveall	1959-64	204	3304	16.20
52	Bake Turner	1962-70	220	3539	16.09
53	George Sauer	1965-70	309	4965	16.07
54	Mac Speedie	1946-52	349	5602	16.05
55	Paul Flatley	1963-70	306	4905	16.03
56	Gary Collins	1962-71	331	5299	16.01
57	Gail Cogdill	1960-70	356	5696	16.00
	Haven Moses	1968-	189	3383	17.90
	Frank Pitts	1965-	172	2874	16.71
	Marlin Briscoe	1968-	179	2897	16.18

TOUCHDOWNS (40)

Rank	Player	Years	TD
1	Don Hutson	1935-45	100
2	**Don Maynard**	1958,60-	88
3	Lance Alworth	1962-72	85
4	Tommy McDonald	1957-68	84
5	Art Powell	1959-68	81
6	**Paul Warfield**	1964-	75
7	Gary Collins	1962-71	70
	Bob Hayes	1965-	70
9	Ray Berry	1955-67	68
	Charley Taylor	1964-	68
11	Jimmy Orr	1958-70	66
12	Bobby Mitchell	1958-68	65
	Sonny Randle	1959-68	65
14	Dante Lavelli	1946-56	62
15	Pete Pihos	1947-55	61
	Billy Howton	1952-63	61
17	Crazy Legs Hirsch	1946-57	60
18	Hugh Taylor	1947-54	58
19	Chris Burford	1960-67	55
	Otis Taylor	1965-	55
21	**Fred Biletnikoff**	1965-	53
22	**Carroll Dale**	1960-	52
	Jerry Smith	1965-	52
24	Del Shofner	1957-57	51
	Charley Hennigan	1960-66	51
26	Ken Kavanaugh	1940-41,45-50	50
	Ray Renfro	1952-63	50
	Frank Clarke	1957-67	50
	Max McGee	1954,57-67	50
	Gary Garrison	1966-	50
31	Alyn Beals	1946-51	49
	Billy Wilson	1951-60	49
33	Kyle Rote	1951-61	48
	Lenny Moore	1956-67	48
35	Pete Retzlaff	1956-66	47
	Joe Morrison	1959-72	47
	Billy Cannon	1960-70	47
38	Bobby Walston	1951-62	46
39	Jim Benton	1938-40,42-47	45
	Lionel Taylor	1959-68	45
41	Buddy Dial	1959-66	44
	Dave Parks	1964-	44
	Roy Jefferson	1965-	44
44	Frank Gifford	1952-60,62-64	43
	Mike Ditka	1961-72	43
46	Gino Cappelletti	1960-70	42
	Warren Wells	1964,67-70	42
48	**Jack Snow**	1965-	41
49	Harlon Hill	1954-62	40
	Jim Mutscheller	1954-61	40
	Boyd Dowler	1959-69,71	40
	Bernie Casey	1961-68	40
	Dan Abramowicz	1967-	38
	Gary Ballman	1962-	37
	Dick Gordon	1965-	36
	Harold Jackson	1968-	34
	Jackie Smith	1963-	34
	John Gilliam	1967-	33
	Gene Washington	1969-	33
	Ben Hawkins	1966-	32

INTERCEPTIONS

(40)

Rank	Player	Years	No.
1	Em Tunnell	1948-61	79
2	Night Train Lane	1952-65	68
3	Dick LeBeau	1959-72	62
	Paul Krause	1964-73	62
5	Bobby Boyd	1960-68	57
	Johnny Robinson	1960-71	57
7	Jack Butler	1951-59	52
	Bobby Dillon	1952-59	52
	Jimmy Patton	1955-66	52
	Larry Wilson	1960-72	52
11	Yale Lary	1952-53,56-64	50
	Don Burroughs	1955-64	50
13	Dave Grayson	1961-70	49
14	**Richie Petitbon**	1959-	48
	Willie Wood	1960-71	48
	Herb Adderley	1961-72	48
17	Jack Christiansen	1951-58	46
	Dave Whitsell	1958-69	46
	Ed Meador	1959-70	46
	Goose Gonsoulin	1960-67	46
21	Erich Barnes	1958-71	45
	Jim Norton	1960-68	45
	Pat Fischer	1961-	45
24	Warren Lahr	1949-59	44
25	**Kermit Alexander**	1963-	43
26	Bobby Hunt	1962-69	42
	Mel Renfro	1964-	42
	Len Barney	1967-	42
29	Don Doll	1949-54	41
	Johnny Sample	1958-68	41
	Jim Johnson	1961-	41
	Willie Brown	1963-	41
33	Tom Keane	1948-55	40
	Ed Sharockman	1962-72	40
	Butch Byrd	1964-71	40
	W. K. Hicks	1964-72	40
	Spider Lockhart	1965-	38
	Miller Farr	1965-	35
	Emmitt Thomas	1966-	35
	Willie Williams	1965-	35

Players active at the end of 1973 are shown in bold face.

LIFETIME LEADERS

PUNT RETURNS

(100)

Rank	Player	Years	Ret.
1	Em Tunnell	1948-61	258
2	**Alvin Haymond**	**1964-**	**253**
3	**Speedy Duncan**	**1964-**	**199**
4	**Ron Smith**	**1965-**	**194**
5	Willie Wood	1960-71	187
6	Woodley Lewis	1950-60	138
7	**Butch Atkinson**	**1968-**	**136**
8	**Kermit Alexander**	**1963-**	**133**
9	Rickie Harris	1965-72	128
10	Hugh McElhenny	1952-64	126
	Yale Lary	1952-53,56-64	126
12	Bill Dudley	1942,45-51,53	124
	Joe Arenas	1951-57	124
14	Abe Woodson	1958-66	123
	Charlie West	**1968-**	**123**
16	Al Carmichael	1953-58,60-61	122
17	Dick James	1956-65	120
	Jon Arnett	1957-66	120
19	Carl Taseff	1951,53-62	117
20	Don Paul	1950-58	113
	Bruce Taylor	**1970-**	**113**
22	George McAfee	1940-41,45-50	112
23	**Bill Thompson**	**1969-**	**111**
24	Claude Gibson	1961-65	110
25	**Mel Renfro**	**1964-**	**108**
26	**Lem Barney**	**1967-**	**107**
27	Johnny Morris	1958-67	104
28	**Bob Hayes**	**1965-**	**102**
	Jake Scott	**1970-**	**95**
	Leroy Kelly	**1964-**	**94**
	Rick Volk	**1967-**	**83**
	Floyd Little	**1967-**	**77**
	Lemar Parrish	**1970-**	**75**

YARDS (1000)

Rank	Player	Years	Yards
1	Em Tunnell	1948-61	2209
2	**Speedy Duncan**	**1964-**	**2182**
3	**Alvin Haymond**	**1964-**	**2148**
4	Bill Dudley	1942,45-51,53	1515
5	George McAfee	1940-41,45-50	1431
6	Willie Wood	1960-71	1391
7	Claude Gibson	1961-65	1381
8	**Ron Smith**	**1965-**	**1302**
9	**Bill Thompson**	**1969-**	**1243**
10	**Butch Atkinson**	**1968-**	**1183**
11	**Bob Hayes**	**1965-**	**1147**
12	**Bruce Taylor**	**1970-**	**1103**
13	Jack Christiansen	1951-58	1084
14	Bosh Pritchard	1942,46-49,51	1072
15	Rodger Bird	1966-68	1063
16	Rickie Harris	1965-72	1029
17	Woodley Lewis	1950-60	1026
18	**Lem Barney**	**1967-**	**1004**
	Leroy Kelly	**1964-**	**990**
	Jake Scott	**1970-**	**974**
	Floyd Little	**1967-**	**859**
	Mel Renfro	**1964-**	**842**
	Charlie West	**1968-**	**820**

AVERAGE RETURNS (8.0)

(Minimum 75 Returns)

Rank	Player	Years	Ret.	Yards	Avg.
1	George McAfee	1940-41,45-50	112	1431	12.78
2	Jack Christiansen	1951-58	85	1084	12.75
3	Claude Gibson	1961-65	110	1381	12.56
4	Bill Dudley	1942,45-51,53	124	1515	12.22
5	Rodger Bird	1966-68	94	1063	11.31
6	Bosh Pritchard	1942,46-49,51	95	1072	11.28
7	**Bob Hayes**	**1965-**	**102**	**1147**	**11.25**
8	**Bill Thompson**	**1969-**	**111**	**1243**	**11.20**
9	**Floyd Little**	**1967-**	**77**	**859**	**11.16**
10	**Speedy Duncan**	**1964-**	**199**	**2182**	**10.97**
11	Vitamin Smith	1949-53	75	814	10.85
12	**Leroy Kelly**	**1964-**	**94**	**990**	**10.53**
13	Abner Haynes	1960-67	85	873	10.27
14	**Jake Scott**	**1970-**	**95**	**974**	**10.25**
15	Tom Watkins	1961-65,67-68	96	970	10.10
16	**Bruce Taylor**	**1970-**	**113**	**1103**	**9.76**
17	Bill Butler	1959-64	88	850	9.66
18	**Lem Barney**	**1967-**	**107**	**1004**	**9.38**
19	Cliff Lewis	1946-51	77	710	9.22
20	Bill Baird	1963-69	88	787	8.94
21	**Butch Atkinson**	**1968-**	**136**	**1183**	**8.70**
22	Johnny Morris	1958-67	104	893	8.59
23	Em Tunnell	1948-61	258	2209	8.56
24	**Lemar Parish**	**1970-**	**75**	**628**	**8.37**
25	Jon Arnett	1957-66	120	981	8.18
26	Richie Harris	1965-72	128	1029	8.04
	Ed Podolak	**1969-**	**56**	**496**	**8.86**
	Jon Staggers	**1970-**	**72**	**570**	**7.92**
	Charlie West	**1968-**	**123**	**820**	**7.80**

TOUCHDOWNS (3)

Rank	Player	Years	TD
1	Jack Christiansen	1951-58	8
2	Em Tunnell	1948-61	5
3	Dick Christy	1958,60-63	4
	Speedy Duncan	**1964-**	**4**
5	Dick Todd	1939-40,42,45-48	3
	Ray McLean	1940,42-47	3
	Bill Dudley	1942,45-51,53	3
	Woodley Lewis	1950-60	3
	Ray Mathews	1951-60	3
	Yale Lary	1952-53,56-64	3
	Ollie Matson	1952,54-66	3
	Bert Zagers	1955,57-58	3
	Bobby Mitchell	1958-68	3
	Claude Gibson	1961-65	3
	Tom Watkins	1961-65,67-68	3
	Leroy Kelly	**1964-**	**3**
	Bob Hayes	**1965-**	**3**
	Rickie Harris	1965-72	3
	Butch Atkinson	**1968-**	**3**
	Ike Hill	**1970-71,73**	**2**
	Floyd Little	**1967-**	**2**
	Lemar Parish	**1970-**	**2**
	Johnny Roland	**1966-**	**2**
	Ron Smith	**1965-**	**2**
	John Staggers	**1970-**	**2**

KICKOFF RETURNS

(100)

Rank	Player	Years	Ret.
1	**Ron Smith**	**1965-**	**256**
2	Abe Woodson	1958-66	193
3	Al Carmichael	1953-58,60-61	191
4	Dick James	1956-65	189
5	Timmy Brown	1959-68	184
6	**Speedy Duncan**	**1964-**	**180**
7	**Alvin Haymond**	**1964-**	**170**
8	Bobby Jancik	1962-67	158
9	**Kermit Alexander**	**1963-**	**153**
10	Ollie Matson	1952,54-66	144
11	Joe Arenas	1951-57	139
12	Woodley Lewis	1950-60	137
13	Clarence Childs	1964-68	134
14	Cannonball Butler	1965-72	133
15	Bill Butler	1959-64	132
16	Bo Roberson	1961-66	130
17	Jon Arnett	1957-66	126
18	Buddy Young	1947-55	125
19	Abner Haynes	1960-67	121
20	Herb Adderley	1961-72	120
21	Dick Christy	1958,60-63	117
22	**Mercury Morris**	**1969-**	**111**
23	Dave Grayson	1961-70	110
	Dave Hampton	**1969-**	**110**
25	**Cecil Turner**	**1968-**	**108**
	Carl Garrett	**1969-**	**108**
27	Walter Roberts	1964-67,69-70	107
28	Bobby Mitchell	1958-68	102
	Rickie Harris	1965-72	102
	Travis Williams	1967-71	102
31	Tom Watkins	1961-65,67-68	101
	Al Nelson	**1965-**	**101**
	Clint Jones	**1967-**	**99**
	Jerry LeVias	**1969-**	**88**
	Preston Pearson	**1967-**	**86**
	Mel Renfro	**1964-**	**85**
	Vic Washington	**1971-**	**84**
	Margene Adkins	**1970-**	**81**
	Don Shy	**1967-**	**81**
	Floyd Little	**1967-**	**80**
	Charlie West	**1968-**	**78**
	Leroy Kelly	**1964-**	**76**

YARDS (2500)

Rank	Player	Years	Yards
1	**Ron Smith**	**1965-**	**6502**
2	Abe Woodson	1958-66	5538
3	Al Carmichael	1953-58,60-61	4798
4	Timmy Brown	1959-68	4781
5	Dick James	1956-65	4676
6	**Speedy Duncan**	**1964-**	**4539**
7	**Alvin Haymond**	**1964-**	**4438**
8	Bobby Jancik	1962-67	4185
9	Joe Arenas	1951-57	3798
10	Ollie Matson	1952,54-66	3746
11	**Kermit Alexander**	**1963-**	**3586**
12	Buddy Young	1947-55	3465
13	Clarence Childs	1964-68	3454
14	Woodley Lewis	1950-60	3325
15	Jon Arnett	1957-66	3110
16	Herb Adderley	1961-72	3080
17	Bo Roberson	1961-66	3057
18	Abner Haynes	1960-67	3025
19	**Mercury Morris**	**1969-**	**2947**
20	Cannonball Butler	1965-72	2931
21	Bill Butler	1959-64	2886
22	**Dave Hampton**	**1969-**	**2877**
23	Dave Grayson	1961-70	2804
24	Travis Williams	1967-71	2801
25	Gale Sayers	1965-71	2781
26	Dick Christy	1958,60-63	2770
27	**Carl Garrett**	**1969-**	**2737**
28	Walter Roberts	1964-67,69-70	2728
29	Lynn Chadnois	1950-56	2720
30	Bobby Mitchell	1958-68	2690
31	**Al Nelson**	**1965-**	**2625**
32	**Cecil Turner**	**1968-**	**2616**
33	Tom Watkins	1961-65,67-68	2510
	Clint Jones	**1967-**	**2426**
	Mel Renfro	**1964-**	**2246**
	Vic Washington	**1971-**	**2178**
	Preston Pearson	**1967-**	**2152**
	Jerry LeVias	**1969-**	**2097**
	Don Shy	**1967-**	**2047**
	Floyd Little	**1967-**	**2045**
	Charlie West	**1968-**	**1991**
	Butch Atkinson	**1968-**	**1833**
	John Gilliam	**1967-**	**1798**
	Margene Adkins	**1970-**	**1784**
	Leroy Kelly	**1964-**	**1784**

AVERAGE RETURNS (25.0)

(Minimum 75 Returns)

Rank	Player	Years	Ret.	Yards	Avg.
1	Gale Sayers	1965-71	91	2781	30.56
2	Lynn Chadnois	1950-56	92	2720	29.57
3	Abe Woodson	1958-66	193	5538	28.69
4	Buddy Young	1947-55	125	3465	27.72
5	Travis Williams	1967-71	102	2801	27.46
6	Joe Arenas	1951-57	139	3798	27.32
7	Steve Van Buren	1944-71	76	2030	26.71
8	Lenny Lyles	1958-69	81	2161	26.68
9	**Mercury Morris**	**1969-**	**111**	**2947**	**26.55**
10	Bobby Jancik	1962-67	158	4185	26.49
11	Bobby Mitchell	1958-68	102	2690	26.37
12	**Dave Hampton**	**1969-**	**110**	**2877**	**26.16**
13	**Alvin Haymond**	**1964-**	**170**	**4438**	**26.11**
14	Ollie Matson	1952,54-66	144	3746	26.01
15	**Al Nelson**	**1965-**	**101**	**2625**	**25.99**
16	Timmy Brown	1959-68	184	4781	25.98
17	Larry Garron	1960-68	89	2299	25.83
18	Clarence Childs	1964-68	134	3454	25.78
19	Herb Adderley	1961-72	120	3080	25.67
20	Pat Studstill	1961-62,64-72	75	1924	25.65
21	**Floyd Little**	**1967-**	**80**	**2045**	**25.56**
22	**Charlie West**	**1968-**	**78**	**1991**	**25.53**
23	Walter Roberts	1964-67,69-70	107	2728	25.50
24	Dave Grayson	1961-70	110	2804	25.49
25	Charley Warner	1963-66	86	2187	25.43
26	**Ron Smith**	**1965-**	**256**	**6502**	**25.40**
27	**Carl Garrett**	**1969-**	**108**	**2737**	**25.34**
28	**Don Shy**	**1967-**	**81**	**2047**	**25.27**
29	**Speedy Duncan**	**1964-**	**180**	**4539**	**25.22**
30	Al Carmichael	1953-58,60-61	191	4798	25.12
31	**Bobby Williams**	**1966-67,69-71**	**77**	**1934**	**25.12**
32	**Preston Pearson**	**1967-**	**86**	**2152**	**25.02**
33	Abner Haynes	1960-67	121	3025	25.00
	John Gilliam	**1967-**	**71**	**1798**	**25.32**
	Butch Atkinson	**1968-**	**74**	**1833**	**24.77**
	Clint Jones	**1967-**	**99**	**2426**	**24.51**
	Cecil Turner	**1968-**	**108**	**2616**	**24.22**
	Dick Gordon	**1965-**	**65**	**1571**	**24.17**

TOUCHDOWNS (3)

Rank	Player	Years	TD
1	Ollie Matson	1952,54-66	6
	Gale Sayers	1965-71	6
	Travis Williams	1967-71	6
4	Bobby Mitchell	1958-68	5
	Abe Woodson	1958-66	5
	Timmy Brown	1959-68	5
7	Buddy Young	1947-55	4
	Cecil Turner	**1968-**	**4**
9	Vitamin Smith	1949-53	3
	Lynn Chadnois	1950-56	3
	Lenny Lyles	1958-69	3
	Charley Warner	1963-66	3
	Ron Smith	**1965-**	**3**
	Dave Hampton	**1969-**	**3**
	Mercury Morris	**1969-**	**3**
	John Gilliam	**1967-**	**2**
	Alvin Haymond	**1964-**	**2**
	Ron Jessie	**1971-**	**2**
	Preston Pearson	**1967-**	**2**
	Mel Renfro	**1964-**	**2**
	Ike Thomas	**1971-**	**2**
	Rocky Thompson	**1971-**	**2**

Players active at the end of 1973 are shown in **bold face.**

LIFETIME LEADERS
PUNTING

PUNTS (300)

	Player	Years	Punts
1	**Bobby Joe Green**	**1960-**	**970**
2	Paul Maguire	1960-70	794
3	**Jerrel Wilson**	**1963-**	**725**
4	Sam Baker	1953,56-69	701
5	**Bobby Walden**	**1964-**	**684**
6	Don Chandler	1956-67	660
7	Pat Studstill	1961-62,64-72	560
8	Curley Johnson	1960-69	556
9	Billy Lothridge	1964-72	532
10	Norm Van Brocklin	1949-60	523
11	Jim Norton	1960-68	518
12	Tommy Davis	1959-69	511
13	Yale Lary	1952-53,56-64	503
14	Ed Brown	1954-65	493
15	Horace Gillom	1947-56	492
16	**Mike Eischeid**	**1966-**	**491**
17	Danny Villanueva	1960-67	488
18	Adrian Burk	1950-56	474
19	**David Lee**	**1966-**	**448**
20	**Larry Seiple**	**1968-**	**419**
21	**Don Cockroft**	**1968-**	**414**
22	**Billy Van Heusen**	**1968-**	**405**
23	Jug Girard	1948-57	397
24	Tom Landry	1949-55	389
25	**Mike Bragg**	**1968-**	**388**
26	**Donny Anderson**	**1966-**	**387**
27	Tom Yewcic	1961-66	369
28	King Hill	1958-69	368
	Ron Widby	**1968-**	**368**
30	**Dennis Partee**	**1968-**	**364**
31	Jerry Norton	1954-64	358
32	Sammy Baugh	1937-52	338
	Pat Richter	1963-70	338
34	**Steve O'Neal**	**1969-**	**337**
35	Gary Collins	1962-71	336
36	**Tom O'Neill**	**1967-**	**317**
37	Bob Waterfield	1945-52	315
38	Mike Mercer	1961-70	307
39	**Spike Jones**	**1970-**	**302**
	Julian Fagan	**1970-**	**299**
	Dave Lewis	**1970-**	**285**
	Steve Spurrier	**1967-**	**230**

PUNT AVERAGE (42.5)

	Player	Years	Avg.
1	Sammy Baugh	1937-52	44.9
2	Tommy Davis	1959-69	44.7
3	**Jerrel Wilson**	**1963-**	**44.5**
4	Yale Lary	1952-53,56-64	44.3
5	Jerry Norton	1954-64	43.8
6	Don Chandler	1956-67	43.5
7	Horace Gillom	1947-56	43.1
8	Norm Van Brocklin	1949-60	42.9
	Bobby Walden	**1964-**	**42.9**
10	Sam Baker	1953,56-69	42.7
	Danny Villanueva	1960-67	42.7
	Billy Van Heusen	**1968-**	**42.7**
13	**Bobby Joe Green**	**1960-**	**42.6**
14	Curley Johnson	1960-69	42.5
	Dennis Partee	**1968-**	**42.5**
	Dave Lewis	**1970-**	**43.7**

POINTS AFTER TOUCHDOWNS

ATTEMPTS (300)

	Player	Years	Att.
1	**George Blanda**	**1949-58,60-**	**863**
2	Lou Groza	1946-59,61-67	834
3	Sam Baker	1953,56-59	444
4	Lou Michaels	1958-69,71	402
5	**Fred Cox**	**1963-**	**387**
6	Bobby Walston	1951-62	384
7	**Jim Bakken**	**1962-**	**375**
8	**Bruce Gossett**	**1964-**	**356**
9	Gino Cappelletti	1960-70	353
10	B. Agajanian	1945,47-49,53-57,60-62,64	351
11	Tommy Davis	1959-69	350
12	**Mike Clark**	**1963-71,73**	**338**
13	**Jim Turner**	**1964-**	**337**
14	Bob Waterfield	1945-52	336
15	**Pete Gogolak**	**1964-**	**331**
16	Gordie Soltau	1950-58	302

GOOD (250)

	Player	Years	Gd.
1	**George Blanda**	**1949-58,60-**	**853**
2	Lou Groza	1946-59,61-67	810
3	Sam Baker	1953,56-59	428
4	Lou Michaels	1958-69,71	386
5	**Fred Cox**	**1963-**	**384**
6	**Jim Bakken**	**1962-**	**369**
7	Bobby Walston	1951-62	365
8	**Bruce Gossett**	**1964-**	**349**
9	Tommy Davis	1959-69	348
10	B. Agajanian	1945,47-49,53-57,60-62,64	343
11	Gino Cappelletti	1960-70	342
12	**Jim Turner**	**1964-**	**333**
13	**Mike Clark**	**1963-71,73**	**325**
14	**Pete Gogolak**	**1964-**	**323**
15	Bob Waterfield	1945-52	315
16	Mike Mercer	1961-70	288
17	Gordie Soltau	1950-58	284
18	Pat Summerall	1952-61	257
	Jan Stenerud	**1967-**	**233**
	Don Cockroft	**1968-**	**211**

PERCENT MADE (95.0)
(Minimum 200 Attempts)

	Player	Years	Gd.	Att.	Pct.
1	Tommy Davis	1959-69	348	350	99.43
2	**Fred Cox**	**1963-**	**384**	**387**	**99.22**
3	**George Blanda**	**1949-58,60-**	**853**	**863**	**98.84**
4	**Jim Turner**	**1964-**	**333**	**337**	**98.81**
5	**Jan Stenerud**	**1967-**	**233**	**236**	**98.72**
6	**Jim Bakken**	**1962-**	**369**	**375**	**98.40**
7	**Don Cockroft**	**1968-**	**211**	**215**	**98.13**
8	**Bruce Gossett**	**1964-**	**349**	**356**	**98.03**
9	Danny Villaneuva	1960-67	236	241	97.92
10	Ben Agajanian	1945,47-49,53-57,60-62,64	343	351	97.72
11	Mike Mercer	1961-70	288	295	97.62
12	**Pete Gogolak**	**1964-**	**323**	**331**	**97.58**
13	Lou Groza	1946-59,61-67	810	834	97.12
14	Pat Harder	1946-53	198	204	97.05
15	Pat Summerall	1952-61	257	265	96.98
16	Gino Cappelletti	1960-70	342	353	96.88
17	Gene Mingo	1960-70	215	223	96.41
18	Sam Baker	1953,56-69	428	444	96.39
19	**Mike Clark**	**1963-71,73-**	**325**	**338**	**96.15**
20	Don Chandler	1956-67	248	258	96.12
21	Lou Michaels	1958-69,71	386	402	96.01
22	Bobby Walston	1951-62	365	384	95.05
	Garo Yepremian	**1966-67,70-**	**178**	**181**	**98.34**
	Curt Knight	**1969-**	**172**	**175**	**98.28**
	Bobby Howfield	**1968-**	**185**	**189**	**97.88**

FIELD GOALS

ATTEMPTS (150)

	Player	Years	Att.
1	**George Blanda**	**1949-58,60-**	**600**
2	Lou Groza	1946-59,61-67	481
3	**Fred Cox**	**1963-**	**370**
4	**Jim Turner**	**1964-**	**356**
5	Lou Michaels	1958-69,71	341
6	**Jim Bakken**	**1962-**	**336**
	Bruce Gossett	**1964-**	**336**
8	Gino Cappelletti	1960-70	333
9	Sam Baker	1953,56-69	316
10	Tommy Davis	1959-69	276
11	**Pete Gogolak**	**1964-**	**275**
12	**Jan Stenerud**	**1967-**	**271**
13	**Mike Clark**	**1963-71,73-**	**232**
14	Gene Mingo	1960-70	220
15	Pat Summerall	1952-61	212
16	B. Agajanian	1945,47-49,53-57,60-62,64	204
17	Mike Mercer	1961-70	195
18	Jim Martin	1950-61,63-64	192
19	**Roy Gerela**	**1969-**	**183**
20	**Mac Percival**	**1967-**	**182**
21	**Curt Knight**	**1969-**	**175**
22	**Garo Yepremian**	**1966-67,70-**	**171**
23	**Horst Muhlmann**	**1969-**	**168**
24	**Tom Dempsey**	**1969-**	**167**
25	**David Ray**	**1969-**	**162**
26	Don Chandler	1956-67	161
27	Danny Villanueva	1960-67	160
28	**Bobby Howfield**	**1968-**	**159**
29	Bobby Walston	1951-62	157
30	**Don Cockroft**	**1968-**	**155**
31	**Errol Mann**	**1968-**	**154**
32	Roger LeClerc	1960-67	152

GOOD (100)

	Player	Years	Gd.
1	**George Blanda**	**1949-58,60-**	**311**
2	Lou Groza	1946-59,61-67	264
3	**Fred Cox**	**1963-**	**230**
4	**Jim Turner**	**1964-**	**220**
5	**Jim Bakken**	**1962-**	**212**
6	**Bruce Gossett**	**1964-**	**208**
7	Lou Michaels	1958-69,71	187
8	**Sam Baker**	**1953,56-69**	**179**
	Jan Stenerud	**1967-**	**179**
10	Gino Cappelletti	1960-70	172
11	**Pete Gogolak**	**1964-**	**163**
12	**Mike Clark**	**1963-71,73-**	**133**
13	Tommy Davis	1959-69	130
14	**Garo Yepremian**	**1966-67,70-**	**114**
15	Gene Mingo	1960-70	112
16	**Roy Gerela**	**1969-**	**111**
17	**Horst Muhlmann**	**1969-**	**109**
18	B. Agajanian	1945,47-49,53-57,60-62,64	104
19	Mike Mercer	1961-70	102
20	**Don Cockroft**	**1968-**	**101**
	Curt Knight	**1969-**	**101**
	David Ray	**1969-**	**101**
23	Pat Summerall	1952-61	100
	Errol Mann	**1968-**	**100**
	Mac Percival	**1967-**	**99**
	Tom Dempsey	**1969-**	**96**
	Bobby Howfield	**1968-**	**92**

PERCENT MADE (50.0)
(Minimum 100 Attempts)

	Player	Years	Gd.	Att.	Pct.
1	**Garo Yepremian**	**1966-67,70-**	**114**	**171**	**66.67**
2	**Jan Stenerud**	**1967-**	**179**	**271**	**66.05**
3	**Don Cockroft**	**1968-**	**101**	**155**	**65.16**
4	**Errol Mann**	**1968-**	**100**	**154**	**64.93**
5	**Horst Muhlmann**	**1969-**	**109**	**168**	**64.88**
6	**Jim Bakken**	**1962-**	**212**	**336**	**63.09**
7	**David Ray**	**1969-**	**101**	**162**	**62.34**
8	**Fred Cox**	**1963-**	**230**	**370**	**62.16**
9	**Bruce Gossett**	**1964-**	**208**	**336**	**61.90**
10	**Jim Turner**	**1964-**	**220**	**356**	**61.79**
11	**Roy Gerela**	**1969-**	**111**	**183**	**60.65**
12	**Dennis Partee**	**1968-**	**70**	**116**	**60.34**
13	**Pete Gogolak**	**1964-**	**163**	**275**	**59.27**
14	Don Chandler	1956-67	94	161	58.38
15	**Bobby Howfield**	**1968-**	**92**	**159**	**57.86**
16	Fred Cone	1951-57,60	59	102	57.84
17	**Curt Knight**	**1969-**	**101**	**175**	**57.71**
18	**Tom Dempsey**	**1969-**	**96**	**167**	**57.48**
19	**Mike Clark**	**1963-71,73-**	**133**	**232**	**57.32**
20	Sam Baker	1953,56-59	179	316	56.64
21	**Jim O'Brien**	**1970-**	**60**	**108**	**55.55**
22	Lou Groza	1946-59,61-67	264	481	54.88
23	Lou Michaels	1958-69,71	187	341	54.83
24	Bob Waterfield	1945-52	60	110	54.54
25	**Mac Percival**	**1967-**	**99**	**182**	**54.39**
26	Danny Villanueva	1960-67	85	160	53.13
27	Mike Mercer	1961-70	102	195	52.30
28	**George Blanda**	**1949-58,60-**	**311**	**600**	**51.83**
29	Gino Cappelletti	1960-70	172	333	51.65
30	Charlie Durkee	1967-68,71-72	52	101	51.48
31	Ben Agajanian	1945,47-49,53-57,60-62,64	104	204	50.98
32	Bobby Walston	1951-62	80	157	50.95
33	Gene Mingo	1960-70	112	220	50.90
34	Gordie Soltau	1950-58	70	138	50.72
35	Roger LeClerc	1960-67	76	152	50.00

Players active at the end of 1973 are shown in **bold face.**

THE CHANGING GAME

AVERAGE POINTS PER GAME

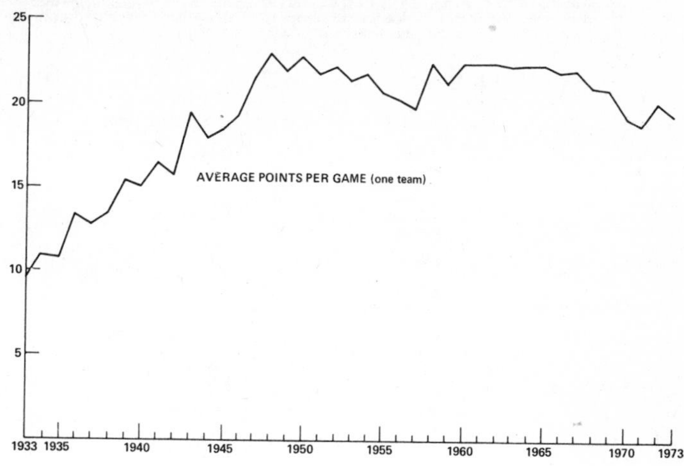

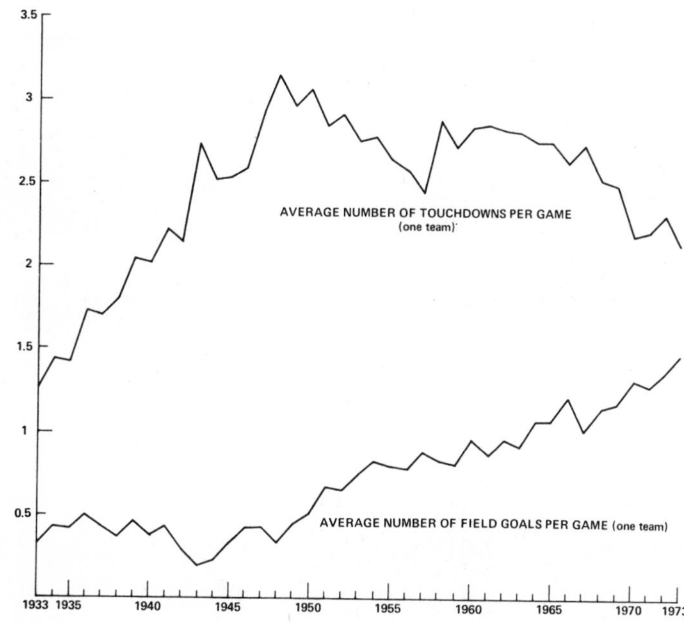

AVERAGE NUMBER OF TOUCHDOWNS PER GAME

AVERAGE NUMBER OF FIELD GOALS PER GAME

FIELD GOAL PERCENTAGE

PASSES-PERCENT COMPLETED

PASSES-PERCENT INTERCEPTED

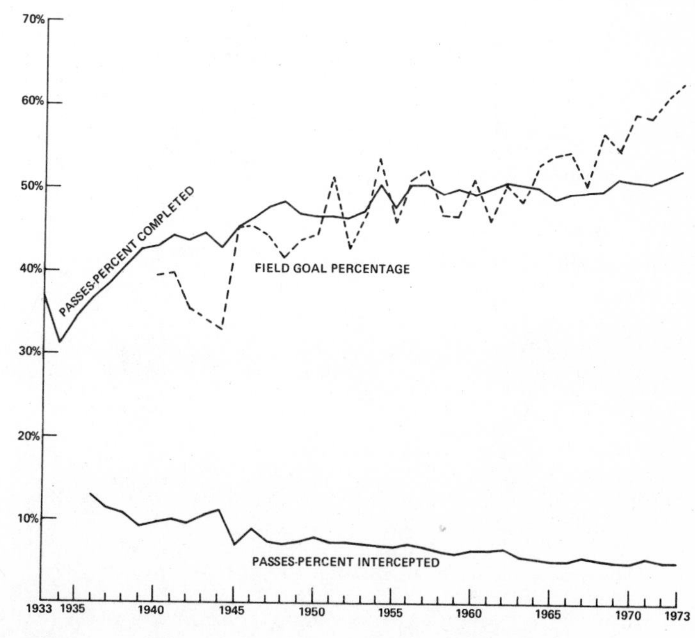

THE COLLEGES — PRO FOOTBALL'S FARM SYSTEM

All men who played in the A.A.F.C., the A.F.L., or the N.F.L. since 1933 are tabulated here by the college(s) they attended. The colleges are listed by conference within the 7 N.C.A.A. regions. The current names of the colleges and the current football conferences are shown. Many of the conferences have more member colleges than are shown here since colleges that have not been attended by any pro football players are not listed; so "only" 497 four year colleges in the United States are listed here. Players who attended more than one college were counted for each college they attended.

EAST – 930

IVY LEAGUE	88
Pennsylvania	25
Columbia	14
Cornell	12
Dartmouth	11
Yale	10
Princeton	9
Brown	5
Harvard	2

EAST COAST CONFERENCE	70
Temple	33
Bucknell	14
Hofstra	6
West Chester State	6
Lehigh	3
Delaware	2
Lafayette	2
LaSalle	2
St. Joseph's-Pa.	2

YANKEE CONFERENCE	44
Boston U.	21
Massachusetts	7
Maine	5
Connecticut	4
Rhode Island	3
New Hampshire	3
Vermont	1

METROPOLITAN INTERCOLLEGIATE CONFERENCE	38
Fordham	34
C.W. Post	2
Kings Point	1
Wagner	1

MIDDLE ATLANTIC CONF.	27
Muhlenberg	6
Western Maryland	6
Albright	4
Delaware Valley	3
Lebanon Valley	2
Franklin & Marshall	2
Ursinus	2
Upsala	1
Dickinson	1

PENNSYLVANIA CONF.	5
Indiana State (Pa.)	2
Bloomsburg State	1
Clarion State	1
Edinboro State	1

INDEPENDENT COLLEGE ATHLETIC CONF.	5
Alfred	2
Hobart	1
Ithaca	1
St. Lawrence	1

LITTLE THREE CONF.	3
Amherst	2
Williams	1

NEW ENGLAND FOOTBALL CONFERENCE	2
Providence	2

EASTERN FOOTBALL CONF.	1
Southern Connecticut St.	1

Other East	647
Pittsburgh	97
Penn State	72
Boston College	58
Syracuse	54
Villanova	50
Duquesne	45
West Virginia	43
Holy Cross	37
Colgate	27
Georgetown	20
George Washington	18
Army	13
N.Y.U.	13
St. Bonaventure	10
Navy	8
Waynesburg	7
Niagara	6
Scranton	6
St. Vincent	6
St. Francis-Pa.	6
Manhattan	5
Rutgers	4
Canisius	4
American International	3
Gettysburg	3
PMC Colleges	3
Springfield	3
St. Anselm's	3
Grove City	3
Geneva	3
Buffalo	2
Northeastern	2
Trinity (Conn.)	2
Arnold	2
Coast Guard	1
Tufts	1
Brandeis	1
C.U.N.Y.-Brooklyn	1
C.U.N.Y.-City	1
Lincoln (Pa.)	1
Westminster	1
Norwich	1
Long Island U.	1

SOUTH – 1606

SOUTHEASTERN CONF.	639
Mississippi	89
Alabama	87
Tennessee	84
Georgia	83
Louisiana State	78
Auburn	58
Kentucky	52
Florida	48
Mississippi State	36
Vanderbilt	24

ATLANTIC COAST CONF.	254
Maryland	50
Duke	44
Wake Forest	39
North Carolina	36
Clemson	33
Virginia	29
North Carolina State	23

MID-EASTERN ATH. CONF.	82
Morgan State	24
Maryland Eastern Shore	21
North Carolina Central	13
North Carolina A & T	11
South Carolina State	10
Delaware State	2
Howard-D.C.	1

SOUTHERN CONFERENCE	74
William & Mary	26
Richmond	21
V.M.I.	9
The Citadel	4
Appalachian State	4
Furman	4
East Carolina	3
Davidson	3

SOUTHERN INTERCOLLEGIATE ATHLETIC CONF.	65
Florida A & M	35
Bethune-Cookman	8
Morris Brown	5
Ft. Valley State	4
Tuskegee	4
Alabama A & M	2
Clark-Ga.	2
Fisk	2
Alabama State	2
Albany State	1

GULF SOUTH CONF.	35
Northwest State-La.	11
Southeastern Louisiana	8
Tennessee-Martin	4
Delta State	3
Mississippi College	3
Troy State	2
Florence State	2
Jacksonville State	1
Livingston	1

CENTRAL INTERCOLLEGIATE ATHLETIC ASS'N	28
Johnson C. Smith	6
Virginia State	6
Norfolk State	5
Virginia Union	5
Elizabeth City State	2
Hampton Institute	2
Shaw	1
Winston-Salem State	1

OHIO VALLEY CONF.	19
Tennessee Tech	5
Murray State	5
Eastern Kentucky	4
Middle Tennessee	2
Austin Peay	1
Morehead State	1
Western Kentucky	1

CAROLINAS CONFERENCE	19
Catawba	8
Presbyterian	5
Elon	3
Lenoir Rhyne	2
Guilford	1

COLLEGE ATHLETIC CONF.	16
Washington-St.L.	7
Washington & Lee	4
Centre	3
Southwestern at Memphis	2

WEST VIRGINIA INTERCOLLEGIATE ATH. CONF.	11
West Virginia Wesleyan	7
Fairmont State	1
West Virginia State	1
West Liberty State	1
West Virginia Tech	1

MASON-DIXON CONF.	2
Hampden-Sydney	2

Other South	362
Miami (Fla.)	53
Georgia Tech	45
Tulane	40
Tennessee State	36
Florida State	33
Southern Mississippi	30
South Carolina	29
Tennessee-Chattanooga	23
Virginia Tech	11
Catholic	8
Howard (Ala.)	8
Morris Harvey	7
Northeast Louisiana	6
Tampa	5
Allen	4
Kentucky State	4
Davis & Elkins	4
Mercer	3
Birmingham-Southern	2
Loyola (N. Orl.)	2
Benedict	1
Edward Waters	1
St. Augustine's	1
Samford	1
Wofford	1
Union (Tenn.)	1
Loyola (Balt.)	1
Mount St. Mary's	1
Oglethorpe	1

MIDWEST – 1604

BIG TEN CONFERENCE	923
Ohio State	122
Purdue	113
Michigan State	110
Minnesota	97
Michigan	95
Wisconsin	84
Indiana	80
Illinois	79
Northwestern	77
Iowa	66

MID-AMERICAN CONF.	104
Miami-Ohio	21
Toledo	18
Ohio U.	18
Bowling Green	16
Western Michigan	14
Kent State	8
Eastern Michigan	7
Central Michigan	2

PRESIDENT'S ATH. CONF.	40
Carnegie-Mellon	14
Case Reserve	12
John Carroll	7
Washington & Jefferson	7

OHIO CONFERENCE	20
Baldwin-Wallace	6
Heidelberg	5
Muskingum	2
Wittenberg	2
Otterbein	2
Ohio Wesleyan	2
Wooster	1

MINNESOTA INTERCOLLEGIATE ATHLETIC CONF.	19
St. Thomas	5
Gustavus Adolphus	4
Minnesota-Duluth	3
St. John's-Minn.	3
Concordia-Moorhead	2
Hamline	2

COLLEGE CONFERENCE OF ILLINOIS & WISCONSIN	19
Illinois Wesleyan	7
Carroll (Wis.)	3
Millikin	3
Augustana	2
North Central	1
North Park	1
Carthage	1
Elmhurst	1

MIDWEST CONFERENCE	11
Ripon	4
St. Olaf	2
Grinnell	2
Lawrence	1
Knox	1
Monmouth	1

INDIANA COLLEGE CONF.	10
Butler	4
Valparaiso	2
Evansville	2
Indiana Central	1
St. Joseph's–Ind.	1

HOOSIER-BUCKEYE CONF.	9
Findlay	4
Manchester	3
Bluffton	1
Defiance	1

WISCONSIN STATE UNIV. CONFERENCE	8
Wis. St.-Superior	2
Wis. St.-LaCrosse	2
Wis. St.-Stevens Point	1
Wis. St.-Oshkosh	1
Wisconsin-Platteville	1
Wisconsin-Stout	1

GATEWAY CONFERENCE	2
Lakeland	1
Northland	1

MICHIGAN INTERCOLLEGIATE ATHLETIC ASS'N.	1
Olivet	1

NORTHERN INTERCOLLEGIATE CONFERENCE	1
St. Cloud State	1

Other Midwest	437
Notre Dame	197
Marquette	37
Cincinnati	33
Detroit	25
Dayton	20
Xavier-Ohio	15
Marshall	15
Southern Illinois	13
DePaul	9
Western Illinois	8
Northern Illinois	7
Youngstown	6
Wayne State	6
Northern Michigan	5
Ball State	4
St. Benedict's	4
St. Ambrose	4
Central State-Ohio	3
Hillsdale	3
Illinois State	2
Parsons	2
St. Norbert	2
Eastern Illinois	2
Loras	2
St. Mary's (Minn.)	2
Ashland	1
Indiana State	1
Lewis	1
Wisconsin-Milwaukee	1
Chicago	1
Detroit Tech	1
Franklin (Ind.)	1
Franklin (Ohio)	1
Lombard	1
Loyola (Chic.)	1
St. Edmonds	1

THE COLLEGES — PRO FOOTBALL'S FARM SYSTEM

MISSOURI VALLEY – 798

BIG EIGHT CONFERENCE	430
Oklahoma	89
Nebraska	84
Missouri	57
Colorado	53
Kansas	44
Oklahoma State	42
Kansas State	35
Iowa State	26

MISSOURI VALLEY CONF.	233
Tulsa	79
North Texas State	33
Memphis State	25
West Texas State	24
Louisville	22
Wichita State	21
New Mexico State	19
Drake	9

NORTH CENTRAL CONF.	33
South Dakota State	11
North Dakota	10
North Dakota State	7
South Dakota	3
Augustana (S.D.)	1
Morningside	1

OKLAHOMA COLLEGIATE ATHLETIC CONF.	20
Central State-Okla.	9
Northeast State-Okla.	3
Langston	3
Cameron State	2
Northwest State-Okla.	1
Southwest State-Okla.	1
East Central State-Okla.	1

MISSOURI INTERCOLLEGIATE ATHLETIC ASS'N.	16
Lincoln (Mo.)	6
NE Missouri State	4
SE Missouri State	3
NW Missouri State	1
SW Missouri State	1
Missouri-Rolla	1

HEART OF AMERICA CONF.	7
Missouri Valley	2
College of Emporia	2
Ottawa (Kan.)	2
Tarkio	1

IOWA INTERCOLLEGIATE ATHLETIC CONF.	6
Luther	2
Central (Iowa)	1
Upper Iowa	1
William Penn	1
Simpson	1

NEBRASKA COLLEGE CONF.	5
Kearney State	3
Wayne State-Neb.	1
Chadron State	1

KANSAS COLLEGE ATHLETIC CONFERENCE	5
Southwestern (Kan.)	2
Tabor	1
McPherson	1
Sterling	1

TRI-STATE INTERCOLLEGIATE CONFERENCE	3
Yankton	3

NEBRASKA INTERCOLLEGIATE ATHLETIC CONF.	3
Doane	1
Hastings	1
Nebraska Wesleyan	1

Other Missouri Valley	37
St. Louis	11
Bradley	9
Oklahoma City	9
Creighton	4
Phillips	2
Iowa Wesleyan	1
Oklahoma Baptist	1

SOUTHWEST – 932

SOUTHWEST ATH. CONF.	539
Texas	92
Arkansas	71
S. M. U.	68
Texas Christian	61
Baylor	59
Texas A & M	58
Houston	49
Texas Tech	42
Rice	39

SOUTHWESTERN ATH. CONF.	184
Grambling	49
Texas Southern	28
Jackson State	27
Southern U.	27
Alcorn A & M	27
Prairie View	22
Mississippi Valley St.	4

LONE STAR CONFERENCE	62
Texas A & I	16
East Texas State	12
Howard Payne	7
Southwest Texas State	7
S. F. Austin State	6
Sam Houston State	6
McMurry	5
Sul Ross State	2
Tarleton State	1

SOUTHLAND CONFERENCE	57
Louisiana Tech.	13
Abilene Christian	11
Lamar Tech	9
Arkansas State	8
Texas-Arlington	7
McNeese State	6
Southwestern Louisiana	3

ARKANSAS INTERCOLLEGIATE CONFERENCE	6
Ouachita Baptist	4
Arkansas Tech	1
Henderson State	1

Other Southwest	84
Hardin-Simmons	25
Arkansas-Pine Bluff	12
Trinity (Texas)	8
Austin	7
Centenary	7
Bishop	6
New Mexico Highlands	6
Wiley	3
Eastern New Mexico	2
St. Mary's (Tex.)	2
Texas-Austin	1
Philander Smith	1
Paul Quinn	1
Corpus Christi	1
Midwestern	1
St. Edward's	1

ROCKY MOUNTAINS – 370

WESTERN ATH. CONF.	235
Arizona State	50
Utah	39
Colorado State	33
Texas-El Paso	32
Arizona	30
Wyoming	23
Brigham Young	18
New Mexico	10

BIG SKY CONFERENCE	57
Idaho	20
Weber State	11
Montana State	8
Montana	8
Northern Arizona	5
Idaho State	4
Boise State	1

GREAT PLAINS ATH. CONF.	16
Kansas State Teachers	7
Nebraska-Omaha	5
Kansas State College	2
Southern Colorado State	1
Ft. Hays Kansas State	1

ROCKY MOUNTAIN ATHLETIC CONFERENCE	6
Adams State	3
Fort Lewis	1
Westminster (Utah)	1
Colorado Mines	1

FRONTIER CONFERENCE	2
Eastern Montana	2

Other Rocky Mountain	54
Utah State	39
Denver	12
Colorado College	2
Regis	1

PACIFIC COAST – 963

PACIFIC - 8 CONFERENCE	590
Southern California	159
U. C. L. A.	80
Stanford	70
Washington	69
Oregon	65
Oregon State	62
Washington State	47
California	38

PACIFIC COAST A.A.	165
San Diego State	45
U. of the Pacific	45
San Jose State	35
Fresno State	17
Los Angeles State	13
Long Beach State	10

FAR WESTERN CONF.	18
San Francisco State	11
Humboldt State	2
Sacramento State	2
Chico State	2
California-Davis	1

SOUTHERN CALIFORNIA INTERCOLLEGIATE CONF.	10
Whittier	5
Occidental	4
Redlands	1

CALIFORNIA COLLEGIATE ATHLETIC ASS'N.	10
Calif. State Polytech	9
Fullerton State	1

PACIFIC NORTHWEST CONF.	9
Linfield	2
Willamette	2
College of Idaho	1
Lewis & Clark	1
Whitworth	1
Pacific (Ore.)	1
Pacific Lutheran	1

EVERGREEN CONFERENCE	2
Eastern Washington St.	1
Central Washington St.	1

Other Pacific Coast	159
St. Mary's	41
Santa Clara	26
San Francisco	26
Nevada	15
Loyola (L.A.)	12
Gonzago	8
Hawaii	7
Calif.-Santa Barbara	7
Portland	4
San Diego	3
Pepperdine	3
Portland State	2
U. S. International	2
Calif. State-Bakersfield	1
California Lutheran	1
Nevada-Las Vegas	1

OTHER PLAYERS – 123

79 players did not attend college.

38 players attended community or junior colleges only.

6 players attended college outside the United States

The Top 20 Colleges

1.	Notre Dame	197
2.	Southern California	159
3.	Ohio State	122
4.	Purdue	113
5.	Michigan State	110
6.	Minnesota	97
	Pittsburgh	97
8.	Michigan	95
9.	Texas	92
10.	Mississippi	89
	Oklahoma	89
12.	Alabama	87
13.	Nebraska	84
	Tennessee	84
	Wisconsin	84
16.	Georgia	83
17.	Indiana	80
	U. C. L. A.	80
19.	Illinois	79
	Tulsa	79

THE HALL OF FAME

1963

Sammy Baugh—Quarterback—Coach
Bert Bell—NFL Commissioner—Coach
Joe Carr—NFL President
Dutch Clark—Quarterback—Coach
Red Grange—Halfback
George Halas—Owner—Coach—End
Mel Hein—Center—League Official—Coach
Pete Henry—Tackle—Coach
Cal Hubbard—Tackle
Don Hutson—End
Curly Lambeau—Founder—Coach—Halfback
Tim Mara—Founder
George Preston Marshall—Founder
Johnny (Blood) McNally—Halfback—Coach
Bronko Nagurski—Fullback
Ernie Nevers—Fullback—Coach
Jim Thorpe—Halfback—Coach

1964

Jimmy Conzelman—Quarterback—Coach—Owner
Ed Healey—Tackle
Clarke Hinkle—Fullback
Mike Michalske—Guard
Art Rooney—Founder
George Trafton—Center

1965

Guy Chamberlin—End—Coach
Paddy Driscoll—Quarterback—Coach
Danny Fortmann—Guard
Otto Graham—Quarterback—Coach
Sid Luckman—Quarterback
Steve Van Buren—Halfback
Bob Waterfield—Quarterback—Coach

1966

Bill Dudley—Halfback
Joe Guyon—Halfback
Arnie Herber—Quarterback
Walt Kiesling—Guard—Coach
George McAfee—Halfback—NFL Game Official
Steve Owen—Coach—Tackle
Shorty Ray—NFL League Official

1967

Chuck Bednarik—Center—Linebacker
Charles Bidwell—Owner
Paul Brown—Coach
Bobby Layne—Quarterback
Dan Reeves—Owner
Ken Strong—Halfback
Joe Stydahar—Tackle—Coach
Em Tunnell—Defensive Back

1968

Cliff Battles—Halfback—Quarterback—Coach
Art Donovan—Defensive Tackle
Crazy Legs Hirsch—Halfback—End
Wayne Millner—End—Coach
Marion Motley—Fullback
Charlie Trippi—Halfback—Quarterback
Alex Wojciechowicz—Center—Linbacker

1969

Turk Edwards—Tackle—Coach
Greasy Neale—Coach—Pre NFL End
Leo Nomellini—Defensive Tackle
Joe Perry—Fullback
Ernie Stautner—Defensive Tackle

1970

Jack Christiansen—Defensive Back—Coach
Tom Fears—End—Coach
Hugh McElhenny—Halfback
Pete Pihos—End

1971

Jimmy Brown—Fullback
Bill Hewitt—End
Bruiser Kinard—Tackle
Vince Lombardi—Coach
Andy Robustelli—Defensive End
Y. A. Tittle—Quarterback
Norm Van Brocklin—Quarterback—Coach

1972

Lamar Hunt—Founder AFL—Owner
Gino Marchetti—Defensive End
Ollie Matson—Halfback
Ace Parker—Quarterback

1973

Ray Berry—End
Jim Parker—Offensive Tackle—Guard
Joe Schmidt—Linbacker—Coach